INTERNATIONAL LAW

INTERNATIONAL LAW

Fifth Edition

EDITED BY

MALCOLM D. EVANS

Professor of Public International Law, University of Bristol

OXFORD

UNIVERSITY PRESS

OXFORD

UNIVERSITY PRESS

Great Clarendon Street, Oxford, OX2 6DP,
United Kingdom

Oxford University Press is a department of the University of Oxford.
It furthers the University's objective of excellence in research, scholarship,
and education by publishing worldwide. Oxford is a registered trade mark of
Oxford University Press in the UK and in certain other countries

Second edition 2006
Third edition 2010
Fourth edition 2014

Impression: 1

Published in the United States of America by Oxford University Press
198 Madison Avenue, New York, NY 10016, United States of America

British Library Cataloguing in Publication Data

Data available

Library of Congress Control Number: 2017964392

ISBN 978-0-19-879183-6

Printed in Great Britain by
Bell & Bain Ltd., Glasgow

OUTLINE CONTENTS

DETAILED CONTENTS

PART I THE HISTORY AND THEORY OF INTERNATIONAL LAW

PART II THE STRUCTURE OF INTERNATIONAL
LEGAL OBLIGATION

PART III THE SUBJECTS OF THE INTERNATIONAL LEGAL ORDER

PART IV THE SCOPE OF SOVEREIGNTY

PART V   RESPONSIBILITY

PART VI RESPONDING TO BREACHES OF INTERNATIONAL OBLIGATIONS

PART VII THE APPLICATION OF INTERNATIONAL LAW

PREFACE TO THE FIFTH EDITION

The first edition of this work appeared in 2003 and although the format, aims, and ambitions of the book have remained largely unchanged over the intervening 15 years, the content has evolved greatly, and continues to do so. The most obvious change in this edition is the addition of an entirely new chapter devoted to International Refugee and Migration Law—a topic of ever increasing importance. Some topics are now addressed by fresh voices, whilst other chapters have been rewritten to reflect—and, most importantly, to reflect upon—the many important developments which have taken place since the previous edition appeared. I am very grateful to each and every contributor to this volume for having synthesized so much into these (relatively) short and (certainly) readable and accessible chapters, which continue to provide authoritative guidance and analysis of the subjects they address. I am also very grateful to the staff at Oxford University Press for their willingness to believe—against all rationality—that this edition could be completed on time. Without their patience, assistance, and occasional cajoling, it would not have been. Of course, I remain immensely grateful also to all those who read and use this book, and I continue to hope that it finds favour as a means of furthering the education and understanding of students, scholars, and practitioners of international law.

It is increasingly the case that international law is being drawn on in domestic law and politics, and the past few years have also seen a marked upturn in recourse to international dispute settlement processes. Whilst at one level this is obviously all very positive, there is also an emerging tendency for States to resort to both domestic and international litigation as part of their broader political strategies, rather than as a genuine means of achieving a peaceful outcome to a contentious situation. Where this will lead us remains to be seen. What is clear is that in an increasingly unstable world, and confronted by further erosions of some of the principal assumptions on which global order has been based for the past 25 years, the need for adherence to the international rule of law becomes ever more pressing. These problems are hardly likely to be remedied by the appearance of a new edition of this work, but it is important to renew and refresh such tools of learning, in the hope that they may be of some assistance to those who seek to further the cause of international law and of international order.

No one has done more to further that cause than Sir Nigel Rodley, who passed away before he was able to complete the revision of his chapter on international human rights law for this edition. I am very grateful to Lyn Rodley who has permitted the publication of his chapter, modestly updated by others, as an *in memoriam* to a man who was an inspiration to us all.

Malcolm D. Evans
January 2018

FROM THE EDITOR'S INTRODUCTION TO THE FIRST EDITION

International law is a rich and varied subject, bearing upon most of the great issues facing individuals and communities. This work aims to capture something of that breadth and diversity by drawing on the knowledge and experience of a broad range of contributors who are intimately engaged in its teaching and practice. It is designed to present the essential elements of the international legal system in a clear and accessible fashion, but seeks to go further, addressing a number of key questions which challenge many of the assumptions upon which the international legal system is founded. It also seeks to provide a succinct introduction to a range of topics that are subject to increasingly detailed international regulation.

Parts I–VI consider the key building blocks of the subject whilst Part VII provides a series of introductory overviews of particular areas of contemporary interest. The structure, coverage, and level of the book are intended to reflect the requirements of undergraduate courses in public international law, although it will also be of use on general courses at the masters' levels as well as being of interest to academics and practitioners.

Although structured to form a coherent presentation of international law, each chapter can be read as a self-contained unit, balancing exposition with argument and reflecting the distinct perspective of its author(s). No attempt has been made to harmonize the views expressed or to produce a single 'voice'. Even if this had been possible, it would have been undesirable. As any teacher—as any lawyer—knows, opinions are best formed through exposure to competing argument. The chapters in this volume combine to address international law from a variety of perspectives: rather than one voice there is a range of voices and a range of opinions. It is to be hoped that this will be a source of stimulation, since the work as a whole aims to be more than just a compendium of knowledge. It aims to be a resource of value to all those interested in probing and testing the international legal enterprise.

NEW TO THIS EDITION

- New chapter on *International Refugee and Migration Law* by Geoff Gilbert and Anna Magdalena Rüsch
- Newly authored chapter on *The Theory and Reality of the Sources of International Law* by Anthea Roberts and Sandesh Sivakumaran
- Newly authored chapter on *International Law and Restraints on the Exercise of Jurisdiction by National Courts of States* by Philippa Webb
- Key new materials and cases covered in this fifth edition include:
  - ICJ decisions in *Application of the Convention on the Prevention and Punishment of the Crime of Genocide (Croatia v Serbia)*; *Maritime Delimitation in the Indian Ocean (Somalia v Kenya), Preliminary Objections*; *Whaling in the Antarctic (Australia v Japan: New Zealand Intervening)*
  - ICC judgment in *Prosecutor v Bemba-Gombo*
  - ECHR judgments in *Al-Dulimi and Montana Management Inc. v Switzerland*; *Hassan v United Kingdom*; *Jaloud v Netherlands*; *Jones and others v the United Kingdom*
  - Arbitral Decisions in *Arctic Sunrise Arbitration (Netherlands v Russia)*; *Bay of Bengal Maritime Boundary Arbitration (Bangladesh v India)*; *South China Sea Arbitration (Philippines v China)*
  - Domestic court judgments, including *Al-Waheed v Ministry of Defence* (UK); *Belhaj and another v Straw and others* (UK); *Benkharbouche v Secretary of State for Foreign and Commonwealth Affairs*; *Bridge of Varvarin Case* (Germany); *Rahmatullah (No. 1) v Ministry of Defence* (UK); *Republic of the Marshall Islands v United States of America et al* (USA); *Serdar Mohammed v Secretary of State for Defence* (UK); *Yukos Capital SARL v OJSC Rosneft Oil Company* (UK)

NOTES ON CONTRIBUTORS

Ademola Abass LLM, PhD, is Head of the Peace and Security Program, the United Nations University, Belgium, and formerly Professor of International Law and International Organization at Brunel University, West London. He researches in Public International Law and Peace and Security, and is the author of *Complete International Law: Text, Cases and Materials,* (2nd edn 2014: Oxford University Press) among others. He has consulted for several international organizations and States. He is a member of the Academic Council on the United Nations Systems and a Fellow of the Cambridge Commonwealth Society.

Dapo Akande is Professor of Public International Law at the University of Oxford, where he is also Co-Director of the Oxford Institute for Ethics, Law and Armed Conflict. He is one of the authors of *Oppenheim's International Law: The United Nations* (2017: Oxford University Press). He is (or has recently been) a member of the board of several journals and institutions including the *American Journal of International Law;* the *European Journal of International Law;* the *African Journal of International and Comparative Law; the British Institute of International and Comparative Law; the American Society of International Law; and the International Centre for Transitional Justice. He is founding editor of the scholarly blog: EJIL:Talk! the blog of the European Journal of International Law.* He has worked as consultant, expert or advisor on various international law issues to international organizations, states and non-governmental organizations.

Alan Boyle is Emeritus Professor of Public International Law at the University of Edinburgh School of Law. His publications include *International Law and the Environment* (with PW Birnie and C Redgwell) (2009: Oxford University Press) and *The Making of International Law* (with C Chinkin) (2007: Oxford University Press). He is a barrister at Essex Court Chambers in London and appears before the ICJ, ITLOS, and PCA.

Matthew Craven is Professor of Public International Law at SOAS University of London. His publications include *The Decolonization of International Law: State Succession and the Law of Treaties* (2007: Oxford University Press) and *The International Covenant on Economic, Social and Cultural Rights: A Perspective on its Development* (1997: Oxford University Press).

James Crawford, AC, SC, FBA is a Judge of the International Court of Justice, and was previously Whewell Professor of International Law, University of Cambridge. As a member of the International Law Commission he was its Special Rapporteur on State Responsibility (1997–2001). His books include *The Creation of States in International Law* (2nd edn, 2006: Oxford University Press); *Brownlie's Principles of Public International Law* (8th edn 2012: Oxford University Press); *State Responsibility: The General Part* (2013: Cambridge University Press) and *Chance, Order, Change: The Course of International Law* (2013: BRILL).

Robert Cryer is Professor of International and Criminal Law at the University of Birmingham. His teaching and research interests are in international law, criminal law, humanitarian law, and legal theory. He is the author of, *inter alia, Prosecuting International Crimes: Selectivity and the International Criminal Law Regime* (with Neil Boister) (2005: Cambridge University Press), *The Tokyo International Military Tribunal: A Reappraisal* (2008: Oxford University Press), and *An Introduction to International Criminal Law and Procedure* (with Håkan Friman, Darryl Robinson, and Elizabeth Wilmshurst) (3rd edn 2014: Cambridge University Press).

Eileen Denza was formerly Assistant Lecturer in Law, Bristol University, a Legal Counsellor to the Foreign and Commonwealth Office, Counsel to the EC Committee of the House of Lords and Visiting Professor of Law at University College London. Her publications include

Diplomatic Law (4th edn 2016: Oxford University Press) and *The Intergovernmental Pillars of the European Union* (2002: Oxford University Press).

Sir Malcolm D Evans KCMG, OBE, is Professor of Public International Law at the University of Bristol. His areas of special interest are the law of the sea and the international protection of human rights, and in particular the freedom of religion and the prevention of torture. His principal publications include *Relevant Circumstances and Maritime Delimitation* (1989: Oxford University Press); *Religion and International Law in Europe* (1997: Cambridge University Press); *Preventing Torture* (1998: Oxford University Press); *Combating Torture in Europe* (2001; 2nd edn, forthcoming, 2018: Council of Europe Press); *The Optional Protocol to the UN Convention against Torture* (with Professor R Murray, *et al*) (2011: Oxford University Press) and numerous edited collections. He is co-General Editor of the *International and Comparative Law Quarterly*, and is currently Chair of the United Nations Subcommittee for Prevention of Torture.

Malgosia Fitzmaurice holds a chair of public international law at the Department of Law, Queen Mary, University of London. She also teaches general international law and the law on the protection of the marine environment at the IMO International Maritime Law Institute at Malta. Her main research interests include international environmental law, indigenous peoples, the law of treaties, the international water law and whaling. She has published widely on these subjects. She has participated in many international conferences and has taught in many law schools abroad, including recently at Berkeley University School of Law and the Sorbonne-Pantheon.

Geoff Gilbert is Professor of Law in the School of Law and Human Rights Centre, University of Essex. He was Editor-in-Chief of the *International Journal of Refugee Law*, 2002–15. He has published widely in the areas of international refugee law, international criminal law, and international human rights law. He has also been a consultant to UNHCR on several occasions and advised various other international organisations working in situations of acute crisis and transition.

Christine Gray, MA, PhD, is Professor in International Law at the University of Cambridge, and a Fellow of St John's College. She is the author of *International Law and the Use of Force* (4th edn, 2018: Oxford University Press) and of *Judicial Remedies in International Law* (1990: Oxford University Press), as well as of many articles on the use of force and on the peaceful settlement of disputes.

Martti Koskenniemi, Professor of International Law, University of Helsinki, Hauser Global Visiting Professor of Law, New York University School of Law and a former member of the International Law Commission. His principal publications include *The Gentle Civilizer of Nations: The Rise and Fall of International Law 1870–1960* (2001: Cambridge University Press) and *From Apology to Utopia: The Structure of International Legal Argument* (2005: Cambridge University Press) (Reissue with a New Epilogue).

Robert McCorquodale is Professor of International Law and Human Rights at the University of Nottingham, barrister at Brick Court Chambers in London, and founding director of Inclusive Law consulting. He is co-author of one of the leading texts in international law, *Cases and Materials on International Law* (6th edn 2016: Oxford University Press), and is on the editorial board of a number of respected academic journals. He has published widely about international law, especially on international human rights law and on the impact of non-State actors on international law, as well as giving advice and training on these issues around the world.

John Merrills, BCL, MA, is Professor of International Law (Emeritus) at the University of Sheffield, a former Dean of the Faculty of Law, and an Associate Member of the *Institut de Droit International*. He is the author of *International Dispute Settlement* (6th edn, 2017: Cambridge University Press), *Human Rights in Europe* (2001: Manchester University Press), *Judge Sir Gerald Fitzmaurice and the Discipline of International Law* (1998: Kluwer Law International) and several other books, as well as numerous articles in law reviews.

Stephen C Neff is the Professor of War and Peace at the University of Edinburgh, specializing in the history of international law. His publications include *Justice Among Nations: A History of International Law* (2014: Harvard University Press); *War and the Law of Nations: A General History* (2005: Cambridge University Press); *The Rights and Duties of Neutrals: A General History* (2000: Manchester University Press); and *Friends But No Allies: Economic Liberalism and the Law of Nations* (1990: Columbia University Press). He writes a regular column, 'Historic Moments', for the *International Judicial Monitor*, on the history of international law.

Phoebe Okowa is Professor of Public International Law at Queen Mary, University of London. She has written extensively in many areas of Public International Law, including the law of State Responsibility, the protection of natural resources in conflict zones, and environmental protection. She is also the co-editor of *Foundations of Public International Law* (Oxford University Press) and a member of the Permanent Court of Arbitration (PCA) at The Hague.

Simon Olleson, MA (Cantab), LLM (NYU), Dip Int Law (Cantab) is a barrister at Three Stone, Lincoln's Inn, London, where he specializes in public international law.

Rose Parfitt, MA (Hons.), PG Dip., MA, PhD, is a Lecturer in Law at Kent Law School. She has taught at institutions including the American University in Cairo, the LSE, Los Andes University, SOAS and the Institute for Global Law and Policy (Harvard Law School), and is currently leading a research project on International Law and the Legacies of Fascist Internationalism at Melbourne Law School, funded by the Australian Research Council. She has published widely in the *London Review of International Law*, *EJIL*, the *Leiden Journal of International Law* and elsewhere. Her book, *Conditional State/ments: A Modular History of International Legal Reproduction*, is coming out in 2018 with Cambridge University Press.

Catherine Redgwell, BA (Hons), LLB, MSc, is Chichele Professor of Public International Law and a Fellow of All Souls College, Oxford, and has published extensively in the international law field, particularly within the areas of environmental law, law of the sea, energy law, and treaty law. She is joint editor of the *British Year Book of International Law* and co-editor of the *Oxford Monographs in International Law* series. She is also Co-Director of the Oxford Martin Programme on Sustainable Oceans.

Anthea Roberts is an Associate Professor at the School of Regulation and Global Governance at the Australian National University. She is a specialist in public international law, investment treaty arbitration and comparative international law. Anthea has served on the Editorial Boards of AJIL, EJIL, ICSID Review and the Journal of World Trade and Investment. She recently authored *Is International Law International?* (2017) and co-edited *Comparative International Law* (2018), both published by Oxford University Press.

Sir Nigel Rodley KBE was Professor of Law and Chair of the Human Rights Centre, University of Essex. A former UN Commission on Human Rights Special Rapporteur on the question of torture (1993-2001), he was a member of the Human Rights Committee established under the International Covenant on Civil and Political Rights since 2001. He served as Chair of the Committee (2013-14). He was also President of the International Commission of Jurists. Honours include a knighthood 'for services to human rights and international law' in 1998 and the American Society of International Law 2005 Goler T Butcher Medal for his 'distinguished contribution to international human rights law'. His many scholarly publications include *The Treatment of Prisoners under International Law* (3rd edn with Matt Pollard, 2009: Oxford University Press).

Anna Magdalena Rüsch, LLM, is an Associate RSD Officer for UNHCR, currently based in Bangkok. She holds a Magister in Law from the University of Vienna as well as an LLM in International Human Rights and Humanitarian Law from the University of Essex. She has published in the areas of international refugee law and international criminal law.

Iain Scobbie, LLB (Hons) (Edin), LLB (Cantab), GDIL (ANU), PhD (Cantab), is professor of public international law at the University of Manchester. He has written on diverse matters such as the jurisprudence and practice of the International Court, legal aspects of the Israel-Palestine question, and the law of armed conflict, as well as the theory of international law.

Sandesh Sivakumaran is Professor of Public International Law at the University of Nottingham. He is the author of *The Law of Non-International Armed Conflict* (2012: Oxford University Press), co-author of *Oppenheim's International Law: United Nations* (2017: Oxford University Press) and *Cases and Materials on International Law* (8th edn 2015: Sweet and Maxwell), and co-editor of *International Human Rights Law* (3rd edn 2017: Oxford University Press). He advises and acts as expert for states, intergovernmental organisations and non-governmental organisations on issues of international law.

Christopher Staker, BA LLB (Hons) (Adelaide), DPhil (Oxford) is a barrister at 39 Essex Chambers in London. Positions that he has previously held include Deputy (Chief) Prosecutor of the Special Court for Sierra Leone (Freetown, Sierra Leone), Principal Legal Secretary at the International Court of Justice (The Hague, Netherlands), Senior Appeals Counsel at the International Criminal Tribunal for the Former Yugoslavia (The Hague), Counsel Assisting the Solicitor-General of Australia, and Counsel in the Office of International Law of the Australian Attorney-General's Department (Canberra, Australia). He has appeared as counsel before international and national courts, including the International Court of Justice, International Tribunal for the Law of the Sea, international criminal courts, and the High Court of Australia.

Surya P Subedi OBE, QC (Hon), DPhil (Oxon.), is Professor of International Law at the University of Leeds and a practising Barrister at Three Stone Chambers, Lincoln's Inn, London. He was the UN Special Rapporteur for Human Rights in Cambodia between 2009 and 2015, and a member of an Advisory Group on Human Rights to the British Foreign Secretary between 2010 and 2015. He has published a number of books, including *International Investment Law: Reconciling Policy and Principle* (3rd edn 2016: Hart Publishing). His name has been designated to serve on the Panels of Arbitrators and of Conciliators of the International Centre for Settlement of Investment Disputes. He was elected to the *Institut de Droit International* in 2011. He is also Chairman of the Board of Editors of the *Asian Journal of International Law* (Cambridge University Press).

Hugh Thirlway, MA, LLB (Cantab.), Dr. en droit, spent most of his career in the legal department of the Registry of the International Court of Justice, including many years as Principal Legal Secretary and Head of Department, but he was also Professor of International Law at the Graduate Institute of International Studies in Geneva, and has served as Visiting Professor at a number of other universities (Leiden, Bristol, Wuhan, Taipei, München etc.). In addition to numerous journal articles, he is the author of the two-volume *Law and Procedure of the International Court of Justice* (originally published in instalments in the BYBIL), as well as *The International Court of Justice* and *The Sources of International Law* (both published by Oxford University Press).

David Turns is Senior Lecturer in International Laws of Armed Conflict at the Defence Academy of the United Kingdom (Cranfield University), previously at the University of Liverpool. He has been a Visiting Professor at the Institute for International Law and International Relations, University of Vienna, and is currently the Chairman of the UK National Group of the International Society for Military Law and the Law of War, a Member of the Society's Board of Directors, and of the International Advisory Board of the *Hungarian Yearbook of International Law and European Law*. He has taught on military staff and legal advisers' courses in several countries and has published widely in the field of international law.

Philippa Webb is Reader (Associate Professor) of Public International Law at King's College London. She is a barrister at 20 Essex Street Chambers, appearing in international courts and English courts in cases involving international law. Philippa was formerly Special Assistant and Legal Officer to ICJ President Rosalyn Higgins, and has held posts at the ICC and UN Headquarters. Her publications include *The Law of State Immunity* (2015, with Lady Fox QC); *Oppenheim's International Law: United Nations* (2017, with Higgins et al); *International Judicial Integration and Fragmentation* (2016), all published with Oxford University Press.

Nigel D White is Professor of Public International Law at the University of Nottingham, formerly Professor of International Law at the University of Sheffield. In addition to publishing numerous articles and essays, he is author of several books including *Keeping the Peace: The United Nations and the Maintenance of International Peace and Security* (2nd edn 1997: Manchester University Press), *The Law of International Organisations* (3rd edn 2017: Manchester University Press), *The UN System: Toward International Justice* (2002: Lynne Rienner), *Democracy Goes to War: British Military Deployments under International Law* (2009: Oxford University Press), and *The Cuban Embargo Under International Law* (2015: Routledge). He has co-authored a number of books including *Collective Security: Theory, Law and Practice* (with Nicholas Tsagourias) (2013: Cambridge University Press). He is also co-editor of a number of leading collections, including *The UN, Human Rights and Post-Conflict Situations* (2005: Manchester University Press), *International Conflict and Security Law* (2005: Cambridge University Press), *European Security Law* (2007: Oxford University Press), *International Law and Dispute Settlement* (2010: Hart), *International Organizations and the Idea of Autonomy* (2011: Routledge), *Counter-Terrorism: International Law and Practice* (2013: Oxford University Press), and *Security and International Law* (2016: Hart). He is co-editor of the *Journal of Conflict and Security Law* published by Oxford University Press.

Chanaka Wickremasinghe is a Legal Counsellor in the Foreign and Commonwealth Office. He was formerly a lecturer in law at Bristol University and a research officer at the British Institute of International and Comparative Law.

Spencer Zifcak is Allan Myers Professor of Law in the Faculty of Law at the Australian Catholic University. He has been a Visiting Fellow at Wolfson College Oxford, Trinity College Dublin and in 2010 was Benjamin Meaker Visiting Professor at the Institute of Advanced Studies at the University of Bristol. His two most recent books are *United Nations Reform: Heading North or South* (2009: Routledge), and with Charles Sampford, *Rethinking International Law and Justice* (2015: Ashgate).

ABBREVIATIONS

AALCC	African Asian Legal Consultative Committee
ACHR	American Convention on Human Rights
AFP	Australian Federal Police
AIA	Advanced Informed Agreement
AJIL	*American Journal of International Law*
API	Application Program Interface
ARIO	Articles on the Responsibility of International Organizations
ARSIWA	Articles on the Responsibility of States for Internationally Wrongful Acts
ASCOBANS	Agreement on the Conservation of Small Cetaceans of the Baltic and North Seas
ASEAN	Association of Southeast Asian Nations
ATCA	Alien Tort Claims Act (US)
AU	African Union
BCN	biological, chemical, nuclear (weapon)
BITs	Bilateral Investment Treaties
BverfGE	*Die Entscheidungen des Bundesverfassungsgerichts*
BYIL	*British Yearbook of International Law*
CAFTA	Central American Free Trade Agreement
CBD	Convention on Conservation of Biological Diversity
CCAMLR	Convention on the Conservation of Antarctic Marine Living Resources
CCSBT	Commission for the Conservation of Southern Bluefin Tuna
CEDAW	Convention on the Elimination of All Forms of Discrimination Against Women
CERD	International Convention on the Elimination of All Forms of Racial Discrimination
CESCR	Committee on Economic, Social and Cultural Rights
CFC	Convention on Fisheries and Conservation of the Living Resources of the High Seas
CFCs	chlorofluorocarbons
CFI	Court of First Instance
CIS	Commonwealth of Independent States
CITES	Convention on International Trade in Endangered Species
CLC	Convention on Civil Liability for Oil Pollution Damage
CMLR	*Common Market Law Review*
COP	Conference of the Parties
CPT	Committee for the Prevention of Torture and Inhuman or Degrading Treatment or Punishment
CSC	Continental Shelf Convention
CSCE	Conference on Security and Cooperation in Europe
DEA	Drug Enforcement Administration
DRC	Democratic Republic of the Congo
DSB	Dispute Settlement Body
DSU	Dispute Settlement Understanding

EAC	East African Community
EBRD	European Bank for Reconstruction and Development
EC	European Community
ECE	(United Nations) Economic Commission for Europe
ECJ	European Court of Justice
ECOMOG	Economic Community of West African States Monitoring Group
ECOSOC	Economic and Social Council
ECOWAS	Economic Community of West African States
ECSI	European Convention on State Immunity
ECtHR	European Court of Human Rights
EEC	European Economic Community
EEZ	Exclusive Economic Zone
EFZ	Exclusive Fishing Zone
EHRR	*European Human Rights Review*
EIA	Environmental Impact Assessment
EJIL	*European Journal of International Law*
EU	European Union
EUROFIMA	European Company for the Financing of Railroad Rolling Stock
FAO	Food and Agriculture Organization
FATF	Financial Action Task Force
FCCC	Framework Convention on Climate Change
FCN	Friendship, Commerce and Navigation (Treaties)
FCO	Foreign and Commonwealth Office
FGM	Female Genital Mutilation
FRY	Federal Republic of Yugoslavia
FSIA	Foreign Sovereign Immunities Act (US)
GA	General Assembly
GAB	General Agreements to Borrow
GATS	General Agreement on Trade in Services
GATT	General Agreement on Tariffs and Trade
GEF	Global Environmental Facility
HCHR	High Commissioner for Human Rights
HIPC	Heavily Indebted Poor Countries
HLPF	High-Level Political Forum
HRC	Human Rights Committee
HRLJ	*Human Rights Law Journal*
HSC	High Seas Convention
IAC	Iraqi Airways Company
IACHR	Inter-American Commission on Human Rights
IAEA	International Atomic Energy Authority
IBRD	International Bank for Reconstruction and Development (World Bank)
ICAO	International Civil Aviation Organization
ICBP	International Council for Bird Preservation
ICC	International Criminal Court
ICCPR	International Covenant on Civil and Political Rights
ICESCR	International Covenant on Economic, Social and Cultural Rights
ICISS	International Commission on Intervention and State Sovereignty
ICJ	International Court of Justice
ICLQ	*International and Comparative Law Quarterly*
ICOMOS	International Council on Monuments and Sites

ICRC	International Committee of the Red Cross
ICSID	International Centre for the Settlement of Investment Disputes
ICTR	International Criminal Tribunal for Rwanda
IDA	International Development Agency
IFAD	International Fund for Agricultural Development
IFC	International Finance Corporation
IGAD	Intergovernmental Authority on Development
IGO	Inter-Governmental Organization
IHL	International Humanitarian Law
IHRL	International Human Rights Law
IHRR	*International Human Rights Reports*
ILA	International Law Association
ILC	International Law Commission
ILM	International Legal Materials
ILO	International Labour Organization
ILR	International Law Reports
IMF	International Monetary Fund
IMO	International Maritime Organization
IMT	International Military Tribunal
IPCC	Intergovernmental Panel on Climate Change
Iran-USCTR	Iran-US Claims Tribunal Reports
ISA	International Seabed Authority
ITC	International Tin Council
ITLOS	International Tribunal for the Law of the Sea
ITO	International Trade Organization
ITTA	International Tropical Timber Agreement
ITU	International Telecommunications Union
IUCN	International Union for the Conservation of Nature
IWRB	International Waterfowl and Wetlands Research Bureau
KAC	Kuwait Airways Corporation
LMO	Living Modified Organism
LNTS	League of Nations Treaty Series
LOAC	Law of Armed Conflict
LOSC	Law of the Sea Convention
LRTAP	Long-Range Transboundary Air Pollution
MAI	Multilateral Agreement on Investment
MARPOL	International Convention for the Prevention of Pollution from Ships
MERCOSUR	Mercado Común del Sur or Mercado Común del Cono Sur
MIGA	Multilateral Investment Guarantee Agency
NAB	New Arrangements to Borrow
NAFO	North Atlantic Fisheries Organization
NAFTA	North American Free Trade Agreement
NAM	Non-Aligned Movement
NATO	North Atlantic Treaty Organization
NGOs	Non-Governmental Organizations
NLM	National Liberation Movement
NYBIL	*Netherlands Yearbook of International Law*
nyr	not yet reported
OAPEC	Organization of Arab Petroleum Exporting Countries
OAS	Organization of American States

OASTS	Organization of American States Treaty Series
OAU	Organization of African Unity
ODIL	*Ocean Development and International Law*
OECD	Organization for Economic Cooperation and Development
OECS	Organization of East Caribbean States
OEEC	Organization for European Economic Cooperation
ONUC	United Nations Operation in the Congo (Organisation des Nations Unies au Congo)
ONUCA	United Nations Observer Group in Central America
OPEC	Organization of Petroleum Exporting Countries
OPRC	Oil Pollution Preparedness and Response Convention
OSCE	Organization for Security and Cooperation in Europe
OSPAR	Convention for the Protection of the Marine Environment of the North-East Atlantic
PCIJ	Permanent Court of International Justice
PIC	Rotterdam Convention on Prior Informed Consent
PLO	Palestine Liberation Organization
PMSC	Private Military Security Company
POPs	Persistent Organic Pollutants
POW	Prisoner of War
PSI	Proliferation Security Initiative
R2P	Responsibility to Protect
Recueil des Cours	*Recueil des cours de l'Académie de droit international*
RFB	Regional Fisheries Body
RFMO	Regional Fisheries Management Organisation
RGDIP	*Revue General de Droit International Public*
RIAA	*Reports of International Arbitral Awards*
RSC	Rules of the Supreme Court (UK)
SADC	South African Development Community
SBDC	Sea-Bed Disputes Chamber
SC	Security Council
SCSL	Special Court for Sierra Leone
SDR	Special Drawing Rights
SFRY	Socialist Federal Republic of Yugoslavia
SIA	State Immunity Act 1978 (UK)
SPS	Sanitary and Phytosanitary Measures
SSA	Straddling Stocks Agreement
SSC	UN Agreement on Straddling Stocks and Highly Migratory Species
STL	Special Tribunal for Lebanon
SUA	Convention on the Suppression of Unlawful Acts Against the Safety of Maritime Navigation
TAC	Total Allowable Catch
TNCs	Transnational Corporations
TPRM	Trade Policy Review Mechanism
TRAFFIC	Trade Records Analysis of Flora and Fauna in Commerce
TRIMs	Trade-Related Investment Measures
TRIPS	Agreement on Trade-Related Aspects of Intellectual Property Rights
TSC	Territorial Sea and Contiguous Zone Convention
TWAIL	Third World Approaches to International Law

UAE	United Arab Emirates
UEMO	Union Economique et Monétaire Ouest-Africaine
UN	United Nations
UNAMIR	United Nations Assistance Mission for Rwanda
UNCAT	Convention against Torture and Other Cruel, Inhuman or Degrading Treatment or Punishment
UNCC	United Nations Compensation Commission
UNCITRAL	United Nations Commission on International Trade Law
UNCLOS	United Nations Conference on the Law of the Sea
UNCTAD	United Nations Conference on Trade and Development
UNDP	United Nations Development Programme
UNEF	United Nations Emergency Force
UNEP	United Nations Environment Programme
UNESCO	United Nations Educational, Scientific and Cultural Organization
UNGA	United Nations General Assembly
UNHCR	United Nations High Commissioner for Refugees
UNICEF	United Nations International Children's Economic Foundation
UNIDO	United Nations Industrial Development Organization
UNITA	União Nacional para a Independência Total de Angola
UNMIK	United Nations Mission in Kosovo
UNOSOM	United Nations Operation in Somalia
UNPROFOR	United Nations Protection Force
UNTAET	United Nations Transitional Administration in East Timor
UNTS	United Nations Treaty Series
UNYB	*United Nations Yearbook*
UPU	Universal Postal Union
VCCR	Vienna Convention on Consular Relations
VCDR	Vienna Convention on Diplomatic Relations
VCLT	Vienna Convention on the Law of Treaties
WEOG	Western Europe and Others Group (Nations)
WHC	World Heritage Convention
WHO	World Health Organization
WIPO	World Intellectual Property Organization
WMD	Weapons of Mass Destruction
WMO	World Meteorological Organization
WTO	World Trade Organization
WWF	World Wildlife Fund
YBIEL	*Yearbook of International Environmental Law*
YBILC	*Yearbook of the International Law Commission*
YIHL	*Yearbook of International Humanitarian Law*

TABLE OF INTERNATIONAL CASES

ETHIOPIA-ERITREA CLAIMS COMMISSION

EUROPEAN COURT OF HUMAN RIGHTS

EUROPEAN COURT OF JUSTICE

WTO/GATT

TABLE OF DOMESTIC
CASES BY COUNTRY

TABLE OF INTERNATIONAL INSTRUMENTS AND OTHER DOCUMENTS

TABLE OF DOMESTIC INSTRUMENTS BY COUNTRY

Statutory Instruments

UNITED STATES

PART I

THE HISTORY
AND THEORY OF
INTERNATIONAL LAW

A SHORT HISTORY OF INTERNATIONAL LAW

Stephen C Neff

SUMMARY

This history will emphasize broad trends in international law, both in the conceptual sphere and in State practice. The discussion will move chronologically, beginning with a cursory look at the ancient world, followed by a rather fuller discussion of the great era of natural law in the European Middle Ages. The classical period (1600–1815) witnessed the emergence of a dualistic view of international law, with the law of nature and the law of nations co-existing (more or less amicably). In the nineteenth century—the least known part of international law—doctrinaire positivism was the prevailing viewpoint, though not the exclusive one. Regarding the inter-war years, developments both inside and outside the League of Nations will be considered. Since the post-1945 period will occupy most of the remainder of this book, this discussion will confine itself to a few historically oriented comments on some of its most general features.

I. INTRODUCTION

It is pleasing to note that the scandalous neglect of the history of international law, which prevailed for so long, has, at long last, begun to be redressed in a significant fashion. There are now, for example, two journals dedicated to the subject. In addition, a series of important monographs have been published in Germany, beginning in 2001. In 2011, a series of 'Studies in the History of International Law' was launched by Brill. In keeping with the tempo of modern technology, there are also two websites devoted to the subject.[1] It may be too early to proclaim the onset of a Renaissance—or, more accurately, a 'naissance'—and there are many large areas yet to be thoroughly explored. But there is no doubt that optimism is in the air and that the future looks brighter than ever.

This short history—inevitably very short history—can give only the most general flavour of the major periods of development of international law. It will accordingly not be possible to give more than the most token attention to developments outside the Western mainstream. Both ideas and State practice will be covered. The ideas chiefly concern what international law was thought to consist of in past times. State practice is concerned with what States actually did. It was the two in combination—if not always in close harmony—that made international law what it became.

---

[1] For a time-line approach to the subject, see http://www.tiki-toki.com/timeline/entry/459289/The-History-of-International-Law/. For a more academic perspective, see the site administered by Tilburg University, at: https://www.tilburguniversity.edu/research/institutes-and-research-groups/i-hilt/.

II. ANCIENT WORLDS

For a vivid indication of how persons from even the most diverse cultures can relate to one another in a peaceful, predictable, and mutually beneficial fashion, it is difficult to top Herodotus's description of 'silent trading' between the Carthaginians and an unnamed North African tribe in about the sixth century BC. When the Carthaginians arrived in the tribe's area by ship, they would unload a pile of goods from their vessels, leave them on the beach, and then return to their boats and send a smoke signal. The natives would then come and inspect the goods on their own, leave a pile of gold, and retire. Then the Carthaginians would return; and, if satisfied that the gold represented a fair price, they would take it and depart. If not satisfied, they would again retire to their ships; and the natives would return to leave more gold. The process would continue until both sides were content, at which the point the Carthaginians would sail away with their gold, without a word exchanged between the two groups. 'There is perfect honesty on both sides', Herodotus assures us, with no problems of theft or conflict (Herodotus, *Histories*, p 336).

This silent trading arrangement may have been successful in its way, but a process of interaction so inflexibly ritualistic and so narrow in subject matter could hardly suffice for political interactions between States, even in ancient times. Most people probably have the feeling that something rather more elaborate is required to merit the grand name of 'international law'. Indeed, the ambiguity of the term 'international law' leads to various different answers to the question of when international law 'began'. If by 'international law' is meant merely the ensemble of methods or devices which give an element of predictability to international relations (as in the silent-trading illustration), then the origin may be placed virtually as far back as recorded history itself. If by 'international law' is meant a more or less comprehensive substantive code of conduct applying to nations, then the late classical period and Middle Ages was the time of its birth. If 'international law' is taken to mean a set of substantive principles applying uniquely to States as such, then the seventeenth century would be the starting time. If 'international law' is defined as the integration of the world at large into something like a single community under a rule of law, then the nineteenth century would be the earliest date (perhaps a trifle optimistically). If, finally, 'international law' is understood to mean the enactments and judicial decisions of a world government, then its birth lies (if at all) somewhere in the future—and, in all likelihood, the distant future at that.

If we take the most restricted of these definitions, then we could expect to find the best evidence for a nascent international law in the three areas of ancient Eurasia that were characterized by dense networks of small, independent States sharing a more or less common religious and cultural value system: Mesopotamia (by, say, the fourth or third millennium BC), northern India (in the Vedic period after about 1600 BC), and classical Greece. Each of these three State systems was characterized by a combination of political fragmentation and cultural unity. This enabled a number of fairly standard practices to emerge, which helped to place inter-State relations on at least a somewhat stable and predictable footing. Three particular areas provide evidence of this development: diplomatic relations, treaty-making, and the conduct of war.[2] A major additional contribution of the Greek city-States was the practice of arbitration of disputes, of which there came to be a very impressive body of practice (Ager, 1996).

It was not inordinately difficult for some of these practices to extend across deeper cultural lines as well. The earliest surviving complete treaty text is between Egypt and the

[2] On the Middle Eastern and Greek practice, see generally Bederman, 2001. On ancient India, see Bhatia, 1977.

Hittite Empire, from the thirteenth century BC. The agreement concerned an imperial division of spheres of influence, but it also dealt with the extradition of fugitives. The problem of good faith and binding force was ensured by enlisting the gods of both nations (two thousand strong in all) to act as guardians (Bederman, 2001, pp 147–50).

With the advent of the great universal religions, far more broadly based systems of world order became possible. One outstanding example was the Islamic empire of the seventh century AD and afterwards. Significantly, the body of law on relations between States within the Muslim world (the Dar al-Islam, or 'House of Islam') was much richer than that regarding relations with the outside world (the Dar al-Harb, or 'House of war'). But even with infidel States and nationals, a number of pragmatic devices evolved to permit relations to occur in predictable ways—such as 'temporary' truces (in lieu of treaties) or safe-conducts issued to individuals (sometimes on a very large scale).[3]

In Western history, the supreme exemplar of the multinational empire was Rome. But the Roman Empire was, in its formative period, a somewhat tentative and ramshackle affair, without an over-arching ethical or religious basis comparable to the Islamic religion in the later Arab empire. That began to change, however, when certain philosophical concepts were imported from Greece (from about the second century BC). The most important of these was the idea of a set of universal principles of justice: the belief that, amidst the welter of varying laws of different States, certain substantive rules of conduct were present in all human societies. This idea first surfaced in the writings of Aristotle (*Rhetoric*, p 1370). But it was taken much further by the philosophers of the Stoic school, who envisaged the entire world as a single 'world city-State' (or *kosmopolis*) governed by the law of nature. Cicero, writing under Stoic influence, characterized this law of nature as being 'spread through the whole human community, unchanging and eternal' (Cicero, *Republic*, pp 68–9).

This concept of a universal and eternal natural law was later adopted by two other groups, the Roman lawyers and the Christian Church, and then bequeathed by them to medieval Europe. The lawyers in particular made a distinction that would have a very long life ahead of it: between a *jus naturale* (or natural law properly speaking) and a *jus gentium* (or law of peoples). The two were distinct, but at the same time so closely interconnected that the differences between them were often very easily ignored. Natural law was the broader concept. It was something like what we would now call a body of scientific laws, applicable not just to human beings but to the whole animal kingdom as well. The *jus gentium* was the human component, or sub-category, of it. Just as the law of nature was universal in the natural world, so was the *jus gentium* universal in the human world.

III. THE MIDDLE AGES: THE NATURAL LAW ERA

The European Middle Ages offers an intriguing picture of dizzying variety and complexity, combined—not always very coherently—with the most sweeping universality. The variety was most apparent in the de-centralized world of feudalism, with its complex and interlocking layers of rights and duties, and its diffusion of governmental powers and jurisdictions. The universality was evident in two major spheres: philosophically and jurisprudentially, in the continued stress on natural law; and politically, in the Holy Roman Empire and in the revival of Roman law which underpinned it.

---

[3] On Islamic views of international law, see generally Khadduri, 1955; and Allain, 2011, pp 394–407.

A. THE UNIVERSALIST OUTLOOK: MEDIEVAL NATURAL LAW

During the Middle Ages, natural-law conceptions, inherited from the classical world, developed under the umbrella of the Catholic Church. But it must be remembered that natural law was not Christian in its inception, but rather was a legacy of the ancient Stoic and Roman legal traditions. The dominant approach—represented outstandingly by Thomas Aquinas—was rationalist in outlook, holding the content of the natural law to be susceptible of discovery and application by means of human reason rather than of revelation.

Natural law is one of the many parts of international law that have never received the systematic study that they merit. In the present context, only a few of its most salient characteristics can be noted.[4] Perhaps its single most outstanding feature was its all-embracing character. It encompassed and regulated the natural and social life of the universe in all its infinite variety—from the movements of the stars in their courses to the gurgling of the four humours through the veins and arteries of the human body, from the thoughts and deeds of all of the creatures of land, sea, and air, to those of human beings and the angels in the heavens. Its strictures applied universally to all cultures and civilizations, past, present, and future.

There continued to be, as in the ancient period, a distinction between the *jus naturale* and the *jus gentium*, though still without any very sharp line between the two. The *jus gentium* was much the lesser of the two. Sometimes it was seen as the detailed application of general principles to the specific conditions of everyday life. Sometimes it was seen as a sort of secondary or 'watered-down' version of natural law, applicable to a frail humanity in its current corrupt and sinful condition. As such, it dealt with such matters as the resort to force. In fact, its most conspicuous achievement was the development of the doctrine concerning just wars, which basically allowed the taking of arms, as a last resort, for the vindication of legal rights.[5]

It must be stressed that this medieval *jus gentium* did not consist entirely, or even primarily, of what would now be called rules of international law. Instead, it was a collection of laws common to all nations, dealing with all aspects of human social affairs—contract, property, crime, and the like. It was more in the nature of an ethical system of universal or trans-cultural scope. Rulers were subject to the strictures of both natural law and the *jus gentium*—but so were private individuals.

B. THE PLURALIST OUTLOOK: THE ITALIAN CITY-STATES

Even if (as the natural-law writers maintained) the whole of human society formed a single moral and ethical community, there was no denying that the world also consisted of a welter of different polities of widely varying degrees of importance—extending all the way from the great empire of Rome itself (ie of Byzantium) to the patchwork of feudal jurisdictions which carpeted Western Europe.

Nowhere was the tension between the universalistic and the pluralistic tendencies of the period more evident, in practice, than in the debates over the legal status of the various 'independent' city-states of northern Italy. These obtained substantial de facto independence from the Holy Roman Empire in the late twelfth century, when the cities of the Lombard League defeated the forces of Emperor Frederick I. There was, however, considerable debate over what this 'independence' really meant. To this conundrum, two of the most prominent medieval lawyers—Bartolus of Sassoferato and his student Baldus of Ubaldis, who both

---

[4] For a good short account of medieval natural-law theory, see generally Gierke, 1938.
[5] For a thorough exposition of medieval just-war theory, see Russell, 1975.

wrote in the fourteenth century—turned their attention. Broadly speaking, the conclusion of Bartolus (largely echoed by Baldus) was that the cities were independent in the sense of being wholly self-governing and independent of one another, but that, in their relations inter se, they continued to be subject to rules of the Empire. Here we see the first glimmer, in European society, of the concept of independence of States operating in conjunction—sometimes very uneasily—with subjection to a larger set of norms governing inter-State relations (Hinsley, 1986, pp 81–2, 88–90, 167–74). For this reason, Bartolus has been called, with some justice, the first theorist of international law (Sereni, 1943, pp 58–63).

C. DEVELOPMENTS IN STATE PRACTICE

It is from the pluralist rather than the universalist side of the great medieval conceptual divide that we must look for innovations in State practice. The reason is easily seen: it is in the day-to-day relation of different States and peoples with one another that the practical problems of law are most likely to arise.

Much of the State practice in the Middle Ages consisted of traditional ways inherited from ancient times. The area of diplomatic relations is an example, with diplomats increasingly being accorded a broad (but not absolute) degree of immunity from judicial process in host States. Beginning in about the eleventh century, European (chiefly Italian) States began to conclude bilateral treaties that spelled out various reciprocal guarantees of fair treatment. These agreements, sometimes concluded with Muslim States, granted a range of privileges to the foreign merchants based in the contracting States, such as the right to use their own law and courts when dealing with one another.

The same process was at work in the sphere of maritime trading. The seafaring community made use of the laws of Oléron (which were actually a series of court decisions from the small island of that name in the Bay of Biscay), and also of a code of rules called the Consolato del Mare, compiled in about the thirteenth century for the maritime community of Barcelona. These codes governed the broad range of maritime activities, including the earliest rules on the rights of neutral traders in wartime.

Certain aspects of the conduct of war witnessed a high level of refinement in the Middle Ages—most notably the law on the ransoming of prisoners of war (a welcome step forward from the alternatives of enslavement and summary killing (Ambühl, 2013)). 'The law of arms' (as it was known) was expounded in the fourteenth century, first by John of Legnano and later by a monk named Honoré de Bonet (or Bouvet), whose book entitled *The Tree of Battles*, of the 1380s, became very influential.[6] Accounts of medieval warfare, however, incline observers to harbour grave doubts as to whether even these practical rules exerted much real influence.

With the European explorations of Africa and, particularly, the New World from the fourteenth century onward, questions of relations with non-European societies assumed an urgent importance—while at the same time posing an immense practical test for the universality of natural law. The Spanish conquest of the Indian kingdoms in the New World sparked especially vigorous legal and moral debates (if only after the fact). The Dominican scholar, Francisco de Vitoria, in a series of lectures at the University of Salamanca delivered in 1539, concluded that the Spanish conquest was justified, on the ground that the Indians had unlawfully attempted to exclude Spanish traders from their kingdoms, contrary to natural-law rules. But he also confessed that his blood froze in his veins at the thought of the terrible atrocities committed by the Spanish in the process.[7]

---

[6] On medieval law on the conduct of war, see Keen, 1965.
[7] Vitoria, Letter to Miguel de Arcos, in *Political Writings*, pp 331–3.

In 1550–51, there occurred one of the major legal confrontations of history, when two prominent figures—Juan Inés de Sepúlveda and Barolomé de las Casas—debated, at length, the lawfulness and legal bases of the Spanish conquests in the New World, under the judgeship of the theologian and philosopher Domingo de Soto. The result, alas, was inconclusive, as Soto declined to render a judgment (Pagden, 2001, pp 77–9).

In short, medieval international law was a jumble of different beliefs and practices—from the rarefied conceptions of the law of nature, to the more serviceable rules by which various communities conducted their actual day-to-day business, from warfare and diplomacy, to buying and selling.

IV. THE CLASSICAL AGE (1600–1815)

In the seventeenth and eighteenth centuries, a new spirit entered into doctrinal thought on international law. This is sometimes put in terms of a secularization of natural-law thought. That, however, is a very misleading characterization, since natural law itself was (and had always been) primarily secular in nature. What was new in the seventeenth century was something quite different: the making of a clear and sharp distinction, for the first time, between the *jus gentium* (or law of nations) and natural law (the law of nature). International law was seen as a kind of alliance or confederation between these two bodies of law, which were now seen as conceptually quite distinct from one another.

The leading figure in the making of this distinction was the Spanish Jesuit writer Francisco Suárez, in a *Treatise on Laws and God the Lawgiver*, published in 1612. The distinction was basically a simple one. The law of nature is universal and eternal. Its basis is reason. Humans did not make this law, but they can apply their gift of rationality to discern its content. The law of nations, in contrast (ie the *jus gentium*), was seen as a purely human creation, a product of human will and initiative. As such, it is subject to alteration from time to time and can vary from place to place. In addition, it is a law that is created by, and is applicable to, relations between States. This law of nations was, in short, international law in our modern sense of that term.

It should be appreciated, though, that international relations were seen to be regulated by both the law of nations and the law of nature. Moreover, the two bodies of law, although conceptually distinct, were seen as operating in close alliance with one another, with natural law at the foundation of the *jus gentium*. The *jus gentium* could depart from natural law in certain respects. It could, for example, permit certain things that natural law forbade—though only in the restricted sense that it could refrain from inflicting punishments of natural-law principles. Illustrations included the capture of private property in wartime and the taking of reprisals. The *jus gentium* could not, however, actually alter the content of natural law.

A. GROTIUS AND HOBBES

If Suárez was the principal innovator of this new way of looking at international law, its best-known expositor was the Dutch writer Hugo Grotius, whose major work *On the Law of War and Peace* was published in Paris in 1625—a work so dense and rich that one could easily spend a lifetime studying it (as a number of scholars have).[8] Grotius's principal

---

[8] Much of the study of Grotius has been by political scientists rather than specifically by international lawyers. For the standard modern biography of Grotius, see Nellen, 2015. For a brief overview of Grotius's legal thought, see Tuck, 1999, pp 78–108. For a more thorough study, see Haggenmacher, 1983.

purpose in this work was to apply the principles of natural law to international affairs. But in the course of his book, he also pointed out many applications of the law of nations as well. Grotius sometimes referred to this as the 'voluntary' law, to emphasize its origin as an expression of human will.

Grotius's writing was hugely influential in European thought for many centuries. As recently as 2008, his authority was invoked by the World Court.[9] Lawyers following his lead—or actually Suárez's lead—became known as 'Grotians'. Sometimes they were called 'eclectics' to reflect the single most outstanding, or defining, feature of the Grotian approach: its dualistic outlook, ie its insistence on international law as a combination of the law of nature and the law of nations. Indeed, the expression 'law of nature and nations' was a common shorthand in the seventeenth and eighteenth centuries for what would later be called simply 'international law'.

The Grotian, or dualistic, view of international law did not go unchallenged. A rival school known as the 'naturalists' rejected the dualistic stance, insisting instead that relations between States are governed exclusively by natural law. The so-called law of nations was asserted to be merely usage, without binding legal force. The leading figure in the naturalist tradition was the English writer Thomas Hobbes, whose master work *Leviathan* was written in 1651, shortly after Grotius's death.

In his writing, Hobbes advanced a picture of natural law, and of the state of nature in which it prevailed, that was radically at odds with that of Grotius and his medieval forebears. Grotius and his followers had regarded the pre-political condition of human society as orderly and law-governed (governed, that is, by natural law). Hobbes, in contrast, saw the pre-political state of nature as a chaotic, even violent, world. Natural law did govern this woeful scene; but natural law was seen to consist, in effect, of a single fundamental right and a single fundamental duty. The right was the right of self-preservation (Hobbes, *Leviathan*, pp 80–4). The duty was the obligation to carry out contracts voluntarily entered into. This obligation to adhere to contracts provided a means of bringing some semblance of order to the primordial chaos of the state of nature. This was the means by which political societies, with well-defined rights and duties, could be brought into being—by way of Hobbes's famous social contract.

Between independent States, however, there was no social contract and no single political society. States, in short, continued to live in a state of nature vis-à-vis one another. But the duty to adhere to contracts still held, and it could enable at least a modicum of order and predictability to emerge. In areas where States had common interests, treaty relations would be feasible. But the Hobbesians, or naturalists, denied that the general customary practices of States could have any such legal force. Only explicit arrangements, consciously and voluntarily assumed by States, could be legally binding (Neff, 2014, pp 166–78).

From a modern vantage point, the divide between the Grotians and the naturalists is not so easily discerned. The reason is that most of the naturalists held a view of natural law that was nearer to Grotius than to Hobbes. The outstanding example is the German natural-law writer Samuel Pufendorf.[10] He had the highest regard for Grotius's ideas about natural law, while firmly denying the validity of the so-called law of nations or customary law. The effect was that the Grotians and the naturalists, in combination, developed and elaborated natural-law thought to an extent far beyond anything that their medieval ancestors had dreamt of. This period became, veritably, the golden age of natural-law thought (or systematic jurisprudence, as it was sometimes termed).

[9] *Sovereignty over Pedra Branca/Pulau Batu Puteh (Malaysia/Singapore), Judgment, ICJ Reports 2008*, p 12, para 53. [10] See generally Samuel Pufendorf, 1934.

The culmination of this systematic natural-law movement came in the mid-eighteenth century, at the hands of the German philosopher Christian Wolff, who fittingly had been trained as a mathematician. He wrote on a number of subjects, including psychology (a term which he popularized) and cosmology (contributing a discourse on the characteristics of the inhabitants of other planets).[11] Prominent in his work was a massive eight-volume treatise on natural law. A supplemental ninth volume treated international law, though entirely through the lens of natural law, with scarcely any attention to State practice. It holds an honourable place on the list of the world's great unread masterpieces.[12]

The most famous and influential writer in the Grotian tradition was the Swiss diplomat Emmerich de Vattel, whose famous exposition of *The Law of Nations* was published in London in 1758. As the first systematic international-law treatise of the modern kind, it would not look drastically out of place on a twenty-first century bookshelf, as the works of Grotius or Wolff certainly would. Instead of setting out a grand philosophical scheme, Vattel's intention was to provide a sort of handbook for lawyers and statesmen. Moreover, its graceful style ensured it a wider usage by lawyers, judges, and lay persons than any other international writing had previously had. It can make a good claim to being the greatest international-law textbook ever written. With it, we stand at the threshold of modern international-law writing.[13]

In a number of ways, Vattel's treatise was a popularization of Wolff's ideas, but it was written in a very different spirit. Where Wolff had been disdainful of the voluntary law, Vattel fully embraced it, cheerfully and candidly expounding it alongside the natural law whenever appropriate. He has been accused of inconsistency—of constantly being on both sides of issues—but that charge is unfair. The fact is that he had two bodies of law to expound, which sometimes provided differing solutions to practical problems. He was generally very forthright about which law he was treating at any given time. It is we who tend to misunderstand the nature of his task because the dualistic mentality of that era is so foreign to us.

The best example of the dualistic 'method' concerned war. The natural law on just wars allowed a State to resort to force in self-help to vindicate a legal right that had actually been violated (or was threatened with violation)—so that, in a given conflict, one side would be fighting justly, and the other one not. The voluntary law, however, was not concerned over which party had the stronger legal claim to use force (ie it did not deal with the *jus ad bellum*, in legal terminology). Instead, it simply treated each side *as if* it had lawfully resorted to war. It then contented itself with regulating the conduct of wars, fixing rules for both parties to apply, on an even-handed basis, in their contention against one another (the *jus in bello*, in the common legal parlance). In effect, then, the natural law saw war in terms of law enforcement and as a sanction for wrongdoing, while the voluntary law, in contrast, saw war more in terms of a duel.

B. THE LAWS OF NATURE AND NATIONS IN ACTION

The writing of Grotius and Hobbes and their followers was not done in a vacuum. Various forces were at work in this period, which served to give this new law of nations a concrete reality. One of the most important of these trends was the emergence (gradual to be sure) of strong central governments, at least in Western Europe, which increasingly gained the upper hand over the older, diffused jurisdictions of the feudal age. Particularly important

---

[11] For Wolff's cosmological views, see Wolff, 1737.   [12] See generally Christian Wolff, 1934.
[13] On Vattel, see generally Jouannet, 1998.

for this trend was the innovation of standing armies in place of the older temporary feudal levies. In addition, these centralizing nation-States were coming to be seen as permanently existing, corporate entities in their own right, separate from the rulers who governed them at any given time—with long-term interests and political agendas of their own.

At least some of the flavour of the medieval natural law survived, however, chiefly in the form of the idea of the existence of something that has come to be called the 'community of States'. The clearest symbol of this was the peace settlement arrived at in Westphalia in 1648, at the conclusion of the Thirty Years War in Germany. It is curious that something called the 'Westphalian system' is sometimes spoken of as a synonym of anarchy or of radical views of absolute State sovereignty—conceptions which actually belong (as will be seen) to the nineteenth century and not to the seventeenth.[14] In reality, the Westphalian settlement was an arrangement reached within the framework of the Holy Roman Empire, with certain prerogatives of the imperial government carefully preserved—ie with the older medieval idea of 'independent' States being subject, at the same time, to certain higher norms. The Peace of Westphalia did, however, provide a sort of template for later times in the way in which it marked out a division of labour (so to speak) between national and international spheres, placing religion carefully in the realm of domestic law.

The idea of a community of States—distinct from, but also analogous to, a community of individual persons—was apparent in sundry other ways in the seventeenth and eighteenth centuries. One of these was in the concept of a balance of power. This was hardly an altogether new idea, but in this period it attained a formal articulation and recognition that it had never had before (most conspicuously in the Peace of Utrecht in 1713, at the conclusion of the War of the Spanish Succession). In conjunction with this concept, the period was one of limited—though also of frequent—warfare. At least in Western Europe, war was largely conducted with trained professional forces, and for limited ends. As a result, European diplomacy bore more resemblance to a meticulous game of chess than to a lurid Hobbesian inferno of mayhem and turmoil. Even warfare often had a ritualistic air, with its emphasis on manoeuvre and siege rather than on pitched battle.

Economic relations manifested much this same combination of cooperation and competitiveness. On the competitive side, this period marked the high tide of mercantilism, with its intense rivalry for trade advantage. But there was also a high degree of cooperation, under an ever-strengthening rule of law, chiefly in the form of a network of treaties of friendship, commerce, and navigation (FCN treaties in the standard legal jargon), which provided a range of safeguards for merchants operating in and trading with foreign countries.

V. THE NINETEENTH CENTURY (1815–1919)

The nineteenth century, extraordinarily, is the least explored area of the history of international law. Its outstanding feature was the rise to dominance of the legal philosophy known as positivism. This conferred onto international law a scientific gloss—or alternatively, in the opinion of some, tied it into a narrow strait-jacket. But positivism did not, or not quite, have the century to itself. A new tendency known as the historical school of law made some important contributions; and natural law, against heavy odds, managed to survive, although in new and unexpected ways.

---

[14] See, for example, the discussion of the 'logic of Westphalia' in Falk, 1975, pp 59–69.

A. 'THE PUBLIC LAW AND SYSTEM OF EUROPE'

With the definitive defeat of revolutionary and imperial France in 1815, the victorious European powers (Britain, Prussia, Russia, and Austria) crafted a new kind of peace settlement, based not merely on the balance of material power between the major States but also on a set of general principles of a more substantive character. These general principles were, to be sure, of a decidedly conservative character. The goal was to craft a continent-wide set of political arrangements that would (they hoped) keep the scourge of revolution from breaking out again.

The peace settlement was to be policed by the major powers—who were, of course, self-appointed to the task—by way of military intervention where necessary. The powers even had a grand name for their enterprise: the 'public law and system of Europe'. This legal order was based on faithful adherence to treaty commitments, together with respect for established laws and legitimate governments and property rights within the States of Europe. But it also included a duty on the part of rulers to 'earn' their legitimacy by providing responsible and efficient government to their peoples and also by cooperating with movements for orderly and peaceful change.

A few of these interventions by the Concert of Europe may be noted briefly. The first ones were in the cause of 'legitimacy' in the 1820s, when there were military interventions to subdue revolutions in Naples and Sardinia (by Austria) and in Spain (by France). Also in the 1820s, the intervention of Britain, France, and Russia in the Greek independence struggle led to independence for the Kingdom of Greece. Great-power involvement similarly led to Belgian independence in the 1830s. Sometimes the powers intervened diplomatically in post-war peace settlements, if the terms imposed on the losing side looked to be too destabilizing for the continent as a whole. This occurred in 1878, when the major powers stepped in to prevent Russia from exacting too harsh a peace against Turkey after a victorious war.

On at least some of these occasions, humanitarian considerations played a part, alongside the more usual political jockeying. The most common cause for concern on this front was the relief of Christian populations that were held to be victims of oppression in the Ottoman Empire. This was certainly one of the motivations for Greek intervention in the 1820s. In 1860, the powers intervened in a communal-violence crisis in the Mount Lebanon area. The most forceful of these great-power humanitarian actions was probably the one in Crete in 1897, when the powers stepped in to stop atrocities and counter-atrocities between Greeks and Turks. In virtually none of these cases was there a pure humanitarian motive, untouched by any other considerations. But some (arguable) precedents were established for later advocates of the lawfulness of humanitarian intervention.

The Concert of Europe 'system' (if it could really be called that) was overtly hegemonic, in modern parlance. There was little sign of any principle of equality of States. Still, the Concert of Europe did at least provide an ideal—if not always the reality—of collective, orchestrated State action for the preservation of international peace. To that extent, it fore-shadowed the post-1945 United Nations. International lawyers, however, never gave it much attention.[15] Instead, their ambitions were directed to another end: to unshackling international law from its natural-law heritage and making it something like a science in the modern sense of that term.

---

[15] For one of the few legal texts to treat this subject, see Dupuis, 1909. See also Simpson, 2004, which devotes considerable attention to the policing practices of the major powers in the nineteenth century.

B. THE POSITIVIST REVOLUTION

On the conceptual front, the major feature of the nineteenth century was the dominant role of positivism. The expression 'positive law' had been in use since the Middle Ages (since at least the fourteenth century) to refer to the man-made law of particular States, in contrast to divine law (ie the commands of God) or natural law. What was new in the nineteenth century, however, was something called a 'positive philosophy', the chief propounder of which was the French social philosopher Auguste Comte. By 'positive', Comte meant something like 'scientific' or 'objective' or 'empirical', in contrast to speculative or religious modes of thought. His new approach stood for the resolute rejection of deductive reasoning from a priori axioms, in favour of empirical, observational, and experimental methods.

Regarding the broader sweep of global history, Comte maintained that the human race had gone through three great historical stages: the theological, the metaphysical, and (now) the 'positive'. In the theological stage, religious ideas had been dominant. In the metaphysical stage, legalistic and jurisprudential thinking had prevailed—meaning, in essence, natural law. But the third age—the 'positive' era (as Comte called it)—was now dawning, promising the true and final liberation of the human mind from the superstitions and dogmas of the past.

In its original form, positivism envisaged the emergence of a sort of technocratic utopia, in which the world would be governed not by clerics or politicians or lawyers (as in the past benighted ages of theology and metaphysics), but rather by engineers and industrialists and financiers. This vision had first been put forward by the eccentric French nobleman, the Comte de St-Simon, in the early nineteenth century.[16] (Auguste Comte's early career, incidentally, included service as St-Simon's secretary.) This early vision, taken to its logical conclusion, envisaged the obsolescence of the nation-State.

This original positivism of St-Simon and Comte was a strange amalgam of technocracy and evangelism. Indeed, positivism actually did become a 'religion of humanity', which had its greatest impact in Brazil (whose national flag is emblazoned with the positivist motto 'Order and Progress'). Not surprisingly, lawyers turned the positive philosophy in a somewhat different direction.

1. The positive philosophy applied to international law

In terms of international law, positivism represented a great ambition: to make international law into a true science, in the image of the natural sciences. That meant that international law must cease to be an expression of how the world should be and become instead an expression of how the world actually is. As such, this new science of international law was—again in the image of the natural sciences—to be value-free, meaning that it was to be a rigorously objective picture of the legal world as it actually was. Evidence of the content of law was to be gathered not from the wispy speculations of philosophers but rather from a close inspection of the actual practice of States—just as chemists and physicists engaged in careful observation and experimentation in order to determine the laws that govern the natural world. Postivism, in short, promoted a rigorously objective and deterministic view of law, ruthlessly shorn of religious and moral and philosophical dogmas.

All of this meant, of course, the rejection of natural law as the basis of international law. Natural law could still be important as an inspiration to law-makers, but it was not accepted by positivist writers as being legally binding in its own right. Stated in modern terminology, it would be said that natural law could be accepted by a positivist as a *material* source of law but not (or no longer) as a *formal* source of law, binding in its own right.

---

[16] On St-Simonism, see generally Manuel, 1956.

Positivism was not a single, monolithic school of thought. It came in three principal versions (which have never received widely known labels) (Neff, 2014, pp 222–43). One of these could be called 'empiricist' because of its belief that the content of law is to be induced from State practice, with customary law as the leading form of international law.[17] A second approach could be called the 'common-will' variant, which emphasized treaties as the primary form of international law. A third approach could be called (with caution) 'voluntarist', since it insisted on voluntary self-restraint by States as the source of international law. What is often called 'positivism' was actually a rather untidy mélange of these three streams of thought (Neff, 2014, pp 243–59). In the present context, only a few of the most salient features of this mélange can be highlighted.

One of the most central aspects of positivism was its close attention to questions of the sources of international law—and, in particular, to the proposition that international law is, fundamentally, an outgrowth or feature of the will of the States of the world. Rules of law are created by the States themselves, by consent, whether express (in written treaties) or tacit (in the form of custom). International law was therefore now seen as the sum total, or aggregation, of agreements which the States of the world happen to have arrived at, at any given time. In a phrase that became proverbial amongst positivists, international law must now be seen as a law *between* States and not as a law *above* States.

International law, in other words, was now regarded as a corpus of rules arising from, as it were, the bottom up, as the conscious creation of the States themselves, rather than as a pre-existing, eternal, all-enveloping framework, in the manner of the old natural law. As a consequence, the notion of a systematic, all-encompassing body of law—so striking a feature of natural law—was now discarded. International law was now seen as, so to speak, a world of fragments, an accumulation of specific, agreed rules, rather than as a single coherent picture. In any area where agreement between States happened to be lacking, international law was, perforce, silent.

Another important effect of positivism was to replace the older, medieval, teleological picture with what might be termed an instrumentalist outlook. That is to say, the law was no longer seen as having any innate goal of its own, or as reflecting any universal master plan. Instead, the law was now regarded, in technocratic terms, as a means for the attainment of goals which were decided on by political processes. Law, in short, was now seen as a servant and not as a master. It was to be a tool for practical workmen rather than a roadmap to eternal salvation.

Closely allied to the consent-based view of international law was the firm insistence of most positivists on the centrality of the State as the principal (or even the sole) subject of international law, ie as the exclusive bearer of rights and duties on the international plane. States were now perceived as possessing what came to be called 'international personality'—and, crucially, as also possessing a set of fundamental rights that must be protected at all times. Foremost of these fundamental rights was the right of survival or self-preservation. This meant that, in emergency situations, States are entitled to take action that would otherwise be contrary to law.

The most dramatic illustration of this point in the nineteenth century occurred in 1837, when the British government, faced with an insurgency in Canada, sent troops into the United States, in pursuit of insurgents who were using that country's territory as a safe haven. They succeeded in capturing the miscreants, killing several persons in the process and destroying a boat named the *Caroline*. The United States vigorously objected to this armed incursion into its territory. Britain justified its action as self-defence. The diplomatic correspondence between the two countries in this dispute produced the classic exposition

---

[17] For a classic exposition of the empiricist variant of positivism, see Oppenheim, 1908.

of the principle of self-defence: action in the face of a crisis that is 'instant, overwhelming, leaving no choice of means, and no moment for deliberation'.[18] This remains today as the canonical statement of the criteria for the exercise by States of self-defence (although it really was a statement of the general principle of necessity rather than of self-defence per se).

The stress on the basic rights of States also gave to positivism a strongly pluralistic cast. Each nation-State possessed its own distinctive set of national interests, which it was striving to achieve in an inherently competitive, even hostile, environment. Each State was sovereign within its territory. And each State's domestic law could reflect that country's own particular history, values, aspirations, traditions, and so forth. It was in this period that the principle of 'the sovereign equality of States' became the fundamental cornerstone—or even the central dogma—of international law, along with the concomitant rule of non-intervention of States into the internal affairs of one another.

A final point is in order concerning the technocratic outlook of positivism. This had the important effect of de-politicizing international law, at least in principle. International lawyers in the nineteenth century became increasingly reluctant to trespass into areas of political controversy. In this regard, they presented a sharp contrast to their natural-law forebears, who had proudly worn the mantle of the social critic. The positivist lawyers were more inclined to see themselves instead as the juridical counterparts of Comte's engineers. In particular, it came to be widely agreed that fundamental national-security interests were questions of politics and not of law—a distinction that Grotius and Vattel would have found difficult to grasp. By the same token, positivism had a strongly non-moralistic flavour.

Nowhere were these features more important than on the subject of war. Positivists tended to regard the rights and wrongs of a State's decision to resort to war as a political rather than a legal issue. They saw war as an inevitable and permanent feature of the inter-State system, in much the way that friction is an inevitable and permanent feature of a mechanical system.

2. The professionalization of international law

The scientific and technocratic and a political ethos of positivism brought a new sense of precision, a business-like character, to the study and practice of international law. One consequence of this was an increasing sense of professionalism and, to a certain extent, of corporate solidarity. An important sign of this was the founding, in 1873, of two major professional bodies in the field, the International Law Association and the Institut de Droit International. This was also the period in which international law became a subject of university studies in its own right, separate from general jurisprudence—and, in particular, from the study of natural law. (This is also a subject which still awaits detailed treatment.)

The nineteenth century was also the period in which major systematic treatises began to be written in the various European languages. Where Vattel had led, many followed. In 1785, Georg Friedrich de Martens wrote an important treatise, which departed from earlier writing in being based primarily on State practice rather than on natural-law doctrine. In English, the most prominent early exposition was by Henry Wheaton, an American diplomat and legal scholar, whose *Elements of International Law* was published in 1836. Its popularity is indicated by the fact that it was translated into French, Spanish, and Italian, with new editions produced for fully a century after the first one. Wheaton was followed in Britain by Robert Phillimore, whose treatise of 1854–61 ran to four volumes (with two further editions). The first major German-language exposition was by Auguste Wilhelm Heffter in 1844 (which ran to eight editions by 1888). The first treatise to be a conscious embodiment of the positive philosophy was by an Argentinian

---

[18] 29 *British and Foreign State Papers*, pp 1137–8.

diplomat, Carlos Calvo, in 1868.[19] This text expanded from two to six volumes over the course of five editions to 1896. The French were slightly later in the field, with a *Précis du droit des gens*, by Théophile Funck-Brentano and Albert Sorel in 1877. More influential was the *Manuel de droit international public* by Henry Bonfils in 1894 (with eight editions by the 1920s). One of the most popular texts was that of the Swiss writer Johann Kaspar Bluntschli, whose exposition in 1868 took the form of a systematic 'code'.[20]

C. DISSIDENT PERSPECTIVES

If positivism was by far the dominant trend in nineteenth-century international law, it fell short of having a complete monopoly. For one thing, natural law—that venerable legacy of the past—showed its resilience, tenaciously surviving in the deeply inhospitable intellectual climate of positivism. Its principal adherent was the Scottish writer James Lorimer. But it also had support from Bluntschli.

In addition, several new approaches to international law were pioneered in the nineteenth century. One of these was liberalism, the essence of which was the centrality of private individuals rather than of States. States were seen as institutions whose function was to promote the rights and interests of private parties, rather than to advance the so-called 'national interest' of the State itself. Liberalism did not attract the explicit support of any important treatise writer, but its impact may be seen in several areas. One was the increased emphasis of freedom of trade in goods, as well as free movement of people and of capital.

Another important feature of liberalism was its focus on what would later be termed human rights. In the nineteenth century, this took the form of an assertion that there was an international minimum standard of treatment, in the area of civil rights, which any person was entitled to receive from any foreign State. This idea, however, met with staunch resistance from positivist writers, most memorably from Calvo, whose 'Calvo Doctrine' insisted on giving the priority to the sovereign right of States to determine their own standards of treatment in their own territories.

A second new school of thought was the nationality school. Its distinguishing feature was the contention that the true collective unit, for purposes of international law, is not the State, but rather the nation. Nations were seen as, essentially, cultural or historical units, bound together by shared languages, literary inheritances, customs, religions, or historical traditions. The best known champion of this was the charismatic Italian idealist (and sometime revolutionary) Giuseppe Mazzini. In the international legal profession, its foremost spokesman was the Italian scholar and political figure Pasquale Mancini. So strong was the Italian connection that this was sometimes referred to as the 'Italian school' of international law. Its most important feature was the contention that there was a kind of natural-law right on the part of nations to form themselves into States.[21] The nationality school's approach thereby became the ancestor of the later law of self-determination of peoples.[22]

A third new approach may be labelled, for lack of a widely known existing term, 'solidarism'. Its core belief was that international law should be based on the interdependence of peoples rather than on the independence of States, as the positivists held. Solidarists thereby sought to mount a frontal challenge to positivism by displacing State sovereignty and independence from their central roles in international law. Solidarism, like liberalism, did not receive systematic doctrinal treatment in the nineteenth century. But its impact was visible in the array of international organizations that began to assemble in this

---

[19] Calvo, 1880–81. For the first edition, in Spanish, see Carlos Calvo, *Derecho internacional teórico y práctico de Europa y América*, 2 vols (Paris: D'Amyot, 1868).   [20] Bluntschli, 1870.
[21] On the nationality school, see Sereni, 1943, pp 155–78.   [22] See Craven and Parfitt, Ch 7 of this book.

period. Its ethos is also evident in the willingness of some lawyers to countenance intervention in the internal affairs of other States, most prominently on humanitarian grounds to protect vulnerable groups from oppression (such as Christians in the Ottoman Empire).

D. THE ACHIEVEMENTS OF THE NINETEENTH CENTURY

One explanation for the remarkable lack of attention by international lawyers to the nineteenth century lies perhaps in the pervasive dominance of doctrinaire positivism over international legal writing generally. There was much, admittedly, that was unattractive about nineteenth-century positivism, particularly to modern eyes—its doctrinaire quality, its narrow horizons, its lack of high ideals, the aura of superficiality raised to the pitch of dogma, its narrowly technocratic character, its ready subservience to power. But it would be wrong to judge it on these points alone because its solid achievements were many. If it lacked the breadth and idealism of natural-law thought, it also discarded the vagueness and unreality that often characterized natural-law thought at its worst. In many ways, positivism was a breath (or even a blast) of fresh air, countering the speculative excesses of natural-law thought. Even if positivism sometimes went too far in the opposite direction, we should nonetheless appreciate the valuable services that it performed in its time.

It is clear from even a cursory survey of the nineteenth century that, when the wills of States were coordinated, impressive results could follow.[23] In the spirit of the St-Simonians, there were various forms of what would come to be called the functional cooperation of States. Progress on this front was most visible in the areas of international communication and transportation: from the international river commissions that were set up to ensure freedom of navigation on the Rhine and Danube Rivers (which had been commercial backwaters since the Middle Ages), to special arrangements for the Suez and Panama Canals, to the founding of the International Telegraphic and Universal Postal Unions (1865 and 1874 respectively). In the spirit of the liberal economists, policies of tariff reduction gathered momentum (with conclusion of the Cobden-Chevalier Treaty in 1860 between France and Britain being the seminal event).

Barriers between States were assiduously broken down in other ways as well. The late nineteenth century became an age of remarkable freedom of movement of peoples, with migration on a massive scale (passports were unnecessary for much of international travel in the period). Capital too moved with great freedom, thanks to the linking of currencies through the gold standard. The period was, in short, a great age of globalization, with the world more closely integrated economically than it would be for many decades thereafter (and in some ways more so than today (see Neff, 1990, pp 38–71)).

The positivist era was also the period in which we first see the international community 'legislating' by way of multilateral treaties, for the most part in areas relating to armed conflict. The first major example of this was the Declaration of Paris of 1856. It restricted the capture of private property at sea, by providing that 'free ships make free goods' (ie that enemy private property could not be captured on a neutral ship). It also announced the abolition of privateering. Within five years, it attracted over 40 ratifications. In 1868, the Declaration of St Petersburg contained a ban on exploding bullets. More importantly, it denounced total-war practices, by stating that the only permissible objective of war is the defeat of the enemy's armed forces. Alongside the law of war—and in some ways in close partnership to it—was the full flowering of the law of neutrality, which, for the first time, emerged in the full light of juridical respectability as a sort of counterpart to the unrestricted right of States to resort to war on purely political grounds.[24]

[23] See generally F S L Lyons, *Internationalism in Europe, 1815–1914* (A. W. Sythoff, 1963).
[24] For the most magisterial exposition of this subject, see Kleen, 1898–1900.

There was 'legislation' in other fields too. On the humanitarian front, the period witnessed a concerted effort by the nations of the world to put an end to slave trading. The culmination of this effort occurred in 1890, when the General Act of the Brussels Conference established an International Maritime Office (at Zanzibar) to act against slave trading. In the less-than-humanitarian sphere of imperialism, the major powers established, by multilateral treaty, the 'rules of the game' for the imperial partitioning of Africa. This took place at the Berlin Conference of 1884–85. (Contrary to the belief of some, that conference did not actually allocate any territories; it established the criteria by which the powers would recognize one another's claims.)

The culmination of nineteenth-century international legislation—and the arrival of parliamentary-style diplomacy and treaty-drafting—came with the two Hague Peace Conferences of 1899 and 1907. The first Conference drafted two major conventions: one on the laws of war and one on the establishment of a Permanent Court of Arbitration (which was actually a roster of experts prepared to act as judges on an ad hoc basis, and not a standing court). The Second Hague Peace Conference, in 1907, was a much larger gathering than the earlier one (and hence less Europe-dominated). It produced 13 conventions on various topics, mostly on aspects of war and neutrality.[25]

Yet another major achievement of the nineteenth century was in the area of the peaceful settlement of disputes. Although it was widely agreed that fundamental security issues were not justiciable, the nineteenth century marked a great step forward in the practice of inter-State arbitration. The trend began with the Jay Treaty of 1794, in which the United States and Britain agreed to set up two arbitration commissions (comprising nationals of each country) to resolve a range of neutrality and property-seizure issues that had arisen in the preceding years. These were followed by a number of ad hoc inter-State arbitrations in the nineteenth century, of which the most famous, again between Britain and the United States, took place in 1871–72, for the settlement of a host of neutrality-related issues arising from the American Civil War.[26]

For all the impressiveness of these achievements, though, the state of the world was well short of utopian. Economic inequality grew steadily even as growth accelerated. The subjection of much of the world to the European imperial powers, together with the 'gunboat diplomacy' that sometimes followed in the wake of legal claims, stored up a strong reservoir of ill-will between the developed and the developing worlds. Nor did the Concert of Europe prove adequate, in the longer term, to the maintenance of international peace. The Franco-Prussian War of 1870–71 proved, all too dramatically, that war between major powers on the continent of Europe was far from unthinkable—and the steady advance in weapons technology and armaments stockpiles promised that future wars could be far more deadly than any in the past. In due course, the Great War of 1914–18 delivered—spectacularly—on that menacing promise.

VI. THE TWENTIETH AND TWENTY-FIRST CENTURIES (1919–)

Since much of this book will cover twentieth-century developments, no attempt will be made at comprehensive coverage here, particularly of the post-1945 period. But certain aspects of both the inter-war and the post-1945 periods which have received comparatively little attention so far will be emphasized.

[25] For an informative and lively account of these conferences, see Tuchman, 1966.
[26] For a detailed and informative account, see Crook, 1975.

A. THE INTER-WAR PERIOD

The carnage of the Great War of 1914–18 concentrated many minds, in addition to squandering many lives. Many persons now held that nothing short of a permanently existing organization dedicated to the maintenance of peace would suffice to prevent future ghastly wars. Their most prominent spokesman was American President Woodrow Wilson. The fruit of their labours was the establishment of the League of Nations, whose Covenant was set out in the Versailles Treaty of 1919. This new system of public order would be of an open, parliamentary, democratic character, in contrast to the discreet great-power dealings of the Concert of Europe. The League was, however, tainted from the outset by its close association with the Versailles peace settlement, an incubus which it never managed to shake off.

1. The League and its supplements

The League was a complex combination of conservatism and boldness. On the side of conservatism was the decision to make no fundamental change in the sovereign prerogatives of nation-States as these had developed up to that time. No attempt was made to establish the League as a world government, with sovereign powers over its member States. Nor did the Covenant of the League prohibit war. Instead, the resort to war was hedged about with procedural requirements—specifically that either a judicial or political dispute-settlement process must be exhausted before there could be war between League member States. On the side of boldness was the Covenant's provision for automatic enforcement action against any League member State resorting to war without observing the peaceful-settlement rules. This enforcement took the form of economic sanctions by all other League member States, a tactic inspired by the Allied blockade of Germany during the Great War.

In due course, two major initiatives supplemented the League's efforts to maintain peace. In 1928, the Pact of Paris was concluded, in which the States parties forswore any resort to war as a means of national policy. The practical effects of this initiative, however, were not impressive. For one thing, no sanctions were provided. It was also carefully understood by the signatories that self-defence action would be permitted—a potentially large loophole. The second initiative was the Stimson Doctrine of 1932, announced by the United States (and named for its Secretary of State at the time) in the wake of Japan's occupation of Manchuria. It held that any situation brought about by aggression would not be accorded legal recognition by the United States. Here, too, the immediate material impact was not great; but it had some precedential value, since the UN General Assembly would later (in 1970) endorse it as a general principle of international relations.[27]

Only on one occasion was the sanctions provision of the Covenant invoked: against Italy for its invasion of Ethiopia in 1935–36. The sanctions failed to save Ethiopia, since the conquest was completed before they could have any serious effect. This failure led to a period of profound soul-searching amongst international lawyers as to what the role of law in the world should be. It similarly led States into desperate searches for alternative sources of security to the League Covenant. A number of countries, such as Switzerland, Belgium, and the Scandinavian States, reverted to traditional neutrality policies. But there were also a number of imaginative proposals for informal, but coordinated, action by States against aggressors (eg Cohn, 1939; Jessup, 1936). There was even a sort of return to ad hoc great-power management, in the form of a collective and coordinated non-intervention policy organized by the major powers at the outbreak of the Spanish Civil War in 1936. Unfortunately, this effort too was largely unsuccessful because of inadequate implementation and great-power rivalry (Watters, 1970).

---

[27] UN Declaration on Friendly Relations between States, GA Res 2625 (24 October 1970).

2. The achievements of the inter-war period

Although the League failed as a protector against aggressors, it would be far wrong to suppose that the inter-war period was a sterile time in international law generally. Precisely the opposite was the case. It was a time of ferment, experiment, and excitement unprecedented in the history of the discipline. A World Court (known formally, if optimistically, as the Permanent Court of International Justice) was established as a standing body, with its seat at The Hague in the Netherlands. It did not have compulsory jurisdiction over all disputes.[28] But it decided several dozen cases, building up, for the first time, a substantial body of international judicial practice. These cases were supplemented by a large number of claims commissions and arbitrations, whose outpourings gave international lawyers a volume of case law far richer than anything that had ever existed before.

The codification of international law was one of the ambitious projects of the period. A conference was convened for that purpose by the League of Nations in 1930, although its fruits were decidedly modest (consisting mainly of clarifications of various issues relating to nationality). The American States achieved rather more in this area, concluding regional conventions in a variety of fields. These included a Convention on Rights and Duties of States in 1933, which included what many lawyers regard as the canonical definition of a 'State' for legal purposes. The American States also concluded conventions on maritime neutrality, civil wars, asylum, and extradition.

The inter-war period also witnessed the first multilateral initiatives on human rights. A number of bilateral conventions for the protection of minorities were concluded between various newly created States and the League of Nations. In the event, these proved not to be very effective; but they set the stage for later efforts to protect minority rights after 1945, as well as human rights generally. The principle of trusteeship of dependent territories was embodied in the mandates system, in which the ex-colonies of the defeated countries were to be administered by member States of the League. This was to be a mission of stewardship—'a sacred trust of civilization'—under the oversight of the League.[29] Finally, the League performed heroic labours for the relief of refugees, in the face of very great obstacles—in the process virtually creating what would become one of the most important components of the law of human rights.

It was a period also of innovative thinking about international law. That the doctrinaire positivism of the nineteenth century was far from dead was made apparent by the World Court in 1927, when it reaffirmed the consensual basis of international law, in the famous (or infamous) *Lotus* case.[30] But positivism also came under attack during this period, from several quarters. One set of attackers were the enthusiasts for collective security, as embodied in the League of Nations. The American scholar Quincy Wright was a notable exemplar. This group were sympathetic to the return of just-war ideas, with the Covenant's restrictions on the resort to war and the provision for collective aid to victims of unlawful war. Their single most striking contention was that neutrality must now be regarded as obsolete.

Within the positivist camp itself, a sweeping revision of nineteenth-century thought was advanced by writers of the Vienna School, led by Hans Kelsen. They discarded the State-centred, consent-based, pluralistic elements of nineteenth-century positivism, while retaining its general scientific outlook. The Vienna School's goal was to reconceive international law—and indeed the whole of law—as a grand, holistic, rationalistic, normative system.[31]

The French lawyer Georges Scelle advanced a broadly similar vision, but from the solidarist (or sociological) vantage point, in contrast to the austere formalism of Kelsen.[32]

---

[28] See Thirlway, Ch 19 of this book.   [29] On the League's experience in this area, see Pedersen, 2015.
[30] *'Lotus' (France v. Turkey), 1927, PCIJ, Ser A, No 10.*   [31] On the Vienna School, see Kunz, 1934.
[32] See Scelle, 1932–34. See also Dupuy, 1990 and Nijman, 2004, pp 192–242.

Scelle in fact provided the first systematic exposition of the solidarist philosophy. In his vision of international law as a global constitutional law, he became the chief intellectual ancestor of the later constitutionalist movement. There was even something of a revival of natural-law thought, most notably in the writings of Louis Le Fur in France and of Alfred Verdross in Austria (who was something of a maverick member of the Vienna School).[33]

In short, the inter-war period did not bring an end to war or aggression. But it was the most vibrant and exciting era in the history of the discipline up to that time (and perhaps since).

B. AFTER 1945

In the immediate aftermath of the Second World War, international law entered upon a period of unprecedented confidence and prestige, for which 'euphoria' might not be too strong a word. International lawyers even found themselves in the (unaccustomed) role of heroic crusaders, with the dramatic prosecutions of German and Japanese leaders for crimes under international law at Nuremberg and Tokyo in the late 1940s (see generally Taylor, 1992; and Cryer and Boister, 2008). At the same time, great plans for the future were being laid.

1. Building a new world

The founding of the United Nations in 1945, to replace the defunct League of Nations, was a critical step in the creation of a new world order. With the UN came a new World Court (the International Court of Justice, or ICJ), though still without compulsory jurisdiction over States. The heart of the organization was the Security Council, where (it was hoped) the victorious powers from the Second World War would continue their wartime alliance in perpetuity as a collective bulwark against future aggressors. (It may be noted that 'United Nations' had been the official name for the wartime alliance.) The UN therefore marked something of a return to the old Concert of Europe approach. The special status of the five major powers (the principal victors in the Second World War, of course) was formally reflected in their possession of permanent seats on the Security Council, together with the power of veto over its decisions.

The UN Charter went further than the League Covenant in restricting violence. It did this by prohibiting not only war as such, but also 'the use of force' in general—thereby encompassing measures short of war, such as armed reprisals. An express exception was made for self-defence. Regarding action against aggressors, the UN was both bolder and more timid than the League had been. It was bolder in that the Charter provided not only for economic sanctions but also for armed action against aggressors. The UN Charter was more timid than the League, however, in that sanctions (whether economic or military) were not mandatory and automatic, as in the League Covenant. The Security Council—dominated by the major powers—was to decide on an ad hoc basis when, or whether, to impose sanctions. The result was to make the UN a more overtly political body than the League had been.

Parallel to this security programme was another one for the promotion of global economic prosperity. The economic-integration effort of the nineteenth century, shattered by the Great War and by the Great Depression of the 1930s, was to be restructured and given institutional embodiments. The International Monetary Fund was founded to ensure currency stability, and the World Bank to protect and promote foreign investment and (in due course) economic development. Trade liberalization would be overseen by a body to be called the International Trade Organization (ITO).

---

[33] See Le Fur, 1932; Verdross, 1927.

In a host of other areas as well, the aftermath of World War II witnessed a huge increase in international cooperation. There scarcely seemed any walk of life that was not being energetically 'internationalized' after 1945—from monetary policy to civil aviation, from human rights to environmental protection, from atomic energy to economic development, from deep sea-bed mining to the exploration of outer space, from democracy and governance to transnational crime-fighting. The cumulative effect was to weld the States of the world in general—and international lawyers in particular—into a tighter global community than ever before. It is easy to understand that, amidst all this hub-bub of activity, a certain triumphalist spirit could pervade the ranks of international lawyers.

The euphoric atmosphere proved, alas, to be very short-lived. Scarcely had the UN begun to function than it became paralysed by Cold War rivalry between the major power blocs—with the notable exception of the action in Korea in 1950–53 (only made possible by an ill-advised Soviet boycott of the Security Council at the relevant time). Nor did the new World Court find much effective use in its early decades. The ITO never came into being (because of a loss of interest by the United States). Plans for the establishment of a permanent international criminal court were also quietly dropped. Nor did the UN Charter's general ban against force have much apparent effect, beyond a cruelly ironic one: of propelling self-defence from a comparative legal backwater into the very forefront of international legal consciousness. Since self-defence was now the only clearly lawful category of unilateral use of force, the UN era became littered with self-defence claims of varying degrees of credibility, from the obvious to the risible. In particular, actions that previously would have been unashamedly presented as reprisals now tended to be deftly re-labelled as self-defence.[34]

All was not gloom, though, by any stretch of the imagination. In non-political spheres, lawyers fared a great deal better, very much in the technocratic spirit of nineteenth-century positivism. The codification of international law, for example, made some major strides, in large part from the activity of a UN body of technical experts called the International Law Commission. The principal areas of law that received a high degree of codification included the law of the sea (with four related conventions on the subject in 1958, replaced in 1982 by a single, broader convention), diplomatic and consular relations (in the early 1960s), human rights (with two international covenants in 1966), and the law of treaties (in 1969).

At the same time, though, it was not so clear that the fundamentals of the subject had changed very much. The basic positivist outlook continued to have great staying power. Some of the most important political and intellectual upheavals of the twentieth century left strangely little mark on international law. Socialism, for example, far from being a major challenge to lawyers, was actually a conservative force. Socialist theorists tended to write more dogmatically in the positivist vein than their Western counterparts did, insisting with particular strength on the upholding of respect for State sovereignty (see Tunkin, 1974).

Nor did the massive influx of developing States onto the world scene bring about any fundamental conceptual upheaval. For the most part, the developing countries readily accepted established ways, although they made some concrete contributions in specific areas. One was the establishment of self-determination as a fundamental, collective human right. Another was in the area of succession to treaties by newly independent States, with the States being given an option of choosing which colonial treaties to retain.

2. New challenges

Around the 1980s, a certain change of atmosphere in international law became evident, as something like the idealism of the early post-war years began, very cautiously, to return.

---

[34] See Gray, Ch 20 of this book.

There were a number of signs of this. One was a sharp upturn in the judicial business of the World Court. This included a number of cases of high political profile, from American policy in Central America to the Tehran hostages crisis to the Yugoslavian conflicts of the 1990s. In the 1990s, the ITO project was revived, this time with success, in the form of the creation of the World Trade Organization (WTO), which gave a significant impetus to what soon became widely, if controversially, known as 'globalization'.[35] Human rights began to assume a higher profile, as a result of several factors, such as the global campaign against South African apartheid and the huge increase in activity of non-governmental organizations.[36]

The end of the Cold War was another vital development, inspiring tangible hopes that the original vision of the UN as an effective collective-security agency might, at last, be realized. The expulsion of Iraq from Kuwait in 1991 lent strong support to this hope. Perhaps most remarkable of all was the rebirth of plans for an international criminal court, after a half-century of dormancy. A statute for a permanent International Criminal Court was drafted in 1998, entering into force in 2002 (with the first conviction handed down in 2012).[37]

In this second round of optimism, there was less in the way of euphoria than there had been in the first one, and more of a feeling that international law might be entering an age of new—and dangerous—challenge. International lawyers were now promising, or threatening, to bring international norms to bear upon States in an increasingly intrusive manner. A striking demonstration of this occurred in 1994, when the UN Security Council authorized the use of force to overthrow an unconstitutional government in Haiti. In 1999, the UN Security Council acquiesced in (although it did not actually authorize) a humanitarian intervention in Kosovo by a coalition of Western powers. It was far from clear how the world would respond to this new-found activism—in particular, whether the various countries would really be content to entrust global security, in perpetuity, to a Concert of Europe-style directorate of major powers.

International legal claims were being asserted on a wide range of other fronts as well, and frequently in controversial ways and generally with results that were unwelcome to some. For example, lawyers who pressed for self-determination rights for various minority groups and indigenous peoples were accused of encouraging secession movements. Some human-rights lawyers were loudly demanding changes in the traditional practices of non-Western peoples. And newly found (or newly rejuvenated) concerns over democracy, governance, and corruption posed, potentially, a large threat to governments all over the world. Some environmental lawyers were insisting that, in the interest of protecting a fragile planet, countries should deliberately curb economic growth. (But which countries? And by how much?) Economic globalization also became intensely controversial, as the IMF's policy of 'surveillance' (a somewhat ominous term to some) became increasingly detailed and intrusive, and as 'structural adjustment' was seen to have potentially far-reaching consequences in volatile societies. Fears were also increasingly voiced that the globalization process was bringing an increase in economic inequality.

VII. CONCLUSION

How well these new challenges will be met remains to be seen. At the beginning of the twenty-first century, it is hard to see the UN 'failing' in the way that the League of Nations did and being completely wound up. No one foresees a reversion to the rudimentary ways of Herodotus's silent traders. But it is not impossible to foresee nationalist or populist

---

[35] See Subedi, Ch 23 of this book.   [36] See Rodley, Ch 25 of this book.
[37] See Cryer, Ch 24 of this book.

backlashes within various countries against what is seen to be excessive international activism and against the élitist, technocratic culture of international law and organization. If there is one lesson that the history of international law teaches, it is that the world at large—the 'outside world', if you will—has done far more to mould international law than vice versa. By the beginning of the twenty-first century, international lawyers were changing the world to a greater extent than they ever had before. But it is (or should be) sobering to think that the great forces of history—religious, economic, political, psychological, scientific—have never before been successfully 'managed' or tamed. And only a rash gambler would wager that success was now at hand. Perhaps the most interesting chapters of our history remain to be written.

REFERENCES

AGER, SL (1996), *Interstate Arbitrations in the Greek World, 337–90 B.C.* (Berkeley, CA: University of California Press).

ALLAIN, J (2011), 'Acculturation Through the Middle Ages: The Islamic Law of Nations and Its Place in the History of International Law', in A Orakhelashvili, *Research Handbook on the Theory and History of International Law*, pp 394–407.

AMBÜHL, R (2013), *Prisoners of War in the Hundred Years War: Ransom Culture in the Late Middle Ages* (Cambridge: Cambridge University Press).

ARISTOTLE (1941), 'Rhetoric', in *The Basic Works of Aristotle* (McKeon, R (ed.)) New York: Random House), pp 1325–451.

BEDERMAN, DJ (2001), *International Law in Antiquity* (Cambridge: Cambridge University Press).

BHATIA, HS (ed) (1977), *International Law and Practice in Ancient India* (New Delhi: Deep and Deep).

BLUNTSCHLI, JC (1870), *Le droit international codifié* (MC Lardy, trans) (Paris: Guillaumin).

BONET, H (1949), *The Tree of Battles* (GW Coopland, trans) (Liverpool: Liverpool University Press).

BONFILS, H (1894), *Manuel de droit international public* (Paris: A Rousseau).

CALVO, C (1880–81), *Le droit international théorique et pratique précédé d'un exposé historique des progrès de la science du droit des gens*, 4 vols (3rd edn, Paris: Pedone-Lauriel).

CICERO, MT (1998), *Republic* (N Rudd, trans) (Oxford: Oxford University Press).

COHN, G (1939), *Neo-neutrality* (AS Kellar and E Jensen, trans) (New York: Columbia University Press).

CROOK, A (1975), *The Alabama Claims: American Politics and Anglo-American Relations, 1865–1872* (Ithaca, NY: Cornell University Press).

CRYER, R and N BOISTER (2008), *The Tokyo International Military Tribunal* (Oxford: Oxford University Press).

DUPUIS, C (1909), *Le principe d'équilibre et le concert européen de la Paix de Westphalie à l'Acte d'Algésiras* (Paris: Perrin).

DUPUY, R-J (1990), 'Images de Georges Scelle', 1 *European Journal of International Law* 235–9.

FALK, RA (1975), *A Study of Future Worlds* (New York: Free Press).

GIERKE, O (1938), *Political Theories of the Middle Age* (FW Maitland, trans) (Cambridge: Cambridge University Press).

GROTIUS, H (1925), *The Law of War and Peace* (FW Kelsey, trans) (Oxford: Clarendon Press).

HAGGENMACHER, P (1983), *Grotius et la doctrine de la guerre juste* (Paris: Presses Universitaires de France).

JOUANNET, E (2012), *The Liberal-Welfarist Law of Nations: A History of International Law* (Cambridge: Cambridge University Press): an intellectual history, covering the period from the eighteenth century onwards.

KOSKENNIEMI, M (2001), *The Gentle Civilizer of Nations: The Rise and Fall of International Law 1870–1960* (Cambridge: Cambridge University Press): contains a vast wealth of information on continental European (particularly French and German) thought in the nineteenth and early twentieth centuries.

NUSSBAUM, A (1954), *A Concise History of the Law of Nations* (rev. edn, New York: Macmillan): a very broad-brush general historical survey of international law, concentrating largely on doctrine.

ORAKHELASHVILI, A (ed) (2011), *Research Handbook on the Theory and History of International Law* (Cheltenham: Edward Elgar): has more on theory than on history; but a broad survey of the subject, from the Middle Ages onward, is provided.

PAGDEN, A (2001), *Peoples and Empires: Europeans and the Rest of the World, from Antiquity to the Present* (London: Phoenix Press): a sweeping survey of the historical (including the legal) evolution of imperialism, with careful attention to legal issues.

TUCK, R (1999), *The Rights of War and Peace: Political Thought and the International Order from Grotius to Kant* (Oxford: Oxford University Press): examines international law in the seventeenth and eighteenth centuries, concentrating on the doctrines of the major thinkers rather than on State practice.

The following works trace the history of certain topics:

ANAND, RP (1983), *Origin and Development of the Law of the Sea: History of International Law Revisited* (The Hague: Martinus Nijhoff).

ANGHIE, A (2005), *Imperialism, Sovereignty and the Making of International Law* (Cambridge: Cambridge University Press).

CROWE, DM (2014), *War Crimes, Genocide, and Justice: A Global History* (New York: Palgrave Macmillan).

DHOKALIA, RP (1970), *The Codification of Public International Law* (Manchester: Manchester University Press).

FREY, LS and ML FREY (1999), *The History of Diplomatic Immunity* (Columbus, OH: Ohio University Press).

GILLESPIE, A (2011), *A History of the Laws of War*, 3 vols (Oxford: Hart).

ISHAY, MR (2008), *The History of Human Rights: From Ancient Times to the Globalization Era* (Berkeley: University of California Press).

MAZZOWER, M (2012), *Governing the World: The History of an Idea* (New York: Penguin)

NEFF, SC (1990), *Friends But No Allies: Economic Liberalism and the Law of Nations* (New York: Columbia University Press).

NEFF, SC (2000), *The Rights and Duties of Neutrals: A General History* (Manchester: Manchester University Press).

NEFF, SC (2005), *War and the Law of Nations: A General History* (Cambridge: Cambridge University Press).

NIJMAN, JE (2004), *The Concept of International Legal Personality: An Inquiry into the History and Theory of International Law* (The Hague: T. M. C. Asser Press).

PAGDEN, A (2015), *The Burdens of Empire: 1539 to the Present* (Cambridge: Cambridge University Press).

RALSTON, JH (1929), *International Arbitration from Athens to Locarno* (London: Oxford University Press).

2

WHAT IS INTERNATIONAL LAW FOR?

Martti Koskenniemi

SUMMARY

The objectives of international law appear differently depending on one's standpoint. International law certainly seeks to realize the political values, interests, and preferences of various international actors. But it also appears as a standard of criticism and means of controlling those in powerful positions. Instrumentalism and formalism connote two opposite sensibilities of what it means to be an international lawyer, and two cultures of professional practice, the stereotypes of 'the advisor' to a powerful actor with many policy alternatives and 'the judge' scrutinizing the legality of a particular international behaviour. Beyond pointing to the oscillation between instrumentalism and formalism as styles of legal thought and practice, however, the question 'what is international law for?' also invokes popular aspirations about peace, justice, and human rights, and thus acts as a platform for an international political community. Whatever its shortcomings, international law also exists as a promise of justice, and thus as encouragement for political transformation.

I. THE PARADOX OF OBJECTIVES

Attempting to answer the question in the title, one first meets with a familiar paradox. On the one hand, it seems indisputable that international law 'has a general function to fulfil, namely to safeguard international peace, security and justice in relations between States' (Tomuschat, 1999, p 23). Or as Article 1 of the UN Charter puts it, the organization has the purpose to 'be a centre for harmonizing the actions of nations in the attainment of . . . common ends' such as international peace and security, friendly relations among nations, and international cooperation. Such objectives seem self-evident and have never been seriously challenged. On the other hand, it is hard to see how or why they could be challenged—or indeed why one should be enthusiastic about them—because they exist at such a high level of abstraction as to fail to indicate concrete preferences for action. What do 'peace', 'security', or 'justice' really mean? As soon as such words are defined more closely, disagreement emerges. To say that international law aims at peace *between States* is perhaps already to have narrowed down its scope unacceptably. Surely it must also seek to advance 'human rights as well as the rule of law domestically inside States for the benefit of human beings . . .' (Tomuschat, 1999, p 23). But what if advancing human rights would call for the destruction of an unjust peace?

In the end, very little seems to depend on any general response to the question 'what is international law for?'. The real problem seems always to be less about whether international law should aim for 'peace', 'security', or 'human rights' than about how to resolve interpretative controversies over or conflicts between such notions that emerge when defending or attacking particular policies. There is no disagreement about the objective of peace in the Middle East between Israel and the Palestinian people. But if asked what 'peace' might mean for them, the protagonists would immediately give mutually exclusive answers. Nor is the 'Asian values' debate about being 'for' or 'against' human rights, but rather about what such rights might be and how they should be translated into social practices in the relevant societies. Therefore, to inquire about the objectives of international law is to study the political preferences of international actors—what it is that *they* wish to attain by international law. And because those preferences differ, the answer to the question in the title can only either remain controversial or be formulated in such broad terms as to contain the controversy within itself—in which case it is hard to see how it could be used to resolve it.

It would thus be wrong to think of the paradox of objectives as a technical problem that could be disposed of by reflecting more closely on the meaning of words such as 'peace', 'security', or 'justice' or by carrying out more sophisticated social or economic analyses about the way the international world is or indeed by drafting definitions of such words in legal instruments. Such notions provide an acceptable response to the question 'what is international law for?' precisely because of their ability to gloss over existing disagreement about political choices and distributional priorities. If they did not work in this way, and instead permanently preferred some choices over other choices, they would no longer provide the neutral platform for peaceful political argument that we expect of them. In accordance with the founding myth of the system, the Peace of Westphalia in 1648 laid the basis for an agnostic, procedural international law whose merit consisted in its refraining from imposing any external normative ideal on the international society. The objectives of that society would now arise from itself and not from any religious, moral, or political notions of the good given externally to it. If there is an 'international community', it is a practical association not designed to realize ultimate ends but to coordinate action to further the objectives of existing communities.[1] Sovereign equality builds on this: because there are no natural ends, every member of the international society is free to decide on its own ends, and to that extent, they are all equal. The law that governs them is not natural but artificial, created by the sovereigns through the processes that are acceptable because neutral. To say that international law is for 'peace', 'security', and 'justice' is to say that it is for peace, security, and justice *as agreed and understood between the members of the system*.[2]

What this means for international legal argument can be gleaned, for instance, from the opinion of the International Court of Justice in the *Reservations* case (1951). Here the Court was called upon to examine the admissibility of reservations to the 1948 Convention on the Prevention and Punishment of the Crime of Genocide. The Court first outlined what seemed a natural consequence of the principles of neutrality and sovereignty, namely that no reservation should be effective against a State that has not agreed to it. To stay with this understanding, however, might have undermined the Convention by creating a system in which some reservations were in force in regard to some States (namely those accepting them) but not against others, while each non-accepting State would be free to regard the

---

[1] This is why it is so easy to discuss it in terms of the ethics of Immanuel Kant, an ethics of universalizable principles of *right action* rather than as instrumental guidelines for attaining the Good. Cf, eg O'Neill, 2000.

[2] This is why Judge James Crawford can conclude that despite Brexit, the Trump election, and the threat from what he calls 'nativism and unilateralism', the 'necessary law of nations' of sovereignty, non-intervention and Pacific settlement is well protected from any backlash, unlike the more substantive 'new' fields of human rights, trade, or environmental law: 'The Current Political Discourse Regarding International Law', 81 *The Modern Law Review* (2018), 1–22.

reservation-making State as not a party to the Convention at all. This would have gone against the universal nature of the Convention. Thus, the Court continued, a State having made a reservation that has been objected to by some of the parties, may still be held a party to the Convention if the reservation is compatible with the 'object and purpose' of the Convention. At this point, then, the Court moved to think of the law expressly in terms of its objectives. However, there were no objectives to the Convention that were independent from the objectives of the *parties* to the Convention. Thus, it was up to each party to make the determination 'individually and from its own standpoint'.[3]

Such an argument defines the objectives of international law in terms of the objectives of the (sovereign) members of the international society—in this case the society formed by the parties to the Genocide Convention—bringing to the fore two types of problems: what will happen in cases where States disagree about the objectives? And why would only State objectives count?

II. CONVERGING INTERESTS?

If no antecedent order establishes a firm priority between what States want, then any controversy about them either will have to remain open, or we shall have to assume that the procedure in which the disagreement is revealed will somehow be able to dispose of it to the satisfaction of all. The latter suggestion embodies the idea of the 'harmony of interests', the presence of an underlying convergence between apparently conflicting State preferences. Under this view, any actual dispute would always be only superficial. At a deeper level, State interests would coalesce and the objective of international law would then be to lead from the former level to the latter.[4]

It is difficult to defend this view against realist criticisms. Why would harmony, instead of conflict, be the true nature of international politics? What evidence is there that, rightly understood, the interests of States and other international actors are compatible? Might the harmony not rather seem a form of wishful thinking that prevents people from clearly seeing where their interests lie, and acting accordingly? Hans Morgenthau, one of the fathers of realist thought in international affairs, attacked the inter-war legalism precisely for having made this mistake. To believe in harmony under the League of Nations had left the world unprepared for Hitler's aggression in 1939 (Morgenthau, 1940, pp 261–84). EH Carr, another powerful realist thinker, described the harmony as an ideological smokescreen: 'Biologically and economically, the doctrine of the harmony of interests was tenable only if you left out of account the interest of the weak who must be driven to the wall, or called in the next world to redress the balance of the present' (Carr, 1946, p 50). Analogous criticisms have been made more recently in response to the emerging nationalism, protectionism and attack on international governance.[5]

[3] *Reservations to the Convention on the Prevention and Punishment of the Crime of Genocide, Advisory Opinion, ICJ Reports 1951*, p 15 at p 26.

[4] This argument, always implicit in moral objectivism and theories of natural law, was made in a dramatic way by Hersch Lauterpacht, speaking at Chatham House in 1941, as bombs were falling over Coventry and his family was being destroyed by the Nazis in Poland: 'The disunity of the modern world is a fact; but so, in a truer sense, is its unity. Th[e] essential and manifold solidarity, coupled with the necessity of securing the rule of law and the elimination of war, constitutes a harmony of interests which has a basis more real and tangible than the illusions of the sentimentalist or the hypocrisy of those satisfied with the existing *status quo*. The ultimate harmony of interests which within the State finds expression in the elimination of private violence is not a misleading invention of nineteenth century liberalism' (Lauterpacht, 1975, p 26).

[5] Eric Posner, 'Liberal Internationalism and the Populist Backlash', University of Chicago: Public law and Legal Theory Working Paper No. 606 (January 2017).

International lawyers have responded to such criticisms in two ways. Some have accepted that only a marginal scope is left by power to law and defined any existing legal regimes as variables dependent on a central power (Schmitt, 1988; Grewe, 2001), or have developed purely instrumental accounts of the use of law in the defence of particular interests or preferences (McDougal, 1953, pp 137–259; Goldsmith and Posner, 2005). Others have sought to articulate the harmony under a more elaborate theory of interdependence or globalization: 'International trade and commerce, international finance, international communication— *all* are essential to the survival of States, and *all* require an international legal system to provide a stable framework within which they may function' (Watts, 2000, p 7). Institutional, procedural, and even linguistic theories have been used to argue that even the articulation of State interests is based on legal notions such as 'sovereignty', 'treaty', and 'binding force' that delimit and define what may count as State interests or even State identity in the first place.[6] Still others have pointed to the myriad of grassroots activities among burgeoning international and non-governmental institutions, citizen groups and companies—a whole transnational "process" that has made it impossible for States to follow their nationalist impulses.[7] In other words, many lawyers have accepted the political realists' premise (that international law is determined by power) but seek to show either that power cannot have its way without international law or that 'power' is in fact a more fluid and complex element of international life than granted by realists and operates by creating practices and expectations of legitimacy from which States cannot extricate themselves without excessive cost.[8]

A first thing to be said about this is that it does highlight that the opposition between 'realism' and 'idealism' is only of limited usefulness. The labels invoke contrasting political sensibilities and different jurisprudential techniques that often merge into each other. Even the hardest 'realism' reveals itself as a moral position (for example by highlighting the priority of the national interest) inasmuch as, 'philosophically speaking, realism is unthinkable without the background of a prior idealistic position deeply committed to the universalism of the Enlightenment and democratic political theory' (Guzzini, 1998, p 16). On the other hand, any serious idealism is able to point to aspects of international reality that support it, and needs such reference in order to seem professionally credible. Much of the realism–idealism controversy is in fact about what element of a many-faceted 'reality' should be chosen as the starting point of one's analysis. Progress in the discipline of international law has then occurred by a new generation of lawyers rejecting the previous one as either 'utopian' because excessively idealist or 'apologist' because too impressed by sovereign power. These critiques are as available today as they were a century ago. Care must be taken not to associate any position or doctrine permanently with either: 'idealism' and 'realism' are best understood as forms of critique and channels for institutional reform in accordance with particular political sensibilities. They are crudely simplifying disciplinary labels, more useful for polemical than analytic purposes.

The second noteworthy aspect of this strategy is that in approving the realist premises it may in fact concede too much—namely that there are definable (political) interests or objectives that it is the point of legal rules to realize. But this may often in fact not be the case (as will be discussed later). In such cases, there is no 'prior' realm of the political to which the law should always pay deference. In fact the determination of the political objective or interest is not independent from seeking to find the legally plausible way of dealing with a matter.[9]

---

[6] See Harold Hongju Koh, 'The Trump Administration and International Law', 56 Washburn Law Journal (2017), 413-469.)

[7] See, eg, Brunnee & Toope 2011.

[8] This is the 'constructivist' explanation of international law's impact on States, much used today in international relations studies. See, eg, Finnemore, 1996. For a discussion, see Brunnee and Toope, 2000, pp 19–74; Kratochwil, 2000, pp 55–9.   [9] This is one of the central arguments in Koskenniemi, 2005.

Many lawyers—and increasingly often political theorists—have, however, made a more ambitious defence of international law. They have argued that, however neutral in regard to political principles, the structure of international law is not devoid of an autonomous normative direction. In their view, international law is accompanied by a cunning logic that slowly socializes initially egoistic States into the law's internationalist spirit.[10] It is possible (though not necessary) to picture this ethic as the 'inner morality of law' that accompanies any serious commitment to work in a legal system.[11] An alternative but parallel approach would be to characterize the system in terms of a 'culture of civility' shared by its administrators and excluding certain types of secrecy, dishonesty, fraud, or manipulation. Such an explanation resonates with international law's emergence in the late nineteenth century as an aspect of optimistic evolutionism among the liberal élites of Europe and North America. It is to assume that by entering into the processes it provides, States come to define not only their objectives but perhaps even their identity by principles offered by international law (Koskenniemi, 2001a).

III. THE SIGNIFICANCE OF STATEHOOD

But the Westphalian myth leaves also unexplained why only *State objectives* count. Ever since Immanuel Kant published his essay on the *Perpetual Peace* (1795), philosophers, political theorists, and lawyers have routinely challenged the State-centrism of the international system, arguing that whatever instrumental value States may have for the coordination of affairs of particular communities, the 'ultimate' members of those communities are individuals and that many other human groups apart from States ('peoples', 'nations', 'minorities', 'international organizations', 'corporations') also play important roles (Westlake, 1910, p 16). Globalization and the crisis of sovereignty have intensified the criticisms of international law as State law from sociological, functional, and ethical standpoints. These critiques have often sought to project a material value or an idea of social justice outside of statehood that they suggest should be enforced by international law (Koskenniemi, 1994, pp 22–9).

The universalizing vocabularies of human rights, liberalism, economic, and ecological interdependence have no doubt complicated inter-sovereign law by the insertion of public law notions such as *jus cogens* and 'obligations owed to the international community as a whole' and by 'fragmenting' the international system into functional institutions (see Section VIII). But no alternative to statehood has emerged. None of the normative directions—human rights, economic or environmental values, religious ideals—has been able to establish itself in a dominating position. On the contrary, what these values may mean and how conflicts between them should be resolved is decided largely through 'Westphalian' institutions. This is not to say that new institutions would not enjoy a degree of autonomy from their members. Human rights and many economic and environmental regimes provide examples of such. The EU has developed into an autonomous system that functions largely outside the frame of international law. How far these other regimes are from that of the EU can, however, be gleaned from the characterization of the WTO system by the Appellate Body in the *Alcoholic Beverages* case (1996):

---

[10] A defence of the view that law socializes States not by constraint but by 'compliance strategies [that] seek to remove obstacles, clarify issues, and convince parties to change their behavior', as well as by 'various manifestations of disapproval: exposure, shaming, and diffuse impacts on the reputations and international relationships of a resisting party', is found in Chayes and Chayes, 1995, pp 109, 110. A more recent, proceduralist defence, insisting on the moral core of the international legal process is Habermas, 2004.

[11] The point about law necessarily containing certain 'aspirations of excellence' without which an order would not be recognized as 'law' in the first place, is made, of course, in Fuller, 1969, especially pp 41–94.

The *WTO Agreement* is a treaty—the international equivalent of a contract. It is self-evident that in an exercise of their sovereignty, and in pursuit of their own respective national interests, the Members of the WTO have made a bargain. In exchange for the benefits they expect to derive as members of the WTO they have agreed to exercise their sovereignty according to commitments they have made in the *WTO Agreement*.[12]

This outlook was reaffirmed by the International Court of Justice in the *Nuclear Weapons* Advisory Opinion in 1996. In response to the question about the lawfulness of the threat or use of such weapons, the Court concluded that whatever the consequences, it could not exclude that such use would be lawful 'in an extreme circumstance of self-defence, when the very survival of a State would be at stake'.[13] 'Benefits' to the States and State survival remain the highest objectives of the system. Bodies such as the European Court of Human Rights or the UN Human Rights Committee recognize that the treaties they administer function in a State-centred world: the margin of appreciation and the wide scope of derogations allow for national security reasons if 'necessary in a democratic society' to operate with notions of 'security' and 'democracy' that are embedded in a world of States.[14]

The defence of international law's State-centredness is thoroughly practical. 'Stated quite simply,' James Brierly once wrote, 'what [international law] tries to do is to define or delimit the respective spheres within which each of the . . . States into which the world is divided for political purposes is entitled to exercise its authority' (Brierly, 1944, p 3). Little of this justification has changed. A form and a process are needed that channel interpretative conflicts into peaceful avenues. This is not to say that non-State values such as 'human rights', 'efficient economies', 'clean environment', or 'democracy' would be unworthy objectives of political action. Disagreement about them has provided the life and blood of international politics especially since the 1990s. The defenders of the State system would only add that such values conflict and that 'States alone have provided the structures of authority needed to cope with the incessant claims of competing social groups and to provide public justice essential to social order and responsibility' (Schachter, 1997, p 22). States may be set aside, of course, by consent or revolution but there are dangers in such transformations, some of which are well known, and something about those dangers results from the single-mindedness of the teleologies pursued by the institutions seeking to replace statehood.

On the other hand, there is no doubt that international politics is far from the Westphalian ideal. The informal networks and epistemic communities that influence international developments beyond the rigid forms of sovereign equality are populated by experts from the developed West. It is hard to justify the attention given and the resources allocated to the 'fight against terrorism' in the aftermath of the attacks on New York and Washington in September 2001 in which nearly 3,000 people lost their lives, while simultaneously six million children under five years old die annually of malnutrition by causes that could be prevented by existing economic and technical resources.[15] More recently, the state of the world has been characterized by massive and increasing inequality. How, for example, should we view data according to which the wealthiest 1 per cent now earn over 50 per

---

[12] *Japan—Taxes on Alcoholic Beverages*, Appellate Body Report (AB–1996–2) DSR 1996: I p 108 (4 October 1996).

[13] *Legality of the Threat or Use of Nuclear Weapons, Advisory Opinion, ICJ Reports 1996*, p 226, paras 96, 101(E).

[14] Or in other words, these mechanisms are only subsidiary: 'The [European Convention on Human Rights] leaves to each contracting State . . . the task of securing the rights and freedoms it enshrines', *Handyside* v *UK*, *Judgment of 7 December 1976, Ser A, No 24*, 1 *EHRR* 737, para 48. As Susan Marks points out, liberal reformers conceive of 'democratization' in terms of reform of *domestic* (and not international) institutions (Marks, 2000, pp 76–100).

[15] 'The State of Food Insecurity in the World 2002', http://www.fao.org/DOCREP/005/Y7352e/Y7352e00. HTM (last visited 24 October 2002).

cent of global wealth, and that the wealth of the richest 62 people has risen by 44 per cent in the past five years since 2010—while at the same time, the wealth of the 'bottom half' fell by 41 per cent. (See 'An Economy for the 1 Per Cent', Oxfam Briefing Paper 210 (18 January 2016). What becomes a 'crisis' in the world and will involve the political energy and resources of the international system is determined in a thoroughly Western-dominated process (Charlesworth, 2002; Orford, 2003).

It is widely believed that the informal and fluid economic, technological, and cultural processes often termed 'governance' rather than 'government' strengthen the political position of the most powerful actors—transnational networks, large corporations, Western developed States—and marginalize public international law (eg Hurrell and Woods, 1999; Arnaud, 2003). Weak States despair over their inability to hold on to achieved positions and privileges by the antiquated rhetoric of sovereignty. But the latter's awkward defence of the conservative system of sovereign equality undermines the extent to which globalization may also open avenues for contestatory transgovernmental action within international civil society, or by what Hardt and Negri call the 'multitude' (Hardt and Negri, 1999, pp 393–413). Today, the supporters of globalization are challenged in the developed West by new types of groups wishing to withdraw from integration (Brexiteers, Trumpists, neo-nationalist and alt-right groups and voters) on the argument that it has benefited only a small elite. There is room for conflict and consensus both *within* and *beyond* the Westphalian system and little political worth lies in deciding a priori in favour of either. Global rules and domestic standards may each be used for progressive or conservative causes. The choice of technique must reflect a historically informed assessment of the effect of particular institutional alternatives.

In the following sections I will try respond to the question 'what is international law for?' by describing its role in a world that is not one of pre-established harmony or struggle but of both cooperation *and* conflict simultaneously. I will argue that international law operates— and should operate—as an instrument for advancing particular claims and agendas *as well as* a relatively autonomous formal technique. This is not to claim political neutrality. Much instrumental thinking about international law today adopts the point of view of the decision-maker in a relatively prosperous State or transnational network, in possession of resources and policy options and seeking guidance on how to fit their objectives within international legality—or to overrule legality with minimal cost. Clearly, international law exists 'for' such decision-makers. But it should not exist exclusively for them. My argument is that there is often a reason to adopt a 'formalist' view on international law that refuses to engage with the question of its objectives precisely in order to constrain those in powerful positions. This seems especially important in a moment when much of the work of international institutions is being challenged by nationalist and illiberal forces. The question 'what is international law for?' needs to be rescued from the context of legal routines and reinstated in the political arenas where it can be used to articulate claims by those who are sidelined from formal diplomacy and informal networks and feel that something about the routines of both is responsible for the deprivations they suffer. In other words, there is reason to defend a legal 'formalism' against a 'pragmatism' that views international law only in terms of the immediate objectives it serves. In order to do that, however, it is necessary first to outline the power of pragmatism.

IV. INTO PRAGMATISM?

The paradox of objectives shows that the formal law of Westphalia cannot be replaced by social objectives or ethical principles without invoking controversies that exist in regard to the latter. 'Whoever invokes humanity wants to cheat', Carl Schmitt once wrote (Schmitt, 1996, p 54), citing the nineteenth-century French socialist Pierre Joseph Proudhon and making a useful point about the use of abstract humanitarianism to label one's political adversary as an enemy of humanity so as to justify extreme measures against him—a point that applied in today's context 'lacks neither lucidity nor relevance' (Kervégan, 1999, p 61). One need not think only of the extreme case of the 'war against terrorism' to canvass the slippery slope from anti-formal reasoning to human rights violation. Quite everyday legal argument assumes the analytical priority of the reasons for the law over the form of the law in a fashion that underwrites Stanley Fish's perceptive dictum: 'once you start down the anti-formalist road, there is no place to stop' (Fish, 1989, p 2).

For example, the right of self-defence under Article 51 of the Charter is formally conditioned by the presence of an 'armed attack'. But what about the case of a *threat* of attack by mass destruction weapons? Here we are tempted to look for guidance from the objective of Article 51. The rationale for allowing self-defence lies, presumably, in the objective of protecting the State. Surely we cannot expect a State to wait for an attack if this would bring about precisely the consequence—the destruction of the State—that the rule was intended to prevent. Because the rule itself is no more valuable than the reason for its existence, we erase the condition of prior armed attack and entitle the State to act in an anticipatory way.[16] Or the other way around: surely formal sovereignty should not be a bar for humanitarian intervention against a tyrannical regime; in oppressing its own population, the State undermines its sovereignty. We honour 'sovereignty' as an expression of a people's self-rule. If instead of self-rule there is oppression, then it would seem nonsensical to allow formal sovereignty to constitute a bar to intervention in support of the people.[17]

Such arguments are based on a thoroughly pragmatic-instrumentalist view of the law, a view that highlights that we do not honour the law because of the sacred aura of its text or its origin but because it enables us to reach valuable human purposes. We follow the emission reduction schedule of chlorofluorocarbons (CFCs) in Article 2 of the 1987 Montreal Protocol on the Protection of the Ozone Layer because we assume that it will reduce the depletion of the ozone layer and the incidence of skin cancer. We honour the domestic jurisdiction clause in Article 2(7) of the UN Charter because we assume it upholds the ability of self-determining communities to lead the kinds of life they choose. But what if it were shown that ozone depletion or skin cancer bears no relationship to the emissions of CFCs, or that domestic jurisdiction merely shields the arbitrary reign of tyrants? In such cases we would immediately look for an equitable exception or a counter-rule so as to avoid the—now unnecessary—costs that would be incurred by bowing to the empty form of the original rule. Article 10(1) of the European Convention on Human Rights provides for freedom of speech. If applying the right would enable the distribution of fascist propaganda, it is always possible to interfere and prohibit it by the counter-rule in Article 10(2) that enables the 'prevention of disorder or crime' and to ensure 'the protection of morals', with a margin of appreciation lying with State authorities. Enabling those authorities to protect 'national security' is indispensable if they are to secure the liberal rights regime. Yet, because setting the 'balance' between security and rights lies with the authorities against whom the rights regime was established, the door to abuse remains open (see Cameron, 2000, pp 62–8).

We often allow the reason for the rule to override the rule. We do this because we believe the rule itself has no intrinsic worth. If it fails to support the purpose for which it was enacted—or worse, prevents its attainment—why should it be honoured? In domestic society, abstract law-obedience can be defended in view of the routine nature of the cases that arise, and the dangers attached to entitling citizens to think for themselves. Such

---

[16] This is the argument for the 'Bush doctrine' of pre-emptive self-defence, as made in the US security strategy, published on 20 September 2002. Cf the text in, eg, *Financial Times*, 21 September 2002, p 4.

[17] This position is often combined with the argument for pro-democratic intervention. For useful analysis, see Chesterman, 2001, pp 88–111.

arguments are weak in the international realm where situations of law-application are few, and disadvantages of obedience often significant. Few States that were economically or politically dependent on Iraq fully implemented the sanctions set up in 1990. Though they were in formal breach of Articles 25 and 48 of the Charter, the UN preferred to look the other way. The EU is not going to give up the prohibition of importation of hormone-treated meat merely because a WTO dispute-settlement organ may have decided it should do so. The importance of the interest in living peacefully with a powerful neighbour and of deciding on national health standards vastly outweighs any consideration about the importance of abstract law-obedience (see Koskenniemi, 2001b).

And yet, there is a dark side to such pragmatic instrumentalism. A legal technique that reaches directly to law's purposes is either compelled to think that it can access the right purpose in some politics-independent fashion—in which case it would stand to defend its implicit moral naturalism—or it transforms itself to a licence for those powers in a position to realize their own purposes to do precisely that. In this way, pragmatism inculcates a heroic mindset: we *can* do it! It is the mindset of well-placed, powerful actors, confident in their possessing the 'right' purpose; the mindset that drove Stalin to collectivization, or the Bush regime to Iraq in 2003. It is the mindset of the civilizing mission and of 'regime change' by force if necessary.

Instrumental action may or may not be acceptable in view of the circumstances and its advisability is typically the object of political controversy. But the instrumentalist mindset—the readiness to act as soon as that seems what one believes useful or good—creates a consistent bias in favour of dominant actors with many policy alternatives from which to choose and sufficient resources to carry out their objectives.[18] To always look for reasons, instead of rules, liberates public authorities to follow their reasoning, and their purposes—hence their frequent aversion against rules in the first place: the International Criminal Court, disarmament or human rights treaties, environmental or law of the sea regimes, and so on (see Byers and Nolte, 2003).

The difficulty with the instrumentalist mindset is that there never are simple, well-identified objectives behind formal rules. Rules are legislative compromises, open-ended and bound in clusters expressing conflicting considerations. To refer to objectives is to tell the law-applier: 'please choose'. There is no doubt that Article 2(4) of the UN Charter aims towards 'peace'. Yet it is equally certain that most people disagree on what 'peace' might mean in a particular case. This is not only about semantic uncertainty. Even apparently unobjectionable objectives such as 'peace' contain a paradox. To be in favour of 'peace' cannot, for example, mean that nobody can ever take up arms. 'Perhaps the most serious problem with outlawing force is that sometimes it is both necessary and desirable' (Watts, 2000, p 10). The UN Charter expressly allows for the use of military force under the authority of the Security Council or in pursuance of the right of self-defence. The positive law of the Charter is both pacifist and militarist—and receives its acceptability by such schizophrenia. Without something like a right to use force in self-defence, aggression would always be rewarded. The European Convention on Human Rights seeks to protect individuals' rights to both freedom and security. But one person's freedom often conflicts with another's security. Whether or not authorities should be entitled to censor prisoners' letters or prohibit the publication of obscene materials, for instance, cannot be reached through instrumental reasoning that would be independent from a political choice (see Koskenniemi, 2000, pp 99–106). The will of the drafters *is* the language of the instrument.

[18] For a description of instrumentalism as a culture, see Binder, 1988, pp 906–9.

Beyond that, there is only speculation about what might be a good (acceptable, workable, realistic, or fair) way to apply it.

Practitioners usually understand international law as being more about routine application of standard solutions, ad hoc accommodation, and compromise than discourse about large objectives. Providing advice to a non-governmental organization or drafting judgments at the International Court of Justice are usually held to require pragmatic reconciliation of conflicting considerations, balancing between 'equitable principles', conflicting rights, or other prima facie relevant aspects of the case at hand. Settlement of the conflicts during the dissolution of the former Yugoslavia in the early 1990s was understood to involve the balancing of conflicting considerations about stability of frontiers and expectations of just change, managing the *uti possidetis* principle together with minority rights for populations left on the wrong side of the boundary.[19] The balance struck between these considerations was in no way dictated by the law but reflected the negotiators' pragmatic assessment of what might work (Lâm, 2000, pp 141–51). At the European Court of Human Rights, individual freedoms are constantly weighted against the need for interference by public authorities. It is established case law that 'an interference must achieve a "fair balance" between the demands of the general interests of the community and the requirements of the protection of the individual's fundamental rights'.[20] In a like manner, the law concerning the delimitation of frontier areas or the sharing of natural resources resolves itself into a more or less flexible cluster of considerations about distributive justice—sometimes described in an altogether open-ended fashion in terms of 'equitable principles' or 'equitable use'—in view of attaining a pragmatically acceptable end-result.[21] And hard cases within the laws of war invariably turn into a contextual assessment of what number of non-combatant casualties might still be within the limits of proportionality by reference to the military objective (military experts and humanitarian lawyers agreeing on the need to 'calculate' (see Kennedy, 2004)).

Few international lawyers think of their craft as the application of pre-existing formal rules or great objectives. What rules are applied and how, which interpretative principles are used and whether to invoke the rule or the exception—including many other techniques—all point to pragmatic weighing of conflicting considerations in particular cases (Corten, 1997). What is sought is something practical, perhaps the 'fairness' of the outcome, as Thomas M Franck has suggested. Under this image, law is not about peace *or* justice, freedom *or* security, stability *or* change, but always about both one *and* the other simultaneously. 'The tension between stability and change, if not managed, can disorder the system. Fairness is the rubric under which the tension is discursively managed' (Franck, 1995, p 7). The lawyer's task is now seen in terms of contextual 'wisdom', or 'prudence', rather than the employment of formal techniques.[22] In a fluid, fragmented world, everything hinges on the sensitivity of the practising lawyer to the pull of contextually relevant considerations.

[19] See Opinions 2 and 3 of the Arbitration Commission of the Peace Conference on the Former Yugoslavia (1992) 31 ILM 1497–1500.

[20] *Fredin v Sweden, Judgment of 18 February 1991, Ser A, No 192*, 13 EHRR 784, para 51; *Lopez Ostra v Spain, Judgment of 9 December 1994, Ser A, No 303–C*, 20 EHRR 277, para 51.

[21] See, eg, Separate Opinion of Judge Jiménez de Aréchaga, *Continental Shelf (Tunisia/Libyan Arab Jamahiriya), Judgment, ICJ Reports 1982*, p 18 at pp 103–8, paras 11–31 and eg the International Convention on the Non-Navigational Uses of International Watercourses, A/RES/51/229 (8 July 1997). I have analysed this 'turn to equity' in, among other places, Koskenniemi, 1999b, pp 27–50.

[22] For a celebration of judicial creativity in this regard, see Lauterpacht, 1958.

V. A TRADITION OF ANTI-FORMALISM

The move to pragmatism emerges from a series of recurrent criticisms of international law's alleged 'formalism'. Pragmatism was supported in the last third of the nineteenth century by the use of a flexible notion of 'civilization' that enabled liberal lawyers to look beyond diplomatic protocol and an outdated natural law. The inter-war lawyers attacked the formalism of sovereignty they projected on pre-war doctrines and advocated (as conservatives) 'tradition' and (as progressives) 'interdependence' as bases for their pragmatic commitment. After the next war, reformist lawyers indicted what they described as the legalistic formalism of the League basing their 'realism' on Cold War themes, either expressly in favour of the West or in a more social-democratic way to support international institutions (see Kennedy, 2000, pp 380–7). Legal realism always had its Hawks and its Doves but for both, it seemed useful to criticize old law for its 'formalism' in order to support 'dynamic' political change.

Interdisciplinary studies in the 1990s highlighted the extent to which the formal validity of a standard was independent from its compliance pull (see, eg, Shelton, 2000). As the law was seen instrumentally, its formality seemed to bear no particular merit: 'hard law' was just one choice among other possible regulative techniques, including soft standards or the absence of any standards at all in cases where the imposition of one's preference seemed within the limits of the possible and preferable given that it might 'minimise transaction and sovereignty costs'.[23] In such debates formal law has nobody speaking in its favour and is indicted as a utopianism supporting conservative causes. Anti-formalism is always a call for transformation: to overrule existing law either because it does not really exist at all, or if it does, because it should not. The debate on soft law and *jus cogens* manifests both of these criticisms and Prosper Weil's famous analysis of the pathological problems (the 'dilution' and 'graduation' of normativity) introduced in international law by such notions was unpersuasive to anti-formalist critics who wanted to realize the good society *now* and had no doubt that they knew how to go about this (see Weil, 1983; Tasioulas, 1996). Avant-garde instrumentalism at the beginning of a new century reads like German public law conservatism a hundred years earlier: over every international rule hangs the sword of *clausula rebus sic stantibus* (see Kaufmann, 1911).

What makes the formalism/anti-formalism debate suspect is the extent to which *anything* may be and has been attacked as 'formalism' (see Kennedy, 2001). The following views, at least, have been so targeted:

(a) rationalistic natural-law theories;

(b) views emphasizing the importance of (formal) sovereignty;

(c) views limiting international law's scope to treaties or other (formal) expressions of consent;

(d) views highlighting the importance of international institutions;

(e) views emphasizing 'rigour' in law-application;

---

[23] For a particularly straightforward instrumental approach, see Posner, 2003. An interdisciplinary research on the recent 'move to law' uses a method of assessing 'legalization' by reference to the standards' obligatory nature, precision, and the presence of a centralized authority. The project examines 'legalization' instrumentally, by concentrating on the conditions under which it constitutes a rational choice. See, eg, Abbott and Snidal, 2001, pp 37–72. Such instrumentalism is not neutral: to assess law from the perspective of rational choice is to occupy the perspective of a small number of actors that actually may choose their options by agendas they set. It celebrates the managerial culture of Western experts at work to advance Western interests.

(f) views stressing the significance of formal dispute-settlement;

(g) views insisting on a clear boundary between law and politics.

The list is by no means exhaustive. In fact, anything can be labelled 'formalism' because the term is purely relational. When a speaker advocates something (a norm, a practice) by its material fullness, the opposite view will inevitably appear to be holding fast to the dead weight of some 'form'. The almost uniformly pejorative use of the term 'formalism' in international law reflects the predominance of the instrumentalist mindset in diplomacy and international politics. The way the legal idiom constructs and upholds the structures of diplomacy and politics is left invisible.

The contrast between instrumentalism and formalism is quite fundamental when seeking to answer the question 'what is international law for?' From the instrumental perspective, international law exists to realize objectives of some dominant part of the community; from the formalist perspective, it provides a platform to evaluate behaviour, including the behaviour of those in dominant positions. The instrumental perspective highlights the role of law as social engineering; formalism views it as an interpretative scheme. The instrumental perspective is typically that of an active and powerful actor in possession of alternative choices; formalism is often the perspective of the weak actor relying on law for protection.

If instrumentalism today needs no particular defence, it may be useful to highlight the twin virtues of formalism. First, it is indispensable. Every standard is always substantive and formal at the same time. The very ideas of treaty and codification make sense only if one assumes that at some point there emerges an agreement, an understanding, a standard that is separate from its legislative background. When States enter an agreement, or when some behaviour is understood to turn from habit into custom, the assumption is that something that was loose and disputed crystallizes into something that is fixed and no longer negotiable. The point of law is to give rise to standards that are no longer merely 'proposed' or 'useful' or 'good', and which therefore can be deviated from if one happens to share a deviating notion of what in fact is useful or good. This is what it means to say that in addition to their acceptability and effectiveness, legal rules should also possess 'validity'. To accept that positive law enjoys that property is not to say anything about how it is recognized in individual rules or standards, nor indeed of whether any actual standard so recognized would possess any particular meaning as against some other putative meaning. Validity indicates a formal property that leaves the norm so characterized a flat, substanceless surface—but a surface without which no 'law' could exist at all.

Secondly, the fact that the legal form is a 'flat substanceless surface' is not politically insignificant. It does something to those it accepts as legal subjects. In a world without or 'before' international law, the acting persons or entities exist as subjects of interests and preferences, both liberated and weighed down by their irreducible particularity. The logic of a social structure between them is a logic of instrumentalism, each subject a *homo economicus*, poised to perpetuate the realization of its idiosyncratic preference. Such actors are completely controlled by the environmental conditions that make interest-fulfilment possible. For them, the external world—including other actors—has no meaning beyond interest-fulfilment: on its own, it is chaotic, incomprehensible. Paradoxically, however, a single-minded instrumentalism is bound to be frustrated in the end: at the mercy of a dangerous and incomprehensible world where every action creates unforeseen consequences, and always falls short of satisfying the ever intensifying interests (eg Foucault, 2005, pp 280–1). This is one of the tragedies of the continuing war in Afghanistan.

By contrast, as legal subjects, actors, as it were, give up their particularity in order to participate in what is general. By recourse to the medium of law that claims 'validity', they are lifted from the tyranny of subjective interests and preferences. The *homo juridicus* in a way decentralizes its own perspective, opening itself to the world at large. In other words, and as thinkers as diverse as Kant, Foucault, and Habermas have pointed out, the political significance of formal law—that is, of law irrespective of what interests or preferences particular legislation might seek to advance—is that it expresses the universalist principle of inclusion at the outset, making possible the regulative ideal of a pluralistic international world. (See Kant, 1999, pp 24–5; Foucault, 2005, pp 280–1; Habermas, 2004. See also Supiot, 2005.) '[O]nly a regime of non-instrumental rules, understood to be authoritative independent of particular beliefs or purposes is compatible with the freedom of its subjects to be different' (Nardin, 1998, p 31). The form of law constructs political adversaries as equals, entitled to express their subjectively felt injustices in terms of breaches of the rules of the community to which they belong no less than their adversaries—thus affirming both that inclusion and the principle that the conditions applying to the treatment of any one member of the community must apply to every other member as well. In the end, competent lawyers may disagree about what this means in practice. But the legal idiom itself reaffirms the political pluralism that underlies the Rule of Law, however inefficiently it has been put into effect. In fact, the failures in the international legal system are always recognized and constructive projects formulated by a prior (though often undisclosed) acceptance of the idea of the rule of formal law. Without that idea, many of the criticisms we all make of the international political world would no longer make sense.

Of course, formal law does not apply itself. Between that form and any decision to project on it meaning 'x' instead of 'y', is a professional technique that may be more or less successful in expressing these regulative ideals. In particular, there is a constant push and pull in the professional world between a *culture of instrumentalism* and a *culture of formalism*. It would be wrong to associate this dialectic with fixed positions representing particular interests or preferences. Instrumental action by lawyers is a necessary part of the search for good rules or institutions beyond the status quo. And any present rules are always also mechanisms to support particular interests and privileges. 'Power' and 'law' are entangled in such complex ways that it is often pointless to interpret particular events as manifesting either one or the other: power works through 'formal rules'—just as, instead of 'naked power', we see everywhere power defined, delimited, and directed by rules.

But the two cultures do play distinct political roles in particular historical situations. As the debates around the fluid dynamism of globalization have demonstrated, formal standards and institutions are often called upon to provide protection for weak actors, and to pose demands on powerful ones.[24] Irrespective of its philosophical justification, there is no magic about formalism as a legal practice, however. It may also come to buttress privilege, apathy, or both. Hence it is important also to focus on instrumentalism and formalism as 'cultures', sensibilities, traditions and frameworks, sets of rituals and self-understandings among institutional actors. As pointed out earlier, the 'heroic' mindset of the *homo economicus* that sees law only as an instrument for *my objectives* often leads to collateral damage, frustration, and tragedy. Against it, I would invoke a practice of formalism, with its associated tropes about valid law, rights, and constitutionalism, less as definite institutional models than as regulative ideals for a profession without which no community could rule itself by standards it recognizes as its own (instead of those of some influential faction). The idea of a universal law needs servants that define themselves as administrators (instead of inventors) of universal standards—the class of lawyers. The traditions and practices of this class are significant only to the extent they remain attached to the 'flat, substanceless surface' of the law.

---

[24] Out of a burgeoning literature, see, eg, Tsagourias, 2000; Koskenniemi, 2009.

VI. INSTRUMENTALISM, FORMALISM, AND THE PRODUCTION OF AN INTERNATIONAL POLITICAL COMMUNITY

Modern international law puts the international lawyer at the heart of the legal system. It is possible to represent that position schematically by reference to the two types of logic at play in the international rule of law. Here is the international relations theorist Hedley Bull:

> The special interests of the dominant elements in a society are reflected in the way in which the rules are defined. Thus the particular kinds of limitations that are imposed on resort to violence, the kinds of agreements whose binding character is upheld, or the kinds of right to property that are enforced, will have the stamp of those dominant elements. But that there should be limits of some kind to violence, and an expectation in general that agreements should be carried out, and rules or property of some kind, is not a special interest of some members of a society but a general interest of all of them. (Bull, 1977, p 55)

So described, law unites an *instrumentalist logic*, one that looks for the realization of objectives through law, with a *formalist logic*, one that establishes standards of behaviour. Now it is obvious that neither logic is fully constraining. The instrumental logic is indeterminate as the objectives always leave a number of possible choices: what does 'peace and security' mean and how should it be realized in the Middle East, for example? Nor is the formalist logic ever fully formal, but always in practice somehow partial and biased. However general the rules of law are, their equal application may appear unjust because the reality to which they are applied is profoundly unequal: should large and small States, democracies, and dictatorships really be treated alike? The form of law is realized in particular rules or decisions that are no longer formal but that always institute a bias in favour of some substantive preferences.

In the *Nuclear Weapons* case (1996), the ICJ was requested by the UN General Assembly to give an Advisory Opinion on the legal status of nuclear weapons. From the perspective of the instrumentalist logic, the relevant regulation (human rights law, environmental law, humanitarian law, and the law concerning the use of force) sought to accomplish several types of objectives: above all protection of human life and the environment, as well as the survival of States. These objectives proved indeterminate, however, and both opponents and supporters of nuclear weapons argued by reference to them: are people better protected with or without nuclear weapons? The instrumental logic did set some limits to what the Court could say, but it did not—indeed could not—fully constrain it. A decision by the Court was needed to bring the instrumental logic to a conclusion.

The formalist logic was equally under-determined. To decide that nuclear weapons were *illegal* would have created a consistent material bias in favour of States in possession of conventional weapons or in de facto possession of undisclosed nuclear weapons. To require the dismantling of disclosed nuclear arsenals would have revolutionized the existing military-political relationships in unforeseen ways. But to decide that nuclear weapons were *lawful* would have maintained the systemic bias in security policy in favour of the Great Powers and gone against the deep-rooted popular sense that the existence of such weapons constitutes a permanent hostage-taking by nuclear weapons States of most of the world's population. Neither illegality nor legality could remain fully within the formalist logic. Both broke through pure form and created one or another type of material preference. Indeed, it was impossible to decide either way without the decision seeming 'biased' from the opposed standpoints. And because the political choice in this case seemed too important for the Court to take, it chose the path of recognizing the insufficiency of both logics: 'the Court considers it does not have sufficient elements to enable it to decide with certainty that the use of nuclear weapons would be necessarily at variance with the principles and rules applicable in armed conflict in any circumstance.'[25]

I have defended elsewhere the Court's silence inasmuch as it protected the need for a sustained *political* condemnation of the killing of the innocent, lifting it from the banal instrumentalism and formalism of modern law (Koskenniemi, 1999a). Irrespective of that position, however, the case illustrates the indeterminacy of both of the two types of logic behind the Rule of Law, as outlined by Bull at the beginning of this section. Neither instrumental calculation nor a purely formal analysis could grasp the status of such weapons: a *decision* was needed that was irreducible to the two logics. Here the decision was silence. In other cases, the Court may have recourse to literalism, balancing, contextualization, and bilateralization, among a host of other techniques, to complete the instrumental and formal structures within which it works (Koskenniemi, 1989, pp 410–21). Each of such techniques is, again, indeterminate. None of them explain why *this* argument was held relevant, why *that* interpretation was chosen. The decision always comes about, as the political theorist Ernesto Laclau has put it, as a kind of 'regulated madness', never reducible to any structure outside it (Laclau, 1996, p 58).

A court's decision or a lawyer's opinion is always a genuinely political act, a choice between alternatives not fully dictated by external criteria. It is even a *hegemonic* act in the precise sense that though it is partial and subjective, it claims to be universal and objective (see further Koskenniemi, 2004a). But it is this very partiality and political nature of the decision that ensures that it is an aspect of, or even a creative moment of, a political community. Here finally is the significance of the under-determination of the two logics behind the Rule of Law. The society upheld by international law is not an effect of instrumental reason, nor even of (some conception) of formal reason *tout court*. It is an effect of decisions that invoke as their justification, and thus offer as valid points of criticism, an idea of (international) community beyond sectorial interests or preferences. An idea of solidarity informs that practice. Of course, such decisions are made under conditions of uncertainty and conflict. They are amenable to criticism from alternative standpoints: there is the solidarity of the lion and that of the antelope. But that this decision-making practice is not the passive reproduction of some globalizing (economic, environmental, humanitarian) structure, projects the international society as a *political community* that seeks to decide for itself what rules govern it. The practice of international law, as Bull suggested, seeks a union of 'dominant elements' with 'general interest'. As such, it remains a terrain in which the never-ending struggle between the two is being waged: hegemony, and critique of hegemony at the same time.

VII. BEYOND INSTRUMENTALISM AND FORMALISM

In other words, although notions such as 'peace', 'justice', or 'human rights' do not fit well within the techniques of legal formalism, and are quite disappointing as behavioural directives, they give voice to individuals and groups struggling for spiritual or material well-being, fighting against oppression, and seeking to express their claims in the language of something greater than merely their personal interests. Law—including international law—has a 'utopian, aspirational face' (Cotterell, 1995, p 17) expressed in large notions such as 'peace', 'justice', or 'human rights' that in countless international law texts appeal to solidarity within community. They do this in three distinct, but related ways.

---

[25] *Legality of the Threat or Use of Nuclear Weapons, Advisory Opinion, ICJ Reports 1996*, p 226, para 95.

First, they redescribe individuals and groups as claimants of rights or beneficiaries of entitlements and in so doing provide them with an identity that they may assert against the homogenizing pull of society's dominant elements. As Karen Knop has pointed out, the treatment of claims of self-determination by marginalized groups such as indigenous peoples in legal institutions has sometimes enabled those groups to be represented by an identity 'that might resonate with those represented' and thus to 'equalize cultures in international law' (Knop, 2002, p 210). Secondly, legal principles give an international voice to communities by allowing them to read their particular grievances as claims of universal entitlement, at the same level as claims made by other members of the community. To be able to say that some act is an 'aggression' or that the deprivation of a benefit is a 'human rights violation' is to lift a private grievance to the level of a public law violation, of concern not only to the victim but to the community. Such notions—and the whole debate about the objectives of international law—act in the political realm to challenge what Norman Geras has termed the 'contract of mutual indifference'—the tendency to regard violations as a private matter between the victim and the perpetrator, and therefore not of concern to others (Geras, 1998). They challenge the way claims are blocked in the international realm as matters of 'security', 'economics', or, for example, 'private law', thus helping to contest dominant discourses and practices that seek to justify themselves by their apolitical self-evidence. And thirdly, to make those claims as *legal* claims (instead of moral aspirations or political programmes) is to imagine—and thus to create—the international world as a set of public institutions within which public authorities should use their power in roughly predictable ways and with public accountability to the community at large.

The fact that public law notions such as *jus cogens* or of obligations *erga omnes* tend to be formulated in such large terms as to restate the paradox of objectives has made them seem quite useless from an instrumental perspective. But, we may now assume, their role may be precisely to counteract the ideological effects of instrumentalism. Again, the *form* of those ideas—of an 'international legal community'—is important in allowing the articulation of the most varied types of claims as more than claims about personal preference, thus integrating the claimants as members of a pluralistic community. 'Self-determination', typically, may be constructed analytically to mean anything one wants it to mean, and many studies have invoked its extreme flexibility. Examined in the light of history, however, it has given form and strength to claims for national liberation and self-rule from the French Revolution to decolonization in the 1960s, the fall of the Berlin Wall, and the political transitions that have passed from Latin America through Eastern Europe and South Africa. 'Peace', too, may be an empty notion, perfectly capable of coexisting with economic deprivation and suppression of human rights. On the other hand, peace movements have been an invaluable aspect of political contestation inasmuch as they 'mobilise support and highlight the inconsistencies in international concepts of peace and security' (Charlesworth and Chinkin, 2000, p 272). Even if 'justice' does lie in the eye of the beholder, without a language of justice, the international struggles for resources, recognition, democracy, or, for instance, 'ending the culture of impunity', would have seemed like so many meaningless games played by diplomats.

In other words, though the question 'what is international law for?' is seldom useful as an aspect of the deliberations over particular problems among international lawyers, it is absolutely crucial as a focus for international law's emancipatory potential. This is why it was significant that the demonstrations against the war in Iraq in 2003 focused on the war's 'illegality'. In this way, the special scandal of Western military action could be articulated as not just the violation of the private interests of Iraqi citizens but as directed against the (legal) community, and thus everyone. The fabricated character of the justifications invoked for the war further highlighted the significance of the claim of the war's formal illegality:

behind the contrast between a morality of 'freedom' and a morality of 'law', there was a deeper question about who should be entitled to rule us and what we can take on trust.

None of this deviates from the need to recognize that while the culture of formalism is a necessary though often misunderstood aspect of the legal craft, as a historical matter, it has often provided a recipe for indifference and needs to be accompanied by a live sense of its political justification. To lift the debate about objectives from diplomatic instruments or academic treatises to the level of political debates is a necessary counterweight to the bureaucratic spirit often associated with formalism. This will enable the reconstruction of international law as a political project. As modern international law arose in the last decades of the nineteenth century, it did so as a part of the élitist politics of European liberal internationalism that expected public opinion and democracy to pave the way for a rationally administered world (see Koskenniemi, 2001a; Pemberton, 2001). The last articulations of that spirit date from the first decade following the Second World War (see, eg, Lauterpacht, 1946). Since then, a gap has been created between the utopian and the pragmatic parts of international law, the former becoming a rather grandiose justification over the latter. But when formalism loses political direction, formalism itself is lost.[26] Hence the turn to pragmatism and instrumentalism. And hence also the more recent 'backlash' against global institutions and the very idea of global rule of law—experienced frequently as rule by an unaccountable expert elite.

The question 'what is international law for?' needs to be resuscitated from the paralysis that infects it because of the indeterminacy of the responses given to it. But this necessitates a reformulation of the relationship of international law to politics, in either of its two guises, as principles and doctrines on the one hand, and as institutional practices on the other. Both political realism and institutional pragmatism arose as reactions to failed expectations about international law's autonomy: realists rejected legal institutions as a sham and told politicians to aim directly at their objectives. Institutionalists were wary of such objectives and instead relied on techniques of adjustment and compromise.

VIII. BETWEEN HEGEMONY AND FRAGMENTATION: A MINI-HISTORY

These reaction formations are intellectually disappointing and politically dubious. Neither provides space for anything but a most formal debate about 'what is international law for?' and no space at all for responding to that question by reference to popular aspirations about peace, order, and justice. A first step in trying to account for such aspirations is to accept that these notions are subject to political controversy and that even as they are formulated in universal terms, they are constantly appropriated by particular agents and interests so as to support their agendas and causes. They are aspects of *hegemonic struggle*, that is to say, part of an argumentative practice in which particular subjects and values claim to represent that which is universal (see Mouffe and Laclau, 2001; Koskenniemi, 2004a). That the question 'what is international law for?' is a terrain of such controversy is a natural aspect of a pluralistic society and a precondition for conceiving its government in democratic terms.

The hegemonic nature of the debate about international law's objectives may be illustrated in terms of its history (see also Koskenniemi, 2004b; Supiot, 2005, pp 275–305). When Spain and Portugal at the end of the fifteenth century divided the non-European world between themselves by reference to a Papal directive, they claimed to be speaking as Christian powers on behalf of humankind as a whole. When the Spanish theologians

---

[26] For a useful reconstruction of Hans Kelsen's formalism in terms of the political project that inspired it, see von Bernstorff, 2001.

Vitoria or Las Casas were later claiming that God had given the Indians a soul just as He had given it to the Spanish, a particular form of Christian scholasticism—Dominican theology—came to speak in terms of universal principles, equally constraining on the Princes and the Indians. And when Hugo Grotius in 1608 challenged the Iberian claims, he was redefining the objectives of international law within a hegemonic struggle that opposed a Reformation-inspired commercial universalism against the *ancien régime* of (Catholic) Christianity. The narrative of international law from those days to the nineteenth century may be depicted as a succession of natural-law arguments that were united by their always emerging from some European intelligentsia that claimed it was speaking on behalf of the world as a whole. When de Emer de Vattel in 1758 formulated his 'necessary law of nations' in terms of the commands of natural reason, and found that it consecrated a balance of power between European sovereigns, he already filled the category of the 'universal' with a profoundly particular understanding that was a part of the (European) Enlightenment.

Since the first appearance of the (modern) international law profession in Europe in the late nineteenth century, that profession imagined itself as, in the words of the Statute of the *Institut de droit international* (1873), the 'juridical conscience of the civilised world'.

This understanding, too, was born in a cultural environment that imagined its own experience—which it labelled 'civilization'—as universal and postulated it as the end-result of the development of societies everywhere. The civilizing mission enthusiastically propagated by late nineteenth-century international lawyers was a hegemonic technique, embedded in an understanding of the law as not simply a technical craft or a set of formal instruments and institutions. It was a spontaneous aspect of 'civilization' which had the natural tendency to become universal.

If the First World War destroyed whatever was left of the civilizing mission, it also gave rise to a series of efforts to articulate anew the universal basis of international law, sometimes in terms of a law-like movement of societies to ever more complex forms of division of labour and interdependence (eg Huber, 1910), sometimes through a reinstatement of the hierarchical principles that were a natural part of legal systems (eg Verdross, 1923). Most of the reconstructive scholarship of the inter-war period, however, simply generalized the legal experience of European societies into the international level, bringing into existence a universal international law through private law analogies, conceiving the Covenant of the League of Nations as a constitution of the world, and by allocating to the juristic class the function of 'filling the gaps' in an otherwise primitive-looking legal system (see Lauterpacht, 1933; Koskenniemi, 1997). The particular European experience with the Rule of Law became the placeholder for the aspirations of peace and justice that lawyers saw were demanded by populations struggling with industrialism and social conflict.

In the more recent post-war era, much of that kind of language—like the political liberalism with which it was associated—has lost credibility. When somebody today claims to be acting on behalf of the 'international community', we immediately recognize the hegemonic technique at work (see Klein, 2001; Feher, 2000; Koskenniemi, 2004a). As against the diplomatic antics of public international law, new specializations today often carry the ideals of universalism and progress. Recently, this has occasioned a lively debate about the 'fragmentation of international law'—the emergence and consolidation of special regimes and technical sub-disciplines: human rights law, environmental law, trade law, humanitarian law, and so on, each field projecting its preferences as universal ones. The result has been increasing normative and jurisdictional conflicts. In its *Tadić* judgment of 1999, the International Criminal Tribunal for the Former Yugoslavia (ICTY) expressly deviated from the practice of the International Court of Justice, as laid out in its *Nicaragua* case in 1986 concerning the attribution of conduct by military irregulars to a State. To move from a standard of 'effective control' to one of 'overall control' significantly enhanced the accountability of foreign States indirectly involved in internal conflicts, constituting a shift of normative preference with respect to one set of international problems.[27] The continuing debate about the relevance of environmental, human rights, or labour standards within the WTO system reflects a search for the relative priority of political objectives within WTO institutions as those priorities have not been set at the level of the relevant agreements themselves. The autonomy invoked by human rights regimes constitutes a subtle manoeuvre by human rights implementation organs to universalize their jurisdiction. 'Dynamic' arguments and the object and purpose test allow the creation of a systemic bias in favour of the protected individuals that could be difficult to justify under traditional law.

Such 'fragmentation' is not a technical problem resulting from lack of coordination. The normative preferences of environmental and trade bodies differ, as do preferences of human rights lawyers and international law 'generalists', and each organ is determined to follow its own preference and make it prevail over contrasting ones. The result is, sometimes, deviating interpretations of the general law, such preferences reflecting the priorities of the deciding organ, at other times the creation of firm exceptions in the law, applicable in a special field (Koskenniemi and Leino, 2002). Such fragmentation is also an aspect of hegemonic struggle where each institution, though partial, tries to occupy the space of the whole. Far from being a problem to resolve, the proliferation of autonomous or semi-autonomous normative regimes is an unavoidable reflection of a 'postmodern' social condition. Its dark side is visible in expert rule and in the backlash against internationalism and global governance witnessed in recent years, especially in the developed world (Koskenniemi 2018).

IX. LEGAL FORMALISM AND INTERNATIONAL JUSTICE

Let me close with four responses to the question 'what is international law for?'. Two are rather straightforward. First, international law exists to advance the values, interests, and preferences that those in dominant positions seek to realize in the world. It is an instrument of power. Secondly, it also gives voice to those who have been excluded from powerful positions and are regularly treated as the objects of other peoples' policies; it provides a platform on which claims about violence, injustice, and social deprivation may be made even against the dominant elements. It is an instrument for the critique of power. To bring these two aspects of international law together means that there is no fixed set of objectives, purposes, or principles that would exist somewhere 'outside' or beyond international law itself, that they are always the objectives of particular actors involved in polemical confrontations. The law is instrumental, but what it is an instrument for cannot be fixed outside the political process of which it is an inextricable part.

This is why, thirdly, international law's objective is always also international law itself. For, as I have tried to argue in this chapter, it is international law's formalism that brings political antagonists together as they invoke contrasting understandings of its rules and institutions. In the absence of agreement over, or knowledge of, the 'true' objectives of political community—that is to say, in an agnostic world—the pure form of international law provides the shared surface—the *only* such surface—on which political adversaries recognize each other as such and pursue their adversity in terms of something shared, instead of seeking to attain full exclusion—'outlawry'—of the other. In this sense, international law's value and its misery lie in its being the fragile surface of political community among social

[27] *Prosecutor v Dusko Tadić*, Judgment, Case No IT-94-1-A, Appeals Chamber, 15 July 1999, 38 ILM 1518, para 137.

agents—States, other communities, individuals—who disagree about their preferences but do this within a structure that invites them to argue in terms of an assumed universality.

But there is a fourth response as well: international law exists as a promise of justice. The agnosticism of political modernity has made the articulation of this teleological view extremely difficult. For the justice towards which international law points cannot be enumerated in substantive values, interests, or objectives. It has no predetermined institutional form. The lawyer's political advocacy and institutional reform-proposals express inadequate and reified images, (partial) points of view. Even when acceptable in their general formulation, as soon as they are translated into particular policies, and start to prefer some interests or values over others, they become vulnerable to the critique of 'false universalism'. For the *homo economicus*, none of this is too important. All that count are the external objectives projected upon the law. If law fails in realizing them, then it loses its authority. The image of law embodied in the metaphor of the *homo juridicus* is quite different. Now law itself—independently of the objectives projected upon it—has authority. This authority comes from the way it describes the international world as a (legal) community where questions of just distribution and entitlement are constantly on the agenda, where claims of legal subjects receive an equal hearing, and where the acts of public officials are assessed by a language of community standards. For the instrumental view, the constraint received from law is justified only in view of the authority of the law's (external) objectives. In the formalist view, law is used to compel because the violations cannot coexist with the aspirations of universality embedded in the legal form. Such violations are singular until the law lifts them from the purely subjective into public illegality:

> Law is the name of the semblance of order—the assembling, the ordering, the establishing of commonality—that is made of our otherwise (subjective) differences when we take, or interpret them to be a world that can be judged, rather than mere subjective experiences. (Constable, 2000, p 95)

But the justice that animates political community is not one that may be fully attained. Not only is law never justice itself, but the two cannot exist side by side. If there is justice, then no law is needed—and if there is law, then there is only a (more or less well-founded) *expectation* of justice. Here is the truth in instrumentalism about positive law being a pointer beyond itself. There is a Messianic structure to international law, the announcement of something that remains eternally postponed. It is this 'to-come' that enables the criticism of the law's own violence, its biases and exclusions. No doubt, law and justice are linked in the activity of lawyers, paradigmatically in the legal judgment. This is the wisdom grasped by legal pragmatism. But the judgment is always insufficiently grounded in law, just as positive law is always insufficiently expressive of justice. In the gap between positive law and justice lies the necessary (and impossible) realm of the politics of law. Without it, law becomes pure positivity, its violence a mere fact of power.

REFERENCES

ABBOTT, K and SNIDAL, D (2001), 'Hard and Soft Law in International Governance', in JL Goldstein, M Kahler, RO Keohane, and A-M Slaughter (eds), *Legalization and World Politics* (Cambridge, MA: MIT Press), pp 37–72.

ARNAUD, A-J (2003), *Critique de la raison juridique 2: Gouvernants sans frontières. Entre mondialisation et post-mondialisation* (Paris: LGDJ).

BINDER, G (1988), 'Beyond Criticism', 55 *U Chi LR* 688–915.

BRIERLY, J (1944), *The Outlook for International Law* (Oxford: Oxford University Press).

BRUNNEE, J and TOOPE, SJ (2011), *Legitimacy and Legality in International Law: An Interactional Account* (Cambridge: Cambridge University Press).

BULL, H (1977), *The Anarchic Society. A Study of Order in World Politics* (London: Macmillan).

BYERS, M and NOLTE, G (2003), *United States Hegemony and the Foundations of International Law* (Cambridge: Cambridge University Press).

CAMERON, I (2000), *National Security and the European Convention on Human Rights* (Stockholm: Iustus).

CARR, EH (1946), *The Twenty Years' Crisis 1919-1939* (London: Macmillan).

CHARLESWORTH, H (2002), 'International Law: A Discipline of Crisis', 65 *MLR* 377–92.

CHARLESWORTH, H and CHINKIN, C (2000), *The Boundaries of International Law. A Feminist Analysis* (Manchester: Manchester University Press).

CHAYES, A and CHAYES, AH (1995), *The New Sovereignty. Compliance with International Regulatory Agreements* (Cambridge, MA: Harvard University Press).

CHESTERMAN, S (2001), *Just War or Just Peace? Humanitarian Intervention and International Law* (Oxford: Oxford University Press).

CONSTABLE, M (2000), 'The Silence of the Law: Justice in Cover's "Field of Pain and Death"', in A Sarat (ed), *Law, Violence and the Possibility of Justice* (Princetown, NJ: Princeton University Press).

CORTEN, O (1997), *L'utilisation du 'raisonnable' par le juge international. Discours juridique, raison et contradictions* (Brussels: Bruylant).

COTTERELL, R (1995), *Law's Community. Legal Theory in Sociological Perspective* (Oxford: Clarendon Press).

CRAWFORD, J (2018), 'The Current Political Discourse Regarding International Law', 81 MLR, 1–22.

FEHER, M (2000), *Powerless by Design. The Age of the International Community* (Durham, NC: Duke University Press).

FINNEMORE, M (1996), *National Interests in International Society* (Ithaca, NY: Cornell University Press).

FISH, S (1989), *Doing What Comes Naturally. Change, Rhetoric, and the Practice of Theory in Literary and Legal Studies* (Oxford: Oxford University Press).

FOUCAULT, M (2005), *Naissance de la biopolitique. Cours au Collège de France 1978–79* (Paris: Gallimard/Seuil).

FRANCK, TM (1995), *Fairness in International Law and Institutions* (Oxford: Oxford University Press).

FULLER, LL (1969), *The Morality of Law* (2nd rev edn, New Haven, CT: Yale University Press).

GERAS, N (1998), *The Contract of Mutual Indifference. Political Philosophy after the Holocaust* (London: Verso).

GOLDSMITH, J and POSNER, E (2005), *The Limits of International Law* (Oxford: Oxford University Press).

GREWE, W (2001), *The Epochs of International Law* (M Byers, trans) (Berlin: De Gruyter).

GUZZINI, G (1998), *Realism in International Relations and International Political Economy* (London: Routledge).

HABERMAS, J (2004), *Der gespaltene Westen* (Frankfurt: Suhrkamp).

HARDT, M and NEGRI, A (1999), *Empire* (Cambridge, MA: Harvard University Press).

HENKIN, L (1989), 'International Law: Politics, Values and Functions', 216 *Recueil des Cours* 9–416.

HUBER, M (1910/1928), *Die soziologischen Grundlagen des Völkerrechts* (Berlin: Rothschild).

HURRELL, A and WOODS, N (1999), *Inequality, Globalization and World Politics* (Oxford: Oxford University Press).

KANT, I (1999), *Critique of Practical Reason* (M Gregor (ed), Introduction by Reath, A) (Cambridge: Cambridge University Press).

KAUFMANN, E (1911), *Das Wesen des Völkerrechts und die Clausula rebus sic stantibus* (Tübingen Mohr).

KENNEDY, D (2000), 'When Renewal Repeats: Thinking Against the Box', 32 *NYU JILP* 335–500.

KENNEDY, D (2004), *The Darker Side of Virtue. Reassessing International Humanitarianism* (Princeton, NJ: Princeton University Press).

KENNEDY, D (2001), 'Formalism', in *The International Encyclopedia of Social & Behavioral Sciences* (The Hague: Kluwer).

KERVÉGAN, J-F (1999), 'Carl Schmitt and "World Unity"', in C Mouffe (ed), *The Challenge of Carl Schmitt* (London: Verso), pp 54–74.

KLEIN, P (2001), 'Les problèmes soulevés par la référence à la communauté inter-nationale comme facteur de legitimite', in O Corten and B Delcourt (eds), *Droit, légitimation et politique extérieure: L'Europe et la guerre du Kosovo* (Brussels: Bruylant), pp 261–97.

KNOP, K (2002), *Diversity and Self-Determination in International Law* (Cambridge: Cambridge University Press).

KOSKENNIEMI, M (1989), *From Apology to Utopia. The Structure of International Legal Argument*, 2005 reissue with new Epilogue (Cambridge: Cambridge University Press).

KOSKENNIEMI, M (1994), 'The Wonderful Artificiality of States', 88 *ASIL Proc* 22–9.

KOSKENNIEMI, M (1997), 'Lauterpacht, The Victorian Tradition in International Law', 8 *EJIL* 215–63.

KOSKENNIEMI, M (1999a), 'The Silence of Law/The Voice of Justice', in L Boisson de Chazournes and P Sands (eds), *International Law, the International Court of Justice and Nuclear Weapons* (Cambridge: Cambridge University Press), pp 488–510.

KOSKENNIEMI, M (1999b) 'The Limits of International Law: Are There Such?', XXVIII *Thesaurus Acroasiarum: Might and Right in International Relations* 27–50.

KOSKENNIEMI, M (2000), 'The Effect of Rights on Political Culture', in P Alston (ed), *The EU and Human Rights* (Oxford: Oxford University Press), pp 99–116.

KOSKENNIEMI, M (2001a), *The Gentle Civilizer of Nations. The Rise and Fall of International Law 1870–1960* (Cambridge: Cambridge University Press).

KOSKENNIEMI, M (2001b), 'Solidarity Measures: State Responsibility as a New International Order?', 72 *BYIL* 339–56.

KOSKENNIEMI, M (2004a), 'International Law and Hegemony: A Reconfiguration', 17 *Cambridge Review of International Affairs*, 197–218.

KOSKENNIEMI, M (2004b), 'Legal Universalism: Between Morality and Power in a World of States', in S Cheng (ed), *Law, Justice and Power: Between Reason and Will* (Stanford, NJ: Stanford University Press), pp 46–69.

KOSKENNIEMI, M (2005), 'International Law in Europe: Between Tradition and Renewal', 16 *EJIL* 113–24.

KOSKENNIEMI, M (2009), 'Miserable Comforters. International Relations as New Natural Law', 15 *EJIR* 395–422.

KOSKENNIEMI, M and LEINO, P (2002), 'The Fragmentation of International Law: Postmodern Anxieties', 16 *LJIL* 533–579.

KOSKENNIEMI, M (2018), 'Conclusion: After Globalization. Engaging the Backlash', in R Schütze & M Gehring (eds), *Governance and Globalization: International Problems—European Solutions* (Cambridge: Cambridge University Press 2018), forthcoming

KRATOCHWIL, F (2000), 'How Do Norms Matter?', in M Byers (ed), *The Role of Law in International Politics. Essays in International Relations and International Law* (Oxford: Oxford University Press), pp 35–68.

LACLAU, E (1996), 'Deconstruction, Pragmatism, Hegemony', in C Mouffe (ed), *Deconstruction and Pragmatism* (London: Verso).

Lâm, MC (2000), *At the Edge of the State: Indigenous Peoples and Self-Determination* (Dobbs Ferry, NY: Transnational).

Lauterpacht, H (1933), *The Function of Law in the International Community* (Oxford: Oxford University Press).

Lauterpacht, H (1946), 'The Grotian Tradition in International Law', 23 *BYIL* 1–53.

Lauterpacht, H (1958), *The Development of International Law by the International Court* (London: Stevens).

Lauterpacht, H (1975), 'The Reality of the Law of Nations', in *International Law, being the Collected Papers of Hersch Lauterpacht*, vol 2, pp 22–51.

Mcdougal, MS (1953), 'International Law, Power and Policy. A Contemporary Conception', 82 *Recueil des Cours* 137–259.

Marks, S (2000), *The Riddle of All Constitutions. International Law, Democracy and the Critique of Ideology* (Oxford: Oxford University Press).

Morgenthau, H (1940), 'Positivism, Functionalism, and International Law', 34 *AJIL* 261–84.

Mouffe, C and Laclau, E (2001), *Hegemony and Socialist Strategy* (2nd edn, London: Verso).

Nardin, T (1983), *Law, Morality and the Relations between States* (Princeton, NJ: Princeton University Press).

O'Neill, O (2000), *Bounds of Justice* (Cambridge: Cambridge University Press).

Orford, A (2003), *Reading Humanitarian Intervention. Human Rights and the Use of Force in International Law* (Cambridge: Cambridge University Press).

Paulus, A (2001), *Die internationale Gemeinschaft im Völkerrecht. Eine Untersuchung zur Entwicklung des Völkerrechts im Zeitalter der Globalisierung* (Munich: Beck).

Pemberton, J-A (2001), *Global Metaphors. Modernity and the Quest for One World* (London: Pluto Press).

Posner, E (2003), 'Do States have a Moral Obligation to Obey International Law?', 55 *Stanford Law Journal* 1901–20.

Posner E (2017), 'Liberal Internationalism and the Populist Backlash', University of Chicago: Public law and Legal Theory Working Paper No. 606.

Schachter, O (1997), 'The Decline of the Nation-state and its Implications for International Law', 35 *Col J of Transnat'l L* 7–23.

Schmitt, C (1988), *Der Nomos der Erde im Völkerrecht des Jus Publicum Europaeum* (3rd edn, Berlin: Duncker & Humblot).

Schmitt, C (1996), *The Concept of the Political* (G Schwab (trans and Introduction)) (Chicago: University of Chicago Press).

Shelton, D (ed) (2000), *Commitment and Compliance. The Role of Non-Binding Norms in the International Legal System* (Oxford: Oxford University Press).

Supiot, A (2005), *Homo juridicus. Essai sur la fonction anthropologique de droit* (Paris: Seuil).

Tasioulas, J (1996), 'In Defence of Relative Normativity: Communitarian Values and the Nicaragua Case', 16 *OJLS* 85–128.

Tomuschat, C (1999), 'International Law: Ensuring the Survival of Mankind on the Eve of New Century', 23 *Recueil des Cours* 1–281.

Tsagourias, N (2000), 'Globalization, Order and the Rule of Law', XI *FYBIL* 247–64.

Verdross, A (1923), *Die Einheit des rechtlichen Weltbildes* (Tübingen: Mohr).

Von Bernstorff, J (2001), *Der Glaube an das Universale Recht. Zur Völkerrechtstheorie Hans Kelsens und seiner Schüler* (Baden-Baden: Nomos).

Watts, Sir A (2000), 'The Importance of International Law', in M Byers (ed), *The Role of Law in International Politics*, pp 5–16.

Weil, P (1983), 'Towards Relative Normativity in International Law?', 77 *AJIL* 413–42.

Westlake, J (1910), *International Law*, vol 2 (2nd edn, Cambridge: Cambridge University Press).

3

A VIEW OF DELFT: SOME THOUGHTS ABOUT THINKING ABOUT INTERNATIONAL LAW

Iain Scobbie

Legal theory is always more or less closely connected with philosophical thinking, political conditions, and ideological currents. As these factors were vastly different in England, Germany and France during the nineteenth century, so legal theory took different directions in these three countries.

Karl Olivecrona, *Law as Fact*
(1971), p 27

[T]heories of law . . . are one of the principal causes of low morale among students of international law.

Ian Brownlie, *International Law at the Fiftieth Anniversary
of the United Nations* (1995), p 22

SUMMARY

International law does not exist in an intellectual vacuum. Our understanding of the nature of international law—of what it is and what it can and should do—is ultimately dependent on theoretical assumptions and presuppositions. These can be latent and unexamined, in which case they are likely to foster only an acritical complacency. As all law has a political dimension, because law attempts to provide authoritative models of how people should behave, it is not surprising that theoretical models of international law encode specific views of the world and of relations between States. These assumptions and presuppositions influence the analysis of substantive issues, thus active engagement with theory is a matter which should neither be ignored nor be simply left behind in the academy.

I. THE PERILS OF PHILOSOPHY

Thinking can be dangerous, much more dangerous than the pseudo-danger envisaged in Professor Brownlie's fatuous assertion that 'there is no doubt room for a whole treatise on the harm caused to the business of legal investigation by theory' (Brownlie, 1983, p 627).[1] Examples of the dangers of thinking are not hard to find. For example, during the Cold War, there was a tendency for some Eastern European analytical legal theorists to focus on logic and formal modes of reasoning (see, eg, Wróblewski, 1974). One supposes that at least partly the decision to do so was rooted in prudence because evaluative substantive or policy analysis could be personally, professionally, and politically dangerous.

Brownlie's assertion simply begs the question. How can one know what there is 'legal' to investigate unless one subscribes to some abstract conception of law? That is a matter for legal theory. It need not provide a watertight definition of what law is and what it is about, but it should at least give basic criteria which enable the identification of what counts as 'legal investigation' in the first place. Further, a disavowal of theory can also denote an unthinking and essentially conservative commitment to a hidden or latent theory that rests content with the status quo and seeks neither to question nor justify either the substance or practice of international law (Warbrick, 1991, pp 69–70).[2] This disinterest simply amounts to a complacent refusal to think about what one is doing, and constitutes an intellectual self-censorship which suppresses analysis and critical evaluation.

If being 'dangerous' takes things too far, thinking should at least be a 'challenge'. How do we know that our beliefs have value unless we examine them and, in particular, their underlying assumptions? These assumptions, these preconceptions, often colour our understanding of the content of international law. As Professor Koskenniemi has observed, a characteristic of contemporary international legal practice is specialization, where discrete sets of substantive issues are packaged into categories such as trade law or environmental law or human rights law and so on. These specializations 'cater for special audiences with special interests and special ethos'. Each contains structural biases in the form of dominant expectations about the values, actors, and solutions appropriate to that specialization, which thus affect practical outcomes. The actors in these different fields conceptualize issues in ways which pull upon these preconceptions to reach solutions which are thought suitable for the specialization (Koskenniemi, 2009a and 2009b: see also Beckett, 2009, and Scobbie, 2009). For example, in discussing the relationship between the law of armed conflict and human rights, Professor Garraway underlines the importance of the analyst's own perspective and presuppositions:

> For human rights lawyers, human rights principles are those that provide the greatest protection to all by introducing a high threshold for any use of force and even if that threshold is crossed, a graduated use of force thereafter. On the other hand, international humanitarian lawyers see this as idealistic and impracticable. As they see it, it would become almost impossible to conduct hostilities legally to which many human rights lawyers would reply that that would be no bad thing! The difficulty is that such an attitude will not abolish armed conflict. (Garraway, 2010, p 509)

Similarly, Professor Kretzmer points out that the doctrine of proportionality employed by the law of armed conflict differs from that employed by human rights law.

---

[1] For Brownlie's antipathy to theory, see further Brownlie, 1981, pp 5–8, and Brownlie, 1995, pp 22ff.

[2] See also Warbrick, 2000, p 621 *passim*, but especially at pp 633–6; and Lasswell and McDougal, 1943, p 207. This was their first co-authored work, and is reprinted as an appendix in Lasswell and McDougal, 1992, vol II, p 1265.

Proportionality in the law of armed conflict concerns collateral damage, and thus permits civilian death and injury, an advance calculation which is an anathema to human rights law. He observes that Additional Protocol II, which regulates non-international armed conflict, makes no reference to proportionality, but that the International Committee of the Red Cross' customary international law study claims it is a principle which applies in this type of conflict (see Henckaerts and Doswald-Beck 2005, Vol I, pp 46–50). Kretzmer comments that this appears to assume that in an internal armed conflict proportionality protects potential victims, but its introduction could instead weaken the protection they might otherwise enjoy under a human rights regime because the armed conflict test of proportionality entrenches as a legitimate expectation that civilians may be killed and injured (see Kretzmer, 2009, pp 17–22).

These examples underline a point made, amongst others, by Professors Allott and Koskenniemi, that as lawyers we must be conscious of what we are doing and why we are doing it and, above all, take responsibility for our arguments. We therefore owe it to ourselves to examine the assumptions and biases we bring with us to our work. As Gertrude Stein cautions, 'If you do write as you have heard it said then you have to change it' (Stein, 1936 (1998a), p 411). Don't worry about Gertrude: she will pop up again later. She often does.

II. THE PROLOGUE—THE VIEW FROM DELPHI

Probably the most widely known fact about the ancient Greek philosopher Socrates, one of the founders of Western philosophy, is the manner of his death. He was condemned to commit suicide, by drinking hemlock, after being tried in Athens for impiety and corrupting youth. In the *Apology*, Plato's account of Socrates' own defence speech at his trial, Socrates recounts that one of his friends had once asked the oracle at Delphi if there was anyone wiser than Socrates, and the priestess replied that no one was (see Plato, 1969, p 49). This was perhaps not the best way for the accused in a capital trial, essentially accused of thought crimes, to ingratiate himself with his jury. Nor, given the nature of the charges against him, was his assertion that he could not abandon philosophy as:

> to let no day pass without discussing goodness and all the other subjects about which you hear me talking and examining both myself and others is really the very best thing a man can do, and that life without this sort of examination is not worth living. (Plato, 1969, pp 71–2)

Socrates was as rashly audacious when, having been found guilty, the prosecutor proposed that he be sentenced to death. Socrates suggested an alternative 'penalty'. Because he had shunned material gain in order to devote himself to persuading Athenians to think of their moral well-being, he thought that Athens should not punish but rather reward him by paying for his upkeep (see Plato, 1969, pp 69–70). Perhaps, given the political context of his trial, he knew he was as good as dead (see, eg, Hughes, 2010, pp 318–25; Waterfield, 2009, pp 173–90).

Pre-Socratic texts are few and fragmentary (see, eg, Gagarin and Woodruff, 1995, and Waterfield, 2000) and no writings by Socrates survive, if indeed there ever were any in the first place. All we know or think we know about what Socrates thought and argued comes from secondary sources, from philosophers such as Plato and Xenophon, and from satirists like Aristophanes. As a result, some contemporary Socratic experts, such as Vlastos, argue that it is unclear what precise ideas should be ascribed to him (Vlastos, 1994).

In *Phaedrus*, Plato places in Socrates' mouth a discussion of the desirability of writing (see Plato, 2002, pp 68–70). He tells the fable of the Egyptian god Theuth who invented writing, and showed it to his fellow-god Thamous who asked him to explain what benefits it would bring. Theuth replied that it would increase the intelligence of Egyptians and improve their memories. Thamous dismissed this justification, arguing that Theuth was committed to writing because he had invented it, and that this commitment had blinded him to its true effect. It would shrivel people's memories. Their trust in the written word would make them remember things 'by relying on marks made by others' rather than on their own mental resources. Writing would simply be a mechanism for jogging the memory, and thus only furnish the appearance of, but not real, intelligence:

> Because your students will be widely read, though without any contact with a teacher, they will seem to be men of wide knowledge, when they will usually be ignorant. And this spurious appearance of intelligence will make them difficult company. (Plato, 2002, p 69)

Thus Socrates argued that anyone who thinks he can help a branch of knowledge to survive by reducing it to writing, or thinks 'that writing will give him something clear and reliable', is wrong:

> there's something odd about writing . . . which makes it exactly like painting. The offspring of painting stand there as if alive, but if you ask them a question they maintain an aloof silence. It's the same with written words: you might think they were speaking as if they had some intelligence, but if you want an explanation of any of the things they're saying and ask them about it, they just go on and on for ever giving the same single piece of information. (Plato, 2002, p 70)

There is an apparent paradox in criticizing the utility of written argument in the course of a written argument (see Waterfield's introduction to Plato, 2002, at pp xxxvii–xlii), but key to Socratic philosophical method is the technique known as *elenchus*, which is a search for truth using dialectic argument. Roughly, this is a form of cross-examination where Socrates' interlocutor makes a claim which Socrates thinks is false and aims to disprove. To do so, Socrates secures agreement to an additional proposition or propositions which he then uses as the basis for further argument which aims at reaching a conclusion which his interlocutor will agree refutes or is incompatible with his initial claim. Accordingly, the optimum method of searching for the truth is by discussion in which claims and counter-claims may be tested and challenged. As Waterfield notes (Plato, 2002, p xxxix), Plato might have thought that the discursive nature of his dialogues should engage the reader in the conversation, which in any case was more concerned with provoking questions than providing answers.

The provocative nature of Socratic method is underlined in the *Apology*. Anytus, one of the prosecutors, had argued that Socrates must be condemned to death because, if not, Athenian youths 'would all immediately become utterly demoralised by putting the teaching of Socrates into practice' (Plato, 1969, p 61). The youths would be demoralized because the aim of Socrates' technique of *elenchus* was to leave his interlocutor in a state of *aporia*, an intellectual impasse which demonstrated to the interlocutor that he could not be sure that he really knew anything about the topic under discussion. To counter Anytus's censure, Socrates employed, again somewhat immodestly, what is sometimes known as the 'gadfly analogy':

> [If] you put me to death, you will harm yourselves more than me . . . If you put me to death, you will not easily find anyone to take my place . . . God has specially appointed me to this city, as though it were a large thoroughbred horse which because of its great size is inclined to be lazy and needs the stimulation of some stinging fly. It seems to me that God has attached me to this city to perform the office of such a fly; and all day long I never cease to settle here, there, and everywhere, rousing, persuading, reproving every one of you. You will not easily find another like me, gentlemen, and if you take my advice you will spare my life. (Plato, 1969, pp 62–3)

The gentlemen comprising the Athenian jury did not agree, and sentenced Socrates to death for impiety and corruption of youth.

This latter charge did not concern sexual impropriety. At that time, among some Athenians, sexual relations between adolescents and older men were socially acceptable. The idea was that the older man would act as a mentor to the younger, take him under his wing to show him how to be a proper Athenian citizen, and perhaps also take him to bed—although these relationships were not widespread but restricted essentially to the upper classes (see, eg, Waterfield, 2009, pp 55–7). Some Victorian philosophers tried to cover this up. For example, in his introduction to *Phaedras*, which considers amongst other things the nature of love, Jowett counsels:

> In this, as in his other discussions about love, what Plato says of the loves of men must be transferred to the loves of women before we can attach any serious meaning to his words. Had he lived in our times he would have made the transposition himself. But seeing in his own age the impossibility of woman being the intellectual helpmate or friend of man . . . seeing that, even as to personal beauty, her place was taken by young mankind instead of womankind, he tries to work out the problem of love without regard to the distinctions of nature (Plato, 1892, p 406).

The charge levied against Socrates that he had corrupted youth concerned, in particular, a young man named Alcibiades. In *Protagoras*, Plato has an unknown friend of Socrates exclaim:

> Hello, Socrates; what have you been doing? No need to ask; you've been chasing around after that handsome young fellow Alcibiades. Certainly when I saw him just recently he struck me as still a fine-looking man, but a man all the same, Socrates (just between ourselves), with his beard already coming. (Plato, 1996, p 3)

It was apparently an intimate relationship and, according to Plato's *Symposium*, they did sleep together. Alcibiades knew, or hoped he knew, what to expect, but these expectations were dashed. Plato has Alcibiades complain that when he and Socrates went to bed 'for all the naughtiness that we'd got up to, I might as well have been sleeping with my father or an elder brother' (Plato, 1994, p 66). Nothing physical took place. Alcibiades' hopes for sexual love were in vain.

This friendship was, nonetheless, one of the reasons why Socrates was sentenced to death, as Alcibiades held less than democratic political ideas in the relentlessly democratic Athens of the fifth century BCE. Rather than be a true mentor and teach Alcibiades how to be a proper Athenian citizen, committed to its rather muscular and aggressive form of democracy, Socrates was thought to have corrupted him by encouraging him to challenge the established order and to favour oligarchy. This was the antithesis of Athenian democracy, and was associated with Athens' political rival, Sparta. Socrates, in one way or another, had corrupted young Athenian men because he encouraged them to question the ways and ideals of their fathers (see, eg, Waterfield, 2009, especially ch 11, and Hughes, 2010).

In this light, Professor Brownlie appears to be a modern Anytus who fears that law students and lawyers might be demoralized by being encouraged to think about the nature of law, and to think for themselves. Perhaps we should reformulate his criticism of legal theory to affirm that there is room for a whole treatise on the harm caused to the business of philosophical investigation by political repression. There are times when thinking, and encouraging thinking, can be dangerous, and which sometimes can be fatal. A more recent example than Socrates is that of Evgeny Pashukanis (1891–1937), the Soviet author of *The General Theory of Law and Marxism* (1924). He was denounced as an 'enemy of the people' and as a 'Trotskyist saboteur' in 1937 and executed without trial. Pashukanis' view that the State would gradually wither away under communism was incompatible with Stalin's claim that socialism had by then been achieved in the Soviet Union (see, eg, Bowring, 2008, pp 146–58, and Head, 2004). Quite simply, the political context may be toxic to a robust and independent evaluation of law's nature, proper aims, and substantive content.

III. LAW, POLITICS, AND INSTRUMENTALISM

It is beyond doubt that the content and conceptions of law, whether international or domestic, bear some relationship to the wider contemporary socio-political context. All law has a political dimension as it aims to provide authoritative models of how those subject to it should behave. Often an issue emerges that is perceived to require regulation, and the contours of its legal analysis are determined by recourse to broadly political values. An early example in international law is Francisco de Vitoria's (c. 1483–1546) *De Indis (On the American Indians)* (1537) which applied scholastic natural law reasoning to undermine the legitimacy of Spanish claims to sovereignty over its American possessions:

> Vitoria's writings on power and the rights of conquest effectively set the agenda for most subsequent discussions on those subjects in Catholic Europe until the late seventeenth century … [A]lthough it is clearly false to speak of Vitoria as the father of anything so generalized and modern as 'International Law', it is the case that his writings became an integral part of later attempts to introduce some regulative principle into international relations.(Vitoria, 1991, p xxviii: *De Indis* is at p 231: see also Brett, 2012, and Tuck, 1999, pp 72–5)

Law and legal theory do not exist in a value-free vacuum but are inevitably concerned with political concerns and conditions,[3] and law inevitably favours some values and interests while ignoring or prejudicing others. In the case of international law, the privileged entities are principally States. Since at least the time of the Peace of Westphalia,[4] global organization has been characterized by the primacy of States as the principal actors on its political stage, making international law in pursuit of their own interests and policies. As Professor Craven has noted:

> notions of State and sovereignty [are] the key architectural features of international relations, whose existence from the Peace of Westphalia onwards is taken to be both 'given' and historically 'constant'. (Craven, 2012, p 864)

Although, in recent years, international legal theory has started to examine the implications of globalization, global governance, and the constitutionalization of the international legal order (see, for instance, works as diverse as Allott, 2002; Berman, 2005; Dunhoff and Trachtman, 2009; Klabbers, Peters, and Ulfstein, 2009; and Slaughter, 2004), the focus of international law remains on the State. The substantive structure and content of international law is asymmetric: it privileges States' interests above all others, relegating those of non-State entities to, at best, a secondary consideration. This asymmetry of the international legal system is reflected in theoretical discussions of international law.

---

[3] For instance, for an overview of the political context of the development of jurisprudential ideas, see Olivecrona, 1971, ch 1; and also Tuck, 1999.

[4] This was constituted by the Peace of Münster (Treaty of Peace between Spain and the Netherlands, signed 30 January 1648: (1648) 1 CTS 1), the Treaty of Münster (Treaty of Peace between the Holy Roman Empire and France, signed 24 October 1648: (1648) 1 CTS 271), and the Treaty of Osnabrück (Treaty of Peace between the Holy Roman Empire and Sweden, signed 24 October 1648: (1648) 1 CTS 198). For an assessment of the influence of the Peace of Westphalia see, eg, Gross, 1948, and Duchhardt, 2012, pp 629–34.

While it should not be surprising that a great deal of international legal theory has been instrumental, aimed at elucidating and explaining the role and conduct of States in the international sphere, another tendency has been more idealistic and is critical of the international system we have.

On the one hand, international legal theory has frequently been employed to provide instrumental methodologies which aim at embedding States' political programmes into the substance of international law—'Legal doctrines dissolve far too easily into thin disguises for assertions of national interests' (Kennedy, 1985, p 371). Clear examples of an instrumental approach to international law are two schools of thought that are principally associated with the antagonistic world views of the USA and the Soviet Union as they each vied for supremacy and power during the Cold War—the New Haven School and Marxist-Leninist theory. Although Soviet theory changed radically after perestroika (see, eg, McWhinney, 1990, and Vereshchetin and Müllerson, 1990, and Tunkin, 2003), instrumentalist approaches did not die with the Cold War, but remain alive and well in contemporary legal theory. Not only has there been a resurgence in interest in the New Haven School (see, eg, Borgen, 2007; Dickinson, 2007; Hathaway, 2007; Koh, 2007; Levit, 2007; Osofsky, 2007; and Reisman, Wiessner, and Willard 2007), but instrumentalism is also located in arguments that international law should, for instance, be liberal (see, eg, Kennedy, 2003, and Slaughter, 1995; compare Alvarez, 2001), be hegemonic (eg Bolton, 2000; Goldsmith and Posner, 2005; and Rabkin, 2005; compare Carty, 2004, and Vagts, 2001), or be Marxist in one way or another (eg Chimni, 2004; Marks, 2008; and Miéville, 2004).

On the other hand, an instrumentalist concentration on the concerns of States has stimulated a counter-reaction which argues, in effect, that international law is something far too important to be left to States. Indeed for some theorists, particularly those associated with the New Stream or New Approaches to International Law group, this appears to amount to a manifesto: 'students of international law should reformulate their sense of cause and effect in international affairs: rejecting reliance upon visions both of State interests that we too often take to propel doctrine and of the law that we take to restrain statesmen' (Kennedy, 1985, p 381).[5]

Perhaps the most radical and extensive contemporary assault on the unchecked focus on the State in the formulation of international law and doctrine is Professor Allott's theory of Social Idealism.[6] For Allott, what matters is humanity rather than a collection of States, the pursuit of whose interests he thinks has all too often harmed people. The primacy of State concerns in the international arena has given rise to the perception that domestic and international affairs are 'intrinsically and radically separate' (Allott 2001, p 244, para 13.105(6)): morality is discontinuous between the domestic and international spheres. Citizens can only participate in international affairs through the mediation of their governments. The State-centric nature of international unsociety (to use Allott's term) and its influence on the conduct of international relations greatly attenuates, if not eliminates, individual moral responsibility for the content and operation of international law. This allows State concerns to trump a demotic humanitarian impulse, as 'governments, and the human beings who compose them, are able to will and act internationally

---

[5] See also Kennedy, 1999 and 2000. Good overviews of New Stream, or New Approaches to International Law, work are Cass, 1996; Paulus, 2001; Purvis, 1991; Rasulov, 2012; and Tushnet, 2005.

[6] For what might be his manifesto, see Allott, 1998, although the Preface to Allott, 2001 might provide an easier understanding of his enterprise; see also Scobbie, 2011, but compare Prager, 1998. The Eminent Scholars archive on the website of the Squire Law Library contains a video of Allott's 2013 lecture 'The True Nature of International Law', and also audio files and transcripts of conversations with him: the portal to this archive is at http://www.squire.law.cam.ac.uk/eminent_scholars/.

in ways that they would be morally restrained from willing and acting internally, murdering human beings by the million in wars, tolerating oppression and starvation and disease and poverty, human cruelty and suffering, human misery and human indignity' (p 248, para 13.105(16)). What we are left with is 'a world fit for governments' (p 249, para 13.109) in which 'international law is left speaking to governments the words that governments want to hear' (p 296, para 16.1).

Some contemporary theorists, however, deny the very existence of a discipline that we can identify as 'international law', as something distinct from other disciplines, particularly politics:

> Our inherited ideal of a World Order based on the Rule of Law thinly hides from sight the fact that social conflict must still be solved by political means and that even though there may exist a common legal rhetoric among international lawyers, that rhetoric must, for reasons internal to the ideal itself, rely on essentially contested—political—principles to justify outcomes to international disputes. (Koskenniemi, 1990, p 7)[7]

This effacement of international law as an entity distinct from politics is, of course, a critique of other theories which see international law as something separate, something distinctly 'legal': it has been challenged (see, eg, Beckett, 2005 and, more generally, MacCormick, 1990). To understand the critique, we must first understand the orthodoxy which engendered it, as social institutions, such as law, often develop dialectically, where a new approach or doctrine emerges as reaction to, or against, the established order. For instance, in the nineteenth century, impressionism originated as a rejection of the historical tradition in French painting (see King, 2006). Théophile Gautier, a prominent and influential nineteenth-century French art critic, was in despair, as he could not understand this new style—'One examines oneself with a sort of horror . . . to discover whether one has become obese or bald, incapable of understanding the audacities of youth' (King, 2006, p 231). This reaction mirrors that of the legal philosopher HLA Hart, who in a 1944 letter to Isaiah Berlin ruminated:

> I have pictures of myself as a stale mumbler of the inherited doctrine, not knowing the language used by my contemporaries (much younger) and unable to learn it . . . (quoted in Lacey, 2004, p 115)

Perhaps an appropriate place to start in considering orthodoxy in theories of international law is with Grotius, often celebrated as the father of international law, as his *De Iure Belli ac Pacis* (*On the Law of War and Peace*) (1625) 'played a decisive part in the emergence of international law as a separate legal discipline' (Haggenmacher, 2012, p 1098). It has been claimed that Grotius' ideas served as a theoretical blueprint for the Westphalian order of international organization, although he died a few years before its creation. Haggenmacher argues that this is only a 'piously nurtured foundational myth . . . [which] is not borne out by the text of Grotius' masterpiece' (2012, p 1099). But if this is what he was not, what was he?

IV. THE VIEW FROM DELFT

Hugo Grotius was born on 15 April 1583 in Delft towards the start of the Eighty Years' War, the war of Dutch independence from Spain, which lasted from 1568–1648, and which was terminated by the Peace of Westphalia. Johannes Vermeer was born towards the end of the war, being baptized in Delft on 31 October 1632. We have no record of his birth date.

---

[7] See also, for instance, Kratochwil, 1989; and Koskenniemi, 1989: for a commentary on both, see Scobbie, 1990.

These two top and tail the rest of this chapter, although our geography and time frame is cast wider than that of the Eighty Years' War.

Like Socrates, Grotius was a dangerous thinker, while Vermeer was socially marginalized as a convert to Catholicism in a predominantly Protestant community. As well as being a lawyer, Grotius was a theologian, and imprisoned for life in 1619 at least partly for his views on the proper relationship between the civil authorities and the church. He escaped from prison in 1621 hidden in a book chest. (Let's try doing that using a Kindle.) Grotius was also a poet, and perhaps one of his more singular poems was 'a *Proof of True Religion* (*Bewys van den Waren Godtsdienst*), designed particularly for the use of seafaring folk, to relieve the tedium of long voyages, and to furnish them with controversial armour to repel the assaults of heathens, Jews, and Mohammedans' (Lee, 1930, pp 35–6).

Hugo Grotius did not invent international law: as Professor Bederman has demonstrated, international law existed in antiquity (Bederman, 2001), but along with writers such as Vitoria and Alberico Gentili (1552–1608: see Scattola, 2012), Grotius is generally seen as one of its founding figures in the modern period. He was not insulated from the politics of his time and place, which were dominated by the protracted revolt of the Dutch United Provinces against their monarch (the king of Spain). A paramount Dutch concern in the early seventeenth century was trade with the East Indies. Grotius was commissioned to defend the military and commercial activity of the Dutch United East India Company in the Far East, including its resort to war as a non-State actor, which led him to write *De Iure Praedae* (*On the Law of Prize*), although this was first published in its entirety only in 1864. One chapter was published in 1609, entitled *Mare Liberum* (*The Free Sea*), at the request of the East Indies Company, in which some of Grotius' relations were directors, with the hope of influencing peace negotiations which were then underway. Subsequently, after his escape from prison, Grotius revised and expanded the theoretical part of *De Iure Praedae* which became *De Iure Belli ac Pacis*. Surviving working papers show that he wanted to contrast his ideas with those of Vitoria (see Haggenmacher, 1990, pp 142–5, and Tuck, 1999, pp 78–83).

Grotius' theory of law marked a break from the scholasticism of Francisco Suárez (1548–1617: see Brett, 2012) and Vitoria. Suárez had rejected the idea that there could be obligation without God, but scholastic natural law embodied an idea of God and the relationship between God and man which could only be considered 'natural' if it were persuasive outside Christian Europe, for instance in the new colonies in America (see Haakonssen, 1996, pp 21–4):

> One of the main points of modern scepticism was that this was not the case. Religious and moral notions were so relative to time and place that no theoretically coherent account could be given of them. Not least, such notions were relative to each person's interest or individual utility. (p 23)

This scepticism was noted by Grotius in the *Prolegomena* to *De Iure Belli Ac Pacis*. He attempted to formulate a theory of natural law which would be impervious to this scepticism, but in doing so he laid the foundations for a secular natural law, arguing that principles of natural law are binding 'though we should even grant, what without the greatest Wickedness cannot be granted, that there is no God, or that he takes no Care of Human Affairs' (*Prolegomena*, para XI, Grotius, 2005, p 38: see also Olivecrona, 1971, pp 13–14). He also rejected the notion that natural law could be identified with either the Old or New Testaments (*Prolegomena*, paras XLIX and LI, Grotius, 2005, pp 47–8). One of Grotius' central concerns was to prove that 'a legal, including an international, order was possible independently of religion' (Haakonssen, 1996, p 30).

Thus it may be argued that Grotius laid the foundations for the secularization of natural law (see Haakonssen, 1985, pp 247–53), although he was not himself irreligious or secular (see, eg, Haggenmacher, 2012, p 1099). Further, he attempted to create an understanding of international law which was not dependent on the doctrine of a single Christian denomination for its validity:

> Grotius had to write outside a single denomination because he sought to fashion a law of nations that could appeal to and bind Catholics, various Protestants and even non-Christians alike. His theory of a law of nations based on the consent of sovereigns was meant to be more or less religiously neutral. (Janis, 1991, p 63; see pp 61–6 generally)

Grotius' conception of the law of nations contained two principal strands. It comprised the *jus gentium*, the law applied by many or all States concerning matters which had an international aspect, and which was rooted in nature and discovered by human reason or which had been disclosed by divine revelation; and the *jus inter gentes*, which arose from States' express or tacit consent (see Bull, Kingsbury, and Roberts, 1990, pp 28–32, and Olivecrona, 1971, pp 23–4). As Grotius stated:

> when many Men of different Times and Places unanimously affirm the same Thing for Truth, this ought to be ascribed to a general Cause; which . . . can be no other than either a just Inference drawn from the Principles of Nature, or an universal Consent. The former shews the Law of Nature, the other the Law of Nations . . . For that which cannot be deduced from certain Principles by just Consequences, and yet appears to be every where observed, must owe its rise to a free and arbitrary Will. (*Prolegomena*, para XLI, Grotius, 2005, p 45)

Accordingly, Grotius opened the avenue for consent-based accounts of law between nations which came to dominate subsequent accounts of the nature of international law as he argued:

> But as the Laws of each State respect the Benefit of that State; so amongst all or most States there might be, and in Fact there are, some Laws agreed on by common Consent, which respect the Advantage not of one Body in particular, but of all in general. And this is what is called the Law of Nations, when used in Distinction to the Law of Nature. (*Prolegomena*, para XVIII, Grotius, 2005, p 39)

Thus a consequence of Grotius' hypothetical rejection of the theological foundations of natural law was that the consent of States became accepted as the basis of the rules of international law. Grotius paved the way for a consensual and secular concept of international law. A theologically based explanation of international law, regardless of the dominant denomination or religion involved, would be radically different in form and content to the existing system. Could it, for example, contain room for human rights in matters such as gender equality, sexual orientation, and freedom of and from religion, and should we expect to find in it elaborate rules on when resort to war could be justified on religious grounds?

V. BUT WHAT IS A THEORY?

Kant provides a useful notion of a theory for our purposes. He defined a theory as:

> A collection of rules, even of practical rules, is termed a theory if the rules concerned are envisaged as principles of a fairly general nature, and if they are abstracted from numerous conditions which, nonetheless, necessarily influence their practical application. Conversely, not all activities are called practice, but only those realizations of a particular purpose which are considered to comply with certain generally conceived principles of procedure . . . [N]o-one can pretend to be practically versed in a branch of knowledge

and yet treat theory with scorn, without exposing the fact that he is an ignoramus in his subject. He no doubt imagines that he can get further than he could through theory if he gropes around in experiments and experiences, without collecting certain principles (which in fact amount to what we term theory) and without relating his activities to an integral whole (which, if treated methodically, is what we call a system). (Kant, 1793 (1970), pp 61–2)

But what does this mean?

It means that the function of a theory is to formulate or guide practice; to provide a relatively abstract framework for the understanding and determination of action. A theory is necessary because it provides us with the intellectual blueprint which enables us to understand the world, or some specific aspect of human affairs. Kant's notion of a system, which comprises an integrated body of knowledge rather than simply a collection of essentially unrelated general rules, underlines the constitutive function of theory. Theory makes data comprehensible by providing a structure for the organization of a given discipline or body of knowledge.

Different types of legal theory have different aims and concerns. For example, analytical theory tends to deal with questions such as the structure of legal systems, its components (such as the nature of rights and duties), legal epistemology (what is legal knowledge?), and legal ontology (does, and how does, law exist?—see, for instance, Arend, 1999, ch 1, especially at pp 28ff; and Franck, 1990, ch 2). Traditionally the ontological argument has dogged international law because of the influence of Austinian imperative theory. Despite, in some quarters (eg Bolton, 2000, pp 2, 4–5, and 48), a lingering attachment to the classical Austinian positivist claim that, because there is no determinate sovereign superior to States capable of promulgating and enforcing its commands, international law is not law but merely amounts to positive morality (see Austin, 1832 (1995), Lecture V, pp 123–5), this view is no longer generally accepted. It seems somewhat bizarre to rely on a discredited nineteenth-century legal philosophy which speaks of the 'sovereign' and is essentially pre-democratic (at least in terms of universal suffrage) as the foundation for a contemporary understanding of law, or for the expression of a hostility to—or even a fear of—the very notion of international law. With the posthumous publication of the works of Jeremy Bentham, it is clear that Austin owed much to Bentham's more sophisticated analysis of law. Further, '[a]lthough there is no question that Bentham had doubts about the law-like character of international law, he was by no means the skeptic that Austin was' (Janis, 2004, p 16, see pp 16–18 generally).

These doubts are now a thing of the past, although some vestiges of the ontological debate remain in theoretical investigations of the sources of international law—the identification of what counts, or should count, as international law, which is, for instance, exemplified in Professor d'Aspremont's examination of formalism and sources (d'Aspremont, 2011) and the debate about relative normativity (see, eg, Beckett, 2001; Roberts, 2001; Tasioulas, 1996; and Weil, 1983). Nevertheless, as Professor Franck (1995, p 6) affirms: 'international law has entered its post-ontological era. Its lawyers need no longer defend the very existence of international law. Thus emancipated from the constraints of defensive ontology, international lawyers are now free to undertake a critical assessment of its content.'

The conceptual exegesis of distinct substantive themes or fields finds expression in works such as Franck's account of the emergence of individualism as a core concept in international law (Franck, 1999); in the numerous applications of New Haven analysis to such diverse topics as the law of the sea (McDougal and Burke, 1962), human rights (McDougal, Lasswell, and Chen, 1969 and 1980), and armed conflict (McDougal and Feliciano, 1994); and in Ragazzi's exegesis of obligations *erga omnes* as rooted ultimately in natural law (Ragazzi, 1997, pp 183–5). Another important strand of contemporary international legal theory is critical theory, that is the ideological critique of the structure and content of international law, often from a position of identity politics such as gender (eg Charlesworth and Chinkin, 2000), race, or Third World Approaches to International Law (eg Anghie, 2005). This can overlap with more normative theory which questions what international law is for and what it should do.

In this chapter, I do not propose to offer anything like a comprehensive account of the diverse theories of international law, or to offer some 'master' theory which trumps all others. We must bear in mind Koskenniemi's cautionary observation about personal predispositions and biases. This propounds that all theoretical positions are, to some degree, subjective. The aim here is much more modest: to offer an outline of some theoretical points and perspectives which should provide a basis for thinking about the nature and function(s) of international law. But we should be clear on one thing: because writers start from different, and often inarticulate, premises about the nature and function of international law, it is not surprising that adhesion to different theoretical presuppositions results in different conclusions about what counts as international law in the first place (Lauterpacht, 1933, p 57).

VI. PROVENANCE AND MEANING

Identifying authorial predispositions is crucial to evaluating the weight to be given to an argument. Indeed, identifying the very author of a text can be decisive in law, in a way alien to other disciplines. For instance, in literature, Foucault argues in favour of the death of the author—the idea that the identity and personality of the author of a work of fiction is irrelevant to the authority and interpretation of the text. He acknowledges:

> I seem to call for a form of culture in which fiction would not be limited by the figure of the author . . . All discourses, whatever their status, form, value, and whatever the treatment to which they will be subjected, would then develop in the anonymity of a murmur. We would no longer hear the questions that have been rehashed for so long: Who really spoke? Is it really he and not someone else? With what authenticity or originality? And what part of his deepest self did he express in his discourse . . . [W]e would hear hardly anything but the stirring of an indifference: What difference does it make who is speaking? (Foucault, 1998, p 222)

Foucault claims that the ascription of an author to a text entails that it 'is not ordinary everyday speech that merely comes and goes . . . On the contrary, it is a speech that must be received in a certain mode and that, in a given culture, must receive a certain status' (p 211). Yet the identity of the person or body promulgating some types of legal texts has precisely this function. The significance of the identity of the actor in law is akin to that of provenance in the art market. Provenance is the chain of proof that demonstrates that an artefact is not a forgery but may be safely attributed to a given artist. Provenance is crucial to valuation: a painting that cannot be shown to have been painted by, say, Manet, does not have the same value as a 'real' attested Manet. (Indeed, Gertrude Stein was displeased when, at the height of the cubist period, her friends Pablo Picasso and Georges Braque signed the other's name to their paintings, as she thought artists should bear responsibility for their own work—see Wagner-Martin, 1995, p 148.)

The value, or significance, of an ostensibly legal document or statement invariably depends on its author; because its author is a judge; because its author is a legislature; because its author is a foreign ministry; and so on. Legal documents and statements are not simply strings of words: rather, they are speech acts—words which are intended to have a practical impact. They are words which are meant to do things and not remain mere utterances. Like making a promise, they constitute an action (an illocutionary act) which does not describe but which is meant to change social reality (see Austin, 1976). When the Athenian jury sentenced Socrates to death, as it was legally empowered to do, its words were meant to have an effect in the real world, particularly for Socrates.

Legal texts, and their authors, only make sense within the context of the system that gives them authority and meaning. Literary, artistic, even philosophical texts, on the other hand, are a great deal more autonomous. At the extreme, as in the case of the fictitious Australian poet Ern Malley whose works were fabricated to satirize modernist poetry, but which now form part of the Australian literary canon, the 'author' need not even exist (see Heyward, 1993). Or reconsider Socrates: he left no writings, but would it matter if 'Socrates', like 'Ern Malley', never existed? Would it matter if he were only a literary device invented by Plato and Xenophon as a vehicle to present their thoughts?

In some circumstances, therefore, to gain a full understanding of a text, it must be located within a framework where it may be properly understood. Some, however, argue that all readings of a text are partial, and that a search for authorial intent, even in law, cannot generate a 'correct' interpretation (eg Balkin, 1986, p 772). There is a degree of truth in this, but it is equally true that legal texts, unlike literary texts, form part of an interlocking system of meaning and are not free radicals that bear the meaning anyone chooses to put upon them. There is a difference between a legal text such as Article 51 of the UN Charter, whose interpretation may be contested in regard to some matters, such as when it would allow a kinetic response (bullets, bombs, and things that go bang) as self-defence in response to a non-kinetic attack (cyber warfare) (see Tallinn Manual, 2013, ch II, and Schmitt, 2012, pp 18–25), and a literary text which can bear any meaning one chooses, such as these lines from Gertrude Stein's poem 'Lifting belly':

> I say lifting belly and then I say lifting belly and Caesars. I say lifting belly gently and Caesars gently. I say lifting belly again and Caesars again. I say lifting belly and I say Caesars and I say lifting belly Caesars and cow come out. I say lifting belly and Caesars and cow come out. (Stein, 1998b, p 410 at p 435)

While most literary critics interpret passages such as this as lesbian eroticism written by Stein for her lover Alice B. Toklas, with the 'cow' being an orgasm for Alice (but see Turner 1999, pp 24–31), reading early Stein, such as 'Lifting belly', generally involves a fruitless search for meaning, because it is an attempt to unlock the sense which she took pains consciously to erase (see Dydo, 2003):

> Stein's true radical legacy lay in her insistence on showing how words and their meanings could be undone; she took it as her right that she had the freedom to use words exactly as she pleased, and in doing so she undermined the relation between words and the world … Janet Flanner remembered: 'A publisher once said to her, "We want the comprehensible thing, the thing the public can understand". She said to him: "My work would have been no use to anyone if the public had understood me early and first."' (Daniel, 2009, p 190)

Indeed, one contemporary commentator thought that Stein had 'outdistanced any of the Symbolists in using words for pure purposes of suggestion—she has gone so far that she no longer even suggests' (Wilson, 1996, p 276, first published 1931). Does this matter? Stein's purpose in writing was to make manifest her 'genius': her work did, and does, not need to 'mean' anything. It exists in, and for, itself—as well as for the Greater Glory of Gertrude.

Legal texts, on the other hand, do need to have an identifiable meaning, or range of acceptable meanings, because the practice of law is an instrumental activity aimed at practical outcomes in the 'real' world. The Socratic (or at least Platonic) idea that the written word is like a painted image as it can only signify one thing entails that words are univocal, and bear one meaning and one meaning alone. This idea that written words 'just go on and on for ever giving the same single piece of information' is simply too reductive. Legal systems are expressed in natural language which cannot fulfil the requirement of univocity because natural language is inherently ambiguous (see, eg, Perelman and Olbrechts-Tyteca, 1969, pp 13–14, para 1, pp 120ff, para 30, and pp 130ff, para 33, and Perelman 1976, pp 34–6, para 24 and pp 114–55, para 56bis). Perelman repeatedly illustrates the non-univocity of natural language using the apparent tautologies 'boys will be boys' or 'business is business'. To give these phrases meaning, different interpretations must be given to the repeated terms whereas in formal logical or mathematical systems such propositions would be meaningless because of the systemic requirement of the principle of identity, which necessitates that terms, or words, are univocal and unambiguous (see, eg, Perelman and Olbrechts-Tyteca, 1969, pp 21ff, para 51, and pp 442–3, para 94, and Perelman, 1976, pp 115–16, para 56bis).

Perelman's theory of rhetoric aims at examining how arguments may persuade and thus assumes that legal arguments can communicate meaning. Drawing on the work of linguistic theorists such as Ferdinand de Saussure (1857–1913), particularly his *Course in General Linguistics* (*Cours de Linguistique Générale*, published posthumously in 1916), some legal theorists argue that all texts are inevitably and radically indeterminate and have no settled meaning (for an account and critique, see Solum, 1987). This has long been a tenet of US legal philosophy. One of the principal strands of American Legal Realism, rule scepticism, argued that this uncertainty lay in the very formulation of rules, and thus judicial decisions could not lay claim to being simply the inexorable application of the law to the issue in question (see Frank, 1949). This is reflected in McDougal and Lasswell's admonition that:

> From any relatively specific statements of social goal (necessarily described in a statement of low-level abstraction) can be elaborated an infinite series of normative propositions of ever increasing generality; conversely, normative statements of high-level abstraction can be manipulated to support any specific social goal. (Lasswell and McDougal, 1943, p 213)

It must be conceded that there cannot be hyper-reality in legal discourse because of the ambiguity of language, but that language must be able to communicate effectively. If law were radically indeterminate then no contract, statute, or treaty could have any determinable meaning, and every criminal conviction is unsafe because of the principle of legality—if all law is indeterminate, then how do we know if/when someone commits a criminal offence? How can there be an effective speech act, if the meaning of that speech cannot be discerned?

While extra-legal factors are undoubtedly taken into account in interpreting an ambiguous text, and in international law the influence of politics in this is well-nigh inescapable, to argue that this means that law inevitably collapses into politics might be to mistake the process for the outcome. Professor Raz draws a distinction between the deliberative and executive stages of legal reasoning. In the former, factors are evaluated to decide what the law should be, and then at the executive stage this solution is incorporated into the law (Raz, 1980, pp 213–14). The drafting of a treaty manifestly falls within the deliberative stage, as does a court's consideration of the proper interpretation of an instrument, but at the executive stage, once the treaty text is finalized, or once the judgment is issued, once the operative speech act takes place, then the political considerations in issue become subsumed within the law.

VII. LIBERAL DEMOCRACY V MARXISM-LENINISM— POLES APART?

It should be clear that the more overtly a writer uncovers his or her theoretical assumptions, the more honest is the writing, because his or her model of international law is exposed on the page for all to see.

To illustrate the formative power of theory, it is convenient to contrast two very different accounts of international law, namely the New Haven School which was elaborated principally by Myres McDougal and Harold Lasswell in Yale Law School, and the pre-perestroika Soviet theory of international law propounded by GI Tunkin. As products of the Cold War, these are primarily of historical interest, but they were distinctive theories of international law which clearly set out to bolster and justify the external projection of the political values of the USA and Soviet Union. Although they thus shared a similar purpose, they embodied profoundly different political aims and objectives: this is abundantly clear in their approach to sources and methodology.

It could be argued that the chasm between the two theories runs deeper, that there is an architectonic difference between the two, as the New Haven School sees law as facilitative whereas Soviet theory amounts to a constitutive theory. Posner explains the facilitative approach as claiming that law provides 'a service to lay communities in the achievement of those communities' self-chosen ends rather than as a norm imposed on those communities in the service of a higher end' (Posner, 1990, p 94). The latter is, of course, the constitutive approach.

McDougal and Lasswell (1981, p 24) defined 'human dignity' as 'a social process in which values are widely and not narrowly shared, and in which private choice, rather than coercion, is emphasized as the predominant modality of power'. Accordingly, the New Haven goal of clarifying and implementing a world order of human dignity could be seen as falling squarely within Posner's notion of a facilitative theory. This is not the case. The *raison d'être* of the New Haven School was the pursuit of an imposed 'higher end', namely, the defence and maintenance of (American) liberal democracy as a bulwark against the spread of communism. This is manifestly a constitutive theory. It is ideological, the attempted globalization of the claim that the USA is morally exceptional and 'endowed by its creator with a special mission, a "manifest destiny", to "overspread" the North American continent and perhaps the world, so as to evangelize it with the twin gospels of American democracy and American capitalism' (Hodgson, 2005, p 20). As Falk observes, New Haven analysis is constructed around an:

> ideological bipolarity of a world order that pits totalitarian versus free societies as the essential struggle of our time, a view that anchors the McDougal and Lasswell jurisprudence in the history of the Cold War era. (Falk, 1995, p 2004)

For McDougal and Lasswell the choice was one between nuclear annihilation and the global promotion of US democratic values (Falk, 1995, p 2002; Duxbury, 1995, pp 195–8). They, in an act of 'ideological partisanship' (Falk, 1995, p 2003), chose the latter.

A. THE NEW HAVEN SCHOOL

The genesis of New Haven lay in the Second World War and the emergence of communism as an international political force. McDougal and Lasswell argued that, when US law schools reopened after the war, they should be 'a place where people who have risked their lives can wisely risk their minds' (Lasswell and McDougal, 1943, p 292). The aim of legal education was to provide systematic training for policy-makers attuned to 'the needs of a free and productive commonwealth':

> The proper function of our law schools is, in short, to contribute to the training of policy-makers for the ever more complete achievement of the democratic values that constitute the professed ends of American polity. (Lasswell and McDougal, 1943, p 206; see also Falk, 1995, p 1993)

These values should be reinforced so that the student applies them automatically to 'every conceivable practical and theoretical situation' (Lasswell and McDougal, 1943, p 244). As lawyers influence or create policy when indicating whether a proposed course of action is or is not lawful (p 209), the law school curriculum should aim towards the implementation of 'clearly defined democratic values in all the areas of social life where lawyers have or can assert responsibility' (p 207). Policy and value permeate law; there are no autonomous or neutral theories of law which can ignore the policy consequences of rules (McDougal and Reisman, 1983, p 122). Therefore:

> In a democratic society it should not, of course, be an aim of legal education to impose a single standard of morals upon every student. But a legitimate aim of education is to seek to promote the major values of a democratic society and to reduce the number of moral mavericks who do not share democratic preferences. The student may be allowed to reject the morals of democracy and embrace those of despotism; but his education should be such that, if he does so, he does it by deliberate choice, with awareness of the consequences for himself and others, and not by sluggish self-deception. (Lasswell and McDougal, 1943, p 212)

Although Lasswell and McDougal initially (1943, *passim*) envisioned the comprehensive application of their theory to reform the entire law school curriculum, it rapidly focused specifically on international law (Duxbury, 1995, p 191). The practical aim of the New Haven School is to advance 'a universal world order of human dignity' which secures the widespread enjoyment of values by individuals. A value is simply 'a preferred event' or, in other words, whatever an individual or decision-maker desires. A full enumeration of values is impossible—'if we were to begin to list all the specific items of food and drink, of dress, of housing, and of other enjoyments, we should quickly recognize the unwieldiness of the task'. McDougal and Lasswell claim that any given value will fall within one or more of the categories that they identify as enlightenment, respect, power, well-being, wealth, skill, affection, and rectitude (McDougal and Lasswell, 1981, p 20: see also Lasswell and McDougal, 1943, pp 217–32; McDougal and Reisman, 1983, p 118; Arend, 1999, p 72; and Duxbury, 1995, p 178). Human dignity, however, is not foundational: 'We postulate this goal, deliberately leaving everyone free to justify it in terms of his preferred theological or philosophical tradition' (McDougal and Lasswell, 1981, p 24: see also Lasswell and McDougal, 1943, p 213).

This goal reflects the New Haven School's basis in, and intended refinement of, the American Legal Realist school of jurisprudence and its intertwining of law and the social sciences, especially economics.[8] Realism rejected formalist accounts of law that claimed to be value-neutral and relied on the logical exegesis of legal principle to explain the operation of the courts and legal system.

---

[8] On American Legal Realism, see Duxbury, 1995, chs 1 and 2; and Feldman, 2000, pp 105–15. More elementary accounts of this school may be found in standard textbooks on jurisprudence, such as Freeman, 2001, ch 9.

Realism, contrary to formalism, laid stress on the social consequences of the law which should be taken into account in judicial decisions, and thus emphasized empiricism. This aimed at determining the real factors involved in judgments beyond the formal appeal to rules, and also at demonstrating the social impact that alternative judicial choices might have. Law was seen as a form of social engineering that could be used as a tool to attain desired societal goals. The New Haven School built on this tradition in American juris-prudence by rejecting the notion that law is merely a system of rules, by trying to achieve a more empirical account of the operation of law in society, and by postulating the instru-mental aim of achieving human dignity (see Morison, 1982, pp 178–88).

The New Haven School displaces the conception of law as a system of rules in favour of one where law is a normative social system which revolves around trends of authoritative decisions taken by authorized decision-makers including, but not restricted to, judges. There is, after all, more to law than what happens in court rooms—'If a legal system works well, then disputes are in large part *avoided*' (Higgins, 1994, p 1, emphasis in origi-nal). International lawyers, giving legal advice that moulds policy and action, are more likely to be in foreign ministries than appearing before the International Court of Justice. Contemporary New Haven doctrine is more radical in its intentions. It claims that its methodology 'can be especially empowering for individuals not associated with the state, a class that classical international law all but disenfranchised'. Applying its techniques, either alone or as part of an interest group, individuals can be involved in influencing the deci-sions that affect their lives (see Reisman, Wiessner, and Willard, 2007, pp 576–8). Law is a continuing process of decisions involving choices aimed at realizing the common value of human dignity:

> the major systems of public order are in many fundamental respects rhetorically unified. All systems proclaim the dignity of the human individual and the ideal of a worldwide public order in which this ideal is authoritatively pursued and effectively approximated. (McDougal and Lasswell, 1981, p 19)

The New Haven process of decisions has been likened to Heraclitus' aphorism that one never steps into the same river twice, because the river moves on. For New Haven ad-herents, because the social context of decisions change, and because the trends and im-plications of past decisions can be unclear, the quest for human dignity necessitates the rejection of a model of law that comprises simply the neutral or impartial application of rules. Rules are:

> inconsistent, ambiguous, and full of omissions. It was Mr. Justice Cardozo who aptly remarked that legal principles have, unfortunately, the habit of travelling in pairs of oppo-sites. A judge who must choose between such principles can only offer as justification for his choice a proliferation of other such principles in infinite regress or else arbitrarily take a stand and state his preference; and what he prefers or what he regards as 'authoritative' is likely to be a product of his whole biography. (Lasswell and McDougal, 1943, p 236)

This, in itself, appears to be a New Haven refinement of the realist notion of the intuitive nature of judicial decision-making. Hutcheson had argued that, in hard cases, the judge does not decide by an abstract application of the relevant rules, but decides intuitively which way the decision should go before searching for a legal category into which the deci-sion will fit—'No reasoning applied to practical matters is ever really effective unless mo-tivated by some impulse' (Hutcheson, 1928–9, p 285). The New Haven School conceded that the application of its method could not overcome discretion or bias on the part of the decision-maker. As a bulwark against this, and thus the tendency to intuitive reductionism advanced by Hutcheson, it counselled that decision-makers should be as self-conscious as possible about their predispositions, and undertake a systematic and comprehensive assessment of policy choices relevant to their decisions as the state of available knowledge allowed (Falk, 1995, p 1999).

Rules are only 'shorthand expressions of community expectations' and thus, like any shorthand, are inadequate as a method of communication (Duxbury, 1995, p 194). Rules simply cannot be applied automatically to reach a decision because that decision involves a policy choice:

> Reference to 'the correct legal view' or 'rules' can never avoid the element of choice (though it can seek to disguise it), nor can it provide guidance to the preferable decision. In making this choice one must inevitably have consideration for the humanitarian, moral, and social purposes of the law. (Higgins, 1994, p 5)

Higgins continues that the New Haven School's articulation of relevant policy factors, and their systematic assessment in decision-making, precludes the decision-maker unconsciously giving preference to a desired policy objective under the guise of it being 'the correct legal rule'.

The realization of preferred values is not, however, the sole factor in decision-making: law does constrain. Recourse must be made to trends of past decisions; and how these relate to the goals the decision-maker wishes to achieve; and how these decisions may be deployed to realize these goals—'the task is to think creatively about how to alter, deter, or accelerate probable trends in order to shape the future closer to his desire' (Lasswell and McDougal, 1943, p 214). Further, these goals can only be achieved if the decision taken is both authoritative and controlling:

> Authority is the structure of expectation concerning who, with what qualifications and mode of selection, is competent to make which decisions by what criteria and what procedures. By control we refer to an effective voice in decision, whether authorized or not. The conjunction of common expectations concerning authority with a high degree of corroboration in actual operation is what we understand by law. (McDougal and Lasswell, 1981, p 22)

More succinctly, Higgins describes law as 'the interlocking of authority with power' (Higgins, 1994, p 5: see also Arend, 1999, pp 77–9).

Thus the New Haven School aims at providing a framework of values and matrix of effective and authoritative decision-making in pursuit of the democratic ideal it favours. In this matrix, the actual and desired distribution of values affects every authoritative decision. In turn, the future distribution of values which stems from these decisions aims to mould and secure community public order to maximize the realization of human dignity (McDougal and Reisman, 1983, p 118).

B. SOVIET THEORY

The other principal Cold War doctrine—the theory of international law sponsored by the Soviet Union, rooted in Marxism-Leninism, and reaching its apogee in the pre-perestroika works of Tunkin (but see Bowring, 2008 for a more nuanced account of Soviet legal theory)—was a diametrical opposite to the New Haven School, both in its professed structure and envisaged political outcome. This orthodoxy, enforced by the Soviet bloc, relied not on the values encompassed in human dignity to explain international law, but on the 'objective' rules of societal development and the historical inevitability of socialism:

> The foreign policy and diplomacy of socialist States is armed with the theory of Marxism-Leninism and a knowledge of the laws of societal development. Proceeding on the basis of a new and higher social system replacing capitalism, they adduce and defend progressive

international legal principles which correspond to the laws of societal development and which are aimed at ensuring peace and friendly cooperation between states and the free development of peoples. (Tunkin, 1974, p 277)[9]

Under Soviet theory, international law was 'under the decisive influence of the socialist States, the developing countries, and the other forces of peace and socialism', and was aimed at 'ensuring peace and peaceful co-existence, at the freedom and independence of peoples, against colonialism in all of its manifestations, and at the development of peaceful international cooperation in the interests of all peoples' (Tunkin, 1974, p 251). The role of international law was to promote human progress, which necessarily led to socialism. Indeed, Soviet writers argued that socialism was the inevitable outcome of social processes and, with its triumph, the State and law (including international law) would be eradicated as these are the products of class division, although there would still be rules of conduct (eg Tunkin, 1974, pp 42, 238: see pp 232ff generally). Until then, international law was 'immortalize[d] . . . as an instrument of struggle between States belonging to opposed social systems' (Damrosch and Müllerson, 1995, p 4) in which the most that could be achieved was peaceful co-existence between capitalist and socialist States.

Soviet theory is squarely based in Marxist-Leninist theory to the extent that, at times, it seems simply to amount to taking the dogma for a walk. Perhaps paradoxically, Soviet theory is much more traditional, more conservative, than the New Haven School, placing its emphasis on rules and State consent to rules, rather than the New Haven realization of values by authorized decision-makers:

> both the Soviet government and Soviet doctrine consistently treated the existing corpus of international law as a system of sufficiently determinate principles and norms which all States are obliged to observe in their mutual relations, in contrast to some Western scholars who find international law to be more or less adaptable and argue that law should fit behaviour rather than the other way around. The Soviet preference for a relatively rigid rule-bound approach was not merely an outgrowth of traditional jurisprudential conventions, but also served political and polemical functions. (Damrosch and Müllerson, 1995, p 9, footnotes omitted)

Soviet theory was rooted in the class struggle, and the Marxist-Leninist tenet that the mode of production within a society (the economic base) is the principal influence on the will of the ruling class, and thus on the social institutions (the superstructure) of that society. Only with the emergence of private property and social classes does the State emerge 'as an organ of the economically dominant class', along with law which constitutes the will of this ruling class in defence of its interests (Kartashkin, 1983, p 81).[10]

Capitalist and socialist States have different interests, and thus wills, given the difference in their socio-economic organization—'the influence of the economic structure of society and its societal laws affects the process of creating norms of international law through the will of a state, since the content of this will basically is determined by the economic conditions of the existence of the ruling class in a given state' (Tunkin, 1974, p 237). While the

[9] For an overview of Marxist theory of law, see Freeman, 2001, ch 12: a clear, succinct, and critical introduction is Collins, 1984. For an account of the early formation of Soviet concepts of international law, see Macdonald, 1998.

[10] See also pp 79–83 generally; and Tunkin, 1974, pp 27, 36, 232ff. Kartashkin (1983, p 81) notes that according to Marxist-Leninist theory, there are five socio-economic formations of society—primitive communal, slave, feudal, capitalist, and communist. Compare Smith's notion of the four stages of society found, for instance, in Smith (1978, pp 14–16): 'in these several ages of society, the laws and regulations with regard to property must be very different' (p 16).

dominant economic class determines the will of a capitalist State, in a socialist State, this comprises 'the will of the entire Soviet people led by the working class' (p 249 and eg p 36). One clear consequence of this divergence in interest is Soviet theory's rejection of 'general principles of law recognized by civilised nations' (Article 38(1)(c) of the Statute of the International Court of Justice) as an independent source of international law. Because of the opposed nature of their socio-economic systems, Tunkin denied the possibility that there could exist normative principles common to socialist and bourgeois legal systems. Even if principles superficially appeared to be common to the two types of system, they were 'fundamentally distinct by virtue of their class nature, role in society, and purposes' (p 199).

A common ideology, however, is unnecessary for the development of international law, but the existence of two opposed social systems places limits on the content of the norms of international law. Because these must be agreed by States on the basis of equality—'only those international legal norms which embrace the agreement of all states are norms of contemporary general international law'—they can be neither socialist nor capitalist (pp 250–1; see also 1974, ch 2, *passim*, and Kartashkin, 1983, pp 96ff).

Consent between States, albeit reflecting the interests of their ruling classes, to specific rules is the keystone of Soviet theory, which, furthermore, recognizes only treaties and custom as sources of international law (Tunkin, 1974, pp 36, 291). There is no room for some authoritative decision-maker to determine or influence the content of international law—for instance, 'The [International] Court does not create international law; it applies it' (p 191). Norm creation necessarily requires State consent, whether express or tacit (p 124 and ch 4, *passim*):

> the majority of states in international relations cannot create norms binding upon other states and do not have the right to attempt to impose given norms on other states. This proposition is especially important for contemporary international law, which regulates relations of states belonging to different and even opposed social systems. (p 128)

In its emphasis on consent which allows international law to bridge between different social systems, Soviet theory is redolent of Grotius' attempt to provide common rules for different 'denominations', although it is stripped of any thought of natural law. Tunkin argues that because natural law theorists of international law undermine its consensual basis, this creates a climate which increases the 'possibilities for an international legal justification of the imperialist policy of *diktat, coercion, and military adventurism*' (p 210).

Tunkin stresses that international law, as it exists between socialist and capitalist States, rests on consensual principles of peaceful co-existence which include the principles of the sovereign equality of States and non-interference in their domestic affairs (pp 29 and 251). The application and implications of these principles differ, however, in the international relations between States from opposed socio-economic systems and in the relations between socialist States inter se. Relations between socialist States are not predicated on the notion of peaceful coexistence but on the principle of socialist or proletarian internationalism (p 47: this doctrine is expounded at length at pp 427ff). Thus Kartashkin maintains that:

> principles of general international law, when applied in relations among socialist countries, expand their shape and acquire new socialist content. They go beyond general principles of international law. For example, the general principle of international law—the equality of states—acquires a new content when applied in relations among socialist states. Parallel to the respect for legal equality, its implementation presupposes the achievement of factual equality of all socialist states and the equalization of their economic level. The principles of socialist internationalism are used by socialist states to strengthen their relations, to protect them from anti-socialist forces, and to ensure the construction of socialism. Thus,

in relations among socialist states two types of norms function—the socialist and general principles and the norms of international law. (Kartashkin, 1983, pp 82–3)

The principle of proletarian internationalism is that of 'fraternal friendship, close coopera-tion, and mutual assistance of the working class of various countries in the struggle for their liberation' (Tunkin, 1974, p 4; see also Butler, 1971, pp 796–7, but compare Hazard, 1971). This manifests itself in principles of socialist legality which, in the relations between socialist States, are *lex specialis* to the norms of general international law (Tunkin, 1974, pp 445–56; see also Osakwe, 1972, p 597). These principles are, 'first and foremost', those of 'fraternal friendship, close cooperation, and comradely mutual assistance' (Tunkin, 1974, pp 434–5; see also Butler, 1971, p 797, and Osakwe, 1972, p 598). Their implementation requires close cooperation between socialist States in foreign and defence policy to secure 'the gains of socialism from possible feeble imperialist swoops' (Tunkin, 1974, p 430).

At its most stark, this aim was expressed in the Brezhnev doctrine, the claim that socialist States could, if necessary, use force to ensure that another socialist State did not divert from socialism and revert to capitalism. This doctrine asserted that a threat to socialism in one State was 'a threat to the security of the socialist community as a whole'[11] and thus a common problem. It therefore constituted 'the joint defense of the socialist system from any attempts of forces of the old world to destroy or subvert any socialist state of this system' (Tunkin, 1974, p 434). Although the Brezhnev doctrine was promulgated following the forcible suppression of moves towards democratization in Czechoslovakia in 1968 (see, eg, Butler, 1971, p 797; Franck, 1970, p 833; and Schwebel, 1972, p 816), this principle of socialist internationalism was employed to justify the Soviet intervention in Hungary in 1956 (Tunkin, 1974, pp 435–6) and its 1980 invasion of Afghanistan (see Brezhnev, 1980, pp 6–9).

C. NEW HAVEN AND SOVIET APPROACHES COMPARED

Accordingly, just as New Haven has the teleological aim of achieving human dignity, and thus the external projection of democratic liberal values, so Soviet theory has the aim of realizing proletarian internationalism, and thus the global triumph of socialism. While New Haven rejects any foundational basis for human dignity, in that it is indifferent to the philosophical positions which individuals may use to justify human dignity, Soviet theory is foundational because it maintains that, by way of objective rules of societal develop-ment, the goal of proletarian internationalism is historically inevitable. In the meantime, according to Tunkin (1974, p 48), common ground must be sought in which competing social systems may peacefully co-exist. Despite opposed theories regarding the nature and function of international law, agreement on specific international legal norms was not im-possible. For instance, the international regulation of human rights occurred despite the absence of a common ideology:

> Marxist-Leninist theory proceeds from the premise that human rights and freedoms are not inherent in the nature of man and do not constitute some sort of natural attributes. Rights and freedoms of individuals in any state are materially stipulated and depend on socio-economic, political and other conditions of the development of society, its achieve-ments and progress. Their fundamental source is the material conditions of society's life. (Kartashkin, 1983, p 95)

---

[11] Brezhnev doctrine as quoted in Schwebel, 1972, pp 816–17; see also Franck, 1970, pp 832–3. Franck argues that the USA foreshadowed the Brezhnev doctrine in its policy towards the Americas—see pp 833–5, and pp 822–35 generally.

McDougal and Lasswell would undoubtedly see this as an example where 'allegedly universal doctrines' such as sovereignty, domestic jurisdiction, and non-intervention are used 'to resist the institutional reconstructions which are indispensable to security'. In this case, the Soviet claim was that the content of internationally agreed human rights fell within the domestic jurisdiction of the implementing State (Tunkin, 1974, pp 82–3). McDougal and Lasswell (1981, p 18) resisted such 'false conceptions of the universality of international law', and argued that the discrediting of such false claims was necessary in order to clarify 'the common goals, interpretations, and procedures essential to achieving an effective international order'.

On the other hand, the policy science approach of New Haven was an anathema to Soviet thinking:

> Even though states may use international law as a support for foreign policy, this does not mean that international law is merged with policy. Mixing international law with policy inevitably leads to a denial of the normative character of international law, that is to say, to a denial of international law, which becomes buried in policy and vanishes as law.
>
> Professor McDougal's concept of the policy approach to international law is an example of this kind of mixing or blending of foreign policy and international law.
>
> … McDougal, while not denying the importance of international law in so many words and sometimes also stressing it, in fact drowns international law in policy. In consequence thereof, international law in McDougal's concept is devoid of independent significance as a means of regulating international relations; it disappears into policy and, moreover, is transformed in to a means of justifying policies which violate international law. (Tunkin, 1974, p 297)

This criticism that New Haven analysis results in the eradication of international law is commonplace (see, eg, Arend, 1996, p 290; Bull, 2002, pp 153–4; and Kratochwil, 1989, pp 193–200). Falk notes that, although not inevitable, the outcome of the application of New Haven analysis to a given issue 'had an uncomfortable tendency to coincide with the outlook of the US government and to seem more polemically driven than scientifically demonstrated' (Falk, 1995, p 2001; see also p 1997, and Koh 2007, p 563). It cannot be doubted that the same was true of Soviet international law, despite its reliance on 'norms'. As Damrosch and Müllerson (1995, pp 8–9) comment:

> The political climate of the Cold War undoubtedly contributed to the sense that the international legal order was far from approaching an optimal or perhaps even minimal level of determinacy. Especially in highly politicized areas such as the use of force or intervention, as well as in many aspects of human rights law, the content and clarity of principles and norms suffered from the fact that states proceeded from opposed interests; while they wanted to delineate parameters for the behaviour of the other side, they were wary of tying their own hands. The positions of the two sides were not only different but often irreconcilable; yet those positions were sometimes dictated more by ideological considerations than by real national interests.

The New Haven tendency to make law malleable in its pursuit of human dignity, McDougal and Lasswell's 'penchant for applying their theory in justification of US foreign policy' (Falk, 1995, p 1997), undoubtedly gives an impression of normative indeterminacy. Could it be argued, however, that this mistakes the anomaly for the paradigm? One of the criticisms of formalism made by realist scholars was that it focused on the judgments of appellate courts which concentrate on contestable points of law (Duxbury, 1995, pp 57, 135–7). Is this not also true of the common impression gained of the New Haven School (and equally of Soviet theory, for that matter)? As Higgins (1994, pp 6–7) notes, New Haven does not require:

> one to find every means possible if the end is desirable. Trends of past decisions still have an important role to play in the choices to be made, notwithstanding the importance of both context and desired outcome. Where there is ambiguity or uncertainty, the policy-directed choice can properly be made.

Koskenniemi has observed that when he worked for the Finnish foreign ministry, politicians seeking international legal advice saw every situation as 'new, exceptional, [a] crisis'. The legal adviser's function was to link this back to precedents, to 'tell it as part of a history', and thus to present it as meshed in 'narratives in which it received a generalizable meaning' in order that the politician 'could see what to do with it' (Koskenniemi, 2005, p 120: compare Charlesworth, 2002b).

The application of most international law is not problematic: standardized rules are applied to standardized situations otherwise, as Franck (1990, p 20) points out, 'for example, no mail would go from one state to another, no currency or commercial transactions could take place . . . [V]iolence, fortunately, is a one-in-a-million deviance from the pacific norm'. Higgins' point appears to be that if ambiguity exists, then the decision-maker can make a choice which implements or is justified by existing legal material. Choice is inevitable in legal decision-making because rules are not fully determined. In these circumstances, Higgins (1994, p 5) thinks it:

> desirable that the policy factors are dealt with systematically and openly. Dealing with them systematically means that all factors are properly considered and weighed, instead of the decision-maker unconsciously narrowing or selecting what he will take into account in order to reach a decision that he has instinctively predetermined is desirable. Dealing with policy factors openly means that the decision-maker himself is subjected to the discipline of facing them squarely.

While one can disagree with the policy factors Higgins thinks relevant, at least this approach has the virtue of making these factors candid. Analysis and evaluation are easier because one knows the factors in play.

VIII. BEYOND THE STATE, ITS INTERESTS, AND INSTRUMENTALISM

Despite their differences, the New Haven and Soviet schools share a common approach: both are instrumental theories of law, aimed at guiding and informing practice while implementing a political programme. Not all legal philosophy has this focus, despite the fact that this might cause disappointment:

> Lawyers and law teachers . . . think (rightly) that legal practice is a practical business, and they expect the philosophy of law to be the backroom activity of telling front-line practitioners how to do it well, with their heads held high. When a philosopher of law asserts a proposition that neither endorses nor criticizes what they do, lawyers and law teachers are often frustrated . . . They cannot accept that legal philosophy is not wholly (or even mainly) the backroom activity of identifying what is good or bad about legal practice, and hence of laying on practical proposals for its improvement (or failing that, abandonment). (Gardner, 2001, p 204)

Much contemporary theory is non-instrumental, and thus detached from the practice of international law. This tendency towards detachment, a perceived disinclination to making clear commitments to anything but being 'critical', has caused adverse comment. For instance, Higgins (1994, p 9) argues that this approach 'leads to the pessimistic conclusion that what international law can do is to point out the problems but not assist in the achievement of goals'. This is precisely the criticism made of Kennedy by Charlesworth (Charlesworth, 2002a). Others have taken a more extreme view, denouncing critical scholars as engendering legal nihilism (eg Carrington, 1984).

Although these criticisms of the critics contain a degree of truth, they fail to give due weight to the idea that reason and knowledge are contextually embedded, that different discourses have different aims and functions. Consider Balkin's epistemologist who engages in a discussion with her colleagues in the philosophy department about the reliability of our knowledge of the passage of time. When, as a result of this discussion, she gets home later than she should and is upbraided by her husband because they are late for a dinner engagement, Balkin observes that it would be beside the point for her to respond using her philosophical arguments to question his knowledge of the passage of time—'in the context of dinner engagements, these speculations are irrelevant and philosophical scepticism is quite out of bounds' (Balkin, 1992, p 752).

Non-instrumental theories of international law are more akin to epistemological arguments regarding the passage of time than the more prosaic knowledge necessary to be prompt for dinner dates. Kennedy, for instance, is much more concerned with the critique of the practice and consequences of the practice of international law than in guiding that practice. As such, he could be seen as falling into an American intellectual tradition:

> Artists and writers began to conceive of themselves as refugees from the American mainstream, the specially endowed inhabitants of a transcendental region sealed off from the hurly-burly of the marketplace, the banality of popular opinion, and the grime of industrialized society. Alienation became the customary and most comfortable posture for American intellectuals; criticism rather than celebration of the dominant American institutions and attitudes became the accepted norm . . . [T]he voluntary withdrawal of American artists and intellectuals into a separate sphere was not peculiar; it was merely part of a major fragmentation that occurred as American society modernized. (Ellis, 1979, p 221)

Nevertheless, an important theme in Kennedy's work (eg 2004) is that individuals should shoulder responsibility for their actions in the international arena, eg in human rights activism. Unfortunately, he also seems to indicate that we can never know the full consequences of our action, which would suggest that we cannot even 'point out the problems'. This could lead to paralysis; a reluctance or refusal to act because we cannot assess the effects of any planned intervention (compare Finnis, 1980, pp 115–17). From Higgins' perspective as a New Haven lawyer, this is indeed a fatal flaw: decisions must be made on the basis of available knowledge with a view to action.

In contrast, Philip Allott, whose work is avowedly iconoclastic (for a range of views, see Allott et al, 2005, and Scobbie, 2011), is essentially a non-instrumentalist critical theorist who demands action. Unlike some tendencies within the New Stream, Allott is imbued with a regenerative idealism, and places his faith in the power of the human mind to reform the future by imagining what that future should be, and then use reason to implement this idea. Human consciousness thus provides the template for human action and human reality, 'We make the human world, including human institutions, through the power of the human mind. What we have made by thinking we can make new by new thinking' (Allott, 2001, p xxvii). Thus at the heart of Allott's project lies an elemental conviction in the power of ideas, of human consciousness, both to structure and to change—to restructure—the world. Allott seeks a 'revolution, not in the streets but in the mind' (p 257, para 14.9) in order to achieve 'a social international society [where] the ideal of all ideals is eunomia, the good order of a self-ordering society' (p 404, para 18.77).

Allott argues for the rejection of the State as the primary unit of authority, and thus for the reconstruction of world affairs. The emphasis in international relations on the centrality of the State is at least a mistake, if not a tragedy, because it encapsulates a fundamental misconception about what matters: it authorizes the pursuit of specifically State interests to the detriment of those of humanity. This structure of international relations, derived from Vattel:

> is not merely a tradition of international law. It implies a pure theory of the whole nature of international society and hence of the whole nature of the human social condition; and it generates practical theories which rule the lives of all societies, of the whole human race. It is nothing but mere words, mere ideas, mere theory, mere values—and yet war and peace, human happiness and human misery, human wealth and human want, human lives and human life have depended on them for two centuries and more. (p 243, para 13.105)

Just as the State is not co-extensive with society, international unsociety, where States dominate, is markedly less representative of humanity.

This was the inevitable outcome of the reception of Vattelian thought in international affairs, which played into the hands of ruling élites (pp 248–9, para 13.106). The conduct of international affairs through the conduit of the State made sovereignty, which projects 'an authority-based view of society', the structural premise of international affairs. This:

> tend[s] to make all society seem to be essentially a system of authority, and . . . to make societies incorporating systems of authority seem to be the most significant forms of society, at the expense of all other forms of society, including non-patriarchal families, at one extreme, and international society, at the other. (p 199, para 12.53)

Thus the notion of the State, organized as sovereign authority over specified territory, trumps membership of other possible societies which are not as exclusive, and whose consciousness and ideals may differ from those of the State (see also Franck, 1999). Moreover, the consciousness of the State is impoverished, concentrating on State rather than human interests. At least in some States, however, the notion of sovereignty has been surpassed by that of democracy which relocates power in society rather than in the simple fiat of authority. This introduces a profound shift in social consciousness as democracy 'seeks to make the individual society-member seek well-being in seeking the well-being of society. Democracy seeks to make society seek well-being in seeking the well-being of each individual society-member' (Allott, 2001, p 217, para 13.31).

International unsociety, on the other hand, has chosen 'to regard itself as the state externalized, undemocratized, and unsocialized' (p 240, para 13.98). The purposes pursued in the world of States are those of States: 'purposes related to the survival and prospering of each of those state-societies rather than the survival and prospering of an international society of the whole human race' (p 247, para 13.105(13)). Morality thus becomes discontinuous between the domestic and international spheres (p 244, para 13.105(6)), and governments are able to act internationally free from the moral restraints that constrain them in domestic affairs, 'murdering human beings by the million in wars, tolerating oppression and starvation and disease and poverty, human cruelty and suffering, human misery and human indignity' (p 248, para 13.105(16)). 'This cannot be how the world was meant to be' (Allott, 2005). Allott's fundamental belief is that international society has the capacity to enable all societies to promote the ever-increasing well-being of themselves and their members:

> It is in international society that humanity's capacity to harm itself can achieve its most spectacular effects. And it is in international society that the ever-increasing well-being of the whole human race can, must, and will be promoted. (p 180, para 12.5)

The State system, and consequent discontinuity between international and domestic affairs, alienates people from international law which 'seems to be the business of a foreign realm, another world, in which they play no personal part' (pp 298–9, para 16.8). It is something, at best, imposed upon them and not something in which they participate, nor forge through the force of their consciousness. International law has not been integrated into the social process of humanity and is 'doomed to be what it has been—marginal, residual, and intermittent' (p 304, para 16.17). As things stand, international law cannot play its proper part in the realization of eunomia—'the good order of a self-ordering society'.

When *Eunomia* was first published, Allott's vision was criticized as utopian. It assumes that a fully socialized international society will be benevolent and eschew conflict, as conflict arises from the competing interests of States. Allott (p xxxii) denies that the criticism of utopianism has any force:

> In response to this criticism, it is surely only necessary to say that our experience of the revolutionary transformation of national societies has been that the past conditions the future but that it does not finally and inescapably determine it. We have shown that we can think ourselves out of the social jungle.

It is equally true that we can think ourselves into that jungle: the betrayal of the idealism of the 1917 Russian revolution by subsequent reigns of terror sometimes aimed, although often not, at the realization of socialism is only one case in point. Allott's presupposition that humanity would develop a more just, loving, and peaceful consciousness—and choose to implement this in its social reality, were it allowed to do so—is difficult to accept without hesitation. His argument is predicated on the belief that bad or wicked choices have been made which have caused human misery. It might be that Allott does not believe in the possibility of 'pure' evil, of wicked acts done in and for themselves. For Allott, human evil might simply be a contingent possibility, the product of a perverted consciousness arising, for instance, from the asocial conduct of international affairs. Accordingly, for Allott, evil might not be a necessary part of the human condition and may be banished through the transformation of human consciousness in the strive for eunomia. This belief, nevertheless, appears to be more an act of faith than a demonstrable proposition (see Scobbie, 2011, pp 191–3).

On the other hand, one consequence of Allott's vision must surely be that of taking responsibility for international society and thus for international law. If Allott's inclusive international society were to be realized, international law would become a matter directly within individual consciousness. Accordingly, individuals (ultimately) rather than the State would determine and thus be responsible for the substantive content of international law. With that responsibility, Allott's hope is that morality would no longer be discontinuous between domestic and international society.

IX. A VIEW OF DELFT

The only landscape that we know Johannes Vermeer painted, *A View of Delft* (c 1660–61), lives in The Hague along with all those international courts and organizations. It hangs in the modest Dutch Classicist setting of the Mauritshuis, the Royal Cabinet of Paintings, and not, for instance, in the more exuberant neo-renaissance exterior, art nouveau interior, of the Peace Palace which houses the International Court of Justice, Permanent Court of Arbitration, and The Hague Academy of International Law. *A View of Delft* is perhaps not as well known as Vermeer's *Girl with a Pearl Earring* (c 1665), which is also in the Mauritshuis, but I think it is the better, and more interesting, painting. It is luminous, with the upper two-thirds of the canvas taken up with a darkening sky.

Art historians have pinpointed that Vermeer painted *A View of Delft* from the upper storey of a building on the Schieweg (Bailey, 2001, p 108). It is also thought that he probably made use of *camera obscura* as an aid in setting out the basic topography of the scene, but the final composition is not a 'photographic' representation of the view from the window on the Schieweg. He reorganized reality, changed perspective, and tonal contrast 'to reinforce the strong friezelike character of the city profile' (Wheelock and Broos, 1995, p 133, see also pp 120–4, Bailey, 2001, pp 109–11, and Westermann, 1996, pp 82–3). The conscious manipulation of elements of composition and perspective was not uncommon with Dutch artists in the eighteenth century (see, eg, Westermann, 1996, pp 75–7). The aim was to highlight and emphasize some aspects at the expense of others in order to produce a more pleasing or dramatic image.

Legal theories are like this: their authors decide the aspects of law they want to discuss and in highlighting some, they downplay or ignore others. In rhetorical theory, this is known as 'presence':

> choice is . . . a dominant factor in scientific debates: choice of the facts deemed relevant, choice of hypotheses, choice of the theories that should be confronted with the facts, choice of the actual elements that constitute facts. The method of each science implies such a choice, which is relatively stable in the natural sciences, but is much more variable in the social sciences.
>
> By the very fact of selecting certain elements and presenting them to the audience, their importance and pertinency to the discussion are implied. Indeed, such a choice endows those elements with a presence, which is an essential factor in argumentation. (Perelman and Olbrechts-Tyteca, 1969, p 116; see pp 115–20)

All theoretical discussions of international law are incomplete in one way or another because different theorists emphasize—give presence to—different aspects of the discipline. They have different concerns, different aims, and different presuppositions—in short, different perspectives—in their thinking about international law.

At the start of this chapter, I identified Socrates as 'one of the founders of Western philosophy', and this discussion has remained within that tradition. While Third World Approaches to International Law (TWAIL), to take one example, has been mentioned, it has not been discussed. That silence should be deafening. All theories distort reality through selection and simplification. Some contemporary—and not so contemporary—theorists argue that these differences are inevitable, because one's whole personality is inextricably involved in one's approach to and understanding of (international) law (see, eg, Kennedy, 2004, and Koskenniemi, 1999; compare Frank, 1949, pp 146–56, and Lasswell and McDougal, 1943, p 236; see also Duxbury, 1995, pp 125–35). Accordingly, there can be no objectivity, no intellectual space beyond the individual analyst—'there is no there there' (Stein, 1938, p 251).

In one of his last books, published posthumously, Professor Judt adverted to the methodological solipsism of identity politics—'Why should everything be about 'me'?'—and continued:

> If everything is 'political,' then nothing is. I am reminded of Gertrude Stein's Oxford lecture on contemporary literature. 'What about the woman question?' someone asked. Stein's reply should be emblazoned on every college notice board from Boston to Berkeley: 'Not everything can be about everything.' (Judt, 2010, pp 189–90)

REFERENCES

ALLOTT, PJ (1998), 'Out of the Looking Glass', 24 *Review of International Studies* 573.

ALLOTT, PJ (2001), *Eunomia: New Order For a New World* (Oxford: Oxford University Press) (first printed in 1990, reprinted 2001 with an extensive new preface).

ALLOTT, PJ (2002), *The Health of Nations: Society and Law Beyond the State* (Cambridge: Cambridge University Press).

ALLOTT, PJ et al (2005), 'Thinking Another World: "This Cannot Be How the World was Meant to Be"', 16 *EJIL* 255, including the following essays:

FRANCK, TM, 'The Fervent Imagination and the School of Hard Knocks', p 343;

HIGGINS, R, 'Final Remarks', p 347;

KNOP, K, 'Eunomia is a Woman: Philip Allott and Feminism', p 315;

KOSKENNIEMI, M, 'International Law as Therapy: Reading The Health of Nations', p 329; and

SCOBBIE, I, 'Slouching Towards the Holy City: Some Weeds for Philip Allott', p 299.

ALVAREZ, JE (2001), 'Do Liberal States Behave Better? A Critique of Slaughter's Liberal Theory', 12 *EJIL* 183.

ANGHIE, A (2005), *Imperialism, Sovereignty and the Making of International Law* (Cambridge: Cambridge University Press).

AREND, AC (1996), 'Toward an Understanding of International Legal Rules', in RJ Beck, AC Arend, and RDV Lugt (eds), *International Rules: Approaches From International Law and International Relations* (New York: Oxford University Press), p 289.

AREND, AC (1999), *Legal Rules and International Society* (New York: Oxford University Press).

AUSTIN, J (1832), in WE Rumble (ed) (1995), *The Province of Jurisprudence Determined* (Cambridge: Cambridge University Press).

AUSTIN, JL (1976), in JO Urmson and M Sbisà (eds), *How to do Things with Words:*

the *William James Lectures Delivered in Harvard University in 1955* (Oxford: Oxford University Press).

BAILEY, A (2001), *Vermeer: a View of Delft* (New York: Henry Holt).

BALKIN, JM (1986), 'Deconstructive Practice and Legal Theory', 96 *Yale LJ* 743.

BALKIN, JM (1992), 'Just Rhetoric?', 55 *MLR* 746.

BECKETT, J (2001), 'Behind Relative Normativity: Rules and Process as Prerequisites of Law', 12 *EJIL* 627.

BECKETT, J (2005), 'Countering Uncertainty and Ending Up/Down Arguments: Prolegomena to a Response to NAIL', 16 *EJIL* 213.

BECKETT, J (2009), 'The Politics of International Law—Twenty Years Later: A Reply', http://www.ejiltalk.org/the-politics-of-international-law-twenty-years-later-a-reply/.

BEDERMAN, DJ (2001), *International Law in Antiquity* (Cambridge: Cambridge University Press).

BERMAN, PS (2005), 'From International Law to Law and Globalization', 43 *Columbia Journal of Transnational Law* 485.

BOLTON, JR (2000), 'Is There Really "Law" in International Affairs?', 10 *Transnational Law and Contemporary Problems* 1.

BORGEN, CJ (2007), 'Whose Public, Whose Order? Imperium, Region, and Normative Friction', 32 *Yale Journal of International Law* 331.

BOWRING B, (2008), 'Positivism Versus Self-determination: the Contradictions of Soviet International Law', in S Marks (ed), *International Law on the Left: Re-examining Marxist Legacies* (Cambridge: Cambridge University Press), p 133.

BRETT, A (2012), 'Francisco de Vitoria (1483–1546) and Francisco Suárez (1548–1617)', in Fassbender and Peters, *Handbook of History*, 1086.

BREZHNEV, L (1980), *On Events in Afghanistan: Leonid Brezhnev's Replies to a Pravda Correspondent* (Moscow: Novosti Press).

BROWNLIE, I (1981), 'The Reality and Efficacy of International Law', 52 *BYIL* 1.

BROWNLIE, I (1983), 'Recognition in Theory and Practice', in RStJ Macdonald and DM Johnston (eds), *The Structure and Process of International Law*, 627.

BROWNLIE, I (1995), 'International Law at the Fiftieth Anniversary of the United Nations: General Course on Public International Law', 255 *Recueil des Cours* 9.

BULL, H (2002), *The Anarchical Society: a Study of Order in World Politics* (3rd edn, Basingstoke: Palgrave).

BULL, H, KINGSBURY, B, and ROBERTS, A (eds) (1990), *Hugo Grotius and International Relations* (Oxford: Clarendon Press).

BUTLER, WE (1971), '"Socialist International Law" or "Socialist Principles of International Relations"?', 65 *AJIL* 796.

CARRINGTON, PD (1984), 'Of Law and the River', 34 *J of Legal Education* 222.

CARTY, A (2004), 'Marxism and International Law: Perspectives for the American (Twenty-First) Century', 17 *Leiden JIL* 247.

CASS, D (1996), 'Navigating the Newstream: Recent Critical Scholarship in International Law', 65 *Nordic JIL* 341.

CHARLESWORTH, H (2002a), 'Author! Author!: A Response to David Kennedy', 15 *Harvard HRJ* 127.

CHARLESWORTH, H (2002b), 'International Law: A Discipline of Crisis', 63 *MLR* 377.

CHARLESWORTH, H and CHINKIN, C (2000), *The Boundaries of International Law: A Feminist Analysis* (Manchester: Manchester University Press).

CHIMNI, BS (2004), 'An Outline of a Marxist Course on Public International Law', 17 *Leiden JIL* 1.

COLLINS, H (1984), *Marxism and Law* (Oxford: Oxford University Press).

CRAVEN, M (2012), 'Colonialism and Domination' in Fassbender and Peters, *Handbook of History*, p 862.

DAMROSCH, LF and Müllerson, R (1995), 'The Role of International Law in the Contemporary World', in LF Damrosch, GM Danilenko, and R Müllerson (eds), *Beyond Confrontation: International Law for the Post-Cold War Era* (Boulder, CO: Westview Press), p 1.

DANIEL, L (2009), *Gertrude Stein* (London: Reaktion Books).

D'ASPREMONT, J (2011), *Formalism and the Sources of International Law: a Theory of the Ascertainment of Legal Rules* (Oxford: Oxford University Press).

DICKINSON, LA (2007), 'Toward a "New" New Haven School of International Law', 32 *Yale Journal of International Law* 547.

DUCHHARDT, H (2012), 'From the Peace of Westphalia to the Congress of Vienna' in Fassbender and Peters, *Handbook of History*, 628.

DUNOFF, JL, and TRACHTMAN, JP (eds) (2009), *Ruling the World? Constitutionalism, International Law and Global Governance* (New York: Cambridge University Press).

DUXBURY, N (1995), *Patterns of American Jurisprudence* (Oxford: Clarendon Press).

DYDO, UE (2003), *Gertrude Stein: The Language that Rises* (Evanston, IL: Northwestern University Press).

ELLIS, JJ (1979), *After the Revolution: Profiles of Early American Culture* (New York: Norton).

FALK, RA (1995), 'Casting the Spell: The New Haven School of International Law', 104 *Yale LJ* 1991.

FASSBENDER, B and PETERS, A (eds) (2012), *The Oxford Handbook of the History of International Law* (Oxford: Oxford University Press).

FELDMAN, SM (2000), *American Legal Thought from Premodernism to Postmodernism: An Intellectual Voyage* (New York: Oxford University Press).

FINNIS, J (1980), *Natural Law and Natural Rights* (Oxford: Clarendon Press).

FOUCAULT, M (1998), 'What is an Author?', in JD Faubian (ed), *Essential Works 1954–84, vol 2, Aesthetics* (New York: New Press), p 203.

FRANCK, TM (1970), 'Who Killed Article 2(4)? or: Changing Norms Governing the Use of Force by States', 64 *AJIL* 809.

FRANCK, TM (1990), *The Power of Legitimacy Among Nations* (Oxford: Oxford University Press).

FRANCK, TM (1995), *Fairness in International Law and Institutions* (Oxford: Clarendon Press).

FRANCK, TM (1999), *The Empowered Self: Law and Society in the Age of Individualism* (Oxford: Clarendon Press).

FRANK, J (1949), *Courts on Trial: Myth and Reality in American Justice* (Princeton, NJ: Princeton University Press).

FREEMAN, MDA (2001), *Lloyd's Introduction to Jurisprudence* (London: Sweet & Maxwell).

GAGARIN, M and Woodruff, P (eds) (1995), *Early Greek Political Thought from Homer to the Sophists* (Cambridge: Cambridge University Press).

GARDNER, J (2001), 'Legal Positivism: 5½ Myths', 46 *American Journal of Jurisprudence* 199.

GARRAWAY, C (2010), '"To Kill or not to Kill"—Dilemmas on the Use of Force', 14 *Journal of Conflict and Security Law* 499.

GOLDSMITH, JL, and Posner, EA (2005), *The Limits of International Law* (New York: Oxford University Press).

GROSS, L (1948), 'The Peace of Westphalia, 1648–1948', 42 *AJIL* 20.

GROTIUS, H (2005) in R Tuck (ed), *The Rights of War and Peace* (Indianapolis: Liberty Fund), available online at Liberty Fund, Online Library of Liberty, http://oll.liberty-fund.org/title/1425.

HAAKONSSEN, K (1985), 'Hugo Grotius and the History of Political Thought', 13 *Political Theory* 239.

HAAKONSSEN, K (1996), *Natural Law and Moral Philosophy: from Grotius to the Scottish Enlightenment* (Cambridge: Cambridge University Press).

HAGGENMACHER, P (1990), 'Grotius and Gentili: a Reassessment of Thomas E. Holland's Inaugural Lecture', in Bull et al, *Hugo Grotius and International Relations*, 133.

HAGGENMACHER, P (2012) 'Hugo Grotius (1583–1645)', in Fassbender and Peters, *Handbook of History*, 1098.

HATHAWAY, OA (2007), 'The Continuing Influence of the New Haven School', 32 *Yale Journal of International Law* 553.

HAZARD, J (1971), 'Renewed Emphasis Upon a Socialist International Law', 65 *AJIL* 142.

HEAD, M (2004), 'The Rise and Fall of a Soviet Jurist: Evgeny Pashukanis and Stalinism', 17 *Canadian Journal of Law and Jurisprudence* 269.

HENCKAERTS, J-M, and DOSWALD-BECK, L (2005), *Customary International Humanitarian Law* (Cambridge: Cambridge University Press).

HEYWARD, M (1993), *The Ern Malley Affair* (London: Faber and Faber).

HIGGINS, R (1994), *Problems and Process: International Law and How We Use It* (Oxford: Clarendon Press).

HODGSON, G (2005), 'The Other American Presidential Election: Choosing A President and Psychoanalyzing A Nation', (Oxford: Europaeum) available at http://www.europaeum.org/files/publications/pamphlets/GodfreyHodgson.pdf.

HUGHES, B (2010), *The Hemlock Cup: Socrates, Athens and the Search for the Good Life* (London: Jonathan Cape).

HUTCHESON, JC (1928–9), 'The Judgment Intuitive: The Function of the "Hunch" in Judicial Decision', 14 *Cornell LQ* 274.

JANIS, MW (1991), 'Religion and the Literature of International Law: Some Standard Texts', in MW Janis (ed), *The*

Influence of Religion on the Development of International Law (Dordrecht: Nijhoff), 61.

JANIS, MW (2004), *The American Tradition of International Law: Great Expectations 1789–1914* (Oxford: Clarendon Press).

JUDT, T (2010), *The Memory Chalet* (London: Heinemann).

KANT, I (1793), 'On the Common Saying: "This May be True in Theory, But it Does Not Apply in Practice"', in H Reiss (ed) (1970), *Kant's Political Writings* (Cambridge: Cambridge University Press), p 61.

KARTASHKIN, V (1983), 'The Marxist-Leninist Approach: The Theory of Class Struggle and Contemporary International Law', in Macdonald and Johnston (eds), *The Structure and Process of International Law*, 79.

KENNEDY, D (1985), 'International Legal Education', 26 *Harvard ILJ* 361.

KENNEDY, D (1999), 'The Disciplines of International Law and Policy', 12 *Leiden JIL* 9.

KENNEDY, D (2000), 'When Renewal Repeats: Thinking Against the Box', 32 *NYU JILP* 335.

KENNEDY, D (2003), 'Tom Franck and the Manhattan School', 35 *NYU JILP* 397.

KENNEDY, D (2004), *The Dark Side of Virtue: Reassessing International Humanitarianism* (Princeton, NJ: Princeton University Press).

KING, R (2006), *The Judgment of Paris: the Revolutionary Decade that Gave the World Impressionism* (New York: Walker and Company).

KINGSBURY B and ROBERTS, A (1990), 'Introduction: Grotian Thought in International Relations', in Bull et al, *Hugo Grotius and International Relations*, 1.

KLABBERS, J, PETERS, A, and ULFSTEIN, G (eds) (2009), *The Constitutionalization of International Law* (Oxford: Oxford University Press).

KOH, HH (2007), 'Is There a 'New' New Haven School of International Law', 32 *Yale Journal of International Law* 559.

KOSKENNIEMI, M (1989), *From Apology to Utopia: The Structure of International Legal Argument* (Helsinki: Finnish Lawyers' Publishing Co).

KOSKENNIEMI, M (1990), 'The Politics of International Law', 1 *EJIL* 4.

KOSKENNIEMI, M (1999), 'Letter to the Editors of the Symposium', 93 *AJIL* 351.

KOSKENNIEMI, M (2005), 'International Law in Europe: Between Tradition and Renewal', 16 *EJIL* 113.

KOSKENNIEMI, M (2009a) 'The Politics of International Law—Twenty Years Later', 20 *EJIL* 7,

KOSKENNIEMI, M (2009b), 'The Politics of International Law—Twenty Years Later', <http://www.ejiltalk.org/the-politics-of-international-law-twenty-years-later>.

KRATOCHWIL, FV (1989), *Rules, Norms and Decisions: On the Conditions of Practical and Legal Reasoning in International Relations and Domestic Affairs* (Cambridge: Cambridge University Press).

KRETZMER, D (2009), 'Rethinking Application of IHL in Non-International Armed Conflict', 42 *Israel Law Review* 1.

LACEY, N (2004), *A Life of HLA Hart: the Nightmare and the Noble Dream* (Oxford: Oxford University Press).

LASSWELL, HD and McDOUGAL, MS (1943), 'Legal Education and Public Policy: Professional Training in the Public Interest', 52 *Yale LJ* 203.

LASSWELL, HD and McDOUGAL, MS (1992), *Jurisprudence For a Free Society: Studies in Law, Science and Policy* (Dordrecht: Martinus Nijhoff).

LAUTERPACHT, H (1933), *The Function of Law in the International Community* (Oxford: Clarendon Press).

LEE, RW (1930), *Hugo Grotius* (Oxford: Oxford University Press).

LEVIT, JK (2007), 'Bottom-Up Lawmaking: Reflections on the New Haven School of International Law', 32 *Yale Journal of International Law* 393.

MacCormick, N (1990), 'Reconstruction after Deconstruction: A Response to CLS', 10 *Oxford JLS* 539.

MacDonald, RStJ (1998), 'Rummaging in the Ruins. Soviet International Law and Policy in the Early Years: Is Anything Left?', in K Wellens (ed) *International Law: Theory and Practice. Essays in Honour of Eric Suy* (The Hague: Martinus Nijhoff), p 61.

MacDonald, RStJ and Johnston, DM (eds) (1983), *The Structure and Process of International Law: Essays in Legal Philosophy Doctrine and Theory* (Dordrecht: Martinus Nijhoff).

McDougal, MS, and Burke, WT (1962), *The Public Order of the Oceans: A Contemporary International Law of the Sea* (New Haven, CT: Yale University Press).

McDougal, MS and Feliciano, FP (1994), *The International Law of War: Transnational Coercion and World Public Order* (Dordrecht: Martinus Nijhoff).

McDougal, MS and Lasswell, HD (1981), 'The Identification and Appraisal of Diverse Systems of Public Order', in MS McDougal and WM Reisman (eds), *International Law Essays* (Mineola, NY: Foundation Press), p 15; first published (1959) 53 *AJIL* 1.

McDougal, MS, Lasswell, HD, and Chen, LC (1969), 'Human Rights and World Public Order: A Framework for Policy-oriented Inquiry', 63 *AJIL* 237.

McDougal, MS, Lasswell, HD, and Chen, LC (1980), *Human Rights and World Public Order: The Basic Policies of an International Law of Human Dignity* (New Haven, CT: Yale University Press).

McDougal, MS and Reisman, WM (1983), 'International Law in Policy-oriented Perspective', in RStJ Macdonald, and DM Johnston (eds), *The Structure and Process of International Law*, 103.

McWhinney, E (1990), 'The 'New Thinking' in Soviet International Law: Soviet Doctrine and Practice in the Post-Tunkin Era', 28 *Canadian YIL* 309.

Marks, S (ed) (2008), *International Law on the Left: Re-examining Marxist Legacies* (Cambridge: Cambridge University Press).

Miéville, C (2004), 'The Commodity-Form Theory of International Law: An Introduction', 17 *Leiden JIL* 271.

Morison, WL (1982), *John Austin* (London: Edward Arnold).

Olivecrona, K (1971), *Law as Fact* (2nd edn, London: Stevens).

Osakwe, C (1972), 'Socialist International Law Revisited', 66 *AJIL* 596.

Osofsky, HM (2007), 'A Law and Geography Perspective on the New Haven School', 32 *Yale Journal of International Law* 421.

Paulus, AL (2001), 'International Law After Postmodernism: Towards Renewal or Decline of International Law?', 14 *Leiden JIL* 727.

Perelman, C (1976), *Logique Juridique: Nouvelle Rhétorique* (Paris: Dalloz).

Perelman, C and Olbrechts-Tyteca, L (1969), *The New Rhetoric: a Treatise on Argumentation* (Notre Dame, IN: University of Notre Dame Press: translation of *La Nouvelle Rhétorique: Traité de l'Argumentation*, 1958).

Plato (1892), in B Jowett (ed), *The Dialogues of Plato, Vol 1* (3rd edn, Oxford: Oxford University Press), available at Liberty Fund, *Online Library of Liberty*, http://oll.libertyfund.org/title/111.

Plato (1969), in H Tredennick (ed), *The Last Days of Socrates* (Harmondsworth: Penguin, rev. edn).

Plato (1994), in R Waterfield (ed), *Symposium* (Oxford: Oxford University Press).

Plato (1996), in CCW Taylor (ed), *Protagoras* (Oxford: Oxford University Press).

Plato (2002), in R Waterfield (ed), *Phaedrus* (Oxford: Oxford University Press).

Prager, CAL (1998), 'Allott in Wonderland', 24 *Review of International Studies* 563.

Posner, RA (1990), *Cardozo: A Study in Reputation* (Chicago: University of Chicago Press).

PURVIS, N (1991), 'Critical Legal Studies in Public International Law', 32 *Harvard JIL* 81.

RABKIN, JA (2005), *Law Without Nations? Why Constitutional Government Requires Sovereign States* (Princeton, NJ: Princeton University Press).

RAGAZZI, M (1997), *The Concept of International Obligations Erga Omnes* (Oxford: Clarendon Press).

RASULOV, A (2012), 'New Approaches to International Law: Images of a Genealogy', in JM Beneyto and D Kennedy (eds), *New Approaches to International Law* (The Hague: TMC Asser Press), p 151.

RAZ, J (1980), *The Concept of a Legal System: An Introduction to the Theory of Legal System* (2nd edn, Oxford: Clarendon Press).

REISMAN, WM, WIESSNER, S, and WILLARD, AR (2007), 'The New Haven School: a Brief Introduction', 32 *Yale Journal of International Law* 575.

ROBERTS, AE (2001), 'Traditional and Modern Approaches to Customary International Law: A Reconciliation', 95 *AJIL* 757.

SCATTOLA, M (2012), 'Alberico Gentili (1552–1608)', in Fassbender and Peters, *Handbook of History*, 1092.

SCHMITT, M (2012), 'International Law in Cyber Space: the Koh Speech and the Tallinn Manual Juxtaposed', 54 *Harvard International Law Journal Online* 13 (2012), available at http://www.harvardilj.org/2012/12/online-articles-online_54_schmitt/.

SCHWEBEL, SM (1972), 'The Brezhnev Doctrine Repealed and Peaceful Co-existence Enacted', 66 *AJIL* 816.

SCOBBIE, I (1990), 'Towards the Elimination of International Law: Some Radical Scepticism about Sceptical Radicalism', 61 *BYIL* 339.

SCOBBIE, I (2009) 'On the Road to Avila?: a Response to Koskenniemi', available at http://www.ejiltalk.org/on-the-road-to-avila-a-response-to-koskenniemi.

SCOBBIE, I (2011) '"The Holiness of the Heart's Affection": Philip Allott's Theory of Social Idealism', in A Orakhelashvili (ed), *Research Handbook on the Theory and History of International Law* (Cheltenham: Edward Elgar), p 168.

SLAUGHTER, AM (1995), 'International Law in a World of Liberal States', 6 *EJIL* 1.

SLAUGHTER, AM (2004), *A New World Order* (Princeton: Princeton University Press).

SMITH, A (1978), in RL Meek, DD Raphael, and P Stein (eds) *Lectures on Jurisprudence* (Oxford: Clarendon Press).

SOLUM, LB (1987), 'On the Indeterminacy Crisis: Critiquing Critical Dogma', 54 *University of Chicago Law Review* 462.

STEIN, G (1936) (1998a), 'The Geographical History of America or The Relation of Human Nature to the Human Mind', in CR Stimpson and H Chessman (eds), *Gertrude Stein: Writings 1932–1946* (New York: Library of America), p 365.

STEIN, G (1938), *Everybody's Autobiography* (London: Heinemann).

STEIN, G (1998b), 'Lifting Belly', in CR Stimpson and H Chessman (eds) *Gertrude Stein: Writings 1903–1932* (New York: Library of America).

TALLINN MANUAL (2013), Schmitt, M (general ed), *Tallinn Manual on the International Law Applicable to Cyber Warfare* (Cambridge: Cambridge University Press) available at http://www.ccdcoe.org/249.html.

TASIOULAS, J (1996), 'In Defence of Relative Normativity: Communitarian Values and the Nicaragua Case', 16 *Oxford JLS* 84.

TUCK, R (1999), *The Rights of War and Peace: Political Thought and the International Order from Grotius to Kant* (Oxford: Oxford University Press).

TUNKIN, GI (1974), *Theory of International Law* (WE Butler, trans) (London: Allen & Unwin).

TUNKIN, GI (2003), *Theory of International Law* (WE Butler, trans) (2nd edn, London: Wildy, Simmonds and Hill).

TURNER, K (ed) (1999), *Baby Precious Always Shines: Selected Love Notes Between Gertrude Stein and Alice B. Toklas* (New York: St Martin's Press).

TUSHNET, M (2005), 'Survey Article: Critical Legal Theory (Without Modifiers) in the United States', 13 *Journal of Political Philosophy* 99.

VAGTS, D (2001), 'Hegemonic International Law', 95 *AJIL* 843.

VERESHCHETIN, VS and MÜLLERSON, R (1990), 'The Primacy of International Law in World Politics', in A Carty and G Danilenko (eds), *Perestroika and International Law: Current Anglo-Soviet Approaches to International Law* (Edinburgh: Edinburgh University Press), p 6.

VITORIA, F (1991) in AR Pagden, J Lawrance, and J Lawrance (eds), *Vitoria: Political Texts* (Cambridge: Cambridge University Press).

VLASTOS, G (1994), 'The Historical Socrates and Athenian Democracy', in Vlastos (Burnyeat, M (ed)), *Socratic Studies* (Cambridge: Cambridge University Press), p 87.

WAGNER-MARTIN, L (1995), '*Favored Strangers': Gertrude Stein and her Family* (New Brunswick: Rutgers University Press).

WARBRICK, C (1991), 'The Theory of International Law: Is there an English Contribution?', in P Allott et al, *Theory and International Law: an Introduction* (London: BIICL), p 49.

WARBRICK, C (2000), 'Brownlie's Principles of Public International Law: An Assessment', 11 *EJIL* 621.

WATERFIELD, R (ed) (2000), *The First Philosophers: the Presocratics and Sophists* (Oxford: Oxford University Press).

WATERFIELD, R (2009), *Why Socrates Died: Dispelling the Myths* (New York: Norton).

WEIL, P (1983), 'Towards Relative Normativity?', 77 *AJIL* 413.

WESTERMANN, M (1996), *A Worldly Art: the Dutch Republic 1585–1718* (New Haven, CT: Yale University Press).

WHEELOCK, AK, and BROOS, B (1995), 'The Catalogue', in AK Wheelock (ed), *Johannes Vermeer* (The Hague: Royal Cabinet of Paintings Mauritshuis), 85.

WILSON, E (1996), *Axel's Castle: A Study of the Imaginative Literature of 1870–1930* (New York: Modern Library, first published 1931).

WRÓBLEWSKI, J (1974), 'Legal Syllogism and Rationality of Judicial Decision', 5 *Rechtstheorie* 33.

FURTHER READING

In addition to the works cited in the bibliography, the following are useful in providing a variety of theoretical perspectives on international law, although this is an enormous and expanding field.

BECK, RJ, AREND, AC, and LUGT, RD (eds) (1996), *International Rules: Approaches From International Law and International Relations* (New York: Oxford University Press): an excellent introductory collection of readings and commentary which covers the principal contemporary schools of international legal thought.

BESSON S, and TASIOULAS, J (eds) (2010), *The Philosophy of International Law* (Oxford: Oxford University Press): contains an excellent set of essays which are firmly rooted in philosophical concerns.

BIANCHI, ANDREA (2016), *International Law Theories: An Inquiry into Different Ways of Thinking* (Oxford: Oxford University Press).

BYERS, M (ed) (2000), *The Role of International Law in International Politics: Essays in International Relations and International Law* (Oxford: Oxford University Press): a collection of essays by distinguished authors which examines the interface between international law and politics. This is for a more advanced audience than Beck although it remains fairly accessible.

KOSKENNIEMI, M (2001), *The Gentle Civilizer of Nations: the Rise and Fall of International Law 1870–1960* (Cambridge: Cambridge University Press): an extensive scholarly analysis of the intellectual history of modern international law.

ORAKHELASHVILI, A (ed) (2011), *Research Handbook on the Theory and History of International Law* (Cheltenham: Edward Elgar): a useful collection of essays.

ORFORD, A, and HOFFMANN, F (eds) (2016), *The Oxford Handbook of the Theory of International Law* (Oxford: Oxford University Press).

RUBIN, AP (1997), *Ethics and Authority in International Law* (Cambridge: Cambridge University Press): a readable and slightly idiosyncratic account of the influence of the naturalist and positivist schools of legal theory on our understanding of international law.

PART II

THE STRUCTURE OF INTERNATIONAL LEGAL OBLIGATION

4

THE THEORY AND REALITY
OF THE SOURCES OF
INTERNATIONAL LAW

Anthea Roberts and Sandesh Sivakumaran[1]

SUMMARY

The classic starting point for identifying the sources of international law is Article 38 of the Statute of the International Court of Justice. Article 38 famously refers to three sources: treaties, customary international law, and general principles of law; as well as two subsidiary means for determining rules of law, namely judicial decisions and the teachings of publicists. However, Article 38 does not adequately reflect how the doctrine of sources operates in practice because it omits important sources of international law while misrepresenting the nature and weight of others. To appreciate how the doctrine of sources operates in practice, international lawyers need to understand how international law is created through a dialogue among States, State-empowered entities, and non-State actors. States are important actors in this process, but they are not the only actors. It is only by understanding this process of dialogue that one can develop a full understanding of the theory—and reality—of the sources of international law.

I. INTRODUCTION

Most of international law is focused on 'primary rules'. These are the rules that set out the rights and obligations of States and other international actors. Examples include the prohibition on the use of force and the obligation to respect human rights. But in order to understand which rules exist, international law also has to have 'secondary rules' that establish the sources of international law. Secondary rules include the rules that are applied to determine the existence and content of the primary rules.[2] They establish the rules

---

[1] School of Regulation and Global Governance (RegNet), Australian National University; and School of Law, University of Nottingham. The first part of this chapter is based on the previous version of this chapter authored by Hugh Thirlway. See generally Thirlway, 2014.

[2] This terminology is adopted from Hart, 1994, who made this distinction in the context of domestic legal systems. In international law, lawyers also distinguish between primary rules (which set out legal obligations) and secondary rules (which set out rules about, for instance, what constitutes a breach and what consequences follow from such a breach). This chapter does not deal with those sorts of secondary rules.

about when and how primary rules are formed, whom they bind, and how they can be changed. In international law, this is referred to as the doctrine of sources.

In domestic legal systems, many legal obligations stem from laws that are passed by parliaments or developed by courts. International law lacks an equivalent legislature for passing laws and it does not have courts with compulsory jurisdiction akin to domestic courts. Instead, legal obligations are based primarily on rules that are created and accepted by actors in the international legal system, principally States. In domestic law, there is usually little dispute about whether a rule exists and instead legal questions often turn on the meaning of the rule and how it applies to the specific facts. By contrast, at the international level, there is often considerable dispute about whether a particular rule exists, in addition to what its meaning is and how it applies to the facts.

The classic starting point for identifying the sources of international law is Article 38 of the Statute of the International Court of Justice (ICJ), which sets out the sources that the Court is to apply when deciding disputes before it. As States, courts and academics routinely resort to Article 38 when seeking to enumerate the sources of international law, Section II of this chapter examines these traditional sources. However, the chapter does not end there. As we will see, that classic conception does not adequately reflect how the doctrine of sources operates in practice.

In Section III, we show that the Article 38 list omits some important sources of law and misrepresents the nature and weight of others. Moreover, as we discuss in Section IV, to appreciate how the doctrine of sources operates in practice, international lawyers need to understand how international law is created through a dialogue among States, State-empowered entities, and non-State actors. States are important actors in this process, but they are not the only actors. It is only by understanding this process of dialogue that one can develop a full understanding of the theory—and reality—of the sources of international law.

II. THE TRADITIONAL THEORY OF THE DOCTRINE OF SOURCES

Article 38 of the ICJ Statute provides:

(1) The Court, whose function is to decide in accordance with international law such disputes as are submitted to it, shall apply:
   (a) international conventions, whether general or particular, establishing rules expressly recognized by the contesting states;
   (b) international custom, as evidence of a general practice accepted as law;
   (c) the general principles of law recognized by civilized nations;
   (d) subject to the provisions of Article 59, judicial decisions and the teachings of the most highly qualified publicists of the various nations, as subsidiary means for the determination of rules of law.

With one exception, the text of Article 38 is the same as that of Article 38 of the Statute of the Permanent Court of International Justice (PCIJ), the predecessor of the ICJ.[3] The exception is the clause in the first paragraph—'whose function is to decide in accordance with international law such disputes as are submitted to it'—which did not appear in the PCIJ Statute. The additional words emphasize that, by applying what is

---

[3] The PCIJ was replaced by the International Court of Justice after the Second World War.

listed in sub-paragraphs (a) to (d), the Court will be applying international law. The implication of these words is that the sources set out in Article 38(1)(a) to (d) constitute recognized sources of international law and, presumably, are the sole sources of international law.

A. TREATIES

The first source of law set out in Article 38(1) of the ICJ Statute is 'international conventions, whether general or particular'. This is another way of referring to treaties. According to the 1969 Vienna Convention on the Law of Treaties (VCLT), a 'treaty' is an international agreement concluded between States in written form and governed by international law, whether or not it is embodied in a single instrument or in two or more related instruments and whatever it happens to be called.[4] The usual way in which a State accepts the obligations provided for in a treaty is to become a party to it through the processes described in Chapter 6, Section III.

A treaty is one of the clearest ways in which rules that are binding on two or more States may come into existence. The VCLT, which largely codifies the customary international law rules on treaties, states the principle in Article 26, under the heading '*Pacta sunt servanda*': 'Every treaty is binding upon the parties to it and must be performed by them in good faith'. On the flipside, a State that is not a party to the treaty is under no obligation as a matter of treaty law to comply with the obligations set therein. As Article 34 of the VCLT puts it: 'A treaty does not create either obligations or rights for a third state without its consent'.[5]

Treaties vary considerably in form. At one end of the spectrum, there are bilateral treaties between two States that deal with a narrow issue, such as a bilateral customs treaty that sets rates of duties and tariffs on various goods. At the other end, there are multilateral treaties with many treaty parties that set out an entire regime governing a particular area, such as the UN Convention on the Law of the Sea or the Vienna Convention on Diplomatic Relations. The former look more like contracts and the latter look more like legislation, but both are binding on the treaty parties as a matter of treaty law.

Even though treaties are only binding on the parties to them, they may also reflect or come to reflect customary international law. When this occurs, States that are not parties to the treaty may be bound by the same substantive obligation as contained in the treaty, but they are bound as a matter of custom rather than treaty. A good example of this comes from the *Military and Paramilitary Activities in and against Nicaragua* case (*Nicaragua* case), in which the International Court of Justice found that it did not have jurisdiction to rule on the relevant treaty, but that the United States was nonetheless bound by the same substantive rules as a matter of customary international law as to which the Court did have jurisdiction.[6]

In addition to creating legal obligations for parties to the treaty, treaty parties may also agree to vary or set aside the rules that customary international law imposes on all States, though such variation or exclusion is only effective between the parties. This power to set aside customary international law is also subject to certain limits, such as the inability for States to contract out of *jus cogens* norms (discussed later).

---

[4] 1969 Vienna Convention on the Law of Treaties, Article 2(1)(a).
[5] But see the exceptions contained in the 1969 Vienna Convention on the Law of Treaties, Articles 35 and 36.
[6] *Military and Paramilitary Activities in and against Nicaragua (Nicaragua v United States of America), Merits, Judgment, ICJ Reports 1984*, pp 392, 424, para 73.

B. CUSTOM

The second source of law set out in Article 38(1) of the ICJ Statute is 'international custom, as evidence of a general practice accepted as law'. This source is also called customary international law or simply custom. International lawyers sometimes refer to 'general international law,' which some take as a synonym for custom and others treat as all non-treaty international law. However, this terminology is confusing, so this chapter instead refers only to custom and general principles as separate sources of law.

It is a near universal characteristic of human societies that many practices that have grown up to regulate day-to-day relationships imperceptibly acquire a status of inexorability: the way things *have* been done becomes the way things *must* be done. The source of custom reflects this process. One approach to custom is to regard it as a form of tacit agreement: States behave towards each other in given circumstances in certain ways, which are found to be acceptable, and thus tacitly assented to, first as a guide to future conduct and then, little by little, as legally determining future conduct. However, this approach is complicated by the fact that custom is also binding on States that did not actively participate in the process of the formation of the custom, provided they did not object to the custom during its formation, as well as States that came into existence after a custom had already been formed.

1. Two elements: State practice and *opinio juris*

Custom is generally considered to be made up of two elements: (1) State practice and (2) *opinio juris sive necessitatis* (opinion as to law or necessity), usually abbreviated to *opinio juris*. State practice refers to general and consistent practice by States, while *opinio juris* means that the practice is accepted as law. Consistent international practice alone does not create a rule of customary international law. The leading statement on the matter comes from the *North Sea Continental Shelf* case, in which the ICJ observed:

> Not only must the acts concerned amount to a settled practice, but they must also be such, or be carried out in such a way, as to be evidence of a belief that this practice is rendered obligatory by the existence of a rule of law requiring it. The need for such a belief, ie the existence of a subjective element, is implicit in the very notion of the *opinio juris sive necessitatis*.[7]

Some authorities view *opinio juris* as requiring that the practice be followed out of a sense of legal obligation,[8] which some international lawyers interpret narrowly to mean that international law is made up of rules of prohibition that are recognized when States feel compelled to respect that prohibition out of a sense of legal obligation. This approach is too narrow and the approach in the ICJ Statute of referring to custom as general practice 'accepted as law' is more accurate. Customary international law rules can prohibit certain conduct, require certain conduct, or permit certain conduct and the nature of *opinio juris* varies accordingly.[9] In some cases, this requires a belief that the practice is followed out

---

[7] *North Sea Continental Shelf, Judgment, ICJ Reports 1969*, p 3, para 77. See also *Continental Shelf (Libyan Arab Jamahiriya/Malta), Judgment, ICJ Reports 1985*, p 13, para 27; *Military and Paramilitary Activities in and against Nicaragua (Nicaragua v United States of America), Merits, Judgment, ICJ Reports 1986*, p 14, paras 183 and 207.

[8] For instance, § 102 of the Restatement (Third) of the Foreign Relations Law of the United States (1987) provides that '[f]or a practice of states to become a rule of customary international law it must appear that the states follow the practice from a sense of legal obligation'.

[9] This approach is captured by the Final Report of the ILA Committee on Formation of Customary (General) International Law on the *Statement of Principles Applicable to the Formation of General Customary International Law* (2010) 7, which provides that '[t]he subjective element [is] usually seen as either the consent of States, or their belief in the legally permissible or (as it may be) obligatory character of the conduct in question'.

of a sense of legal obligation (for rules prohibiting or requiring certain conduct), while in others, it requires a belief that the practice is permitted (for rules permitting certain conduct). The touchstone is that the practice has to be 'accepted as law'.

2. State practice

The content of State practice

States are abstract entities. Thus, State practice refers to the practice of State organs, such as the judiciary, the legislature, the executive, the military, and State officials such as the Head of State. It includes, but is not limited to, diplomatic correspondence, public statements by State officials (eg the President, Prime Minister, Secretary of State, Foreign Minister, and Attorney-General), executive actions and practices, official manuals that govern State actions (eg military manuals on the law of armed conflict), legislation, case law, and statements and votes of States in international fora.

All relevant practice of a State is to be considered. If the practice is inconsistent—for example, one State organ acts in one way and another State organ acts in a different way—the contribution of the individual State's practice to the general 'State practice' element of custom may be reduced or discounted.[10]

There is some dispute about which evidence counts as State practice and which as *opinio juris*. Some authors distinguish between actions (State practice) and statements (*opinio juris*) (D'Amato, 1971, pp 89–90, 160). On this theory, a State respecting or violating an individual's human rights (such as affording an individual due process or arbitrarily detaining them) would amount to State practice, whereas a State making a statement affirming the existence of a human right or condemning human rights violations (such as affirming the right to due process or condemning arbitrary detention), or explaining its vote on a General Assembly resolution concerning human rights, would amount to *opinio juris*. Other authors object to this distinction and instead see both actions and statements as amounting to State practice.[11] This can sometimes result in double counting where, for instance, acceptance of a General Assembly resolution is taken as evidence of both State practice and *opinio juris*.

Consistency, generality, and duration of practice

There are no set rules on the consistency, generality, or duration of practice required to create a custom. This 'cannot be mathematically and uniformly decided. Each fact requires to be evaluated relatively according to the different occasions and circumstances.'[12]

The settled practice required to establish a rule of customary law does not need to be the practice of every single State of the world, as long as it is relatively widespread, representative, and consistent. The requirement that the practice be widespread cannot be quantified; it will depend on the issue and circumstances in question. The requirement that the practice be representative necessitates looking at whether the practice is followed by States that are geographically, economically, and geopolitically diverse. For instance, if only Western European States follow or accept a practice, it is difficult to claim that it amounts to a rule of customary *international* law.

In judging generality and consistency, it is important to look at both actions and reactions of States. State practice (and *opinio juris*) are two-sided; one State asserts a right, either explicitly or by acting in a way that impliedly constitutes such an assertion, and the

---

[10] ILC, Draft Conclusion 7 of the Draft Conclusions on Identification of Customary International Law, A/71/10, para 62.

[11] Restatement (Third) of the Foreign Relations Law Of The United States (1987), §102; Akehurst, 1974–75, pp 1, 2, 35.

[12] *North Sea Continental Shelf, Judgment, ICJ Reports 1969*, p 3, Dissenting Opinion of Judge Tanaka, 175.

State or States affected by the claim then react by affirming the legality of the action, objecting to it, or acquiescing. These actions and reactions tend to support the claimed right if no protest is made, or exclude the claimed right if there is a protest. Affirmation of the legality of the action helps to create a customary rule clearly and quickly, but mere acquiescence may be sufficient depending on the circumstances. The accumulation of instances of the one kind (protest) or the other (affirmation or acquiescence) constitutes the overall practice required for determining the existence of a customary rule.

One problem that exists in this regard is when there is a divergence between what States say and what they do, for example, when they assert that a particular rule of customary law exists but their practice is inconsistent with or contrary to that rule. In the field of human rights law, for example, the domestic law of practically every State of the world prohibits torture, and States are generally agreed that there is a rule of customary international law forbidding it. Yet there is no doubt that torture continues to be widely practised. Can a rule of customary international law exist if it suffers from this sort of inconsistent practice? In relation to this point, in connection with whether a customary rule prohibiting the use of force exists even though States clearly use force in violation of such a rule, the ICJ in the *Nicaragua* case explained that:

> The Court does not consider that, for a rule to be established as customary, the corresponding practice must be in absolutely rigorous conformity with the rule. In order to deduce the existence of customary rules, the Court deems it sufficient that the conduct of States should, in general, be consistent with such rules, and that instances of State conduct inconsistent with a given rule should generally have been treated as breaches of that rule, not as indications of recognition of a new rule. If a State acts in a way prima facie inconsistent with a recognized rule, but defends its conduct by appealing to exceptions or justifications contained within the rule itself, then whether or not the State's conduct is in fact justifiable on that basis, the significance of that attitude is to confirm rather than to weaken the rule.[13]

Another difficulty occurs when an issue is new and very little practice has had time to accrue. In this regard, the ICJ in the *North Sea Continental Shelf* case held that:

> [A]lthough the passage of only a short period of time was not necessarily a bar to the formation of a new rule of customary international law on the basis of what was originally a purely conventional rule, it was indispensable that State practice during that period, including that of States whose interests were specially affected, should have been both extensive and virtually uniform in the sense of the provision invoked and should have occurred in such a way as to show a general recognition that a rule of law was involved.[14]

Some authors have argued that, when dealing with new areas of practice like space exploration, it is possible to have 'instant custom' based on evidence such as declarations in widely accepted General Assembly resolutions (Cheng, 1965). However, this approach is controversial and has not been generally accepted. As has been pointed out (Crawford and Viles, 1994, p 93): 'Custom is developed by a dialogue in time. By definition, therefore, instant custom is excluded. Like good coffee, international law has to be brewed.' How long it takes to brew depends on the generality and consistency of the practice.

---

[13] *Military and Paramilitary Activities in and against Nicaragua (Nicaragua v United States of America)*, Merits, Judgment, ICJ Reports 1986, p 14, para 186.

[14] *North Sea Continental Shelf*, Judgment, ICJ Reports 1969, pp 3, 43, para 74.

Practice of parties to treaties

Multilateral treaties and declarations by international fora such as the General Assembly can declare existing customs, crystallize emerging customs, and generate new customs.[15] For example, human rights law has grown largely through the adoption of wide-ranging international conventions. Since almost all States have ratified some of these conventions, it is widely argued that their conventional provisions are binding also on non-parties on the basis that they amount to customary international law. In determining whether a treaty obligation reflects a customary obligation, it is necessary to look at the practice of both States that are not parties to the treaty, to determine whether they view themselves as bound by the rule, as well as parties to the treaty. However, conforming practice by States parties to a treaty can be ambiguous (Baxter, 1970, p 64).

The latter point arose in the *North Sea Continental Shelf* case, when the ICJ had to consider whether a rule of maritime delimitation laid down in the 1958 Geneva Convention on the Continental Shelf had become a rule of customary international law. The Court noted that a number of instances of delimitation complying with the rule were delimitations effected by States parties to the Convention, that those States 'were therefore presumably . . . acting . . . in the application of the Convention', and therefore '[f]rom their action no inference could legitimately be drawn as to the existence of a rule of customary law . . .'[16] Where a treaty is widely adopted, it is more likely to reflect custom, but it can also be more difficult to identify whether treaty parties are following it out of a sense of treaty or customary obligation.

Specially affected States

The issue of specially affected States is also controversial. Specially affected States are those States that are 'specially affected' by the purported rule. The ICJ indicated in the *North Sea Continental Shelf* case that the practice of specially affected States must be given special consideration in determining the existence and content of customary international law.[17] But this leaves open the question of which States are specially affected on any particular issue. That question arose in the case concerning the *Legality of the Threat or Use of Nuclear Weapons*:[18] was the practice of the States that possessed nuclear weapons more significant than that of the States which did not? Which States could be understood as specially affected in this context—the ones that might use nuclear weapons or the ones that might have such weapons used against them? The Court did not comment directly on this point.[19] But this doctrine has been critiqued for providing a cover for dominant States to play a disproportionate role in the formation or otherwise of customary international law. For instance, one author (Danilenko, 1993, p 96) argues:

> [T]he notion of 'specially affected States' may be used as a respectable disguise for 'important' or 'powerful' States which are always supposed to be 'specially affected' by all or almost all political-legal developments within the international community.

3. *Opinio juris*

The idea that, in order to constitute custom, State practice has to be accompanied by a belief by the acting States that they are adhering to an *existing* rule of law creates a number of difficulties. First, States are abstract entities and thus do not have 'beliefs'. As such,

---

[15] Ibid, pp 3, 39, paras 63 and 41, para 71.   [16] Ibid, p 3, para 76.   [17] Ibid, p 3, para 74.
[18] *Legality of the Threat or Use of Nuclear Weapons, Advisory Opinion, ICJ Reports 1996*, p 226.
[19] But see ibid, pp 226, 535, Dissenting Opinion of Judge Weeramantry.

when attempting to adduce what States believe, we have to look at their actions and words. Second, how can a practice ever develop into a customary rule if States have to believe the rule already exists before their practice can be significant for the creation of the rule? Is it sufficient if initially States act in the *mistaken* belief that a rule already exists, a case of a shared mistake producing law? Or is it the case that the States initially acting assert that this is the law (whether they believe it to be or not) and, if others accept that assertion as law, it becomes so?

The latter approach makes more sense. A good example of this is the Truman Proclamation in 1945 in which the United States asserted for the first time that coastal States had a right to utilize natural resources in the subsoil and seabed of the continental shelf that was contiguous to their coastlines.[20] Within a very short period of time, the Proclamation went from one State's declaration to customary international law based on other States' acceptance of, or acquiescence to, the assertion and its incorporation into multilateral treaties. In making the Proclamation, US government actors did not mistakenly believe that it reflected existing law. Instead, they made an assertion about what the law should be and what the United States was prepared to treat the law as being (for itself and for others) going forward. *Opinio juris* was not based on a mistaken belief but rather a conscious articulation of a legal claim (Crawford and Viles, 1994, p 92).

Understood in this way, the function of *opinio juris* is to separate out practice that is, or is asserted to be, legally permitted or required, as opposed to being undertaken merely out of courtesy or comity. As the ICJ put it in the *North Sea Continental Shelf* case: 'The frequency, or even habitual character of the acts is not in itself enough. There are many international acts, for example, in the field of ceremonial and protocol, which are performed almost invariably, but which are motivated only by considerations of courtesy, convenience or tradition, and not by any sense of legal duty.'[21] A common example given is humanitarian assistance. Many States give humanitarian assistance after a crisis, but they typically treat this as something they do out of a sense of morality or comity, not legal obligation. On this approach, actions can form custom only if accompanied by an articulation of the legality of the action, ie an articulation that the action is permitted or required by international law. This approach focuses attention on statements of belief, rather than actual beliefs, which is useful when dealing with abstract entities. The focus also explains how a custom can emerge, and how customary rules can change over time, based on new or changing articulations of legality.

4. The relativity of custom

General custom

An important difference between customary international law and treaties is that custom is binding on all States, whereas, as we have seen, treaty law is binding only on the parties to the particular treaty. A State that relies in a dispute on a rule of treaty law has to establish that the treaty binds the other party to the dispute. By contrast, if a claim is based on general customary international law, it is sufficient to establish that the customary rule exists. There is no need to show that the other party has accepted it, or participated in the practice from which the rule derives. There are two exceptions to this general position:

(1) *special* or *local* customary law, which is binding on only a defined group of States; and

(2) the *persistent objector* doctrine, by which a State that has persistently objected to a customary rule during (not only subsequently to) its formation is not bound by that rule.

[20] The Truman Proclamation of 28 September 1945, Presidential Proclamation No. 2667, 3 CFR 67 (1945–1948 Compilation).   [21] *North Sea Continental Shelf, Judgment, ICJ Reports 1969*, p 3, para 77.

Special or local custom

As regards *local* custom, an oft-cited example relates to the practice of diplomatic asylum in Latin America, whereby the States of the region recognize the right of the embassies of other States of the region to give asylum to political fugitives. Such a rule is purely local in that it could not successfully be asserted in favour of, or against, States outside the region: for example, neither the British Embassy in a South American capital, nor the embassy of a South American State in London, would be regarded as entitled to offer asylum to political fugitives. But such a local customary rule would not be applicable against a Latin American State that has objected to such a rule, as the International Court of Justice found to be the case with respect to Peru in the *Asylum* case.[22] It is also possible for a *special* custom to exist between just two States.[23]

Persistent objectors

According to the persistent objector doctrine, a State which objected consistently to a rule of law while it was still in the process of becoming such a rule can continue to 'opt out' of the application of the rule even after it has acquired the status of a rule of general customary law. This notion is usually traced back to the *Fisheries* case between the UK and Norway, which concerned the legality of the baselines drawn by Norway around its coasts in order to calculate the breadth of its territorial sea. The UK argued that the Norwegian baselines were inconsistent with a rule of customary law referred to as the 'ten-mile rule', but the Court was not satisfied that any such general rule of customary law existed. It then added: 'In any event the ten-mile rule would appear to be inapplicable as against Norway inasmuch as she has always opposed any attempt to apply it to the Norwegian coast.'[24]

Subsequent objectors

In order to opt out of a customary rule, a State has to oppose the rule *during* its formation. If it only objects subsequently, the State will be taken as bound by the existing customary rule. The lack of a subsequent objector doctrine helps to explain why new States, for instance States that were decolonized or States that have emerged after the break-up of a broader union like the Union of Soviet Socialist Republics, are held to be bound by existing customary international law. Even though they did not have the option of persistently objecting during the formation of such customary rules, they are not permitted to opt out of the custom on the basis of being subsequent objectors. This rule has been critiqued for permitting the rules that were developed by colonial powers to remain in effect even after decolonization occurred, despite objection by some of the newly independent States. If enough States object to a rule, it may be possible for those States to undermine the existence of a customary international law rule or create sufficient State practice and *opinio juris* in favour of a new customary rule. However, if only isolated objection occurs, it is likely to be discounted as subsequent objection.

C. GENERAL PRINCIPLES OF LAW

When Article 38 of the PCIJ Statute was being drafted, the Committee of Jurists that was appointed to draw up the Statute was concerned that, in some cases, the future Court might find that no treaty or customary law rule governed the issues in dispute before it. It

---

[22] *Asylum, Judgment, ICJ Reports 1950*, p 266 at pp 277–8.
[23] *Right of Passage over Indian Territory, Merits, Judgment, ICJ Reports 1960*, p 6 at p 39.
[24] *Fisheries, Judgment, ICJ Reports 1951*, p 116 at p 131.

was thought undesirable, and possibly inappropriate in principle, that the Court should be obliged to declare what is known as a *non liquet*—a finding that a particular claim could neither be upheld nor rejected, for lack of any existing applicable rule of law.[25]

The extent to which international legal relations were governed in the 1920s, at the time of the Committee's work, by anything beyond treaties and custom, is unclear, but the Committee was able to agree that, failing one of those sources, the Court should apply 'the general principles of law recognized by civilized nations'. While the PCIJ and ICJ have made mention of certain principles,[26] it seems that neither has based a decision directly on such general principles.

There is no unanimity among scholars as to the nature of the principles that may be invoked under this head. There are broadly two possible interpretations. According to one interpretation, general principles are those which can be derived from a comparison of the various systems of domestic law, and the extraction of such principles as appear to be shared by all, or a majority, of them.[27] This interpretation gives force to the reference to the principles being those 'recognized by civilized nations', although the term 'civilized' is now out of place. In line with this interpretation, parties to cases before the ICJ have at times invoked comparative studies of municipal law.[28]

An alternative interpretation is that the principles to be applied by the International Court of Justice also include general principles applicable directly to *international* legal relations and general principles applicable to legal relations *generally*. Some of these are in effect assertions of secondary rules, such as the principle *pacta sunt servanda* or the principles governing the relationship between successive treaties that the special prevails over the general and that the later prevails over the earlier.

For some scholars, the 'general principles of law' justify appeal to ethical concepts, as deriving from 'the universal juridical conscience . . . as the ultimate material "source" of all law';[29] but this remains a minority view, and difficult to square with the origins of the concept.

D. JUDICIAL DECISIONS AND THE TEACHINGS OF PUBLICISTS

Article 38(1) makes a clear distinction between the sources of international law in paragraphs (a) to (c), and judicial decisions and the teachings of the most highly qualified publicists as 'subsidiary means for the determination of rules of law' in paragraph (d).

---

[25] This is to be distinguished from a finding that a particular claim is not supported by a positive rule of law.

[26] See, for example, *Corfu Channel, Merits, Judgment, ICJ Reports 1949*, p 4 at p 22; *Reservations to the Convention on the Prevention and Punishment of the Crime of Genocide, Advisory Opinion, ICJ Reports 1951*, p 15 at p 23; *Nuclear Tests (Australia v France), Judgment, ICJ Reports 1974*, p 253 at p 268, and *(New Zealand v France), Judgment, ICJ Reports 1974*, p 457 at p 473.

[27] A pioneering and influential work on this subject was Lauterpacht, 1927. A clearer statement of the derivation of general principles from national systems is to be found in the Rome Statute of the International Criminal Court: 'general principles of law derived by the Court from national laws of legal systems of the world' (Article 21(1)(c)). On the dangers of analogy from municipal systems, see Thirlway, 2002, pp 268–405.

[28] In the case of *Right of Passage over Indian Territory, Merits, Judgment, ICJ Reports 1960*, p 6, Portugal argued that general principles of law supported its right to passage from the coast to its enclaves of territory, and adduced a comparative study of the provisions in various legal systems for what may be called 'rights of way of necessity'. When for the first time an application was made by a State (Malta) to intervene in a case between two other States (Tunisia and Libya) on the basis of having an interest which might be affected by the decision in the case (a possibility referred to in Article 62 of the Court's Statute), Malta similarly relied on a comparative law study showing the conditions and modalities of intervention in judicial proceedings in various national courts.

[29] Separate Opinion of Judge Cançado Trindade, *Pulp Mills on the River Uruguay (Argentina v Uruguay), Judgment, ICJ Reports 2010*, p 14 at p 156, para 52.

The reason for this is evident: if a rule of international law is stated in a judicial decision, or in a textbook, it will be stated as a rule deriving either from treaty, custom, or general principles. The judge, or the author of the textbook, will not assert that the rule stated is law *because* the judge or textbook writer has stated it; he or she will state it because it is considered to derive from one of the three sources.

In the early days of the development of international law, the teachings of publicists carried considerably more weight than do the authors of even the most respected textbooks of today. Historically, teachings of publicists exercised a profound influence on the development of international law.[30] Today, certain teachings of publicists remain influential, but only a fraction of what is published carries this sort of weight and, even then, not to the same extent as in the past. States involved in a dispute, or their counsel, will often cite the leading textbooks and monographs in support of their claims, as will arbitral tribunals in their awards, international criminal courts in their judgments, and individual judges of the ICJ in separate or dissenting opinions. The ICJ itself rarely quotes teachings.

The reference in Article 38(1)(d) to judicial decisions includes the decisions of the ICJ itself. The ICJ refers more frequently than it once did to arbitral decisions and judgments of other courts and tribunals, and habitually cites its own previous decisions. The Court has, however, made clear that, in accordance with Article 59 of its Statute which provides that '[t]he decision of the Court has no binding force except between the parties and in respect of that particular case', it does not regard its previous decisions as binding precedents. In one case the Court explained that '[i]t is not a question of holding [the parties to the current case] to decisions reached by the Court in previous cases. The real question is whether, in this case, there is cause not to follow the reasoning and conclusions of earlier cases.'[31]

The scope of Article 38(1)(d) is not limited to decisions of the ICJ. It includes decisions of other international and regional courts and tribunals as well as the decisions of domestic courts. The weight to be given to any judicial decision will depend on a number of factors, including the identity of the court or tribunal and the quality of reasoning of the decision.

Domestic court decisions are unique within the doctrine of sources because of their ability to wear two hats, representing: (1) the practice of the forum State, which may be relevant to the determination of custom and the interpretation of treaties; and (2) a subsidiary means of determining international law, capable of stating international norms with more authority than attends the practice of a single State (Roberts, 2011, p 59). This dual role creates a question mark over the extent to which domestic courts should understand their own role, and be understood by others, as functioning as national actors that seek to create and shape international norms or international actors that seek to impartially enforce international law (Roberts, 2011, pp 59–60).

In the *Arrest Warrant* case, the question before the ICJ was whether incumbent Foreign Ministers enjoy absolute immunity from prosecution in other States for crimes allegedly committed during their period of office, or whether there is an exception to this rule in the case of war crimes and crimes against humanity. The parties both relied on decisions on the point by the UK House of Lords in the *Pinochet* case[32] and the French *Cour de cassation* in

---

[30] Writing in 1965, Clive Parry (1965, p 3) observed that the 'books and the opinions of the nineteenth century seem often to resemble catalogues of the praises of famous men. "Hear also what Hall sayeth. Hear the comfortable words of Oppenheim" is an incantation which persists even into this century.'

[31] *Land and Maritime Boundary between Cameroon and Nigeria, Preliminary Objections, Judgment, ICJ Reports 1998*, p 275, para 28.

[32] *R v Bow Street Metropolitan Stipendiary, ex parte Pinochet Ugarte (Amnesty International Intervening) (No 3)* [1999] UKHL 17; [2000] 1 AC 147; [1999] 2 All ER 97.

the *Qadaffi* case.[33] The statements of international law in those decisions could have been regarded as 'subsidiary means' for the determination of the customary law on the subject; they were, however, presented as evidence of State practice, and the Court dealt with them as such.[34] The Court referred to the 'few' decisions of national courts on the question; the paucity of practice was obviously relevant to the question whether a customary rule had become established. But if the decisions had been classified as 'subsidiary means' under Article 38(1)(d), the only question would have been whether they correctly stated the law, not whether they represented a widespread practice of national judicial bodies.

III. THE MODERN REALITY OF THE DOCTRINE OF SOURCES

Article 38(1) has been much criticized as a list of the sources of international law. It has often been suggested that it is inadequate, out of date, or ill-adapted to modern international relations. In this section, we discuss some of the ways in which the sources of international law do not work in practice in the way in which they are presented in Article 38(1). Some sources of international law are missing from the list, such as unilateral declarations. Meanwhile, the nature and relative weight of other sources is misrepresented. For instance, custom is often found in ways that significantly depart from the traditional theory, and judicial decisions have significantly more weight in practice than their 'subsidiary' label in Article 38(1) would suggest. It is important to understand these nuances in order to appreciate the modern reality of the doctrine of sources.

A. WHAT IS MISSING FROM ARTICLE 38(1)

In practice, the sources of international law are not limited to treaties, custom, and general principles; and the subsidiary means for determining the law do not consist solely of judicial decisions and the teachings of publicists. There are a whole host of other materials that are relevant insofar as international law obligations are concerned.

1. Unilateral declarations

Certain unilateral declarations on the part of a State bind the State that makes them. In the *Nuclear Tests* case, the ICJ observed that:

> It is well recognized that declarations made by way of unilateral acts, concerning legal or factual situations, may have the effect of creating legal obligations . . . When it is the intention of the State making the declaration that it should become bound according to its terms, that intention confers on the declaration the character of a legal undertaking . . .[35]

It is the intention of the State making the declaration that is crucial, and many declarations are not binding because the issuing State did not intend to be bound by them. The form the declaration takes is not determinative, with binding unilateral declarations arising out of diplomatic notes, letters, and communiqués from the President of a State, as well as public

---

[33] *SOS Attentat and Castelnau d'Esnault* v *Qadaffi, Head of State of the State of Libya*, France, Court of Cassation, criminal chamber, 13 March 2000, No 1414.

[34] *Arrest Warrant of 11 April 2000 (Democratic Republic of Congo* v *Belgium), Preliminary Objections and Merits, Judgment, ICJ Reports 2002*, p 3, paras 57, 58.

[35] *Nuclear Tests (Australia* v *France), Judgment, ICJ Reports 1974*, p 253, para 43. See also ILC, Guiding Principles Applicable to Unilateral Declarations of States Capable of Creating Legal Obligations, Principle 1.

speeches.[36] The legal effects of the declaration depend on the substance of the declaration, the circumstances surrounding the making of the declaration, and the reactions to which the declaration gives rise.[37]

2. Resolutions of the UN Security Council

Under Article 25 of the UN Charter, 'The Members of the United Nations agree to accept and carry out the decisions of the Security Council in accordance with the present Charter.' This rule only applies to 'decisions' of the UN Security Council, not recommendations, findings, or opinions. A 'decision' may form only one part of a resolution and is indicated through use of the language that the Security Council 'decides' X or Y. Security Council resolutions do not constitute an independent source of law per se because their legal force derives from the Charter, that is to say, a treaty. These obligations are not only binding, they also prevail over other inconsistent international law obligations.[38]

The Security Council was not very active during the Cold War because of divisions between blocs of States and the threat or use of the power to veto draft resolutions by the permanent members of the Security Council (China, France, Russia, the United Kingdom, and the United States). However, since the end of the Cold War, and particularly since the attacks of 11 September 2001, the Security Council has used its powers to set up elaborate regulatory regimes, sometimes with direct effects on individuals. One example of this sort of law-making by the Security Council is Resolution 1373 (2001), which required all States to take a variety of measures to combat terrorism, including criminalizing certain acts and freezing assets (Szasz, 2002; Talmon, 2005). Another example is Resolution 827 (1993), in which the Security Council decided to establish the International Criminal Tribunal for the former Yugoslavia, which permitted international criminal prosecutions to be brought against individuals (Boyle and Chinkin, 2007, pp 111–12).

3. *Jus cogens* norms

Jus cogens norms are 'peremptory' legal norms from which no derogation is permitted. According to Article 53 of the VCLT: 'a peremptory norm of general international law is a norm accepted and recognized by the international community of States as a whole as a norm from which no derogation is permitted and which can be modified only by a subsequent norm of general international law having the same character.'[39]

Scholars disagree over whether *jus cogens* norms are part of customary international law. For instance, one author argues that custom is a suitable source for peremptory norms because it serves as a vehicle for generally binding international law on important moral issues (Brownlie, 2008, pp 510–12). By contrast, another author takes issue with the concept of *jus cogens* norms, arguing that they are not truly customary because they can be asserted despite a lack of State practice and consent by States (Weil, 1983). To the extent that *jus cogens* represent a subset of customary international law norms, they can be considered as coming under Article 38(1)(b) as 'general practice accepted as law'.

---

[36] ILC, Guiding Principles Applicable to Unilateral Declarations of States Capable of Creating Legal Obligations, Commentary to Principle 5, para 2.

[37] *Nuclear Tests (Australia v France), Judgment, ICJ Reports 1974*, p 253, para 51; ILC, Guiding Principles Applicable to Unilateral Declarations of States Capable of Creating Legal Obligations, Principle 3.

[38] According to Article 103 of the UN Charter, 'In the event of a conflict between the obligations of the Members of the United Nations under the present Charter and their obligations under any other international agreement, their obligations under the present Charter shall prevail.'

[39] For current work on this topic by the International Law Commission, see http://legal.un.org/ilc/guide/1_14.shtml.

Exactly which norms amount to *jus cogens* norms is still subject to some controversy.[40] The International Court of Justice has identified certain *jus cogens* norms, including the 'norm prohibiting genocide'[41] and 'the prohibition of torture'.[42] In addition, the International Law Commission has identified as *jus cogens* norms the prohibitions of aggression, slavery, racial discrimination, and crimes against humanity, and the right to self-determination.[43] The peremptory status of these norms derives from the importance of their normative content to the international community.

Jus cogens norms are sometimes linked to norms that create 'obligations *erga omnes*', which are obligations that are owed to the international community as a whole rather than to a specific State. One of the consequences of finding that an obligation is *erga omnes* is that any State may react to its violation by, for instance, bringing a case against the offending State, not just the State or States directly injured or affected by the violation.[44]

The precise consequences of *jus cogens* norms are also not fully agreed upon. One thing that is clear is that, as no derogation is permitted from *jus cogens* norms, '[a] treaty is void if, at the time of its conclusion, it conflicts with a peremptory norm of general international law' and, '[i]f a new peremptory norm of general international law emerges, any existing treaty which is in conflict with that norm becomes void and terminates.'[45]

4. Resolutions of the UN General Assembly

General Assembly resolutions are not an independent source of law. As a general rule, General Assembly resolutions are not binding on States. Article 10 of the UN Charter provides that the General Assembly 'may discuss any questions or any matters within the scope of the present Charter', and, subject to one exception,[46] 'may make recommendations to the Members of the United Nations or to the Security Council or to both on any such questions or matters'. Certain resolutions might be binding on UN member States, such as on budgetary matters, but the source for the binding nature of those resolutions is the UN Charter, a treaty.[47] Other resolutions might be binding on subsidiary bodies of the General Assembly, but that is due to internal UN law.

The fact that General Assembly resolutions are generally understood to be non-binding does not mean that they are without value insofar as the sources of international law are

[40] For a light-hearted, but well-reasoned, debunking of the whole concept, see D'Amato, 1990.
[41] See *Application of the Convention on the Prevention and Punishment of the Crime of Genocide, Preliminary Objections, ICJ Reports 1996*, p 595, para 31; *Armed Activities on the Territory of the Congo (New Application: 2002) (Democratic Republic of the Congo v Rwanda), Jurisdiction and Admissibility, Judgment, ICJ Reports 2006*, p 6, para 64.
[42] *Questions relating to the Obligation to Prosecute or Extradite (Belgium v Senegal), Judgment, ICJ Reports 2012*, p 422, para 99.
[43] ILC, Draft Articles on the Responsibility of States for Internationally Wrongful Acts, Commentary to Draft Article 26, para 5.
[44] See *Barcelona Traction, Light and Power Company, Limited, Second Phase, Judgment, ICJ Reports 1970*, p 3, paras 33–5 and para 91. This assimilation is by no means self-evident; the Commentary to the ILC Articles on State Responsibility suggests that there is at least 'a difference in emphasis' (Commentary to Article 40, Part I, para (7)).   [45] 1969 Vienna Convention on the Law of Treaties, Articles 53 and 64.
[46] The exception is contained in Article 12 of the UN Charter: 'While the Security Council is exercising in respect of any dispute or situation the functions assigned to it in the present Charter, the General Assembly shall not make any recommendation with regard to that dispute or situation unless the Security Council so requests.'
[47] Article 17(1) of the UN Charter provides that '[t]he General Assembly shall consider and approve the budget of the Organization'.

concerned. There is a nuanced relationship between General Assembly resolutions and the sources of international law. Certain treaties are adopted by the General Assembly, in a resolution, and opened for signature by States.[48] The General Assembly also encourages States to ratify particular treaties. General Assembly resolutions have led to the elaboration of treaties.[49] They can also be understood as 'authoritative interpretations by the Assembly of the various principles of the United Nations Charter depending on the circumstances' (Shaw, 2017, p 86).

Insofar as customary international law is concerned, certain resolutions are considered to reflect custom.[50] The ICJ has noted that:

> General Assembly resolutions, even if they are not binding, may sometimes have normative value. They can, in certain circumstances, provide evidence important for establishing the existence of a rule or the emergence of an *opinio juris*. To establish whether this is true of a given General Assembly resolution, it is necessary to look at its content and the conditions of its adoption; it is also necessary to see whether an *opinio juris* exists as to its normative character. Or a series of resolutions may show the gradual evolution of the *opinio juris* required for the establishment of a new rule.[51]

The evidentiary weight of a specific resolution depends on a number of factors, including the clarity or ambiguity of the substance of the resolution; the voting pattern, that is to say the number of States that voted in favour of, against, or abstained on, the resolution; and its affirmation in later resolutions. States' votes in respect of a resolution can constitute *opinio juris*,[52] which can give rise to a rule of customary international law. In none of these cases, though, are the resolutions independently binding *as resolutions*.

It is important to note, however, that this characterization of the value of General Assembly resolutions partly reflects a power struggle among States as to the law-making power of different venues and sources. In the early years of the United Nations, Western States dominated the General Assembly. During this period, these States used these resolutions to do more than simply make 'recommendations'. For instance, when the Security Council was unable to adopt resolutions on the maintenance of international peace and security due to the veto, the United States urged resort to General Assembly resolutions through the Uniting for Peace resolution.[53] Following decolonization, the composition of the General Assembly changed radically and developing States became the majority. These States attempted to use their numerical superiority to push through developments in international law, including resolutions establishing the New International Economic Order. Western States responded by reasserting that General Assembly resolutions were non-binding and key powers, like the United States, sought to shift law-making to other arenas where they had a greater voice, like the Security Council.

---

[48] For example, the Convention against Torture and Other Cruel, Inhuman or Degrading Treatment or Punishment was adopted and opened for signature, ratification, and accession by GA Res 39/46 (1984).

[49] For example, the Universal Declaration of Human Rights, annexed to GA Res 217A (III) (1948), led to the drafting and adoption of the International Covenant on Economic, Social and Cultural Rights and the International Covenant on Civil and Political Rights.

[50] For example, the Declaration on Principles of International Law concerning Friendly Relations and Co-operation among States in accordance with the Charter of the United Nations, GA Res 2625 (XXV) (1970).

[51] *Legality of the Threat or Use of Nuclear Weapons, Advisory Opinion, ICJ Reports 1996*, p 226, 254, para 70.

[52] *Military and Paramilitary Activities in and against Nicaragua (Nicaragua v United States of America), Merits, Judgment, ICJ Reports 1986*, pp 14, 99, para 188.   [53] UNGA Res 377(V), 3 November 1950.

B. WHAT IS MISLEADING IN ARTICLE 38(1)

1. Customary international law

State focus

Article 38(1)(b) refers to 'international custom, as evidence of a general practice accepted as law'. The language is neutral. However, as seen in Section II, the term 'general practice' has been taken to mean 'State practice' and 'accepted as law' the *opinio juris* of States.[54] By and large, the practice and *opinio juris* of non-State actors tend to be left out of the formation of custom, although suggestions have been made to include the practice and *opinio juris* of other actors.

Traditional custom, modern custom, and custom by assertion

Implicit in the reference to 'international custom' in Article 38(1)(b) is that there is only one type of customary international law. However, it may be better to understand custom as existing on a spectrum between what may be called 'traditional' custom, which is based on an inductive methodology, and 'modern' custom, which is based on a deductive methodology (Roberts, 2001).

Traditional custom results from general and consistent practice followed by States from a sense of legal obligation or permission. It focuses primarily on State practice in the form of inter-State interaction and acquiescence. *Opinio juris* is a secondary consideration invoked to distinguish between legal obligations and non-legal commitments or practices. Traditional custom is evolutionary and is identified through an inductive process in which a general custom is derived from specific instances of State practice. This approach is evident in the *S.S. Lotus* case, where the PCIJ inferred a general custom about objective territorial jurisdiction over ships on the high seas from previous instances of State action and acquiescence.[55]

By contrast, modern custom is derived by a deductive process that begins with general statements of rules rather than particular instances of practice. This approach emphasizes *opinio juris* rather than State practice because it relies primarily on statements about what the law is rather than concrete actions by States. Modern custom can develop quickly because it is often deduced from multilateral treaties and declarations by international fora such as the General Assembly. An example of the deductive approach is the Merits Judgment in the *Nicaragua* case. In that case, the International Court of Justice paid lip service to the traditional test for custom but derived customary rules prohibiting the use of force and intervention into other States from statements such as General Assembly resolutions as well as the attitude of States toward such resolutions. The Court did not undertake a serious inquiry into the *actual practice* of States with respect to the use of force, such as using or failing to use force, as distinct from *statements* by States about the legality of using force. Instead, the Court held that it was sufficient for conduct to be generally consistent with statements of international rules, provided that instances of inconsistent practice had been treated as breaches of the rule concerned rather than as generating a new rule.[56]

This divergence in custom has been rationalized by analysing the requirements of State practice and *opinio juris* on a sliding scale (Kirgis, 1987). At one end, highly consistent

---

[54] The ILC, in Draft Conclusion 4(1) of the Draft Conclusions on Identification of Customary International Law A/71/10, para 62, provides that '[t]he requirement, as a constituent element of customary international law, of a general practice means that it is primarily the practice of States that contributes to the formation, or expression, of rules of customary international law'.

[55] *S.S. 'Lotus', Judgment No 9, 1927, PCIJ, Ser A, No 10*, at pp 18, 29.

[56] *Military and Paramilitary Activities in and against Nicaragua (Nicaragua v United States of America), Merits, Judgment, ICJ Reports 1986*, p 14, para 186.

State practice can establish a customary rule without requiring much evidence of *opinio juris*. However, as the frequency and consistency of State practice decline, a stronger showing of *opinio juris* will be required. The exact trade-off between State practice and *opinio juris* will depend on the importance of the activity in question and the reasonableness of the rule involved. An objection to this approach is that it reinterprets the concept of custom so as to produce the 'right' answers (Simma and Alston, 1988–89). Another approach to the divergence in custom has been to argue that many of the rules that fit the category of modern custom would be better understood as general principles of law (Simma and Alston, 1988–89).

It may be that traditional and modern custom line up with international rules that are more facilitative or moral in nature. At one extreme, there are completely facilitative rules, which promote coexistence and cooperation but do not deal with substantive moral issues (such as that ships must pass on the left). At the other extreme, there are laws that are primarily moral rather than facilitative (such as some human rights obligations) and peremptory rules that prohibit actions whether or not they affect coexistence and cooperation (such as *jus cogens* norms, eg prohibiting genocide). Facilitative customs may rely more heavily on the traditional approach because they turn a description of past practice into a prescriptive requirement for future action. Moral customs may rely more heavily on the modern approach because they prescribe future action based on normative evaluations of ideal practice rather than accurate descriptions of past practice.

In some cases, instead of adopting an inductive traditional approach or a deductive modern approach, the existence of a customary rule is simply asserted. For example, the ICJ has found that provisions of the International Law Commission's Articles on State Responsibility reflect customary international law.[57] The Court made the determinations in passing and did not set out any State practice or *opinio juris* to demonstrate the customary status of the rules.

Indeed, in practice, it is rare for the practice and *opinio juris* of all States, or even a majority of States, to be considered in the determination of custom. One such rare example is the International Committee of the Red Cross' study on *Customary International Humanitarian Law*, which consists of one volume of rules and one volume of practice, the latter totalling more than 4,000 pages (Henckaerts and Doswald-Beck, 2005). But when the practice and *opinio juris* of States *is* set out in a transparent manner, the methodology by which the rule has been determined becomes open to criticism.[58] The *Customary International Humanitarian Law* study is very much the exception. Far more frequently, the identification of a customary rule involves focusing on a small number of States, with the practice of these States being said to reflect a broader, more general practice. In many cases, international lawyers derive custom based primarily on the practice of a handful of core Western States, often with a primary focus on English-language and sometimes French-language sources. As a result, the practice of non-Western States and smaller and less powerful States, as well as non-Anglophone/Francophone sources, are often left out of, or insufficiently considered in, the analysis. Sometimes this process of privileging and marginalizing different practice and sources may occur for practical reasons, such as the limited linguistic capacity of the decision-maker, the time-sensitive nature of the inquiry, or because the practice of certain States is easier to find. At other times, it might occur for ideological reasons with some international lawyers showing a tendency to discount the practice of un-likeminded States because they do not like the practices of those States. Whatever the reasons, this pattern of

---

[57] Eg *Application of the Convention on the Prevention and Punishment of the Crime of Genocide (Bosnia and Herzegovina v Serbia and Montenegro), Judgment, ICJ Reports 2007*, pp 43, 217, para 420.

[58] The Study was criticised by the US: Bellinger III and Haynes II, 2007. See Section IV C 3.

privileging the practice of and sources from certain States manifests itself in many places in international law (Roberts 2017, pp 165–85; 254–75).

In practice, then, instead of involving a thorough analysis of general and consistent State practice, customary rules are often claimed following analysis of the practice of a small number of States, deduced from a pre-existing rule, or asserted without explanation. In addition, States and other courts often refer to the decisions of international or national courts to prove customary international law, even if those courts did not undertake a full analysis of State practice and *opinio juris* themselves. The tendency is to cite to some other authority that has 'found' a custom rather than to try to 'find' a custom oneself. One reason for this is that the test for custom is so exacting that it is almost impossible to apply faithfully. As a result, it is all too easy to claim that a particular rule is one of customary international law; at the same time, it is also easy to dispute the existence of a customary rule on the basis that the practice examined is insufficient to live up to the exacting standards of Article 38(1)(b).

2. Judicial decisions and the teachings of publicists

A second aspect of Article 38(1) that is misleading is the seemingly clear division between sources of international law on the one hand and subsidiary means for the determination of rules of law on the other hand.

Judicial decisions are mentioned in Article 38(1), but they are relegated to the status of a subsidiary means and placed at the same level as teachings of publicists. Yet, judicial decisions occupy a more important place in the practice of international law than Article 38(1) would suggest (Boyle and Chinkin, 2007, pp 263–312). Courts and tribunals interpret and apply the law; they do not create it. However, it is through interpretation that the law develops (Venzke, 2012). There is a fine line between development of the law through interpretation and creation of the law, and international law has developed considerably as a result of judicial decisions.[59] For example, the idea that international organizations have international legal personality stems from the ICJ's Advisory Opinion on *Reparation for Injuries Suffered in the Service of the United Nations*;[60] and the rules on reservations to treaties in the VCLT are based on the ICJ's advisory opinion on *Reservations to the Convention on the Prevention and Punishment of the Crime of Genocide*.[61] In practice, judicial decisions do not solely evidence the law.

Judicial decisions also play a crucial role insofar as customary international law is concerned. Judicial decisions identify rules of customary international law. They also crystallize customary rules. In the *Nicaragua* case, the ICJ found that the rules in Article 3 common to the four Geneva Conventions of 1949 and applicable in non-international armed conflicts were 'elementary considerations of humanity' and applicable also in international armed conflicts.[62] The Court did not set out any State practice or *opinio juris* for the finding, a finding which Judge Sir Robert Jennings described in his Dissenting Opinion as 'not a matter free from difficulty'.[63] The finding was also criticized by leading commentators. However, over time, the holding has become universally accepted and it is likely that common Article 3 passed into customary international law in large part *because*

---

[59] See for example Lauterpacht, 1958 and Tams and Sloan, 2013.

[60] *Reparation for Injuries Suffered in the Service of the United Nations, Advisory Opinion, ICJ Reports 1949*, p 174.

[61] *Reservations to the Convention on the Prevention and Punishment of the Crime of Genocide, ICJ Reports 1951*, p 15.

[62] *Military and Paramilitary Activities in and against Nicaragua (Nicaragua v United States of America), Merits, Judgment, ICJ Reports 1986*, pp 14, 104, para 218.

[63] Ibid, p 14, Dissenting Opinion of Judge Sir Robert Jennings, p 537.

of the *Nicaragua* judgment. In addition, as Hersch Lauterpacht observed, '[m]any an act of judicial legislation may in fact be accomplished under the guise of the ascertainment of customary international law' (Lauterpacht, 1958, p 368). Insofar as custom in particular is concerned, judicial decisions do far more than simply identify pre-existing rules.

By contrast to the increasing importance of judicial decisions, teachings of publicists are declining in importance. Putting academic writings on a par with judicial decisions in the statutes of the PCIJ and ICJ might be understood as a way of trying to balance the common law and civil law domestic traditions that underlie international law. Although the judge is the primary protagonist in the common law tradition, this honour is accorded to the teacher-scholar in the civil law tradition. The declining importance of teachings might suggest a broader recalibration within international law to becoming more common law-like. One reason for this is a relative shift in the availability and perceived importance of judicial decisions. Now that there exists a much greater body of judicial and arbitral decisions enunciating rules of international law, the emphasis in practice has shifted toward the contribution made by such decisions and away from the views of 'the most highly qualified publicists of the various nations'. This is the case even if the judge and the academic are one and the same person.

However, certain teachings continue to be influential. Teachings of publicists have given rise to new ideas which have since become orthodox (Sivakumaran, 2017a). In particular, in areas where States have been reluctant to articulate legal norms, or a standoff between different approaches exists, and no courts have jurisdiction, academic writings may play a crucial role. A good example of this is the Tallinn Manual on the International Law applicable to Cyber Warfare (Schmitt, 2013), a manual drawn up by an expert group, which dominates discussion on the issue. International law textbooks and treatises also shape the thinking of future generations of international lawyers and are often used by international lawyers in practice. More generally, publicists are part of the community of international lawyers and the teachings of publicists are part of the interaction between members of the community.

IV. THE DYNAMIC NATURE OF LAW-MAKING

Article 38(1) refers to States, courts, and publicists. It thus identifies some of the key actors that are involved in the making and evidencing of international law. However, since the Article was drafted, many other actors have emerged to play a central role in the making and shaping of international law. To understand the different types of actors that are involved in this process, and the way in which they create international law through a dialogic interaction, we start in this section by distinguishing among States, State-empowered entities, and non-State actors and explain how international law often evolves from dialogue among these actors (Roberts and Sivakumaran, 2012; Sivakumaran, 2017b). We then turn to examples of how this dialogue plays out with respect to treaties and custom as well as other materials that affect States' obligations, namely Draft Articles of the International Law Commission (ILC) and General Comments and Views of UN human rights treaty bodies.

A. STATES, STATE-EMPOWERED ENTITIES, AND NON-STATE ACTORS

States remain the most important actors in making and shaping international law. By and large, States conclude treaties and it is the practice and *opinio juris* of States, and possibly other actors, that go to the formation of customary international law. As former ICJ

President Rosalyn Higgins (1993, p 39) has put it: 'States are, at this moment in history, still at the heart of the international legal system.' But States are not the only actors that help to create international law.

States also empower other entities to help create, develop, interpret, apply, and propose changes to the law. These State-empowered entities are usually created and empowered on the international plane by two or more States and granted authority to make decisions or take actions. Examples include the ICJ, the ILC, the International Tribunal for the Law of the Sea, UN human rights treaty bodies, the World Trade Organization (WTO), conferences of parties in international environmental law, and the United Nations High Commissioner for Refugees. In some cases, however, States empower an entity that already exists to carry out particular functions. An example is some of the functions that States have empowered the ICRC to undertake. State-empowered entities fall between the categories of States and non-State actors. They are not States but, because of their empowerment by States, they should not be understood purely as non-State actors.

In certain circumstances, various non-State actors may also play a role in shaping and interpreting international law. These include non-governmental organizations, individual publicists, and national liberation movements. This view has been endorsed by members of the New Haven school (eg Reisman, 1992, p 122), and modern positivists (eg Simma and Paulus, 1999, p 306).[64] However, it is generally recognized that the role of such non-State actors is less influential than those of both States and State-empowered entities.

B. DIALOGUE AMONG DIFFERENT INTERNATIONAL ACTORS

Together, States, State-empowered entities, and non-State actors comprise a community of actors that make and shape international law. This community resembles the idea that international law involves an interpretive community in which various actors make and assess assertions about the existence and content of international law (Johnstone, 1991; Johnstone, 2005), though it extends beyond matters of interpretation. It also bears some resemblance to the notion of the 'invisible college of international lawyers', though the focus there is on international lawyers per se rather than other actors such as States and international courts (Schachter, 1977).

There are disputes about which actors comprise the community of international actors that make and shape international law. For instance, some States would argue that only States have the power to make international law, so other actors are not legitimate members of the community. Similarly, some State-empowered entities might view themselves as having a legitimate role in the community, but seek to exclude or downplay the role of non-State actors. Some international legal schools of thought take a broad approach to this question. For instance, in assessing the existence of international law, the New Haven (Yale) school advocates look beyond State practice to:

> the aggregate actual decision process, comprised, as it is, of governments, inter-governmental organizations, non-governmental organizations and, in no small measure, the media. All the actors, who assess, retrospectively or prospectively, the lawfulness of international actions and whose consequent reactions shape the flow of events, now constitute, in sum, the international legal decision process.[65]

The exact composition of the community varies depending on the subject matter at hand. On a matter of international human rights law, for example, the community would include States, regional human rights courts, UN human rights treaty bodies, special procedures

---

[64]   Reisman, 1992, p 122; Simma and Paulus, 1999, p 306.   [65]   Reisman, 2000, p 13.

mandate-holders of the UN Human Rights Council, human rights non-governmental organizations, and human rights academics. If the issue is at the intersection of trade law
and human rights, the community might also include the WTO, trade law academics,
and others. Instead of being a single community, there are multiple communities of international actors and sometimes tensions exist between and within these communities.[66]
For instance, international human rights lawyers and international humanitarian lawyers
sometimes clash over whether a particular issue is regulated by international human rights
law or international humanitarian law. This is not always solely a disagreement about the
substantive law but also one of legal cultures, expertise, and value judgements.

The various actors within the community engage in a dialogue with one another over
the making and shaping of international law, including the creation and interpretation of
treaties, the formation and identification of custom, and the conclusion of a whole host of
other materials. It is through this dialogue that some actors propose the existence, content,
or application of particular international law norms and other actors react to confirm or
contest that assertion of international law. This represents a delicate balancing act. In some
instances, the responding actors agree with the claim about the existence or content of international law. In other instances, they contest the claim. In still other instances, the responding actors go further and contest the authority of the initial actor to play a role in creating or
interpreting international law. For example, if States take the view that a State-empowered
entity has pushed the law or its authority too far, States will sometimes react not only by
rejecting the interpretation of the law put forward by the entity but also by limiting or down-
playing the general authority of the State-empowered entity or narrowing its mandate. In
most instances, however, States either accept or acquiesce in the work of State-empowered
entities, which works to reaffirm the authority of these bodies and permits their work to
play an important role in the formation of international law. As in customary international
law, the existence or content of international law is gleaned from the accumulation of these
actions, assertions, and reactions. Unlike the traditional theory of custom, however, this process involves States, State-empowered entities, and non-State actors; and the interactions are
not limited to actions by States or the identification of customary rules.

C. DIALOGUE WITH RESPECT TO THE TRADITIONAL SOURCES OF INTERNATIONAL LAW

1. Creation of treaties

States play the predominant role insofar as the conclusion of treaties is concerned; however, other actors within the community also have a role to play, including in the formation of the treaties themselves. Major conventions have been based on drafts prepared by
the International Law Commission, such as the Vienna Convention on the Law of Treaties
(1969) and the Vienna Convention on Diplomatic Relations (1961). Other major treaties,
notably the original drafts of the Geneva Conventions (1949) and Additional Protocols
(1977), were prepared by the ICRC and put before States at the diplomatic conferences of
1949 and 1974–7 respectively. In the process of preparing the drafts, the ICRC consulted
inter alia government experts and Red Cross experts and, in this way, a variety of actors
took part in the dialogic process described earlier.

---

[66] This issue touches upon both the fragmentation of international law into different subfields and different
institutions, see Fragmentation of International Law: Difficulties Arising from the Diversification and
Expansion of International Law, Report of the Study Group of the International Law Commission, Finalized
by Martti Koskenniemi, A/CN.4/L.682 (13 April 2006); as well as the idea that international law is made up of
a 'divisible' college of international lawyers. See Roberts, 2017, pp 1–17.

The preparation of draft treaties can be particularly influential as, oftentimes, the overall shape and approach of a convention is set, with the diplomatic conference merely adding, removing, and modifying particular provisions. Terminology used by the original drafters is often carried forward into the treaty and becomes an accepted part of international law. This is true, for example, of terms such as 'contracting state', 'provisional application', and 'consent to be bound' in the Vienna Convention on the Law of Treaties (Pronto and Wood, 2010, p 4). It is also true of concepts like 'complementarity' in the Rome Statute of the International Criminal Court.

In some cases, non-State actors participate at diplomatic conferences at which treaties are adopted. For example, national liberation movements were participants at the diplomatic conference that gave rise to the Additional Protocols to the Geneva Conventions. Non-governmental organizations were participants at the Rome Conference which adopted the Statute of the International Criminal Court (1998) and played a particularly influential role. Some treaties also permit ratification and accession by non-State actors. For example, international organizations and regional integration organizations are able to participate in certain treaties.[67] National liberation movements engaged in a war of national liberation against a State party to Additional Protocol I are able to submit a unilateral declaration to the depositary undertaking to apply the Geneva Conventions and Additional Protocol.[68]

2. Interpretation of treaties

Treaties need to be interpreted and the interpretation of a treaty can greatly affect both the content and nature of an obligation. For example, Article 2(1) of the ICCPR provides that '[e]ach State Party to the present Covenant undertakes to respect and to ensure to all individuals within its territory and subject to its jurisdiction the rights recognized in the present Covenant . . .' But what do the words 'within its territory and subject to its jurisdiction mean'? Is the 'and' conjunctive or disjunctive? The interpretation of the words can make a significant difference to the extent of States parties' obligations (ie it could limit obligations to individuals who are within a State's territory *and* subject to its jurisdiction, or it could extend obligations to individuals who are within a State's territory as well as individuals who are not within its territory but who are subject to its jurisdiction). As such, the interpreter of a treaty holds considerable power. States parties to a treaty are authoritative interpreters of that treaty. However, States often also empower other actors to interpret and apply treaties.

Some constituent instruments of international organizations refer to particular organs of the organization to issue interpretations. For example, the International Monetary Fund Articles of Agreement provide that '[a]ny question of interpretation of the provisions of this Agreement arising between any member and the Fund or between any members of the Fund shall be submitted to the Executive Board for its decision'.[69] Many treaties empower an international court or tribunal to interpret and apply their terms.[70] The interpretation of a treaty on the part of a court or tribunal will be binding on the parties to the particular case, but will also be highly influential for other parties to the treaty. The interpretations of other actors may also be influential. For example, although falling into the category of teachings of publicists, the ICRC's article-by-article Commentaries on the Geneva Conventions have been described by the ICTY Appeals Chamber as 'authoritative'.[71]

---

[67] For example, UN Convention on the Law of the Sea, Annex IX; UN Convention on the Rights of Persons with Disabilities, Article 44.   [68] Additional Protocol I, Article 96(3).

[69] Articles of Agreement of the International Monetary Fund, Article XXIX(a).

[70] Eg Convention on the Prevention and Punishment of the Crime of Genocide, Article IX.

[71] *Prosecutor v Tadić, Judgment*, Case No IT–94–1–A, Appeals Chamber, 15 July 1999, para 93.

A range of actors can thus properly interpret a treaty. If the interpretation of one actor is accepted by others, a shared view of the law emerges. By contrast, given the decentralization of the international system, multiple interpretations of a treaty provision by different actors can also exist. There is not always a nice, neat solution. In some cases, international courts or arbitral tribunals may adopt a particular interpretation of a treaty and the treaty parties may reject that interpretation. For instance, in response to broad interpretations adopted by certain international arbitral tribunals under the North American Free Trade Agreement (NAFTA), the NAFTA treaty parties issued a joint interpretation clarifying that they held a narrower understanding of the treaty terms.[72] Subsequent NAFTA tribunals have largely followed the treaty parties' interpretation. By contrast, some States have explicitly adopted some approaches adopted by arbitral tribunals into their subsequent investment treaties and models, which works to confirm the interpretations adopted by these arbitral tribunals.

3. Custom

Although the elements that go to the *formation* of custom (State practice and *opinio juris*) are those of States and possibly other actors, the *identification* of custom is often left to State-empowered entities such as the ICJ and the ILC. Although these bodies are meant to identify custom based on State practice and *opinio juris*, as we have seen, they often end up declaring the existence or absence of custom through a deductive process or pure assertion without a strong inductive basis.

However, that is not the end of the process. Following the identification of a customary rule by a State-empowered entity, a dialogue often ensues with States, other State-empowered entities, and non-State actors responding to that assertion about the existence or content of international law to either confirm or contest the assertion.

A good example is the ICRC's study on *Customary International Humanitarian Law*. This study identified 161 rules of customary international humanitarian law, the vast majority of which were found to be applicable in international and non-international armed conflicts alike. Following its publication, the United States issued a response in which it took issue with certain aspects of the study (Bellinger III and Haynes II, 2007). It contested the customary nature of certain rules, such as '[t]he use of methods or means of warfare that are intended, or may be expected, to cause widespread, long-term and severe damage to the natural environment is prohibited' (Bellinger III and Haynes II, 2007, pp 455–60). And it set out some concerns over the methodology of the study, including that there was insufficient State practice for many of the rules proffered as customary law, that there was 'too much emphasis on written materials, such as military manuals . . . as opposed to actual operational practice by States during armed conflict', and that insufficient account was taken of the practice of specially affected States (Bellinger III and Haynes II, 2007, pp 544–60). If other States and international actors had followed suit, contesting the study's findings and methodology, the study might not have become influential. Instead, many other actors cited the study with approval and adopted its findings that particular rules reflected customary international law, including States, international

---

[72] In NAFTA, the treaty parties created a Free Trade Commission made up of representatives from the NAFTA treaty parties that had the power to issue joint interpretations that were binding on NAFTA tribunals. However, even in the absence of such a provision, the subsequent agreements and practice of treaty parties is relevant to the interpretation of the treaty. See 1969 Vienna Convention on the Law of Treaties, Article 31(3) (a) and (b).

courts, domestic courts, academics, and other entities.[73] In practice, the study has become the starting point for any discussion on customary international humanitarian law and a shortcut for doing the firsthand work oneself.

Similarly, once a leading court or tribunal finds that a particular rule is one of customary international law, other courts, tribunals, States, and academics frequently cite that finding without carrying out the analysis themselves. Indeed, the Special Tribunal for Lebanon has indicated that '[t]he combination of a string of decisions [of international courts and tribunals] . . . coupled with the implicit acceptance or acquiescence of all the international subjects concerned, clearly indicates the existence of the practice and *opinio juris* necessary for holding that a customary rule of international law has evolved'.[74] Although not an orthodox statement of the theory of customary international law, the quote captures much of the reality of the identification of custom in practice. Custom is often identified by international courts and tribunals and, if States and other actors do not protest, it often becomes accepted, particularly if other entities cite it with approval.

If States disagree with a position taken by an international court, they can also push back against the ruling and adopt a different approach going forward. A good example of this is the *S.S. Lotus* case in which the Permanent Court of International Justice held that the flag State of a ship that was injured in a collision had authority to prosecute the captain of the ship that caused the collision on the basis that a ship is an extension of a State's territory and so effects felt by the ship are felt within that flag State's territory.[75] This proposition was reversed by States in the 1982 UN Convention on the Law of the Sea.[76]

D. OTHER MATERIALS AFFECTING STATES' OBLIGATIONS

The dialogue among States, State-empowered entities, and other actors applies also in respect of a host of other materials that affect States' obligations. Examples of such materials are analysed below, namely Draft Articles of the International Law Commission and General Comments and Views of UN human rights treaty bodies. Draft Articles are particularly influential in international law, as is the work product of human rights treaty bodies in international human rights law.

1. Draft Articles of the International Law Commission

The International Law Commission is an expert body established and empowered by the General Assembly.[77] It has as its mandate 'the promotion of the progressive development of international law and its codification'.[78] One of the principal forms of the ILC's work is 'draft Articles'.[79] Draft Articles are often part-codification and part-progressive development and it is not always apparent which aspects of them are codification and which are progressive development. They are soft in form and are not binding as such; however, they may contain binding elements, namely when particular draft Articles reflect existing customary international law or become a catalyst for such rules to be accepted.

---

[73] Eg Colombia, *Comando General de la Fuerzas Armadas, Manual de Derecho Operacional*, Manual FF.MM 3–41 Público (2009); *Prosecutor v Bemba-Gombo, Judgment pursuant to Article 74 of the Statute*, Case No ICC-01/05–01/08, 21 March 2016, para 152; *Hamdan v Rumsfeld* 548 US 557 (2006), per Justice Stevens; *Public Committee against Torture in Israel and Palestinian Society for the Protection of Human Rights and the Environment* v *Israel and ors*, HCJ 769/02, 13 December 2006, para 23; Report of the Secretary-General's Panel of Experts on Accountability in Sri Lanka, 31 March 2011, para 183.

[74] Case No. CH/AC/2010/02, Decision on Appeal of Pre-Trial Judge's Order regarding Jurisdiction and Standing, 10 November 2010, para 47.   [75] *S.S. 'Lotus', Judgment No 9, 1927, PCIJ, Ser A, No 10*, at p 18.

[76] UN Convention on the Law of the Sea, Article 97.   [77] General Assembly Res 174(II) (1947).

[78] Statute of the International Law Commission, Article 1(1).

[79] Statute of the International Law Commission, Article 20.

Many draft Articles have been highly influential notwithstanding their soft form (Boyle and Chinkin, 2007, pp 171–83). The Articles on State Responsibility, for example, have been cited numerous times by international, regional, and domestic courts,[80] and in the teachings of publicists. Indeed, even prior to the adoption of the Draft Articles, they had been cited with approval by courts and tribunals, including the ICJ.[81] There is thus a paradox between the (soft) form of ILC's draft Articles and their authority (Caron, 2002).

The ILC's work garners significant respect partly because the body is empowered by States, partly because the ILC members are typically well-respected international lawyers (often academics and former government international lawyers), and partly because it produces rigorous outputs. In addition, the way in which the ILC works involves a dialogue with States, which adds to the weight of the Commission's ultimate work product. At the outset of the Commission's work, it requests States, and sometimes other actors,[82] to furnish information on the subject under consideration.[83] Draft articles are circulated to States,[84] and sometimes other actors, for their comments; and the ILC is obliged to take these comments into consideration when preparing its final draft.[85] The Commission's work is also discussed annually in the Sixth (Legal) Committee of the General Assembly. In some cases, the General Assembly adopts a resolution taking note of the final work product, as it did with respect to the Draft Articles on State Responsibility, and in other cases the work product forms the basis of treaty negotiations, as occurred with the Vienna Convention on the Law of Treaties (1969) and the Vienna Convention on Diplomatic Relations (1961).[86]

At the same time, certain other work products of the ILC have not had any significant influence, such as the Draft Articles on the Status of the Diplomatic Courier and the Diplomatic Bag not Accompanied by Diplomatic Courier (1989). It is difficult to determine exactly why certain outputs prove influential while others are neglected. Much depends on the reception of the ILC's work product by other members of the community of international lawyers.

2. General Comments and Views of UN human rights treaty bodies

Many actors contribute to the creation and shaping of international human rights law. Of particular importance is the work-product of UN human rights treaty bodies, which like the International Law Commission are State-empowered entities. The core international human rights treaties established a treaty body, which examines the progress made by States parties in the implementation of the treaty.[87] These treaty bodies issue 'General Comments' or 'General Recommendations' in which they set out their interpretation of

---

[80] See 'Responsibility of States for internationally wrongful acts: Compilation of decisions of international courts, tribunals and other bodies', UN Doc A/62/62 and Add.1; and the updates thereto.

[81] Eg *Gabčíkovo-Nagymaros Project (Hungary/Slovakia), Judgment, ICJ Reports 1997*, p 7, paras 47, 50–3, 58, 79, 83.

[82] Eg International organizations were requested to furnish information as regards the Draft Articles on the Responsibility of International Organizations. *Yearbook of the International Law Commission 2002*, vol II (Part Two), p 96 para 488.   [83] Statute of the International Law Commission, Articles 16(c) and 19(2).

[84] Ibid, Articles 16(h) and 21.   [85] Ibid, Articles 16(i) and 22.

[86] Pursuant to Article 23 of the ILC Statute, the ILC may recommend to the General Assembly: '(a) To take no action, the report having already been published; (b) To take note of or adopt the report by resolution; (c) To recommend the draft to Members with a view to the conclusion of a convention; (d)   To   convoke   a conference to conclude a convention.'

[87] Eg Convention on the Rights of the Child (1989), Article 43(1). Exceptionally, the Committee on Economic, Social and Cultural Rights was established pursuant to ECOSOC Res 1985/17 rather than by the International Covenant on Economic, Social and Cultural Rights.

provisions of the relevant treaty and other issues relating to the treaty, such as on reservations and State succession.[88] Treaty bodies also issue 'Views', namely decisions that set out the treaty body's findings on violations alleged by the author of an individual communication. Through General Comments and Views, treaty bodies often advance a particular interpretation of the law and seek to assert the breadth and depth of their authority. Sometimes States push back, either on the specific interpretation or on the authority of the treaty bodies to weigh in on particular issues or to resolve them authoritatively.

General Comments are prepared by the relevant treaty body, with drafts being shared with States parties to the treaty and other stakeholders, such as special procedures mandate holders, national human rights institutions, NGOs, and academics.[89] Comments received are then considered by the treaty body; and treaty bodies have amended draft General Comments in light of comments received. Once adopted, General Comments are used by States, domestic and international courts, and other entities; and through this usage, a shared view of the law can come into being. On a few occasions, following the adoption of a General Comment, some States parties have issued observations in which they express their disagreement with certain aspects of the General Comment. Depending on the reactions of other members of the community of international actors, this difference of opinion may prevent a shared view of the law from emerging.

A good example of this dialogic process, and the push and pull among certain treaty bodies and States over the substance of international law and which actors play an authoritative role in interpreting it, is the UN Human Rights Committee's General Comment 24. In that General Comment, the Committee made certain statements about when reservations would be incompatible with the ICCPR and what the consequences of such a finding would be. The Committee also stated that '[i]t necessarily falls to the Committee to determine whether a specific reservation is compatible with the object and purpose of the Covenant'.[90] In response, the French, UK, and US governments submitted observations rejecting the Committee's interpretation as a matter of international law and objecting to the Committee's claim to being able to decide these issues authoritatively.[91] The International Law Commission would later add its voice to the debate.[92]

The legal status of both General Comments and Views is contested. They are not binding, but they cannot simply be dismissed or ignored; they are often described as 'authoritative'. In the case of Views, the Human Rights Committee has indicated that '[t]he views of the Committee under the Optional Protocol [to the ICCPR] represent an authoritative determination by the organ established under the Covenant itself charged with the interpretation of that instrument'.[93] For its part, the International Court of Justice has indicated that 'it believes that it should ascribe great weight to the interpretation adopted by this independent body [the Human Rights Committee] that was established specifically to supervise the application of that treaty [the ICCPR]'.[94] This means that 'there is a strong

---

[88] See HRI/GEN/1/Rev.9 (Vol. I), 27 May 2008; HRI/GEN/1/Rev.9 (Vol. II), 27 May 2008. More recent General Comments and General Recommendations are accessible at: http://www.ohchr.org/EN/HRBodies/Pages/TBGeneralComments.aspx.

[89] Report of the Chairs of the human rights treaty bodies on their twenty-seventh meeting, A/70/302, 7 August 2015, para 91.   [90] General Comment 24, para 18.

[91] Observations of France, the UK, and the US, in response to Human Rights Committee General Comment 24. Human Rights Committee, Report on the Work of Its Fifty-First Session, A/51/40 (1997) Annex VI, para 14; Human Rights Committee, Report on the Work of Its Fiftieth Session, A/50/40 (1996) 126 and 130.

[92] ILC, Report on the Work of Its Sixty-Third Session, UN Doc A/66/10/Add.1 (2011) 524–42.

[93] Human Rights Committee, General Comment No 33, CCPR/C/GC/33, 5 November 2008, para 13.

[94] *Ahmadou Sadio Diallo (Republic of Guinea v Democratic Republic of the Congo), ICJ Reports 2010*, pp 639, 664, para 66.

presumption that they are correct, they must be given serious consideration, and there must be a sound, legal reason for disagreeing with them' (Higgins, 2017, Vol II, pp 129, 135). However, the precise status of Views and General Comments remains controversial.[95]

V. CONCLUSION: EXPLAINING THE DISCONNECT BETWEEN THEORY AND PRACTICE

The doctrine of sources presents a puzzle. States, courts, and academics routinely refer to Article 38 when setting forth the sources of international law. Yet, in significant ways, Article 38 is incomplete and does not always present an accurate reflection of practice. It reflects a highly statist approach to sources that clearly distinguishes between sources of international law that are (at least ostensibly) based on State consent (treaties, custom, and general principles) and subsidiary sources that are not based on State actions per se (judicial decisions and teachings of publicists). The reality is much more nuanced.

The theoretically strict division between the sources of international law and the subsidiary means for determining the law is, in practice, far from clear. And a whole host of materials that are not to be found in Article 38 also affect the content of States' international law obligations. International law is created through a dialogue among States, State-empowered bodies, and non-State actors. States play a leading role in this process, but they are not the only actors. Increasingly, State-empowered bodies have been created and play a significant—and sometimes decisive—role in identifying, interpreting, and applying international law. In some instances, non-State actors also participate in the process.

Why then does a disconnect persist between the theory and reality of the sources of international law? That question does not admit an easy answer. One reason may lie in the different ways lawyers justify international laws or sources through resort to ideas of descriptive accuracy and normative appeal. In an ideal world, a source of law or a particular legal norm would be both descriptively accurate (ie it would reflect what actually happens and thus be both descriptively and predictively accurate) and normatively appealing (ie it would reflect notions of what should happen based on some external normative principles such as principles of procedural or substantive morality). In practice, there is often tension between these two values.

Take custom as an example. The theory of custom sounds normatively appealing because it requires general and consistent State practice, which suggests that it is justified because it is developed through a representative process that incorporates broad State consent. In reality, however, international lawyers often find custom based on a very limited (and sometimes not representative) assessment of State practice. The theory of custom sounds normatively appealing, but it is not at all descriptively accurate in terms of describing the actual process of finding custom. However, if one were to attempt to formulate a rule for determining custom that was descriptively accurate, it would not be normatively appealing.

A similar tension might exist with respect to the role of State-empowered bodies and non-State actors in the formation of international law. International law is often normatively justified on the basis that is derived from State consent. In practice, however, it is frequently developed through a dialogue among States, State-empowered bodies, and

---

[95] For instance, the US has indicated that 'the views of the [Human Rights] Committee should be carefully considered by the States Parties. Nevertheless, they are neither primary nor authoritative sources of law and the impression should not be given that they are being cited as such.' Observations of the United States of America on the Human Rights Committee's Draft General Comment 35: Article 9, 10 June 2014.

non-State actors in a way that exhibits a much more attenuated relationship to State consent. Openly acknowledging this fact may result in a theory of sources that is more descriptively accurate. But it would require a new normative justification because it suggests that international law is not based as clearly and directly on State practice and State consent as traditional theories of international law suggest.

This dynamic is reminiscent of Martti Koskenniemi's description of international legal argument as oscillating between being a mere apology for State power (and thus being descriptively accurate) and being utopian and unachievable (and thus being normatively appealing) (Koskenniemi, 1989). The doctrine of sources aims to be normatively appealing, but it is utopian and unachievable. An account of the real way in which sources are often identified may be more descriptively accurate, and also possibly more normatively appealing on some dimensions (such as arguments about the inclusion of civil society creating a democratizing effect), but it would lack normative appeal on key metrics (such as how inclusive and representative it is in terms of the State practice considered).

Whatever the reasons for this disconnect, international lawyers seeking to master the doctrine of sources need to understand both its theory and its reality. In doing so, international lawyers need to learn to talk the talk, and walk the walk, of the sources of international law and gain an awareness that there is often a gulf between the two. In the vein of Martti Koskenniemi, one needs to be able to play the game and critique the game and one needs to know when to do each one. It is the tension and ambiguity between theory and practice, along with sources' gatekeeping function, that keeps so many international lawyers returning to the doctrine of sources as an important subject to focus on in international law.

REFERENCES

AKEHURST, M (1974-75), 'Custom as a Source of International Law', *British Yearbook of International Law* 1

BAXTER, RR (1970), 'Treaties and Custom', 129 *Recueil des Cours* 27.

BELLINGER III, JB and HAYNES II, WJ (2007), 'A US Government Response to the International Committee of the Red Cross Study *Customary International Humanitarian Law*', 89 *IRRC* 443.

BOYLE, A and CHINKIN, C (2007), *The Making of International Law* (Oxford: Oxford University Press).

BROWNLIE, I (2008), *Principles of Public International Law* (7th edn, Oxford: Oxford University Press).

CARON, DD (2002), 'The ILC Articles on State Responsibility: The Paradoxical Relationship between Form and Authority', 96 *AJIL* 857.

CHENG, B (1965), 'United Nations Resolutions on Outer Space: "Instant" Customary Law?', 5 *Indian JIL* 23.

CRAWFORD, J and VILES, T (1994), 'International Law on a Given Day', in K Ginther et al (eds), *Völkerrecht zwischen normativem Anspruch und politischer Realität* 45, reprinted in J Crawford (2002), *International Law as an Open System* (London: Cameron May), p 69.

D'AMATO, A (1971), *The Concept of Custom in International Law* (Ithaca: Cornell University Press).

D'AMATO, A (1990), 'It's a Bird, It's a Plane, It's *Jus Cogens*', 9 *Conn JIL* 1.

DANILENKO, G (1993), *Law-Making in the International Community* (Dordrecht: Martinus Nijhoff).

HART, HLA (1994), *The Concept of Law* (2nd edn, Oxford: Clarendon Press).

instruments will tend to legitimize conduct, and make the legality of opposing positions harder to sustain (Chinkin, 1989, p 866). Formally non-binding resolutions and declarations may additionally acquire binding legal character as elements of a treaty-based regulatory regime,[13] or constitute a 'subsequent agreement between the parties regarding the interpretation of the treaty or the application of its provisions',[14] or influence the development and application of treaties or general international law.[15]

The recognition that non-binding soft law instruments may have legally significant effects does not entail rewriting the law of treaties or expanding the sources of international law; still less does it require us to engage in the 'deformalization of the ascertainment of international legal rules'.[16] To argue otherwise is to miss the point. The point is that treaties, soft law, general principles, and custom interact and supplement each other. What matters is to understand that there is an interaction, even when the instrument itself is formally non-binding.

It is certainly a fallacy to dismiss these various forms of soft law as not law and therefore of no importance: they can and do contribute to the process of international law-making and the evolution of treaty-based regimes, as the examples considered later will show. Nor is reliance on soft law to be confused with the application of *lex ferenda* or 'evolving law'.[17] If it is true that some soft law instruments—like treaties that are not yet in force—are part of the process by which customary law evolves, then it is equally true that in the evolutionary stage they have not yet generated actual law, and we should not pretend otherwise. Identifying when law in the making has become law is of course precisely the point on which States and international lawyers will often disagree, but it is precisely at that point that 'soft law' is in reality no longer soft. Our focus in this chapter is on soft law as one element in the law-making process precisely because it leads to law, not to something less than law.

II. WHAT IS SOFT LAW?

'Soft law' has a range of possible meanings (Baxter, 1980; Chinkin, 1989; Dupuy, 1991; Sztucki, 1990; Hillgenberg, 1999). From a law-making perspective the term 'soft law' is simply a convenient description for a variety of non-legally binding but normatively worded instruments used in contemporary international relations by States and international organizations. It encompasses, inter alia, inter-State conference declarations such as the 1992 Rio Declaration on Environment and Development; UN General Assembly instruments such as the 1948 Universal Declaration of Human Rights, the 1970 Declaration on the Principles of Friendly Relations Among States, or the 2007 Declaration on the Rights of Indigenous Peoples, or other resolutions dealing with outer space, the deep seabed, decolonization, or natural resources; or codes of conduct, guidelines, and recommendations of international organizations, such as UNEP's 1987 Guidelines on Environmental Impact Assessment, FAO's Code of Conduct on Responsible Fisheries, or many others adopted by IMO, IAEA, FAO and so on.

---

[13] Eg under the 1982 UN Convention on the Law of the Sea, Articles 210–11, or the 1994 Nuclear Safety Convention, on which see later in the chapter.

[14] See 1969 Vienna Convention on the Law of Treaties, Article 31(3)(a).

[15] See *Gabčíkovo-Nagymaros Dam Case, Judgment, ICJ Reports 1997*, p 7, para 140.

[16] D'Aspremont, 2011, p 129, argues that it does.

[17] *OSPAR Arbitration* (2003) PCA, paras 101–4. On the applicability of evolving law see the very sensible comments by McDorman, 2004.

Soft law in this sense can be contrasted with hard law, which is always binding. Seen from this angle, the legal form is decisive: treaties which have entered into force are by definition hard law, at least for the parties. So, in principle, are UN Security Council resolutions adopted under Chapter VII of the UN Charter, because all UN member States have agreed to accept and carry out these decisions.[18] If the form is that of a non-binding agreement, such as the Helsinki Accords (Schachter, 1977) or a UN General Assembly resolution or declaration,[19] it will not be a treaty for precisely that reason and we will have what is in effect a 'soft' agreement. Of course, the question whether an agreement is a binding treaty is not necessarily easy to answer, as we can observe in the *Qatar-Bahrain Maritime Delimitation* case.[20] The test is one of substance and intent; the label attached to the instrument is not decisive. Moreover, an agreement involving a State and another entity may be binding, even if it is not a treaty,[21] so the distinction between hard and soft agreements is not simply synonymous with the distinction between treaties and other instruments. Furthermore, once soft law begins to interact with binding instruments its non-binding character may be lost or altered.

As we have seen, reliance on soft law as part of the law-making process takes a number of different forms. While the legal effect of declarations, resolutions, guidelines, and other soft law instruments is not necessarily the same, it is characteristic of nearly all of them that they are negotiated and often carefully drafted statements, which are in some cases intended to have some normative significance despite their non-binding, non-treaty form. There is at least an element of good faith commitment,[22] evidencing in some cases a desire to influence State practice or expressing some measure of law-making intention and progressive development. In this sense non-binding soft law instruments are in some cases not fundamentally different from those multilateral treaties which serve much the same law-making purposes. They may also be both an alternative to and part of the process of multilateral treaty-making. In the following sections we will explore the uses of soft law and consider what legal effect it may have.

III. A CHOICE OF TREATIES OR SOFT LAW?

The literature identifies at least four reasons why soft law instruments represent an alternative to law-making by treaty (Chinkin, 1989, p 850; Abbott and Snidal, 2000, p 421; Hillgenberg, 1999, p 499; Neuhold, 2010, p 40). First, it may be easier to reach agreement when the form is non-binding. It can enable States to take on commitments that otherwise they would not, or to formulate them in a more precise and detailed form that could not at that point be agreed in a treaty. The soft law approach thus allows States to tackle a problem collectively at a time when they do not want to shackle their freedom of action. Their legal commitments, and the consequences of any non-compliance, are more limited.

[18] UN Charter, Article 25.
[19] In UN practice a 'declaration' is used in preference to a 'resolution' when 'principles of great and lasting importance are being enunciated'. See UN Doc E/CN.4/L.610 (1962) cited in Cheng, 1965, p 32.
[20] *Maritime Delimitation and Territorial Questions between Qatar and Bahrain, Jurisdiction and Admissibility, Judgment, ICJ Reports 1994*, p 112.
[21] See *Anglo-Iranian Oil Co, Preliminary Objections, ICJ Reports 1952*, p 93.
[22] Separate Opinion of Judge Lauterpacht, *Voting Procedure on Questions relating to Reports and Petitions concerning the Territory of South West Africa, Advisory Opinion, ICJ Reports 1955*, p 118: 'The State in question, while not bound to accept the recommendation, is bound to give it due consideration in good faith.' See also Virally, 1956, pp 85–91. A soft law declaration may result in binding unilateral obligations: see *OSPAR Arbitration* (2003) PCA, para 90.

In this context soft law has been a useful instrument for developing international law in relatively new fields such as human rights or environmental protection.

Secondly, soft law instruments will normally be easier to supplement, amend, or replace than treaties, since all that is required is the adoption of a new resolution by the relevant international institution (Aust, 1986, p 791). Treaties take time to replace or amend, and the attempt to do so can result in an awkward and overlapping network of old and new obligations between different sets of parties. The important point is that soft law is often relied on to provide the detailed technical rules and standards required to implement international regulatory regimes concerned with safety, pollution, resource conservation, and so on. Because they are often based on expert advice, and may need to change frequently to reflect changes in policy or in the underlying science, there is little point putting these rules and standards into the text of a treaty.

Thirdly, it may be easier for some States to adhere to non-binding instruments because they can avoid the domestic treaty ratification process, and perhaps escape democratic accountability for the policy to which they have agreed. In this context the benefits of soft law are essentially domestic and constitutional in character. Of course this very feature may also make it comparably harder to implement such policies if public funding, legislation, or public support is necessary. A new government may also find it easier to repudiate soft law commitments, so other governments may wish to be careful about relying on them.

Finally, soft law instruments may provide more immediate evidence of international consensus on an agreed text than a treaty. The UN General Assembly resolution on the law of State responsibility is a good example.[23] Although views within the International Law Commission and the UN Sixth Committee on the eventual form of the ILC Draft Articles were divided, both bodies recommended that the UNGA 'take note' of the Draft Articles, in the expectation that in this form they would 'exert an influence on the crystallization of the law of State responsibility through application by international courts and tribunals and State practice,' deferring for later a decision on whether to proceed with a codification treaty (Crawford and Olleson, 2005, p 959). Much of it was already existing law, or had become accepted as law during the process of codification, a conclusion which international courts have done nothing to dispel.[24]

It cannot be said that the ILC's State responsibility articles are unsuited to adoption in the form of a multilateral treaty; on the contrary they are drafted as if in treaty form. An UNGA resolution may in this case be more effective than a treaty for two reasons. Firstly, a treaty runs the risk of securing only a relatively small number of parties; its impact may also be qualified by reservations and the need to wait for ratification and entry into force. Second, referring the Draft Articles to a diplomatic conference might re-open debates on a text which already rests on a delicate compromise between differing views (Crawford and Olleson, 2005, p 961, and Koskenniemi, 2001, p 341). It would thus be better for States simply to endorse a consensus in the Commission and then argue about the status of the rules in their dealings with each other and in litigation. In this case, the form of the articles is more significant for what it tells us about the process of international law-making than about the nature or legal status of the rules themselves.

If we look at the more recent work of the ILC, it can be seen that the multilateral treaty is no longer the Commission's preferred instrument for the codification of international law. Although Articles 17 and 23 of the Statute of the Commission refer expressly to the conclusion of conventions, other possibilities are left open. Since 2001, soft law outcomes

---

[23] UNGA Res 56/83 (2001).
[24] *Gabčíkovo-Nagymaros Dam Case, ICJ Reports 1997*, p 7. See Crawford, 2002, pp 1–60.

have increasingly been used.[25] Even the re-examination of the law and practice on reservations to treaties has concluded with the adoption of soft law guidelines.[26]

One important feature of the treaty as an instrument of codification is that States have significant input into the treaty negotiations and they have sometimes made substantial changes to ILC drafts.[27] This renegotiation does not necessarily happen when the UN General Assembly simply adopts or takes note of a declaration of principles drafted by the Commission. A treaty basis may also be required when creating new international organizations or institutions, such as the International Criminal Court, or for dispute settlement provisions, while for some States ratified treaties become part of their national law, and adoption of a text in this form becomes a convenient way of changing national law. The latter point explains why these States ultimately favoured adoption of a treaty on the law of State immunity, rather than a simple declaration. But even for new law, non-binding instruments may still be useful if they can help generate widespread and consistent State practice and/or provide evidence of *opinio juris* in support of a new customary rule. There are good examples of UN General Assembly resolutions and intergovernmental declarations having this effect in the *Nicaragua Case*,[28] the *Nuclear Weapons Advisory Opinion*,[29] and the *Western Sahara Advisory Opinion*.[30]

What all of this suggests is that the non-binding form of an instrument is of relatively limited relevance in the context of customary international law-making. Treaties do not generate or codify customary law because of their binding form but because they either influence State practice and provide evidence of *opinio juris* for new or emerging rules, or because they are good evidence of what the existing law is.[31] In many cases this is no different from the potential effect of non-binding soft law instruments. Both treaties and soft law instruments can be vehicles for focusing consensus on rules and principles, and for mobilizing a consistent, general response on the part of States. Depending upon what is involved, treaties may be more effective than soft law instruments for this purpose because they indicate a stronger commitment to the principles in question and to that extent they may carry greater weight than a soft law instrument, but the assumption that they are necessarily more authoritative is misplaced.

To take one final example, the 1992 Rio Declaration on Environment and Development both codifies existing international law and seeks to develop new law (Viñuales, 2015). It is not obvious that a treaty with the same provisions would carry greater weight or achieve its objectives any more successfully. On the contrary, it is quite possible that such a treaty would, several years later, still have far from universal participation, whereas the 1992 Declaration secured immediate consensus support, with such authority as that implies. This does not mean that the Rio Declaration itself is binding law. Its value, like certain other soft law declarations, is evidential: it tells us what States believe the law to be in certain cases, or in others what they would like it to become or how they want it to develop. The Declaration's legal significance can

---

[25] On the comparative advantages of different forms see Crawford, 2002, pp 58–60.

[26] ILC, *Guide to Practice on Reservations to Treaties*, sixty-third session (2011) GAOR A/66/10/Add.1.

[27] Eg the 1969 Vienna Convention on the Law of Treaties and the 1997 International Convention on the Non-navigational Uses of International Watercourses.

[28] *Military and Paramilitary Activities in and against Nicaragua, Merits, ICJ Reports 1986*, p 14 ('*Nicaragua Case*').

[29] *Legality of the Threat or Use of Nuclear Weapons Advisory Opinion, ICJ Reports 1996*, p 226 ('*Nuclear Weapons Case*').   [30] *Western Sahara, Advisory Opinion, ICJ Reports 1975*, p 12.

[31] See especially *North Sea Continental Shelf Case, ICJ Reports 1969*, p 3; *Nicaragua Case, ICJ Reports 1986*, p 14; *Libya/Malta Continental Shelf Case, ICJ Reports 1985*, p 14.

therefore only be properly appreciated in conjunction with an examination of the pre-existing customary and treaty law, and the subsequent development of State practice, further treaties, protocols, regulations, and judicial decisions. It has had significant impact in all of these areas of law-making; many of the Rio principles have been re-ferred to by the ILC in support of the Draft Articles relating to transboundary harm,[32] and the Declaration appears to be one of the 'great number of instruments' setting out norms of international environmental law to which the ICJ referred in the *Gabčíkovo-Nagymaros Dam* case,[33] and on which the Court also relied explicitly in its *Nuclear Weapons* Advisory Opinion.[34]

IV. SOFT LAW AS PART OF THE MULTILATERAL TREATY-MAKING PROCESS

Some non-binding soft law instruments are significant because they are the first step in a process eventually leading to conclusion of a multilateral treaty. Others contribute to the interpretation and amplification of treaties. Some do both. In the human rights context non-binding declarations have been used almost since the inception of the UN itself.[35] The key instruments nearly all began in soft law form but are now incorporated in the multilateral treaties which today form the corpus of international human rights law. Once that transformation was achieved the declarations themselves ceased in most cases to have any further relevance. The one exception is the first and most important: the Universal Declaration of Human Rights.

The Universal Declaration was the earliest internationally endorsed statement of what UN member States regarded as human rights.[36] In the words of the chair of the Human Rights Commission: 'It is not a treaty; it is not an international agreement. It is not and does not purport to be a statement of law or of legal obligation.'[37] It is plainly soft; but is it in any sense law? Yes, in at least two, possibly three, senses. First, it represents a common understanding by UN member States of the human rights provisions of the UN Charter.[38] As such it is relevant to interpretation of the Charter and to the development of human rights law by the UN. Second, some of its provisions express 'general principles of law' rec-ognized as sources of international law by Article 38(1)(c) of the Statute of the ICJ (Meron, 1991, pp 88–9). As such they can be taken into account and applied by courts. The right of access to justice is one example of such principles.[39] A third, but more contested, view is that, whatever its initial status, the UDHR has created a customary international law of human rights (Hannum, 1995–6, p 287; Sohn, 1982, p 17).[40] Even if this is not true of the

---

[32] The commentaries to the 2001 Articles on Transboundary Harm and the 2006 Principles on the Allocation of Loss draw upon Principles 2, 7, 10, 11, 13, 15, 16, 17, 18, and 19. See ILC Report (2001) GAOR A/56/10; id (2006) GAOR A/61/10, paras 51–67.   [33] *ICJ Reports 1997*, p 7, para 140.

[34] *ICJ Reports 1996*, p 226, paras 29–30, and see also Dissenting Opinions of Judges Weeramantry and Palmer in the *Request for an Examination of the Situation, ICJ Reports 1995*, p 288. See also *Iron Rhine Arbitration*, PCA 2005, para 59; *Kishenganga Arbitration (Partial Award)* PCA 2013, para 449.

[35] More recent examples include the UN Declaration on the Rights of Indigenous Peoples, UNGA Res 61/295 (2007) on which see Barelli, 2009.

[36] UNGA Res 217A (III). Forty-eight States voted in favour; none against; eight abstained.

[37] Quoted in M Whiteman, I *Digest of International Law* 55 (1963).The Chair was Eleanor Roosevelt.

[38] UN Charter, Articles 1(3) 55, 56, 62, and 76. See Hannum, 1995–6, p 287.

[39] See *Golder v. United Kingdom*, 1 EHRR 1975, p 524.

[40] Compare the more nuanced position in Meron, 1991, pp 82–90.

whole declaration, some of its provisions have undoubtedly become customary international law, including freedom from genocide, slavery, and torture.[41]

Moreover, regardless of the status of the Declaration itself, or of the rights it sets forth,
it has provided the essential negotiating foundation for the UN's two principal human
rights treaties, the International Covenants on Civil and Political Rights and on Economic,
Social and Cultural Rights. The negotiations lasted 18 years, and they resulted in the creation of two distinct categories of human rights, formulated differently and with different
compliance machinery, but the core principles were those laid down in 1948. Not all States
are parties to the 1966 UN Covenants, however, and it is in that context that the UDHR
remains relevant in contemporary international law.

Aspirational declarations on human rights do not necessarily have normative effect or
lead to treaty negotiations.[42] As one commentator has observed, 'At the time of their adoption most UN resolutions on human rights are promotional rather than restatements or reaf-
firmations of legal norms. However, to suggest that they do not contribute to law-making is
to underestimate the impact of "merely" moral or political statements in the area of human
rights' (Joyner, 1997, p 147). Since 1948, UN law-making in the human rights field has largely
followed the same pattern: first a declaration is adopted, then a treaty is negotiated.[43] In some
cases the treaty follows within a few years (eg the 1965 Convention on the Elimination of All
Forms of Racial Discrimination); in others it has taken 30 years (eg the 1989 Convention on
the Rights of the Child) for negotiations on a binding instrument to be concluded.

There are many other examples of UN resolutions initiating a process of international
law-making, for example on outer space, the deep seabed, and climate change.[44] IAEA
Guidelines[45] formed the basis for the rapid adoption of the 1986 Convention on Early
Notification of a Nuclear Accident following the Chernobyl accident; UNEP Guidelines
on Environmental Impact Assessment[46] were substantially incorporated in the 1991 ECE
Convention on Environmental Impact Assessment in a Transboundary Context; and
UNEP's Guidelines on Land-based Sources of Marine Pollution[47] provided a model for
regional treaties.[48]

There are also well-known instances of General Assembly resolutions interpreting
and applying the UN Charter, including those dealing with decolonization or the use of
force.[49] The ILC commentary to what is now Article 31(3)(a) of the Vienna Convention

---

[41] See *Questions relating to the Obligation to Prosecute or Extradite (Belgium v Senegal), Judgment, ICJ
Reports 2012*, p 442, para 99; *Application of the Convention on the Prevention and Punishment of the Crime of
Genocide (Bosnia and Herzegovina v Serbia and Montenegro), ICJ Reports 2007*, p 43, para 161.

[42] See, eg, the 1993 Vienna Declaration and Programme of Action on Human Rights, and other examples
quoted in Joyner, 1997, pp 146–7.

[43] See, eg, 1959 Declaration on the Rights of the Child, UNGA Res 1386 (XIV); 1963 Declaration on the
Elimination of Racial Discrimination, UNGA Res 1904 (XVIII); 1967 Declaration on the Elimination of
Discrimination Against Women, UNGA Res 2263 (XXII); 1973 Declaration Against Torture, UNGA Res 3059
(XXVIII).

[44] 1963 Declaration of Legal Principles Governing the Activities of States in the Exploration and Use of
Outer Space, UNGA Res 1962 (XVIII); 1970 Declaration of Principles Governing the Sea Bed and Ocean Floor
and Subsoil Thereof Beyond the Limits of National Jurisdiction, UNGA Res 2749 (XXV); 1988 Resolution on
Protection of Global Climate for Present and Future Generations of Mankind, UNGA Res 43/53.

[45] IAEA/INFCIRC/321 (1985).   [46] UNEP/GC14/25 (1987).   [47] UNEP/WG.120/3 (1985).

[48] See, eg, 1990 Kuwait Protocol for the Protection of the Marine Environment Against Marine Pollution
from Land-based Sources.

[49] 1960 Declaration on the Granting of Independence to Colonial Countries and Peoples, UNGA Res 1514
(XV); 1970 Declaration on Principles of International Law Concerning Friendly Relations and Co-operation
Among States in Accordance with the Charter of the United Nations, UNGA Res 2625 (XXV). See *Western
Sahara, Advisory Opinion, ICJ Reports 1975*, p 12; *Military and Paramilitary Activities in and against Nicaragua
(Nicaragua v United States of America) Merits, Judgment, ICJ Reports 1986*, p 14.

on the Law of Treaties notes simply that '... an agreement as to the interpretation of a provision reached after the conclusion of the treaty represents an authentic interpretation by the parties which must be read into the treaty for purposes of its interpretation'.[50] That agreement does not have to be binding.[51] Provided they are adopted by consensus, soft law resolutions may constitute either a subsequent agreement on interpretation of a treaty, or subsequent practice, pursuant to Articles 31(3)(a) and (b) respectively.[52] If the parties subsequently wish to add to or change their previous interpretation or practice they are free to do so by the simple expedient of adopting another resolution. There are limits to this possibility however. Soft law resolutions cannot change the object and purpose of a treaty nor can they formally amend it.[53]

Resolutions of treaty bodies help to ensure a common understanding of what a treaty requires and may provide the detailed rules and technical standards required for implementation by the parties.[54] Non-binding WHO and FAO standards may thus become 'international standards, guidelines or recommendations' for the purpose of judging compliance with the WTO Sanitary and Phytosanitary Agreement.[55] In the *Pulp Mills* case, the ICJ had to interpret references to 'guidelines and recommendations of international technical bodies' in Article 41 of the 1975 Statute of the River Uruguay. The parties relied, inter alia, on WHO standards for air and water pollution. These are not binding on States, but as the ICJ indicated they are 'to be taken into account by the State so that the domestic rules and regulations and the measures it adopts are compatible with those guidelines and recommendations'.[56]

The preamble to the 1994 Nuclear Safety Convention also recognizes that internationally formulated safety guidelines 'can provide guidance on contemporary means of achieving a high level of safety'. IAEA guidelines would be the obvious starting point for determining what constituted the 'appropriate steps' with regard to safety controls required by Articles 10–19 of the Convention (Boyle and Redgwell, 2018, ch 9). These internationally agreed standards are essential in giving hard content to the overly general and open-textured terms of regulatory or framework treaties (Contini and Sand, 1972). The detailed rules can easily be changed or strengthened as scientific understanding develops or as political priorities change.

FAO has made use of a mixture of hard and soft law instruments to promote implementation of the fisheries provisions of the 1982 UNCLOS. The 1993 Agreement to Promote Compliance with Conservation Measures on the High Seas is a binding treaty, but it forms an integral part of the non-binding 1995 Code of Conduct on Responsible Fishing, which is itself further implemented by other measures including the 2001 Plan of Action on

---

[50] ILC, 'The Law of Treaties', commentary to Article 27, at para (14) in Watts, 1999, vol II, p 689.

[51] See *Kasikili/Sedudu Island (Botswana/Namibia) Judgment, ICJ Reports 1999*, pp 1075–6, paras 47–51 and the case law cited at para 50. See also, Preliminary Conclusions by the Chairman of the Study Group on the Subject of Treaties over Time, ILC, Report on the work of its sixty-third session (2011) *General Assembly, Official Records, Sup. No 10* (A/66/10) pp 281–4.

[52] *Whaling in the Antarctic (Australia v Japan: New Zealand Intervening), Judgment, ICJ Reports* 2014, p 226, paras 46, 83.   [53] Ibid, p 226, para 56.

[54] Rose, 2012, gives a good account of how soft law guidance has been used by the OECD to help governments and national courts implement the 1997 Bribery Convention.

[55] 1994 SPS Agreement, article 3.

[56] *ICJ Reports 2010*, para 62. See also para 197. Unusually for an international organization, WHO may adopt 'regulations' which will be binding on all member States except those who register an objection, but this power is rarely used, and in practice non-binding recommendations have become the main regulatory instrument: see 1948 WHO Constitution, articles 21–23; Fidler, 1998, p 1079; Burci and Vignes, 2004, pp 124–55.

Illegal, Unreported and Unregulated Fishing, also a soft law instrument. Negotiated in the same manner as treaties, and adopted by consensus in FAO,[57] these non-binding 'voluntary instruments' are aimed at regional fisheries organizations and the fishing industry as well as States, but in part they also reiterate, interpret, and amplify relevant provisions of UNCLOS and the 1995 Fish Stocks Agreement. The scope of the Code is broader than either of these treaties, however. It contains some elements which are unlikely to find their way into a binding agreement, and others which could not be agreed on as part of the UN Fish Stocks Agreement. The 1993 Agreement and the 1995 Code were negotiated in parallel with the Fish Stocks Agreement, and all three 'can be viewed as a package of measures that reinforce and complement each other' (Moore, 1999, pp 91–2). Reviewing the effect of all these inter-related measures, a former FAO legal adviser concludes: 'There can be little doubt that the sum total of the changes introduced has substantially strengthened the regime of the 1982 UN Convention, leaving aside the question whether there has been a *de facto* amendment of it in some respect' (Edeson, 1999, p 165; 2003, p 165).

These examples all point to the conclusion that the non-binding force of soft law can be over-stated. In many of the examples earlier in the chapter, States are not free to disregard applicable soft law instruments: even when not incorporated directly into a treaty, they may represent an agreed understanding of its terms. Thus, although of themselves these instruments are not legally binding, their interaction with related treaties may transform their legal status into something more.

V. SOFT LAW AND CUSTOMARY LAW

Non-binding instruments may also serve law-making purposes if they generate widespread and consistent State practice and/or provide evidence of *opinio juris* in support of a customary rule.[58] Whether they do so will depend on various factors which must be assessed in each case. A potentially law-making resolution or declaration need not necessarily proclaim rights or principles *as law*, but as with treaties, the wording must be 'of a fundamentally norm-creating character such as could be regarded as forming the basis of a general rule of law'.[59] The context within which soft law instruments are negotiated and the accompanying statements of delegations will also be relevant if assessing the *opinio juris* of States.[60] Lastly, the degree of support is significant. A resolution adopted by consensus or by unanimous vote will necessarily carry more weight than one supported only by a majority of States.[61] Resolutions opposed by even a small number of States may have no law-making effect if those States are the ones most immediately affected.[62] The attempt by the General Assembly in the 1970s to change the law on expropriation of foreign

---

[57] However some States expressed significant reservations when adopting the Plan of Action: see FAO, *Report of the Committee on Fisheries*, 24th Session (2001).

[58] See, eg, *Nicaragua Case, ICJ Reports 1986*, p 14; *Nuclear Weapons Advisory Opinion, ICJ Reports 1996*, p 226; *Western Sahara Advisory Opinion, ICJ Reports 1975*, p 12.

[59] *North Sea Continental Shelf, ICJ Reports 1969*, p 3, para 72 and see Lowe, 1999; Brownlie, 1979, pp 260–2.

[60] See, eg, *Libya/Malta Continental Shelf Case, ICJ Reports*, p 14, paras 43–4, 49, and 58, where the Court draws upon the negotiating record of the 3rd UN Conference on the Law of the Sea.

[61] *Whaling in the Antarctic (Australia v Japan: New Zealand Intervening), Judgment, ICJ Reports* 2014, p 226, paras 46, 83.

[62] See on this point the cautionary dissent of Schwebel in the *Legality of the Threat or Use of Nuclear Weapons, ICJ Reports 1996*, p 226, noting that, '[i]f a resolution purports to be declaratory of international law, if it is adopted unanimously (or virtually so, qualitatively as well as quantitatively) or by consensus, and if it corresponds to State practice, it may be declaratory of international law'.

investments is a well-known example of the inability of majorities of States to legislate for minorities in this fashion.[63] The General Assembly's ban on deep seabed mining outside the framework of UNCLOS is another. In this case, the minority of objecting States established their own parallel regime, until eventually a compromise agreement was reached.[64]

In an international system where the consent or acquiescence of States is still an essential precondition for the development of new law or changes to existing law, these examples show that opposing votes matter. Even if such resolutions do change the law for States which vote in favour, it is clear that they do not do so for the dissenting minority. Moreover, even consensus adoption will not be as significant as it may at first appear if accompanied by statements which seriously qualify what has been agreed, or if it simply papers over an agreement to disagree without pressing matters to a vote. For all these reasons, the adoption of resolutions by international organizations or of declarations by States should not be confused with law-making per se.

Professor Cheng has argued that, if appropriately worded, General Assembly resolutions can create 'instant' customary law (Cheng, 1965). In his view the clearly articulated expression of *opinio juris* through the medium of a non-binding resolution or declaration may be enough, without further State practice, to afford evidence of a new rule of customary or general international law. For anyone seeking to use the UN General Assembly as a law-making instrument this is an attractive but generally unsustainable argument. Cheng himself rightly cautions against the facile assumption that UNGA resolutions make law, and his view of instant law-making is limited to very specific circumstances. Firstly, it depends on a strong consensus in favour of such a resolution.[65] Secondly, it requires appropriate wording. In his view, the principal UNGA resolutions on outer space fail this test, because they merely articulate principles by which States 'should be guided',[66] rather than potentially normative rules. In this respect they compare unfavourably with, for example, the rights proclaimed in the Universal Declaration of Human Rights or the Declaration on the Granting of Independence to Colonial Territories and Peoples. However, neither of these resolutions was adopted by consensus and it is very doubtful that their impact has ever been instantaneous. Cheng was also writing before any of the leading modern ICJ cases on the creation of customary law were decided, and even his cautious formulation may now be too generous. The jurisprudence is not favourable, it must be said, to notions of instant law-making, but stresses instead the need for subsequent confirmatory practice, or at least the absence of contrary practice.[67]

If the resolutions on outer space did not make instant law, and were designed to be replaced by treaties,[68] why adopt them at all? Apart from important practical considerations

---

[63] See 1974 Charter of Economic Rights and Duties of States, UNGA Res 3281 (XXX) and *Texaco Overseas Petroleum Co v Libyan Arab Republic,* 53 ILR (1977) p 422, paras 80–91. One hundred and twenty States voted for the Resolution, six voted against, and ten abstained.

[64] The 1970 Declaration of Principles Governing the Seabed and Ocean Floor etc, UNGA Res 2749 (XXV) was adopted by 108 votes in favour with 14 abstentions. For an account of the subsequent disagreements over the legal status of the deep seabed and the Reciprocating States regime established by Western States, see Churchill and Lowe, 1999, pp 224–35.

[65] Resolutions 1721 (XVI)(1961) and 1962 (XVIII)(1963) were agreed first by the USA and USSR (the only space States at that time) then adopted unanimously by the Outer Space Committee, the 1st Committee, and the UNGA.

[66] UNGA Res 1962 (XVIII)(1963). The wording of Res 1721 (XVI) is even weaker: 'The General Assembly . . . commends to States for their guidance . . . the following principles.'

[67] See especially *North Sea Continental Shelf Case, ICJ Reports 1969,* p 3 and *Nicaragua Case, ICJ Reports 1986,* p 14. But the *Gabčíkovo-Nagymaros Dam Case, ICJ Reports 1997,* p 7 may be more favourably inclined to instant law-making.   [68] See now the 1967 Outer Space Treaty and the 1979 Moon Treaty.

of simplicity and speed of adoption compared to treaties, the importance of resort to the UNGA lies in the collective affirmation which is thereby provided for a legal regime otherwise only impliedly asserted by the space States. The resolutions provided both a record of what all States believed the relevant rules either were or should be, and evidence of *opinio juris* demonstrating the law-making significance of their earlier practice. As Brownlie (1991, p 204) observes, 'In the face of a relatively novel situation the General Assembly provides an efficient index to the quickly growing practice of States.' Elsewhere he refers to the 'decisive catalytic effect' which such resolutions may have on State practice (Brownlie, 1979, p. 261).

In those circumstances it would be safe for space States to proceed on the assumption that there would be no opposition to activities conducted in conformity with the principles endorsed by the resolutions. That these principles were subsequently reaffirmed in treaty form shows both the value of soft law precedents as a prelude to later agreement on a more detailed international regime, and the preference for treaties as a means of stabilizing the law within an appropriate institutional framework once the views and practice of States are settled. This may suggest a perception that soft law is too fragile an instrument to sustain the long-term regulation of common areas such as space or the deep seabed,[69] but it is certainly an effective starting point when States need reassurance before commencing novel and previously unregulated activities.

The adoption of non-binding resolutions or declarations can also lead to changes in the existing law, in some cases quite quickly. The termination of driftnet fishing on the high seas is a good example of the successful use of UNGA resolutions in this way.[70] Although the resolutions themselves have no legal force, and do not make 'instant' law, the widespread opposition to such fishing has been effective in pressuring the small number of States involved to comply with the resolutions and phase out the use of driftnets. Such changes in the law can of course only come about as a result of changes in practice by those States most closely involved. Moreover, even States which initially voted against such resolutions may eventually conform to the general will. The initial opposition of colonial powers to UN resolutions on self-determination soon faded, and as the *Western Sahara* and *East Timor* cases show,[71] former colonial States have become the principal advocates of self-determination for their former colonies.

Why use non-binding resolutions for such purposes? Negotiating a global treaty on driftnets would have taken as long or longer; it would not have entered into force until there were enough ratifications, and if the relevant States failed to become parties they would not be bound anyway. In the latter case the law would not change unless these States changed their practice, which is no less true of the non-binding resolutions adopted by UNGA. In such cases, if the consensus for a change in practice is strong enough, a treaty is not necessary. If it is not strong enough a treaty will not necessarily strengthen it. If the weakness of soft law is that States are not obliged to comply, the same is no less true of an unratified or poorly ratified treaty. Whether a treaty changes the customary law will still depend on how far it influences the practice of non-party States, rather than on its binding force.

---

[69] The USSR had from the start argued in favour of a treaty; Cheng, 1965, at p 31 surmises that it agreed to the adoption of a resolution out of concern that any treaty might be vetoed by the US Senate.

[70] UNGA Res 44/225, 22 December 1989 and UNGA Res 46/215, 20 December 1991 on Large Scale Pelagic Driftnet Fishing, and other instruments collected in FAO, *Legislative Study 47: The Regulation of Driftnet Fishing on the High Seas* (Rome, 1991). See Kaye, 2001, pp 188–94.

[71] *Western Sahara, Advisory Opinion, ICJ Reports 1975*, p 12; *East Timor (Portugal v Australia) Judgment, ICJ Reports 1995*, p 90.

VI. TREATIES AS SOFT LAW

An alternative view of soft law focuses not on its non-binding character but on the contrast between 'rules', involving clear and reasonably specific commitments which are in this sense hard law (eg 'No State may validly purport to subject any part of the high seas to its sovereignty') and 'norms' or 'principles', which, being more open-textured or general in their content and wording, can thus be seen as soft, even when contained in a binding treaty.

The point was made many years ago by the late Judge Baxter that some treaties are soft in the sense that they impose no real obligations on the parties (Baxter, 1980). Here it is the *formulation* of the provision which is decisive in determining whether it is hard or soft, not its form as a treaty or binding instrument. Though formally binding, the vagueness, indeterminacy, or generality of their provisions may deprive them of the character of 'hard law' in any meaningful sense. The 1992 Framework Convention on Climate Change provides a good example. Adopted by consensus at the Rio Conference, this treaty imposes some commitments on the parties, but its core articles, dealing with policies and measures to tackle greenhouse gas emissions, are so cautiously and obscurely worded and so weak that it is doubtful whether any real obligations are created.[72] Moreover, whatever commitments have been undertaken by developing States are also conditional on performance of commitments by developed State parties to provide funding and transfer of technology.[73] The hard content for this framework agreement is provided by the subsequent protocol agreed at Kyoto in 1997.

Such treaty provisions are almost impossible to breach and in that limited sense Judge Baxter is justified in calling them soft law. More of a political bargain than a legal one, these are 'soft' undertakings of a very fragile kind.[74] They are not normative and cannot be described as creating law in any meaningful sense. This is probably true of many treaties, a point recognized by the International Court in the *North Sea Continental Shelf* case when it specified that one of the conditions to be met before a treaty could be regarded as lawmaking is that it should be so drafted as to be 'potentially normative' in character.[75] But that begs an obvious question: what do we mean by 'potentially normative'? A treaty does not have to set out 'rules' or 'obligations' to have normative effect: it may also be drafted in the form of 'principles' by which the parties have agreed to be guided.

The Convention on Climate Change once again provides a good example. Indeed, given how weak the rest of the treaty is, the 'principles' found in Article 3 are arguably the most important 'law' in the whole agreement because they prescribe how the regime for regulating climate change is to be developed by the parties. It is worth quoting the main elements of this provision:

Article 3: Principles
    In their actions to achieve the objective of the Convention and to implement its provisions, the parties shall be guided, *inter alia*, by the following:

1. The Parties should protect the climate system for the benefit of present and future generations of humankind . . . on the basis of equity and in accordance with their common but differentiated responsibilities . . .

---

[72] Especially Articles 4(1) and (2). The United States' interpretation of these Articles was that 'there is nothing in any of the language which constitutes a commitment to any specific level of emissions at any time . . .' The parties determined at their first meeting in 1995 that the commitments were inadequate and they agreed to commence negotiation of the much more specific commitments now contained in the 1997 Kyoto Protocol.   [73] Article 4(7).
[74] See also the 2015 Paris Agreement and Bodansky, 2016, p 306; Rajamani, 2016, p 337.
[75] *North Sea Continental Shelf, Judgment, ICJ Reports 1969*, p 3, para 72.

2. The Parties should take precautionary measures to anticipate, prevent, or minimise the causes of climate change and mitigate its adverse effects . . .

3. The Parties have a right to, and should, promote sustainable development . . .

These elements of Article 3 are all drawn directly from the non-binding Rio Declaration on Environment and Development; they reflect principles which are not simply part of the Climate Change Convention, but which have been more widely endorsed and applied by States. They are not expressed in obligatory terms: the use of 'should' qualifies their application, despite the obligatory wording of the chapeau sentence. All of these principles are open-textured in the sense that there is content is undefined and they leave much room for interpretation and elaboration. They are not at all like rules requiring States to conduct an environmental impact assessment, or to take measures to prevent harm to other States.

Given their explicit role as guidance and their softer formulation, the 'principles' in Article 3 are not necessarily binding rules which must be complied with or which entail responsibility for breach if not complied with; yet, despite all these limitations they are not legally insignificant.[76] At the very least Article 3 is relevant to interpretation and implementation of the Convention as well as creating expectations concerning matters which must be taken into account in good faith in the negotiation of further instruments.

Article 3 takes a novel approach to environmental protection, but in the context of a dynamic and evolutionary regulatory regime such as the Climate Change Convention it has the important merit of providing some predictability regarding the parameters within which the parties are required to work towards the objective of the Convention. In particular, they are not faced with a completely blank sheet of paper when entering subsequent protocol negotiations or when the Conference of the Parties takes decisions under the various articles empowering it to do so. Thus it is significant that the relevance of Article 3 was reiterated in the mandate for negotiation of the Kyoto Protocol,[77] and is referred to in the preamble to the Protocol. It is a nice question whether the parties collectively are entitled to disregard the principles contained in Article 3, or what the legal effect of decisions which do so may be,[78] but however weak it may seem, parties whose interests are affected do have a right to insist on having the principles of Article 3 taken into account (Rajamani, 2012). As we shall see in the following section, sustainable development, intergenerational equity, or the precautionary principle, are all more convincingly seen in this sense: not as binding obligations which must be complied with, but as principles, considerations, or objectives to be taken account of—their wording may be soft, but they are still law.

VII. SOFT LAW GENERAL PRINCIPLES

The idea that general norms or principles can affect the way courts decide cases or the exercise of discretionary powers by an international organization is not confined to treaty regimes. Indeed, in modern international relations such general norms or principles are probably more often found in non-binding declarations or resolutions of international organizations than in the provisions of multilateral treaties. The Universal Declaration of Human Rights remains one of the most influential examples of soft law of this kind (see earlier). International courts have of course always had the power under Article 38(1)(c) of

---

[76] See the debate between Sands and Mann in Lang, 1995, pp 53–74.

[77] The so-called 'Berlin mandate': Decision 1/CP.1, in *Report of the Conference of the Parties on its 1st Session*, UN Doc FCCC/CP/1995/7/Add.1.

[78] Arguably the principle of common but differentiated responsibility has been departed from in the 2015 Paris Agreement. But the Paris Agreement is itself a treaty, and as such can override or depart from the UN Framework Convention.

the ICJ Statute to refer to general principles of law. In most cases this entails borrowing by analogy from common elements of national law, such as non-discrimination or the right to a fair hearing.[79] In essence, resort to general principles of this kind is judge-made law.

However, it is also possible for States to adopt general principles not derived from national law, with the intention that courts and States should apply them when relevant. Such general principles do not have to create rules of customary law to have legal effect. Rather, their importance derives principally from the influence they can exert on the interpretation, application, and development of other rules of law. As we saw earlier, Article 31(3) of the 1969 Vienna Convention on the Law of Treaties requires subsequent agreements, practices, and rules of international law to be taken into account when interpreting a treaty (McLachlan, 2005; Boyle, 2005, pp 572–4). This provision appears to include reference to general principles as an aid to treaty interpretation.[80] If that is correct, soft law declarations such as the 1992 Rio Declaration on Environment and Development or the 1948 Universal Declaration of Human Rights will have to be taken into account insofar as they articulate general principles agreed by consensus. The point is not confined to treaty interpretation, however. A general principle of this kind may also influence the interpretation and application of customary law.

The precautionary approach (or principle) endorsed by consensus in Principle 15 of the 1992 Rio Declaration on Environment and Development is a case in point. The precautionary approach is a common feature of almost all the Rio and post-Rio global environmental agreements. Principle 15 of the Rio Declaration provides as follows:

> *Principle 15*: In order to protect the environment, the precautionary approach shall be widely applied by states according to their capabilities. Where there are threats of serious or irreversible damage, lack of full scientific certainty shall not be used as a reason for postponing cost-effective measures to prevent environmental degradation.

Its purpose is thus to make greater allowance for uncertainty in the regulation of environmental risks and the sustainable use of natural resources.

Some writers and governments have argued that the precautionary principle or approach is a rule of customary international law, but international courts and most governments have been noticeably hesitant to accept this characterization.[81] If, alternatively, the precautionary principle is viewed simply as a general principle of law, on which decision-makers and courts may rely when deciding cases and interpreting treaties, then its subsequent use by national and international courts and by international organizations is easier to explain. In the *Pulp Mills* case both parties relied on the 'precautionary approach' primarily as a general principle whose significance lay in its impact on the interpretation and application of the 1975 Statute of the River Uruguay. The Court accepted that 'a precautionary approach may be relevant to the interpretation and application of the provisions of the Statute,'[82] but it is also relevant to interpretation and application of existing rules of customary international law. Thus, as Brownlie observes, 'The point which stands out is that some applications of the principle,

---

[79] *S.W. Africa Case, ICJ Reports 1966*, pp 294–301 (Judge Tanaka); *Golder v UK, ECtHR 1975, Ser A, No 18*, paras 10–36, but cf Dissenting Opinion of Judge Fitzmaurice, paras 18–46 and 48 and see generally Cassese, 1986, pp 170–4; Cheng, 1953; Friedmann, 1963.

[80] Thus in *Golder* the ECtHR referred to access to a court as a 'general principle of law' when interpreting Article 6 of the European Convention on Human Rights. Note, however, that general principles cannot override or amend the express terms of a treaty: see *Beef Hormones Case* (1998) WTO Appellate Body, paras 124–5.

[81] See, eg, *Beef Hormones Case (1998) WTO Appellate Body*, paras 120–5; *Southern Bluefin Tuna cases (Provisional Measures) (1999) ITLOS Nos 3 & 4*, paras 77–9; *Pulp Mills on the River Uruguay, Merits, Judgment, ICJ Reports 2010*, p 51, para 164. Compare *Advisory Opinion on Responsibilities and Obligations of States Sponsoring Persons and Entities with Respect to Activities in the Area, ITLOS Seabed Disputes Chamber 2011*, para 131.

[82] *ICJ Reports 2010*, p 51, para 164. See also *Responsibilities and Obligations of States Sponsoring Persons and Entities with Respect to Activities in the Area, Advisory Opinion, ITLOS Reports 2011*, p 10, para 131.

which is based on the concept of foreseeable risk to other states, are encompassed within existing concepts of state responsibility' (Brownlie, 2003, p 276). The ILC special rapporteur on transboundary harm has taken the same view, concluding that the precautionary principle is already a component of customary rules on prevention of harm and environmental impact assessment, 'and could not be divorced therefrom'.[83]

Much the same could be said of sustainable development, on which the parties in *Pulp Mills* also relied. Lowe (1999, p 31) makes the essential point with great clarity:

> Sustainable development can properly claim a normative status as an element of the process of judicial reasoning. It is a meta-principle, acting upon other rules and principles—a legal concept exercising a kind of interstitial normativity, pushing and pulling the boundaries of true primary norms when they threaten to overlap or conflict with each other.

In the case law sustainable development thus becomes a mediating principle between the right to development and the duty to control sources of environmental harm.[84] Modifying norms or principles need not impose obligations or regulate conduct, they do not depend on State practice, and they do not need the same clarity or precision as rules. What gives general principles of this kind their authority and legitimacy is simply the endorsement of States—*opinio juris* in other words.[85]

Such principles have legal significance in much the same way that Dworkin uses the idea of constitutional principles.[86] They lay down parameters which affect the way courts decide cases or how an international institution exercises its discretionary powers. They can set limits, or provide guidance, or determine how conflicts between other rules or principles will be resolved. They may lack the supposedly harder edge of a 'rule' or 'obligation', but they should not be confused with 'non-binding' or emerging law. That is perhaps the most important lesson to be drawn from the ICJ's references to sustainable development in the *Gabčíkovo-Nagymaros Dam* and *Pulp Mills* cases.[87] Even if sustainable development is not in the nature of a legal obligation, it does represent a policy goal or principle that can influence the outcome of litigation and the practice of States and international organizations, and it may lead to significant changes and developments in the existing law.[88]

These examples show that subtle changes in the existing law and in existing treaties may come about through reliance on such general principles. In any system of law the ability to make changes on a systemic basis is important. How else could this be done in international law? New *rules* of customary law are not appropriate to the elaboration of general principles of this kind and could not be created quickly enough; moreover, a treaty endorsing the precautionary principle or sustainable development would only bind the parties. A binding resolution of the UNSC may be a possible option, but only where questions of international peace and security are at stake. Thus the consensus endorsement by States of a general principle enshrined in a soft law declaration is an entirely sensible solution to such law-making challenges.

---

[83] Report of the ILC, Fifty-Second Session, A/55/10, para 716.

[84] See the ICJ's references to sustainable development in the *Gabčíkovo-Nagymaros Dam Case, ICJ Reports 1997*, p 7, para 140; *Pulp Mills on the River Uruguay Case (Interim Measures), ICJ Reports 2006*, p 113, para 80; *Pulp Mills on the River Uruguay Case (Merits), ICJ Reports 2010*, p 14, paras 177 and 184, and see Barrall, 2012, p 377.

[85] Lowe, 1999, p 33, dispenses even with *opinio juris*, but unless such norms emerge from thin air at the whim of judges the endorsement of States must be a necessary element. All the norms Lowe relies on do in fact have such endorsement.   [86] Dworkin, 1977. This argument is developed by Sands, 1995.

[87] See n 84.

[88] See for example the inclusion of provisions on sustainable use or sustainable development in the 1994 WTO Agreement, the 1995 UN Fish Stocks Agreement, and the 1997 UN Convention on International Watercourses.

VIII. CONCLUSIONS

Soft law is manifestly a multi-faceted concept, whose relationship to treaties, custom, and general principles of law is both subtle and diverse. At its simplest, soft law facilitates progressive evolution of customary international law. It presents alternatives to law-making by treaty in certain circumstances; at other times it complements treaties, while also providing different ways of understanding the legal effect of different kinds of treaty. Those who maintain that soft law is not law have perhaps missed some of the points made here; moreover those who see a treaty as necessarily having greater legal effect than soft law have perhaps not looked hard enough at the 'infinite variety' of treaties, to quote Baxter once more. Soft law has generally been more helpful to the process of international law-making than it has been objectionable, and that is the key point. It is inconceivable that modern treaty regimes or international organizations could function successfully without resort to soft law. Nor is it likely that the ICJ will take a different view, given the way soft law is used by parties to international litigation to legitimize their legal arguments.

In the *Pulp Mills* case, for example, Argentina and Uruguay relied, inter alia, on the 1992 Rio Declaration on Environment and Development, UNEP's 1987 Goals and Principles of Environmental Impact Assessment, and the ILC's 2002 Draft Articles on Prevention of Transboundary Harm.[89] Given the outcome of the case, they were not wrong to do so. In the absence of hard law, litigators will inevitably turn to whatever best supports their case, even if it is soft law.

REFERENCES

ABBOTT, K, and SNIDAL, D (2000), 'Hard and Soft Law in International Governance' 54 *International Organisation* 421.

ALVAREZ, J (2005), *International Organizations as Law-Makers* (Oxford: Oxford University Press), pp 597–600.

AUST, A (1986), 'The Theory and Practice of Informal International Instruments', 35 *ICLQ* 787.

BARRALL, V (2012), 'Sustainable Development in International Law: Nature and Operation of an Evolutive Legal Norm', 23 *EJIL* 377.

BARELLI, M (2009), 'The Role of Soft Law in the International Legal System', 58 *ICLQ* 957.

BAXTER, RR (1980), 'International Law in 'Her Infinite Variety', 29 *ICLQ* 549.

BODANSKY, D (2016) 'The Paris Climate Change Agreement: A New Hope?' 110 *AJIL* 306.

BOYLE, AE (2005) 'Further Development of the Law of the Sea Convention: Mechanisms for Change', 54 *ICLQ* 563.

BOYLE, AE (2018) 'The Choice of a Treaty: Interaction between Hard Law and Soft Law in United Nations Law-Making', in D Malone, S Chesterman, and S Villalpando (eds) *Oxford Handbook of UN Treaties* (Oxford: Oxford University Press).

Boyle, AE, and Freestone, D (eds) (1999) *International Law and Sustainable Development: Past Achievements and Future Prospects* (Oxford: Oxford University Press).

BOYLE, AE, and REDGWELL, C (2018) *International Law and the Environment* (4th edn, Oxford: Oxford University Press).

---

[89] The Court noted that the UNEP Goals and Principles, UNGA Res 42/184 (1987) constitute guidance issued by an 'international technical body' and therefore have to be taken into account under Article 41 of the Statute of the River Uruguay. See *ICJ Reports 2010*, p 61, para 205. Except when noting the submissions of the parties the Court made no specific reference to the ILC Draft Articles or to the Rio Declaration, but its judgment affirms the legal status of the relevant provisions of both texts.

BROWNLIE, I (1979) 'The Legal Status of Natural Resources', 162 *Recueil des Cours* 245.

BROWNLIE, I (1991) *Basic Documents on International Law* (3rd edn, Oxford: Oxford University Press).

BROWNLIE, I (2003) *Principles of Public International Law* (6th edn, Oxford: Oxford University Press).

BURCI, GL, and VIGNES, C-H (2004) *WHO* (The Hague: Kluwer), pp 124–55.

CASSESE, A (1986) *International Law in a Divided World* (Oxford: Oxford University Press).

CHENG, B (1965) 'United Nations Resolutions on Outer Space: 'Instant' Customary Law?' 5 *Indian J Int L* 23–48 (reprinted in B Cheng (ed) (1982) *International Law Teaching and Practice* (London: Stevens), p 237).

CHINKIN, CM (1989) 'The Challenge of Soft Law: Development and Change in International Law', 38 *ICLQ* 850.

CHURCHILL, RR, and LOWE, AV (1999) *The Law of the Sea* (3rd edn, Manchester: Manchester University Press).

CONTINI, P, and SAND, P (1972) 'Methods to Expedite Environment Protection: International Ecostandards' 66 *AJIL* 37.

CRAWFORD, J (2002) *The International Law Commission's Articles on State Responsibility* (Cambridge: Cambridge University Press).

CRAWFORD, J, and OLLESON, S (2005) 'The Continuing Debate on a UN Convention on State Responsibility', 54 *ICLQ* 959.

D'ASPREMONT, J (2008), 'Softness in International Law: A Self-Serving Quest for New Materials' 19 *EJIL* 1075.

D'ASPREMONT, J (2011), *Formalism and the Sources of International Law* (Oxford: Oxford University Press).

DUPUY, P-M (1991) 'Soft Law and the International Law of the Environment' 12 Michigan *JIL* 420.

DWORKIN, R (1977) *Taking Rights Seriously* (London: Duckworth).

EDESON, W (1999) in Boyle and Freestone, *International Law and Sustainable Development*, 165.

EDESON, W (2003) 'Soft and Hard Law Aspects of Fisheries Issues', in M Nordquist, G Moore, and S Mahmoudi (eds) *The Stockholm Declaration and Law of the Marine Environment* (The Hague: Nijhoff), p 165.

FAO (1991) *The Regulation of Driftnet Fishing on the High Seas: Legal Issues* (Rome: FAOC).

FASTENRATH, U (1993) 'Relative Normativity in International Law', 4 *EJIL* 305

FIDLER, S (1998) 'The Future of the WHO: What Role for International Law?' 32 *Vand JTL* 1079.

FRIEDMANN, W (1963) 'The Uses of General Principles in the Development of International Law', 57 *AJIL* 279.

HANNUM, H (1995–6) 'The Status of the Universal Declaration of Human Rights in National and International Law' 25 Georgia J Int & *Comp L* 287.

HILLGENBERG, H (1999) 'A Fresh Look at Soft Law', 10 *EJIL* 499.

Joyner, C (ed) (1997) *The United Nations and International Law* (Cambridge: Cambridge University Press)

KAYE, S (2001) *International Fisheries Management* (The Hague: Kluwer Law International).

KLABBERS, J (1996) 'The Redundancy of Soft Law', 65 Nordic *JIL* 167.

KOSKENNIEMI, M (1992) 'Breach of Treaty or Non-Compliance? Reflections on the Enforcement of the Montreal Protocol' 3 *YbIEL* 123.

KOSKENNIEMI, M (2001) 'Solidarity Measures: State Responsibility as a New International Order', 72 *BYbIL* 341.

KOSKENNIEMI, M (2009) 'The Politics of International Law', 20 *EJIL* 7.

Lang, W (ed.) (1995) *Sustainable Development and International Law* (The Hague: Kluwer Law International).

LOWE, AV (1999) 'Sustainable Development and Unsustainable Arguments' in Boyle and Freestone, *International Law and Sustainable Development*, p 18.

McDorman, T (2004) 'Access to Information under Article 9 of the OSPAR Convention' 98 *AJIL* 330.

McLachlan, C (2005) 'The Principle of Systemic Integration and Article 31(3)(c) of the Vienna Convention', 54 *ICLQ* 279.

Meron, T (1991) *Human Rights and Humanitarian Norms as Customary Law* (Oxford: Oxford University Press).

Moore, G (1999) 'The Code of Conduct for Responsible Fisheries', in E Hey (ed) *Developments in International Fisheries Law* (The Hague: Nijhoff), p 85.

Neuhold, HP, (2010) 'The Inadequacy of Law-Making by International Treaties: 'Soft Law' as an Alternative?' in R Wolfrum and V Roben (eds) *Developments of International Law in Treaty Making* (Berlin: Springer-Verlag GmbH & Co.), p 50.

Rajamani, L (2012) 'The Durban Platform for Enhanced Action and the Future of the Climate Regime', 61 *ICLQ* 501.

Rajamani, L (2016) 'The 2015 Paris Agreement: Interplay Between Hard, Soft and Non-Obligations' 28 *J Env L* 337.

Rose, C (2012) 'The UK Bribery Act 2010 and Accompanying Guidance', 61 *ICLQ* 485.

Sands, P (1995) 'International Law in the Field of Sustainable Development', in Lang, *Sustainable Development*, p 53.

Schachter, O (1977), 'The Twilight Existence of Non-Binding International Agreements', 71 *AJIL* 296.

Sohn, L (1982), 'The New International Law: Protection of the Rights of Individuals Rather than States', 32 *Am ULR* 1

Sztucki, J (1990), 'Reflections on International 'Soft Law', in J Ramberg et al (eds) *Festskrift till Lars Hjerner: Studies in International Law* (Stockholm: Norstedts), p 549.

Viñuales, J (ed) (2015), *The Rio Declaration on Environment and Development: A Commentary* (Oxford: Oxford University Press).

Virally, M (1956) 'Valeur juridique des recommandations' Annuaire Français de Droit International 66–99.

Watts, AD (ed) (1999) *The International Law Commission, vol II* (Oxford: Oxford University Press), p 689.

Weil, P (1983) 'Towards Relative Normativity in International Law', 77 *AJIL* 411.

FURTHER READING

Baxter, RR (1980), 'International Law in 'Her Infinite Variety', 29 *ICLQ* 549: a classic account of the diversity of treaties and their legal effect.

Charney, J (1993), 'Universal International Law', 87 *AJIL* 529: one of the best analyses of the evolution of general international law through soft law, although it does not use the term.

Cheng, B (1983), 'Custom: The Future of General State Practice in a Divided World', in RStJ Macdonald and DM Johnston (eds) *The Structure and Process of International Law* (Dordrecht: Martinus Nijhoff), pp 513–54: a sceptical treatment of the idea that General Assembly resolutions can be instant customary international law.

Chinkin, CM (1989), 'The Challenge of Soft Law: Development and Change in International Law', 38 *ICLQ* 850: remains one of the best discussions of the subject.

Sloan, B (1987), 'General Assembly Resolutions Revisited', 58 *BYBIL* 39: the classic account of the legal effect of UN General Assembly resolutions, but now dated.

6

THE PRACTICAL WORKING OF THE LAW OF TREATIES

Malgosia Fitzmaurice

SUMMARY

This chapter considers key structural questions and fundamental problems relating to the law of treaties. The structural matters considered include the concept of a treaty; the anatomy of treaties (including the making of treaties; authority to conclude treaties; expression of consent to be bound; invalidity of treaties (non-absolute grounds for invalidity of treaties, absolute grounds for invalidity of treaties, amendment and modification); suspension and termination).

The key issues addressed include the scope of legal obligation (the principle *pacta sunt servanda*, treaties, and third States); interpretation and reservation to treaties (including interpretative declarations); and finally, problems concerning the grounds for termination (such as supervening impossibility and material breach) and fundamental change of circumstances (*rebus sic stantibus*). The chapter takes into consideration the theory and practice of the law of treaties, with an extensive analysis of the relevant case law of various international courts and tribunals, placing special emphasis on the jurisprudence of the International Court of Justice (ICJ).

I. INTRODUCTION

Treaties are one of the means through which States deal with each other and a precise method of regulating relations between States. Treaties almost exclusively regulate some areas of international law, such as environmental law, while they are of the utmost importance in others, such as international economic relations, and play a decisive role in the field of human rights. International trade and international investments as well as international communication are unimaginable without treaties. Thus knowledge of the law of treaties is essential to an understanding of how international relations and international law work. That law is codified in the 1969 Vienna Convention on the Law of Treaties (the VCLT), the provisions of which will be presented and analysed in this chapter.

II. BASIC CONCEPTS AND STRUCTURES

A. WHAT IS A TREATY?

VCLT Article 2(2) defines a treaty as '[a]n international agreement concluded between States in written form and governed by international law, whether embodied in a single instrument or in two or more related instruments and whatever its particular designation'.

The term 'treaty' is used generically (Aust, 2013, p 10) and a treaty may be described in a multitude of ways. The International Law Commission (ILC) said:

> In addition to a 'treaty', 'convention', and 'protocol', one not infrequently finds titles such as 'declaration', 'charter', 'covenant', 'pact', 'act', 'statute', 'agreement', 'concordat', whilst names like 'declaration', 'agreement', and 'modus vivendi' may well be found given both to formal and less formal types of agreements. As to the latter, their nomenclature is almost illimitable, even if some names such as 'agreement', 'exchange of notes', 'exchange of letters', 'memorandum of agreement', or 'agreed minute', may be more common than others . . . there is no exclusive or systematic use of nomenclature for particular types of transaction.[1]

The question 'what is a treaty?' is one of the most vexing legal issues in the law of treaties. Usually this question appears in litigating of cases, mostly before international courts and tribunals; national courts have also dealt with this matter. There is a great variety of case law concerning this subject matter and it is almost impossible to draw some definitive conclusions. One of the most difficult and unresolved problems is the question of the intention of parties in relation to the bindingness of an instrument, ie whether it is a treaty or not. The Vienna Convention does not require that a treaty be in any particular form or comprise any particular elements, so if there is a dispute concerning the status of a document—eg a joint communiqué—as a treaty, an objective test is used to determine the question, taking into account its actual terms and the particular circumstances in which it was made. For example, minutes of a meeting can comprise a treaty. In the *Qatar* v *Bahrain* case the International Court of Justice (ICJ) said:

> The Court does not find it necessary to consider what might have been the intentions of the Foreign Minister of Bahrain or, for that matter those of the Foreign Minister of Qatar. The two ministers signed a text recording commitment accepted by their Governments, some of which were to be given an immediate application. Having signed such a text, the Foreign Minister of Bahrain is not in the position subsequently to say that he intended to subscribe only to a 'statement recording political understanding', and not to an 'international agreement'.[2]

---

[1] *YBILC* (1966), vol II (part two), p 188. See also in *Customs Régime between Germany and Austria (Protocol of 19 March 1931), Advisory Opinion, 1931, Ser A/B, No 41*, p 47 where the Court stated: '. . . it is well known that such engagements may be taken in the form of treaties, conventions, declarations, agreements, protocols, or exchanges of notes', p 47). See also *Ahmad and Aswat* v *Government of the United States of America* [2006] EWHC 2927 (Admin), para 76, where Diplomatic Notes issued by the US government were found to be binding.

[2] *Maritime Delimitation and Territorial Questions between Qatar and Bahrain, Jurisdiction and Admissibility, Judgment, ICJ Reports 1994*, p 112, para 27. See also *Land and Maritime Boundary between Cameroon and Nigeria (Cameroon v Nigeria; Equatorial Guinea Intervening), Judgment, ICJ Reports 2002*, p 303 in which the Court analysed two documents: the 1975 Maroua Declaration and the 1971 Youndé II Declaration. On the basis of the manner in which these Declarations were concluded (signed by the Heads of Cameroon and Nigeria), the Court stated as follows: '[t]he Court considers that the Maroua Declaration constitutes an international agreement concluded between States in written form and tracing a boundary; it is thus governed by international law and constitutes a treaty in the sense of the Vienna Convention on the Law of Treaties . . . and which in any case reflects customary international law in this respect' (para 263).

The question of the variety of forms was also considered by the Arbitral Tribunal in the 2015 *Philippines* v *China Award (Award on Jurisdiction and Admissibility)*.[3] The Tribunal acknowledged that a treaty may assume a variety of forms and that the form is not decisive of its status as an agreement establishing legal obligations between the parties (para 214). The difficulty (if not impossibility) of formulating a firm definition of a treaty, and consequently the reliance on the frequently inconsistent pronouncements of international courts and tribunals, contributes to uncertainty for States regarding international obligations. Such a situation is exemplified by the recent Judgment of the International Tribunal for the Law of the Sea (ITLOS) in the *Bangladesh/Myanmar* case,[4] where the legal character of minutes was again at issue. In this case, the ITLOS, having examined the two sets of Agreed Minutes in question, proceeded in an entirely different manner from the ICJ and reached the opposite conclusion. There are fundamental differences in reasoning relating to essentially very similar sets of documents. The ICJ was firmly of the view that the Agreed Minutes in question created rights and obligations for States and thus constituted an international agreement. The ITLOS, on the other hand, having analysed two sets of fairly detailed and precise Agreed Minutes (dating from 1974 and 2008), was of the view they were nothing more than a record of two meetings. Such disparities in decisions regarding very similar cases must cause uncertainty and tension in inter-State relations.

Another fundamental difference between the findings relates to the question of the intention of the parties. In the *Qatar* v *Bahrain* case the ICJ was adamant that the intentions of States as to the nature of an instrument were of no interest to the Court, which based its decision entirely on the objective text of the document before it.

The ITLOS, however, took a different stand on this matter. It said:

> From the beginning of the discussions Myanmar made it clear that it did not intend to enter into a separate agreement on the delimitation of territorial sea and that it wanted a comprehensive agreement covering the territorial sea, the exclusive economic zone and the continental shelf.[5]

Similarly, the Arbitral Tribunal in the *Philippines* v *China* case stressed the importance of the intention of the parties to establish rights and obligations, pointing out that, '[t]o constitute a binding agreement, an instrument must evince a clear intention to establish rights and obligations between the parties. Such clear intention is determined by reference to the instrument's actual terms and the particular circumstances of its adoption. The subsequent conduct of the parties to an instrument may also assist in determining its nature.'[6]

The ITLOS in the *Bangladesh/Myanmar* case also stressed that the fact that both parties had not submitted the Agreed Minutes to their domestic constitutional procedures in regard to the conclusion of treaties was an indication that the Agreed Minutes were not to be considered as legally binding.[7] According to VCLT Article 46, however, a State may not invoke the fact that its consent to be bound by a treaty has been expressed in violation of a provision of its internal law regarding competence to conclude treaties as invalidating

---

[3] *Philippines* v *China Award (Award on Jurisdiction and Admissibility)* Award of 1 October 2015, *PCA Case No 2013–19*.

[4] *Delimitation of the Maritime Boundary in the Bay of Bengal (Bangladesh/Myanmar)*, Judgment, *ITLOS Reports 2012*, p 12.

[5] Ibid, para 92.

[6] *Philippines* v *China Award (Award on Jurisdiction and Admissibility)* Award of 1 October 2015, *PCA Case No 2013–19*, para 213.

[7] *Delimitation of the Maritime Boundary in the Bay of Bengal (Bangladesh/Myanmar)*, Judgment, *ITLOS Reports 2012*, p 12, para 97.

its consent unless that violation was manifest and concerned a rule of its internal law of fundamental importance. This was confirmed by the ICJ in the *Cameroon v Nigeria* case.[8] Again, there seems to be a difference of approach between the ICJ and ITLOS on this point.

The issue of what a treaty is was also considered by the ICJ in the 2017 *Maritime Delimitation in the Indian Ocean (Somalia v Kenya) (Preliminary Objections)* case, where the question of the legal status of the Memorandum of Understanding (MOU) arose. The Minister for Foreign Affairs of the Government of Kenya and the Minister for National Planning and International Cooperation of the Transitional Federal Government of Somalia signed a 'Memorandum of Understanding between the Government of the Republic of Kenya and the Transitional Federal Government of the Somali Republic to grant to each other No Objection in respect of submissions on the Outer Limits of the Continental Shelf beyond 200 Nautical Miles to the Commission on the Limits of the Continental Shelf'. This MOU was registered with the Secretary-General of the United Nations according to Article 102 of the United Nations Charter. The Court stated that the MOU is a written document, in which Somalia and Kenya recorded their agreement on certain points governed by international law.[9] It first analysed the power of the Somalian Minister to enter into an agreement and whether the signature could be a final expression of consent to be bound. Relying on the full powers of the Minister and the clear statement in the MOU ('this Memorandum of Understanding shall enter into force upon its signature'), the Court concluded that the Minister had the power to bind the State upon the signature and did not require ratification as provided for by Somalian law (relying on the *Cameroon/Nigeria* case). However, having interpreted the substantive provisions of the MOU (its object and purpose and in particular its sixth paragraph) in accordance with Articles 31 and 32 of the VCLT, the Court decided that the MOU was not intended to establish a procedure for the settlement of the maritime boundary dispute between the parties:

> The Court has concluded that the sixth paragraph of the MOU, read in its context and in light of the object and purpose of the MOU, sets out the expectation of the Parties that an agreement would be reached on the delimitation of their continental shelf after receipt of the CLCS's recommendations. It does not, however, prescribe a method of dispute settlement. The MOU does not, therefore, constitute an agreement 'to have recourse to some other method or methods of settlement' within the meaning of Kenya's reservation to its Article 36, paragraph 2, declaration, and consequently this case does not, by virtue of the MOU, fall outside the scope of Kenya's consent to the Court's jurisdiction.[10]

The question of creating legally binding obligations through a communication alleged to be an international agreement has also arisen in relation to the Communication of 16 March 2016 to the European Parliament, the European Council, and the Council entitled 'Next operational steps in EU-Turkey cooperation in the field of migration' ('the communication of 16 March 2016'). The European Commission stated that, on 7 March 2016, the '[European Union] leaders [had] warmly welcomed the additional proposals made by [the Republic of] Turkey and [had] agreed to work with Turkey on the basis of a set of six principles', that 'the President of the European Council [had been] requested to take forward these proposals and work out the details with Turkey before the March European Council', and that 'this Communication [set] out how the six principles should be taken forward, delivering on

---

[8] *Land and Maritime Boundary between Cameroon and Nigeria (Cameroon v Nigeria: Equatorial Guinea Intervening), Judgment, ICJ Reports 2002,* p 303, para 265.

[9] *Maritime Delimitation in the Indian Ocean (Somalia v Kenya), Preliminary Objections, 2 February 2017, nyr,* para 42.

[10] *Maritime Delimitation in the Indian Ocean (Somalia v Kenya), Preliminary Objections, 2 February 2017, nyr,* paras 105–6.

the full potential for [European Union]-[Republic of] Turkey cooperation while respecting European and international law'.[11] The communiqué was alleged to be a treaty within the meaning of Article 2 of the 1969 VCLT and of Article 218 of the Treaty on the Functioning of the European Union (TFEU). The European Council argued, *inter alia*, 'that, to the best of its knowledge, no agreement or treaty in the sense of Article 218 TFEU or Article 2(1)(a) of the Vienna Convention on the law of treaties of 23 May 1969 had been concluded between the European Union and the Republic of Turkey' and that the EU-Turkey statement, published by means of Press Release No 144/16, was merely 'the fruit of an international dialogue be-tween the Member States and [the Republic of] Turkey and—in the light of its content and of the intention of its authors—[was] not intended to produce legally binding effects nor con-stitute an agreement or a treaty' (para 27). The Court agreed that, not having been concluded by the European Council, the communiqué was not an international treaty between the EU and Turkey (para 46). The Court considered the expression 'Members of the European Council' and the term 'EU', contained in the EU-Turkey statement published in Press Release No 144/16, referred to the Heads of State or Government of the European Union, not the European Council (para 69), and so was not 'a measure adopted by the European Council, or, moreover, by any other institution, body, office or agency of the European Union, or as revealing the existence of such a measure that corresponds to the contested measure'. Even if an international agreement had arisen from the meeting, it would have been between 'the Heads of State or Government of the Member States of the European Union and the Turkish Prime Minister', not the EU and Turkey (paras 71 and 72).

Since a treaty is a method of creating binding legal obligations, there must also be an intention to create legal relations. The Rapporteur of the ILC stated that the element is implicitly present in the phrase 'governed by international law'.[12] There are some interna-tional acts that may assume the form of international agreements but which were never in-tended to create legal obligations, such as the 1975 Final Act of the Conference on Security and Cooperation in Europe.[13]

Such Acts are sometimes called 'soft law'[14] and their legal status is not clear. However, as they are not legally binding, they are not enforceable in the courts. They cannot be ignored, however, since soft law may 'harden' into a treaty[15] or become a norm of interna-tional customary law. Some authors see 'soft law' as a more flexible alternative to treaty-making (Boyle, 2000) though others consider the whole concept misconceived, both in that if it is not binding, it is not law, and that it creates an expectation of compliance while simultaneously undermining the authority of law (Weil, 1983).

Finally, in the *Nuclear Test* cases,[16] the ICJ made it clear that unilateral statements of States can have binding effect if the intention that they be legally binding is clear; that there is clear evidence regarding the circumstances in which they are made; and that the

---

[11] *NF v Council*, Case T-192/16, 28 February 2017. http://curia.europa.eu/juris/document/document.jsf?te xt=&docid=188483&pageIndex=0&doclang=en&mode=lst&dir=&occ=first&part=1&cid=426840.

[12] Fourth Report on the Law Treaties, *YBILC* (1965), vol II, p 12.

[13] The Act stated that it was not eligible for registration under UN Charter Article 102 and was generally understood not to have binding force. The failure to register a treaty under UN Charter Article 102 does not mean that the instrument in question is not a treaty, whilst the act of registration does not mean that it is. For example, the 1957 Declaration by Egypt concerning the nationalization of the Suez Canal was registered by the Egyptian government but was not a treaty.

[14] Other examples include the 1972 Stockholm Declaration on Human Environment and the 1992 Rio Declaration on Environment and Development. On soft law generally, see Ch 5 of this book.

[15] Eg the 1988 Baltic Sea Ministerial Declaration and the 1992 Baltic Sea Declaration hardened into the 1992 Convention on the Protection of the Baltic Sea and the Baltic Sea Area ('The Helsinki Convention').

[16] *Nuclear Tests (Australia v France), Judgment, ICJ Reports 1974*, p 253, paras 42–3. The need for intention was reiterated by the Court in *Frontier Dispute, Judgment, ICJ Reports 1986*, p 554, para 39.

question is approached with due caution. However, it has been argued that there is little evidence to support the Court's view and, in any case, there was insufficient evidence of intent on the facts of the case.

B. THE VIENNA CONVENTIONS

The 1969 Vienna Convention on the Law of Treaties was opened for signature on 23 April 1969 and entered into force on 27 January 1980. It was the product of the International Law Commission[17] and the UN Conference on the Law of Treaties that met at Vienna from 26 March to 24 May 1968, and from 9 April to 22 May 1969. The 1978 Vienna Convention on Succession of States in Respect of Treaties is in force but not all of its rules are considered to represent customary international law.

The 1986 Vienna Convention between States and International Organizations or between Organizations adapts the rules of the 1969 Convention to its subject matter and, although not in force, is considered to reflect customary international law. The present chapter is based mainly on the provisions of the 1969 Vienna Convention.

1. The scope of the Vienna Convention

The Vienna Convention regulates treaties concluded between States (Article 1) and in written form (Article 2(1)(a)). This does not mean that oral agreements have no effect under international law or that principles found in the VCLT do not apply to such agreements, merely that they are not governed by the VCLT itself. Questions of succession to treaties, State responsibility, and the effect of the outbreak of hostilities on treaties are also excluded from its scope (Article 73). Furthermore, the Convention is not retroactive and only applies to treaties concluded after its entry into force (Article 4). It acts as a residual rule, ie it is applicable unless a particular treaty provides otherwise; or unless the parties agree otherwise; or if a different intention is otherwise established. Although the VCLT does not apply to treaties between States and international organizations per se, those of its provisions that reflect rules of international customary law do apply to such treaties (Article 3(b)). Moreover, the provisions of the VCLT apply as between States parties to the VCLT as regards treaties to which other forms of subjects of international law (such as international organizations) are also parties (Article 3(c)).

2. The Vienna Convention and customary law

There are two problems concerning the relationship between the Vienna Convention and international customary law: (i) which provisions of the Vienna Convention codified customary law and which constituted progressive development; and (ii) how does customary law relating to treaties operate?

It is difficult, if not impossible, to answer the first of these questions. Certain provisions of the Convention that represented progressive development at the time of its signing—such as reservations and modification of treaties—were probably already within the body of international customary law by the time of its entry into force (Sinclair, 1984, pp 10–21). In the *Gabčíkovo-Nagymaros Project* case the ICJ identified the rules concerning termination and suspension of treaties as codificatory[18] and in the *Kasikili/Sedudu Island* case it said that the rules of interpretation reflected customary international law.[19]

---

[17] The Special Rapporteurs of the Commission were Professors Briely and Lauterpacht, Sir G Fitzmaurice, and Sir H Waldock.

[18] *Gabčíkovo-Nagymaros Project (Hungary/Slovakia), Judgment, ICJ Reports 1997*, p 7, para 46.

[19] *Kasikili/Sedudu Island (Botswana/Namibia), Judgment, ICJ Reports 1999*, p 1045, para 18.

As to the second problem, Articles 3(b), 4, 38, and 43 combine to provide that when the provisions of the Convention are inapplicable the rules of international customary law (or in some instances general principles of law) with the same legal content may be applicable. The most significant is Article 4 concerning the non-retroactive effect of provisions of the VCLT that were not reflective of customary law.

A different area of research, which thematically belongs to sources of international law, is the role of treaties in codification, crystallization, and originating of a norm of customary international law.[20]

III. THE ANATOMY OF A TREATY

A. THE MAKING OF TREATIES

Treaties are by far the most important tools of regulating international relations. They may be concluded between States, between States and international organizations, and between international organizations. International organizations, in particular the UN, play a most important role in international law-making as initiators of treaties and as a source of expertise.

B. AUTHORITY TO CONCLUDE TREATIES

VCLT Articles 7 and 8 concern the making of treaties. A most important issue is that of full powers,[21] the holder of which is authorized to adopt and authenticate the text of a treaty and to express the consent of the State to be bound by a treaty, although there are a growing number of treaties, particularly bilateral treaties, which are concluded in a simplified form that does not require the production of full powers (for example exchange of notes). The general rule expressed in the VCLT (Article 7, paragraph 1(a) and (b)) is that a person is considered as representing a State for the purpose of expressing the consent of the State to be bound by it if he or she produces appropriate full powers, or it appears from the practice of the States concerned or from other circumstances that their intention was to consider that person as representing the State for such purposes and to dispense with full powers. There is, however, a group of persons who, by virtue of their functions and without having to produce full powers, are considered to have such authority, these being: Heads of State, Heads of Government, and Ministers for Foreign Affairs; heads of diplomatic missions, for the purpose of adoption of the text of a treaty between the accrediting State and the State to which they are accredited; representatives accredited by States to an international organization or one of its organs, for the purpose of adopting the text of a

---

[20] In relation to this question see, eg, *North Sea Continental Shelf Cases (Federal Republic of Germany v Denmark; Federal Republic of Germany v the Netherlands) Judgment, ICJ Reports 1969*, p 3; *Military and Paramilitary Activities in and against Nicaragua (Nicaragua v United States of America). Merits, Judgment. ICJ Reports 1986*, p 14; see also the 2000 ILA Report on Formation of Customary (General) International Law. The ILC has on its agenda a topic entitled 'Identification of customary international law' (Sir Michael Wood, a Special Rapporteur). The relationship between treaties and customary international law was dealt with in his Third Report at the sixty-seventh session.

[21] Defined in Article 2(1)(c) as a 'Document emanating from the competent authority of a State designating a person or persons to represent a State for negotiating, adopting or authenticating the text of a treaty, for expressing consent of the State by a treaty, or for accomplishing any other acts with respect to a treaty'. See also *Case Concerning the Land and Maritime Boundary between Cameroon and Nigeria (Cameroon v Nigeria; Equatorial Guinea Intervening), Judgment, ICJ Reports 2002*, p 303.

treaty in that conference, organization, or organ (Article 7(2)). The ICJ in the *Cameroon* v
Nigeria case confirmed this rule.[22] In 2006 in the *Democratic Republic of Congo* v *Rwanda*
the Court examined the powers of the 'Big Three' (the Head of State, Head of Government,
and Minister for Foreign Affairs) to bind the States and, after having again confirmed the
'well established rule', went on to say: '[t]he Court notes, however, that with increasing
frequency in modern international relations other persons representing a State in specific
fields may be authorised by that State to bind it by their statements in respect to matters
falling within their purview. This may be true, for example, of holders of technical ministerial portfolio exercising powers in their field of competence in the area of foreign relations,
and even of certain officials.'[23]

These developments in international law were not reflected in the approach taken by
the ITLOS in the *Bangladesh/Myanmar* case where it adhered to the traditional rule,
saying that:

> the head of the Burmese delegation, Commodore Hlaing, a naval officer, could not be
> considered as representing Myanmar for the purpose of expressing consent to be bound
> by a treaty as he was not one of the holders of high-ranking office in the State referred
> to in article 7, paragraph 2, of the Vienna Convention. Furthermore, the circumstances
> described in article 7, paragraph 1, of the Vienna Convention do not apply in the pres-
> ent case since Commodore Hliang did not have full powers issued by the Government of
> Myanmar and there were no circumstances to suggest that it was the intention of Myanmar
> and Bangladesh to dispense of full powers.[24]

Full powers have to be distinguished from credentials, which are submitted to an international organization or a government hosting an international conference by a delegate attending to negotiate a multilateral treaty. Credentials only authorize the delegate to adopt
the text of a treaty and to sign a Final Act. Signing the treaty itself requires full powers or
specific instructions from government. Full powers and credentials may be combined in
one document.

Where an unauthorized person purports to conclude a treaty Article 8 provides that
the action is without legal effect, unless subsequently confirmed by the State. On the other
hand, Article 47 provides that where an authorized representative of a State expresses consent to be bound although instructed by their State not to do so, this does not invalidate
that consent, unless the limitation on their authority was notified to other negotiating
States beforehand.

The issue of the authority to sign a binding agreement was raised in the *Maritime
Delimitation in the Indian Ocean case (Somalia* v *Kenya) (Preliminary Objections)*. In this
case there was a question of the authority of the Somali Minister for National Planning
and International Cooperation to bind internationally Somalia by signing of the MOU.
He presented full powers signed by the Prime Minister of the Transnational Federal
Government of Somalia. The Court satisfied itself that as a matter of international law, the
Somali Minister properly represented Somalia in signing the MOU on its behalf (para 43
of the Judgment).

[22] *Land and Maritime Boundary between Cameroon and Nigeria (Cameroon* v *Nigeria; Equatorial Guinea Intervening), Judgment, ICJ Reports 2002*, p 303, para 265.

[23] *Armed Activities on the Territory of the Congo (New Application: 2002) (Democratic Republic of Congo* v *Rwanda) Jurisdiction of the Court and Admissibility of the Application, ICJ Reports 2006*, p 6, para 47.

[24] *Delimitation of the Maritime Boundary in the Bay of Bengal (Bangladesh/Myanmar), Judgment, ITLOS Reports 2012*, p 12, para 83.

C. EXPRESSION OF CONSENT TO BE BOUND

The role of the expression of consent by States to be bound by a treaty is to constitute a mechanism by which the treaty becomes a juridical act. According to Article 11, 'The consent of a state to be bound by a treaty may be expressed by signature, exchange of instruments constituting a treaty, ratification, acceptance, approval or accession, or by any other means if so agreed.' Article 11 lists a number of particular means of expressing consent to be bound, while also allowing parties to adopt any other means on which they agree. The precise method is, therefore, for the parties to a treaty to decide amongst themselves.

The legal effect of signature of a treaty depends upon whether or not it is subject to ratification, acceptance, or approval. If it is, then signature constitutes an intermediate step, indicating that the delegates have agreed upon the text and are willing to accept it. Signature under these circumstances does not express the final consent to be bound and the signing of a treaty does not impose any obligation on a State to ratify it or even, in the absence of an express term to this effect, to submit it to the national legislator for consideration. However, the initial signature also constitutes a juridical act in the sense that by its signature each State accepts certain legal consequences, for example under VCLT Articles 18, 24(4), and 25. The intermediate stage between signature and ratification enables States to promulgate necessary legislation or obtain necessary parliamentary approval. Ratification conforms to the democratic principle that the government should consult public opinion either in parliament or elsewhere before finally approving a treaty (Shearer, 1994, p 414).

1. Signature

Signature only expresses consent to be bound when it constitutes the final stage of a treaty-making process. Article 12 lists a variety of possible means to express consent to be bound by signature, including signature *ad referendum*. This commonly indicates either that the signatory State is currently unable to accept the terms of the treaty, or that the plenipotentiary concerned had no definitive instructions in the matter. Signature *ad referendum* becomes a full signature if subsequently confirmed by the State concerned. Article 12 also provides that initialling a treaty constitutes signature when it is established that the negotiating State so agreed. In the *Maritime Delimitation in the Indian Ocean case (Somalia v Kenya) Preliminary Objections*, the ICJ reiterated that a treaty can enter into force upon signature and the signature can represent a valid consent to be bound by treaty (para 47).

2. Ratification

Ratification is understood as a formal, solemn act on the part of a Head of State through which approval is given and a commitment to fulfil its obligations is undertaken, although the significance of the act at the international level has changed over time. As Judge Moore said in 1924, the older view that treaties might be regarded as binding before they had been ratified was now 'obsolete, and lingers only as an echo from the past'.[25]

VCLT Article 2(1)(b) provides that '"ratification", "acceptance", "approval" and "accession" mean in each case the international act so named whereby a state establishes on the international plane its consent to be bound by a treaty'. Despite the use of the word 'means', this does not define ratification, but indicates its effect. Article 14 provides that consent to be bound is expressed by ratification if: (a) the treaty expressly so provides; (b) the negotiating States otherwise agree that ratification is necessary; (c) the treaty has been signed subject to ratification; or (d) an intention to sign subject to ratification appears from the full powers or was expressed during negotiations.

---

[25] *Mavrommatis Palestine Concessions, Judgment No 2, 1924, PCIJ, Ser A, No 2, p 57.*

Ratification is unconditional and, unless the treaty in question provides otherwise, is not dependent on the receipt or deposit of instruments of ratification by other States. Some support for a relatively relaxed approach to the formalities of ratification can be gleaned from the attitude of the ICJ in the *Nicaragua* case, where Nicaragua's failure to ratify the Statute of the former Permanent Court of International Justice and convert 'potential commitment to effective commitment' was seen as being rectified by its ratification of the ICJ Statute.[26]

3. Accession

This means of consent to be bound is regulated by VCLT Article 15 and refers to the means by which a State expresses its consent to become a party to a treaty that it was not in a position to sign.[27] A State can only accede to a treaty if the treaty so provides or the parties agree. Treaties setting up regional regimes may often permit accession by invitation.[28] Can a State accede to a treaty that is not yet in force? The International Law Commission has pointed out that:

> An examination of the most recent treaty practice shows that in practically all modern treaties which contain accession clauses the right to accede is made independent of the entry into force of a treaty, either expressly, by allowing accession to take place before the date fixed for the entry into force of the treaty, or impliedly, by making the entry into force of the treaty conditional on the deposit, *inter alia*, of instruments of accession.[29]

4. Acceptance and approval

These are recognized and widely used methods of expressing consent to be bound and are regulated by VCLT Article 14(2). There are no great differences between signature subject to acceptance or approval and signature subject to ratification. The use of these methods of consent to be bound was intended to simplify procedures by, for example, avoiding constitutional conditions that might require obtaining parliamentary authority prior to ratification. The rules applicable to ratification apply to acceptance and approval (Aust, 2013, p 100) and, unless provided otherwise, acceptance and approval have the same legal effect as ratification. Expressing consent to be bound by acceptance or approval without prior signature is analogous to accession. In many of the more recent conventions concluded under the auspices of the UN, such as the 1997 UN Convention on the Law of the Non-Navigational Uses of International Watercourses,[30] all means of consent to be bound are listed as available options.

5. New developments regarding consent to be bound ('by any other means if so agreed', Article 11 of the 1969 Vienna Convention)

Developments in treaty-making between States have resulted in the evolution of certain techniques, the legal character of which is unclear, but which may involve consent to be bound by a treaty being given in a more informal fashion. One such technique is the method of a 'tacit approval' which is based on a principle that a State is bound by a decision of an organ of established by a multilateral treaty unless it 'opts out'. This practice is

---

[26] *Military and Paramilitary Activities in and against Nicaragua (Nicaragua v United States of America), Jurisdiction and Admissibility, Judgment, ICJ Reports 1984*, p 392.

[27] Very rarely it can be the principal means of expressing consent to be bound, as in the often cited yet isolated example of the 1928 General Act for the Pacific Settlement of International Disputes.

[28] Eg 1992 Convention on the Protection of the Marine Environment of the Baltic Sea Area.

[29] *YBILC* (1966), vol II (part two), p 199. [30] (1997) 36 ILM 700.

adopted by many international agreements and has been particularly developed in treaties concluded under the auspices of the International Maritime Organization, such as the procedure of amending the annexes in the Convention on the Prevention of Pollution from Ships (MARPOL 73/78). At times, the changes to the obligations of States parties brought about by means of such informal amendment procedures can be very considerable. Therefore, in some States such changes may be submitted to a national approval procedure, as if they were a formal amendment to the treaty concerned.

Another new development regarding consent to be bound is connected to the advent of Multilateral Environmental Agreements (MEAs), which frequently empower their organs, known as the Conference of the Parties (COPs) or Meeting of the Parties (MOPs), to adopt the decisions which further develop or specify the obligations of State parties, which were not agreed upon by the parties at the time of the conclusion of the MEAs. The powers of the COPs/MOPS to do this are based on so-called 'enabling clauses' in the MEAs, which provide that certain obligations will be specified by these organs in such a fashion. In some cases COPs/MOPs have adopted decisions (such as the establishment of rather complex compliance mechanisms) even without an enabling clause. Therefore decisions of COPs/MOPs can, in practice, reformulate the obligations of States without them giving their formal consent to be bound.

D. INVALIDITY OF TREATIES

The grounds for invalidity of treaties within the VCLT can be divided into two groups: relative grounds in Articles 46–50 and absolute grounds in Articles 51–3.[31] The main difference between these grounds is that the relative grounds render a treaty voidable at the insistence of an affected State whereas the absolute grounds mean that the treaty is rendered void *ab initio* and without legal effect. The Vienna Convention does not differentiate between bilateral and multilateral treaties. However, in the case of bilateral treaties the legal effect of establishing a relative ground of invalidity has the same legal effect as establishing absolute invalidity: the treaty falls (Sinclair, 1984). In the case of multilateral treaties, however, establishing an absolute ground means that the treaty has no legal force at all whereas establishing a relative ground—meaning that the consent of a particular State to a multilateral treaty is vitiated—does not affect the validity of the treaty as a whole as between the other remaining parties (Article 69(4)).

Article 45 as a ground of the invalidity of the treaty (internal law of a State) was explained in the *Cameroon* v *Nigeria* case, where Nigeria argued that Cameroon should have known about its internal law. The Court was of the view that there is 'no general legal obligation for States to keep themselves informed of legislative and constitutional developments in other States which are, or may become important for the international relations of these States'.[32]

Article 46 concerns the failure to comply with internal law regarding competence to conclude a treaty, and provides that this may only be a ground for invalidating consent to be bound if that failure was 'manifest'. In the *Cameroon* v *Nigeria* case, Nigeria argued that '. . . it should have been "objectively evident" to Cameroon, within the meaning of

---

[31] Sinclair divides cases of invalidity into three groups, concerning: the capacity of the parties (Articles 46–7); the validity of consent to be bound (Articles 48–50); and the lawfulness of the object of the treaty (Articles 51–3) (Sinclair, 1984, p 160).

[32] *Land and Maritime Boundary between Cameroon and Nigeria (Cameroon* v *Nigeria; Equatorial Guinea Intervening), Judgment, ICJ Reports 2002*, p 303, para 266. See also *Marine Delimitation in the Indian Ocean (Somalia* v *Kenya), Preliminary Objection, 2 February 2017, nyr*, para 49.

Article 46, paragraph 2 of the VCLT that the Nigerian Head of State did not have unlimited powers'[33] but the Court, while accepting that '[t]he rules concerning the authority to sign treaties are constitutional rules of fundamental importance', took the view that '. . . a limitation of a Head of State's capacity in this respect is not manifest in the sense of Article 46, paragraph 2, unless at least properly publicized. This is particularly so because Heads of States belong to the group of persons who, in accordance with Article 7, paragraph 2, of the Convention . . . are considered as representing the State.'[34]

Article 47 is similar, concerning cases in which the representatives purporting to conclude a treaty were acting beyond the scope of their instructions.[35] Article 48 concerns error as a vitiating ground, and follows the approach of the ICJ in the *Temple* case. In that case, Thailand argued that the boundary line indicated on a map annexed to a treaty was in error since it did not follow the watershed line that was prescribed by the treaty text. The Court rejected this argument, saying:

> It is an established rule of law that the plea of error cannot be allowed as a vitiating consent if the party advancing it contributed by its conduct or error, or could have avoided it, or the circumstances were such as to put party on notice of a possible error. The Court considers that the character and qualifications of persons who saw Annex I map on the Siamese side would alone make it difficult for Thailand to plead error in law . . .[36]

Articles 49 and 50 concern fraud and corruption. There is a paucity of materials relating to these Articles, though as far as corruption is concerned, the ILC observed that only an act calculated to exercise a substantial influence on the disposition of a representative to conclude a treaty could be invoked as a reason to invalidate an expression of consent that had subsequently been given.[37]

Turning from the relative to the absolute grounds for invalidity, Article 51 deals with the coercion of a representative, Article 52 the coercion of a State, and Article 53 the conflict with norms of *jus cogens*. In all these cases a treaty is void *ab initio*, in the latter case by virtue of its conflicting with international public policy (the consequences of which are addressed in Article 71). Practice in relation to all these Articles is limited. The classic example relating to Article 51, the coercion of a representative, concerns the pressure exerted by Göring and Ribbentrop upon President Hacha of Czechoslovakia to sign a treaty with Germany establishing a German protectorate over Bohemia and Moravia in 1939. There is a clear link between Article 52—the coercion of a State—and the prohibition of the use of force under international law. Iceland advanced a claim of this nature in the 1973 *Fisheries Jurisdiction* case and the ICJ stated that:

> There can be little doubt, as implied in the Charter of the United Nations and recognised in Article 52 of the Vienna Convention on the Law of Treaties, that under contemporary international law an agreement concluded under the threat or use of force is void . . .[38]

---

[33] *Land and Maritime Boundary between Cameroon and Nigeria (Cameroon v Nigeria; Equatorial Guinea Intervening), Judgment, ICJ Reports 2002*, p 303, para 258.

[34] *Land and Maritime Boundary between Cameroon and Nigeria (Cameroon v Nigeria; Equatorial Guinea Intervening), Judgment, ICJ Reports 2002*, p 303, para 265.

[35] YBILC (1966), vol II (part two), p 243.

[36] *Temple of Preah Vihear, Merits, Judgment, ICJ Reports 1962*, p 6 at p 26.

[37] YBILC (1966), vol II (part two), p 244.

[38] *Fisheries Jurisdiction (United Kingdom v Iceland), Jurisdiction of the Court, Judgment, ICJ Reports 1973*, p 3, para 24. However, on the facts of the case the Court concluded that '[t]he history of negotiations which led up to the 1961 Exchange of Notes reveals that these instruments were freely negotiated by the interested parties on the basis of the perfect equality and freedom of decision on both sides'.

E. AMENDMENT AND MODIFICATION

The growth in number of multilateral treaties resulted in the necessity of devising amendment procedures and, in order to make amendment procedures more flexible, modification procedures. These are addressed in VCLT Articles 39–41. The ILC explained that amendment is a formal matter introducing changes into the treaty text whereas modification is a less formal procedure which affects only certain parties to a treaty.[39] However, in practice it is often difficult to distinguish between these two procedures (Sinclair, 1984, p 107).

Amendments to treaties should be distinguished from the revision of a treaty. Revision is a more comprehensive process resulting in changes to a treaty. However, a diplomatic conference is often needed both to revise and to amend a treaty, as, for example, in the case of the 1992 Convention on the Protection of the Marine Environment of the Baltic Sea (the '1992 Helsinki Convention').[40] Amendments are subject to approval by the parties to the treaty. However, some treaties—such as the Helsinki Convention—contain technical annexes, which may, if the treaty so provides, be amended by a simplified system whereby an amendment to an annex is deemed to have been accepted at the end of a specified period unless in the meanwhile any State party has submitted a written objection to the depositary.

F. TERMINATION AND SUSPENSION OF THE OPERATION OF TREATIES

The general provisions on suspension and termination of treaties are set out in VCLT Articles 54–59. Termination of a treaty may result from the grounds of termination that are internal to the treaty as well as from grounds external to the treaty. The 'internal' grounds will be considered here. The 'external grounds', concerning breach of obligations, will be considered later. As regards the 'internal' grounds for termination or suspension, the general rule in Article 54 is that a treaty may be terminated or a party may withdraw from a treaty in accordance with the provisions of the treaty itself or at any time by consent of all parties following consultations. Article 57 provides that the operation of a treaty with regard to all parties or to a particular party may be suspended in accordance with the provisions of the treaty in question.

Some treaties provide that they will remain in force only for a specific period of time whereas others provide for termination by a resolution of the contracting parties. As to withdrawal from a treaty, some treaties provide for a period of notice while others do not. For example, the 1992 Helsinki Convention provides that at any time after the expiry of five years from the date of its entry into force any party may, by giving written notification to the depositary, withdraw from the Convention. Withdrawal takes effect on the thirtieth day of June of the year following the year in which the depositary was notified of the withdrawal.

VCLT Article 58 provides for suspension of the operation of a multilateral treaty by agreement between certain parties only. This Article must be read in conjunction with Article 41 which provides for the modification of treaty provisions between certain parties only. Article 59 covers the case of tacit termination of a treaty. There is a particular problem concerning the relationship between tacit termination in accordance with Article 59 and Article 30, which concerns the effect of successive treaties relating to the same subject matter and which relates to cases in which the parties clearly intended the earlier treaty to be abrogated or its operation wholly suspended by the conclusion of the subsequent treaty.

---

[39] *YBILC* (1966), vol II (part two), p 232.

[40] 'A conference for the purpose of a general revision of or an amendment to this Convention may be convened with the consent of the Contracting Parties or the request of the Commission' (Article 30).

IV. THE SCOPE OF LEGAL OBLIGATIONS

A. THE PRINCIPLE *PACTA SUNT SERVANDA*

The principle *pacta sunt servanda* is enshrined in Article 26 of the VCLT which provides that '[e]very treaty in force is binding upon the parties to it and must be performed by them in good faith'. Good faith is itself a legal principle and forms an integral part of the *pacta sunt servanda* principle.[41]

The fundamental importance of *pacta sunt servanda* was confirmed by the ICJ in the 1997 *Gabčíkovo-Nagymaros* case, which, generally speaking, advocated its strict observance. The case concerned the implementation of a 1977 treaty providing for the construction of a hydro-electric scheme along stretches of the Danube in Hungary and Slovakia. Hungary argued that the conduct of both parties indicated that they had repudiated this bilateral treaty, which, therefore, had come to an end. The Court, however, took the view that the reciprocal wrongful conduct of both parties 'did not bring the Treaty to an end nor justify its termination'.[42] The effect of breaching treaty obligations will be considered later, but at this point it should be noted that, despite both parties being in fundamental breach of important elements of their treaty obligations, the Court thought the 1977 Treaty 'cannot be treated as voided by unlawful conduct'.[43]

The Court made a direct reference to the principle *pacta sunt servanda*, saying that '[w]hat is required in the present case by the rule *pacta sunt servanda*, as reflected in Article 26 of Vienna Convention of 1969 on the Law of Treaties, is that the parties find solution within the co-operative context of the Treaty'.[44] The Court observed that the two elements in Article 26—the binding force of treaties and the performance of them in good faith—were of equal importance and that good faith implied that, 'in this case, it is the purpose of the Treaty, and the intentions of the parties in concluding it, which should prevail over its literal application. The principle of good faith obliges parties to apply it in a reasonable way in such a manner that its purpose can be realized.'[45]

These are far-reaching statements and, while they may have been particularly suited to the issues in the *Gabčíkovo-Nagymaros* case itself, it is still impossible to determine the extent to which they bear upon the application of the principle *pacta sunt servanda* in the law of treaties in general.

B. TREATIES AND THIRD STATES

The issue of treaties and non-State parties—third States—are addressed in VCLT Articles 34–38. The fundamental rule concerning the relationship between treaties and third States is expressed by the maxim *pacta tertiis nec nocent nec prosunt*, enshrined in Article 34. The Convention then deals with an obligation (Article 35) and a right (Article 36—often referred to as stipulations *in favorem tertii*) arising from a treaty for a third State. As to the obligation, the requirements are so strict that, when fulfilled, they in fact amount to the existence of a collateral agreement between the parties to the treaty and the third State and it is this collateral agreement, rather than the original treaty, which is the legal basis for the third State's obligation.

There are procedural differences in the establishment of an obligation and of a right. The third State must accept an obligation in writing, whereas in a case of the right, the assent of

---

[41] *YBILC* (1966), vol II (part two), p 211.
[42] *Gabčíkovo-Nagymaros Project (Hungary/Slovakia), Judgment, ICJ Reports 1997*, p 7, para 114.
[43] Ibid, para 133.   [44] Ibid, para 142.   [45] Ibid.

the third State(s) is presumed, unless the treaty provides otherwise or there are indications to the contrary. Any obligation arising for a third State can be revoked or modified only with the consent of the parties to the treaty and of the third State, unless it is established that they agreed otherwise. Any right arising for a third State can be revoked or modified only by the parties if it is established that the right was intended to be revocable or subject to modification without the consent of the third State. Caution is usually recommended when considering whether a treaty has given rise to stipulations *in favorem tertii*. As the PCIJ said:

> It cannot be lightly presumed that stipulations favourable to a third State have been adopt-ed with the object of creating an actual right in its favour. There is, however, nothing to prevent the will of sovereign States from having this object and this effect. The question of the existence of a right acquired under an instrument drawn between other States is there-fore one to be decided in each particular case: it must be ascertained whether the States which have stipulated in favour of the third State meant to create for that State an actual right which the latter has accepted as such.[46]

Nothing in the VCLT prevents a rule set out in a treaty from becoming binding upon third States as a customary rule of international law if recognized as such (Article 37). However, the VCLT does not deal specifically with the question of whether the objective regimes created by treaties are binding only on States parties to those instruments or whether they are valid as against the entire international community—are valid *erga omnes*. Examples of such treaties would include those providing for the neutrality or demilitarization of a certain territory or area, or establishing freedom of navigation in international waterways such as the Suez Canal, Kiel Canal, and the Turkish Straits.[47]

V. GENERAL PRINCIPLES OF INTERPRETATION

A. GENERAL ISSUES

'There is no part of the law of treaties which the text writer approaches with more trepi-dation than the question of interpretation' (McNair, 1961). The complex issue of treaty interpretation will be discussed in the light of the work of the ILC during its codification of the law of treaties, the principles of interpretation included in the Vienna Convention, and the jurisprudence of the international and national courts and tribunals, with special regard to the case law of the ICJ. The purpose of interpretation is to establish the meaning of the text that the parties intended it to have 'in relation to circumstances with reference to which the question of interpretation has arisen' (Oppenheim, 1992).

Basing himself on the jurisprudence of the World Court,[48] the ILC's Rapporteur, Fitzmaurice (Fitzmaurice, 1951) drew up the following comprehensive set of principles of interpretation:

Principle I: actuality of textuality—that treaties are to be interpreted as they stand, on the basis of their actual texts.

Principle II: the natural and ordinary meaning—that, subject to principle of contem-poraneity (where applicable), particular words and phrases are to be given their normal,

---

[46] *Free Zones of Upper Savoy and the District of Gex, Judgment, 1932, PCIJ, Ser A/B, No 46,* p 96 at pp 147–8.

[47] The ILC took the view that Article 36(1) provided sufficient basis for rights to be accorded to all States and Article 38 a sufficient basis for the establishment of treaty rights and obligations *erga omnes*. For criticism see Chinkin, 1993.   [48] *YBILC* (1966), vol II (part two), p 220.

natural, and unstrained meaning in the context in which they occur. This principle can only be displaced by direct evidence that the terms used are to be understood in manner different to their natural and ordinary meaning, or if such an interpretation would lead to an unreasonable or absurd result.

Principle III: integration—that treaties are to be interpreted as a whole. This principle is of fundamental importance and means that individual parts, chapters, or sections of a treaty are not to be interpreted out of their overall context.

The remaining principles take effect subject to the three principles outlined in the preceding paragraphs. There are:

Principle IV: effectiveness (ut magis valeat quam pereat)—that treaties are to be interpreted with reference to their declared or apparent objects and purposes; and particular provisions are to be interpreted so as to give them the fullest effect consistent with the normal sense of the words and with the text as a whole in such a way that a reason and meaning can be attributed to every part of the text.

Principle V: subsequent practice—that recourse may be had to subsequent practice of parties relating to the treaty.

Principle VI: contemporaneity—that the terms of a treaty must be interpreted in the light of linguistic usage current at the time when the treaty was concluded.

In general, there are three main schools of interpretation: the subjective (the 'intention' of parties) approach; the objective (the 'textual') approach, and the teleological (or 'object and purpose') approach. These schools of interpretation are not mutually exclusive (Sinclair, 1984) and the VCLT draws on all three. It is the reconciliation of the objective and the subjective approaches that is the most difficult, controversial, and, some would say, impossible task (Koskenniemi, 1989). For the ILC, the starting point was the text rather than the intention of the parties,[49] since it presumed that the text represented a real expression of what the parties did in fact intend. It also appears that the ICJ's preferred method of interpretation is reliance on the text of a treaty.

B. PRACTICE

VCLT Article 31(1) provides:

> A treaty shall be interpreted in good faith in accordance with the ordinary meaning to be given to the terms of the treaty in their context and in the light of its object and purpose.

The ICJ has acknowledged this to constitute international customary law.[50] The underlying principle is that a treaty will be interpreted in good faith. The 'rule' (in the singular) of interpretation is a procedure consisting of three elements: the text, the context, and the object and purpose. The context of a treaty is set out in some detail in Article 31(2) and embraces any instrument of relevance to the conclusion of a treaty, as well as a treaty's preamble and annexes. There is no hierarchy between the various elements of Article 31; rather, they reflect a logical progression, 'nothing more' (Aust, 2013, p 208).

---

[49] Ibid.

[50] *Territorial Dispute (Libyan Arab Jamahiririya/Chad), Judgment, ICJ Reports 1994*, p 6, para 41; *Oil Platforms (Islamic Republic of Iran v United States of America), Preliminary Objections, Judgment, ICJ Reports 1996*, p 803, para 23; *Kasikili/Sedudu Island (Botswana/Namibia), Judgment, ICJ Reports 1999*, p 1045, para 18 (for which see Fox, 2010).

The Court has consistently adhered to the textual interpretation as being the most important. In the *Libya/Chad* case, the Court stated that:

> Interpretation must be based above all upon the text of a treaty. As a supplementary measure recourse may be had to means of interpretation such as the preparatory work of the treaty.[51]

Article 31 reflects the principle that a treaty has to be interpreted in good faith that is the embodiment of the principle *pacta sunt servanda*. The determination of that ordinary meaning of term is undertaken in the context of a treaty and in the light of its object and purpose. A good example is the Advisory Opinion *On the Interpretation of the Convention of 1919 Concerning Employment of Women During the Night*. Article 3 of that Convention ('women without distinction of age shall not be employed during the night in any public or private industrial undertaking, or in any branch thereof, other than an undertaking in which members of the same family are employed') left unclear its application to certain categories of women other than manual workers. The Court said:

> The wording of Article 3, considered by itself, gives rise to no difficulty; it is general in its terms and free from ambiguity or obscurity. It prohibits the employment during the night in industrial establishments of women without distinction of age. Taken by itself, it necessarily applies to the categories of women contemplated by the question submitted to the Court. If, therefore, Article 3 . . . is to be interpreted in such a way as not to apply to women holding posts of supervision and management and not ordinarily engaged in manual work, it is necessary to find some valid ground for interpreting the provision otherwise than in accordance with the natural sense of words. The terms of Article 3 . . . are in no respect inconsistent either with the title, or with the Preamble, or with any other provision of the Convention. The title refers to 'employment of women during the night'. The Preamble speaks of 'women's employment during the night'. Article 1 gives a definition of 'an industrial undertaking'. Article 2 states what is meant by the term 'night'. These provisions, therefore, do not affect the scope of Article 3, which provides that 'women shall not be employed during the night either in any public or private industrial undertaking, or in any branch thereof'.[52]

This might be compared with the views of Judge Anzilloti, who argued that '[i]f article 3, according to the natural meaning of its terms, were really perfectly clear, it would be hardly admissible to endeavour to find an interpretation other than that which flows from the natural meaning of its terms'.[53] He thought that only the intention of the parties should have been used to determine the correct interpretation.

Another problem concerns what is to count as subsequent practice for the purposes of interpretation, the use of which is sanctioned as forming a part of the context of the treaty by Article 31(3). The ILC has undertaken in 2013 a project on subsequent practice (Professor Georg Nolte—a Special Rapporteur). In 2016, text of the draft conclusions were provisionally adopted by the Drafting Committee on first reading. In the *Kasikili/Sedudu Island* case the Court adhered to the ILC's view that the subsequent practice of parties to a treaty constitutes an element to be taken into account when determining its meaning,[54] but it took a narrow approach to what comprises subsequent practice and did not take account of unilateral acts of the previous authorities of Botswana on the grounds that these were for internal purposes only and unknown to the Namibian authorities. The Court also considered the relevance of an alleged 'subsequent agreement' between the previous

---

[51] *Territorial Dispute*. The use of supplementary material is considered later in this chapter.

[52] *Interpretation of the Convention of 1919 Concerning Employment of Women During the Night, Advisory Opinion, 1932, PCIJ, Ser A/B, No 50*, p 365 at p 373.   [53] Dissenting Opinion of Judge Anzilloti, ibid, p 383.

[54] *Kasikili/Sedudu Island (Botswana/Namibia), Judgment, ICJ Reports 1999*, p 1075, para 49.

authorities in Namibia and Botswana as only amounting to 'collaboration' over matters concerning the border and not having any effect on the interpretation of the treaty in question.[55] However, the Court was prepared to accord such material some role, noting them as facts which supported the interpretation of the 1890 Treaty in accordance with the ordinary meaning of its terms.[56] This is a usage not explicitly foreseen by the VCLT.

The issue of the importance of subsequent practice of States arose in connection with the interpretation of the term '*comercio*' (commerce) in the 2009 *Costa Rica v Nicaragua* case. The Court said:

> This does not, however, signify that, where a term's meaning is no longer the same as it was at the date of conclusion, no account should ever be taken of its meaning at the time when the treaty is to be interpreted for purposes of applying it.

On the one hand, the subsequent practice of the parties, within the meaning of Article 31(3)(b) of the Vienna Convention, can result in a departure from the original intent on the basis of a tacit agreement between the parties. On the other hand, there are situations in which the parties' intent upon conclusion of the treaty was, or may be presumed to have been, to give the terms used—or some of them—a meaning or content capable of evolving, not one fixed once and for all, so as to make allowance for, among other things, developments in international law. In such instances it is indeed in order to respect the parties' common intention at the time the treaty was concluded, not to depart from it, that account should be taken of the meaning acquired by the terms in question upon each occasion on which the treaty is to be applied.[57]

The issue of subsequent practice has also arisen in the *Whaling in the Antarctic* case[58] in relation to the resolutions adopted by the International Whaling Commission (IWC). Australia argued that the resolutions had to be taken into account in interpreting the Convention because they comprised 'subsequent agreement between the parties regarding the interpretation of the treaty' and 'subsequent practice in the application of the treaty which establishes the agreement of the parties regarding its interpretation' in the sense codified by the Vienna Convention on the Law of Treaties (Articles 31(3)(a)–(b)). Only some of the relevant resolutions were adopted by consensus and others, including Resolution 1995-9 in particular, were adopted by mere majority, and without the concurrence of Japan. The Court concluded that those resolutions adopted by consensus did not sufficiently establish Australia and New Zealand's restrictive interpretation of the scope of permissible lethal means in scientific research, while others, like Resolution 1995-9, could not be accepted here as authoritative guides to the interpretation of the Convention. In the Court's words:

> Australia and New Zealand overstate the legal significance of the recommendatory resolutions and Guidelines on which they rely. First, many IWC resolutions were adopted without the support of all States parties to the Convention and, in particular, without the concurrence of Japan. Thus, such instruments cannot be regarded as subsequent agreement to an interpretation of Article VIII, nor as subsequent practice establishing an agreement of the parties regarding the interpretation of the treaty within the meaning of [VCLT 31(3) (a) (b)]. (para. 83) of the Judgment.[59]

---

[55] See generally ibid, paras 52–79.   [56] Ibid, para 80.

[57] *Dispute regarding Navigational and Related Rights between Costa Rica and Nicaragua*, Judgment of 13 July 2009, para 64.

[58] *Whaling in the Antarctic (Australia v Japan: New Zealand Intervening)*, Judgment, ICJ Reports 2014, p 226. See Fitzmaurice, 2016, pp 55–138.   [59] See Arato, 2014.

C. TRAVAUX PRÉPARATOIRES

VCLT Article 32 makes it clear that supplementary means of interpretation—including *travaux préparatoires*, preparatory work—may be used either to confirm the meaning of the treaty or as an aid to interpretation where, following the application of Article 31, the meaning is ambiguous or obscure or leads to a result which is manifestly absurd or unreasonable. Both the *Employment of Women During the Night* Advisory Opinion and the *Kasikili/Sedudu* case, considered in n 50 in this chapter, illustrate the use of supplementary means to confirm an interpretation arrived at on the basis of Article 31. It is the use of preparatory work as a supplementary means of interpretation that gives rise to most difficulties, as is illustrated by the jurisdictional phases of the *Qatar v Bahrain* case.

The problem in this case centred on whether Qatar and Bahrain had ever entered into an agreement that would permit one of them to bring their case before the ICJ without the express approval of the other. The ICJ first decided that the fragmentary nature of the preparatory work meant that it could only be used with caution but noted that:

> the initial . . . draft expressly authorised a seisin by one or other of the parties and that that formulation was not accepted. But the text finally adopted did not provide that the seisin of the Court could only be brought about by the two parties acting in concert, whether jointly or separately. The Court is unable to see why abandonment of a form of words corresponding to the interpretation given by Qatar . . . should imply that they must be interpreted in accordance with Bahrain's thesis. As a result, it does not consider the *travaux préparatoires*, in the form in which they have been submitted to it—ie limited to the various drafts . . . —can provide it with conclusive supplementary elements for the interpretation of the text adopted; whatever may have been the motives of each of the parties, the Court can only confine itself to the actual terms of the Minutes as the expression of their common intention, and to the interpretation of them which it has already given.[60]

The Court concluded that a unilateral application was legitimate. Judge Schwebel criticized this, arguing that the Court's interpretation did not reflect the common intention of the parties. He argued that the Court's view that the preparatory work did not provide conclusive supplementary elements was unconvincing, observing that:

> since deletion of the specification, 'either of the two parties may submit the matter to the International Court of Justice' in favour of the adopted provision 'the two parties may submit the matter . . .' surely manifested Bahrain's intention that 'either of the two parties' may *not* submit the matter, the Court's inability to see so plain a point suggests to me an unwillingness to do so.[61]

He considered that 'the requisite common, ascertainable intention of the parties to authorize unilateral reference to the Court is absent. Its absence is—or should be have been—determinative'[62] and concluded that:

> What the text and context of the Doha Minutes leaves unclear is, however, crystal clear when those Minutes are analysed with the assistance of the *travaux préparatoires* . . . the preparatory work of itself is not ambiguous; on the contrary, a reasonable evaluation of it sustains only the position of Bahrain.[63]

---

[60] *Maritime Delimitation and Territorial Questions between Qatar and Bahrain, Jurisdiction and Admissibility, Judgment, ICJ Reports 1995*, p 6, para 41.

[61] Dissenting Opinion of Judge Schwebel, ibid, p 27 at p 36.   [62] Ibid, p 37.

[63] Ibid, pp 38–9. For similar analyses see the Dissenting Opinions of Judges Shahabuddeen, ibid, p 51 and Koroma, ibid, p 67.

D. THE OBJECT AND PURPOSE OF A TREATY

Article 31 of the Vienna Convention stipulates that a treaty should be interpreted 'in the light of its object and purpose' but this is a vague and ill-defined term, making it an unreliable tool for interpretation. Indeed, the ILC itself voiced certain doubts as to the usefulness of this criterion, particularly as regards reservations[64] (a topic considered later in Section VI). A further problem concerns the relationship between the 'object and purpose' of a treaty and the principle of effectiveness, which is considered in Section V E. The object and purpose of a treaty, and whether this can evolve over time, was debated in the *Whaling in the Antarctic* case. Australia sought to rely on an evolutive interpretation of the Preamble to the International Convention of the Regulation of Whaling (ICRW), arguing that terms such as 'safeguard', 'protection', and 'common interest' must now be interpreted to imply the preservation of all species of whales. Japan relied on a more static approach, pointing to the orderly regulation of the whaling industry and the protection of whales, the ordinary meaning of which, it suggested, indicated that 'whaling operations should be confined to those species best able to sustain exploitation in order to give an interval for recovery to certain species of whales now depleted in numbers', thus permitting certain species to be exploited in a sustainable manner.

The Court noted that whilst '[a]mendments to the Schedule and recommendations by the IWC may put an emphasis on one or other objective pursued by the Convention', they 'cannot alter its object and purpose'.[65]

It also had to consider the 'object and purpose' of Article VIII of the ICRW, which regulates scientific whaling and the issuance of permits by the States parties to the Convention. The Court took the view that Article VIII was an integral part of the Convention and its meaning should be determined on an objective basis. As a result, contracting governments were not entitled to issue permits based on their own unilateral determinations of whether such whaling was for the purposes of scientific research. Rather, such whaling programmes had to reflect accepted scientific practice and the criteria adopted by the IWC and only be carried out for scientific research purposes. It did not however spell out what was meant by 'scientific research'.[66]

E. THE PRINCIPLE OF EFFECTIVENESS

The principle of effectiveness, enshrined in the maxim *magis valeat quam pereat*, was acknowledged by the ILC, which observed that '[w]hen a treaty is open to two interpretations one of which does and the other does not enable the treaty to have appropriate effects, good faith and the objects and purposes of the treaty demand that the former interpretation should be adopted'.[67]

Although the principle of effectiveness can operate as an element within the 'object and purposes' test, it is not limited to this role and, as Thirlway notes, the ICJ has used it to ascertain the intention underlying the treaty and as a starting point for a broader discussion. It also operates in the broader context of giving effect to the terms of a text.

The principle of effectiveness has two meanings. The first is that all provisions of the treaty or other instrument must be supposed to have been intended to have significance

---

[64] First Report on the Law of Treaties, *YBILC* (1962), vol II, pp 65–6.

[65] *Whaling in the Antarctic (Australia v Japan: New Zealand Intervening), Judgment, ICJ Reports* 2014, p 226, para 56.

[66] This was criticized in the Dissenting Opinion of Judge Bennouna, who thought it a 'perilous exercise' to determine the purpose of a given activity without having first clarified what this activity consists of.

[67] *YBILC* (1966), vol II (part two), p 219.

and to be necessary to express the intended meaning. Thus an interpretation that renders a text ineffective and meaningless is incorrect. The second operates as an aspect of the 'object and purposes' test, and it means that the instrument as a whole and each of its provisions must be taken to have been intended to achieve some end, and that an interpretation that would make the text ineffective to achieve that object is also incorrect. Thirlway observes that this latter approach is similar to the 'object and purpose' criterion, and 'has therefore, like this criterion, to be employed with discretion' (Thirlway, 1992).

F. THE DYNAMIC (EVOLUTIVE) INTERPRETATION OF TREATIES AND THE EUROPEAN COURT OF HUMAN RIGHTS (ECTHR)

One of the most contentious, disputed, and discussed issues in treaty interpretation is the so-called dynamic (evolutive) interpretation of treaties, which in particular has been developed in the jurisprudence of the European Court of Human Rights. The basis for such as an interpretative method is predicated upon the principle that the treaty is a living instrument. There are several cases (such as *Tyrer* (1975), *Golder* (1978), and *Marckx* (1979)) in which the Court decided to override the consent of the parties in the name of 'the interests served by the protection of the human rights and fundamental freedoms guaranteed by the Convention', which 'extend beyond individual interests of the parties concerned'. This resulted in the establishment by the parties to the Convention of the 'standards forming part of the public law of Europe'. First of all, the interpretative method of the ECtHR derives from the special legal nature of this Convention and the obligations, which doctrinal basis was enunciated in the 1965 *Austria* v *Italy* case. The Court also stressed the 'essentially objective character' of the 'obligations undertaken by the High Contracting Parties'. The 'objective legal order' 'benefits from the "collective enforcement"'. However, such an interpretative method was a subject of much criticism (eg by Sinclair and Fitzmaurice) as overriding intention and the consent to be bound of the parties to the Convention, and introducing the element of uncertainty for the parties due to much more extensive interpretation of the provisions of the Convention. There are other international judicial bodies which to a certain degree adopted such a method, such as, for example, within the World Trade Organization (WTO).

The issue of whether the ICRW was an evolving (dynamic) instrument and whether resolutions of the IWC could 'evolve' the Convention was also debated during the *Whaling in the Antarctic* case. The Court, noting that the substantive provisions concerning the regulation of whaling were to be found in the Schedule to the Convention rather than the Convention itself, observed that '[t]he Commission has amended the Schedule many times. The functions conferred on the Commission have made the Convention an evolving instrument . . .'[68] Thus whilst the objects and purposes of the Convention are not susceptible to evolution, the regulatory framework through which it achieves those objects and purposes may be so.

G. PLURILINGUAL TREATIES

A further problem concerns the interpretation of treaties drawn up in more than one language. The ILC observed that:

> the majority of more formal treaties contain an express provision determining the status of the different language versions. If there is no such provision, it seems generally accepted

---

[68] *Whaling in the Antarctic (Australia v Japan: New Zealand Intervening), Judgment, ICJ Reports* 2014, p 226, para 45.

that each of the versions in which the text of the treaty was 'drawn' up is to be considered authentic, and therefore authoritative for the purpose of interpretation. Few plurilingual treaties containing more than one or two articles are without some discrepancy between the texts . . . the plurality of texts may be a serious additional source of ambiguity or obscurity in the terms of the treaty. On the other hand, when meaning of terms is ambiguous or obscure in one language, but it is clear and convincing as to the intentions of the parties in another, the plurilingual character of the treaty facilitates interpretations of the text the meaning of which is doubtful.[69]

In the *Mavrommatis Palestine Concession* case, the ICJ had to interpret the phrases 'public control' and 'contrôle public' in the French and English authentic language texts of the Palestine Mandate. The Court said:

> Where two versions possessing equal authority exist one of which appears to have a wider bearing than the other, it is bound to adopt the more limited interpretation which can be made to harmonise with both versions and which, as far as it goes, is doubtless in accordance with the common intention of the parties.[70]

The matter is covered by VCLT Article 33, which reflects these general approaches to the problem.

In conclusion, it may be said that there are numerous examples of the difficulties concerning the treaty interpretation. Such an example is the interpretation of Article 18 of the 1929 Geneva Convention on the Treatment of Prisoners of War, which provides that prisoners were to salute the officers of the captor country. In 1944, this clause was the subject of an interpretative dispute. In the period between 1939 and 1944, allied prisoners of war in Germany saluted their German captors in a classical manner, by touching their hands to the visors of their caps. Article 18 of the Convention is silent as to whether the salute be returned, which is a universal military tradition: 'a salute unreturned is like the sound of one hand clapping' (Vagts, 1993, p 490). After the failed attempt at Hitler's assassination (20 July 1944), regular German army troops were ordered to salute prisoners of war in a Nazi style, which resulted in protests from the British. Eventually, due to the services of the International Committee of the Red Cross, the issue was resolved and prisoners permitted to use the salute prevalent in their own army.[71]

VI. RESERVATIONS TO TREATIES

A. THE *GENOCIDE CONVENTION* CASE

Reservations to multilateral treaties are one of the most problematic issues in the law of treaties. According to VCLT Article 2(d): 'Reservation means a unilateral statement, however phrased or named, made by a State, when signing, ratifying, accepting, approving or

---

[69] *YBILC* (1966), vol II (part two), pp 224–5.

[70] *Mavrommatis Palestine Concessions, Judgment No 2, 1924, PCIJ, Ser A, No 2,* p 19.

[71] Example from Vagts (1993, p 490) who comments: 'Thus we find interpretation of the Convention being presented and considered by persons far away from the original negotiating process. Most of them were not lawyers and they had no access to *travaux préparatoires* (which, as so often happens, would not have been helpful). There was no decision-maker to force a solution upon the parties. Yet it is apparent that the parties in dispute, although coming from different and at the time violently hostile states, did share assumptions about what a "salute" was, and when and how one should be rendered. Indeed, it seems likely the professional and traditional German officers had more in common on this point with their British counterparts than with their Nazi colleagues.'

acceding to a treaty, where, it purports to exclude or to modify the legal effect of certain provisions of the treaty in their application to that State.'

In its role as a treaty depository, the League of Nations had only allowed reservations that were accepted by all contracting parties to a treaty; otherwise it treated both the reservations and the signatures or ratifications to which they were attached as null and void. The Pan-American Union adopted a different, more flexible approach, the gist of which was that a treaty was considered to be in force as between a reserving State and States that accepted the reservation but not in force as between a reserving State and States that did not accept the reservation.

The modern approach is derived from the 1951 Advisory Opinion of the ICJ in the *Reservation to the Convention on Genocide* case, the principal features of which were that:

> A State which has made and maintained a reservation which has been objected to by one or more of the parties to the Convention but not by others, can be regarded as being a party to the Convention if the reservation is compatible with the object and purpose of the Convention; otherwise, that State cannot be regarded as being a party to the Convention.[72]

The Court added that:

> If a party to the Convention objects to a reservation which it considers to be incompatible with the object and purpose of the Convention, it can in fact consider that the reserving State is not a party to the Convention . . . if on the other hand, a party accepts the reservation as being compatible with the object and purpose of the Convention, it can in fact consider that the reserving State is a party to the Convention.[73]

It has to be said that although the Court's approach was subsequently reflected in the VCLT, the Court had made it clear that it was expressing its views on the operation of reservations only in relation to the Genocide Convention, noting that:

> In such a Convention the contracting States do not have any interests of their own; they merely have, one and all, a common interest, namely the accomplishment of those high purposes which are the *raison d'être* of the convention. Consequently in a convention of this type one cannot speak of individual advantages or disadvantages to States, or of the maintenance of a perfect contractual balance between rights and duties.[74]

And that:

> The object and purpose of the Genocide Convention imply that it was the intention of the General Assembly and of States which adopted it that as many States as possible should participate. The complete exclusion from the Convention of one or more States would not only restrict the scope of its application, but would detract from the authority of the moral and humanitarian principles which are its basis.[75]

It was for these reasons that the Court departed from the more rigid system operated by the League of Nations, which some judges had considered to reflect international customary law.[76] However, it was the General Assembly itself which requested that the UN

---

[72] *Reservations to the Convention on the Prevention and Punishment of the Crime of Genocide, Advisory Opinion, ICJ Reports 1951*, p 15 at p 29. See also *Armed Activities on the Territory of the Congo (New Application: 2002), (Democratic Republic of the Congo v Rwanda), Jurisdiction of the Court and Admissibility of the Application*; see also Joint Separate Opinion of Judges Higgins, Kooijmans, Elaraby, Owada, and Simma, *ICJ Reports 2006*.

[73] Ibid.   [74] Ibid, p 23.   [75] Ibid, p 24.

[76] See Joint Dissenting Opinion of Judges Guerrero, Sir Arnold McNair, Read, and Hsu Mo, ibid, p 31.

Secretary-General adopt this new approach when acting in his capacity as depositary of multilateral treaties.[77]

The question of a reservation to Article IX of the Genocide Convention was a subject matter of the *Democratic Republic of Congo* v *Rwanda* case. The Democratic Republic of Congo (DRC) argued that the reservation made by Rwanda to Article IX of the Genocide Convention (ie to the submission of disputes arising from the interpretation of this Convention to the ICJ) was against the spirit of Article 53 of the 1969 VCLT as it prevented 'the . . . Court from fulfilling its noble mission of safeguarding peremptory norms'.[78] The Court, however, decided that 'the prohibition of genocide, cannot of itself provide a basis for jurisdiction of the Court to entertain that dispute. Under the Court's Statute that jurisdiction is always based on the consent of the parties'.[79] This prompted a powerful Joint Separate Opinion by Judges Higgins, Koojimans, Elaraby, Owada, and Simma, who, in light of recent developments in relations to reservation in general and to human rights treaties, were of the view that '[i]t is thus not self-evident that a reservation to Article IX could not be regarded as incompatible with the object and purpose of the Convention and we believe that this is a matter that the Court should revisit for further consideration'.[80]

B. THE REGIME OF THE 1969 VIENNA CONVENTION

The Court's approach is reflected in VCLT Article 19 and so attempts to strike a balance between ensuring the integrity of a treaty while encouraging universal participation. Article 20(4) tips the balance towards widening participation by providing that even if a State party objects to a reservation attached to the signature or ratification of another State, the treaty will nevertheless enter into force and the reservation be effective between them unless 'a contrary intention is definitely expressed by an objecting State'. Moreover, the idea that the approach in the *Genocide Convention* case should be limited to those treaties where there was no particular advantage or disadvantage for an individual State was abandoned and Article 20(5) provides that a reservation is considered to have been accepted by a State if it has not objected to it within 12 months of being notified of it, unless the reservation concerns the constituent instrument of an international organization, or the treaty in question provides otherwise.

Again following the *Genocide Convention* case, VCLT Article 19(c) provides that a State may not submit a reservation which is 'incompatible with the object and purpose of the treaty'. This criterion is vague and difficult to grasp. However, reservations of general character are considered to be incompatible with the 'object and purpose' of a treaty.[81] While reservations to treaty provisions which codify international customary law are possible,[82] there is no doubt that reservations to provisions reflecting norms of *jus cogens* are not.

---

[77]   GA Res 598 (VI), 12 January 1952.

[78]   *Armed Activities on the Territory of the Congo (New Application: 2002) (Democratic Republic of Congo v Rwanda) Jurisdiction of the Court and Admissibility of the Application, ICJ Reports 2006,* p 6, para 56.

[79]   Ibid, para 64.

[80]   Joint Separate Opinion of Judges Higgins, Koojimans, Elaraby, Owada, and Simma, ibid, para 29.

[81]   See, before the European Court of Human Rights, *Belilos* v *Switzerland, Judgment of 29 April 1988, Ser A, No 132,* para 55.

[82]   See, eg, *North Sea Continental Shelf, Judgment, ICJ Reports 1969,* p 3, paras 29 and 72 which seem to accept the possibility. But cf UN HRC General Comment No 24(52) on issues relating to reservations made upon ratification or accession to the Covenant or Optional Protocols thereto, or in relation to declarations under Article 41 of the Covenant, 11 November 1994 (for text see (1995) 15 *HRLJ* 262) which argues that reservations to provisions in human rights treaties which represent customary international law are not permissible. This is considered further later.

How are those reservations which are incompatible with the object and purpose of a treaty distinguished from those which are not? There are two schools of thought: the permissibility school and the opposability school. The permissibility school is based on a two-stage assessment procedure: first, the reservation must be objectively assessed for compatibility with the object and purpose of the treaty. If it is not compatible, acceptance by other States cannot validate it.[83] If, however, the reservation is compatible with the object and purpose of the treaty, the parties may decide whether to accept or object to the reservation on whatever other grounds they wish, such as for political reasons. The opposability school bases the validity of the reservation entirely upon whether it has been accepted by other parties and sees the compatibility test as merely a guiding principle for the parties to contemplate when considering whether to accept or object to the reservation.[84]

Some treaties attempt to deal with this question on a treaty-by-treaty basis. For example, the 1965 International Convention on Elimination of All Forms of Racial Discrimination, Article 20, uses a mathematical test, providing that a reservation is incompatible with the 'object and purpose' of the treaty if at least two-thirds of the contracting parties object to it.

The *Restrictions to the Death Penalty* Advisory Opinion concerned a reservation made by Guatemala to the prohibition of the infliction of capital punishment 'for political offenses or related common crimes' found in Article 4(4) of the 1969 American Convention on Human Rights, which is a non-derogable provision. Faced with the question whether a reservation was permissible in the light of the object and purpose of the Convention, the Inter-American Court of Human Rights said that:

> a reservation which was designed to enable a State to suspend any of the non-derogable fundamental rights must be deemed incompatible with the object and purpose of the Convention and, consequently, not permitted by it. The situation would be different if the reservation sought merely to restrict certain aspects of a non-derogable right without depriving the right as a whole of its basic purpose. Since the reservation . . . does not appear to be of a type that is designed to deny the right to life as such, the Court concludes that to that extent it can be considered, in principle, as being not incompatible with the object and purpose of the Convention.[85]

One unresolved question concerns the legal effect of having attached an impermissible reservation to a signature or ratification. There are two possible solutions: the first is that unless it is withdrawn, a State making an impermissible reservation will not be considered a party to a treaty. The second is that the impermissible reservation may be severed and the State be bound by the treaty in its entirety. Although, as will be seen in Section VII, there is some practice supporting the severability approach in the human rights sphere, it is difficult to see how the reservation can legitimately be severed if the consent to be bound is made expressly subject to such a reservation, albeit an impermissible one.

C. GUIDE TO PRACTICE ON RESERVATIONS TO TREATIES

At its 3125th Meeting on 11 August 2011 the International Law Commission completed its work on reservation to treaties, which had commenced in 1993, and recommended to the General Assembly that it take note of its Guide to Practice on Reservations to

---

[83] UN Doc A/CN.4/470 (30 May 1995) (First Report on Reservations), p 49, para 102. See also *YBILC* (1995), vol II (part two), p 101.   [84] Ibid.
[85] *Restrictions to the Death Penalty*, Advisory Opinion, Inter-American Court of Human Rights, AO OC-3/83, 8 September 1983, para 61, (1984) 23 ILM 320, p 341.

Treaties.[86] The Guide deals with all aspects of reservations—including in Section 4.5 the consequences of invalid reservations—and, unlike the 1969 VCLT, it also considers the meaning and effect of interpretative declarations.

The purpose of the Guide to Practice is to provide assistance to practitioners of international law—decision-makers, diplomats, and lawyers (including those who plead cases before national courts and tribunals)—who are faced with problems concerning the permissibility and effects of reservations to treaties and interpretative declarations, explaining the VCLT and supplementing it by addressing some *lacunae*. Some sections of the Guide reproduce VCLT while some are *de lege ferenda*; in some cases, guidelines are based on practices that have developed in the margins of the Vienna Conventions; other guidelines are simply recommendations and are meant only to encourage.[87]

The Guide to Practice is divided into five parts. Part 1 is devoted to the definition of reservations and interpretative declarations and to the distinction between these two types of unilateral statement (it also includes an overview of various unilateral statements, made in connection with a treaty, that are neither reservations nor interpretative declarations). Part 2 sets out the form and procedure to be used in formulating reservations and interpretative declarations and reactions thereto. Part 3 concerns the permissibility of reservations and interpretative declarations and reactions thereto and sets out the criteria for the assessment of permissibility. Part 4 sets out the legal effects produced by reservations and interpretative declarations, depending on whether they are valid (in which case a reservation is 'established' if it has been accepted) or not; this part also includes the effects of objections to and acceptances of reservations. Part 5 supplements the only provision of the 1978 Vienna Convention on Succession of States in respect of Treaties that deals with reservations, this being Article 20 which provides for the continuity of a reservation to a treaty in the case of succession by a newly independent State. The Guide also addresses situations in which States unite or separate as well as issues raised by objections to or acceptances of reservations and by interpretative declarations in relation to succession of States.[88]

D. THE PROBLEM OF RESERVATIONS TO HUMAN RIGHTS TREATIES

The system of reservations found in the Vienna Convention was supposed to be comprehensive, but it became clear in the 1980s that the system was difficult to apply, particularly as regards the compatibility of reservations to human rights treaties with their 'object and purpose', and in 1993 the topic of the Law and Practice Relating to Reservations to Treaties was added to the ILC's agenda (see Section VI C in this chapter). Human rights treaties are not contractual in nature and do not only create rights and obligations between States on the traditional basis of reciprocity, but also establish relationships between States and individuals. Several undecided issues had to be solved: were all reservations made by States permissible?[89] If not, who decides on their permissibility? What are the legal effects

---

[86] Sixty-third session (26 April–3 June and 4 July–12 August 2011), Suppl 10. The ILC Special Rapporteur on the topic, Professor Pellet, produced 17 Reports on the subject. For a full overview see http://legal.un.org/ilc/summaries/1_8.htm.

[87] See 'Symposium: the International Law Commission's Guide to Practice on Reservations to Treaties', (2013) 24 *EJIL* 1055–152.

[88] The Guide to Practice has prompted many comments from States, with particular concerns being expressed regarding Guideline 2.3.1 and 2.3.2 on the acceptance of and objection to 'late reservations' and to Section 4.5 on the 'Consequences of an Invalid Reservation'.

[89] For further discussion of this see Pellet and Muller, 2011.

of accepting or rejecting a reservation or of having made an impermissible reservation? Broadly speaking there are two main approaches: one illustrated by the approach of the UN Human Rights Committee (the HRC) that stresses the inadequacies of the VCLT regime and the other that considers that regime absolutely satisfactory.

There are very few international bodies, other than the European Court of Human Rights and the Inter-American Court of Human Rights, that have an institutionalized procedure to decide upon the permissibility of reservations. In the *Belilos* case the European Court of Human Rights decided that a declaration made by Switzerland when ratifying the ECHR was in fact a reservation of a general character and therefore impermissible under the terms of ECHR Article 64. The Court severed the reservation and decided that Switzerland was bound by the Convention in its entirety.[90] Similarly, in the *Loizidou* case the European Court of Human Rights considered that Turkish reservations to the jurisdiction of the Commission and Court to consider applications relating to activities in Northern Cyprus were invalid and severable, meaning that such applications could be considered by the Strasbourg organs, notwithstanding the intention of Turkey to prevent this.[91]

The question of reservations to human rights treaties was considered by the UN HRC in a controversial General Comment No 24 (1994).[92] The HRC is the body established under the 1966 ICCPR and has the task of overseeing compliance by States parties with their obligations under the Covenant. In its General Comment, the Committee took the view that the Vienna Convention provisions, which give a role to State objections in relation to reservations, are inappropriate in the context of human rights treaties, which do not comprise a web of inter-State reciprocal exchanges of mutual obligations but are concerned with endowing individuals with rights. The HRC took the view that reservations offending peremptory norms would not be compatible with the object and purpose of the Covenant and raised the question of whether reservations to non-derogable provisions of the Covenant were compatible with its object and purpose. It expressed the view that reservations to the system of individual communications to the Committee established under the first Optional Protocol to the Covenant would not be compatible with its object and purpose. The HRC also took the view that it was the Committee itself which should determine whether a specific reservation was compatible with the object and purpose of the Covenant.

The General Comment provoked strong reaction, including from the UK and USA, who considered VCLT Article 19(c) both adequate and applicable to reservations to human rights treaties and considered it for States parties to determine whether a reservation is compatible with the object and purpose of that treaty rather than the Committee. Moreover, the USA stressed that reservations formed an integral part of the consent to be bound and are not severable. The Committee, however, affirmed its General Comment in the *Rawle Kennedy* case, though it was questioned by a number of members who in a Dissenting Opinion observed that:

> The normal assumption will be that the ratification or accession is not dependent on the acceptability of the reservation and the unacceptability of the reservation will not vitiate the reserving State's agreement to be party to the Covenant. However, this assumption cannot apply when it is abundantly clear that the reserving State's agreement to becoming party to the Covenant is *dependent* on the acceptability of the reservation. The same applies with reservations to the Optional Protocol.[93]

---

[90] *Belilos* v *Switzerland, Judgment of 29 April 1988, Ser A, No 132*, paras 52–5, 60.

[91] *Loizidou* v *Turkey (Preliminary Objections), Judgment of 23 March 1995, Ser A, No 310*, paras 15, 27, 89, 90, 95.   [92] See n 37.

[93] *Rawle Kennedy* v *Trinidad and Tobago*, Comm No 845/1999, Decision, 2 November 1999, UN Doc A/55/40, vol II, Annex XI, A, Individual Dissenting Opinion of Judges Ando, Bhagwati, Klein, and Kretzmer, para 16.

However, in his Second Report as ILC Special Rapporteur, Pellet argued that the system of the Vienna Convention is adequate to address reservations in human rights treaties[94] and has recently noted that the practice of human rights bodies is not uniform and, for example, the Committees of the Conventions on Elimination of Discrimination against Women and International Convention on the Elimination of All Forms of Racial Discrimination attempt to persuade States to withdraw offending reservations rather than to decide on impermissibility.[95] It is, then, clear that there is a significant ongoing controversy surrounding this question.

This was confirmed by the 2007 meeting between the ILC and human rights bodies regarding reservations to human rights treaties.[96] During this meeting the representatives of several human rights bodies as well as the members of the Commission presented their views on this issue. During the discussion several issues were raised, the most important being the invalidity of reservation to treaties. Although the special character of human rights treaties was noted, a view was expressed that there were other areas such as environmental protection which also had special characteristics. However, a distinctive feature of human rights treaties was the presence of the human rights bodies. It was observed, nevertheless, that the law of treaties generally and the regime set up under Article 19 of the VCLT were applicable and adequate to deal with reservations to human rights treaties, but should be applied in 'an appropriate and suitably adopted manner'. The heart of the discussion was the issue of the delicate balance between the integrity and universality of treaties in respect of reservations. All participants were in agreement as to the competence of the human rights bodies to assess the validity of reservations. The most important issue was so-called 'reservation dialogue' between the reserving State and the human rights body. Taking a 'dialogue approach' best reflected the underlying political situation concerning reservations while giving human rights bodies the opportunity to exercise pragmatism (which is a particular feature of their policy towards reservations) and discretion. However, the question of the severance of an offending reservation from the consent to be bound by a treaty remained an unresolved problem in cases where it was impossible to ascertain the intention of the States parties in this respect. On one hand, some human rights bodies supported their right to severe reservations; on the other hand, some participants adhered to the view that the principle of sovereignty must prevail.

In his final Report, Pellet further analysed the so-called 'reservations dialogue'.[97] According to Pellet, the reservations regime of the VCLT is so flexible that it leaves room for dialogue between the key players (the author of the reservation on one hand, and the other contracting States or international organizations and any monitoring bodies on the other). However, the VCLT does not provide a legal framework for such a dialogue, in which the Human Rights Treaty bodies have a leading role by drawing the attention of States parties to those reservations which they find dubious or outdated in order to encourage the reserving State to modify or withdraw them.[98] However, as Pellet says, such a dialogue does not often result in a satisfactory solution. Therefore, in the Addendum to his final Seventeenth Report Pellet suggested that, following the precedent set by the Council

---

[94] For a summary see *YBILC* (1997), vol II, pp 53–4, 57.

[95] A Pellet, *Eighth Report on Reservations to Treaties*, ILC, Fifty-fifth Session (2003), A/CN.4/535, paras 17–27.

[96] See Annex to A Pellet, *Fourteenth Report on Reservation to Treaties*, ILC, Sixty-first Session (2009), A/CN.4/614, pp 27–34.

[97] A Pellet, *Seventeenth Report of Reservations to Treaties*, ILC Sixty-third Session (2011), A/CN.4/647.

[98] The 'reservation dialogue' is frequently conducted during review of the periodic reports submitted to the Treaty Bodies by the States parties, at which both are present.

of Europe, an impartial body—a 'reservations and objections to reservations assistance mechanism'—should be established to assist in a case of a stalemate.[99] However, after considering the matter in some depth, the ILC did not pursue this. It did, however, include an Annex to the Guide to Practice, entitled 'Conclusions on the Reservations Dialogue', which offers guidance on how such a 'dialogue' might be facilitated and which recommends that '[t]he General Assembly call upon States and international organizations, as well as monitoring bodies, to initiate and pursue such a reservations dialogue in a pragmatic and transparent manner'.

E. INTERPRETATIVE DECLARATIONS

Interpretative declarations are not addressed by the VCLT. They are, however, frequently appended to treaties by governments at the time of signature, ratification, or acceptance. They are explanatory in character, setting out how a State understands its treaty obligation when expressing its consent to be bound. However, such declarations must be subject to close scrutiny. If they change the scope of the obligation, they cease to be declarations and become reservations. The legal effect of interpretative declarations depends upon whether they aim to offer an interpretation of the treaty that may subsequently be proved incorrect (a 'mere interpretative declaration') or whether they offer an interpretation that is to be accepted by others (a 'qualified interpretative declaration').

In practice, distinguishing between reservations and forms of interpretative declarations can be a very daunting task and the ILC Guide to Practice on Reservation to Treaties does now seek to provide some helpful guidance. First, it defines an interpretive declaration as a 'unilateral statement, however phrased or named, made by a State or an international organization, whereby a State or that organisation purports to specify or clarify the meaning or scope of a treaty or of certain of its provisions'.[100] It then says that '[t]he character of a unilateral statement as a reservation or as an interpretative declaration is determined by the legal effect that its author purports to produce'[101] and, in determining this, '. . . the statement should be interpreted in good faith in accordance with the ordinary meaning to be given to its terms, with a view to identifying therefrom the intention of its author, in light of the treaty to which it refers'.[102] While '[t]he phrasing or name of a unilateral statement provides an indication of the purported legal effect',[103] what it is called by the declaring State would not seem to be definitive, even though it is the intention of the declaring State that is to be determined. Despite this additional guidance, distinguishing between a reservation and an interpretive declaration remains a difficult task.

VII. PROBLEMS CONCERNING THE GROUNDS FOR TERMINATION

This section will consider some specific issues concerning the external grounds for terminating or suspending a treaty, these being material breach, supervening impossibility of performance, and fundamental change of circumstances.

---

[99] A Pellet, *Seventeenth Report of Reservations to Treaties*, ILC sixty-third session (2011), A/CN.4/647/Add.1, paras 85–101.   [100] Guideline 1.2.
[101] Guideline 1.3.   [102] Guideline 1.3.1.   [103] Guideline 1.3.2.

A. MATERIAL BREACH

VCLT Article 60 regulates the consequences of a breach of a treaty obligation deriving from the law of treaties, rather than from the law of State responsibility (see Simma and Tams, 2012). The guiding principle is that of reciprocity. The ILC took a cautious approach to material breach, considering that a breach of a treaty, however serious, did not *ipso facto* put an end to a treaty but that within certain limits and subject to certain safeguards the right of a party to invoke the breach of a treaty as a ground for terminating it or suspending its operation must be recognized, and Article 60 takes the same approach.

Taking a strict approach to the effect of a material breach aims at striking a balance between the need to uphold the stability of treaties and the need to ensure reasonable protection for the innocent victim of a breach, though it may appear that the stability of treaties is the first priority. It is certainly true that the ICJ takes a restrictive approach to the application of Article 60. For example, in the *Gabčíkovo-Nagymaros* case it responded to Hungary's claim that Slovakia's actions in relation to other treaties had a bearing upon the assessment of Hungary's own actions by saying that '[i]t is only material breach of the treaty itself, by a State party to that treaty, which entitles the other party to rely on it as a ground for terminating the treaty'.[104] The Court explained that, while the violation of any other treaty or rules of general international law might justify an injured State taking other measures, such as countermeasures, it did not constitute a ground for termination of the treaty under the law of treaties.

This case is also illustrative of what comprises a material breach. Hungary relied on the construction of a bypass canal in pursuance of a plan known as 'Variant C' by Czechoslovakia, and which was unauthorized by the original 1977 Treaty between the parties, as the basis for invoking material breach of that treaty. Czechoslovakia claimed that its plans were justified as a legitimate response to prior breaches of the treaty by Hungary. The Court found that Czechoslovakia had indeed violated the 1977 Treaty when it diverted the waters of the Danube into the bypass canal in October 1992 but that the construction of the works prior to this had not been unlawful. Thus the notification by Hungary in May 1992 that it was terminating the 1977 Treaty for material breach was premature, as no breach had yet occurred. Moreover, the Court took the view that by attempting to terminate the 1977 Treaty by means of a declaration issued on 6 May 1992 with effect as of some 19 days later on 25 May 1992, Hungary had not acted in accordance with the principle of good faith and therefore had by its own conduct prejudiced its right to terminate the 1977 Treaty. The Court stated that:

> This would still have been the case even if Czechoslovakia, by the time of the purported termination, had violated a provision essential to the accomplishment of the object or purpose of the Treaty.[105]

In the later case concerning the *Application of the Interim Accord of 13 September 1995* Greece attempted to invoke the material breach of a treaty obligation (VCLT Article 60(3)(b)) and countermeasures as subsidiary defences in order to justify its disregard for its obligations under the Interim Accord not to oppose the former Yugoslav Republic of Macedonia's application of membership of an international organization, in this case, NATO. Greece argued that the applicant was in material breach since it had displayed

---

[104] *Gabčíkovo-Nagymaros Project (Hungary/Slovakia), Judgment, ICJ Reports 1997*, p 7, para 106.
[105] Ibid, para 110.

a particular symbol in contravention of Article 7(2) of the Interim Accord, but this was rejected by the Court.[106]

The relationship between the material breach of a treaty and the law of State responsibility, and particularly with countermeasures, is extremely problematic. Although not resolved by the ILC in its work on the law of treaties it appears that its intention was that the two regimes should coexist and the ILC's Commentary to its Articles on State Responsibility reflect this, indicating that State responsibility does not deal with the 'consequences of breach for the continual or binding effect of the primary rule (eg the right of an injured State to terminate or suspend a treaty for material breach, as reflected in Article 60 of the Vienna Convention on the Law of Treaties)'. The Special Rapporteur, James Crawford, explained that:

> There is thus a clear distinction between action taken within the framework of the law of treaties (as codified in the Vienna Convention) and conduct raising questions of State responsibility (which are excluded from the Vienna Convention). The law of treaties is concerned essentially with the content of primary rules and with the validity of attempts to alter them; the law of State responsibility takes as given the existence of primary rules (whether based on a treaty or otherwise) and is concerned with the question whether the conduct inconsistent with those rules can be excused and, if not, what consequences of such conduct are. Thus it is coherent to apply the Vienna Convention rules as to the materiality of breach and the severability of provisions of a treaty in dealing with issues of suspension, and the rules proposed in the Draft articles as to proportionality etc, in dealing with countermeasures.[107]

This finds reflection in the approach taken by the ICJ in the *Interim Accord* case, where it considered whether the actions of Greece might be justifiable as both under the law of treaties and as a countermeasure under the rules of State responsibility.[108]

B. SUPERVENING IMPOSSIBILITY OF PERFORMANCE

This ground for termination is well established and uncontested. VCLT Article 61 limits this ground to the 'permanent disappearance or destruction of an object indispensable for the execution of a treaty' and it cannot be invoked by a party that was itself instrumental in causing these circumstances to come about by the breach of its treaty

---

[106] The Court concluded that 'the only breach which has been established is the display of a symbol in breach of Article 7, paragraph 2, of the Interim Accord, a situation which ended in 2004. The Court considers that this incident cannot be regarded as a material breach within the meaning of Article 60 of the 1969 Vienna Convention.' See *Application of the Interim Accord of 13 September 1995 (the former Yugoslav Republic of Macedonia* v *Greece), Judgment of 5 December 2011, ICJ Reports 2011*, p 644, para 163.

[107] Third Report on State Responsibility, A/CN.4507/Add.3.

[108] Having rejected the argument based on material breach under the VCLT, the Court then rejected the argument based on countermeasures: 'the Court is not persuaded that the Respondent's objection to the Applicant's admission was taken for the purpose of achieving the cessation of the Applicant's use of the symbol prohibited by Article 7, paragraph 2'. See *Application of the Interim Accord of 13 September 1995 (the former Yugoslav Republic of Macedonia* v *Greece), Judgment of 5 December 2011, ICJ Reports 2011*, p 644, para 164. The complex nature of the relationship between material breach of a treaty and countermeasures has been evidenced by the Russian Federation's decision to suspend and in one case terminate various nuclear-related agreements between itself and the United States of America. Russia's unilateral decisions have raised several questions with regard to the unclear relationship between the law of treaties and countermeasures. Hofer, 2016, http://www.ejiltalk.org/russias-unilateral-suspension-of-the-2013-agreement-on-nuclear-cooperation-with-the-united-states/.

obligations. Once again, the ICJ has taken a strict approach. In the *Gabčíkovo-Nagymaros* case Hungary argued that the essential object of the 1977 Treaty was a joint economic investment, which was inconsistent with environmental considerations and had ceased to exist, rendering the 1977 Treaty impossible to perform. The Court observed that if the joint exploitation of the investment was no longer possible, this was because of Hungary's failure to perform most of the works for which it was responsible under the 1977 Treaty and, as indicated, impossibility of performance cannot be invoked by a party as a ground for terminating a treaty when it is the result of that party's own failure to perform its treaty obligations.

C. FUNDAMENTAL CHANGE OF CIRCUMSTANCES

Fundamental change of circumstances as a ground for the termination of a treaty is controversial. The principle of stability of contractual obligations and the conviction that 'it is a function of the law to enforce contracts or treaties even if they become burdensome for the party bound by them' militates against it (*Oppenheim's International Law*, 1992) but this needs to be balanced against the view that '[o]ne could not insist upon petrifying a state of affairs which had become anachronistic because it is based on a treaty which either does not contain any specific clause as to its possible termination or which even proclaimed itself to be concluded for all times to come' (Nahlik, 1971). VCLT Article 62 takes a particularly cautious approach. It accepts that termination on these grounds is possible, but it is of limited scope. It may not be invoked in relation to a treaty, which establishes a boundary; and, as with Article 61, a State may not invoke Article 62 if the change was caused by a breach of its own international obligations, either under the treaty in question or any other international agreement.

The ICJ has taken a very cautious approach to this principle. In the *Fisheries Jurisdiction* case it said:

> International law admits that a fundamental change of circumstances which determined the parties to accept a treaty, if it has resulted in a radical transformation of the extent of obligation imposed by it, may, under certain conditions, afford the party affected a ground for invoking the termination or suspension of a treaty. This principle, and the conditions and exceptions to which it is subject, have been embodied in Article 62 of the Vienna Convention on the Law of Treaties, which may in many respects be considered as a codification of existing customary law on the subject of termination of a treaty relationship on account of changed circumstances.[109]

The *Gabčíkovo-Nagymaros* case again illustrates the Court's approach. Hungary identified several 'substantive elements' that had been present when the 1977 Treaty had been concluded but which it claimed had changed fundamentally when it issued its notice of termination in May 1992, these being: the whole notion of socialist economic integration which underpinned the 1977 Treaty; the replacement of a joint and unified operational system with separate unilateral schemes; the emergence of market economies in both States; the Czechoslovakian approach that had turned a framework treaty into an immutable norm; and, finally, the transformation of a treaty inconsistent with environmental protection into a prescription for environmental disaster.[110]

---

[109] *Fisheries Jurisdiction (United Kingdom v Iceland), Jurisdiction of the Court, Judgment, ICJ Reports 1973*, p 3, para 36 (see Fitzmaurice, 2012).

[110] *Gabčíkovo-Nagymaros Project (Hungary/Slovakia), Judgment, ICJ Reports 1997*, p 7, para 95.

The Court concluded that while the political situation was relevant to the conclusion of the 1977 Treaty, its object and purpose—the joint investment programme for
the production of energy, the control of floods, and the improvement of navigation on
the River Danube—were not so closely linked to political conditions that the political changes in central Europe had radically altered the extent of obligations still to be
performed.[111] The Court drew the same conclusion regarding the changes in economic
systems, concluding that even if by 1992 the projected profitability of the scheme had
declined, it had not done so to an extent that would transform the nature of the parties'
obligations. Likewise, developments in environmental knowledge and environmental
law were not completely unforeseen. Having analysed the parties' arguments the Court
concluded that 'the changed circumstances advanced by Hungary are, in the Court's
view, not of such nature, either individually or collectively, that their effect would radically transform the extent of the obligation still to be performed in order to accomplish
the Project'.[112] The Court therefore interpreted VCLT Article 62 strictly, believing that a
'fundamental change of circumstances must have been unforeseen; the existence of the
circumstances at the time of the Treaty's conclusion must have constituted an essential
basis of consent of the parties to be bound by the Treaty' and that 'the stability of treaty
relations requires that the plea of fundamental change of circumstances be applied only
in exceptional cases'.[113]

VIII. CONCLUSION

This chapter has presented the main issues of treaty law found in the 1969 Vienna
Convention on the Law of Treaties. It has attempted to illustrate the application and
interpretation of the Convention in practice through the case law, in particular that of
the International Court of Justice. Although rightly considered as one of the greatest
accomplishments of the ILC, the Vienna Convention does not cover all possible areas
and issues, particularly the question of reservation to human rights treaties and the
relationship between State responsibility and material breach. The law of treaties is a
classical yet constantly developing branch of international law. Treaties are the main
tool of relations between States and therefore it is only to be expected that the rules
that govern their application are not static but constantly evolve and reflect the development of other branches of international law. Indeed, the law of treaties has become
a particularly dynamic subject and the International Law Commission has currently
two projects on the law of treaties on its agenda. These are: 'subsequent agreements and
subsequent practice in relation to the interpretation of treaties';[114] and 'the provisional
application of treaties'.[115] It is clear, then, that there are further important developments to come.

[111] Ibid.   [112] Ibid, para 104.   [113] Ibid.
[114] The ILC decided to commence work on this topic in 2008, which until 2012 was known as 'treaties over
time', with Mr Georg Nolte as Special Rapporteur. Up to 2016, the Special Rapporteur in relation to subsequent
practice had presented four reports and a set of 13 draft conclusions, which the Commission adopted at the
first reading.
[115] The ILC decided to commence work on this topic in 2012, with Mr Juan Gomez-Robledo as Special
Rapporteur. Up to 2016, the Special Rapporteur in relation to provisional application of treaties had presented
four reports and ten draft guidelines.

REFERENCES

ARATO, J (2014), 'Subsequent Practice in the Whaling Case, and What the ICJ Implies about Treaty Interpretation in International Organizations', *EJIL* Talk!, 31 March 2014, www.ejiltalk.org.

AUST, A (2013), *Modern Treaty Law and Practice* (3rd edn, Cambridge: Cambridge University Press).

BOYLE, A (2000), 'Some Reflections on the Relationship of Treaties and Soft Law', in V Gowlland-Debbas (ed), *Multilateral Treaty Making* (The Hague: Martinus Nijhoff), p 25.

CHINKIN, C (1993), *Third Parties in International Law* (Oxford: Oxford University Press).

FITZMAURICE, SIR G (1951), 'Treaty Interpretation and Certain Other Treaty Points, 1947–1951', 22 *BYIL* 1.

FITZMAURICE, M (2012), 'Exceptional Circumstances and Treaty Commitments', in DB Hollis (ed), *The Oxford Guide to Treaties* (Oxford: Oxford University Press), p 605.

FITZMAURICE, M (2016), 'The Whaling Convention and Thorny Issues of Interpretation', in M Fitzmaurice and D Tamada (eds), *Whaling in the Antarctic: Significance and Implications of the ICJ Judgment* (Leiden: Brill/Nijhoff), pp 55–138.

FOX, H (2010), 'Article 31(3)(a) and (b) of the Vienna Convention and the *Kasikili/Sedudu Island Case*', in M Fitzmaurice, O Elias, and P Merkouris, *Treaty Interpretation and the Vienna Convention on the Law of Treaties 30 Years On* (Leiden/Boston: Martinus Nijhoff), p 59.

HOFER, A (2016), 'Russia's Unilateral Suspension of the 2013 Agreement on Nuclear Cooperation with the United States', *EJIL Talk!*, 26 October 2016.

KOSKENNIEMI, M (1989), *From Apology to Utopia; The Structure of International Legal Argument* (2005 reissue, Cambridge: Cambridge University Press).

MCNAIR, AD (1961), *The Law of Treaties* (2nd edn, Oxford: Clarendon Press).

NAHLIK, SE (1971), 'The Grounds of Invalidity of and Termination of Treaties', 65 *AJIL* 747.

OPPENHEIM, L (1992), Jennings, Sir R and Watts, Sir A (eds), *Oppenheim's International Law* (9th edn, Harlow: Longman).

PELLET, A and MULLER, D (2011), 'Reservations to Treaties: An Objection to a Reservation is Definitely not an Acceptance', in E Cannizzaro (ed), *The Law of Treaties Beyond the Vienna Convention* (Oxford: Oxford University Press), p 37.

SHEARER, IA (1994), *Starke's International Law* (11th edn, London: Butterworths).

SIMMA, B and TAMS, C (2012), 'Reacting to Treaty Breaches', in Hollis, *The Oxford Guide to Treaties*, p 576.

SINCLAIR, SIR I (1984), *The Vienna Convention on the Law of Treaties* (2nd edn, Oxford: Oxford University Press).

THIRLWAY, H (1992), 'The Law and Procedure of the International Court of Justice, 1960–1989', Part Three, 63 *BYIL* 1.

VAGTS, D (1993), 'Treaty Interpretation and the New American Ways of Law Reading', 4 *EJIL* 472.

WEIL, P (1983), 'Towards Relative Normativity in International Law', 77 *AJIL* 413.

FURTHER READING

BIANCHI, A, PEAT, D, and WINDSOR, M (2015) (eds), *Interpretation in International Law* (Oxford: Oxford University Press): offers an original approach to treaty interpretation. Contributors provide fresh thinking on the functions, rules, and strategies of interpretation.

BJORGE, E (2014), *The Evolutionary Interpretation of Treaties* (Oxford: Oxford University Press): investigates the contentious issue of the interpretation of treaties in light of changing conditions and subsequent development of international law, arguing that evolutionary interpretation of treaties should be understood as the natural corollary of the parties' intentions.

CANNIZZARO, E (2011), *The Law of Treaties Beyond the Vienna Convention* (Oxford: Oxford University Press): a collection of essays on challenging aspects of the law of treaties.

CORTEN, O and KLEIN, P (eds) (2011), *The Vienna Convention on the Law of Treaties: A Commentary* (New York: Oxford University Press): a detailed commentary on the Vienna Convention.

DISTEFANO, G, GAGGIOLI, G, and HECHE, A (eds) (2016), *La convention de Vienne de 1978 sur la succession d'Etats en matière de traités: Commentaire article par article et études thématiques*, 2 volumes (Bruxelles: Emile Bruylant): analyses in great detail the contributions and shortcomings of this Convention in the light of the preparatory work as well as recent practice and how the Convention could have given rise to customary principles and rules in this field.

DÖRR, O and SCHMALENBACH, K (2012), *Vienna Convention on the Law of Treaties: A Commentary* (Berlin: Springer): an in-depth commentary on the VCLT.

FITZMAURICE, M and ELIAS, O (2005), *Contemporary Issues in the Law of Treaties* (Utrecht: Eleven International Publishing): a collection of essays dealing with some pertinent and often unresolved issues of the law of treaties.

FITZMAURICE, M, ELIAS, O, and MERKOURIS, P (eds) (2010), *Treaty Interpretation and the Vienna Convention on the Law of Treaties 30 Years On* (Leiden/Boston: Martinus Nijhoff Publishers): an in-depth study on approaches to interpretation in the VCLT and on subsequent developments.

GARDINER, R (2015), *Treaty Interpretation* (2nd edn, Oxford: Oxford University Press): an in-depth study of treaty interpretation, based on meticulous analysis of Article 31 of the 1969 Vienna Convention on the Law of Treaties, including the historical development of treaty interpretation; the work of the International Law Commission; relevant case law; and the views of doctrine.

HOLLIS, DB (ed) (2012), *The Oxford Guide to Treaties* (Oxford: Oxford University Press): this provides a comprehensive guide to treaties, on the rules and practices surrounding the making, interpretation, and operation of these instruments.

KLABBERS, J (1996), *The Concept of Treaty in International Law* (The Hague: Kluwer Law International): a highly original study of the law of treaties, often controversial but very thought provoking. It includes an overview of relevant jurisprudence of the International Court of Justice.

LESTSAS, G (2007), *A Theory Interpretation of the European Convention on Human Rights* (Oxford: Oxford University Press).

MCNAIR, AD (1961), *The Law of Treaties* (2nd edn, Oxford: Clarendon Press): the classical treatise on the law of treaties.

MERKOURIS, P (2015), *Article 31(3)(C) VCLT and the Principle of Systemic Integration: Normative Shadows in Plato's Cave* (Leiden: Brill/Martinus Nijhoff): the author tackles a provision on treaty interpretation that has risen in prominence, Article 31(3)(c) VCLT. Through an examination of both its written and unwritten elements, the book's premise is that the 'proximity criterion' is the optimal way of understanding and utilizing this provision, that conflict resolution principles may be of use within Article 31(3)(c), and, finally, that the principle of systemic integration is indispensable not only for interpreting treaty provisions but customary international law as well.

NOLTE, G (ed) (2013), *Treaties and Subsequent Practice* (Oxford: Oxford University Press): explores subsequent practice in treaty interpretation and in general international law. It provides a comprehensive treatment of this topic by eminent commentators, combining contributions which focus on practical cases with chapters examining the theoretical underpinnings of treaty interpretation.

ORAKHELASHVILI, A and WILLIAMS, S (eds) (2010), *40 Years of the Vienna Convention on the Law of Treaties* (London: British Institute of International and Comparative Law): an evaluation of the VCLT, containing detailed analysis of unresolved issues.

PADDEU, F (2018), *Justification and Excuse in International Law: Concept and Theory of General Defences* (Cambridge: Cambridge University Press): analyses the distinction between justifications and excuses in case of international wrong-doing and shows that the distinction is not only possible in international law, but also would have important practical implications.

PELLET, A and MÜLLER, DS (eds) (2011), 'Reservations to Human Rights Treaties: Not Absolute Evil . . . ', in U Fastenrath et al (eds), *From Bilateralism to Community Interest: Essays in Honour of Bruno Simma* (Oxford: Oxford University Press), p 521.

QUAST MERTSCH, A (2012), *Provisionally Applied Treaties: Their Binding Force and Legal Nature* (Leiden: Brill/Martinus Nijhoff): examines the binding force and legal nature of treaties during the period of their provisional application, a subject whose significance in practice is not reflected in the relatively limited attention it receives in academic writing. It analyses academic opinion and international practice (including especially the manifestations of the intentions of the parties) on the subject.

REUTER, P (1995), *Introduction to the Law of Treaties* (J Moco and P Haggenmacher (trans)) (London: Kegan Paul International): presents an in-depth study of the 1986 Convention on the Law of Treaties between States and International Organizations or between International Organizations.

SINCLAIR, SIR I (1984), *The Vienna Convention on the Law of Treaties* (2nd edn, Manchester: Manchester University Press): a classical book on the 1969 Vienna Convention on the Law of Treaties that also includes practice of States and the overview of the ILC's work on the codification of the Convention.

VENZKE, I (2014), *How Interpretation Makes International Law: On Semantic Change and Normative Twists* (2nd edn, Oxford: Oxford University Press): an important contribution to the debate on interpretation of treaties.

VILLIGER, M (1997), *Customary Law and Treaties, A Manual on the Theory and Practice of the Interrelation of Sources* (2nd edn, Zurich: Schulthess Polygraphischer Verlag and The Hague: Kluwer Law International): a systematic and erudite study on written and unwritten international law.

VILLIGER, M (2009), *Commentary on the Vienna Convention on the Law of Treaties* (Leiden/Boston: Martinus Nijhoff Publishers): an in-depth commentary.

ZIEMELE, I (ed) (2004), *Reservations to Human Rights Treaties and the Vienna Convention Regime, Conflict, Harmony or Reconciliation* (The Hague: Martinus Nijhoff): gives a comprehensive overview of the practice of human rights bodies in relation to reservations, as well a theoretical background.

PART III

THE SUBJECTS OF THE INTERNATIONAL LEGAL ORDER

7

STATEHOOD, SELF-DETERMINATION, AND RECOGNITION

Matthew Craven and Rose Parfitt

SUMMARY

The idea that international law's primary function is to regulate the relations among States has long been an axiomatic feature of the discipline. Yet this apparently straightforward description only thinly veils a longstanding problem. In one direction, the existence of a society of independent States appears to be a necessary presupposition for the discipline—something that has to precede the identification of rules of international law, as produced through the mutual interaction of its members. In another direction, however, statehood is clearly a product of international law, following from the need for certain rules to determine which political communities can rightfully claim the prerogatives of sovereignty. The apparent contradiction here has shaped many facets of the discourse of international law since the nineteenth century, demarcating debates as to the character of statehood (whether factual or normative) and the implications of self-determination (whether determined or determining) and of recognition (whether declaratory or constitutive). Yet these are not merely abstract, theoretical debates. Instead, these contradictions were thrown up as a consequence of the establishment, and subsequent dismantlement, of European colonial empires, during which process the model of the European nation-State was exported as the principal mode of political organization for all people everywhere in the world. This is to prompt a series of reflections: why has statehood come to assume such a central and powerful role in the world today, in which there appears to be 'no alternative' to either being part of a State or the object of its coercive power? Why has the normative 'pull' (and material 'push') of an institution whose origins lie in the very specific historical, geographical, and cultural context of sixteenth-century Western Europe, proved to be so irresistible? What, if anything, changed with the emergence of a right of peoples to self-determination in the mid-twentieth century, together with the (rhetorical?) abandonment of the 'standard of civilization' as a mode of determining which communities would be recognized as subjects of international law and which would not? Finally, we also reflect upon the question whether, in an era of acute transnational inequality, instability, and violence, the continued enthusiasm for 'secession' really offers an antidote to the pathologies of statehood. Is the problem one of individual 'State failure', such that new States might 'succeed'? Or does the State's increasing incapacity to fulfil its promises of order and justice signal the beginning of the end for an institution once hailed widely, by Hegel and his followers, as the universal apotheosis of individual rationality, freedom, and 'self-consciousness'?

I. INTRODUCTION

It is a remarkable feature of our contemporary understanding of the world that if forced to describe it, we would normally do so in one of two ways. One would be in terms of its physical and biological geography (a description of continents, oceans, climate, and plant or animal life-forms); the other in terms of its political geography, as being a world divided systematically and uniformly by reference to the territorial parameters of States (as one would find marked by colours within an atlas). That the second form of representation appears significant is to mark the extraordinary power that that idea of the State has come to play in the formation of our social, political, economic, and cultural world view. Not only is it now an apparently universal institution, but its very centrality in the structures of consciousness by which we construct the social world is to render it, as Bourdieu puts it, almost 'unthinkable' (Bourdieu, 2014, p 4). The languages through which we might want to describe it—like international law—are often the languages that the State itself has produced.

However much we may take its presence for granted in an era in which virtually the entire surface of the earth is now covered in nation-States, this incredibly powerful and monolithic way of organizing collective life has not been a permanent feature in history. If, for the sake of argument, we identify States simply with the existence of 'political communities', then States have been around for centuries, even millennia—from the ancient city-State of Athens (c. 508–322 BCE) to the Kingdom of Aksum (c. 100–940 CE) to the Chinese Empire (c. 221 BCE–1912 CE). They have, however, also changed much over this time (Tilly, 1992; Spruyt, 1994). Broadly speaking, until about 200 years ago, the distribution of political authority around the globe could largely be described in terms of its relative intensity. High levels of loyalty and allegiance to the 'sovereign' were concentrated in 'centres of power' within denser urban sites, which then shaded off in the more remote frontier zones at the outer edges of the realm. Today, by contrast, we inhabit a global order framed in terms of an undeniably Western European model of the nation-State, characterized by the possession of determinate boundaries, centralized bureaucratic structures, and a single, uniform system of law (Weber, 1978; Giddens, 1985). The purchase of this institution upon the political imagination has been such that not only does the daily routine of 'politics' remain firmly embedded within its frame (institutionalized, for example, in parliamentary debates, elections, and campaigns for office), but that even movements of resistance tend to adopt it as their principal mode of emancipation.

This is to prompt a series of questions: what is it about the idea of the State that makes its 'status' so ubiquitously desirable? From the eccentric 'micro-nation' projects of Liberland, North Sudan, Enclava, and Sealand, to the international jihadist group which styles itself ISIS or 'Islamic State', to oppressed peoples within States like the Kurds and the Oromo, to former colonies like Palestine and Western Sahara which have been denied the right to self-determination through military occupation, the desire to become a 'State' appears to be the uniform objective. So why is collective liberation so consistently narrated in the language of statehood? And why does opposition to the State appear to resolve itself so regularly in the emergence of yet another State?[1]

Yet even as independence movements—in places as diverse as Bougainville, Chechnya, Catalonia, Nagorno-Karabakh, Somaliland, Scotland, or West Irian—continue to re-affirm the singularity of the State as the primary mode of political organization, they also threaten

---

[1] Some recent examples: the independence of Abkhazia and South Ossetia, officially parts of Georgia, was declared, by decree, by Russia on 26 August 2008; the 'Independent state of Azawad' was declared in northern Mali on 6 April 2012; the 'Republic of Crimea' declared its independence from Ukraine on 11 March 2014.

it in doing so. Not only do such secessionist movements challenge the integrity of the State against which they assert their independence; they also pose a challenge to the broader international order within which each State necessarily locates itself and upon which it relies for its legitimacy. Not all such movements turn out in the same way of course. In some cases, claims to independence are given the definitive seal of statehood by membership in the United Nations (eg Eritrea 1993). In others, effective self-government continues, yet the claim to independent statehood goes decisively unrecognized (eg Somaliland 1996–). Still other attempts at forming new sovereign States survive in an apparent twilight zone of partial recognition (eg Kosovo 2009–, Palestine 1988–). At such moments, international lawyers are often asked for advice. Is it right or proper for other States to recognize such claims? What are the implications for doing so, or indeed for refusing such recognition? How far does institutional membership go to determine the outcome in such cases? What consideration should be given to the democratic credentials of the new State or the role played by human rights? This, at first, seems appropriate. After all, international lawyers are supposed to possess some special kind of expertise in this area, one that is sought not only by those concerned with the distributional consequences of any political change, but by the public at large. International law is, indeed, usually defined as the law that applies as between sovereign States, and international lawyers have spent an inordinate amount of time on the attempt to determine what they are, how they come into being, and how they change. Yet on closer inspection, this faith in international law as a source of definitive answers to questions about the who, what, why, and how of statehood—questions with huge implications for the territories and populations involved—is undercut by the very proximity of the problem to the language and practice of international law itself. The 'State' is almost too self-evident.

An initial difficulty here is that the central position assigned to States in the formation of rules of international law has created something of a logical impasse for international lawyers when they attempt to conceptualize how that same law might regulate States' existence or demise. An early attempt to do so is to be found in Lassa Oppenheim's dizzyingly circular explanation in his classic *Treatise* of 1905:

> The conception of International Persons is derived from the conception of the Law of Nations. As this law is the body of rules which the civilised states consider legally binding in their intercourse, every state which belongs to the civilised states, and is, therefore, a member of the Family of Nations, is an International Person. (Oppenheim, 1905, p 99)

In this formulation, States are entities that possess international personality under international law, and they do so because international law lays down that this should be so. But international law is, in turn, merely the 'body of rules' which the States consider to be 'binding in their intercourse' with one another. The legal personality of the State then, is seen to be a product of the law of which it (the State) is deemed to be the author. As a form of 'bootstraps' argument, this was clearly an unsatisfactory formulation, but it is important to recall that its origin was found in a determination, on the part of those such as Oppenheim, to try to demonstrate that international law could be regarded as a 'positive' branch of law, notwithstanding the absence of a super-sovereign from which normatively binding 'commands' could derive (the critique launched by John Austin in 1832; see Austin, 1995, p 123), without resort to the kinds of normative presuppositions associated with the 'natural law' thinking of the previous three centuries. And the centrality of the State in the organization and ordering of international society was, for international lawyers working in that vein, largely a pre-supposition rather than a conclusion.

A little more than a hundred years later, however, talk of both the exclusivity of States as subjects of international law and of States as primary actors in international relations is regarded as an increasingly antiquated proposition. Within international law itself, international organizations, individuals, minorities, corporations, and even animals and rivers have all made the transition from being the object of international law to agents in possession of some kind of international 'subjectivity' or 'personality' (see Johns (ed), 2010). Non-State actors (whether NGOs or international organizations) are playing an increasingly important role in treaty-making, and the figure of the 'international community' is repeatedly invoked (in the context, for example, of the elaboration of *erga omnes* obligations) as an entity having some, albeit still rather vague, legal status.[2] 'Statism', indeed, is increasingly used as a derogatory label, attached to any approach that is seen to prioritize the interests of States over those of the individuals, communities, and environments over which they exert authority (see Marks, 2006).

At the same time, however, the story of the gradual 'decline of the nation-State' is often told with a hint of nostalgia. Writing in 1998, for example, Oscar Schachter observed that the growth, and increased mobility, of capital and technology, the formation of 'new social identities' (forged as much by transnational drugs traffickers and arms traders as by international NGOs), and the emergence of 'failed States' (see later) posed enormous challenges to the idea of a global order of States regulated by rules of international law (Schachter, 1998, pp 10–16). Nonetheless, despite the trends, Schachter concluded that 'it [was] most unlikely that the State will disappear in the foreseeable future'. Not only has the State provided the structures of authority needed to cope with the 'incessant claims of competing societal groups', he argued, but it still promises dignity and protection for the individual with access to common institutions and the equal protection of the law (Schachter, 1998, p 22). For Schachter, then, the key question was not so much whether the State as such would survive, but whether international law would be able to adjust to such phenomena and respond to the changing demands of the environment in which it operated.

Whether or not one accepts Schachter's diagnosis, or indeed his confidence for the future, there are two broad themes interwoven in his analysis that are widely shared. One is a factual or sociological reflection on the changing character of international society and the declining power or authority of the nation-State, witnessed by the emergence of alternative schemes of legal responsibility and a broadening of the range of international actors.[3] The other is a normative or ethical variant which regards the tradition of State 'sovereignty' as an archaic impediment to the pursuit of humanitarian or other cosmopolitan agendas (human rights, environmental protection, criminal justice, etc) and which has often been called upon to legitimate interventionist policies aimed specifically at undermining the exclusive authority of the State.[4] To pose this opposition in the form of a question: is the authority of the State objectively speaking 'in decline', or does that authority *need* to be challenged in order, for example, to 'protect' vulnerable populations? In some ways, of course, these two forms of reflection work against each other: the first seeing States as increasingly marginalized by social forces that escape their regulative or coercive capabilities; the second believing that States retain an authority that needs to be dismantled before emancipatory agendas may be put in place. Where they meet, furthermore, is in an alarming vision of global order in which the State as political agent, instructed with the task of

[2] See, eg, ILC Articles on the Responsibility of States for Internationally Wrongful Acts (2001) Articles, 33, 42, and 48.

[3] See, eg, proposals relating to the development of 'Global Administrative Law' (Kingsbury, Krisch, and Stewart 2005), and other initiatives directed towards the development of the accountability of non-State actors more generally (Clapham, 2006).

[4] See, eg, Orford's genealogical account of the relationship between the Responsibility to Protect and the development of international executive authority (Orford, 2011).

'mediating' between the individual and the general interest, has neither the ability nor the competence to resist the incursions of a global 'community' that claims both power and justice on its own side.[5]

Before we settle upon such a conclusion, however, we might also want to consider an alternative narrative here—that concerns the way in which the State, as the principal mode, or technology, of social and political organization was, and continues to be, globalized (Badie, 2000). Rather than focusing on its supposedly imminent decline, we might reflect, rather, on the possibility that the State-project was never complete—that having been exported to the non-Western world during decolonization, it has become the persistent object of a host of projects (humanitarian, political, economic, and legal) associated with making the world into a world of nation-States, to shore them up, save them from 'failure', and mute their pathologies. From that standpoint, the role of international law has not been to advance its decline, but rather to 'perform' the State and produce it as an 'effect' of rule (Mitchell, 1999). And if that is the case then we should be equally concerned with material or 'distributive' consequences of that particular way of organizing the world—of the forms of domination or exploitation it has brought in its wake, and the other ways of 'being in the world' that it has foreclosed. These are questions to which we will return throughout this chapter, beginning first with a look at the emergence of the ideas of statehood, recognition, and self-determination between the sixteenth and nineteenth centuries.

II. HISTORY

At the beginning of the Fourth Edition of his influential *Treatise on International Law*, prepared for publication in 1895, shortly before his death, William Hall offered a succinct definition:

> International law consists in certain rules of conduct which modern civilised states regard as being binding on them in their relations with one another with a force comparable in nature and degree to that binding the conscientious person to obey the laws of his country, and which they also regard as being enforceable by appropriate means in case of infringement. (Hall, 1895, p 1)

This statement—typical of the positivist tradition which emerged in the late nineteenth century (Koskenniemi, 2001)—is remarkable in several respects. To begin with, there is the question of tone: this is not the beginning of an enquiry, or a speculation that has to be situated in some historical context. There is no attempt to locate his subject in contemporary debate or practice. This is international law written as science. International law, here, is not merely a language, or a way of describing certain activities or practices. It is already a thing with definite content, there to be described. The content of international law was to be found, in turn, in rules of conduct which Sates, as a matter of fact, regarded as binding upon them. This definition did not rely on some anterior normative order (whether centred on God or the inherent rationality of 'mankind' as in the natural law tradition of Vattel, Grotius, and others). Nor did it require any attempt to engage with the complex of social and political relations that, over the course of centuries, had come to constitute the authority of each the States of the 'Family of Nations', such that each could indeed be regarded as an individual, sui generis 'person'. For Hall, international law was simply to be

---

[5] See Hardt and Negri, 2000, p 15: 'Empire is formed not on the basis of force itself but on the basis of the capacity to present force as being in the service of right and peace.'

located in an empirical practice of consent and obligation. At the heart of this practice, of course, was the 'modern civilized State'—in practice, the European or (in the Americas) neo-European State—whose actions were both the object and measure of this science. One needed a community of civilized States for there to be rules of conduct. And in order that their commitments should be binding, those States required the necessary will and a capacity to understand that those commitments warranted enforcement 'by appropriate means'. Imagining the State in this way—essentially as a male, Western European individual subject of law 'writ large', to adopt Plato's formation[6]—and placing it at the centre of a global normative universe, allowed an elaborate architecture of legal rules to be described and generated around it.

It is notable, furthermore, that in this definition, and in his *Treatise* more generally, Hall avoids the term 'sovereignty' almost completely, except in relation to those matters which were presumptively 'internal' such as might engage the relationship between the State and its subjects. In place of the word 'sovereignty' when describing the authority, rights, and duties of the State, he used the term 'personality'. What was significant about this choice of language was the fact that the term 'personality' assumed the existence of a systemic order that attributed a range of competences to certain designated actors. Just as a corporation might be assigned a specific set of legal capacities under municipal law—such as the capacity to sue and be sued—so, in the case of States, they would be 'accorded' certain capacities in international law—indeed, the fullest set of international rights and duties that it was possible to possess. Once statehood came to be separated from 'international personality' in this way, the State was no longer understood as carrying with it certain natural rights or prerogatives.[7] Instead, 'the State' was now used as a descriptive term, referring to an entity which possessed a specific set of 'objective' characteristics, and which could then be accorded the set of rights and duties (comprising its 'personality') on that basis.[8] In contrast to the Vattelian idea of States enjoying a natural liberty in a state of nature, for Hall and his colleagues this liberty of action was one 'subject to law' (Hall, 1895 p 24).

At the time in which Hall was writing, nearly all treatises on international law began in similar manner and would be followed by one or more chapters containing an extemporized discussion of the State as the primary subject of international law (see Westlake, 1904; Twiss, 1884; Lawrence, 1895; Wheaton, 1836; Phillimore, 1871; Rivier, 1896; Fiore, 1890; Bonfils, 1894). Typically this section or chapter would seek to define what was meant by a State for purposes of international law, determine who or what would count for such purposes, and address matters of classification (distinguishing perhaps between 'sovereign' or 'semi sovereign' States, and identifying vassals, protectorates, condominia, and unions as particular classes). Comment would routinely be passed on difficulties of nomenclature—debating whether everything called a State could be treated as a State and whether States differed from 'nations'. In the process, there would usually also be some associated reflections upon the notion of 'sovereignty' and what that might mean in the context of international relations, and of the putative role that 'recognition' might play. Once, in other words, the issue of who the subjects of law were had been established, together with the framework for determining the extent and scope of their rights and obligations

[6] *Plato's Republic*, 2004, p 121.
[7] The remainder of such an idea is to be found in the recognition, within the UN Charter, of the 'inherent' right of self-defence. See Article 51 UN Charter.
[8] See O'Connell, 1970, Vol I, p 80: 'It is clear that the word "person" is used to refer to one who is a legal actor, but that it is of no assistance in ascertaining who or what is competent to act. Only the rules of international law may do this, and they may select different entities and endow them with different legal functions, so it is a mistake to suppose that merely by describing an entity as a "person" one is formulating its capacities in law.'

(ie the question of sources), those principles could then be applied to a range of more concrete matters such as the law of the sea, the protection of nationals abroad, or belligerent relations.

The fact that this discussion of States and their character was always the starting point, for these jurists, was significant in more ways than one. In one respect, it reflected a new determination, on the part of 'professional' international lawyers, to ground international law in State practice and consent rather than in the inherited tradition of natural rights. In another respect, however, it also illustrated the way in which 'the State' had come to supplant other ways of describing political society—whether that be in terms of the people, the nation, civil society, the sovereign, the monarch, or the multitude. Whilst Hall, like many others, continued to use Bentham's terminology in describing his subject matter ('international law'), he no longer attributed any particular significance to the 'nation' as such.

Even if Hall and others of the positivist persuasion sought to mark themselves out from their 'naturalist' intellectual predecessors, they nevertheless uniformly saw themselves as working in a well-established tradition with its roots in the Roman Law notion of the *jus gentium*, as subsequently received and modified through the work of Suarez, Ayala, Gentili, Grotius, Bynkershoek, Pufendorf, Wolff, and de Vattel, among others. In many respects, what seemed to tie these classic works together as a single tradition was twofold. In the first place, these authors all sought to identify the existence of a law that both transcended and bound the sovereign, whether that found its origin in principles derived from natural law or from the more immediate practice of sovereigns in their relations inter se. Secondly, these treatises all assumed the existence of a plurality of sovereign subjects whose 'external' relations were regulated by the terms of this *jus gentium*. A key moment in this story, as it was to be later narrated, was the moment at which this plurality—the 'Family of Nations'—was to appear; and, without exception, that moment was identified with the birth of a secular international society within Europe, the inauguration of which was marked by the Peace of Westphalia of 1648. For it was at this point, it was argued, that a nascent international community finally emerged from the shadow of the Holy Roman Empire and from the coercive authority of the Catholic Church (Hall, 1895, pp 55–60).

The emphasis given to the Peace of Westphalia by the likes of Hall made it possible to think of international society straightforwardly as a society of independent sovereigns and their subordinates. But this, of course, said very little about the State itself as an idea, or about the many transformations it underwent over the centuries. Machiavelli's account in *The Prince* had suggested that the archetypal sixteenth-century sovereign existed 'in a relationship of singularity and externality, of transcendence, to his principality' (Foucault, 2007, p 91). Since the Prince could receive his principality by inheritance, acquisition, conveyance, or conquest, there was nothing but a synthetic link between the two. The principality, including both its territory and population, stood in a quasi-feudal relation to the Prince's individual authority; it had no separate meaning or significance. International relations could thus be understood almost exclusively in terms of the rights, possessions, and entitlements of the person of the sovereign.

By the time at which Grotius and Pufendorf were writing in the mid-seventeenth century, however, two new traditions of thought had started to emerge. One of these, marked by invocation of the idea of the social contract (partially present in the work of Grotius, but given much more concrete form in the work of Hobbes and Locke a little further towards the end of the 1600s), sought to forge a definitive link between the people (understood as a community of individuals or as a 'multitude') and the sovereign (the individual or group of people who were endowed with the right to rule). From this point on, those entitled to exercise the prerogatives of sovereignty (what we now call the 'government') could plausibly be separated from the place in which sovereignty was located (what we now associate with the 'State'). The other tradition, which was associated with the emergence of mercantilist thought in the seventeenth century, began conceptualizing the territory and people in terms of a unit of economic activity (Foucault, 2007). Since sovereignty, as Locke in particular was to aver, was underpinned by the appropriation and use of land,[9] the idea developed that the exercise of sovereign rights ought to be oriented in that direction: the people should be governed (put to work) and not merely ruled. This involved not only bringing the population as a productive resource within the boundaries of governmental action (eg through the regulation of migration and vagrancy and the introduction of 'poor laws'). It also pointed to a concern for the maximization of the productive output of land. In Europe, this led to the forcible 'clearing' of traditional land-holdings. Outside Europe, it legitimized the creation of new settler colonies on the grounds that the so-called 'savages' of the 'new world' had failed to appropriate and use the land they inhabited productively, and therefore had no legal claim over it (see, eg, Bhandar, 2014).

Central to the development, in the seventeenth century, of this new 'art of government' (*raison d'état*, as it became known) was an idea of the 'State' that had both objective and subjective characteristics. In an objective sense, the State was increasingly coming to be understood in terms of a set of identifiable characteristics (later to be understood as 'criteria'), including territory, population, and government, and yet which assumed an identity that was somehow greater than, or at least independent of, the sum of its parts. Governments might come and go, for example, but the State, so long as it retained the core elements, would remain the same. In a subjective sense, on the other hand, the State was increasingly understood as possessing some immanent end—whether that was simply to maintain common peace and security, or to further the cause of society. Both of these strands of thought came neatly to be expressed in Pufendorf's definition of the State as a 'compound Moral person, whose will being united and tied together by those covenants which before passed amongst the multitude, is deemed the will of all, to the end that it may use and apply the strength and riches of private persons towards maintaining the common peace and security' (Pufendorf, *On the Law of Nature and Nations*, Bk VII, c 2, s 13).

A significant feature of Pufendorf's definition here—anticipated in Hobbes' description of the Leviathan—was the personification of the State as a moral entity in its own right. To describe the State as a 'person' in this way had several obvious consequences. In the first instance, it encouraged the ascription to the State of certain passions, interests, and motivations that went beyond the strictly instrumental task of preserving peace and good order, or defending the realm from external attack. As Wolff would later argue, for example, the State was duty-bound to seek its own 'self-perfection' by maximizing its wealth and prestige—a task which necessitated the development of new systems of knowledge (statistics) and the bureaucratic organization of social and economic affairs to that end (police). In the second place, the move towards personifying the State also encouraged the development, in the hands of Vattel in particular, of what has become known as the 'domestic analogy' in which States were to be understood as being in a position analogous to individuals prior to the establishment of civil society, seeking security and community in their relations with others. For Vattel, thus, States existed in a state of nature, enjoying the same rights 'as nature gives to men for the fulfilment of their duties' (Vattel, 1758, p 4) and such natural liberties as befitted their character. The law of nations provided the structure by which that freedom and equality was to be preserved and promoted within the frame of a wider international society.

[9] Locke, 1690, pp 18–30. See also Vattel, pp 37–8: 'The whole earth is designed to furnish sustenance for its inhabitants; but it cannot do this unless it be cultivated. Every Nation is therefore bound by the natural law to cultivate the land which has fallen to its share.'

In many respects, it is difficult to underestimate the enduring significance of Vattel's appealingly simplistic account of the State in international relations. However far international thought may have moved, today, away from the idea of States enjoying certain natural prerogatives, or of sovereignty being sharply demarcated between internal and external domains, the idea that the world could be described in terms of States as a sociological category of 'person', possessing a distinct 'will', 'mentality', or 'motivation' that may encourage them to interact with one another in certain determinate ways, is one that endures to this day. This is no more clearly demonstrated than in the 'rational choice' analytics that is deployed, in some quarters, to detail the process and efficacy of international law today (eg Goldsmith and Posner, 2006).

Nevertheless, for those, like Hall, receiving this tradition in the nineteenth century, there were always evident complexities that had to be negotiated. To begin with, it was not exactly easy to translate this monadic description of international society as a society of 'free and independent' nations into practice at the time. Writing in the middle of the century, for example, Phillimore was to identify 11 different categories of State, four of which were 'peculiar' cases (Poland, Belgium, Greece, and Egypt), the rest of which included, in addition to States under one sovereign, two categories of Unions, States that took the form of Free Towns or Republics, Tribute-paying States (Vassals), and two further categories of States under different forms of Protectorate. Further to this, there was the complex phenomenon of the German Confederation (a loose alliance of 70 independent 'States') to be explained (Phillimore, 1871, p 101). This was, on no account, a uniform scheme of political organization.

Adding to the complexity, by the end of the nineteenth century, international lawyers were increasingly concerned as to how their received tradition of sovereignty might apply to the non-European world (a concern that was taken up explicitly in 1879 by the newly formed Institut de Droit International[10]). The problem faced by the Institut's members was this: in their desire to avoid the abstract rationalism of natural law and locate international rights and obligations instead in the empiricism of practice and custom, international lawyers had come to speak about international law in specifically European terms. At a time in which the idea of the nation as a cultural and linguistic community was emerging in a specifically political form (demanding an alignment between nation and State), it seemed obvious that the international relations of such a community of nation-States would be imbued with, or built upon, the same consciousness of history and tradition. Custom seemed to imply some kind of social consensus, and consensus a commonality of understanding and outlook (what Westlake referred to as a 'juridical consciousness') that could only readily be supposed in relation to 'civilized' communities in Europe (or those communities of 'European origin' elsewhere). For some, in fact, international law was actually more properly described as the Public Law of Europe, as in the work of those such as Martens (1864), Heffter (1857), and Klüber (1851).

Yet for all this, international lawyers in the nineteenth century were also aware of the long history of treaty-making with all manner of local sovereigns in Asia, Africa, and elsewhere, the form of which seemed to suppose that those relations were to be governed by the terms of international law (see Alexandrowicz, 1967; Anghie, 2005). Indeed, the fact that from the early 1880s onwards European exploration of the interior of Africa was to be marked, amongst other things, by the systematic and widespread conclusion of treaties with local kings and chiefs providing for 'protection' or for the cession of sovereignty only made the issue more pressing. How might an exclusively European system of public law

---

[10]   Twiss, 1879–1880, p 301. See generally Koskenniemi, 2001, pp 98–178.

conceive of such arrangements? And what might this imply as regards the status of those communities?

It was at this point that the language of 'civilization' (Said, 1979) was to invest itself in the realm of law. Although few international lawyers at the time explicitly introduced into their definitions of the State a requirement that they be 'civilized',[11] the existence of an implicit 'standard of civilization' ran throughout most their work in relation to recognition or territorial title, or when describing the character of international law (Gong, 1984; Anghie, 2005). Thus, for example, whilst Hall spoke in quite abstract terms about the 'marks of an independent state' (being permanently established for a political end, possessing a defined territory, and being independent of external control) he was still to make clear that international law consisted of those rules of conduct which 'modern *civilised* states' regarded as being binding upon them (Hall, 1895, p 1). One could not, in other words, assume that simply because there existed treaty relations with non-European States such as China or Japan, that those latter States were to be regarded as having the same rights and privileges as European States. As Lawrence was to note:

> there are many communities outside the sphere of International Law, though they are independent states. They neither grant to others, nor claim for themselves the strict observance of its rules. Justice and humanity should be scrupulously adhered to in all dealings with them, but they are not fit subjects for the application of legal technicalities. It would, for instance, be absurd to expect the king of Dahomey to establish a Prize Court, or to require the dwarfs of the central African forest to receive a permanent diplomatic mission. (Lawrence, 1895, p 58)

By and large, thus, international lawyers began to differentiate in their accounts between those 'normal' relations that pertained between European States and those that characterized relations with other political communities on the outside. Beyond Europe, the treaties that put in place regimes of protection or for consular jurisdiction and extraterritoriality, or those that purported to 'cede' territory, took the *form* of agreements between sovereign States; their substance, however, was to deny any such pretension.

Yet there was a difficulty here. Even if non-European States did not possess a sovereignty equivalent to that of European States, to deny them status of any kind would have put in question the validity of the agreements—treaties of cession, boundary agreements, concessions, and so on—upon which European privileges seemed to depend (Koskenniemi, 2005, pp 136–43; Anghie, 2005, pp 76–82). Some position within the broader framework of international law therefore had to be found for them; they had to be simultaneously included yet excluded from the realm of international law.[12] Some jurists responded by differentiating between legal relations, as might exist between European States, and non-legal, moral, or ethical propositions that were said to govern relations with the non-civilized world (Westlake, 1894, pp 137–40). Others made a distinction between States enjoying full membership and those enjoying merely partial membership in the family of nations (Wheaton, 1866; Oppenheim, 1905). Still others drew a line between 'plenary' and partial recognition

---

[11] See, eg, Phillimore, 1871, p 94. Occasionally, the point was made more explicit. See Westlake, 1984, pp 102–3; Lawrence, 1895, p 58.

[12] Schmitt, 1974, p 233, examining Rivier's *Lehrbuch des Volkerrechts* (1889) notes that his overview of 'current sovereign states' included 25 States in Europe, 19 in the Americas, then 'states in Africa' including the Congo Free State, the Free State of Liberia, the Orange Free State, the Sultanate of Morocco, and the Sultanate of Zanzibar. Schmitt notes that in respect of the latter category these were called States but the word sovereign was avoided, and in the case of Morocco and Zanzibar, Rivier had noted that 'obviously' they did 'not belong to the community of international law'. Schmitt asks pithily: 'Why were they even included in the enumeration?'

(Lorimer, 1883, pp 101–23). There was agreement on one point, however, namely that in order to be admitted into the family of nations, those aspirant States had to demonstrate their 'civilized' credentials. To be 'civilized', furthermore, largely meant the creation of institutions of government, law, and administration modelled upon those found in Western Europe (Westlake, 1894, pp 141–3; Mill, 1861, pp 161–3). This was a message fully understood in Japan, whose rapid process of 'Westernization' in the latter half of the nineteenth century eventually allowed it to rid itself of the regimes of consular jurisdiction that had been put in place in order to insulate Western merchants and traders from the application of local law. Only once this 'badge of imperfect membership' had been removed was Japan understood to have become a full member of international society (Westlake, 1894, p 46).[13]

These assumptions, it has to be said, by no means disappeared overnight—if they can be said to have disappeared at all. In the wake of the First World War, many of them were remodelled and given institutional form under the League of Nations. Article 38(3) of the Statute of the Permanent Court of International Justice, for example, referred to 'the general principles of law recognized by *civilised* nations'—a phrase that was incorporated directly, in 1945, into the present Statute of the ICJ at Article 38(1)(c). The theme was maintained even more explicitly in the institutions of the Mandate system designed, by the League, to deal with the situation of the colonies and territories extracted from Germany and the Ottoman Empire under the terms of the various peace treaties. Under Article 22 of the Covenant of the League, 'advanced nations' (viz Britain, France, Belgium, Australia, New Zealand, South Africa, and Japan) were entrusted with the task of exercising 'tutelage' on behalf of the League over those colonies and territories described as 'inhabited by peoples not yet able to stand by themselves under the strenuous conditions of the modern world'. The purpose of this 'sacred trust' was to advance the 'well-being and development of such peoples', with the precise implications of this phrase depending on a classification set out within that same article. Certain territories (designated as 'Class A' Mandates) were regarded as having 'reached a stage of development where their existence as independent nations can be provisionally recognized', in which case the Mandatory Power was to provide administrative advice and assistance 'until such time as they are able to stand alone'. This category included those territories in the Middle East separated from the Ottoman Empire (Iraq, Palestine and Transjordan, Syria, and Lebanon). 'Class B' territories (those in Africa with the exception of South-West Africa) were to be subject to significantly more intensive degrees of administrative control without any explicit expectation of independence, and 'Class C' territories (Pacific Islands and South West Africa) were those declared to be 'best administered under the laws of the Mandatory as integral portions of its territory', subject to certain safeguards 'in the interests of the indigenous population' (see Anghie, 2005, pp 115–95).

Whilst, as Schwarzenberger suggested, the Mandate system came very close to being a mechanism for the continuation of colonialism 'by other means' (Schwarzenberger, 1950, p 134), the very decision to employ 'other means' was significant. To begin with, the institution of international trusteeship seemed to make clear that Mandate powers were not acquiring such territories as 'colonies', and therefore could not be taken to enjoy the normal

---

[13] A contrast might be drawn here with the rather slower progress made in the case of China. The Nine Power Treaty of 1922 sought to guarantee the 'Open Door' policy in China (by which was meant 'equality of opportunity in China for the trade and industry of all nations') to be secured by barring any agreement that might secure special commercial privileges for any one State. A special Commission was set up to examine the question as to whether the continuation of extraterritorial privileges was justified. It reported back in 1926 concluding that although progress had been made, more was needed before such regimes could be suspended. See Summary and Recommendations of the Report of the Commission on Extraterritoriality in China, 1926, in (1927) 21 *AJIL*, Supplement 58.

rights of sovereignty in relation to such territories. But if that was the case, it posed the obvious question as to where sovereignty lay (Wright, 1930). The territories themselves could barely be described as sovereign in their own right, as otherwise the restrictions on their independence would have been inexplicable. Some other status had to be devised for them, or at least some language that avoided the problematic implications of the notion of 'sovereignty'. This, of course, was not a problem solely related to the institution of the Mandate, but was equally relevant to the authority exercised by the League of Nations itself—how might its powers be described within an international order comprising sovereign States?

Whether or not as a consequence of reflecting upon such problems, international lawyers writing at the time of the League began to regard the notion of sovereignty and its correlates (sovereign equality and domestic jurisdiction), not as something integral to their understanding of international law, but rather as an obstacle to be overcome. For many, a fixation with the idea of sovereignty as both indicative of the absence of any higher authority, and as the source of law (understood, perhaps, in Austinian terms as the command of the sovereign) had left the discipline not only in a condition of internal contradiction,[14] but ill-equipped to deal with a world of new international institutions and novel forms of governance. Writing in 1928, for example, Brierly joined the emerging chorus, dismissing the idea of sovereignty as 'an idolon theatre' that bore little relation to the way in which States and other 'international persons' related to one another in practice (Brierly, 1924, p 13). If 'sovereignty' was to be retained as an idea it had to undergo nothing less than a conceptual transformation. One place in which the contours of such a transformation can be discerned is in the *Wimbledon* case, which came before the PCIJ in 1923. The case dealt with a claim made by Germany that the granting of an unfettered right of passage to vessels of all nationalities through the Kiel canal—a right stemming from the punitive terms of the Treaty of Versailles, concluded between German and the Allied and Associated Powers at the end of the First World War—would 'imply the abandonment by Germany of a personal and imprescriptible right, which forms an essential part of her sovereignty'. The Court responded by stating that it:

> decline[d] to see in the conclusion of any Treaty by which a State undertakes to perform or refrain from performing a particular act an abandonment of its sovereignty. No doubt any convention creating an obligation of this kind places a restriction on the exercise of sovereign rights of the State, in the sense that it requires them to be exercised in a certain way. But the right of entering into international engagements is an attribute of State sovereignty.[15]

Sovereignty, in other words, was not to be understood as an unfettered freedom from external constraint, but rather as a way of describing a capacity for binding others to, and being bound by, international law. It was no longer something that had any innate content (such as describing certain natural rights or prerogatives), nor something that could be raised as an objection to those obligations once entered into.[16] It was merely

---

[14] Kennedy, 1997, p 114 associates a scepticism of sovereignty with positivism: 'To fulfil their polemical mission, to render plausible a legal order among sovereigns, the philosophy which sets this question, which makes sovereigns absolute or requires a sovereign for legal order, must be tempered, if not rejected. As a result, to inherit positivism is also to inherit a tradition of response to the scepticism and deference to absolute state authority, which renders legal order among sovereigns *implausible* in the first place.'

[15] S.S. 'Wimbledon', Judgments, 1923, PCIJ Rep, Ser A, No 1, p 25.

[16] See also *Military and Paramilitary Activities in and against Nicaragua (Nicaragua v United States of America), Merits, Judgment, ICJ Reports 1986*, p 14, para 131: 'A state . . . is sovereign for purposes of accepting a limitation of its sovereignty.'

a way of describing those remaining powers and liberties afforded to the State under international law.

This new way of thinking was undoubtedly helpful in several respects. To begin with, it allowed a dissociation between the possession of 'sovereign rights' on the one hand and the actual order of power on the other. This meant that territories under belligerent occupation,[17] subject to a treaty of Protection or placed under the administration of a Mandatory Power, for instance, could be conceived as being subject to the governmental authority of another State, yet not part of its territorial sovereignty. Sovereignty in such cases survived in suspended form. It also disposed of the problem of sovereign equality and domestic jurisdiction: States could regard themselves as equal, so long as it was clear that 'equality' meant an equal capacity to enjoy rights and bear obligations. They also retained a right of domestic jurisdiction so far as this described a residual domain of freedom left untrammelled by the constraints of external obligation.[18] It was only a short move from here to the position adopted by Kelsen, amongst others, who came to the conclusion that States were nothing but legal orders, described fully and completely in terms of propositions of law.[19]

However, this determination to formalize statehood and functionalize sovereignty coexisted uneasily with the normative zeitgeist of the post-First World War era—namely the principle of 'national self-determination'. This principle, advanced, in particular, by President Woodrow Wilson in 1918 (see later), implied a substantive conception of the State rooted in ideas of community and cultural homogeneity, determined for the most part by religious or linguistic markers. The sovereignty that this idea demanded—a sovereignty realized most concretely in the new system of 'national States' and 'national minorities' set up in Eastern Europe—was not one that could be regulated from outside, but inhered in a determinate people with values and interests that required protection and advancement. Ironically, these simultaneous currents—the promotion of national self-determination and the juridification of sovereignty—left legal doctrine in much the same bind as it had found itself half a century before at the height of the positivist reaction against natural law theory. Systematically cut through by an opposition between two ideas of statehood (one formal, the other substantive) and two ideas of sovereignty (one innate, the other attributed or delegated), neither of which could attain ascendency, inter-war jurists within the West found it no less impossible to avoid the trap of analytical contradiction than their teachers had done (Koskenniemi, 2005, pp 59–60, 224–33). This opposition, as we shall see, was to continue to infect the mainstream discussion of statehood through the period of decolonization and on into the new millennium—its presence being felt in debates as to the relationship between self-determination and *uti possidetis* (whether 'people' determined the territory, or the territory the people) and, of course, in discussions over the implications of recognition (whether it was 'constitutive' or 'declaratory'). The key observation here, however, is not simply to note the pervasiveness of a set of contradictory undercurrents that underpin the legal formation of statehood in international law, but to note that many of these contradictions were to appear for a particular reason—that this

---

[17] See Article 43 Hague Regulations 1907.

[18] See, eg, *Nationality Decrees in Tunis and Morocco, Advisory Opinion, 1923, PCIJ, Ser B, No 4*, p 24: 'The question whether a certain matter is or is not solely within the jurisdiction of a state is an essentially relative question; it depends upon the development of international relations.'

[19] Kelsen, 1942, pp 64–5: 'The State is not its individuals; it is the specific union of individuals, and this union is the function of the order which regulates their mutual behaviour . . . One of the distinctive results of the pure theory of law is its recognition that the coercive order which constitutes the political community we call a state, is a legal order. What is usually called the legal order of the state, or the legal order set up by the state, is the state itself.'

was the means by which European statehood could be globalized and made the universal mode of political organization and emancipation. They give expression, in other words, to how the State comes to be positioned as both an object of desire as well as a presupposition of the order through which it is produced.

III. DEFINING AND RECOGNIZING THE STATE

One of the most concrete manifestations of the shift in legal thought described earlier—from the idea of States existing in a Vattelian state of nature between whom a thin architecture of legal relations came to be established, to one in which States were understood to exist as legal entities endowed with certain competences by international law—can be found in the increasing concern to identify those 'marks' or 'criteria' by which statehood could be measured. For Vattel and other natural law scholars, describing or defining the State was primarily a matter of trying to capture the plurality of different kinds of political communities existing in Europe in the middle of the eighteenth century. For those undertaking the same exercise 100 or 200 years later, however, the project of description had taken on a different character, concerning itself less with describing and indexing those communities that existed as a matter of sociological fact, and more with the task of prescribing how much sovereignty—how much 'international personality' in the form of rights and duties—they should enjoy.

One result of this shift in emphasis was that the terms of description became more explicitly exclusionary as time went by. Thus, when Wheaton in 1866 endorsed Cicero's classic definition of the State as 'a body political, or society of men, united together for the purpose of promoting their mutual safety or advantage by their combined strength' he also took trouble to specify what entities were not included in this category. It did not include, as far as he was concerned, corporations created by the State itself, for instance, nor 'voluntary associations of robbers or pirates', nor 'unsettled horde[s] of wandering savages', nor indeed nations since the State 'may be composed of different races of men' (Wheaton 1866, s 17). Oppenheim's 1905 definition—much closer to the definition which the signatories of *Montevideo Convention on the Rights and Duties of States* settled on in 1933 (see later)—was similarly exclusionary in nature. 'A State proper', he wrote, 'is in existence when a people is settled in a country under its own Sovereign Government.' By this definition '[a] wandering people, such as the Jews were while in the desert for forty years . . . is not a State'. Likewise '[a]n anarchistic community' would be excluded from statehood by its lack of a government; and 'so-called Colonial States' were excluded by their lack of 'sovereignty', a term that referred to 'independence all round, within and without the borders of the country' (Oppenheim, 1905, pp 100–1). The definition of the State thus became a vehicle not merely for purposes of description (providing an analytical framework for understanding the character of international society for purposes of law) but also for purposes of distinguishing between those political communities that might properly be regarded as subjects of international law and those that would not. For some, this shift in orientation was decisive. As O'Connell was later to suggest (1970, p 81): 'the proposition "France is a State" is not a description or a definition but merely a conclusion to a train of legal reasoning.'

This shift from fact to law (or, if you prefer, from description to prescription) was, nevertheless, to have a particular context. In the first half of the nineteenth century a series of revolutionary wars had inspired a number of independence movements around the world (Belgium, Greece, Haiti, Mexico, Chile, and a host of other Latin American republics) in which claims to statehood grounded in the 'mere fact' of their independence were routinely opposed by the former colonial powers. In this context, international lawyers began to turn to the doctrine of recognition (a doctrine that had previously been employed largely for purposes of identifying a condition of belligerency or insurgency). Even if the independent existence of States was merely a question of fact, they reasoned, it was difficult to judge the legitimacy of such claims except by reference to the competing claims of other States. In case of secession, for example, it was understood that to recognize a new State before the moment at which it had fully established its independence was not merely to offend the sensibilities of the State attempting to suppress the rebellion, but constituted also an act of unlawful intervention. This encouraged a differentiation between the existence of States understood in terms of their internal effectiveness, and the question of their membership in the wider international community which would be determined by the practice of recognition. Wheaton (1866, s 21, p 28) distinguished, thus, between internal and external sovereignty for such purposes:

> So long, indeed, as the new State confines its action to its own citizens, and to the limits of its own territory, it may well dispense with such recognition. But if it desires to enter into that great society of nations, all the members of which recognize rights to which they are mutually entitled, and duties which they may be called upon reciprocally to fulfil, such recognition becomes essentially necessary to the complete participation of the new State in all the advantages of this society.

What this distinction immediately suggested was that questions of status, on the one hand, and of participation in international society, on the other, were ultimately separable, with the practice of recognition being relevant to the latter, but not the former. The ensuing hypothesis that there might be States which possessed 'internal sovereignty', but yet which did not participate in the 'great society of nations', found, furthermore, concrete expression in the postulated divide between the European and non-European worlds at the time. This allowed European international lawyers at the time to acknowledge and rationalize the existence of the Ottoman, Chinese, Japanese, and Ethiopian Empires, for example, as independent political communities, without needing to accept that they were, as a consequence, subjects of international law in the fullest sense. As non-European jurists well understood, however (see Becker Lorca, 2015), this new 'constitutive' doctrine of recognition gave those States whose sovereignty was not in question an immense degree of power in determining whether 'outsiders' should be allowed 'within the pale of those rights and duties, which civilised Nations are . . . entitled reciprocally to claim from each other', as the British foreign secretary George Canning put it (quoted in Grewe, 2000, p 499).[20] It was here that the 'standard of civilization' came into its own as an instrument of international law. In addition to having failed to organize themselves collectively in such a way as to resemble States in an 'objective' sense, 'savage tribes', having been judged incapable of comprehending the rules of international law, could also be denied recognition. This judgement was usually based on their alleged inability to comprehend the rules of international law, and presumed incapacity, therefore, to 'reciprocate' any such recognition (Lorimer, 1883–84, p 117). By contrast, entities like the Chinese Empire which did, up to a point, seem State-like in their appearance, could, it was agreed, be 'partially' recognized, and hence granted some but not all the rights associated with sovereign statehood (Westlake, 1914, p 82).

[20] Wheaton, 1866, s 21: 'until such recognition becomes universal on the part of the other States, the new State becomes entitled to the exercise of its external sovereignty as to those states only by whom that sovereignty has been recognized'; Lorimer, p 106: 'Though recognition is often spoken of as admission into the family of nations, it leaves the State which has claimed and obtained it from one State only, in the same position in which it formerly stood to every other State.'

Whilst this nineteenth-century practice, however, seemed to rely upon a differentiation between the question of sovereign status on the one hand and that of participation in the international community on the other, it was always clear that the ultimate objective was to achieve congruence between the two. What was ultimately envisaged was a truly global system of inter-State law governed by the principles of sovereign equality and territorial integrity. And so far as that was the objective, participation within that system could not remain dependent upon the benevolence or discretion of imperial powers, but would have to be conditioned upon the pure fact of a State's independent existence. In the early twentieth century, thus, international lawyers began to distance themselves from what they saw to be the nineteenth-century 'constitutive' approach to recognition and embraced, instead, a 'declaratory' approach the gist of which was to declare that a State would exist for purposes of international law at the moment in which it existed 'in fact'. This indeed was the platform adopted by members of the Pan-American Union when they came to draft what is now taken to be the seminal definition of statehood in the *Montevideo Convention on the Rights and Duties of States* in 1933. There, they insisted that the 'political existence of the state'—which they took to be entities possessed of a permanent population, defined territory, government, and a capacity to enter relation with other States—'is independent of recognition by other states'. 'Even before recognition,' Article 3 provides, 'the state has the right to defend its integrity and independence, to provide for its conservation and prosperity, and consequently to organize itself as it sees fit, to legislate upon its interests, administer its services, and to define the jurisdiction and competence of its courts.'

If the authors of the Montevideo Convention clearly aspired to eliminate the role of recognition as a determinant in the enjoyment of the prerogatives of sovereignty, they nevertheless left on the table the question as to how one might conceive the existence of the State for such purposes—was it a mere pre-supposition of international law? Or rather a legally determined status? Were the criteria legal or factual? And how might one understand the relationship between the two? The title of Crawford's influential book on the subject, *The Creation of States in International Law*, would appear to attribute a decisively constitutive role to international law in this question. The obvious objection, as suggested earlier, is that States are clearly not 'created' by international law in the same sense that a cabinet maker might craft a piece of furniture. Rather, they emerge through sustained political action and agitation—frequently violent—in which political independence is wrested from forces sustaining the political status quo. Indeed, international lawyers (Crawford included) are aware of as much, and routinely place emphasis upon the importance of 'effectiveness on the ground', so to speak, for purposes of determining the existence or otherwise of a State. This would seem to suggest, accordingly, that the role of law is, in practice, almost entirely *ex post facto*; indeed, that that 'sovereignty' itself should be understood as 'a political fact for which no purely legal authority can be constituted' (Wade, 1955, p 196).

In giving his book this title, however, Crawford was not being naïve. What he was arguing against was an exclusively 'empirical' notion of statehood. For, as he points out, however important 'effectiveness' might be, a State is not, as he puts it, 'a fact in the sense that a chair is a fact'; rather, it is 'a legal status attaching to a certain state of affairs by virtue of certain rules or practices' (Crawford, 2006, p 5). A closer analogy therefore might be the status of 'criminality', which is generated through the institutions and structures of the criminal law, or that of 'insanity', formed through the discipline of psychiatry (Foucault, 2006). Just as 'thief' is a designation appropriate only once it has been determined that the person concerned has unlawfully appropriated the property of another, so the label 'State' makes little sense unless the legal framework within which the powers and competences associated with statehood, and the manner in which they can be acquired, has already been determined (Kelsen, 1942). Both 'fact' and 'law' play a role, in other words, and 'effectiveness', as the summative expression of those facts deemed to be legally relevant, is understood to act as the hinge between the two.

Crawford's assumption here that it is the legal order that accords 'statehood' to those entities that possess the requisite characteristics largely depends upon the hypothesis that States are constituted through essentially consensual processes. The emergence of 12 new Republics out of the defunct Soviet Union in the early 1990s, for example, posed relatively few problems on this score for the simple reason that Russia had effectively renounced, in the Alma Ata Declaration and Minsk Accord,[21] any legal interest or claims to sovereignty over those regions (Mullerson, 1993). Here, one could conceive of the parent State either 'delegating' sovereign authority to the nascent regimes, or simply creating the necessary legal 'space' through the evacuation of its own claim to sovereignty, allowing the new States then to assert their rights over the territories and populations concerned.[22] In a similar manner, one might also understand the process of decolonization to have been enabled through the 'suspension' of metropolitan States' claims to sovereignty over non-self-governing territories, which thereby created the necessary space for the exercise of 'self-determination' (see later).

Yet in many cases the issue is not one of the consensual devolution of sovereign authority (viz the *granting* of independence) but rather of the assertion of a new claim to statehood, out of a condition of dispute or conflict. Whatever legal rules might be put in place, in a world already fully demarcated in terms of sovereign jurisdiction (in which there are no longer any 'white spaces on [the] map' (Nesiah, 2003) within which new States might emerge) the process of 'creation' can only be achieved by way of displacing in some manner the prior claims to sovereignty of another, already existing State. In that sense, unless existing claims to territorial sovereignty are lifted or suspended in some way, the emergence of a new State cannot be achieved without some measure of illegality.

It was always evident, of course, that if States were to be regarded as actors endowed with personality by a superordinating legal order, it was necessary to set out somewhere the terms under which this 'attribution' of authority might take place and the consequences of it. Strange as it may seem, however, the process of codifying the rights and duties of States has never been completed to any satisfactory degree. In 1949 the United Nations' International Law Commission (ILC) did produce a *Draft Declaration on the Rights and Duties of States*,[23] which went some way towards summarizing what the legal implications of statehood might be. Even though this draft was not, in the end, adopted by the General Assembly, it remains the most complete attempt to summarize the relationship between statehood and personality. Alongside a list of ten duties the Draft Declaration includes four rights: 'the right to independence and hence to exercise freely, without dictation by any other States, all its legal powers, including the choice of its own form of government' (Article 1); 'the right to exercise jurisdiction over its territory and over all persons and things therein, subject to the immunities recognized by international law' (Article 2); the

---

[21] Agreement Establishing the Commonwealth of Independent States (Minsk Accord), 8 Dec 1991, 31 ILM (1992) 143; Alma Ata Declaration, 21st December 1991, ibid, p 148.

[22] One may note here, that the answer often depends upon the stance adopted in relation to the role of recognition. See, eg, Hall, 1895, p 88: 'Of course recognition by a parent state, by implying an abandonment of all pretensions over the insurgent community, is more conclusive evidence of independence than recognition by a third power, and it removes all doubt from the minds of other governments as to the propriety of recognition by themselves; but it is not a gift of independence; it is only an acknowledgement that the claim made by the community to have definitively established its independence.'

[23] GA Res 375(VI), 6 December 1949, Annex.

right to 'equality in law with every other State' (Article 5); and the 'right of individual and collective self-defence against armed attack' (Article 12). Each of these does indeed seem to describe powers possessed *only* by States—to which may be added, perhaps, a plenary competence to perform legal acts such as conclude treaties; a right not to be subject to compulsory international process or dispute settlement without consent; and the benefit of a presumption that States enjoy an 'unlimited freedom' subject only to those constraints determined by law (the '*Lotus*' principle) (Crawford, 2006, pp 40–1). Taken together, these may give some indication as to why statehood remains such an attractive proposition for oppressed peoples and territories in particular—from the Irish to the Albanian population of Kosovo, and from the Palestinians to the Sahrawi and the Rohingyas.

Whilst drafting the Declaration, the International Law Commission also briefly discussed the merits of seeking a new definition of the State for purposes of international law. The general reaction, at that time, was that such a project was either unnecessary as being self-evident, or indeed too controversial (the concern being that it would only have salience as regards 'new' rather than 'old' States). In part at least it was informed by the fact that the Pan American Union had already drafted the *Montevideo Convention on the Rights and Duties of States*, Article 1 of which set out a basic definition which, if not definitive, could be taken as the starting point for most discussions of territorial status. Article 1 provides as follows:

> The State as a person of international law should possess the following qualifications:
>
> (a) a permanent population;
> (b) a defined territory;
> (c) government; and
> (d) capacity to enter into relations with other states.

For all its significance, given that Article 1 is, in effect, all we have in terms of an accepted definition of statehood, its precise implications remain obscure. In the first place, the 'capacity to enter into relations with other states' seems to be a conclusion rather than a starting point, and there is no mention of other putatively relevant matters such as independence, legitimacy, democracy, or self-determination. Precisely what Article 1 'declares', furthermore, requires some interpretive work. As a legal prescription, its terms appear to be either too abstract or too strict. They are too abstract in the sense that to say that an entity claiming to be a State needs to be able to declare itself as having people, territory, and a form of government is really to say very little, and certainly does nothing to guide responses to claims by aspirant States such as Chechnya, Kosovo, Northern Cyprus, Palestine, or Catalonia. Certainly it may exclude Wheaton's private corporation or his nomadic society, but one may ask what else? And to what end?

Analytically, the definition would seem to require one of two things: either a quantitative measure of intensity (so instead of merely necessitating the existence of a people, a territory, and something that describes itself as a government, it requires that these qualities are possessed in sufficient degree), or a qualitative measure (so that claims to statehood must be justified on the basis of some external standard, by responding to a principle of self-determination, for example, or being capable of substantiation without impinging upon the rights and duties of other sovereign States). But both of these measures—of intensity and justification—seem then to demand too much. The measure of intensity seems to require the articulation of a 'threshold' evaluation the establishment of which would be to deny the very 'factual' character that it seeks to express—who could say in advance, without lapse into arbitrariness, how much territory, or how many people, are required in order to create a State? Surely what would matter is whether it is capable of surviving as an independent State, and that, presumably, is something to be determined after the fact so to speak. The measure of justification has a similar problem; it seems to rely upon the prior establishment of internationally recognized regimes of entitlement and responsibility (recognized claims over territory or rights in relation to nationals) the validity of which would assume that the State as a legal subject is already in existence. In either case, the problem is how one moves from fact to law, or from cognition of the existence of something that calls itself a State to its legal recognition without, in a sense, assuming that the thing being offered the imprimatur of 'legality' is not somehow already legally existent. Let us now look in more detail at how this problem plays out in relation to each of the four accepted 'criteria' for statehood.

A. POPULATION

As suggested earlier, one of the critical ideas accompanying the development of the idea of the State was that the populace should not be understood merely as the accidental objects of a sovereign's authority, but that they also partook of that sovereignty. Increasingly, indeed, as the nation-State emerged, in the late eighteenth and nineteenth centuries, as the dominant rubric for organizing collective and inter-communal life, 'the people' came to be regarded as the immediate object of an emergent art of government, for which Lincoln's phrase 'government by the people, for the people, and of the people' was an obvious cumulative expression. A State's population, by the start of the nineteenth century, was not merely a source of wealth and power for the sovereign; nor was it only a means by which the State could ultimately secure itself in competition with other States (through the drafting of troops and the cooption of labour for the production of wealth, for example). In addition, and perhaps even more importantly, the people provided the rationale for government itself: the purpose of government (and hence of the State as a whole) was, above all, the promotion of the prosperity and happiness of the populace.

That the State gradually came to have this immanent end encouraged the idea that, to be politically and economically viable, it needed to be of sufficient size (Hobsbawm, pp 29–39). The smaller, more 'backward', nationalities, as Mill was to aver, were much better off being absorbed into larger nations, rather than 'sulk on [their] own rocks . . . cut off from the general movement of the World' (Mill, *Considerations on Representative Government*, 1861, pp 363–4). Unification became, thus, the dominant theme of nation-building in the nineteenth century, so much so that the claims of those such as the Fenians in Ireland or the Bretons in France were routinely disparaged. This was an idea that had not entirely been shaken off by the early part of the twentieth century, as doubt continued to be expressed as to whether small States such as Luxembourg or Liechtenstein, for example, could properly be regarded as independent States. Liechtenstein, indeed, was denied membership of the League of Nations in 1920, on the formal grounds of its lack of independence from Austria (to whom it had 'delegated' certain customs and postal duties under Agreement). Underlying that rationale, however, was an evident concern over its size and the political implications of allowing micro-States the same voting rights as other, bigger States in the organs of the League (Duursma, 1996, pp 173–4). Later practice in the context of the United Nations, however, has suggested that this concern is no longer quite what it used to be. In contrast to the League of Nations, statehood is a prerequisite for membership of the United Nations. Yet States such as Andorra, Monaco, Brunei, Kiribati, Nauru, Palau, Vanuatu, and the Marshall Islands sit alongside Liechtenstein in today's General Assembly, all of them with populations of under 1 million. This has led most scholars of statehood to conclude that, when it comes to the criterion of population, there is no minimum threshold.

The alternative, then, to a threshold 'population' is the idea that the people in question must enjoy exclusive relations of nationality with the nascent State. This was an idea, during the early years of the twentieth century, that informed the concerted attempt to use the concept of nationality (under the banner of 'national self-determination') to demarcate the populations of different States by re-drawing boundaries, instituting plebiscites, and engaging in compulsory population exchanges (Berman, 2012). But as much as this practice pointed to the desire on the part of the policy-makers at the time to ensure that the 'nation' and the 'State' be made congruent, it was also made clear that the competence to confer and withhold nationality was a matter falling essentially within the domestic jurisdiction of States. That is to say, international law neither required the conferral of nationality in any particular case nor prohibited its withdrawal.[24] Aside from occasional attempts to deal with the problem of statelessness, the only context in which international law has involved itself in issues of nationality is in relation to the question of diplomatic protection, and specifically in the context in which one State has sought to rely upon a contested bond of nationality when bringing a claim against another State.[25] To the extent, then, that the conferral of nationality has tended to be regarded as a sovereign right, it would seem to be a consequence, rather than a precondition, of statehood. Moreover, as the toleration of multiple nationality has increased (see Franck, 1999, pp 61–75) even the theoretical possibility that the bond of nationality might be regarded as a legally effective determinant of the criterion of 'population' has almost entirely disappeared.

In fact, the almost total conceptual separation between statehood and the idea of a constitutive population was marked in the second opinion of the Badinter Commission in 1992 in which the Commission suggested, in the context of the collapse of the Socialist Federal Republic of Yugoslavia, that one of the possible implications of the principle of self-determination was that the individuals concerned should have a right to choose their own nationality.[26] That this offered the possibility that a majority of the population of a new State might 'opt' for the nationality of a neighbouring State was treated as largely irrelevant for purposes of determining whether the new State met the conditions necessary for its own legal existence. Rather than being a condition of statehood, thus, the existence of a 'population' seems to be cast in almost metaphorical terms—the population must exist 'as if' in relationship to an order of government over territory, in which their presence as objects of coercion is necessary, but their identity as participants in that political community remains indeterminate.

B. TERRITORY

Much of what has just been argued in relation to the criterion of population also applies in relation to that of territory. In the same sense that statehood seems not to be contingent upon any threshold level of population, so also it is hard to discern any specific condition concerning possession, on the part of the nascent State, of sufficient portions of land. Monaco has a territory of less than 1.95 km^2 and the Vatican City (a 'non-member State' at the UN) less than 0.5 km^2 (Duursma, 1996, p 117). At the same time, it is clear that the real issue in most cases is not size, nor indeed the mere factual possession or control over territory (possession may always be 'adverse', of course, as in cases of belligerent occupation), but rather the ability to rightfully claim the territory as a domain of exclusive authority. If,

---

[24] *Nationality Decrees in Tunis and Morocco, Advisory Opinion, 1923, PCIJ, Ser B, No 4,* p 24.

[25] *Nottebohm, Second Phase, Judgment, ICJ Reports 1955,* p 4.

[26] See also Articles 1 and 11, ILC Draft Articles on Nationality of Natural Persons in Relation to the Succession of States (1999).

as Arbitrator Huber put it in the *Island of Palmas Case*, sovereignty signifies independence, and independence 'in regard to a portion of the globe . . . the right to exercise therein, to the exclusion of any other State, the function of a State',[27] then the existence or absence of competing claims to sovereignty would appear to be key.

However, if what is required of new States is the possession of territory that is otherwise 'unclaimed' or 'undisputed' then, unless one were to be able to identify the territory in question as *terra nullius* (unoccupied territory),[28] or territory which has been explicitly or tacitly 'ceded' to it, then it is very difficult to see how any such nascent State could fulfil such a criterion. Prior to the mid-nineteenth century, it was routinely assumed by international lawyers that 'distant' lands 'inhabited only by natives', as Judge Huber put it in the Island of Palmas Arbitration of 1928, were, in effect, unoccupied—or, at least, occupied by a community which did not count as a 'population'. *Terra nullius* was, thus, the legal doctrine which legitimized the conquest of vast swathes of territory, including the whole of Australia, none of which was ceded. Today, however, that doctrine has been wholly discredited (Moreton-Robinson, 2015)—giving rise in the Australian context, at least, to an entire new right of 'native title'.[29] With the important exception of Indigenous conceptions of 'self-determination' (see later), the effect of this has been to ensure that claims to statehood in the post-decolonization era are almost routinely oppositional, and rendered in the language of secession.

Even if we were to accept the idea that territory is somehow foundational to the question of statehood, the position requires further nuance. It has long been accepted, for example, that the absence of clearly delimited boundaries is not a prerequisite for statehood. Albania, for example, was admitted to the League of Nations in 1920 despite the fact that its frontiers had yet to be finally fixed, the subsequent delimitation of which came to be the subject of an Advisory Opinion of the PCIJ in the *Monastery of Saint Naoum* case of 1924.[30] Reflecting on this practice, the International Court of Justice subsequently affirmed in the *North Sea Continental Shelf* cases that:

> The appurtenance of a given area, considered as an entity, in no way governs the precise delimitation of its boundaries, any more than uncertainty as to boundaries can affect territorial rights. There is for instance no rule that the land frontiers of a State must be fully delimited and defined, and often in various places and for long periods they are not . . .[31]

What this appears to suggest is that the border and the territory of the State are effectively two different things (notwithstanding the 'Montevideo' stipulation that a State's territory must be 'defined'). Borders, on one side, seem to be the consequence rather than the cause of an acknowledgment that the possession of territory by some entity is legitimate. Their delimitation, after all, proceeds on the assumption that there are legitimate entitlements on either side. Territory, by contrast, seems to be a pre-condition for the assertion of rights of property in relation to space insofar as it concerns the very existence of the legal subject.

This distinction between the territory of a State and its boundaries is an undoubtedly appealing one. It opens up the possibility, in particular, of addressing ongoing disputes over the location of borders (often determined by reference to the classical 'modes' by

---

[27] *Island of Palmas Case* (1928) 2 RIAA 829.

[28] For a discussion of this notion in the context of Western Sahara, see *Western Sahara, Advisory Opinion, ICJ Reports 1975*, p 12, paras 79–81.

[29] See *Mabo and Ors v Queensland (No 2)* (1992) 175 CLR 1, especially Judgment of Justice Brennan; Native Title Act No 100 (1993). [30] *Monastery of Saint-Naoum, Advisory Opinion, 1924 PCIJ, Ser B, No 9*.

[31] *North Sea Continental Shelf, Judgment, ICJ Reports 1969*, p 3, para 46.

which territory might be acquired such as discovery, cession, annexation, occupation, or prescription[32]) without, in the process, continually calling into question the identity of the States whose borders are the subject of dispute. It would be almost absurd to argue, for example, that the alteration of the UK's jurisdiction that occurred as a consequence of its assertion of sovereignty over the Island of Rockall in 1972 (following an earlier claim to its 'possession' in 1955) was such as to affect its legal identity and therefore require it to apply afresh for membership in the UN.

At the same time, however, it is clear that radical changes to borders can sometimes have precisely that effect. In 1992, for example, Serbia-Montenegro was denied the right to style itself, in the form of the 'Federal Republic of Yugoslavia', as the continuation of the collapsed Socialist Federal Republic of Yugoslavia (in the same way that Russia represented itself as the continuation of the former USSR). The international community refused to accept its claim that Croatia, Bosnia-Herzegovina, Macedonia, and Slovenia had 'seceded' from Yugoslavia, leaving Serbia-Montenegro as its remaining 'rump' State. On the contrary, the Badinter Commission in 1991 characterized the situation as one of Yugoslavia's 'dissolution' rather than secession, and in consequence, Serbia-Montenegro was forced, like the other former Yugoslav States, to reapply for UN membership as a different State (see Blum, 1992).

Borders, as this suggests, are not merely lines on the ground, or ways of delimiting spheres of public jurisdiction. Instead, they serve to delimit both the identity and existence of a political order by means of its separation from others—the 'non-democratic condition of democracy' as Balibar (2004) puts it. The supposition, thus, that the existence of borders and the existence of territory are radically different things is hard to sustain. In case of the emergence of Israel in 1948, for example, it was not merely the case that *some* of its borders were in question at the time of its recognition and admission to the United Nations, but *all of them*, given that it had been carved out of the defunct Mandate for Palestine. What was undoubtedly of significance here was the general atmosphere of uncertainty that had been generated, amongst other things, by the Security Council's failure to endorse the General Assembly's earlier plan for Palestine's partition, outlined in Resolution 181(II) of 1947, and the apparent termination of the Mandate occasioned by the unilateral withdrawal of the British administration. Since the status of Palestine, as a former mandated territory awaiting recognition, was *itself* in flux at that time, there appeared to be no 'effective' interlocutor able to claim that recognition of the new State of Israel constituted a violation of its own territorial sovereignty (even though there were clearly arguments to be made on the part of the Palestinian population generally). The result was such as to allow a space for recognition of the State of Israel to open up without, it seems, the kinds of qualms associated with premature recognition that would naturally have arisen in other contexts. This move was not, of course, universally welcomed. Far from recognizing Israel as a State, the Arab States launched a war against it, the result of which was Israel's occupation of a still larger area of mandatory Palestine. Israel's application for UN membership was accepted nonetheless on 11 May 1949, although even these newly enlarged borders had yet to be fully confirmed. What this example seems to suggest is that the criterion of territory, like that of population, operates less as an empirical observation as to the existence of an accepted factual condition, than again as a metaphorical assertion: the State must exist 'as if' it possessed territory with determinate boundaries. If that is so, then it might also be the case that it is in the theatrical performance of statehood—through, amongst other things, the rituals of recognition, admission, flying the flag, building walls, and policing borders—that States come to acquire the territory that supposedly conditions their existence (Brown, 2010).

---

[32] For a classical account of the modes of acquisition of territory see Jennings, 1963.

C. INDEPENDENT GOVERNMENT

For all of the aporias associated with the requirements of territory and population, those addressing the criteria for statehood are unified on one matter above all else: that the criteria for statehood are ultimately directed towards the recognition of 'effective' governmental entities.[33] Effectiveness in this context is generally taken to mean that the government of a putative State must demonstrate unrivalled possession and control of public power (whatever the specificities of that might be in any particular setting) throughout the territory concerned. Once that unrivalled possession is established, recognition of statehood may follow. This emphasis upon governmental effectiveness forms a key part of Crawford's thesis. Given that 'nationality is dependent upon statehood, not vice versa' and that territory is defined 'by reference to the extent of governmental power exercised', 'there is a good case', he suggests, 'for regarding government as the most important single criterion of statehood, since all the others depend upon it' (Crawford, 2006, p 56).

Crawford's argument doesn't stop here, though. His purpose is not simply to point out that, as the Commission of Jurists maintained in the *Aaland Islands* case, a new State only comes into existence once it is 'strong enough to assert [itself] throughout the territories of the state without the assistance of foreign troops.'[34] Rather, it is to suggest that this criterion of effectiveness operates as a legal principle in its own right, the effect of which is conditioned by other relevant principles of international law, and in particular by norms having the status of *jus cogens* such as the right of peoples to self-determination and the prohibition on the use of force. This leads Crawford to a hypothesis which cuts in two directions. On the one hand, he maintains that the reason why certain relatively effective political entities, such as the Turkish Republic of Northern Cyprus or Southern Rhodesia, were not recognized as independent States was that to have offered such recognition would have violated certain *jus cogens* norms. On the other hand, he also argues that where *jus cogens* norms like self-determination do apply, they are able to displace the criterion of effectiveness, allowing certain 'ineffective' States to be recognized nonetheless.

In this latter context, Crawford cites, by way of illustration, the case of the Belgian Congo, which was granted a hurried independence in 1960 as the Republic of the Congo in circumstances in which little preparation had been made for independence and in which public order broke down shortly after (with secessionist factions seeking their own independence in Katanga and elsewhere). Belgian troops were reintroduced into the territory under the guise of humanitarian intervention and the United Nations responded by establishing ONUC (the United Nations Operation in the Congo) for purposes of restoring order whose mission continued until 1964. As Crawford puts it '[a]nything less like effective government it would be hard to imagine. Yet despite this there can be little doubt that in 1960 the Congo was a state in the full sense of the term' (Crawford, 2006, p 57). Its admission to the United Nations for membership had already been approved and UN action had been taken on the basis of preserving the 'sovereign rights of the Republic of the Congo'. Crawford suggests ultimately that there were three possible ways of interpreting this practice: (i) that the international recognition of the Congo was simply premature because it did not possess an effective government; (ii) that international recognition of the Congo had the effect of creating a State despite the fact that it was not properly qualified (ie that recognition was thereby 'constitutive'); or (iii) that the requirement of 'government' was, in certain particular contexts, less stringent than might otherwise be thought.

---

[33] Lauterpacht, 1947, pp 340–1: 'The principal and probably the only essential condition of recognition of States and governments is effectiveness of power within the State and of actual independence of other States. Other conditions are irrelevant to the true purposes and nature of recognition.'

[34] LNOJ, Sp Supp 4 (1920) pp 8–9.

Crawford's clear preference is for the third of these three options and he explains the position as follows:

> [B]y withdrawing its own administration and conferring independence on local authorities, Belgium was precluded from denying the consequences of its own conduct. Thereafter there was no international person as against whom recognition of the Congo could be unlawful. It is to be presumed that a new State granted full and formal independence by a former sovereign has the international right to govern its territory.... On the other hand, in the secessionary situation the position is different. A seceding entity seeks statehood by way of an adverse claim, and in general statehood can only be obtained by effective and stable exercise of governmental powers. (Crawford, 2006, pp 57–8)

It is important to understand the role assigned to the idea of effectiveness here. To begin with, it is presented as a general principle of international law—it is not, in that sense, a 'law creating fact' (as might be expressed in the phrase *ex factis ius oritur*), but simply a circumstantial trigger that produces certain legal consequences. Effectiveness, furthermore, is not sufficient on its own: just as some effective entities have not been recognized as States (such as Taiwan, whose recognition as an independent State has been almost permanently deferred as a consequence of the claims made by China over its territory), so also other less-than-effective entities have continued to be regarded as States despite that condition (and one may mention here both States under a condition of belligerent occupation such as the Baltic Republics between 1940 and 1990 and Kuwait in 1990–91, and States which, like Lebanon and Burma in the 1970s, have experienced extended periods of internal turmoil). Effectiveness, in other words, is supposed to operate as a principle the parameters of which are legally determined and may, at that level, interact with other relevant principles.

Yet it is equally clear that the further one goes in seeking to juridify the condition of 'effective government', the more clearly one exposes the inevitable tension between a legal principle that seeks to allow for the recognition of new aspirant entities once they have become legal 'facts', so to speak, and one that prohibits any such recognition as a violation of the territorial sovereignty of the State from which that entity is to emerge. In the nineteenth century, the criterion of effectiveness was intimately linked with the idea of premature recognition. If a third State were to recognize an insurgent movement as an independent State before the moment at which they had fully established themselves, that recognition would constitute 'a wrong done to the parent State' and, indeed, 'an act of intervention' (Hall, 1895, p 89).[35] European powers were, thus, very cautious when addressing the recognition of the new States in South America, for example, frequently modulating their response by reference to what seemed to be happening on the ground. Usually the insurgent communities were initially recognized *de facto*, with *de jure* recognition coming only once it was clear that Spain had given up the fight. The importance of effectiveness, in such a context, was found in the way in which it served to mark the moment at which the rights of the parent State gave way in the face of those of the secessionist movement. But an examination of the practice indicates that effectiveness never really meant quite the same thing in every place.[36] What

---

[35] In practice, even the intermediary step of recognizing insurgents as belligerents, as Britain and France did in relation to the secessionist States in the American Civil War of 1861–65, was frequently treated as an unjustified intervention.

[36] *Island of Palmas Case* (1928) 2 RIAA 829 per Huber: 'Manifestations of territorial sovereignty assume . . . different forms according to conditions of time and place. Although continuous in principle, sovereignty cannot be exercised in fact at every moment on every point of a territory. The intermittence and discontinuity compatible with the maintenance of the right necessarily differ according as inhabited or uninhabited regions are involved, or regions enclosed within territories in which sovereignty is incontestably displayed or again regions accessible from, for instance, the high seas.'

was required in order to establish territorial sovereignty depended upon the nature and strength of rival claims. Thus, a relatively ineffective Congo Free State, for example, could garner recognition in 1885 simply because of the apparent absence of any other recognized sovereign whose rights would be impeded in the process (the local communities having, it was claimed, 'conceded' their sovereignty to King Leopold by way of treaties of protection). Considerably more was required for the recognition of the new Republics in Latin America when it was the sovereignty of another European power (Spain) being displaced. For all the subtle modulations of this early practice, however, such arguments clearly became more problematic in the course of the twentieth century once it came to be accepted that the use of force was no longer a legitimate means of acquiring title to territory.[37]

Given that the general prohibition on the use of force seems to prohibit also the annexation of territory, it is very hard to see how one might legitimate the establishment of a State on the territory of another by such means (*ex inuria ius non oritur*). Even though the unilateral use of force was still, under the League of Nations, merely restricted rather than prohibited outright (as it has been since 1945), the case of Manchukuo offers a useful illustration. When Japan invaded the Chinese territory of Manchuria in 1931 and declared a new, supposedly independent State of 'Manchukuo' in its place, the Lytton Commission was dispatched there by the League of Nations on a fact-finding mission. The Commission concluded that the Japanese action was inconsistent with both the League's Covenant and the Kellogg-Briand Pact (Japan and China being signatories to both) and that Manchukuo itself, far from being independent, remained largely under Japanese control. This report underpinned the subsequent articulation of the 'Stimson doctrine', the substance of which affirmed the refusal of the United States (and those States which followed it) to 'admit the legality of any situation *de facto* . . . which may impair . . . the sovereignty, the independence, or of the territorial and administrative integrity of the Republic of China' when that situation had been brought about by means contrary to the Pact of Paris.[38] Several League of Nations resolutions were adopted on this basis calling for the non-recognition of 'Manchuko' and the 'state' was finally dismantled in 1945, following Japan's defeat in the Second World War. Likewise, the Turkish Republic in Northern Cyprus, established as a purportedly independent State following the Turkish intervention in 1974, has consistently been denied recognition, principally, once again, on the basis that its creation was the product of an unlawful military intervention.[39] Similar arguments were also put forward by Bosnia in its memorial in the *Genocide* case which maintained that the Republica Srpska was not a State, in part at least because its creation was associated with a violation of the prohibition on the use of force on the part of Serbian forces.[40]

It is worth noting, in this context, that the prohibition on the use of force has been instrumental not merely in resisting the establishment of 'puppet' regimes, but also in preserving the formal 'continuity' of States during periods of occupation. The Baltic Republics (Estonia, Latvia, and Lithuania), for example, were occupied by the Soviet Union in 1940 and incorporated into the Union. A good many States refused to recognize the legality of the incorporation (Ziemele, 2005, pp 22–7) and when in 1990 the Supreme Councils of the three Baltic States resolved to 're-establish' their independence (which involved the re-invocation of laws pre-dating the occupation and the rejection of obligations assumed on their behalf by the Soviet Union) the EC adopted a Declaration welcoming 'the restoration of sovereignty and independence of the Baltic states which they had lost in 1940' and

---

[37] See Article 2(4) UN Charter; Declaration of Principles of International Law Concerning Friendly Relations and Co-operation among States in Accordance with the Charter of the UN, GA Res 2625(XXV), (24 October 1970), Principle 1. See generally Korman, 1996.   [38] 1 Hackworth 334.

[39] See *Cyprus v Turkey* [GC] no 2571/94, ECHR 2001-IV, 120 ILR 10.

[40] Memorial of the Government of the Republic of Bosnia and Herzegovina, 15 April 1994, p 264.

resolving to re-establish diplomatic relations with them.[41] The prohibition on the use of force, in other words, seems to work not only as a way of denying the recognition to what might otherwise be regarded as effective entities, but also as a way of keeping alive (as a formal idea at least) States which have been the subject of occupation and annexation and which are, to all intents and purposes, therefore 'ineffective'. One may recall, to cite another pertinent example, that the first Gulf War of 1990 was authorized by the Security Council in Resolution 678 (29 November 1990) on the basis of seeking to protect and secure the territorial integrity and political independence of Kuwait. The presumptive illegality of Iraq's invasion of Kuwait made it possible to presuppose the latter's continued existence as a State and in this way to authorize intervention on the basis of collective self-defence, despite the fact that Kuwait's government had been effectively displaced by that of Iraq.

The question remains, however, as to what will become of the principle of governmental effectiveness if it really is, as Crawford suggests, being systematically displaced by the emergence of *jus cogens* norms—in the post-1945 period in particular. On one side, one may note an increased willingness to recognize as States (for one reason or another) entities that are in some respects ineffective. One may recall in recent years, for example, that both Bosnia-Herzegovina and Croatia were recognized by the EC as independent States in 1992 at a time at which the governments concerned had effective control over only a portion of the territory in question (Rich, 1993). On the other side, however, it is hard to think of many examples of new States emerging and being recognized simply because they have managed to secure their independence 'effectively'—that is, as a matter of fact. Over the past decade alone, Abkhazia, South Ossetia, Azawad, South Sudan, Donetsk, and several other entities—not to mention 'Islamic State', and of course 'North Sudan'—have all declared their independence under governments (or at least under leaders) which arguably did possess 'effective' control over a particular territory, and yet none of these entities has been recognized as a State by more than a few members of the international community. At the time of writing, it seems imminent that Catalonia and Iraqi Kurdistan are about to do the same. Even when it does seem possible that a new State has emerged—in the disputed case of Kosovo, for example, which declared its independence in 2008—the principle of effectiveness is not usually employed as the definitive explanation. Other frameworks, such as consent, self-determination, or disintegration, are usually deployed in its place as a means of displacing the claims of the territorial sovereign. Arguably the most problematic cases were those of Bangladesh and Eritrea, the recognition of which could not easily be framed in terms of the standard understanding of self-determination. Yet even here, commentators have tended to seek some other interpretive framework for explaining such practice: relying, for example, on the idea that Eritrea had been unlawfully seized by Ethiopia, and that Bangladesh had been effectively governed as a non-self-governing territory by Pakistan (a case 'approximating' colonial rule) and could therefore claim a right of self-determination.

This tendency towards the promotion of an exclusively 'juridical' idea of statehood in which questions of effectiveness are routinely subordinated by reference to other legal principles has been noted in the work of Jackson and Kreijen, among others. For Jackson (1990, pp 21–31), decolonization marked the moment at which the notion of sovereignty increasingly took on a negative cast (as implying merely freedom from external interference as opposed to a positive capacity to act), leading to the recognition of what he calls 'quasi-states'. These are States which, because of their precipitous independence, were given the imprimatur of statehood before they had developed the necessary internal capacity for

---

[41] 7/8 Bull EC (1991) 1423.

political self-government and economic independence—that is, before they had become effective. A similar stance is adopted by Kreijen, who speaks of this change in terms of the 'transformation of the notion of independence from an inherently material concept based on internal sovereignty to a mere formal legal condition primarily depending on external recognition' (Kreijen, 2002, p 92). For Kreijen, this 'juridification of statehood' was a situation that demanded ameliorative action on the part of the international community, through the recognition of a right to development, or the reintroduction of the notion of trusteeship into international law.

Such reflections draw, obviously enough, upon themes embedded within the old nineteenth-century 'standard of civilization', and those same themes have been given further impetus in more recent debates over so-called 'failed' or 'fragile' States. The origin of this debate can be traced back to an influential article by Helman and Ratner (1992), in which they were to identify, as a new phenomenon in international relations, a class of 'failed' or 'failing states'. Failed States, for their purposes, were States such as those like Somalia, Sudan, Liberia, and Cambodia, in which (in their terms again) civil conflict, government breakdown, and economic privation imperilled their own citizens and threatened their neighbours 'through refugee flows, political instability, and random warfare'. The designation of such States as 'failed', of course, was not simply a neutral exercise in description or diagnosis, but formed a necessary prelude for the adumbration of a series of intrusive policy recommendations the central feature of which was the proposed introduction of a system of 'United Nations Conservatorship' along the lines subsequently established in East Timor, Bosnia-Herzegovina, and Kosovo for purposes of national, post-conflict reconstruction.

Whilst for Helman and Ratner the idea of State 'failure' was one that recommended reconstructive activity, in other hands it has formed the basis for advocacy of a 'preventive' system including the imposition of sanctions upon such States and their exclusion from membership in international organizations (Rotberg, 2002). In some cases, indeed, the notion has even been employed as the basis for a refusal to recognize or implement treaty obligations.[42] As Simpson points out, such ideas are redolent of those abounding at the end of the nineteenth century in which critical differentiations were made between different kinds of State and other polities (deemed 'civilized', 'semi-civilized', or 'barbarous') for the purpose of legitimating a range of different kinds of intervention (Simpson, 2004, pp 240–2). On such a view the re-emergence of this 'liberal anti-pluralist' theme within international legal doctrine (in which the principles of territorial sovereignty and sovereign equality are routinely downplayed or excised) recalls the intellectual structures of nineteenth-century imperialism (Gordon, 1997). Yet it is also run through with many of the same kinds of contradictions. Just as nineteenth-century international lawyers struggled with the problem of having to simultaneously recognize and deny the status of political communities in the extra-European world, so those invoking the notion of State 'failure' seem to maintain in place the idea that they are indeed still States for purposes of attributing responsibility for their condition, yet not entitled to the normal prerogatives of sovereignty that the intervening States would expect for themselves. As Crawford succinctly concludes, '[t]o talk of States as "failed" sounds suspiciously like blaming the victims' (Crawford, 2006, p 722).

One way to make sense of this discourse of failure, however, is to notice how it subtly shifts attention away from standard questions as to the 'intensity' and 'exclusivity' of

---

[42] See Yoo, Memorandum, 9 January 2002 explaining that the Geneva Conventions did not apply because Afghanistan was a failed State.

governmental effectiveness towards its implicit content. According to Crawford, 'international law lays down no specific requirements as to the nature and extent of [governmental] control, except that it include some degree of maintenance of law and order and the establishment of basic institutions' (Crawford, 2006, p 56). Yet this definition clearly offers little assistance in the task of distinguishing a government from some other kind of social arrangement—whatever 'government' is not. One might ask, in that respect, what type of control counts as 'law and order', and what administrative arrangements meet the benchmark of 'basic institutions'? One does not have to dig too deeply, in fact, to find an answer. In a wealth of cases, from the 'unequal treaties' concluded with the Chinese Empire in the late nineteenth century, to the 'minorities treaties' concluded with the 'national States' of Central and Eastern Europe after the First World War, to much more recent efforts at 'State-building' in the Balkans and elsewhere, States have only been recognized as such if, and to the extent that, they have put in place an administrative regime that is capable of protecting a narrow set of individual rights—to personal security, to equal treatment, and to the protection of property (Parfitt, 2016). The implicit telos of 'government', in such cases, has been the establishment of such minimal conditions as might be required to enable global commerce to progressively extend its reach alongside, and within, the armature of the State.

What was evidently missing from this was any sense that governments might be assessed on their willingness and capacity to minimize hunger or poverty, redistribute wealth, offer universal free education, or protect the environment. Even the recent trend towards conditioning recognition upon the implementation of provisions concerning human rights— as in Kosovo and Bosnia-Herzegovina, for example—manifests the same orientation. For example, the ill-fated Comprehensive Proposal for the Kosovo Status Settlement, proposed in February 2007 by the then-UN Special Envoy Martti Ahtisaari, suggested that Kosovo should, as a condition of its recognition as an independent State, commit itself to becoming 'a multi-ethnic society', governing itself 'democratically and with full respect for the rule of law through its legislative, executive and judicial institutions'. In addition, furthermore, to protecting 'the highest level of human rights', it was also expected to create 'an open market with free competition', compliance with which would be subject to ongoing 'supervision' by the 'international community'.[43] 'Effective government', here, retains the same valence 'effective occupation' did in the 1885 Berlin Act's stipulations regarding the validity of European claims to sovereignty in the Congo Basin—it requires the creation and maintenance of a minimal legal framework required for commodity production and exchange. And it is in that connection that the implicit sub-text of the regime of statehood begins to become apparent: to be a State is to be capable of participating in the global market, and enabling the continued reproduction of conditions that underpin the unequal global distribution of wealth, power, and pleasure (Parfitt, forthcoming, 2018).

D. RECOGNITION

If, as suggested earlier, one of the primary objectives of the Pan American Union in drafting the Montevideo criteria was to marginalize, or even eliminate, the practice of recognition as a way of regulating the admission of non-European States into the international legal order, it could not succeed in rendering 'statehood' an entirely objective category. After all, as critics of the 'declaratory' position have argued, however confidently a political community might believe itself to have fulfilled the criteria for statehood, it is only through acceptance of that fact by other States that this belief becomes effective. To such

---

[43] Ahtisaari Plan, (2007) Article 1, 'General Principles', paras 1.1–1.4, 1.11.

critics, it is meaningless to assert that Somaliland, the 'Republic of Artsakh', or indeed 'Islamic State' *are* States if no other States are prepared to treat them as such. Those, by contrast, who continue to defend the declaratory approach point to the political and discretionary character of recognition—to the fact that, as in the *Tinoco Arbitration*, a State like the UK may refuse to recognize another (government in that case) not because of any perceived defect in origin or competence, but simply because it does not wish to have diplomatic relations with it.[44] The determinants of statehood must, they argue, be posited as anterior to the practice of recognition (even if the latter may be thought to provide evidence for the former), simply in order to guard against the risk that recognition might be deployed (or withheld) for political purposes. The real difficulty arrives, of course, when it comes to entities like Palestine and, more recently, Kosovo, which are both recognized and unrecognized by numerous States. Are they States for the purposes of some members of the international community and not for others, as the constitutive position would suggest? Or are they States regardless of their non-recognition by other members of that community, having met the criteria for statehood as judged by some external arbiter, as the declaratory position would suggest—without, however, supplying a satisfactory answer as to who, if not States themselves, that arbiter must be?

To a large extent these respective positions on the question of recognition turn not so much on the question of whether the existence of a State is a self-expressive fact, or upon the fulfilment or lack thereof of the requisite criteria, but upon the analytical relationship between the two elements of 'status' and 'relations'. In one (the declaratory approach) these are kept distinct: the question of status has to be determined prior to the creation of relations with others. Only those entities fulfilling the requisite criteria can be said to have the capacity to enter into legal relations with others as States. In the other, the two issues are merged such that the existence or otherwise of such relations becomes the mode by which status is determined. Only those entities having relations with other States can be assumed to have the legal capacity to do so. The difficulty with the declaratory position is that it seeks to maintain both the idea that the creation of States is rule-governed, and that the conferral or withholding of recognition is an essentially political and discretionary act. To postulate the existence of a rule, but then deny it any ground for being applied is to rely rather heavily upon the self-executory character of formal rule. The difficulty with the constitutive position, by contrast, is that it seeks to maintain that the conferral or withholding of recognition is a legal act (or at least one with legal effects) but that in the absence of either a 'duty to recognize' (as asserted by Lauterpacht, 1947) or of the existence of an agency competent to adjudicate (as asserted by Dugard, 1987), then allows the question of status to become entirely dependent upon the individual position of the recognizing States. The best one could say from a constitutive position, in any particular context, was that a political community was 'more or less' a State.

For the most part, although many profess to prefer the 'declaratory approach',[45] doctrine on recognition remains fundamentally ambivalent on most of these key questions.[46] There are two particular difficulties. To begin with, it is clear that recognition of another State will have

---

[44] *Tinoco Arbitration (Costa Rica v Great Britain)* (1923) 1 RIAA 369; (1924) 18 AJIL 147, p 154.

[45] Article 3: 'The political existence of the state is independent of recognition by the other states'; and article 6: 'The recognition of a state merely signifies that the state which recognizes it accepts the personality of the other with all the rights and duties determined by international law.' See also, Badinter Commission, Opinions 8 and 10, 92 ILR 201, 206 (1992).

[46] See Brownlie, 1982, p 197: 'in the case of "recognition", theory has not only failed to enhance the subject but has created a *tertium quid* which stands, like a bank of fog on a still day, between the observer and the contours of the ground which calls for investigation.'

certain legal implications: it implies, at the very least, a commitment to respect the sovereignty and territorial integrity of the State it has recognized and will also have a range of domestic legal consequences as might concern the recognition of its law and legal transactions occurring within its jurisdiction. By the same token, it is almost universally held that recognition will not necessarily imply a willingness to enter into diplomatic relations with that other State, nor indeed a recognition of its government (prior to 2001, for example, only three States recognized the Taliban as the government of Afghanistan, yet there was no doubt that all recognized the State of Afghanistan). But it is not always easy to dissociate the fact of recognition from the idea of political approval. In the context of governmental recognition (relevant primarily in case of those governments establishing their authority by unconstitutional means) this issue led to the enunciation by the Mexican Secretary of Foreign Relations of what became known as the 'Estrada Doctrine', the effect of which was to recommend the recognition of all effective governments irrespective of the means by which they came to power (Jessup, 1931). However, it was inevitable that there would always be questions of interpretation in cases in which two (or more) rival governments found themselves competing for power. It is perhaps no wonder, then, that the policy of formal governmental recognition has gradually be abandoned (for a critique, see Talmon, 1998, pp 3–14).

The difficulty of separating law from policy/politics, however, has not been confined to governmental recognition, but has also influenced practice in relation to the recognition of States. Whilst, as we have seen, non-recognition has often been employed as a way of signalling the international community's condemnation of attempts to subvert processes of self-determination or to establish new States by recourse to force, the fact that it is also still seen to be an essentially 'discretionary act that other States may perform when they choose and in the manner of their own choosing'[47] makes it a somewhat haphazard semeiotic device. In an enlightening typology, Warbrick (1997, pp 10–11) explains that the mere statement 'We (State A) do not recognize entity X as a State' has at least five possible meanings:

(1) We take no decision, one way or another, about recognizing X [in A's eyes, X may or may not be a State];

(2) We have chosen not to recognize X (although we could do) for political reasons not related to X's status [by implication, A does consider X to be a State];

(3) We do not recognize X because it would be unlawful/premature for us to do so [A does not regard X as legally a State];

(4) We do not recognize X, although it might (appear to) be a State, because there are customary law obligations or specific treaty obligations which prohibit us from doing so;

(5) We do not recognize X, although it might (appear to) be a State, because there is a specific obligation imposed by the Security Council not to do so.

Much would seem to depend, thus, upon how the recognizing State characterizes or understands its own actions. Only by looking behind the refusal to recognize might one determine a difference in stance, for example, between the refusal to recognize the Turkish Republic of Northern Cyprus or, more recently, the 'breakaway Republics' of Abkhazia and South Ossetia (informed, it seems, by a reflection upon the illegality—respectively—of the Turkish intervention in Cyprus and Russian intervention in Georgia) and the similar refusal to recognize the former Yugoslav Republic of Macedonia in early 1992 (informed, it

---

[47] Badinter Commission, Opinion No 10 of 1992, 92 ILR 206, p 208.

seems, by an unwillingness to prejudice diplomatic relations with Greece). In some cases, however, the position is simply opaque. It was never entirely clear, for example, whether those Arab States which refused to recognize the State of Israel before 1993 really believed that Israel *was* not a State (and hence was not bound by the various treaty obligations to which it was a party), or whether they merely desired to make clear that it *should* not exist as a State, even if it did so in fact. If it is necessary to read recognition policy symptomatically—that is, as an expression of a particular standpoint that might, or might not, be made explicit—then it becomes increasingly difficult to disentangle those considerations that bear upon the question of legal status, and those that apparently do not.

Bearing this out, even States taking a firm position in seeking to avoid recognition of a State (and hence avoid any sense of condoning its existence) have found themselves, in practice, unable or unwilling to live with the consequences. In refusing to recognize Israel, for example, few of the Arab States were willing to accept as a consequence of that non-recognition that Israel was not bound by the Geneva Conventions of 1949 in relation to its occupation of the West Bank and Gaza, or that it was otherwise free to ignore general principles of international law governing the use of force. More generally, domestic courts have also frequently sought to avoid the consequences of non-recognition policies, and have resorted to a variety of different expedients to allow judicial cognition of the laws of what are formally unrecognized States. In the *Carl Zeiss* case, for example, the House of Lords avoided the obvious consequences of the British government's refusal to recognize the German Democratic Republic by treating the legislative acts of the GDR as essentially those of the USSR.[48] Similarly, in *Hesperides Hotels*, Lord Denning adopted a policy, already well established in the United States, of allowing recognition of the laws of unrecognized States (in that case the Turkish Republic of Northern Cyprus) insofar as they related to 'the day to day affairs of the people, such as their marriages, their divorces, their leases, their occupations and so forth'.[49] In the UK, in fact, this latter policy has come to find formal expression in the Foreign Corporations Act of 1991 which states that foreign corporations having status under the laws of an unrecognized State may nevertheless be treated as a legal person if those laws are 'applied by a settled court system in that territory'. In each of these cases, an important consideration seems to have been a concern to insulate the 'innocent' population from the 'illegalities' associated with the claims to authority on the part of their governments. But they also illustrate in some ways a continued prevarication between the need, on the one hand, to recognize 'effective' entities whilst, on the other, to ensure at least the semblance of some commitment to the legal values that a refusal to recognize might have embodied. Just as, in the past, the distinction between recognition *de jure* and recognition *de facto* allowed States the opportunity to have dealings with insurgent governments without, at the same time, being seen to implicate themselves overtly in an act of intervention, so also the more recent practice of recognizing the acts of certain governments whilst not recognizing their claims to statehood underlines the point made earlier, that legal doctrine has consistently sought to embed both law and fact within itself—at the price of an apparently chronic normative instability.

To illustrate the point, if doctrine on statehood and recognition seems to admit the necessity of a constructive ambiguity, perhaps the most obviously anomalous (or is that representative?) case is that of Taiwan, or the 'Republic of China' (ROC), as it is known officially (Crawford, 2006, pp 198–221). In 1949, the Nationalist government of what was then the Republic of China, the Kuomintang, fled mainland China during the civil war

---

[48] *Carl-Zeiss-Stiftung* v *Rayner & Keeler Ltd (No 2)* [1967] 1 AC 853. See also *Gur Corporation v Trust bank of Africa* [1987] 1 QB 599. [49] *Hesperides Hotels Ltd* v *Aegean Turkish Holidays Ltd* [1978] QB 205, p 218.

and took up residence on the island of Taiwan. Until 1971, it continued to be recognized as the official Chinese government, to the extent of occupying China's permanent seat on the Security Council. In 1971, however, Taiwan was removed from the United Nations and its seat was taken up, instead, by the Government of the People's Republic of China (PRC), which had been in *de facto* control of mainland China since 1949, and gradually from the late 1970s onwards States transferred their recognition from the government of the ROC to that of the PRC. The government of Taiwan (the ROC) has never entirely renounced its claim to being the government of China as a whole, however; and nor has it, for this reason, asserted its existence as an independent State unequivocally. Taiwan, nevertheless, has many dealings with other States, largely on the same basis as any other State (but without the same diplomatic privileges). Taiwanese government agencies are often regarded as having legal status in other countries and a capacity to sue and be sued. It is a party to a number of treaties and has membership in the WTO (as a 'Separate Customs Territory' under the name 'Chinese Taipei'). In the UK, Taiwanese corporations are allowed to do business under the terms of the 1991 Foreign Corporations Act 'as if' Taiwan were a recognized State, and in the US relations have largely been 'normalized' under the terms of the Taiwan Relations Act 1979 which seeks to implement the policy of maintaining 'unofficial relations'. So extreme is the mismatch between Taiwan's formal claims and effective status that '[i]t is surprising', as Crawford observes 'it does not suffer from schizophrenia', (Crawford, 2006, p 220). The same might be said of international lawyers more generally.

IV. SELF-DETERMINATION

As we have already seen, one of the key characteristics of the idea of the State as it was to emerge in social and political thought from the time of Grotius onwards was that it was never solely reducible to the authority of the ruler or government of the time. The idea of the State was always organized by reference also to a community, society, or nation in relation to which governmental authority would be exercised. It is no accident, thus, that 'international law' acquired the designation attributed to it by Bentham, rather than 'inter-State' law or 'inter-sovereign' law, for example. The *jus gentium* was always seen as the law between nations or societies as much as a law between sovereigns, and the term *civitas* or *respublica* more often than not merely denoted the internal relationship between one thing and the other. Nevertheless, there were two immanent traditions of thought which informed this relationship between nation and State as they were to develop (Skinner, 2004, pp 368–413). One of these was a tradition of civic republicanism that conceived of sovereign authority as a product of relations between individuals existing within the frame of a pre-conceived society (exemplified most clearly in the theory of the social contract). The other was a 'communitarian' or 'romantic' tradition that emphasized the corporate character of the society or nation, the institutional expression of which would be the State (exemplified in Pufendorf's characterization of the State as a 'moral person'). In both cases, the 'nation' remained an important idea—on one side as the social frame that would emerge out of the contract of sovereignty; on the other side as a natural community endowed with certain innate ends and prerogatives (and, indeed, perhaps an independent 'will'). In neither case, however, was the nation entirely reducible to the State itself.

As noted earlier, over the course of the nineteenth century, and in particular in the immediate aftermath of the First World War, these two themes came to be summarized in a single verbal expression, that of 'national self-determination'. Far from resolving the tension between them, however, the various iterations of this idea merely internalized and reproduced the two traditions. Those who associated themselves with the tradition of civic republicanism (with its roots in the enlightenment and the work of those such as Kant), conceived of self-determination primarily in terms of representative self-government: it being the promotion of individual liberty through the technique of self-rule that was sought. Here, the nation was not so much a condition or pre-supposition, but something that was to be developed through a practice of self-rule marshalled by the State—it was the State, as Bourdieu put it, that was charged with making the nation, rather than the other way round (Bourdieu, 2014, pp 346–52). By contrast, the version of self-determination that came to be associated, in the early part of this period, with emergent nationalist thought in Latin America, Greece, Germany, Italy, and elsewhere (sustained in the work of Herder, Fichte, and Mazzini amongst others) insisted that if this principle was to be realized, it was the nation that came first, and the State had to be mapped around it. It was, thus, the perfection of national society (whether determined by reference to racial, ethnic, religious, linguistic, or historic homogeneity) that was to be sought in the promotion of its self-determination. These two concepts of self-determination presented very different challenges to the existing order of sovereign States. The first presented a challenge to the authority of those governments which sought to represent the will of their populations externally without necessarily being willing to make themselves responsible to them internally. The second offered an 'external' challenge to the spatial ordering of a dynastic European society and its failure to map itself congruously with the geography of 'nations' as they were to perceive themselves. These were not identical challenges by any means: the former appeared to confront the sovereign's authority with a criterion of legitimacy founded upon a rationalistic conception of representation, whereas the latter appeared to challenge even representative authority with a claim to power based upon group identity (Berman, 1988–89, p 58). In either sense, however, national self-determination was clearly the language of change and reform (see Cobban, 1945), at least until the full horror of its potential became clear, in later years, in the doctrines of *lebensraum*, *spazzio vitale*, and *Hakkō ichiu*.

It was in the reconstruction of Europe in the aftermath of the 1914–18 War, however, that the principle of national self-determination was to obtain its most concrete institutional expression. The agenda had been set by President Wilson in his speech to Congress in 1918 in which he famously set out the 'Fourteen Points' which he believed should inform the peace process. None of these points referred explicitly to the principle of national self-determination, but it was nevertheless made clear that boundaries in the new Europe should be configured so far as possible by reference to 'historically established' relations of nationality and allegiance. The Polish State was resurrected, Czechoslovakia and a Serb-Croat-Slovene State created out of the former Austro-Hungarian Empire, and various other border adjustments made with provision for plebiscites in various locations. In many respects, however, it was an imperfect plan. On the one hand, it was always evident that the task of aligning political boundaries around the various 'nations' of Europe would be 'utterly impracticable', not simply because of the difficulties of determining which 'nation' deserved a State, but also because of their dispersed character (Hobsbawm, 1992, pp 131–41). This recommended two expedients—one being the forcible transfer of certain populations (between Greece and Turkey, for example[50]), the other being the institution of minority protection regimes within the various Peace Treaties in order to safeguard the position of those residual national communities that found themselves suddenly cut adrift from the 'kin State' to which they were thought naturally to belong (Fink, 2004; Claude, 1955, pp 12–30). On the other hand, it was also evident that the Wilsonian project of

---

[50] Convention Concerning the Exchange of Greek and Turkish Populations, Lausanne, 30 January 1923.

self-determination was destined to be geographically limited—national self-determination was not something that was envisaged as being applicable in relation to the victorious powers themselves (eg for the Flemish, the Irish, or Basques) or, indeed, to any of their colonies. Notwithstanding the promises made to Arab nationalists during the War, and the many non-European nations which sought recognition of their territorial claims at the Paris Peace Conference—from Ho Chi Minh on behalf of Vietnam, then part of French Indochina, to Şerif Pasha, representing the Society for the Ascension of Kurdistan—the closest thing to 'national self-determination' implemented outside Europe was the institution of the Mandate System.

If national self-determination was merely the implicit and rather contradictory premise behind the reorganization of Europe after the First World War, it became a very much more explicit part of the settlement after the Second World War, though on quite different terms. The UN Charter identified respect for the principle of equal rights and self-determination of peoples as being one of the purposes of the Organization (Article 1). Meanwhile, Chapter XI of the Charter underlined the duty of administering States to foster self-government, development, and the political, economic, social, and educational 'advancement' of those peoples which had 'not yet attained a full measure of self-government'. In effect, while Chapter XII transformed the League's 'mandated territories' (and some others) into 'trust territories' under its 'administration and supervision', Chapter XI undertook (even to the extent of reproducing the language of the 'sacred trust') to transform *all* remaining colonies into the equivalent of 'Class A' mandated territories, whose 'free political institutions' metropolitan powers were duty-bound to 'develop' on a 'progressive' basis (Article 73). The populations of such 'non-self-governing territories' had other ideas, however, and by 1960 decolonization was well under way. As was made clear by the newly enlarged General Assembly in a series of resolutions beginning with the Declaration on the Granting of Independence to Colonial Territories of 1960, 'self-determination' was a right belonging to all colonies, entailing an obligation to take 'immediate steps . . . in Trust and Non-Self-Governing Territories or all other territories which have not yet attained independence, to transfer all powers to the peoples of those territories, without any conditions or reservations'.[51] Over the course of the next 30 years most of those territories identified as 'non-self-governing' by the United Nations were to acquire their independence and become, as an important marker of their new status, members of the United Nations.

Whilst decolonization was obviously to transform the membership of the UN, and radically re-shape the character and nature of its activities, the scope of the right of peoples to self-determination which emerged remained unclear for some time. In one direction, the question whether self-determination was a principle applicable only in the context of decolonization, or whether it might also legitimate secession in other contexts, remained unanswered. Apart from the problematic example of Bangladesh, which having seceded from Pakistan received UN membership in March 1972, UN practice seemed limited in that sense, but limited in a way that seemed to speak of pragmatism rather than principle. If what was in contemplation was the 'self-determination' of 'all peoples', as Article 1(1) of the two UN Covenants on Human Rights affirmed in 1966,[52] then why did practice seem to restrict it only to those overseas territories that had formed part of the maritime empires of European States? Was it only in that context that one could speak of peoples being non-self-governing or subject to oppression or alien rule? And where (as the Ibo in Biafra and the Katanganese in Congo wondered) had the word 'national' gone?

---

[51] GA Res 1514, (14 December 1960), para 5. See also, GA Res 1541, (15 December 1960).
[52] International Covenant on Civil and Political Rights (1966), Article 1(1); International Covenant on Economic, Social and Cultural Rights (1966), Article 1(1).

It soon became apparent in the 1960s that the right to self-determination, understood as a right to opt for independent statehood, was not allocated on the basis of ethnic or linguistic homogeneity, but rather on the basis of pre-existing—that is, colonial—administrative boundaries. In some instances, the external boundaries of the colony defined the presumptive unit of self-determination—as, for example, in the case of Ghana or the Belgian Congo. In other cases, the extent of that unit was determined by reference to the internal boundaries that demarcated the different administrative units of a single colonial power, such as the boundary between Uganda and Tanganyika, for example. The principle, in this second case, came to be expressed in the phrase *uti possidetis iuris* ('as you possess under law') and had its origins in the somewhat hazy practice of boundary delimitation in Latin America. Following its implicit endorsement by the Organisation of African Unity's Heads of State and Government in 1964,[53] it subsequently came to be affirmed as 'a general principle . . . logically connected with the phenomenon of obtaining independence, wherever it occurs' whose 'obvious purpose is to prevent the independence and stability of new States being endangered by fratricidal struggles'[54] (see generally Shaw, 1996). While it did provide a way of resolving the prior question of who 'the people' were, enabling them then to decide collectively on the shape of their political future, precisely what 'logic' strictly required obeisance to the inherited parameters of colonial administration was not clear (Mutua, 1995). Certainly, however, an awareness of the role played by the minorities regime and by nationalism more generally in triggering the Second World War, and subsequent genocidal practices, played no small part in the gradual abandonment of the idea of 'national' self-determination in favour of a self-determination of 'peoples'.

In many ways—as divided peoples like the Kurds, Zulu, and Tamils; ethnic minorities within the new States like the Rohingya and the Lozi; and Indigenous peoples throughout Australia, New Zealand, Canada, and elsewhere could hardly fail to notice—the implementation of self-determination proved, in practice, to deliver far less than it had promised. If, as Berman puts it, the principle of self-determination challenged some of the most basic assumptions of legal thought 'by posing the problem of law's relationship to sources of normative authority lying beyond the normal rules of a functioning legal system' (Berman, 1988–89, p 56), by the 1980s it had already assumed a quiescent form. The more it came to be identified as a prosaic institutional practice, or as a pragmatic obeisance to the determined character of existing boundaries, the less dangerous (and indeed less emancipatory) it seemed. As the Supreme Court of Canada subsequently clarified in 1992, the right *to be* a State (or at least to include that option on the list of possible outcomes) was, according to extant customary international law, possessed only in 'exceptional' situations, those being 'at best' in 'situations of former colonies; where a people is oppressed, as for example under foreign military occupation; or where a definable group is denied meaningful access to government to pursue their political, economic, social and cultural development'—the latter situation remaining, as we shall see, extremely contested.[55] In all other situations, the right to self-determination was an 'internal' one, amounting to 'a people's pursuit of its political, economic, social and cultural development within the framework of an existing State' (para 126). Only through this distinction between 'external' and 'internal' self-determination, coupled with an increased emphasis placed upon the intrinsic relationship between 'internal' self-determination and the protection of individual and collective human rights (Cassese, 1995, pp 101–40; McCorquodale, 1994), can it now be construed as a right of 'all peoples'.

---

[53] 'Cairo Declaration on Boundaries', Organisation of African Unity Heads of State and Government, Cairo, July 1964, AHG/Res 16(1) 1964.   [54] *Frontier Dispute, Judgment, ICJ Reports* 1986, p 554, para 20.
[55] Supreme Court of Canada, *Reference re Secession of Quebec* [1998] 2 SCR 217, para 138.

Yet if self-determination does, nonetheless, amount to a right to statehood at least in the 'exceptional' cases of colonialism and military occupation, this leaves open the question of how that right can be squared with the rights of existing States, and in particular with the right to territorial integrity. For some colonial powers, after all, the colony was still largely regarded as an inherent part of the metropolitan State (very much more so for Portugal and France, for example, than for Britain) the separation of which necessarily implied some diminution of the sovereign claims of the colonial powers. If this made the ('external') right of self-determination a difficult one to assert, the yet-to-be-determined status of claimant 'people' made it still harder. By its nature, the right of self-determination seemed to speak of a process of determining future status, rather than a status in its own right. This, as Berman notes, posed the question as to how international law could possibly 'recognize a right accruing to an entity which, by its own admission, lack[ed] international legal existence?' (Berman, 1988–89, p 52). The answer to that question, as it was to emerge during decolonization, seemed to be that self-determination had a suspensive capacity the effect of which was to displace claims to sovereignty on the part of the parent State, and affirm, somewhat obscurely, the nascent claims to sovereignty on the part of the people whose future had yet to be determined. There was, in fact, a model for this idea already in place, and which had already informed some of the practice of the ICJ in its deliberations on the question of sovereignty in case of Protected States (such as Morocco)[56] and Mandate territories. In the case of the latter, as McNair was to put it, the question of sovereignty seemed to lie in 'abeyance'.[57] The rights of the Mandatory Power, he suggested, were not those of a sovereign, but rather those enjoyed in virtue of agreement, to be exercised by way of the 'sacred trust' spoken of in Article 22 of the Covenant. Independence thus in no way implied a loss of sovereignty, or a violation of the principle of territorial integrity, on the part of the Mandatory Power, but rather the fruition of a status temporarily subordinated by the fact of colonial administration. In that respect, the most remarkable feature of the process of decolonization was the much more generalized, and quasi-legislative, statement found in the General Assembly's Declaration on Friendly Relations[58] which declared that 'the territory of a colony or other non-self-governing territory has, under the Charter of the United Nations, *a status separate and distinct from the territory of the State administering it*' (emphasis added). When approached from this angle, any apparent tension that existed between the General Assembly's espousal of the principle of self-determination and its simultaneous reaffirmation of the principle of territorial integrity could be resolved by means of re-casting the relationship between the colonizer and the colonized.

If the principle of self-determination implied a suspension of claims to sovereignty on the part of the metropolitan State, it also entailed the non-recognition of attempts to subvert that process. Thus, for example, when a minority white regime in what was then Southern Rhodesia declared its independence from Britain in 1965, its unilateral declaration of independence was immediately condemned by both the UN General Assembly[59] and the Security Council. The latter called upon States not to recognize the 'illegal racist minority regime', and provided for a regime of sanctions to be imposed.[60] Similarly, but in a different context, when the South African government, in pursuit of its policy of apartheid, established the Bantusans of Transkei, Ciskei, Venda, and Bophuthatswana in

[56] *Case Concerning rights of nationals of the United States of America in Morocco, Judgment, ICJ Reports 1950,* p 172, at p 188 where, despite the French Protectorate, Morocco was declared to be 'a sovereign state'.
[57] *International Status of South West Africa, Advisory Opinion, ICJ Reports 1950,* p 146, Separate Opinion of Judge McNair, p 150.   [58] GA Res 2625 (XXV), (24 October 1970).
[59] GA Res 2379 (SSVI), (28 October 1968).
[60] SC Res 232 (16 December 1966); SC Res 235 (29 May 1968).

the years 1976–81 under the pretext that this constituted an implementation of the principle of 'self-government', those claims were again rejected, with the General Assembly and Security Council condemning their establishment and calling for non-recognition.[61] Only in cases in which the subversion of self-determination came at the hands of another 'newly independent state' (eg Goa, West Irian, East Timor, and Western Sahara) was the reaction somewhat more muted or equivocal. The rubric of anti-colonialism, it seems, had somewhat less purchase in such cases.

Whilst self-determination was the principal mode through which decolonization was to be pushed forward in the 1950s and 60s, its significance was not to be confined to that era. On the one hand, there remained—and remain—several colonial and/or territories still under military occupation, for whom the enjoyment of a widely acknowledged right to 'external' self-determination continues to be thwarted. Whereas the statehood of Namibia, first a German colony and then a South African mandated territory, was finally recognized in 1990, and whereas East Timor, once a Portuguese colony, at last achieved a troubled independence from Indonesian rule in 1999, the same cannot be said either for Western Sahara (a former Spanish colony, now occupied by Morocco), or, perhaps most notoriously of all, for Palestine. As Drew has pointed out, the turn to peace negotiations has arguably contributed to the problem, amongst other things by equalizing the status of the two negotiating partners (Israel and the Occupied Palestinian Territories) and, in doing so, relinquishing the particular content of self-determination, whose purpose it is to elevate the rights of occupied people above the rights of the occupying power (Drew, 2001, p 681).

On the other hand, however, the international community has become increasingly troubled, particularly since the fall of the Berlin Wall in 1989, by a spiralling number of intractable conflicts fought in the name of self-determination, and yet where a right of 'external' self-determination was not thought to apply in the classical sense. In the immediate aftermath of the collapse of Communism the customary distinction between 'external' and 'internal' self-determination was protected, in large part through a resort to the terminology of 'dissolution' or of 'consent'. Thus, whilst many of the new States which emerged from behind the 'iron curtain' in the late 1980s and early 1990s employed the language of self-determination—holding plebiscites or national polls by way of authorization, and in some cases even making a capacity to speak the 'national' language a determinant of subsequent citizenship (Cassese, 1995, pp 257–77)—the idea that this practice might have instanced a displacement of the principle of territorial integrity was carefully avoided. In the case of the USSR itself, for example, while widespread and violent demands for independence from Soviet rule, unleashed during the period of Perestroika, were certainly a cause of the USSR's collapse, the fact that Russia had effectively renounced, in the Alma Ata Declaration and Minsk Accords,[62] any legal interest or claims to sovereignty over those regions was to lend the process the aura of a consensual 'parting of ways' (Mullerson, 1993). The two agreements themselves suggested that the Soviet Union had, in fact, 'ceased to exist', allowing for the emergence to independence of 12 of the 15 former Soviet Republics within a loose confederation (the Commonwealth of Independent States) out of the ashes of a now defunct State. That Russia was to claim shortly afterwards that it was in fact 'continuing' the legal existence of the USSR (retaining importantly the privileges of the latter within the UN) did not, ultimately, profoundly change the analysis apart from suggesting that the process was better seen as one of consensual secession than of disintegration. Elsewhere, the three Baltic States asserted their independence separately on the grounds

---

[61] GA Res 31/6A (26 October 1976); SC Res 402, (22 December 1976).
[62] Agreement Establishing the Commonwealth of Independent States (Minsk Accord), 8 December 1991, 31 ILM (1992) 143; Alma Ata Declaration, 21 December 1991, ibid, p 148.

of their unlawful annexation by the USSR in 1940, and the former Warsaw Pact States, Hungary, Romania, Poland, and Bulgaria, were seen to have merely 'transitioned' from Soviet control to full independence through the medium of a change of government.

The case of the Socialist Federal Republic of Yugoslavia was probably the most reveal-ing however (see Radan, 2002). Prior to 1989, Yugoslavia had (like the USSR itself) been a federal State comprising six Republics, representing the major 'nationalities', and two autonomous enclaves (Kosovo and Vojdvodina), each of which had representation in the administration of the Federation. The death of President Tito in 1980 was followed by a power struggle within the Federation culminating in declarations of independence being announced on the part of Slovenia and Croatia in 1991. Both declarations recalled the principle of national self-determination (which itself had some recognition in the Federal Constitution). These initiatives, however, were forcibly resisted and the subsequent vio-lence that was then to engulf first Croatia and then Bosnia-Herzegovina was so severe that it led to the dispatch of peacekeeping forces (UNPROFOR), the establishment of the International Criminal Tribunal for the Former Yugoslavia, and the later submission of claims of genocide to the International Court of Justice.

One of the key questions here for other States was whether or not to recognize the state-hood of the entities emerging from the conflict. Doing so had several important implica-tions as regards the characterization of the then-ongoing conflict (whether, for example, it was an international rather than merely an internal armed conflict (see Gray, 1996)). In terms of the relationship between statehood and self-determination, however,[63] the ques-tion of recognition brought into play the possibility that a 'post-colonial' right of seces-sionary self-determination might be sanctioned in the process, the implications of which would extend far beyond the confines of the conflict itself. Sensing that there were a num-ber of delicate issues involved, the States of the European Economic Community (EEC) formed a Conference on Yugoslavia which, in 1991, established what became known as the 'Badinter Commission' (so named after its Chairman Robert Badinter, President of the French Constitutional Court) to provide advice on the legal issues arising from Yugoslavia's imminent implosion (see Craven, 1995; Terrett, 2000). In the autumn of 1991 the Badinter Commission issued two significant Opinions that set the stage for the subsequent inter-national recognition of Croatia, Slovenia, and Bosnia-Herzegovina, and, somewhat later, that of Macedonia. The key advice given by the Badinter Commission, having specifically been asked about the implications of the principle of self-determination, was to declare that the former SFRY was 'in the process of disintegration' on the basis that the Federal organs could no longer wield effective power (the suggestion being that the remainder of those Federal organs, and in particular the Yugoslav National Army, had effectively been co-opted by the Serbian government).

Perhaps what is most interesting about this Opinion, however, is what it left out. What the Commission signally did not say was that the 'nationalities' within the Federation possessed a right of secessionary self-determination. On the contrary, it remained re-markably silent on the matter of self-determination except to note the responsibilities of the new States towards the human rights of their future minorities. The Commission's general reluctance here, no doubt, was informed by the sense that the recrudescent eth-nic nationalism that underpinned these claims to independence, if encouraged, would only exacerbate the conflict still further. Caught thus in a position of neither want-ing to ally itself with the Milosević regime, whose campaign of violence had been pur-sued under the banner of the preservation of the territorial integrity of Yugoslavia,

---

[63] See on this Koskenniemi, 1994a.

nor wanting to provide a continuing justification for inter-ethnic violence in the name of national self-determination, the Commission's determination that the Federation was in the process of dissolution was thus a dextrous act. Its effect was to provide a necessary analytical space within which the recognition of the six emergent Republics could take place without risk of undermining respect for the principle of territorial integrity. Indeed, in its second Opinion the Badinter Commission reaffirmed the principle of *uti possidetis* explicitly, making clear in the process that the entities emerging from the former Yugoslavia were to be those that already had enjoyed administrative recognition within the Federation.

The solution proposed by the Commission was always to leave a certain ambiguity as to the status of Kosovo, which had possessed a degree of administrative independence within the Federal structure, yet had not been one of its constituent Republics. Whether the principle of *uti possidetis*, as it has come to be construed, was sufficiently subtle as to enable an effective distinction to be made between different kinds of internal administrative borders is perhaps an open question. But the case of Kosovo poses a slightly different set of questions insofar as it is held up by some as an illustration of the possibility, alluded to by the Supreme Court of Canada (see earlier in the chapter), that a 'external' right of self-determination may emerge in a context in which a people is systematically and violently denied its right to 'internal' self-determination (Williams, 2003). This amounts, as we shall see in Section V, to the argument that there has come to exist, as a matter of post-Cold War international law, a right of 'remedial' secessionary self-determination.

V. DEMOCRACY AND HUMAN RIGHTS

If the collapse of Communism in Central and Eastern Europe challenged the international community to find a way to uphold international law's uneasy balance between the promises of self-determination and the preservation of State sovereignty, it also presented it with an opportunity. For, from its very earliest articulation, the idea of self-determination has appeared to give expression to one simple idea—that, as Wilson was to put it, 'governments derive all their just powers from the consent of the governed'.[64] Whilst undoubtedly a latent idea in most schemes of political organization through the twentieth century, it has in recent years been given further legal impetus in the idea that there exists an 'emerging right to democratic governance' in international law (Franck, 1996; Fox and Roth, 2000)—the source of which is traced to the linkage between the principle of self-determination and the individual rights of political participation (Article 25 ICCPR) and evidenced in the emerging practice of multilateral election monitoring and other initiatives designed to promote democracy and human rights ('low intensity democracy' as Marks puts it (Marks, 2003)).

There are two plausible ways in which this concern for democracy and human rights may impinge upon the question of statehood: one as an additional 'condition' that needs to be met before independence may be recognized (one of the earliest examples being Fawcett's interpretation of the Southern Rhodesian crisis in 1965 (Fawcett, 1965–66)); the other as a basis for the exercise of self-determination on the part of a community suffering oppression or systematically excluded from access to government (sometimes referred to, as noted earlier, as 'remedial secession'). In respect of the first, there is some evidence to

---

[64] President Woodrow Wilson, Second Inaugural Address, 5 March 1917.

suggest that, in Europe at least, States have been keen to incorporate questions concerning human rights and democracy into their decision-making on recognition. Thus, shortly after the beginning of the conflict in Yugoslavia in 1991, the EC Member States convened at an extraordinary EPC ministerial meeting to adopt a common policy on the recognition of States emerging from the Soviet Union and Yugoslavia. The result was a set of guidelines in which they affirmed 'their readiness to recognise, subject to the normal standards of international practice and political realities in each case, those new states which . . . have constituted themselves on a democratic basis'.[65] Further to this, they set out several additional conditions, including: (1) respect for the provisions of the UN Charter and the Helsinki Final Act 'especially with regard to the rule of law, democracy and human rights'; (2) guarantees for the rights of ethnic and national groups and minorities; (3) respect for the inviolability of existing borders; (4) acceptance of all relevant arms control commitments; and (5) a commitment to settling all future questions of State succession and regional disputes by agreement. In the event, these guidelines were very loosely applied. The recognition of Croatia, for example, proceeded in early 1992 despite the fact that the Badinter Commission had found that it had not fully complied with the relevant conditions. By contrast, the recognition of Macedonia was held up not on the grounds of its failure to meet these conditions, but rather as a consequence of an ongoing dispute with Greece over its name.[66] Thus, while considerable enthusiasm remains for the idea that the new States acquiring their independence would remain bound by all pre-existent human rights treaty commitments that were formally applicable to that territory (Kamminga, 1996; Craven, 2007, pp 244–56), commentators remain cautious as to the legal significance of the Guidelines when taken by themselves (Murphy, 2000, p 139).

When placed in the context of other developments, however, the picture looks rather different. For example, in the 1990s several regimes of international territorial administration were put in place, both in Eastern Europe (in Bosnia-Herzegovina and Kosovo) and elsewhere (in East Timor, for example), in the wake of wars characterized by widespread abuses of human rights and international humanitarian law, which placed the task of securing the rule of law and the protection of human rights at centre stage (Wilde, 2008). As some have argued, such regimes seemed to function as institutional precursors to independence in such a way as to be evidence of a new emerging doctrine of 'earned sovereignty'—earned in the sense of being phased, conditional, and perhaps even constrained. 'Sovereignty', on this view, is no longer a right of States or colonized/occupied peoples but rather a 'bundle of rights' available to be allocated, by the 'international community' and by degrees, depending on the extent to which such conditions are met (Williams, Scharf, and Hooper, 2002–03). Yet as critics of this 'earned sovereignty' approach have noted, whatever the perceived merits of such an agenda, and however far this may be thought to open out a new realm of policy alternatives, it is hard to shake off the sense that this amounts to anything other than a new 'standard of civilization'—that is, a highly selective reinstitution, under UN auspices, of the old Mandate/Trusteeship arrangement in which territories were 'prepared' for independence under the tutelage of colonial masters (Drew, 2007, 87–92; Wilde, 2001, pp 261–2).

Just as there is a certain hesitancy about the role that considerations of democracy and human rights might play in the recognition of new States, so also there is significant equivocation over the extent to which those considerations might serve as a basis for

---

[65] Declaration on the 'Guidelines on the Recognition of New States in Eastern Europe and in the Soviet Union' (1992) 31 ILM 1486.

[66] See *Application of the Interim Accord of 13 September 1995 (The former Yugoslav Republic of Macedonia v Greece), Judgment, ICJ Reports 2011,* p 644.

legitimating secession. As we have seen, in its Advisory Opinion concerning the seces-sionist claims of Quebec, the Canadian Supreme Court had asserted that the international law right to self-determination gave a right to external self-determination in situations 'where a people is oppressed' or where 'a definable group is denied meaningful access to government to pursue their political, economic, social and cultural development'.[67] It was to conclude, however, that Quebec 'did not meet the threshold of a colonial people or an oppressed people' and since the Quebecers had not been denied 'meaningful ac-cess to government' they did not enjoy the right to effect the secession of Quebec from Canada unilaterally. Rather, they enjoyed a (Constitutional) right to negotiate the terms of a separation.

A somewhat different context was to pertain, however, in the case of Kosovo when the International Court of Justice was requested by the General Assembly to consider the lawfulness of its Declaration of Independence of 2008.[68] As was detailed in the evidence presented to the Court (and had earlier been highlighted by the ICTY in the *Milutinović* case[69]) the Kosovo Albanians had been the object of discrimination, repression and vio-lence throughout the 1990s, and in particular during the violence of 1998–99 which had itself ultimately led to the adoption of Security Council Resolution 1244 (1999) and the establishment of UNMIK. Whilst, as several judges pointed out in their Separate Opinions (eg Judges Yusuf and Scpúlveda-Amor), the Court might naturally have been led to con-sider whether, in the circumstances, the population enjoyed a right of remedial secession, the majority evaded the question entirely; they focused rather on the narrowest of issues— whether the authors of the Declaration had acted in violation of international law (which, it found, they had not). That this resolved neither the issue as to whether the Kosovars had a right to external self-determination, nor whether the subsequent recognition of its independence might constitute a violation of Serbian sovereignty, was to leave Kosovo ultimately in a state of limbo (recognized by 115 States as of February 2017, but unrecog-nized by many others).

One reason for caution on the part of the International Court, no doubt, related to the fact that it wanted to avoid setting some kind of precedent in light of the various movements that were seeking independence in the region around the Black Sea and the Caucasus. Between 1990 and 2014 at least seven purported new States declared their independence in this region, starting with the 'Pridnestrovian Moldavian Republic' or 'Transnistria', which declared its independence from Moldova on 2 September 1990, and the 'Republic of Artsakh' (more commonly known as Nagorno-Karabakh), on 2 September 1991 in territory claimed both by Armenia and Azerbaijan. Then, in mid-2008, two na-scent States—the 'Republic of Abkhazia' or 'Apsny' and the Republic of South Ossetia, also known as 'Alania'—declared their independence from Georgia with strong Russian support. Transnistria and Artsakh have been recognized either not at all (in the case of the latter) or (in the case of Transnistria) by their fellow separatist entities in the so-called 'Community for Democracy and Rights of Nations' formed by these four renegade re-publics. By contrast, both Abkhazia and South Ossetia were immediately recognized by Russia, along with a handful of other States (such as Nauru and Venezuela). Finally (at least for the moment), in 2014, the 'Republic of Crimea', the Donetsk Peoples' Republic' and the 'Luhansk People's Republic' all declared their independence from Ukraine.

---

[67] *Reference re Secession of Quebec* [1998] 2 SCR 217, para 138.

[68] *Accordance with International Law of the Unilateral Declaration of Independence in Respect of Kosovo, Advisory Opinion, ICJ Reports 2010,* p 403.

[69] *Prosecutor* v *Milutinović et al, Judgment,* Case No IT-05–87-T, Trial Chamber III (26 February 2009).

In all of these cases, the assertion of a right to self-determination was accompanied by allegations of ethnically motivated oppression on the part of the State from which they wanted to secede. These claims have, in case of the Georgian and Ukrainian entities, been supported by the Russian government. Explaining Russia's recognition of Abkazia and South Ossetia's independence, for example, Russian Prime Minister Dmitry Medvedev insisted that in doing so his country had been acting on the basis of 'their freely expressed desire for independence . . . based on the principles of the United Nations Charter' as well as with 'international precedents for such a move', specifically the recognition of Kosovo's independence by 'Western countries'. 'In international relations,' Medvedev warned, 'you cannot have one rule for some and another rule for others.'[70] The question remains, however, as to whether ethnic Abkhazians, Ossetians, and (in Crimea, Donetsk, and Luhansk) ethnic Russians have, indeed, been the subject of 'ethnic cleansing' on the part of Georgia and Ukraine, respectively, sufficient to justify their claims to external self-determination; and how any response to that question might take account, also, of similar allegations regarding the 'ethnic cleansing' of Georgians, Ukrainians, Ukrainian Tartars, and others in the territories concerned. According to Georgia, for example, in its application to the ICJ, '[t]he Russian Federation's support of separatist elements within the Ossetian and Abkhaz ethnic minorities and their *de facto* authorities has the effect of denying the right of self-determination to the ethnic Georgians remaining in South Ossetia and Abkhazia.'[71] Ukraine, in similar vein, alleges systematic discrimination by Russia both prior to and in the wake of the annexation against Crimea's Tartar population amounting, in its terms, to 'collective punishment' and 'collective erasure'.[72]

What is most striking, of course, has been the spectre of Russian intervention, both direct and indirect, in all of these secessionist enterprises, with the exception only of Artsakh/Nagorno-Karabakh. Whilst in all cases the declarations of independence had been underpinned by referenda (the Transnistrian referendum only being held, however, several years after the event in 2006), those referenda have nevertheless been widely condemned as having been underpinned by a climate of intimidation allegedly engineered, in each case, to ensure a favourable vote. Indeed, so violent and extensive has Russia's involvement in these secessionist movements been that both Georgia and Ukraine have brought cases against Russia before the ICJ, as noted earlier, alleging the latter's violation of the Convention on the Elimination of All Forms of Racial Discrimination and, in Ukraine's case, also of the Convention for the Suppression of the Financing of Terrorism.

Of particular note, here, is the case of Crimea, which stated its intention, prior to the holding of the referendum, that if a majority returned a vote in favour of independence, it would simultaneously seek integration into the Russian Federation. Two days after that 'yes' vote was received in the referendum on 16 March, the self-declared Republic of Crimea concluded a treaty with Russia to bring this about. Given that the referendum in Crimea was not only unconstitutional under Ukrainian law, but also held in a situation in which masked Russian troops had already seized hold of and dissolved the Crimean Supreme Council (Crimea's regional parliament), neither its pro-independence vote nor the subsequent treaty with Russia has been recognized by the international community

---

[70] Dmitry Medvedev, 'Why I had to recognise Georgia's breakaway regions', *Financial Times*, 27 August 2008, p 9.

[71] *Application of the International Convention on the Elimination of All Forms of Racial Discrimination*, Application Instituting Proceedings at the International Court of Justice, *Georgia* v *Russian Federation*, 12 August 2008, p 10, para 14.

[72] *Terrorism Financing and Racial Discrimination in Ukraine*, Application Instituting Proceedings at the International Court of Justice, *Ukraine* v *Russian Federation*, 16 January 2017, p 27.

(as the General Assembly underscored in its Resolution 68/262 (27 March 2014)). Crimea is now widely understood to have been unlawfully annexed by the Russian Federation.[73]

Whilst the majority of the international community has looked on at these developments with some dismay (see, for example, Resolution 382 of the NATO Parliament Assembly in respect of Georgia, General Assembly Resolution 68/262 in respect of Ukraine, and the European Parliament's resolution in support of Moldovan sovereignty),[74] the shadow cast by the Kosovo case is unmistakable. Not only does it appear to have given impetus to the holding of unauthorized/illegal referenda (an issue, at the time of writing, being confronted both by Spain in respect of Catalonia and Iraq in respect of its Kurdistan Region) but it has clearly opened the door to a new form of 'interventionist self-determination' that arguably finds its origins in a melding of the doctrine of humanitarian intervention on the one hand, and that of remedial self-determination on the other.

VII. CONCLUSION

In an article written in the early 1990s, Martti Koskenniemi reflected upon the contemporary resonance of Engel's notion of the 'withering away' of the State. In Koskenniemi's view, there were two versions of this thesis in circulation. One was a 'sociological' version that, on observing the recent globalization of politics, argued that 'states are no longer able to handle problems such as massive poverty, pollution of the atmosphere, or even their own security' without entering into forms of cooperation that entail the 'gradual dissolution of sovereignty' (Koskenniemi, 1994b, p 22). The other was an 'ethical' version that regarded statehood as a form of 'morally indefensible egotism' that serves either to create and perpetuate 'artificial distinctions among members of the human community' or to justify the use of State apparatus for oppression. Each of these critiques stresses the artificiality of the State as an idea or institution; each also sees its withering away as essentially beneficial. As we have seen, these two standpoints are not external to the State, but rather run through the discourses on sovereignty, self-determination, legitimacy, and recognition that constitute it. There is a constant equivocation, in all such discussions, as to whether the world is to be taken 'as it is' (in which we might be inclined to treat statehood as a question of fact, effectiveness as the primary condition, recognition as declaratory, and sovereignty as innate), or as something which must be engineered to correspond to those values which we take to be universal and necessary (in which case, we might treat statehood as being a matter of law, self-determination or democratic legitimacy as primary conditions, recognition as quasi-constitutive, and sovereignty as delegated or conditional). To note the equivocation here, however, is to underscore what Koskenniemi sees as the untenable character of either position. On the one hand the ethics in question will always be

---

[73] One should also note continued Russian presence/involvement in a number of the other entities in question, which ranges from the issuing of Russian passports to (ethnically Abkhazian, Ossetian, and Russian) Georgian and Ukrainian citizens in these areas to the outright seizure by Russian soldiers of institutional control and State territory.

[74] 'The Situation in Georgia', 2010 NATO Parliament Assembly, Res 382 refers to 'Georgia's occupied territories of Abkhazia and South Ossetia', while in GA Res 68/262 of 27 March 2014, the General Assembly called upon 'all States to desist and refrain from actions aimed at the partial or total disruption of the national unity and territorial integrity of Ukraine' and upon 'all States, international organizations and specialized agencies not to recognize any alteration of the status of the Autonomous Republic of Crimea and the city of Sevastopol' arising from the flawed referendum of 2016 (paras 2 and 6); European Parliament resolution on Moldova (Transnistria), 25 October 2016, 'denounced the attempt in the Moldovan region of Transnistria to establish its independence in a unilateral way by organising a so-called referendum'.

situational, a product of certain social conditions arising at a particular point in time; on the other hand, what we call social reality itself 'is in the last resort an ethical construction' dependent upon our willingness to act 'as if' the world were really like that. In his view, therefore, the State 'as a pure form' is valuable as a 'location' or 'language' within which 'we can examine the consequences and acceptability of the various jargons of authenticity', as he calls them, which seek to challenge the State's normative universality and 'set them in a specific relationship so as to enable political action' (Koskenniemi, 1994b, p 28).

One of the themes developed in this chapter, however, has been to explain how many of these seemingly abstract theoretical arguments about recognition, statehood, or sovereignty arose in a specific historical, geographical, and cultural context. However much these phenomena may have been 'globalized' over the past five centuries, the fact remains that the sovereign State is a Western European invention, whose universality came to be theorized in and through Europe's encounter with the non-European world from the late sixteenth century onwards. As we saw earlier, the difficulties involved—in nineteenth-century jurisprudence in particular—in seeking to delimit the scope of international law by reference to the pre-existence of (European) nation-States, while simultaneously employing a prescriptive notion of statehood to supervise 'entry' into the family of nations, conditioned many of the theoretical puzzles that subsequently emerged.

Yet for those located in the non-European world—perhaps for Indigenous peoples most acutely—as well as for those groups who continue to find themselves on the margins of the State, the problem is not merely a theoretical one. On the contrary, the assumptions about land ('territory'), subjectivity ('population'), order ('government'), and community ('independence') that comprise the State are not only conceptually incompatible with alternatives; they are also destructive, in a material sense, of the societies and environments to which those alternatives refer (Black, 2011; Borrows, 2002; Rivera, 1984; Simpson, 2014; Watson, 2015). The language of statehood is *itself* a 'jargon of authenticity' from this perspective. For Marxist, 'Third World', feminist, queer, Indigenous, and many other 'situated' observers of international law (Haraway, 1988, p 590), it was and remains difficult to accept the idea that the State is simply normatively indeterminate, whether as a concept or as a practice (Miéville, 2005; Chimni, 2017; Charlesworth and Chinkin, 2000; Ruskola, 2010; Coulthard, 2014). All refer, in one form or another, to the presence of what might be called a 'structural bias' (Koskenniemi, 2005, pp 606–15) in the language and practice of statehood that, in practice, privileges certain kinds of politics, certain ways of being in the world, and certain orders of power and wealth (Scott, 1998). This, undoubtedly, provides part of the rationale behind the establishment of an entity like the Democratic Federation of Northern Syria or 'Rojava', an avowedly non-State region governed on the basis of 'a new social contract' led by principles of gender equality, environmental sustainability, and 'democratic autonomy'.[75]

As to why, elsewhere in the world, statehood continues to hold out the ultimate promise of collective emancipation, one answer may be found in the way in which the old imperial language of hierarchy, civilization, and progress has come to be translated into the (supposedly) more technical language of economics and, in particular, of development (Pahuja, 2011). The nation-State, in this sense, continues to be presented as an object of work, that has to be sustained, supported, performed, and 'perfected' (to invoke Wolff) through initiatives, for example, to promote good governance, the rule of law, economic growth, and human rights. This new articulation of the State's objectives has, in turn, encouraged the emergence of a 'muscular humanitarianism' (Orford, 2003), legitimating intervention

---

[75] *Self-Rule in Rojava, Charter of the Social Contract*, 29 January 2014, available at https://peaceinkurdistancampaign. com/charter-of-the-social-contract/ (accessed 28 October 2017).

not because of a State's egregious pathologies but perhaps because it is not pathological enough. As the pressure on the world's physical 'resources' continues to mount, however, the 'perfectability' of the State is thrown increasingly into doubt. In this context, the 'turn to secession'—the flight from the disappointments of an existing State towards the promises held out by a new one—may turn out to be one of this century's greatest ironies.

REFERENCES

ALEXANDROWICZ, C (1967), *An Introduction to the History of the Law of Nations in the East Indies* (Oxford: Clarendon Press).

ANGHIE, A (2005), *Imperialism, Sovereignty and the Making of International Law* (Cambridge: Cambridge University Press).

AUSTIN, J (1995), *The Providence of Jurisprudence Determined* (Cambridge: Cambridge University Press).

BADIE, B (2000), *The Imported State: The Westernization of the Political Order* (Stanford: Stanford University Press).

BALIBAR, E (2004), *We the People of Europe: Reflections on Transnational Citizenship* (Princeton: Princeton University Press).

BECKER LORCA, A (2015), *Mestizo International Law: A Global History 1842–1933* (Cambridge: Cambridge University Press).

BERMAN, N (1988–89), 'Sovereignty in Abeyance: Self-Determination and International Law', 7 *Wisc ILJ* 51.

BERMAN, N (2012), *Passion and Ambivalence* (Martinus Nijhoff/Brill).

BHANDAR, B (2014), 'Property, Law, and Race: Modes of Abstraction', 4 *UC Irvine Law Review* 203.

BLACK, CF (2011), *The Land is the Source of the Law: A Dialogic Encounter with Indigenous Jurisprudence* (London, New York: Routledge).

BLUM, Y (1992), 'UN Membership of the "New" Yugoslavia: Continuity or Break?' 86 *AJIL* 830.

BONFILS, H (1894), *Manuel de Droit International Public* (Paris: Rousseau).

BORROWS, J (2002), *Recovering Canada: The Resurgence of Indigenous Law* (Toronto: University of Toronto Press).

BOURDIEU, P (2014), *On the State: Lectures at the Collège de France 1989–1992* (Cambridge: Polity Press).

BRIERLY, J (1924), 'The Shortcomings of International Law', 5 *BYIL* 13.

BROWN W (2010), *Walled States, Waning Sovereignty* (New York: Zone Books).

BROWNLIE, I (1982), 'Recognition in Theory and Practice', 53 *BYIL* 197.

CASSESE, A (1995), *Self-Determination of Peoples: A Legal Reappraisal* (Cambridge: Cambridge University Press).

CHARLESWORTH, H and CHINKIN, C (2000), *The Boundaries of International Law: A Feminist Analysis* (Manchester: Manchester University Press).

CHIMNI, BS (2017), *International Law and World Order: A Critique of Contemporary Approaches* (2nd edn, Cambridge: Cambridge University Press).

CLAPHAM, A (2006), *Human Rights Obligations of Non-State Actors* (Oxford: Oxford University Press).

CLAUDE, I (1955), *National Minorities; an International Problem* (Cambridge: Harvard University Press).

COBBAN, A (1945), *National Self-Determination* (Oxford: Oxford University Press).

COULTHARD, G (2014), *Red Skin, White Masks: Rejecting the Colonial Politics of Recognition* (Minneapolis: University of Minnesota Press).

CRAVEN, M (1995), 'The European Community Arbitration Commission on Yugoslavia', 67 *BYIL* 333.

CRAVEN, M (2007), *The Decolonization of International Law: State Succession and the*

Law of Treaties (Oxford: Oxford University Press).

CRAWFORD, J (2006), *The Creation of States in International Law* (2nd edn, Oxford: Oxford University Press).

DREW, C (2001), 'The East Timor Story: International Law on Trial', 12 *EJIL* 651.

DREW, C (2007), 'The Meaning of Self-determination: "The Stealing of the Sahara" Redux?', in K Arts and P Pinto Leite, *International Law and the Question of Western Sahara* (Leiden: IPJET), p 87.

DUGARD, J (1987), *Recognition and the United Nations* (Cambridge: Cambridge University Press).

DUURSMA, JC (1996), *Fragmentation and the International Relations of Micro States* (Cambridge: Cambridge University Press).

FAWCETT, JES (1965–66), 'Security Council Resolutions on Rhodesia', 41 *BYIL* 103.

FINK, C (2004), *Defending the Rights of Others: The Great Powers, the Jews, and International Minority Protection* (Cambridge: Cambridge University Press).

FIORE, P (1890), *Le Droit International Codifié et sa Sanction Juridique*, trans Chrétien (Paris: Chevalier-Marescq).

FOUCAULT, M (2006), *Psychiatric Power: Lectures at the College De France, 1973–1974* (Palgrave Macmillan).

FOUCAULT, M (2007), *Security, Territory, Population: Lectures at the College de France 1977–1978* (Palgrave Macmillan).

FOX, GH and ROTH, BR (eds) (2000), *Democratic Governance and International Law* (Cambridge: Cambridge University Press).

FRANCK, T (1996), 'Clan and Superclan: Loyalty, Identity and Community in Law and Practice', 90 *AJIL* 359.

FRANCK, T (1999), *The Empowered Self: Law and Society in an Age of Individualism* (Oxford: Oxford University Press).

GIDDENS, A (1985), *The Nation-State and Violence* (Cambridge: Polity Press).

GOLDSMITH, J and POSNER, E (2006), *The Limits of International Law* (Oxford: Oxford University Press).

GONG, G (1984), *The Standard of Civilization in International* Society (Oxford: Clarendon Press).

GORDON, R (1997), 'Saving Failed States: Sometimes a Neo-colonialist Notion', 12 *American ULILP* 904.

GRAY, C (1996), 'Bosnia and Herzegovina: Civil War or Inter-State Conflict?' 67 *BYIL* 155.

GREWE, WG (2000[1984]), *The Epochs of International Law*, trans M Byers (Berlin, New York: Walter de Gruyter).

HALL, W (1895), *A Treatise on International Law* (Oxford: Clarendon Press).

HARAWAY, D (1988), 'Situated Knowledges: The Science Question in Feminism and the Privilege of Partial Perspective', 14 *Feminist Studies* 575.

HARDT, M and NEGRI, A (2000), *Empire* (Cambridge, MA: Harvard University Press).

HEFFTER, A-G (1857), *Le droit international publique de l'Europe* (Berlin, Paris: Cotillon).

HELMAN, G and RATNER, S (1992–93), 'Saving Failed States', 89 *Foreign Policy* 3.

HOBBES, T, (1957, first published 1651), *Leviathan; or The Matter, Forme and Power of a Commonwealth Ecclesiastical and Civil*, M Oakeshott (ed) (Oxford: Blackwell).

HOBSBAWM, E (1992), *Nations and Nationalism since 1780* (2nd edn, Cambridge: Cambridge University Press).

JACKSON, R (1990), *Quasi-States: Sovereignty, International Relations and the Third World* (Cambridge: Cambridge University Press).

JENNINGS, R (1963), *The Acquisition of Territory in International Law* (Manchester: Manchester University Press).

JESSUP, P (1931), 'The Estrada Doctrine', 25 *AJIL* 719.

Johns, F (ed) (2010), *International Legal Personality* (Farnham: Ashgate).

Kamminga, M (1996), 'State Succession in Respect of Human Rights Treaties', 7 *EJIL* 469.

Kelsen, H (1941–42), 'The Pure Theory of Law and Analytical Jurisprudence', 55 *Harv LR* 44.

Kennedy, D (1997), 'International Law and the Nineteenth Century: History of an Illusion', 17 *Quinnipiac Law Review* 99.

Kingsbury, B, Krisch, N, and Stewart, R (2005), 'The Emergence of Global Administrative Law', 68 *Law and Contemporary Problems* 15.

Klüber, J (1851), *Europäisches Völkerrecht* (2nd edn, Schotthausen: Hurter).

Korman, S, (1996) *The Right of Conquest: The Acquisition of Territory by Force in International Law and Practice* (Oxford: Oxford University Press).

Koskenniemi, M (1994a), 'National Self-Determination Today: Problems of Legal Theory and Practice', 43 *ICLQ* 241.

Koskenniemi, M (1994b), 'The Wonderful Artificiality of States', 88 *ASIL Proceedings* 22.

Koskenniemi, M (2001), *The Gentle Civiliser of Nations: The Rise and Fall of International Law 1870–1960* (Cambridge; Cambridge University Press).

Koskenniemi, M (2005), *From Apology to Utopia: The Structure of International Legal Argument* (2nd edn, Cambridge: Cambridge University Press).

Kreijen, G (2002), 'The Transformation of Sovereignty and African Independence: No Shortcuts to Statehood', in G Kreijen (ed), *State Sovereignty and International Governance* (Oxford: Oxford University Press), p 45.

Lauterpacht, H (1947), *Recognition in International Law* (Cambridge: Cambridge University Press).

Lawrence, T (1895), *The Principles of International Law* (Boston: DC Heath and Co).

Locke, J (1690), *Second Treatise of Government*, ed McPherson (Indianapolis: Hackett Publishing Co, 1980).

Lorimer, J (1883), *The Institutes of the Law of Nations* (Edinburgh: W Blackwood).

Machiavelli, N (1532), *The Prince* (trans G Bull 1961).

McCorquodale, R (1994), 'Self-Determination: A Human Rights Approach', 43 *ICLQ* 857.

Marks, S (2003), *The Riddle of All Constitutions: International Law, Democracy and the Critique of Ideology* (Oxford: Oxford University Press).

Marks, S (2006), 'State-Centrism, International Law, and the Anxieties of Influence', 19 *Leiden JIL* 339.

Martens, G de (1864), *Précis du droit des gens moderne de l'Europe* (2nd edn, Paris: Guillaume).

Miéville, C (2005), *Between Equal Rights: A Marxist Theory of International Law* (Leiden, Boston: Brill).

Mill, JS (1861), *Considerations on Representative Government*, (London: Holt & Co).

Mitchell, T (1999), 'Society, Economy, and the State Effect', in G Steinmetz (ed), *State/Culture: State-Formation after the Cultural Turn* (Cornell: Cornell University Press), p 76.

Moreton-Robinson, A (2015), *The White Possessive: Property, Power and Indigenous Sovereignty* (Minnesota: University of Minnesota Press).

Mullerson, R (1993), 'The Continuity and Succession of States by Reference to the Former USSR and Yugoslavia', 42 *ICLQ* 473.

Murphy, S (2000), 'Democratic Legitimacy and the Recognition of States and Governments', in GH Fox and BR Roth (eds) *Democratic Governance and International Law* (Cambridge: Cambridge University Press), p 123.

Mutua, M (1995), 'Why Redraw the Map of Africa? A Moral and Legal Inquiry' 16 *Michigan JIL* 1113–76.

NESIAH, V (2003), 'Placing International Law: White Spaces on a Map', 16 *Leiden JIL* 1.

O'CONNELL, D (1970), *International Law* (2nd edn, London: Stevens & Sons), I.

OPPENHEIM, L (1905), *International Law: A Treatise* (London: Longmans, Green & Co.).

ORFORD, A (2003), *Reading Humanitarian Intervention: Human Rights and the Use of Force in International Law* (Cambridge: Cambridge University Press).

ORFORD, A (2011), *International Authority and the Responsibility to Protect* (Cambridge, Cambridge University Press).

PAHUJA, S (2011), *Decolonizing International Law: Development, Economic Growth and the Politics of Universality* (Cambridge: Cambridge University Press).

PARFITT, R (2016), 'Theorizing Recognition and International Personality', in A Orford and F Hoffman (eds), *The Oxford Handbook of the Theory of International Law* (Oxford: Oxford University Press), p 583.

PARFITT, R (forthcoming 2018), *Conditional State/ments: Modular History, International Law and Sovereign Inequality* (Cambridge: Cambridge University Press).

PHILLIMORE, R (1871), *Commentaries on International Law* (London: Butterworths), I–III.

PLATO'S REPUBLIC (2004), trans CDC Reeve (Indianapolis: Hackett).

PUFENDORF, S, *De jure naturae et gentium libri octo* (1698 trans Oldfather and Oldfather, Oxford: Clarendon Press, 1934).

RADAN, P (2002), *The Breakup of Yugoslavia and International Law* (London: Routledge).

RICH, R (1993), 'Recognition of States: The Collapse of Yugoslavia and the Soviet Union', 4 *EJIL* 36.

RIVERA CUSICANQUI, S (1984), '*Oprimidos pero no vencidos': Luchas del Campesinado Aymara y Qhechwa, 1900–1980* (La Paz: Instituto de Investigaciones de las Naciones Unidas para el Desarrollo Social).

RIVIER, A (1896), *Principes du Droit des Gens* (Paris: Rousseau).

ROTHBERG, R (2002), 'Failed States in a World of Terror', 81 *Foreign Affairs* 127.

RUSKOLA, T (2010), 'Raping Like a State', 57 *UCLA Law Review* 1477.

SAID, E (1979), *Orientalism* (New York: Random House).

SCHACHTER, O (1998), 'The Decline of the Nation-State and its Implications for International Law', 36 *Col JTL* 7.

SCHMITT, C (2003), *The Nomos of the Earth* (1974 trans G Ulmen) (New York: Telos Press).

SCHWARZENBERGER, G (1950), *A Manual of International Law* (2nd edn, London: Stevens).

SCOTT, J (1998), *Seeing Like a State* (New Haven: Yale University Press).

SHAW, M (1996), 'The Heritage of States: The Principle of *Uti Possidetis Juris* Today', 67 *BYIL* 75.

SIMPSON, A (2014), *Mohawk Interruptus: Political Life Across the Borders of Settler States* (Chapel Hill: Duke University Press).

SIMPSON, G (2004), *Great Powers and Outlaw States: Unequal Sovereigns in the International Legal Order* (Cambridge: Cambridge University Press).

SKINNER, Q (2004), *Visions of Politics*, Vol II (Cambridge: Cambridge University Press).

SPRUYT, H (1994), *The Sovereign State and its Competitors* (Princeton: Princeton University Press).

TALMON, S (1998), *Recognition of Governments in International Law* (Oxford: Clarendon Press).

TERRETT, S (2000), *The Dissolution of Yugoslavia and the Badinter Arbitration Commission* (Aldershot: Ashgate).

TILLY, C (1992), *Coercion, Capital and European States: AD 990–1992* (Malden, MA: Blackwell).

TWISS, T (1884), *Law of Nations Considered as Independent Political Communities* (Oxford: Clarendon Press).

VATTEL, E DE (1916), *The Law of Nations or the Principles of Natural Law* ([1758 trans G Fenwick] Washington: Carnegie Institute).

WADE, H (1955), 'The Basis of Legal Sovereignty', 13 *CLJ* 172.

WARBRICK, C (1997), 'Recognition of States: Recent European Practice', in MD Evans (ed), *Aspects of Statehood and Institutionalism in Contemporary Europe* (Aldershot: Dartmouth Publishers), p 9.

WATSON, I (2015), *Aboriginal Peoples, Colonialism and International Law: Raw Law* (Abingdon, Oxon: Routledge).

WEBER, M (1978), *Economy and Society* (Berkeley: University of California Press), Vols I and II.

WESTLAKE, J (1894), *Chapters on the Principles of International Law* (Cambridge: Cambridge University Press).

WESTLAKE, J (1904), *International Law* (Cambridge: Cambridge University Press).

WESTLAKE, J (1914), *The Collected Papers of John Westlake on Public International Law* (ed L Oppenheim, Cambridge: Cambridge University Press).

WHEATON, H (1936), *Elements of International Law* ([1866] Oxford: Clarendon Press).

WILDE, R (2001), 'From Danzig to East Timor and Beyond: the Role of International Territorial Administration', 95 *AJIL* 583.

WILDE, R (2008), *International Territorial Administration: How Trusteeship and the Civilising Mission Never Went Away* (Oxford: Oxford University Press).

WILLIAMS, P (2003), 'Earned Sovereignty: The Road to Resolving the Conflict over Kosovo's Final Status', 31 *Denver JILP* 387.

WILLIAMS, P, SCHARF, M, and HOOPER, J (2002–3), 'Resolving Sovereignty-Based Conflicts: The Emerging Approach of Earned Sovereignty', 31 *Denver JILP* 349.

WRIGHT, Q (1930), *Mandates under the League of Nations* (Chicago: The University of Chicago Press 1930).

ZIEMELE, I (2005), *State Continuity and Nationality: The Baltic States and Russia* (Leiden: Martinus Nijhoff).

FURTHER READING

ANGHIE, A (2005), *Imperialism, Sovereignty and the Making of International Law* (Cambridge, Cambridge University Press): a hugely influential account of the colonial origins of modern international law. A central text in Third World Approaches to International Law (TWAIL).

BERMAN, N (1988–89), 'Sovereignty in Abeyance: Self-Determination and International Law', 7 *Wisc ILJ* 51: the foremost author on the subject of nationalism and international law—here turning to the subject of self-determination.

COULTHARD, G (2014), *Red Skin, White Masks: Rejecting the Colonial Politics of Recognition* (Minneapolis: University of Minnesota Press): a vitally important critique of Western liberal practices of recognition from the standpoint of the struggle for Indigenous self-determination in Canada.

CRAWFORD, J (2006), *The Creation of States in International Law* (Oxford: Clarendon Press): a monumental, encyclopaedic work that remains the key reference point on the subject of statehood.

JOHNS, F (ed) (2010), *International Legal Personality* (Farnham: Ashgate): a comprehensive collection of essays on the question of international legal personality that pushes the question far beyond the standard categories.

KNOP, K (1993), 'Re/Statements: Feminism and State Sovereignty in International Law', 3 *Transnational Law and Contemporary Problems* 293: an early, but important, feminist critique of State sovereignty and the way in which it renders women 'analytically invisible'.

KOSKENNIEMI, M (2005), *From Apology to Utopia: The Structure of International Legal Argument* (2nd edn, Cambridge: Cambridge University Press): a challenging structuralist critique that lays out the indeterminacy of legal argumentation on the question of sovereignty (especially ch 4).

LAUTERPACHT, H (1947), *Recognition in International Law* (Cambridge: Cambridge University Press): dated, and inevitably stamped with his own idiosyncrasies, yet still the best account of the doctrinal debate over recognition.

MARKS, S (2003), *The Riddle of All Constitutions: International Law, Democracy and the Critique of Ideology* (Oxford: Oxford University Press): an important critique of the right to democracy in international law as a form of ideology.

NESIAH, V (2003), 'Placing International Law: White Spaces on a Map', 16 *Leiden JIL* 1: a critique of the way in which the statist paradigm forecloses the self-determination options available to nomadic communities (of Western Sahara in this case).

SIMPSON, G (2004), *Great Powers and Outlaw States: Unequal Sovereigns in the International Legal Order* (Cambridge: Cambridge University Press): traces the persistence of the idea of sovereign inequality and imperialism in international law.

WILDE, R (2008), *International Territorial Administration: How Trusteeship and the Civilising Mission Never Went Away* (Oxford: Oxford University Press): the most comprehensive and effective account of the historic and contemporary practice of International Territorial Administration.

8

INTERNATIONAL
ORGANIZATIONS

Dapo Akande

SUMMARY

This chapter examines the legal framework governing international organizations. It begins with an examination of the history, role, and nature of international organizations. It is argued in the chapter that although the constituent instruments and practices of each organization differ, there are common legal principles which apply to international organizations. The chapter focuses on the identification and exploration of those common legal principles. There is an examination of the manner in which international organizations acquire legal personality in international and domestic law and the consequences of that legal personality. There is also discussion of the manner in which treaties establishing international organizations are interpreted and how this differs from ordinary treaty interpretation. The legal and decision-making competences of international organizations are considered, as are the responsibility of international organizations and their privileges and immunities. Finally, the chapter examines the structure and powers of what is the leading international organization—the United Nations (UN).

I. INTRODUCTION

A distinctive feature of modern international affairs is the large number of international organizations through which States seek to achieve cooperation. This chapter looks at the place occupied by international organizations within the international legal system and sketches the legal framework governing their activities. It also describes the structure and activities of the leading global international organization—the United Nations (UN).

A. HISTORY AND ROLE OF INTERNATIONAL ORGANIZATIONS

International organizations were first created in the nineteenth century as a means of conducting international relations and fostering cooperation between States. They evolved from the ad hoc multilateral conferences convened by States to deal with particular situations—such as the Congress of Vienna (1815) which settled issues arising from the end of the Napoleonic wars—into institutions in which member States not only met regularly but which also possessed organs that functioned on a permanent basis. The early international organizations dealt with technical, non-political matters and included Commissions regulating European rivers such as the Rhine, the International Telegraphic Union (1865), and the Universal Postal Union (1874). The League of Nations, created in 1919 after the First World War, was the forerunner of the UN and was the first international organization established to deal with general political and other relations between States and which aspired to universal membership.

International organizations now play a significant role in international affairs generally and in the development of international law specifically. They exist in practically all fields of endeavour, ranging from general political cooperation to protection of the environment, defence, provision of humanitarian and development assistance, promotion of trade, etc. It is a reflection of the significant role that international organizations play in international affairs and in the exercise of public power that attention is now being paid to the question of what the limits of their powers are and the principles relating to when and how these organizations may be held accountable or responsible for the exercise of such powers.[1]

Within their diverse fields of operation, international organizations perform a number of functions. These include:

- Providing a forum for identifying and deliberating upon matters of common interest;
- Providing a forum for developing rules on matters of common interest;
- Acting as vehicles for taking action on international or transnational problems;
- Providing mechanisms for promoting, monitoring, and supervising compliance by States and non-State actors with agreed rules and policies as well as for gathering information regarding the conditions in and practices of States and non-State actors;
- Providing a forum for the resolution of international disputes.

B. DEFINITION, DISTINCTIONS, AND DIFFERENCES

Given the variety of organizations that are international in character, it is difficult to lay down a satisfactory and all-encompassing definition which distinguishes those organizations considered as 'international organizations' under international law from other types of organizations (Klabbers, 2015, p 6). Article 2(a) of the International Law Commission's 2011 Articles on the Responsibility of International Organizations (ARIO) provides that:

> 'international organization' means an organization established by a treaty or other instrument governed by international law and possessing its own international legal personality. International organizations may include as members, in addition to States, other entities . . .[2]

This definition embodies the key criteria for identifying whether an entity is an international organization. First, such an entity must be composed predominantly of States and/or other international organizations, though the membership may extend to other entities as well. Secondly, the entity must be established under international law. Although international organizations are usually created by treaty, they can also be created by other means, such as the resolution of another international organization, the resolution of a conference of States, or joint unilateral acts of States. Examples of organizations created

---

[1] See generally, Reinisch, 2001; Blokker, 2011; ILA Committee Report, 2004; ILA Study Group Report, 2012; and ILC Report, 2011, ch V, 'Responsibility of International Organizations'.

[2] ILC Report, 2011, p 54.

other than by treaty include the Organization for Security and Cooperation in Europe (OSCE) and the Organization of the Petroleum Exporting Countries (OPEC). Thirdly, for an entity to be an international organization it must have a will that is distinct and separate from that of the members. This is usually manifested in practice in at least one of the organs of the organization being autonomous from the members or possessing the ability to operate on a majority basis. It is having a 'distinct will' that justifies the conferral of separate legal personality.

The criteria set out in the preceding paragraph distinguish intergovernmental organizations which are the subject of this chapter from other types of international associations such as international non-governmental organizations and international public corporations. The key factor distinguishing international or intergovernmental organizations, such as the UN or the World Trade Organization (WTO), from international non-governmental organizations, such as Amnesty International or Greenpeace, is that the former are composed predominantly of States (and other intergovernmental organizations) while the latter are composed of private entities though they operate in more than one country. International public corporations or joint inter-State enterprises are entities jointly created by a number of States for the performance of commercial functions. Examples include the European Company for the Financing of Railway Rolling Stock (EUROFIMA) or Air Afrique (an airline established by 11 West African States). While international organizations are entities created under international law and have international legal personality, joint inter-State enterprises are formally established under the corporate law of one of the member States, even though the enterprise may have its roots in a treaty.

Despite sharing a common definition, there are many differences between international organizations. The most obvious differences concern membership and functions. Membership may either be universal (open) or closed. Universal organizations are open to all States and examples include the UN and its specialized agencies (see Section VII A.2 of this chapter). Closed organizations limit membership to those States fulfilling certain specified criteria. Examples of closed organizations include those whose membership is based on geographic criteria (eg regional organizations such as the Organization of American States (OAS) and the African Union (AU)) or economic criteria (eg OPEC and the Organization for Economic Cooperation and Development (OECD)). Some international organizations, such as the UN, have general functions within broad areas whereas the functions of others are restricted to particular fields, such as telecommunications, labour, health, or trade. Membership and function can be combined in various ways: some closed regional organizations exercise general functions (eg the OAS and the Council of Europe), while some universal organizations only have competence in limited fields (eg the UN specialized agencies and the WTO).

In considering whether or not a body or institutional structure qualifies as an international organization, one must consider the substance of the structure established by States rather than whether it is formally designated as an international organization. The key is whether the criteria outlined are fulfilled rather than the designation of the organization. Therefore, the more informal institutional arrangements established by some multilateral environmental treaties[3] and which are composed simply of: (i) a conference of the parties to the relevant treaty (COP) which meet regularly; (ii) one or more subsidiary bodies of the COP; and (iii) a secretariat which services the work of the COP and subsidiary bodies, may qualify as international organizations when they have a will distinct from those of the

---

[3] Eg the London Convention on the Prevention of Marine Pollution by Dumping of Wastes and other Matter (1972), the UN Framework Convention on Climate Change (1992), and the Kyoto Protocol (1997). See further, Churchill and Ulfstein, 2000, pp 623–5.

members. In some cases, these 'institutions' have even entered into treaties with States or other international organizations (Churchill and Ulfstein, 2000).

C. IS THERE A COMMON LAW OF INTERNATIONAL ORGANIZATIONS?

Given their great diversity, the existence of a common law applicable to international organizations has been questioned. On one view, since the law governing each organization derives from its own constituent instrument and practices (its 'constitution'), each will be governed by different legal principles which can only be applied by analogy to other organizations. It is true that these 'constitutions' regulate many matters, such as membership, competences, and financing, in differing ways. However, it is equally true that customary international law and, to a much lesser degree, treaties have generated principles of general application to international organizations. These common principles concern matters such as the legal personality of international organizations, implied competences, interpretation of constituent instruments, employment relations, immunities and privileges, and the liability and responsibility of the organization and its member States (see ILC Report, 2011, ch 5). These common principles apply in the absence of any contrary principle provided for in the law of the particular organization, and as regards liability and responsibility may even apply despite contrary provisions in the internal law of the organization. It is also accepted that the solutions adopted by one organization to a problem have a relevance to the approach to be taken to an analogous problem in another. The following sections outline the most important elements of this common law applicable to international organizations.

II. LEGAL PERSONALITY

In considering the legal position of international organizations it is useful to start by considering whether such entities possess legal personality and, if so, what the consequences of that legal personality are. Since international organizations usually operate both on the international plane and in national territories, one must consider whether these organizations possess international legal personality and legal personality in domestic law. Section II A examines the meaning of international legal personality and the sources of that personality for international organizations, especially in cases in which it is not expressly provided for in the constituent instrument of that organization. It also examines the consequences for international organizations of the possession of international legal personality. Section II B considers whether non-member States of an international organization are bound to recognize its legal personality. Section II C examines the obligation of member States to confer personality in domestic law and the various techniques used by States to confer such personality.

A. PERSONALITY IN INTERNATIONAL LAW

1. The meaning of international legal personality

To say that an entity has international legal personality is to say that the entity is a bearer of rights and duties derived from international law. Although it was often asserted in the nineteenth and early twentieth centuries that States were the only subjects of international law, it was decisively established in the *Reparation for Injuries* Advisory Opinion that other entities, particularly international organizations, also possess international legal personality. The case arose out of the murder of a UN mediator in Jerusalem by a Jewish group.

The UN General Assembly requested an opinion from the International Court of Justice on whether the UN had the capacity to bring an international claim (against Israel) for the purpose of obtaining reparation for injuries done to the organization and its agents. While Article 104 of the Charter imposes an obligation on UN member States to confer legal personality on the Organization within their *domestic* legal systems, there is nothing in the Charter which expressly grants *international* personality to the UN. Nevertheless, the Court found that the UN possesses international legal personality, arguing that this was necessary for the fulfilment of its functions. The Court also deduced legal personality from the powers and rights that had been given to the UN (the power of decision-making, domestic legal personality, immunities and privileges, and treaty-making powers) under the Charter. The Court noted that the Organization 'occupies a position in certain respects in detachment from its members' and that:

> the Organization was intended to exercise and enjoy, and is in fact exercising and enjoying, functions and rights which can only be explained on the basis of the possession of a large measure of international personality and the capacity to operate on the international plane.[4]

To say that international organizations possess international legal personality tells us that they are capable of possessing international rights, capacities, or duties. However, apart from a few specific capacities indicated in Section II A3 of this chapter, possession of international legal personality does not define the particular capacities, rights, or duties that any particular organization possesses nor does it indicate that they possess the same capacities, rights, or duties (Gazzini, 2011, p 43).

2. The sources of international legal personality for international organizations

Although treaties establishing universal international organizations do not usually provide expressly that they possess international legal personality, there are treaties dealing with closed international organizations which do so.[5] Where there is no express treaty basis, international personality may be deduced by other means.

There are two basic schools of thought regarding the method by which the personality is to be established in the absence of an express treaty provision. The first school—the will theory—asserts that the personality of an international organization is derived from the will of the members to confer such personality. This conferral is done expressly in the constitutive instrument of the organization or may be deduced from the capacities, powers, rights, and duties bestowed to the organization (Schermers and Blokker, 2011, para 1565; Reinisch, 2000, pp 54–9; Sands and Klein, 2009, para 15-006). According to this school of thought, an international organization will only have personality if its members intended it to have such personality or if it can be asserted that such personality is necessary for the fulfilment of the functions ascribed to it by its members. The second school—the objective approach—asserts that an international organization has international legal personality as long as certain objective criteria set out by law are fulfilled (Seyersted, 1964; Rama Montaldo, 1970). Thus personality is not derived from the will of the members but from the presence of the criteria stated earlier in the definition of an international organization.[6]

---

[4] *Reparation for Injuries Suffered in the Service of the United Nations, Advisory Opinion, ICJ Reports 1949*, p 174 at p 179.

[5] Examples include the Treaty on European Union (as amended by Lisbon Treaty), Article 47; EC Treaty, Article 210; European Coal and Steel Community Treaty, Article 6; Agreement Establishing the African Development Bank, Article 50.

[6] Amerasinghe, 2005, p 83 tries to merge both schools by arguing that the intention required is not subjective but objective and to be found in the circumstances surrounding the creation of the organization.

There has been much debate regarding which of these two approaches was taken by the Court in the *Reparation for Injuries* Advisory Opinion. In that case, the Court made reference on more than occasion to the intention of the parties in ascribing legal personality to the UN. However, this does not necessarily mean that the Court adopted the will theory.

What the Court seemed to be saying was that the intention of the members to ascribe certain rights, functions, and characteristics to the UN could only be given effect if the organization possessed its own legal personality. This is not inconsistent with saying that the members had ascribed characteristics to the organization which satisfied the criteria required for conferring international personality. While the key factor is the possession of those characteristics, they necessarily arise out of the will of the members. Thus, there is no radical difference between the two schools if one accepts that the characteristics which confer international legal personality on international organizations must necessarily be conferred on it by its members. Once those characteristics are conferred (by the will of the members through its constituent instrument or subsequent practice), the rules of international law confer international personality on the organization with all the consequences that this entails. Arguably, all that the Court did in the *Reparation for Injuries* Advisory Opinion was to search to see if the characteristics necessary for international personality (and which are predetermined by international law) had been conferred on the UN by its members.[7]

3. The consequences of the possession of international legal personality by international organizations

Possessing international legal personality means that an organization possesses rights and duties in international law, but this does not usually tell us the particular rights and capacities possessed by a particular organization. However, there are certain consequences which flow from the possession of international legal personality by an international organization.

(1) Personality distinguishes the collective entity (the organization) from the members. In particular, legal personality separates out the rights and obligations of the organization from those of the members (Lauterpacht, 1976, p 407; Oppenheim, 2017, §11.13).

(2) Personality entitles the organization to bring a claim in international law for the purpose of maintaining its own rights.[8] Such claims by international organizations will be brought through the mechanisms which exist in international law for the settlement of international disputes and can only be made in an international tribunal if that the tribunal has jurisdiction to deal with the case.

(3) Personality entails the consequence that an international organization is responsible for the non-fulfilment of its obligations (Article 3 ARIO 2011). Personality also gives rise to a presumption that members of the organization are not liable with respect to the obligations *of the organization*, although this presumption can be displaced (see Section V of this chapter).[9] Members remain liable for *their own obligations* and that responsibility may arise in the same set of circumstances where the organization is also responsible.

---

[7] See text at n 4. In the sentences following that quote the Court states that the UN 'could not carry out the intention of its founders if it were devoid of legal personality. It must be acknowledged that its Members, by entrusting certain functions to it, with attendant duties and responsibilities, have clothed it with the compliance required to enable those functions to be effectively discharged.'

[8] Schermers and Blokker, 2011, para 1856 argue that this capacity is an implied power but one possessed by all international organizations.

[9] See ILC Commentary Article 62 ARIO, ILC Report, 2011, p 163, paras 2–3.

These first three consequences are inherent in the very notion of international legal personality and apply to any international legal person. However, there are other consequences of the personality of international organizations which do not apply to all international legal persons but result from the nature of personality possessed by international organizations.

(4) Customary international law confers, at least within the host State, certain privileges and immunities on international organizations that are necessary for the efficient and independent functioning of the organization (see further Section VI of this chapter). As Higgins (1994, p 91) puts it, 'members—and *a fortiori* the headquarters State—may not at one and the same time establish an organization and fail to provide it with those immunities that ensure its role as distinct from that of the host State.'

(5) International organizations possess a power to conclude agreements which are subject to the law of treaties.[10] Although the question whether a particular treaty or type of treaty is within the competence of any particular organization depends on its implied powers (Webb, 2014, p 570), every organization at least has the competence (where not expressly denied) to enter into certain types of treaties. These include host State agreements and treaties for the purpose of settling claims by and against the organization.[11]

B. OBJECTIVE LEGAL PERSONALITY AND RELATIONS WITH NON-MEMBER STATES

Given that international organizations are created by treaties—which do not bind non-parties without their consent[12]—it might be argued that the personality of an international organization is only binding on members.[13] This would mean that non-members would only be bound to accept that personality where they have 'recognized' the organization as a legal person. However, the better view is that the personality of international organizations is in fact objective, which means that it is opposable to non-members and that non-members are bound to accept that organization as a separate legal person.[14]

In the *Reparation for Injuries* Opinion, the Court had to consider whether the UN could bring a claim against a State (Israel) which was not a member of the Organization. It took the view that:

> fifty States, representing the vast majority of the members of the international community, had the power, in conformity with international law, to bring into being an entity possessing objective international personality and not merely personality recognised by them alone... .[15]

Thus, international organizations with a membership consisting of the vast majority of the international community possess objective international personality. However, it is important to note that the Court did not say that *only* such organizations possess objective personality and there are good reasons of practice and principle for concluding that

---

[10] Vienna Convention on the Law of Treaties between States and International Organizations or between International Organizations (1986), preambular para 11.

[11] See *Reparation for Injuries Suffered in the Service of the United Nations, Advisory Opinion, ICJ Reports 1949*, p 174 at p 181.   [12] Vienna Convention on the Law of Treaties (1969), Article 34.

[13] See *Third Restatement*, 1987, para 223.   [14] See ILC Report, 2011, p 76, para 9.

[15] *Reparation for Injuries Suffered in the Service of the United Nations, Advisory Opinion, ICJ Reports 1949*, p 174 at p 185.

the personality possessed by any international organization is objective and opposable to non-members. In practice, 'no recent instances are known of a non-member State refusing to acknowledge the personality of an organization on the ground that it was not a member State and had not given the organization specific recognition' (Amerasinghe, 2005, p 87). Furthermore, domestic courts of non-member States do acknowledge the international personality of international organizations.[16] As a matter of principle, the personality of international organizations derives from the effect that customary international law (which is binding on all States) ascribes to their characteristics. Thus, once international law ascribes personality to an organization, a subject of international law is created with its own rights and its own duties.

C. PERSONALITY IN DOMESTIC LAW

1. The obligation to confer domestic legal personality

Since international organizations also operate within the territory of States, they usually need to possess domestic legal personality, including the capacity to perform legal acts in domestic law. For example, international organizations will need to be able to enter into contracts, own property, and institute legal proceedings. Many treaties establishing international organizations provide that they are to have the necessary legal capacities in domestic law, for example UN Charter, Article 104. Even where there is no express treaty obligation, there may be an implied obligation for members to provide the organization with such domestic capacities as are necessary to allow it to function effectively (Reinisch, 2000, p 44).

2. The manner in which domestic legal personality is recognized

States confer domestic legal personality on international organizations in various ways. The technique used depends in part on the relationship between international law and the national law of the State concerned (Oppenheim, 2017, §§11.28–11.29). The technique also varies between member States of an organization and non-members. In member States which adopt a more monist tradition of the relationship between international law and national law, the domestic personality is often taken to flow directly from the treaty provision requiring the conferment of such personality. This position has been taken in: (i) the USA and Belgium[17] with respect to the UN; (ii) the Netherlands with respect to the UN Relief and Rehabilitation Administration;[18] and (iii) Italy with respect to the North Atlantic Treaty Organization (NATO).[19]

In member States in which treaties do not form part of domestic law such treaty obligations will usually need to be transformed into national law by a national instrument. This is the technique adopted in common law countries like the UK, where the International Organizations Act 1968 provides that the Executive may by Order in Council confer the legal capacities of a body corporate on any international organization of which the UK is a member.[20]

Thus in the UK, the House of Lords in *JH Rayner (Mincing Lane) Ltd* v *Department of Trade and Industry* stressed that the legal persona of the International Tin Council (ITC)

---

[16] Eg *International Tin Council v Amalgamet* (1988) 80 ILR 31; 524 NYS 2d 971.

[17] *Manderlier v Organisation des Nations Unies & Etat Belge (Ministre des Affaires Etrangères)* (1972) 45 ILR 446; *UN v B* (1952) 19 ILR 490.   [18] *UNRRA v Daan* (1949) 16 ILR 337.

[19] *Branno v Ministry of War* (1955) 22 ILR 756.

[20] International Organizations Act 1968, s 2(a). Similar legislation exists in the USA, Australia, Canada, and New Zealand.

in English law was created not by the constituent agreement of the organization but by the domestic legislation. According to Lord Oliver:

> Without the Order in Council the I.T.C. had no legal existence in the law of the United Kingdom . . . What brought it into being in English law was the Order in Council and it is the Order in Council, a purely domestic measure, in which the constitution of the legal persona is to be found and in which there has to be sought the liability of the members which the appellants seek to establish, for that is the act of the ITC's creation in the United Kingdom.[21]

The consequence of this was that the liability of members for the organization's debts depended on domestic legislation rather than on the position in international law.

The legal personality of international organizations will also be recognized by the courts of non-member States. Under private international law domestic courts will recognize the legal status and capacities of an organization created by foreign law. Similarly, since an international organization has personality under the law of its creation—international law—that personality will be recognized by domestic courts.[22]

In the UK, it has been held that the legal personality of an international organization of which the UK is not a member will be recognized where the organization has been accorded legal personality under the law of the host State or of another member State[23] rather than by virtue of international law and the relevant constituent treaty. Taken to its logical conclusion, this approach would have the unfortunate consequence that the law governing the status and capacities of the organization would be the foreign domestic law. Happily, the High Court in *Westland Helicopters Ltd* v *Arab Organization for Industrialization*[24] held that while the personality of an international organization of which the UK was not a member would only be recognized in the UK if a foreign State had accorded that organization personality in its domestic law, the law governing the status and capacities of the organization is international law, including the relevant treaties.

III. INTERPRETATION OF CONSTITUENT INSTRUMENTS

Treaties which establish international organizations set out both the purposes, structure, and competences of the organization as a whole and the particular functions and powers granted to its individual organs. These treaties define the position of the organization towards its members as well as the relationship between the individual organs. Although they are not party to such treaties, international organizations are bound by their constituent instruments.[25] In many cases, these treaties also create rights and impose obligations between the members. Finally, they may to some degree define the relationship between the organization and third parties. Consequently, the manner in which they are interpreted is of considerable importance. The following subsections consider: (i) who is empowered to interpret constituent treaties of international organizations; and (ii) the relevant principles of treaty interpretation.

---

[21] [1989] 3 WLR 969, 1012c.

[22] See *International Tin Council v Amalgamet* (1988) 80 ILR 31; 524 NYS 2d 971; *Arab Organization for Industrialisation and others v Westland Helicopters Ltd and others* (1987) 80 ILR 622.

[23] *Arab Monetary Fund v Hashim* [1990] 1 All ER 685. A similar approach was taken in the US case *In Re Jawa Mahmoud Hashim* (1995) 107 ILR 405.

[24] *Westland Helicopters Ltd* v *Arab Organization for Industrialization* [1995] 2 All ER 387; 108 ILR 564.

[25] *Interpretation of the Agreement of 25 March 1951 between the WHO and Egypt, Advisory Opinion, ICJ Reports 1980*, p 73, para 37.

A. WHO IS EMPOWERED TO INTERPRET?

Since the organs of international organization will need to have some appreciation of the scope of their functions and powers in order to carry them out, these organs will necessarily and routinely have to interpret the treaty setting up the international organization. In the *Certain Expenses* Advisory Opinion, the ICJ accepted that 'each organ [of the UN] must, in the first place at least, determine its own jurisdiction'.[26] Interpretations by organs will take place either formally and explicitly (eg in a legal act of the organ)—particularly in cases where dispute arises as to the meaning of particular provisions—or impliedly as a result of the practice of the organ in question. Some constituent treaties provide for formal and definitive interpretations by a particular organ. This is particularly common with respect to international financial institutions where there is often an obligation to submit questions of interpretation to the Executive Board, Board of Directors, or the Board of Governors of the institution for decision.[27] In such circumstances, the interpretations given by these organs are binding, at least on the parties to the dispute, if not on all members and other organs. Where there is no formal power of interpretation given, and interpretation arises simply in the course of the work of the organization, such interpretations are not binding on member States. In the same way that organs will have to interpret constituent treaties in the course of their functions, members will similarly have to do so (Tzanakopoulos, 2011, ch 5).

Judicial or arbitral tribunals may also have occasion to interpret constituent instruments. Such bodies may be created to deal with legal issues which arise within the system of the international organization in question. Examples include the Court of Justice of the European Union and the International Tribunal for the Law of the Sea. International organizations do not have standing to be parties in contentious cases before the ICJ although UN organs and UN specialized agencies may request Advisory Opinions from the ICJ on legal questions arising within the scope of their competence, including the interpretation of their constituent instruments.[28] In the case of specialized agencies, this competence to request Advisory Opinions will be contained in agreements concluded with the UN or in their constituent instruments.[29] The ICJ may also have to interpret the constituent instrument of international organizations in contentious cases between States, where such a case raises questions relating to the rights and obligations of States arising from such treaties.

The constituent treaties may also provide for disputes arising thereunder to be referred to international arbitration.[30] Alternatively, an arbitral tribunal established under a treaty or contract between an international organization and a third party may have to interpret the constitution of that organization.[31] As has already been seen, national courts may also have to construe the constituent instruments of international organizations.

---

[26] *Certain Expenses of the United Nations, Advisory Opinion, ICJ Reports 1962*, p 151 at p 168.

[27] Eg IMF Articles of Agreement, Article XXIX(a); IBRD Articles of Agreement, Article IX(a); Agreement Establishing the Asian Development Bank, Article 59.

[28] Although there are implications to the contrary in the *Legality of the Use by a State of Nuclear Weapons in Armed Conflict, Advisory Opinion, ICJ Reports 1996*, p 66, para 28, the better view is that an authorized UN specialized agency is always entitled to request an advisory opinion on the interpretation of its constituent instrument. See Akande, 1998, pp 452–7.

[29] Eg WHO Constitution, Article 76; IMO Constitution, Article 66.

[30] Eg Universal Postal Unison Constitution, Article 39.

[31] See *Westland Helicopters v Arab Organization for Industrialization et al* (1989) 80 ILR 595.

B. WHAT ARE THE RELEVANT PRINCIPLES OF INTERPRETATION TO BE APPLIED?

Since the constituent instruments establishing international organizations are usually treaties, interpretation is governed by Articles 31 and 32 of the Vienna Convention on the Law of Treaties (see Fitzmaurice, Ch 6 of this book). Article 5 of that Convention expressly states that the Convention applies to such treaties and in the *Nuclear Weapons Advisory Opinion (Request by WHO)* the ICJ stated that:

> From a formal standpoint, the constituent instruments of international organizations are multilateral treaties, to which the well-established rules of treaty interpretation apply.[32]

However, the ICJ has noted that constituent instruments have 'certain special characteristics'[33] and that:

> the constituent instruments are also treaties of a particular character; their object is to create new subjects of law endowed with a certain autonomy, to which the parties entrust the task of realizing common goals. Such treaties can raise specific problems of interpretation, owing, *inter alia*, to their character which is conventional and at the same time institutional; the very nature of the organization created, the objectives which have been assigned to it by its founders, the imperatives associated with the effective performance of its functions, as well as its own practice, are all elements which may deserve special attention when the time comes to interpret these constituent treaties.[34]

To the extent that constituent instruments are in some senses 'constitutions', the general rules of treaty interpretation have to be applied differently when such treaties are under consideration (Lauterpacht, 1976, p 416; Amerasinghe, 2005, p 59). It is these differences that are focused on next.

1. The role of objects and purposes—the principle of effectiveness

Article 31 of the Vienna Convention provides that:

> A treaty shall be interpreted in good faith, in accordance with the ordinary meaning to be given to the terms of the treaty in their context and in the light of its object and purpose.

The ICJ has stated that 'interpretation must be based above all upon the text of the treaty'[35] and generally speaking, the objects and purpose of a treaty are subsidiary to the text (Aust, 2013, p 209). However, when interpreting constituent instruments of international organizations special prominence is given to the objects and purposes of the instrument and of the organization. In the *Nuclear Weapons* Advisory Opinion the Court spoke of 'the very nature of the organization created, the objectives which have been assigned to it by its founders, the imperatives associated with the effective performance of its functions' as elements which may 'deserve special attention' in interpreting the constituent instruments of international organizations. Likewise in the *Reparation for Injuries* Advisory Opinion, the Court stated that 'the rights and duties of an entity such as the Organization must depend on its purposes and functions as specified or implied in its constituent

---

[32] *Legality of the Use by a State of Nuclear Weapons in Armed Conflict (Request by WHO), Advisory Opinion, ICJ Reports 1996*, p 66, para 19.

[33] *Certain Expenses of the United Nations, Advisory Opinion, ICJ Reports 1962*, p 151 at p 157.

[34] *Legality of the Use by a State of Nuclear Weapons in Armed Conflict, Advisory Opinion, ICJ Reports 1996*, p 66, para 19.

[35] *Territorial Dispute (Libya/Chad), Judgment, ICJ Reports 1994*, p 21, para 41.

documents or developed in practice'.[36] Frequently, the Court 'will seek to determine what are the purposes and objectives of the organization and will give to the words in question an interpretation which will be most conducive to the achievement of those ends' (Lauterpacht, 1976, p 420). This is known as the principle of effectiveness. The primary example of this principle is the doctrine of implied powers, by which an organization is deemed to have those powers that are necessary for achieving its purposes even in the absence of words in the text which indicate that the organization is to have such a power (Section IV A of this chapter).

2. The role of subsequent practice

The practice of the organization is often given a special role and is used not only in cases where the text of the agreement is ambiguous but also in cases of silence and to graft new rules on to the constituent instrument. The justification for this is that such treaties must be regarded as living instruments and be interpreted in an evolutionary manner, permitting the organization to fulfil its purposes in changing circumstances (Kadelback, 2012, p 79). A well-known example of this is the *Namibia* Advisory Opinion,[37] where the Court, relying on the consistent practice of the Security Council and its members, held that an abstention by a permanent member of the Security Council was a 'concurring vote' within the meaning of Article 27(3) of the UN Charter and not a veto. Similarly, in the *Reparation for Injuries* Advisory Opinion the Court referred to the practice of the UN and the fact that it had entered into treaties as confirming the legal personality of the Organization.[38]

Reference to the practice of the parties as a means of treaty interpretation is permitted by the Vienna Convention, Article 31(3)(b). However, the Court has also drawn on the practice of the organs of the organization. This is significant since some organs are not composed of all the organization's members and, even if they are, many operate on the basis of majority voting. Thus, the practice of the organs of an organization may not reflect the position of all parties to the treaty. Where some members object to the practice of an organ, allowing that practice to influence interpretation or development of new rules amounts to imposing new obligations on the minority without their consent. This is contrary to the general principle of international law that obligations can only arise from express or implied consent and some judges of the ICJ have counselled against this approach.[39] Some authors claim there is an independent rule permitting the use of the practice of organs which members of organizations must be deemed to have accepted (Lauterpacht, 1976, p 460; Kadelback, 2012, p 86). However, subsequent practice of a majority within an organ must not be used as a means of constitutional amendment (Amerasinghe, 2005, p 54; Lauterpacht, 1976, p 465). It is noteworthy that in practically all cases where the ICJ has referred to subsequent practice of organs it has simply been used as a means of confirming an interpretation already arrived at using other methods of interpretation. Subsequent practice of organs should therefore be confined to cases where it establishes the agreement of the parties, confirms a result already reached, or to cases where other methods of interpretation lead to an ambiguity or an unreasonable result.

---

[36] *Reparation for Injuries Suffered in the Service of the United Nations, Advisory Opinion, ICJ Reports 1949*, p 174 at p 180.

[37] *Legal Consequences for States of the Continued Presence of South Africa in Namibia (South West Africa) notwithstanding Security Council Resolution 276 (1970), Advisory Opinion, ICJ Reports 1971*, p 16, paras 20–2.

[38] *Reparation for Injuries Suffered in the Service of the United Nations, Advisory Opinion, ICJ Reports 1949*, p 174 at p 179.

[39] See the Separate Opinion of Judge Spender in *Certain Expenses of the United Nations, Advisory Opinion, ICJ Reports 1962*, p 151 at p 197.

IV. POWERS OF INTERNATIONAL ORGANIZATIONS

In addition to the powers expressly conferred on international organizations by their constituent treaties these organizations also possess powers which are implied. This section examines the basis for those implied powers. It then surveys the kinds of decision-making powers possessed by international organizations, and finally examines the legal consequences when organizations act beyond their powers.

A. IMPLIED POWERS

In the *Reparation for Injuries* Advisory Opinion, the ICJ stated that:

> Under international law, an Organization must be deemed to have those powers which, though not expressly provided in the Charter, are conferred upon it by necessary implication as being essential to the performance of its duties.[40]

This doctrine of implied powers has been applied by the ICJ in a number of cases. In the *Reparation for Injuries* Advisory Opinion, the Court held that the UN was entitled to present an international claim on behalf of its agents even though such a power is not stated in the Charter. Likewise, in the *Certain Expenses* Advisory Opinion,[41] the Court held that the UN Security Council and General Assembly were competent to establish peacekeeping operations although that concept is not mentioned in the Charter.

Implied powers are not restricted to those powers necessary for carrying out express powers or functions. On the contrary, ICJ jurisprudence shows that powers can be implied whenever they are 'essential' for the fulfilment of the organization's objects and purposes. Furthermore, 'essentiality' does not mean that the power to be implied must be 'indispensably required' (Lauterpacht, 1976, pp 430–2; Oppenheim, 2017, §9.09). The Court has been rather liberal in its approach and has been willing to imply a power where it would 'promote the efficiency of the Organization'.[42] The main limitation is that the power must be directed at achieving the aims and purposes of the organization. As the ICJ stated in *Certain Expenses* Advisory Opinion:

> When the Organization takes action which warrants the assertion that it was appropriate for the fulfilment of one of the stated purposes of the United Nations, the presumption is that such action is not *ultra vires* the Organization.[43]

B. DECISION-MAKING POWERS

International organizations are often given the power to take decisions relating to their spheres of activity. Some decisions relate to the internal workings of the organization itself and are directed at the organs of the organization—for example, decisions approving the budget, staff regulations, rules of procedure, or decisions establishing subsidiary organs. Other decisions are taken in the course of carrying out the tasks entrusted to the organization and are directed at the members of the organization or, exceptionally, at third parties such as individuals and other non-State entities. Examples include decisions of the World

---

[40] *Reparation for Injuries Suffered in the Service of the United Nations, Advisory Opinion, ICJ Reports 1949*, p 174 at p 182.

[41] *Certain Expenses of the United Nations, Advisory Opinion, ICJ Reports 1962*, p 151 at p 177.

[42] Akande, 1998, p 444.

[43] *Certain Expenses of the United Nations, Advisory Opinion, ICJ Reports 1962*, p 151 at p 168.

Health Organization (WHO) setting standards with respect to pharmaceutical and other products; decisions of the UN Security Council imposing sanctions on a State; and decisions of the ICAO Council relating to safety standards for international aviation.

In determining whether or not a particular decision of an international organization is legally binding on its addressee one must consider, first, whether that organ or organization is empowered by its constitution (expressly or impliedly) to take binding decisions, and secondly, whether the language of the decision reveals an intention on the part of the organ to issue a binding decision.

Some constituent treaties expressly confer on organizations the power to issue decisions binding on their members. For example, Article 25 of the UN Charter obliges members to carry out decisions of the Security Council and under Article 22 of the WHO Constitution regulations adopted by the World Health Assembly are binding, unless a member opts out of the regulation *ab initio*.

Since international organizations do not generally have law-making powers, they are usually given power to take non-binding decisions which may take a number of forms. The most common is the power to make *recommendations* to members concerning matters within the scope of the organization (eg UN General Assembly under Articles 10–14 of the UN Charter). Other decisions may be *determinations* consisting of findings of facts or characterizations, or formal *declarations* of principles which the organ considers applicable in a particular area. Since these decisions are not binding, they do not, of themselves, create obligations for member States.

However, the non-binding nature of decisions does not mean that a particular decision is devoid of legal effect for members. Some constituent instruments oblige members to consider recommendations in good faith. For example, the International Labour Organization (ILO) and UN Educational, Scientific and Cultural Organization (UNESCO) Constitutions (Articles 19(6) and Articles 4(4) and 8 respectively) require member States to submit recommendations to their competent national authorities for consideration and to report back to the organization on action taken. Furthermore, a separate international treaty may contain an obligation to have regard to (and possibly to comply with) non-binding decisions of an international organization. For example, the WTO Agreement on Sanitary and Phytosanitary Measures (SPS), Article 3 encourages members to base their SPS measures on standards adopted by other international organizations. Although members are not required to confirm these standards, measures in conformity are presumed to comply with the relevant WTO provisions.[44] Likewise, a number of provisions of the UN Convention on the Law of the Sea (eg Articles 22 and 211–21) require States to comply with standards adopted by the 'competent international organization' (usually the IMO). Additionally, it is arguable that there is a presumption that members acting in accordance with a relevant decision of an international organization are acting lawfully at least as between the members of that organization.

Finally, non-binding decisions of international organizations may contain rules of law which are or become binding through other processes of international law. Resolutions of the UN General Assembly which are couched in declaratory terms are a good example.[45] Where such declarations elaborate on rules contained in the constituent treaty of the organization or other treaties adopted within the organization they may be regarded as authoritative interpretations of the treaty in question or, alternatively, as subsequent practice

---

[44] *Beef Hormone Case*, Appellate Body Report, WT/DS26/AB/R, WT/DS48/AB/R (16 January 1998).
[45] Eg Universal Declaration of Human Rights, GA Res 217A (1948); Declaration of Principles of International Law Concerning Friendly Relations Among States, GA Res 2625 (1970).

establishing the agreement of the parties to the treaty.[46] Furthermore, such resolutions may be declaratory of pre-existing rules of customary international law. Alternatively, such resolutions may play a role in the formation of *new* customary rules so that the rules contained therein may come to be regarded as binding. As the ICJ noted in the *Nuclear Weapons* Advisory Opinion:

> General Assembly resolutions, even if they are not binding, may sometimes have normative value. They can, in certain circumstances, provide evidence important for establishing the existence of a rule or the emergence of an *opinio juris*. To establish whether this is true of a given General Assembly resolution, it is necessary to look at its content and the conditions of its adoption; it is also necessary to see whether an *opinio juris* exists as to its normative character. Or a series of resolutions may show the gradual evolution of the *opinio juris* required for the establishment of a new rule.[47]

Thus while some international organizations have the competence to adopt decisions which are binding on member States and others, most do not possess this power. However, non-binding decisions of international organizations are not without legal effect and the rules contained in those decisions may be binding through a link with other treaties or under customary international law.

C. *ULTRA VIRES* DECISIONS OF INTERNATIONAL ORGANIZATIONS

What is the effect of a decision that is beyond the powers (*ultra vires*) of the organ or the organization? Are these decisions legally effective, despite their illegal foundation, or are such decisions nullities and therefore of no effect at all (void *ab initio*)? A middle position might perhaps be taken whereby such decisions are voidable, meaning that they are effective until they are set aside by a competent body. Whatever view is taken, the question arises how it is to be determined whether a particular decision is *ultra vires* or not. Very few international organizations have, like the EU, a judicial system competent to compulsorily adjudicate on the legality of acts of the organs of the organization. There is, for example, no general procedure by which the ICJ can consider the legality of decisions of the UN or its specialized agencies. However, such questions may be raised in ICJ advisory opinions requested by the organ or organization or may arise incidentally in a contentious case between States (Akande, 1997).

Review by the ICJ of the legality of decisions by the UN occurred in the *Certain Expenses* Advisory Opinion,[48] where the General Assembly requested an opinion from the Court on whether expenditures related to UN peacekeeping missions were expenses of the UN within the meaning of Article 17 of the Charter. If they were, member States had an obligation to contribute to the costs of such missions. In considering that question, the Court felt it necessary to consider whether the peacekeeping operations in question had been lawfully established by the Security Council and the General Assembly.

In the *Namibia* Advisory Opinion,[49] the Court was asked to consider the legal consequences for States of the continued presence of South Africa in Namibia following the

---

[46] Article 31(3)(c) Vienna Convention on the Law of Treaties.

[47] *Legality of the Use by a State of Nuclear Weapons in Armed Conflict, Advisory Opinion, ICJ Reports 1996*, p 66, para 70. See also *Military and Paramilitary Activities in and Against Nicaragua (Nicaragua* v *United States), Merits, Judgment, ICJ Reports 1986*, p 14 at pp 99ff.

[48] *Certain Expenses of the United Nations, Advisory Opinion, ICJ Reports 1962*, p 151 at pp 156–68.

[49] *Legal Consequences for States of the Continued Presence of South Africa in Namibia (South West Africa) notwithstanding Security Council Resolution 276 (1970), Advisory Opinion, ICJ Reports 1971*, p 16, paras 45–53.

termination of South Africa's mandate for the territory by the General Assembly and the decision by the Security Council in Resolution 276 that States had an obligation to refrain from dealing with South Africa in regard to that territory. The Court stated that while there was no established procedure of judicial review within the UN system, the Court was competent and would review the legality of the relevant decisions of the General Assembly and the Security Council. In both cases just referred to, the Court found the relevant decisions to be lawful.

In addition to 'incidental' judicial review by international tribunals of the legality of acts of international organizations, there is the possibility that national and regional courts may also be called upon to decide, indirectly, on the legality of acts of international organizations (see Reinisch, 2010). This may happen when challenges occur in domestic legal systems to national measures implementing the decision of an international organization. There have been several cases where national courts and regional courts like the European Court of Justice or the European Court of Human Rights have been asked to invalidate, or find unlawful, national measures implementing decisions of the UN Security Council to impose sanctions under its powers under Chapter VII of the UN Charter (Tzanakopoulos, 2010). In some cases, the national measure is challenged based on a lack of compliance with domestic law. However, in other cases the challenge is based on the failure of the challenged measure (the sanctions) to comply with international law standards, particularly those established by international human rights law. In these cases, the decision of the court is, in strict terms, about the legality of the domestic implementing act. However, since those acts are based on, and even mirror, decisions of the UN Security Council, the decision, in reality, constitutes a review of the Security Council's decision. The most extreme example of a tribunal engaging in such review is the decision of the Grand Chamber of the European Court of Justice (ECJ) in *Kadi II* that the imposition of targeted sanctions against a person alleged to have links with Al-Qaeda was inconsistent with his fundamental rights as there was insufficient evidence of his involvement with Al-Qaeda.[50] The European Court of Human Rights has stated that since the UN Charter includes the achievement of international cooperation in promoting and encouraging respect for human rights and fundamental freedoms among its purposes, the Court will presume that the Security Council does not intend to violate fundamental principles of human rights when interpreting resolutions of the Council which impose obligations on UN member States.[51] However, in one recent case, the Court has declared the actions of a State, acting in compliance with a decision of the Council to impose sanctions on a terrorist suspect, to be contrary to the provisions of the European Convention of Human Rights.[52] Although not quite a review of the Council's decisions, the Court has shown a willingness to disregard and not apply those aspects of a Security Council decision that do not conform to fundamental rights.

The dearth of established procedures for reviewing the legality, under international law, of decisions of international organizations makes the view that illegal decisions are voidable (Osieke, 1983, p 255) problematic. In effect, it would mean that illegal decisions stand unless, by accident, there is the possibility of review. This is clearly unsatisfactory, and the

---

[50] See *Commission, Council, United Kingdom v Yassin Abdullah Kadi (Kadi II)* Joined cases C-584/10P; C-593/10P; C-595/10P (July 2013) (European Court of Justice).

[51] *Al-Jedda v the United Kingdom* [GC], no 27021/08, ECHR 2011; 53 *EHRR; Nada v Switzerland*, no 10593/08, Judgment of 12 September 2012, ECHR 2012.

[52] *Al-Dulimi and Montana Management Inc. v Switzerland* [GC], no 5809/08, ECHR 2016. See Milanovic, 2016; Peters, 2016.

better view is that *ultra vires* decisions—but not those merely suffering some minor procedural defect—are a nullity.[53] As Judge Morelli said in the *Certain Expenses* case:

> In the case of acts of international organizations . . . there is nothing comparable to the remedies existing in domestic law in connection with administrative acts. The consequence of this is that there is no possibility of applying the concept of voidability to the acts of the United Nations. If an act of an organ of the United Nations had to be considered as an invalid act, such invalidity could constitute only the *absolute nullity* of the act. In other words, there are only two alternatives for the acts of the Organization: either the act is fully valid, or it is an absolute nullity, because absolute nullity is the only form in which invalidity of an act of the Organization can occur.[54]

Thus, where a decision is illegal, a State is free to depart from it.[55] However, there is always the risk that the decision might later be found to be lawful and the non-compliant State in breach of its obligations.

It must be noted that given the limited opportunities for judicial review, the principle that *ultra vires* acts are void *ab initio* might undermine the certainty of decisions of international organizations and permit States to seek to evade their treaty obligations. However, this danger is reduced by the presumption, already referred to, that acts of international organizations directed at the fulfilment of the purposes of the organization are valid, meaning that the burden of proof is on the State arguing otherwise. Additionally, mere procedural defects do not render decisions invalid. The combination of these principles is sufficient to ensure stability.

In addition to the prospect that a decision of an international organization which was adopted beyond the powers of that organization might be void, the organization might be responsible under international law for a breach of its obligations where the illegal decision is in violation of an international obligation owed by the organization (Tzanakopoulos, 2011, Part I).

V. RESPONSIBILITY OF INTERNATIONAL ORGANIZATIONS

International organizations are subjects of international law and therefore have their own obligations under international law. What happens when an international organization breaches these obligations? As was pointed out earlier, one of the consequences of the separate legal personality possessed by international organizations is that these organizations are responsible under international law for breaches of their international obligations.

However, questions relating to the responsibility for internationally wrongful acts become particularly tricky in cases where the act said to be in breach of international law was performed by an organ of a State that is acting, in the general context where the violation occurred, at the behest of an international organization or as part of an operation of that organization. Such questions may arise, for example, in cases where State armed forces act as part of a peacekeeping or peace-enforcement operation that is authorized by an international organization.

---

[53] The constitution of the organization might provide that wrongful decisions become void only following the determination of a competent body. See Osieke, 1983, pp 244–5.

[54] *Certain Expenses of the United Nations Advisory Opinion, ICJ Reports 1962*, p 151 at p 222.

[55] See Separate Opinion of Judge Gros, *Interpretation of the Agreement of 25 March 1951 between the WHO and Egypt, Advisory Opinion, ICJ Reports 1980*, p 73 at p 104.

As a result of the separate legal personality of international organizations, there is a presumption that members of the organization are not liable with respect to the obligations of the organization, although this presumption can be displaced.[56] The principle that members of the organization are not liable for its obligations is illustrated by the *International Tin Council* (ITC) cases. These cases arose out the failure of the ITC—an international organization established to control the price of tin on the world markets—to meet its commercial obligations. The ITC operated a buffer stock of tin and bought tin when prices were low (thus creating a demand) and sold when prices were high. The organization was empowered to borrow money to finance these transactions. As a result of a persistent drop in the price of tin, the organization was no longer in a position to carry out trading and defaulted on a number of contracts with tin brokers and commercial bankers. These parties brought an action in England (and elsewhere) seeking, amongst other things, to hold the members of the ITC liable for its debts. These actions were dismissed at all levels of the English courts on the ground that the personality of the organization precluded holding the members liable. The House of Lords relied primarily on English domestic law[57] while the majority in the Court of Appeal reached the same conclusion on the basis of international law.[58]

In 2011, the ILC adopted a set of Articles on the Responsibility of International Organizations (ARIO)[59] mapping out the field. The ARIO is modelled after the ILC's Articles on State Responsibility (see Crawford and Olleson, Ch 14 of this book). In most areas, the ILC has taken the same approach that it took with regard to State responsibility, even using similar wording in many of the corresponding articles. Article 3 of the ILC's Articles states that '[e]very internationally wrongful act of an international organization entails the international responsibility of the international organization'. As is the case with State responsibility, an international organization commits an internationally wrongfully act when (i) conduct is attributable to that organization under international law and (ii) that conduct constitutes a breach of an international obligation of that international organization (Article 4 ARIO). The ILC has adopted similar rules (when compared with State responsibility) with regard to attribution, breaches of international obligations, circumstances precluding wrongfulness, the content of international responsibility, and the implementation of the international responsibility of international organization.

The work of the ILC on the ARIO was the subject of a number of criticisms.[60] It was argued that since the mandates and functions of international organizations are very different, it is unreasonable to apply a single set of rules to all of them. Secondly, it is argued that the ARIO rely too greatly on the law of State responsibility and do not recognize sufficiently the differences between a State and an international organization. Thirdly, it has been noted that in many areas, there is very little practice with regard to the responsibility of international organizations and it is therefore not clear where rules contained in the ARIO are derived from apart from the analogy with State responsibility. Some of these criticisms go too far and were responded to by the ILC in its commentary to the ARIO

---

[56] See ILC Commentary to Article 62 ARIO, ILC Report, 2011, p 163, paras 2–3.

[57] *JH Rayner v Department of Trade and Industry* [1988] 3 All ER 257; [1989] 3 WLR 969 (HL).

[58] [1988] 3 All ER 257 (CA), particularly Ralph Gibson LJ at 353. Likewise in the *Arab Organization for Industrialisation and others* v *Westland Helicopters Ltd and others* 80 ILR 622, Court of Justice, Geneva (1987); Swiss Federal Supreme Court (1988), the Swiss courts held the member States of the organization were not bound by the obligations undertaken by the organization towards a private entity.

[59] ILC Reports, 2011, ch V.

[60] See, eg, Blokker, 2011; Boon, 2011. See also *Legal Responsibility of International Organizations in International Law*, Meeting Summary, Chatham House, 11 February 2011, available at http://www.chathamhouse.org/publications/papers/view/109605.

(ILC Report 2011, pp 69–71).[61] Although international organizations are very different, the same is true for States (and individuals as well as corporations). It is not at all clear why the differences between international organizations should mean that there are different rules of responsibility for that category. Any justifiable differences can be preserved by making room for *lex specialis* regimes in particular cases (see Article 64 ARIO). In addition, though the ARIO follows the scheme for State responsibility, there are notable differences between States and international organizations that have warranted a different approach in some parts of the regime of responsibility of international organizations or which have required special attention.

One area which has required special attention is the division of responsibility between international organizations and their member States. Often, international organizations act through their members and this raises the question whether the acts of the members (or the organs of the members) when acting within the context of the organization will create responsibility for the State or for the organization. The general rule with regard to attribution of acts to an international organization is that the conduct of organs or agents of the organization are to be regarded as that of the organization when the organ or agent acts in the performance of their functions (Article 6 ARIO). However, there are circumstances when States lend their organs to an international organization, with the result that those organs become organs of the international organization, but they also remain organs of the lending State because they still act, in part, on behalf of the State. The question that arises in such a case is whether the act of the organ is to be attributed to the international organization or to the lending State. This question is of importance in the context of peacekeeping because, although UN peacekeeping forces are subsidiary organs of the UN, the troops are contributed by States and these States retain jurisdiction and some degree of control over their troops. Article 7 of the ARIO provides that:

> The conduct of an organ of a State or an organ of or agent of an international organization that is placed at the disposal of another international organization shall be considered under international law an act of the latter organization if the organization exercises effective control over that conduct.

Therefore, whether the UN is legally responsible for the acts of peacekeeping or peace-enforcement forces will depend on the effectiveness of factual control exercised by the UN over the troops in question and over their conduct (Oppenheim, 2017, ch 13, sec 9.1). The key test is not whether the organization has ultimate authority or control over the forces, as was held by the ECtHR in *Behrami v France* and *Saramati v France, Germany and Norway*,[62] but rather whether the organization has actual operational control of the activity in question. Since UN peacekeepers often continue to act within their national chain of command as well, the troop-contributing State will be responsible in cases where it is that State that has directed the activities of the forces in question. To assert otherwise, as the European Court of Human Rights did, is to suggest that States 'can retain actual control over their forces [assigned to UN action] and at the same time have absolutely no liability for anything that these forces do, since their actions are supposedly attributable solely to the UN' (Milanović and Papić, 2009). This is an untenable position. Happily, in the later *Al-Jedda* case, the ECtHR recognized that the test of attribution set out by the ILC is effective control (though it did not actually overrule its earlier decision in *Behrami*).[63] Also,

---

[61] See Wood, 2013.

[62] *Behrami v France and Saramati v France, Germany and Norway* (Dec) [GC], nos 71412/01 and 78166/01, 2 May 2007; 45 *EHRR* 85.

[63] *Al-Jedda v the United Kingdom* [GC], no 27021/08, ECHR 2011; 53 *EHRR* 23, para 84.

there is no reason to assume that there may not be dual or multiple attribution. Attribution of conduct to an international organization on the basis of effective control does not mean that the act of the organ is not also attributable to the State.[64]

Member States may not escape responsibility for breaches of their own (ie the members') obligations simply by causing the organization to perform an act which, if performed by the member State, would be a breach of the member's obligation (Article 60 ARIO). Thus, the ECtHR has held that States parties to the ECHR cannot free themselves from obligations under that Convention by transferring functions to an international organization. In such cases, 'the State is considered to retain Convention liability in respect of treaty commitments subsequent to the entry into force of the Convention'.[65] This principle is important as it prevents States circumventing their international obligations through the creation of an international organization which is then conferred with competence to act in the area in question.

Where an international organization is responsible for an internationally wrongful act it has an obligation to make reparation for the injury caused by the wrong (Article 30 ARIO). However, the mechanisms by which such responsibility can be established, and through which injured parties can obtain redress against international organizations, remain undeveloped. As will be seen in the following section, such organizations are usually immune from the jurisdiction of domestic courts. Furthermore, international organizations cannot be parties to contentious cases before the International Court of Justice and there are few standing tribunals with competence to decide cases involving international organizations. Therefore the quest to enhance the accountability of these organizations must not only involve an elucidation of the relevant principles of responsibility but also the development of mechanisms through which that responsibility can be determined.

VI. PRIVILEGES AND IMMUNITIES

International organizations require certain privileges and immunities for the effective performance of their tasks. These immunities are granted to preserve the independence of the organization from its member States and to secure the international character of the organization. They ensure that no member State is able to interfere unilaterally through its legislative, executive, or judicial branches with the workings of an international organization set up to act in the common interests of members. This section considers the sources and content of the privileges and immunities of international organizations.

A. SOURCES OF PRIVILEGES AND IMMUNITIES

The privileges and immunities of international organizations may be derived from a number of sources (Oppenheim, 2017, §§16.01–16.18).

1. Treaties

There are three types of treaties which deal with the privileges and immunities of international organizations. First, the constituent instrument of the organization often includes

---

[64] Ibid, para 80; see Dannenbaum, 2010, asserting that effective control is held by entity/entities with power to prevent violations. See now also the decision of the Netherlands Supreme Court in *Netherlands* v *Nuhanović*, 6 September 2013.

[65] *Bosphorus Hava Yollari Turizm ve Ticaret Anonim Sirketi* v *Ireland* [GC], no 45036/98 ECHR, 2005-VI, pp 157–8.

provisions requiring member States to grant the organization immunities. Such provisions are usually very basic and, like Article 105 of the UN Charter, only contain a general statement that the organization, its officials, and representatives of members are to enjoy such privileges and immunities as are necessary for the exercise of their functions.[66]

Second, there are general multilateral agreements dealing with the immunities of particular international organizations or groups of organizations. These types of agreements are regarded as a necessary supplement to the more basic provisions in the constituent instruments. The leading examples include the 1946 General Convention on the Privileges and Immunities of the UN and the 1947 Convention on the Privileges and Immunities of the Specialized Agencies.[67]

The third type of treaties are bilateral agreements between international organizations and individual States which set out specific privileges and immunities. They are most commonly concluded between the organization and a State in which the former (or an organ of the organization) is situated (eg headquarters agreements) or with States in which the organization is to perform a particular mission, such as a peacekeeping or fact-finding activity (eg Status of Forces Agreements). Such States need not be members of the organization.[68]

2. Customary international law

In the absence of a treaty obligation, customary international law requires States to grant privileges and immunities to international organizations.[69] This has been recognized both by the domestic courts of member States of an organization and by those of non-member States which have consented to the organization functioning in their territory.[70] The obligation is one of good faith and only requires the 'provision of what is necessary for an organization to perform its functions' (Higgins, 1994, p 91).

3. National law

Since privileges and immunities are to be enjoyed within the national legal order (see generally Reinisch, 2013), many States have enacted domestic legislation governing their

[66] See also ILO Constitution, Article 40; WHO Constitution, Article 12; Council of Europe Statute, Article 4(a); OAS Charter, Articles 133 and 134. However, the constitutional texts of international financial institutions contain fairly elaborate provisions. See, eg, IBRD Articles of Agreement, Article VII; IMF Articles of Agreement, Article IX; EBRD Constitution, Articles 46–55.

[67] Similar treaties exist within the OAS, Council of Europe, European Communities, League of Arab States, and the OECD.

[68] For a long time Switzerland was not a member of the UN but had an agreement with the UN regarding the UN's office in Geneva.

[69] See Reinisch, 2000, pp 145ff; Higgins, 1994, pp 90–4; *Third Restatement*, 1987, para 467(1); Amerasinghe, 2005, pp 344–8; Möldner, 1995, p 1328. But see Sands and Klein, 2009, para 15–039, who only accept such a customary obligation in some cases. For an extensive study which argues that customary international law does not provide immunity to international organizations (but which also cites several cases to the contrary), see Wood, 2014.

[70] See *X et al v European School Munich II* (Bavarian Administrative Court, Germany, 1995), referred to by Reinisch, 2000, pp 150–1; *Iran-United States Claims Tribunal v AS*, 96 ILR 321, 329 (Netherlands Supreme Court, 1985); *ESOC Official Immunity Case* 73 ILR 683 (Federal Labour Court, FR Germany, 1973); *Branno v Ministry of War*, 22 ILR 756 (Court of Cassation, Italy, 1954); *International Institute of Agriculture v Profili*, 5 ILR 413 (Court of Appeal, Italy, 1930). Courts of States other than the host State have held that they are not obliged to grant immunities to international organizations in the absence of a treaty. See *Bank Bumiputra Malaysia BHD v International Tin Council*, 80 ILR 24 (High Court, Malaysia, 1987); *International Tin Council v Amalgamet*, 80 ILR 31 (New York Supreme Court, 1988); *ECOWAS v BCCI*, 113 ILR 473 (Court of Appeal of Paris, France, 1993). See also *Tissa Amaratunga v Northwest Atlantic Fisheries Organisation*, 30 September 2010, 2010 Can LII 346 (Nova Scotia Supreme Court, Canada).

being granted. The relevant legislation in the UK is the International Organizations Act 1968, which provides that the Executive may by subsidiary legislation (Order in Council) grant the stated privileges and immunities to international organizations of which the UK is a member.

B. SCOPE OF PRIVILEGES AND IMMUNITIES

The particular privileges and immunities which a State is to grant an international organization flow from the source of the obligation, which will most commonly be a treaty. Despite the impressive number of treaties providing for the privileges and immunities, there are remarkable similarities in their content. This has permitted rules of customary international law to develop. However, these similarities relate to general matters and details vary from treaty to treaty.

   Who is entitled to the immunity? Most treaties accord privileges and immunities to three categories of person: first, to the organization itself; secondly, to officials of the organization (including experts on mission for the organization); thirdly, to representatives of member States (or exceptionally of other bodies) of the organization. This chapter considers only the privileges and immunities of the organization itself since the personal immunities of international officials and State representatives are considered by Wickremasinghe in Ch 12 of this book. The five main privileges and immunities conferred on international organizations are considered in the following sections.

1. Immunity from jurisdiction

International organizations are usually granted absolute immunity from the judicial jurisdiction of States.[71] This immunity from jurisdiction prevents law suits against organizations before domestic courts unless they have waived their immunity by consenting to the proceedings. As has been the case with State immunity, there has been pressure to restrict the absolute nature of the immunity granted to international organizations. It has been argued that according such immunity may cause injustice where individuals have no other means of obtaining redress.[72] One particularly notorious case is the Haiti Cholera incident, where the UN was accorded immunity from the jurisdiction of the domestic courts in a case where individuals sought compensation for harm arising from the outbreak of cholera in Haiti in 2010, which had been assessed by experts as having been introduced by UN peacekeepers into that country, and which led to thousands of deaths.[73]

   In order to prevent injustice, a number of domestic courts have applied to international organizations the concept of restrictive immunity, granting them jurisdictional immunity only in relation to acts *jure imperii* (in the exercise of sovereign authority) rather than acts *jure gestionis* (done privately).[74] Alternatively, it has been argued that the grant of immunity should be conditional on the presence of alternative methods of resolving disputes involving international organizations (Gaillard and Pingel-Lenuzza, 2002). The invocation of this obligation is intended to pressure the organization and its member States to

---

[71] For example, Article II, Section 2 of the 1946 Convention on the Privileges and Immunities of the UN.

[72] See the arguments advanced by the applicants in *Waite and Kennedy* v *Germany* [GC], no 26083/94, ECHR 1999-I, and in *Association of Citizens 'Mothers of Srebrenica'* v *Netherlands & United Nations*, Rechtbank 's-Graveenhage [the Hague, District Court], 10 July 2008, 295247/HA ZA 07-2973.

[73] See *Delema Georges et al* v *The United Nations et al*, 834 F 3d Supp 88 (2nd Cir, 2016). In 2016, the UN, despite maintaining its legal position, acknowledged its role in the introduction of cholera and began to provide material assistance to affected communities.

[74] See Reinisch, 2000, pp 185–205 who notes that this trend is most common in Italy.

ensure that the organization provides adequate dispute-settlement obligations. The first approach, which relies on an analogy with State immunity, is based on the misapprehension that since international organizations are composed of States they are to be placed in the same position as foreign States. This approach is incorrect for at least two reasons. First, it is contrary to the express provisions of the relevant treaties. Secondly, international organizations are not sovereign entities and do not exercise sovereign authority. Their immunity is not granted to protect sovereign or public acts but is functional and granted in respect of acts done in the exercise of their functions. Such functions and acts may well be commercial and so classified as private if carried out by a State. Thus immunity may arise for an international organization in cases where a foreign State will be denied immunity. For example, employment disputes fall within the immunity of an international organization even if the relations with the particular employee might be classified as *jure gestionis*.

The second approach, which conditions immunity on the existence of alternative dispute resolution mechanisms, is not in accordance with the treaties providing immunity. Although such treaties may provide an obligation for the organization to make provision for alternative modes of dispute settlement (eg Article 29, UN Convention, discussed later) that obligation is not expressed as limiting the immunity of the organization before domestic courts. The two obligations (that of the organization to find alternative methods of dispute settlement and that of the State to accord immunity) are independent of each other.[75] However, in some cases, the ECtHR has held that where member States create an international organization and accord such organization immunity from domestic legal process without creating alternative methods of dispute settlement, this may amount to a violation, on the part of the members, of their obligation to provide access to a court.[76] In a more recent case, the ECtHR has declared that measures taken by a High Contracting Party which reflect generally recognized rules of international law on the immunity of international organizations cannot, in principle, be regarded as imposing a disproportionate restriction on the right of access to a court, since some restrictions on access to the courts are inherent in the right.[77] It may be that since the facts of that case arose out of the exercise by the UN Security Council of its powers to maintain international peace and security, the Court took the view that this aim was a sufficient counterweight to the denial of access to the Court. Alternatively, it may be thought that in cases where it is sought to hold international organizations responsible, in a domestic court, for acts occurring outside the territory of that State, and those acts are covered by immunity, the domestic forum does not have jurisdiction such as to be able to provide access to court.

It should be noted that some international organizations are not granted absolute immunity by the relevant treaties. In particular, constituent instruments of a number of international financial institutions such as the World Bank (IBRD) do not extend immunity to certain kinds of actions. This is because these organizations operate in the commercial world where it is felt necessary to permit creditors to institute actions in some instances.

2. Immunity from execution

International organizations also enjoy immunity from measures of execution. This prevents the seizure or even the pre-judgment attachment of its property or other assets. It is important to note that a waiver of jurisdictional immunity does not include a waiver of the enforcement jurisdiction which must be given expressly and separately. In some cases,

---

[75] *Association of Citizens 'Mothers of Srebrenica' v Netherlands & United Nations*, Rechtbank 's-Graveenhage, July 10, 2008, 295247/HA ZA 07–2973, para 5.15.

[76] *Waite and Kennedy v Germany* [GC], no 26083/94, ECHR 1999-I.

[77] *Stichting Mothers of Srebrenica and Others v The Netherlands* (Dec), no 65542/12, ECHR 2013.

particularly as regards international financial institutions, the immunity from execution granted by the relevant treaty only applies before the delivery of final judgment.

3. Inviolability of premises, property, and archives

Practically all relevant treaties provide that the premises of an international organization are to be inviolable and that its property and assets are to be immune from search, requisition, confiscation, or other forms of interference by State authorities.[78] Thus, national authorities may not enter such premises without the consent of the international organization, even when a crime has been committed on the premises or a criminal is sheltering there. The treaties also impose an obligation on the national authorities to exercise due diligence in protecting those premises from acts of third parties.

The archives (documents) of an international organization are usually inviolable wherever located.[79] This ensures the confidentiality of communications within and with the international organization, enabling it to function effectively and independently. Consequently, international organizations are not obliged to produce their official documents, or other documents held by them, in proceedings before national courts. In one of the Tin Council cases—*Shearson Lehman Bros* v *Maclaine Watson & Co*[80]—the House of Lords held that documents issued by an international organization, but which had been communicated to third parties by officials of the organization, did not benefit from these principles. This decision has been criticized because the documents were sent by the organization to the States in their capacity as members—not as third parties—and in relation to the work of the organization (Higgins, 1994, pp 93–4). Plainly, the confidentiality of such documents requires protection as otherwise the inviolability of the archives would relate only to documents prepared by the organization's secretariat and kept within it. It would fail to cover all the documents needed by an organization for work, since international organizations are made up of various organs.

4. Currency and fiscal privileges

Since many international organizations exercise their functions in a number of countries, they will need to transfer funds. Several treaties provide that such transactions are to be free from financial restrictions. For example, the UN Convention provides that the organizations (a) 'may hold funds, gold or currency of any kind and operate accounts in any currency' and (b) may freely transfer their 'funds, gold or currency from one country to another or within any country and to convert any currency held by them into any other currency'.[81] International organizations are usually exempt from direct taxation of their assets, income, and property as well as from customs duties and other import and export restrictions in respect of articles for official use.[82] However, this does not extend to charges for public utility services or excise duties or sales taxes.

5. Freedom of communication

It is commonly provided that official communications by international organizations shall be accorded treatment at least as favourable as that accorded to foreign governments.[83] In

---

[78] UN Convention 1946, Article II, Section 3; Specialized Agencies Convention 1947, Article III, Section 5.
[79] UN Convention 1946, Article II, Section 4; Specialized Agencies Convention 1947, Article III, Section 6.
[80] *Shearson Lehman Bros* v *Maclaine Watson & Co*, 77 ILR 107 (1987).
[81] UN Convention, Article II, Section 5; Specialized Agencies Convention, Article III, Section 7.
[82] UN Convention, Article II, Section 7; Specialized Agencies Convention, Article III, Section 9.
[83] UN Convention, Article III, Section 9; Specialized Agencies Convention, Article IV, Section 11; IBRD Articles of Agreement, Article VII(7).

addition it is sometimes provided that no censorship shall be applied to official communications of the organization and that the organization shall have the power to use codes as well as couriers and bags having the same status as diplomatic couriers and bags.[84]

6. Conclusions on privileges and immunities

International organizations should not use their privileges and immunities to circumvent either the domestic laws of States or their responsibility towards third parties. In order to prevent immunity being used to avoid legal responsibility, Article 29 of the UN Convention provides that '[t]he United Nations shall make provisions for appropriate modes of settlement of (a) disputes arising out of contracts or other disputes of a private law character to which the United Nations is a party . . . '. In practice, international organizations will often include arbitration clauses in contracts that they enter into. Furthermore, most organizations have a system for the settlement of employment disputes, which includes recourse to an international administrative tribunal.

Finally, it must be remembered that international organizations remain responsible in international law for breaches of their obligations even if they are immune from process before domestic courts. As the ICJ has stated, 'the question of immunity from legal process is distinct from the issue of compensation for any damages incurred as a result of acts performed by the UN or by its agents acting in their official capacity.'[85]

VII. THE UN SYSTEM

The remainder of this chapter will look at the structure and powers of what is perhaps the leading family of international organizations—the UN system. The UN was established after the Second World War with very broad aims, including: (i) the maintenance of international peace and security; (ii) the development of friendly relations among nations; (iii) international cooperation in solving international problems of an economic, social, cultural, or humanitarian character; and (iv) the promotion of human rights (Article 1 UN Charter). The work of the UN and its specialized agencies touches on practically every area of human life and endeavour.

A. THE STRUCTURE OF THE UN

Like all international organizations, the UN is composed of a number of organs. In addition, the UN system comprises a family of international organizations which share certain common institutions and practices.

1. The UN organs

Article 7 of the UN Charter identifies two types of organs within the UN: principal organs and subsidiary organs. Article 7(1) lists the six principal organs of the UN: (i) the General Assembly; (ii) the Security Council; (iii) the Economic and Social Council (ECOSOC); (iv) the Trusteeship Council; (v) the International Court of Justice; and (vi) the Secretariat. The structure and powers of each of these organs shall be discussed later. Article 7(2) provides that 'such subsidiary organs as may be found necessary may be established in accordance with the present Charter'. While the list of principal organs is exhaustive, and

---

[84] UN Convention, Article III, Sections 9 and 10; Specialized Agencies Convention, Article IV, Section 12.
[85] *Difference Relating to Immunity from Legal Process, Advisory Opinion, ICJ Reports 1999*, p 62, para 66.

no such organs may be established or wound up except by amendment of the Charter, subsidiary organs can always be created by the principal organs. Their lifespan is determined by the principal organ that has established them.

The powers, functions, and composition of the principal organs are determined by the Charter, while those of subsidiary organs are determined by the principal organ that establishes them. Subsidiary organs established by the General Assembly include the Human Rights Council, the International Law Commission, the UN Environment Programme (UNEP), the Office of the UN High Commissioner for Refugees (UNHCR), UNICEF, and the UN Development Programme (UNDP). Subsidiary organs set up by the Security Council include peacekeeping missions, Sanctions Committees, the International Criminal Tribunals for the Former Yugoslavia and Rwanda, and the UN Compensation Commission (UNCC).

In most cases, a principal organ will confer some of its powers on a subsidiary organ that it creates. However, a principal organ may be entitled to confer on the subsidiary organ powers which it does not itself possess where the power to establish such a subsidiary organ is necessary for the performance of the functions of the principal organ (Sarooshi, 1996, pp 426–31; Oppenheim, 2017, §6.18). Thus, both the General Assembly and the Security Council have established subsidiary organs that have judicial powers even though they themselves do not have such powers. The legality of their doing so was confirmed by the ICJ in the *Administrative Tribunal* Advisory Opinion[86] and by the Appeals Chamber of the International Criminal Tribunal for the Former Yugoslavia.[87] Moreover, in the *Administrative Tribunal* case it was held that the General Assembly was bound to give effect to the awards of the Administrative Tribunal thus confirming that a principal organ can establish a subsidiary organ with powers to bind the principal organ.

2. The specialized agencies

The Charter also refers to another type of body known as specialized agencies. Unlike the subsidiary organs, these are international organizations in their own right. They are established by separate treaties and brought into relationship with the UN by agreement (Articles 57 and 63). They operate in particular technical fields and, like the UN, are open organizations with worldwide membership and responsibilities (Oppenheim, 2017, ch 7). There are currently 17 specialized agencies.[88]

Although they are independent international organizations, the UN Charter provides that the UN may coordinate their activities (Articles 57–60), principally through

---

[86] *Effects of Awards of Compensation made by the United Nations Administrative Tribunal*, Advisory Opinion, *ICJ Reports* 1954, p 47.

[87] *Prosecutor v Tadić*, Decision on the Defence Motion for Interlocutory Appeal on Jurisdiction (Interlocutory Appeal), Case No IT–94–1–AR72 (2 October 1995); 105 ILR 419, 470–1.

[88] These are: (1) the International Labour Organization (ILO); (2) the Food and Agriculture Organization (FAO); (3) the UN Educational, Scientific and Cultural Organization (UNESCO); (4) the World Health Organization (WHO); (5) the International Bank for Reconstruction and Development (IBRD or World Bank)—within the World Bank group are three agencies which are also specialized agencies but are run together with the World Bank; (6) the International Development Association (IDA); (7) the International Finance Corporation (IFC); (8) the Multilateral Investment Guarantee Agency (MIGA); (9) the International Monetary Fund (IMF)—the IMF is separate from the World Bank but closely related as another 'Bretton Woods' Institution; (10) the International Civil Aviation Organization (ICAO); (11) the Universal Postal Union (UPU); (12) the International Telecommunications Union (ITU); (13) the World Meteorological Organization (WMO); (14) the International Maritime Organization (IMO); (15) the World Intellectual Property Organization (WIPO); (16) the International Fund for Agricultural Development (IFAD); (17) the UN Industrial Development Organization (UNIDO).

ECOSOC. In practice, coordination and cooperation are achieved through the UN System Chief Executives Board for Coordination (CEB), composed of the executive heads of the organizations within the UN, and its High Level Committees. Development assistance is coordinated by UNDP (Oppenheim, 2017, §§7.43–7.45; 17.56–17.66).

In the *Nuclear Weapons Advisory Opinion (WHO Request)*,[89] the ICJ, relying on what it termed the 'logic of the overall system contemplated by the Charter', appeared to suggest that overlap within the UN system should be avoided. According to the Court, the Charter 'laid the basis of a "system" designed to organize international co-operation in a coherent fashion by bringing the UN, invested with powers of a general scope, into relationship with various autonomous and complementary organizations, invested with sectorial powers'. The Court stated that the WHO 'cannot encroach on the responsibilities of other parts of the UN system'. Thus, since questions of disarmaments and arms regulations are within the competence of the UN itself they were held to be outside the competence of the specialized agencies.

However, the constitutions of the specialized agencies and their practice show that legitimate overlap can and does exist in the work of the specialized agencies. For example, both the WHO and the ILO are competent to deal with health of workers. Likewise IMO, UNEP, and the International Atomic Energy Agency cooperate regarding transportation of nuclear fuel by sea (Akande, 1998).

3. Treaty bodies

A variety of treaties concluded under the auspices of the UN establish bodies which maintain very close relations with the UN and are considered as UN bodies (Oppenheim, 2017, §§6.43–6.45). Examples include the various committees set up by human rights treaties to monitor compliance with the obligations they contain, such as the Human Rights Committee and the Committee Against Torture. These bodies only act in relation to those States which are parties to these treaties. They meet in the UN, are serviced by the UN Secretariat, and submit reports to the General Assembly.

B. PRINCIPAL ORGANS OF THE UN

1. The General Assembly

The General Assembly is the plenary organ of the UN and is the only principal organ composed of all member States (Article 9). It is a deliberative, not legislative body and unlike the Security Council meets annually in regular session, the main part of which usually takes place between September and December (Article 20). It may also meet in special session outside its regular sessions. At its regular sessions, most agenda items are allocated to one of the six main committees (eg Disarmament and International Security; Economic and Social; Financial; Legal), where substantive discussion and decision-taking occurs.

There are also two procedural and two standing committees. The procedural committees, which unlike the main committee are not composed of all UN members, are the General Committee (responsible for organizing the work of the session and for deciding on the agenda) and the Credentials Committee (which examines the credentials of representatives of member States). The standing committees—the Advisory Committee on Administrative and Budgetary Questions and the Committee on Contributions—assist the Fifth Committee with financial matters and are composed of experts rather than representatives of member States.

---

[89] *Legality of the Use of Nuclear Weapons in Armed Conflict, Advisory Opinion, ICJ.*

The Assembly has competence to discuss and make recommendations upon the very broad range of matters falling within the scope of the Charter (Article 10). However, it can only make binding decisions on internal administrative matters. Articles 11–17 of the Charter specifically provide that the General Assembly has competence with regard to peace and security, promoting human rights, and international cooperation in political, economic, social, cultural, educational, and health fields. However, the Assembly may not make recommendations concerning disputes or situations in respect of which the Security Council is exercising its functions unless requested to do so by the Council (Article 12) and, together with the UN as a whole, it may not intervene 'in matters which are essentially within the domestic jurisdiction of any State' (Article 2(7)). Voting in the Assembly is on the basis of one member one vote. Decisions on important questions must be adopted by two-thirds of members present and voting. There is a non-exhaustive list of such important questions. Other decisions are to be taken by simple majority (Article 18).

2. The Security Council

The Security Council is composed of 15 member States of the UN. There are five permanent members of the Council (China, France, Russia, the UK, and the USA) and ten which are elected by the Assembly for two-year terms (Article 23). Its competence is mainly (though not exclusively) limited to issues concerning the maintenance of international peace and security, for which it bears primary responsibility within the UN system (Article 24). Although each member has one vote, decisions on non-procedural matters must be adopted by the affirmative vote of nine members and include the concurring vote of the permanent members, who therefore possess a veto with respect to substantive decisions. Abstentions, however, are not deemed to be vetoes.[90] The powers of the Security Council with regard to the maintenance of peace and security and in regard to dispute settlement are explored by Merrills and Gray in Chs 18 and 20 of this book. It suffices here to note that the Council has the power to adopt decisions which are binding on members of the UN (Article 25).

3. The ECOSOC

ECOSOC is the primary organ responsible for economic and social matters within the UN. It is composed of 54 members who serve for three years; each member has one vote. ECOSOC can make or initiate studies in the area of its competence and make recommendations to the General Assembly, the member States, or the specialized agencies on such matters (Article 62). ECOSOC has special responsibility for the promotion of human rights. It has been active in preparing treaties in the human rights areas (eg the International Covenant on Civil and Political Rights). It also has responsibilities regarding the specialized agencies, concerning their relations with the UN and the coordination of their activities.

ECOSOC has created a number of subsidiary organs: five regional commissions—for Africa, Asia Pacific, Europe, Latin America and the Caribbean, and Western Asia—and nine functional Commissions dealing with particular topics, including the Commission on Sustainable Development and the Commission on the Status of Women. ECOSOC also has a few standing committees (eg the Commission on Human Settlements and the Commission on Transnational Corporations) and a number of standing bodies of experts.

---

[90] *Legal Consequences for States of the Continued Presence of South Africa in Namibia (South West Africa) notwithstanding Security Council Resolution 276 (1970), Advisory Opinion, ICJ Reports 1971*, p 16, paras 20–2.

4. The International Court of Justice

This is the principal judicial organ of the UN and is considered by Thirlway in Ch 19 of this book.

5. The Secretariat

The Secretariat consists of the staff of the UN and is headed by the Secretary-General. It services the work of the UN organs, except the ICJ, and carries out other functions that they assign to it. In addition, the Secretary-General may bring to the attention of the Security Council any matter which he considers may threaten international peace and security (Article 99). Members of the Secretariat are to be independent of governments and may not seek or receive instructions from them (Article 100).

6. Trusteeship Council

The Trusteeship Council was set up to administer the trusteeship system established by Chapter XII of the Charter. This concerned the administration of territories that had been League of Nations mandates (ie territories taken from Germany and Turkey following the First World War) and territories 'detached from enemy States as a result of the Second World War' (Article 77) with the objective of promoting the advancement of the inhabitants and their progressive development towards self-government and independence. The work of the Council was suspended in 1994 when the last of the Trust territories, Palau, achieved independence.

VIII. CONCLUSION

Despite the diversity in the nature and tasks of international organizations, it has proved possible to identify some common legal principles which govern these organizations. However, it cannot be forgotten that the structure, functions, and powers of each organization are primarily to be derived from the treaty setting up the organization and the practice which has built up regarding that organization.

That States have created new international organizations to deal with emerging problems in international affairs is principally the result of three factors. First, there is the realization that a number of problems faced by States and their populations can only be resolved or can best be resolved through international cooperation. Secondly, there is the realization that such cooperation often needs to be multilateral. Thirdly, it is clear that such cooperation needs to be permanent. The heightened awareness by States of these points and the increasing emergence of 'global problems' mean that there is likely to be an increase not only in the number of international organizations but also in the powers and functions accorded to those organizations. However, together with this increasing delegation of public powers by States to international organizations, it is likely that greater attention will be paid to developing means to hold these organizations accountable for the exercise of such powers.[91] This is a process that has already generated much interest and will involve careful analysis of the limits of the powers of international organizations.

---

[91] See generally, Reinisch, 2001; ILA Committee Reports, 1996–2000; and ILC Reports 2009.

REFERENCES

AKANDE, D (1997), 'The International Court of Justice and the Security Council: Is there Room for Judicial Control of Decisions of the Political Organs of the United Nations?', 46 *ICLQ* 309.

AKANDE, D (1998), 'The Competence of International Organizations and the Advisory Jurisdiction of the International Court of Justice', 9 *EJIL* 437.

AMERASINGHE, CF (2005), *Principles of the Institutional Law of International Organizations* (2nd edn, Cambridge: Cambridge University Press).

AUST, A (2013), *Modern Treaty Law and Practice* (3rd edn, Cambridge: Cambridge University Press).

BLOKKER, N (2011), 'Preparing Articles on Responsibility of International Organizations: Does the International Law Commission Take International Organizations Seriously? A Mid-Term Review', in J Klabbers and A Wallendahl (eds), *Research Handbook on the Law of International Organizations* (Cheltenham: Edward Elgar).

BOON, KE (2011), 'New Directions in Responsibility: Assessing the International Law Commission's Draft Articles on the Responsibility of International Organizations', 37 *Yale JIL Online* 8.

CHURCHILL, RR and ULFSTEIN, G (2000), 'Autonomous Institutional Arrangements in Multilateral Environmental Agreements: A Little-Noticed Phenomenon in International Law', 94 *AJIL* 623.

DANNENBAUM, T (2010), 'Translating the Standard of Effective Control into a System of Effective Accountability: How Liability Should be Apportioned for Violation of Human Rights by Member State Troop Contingents Serving as United Nations Peacekeepers', 51 *Harvard JIL* 113.

GAILLARD, E and PINGEL-LENUZZA, I (2002), 'International Organizations and Immunity from Jurisdiction: To Restrict or to Bypass', 51 *ICLQ* 1.

GAZZINI, T (2011), 'Personality of International Organizations', in Klabbers and Wallendahl, *Research Handbook on the Law of International Organizations*.

HIGGINS, R (1994), *Problems and Process: International Law and How We Use It* (Oxford: Oxford University Press).

HIGGINS, R, WEBB, P, AKANDE, D, SIVAKUMARAN, S, and SLOAN, J (2017), *Oppenheim's International Law: United Nations* (Oxford: Oxford University Press).

ILA COMMITTEE REPORT (2004), Final Report of the International Law Association Committee on Accountability of International Organization, *Report of the 71st Conference of the ILA held at Berlin*, p 164 (previous reports of the Committee also available via http://www.ila-hq.org/en/committees/index.cfm/cid/9).

ILA STUDY GROUP REPORT (2012), Report of the International Law Association Study Group on the Responsibility of International Organization, (Sofia Conference) (available via http://www.ila-hq.org/en/committees/study_groups.cfm/cid/1019).

ILC REPORT (2011), *Report of the International Law Commission on the Work of its 63rd Session* (UN Doc A/66/10).

KADELBACH, S (2012), 'The Interpretation of the Charter', in B Simma (ed), *The Charter of the United Nations: A Commentary* (Oxford: Oxford University Press).

KLABBERS, J (2015), *An Introduction to International Organizations Law* (3rd edn, Cambridge: Cambridge University Press).

LAUTERPACHT, H (1976), 'The Development of the Law of International Organizations by the Decisions of International Tribunals', 52 *Recueil des Cours* 377.

MILANOVIĆ, M and PAPIĆ, T (2009), 'As Bad As It Gets: The European Court Of Human Rights' *Behrami and Saramati* Decision and General International Law', 58 *ICLQ* 267.

MILANOVIĆ, M (2016), 'Grand Chamber Judgment in Al-Dulimi v. Switzerland', *EJIL:Talk!* 23 June 2016.

MÖLDNER, M (2012), 'International Organizations or Institutions, Privileges and Immunities', in R Wolfrum (ed), *Max Planck Encyclopedia of Public International Law* (Oxford: Oxford University Press).

PETERS, A (2016), 'The New Arbitrariness and Competing Constitutionalisms: Remarks on ECtHR Grand Chamber Al-Dulimi', *EJIL:Talk!* 30 June 2016.

OSIEKE, E (1983), 'The Legal Validity of Ultra Vires Decisions of International Organizations', 77 *AJIL* 239.

RAMA MONTALDO, M (1970), 'International Legal Personality and Implied Powers of International Organizations', 44 *BYIL* 111.

REINISCH, A (2000), *International Organizations in Domestic Courts* (Cambridge: Cambridge University Press).

REINISCH, A (2001), 'Securing the Accountability of International Organizations', 7 *Global Governance* 131.

REINISCH, A (ed) (2010), *Challenging Acts of International Organizations Before National Courts* (Oxford: Oxford University Press).

REINISCH, A (ed) (2013), *The Privileges and Immunities of International Organizations in Domestic Courts* (Oxford: Oxford University Press).

REINISCH, A and KLEIN, P (eds) (2009), *Bowett's Law of International Institutions* (6th edn, London: Sweet & Maxwell).

SAROOSHI, D (1996), 'The Legal Framework Governing United Nations Subsidiary Organs', 67 *BYIL* 413.

SCHERMERS, HG and BLOKKER, N (2011), *International Institutional Law* (5th rev edn, The Hague: Martinus Nijhoff).

SEYERSTED, F (1964), 'International Personality of Intergovernmental Organizations: Do Their Capacities Really Depend upon Their Constitutions?', 4 *IJIL* 1.

THIRD RESTATEMENT (1987), *Third Restatement of the Law: The Law of Foreign Relations of the United States*, vol 1 (St Pauls, MN: American Law Institute Publishers).

TZANAKOPOULOS, A (2010), 'Domestic Court Reactions to UN Security Council Sanctions' in A Reinisch (ed), *Challenging Acts of International Organizations Before National Courts* (Oxford: Oxford University Press).

TZANAKOPOULOS, A (2011), *Disobeying the Security Council: Countermeasures Against Wrongful Sanctions* (Oxford: Oxford University Press).

WEBB, P (2014), 'Treaties and International Organizations: Uneasy Analogies', in C Tams, T Tzanakopoulos, and A Zimmermann (eds), *Research Handbook on the Law of Treaties* (Cheltenham: Edward Elgar).

WOOD, M (2013), '"Weighing" the Articles on Responsibility of International Organisations', in M Ragazzi (ed), *The Responsibility of International Organisations. Essays in Memory of Sir Ian Brownlie* (The Hague: Martinus Nijhoff).

WOOD, M (2014), 'Do International Organizations Enjoy Immunity under Customary International Law', 10 *International Organizations Law Review*.

FURTHER READING

ALVAREZ, JE (2005), *International Organizations as Law-makers* (Oxford: Oxford University Press): this considers the law-making and dispute-settlement functions of international organizations.

AMERASINGHE, CF (2005), *Principles of the Institutional Law of International Organizations* (2nd edn, Cambridge: Cambridge University Press): provides an excellent overview of the law relating to international organizations.

BEKKER, PHF (1994), *The Legal Position of Intergovernmental Organizations: A Functional Necessity Analysis of Their Legal Status and Immunities* (Dordrecht: Martinus Nijhoff): a good introduction to the legal status, privileges, and immunities of international organizations.

HIGGINS, R, WEBB, P, AKANDE, D, SIVAKUMARAN, S, and SLOAN, J (2017), *Oppenheim's International Law: United Nations* (Oxford: Oxford University Press): a comprehensive treatment of the law of the United Nations, covering both the institutional law and the law relating to the activities of the organization.

KLABBERS, J and WALLENDAHL, A (eds) (2011), *Research Handbook on the Law of International Organizations* (Cheltenham: Edward Elgar): a detailed examination of various issues relating to the law of international organizations.

RAGAZZI, M (ed), (2013), *The Responsibility of International Organizations. Essays in Memory of Sir Ian Brownlie* (The Hague: Martinus Nijhoff).

REINISCH, A (2000), *International Organizations in Domestic Courts* (Cambridge: Cambridge University Press): an excellent consideration of the legal issues which arise when international organizations sue and are sued in domestic courts.

SANDS, P and KLEIN, P (eds) (2009), *Bowett's Law of International Institutions* (6th edn, London: Sweet & Maxwell): this provides an excellent overview of the structure of the leading international organizations as well as of the common legal issues relating to these organizations.

SCHACHTER, O and JOYNER, J (eds) (1995), *United Nations Legal Order*, 2 vols (Cambridge: Cambridge University Press): a detailed examination of the structure of the UN and its specialized agencies, considering the competence of these organizations in a variety of areas.

SCHERMERS, HG and BLOKKER, N (2011), *International Institutional Law* (5th rev edn, The Hague: Martinus Nijhoff): a detailed examination of the law relating to international organizations.

SIMMA, B (ed) (2012), *The Charter of the United Nations: A Commentary* (3rd edn, Oxford: Oxford University Press): an article-by-article analysis of the Charter of the UN.

SLOAN, B (1991), *United Nations General Assembly Resolutions in Our Changing World* (Ardsley, NY: Transnational Publishers): a very good consideration of the status of UN General Assembly resolutions.

WELLENS, K (2002), *Remedies Against International Organizations* (Cambridge: Cambridge University Press): an overview of the law relating to responsibility of international organizations.

WHITE, N (2005), *The Law of International Organizations* (2nd edn, Manchester: Manchester University Press): this provides an excellent overview of the law relating to international organizations.

9

THE INDIVIDUAL AND THE INTERNATIONAL LEGAL SYSTEM

Robert McCorquodale

SUMMARY

This chapter explores the role of the individual in the international legal system today. It considers the extent to which the individual, including groups of individuals, is an independent participant in this system. This participation is explored by reference to the direct rights and responsibilities of individuals under the international legal system, their capacity to bring international claims, and their ability to participate in the creation, development, and enforcement of international law. Particular examples from a wide range of areas of international law, including international human rights law, international criminal law, and international economic law, will be used to show the conceptual and practical participation of individuals in the international legal system. The conclusion reached is that individuals are participants in that system, and are not solely objects that are subject to States' consent, though their degree of participation varies depending on the changing nature of the international legal system.

I. INTRODUCTION

The issue of the role of the individual in international law has been a part of the debate over the nature of the international legal system for centuries. In 1532 Francisco de Vitoria considered that the indigenous peoples of South America had some claim to protection under international law (Anaya, 2004; Paust, 2011) and, in the twenty-first century, the entry into force of the International Criminal Court confirmed the customary international law position of the direct responsibility of individuals under international law for certain actions (see Cryer, Ch 24 of this book), and the actions of individuals were significant in leading to constitutional changes and international actions worldwide.

However, for much of this time the dominant view has been that individuals had no effective independent role in the international legal system. Their role was wholly determined by States and was entirely subject to States' consent (Remec, 1960; Tornaritis, 1972). The developments in international law into the twenty-first century have been the main reason why the issue of the role of individuals in the international legal system has again come to prominence.

A. THE INDIVIDUAL

'The individual' is defined and conceived in a number of different ways in the international legal system. It clearly includes each human being. When human beings (usually known in law as 'natural persons') have any involvement in the international legal system, it is often as part of a group of natural persons acting together. For example, groups of indigenous people and groups who have the right of self-determination are natural persons who act together in regard to some international legal issues. As such, they should be considered to be 'individuals' within the international legal system. Natural persons do form groups due to common interests, such as non-governmental organizations (eg Amnesty International, Oxfam), although these groups are legally separate entities from natural persons. Corporations are also separate entities that are formed to further the common interests of natural persons, and all legal systems recognize the existence and activities of corporations and acknowledge them as non-natural legal persons (Dine, 2000; Muchlinski, 2007). Therefore, the notion of 'individuals' could include all these types of legal person, natural and non-natural.

This chapter takes the concept of 'the individual' within the international legal system to include all those natural and non-natural persons acting separately and as groups.[1] The justification for taking such a view is that the international legal system is primarily a State-based system. The roles of any natural and non-natural persons in this system are compared with that of the State, with a definition based on what they are not—ie non-States—being problematic (Alston, 2005). Consequently, excluded from this concept of 'the individual' are States and also those entities who have authority and power that is State-like, such as intergovernmental organizations (eg the UN), armed opposition groups who control territory (see an example in *Elmi* v *Australia*),[2] or sub-State units in a federal State. In order to clarify as comprehensively as possible the role of the individual in the international legal system, this chapter considers as wide and as diverse a range of 'individuals' acting within that system as possible.

B. INDIVIDUALS IN THE INTERNATIONAL LEGAL SYSTEM

The international legal system is traditionally constructed as a State-based system with State sovereignty being supreme. The dominant positivist theories of international law confirm that construction, as their view is that '[s]ince the Law of Nations is a law between States only and exclusively, States only and exclusively are subjects of the Law of Nations' (Oppenheim, 1905, p 341). A 'subject' of the international legal system has direct rights and responsibilities under that system, can bring international claims, and, it is argued, is able to participate in the creation, development, and enforcement of international law. Historically, under this dominant view, any role of the individual in the international legal system is purely as an 'object' of that system and not as a 'subject'.[3] In their view, individuals

---

[1] This definition is similar to that adopted under the European Convention on Human Rights, see Committee of Ministers, 2001.

[2] *Elmi* v *Australia*, UN Committee Against Torture, No 120/1998, 7 *IHRR* 603.

[3] It was argued by the Chinese delegate (Mr Hsu) to the UN General Assembly's Sixth Committee in October 1954 that '[a]n individual who had no State to protect him was entitled to a direct international remedy. Moreover, while international delinquents, such as pirates or offenders against the peace and security of mankind, had been accepted as subjects of international law, it would be strange if stateless persons in need of protection would be regarded as outside its scope' (my thanks to Professor Sir Eli Lauterpacht for this material).

are objects, either in the same sense as territory or rivers are objects of the system because there are (State-created) legal rules about them, or in the sense that they are beneficiaries under the system, so that treaties on, for example, diplomatic persons or commerce indirectly benefit individuals.

This traditional approach is now largely discredited. The reality is that there are many actors in the international legal system in addition to States and these actors have some international legal personality. The International Court of Justice (ICJ) clarified the issues of international personality, and what is a 'subject' of the international legal system, in its *Reparations for Injuries* Opinion:

> The subjects of law in any legal system are not necessarily identical in their nature or in the extent of their rights, and their nature depends on the needs of the community. Throughout its history, the development of international law has been influenced by the requirements of international life, and the progressive increase in the collective activities of States has already given rise to instances of action upon the international plane by certain entities which are not States ... In the opinion of the Court, the [United Nations] Organisation was intended to exercise and enjoy, and is in fact exercising and enjoying, functions and rights which can only be explained on the basis of the possession of a large measure of international personality and the capacity to operate upon an international plane ... That is not the same thing as saying that it is a State, which it certainly is not, or that its legal personality and rights and duties are the same as those of a State ... It does not even imply that all its rights and duties must be upon the international plane, any more than all the rights and duties of a State must be upon that plane. What it does mean is that it is a subject of international law and capable of possessing international rights and duties, and that it has capacity to maintain its rights by bringing international claims.[4]

This is an important statement of international legal principles. It directly links being a subject of international law with international legal personality. It clarifies that there can be subjects of the international legal system that are not States. These subjects do not all possess the same rights and duties, and not all of these rights and duties need to be on the international plane alone. It also explains how the international legal system has developed, and continues to develop, in ways that allow non-States to have international legal personality and so to act independently in the international legal system (Nijman, 2004; Peters, 2016). In this Opinion the ICJ applied these principles to the position of the UN itself to decide that it did have international legal personality. A later ICJ opinion[5] applied these principles to other international (intergovernmental) organizations.

The ICJ Opinion on Reparations clearly sets out broad principles that could be applied to any non-State actor (and thus applies to the individuals considered in this chapter) on the international plane. It recognizes that, while the State is the primary subject of the international legal system, the subjects of that system can change and expand depending on the 'needs of the [international] community' and 'the requirements of international life'. It does not say whether these 'needs' and 'requirements' are solely determined by States (as the dominant theories of international law would suggest) or by other means. After all, the term 'the international community' in the Opinion is

---

[4] *Reparation for Injuries Suffered in the Service of the United Nations, Advisory Opinion, ICJ Reports 1949,* p 174 at pp 178–9.

[5] *Legality of the Use of Nuclear Weapons in Armed Conflict, Advisory Opinion, ICJ Reports 1996,* p 66.

expressly not limited to an international community of States alone (in comparison to the Vienna Convention on the Law of Treaties, Article 53) and so should include States and non-States. It certainly indicates that there can be subjects of the international legal system that are not States.

Some writers have argued that, rather than the State being the primary 'subject' of the international legal system, the primary 'subject' is the individual (Scelle, 1932). They argue, for example, that individuals are the real actors beneath the State, as the State itself does not exist without individuals. A variation on this idea is that of Hersch Lauterpacht, one of the most influential British international lawyers of last century, who argued that individuals could become subjects of the international legal system. He considered that the claim of the State to unqualified exclusiveness in the field of international relations was not tenable, especially as:

> Fundamental human rights are rights superior to the law of the sovereign State … [and must lead to the] consequent recognition of the individual human being as a subject of international law. (Lauterpacht, 1950, p 72)

A middle path has been suggested in which individuals are objects when acquiring international rights and subjects when exercising them (Parlett, 2011), though Anne Peters takes a different approach:

> The individual has become a primary subject (person) of international law. Individuals not only have numerous 'subjective' international rights (in the plural) but are also further entitled to international legal subjectivity (international legal personality) in virtue of their personhood on the basis of customary international law and general principles of law and as an aspect of their human right to legal personality. Put differently, the international legal personality of human beings is rooted in Art. 16 ICCPR and already forms a general principle of law. (Peters, 2016, p 8)

Philip Allott adopts a broader view in which he sees international society as not being composed of States but as arising from the 'self-creating' of all human beings (Allott, 1992). So these writers would argue that the nature of the international legal system and the 'needs' of the international community have meant that individuals are subjects—the primary or only subjects—of the international legal system.

Of course, individuals are necessary for an entity to be recognized as a State, in the sense that an entity must have 'a population' to be a State (see Craven and Parfitt, Ch 7 of this book). In any event, the State is a legal fiction and so it cannot act by itself. Instead individuals and groups act on behalf of the State and in the State's name.[6] Thus individuals are at the very core of the international legal system, no matter how that system is defined. Yet this does not necessarily make them 'subjects' or 'objects' of this system.

The 'subject' v 'object' dichotomy has been criticized by a number of writers, not least because it privileges certain voices and silences others (eg Koskenniemi, 1989; Charlesworth and Chinkin, 2000; Anghie, 2005).

Rosalyn Higgins offers an alternative approach, arguing that: the whole notion of 'subjects' and 'objects' has no credible reality, and, in my view, no functional purpose. We have erected an intellectual prison of our own choosing and then declared it to be an unalterable constraint. (Higgins, 1994, p 49; see also Higgins, 1979)

---

[6] Though the individual, in his/her private capacity, remains distinct from the actions he/she takes on behalf of the State (Geuss, 2007).

Rather, she prefers the idea of the 'participant' in the international legal decision-making process. She explains this by use of an example:

> The topics of minimum standard of treatment of aliens, requirements as to the conduct of hostilities and human rights, are not simply exceptions conceded by historical chance within a system that operates as between States. Rather, they are simply part and parcel of the fabric of international law, representing the claims that are naturally made by individual participants in contradistinction to state-participants. (Higgins, 1994, p 50)

Under this view, there are many participants in the international legal system, in the sense that there are many different entities, from States and international organizations to transnational corporations and natural persons, who engage in international activity (or 'upon an international plane', to use the ICJ's words set out earlier in this section in the *Reparations for Injuries* Opinion). Participation may be extensive and over a wide range of international matters or it can be limited to a few issues. Participation will depend on the particular area of the international legal system concerned and the activity and involvement of entities in that area, rather than on the determination by States (and only States) as to whether any non-States are 'subjects' for a specific purpose. As the international community changes and the 'needs' or areas governed by international law develop, then so will participation in the international legal system.

This argument for considering individuals as 'participants' in the international legal system, rather than as 'objects' or 'subjects', is a compelling and practical one. Indeed, the notion of participation as a valuable framework to explore involvement in the international legal system (and thus as a means to determine if individuals have a voice in the system) has been applied effectively by Karen Knop from a different conceptual standpoint to that of Higgins (Knop, 2002). At the same time, this framework is still consistent with the dominant State-based concept of the international legal system, as participation in the system could be viewed as largely dependent on State consent and falls within the broad legal principles expressed by the ICJ in its *Reparations for Injuries* Opinion. Therefore, participation as a framework for considering the role of individuals in the international legal system is flexible and open enough to deal with developments in that system over the centuries, and is not constricted to a State-based concept of that system or to appearances before international bodies. Accordingly, if it can be shown that individuals are exercising and enjoying 'in fact' (to use the ICJ's words) certain rights, privileges, powers, or immunities in the international legal system then they can be presumed to be acting as international legal persons (Meron, 2006; Boyle and Chinkin, 2007) and are sources of international law (McCorquodale, 2017).

Of course, these individuals do not all share the same aims or values across the international community. They can reflect the hierarchies and political agendas within States, and can be captive to States and to power. Yet the decision to participate on the international plane is made by the particular individual and is not dictated by States' views, though it may be prompted by State action (eg to seek investment in a national industry) or State inaction (eg to fill the need for a secretariat of a treaty body). The degree of participation by an individual will vary, often depending on its own resources, its functions, and the attitude of other participants, including States (Puvimanasinghe, 2007).

It is the extent of that participation in the international legal system by individuals, and the State's role in determining the degree of participation, that will be considered in this chapter. This will be examined by reference to the direct rights and responsibilities of individuals under the international legal system, their capacity to bring international claims, and their ability to participate in the creation, development, and enforcement of international law as independent participants.

II. INTERNATIONAL RIGHTS AND RESPONSIBILITIES

A. INDIVIDUAL RIGHTS

The Permanent Court of International Justice (PCIJ) had to consider in *Jurisdiction of the Courts of Danzig* whether it was possible for individuals to have rights under international law. It held:

> [I]t cannot be disputed that the very object of an international agreement, according to the intention of the contracting parties, may be the adoption by the parties of some definite rules creating individual rights and obligations and enforceable by the national courts.[7]

While this Opinion confirmed that individuals can have rights in the international legal system, these rights will not all be of the same nature. As Wesley Hohfeld (1913) demonstrated, a 'right' can mean a claim-right, a privilege, a power, or an immunity (or a number of these at once). In some instances, the right of the individual within the international legal system is of the nature of the ability to bring a claim (a claim-right) against the State (see further later in this chapter). However, many of the rights of individuals in the international legal system are more in the nature of an immunity from action against them, such as those that arise due to their status as prisoners of war (see Turns, Ch 27 of this book), or a privilege, such as the liberty to travel on the high seas without interference (see Evans, Ch 21 of this book). In the same way, States have a variety of rights within the international legal system, not all of which enable claims to be brought. The rights of individuals and the rights of States in the international legal system are not identical but, while they may overlap or interact (such as under international humanitarian law in relation to use of force on a territory affecting combatants and non-combatants—see Turns, Ch 27 of this book), they are distinct rights.

The area where individual rights are most developed is in relation to human rights, which include both rights of individuals and of groups, and which are now a matter of international law. At one time governments dealt with those within their jurisdiction as they wished and resisted all criticisms of their actions by claiming that human rights were matters of 'domestic jurisdiction' (under Article 2(7) UN Charter) and the responsibility of each State alone. However, human rights are now an established part of the international legal system with an institutional structure, including supervisory mechanisms to check compliance with legal obligations, and with a defined content of human rights (see Rodley, Ch 25 of this book). Every State has ratified at least one treaty containing legal obligations to protect human rights and all States have acknowledged that 'the promotion and protection of all human rights is a legitimate concern of the international community'.[8]

This acknowledgement that human rights are a legitimate concern of the international community has a direct effect on State sovereignty, in that one aspect of each State's control and authority over its activities on its territory and within its jurisdiction is now subject to international legal review. This applies when a State has expressly agreed to this review by ratifying a treaty protecting human rights. It also applies when the protection of a human right has become a matter of customary international law or *jus cogens*, which can happen without a State having any express practice on the issue. Some human rights create legal obligations on States that the State cannot evade by contrary practice. For example, the ICJ took the view that South Africa was bound by international obligations in relation to racial

---

[7] *Jurisdiction of the Courts of Danzig, Advisory Opinion, 1928, PCIJ, Ser B, No 15*, pp 17–18.
[8] Vienna Declaration (1993) 32 ILM 1661, para 4.

discrimination despite its clear contrary practice[9] and also that all States must comply with the right of self-determination.[10]

Thus States have, by treaty and other practice, placed human rights for individuals (including groups of individuals) within the international legal system. There are problems with the way international human rights law has been created, such as the conception that rights are only held in relation to a centralized State (Otto, 1997) and the general exclusion of individuals from direct responsibility for human rights violations (see later). Nevertheless, international human rights law is significant in terms of demonstrating that individuals have rights within the international legal system.

Individuals also have rights in the international legal system outside the specific context of international human rights law. For example, within international humanitarian law, individuals have certain rights depending on their status as, for example, prisoners of war or non-combatants (see Turns, Ch 27 of this book).[11] Many of these individual rights are now considered to be customary international law or even *jus cogens*. Yet the rights of individuals within the international legal system were all initially determined and placed within that system by States. States decided and agreed that these rights were rights within that system and not solely rights within a national legal system. Martti Koskenniemi concludes from this that the creation of these rights of individuals by States, particularly within international human rights law, affirms the position of States as the sole rights-holder in the international legal system:

> By establishing and consenting to human rights limitations on their own sovereignty, states actually define, delimit, and contain those rights, thereby domesticating their use and affirming the authority of the state as the source from which such rights spring. (Koskenniemi, 1991, p 406)

Contrary to this view, each State, as demonstrated earlier, no longer has complete control over the continuance, development, and interpretation of individuals' rights, and the rights of individuals are distinct from the rights of States. Thus a number of the rights of individuals in the international system are now, to some extent, separate from the specific control and direction of States, at least as they are protected by customary international law (or by *jus cogens*), and are independent rights within the international legal system. It can be concluded, therefore, that, although originally based on the agreement of States, individuals now have some distinct rights in the international legal system, ranging from a person's right to freedom from torture to the protection of a group of individuals under the right of self-determination.

B. INDIVIDUAL RESPONSIBILITY

Responsibility in the international legal system is generally considered to mean a legal obligation that, if breached, can give rise to international consequences (see Crawford and Olleson, Ch 14 of this book). Even though individuals have been a part of international activity for centuries, from trading to colonizing, generally the actions of individuals did

---

[9] *Legal Consequences for States of the Continued Presence of South Africa in Namibia (South West Africa) notwithstanding Security Council Resolution 276 (1970), Advisory Opinion, ICJ Reports 1971*, p 16, paras 21–2.

[10] *East Timor Case (Portugal v Australia), Judgment, ICJ Reports 1995*, p 90, *Legal Consequences of the Construction of a Wall in the Occupied Palestine Territory, Advisory Opinion, ICJ Reports 2004*, p 136, paras 118 and 122.

[11] Cf *Bridge of Varvarin Case*, German Federal Constitutional Court, 13 August 2013, BvR 2660/06.

not give rise to any international responsibility on them; it only arose when those actions were attributed to the State and then the State was internationally responsible.[12]

The development of individual responsibility for certain crimes under both international criminal law and international humanitarian law illustrates the lineage of individual responsibility in the international legal system, with a full discussion of these areas found elsewhere in this book. Both piracy and slavery were widely seen as offences against the whole international community, for which individuals were directly responsible (Ratner and Abrams, 2009; Martinez, 2012). The justification for this was that 'the pirate and the slave trader … [are each] *hostis humani generis*, an enemy of all mankind'.[13] Individuals, even when acting as part of the organs of the State and under orders from the State, are independently responsible within the international legal system for certain actions. This was neatly summarized by the Nuremberg International Military Tribunal:

> Crimes against international law are committed by men, not by abstract entities [of States], and only by punishing individuals who commit such crimes can the provisions of international law be enforced.[14]

This individual responsibility, which is based on both customary international law and treaties, is now enforced (where there is jurisdiction) through international criminal courts and tribunals (see Cryer, Ch 24 of this book). Prior to this, the individual responsibility still existed, and was occasionally enforced in national courts,[15] even though no international judicial body enforced it. In the same way, State responsibility exists even where no other State takes action to enforce it (such as seen in the lack of any legal action after the Chernobyl nuclear power plant explosion in 1986). Thus, even though it was necessary for States to agree to the decisions or treaties that created these recent international criminal tribunals and courts, the individual responsibility under international law still existed independently of these agreements.[16] The responsibility arose through customary international law and no one State now has the ability to limit this responsibility, at least with regard to acts such as piracy and genocide. Roger O'Keefe clarifies this:

> If individual criminal responsibility under international law for the violation of certain rules of customary law is conceptually possible, individual criminal responsibility under international law for the violation of specific treaty provisions should also be possible, and indeed is so. (O'Keefe, 2015, para 2.68)

However, the victims of actions that are contrary to international criminal law are not yet able to bring actions directly against the perpetrator to the international criminal courts and tribunals (where there is jurisdiction), as they must rely on States or on independent prosecutors to do so. However, victims of violations of international criminal law could seek reparations in some courts and tribunals, such as under Article 75 of the Statute of the International Criminal Court (Schabas, 2011; Henckaerts, 2007).

There have also been significant developments in international law in relation to the responsibilities of corporations for breaches of international law. The adoption by the UN Human Rights Council of the Guiding Principles on Business and Human Rights

---

[12] See *United States Diplomatic and Consular Staff in Tehran, Judgment, ICJ Reports 1980*, p 3.

[13] *Filartiga* v *Peña-Irala*, 630 F.2d 876 (US 2nd Cir 1980).

[14] *Nuremberg Judgment* (1948) 22 Trial of the Major War Criminals before the International Military Tribunal 466.   [15] Eg *Attorney-General of the Government of Israel* v *Eichmann* (1961) 36 ILR 5.

[16] Article 58 of the International Law Commission's Articles on State Responsibility, 2001, provides that '[t]hese Articles are without prejudice to any question of the individual responsibility under international law of any person acting on behalf of a State'. See Clapham, 2010.

(UN Guiding Principles, 2011) makes clear that corporations have responsibilities for the harm that they do and must mitigate adverse human rights impacts. This is conceived by the Guiding Principles as being generally a voluntary responsibility and not a legally enforceable one (unless States create national laws to enforce it). However, it is possible that the breadth of the concept of 'human rights due diligence' used in the Guiding Principles, together with actions by States and claims being brought by victims in this area, will lead to increased remedies for individuals affected by a corporation's actions (Mares, 2012; Lindsay et al, 2013). These developments are just part of the broader understanding that corporations are significant participants in international law-making (Alvarez, 2011).

There are limits to the responsibility of individuals under international law. For example, international human rights law is still crafted in terms of the responsibilities of States, and actions by individuals that affect other individuals (such as actions by corporations) are not dealt with by international human rights law unless they can be attributed to the State (Joseph, 2010). Yet corporations have been held to be capable of international responsibility for human rights violations[17] or as having a shared responsibility with States for such actions (Hemphill and White, 2016).

Yet a possibility of extending the responsibility of individuals under international law is seen in Security Council Resolution 1373 (2001), passed after the international terrorist actions in the USA in September 2001, where the Security Council declared that:

> [A]cts, methods, and practices of terrorism are contrary to the purposes and principles of the United Nations and that knowingly financing, planning and inciting terrorist acts are also contrary to the purposes and principles of the United Nations.

As this paragraph (also repeated in later resolutions) does not refer to crimes against humanity or other acknowledged areas of individual responsibility under international law, it must be asserting that terrorist actions per se give rise to individual responsibility. There is no requirement in the Resolution to link those activities to a State for there to be international responsibility. While Security Council resolutions are not automatically international law, they can indicate the direction that international law may be headed. It appears, therefore, that certain actions by individuals (being terrorist actions) could be in breach of international law and so give rise to international responsibility by those individuals.

The importance of establishing responsibility of individuals for international crimes is that it demonstrates that there are some actions by individuals that lead to direct international responsibility on an individual. The individual is responsible without any need to link the individual with the State. This draws a clear distinction between the individual and the State in terms of international responsibility.

III. INTERNATIONAL CLAIMS

A. BRINGING INTERNATIONAL CLAIMS

The conceptual understanding that individuals have rights and responsibilities in the international legal system does not automatically mean that they have the ability to bring international claims to assert their rights or are able to claim an immunity to prevent their responsibilities being enforced (on immunities, see Webb, Ch 11 and Wickremasinghe, Ch

---

[17] *Kaliña and Lokono Peoples* v *Suriname, Merits, Reparations and Costs, Judgment of 25 November 2015, Ser C, No 309*, para 224.

12 of this book). Thus the PCIJ declared that 'it is scarcely necessary to point out that the capacity to possess civil rights does not necessarily imply the capacity to exercise those rights oneself'.[18] Instead, the conclusion reached by most writers is that 'individuals are extremely handicapped in international law from the procedural point of view' (Higgins, 1994, p 51). Many of the international institutions that determine claims, such as the ICJ, are barred to individuals, even though a significant number of their cases arise from actions by, or against, individuals. This was seen most starkly in the *East Timor* case,[19] where the claims of the East Timorese themselves could not be brought to, or directly considered by, the ICJ.

Traditionally, the only means available for individuals to bring a claim within the international legal system has been when the individual is able to persuade a government to bring a claim on the individual's behalf and that it was not the individual's international rights that are being asserted but the State's own rights.[20] However, the ICJ has clarified that there are individual rights that may be invoked in the Court.[21]

The justification that a State has to assert this type of claim is through the linkage of nationality.[22] The international legal system has developed intricate rules regarding the nationality of people in terms of their relationship to States, as determined by the degree of connection individuals have to the territory of a State (see Staker, Ch 10 of this book). Even then, this nationality connection may be insufficient if there are other international rules that override it or if the State chooses not to take action. Indeed, the ICJ has stated that:

> [t]he State must be viewed as the sole judge to decide whether its protection will be granted, to what extent it is granted, and when it will cease … Should the natural or legal persons on whose behalf it is acting consider that their rights are not adequately protected, they have no remedy in international law.[23]

This position was challenged in the UK in a case arising from the internationally unlawful detention by the USA of prisoners in Guantánamo Bay from the time of the Afghanistan conflict in 2001. In *Abbasi v Secretary of State for Foreign and Commonwealth Affairs*[24] the applicant (a British national) sought judicial review of the adequacy of the diplomatic actions of the British government with the US government concerning his detention in Guantanamo Bay. The UK Court of Appeal found that there was a legitimate expectation (though a limited one) by nationals that their government would make representations to another government to assist them and the courts could thus consider the diplomatic activity of the UK government. In this instance, the Court found that the UK government's actions were sufficient, yet it also expressed its very deep concern about the violation of international law that was occurring in Guantánamo Bay.

---

[18] *Appeal from a Judgment of the Hungaro/Czechoslovak Mixed Arbitral Tribunal, Judgment, 1933, PCIJ, Ser A/B, No 61*, p 208 at p 231.

[19] *East Timor Case (Portugal v Australia), Judgment, ICJ Reports 1995*, p 90.

[20] *Panevezys-Saldutiskis Railway, Judgment, PCIJ, Ser A/B, No 76*, p 4.

[21] Cf *LaGrand (Germany v United States of America), Merits, Judgment, ICJ Reports 2001*, p 466, para 42. See also *Jadhav Case (India v Pakistan), Provisional Measures, Order of 18 May 2017, ICJ Reports 2017*, nyr, para 48: 'The Court considers that these [provisional] measures [ordered] are aimed at preserving the rights of India and of Mr Jadhav under Article 36, paragraph 1 of the Vienna Convention.'

[22] There are some instances where a State might be able to bring a claim on behalf of the international community (of States and non-States): see International Law Commission (2001), Article 48.

[23] *Barcelona Traction, Light and Power Company, Limited, Second Phase, Judgment, ICJ Reports 1970*, p 3, paras 78–9.

[24] *Abbasi v Secretary of State for Foreign and Commonwealth Affairs* [2002] EWCA Civ 1316, 19 September 2002; (2003) 42 ILM 358.

This position, by which the individual could not assert claims directly to international bodies, began to change during the twentieth century. A series of international bodies were established in the early part of that century as a means to settle conflicts between States and included in their powers was the ability to consider claims by individuals. These bodies included the Central American Court of Justice, the Mixed Arbitral Tribunals in Europe, the minority protections offered by the League of Nations, and the dispute mechanisms of the International Labour Organization (Butler, 2007; Parlett, 2011). In the second half of that century, the vast growth of international human rights supervisory bodies and international commercial arbitral bodies has taken the issue of individuals bringing international claims to a higher level.[25] Indeed, the fact that a dispute over territory between a State and an armed non-State actor could be determined by an international arbitration, as happened between the government of Sudan and the Southern Sudan People's Liberation Movement at the Permanent Court of Arbitration in 2009,[26] is an example of this significant development.

Rather than set out the detailed provisions of the large number of treaties or other documents that enable individuals to bring claims in an international context, the rest of this section will summarize the main aspects of the key areas of international law in which individuals can bring claims: international human rights law and international economic law. However, it should be noted that individuals can also bring international claims in other areas, for example, employees of some international organizations may bring claims against that organization to an international body (Hunt, 2010). The ability to bring these claims is also a method by which individuals can create international law.

B. INTERNATIONAL HUMAN RIGHTS LAW

Within international human rights law, a number of treaties permit individuals to bring claims against a State, alleging violations of their human rights, before both international and regional bodies. This is an extraordinary development in the international legal system away from a position in which a State's actions on its own territory were not subject to international review. Claims can be brought by individuals against the State of which they are a national and against a State in whose jurisdiction they happen to be, even if temporarily, irrespective of whether they are a national of that State.[27] In most instances, the individual is a direct party to the proceedings before the international body (with most proceedings being conducted by written submissions). Decisions can be made, or 'views' given, by international bodies in which States are found to be in violation of their human rights obligations and remedies are indicated. These remedies range from monetary compensation to ordering the State to conduct investigations into the violations (Shelton, 2015).

Despite all of this, the State is still an intermediary, or directly involved, in these international claims by individuals. Such claims cannot be brought unless the relevant State has ratified the relevant treaty (whether a human rights treaty or a treaty establishing an international organization which facilitates claims by individuals), or the State has accepted the relevant Article of the treaty that allows individuals to bring the claim. In addition, no international claim can be brought by an individual unless he or she has exhausted

---

[25] See the International Law Commission Reports on Diplomatic Protection and its changes over time: UN Doc A/CN.4/484 (1998) and UN Doc A/CN.4/506 (2000).

[26] *Abyei Arbitration (The Government of Sudan v Sudan Peoples' Liberation Movement/Army)* Permanent Court of Arbitration, Final Award, 22 July 2009, 48 ILM 1258.

[27] Eg *Soering v United Kingdom, Judgment of 7 July 1989, Ser A, No 161, 11 EHRR* 439.

domestic remedies in the relevant State. The reason for the latter is to enable States to resolve the issues at national level first, with the international bodies only being involved after all proceedings or other action at the State level have been effectively exhausted. Thus it might initially appear as if there is no independent ability for individuals to bring claims before international human rights bodies.

However, there are some aspects to these individual claims that show, in practice, some independent ability for individuals to bring international claims in this area. First, under the European Convention on Human Rights (ECHR) and the American Convention on Human Rights (ACHR) individuals can appear and bring their claims direct to the relevant Court. In addition, ratification of the ECHR is effectively required before a State can be a member of the EU (Douglas-Scott, 2011). Thus, in practice, European States are no longer able to prevent individual claims under that regional human rights system, which means that there are now about 800 million individuals who have the right to bring international claims under that treaty. Further, even if a State is not party to a particular human rights treaty, some international bodies, such as the Inter-American Commission on Human Rights and the UN Human Rights Council, can still, on the basis of individuals' claims revealing a consistent pattern of gross and reliably attested violations of human rights, make public conclusions about that State's human rights record.

Second, the link between nationality and the ability to bring claims is no longer essential. The relevant link is now jurisdiction. If a State has jurisdiction over an individual, which can include where that individual is not a national of that State and even where that State's jurisdiction over the individual is unlawful,[28] then an individual can bring a claim against that State if that State has ratified a relevant human rights treaty. The State of which that individual is a national does not have to be a party to the treaty and the individual could be a stateless person. This has meant that, in practice, States are now subject to a wider number of claims by individuals before international bodies. This represents 'a momentous advance in the world community' (Cassese, 1986, p 102).

Third, these treaties give individuals the procedural capacity to bring international claims. While this is a restricted capacity as it is dependent on State consent (as seen earlier), it does have significant practical effects. States rarely ignore the individual's claim to an international body. Rather, they often respond to the claim at some length (though the practice is by no means universal), especially as, if they do not respond, the international body will still consider the matter, as there is some onus on the State to prove that there has been no violation.[29] When an international human rights body reaches a conclusion in relation to an individual's claim then States usually treat this conclusion as a serious matter that requires some response. If the conclusion is that there is no violation of a human right then the State will ensure that the media is aware of this. If the conclusion is that there has been a violation, then the State will respond in some way, from amending the relevant law or practice to making a derogation from the relevant provision (should this be possible) or offering a justification for their actions. Sometimes a State will even seek to denounce the treaty and criticize the international body: Peru, for example, withdrew its acceptance of the jurisdiction of the Inter-American Court of Human Rights before later re-accepting it after a change of national government. Very rarely will the State not respond at all. So these individual claims are treated seriously by States, in the same way as a claim brought against a State by another State before an international body is treated seriously.

Finally, the conclusions reached by international human rights bodies about individual claims can have practical effects on a State through the adoption of those conclusions by

---

[28] *Loizidou* v *Turkey (Preliminary Objections)*, Judgment of 23 March 1995, Ser A, No 310, 20 *EHRR* 99.

[29] *Bleier* v *Uruguay*, decision of 29 March 1982 1 *Selected Decisions of the Human Rights Committee* 109.

national courts and by other international bodies whose decisions are legally binding on a State. The latter is seen in the approach taken by the Court of Justice of the European Union, which decided that 'respect for fundamental [human] rights forms an integral part of the general principles of [European] Community law protected by the Court of Justice'.[30] It has applied this principle, for example, to restrict decisions by the UN Security Council on terrorism matters that did not take account of human rights.[31] Thus the practical effects of individuals being able to bring claims before international human rights bodies are such as to place effective limits upon a State's ability to control or restrict those claims. The State's role as an intermediary, or barrier, between the individual and an international human rights body, while still crucial for an individual to be able to bring a claim, is, in practice, permeable.

C. INTERNATIONAL ECONOMIC LAW

One of the areas of significant growth in the international legal system since the latter part of the twentieth century has been international economic law. Part of this growth has included the creation and development of mechanisms by which individuals, usually corporations, can bring claims against States. These mechanisms were initially ad hoc arbitration bodies and inter-State bodies to which individuals had access, for example, the Iran-US Claims Tribunal and the UN Compensation Commission. They now include institutional bodies (both treaty-based and non-treaty-based) with established procedures, such as under the International Chamber of Commerce and the International Centre for the Settlement of Investment Disputes and through the model law of the UN Commission on International Trade Law (see Subedi, Ch 23 of this book).

Each of these mechanisms allows individuals to bring claims against a State to an international body, which makes a decision, usually legally binding and enforceable, in relation to the claim (Redfern, Hunter, Blackaby, and Partasides, 2015). Most of the disputes between individuals and States in this area are now resolved by a combination of public and private international law, with decisions of international bodies enforced through national law, often as a consequence of a treaty obligation (such as the New York Convention on the Recognition and Enforcement of Foreign Arbitral Awards 1958).

In international economic law, as with international human rights law, it is the State that enables the individual to bring a claim either by ratifying the relevant treaty and/or through a contract agreed specifically by the State with the individual. However, in this area of law the ability of the State to refuse to allow individuals to bring international claims is often quite limited. In many instances the State, particularly a developing State, has little ability to resist an individual's (usually a transnational corporation) request to be able to bring an international claim (or to ratify the relevant treaty to enable such a claim to be made). This is because the economic power of such individuals is far greater than that of many States. In addition, many economically powerful States will place pressure on other States to allow (eg by ratifying the relevant treaty) individuals to bring these claims due to the influence of the individual in that economically powerful State, and individuals are making claims and participating in international law in a dynamic manner.

Many of the claims brought by States to international economic legal bodies, such as under the dispute settlement procedures of the World Trade Organization (WTO), are

---

[30] *Internationale Handelsgesellschaft* v *Einfur und Voratsstelle Getreide*, Case 11/70 [1970] ECR 1125, para 4.

[31] *Kadi and Al Barakaat International Foundation* v *Council*, Joined Cases 402/05 and 415/05, [2008] ECR I-6351 and *Commission, Council, United Kingdom* v *Yassin Abdullah Kadi (Kadi II)* Joined Cases C-584/10P; C-593/10P; C-595/10P, [2010] ECR II-5177.

initiated, sponsored, and prosecuted in effect by the individual corporations—and individuals with the relevant nationality—that are affected by the trade action that is the subject of the claim (Croley and Jackson, 1996; Charnovitz, 2001). Examples of the driving role of corporations in directing litigation under the WTO include Kodak and Fuji representatives being on the US and Japanese delegations on a case affecting them, and the large banana corporations convincing the USA and the EU to litigate about the trade in bananas from the Caribbean, despite the very few bananas produced in the USA and the EU (Tietje and Nowrot, 2004; Brown and Hoekman, 2005). Indeed, the drafting of key international economic treaties is often done at either the instigation of, or with the direct involvement of, transnational corporations, as seen in the Agreement on Trade-Related Aspects of Intellectual Property Rights 1994. Further, the World Bank has created an Inspection Panel, which allows individuals who believe that they will be affected detrimentally by a project in a State that is to be funded by the World Bank to ask the Panel to investigate their claim (Alfredsson and Ring, 2001). The Bank can do this even if the State is opposed to such investigation. A similar system is operated by the Asian Development Bank and the Inter-American Development Bank. This pressure from individuals for more control over international activity in the economic area will increase with globalization.

The major economic region of Europe provides the opportunity for individuals to bring claims to an international body. In *Van Gend en Loos* the European Court of Justice held:

> The European Economic Community [now European Union] constitutes a new legal order of international law for the benefit of which the States have limited their sovereign rights, albeit within limited fields, and the subjects of which comprise not only Member States but also their nationals. Independently of the legislation of Member States, Community law therefore not only imposes obligations on individuals but is also intended to confer upon them rights which become part of their legal heritage. These rights arise not only where they are expressly granted by the Treaty, but also by reason of obligations which the Treaty imposes in a clearly defined way upon individuals as well as upon the Member States and institutions of the Community.[32]

This decision highlights the limitations on the ability of EU Member States to prevent claims by individuals under European law. Though there are some situations in which the individual can bring a claim directly to the Court, in fact the main avenue for individuals to bring claims under the EU treaties is in their national courts. There is also indirect access to the Court of Justice, as most cases are brought to the Court by national courts seeking an interpretation from the Court in relation to EU treaty issues arising in the individual claim before that national court (Treaty Establishing the European Union, Article 267).

The ability of individuals (mainly corporations) to bring international claims in international economic law is now considerable. The main participants in a number of areas of international economic law are primarily States and corporations, and they are often acting on equal terms. In negotiation of contracts where a transnational corporation is involved, an agreement on a dispute settlement mechanism is vital. Invariably this will be an international body to which the corporation can bring a claim and obtain an enforceable judgment. That judgment by an international body can be affected by the nature of the

---

[32] *Van Gend en Loos*, Case 26/69 [1969] ECR 419.

claim being brought by the individual and their rights (McLachlan, Shore, and Weiniger, 2017). For most States that seek to encourage foreign investment, such an agreement allowing international dispute settlement is necessary and is not able to be rejected. Indeed, the State of nationality is not even asserting its own rights, as has been acknowledged by investment arbitration tribunals:

> [W]hen a State claimed for a wrong done to its national [in international law] it was in reality acting on behalf of that national, rather than asserting a right of its own. The pretence that it was asserting a claim of its own was necessary, because the State alone enjoyed access to international dispute settlement and claims machinery. However, there is no need to continue that fiction in a case in which the individual is vested with the right to bring claims of its own [as in international economic law]. In such a case there is no question of the investor claiming on behalf of the State. The State of nationality of the Claimant does not control the conduct of the case. No compensation which is recovered will be paid to the State. The individual may even advance a claim of which the State disapproves or base its case upon a proposition of law with which the State disagrees . . . It can be seen that the international protection for investment is really giving substantive rights to individuals that cannot be overridden by States, and a claim might not even be able to be prevented by the home State of the individual corporation.[33]

What now occurs is that the individual decides to file a claim, argues directly with the State, keeps the proceeds of the claim, has direct access to an international tribunal (usually without having to exhaust domestic remedies), and is the real actor in the international legal system. Thus, to all intents and purposes, individuals now have an independent capacity to ensure that they can bring an international claim in some areas of international economic law, which is a dramatic development in the last few decades.

IV. CREATION, DEVELOPMENT, AND ENFORCEMENT OF INTERNATIONAL LAW

One of the essential aspects of an international legal person is 'the capacity to participate in international law-making and to enforce rules of international law' (Orakhelashvili, 2001, p 256). From the classical definition of the sources of international law found in Article 38 of the Statute of the ICJ, where State practice and State treaty-making are pre-eminent, to the laws on territory and jurisdiction being about State boundaries, it is the State that appears to decide exclusively on the creation, development, and enforcement of international law. Even the definition of which entity is a State is decided (through the process of recognition) by other States. An initial focus on groups occurred in the early part of the twentieth century on minorities within and across States, as minorities have 'made a significant and fundamental contribution to precisely that [international legal] system, as they are among the oldest challenges of international (legal) relations between empires, cities and States' (Nijman, 2012, p 118). It is necessary to see the extent to which individuals have been involved in the creation, development, and enforcement of international law.

---

[33] *Corn Products International Inc* v *United Mexican States*, ICSID Case No ARB (AF)/04/1, *Decision on Responsibility*, Award, 15 January 2008, paras 173–4. Note also *Urbaser SA* v *Argentina*, ICSID Case No ARB/07/26, 8 December 2016, where the Tribunal commented that '[t]he protection of [the] universal basic human right [to water] constitutes the framework within which [investor] Claimants should frame their expectations' (para 624).

A. RIGHT OF SELF-DETERMINATION

One area where the role of the individual can be seen as a challenge to the State-based system and where individuals have been involved in the creation, development, and enforcement of international law is with respect to the right of self-determination. Article 1 of both the International Covenant on Economic, Social and Cultural Rights and the International Covenant on Civil and Political Rights provides that 'all peoples have the right of self-determination. By virtue of that right they freely determine their political status and freely pursue their economic, social and cultural development.' This right is a collective right, that is, a right of a group of individuals as a group (Chirwa, 2016). Its importance in relation to this chapter is that it is a part of the international legal system where the priority is given to groups of individuals and not to States. While the definition of the right of self-determination, including its limitations, has been drafted by States and a number of decisions about its exercise, such as whether to recognize a self-determining entity as a State, are decided by States, much of its development has been by individuals acting as a group.

This can be shown in a number of ways: from its development beyond a legal justification for decolonization (which operated largely within a State-based structure) to its application outside the colonial context to independent States and internal self-determination; and its emphasis on the right of the people to decide their own destiny (McCorquodale, 1994). Some of these aspects were explained by Judge Nagendra Singh in the *Western Sahara* Opinion, when he said that:

> [T]he consultation of the people of a territory awaiting decolonization is an inescapable imperative ... Thus even if integration of territory was demanded by an interested State, as in this case, it could not be had without ascertaining the freely expressed will of the people—the very *sine qua non* of all decolonization.[34]

Indeed, the British government, one of the largest colonizers, went further when it stated: '[A]s the [United Nations] Charter and the two International Covenants expressly declare, [it is] a right of peoples. Not States. Not countries. Not governments. Peoples.'[35] It can be seen that 'the peoples in whom [the] right is vested are not inherently or necessarily represented by States or by governments of States' (Crawford, 1988, p 166).

In fact, so successful have groups of individuals been in relation to the right of self-determination that new States have arisen despite the expressed wish of some very powerful States that this should not happen (eg in the early stages of the break-up of the former Yugoslavia) and States are now forced to accept that self-determination applies to groups within States.[36] Indeed, it could be considered that the right of self-determination has changed the international legal system significantly, as even the elements taken into consideration as to whether an entity is a State now include whether that entity complies with the right of self-determination. With all the restrictions that States can bring to the exercise of the right of self-determination, its development has been beyond the control of States and its enforcement has frequently been due to the persistence of individuals and not of States. While there remain concerns about the abuse of the right and the unequal impact of the right, especially on women (Charlesworth and Chinkin, 2000), the participation of peoples in this area opens the possibility of a less State-based and territorial idea

---

[34] *Western Sahara, Advisory Opinion, ICJ Reports 1975*, p 12 at p 81.
[35] Statement by the UK representative to the UN Commission on Human Rights (Mr H Steel), 9 February 1988 (1988) 59 *BYIL* 441.
[36] *Reference Re Secession of Quebec*, Canadian Supreme Court (1998) 37 ILM 1340.

of the right of self-determination (Knop, 2002; Saul, 2011; Wilde, 2011). The power of individuals as a group is expressed by Judge Ammoun in the *Namibia* Opinion:

> Indeed one is bound to recognize that the right of peoples to self-determination, before being written into charters that were not granted but won in bitter struggle, had first been written painfully, with the blood of the peoples, in the finally awakened conscience of humanity.[37]

B. INDIGENOUS PEOPLES

Another area of international law where the 'conscience of humanity' has been awakened is in relation to indigenous peoples. Although their international legal status had been acknowledged in the sixteenth century and some national courts considered them as communities distinct from States, it was not until late in the twentieth century that substantial renewed consideration was given to their position in the international legal system (Anaya, 2004). Most significantly, there is the UN Declaration on the Rights of Indigenous Peoples 2007. This Declaration's importance also lies in the fact that the process of its creation and development was largely outside the sole control of States. It was drafted with a significant degree of participation by indigenous peoples, who were, in the drafting process, acting on almost equal terms to State representatives. This process was revolutionary in the UN system (Lâm, 2000; Xanthaki, 2009).

Process and procedure, as discussed in relation to human rights, are significant aspects of the international legal system in terms of clarification of the participants in that system. In addition, the Declaration (even when it was a draft) assisted national and international courts in upholding the rights and separate status of indigenous peoples.[38]

C. NON-GOVERNMENTAL ORGANIZATIONS

The participation of individuals, usually as groups or peoples, in the creation, development, and enforcement of international law in the areas of self-determination and indigenous peoples has been fostered by the growing role of non-governmental organizations (NGOs). These organizations, which are part of international civil society, have had an increasingly crucial effect on the creation, development, and enforcement of many parts of the international legal system. Even in earlier centuries their role was relevant, as seen in the activities of the Anti-Slavery Society being crucial to the abolition of slavery and the role of women's groups (Bianchi, 1997). In more recent times NGOs have been important in the creation of international law, with, for example, NGOs assisting in the drafting of the Convention on the Rights of the Child, as acknowledged in the *travaux préparatoires* of that treaty, and the Convention on the Conservation of Migratory Species of Wild Animals 1979 (Bowman, 1999), the organization of a systematic campaign towards the adoption of the Convention Against Torture and other related documents (Van Boven, 1990), the creation of the International Criminal Court (Pace and Thieroff, 1999), the banning of landmines (Anderson, 2000), and reform of the environmental impacts of the World Bank's lending policies (Rossi, 2010), as well as fostering proposals for the establishment of a UN High Commissioner for Human Rights (Clapham, 1994).

---

[37] *Legal Consequences for States of the Continued Presence of South Africa in Namibia (South West Africa) notwithstanding Security Council Resolution 276 (1970), Advisory Opinion, ICJ Reports 1971,* p 16 at p 74.

[38] See *Cal v Attorney-General* (Claim 121/2007), Supreme Court of Belize, 18 October 2007, and Inter-American Court of Human Rights, *Case of the Saramanka People v Suriname, Preliminary Objections, Merits, Reparations and Costs, Judgment of 28 November 2007, Ser C No 173.*

There are two areas of the international legal system where the law has developed primarily as a response to the activities of NGOs. These are international humanitarian law, where the role of the International Committee of the Red Cross (ICRC)—a hybrid NGO—has been crucial, and issues relating to labour conditions, where trade unions and employer organizations have played a significant role. The ICRC has the express acknowledgement of its role in the Geneva Conventions 1949 and the 1977 Protocols. For example, States can entrust the fulfilment of their duties to the ICRC (common Article 10 (or 11) of the Conventions), they must cooperate with the ICRC during conflicts (Article 81 Geneva Prisoner of War Convention), and before any proposed amendment by a State to the Protocols can be acted upon, the ICRC must be consulted (Article 97 Protocol I and Article 24 Protocol II). Non-State groups can also be parties to these Conventions,[39] and generally help to develop international humanitarian law (Roberts and Sivakumaran, 2012). Similarly, trade unions and employer organizations are institutionally part of the International Labour Organization, which has adopted many treaties and other international documents. Of similar power, but with a less institutional role, have been the activities of environmental NGOs, who are a vital element in the creation and sustenance of international environmental law (Cullen and Morrow, 2001) and the roles of health foundations in the expansion of public/private partnerships in international health law (Burci, 2009).

The roles that NGOs play in relation to the development of international law are numerous. They include 'elaborating further interpretative rules in connection with already existing international instruments ... [which have come to be] referred to as ... authoritative sources' (Van Boven, 1990, p 357). They are involved in international decision-making, usually indirectly, by their participation in international fora, from the UN itself to its agencies and as a distinct part of international conferences, as well as being claimants in national courts seeking to clarify international obligations (Noortmann, 2015). Indeed, NGOs can be 'sought-after participants in a political process ... that allow NGOs to move from the corridors to the sessions' (Knop, 1993). Sometimes this participation can be important as a balance against States' views, as seen in the Bangkok NGO Declaration on Human Rights that appeared successfully to reduce the impact of the Asian States' Declaration in relation to cultural relativism (Steiner and Alston, 2000, p 549), and sometimes NGOs act in opposing ways due to their different objectives (eg during the Beijing Conference on Women—Otto, 1999). Sometimes NGOs are essential to the continuing operation of some international bodies, as the African Commission on Human Rights has acknowledged (Motala, 2002), due to their provision of information, people, and resources. In the area of international environmental law, the role of NGOs has been particularly crucial, for example, in relation to the protection of birds:

> [T]he role of [NGOs] has proved to be of vital importance. Not only have they regularly pressed for the adoption of agreements ... they have frequently shown a willingness to undertake much of the preliminary drafting work necessary to make such projects a reality. Insofar as these agreements, once concluded, have required to be sustained by technical resources and expertise, NGOs have been prominent in the provision of such support ... [In relation to one treaty,] one such [NGO] has also provided the administrative infrastructure for the establishment of a secretariat. (Bowman, 1999, p 298)

---

[39] For example, on 21 June 2015 the Polisario Front, on behalf of the people of Western Sahara, agreed to apply the 1949 Geneva Conventions and the Additional Protocol I to the armed conflict between it and Morocco, which was accepted by the depository State (Switzerland): http://armedgroups-internationallaw.org/2015/09/02/unilateral-declaration-by-polisario-under-api-accepted-by-swiss-federal-council.

The terms of the treaties that are eventually ratified are often drafted and negotiated by NGOs. The participation of NGOs in the treaty process itself also ensures greater transparency and accountability of States for their negotiating positions. To look solely at the end process (ie the ratified treaty) without any examination of the process by which that law is made ignores the discursive context, power structures, and interests involved in international law-making. This powerful role has been recognized at times, with NGOs being parties, with States, to Memoranda of Understanding (which are international agreements, although they are not treaties) concerning conservation measures about particular species, with responsibilities being placed on both States and NGOs under these Memoranda (Bowman, 1999). NGOs, as part of civil society, are acknowledged in the Guiding Principles on Business and Human Rights as having a role in applying those Principles (McCorquodale, 2013).

NGOs are also active participants in the enforcement of international law. In many instances they assist individuals to bring international claims, or bring claims themselves, and they provide information to international bodies that will often not be provided by States (Charnovitz, 2006). These roles of NGOs are accepted now in practice by States and by the rules of procedure of the international bodies, and are even specifically referred to in some treaties (eg Article 45 of the Convention on the Rights of the Child) and in monitoring compliance (eg Aarhus Convention on Access to Information, Public Participation in Decision-Making and Access to Justice in Environmental Matters 1998—Ryngaert and Noortmann, 2010). NGOs have regularly brought *amicus curiae* information to international bodies, whereby they have sought to assist the international bodies in making decisions in cases brought by others against a State, and acted to implement the State's policies, such as with development and humanitarian aid (Rossi, 2010).

At the same time, NGOs and individuals have used national legal systems to enforce international legal obligations of States (Vazquez, 1992). In addition, NGOs operate as fact-finding bodies, lobbyists, and advocates in a way that generates publicity about violations of international law. These can be a most effective means of enforcing compliance with international law by States in an international legal system where other forms of enforcement are often lacking or rarely operate. NGOs can also have such a powerful effect on States that some States will act directly against them, even if this is in breach of international law. For example, the persistent activities of Greenpeace, an environmental NGO, against French nuclear testing in the South Pacific led to the French government ordering some of its agents to sink the Greenpeace ship 'Rainbow Warrior' in a New Zealand harbour. As a consequence of this breach of international law, France had to pay compensation to New Zealand for interference in its sovereignty (though not to Greenpeace) and had to send its agents to a remote Pacific island.[40]

It is beyond doubt that NGOs have participated in the creation, development, and enforcement of international law. They have brought new ideas, sustained focus and pressure, and effective means of action in the international legal system (Rajagopal, 2003; Lindblom, 2005). They offer an alternative voice to States, though they share the problems of lack of legitimacy, few democratic processes, and the limited representativeness of many States (Cullen and Morrow, 2001; Bennoune, 2012). They provide a means to hold States and State-based organizations to account and they seek to increase the transparency of international decision-making (Charnovitz, 2006). The importance of their roles has been acknowledged in the European Convention on the Recognition of the Legal Personality of International NGOs 1991 and the UN Declaration on the Rights of Human Rights Defenders 1998. Much of NGOs' activity is only possible because States allow it to happen,

---

[40] *Rainbow Warrior (France/New Zealand)* (1990) 20 RIAA 217; 82 ILR 499.

such as participation in international fora, but not all of it is controlled by, or controllable by, States. As a consequence a 'peculiar process of interaction between traditional law mechanisms and transnational social processes with the mediation of non-State actors has become a novel method of law-making and law enforcement' (Bianchi, 1997, p 201). NGO participation may be a novel method of international law-making but it is now an accepted method.

As mentioned, NGO activity is part of the individual's role in civil society. Individuals can also act without the legal framework of an NGO. For example, the inspiration behind the creation of the ICRC came from one individual's activity in response to an armed conflict, and groups of individuals can prompt international action, such as the international condemnation of South Africa's apartheid system. In more recent years, the role of social media, especially in the formation of protests against the State, can have an effect on international legal responses, including humanitarian intervention, as occurred in north Africa in 2011 (Cottle, 2011 and see Zifcak, Ch 16 of this book).

D. JURISTS

The role of jurists, or individual writers on international law, has had a long-term effect on international law. Jurists have been given a special position in the creation, development, and enforcement of international law, with Article 38(d) of the ICJ Statute authorizing the ICJ to apply 'the teachings of the most highly qualified publicists of the various nations as [a] subsidiary means for the determination of rules of [international] law'. Their influence can be specific, such as their influence on the inclusion of persecutions on the basis of gender being considered as crimes against humanity (Bianchi, 1997), on the drafting of the Siracusa Principles on derogations and the Limburg Principles on economic, social, and cultural rights, and on decisions of international bodies. It can also be general, such as the roles of individual jurists regarding the various draft Articles of the International Law Commission. The roles of jurists as experts on international law, from membership of international bodies, such as the ICJ and international human rights bodies, to advising States and being members of expert panels in international organizations (from the World Health Organization to the Atomic Energy Agency), is also important.

From the earliest philosophers, the understanding of what the nature of international law is has been a crucial part of the development of rules and principles in the international legal system. Allott has shown how the ideas of Vattel 'determined the course of history' (Allott, 1989, p 14), as Vattel propounded a sovereignty theory of the State (in contrast to the more inclusive 'all humanity' idea that had been expounded earlier), which now forms the basis of much of the dominant view of international law.

Indeed, much of our understanding of what the international legal system is, and the role of individuals in it, is affected by the writings of jurists. For example, jurists who adopt a positivist approach to the international legal system, although generally considering that the individual has no independent role from that of the State, have been important in identifying rules of customary international law and persuading States that these rules legally bind them (Oppenheim, 1905). It has been argued that the positivist concept of international law as a State-based process 'is incapable of serving as the normative framework for present or future political realities ... new times call for a fresh conceptual and ethical language' (Tesón, 1992, pp 53–4). Some of the fresh conceptual and ethical language that has been suggested includes the application of feminist theory to the international legal system, which shows the limitations of the State as a framework for engagement in gender issues (Charlesworth, Chinkin, and Wright, 1991), and a recognition that relying on constant binary oppositions, such as State v non-State, cannot produce a coherent international legal system (Koskenniemi, 1989). Other jurists consider that 'the burgeon-ing canon of individual rights has begun to crack open the previously encrusted [posi-tivist] Vatellian system' (Franck, 1999, p 281) and that 'we should adjust our intellectual framework to a multi-layered reality consisting of a variety of authoritative structures ... [in which] what matters is not the formal status of a participant ... but its actual or prefer-able exercise of functions' (Schreuer, 1993, p 453). Others reject the current conceptual parameters and argue for a new understanding of international society (Allott, 2001).

Each of these conceptual approaches seeks to explain the law-making processes of the international legal system and, in so doing, offers reflections on the role of the individual in that system. These approaches have occasionally been taken up by States and others in ways that have affected the development of international law (eg in ICJ decisions and UN resolutions), as well as by national courts, whose decisions can become examples of State practice to form customary international law and develop international law in their interpretation of treaties (Roberts, 2011). A specific example is found in the speech of the UN Secretary-General, Kofi Annan, on the award of the Nobel Peace Prize 2001 to him and to the UN:

> Over the past five years, I have often recalled that the United Nations' Charter begins with the words: 'We the peoples'. What is not always recognized is that 'We the peoples' are made up of individuals whose claims to the most fundamental rights have too often been sacrificed in the supposed interests of the State or the nation ... In this new century, we must start from the understanding that peace belongs not only to States or peoples, but to each and every member of those communities. The sovereignty of States must no longer be used as a shield for gross violations of human rights. Peace must be made real and tangible in the daily existence of every individual in need. Peace must be sought, above all, because it is the condition for every member of the human family to live a life of dignity and secu-rity ... Throughout my term as Secretary-General, I have sought to place human beings at the centre of everything we do—from conflict prevention to development to human rights. Securing real and lasting improvement in the lives of individual men and women is the measure of all we do at the United Nations. (Annan, 2001, pp 2–3)

Therefore, it can be seen that, in various ways, individuals have had, and continue to have, an important part in the creation, development, and enforcement of international law. This has been by groups of individuals, from peoples with the right of self-determination and indigenous peoples, to NGOs, and jurists have also had an influence. It can also be seen in the contribution of women and men throughout the centuries who offer new ideas and practical applications in relation to international law.

V. CONCLUSIONS

The role of the individual in the international legal system remains a contentious one. The extent of this role can depend on how the nature of the system is conceptualized and ap-plied, as well as an understanding of diverse areas of international law. In most cases the crucial issue is whether the individual has an independent role in the system or whether the individual's role is solely dependent on State consent.

In approaching these issues, a broad definition of the 'individual' has been adopted, with the understanding that 'participation' in the international legal system (as against the 'sub-ject' v 'object' stricture) is the relevant context for considering the role of the individual. This has opened up more possibilities to discover the conceptual and practical role of the indi-vidual in the system. It has been shown that individuals do have considerable international rights and responsibilities in the system, a number of which are independent from a State's ability to control or determine them. The vast array of international claims available to individuals are largely still within the control of States in principle, though not in practice.

It is clear that the individual has been a crucial factor in the creation, development, and enforcement of international law. As the ICJ noted in its *Reparations for Injuries* Opinion (see Section I B of this chapter), the 'needs of the [international] community' and 'the requirements of international life' have ensured that the individual has a continuing role in the international legal system. In addition, individuals, by their actions, influence not only the concept and content of international law but also the way it is applied by States and the extent and manner by which a State consents to rules of international law (McCorquodale, 2004). Individuals can begin to contribute to the development of customary international law as their participation affects the practice of international law, including the possibility that an agreement between a State and an individual may be considered to be an international law agreement or a treaty. Indeed, 'the proposal that individuals ought to be included in the process of customary international law formation is both theoretically grounded and technically feasible' (Ochoa, 2007, p 169; Müller, 2008). As Judge Cançado Trindade, then President of the Inter-American Court of Human Rights, noted:

> The doctrinal trend which still insists in denying to individuals the condition of subjects of international law is ... unsustainable [and] that conception appears contaminated by an ominous ideological dogmatism, which had as the main consequence to alienate the individual from the international legal order. It is surprising—if not astonishing—besides regrettable, to see that conception repeated mechanically and ad nauseam by a part of the doctrine, apparently trying to make believe that the intermediary of the State, between the individuals and the international legal order, would be something inevitable and permanent. Nothing could be more fallacious.[41]

Individuals may not yet be participating in the international legal system to the same extent as States or on an equal footing with them but the trend is clear: the role of the individual in this system is continuing to expand, often despite the wishes of States. Indeed, it might be argued that this participation of the individual in the international legal system 'reflects a strength in the system's potential to respond flexibly to the needs of the international community' (Parlett, 2011, p 369). If, as Annan asserts, the ultimate foundation of the international legal system is 'We, the Peoples', then the role of each State is not to ensure and perpetuate its own power but to enable every individual to live a life of dignity and security and so to ensure human flourishing. The interests of individuals must count for more than the interests of States.

REFERENCES

ALFREDSSON, G and RING, R (2001), *The Inspection Panel of the World Bank* (The Hague: Martinus Nijhoff).

ALLOTT, P (1989), *International Law and International Revolution: Reconceiving the World* (Hull: Hull University Press).

ALLOTT, P (1992), 'Reconstituting Humanity—New International Law', 3 *EJIL* 219.

ALLOTT, P (2001), *Eunomia: New Order for a New World* (rev edn, Oxford: Oxford University Press).

---

[41] *Juridical Status and Human Rights of the Child, Advisory Opinion OC-17/02 Ser A, No 17* (28 August 2002), (2004) 11 IHRR 510, Concurring Opinion of Judge Cançado Trindade, paras 26–7.

ALSTON, P (2005), *Non-State Actors and Human Rights* (Oxford: Oxford University Press).

ALVAREZ, J (2011), 'Are Corporations "Subjects" of International Law', 9 *Santa Clara JIL* 1

ANAYA, J (2004), *Indigenous Peoples in International Law* (2nd edn, Oxford: Oxford University Press).

ANDERSON, K (2000), 'The Ottawa Convention Banning Landmines, The Role of International Non-Governmental Organisations and the Idea of International Civil Society', 11 *EJIL* 91.

ANGIE, A (2005), *Imperialism, Sovereignty and the Making of International Law* (Cambridge: Cambridge University Press)

ANNAN, K (2001), 'We Can Love What We Are Without Hating What—and Who—We Are Not', Nobel Peace Prize Lecture, 10 December 2001, http://www.un.org/News/Press/docs/2001/sgsm8071.doc.htm.

BENNOUNE, K (2012), 'Productive Tensions: Women's NGOs, the "Mainstream" Human Rights Movement and International Lawmaking, in C Bailliet (ed), *Non State Actors, Soft Law and Protective Regimes: From the Margins* (Cambridge: Cambridge University Press).

BIANCHI, A (1997), 'Globalization of Human Rights: The Role of Non-State Actors', in G Teubner (ed), *Global Law Without a State* (Aldershot: Dartmouth).

BOWMAN, M (1999), 'The Global Protection of Birds', 11 *Journal of International Environmental Law* 87.

BOYLE, A and CHINKIN, C (2007), *The Making of International Law* (Oxford: Oxford University Press).

BROWN, C and HOEKMAN, B (2005), 'WTO Dispute Settlement and the Missing Developing Country Case: Engaging the Private Sector', 8 *J Int'l Econ. L* 861.

BURCI, GL (2009), 'Public/Private Partnerships in the Public Health Sector', 6 *International Organization LR* 359.

BUTLER, I (2007), *Unravelling Sovereignty: Human Rights and the Structure of International Law* (Groningen: Intersentia).

CASSESE, A (1986), *International Law in a Divided World* (Oxford: Clarendon Press).

CHARLESWORTH, H and CHINKIN, C (2000), *The Boundaries of International Law: A Feminist Analysis* (Manchester: Manchester University Press).

CHARLESWORTH, H, CHINKIN, C, and WRIGHT, S (1991), 'Feminist Approaches to International Law', 85 *AJIL* 631.

CHARNOVITZ, S (2001), 'Economic and Social Actors in the World Trade Organization', 7 *ILSA J of International and Comparative Law* 259.

CHARNOVITZ, S (2006), 'Non-Governmental Organizations and International Law', 100 *AJIL* 348.

CHIRWA, D (2016), 'Group Rights and the Protection of Economic, Social and Cultural Rights in Africa', in D Chirwa and L Chenwi (eds), *The Protection of Economic, Social and Cultural Rights in Africa* (Cambridge: Cambridge University Press).

CLAPHAM, A (1994), 'Creating the High Commissioner for Human Rights: The Outside Story', 5 *EJIL* 556.

CLAPHAM, A (2010), 'The Role of the Individual in International Law', 21 *EJIL* 25.

COMMITTEE of MINISTERS (2001), Report of the Evaluation Group on the European Court of Human Rights, 22 *HRLJ* 308.

COTTLE, S (2011), 'Media and the Arab Uprisings of 2011', 12 *Journalism* 647.

CRAWFORD, J (ed) (1988), *The Rights of Peoples* (Oxford: Oxford University Press).

CROLEY, S and JACKSON, J (1996), 'WTO Dispute Procedures, Standard of Review and Deference to National Governments', 90 *AJIL* 193.

CULLEN, H and MORROW, K (2001), 'International Civil Society in International Law: The Growth of NGO Participation', 1 *Non-State Actors in International Law* 7.

DINE, J (2000), *The Governance of Corporate Groups* (Cambridge: Cambridge University Press).

DOUGLAS-SCOTT, S (2011), 'The European Union and Human Rights after the Treaty of Lisbon', 11 *HRLR* 645.

FRANCK, T (1999), *The Empowered Self: Law and Society in the Age of Individualism* (Oxford: Oxford University Press).

GEUSS, R (2007), *History and Illusion in Politics* (Cambridge: Cambridge University Press).

HEMPHILL, T and WHITE, G (2016), 'The World Economic Forum and Nike: Emerging "Shared Responsbility" and Institutional Control Models for Achieving a Socially Responsible Chain', 1 *Business and Human Rights Journal* 2.

HENCKAERTS, J-M (2007), 'Concurrent Application of International Human Rights Law and International Humanitarian Law', 1 *Human Rights and International Legal Discourse* 95.

HIGGINS, R (1979), 'Conceptual Thinking about the Individual in International Law', 11 *New York Law School Law Review* 11.

HIGGINS, R (1994), *Problems and Process: International Law and How We Use It* (Oxford: Oxford University Press).

HOHFELD, W (1913), 'Fundamental Legal Conceptions as Applied to Judicial Reasoning', 23 *Yale LJ* 16.

HUNT, S (2010), 'Human Rights Accountability of International Organisations vis-à-vis their Staff: The United Nations', in J Wouters, E Brems, S Smis, and P Schmitt (eds), *Accountability for Human Rights Violations by International Organizations* (Antwerp: Intersentia).

INTERNATIONAL LAW COMMISSION (2001), *Articles on Responsibility of States for Internationally Wrongful Acts*, 53rd Session, UN Doc A/CN.4/L.602/Rev.1, 26 July 2001, available at http://www.un.org/law/ilc.

JOSEPH, S (2010), 'Scope of Application', in D Moeckli, S Shah, and S Sivakumaran (eds) *International Human Rights Law* (Oxford: Oxford University Press).

KNOP, K (1993), 'Re-statements: Feminism and State Sovereignty in International Law', 3 *Transnational and Contemporary Legal Problems* 293.

KNOP, K (2002), *Diversity and Self-Determination in International Law* (Cambridge: Cambridge University Press).

KOSKENNIEMI, M (1989), *From Apology to Utopia: The Structure of International Legal Argument*, 2005 reissue (Cambridge: Cambridge University Press).

KOSKENNIEMI, M (1991), 'The Future of Statehood', 32 *Harvard ILJ* 397.

LÂM, MC (2000), *At the Edge of the State: Indigenous Peoples and Self-Determination* (Ardsley, NY: Transnational Publishers).

LAUTERPACHT, H (1950), *International Law and Human Rights* (London: Stevens).

LINDBLOM, A-K (2005), *Non-Governmental Organisations in International Law* (Cambridge: Cambridge University Press).

LINDSAY, R, MCCORQUODALE, R, BLECHER, L, BONNITCHA, J, CROCKETT A, and SHEPPARD, A (2013), 'Human Rights Responsibilities in the Oil and Gas Sector: Applying the UN Guiding Principles', 6 *Journal of World Energy Law and Business* 1.

MCCORQUODALE, R (1994), 'Self-Determination: A Human Rights Approach', 43 *ICLQ* 857.

MCCORQUODALE, R (2004), 'An Inclusive International Legal System', 17 *Leiden JIL* 477.

MCCORQUODALE, R (2013), 'Pluralism, Global Law and Human Rights: Strengthening Corporate Accountability for Human Rights Violations', 2 *Global Constitutionalism* 287.

MCCORQUODALE, R (2017), 'Sources and the "Subjects" of International Law: A Plurality of Law-Making Participants', in S Besson and J d'Aspremont (eds), *Oxford Handbook on the Sources of International Law* (Oxford: Oxford University Press).

McLachlan, C, Shore, L, and Weiniger, M (2017), *International Investment Arbitration* (2nd edn, Oxford: Oxford University Press).

Mares, R (ed) (2012), *Siege or Cavalry Charge? The UN Mandate on Business and Human Rights* (The Hague: Martinus Nijhoff).

Martinez, JS (2012), *The Slave Trade and the Origins of International Human Rights* (Oxford: Oxford University Press).

Meron, T (2006), *The Humanization of International Law* (Boston: Brill Academic).

Motala, A (2002), 'Non-Governmental Organisations in the African System', in M Evans and R Murray (eds), *The African Charter on Human and Peoples' Rights* (1st edn, Cambridge: Cambridge University Press).

Muchlinski, P (2007), *Multinational Enterprises and the Law* (2nd edn, Oxford: Oxford University Press).

Müller, T (2008), 'Customary Transnational Law: Attacking the Last Resort of State Sovereignty', 15 *Ind J of Global Legal Studies* 19.

Nijman, J (2004), *The Concept of International Legal Personality* (The Hague: TMC Asser Press).

Nijman, J (2012), 'Minorities and Majorities' in B Fassbender and A Peters (eds), *The Oxford Handbook of the History of International Law* (Oxford: Oxford University Press).

Noortmann, M (2015), 'NGOs: Recognition, Roles, Rights and Responsibilities', in M Noortmann, A Reinisch, and C Ryngaert (eds) *Non-State Actors in International Law* (Oxford: Hart).

Ochoa, C (2007), 'The Individual and Customary International Law Formation', 48 *Va J Int'l L* 119.

O'Keefe, R (2015), *International Criminal Law* (Oxford: Oxford University Press).

Oppenheim, L (1905), *International Law*, vol 1 (London: Longmans).

Orakhelashvili, A (2001), 'The Position of the Individual in International Law', 31 *California Western ILJ* 241.

Otto, D (1997), 'Rethinking Universals: Opening Transformative Possibilities in International Human Rights Law', 18 *Aust YBIL* 1.

Otto, D (1999), 'A Post-Beijing Reflection on the Limitations and Potential of Human Rights Discourse for Women', in K Askin and D Koenig (eds), *Women and International Human Rights Law*, vol 1 (Ardsley, NY: Transnational Publishers).

Pace, W and Thieroff, M (1999), 'Participation of Non-Governmental Organisations', in R Lee (ed), *The International Criminal Court* (The Hague: Kluwer).

Parlett, K (2011), *The Individual in the International Legal System* (Cambridge: Cambridge University Press).

Paust, J (2011), 'Nonstate Actor Participation in International Law and the Pretence of Exclusion', 51 *Virginia JIL* 977.

Peters, A (2016), *Beyond Human Rights: The Legal Status of the Individual in International Law* (Cambridge: Cambridge University Press).

Puvimanasinghe, S (2007), *Foreign Investment, Human Rights and the Environment* (Leiden: Brill Academic).

Rajagopal, B (2003), *International Law from Below* (Cambridge: Cambridge University Press).

Ratner, S and Abrams, J (2009), *Accountability for Human Rights Atrocities in International Law* (3rd edn, Oxford: Oxford University Press).

Redfern, A, Hunter, M, Blackaby, N, and Partasides, C (2015), *Law and Practice of International Commercial Arbitration* (6th edn, Oxford: Oxford University Press).

Remec, P (1960), *The Position of the Individual in International Law According to Grotius and Vattel* (The Hague: Martinus Nijhoff).

ROBERTS, A (2011), 'Comparative International Law? The Role of National Courts in Creating and Enforcing International Law', 60 *ICLQ* 57.

ROBERTS, A and SIVAKUMARAN, S (2012), 'Lawmaking by Nonstate Actors: Engaging Armed Groups in the Creation of International Humanitarian Law', 37 *Yale JIL* 107.

ROSSI, I (2010), *Legal Status of Non-Governmental Organizations in International Law* (Antwerp: Intersentia).

RYNGAERT, C and NOORTMANN, M (2010), 'New Actors in Global Governance and International Human Rights Law', 4 *Human Rights and International Legal Discourse* 5.

SAUL, B (2011), 'The Normative Status of Self-Determination in International Law: A Formula for Uncertainty in the Scope and Content of the Right?', 11 *HRLR* 609.

SCELLE, G (1932), *Précis de droit des gens* (Paris: Recueil Sirey).

SCHABAS, W (2011), *Introduction to the International Criminal Court* (4th edn, Cambridge: Cambridge University Press).

SCHREUER, C (1993), 'The Waning of the Sovereign State: Towards a New Paradigm for International Law', 4 *EJIL* 447.

SHELTON, D (2015), *Remedies in International Human Rights Law* (3rd edn, Oxford: Oxford University Press).

STEINER, H and ALSTON, P (2000), *International Human Rights in Context*

(2nd edn, Oxford: Oxford University Press).

TESÓN, F (1992), 'The Kantian Theory of International Law', 92 *Col LR* 53.

TIETJE, C and NOWROT, K (2004), 'Forming the Centre of a Transnational Economic Legal Order? Thoughts on the Current and Future Position of Non-State Actors in WTO Law', 5 *European Business Organization LR* 321.

TORNARITIS, C (1972), *The Individual as a Subject of International Law* (Nicosia: Public Information Office).

UNITED NATIONS (2011), Special Representative to the Secretary-General's Report to the United Nations Human Rights Council, *Guiding Principles on Business and Human Rights: Implementing the United Nations 'Protect, Respect and Remedy' Framework* (21 March 2011), A/HRC/17/L.17/Rev.1.

VAN BOVEN, T (1990), 'The Role of Non-Governmental Organizations in International Human Rights Standard-Setting: A Prerequisite for Democracy', 20 *California Western ILJ* 207.

VAZQUEZ, C (1992), 'Treaty-Based Rights and Remedies of Individuals', 92 *Col LR* 1082.

WILDE, R (2011), 'Self-Determination, Secession, and Dispute Settlement after the Kosovo Advisory Opinion', 24 *Leiden JIL* 149.

XANTHAKI, A (2009), 'Indigenous Rights in International Law over the Last 10 Years and Future Developments', 10 *Melbourne JIL* 27.

FURTHER READING

It is in the nature of the topic that the vast amount of relevant literature in this area is found in articles and book chapters many of which are referred to in the text and listed in the References section. The publications of particular note are:

ALSTON, P (2005), *Non-State Actors and Human Rights* (Oxford: Oxford University Press).

CANÇADO TRINDADE, A (2011), *The Access of Individuals to International Justice* (Oxford: Oxford University Press).

CLAPHAM, A (2006), *Human Rights Obligations of Non-State Actors* (Oxford: Oxford University Press).

DUPUY, P-M and VIERUCCI, L (2008), *NGOs in International Law* (Cheltenham, Edward Elgar).

McCorquodale, R (2011), *International Law Beyond the State* (London: CMP Publishing).

Nørgaard, C (1962), *The Position of the Individual in International Law* (Copenhagen: Munksgaard).

Parlett, K (2011), *The Individual in the International Legal System* (Cambridge: Cambridge University Press).

Peters, A (2016), *Beyond Human Rights: The Legal Status of the Individual in International Law* (Cambridge: Cambridge University Press).

Portmann, R (2010), *Legal Personality in International Law* (Cambridge: Cambridge University Press).

PART IV

THE SCOPE OF SOVEREIGNTY

10

JURISDICTION

Christopher Staker

SUMMARY[1]

Each State has the right to regulate its own public order, and to that end it is entitled to legislate for everyone within its territory. But States are also entitled to legislate for their nationals, and some actions extend over national boundaries; and there are accordingly situations in which two or more States may seek to apply their laws to the same conduct. This chapter is concerned with the principles of international law that regulate the right of States to apply their laws to conduct, and with the resolution of disputes arising from overlapping jurisdictional claims, and also with the problems of enforcing national laws.

I. INTRODUCTION

A. THE MEANING OF 'JURISDICTION'

'Jurisdiction' is the term that describes the limits of the legal competence of a State or other regulatory authority (such as the European Union (EU)) to make, apply, and enforce rules of conduct upon persons. It 'concerns essentially the extent of each state's right to regulate conduct or the consequences of events'.[2]

States regulate conduct in this sense in various ways, which may involve any of the branches of government. Thus, the Legislature may lay down rules by statute, or the Executive may do so by order. Laws on the provocation of religious hatred, and statutory instruments forbidding the export of certain goods to certain countries, are obvious examples. Some laws are less obviously prescriptive, but are nonetheless equally part of the structure of the social order: for example, laws regarding the qualifications for the acquisition of a State's nationality or determining the circumstances in which contractual obligations may be avoided, or describing the conditions upon which a person will be liable to pay taxes to the State. States also regulate conduct by means of the decisions of their courts, which may order litigating parties to do or abstain from doing certain things. So, too, may the State's administrative bodies, which may apply rules concerning, for example, the issuance of licences to export goods to certain countries. The police, and other

---

[1] Professor Vaughan Lowe was the sole author of this chapter as it appeared in the first and second editions, and co-author of the chapter as it appeared in the third edition, of this book. The chapter in this present edition retains substantial amounts of the original text.　　　　[2] *Oppenheim's International Law*, 1992, p 456.

law-enforcement agencies, are also involved, in the arrest and detention of persons and the seizure of goods. All of these activities are in principle regulated by the rules of international law concerning jurisdiction.

The term 'jurisdiction' is also commonly used in international law to describe the scope of the right of an international tribunal, such as the International Court of Justice or the International Criminal Court, to adjudicate upon cases and to make orders in respect of the parties to them. In abstract terms, the jurisdiction of States and the jurisdiction of tribunals are both instances of the concept of the scope of the powers of a legal institution; but it is traditional, and practically useful, to distinguish between them and to treat them separately. The jurisdiction of international tribunals is, accordingly, not treated in this chapter.

B. THE SIGNIFICANCE OF THE PRINCIPLES OF JURISDICTION

The legal rules and principles governing jurisdiction have a fundamental importance in international relations, because they are concerned with the allocation between States, and other entities such as the EU, of competence to regulate daily life—that is, the competence to secure the *differences* that make each State a distinct society. Inasmuch as they determine the reach of a State's laws, they may be said to determine what the boundaries of that State's particular public order are. For instance, the rejection by western States of the *fatwah* issued against Salman Rushdie was, in essence, a denial that the jurisdiction of the Iranian authorities extended so far as to regulate conduct in the UK.[3] There are many other examples of contested jurisdictional claims, perhaps less spectacular but affecting a much wider range of interests. For example, the USA has at various times enacted laws that purport to forbid foreign businesses, based outside the USA, to trade with certain States such as the former Soviet Union, Iran, and Cuba. Those laws have imposed significant economic costs and disadvantages on non-US companies; and they raise the question of the propriety—indeed, the legality—of one State purporting to forbid persons in another State to do things that are perfectly lawful in the State where those persons are located.

Similarly, as the principles governing jurisdiction define the limits of the State's coercive powers, they effect one of the most important delineations of the different societies into which the world is divided. It is these principles that dictate that the executive and judicial authorities of one State have no right to operate in the territory of another State without the latter's consent. It was thus necessary, for instance, for France and the UK to conclude an agreement allowing the customs and immigration officers of each to operate in the territory of the other in relation to the Channel Tunnel,[4] and for the Netherlands and the UK to conclude an agreement to permit the Scottish court to sit at Camp Zeist in the Netherlands to hear the cases against the Libyan nationals accused of blowing up a US aeroplane in the skies above Lockerbie in Scotland.[5]

In view of their significance, it is not surprising that the principles governing jurisdiction have attracted considerable attention from jurists over the years. In fact, however, international controversy over the limits of jurisdiction, which was intense in the four or five decades after 1945, seems to have abated somewhat during recent years.

---

[3] It appears that it was technically a religious authority, rather than what in western terms would be thought of as a typically 'governmental' authority, that issued the *fatwah*. This raises the interesting question of the limits of the notion of 'the State' for the purposes of State responsibility. On this question see Part V of this book and see *United States Diplomatic and Consular Staff in Tehran, Judgment, ICJ Reports 1980*, p 3.

[4] See the Sangatte Protocol, 25 November 1991, Cm 1802; (1991) 62 *BYIL* 623–5.

[5] See the Agreement concerning a Scottish Trial in the Netherlands, 18 September 1998, UKTS No 43 (1999); 117 ILR 664, 666, 673. See also Aust, 2000.

Before turning to the examination of those principles in more detail, it is necessary to say a word about the framework within which jurisdictional principles are analysed by international lawyers.

C. THE DOCTRINAL ANALYSIS OF JURISDICTION

Jurisdiction, as a topic of international law, has a less solid and universal basis than is often supposed. English-language monographs typically devote a chapter to the topic,[6] as they have done since the late nineteenth century:[7] continental monographs, on the other hand, have tended to adopt a rather different approach, regarding jurisdiction as an aspect of statehood or territory or the law of the sea or of some other aspect of international law. There is, on this continental approach, no comprehensive, consolidated statement of all of the principles of jurisdiction.[8] It is notable that there is, for example, no volume devoted to jurisdiction in Verzijl's great treatise, *International Law in Historical Perspective*. That pattern appears to be changing. In 1968 the Council of Europe produced a *Model Plan for the Classification of Documents concerning State Practice in the Field of Public International Law*,[9] which distributed the treatment of jurisdiction under a number of different headings, including 'Personal Jurisdiction', 'State Territory and Territorial Jurisdiction', and 'Seas, Waterways, Ships', in line with the continental approach. In 1997, that plan was revised,[10] and jurisdiction now has its own separate chapter in the Model Plan, divided up as follows:

Part Eight: Jurisdiction of the State

I. *Bases of jurisdiction*

   A. Territorial principle

   B. Personal principle

   C. Protective principle

   D. Universality principle

   E. Other bases

II. *Types of jurisdiction*

   A. Jurisdiction to prescribe

   B. Jurisdiction to adjudicate

   C. Jurisdiction to enforce

III. *Extra-territorial exercise of jurisdiction*

   A. General

   B. Consular jurisdiction

   C. Jurisdiction over military personnel abroad

   D. Others (artificial islands, *terrae nullius*, etc)

IV. *Limitations upon jurisdiction (servitudes, leases, etc)*

V. *Concurrent jurisdiction*

---

[6] See, eg, the texts by Oppenheim, 1992; Crawford, 2012; O'Connell, 1970.
[7] See, eg, the texts by Twiss, 1884 and Hall, 1895.   [8] See, eg, Verhoeven, 2000.
[9] Council of Europe Res (68) 17 (28 June 1968). This scheme is used to arrange the survey of United Kingdom Materials on International Law, in each year's *British Yearbook of International Law (BYIL)*.
[10] Council of Europe Res (97) 11 (12 June 1997).

While European doctrine thus seems to be moving towards the traditional 'English' approach, there are signs of a different development in the USA. The great *Digests* of US practice, edited by Marjorie Whiteman, Marian Nash, and others, had until 1988 separate chapters on jurisdiction, in accordance with the traditional approach. The more recent volumes, published (after a gap in publication) from 2001 onwards, do not. These volumes distribute material on jurisdiction under headings such as 'taxation' and 'international criminal court'. The shift may appear insignificant; and it may prove to be so. It may, however, signal a change in attitude to the very nature of jurisdiction. Whereas in the past jurisdiction was seen, both in the 'English' and the continental views, as a matter of the reach of the authority of a State, this development in US doctrine appears to treat jurisdiction as an aspect of the substantive topic that is regulated. If this trend persists the principles of jurisdiction may fragment, so that States may assert a more extensive jurisdiction over, say, tax matters and 'terrorist' offences than they do over unlawful arms sales and other crimes. Should that happen, and should the assertions of jurisdiction be recognized in international law, the near-inevitable result is that jurisdictional claims will steadily expand, and that the States most interested in regulating particular areas of conduct will increasingly apply their laws to activities outside their own borders and within the borders of other States—much in the manner of the Rushdie *fatwah*. For purposes of this chapter, however, the approach of the Council of Europe scheme will be adopted.[11]

1. Types of jurisdiction

The first section of the Council of Europe Model Plan, 'Bases of jurisdiction', is concerned with the ambit of a State's laws: that is, with its jurisdiction to prescribe rules, or its 'legislative' or 'prescriptive' jurisdiction, as it is sometimes called. The second section, 'Types of jurisdiction', somewhat illogically steps up to a higher level of abstraction and distinguishes between, on the one hand, the jurisdiction to prescribe rules and, on the other hand, the jurisdiction to enforce them, or 'enforcement jurisdiction' as it is commonly known. Thus, the UK may enact a law forbidding, say, murder and make that law applicable to all British citizens wherever in the world they might be. That would fall within the UK's prescriptive jurisdiction, in accordance with what is called the 'nationality' or 'personal' principle (Section I B in the Council of Europe scheme). But if a British citizen were to commit murder in, say, Argentina, the UK authorities would have no right to enter Argentina and arrest the murderer; and if they did so they would violate Argentinean sovereignty.[12] The UK's enforcement jurisdiction, like that of every other State, is in principle limited to its own territory. That is why States need to seek the extradition of persons accused of committing crimes within their jurisdiction, in circumstances where the accused is living in another State.

There is another 'Type of jurisdiction' identified in the Council of Europe scheme, and in similar frameworks adopted elsewhere:[13] that is the 'jurisdiction to adjudicate', or 'adjudicative jurisdiction', or 'curial jurisdiction'. This refers to the right of courts to receive, try, and determine cases referred to them. However, problems arising where the

---

[11] Of course, as in the case of all areas of the law, shifts in thinking over time can be expected in any event. See, for example, Mills (2014).

[12] For an example of such a violation see *Attorney-General of the Government of Israel* v *Adolf Eichmann* (1961) 36 ILR 5.

[13] See, eg, the American Law Institute's *Restatement of the Law: the Foreign Relations Law of the United States*, 3rd edn, 1987; Akehurst, 1972–3, pp 145–217.

courts of more than one State are seized of the same subject matter (for instance where two disputing parties each commence proceedings against the other in different States in respect of the same dispute) are usually considered within the realm of private international law. Insofar as parties choose to submit to the jurisdiction of a national court, there can be no cause for complaint unless one or more of the parties is subject to an order made under the law of another State, obliging them not to submit to the foreign court. If such an antisuit order is made, there is a clash of prescriptive jurisdictions, as there is if two or more courts hear the same case and issue conflicting orders.[14] For purposes of public international law, all of this can largely be analysed in terms of prescriptive and enforcement jurisdiction. A separate category of 'jurisdiction to adjudicate' is therefore not considered in this chapter.

2. Other jurisdictional issues

The third category in the Council of Europe scheme, 'Extra-territorial exercise of jurisdiction', is concerned with the exceptional circumstances in which a State is entitled to exercise its enforcement jurisdiction (and with it, by necessary implication, its legislative jurisdiction) in the territory of another State. A common example in NATO States is the network of arrangements under which troops of one NATO State are stationed in another, but subject to the control of their home State authorities, so that, for instance, US military police will have the right to arrest and imprison members of US forces on military bases in the UK.

The fourth and fifth of the Council of Europe 'Types' are of a rather different kind. The 'Limitations upon jurisdiction' instanced by servitudes and leases are limitations that arise when a particular piece of territory is 'leased' to another State (as part of Hong Kong was leased by China to the UK from 1898 to 1997, as the Panama Canal Zone was leased by Panama to the USA from 1903 to 1977, and as Guantánamo Bay has since 1903 been, and still is, leased by Cuba to the USA), and under the terms of the lease the territorial sovereign permits the lessee to exercise exclusive jurisdiction over the area. This is not so much a 'type' of jurisdiction as a particular consequence of the temporary transfer or alienation of rights of sovereignty over areas of State territory, and it will not be further discussed here.[15] The final category, 'Concurrent jurisdiction', concerns the issues that arise when two or more States are entitled to exercise legislative (or, rarely, enforcement) jurisdiction in relation to the same factual circumstances.[16]

---

[14] See 'The Principles for Determining When the Use of the Doctrine of *forum non conveniens* and Anti-suit Injunctions is Appropriate', Institut de Droit International, *Annuaire*, vol 70–I (2002–2003), p 14.

[15] See further Craven and Parfitt, Ch 7 in this book.

[16] Consideration of issues of jurisdiction have also arisen in the context of Article 1 of the European Convention on Human Rights (ECHR), which provides that '[t]he High Contracting Parties shall secure to everyone within their jurisdiction the rights and freedoms defined in Section I of this Convention'. The question whether the ECHR applies to acts of agents of an ECHR contracting State performed outside that State's territory will thus depend on whether persons affected by those acts are within the 'jurisdiction' of the State to which those agents belong, for purposes of Article 1 of the ECHR. That issue overlaps with, but is not the same as, the question with which this chapter is concerned. The European Court of Human Rights has held that the ECHR may apply to acts of a contracting State's agents performed outside its territory in certain circumstances, for instance, situations where the contracting State's agents operating outside its territory exercise 'total and exclusive control' or 'full and exclusive control' over an individual; or certain situations when, as a consequence of military action, a contracting State exercises effective control of an area outside its national territory. See, for instance, *Al-Skeini and Others* v *the United Kingdom* [GC], no 55721/07, ECHR 2011; *Jaloud* v *Netherlands* [GC], no 47708/08, ECHR 2014; (2015) 60 EHRR 29; *Al-Waheed* v *Ministry of Defence* [2017] UKSC 2; [2017] 2 WLR 327.

II. PRESCRIPTIVE JURISDICTION

To whom may a State extend its laws? Whom may the State order to do this, or not to do that? Or, to ask a question of a slightly different kind, who may be deemed by a State to be, say, a citizen, or 'married', or 'an infant'; or how far may a State rule that a particular ceremony counts as a valid wedding, or divorce; what, in other words, are the limits of the right of a State to impose legal characterizations upon persons or events? These are all questions about the reach, the ambit or scope, of a State's laws; that is, about the limits of its prescriptive or legislative jurisdiction.

Before turning to the principles that explain the bases upon which States are entitled to exercise prescriptive jurisdiction, it is necessary to refer to a tiresome and oddly persistent fallacy that arose from an early case in the Permanent Court of International Justice (PCIJ). The case concerned a collision on the high seas (ie that part of the sea that is beyond the territorial jurisdiction of every State), between the French steamer, the *Lotus*, and the Turkish steamer, the *Boz-Kourt*, which resulted in eight deaths. When the *Lotus* entered Constantinople, the Turkish authorities prosecuted M Demons, the officer of the watch on the *Lotus*. Proceedings were also instituted against the captain of the Turkish ship. France objected to the proceedings against M Demons on the ground that no State is entitled to extend its law to foreign ships on the high seas, and that Turkey, accordingly, was not entitled to prosecute M Demons. The PCIJ held that Turkey was entitled to prosecute. The passage in question is so often quoted, and so much misunderstood, that it is worthwhile reproducing it here. The Court said:[17]

> the first and foremost restriction imposed by international law upon a State is that—failing the existence of a permissive rule to the contrary—it may not exercise its power in any form in the territory of another State. In this sense jurisdiction is certainly territorial; it cannot be exercised by a State outside its territory except by virtue of a permissive rule derived from international custom or from a convention.

That proposition is not controversial. It asserts that a State's *enforcement* jurisdiction is in principle confined to the State's territory (a point considered further in this chapter in Section III). In the *Lotus* case, this was not an issue. Turkish authorities had not gone out on to the high seas to arrest M Demons: they had waited until the *Lotus* entered a Turkish port and so came within Turkish territory and thus within Turkish enforcement jurisdiction. The question was whether having arrested M Demons in Turkey he, as a French citizen, could then be prosecuted by the Turkish authorities for his acts outside Turkish territory, on the high seas. The Court continued, addressing itself to this question, as follows:[18]

> It does not, however, follow that international law prohibits a State from exercising jurisdiction in its own territory, in respect of any case which relates to acts which have taken place abroad, and in which it cannot rely on some permissive rule of international law. Such a view would only be tenable if international law contained a general prohibition to States to extend the application of their laws and the jurisdiction of their courts to persons, property and acts outside their territory, and if, as an exception to this general prohibition, it allowed States to do so in certain specific cases. But this is certainly not the case under international law as it stands at present. Far from laying down a general prohibition to the effect that States may not extend the application of their laws and the jurisdiction of their courts to persons, property and acts outside their territory, it leaves them in this respect a wide measure of discretion which is only limited in certain cases by prohibitive rules . . .

---

[17] 'Lotus', *Judgment No 9, 1927, PCIJ, Ser A, No 10*, pp 18–19.   [18] Ibid, p 19.

That passage has been read as indicating that a State may extend the reach of its prescriptive jurisdiction as it chooses, except in circumstances where it can be shown that some rule of international law specifically prohibits it from doing so. A moment's thought will indicate that it is extremely improbable that this is what the Court meant to say. Suppose, for example, that Zimbabwe were to enact a law that made it an offence for anyone, of whatever nationality and wherever in the world they might be, to make a complaint to a UN body alleging that any State had violated its international human rights obligations; and suppose that a British citizen, on holiday in Zimbabwe, was arrested and charged with breaking that law by writing to the UN Human Rights Committee from his home in Birmingham with a complaint that, say, Iraq had violated its obligations.[19] Could it really be supposed that the onus would be upon the UK to prove that some prohibitive rule of international law forbade such exercises of legislative jurisdiction by Zimbabwe?

There are many reasons for thinking that international law does not impose the burden of proof upon those objecting to egregious assertions of jurisdiction over foreigners outside the territory of the legislating State. Two are of particular relevance here. First, in more than a century of objections to exercises of extraterritorial jurisdiction, from the *Cutting* case[20] onwards, there seems to be not a single instance of an objecting State either seeking to prove that there existed a prohibitive rule forbidding the contested exercise of extraterritorial jurisdiction, or indicating that it might consider itself to be under any legal obligation to do so. When States object to exercises of jurisdiction, they simply assert that the other State has 'no right' to exercise jurisdiction in the way that it claims. State practice is consistently based upon the premise that it is for the State asserting some novel extraterritorial jurisdiction to prove that it is entitled to do so. Secondly, the argument in favour of the alleged presumption of freedom is fallacious. In the *Lotus* case the Court argued that:

> International law governs relations between independent States. The rules of law binding upon States therefore emanate from their own free will as expressed in conventions or by usages generally accepted as expressing principles of law and established in order to regulate the relations between these co-existing independent communities or with a view to the achievement of common aims. Restrictions upon the independence of States cannot therefore be presumed.[21]

Even if the characterization of international law as fundamentally consensual is accepted, it does not follow that a sovereign State is free to do what it wishes. The sovereign equality of States is equally a fundamental principle of international law. Claims by one State to prescribe rules for persons in another State encroach upon the right of the State where those persons are based to exercise jurisdiction itself over those persons within its territory.

There are two States—two 'co-existing independent communities'—involved, and there plainly can be no presumption that the one asserting extraterritorial jurisdiction is entitled to prevail in the event of a conflict, and to impose its laws on persons within the territory of another State.

The best view is that it is necessary for there to be some clear connecting factor, of a kind whose use is approved by international law, between the legislating State and the conduct that it seeks to regulate. This notion of the need for a linking point, which has been adopted by some prominent jurists,[22] accords closely with the actual practice of States. If

---

[19] An extreme example: Zimbabwe has not, as far as I know, enacted any such law. The USA, however, has enacted a law in somewhat similar terms: see n 68.

[20] *Foreign Relations of the United States*, 1887, p 751; 1888, II, pp 1114, 1180.

[21] *'Lotus'*, Judgment No 9, 1927, PCIJ, Ser A, No 10, p 18.

[22] See the discussion in *Attorney-General of the Government of Israel* v *Adolf Eichmann* (1961), 36 ILR 5.

there exists such a linking point, one may presume that the State is entitled to legislate; if there does not, the State must show why it is entitled to legislate for anyone other than persons in its territory and for its nationals abroad (who are covered by the territorial and the national principles respectively).

There are two of these linking points, or 'Bases of jurisdiction', or 'principles of jurisdiction' (the terms mean the same thing) that are firmly established in international law: territoriality and nationality.

A. THE TERRITORIAL PRINCIPLE

The territorial principle is a corollary of the sovereignty of a State over its territory. That sovereignty entails the right of the State to prescribe the laws that set the boundaries of the public order of the State. It is taken for granted that foreign visitors to a State are bound by the State's criminal law in the same way as everyone else in the State. It may be less obvious, but it is no less true, that States may impose the entirety of their laws—economic, social, cultural, or whatever—upon everyone within their territories. In practice, States generally exercise this power with moderation. While the basic principle is that everyone within the territory is equally obliged to obey the law, those laws may be drafted so as to exempt people who are merely visiting the State from certain obligations, such as obligations to pay income tax or to perform compulsory military service (and equally, so as to exclude them from certain rights, such as the right to vote, or to social security payments). Exactly how and where these lines are drawn is a matter for each State to decide, subject to its treaty commitments and its duty to respect basic human rights.

The 'territory' of the State includes not only its land territory but also both its territorial sea, which extends up to 12 n. miles from its coast, and the airspace above its land and sea territory. States may thus legislate for ships off their coasts, and for aircraft in their skies. It was the latter right that entitled the UK to prosecute the Libyan nationals accused of blowing up a US aircraft in the skies above Lockerbie, Scotland, in 1988. Again, in practice States usually leave the prescription of rules applicable on board ships or aircraft to the State of registry of the craft,[23] asserting jurisdiction only in exceptional cases. The routine application of the customs and excise laws of the territorial State is a common exception to this pattern, which is one reason why duty-free sales cease shortly before the craft arrives at its destination. States enjoy 'plenary' jurisdiction over their territory. That is to say, subject to their duties under human rights laws and similar constraints, they may legislate as they please, on any matter whatsoever. At sea, States enjoy an additional but functionally limited jurisdiction.

Beyond the 12 n. mile territorial sea they may claim a 12 n. mile contiguous zone, in which they can exercise jurisdiction in relation to customs, fiscal, sanitary, and immigration matters, and also in order to safeguard submarine archaeological sites. Subject to certain limitations, they may also assert jurisdiction over the exploration for and exploitation of living and non-living resources (such as fish and oil) and energy, over the establishment of artificial islands and structures, and over pollution and scientific research, in an Exclusive Economic Zone (EEZ) that extends up to 200 n. miles from the coast. And they may assert full civil and criminal jurisdiction over installations, such as oil rigs, set up on their continental shelves or in their EEZs in order to exploit seabed resources. These zones that lie beyond the territorial sea are not part of the territory of the State; but the coastal State is permitted to exercise limited jurisdiction in them, in contrast to the position on

[23] See, for example, the handling of the problem of drunks on aircraft: (2003) 74 *BYIL* 681.

the high seas (and in outer space) where, in principle, craft and those on board them are subject to the jurisdiction only of the State of registry (the 'flag' State).[24]

Most acts, most bank robberies, weddings, and daily struggles to earn a living, take place squarely within the territory of a single State. The territorial principle is entirely adequate to sustain jurisdiction over such acts. Indeed, in the domestic law of many States there is a presumption that the State's laws, in particular its statutes, apply throughout the State's territory but not outside that territory, unless there is clear indication that the law is intended to apply outside the territory. Some acts, however, straddle more than one jurisdiction. The Lockerbie bomb is said to have been loaded aboard the aircraft in Malta, before it entered the UK; the September 11th attacks are said to have been planned and prepared by people in a number of different countries. Which State has jurisdiction? One solution would be to allow each State to exercise jurisdiction over the particular fragment of the greater scheme that was located within its territory: one State might prosecute the offence of loading a bomb on board an aircraft, another the offence of causing an explosion on board an aircraft, another murder, and so on. Whatever theoretical tidiness might be preserved by such an approach, it has no practical merits to commend it. It is more efficient if the investigation and prosecution of an offence is concentrated largely in the hands of a single State. That is what States in fact do. Territorial jurisdiction has spawned two variants to cope with such situations. They are commonly known as subjective territorial jurisdiction and objective territorial jurisdiction.

1. Subjective territorial jurisdiction

'Subjective territorial jurisdiction' is the name given to the exercise of prescriptive jurisdiction by a State in circumstances where it applies its law to an incident which is initiated within its territory but completed outside its territory. The prosecution for murder of bombers by the State in which they put the bomb on board an aircraft, even though the bomb exploded in the airspace of another State, is an example.

2. Objective territorial jurisdiction

'Objective territorial jurisdiction' is the name given to the exercise of prescriptive jurisdiction by a State in circumstances where it applies its law to an incident that is completed within its territory, even though it was initiated outside its territory. The prosecution for murder of bombers by the State in whose airspace a bomb on board an aircraft exploded, even though the bomb had been loaded onto the aircraft in another State, is an example. The *Lotus* case is another example. Ships (and aircraft) are treated for jurisdictional purposes much as if they are pieces of floating territory of the State of registration, although they are, in law, quite clearly not parts of the State's territory. The act of the *Lotus* in colliding with the Turkish ship was, therefore, an act completed within Turkish territorial jurisdiction—literally, within the Turkish ship—and accordingly liable to be prosecuted by the Turkish authorities.

Both subjective and objective territorial jurisdiction are routinely asserted by States, in order to secure the application of their laws to all elements of offences that they wish to prosecute. In English law, examples include *DPP v Doot*,[25] *DPP v Stonehouse*,[26] and *Liangsiriprasert v Government of the United States of America*.[27]

---

[24] See the UN Convention on the Law of the Sea, 1982, Articles 2, 33, 56, 60, 92, 303. For the case of ships having no nationality, see, for instance, *United States v Bravo*, 480 F.3d 88 (2007). Developments have been anticipated in relation to jurisdiction over activities in outer space with the emergence of private travel in that realm. See Hobe, 2007; Blount, 2007.   [25] *DPP v Doot* [1973] AC 807; [1973] 1 All ER 940 (HL).

[26] *DPP v Stonehouse* [1978] AC 55; [1977] 2 All ER 909 (HL).

[27] *Liangsiriprasert v Government of the United States of America* [1991] 1 AC 225; [1990] 2 All ER 866 (PC).

3. The 'effects' doctrine

Exercises of subjective territorial jurisdiction have not proved problematic; but the same cannot be said for exercises of objective territorial jurisdiction. There is little difficulty with cases where distinct physical elements of the overall crime take place within the jurisdiction of different States. But some States, notably the USA, have sought to extend the concept much further. The clearest example of this is the so-called 'effects' doctrine, developed first in the context of US antitrust law. In the *Alcoa* case, *US* v *Aluminium Co of America*,[28] the USA asserted jurisdiction over the conduct of a non-US company that was a member of a cartel whose activities were intended to affect imports to or exports from the USA, and actually did so. The significance of the decision was that it did not depend upon the commission of physical acts within US territory: the intentional production of economic 'effects' within the USA was sufficient.

This idea reached what is perhaps its fullest expression in the *Uranium Antitrust* litigation, which surfaced in the English courts in *Rio Tinto Zinc Corp* v *Westinghouse Electric Corp*.[29] There, uranium producers in a number of States, including the UK, formed, with the knowledge or encouragement of their national governments, a cartel, primarily in order to maintain the world market price of uranium. This was in response to a protectionist US law that had effectively shut them out of the US market, which amounted to more than two-thirds of the world market. Meanwhile, Westinghouse, a US company, had contracted to sell uranium to a public utility in the USA, at a price set some years earlier, but needed to buy the uranium on the world market. The cartel's success in maintaining the market price of uranium was such that Westinghouse could not afford to fulfil the contract. Westinghouse was sued for $2bn; and it in turn sued some members of the cartel for $6bn, under a provision of US antitrust law that allows those injured by cartels to recover treble damages. Here, US law was to be applied to non-US companies, in respect of their acts outside the USA, at a time when they were forbidden by US law to trade in the USA. The only jurisdictional link was the 'effect' of the cartel upon the USA: there was no intraterritorial conduct in the USA at all. It is the reliance upon economic repercussions within the territory, rather than upon some element of intraterritorial conduct, that distinguishes the 'effects' doctrine in its pure form from objective territorial jurisdiction, which does require some intraterritorial conduct. The assertion of extraterritorial jurisdiction by the USA in this case was met with strong protests from many other States.

It is sometimes said that other States also assert jurisdiction on the basis of the 'effects' doctrine. There is some truth in this. States such as France and Germany, and the EC in cases such as *Woodpulp*,[30] have adopted laws or decisions that appear to involve such an assertion; but on a closer inspection it is clear that such laws are usually applied only in circumstances where there is some element of intraterritorial conduct. In cases where environmental pollution in one State causes physical damage in the territory of another, the jurisdiction of the latter in respect of the matter may be analysed in terms of objective territorial jurisdiction, rather than the 'effects' doctrine.[31]

---

[28] *United States* v *Aluminium Co of America*, 148 F.2d 416 (1945).
[29] *Rio Tinto Zinc Corp* v *Westinghouse Electric Corp* [1978] 1 All ER 434 (HL); and see Lowe, 1983.
[30] *Ahlström Osakeyhtiö* v *Commission*, Cases 89/85 [1988] ECR 5193. See also *InnoLux* v *European Commission*, Case C-231/14P, [2015] 5 CMLR 13; Chan, 2015. In relation to India, see Chaudhry and Mahajan, 2011; Jain, 2012.   [31] Cf Ellis, 2012.

B. THE NATIONAL PRINCIPLE

States have an undisputed right to extend the application of their laws to their citizens (that is, those who have the nationality of the State), wherever they may be. This type of jurisdiction has a longer history than jurisdiction based upon the territorial principle. Rulers asserted jurisdiction over those who owed allegiance to them even before the rulers' control over their land territory was consolidated to the point where they could be said to assert territorial jurisdiction. Nonetheless, the advent of the European territorial State as the paradigmatic unit of the international legal order has long since given territorial jurisdiction pre-eminence. Jurisdiction based on nationality is used relatively infrequently.

States are in principle left free to decide who are their nationals, and to lay down the conditions for the grant of nationality in their own laws. One common basis for this has been to accord nationality to anyone born in the territory; except, perhaps, in cases where the mother's presence is merely transient—for example, as a passenger on a ship or aircraft transiting the State's territory. This basis of nationality is sometimes known as the *jus soli*. Another common basis is to accord nationality to children one or both of whose parents are themselves nationals of the State. This is sometimes known as the *jus sanguinis*. The nationality law of a State may apply a combination of variations of both of these principles.[32] States also commonly provide for the conferral of nationality by naturalization, the process in which those who fill whatever residential and other requirements the State may lay down apply to become nationals of the State. States typically also provide for the circumstances in which nationality is lost. For instance, a State's nationality legislation may provide that a person will cease to be a national of that State if they apply for and are granted the nationality of another State, and may provide for the possibility of voluntary renunciation of nationality. It is not uncommon for people to have two nationalities, one derived from the nationality of their parents, the other from the place where they were born, or one nationality that they acquired at birth and another that they subsequently obtained by naturalization. Such people are known as 'dual nationals'. Some people may have three, or even more, nationalities.

The nationality of companies is also a matter for each State to determine under its own laws; but here the practice is more complex. As the International Court noted in the *Barcelona Traction* case,[33] there is a divergence in State practice. Broadly speaking, there is a tendency for common law States to accord nationality to companies on the basis of their incorporation in the territory of the State, regardless of where the actual business or management of the company is carried out. In contrast, at least some civil law States confer their nationality not on the basis of the place of incorporation but rather on the basis of the place where the company has the seat of its management. As companies may be formally incorporated in one State for tax reasons, but maintain their actual business or management elsewhere, this is a significant point. In contrast to individuals it seems that companies cannot change their nationality, for example by naturalization. They can only achieve a comparable result, by dissolving the company and transferring all of its assets and responsibilities to a new company in another State. This is, however, more a matter of corporate succession than of a change of nationality.

The freedom of States to fix the conditions for the grant of nationality extends also to ships and aircraft. The same is true of comparable structures, such as offshore oil rigs

---

[32] See, for instance, the British Nationality Act 1981, s 1 (acquisition by birth or adoption), s 2 (acquisition by descent).

[33] *Barcelona Traction, Light and Power Company, Limited, Second Phase, Judgment, ICJ Reports 1970*, p 3.

(which appear to be regarded as having the nationality of the State of registry while they are in transit, even though they fall under the jurisdiction of the coastal State while they are actually operating on the continental shelf). Typical conditions might include a requirement that the vessel operates from a home port in the State, or has a certain proportion of the owners, or perhaps of the crew, having the nationality of the State. In this respect, many States tend to be more restrictive in granting nationality to ships and aircraft than they are in granting nationality to companies.

This freedom to determine nationality is not absolute. The existence of limitations upon the international effectiveness of grants of nationality was discussed by the International Court in the *Nottebohm* case,[34] which is sometimes supposed to be authority for the proposition that a genuine and close link between the individual and the national State is necessary if nationality is to be effective: ie if other States are to be obliged to accept it as an adequate basis for the State to treat the individual as its national. The Court did not say that. It did hold that nationality should, in principle, be the juridical expression of a close factual link between the individual and the national State. But the Court was not concerned with the effectiveness of nationality in general, but only with the much narrower issue of its effectiveness as the basis for diplomatic protection. The Court was not even concerned with the general question of the right of a national State to exercise diplomatic protection. The Court limited itself to the particular question whether a State with which a naturalized citizen has no real links can exercise diplomatic protection on behalf of the citizen against another State with which the citizen, while not a national of that State (Nottebohm was not a dual national), does have close and real links. The decision was, accordingly, of no relevance whatever to the question of the efficacy of nationality for jurisdictional purposes. Indeed, as Nottebohm had himself chosen to become a naturalized citizen of a State, Liechtenstein, with which he had no real links, it is difficult to see any ground on which Liechtenstein could be denied the right to impose its laws upon Nottebohm in accordance with the nationality principle.

One may also note that on the one occasion, post-*Nottebohm*, when the International Court was invited to rule that grants of nationality not underpinned by some close factual connection with the putative national State were ineffective, it did not do so, but instead reaffirmed that it is for each State to fix the conditions for the grant of its nationality.[35] There are, no doubt, limits to this freedom. The mass imposition of nationality upon unwilling people, or nationality obtained by fraud or corruption, or a nationality acquired for vessels in order to circumvent legal regulations based upon the nationality of ships, for example, might in certain circumstances be held not to be effective. For practical purposes, however, States remain free to decide who are their nationals. (It should also be noted that it is arguable that the exercise of legislative jurisdiction based upon nationality is not a matter for international law at all. The way that a State treats its nationals is—questions of human rights apart—in general not a matter for international law. If a State were to legislate for persons who were indisputably its nationals, who could complain?)

In practice, States now rarely exercise legislative jurisdiction specifically on the basis of nationality.[36] They tend to do so in order to prohibit serious offences which not only disturb the peace of the place where they are committed, but also signal a characteristic of the offender in which the national State has an interest. For example, a State would plainly

---

[34] *Nottebohm, Second Phase, Judgment, ICJ Reports 1955*, p 4.

[35] See the *Constitution of the Maritime Safety Committee of the Inter-Governmental Maritime Consultative Organization, Advisory Opinion, ICJ Reports 1969*, p 150.

[36] But see, for instance, *United States v Clark*, 435 F.3d 1100 (2006). For an argument that nationality jurisdiction should be used more frequently see Arnell, 2001.

have an interest in forbidding its nationals to engage in bribery of officials of other countries while abroad, or to commit sexual crimes abroad.[37] A State might also for instance decide to tax its citizens resident abroad on their income earned abroad.[38]

There is an increasing tendency for States to extend the extraterritorial application of their laws not only to nationals but to residents, in order to make the repression of serious crimes more effective. The UK's Crime (International Co-operation) Act 2003 introduced such provisions into ss 63B and 63C of the Terrorism Act 2000.[39] States may also apply their own laws (including human rights law) to extraterritorial acts of their own governmental authorities, or persons contracted by or under the authority of their own governmental authorities.[40]

C. THE PROTECTIVE PRINCIPLE

It has long been recognized that when essential interests of the State are at stake States need to, and will, act in order to preserve themselves. Accordingly, when vital issues are threatened, even if by non-nationals acting outside the territory of the State, the State's interests are engaged and it may exercise its legislative jurisdiction over them.[41] The counterfeiting of a State's currency is a typical example, as is an extraterritorial conspiracy to evade the State's immigration laws.

The category of vital interests is not closed. The USA has asserted jurisdiction over foreigners on the high seas on the basis of the protective principle, in cases such as *US v Gonzalez*,[42] and in statutes such as the 1986 Maritime Drug Law Enforcement Act (see Murphy, 2003).[43] It argues that the illegal trade in narcotics constitutes so severe a threat to US society that the protective principle allows this extension of its jurisdiction. Other States have acquiesced in this US move; but they have tended not to follow it but rather to extend their jurisdiction by means of treaty arrangements concerning the suppression of unlawful drug trafficking.

The rationale of the protective principle is clearly linked to the protection of vital State interests. Accordingly, while the category is not closed, the potential for its expansion is limited. Whereas States could, in principle, apply any law that they might choose to their nationals, by no means every law could be given extraterritorial scope under the protective principle. That is why offences against, for example, a State's competition laws are not prosecuted on the basis of this principle but are instead explained as applications of the territorial principle or the 'effects' doctrine. That said, the overblown rhetoric with which

---

[37] See the examples in n 39 in this chapter.   [38] The USA adopts this approach.

[39] See for instance the UK's Bribery Act 2010, extending the criminal provisions of that Act to persons having a 'close connection' with the UK, defined as persons with different types of British nationality, British subjects, British protected persons, UK residents, bodies incorporated in the UK, and Scottish partnerships. A similar example is the US Foreign Corrupt Practices Act §78dd-2, applying the Act extraterritorially to US 'domestic concerns', defined to include US citizens, residents, and corporations. See also the UK Sexual Offences Act 2003, ss 9, 72, which have application in relation to UK residents as well as UK citizens. See also Ratner, 2003. Cf Arnell, 2001, p 984. See also, for instance, *XYZ v The Commonwealth* [2006] HCA 25 (High Court of Australia).

[40] See, for instance, *Al-Skeini and Others v the United Kingdom* [GC], no 55721/07, ECHR 2011; (2011) 53 EHRR 18 ; *Al-Jedda v the United Kingdom* [GC], no 27021/08, ECHR 2011; 53 EHRR 23; *Smith v Ministry of Defence* [2013] UKSC 41, [2013] 3 WLR 69; cf *R v Hape* 2007 SCC 26; [2008] 1 LRC 551; 143 ILR 140; *Munaf v Geren* 553 US (2008); *United States v Passaro*, 577 F.3d 207 (2009); *R (Smith) v Oxfordshire Assistant Deputy Coroner* [2010] UKSC 29; [2011] AC 1. See also Ryngaert, 2008.

[41] See for instance German Criminal Code, Section 5.   [42] *US v Gonzalez* 776 F.2d 931 (1985).

[43] See also for instance *US v Reumayr*, 530 F.Supp 2d 1210 (2008), 1221–2 and the cases there cited; *US v Yousef*, 327 F.3d 56 (2003), 110–11.

governments from time to time describe their attempts to combat various 'threats' to the State, or to civilized values or to the world order or whatever, must take their toll. The pressure to expand the use of this principle, and the danger of unshackling it from the protection of truly *vital* interests and of permitting its use for the convenient advancement of important interests, is clear.

D. THE UNIVERSAL PRINCIPLE

Some crimes are regarded as so heinous that every State has a legitimate interest in their repression. That is the traditional explanation of universal jurisdiction.[44] But given that the first, and one of the most firmly established, of the instances of crimes covered by the universal principle is piracy, one may wonder if the traditional explanation is entirely satisfactory.

It is probably more accurate to say that there are two strands running together to make up the universal principle. One is the strand that is indeed made up of heinous crimes, such as genocide, crimes against humanity, and serious war crimes,[45] all of which are subject to universal jurisdiction.[46] The second is crimes that are serious, and which might otherwise go unpunished. Piracy—which means simply an unauthorized act of violence or depredation committed by a private vessel on the high seas against another vessel, for private ends—may involve relatively minor uses of force; and not every act of piracy can properly be described as heinous. Yet for centuries, piracy was covered by universal jurisdiction, but murder, armed robbery, rape, and arson on land, which could surely be equally heinous, were (and are) not. The justification for universal jurisdiction over pirates is not so much that piracy is inherently heinous, and on a par with genocide and war crimes, as the fact that because pirates operate on the high seas it is very easy for them to evade the jurisdiction of any State that might have jurisdiction over them on some other basis (for example, the flag State of their ship, or their national State), unless any State that happens to have them within its jurisdiction is entitled to try them.[47]

This point is not trivial. One might argue that the principle could be extended to justify assertions of jurisdiction over others who commit serious crimes in places beyond the territorial jurisdiction of the State. Crimes committed in Antarctica would be one example (which the USA has in fact addressed by making certain acts, such as murder, committed by or against US nationals in Antarctica, subject to US jurisdiction).

Universal jurisdiction has undergone something of a renaissance in recent years.[48] Belgium is one of a number of States that have enacted laws providing for universal jurisdiction over particularly serious offences such as war crimes (see Reydams, 2003a). In the *Arrest Warrant* case[49] the Democratic Republic of the Congo complained that Belgium

---

[44] See, eg, *US v Yunis*, 681 F.Supp 896 (1988); *Arrest Warrant of 11 April 2000 (Democratic Republic of the Congo v Belgium), ICJ Reports 2002*, p 3; (2002) 41 ILM 563.

[45] The catalogue of crimes subject to universal jurisdiction is not yet definitively enumerated: for the view that it does not include terrorism, see *US v Yousef*, 327 F.3d 56 (2003) at 108.

[46] The extent to which crimes are subject to universal civil jurisdiction, in addition to universal criminal jurisdiction, may be an emerging issue: see, for instance, Donovan and Roberts, 2006.

[47] See again the *Yunis* case (n 44). See further Goodwin, 2006. For a recent practical example of jurisdictional issues relating to piracy, see, for instance, Treves, 2009. The same argument might apply to any ship on the high seas that is without any nationality: compare *United States v Bravo* 480 F.3d 88 (2007).

[48] See *The Princeton Principles on Universal Jurisdiction* (2001), and the *Cairo-Arusha Principles on Universal Jurisdiction in Respect of Gross Human Rights Offences* (2002). However, the resurgence has not been without criticism: see, for instance, Jalloh, 2010.

[49] *Arrest Warrant of 11 April 2000 (Democratic Republic of the Congo v Belgium), ICJ Reports 2002*, p 3.

had issued a warrant for the arrest of the DRC's acting Minister of Foreign Affairs, Mr Yerodia, charging him with provoking massacres of Tutsi civilians, contrary to the Belgian War Crimes Act. There were no links between Belgium and the alleged offence or offender. The case was decided on grounds of the Foreign Minister's immunity, but some of the Separate and Dissenting Opinions discuss the validity of Belgium's claim to universal jurisdiction. The Opinions differ, but are mostly supportive of Belgium's claim.[50] However, the Belgian law on universal jurisdiction was repealed in 2003. The overlap between crimes of universal jurisdiction and treaty-based extensions of jurisdiction is considered further in the next section.

E. TREATY-BASED EXTENSIONS OF JURISDICTION

If the territorial principle, in all its variants, is overwhelmingly the most important principle in the day-to-day application of a State's laws, much the most important basis for the assertion of extraterritorial jurisdiction is now the large, and constantly growing, network of treaties in which States cooperate to secure the effective and efficient subjection to the law of offences of common concern.

Most of these treaties follow the same broad pattern. A particular offence or range of offences is defined. For example, Article 1 of the 1971 Montreal Convention for the Suppression of Unlawful Acts against the Safety of Civil Aviation (which was at the centre of the *Lockerbie* case in the International Court of Justice)[51] states that a person commits an offence if he unlawfully and intentionally performs an act of violence against a person on board an aircraft in flight if that act is likely to endanger the safety of that aircraft, or if he commits certain other specified acts. The Convention then goes on to require all States parties to make such acts punishable by severe penalties and to assert their jurisdiction over such offences if they are committed in certain specific circumstances, including offences committed in the territory of the State or on board an aircraft registered in the State, and offences committed in cases where the aircraft lands in the State's territory with the alleged offender still on board. Most significant of all is the obligation to provide for jurisdiction over offences in every case where the alleged offender is *found* within the State's territory, regardless of the offender's nationality or of the place where the offence was committed. This is a crucial element in what is often known as the *aut dedere, aut judicare* provision, which stipulates that in every case where an alleged offender is found within the State's territory the State must either extradite that person to face trial in another State that seeks the person for the purposes of prosecution (and for this purpose, the Convention offences are deemed by the Convention to be included in the lists of extraditable crimes that appear in any extradition treaties that may be in force between the two States), or if it does not extradite, it must submit the case to its competent authorities for the purpose of prosecution. In *Questions relating to the Obligation to Prosecute or Extradite*,[52] the International Court found that Senegal had breached such an obligation found in Article 7 of the 1984 Torture Convention.

---

[50] See also for instance *Jorgic v Germany*, no 74613/01, ECHR 2007-III; (2008) 47 *EHRR* 6, paras 25, 48–54, 67–9; *Ould Dah v France* (Dec), no 13113/03, ECHR 2009; (2013) 56 *EHRR* SE17.

[51] See *Questions of Interpretation and Application of the 1971 Montreal Convention arising from the Aerial Incident at Lockerbie, Provisional Measures, Orders of 14 April 1993, ICJ Reports 1992*, pp 3, 114; 94 ILR 478; *Preliminary Objections, Judgment, ICJ Reports 1998*, pp 9, 115; 117 ILR 1.

[52] *Questions relating to the Obligation to Prosecute or Extradite (Belgium v Senegal), Judgment, ICJ Reports 2012*, p 442.

Thus, the aim is to ensure that alleged offenders do not escape prosecution; and the Convention does this in part by creating what is in essence a form of universal jurisdiction as between the parties (O'Keefe, 2004). (It is, strictly speaking, only applicable between the parties. In theory, if an alleged offender was prosecuted for an offence outside the territory of, and not on an aircraft registered in, the prosecuting State, and the national State of the alleged offender was not a party to the Convention, it could object to the assertion of jurisdiction over its citizen. There do not appear to have been any such protests, however.)

There are many conventions that follow a similar pattern, most of them designed to counter various forms of terrorist activity or internationally organized crime. Some, such as the 1979 International Convention Against the Taking of Hostages, have introduced a different, wider range of circumstances in which States parties must establish their jurisdiction over offences defined in the convention. The 1979 Hostages Convention stipulates that States parties must establish their jurisdiction over convention offences committed: in the State's territory, or on board a ship or aircraft registered in the State; or by any of its nationals (and, if the State considers it 'appropriate', also by any stateless persons who have their habitual residence in its territory); or 'in order to compel that State to do or abstain from doing any act'; or with respect to a hostage who is a national of that State, 'if that State considers it appropriate'. The last two circumstances are particularly interesting.

In the last circumstance, jurisdiction is based on the nationality of the victim, a ground often known as the 'passive personality' principle, which will be discussed later in this chapter. It would allow a State to prosecute someone who took one of that State's citizens hostage in a foreign State. The other extension of jurisdiction, to States which are the target of the hostage-taker's pressure, would allow, for example, Israel to prosecute someone who took a non-Israeli Jew hostage in order to bring pressure upon Israel—a scenario similar to the hijacking of the *Achille Lauro* in 1985,[53] in which a Jewish US citizen was killed as part of a campaign to pressurize Israel. Striking as such bases of jurisdiction might be, in the context of the treaty their effect is less dramatic. The general *aut dedere, aut judicare* principle requires the State to prosecute *every* alleged offender found within its territory, if it does not extradite the person. The law of States parties must therefore provide for jurisdiction over offenders whether or not the offence was committed within the State's territory or ships or aircraft, or by or against a national of the State, or in order to compel the State to do something. The broad grounds of treaty jurisdiction are all in effect swallowed up within the quasi-universal jurisdiction that the *aut dedere, aut judicare* principle requires. What the treaty regime does add, however, is a clear entitlement of States whose links with the offence fall within one of the specified grounds to seek the extradition of the alleged offender.[54] The treaty provisions have the important practical effect of extending the range of States acknowledged as having a legitimate interest in the prosecution of the alleged offender.

These treaty-based extensions of jurisdiction have induced some parallel developments in the unilateral practice of States. For example, after the 1985 *Achille Lauro* incident, the USA followed the broad approach of these international treaties by enacting the 1986 Omnibus Diplomatic Security and Anti-Terrorism Act, which asserted jurisdiction over physical attacks on US citizens outside the USA. (It is interesting to note

---

[53] See (1985) 24 ILM 1509. See also Cassese, 1989.

[54] In the case of an *aut dedere, aut judicare* provision in a human rights treaty for alleged violations of which there is a right of individual complaint, a victim of an alleged human rights violation may also be able to complain that the State in which the alleged perpetrator is present has failed to extradite or prosecute: see for example *Guengueng et al v Senegal*, Committee Against Torture, Communication No 181/2001, decision of 19 May 2006, CAT/C/36/D/181/2001.

that this development was recorded in the *Cumulative Digest of United State Practice in International Law 1981–88* under the heading 'Jurisdiction Based on Universal and Other State Interests'—an indication of an increasingly robust approach to extraterritorial jurisdiction over terrorists.)

There is a discussion as to the extent to which instances of the principle of *aut dedere, aut judicare* are not merely treaty-based extensions of jurisdiction, but a part of customary international law (so that the obligation will apply to all States, whether or not the State is a party to a treaty which may merely reflect what is in any event a rule of customary international law).[55] Even in cases where the principle of *aut dedere, aut judicare* may not apply, there is still the question as to the extent to which customary international law still permits States to exercise criminal jurisdiction over crimes committed outside its territory by persons who are not its nationals, in exercise of the principle of universal jurisdiction.

For instance, the Statute of the International Criminal Court (ICC) gives that international court jurisdiction over genocide, war crimes, and crimes against humanity, as set out in that statute. Some of those crimes also fall within the scope of earlier international treaties (such as the Geneva Conventions and Torture Convention), such that these crimes are subject to the principle of *aut dedere, aut judicare* by virtue of those earlier treaties. However, although the ICC Statute embodies a principle of 'complementarity' (the effect of which is that the ICC will deal with crimes within its jurisdiction only where national authorities are unwilling or unable to do so), it does not itself contain an express principle of *aut dedere, aut judicare*, nor does it expressly provide that States have universal jurisdiction over such crimes. Nevertheless, various States have adopted legislation implementing the ICC Statute domestically, giving their national authorities and national courts some type of universal jurisdiction over such crimes.[56] Some States may even permit universal jurisdiction to be exercised in respect of conduct committed outside its territory where the alleged offender who is not a national of that State is not even present in that State, so that an exercise of universal jurisdiction requires a request for that person's extradition.[57] Other States have adopted more restrictive solutions.[58]

Some States appear to consider that unfettered exercises of universal jurisdiction may lead to difficulties in practice. In 2003 the Belgian legislation was amended so that prosecutions of serious violations of international humanitarian law committed extraterritorially require a link connecting the violations with Belgium, as the State exercising jurisdiction.[59] In 2011, the UK legislated to require the consent of the Director of Public

[55] See International Law Commission, Fourth report on the obligation to extradite or prosecute, Zdzislaw Galicki, Special Rapporteur, 31 May 2011, A/CN.4/648.

[56] For instance, the relevant national legislation in Australia, Canada, Germany, Netherlands, and New Zealand.

[57] For instance, Spain sought the extradition from the UK of former Chilean President Pinochet in respect of charges of crimes committed primarily in Chile: see *R v Bow Street Metropolitan Stipendiary Magistrate, ex parte Pinochet Ugarte (No 3)* [2000] 1 AC 147, discussing universal jurisdiction under the Torture Convention. In the *Arrest Warrant* case (n 49 in this chapter), Belgium had issued an international arrest warrant for the former Minister for Foreign Affairs of the Democratic Republic of the Congo.

[58] For instance, the UK International Criminal Court Act 2001, especially ss 51, 58, 68, extends jurisdiction to UK citizens and residents, persons subject to UK service jurisdiction, as well as 'a person who commits acts outside the United Kingdom at a time when he is not a United Kingdom national, a United Kingdom resident or a person subject to UK service jurisdiction and who subsequently becomes resident in the United Kingdom'.

[59] See Reydams, 2003b. See also *Jiménez Sánchez and ors v Gibson and ors*, Appeal Judgment, No 1240/2006; ILDC 993 (ES 2006) (Spain, Supreme Court, Criminal Chamber) (but compare the earlier decision of the Spanish Constitutional Tribunal in the *Guatemala Genocide* case (2006) 100 *AJIL* 207). Such a link might be the nationality or residence of the victim or the presence of the accused person in the territory of the State exercising jurisdiction.

Prosecutions for private prosecutions to be brought in respect of specified international crimes.[60] A Spanish court has also suggested that universal jurisdiction should be exercised only where the territorial State and the ICC fail to act.[61]

In addition to universal criminal jurisdiction, in the USA the Alien Tort Statute (ATS or Alien Tort Claims Act) permits civil claims by aliens for damages in tort for 'violation of the law of nations or a treaty of the United States'.[62] Over the last decades numerous civil claims have been brought under this legislation in US courts, against defendants who are not US citizens in respect of conduct committed outside the USA in alleged breach of international law, in particular international criminal law or human rights law. However, in *Kiobel* v *Royal Dutch Petroleum Co*, the US Supreme Court held that the presumption against extraterritoriality applies to claims under the Alien Tort Statute, and that it did not in that case permit relief for violations of the law of nations occurring outside the USA. The Supreme Court said in that case that 'there is no indication that the ATS was passed to make the USA a uniquely hospitable forum for the enforcement of international norms'.[63] While the Supreme Court thereby significantly reduced the scope of the ATS, it is too early to know exactly to what extent. The court stated in its conclusion that 'even where the claims touch and concern the territory of the USA, they must do so with sufficient force to displace the presumption against extraterritorial application' and that for this purpose 'it would reach too far to say that mere corporate presence suffices'.[64] As Justice Alito said in a concurring opinion, 'This formulation obviously leaves much unanswered'. Whether the 'touch and concern' test will prove to be something similar to the 'effects' doctrine discussed earlier, or something much narrower, remains to be seen.

F. CONTROVERSIAL BASES OF PRESCRIPTIVE JURISDICTION

The bases of jurisdiction described in the preceding section are generally accepted in State practice. There are certain other bases that have been advanced by States from time to time, which have not found general acceptance. These are instances of States considering that the link between them and the conduct that they seek to regulate is sufficient to warrant the exercise of prescriptive jurisdiction. The objections of other States, however, operate to preclude the emergence of a 'general practice accepted as law' and the consequent establishment of the claimed basis of jurisdiction in customary international law.

1. Passive personality

One of the oldest controversial bases of prescriptive jurisdiction is the so-called 'passive personality' principle: that is, the principle that would allow the national State of the victim of an offence to assert prescriptive jurisdiction. That principle lay behind the controversy that arose in 1885 when Mr AK Cutting, a citizen of the USA, was imprisoned in Mexico and charged with having libelled a Mexican citizen in a paper published in the USA. In his annual address to Congress in 1886, President Grover Cleveland recalled that the incident 'disclosed a claim of jurisdiction by Mexico novel in our history, whereby any offense committed anywhere by a foreigner, penal in the place of its commission, and of which a Mexican is the object, may, if the offender be found in Mexico, be there tried and punished in conformity with Mexican laws'. He went on to say that '[t]he admission of

---

[60] Police Reform and Social Responsibility Act 2011, s 153. Cf *Re Gorbachev*, City of Westminster Magistrates Court (2011) 82 *BYIL* 570.

[61] *Peruvian Genocide Case*, Spain, Supreme Court, 20 May 2003, 141 ILR 720.

[62] See for instance Henner, *Human Rights and the Alien Tort Statute* (2009).

[63] *Kiobel* v *Royal Dutch Petroleum Co*, 133 S Ct 1659 (2013), p 12.   [64] Ibid, p 14.

such a pretension would be attended with serious results, invasive of the jurisdiction of this Government and highly dangerous to our citizens in foreign lands. Therefore I have denied it and protested against its attempted exercise as unwarranted by the principles of law and international usages.' It is a perfect example of a protest against an excessive jurisdictional claim. It will be noted that the USA assumed that the burden lay upon Mexico to prove its entitlement to exercise jurisdiction in this way; no attempt was made by the USA to establish a 'prohibitive rule' of the kind that is sometimes said to be required by the *Lotus* case.

Claims to jurisdiction based upon the passive personality principle have continued to be made. For example, in 1975 the USA again had cause to protest against assertions of passive personality jurisdiction, on that occasion by Greece.[65] There is, however, a trend in favour of accepting it. As one of the Separate Opinions in the *Arrest Warrant* case noted, '[p]assive personality jurisdiction, for so long regarded as controversial . . . today meets with relatively little opposition, at least so far as a particular category of offences is concerned.'[66] The qualification is important. Passive personality jurisdiction is indeed widely tolerated when used to prosecute terrorists. Whether it would be as acceptable if used to prosecute, for example, adulterers and defamers is another matter.

2. National technology

One of the most imaginative, and least successful, attempts to extend the scope of legislative jurisdiction was made by the USA in the 1980s. In the course of its attempts to prohibit trade with the Soviet Union, following the imposition of martial law in Poland, the USA made it a criminal offence for anyone, regardless of their nationality or State of residence, to export to the Soviet Union goods that contained more than a certain proportion of components of US origin or which had been created using US technology. This was an attempt to assert jurisdiction on the basis of the 'nationality' of technology (a concept unknown in international law); and it was vigorously resisted by the European States whose nationals bore the brunt of the prohibition. The main European protest appears in the Comments of the European Community dated 12 August 1982.[67] Again, however, the refusal of other States to accept the right of the USA unilaterally to impose its law on anyone who handles US technology has not prevented the acceptance of that basis of jurisdiction on an agreed basis in international treaties. For example, States appear to have been willing to conclude agreements relating to transfers of nuclear materials, under which the consent of the supplying State is required in the event of subsequent transfers of the material.

3. Unprincipled assertions of jurisdiction

From time to time, States are tempted to assert an extended extraterritorial jurisdiction in a manner that appears to be almost totally unprincipled. One of the most startling examples is to be found in the US Military Order of 13 November 2001, concerning the detention at a US base, Guantánamo Bay in Cuba, of 'international terrorists' seized by the USA in Afghanistan. Section 7 of that Order stipulates, in relation to detained individuals, that:

> the individual shall not be privileged to seek any remedy or maintain any proceeding, directly or indirectly, or to have any such remedy or proceeding sought on the individual's behalf, in (i) any court of the United States, or any State thereof, (ii) any court of any foreign nation, or (iii) any international tribunal.[68]

---

[65] See the *Digest of United States Practice in International Law 1975*, p 339.

[66] *Arrest Warrant of 11 April 2000 (Democratic Republic of the Congo v Belgium), ICJ Reports 2002*, p 3, Joint Separate Opinion of Judges Higgins, Kooijmans, and Buergenthal, p 11; *Lozano v Italy*, Appeal Judgment, Case No 31171/2008; ILDC 1085 (IT 2008) 24 July 2008. [67] (1982) 21 ILM 891.

[68] 66 FR 57831.

It is not clear whether this curiously drafted Order was intended to prevent the making of applications to bodies such as the Inter-American Commission of Human Rights;[69] but insofar as it is intended to forbid non-US citizens to make such applications, it is difficult to see that even the protective principle could be stretched so far as to justify this provision, even if it were otherwise compatible with the USA's international obligations.

G. INADEQUACIES OF THE TRADITIONAL APPROACH

The traditional approach to the bases of jurisdiction is beset by considerable difficulty in practice. Two problems stand out. First, the problem of locating acts; and second, the problem of reconciling conflicts when two or more States have concurrent jurisdiction.

1. The difficulty of locating acts

The territorial principle, both in its plain form and its objective and subjective variants, presupposes that it is clear *where* an act is committed; but that is far from always the case. Take, for example, the case of the hijacking of an aircraft. If control over an aircraft registered in State A is seized while the aircraft is in the airspace of State B, is the hijack 'committed' (or, rather, *still being* committed) when the aircraft lands in State C? And, to take another example, suppose that individuals in States L and M conspire by fax, telephone, and e-mail to import narcotics into State K, but that only one of them ever sets foot in State K. Could each of States K, L, and M assert jurisdiction over the entire conspiracy and all of the participants?[70]

As a matter of domestic law (the law under which the accused will, of course, be tried), it is evident that much will depend upon the particular way in which the crime with which they are charged is defined. The English courts have distinguished between 'conduct' crimes and 'result' crimes, the former focusing upon what is actually done and the latter upon the consequences of what is done, in a manner that lends itself respectively to the application of the subjective and objective variants of territorial jurisdiction.[71]

While such approaches may be sufficient to enable national courts to overcome any difficulties that they may have in determining the reach of the laws that they have to apply, it does not answer the question whether the jurisdictional reach asserted in those laws is in conformity with international law. Indeed, the drafting of national laws may aggravate the problem. It is quite possible to redraft every offence so as to make it a crime to enter the State having done *x*, *y*, or *z* before entry. For example, the customs laws of some Commonwealth States made it an offence for ships to enter the territorial sea *having broken* a bulk cargo into smaller parcels on the high seas (such breaking being almost invariably the prelude to smuggling of goods ashore). Was that an extension of the State's jurisdiction onto the high seas? Or was it an assertion of jurisdiction over acts that took place within the State's territory? A slightly different issue was raised in the 1920s by the US Prohibition Law, which sought to forbid the importation of alcohol into the USA. That law was applicable to foreign cruise ships entering US ports from the high seas. Did that therefore mean that the US was forbidding those ships to carry alcohol on the high seas? That was certainly the practical effect of the enforcement of the Prohibition Law; but was it the proper juridical characterization of that law?

There is no clear theoretical answer to this problem. As usual, however, there is much to be said for falling back on common sense. Where other States consider that the

---

[69] To its credit the Inter-American Commission acted anyway: see (2002) 41 ILM 532. So did the US Supreme Court: see *Rasul* v *Bush*, 542 US 466 (2004).   [70] See further Blackmore, 2006.
[71] See the cases referred to in nn 25–27 of this chapter; Hirst, 2003.

jurisdictional claim has gone too far—as they did in relation to the application of the Prohibition Law to foreign cruise ships,[72] but not in relation to the laws on the breaking of bulk cargo—they will protest. Those protests generally hold jurisdictional claims within reasonable bounds. If other States choose to acquiesce in the claim, it will become established in customary law.[73]

There was much speculation that the internet would lead to near-unimaginable difficulties concerning jurisdiction. In fact international law appears to have accommodated crimes in cyberspace with barely the flicker of a monitor: the regime under the 2001 Council of Europe Convention on Cybercrime[74] is based upon the traditional territorial and national principles of jurisdiction. However, issues remain, and are likely to increase as technology evolves.[75]

2. The difficulty of overlapping jurisdiction

All of the examples cited in the previous section in fact involve overlapping jurisdiction: that is, more than one State can make out a claim on the basis of established principles of international law to apply its laws to the conduct in question. That is why the cases are problematic: it is unlikely that a State will complain about the assertion of jurisdiction over an individual unless there is some other State that might more appropriately assert jurisdiction. In the 'Prohibition' cases, for example, the protesting European States thought it right that the flag State, and not the State of each port at which a cruise ship might call, should decide whether or not the ship could carry alcohol on board.[76]

Instances of 'overlapping', or 'concurrent', jurisdiction give rise to the question of priority. If the applicable laws diverge, which is to prevail? In some cases it may appear clear which law is to yield. There is a considerable body of practice supporting the view that a State may not require anyone outside its territory to do an act that would violate the criminal law of the place where the act would be done. Thus, courts in the USA allow what is sometimes known as the 'foreign sovereign compulsion' defence. For example, the court may excuse a failure to produce documents in pursuance of an order of the court, if the failure results from a prohibition on disclosure under the criminal law of the State where the documents are located.[77] (This defence is not available in circumstances where the duty of non-disclosure arises under the civil, rather than the criminal, law of the territorial State.)[78]

Some States have sought to utilize the foreign sovereign compulsion defence by enacting laws that oblige persons in their territory to do or not to do certain things. For instance, the UK enacted the Protection of Trading Interests Act 1980 (a more powerful successor to the Shipping Contracts and Commercial Documents Act 1964), under which the Secretary of State may order any person in the UK not to comply with orders from

---

[72] The dispute was largely settled by an accommodation in the series of bilateral 'Liquor treaties' made with the USA.
[73] For an application of acquiescence as a basis for jurisdiction see *US* v *Suerte*, 291 F.3d 36 (2002), *Digest of United States Practice in International Law 2002*, p 133.
[74] ETS No 185; 41 ILM 282 (2002). See Article 22.1.d.
[75] See, for instance, Svantesson, 2017; Bigos, 2005; Schultz, 2008; Levin, Doran, and Maria, 2012; Narayanan, 2011–12 (who considers the possible solutions to State jurisdiction over cloud computing to include extraterritorial application of domestic regulations, international cooperation, harmonization, and a sort of 'law of the cyber sea'). See also the *Tallinn Manual on the International Law Applicable to Cyber Warfare*, 2013, 15–26.
[76] Compare that situation with the case of *US* v *Neil*, 312 F.3d 419 (2002), *Digest of United States Practice in International Law 2002*, p 131. [77] See, eg, *Société Internationale* v *Rogers*, 357 US 197 (1958).
[78] See, eg, *US* v *First National City Bank*, 396 F.2d 897 (1968).

a foreign court for the production of evidence or, indeed, with substantive orders made on the basis of extraterritorial jurisdiction by a foreign State. The powers under the Act were invoked in 1982 in order to forbid British businesses to comply with US orders not to supply goods to the Soviet Union for use in connection with the construction of the Siberian gas pipeline, during the so-called 'pipeline' dispute[79]—an unusual example of one NATO State making it a criminal offence to comply with the law of another NATO State in respect of dealings with the Soviet Union during the Cold War. Similar laws, often known as 'blocking' statutes, have been adopted by a number of other States including Australia, Belgium, Canada, Denmark, Finland, France, Germany, Italy, Japan, the Netherlands, New Zealand, Norway, the Philippines, South Africa, Switzerland, and—the most dramatic measure of all—the European Community.[80]

Blocking statutes are no solution to jurisdictional conflicts. Quite apart from the fact that they represent a degree of friction in the international system that inevitably impairs its efficiency, they do nothing to overcome the problem of what might be called 'prudential compliance'. Even though an extraterritorial measure may be patently unlawful as a matter of international law, and though it is possible that a person may at some point be ordered not to comply with it, the risk of the legislating State imposing sanctions for non-compliance is so great that anyone caught by the extraterritorial claim must, if they are prudent, organize their affairs so as to comply with the law. European businesses, for example, often organize transactions so as to comply with US law, even though the USA may have no legitimate claim to jurisdiction over them; and the converse is increasingly true of US companies in relation to EU law.

Jurisdictional disputes continue to arise, though their forms change. Thus, in 1996 the USA enacted laws providing for sanctions against Cuba (the Helms-Burton Act) and against Iran and Libya (the D'Amato Act). Those laws contained a range of extraterritorial measures, including the imposition of sanctions upon non-US businesses which purchased, in good faith and for full value, property in Cuba that had been confiscated in the 1960s from US owners who had not been compensated for the takings. These measures provoked a strong response from the European Community, resulting in an uneasy stand-off when the full implementation of the American laws was suspended.[81]

The States that claim extraterritorial jurisdiction are by no means always and wholly insensitive to the views of other States. US courts, in particular, have developed what they call the 'balancing of interests' approach to jurisdiction of conflicts. This approach has a number of variants, which may be seen in the leading cases such as *Timberlane*, *Mannington Mills*, and *Hartford Fire Insurance*.[82] Broadly speaking, under this approach the court considers the nature and extent of the USA's interest in having its law applied, and the interests of the other State in not having US law applied, and also factors such as the nationalities of the parties involved and the nature of their links with the USA. It then decides whether, on balance, it is right to apply US law or to exercise judicial restraint. Not surprisingly, it is practically invariably decided to apply US law. Nonetheless, there is no doubt that judges in US courts are now more sensitive to the constraints of international law and the demands of international comity than they were in the 1960s and 70s.[83]

---

[79] See the symposium in (1984) 27 *German Yearbook of International Law* 11–142. Cf Killman, 2004.

[80] See European Community Council Regulation (EC) 2271/96, published in (1996) OJ L309. For other measures, see Lowe, 1983.   [81] See Lowe, 1997.

[82] The cases are discussed in *Hartford Fire Insurance Co v California*, 509 US 764;113 S Ct 2891 (1993); and Lowenfeld, 1995.

[83] See the decision of the Supreme Court in *F Hoffmann-La Roche Ltd v Empagran SA*, 542 US 155; 124 S Ct 2359 (2004).

There are more satisfactory approaches to a solution to jurisdictional conflicts than uni-lateral restraint and blocking statutes. Sometimes States may be able to harmonize their policies[84] so that even though their jurisdictional claims may overlap, individuals affected by those laws are not subjected to conflicting demands. Sometimes, States may be able to establish consultation procedures in order to seek to eliminate on a case-by-case basis extraterritorial applications of laws which would cause difficulty for the State in whose territory the regulated conduct occurs. A good example of this is the antitrust cooperation procedure established by the European Community and the USA.[85] Such steps have, in re-cent years, done much to defuse disputes over jurisdiction, which are now somewhat less common and less acute than they were in the 1980s—though whether this trend is any-thing more than temporary remains to be seen. Ultimately, however, it must be recognized that jurisdictional conflicts are conflicts over the right to prescribe the rules that make up the public order of the State. Whatever solution is adopted, it must be a solution that ensures the right of every State, as an equal sovereign, to decide for itself upon the precise nature of that public order, to the extent that it can do so without invading and subverting the right of other States to do likewise.

III. THE FUNDAMENTAL PRINCIPLE GOVERNING ENFORCEMENT JURISDICTION

In contrast to the principles governing the exercise of prescriptive jurisdiction, the inter-national law governing the exercise of enforcement jurisdiction is clear and simple. There is one basic principle: enforcement jurisdiction may not be exercised in the territory of any other State without the consent of that State. In other words, enforcement jurisdiction is in principle limited to the territory of the State concerned. (In fact, those two proposi-tions are not precisely the same: there are areas outside the territory of a State that do not fall within the territory of another State—for example, the high seas, and the exclusive economic zones of other States.)

One particular application of this principle is that the courts of one State will generally not enforce the public laws of another. 'Public laws', in this context, means not only crimi-nal laws but also laws relating to matters such as taxation, that are quintessentially mani-festations of the State's sovereign power, rather than laws that lay down the ground rules for the creation of rights and duties between individuals, in the way that, say, contract, family, and land law do. The most difficult laws to classify on this basis are tort laws. These are in some respects private, but may also be viewed as laws by which the State prescribes rules of conduct for society, in the same way that it does in its criminal law, but leaving the enforcement of those rules up to private parties. This dual nature of tort law is most evident in US antitrust laws, where those injured by unlawful anticompetitive practices are enabled to recover treble damages, as an incentive to act as 'private attorneys general' in the enforcement of the laws. For that reason, English courts have refused to enforce US antitrust laws.[86]

---

[84] For instance, through international treaties, or measures adopted in the context of regional organizations such as the EU: see, for instance, Mitsilegas, 2009.

[85] EC-US Agreement on the Application of Positive Comity Principles in the Enforcement of their Competition Laws, OJ L173 of 18 June 1998.

[86] See the submissions of the Attorney-General in *Rio Tinto Zinc* v *Westinghouse Corp* [1978] AC 547 (HL). Cf *Lewis* v *Eliades* [2003] EWCA Civ 1758.

It is unusual, but not unknown, for one State to give another permission to exercise enforcement jurisdiction in its territory. Perhaps the most significant agreements of this kind in recent years are the so-called 'ship rider' agreements made, for example, by the USA with a number of Caribbean States, under which US navy vessels may in certain circumstances enter the territorial seas of the other party in order to pursue and arrest vessels suspected of being engaged in the illicit traffic in narcotic drugs. Similar agreements have been prepared on a multilateral basis in order to facilitate international action against narcotics traffic and (in the 2005 amendments to the 1988 Convention for the Suppression of Unlawful Acts Against the Safety of Maritime Navigation) against terrorism.

Ordinarily, where an alleged offender who is sought for the purposes of prosecution is within the territory of another State, the State that seeks that person must request the State where he is found to surrender him or her. Many States are, under their own domestic law, bound not to surrender individuals except in accordance with an extradition agreement that is in force with the requesting State. In addition, some States are bound under their own law not to surrender their nationals to foreign States under any circumstances. There is a rich body of international law and practice concerning the interpretation and application of extradition treaties, but shortage of space precludes its discussion here.

It is not unknown for States to attempt to obtain custody of alleged offenders without going through the formalities of extradition procedures—or, indeed, any other formalities. For example, individuals are sometimes simply transported over national borders into the hands of law-enforcement officers on the other side. This appears, for example, to have been the way in which many members of the European terrorist organizations such as the Red Brigades and the Baader-Meinhof Gang were moved around Europe in the 1970s. On occasion, States have gone further, and themselves seized wanted persons from the territory of another State.[87] Such actions patently violate the territorial sovereignty of the State from which the persons are seized. If that State should retrospectively 'consent' to the seizure, that may cure the illegality; alternatively, the State may declare that it does not intend to pursue the question of the violation, and will regard the matter as closed. This seems to have happened, for instance, in relation to the seizure, apparently by agents of the government of Israel, of Adolf Eichmann from Argentina. Initially unaware of Eichmann's abduction, the government of Argentina subsequently agreed to abandon its claim for reparation for the violation of its territorial sovereignty.

What is the position if a State seizes an accused person, in violation of territorial sovereignty of another State, and then puts that person on trial in its own courts? As a matter of international law, one might say that the subsequent trial compounds the violation of the other State's territorial sovereignty; and even if that State acquiesces, as Argentina did in the trial of Eichmann, there is at least the possibility that the national State of the abducted individual might complain that its rights, too, have been violated. As far as the individual is concerned, the position is less clear. In some States the illegality of the abduction may, as a matter of the domestic law of the State, preclude the trial of the individual. In most States, however, it is likely that the illegality of the abduction will be regarded as a matter to be handled by the Executive, if and when the State from which the defendant is taken complains, but not a matter that the trial court needs to take into account. So, for example, in the USA the most egregious violation of international law appears to be insufficient to constitute a bar to the trial of the abducted defendant: even the sand-bagging of suspects and the smuggling of their comatose bodies back to the USA was held to be no obstacle to their trial before a US court, on the curious ground that the individuals did not enjoy

---

[87] Or tried to ship them abroad in wooden crates: see the two episodes noted in Harris, 2004, p 369.

the protection of US Constitutional safeguards while they were outside US territory.[88] The English courts adopt a somewhat different approach. Having long taken the view that it was no concern of the court how the defendant happened to have arrived before it, in more recent years the courts have moved towards the view that the forcible abduction of defendants in violation of agreed procedures may be so serious as to amount to an abuse of process, in which case their trial should not proceed.[89] Such a finding will, however, be unusual, and be made only where the British police or prosecuting authorities have themselves acted illegally or colluded in unlawful procedures in order to secure the presence of the defendant in the UK, or have violated international law or the law of a foreign State or otherwise abused their powers.[90]

IV. CONCLUSION

This chapter has surveyed, albeit briefly, the principles of international law governing exercises of legislative and enforcement jurisdiction. These are truly principles, and not rules. The difficulties of applying the principles rigidly have been noted, and are implicit in the nature of jurisdiction. It is not possible to devise strict rules that would divide jurisdiction between sovereign States in any practical manner. The solution to jurisdictional problems has to be found by increasing the sensitivity of States to the constraints imposed by international law, and also to the fact that the interests of other States demand respect. It should be clear that if in any case the exercise by one State of its jurisdiction threatens to subvert the laws that another State has enacted to regulate life in its own territory, in the exercise of its sovereign right to choose how to organize life within its borders, the boundaries of lawful jurisdiction have been over-stepped. If States wish to do more than they are able to do within the limits of the jurisdiction allowed to them, they must first seek the agreement and cooperation of other States.

REFERENCES

AKEHURST, M (1972–3), 'Jurisdiction in International Law', 46 *BYIL* 145–217.

ARNELL, P (2001), 'The Case for Nationality-Based Jurisdiction', 50 *ICLQ* 955.

AUST, AI (2000), 'Lockerbie: The Other Case', 49 *ICLQ* 278.

BIGOS, O (2005), 'Jurisdiction over Cross-boundary Wrongs on the Internet', 54 *ICLQ* 585.

BLACKMORE, JDA (2006), 'The Jurisdictional Problem of the Extraterritorial Conspiracy', 17 *Criminal Law Forum* 71.

BLOUNT, P ET AL (2007), 'Jurisdiction in Outer Space: Challenge of Private Individuals in Space', 33 *Journal of Space Law* 299.

CASSESE, A (1989), *Terrorism, Politics and The Law* (Cambridge: Polity Press).

---

[88] See *US v Toscanino*, 500 F.2d 267 (1974); *US v Verdugo-Urquidez*, 494 US 259 (1990); *US v Alvarez-Machain*, 504 US 655,112 S Ct 2188 (1992). Cf *Sosa v Alvarez-Machain*, 542 US 692 (2004).

[89] *Bennett v Horseferry Road Magistrates' Court* [1994] 1 AC 42; [1993] 3 All ER 138 (HL). And see the South African case of *State v Ebrahim* (1992) 31 ILM 888.

[90] *R v Staines Magistrates Court, ex parte Westfallen* [1998] 4 All ER 210.

CHAN, A (2015), 'InnoLux Corp v European Commission: Establishment of the Effects Doctrine in Extra-territoriality of EU Competition Law?', 36 *European Competition Law Review* 463.

CHAUDHRY, S and MAHAJAN, K (2011), 'The Case for an Effective Extraterritorial Competition Commission of India in Light of International Practices', 32 *European Competition Law Review* 314.

CRAWFORD, J (2012), *Brownlie's Principles of Public International Law* (8th edn, Oxford: Oxford University Press).

DONOVAN, D and ROBERTS, A (2006), 'The Emerging Recognition of Universal Civil Jurisdiction', 100 *AJIL* 142.

ELLIS, J (2012), 'Extraterritorial Exercise of Jurisdiction for Environmental Protection: Addressing Fairness Concerns', 25 *Leiden JIL* 397.

GOODWIN, J (2006), 'Universal Jurisdiction and the Pirate: Time for an Old Couple to Part', 39 *Vand J Transnat'l L* 973.

HALL, W (1895), *A Treatise on International Law* (5th edn, Oxford: Clarendon Press).

HARRIS, DJ (2004), *Cases and Materials on International Law* (6th edn, London: Sweet & Maxwell).

HENNER, P (2009), *Human Rights and the Alien Tort Statue* (Chicago: American Bar Association).

HIRST, M (2003), *Jurisdiction and the Ambit of the Criminal Law* (Oxford: Oxford University Press).

HOBE, S et al (2007), 'Space Tourism Activities: Emerging Challenges to Air and Space Law', 33 *Journal of Space Law* 359.

JAIN, A (2012), 'Extraterritorial Jurisdiction of Competition Commission of India', 19 *Journal of Financial Crime* 112.

JALLOH, C (2010), 'Universal Jurisdiction, Universal Prescription? A Preliminary Assessment of the African Union Perspective on Universal Jurisdiction', 21 *Criminal Law Forum* 1.

KILLMAN, E (2004), 'Enforcement of Judgments and Blocking Statutes', 53 *ICLQ* 1025.

LEVIN, D, DORAN, S, and MARIA, LA (2012), 'Megaupload and Criminal Charges', 4 *Revista Española de Relaciones Internacionales* 23.

LOWE, V (1983), *Extraterritorial Jurisdiction* (Cambridge: Grotius).

LOWE, V (1997), 'US Extraterritorial Jurisdiction: The Helms-Burton and D'Amato Acts', 46 *ICLQ* 378–90.

LOWENFELD, A (1995), 'Conflict, Balancing of Interests, and the Exercise of Jurisdiction to Prescribe: Reflections on the *Insurance Antitrust Case*', 89 *AJIL* 42.

MILLS, A (2014), 'Rethinking Jurisdiction in International Law', 84 *BYIL* 187.

MITSILEGAS, V (2009), 'The Third Wave of Third Pillar Law. Which Direction for EU Criminal Justice?', 34 *European Law Review* 523.

MURPHY, S (2003), 'Extraterritorial Application of US Laws to Crimes on Foreign Vessels', 97 *AJIL* 183.

NARAYANAN, V (2011–12), 'Harnessing the Cloud: International Law Implications of Cloud Computing', 12 *Chi J Int'l L* 783.

O'CONNELL, DP (1970), *International Law* (2nd edn, London: Stevens).

O'KEEFE, R (2004), 'Universal Jurisdiction: Clarifying the Basic Concept', 2 *Journal of International Criminal Justice* 735.

OPPENHEIM, L (1992), JENNINGS, SIR R, and WATTS, SIR A (eds), *Oppenheim's International Law* (9th edn, Harlow: Longman).

RATNER, S (2003), 'Belgium's War Crimes Statute. A Postmortem', 97 *AJIL* 888.

REYDAMS, L (2003a), *Universal Jurisdiction: International and Municipal Legal Perspectives* (Oxford: Oxford University Press).

REYDAMS, L (2003b), 'Belgium Reneges on Universality: The 5 August 2003 Act on Grave Breaches of International Humanitarian Law', 1 *Journal of International Criminal Justice* 679.

RYNGAERT, C (2008), 'Litigating Abuses Committed by Private Military Companies', 19 *EJIL* 1035.

SCHULTZ, T (2008) 'Carving up the Internet: Jurisdiction, Legal Orders, and the Private/Public International Law Interface', 19 *EJIL* 799.

SVANTESSON, DJB (2017), *Solving the Internet Jurisdiction Puzzle* (Oxford: Oxford University Press).

TREVES, T (2009), 'Piracy, Law of the Sea, and Use of Force: Developments off the Coast of Somalia', 20 *EJIL* 399.

TWISS, SIR T (1884), *On the Rights and Duties of Nations in Times of Peace* (Oxford: Clarendon Press).

VERHOEVEN, J (2000), *Droit International Public* (Bruxelles: Larcier).

FURTHER READING

Curiously, there is no satisfactory modern monograph on jurisdiction. There are, however, some good articles that discuss the basic principles of jurisdiction in international law in the light of the various disputes that have arisen over the years:

AKEHURST, M (1972–73), 'Jurisdiction in International Law', 46 *BYIL* 145.

BOWETT, DW (1982), 'Jurisdiction: Changing Patterns of Authority over Activities and Resources', 53 *BYIL* 1.

LOWE, V (1981), 'Blocking Extraterritorial Jurisdiction: The British Protection of Trading Interests Act, 1980', 75 *AJIL* 257.

LOWE, V (1985), 'The Problems of Extraterritorial Jurisdiction: Economic Sovereignty and the Search for a Solution', 34 *ICLQ* 724.

MANN, FA (1964–I), 'The Doctrine of Jurisdiction in International Law', 111 *Recueil des Cours* 1.

MANN, FA (1984–III), 'The Doctrine of International Jurisdiction Revisited after Twenty Years', 186 *Recueil des Cours* 9.

SCHLOSSER, P (2000), 'Jurisdiction and International Judicial and Administrative Co-operation', 284 *Recueil des Cours* 9.

11

INTERNATIONAL LAW AND RESTRAINTS ON THE EXERCISE OF JURISDICTION BY NATIONAL COURTS OF STATES

Philippa Webb

SUMMARY

Three restraints—State immunity, act of State, and non-justiciability—are invoked by States to avoid the exercise of jurisdiction by domestic or foreign courts. These three 'avoidance techniques' are underpinned by the idea that States are independent and equal and should therefore not be subject to the jurisdiction of another State, or even their own State if the matter is considered inappropriate for judicial scrutiny. This chapter examines the three doctrines, focusing on the operation of the restrictive doctrine of State immunity. This is an evolving area in which the decisions of national and international courts have a strong influence on the development of international law.

I. OVERVIEW

The principle of the sovereign equality of States is 'one of the fundamental principles of the international legal order'.[1] Respect for sovereign equality results in the obligation of non-intervention in the internal affairs of another State and a prohibition on the settlement of disputes without the consent of all the States involved. At the same time, States are no longer untouchable and various exceptions and limitations on their ability to be held to account are being developed in domestic law, treaty law, and customary international law.

This chapter discusses three techniques for avoiding judicial scrutiny of a foreign State's activities in the 'forum State' (that is, the State where the proceedings are brought). These three 'avoidance techniques' are immunity, act of State, and non-justiciability (see generally, Collins, 2017).

---

[1] *Jurisdictional Immunities of the State (Germany v Italy: Greece Intervening)*, Judgment, ICJ Reports 2012, p 99, para 57. See also Article 2(1) of the United Nations Charter. This chapter has drawn upon the excellent chapter by Lady Hazel Fox QC in previous editions of this textbook.

States have moved from an absolute to an increasingly restrictive approach (with the exception of China).[2] This means that most States recognize exceptions to State immunity related to commercial and private law activities of States. State immunity serves two purposes: first, it prevents the forum court from exercising jurisdiction to inquire further into the claim; and second, it removes the claim to another process of settlement, usually to settlement through diplomatic channels or perhaps to proceedings in the foreign State's own court. Because immunity brings a halt to proceedings it is, from a potential defendant's point of view, the most effective avoidance technique.

The other two techniques—act of State and non-justiciability—may be raised in proceedings where private persons or a foreign State is a party. Act of State is a defence to the substantive law requiring the forum court to exercise restraint in the adjudication of disputes relating to legislative or other governmental acts which a foreign State has performed within its territorial limits. Non-justiciability bars a national court from adjudicating certain issues, particularly international relations between States, due to a lack of judicial or manageable standards for determining them.

II. STATE IMMUNITY

A. DEVELOPMENT OF THE COMMON LAW RELATING TO STATE IMMUNITY

The law relating to immunity in common law jurisdictions first developed in cases involving warships. In the leading case of *The Schooner Exchange* v *McFaddon*,[3] the US Supreme Court rejected a creditor's claim for attachment and ordered the release of a vessel which was undergoing repairs in Philadelphia. The formerly private ship had been seized under a decree of the French Emperor Napoleon and converted into a public armed ship. The court held that a State warship was immune from arrest and process in the courts of another State. Marshall CJ stated the immunity was upon the consent of the territorial State to waive its exclusive jurisdiction. His subtle reconciliation of the territorial State's jurisdiction and the foreign State's independence was expressed as follows:

> This perfect equality and absolute independence of sovereigns and this common interest impelling them to mutual intercourse and an interchange of good offices with each other, have given rise to a class of case in which every sovereign is understood to waive the exercise of a part of that complete exclusive territorial jurisdiction, which has been stated to be the attribute of every nation.[4]

The English Court of Appeal in *The Parlement Belge* applied the ruling in the *Schooner Exchange* more widely to cover all ships of a foreign State regardless of whether they were engaged in public service or trade.[5] The absolute rule, declared in *The Parlement Belge*,

---

[2] *Democratic Republic of the Congo and Others* v *FG Hemisphere Associates LLC* [2011] HKCFA 42.

[3] *The Schooner Exchange* v *McFaddon* (1812) Cranch 116 (US).

[4] The release of the Argentinian warship, the *ARA Libertad*, after its arrest to enforce an outstanding commercial judgment given by both the New York and Ghana courts indicates this continued enforceability of the international law obligation to respect the immunity of a foreign State's warship. See '*ARA Libertad*' (*Argentina* v *Ghana*), *Provisional Measures, Order 15 December 2012, ITLOS Reports 2012*, p 332; 27 September 2013, Agreement between Argentina and Ghana settling the dispute.

[5] *The Parlement Belge* (1879–90) 5 Prob Div 197 (CA); a packet boat owned by the King of the Belgians involved in a collision in the port of Dover was held to enjoy State immunity although at the time it was carrying both royal mail and passengers and merchandise for hire.

treating all acts of a foreign State as immune, continued to be observed in English law and applied by English courts until the 1970s.[6]

By the late 1970s, the restrictive approach to immunity began to emerge. In 1977, the Privy Council in *The Philippine Admiral*[7] reinterpreted *The Parlement Belge*, declaring that it had not laid down the wide proposition that 'a sovereign can claim immunity for vessels owned by him even if they are admittedly being used wholly or substantially for trading purposes'. It rejected a plea of immunity in respect of *in rem* proceedings (ie proceedings for attachment and sale directed against the vessel itself) brought for goods supplied to a vessel operated as an ordinary trading ship in which the Philippine government retained an interest. The next year the Court of Appeal in *Trendtex v Central Bank of Nigeria*[8] rejected immunity in proceedings against the Central Bank of Nigeria for failure to honour a commercial letter of credit.[9] The court was unanimous in its view that the bank, by the terms of its establishment, was an independent entity and not to be treated as part of the State of Nigeria; it held by a majority that English law recognized no immunity in respect of proceedings brought for a commercial activity such as the issue of a letter of credit. In accepting a restrictive doctrine of immunity in the common law—a move which was confirmed by the House of Lords in *I Congreso del Partido*[10]—the English courts were influenced by legal developments elsewhere, such as in the United States (US).

In 1952, the US State Department announced in the Tate letter that in future US policy would follow the restrictive doctrine of State immunity. In 1976, in part responding to the need of commercial banks financing sovereign States' debt to have legal recourse, the US Congress enacted the Foreign Sovereign Immunities Act (FSIA), which was the first legislation to introduce the restrictive doctrine into the common law. Two years later, in 1978, the UK enacted its own State Immunity Act (SIA). The SIA has served as the model for many jurisdictions, including Singapore, Pakistan, and South Africa. The 2004 United Nations Convention on Jurisdictional Immunities of States and their Property (see Section II C) closely followed the SIA in its structure and formulation of exceptions and the UK provided strong support for the negotiation and drafting of the Convention.

B. DEVELOPMENT IN CIVIL LAW JURISDICTIONS

With the increased participation of States in trading activities following the First World War, there was dissatisfaction with the denial of legal redress against States for such commercial activities. Certain civil law countries, especially in Italy, Belgium, and the Egyptian mixed courts, led the way in adopting a restrictive doctrine of immunity. States enjoyed immunity for proceedings relating to acts committed in exercise of sovereign authority (*acta jure imperii*) but not for trading activities or acts which a private person may perform (*acta jure gestionis*). In 1963, in a magisterial decision surveying State practice, bilateral

---

[6] *The Cristina* [1938] AC 485 (HL) per Lord Atkin at 491. Attempts to confine immunity to the central government of the State, or to exclude departments or agencies which enjoyed separate legal personality (*Baccus SRL v Servicio Nacional del Trigo* [1957] 1 QB 438; 28 ILR 160 (CA)), or to treat consent of the State given in an agreement prior to the dispute as constituting waiver of immunity (*Kahan v Pakistan Federation* [1951] 2 KB 1003; 18 ILR 210 (CA)), were all unsuccessful in the English courts.

[7] *The Philippine Admiral* [1977] AC 373; [1976] 1 All ER 78; 64 ILR 90 (PC).

[8] *Trendtex Trading Corporation v Central Bank of Nigeria* [1977] 1 QB 529; [1977] 1 All ER 881; 64 ILR 111 (CA).

[9] A letter of credit is an undertaking given by a bank to pay a certain sum of money on receipt of documents of title and transport relating to a particular consignment of goods; it may be enforced against the bank independently of the solvency or any refusal to pay on the part of the consignor.

[10] *I Congreso del Partido* [1983] 1 AC 244; [1981] 2 All ER 1064 at 1074; 64 ILR 307 (HL).

and multilateral treaties, and legal writing, the German Federal Constitutional Court declared that international law permits a restrictive doctrine of State immunity and that the proper criterion for the distinction between sovereign and private acts is the *nature* of the act, not its purpose. The German court allowed proceedings by a builder to recover the cost of repair carried out on the Iranian Embassy, holding the repair contract to relate to a non-sovereign act and hence not to be immune.[11]

Further support for the restrictive doctrine is found in the 1926 Brussels Convention for the Unification of Certain Rules concerning the Immunities of Government Vessels and its 1934 protocol, providing that State-owned or operated ships used exclusively for non-governmental commercial purposes do not enjoy immunity and are subject to the same legal rights and obligations as ships owned or operated by private persons for the purposes of trade. In 1972, the European Convention on State Immunity (ECSI) was adopted, which introduced a number of exceptions to immunity from adjudication broadly on the restrictive doctrine.

C. SOURCES OF THE INTERNATIONAL LAW OF STATE IMMUNITY, INCLUDING THE 2004 UN CONVENTION

Until 2004, there was no universal international treaty on State immunity. The 1926 Brussels Convention, mentioned earlier and ratified by 29 States, merely removed immunity in respect of State-owned or operated ships and their cargoes engaged in trade. And only eight States (Austria, Belgium, Cyprus, Germany, Luxembourg, Netherlands, Switzerland, and the UK) are parties to the 1972 ECSI. Nor, until 2002, was there any direct ruling on State immunity by an international court.

The position has changed in the past two decades. First, the International Court of Justice has delivered a number of important Judgments on the customary international law relating to immunity:[12] in the *Arrest Warrant of 11 April 2000* the International Court upheld the immunity from criminal jurisdiction of an incumbent Minister for Foreign Affairs accused of inciting genocide;[13] in *Certain Questions of Mutual Assistance in Criminal Matters,* the Court considered the immunity of the Djibouti Head of State and State officials in relation to acts taken by French authorities in course of a criminal investigation;[14] in the *Obligation to Prosecute or Extradite*, it examined the extent to which universal jurisdiction was exercisable against a former Head of State accused of torture who had sought refuge in a third State, Senegal;[15] and in *Jurisdictional Immunities*, it reviewed the law of State immunity in a claim brought by Germany against Italy (with Greece intervening) for the disregard of State immunity by Italian courts in proceedings relating to war damage caused by Nazi Germany during the Second World War.[16] At the time of writing, two cases are pending before the International Court involving questions of immunity: in *Immunities and Criminal Proceedings*, Equatorial Guinea instituted proceedings

---

[11] *Empire of Iran Case*, 45 ILR 57 at 80 (German Federal Constitutional Court, 30 April 1963).

[12] The ICJ case *Certain Criminal Proceedings in France (Republic of the Congo v France)* concerned the immunities of the President and the Minister of the Interior of the Republic of the Congo, but the case was withdrawn at the request of the Republic of the Congo in 2010. See *Certain Criminal Proceedings in France (Republic of the Congo v France), Order of 16 November 2010, ICJ Reports 2010*, p 635.

[13] *Arrest Warrant of 11 April 2000 (Democratic Republic of Congo v Belgium), ICJ Reports 2002*, p 3.

[14] *Certain Questions of Mutual Assistance in Criminal Matters (Djibouti v France), Judgment, ICJ Reports 2008*, p 177.

[15] *Questions relating to the Obligation to Prosecute or Extradite (Belgium v Senegal), ICJ Reports 2012*, p 442.

[16] *Jurisdictional Immunities of the State (Germany v Italy: Greece Intervening), ICJ Reports 2012*, p 99. See Van Alebeek, 2012; Keitner, 2013; McGregor, 2013.

against France, accusing it of violating the immunity from criminal jurisdiction of the Second Vice-President and the legal status of the building which houses the Embassy of Equatorial Guinea in France; and in *Certain Iranian Assets*, Iran has brought proceedings against the US for, *inter alia*, the alleged failure of the latter to respect the immunity of the Iranian Central Bank and other Iranian entities. Various enforcement proceedings have been brought in the US against these Iranian entities pursuant to legislation that makes an exception to the FSIA for 'State sponsors of terrorism', resulting in punitive damages worth billions of dollars.

Second, on 16 December 2004 the UN General Assembly adopted the first international convention on State immunity: the UN Convention on the Jurisdictional Immunities of States and their Property (UN Convention or UNCSI). UNCSI enshrines the restrictive doctrine of State immunity in regard to civil and commercial proceedings in national courts.

At the time of writing, UNCSI was not yet in force. It has 21 parties of the required 30 to enter into force under Article 30 of the Convention. It has nonetheless proved to be influential on the development of the law of State immunity and certain of its provisions are regarded as codifying customary international law (see later).

UNCSI was the culmination of 35 years of work by the International Law Commission (ILC), the Sixth Committee of the UN General Assembly, and the Ad Hoc Committee on Jurisdictional Immunities of States and their Property. Negotiations were difficult at times, and the decades of work on the Convention have been recognized by judges and academic commentators as evidence of where international consensus exists, and where it remains elusive, on certain issues.

Five substantive issues divided States' views on the draft Convention in the 1990s:

(i)   How to define the concept of a State for the purposes of immunity;

(ii)   What the criteria are for determining the commercial character of a contract or transaction;

(iii) The concept of a State enterprise or other entity in relation to commercial transactions;

(iv)   The nature and extent of an exception to State immunity for contracts of employment;

(v)   The nature and extent of measures of constraint that can be taken against State property.

These issues were debated in various Working Groups and in 1999, two more issues were added for consideration:

(vi)   What form the outcome of the ILC's work should take (eg convention, model law, guidelines);

(vii) Whether there is an exception to State immunity for violation of *jus cogens* norms.

In 2002, the Working Group reached compromise solutions on the outstanding issues and published a revised text. It decided that the question of an exception to immunity for violations of *jus cogens* norms was not 'ripe enough' for codification. In 2004, the General Assembly adopted the text as UNCSI.

The starting point of UNCSI is Article 5: 'A State enjoys immunity, in respect of itself and its property, from the jurisdiction of the courts of another State subject to the provisions of the present Convention.' The rest of the Convention can be seen as a means of defining the meaning and exceptions to this principle.

UNCSI is divided into five parts. Part I (Introduction) sets out the use of terms, including the meaning of 'court', 'State', 'commercial transaction'. Article 3 clarifies that UNCSI is without prejudice to the privileges and immunities enjoyed by diplomatic and other missions and persons connected with them, the immunity of heads of State *ratione personae*, and aircraft or space objects owned or operated by a State. Article 4 provides for the non-retroactivity of the Convention.

Part II (General Principles) sets out the rules relating to express waiver, participation in court proceedings by the foreign State, and counterclaims. UNCSI follows the widespread practice of treating separately immunity from adjudication (Part III) and immunity from enforcement (Part IV).

Part III contains eight types of proceedings in which State immunity cannot be invoked. These exceptions are modelled on—but not identical to—the ECSI, the US FSIA, and the UK SIA. The exceptions include commercial transactions, employment contracts, personal injuries and damage to property, ownership, possession, and use of property, intellectual and industrial property, participation in companies, ships in commercial use, and arbitration agreements.

Part IV deals with immunity from measures of constraint in connection with proceedings before a court. It contains separate rules on pre-judgment (Article 18) and post-judgment (Article 19) measures of constraint. Article 21 lists five categories of State property immune from attachment, arrest, or execution. Part V contains miscellaneous provisions and Part VI contains the standard final provisions.

The 21 States parties are mainly from western Europe and the commercially developed parts of the Middle East. But the relatively low number of parties belies its influence as evidence of State practice and *opinio juris* on the law of State immunity. Certain of its provisions have been held by international and national courts to reflect customary international law. Even where a court may doubt the Convention's customary status, reference to UNCSI has become routine in proceedings involving issues of immunity.

UNSCI's provisions are enacted as national legislation by States including Japan, Spain, and Sweden. States may also enact provisions only in part, such as the French 2016 law that draws on UNSCI's Part IV provisions on enforcement measures. Russia, a signatory to the Convention, has a 2016 law that adopts the restrictive doctrine in a manner similar to UNCSI. China, also a signatory, has rejected the presumption that signing the Convention endorses the restrictive doctrine. The Office of the Commissioner of the Ministry for Foreign Affairs has explained in the context of litigation:[17]

> China signed the Convention on 14 September 2005, to express China's support of the . . . coordination efforts made by the international community. However, until now China has not yet ratified the Convention, and the Convention itself has not yet entered into force. Therefore, the Convention has no binding force on China, and moreover it cannot be the basis of assessing China's principled position on relevant issues.
>
> After signature of the Convention, the position of China in maintaining absolute immunity has not been changed, and has never applied or recognized the so-called principle or theory of 'restrictive immunity'.

The UK, another signatory but not a party, has not made any attempt to modify its legislation on State immunity, but the courts have paid careful attention to UNCSI. The general approach has been to examine UNCSI on a provision-by-provision basis (including the *travaux préparatoires*) to assess whether it reflects customary international law. In 2006, Lord Bingham in *Jones* v *Saudi Arabia* cited UNCSI as evidence that there is no exception to State immunity from civil proceedings for violations of *jus cogens* norms such as torture.

---

[17] *Democratic Republic of Congo and others* v *FG Hemisphere Associates LLC* [2011] HKCFA 43.

He observed: 'Despite its embryonic status, this Convention is the most authoritative state-ment available on the current international understanding of the limits of state immunity in civil cases, and the absence of a torture or jus cogens exception is wholly inimical to the claimants' contention'.[18] Lord Hoffmann also found UNCSI relevant, noting that 'It is the result of many years work by the International Law Commission and codifies the law of state immunity'.[19]

In 2017, the UK Supreme Court in Belhaj v Straw; Rahmatullah (No. 1) v Ministry of Defence referred to the words 'interests or activities' in Article 6(2)(b) of UNCSI. The ques-tion was whether these words extended the basis for the indirect impleading of a State beyond a state's property and rights and, if so, whether this represented the 'current con-sensus of nations'.[20] Lord Mance observed that in Jones v Saudi Arabia the question had been about the existence of an exception to immunity from civil proceedings for torture, which was 'a fundamental question which the Convention, however embryonic, could be expected to cover'.[21] However, '[t]o attach equivalent relevance to the use in a Convention with no binding international status of the ambiguous terminology of article 6(2)(b) is to take Lord Bingham's words out of context'.[22] After analysing the travaux of Article 6, Lord Mance concluded that the concept of 'interests' could not be carried so far as to cover 'reputational or like disadvantage' to a State and indirect impleading needed some specifi-cally legal effect on the State.[23]

The European Court of Human Rights has been willing to embrace UNCSI as an expres-sion of customary international law, in particular Article 11 on the employment contract exception to State immunity, and has held that UNCSI (or its specific provisions) reflect customary international law applicable to any State that has not objected to UNCSI's adop-tion;[24] has not objected to the adoption of a specific rule in the ILC Draft Articles;[25] signed UNCSI;[26] or was in the process of ratifying UNCSI.[27]

According to the ECtHR, a state's participation in the negotiation or adoption of UNCSI makes it 'possible to affirm that [a draft Article] applies to the respondent state under customary international law'.[28] In the Oleykinov Judgment, the Court held that Russia ap-pears to have accepted restrictive immunity as a principle of customary international law even prior to its signature of UNCSI by not (persistently) objecting to the 1991 ILC Draft Articles.[29]

The ICJ, in Jurisdictional Immunities, took a more circumspect approach to UNCSI as a reflection of customary international law. The ILC work, negotiations, signing, ratifi-cation, and application of the Convention may constitute evidence of State practice and opinio juris:[30]

---

[18] Jones v Ministry of Interior for the Kingdom of Saudi Arabia and Ors [2006] UKHL 26, Lord Bingham, para 26.

[19] Ibid, Lord Hoffman, para 45.

[20] Belhaj and another v Straw and others; Rahmatullah (No 1) v Ministry of Defence and another [2017] UKSC 3, Lord Sumption, para 195.

[21] Ibid, Lord Mance, para 25.   [22] Ibid.   [23] Ibid, paras 26, 29, 195.

[24] Cudak v Lithuania [GC], no 15869/02, ECHR 2010, paras 66–7; Naku v Lituania and Sweden, no 26126/07, 8 November 2016, para 60.

[25] Wallishauser v Austria, no 156/04, 17 July 2012, para 69.

[26] Oleynikov v Russia, no 36703/04, 14 March 2013, para 67.

[27] Sabeh El Leil v France [GC], no 34869/05, 29 June 2011, para 58.

[28] Cudak v Lithuania [GC], no 15869/02, ECHR 2010, para 67.

[29] Oleynikov v Russia, no 36703/04, 14 March 2013, paras 67–8.

[30] Jurisdictional Immunities of the State (Germany v Italy: Greece Intervening), Judgment, ICJ Reports 2012, p 99, para 55.

In the present context, State practice of particular significance is to be found in the judgments of national courts faced with the question whether a foreign State is immune, the legislation of those States which have enacted statutes dealing with immunity, the claims to immunity advanced by States before foreign courts and the statements made by States, first in the course of the extensive study of the subject by the International Law Commission and then in the context of the adoption of the United Nations Convention. *Opinio juris* in this context is reflected in particular in the assertion by States claiming immunity that international law accords them a right to such immunity from the jurisdiction of other States; in the acknowledgment, by States granting immunity, that international law imposes upon them an obligation to do so; and, conversely, in the assertion by States in other cases of a right to exercise jurisdiction over foreign States.

The ICJ considered Articles 12 (territorial tort) and 19 (immunity from post-judgment measures of constraint) of UNCSI, while carefully noting that the provisions of UNCSI are 'relevant only in so far as their provisions and the process of their adoption and implementation shed light on the content of customary international law'.[31]

In sum, international and national courts have been treating UNCSI as a useful, but not always definitive, starting point for their analysis of the law on State immunity. The belief that the Convention would have a harmonizing effect on law and practice (preambular para 3 of UNCSI) is thus more realistic than the slow rate of ratifications suggests.

D. THE FEATURES OF STATE IMMUNITY

1. The plea as a bar to the judicial power of the forum state in respect of proceedings before a court

The plea of immunity primarily concerns the civil jurisdiction of a State's courts, though the *enforcement* of that power may involve the exercise of criminal jurisdiction (eg arrest, detention, and prosecution of the defendant). The plea does not relate to the *legislative* power of the State—the State's jurisdiction to prescribe laws—which goes more to the plea of non-justiciability and act of State (see later in this chapter).

The main significance of a plea of State immunity relates to its effect upon the jurisdiction of a forum court, whether in criminal, civil, family, or other matters, including administrative tribunals. The position regarding arbitral tribunals is different because they derive their authority directly from the consent of the parties. Given that an arbitral tribunal does not have any means through which to give effect to its award, it falls to the State and its courts to enforce an arbitral award, and the plea of State immunity may have a relevance even as regards arbitral proceedings (see later).

International tribunals

State immunity is not generally a bar to proceedings before an international tribunal where States enjoy equal standing and which is not operated within one State's legal system. Where the authority of the international tribunal derives from a UN Security Council resolution made under Chapter VII which imposes binding obligations on all States, State immunity is no bar to prosecution of a State official. Thus President Milosević of the former Yugoslavia and Prime Minister Kambanda of Rwanda were prosecuted in the International Criminal Tribunals for the former Yugoslavia (ICTY) and the International Criminal Tribunal for Rwanda (ICTR). President Al-Bashir of Sudan is wanted by the

---

[31] Ibid, para 66.

International Criminal Court (ICC) for crimes including genocide. President Taylor of Liberia was held to enjoy no immunity from the jurisdiction of the Special Court for Sierra Leone (SCSL) because that court ruled that 'the principle of State immunity derives from the equality of States and therefore has no relevance to international criminal tribunals which are not organs of a State but derive their mandate from the international community'.[32]

It may be necessary, however, to make a distinction between the accused State official whose claim to immunity will have no force before an international tribunal and the position of the State to which such official belongs when questions of enforcement of the tribunal's orders are concerned. Such distinctions may be particularly relevant in respect of 'mixed' or 'hybrid' courts that combine international and national elements. And, in any event, the effective operation of international tribunals remains dependent on the cooperation of States, as evidenced by the failure of States parties to the ICC to arrest President Al-Bashir when he was on their territory.[33]

2. Waiver of immunity

Immunity may be waived by the defendant State and the forum court will have jurisdiction to proceed against it (or its official or agency or instrumentality). Contemporary law on immunity has broadened the occasions in which waiver may be made, but three conditions remain: (i) that consent to waive the immunity must be given by the State itself, not by the agency or individual performing the sovereign act on the State's behalf; (ii) that its expression be unequivocal and certain; (iii) that waiver of immunity from execution requires a separate waiver from immunity from adjudication.

US law interprets these requirements to permit implied as well as express consent to waive both immunity from jurisdiction and from execution, but waiver of immunity from pre-judgment attachment of a State's property must be by express consent.[34] English law is narrower; it has abandoned the strict requirement that submission be made in the face of the court (to the judge hearing the case), but still requires that waivers to immunity from both jurisdiction and execution be given separately and in writing.[35] Once a waiver is given by, for example, instituting proceedings, it is irrevocable, unless it is revoked in accordance with its own terms or with the consent of the all the parties to the waiver agreement.[36] Waiver of immunity must be distinguished from submission to the jurisdiction of a national court; a general waiver of immunity does not amount to a submission to the jurisdiction of the English courts as required by s 2(1) SIA.[37]

Implied waiver: A State may waive its immunity through its actions rather than words. Section 2 of the UK SIA provides for four ways in which a State may give or be deemed to

---

[32] *Prosecutor* v *Charles Taylor*, Appeals Chamber, No SCSL–2003–01–I, Judgment of 31 May 2004; 128 ILR 239. Liberia initially challenged this decision, filing an application against Sierra Leone before the International Court of Justice asserting that the Special Court was not a UN organ, nor established as an international criminal court, and that the Special Court 'cannot impose legal obligations on States that are not parties to the Agreement between Sierra Leone and the United Nations'. However, in 2006 Liberia requested that he be tried by the Special Tribunal and on 30 May 2012 Taylor was convicted of war crimes and supporting the commission of atrocities committed by rebel forces in the civil war in Sierra Leone. Taylor has lodged an appeal against his 50-year imprisonment sentence.

[33] See Wickremasinghe, Ch 12 of this book.   [34] See US FSIA ss 1605(a)(1), 1610(a)(1) and (d)(1).

[35] Consent that UK law shall apply is not to be regarded as submission to jurisdiction (SIA s 2(2)).

[36] *High Commissioner of Pakistan in UK* v *National Westminster Bank* [2015] EWHC (Ch) holding that waiver by institution of proceedings extends to all subsequent procedural steps and any appeal.

[37] *Svenska Petroleum Exploration AB* v *Government of the Republic of Lithuania & Anor* [2006] EWCA Civ 1529; [2007] 2 WLR 876, confirming [2005] EWHC 2437 (Comm); [2006] 1 All ER 731 (Gloster J).

give consent to proceedings: submission after the dispute, by prior written agreement, by institution of proceedings, or by intervening or 'taking any step in the proceedings' other than to claim immunity or to assert an interest in property in certain cases. Article 8 of UNCSI provides that a State does not waive immunity if its sole purpose was to intervene to invoke immunity or to assert a right or interest in property at issue in the proceedings or if its representative appears as a witness. If a State fails to enter an appearance before a foreign court, this shall also not be interpreted as consent to the exercise of jurisdiction by the court (Article 8(4), UNCSI).

A specific case of implied waiver is where a State enters into an arbitration agreement. 'Arbitration is a consensual procedure and the principle underlying s 9 [SIA] is that, if a State has agreed to submit to arbitration, it has rendered itself amenable to such process as may be necessary to render the arbitration effective.'[38] The key question is whether consent to arbitration also constitutes waiver of enforcement of the award against the State's property either by the courts of the State where the arbitration is held or by courts elsewhere.[39] Most States (including the UK) and the UNCSI (Article 17) limit the scope of the arbitration waiver to the supervisory jurisdiction of a court in support of the arbitration agreement and the arbitral proceedings, and require additional and express waiver for enforcement proceedings (Fox and Webb, 2015, p 397).

3. A procedural plea to the jurisdiction of the court, not an exemption from responsibility

A State's enjoyment of immunity is separate to the question of whether it has committed an internationally wrongful act giving rise to its responsibility. The ICJ has explained that:

[t]he rules of State immunity are procedural in character and are confined to determining whether or not the courts of one State may exercise jurisdiction in respect of another . . . . It regulates the exercise of jurisdiction in respect of particular conduct and is thus entirely distinct from the substantive law which determines whether that conduct is lawful or unlawful.[40]

State responsibility concerns the extent to which the acts of a person, natural or legal, may be attributed to a State, whereas immunity acts as a bar to the acts of one State being subject to the jurisdiction of another. The entitlement to immunity is, therefore, not lost due to the gravity of the alleged injury, its criminal nature under international law, or the lack of alternative means of securing redress.[41] The underlying responsibility of the defendant State remains unaffected by the grant of immunity, even though this may result in no remedy being available and the avoidance of responsibility. Where immunity is waived the claim can, of course, be decided by the application of the law in the ordinary way.

---

[38] *Svenska Petroleum Exploration AB* v *Lithuania and Another* [2006] EWCA Civ 1529; [2007] 2 WLR 876 per Moore-Bick LJ at 913.

[39] *Creighton* v *Qatar*, France Court of Cassation, ch civ.1, 6 July 2000 (see Pingel, 2000), but cf *Commisimpex* v *Republic of the Congo*, No 13–17.751, Court of Cassation, 1st Chamber, 13 May 2015 (holding that waiver of immunity for execution has to be express). In *Orascom Telecom Holding SAE* v *Republic of Chad & Ors* [2008] EWHC 1841 (Comm); 2 Lloyds Rep [2008] 397, para 49 Stanley Burnton J refused to construe a foreign State's submission to arbitration and the signing of terms of reference containing express reference to ICC Rules Article 28(6) to constitute waiver so as to expand the waiver of immunity beyond the commercial purposes exception in SIA s 13(4).

[40] *Jurisdictional Immunities of the State (Germany* v *Italy: Greece Intervening), Judgment of 3 February 2012*, p 99, paras 58, 93.

[41] Ibid, para 101.

4 The nature of the proceedings in the national court

Immunity from civil proceedings

A general rule of immunity from civil jurisdiction subject to exceptions for acts of a private law or commercial nature—the restrictive doctrine—is applied by the majority of States and enshrined in UNCSI. The restrictive doctrine distinguishes between acts undertaken by the foreign State in the exercise of its sovereign authority (*acta jure imperii*)— such as acts of the armed forces, police, diplomatic and political agents, and agencies of the foreign State which continue to attract immunity—and acts of a commercial or private law nature (*acta jure gestionis*), such as the sale of goods, contracts of employment, loans, and financial arrangements which do not attract immunity. See further Section II F on the exceptions to immunity from civil proceedings.

Immunity from criminal proceedings

The immunity of a foreign State in respect of foreign criminal proceedings remains generally absolute (Institut de droit international, 2009). As for State officials, however, there is a strong view that perpetrators of international crimes should not go unpunished. At the same time, the extent to which the House of Lords Judgment in *Pinochet (No. 3)* has established a human rights exception to immunity *ratione materiae* is much less certain.[42] With hindsight, *Pinochet (No. 3)* is beginning to look like the high-water mark for the setting aside of immunity in the face of allegations of grave human rights violations. Nonetheless, the ILC has adopted a Draft Article 7 in its 2017 session, which states that immunity *ratione materiae* shall not apply in respect of the following crimes under international law: crime of genocide, crimes against humanity, war crimes, crimes of apartheid, torture, and enforced disappearance.[43]

E. DEFINITION OF THE STATE FOR THE PURPOSE OF STATE IMMUNITY

There is variation among jurisdictions in how they define 'the State'. The definition of the State is important as regards its own position as a defendant in proceedings and also because the relationship between a separate entity and the State helps determine the extent to which that entity may enjoy immunity.

1. The state

The term 'State' refers to sovereign and independent States, though certain entities may be treated as States even if they lack one or more of the conditions of statehood, such as Vatican City (Fox and Webb, 2015, p 341). The Kurdistan Regional Government of Iraq has been treated as a separate entity, not a State.[44]

2. Constituent units

Constituent units and political subdivisions are treated as separate entities under the SIA and only enjoy immunity when exercising sovereign powers in the accordance with s 14(2)(a) and (b). The SIA does not distinguish between constituent units and political

---

[42] *R v Bow Street Metropolitan Stipendiary, ex parte Pinochet Ugarte (Amnesty International Intervening) (No 3)* [1999] UKHL 17; [2000] 1 AC 147 for which see Fox, 1999. See further Wickremasinghe, Ch 12 of this book and Foakes, 2014.

[43] UN Doc A/72/10 (2017), Chapter VII, Part C.

[44] This was common ground between the parties in *Pearl Petroleum Co Ltd v The Kurdistan Regional Government of Iraq* [2015] EWHC 3361 (Comm).

subdivisions of a federal State. This differs from the US FSIA, which expressly states that political subdivisions are included in s 1603, which defines a 'State' for the purposes of immunity.

3. Separate entity

Under s 14(1) of the UK SIA, the definition of the 'State' does not include reference to separate entities. Separate entities are generally not entitled to immunity from adjudicative jurisdiction and consequently do not enjoy immunity from execution. However, under s 14(2) a separate entity may enjoy immunity 'if the proceedings relate to anything done by it in the exercise of sovereign authority and the circumstances are such that a State would have been so immune'.[45] If a separate entity (other than the central bank or other monetary authority) submits to the jurisdiction of the English court in proceedings where it is entitled to such immunity under s 14(2), it enjoys the same immunity as the State.[46] This requires an English court to engage in an extensive review of the past and present operations of an entity to determine which factor—the extent of the foreign State's control or the functions of the entity in conformity with private law of the forum State—is to prevail.[47]

The US FSIA, on the other hand, treats all instrumentalities and agencies as coming within the definition of the 'State' for the purposes of immunity though subject to some qualifications regarding procedure and enforcement against agency property. Other jurisdictions distinguish between the central organs or departments of government which enjoy immunity and other State agencies. UNCSI, Article 2(1)(b)(iii) defines 'State' as including 'agencies or instrumentalities of the State or other entities, to the extent that they are entitled to perform *and* are actually performing acts in the exercise of sovereign authority' (emphasis added).

When it comes to immunity from enforcement, s 13(2)(b) of the UK SIA provides that the property of the 'State' enjoys immunity from the enforcement of a judgment or award. Under s 14(3), this immunity extends to a separate entity only if it would have been entitled to immunity under s 14(2) if it had not submitted to the jurisdiction of the English court. Otherwise, a separate entity (other than a central bank or monetary authority) does not enjoy immunity from enforcement.[48] Under the FSIA, the approach is more straightforward. The property in the US of a foreign 'State' includes the property of an agency or instrumentality and it is immune, subject to certain exceptions that apply to foreign States in the FSIA (Stewart, 2005).

4. Representatives of the state

In English law, the Court of Appeal in *Propend* held that the word 'government' in SIA, s 14(1) has to be construed as affording to individual employees or officers of a foreign State protection under the same cloak as protected the State itself. The protection afforded to States by the SIA would be undermined if employees or officers of the State could be sued

---

[45] *Kuwait Airways Corporation (No 1)* v *Iraqi Airways Co.* [1995] 1 WLR 1147 (HL).

[46] Fox and Webb, 2015, p 218. Section 13(1)–(4) UK SIA would apply.

[47] See, for example, *Trendtex Trading Corporation* v *Central Bank of Nigeria* [1977] 1 QB 529, where such an exercise was with regard to the separate status of the Central Bank of Nigeria. SIA s 14(4) now provides that the central bank of a State, irrespective of whether it is a department or a separate entity, is to be treated as if it were the State for the purposes of enforcement. See also the Privy Council *La Générale des Carrières et des Mines (Appellant)* v *F.G. Hemisphere Associates LLC* [2012] UKPC 27 which identified a separate entity as 'enjoying a hybrid status' and declared that in determining its status there should be applied a 'strong presumption . . . that its separate status should be respected'.

[48] Dickinson, A (2008), 'State Immunity and State-Owned Enterprises', Report prepared for the Special Representative of the UN Secretary-General on business and human rights, p 16.

as individuals for matters of State conduct in respect of which the State they were serving had immunity.[49] Thus the exceptions which apply to the State are applicable to officers of the State. *Propend* was affirmed by the House of Lords in *Jones v Saudi Arabia*, with the Lords holding that State immunity applied both to an organ (Ministry of the Interior) and to individuals acting in an official capacity. Lord Bingham declared that '[a] State can only act through its servants and agents; and their official acts are the acts of the state; and the state's immunity in respect of them is fundamental to the principle of state immunity'.[50]

In US law, the definition of a 'foreign state' includes 'an agency or instrumentality of a foreign state', which in turn 'means any entity—(1) which is a separate legal person, corporate or otherwise' (FSIA s 1605 (a)–(b)). Conflicting decisions in the federal circuit courts as to whether the definition included 'natural persons' were resolved in 2010 by the Supreme Court determining that, there being no evidence of the intent to include individual officials within the meaning of 'agency or instrumentality', the FSIA had not replaced the common law with respect to the immunity of individual officials, according to which the State Department, on the request of the foreign State, determines whether the official was acting in an official capacity (and so entitled to immunity) or not when undertaking the act in question.[51] In effect, while the conduct of a foreign official might still be construed as an act of the State for which there is no immunity (as it has been lifted by the FSIA), the State officials themselves might enjoy a greater degree of immunity than that of the State itself, including immunity from criminal prosecution for international crimes.[52]

UNCSI Article 2(1)(b) defines 'State' to include 'representatives of the State acting in that capacity'. UNCSI is silent as to whether it applies to the armed forces of a State. However, on introducing the Convention for adoption by the Sixth Committee of the UNGA, the Chairman of the ad hoc committee, Professor Gerhard Hafner, stated his belief that a general understanding had always prevailed that military activities were not covered by the Convention.[53]

F. EXCEPTIONS TO IMMUNITY FROM JURISDICTION

1. The exceptions to immunity from civil jurisdiction of a foreign State

Today there is widespread acceptance that the State immunity from jurisdiction is subject to exceptions, whereas immunity from enforcement jurisdiction remains largely absolute.[54]

---

[49] Cf *Propend Finance Pty v Sing* (1997), 111 ILR 611, affirmed in *Jones v Ministry of Interior for the Kingdom of Saudi Arabia and Ors* [2006] UKHL 26; [2007] 1 AC 270, paras 30, 78.

[50] *Jones v Minister of Interior of Kingdom of Saudi Arabia* [2007] 1 AC 270, para 30.

[51] *Samantar v Yousuf*, 130 S Ct 2278 (2010), 2287–9.

[52] On remand in the *Samantar* case, the Fourth Circuit Court of Appeals, controversially, held the defendant was not entitled to immunity in respect of participation in torture and extrajudicial killing by the governing military regime, holding foreign official immunity did not extend to violations of *jus cogens*, even if the acts were performed in the defendant's official capacity (*Yousuf v Samantar*, 699 F.3d 763 (4th Cir 2012)). In March 2013 the defendant petitioned the Supreme Court to consider whether a foreign official's common law immunity for acts performed on behalf of a foreign State is abrogated if those official acts violate norms of *jus cogens* but this request was subsequently denied. See further Wickremasinghe, Ch 12, Section VI of this book.

[53] He referred to the 1991 ILC Commentary on Draft Article 12 (the exception relating to personal injuries and damage to property), stating it did not apply to situations of armed conflict. Finland, Norway, and Sweden deposited declarations upon ratification excluding military activities both during an armed conflict and activities performed in the course of official duties.

[54] The ICJ in *Jurisdictional Immunities of the State (Germany v Italy: Greece Intervening), Judgment, ICJ Reports 2012*, p 99, para 113 observed that 'the immunity from enforcement enjoyed by States in regard to their property situated on foreign territory goes further than the jurisdictional immunity enjoyed by those same States before foreign courts'.

Widely recognized exceptions include proceedings relating to contracts which a private party may enter, or which are of a commercial nature, contracts of employment other than those with nationals of the sending State engaged in public service, immovable property, personal injuries, damage or loss to property of a tangible nature, and proceedings relating to the operation of seagoing ships and their cargo. The US FSIA stands alone in removing immunity for claims in respect of expropriation of property contrary to international law. Only the US and Canada have a 'terrorism exception' to immunity that allows States designated as 'sponsors of terrorism' or 'supporters of terrorism' to be sued in domestic courts.[55] Iran has recently brought proceedings against the US in the ICJ alleging that the US has violated international law by denying immunity to Iran in such litigation.[56]

Commercial transactions

The most well-known exception relates to commercial transactions between a private party and the foreign State. It has proven difficult to define the criteria for distinguishing a commercial transaction from one 'in exercise of sovereign authority'. As explained in the *Empire of Iran* case, 'the generally recognized sphere of sovereign activity' which remains immune 'includes the activities of the authorities responsible for foreign and military affairs, legislation, the exercise of police power and the administration of justice'. While the significance of the distinction was recognized by the ICJ in the *Jurisdictional Immunities* case, and that 'States are generally entitled to immunity in respect of *acta jure imperii*',[57] the Court provided no criteria for distinguishing between them, other than that 'the acts in question fall to be assessed by reference to the law governing the exercise of sovereign power *(jus imperii)* or the law concerning non-sovereign activities of a State, especially private and commercial activities *(jus gestionis)*'.[58] However, examples of the retention of immunity for acts in the exercise of sovereign immunity can be found in the careful drafting of exceptions to State immunity.[59]

The competence of civil courts, such as in France, is restricted to civil and commercial matters, and does not extend to public and administrative matters; it is, therefore, not that difficult to apply the civil court's criterion of an act or transaction in which an individual may engage, as opposed to *'un acte de puissance publique ou un acte qui a été accompli dans l'intérêt d'un service public'* to proceedings brought against a foreign State. Article 4 of ECSI allows an exception for proceedings relating to an obligation of a State by virtue of a *contract*—a contract being a legal transaction in which a private person may engage. Applying the same approach to non-contractual claims of a private law character, immunity was refused by the Austrian Supreme Court when sought by the US in respect of a claim for damages arising out of a road accident due to the negligence of an embassy driver when collecting the mail of the US air attaché.[60] The court distinguished a sovereign

---

[55] 28 USC § 1605A (US); Justice for Victims of Terrorism Act, SC 2012, c 1, s 2 (Canada).

[56] *Certain Iranian Assets (Iran v US)*, Application filed on 15 June 2016.

[57] *Jurisdictional Immunities of the State (Germany v Italy: Greece Intervening)*, Judgment of 3 February 2012, p 99, para 61.

[58] Ibid, para 60. Cf the Court's ruling in respect of immunity from enforcement that the cultural Centre Villa Vigoni, 'intended to promote cultural exchanges between Germany and Italy', was 'being used for governmental purposes that are entirely non-commercial and hence for purposes falling within Germany's sovereign functions' (ibid, para 119).

[59] Thus agreements to which States are the sole parties are excluded from the exception for commercial transactions (SIA s 3(2), UNCSI Article 10(2)(a); contracts of employment with diplomats and agents excluded from the employment exception SIA s. 16(1)(a), UNCSI, Article 11(2)(b); warships and naval auxiliaries excluded from the exception for State ships SIA s 10 and UNCSI Article 16(2)).

[60] *Holubek v The Government of United States*, Austrian Supreme Court, 10 February 1961, 40 ILR 73.

act from a private one, such as the operation of a motor car and the use of public roads, where the relationship between the parties was on the basis of equality with no question of supremacy, rather than subordination; in applying the distinction the court looked to the nature of the act of driving as opposed to its purpose, being the collection of mail between government departments.

Common law courts are usually not of limited competence and consequently have no national practice as to what constitutes an act performable by a private person as opposed to a State. But mindful of the underlying rationale of the restrictive doctrine—that States which engage in trade should be amenable to jurisdiction—they have applied a test of commerciality in determining the non-immune nature of the proceedings. Questions concerning contracts made in the territory of the foreign State and governed by its administrative law are expressly excluded from the commercial transaction exception in the UK SIA s 3(2).

Section 1605(a)(2) of the US FSIA removes immunity where claims are based upon a commercial activity and s 1603(d) provides that '[t]he commercial character of an activity shall be determined by reference to the nature of the course of conduct or particular transaction or act, rather than by any reference to its purpose'. Commerciality is not defined by the FSIA and inconsistent decisions have been given in proceedings relating to development of natural resources, foreign assistance programmes, and government exchange control. Thus US courts have held immune the cancellation of an agreement licensing the export of rhesus monkeys,[61] and mistreatment by police resulting from a whistle-blowing complaint made in the course of employment under contract in a hospital;[62] and held non-immune a technical assistance contract under which the contractor enjoyed diplomatic immunities and tax exemption,[63] a foreign government's undertaking to reimburse doctors and the organ bank for kidney transplants performed on its nationals in US hospitals,[64] and a restriction on the payment of government-issued bonds due to a shortage of foreign reserves.[65] US courts have avoided determining whether the leasing of prisoners of war as slave labour by the Nazi regime to German industrial concerns constituted a commercial activity.[66]

To avoid such difficulties, ECSI, the UK SIA, and similar legislation of other Commonwealth States use a listing method by which proceedings relating to specific categories of commercial transactions are listed as non-immune; s 3 of the UK SIA lists as non-immune commercial transactions 'sale of goods or supply of services, and 'loans or other transaction for the provision of finance, guarantee or indemnity of any such transaction or of other financial obligation' (s 3(3)(a) and (b)) (such transactions are not qualified by the condition 'otherwise than in the exercise of sovereign activities');[67] and both the SIA and ECSI also make non-immune proceedings relating to certain contracts of employment, to participation in companies or associations, and to claims relating to patents, trademarks, and other intellectual property rights (ECSI Articles 5, 6, and 8; SIA ss 4, 7, and 8). The listing approach is also adopted by UNCSI, which sets out exceptions for commercial transactions (Article 10), contracts of employment (Article 11), ownership and use of property (Article 13), intellectual and industrial property (Article 14), companies (Article 15), and ships (Article 16).

---

[61] *Mol Inc* v *Peoples Rep of Bangladesh*, 736 F.2d 1326 (9th Cir 1994) cert denied 105 S Ct 513.

[62] *Saudi Arabia* v *Nelson*, 123 L Ed 2d 47 (Sup Ct 1993); 100 ILR 544.

[63] *Practical Concepts* v *Republic of Bolivia*, 811 F.2d 1543 (DC Cir 1987); 92 ILR 420.

[64] *Rush-Presbyterian-St Luke's Medical Center* v *the Hellenic Republic*, 877 F.2d 574 (7th Cir 1989) cert denied 493 US 937; 101 ILR 509.

[65] *Republic of Argentina* v *Weltover*, 504 US 607 (1992); 100 ILR 509.

[66] *Princz* v *Federal Republic of Germany*, 26 F.3d 1166; (DC Cir 1994); 33 ILM 1483.

[67] *Orascom Telecom Holding SAE* v *Republic of Chad & Ors* [2008] EWHC 1841 (Comm) 2 Lll Rep [2008] 397, citing Lord Diplock in *Alcom Ltd* v *Republic of Colombia* [1984] 1 AC 580, 603.

Even with this method, challenging cases regularly come before the English courts. Cases such as *I Congreso del Partido* (whether disposal of a cargo by a State agency contrary to terms of the contract of carriage on orders of the State for political reasons was immune)[68] and *Kuwait Airways Corp v Iraqi Airways Co* (whether seizure and transfer of Kuwaiti aircraft to Iraq after the invasion of Kuwait with a view to incorporation in the Iraqi civil airfleet was immune)[69] demonstrate the difficulty of distinguishing a commercial transaction from an act in exercise of sovereign authority. The accepted solution applied by English courts is to determine the *nature* and not the purpose of the activity. But when applied to determine the nature of the funds held in a bank account of a diplomatic embassy this test proved arbitrary; such funds could be treated as being used for the purchase of goods and services—clearly commercial acts—or more broadly for the discharge of diplomatic functions, which were clearly activities in exercise of sovereign authority.[70]

Faced with these difficulties, Lord Wilberforce reformulated the test as requiring a court to consider:

> ... the whole context in which the claim against the State is made, with a view to deciding whether the relevant act(s) on which the claim is based should, in that context, be considered as fairly within an area of activity, trading or commercial or otherwise of a private law character, in which the State has chosen to engage or whether the relevant activity should be considered as having been done outside the area and within the sphere of governmental or sovereign activity.[71]

Therefore, when deciding cases both under the SIA[72] and under the common law, a purposive construction of the public/private criterion is now applied which takes account of the whole context, including the place where the persons are alleged to have committed the acts and those who were designed to benefit from the conduct complained of. Thus, for example, and although by their nature the acts in question were ones which a private person might have committed, proceedings brought against visiting US forces were barred since on the facts of the cases those acts had been performed in the exercise of sovereign authority by reason of their having been undertaken by service personnel and in pursuance of the purpose of maintaining an efficient fighting force.[73]

The relevance of purpose as well as the nature of the transaction was much debated by the ILC and its final formulation of UNCSI Article 2(2) reads as follows:

> In determining whether a contract or transaction is a 'commercial transaction' under paragraph 1 (c), reference should be made to the nature of the contract or transaction, but its purpose should also be taken into account if the parties to the contract or transaction have so agreed, or, if in the practice of the State of the forum, that purpose is relevant to determining the non-commercial character of the contract or transaction.

---

[68] *I Congreso del Partido* [1983] 1 AC 244; [1981] 2 All ER 1064; 64 ILR 307 (HL).

[69] *Kuwait Airways Corp v Iraqi Airways Co* [1995] 3 All ER 694; 103 ILR 340 (HL).

[70] In *Alcom Ltd v Republic of Colombia* the Court of Appeal adopted the first view [1983] 3 WLR 906; [1984] 1 All ER 1 and the House of Lords the second [1984] AC 580; [1984] 2 WLR 750; [1984] 2 All ER 6 (HL). See also *NML Capital Ltd v The Republic of Argentina* [2011] UKSC 31, where the Supreme Court was split on whether the commercial nature of the underlying transaction rendered enforcement proceedings in respect of a judgment given in New York 'commercial' or 'sovereign' in nature.

[71] *I Congreso del Partido* [1983]1 AC 244; [1981] 2 All ER 1064, 1074; 64 ILR 307 (HL).

[72] *Propend Finance Pty Ltd v Sing*, 111 ILR 611, 2 May 1997 (CA).

[73] *Holland v Lampen-Wolfe* [2000] 1 WLR 1573; [2000] 3 All ER 833; 119 ILR 367 (HL) concerning a complaint of libel contained in a report of a supervising officer of a civilian lecturer engaged to give a course to visiting US forces; *Littrell v USA (No 2)* [1994] 4 All ER 203; [1995] 1 WLR 82; 100 ILR 438 (CA) concerning a claim of medical negligence against a service doctor treating an airman on a US base in the UK.

The reference to purpose, designed to accommodate developing States' wish to retain immunity for contractual transactions vital to their economy or for disaster prevention or relief, has resulted in a complex piece of drafting strengthening the defendant's immunity by which the national court may be required to engage in a four-stage exercise in determining whether it has jurisdiction in a commercial transaction under Article 2(1)(c) (iii).[74] The Annex of Understandings contains nothing specific with regard to this Article and it would seem that the ambiguities present in the Article constitute an open invitation for reservation or interpretative declaration to any State proposing to give effect to the Convention in its law by ratification. However, it should not be forgotten that the Working Group of the ILC itself in 1999, after an exhaustive review of the whole subject, concluded that 'the distinction between the so-called nature and purpose tests might be less significant in practice than the long debate about it might imply'.[75]

Employment contract exception

There is also widespread acceptance of an exception to State immunity for employment disputes brought by employees that do not touch on the 'three R's' (recruitment, renewal, or reinstatement) and do not implicate the sovereign activities of the State, such as national security (Webb, 2016). These cases tend to arise when locally recruited employees of a foreign embassy sue for unfair dismissal or discrimination.

The UK SIA is one of the strictest statutes in the world when it comes to the scope for employees to sue a State under the employment contract exception, being matched only by the legislation of South Africa, Pakistan, and Malawi. The recent *Benkharbouche and Janah* cases[76] exposed sharp differences between UK and international and regional requirements: in particular, SIA ss 4(2) and 16(1)(a) as compared to ECHR Article 6 and the EU Charter of Fundamental Human Rights Articles 45 and 47.

In *Janah*, two Moroccan nationals were employed as domestic workers by the Libyan Embassy and Sudanese Embassy in London. Both women were dismissed from their employment and brought claims against Libya and Sudan, respectively. Ms Janah's claims related to failure to pay the National Minimum Wage, breaches of the Working Time Regulations, failure to provide her with payslips or a contract, unfair dismissal, discrimination, and harassment. By the time the case came before the Supreme Court, only Ms Janah participated and it was left to the UK Secretary of State to make the counter-arguments.

The key question was whether ss 4(2)(b) and 16(1)(a) of the SIA are consistent with the ECHR and the EU Charter of Fundamental Human Rights. Section 4(2)(b) provides that a State is immune as respects proceedings relating to a contract of employment between a State and a person who at the time of the contract is neither a national of the UK nor resident there; s 16(1)(a) has the effect that a State is immune as respects proceedings concerning the employment of members of a diplomatic mission, including its administrative, technical, and domestic staff. The Supreme Court had to decide whether these provisions have any basis in customary international law.

Ms Janah's case was that ss 4(2)(b) and 16(1)(a) of the SIA are incompatible with Article 6 of the ECHR because 'they unjustifiably bar access to a court' to determine her claims.[77]

---

[74] These stages being to consider the nature of the transaction, first in the absence and second in the presence of evidence of the purpose of the transaction; third, to take account of such purpose where an agreement of the parties so as to take such purpose into account is proved; and fourth, to have regard to purpose if it is relevant in the practice of the forum State, *not* of its law, in determining the non-commercial character of the transaction.

[75] See A/CN.4/L.576, para 60.

[76] *Benkharbouche v Secretary of State for Foreign and Commonwealth Affairs and Secretary of State for Foreign and Commonwealth Affairs and Libya v Janah* [2017] UKSC 62.

[77] Ibid, para 13.

In particular, the immunities being conferred by the SIA on Libya and Sudan were no longer required as a matter of obligation by customary international law. According to Lord Sumption:

> The employment of Ms Janah and Ms Benkharbouche were clearly not exercises of sovereign authority, and nothing about their alleged treatment engaged the sovereign interests of their employers. Nor are they seeking reinstatement in a way that would restrict the right of their employers to decide who is to be employed in their diplomatic missions. As a matter of customary international law, therefore, their employers are not entitled to immunity as regards these claims. It follows that so far as sections 4(2)(b) or 16(1)(a) of the State Immunity Act confer immunity, they are incompatible with article 6 of the Human Rights Convention.[78]

As a result, ss 4(2)(b) and 16(1)(a) of the SIA were disapplied to the claims derived from EU law (discrimination, harassment, breach of the Working Time Regulations). The Supreme Court upheld the Court of Appeal's declaration of incompatibility under s 4 of the Human Rights Act 1998. It is now up to Parliament to remove the incompatibility by revising the SIA, the text of which has not been changed since it was enacted four decades ago.

Non-commercial torts

In addition to the various exceptions linked to commercial activities, UNCSI and State practice in legislation and court decisions allow an exception for certain non-contractual delictual activities of a foreign State. Article 12 of UNCSI contains an exception from immunity in civil proceedings which 'relates to pecuniary compensation for death or injury to the person, or damage to or loss of tangible property, caused by an act or omission which is alleged to be attributable to the State, if the act or omission occurred in whole or in part in the territory of that other State, and if the author of the act or omission was present in that territory at the time of the act or omission'. Three points may be made. First, the scope of the exception is narrow, being confined to physical infliction of damage to the person or property with its origin derived from insurable risks arising from physical injuries and damage resulting from traffic accidents; proceedings relating to false, defamatory, or negligent statements are not included. Second, the exception only relates to wrongful conduct of a foreign State committed in the territory of the forum State.[79] Third, the exception in UNCSI and common law legislation contains no requirement that the injury or damage be caused in the course of commercial activity; injury or damage resulting from an act in exercise of sovereign authority is recoverable, as for example proceedings for State-ordered assassination of a political opponent which has been held non-immune under a similar tort exception in the US FSIA. The ICJ was careful in *Jurisdictional Immunities* not to 'resolve the question whether there is in customary international law a "tort exception" to State immunity applicable to *acta jure imperii* in general'.[80]

---

[78] Ibid, Lord Sumption, para 76.

[79] The UK SIA s 5 merely refers to '(a) the death or personal injury; or (b) damage to or loss of tangible property, caused by act or omission in the United Kingdom'; the US FSIA s 1605(a)(5) is similar with the personal injury, death, or damage to or loss of property occurring in the USA (but excludes any claim based on failure of any State official or employee to exercise or perform a discretionary function); the UN Convention Article 12, following ECSI Article 11, is even stricter, limiting proceedings to where the author is present in the forum State at the time when the facts occurred.

[80] *Jurisdictional Immunities of the State (Germany v Italy: Greece Intervening), Judgment of 3 February 2012*, p 99, para 65.

Not all jurisdictions accept such a wide removal of State immunity for non-contractual claims; in a case relating to immunity in respect of an assault by a soldier of the foreign State while within the territory of the forum State, the European Court of Human Rights, after a survey of State practice, concluded that a 'trend in international and comparative law towards limiting State immunity in respect of personal injury caused by an act or omission within the forum State' refers primarily 'to "insurable" personal injury, that is incidents arising out of ordinary traffic accidents, rather than matters relating to the core area of State sovereignty such as the acts of a soldier on foreign territory which, of their very nature, may involve sensitive issues affecting diplomatic relations between States and national security'.[81]

Decisions by Italian courts applying this 'territorial tort' exception to award damages for forcible deportation and forced labour of an Italian national by German military authorities during the Second World War led to Germany bringing the *Jurisdictional Immunities* case to the ICJ.[82] After an extensive survey of State practice, the Court upheld Germany's immunity: 'State practice in the form of judicial decisions supports the proposition that State immunity for *acta jure imperii* continues to extend to civil proceedings for acts occasioning death, personal injury or damage to property committed by the armed forces and other organs of a State in the conduct of armed conflict, even if the relevant acts take place on the territory of the forum State'.[83]

2. Jurisdictional connection with the forum state

The limitation of the personal injuries exception to acts committed in the forum territory highlights the general question whether the jurisdiction of national courts over foreign States is conditional on some close link with the territory of the forum State. Both ECSI and the US FSIA require that there be a nexus or jurisdictional connection with the forum State in respect of each of the recognized exceptions to State immunity. That jurisdictional connection for some exceptions, as with employment contracts and personal injuries, is stricter than those recognized in private international law for private party litigation. The UK and other common law jurisdictions have also accepted additional jurisdictional links for the employment, tort, and other exceptions; only in respect of the commercial transaction, arbitration, and State ships exceptions is there an absence of a connection other than those required in ordinary litigation for the exercise of extraterritorial personal jurisdiction under Civil Procedure Rules, r 6.26 (formerly RSC Order 11, r 1) or like common law procedures. The UK Supreme Court in *NML* v *Argentina* endorsed the omission in s 3(1)(a) of a jurisdictional link between the foreign State's commercial transaction and the UK jurisdiction. In the leading judgment Lord Phillips said, and with which point all their Lordships concurred:

> I can see no justification for giving section 3(1)(a) a narrow interpretation on the basis that it is desirable to restrict the circumstances in which it operates to those where the commercial transaction has a link with the United Kingdom. The restrictive doctrine of sovereign immunity does not restrict the exemption from immunity to commercial transactions that are in some way linked to the jurisdiction of the forum.[84]

---

[81] *McElhinney* v *Ireland and the UK* [GC], no 31253/96, para 38, ECHR 2001-XI, 34 *EHRR* 13.

[82] *Ferrini* v *Greece and Germany* (Dec), no 59021/00, ECHR 2002-X, 129 ILR 537; see also *Distomo Massacre Case*, Germany Federal Constitutional Court, 15 February 2006, 135 ILR 185.

[83] *Jurisdictional Immunities of the State (Germany v Italy: Greece Intervening)*, Judgment of 3 February 2012, p 99, para 77.

[84] *NML Capital Ltd* v *The Republic of Argentina* [2011] UKSC 31, para 39.

UNCSI adopts a neutral position, referring in Article 10(1) to the determination of jurisdiction over the commercial transaction exception to 'the applicable rules of private international law' of the forum State.[85]

For proceedings which are clearly identical to those brought in private litigation, there may be no need to require any special additional jurisdictional link where the defendant is a foreign State. But for proceedings which relate to conflicts of jurisdiction between States, the plea of immunity serves to demarcate the limits of State jurisdiction exercisable over the public acts of another State.

G. IMMUNITY FROM ENFORCEMENT

A foreign State is largely immune from forcible measures of execution against its person or property, and the rules on immunity from enforcement must be applied separately from those on immunity from jurisdiction.[86]

1. Immunity of the person of the state or representatives from coercive measures

Immunity from coercive measures against the personal representative of the State remains absolute. As confirmed by the ICJ in the *Arrest Warrant* case, no Head of State, Head of Government, or Minister for Foreign Affairs while in office may be arrested by order of the court of another State, nor may preliminary measures such as the issue or international circulation of an arrest warrant be taken against such persons.[87] The immunity *ratione materiae* enjoyed by such officials is an important element of the State's own immunity enabling it to function effectively. In *Djibouti v France,* the ICJ explained the expected behaviour of a State seeking to invoke the immunity of its officials: 'the State which seeks to claim immunity for one of its organs is expected to notify the authorities of the other State concerned, whether through diplomatic exchanges or before a French judicial organ.' The Court noted that 'this would allow the court of the forum State to ensure that it does not fail to respect any entitlement to immunity and might thereby engage the responsibility of that State. Further the State notifying a foreign court that judicial process should not proceed, for reasons of immunity against its State organs, is assuming responsibility for any internationally wrongful act at issue committed by such organs'.[88]

No injunction or order for specific performance may be directed against a foreign State on pain of penalty if not obeyed. Thus the Netherlands Supreme Court has ruled that it has no jurisdiction to declare a foreign State bankrupt:

> Acceptance of this jurisdiction would imply that a trustee in bankruptcy with far-reaching powers could take over the administration and the winding up of the assets of a foreign power under the supervision of a Dutch public official. This would constitute an unacceptable infringement under international law of the sovereignty of the foreign State concerned.[89]

---

[85] See also ILC Commentary to Article 10(1), para (3) and (4).

[86] *Jurisdictional Immunities of the State (Germany v Italy: Greece Intervening), Judgment of 3 February 2012,* p 99, para 113.

[87] *Arrest Warrant of 11 April 2000 (Democratic Republic of Congo v Belgium), Preliminary Objections and Merits, Judgment, ICJ Reports 2002,* p 3, paras 62–71. In the case concerning *Certain Criminal Proceedings in France (Republic of Congo v France)* brought in 2003 the applicant State claimed that the initiation of a criminal investigation by the French court without service on the foreign State constituted a violation of a serving Head of State's immunity. This case was discontinued in 2010. See *Certain Criminal Proceedings in France (Republic of the Congo v France), Order of 16 November 2010, ICJ Reports 2010,* p 635.

[88] *Certain Questions of Mutual Assistance in Criminal Matters (Djibouti v France), ICJ Reports 2008,* p 177, para 196.

[89] *WL Oltmans* v *The Republic of Surinam,* Netherlands Supreme Court, 28 September 1990 (1992) 23 *NYIL* 442 at 447.

For the same reason, the UK SIA s 13(1) prohibits the imposition of any penalty by way of committal or fine in respect of any failure or refusal by the State to disclose information or produce any document, and s 13(2) the giving of any relief against a State by way of injunction or order for specific performance or recovery of land or other property.

2. Immunity of state property from coercive measures

State practice and UNCSI recognize an exception to the general rule of immunity from enforcement in respect of State property in use for commercial purposes.[90] English law permits the recognition and enforcement of a foreign judgment given against a State (other than the UK or the State to which that court belongs), provided the foreign court would have had jurisdiction if it had applied the UK rules on sovereign immunity set out in SIA ss 2 to 11,[91] but execution without the consent of the State remains solely in respect of State property shown to be 'in use or intended for use for commercial purposes' (SIA s 13(4)).

UNCSI draws a distinction between measures of enforcement against the property of a State that are taken pre-judgment and post-judgment; the rule of immunity is absolute in both scenarios unless the State has consented, or allocated or earmarked the property for the satisfaction of the claim. An additional exception to immunity, somewhat narrower than SIA s 13(4), is permitted in respect of post-judgment measures for State property in use for commercial purposes, Article 19(c) UNCSI.

In *Jurisdictional Immunities*, the ICJ, when deciding whether Germany's immunity from enforcement had been infringed by the Italian court's imposition of a legal charge on the Villa Vigoni owned by the German government, referred to Article 19 UNCSI. Without deciding whether it reflected current customary international law, the ICJ noted that it provided for three exceptions to immunity—express consent, allocation by the State, and the use of State property 'for an activity not pursuing governmental non-commercial purposes'. Finding that Villa Vigoni was used for cultural purposes, the Court concluded that it was used entirely for non-commercial governmental purposes and was thus immune from measures of constraint.[92]

3. State property generally recognized as immune

Diplomatic and military property have generally been recognized as categories of State property used for sovereign purposes and consequently have enjoyed immunity from seizure, even when there is a general waiver by the State of its immunity from enforcement. The property of central banks has also been recognized as enjoying special immunity in numerous jurisdictions. UNCSI adds two relatively new categories: property forming part of the cultural heritage of a State or of its archives, and property forming part of an exhibition of objects of scientific, cultural, or historical interest (Articles 21(1)(d) and (e)).[93]

Property of the diplomatic mission

In the *Philippine Embassy* case, immunity was recognized when attachment was sought of the account of the Philippine diplomatic mission in Bonn to satisfy a judgment for unpaid rent of an office. Article 22(3) of the Vienna Convention on Diplomatic Relations states:

---

[90] The principle was stated four decades ago in *The Philippine Embassy Bank Account* case, German Federal Constitutional Court, 13 December 1977, 46 *BverfGE*, 342; 65 ILR 146, 184.

[91] Civil Jurisdiction and Judgments Act 1982 s 31, *NML Capital Ltd v The Republic of Argentina* [2009] 1 Lloyd's Rep 378, reversed [2010] EWCA Civ 41; appeal allowed [2011] UKSC 31. For registration of a judgment against the UK see SIA Part II ss 18–19; no procedure is available for registration of a judgment given by a court against a State to which that court belongs, *AIC Ltd v Federal Government of Nigeria and Attorney-General of Federation of Nigeria* [2003] EWHC 1357 (QB); 129 ILR 871.

[92] *Jurisdictional Immunities of the State (Germany v Italy: Greece Intervening), Judgment of 3 February 2012*, p 99, paras 118–20.

[93] The immune categories may lose their immunity by express consent or specific allocation.

'[t]he premises of the mission, their furnishings and other property thereon and the means of transport of the mission shall be immune from search, requisition, attachment or execution.'

Although the bank account of the mission is not expressly mentioned in the Vienna Convention, State practice, confirmed by Article 21(1)(a) of UNCSI which refers to 'any bank account', overwhelmingly recognizes that an account of a diplomatic mission held in a bank in the forum State enjoys immunity unless it can be affirmatively shown that the sums deposited have been specifically allocated to meet commercial commitments.

Military property

Ships of war were recognized as immune from local jurisdiction from the eighteenth century or earlier, but the modern category of military property, as defined in UNCSI as 'property of a military character or used or intended for use in the performance of military functions' (Article 21(1)(b)), is capable of a wider meaning.[94] The US FSIA adopts a similar definition of property used or intended to be used 'in connection with a military activity', which includes not only all types of armaments and their means of delivery but also basic commodities such as food, clothing, and fuel to keep a fighting force operative.[95] The existence of such an immune category exposes sales of military equipment to a plea of immunity from jurisdiction. Such a possibility would seem to be avoided in English law and come within the SIA s 3 definition of a commercial transaction provided the sale is in ordinary private law form and not pursuant to an agreement between States.

Central bank property

It is widely accepted that central bank property enjoys immunity in all circumstances because it is assumed to be used for government non-commercial purposes. Several jurisdictions support this position, including the UK, China, Japan, and South Africa, and it is codified in UNCSI Article 21. It is generally accepted that, at the very least, central bank property is immune in circumstances where it is in fact used for 'central banking functions/purposes', and that this immunity is only lifted if the primary or sole purpose for which the property is held is commercial. The US FSIA s 1611(b)(1), for example, extends a priori immunity from execution only to property of a central bank 'held for its own account'. This is intended and taken to mean that the funds 'are used or held in connection with central banking activities, as distinguished from funds used solely to finance the commercial transactions of other entities or of foreign states'.[96]

In a case relating to State property held by a private corporation in the name of the State's central bank, the English court construed the term 'property of the State' in the SIA to 'include all real and personal property and will embrace any right, interest, legal, equitable or contractual in assets that might be held by a State or any "emanation of the State" or central bank or other monetary authority that comes within sections 13 and 14 of the Act'.[97] The growing practice of placing of excess foreign exchange reserves in

---

[94] The UNGA Ad Hoc Committee decided in view of the uncertainty of the law to exclude aircraft and space objects by stating in Article 3 that the 2004 UN Convention is without prejudice to the immunities enjoyed by a State under international law with respect to aircraft and space objects owned or operated by a State. This would seem to exclude this type of State property from the category of military property declared immune in Article 19(1)(c).

[95] FSIA s 1611(b)(2); Legislative History of the Foreign Sovereign Immunities Act 1976, House Report No 94–1487, 94th Cong, 2nd Sess 12 reproduced in (1976) 15 ILM 1398, 30–1.

[96] *Jurisdiction of United States Courts in Suits Against Foreign States*, H Rep No 94–1487, 94th Cong. reproduced in (1976) 15 ILM 1398, 1414.

[97] *AIG Capital Partners Inc & Anor* v *Kazakhstan (National Bank of Kazakhstan intervening)* [2005] EWHC 2239 (Comm); [2006] 1 All ER (Comm) 1; [2006] 1 WLR 1420; 129 ILR 589.

Sovereign Wealth Funds, often with a declared purpose of 'use for future generations', has raised issues relevant to their enjoyment of immunity from enforcement, particularly where invested in equities, derivatives, or short-term commercial assets (Truman, 2007). Such Sovereign Wealth Funds, whether held in the name of the State or its central Bank, currently enjoy, under US, UK, and Chinese legislation and UNCSI, complete immunity from enforcement. Where, however, such a Fund is used for wealth enhancement by 'playing the markets', it would seem arguable, at least as regards the fees of brokers, banks, and other third parties which such transactions generate, that for the purposes of attachment these credits in the Fund might be treated as for 'commercial purposes' despite the overall long-term intention of the Fund to serve as a reserve for the State and its people.

Cultural heritage of the state

The immunity accorded to the cultural heritage of the State is designed to deter pillage and illegal export of scientific, cultural, or historical treasures (Gattini, 2008). The immunity of property forming part of the cultural heritage of a State is complicated by applicable laws of ownership, State regulation of privately owned national treasures, and claims of individuals to property expropriated in time of armed conflict.[98] Where the presence of cultural objects is restricted to their temporary public exhibition, State practice seems more favourable to conferring immunity. In 2004 the Swiss Ministry of External Affairs declared that cultural property of a State on exhibition was immune and overruled a court order on the application of a creditor of Russia, the Swiss trading company NOGA, for the seizure of paintings from the Moscow's Pushkin Museum on exhibition in Switzerland, and ordered their return to Russia.[99] The US Immunity Seizure Act of 1966 and the UK Tribunals and Courts Act 2007 Part 6 confer protection from seizure or attachment on objects in possession of a foreign State sent for exhibition subject to prior notification of their intended exhibition, though the UK Act does not bar museums in the UK or lenders being subject to proceedings, other than specific restitution, in respect of exhibited works of art.

4. Proof of property in use for sovereign purposes

Whereas it is relatively easy to determine that a seagoing vessel equipped with guns and manned by Naval personnel is not to be treated as property in commercial use, it is more difficult to ascertain the character of funds held in the name of a State.

A key issue is what evidence is available to establish the intended commercial use of State property. In the *Philippine Embassy* case the German court considered that it would constitute unlawful interference in matters within the exclusive competence of the sending State for any inquiry, beyond obtaining the Ambassador's certificate, to be instituted as to the intended use of funds held in a diplomatic mission's bank account. The position is similar in English law. Under s 13(4) of the SIA, property in use or intended use for commercial purposes is made subject to attachment; s 17 defines 'commercial purposes' to mean 'purposes of such transactions or activities as are mentioned in section 3(3)', that is, use in relation to a sale of goods or supply of services, a transaction for provision of

---

[98] The ruling by the US Supreme Court in *Republic of Austria v Altmann* 541 US 677 (2004), that there was no limitation on the retroactive operation of the FSIA, renders applicable the restrictive doctrine including the expropriation exception to State immunity in s 1605(a)(3) to such claims for war damage. In that case Austria sought to rely on the rule of absolute immunity in force prior to 1952 as a bar to a claim by the owner of several Klimt paintings confiscated by the Nazis and exhibited by the Austrian national gallery.

[99] RSDIE 14 (2004) 674.

finance, or a commercial, industrial, professional, or industrial activity. In a case seek-ing attachment of a diplomatic mission's account for unpaid surveillance equipment, the English Court of Appeal construed the statutory words 'intended use for commercial purposes' as covering commercial transactions entered into by the Ambassador; but the House of Lords declared the current account of a foreign diplomatic mission was held for the sovereign purpose of meeting the expenses of the mission and was not suscep-tible of anticipatory dissection into the various uses, commercial as well as sovereign, to which monies drawn on it might be used in the future. Only specific earmarking of a fund for present or future commercial use, the House of Lords held, would meet the exception to immunity from execution provided in the SIA for commercial property in use or intended use for commercial purposes (SIA s 13(4)).[100] A modification of this strict requirement was permitted in *Orascom*; a London bank account (not of the diplo-matic mission) into which the oil revenues of a foreign State were paid for the purpose of discharging a commercial debt owed to World Bank with the surplus, if any, to be held for general use including sovereign purposes, was treated as an account for commercial purposes and non-immune.[101]

In *SerVaas*, a company sought enforcement of a Third Party Debt Order against the debts payable to Iraq to recover money due under an agreement with the previous Iraqi regime. Iraq argued that the money due to the State was immune from execution by virtue of the SIA s 13(2)(b), (4). The Supreme Court, having regard to a certificate of the Head of Mission of the Embassy of Iraq which declared that Iraq's share had never been used, was not in use, and was not intended to be for use for any commercial purpose, held unani-mously that any the debts were not 'connected to, or destined for use in, any mercantile or profit-making activity in Iraq' and therefore did not fall within the 'commercial purpose' exception.[102]

Another difficult case was *LR Avionics Technologies Ltd* v *The Federal Republic of Nigeria*.[103] The Federal Republic of Nigeria was the owner of office premises at 56/57 Fleet Street in London. It granted a lease to a company called Online Integrated Solutions Ltd for the purpose of providing visa and passport services (although other office use was also permitted) in exchange for an annual rent of £150,000. When an Israeli company sought to enforce an award against Nigeria by attaching the Fleet Street property, Nigeria's Acting High Commissioner issued a certificate which stated that the property was 'in use . . . for commercial purposes'. The court held that the leas-ing of foreign-State-owned premises to a third party for the facilitation of passport and visa applications did not fall within 'in use . . . for commercial purposes' under s 13(4) of the SIA.

5. Mixed bank accounts

English courts have held that funds held for both sovereign and commercial purposes in a mission's bank account remain immune unless a specific account is opened or specific allocation made for a commercial purpose.[104] Belgian courts have upheld the presumption that assets of a diplomatic mission were in use or intended use for

---

[100] *Alcom v Republic of Colombia* [1984] AC 580; [1984] 2 WLR 750; [1984] 2 All ER 6 (HL).

[101] *Orascom Telecom Holding SAE v Republic of Chad & Ors* [2008] EWHC 1841 (Comm); 2 Lll Rep [2008] 397. To the same effect, *EM Ltd v Republic of Argentina* 473 F.3d 463 (2d Cir 2007).

[102] *SerVaas Inc v Rafidian Bank and others* [2012] UKSC 40, para 32 (per Lord Clarke).

[103] *LR Avionics Technologies Ltd v The Federal Republic of Nigeria* [2016] EWHC 1761 (Comm).

[104] *Orascom Telecom Holding SAE v Republic of Chad & Ors* [2008] EWHC 1841 (Comm); 2 Lll Rep [2008] 397. To the same effect, *EM Ltd v Republic of Argentina* 473 F.3d 463 (2d Cir 2007).

sovereign purposes and hence immune.[105] A US District Court, however, allowed attachment of a mixed diplomatic bank account; exemption of mixed accounts would in the court's view create a loophole, for any property could be made immune by using it, at one time or other, for some minor public purpose.[106] A later decision by a US court refused attachment of a mixed bank account holding that such attachment would be contrary to the US's obligation under Article 25 of the Vienna Convention on Diplomatic Relations.

6. The requirement of a connection between the state property to be attached and the subject matter of the proceedings

There is a division in State practice on whether there needs to be a connection between the State property to be attached and the subject matter of the proceedings. The US FSIA requires that the State property 'is or was used for the commercial activity upon which the claim was based' (s 1610(a)(2)). This restriction does not appear in the UK SIA. This requirement of a connection between the property and the claim restricts considerably the scope of the execution permitted against the property of a foreign State. The FSIA only imposes the connection condition when execution is sought against a State, but not when against an agency or instrumentality (in which case all property used for commercial activity is permitted).[107]

The provisions in UNCSI dealing with this issue were much debated. Article 19(c) makes post-judgment measures against the property of the State subject to three requirements: the property (i) is to be in use or intended use by the State for other than governmental non-commercial purposes; (ii) is to be in the territory of the forum State; and (iii) must have a connection with the entity against which the proceeding was directed. This Article is accompanied by three annexed Understandings, defining 'entity' as one enjoying independent legal personality and 'property' as 'broader than ownership or possession', and, in order to prevent evasion of the State of its liability to meet its judgments, reserving the position under national laws as to 'piercing the veil'. These provisions would seem to broaden the scope of State property over which measures of constraint are allowed beyond the narrow confines found in the US FSIA of State property which is the subject matter of the proceedings.

III. ACT OF STATE

The second 'avoidance technique' is known as act of State or 'foreign act of State'. The principle, as stated in *Underhill v Hernandez*,[108] is that the courts of one State will not sit in judgment on the acts of the government of another done within its territory. Both act of State and non-justiciability (discussed in Section IV) give effect to a policy of 'judicial restraint or abstention'.[109]

---

[105] *Leica AG v Central Bank of Iraq*, 15 February 2000, Brussels Ct of Appeal, J des trib (2001) 6; *Iraq v Vinci Constructions*, 4 October 2002, Brussels Ct of Appeal, J des trib (2003) 318; 127 ILR 101; *Dumez v Iraq*, French Ct of Cassation, 15 July 1999; 27 ILR 144. See 27 April 2017 judgment (No 48/2017) of the Belgian Constitutional Court largely confirming the validity of the Act of 23 August 2015 which set outs a system of prior authorization by the Judge of Seizures for all seizures of property belonging to a foreign State or an international organization.

[106] *Birch Shipping Corp v Embassy of United Republic of Tanzania*, 507 F.Supp 311 (DDC 1990); 63 ILR 524.

[107] US FSIA s 1610(b)(2).   [108] *Underhill v Hernandez* 168 US 250 (1897).

[109] *Buttes Gas and Oil Co v Hammer (No 3)* [1982] AC 888, 931F–934C per Lord Wilberforce.

Whereas there is no exception to State immunity for serious violations of international law, even of *jus cogens* character, courts have accepted and applied a public policy limitation on act of State where fundamental human rights violations are in issue. This may be explained by the procedural/substantive distinction that courts apply. Immunity is seen as a procedural plea. In *Jones* v *Ministry of Interior for the Kingdom of Saudi Arabia* the court held that Saudi Arabia was immune in relation to a claim brought by British nationals for alleged acts of torture committed in a Saudi prison on the orders of the Ministry of the Interior of Saudi Arabia.[147] Lord Hoffman explained how, in the view of the Supreme Court, no conflict arose between immunity and human rights: 'To produce a conflict with state immunity, it is therefore necessary to show that the prohibition on torture has generated an ancillary procedural rule which, by way of exception to State immunity entitles or perhaps requires states to assume civil jurisdiction over other states in cases in which torture is alleged. Such a rule may be desirable . . . [b]ut contrary to the assertion of the minority in *Al-Adsani*, it is not entailed by the prohibition of torture.'[148] As Lord Bingham in the same case succinctly stated: 'The International Court of Justice has made plain that breach of a *jus cogens* norm of international law does not suffice to confer jurisdiction (*Democratic Republic of the Congo* v *Rwanda,* ICJ, 3 February 2006, para 64)'.[149]

The ICJ took the same approach in *Jurisdictional Immunities* in 2012. Italy had put forward three strands of argument: first, that there is no immunity in international law when a State has committed serious violations of international humanitarian law amounting to war crimes and crimes against humanity; second, that there is no State immunity for violations of norms of *jus cogens* character; third, that the denial of immunity is justified because all other attempts to obtain reparations for the victims had failed.[150] The ICJ in deciding against Italy's claim dismissed all three arguments and also rejected Italy's contention that the combined effect of the three lines justified an exception to State immunity. In doing so the ICJ based its reasoning on the straightforward proposition that the plea of immunity was a procedural plea independent of the issues raised in the Italian claim relating to State responsibility and their determination. The Court stated:

> The rules of State immunity are procedural in character and are confined to determining whether or not the courts of one State may exercise jurisdiction in respect of another State. They do not bear upon the question whether or not the conduct in respect of which the proceedings are brought was lawful or unlawful.[151]

Earlier, the Court had noted:

> . . . that Italy, in response to a question posed by a member of the Court, recognized that those acts had to be characterized as *acta jure imperii*, notwithstanding that they were unlawful. The Court considers that the terms '*jure imperii*' and '*jure gestionis*' do not imply

---

[147] *Jones* v *Ministry of Interior for the Kingdom of Saudi Arabia and Ors* [2006] UKHL 26; [2007] 1 AC 270. For the case before the European Court of Human Rights, see *Jones and Others* v *the United Kingdom*, nos 34356/06 and 40528/06, ECHR 2014.

[148] Ibid, para 45.

[149] Ibid, para 24. Had the alleged acts of torture taken placed within the UK, rather than in a Saudi prison, the territorial tort exception in SIA s 5, which is also found in Article 12 of the UN Convention, might have been applicable. Expanding the tort exception to include international crimes causing death or injuries to the person attracted considerable support at the 2009 Naples Session of the Institut de droit international, but was not, however, included in the final resolution adopted. See Institut de droit, Naples, 2009 Resolution on International Crimes and Immunities from Jurisdiction of States and their Agents (Rapporteur Lady Fox), ADI vol 73 and see Salmon, 2009.

[150] Italy also had an argument based on the territorial tort exception to immunity.

[151] *Jurisdictional Immunities of the State (Germany* v *Italy: Greece Intervening), Judgment of 3 February 2012,* p 99, para 93.

that the acts in question are lawful but refer rather to whether the acts in question fall to be assessed by reference to the law governing the exercise of sovereign power *(jus imperii)* or the law concerning non-sovereign activities of a State, especially private and commercial activities *(jus gestionis)*. To the extent that this distinction is significant for determining whether or not a State is entitled to immunity from the jurisdiction of another State's courts in respect of a particular act, it has to be applied before that jurisdiction can be exercised.[152]

In Judgment 238 of 22 October 2014, the Italian Constitutional Court held that Italy's compliance with the ICJ's *Jurisdictional Immunities* Judgment was unconstitutional. The Italian court declared that compliance with the ICJ's ruling entailed a disproportionate restriction on the right of access to court (enshrined in Article 24 of the Italian Constitution). Respect for State immunity could not bar access to court where Article 14 applied and the commission of crimes against humanity and war crimes was alleged. The Constitutional Court did not challenge the ICJ Judgment as a statement of customary international law; it instead refused to allow the Judgment to have legal effects at the domestic level.[153]

VI. CONCLUSION

The pendulum continues to swing between protecting the activities of States from judicial scrutiny and calling for greater accountability and remedies for violations of international law. The public policy limitation to act of State is now well established, and has been applied in cases involving allegations of human rights violations. Similarly, the scope of non-justiciability has narrowed over time, with judges being more willing to scrutinize a wide range of activities undertaken by States. A human rights exception to State immunity has been repeatedly rejected by courts, including the ICJ in *Jurisdictional Immunities*. But there is potential for human rights to be litigated through existing exceptions to State immunity, such as the commercial or employment exceptions.[154] And the law will continue to evolve through the accretion of State practice, reflecting the values and priorities of States and their constituents as they attempt to strike the balance between immunity and accountability.

REFERENCES

ALEBEEK, R VAN (2012), 'Jurisdictional Immunities of the State (Germany v Italy): On Right Outcomes and Wrong Terms', 55 *German Yearbook of International Law* 281.

COLLINS, L (Gen ed) (2017), *Dicey, Morris and Collins on Conflicts of Laws* (15th edn, London: Thomson Sweet & Maxwell).

FOAKES J, *The Position of Heads of State and Senior Officials in International Law* (Oxford: Oxford University Press, 2014).

FOX, H (1999), 'The *Pinochet Case No 3*', 48 *ICLQ* 687.

---

[152] Ibid, para 60. See scepticism about the procedural/substantive distinction in Fox and Webb, 2015, ch 2.

[153] The Court declared unconstitutional the relevant provisions of Law No 5 of 2013 and Law No 848 of 1957 ratifying the UN Charter (insofar as it required compliance with the ICJ Judgment in *Jurisdictional Immunities*).

[154] The recent Supreme Court judgment in *Reyes* v *Al-Malki* [2017] UKSC 61, although on diplomatic immunity, contains interesting analysis by Lady Hale and Lords Clarke and Wilson on the incompatibility of diplomatic immunity with human trafficking and the need to take a broad view of the 'professional and commercial activity' exception to diplomatic immunity in Article 31(1)(c) of the Vienna Convention on Diplomatic Relations.

Fox, H and Webb, P (2015), *The Law of State Immunity* (3rd rev edn, Oxford: Oxford University Press).

Gattini, A (2008), 'The International Customary Law Nature of Immunity from Measures of Constraint for State Cultural Property on Loan', in I Buffard, J Crawford, A Pellet, and S Wittich (eds) (2011), *International Law between Universalism and Fragmentation: Festschrift in Honour of Gerhard Hafner* (The Hague: Martinus Nijhoff), p 421.

Institut De Droit, Naples (2009), *Resolution on International Crimes and Immunities from Jurisdiction of States and their Agents* (Rapporteur Lady Fox), ADI vol 73.

Keitner, C (2013), 'Germany v Italy and the Limits of Horizontal Enforcement: Some Reflections from a United States Perspective', 11 *J Int'l Crim Just* 167.

McGregor, L (2013), 'State Immunity and Human Rights: Is There a Future after Germany v. Italy?', 11 *J Int'l Crim Just* 25.

Pingel, N (2000), '*Creighton v Qatar*', JDI 1054.

Salmon, J (2009) 'La Résolution de Naples de L'Institut de droit international sur les immunités de juridiction de l'Etat et de ses agents en cas de crimes internationaux (10 Septembre 2009)', *Belg Rev DI* 316.

Stewart, DP (2005), 'The UN Convention on Jurisdictional Immunities of States and their Property', 99 *AJIL* 194.

Truman, EM (2007), 'Sovereign Wealth Funds: The Need for Greater Transparency and Accountability', *Peterson Institute Policy Brief* BP 07-6.

Webb, P (2016), 'The Immunity of States, Diplomats and International Organizations in Employment Disputes: The New Human Rights Dilemma?', 27 *EJIL* 745.

FURTHER READING

Akande, D and Shah, S (2010), 'Immunities of State Officials, International Crimes, and Foreign Domestic Courts', 21 *EJIL* 815: analyses the arguments for and against an international crimes exception to immunity of State officials, placing it in the context of the relationship between the immunity of States and those who act on their behalf.

Brownlie, I (2008), *Principles of Public International Law* (7th edn, Oxford: Oxford University Press): sets out his proposed alternative solution to the application of the *jure imperii/jure gestionis* dichotomy with two sets of countervailing criteria which were to be balanced in determining the nature of the act of the foreign State.

Dickinson, A, Lindsay, R, and Loonam, JP (2004), *State Immunity: Selected Materials and Commentary* (Oxford: Oxford University Press): commentary on the State immunity legislation of the UK and US, drawing comparisons to the UNCSI.

Fox, H and Webb, P (2015), *The Law of State Immunity* (3rd rev edn, Oxford: Oxford University Press): an in-depth examination of the topic of State immunity, with emphasis on the practice of the UK and US and the significance of UNCSI.

Hafner, G, Kohen, M, and Breau, S (eds) (2006), *State Practice regarding State Immunities: La pratique des Etats concernant les immunités des Etats in English and French* (Strasbourg: Council of Europe).

Juratowitch, B (2014), 'Fora Non Conveniens for Enforcement of Arbitral Awards against States', 63(2) *ICLQ* 477: discusses recent cases on enforcement of arbitral awards and the doctrine of *forum non conveniens*, which can also serve as an avoidance technique for defendants (whether States, people, or companies).

Lauterpacht, H (1951), 'The Problem of Jurisdictional Immunities of Foreign States', 28 *BYIL* 220: a classic piece on State immunity, expressing scepticism regarding the absolute doctrine.

McGoldrick, D (2010), 'The Boundaries of Justiciability', 59 *ICLQ* 981: analyses trends in the approach of English courts to non-justiciability, given the growing importance of human rights and the rule of law.

McLachlan, C (2014), *Foreign Relations Law* (Cambridge: Cambridge University Press): considers the three avoidance techniques discussed in this chapter by looking at the distribution of the foreign relations power between branches of government, the impact of the foreign relations power on individual rights, and the treatment of the foreign State within the domestic legal system.

Mizushima T (2010), 'The Enactment of Japan's State Immunity Act in 2009', 53 *Jap YBIL*: precise analysis of one of the early pieces of legislation to implement UNCSI (in advance of ratification by Japan).

O'Keefe, R and Tams, C J (eds) (2013), *The UN Convention on Jurisdictional Immunities of States and Their Property: A Commentary* (Oxford: Oxford University Press): article-by-article analysis of UNCSI, drawing on the *travaux* as well as State practice and academic commentary.

Peters, A et al (eds) (2015), *Immunities in the Age of Global Constitutionalism* (Leiden: Brill): analyses new trends and challenges for the immunities of States, their officials, and international organizations within the framework of global constitutionalism and multilevel governance.

12

IMMUNITIES ENJOYED BY OFFICIALS OF STATES AND INTERNATIONAL ORGANIZATIONS

Chanaka Wickremasinghe

SUMMARY

This chapter seeks to explain the immunities enjoyed by various categories of officials of States and international organizations involved in the conduct of international relations.[1] It sets out the broad rationale underlying these immunities as being to facilitate the processes of communication between States on which international relations and cooperation rely. The law relating to the various categories of officials is then considered in turn, noting in particular the extent of the immunities from jurisdiction which they enjoy.

Finally, the question of the inter-relation of the law on immunities (which developed largely as a 'self-contained regime') with recent developments in the field of international criminal law is considered. The discussion focuses on the challenges to immunities which are presented by measures to end the impunity of those who commit the most serious international crimes, such as through the development of extraterritorial jurisdiction and the establishment of international criminal courts and tribunals. A range of judicial decisions, such as the House of Lords decision in the *Pinochet No 3* case, the judgments of the International Court of Justice in the *Arrest Warrant* and *Jurisdictional Immunities of the State* cases, and the decisions of the International Criminal Court relating to the arrest warrant in the *Al Bashir* and *Qadhafi* cases, are reviewed in order to consider how international law has sought to reconcile these apparently conflicting priorities.

[1] The views expressed here are purely personal. I am grateful to Sir Michael Wood, Sir Daniel Bethlehem, Chris Whomersley, Diana Brooks, Doug Wilson, and Sir Malcolm Evans for helpful suggestions and improvements to earlier drafts.

I. INTRODUCTION

The primary focus of this chapter is on the immunities which officials of States and international organizations enjoy from the jurisdiction of other States, which are broadly contained within the framework of diplomatic law.[2] For these purposes diplomatic law means the law by which international relations are conducted, and the processes of communication at the public international level are facilitated. Such communication can occur by a variety of means and in a number of settings. It includes both eye-catching, single events such as State visits and summits between Heads of State, as well as the more everyday work of foreign ministries, diplomatic missions, consular posts, and international organizations (James, 1991). The setting for such international communication ranges from simple ad hoc bilateral meetings of State officials to permanent institutionalized cooperation in large international organizations such as the UN and its specialized agencies.

Diplomatic law has ancient roots, and today comprises a large and, in many respects, highly developed body of law, derived from a variety of sources. For present purposes these include the 1961 Vienna Convention on Diplomatic Relations (VCDR), the 1963 Vienna Convention on Consular Relations (VCCR), and the 1969 Convention on Special Missions. Additionally, in relation to international organizations there is a large number of treaties which deal with both the privileges and immunities of representatives of States to international organizations and the privileges and immunities of officials and experts of those organizations. The best known examples of these treaties are the 1946 Convention on the Privileges and Immunities of the UN, and the 1947 Convention on the Privileges and Immunities of the Specialized Agencies. A further important component of diplomatic law is the Convention on the Prevention and Punishment of Crimes against Internationally Protected Persons, including Diplomatic Agents 1973.[3]

However, diplomatic law is not fully codified, and certain categories of those engaged in the conduct of international relations therefore enjoy immunity only by virtue of customary international law. For example, as we shall see, the law governing the privileges and immunities of foreign Heads of State and other senior government officials remains largely uncodified at the international level. In addition to this body of treaties and custom which sets out the primary rules of diplomatic law, it is important to review the extensive body of judicial decisions of both international and national courts and tribunals in which those rules have been interpreted and applied.

In earlier eras, when the range of diplomatic communication was less developed, its governing law was less sophisticated and the rationales on which that law rested were broad approximations. In the modern era, however, the legal fiction of extraterritoriality of foreign missions has now been discredited (Crawford, 2012, p 397). The 'representative theory' (ie the identification of representatives of a sending State with the State itself) has been subjected to more rigorous rationalization, but continues to contribute to the rationale

---

[2] Whilst the primary focus will be on diplomatic law, its interaction with other more recent developments in international law, including in human rights law and international criminal law, will be considered in a number of the subsequent sections of this chapter.

[3] For text see (1974) 13 ILM 41. This Convention comprises an important aspect of the duty of protection States owe to officials of States and international organizations engaged on international business, providing for broad extraterritorial jurisdiction in respect of crimes relating to attacks on these persons. For a commentary on its drafting and negotiation see Wood, 1974.

of jurisdictional immunities.[4] However, it is now the 'functional necessity' theory which provides the most convincing explanation of much of the modern law of diplomacy.[5] This recognizes that international cooperation between States, from which political, economic, social, and cultural benefits flow, is entirely dependent on effective processes of communication. It is therefore essential that international law should protect and facilitate those processes, and it is to that end that modern diplomatic law seeks to ensure an appropriate balance between the interests of the sending and receiving States. Professor Denza (2016, p 1) observes:

> Diplomatic law in a sense constitutes the procedural framework for the construction of international law and international relations. It guarantees the efficacy and security of the machinery through which States conduct diplomacy, and without this machinery States cannot construct law whether by custom or by agreement on matters of substance.

The primary aspect of diplomatic law on which this chapter will concentrate is the grant of immunity from local jurisdiction. In this respect it is important to note that international law recognizes two basic types of immunity from jurisdiction in relation to officials of States and international organizations.

The first is immunity *ratione personae*, ie immunity enjoyed by certain categories of State officials by virtue of their office. The functions of certain key offices of State are so important to the maintenance of international relations that they require immunity for their protection and facilitation.[6] These immunities cover both the official and the private acts of such office-holders, since interference with the performance of the official functions of such a person can result from the subjection of either type of act to the jurisdiction of the receiving State (eg if a diplomat is arrested it will interfere with his ability to perform his official functions whatever the reason for his arrest). These categories of official enjoy complete personal inviolability (including freedom from arrest and/or detention) and absolute immunity from criminal jurisdiction. Immunity from civil jurisdiction may also be recognized (though given the less coercive nature of civil jurisdiction, this immunity may be limited in respect of certain purely private actions of members of certain categories of official).[7] However, because immunities *ratione personae* attach only to enable the proper functioning of particular offices of State, rather than to benefit the office-holder individually, they lapse when the office-holder leaves office.

The second type of immunity is immunity *ratione materiae*—these immunities attach to the official acts of State officials. They are derivative from the principle of State immunity, which precludes the courts of one State adjudicating upon the acts of another State without its consent. Such immunities are, therefore, determined by reference to the nature of the acts in question rather than by reference to the particular office of the official who performed them. As such they cover a narrower range of acts than immunities *ratione personae*, but

---

[4] The representative theory suggests that diplomats, as representatives of the sending State, should enjoy the same immunities as the State does itself. The preamble of the VCDR states that: '. . . the purpose of such privileges and immunities is not to benefit individuals but to ensure the efficient performance of the functions of diplomatic missions as representing States . . .'. In any event it might also be noted that the immunities of States themselves are now more limited and are increasingly based on function rather than simply on status.

[5] See introductory comments to Section II of the ILC Commentary on its final draft Articles, *YBILC* (1958), vol II, pp 94–5; see also comments of Sir Gerald Fitzmaurice, *YBILC* (1957), vol I (part two), para 10.

[6] See, eg, the preamble to the VCDR and the judgment of the ICJ in *Arrest Warrant of 11 April 2000 (Democratic Republic of Congo v Belgium), Preliminary Objections and Merits, Judgment, ICJ Reports 2002*, p 3.

[7] Denza, 2016, pp 232–4 notes how, historically, the immunities of diplomats from civil jurisdiction were less readily accepted than immunities from criminal jurisdiction.

cover a wider range of actors—indeed, they potentially apply to the official acts of all State officials. Furthermore, because they relate to the nature of the act in question, the immunity for such official acts subsists even after the individual who performed has ceased to have any official functions. Thus a former State official can benefit from such immunity in respect of his official acts performed while in office, even after he has left office.

It is important to note that both of these types of immunity operate simply as procedural bars to jurisdiction, and can be waived by appropriate authorities of the sending State, thus enabling the courts of a foreign State to assert jurisdiction.

The related, but conceptually distinct, doctrines of non-justiciability and/or act of State are not dealt with here. Non-justiciability is sometimes confusingly described as 'subject-matter immunity', but is in fact distinct from procedural immunity, since it essentially asserts that the subject matter of the claim is in fact governed by international law (or, in some cases, foreign public law) and therefore falls outside the competence of national courts of other States to determine.[8] A plea of non-justiciability requires the court to give closer examination to the basis of the proceedings than when it deals with a procedural immunity. However, further confusion may arise from the fact that these various forms of objection to jurisdiction are not mutually exclusive, but can in fact exist simultaneously (see Barker, 1998). Cases where different grounds for objection to jurisdiction coexist will usually be dismissed on the basis of a procedural immunity, since that question must be decided at the outset of proceedings, and will often be the simplest means of bringing the proceedings to an end.[9]

Despite the considerable constraint which procedural immunities (and other privileges of foreign diplomatic missions) place on the territorial jurisdiction of a receiving State, States generally observe them scrupulously. Perhaps more surprisingly, despite certain notorious cases of their abuse, there is no substantial body of opinion which advocates their abolition or restriction. For example, in response to the *St James's Square Incident* of 1984 (in which a police officer was killed by a shot fired from within the Libyan People's Bureau in London, while she was patrolling a political demonstration outside the Bureau), both the Foreign Affairs Committee of the UK Parliament and the UK government considered whether amendment of the VCDR should be sought, but rejected this on the grounds that it was neither practicable nor desirable.[10]

The generally high level of compliance with diplomatic law is usually ascribed to the reciprocal nature of diplomatic exchange (see, eg, Higgins, 1985). Since each State is both a sending State and a receiving State, each State has an interest in maintaining the proper equilibrium between the rights of sending and receiving States. This explains the restraint shown both by receiving States in respecting the privileges and immunities of foreign missions, and by members of diplomatic missions in their conduct while abroad.

---

[8] See *Buttes Gas and Oil Co v Hammer* [1982] AC 888 (HL). For the limits of this doctrine see the case of *Kuwait Airways Corp v Iraqi Airways Co (No 2)* [2002] UKHL 19, 16 May 2002 and *Belhaj v Straw* [2017] UKSC 3. For the application of the doctrine of non-justiciability alongside questions of the immunity of a former State official see the dissenting speech of Lord Lloyd in the *Pinochet (No 1)* case [1998] 3 WLR 1456, 194–6 and discussed by Denza, 1999, pp 956–8.

[9] Procedurally non-justiciability/act of State is considered more as a substantive defence rather than simply a procedural bar to the jurisdiction of the court, and may therefore be considered at a later stage of proceedings—eg the judgment of Lord Goff in *Kuwait Airways Corp v Iraqi Airways Co (No 1)* [1995] 1 WLR 1147 (HL). For the obligation of a court to consider the plea of immunity *in limine litis* see *Difference Relating to Immunity from Legal Process of a Special Rapporteur of the Commission on Human Rights, Advisory Opinion, ICJ Reports 1999*, p 62.

[10] See *Abuse of Diplomatic Privileges and Immunities*, FAC First Report 1984–5 (HC 127), paras 53–7, and the Government's Reply (Misc No 5 (1985), Cmnd 9497), paras 9–11.

It should be noted that diplomatic law has grown up largely as a 'self-contained regime', setting out the rights and obligations of receiving States and sending States, and with its own remedies available in cases of abuse. This has been observed by the ICJ[11] and is also reflected in the ILC Articles on State Responsibility, Article 50 of which provides that States are not permitted to infringe the inviolability of diplomatic and consular agents, premises, archives, and documents when taking countermeasures (Crawford, 2002, pp 50 and 288–93). However, as will be seen in Section VII of this chapter, the interaction of diplomatic law with recent developments in other areas of international law, and particularly in international criminal law, has raised difficult problems which have yet to be fully answered.

II. DIPLOMATIC RELATIONS

The primary, though not exclusive, means of communication between governments is through the establishment of diplomatic relations, usually involving the exchange of permanent diplomatic missions. A diplomatic mission is of course in a position of considerable vulnerability, being located in territory over which another State exercises jurisdiction, and thus having limited means available to it for ensuring its own security. From the earliest times, therefore, international society has recognized the need to protect diplomatic agents so as to enable diplomatic exchange (Young, 1964; Barker, 1996, pp 32–55). The rules of international law which govern the establishment and maintenance of such diplomatic relations are now codified in the 1961 Vienna Convention on Diplomatic Relations (VCDR). With over 190 parties, the VCDR is amongst the most widely ratified of all multilateral treaties, and it is probable that even those of its aspects which were originally progressive developments of the law now reflect customary international law.[12] The VCDR has thus been extraordinarily successful in its aim to create a comprehensive legal framework for the conduct of diplomatic relations.[13]

A. THE SCHEME OF THE VIENNA CONVENTION ON DIPLOMATIC RELATIONS

The VCDR seeks to establish a proper balance of the rights of sending and receiving States. The founding principle set out in Article 2 is that diplomatic relations take place by mutual consent. Article 3 then sets out the primary functions of a diplomatic mission:

(a) to represent the sending State;

(b) to protect the interests of the sending State and its nationals;

(c) to negotiate with the government of the receiving State;

---

[11] See *United States Diplomatic and Consular Staff in Tehran, Judgment, ICJ Reports* 1980, p 3, paras 86–7.

[12] Ibid, paras 45 and 62. For a summary of the main issues on which the VCDR represented progressive development of the law at the time of its negotiation, see Denza, 2016, pp 2–5.

[13] Denza, 2016, pp 1–2 suggests three reasons to explain the success of the VCDR. First, that the law in this area is both long-established and has been relatively stable for a considerable time. Secondly, the important role played by reciprocity in the maintenance of the rules. Thirdly, the careful attention paid in the drafting processes of the ILC and in the Vienna Conference itself to producing a text which could command the general approval of States.

(d) to ascertain and report to the government of the sending State on the conditions and developments in the receiving State;

(e) to promote friendly relations between the sending State and the receiving State, and to develop their economic, cultural, and scientific relations.

The next part of the Convention (Articles 4–19) deals with various procedural questions in relation to the establishment of diplomatic relations, and in particular the appointment and accreditation of diplomatic agents. The consent of the receiving State is required in the form of a prior *agrément* for the appointment of the head of mission. Denza (2016, p 40) observes:

The justification for the requirement lies in the particular sensitivity of the appointment of a head of mission and the need, if a head of mission is effectively to conduct diplomacy between two States, for him to be personally acceptable to both of them.

In relation to other diplomatic agents (except defence attachés) the sending State does not have to obtain the prior consent of the receiving State (Article 7). Nevertheless, the sending State must provide to the receiving State notification (and, as far as possible, prior notification) of the arrival and final departure (or termination of the functions) of all members of missions (Article 10).[14] Furthermore the receiving State is, at any time (including before their arrival in the receiving State), entitled to inform the sending State that the head of the mission or any other member of a mission is *persona non grata*, or unacceptable, without giving reasons for doing so (Article 9).[15] In such cases the sending State must recall the person or terminate his functions. If the sending State fails to respond the receiving State may, after a 'reasonable period', treat the person as no longer enjoying diplomatic privileges and immunities.

Articles 20–8 concern the privileges and facilities which the sending State must grant to the mission itself. Thus under Article 22 the premises of the mission are inviolable, and agents of the receiving State are not entitled to enter them without the consent of the head of the mission. During the drafting work of the ILC and also during the negotiation of the VCDR, it was considered whether there should be any exceptions to this rule in times of extreme emergency. However, such proposals were overwhelmingly rejected on the grounds that the power of appreciation as to whether one of the exceptions was applicable to a given situation would belong to the receiving State, and that this might lead to abuse. In 1984 during the *St James's Square Incident* the UK

[14] It now appears that the UK courts will not consider that notification is a prerequisite to the entitlement of diplomatic status, *R v Home Secretary, ex parte Bagga* (1990) 88 ILR 404: but see also the earlier cases of *R v Governor of Pentonville Prison, ex parte Teja* (1971) 52 ILR 368, *R v Lambeth Justices, ex parte Yusufu* (1985) 88 ILR 323, and *R v Governor of Pentonville Prison, ex parte Osman (No 2)* (1988) 88 ILR 378—in relation to the latter see also the certificate of the Foreign and Commonwealth Office (FCO) in (1988) 59 *BYIL* 479. In *Al Attiyah v Bin-Jasim Bin-Jaber Al Thani* [2016] EWHC 212 (QB) the Court refused to exercise jurisdiction over a challenge to the entitlement of an individual to diplomatic status, where the Court had before it evidence of his appointment by the sending States duly certified by FCO. The decision was subsequently approved by the Court of Appeal in *Al-Juffali v Estrada* [2016] EWCA Civ 176.

[15] In its Reply to the Foreign Affairs Committee (n 10 of this chapter, paras 689–90) the government set out its policy in respect of the kinds of behaviour which would lead to a declaration of *persona non grata*, which included matters such as espionage and incitement to violence, as well as other criminal offences. In addition, a serious view would be taken of reliance on diplomatic immunity to evade civil liabilities. Finally the government also stated a new policy in relation to parking offences, under which persistent failure to pay parking fines would lead to a review of a person's acceptability as a member of a mission. Denza, 2016, p 72 notes how the number of parking tickets cancelled on grounds of diplomatic immunity fell from over 100,000 in 1984, to just over 2,300 in 1993.

government scrupulously respected the inviolability of the Libyan Mission throughout, notwithstanding the outrage that had been perpetrated from there, and the premises were not entered until after the severance of diplomatic relations and the vacation of the premises.[16]

Furthermore, under Article 22(2) the receiving State is under a special duty to take all appropriate steps to protect the premises of the mission against all intrusion, and to prevent disturbances to the peace of the mission or impairment of its dignity. Thus in the *Tehran Hostages* case, although those who attacked the US Embassy and Consulates were not acting on behalf of Iran in the initial phase, Iran was nonetheless responsible for having failed to take appropriate steps to protect the premises and their occupants.[17]

In relation to the duty to prevent any disturbance of the peace of the mission or impairment of its dignity in normal times, the question of whether to allow peaceful political demonstrations outside diplomatic missions may require the receiving State to strike a balance between rights of political expression and the maintenance of its obligations towards the sending State.[18]

Similarly under Article 24 the archives of the mission are inviolable.[19] In addition, Article 27 provides for the free communication of the mission, including the inviolability of official correspondence, free use of diplomatic bags for diplomatic documents and articles for official use, and the protection from interference of diplomatic couriers.

---

[16] During the inquiry into the incident by the Foreign Affairs Committee two possible grounds of entry into the mission were examined. First, whether there had been a material breach of treaty by Libya entitling the UK to repudiate it and enter the premises. This was rejected on the basis that the VCDR is a self-contained regime, with its own remedies in case of breach. The second question was whether the UK would have had a right to enter the premises under the doctrine of self-defence. The Legal Adviser to the Foreign and Commonwealth Office told the Committee that self-defence would in principle be available in respect of both action directed against the State and action directed against its nationals. However, he believed the circumstances of this case did not justify forcible entry on the grounds of self-defence, as the criteria specified in the *Caroline* case were not met. The Committee accepted the latter conclusion but made no comment on the general point as to the applicability of self-defence as a ground for entering diplomatic premises (n 9 of this chapter, paras 94–5). Mann (1990, pp 333–7) argued that the inviolability of premises is conditioned by the lawfulness of their use, and so the government had the right, and the duty, to enter the premises, to search for and remove any weapons held there.

[17] *United States Diplomatic and Consular Staff in Tehran, Judgment, ICJ Reports 1980,* p 3, paras 62–8. During the second period when the Court found that through its support of the hostage-takers, Iran was directly responsible for their actions, it violated, *inter alia,* paras (1) and (3) of Article 22 VCDR (ibid, para 77).

[18] In its Reply to the Foreign Affairs Committee (n 10 of this chapter, para 39(e)) the government explained that in most cases this was left to the police, who tended to manage such situations by, for example, keeping demonstrators on the opposite side of the road to the mission premises.

[19] A violation of Article 24 was found in *United States Diplomatic and Consular Staff in Tehran, Judgment, ICJ Reports 1980,* p 3. For the question of whether inviolability extends to documents which have been removed from the mission and are subsequently used in legal proceedings see *Shearson Lehman Brothers Inc v Maclaine Watson and Co, International Tin Council Intervening* [1988] 1 WLR 16 and Mann, 1990, pp 328–9. See also the pre-VCDR Canadian case of *Rose v The King* (1947) 3 DLR 710 in which documentary evidence of espionage against accused persons in criminal proceedings was held to be admissible notwithstanding that it had been stolen from the Russian Embassy and inviolability had not been waived. In the case of *Fayed v Al-Tajir* (CA [1987] 3 WLR 102) an internal memorandum of an embassy in London was found to be protected by absolute privilege as a diplomatic document, leading to a dismissal of a libel action based on the contents of the document. In the recent case of *R (Bancoult) v Secretary of State for Foreign and Commonwealth Affairs (No 3)* [2014] EWCA Civ 708, the Court of Appeal (reversing the Administrative Court on this point) ruled that a reporting cable from the US Embassy in London back to the State Department, which had been leaked to the world at large through the 'Wikileaks' website (ie without the consent of the USA), did not retain inviolability under Articles 24 and 27(2) of the VCDR and was therefore admissible. This decision was under appeal at the time of writing.

Articles 29–39 deal with the privileges and immunities enjoyed by members of the mission. As well as jurisdictional immunities (considered in the next section of this chapter), these include other matters such as the inviolability of the private residence of a diplomatic agent, exemption from taxes and customs duties, and exemption from national service requirements in the receiving State. Thus members of diplomatic missions enjoy wide protections from interference by the receiving State, which must be given effect in national law, this being done in the UK by the Diplomatic Privileges Act 1964. However, it is important to emphasize that the rights and privileges are not granted for the personal benefit of the individuals concerned, but to ensure the efficient performance of the functions of the diplomatic mission.

By way of *quid pro quo* for the enjoyment of privileges and immunities, members of diplomatic missions owe certain duties towards the receiving State. These are:

(a) the duty to respect the laws and regulations of the receiving State (Article 41(1));

(b) the duty not to interfere in the internal affairs of the receiving State (Article 41(1));

(c) all official business of the communication by the mission with the receiving State should be through the Ministry of Foreign Affairs of the receiving State, or with such other ministries as may be agreed (Article 41(2));

(d) the premises of the mission must be not be used in any manner incompatible with the functions of the mission (Article 41(3));

(e) a diplomatic agent must not practise for personal profit any professional or commercial activity in the receiving State (Article 42).

Finally in Articles 43–6 the Convention deals with arrangements on the termination of diplomatic functions and on severance of diplomatic relations.

B. JURISDICTIONAL IMMUNITIES

The VCDR recognizes various categories of staff members of diplomatic missions, each enjoying immunity from jurisdiction to a different extent:

(a) diplomatic agents (ie the head of the mission and other members of the diplomatic staff) and their families (provided that they are not nationals of the receiving State (Article 37(1)) enjoy immunities *ratione personae*, ie by virtue of their office. Thus they are granted personal inviolability, including freedom from arrest and detention (Article 29),[20] and absolute immunity from criminal jurisdiction (Article 31). A diplomatic agent is also immune from civil and administrative jurisdiction,[21] except in three types of case:

(i) a real action relating to immovable property situated in the territory of the receiving State, unless he holds it on behalf of the sending State for the purposes of the mission;[22]

---

[20] A further aspect of inviolability is the duty to protect diplomatic agents, on which see also the Convention on the Prevention and Punishment of Crimes against Internationally Protected Persons (earlier). For clear breaches of both limbs of Article 29 see *United States Diplomatic and Consular Staff in Tehran, Judgment, ICJ Reports 1980*, p 3, paras 62–3 and 77. Self-defence or an overriding duty to protect human life appears to provide a limited exception. See ibid, para 86 and Denza, 2016, pp 221–3.

[21] This includes civil proceedings concerning private matters. See, eg, the Australian case of *De Andrade* v *De Andrade* (1984) 118 ILR 299, in which the immunity of a diplomat was upheld in relation to divorce and custody proceedings; see also *Re P* [1998] 1 FLR 624 and 1 FLR 1026. But see also *Al-Juffali* v *Estrada* [2016] EWCA Civ 176.

[22] See Denza, 2016, pp 239–47. On the difficult issue of whether the private residence of a diplomat is included within the exception, see *Intpro Properties* v *Sauvel* [1983] 2 WLR 908. The private residence of a diplomat is, however, inviolable by virtue of Article 30 (considered in *Reyes* v *Al-Malki* [2017] UKSC 61).

(ii) an action relating to succession in which the diplomatic agent is involved as executor, administrator, heir, or legatee as a private person and not on behalf of the sending State;

(iii) an action relating to any professional or commercial activity exercised by the diplomatic agent in the receiving State outside his official functions.[23]

(b) Administrative and technical staff and their families, who are not nationals or permanent residents of the receiving State enjoy similar personal inviolability and immunity from criminal jurisdiction to diplomatic agents. However, their immunity from civil jurisdiction does not extend to acts performed outside the course of their duties (Article 37(2)).[24]

(c) Service staff who are not nationals or permanent residents of the receiving State enjoy immunity *ratione materiae*, in respect of acts performed in the course of their duties (Article 37(3)).

(d) Diplomatic agents representing the sending State but who are in fact nationals or permanent residents of the receiving State, also enjoy immunity *ratione materiae* in respect of official acts performed in the exercise of their functions (Article 38(1)).[25]

(e) All members of diplomatic missions who enjoy immunities while in office enjoy a subsisting immunity *ratione materiae* with respect to acts performed in the exercise of their functions as members of the mission even after they have left office (Article 39(2)).[26]

It might be noted that generally immunities under the VCDR operate only in respect of the jurisdiction of the receiving State. However, the provisions of Article 40 can be distinguished in that third States must accord diplomatic agents (and their family members) inviolability and such immunities as may be required to ensure their transit or return while en route to and from post.[27]

C. REMEDIES IN CASES OF ABUSE

While the immunities set out in the previous section impose a considerable derogation from the jurisdiction of receiving States, the VCDR seeks to redress the balance, at least partially, by providing for certain remedies in cases of abuse. Jurisdictional immunities operate purely at the procedural level, by barring the adjudicative powers of the local courts in respect of the holder, but they do not in themselves amount to substantive exemptions from the law itself. Indeed, as we have seen, members of diplomatic missions are under a duty to respect the law of the receiving State. Therefore where such immunity is waived, the local courts may enjoy jurisdiction within the usual bounds set by international law. Article 32 of the VCDR deals with the question of waiver, setting out: (a) that waiver is a prerogative of the sending State (not the diplomatic agent in question) (Article 32(1)); (b) that waiver must always be express (Article 33(2)); and (c) that waiver from jurisdiction in

---

[23] For discussion, albeit obiter, of the scope of this exception see *Reyes v Al-Malki* [2017] UKSC 61.

[24] See, eg, *Re B* (2002) 145 ILR 516.

[25] See *Al-Juffali v Estrada* [2016] EWCA Civ 176.

[26] See the German Constitutional Court case of the *Former Syrian Ambassador to the GDR* (1997) 115 ILR 596; see also the *Pinochet* case discussed later in this chapter. For further explanation see Dinstein, 1966.

[27] See the Netherlands case, *Public Prosecutor v JBC* (1984) 94 ILR 339. In a recent UK case, a diplomat accredited to the Ethiopian Embassy in Washington was prosecuted and convicted of the importation of drugs whilst on a holiday in Europe. The judge of the Crown Court rejected the defendant's plea of immunity as she was not travelling through London to resume her diplomatic functions in Washington (*R v Wondemagegne* 12 July 2012—ruling on file with the author).

respect of civil or administrative proceedings does not, in itself, imply waiver from execution of the judgment (Article 33(4)).[28]

However, waivers remain in the discretion of the sending State,[29] and in the event that it refuses, the receiving State must rely on the broader remedy of withdrawing its consent, either in respect of a particular member of the mission by declaring him or her *persona non grata* or, in a particularly egregious case, by breaking off diplomatic relations.

III. CONSULAR RELATIONS

The role of consuls is to represent the sending State, and to promote and/or protect its interests in the receiving State, but with the emphasis of that role on technical and administrative matters rather than political matters (in which diplomatic staff specialize). Consuls often deal with private interests, such as assistance to nationals of the sending State in the receiving State and the promotion of trade, rather than the public interests of the sending State. Nevertheless, generalizations about consular relations must be treated cautiously since the range of consular functions, as set out in VCCR, Article 5, is very broad. It can include:

(a) protecting in the receiving State the interests of the sending State and its nationals;[30]

(b) assisting nationals of the sending State in need of help in the receiving State;

(c) obtaining appropriate legal assistance for nationals of the sending State before tribunals and other authorities of the receiving State;

(d) assistance to vessels and aircraft of the sending State and their crews, as well as exercising rights of supervision and inspection thereof;

(e) promoting trade between the two States;

(f) issuing passports and/or visas and other notarial functions;

(g) promoting cultural exchange.

Though international law on consular relations has ancient roots, the modern law first developed in a vast web of bilateral consular treaties in the nineteenth and twentieth centuries. Yet so varied were these treaty provisions that it was believed that (unlike the law of diplomatic relations prior to 1961) customary international law played only a very limited role in the establishment and maintenance of consular relations. However, following work by the ILC in the late 1950s and early 1960s, the 1963 Vienna Convention on Consular Relations (VCCR) sought to consolidate and codify a basic body of rules. While the VCCR does establish a widely accepted benchmark for consular relations[31] it expressly states that it shall not affect existing agreements between States, or prevent States from varying its provisions in their future agreements (Article 73).[32]

---

[28] By way of an exception to Article 32(1) and (2), Article 32(3) provides that a waiver will be implied in respect of counterclaims which are directly related to the principal claim in proceedings commenced by the holder of the immunity.

[29] For examples of practice see also Denza, 2016, pp 284–6.

[30] On the VCCR system of consular protection of nationals of the sending State, see *LaGrand (Germany v USA), Merits, Judgment, ICJ Reports 2001*, p 466, para 74. In the context of UK public law see also *R (Abbasi) v Secretary of State for Foreign and Commonwealth Affairs* [2002] EWCA Civ 1598.

[31] For example in *United States Diplomatic and Consular Staff in Tehran, Judgment, ICJ Reports 1980*, p 3, para 62 the ICJ found that the protection of consular staff and property under the VCCR also reflected rules of customary international law.

[32] Similarly under the UK implementing legislation, the Consular Relations Act 1968, the relevant provisions of the VCCR are implemented by and scheduled to the Act, but by virtue of s 3 any international agreement of the UK under which consular privileges and immunities differ from the VCCR standard may be given effect by Order in Council.

The scheme of the VCCR is not unlike the VCDR, dealing with: the establishment and conduct of consular relations (Articles 2–24); the end of consular functions (Articles 25–7); facilities, privileges, and immunities relating to a consular post (Articles 28–39); facilities, privileges, and immunities relating to consular officers and other members of a consular post (Articles 40–57); the regime relating to honorary consuls (Articles 58–68); and general provisions (Articles 69–73).

The differences in the functions of consuls, as compared to diplomats, explain the differences in the extent of immunities from jurisdiction that are generally granted to consuls.[33] Consular officers enjoy a more limited personal inviolability—they may not be arrested or detained pending trial, except in the case of a grave crime[34] and pursuant to a decision by the competent judicial authority (Article 41). In relation to immunity from jurisdiction, consular officers enjoy only immunity *ratione materiae*, ie in respect of acts performed in the exercise of their consular functions (Article 43).[35]

IV. SPECIAL MISSIONS

In addition to the communication between governments that is enabled through the establishment of permanent diplomatic missions, an important means of carrying out particular items of inter-governmental business is through the use of special missions (sometimes called ad hoc diplomacy). The advantages of conducting international relations in this way are various. One is that it is a way of enabling direct contact between senior office-holders or those with particular specialisms or expertise in the respective countries (eg the UK currently has a number of roving special representatives, including one for climate change, whose interlocutors in other States will include individuals beyond the classical diplomatic channel between an Embassy and the Ministry of Foreign Affairs of the receiving State). Another aspect for some countries may be that ad hoc diplomacy may contribute to saving some of the costs of maintaining an extensive network of large diplomatic missions overseas. Special missions offer an important degree of flexibility to States in maintaining their international relations. In practice therefore special missions may vary considerably in appearance—ranging from missions involving the Head of State in person on matters of great political moment, to missions consisting of relatively junior officials concerned with a purely technical matter between the sending and receiving States.

While the use of ad hoc diplomacy of this sort in fact pre-dates the establishment of the present system of permanent diplomatic missions, the legal status of such missions has begun to attract greater attention in recent years. There is a growing body of State practice, including national legislation, decisions from national courts, and governmental statements (Wood, 2012).[36]

---

[33] Though in its practice with certain States, the UK has been willing to agree that the diplomatic standard of privileges and immunities should be extended to consular officers—see, eg, Consular Relations (Privileges and Immunities) (People's Republic of Bulgaria) Order 1970 (SI 1970/1923); Consular Relations (Privileges and Immunities) (People's Republic of China) Order 1984 (SI 1984/1978); Consular Relations (Privileges and Immunities) (Polish People's Republic) Order 1978 (SI 1978/1028); and Consular Relations (Privileges and Immunities) (USSR) Order 1970 (SI 1970/1938). For comparable US practice see Lee and Quigley, 2008, pp 463–9.

[34] The term 'grave crime' is not defined under the VCCR. However, the UK Consular Relations Act 1968 defines it as any crime punishable by up to a term of five years' imprisonment (s 1(2)).

[35] Determining what constitutes an 'official act' for these purposes can raise difficult questions of characterization. See Lee and Quigley, 2008, pp 440–61.

[36] See also the survey of State practice in *R (Freedom and Justice Party and others) v Secretary of State for Foreign and Commonwealth Affairs and the Director of Public Prosecutions* [2016] EWHC 2010 (Admin).

The ILC considered the topic of special missions following its work on diplomatic and consular relations, resulting in the 1969 UN Convention on Special Missions. The Convention seeks to set out in some detail norms for the conduct of ad hoc diplomacy, including the privileges and immunities which attach to special missions. The Convention does not have wide participation[37] and there is some question as to whether all of its provisions reflect customary international law. While the basic principles are not in doubt, Sir Arthur Watts has suggested that the main reason for the limited success of the Convention appears to be its inflexibility, in that it seeks to apply a single standard of treatment to all kinds of missions (see Watts, 1999, pp 344–5). There may also have been some concerns arising from the definition of special missions, as well as some practical difficulties arising from the temporary nature of such missions.

The Convention broadly follows the familiar scheme of the VCDR and VCCR. It sets out firmly the principle of mutual consent as underlying ad hoc diplomacy (Articles 2 and 3), and then deals with procedural questions for the sending and conduct of special missions (Articles 2–19). It sets out the facilities, privileges, and immunities of missions (Articles 22–8) and of their members and other staff (Articles 29–48).

Substantive aspects of the Convention also resemble the VCDR; hence for the purposes of jurisdictional immunities the staff are divided into broadly similar categories enjoying immunities to a similar extent.[38] Members of special missions are under an obligation to respect local law (Article 47). Also in cases of abuse the remedies of the receiving State are similar to those under the VCDR, including seeking waiver (Article 41), declaration of *persona non grata* (Article 12), or bringing the mission to an end (Article 20(1)(e)). Finally it might be noted that the Convention provides that such additional privileges and immunities as may be required under international law apply to the Head of the sending State, the Head of its government, its Minister for Foreign Affairs, and other persons of high rank when on a special mission (Article 21).[39]

The fact that relatively few States are parties to the Special Missions Convention means that a good part of the case law and other State practice pertains to the customary international law of special missions. Crawford sums up the position as follows:

> The Convention has influenced the customary rules concerning persons on official visits (special missions) which have developed largely through domestic caselaw. The Convention confers a higher scale of privileges and immunities upon a narrower range of missions than extant customary law, which focuses on the immunities necessary for the proper conduct of the mission, principally inviolability and immunity from criminal jurisdiction. (Crawford, 2012, p 414)[40]

---

[37] There are currently 38 parties. The UK signed the Convention on 17 December 1970, but has not ratified it.

[38] Under Articles 29 and 31, 'representatives of the sending State in the special mission and members of its diplomatic staff' enjoy personal inviolability and jurisdictional immunities equivalent to those of diplomatic agents under the VCDR (save that in respect of immunity from civil jurisdiction a further exception is made in relation to road traffic accidents outside the official functions of the person concerned). Family members, administrative and technical staff, service staff, and members of the mission who are nationals of the receiving State all enjoy equivalent immunities to those under the VCDR (see Articles 39, 36, 37, and 40 respectively). Temporally immunities are limited to the duration of the mission, save that immunity *ratione materiae* in relation to official acts continues to subsist even after the mission has come to an end (Article 44(2)).

[39] However, it is not clear what additional privileges and immunities this might entail. See *Satow's Diplomatic Practice* (2009, p 190).

[40] See also Wood, 2012 for a survey of State practice from Austria, Belgium, Finland, France, Germany, the Netherlands, the UK, and the USA, leading to the conclusion that '[t]here now appears to be a "settled answer" to the question of the customary law on the immunities of special missions'.

Thus the members of a special mission will enjoy personal inviolability and unqualified immunity *ratione personae* from criminal jurisdiction, as well as such immunity from civil and administrative jurisdiction as is necessary for them to carry out the functions of their mission. Such immunity should in principle last only for so long as is functionally necessary for the achievement of the special mission, but not longer. In addition immunity *ratione materiae* will attach to the official acts of the members of the special mission performed during the mission, which will in principle subsist even after the special mission has been completed.

By way of illustration it may be helpful to consider some recent UK practice in relation to special missions.[41] Whilst there have been a number of recent cases in which a court of first instance has had to consider whether a foreign visitor enjoys immunity as being on a special mission,[42] the issue of special mission immunity was considered in some detail by the High Court (on appeal from the Magistrates' Court) in the case of *Khurts Bat* v *Investigating Judge of the Federal Court of Germany*.[43] In that case a Mongolian official visiting the UK in the hope of arranging official meetings once there, but without having obtained UK consent to his presence in the UK for those purposes, claimed that he was immune from extradition proceedings in the UK on the basis that he was on a special mission. The High Court accepted that special mission immunity was governed by customary international law, which for these purposes was part of the common law. The court started from the definition of a special mission in Article 1 of the 1969 Convention:

> A 'special mission' is a temporary mission, representing the State, which is sent by one State to another State *with the consent of the latter* for the purposes of dealing with it on specific questions or performing in relation to it a specific task (emphasis of the court).[44]

The court found that it was vital that the prior consent of the receiving State should be obtained, and that it is consent to a special mission as such. As neither of these conditions was satisfied in the instant case, the court rejected the claim for special mission immunity. In doing so the court held that the question of consent by the UK (ie as the receiving State) was—like the question of whether or not the UK had agreed to the accreditation of a member of a permanent diplomatic mission—a matter that was exclusively for decision by the government and not the courts. It was therefore a question on which the government could provide conclusive evidence to the court by means of a certificate.

Subsequently,[45] the UK government sought to set out a clearer process for decision-making on the question of special missions. Prior to the *Khurts Bat* decision the question of

---

[41]   As the UK is not a party to the Special Missions Convention, this practice is based on the UK's obligations under customary international law.

[42]   See judgment of the Bow Street Magistrates' Court in the case of *Bo Xilai* (2005) 128 ILR 713 (8 November 2005) concerning a Minister of International Trade who was part of a delegation on a State visit led by the then Chinese President; see also that of the Westminster Magistrates' Court in *Re: Ehud Barak*, 29 September 2009 (not yet reported), concerning a visiting Defence Minister visiting the UK for official engagements with the British government. See also the unreported cases in the City of Westminster Magistrates' Court of *Court of Appeal of Paris* v *Durbar* (16 February 2008) and *Re Mikhael Gorbachev* (2011) 82 *BYIL* 570 (30 March 2011).

[43]   *Khurts Bat* v *Investigating Judge of the Federal Court of Germany* [2011] EWHC 2029 (Admin). For comment see Sanger, 2013.

[44]   Ibid, para 29.

[45]   The issue of special mission immunity arose again in October 2011 during a visit to London of the then Israeli Leader of the Opposition, Tzipi Livni, on an invitation for official talks from the British Foreign Secretary. A would-be private prosecutor sought the consent of the Director of Public Prosecutions (DPP) to the issue of an arrest warrant in respect of Ms Livni in relation to allegations of war crimes committed during the time that she was Foreign Minister of Israel. Following the issue of a certificate by the Foreign and Commonwealth Office (FCO) confirming that it had consented to her visit as a special mission, the DPP declined to consent to the issue of the warrant, issuing a statement explaining that the FCO certificate was conclusive evidence that Ms Livni was on a special mission. See CPS statement of 6 October 2011 at http://blog.cps.gov.uk/2011/10/cps-statement-in-relation-to-ms-tzipi-livinis-visit-to-the-uk.html.

special mission status had often been left to be implied from the circumstances of each case, leading in some cases to an undesirable potential for uncertainty. In a Written Ministerial Statement to Parliament,[46] the Foreign Secretary therefore set out the government's view of what a special mission was but, referencing the *Khurts Bat* case, also noted that not all official visitors would necessarily be entitled to special mission status. The intention was to establish a new procedure, initially on a pilot basis, so that the question of the government's consent to a visit as a special mission could be expressly addressed before the arrival of its members in the UK. To that end, foreign diplomatic missions in London were invited to submit details of forthcoming official visits from their respective sending States, where those States required clarity on whether the UK would consent to the visit as a special mission.[47]

However, in 2015 proceedings were brought to challenge the government's decision to consent to the visit of the Egyptian Chief of Defence Staff to the UK on official business on the grounds that special mission immunity was not part of customary international law and should not be given effect in the UK as part of the common law. In a lengthy and closely reasoned judgment the Divisional Court held that special mission immunity is a requirement of customary international law, and that is given effect in the common law.[48]

V. HOLDERS OF HIGH-RANKING OFFICES, SUCH AS HEADS OF STATE, HEADS OF GOVERNMENT, AND MINISTERS FOR FOREIGN AFFAIRS

A. HEADS OF STATE

In previous eras when most States were governed by personal sovereigns such as monarchs or emperors, there was a close identity in international law between such persons and their States. However, modern international law tends to consider the rights and competences of Heads of State as attaching to them in their capacity as the highest representatives of their States, rather than inherently in their own right (Watts, 1994, pp 35–7). That said, international law recognizes that the Head of State may exercise a number of important powers in international relations *ex officio*, including the sending and receiving of diplomats and consuls, and the conclusion of treaties.[49]

---

[46] Hansard HC Deb, 4 March 2013, Col 55–6WS.

[47] The process has generated some practice; see, eg, Hansard HC Deb, 12 July 2013 Col 427–30W. The administrative nature of the process should be noted and that whilst it can establish whether or not the government has expressly consented to a particular visit as a special mission in advance, the legal consequences of such consent clearly remain matters of law which may ultimately be determined by the courts. Similarly, if a sending State chooses not to use the administrative process, that will not necessarily be determinative of the legal status of a subsequent official visit—thus, for example, the Rwandan General Karenzi Kareke asserted special mission immunity following his arrest in London in 2015 under a European Arrest Warrant issued by a Spanish magistrate, although ultimately the arrest warrant was lifted for other reasons.

Interestingly, in a parallel development in the Netherlands, the Dutch government wrote to the Dutch parliament setting out its view of its obligations under customary international law to grant immunity to members of foreign official missions (see letter of 26 April 2012 from the Minister of Foreign Affairs and the State Secretary for Security and Justice to the Senate and House of Representatives on the immunity of members of foreign official missions).

[48] *R (Freedom and Justice Party and others)* v *Secretary of State for Foreign and Commonwealth Affairs and the Director of Public Prosecutions* [2016] EWHC 2010 (Admin). However as the case is under appeal at the time of writing, further comment must await the findings of the Court of Appeal.

[49] See, eg, 1969 VCLT, Article 7 and *Land and Maritime Boundary between Cameroon and Nigeria (Cameroon v Nigeria: Equatorial Guinea Intervening), ICJ Reports 2002*, paras 263–8.

The immunity of Heads of State from the jurisdiction of foreign States remains largely uncodified at the international level, but it has undergone some important changes in modern times. During earlier times when international law closely identified a Head of State with his or her State, the absolute doctrine of 'sovereign immunity' prevailed. However, more recently, as the restrictive doctrine of immunity in relation to States has developed, more distinct rules in relation to Heads of State have also developed (Watts, 1994, pp 52–66).[50]

The International Court of Justice has recently reaffirmed aspects of the law as regards personal inviolability and immunity from criminal jurisdiction, in the following terms:

A Head of State enjoys in particular 'full immunity from criminal jurisdiction and inviolability' which protects him or her 'against any act of authority of another State which would hinder him or her in the performance of his or her duties'. Thus the determining factor in assessing whether or not there has been an attack on the immunity of the Head of State lies in the subjection of the latter to a constraining act of authority . . . The Court recalls that the rule of customary international law reflected in Article 29 of the Vienna Convention on Diplomatic Relations, while addressed to diplomatic agents, is necessarily applicable to Heads of State. This provision reads as follows:

'[t]he person of a diplomatic agent shall be inviolable. He shall not be liable to any form of arrest or detention. The receiving State shall treat him with due respect and shall take all appropriate steps to prevent any attack on his person, freedom or dignity.'

This provision translates into positive obligations for the receiving State as regards the actions of its own authorities, and into obligations of prevention as regards possible attacks by individuals or other third parties. In particular, it imposes on receiving States the obligation to protect the honour and dignity of Heads of State, in connection with their inviolability.[51]

Further evidence of the relevant principles of customary international law can also be found in the practice of national courts, as well as in relevant national legislative provisions.

In the UK, s 20 of the State Immunity Act 1978 essentially equates the position of a foreign Head of State with the head of a diplomatic mission. Thus a foreign Head of State (whether on an official or a private visit) will enjoy complete personal inviolability and absolute immunity from criminal jurisdiction *ratione personae*.[52] Immunity from civil jurisdiction is potentially more complex in that it involves determining whether the act in question was performed by

---

[50] For a US perspective on this development see *Tachiona and others* v *Mugabe and others* 169 F.Supp 2d 259 (2001) (although the Court of Appeals (2nd Circuit) did not follow the same line of reasoning in its decision of 6 October 2004, 386F.3d 205). See also *Wei Ye* v *Jiang Zemin* 383F.3d 620. More recently, following the decision of the Supreme Court in *Samantar* v *Yousuf*, 130 S Ct 2278 (2010) that the immunity of individuals is not governed by the Foreign Sovereign Immunities Act, this issue will now usually focus on any 'suggestion of immunity' filed by the State Department—see, for example, *Habyarimana* v *Kagame*, Court of Appeals 696 F.3d 1029 (10th Circuit, 2012) and *Manoharan* v *Rajapaksa*, Court of Appeals (DC Circuit), 29 March 2013.

[51] *Case concerning Certain Questions of Mutual Assistance in Criminal Matters (Djibouti* v *France) Judgment of 4 June 2008*, paras 170 and 174. On the facts of the case the Court found that an invitation to a Head of State to testify in the course of criminal proceedings (without any suspicion attaching to him) did not violate his inviolability. However, the Court also found that had the French authorities passed confidential information regarding the witness summons to the Press, in the context of an official visit by the Djiboutian Head of State, this could constitute a failure in its obligation to protect his honour and dignity. On the other hand, see *Aziz* v *Aziz and others* [2007] EWCA Civ 712 in which the English Court of Appeal rejected an application by a Head of State for parts of a judgment to which he was not a party to be kept secret, in order to avoid the revelation of personal information about him. In similar vein see *Harb* v *King Fahd* [2005] EWCA Civ 632, discussed in n 53 in this chapter.

[52] See, eg, judgment of the Bow Street Magistrates' Court in *Mugabe* of 14 January 2004 (2004) 53 *ICLQ* 770.

the Head of State in his or her official capacity as an organ of the State, or whether it was performed in his or her personal capacity. In relation to the acts of a Head of State performed in his public capacity, the provisions in Part I of the Act (relating to the immunity of State itself, and considered in the previous chapter) will be applicable. For all other acts Heads of State will enjoy immunity from civil jurisdiction subject to the three exceptions noted in respect of Article 31(1) VCDR.[53] Finally it should be noted that the immunities of a Head of State can be waived, either by the Head of State himself or herself, or by his or her State.

On the other hand, when a Head of State leaves office, the House of Lords has found that he or she will enjoy immunities on the same basis as a former diplomat, and in particular subsisting immunity *ratione materiae* for his or her official acts (as per Article 39(2) VCDR). The extent of this immunity was of course the subject of detailed scrutiny in the *Pinochet* case (examined later in this chapter).

B. HEADS OF GOVERNMENT AND MINISTERS FOR FOREIGN AFFAIRS

Heads of Government and Ministers for Foreign Affairs enjoy immunity from jurisdiction *ratione personae* under international law to the same extent as Heads of State, since they perform comparable functions in representing their States in international relations.[54] The position in relation to the personal inviolability and immunity from criminal jurisdiction of serving Foreign Ministers was clarified by the International Court of Justice in the *Arrest Warrant* case.[55]

The case concerned the issue by a Belgian magistrate of an international warrant for the arrest of the incumbent DRC Foreign Minister[56] for his alleged involvement in grave

---

[53]   See, eg, Laddie J in *BCCI* v *Price Waterhouse* [1997] 4 All ER 108, in which certain acts of Sheikh Zayed of Abu Dhabi were immune from suit under s 20 as he was Head of State of the UAE, notwithstanding that the acts in question were not performed in that capacity. This was so even though Sheikh Zayed was simultaneously head of one of the constituent units of the UAE, and his acts may have been performed in a public capacity in that respect. In the case of *Harb* v *HM King Fahd bin Abdul Aziz* [2005] EWCA Civ 632 the President of the Family Division of the High Court upheld a Head of State's assertion of immunity in relation to proceedings for ancillary relief in matrimonial proceedings. The applicant appealed, but King Fahd died before the Court of Appeal could hear the appeal, thus bringing the proceedings to an end (see [2005] EWCA Civ 1324). However, the Court of Appeal had already by that stage ruled that the duty of the forum State to protect a Head of State from 'any attack on his person, freedom or dignity' (Article 29 VCDR) did not entail that the proceedings in which King Fahd was asserting immunity must be held in private.

Another aspect of the assimilation of a Head of State with the position of a head of a diplomatic mission, namely the extension of immunities to members of the family, was considered in the case of *Apex Global Management Ltd* v *Fi Call Ltd and others* [2013] EWCA Civ 642. A half-brother of the current King of Saudi Arabia (and son of the former King) and his son both claimed immunity in civil proceedings on the basis they were 'members of the family forming part of the household' of the King, as per s 20(1)(b) of the State Immunity Act. The Court found that they could not be considered as 'forming part of the household' of the King for these purposes.

Separately, it may be noted that the government of South Africa extended immunity to the wife of the then President Mugabe of Zimbabwe in relation to an alleged assault in South Africa in August 2017 (http://www.dirco.gov.za/docs/2017/media0820.htm), though it is understood a challenge to this decision was subsequently launched before the South African courts.

[54]   In principle, their official acts, like those of other State officials, will also be protected by immunity *ratione materiae* which subsists even after they have left office: see Sections VI and VIII B of this chapter.

[55]   *Arrest Warrant of 11 April 2000 (Democratic Republic of Congo* v *Belgium), Preliminary Objections and Merits, Judgment, ICJ Reports 2002*, p 3. For comments see Cassese, 2002; Wirth, 2002; Spinedi, 2002; Sir Robert Jennings, 2002; Stern, 2002; Schreuer and Wittich, 2002; McLachlan, 2002.

[56]   In fact whilst he was the incumbent Foreign Minister at the material time, ie at the point the arrest warrant was issued, he subsequently left that office to become the Minister of Education and by the time of the judgment he held no ministerial portfolio at all.

breaches of the Geneva Conventions and the Additional Protocols thereto, and crimes against humanity. The relevant Belgian statute provided for universal jurisdiction in the Belgian courts over these crimes (ie wherever and by whomsoever they were committed) and provided that 'the immunity attaching to the official capacity of a person shall not prevent the application of the present law'.[57]

The ICJ upheld DRC's complaint that the issue of the arrest warrant was a violation of the immunity from criminal jurisdiction and the personal inviolability which an incumbent Foreign Minister enjoys under international law. The Court based this conclusion chiefly on the functions exercised by a Foreign Minister in international relations. The Court noted that he or she is in charge of his or her government's diplomatic activities, and represents it in international negotiations and meetings, as well as having powers under international law to act on behalf of and to bind the State in, for example, treaty relations, simply by virtue of his or her office. Such functions required that a Foreign Minister should be able to travel internationally freely and to be able to be in constant communication with his or her government and its diplomatic missions around the world. Such considerations led the Court to consider that Foreign Ministers enjoyed complete personal inviolability and absolute immunity from criminal jurisdiction *ratione personae*, throughout the duration of their office. In that respect it was irrelevant whether the acts in question were private or official, or that they were performed prior or subsequently to the Foreign Minister in question assuming office, or whether the Foreign Minister was in the forum State on a private or an official visit.

Three further points should be noted about the extent of the immunity from jurisdiction of an incumbent Foreign Minister under the judgment.[58] First, it might be noted that Foreign Ministers may rely upon their immunities in any State, whereas, for example, diplomatic immunity is largely limited to immunity from the courts of the receiving State. Secondly, attention might be drawn to the fact that the Court found specifically that there was no exception to the immunity of a serving Foreign Minister from the criminal jurisdiction of national courts in respect of international crimes, such as war crimes or crimes against humanity. Thirdly, the immunity of a Foreign Minister can be waived by his own State.

Though the Court's findings are strictly speaking confined to the immunities enjoyed by Foreign Ministers, it seems clear that similar immunities apply, perhaps *a fortiori*, to Heads of Government.[59] How far such immunities can also be extended to other Ministers or officials may depend on analogous reasoning, based on the involvement of such persons in international relations.[60] Thus, for example, in the UK, decisions at first instance have

---

[57] *Act concerning the Punishment of Grave Breaches of International Humanitarian Law* of 10 February 1999 (1999) 38 ILM 921. The Act has since been substantially amended and this provision removing immunity has been repealed.

[58] The Court's comments, strictly speaking obiter dictum, on the extent of the subsisting immunity *ratione materiae* of a Foreign Minister after he has left office are considered in Section VIII of this chapter.

[59] See, eg, the US case of *Saltany v Reagan and others* (1988) 80 ILR 19, affirmed (1989) 87 ILR 680. For a contrasting view on scope of immunity *ratione materiae* see Douglas, 2012.

[60] This is in issue in a current case before the ICJ in which Equatorial Guinea alleges that the French authorities have failed to respect the immunity *ratione personae* enjoyed by the Second Vice-President of Equatorial Guinea in charge of Defence and State Security in the institution of criminal proceedings in France against him on charges of corruption (http://www.icj-cij.org/en/case/163).

It might be noted that in the ILC, the Second Report of Special Rapporteur Escobar Hernandez on the 'Immunity of State Officials from Foreign Criminal Jurisdiction', 4 April 2013 (A/CN.4/661) has proposed limiting immunity *ratione personae* in this respect to the so-called 'Troika', ie the Head of State, Head of Government, and Minister of Foreign Affairs, leaving other high-ranking official visitors to be protected only by special mission immunity which would not extend therefore to visits in a private capacity (see paras 59–68). This position has been adopted by the ILC on first reading (albeit with considerable doubt being expressed within the ILC)—see ILC Report 2013, ch V—but has attracted criticism by some States.

recognized that such immunities extend to a visiting Defence Minister,[61] and to a visiting Minister of Commerce (whose portfolio included responsibility for international trade).[62] Nevertheless it is not yet clear where the lines should properly be drawn, and the task is not made easier by the different ways in which different governments organize themselves internally. In any event, other ministers or senior officials will enjoy immunities when on official visits as members of special missions.

VI. THE IMMUNITIES OF OTHER STATE OFFICIALS

The immunities discussed in Sections II–V of this chapter appear to be the principal regimes of immunities which international law requires should be granted *ratione personae* in respect of particular categories of State official.[63] However, under the doctrine of State immunity, in principle all State officials (and former State officials[64]) enjoy immunity *ratione materiae* from foreign jurisdiction for their official acts. The rationale for this is that a State as an entity can only act through the agency of individuals working on its behalf. The official acts of those individuals can engage the international responsibility of the State, and they can only be challenged in a way that is consistent with international law. In broad terms a national court of one State is therefore precluded from adjudicating upon the official acts of State officials of another State.

It is convenient to examine this proposition first in relation to civil jurisdiction and then to criminal jurisdiction. It seems clear that the immunity of State officials in respect of their official acts from the civil jurisdiction of the courts of other States should be upheld, where the effect of proceedings would be to undermine or render nugatory the immunity of the employer State.[65] In other words, it prevents an applicant from seeking to circumvent State immunity by adopting the tactic of suing the individual carrying out the business of State. This is reflected in the 2004 UN Convention on the Jurisdictional Immunities of States and Their Property.[66]

In the UK this proposition finds support in both the common law[67] and some recent cases under the State Immunity Act 1978. Thus in *Propend Finance* v *Sing* the Commissioner of the Australian Federal Police (AFP) was permitted to claim State immunity, in connection with contempt proceedings for an alleged breach of an undertaking committed by an AFP

---

[61] See judgment of the Bow Street Magistrates' Court in the case of *Mofaz*, 12 February 2004 (2004) 53 *ICLQ* 771–3. See also *Re: Ehud Barak*, 29 September 2009 (see Franey, 2011, p 131). On the other hand in the *Khurts Bat* case the administrative head of the National Security Office of Mongolia was found to be outside the 'narrow circle' of those entitled to immunity *ratione personae*, as his position was simply not sufficiently senior in the structure of the Mongolian State.

[62] See judgment of the Bow Street Magistrates' Court in the case of *Bo Xilai* (2005) 128 ILR 713 (8 November 2005).

[63] Additional categories would be State officials who staff permanent representations to international organizations. Their status, privileges, and immunities will depend on the particular arrangements made under relevant treaties on privileges and immunities as well as the Headquarters Agreement of the organization in question: see for example El-Erian and Scobbie, 1998, pp 857–67.

[64] See for example Article 39(2) VCDR in relation to former members of diplomatic missions, and the treatment of the immunities of former Heads of State in *Pinochet No 3* [1999] 2 WLR 827, discussed in Section VIII B of this chapter.

[65] See Lord Browne-Wilkinson in *Pinochet No 3* [1999] 2 WLR 827, 847F.

[66] Thus in defining the 'State' (the beneficiary of immunity under the Convention) it includes in Article 1(b) (iv) 'representatives of the State acting in that capacity'.

[67] See, eg, *Twycross* v *Dreyfus* (1877) 5 Ch D 605; *Rahimtoola* v *Nizam of Hyderabad* [1958] AC 379; also *Zoernsch* v *Waldock* [1964] 2 QB 352. See Whomersley, 1992.

officer accredited as a diplomatic agent to the Australian High Commission in London. The Court of Appeal held:

> The protection afforded by the Act of 1978 [ie the State Immunity Act 1978] to States would be undermined if employees, officers or (as one authority puts it) 'functionaries' could be sued as individuals for matters of State conduct in respect of which the State they were serving had immunity. Section 14(1) must be read as affording individual employees or officers of a foreign State protection under the same cloak as protects the State itself.[68]

The House of Lords approved this formulation of the principle in the case of *Jones v Ministry of the Interior of the Kingdom of Saudi Arabia*, in the context of civil proceedings relating to allegations of torture against Saudi Arabia and certain of its officials.[69] Lord Bingham drew the following conclusions as relevant: (1) that the individual defendants were at the material times acting or purporting to act as servants or agents of the State; (2) that their acts were accordingly attributable to the State; (3) that no distinction could be made between the claim against the State and the claim against the individual defendants; and (4) that none of the claims fell within any exception to immunity under the State Immunity Act 1978.[70] The court went on to find that the *jus cogens* nature of the prohibition of torture did not of itself operate to enable a third State to assert civil jurisdiction in the face of State immunity, and that there was currently no generally accepted exception to State immunity from civil jurisdiction in relation to breaches of international law.

The claimants subsequently brought proceedings against the UK government in the European Court of Human Rights, arguing that the judgment of the House of Lords upholding the immunity of the defendants violated the claimants' right of access to a court and to a fair trial under Article 6 of the European Convention on Human Rights (ECHR). The court found that the immunity enjoyed by the defendants reflected generally recognized rules of public international law, and as such could not be regarded as an unjustified or disproportionate restriction on the claimants' rights. However the court noted that in the light of developments currently underway in this area of public international law, this is a matter which needs to be kept under review by the contracting States of the ECHR.[71]

In contrast to the interpretation by the UK courts of the State Immunity Act in this respect, in 2010 the US Supreme Court reversed the practice of a number of lower courts[72] and found that the immunity *ratione materiae* enjoyed by individuals (whether current or former officials) is not governed by the US Foreign Sovereign Immunities Act (1976).[73] Instead the immunity of individuals in US law remains regulated by the common law, and in this respect it is open to the US government to make a 'suggestion of immunity'

[68] *Propend Finance v Sing* 111 ILR 611 at 669. For criticism see Barker, 1998. But see also the US cases of *Chuidian v Philippine National Bank* (1990) 92 ILR 480 and *Herbage v Meese* (1990) 98 ILR 101. Also the Canadian cases of *Jaffe v Miller* (1993) 95 ILR 446 and *Walker v Baird* (1994) 16 OR (3d) 504. Other cases from the UK include *Re P (No 2)* (1998) 114 ILR 485, and under the common law of State immunity *Holland v Lampen-Wolfe* [2000] 1 WLR 1548.

[69] *Jones v Ministry of Interior for the Kingdom of Saudi Arabia and Ors* [2006] UKHL 26; [2007] 1 AC 270. See also *Al Attiyah v Bin-Jasim Bin-Jaber Al Thani* [2016] EWHC 212 (QB).

[70] *Jones v Ministry of Interior for the Kingdom of Saudi Arabia and Ors* [2006] UKHL 26; [2007] 1 AC 270, para 13.

[71] *Jones and Others v the United Kingdom*, nos 34356/06 and 40528/06, ECHR 2014.

[72] See for example the case of *Belhas v Ya'alon*, US Court of Appeals (DC Circuit), 515 F.3d 1279, 15 February 2008, which had found that a former senior member of the Israeli Defence Force enjoyed immunity under the FSIA in respect of civil proceedings arising from alleged war crimes.

[73] See the case of *Samantar v Yousuf*, 130 S Ct 2278 (2010).

which the courts will invariably follow.[74] The *Samantar* case concerned a former Prime Minister of Somalia accused of serious human rights abuses during his period in office. After the Supreme Court's judgment, the case was remitted for further determination, and the State Department issued a Suggestion of Immunity finding that Samantar did not enjoy immunity because there was currently no government of Somalia recognized by the USA able to assert the immunity on his behalf. The State Department also offered the view that, given Samantar's adoption of US residence, it was incumbent on him to accept the values of American society. Interestingly, the Court of Appeals of the Fourth Circuit subsequently held that it was not bound by the terms in the Suggestion of Immunity, but rather found that Samantar did not enjoy immunity because the allegations against him were of breaches of norms of *jus cogens*, and that there was an exception to immunity in this respect. Samantar subsequently sought certiorari in the Supreme Court; however, that was denied despite there being by then a government of Somalia that was recognized by the US, and which had asserted immunity on Samantar's behalf.

Turning to the application of immunity *ratione materiae* in relation to criminal jurisdiction, a useful starting point is the ongoing work of the International Law Commission. The first Special Rapporteur on the topic (Ambassador Kolodkin) addressed the law and practice on immunity *ratione materiae* rather clearly. In his Second Report the Special Rapporteur set out the traditional rationale for immunity *ratione materiae*, but then considered whether as a matter of customary international law there were any exceptions to this form of immunity, for example, in relation to international crimes or human rights abuses.[75] He noted that there were various attempts at justifying such an exception: (i) that such objectionable acts could not be considered to be 'official acts' for the purposes of immunity; (ii) that official act immunity is incompatible with individual criminal responsibility in international criminal law; (iii) that the *jus cogens* nature of these prohibitions in question prevailed over immunity; (iv) that there is a customary international law exception to immunity in relation to international crimes; (v) that the availability of universal jurisdiction for the gravest crimes was incompatible with immunity. However, he found none of these propositions persuasive. The only case in which he found there was an absence of immunity was 'where criminal jurisdiction is exercised by a State in whose territory an alleged crime has taken place, and this State has not given its consent to the performance in its territory of the activity which led to the crime and to the presence in its territory of the foreign official who committed the alleged crime'.[76]

The ILC's second Special Rapporteur, Professor Escobar Hernandez, has taken a different approach to the question of exceptions to immunity from immunity *ratione materiae*, and proposed that such immunity should not apply to extensive list of crimes, including genocide, crimes against humanity, war crimes, torture, enforced disappearances, corruption-related crimes, and crimes against the person and property

[74] For some other recent examples of suggestions of immunity in this respect see the Suggestion of Immunity filed on 7 September 2012 in the case *Jane Doe v Ernesto Zedillo Ponce de Leon* in US District Court of Connecticut, providing that the former Mexican President Zedillo enjoyed continuing immunity for his official acts whilst he was in office. The District Court upheld his immunity in line with the Suggestion in a judgment of 18 July 2013. See also the Suggestion of Immunity of 17 December 2012 filed in the case of *Rosenberg et al v Lashkar e Taiba*, in which the immunity of two former Directors of Pakistan's Inter-Service Intelligence Directorate in a suit concerning the terrorist attacks in Mumbai in 2008 was at issue. See also Koh, 2011; Bellinger, 2011.

[75] Respectively UN Doc A/CN.4/631 and A/CN.4/646.

[76] Second Report of Special Rapporteur Kolodkin (UN Doc A/CN.4/646), para 94. For a review of relevant practice see Franey, 2011, pp 157–285.

committed on the territory of the forum State.[77] However, the juridical basis for this proposal is not clear, being based on supposed 'trends' in State practice identified by the Special Rapporteur. In fact, the survey of State practice she provides is unconvincing and ultimately appears to be based more on policy prescription than legal analysis, and it is therefore submitted that her analysis is an insufficient foundation to support such an extensive proposal.[78]

Turning to the modalities of immunity, these were addressed by Ambassador Kolodkin in his Third Report (at the time of writing, Professor Escobar Hernandez has not yet done so). Of particular interest is his finding that because immunity *ratione materiae* is an immunity of the State and not of the individual, the State which the official serves must assert immunity *ratione materiae* in any case before it can be given effect. An assertion by an individual official alone is not sufficient. Nor is there any obligation on the court to raise immunity *ratione materiae* proactively or *proprio motu* in relation to criminal proceedings. Interestingly, he suggests that a waiver of immunity *ratione materiae* could be implied as well as express, and, despite subjecting the proposition to some scrutiny, he appears to accept a waiver by consenting to be bound by a relevant international agreement is possible.

It is pertinent to note that in broad terms the applicability of immunity *ratione materiae* in criminal proceedings appears to be accepted by the UK courts. To the extent that the immunities *ratione materiae* of a former Head of State are a manifestation of this more general immunity, it might be noted that in *Pinochet No 3* it was suggested that such immunity could be asserted successfully to bar proceedings in respect of most crimes (with the important exception of torture contrary to the UN Convention against Torture) where these are committed in the performance of the functions of government.[79]

The point was given further consideration by the High Court in the case of *Khurts Bat*. The case arose in relation to extradition proceedings commenced by Germany in respect of an alleged abduction and serious bodily injury, which in large part took place on German soil. Mongolia intervened (a) indicating that it had accepted responsibility for Khurts' actions on the plane of international law (an official apology had been submitted to Germany), and (b) asserting immunity *ratione materiae* on his behalf. The court accepted the broad principle of immunity *ratione materiae*, but noted the finding of Special Rapporteur Kolodkin that an exception to immunity from criminal jurisdiction might exist, where the acts in question took place on the territory of the forum State, in circumstances where the forum State had neither given its consent to the presence of the official on its territory nor to the activities under investigation. Finding that the authorities were broadly, but not unanimously, supportive of that proposition, the court found that Khurts did not benefit from immunity *ratione materiae* in the instant case. However it might be noted that the ILC has not adopted an exception for such territorial crimes in the forum State.[80]

---

[77] See Fifth Report of Special Rapporteur Escobar Hernandez (UN Doc A/CN.4/701).

[78] In fact the Special Rapporteur's proposal was amended significantly following consideration by the ILC, and even then the fact that the ILC could only provisionally adopt this more limited proposal after a vote in which a significant minority voted against it, suggests the matter remains strongly contested (see further Section VIII B).

[79] Thus Lord Hope found that immunity *ratione materiae* of a former Head of State could be relied upon in relation to charges of conspiracy to murder—see [1999] 2 WLR 827, 881, and 887. See also the speeches of Lords Browne-Wilkinson and Hutton, at 848 and 888 respectively. On the other hand, Lord Millett expressly found that immunity *ratione materiae* is not available in respect of an offence committed in the forum State (at 913). See also *Wei Ye v Jiang Zemin* 383F.3d 620.

[80] ILC Report 2017, p 188 (para 24 of the commentary to draft Article 7).

VII. OFFICIALS OF INTERNATIONAL ORGANIZATIONS

While the immunities of international organizations have been inspired by the immunities granted to States and their officials, they differ in some respects, reflecting the important differences between international organizations and States.[81] In the normal course of events an international organization will not have its own territory, but rather be based on territory over which a State exercises jurisdiction (special cases of international administration such as, for example, the UN administration of Kosovo or in East Timor are not considered here). An international organization will not have its own population, from which its officials are chosen, but instead will employ persons who hold the nationality (with its attendant rights and obligations) of a State. Finally an international organization will not generally perform all the functions of government, with a full legal system of its own. Rather it will have its own institutional law, but will have to rely upon the local law in respect of other matters such as, for example, the maintenance of public order through the exercise of criminal jurisdiction.

Both diplomatic immunities and the immunities of international organizations arise from considerations of functional necessity, and as we shall see, the former have inspired the latter in some respects. However, it does not follow that they should be identical in extent. Jenks suggests that there are three major differences between diplomatic immunities and those of international officials (Jenks, 1961, p xxxvii). First, it is unusual for a diplomatic agent to have the nationality of the receiving State and in such situations as we have seen the scope of the immunities he enjoys can be restricted by the receiving State to his or her official activities only. On the other hand, for officials of international organizations[82] it may be especially important that they enjoy immunities against their own States of nationality.[83] Secondly, whereas a diplomatic agent may be immune from legal process in the receiving State, he or she will remain subject to legal process in the sending State. In relation to officials of international organizations there is no sending State as such, and thus appropriate procedures may have to be adopted, either through some international disciplinary procedure established by the organization, or through waiver of immunity. Thirdly, the principle of reciprocity, which plays such an important role in the maintenance of diplomatic law between States, cannot operate in the same way in respect of international organizations. Thus Jenks rejects a simple assimilation of the immunities of international organizations with diplomatic immunities, in favour of looking at the former on their own merits as based upon their particular functional needs.

---

[81] See para 7 of the General Commentary on the ILC Draft Article on the Responsibility of International Organisations with commentaries (2011) http://legal.un.org/ilc/texts/instruments/english/commentaries/9_11_2011.pdf.

[82] Under relevant instruments additional categories of persons may benefit from similar immunities (though not identical in every respect); see, for example, the position of 'experts on mission' under the 1946 Convention on the Privileges and Immunities of the UN.

[83] Not all States accept that their own nationals when employed by international organizations enjoy the full range of immunities enjoyed by the officials who hold other nationalities. However, such limitations often concern fiscal immunities or exemptions from national service rather than immunity from legal process. For examples of the general rule see the ICJ Advisory Opinions in the *Applicability of Article VI, Section 22 of the Convention on the Privileges and Immunities of the United Nations, Advisory Opinion, ICJ Reports 1989*, p 177 ('*Mazilu*') and *Difference Relating to Immunity from Legal Process of a Special Rapporteur of the Commission on Human Rights, Advisory Opinion, ICJ Reports 1999*, p 62 ('*Cumaraswamy*').

It is of course impossible to survey the range of international organizations, and the immunities of each will be governed by their own treaty provisions.[84] Only the immunities of personnel of the UN are considered here, as illustrative rather than generally applicable (see further Michaels, 1971). In broad terms the Convention on the Privileges and Immunities of the UN 1946 divides staff members of the UN into three categories:

(a) the Secretary-General and the Assistant Secretaries-General shall be accorded ambassadorial status, and enjoy equivalent immunities *ratione personae* (Article V, s 19);

(b) all other officials of the Organization enjoy immunity from legal process in respect of their official acts, ie immunity *ratione materiae* (Article V, s 18(a)); and

(c) experts on mission (ie persons who undertake temporary missions for the UN) who enjoy immunity from suit for their official acts (*ratione materiae*), as well as—in view of their need to travel freely in performance of their mission—a specific grant of personal inviolability (Article VI, s 22).[85]

The Convention makes clear that the immunities of officials and experts are granted not for their personal benefit, but for the benefit of the Organization. The Secretary-General thus has the right *and the duty* to waive immunity of any official where the immunity would in his or her opinion impede the course of justice and can be waived without prejudice to the interests of the Organization (Article V, s 20).[86]

Given that most officials and experts of the UN only enjoy immunity *ratione materiae* in respect of their official acts, an important question is who should determine whether any particular act is an 'official act'. In many of the cases which might concern the exercise of ordinary criminal jurisdiction it will be possible to say that the offence is not an official act, and so the question of immunity does not arise. Thus, for example, when during the Cold War there were a number of cases in which international officials were accused of espionage in the USA, they were unable to claim immunity as the activities in question were not official activities.[87] However, in other cases, where there may be some dispute as to the nature of an act, it is necessary to ask whether that issue should be determined by the Secretary-General on behalf of the Organization, or the relevant national court as part of its task in applying the immunity. In the *Cumaraswamy* case, the ICJ gave a rather nuanced answer to the question, stating that:

> When national courts are seised of a case in which the immunity of a UN agent is in issue, they should immediately be notified of any finding by the Secretary-General concerning that immunity. That finding and its documentary expression creates a presumption which can only be set aside for the most compelling reasons and is thus to be given the greatest weight by the national courts.[88]

---

[84] Though in relation to most officials of international organizations there is considerable uniformity in the relevant treaty provisions, they enjoy immunity from jurisdiction *ratione materiae*, ie in relation to their official acts, whilst provision is often made for certain high officials to be granted a wider immunity *ratione personae* whilst in office. In relation to international organizations of which the UK is a member their immunities may be given effect in the UK by Order in Council made under the International Organizations Act 1968.

[85] The immunity from arrest of an expert on mission was given consideration in the case of *R v KL* [2014] EWCA Crim 1729 in which the defendant, a Nepalese army officer and member of a UN Observer Mission in South Sudan, was arrested in the UK whilst on leave from the UN service in relation to allegations of torture in Nepal prior to and separate from his service for the UN. The Court of Appeal expressed doubt as to his entitlement to immunity from jurisdiction in these circumstances, but in any event found that the UN had validly waived any immunity he may have enjoyed (paras 76–101).

[86] See *R v KL* [2014] EWCA Crim 1729.

[87] See, eg, *US v Coplon* 84 F.Supp 472 (1949); *US v Melekh* 190 F.Supp 67 (1960); and *US v Egorov* 222 F.Supp 106 (1963). In another context see also the case of *Westchester County v Ranollo* (1946) 13 ILR 168.

[88] *Difference Relating to Immunity from Legal Process of a Special Rapporteur of the Commission on Human Rights, Advisory Opinion, ICJ Reports 1999*, p 62, para 61. For comment see Wickremasinghe, 2000.

The Court thus sought to balance the interests of the organization and the local jurisdiction, though, in the final analysis, it is the local court which must decide whether there are compelling reasons to rebut the presumption established by the Secretary-General's finding.

VIII. THE SCOPE OF IMMUNITIES FOR SERIOUS CRIMES UNDER INTERNATIONAL LAW—IMMUNITY AND IMPUNITY DISTINGUISHED

None of the immunities which have been considered are for the benefit of any particular individual or group of individuals, but rather are for the benefit of the State/international organization which they represent. Thus the sending State/employer international organization can waive any of these immunities, thereby consenting to the jurisdiction of the courts of another State over the official in question. This applies whether the immunity in question arises *ratione personae* or *ratione materiae*.

However, in a parallel development, the scope of international law has now broadened from an almost exclusive concern with the rights and duties of States, so that it now also imposes a considerable body of obligations in respect of individuals. Of particular interest for present purposes is the evolution of individual criminal responsibility under international law for a number of serious international crimes which offend international public order. As Sir Arthur Watts (1994, p 82) points out:

> For international conduct which is so serious as to be tainted with criminality to be regarded as attributable only to the impersonal State and not to the individuals who order or perpetrated it is both unrealistic and offensive to common notions of justice.

Furthermore, recent years have seen a determination within international society to put an end to the impunity of the perpetrators of such crimes, through the development of extraterritorial jurisdiction and the establishment of international criminal tribunals. In a further development, and in line with the general trend to seek to rationalize all regimes of privilege or immunity (which is observable in other areas of international and national law), the immunities of State officials in respect of international crimes have been subject to particularly keen scrutiny in recent years.

Exactly how these apparently conflicting priorities in the law should be integrated is still being worked out. Simple attempts at seeking to choose between them on the basis of hierarchy by means of the *jus cogens* or *erga omnes* nature of the primary prohibitions of the criminalized conduct appear not to provide answers, particularly in respect of procedural obligations of States—a point that has recently been underlined by the decision of the International Court of Justice in the *Jurisdictional Immunities* case.[89] Nevertheless in recent years the law has undergone, and may still be undergoing, considerable re-examination and some significant revisions. What follows therefore does not attempt to prescribe what the law ought to be, but simply seeks to describe the law as it is in its current stage of development.

---

[89] See, eg, the ECtHR case of *Al-Adsani* v *UK* [GC], no 35763/97, ECHR 2001-XI, 34 *EHRR* 11, which dealt with the question of the immunity of the State itself from civil jurisdiction. See also Article 98(1) of the Statute of the International Criminal Court.

A. IMMUNITIES *RATIONE PERSONAE*

In the *Arrest Warrant* case the ICJ was concerned with the immunity *ratione personae* of a serving Foreign Minister, and concluded that under customary international law no exception to that immunity exists in respect of war crimes or crimes against humanity. The Court based this upon its review of national legislation[90] and those few decisions of higher courts in national legal systems on the point.[91] One of these was the decision of the French *Cour de Cassation* in the *Qadaffi* case (Zeppala, 2001), in which the immunity of a serving Head of State was found to operate in respect of allegations of his involvement in international terrorism.[92] The other major case referred to is the decision of the House of Lords in the *Pinochet* case, in which in a number of dicta their Lordships suggested that the immunity *ratione personae* of serving Heads of State and serving Ambassadors (unless waived) could be relied upon in proceedings for international crimes.[93]

Thus it seems that based on general principle the immunity *ratione personae* of certain incumbent high State officials, including Heads of State, Heads of Government, Foreign Ministers, and diplomatic agents and members of special missions, are, in the absence of waiver by the sending State, an absolute bar to the criminal jurisdiction of the national courts for the duration of their office/mission,[94] even in relation to these serious international crimes. The reason for this is that the functions which these officials serve in maintaining international relations are such that they should not be endangered by the subjection of such officials (while they are in office) to the criminal jurisdiction of another State.

However, in the *Arrest Warrant* case the ICJ also stressed that immunity was not the same as impunity. In this respect it noted four circumstances in which the availability of immunity *ratione personae* of incumbent office-holders would not prevent their prosecution:

(i) where the office-holder in question is prosecuted by the courts of his or her own State;

(ii) where immunity is waived by the office-holder's State;

(iii) when the office-holder leaves office, he or she may be prosecuted by the court of another State (provided that in other respects it has jurisdiction in accordance with international law) in respect of his or her acts prior to or subsequent to his or her period of office, or for his or her private acts during his period of office; and

(iv) by certain international criminal courts, provided that they have jurisdiction.

---

[90] In this respect the former Belgian Act of 10 February 1999 under which immunities were not admissible in respect of war crimes, crimes against humanity, and genocide, appeared exceptional and so could not be relied upon as sufficient evidence in itself of an emerging rule of general international law. A point underlined by the fact that this provision was repealed and the Act as whole was substantially amended following the Court's judgment and diplomatic pressure from other States.

[91] Subsequent cases which also support the findings of the ICJ are *Tachiona and others* v *Mugabe and others* 169 F.Supp 2d 259 (2001) and *Wei Ye* v *Jiang Zemin* 383F.3d 620; similarly the trio of cases from the Bow Street Magistrates' Court, *Mugabe* of 14 January 2004 (2004) 53 *ICLQ* 770, *Mofaz*, 12 February 2004 (2004) 53 *ICLQ* 771–3, and *Bo Xilai*, 8 November 2005 (128 ILR 713) as well as the case of *Re Ehud Barak* from the Westminster Magistrates' Court (*Re Ehud Barak*, 29 September 2009 (not yet reported)).

[92] *Qadaffi* case (2001) 125 ILR 490.

[93] See the speeches of Lord Browne-Wilkinson at 844E–G; Lord Hope at 886G–H; Lord Saville at 903F–G; Lord Millett 913 E–G; and Lord Phillips at 924C–D.

[94] Heads of State, Heads of Government, and Foreign Ministers appear to enjoy immunities in respect of all foreign States (ie *erga omnes*), whereas the immunities under the VCDR and the Special Missions Convention are primarily enjoyed only in the receiving State (though they also provide for privileges and immunities whilst in transit).

two of these circumstances are relatively uncontroversial and are well-established
ational law, and need little further comment here.[95] However, the latter two cir-
:es form the basis of the consideration of the following subsections.

B. IMMUNITIES *RATIONE MATERIAE*

The prelude to the re-examination of immunities *ratione materiae* in relation to serious
crimes under international law was the arrest of the former President of Chile, General
Pinochet, in 1998. Pinochet was arrested while temporarily in London for medical treatment, following a request by Spain for his extradition in connection with charges of *inter
alia* the widespread use of torture during his period of office as Head of State of Chile.
Eventually the House of Lords had to consider whether Pinochet could resist extradition
by relying on his subsisting immunity *ratione materiae*, ie in respect of official acts he
performed while he was Head of State, notwithstanding that he was no longer in office.

Trying to distil the *ratio decidendi* of the judgment of the House of Lords is complicated
not only by the nature of the case, but also by the fact the reasoning in each of the speeches
of the six judges in the majority differs. A full treatment is therefore beyond the scope of
this chapter.[96] The court was faced on the one hand with allegations of the crime of torture
under the Torture Convention, which is defined so as to require official involvement,[97]
and on the other with Pinochet's claim to immunity *ratione materiae*. By a majority of six
to one the House rejected the plea of immunity in respect of the torture allegations.

Put briefly, three of their Lordships relied upon an implied waiver of the immunity
ratione materiae, which it found States parties to the Torture Convention must have intended.[98] If this were otherwise the international criminalization of torture under the
Convention would have been rendered largely ineffective, as anybody charged with torture
would (in the absence of waiver) be able to rely on official act immunity.

However, the speeches of the other three of their Lordships in the majority appear to have
been more broadly based. They suggest that individual responsibility for serious crimes in
international law cannot be opposed by reliance upon the immunity *ratione materiae* of former Heads of State. That form of immunity only covers official acts in order to ensure that the
immunities of the State itself are not undermined by proceedings against its former Head. The
purpose of the immunity is therefore to ensure that the national courts of one State do not adjudicate on the responsibility of another State without the consent of the latter. However, these
judges found that as such immunity is concerned with the responsibility of the State, it cannot
be invoked in respect of an individual's own criminal responsibility in international law.[99]

---

[95] It might be noted in respect of (i) that the immunities *ratione personae* of certain high officials of
international organizations can be opposed to the jurisdiction of the courts of their own State of nationality.

[96] The case is the subject of a considerable literature, including: Warbrick, Salgado, and Goodwin, 1999; Fox,
1999; Barker, 1999; Denza, 1999; Dupuy, 1999; Dominicé, 1999; Cosnard, 1999; Chinkin, 1999; Van Alebeek, 2000.

[97] See Article 1(1) of the UN Convention Against Torture and other Cruel, Inhuman or Degrading
Treatment of Punishment 1984, which defines torture as the intentional infliction of pain or suffering for
various purposes, 'when such pain or suffering is inflicted by or at the instigation of or with the consent or
acquiescence of a public official or other person acting in an official capacity'.

[98] See the speeches of Lord Browne-Wilkinson at 847; Lord Hope (who found the exception to immunity
ratione materiae applied only in respect of a systematic or widespread torture) at 882–7; and Lord Saville at 904.

[99] Lord Hutton accepted the fact that the allegations of torture concerned acts in the performance of
public functions, but found that 'certain crimes are so grave and so inhuman that they constitute crimes
against international law and that the international community is under a duty to bring to justice a person
who commits such crimes'. He then held that individual criminal liability in respect of such crimes was quite
distinct from the question of State responsibility which underlay immunities *ratione materiae* (at 887–902).
Lord Millett found the existence of immunity *ratione materiae* simply inconsistent with the development
of serious crimes of *jus cogens* nature for which extraterritorial jurisdiction was available (at 909–14). Lord
Phillips similarly found that the development of international crimes and extraterritorial jurisdiction could
not coexist with immunity *ratione materiae* (at 924).

In line with the usual rules of *stare decisis,* the narrower reading of the *Pinochet* case based on implied waiver under the Torture Convention has subsequently been endorsed by the Court of Appeal. It is submitted, therefore, that the *Pinochet* case is authority in English law[100] for the proposition that there is an exception to immunity from criminal jurisdiction *ratione materiae* enjoyed by former Heads of State in respect of acts of official torture, where the relevant State or States are parties to the Torture Convention. It might also be noted that their Lordships found that since the development of individual criminal responsibility in respect of torture under the Convention represents a distinct basis of responsibility to which official act immunity does not extend, Pinochet's immunity *ratione materiae* from civil process was unaffected. Beyond this it is difficult to draw further conclusions.

Whether the exception to immunity found in the *Pinochet* case can be extended in respect of other international crimes and/or in respect of other immunities *ratione materiae* enjoyed by officials or former officials has been much debated, but firm conclusions have so far eluded international consensus. In this respect it should be recalled that the International Court of Justice in its judgment in the *Arrest Warrant* case also commented on this issue, though these comments are strictly speaking *obiter* since this case was concerned with the immunities *ratione personae* of a serving Foreign Minister. The majority of the Court found that a former Foreign Minister would be liable to prosecution in the courts of another State for the acts he performed during his period of office in his private capacity.[101] If this is taken as a broad statement of the principle that a former Foreign Minister enjoys a subsisting immunity *ratione materiae* for his official acts, it may be unsurprising. However, this passage of the judgment has been the subject of criticism for the narrowness of its formulation (McLachlan, 2002) and some have even drawn from it the implication that the subsisting immunity of a former Foreign Minister would be applicable in respect of serious international crimes such as war crimes and crimes against humanity (Wirth, 2002; Spinedi, 2002). If this latter point is what the Court intended then it might suggest that a narrow reading should be given to the decision of the House of Lords in the *Pinochet* case.[102] On the other hand, it should be noted that in their Joint Separate Opinion Judges Higgins, Kooijmans, and Buergenthal suggest that the current trend of State practice is that serious international crimes are not covered by the immunities *ratione materiae* of former State officials.[103]

Subsequently, the Swiss case of *Nezzar*[104] concerned an Algerian accused of atrocities amounting to crimes against humanity and war crimes during his service as an Army General, the Defence Minister, and part of the collective Presidency of Algeria in the early 1990s. A criminal complaint was brought in Switzerland during the temporary presence of the accused there. When the Swiss Ministry of Foreign Affairs were asked for their view on immunity they provided an answer in line with the *Arrest Warrant* Judgment to the effect that as a former State official he enjoyed an ongoing immunity for his official acts. The

---

[100] See *R* v *KL* [2014] EWCA Crim 1729, paras 25–39.

[101] *Arrest Warrant of 11 April 2000 (Democratic Republic of Congo v Belgium), Preliminary Objections and Merits, Judgment, ICJ Reports 2002,* p 3, para 61.

[102] In *Jurisdictional Immunities of the State (Germany v Italy: Greece Intervening), Judgment of 3 February 2012,* para 87, the ICJ certainly seem to have given the *Pinochet* judgment a narrow reading based on the particular language of the Torture Convention.

[103] *Arrest Warrant of 11 April 2000 (Democratic Republic of Congo v Belgium), Preliminary Objections and Merits, Judgment, ICJ Reports 2002,* p 3, Joint Separate Opinion, para 85. See also Akande (2004, p 415) who concludes that 'immunity *ratione materiae* does not exist with respect to domestic criminal proceedings for any of the international crimes set out in the Statute of the ICC'.

[104] *A* v *Ministère public de la Confédération, Swiss Federal Criminal Court,* 25 July 2012.

Swiss Federal Criminal Court, however, rejected the claim to immunity *ratione materiae* on the basis that it would be inconsistent with the international criminalization of crimes as serious as those charged in the instant case.

Despite the apparent breadth of the ruling in this case, Professor Wuerth points out that it may be distinguishable in that Algeria did not assert immunity on behalf of Nezzar, and as we have seen there is some authority for saying that in the case of immunity *ratione materiae* the State must assert that immunity. Thus she concludes that *Pinochet* remains the only case where immunity has been denied in criminal proceedings in the face of an assertion of immunity by the State in whose service the defendant official or former official was acting at the time of the allegations (Wuerth, 2012, 2013). In similar vein, Professor O'Keefe is cautious about the broader significance of the *Pinochet* precedent.[105]

As noted earlier, the International Law Commission has been engaged in work on this subject for the past decade. In her Fifth Report the Second Special Rapporteur, Professor Escobar Hernandez, effectively proposed that that immunity *ratione materiae* should not apply in relation to the crimes of genocide, crimes against humanity, war crimes, torture, and enforced disappearance, as well as crimes of corruption and crimes resulting in harm to persons or property in the forum State.[106] However the issue proved divisive in the ILC itself, and a reduced version of the Special Rapporteur's proposal was only provisionally adopted by the ILC after a vote, and even then in the face of significant opposition among some members to the idea of a generally expressed provision on exceptions to immunity in respect of international crimes.[107] The provisionally adopted text of Draft Article 7 provides that immunity *ratione materiae* shall not apply in relation to genocide, crimes against humanity, war crimes, apartheid, torture, and enforced disappearance.[108] The crimes are defined by reference to their definitions in a number of treaties. When this text was discussed by States in the UN General Assembly's Sixth Committee in 2017, it was strongly criticized by many States as being arbitrary and not supported in State practice and as such it could not amount to a codification of existing law. Given the vote in the ILC and the criticisms and doubts expressed by States in the Sixth Committee, it may be hoped that the ILC will consider the text further and seek to bring forward a proposal that can command consensus. Whatever else may be said, for present purposes it is submitted that the divisions around Draft Article 7 as it is provisionally adopted in 2017 on first reading demonstrate that it cannot be said to reflect the existing law.

C. IMMUNITIES BEFORE INTERNATIONAL CRIMINAL COURTS

The development of international criminal courts has clearly been a major step in combating impunity for serious international crimes. While a detailed discussion of the question of immunities before such courts is beyond the scope of this chapter, the broad principles will be outlined. As we have noted, the ICJ suggested that immunities would not in principle be available before international courts providing that they have jurisdiction. An apparently similar finding was made by the Appeals Chamber of the Special Court of Sierra Leone.[109] Indeed the Statutes of the Nuremberg and Tokyo Tribunals, the International Criminal Tribunal for the Former Yugoslavia (ICTY), the International Criminal Tribunal for Rwanda (ICTR), the Rome Statute of the International Criminal Court (ICC), and the

---

[105] O'Keefe (2015), paras 10.72–10.84.   [106] UN Doc A/CN.4/701.
[107] See Report of the International Law Commission at its 69th Session (UN Doc A/72/10), pp 163–5 and 171–3.
[108] Ibid, pp 177–191.
[109] See *The Prosecutor* v *Charles Taylor*, Case No SCSL-2003–01-I (31 May 2004).

Statute of the Special Court for Sierra Leone (SCSL) all contain express provisions to the effect that the official capacity of an individual shall in no case exempt them from criminal responsibility.[110] However, it should be noted that in general those provisions appear to be aimed at the non-application of substantive defences based on official position, rather than the procedural immunities under consideration. By contrast, Article 27(2) of the Rome Statute is express in providing that immunities in international law shall not be a bar to the jurisdiction of the ICC.

Nevertheless, as Professor Akande has persuasively argued, this picture requires some further elaboration in view of the range of different international criminal tribunals which currently exist (Akande, 2004). In particular the question of whether an individual can rely on immunities in international law before an international court will, as a first step, require a consideration of the basis on which the court was established as well as the provisions of its constitutive statute. Moreover, since these international courts will require the assistance of national authorities and national courts in matters such as arresting and transferring suspects, providing evidence, and other forms of cooperation, there are also questions as to the availability of immunities before relevant national authorities in these situations.

In this respect the ICTY and ICTR, which were established by the Security Council pursuant to its mandatory powers under Chapter VII of the UN Charter, may be distinguished from tribunals established by treaty. The removal of the immunity of defendants in the Statutes of these two Tribunals not only entitles the Tribunals themselves to adjudicate over such individuals, but it also provides a legal basis for all member States of the UN to deny immunity to such persons when arresting or transferring them pursuant to Orders of the Tribunals. At the same time, however, it should also be noted that the Appeals Chamber of the ICTY has for example recognized the immunities of State officials *ratione materiae*, exempting them from a requirement to produce documents in evidence which they held by virtue of their official position.[111]

As a body established by treaty, the ICC is in a different position, since States must consent to be bound by the Rome Statute before they are bound by it. While the Rome Statute appears to limit the immunities available to defendants in proceedings before the ICC itself (Article 27(2)), it is not clear that this provision can restrict the immunities of officials of States that are not parties to the Rome Statute, unless, of course, there is a waiver by the relevant State, or a binding resolution of the Security Council to this effect. In relation to the availability of immunities to proceedings before national authorities and national courts, relating to requests by the ICC for surrender and assistance, it should be noted that Article 98(1) of the Rome Statute also preserves the State and diplomatic immunities of officials and property of third States.[112] In other words, officials of a State which is not a party to the Rome Statute may be able to claim immunity in respect of their arrest and transfer to the Court, whereas a State party to the Rome Statute has in effect waived such immunities in respect of its own officials both before the ICC itself and in the courts of other States

---

[110] See Article 7 of the Charter of the International Criminal Tribunal of Nuremberg and Article 6 of the Charter of the Tokyo Tribunal. See Article 7(2) of the Statute of the ICTY; Article 6(2) of the Statute of the ICTR; Article 27 of the Statute of the ICC; and Article 6(2) of the Statute of the Special Court for Sierra Leone.

[111] See *Prosecutor* v *Blaskić*, Judgment, Case No IT-95-14-T, Trial Chamber (3 March 2000); 110 ILR 609. However, see also the case of *Prosecutor* v *Krstić*, Judgment, Case No IT-98-33-A, Appeals Chamber (19 April 2004). For comment see Akande, 2004, p 418.

[112] Thus Article 98(1) states: 'The Court may not proceed with a request for surrender or assistance which would require the requested State to act inconsistently with its obligations under international law with respect to the State or diplomatic immunity of a person or property of a third State, unless the Court can first obtain the cooperation of that third State for the waiver of the immunity.'

parties in respect of their cooperation with the ICC. However, there may be a further layer of complexity in cases which are referred to the Court by the Security Council, depending on the terms of such referral.

The first decision of the ICC to deal with these issues was the decision of the Pre-Trial Chamber on the arrest warrant sought by the Prosecutor in the case of *The Prosecutor* v *Omar Hassan Ahmad Al Bashir*.[113] As is well known, the Prosecutor sought the arrest of President Al Bashir, the serving Head of State of Sudan, for war crimes, crimes against humanity, and genocide. In the event the Court issued two warrants in respect of five counts of crimes against humanity, two counts of war crimes, and three counts of genocide.[114] It dealt with the immunity issue in a short passage that found that the position of Al Bashir, as Head of a State which was not a party to the Rome Statute, had no effect on the jurisdiction of the Court over the case. In support of this finding it considered that: (i) putting an end to impunity was a core goal of the Rome Statute; (ii) Article 27 of the Rome Statute sought to give effect to this goal with specific language limiting exemptions and immunities attaching to persons by reason of their office; (iii) on the basis of the clear language of Article 27, there was no need to examine other sources of law; and (iv) in referring the situation in Darfur to the ICC, the Security Council accepted that the investigation and any resulting prosecutions would accord with the provisions of the Rome Statute as a whole. Thus it was clear that Al Bashir's position as Head of State was not a bar to the jurisdiction of the Court.

The more complex issue seems to be what steps States may or must take in execution of the warrants.[115] Although the Court did not expressly address the application of Article 98(1), it did consider that Sudan was obliged 'to cooperate fully with and provide any necessary assistance to the Court' by virtue of Security Council Resolution 1593 (2005), a binding resolution under Chapter VII of the UN Charter and given primacy over other obligations by virtue of Article 103 of the Charter.[116] The Court ordered that the arrest warrant be served on all States parties to the Rome Statute, and all members of the Security Council that are not States parties to the Rome Statute, with a request for the arrest and surrender of Al Bashir. While the reasoning of the Court is concise, it might suggest that the effect of Resolution 1593 (2005) is to assimilate the position of Sudan with that of a State party, which by virtue of Article 27 cannot assert immunity to oppose arrest proceedings at the national level. If that is the case, then clearly States parties are under an obligation to comply with request for arrest and surrender under Article 89 of the Rome Statute.[117]

---

[113]   *The Prosecutor* v *Omar Hassan Ahmad Al Bashir*, 4 March 2009, Case No ICC-02/05–01/09.

[114]   See decisions of Pre-Trial Chamber I of 4 March 2009 (ref ICC 02/05–01/09–3) and 12 July 2010 (ref ICC 02/05–01/09–94) respectively.

[115]   Gaeta, 2009 and Akande, 2009.

[116]   Paragraph 2 of UNSCR 1593 provides: '*Decides* that the Government of Sudan and all other parties to the conflict in Darfur, shall cooperate fully with and provide any necessary assistance to the Court and the Prosecutor pursuant to this resolution and, while recognizing that States not party to the Rome Statute have no obligation under the Statute, *urges* all States and concerned regional and other international organizations to cooperate fully.'

[117]   In this respect see the Judgments of the Pre-Trial Chamber in relation to Malawi (13 December 2011), Chad (13 December 2011), DRC (9 April 2014), and South Africa (6 July 2017), finding that these States had failed in the obligation of cooperation in failing to arrest Bashir when he visited them. For comment see Knottnerus, 'The Immunity of Al-Bashir: The Latest Twist in the Jurisprudence of the ICC', *EJILTalk!* 15 November 2017.

It might be noted that following the Court's decision in 2009, the UK made an Order in Council based on the enabling powers in both s 23(5) of the International Criminal Court Act 2001 and s 1 of the United Nations Act 1946, providing that State or diplomatic immunities will not prevent proceedings in the UK for the arrest and delivery of persons alleged to have committed an ICC crime as a result of the referral of the situation in Darfur under UNSCR 1593 (see the International Criminal Court (Darfur) Order 2009, SI 699/2009).

The effect on non-States parties other than Sudan would depend upon the interpretation of relevant Security Council resolutions.[118]

IX. CONCLUSION

Thus we have seen that in modern diplomatic law there has been considerable movement towards the rationalization of immunities, so that it is now clear that they are not granted for the personal benefit of their holders. Instead they are granted on a functional basis, to facilitate the processes of communication and cooperation in international relations. Carefully considered legal regimes have been created in which the interests of sending and receiving States have been balanced. There is a general acceptance that without these immunities their holders could be impeded from effective performance of these important functions, the purpose of which serves the international public interest. Following its codification in the 1960s, diplomatic law has, for the most part, constituted a well-observed and stable body of rules.

At the same time greater consensus has developed and continues to develop on the standards of governance of those exercising public power, and in particular recently on the criminalization of the gravest excesses in this respect. The wholesale exemption of those who commit such crimes in connection with public purposes would clearly be contradictory. The establishment of the International Criminal Court, in relation to which immunities are not available (except as provided for in Article 98 of the Rome Statute), is clearly a hugely significant step for international law.

However, the resolution of these conflicting priorities at the national level is still being worked out, and an authoritative statement of the law is not possible at this point. There appears to be a considerable degree of consensus that immunities *ratione personae* attaching to certain offices will render their holders immune from national proceedings, but not necessarily from international proceedings where, for example, States have accepted the jurisdiction of an international court, or where the UN Security Council using its mandatory powers has removed such immunity. On the other hand once such office-holders have left office, they will enjoy a general immunity in respect of their official acts *ratione materiae*, but exceptionally it appears that in respect of certain international crimes, notably torture as provided for under the Torture Convention, they might not be so immune.

REFERENCES

AKANDE, D (2004), 'International Law Immunities and the International Criminal Court', 98 *AJIL* 407.

AKANDE, D (2009), 'The Legal Nature of Security Council Referrals to the ICC and its Impact on Al Bashir's Immunity', 7 *J Int'l Crim Just* 333.

BARKER, JC (1996), *The Abuse of Diplomatic Privileges and Immunities: A Necessary Evil?* (Aldershot: Dartmouth).

---

[118] A full treatment of all the issues raised (both legal and diplomatic) is beyond the scope of this chapter. It should be noted that the case has resulted in considerable diplomatic activity. President Bashir's ability to travel internationally has been severely curtailed. On the other hand, there is an ongoing process of discussion in the African Union which touches on many of the issues raised here culminating in that adoption in January 2017 of the ICC Withdrawal Strategy (Labuda, 'The African Union's Collective Withdrawal from the ICC: Does Bad Law Make Good Politics?', *EJIL Talk!* 15 February 2017). So far, Burundi has withdrawn with effect from October 2017, whereas decisions to withdraw by Gambia and South Africa have been subsequently reversed.

BARKER, JC (1998), 'State Immunity, Diplomatic Immunity and Act of State: A Triple Protection Against Legal Action', 47 *ICLQ* 950.

BARKER, JC (1999), 'The Future of Former Head of State Immunity after *ex parte Pinochet*', 48 *ICLQ* 937.

BELLINGER, J (2011), 'The Dog that Caught the Car: Observations on the Past, Present and Future Approaches of the Office of the Legal Adviser to Official Acts Immunities', 44 *Vanderbilt Journal of Transnational Law* 819.

CHINKIN, C (1999), 'Ex Parte Pinochet Ugarte (No 3), Casenote', 93 *AJIL* 703.

COSNARD, M (1999), 'Quelques observations sur les décisions de la Chambre des Lords dans l'Affaire *Pinochet*', 103 *RGDIP* 309.

CRAWFORD, J (2002), *The International Law Commission's Articles on State Responsibility* (Cambridge: Cambridge University Press).

CRAWFORD, J (2012), *Brownlie's Principles of Public International Law* (8th edn, Oxford: Clarendon Press).

DENZA, E (1999), '*Ex Parte Pinochet*: Lacuna or Leap?', 48 *ICLQ* 949.

DENZA, E (2016), *Diplomatic Law* (4th edn, Oxford: Clarendon Press).

DINSTEIN, Y (1966), 'Diplomatic Immunity from Jurisdiction *Ratione Materiae*', 15 *ICLQ* 76.

DOMINICÉ, C (1999), 'Quelques observations sur l'immunité de juridiction pénale de l'ancien Chef d'État', 103 *RGDIP* 297.

DOUGLAS, Z (2012), 'State Immunity for the Acts of State Officials', 82 *BYIL* 281.

DUPUY, P-M (1999), 'Crimes et immunités', 103 *RGDIP* 289.

EL-ERIAN, A and SCOBBIE, I (1998), 'International Organisations and International Relations', in R-J Dupuy (ed), *A Handbook on International Organisations* (2nd edn, Dordrecht: Martinus Nijhoff).

FOX, H (1999), 'The *Pinochet No 3* Case', 48 *ICLQ* 687.

FRANEY, E (2011), *Immunity, Individuals and International Law* (Saarbrücken: Lambert Academic Publishing).

GAETA, P (2009), 'Does President Al Bashir Enjoy Immunity from Arrest?', 7 *J Int'l Crim Just* 315.

HIGGINS, R (1985), 'The Abuse of Diplomatic Privileges and Immunities: Recent United Kingdom Experience', 79 *AJIL* 641.

JAMES, A (1991), 'Diplomatic Relations and Contacts', 62 *BYIL* 347.

JENKS, CW (1961), *International Immunities* (London: Stevens).

JENNINGS, SIR ROBERT (2002), 'Jurisdiction and Immunity in the ICJ Decision in the *Yerodia* Case', 4 *International Law Forum* 99.

KOH, HH (2011), 'Foreign Official Immunity after *Samantar*: A United States Government Perspective', 44 *Vanderbilt Journal of Transnational Law* 1141.

LEE, LT and QUIGLEY, J (2008), *Consular Law and Practice* (3rd edn, Oxford: Clarendon Press).

MCLACHLAN, C (2002), '*Pinochet* Revisited', 51 *ICLQ* 959.

MANN, FA (1990), '"Inviolability" and Other Problems of the Vienna Convention on Diplomatic Relations', in FA Mann, *Further Studies in International Law* (Oxford: Clarendon Press).

MICHAELS, DB (1971), *International Privileges and Immunities: a Case for a Universal Statute* (The Hague: Martinus Nijhoff).

ROBERTS, I (ed) (2009), *Satow's Diplomatic Practice* (6th edn, Oxford: Oxford University Press).

SANGER, A (2013), 'Immunity of State Officials from the Criminal Jurisdiction of a Foreign State', 62 *ICLQ* 193.

SCHREUER, C and WITTICH, S (2002), 'Immunity v Accountability: the ICJ's Judgment in the *Yerodia* Case', 4 *International Law Forum* 117.

SPINEDI, M (2002), 'State Responsibility v Individual Responsibility for International Crimes: *Tertium Non Datur*', 13 *EJIL* 895.

STERN, B (2002), 'Les dits et non dits de la Cour Internationale de Justice dans l'affaire RDC contre Belgique', 4 *International Law Forum* 104.

VAN ALEBEEK, R (2000), 'The *Pinochet* case: International Human Rights Law on Trial', 71 *BYIL* 29.

WARBRICK, CJ, SALGADO, EM, and GOODWIN, N (1999), 'The *Pinochet* Cases in the United Kingdom', 2 *YIHL* 1.

WATTS, SIR ARTHUR (1994), 'The Legal Position in International Law of Heads of States, Heads of Governments and Foreign Ministers', 247 *Recueil des Cours* 9.

WATTS, SIR ARTHUR (1999), *The International Law Commission 1949–1998 Vol I* (Oxford: Oxford University Press).

WHOMERSLEY, C (1992), 'Some Reflections on the Immunity of Individuals for Official Acts', 41 *ICLQ* 848.

WICKREMASINGHE, C (2000), 'The Advisory Opinion on the Difference Relating to Immunity from Legal Process of Special Rapporteur of the Commission on Human Rights', 49 *ICLQ* 724.

WIRTH, S (2002), 'Immunity for Core Crimes? The ICJ's Judgment in the *Congo* v *Belgium* Case', 13 *EJIL* 877.

WOOD, M (1974), 'The Convention on the Prevention and Punishment of Crimes against Internationally Protected Persons, including Diplomatic Agents', 23 *ICLQ* 791.

WOOD, M (2012), 'The Immunity of Official Visitors', 16 *Max Planck Yearbook of UN Law* 35.

WUERTH, I (2012), '*Pinochet*'s Legacy Reassessed', 106 *AJIL* 731.

WUERTH, I (2013), 'Foreign Official Immunity: Invocation, Purpose and Exceptions', 23 *Swiss Review of International and European Law* 207.

YOUNG, E (1964), 'The Development of the Law of Diplomatic Relations', 40 *BYIL* 141.

ZEPPALA, S (2001), 'Do Heads of State Enjoy Immunity from Jurisdiction for International Crimes? The *Ghaddafi* Case before the French *Cour de Cassation*', 12 *EJIL* 595.

FURTHER READING

Consuls

LEE, LT and QUIGLEY, J (2008), *Consular Law and Practice* (3rd edn, Oxford: Clarendon Press): the standard guide to consular law.

Diplomats

DENZA, E (2016), *Diplomatic Law* (4th edn, Oxford: Clarendon Press): the definitive guide to the Vienna Convention on Diplomatic Relations.

ROBERTS, I (ed) (2016), *Satow's Diplomatic Practice* (7th edn, Oxford: Oxford University Press): an up-to-date and very readable edition of a classic work, containing a wealth of information and practice.

Special missions

WOOD, M (2012), 'The Immunity of Official Visitors', 16 *Max Planck Yearbook of UN Law* 35: A thorough and thoughtful survey of customary international law and recent State practice on this under-explored subject—an important addition to the literature.

Heads of state, heads of government, and foreign ministers

FOAKES, J (2014), *The Position of Heads of State and Senior Officials in International Law* (Oxford: Clarendon Press): a balanced and thoughtful discussion of the law and practice, which updates Sir Arthur Watts' work (see below).

WATTS, SIR ARTHUR (1994), 'The Legal Position in International Law of Heads of State, Heads of Governments and Foreign Ministers', 247 *Recueil des Cours* 9: a very readable survey of the law and its underpinning at that date.

Officials of international organizations

ZACKLIN, R (1998), 'Diplomatic Relations: Status Privileges and Immunities' and SCOBBIE, I (revising El-Erian, A), 'International Organisations and International Relations', both in R-J Dupuy (ed), *A Handbook on International Organisations* (2nd edn, Dordrecht: Martinus Nijhoff), pp 293–313 and 831–67, respectively.

The interplay of international criminal law and the law of immunities

O'KEEFE, R (2015), *International Criminal Law* (Oxford: Clarendon Press): chapter 10 of this work provides a clear-minded, if critical, analysis of recent developments on this issue.

VAN ALEBEEK, R (2008), *The Immunity of States and Their Officials in International Criminal Law and International Human Rights Law* (Oxford: Clarendon Press): an interesting attempt to bring coherence to the various legal strands of the issues.

Work of the international law commission on 'immunity of state officials from foreign criminal jurisdiction'

An Analytical Guide to this work can be found at: http://legal.un.org/ilc/guide/4_2.shtml, comprising three Reports of the first Special Rapporteur, Amb. Kolodkin, and currently five Reports of the second Special Rapporteur, Madam Escobar Hernandez, as well as a useful, if now dated, Memorandum of the Secretariat (UN Doc A/CN.4/596) and the Reports of the Drafting Committee and Comments of States.

Pinochet

There is an abundance of literature on this case; a starting point might be:

WARBRICK, CJ, SALGADO, EM, and GOODWIN, N (1999), 'The *Pinochet* cases in the United Kingdom', 2 *YIHL* 1.

For some of the legal policy issues at stake see:

BIANCHI, A (1999), 'Immunity versus Human Rights: The *Pinochet* Case', 10 *EJIL* 237.

DENZA, E (1999), '*Ex parte Pinochet*: Lacuna or Leap', 48 *ICLQ* 949.

Immunities before the ICC

AKANDE, D (2004), 'International Law Immunities and the International Criminal Court', 98 *AJIL* 407.

13

THE RELATIONSHIP BETWEEN INTERNATIONAL AND NATIONAL LAW

Eileen Denza

SUMMARY

Enormous growth in the substance of international law implies that it is now mostly applied and enforced by national authorities and courts. International tribunals are clear that in case of conflict the international rule prevails, but they will not invalidate national law and have traditionally regarded as a domestic matter how the correct international result is achieved. For national legislatures and courts, by contrast, their mandate derives from their national constitution. Constitutional provisions are complex and infinitely varied and do not give clear answers to many problems which arise in national courts. There is no prospect of a harmonized approach to the relationship between international and national law, but it is possible to identify factors conducive to the avoidance of conflict. These include close involvement of international lawyers in the treaty-making and ratification process, attention at the time of ratification to implementation questions, teaching of international law as part of professional training of judges, and expert assistance to national courts when international law questions arise.

I. INTRODUCTION

The law of nations was until the twentieth century concerned mainly—though never exclusively—with the conduct of sovereign States and relations between those States. Now, however, it permeates and radically limits and conditions national legal orders, its rules are applied and enforced by national authorities, and national courts are often asked to resolve its most fundamental uncertainties. Yet international law does not itself prescribe how it should be applied or enforced at the national level. It asserts its own primacy over national laws, but without invalidating those laws or intruding into national legal systems, requiring a result rather than a method of implementation. National constitutions are therefore free to choose how they give effect to treaties and to customary international law. Their choice of methods is extremely varied. Can it be shown that certain constitutional approaches are based on greater deference to international law or help to reduce conflict between legal orders? If not, are there other general factors conducive to greater mutual understanding and to resolving the practical problems of coexistence?

II. THE APPROACH OF INTERNATIONAL COURTS AND TRIBUNALS

The jurisdiction given to international courts and tribunals is normally limited to the determination of questions of international law. In theory, nothing prevents States from referring to international arbitration or adjudication an issue of national law, but questions of national law usually arise before international tribunals only if relevant to the construction of an international agreement or to the establishment of breach of an international obligation.

The Permanent Court of International Justice in the cases of *The Serbian Loans*[1] and *The Brazilian Loans*[2] explored the nature of its competence, under a Special Agreement between France and the Kingdom of the Serbs, Croats and Slovenes, to construe terms of a loan contract between the Kingdom and French bondholders. The Court observed that while its main function was to decide disputes between States on the basis of international law, it also had jurisdiction to determine 'the existence of any fact which, if established, would constitute a breach of an international obligation'. This jurisdiction included questions of municipal law, but the Court made clear that it could not undertake its own construction of national laws, with the danger of contradicting rulings of national tribunals. It said:

> It would be a most delicate matter to do so, especially in cases concerning public policy and in cases where no relevant provisions directly relate to the questions at issue. It is French legislation, as applied in France, which really constitutes French law . . .

In the *Nottebohm* case[3] the International Court of Justice had to determine whether Liechtenstein was entitled to exercise a right of diplomatic protection of Nottebohm—a German national by birth who had become a naturalized citizen of Liechtenstein but without having any real connections with that State. States are entitled to exercise diplomatic protection of their nationals, and international law does not impose limitations on the right of a sovereign State to determine who are its nationals. The Court emphasized, however, that the issue in the case was not the domestic law validity of Nottebohm's naturalization, but whether the grant of nationality by Liechtenstein produced international legal effects which must be recognized by Guatemala.

A. WHERE NATIONAL LAW CAUSES BREACH OF INTERNATIONAL LAW

International tribunals have consistently held that in the event of conflict between international obligations and national law, the international rule prevails. This was set out in the draft Declaration on Rights and Duties of States prepared by the International Law Commission and endorsed in 1949 by the UN General Assembly. Article 13 provides:

> Every state has the duty to carry out in good faith its obligations arising from treaties and other sources of international law, and it may not invoke provisions in its constitution or its laws as an excuse for failure to perform this duty.[4]

The rule was restated in Article 27 of the Vienna Convention on the Law of Treaties[5] as follows:

> *Internal law and observance of treaties*
> A party may not invoke the provisions of its internal law as justification for its failure to perform a treaty. This rule is without prejudice to Article 46.

---

[1] *Serbian Loans, Judgment No 14, 1929, PCIJ, Ser A, No 20.*
[2] *Brazilian Loans, Judgment No 15, 1929, PCIJ, Ser A, No 21.*
[3] *Nottebohm, Second Phase, Judgment, ICJ Reports 1955*, p 4.   [4] GA Res 375 (IV).
[5] UKTS No 58 (1980), Cmnd 7964.

Article 46 permits a State to argue that its consent to a treaty was invalidated by violation of its internal law only where 'that violation was manifest and concerned a rule of its internal law of fundamental importance'.

The Permanent Court of International Justice, in the *Exchange of Greek and Turkish Populations* case,[6] stated that it was self-evident that a State which had assumed international obligations was bound to make necessary modifications in its legislation to ensure their fulfilment. The need for effective implementation of international human rights obligations in national law so that they can be relied on by individuals is particularly obvious, and the primacy of international obligations over conflicting national law has often been reaffirmed by human rights tribunals. The Inter-American Court of Human Rights, for example, in an Advisory Opinion on *International Responsibility for the Promulgation and Enforcement of Laws in Violation of the Convention* said:

> Pursuant to international law, all obligations imposed by it must be fulfilled in good faith; domestic law may not be invoked to justify non-fulfilment. These rules may be deemed to be general principles of law and have been applied by the Permanent Court of International Justice and the International Court of Justice even in cases involving constitutional provisions . . .[7]

International tribunals will not, however, declare national laws invalid—merely that these laws or the way in which they have been applied are inconsistent with international law. Thus the Inter-American Court of Human Rights, in the Advisory Opinion just cited made clear that its Opinion related:

> . . . only to the legal effects of the law under international law. It is not appropriate for the Court to rule on its domestic legal effect within the State concerned. That determination is within the exclusive jurisdiction of the national courts and should be decided in accordance with their laws.[8]

The International Court of Justice in the *LaGrand* case[9] was required to consider the consequences of the admitted failure by the USA to give timely notification to two German nationals of their right to consular protection under Article 36 of the Vienna Convention on Consular Relations. Notwithstanding a provisional order from the ICJ asking the USA to 'take all measures at its disposal' to stay execution of Walter LaGrand until the case brought by Germany had been decided,[10] he was executed as scheduled. On the merits, Germany later argued, *inter alia*, that the US constitutional rule of 'procedural default' (under which a procedural failing which had not been raised at State level could not be argued at federal level) violated Article 36 of the Vienna Convention, which required the USA to give full effect to the purposes for which the rights to notification and consular access are intended. The ICJ emphasized that:

> In itself, the rule does not violate Article 36 of the Vienna Convention. The problem arises when the procedural default rule does not allow the detained individual to challenge a conviction and sentence by claiming, in reliance on Article 36, paragraph 1 of the Convention, that the competent national authorities failed to comply with their obligation to provide the requisite consular information 'without delay', thus preventing the person from seeking and obtaining consular assistance from the sending State.[11]

[6] *Exchange of Greek and Turkish Populations, Advisory Opinion, 1925, PCIJ, Ser B, No 10.*
[7] *Advisory Opinion, OC-14/94, Ser A, No 14 (9 December 1994), para 35, 116 ILR 320.*   [8] Para 34.
[9] *LaGrand (Germany v United States of America), Merits, Judgment, ICJ Reports 2001*, p 466. See Mennecke and Tams, 2002.
[10] *LaGrand (Germany v United States of America), Provisional Measures, Order of 3 March 1999, ICJ Reports 1999*, p 9.
[11] *LaGrand (Germany v United States of America), Merits, Judgment, ICJ Reports 2001*, p 466, paras 79–91.

The Court held that an apology for any future violations of Article 36 would be inadequate reparation, and that the USA must allow review and reconsideration of a conviction and sentence in the light of the violation of the rights in the Convention. They stressed, however, that this obligation could be carried out in various ways, and that '[t]he choice of means must be left to the United States'.[12]

In the case of *Avena* the Court noted that the procedural default rule had not been revised, and refined its views, saying:

> It follows that the remedy to make good these violations should consist in an obligation on the United States to permit review and reconsideration of these nationals' cases by the United States courts . . . with a view to ascertaining whether in each case the violation of Article 36 committed by the competent authorities caused actual prejudice to the defendant in the process of administration of criminal justice.[13]

In response, President Bush ordered US courts to review the cases of 49 Mexicans under sentence of death. But on a further application by one of those covered by the *Avena* decision and again in the face of an order from the International Court calling for a stay of execution, the US Supreme Court in the case of *Medellin v Texas*[14] by majority ruled that the ICJ ruling did not constitute enforceable US federal law and that the President had no constitutional authority to alter this position so as to overrule the procedural default rule. Texas executed Medellin in full knowledge that this represented a violation of the international obligations of the USA.[15]

B. INTERNATIONAL LAW LOOKS MAINLY TO THE RESULT

Traditionally, international tribunals and supervisory bodies have concerned themselves only with the result in the specific case where there has been a complaint of breach. The method of national implementation of international obligations has been regarded as an internal affair. There are, however, signs of a more intrusive approach.

In the European Community law context, the European Court of Justice from the outset went beyond asserting the primacy of a European Community treaty or secondary obligation. In the case of *Costa v ENEL*,[16] the ECJ did not limit itself to saying that Italy was in breach of its Community law obligations because its courts upheld a later national measure which was inconsistent with these obligations. It held that:

> By contrast with ordinary international treaties, the EEC Treaty has created its own legal system which, on the entry into force of the Treaty, became an integral part of the legal systems of the Member States . . .

and that:

> the law stemming from the Treaty, an independent source of law, could not, because of its special and original nature, be overridden by domestic legal provision, however framed,

---

[12] Ibid, para 125.

[13] *Avena and Other Mexican Nationals (Mexico v United States of America)*, Judgment, ICJ Reports 2004, p 12, para 121. See Shelton, 2004.

[14] *Medellin v Texas* (2008) 552 US 491, noted in (2008) 102 *AJIL* 859.

[15] For the restrained reaction of the ICJ, see Judgment in *Request for Interpretation of the Judgment of 31 March 2004 in the Case concerning Avena and Other Mexican Nationals (Mexico v United States of America)*, Judgment of 19 January 2009 paras 47–59. It follows that in the US legislation would be required to ensure compliance with the obligations of consular notification and access, and this has not yet happened.

[16] *Costa v ENEL* Case 6/64 [1964] ECR 585.

without being deprived of its character as Community law and without the legal basis of the Community itself being called into question.

This formulation of the supremacy of Community and now European Union (EU) law—not self-evident on the face of the Treaties—is among the features distinguishing EU law from international law (Craig and de Búrca, 2007, ch 8; Slaughter and Burke-White, 2007). In consequence of the more intrusive nature of the EU legal order Member States may be accountable for the methods by which they implement EU legislation. The European Commission is charged with ensuring that the provisions of the Treaties are applied, and has vigorously monitored methods of national implementation.

In the field of international criminal law, it is now common for treaties not merely to permit but to require the assumption of criminal jurisdiction at national level, and to set out a uniform definition of certain criminal offences in such a way that detailed changes in national law are required. Under the 1984 UN Convention against Torture and Other Cruel, Inhuman or Degrading Treatment or Punishment,[17] for example, there is first a uniform definition of torture for the purposes of the Convention. Secondly, there is a requirement for each party to take effective legislative, administrative, judicial, or other measures to prohibit torture within its own jurisdiction and to ensure that all acts of torture are offences under its criminal law. Thirdly, a party must establish a wider extraterritorial jurisdiction on grounds such as the nationality of the alleged offender where it does not extradite an alleged offender taken into custody in its territory. The requirements imposed on national laws by successive treaties in the field of international criminal law are increasingly detailed. The Statute of the International Criminal Court does not impose express requirements on parties to incorporate international criminal offences in domestic law, but the principle of complementarity (whereby the ICC assumes jurisdiction only where parties fail in their primary responsibility to prosecute) ensures that parties give close attention to national implementation of its rules.[18]

The Convention against Torture, like earlier human rights conventions, establishes a Committee whose functions include monitoring national implementation. Parties must report to the Committee against Torture, on the measures taken. The Committee comment on the effectiveness of national implementing measures, and may make any criticisms public (along with observations by the State concerned) in its own annual report. Governments must therefore give careful thought to implementation before ratification rather than simply leave to their courts the task of giving effect to the Convention within the context of national criminal law. Other modern conventions—on for example non-proliferation of biological or chemical weapons or protection of the environment—also require for proper implementation supervision or inspection mechanisms at national level for which no international model law can be prescribed.[19]

The need for precise national implementation in criminal matters has been highlighted by the difficulty in controlling piracy off the coast of Somalia. Customary international law permits national arrest and punishment of any pirates apprehended on the high seas—but in addition to problems in the arrest of pirates, it has been found that even States willing to try and to punish pirates lack the necessary national criminal jurisdiction. The international maritime community regard it as urgent that international conventions which plug this gap are widely ratified and effectively enforced at national level.[20]

---

[17] UKTS No 107 (1991), Cm 1775.

[18] See Third Report of ICC Committee of the International Law Association, Rio de Janeiro (2008).

[19] See generally Ulfstein, 2007. For a curious application of US federal implementing legislation, see *Bond v US* (2014), 572 US; 134 S Ct 2077 (2014).

[20] UN SC Res 1846 (2 December 2008) has addressed these problems.

III. THE APPROACH OF NATIONAL PARLIAMENTS
AND NATIONAL COURTS

While the principles applied by international tribunals to the relationship between international and national law are uniform and reasonably straightforward, this is not so with the approaches taken by national parliaments or by national courts. For each national legislature and court, the relationship is determined by its own constitution. National bodies do not dispute what is said by international tribunals as to the position in international law, but they perceive the way in which international law is integrated into and applied within their own legal order as being their own constitutional affair. Other States do not question this autonomy, and international tribunals—as illustrated in Section II of this chapter—regard national laws and constitutional methods as outside their competence.

Scholars have put forward various theories to explain the relationship between international and national law. Most persistent have been the theories of monism and of dualism. For the monists, there is a single legal system with international law at its apex and all national constitutional and other legal norms below it in the hierarchy. There is no need for international obligations to be 'transformed' into rules of national law, and in case of conflict, the international rule prevails. The fact that national organs do not behave according to such rules indicates the weakness of international law, but does not invalidate the theory. According to Kelsen, the leading exponent of the monist theory, it was based not on scientific observation, but on ethical considerations (Kelsen, 1920).

Under the dualist theory, international law and national law operate on different levels. International law is a horizontal legal order based on and regulating mainly relations and obligations between independent and equal sovereign States. To the extent that to be effective it requires to be applied at national level, it is for each State to determine how this is done. If the international rule confers rights or obligations on individuals or entities created under national law, the national legislature may 'transform' it into a rule of national law, and the national judge will then apply it as a rule of national or domestic law.

Neither theory has influenced the development or revision of national constitutions, national debates about ratification of international agreements, or decisions of national courts on questions of international law. Except as shorthand indications of the general approach within a particular State to implementation of international rules, the theories are not useful in clarifying the relationship between international law and national laws. They suggest that there are only two methods of approach and that one or other theory must be 'correct' or at least preferable. Neither of these impressions is helpful. There are almost as many ways of giving effect to international law as there are national legal systems. To classify a State as 'monist' or 'dualist' does not assist in describing its constitutional approach to international obligations, in determining how its government and parliament will adopt or implement a new treaty, or in predicting how its courts will approach the complex questions which arise in litigation involving international law.

IV. THE SPECTRUM OF CONSTITUTIONAL RULES

Six States have been chosen as examples spanning the spectrum from monism to dualism and as reflecting constitutions emerging, or undergoing revision, at different historical periods. They are the Netherlands, Germany, France, Russia, the USA, and the UK. In each of these, the approach to international law reflects the historical background to the development, adoption, or revision of the constitution.[21]

These brief accounts of constitutional frameworks give only a partial account of rules which have been extensively interpreted and supplemented by the practice of national legislative, executive, and judicial organs. Only in the light of that practice and jurisprudence can one assess how practical problems are dealt with in each national context.

A. THE NETHERLANDS

The provisions in the Netherlands Constitution, as revised in 1953 and most recently in 2008, are based on two elements—a very strong degree of parliamentary control of the approval of all treaties before the Netherlands becomes bound, and a clear hierarchical superiority of treaties thus ratified over both prior and subsequent laws and statutory regulations. Article 94 of the Constitution provides for the supremacy of treaties binding on all persons in the Netherlands over prior and subsequent national law, but Article 91 makes this supremacy conditional on the treaty having been approved by the States-General. Such approval may be express or tacit. Some categories of treaties are exempted by statute from the requirement of parliamentary approval. Where any provision in a treaty conflicts or may conflict with the Constitution, a two-thirds majority in both Houses of the States-General is required for approval. Under Article 120, Netherlands courts may not review the compatibility of a treaty with the Constitution, though in other respects they interpret and apply the treaty as national law. Article 93 further provides that treaties and resolutions of international organizations which may become binding on all persons by virtue of their contents become binding after they are published. These provisions do not apply to customary international law which is not given the same precedence over national law.

Article 90 of the Constitution requires the government to promote the development of the international legal order. This, however, gives the government no mandate to override careful scrutiny by the States-General, and before approval of treaties, lawyers, and other negotiators are cross-examined in Parliamentary Committees over the detail of their texts to an extent unparalleled elsewhere in Europe. Van Dijk and Tahzib comment on this system of scrutiny:

> Thus a fair balance is achieved between the primary duty of the Government to promote the international legal order and Parliament's control over the way this duty is exercised.[22]

B. GERMANY

The 1949 German Basic Law (Grundgesetz), reflecting the German experience of National Socialism and the Second World War, provides in Article 25 that:

> The general rules of public international law shall be an integral part of federal law. They shall take precedence over the laws and shall directly create rights and duties for the inhabitants of the federal territory.

---

[21] For a wider cross-section of approaches see Nijman and Nollkaemper (eds), 2007 (in particular Peters, 2007, pp 254–70; Sloss, 2009; and Shelton, 2011).

[22] Van Dijk and Tahzib, 1994, p 125. See also van Panhuys, 1953; Schermers, 1987; Leigh, Blakeslee, and Ederington (eds), 1999; Peters, 2007, pp 304–5; Shelton, 2011, p 407.

Articles 23 and 24 of the Basic Law permit the Federation by legislation to transfer sovereign powers to intergovernmental institutions, in particular to the EU established by the Treaty on European Union signed at Maastricht in 1992, and to a system of mutual collective security in order to 'bring about and secure a peaceful and lasting order in Europe and among the nations of the world'. Article 26 makes it unconstitutional to carry out acts with the intention of disturbing peaceful relations between nations, especially preparation of an aggressive war.

Article 59, however, provides that:

> (2) Treaties which regulate the political relations of the Federation or relate to matters of federal legislation shall require the consent or participation, in the form of a federal law, of the bodies competent in any specific case for such federal legislation . . .

Under German constitutional practice, Parliament may be involved in treaty negotiations, and policy issues may be discussed in the Foreign Affairs Committee of the Bundestag or in that of the Bundesrat. The treaties regarded as regulating the political relations of the Federation are those which might affect the existence, independence, status, or role of the German State. Ultimate control of new treaties lies with the Federal Constitutional Court (Bundesverfassungsgericht) and its decision in the matter binds all State organs. The court has stated that a fundamental objective of the Grundgesetz is to enable fulfillment of Germany's obligations under international law.

The role of the Federal Constitutional Court was of central importance to Germany's position as the last member State to ratify the Maastricht Treaty in 1993. Even following adoption of the new Article 23 of its Basic Law as the basis for participation in the new EU, Germany was unable to ratify until the Constitutional Court had ruled in the case of *Brunner* v *European Union Treaty*. Brunner argued that the integration to be effected by the Treaty would lead to 'development towards the covert and irrevocable institution of a European federal state'. On this, the court said:[23]

> Germany is one of the 'Masters of the Treaties' which have established their adherence to the Union Treaty concluded 'for an unlimited period' . . . with the intention of long-term membership, but could also ultimately revoke that adherence by a contrary act. The validity and application of European law in Germany depend on the application-of-law instruction of the Accession Law. Germany thus preserves the quality of a sovereign State in its own right and the status of sovereign equality with other States . . .

A similar review of the implications of the 2007 Treaty of Lisbon was carried out by the Constitutional Court, and the court insisted on further national legislation to elaborate parliamentary rights of control before German ratification.[24]

In the *Görgülü* case, the Federal Constitutional Court clarified that international agreements—and in particular the European Convention on Human Rights (ECHR)—have the status of a federal statute but do not prevail in case of conflict with the Basic Law. The Basic Law must, however, be construed in accordance with the ECHR as interpreted by the European Court of Human Rights.[25]

---

[23] *Brunner* v *European Union Treaty* [1994] 1 CMLR 57, para 55. See also Schwarze, 1994, 1995, 2001; Treviranus and Beemelmans, 1995.

[24] BVerfG, 2 BvR 2/08, 30.6.2009 and Press Release no 72/2009. On the 'cooperative relationship' between German and international courts, particularly on human rights, see Paulus, 2007.

[25] *Görgülü* case, BVerfGE 111, 307, 2 BvR 148/04 (Order of 14 October 2004); 1BvR 1664/04 (Order of 5 April 2005); 1BvR 2790/04 (Order of 10 June 2005); Shelton, 2011, p 240.

C. FRANCE

The 1958 Constitution of the Fifth Republic also requires careful control of the ratification of treaties. Article 53 provides that:

> Peace treaties, commercial treaties, treaties or agreements concerning international organizations, those which impose a financial burden on the State, those which modify legislative provisions, those concerning personal status, those which effect cession, exchange or addition of territory, may not be ratified or approved except by virtue of a law.

Under Article 54, if the Constitutional Council (*Conseil Constitutionnel*) declares that an international commitment contains provision adverse to the Constitution, authorization to ratify may be given only after amendment of the Constitution. Amendment under the terms of this provision has been made for the ratification of the Treaties of Maastricht, Amsterdam, and Lisbon, and for the ratification of the Statute of the International Criminal Court.[26] The 2008 amendment adopted by both Houses of Parliament which permitted French ratification of the Treaty of Lisbon followed the French rejection by referendum of the draft Constitutional Treaty for the European Union—but in spite of the similarities between the two, no second referendum was permitted. In 1985 the Constitutional Council concluded that Protocol No. 6 to the European Convention on Human Rights and Fundamental Freedoms on the Abolition of the Death Penalty was not in conflict with the Constitution and, in particular, that it was not inconsistent with the essential conditions for national sovereignty (Favoreu, 1985). Article 55 provides that treaties duly ratified have, after publication, an authority superior to legislation. Only in 1989, however, did the Conseil d'Etat accept that this superiority applied not only to earlier but also to later national legislation (Eisemann and Kessedijan, 1995). In this context a specific treaty provision must be shown to have direct effect before it may be invoked by a party to litigation in French courts (Errera, 2008).

Under French practice, the Minister for Foreign Affairs may issue an interpretation of a treaty provision to a court, and this interpretation can be relied on in later cases involving the same provision if it is of general application and binding on the court.[27] In the case of *Kandyrine de Brito Paiva*,[28] the Conseil d'Etat invited submission of an *amicus curiae* brief from Gilbert Guillaume[29] to assist in resolution of a conflict between ECHR—which prohibits discrimination on the basis of nationality in regard to the right to property—and the Agreement of 1997 between France and Russia which settled pre-1917 claims but limited distribution of assets to French nationals. The claimant had inherited a claim in respect of a loan from his French great-uncle but was himself Portuguese. The court held that there was no conflict between the two treaties since the ECHR had to be interpreted in the light of the bilateral treaty, but that any conflict between treaties should be resolved in the light of national constitutional rules and principles.

D. RUSSIA

In 1993, after a prolonged battle between the Constitutional Commission and President Yeltsin, the Russian Federation adopted a constitution to reflect the newly democratic

---

[26] Constitutional Law of 8 July 1999, No 99–568. See Errera in House of Lords EU Committee, 6th Report 2003–04, HL Paper 47 *The Future Role of the European Court of Justice*, QQ 161–8 and Supplementary Notes, 2008; Bell, 2005.

[27] *Affaire Barbie*, 100 ILR 330.

[28] Conseil d'Etat No. 3036/78, 28 Revue française de droit administratif 17 (2012); (2012) 106 *AJIL* 353.

[29] Former Legal Adviser to the Ministry of Foreign Affairs, Judge of the ICJ, and member of the Conseil d'Etat.

character of Russia and a new acceptance of the international legal order. Article 86 of the Constitution gives the President of Russia the power to negotiate and conclude treaties. Article 106 provides for both Chambers of Parliament (the Duma and the Federal Council) to give consent to treaties by federal law. The meaning of these provisions was later clarified by the 1995 Federal Law on International Treaties which reflected accession by Russia to the Vienna Convention on the Law of Treaties. As with most national constitutions, publication is essential for a treaty to carry binding force in Russian law, and the treaty must be binding under international law.[30]

Under Article 15.4 of the 1993 Constitution:

> The generally recognized principles and norms of international law and the international treaties of the Russian Federation shall constitute part of the legal system. If an international treaty of the Russian Federation establishes other rules than those stipulated by the law, the rules of the international treaty shall apply.

This provision gives clear priority to both customary international law and treaties in force for Russia over both earlier and later national laws. It marked a radical change from the position under the 1977 Constitution of the Soviet Union which did not permit treaties to be invoked before domestic courts. The numerous treaties on human rights which the Soviet Union had so freely ratified without reservation suddenly became enforceable in Russian courts. Russian courts apply principles of international law directly—particularly the ECHR and its case law—though hampered by limited judicial independence, the lack of professional training in international law, and the shortage of relevant materials in Russian translation.

Article 15.4 does not, however, give international law priority over the Russian Constitution. The Constitutional Court may review the compatibility with the Constitution of treaties not yet in force for Russia, and also of international decisions interpreting treaties already in force (Danilenko, 1994; Butler, 2002; Danilenko, 1999; Zimnenko, 2007; Petrov and Kalinchenko, 2011). This was emphasized by the Russian Constitutional Court in response to the judgment of the Grand Chamber of the European Court of Human Rights in the case of *Markin* v *Russia*[31] finding that Russia was in breach of Article 14 of the ECHR in refusing equal treatment regarding parental leave to a military serviceman. The President recommended that Russia should follow the approach taken by the German Constitutional Court in the *Görgülü* case.[32]

In 2015 the Russian Constitutional Court assumed the power to declare that an international decision inconsistent with the Russian Constitution is 'impossible to implement'. This power was exercised for the first time in 2016 when the Constitutional Court ruled[33] that it was 'impossible to implement' the ECtHR final judgment in *Anchugov and Gladkov* v *Russia*[34] which had declared that Russia's constitutional blanket ban on voting rights for convicted prisoners was inconsistent with Protocol 1 to the ECHR. The Russian Constitutional Court based its judgment on stating that Russia's consent to be bound by Protocol 1 to the ECHR was invalid since at the time of ratification it was not understood that the right to vote could not be restricted in regard to convicted prisoners. It further maintained that under Article 31 of the Vienna Convention on the Law of Treaties Russia could disregard a decision of the ECtHR which gave an interpretation of the ECHR

---

[30] Decree No 10 of the Plenum of the Supreme Court of the Russian Federation, 5 October 2003.
[31] Application No 30078/06. See analysis and comment at (2013) 106 *AJIL* 836.
[32] See n 25 in this chapter.
[33] Ruling of 19 April 2016 No 12-II/2016. See analysis and comment in (2017) 111 *AJIL* 461.
[34] *Anchugov and Gladkov* v *Russia*, nos 11157/04 and 15162/05, 4 July 2013.

contrary to the ordinary meaning of a provision in context and in the light of its object and purpose. The Russian ruling should not be seen as a protest, and there were ways—falling short of amendment to the Russian Constitution—whereby compliance with the ECtHR decision might be achieved.

Russian courts interpret treaties in accordance with the Vienna Convention on the Law of Treaties, but may apply for assistance from the Ministry of Foreign Affairs or the Ministry of Justice.[35]

E. THE USA

Under Article II s 2 of the Constitution of the USA, adopted in 1787 when the original confederal system was replaced by a fully federal system, the President:

> shall have Power, by and with the Advice and Consent of the Senate, to make Treaties, provided two thirds of the Senators present concur ...

It is clear that 'Advice and Consent' was intended to require consultation of the Senate during negotiations, but following one unhappy experience, the first President, George Washington, limited consultation to approval of treaties before ratification. The independent power of the Senate to reject or delay approval of treaties submitted by the executive is substantial.

Article VI s 2 further provides that:

> This Constitution, and the Laws of the United States which shall be made in Pursuance thereof; and all Treaties made, or which shall be made, under the authority of the United States, shall be the Supreme Law of the Land, and the Judges in every State shall be bound thereby, any Thing in the Constitution or Laws of any State to the Contrary notwithstanding.

International law was accepted as part of the law of the individual States, and following the formation of the USA it was also accepted as part of federal law without the need for incorporation by Congress or by the President—thought this has recently been questioned. International law is, however, regarded as subject to the Constitution and thus, at national level, to 'repeal' by later US law. Wherever possible a US statute is construed so as not to conflict with international law.[36]

International law and international agreements binding the USA may be interpreted and enforced by US courts. According to the Third Restatement of the Foreign Relations Law of the United States:

> (2) Cases arising under international law or international agreements of the United States are within the Judicial Power of the United States and, subject to Constitutional and statutory limitations and requirements of justiciability, are within the jurisdiction of the federal courts.
>
> (3) Courts in the United States are bound to give effect to international law and to international agreements of the United States, except that a 'non-self-executing' agreement will not be given effect as law in the absence of necessary implementation.[37]

Determinations of international law by the Supreme Court, including review of State laws on grounds of inconsistency with international law, are binding on the States and on State

---

[35] Shelton, 2011, p 523.

[36] In *Al Bihani* v *Obama*, US Court of Appeals No 09–5051, (2010), however, the Court found that Congress did not intend the international laws of war to constrain the President's war powers as defined under statute.

[37] Chapter 2 Status of International Law and Agreements in United States Law, s 111.

courts. There are complex rules of constitutional law and practice determining whether an agreement is 'self-executing' in the USA, and these have little regard to international rules of treaty interpretation. They were applied by the Supreme Court in the case of *Medellin* v *Texas*, described in Section II A (n 14) of this chapter, where the majority held that a judgment of the International Court of Justice did not constitute a self-executing obligation in the USA.[38] In response, a Joint Task Force of the American Bar Association and the American Society of International law on Implementing Treaties under US Law studied *Medellin* and in its Report recommended expedited legislation where there was imminent risk of treaty-breach by the USA and, for future treaties, better identification by the executive and the Senate of self-executing provisions and delay in bringing a treaty into force until other provisions were implemented by legislation.[39]

On ratifying the International Covenant on Civil and Political Rights in 1992, the US government attached a declaration stating that Articles 1 through 27 of the Covenant were not self-executing, and there has been no implementing legislation. The US Senate, in giving 'advice and consent' to a treaty, now states which of its provisions are self-executing. Where an agreement is given effect in US law, it is the implementing legislation, not the agreement, which is regarded as US law.[40]

Under US judicial practice, great weight is given to views on questions of international law expressed by the US government, whether by way of *amicus curiae* briefs, interventions as a party, or 'executive suggestions', mainly so that the USA should speak with one voice on such questions.

The receptiveness of the USA to international law has, however, been challenged both at federal and at State level by a series of bills which would prohibit use of international and foreign law. A typical example was the Oklahoma 'Save our State' resolution which would have prohibited the State courts from considering international law. Most of these bills have been struck down as unconstitutional, but they betray ignorance of their practical implications and send a damaging message abroad.[41]

F. THE UK

Under the unwritten constitution of the UK, Parliament has the supreme power to establish and to change the law of the UK. The conduct of foreign affairs, including the conclusion and termination of treaties, remains under the royal prerogative—which means that it is carried out by the government of the day, who are broadly accountable to Parliament.

Customary international law has long been regarded as part of the law of England and of Scotland without any need for specific incorporation, and this rule has also applied in Commonwealth States as part of the common law.[42] The modern approach states rather that 'international law is not a part of, but is one of the sources of the common law'.[43] Treaties, however, are not regarded as a source of rights or obligations in domestic law. The reason is that otherwise it would be open to the executive to alter national law by a treaty instead of through the enactment of legislation and thus to bypass the supremacy of Parliament. It is in theory open to the executive to assume international legal

---

[38] See nn 14 and 15.

[39] Report at http://www.americanbar.org/content/dam/aba/migrated/leadership/2010/midyear/daily_journal/108C.authcheckdam.pdf.

[40] Third Restatement of the Foreign Relations Law of the US. See also Jackson, 1987; Riesenfeld and Abbott, 1994; Aust, 2013, pp 174–6.

[41] See Fellmeth, 2012; Shelton, 2011, esp. pp 655–9; Bradley, 2014; Sloss, Ramsey and Dodge, 2011.

[42] For the position in Canada, for example, see *R* v *Hape* [2008] 1 LRC 551, paras 34–46.

[43] Per Lord Sumption in *Belhaj* v *Straw* [2017] UKSC 3, para 252.

commitments, but these will not be given effect within the national legal system if they require changes in the law or the jurisdiction of the UK or the payment of money (which must be voted by Parliament). The executive may conclude treaties which do not involve changes in domestic law—for example Treaties of Friendship or Investment Promotion and Protection Agreements.

The position was expressed succinctly by Lord Templeman thus in a case which followed the collapse in 1985 of the International Tin Council and the attempts of its creditors through UK courts to recover their losses from its member States:

> A treaty is a contract between the governments of two or more sovereign States. International law regulates the relations between sovereign States and determines the validity, the interpretation and the enforcement of treaties. A treaty to which Her Majesty's Government is a party does not alter the laws of the United Kingdom. A treaty may be incorporated into or alter the laws of the United Kingdom by means of legislation. Except to the extent that a treaty becomes incorporated into the laws of the United Kingdom by statute, the courts of the United Kingdom have no power to enforce treaty rights and obligations at the behest of a sovereign government or at the behest of a private individual.[44]

Under Part 2 of the Constitutional Reform and Governance Act 2010,[45] which replaced the constitutional convention, formerly known as the Ponsonby rule, all treaties subject to ratification are laid before Parliament for 21 days on which it is sitting. It has, however, almost never happened that for a treaty—even an important one—not requiring any change in UK law, Parliament has pressed for a debate. The 2010 Act prohibits the government from ratifying if the House of Commons vote against it, and imposes conditions if the House of Lords vote against.[46] The Foreign and Commonwealth Office since 1996 accompany the treaty with an Explanatory Memorandum highlighting issues of significance.[47] Where the treaty requires changes in UK law or payment of money, the government also secure passage of the necessary changes—whether by Act of Parliament or by secondary legislation—before the treaty is brought into force for the UK. The government never deliberately assumes international commitments without being able to give internal effect to them. These constitutional constraints have meant that the UK has rarely been found in breach of its commitments.[48] Violations of the ECHR found against the UK are a very small proportion of the individual complaints brought, and the Human Rights Act 1998[49] was designed to reduce their number by providing a more effective system of domestic application.

Parliament may, however, decide as sovereign to violate treaty commitments. This was made clear by the Lord Chancellor in the context of the question of the response by the UK to a judgment of the European Court of Human Rights declaring unlawful the total ban on allowing prisoners to vote. The government accepted its international legal duty to implement this decision, but draft legislation presented to Parliament permitted it the choice of non-compliance.[50]

---

[44] *JH Rayner* v *Department of Trade and Industry* [1988] 3 All ER 257; 81 ILR 670.   [45] C 25.

[46] For detail, see Barrett, 2011. House of Commons Note SN/1A/5855, Parliament's new statutory role in ratifying treaties.

[47] For the new arrangements, see *Hansard*, HC, vol 576 (16 December 1996) WA 1101, (1996) *BYIL* 746 and 753.

[48] For UK practice see Aust, 2013, pp 168–71.

[49] C 42, especially s 3.

[50] Evidence to HL Select Committee on the Constitution 21 November 2012, QQ 2–7. The Lord Chancellor cited Lord Hoffmann's judgment in *R* v *Secretary of State for the Home Department ex parte Simms* [2000] 2 AC 115.

The UK government does not direct the courts on questions of international law. On request from the court or from a party to litigation, however, the Foreign and Commonwealth Office issues certificates on points of fact peculiarly within the knowledge of the government—for example, whether an entity is recognized as a State or government and whether an individual has been notified and received as a diplomat. These are accepted as conclusive. Where a point of international law of interest to the government is in issue in litigation, the Attorney-General may nominate counsel to assist the court as *amicus curiae*. But although counsel so nominated may be assisted by government legal advisers, he or she is not directly instructed and remains an independent 'friend of the court'.

These brief and superficial surveys illustrate that at the stage of national acceptance as well as of national judicial application of international law obligations, the methods employed do not turn on any universally applicable theory of the relationship. They turn rather on the relationship between the executive, legislative, and judicial organs of each State, on how a potential new international obligation should be democratically scrutinized, on how subsequent application can be effectively guaranteed, and on whether the national courts are independent of the executive in determining issues of international law.

V. SOME PROBLEMS WHICH ARISE IN NATIONAL COURTS

Examination of cases in national courts where the question of the relationship between international and national law has been raised shows the extreme diversity of the issues which present themselves. In many cases these issues are not capable of easy resolution in terms of national constitutions, far less in terms of general theories.

A. DOES A RULE OF CUSTOMARY INTERNATIONAL LAW PREVAIL OVER CONFLICTING NATIONAL LAW?

It seems that all national legal systems accept customary international law as an integral part of national law. Incorporation is specifically provided for in some constitutions, but in others which make no express provision the result is the same. The nature of customary international law as part of Scots law was examined for the first time in 1999 by the Appeal Court of the High Court of Justiciary in two criminal cases where the defendants, charged with sabotage against Britain's nuclear weapons, argued as 'reasonable excuse' for their conduct the international illegality of holding these weapons. The court held, without citing Scottish authority since there was none, that a 'rule of customary international law is a rule of Scots law'. It was not a fact to be established (like foreign law) by expert evidence, but was to be argued by submission and decided by the judge.[51]

English courts, however, found themselves for many years precluded from applying modern customary international law rules on restricted State immunity because the old rule of absolute State immunity had become embedded, or 'transformed' into English common law by judicial decisions. Under the rules on precedent, the judges maintained that these could be reversed only by the House of Lords as the supreme appellate body. Eventually Lord Denning, presiding over the Court of Appeal in the case of *Trendtex Trading Corporation Ltd* v *Central Bank of Nigeria*, persuaded one of his two judicial

---

[51] Cases of *John v Donnelly* and *Lord Advocate's Reference No 1, 2000*, 2001 SLT 507 (*Greenock anti-nuclear activists*), described in Neff, 2002.

colleagues that this attitude was wrong. Customary international law was incorporated into English law so that when its rules changed, English law also changed. Lord Denning said:

> International law does change, and the courts have applied the changes without the aid of any Act of Parliament. Thus, when the rules of international law were changed (by the force of public opinion) so as to condemn slavery, the English courts were justified in applying the modern rules of international law . . . [52]

National courts seldom set aside national law because of its conflict with customary international law, but the Court of Justice of the EU—functioning at a level intermediate between the international legal order and national legal orders—set out criteria under which it might review Union law for consistency with customary international law. In the *Air Transport Association of America* case,[53] the Court held that customary rules could be relied on by an individual as against an EU act insofar as, first, the rules were capable of calling into question the competence of the Union to adopt the act challenged and, secondly, the act was liable to affect rights or to create EU obligations. It then held that application of the EU's carbon-trading scheme to international flights by non-EU airlines landing or taking off from territory of the Member States was consistent with customary international law principles regarding sovereignty and jurisdiction.

B. WHAT IS THE MEANING OF AN INTERNATIONAL LAW RULE IN THE CONTEXT OF DOMESTIC LAW?

In most cases, the national court does not merely decide whether to apply a rule of international law, but on the effect of the international rule in the domestic law context where it arises. Thus, in the Scottish nuclear weapons protesters cases described in Section V A (n 52) of this chapter, holding that international law was part of Scots law was not the end of the matter. The court had then to consider whether the holding of nuclear missiles was lawful under international law—a question which had been carefully avoided by the International Court of Justice[54]—and further whether international law gave individuals a right of forcible intervention to stop international crimes such as would amount to a defence of 'necessity' under Scots criminal law. The Appeal Court held that the conduct of the UK government was not illegal and that international law conferred no right of forcible intervention on individuals. The UK House of Lords, dismissing claims by protesters against the impending conflict in Iraq that they were 'preventing crime', held in the case of *R v Jones*[55] that, although a crime of aggression existed in international law, it did not follow automatically that 'aggression' was an offence in domestic law. Aggression was a crime committed by a State, not precisely defined under international law, and it would be contrary to modern constitutional practice for English courts to treat it as a crime in English law without specific statutory authority. As to the argument that the crime under international law had been tacitly assimilated into domestic law, Lord Bingham maintained that it was 'very relevant not only that Parliament has so far refrained from taking this step but also that it would draw the courts into an area which, in the past, they have entered, if at all, with reluctance and the utmost circumspection.'

---

[52] *Trendtex Trading Corporation Ltd* v *Central Bank of Nigeria* [1977] 1 QB 529; [1977] 1 All ER 881. For critical comment, see Collier, 1989.

[53] *Air Transport Association of America, American Airlines Inc, Continental Airlines Inc, United Airlines Inc* v *Secretary of State for Energy and Climate Change*, Case C-366/10 [2012] 2 CMLR 4; Denza, 2012.

[54] *Legality of the Threat or Use of Nuclear Weapons, Advisory Opinion, ICJ Reports 1996*, p 226.

[55] *R v Jones* [2006] UKHL 16. See also remarks of US Court of Appeals in *Hamdan* v *US*, Judgment of 16 October 2012, No 11–1257.

In 2004 the US Supreme Court in *Rasul* v *Bush*,[56] in order to determine whether they had jurisdiction to review the legality of the detention of prisoners in the Guantánamo Bay Naval Base in Cuba, applied the terms of the Lease Agreement of 1903 under which Cuba conferred on the USA 'complete jurisdiction and control' over the Base while retaining ultimate sovereignty. The majority inferred from the Agreement that the relevant statute should be construed to give US federal courts jurisdiction.

In 2010 The US Supreme Court in the case of *Abbott* v *Abbott* had to construe the term 'rights of custody' in the Hague Convention on the Civil Aspects of Child Abduction to determine whether a father with a *ne exeat* right under Chilean law restricting removal of his son from Chile without his consent was entitled to demand his return under the Convention. The Supreme Court had regard to the object and purpose of the Convention, the negotiating history, the views of the State Department and decisions of courts in other contracting States in deciding that a *ne exeat* right amounted to a right of custody.[57]

US courts were authorized directly to determine questions of international law by the Alien Tort Statute 1789,[58] which confers original jurisdiction on federal district courts to determine 'any civil action by an alien for a tort only, committed in violation of the law of nations or a treaty of the United States'. After the rediscovery of this statute in the celebrated case of *Filartiga* v *Peña-Irala*,[59] where the plaintiff claimed damages for the torture of his son in Paraguay, the courts were invited in many cases to decide whether conduct which had taken place abroad violated modern rules of international law. The Supreme Court, however, in 2004, in the case of *Sosa* v *Alvarez-Machain*,[60] placed a narrow construction on the statute. They held that it was intended to be a jurisdictional statute covering causes of action where in 1789 the common law imposed personal liability—offences against ambassadors, violation of safe-conducts, and piracy. New violations of international law were not entirely excluded, but the courts should be cautious in finding new private rights on the basis of the law of nations. In the case of *Kiobel* v *Royal Dutch Petroleum*[61] the Supreme Court held further that the statute was not intended to have extraterritorial application and could not be invoked by Nigerian nationals in regard to conduct abroad by the Nigerian subsidiary of a Dutch/British oil company. The majority said that the statute was intended to avoid friction for the US in foreign relations and not to make the USA a forum for litigating violations of international law in the territory of foreign sovereigns.

C. IS THE INTERNATIONAL RULE DIRECTLY APPLICABLE AND DIRECTLY EFFECTIVE?

International courts often have to determine whether an international rule—usually a treaty provision—is directly applicable, so that no further implementing action is required for it to be legally binding at national level. This question is often cast in terms of whether the treaty is 'self-executing'—an expression which may under national law depend solely on construction of the treaty or may also (particularly in the USA) turn on internal constitutional practice. A different question is whether the rule is directly effective—so that an individual may rely on it as a source of rights at national level. The distinction between direct applicability and direct effect has been clarified by the jurisprudence of the European

---

[56] *Rasul* v *Bush* (2004) 542 US 466.
[57] 130 S Ct 1983. See (2010) 59 ICLQ 1158; (2011) 105 *AJIL* 108.   [58] 28 USC §1350.
[59] *Filartiga* v *Peña-Irala*, 630 F.2d 876 (1980); 577 F.Supp 860.
[60] *Sosa* v *Alvarez-Machain* 124 S Ct 2739, 29 June 2004. For a full account and comment see Roth, 2004.
[61] US S Ct, 17 April 2013. See earlier discussion in (2012) 106 *AJIL* 509–71 and 862–5. For comprehensive analysis of the case and its implications see Wuerth, 2013b, Agora, 'Reflections on *Kiobel*' (2013) 107 *AJIL* 829.

Court of Justice. Contrary to what is sometimes suggested, the ECJ did not invent the doctrine of direct effect, which can be traced back to rulings of the Permanent Court of International Justice and to cases in European jurisdictions, but it did lay down criteria to be uniformly applied throughout the European Union. It is this uniformity which is one of the most striking features distinguishing EU from public international law.

The cases of *Breard* v *Pruett, Breard* v *Greene* were almost identical to the *LaGrand* case described in Section II A of this chapter.[62] Breard was a national of Paraguay convicted of murder by a Virginia court in the USA. A few days before he was to be executed, Paraguay brought proceedings before the International Court of Justice, on the ground that the authorities had failed to inform him of his rights to consular protection under Article 36 of the Vienna Convention on Consular Relations. The ICJ issued an interim order requesting that the USA should take all measures to suspend the execution pending its final decision.[63] On the day of the execution, the Supreme Court considered petitions seeking a stay. Among the issues was whether Article 36 of the Vienna Convention requiring notification to a person arrested of his rights to consular access and protection, was directly effective in a national court. On this, the Supreme Court held that:

> neither the text nor the history of the Vienna Convention clearly provides a foreign nation a private right of action in United States courts to set aside a criminal conviction and sentence for violation of consular notification provisions.[64]

The Supreme Court denied the petitions and Breard was executed in the face of the ICJ's order. The Supreme Court followed the *Breard* ruling in the case of *Sanchez-Llamas* v *Oregon*[65] notwithstanding intervening decisions of the International Court of Justice casting doubt on the application of domestic procedural rules where Article 36 had been violated. Chief Justice Roberts denied that the interpretation of the International Court was binding on US courts, saying:

> If treaties are to be given effect as federal law under our legal system, determining their meaning as a matter of federal law 'is emphatically the province and duty of the judicial department' headed by the 'one supreme Court' established by the Constitution.

In *Medellin* v *Texas*, described in Section II A (n 14) of this chapter,[66] the Supreme Court held further that a judgment by the International Court of Justice in the *Avena* case[67] did not create directly enforceable domestic law. The conflict between entitlement under international law and US state law has continued and been confirmed by the case of *Leal Garcia* v *Texas*.[68]

A similar issue was raised in the case of *US* v *Alvarez-Machain* in 1992. Alvarez-Machain, a national of Mexico, was abducted in an operation for which the US Drug Enforcement Administration (DEA) was responsible. Charged with kidnap and murder of a DEA agent, he argued that his forcible abduction constituted outrageous conduct in violation of customary international law and that US courts therefore lacked jurisdiction to try him. The Supreme Court accepted that the abduction, against which Mexico had protested, violated general international law principles. This violation did not, however, give the defendant a free-standing right to contest jurisdiction. Nor could the US–Mexico Extradition Treaty

---

[62] See text at n 10 of this chapter.

[63] *Vienna Convention on Consular Relations (Paraguay v United States of America), Provisional Measures, Order of 9 April 1998, ICJ Reports 1998*, p 248.

[64] 134 F.3d 615 (1998); 118 ILR 23.   [65] *Sanchez-Llamas* v *Oregon* (2006) 548 US 331.

[66] *Medellin* v *Texas* (2008) 552 US 491.   [67] See n 13.

[68] 131 S Ct 2966 (2011); Charnovitz, 2012.

be read as including an implied term prohibiting abduction or prosecution when the defendant's presence was obtained by means outside the Treaty.[69]

In the following year a similar situation arose in the English case of *Bennett v Horseferry Road Magistrates' Court*. There the presence of the accused resulted from abduction by South African police in collusion with English police. The House of Lords held that the courts should decline as a matter of discretion to exercise criminal jurisdiction. Lord Bridge said:

> Where it is shown that the law enforcement agency responsible for bringing a prosecution has only been enabled to do so by participating in violations of international law and of the laws of another state in order to secure the presence of the accused within the territorial jurisdiction of the court, I think that respect for the rule of law demands that the court take cognisance of that circumstance.[70]

D. DOES A TREATY PREVAIL OVER INCONSISTENT NATIONAL LAW?

On the whole, national constitutions give clear directions to their courts on questions of priority, though they differ. For the UK and for its former dependencies which continued to follow its approach on becoming independent States within the Commonwealth, an unincorporated treaty cannot prevail over a conflicting statute, whether the statute is earlier or later in time. Under Article 55 of the French Constitution, by contrast, duly ratified and published treaties take precedence over national laws, whether earlier or later. The Constitutional Council in 1988 examined a complaint by candidates in elections to the National Assembly requesting annulment of elections in a particular constituency on the ground that the French Law of 11 July 1986 prescribing the procedure for elections violated Article 3 of the First Additional Protocol to the European Convention on Human Rights and Fundamental Freedoms, signed in 1950. This requires that elections should take place 'under conditions which will ensure the free expression of the opinion of the people in the choice of the legislature'. The Constitutional Council held, however, that the 1986 Law was not inconsistent with Protocol No. 1.

The Russian Constitution of 1993, as explained earlier, gives priority to customary international law and treaties over inconsistent Russian national laws. Article 17 of the Constitution further guarantees human rights in conformity with generally recognized principles of international law. In the *Case Concerning Certain Normative Acts of the City of Moscow and Some Other Regions*,[71] the Constitutional Court reviewed the legality of local acts reintroducing a residence permit requirement in the light of Article 17. The court held that they were inconsistent with the right to freedom of movement and choice of place of residence guaranteed under Article 12 of the International Covenant on Civil and Political Rights, by Protocol No. 4 to the ECHR and by general principles of international law.

Under the US Constitution an act of Congress supersedes an earlier rule of international law if it is clear that this was the intention of the domestic law and the two cannot fairly be reconciled. Thus in the *Breard* case, described in Section V C of this chapter, the Supreme Court found that even if Breard had a right to consular assistance on the basis

---

[69] *US v Alvarez-Machain* (1992) 504 US 655. For the sequel, see *Sosa v Alvarez-Machain*, in the previous section.

[70] *Bennett v Horseferry Road Magistrates' Court* [1993] 3 All ER 138, 155.

[71] VKS 1996 No 2, described in Danilenko, 1999, pp 57, 64.

of Article 36 of the Vienna Convention on Consular Relations, it had been superseded in 1996 by the express terms of the Antiterrorism and Effective Death Penalty Act, providing that a petitioner in federal courts alleging that he was held in violation of treaties of the USA would not, as a general rule, be afforded an evidentiary hearing on his claim if he had failed to develop the factual basis of his claim in State courts.[72]

The courts of the US, like those of other States, usually go to considerable effort to avoid conflict between national rules and international obligations. The approach of English courts was set out by Lord Denning in *Saloman v Commissioners of Customs and Excise*, where he said of a treaty which could not directly be relied on but which formed part of the background to the statutory provision in issue:

> I think we are entitled to look at it because it is an instrument which is binding in international law and we ought always to interpret our statutes so as to be in conformity with international law.[73]

The case of *Alcom v Republic of Colombia and others*[74] in 1984 raised the question whether execution of a judgment could take place against the ordinary bank account of a diplomatic mission. This had not been expressly regulated by any UK statute. The House of Lords accepted, largely on the basis of a 1977 judgment of the German Constitutional Court in proceedings against the Philippine Republic, that international law required such immunity from enforcement. Lord Diplock observed that the position in international law at the date of the State Immunity Act did not conclude the question of construction, and said:

> It makes it highly unlikely that parliament intended to require United Kingdom courts to act contrary to international law unless the clear language of the statute compels such a conclusion; but it does not do more than that.

A similar approach was taken by the Southern District Court of New York in *US v The Palestine Liberation Organization and others*, which held that the US Anti-Terrorism Act 1988 did not supersede the 1946 Headquarters Agreement between the UN and the USA. The court emphasized that precedence of a later statute over a treaty occurred only where the two were irreconcilable and Congress had clearly shown an intent to override the treaty in domestic law, stating that:

> unless this power is clearly and unequivocally exercised, this court is under a duty to interpret statutes in a manner consonant with existing treaty obligations. This is a rule of statutory construction sustained by an unbroken line of authority for over a century and a half.[75]

E. CAN A TREATY PREVAIL OVER A NATIONAL CONSTITUTIONAL NORM?

There are many instances where a national constitutional court has reviewed the compatibility with the national constitution of a treaty before its ratification. The French and German Constitutions were each amended to ensure the compatibility of the Treaty on European Union signed at Maastricht and succeeding EU Treaties with the national constitutional order. By the European Communities Act 1972 the UK also amended its

---

[72] 118 ILR 23, 33–4.
[73] *Saloman v Commissioners of Customs and Excise* [1967] 2 QB 116. See also Lord Denning in *Corocraft Ltd and another v Pan American Airways Inc* [1969] 1 QB 616.
[74] *Alcom v Republic of Colombia and others* [1984] 2 All ER 6.
[75] *US v The Palestine Liberation Organization and others*, 695 F.Supp 1456 (1988); 82 ILR 282.

constitution in order to accept features of the Community legal order—in particular direct applicability and direct effect—which were inconsistent with its own general approach to the implementation of international obligations. While the European Union (Withdrawal) Bill if enacted would make EU legislation in operation on exit day part of UK domestic law and would preserve its direct effect and supremacy in the UK, the Bill also provides that 'the principle of the supremacy of EU law does not apply to any enactment or rule of law passed or made after exit day'.[76]

With the possible exception of the Netherlands Constitution, there appears to be no example of a national legal order requiring the supremacy of international legal obligations over the national constitution. The transparent procedures used before the acceptance of treaties by most States have ensured that direct conflicts between national constitutions and treaties in force have been rare. In 1974, however, the German Federal Constitutional Court in the *Internationale Handelsgesellschaft* case[77] considered the possibility that European Community law might infringe constitutional rights guaranteed under the German Constitution. The court said that so long as [solange] the Community did not have its own catalogue of fundamental rights, the German courts must reserve the right to examine the compatibility of Community law with the fundamental rights in the German Constitution. The judgment (known colloquially as the *Solange* judgment) appeared to challenge the supremacy of European Community law, and it gave rise to successive and prolonged attempts by the Commission of the European Communities, by Germany, and by some other Member States to secure accession by the Community and then the Union to the European Convention on Human Rights. It confirms that for German courts, their own constitution, as amended to provide for acceptance of specific treaties, is their supreme law. This approach has been confirmed by the *Görgülü* case described in Section IV B of this chapter.[78] In 2016 the Constitutional Court of Hungary concluded that it was entitled to review the compatibility of European Union law with fundamental rights and sovereignty as guaranteed by the Hungarian Constitution.[79]

While European law may be compared with international law so far as national legal systems are concerned, in its implementation of its international obligations it should be compared with national legal systems. The European Court of Justice in the *Kadi* case,[80] considering the relationship between the international legal order and the Community legal order, in order to decide whether it could review the legality of Community measures implementing a Security Council resolution on sanctions, also began with its own basic constitutional charter, the European Community Treaty, and fundamental rights as general principles of law guaranteed by the Court. It stressed that:

> the obligations imposed by an international agreement cannot have the effect of prejudicing the constitutional principles of the EC Treaty, which include the principle that all Community acts must respect fundamental rights, that respect constituting a condition of their lawfulness . . .

Review of a Community implementing instrument would, however, not entail any challenge to the primacy of the Security Council resolution in international law.

---

[76] Clause 5.

[77] *Internationale Handelsgesellschaft* v *Einfur und Voratsstelle Getreide*, Case 11/70 [1970] ECR 1125; [1974] 2 CMLR 540.

[78] Note 26.

[79] Decision 22/2016 (XII 5) AB on the interpretation of Article B (2) of the Fundamental Law, analyzed in (2017) 111 *AJIL* 468.

[80] *Kadi and Al Barakaat International Foundation* v *Council*, Joined Cases 402/05 and 415/05 [2008] ECR I-6351, paras 280–330. See Denza, 2013, pp 185–7.

F. SHOULD THE EXECUTIVE DIRECT OR GUIDE THE NATIONAL COURT?

In most States this question is not dealt with in constitutional provisions, but is clear from practice. National judges cannot have up-to-date knowledge of international law, even where it forms part of their training. Except where there are practising lawyers with this expertise, or where international law teachers may appear as advocates, the main source of expert advice are the lawyers working continuously for the government on international law. National courts generally seek to avoid conflicts with international obligations which would embarrass their governments. They accept that it is highly desirable that on questions of recognition, jurisdiction, and immunity the State should speak with one voice.

In a large number of States—notwithstanding any principle of separation of powers—the executive will direct a national court on questions of international law—particularly on diplomatic and State immunity. In France, for example, the Conseil d'Etat would until recently normally seek guidance from the Ministry of Foreign Affairs on the construction of an international agreement, particularly if it saw a danger of embarrassment to the government. French courts may, however, decide that a reference is unnecessary because the treaty is clear (*acte clair*) and may dissent from the advice given (de la Rochère, 1987).[81] In the USA, although the courts have general powers to determine questions of international law, it is usual for the executive to give assistance in sensitive cases, either through *amicus curiae* briefs, interventions, or 'executive suggestions'. In the legal battles over Concorde's access to Washington and New York, culminating in the case of *Air France and British Airways v Port Authority of New York and New Jersey* in the US District and appellate courts, *amicus curiae* briefs from the US government to the courts on international obligations under the bilateral air services agreements with the UK and with France were crucial to the airlines' success and so to Concorde's entry into commercial service (Owen, 1997, ch 10). By the Foreign Sovereign Immunities Act,[82] the US government sought to delegate to its courts determination of questions of State immunity which had often proved politically sensitive. But the State Department has made clear that residual common law State immunity remains in some areas and that in these areas it may still file *amicus curiae* briefs and will expect US courts to defer to its views.[83] In *Habyarimana v Kagame*[84] the US Court of Appeals, citing earlier cases, accepted as conclusive the determination of the executive that the Head of State of Rwanda was immune from suit even for acts committed prior to assuming office.

In the UK, the executive are constrained by the independence of the courts from offering direction on questions of law. On questions of fact peculiarly within the knowledge of the government it is practice to provide certificates on request, and statutes such as the Diplomatic Privileges Act 1964[85] and the State Immunity Act 1978[86] expressly provide for such certificates to be given 'by or under the authority of the Secretary of State' and for their conclusive effect. In cases of importance for the government, the Attorney-General may nominate counsel to act as an independent *amicus curiae*—as in the case of *Alcom v Colombia* described in Section V D of this chapter and in the *Pinochet* case.[87]

---

[81] See *Gisti* case, Conseil d'Etat, 29 June 1990, 111 ILR 499; *Agyepong* case, Conseil d'Etat, 2 December 1994, 111 ILR 531. In the case of *Beaumartin v France, Judgment of 24 November 1994, Ser A, No 296-B*; 19 *EHRR* 485 the European Court of Human Rights held that the practice was incompatible with the right, under Article 6 of the ECHR, of access to 'an independent and impartial tribunal established by law'.

[82] 28 USC § 1603.   [83] See US *amicus* brief in *Matar v Dichter*, No. 07–2579-cv, 19 December 2007.

[84] 821 F.Supp 2d 1244.

[85] C 81, s 4. For examples, and for US practice see Denza, 2016, pp 255–7 and 322–3.   [86] Section 21.

[87] *R v Bow Street Metropolitan Stipendiary, ex parte Pinochet Ugarte (No 1)* [1999] UKHL 52; [1998] 3 WLR 1456. On the contrasting approaches of US and UK courts, see Collins, 2002.

Although international law does not prescribe what guidance the executive should give a domestic court, assistance may be derived from the Advisory Opinion of the International Court of Justice in the *Cumaraswamy* case.[88]

G. SHOULD A NATIONAL COURT APPLY A FOREIGN LAW WHICH CONFLICTS WITH INTERNATIONAL LAW?

The six questions described in preceding Sections A–F raise questions about the application of international law within each national legal order and, generally speaking, answers are provided by national constitutional law and practice. Two other questions often arise for which no direct answers are given in national constitutions. The first concerns the effect of a foreign law or executive action which is alleged to contravene international law. To answer this question the national court is required not merely to ascertain the content of international law but to decide whether it has been violated by the act of another State and, if so, the effect of that illegal act within its own legal order.

The doctrine of judicial deference to the acts of another sovereign has been most extensively developed by the courts of the USA. The classic statement of the rule, in 1897, was in *Underhill* v *Hernandez*, where the Supreme Court said:

> [E]very sovereign state is bound to respect the independence of every other sovereign state, and the courts of one country will not sit in judgment on the acts of the government of another, done within its own territory.[89]

The rule has often been applied in the context of acts of expropriation alleged to violate international law, and US courts have adopted a flexible approach designed not to hinder the executive and legislative branches in their conduct of foreign policy. The 'act of State' doctrine was re-examined by the Federal Court of Appeals in 1983 in the context of claims of corruption and anti-competitive practices in the context of an award of a concession to exploit offshore oil. In the case of *Clayco Petroleum Corporation* v *Occidental Petroleum Corporation and others* the court confirmed its applicability. The grant of a concession to exploit natural resources was inherently a sovereign act which no private person could perform, and 'the purpose of the doctrine is to prevent the judiciary from interfering with the political branch's conduct of foreign policy'.[90] By contrast, the US Court of Appeals refused to apply the doctrine in the case of *Republic of the Philippines* v *Marcos and others*, where the successor government of the Philippines sought to prevent further misappropriation of real properties in New York illegally acquired by Marcos when he was President. The court emphasized that any misappropriation had been a purely private act, that Marcos was no longer President of the Philippines, and that the present government of the Philippines actively sought the assistance of the US courts. This action by the new government was not expropriation:

> The complaint seeks recovery of property illegally taken by a former head of state, not confiscation of property legally owned by him.[91]

The House of Lords re-examined the rule in *Kuwait Airways Corporation* v *Iraqi Airways*.[92] The case resulted from the taking by Iraqi forces during their 1990 invasion of

---

[88] *Difference Relating to Immunity from Legal Process of a Special Rapporteur of the Commission on Human Rights, Advisory Opinion, ICJ Reports 1999*, p 62, paras 60–2 and in Separate Opinion of Judge Oda.

[89] *Underhill* v *Hernandez* 168 US 250, 18 S Ct 83n (1897).

[90] *Clayco Petroleum Corporation* v *Occidental Petroleum Corporation and others* 712 F.2d 404 (1983); 81 ILR 522.

[91] *Republic of the Philippines* v *Marcos and others* 806 F.2d 344 (1986); 81 ILR 581.

[92] *Kuwait Airways Corporation* v *Iraqi Airways Co (No 2)* [2002] UKHL 19; [2002] 3 All ER 209. See Note in (2002) 73 *BYIL* 400. The reasoning was criticized by Carruthers and Crawford, 2003.

ten commercial aircraft belonging to Kuwait Airways Corporation (KAC) and their transfer, by decree of the Revolutionary Command Council, to the State-owned Iraqi Airways Company. Some of the aircraft were later destroyed by coalition bombing during the conflict to liberate Kuwait and others were flown to and sheltered by Iran. KAC claimed the return of the aircraft or payment of their value, and damages. To determine liability under English law it was necessary to apply the law of Iraq and thus to determine the validity of the decree of the Revolutionary Command Council. It was clear that the invasion of Kuwait and the seizure of its assets violated fundamental rules of international law including binding Security Council resolutions. Lord Nicholls went on to say, at paragraph 29:

> Such a fundamental breach of international law can properly cause the courts of this country to say that, like the confiscatory decree of the Nazi government of Germany in 1941, a law depriving those whose property has been plundered of the ownership of their property in favour of the aggressor's own citizens will not be enforced or recognized in proceedings in this country. Enforcement or recognition of this law would be manifestly contrary to the public policy of English law. For good measure, enforcement or recognition would also be contrary to this country's obligations under the UN Charter. Further, it would sit uneasily with the almost universal condemnation of Iraq's behaviour and with the military action, in which this country participated, taken against Iraq to compel its withdrawal from Kuwait. International law, for its part, recognizes that a national court may properly decline to give effect to legislative and other acts of foreign states which are in violation of international law . . .

A similar approach was adopted by the UK Court of Appeal in *Yukos Capital* v *OJSC Rosneft*,[93] in which the Court held that they were not precluded from challenging a Russian court decision on the ground that it had been secured through a judicial process lacking independence.

The overlapping doctrines of act of State as applied in the UK, the US, and several other jurisdictions were comprehensively reviewed and analysed by the UK Supreme Court in the *Belhaj* case.[94] Belhaj and his wife alleged that UK security services cooperated with US and Libyan authorities to surrender them to Libya where Belhaj was tortured and held for six years. Rahmatullah, whose appeal was joined with that of Belhaj, was surrendered from UK into US custody and alleged that he was then tortured and held for ten years in the US air base at Bagram in Afghanistan. All seven Supreme Court judges clearly distinguished between foreign act of State in the sense now under discussion, which, according to Lord Mance in paragraph 7 of his leading judgment, 'requires a domestic court to accept without challenge the validity of certain foreign state acts', and the other sense—discussed in Section V H—of 'a broader principle of non-justiciability, whereby the domestic court must simply declare itself incompetent to adjudicate'. There are differences between Lord Mance and the separate judgments of Lord Neuberger and Lord Sumption as to whether the 'recognition' aspect of the act of State doctrine should be sub-divided between acceptance of a foreign legislative act and acceptance of an executive act. But all seven judges agreed that the doctrine was subject to exceptions on grounds of public policy and that the most important of these applied to the breaches of fundamental human rights alleged by Belhaj and Rahimtoola—in particular torture and prolonged detention without judicial review. All seven judges also agreed in dismissing the existence of a separate doctrine whereby UK courts should abstain from adjudicating on a foreign act where this would embarrass the UK government in the conduct of its international relations.

---

[93] *Yukos Capital* v *OJSC Rosneft*, [2014] EWHC 1288 (Comm).
[94] *Belhaj and another* v *Straw and others; Rahmatullah (No 1)* v *Ministry of Defence and another* [2017] UKSC 3.

Although the US and English cases on this form of 'act of State' have developed on parallel tracks, a comparison shows that the US cases are based more closely on deference to the views of the executive, so that the State may speak with a single voice, while the English courts seek rather to apply public and private international law themselves. The distinction between the US and the UK doctrines of 'foreign act of State' has been clearly drawn in the UK Supreme Court judgments in *Belhaj*.

H. ARE THERE QUESTIONS OF INTERNATIONAL LAW WHICH NATIONAL COURTS SHOULD DECLINE TO ANSWER?

Generally speaking, where questions of international law arise before national courts, they are either (as with immunity) an essential preliminary to assumption of jurisdiction over the claim or criminal charge, or they are incidental to the construction of a national statute or a claim brought under national law. The court, with whatever assistance it can secure from counsel or from its ministry of foreign affairs, must do the best it can. Sometimes, however, where a question of international law is central to the claim, English and US courts have held that they are in effect not competent to answer it. The classic statement of this principle of 'judicial restraint' was the judgment of Lord Wilberforce in the House of Lords in the case of *Buttes Gas and Oil Co v Hammer*.[95] On its face the claim was one of defamation and the defence was justification. But the real underlying dispute was over the extent of the territorial waters of Sharjah in the Persian Gulf and the right to exploit natural resources below these waters, and could not be decided without investigation of the conduct of Umm al Qaiwain, Iran, and the UK as well as Sharjah. Lord Wilberforce, with the support of his judicial colleagues, found that for an English court there were no judicial standards to judge the issues of international law and that:

> the court would be in a judicial no-man's land; the court would be asked to review transactions in which four sovereign states were involved, which they had brought to a precarious settlement, after diplomacy and the use of force, and to say that at least part of these were 'unlawful' under international law.

The principle of judicial restraint was considered in the successive *Pinochet* cases before the House of Lords. In the first case Lord Slynn and Lord Lloyd—both of whom held that General Pinochet was immune as a former Head of State—also maintained that the rule was applicable. Lord Lloyd said assumption of jurisdiction would imperil relations between governments and that:

> we would be entering a field in which we are simply not competent to adjudicate. We apply customary international law as part of the common law, and we give effect to our international obligations so far as they are incorporated in our statute law; but we are not an international court.[96]

---

[95]   *Buttes Gas and Oil Co v Hammer* [1982] AC 888; 64 ILR 273 and 331.

[96]   *R v Bow Street Metropolitan Stipendiary, ex parte Pinochet Ugarte (No 1)* [1998] UKHL 41; [2000] AC 61; [1998] 4 All ER 897; [1998] 3 WLR 1456, 1495.

[97]   *R v Bow Street Metropolitan Stipendiary, ex parte Pinochet Ugarte (Amnesty International Intervening) (No 3)* [1999] UKHL 17; [2000] 1 AC 147; [1991] 2 All ER 97; [1999] 2 WLR 827; 119 ILR 135. See, on the question of act of State, Denza, 1999. See also *Campaign for Nuclear Disarmament v The Prime Minister* [2002] EWHC 2759 (QB) and Note in (2002) 73 *BYIL* 444.

[98]   *The Republic of Ecuador v Occidental Exploration and Production Company* [2005] EWHC 774 (Comm). See also the judgment of the Court of Appeal at [2007] EWCA Civ 456.

Lord Nicholls and Lord Steyn held, however, that the doctrine did not apply. Lord Steyn maintained that the charges against General Pinochet were already in 1973 condemned as high crimes by customary international law and that it would be wrong for English courts to extend the doctrine of judicial restraint in a way which ran counter to customary international law at the relevant time. In the third *Pinochet* case before the House of Lords[97] judicial restraint was given short shrift.

The English High Court also gave a narrow interpretation to non-justiciability in 2005 in *The Republic of Ecuador* v *Occidental Exploration and Production Company*.[98] Aikens J described the doctrine as establishing 'a general principle that the municipal courts of England and Wales do not have the competence to adjudicate upon rights arising out of transactions entered into independent sovereign States between themselves on the plane of international law'. He held that it did not apply so as to prevent the court from determining a challenge by Ecuador under the UK Arbitration Act 1996 to an Award made pursuant to a Bilateral Investment Treaty between the USA and Ecuador. The Court of Appeal agreed with his analysis.

In *Mbasogo (President of the State of Equatorial Guinea)* v *Logo*,[99] the English Court of Appeal dismissed a claim for damages arising from an attempted private coup, holding that it was non-justiciable since it involved the exercise or assertion of a sovereign right. English courts had no jurisdiction to enforce the public law of a foreign State. The English Administrative Court also declined to review the UK government's decision to ratify the Treaty of Lisbon without a referendum in the case of *R (Wheeler)* v *Office of the Prime Minister*, denying the existence of an implied promise giving rise to a legitimate expectation. The court held that '[t]he subject-matter, nature and context of a promise of this kind took place in the realm of politics, not of the courts, and the question whether the government should be held to such a promise is a political rather than a legal matter'.[100]

The doctrine of judicial restraint has been strongly criticized by Rosalyn Higgins (Higgins, 1991, pp 273–4). But the approach is parallel to the restraint shown by the Permanent Court of International Justice in the extract from the *Serbian Loans* and *Brazilian Loans* cases cited at the outset of this chapter. It may also be seen as similar to the rule of *forum non conveniens* in private international law whereby courts defer to domestic courts of another State.

In the *Belhaj* case described in the previous section, the House of Lords considered whether the doctrine applied given that a decision on the merits of the claims would necessarily involve adjudication on the lawfulness of the acts of the other States implicated— in particular Libya and the US. The clearest analysis of the principle in the light of the precedents was given by Lord Sumption who said:[101]

> In all the cases cited, the claimant relied on a recognised private law cause of action, and pleaded facts which disclosed a justiciable claim of right. But the private law cause of action failed because, once the cause of action was seen to depend on the dealings between sovereign states, the court declined to treat it as being governed by private law at all . . .

and that:

> Once the acts alleged are such as to bring the issues into the issues into the 'area of international dispute' the act of state doctrine is engaged.

There were differences among the judges as to whether violations of international law or fundamental human rights implied that the doctrine did not apply or constituted an

---

[99] *Mbasogo (President of the State of Equatorial Guinea)* v *Logo* [2006] EWCA Civ 1370, [2007] QB 846.
[100] [2008] UKHL 20. See also McGoldrick, 2010 and Nicholson, 2015.
[101] *Belhaj and another* v *Straw and others* [2017] UKSC 3, para 234.

exception. Lord Sumption said that this did not matter—what mattered is that the un-derlying principle should be clear, coherent, and in line with contemporary standards. It would be 'contrary to the fundamental requirements of judicial administration by an English court to apply the foreign act of state doctrine to an allegation of civil liability for complicity in acts of torture by foreign states'.[102] Notwithstanding the differences in analy-sis of the doctrine in the judgments of Lord Mance and Lord Neuberger, all seven judges concurred in this result.

VI. CONCLUSION: ELEMENTS OF A HAPPY RELATIONSHIP

Several of the constitutional provisions described in this chapter have been revised in re-cent years in order more effectively to integrate international law into the national legal order. There is continuous cross-fertilization in attempts to remedy perceived weaknesses. The extent to which this now happens in the superior courts in the UK has been vividly described by Lord Bingham, who summed up as follows:

> If we believe, as we probably do, that peace and good order in the world depend to a large extent on the observance of legal rules, on the international as on the national place, the contribution made by national courts, not least our own, is one of which we . . . may be proud.[103]

But on the other hand there have been signs in a few States—Germany, Russia, the USA, and the UK are mentioned in this chapter—of renewed emphasis on the supremacy of national constitutions and of popular suspicion of adverse judgments from international courts.

It is unrealistic to suggest that any fundamental harmonization of national constitu-tional provisions is practicable. So long as national constitutions reflect the history and identity of independent States, and so long as international law itself remains in general non-intrusive as to how it is applied and enforced at national level, there will be infinite variety in national systems.

It is difficult even to suggest criteria on which a 'scoreboard' of impressive and failing performers could be drawn up. If, for example, the criterion is the production of judg-ments on general questions of international law which carry weight in other jurisdictions, one would rate Germany at the highest level. The laconic judgments of French courts, however correct, lack wider appeal because there is little evidence of the legal reasoning behind them. Judgments of the UK House of Lords and the US Supreme Court probably carry less weight abroad because the courts have so often been openly divided on funda-mental questions—*Breard, Alvarez-Machain, Pinochet*, to name only three discussed in this chapter.[104] Receptiveness to decisions in other States could be a criterion—in most jurisdictions there is increasing readiness to take into account cases from other jurisdic-tions, even though primary reliance on national precedents has led to some divergence of international law into separate streams.[105] Adverse judgments from international tribu-nals might be another criterion—and for the UK this was undoubtedly a factor in chang-ing its system of enforcing the European Convention on Human Rights in its domestic legal order. But an objective assessment on this basis would need to take in readiness to accept exposure to international assessment. The UK accepted the right of individual

---

[102] Ibid, paras 249–59, 262.   [103] Bingham, 2010, p 54.
[104] On *Pinochet's* influence, see Wuerth, 2013a.   [105] See Roberts, 2011.

petition under the Convention at an early stage and is now the only Permanent Member of the Security Council to accept the compulsory jurisdiction of the International Court of Justice.

In the absence of any identification of the ideal relationship between international law and national law, five factors will be proposed as generally conducive to the avoidance of conflict. They are:

(1) close involvement in the treaty-making process of lawyers with knowledge both of their own legal systems and of international law;

(2) close attention to questions of national implementation during the treaty-making process and before ratification;

(3) detailed parliamentary scrutiny of important treaties before national ratification;

(4) teaching of international law as a compulsory element of a law degree and of professional training; and

(5) involvement of specialist international lawyers as counsel and as *amici curiae* whenever difficult questions of international law arise in national courts.

Some of these suggestions go to 'the reality of legal culture' (Higgins, 1991, pp 266–8). All of them call for openness to international law, including its imperfections, its uncertainties, and its rapid shifts. The motto for national law-makers and judges might well be 'only connect'.

REFERENCES

Aust, A (2013), *Modern Treaty Law and Practice* (3rd edn, Cambridge: Cambridge University Press).

Barrett, J (2011), 'The United Kingdom and Parliamentary Scrutiny of Treaties: Recent Reforms', 60 *ICLQ* 225.

Bell, J (2005), 'French Constitutional Council and European Law', 54 *ICLQ* 735.

Bingham, T (2010), *Widening Horizons: The Influence of Comparative Law and International Law on Domestic Law* (Hamlyn Lectures, Cambridge: Cambridge University Press).

Bradley, C (2014), *International Law in the US Legal System* (Oxford, New York: Oxford University Press).

Butler, W (2002), *The Law of Treaties in Russia and the Commonwealth of Independent States* (Cambridge, New York: Cambridge University Press).

Carruthers, JM and Crawford, EB (2003), 'Kuwait Airways Corporation *v* Iraqi Airways Company', 52 *ICLQ* 761.

Charnowitz, S (2012), 'Correcting America's Continuing Failure to Comply with the Avena Judgment', 106 *AJIL* 572.

Collier, J (1989), 'Is International Law Really Part of the Law of England?', 38 *ICLQ* 924.

Collins, L (2002), 'Foreign Relations and the Judiciary', 51 *ICLQ* 485.

Craig, P and De Búrca, G (2007), *EU Law: Text, Cases and Materials* (3rd edn, Oxford: Oxford University Press).

Danilenko, G (1994), 'The New Russian Constitution and International Law', 88 *AJIL* 451.

Danilenko, G (1999), 'Implementation of International Law in CIS States: Theory and Practice', 10 *EJIL* 51.

De La Rochère, D (1987), in Jacobs and Roberts (eds), p 39.

Denza, E (1999), 'Ex parte Pinochet: Lacuna or Leap?', 48 *ICLQ* 687.

DENZA, E (2012), 'International Aviation and the EU Carbon Trading Scheme: Comment on the *Air Transport Association of America Case*', 37 *European Law Review* 314.

DENZA, E (2013), 'Placing the European Union in International Perspective', in M Adams, de Waele, J Meeusen, and G Straetmans (eds), *Judging Europe's Judges: The Legitimacy of the Case Law of the European Court of Justice Examined* (Oxford: Hart).

DENZA, E (2016), *Diplomatic Law* (4th edn, Oxford: Oxford University Press).

EISEMANN, P-M and KESSEDIJAN, C (1995), in Leigh and Blakeslee (eds), p 1.

ERRERA, R (2008), 'Domestic Courts and International Law, the Law and Practice in France', paper given to Colloquium on International Law in Domestic Courts, organized by Amsterdam Center for International Law.

FAVOREU, L (1985), XXXI *Annuaire Français de Droit International* 868.

FELLMETH, A (2012), 'U.S. State Legislation to Limit Use of International and Foreign Law', 106 AJIL 107.

HIGGINS, R (1991–V), 'International Law and the Avoidance, Containment and Resolution of Disputes', 230 *Recueil des Cours* 273–4.

JACKSON, J (1987), in Jacobs and Roberts (eds), p 141.

JACOBS, F and ROBERTS, S (eds) (1987), *The Effect of Treaties in Domestic Law* (London: Sweet & Maxwell).

KELSEN, H (1920), *Das Problem der Souveränitat und die Theorie des Völkerrechts-Beitrag zu einer reinen Rechtslehre* (Tübingen: JC Mohr).

LEIGH, M and BLAKESLEE, MR (eds) (1995), *National Treaty Law and Practice*, vol 1 (Washington, DC: ASIL).

LEIGH, M, and BLAKESLEE, and EDERINGTON, LB (eds) (1999), *National Treaty Law and Practice*, vol 2 (Washington, DC: ASIL).

McGOLDRICK, D (2010), 'The Boundaries of Justiciability', 59 *ICLQ* 981.

MENNECKE, M and TAMS, C (2002), 'The LaGrand Case', 51 *ICLQ* 449.

NEFF, S (2002), 'International Law and Nuclear Weapons in Scottish Courts', 51 *ICLQ* 171.

NICHOLSON, M (2015), 'The Political Unconscious of the English Foreign Act of State', 64 *ICLQ* 743.

NIJMAN, J and NOLLKAEMPER, A (eds) (2007), *New Perspectives on the Divide Between National and International Law* (Oxford: Oxford University Press).

OWEN, K (1997), *Concorde and the Americans* (Shrewsbury: Airlife Publishing).

PAULUS, A (2007), 'The Emergence of the International Community and the Divide Between International and Domestic Law', in Nijman and Nollkaemper (eds), p 216.

PETERS, A (2007), 'The Globalization of State Constitutions', in Nijman and Nollkaemper (eds), p 251.

PETROV, R and KALINCHENKO, P (2011), 'The Europeanization of Third Country Judiciaries through the Application of the EU Acquis: the Cases of Russia and Ukraine', 60 *ICLQ* 325.

RIESENFELD, S and ABBOTT, F (eds) (1994), *Parliamentary Participation in the Making and Operation of Treaties* (The Hague: Nijhoff/Kluwer).

ROBERTS, A (2011), 'Comparative International Law? The Role of National Courts in International Law', 60 *ICLQ* 57.

ROTH, B (2004), 'Note on *Sosa v Alvarez-Machain*', 98 *AJIL* 798.

SCHERMERS, H (1987), in Jacobs and Roberts (eds), p 109.

SCHWARZE, J (1994), 'La ratification du traité de Maastricht en Allemagne, l'arrêt de la Cour constitutionnelle de Karlsruhe', *Revue du Marché Commun* 293.

SCHWARZE, J (1995), 'Towards a Common European Public Law', 2 *European Public Law* 227.

SCHWARZE, J (ed) (2001), *The Birth of a European Constitutional Order* (Baden-Baden: Nomos).

SHELTON, D (2004), 'Note on *Avena and Other Mexican Nationals*', 98 *AJIL* 559.

SHELTON, D (2011), *International Law and Domestic Legal Systems* (Oxford, New York: Oxford University Press).

SLAUGHTER, A-M and BURKE-WHITE, W (2007), 'The Future of International Law is Domestic (or, The European Way of Law)' in Nijman and Nollkaemper (eds), p 110.

SLOSS, DL (ed) (2009), *The Role of Domestic Courts in Treaty Enforcement: A Comparative Study* (Cambridge, New York: Cambridge University Press).

SLOSS, DL, RAMSEY, MD, and DODGE, WS (2011), *International Law in the US Supreme Court: Continuity and Change* (Cambridge, New York: Cambridge University Press).

TREVIRANUS, H and BEEMELMANS, H (1995), in Leigh and Blakeslee (eds), p 5.

ULFSTEIN, G (ed, in collaboration with T Marauhn and A Zimmermann) (2007), *Making Treaties Work* (Cambridge: Cambridge University Press).

VAN DIJK, P and TAHZIB, BG (1994), in Riesenfeld and Abbott (eds), p 109.

VAN PANHUYS, JHF (1953), 'The Netherlands Constitution and International Law', 47 *AJIL* 537.

WUERTH, I (2013a), '*Pinochet*'s Legacy Reassessed', 106 *AJIL* 731.

WUERTH, I (2013b), '*Kiobel* v. *Royal Dutch Petroleum Co*: The Supreme Court and the Alien Tort Statute', 107 *AJIL* 601.

ZIMNENKO, BL (2007), *International Law and the Russian Legal System*, WE Butler (ed and trans) (Utrecht: Eleven International Publishing).

FURTHER READING

AUST, A (2013), *Modern Treaty Law and Practice* (3rd edn, Cambridge, Cambridge University Press), ch 10, 'Treaties and Domestic Law': a clear introduction.

CAI, C (2016), 'International Law in Chinese Courts during the Rise of China', 110 *AJIL* 269: historical and political comment on the silence of China's Constitution on international law, and an account of practice.

CASSESE, A (2005), *International Law* (2nd edn, Oxford: Oxford University Press), ch 12, 'The Implementation of International Rules within National Systems': thorough account of theory and practice in many States.

LEIGH, M, BLAKESLEE, MP, and EDERINGTON, LB (eds) (1999), *National Treaty Law and Practice* (Washington, DC: ASIL): an extensive comparative survey.

NIJMAN, J and NOLLKAEMPER, A (eds) (2007), *New Perspectives on the Divide Between National and International Law* (Oxford: Oxford University Press): a critical analysis of theories.

NOLLKAEMPER, A (2011), *National Courts and the International Rule of Law* (Oxford: Oxford University Press): an extensive and perceptive analysis of cases from the perspective of the rule of law.

RIESENFELD, S and ABBOTT, F (eds) (1994), *Parliamentary Participation in the Making and Operation of Treaties* (The Hague: Nijhoff/Kluwer).

SHELTON, D (ed) (2011), *International Law and Domestic Legal Systems* (Oxford, New York: Oxford University Press): a wide-ranging survey of constitutional provisions and practice.

PART V

RESPONSIBILITY

14

THE CHARACTER AND FORMS OF INTERNATIONAL RESPONSIBILITY

James Crawford and Simon Olleson

SUMMARY

On the international plane, responsibility is the necessary corollary of obligation: every breach by a subject of international law of its international obligations entails its international responsibility. This chapter starts by giving an overview of different forms of responsibility/liability in international law before examining the general character of State responsibility. Due to the historical primacy of States in the international legal system, the law of State responsibility is the most fully-developed branch of responsibility and is the principal focus of the chapter. In contrast, although the International Law Commission, broadly following the scheme of the 2001 Articles on State Responsibility, adopted Articles on Responsibility of International Organizations in 2011, the responsibility of international organizations remains an under-developed area; it is considered only briefly, as is the potential responsibility under international law of other international actors.

The law of State responsibility deals with three general questions: (1) has there been a breach by a State of an international obligation; (2) what are the consequences of the breach in terms of cessation and reparation; (3) who may seek reparation or otherwise respond to the breach as such, and in what ways? As to the first question, this chapter discusses the constituent elements of attribution and breach, as well as the possible justifications or excuses which may preclude responsibility. The second question concerns the various secondary obligations which arise upon the commission of an internationally wrongful act by a State, and in particular the forms of reparation. The third question concerns issues of invocation of responsibility, including the taking of countermeasures.

I. THE SCOPE OF INTERNATIONAL RESPONSIBILITY: INTRODUCTION AND OVERVIEW

Article 1 of the Articles on Responsibility of States for Internationally Wrongful Acts (ARSIWA or 'the Articles on State Responsibility'), adopted by the International Law Commission in 2001,[1] provides: 'Every internationally wrongful act of a State entails the international responsibility of that State.'[2] Due to the historical development of international law, its primary subjects are States. It is on States that most obligations rest and on whom the burden of compliance principally falls. For example, human rights conventions, though they confer rights upon individuals, impose obligations upon States. If other legal persons have obligations in the field of human rights, it is only by derivation or analogy from the human rights obligations accepted by States (see Alston, 2005; Clapham, 2006; McCorquodale, Ch 9 in this book). State responsibility is the paradigm form of responsibility on the international plane.

But there can be international legal persons other than States, as the International Court of Justice (ICJ) held in *Reparation for Injuries*.[3] Being a subject of any legal system involves having responsibilities as well as rights. Thus it would seem unproblematic to substitute the words 'international organization' or 'international legal person' for 'State' in Article 1 of the Articles on State Responsibility; that basic statement of principle would seem equally applicable by definition to all international legal persons.

In relation to international organizations, at least, a corollary of their undoubted capacity to enter into treaties with States or with other international organizations is that they are responsible for breaches of the obligations undertaken; this follows from the principle *pacta sunt servanda*.[4] The same is true for breaches of applicable general international law.

The potential responsibility of international organizations under general international law was affirmed by the International Court in the *Cumaraswamy* Advisory Opinion.[5] But there are serious difficulties of implementation, since the jurisdiction of international

---

[1] Articles on the Responsibility of States for Internationally Wrongful Acts, adopted by the ILC on 10 August 2001: Report of the International Law Commission, Fifty-third Session, A/56/10, Chapter IV; YILC 2001, vol II(2), pp 26–30. The General Assembly took note of the Articles, recommended them to the attention of governments, and annexed them to GA Res 56/83 (10 December 2001). For subsequent consideration, see Crawford, 2013, pp 42–4; GA Res 68/104 (16 December 2013); and GA Res 71/133 (13 December 2016). The Articles and the Commentaries are reproduced in Crawford, 2002 (the Articles at pp 61–73) and the Articles alone in Evans, 2017, pp 518–26.

[2] See also the often quoted dictum of the Permanent Court of International Justice in *Factory at Chorzów, Jurisdiction, Judgment No 8, 1927, PCIJ, Ser A, No 9*, p 21: 'It is a principle of international law that the breach of an engagement involves an obligation to make reparation.' See also *Jurisdictional Immunities of the State (Germany v Italy (Greece intervening)), Judgment, ICJ Reports 2012*, p 99, para 136, where the ICJ observed that 'responsibility is automatically inferred from the finding that certain obligations have been violated'. Article 1 ARSIWA was endorsed as reflecting customary international law by a Special Chamber of ITLOS in *Delimitation of the Maritime Boundary between Ghana and Côte d'Ivoire in the Atlantic Ocean (Ghana/Côte d'Ivoire)*, Judgment of 23 September 2017, para 558.

[3] *Reparation for Injuries Suffered in the Service of the United Nations, Advisory Opinion, ICJ Reports 1949*, p 174 at p 179.

[4] See Vienna Convention on the Law of Treaties between States and International Organizations or Between International Organizations (1986), Article 26; cf Morgenstern, 1986, pp 13–16, 32–6, 115.

[5] *Difference Relating to Immunity from Legal Process of a Special Rapporteur of the Commission on Human Rights, Advisory Opinion, ICJ Reports 1999*, p 62, para 66.

courts and tribunals has been developed largely by reference to States and not international organizations.[6]

Between 2002 and 2011, the ILC attempted to pull together the relatively sparse international practice in relation to the responsibility of international organizations. In doing so, it based itself to a large extent upon the model of the Articles on State Responsibility; the Articles on Responsibility of International Organizations (ARIO), adopted by the ILC in 2011,[7] adopt and adapt many of the formulations of the Articles on State Responsibility. But there are also some major differences, reflecting the differences in structure and function as between States and international organizations.[8]

The position so far as the international responsibility of individuals, corporations, non-governmental organizations, and other groups are concerned is far less clear. Despite the fact that international law may confer rights directly upon individuals, even outside the field of international human rights law,[9] it is doubtful whether they are 'subjects' of international law in any meaningful sense, and so far no general regime of responsibility has developed to cover them.

The international responsibility of individuals has only developed in the criminal field, and then only in comparatively recent times. True, piracy has been recognized as a 'crime against the law of nations' for centuries. But it is better to see this as a jurisdictional rule allowing States to exercise criminal jurisdiction for pirate attacks on ships at sea rather than a rule conferring 'legal personality' on pirates.[10] One does not acquire international legal personality by being hanged at the yardarm.

[6] Thus special provision has had to be made for the EU, which is not a State, so that it could be a party to contentious proceedings under the 1982 UN Convention on the Law of the Sea (see Article 305 and Annex IX) and under the WTO dispute settlement mechanism. See generally Wellens, 2002 and Klabbers, 2015. Similarly, Article 17 of Protocol 14 to the European Convention of Human Rights (2004) provided for the amendment of Article 59 of the Convention so as to permit the EU to become a party by accession. A draft accession agreement was finalized on 5 April 2013; upon the draft text of the accession agreement being submitted to the Court of Justice of the European Union for its opinion prior to signature, the Court held that accession by the EU to the ECHR was not compatible with EU law: see CJEU, Opinion 2/13, *EU Accession to the ECHR*, 18 December 2014.

[7] Articles on Responsibility of International Organizations (ARIO), Report of the International Law Commission, Sixty-third Session, A/66/10 (2011), Chapter V; YILC 2011, vol II(2), reproduced in Evans, 2017, pp 552–63. For consideration by the General Assembly, see GA Res 66/100 (9 December 2011); GA Res 69/126 (10 December 2014) and GA Res 72/XX (XX December 2017).

[8] In addition, Part Five ARIO (Articles 58–63) deals with the question of State responsibility in connection with the acts of international organizations. It attempts to frame rules dealing with questions, paralleling those in Part One, Chapter IV ARSIWA, as regards aid or assistance, direction and control, and coercion by a State in relation to the internationally wrongful act of an international organization (Articles 58–60). In addition, it contains rules applicable to the situation in which a member State seeks to avoid compliance with its own international obligations by procuring an act of the international organization to do what it itself is unable to do (Article 61), and a provision in relation to the acceptance of responsibility by a State for the internationally wrongful act of an international organization (Article 62). Article 63 is a saving clause, which makes clear that the preceding provisions of Part Five are 'without prejudice to the international responsibility of the international organization which commits the act in question, or of any State or other international organization'. These provisions undoubtedly constitute progressive development, rather than codification of existing customary international law.

[9] *Jurisdiction of the Courts of Danzig, Advisory Opinion*, 1928, PCIJ, Ser B, No 15, pp 17–21; *LaGrand (Germany v United States of America), Merits, Judgment*, ICJ Reports 2001, p 466, para 77; *Avena and Other Mexican Nationals (Mexico v United States of America), Judgment*, ICJ Reports 2004, p 12, para 40.

[10] See the Separate Opinion of Judge Moore in *The 'Lotus'*, Judgment No 9, 1927, PCIJ, Ser A, No 10, p 70; United Nations Convention on the Law of the Sea 1982, Articles 101–7; Rubin, 1998; Jennings and Watts, 1992, vol 1, pp 746–55; and see Evans, Ch 21 of this book.

Since the Second World War, by contrast, real forms of individual criminal responsibility under international law have developed. First steps were taken with the establishment of the Nuremberg and Tokyo war crimes tribunals and the conclusion of the Genocide Convention in the immediate post-war period; after the end of the Cold War there followed, in rapid succession, the creation by Security Council resolution of the International Criminal Tribunal for Yugoslavia (ICTY) (1992) and the International Criminal Tribunal for Rwanda (ICTR) (1994), and the adoption of the Rome Statute of the International Criminal Court (ICC) (1998), which entered into force on 1 July 2002. Further, various 'mixed' or 'hybrid' international criminal tribunals have been set up for, *inter alia*, Bosnia-Herzegovina (2004–), East Timor (2000–2006), Sierra Leone (2002–2013), Kosovo (2000–), Cambodia (2003–), and Lebanon (2007–).[11]

On the other hand, so far there has been no development of corporate criminal responsibility in international law. Under the two ad hoc Statutes and the Rome Statute only individual persons may be accused. The Security Council often addresses recommendations or demands to opposition, insurgent, or rebel groups—but without implying that these have separate personality in international law. Any international responsibility of members of such groups is probably limited to breaches of applicable international humanitarian law or even of national law, rather than general international law. Similarly, if rebel groups succeed in becoming the government of the State (whether of the State against which they are fighting, or of a new State which they succeed in creating), that State may be responsible for their acts (ARSIWA, Article 10). But if they fail, the State against which they rebelled is in principle not directly responsible for their actions, and any possibility of collective responsibility for their acts fails with them.[12]

It is also very doubtful whether 'multinational corporations' are subjects of international law for the purposes of responsibility, although steps are being taken to develop voluntary adherence to human rights and other norms by corporations.[13] From a legal point of view, so-called multinational corporations are better regarded as groups of corporations, each created under and amenable to the national law of their place of incorporation as well as to any other national legal system within which they operate.

Thus, although Article 58 of the ILC's Articles on State Responsibility reserves in general terms the possibility of 'individual responsibility under international law of any person acting on behalf of a State',[14] a reservation which is not limited to criminal responsibility, so far there has been virtually no development in practice of civil responsibility of individuals or corporations for breaches of international law as such. Only the USA has legislation dealing (in a very uneven way) with this issue; in recent years the scope of application of that

---

[11] See also the Extraordinary African Chambers (2013–), set up within the court system of Senegal pursuant to an agreement with the African Union in order to try international crimes committed in Chad between 1982 and 1990 under the regime of the former Chadian President Hissène Habré.

[12] Although in the context of investment treaty arbitration, States have on occasion been held to have breached specific treaty obligations requiring 'full protection and security' for investors as a result of the State's own failure to exercise due diligence in protecting them against the actions of insurgent groups: see, eg, *Ampal-American Israel Corporation v Arab Republic of Egypt (ICSID Case No ARB/12/11)*, Decision on Liability and Heads of Loss of 21 February 2017, paras 240–5, 283–90; *Asian Agricultural Products Ltd v Republic of Sri Lanka (ICSID Case No ARB/87/3)*; Award of 27 June 1990; (1997) 4 ICSID Reports 250.

[13] See, eg, *Guiding Principles on Business and Human Rights: Implementing the United Nations 'Protect, Respect and Remedy' Framework* (2011) A/HRC/17/31, Annex, endorsed by the Human Rights Council by HRC Res 17/4 (16 June 2011), and the work (2011–) of the Working Group on the issue of human rights and transnational corporations and other business enterprises set up by the Human Rights Council to monitor implementation of the *Guiding Principles*. Generally, see De Schutter, 2006. On the problems of establishing international responsibility of corporations, see Ratner, 2001.

[14] See likewise ARIO, Article 66.

legislation has been severely curtailed.[15] As the dissenting judges in the *Arrest Warrant* case pointed out in 2002, at a time when the interpretation of the jurisdiction under the Alien Tort Claims Act (ATCA) was perhaps at its highest point, that legislation could be seen as 'the beginnings of a very broad form of extraterritorial jurisdiction' in civil matters; however, they added that although 'this unilateral exercise of the function of guardian of international values has been much commented on, it has not attracted the approbation of States generally'.[16]

The development of international criminal law is considered by Cryer in Ch 24. In this chapter we examine the foundational rules of State responsibility—in particular the bases for and consequences of the responsibility of a State for internationally wrongful acts. Questions of the implementation of such responsibility by an injured State or by other interested parties, as well as possible responses (retorsion, countermeasures, sanctions) are dealt with only briefly; they are discussed in greater detail in other chapters (see Okowa, Ch 15 and White and Abass, Ch 17). To a large extent, similar principles apply to the responsibility of international organizations, with appropriate adjustments to take account of their particular nature; to the extent that the applicable rules differ significantly, they are likewise noted later in this chapter.

II. STATE RESPONSIBILITY: ISSUES OF CLASSIFICATION AND CHARACTERIZATION

The category 'State responsibility' covers the whole field of the responsibility of States for internationally wrongful conduct. It amounts, in other words, to a general law of wrongs. But what is a breach of international law by a State depends on what its international obligations are, and especially as far as treaties are concerned, these vary from one State to the next. There are a few treaties (the United Nations Charter, the 1949 Geneva Conventions, and some international human rights treaties) to which virtually every State is a party;

---

[15] Private parties (US or foreign) can in principle be sued for torts occasioned 'in violation of the law of nations' committed against aliens, under the unusual jurisdiction created by the Alien Tort Claims Act (28 USC §1350). The US cases have distinguished between corporate complicity with governmental violations of human rights, and those violations (eg genocide, slavery) which do not require any governmental involvement or State action: see, eg, *Kadić v Karadžić* 70 F.3d 232 (1995) (2nd Cir 1995); 104 ILR 135. The existence of jurisdiction under ATCA to hear claims of breach of fundamental human rights norms survived scrutiny by the Supreme Court in *Sosa v Alvarez-Machain* 124 S Ct 2739; 542 US 692 (2004), although its scope was somewhat reduced. Its scope of application was however severely limited in *Kiobel v Royal Dutch Petroleum Company* 133 S Ct 1659; 569 US (2013), in which the Supreme Court held that, in light of the presumption against extraterritorial application of statutes, ATCA does not normally provide a cause of action in relation to conduct in breach of international law occurring outside the USA. The Supreme Court did not in the end decide in *Kiobel* the question (for which certiorari was originally granted) whether, in any event, corporations can be liable under ATCA, and there remains a split in the decisions on that issue in the lower courts. In addition to ATCA, civil claims based upon or relating to a breach of international law abroad can be brought before the US courts in certain narrowly defined circumstances: the Torture Victims Protection Act 1991 (28 USC 1350) creates a cause of action against individuals in relation to torture or extrajudicial killing 'under actual or apparent authority, or color of law, of any foreign nation'; after a divergence of views among the Courts of Appeals, the question whether the TVPA can be applied to corporations has been resolved in the negative by the decision of the Supreme Court in *Mohamad v Palestinian Authority*, 132 S Ct 1702; 566 US (2012). The Supreme Court held that, in light of its use of the word 'individual', the scope of the TVPA is restricted to natural persons.

[16] *Arrest Warrant of 11 April 2000 (Democratic Republic of Congo v Belgium), Preliminary Objections and Merits, Judgment, ICJ Reports 2002*, p 3, Separate Opinion of Judges Higgins, Kooijmans, and Buergenthal, para 48.

otherwise each State has its own range of bilateral and multilateral treaty obligations. Even under general international law, which might be expected to be virtually uniform for every State, different States may be differently situated and thus *de facto* may have different re-sponsibilities—for example, upstream States rather than downstream States on an inter-national river, capital importing and capital exporting States in respect of the treatment of foreign investment, or States on whose territory a civil war is raging as compared with third parties to the conflict. In other words, there is no such thing as a uniform code of international law, reflecting the obligations of all States.

On the other hand, the underlying concepts of State responsibility—attribution, breach, excuses, consequences—seem to be general in character. Particular treaties or rules may vary these underlying concepts in particular respects, but otherwise they are assumed and they apply unless excluded.[17] These background or standard assumptions underlying international responsibility and on the basis of which specific obligations of States exist and are applied are set out in the ILC's Articles on State Responsibility. The Articles are the product of more than 40 years' work by the ILC on the topic, and in common with other ILC texts they involve both codification and progressive development (Crawford, 2013, pp 35–42; *Symposium*, 2002, p 96; *AJIL* pp 773–890). They are the focus of what follows.

A. RESPONSIBILITY UNDER INTERNATIONAL OR NATIONAL LAW?

Evidently State responsibility can only be engaged for breaches of international law, that is, for conduct which is internationally wrongful because it involves some violation of an in-ternational obligation applicable to and binding on the State. A dispute between two States concerning the breach of an international obligation, whether customary or treaty-based, concerns international responsibility, and this will be true whether the remedy sought is a declaration that conduct is wrongful, cessation of the conduct, or compensation for damage suffered. On the other hand, not all claims brought against a State involve interna-tional responsibility, even if international law may be relevant in some way. For example, if a State is sued in relation to a commercial transaction in a national court, international law helps to determine the extent of the defendant State's immunity from jurisdiction and from measures of enforcement, but the underlying claim will derive from the applicable law of the contract. There is thus a distinction between State responsibility for breaches of international law, and State liability under national law. One does not entail the other.

---

[17] ARSIWA, Article 55 (*lex specialis*). For examples of a *lex specialis* see, eg, the provisions of the WTO Agreements excluding compensation for breach and focusing on cessation, and (perhaps) Article 41 of the European Convention on Human Rights which appears, at least in some circumstances, to give States an option to pay compensation rather than providing restitution in kind; nevertheless they remain bound by Article 46 of the European Convention to abide by the judgments of the European Court, and in that regard to take, under the supervision of the Committee of Ministers, 'the general and/or, if appropriate, individual measures to be adopted in their domestic legal order to put an end to the violation found by the Court and to redress so far as possible the effects' (*Scozzari and Giunta* v *Italy* [GC], nos 39221/98 and 41963/98, para 249, ECHR 2000-VIII). After initial hesitations (see, eg, *Ireland* v *UK, Judgment of 18 January 1978, para 187, Ser A, No 25*), the practice of the European Court of Human Rights appears to be evolving, at least in relation to certain types of breach, towards a requirement of real restitution by way of just satisfaction, rather than merely the payment of compensation: see, eg, *Assanidze* v *Georgia* [GC], no 71503/01, paras 202–3 ECHR 2004-II; *Ilaşcu and Others* v *Moldova and Russia* [GC], no 48787/99, para 490, ECHR 2004-VII; *Sejdovic* v *Italy* [GC], no 56581/00, paras 125–6, ECHR 2006-II; *Verein gegen Tierfabriken Schweiz (VgT)* v *Switzerland (No 2)* [GC], no 32772/02, paras 85–90, ECHR 2009-IV; *Hirsi Jamaa* v *Italy* [GC], no 27765/09, paras 209–11, ECHR 2012-II; for an apparent retreat as regards the power of the Court to order (rather than recommend) the adoption of the individual measures required to remedy a breach, see the judgment of a closely divided Grand Chamber and the dissenting opinions in *Moreira Ferreira (No 2)* v *Portugal* [GC], no 19867/12, 11 July 2017.

Even at the international level, not all claims brought by one State against another necessarily involve State responsibility; in addition to claims alleging breach of an obligation or as to the reparation required for a breach, the category of international claims also covers, *inter alia*, disputes relating solely to the proper interpretation of a treaty, and disputes as to sovereignty over territory or maritime delimitation.[18] Claims of responsibility were traditionally brought directly between States at the international level, or (much less often) before an international court or tribunal. Both these avenues remain but there is now a further range of possibilities. For example, in some cases individuals or corporations are given access to international tribunals and can bring claims of State responsibility in their own right, eg for breach of the European Convention on Human Rights before the European Court of Human Rights, or for breach of a bilateral or multilateral investment protection treaty before an arbitral tribunal established under the treaty. Whether such international claims may also be enforced in national courts depends on the approach of the national legal system to international law in general (see Denza, Ch 13) and on the rules of State immunity (see Webb, Ch 11). In certain circumstances it is possible for responsibility claims to be 'domesticated', and the principles of subsidiarity and complementarity indicate an increasing role for national courts in the implementation and enforcement of international standards.[19] But the interaction between rules of jurisdiction and immunity and the relation between national and international law make this a complex area. For the sake of simplicity, this chapter will be confined to claims of State responsibility brought at the international level.

B. TYPOLOGY OF STATE RESPONSIBILITY

National legal systems often distinguish types or degrees of liability according to the source of the obligation breached—for example, crime, contract, tort, or delict.[20] In international law it appears that there is no general distinction of this kind. As the arbitral tribunal said in the *Rainbow Warrior* case:

the general principles of International Law concerning State responsibility are equally applicable in the case of breach of treaty obligation, since in the international law field there is no distinction between contractual and tortious responsibility, so that any violation of a State of any obligation, of whatever origin gives rise to State responsibility.[21]

[18] In setting out (apparently exhaustively) the categories of disputes as to which a State may choose to accept the jurisdiction of the Court, Article 36(2) of the Statute of the International Court of Justice (the Optional Clause), mentions, in addition to disputes involving questions of responsibility (ie 'the existence of any fact which, if established, would constitute a breach of an international obligation'; and 'the nature or extent of the reparation to be made for the breach of an international obligation' (paragraphs (c) and (d)), disputes as to 'any question of international law' and disputes relating to 'the interpretation of a treaty' (paragraphs (a) and (b)). Neither of those latter types of dispute necessarily involve questions of responsibility (although claims of responsibility may form a part of the wider dispute in a particular case).

[19] For consideration of the extent to which domestic courts may contribute to the development of the law of international responsibility, including consideration of application of the Articles by domestic courts, see Olleson, 2013 and Wittich, 2013.

[20] Cf the division of sources of obligation in Roman law into contract, delict, and quasi-contract/unjust enrichment: D.1.1.10.1 (Ulpian): 'Iuris praecepta sunt haec: honeste vivere, alterum non laedere, suum cuique tribuere' ('the principles of law are these: to live honourably, not to harm any other person, and to render to each his own').

[21] *Rainbow Warrior (France/New Zealand)*, (1990) 20 *RIAA* 217, para 75; for the arguments of the parties, see paras 72–4. See also the ICJ in *Gabčíkovo-Nagymaros Project (Hungary/Slovakia), Judgment, ICJ Reports 1997*, p 7, paras 46–8, especially para 47: 'when a State has committed an internationally wrongful act, its international responsibility is likely to be involved whatever the nature of the obligation it has failed to respect', citing what is now ARSIWA, Article 12: 'There is a breach of an international obligation by a State when an act of that State is not in conformity with what is required of it by that obligation, *regardless of its origin or character*' (emphasis added).

To this extent the rules of State responsibility form the basis for a single system, having no precise equivalent in national legal systems. The reason is that international law has to address a very broad range of needs on the basis of rather few basic tools and techniques. For example, treaties perform a wide variety of functions in the international system—from establishing institutions in the public interest and rules of an essentially legislative character, to making specific contractual arrangements between two States. Unlike national law, however, there is no categorical distinction between the legislative and the contractual. What is crucial is the structure of the specific obligations imposed (that is, whether, on analysis, they are owed bilaterally between pairs of States or multilaterally to all States parties), and whether they can be properly characterized as having been established for the protection of some common or collective interest (whether of the group of States parties to the treaty, or the international community as a whole).

The Tribunal in the *Rainbow Warrior*[22] arbitration and the International Court in the *Gabčíkovo-Nagymaros Project*[23] case both held that in a case involving the alleged breach of a treaty obligation, the general defences available under the law of State responsibility coexist with the rules of the law of treaties laid down in the 1969 Vienna Convention on the Law of Treaties.[24] But the two sets of rules perform different functions. The rules of the law of treaties determine when a treaty obligation is in force for a State and what it means, that is, how it is to be interpreted. The rules of State responsibility determine when a breach of such an obligation has occurred and what the legal consequences of that breach are in terms of such matters as reparation. There is some overlap between the two but they are legally and logically distinct. A State faced with a material breach of a treaty obligation can choose to suspend or terminate the treaty in accordance with the applicable rules of treaty law, thus releasing itself from its obligation to perform its obligations under the treaty in future (VCLT, Article 60). But doing so does not prevent it also from claiming reparation for the breach.[25]

In addition, national legal systems also characteristically distinguish 'civil' from 'criminal' responsibility, with the latter characteristically involving repression and punishment. By contrast there is little or no State practice allowing for 'punitive' or 'penal' consequences of breaches of international law. For instance, in 1976, Chilean agents killed a former Chilean minister, Orlando Letelier, and one of his companions by a car bomb in Washington, DC. The US courts subsequently awarded both compensatory and punitive damages for the deaths, acting under the local torts exception of the Foreign State Immunity Act.[26] But the local judgment was practically unenforceable.[27] Subsequently, as

---

[22] *Rainbow Warrior (France/New Zealand)*, (1990) 20 *RIAA* 217, para 75.

[23] *Gabčíkovo-Nagymaros Project (Hungary/Slovakia), Judgment, ICJ Reports 1997*, p 7, paras 46–8.

[24] See also *Application of the Interim Accord of 13 September 1995 (the former Yugoslav Republic of Macedonia v Greece), Judgment of 5 December 2011, ICJ Reports 2011*, p 644, in which the Court (at paras 144–65) rejected various arguments put forward by the respondent State based on alleged breaches by the applicant State of its international obligations under both the law of treaties (the so-called *exceptio inadimpleti contractus* and material breach of treaty under Article 60 VCLT) and the law of State responsibility (countermeasures) by which the respondent State had attempted to justify its own failure to comply with its international obligations.

[25] In other words, a State can terminate a treaty for breach while claiming damages for breaches that have already occurred: see VCLT, Articles 70(1)(b), 72(1)(b), 73.

[26] See *Letelier v Republic of Chile*, 488 F.Supp 665 (1980); 19 ILM 409; 63 ILR 378 (District Court, DC) for the decision on State immunity, and see 502 F.Supp 259 (1980); 19 ILM 1418; 88 ILR 747 (District Court, DC) for the decision as to quantum; the Court awarded the plaintiffs approximately $5 million, of which $2 million was punitive damages.

[27] The Court of Appeals for the 2nd Circuit, reversing the District Court, refused to allow enforcement against the Chilean national airline: 748 F.2d 790 (1984); the Supreme Court denied certiorari: 471 US 1125 (1985).

part of the restoration of relations between the USA and Chile following the latter's return to democracy, it was agreed that a bilateral commission would determine the amount of compensation payable as an *ex gratia* settlement without admission of liability. Under the terms of reference of the Commission, the damages were to be assessed 'in accordance with applicable principles of international law, as though liability were established'.[28] The Commission awarded sums only on a compensatory basis for loss of income and moral damage; the Separate Opinion of the Chilean member of the Commission made clear that punitive damages were not accepted in international law.[29]

The draft of the Articles on State Responsibility adopted on first reading in 1996 sought to introduce the notion of 'international crimes' of States.[30] It was not envisaged that States could be fined or otherwise punished—no State has ever been accused of a criminal offence before an international court, even where the conduct involved aggression or genocide. In 1998, the concept of 'international crimes of States' was set aside, contributing to the unopposed adoption of the Articles on State Responsibility by the ILC in 2001. The episode suggests that State responsibility is an undifferentiated regime, which does not embody such domestic classifications as 'civil' and 'criminal'; the International Court endorsed this approach in the *Bosnian Genocide* case.[31]

But this does not prevent international law responding in different ways to different kinds of breaches and to their different impacts on other States, on individuals, and on international order. First, individual State officials have no impunity if they commit crimes under international law, even if they may not have been acting for their own individual ends.[32] Secondly, the Articles on State Responsibility make special provision for the consequences of certain serious breaches of peremptory norms of general international law (*jus cogens*). A breach is serious if it involves a 'gross or systematic failure by the responsible State to fulfil' such an obligation (Article 40(2)). The major consequence of such a breach is not any form of penal consequence for the responsible State, but rather the obligation on all other States to refrain from recognizing as lawful the situation thereby created or from rendering aid or assistance in maintaining it (Article 41(2)). In addition, States must cooperate to bring the serious breach to an end 'through any lawful means' (Article 41(1)); the principal avenues for such cooperation are through the various international organizations, in particular the Security Council, whose powers to take measures

---

[28]   *Re Letelier and Moffitt* (1992), 88 ILR 727, 731.

[29]   Ibid, p 741. The resulting award was paid to the victims' heirs on condition that they waived their rights under the domestic judgment.

[30]   For the text of former Article 19 see Crawford, 2002, pp 352–3.

[31]   *Application of the Convention on the Prevention and Punishment of the Crime of Genocide (Bosnia and Herzegovina v Serbia and Montenegro), Merits, Judgment, ICJ Reports 2007*, p 43, paras 65–6.

[32]   At the international level see Statute of the ICTY, Articles 7(2), 7(4); Statute of the ICTR, Articles 6(2), 6(4); Rome Statute of the ICC, Articles 27, 33. At the national level see *R v Bow Street Metropolitan Stipendiary, ex parte Pinochet Ugarte (Amnesty International Intervening) (No 3)* [1997] UKHL 17; [2000] 1 AC 147. However, the ICJ has held that serving Foreign Ministers (and by implication, serving Heads of State and other senior ministers) while in office have absolute jurisdictional immunity from prosecution in the national courts of other States: *Arrest Warrant of 11 April 2000 (Democratic Republic of Congo v Belgium), Preliminary Objections and Merits, Judgment, ICJ Reports 2002*, p 3, paras 51–61. The Court protested that this immunity did not involve impunity, *inter alia*, because of the possibility of prosecution at the international level, or prosecution by the national State. The jurisdictional immunity apparently lasts only so long as the individual holds office: cf, however, paras 60–1, and compare with the Separate Opinion of Judges Higgins, Kooijmans, and Buergenthal, para 89. As a matter of English law, officials of a foreign State who, in the performance of their functions, commit crimes abroad contrary to international law enjoy immunity before the English courts when faced with *civil* claims in relation to those acts, even if the acts of which they are accused constitute a breach of a peremptory norm of international law (*jus cogens*): *Jones v Ministry of Interior for the of Kingdom of Saudi Arabia and Ors* [2006] UKHL 26; [2007] 1 AC 270.

to restore international peace and security substantially overlap with these provisions (Koskenniemi, 2001).

In the Advisory Opinion on *Legal Consequences of the Construction of a Wall in the Occupied Palestine Territory*, the ICJ discussed the existence of such consequences for third States as a result of the breaches by Israel of the right of self-determination and certain obligations under international humanitarian law. The Court made no express reference to Articles 40 and 41 of the Articles; rather it reasoned first that the norms in question constituted rights and obligations *erga omnes* (ie were owed to the international community as a whole) and then held that '[g]iven the character and the importance of the rights and obligations involved', other States were under obligations not to recognize the illegal situation resulting from the construction of the Wall and not to render aid and assistance in maintaining the situation thereby created, as well as an obligation 'while respecting the United Nations Charter and international law to see to it that any impediment, resulting from the construction of the wall, to the exercise by the Palestinian people of its right to self-determination is brought to an end'.[33] In addition, the Court was of the view that the 'United Nations, and especially the General Assembly and the Security Council, should consider what further action is required to bring to an end the illegal situation resulting from the construction of the wall . . .'[34]

By contrast, in *Jurisdictional Immunities of the State*, the Court openly referred to Article 41 of the Articles and appeared to endorse the norms it contains imposing obligations on third States as reflecting customary international law, observing that:

> recognizing the immunity of a foreign State in accordance with customary international law does not amount to recognizing as lawful a situation created by the breach of a *jus cogens* rule, or rendering aid and assistance in maintaining that situation, and so cannot contravene the principle in Article 41 . . .[35]

Quite apart from collective enforcement and the obligations which may arise for third States, the possibility remains of unilateral action by individual States against States responsible for such serious breaches as genocide, war crimes, or denial of fundamental human rights.[36] Further, at least as regards certain categories of obligations which protect fundamental 'community' interests, it is possible that States to which the obligation is owed may invoke the responsibility of the wrongdoing State even if they have themselves suffered no injury save the legal injury resulting from the violation of the norm in question.

III. THE ELEMENTS OF STATE RESPONSIBILITY

As already noted, the international responsibility of a State arises from the commission of an internationally wrongful act. An internationally wrongful act presupposes that there is conduct, consisting of an action or omission, that: (a) is attributable to a State under international law; and (b) constitutes a breach of the international obligations of that State (ARSIWA, Article 2). In principle, the fulfilment of these conditions is a sufficient basis for international responsibility, as has been consistently affirmed by international courts

---

[33] *Legal Consequences of the Construction of a Wall in the Occupied Palestine Territory*, Advisory Opinion, *ICJ Reports 2004*, p 136, para 159.

[34] Ibid, para 160.

[35] *Jurisdictional Immunities of the State (Germany v Italy; Greece Intervening), ICJ Reports 2012*, p 99, para 93.

[36] For instance, States may adopt measures which are not inconsistent with their international obligations (retorsion). Further, in the case of breach of certain types of obligation, States which themselves are not injured by the breach may be able to take countermeasures; see, for instance, the catalogue of State practice discussed in the Commentary to ARSIWA, Article 54. The ILC left the question open for future development.

and tribunals.[37] In some cases, however, the respondent State may claim that it is justified in its non-performance, for example, because it was acting in self-defence or was subject to a situation of *force majeure*. In international law such defences or excuses are termed 'circumstances precluding wrongfulness'. They will be a matter for the respondent State to assert and prove, not for the claimant State to negative.

The three elements—attribution, breach, and the absence of any valid justification for non-performance—will be discussed in turn before we consider the consequences of State responsibility, in particular for the injured State or States.

A. ATTRIBUTION OF CONDUCT

Although they seem real enough to their citizens (and, normally, to others), States are juridical abstractions. Like corporations in national law, they necessarily act through organs or agents.[38] The rules of attribution under the law of State responsibility (ARSIWA, Articles 4–11) specify the actors whose conduct may engage the responsibility of the State, either generally or in specific circumstances. It should be stressed that the issue here is one of responsibility for breaches of international obligations of the State. It does not concern other issues for which a process of attribution may be necessary, for instance which officials can enter into those obligations in the first place.[39] Only senior officials of the State (the Head of State or Government, the Minister of Foreign Affairs, and diplomats in certain circumstances: see VCLT, Article 7) have inherent authority to bind the State; other officials act upon the basis of express or ostensible authority (VCLT, Article 46).[40] By contrast, any

---

[37] See *Phosphates in Morocco, Preliminary Objections, Judgment, PCIJ, Ser A/B, No 74*, p 10; *United States Diplomatic and Consular Staff in Tehran, Judgment, ICJ Reports 1980*, p 3, para 56; *Military and Paramilitary Activities in and against Nicaragua (Nicaragua v United States of America), Merits, Judgment, ICJ Reports 1986*, p 14, para 226; *Gabčíkovo-Nagymaros Project (Hungary/Slovakia), Judgment, ICJ Reports 1997*, p 7, para 78; and *Application of the Convention on the Prevention and Punishment of the Crime of Genocide (Bosnia and Herzegovina v Serbia and Montenegro), Merits, Judgment, ICJ Reports 2007*, p 43, para 385, where the Court referred to 'the well-established rule, one of the cornerstones of the law of State responsibility, that the conduct of any State organ is to be considered an act of the State under international law, and therefore gives rise to the responsibility of the State if it constitutes a breach of an international obligation of the State'; see also para 149. See also *Dickson Car Wheel Company* (1931) 4 *RIAA* 669, 678.

[38] *German Settlers in Poland, Advisory Opinion, 1923, PCIJ, Ser B, No 6*, p 22.

[39] For consideration of the role of attribution in public international law generally, including the law of State responsibility, see Olleson, 2016, pp 458–70.

[40] See also *Maritime Delimitation and Territorial Questions between Qatar and Bahrain, Jurisdiction and Admissibility, ICJ Reports 1994*, p 112, paras 26–7; *Land and Maritime Boundary between Cameroon and Nigeria (Cameroon v Nigeria: Equatorial Guinea Intervening), Merits, Judgment, ICJ Reports 2002*, p 303, paras 264–8. For an analogous question as to whether the position taken by organs of the constituent entities of a federal State is capable of giving rise to a 'dispute as to the meaning or scope' of a prior judgment sufficient to form the basis for a request for interpretation under Article 60 of the Statute of the ICJ, see *Request for Interpretation of the Judgment of 31 March 2004 in the Case concerning Avena and Other Mexican Nationals (Mexico v United States of America), Provisional Measures, Order of 16 July 2008, ICJ Reports 2008*, p 311. The Court held that the refusal of the courts of certain constituent states of the USA to give effect to the Court's judgment in *Avena*, as well as the decision of the Supreme Court that the judgment was not directly enforceable as a matter of domestic constitutional law, were sufficient to give rise to the appearance of the existence of a 'dispute' within the meaning of Article 60; this was held to be the case despite the statement of the federal executive authorities that they did not dispute the meaning and effects of the ICJ's judgment in *Avena* to the effect that the USA was under an obligation to allow reconsideration and review of the convictions (ibid, paras 55–6). Subsequently, the Court refused the request for interpretation on other grounds: see *Request for Interpretation of the Judgment of 31 March 2004 in the Case concerning Avena and Other Mexican Nationals (Mexico v United States of America) (Mexico v United States of America), Judgment, ICJ Reports 2009*, p 3, paras 43–6; although in doing so it did not depart from its finding made at the provisional measures stage as to the existence of a dispute, its discussion of the issue casts some doubt on whether the position taken by the courts of the USA was sufficient given the position taken by the federal executive: see paras 31–42.

State official, even at a local or municipal level, may commit an internationally wrongful act attributable to the State—the local constabulary torturing a prisoner,[41] for example, or the local mayor requisitioning a factory.[42]

A State does not normally guarantee the safety of foreign nationals on its territory, the security of their property, or the success of their investments. In terms of any injury suffered, there has to be some involvement by the State itself—in effect, by the government of the State—in the conduct of which complaint is made. A State will generally only be liable for the conduct of its organs or officials, acting as such (ARSIWA, Article 4; Commentary, Crawford, 2002, pp 94–9). Purely private acts will not engage the State's responsibility, although the State may in certain circumstances be liable for its failure to prevent those acts, or to take action to punish the individuals responsible.[43] On the other hand, the scope of State responsibility for official acts is broad, and the definition of 'organ' for this purpose comprehensive; it includes 'all the individual or collective entities which make up the organization of the State and act on its behalf'.[44] There is no distinction based on the level of seniority of the relevant officials in the State hierarchy; as long as they are acting in their official capacity, responsibility is engaged. In addition, there is no limitation to the central executive; responsibility may be engaged for acts of federal, provincial, or even local government officials. The classification of powers is also irrelevant: in principle, the concept of 'organ' covers legislatures, executive officials, and courts at all levels.[45]

Under Article 4, the primary consideration for characterization of a person or entity as an organ is their formal status under the State's domestic law (so-called 'de jure organs').[46] In addition, the conduct of what are usually referred to as 'de facto' organs[47] may, exceptionally, be attributable to the State in the same manner:

> [. . .] persons, groups of persons or entities may, for purposes of international responsibility, be equated with State organs even if that status does not follow from internal law, provided that in fact the persons, groups or entities act in 'complete dependence' on the State, of which they are ultimately merely the instrument. In such a case, it is appropriate to look beyond legal status alone, in order to grasp the reality of the relationship between the person taking action, and the State to which he is so closely attached as to appear to be nothing more than its agent: any other solution would allow States to escape their international responsibility by choosing to act through persons or entities whose supposed independence would be purely fictitious.[48]

---

[41] See, eg, *Velásquez-Rodríguez v Honduras*, Merits, Judgment of 29 July 1988, Ser C, No 4, 95 ILR 259, para 183 ('not all levels of the Government of Honduras were necessarily aware of those acts, nor is there any evidence that such acts were the result of official orders. Nevertheless, those circumstances are irrelevant for the purposes of establishing whether Honduras is responsible under international law'). See also p 296, para 170.

[42] *Elettronica Sicula SpA (ELSI)*, Judgment, ICJ Reports 1989, p 15.

[43] *Janes (US v Mexico)* (1926) 4 RIAA 82; cf *Noyes (US v Panama)* (1933) 6 RIAA 308. For a modern example, see, eg, *Ampal-American Israel Corporation v Arab Republic of Egypt (ICSID Case No ARB/12/11)*, Decision on Liability and Heads of Loss, 21 February 2017, paras 240–245, 283–290.

[44] Commentary to Article 4, paragraph (1). Article 4 and the Commentary were cited with approval in *Application of the Convention on the Prevention and Punishment of the Crime of Genocide (Bosnia and Herzegovina v Serbia and Montenegro)*, Merits, Judgment, ICJ Reports 2007, p 43, para 388.

[45] ARSIWA, Article 4. See also *LaGrand (Germany v United States of America)*, Provisional Measures, Order of 3 March 1999, ICJ Reports 1999, p 9, para 28: 'Whereas the international responsibility of a State is engaged by the action of the competent organs and authorities acting in that State, whatever they may be.'

[46] See ARSIWA, Article 4(2); exceptionally, it may be appropriate to look behind the formal characterization of an entity under domestic law: see Commentary to Article 4, para (11) (Crawford, 2002, p 98), and for discussion, see Crawford and Mertenskötter, 2015, pp 28–30.

[47] *Application of the Convention on the Prevention and Punishment of the Crime of Genocide (Bosnia and Herzegovina v Serbia and Montenegro)*, Merits, Judgment, ICJ Reports 2007, p 43, para 390.

[48] Ibid, para 392.

In addition to the acts or omissions of organs (*de jure* or *de facto*), the conduct of persons or entities exercising elements of governmental authority is attributable to the State, provided they were acting in exercise of the governmental authority conferred on them (ARSIWA, Article 5); a State cannot avoid responsibility for particular conduct by privatizing or delegating what are properly governmental functions to persons or individuals which do not formally constitute its organs. The touchstone for attribution in this context is that the person or entity was in fact exercising governmental authority in carrying out the conduct in question.

Acts or omissions of any State organ (*de jure* or *de facto*), or of persons or entities exercising elements of governmental authority, are attributable to the State provided they were acting in that capacity at the time; that is the case even if they may have been acting *ultra vires* or in contravention of instructions.[49] Indeed, the State may be responsible for conduct which is clearly in excess of authority, if the official has made use of an official position. For example, in *Caire*, a French national in Mexico was killed by members of the Mexican army after he had refused their demands for money. The tribunal held that, for the *ultra vires* acts of officials to be attributable to the State, 'they must have acted at least to all appearances as competent officials or organs, or they must have used powers or methods appropriate to their official capacity'.[50] In the circumstances the responsibility of the State was engaged 'in view of the fact that they acted in their capacity of officers and used the means placed at their disposition by virtue of that capacity'.[51] Similarly, in *Youmans*, US citizens cornered in a house by a mob were killed after soldiers sent to disperse the crowd, contrary to orders, opened fire on the house, forcing the inhabitants out into the open. The Tribunal held that there was State responsibility given that 'at the time of the commission of these acts the men were on duty under the immediate supervision and in the presence of a commanding officer'. The Tribunal went on to comment that:

> Soldiers inflicting personal injuries or committing wanton destruction or looting always act in disobedience of some rules laid down by superior authority. There could be no liability whatever for such misdeeds if the view were taken that any acts committed by soldiers in contravention of instructions must always be considered as personal acts.[52]

By contrast, a State is not in general responsible for the acts of mobs or of private individuals as such. Their conduct may, however, be attributable if the State acknowledges and adopts (or in common law terminology 'ratifies') their acts as its own (ARSIWA, Article 11). In the *Tehran Hostages* case, the International Court held that although initially the students who took control of the US Embassy in Tehran were not acting as agents of Iran, a subsequent decree of Ayatollah Khomeini endorsing the occupation of the embassy:

> translated continuing occupation of the Embassy and detention of the hostages into acts of [Iran]. The militants, authors of the invasion and jailers of the hostages, had now become agents of the Iranian State for whose acts the State itself was internationally responsible.[53]

Similarly, the State will be responsible if the authorities act in collusion with the mob, or participate in the mob violence. However, international tribunals generally require strong evidence of such collusion.[54]

---

[49] Article 7 ARSIWA; see also the final words of Article 5 ARSIWA. For an illustration, see *Union Bridge Company (USA v Great Britain)* (1924) 6 *RIAA* 138.

[50] *Caire (France v Mexico)* (1929) 5 *RIAA* 516, 530.   [51] Ibid, 531.

[52] *Youmans (USA v Mexico)* (1926) 4 *RIAA* 110; (1927) 21 *AJIL* 571, para 14.

[53] *United States Diplomatic and Consular Staff in Tehran, Judgment, ICJ Reports 1980*, p 3, paras 73–4.

[54] *Janes (USA v Mexico)* (1926) 4 *RIAA* 82.

In addition, conduct which is not attributable to a State because it was carried out by persons acting in a purely private capacity may nonetheless result in the State's international responsibility because the State failed in some obligation to prevent the conduct in question. However, in such a case, responsibility arises as a result of the State's own failings. For instance, in the *Tehran Hostages* case, Iran was held to have breached its special obligation of protection of the embassy and consular premises and personnel, even prior to its adoption of the acts of the occupying students.[55]

Like other systems of law, international law does not limit attribution to the conduct of the regular officials or organs of the State; it also extends to conduct carried out by others who are authorized to act by the State or at least who act under its actual direction or control. In the *Nicaragua* case, the International Court stated that:

> For this conduct [of the *contra* rebels] to give rise to legal responsibility of the USA, it would in principle have to be proved that that State had *effective control* of the military or paramilitary operations in the course of which the alleged violations were committed.[56]

The Articles on State Responsibility follow this approach: under Article 8, conduct of a person or group of persons is attributable to the State 'if the person or group of persons is in fact acting on the instructions of, or under the direction or control of, that State in carrying out the conduct' (ARSIWA, Article 8; Commentary, Crawford, 2002, pp 110–13); and it was reaffirmed by the International Court in *Bosnian Genocide*, as concerns the attribution to the FRY of the conduct of the Bosnian Serb forces and paramilitary groups.[57] There the Court disapproved the test of 'overall control' proposed by the Appeals Chamber of the ICTY in *Tadić*,[58] observing that:

> the 'overall control' test has the major drawback of broadening the scope of State responsibility well beyond the fundamental principle governing the law of international responsibility: a State is responsible only for its own conduct, that is to say the conduct of persons acting, on whatever basis, on its behalf . . . [T]he 'overall control' test is unsuitable, for it stretches too far, almost to breaking point, the connection which must exist between the conduct of a State's organs and its international responsibility.[59]

As this passage illustrates, the governing principle is that of independent responsibility: the State is responsible for its own acts, ie for the acts of its organs and agents, and not for the acts of private parties, unless there are special circumstances warranting attribution to it of such conduct.

The same applies where one State is somehow implicated in the conduct of a third State, whether by aiding or assisting the other State in breaching an obligation owed by both of them, or by coercing or exercising direction and control over the other State to that end— indeed it applies *a fortiori*, since the third State will ordinarily be responsible for its own acts in breach of its own international obligations (ARSIWA, Articles 16–19).

---

[55] *United States Diplomatic and Consular Staff in Tehran, Judgment, ICJ Reports 1980*, p 3, para 63.

[56] *Military and Paramilitary Activities in and against Nicaragua, Merits, Judgment (Nicaragua v United States of America), ICJ Reports 1986*, p 14, para 115 (emphasis added).

[57] *Application of the Convention on the Prevention and Punishment of the Crime of Genocide (Bosnia and Herzegovina v Serbia and Montenegro), Merits, Judgment, ICJ Reports 2007*, p 43, paras 402–7.

[58] *Prosecutor v Tadić, Judgment*, Case No IT-94-1-A, Appeals Chamber, 15 July 1999, 38 ILM 1518, para 145.

[59] *Application of the Convention on the Prevention and Punishment of the Crime of Genocide (Bosnia and Herzegovina v Serbia and Montenegro), Merits, Judgment, ICJ Reports 2007*, p 43, para 406.

But there is another facet to the principle of independent responsibility: a State cannot hide behind the involvement of other States. It is responsible if and to the extent that it contributed to that wrongful conduct by its own acts. Thus in *Nicaragua*, the acts of the *contras* were not as such attributable to the USA, but the USA was held responsible for its own conduct (in itself internationally wrongful) in training and financing the *contras* and in carrying out some specific operations, including the mining of a Nicaraguan harbour.[60] Likewise if a number of States act together in administering a territory, each will be responsible for its own conduct as part of the common enterprise.[61]

In another, and rather special, form of parallelism, the State will be responsible for the conduct of an insurrectional movement which subsequently becomes the government of that State (or, if they are a secessionary movement, of the new State they are struggling to create) (ARSIWA, Article 10; Commentary, Crawford, 2002, pp 116–20; and see Dumberry, 2006; Crawford, 2013, pp 170–81). The rule is to some extent anomalous, since it determines the attribution of conduct not by events at the time of that conduct but by reference to later contingencies—the success or failure of the revolt or secession. But the principle is established, and is reflected in Article 10 of the ILC Articles.[62] Further, a State may exceptionally be held responsible for the actions of persons exercising elements of governmental authority in the absence or default of the official authorities (ARSIWA, Article 9; Commentary, Crawford, 2002, pp 114–15; Crawford, 2013, pp 166–9). For instance, in *Yeager*, immediately after the revolution in Iran in 1979 the claimant had been detained for several days by 'revolutionary guards' and had then been evacuated from the country; the US–Iran Claims Tribunal held that, although the guards were not recognized under internal law as part of the State apparatus, they were in fact exercising public functions in the absence of the previous State apparatus: Iran was thus held responsible for their acts.[63]

The question of attribution of conduct in the field of responsibility of international organizations has somewhat different contours. As just discussed, in the law of State responsibility, there are a number of ways in which the conduct of organs, instrumentalities, and even, in some circumstances, private parties may be attributed to the State. By contrast, given the different structure of international organizations—which are functional entities, not territorial communities—the 'general rule' is that conduct must be that of an organ or agent of the international organization, acting in the performance of its functions (ARIO, Article 6). This 'functional' criterion underlying attribution of conduct to an international

---

[60] *Military and Paramilitary Activities in and against Nicaragua (Nicaragua v United States of America)*, *Merits, Judgment, ICJ Reports 1986*, p 14, in particular paras 75–80, 238, 242, 252, 292(3)-(6).

[61] Cf *Certain Phosphate Lands in Nauru (Nauru v Australia)*, *Preliminary Objections, ICJ Reports 1992*, p 240, where the International Court left the question of possible apportionment of any compensation found to be due between the other implicated States to the merits stage.

[62] In *Application of the Convention on the Prevention and Punishment of the Crime of Genocide (Croatia v Serbia), Judgment, ICJ Reports 2015*, p 3, where the issue was whether Serbia had been bound by the Genocide Convention in relation to events prior to it becoming a party thereto in 1992, the ICJ (at para 104) abstained from expressing a view as to the extent to which the rule embodied in Article 10(2) ARSIWA reflects customary international law, observing that the rule in any event concerned only with the attribution of acts to a new State, and does not have the effect of creating obligations binding upon either the new State or the movement that succeeded in establishing that new State.

[63] *Yeager v The Islamic Republic of Iran* (1987) 82 ILR 178. Cf, however, *Short v The Islamic Republic of Iran* (1987) 82 ILR 148 and *Rankin v The Islamic Republic of Iran* (1987) 82 ILR 204 (decided on the basis that the claimants had failed to prove that their departure was caused by actions attributable to Iran, rather than the general turmoil accompanying the revolution).

organization has parallels in other areas of the law, in particular as concerns the immunity from jurisdiction of the officials or agents of international organizations.[64]

The addition of the notion of agents to that of organs substantially widens the basis of attribution as compared to the corresponding rules of State responsibility. As a result it effectively subsumes the other bases of attribution. For instance, an individual who does not have any official status within an international organization but carries out conduct upon its instructions or under its direction and control will be regarded as its agent and the conduct will be attributable to the organization on that basis.

As a result of the dominant role played by the rule permitting attribution of the conduct of organs and agents of international organizations, the Articles on Responsibility of International Organization contain only two alternative bases for the attribution of conduct to an international organization: first, in a similar fashion to the position under the law of State responsibility, conduct will be attributable if it has been acknowledged and adopted by the international organization as its own (ARIO, Article 9); second, conduct may be attributed to an international organization on the basis that the conduct is that of the organ of a State or the organ or agent of another international organization which has been placed at the disposal of the international organization and over which the international organization exercises 'effective control' (ARIO, Article 7). However, in contrast to the other provisions dealing with attribution, the purpose of this rule is not to determine *whether* particular conduct is attributable as such; rather it addresses the question of which of two entities (the 'borrowing' international organization or the 'lending' State (or international organization)) is the relevant one for purposes of attribution.

That provision is of particular relevance in the context of the attribution of the conduct in breach of applicable international obligations of national contingents assigned to United Nations peacekeeping missions. Whether or not the conduct in question is to be attributed to the United Nations or to the contributing State turns on the relative degree of 'effective control' in fact exercised by those entities over the conduct in question. That in turn depends upon a number of factors, including the mandate of the peacekeeping mission, any agreement between the United Nations and the contributing State as to the terms on which troops were to be placed at the disposal of the United Nations, the extent

---

[64] See Article 105 UN Charter; Convention on the Privileges and Immunities of the United Nations, 13 February 1946, (the General Convention), Article V, Section 18 (as regards UN officials) and Article VI, Section 22 (as regards experts on mission), and Convention on the Privileges and Immunities of the Specialized Agencies, 21 November 1947, Article VI, Section 19 (as regards officials of the specialized agencies) and the various Annexes in relation to experts on mission of the specialized agencies). See also *Applicability of Article VI, Section 22, of the Convention on the Privileges and Immunities of the United Nations, Advisory Opinion, ICJ Reports 1989*, p 177, in which the ICJ, in concluding that Special Rapporteurs of the former Sub-Commission on the Prevention on Discrimination and the Protection of Minorities enjoyed the privileges and immunities accorded to an expert on mission under the General Convention (para 55), observed that '[t]he essence of the matter lies not in their administrative position, but in the nature of their mission' (para 47). Similarly, in the *Cumaraswamy* Advisory Opinion, the Court held that Special Rapporteurs of the Human Rights Commission are entitled to the privileges and immunities accorded to experts on mission under the General Convention, observing: 'what is decisive is that they have been entrusted with a mission by the United Nations and are therefore entitled to the privileges and immunities provided for in Article VI, Section 22, that safeguard the independent exercise of their functions': *Difference Relating to Immunity from Legal Process of a Special Rapporteur of the Commission on Human Rights, Advisory Opinion, ICJ Reports 1999*, p 62, para 43. Whether the agent was carrying out functions on behalf of an organization is also the criterion on the basis of which the question of whether an international organization may bring a claim by way of 'functional protection' in relation to injuries caused to the agent is to be determined: see *Reparation for Injuries Suffered in the Service of the United Nations, Advisory Opinion, ICJ Reports 1949*, p 174 at pp 177, 180, 181–4. See further ARSIWA, Article 9.

to which the troops remain subject to the command and jurisdiction of the contributing State, and whether United Nations command and control was effective.

The appropriate test to be applied in these circumstances has given rise to controversy. In 2007, the Grand Chamber of the European Court of Human Rights in *Behrami and Behrami v France; Saramati v France, Germany and Norway* determined that the United Nations exercised a sufficient degree of control over troops forming part of KFOR in Kosovo that their actions were to be attributed to the United Nations, such that the Court had no jurisdiction *ratione personae* over the applicant's claims; in doing so, it applied a test of whether the United Nations Security Council 'retained ultimate authority and control so that operational command only was delegated'.[65]

Subsequently, a similar question, whether the actions of UK troops forming part of the multinational force in Iraq authorized by SC Resolution 1546 (8 June 2004) were to be attributed to the United Nations, rather than the UK, came before the House of Lords in *R (Al-Jedda) v Secretary of State for Defence*.[66] While apparently accepting the correctness of the 'ultimate authority and control' approach, the House distinguished the case before it on the facts, and held, on the basis of the wording of the relevant Security Council resolutions, that UK troops in Iraq could not realistically be said to be subject to UN authority and control.

In its Commentary on the Articles on Responsibility of International Organizations, the ILC noted that the UN Secretary-General had distanced himself from the approach taken in *Behrami*, and gently criticized the approach of the European Court on the basis that 'when applying the criterion of effective control, "operational" control would seem more significant than "ultimate" control, since the latter hardly implies a role in the act in question'.[67]

Subsequently, when *Al-Jedda* came before the European Court, the Grand Chamber appears to have retreated at least implicitly from its previous position. In rejecting the argument of the UK government that the actions of UK troops should be regarded as attributable to the United Nations, the Grand Chamber followed the approach of the House of Lords in distinguishing *Behrami* on the facts, although it appeared to continue to endorse the actual result in *Behrami*.[68] At the same time it avoided taking a firm position on whether the applicable test was that of ultimate authority and control (as suggested in *Behrami*), or effective operational control over the relevant conduct of troops (as suggested by the ILC), merely finding that, in the circumstances, neither test was fulfilled.[69]

The matter was taken further by the decision of the Dutch Supreme Court of 6 September 2013 in the so-called *Dutchbat* case.[70] A Dutch battalion serving as part of UNPROFOR

---

[65] *Behrami and Behrami v France; Saramati v France, Germany and Norway* (Dec) [GC], nos 71412/01 and 78166/01, 2 May 2007, para 133. See also *Kasumaj v Greece* (Dec), no 6974/05, 5 July 2007; *Gajić v Germany* (Dec), no 31446/02, 28 August 2007; *Beric v Bosnia and Herzegovina* (Dec), no 36357/04, ECHR 2007-XII. In *Behrami*, the Court did not need to address the extent to which the conduct might be attributable to both the UN and the contributing States.

[66] *R (Al-Jedda) v Secretary of State for Defence* [2007] UKHL 58; [2008] 1 AC 332.

[67] ARIO, Commentary to Article 7, para (10); Report of the International Law Commission, Sixty-third Session, A/66/10, 90–1; YILC 2011, vol II(2).

[68] *Al-Jedda v the United Kingdom* [GC], no 27021/08, ECHR 2011, para 83.

[69] Ibid, para 84. The Grand Chamber continued to refer only to the ILC's 2004 draft commentary (ibid, para 56), and made no reference to the ILC's criticism of the decision in *Behrami*, which had already appeared in the Commentary to Draft Article 6 (as it then was) adopted on first reading in 2009: see Commentary to Draft Article 6, paras (9)–(11), Report of the International Law Commission, Sixty-first Session, A/64/10, 67–9; YILC 2009, vol II(2).

[70] *State of the Netherlands v Nuhanović*, First Chamber, Supreme Court of the Netherlands, 6 September 2013.

in Bosnia was involved in a decision to expel three Bosnian men from a compound at Srebrenica. Despite Dutch attempts to negotiate safe passage with the commander of the Bosnian Serb militia (Mladić) the three men were shortly afterwards murdered by the militia. The Dutch government argued that responsibility lay with the United Nations exclusively. Affirming on cassation the decision of the Hague Court of Appeal, the Supreme Court held that the Dutch government was civilly responsible for their deaths. It said:

> [I]nternational law, in particular article 8 [ARIO] in conjunction with article 48(1) [ARIO], does not exclude the possibility of dual attribution of given conduct. For the purpose of deciding whether the State had effective control it is not necessary for the State to have countermanded the command structure of the United Nations by giving instructions to Dutchbat or to have exercised operational command independently. It is apparent from the Commentary on article 7 [ARIO] that the attribution of conduct to the seconding State or the international organization is based on the factual control over the specific conduct, in which all factual circumstances and the special context of the case must be taken into account.[71]

In the circumstances it was unnecessary to determine whether the United Nations was also responsible. The Court robustly rejected the argument that its decision would deter governments from engaging in peacekeeping operations and that a policy of restraint should be followed. On that basis, the Court said:

> [t]here would be virtually no scope for the courts to assess the consequences of the conduct of a troop contingent in the context of a peace mission, in this case the conduct of which Dutchbat and hence the State are accused. Such far-reaching restraint is unacceptable. Nor is this altered by the fact that the State expects this to have an adverse effect on the implementation of peace operations by the United Nations, in particular on the willingness of member States to provide troops for such operations. This should not, after all prevent the possibility of judicial assessment in retrospect of the conduct of the relevant troop contingent.[72]

B. BREACH OF AN INTERNATIONAL OBLIGATION

The second element of responsibility is breach of an international obligation of the State. Here an initial distinction is drawn between State responsibility arising in the context of direct State-to-State wrongdoing and State responsibility arising in the context of diplomatic protection (injury to aliens or their property). This is so even though the relevant obligations may be contained in a treaty, the breach of which in principle engages direct State-to-State responsibility. The International Court was careful to preserve the distinction in the *ELSI* case, where the USA sought to base its action on breach of a bilateral treaty: nonetheless, the Chamber said, its claim was in the nature of diplomatic protection and was thus subject to the normal requirements applicable to such a claim, including the exhaustion of local remedies.[73]

---

[71] Ibid, paras 3.11.2–3.   [72] Ibid, para 3.18.3.
[73] *Elettronica Sicula SpA (ELSI), Judgment, ICJ Reports 1989*, p 15, para 52. Compare *Arrest Warrant of 11 April 2000 (Democratic Republic of Congo v Belgium), Preliminary Objections and Merits, Judgment, ICJ Reports 2002*, p 3, para 40. In *Armed Activities on the Territory of the Congo (Democratic Republic of the Congo v Uganda), ICJ Reports 2005*, p 168 it was held, in relation to counterclaims of mistreatment of persons within the grounds of the embassy of the respondent State, that to the extent that the claims were based on alleged breaches of the Vienna Convention on Diplomatic Relations due to mistreatment of diplomats of the respondent State and violations of the inviolability of its embassy, they were not claims having the character of diplomatic protection as they sought reparation for direct injury to the respondent State itself (paras 330–1). By contrast, insofar as the counterclaims were brought in respect of individuals not having diplomatic status, they fell under the rubric of diplomatic protection.

Many of the issues which arise in the context of diplomatic protection (nationality of claims, exhaustion of local remedies)[74] do not arise in the context of direct State-to-State disputes. The only issue in these direct State-to-State cases is whether conduct attributable to State B causes legal harm to State A in breach of international law. If so, responsibility is prima facie engaged.

On its face, the requirement that there should be a breach of an international obligation of the State seems obvious enough. However, a number of questions arise: for example, causation, the notion of injury, the time factor (rules concerning non-retrospectivity of international law and acts continuing in time), and so on.

An important preliminary point should be made: international law is a distinct system, separate from national legal systems. In its own terms it prevails over national law in the event of conflict, and this is so irrespective of the approach taken by the national legal system. Several consequences follow. First, a State cannot invoke its own municipal law as a justification for refusal or failure to comply with its international obligations, whether under a treaty or otherwise.[75] The fact that an act or omission is lawful (or unlawful) under national law does not prejudge the question of its lawfulness or otherwise under international law.[76] Second, the content of municipal law is considered a matter of fact for international law;[77] in theory, the two live in distinct spheres, communicating via the rules of evidence. Third, a State cannot seek to invalidate the entry into force of international obligations by reference to municipal law constraints which it failed to observe.[78]

Of course, conduct attributable to a State may consist of both actions and omissions; breach of international obligations by omission (or by a combination of acts and omissions) is relatively common.[79] For instance in the *Tehran Hostages* case, the International Court held that the responsibility of Iran was due to the 'inaction' of its authorities which 'failed to take appropriate steps' in circumstances where such steps were evidently called for.[80]

---

[74] See the ILC's Articles on Diplomatic Protection (2006); Report of the International Law Commission, 58th Session (2006), A/61/10, ch IV; YILC 2006, vol II(2), reproduced in Evans, 2017, pp 538–41. For consideration by the General Assembly, see GA Res 61/35 (4 December 2006); GA Res 62/67 (6 December 2007); GA Res 65/27 (6 December 2010); GA Res 68/113 (16 December 2013); and GA Res 71/142 (13 December 2016). See further Okowa, Ch 15 in this book.

[75] *Greco-Bulgarian 'Communities', Advisory Opinion, 1930, PCIJ, Ser B, No 17*, p 32; ARSIWA, Articles 3, 32. For a slightly different manifestation of the same principle in relation to the obligation to comply with a judgment of the ICJ, see also *Request for Interpretation of the Judgment of 31 March 2004 in the Case concerning Avena and Other Mexican Nationals (Mexico v United States of America), Judgment, ICJ Reports 2009*, p 3, para 47: 'considerations of domestic law which have so far hindered the implementation of the obligation incumbent upon the United States, cannot relieve it of its obligation.'

[76] *Elettronica Sicula SpA (ELSI), Judgment, ICJ Reports 1989*, p 15, para 73. *Compañía de Aguas del Aconquija and Vivendi Universal v Argentine Republic (ICSID Case No ARB/97/3)*, Decision on Annulment, 3 July 2002, 41 ILM 1135.

[77] *Certain German Interests in Polish Upper Silesia, Merits, Judgment No 7, 1926, PCIJ, Ser A, No 7*, p 19.

[78] *Free Zones of Upper Savoy and the District of Gex, Judgment, 1932, PCIJ, Ser A/B, No 46*, p 96 at p 167 and see ibid, at p 170; *Legal Status of Eastern Greenland, Judgment, 1933, PCIJ, Ser A/B, No 53*, p 22 at p 71, and the Dissenting Opinion of Judge Anzilotti, pp 91–2. In relation to the law of treaties, see VCLT, Articles 27, 46; and *Land and Maritime Boundary between Cameroon and Nigeria (Cameroon v Nigeria: Equatorial Guinea Intervening), Judgment, ICJ Reports 2002*, p 303, paras 264–8.

[79] Cf ARSIWA, Article 2, and Commentary to Article 1, paras 1 and 8; Commentary to Article 2, para 4.

[80] *United States Diplomatic and Consular Staff in Tehran, Judgment, ICJ Reports 1980*, p 3, paras 63, 67. See also *Velásquez-Rodríguez v Honduras, Merits, Judgment of 29 July 1988, Ser C, No 4*, 95 ILR 259, para 170: 'under international law a State is responsible for the acts of its agents undertaken in their official capacity and for their omissions . . .'; *Affaire relative à l'acquisition de la nationalité polonaise (Germany v Poland)* (1924) 1 RIAA 425.

1. Fault, harm, and damage

There has been a major debate about whether international law has a general requirement of fault. The debate is between those who maintain that international law requires some fault on the part of the State if it is to incur responsibility and supporters of so-called 'objective responsibility'. The case law tends to support the objective school. Thus in *Caire*, the arbitral tribunal affirmed 'the doctrine of the "objective responsibility" of the State, that is, the responsibility for the acts of its officials or organs, which may devolve upon it despite the absence of any "*faute*" on its part'.[81] However, there are statements which may be seen as going the other way. In the *Corfu Channel* case, the International Court held that:

> It is clear that knowledge of the minelaying cannot be imputed to the Albanian Government by reason merely of the fact that a minefield discovered in Albanian territorial waters caused the explosion of which the British warships were victims . . . [I]t cannot be concluded from the mere fact of the control exercised by a State over its territory and waters that that State necessarily knew, or ought to have known, of any unlawful act perpetrated therein, nor yet that it necessarily knew, or should have known, the authors. This fact, by itself and apart from other circumstances, neither involves *prima facie* responsibility nor shifts the burden of proof.[82]

In that case Albania's responsibility was upheld on the basis that (according to the evidence gathered, including by an expert commission) Albania must have known that the mines had been recently laid and nonetheless, in breach of its international obligations, failed to warn ships passing through the strait of their presence.

When scholarly debate bogs down around some dichotomy such as 'responsibility for fault'/'objective responsibility', something has almost always gone wrong. Here the problem is one of level of analysis: there is neither a rule that responsibility is always based on fault, nor one that it is always independent of it—indeed, there appears to be no presumption either way. This is hardly surprising in a legal system which has to deal with a wide range of problems and disposes of a limited armoury of techniques. But in any event circumstances alter cases, and it is illusory to seek for a single dominant rule. Where responsibility is essentially based on acts of omission (as in *Corfu Channel*), considerations of fault loom large. But if a State deliberately carries out some specific act, there is less room for it to argue that the harmful consequences were unintended and should be disregarded. Everything depends on the specific context and on the content and interpretation of the obligation said to have been breached.

Thus the ILC Articles on State Responsibility endorse a more nuanced view. Under Articles 2 and 12, the international law of State responsibility does not require fault before an act or omission may be characterized as internationally wrongful. However, the interpretation of the relevant primary obligation in a given case may well lead to the conclusion that fault is a necessary condition for responsibility in relation to that obligation, having regard to the conduct alleged.[83]

---

[81] *Caire (France v Mexico)* (1929) 5 *RIAA* 516, 529.

[82] *Corfu Channel, Merits, Judgment, ICJ Reports 1949*, p 4 at p 18. See also *Home Missionary Society (USA v Great Britain)* (1920) 6 *RIAA* 42.

[83] ARSIWA, Articles 2 and 12; Commentary, Crawford, 2002, pp 83–5, 125–30. See further, Crawford, 2013, pp 93, 113–14, 217–20. For example, in order for State responsibility to arise for acts which are attributable to a State under Article II of the 1948 Genocide Convention, various specific mental elements must be shown (see *Application of the Convention on the Prevention and Punishment of the Crime of Genocide (Bosnia and Herzegovina v Serbia and Montenegro), ICJ Reports 2007*, p 43, para 187); most notably, these include proof of the specific intent (*dolus specialis*) to destroy, in whole or in part, a national, ethnic, racial, or religious group as such: see paras 187–90 and 198; and see also paras 292–7; 319; 334; 354; 370–8; see similarly *Application of the Convention on the Prevention and Punishment of the Crime of Genocide (Croatia v Serbia), Judgment, ICJ Reports 2015*, p 3, paras 132–48, 402–40; 448 and 500–15.

Similarly, there has been an intense debate concerning the role of harm or damage in the law of State responsibility. Some authors (and some governments) have claimed that the State must have suffered some form of actual harm or damage before responsibility can be engaged (Bollecker-Stern, 1973). Once more, the ILC Articles leave the question to be determined by the relevant primary obligation: there is no *general* requirement of harm or damage before the consequences of responsibility come into being. In some circumstances, the mere breach of an obligation (which may be seen as involving 'legal' injury) will be sufficient to give rise to responsibility; this is the case, for instance, of even a minor infringement of the inviolability of an embassy or consular mission. On the other hand, in the context for example of pollution of rivers, it is necessary to show some substantial impact on the environment or on other uses of the watercourse before responsibility will arise.[84]

A corollary of this position is that there may have been a breach of international law but no material harm may have been suffered by another State or person in whose interest the obligation was created. In such cases international courts frequently award merely declaratory relief on the ground that nothing more is required.[85] However, in such circumstances, the main point of asserting responsibility may be for the future, to avoid repetition of the problem, rather than to obtain compensation for the past.

2. Continuing wrongful acts and the time factor

The basic principle is that a State can only be internationally responsible for breach of a treaty obligation if the obligation is in force for that State at the time of the alleged breach. It is therefore necessary to examine closely at what point an obligation entered into force, or at what point the obligation was terminated or ceased to bind the State.

For example in *Mondev*,[86] a claim was brought by a Canadian company alleging breach of the NAFTA Chapter 11 investment protection provisions by the USA. The claimant alleged that by various actions of the Boston city authorities the value of the applicant's interests in building and development projects had effectively been expropriated. But all of these actions took place before NAFTA's entry into force on 1 January 1994: the only later events were decisions of US courts denying Mondev's claims under US law. The Tribunal

---

[84] Thus the mere risk of future harm was held not to constitute a sufficient basis for responsibility in the *Lac Lanoux Arbitration* (1957) 24 ILR 101. In *Gabčíkovo-Nagymaros Project (Hungary/Slovakia), Judgment, ICJ Reports 1997*, p 7, the ICJ held that preparations for the diversion of the Danube on the territory of one State did not involve a breach of treaty until the diversion went ahead (and caused damage to the other State). See further, Crawford, 2013, pp 233–5. Similarly, a claim of breach of the obligation of prevention of transboundary harm (ie the obligation on States under customary international law to use all available means to avoid activities within their territory or in areas under their jurisdiction which cause significant damage to the environment of another State (see *Pulp Mills on the River Uruguay (Argentina v Uruguay), Judgment, ICJ Reports 2010 (I)*, p 14, para 101)) requires that significant harm be proved: see *Certain Activities carried out by Nicaragua in the Border Area (Costa Rica v Nicaragua); Construction of a Road in Costa Rica along the San Juan River (Nicaragua v Costa Rica), ICJ Reports 2015*, p 665, paras 118–20, 192–6, 203–7, 211–13, 216, 217. For an example of a treaty provision explicitly requiring damage, see, eg, Article 139(2) of the 1982 United Nations Convention on the Law of the Sea, which imposes liability in the event that damage is caused as a result of a failure by a State to carry out its responsibility to ensure compliance with the regime applicable to deep sea bed mining in the Area; see further ITLOS Seabed Disputes Chamber, *Responsibilities and Obligations of States Sponsoring Persons and Entities with Respect to Activities in the Area, Advisory Opinion, ITLOS Reports 2011*, p 10, paras 178–84; but see also para 210 as regards the continuing role of the customary rules of State responsibility in respect of a breach not causing damage.

[85] The *'I'm Alone'* (1935) 3 RIAA 1609, 1618; see also *Corfu Channel, Merits, Judgment, ICJ Reports 1949*, p 4 at pp 35–6, in which the ICJ made such a declaration in relation to Albania's claim of violation of its sovereignty as the result of the mine-sweeping operations carried out within its territorial waters by British warships.

[86] *Mondev International Ltd v United States of America (Case No ARB(AF)/99/2)*, Award of 11 October 2002, ICSID Reports, vol 6, 192.

held that NAFTA could not be applied retrospectively to actions prior to its entry into force. This left open the possibility of a claim of denial of justice in respect of the court decisions after NAFTA came into force, but the Tribunal concluded that the courts had not in any way acted improperly, and thus that there had been no denial of justice.

The relevant principle is stated in Article 13 of the ILC Articles: 'An act of a State does not constitute a breach of an international obligation unless the State is bound by the obligation in question at the time the act occurs.' The principle is clear enough, but its application may cause problems, in particular regarding changes in customary international law obligations, when it may not be clear precisely when an old customary rule was replaced by a new one.[87] For example, slavery was not always unlawful under international law, yet claims are sometimes made for reparation for persons or groups whose lives were affected by slavery and the slave trade.[88]

Another problem involves determining exactly when, or during what period, a wrongful act occurs. Wrongful acts can continue over a period of time—for instance the continued detention of diplomatic and consular personnel in the *Tehran Hostages* case, or the forced or involuntary disappearance of a person contrary to human rights norms.[89] Other wrongs may be instantaneous, even though their effects may continue after the point of breach. For example, an unlawful killing or a law expropriating property have effect at a specific moment; the breach occurs at the moment the victim is killed or the property is taken, and this even though the effects of these breaches are enduring. In general, such continuing consequences concern the scope of reparation, not whether there has been a breach in the first place.[90]

These distinctions may also be significant when it comes to issues of the jurisdiction of courts in cases concerning responsibility. For example, under the ECHR, claims can only be brought against a State party concerning breaches occurring after the Convention entered into force for that State. But it may be—depending on how one characterizes the conduct—that a breach which was initially committed by a State before it became a party continues thereafter and to that extent falls within the jurisdiction *ratione temporis* of the Court. For example, the circumstances of the *Loizidou* case before the European Court of Human Rights went back to the Turkish intervention in Cyprus in 1974, after Turkey became a party to the Convention but long before it accepted the right of individual petition. But the continuing exclusion of Mrs Loizidou from access to her property in the Turkish-controlled north continued after that date and could be dealt with by the Court.[91]

C. CIRCUMSTANCES PRECLUDING WRONGFULNESS: DEFENCES OR EXCUSES FOR BREACHES OF INTERNATIONAL LAW

Although conduct may be clearly attributable to a State, and be clearly inconsistent with its international obligations, it is possible that responsibility will not follow. The State may be able to rely on some defence or excuse: in the Articles on State Responsibility these are collected under the heading of 'Circumstances precluding wrongfulness' in Chapter V of Part

---

[87] See, eg, *Fisheries Jurisdiction (United Kingdom v Iceland), Merits, Judgment, ICJ Reports 1974*, p 3.

[88] *Le Louis* (1817) 2 Dodson 210.

[89] See, eg, the judgment of the Inter-American Court of Human Rights in *Blake v Guatemala, Merits, Judgment of 24 January 1998, Ser C, No 36* (1998).

[90] ARSIWA, Article 14; Commentary, Crawford, 2002, pp 135–40. See further, Crawford, 2013, pp 253–65.

[91] See *Loizidou v Turkey (Preliminary Objections), Judgment of 23 March 1995, Ser A, No 310*, 20 EHRR 99 and *Merits, RJD 1996–VI*, 23 EHRR 513; see also *Papamichalopoulos v Greece, Judgment of 24 June 1993, Ser A, No 260–B* (European Court of Human Rights).

One. Chapter V is essentially a catalogue or compilation of rules that have been recognized as justifying or excusing non-compliance by a State with its international obligations, and it is not exclusive.[92] It should be noted that none of the circumstances precluding wrongfulness can operate to excuse conduct which violates a peremptory norm (ARSIWA, Article 26): one cannot plead necessity to justify invading Belgium, for example.[93]

1. Consent

Valid consent by a State to action by another State which would otherwise be inconsistent with its international obligations precludes the wrongfulness of that action as against the consenting State (ARSIWA, Article 20). This is consistent with the role of consent in international relations generally: thus a State may consent to military action on its territory which (absent its consent) would be unlawful under the United Nations Charter. More mundanely, a State may consent to foreign judicial inquiries or arrest of suspects on its territory.[94] However, the scope of any consent in fact given by a State needs to be carefully examined and normally will be strictly construed.[95] Further, consent only goes so far: a State cannot waive the application of what in national law would be called mandatory rules and in international law are known as peremptory norms. Thus a State cannot (by treaty or otherwise) consent to or legitimize genocide, a situation expressly provided for in the ILC's formulation of the defence of consent; consent must be 'valid' (ARSIWA, Article 20; cf Article 26). Further, consent will only preclude the wrongfulness of conduct with regard to the consenting State; if the obligation breached is owed in parallel to more than one State, the wrongfulness of the act will not be precluded with regard to those States that have not consented.[96]

2. Self-defence

In certain circumstances, a State may permissibly disregard other international obligations while acting in self-defence in accordance with the Charter of the United Nations (ARSIWA, Article 21). The point was implicitly recognized by the International Court in the *Nuclear Weapons* Advisory Opinion, when it distinguished between per se restrictions on the use of force, whatever the circumstances—in another formulation, 'obligations of total restraint'—and considerations which, even if mandatory in time of peace, might be overridden for a State facing an imminent threat and required to act against it in self-defence.[97]

3. *Force majeure*

In common with most legal systems, international law does not impose responsibility where the non-performance of an obligation is due to circumstances entirely outside the control of the State. This defence obviously needs to be tightly circumscribed, and Article

---

[92] Specific defences or excuses may be recognized for particular obligations: eg Article 17 of the 1982 Convention on the Law of the Sea. Cf ARSIWA, Article 55.

[93] As Chancellor von Bethmann-Hollweg did before the Reichstag in 1914: see Crawford, 2002, p 178. See further, Crawford, 2013, ch 9. Generally see Paddeu, 2017.

[94] See, eg, *Savarkar (Great Britain v France)* (1911) 11 *RIAA* 243.

[95] See, eg, the careful consideration given by the ICJ to the scope and extent of the DRC's consent to the presence of Ugandan troops on its territory in *Armed Activities on the Territory of the Congo (Democratic Republic of the Congo v Uganda)*, Judgment, *ICJ Reports 2005*, p 168.

[96] See, eg, *Customs Régime between Germany and Austria, 1931*, Advisory Opinion, PCIJ, Ser A/B, No 41, p 37.

[97] On per se restrictions see *Legality of the Threat or Use of Nuclear Weapons*, Advisory Opinion, ICJ Reports 1996, p 226, paras 39, 52; on 'obligations of total restraint', see para 30.

23(1) of the ILC Articles provides that *force majeure* is a defence only where 'the occurrence of an irresistible force or of an unforeseen event, beyond the control of the State, [makes] it materially impossible in the circumstances to perform the obligation'. The defence of *force majeure* is further circumscribed by the limitations in Article 23(2), which provide that *force majeure* will not apply if either the situation 'is due, either alone or in combination with other factors, to the conduct of the State invoking it', or if, as a result of assessment of the situation and the obligation in question, the State seeking to invoke *force majeure* is to be regarded as having assumed the risk of the situation occurring.

4. Distress and necessity

The two circumstances of distress and necessity have much in common in that they both excuse conduct which would otherwise be wrongful because of extreme circumstances. According to Article 24, distress operates to excuse conduct where the author of the act 'had no other reasonable way . . . of saving the author's life or the lives of other persons entrusted to the author's care'. By contrast, necessity operates to excuse conduct taken which 'is the only means for the State to safeguard an essential interest against a grave and imminent peril'. Distress and necessity are to be distinguished from *force majeure* in that violation of the obligation in question is theoretically avoidable, although absolute compliance of the State with its international obligations is not required; a State is not normally required to sacrifice human life or to suffer inordinate damage to its vital interests in order to fulfil its international obligations.

The possibilities of abuse are obvious, in particular for invocation of necessity, and in the ILC Articles both circumstances are narrowly confined. Thus reliance on them is precluded if the State has in some way contributed to the situation which it is seeking to invoke to excuse its conduct. Further, the invoking State can only excuse conduct which is not unduly onerous for other States. Reliance on distress is precluded if the act in question 'is likely to create a comparable or greater peril' (ARSIWA, Article 24(2)(b)). Likewise, the invocation of a state of necessity is precluded if the action would 'seriously impair an essential interest of the State or States towards which the obligation exists, or of the international community as a whole' (ARSIWA, Article 25(1)(b)).

Argentina has sought to rely on a state of necessity as justifying the measures it adopted to deal with the Argentine financial crisis between 1999 and 2002; those measures have given rise to a large number of claims by foreign investors under bilateral investment treaties. In the majority of cases, the plea of necessity has been rejected on the grounds that the financial crisis and its potential consequences were not sufficiently serious to be regarded as imperilling an 'essential interest' and the situation did not involve a 'grave and imminent peril'; in any case, it has been held that the measures adopted were not the 'only way' for Argentina to deal with the crisis, there were other lawful means at its disposal in that regard, and Argentina had contributed to the situation.[98]

---

[98] See, eg, *CMS Gas Transmission Company* v *Argentine Republic (ICSID Case No ARB/01/8)*, Award of 12 May 2005; *Enron Corporation and Ponderosa Assets LP* v *Argentine Republic (ICSID Case No ARB/01/3)*, Award of 22 May 2007; *Sempra Energy International* v *Argentine Republic (ICSID Case No ARB/02/16)*, Award of 28 September 2007; *BG Group plc* v *Republic of Argentina*, Final Award of 24 December 2007. Cf *LG&E Energy Corp, LG&E Capital Corp, LG&E International Inc* v *Argentine Republic (ICSID Case No ARB/02/1)*, Decision on Liability of 3 October 2006, in which the Tribunal concluded that a state of necessity had existed for at least part of the period in question. The Award in *CMS* was the subject of an application for annulment; the ad hoc Committee, although finding various defects in the reasoning of the Tribunal, declined to annul the Award: *CMS Gas Transmission Company* v *Argentine Republic (ICSID Case No ARB/01/8)*, Decision on Annulment of 25 September 2007. Many of the other decisions against Argentina have also been the object of applications for annulment, with varying degrees of success.

Although where either distress or a state of necessity is found to have been established the wrongfulness of the act is precluded, other States are not necessarily expected to bear the consequences of another State's misfortune; the invoking State may have to pay compensation for any material loss caused to the State or States to which the obligation breached was owed (Article 27(b)).[99]

5. Countermeasures

As the International Court affirmed in the *Gabčíkovo-Nagymaros Project* case, countermeasures taken by a State in response to an internationally wrongful act of another State are not wrongful acts, but are recognized as a valid means of self-help as long as certain rather stringent conditions are respected.[100] Countermeasures as described in the ILC Articles only cover the suspension of performance by a State of one or more of its obligations; they are to be distinguished from acts of retorsion which, since they are by definition not a breach of the obligations of the State adopting them, cannot give rise to State responsibility and therefore require no justification. Certain obligations, such as that to refrain from the use of force, those protecting fundamental human rights and of a humanitarian character prohibiting the taking of reprisals, and those under other peremptory norms may not be suspended by way of countermeasure.[101]

6. Consequences of invoking a circumstance precluding wrongfulness

Although the wrongfulness of an act may be precluded by international law, that is not the end of the question. First, the wrongfulness of the act will only be precluded so long as the circumstance precluding wrongfulness continues to exist. For instance, if State A takes countermeasures in response to a breach by State B of obligations owed to State A, if State B recommences performance of its obligations State A must terminate its countermeasures; if it does not, it will incur responsibility for the period from which the countermeasure was no longer justified (ARSIWA, Article 27(a); and see Articles 52(3)(a) and 53). Secondly, the preclusive effect may be relative rather than general: again, this is obviously true of countermeasures, where conduct which is justified vis-à-vis a wrongdoing State will not or may not be justified *erga omnes*.

IV. THE CONTENT OF INTERNATIONAL RESPONSIBILITY

Upon the commission of an internationally wrongful act, certain secondary obligations arise by operation of law. These are codified in Part Two, Chapter I of the ILC Articles,

---

[99] Cf *LG&E Energy Corp, LG&E Capital Corp, LG&E International Inc* v *Argentine Republic (ICSID Case No ARB/02/1)*, Decision on Liability of 3 October 2006, in which the Tribunal held that no compensation was payable to the investor in relation to the period during which it held that a state of necessity had existed.

[100] The conditions required by the ARSIWA in order for countermeasures to be lawful are: they must be taken to induce compliance with the obligations contained in Part Two of the Articles (reparation, cessation . . .) (Article 49(1)(a)); there must have been a request to the wrongdoing State to fulfil its obligations in this regard (Article 49(1)(b); the countermeasures must be as far as possible reversible (Article 49(3)); they must be proportionate (Article 51); and notification must have been given of the decision to take countermeasures accompanied by an offer to negotiate (Article 52(1)). For the recognition of all but the last of these conditions as customary see *Gabčíkovo-Nagymaros Project (Hungary/Slovakia), Judgment, ICJ Reports 1997*, p 7. Generally see Crawford, 2013, ch 21.

[101] Article 50(1) ARSIWA; in addition, obligations under any applicable dispute settlement procedure and in relation to the inviolability of diplomatic or consular agents, premises, archives, and documents may likewise not be the object of countermeasures: Article 50(2) ARSIWA.

which identifies two main categories, the obligations of cessation and reparation. The equal emphasis on these involves an important insight. Issues of State responsibility are not only backward-looking, concerned at obtaining compensation for things past. They are at least as much concerned with the restoration of the legal relationship which has been threatened or impaired by the breach—ie with the assurance of continuing performance for the future. This is particularly clear where the individual breach may not have in itself caused any great amount of harm but where the threat of repetition is a source of legal insecurity. It can be seen in matters as diverse as the protection of embassies and of the environment. In these and other contexts, the relevant rules exist to protect ongoing relationships or situations of continuing value. The analogy of the bilateral contract, relatively readily terminated and replaceable by a contract with someone else, is not a useful one even in the context of strictly bilateral inter-State relations, and *a fortiori* where the legal obligation exists for the protection of a wider range of (non-synallagmatic) interests.

Thus the fact that the responsible State is required to make reparation for a breach does not mean that it can disregard its obligation for the future, effectively buying its way out of compliance; when an obligation is breached, it does not disappear.[102] The obligation continues to bind the responsible State, which remains obliged to perform it (ARSIWA, Article 29). As a corollary, in the case of a continuing wrongful act, the responsible State is under an obligation to bring that act to an end (Article 30(a)). In certain circumstances it may even be incumbent upon the responsible State to offer appropriate assurances and guarantees of non-repetition of the act in question to the State to which the obligation is owed (Article 30(b)).

The point was made by the International Court in the *LaGrand* case, which concerned the USA's non-observance of obligations of consular notification under Article 36 of the Vienna Convention on Consular Relations. The particular occasion of Germany's complaint was the failure of notification concerning two death row inmates who (notwithstanding their German nationality) had hardly any connection with Germany; but there was a wider concern as to the USA's compliance with its continuing obligations of performance under the Consular Relations Convention. Indeed the USA accepted this, and spelled out in detail the measures it had taken to ensure compliance for the future. In consequence the Court held:

> that the commitment expressed by the United States to ensure implementation of the specific measures adopted in performance of its obligations under Article 36, paragraph 1(b), must be regarded as meeting Germany's request for a general assurance of non-repetition.[103]

In its subsequent practice, whilst recognizing its power in an appropriate case to order a State to give assurances and guarantees of non-repetition, the International Court has

---

[102] Even in the case of a material breach of a treaty obligation within the meaning of Article 60(3) VCLT, which may permit other parties to terminate or suspend the operation of the treaty, Article 65 VCLT imposes a requirement that notice be given to that effect, which, except in cases of special urgency, will not take effect for at least three months. Further, Article 70 VCLT makes clear that the termination of a treaty operates only prospectively so as to release the parties from their future obligations of performance under the treaty, and does not affect any right, obligation, or situation created through the execution of the treaty prior to its termination, whilst Article 72 VCLT provides that a suspension only relieves the relevant States parties from further performance during the period of the suspension, and does not otherwise affect the legal relations between them established by the treaty.

[103] *LaGrand (Germany v United States of America), Merits, Judgment, ICJ Reports 2001*, p 466, para 124; see also the *dispositif*, para 128(6); see also *Avena and Other Mexican Nationals (Mexico v United States of America), Judgment, ICJ Reports 2004*, p 12, paras 149–50.

declined to do so on the basis that, '[a]s a general rule, there is no reason to suppose that a State whose act or conduct has been declared wrongful will repeat that act or conduct in the future, since its good faith is to be presumed';[104] it has accordingly made clear that an order requiring a responsible State to offer assurances of non-repetition, or to take specific measures to ensure that a wrongful act is not repeated, should only be made when there are 'special circumstances' justifying such a course of action.[105]

But questions of reparation also arise, especially where actual harm or damage has occurred, and under international law the responsible State is obliged to make full reparation for the consequences of its breach, provided that these are not too remote or indirect. The linkage between breach and reparation is made clear, for example, in Article 36(2) of the Statute of the International Court, which specifies among the legal disputes as to which a State may accept the Court's jurisdiction:

(c) the existence of any fact which, if established, would constitute a breach of an international obligation;

(d) the nature or extent of the reparation to be made for the breach of an international obligation.

This link was spelled out in a classic passage by the Permanent Court in the *Factory at Chorzów* case, in the context of a jurisdictional provision conferring jurisdiction on the Court over 'differences of opinion arising from the interpretation and the application' of particular treaty provisions:

It is a principle of international law that the breach of an engagement involves an obligation to make reparation in an adequate form. Reparation therefore is the indispensable complement of a failure to apply a convention and there is no necessity for this to be stated in the convention itself. Differences relating to reparations, which may be due by reason of failure to apply a convention, are consequently differences relating to its application.[106]

There is no need for a specific mandate to an international court or tribunal to award reparation, if it has jurisdiction as between the parties in the matter: a dispute as to the interpretation or application of a treaty covers a dispute as to the consequences of its breach and thus the form and extent of reparation.

The underlying principle is that reparation must wipe out the consequences of the breach, putting the parties as far as possible in the same position as they would have been if the breach had not occurred. In order to achieve that, reparation may take several forms, including but not limited to monetary compensation. Again, both points were made by the Permanent Court in a later stage of the *Chorzów* case:

The essential principle contained in the actual notion of an illegal act—a principle which seems to be established by international practice and in particular by the decisions of arbitral tribunals—is that reparation must, so far as possible, wipe out all the consequences of

---

[104] *Dispute regarding Navigational and Related Rights (Costa Rica v Nicaragua), Judgment, ICJ Reports 2009,* p 213, para 150.

[105] Ibid; see also *Pulp Mills on the River Uruguay (Argentina v Uruguay), ICJ Reports 2010 (I),* p 14, para 278; *Application of the Interim Accord of 13 September 1995 (former Yugoslav Republic of Macedonia v Greece), Judgment, ICJ Reports 2011,* p 644, para 168); *Jurisdictional Immunities of the State (Germany v Italy (Greece intervening)), Judgment, ICJ Reports 2012,* p 99, para 138; *Certain Activities carried out by Nicaragua in the Border Area (Costa Rica v Nicaragua); Construction of a Road in Costa Rica along the San Juan River (Nicaragua v Costa Rica), ICJ Reports 2015,* p 665, para 141; cf also ibid, at para 227.

[106] *Factory at Chorzów, Jurisdiction, Judgment No 8, 1927, PCIJ, Ser A, No 9,* p 21.

the illegal act and reestablish the situation which would, in all probability, have existed if that act had not been committed. Restitution in kind, or, if this is not possible, payment of a sum corresponding to the value which a restitution in kind would bear; the award, if need be, of damages for loss sustained which would not be covered by restitution in kind or payment in place of it—such are the principles which should serve to determine the amount of compensation due for an act contrary to international law.[107]

As this passage suggests, in theory at least, international law has always placed restitution as the first of the forms of reparation; it is only where restitution is not possible that other forms are substituted. This contrasts with the common law approach, under which money was taken to be the measure of all things and specific performance or restitution in kind were historically somewhat exceptional. In practice the two approaches are tending to converge—on the one hand, it is not infrequently found that specific restitution is not possible or can only be made in an approximate form in international law, while courts in the common law tradition have been expanding the scope of non-pecuniary remedies.

The basic requirement of compensation is that it should cover any 'financially assessable damage' flowing from the breach (ARSIWA, Article 36). In many cases (especially those involving loss of life, loss of opportunity, or psychiatric harm), the process of quantification is approximate and may even appear arbitrary; however, as in domestic legal systems, the difficulty in quantifying intangible loss has never had as a consequence that no compensation is payable.[108] By contrast in cases involving loss of property (including expropriation) a market for the property may exist which will give greater guidance. In addition, issues such as loss of profits may arise: provided they are clearly established, these may be compensable. Compensation may be supplemented by the award of interest (including, if necessary, compound interest); after some prevarication, the ILC decided to treat the issue of interest in a separate article (ARSIWA, Article 38; Commentary, Crawford, 2002, pp 235–9).

Although international tribunals have been moving towards a more realistic appreciation of issues of compensation (Gray, 1987, pp 77–95; Crawford, 2013, ch 17)—and of remedies more generally—it remains the case that many international disputes have a distinctly symbolic element. The claimant (whether a State or some other entity) may seek vindication more than compensation, and this is recognized in the international law of reparation by the protean remedy of 'satisfaction'. According to Article 37(2) of the ILC Articles, satisfaction 'may consist in an acknowledgement of the breach, an expression of regret, an apology or another appropriate modality'. In many cases before international courts and tribunals, an authoritative finding of the breach will be held to be sufficient satisfaction: this was the case in terms of Albania's claim that the UK had violated its sovereignty by conducting certain mine-sweeping operations in its territorial waters in the *Corfu Channel* case,[109] and it has been held to be the situation in innumerable human

---

[107] *Factory at Chorzów, Merits, Judgment No 13, 1928, PCIJ, Ser A, No 17*, p 47.

[108] See, eg, the classic statement by Umpire Parker in relation to non-material damage in *The S.S. 'Lusitania'* (USA v Germany) (1923) 7 RIAA 32, 40: 'That one injured is, under the rules of international law, entitled to be compensated for an injury inflicted resulting in mental suffering, injury to his feelings, humiliation, shame, degradation, loss of social position or injury to his credit or to his reputation, there can be no doubt, and such compensation should be commensurate to the injury. Such damages are very real, and the mere fact that they are difficult to measure or estimate by money standards makes them none the less real and affords no reason why the injured person should not be compensated therefore as compensatory damages.' That approach has been approved and applied by the ICJ in assessing the compensation due for non-material injury resulting from the wrongful arrest, detention and eventual expulsion by the respondent State of a national of the claimant State in breach of applicable international human rights obligations: see *Ahmadou Sadio Diallo (Republic of Guinea v Democratic Republic of the Congo), Compensation, Judgment, ICJ Reports 2012*, p 324, paras 18–25.

[109] *Corfu Channel, Merits, Judgment, ICJ Reports 1949*, p 4 at p 25 and pp 35–6.

rights cases, including some where more substantial remedies might have seemed justified (Shelton, 2015, pp 255–68). Similarly, in the *Bosnian Genocide* case, the ICJ held that
the FRY had breached its obligation to prevent genocide in relation to the massacre at
Srebrenica. Having recognized that restitution was not possible and that compensation
was not appropriate given the lack of the necessary 'sufficiently direct and causal nexus'
between the FRY's breach of the obligation and the massacre,[110] it held that a declaration
constituted 'in itself appropriate just satisfaction'.[111]

On the other hand, in a situation in which the breach is a continuing one, a declaration of breach and that the responsible State is under a duty to put an end to it may take
on some of the characteristics of an injunction, albeit that there are few mechanisms
to ensure enforcement or compliance. Thus in *Avena*, the ICJ held that the USA had
breached its obligations under the Vienna Convention on Consular Relations in relation
to a number of Mexican nationals who had been convicted and sentenced to death by
failing to inform them of their right to have the consular authorities notified. The Court
made declarations as to the specific violations of the Vienna Convention,[112] and further
held that appropriate reparation consisted in a declaration that the USA was 'to provide, by means of its own choosing, review and reconsideration of the: convictions and
sentences of the Mexican nationals'.[113] Similarly, in *Bosnian Genocide*, the Court concluded that there had been a failure to comply with the obligation to punish genocide.
The Court in that regard made a declaration not only of the fact of the breach, but also
ordered that Serbia 'should immediately take effective steps to ensure full compliance'
with its obligation to punish, and 'to transfer individuals accused of genocide [. . .] for
trial by the International Criminal Tribunal for the former Yugoslavia, and to co-operate
fully with that Tribunal'. Likewise, in *Jurisdictional Immunities of the State*, the Court
found a violation by Italy of its international obligations as a result of decisions of the
Italian courts holding that Germany was not entitled to immunity in respect of atrocities
committed against Italian nationals by the Nazis during the Second World War. By way
of remedy, the Court made declarations as to the breaches,[114] as well as declaring that
by way of restitution, Italy must 'by enacting appropriate legislation, or by resorting to
other methods of its choosing, ensure that the decisions of its courts and those of other
judicial authorities infringing the immunity which the Federal Republic of Germany
enjoys under international law cease to have effect'.[115] By contrast, it declined to make
any declaration that Italy's international responsibility was engaged as a result, on the
basis that such a declaration 'would be entirely redundant, since that responsibility is
automatically inferred from the finding that certain obligations have been violated'.[116]
As was noted in Section II B, if the conduct in question constitutes a serious breach
of an obligation arising under a peremptory norm of general international law certain
additional consequences arise for all other States under Article 41—in particular, the
obligation not to recognize as lawful the situation created and not to render aid or assistance in its maintenance.

---

[110] *Application of the Convention on the Prevention and Punishment of the Crime of Genocide (Bosnia and
Herzegovina v Serbia and Montenegro), Merits, Judgment, ICJ Reports 2007*, p 43, paras 460–2.

[111] Ibid, paras 463 and 471(5) and (9).

[112] *Avena and Other Mexican Nationals (Mexico v United States of America), ICJ Reports 2004*, p 12, paras
153(4)–(8).

[113] Ibid, para 153(9).

[114] *Jurisdictional Immunities of the State (Germany v Italy (Greece intervening)), Judgment, ICJ Reports 2012*,
p 99, paras 135 and 139(1)–(3).

[115] Ibid, para 139(4); and see para 137.   [116] Ibid, para 136.

V. INVOCATION OF RESPONSIBILITY: RESPONSES BY THE INJURED STATE AND OTHER STATES

Although international responsibility is deemed to arise directly by operation of law on the occurrence of a breach, for practical purposes that responsibility has to be invoked by someone. It may be invoked by the injured State or other party, or possibly by some third State concerned with the 'public order' consequences of the breach. Part Three of the ILC Articles deals with this important issue but in a non-exclusive way. In particular, while the Articles acknowledge the possibility that the responsibility of a State may be invoked by an injured party other than a State (eg by an individual applicant to the European Court of Human Rights), Article 33(2) leaves issues of the rights of persons or entities other than States which may arise as the result of a breach of an international obligation (including the right of invocation) for treatment elsewhere. The scope of Parts Two and Three is thus narrower than that of Part One of the Articles: Part One deals with the conditions for *all* breaches of international law by a State in the field of responsibility, whereas Part Two is formally limited to defining the content of international responsibility and the obligations which arise as a consequence which are owed to another State or States or the international community as a whole,[117] and Part Three by its terms is concerned only with the invocation of that responsibility of a State by another State or States.

Even so, the subject of Part Three is a large and controversial one. To what extent is a State to be considered as injured by a breach of international law on the part of another State? And if not individually injured, to what extent might it nevertheless demand remedies for the breach—with the inferential consequence of countermeasures if such remedies are not forthcoming? Given that international law includes not only bilateral obligations analogous in national systems to contract and tort (or delict), but also obligations intended to protect vital human interests of a generic kind (peace and security, the environment, sustainable development), the questions dealt with in Part Three could scarcely be more important.

They are primarily addressed through two articles. One (Article 42) defines in relatively narrow and precise terms the concept of the 'injured State', drawing in particular on the analogy of VCLT Article 60(2).[118] The second (Article 48) deals with the invocation of responsibility in the collective interest, in particular with respect to obligations owed to the international community as a whole, giving effect to the Court's dictum in the *Barcelona Traction* case, set out later in this section. The former category covers the breach of an obligation owed to a State individually. Also treated as 'injured States' are those States which

---

[117] For recognition of the point, see, eg, *Archer Daniels Midland Company and Tate & Lyle Ingredients Americas, Inc.* v *United Mexican States* (ICSID Case No ARB(AF)/04/05), Award of 21 November 2007, para 118; *Wintershall Aktiengesellschaft* v *Argentina* (ICSID Case No ARB/04/14), Award of 8 December 2008, paras 112–13; *Micula* v *Romania* (ICSID Case No ARB/05/20), Award of 11 December 2013, fn 172. Nevertheless, it appears that in principle, and apart from any relevant *lex specialis*, the content of the relevant obligations which arise upon breach of an international obligation are no different where the obligation is owed to and invoked by an individual or corporation, and the provisions of Part Two of the Articles have frequently been referred to and applied (whether or not by analogy) by human rights bodies and by tribunals in investment treaty arbitrations.

[118] Article 60(2) provides as follows: A material breach of a multilateral treaty by one of the parties entitles: the other parties by unanimous agreement to suspend the operation of the treaty in whole or in part or to terminate it either: in the relations between themselves and the defaulting State; or as between all the parties; a party specially affected by the breach to invoke it as a ground for suspending the operation of the treaty in whole or in part in the relations between itself and the defaulting State; any party other than the defaulting State to invoke the breach as a ground for suspending the operation of the treaty in whole or in part with respect to itself if the treaty is of such a character that a material breach of its provisions by one party radically changes the position of every party with respect to the further performance of its obligations under the treaty.

are particularly affected by the breach of a multilateral obligation, either because they are 'specially affected' or because the obligation is integral in character, so that a breach affects the enjoyment of the rights or the performance of the obligations of all the States concerned.

The contrast is with the 'other States' entitled to invoke responsibility, which are specified in Article 48(1):

Any State other than an injured State is entitled to invoke the responsibility of another State . . . if:

(a) the obligation breached is owed to a group of States including that State, and is established for the protection of a collective interest of the group; or

(b) the obligation breached is owed to the international community as a whole.

Article 48(1)(b) reflects the distinction drawn by the International Court in *Barcelona Traction* between on the one hand, 'bilaterizable' obligations and on the other, obligations owed to the international community as a whole (sometimes called obligations '*erga omnes*'), a category that encompasses most, if not all, peremptory norms of international law. In the case of the latter type of obligations:

By their very nature [they] are the concern of all States. In view of the importance of the rights involved, all States can be held to have a legal interest in their protection . . .[119]

The Court gave a number of examples of such obligations, including the prohibition of acts of aggression and genocide and 'the principles and rules concerning the basic rights of the human person, including protection from slavery and discrimination'.[120] Since then, the Court has also recognized the right of self-determination,[121] those obligations of international humanitarian law which it had previously described as 'intransgressible principles of international customary international law',[122] and the prohibition of torture[123] as falling within the category.

Article 48(1)(a) covers obligations owed to a group of States and 'established for the protection of a collective interest of the group'; the prime examples are obligations under multilateral treaties protecting 'community' interests, for instance obligations under human rights treaties, and certain treaty obligations in the field of environmental law. The primary

---

[119] *Barcelona Traction, Light and Power Company, Limited, Second Phase, Judgment, ICJ Reports 1970*, p 3, para 33.

[120] Ibid, para 34. For reaffirmation of the *erga omnes* nature of the prohibition of genocide, see *Application of the Convention on the Prevention and Punishment of the Crime of Genocide (Bosnia and Herzegovina v Yugoslavia), Preliminary Objections, ICJ Reports 1996*, p 595, para 31; *Armed Activities on the Territory of the Congo (New Application: 2002) (Democratic Republic of the Congo v Rwanda), Provisional Measures, Order of 10 July 2002, ICJ Reports 2002*, p 219, para 71; and *Application of the Convention on the Prevention and Punishment of the Crime of Genocide (Croatia v Serbia), Judgment, ICJ Reports 2015*, p 3, para 87.

[121] See *East Timor (Portugal v Australia), Judgment, ICJ Reports 1995*, p 90, para 29. See also *Legal Consequences of the Construction of a Wall in the Occupied Palestine Territory, Advisory Opinion, ICJ Reports 2004*, p 136, para 155.

[122] Ibid, para 157; the quoted passage is from the *Legality of the Threat or Use of Nuclear Weapons, Advisory Opinion, ICJ Reports 1996*, p 266, para 79. In *Jurisdictional Immunities of the State (Germany v Italy; Greece Intervening), Judgment, ICJ Reports 2012*, p 99, paras 93–7, the Court deliberately abstained from taking a position as to whether the 'rules of the law of armed conflict which prohibit the murder of civilians in occupied territory, the deportation of civilian inhabitants to slave labour and the deportation of prisoners of war to slave labour' constitute rules of *jus cogens*, reasoning that, even assuming that were so, in any case there was no conflict between the *jus cogens* character of the relevant norms and the rules on State immunity.

[123] *Questions Relating to the Obligation to Prosecute or Extradite (Belgium v Senegal), Judgment, ICJ Reports 2012*, p 422, para 99.

beneficiaries of such obligations are either individuals in the case of the former, or the group of States as a whole in the case of the latter.[124] Obligations of this type deriving from a treaty are sometimes referred to as obligations *erga omnes partes*.

By definition the States falling within the situations covered by Article 48(1) will not normally have suffered any injury, save the purely 'legal' injury resulting from the very violation of the norm in question. As a consequence, the ILC proposed that in invoking the responsibility of the wrongdoing State on this basis, they should be limited to claiming cessation of continuing wrongful acts and assurances and guarantees of non-repetition, as well as performance of the obligation of reparation 'in the interest of the injured State or the beneficiaries of the obligation breached' (Article 48(2)(a) and (b)).

As yet, the ILC's proposal as to obligations *erga omnes*, although founded on the dictum of the Court in *Barcelona Traction*, has found limited support in State practice.[125] However, as concerns obligations *erga omnes partes*, in *Questions Relating to the Obligation to Prosecute or Extradite*, a dispute arising under the Convention Against Torture (one of the paradigm examples of a multilateral treaty establishing obligations in the collective interest), the International Court substantially endorsed the approach proposed by the ILC in Article 48(1)(b) although it did so without expressly referring to the Articles. In rejecting the objection to the admissibility of Belgium's claim invoking the responsibility of Senegal for failure to comply with its obligations under the Convention in respect of Hissène Habré, the former President of Chad, who was accused of various acts of torture, the Court observed:

> The States parties to the Convention have a common interest to ensure, in view of their shared values, that acts of torture are prevented and that, if they occur, their authors do not enjoy impunity. The obligations of a State party to conduct a preliminary inquiry into the facts and to submit the case to its competent authorities for prosecution are triggered by the presence of the alleged offender in its territory, regardless of the nationality of the offender or the victims, or of the place where the alleged offences occurred. All the other States parties have a common interest in compliance with these obligations by the State in whose territory the alleged offender is present. That common interest implies that the obligations in question are owed by any State party to all the other States parties to the Convention. All the States parties 'have a legal interest' in the protection of the rights involved [. . .]. These obligations may be defined as 'obligations *erga omnes partes*' in the sense that each State party has an interest in compliance with them in any given case.
>
> The common interest in compliance with the relevant obligations under the Convention against Torture implies the entitlement of each State party to the Convention to make a claim concerning the cessation of an alleged breach by another State party. If a special interest were required for that purpose, in many cases no State would be in the position to make such a claim. It follows that any State party to the Convention may invoke the responsibility of another State party with a view to ascertaining the alleged failure to comply with its obligations *erga omnes partes* [. . .], and to bring that failure to an end.[126]

[124] This does not exclude the possibility that one or more States may be injured in the sense of ARSIWA, Article 42 by a breach of an environmental protection norm. Rather, as demonstrated by the fact that cessation is sought in the interests of the beneficiaries of the obligation, Article 48 seeks, without prejudice to that possibility, to articulate the possible interest of other States in compliance with the obligation in question.

[125] But see the comments of Judge Simma in *Armed Activities on the Territory of the Congo (Democratic Republic of the Congo v Uganda), Judgment, ICJ Reports 2005*, p 168, Separate Opinion, paras 32–41.

[126] *Questions Relating to the Obligation to Prosecute or Extradite (Belgium v Senegal), Judgment, ICJ Reports 2012*, p 422, paras 68–9. The Court went on to declare that Senegal was under an obligation to cease its continuing wrongful act, and was therefore required to 'take without further delay the necessary measures to submit the case to its competent authorities for the purpose of prosecution, if it does not extradite Mr. Habré': para 121; and see para 122(6).

The Court's reference to the 'legal interest' in protection of the rights involved, in support of which the Court provided a reference to its dictum in the *Barcelona Traction* case, suggests an acceptance of the same approach in respect of obligations *erga omnes*.

Part Three of the ILC Articles goes on to consider a number of related questions, for example, the consequences of invocation of responsibility by or against several States, circumstances such as waiver or delay where a State may be considered to have lost the right to invoke responsibility, as well as that ultimate form of invocation, the taking of countermeasures in response to an international wrongful act which remains unredressed and unremedied. Some of these issues are dealt with elsewhere in this book.

VI. FURTHER DEVELOPMENT OF THE LAW OF INTERNATIONAL RESPONSIBILITY

As we have seen, there has traditionally been a tendency to view international responsibility as, in the first place, essentially a bilateral matter, without wider consequences for others or for the international system as a whole, and, in the second place, as quintessentially an inter-State issue, separated from questions of the relations between States and individuals or corporations, or from the rather unaccountable world of international organizations. This approach works well enough for bilateral treaties between States or for breaches of general international law rules which have an essentially bilateral operation in the field of intergovernmental relations. But international law now contains a range of rules which cannot be broken down into bundles of bilateral relations between States but cover a much broader range. How can these be accommodated within the traditional structure of State responsibility? The attempt to develop the law beyond traditional paradigms was the greatest challenge facing the ILC, and constitutes one of the more fascinating fields of a rapidly developing—and yet precarious—international order. In the more than a decade and a half since the adoption of the Articles, at least some of the progressive steps proposed by the ILC are now becoming accepted.

REFERENCES

ALSTON, P (2005), *Non-State Actors and Human Rights* (Oxford: Oxford University Press).

BOLLECKER-STERN, B (1973), *Le préjudice dans la théorie de la responsabilité internationale* (Paris: Pedone).

CLAPHAM, A (2006), *Human Rights Obligations of Non-State Actors* (Oxford: Oxford University Press).

CRAWFORD, J (2002), *The International Law Commission's Articles on State Responsibility; Introduction, Text and Commentaries* (Cambridge: Cambridge University Press).

CRAWFORD, J (2013), *State Responsibility. The General Part* (Cambridge: Cambridge University Press).

CRAWFORD, J and MERTENSKÖTTER, P (2015), 'The Use of the ILC's Attribution Rules in Investment Arbitration', in M Kinnear et al (eds), *Building International Investment Law: The First 50 Years of ICSID* (The Hague: Kluwer Law International), p 27.

DE SCHUTTER, O (2006), *Transnational Corporations and Human Rights* (Oxford: Hart Publishing).

DUMBERRY, P (2006), 'New State Responsibility for Internationally Wrongful Acts by an Insurrectional Movement', 17(3) EJIL, 605.

EVANS, MD (2017), Blackstone's International Law Documents (13th edn, Oxford: Oxford University Press).

GRAY, C (1987), Judicial Remedies in International Law (Oxford: Clarendon Press).

JENNINGS, RY and WATTS, A (1992), Oppenheim's International Law (9th edn, London: Longman).

KLABBERS, J (2015), An Introduction to International Organizations Law (3rd edn, Cambridge: Cambridge University Press).

KOSKENNIEMI, M (2001), 'Solidarity Measures: State Responsibility as a New International Order?', 72 BYIL 337.

MORGENSTERN, F (1986), Legal Problems of International Organizations (Cambridge: Grotius).

OLLESON, S (2013), 'Internationally Wrongful Acts in the Domestic Courts: The Contribution of Domestic Courts to the Development of Customary International Law Relating to the Engagement of International Responsibility', 26 LJIL 615.

OLLESON, S (2016), 'Attribution in Investment Treaty Arbitration', (2016) 31 ICSID Review—FILJ 457.

PADDEU, F (2017), Justification and Excuse in International Law. Concept and Theory of General Defences (Cambridge: Cambridge University Press).

RATNER, SR (2001), 'Corporations and Human Rights: A Theory of Legal Responsibility', 111 Yale LJ 443.

RUBIN, AP (1998), The Law of Piracy (2nd edn, Irvington-on-Hudson, NY: Transnational Publishers).

SHELTON, D (2015), Remedies in International Human Rights Law (3rd edn, Oxford: Oxford University Press).

WELLENS, K (2002), Remedies against International Organizations (Cambridge: Cambridge University Press).

WITTICH, S (2013), 'Domestic Courts and the Content and Implementation of State Responsibility', 26 LJIL 643.

FURTHER READING

BODANSKY, D, CROOK, J, ROSENSTOCK, R, BROWN WEISS, E, BEDERMAN, DJ, SHELTON, D, CARON, DD, and CRAWFORD, J (2002), 'Symposium: The ILC's State Responsibility Articles', 96 AJIL 773–890: a collection of responses to the adoption of the ILC's Articles on State Responsibility.

CRAWFORD, J (2002), The International Law Commission's Articles on State Responsibility; Introduction, Text and Commentaries (Cambridge: Cambridge University Press): the ILC's Articles on State Responsibility and authoritative commentaries adopted in 2001, together with an introduction and analytical tools, including an index and table of cases.

CRAWFORD, J (2013), State Responsibility: The General Part (Cambridge: Cambridge University Press): a comprehensive account of the law and practice; appends the main texts.

CRAWFORD, J and OLLESON, S (2005), 'The Continuing Debate on a UN Convention on State Responsibility', 54 ICLQ 959: an account of the debate in the Sixth Committee of the General Assembly in late 2004 as to whether the ILC's Articles on State Responsibility should be transformed into a multilateral convention.

CRAWFORD, J, PELLET, A, and OLLESON, S (eds) (2010), The Law of International Responsibility (Oxford: Oxford University Press): a collection of essays by expert academics and practitioners, covering an overview of the entirety of the field of international responsibility.

DUPUY, P-M, NOLTE, G, SPINEDI, M, SICILIANOS, L-A, WYLER, E, TAMS, CJ, GATTINI, A, SCOBBIE, I, ALLAND, D, and KLEIN, P (2002), 'Symposium: Assessing the Work of the International Law Commission on State Responsibility', 13 *EJIL* 1037–256: a stimulating collection of essays on the ILC's Articles on State Responsibility, with particular emphasis on the 'serious breaches' provisions and the multilateral aspects of invocation.

OLLESON, S (2016), 'Attribution in Investment Treaty Arbitration', (2016) 31 *ICSID Review—FILJ* 457: an examination of the operation of the principles of attribution under the law of State responsibility in the specific context of investment treaty arbitration.

RAGAZZI, M (2005), *International Responsibility Today. Essays in Memory of Oscar Schachter* (Leiden: Nijhoff): a useful collection of 36 essays by specialists covering general and special issues in the field of responsibility.

WITTICH, S (2013), 'Domestic Courts and the Content and Implementation of State Responsibility', 26 *LJIL* 643.

WEBSITES

http://www.lcil.cam.ac.uk/projects/state-responsibility-project
Collection of materials on State responsibility, including the reports of the last Special Rapporteur, and various articles.

http://www.un.org/law/ilc
Official website of the International Law Commission, maintained by the United Nations Secretariat. Collection of materials on the codification of State responsibility by the Commission.

15

ISSUES OF ADMISSIBILITY AND THE LAW ON INTERNATIONAL RESPONSIBILITY

Phoebe Okowa

SUMMARY

This chapter examines the legal regime governing the admissibility of claims in international adjudication. A central element in the admissibility of claims is the requirement that a litigant should be able to establish a legal interest in respect of the claim brought before an international tribunal. Specific attention is therefore paid to the mechanisms for establishing a legal interest, drawing a distinction between claims brought by States in their own right and those on behalf of their nationals. The role of nationality is examined and the problems posed by competing claims in relation to multiple nationalities are explored. The unique nature of the problems raised in extending diplomatic protection to corporations and shareholding interests is considered in light of the jurisprudence of international tribunals. The emergence of a large category of obligations designed to protect community values and which do not fit within a private rights model pose particular problems for an international adjudication framework, which is largely bilateral in character. These categories remain ill-defined and the consequences of their breach are largely underdeveloped. Special consideration is therefore given to the perennial difficulties involved in establishing legal interest in the case of obligations *erga omnes*, designed to protect collective interests and therefore owed to a multiplicity of States. These difficulties, it is suggested, are compounded by the fact that the development of obligations *erga omnes* have not been accompanied by any discernible refinement of the mechanisms for their enforcement. The final section considers the extent to which the operation of the rule on exhaustion of local remedies may operate to affect the admissibility of a claim. The parameters of the rule are explored and circumstances when, as a matter of policy, it ought to be regarded as inapplicable are discussed.

I. INTRODUCTION

The legal basis for the imposition of responsibility as well as the excuses that may exonerate a State from responsibility are discussed in the previous chapter. The concern in this chapter is essentially twofold. First, to identify the State or States that could be described as having *locus standi* in relation to a given wrong. Second, to consider the application of other rules of international law that may operate to preclude the admissibility of a claim before an international tribunal even if a cause of action and legal interest are clearly established. Although the grounds for the imposition of responsibility and issues of admissibility generally tend to be treated as discrete topics in much of the literature, there is nevertheless a close relationship between them. The admissibility of a claim has a close relationship with the rule justifying the imposition of responsibility, for who has standing to sue in respect of a wrong is to a large extent determined by the nature and content of the obligation, the manner of breach, and the range of interests the obligation is designed to protect. As a preliminary matter, a litigant State must be able to establish that an obligation owed to it has been breached. In theory, where the obligation breached is designed to protect community values, it is easier for a claimant State to establish legal interest by demonstrating that it is within the zone of protection afforded by that obligation (Thirlway, 1995, pp 49–58; Crawford, Pellet, and Olleson, 2010, p 1024).[1] But as will be immediately apparent from the following discussion, the legal framework for protecting community obligations lacks intellectual coherence and the modalities for their implementation are fraught with practical difficulties.

II. LEGAL INTEREST AS A PREREQUISITE TO ADMISSIBILITY OF CLAIMS

In general, international law like most other legal systems insists that only those claimants who have a demonstrable interest may bring an action in respect of a wrong. The matter was considered at length in the *South West Africa* cases and it provides a good place to start the inquiry. The applicant States brought a claim before the International Court challenging the compatibility of South Africa's policy of apartheid in South West Africa with its obligations under the League Mandate. The International Court of Justice (ICJ) rejected the applicants' claim principally on the basis that they had no legal right or interest in respect of the subject matter of the dispute brought by them.[2] Ethiopia and Liberia had argued that South Africa's policy of racial discrimination in South West Africa was an express violation of its obligations as trustee under the League mandate. The Court took the view that the obligations, in respect of which Ethiopia and Liberia were bringing claims, were owed to the League of Nations and not to its individual members, and as such the applicant States had no *locus standi* in respect of the matter. Although the correctness of the interpretation of the mandate by the Court has been doubted (Dugard, 2004, para

---

[1] The practice of the ICJ unfortunately paints a different picture. In its jurisprudence, the Court has maintained a distinction between the existence of legal interest and the ability to invoke the jurisdictional provisions of the Court. The existence of a legal interest does not necessarily mean that a State will be entitled to bring a claim and other jurisdictional factors may operate to exclude the claim. See *East Timor* case (*Portugal v Australia*), *Judgment, ICJ Reports 1995*, p 90, para 29.

[2] *South West Africa, Second Phase, Judgment, ICJ Reports 1966*, p 6, para 99; see ILC Commentary to Draft Article 48 (para 7), Official Records of the General Assembly, Fifty-sixth Session, Supplement No 10 (A/56/10) Chapter V.

38), the point of principle has few detractors; there is a consensus that perhaps with the exception of *erga omnes*, only those who are designated as beneficiaries of international obligations have a right to enforce them.[3] In the *Nicaragua* case, the International Court denied that the USA could rely on alleged breaches of obligations which Nicaragua owed to the Organization of American States (OAS) as opposed to the USA as an individual member, as a justification for imposing countermeasures on Nicaragua. In the event, the obligations in question were found to be in the nature of a political pledge rather than a legal commitment. The Court nevertheless pointed out that:

> even supposing that such a political pledge had the force of a legal commitment it could not have justified the United States insisting on the fulfilment of a commitment made not directly towards the United States but towards the organisation, the latter alone being empowered to monitor the implementation.[4] In one sense, both the *Nicaragua* and *South West Africa* cases flow logically from the principle that organisations have a separate legal entity from their members and breaches of duties owed to them cannot be conflated with those owed to individual members.

A. RATIONALE OF INTERNATIONAL LAW RULES ON *LOCUS STANDI*

Several reasons may be detected in the various rules underpinning *locus standi* in international law. The first and most obvious can in part be explained by the nature of international law as a law primarily between States, and as a consequence only States in general have procedural capacity to bring an action before an international tribunal. Thus, except for those limited situations where individuals, corporations, or other legal entities have been granted access under existing treaties, they have no standing and their claims must be channelled through the State of their nationality.[5] In this respect, there is something artificial about international law rules on *locus standi*, for even when it is the individual who has been injured, the traditional view proceeds on the premise that it is the State of which that individual is a national that is wronged and who can therefore bring an action in respect of the wrong (Leigh, 1971, p 453; Crawford, 2012, p 702).

Second, general international law rules on standing reflect *the jus dispositivum* view of international law and in particular the role of international tribunals, this being primarily that of settling disputes between States on a private rights model. Although there has been a consistent jurisprudence recognizing that a large number of obligations do not fit into private rights model, in particular those designed to protect community interests, international law has tended to exclude standing where an applicant State's interest is a general vindication of community values.[6] A related rationale of the rules on *locus standi*, it could be argued, is to provide an orderly framework for the resolution of disputes and to avoid wherever possible overlapping claims or those that are entirely unmeritorious.

---

[3] *Barcelona Traction, Light and Power Company, Limited, Second Phase, Judgment, ICJ Reports 1970*, p 3, para 35. See also Crawford, 2013, p 542.

[4] *Military and Paramilitary Activities in and against Nicaragua (Nicaragua v United States of America), Merits, Judgment, ICJ Reports 1986*, p 14, para 262.

[5] The many jurisdictional issues that arise in this context are strictly speaking beyond the scope of the present inquiry and have been extensively dealt with in the literature on jurisdiction of international tribunals. See Fitzmaurice, 1986, pp 427–575; Rosenne, 1997.

[6] See *Barcelona Traction, Light and Power Company, Limited, Second Phase, Judgment, ICJ Reports 1970*, p 3 and *East Timor (Portugal v Australia), Judgment, ICJ Reports 1995*, p 90.

Enforcement through adjudication also serves a secondary purpose of making regimes credible and providing a systemic framework for holding parties to their bargains. Nationality in this context provides a convenient basis for channelling claims. The focus on nationality though is not without its flaws. It could be argued that the right of diplomatic protection lacks a democratic spirit at its core and only serves to perpetuate existing inequalities in the system of human rights protection. Those most at risk from violations of fundamental rights are the displaced, refugees, and stateless persons; in the absence of a progressive and generous interpretation of citizenship they are largely left without a remedy. Moreover, a considerable body of empirical evidence illustrates the gross inequality in the capacity of States to protect their citizens and there is nothing in the structure of international law to mitigate these inequalities.

Thirdly, the rules on admissibility attempt to strike a balance between the need for international oversight over the performance of obligations but also respect for the sovereignty of States, and that, as a result, international tribunals remain forums of last resort, only coming into play when a definitive outcome has proved impossible through national institutions. Thus, rules on exhaustion of local remedies can in part be explained by reference to the territorial character of jurisdiction. The decisions in the *Nottebohm*[7] and *Barcelona Traction* cases[8] also manifest a particular sensitivity to the right of the territorial State to deal with matters occurring on its territory.

The twenty-first century has witnessed a general retreat from the *jus positivum* view of international law and the acceptance of obligations said to reflect community values, protecting common interests and going beyond the bilateral character of international law. These obligations protecting extra-State interests do not fit within a bilateral or private rights framework and pose a particular challenge for the traditional rules on admissibility of claims. These obligations transcend individual State interests, and the need to protect them through international claims has long been recognized as necessary to protect the underlying community values.[9] The obligations, principally in the field of human rights, protection of the environment, and the preservation of peace and security, may affect the interests of the international community at large without affecting the interests of any one particular State.[10] Extended notions of *locus standi* have been proposed *de lege ferenda* in order to make the protection of these values credible. Thus, there is increasingly a presumption that all States have a general interest in the legality of actions that affect community interests, even if the precise implications are yet to be worked out.[11]

B. MODALITIES OF ESTABLISHING LEGAL INTEREST

Given international law's conception of standing as a vindication of primarily private rights, it comes as no surprise that for a claim to be admissible, the applicant State must demonstrate that it has a legal interest in the matter. At a general level, legal interest is

---

[7] *Nottebohm, Second Phase, Judgment, ICJ Reports 1955*, p 4.

[8] *Barcelona Traction, Light and Power Company, Limited, Second Phase, Judgment, ICJ Reports 1970*, p 3.

[9] See, for example, *SS 'Wimbledon', Judgments, 1923, PCIJ, Series A, No 1* in which the UK, France, Italy, and Japan were able to bring a claim against Germany for denying access to the Kiel Canal. Of the applicant States, Italy and Japan were not directly injured themselves but they were allowed to bring the claim because of the collective interests that all maritime States had in the Kiel Canal.

[10] Although there has been a general recognition of obligations *erga omnes*, there is not a single case in which an applicant State has successfully brought a claim designed to enforce community values.

[11] See ILC Articles on the Responsibility of States for Internationally Wrongful Acts (ARSIWA), Article 48; Crawford, 2013, p 370; Simma, 1994, p 217.

defined by reference to the obligation breached; not quite a distinct issue but part of the definition of the cause of action—the party to whom the obligation is owed is the party entitled to claim. In determining the *locus standi* of a State, a distinction is usually maintained between injury to direct interests and those that affect indirect interests (principally injury to nationals whether natural, corporate, or other legal entity recognized by municipal law). There is a presumption that State protection of its sovereign rights is inherent and a State must be taken to have a legal interest in respect of those wrongs that affect its direct interests. Although the distinction between direct and indirect interests is well established in the literature, and in the jurisprudence of international tribunals, the dividing line between them is not always easy to determine, especially with regard to mixed claims where there are elements of direct injury to a State's own interests as well as injury to its nationals (Meron, 1959, pp 87–8; Wittich, 2001, pp 121–87). In practice, it is accepted that damage to a State's warships, diplomatic missions, members of its armed forces, the executive (including the Head of State), and State property are examples of injuries which qualify as direct interests. Cases of direct injury to a State's interests are rare and, when they occur, hardly controversial.

III. THE BASES OF DIPLOMATIC PROTECTION

A. INDIRECT CLAIMS: DETERMINING NATIONALITY

Where injury is suffered by a natural person or other legal entity recognized by municipal law, the general view is that the right to bring a claim in respect of the wrong lies with the State of the victim's nationality. It is the bond of nationality that creates the necessary link between a State and the injury in respect of which a claim is brought.

In the *Mavrommatis* case, the Permanent Court observed that:

> It is an elementary principle of international law that a State is entitled to protect its subjects, when injured by acts contrary to international law committed by another State, from which they have been unable to obtain satisfaction through ordinary channels. By taking up the case of one of its subjects and by resorting to diplomatic protection or international judicial proceedings on his behalf, a State is in reality asserting its own rights—rights to ensure, in the person of its subjects, respect for the rules of international law.[12]

Since the exercise of diplomatic protection is generally viewed as the right of the State, the argument has consistently been made that reliance on the right is within the absolute discretion of States (Borchard, 1915, p 29; Oppenheim, 1992, p 934; Malanczuk, 1997, p 257; Dugard, 2000, p 213; ILA, Report of the 69th Conference, 2000; Crawford, 2013, p 571). It is further accepted that the decision whether to exercise the discretion or not is invariably influenced by political considerations rather than the legal merits of the particular claim. The point was made by the International Court when it noted that:

> within the limits prescribed by international law, a State may exercise diplomatic protection by whatever means and to whatever extent it thinks fit, for it is its own right that the State is asserting. Should the natural or legal person on whose behalf it is acting consider that their rights are not adequately protected, they have no remedy in international law. All they can do is resort to municipal law, if means are available, with a view to furthering their cause or obtaining redress. The municipal legislator may lay upon the State an obligation

---

[12] *Mavrommatis Palestine Concessions, Judgment No 2, 1924, PCIJ, Ser A, No 2,* p 12.

to protect its citizens abroad, and may also confer upon the national a right to demand the performance of that obligation, and clothe the right with corresponding sanctions. However, all these questions remain within the province of municipal law and do not affect the position internationally.

The State must be viewed as the sole judge to decide whether its protection will be granted, to what extent it is granted, and when it will cease. It retains in this respect a discretionary power the exercise of which may be determined by considerations of a political or other nature, unrelated to the merits of the particular case. Since the claim of the State is not identical with that of the individual or corporate person whose cause is espoused, the State enjoys complete freedom of action.[13] These propositions have been confirmed in the subsequent case law of the International Court[14] and virtually all Commonwealth jurisdictions that have considered the matter. (McLachlan, 2014, p 358)

In *Abbasi* v *Secretary of State for Foreign and Commonwealth Affairs*,[15] the applicant, who was detained by the US authorities at Guantánamo Bay, sought judicial review to compel the UK Foreign Office to take up his case and make appropriate representations on his behalf to the US government. In the alternative, he asked that the UK government be compelled to give an explanation as to why representations on his behalf had not been undertaken. The English Court of Appeal, after an extended review of authorities, confirmed the orthodox position that diplomatic protection was a right of States and that it did not as such give rise to an enforceable duty under English law. However, it noted that this discretion was subject to judicial oversight, especially if it could be shown that the decision was irrational or contrary to the rules of natural justice.

It has always been maintained that because the right is discretionary, there is in principle no obligation on the part of the State to transmit the damages obtained to any of the individuals concerned. However, it is suggested that the tectonic shift in favour of individual rights of late make it very likely that such a proposition is no longer tenable in most democratic States; indeed, there is little evidence that States have in practice withheld remedies from nationals on whose behalf they were claiming. Whatever may be the position in strict law, it is arguable that there is at least a moral duty on the State to transmit compensation. Furthermore, insofar as the right of protection is characterized as that of the State, the State espousing a claim may choose to do so even in the face of opposition from the injured individual. It is principally for this reason that those tribunals and jurists who have considered the issue have rejected the so-called *Calvo clause*, the terms of which allowed certain natural and corporate persons to waive the right of diplomatic protection (Shea, 1955).

The discretionary character of diplomatic protection has in recent years been subjected to trenchant criticism, as incompatible with an international system committed to human rights. It has therefore been proposed that the right of diplomatic protection should be seen as a legal duty exercisable by the State on behalf of the injured individual.[16] This position finds some support in national constitutions which provide for a right of protection

---

[13] *Barcelona Traction, Light and Power Company, Limited, Second Phase, Judgment, ICJ Reports 1970*, p 3, paras 78–9.

[14] *LaGrand (Germany v United States of America), Merits, Judgment, ICJ Reports 2001*, p 466

[15] *Abbasi v Sec of Foreign and Commonwealth Affairs and Sec of Home Office* [2002] EWCA Civ 1598, 6 November 2002.

[16] Bennouna, *Preliminary Report on Diplomatic Protection*, 1998, paras 34–7, 65–6; Dugard, 2000, paras 17 and 61–74.

which is enforceable even against the State of which the person is a national.[17] In practice though, constitutional entrenchment does not radically improve the position of aggrieved individuals. The right as interpreted in domestic cases still grants the executive a wide discretion and in many cases the individual is entitled to no more than an expectation that his request for diplomatic representation will be treated fairly by the executive (McLachlan, 2014, pp 363–74). For instance, in *Kaunda and others v President of the Republic of South Africa and others*[18] the South African Constitutional Court recognized that the right to request diplomatic protection was a constitutional entitlement under the South Africa constitution but it went on to hold that its actual exercise was a matter of foreign policy and therefore within the discretion of the executive branch. The decision in *Kaunda* has been confirmed in two subsequent decisions of the Supreme Court of South Africa. In *Rootman v President of the Republic of South Africa*,[19] the Supreme Court refused a request by the applicant that the South African government be compelled to take steps to assist him in securing the execution of a money judgment in his favour, granted by the Pretoria High Court, against the government of the Democratic Republic of Congo (DRC). The applicant had argued that the rule of law created an expectation that the State would assist a citizen to enforce his or her rights. The Court, however, noted that although the State may engage in diplomatic negotiations with a foreign State to secure the rights of its citizens, it could not be compelled to do so. The securing of individual rights has to be weighed against other competing factors such as the overriding interests of the State which may militate against diplomatic protection. Customary international law also permits States to exclude whole groups of nationals from diplomatic protection, such as deserters and persons serving in foreign armed forces.

In *Omar Khadr v The Prime Minister of Canada*, the applicant argued that the failure of the Canadian government to make representations to the US government that he be released from Guantánamo Bay was a violation of his rights under the Canadian Charter of Rights and Freedoms. This was contested by the Canadian government, which argued that it had an 'unfettered discretion to decide whether to request the return of a Canadian citizen detained in a foreign country, this being a matter within its exclusive authority to conduct foreign affairs'. The Court was therefore called upon to examine whether Canada had a legal duty to protect Mr Khadr and what the ambit of that duty might be. The Canadian Supreme Court concluded that, in general, the right of protection was not enforceable as it fell within the executive's conduct of foreign policy. However, the Court would intervene

---

[17] Examples include the constitutions of Albania, Belarus, Bosnia and Herzegovina, Bulgaria, Cambodia, China, Croatia, Estonia, Georgia, Guyana, Hungary, Italy, Kazakhstan, Lao People's Democratic Republic, Latvia, Lithuania, Poland, Portugal, Republic of Korea, Romania, Russian Federation, Spain, the Former Yugoslav Republic of Macedonia, Turkey, Ukraine, Vietnam, and Yugoslavia. See Dugard, 2000, para 80.

[18] *Kaunda and others v President of the Republic of South Africa and others*, Case CCT 23/04, 2005 (4) SA 235 (CC).

[19] *Rootman v President of the Republic of South Africa*, Case 016/06, [2006] SCA 80 (RSA). See also *Van Zyl v Government of the Republic of South Africa*, Case 170/06, [2007] SCA 109 (RSA), rejecting the applicant's argument that they had a constitutional right to diplomatic protection and the government a corresponding obligation to provide such protection, including the submission of claims to international arbitration or adjudication before the international court. The court, although conceding that the exercise of diplomatic protection remained the prerogative of state, was prepared to accept that this may in fact entail a duty to exercise such protection where the fundamental rights of the citizen was involved. In deciding whether or not to take up the case of one of its nationals, the government was expected to act rationally. The court also noted that as the right of diplomatic protection was derived from the constitution as an aspect of citizenship, the South African government could not be expected to intervene where the wrong had been done not to South African citizens but to a foreign company in respect of which they had an interest.

if the government's position was irrational or contrary to a legitimate expectation. The Court concluded that in the specific circumstances of the case, the failure to exercise diplomatic protection was a violation of the applicant's rights to life, liberty, and security of the person.[20] The Supreme Court explained that the rule of law entailed an expectation that all government action was potentially subject to the Charter and the individual rights which it guaranteed. The Crown prerogative in the conduct of foreign affairs was also subject to the Charter.[21]

The decisions of national courts on these constitutional provisions support the thesis that general international law as it stands does not contain an enforceable legal duty of diplomatic protection.[22] Human rights obligations and treaties protecting the economic interests of individuals have nevertheless substantially eroded the centrality of diplomatic protection as a mechanism for the protection of aggrieved individuals by creating directly enforceable rights even as against the State of which the individual is a national.[23] Moreover, the right of diplomatic protection, even when provided for in a constitution, is by its own terms self-limiting—it only extends to nationals and expressly excludes persons lacking formal ties of citizenship. In *Al-Rawi*, the English Court of Appeal accepted that international law on nationality decides who is entitled to diplomatic protection and therefore a person who is not a British national is not entitled to the protection of the State. The arguments that a State has a duty to secure fundamental rights for all those on its territory failed on the premise that the alleged violations occurred extra-territorially in circumstances where the State was not complicit. As part of the progressive development of international law, ILC Draft Article 8(2) had extended the right of diplomatic protection to refugees when that person, 'at the date of injury and at the date of the official presentation of the claim is lawfully and habitually resident in that state'. The Court of Appeal in *Al-Rawi* considered this argument but found it unpersuasive since the alleged harm to Al-Rawi occurred extra-territorially and in circumstances when the UK government was not complicit.[24]

Indeed, for many years, it was widely assumed that the centrality of the law on diplomatic protection would quietly fall into desuetude. In relation to protection of foreign investments, many States and corporations were increasingly realizing that their interests were better protected through bilateral investment treaties. The consensus around free market economics also created a more favourable environment for foreign investments and less interest in the processes of expropriation. Furthermore, it was argued that broad

---

[20] *Omar Khadr v The Prime Minister of Canada* 2009 FCA 246.

[21] However, in *Ilaşcu and Others v Moldova and Russia* [GC], no 48787/99, ECHR *2004-VII* the European Court of Human Rights took the view that duty to make representations including judicial claims may be legally mandatory as a consequence of a State's obligations in Article 1 of the ECHR to 'secure to everyone within its jurisdiction' the rights guaranteed by the convention. In relation to the detention of the applicants in the Transdniestrian Republic controlled by the separatists, the Court took the view that Moldova was under an obligation to make representations to Russia and the separatists to try and secure their release. Failure to do so was a violation of the obligations in Article 1 of the ECHR.

[22] *Kaunda and others v President of the Republic of South Africa and others*, Case CCT 23/04, 2005 (4) SA 235 (CC). In the *Hess Decision*, BverfGE, 55, 349, 90 ILR 386, the German Federal Constitutional Court upheld the existence of a federal constitutional right to diplomatic protection but denied that it was required by customary international law. See also *Abbasi v Sec of Foreign and Commonwealth Affairs and Sec of Home Office* [2002] EWCA Civ 1598, 6 November 2002. Federal Court of Australia in *Hicks v Ruddock* [2007] FCA 299, para 93, did not rule out the possibility that a right of diplomatic protection may in fact be enforceable.

[23] *LaGrand (Germany v United States of America), Merits, Judgment, ICJ Reports 2001*, p 466.

[24] *Al-Rawi and Others v The Secretary of State for Foreign and Commonwealth Affairs* [2006] EWCA Civ 1279.

acceptance of the universality of human rights rendered any special regimes of protection redundant; but these arguments of redundancy are increasingly open to challenge. There has been a marked increase in the disregard for due process requirements in the fight against terrorism even by democracies otherwise committed to the rule of law. It is not surprising that the largest number of cases challenging detention orders and seeking diplomatic protection have been from detainees held by the United States at Guantánamo Bay (McLachlan, 2014, pp 358–71).

It is suggested that for all its shortcomings, diplomatic protection continues to play an important role as a default mechanism for the enforcement of claims when no other remedies are available. A better view, it is suggested, is to see diplomatic protection and enforcement mechanisms in human rights instruments as operating in parallel, serving related—but at times discrete—objectives. For example, vindication of the rule of law may require that an action be brought on the international plane by a State even in the face of opposition by the wronged individual (Brierly, 1928, p 48; Dugard, 2000, para 73; Crawford, 2013, pp 584–7). It must also be accepted that States may have wider concerns going beyond the immediate interests of the wronged individual; these interests will at times be better served by exercising the discretion not to bring an action on the international plane. Where the exercise of its discretion results in the denial of a fundamental right, it is suggested that the right of the State should be subordinated to the rights of the aggrieved individual. The existence of a human rights obligation, it is suggested, creates a strong expectation that the State will exercise its discretion in support of the aggrieved individual.

B. ESTABLISHING NATIONALITY FOR PURPOSES OF DIPLOMATIC PROTECTION

1. Natural persons

It is generally accepted that the conferment of nationality is prima facie a matter which falls within the jurisdiction of a State as an attribute of its sovereignty, and in general there is a presumption that nationality granted by a State in accordance with its domestic law is valid for all purposes, including entitlement to bring a claim on the international plane. There is nevertheless considerable, if not universal, support for the view that the validity of any nationality so conferred on the international plane is a question of international law, and will only be opposable to other States if it has been granted in a manner that conforms to international law criteria.[25] In particular, for nationality to provide a valid basis for the exercise of diplomatic protection, it must have been granted in a manner consistent with principles of international law. For this reason, a grant of nationality may be disregarded on the international plane or treated as a nullity, if it has been made in excess of jurisdictional limits placed by international law, such as the extension of nationality laws to foreigners who owe no allegiance to the State granting nationality. Dugard has also suggested that international law retains a reserve power to disregard nationality laws that are discriminatory in character, or inconsistent with fundamental principles of human rights.[26] Most authorities also agree that nationality will be invalid if it has been acquired *mala fides*, or on the basis of a tenuous connection, such as extending nationality laws to aliens in transit.[27]

---

[25] See *Nottebohm, Second Phase, Judgment, ICJ Reports 1955*, p 4.

[26] According to Dugard, nationality laws should be disregarded if they discriminate on the basis of race, gender, or religious affiliation. Dugard, 2000, para 104. See also Oppenheim, 1992, pp 856 and 874; Brownlie, 2008, pp 386 and 388.

[27] Dugard, 2000, para 104; Littlefield, 2009, pp 1461–82.

The precise role of international law in determining nationality for purposes of dip-lomatic protection is, however, not free from controversy (Crawford, 2013, pp 574–80). In general, two diametrically opposed positions seem to have emerged in the literature. The first proceeds on the premise that questions of nationality must be settled by way of *renvoi* to municipal law, and in principle the validity of nationality conferred by a State in accordance with the requirements of its internal law must be treated as conclusive since international law does not as such have a law on nationality.[28] The second position denies conclusiveness to municipal law criteria, and takes as its starting point the view that the validity of nationality on the international plane is a question of international law. In par-ticular, for nationality to be valid on the international plane it must be firmly grounded on the existence of a genuine link between the claimant State and the individual on whose behalf he claims (Brownlie, 2008, p 398; Fitzmaurice, 1957, pp 196–201).

Proponents of the second position argue that although the grant of nationality is a pre-rogative of States and therefore a question of domestic law, like most unilateral acts per-formed on the municipal plane, questions of ultimate validity on the international plane must be determined by reference to international standards if the rule of law is to be main-tained.[29] This position received explicit support in Article 1 of the 1930 Hague Convention on Certain Questions Relating to the Conflict of Nationality Laws, which provided that '[i]t is for each State to determine under its own law who are its nationals'—but with the proviso that:

> This law shall be recognized by other States in so far as it is consistent with international conventions, international custom, and the principles of law generally recognized with regard to nationality.[30]

Although most writers agree that international law must retain some quality control in matters of nationality, the precise nature of this oversight is the subject matter of disagree-ment. There is consensus that international law must retain a reserve power to disregard nationality claims that are fraudulent in origin, discriminatory, or in clear violation of gen-erally accepted jurisdictional principles. Beyond that, it is controversial whether—at least in the context of diplomatic protection—international law requires that there should be a genuine or effective link between the State and the national on whose behalf it is claiming (Crawford, *Brownlie's Principles*, 2012, p 706).

2. The requirement of the genuine link

In the *Nottebohm* case the International Court was of the view that for nationality to be a valid basis of diplomatic protection on the international plane, it must be based on a genuine link between the wronged individual and the State on whose behalf it was claim-ing. It said that:

> A State cannot claim that the rules [pertaining to the acquisition of nationality] which it has thus laid down are entitled to recognition by another State unless it has acted in conformity with this general aim of making the legal bond of nationality accord with the individual's genuine connection with the State which assumes the defence of its citizens by means of protection as against other States.

---

[28] *Nottebohm* case, *Second Phase, Judgment, ICJ Reports 1955*, p 4, Dissenting Opinions of Judges Klaestad (p 30), Reid (p 42), and Guggenheim (p 54).

[29] *Flegenheimer Claim* (1958) 25 ILR 91, 96–112; Oppenheim, 1992, p 855.

[30] 179 LNTS 89.

The Court listed the following as indispensable elements of valid nationality for purposes of diplomatic protection:

> A legal bond having as its basis a social fact of attachment, a genuine connection of existence and sentiments, together with the existence of reciprocal rights and duties. It may be said to constitute a juridical expression of the fact that the individual upon whom it is conferred, either directly by the law or as a result of an act of the authorities, is in fact more closely connected with the population of the State conferring nationality than with that of any other State.[31]

In State and arbitral practice, the requirement of a genuine link was not without precedent, and had been applied to cases of diplomatic protection involving dual or multiple nationality as a mechanism for prioritizing the claim of the State with the most effective connection (Brownlie, 2008, p 407). In the *Nottebohm* case, the Court refused to confine its application to those situations. The majority were of the view that a genuine link was a general requirement, a necessary condition for all claims grounded on nationality.[32]

This decision has been controversial and in the literature and subsequent judicial decisions attempts have been made either to distinguish it, or to limit its application to the facts of the case. In the *Flegenheimer* case, the Italian-USA Commission confined the application of the genuine link requirement to cases involving dual nationals.[33] In the *Barcelona Traction* case, the International Court refused to extend the genuine link requirement to corporations, and further, refrained from expressing an opinion on the correctness of the genuine link requirement as a matter of general international law.[34] A number of reasons have been advanced in support of the view that the *Nottebohm* case was not laying down general rules of international law applicable to all cases of nationality. First, there was considerable evidence before the Court that the processes of naturalization by which Nottebohm had acquired his citizenship were probably in bad faith. Dugard has therefore suggested that finding the links between Nottebohm and Liechtenstein to be tenuous provided the Court with a convenient excuse to avoid acknowledging a nationality claim that was tainted by bad faith without having to pass judgment on a government's competence to confer nationality under its own domestic law (Dugard, 2000, para 108).

Secondly, there is no doubt that the Court was influenced by the unique factual context of the dispute. Nottebohm's links with Guatemala were close and long-standing, spanning over a period of some 34 years. On the other hand his connections with Liechtenstein were weak and transitory and, given the circumstances, the Court thought it inequitable to allow Liechtenstein to exercise diplomatic protection as against Guatemala.[35] It is for this reason that in much of the subsequent literature the argument has been made that the Court was not dealing with the question of the validity of Nottebohm's application as against the whole world but more specifically against Guatemala. Indeed many authorities have doubted whether the Court would have reached the same conclusion if the case had been brought by Liechtenstein against some third State with whom Nottebohm had no connection (Crawford, 2013, p 574; Harris, 1998, p 594).

---

[31] *Nottebohm, Second Phase, Judgment, ICJ Reports 1955*, p 4 at p 23.
[32] Ibid.
[33] *Flegenheimer Claim* (1958), 25 ILR, 148–50.
[34] *Barcelona Traction, Light and Power Company, Limited, Second Phase, Judgment, ICJ Reports 1970*, p 3, para 70.
[35] *Nottebohm, Second Phase, Judgment, ICJ Reports 1955*, p 4 at p 26.

It is also possible to argue that although in formal terms the Court was faced with a claim of a person possessing only one nationality, it approached the case as if Nottebohm was a national of both States but with his real and effective nationality being that of Guatemala. If this were so, the *Nottebohm* decision is in keeping with the long-held view that where a person possesses two nationalities, it is the effective nationality that is determinant[36] and the State of second nationality cannot bring a claim against the State of effective first nationality where a genuine link exists.

The Court's formal conclusion that nationality must be supported by a 'genuine link' in order to be opposable in the field of diplomatic protection has also been criticized for two reasons. First, it has been argued that as a matter of policy, it is desirable that the test for nationality be capable of objective determination. The requirement of a genuine link introduces into this area of law a vague and uncertain test and is therefore open to abuse.[37] Second, that by denying the validity of certain forms of nationality, it has the practical effect of severely restricting the scope of diplomatic protection. It has been argued that it is undesirable as a matter of policy that a wrong should go without redress simply because the links between the State and the national on whose behalf he is claiming are weak.[38] In its decision in the *Ahmadou Sadio Diallo* case,[39] the International Court was not particularly troubled by the genuine link requirement when treating as admissible Guinea's claims against the Democratic Republic of Congo (DRC). Guinea had instituted proceedings by way of diplomatic protection on behalf of Ahmadou Sadio Diallo, a businessman of Guinean nationality who had been resident in the DRC for 32 years. His connections with Guinea were at best tenuous, yet the Court's approach to the nationality question was in marked contrast to that taken in the *Nottebohm* case.[40] That Guinea was able to bring this action without any challenge by the respondent State or adverse comment by the Court is a further indication of the prevailing uncertainty as to the exact reach of the 'genuine link' requirement. Until his expulsion from the DRC, it appears that all of Mr Diallo's links for a period of 32 years were with that State—a period not dissimilar to the 34-year link between Nottebohm and Guatemala in the *Nottebohm* case. The *Diallo* decision lends some support to the view that the *Nottebohm* decision should be confined to its own facts and not treated as laying down rules of general application.[41]

3. Some conclusions

Notwithstanding the authoritative decision of the majority judgment in the *Nottebohm* case, there is no general support for the genuine link requirement in State practice. This is not to say that there is no role for international law in matters of nationality. A limited reserve power to exclude certain nationality claims is generally argued for in cases of manifest fraud, instances where nationality has been extended in bad faith, or where the grant of nationality is incompatible with fundamental principles, such as those prohibiting racial discrimination (Crawford, 2012, p 706).

---

[36] *Canevaro* case (Permanent Court of Arbitration) (1912) 11 *RIAA* 397; *Merge* claim (1955) 22 ILR 443; *Esphanian* v *Bank Tejarat* (1983) 2 Iran-USCTR 157.

[37] Dissenting Opinion of Judge Reid, *Nottebohm, Second Phase, Judgment, ICJ Reports 1955*, p 4 at p 46.

[38] See Dissenting Opinion of Judge ad hoc Guggenheim, pp 63–4 and see Brownlie, 2008, pp 417–18.

[39] *Ahmadou Sadio Diallo (Republic of Guinea* v *Democratic Republic of Congo), Preliminary Objections*, Judgment of 24 May 2007.

[40] Ibid, para 41. Although it is perhaps significant that Mr Diallo, unlike Nottebohm, was born in Guinea of Guinean parents and lived there for his first 17 years. See application instituting proceedings, p 31.

[41] For the exercise of diplomatic protection in the absence of a genuine link see *LaGrand (Germany* v *United States of America), Merits, Judgment, ICJ Reports 2001*, p 466. See also Douglas, 2009, p 313; Okowa, 2008.

C. THE NATIONALITY OF CORPORATIONS

As in the case of individuals, international law proceeds on the premise that it is the State of which it is a national which may exercise diplomatic protection on behalf of a company. The general difficulty in this area is in deciding what criteria may be employed to determine the nationality of corporations. The law is not helped by the existence of largely contradictory and incompatible principles in both the literature and in the jurisprudence of international tribunals.

In the *Barcelona Traction* case, the International Court concluded that the nationality of a company had to be determined by reference to the laws of the State in which it was incorporated or had its registered office. The majority were of the view that the simple fact of incorporation under the law of a State was conclusive. Moreover, the majority thought that it was not necessary to lift the corporate veil in order to determine the economic reality of a company, even if this indicated that it had links with a State other than that of incorporation. The Court thus denied Belgium the right to bring an action in respect of wrongs done to a Canadian company, in circumstances where the majority of the shareholders were Belgian. In rejecting Belgium's claim, the Court noted that a company, as an institution of municipal law, was an entity distinct from its shareholders. As such, where a wrong was done to the company, while the interests of the shareholders might be affected it was the company alone that had the right to maintain an action in international law. It noted that:

> whenever shareholder's interests are harmed by an act done to the company, it is to the latter that he must look to institute appropriate action; for although two separate entities may have suffered from the same wrong, it is only one entity whose rights have been infringed.[42]

However, the majority of the Court thought there were a number of instances in which the State of which the shareholders were nationals might be entitled to bring a claim on the international plane. This included those situations where the direct rights of shareholders were affected. Examples given by the Court included: (a) their rights to dividends; (b) the right to attend and vote at general meetings; and (c) the right to share in the assets of the company after liquidation.[43]

Some judges thought that shareholders may be entitled to diplomatic protection in cases where the company had the nationality of the respondent State. The Court refrained from expressing an opinion on the correctness of this proposition, noting that the issue did not arise on the facts of the case since it was Canada, not Spain, which was the country of nationality of the company.[44] However, the correctness of the proposition is in any event open to challenge. First, it ignores the traditional rule that a State is not guilty of violating international law when it harms one of its own nationals.[45] Secondly, it is difficult to reconcile it with the argument advanced by the majority that, when a wrong is done to a company, the interests of the shareholders may be affected but only the company has rights which are capable of legal protection. If shareholders are entitled to protection in the situation where the wrong is done to the company by the state of incorporation and therefore to its own national, what is the precise legal basis of the protection? Is there a process here by which mere interests are transformed into rights capable of legal protection?

---

[42] *Barcelona Traction, Light and Power Company, Limited, Second Phase, Judgment, ICJ Reports 1970*, p 3, para 44.   [43] Ibid, para 47. See also Lowe, 2002, p 275; Watts, 1996, p 435.
[44] Ibid, para 92. There is, however, support for this view in the jurisprudence of the Iran-USA Claims tribunal, eg *Starrett Housing Corporation et al v Government of the Islamic Republic of Iran et al* (1983) 4 Iran-USCTR 122.   [45] See ibid, Separate Opinion of Judge Jessup, p 162 at p 192, para 52.

The Court also thought that shareholders may be entitled to protection where the company had ceased to exist.[46] On the facts, the Court took the view that although the Barcelona Traction Company was in receivership, it was formally still in existence, and for this reason Belgium could not exercise protection on behalf of the shareholders. Other judges were prepared to extend diplomatic protection in those instances where, although a company was still formally in existence, it had become practically paralysed.[47]

The Court advanced some policy-based justifications to support its conclusions.[48] In rejecting the claims of Belgium, the Court denied that shareholders were vested with any general right of protection. It noted that extension of protection to shareholders, by exposing the allegedly wrong-doing State to a wide range of claimants, could introduce an element of uncertainty and insecurity in international economic relations. The Court was also concerned with the practical difficulty of ascertaining shareholding interests since such shares frequently change hands, and in many instances it could be difficult to determine which State was entitled to exercise protection, especially where the nominee and beneficiaries were from different States.[49] Moreover, given the fluid character of the shares, ascertaining the legal interest may be particularly difficult, since for a right of protection to exist nationality must be continuous (a point examined subsequently). In the *Barcelona Traction* case itself, there was some doubt whether the Belgian interest in the shares had been continuous and in particular whether Belgium could have satisfied the test at the time of the injury. The decision is therefore an unequivocal authority in support of the view that, when a company is injured, it is the national State of the company alone that may bring an action and shareholders as a category are not entitled to diplomatic protection. However, it is clear that some judges were prepared to extend protection to shareholders. Moreover, a number of them favoured a different test for corporations and would have applied the genuine link test as formulated in the *Nottebohm* case, with the result that the State of incorporation would not have an automatic right of protection in the absence of some tangible connection. Such a genuine link could be demonstrated by proving that the majority of shareholders were from the State asserting the right of diplomatic protection. Furthermore, there is evidence that in practice, States have been prepared to extend diplomatic protection to shareholding interests in foreign corporations, and such a right has been unequivocally advocated by the ILA in its 2000 report on the law of diplomatic protection (Douglas, 2009, p 397). There is also evidence that States have been reluctant to extend protection to companies incorporated in their territory in the absence of substantial link with the national economy. However, the law in this area cannot be stated with certainty. In the *Oil Platforms* case, Iran denied that the USA had the right as a matter of international law to extend diplomatic protection to US-flagged but foreign-owned merchant ships, on the basis that there was an absence of a genuine link between the ships and the US government as required by international law.[50] The Court's judgment, however, does not suggest that it was particularly troubled by the absence of a genuine link with the USA.[51]

---

[46] Ibid, paras 64–8.

[47] See, eg, ibid, Separate Opinion of Judge Fitzmaurice, p 65 at pp 72–5, paras 14–20.

[48] Ibid, paras 94, 96.

[49] There was some evidence before the Court that the ultimate beneficiaries of the shareholding interest in the *Barcelona Traction* case were themselves non-Belgian.

[50] See *ICJ Pleadings, Oil Platforms (Islamic Republic of Iran v United States of America)*, Reply and Defence to Counter Claim submitted by the Islamic Republic of Iran, vol I, pp 202–14 (10 March 1999).

[51] *Oil Platforms (Islamic Republic of Iran v United States of America)*, Judgment, ICJ Reports 2003, p 161, *passim*.

The protection of corporations and shareholding interests received extended consideration by the ICJ in the *Case Concerning Ahmadou Diallo*, its first significant decision on this point since the *Barcelona Traction* case.[52] Mr Diallo, it will be recalled, had been settled in Zaire for 32 years. During this time, he had established two companies which were at the centre of the dispute: Africom-Zaire and Africontainers-Zaire. In the course of their business dealings, the DRC, as well as several mining and oil companies operating in the DRC, became indebted to Mr Diallo's companies. The attempts by Mr Diallo and his companies to sue, and recover the monies owed, received unfavourable treatment from the Congolese authorities and his attempts at litigation in the Congolese courts were largely fruitless. Guinea argued that the decision of the Congolese authorities to expel Mr Diallo in November 1995 was taken in order to irrevocably frustrate his efforts to enforce a judgment obtained by him against Zaire Shell for the sum of 60 billion dollars. The DRC raised a number of preliminary objections. It argued that Guinea lacked standing to bring the application, insofar as it related to wrongs allegedly done to Africom-Zaire and Africontainers-Zaire, these being Congolese companies. The DRC relied directly on the *Barcelona Traction* case in support of its arguments that the two companies were corporations under Zairean law, with rights distinct and separate from those of Mr Diallo, a shareholder. DRC argued that positive international law did not entitle a State to bring an action in respect of a wrong done to a shareholder in a company registered in another State. It further denied that international law recognized a process of 'substitution' whereby the rights of a company could be assigned to a shareholder for purposes of litigation, when the State whose responsibility is at issue is also the national State of the company.

The Court accepted that that Mr Diallo's direct rights as a shareholder in the two companies were affected and as a result Guinea had *locus standi* to bring the claims. It drew a distinction between Mr Diallo's rights and those of the company, and concluded that Guinea as the national State was entitled to exercise diplomatic protection in relation to his shareholding interests. The right to protect shareholders' direct interests was explicitly recognized by the majority in the *Barcelona Traction* case.

It was previously noted that in its judgment in the *Barcelona Traction* case, the ICJ left unresolved the question of whether shareholders were entitled to diplomatic protection if the company had the nationality of the wrong-doing State. In the *Diallo* case, Guinea's third claim rested squarely on the alleged existence of this exception, claiming a right of diplomatic protection by way of substitution on the ground that the wrong-doing State was the State of nationality of Africom-Zaire and Africontainers-Zaire, the companies concerned.

The Court categorically denied the existence of this exception as a matter of customary international law.[53] In support of its claim for a right of diplomatic protection by way of substitution, Guinea had relied on arbitral awards, decisions of the European Commission on Human Rights, ICSID jurisprudence, and bilateral treaties for the promotion and protection of investment disputes, which had recognized protection of shareholding interests, where the respondent State was also the national State of the company (Douglas, 2009, p 397). The Court regarded these arbitral awards and treaty provisions as *lex specialis*, stating that they did not support a general right of diplomatic protection by way of substitution.[54]

---

[52] *Ahmadou Sadio Diallo (Republic of Guinea v Democratic Republic of Congo), Preliminary Objections,* Judgment of 24 May 2007.

[53] Ibid, para 89. This aspect of the judgment was followed by the South African Supreme Court in *Van Zyl v Government of the Republic of South Africa*, Case 170/06, [2007] SCA 109 (RSA).

[54] Ibid, para 90.

It distinguished its earlier decision in the *Elettronica Sicula* case, where a chamber of the Court had allowed the USA to bring a claim in respect of a wrong done to an Italian company, the shares of which were held by two American corporations,[55] on the grounds that it was not based on general international law but on treaty provisions which allowed protection of shareholding interests in the circumstances that had arisen.

In its Draft Articles on Diplomatic Protection, the ILC had considered a more limited exception, allowing protection of shareholding interests only where a company's incorporation in a respondent State was a mandatory condition of doing business in that country. The Court noted that, on the facts before it, there was no evidence that Africom-Zaire and Africontainers-Zaire had been incorporated in Zaire (DRC) as a condition of doing business there. It therefore expressed no opinion on the validity of the ILC's proposed exception as a matter of customary law.

Thus, more than 40 years after its landmark decision in the *Barcelona Traction* case, the Court has reaffirmed that judgment in almost all respects. The significance of the Court's judgment should not, however, be exaggerated. The Court itself noted that the role of diplomatic protection has largely fallen into disuse since most issues relating to diplomatic protection of corporations and shareholding interests are now dealt with comprehensively in international treaties.[56] The significant delays that accompany claims arising by way of diplomatic protection also account for the lack of interest in this process. The litigation in the *Barcelona Traction* case lasted almost two decades, while in the *Diallo* case, it took more than ten years to reach the final judgment.

D. APPLYING THE NATIONALITY RULE

1. Nationality must be continuous

To the extent that the State exercising the right of diplomatic protection is acting on its own behalf and not as agent of the injured national, it is generally said to be a requirement that the nationality must be continuous. This is logical, since it is the bond of nationality which establishes the State's interest in the claim. Thus the claim must belong to a person or group of persons, having the nationality of the claimant State from the time of the injury until the making of the award. Therefore, in cases of subrogation and assignment, it is arguable that the nominee or assignee should have the same nationality as the original holder of the title. Many authorities nevertheless state that the rule should have no application where there has been a forced or involuntary change of nationality, for instance through a process of State succession or changes in a State's frontiers (Crawford, *Brownlie's Principles*, 2012, p 703; Crawford, 2013, p 577). The argument has also been made that the rule should be applied flexibly where the protection of financial interests is at issue as these frequently change hands and the ties of nationality are unlikely to be of much significance. It is also suggested that the rule should have no application in proceedings which have as their object the protection of fundamental human rights, although this may largely stem from independent duties on the State to secure the human rights of all those on its territory and not a logical application of the law on diplomatic protection to serious cases.

2. Diplomatic protection and the problem of multiple nationality

Cases of multiple nationalities present particular problems, for they involve decisions concerning which of the potentially competing claimants should be entitled to exercise

---

[55] *Elettronica Sicula SpA (ELSI), Judgment, ICJ Reports 1989*, p 15.
[56] Ibid, para 88.

diplomatic protection. They also involve the difficulty of deciding whether one State of nationality can maintain a claim against a second State of nationality. A number of rules have emerged in State practice to deal specifically with such problems.

Two broad principles are widely accepted as regulating diplomatic protection in this area. First, diplomatic protection of dual or multiple nationals is governed by the principle of real or dominant nationality, and where there is a conflict, the nationality based on an effective link is usually treated as decisive.[57] This principle has been explicitly endorsed in the jurisprudence of international tribunals, including the Iran-USA Claims Tribunal.[58] It has also been adopted without qualification in claims brought before the UN Compensation Commission, which considered claims against Iraq arising out of its invasion of Kuwait in 1991:[59] applying the effective nationality test, the Commission was prepared to admit claims by Iraqi nationals who also possessed valid and therefore the effective nationality of another State.

Secondly, where the application of the test indicates that the national has equally strong ties with two or more States, neither should be permitted to exercise diplomatic protection on his behalf against the other State of which he is a national, the rule of international law being that one does not have a remedy on the international plane against one's own State.[60] Moreover, to allow protection in circumstances where the national has strong ties with both States would undermine the sovereign equality of States; it is in any case a cardinal rule that the exercise of diplomatic protection must be consistent with other principles of international law. In deciding which of the nationalities is to be treated as dominant or effective, tribunals have paid regard to factors such as whether the nationality was acquired at birth, the residence or domicile of the national, date of naturalization, language, employment and financial interests, whether the nationality was acquired *bona fides*, and whether the national was precluded from denying a nationality that he had in everyday dealings held out as his own.[61]

3. Claims against third States

There is authority for the view that the principle of dominant or effective nationality has no application where any of the national States of a dual national wish to protect that national against a third State (Crawford, 2012, p 710). In the *Salem* case, the Tribunal held that:

> the rule of international law [is] that in the case of dual nationality a third power is not entitled to contest the claim of one of the two powers whose national is interested in the case by referring to the nationality of the other power.[62]

It is difficult to mount a principled defence for the exclusion of the effective nationality rule in these circumstances, unless one believes the rule is no more than a vehicle for resolving competing claims in cases involving dual nationals and there is no justification for its application outside those contexts. However, it may be taken as another indication that international *lex lata* is not too wedded to the requirement of a genuine link.

---

[57] Eg *Canevaro* case (1912) 11 *RIAA* 397.

[58] *Esphanian v Bank Tejarat* (1983) 2 Iran-USCTR 157, 166. The decision in the *Salem* case (1932) 2 *RIAA* 1161 provides an isolated example rejecting the dominant/effective nationality test.

[59] UN Doc S/AC.26/1991/7 Rev1, para 11.

[60] See *Merge* claim (1955) 22 ILR 443 and see Dugard, 2000, p 53; Brownlie, 2008, p 400–2.

[61] See the *Hein* case, *Annual Digest and Reports of Public International Law Cases* 1919–22, Case No 148, p 216; *Canevaro* case (1912) 11 *RIAA* 397.   [62] *Salem* case (1932) 2 *RIAA* 1161, 1188.

4. Some issues concerning protection of shareholding interests

In the *Barcelona Traction* case, several judges thought shareholders had an independent right of protection under international law but there were fundamental differences concerning the precise nature of that right. Some thought that shareholders should be regarded as having a secondary right of protection which could be activated if the national State of the company had failed to act on its behalf.[63] The majority, however, rejected this, arguing that a secondary right could only come into existence once the primary right had been extinguished, and the failure of a State to exercise a primary right did not necessarily extinguish it.[64] Furthermore, the Court noted that the national State of the company is perfectly free to decide on the method and extent of protection it should grant to a company having its nationality. It may for instance decide to settle the claim, and to reopen these settlements by granting shareholders either a parallel or subsidiary right would substantially undermine the security of international economic transactions.[65]

Another argument in support of extending protection to shareholders is that the genuine link requirement formulated in the *Nottebohm* case also applies to the protection of companies, so that only in cases where there is such a link can the State of incorporation bring a claim. The existence of a shareholding interest, it is then argued, provides the best evidence of the genuine link requirement, especially in those instances where the shareholders are from the State claiming a right of protection or where the board of directors has ties of nationality with the claimant State. In the *Barcelona Traction* case, for instance, Judge Jessup denied that Canada had a right to exercise diplomatic protection by virtue of the company's incorporation in that State, in the absence of some demonstrable link. He noted that:

> If a State extends its diplomatic protection to a corporation to which it has granted a charter of convenience while at the same time similar diplomatic assistance is being extended by another State whose nationals hold 100% of the shares, the situation might be considered analogous to cases of dual nationality of natural persons—*Nottebohm* principle applies equally here.[66]

In State practice and the jurisprudence of international tribunals there are numerous instances where States have been prepared to intervene and exercise diplomatic protection in respect of shareholding interests in foreign corporations (Douglas 2009, p 397; Oppenheim, 1992, p 322). In the *Barcelona Traction* case the ICJ treated these instances as *lex specialis*, based as it were on the terms of the instruments establishing them. However, in a curious judgment in the 1989 *ELSI* case, and without any reference to the *Barcelona Traction* case, the USA was permitted to exercise diplomatic protection in respect of injury to an Italian company, which was wholly owned by two US subsidiaries. Although Italy raised objections, the Court was untroubled by them, and preferred to dispose of the claim on the basis that there had been no violation of the treaty obligations relied on by the USA.[67]

---

[63] *Barcelona Traction, Light and Power Company, Limited, Second Phase, Judgment, ICJ Reports 1970*, p 3, Separate Opinion of Judge Fitzmaurice, p 65 at p 96, para 53.

[64] *Barcelona Traction, Light and Power Company, Limited, Second Phase, Judgment, ICJ Reports 1970*, p 3, para 96.   [65] Ibid, para 97.

[66] Ibid, Separate Opinion of Judge Jessup, p 162 at p 170, para 19.

[67] *Elettronica Sicula SpA (ELSI), Judgment, ICJ Reports 1989*, p 15, para 101. But cf the Dissenting Opinion of Judge Oda, p 83, who questioned the right of the USA to exercise diplomatic protection on behalf of shareholders in an Italian company when that company had not ceased to exist.

It would therefore seem that notwithstanding the opinion of the majority in the *Barcelona Traction* case, there is a substantial body of international practice and jurisprudence in support of the protection of shareholding interests. However, a number of problems remain, in particular with regard to the precise circumstances when shareholders may be entitled to protection, the range of interests capable of protection, and the modalities of reconciling competing claims (Lowe, 2002).

5. Exclusion of the nationality rule

The nexus of nationality is not required in all instances and its application may be waived by treaty or other ad hoc arrangements, such as delegation of the right of protection to another sovereign. Treaties may also extend a general right of protection to non-nationals. The most significant development in this respect relates to Article 8C of the Treaty of the EU, which creates a treaty-based right of diplomatic protection for all EU nationals within the jurisdiction of a Member State irrespective of nationality (Dugard, 2004, para 8). Other subjects of international law, such as international organizations, may be entitled to exercise such functional protection for those in their service unencumbered by considerations of nationality (Crawford, 2013, p 593). In the *Reparations* case, the ICJ thought nationality irrelevant in cases where the UN brings a claim in respect of injuries to agents of the organization incurred in the course of their duties. The Court justified the right of protection in the following terms:

> In order that the agent may perform his duties satisfactorily, he must feel that this protection is assured to him by the Organization, and that he may count on it. To ensure the independence of the agent, and, consequently, the independent action of the organization itself, it is essential that in performing his duties he need not have to rely on any protection than that of the organization . . . In particular, he should not have to rely on the protection of his own State. If he had to rely on that State, his independence might well be compromised.[68]

The claim in these instances could even be addressed to the State of the victim's nationality. Examples of other instances where the nationality of claims rule has been regarded as generally inapplicable include situations where claims have been brought on behalf of aliens in the service of the claiming State:[69] stateless persons; non-nationals forming a minority in a group of national claimants; refugees and non-nationals with long-term residence in the State espousing diplomatic protection (Oppenheim, 1992, p 515). In *Al-Rawi and others* v *The Secretary of State for Foreign and Commonwealth Affairs*[70] the English Court of Appeal denied that a sovereign State possessed standing to exercise diplomatic protection on behalf of resident aliens or refugees. It concluded that Article 8 of the ILC Draft Articles on Diplomatic Protection,[71] which envisaged protection for stateless persons and refugees habitually resident in a claimant State, was, strictly speaking, *lex ferenda* and an exercise in the progressive development of the law and not its restatement. *Al-Rawi* is, however, a decision of a domestic court and, to the extent that it is at odds with the weight of authority

---

[68] *Reparation for Injuries* case (*Advisory Opinion*), *ICJ Reports 1949*, p 174 at pp 179, 181–4.

[69] See for example *The M/V Saiga No 2 (Saint Vincent and the Grenadines* v *Guinea)*, ITLOS Case No 2, Judgment of 1 July 1999, in which the International Tribunal for the Law of the Sea accepted that the flag State had the right to protect non-national crew members.

[70] *Al-Rawi and Others* v *The Secretary of State for Foreign and Commonwealth Affairs* [2006] EWCA Civ 1279, paras, 63, 64, 89, and 115ff.

[71] See Seventh Report of the ILC Rapporteur on Diplomatic Protection, 7 March 2006, Fifty-eighth Session, A/CN.4/567.

in public international law, cannot be regarded as decisive on this point. Article 48(2)(b) of the ILC Articles on State Responsibility entitle States to bring claims and seek reparation including on behalf of non-nationals in respect of *erga omnes* obligations unencumbered by the requirements of nationality. However, despite support for extending the category of persons protected under diplomatic protection, States remain very reluctant to extend diplomatic protection in the absence of the formal ties of citizenship. The weight of authority on close analysis is in fact in support of *Al-Rawi* (McLachlan, 2014).

IV. ADMISSIBILITY IN CASES CONCERNING OBLIGATIONS OWED TO A PLURALITY OF STATES

A. INTRODUCTION

The obligations forming the basis of claims considered in the previous sections have been in the nature of distinct bilateral duties; they are either owed directly to the State or indirectly through persons having its nationality. In both instances, the legal interest takes the form of a private law claim; the wronged State must demonstrate either a direct injury to its interests or those of its nationals. Much of the traditional law on State responsibility has been concerned precisely with the enforcement of these bilateral rights and duties; the *jus dispositivum* character of international law guaranteed that only those directly affected could enforce those claims. The category of obligations considered in this section takes two forms. The first are obligations *erga omnes partes* owed to a State under a treaty instrument, and which have the objective of protecting the collective interests of all the parties. As long as the injury or violation is within the scope of the protected interests, any of the States parties to the treaty instruments has a prima facie right to make representations or bring a claim. For instance, States parties to regional human rights treaties invariably have a right to make representations even if the affected individuals are not their nationals. Other treaties creating zones of collective interests include regional nuclear-free zone treaties, regional environmental treaties, and regional instruments for economic integration.[72]

The second variation concerns the so-called *erga omnes* obligations proper which are owed to the international community as a whole. There has long been a consensus, at least since the Second World War, that international law may have an interest in creating obligations for the benefit of individuals and other non-State entities, such as units of self-determination, international organizations, etc. Other obligations in this category rest on the premise that certain values are fundamental, and are therefore owed to the international community as a whole. The protection of these values may coincide with individual State interests, as in the case of aggression, but in most cases they usually transcend such interests. As a result, the international system may recognize a role for third States in their enforcement even if they are not directly injured. An implicit feature of this category of obligations is that the specific requirements of legal interest based either on direct injury or ties of nationality are dispensed with.

In an often cited passage, the International Court of Justice in the *Barcelona Traction* case accepted that there were gradations of obligations in the international system, and that implicitly these qualitative differences may call for or justify different responses by members of the international community. It observed that:

---

[72] For relevant treaties see for instance South Pacific Nuclear Treaty (Raratonga, 1985) (1985) 24 ILM 1442; Treaty of Tlatelolco on the Prohibition of Nuclear Weapons in Latin America (1967) 634 UNTS 281; Africa Nuclear Free Zone Treaty (1996) 35 ILM 698; ASEAN Nuclear Free Zone Treaty 1996, 35 ILM 635.

An essential distinction should be drawn between obligations of a State towards the inter-national community as a whole and those arising vis-à-vis another State in the field of diplomatic protection. By their very nature the former are the concern of all States in view of the importance of the rights involved, all States can be held to have a legal interest in their protection, they are obligations *erga omnes*. Such obligations derive for example in contemporary international law, from the outlawing of aggression, and of genocide, as also from the principles and rules concerning the basic rights of the human person, including protection from slavery and racial discrimination. Some of the corresponding rights of protection have entered into the body of general international law[73] while others are con-ferred by international instruments of a universal or quasi-universal character.[74]

The Court's pronouncements on the *erga omnes* character of obligations were, strictly speaking, *obiter* since no such rights were involved on the facts, but the literature accepted that, at least at the level of primary rules, international obligations fell into two distinct categories: those in the nature of a civil law right and which were owed to individual States, and those which created a regulatory framework for dealing with public order concerns and were therefore owed to the international community as a whole (Tams, 2005; Ragazzi, 1997).

The Court's declaration has unfortunately not been followed with practical mechanisms for the enforcement. In particular, there is no consensus on whether a distinct category of secondary rules has also come into operation and directed at the enforcement of *erga omnes* obligations. It remains a moot point whether international law recognizes litigation in the public interest, and in particular whether States have a legal interest to enforce com-munity values through the processes of adjudication. For convenience, *erga omnes* rights as treaty rights and under customary law are considered separately.

B. TREATY INSTRUMENTS PROTECTING COLLECTIVE INTERESTS

It has long been recognized that States may have an interest in the observance of treaty instruments to which they are a party even without being directly affected. For example, Article 60 of the Vienna Convention on the Law of Treaties entitles States parties to ter-minate a treaty on account of material breach. Similarly, Article 42 of the ILC's Articles on State Responsibility explicitly recognizes the interests of States in ensuring compli-ance with treaty instruments to which they are a party. The obligations are described as interdependent with the result that non-compliance by any one party automatically affects the interests of all other parties to the treaty instrument. The Commission's approach is to create different degrees of 'affectedness', and the forms of responses that States may be entitled to adopt are determined by the degree to which they are affected by the breach.[75]

Arguably, there is no reason in principle why a State should not bring an action for the sole purpose of enforcing the rule of law on the basis of a treaty instrument or customary law. It should in principle have the right to do so even if it has suffered no material injury itself, or in the person of its national. Thus, leaving aside the problematic question whether international law recognizes an *actio popularis*, it could be said that at least in respect of

---

[73] See *Reservations to the Convention on the Prevention and Punishment of the Crime of Genocide*, Advisory Opinion, *ICJ Reports 1951*, p 23.

[74] *Barcelona Traction, Light and Power Company, Limited, Second Phase, Judgment, ICJ Reports 1970*, p 3, paras 33–4.

[75] ILC ARSIWA Articles 42 and 48 envisage a distinct role for States in enforcing obligations *erga omnes* including a right to bring an action and obtain compensation on behalf of an injured State.

those obligations contained in multilateral treaties, to which a large number of States are parties, the public interest concerns are readily met by the recognition that all parties to such instruments may bring an action for their enforcement. The International Court has explicitly endorsed *locus standi* in the case of *erga omnes partes* (as opposed to *erga omnes, stricto sensu*) in *Questions relating to the Obligation to Prosecute or Extradite (Belgium* v *Senegal)* under the UN Convention against Torture. Referring to obligations under the Torture Convention, the Court noted that:

> The common interest in compliance with the relevant obligations under the Convention against Torture implies entitlement of each State Party to the Convention to make a claim concerning the cessation of an alleged breach by another State Party. If a special interest were required for that purpose, in many cases no State would be in a position to make such a claim. It follows that any State Party to the Convention may invoke the responsibility of another State Party with a view to ascertaining the alleged failure to comply with its obligations *erga omnes partes*, such as under Article 6, paragraph 2, and Article 7, para 1, of the Convention, and to bring that failure to an end.[76]

In the *Whaling in the Arctic* case, the International Court recognized the right of Australia and New Zealand to bring a case against Japan for violations of obligations under the Whaling Convention, to which they were party, even though neither of the two States could claim to be particularly affected by the Japanese whaling activities.[77]

C. LITIGATION IN THE PUBLIC INTEREST AND THE ENFORCEMENT OF *ERGA OMNES* OBLIGATIONS *STRICTO SENSU*

What is to be the position where public interest is provided for as a matter of customary law as opposed to a treaty instrument? Is access to justice an imperative consequence of the recognition of obligations *erga omnes*? Those supporting the existence of an *ordre public* see the recognition of a public interest framework for their enforcement as a logical consequence of the recognition of *erga omnes* obligations, operating as a collective guarantee of the values underpinning the Conventions.[78] In Roman law it was always accepted that a plaintiff could bring an action before a court if it was in the public interest, and there was no requirement that the plaintiff should demonstrate a specific injury to its own interests before commencing litigation. Most systems of law have adopted in some form mechanisms for protecting collective interests and the initial trajectory of *erga omnes* obligations created much anticipation that it would also be backed by a system of public enforcement. Despite considerable interest in the subject in the academic literature, the question of enforcement has largely received a cool reception in international dispute settlement fora (Cancado Trinidade, 2010). The matter was considered by the International Court in the *South West Africa* cases. The applicant States, Liberia and Ethiopia, had argued that in order to be effective, the mandate for South West Africa should be interpreted in a way that would recognize their own right to bring an action, even though the obligations in question were not owed to them as individual members of the League but rather to the League itself. It was not contested that the applicant States had not suffered direct injury on account of South Africa's policy of apartheid, which they were challenging; instead they

---

[76] *Questions relating to the Obligation to Prosecute or Extradite (Belgium* v *Senegal), Judgment, ICJ Reports 2012*, p 442, paras 69–70.

[77] *Whaling in the Antarctic (Australia* v *Japan: New Zealand Intervening), Judgment, ICJ Reports* 2014, p 226.

[78] See *Whaling in the Antarctic (Australia* v *Japan: New Zealand Intervening), Judgment, ICJ Reports* 2014, p 226, Separate Opinion of Judge Cancado Trindade.

were indirectly asking for the recognition of a process of collective enforcement exercisable at the behest of any member of the international community. The Court rejected this argument and observed that:

> Looked at in another way moreover, the argument amounts to a plea that the Court should allow the equivalent of an *actio popularis*, or right resident in any member of a community to take legal action in vindication of public interest. But although a right of this kind may be known to certain municipal systems of law, it is not known to international law as it stands at present: nor is the Court able to regard it as imported by the 'general principles of law' referred to in Article 38, paragraph 1 (c) of its Statute.[79]

The extreme reticence shown by the Court in extending standing to vindicate community interests generated much disquiet in the international community, especially from African States, and in the academic literature there was a sustained effort to discredit the decision. The subsequent jurisprudence of the Court however confirms that the decision was not an aberration and the Court has without exception continued to affirm this narrow approach to questions of *locus standi*, rejecting any overarching concept of public interest litigation.

Its next most important judgment on the subject, was in the *Barcelona Traction* case.

Again, the Court did not regard its recognition of *erga omnes* obligations as necessarily creating a parallel right of an *actio popularis*. The right of enforcement in the Court's view only existed in those instances where the obligation was strictly speaking binding *erga omnes partes*. It observed that:

> With regard more particularly to human rights, to which reference has already been made in paragraph 34 of this judgment, it should be noted that these include protection against denial of justice. However, on the universal level, the instruments which embody human rights do not confer on States the capacity to protect the victims of infringements of such rights irrespective of their nationality. It is therefore still on the regional level that a solution to this problem has had to be sought; thus within the Council of Europe, of which Spain is not a member, the problem of admissibility encountered by the claim in the present case has been resolved by the European Convention on Human Rights, which entitles each State which is a party to the Convention to lodge a complaint against any other contracting State for the violation of the Convention, irrespective of the nationality of the victim.[80]

This conclusion, like the earlier judgment in the *South West Africa Cases*, is problematic because it has the effect of depriving the *erga omnes* regime of much practical significance. There are few instruments of general application which provide for the enforcement of *erga omnes* obligations. This lack of realistic mechanisms for enforcement has the unfortunate effect of rendering these obligations largely theoretical.

Moreover the Court has further taken the view that the *erga omnes* character of an obligation does not trump the jurisdictional barriers that attach to international adjudication, and in the absence of consent to the jurisdiction of the International Court, the Court will simply not entertain a claim notwithstanding *the erga omnes* character of the obligation giving rise to it (Schachter, 1991, p 210; Crawford, 2012, pp 596–7).

This much is clear from the ICJ decision in the *East Timor* case in which Portugal brought an action against Australia arguing that by entering into a treaty with Indonesia regarding the delimitation of the East Timorese continental shelf, Australia had interfered

---

[79] *South West Africa, Second Phase, Judgment, ICJ Reports 1966*, p 6, para 88. Judge Jessup who delivered a strong dissent was nevertheless disinclined to accept a general right of *actio popularis*.

[80] *Barcelona Traction, Light and Power Company, Limited, Second Phase, Judgment, ICJ Reports 1970*, p 3, para 91.

with the right of East Timorese people to self-determination, a right whose *erga omnes* character was impeccable. Yet a substantive judgment on the matter required the Court to rule on the legality of Indonesia's invasion of East Timor and the subsequent jurisdictional authority enjoyed by Indonesia over the East Timorese. Indonesia was not a party to the dispute, nor had it accepted the Court's jurisdiction. It was therefore immediately apparent that the Court was being asked to rule on the rights and obligations of a third party to the dispute contrary to its previous jurisprudence as laid down in the *Monetary Gold* case. Portugal argued that limitations on the Court's jurisdiction under the *Monetary Gold* principle had no application in view of the *erga omnes* character of the obligations involved. The Court rejected the claim and observed that:

> Portugal's assertion that the right of peoples to self-determination as it evolved from the Charter and from the UN practice has an *erga omnes* character is irreproachable. The principle of self-determination of peoples has been recognised in the United Nations Charter and in the jurisprudence of the Court. It is one of the essential principles of contemporary international law. However, the Court considers that the *erga omnes* character of a norm and the rule of consent are two different things. Whatever the nature of the obligations invoked, the Court could not rule on the lawfulness of the conduct of a State when its judgment would imply an evaluation of the lawfulness of the conduct of another State which is not a party to the case. Where this is so, the Court cannot act even if the right in question is a right *erga omnes*.[81]

In *Armed Activities in the Territory of the Congo (DRC v Rwanda)*, the Court confirmed its previous jurisprudence. It noted that the *erga omnes* character of the obligations under the Genocide Convention did not give the Court jurisdiction to entertain a dispute in the absence of the parties' consent.[82]

Nevertheless, in its Advisory Opinion on the *Legal Consequences of the Construction of a Wall in the Occupied Palestinian Territory*, the Court came quite close to recognizing the existence of an *actio popularis*. Referring to Israeli violations of the rights of the Palestinian people to self-determination, it observed that:[83]

> Given the character and importance of the rights and obligations involved, the Court is of the view that all States are under an obligation not to recognize the illegal situation resulting from the construction of the wall . . . They are also under an obligation not to render aid or assistance in maintaining the situation created by such construction. It is also for all States, while respecting the United Nations Charter and international law, to see to it that any impediment, resulting from the construction of the wall, to the exercise by the Palestinian people of its right of self-determination is brought to an end.

The standing of all States to enforce community norms was advanced by Judge Simma two years later in *Armed Activities in the Territory of the Congo (DRC v Uganda)*. The Court had refused to entertain Uganda's counterclaim concerning the alleged mistreatment by Congolese soldiers of persons whose nationality had not been established. Judge Simma argued that the Court should have entertained the claim since the obligations in question were binding *erga omnes*. He said that:[84]

---

[81] *East Timor (Portugal v Australia), Judgment, ICJ Reports 1995*, p 90, para 29.

[82] *Armed Activities on the Territory of the Congo (New Application: 2002) (Democratic Republic of the Congo v Rwanda), Jurisdiction and Admissibility, Judgment, ICJ Reports 2006*, p 6, paras 28–70.

[83] *Legal Consequences of the Construction of a Wall in the Occupied Palestine Territory, Advisory Opinion, ICJ Reports 2004*, p 136, para 159.

[84] *Armed Activities on the Territory of the Congo (Democratic Republic of the Congo v Uganda), Judgment, ICJ Reports 2005*, p 168, Separate Opinion of Judge Simma, pp 347–8.

the question of standing of a claimant state for violations of human rights committed against persons which might or might not possess the nationality of that state, the jurisdiction of the Court not being at issue, the contemporary law of state responsibility provides a positive answer as well . . . The obligations deriving from the human rights cited above and breached by the DRC are instances *par excellence* of obligations that are owed to a group of States including Uganda, and are established for the protection of a collective interest of the States parties to the Covenant.

Further obstacles in the path of litigation *actio popularis* have been noted. Schachter, for instance, has suggested that States are reluctant to set precedents which could be used in future litigation against them and so they are unlikely to lodge claims even in respect of *erga omnes* obligations unless their direct interests were involved. Moreover, he warns that there is a real risk that an expansive concept of *actio popularis* is likely to deter even further State acceptance of the International Court's compulsory jurisdiction; and those States who accept compulsory jurisdiction will invariably protect themselves from its consequences by making reservations against *actio popularis* suits (Schachter, 1991, p 212). In any case, it is abundantly clear from the few occasions on which the International Court has considered the matter that it has been particularly reticent to acknowledge public interest litigation as a means of enforcing *erga omnes* obligations (Tam, 2005).

The Articles finally adopted by the ILC in 2001 explicitly recognize the right of States other than those directly injured to bring an action in the public interest.[85] Two situations were contemplated: 'where the obligation breached is either owed to a group of States including that State bringing the action and is established for the protection of a collective interest of the group' (*erga omnes partes*). The second instance encompassed general *erga omnes* obligations—obligations owed to the international community as a whole. Article 48 was not universally accepted; some States were concerned that it would encourage pointless litigation, a problem likely to be aggravated by the decentralized nature of adjudication of claims in the international system. The Special Rapporteur in the Commentary to Article 48 acknowledged that the Article involved elements of progressive development of the law insofar as it entitled States to bring claims for restitution and reparation on behalf of the beneficiaries of the obligation even when they were not directly affected. The Articles were commended to States by the UN General Assembly in GA Resolution 56/83 (12 December 2001), but it remains an open question whether this positive endorsement will be reflected in actual State behaviour (Crawford and Olleson, 2005). There is to date no evidence that States have been particularly emboldened by Article 48 in bringing *erga omnes* claims. In a case brought by the Marshall Islands against the United Kingdom concerning obligations to negotiate with a view to the cessation of

---

[85] Article 48 provides:

1. Any State other than an injured State is entitled to invoke the responsibility of another in accordance with Para 2 if:
    (a) the obligation breached is owed to a group of States including that State, and is established for the protection of a collective interest of the group; or
    (b) the obligation breached is owed to the international community as a whole.
2. Any State entitled to invoke responsibility under paragraph 1 may claim from the responsible State:
    (a) cessation of the internationally wrongful act, and assurances and guarantees of non-repetition in accordance with Article 30; and
    (b) performance of the obligation of reparation in accordance with the preceding articles, in the interest of the injured State or of the beneficiaries of the obligation breached.
3. ...

the nuclear arms race and nuclear disarmament, the Marshall Islands based its application not only on UK obligations under Article IV of the Non-Proliferation Treaty (NPT) but also on the *erga omnes* character of the obligations prohibiting the use of nuclear weapons. It argued that it had a clear interest deriving 'from its status as a party to an interdependent treaty—the NPT—a treaty whose breach is of such a character as radically to change the position of all the other states to which the obligation is owed with respect to the further performance of the obligation'. Finally, and invoking Article 48 of the ILC Articles, the Marshall Islands argued that its standing 'derives from its status as a member of the international community reacting against a breach of an *erga omnes* obligation'.[86] In the event, the ICJ did not consider the substance of these arguments, finding that it lacked jurisdiction to hear the case.[87]

V. ADMISSIBILITY OF CLAIMS AND THE RULE ON EXHAUSTION OF LOCAL REMEDIES

A. INTRODUCTION

There is almost universal consensus that in the absence of an agreement to the contrary, a claim is inadmissible on the international plane unless the alien or legal person on whose behalf a claim has been brought has exhausted local remedies in the putative respondent State. The rule has been endorsed in the literature as a rule of customary law and its normative quality has been accepted by international tribunals.[88]

A number of reasons have been put forward in support of the rule. The first is a logical consequence of the sovereignty of States in respect of matters occurring on their territory.

It is therefore generally accepted that out of respect for sovereignty, a State must be given the first opportunity to exercise jurisdiction in respect of matters occurring in its territory. There is a presumption that the wronged national, by voluntarily bringing himself within the jurisdiction of the respondent State, must be taken to have assumed the risk of having local law applied to him.

The second reason rests on considerations of practical convenience. It would be both expensive and futile to bring small claims before an international forum when there is a possibility of expeditious redress before local tribunals. It has also been suggested that in these instances the local courts are better placed to evaluate the facts and the evidence, as well as deciding on the appropriate methods of compensation (Crawford, 2012, pp 710–11). They are therefore clearly more appropriate fora for the settlement of these disputes than the international arena.

Thirdly, in a number of instances, it is the failure to provide local redress for breach of an international obligation that engages the responsibility of the State. There can be no claim on the basis of denial of justice until local remedies have been exhausted. In this instance failure to exhaust local remedies is not so much a bar to the admissibility of the claim; rather it operates to determine the existence of responsibility, since until such remedies have been exhausted and found to be wanting no case for violation of international law can be made.

---

[86]   Memorial of The Marshall Islands, 16 March 2015, para 103.

[87]   *Obligations Concerning Negotiations Relating to Cessation of the Nuclear Arms Race and to Nuclear Disarmament (Marshall Islands* v *United Kingdom), Preliminary Objections, ICJ Reports 2016*, nyr.

[88]   See, eg, *Ahmadou Sadio Diallo (Republic of Guinea* v *Democratic Republic of Congo), Preliminary Objections*, Judgment of 24 May 2007, paras 42–4.

B. THE CONTENT OF THE RULE

What are the parameters of the rule requiring exhaustion of local remedies and when and in what circumstances is it discharged? The first general observation is that the rule only applies in those instances where the State brings a claim on behalf of a national. As a matter of principle, a State bringing a claim to protect its direct interests is not obliged to exhaust such remedies. Although there is nothing to preclude it from doing so, and in particular circumstances it may in fact be convenient to explore the availability of remedies in the local courts.

Second, there is considerable support for the view that the obligation to exhaust local remedies relates only to legal remedies, and would exclude remedies that are discretionary or that are available as a matter of grace (Brownlie, 2008, p 495; Brierly, 1963, p 281). It also seems to be a general requirement that the national in question must exhaust the remedies available to their fullest extent. In particular, they must raise before local courts all the arguments that they may wish to bring before international tribunals,[89] as well as appeal procedures provided for under local law.[90]

It seems perfectly logical that as a corollary there is no obligation to exhaust local remedies where these are unavailable in practice or are unlikely to yield any concrete results. Nevertheless the decision whether legal remedies are unavailable in a particular legal system is a contentious one, and it remains unclear how far the foreign national is expected to test the options under national law before reaching the conclusion that they are bound to be futile. In the *Interhandel* case, brought by Switzerland before the International Court, the Court concluded that as Interhandel's suit was still pending before US courts, local remedies had not been exhausted.[91] The conclusion on the face of it appeared harsh, since the corporation had been involved in litigation in US courts for a period of almost ten years before proceedings were commenced by Switzerland before the International Court.

The jurisprudence of international tribunals indicates that local remedies will generally be regarded as unavailable if the applicant, although granted a right of appeal on a point of law, chooses not to exercise it, because the precise point raised has previously been decided by a higher court to the detriment of a litigant. Similarly, local remedies are treated as unavailable if an appeal would lie on a point of fact, but appellate courts lack the power to review points of fact.[92] In the case of Georgia against Russia, the Grand Chamber of the European Court of Human Rights confirmed that the rule on exhaustion of local remedies does not in 'principle apply where the applicant government complains of a practice as such with the aim of preventing its continuation or recurrence but does not ask . . . the Court to give a decision on each of the facts put forward as proof or illustrations of that practice'. Furthermore that the rule does not apply 'where an administrative practice, namely a repetition of acts incompatible with the Convention, and official tolerance by the State has been shown to exist and is of such a nature as to make proceedings futile'.[93] In other words, the remedy available must present a reasonable possibility of redressing the personal claim of the litigant (Crawford, 2013, p 581; Dugard, 2002, para 45).

---

[89]   *Finnish Ships Arbitration*, 1934, 3 RIAA 1479; *Elettronica Sicula SpA (ELSI), Judgment, ICJ Reports 1989,* p 15.   [90]   *Ambatielos Claim*, 1956, 12 RIAA 83.

[91]   *Interhandel, Preliminary Objections, Judgment, ICJ Reports 1959,* p 6.

[92]   *Finnish Ships Arbitration*, 1934, 3 RIAA 1479; *Panevezys-Saldutiskis Railway, Judgment, 1939, PCIJ, Ser A/B, No 76,* p 4 at p 18.

[93]   *Georgia v Russia (I) [GC], no 13255/07, ECHR 2014 (extracts), para 125.*

C. THE APPLICATION OF THE RULE IN THE CONTEXT OF MIXED CLAIMS

The rule requiring the exhaustion of local remedies only applies in those instances where the State brings forward a claim on behalf of a national, and not when it claims on its own behalf. The rule therefore rests on the assumption that it will always be easy to distinguish between these two situations. While it is usually possible to maintain the distinction, there are many cases where the dividing line is not so clear, especially when the wrong simultaneously injures both the national and the State's own direct interests. In these instances, it becomes difficult to decide whether the rule requiring the exhaustion of local remedies applies. Moreover, it is not uncommon for applicant States to seek a declaration or an interpretation of a treaty and damages in respect of an injury to their nationals in the same proceedings. Dugard, in his second report on diplomatic protection, suggested that in respect of such mixed claims, the exhaustion of local remedies rule should only apply if the claim is overwhelmingly concerned with injury to the national (Dugard, 2001, paras 19–24).

There is some support in the jurisprudence of international tribunals for the *preponderance* of interests test in the case of mixed claims. In the *Interhandel* case, Switzerland had insisted on the non-applicability of the local remedies rule, arguing that its claim concerned the failure of the US authorities to apply the terms of an applicable treaty, that had caused it direct harm. In rejecting the claim, the Court noted that the dispute was essentially one in which:

> the Swiss Government appears as having adopted the cause of its national Interhandel, for the purpose of securing restitution to that company of assets vested by the government of the USA.

It further observed that:

> one interest, and one alone of Interhandel has induced the Swiss Government to institute proceedings, and that this interest is the basis for the present claim and should determine the scope of the action brought before the Court by the Swiss Government in its alternative as well as principal form.[94]

In the *ELSI* case, the Chamber of the International Court of Justice rejected the argument of the USA that, insofar as the claim was founded on breach of a treaty obligation, it should be treated as an instance of direct injury to State interests rather than a claim made on behalf of a national for purposes of the local remedies rule. In rejecting the argument, the Chamber observed that:

> the matter which colours and pervades the United States Claim as a whole is the alleged damage to Raytheon and Machlett [United States Corporations].[95]

The correctness of this proposition is difficult to fault, for even claims brought exclusively on behalf of nationals usually originate in some kind of non-compliance with a treaty obligation owed to the applicant State. The fact that a breach of a treaty is at issue cannot therefore be regarded as a reliable test (if at all) for distinguishing between direct injury to a State's interests and those cases where it claims on behalf of a national.

Theodore Meron suggested that in deciding on the nature of the claim, it is necessary to have regard to the real interests and goals of the litigant State. Is the State primarily pursuing its own interests or is the action really a claim brought on behalf of a national? If the claim is primarily concerned with injury to a national, then the rule will operate to exclude the

---

[94] *Interhandel, Preliminary Objections, Judgment, ICJ Reports 1959*, p 6 at p 29.
[95] *Elettronica Sicula SpA (ELSI), Judgment, ICJ Reports 1989*, p 15, para 91.

admissibility of the claim including any secondary elements, which strictly speaking are in the nature of inter-State claims (Crawford, 2013, p 584; Meron, 1959, p 87). There is also general recognition that claims, which are primarily about treaty interpretation and application, are direct State claims even if they arise in circumstances also affecting the rights of a private person[96] (Oppenheim, 1992, p 523). The subject matter of the dispute may also provide a useful guide to the true character of the claim. Thus injuries to diplomatic or consular staff,[97] or State property,[98] will generally be regarded as direct claims and therefore not subject to the local remedies rule. Although not conclusive, the nature of the remedy sought may also be a useful indicator in claims presenting mixed elements (Adler, 1990, p 652; Dugard, 2001, paras 29–30). There is considerable justification in looking at the essence of the claim and characterizing it by paying regard to its principal objectives. However, a rigid application of the predominance test may preclude valid claims by governments, especially when in the circumstances they are unlikely to obtain any local remedies for breach of their treaty rights (Fitzmaurice, 1961, p 37; Thirlway, 1995, pp 85–90). Moreover, the *dominance test* ignores the fact that a State may have a legal interest of its own to protect, such as vindicating the values underpinning the treaty regime, and which are unlikely to be satisfied by any material compensation or restitution of property in national courts.

D. A RULE OF SUBSTANCE OR PROCEDURE?

Is the rule requiring exhaustion of local remedies a rule of procedure or substance? There has been considerable discussion in the literature as to the precise character of the rule requiring exhaustion of local remedies, and in particular whether it is a rule of substance or procedure. This seemingly sterile debate on closer analysis has important normative consequences, and therefore merits close attention.

A number of different positions have been adopted. The first characterizes the rule as one of substance and proceeds from the premise that the exhaustion of local remedies is not so much a condition of admissibility of claims; rather, it determines the very existence of responsibility. On this view, until local remedies have been exhausted and found wanting, there can be no international 'delict' to engage the responsibility of the State.[99]

The second position treats the rule as a procedural prerequisite to the admissibility of a claim. On this view the responsibility of a State is engaged and complete from the time of the wrongful act, but redress on the international plane cannot be effected until local remedies have been exhausted.

The third position distinguishes between different kinds of wrongs that may cause injury to a national on whose behalf a claim is subsequently brought. On this view, where the national is injured by a violation of a rule of domestic law, no question of international responsibility arises until local remedies have been exhausted. Only then can a claim be brought on the international plane for denial of justice. Here exhaustion of local remedies is substantive, for until such remedies have failed there can be no question of responsibility on the international plane. Proponents of this third position distinguish the situation where the national is injured by what is clearly a rule of international law. Here, the responsibility of the respondent State is activated from the time of the injury. In this

---

[96] See *Avena and other Mexican Nationals (Mexico v United States of America), Judgment, ICJ Reports 2004,* p 12, paras 35–6.

[97]   *United States Diplomatic and Consular Staff in Tehran, Judgment, ICJ Reports 1980,* p 3.

[98]   *Corfu Channel, Merits, Judgment, ICJ Reports 1949,* p 4.

[99]   Ago, R, 'Sixth Report on State Responsibility', *YBILC* (1977), vol II (part one), pp 22–3.

instance, the requirement that local remedies have to be exhausted must be seen as no more than a procedural prerequisite to the admissibility of a claim on the international plane, and does not as such affect the origin of responsibility.

This debate as to the nature of the local remedies rule may have implications for other related rules of admissibility, such as the requirement that the applicant State must demonstrate the continuous nationality of the claim. It has been noted that for a claim to be admissible on the international plane it must be national in origin. In other words, from the time of the injury until the making of the award, the claim must belong to persons having the nationality of the claimant State. The exact time when a wrong ripens for purposes of responsibility also depends on whether one adopts the procedural or substantive position and therefore has implications for the rule on continuous nationality of claims.

Second, if the rule determines the origin of responsibility, it operates as a bar to States wishing to seek declaratory judgments or interpretation of treaties in circumstances where injured nationals have not exhausted local remedies since, until such remedies have been exhausted, there can be no question of responsibility.

Finally, Dugard has suggested that the rule may also affect the *temporis* jurisdiction of international tribunals in those instances where States have stated that their acceptances of the Court's jurisdiction will only be effective after a specified date (Dugard, 2001, para 33). On the procedural view, the effective time for jurisdictional purposes is the occurrence of the injury. On the substantive view, the effective time will be after the exhaustion of local remedies. Thus a claim may be admissible or inadmissible depending on which view of the rule one adopts.

E. WHICH VIEW REPRESENTS THE LAW?

The answer to this question must surely be speculative, and has to be approached as a matter of principle rather than on the basis of State and arbitral practice since no international decision has explicitly addressed the issue and the positions adopted by governments have been largely partisan and influenced by the exigencies of litigation. However, the decisions in the *German Interests in Polish Upper Silesia*,[100] *Chorzow Factory*,[101] and *Phosphates in Morocco*[102] cases provide strong evidence in support of the procedural position. In both cases the Court reached the conclusion that responsibility was incurred immediately following on the wrongful act, rather than after the exhaustion of local remedies.

As a matter of principle, it is difficult to mount a spirited defence of the substantive position. It proceeds on the premise that the determination of whether a breach of international law takes place depends not on the international norm but on the procedures of local tribunals. This potentially undermines the values that inform the applicable legal regime (Dugard, 2001, paras 56 and 63; Amerasinghe, 1990, p 328). Non-compliance with an obligation threatens the integrity of the applicable norm irrespective of whether local remedies have been exhausted or not. As Judge Lauterpacht noted in the *Norwegian Loans* case:

> the exhaustion of local remedies cannot itself bring within the province of international law a dispute which is otherwise outside its sphere. The failure to exhaust local remedies may constitute a bar to the jurisdiction of the court; it does not affect the intrinsically international character of a dispute.[103]

[100] *Certain German Interests in Polish Upper Silesia, Merits, Judgment No 7, 1926, PCIJ, Ser A, No 7.*
[101] *Factory at Chorzow, Merits, Judgment No 13, 1928, PCIJ, Ser A, No 17.*
[102] *Phosphates in Morocco, Judgment, 1937, PCIJ, Ser A/B, No 74, p 10.*
[103] *Certain Norwegian Loans, Judgment, ICJ Reports 1957, p 9, Separate Opinion of Judge Lauterpacht, p 34 at p 38.*

Secondly, it is generally accepted that States may agree by treaty to exclude the operation of a rule. The validity of such agreements was accepted without qualification in the *ELSI* case. Dugard has suggested that the validity of such waiver is difficult to defend, if one adopts the substantive view, since it is tantamount to saying that States can agree to make something delictual when ordinarily it would not be a breach unless and until it has given rise to subsequent denial of justice (Dugard, 2001, para 33). For this reason most authorities consider the exhaustion of local remedies to be a rule of procedure. The State incurs international responsibility from the moment of the wrongful act but the right to bring an international claim is suspended until the State has had the opportunity to remedy the situation.

F. THE EXCLUSION OF THE LOCAL REMEDIES RULE

There can be no obligation to exhaust local remedies if there are no local remedies to exhaust (Fitzmaurice, 1961, p 59). In order to be considered effective, the local remedy must have the capacity to remedy the complaint. Clearly, when the conduct giving rise to the injury does not violate local law, there will be no local remedies and the matter can immediately be taken up on the international plane. The argument has also been made that there is no obligation to exhaust local remedies in cases where public international law does not permit the respondent State to exercise jurisdiction in the first place (Brownlie, 2008, p 495; O'Connell, 1970, p 951). Thus an attempt to exercise jurisdiction over an alien in circumstances where international law does not grant jurisdiction would clearly be a nullity, and there is considerable merit in the argument that no obligation to exhaust local remedies arises.[104]

Many authorities argue that there is no obligation to exhaust local remedies where there is no voluntary link between the injured individual and the respondent State (Dugard, 2002, para 83). Thus, the argument has been made that in principle there should be some degree of connection between the injured individual and the respondent State and that the obligation is therefore dispensed with where the links are transitory or clearly involuntary. Examples would include air crash victims involuntarily or fortuitously injured by events in the respondent State. On the other hand, it can be argued that it is precisely such cases that local courts are particularly suitable for, given the multiple character of the claims and the clear local interest in the dispute.

Finally, the requirement to exhaust local remedies may be formally dispensed with by a treaty. Many international treaties provide that in the event of a dispute between the State and a foreign legal person, the dispute is to be referred to arbitration. Tribunals considering the issue have reached the conclusion that where provision is expressly made for arbitration, then there will clearly be no obligation to exhaust local remedies (Crawford, *Brownlie's Principles*, 2012, p 715).

VI. CONCLUSION

The preceding discussion has attempted to isolate the main legal grounds governing the admissibility of claims. These conditions are not context specific; they operate in most cases where the responsibility of a state is called into question in an international forum. The requirement of exhaustion of local remedies will invariably govern the admissibility of most claims unless, on the facts, a specific waiver is in operation. The discussion on *erga*

---

[104] See *Barcelona Traction, Light and Power Company, Limited, Second Phase, Judgment, ICJ Reports 1970*, p 3, Separate Opinion of Judge Fitzmaurice, p 65 at pp 103–10, paras 66–83.

omnes obligations is largely tentative; protestations about their normative significance have unfortunately not been met by a workable framework for their enforcement. The work of the International Law Commission, completed in 2001, represents the most significant advance yet, insofar as it provides for a coherent regime for the enforcement of these obligations. Yet even the Commission's proposals especially in Article 48 are clearly stated in *de lege ferenda* terms and their effectiveness will ultimately depend on their reception in State practice. In this regard the significance of the Marshall Islands' arguments in the *Nuclear Non-proliferation* case should not be underestimated; it is the first positive attempt to invoke Article 48 of the ILC's Articles as establishing *locus standi* in respect of *erga omnes* obligations.

It is to be regretted though that despite a fairly extensive jurisprudence, the rules governing the nationality of claims, in particular the criteria for nationality, in the context of diplomatic protection cannot be stated with certainty. The work then of the International Commission on the law governing diplomatic protection has consolidated and clarified the law on many important issues and is to be welcomed.

This brief survey does not purport to be a complete account of the infinite variety of circumstances that may legally operate to preclude the admissibility of a claim. Some of these, such as inadmissibility on account of 'waiver', have received attention in the literature, including in the work of the International Law Commission (Crawford, 2002, pp 266–9). Other grounds of preclusion—such as a finding that the dispute is without object;[105] that the applicant State has itself indulged in the same wrongful act in respect of which it now complains (the 'clean hands' doctrine);[106] that the applicant has acquiesced in wrongful conduct forming the subject matter of the dispute;[107] or that the chosen forum is inappropriate (especially where the applicant State has instituted proceedings in a forum other than that nominated by the treaty)—are closely intertwined with the merits, and may therefore be treated either as issues of admissibility or as substantive grounds for defeating the claim at the merits stage. Moreover, in certain cases, the operation of estoppel may preclude the examination of a particular issue even in circumstances when the claim itself has been found to be admissible.[108] The survey is also undertaken without prejudice to the *lex specialis* regimes governing the protection of corporations or their shareholders under international economic treaties and protection mechanisms in human rights instruments.[109]

---

[105] *Northern Cameroons, Preliminary Objections, Judgment, ICJ Reports 1963*, p 15.

[106] See *ICJ Pleadings, Oil Platforms (Islamic Republic of Iran v United States of America)*, Counter Memorial and Counter Claim Submitted by the United States of America, Part VI, pp 161–79 (23 June 1997) and Reply and Defence to Counter Claim submitted by the Islamic Republic of Iran, vol I, pp 187–98 (10 March 1999); *Gabčíkovo-Nagymaros Project (Hungary/Slovakia), Judgment, ICJ Reports 1997*, p 7, para 133; Dugard, 2005, *passim*.

[107] *ICJ Pleadings, Passage through the Great Belt (Finland v Denmark)*, Counter-memorial of the Government of the Kingdom of Denmark, Vol I, p 248 (May 1992).

[108] Eg *Temple of Preah Vihear, Merits, Judgment, ICJ Reports 1962*, p 6 at pp 22–3.

[109] In many cases these contain express provisions where parties agree to waive their right to diplomatic protection. Article 27 of the 1965 Convention on the Settlement of Investment Disputes, 575 UNTS 159, is particularly apt. It reads: 'No Contracting State shall give diplomatic protection, or bring an international claim, in respect of a dispute which one of its nationals and another Contracting State shall have consented to submit or shall have submitted to arbitration under this Convention, unless such other Contracting State shall have failed to abide by and comply with the award rendered in such dispute.'

REFERENCES

ADLER, M (1990), 'The Exhaustion of the Local Remedies Rule after the International Court of Justice's Decision in ELSI', 39 *ICLQ* 641.

AMERASINGHE, CF (1990), *Local Remedies in International Law* (Cambridge: Grotius).

BORCHARD, EM (1915), *The Diplomatic Protection of Citizens Abroad* (New York: Banks Law Publishing Co).

BRIERLY, JL (1928), 'The Theory of State Complicity in International Claims', 9 *BYIL* 48.

BRIERLY, JL (1963), *The Law of Nations* (6th edn, Oxford: Clarendon Press).

BROWNLIE, I (2008), *Principles of Public International Law* (7th edn, Oxford: Clarendon Press).

CANCADO TRINDADE, AA (2010), *International Law for Humankind: Towards a New* Jus Gentium (The Hague: Martinus Nijhoff).

CRAWFORD, J (2002), *The International Law Commission's Articles on State Responsibility* (Cambridge: Cambridge University Press).

CRAWFORD, J (2012), *Brownlie's Principles of Public International Law* (8th edn, Oxford: Clarendon Press).

CRAWFORD, J (2013), *State Responsibility: The General Part* (Cambridge: Cambridge University Press).

CRAWFORD, J and OLLESON, S (2005), 'The Continuing Debate on a UN Convention on State Responsibility', 54 *ICLQ* 959.

CRAWFORD, J, PELLET, A, and OLLESON, S (2010), *The Law of International Responsibility* (Oxford: Oxford University Press).

DOUGLAS, Z (2009), *The International Law of Investment Claims* (Cambridge: Cambridge University Press).

DUGARD, J (2000), *First Report on Diplomatic Protection*, UN Doc A/CN.4/506.

DUGARD, J (2001), *Second Report on Diplomatic Protection*, UN Doc A/CN.4/514.

DUGARD, J (2002), *Third Report on Diplomatic Protection*, UN Doc A/CN.4/523.

DUGARD, J (2004), *Fifth Report on Diplomatic Protection*, UN Doc A/CN.4/538.

DUGARD, J (2005), *Sixth Report on Diplomatic Protection*, UN Doc A/CN.4/546.

FITZMAURICE, G (1957), 'The General Principles of International Law, Considered from the Standpoint of the Rule of Law', 92 *Recueil des Cours* 1.

FITZMAURICE, G (1961), 'Hersch Lauterpacht—The Scholar as Judge', 38 *BYIL* 37.

FITZMAURICE, G (1986), *The Law and Procedure of the International Court of Justice*, vol II (Cambridge: Grotius).

HARRIS, DJ (1998), *Cases and Materials on International Law* (5th edn, London: Sweet & Maxwell).

LEIGH, GIF (1971), 'Nationality and Diplomatic Protection', 20 *ICLQ* 453.

LITTLEFIELD, S (2009), 'Citizenship, Identity and Foreign Policy: The Contradictions and Consequences of Russia's Passport Distribution in the Separatist Regions of Georgia', 61 *Europe Asia Studies* 1461.

LOWE, AV (2002), 'Shareholders Rights from Barcelona to ELSI', in N Ando, E McWhinney, and R Wolfrum (eds), *Essays in Honor of Judge Oda* (The Hague: Kluwer), p 65.

LOWE, AV and FITZMAURICE, M (1996), *Fifty Years of the International Court of Justice* (Cambridge: Cambridge University Press).

MCLACHLAN, C (2014), *Foreign Relations Law* (Cambridge: Cambridge University Press).

MALANCZUK, P (1997), *A Modern Introduction to International Law* (London: Routledge).

MERON, Y (1959), 'The Incidence of the Rule of Exhaustion of Local Remedies', 35 *BYIL* 83.

O'CONNELL, DP (1970), *International Law* (2nd edn, London: Stevens).

OKOWA, P (2008), 'Case Concerning Ahmadou Sadio Diallo (Republic of Guinea v DRC), Preliminary Objections', 57 *ICLQ* 219.

OPPENHEIM, L (1992), *Oppenheim's International Law* (9th edn, London: Longman).

RAGAZZI, M (1997), *The Concept of International Obligations Erga Omnes* (Oxford: Oxford University Press).

ROSENNE, S (1997), *The Law and Practice of the International Court, 1920–1996* (3rd edn, The Hague: Nijhoff).

SCHACTER, O (1991), *International Law in Theory and in Practice* (Dordrecht: Martinus Nijhoff).

SHEA, D (1955), *The Calvo Clause* (Minneapolis, MN: University of Minnesota Press).

SIMMA, B (1994), 'From Bilateralism to Community Interest in International Law', 250 *Recueil des Cours* 217.

TAMS, C (2005), *Enforcing Obligations Erga Omnes in International Law* (Cambridge, Cambridge University Press).

THIRLWAY, H (1995), 'Law and Procedure of the International Court of Justice', 66 *BYIL* 4.

WATTS, A (1996), 'Nationality of Claims: Some Relevant Concepts', in Lowe and Fitzmaurice, *Fifty Years of the International Court of Justice*, p 424.

WITTICH, S (2001), 'Direct Injury and the Incidence of the Local Remedies Rule', 5 *Austrian Rev of Int'l and European L* 121.

FURTHER READING

AMERASINGHE, CF (1990), *Local Remedies in International Law* (Cambridge: Grotius): a comprehensive survey of the law including an in-depth study of the main doctrinal controversies.

CANCADO TRINDADE, AA (1983), *The Application of the Rule of Exhaustion of Local Remedies in International Law* (Cambridge: Cambridge University Press): a useful account of the rule with detailed illustrations from the jurisprudence of human rights tribunals, but rather dated.

DE HOOGH, AJJ (1996), *Obligations Erga Omnes and International Crimes: A Theoretical Inquiry into the Implementation and Enforcement of the International Responsibility of States* (The Hague: Kluwer): a detailed inquiry into the perennial difficulties surrounding the enforcement of *erga omnes* obligations.

INTERNATIONAL LAW ASSOCIATION (2000), *Committee on Diplomatic Protection of Persons and Property, Report of the Sixty-Ninth Conference* (London): a comprehensive and interesting examination of a wide range of issues relating to diplomatic protection.

PARRY, C (1956), 'Some Considerations Upon the Protection of Individuals in International Law', 90 *Recueil des Cours* 657: a good analysis of the law on diplomatic protection and includes some consideration of claims brought by international organizations.

TAMS, C (2005), *Enforcing Obligations Erga Omnes in International Law* (Cambridge, Cambridge University Press).

WARBRICK, C (1988), 'Protection of Nationals Abroad: Current Legal Problems', 37 *ICLQ* 1002: a useful analysis of some of the problematic aspects of diplomatic protection.

16

THE RESPONSIBILITY TO PROTECT

Spencer Zifcak

SUMMARY

The responsibility to protect has succeeded humanitarian intervention as the primary conceptual framework within which to consider international intervention to prevent the commission of mass atrocity crimes. First conceived in 2001, the doctrine has obtained international recognition in a remarkably short time. Its acceptance by the UN World Summit of political leaders in 2005, and later by the UN Security Council, provided the foundation for its further elaboration in international relations theory and political practice. This chapter provides the background to the new doctrine's appearance with a survey of the existing law and practice with respect to humanitarian intervention. It traces the subsequent intellectual and political development of the responsibility to protect both before and after the adoption of the World Summit resolutions that embodied it. This analysis discloses that debate about the doctrine has been characterized by significant differences of opinion and interpretation between nations of the North and the South. Four country case studies follow to illustrate and elaborate upon those differences. In that context, the chapter concludes with a detailed consideration of the contemporary standing of the doctrine in international law.

I. INTRODUCTION

The genocide in Rwanda and ethnic cleansing in the Balkans in the 1990s left the international community's political leadership with a formidable dilemma. Plainly, the international community could no longer stand by while mass atrocities were committed. The cost in human rights and human life was simply too great. At the same time, however, the UN Charter's core commitment to national sovereignty seemed an insuperable obstacle to international intervention in conflicts that took place entirely within the boundaries of a State. Non-interference in a nation's domestic affairs remained the cardinal rule underpinning the global legal order. If, therefore, the call 'never again' were to be made meaningful, new thinking and greater resolve were needed to chart the perilous waters between these apparently irreconcilable legal principles and political commitments.

The dilemma itself was not new. Debates about humanitarian intervention had taken place over centuries (Chesterman, 2001). Nevertheless, the impetus had seemed greater, and the scale of recent atrocities, not least in Kigali and Srebrenica, had shocked the world's conscience. The widespread and rapid acceptance of the understanding that individuals, just as much as States, should be regarded as the subjects of international law and, therefore, that they were deserving of its protection, had elevated human rights concerns to the top table of international political, legal, and academic deliberation (Alston and MacDonald, 2008; Fabri, 2008; Peters, 2009).

It was largely by way of cracking that seemingly intractable problem that the idea that nations individually have a responsibility to protect their own citizens and that collectively they may take action to protect those in peril elsewhere has recently been developed and elaborated.[1] As I will argue, the 'responsibility to protect' (R2P) has not yet crystallized into a norm of international law. Yet its advance as a widely considered and broadly accepted political doctrine has been rapid. In the remainder of this chapter I trace this advance and assess the doctrine's contemporary legal and political standing. To do that effectively, it may help to contextualize the issue by examining briefly the legal position with respect to its predecessor conception—humanitarian intervention (Evans, 2006).

II. HUMANITARIAN INTERVENTION IN INTERNATIONAL LAW

The prima facie position with respect to military interventions undertaken for humanitarian purposes appears to be as follows.[2] Pursuant to Article 2(4) of the United Nations (UN) Charter:

> All states shall refrain in their international relations from the threat or use of force against the territorial integrity and political independence of any state, or in any other manner inconsistent with the purpose of the United Nations.

This injunction against the use of force is reinforced by the terms of Article 2(7) which declares: 'Nothing in the present Charter shall authorize the UN to intervene in matters which are essentially within the domestic jurisdiction of any state.' The principle of non-intervention, together with that of the sovereign equality of States, is designed to ensure that each State respects the prerogatives and entitlements of every other State.

There are only two exceptions in the Charter to the Article 2(4) prohibition. First, Chapter VII of the Charter empowers the Security Council to authorize the use of force in response to threats and breaches of international peace and security. Pursuant to Article 39, therefore, the Security Council may make recommendations as to what measures, including the use of armed force, should be taken to address an identified threat to international peace and security or to any act of aggression. Secondly, in accordance with Article 51, member States of the United Nations may take measures, whether individually or collectively, in pursuit of their inherent right to self-defence should they be subject to armed attack. Such action in self-defence may continue until the Security Council itself has instituted whatever further measures are necessary to maintain international peace and security.

When laid down plainly in this way, it is apparent that the express terms of the Charter do not readily embrace either humanitarian intervention or a responsibility to protect

---

[1] See the International Commission on Intervention and State Sovereignty (2001), *The Responsibility to Protect: Report of the International Commission on Intervention and State Sovereignty*, Ottawa: International Development Research Centre.

[2] See generally, Chesterman, 2001, ch 2; Wheeler, 2004; Welsh, 2004.

(Gray, 2018, ch 2; Gray, Ch 20 of this book). The principle of non-intervention stands steadfastly in their path. The UN Declaration on Friendly Relations of 1970 states the duty in similar and compelling fashion:[3]

> No State or group of states has the right to intervene directly, or indirectly, for any reason whatsoever in the international external affairs of any other State. Consequently, armed intervention and all other forms of interference or attempted threats against the personality of the state or against its political, economic and cultural elements are in violation of international law.

Of course, the Charter's provisions are capable of competing interpretations. These can occupy the full spectrum from the literal to the liberal. International lawyers, for example, have argued that, despite what appear to be the plain words of the Charter text, a doctrine of humanitarian intervention may be insinuated into its interstices (Chesterman, 2001, p 47; Holzgrefe, 2003, p 53). One argument made is that Article 2(4) prohibits the use of force only against 'the territorial integrity or political independence of a state'. If, therefore, force is used in the pursuit of some other objective, particularly one that is consistent with the objects of the Charter, it may be permissible. A humanitarian intervention, properly conducted, may pose no long-term threat either to the territorial integrity or political autonomy of a State. Its sole purpose may be said to be to prevent the further commission of atrocities pending the restoration of stability.

Such an interpretation faces great difficulty, however, because it creates the prospect of a damaging ambiguity in the Charter's interpretation. Even a brief look at the *travaux préparatoires*, as a means of resolving such an ambiguity, demonstrates clearly that such an adventurous interpretation of the qualification has little if any plausible foundation. Instead, the original aim of the non-intervention principle appears to have been to protect smaller States and the words 'territorial integrity and political independence' were added as supplements to, not as detractions from, the general prohibition on the use of force.

Next, it may be suggested that the use of force is permitted so long as it is not, in the terms of Article 2(4), 'in any other manner inconsistent with the purposes of the United Nations'. Clearly, if the objective of the intervention is to prevent gross violations of human rights, it could not be said to be anything other than consistent with the Charter's fundamental purposes. The argument runs into immediate problems, however, not the least of which is that even if the disputed intervention is aimed at protecting and preserving the human rights of the afflicted people of a nation, the Charter's express prohibition of infringements upon the territorial integrity and political independence of a sovereign State still stands. It is unlikely that a vague reference to humanitarian purpose is sufficient to displace it.

Alternatively, a right or obligation of humanitarian intervention may arise in consequence of its progressive acceptance as part of customary international law (Cassese, 1999; Chesterman, 2001, ch 2; Corten, 2008). There are significant methodological and practical difficulties, however, that stand in the way of humanitarian intervention's recognition as a customary rule. The International Court of Justice, for example, has had only limited opportunity to develop the rules governing the use of force.[4] Insofar as the Court has considered the matter, it has come down steadfastly against any broadly applicable doctrine of

---

[3] Declaration on Principles of International Law Concerning Friendly Relations and Co-operation among States in accordance with the Charter of the United Nations, 24 October 1970, Article 1.

[4] See, in particular, *Military and Paramilitary Activities in and against Nicaragua (Nicaragua v United States of America), Merits, Judgment, ICJ Reports 1986*, p 14; *Legality of Use of Force (Yugoslavia v Belgium), Provisional Measures, Order of 2 June 1999, ICJ Reports 1999*, p 124.

permissible intervention. Nations themselves are not often clear or straightforward about their motivations for acting, and mix legal justifications with political and security concerns in a way that makes the interpretation of State action an uncertain exercise. The UN's norm-creating bodies, in particular the Security Council and General Assembly, may not always be at one in their judgment of events, raising complex questions about the weight to be given to the opinions of each and the relative merits of both.

Such methodological difficulties have plainly been present in the most recent examples of international military interventions claimed to have had a humanitarian foundation. These are worth examining more closely. Two classes of case may be identified: those where the UN Security Council has sanctioned purported humanitarian interventions and those where it has not.

A. INTERVENTION WITH SECURITY COUNCIL AUTHORIZATION

In the first category are the cases of international intervention in Somalia, Rwanda, and Bosnia (see Weiss, 2007; Evans, 2008; Welsh, 2008). The Somali operation was justified principally on the basis that the obstacles being placed in the way of urgently required humanitarian assistance to the country's distressed population were, in the opinion of the Security Council, such as to constitute a threat to international peace and security. The Council, therefore, authorized the international community pursuant to Chapter VII to use all necessary means to establish a secure environment for international relief operations.[5] The UN Secretary-General later expressed his opinion that the Somali operation constituted a new precedent for the Council. It had, for the first time, authorized a military intervention for purely humanitarian purposes.[6]

All too late, the Security Council authorized French military intervention to prevent further mass atrocities in Rwanda. It had previously determined that the Rwandan genocide had constituted a threat to international peace and security and that safe havens were therefore required for those fleeing the genocide. In its primary resolution the Council also referred specifically to the wider disruption to cross-border security that had been created by the mass internal displacement of Rwandan citizens. Again, the Council authorized all necessary means to achieve the primary humanitarian objective. To that end, it instructed the French interveners to create a safe haven in which those fleeing the wider conflict could find security.[7] The French were also clear that any intervention on their part had to be founded upon the Security Council's mandate, even if delay were the result.[8]

The Security Council's many resolutions in relation to Bosnia and Herzegovina were directed principally at ending civil conflict consequent upon the dissolution of the former Yugoslavia rather than having a primarily humanitarian objective, although the latter remained significant. Resolution 770 (1992), for example, called upon States to take the measures necessary to facilitate the delivery of humanitarian aid and assistance to Sarajevo and other parts of the country as needed. It went further to authorize the UN intervention force to act in self-defence where necessary in order to reply to bombardments of established safe havens or to armed incursion into them and to take all necessary measures, including the use of air power in and around the internationally protected safe areas, to support its protective objective.[9] Again these resolutions proceeded from the Council's

---

[5] SC Res 794 (3 December 1992).   [6] 1993 *UNYB* 51.   [7] SC Res 929 (22 June 1994).
[8] 40 *Annuaire Français de Droit International Public* (1998) 429–30.
[9] SC Res 770 (13 August 1992) and see further SC Res 814 (26 March 1993); SC Res 816 (31 March 1993); SC Res 844 (19 June 1993); and SC Res 871 (2 October 1993).

earlier determination that the conflict in Bosnia and Herzegovina constituted a threat to international peace and security.

These three cases suggest that since 1990, a highly circumscribed recognition of a right of humanitarian intervention may have been developing gradually within customary international law. The legal preconditions for such a nascent right were first that an existing or potential humanitarian catastrophe must be identified. Secondly, the catastrophe and its wider effects must be such as to constitute, in the opinion of the Security Council, a threat to international peace and security. Thirdly, the Security Council must explicitly authorize any subsequent military intervention. Fourthly, and implicitly, the authorization and conduct of the intervention must be an act of last resort (see Gazzini, 2005, p 174; Corten, 2008, p 106).

B. INTERVENTION WITHOUT SECURITY COUNCIL AUTHORIZATION

Following the defeat of the Iraqi army in Kuwait and its subsequent withdrawal from that country, in 1991 the Kurdish peoples in the north of the country sought to assert their right to political independence. This uprising was met with brute military force by troops loyal to the Hussein regime and, after it was put down, the government embarked upon further, genocidal, repression of the Kurdish population. In response, the Security Council adopted Resolution 688. The resolution condemned the repression of the Iraqi civilian population, demanded that Iraq end this oppression, and insisted that Iraq allow international humanitarian organizations immediate access to all those in need of assistance. The Council also appealed to all member States and humanitarian organizations to continue their humanitarian relief efforts. Despite its strong language, however, the resolution did not contain any express authorization for military action pursuant to Chapter VII.[10]

Nevertheless, on the same day, the US administration announced that it would commence dropping food and other forms of material aid over Northern Iraq in partnership with France and the United Kingdom. Then, 11 days later, when it appeared as if the aid effort was being substantially compromised by mountainous and inhospitable terrain into which the aid was being delivered, President Bush announced unilaterally that US troops would enter Northern Iraq in order to establish safe havens for the beleaguered Kurdish population.

When these interventions were challenged by Iraq in the Security Council, the coalition partners contended that their actions were justified on purely humanitarian grounds. They also sought to establish legal legitimacy for their interventions by arguing that Resolution 688 had provided implicit legal authorization for them. The argument that humanitarian intervention might legally be supported by such implicit authorization was difficult to justify. This was because the express terms of the relevant resolution did not appear to allow for such an expansive interpretation. The resolution itself was the first of 14 that had not been adopted under Chapter VII. And in the Council debates that led to its adoption, the prospect of military intervention had never explicitly been contemplated. However strongly based on humanitarian concern, then, the arguments put in favour of the right of a State or States to engage unilaterally in humanitarian intervention without express Security Council authorization seemed, at least at that stage, to have only the most tenuous foundation.

The question as to the legality of unilateral humanitarian intervention emerged for consideration again in 1999 in relation to the controversial intervention by NATO in defence

---

[10] SC Res 688 (5 April 1991).

of the ethnic Albanian people of Kosovo.[11] So as to protect the Kosovar Albanians from violence and ethnic cleansing at the hands of Serbian forces, NATO conducted some thousands of bombing raids on Kosovo and surrounding areas over several months. Prior to this, the Security Council had adopted three resolutions concerning the deteriorating military and humanitarian situation.

Resolution 1160 condemned the use of excessive force by Serbian police, imposed an arms embargo, and expressed support for a political solution based on the territorial integrity of the FRY with greater autonomy for the Kosovar Albanians.[12] Resolution 1199 recognized the deteriorating humanitarian situation, one that had already resulted in numerous civilian casualties and the displacement of 230,000 people from their homes. It declared the situation as one constituting a threat to international peace and security and, acting under Chapter VII, demanded a ceasefire and action to improve the humanitarian position.[13] In Resolution 1203, finally, the Council decided that should the concrete measures it had demanded not be taken, and should Serbia not comply with the terms of the agreement reached with NATO and the Organization for Security and Co-operation in Europe (OSCE) to end the hostilities, it would *consider* further action and additional measures to maintain or restore peace and stability in the region.[14] These resolutions fell far short of authorizing any international military intervention to achieve that aim.

Certainly, the Council had determined that the deterioration of the situation in Kosovo threatened regional peace and security. And, in Resolution 1199, the Council had demanded an immediate end to hostilities and the maintenance of a ceasefire. It had also demanded immediate measures to avert an imminent catastrophe. Not once, however, had the Council authorized the use of force by the international community in order to advance these objectives. Instead, in Kosovo, NATO took upon itself the task of pursuing and achieving them without further reference to the Council.

The bare bones of NATO's legal argument were straightforward. The Security Council had adopted resolutions under Chapter VII that demanded that the Yugoslavian authorities halt their brutal repression of ethnic Albanians. The authorities had refused to comply with these resolutions and the prior, brokered agreements to which they referred. Consequently, NATO member States presumed unilaterally to act in support of those resolutions by intervening to prevent further violations.

However forcefully legal arguments in favour of the NATO action were put, formidable obstacles remained in the path of their acceptance. The argument that NATO's intervention was implicitly justified as a means of enforcing prior Security Council resolutions again was weak. This was because the wording of the resolutions did not at all appear to authorize any subsequent unilateral military action and it left for the Council's further consideration any decision as to what additional measures might be necessary to pursue and enforce its demands (Corten, 2008). Quite apart from this, the idea that a State or group of States could or should act unilaterally to enforce Council resolutions without any subsequent Council involvement or authorization could open the door to opportunistic interventions of any and every kind.[15] Finally, even if it had been accepted prior to Kosovo that the protection of non-derogable human rights had achieved the status of *jus cogens* and therefore obliged the UN to protect them, it by no means followed that the unilateral employment of military force to secure them, outside the UN, had also become part of customary international law (Alston and MacDonald, 2008).

[11] See Simma, 1999; Chinkin, 2000; Thakur, 2011a.   [12] SC Res 1160 (31 March 1998).
[13] SC Res 1199 (23 September 1998).   [14] SC Res 1203 (24 October 1998).
[15] See to similar effect the statement by the Permanent Representative of India during Security Council debate, SC/1035 (24 March 1999), p 3 at p 10.

Considering this, the conclusion of the Independent Commission Report on Kosovo (2000) is apt:

> Far from opening up a new era of humanitarian intervention the Kosovo experience seems, to this Commission at least, to teach a valuable lesson of skepticism and caution. Sometimes, and Kosovo is such an instance, the use of military force may become necessary to defend human rights. But the grounds for its use in international law urgently need clarification and the tactics and rules of engagement for its use needs to be improved. Finally, the legitimacy of such use of force will always be controversial, and will remain so, as long as we intervene to protect some people's lives but not others.

III. THE BIRTH OF THE RESPONSIBILITY TO PROTECT

In the decade following Kosovo, there had been no significant instances of humanitarian military interventions in which the international community engaged. State practice, therefore, provided no further guidance as to the doctrine's further development in international law. At the same time, however, conceptual developments have been quick. These developments have focused not upon humanitarian intervention per se, but rather on a bold endeavour, by those concerned to prevent mass atrocity crimes, to craft a new, more thoughtful, and more measured doctrine to build upon and at the same time differentiate it from its humanitarian predecessor. In just a few years the idea of humanitarian intervention has been displaced by what has come to be known as the responsibility to protect (R2P).

Speaking in an address to the UN General Assembly in 1999, then UN Secretary-General Kofi Annan challenged member States to resolve what he saw as the conflict between the principle of non-interference with State sovereignty, embodied in Article 2(4) of the Charter, and the responsibility of the international community to respond to massive human rights violations and ethnic cleansing. He posed what he described as a tragic dilemma:

> To those for whom the greatest threat to the future of the international order is the use of force in the absence of a Security Council mandate, one might ask . . . in the context of Rwanda: if in those dark days and hours leading up to the genocide a coalition of states had been prepared to act in defence of the Tutsi population, but did not receive prompt Security Council authorization, should such a coalition have stood aside and allowed the horror to unfold?
>
> To those for whom the Kosovo action heralded a new era when States and groups of States can take military action outside the established mechanisms for enforcing international law, one might ask: is there not a danger of such interventions undermining the imperfect, yet resilient, security system created after the Second World War, and of setting dangerous precedents for future interventions without a clear criterion to decide who might invoke these precedents, and in what circumstances?[16]

To steer between the Scylla and Charybdis of the problem, Annan argued that the Security Council must be able to agree on effective action to defend fundamental human rights. He proposed that the core challenge to the Council in the twenty-first century was: 'To forge

---

[16] Address by Kofi Annan to the 54th Session of the UN General Assembly, 20 September 1999.

unity behind the principle that massive and systematic violations of human rights—wherever they may take place—should not be allowed to stand.'

The Secretary-General's call to action met with a mixed and in some places hostile response in the General Assembly. Nevertheless, it prompted the Canadian government, in a singular initiative, to form an international panel of experts, the International Commission on Intervention and State Sovereignty (ICISS), to address the problem. The Commission consulted widely with governments, non-governmental organizations, intergovernmental organizations, universities, and think-tanks. On the basis of these extensive consultations, it produced its final report, *The Responsibility to Protect*.[17] The report radically altered the terms of the ensuing political debate in three inter-related ways.

First, it re-conceptualized forcible international action in defence of peoples at risk of mass atrocity. The international community would no longer engage in 'humanitarian intervention' but would instead exercise a broader responsibility to protect nations at risk of failure and descent into violence. Secondly, the new approach attributed primary responsibility for taking action to prevent humanitarian disaster upon the sovereign government of the nation in which it might occur. Only if and when that responsibility had not been exercised would the larger global community's parallel responsibility to intervene in the national and international interest be engaged. Thirdly, new rules of engagement should be developed to ensure that any such intervention would have the maximum possible opportunity for success.

The Commission asserted, more in hope than expectation given its novelty, that the responsibility to protect reflected an emerging norm of international law and behaviour:

> Based on our reading of state practice, Security Council precedent, established norms, guiding principles, and evolving customary international law, the Commission believes that the Charter's strong bias against military intervention is not to be regarded as absolute when decisive action is required on human protection grounds.[18]

As to the vexed question of military intervention, ICISS recommended that it should take place pursuant to authorization by the Security Council and only then after the careful consideration of five criteria of legitimacy. These were that:

- The threatened harm must be serious; ie it must involve genocide, war crimes, crimes against humanity, or ethnic cleansing.
- The primary purpose of the intervention must be to halt the threatened humanitarian catastrophe.
- Military intervention must be adopted only as a measure of last resort.
- The proposed military action must be proportionate to the threat.
- The adverse consequences flowing from the military intervention should clearly be less than the consequences of inaction (see Evans, 2008, p 139).

Finally, ICISS developed its conceptual framework by proposing that three different forms of responsibility were engaged. The responsibility to protect should best be exercised initially through prevention. This 'responsibility to prevent' spoke to the need to take every reasonable step to ensure that predicted humanitarian catastrophes would not occur. Preventive strategies such as good governance and human rights, together with international aid and development assistance, should be the first to be deployed. Next, 'the

---

[17] International Commission on Intervention and State Sovereignty (2001), *The Responsibility to Protect: Report of the International Commission on Intervention and State Sovereignty*, Ottawa, International Development Research Centre.   [18] Ibid, p 16.

responsibility to react' emphasized that in the exercise of its preventive role, the international community should always prefer non-forcible measures, such as diplomatic negotiations and economic sanctions, to instigating armed intervention. Once a crisis had been averted, whether militarily or otherwise, a *'responsibility to rebuild'* would be assumed. In this, the international community would involve itself in peacekeeping, economic and social reconstruction, constitutional renewal, and other similar developmental initiatives.

The central thrust of the report, then, was upon the prevention of conflict through a range of non-military measures that would likely entail significant transfers of wealth, expertise, and opportunity from developed to developing countries. It would involve taking Third World development seriously. Only when such measures had failed to avert an anticipated humanitarian crisis would more coercive means be considered.

IV. THE 2005 WORLD SUMMIT

A. TOWARDS THE 2005 WORLD SUMMIT

Three years after ICISS had reported, its recommendations received powerful endorsement from the Secretary-General's High-Level Panel on Threats, Challenges and Change (HLP). The Panel adopted the conceptual framework embodied in the idea of the responsibility to protect. It favoured the ICISS's conclusion that any such responsibility should be exercised only with the endorsement of the Security Council. And it incorporated, with some minor alterations, the legitimacy criteria that had been set down in the original report.[19]

Addressing the relevant legal issues, the HLP observed that the Charter reaffirmed a fundamental faith in human rights but did not do much to protect them. Article 2(7) prohibits intervention in matters that are essentially within the jurisdiction of any State. Nevertheless, the Panel asserted that the principle of non-intervention embodied in that Article could not be used to shield nations from the consequences of State-sponsored genocidal acts or other atrocities. These should properly be considered as threats to international peace and security under Article 24 and, as such, might with legal justification provoke a response from the Security Council:

> We endorse the emerging norm that there is a collective international responsibility to protect, exercisable by the Security Council, authorizing military intervention as a last resort, in the event of genocide and other large-scale killing, ethnic cleansing or serious violations of international humanitarian law which sovereign governments have proved powerless or unwilling to prevent.[20]

Taking his lead from the HLP, the Secretary-General recommended that the World Leaders' Summit in 2005 adopt the responsibility to protect.[21] Even so, it was unclear whether his recommendation would survive the exhaustive and exhausting negotiations that would occur in the six months preceding the Summit. The principal line of objection was clear. Some States would argue strongly in favour of the international community's entitlement to intervene in the face of genocide, crimes against humanity, and other mass atrocities

---

[19] *A More Secure World: Our Shared Responsibility*, the Report of the High-Level Panel on Threats, Challenges and Change, UN Doc A/59/565, 2004.

[20] Ibid; and for an analysis of the assertion see Corten, 2008, p 127.

[21] *In Larger Freedom: Towards Development, Security and Human Rights for All*, Report of the Secretary-General, UN Doc A/59/2005, 2005, p 35.

committed by a State. Others, however, would maintain that the Security Council was prohibited legally from authorizing coercive action against sovereign nations in relation to any matter that occurred within their borders. As the Permanent Representative of Algeria put the matter in an early discussion on the Secretary-General's report:

> interference can occur with the consent of the State concerned … we do not deny that the United Nations has the right and duty to help suffering humanity. But we remain extremely sensitive to any undermining of our sovereignty, not only because sovereignty is our last defence against the rules of an unequal world, but because we are not taking part in the decision making process of the Security Council.[22]

Generally speaking, the Western Europe and Others Group (WEOG) nations supported the inclusion of a resolution in favour of the responsibility to protect in the World Summit outcome document. The United States, however, had significant reservations. A powerful bloc in the Non-Aligned Movement (NAM) either opposed its inclusion or sought significant amendments to the basic principles that had been set down. Several Latin American nations also expressed their disquiet. The most interesting and crucial aspect of these pre-summit discussions was the strong support for the doctrine provided by the nations of Africa. In a sense, this was not surprising. It has been in Africa—perhaps more than in any other region of the world—that mass violations of human rights of the kind sought to be prevented here, have occurred. African nations had first-hand, or near-hand, experience of the atrocities and consequent human suffering with which the doctrine was concerned, and an intimate and devastating knowledge of the consequences of both State and international failure.[23] In this context, the Tanzanian President had made the case plainly:

> We must now stop misusing the principles of sovereignty and non-interference in the internal affairs of states to mark incidents of poor governance and unacceptable human rights abuses … In the aftermath of the genocide in Rwanda, and in light of the massive influx of refugees in the Great Lakes Region, it is inevitable to conclude that the principle of non-intervention in the internal affairs of a state can no longer find unqualified, absolute legitimacy … Governments must first be held responsible for the life and welfare of their people. But, there must also be common agreed rules and benchmarks that would trigger collective action through our regional organizations and the United Nations against governments that commit unacceptable human rights abuses.[24]

B. THE WORLD SUMMIT RESOLUTION

Under heavy pressure to adopt some form of the responsibility to protect formula, diplomatic representatives in New York haggled into the last week before the Summit to try to find the words that might permit a compromise text to go to the world's leaders for endorsement.[25] After frenzied last minute negotiations, the final text was concluded. It was hedged with qualifications and therefore weaker than that which had been proposed

---

[22] Abdallah Baali, Permanent Representative of Algeria, Statement to the Informal Thematic Consultations of the General Assembly to Discuss the Four Clusters Contained in the Secretary-General's Report 'In Larger Freedom', Cluster III: Freedom to Live in Dignity, 19 April 2005.

[23] For that reason the African Union had previously inserted a provision embodying a doctrine resembling the responsibility to protect into its Constitutive Act. See Article 4(h).

[24] President of Tanzania, Benjamin Mkapa, address to the First Summit of the International Conference on the Great Lakes, Dar-es-Salaam, November 2004.

[25] As to the General Assembly Debate prior to the World Summit see Bellamy, 2008; Zifcak, 2009, ch 6.

in the ICISS and HLP reports. Nevertheless, the very fact that the concept and principle had been agreed to at the World Summit represented a substantial success. The concluded wording was as follows:

> 138. Each individual State has the responsibility to protect its populations from genocide, war crimes, ethnic cleansing and crimes against humanity. This responsibility entails the prevention of such crimes, including their incitement, through appropriate and necessary means. We accept that responsibility and will act in accordance with it ...
>
> 139. The international community, through the United Nations, also has the responsibility to use appropriate diplomatic, humanitarian and other peaceful means, in accordance with Chapters VI and VII of the Charter, to help protect populations from genocide, war crimes, ethnic cleansing and crimes against humanity. In this context, we are prepared to take collective action, in a timely and decisive manner, through the Security Council, in accordance with the Charter, including Chapter VII, on a case-by-case basis and in cooperation with relevant regional organizations as appropriate, should peaceful means be ineffective ... We stress the need for the General Assembly to continue considerations of the responsibility to protect populations from genocide, war crimes, ethnic cleansing and crimes against humanity and its implications, bearing in mind the principles of the Charter and international law. We also intend to commit ourselves, as necessary and appropriate, to helping states build capacity to protect their populations from genocide, war crimes, ethnic cleansing and crimes against humanity and to assisting those which are under stress before crises and conflicts break out.[26]

Despite this success, a close look at the Summit resolution makes it plain that several of the doctrine's underlying principles were likely to be qualified heavily in practice. In the process of negotiating the final text, victory went to those favouring the acceptance of the new doctrine. However, those opposing it, whether absolutely or conditionally, managed to extract substantial concessions. A close reading of the text reveals the following qualifications:

- The crimes in relation to which a responsibility to protect may arise were limited to genocide, war crimes, ethnic cleansing, and crimes against humanity. A suggestion from the United States that an additional phrase 'or other major atrocities' be added to avoid further definitional argument was not adopted.
- The international community was enjoined in the first instance to exercise its responsibility by using all appropriate diplomatic, humanitarian, and other peaceful means in accordance with the Charter. Collective action could be triggered only when such peaceful means are considered to have been inadequate.
- The international community, in its Summit embodiment, indicated that it was 'prepared to take collective action'. Following from an American recommendation, the words 'we recognize our shared responsibility to take collective action' were removed.
- Collective action by the international community must be authorized by the Security Council in accordance with the terms of Chapter VII of the Charter. The idea, referred to briefly by the HLP, that there may be certain circumstances in which intervention might be countenanced without such authorization did not make its way into the text.
- No criteria of legitimacy were set down. Instead, the international community, through the United Nations, would determine on a 'case-by-case' basis whether

[26] 2005 World Summit Outcome, UN Doc A/60/L.1.

collective action to defend populations from criminal activities is required. This was a late insertion, at the behest of the United States and China.

- Collective action under Chapter VII would be considered only where national authorities 'manifestly fail to protect their populations' from the relevant crimes. This was a standard considerably higher than that initially suggested.

- A recommended constraint—that the permanent members of the Security Council (P-5) should refrain from exercising the veto in cases of genocide, war crimes, ethnic cleansing, and crimes against humanity—was rejected.

There was no doubt that the formal recognition of the new doctrine of the responsibility to protect by the world's political leadership stood as one of the principal achievements of the World Summit. However, as is plain from this analysis of the resolution's text, there remained ample room for argument as to its meaning, standing, and exercise (Focarelli, 2008).

V. POST-WORLD SUMMIT RECOGNITION OF R2P

Since the World Summit, the most significant development with respect to the responsibility to protect has been its recognition by the Security Council. In the context of a debate upon the protection of civilians in armed conflict, the Security Council approved Resolution 1674 dealing with all aspects of that question, including the promotion of economic growth, poverty eradication, national reconciliation, good governance, democracy, the rule of law, and the protection of fundamental human rights.[27] This resolution reaffirmed 'the provisions of paragraphs 138 and 139 of the 2005 World Summit Outcome Document regarding the responsibility to protect populations from genocide, war crimes, ethnic cleansing and crimes against humanity'. Apart from the normative importance of this reaffirmation, the adoption of the resolution marked the first occasion upon which the Security Council acknowledged expressly that its role may extend not just to the prevention of threats to international peace and security but also to the cessation of mass atrocities taking place within State borders.

Soon after, without any further elaboration of the doctrine, the Security Council invoked the new norm for the first time—in relation to the situation in Darfur. In Resolution 1706, the Council resolved, among other things, to deploy a UN peacekeeping force in Darfur and sought the consent of the Sudanese government to do so.[28] In its preliminaries, Resolution 1706 recalled Resolution 1674 and its endorsement of the terms of the World Summit Outcome in this respect. It reaffirmed the Council's strong commitment to the sovereignty, unity, independence, and territorial integrity of Sudan but made clear its view that the nation's sovereignty would not be adversely affected by the transition to a UN force devoted to the cause of peace. In the preamble of Resolution 1973 with respect to the Libyan intervention in 2011, the Council reiterated the responsibility of the Libyan authorities to protect the population and reaffirmed that the parties to the conflict bore the primary responsibility for ensuring the protection of civilians.[29] A similar reaffirmation followed in the Council Resolution on Côte d'Ivoire.[30] In Security Council resolutions, as at 2017, there have been preambular references to R2P on more than 50 occasions.

---

[27] SC Res 1674 (28 April 2006).   [28] SC Res 1704 (25 August 2006).
[29] SC Res 1973 (17 March 2011).   [30] SC Res 1975 (30 March 2011).

VI. THE SECRETARY-GENERAL'S ELABORATION OF THE RESPONSIBILITY TO PROTECT

The World Summit resolutions with respect to R2P, although adopted by consensus, were highly general in nature and much work remained to be done to put flesh on their bones. To assist with this task Ban Ki-Moon appointed Professor Edward Luck to be his special adviser on the subject, and Luck went to work to make the doctrine comprehensible and concrete. The product was the Secretary-General's report to the General Assembly on the implementation of the responsibility to protect, which was tabled in January 2009.[31]

The report made clear that Kofi Annan's successor was also committed to the doctrine. It contained a detailed encapsulation and explication of the new doctrine's principal parameters. It drew heavily on the work of ICISS and the HLP but its cast was much more pragmatic. In elaborating upon it, a three-Pillar approach to its implementation was proposed.

Pursuant to the first Pillar, the nation in which a humanitarian catastrophe is in prospect must assume responsibility for taking timely and appropriate preventative measures. These may include intensive diplomatic steps to mediate impending conflict, the adoption of anti-corruption strategies, the early prosecution of those engaging in violent activity, the promotion of human rights, and efforts to secure the rule of law and establish more effective governance. The second Pillar involved calibrated reaction by the international community. Here, concerted and well-targeted assistance in the form of development aid, foreign investment, technical assistance, economic incentives, rapid police responsiveness, and more general capacity-building would be crucial. Under the third Pillar, such measures may be supplemented initially by 'soft' coercion that may include international fact-finding, the deployment of peacekeepers, the imposition of arms embargoes, the application of diplomatic and economic sanctions, and the creation of safe havens and no-fly zones. Then, when all else had failed, the Security Council could authorize military intervention as the measure of last resort.

The Secretary-General sought to clarify certain issues about which there had been considerable confusion or dissension since the World Summit. He made clear that R2P applies only in relation to cases of genocide, war crimes, crimes against humanity, and ethnic cleansing. It does not detract from existing international commitments under international humanitarian law, human rights law, or refugee law. Collective action in the use of force must be undertaken with the authority of the Security Council and in accordance with Chapter VII of the Charter. R2P provides no support, therefore, for unilateral military interventions. The doctrine is to be distinguished from 'humanitarian intervention'. Humanitarian intervention, the report said, posed a false choice between either standing by in the face of catastrophe or deploying coercive military force to protect populations that were threatened. R2P sought to overcome this binary divide by recasting sovereignty as responsibility and then defining in some detail what the respective duties and obligations of nations and the international community to prevent humanitarian catastrophes should be.

The Secretary-General presented yearly reports on R2P from 2010 to 2017. Of these, three were of particular importance. In 2012, Ban Ki-Moon presented his report on 'timely and decisive response'.[32] The report was significant because it was the first to be directed at illuminating the parameters and practice of coercive intervention. It was also the first in

---

[31] Report of the Secretary-General, *Implementing the Responsibility to Protect*, UN Doc A/63/677; Luck, 2009.

[32] Report of the Secretary-General, *Responsibility to Protect: Timely and Decisive Response*, UN Doc A66/874.

which the Secretary-General could address disagreements that had emerged in the course of the UN-sanctioned NATO intervention in Libya.

The report set down five key lessons that had been learnt from the experience of the doctrine's implementation:

- While each instance of its application had been distinct, the doctrine's principles could and should be applied uniformly. Its mechanisms and methods, however, had necessarily to be shaped by circumstances on the ground.

- The Security Council had become more actively engaged than previously in responding to gross human rights violations.

- A more integrated and nuanced understanding of how the three Pillars related to one another was required. None of the Pillars was likely to stand on its own. The purpose of Pillar 3 intervention, for example, was directed primarily to enabling national authorities to resume their responsibility to protect their own peoples in conformity with the legal obligations inherent in Pillar 1.

- Any effective and integrated strategy was likely to involve elements of response and prevention. Capacity building, through the establishment of independent commissions of inquiry, for example, embraced elements of both.

- Finally, the role of partners, in particular regional intergovernmental organizations, was invaluable. Every effort should be made to strengthen the ties between the two in a concerted endeavour to prevent mass atrocity crimes.

Traversing the more uncertain terrain of coercive intervention, the Secretary-General's report was at pains to point out that Pillar 3 interventions did not necessitate the application of military force. A comprehensive range of less intensive measures was available, including sanctions, the restriction of scientific and technical co-operation, the constraint or severance of diplomatic ties, and controlling the availability of high value commodities or weapons. Even under s 42 of the UN Charter, military intervention could be left as a last resort, for example in favour of sanctions or the establishment of security and no-fly zones.

Recognizing that there had been disagreement amongst the members of the Security Council as to the means and ends of the international community's military intervention in Libya one year before, the Secretary-General remarked diplomatically that:

> the Security Council decided to authorize the use of force after most of its members had come to the conclusion that a series of peaceful measures had proven inadequate. Some member states, however, have contended that non-coercive measures were not given sufficient time to demonstrate results . . . Others have expressed the view that those charged with implementing Council resolution 1973 exceeded the mandate they were given by the Council. Whatever the specific merits of the arguments, it is important that the international community learns from these experiences and that concerns expressed by member states are taken into account in the future.[33]

The Secretary-General's next substantive report was delivered in 2015. It was entitled *A Vital and Enduring Commitment: Implementing the Responsibility to Protect*.[34] Coming ten years after the adoption of the doctrine in 2005, the report sought to gather together the key lessons that had been learnt during that decade. The Secretary-General noted that

[33] UN Doc A/66/874 (25 July 2012), para 54.
[34] Report of the Secretary-General, *Responsibility to Protect: A Vital and Enduring Commitment: Implementing the Responsibility to Protect*, UN Doc A/69/981 (13 July 2015).

despite the best endeavours of R2P's founders, practitioners, and supporters, mass atrocity crimes continued to be committed in far too many countries. As the primary examples he cited the situations in the Central African Republic, South Sudan, Sudan, the Democratic Republic of the Congo, Syria, Libya, Yemen, and the Democratic People's Republic of Korea.

Nevertheless Ban Ki-Moon remarked upon several positive, evolutionary developments that had been consolidated during the decade. An increasing number of States had become parties to international legal instruments with respect to genocide, war crimes, crimes against humanity, and ethnic cleansing. Within the UN, an atrocity crime perspective had been integrated into conflict prevention, development cooperation, peacekeeping, and peacebuilding. States had strengthened their focus on building capacity in nations at risk of failure. In several countries there had been promising examples of initiatives to strengthen electoral commissions and human rights institutions, to reinforce human rights protection and respect for international humanitarian law in security sector reform, and to encourage freedom of the press and other mechanisms designed to counter incitement to discrimination, hostility, and violence. The Security Council had adopted 30 resolutions and six presidential statements that referred to the responsibility to protect that demonstrated strong support for the principle. Acting under Chapter VII of the UN Charter, the international community had begun to employ more robust tools, including sanctions that had been designed to discourage the targeting of civilians. The UN had established peacekeeping missions with a strong commitment to the protection of civilians at risk.

The Secretary-General, however, could hardly fail to acknowledge that in the doctrine's first decade, significant failures had occurred in the implementation of R2P. Mass atrocity crimes continued unabated. Of all the factors that had contributed to this situation, the Secretary-General singled out the lack of the political will to act as the most significant:

> While prevention is the preferred approach to implementing the responsibility to protect, it does not always succeed. Experience in the last decade demonstrates that timely and decisive response remains essential to protecting populations and that a collective response can dampen the determination of potential perpetrators to commit atrocity crimes. However, the record shows a lack in both the political will and cohesion of the international community, which has compromised the pursuit of a consistent and timely response to protecting populations.[35]

In that context, he called upon the Security Council to act earlier to address situations of concern before they escalate into intractable conflicts, to provide strong backing for preventive diplomacy and mediation, and to ensure that perpetrators of atrocity crimes were held to account for their actions. He also encouraged the permanent members of the Security Council to refrain from their use of the veto in circumstances where mass atrocities were in contemplation or had already commenced.

The 2016 report was Ban Ki-Moon's final one. Perhaps therefore because he had little to lose, this report was considerably more assertive in its support for R2P and frank in its assessments of its shortcomings.[36] The Secretary-General began by noting some further positive developments. The imperative to combat mass atrocity crime within the framework of R2P, he said, had been widely accepted. It had become a key agenda item at

---

[35] Report of the Secretary-General, *Responsibility to Protect: A Vital and Enduring Commitment: Implementing the Responsibility to Protect*, UN Doc A/69/981 para 36.

[36] Report of the Secretary-General, *Mobilising Collective Action: The Next Decade of the Responsibility to protect*, UN Doc A/70/999 (22 July 2016).

intergovernmental forums both within and beyond the United Nations. New structures, including more than 40 national R2P focal points, had been created at national, regional, and international levels to encourage the fulfillment of the international community's collective responsibility to combat crimes against humanity. The UN had adopted the 'Human Rights Up Front' initiative, the purpose of which was to sensitize every instrumentality and division of the Organization to human rights concerns, including the imperative to detect and prevent the commission of mass atrocity crimes. At the same time, however, the incidence of crimes against humanity had regrettably increased. Ban Ki-Moon remarked somewhat despondently that:

> Over the past few years, however, we have drifted off-track, threatening to reverse years of progress. The frequency and scale of atrocity crimes have increased and will likely continue to do so unless the international community takes more determined and consistent action to fulfil its responsibility to protect. Research demonstrates that in 2014 the number of deaths caused by armed conflict and atrocity crimes exceeded 100,000—its highest level since 1994—driven in large part by the increased targeting of civilians. Over the past two years, civilian populations in the Central African Republic, Iraq, South Sudan, the Sudan, Syria and Yemen have been subjected to systematic violence that could constitute atrocity crimes. In Syria alone, more than a quarter of a million people have been killed and more than 11 million displaced by a civil war in which government forces and non-State armed groups have paid scant regard to their legal obligations to civilians. Sexual and gender-based violence . . . also continues to be prevalent.[37]

The Secretary-General singled out three trends he thought were particularly worrying in this context. In many armed conflicts the combatants had proceeded in blatant disregard of international law, especially international humanitarian law. The deliberate targeting of civilians had become commonplace. Member States, while recognizing the necessity for preventative measures, had insufficiently translated that recognition into practical action. The deployment of peacekeeping forces, for instance, had all too often been delayed, and the provision of the money needed for effective peacekeeping lagged well behind that which was required. Armed conflicts had frequently been exacerbated by the intervention of third party nations seeking to advance their own strategic interests at the expense of domestic populations. Such external actors had been responsible, for instance, for the provision of heavy weaponry to parties involved in civil war and for shielding the perpetrators of serious crime.

Ban Ki-Moon made three key recommendations to render the responsibility to protect more credible and practical. Far greater emphasis, he asserted, should be given to effective prevention. For that to succeed, the analysis and assessment of potentially dangerous situations must be improved. The UN itself had taken significant steps in this direction with the publication of its influential 'Framework for the Analysis of Atrocity Crimes',[38] and with the implementation of its comprehensive 'Human Rights Up Front' initiative.[39]

Next, the international community should place greater emphasis on capacity-building and non-military forms of intervention to protect populations at risk of mass atrocity crime. These, the Secretary-General proposed, might include fact-finding, monitoring, reporting and verification, commissions of inquiry, public advocacy, quiet diplomacy,

---

[37] Report of the Secretary-General, *Mobilising Collective Action: The Next Decade of the Responsibility to Protect*, UN Doc A/70/999, para 8.

[38] United Nations, 'Framework of Analysis for Atrocity Crimes: A Tool for Prevention', 2014.

[39] See Deputy Secretary-General's remarks at briefing of the General Assembly on Human Rights Up Front, 17 December 2013.

conciliation and arbitration, humanitarian assistance and protection, the protection of refugees and internally displaced peoples, and consent-based peacekeeping.

Finally, the Security Council's orientation to potential conflict situations should also change to give far higher priority than previously to prevention and early intervention. This it could do by developing closer relationships with companion UN bodies such as the Human Rights Council, the Human Rights Treaty Body system, and the Peacebuilding Commission. Focusing as they do on existing and potential abuses of human rights, the work of these bodies and their rapporteurs could play an immensely valuable role in alerting the Security Council to risks of mass atrocity crime in nations on which they held a watching brief. The Council should also be open to the work and recommendations of civil society organizations. These organizations, he observed, were often the first to detect worrying developments at the national and local levels. Their work could play an important part in contributing to early warning mechanisms through which national and intergovernmental organizations receive critical information concerning potentially inflammatory situations. The P-5 members of the Security Council, the Secretary-General opined more in hope than expectation, should consider seriously the voluntary abandonment of the exercise of the veto when deliberating upon the commission of crimes against humanity. The fact that in the Security Council Russia had exercised its veto power in relation to eight different draft resolutions regarding the Syrian conflict was no doubt influential in the formulation of that recommendation.

VII. CASE STUDIES

A. LIBYA

Early in 2011, the new responsibility to protect doctrine faced the first serious test of its application in the wake of the 'Arab Spring' uprisings in Libya and Syria—and their savage repression by dictatorial regimes. Would the international community's in-principle commitment to prevent mass atrocities translate into practical, effective, international action (Zifcak, 2012)?

The military intervention in Libya in 2011, pursuant to Security Council Resolution 1973, presented considerable dangers for the future of R2P.[40] This was the first international military intervention with an R2P focus. Its purpose was to protect the peoples of Benghazi against gross human rights abuses planned and commenced by the Gaddafi regime. The risks attached to failure were considerable. If the intervention were to fail, the entire idea of a responsibility to protect could be called into question.

In the event, the immediate objective of protecting Libyan civilians from the grave human rights abuses threatened by the Gaddafi government was achieved. With the assistance of NATO bombardment, the country fell to Libyan rebels. The citizens of Benghazi were spared the massacre that in all likelihood had awaited them. The bombardment ensured that Colonel Gaddafi would not regain control and that, at least for the then foreseeable future, the civilian population would be safe under the umbrella of the government of the former opposition National Transitional Council.

The fact of military victory on the ground was sufficient to justify the initial, but in hindsight highly premature, conclusion that the Libyan R2P operation had succeeded (Evans, 2011; Thakur, 2011a). This was despite strong protests as to its conduct lodged, not

---

[40] SC Res 1973 (17 March 2011).

without reason, by those members of the Security Council that abstained from the vote on Resolution 1973.[41]

It was not just the military win that seemed to secure R2P as an international political doctrine of considerable importance. The Libyan success had a number of novel aspects, each of which seemed to consolidate the doctrine's gains (Bellamy, 2011; Adams, 2012). Unlike preceding humanitarian interventions, the Libyan one was founded upon a resolution of the UN Security Council with explicit preambular reference to its conformity with R2P. This was not a unilateral intervention by Western forces such as that which had created such enormous legal controversy in Kosovo. The role of regional organizations was even more important.[42] The Arab League, in particular, took firm action against Libya, condemning the government's attitudes and actions and expelling the country from its membership. Importantly, success in Libya also came without the imposition of 'boots on the ground'.

At the same time, the intervention revealed certain deficits in the manner of its implementation. The most severe criticism of the Libyan case related to 'mission creep'. Those members of the Security Council who abstained from the vote on Resolution 1973 attacked forcefully what they saw as the abuse of the Council's mandate. In their view there was no way in which the relevant resolution could have permitted the transformation of the mission from the protection of civilians to the objective of regime change (Bellamy and Williams, 2016, ch 34).

Consequently, reservations were expressed as to the legality of the transformation. Here, the argument was that Resolution 1973 could not be stretched to cover actions such as intervention in a civil war, the assassination of a government's leadership, and the overthrow of the regime.[43] Security Council endorsement was critical to underpin the legality of the intervention but the actions of the coalition forces were said by the BRICS countries Russia and China to take the intervention beyond the Resolution's terms and, therefore, possibly beyond what the UN Charter could be interpreted to allow. Further, Russia, China, India, and Brazil all objected strongly to the alteration of NATO's military stance from the relative neutrality of civilian protection to evident partiality in taking the rebel side.[44]

Nevertheless, considerable optimism surrounded the subsequent elections for the first Libyan government. It seemed as if the country could take a democratic turn, much as its neighbour Tunisia had done.

Tragically, in ensuing years Libya fell instead into a state of semi-anarchy.[45] Even as late as 2017, the capital Tripoli remained under the control of multiple armed groups. Most were aligned with the internationally recognized government, the Presidency Council, on the one hand, or on the other with the military opposition and alternative government, the Misrata Third Force. Armed groups of every complexion had continued to fight for the advancement of their sectional interests, provoking clashes in contested areas throughout the city and its environs. Ordinary crime and lawlessness had spread widely in the city, with kidnappings and robberies adversely affecting citizens' freedom of movement. In Benghazi, within the space of a month in early 2017, four bomb blasts in succession had killed four people and injured more than 30 others. One of the bombings was directed at the city's chief of police and another at a senior commander in the Libyan National Army, the military arm of the putative government. Fighting between the Libyan National Army and

---

[41] UN Doc S/PV.6498 (17 March 2011).   [42] SC Res 1973 (17 March 2011).

[43] UN Doc S/PV.6566 (27 June 2011), Mr Mashabane (South Africa).

[44] See, eg, UN Doc S/PV.6528 (4 May 2011), Mr Churkin (Russian Federation) and Mr Baodong (China).

[45] 'Libya: Events of 2016', World Report 2017, *Human Rights Watch*.

Misrata had commenced and continued unabated in the oil crescent region and the Sabha area of the country.

Tens of thousands of refugees from Somalia, Sudan, and Libya poured through the country to the Mediterranean in search of safety and security in Europe. The refugees were deeply unpopular with the local population. On 15 August 2017, the UN Special Rapporteur on extra-judicial or summary or arbitrary executions reported that refugees and migrants in Libya faced abuse and extreme violence, with some 'being deliberately killed and others . . . dying as a result of torture, malnutrition and medical neglect'.[46]

Throughout the years since the NATO-led intervention, the Libyan situation remained chaotic. The international community had paid dearly for the neglect of its 'responsibility to rebuild' the Libyan nation in the immediate aftermath of the 2011 intervention. As to this, Anne-Marie Slaughter, the former President of the American Society of International Law and Foreign Policy Adviser to Hillary Clinton, said recently:

> Although I remain committed to the responsibility to protect, the doctrine that commits the international community to stopping a government from committing genocide, crimes against humanity or systematic war crimes against its own people, I would not now support a humanitarian action against a government that did not include extensive plans for the post military phase. I would also want to be clear-headed in advance that deeply distasteful compromises with the same government may be necessary.[47]

B. SYRIA

It was substantially owing to reservations by Russia, and the other BRICS countries (Brazil, India, China, and South Africa), concerning the conduct of the Libyan intervention that, in the first year of the Syrian conflict, three draft Security Council resolutions recommending various degrees of condemnation and international intervention in response to the worsening Syrian crisis were vetoed by Russia and China. In 2014 a fourth resolution, referring the Syrian situation to the International Criminal Court (ICC) for investigation, was also vetoed. The Russian foreign minister, Sergei Lavrov, explained that as a result of NATO over-reach, Russia 'would never allow the Security Council to authorize something similar to what happened in Libya'.

A fundamental question that Security Council members had to address with respect to Syria was whether or not a direct military intervention of the kind undertaken in Libya was likely to achieve its objective—without causing more harm to the civilian population than might otherwise occur. At the time a decision to intervene could have been taken, that is within the first year of the civil war, the considerations for and against would have been finely balanced. By the second year, the likely answer to the question had turned into a 'no' (Zifcak, 2012).

In the early months of the Syrian conflict, the government of Bashar Al-Assad had substantial military resources; its military command and security intelligence services were, with the exception of some notable defections, cohesive and loyal to the government; and the President still retained the confidence of a substantial proportion of the population. Recruits and advisers from Palestine, Lebanon, Iran, and Iraq had bolstered government forces. A steady flow of weapons had continued to arrive from Russia and Iran. As the war

---

[46] UN Doc A/72/335, 'Unlawful Deaths of Refugees and Migrants', Report of the Special Rapporteur of the Human Rights Council on Extra-Judicial, Summary and Arbitrary Executions, 15 August 2017.

[47] *Prospect*, June 2017, p 43.

intensified throughout 2013, however, the Syrian rebellion strengthened. The opposition, similarly, consisted of many thousands of fighters. Swathes of the north and central regions became no-go areas for Syrian government fighters. The rebels began to launch wave after wave of attacks upon suburban areas of Damascus and Aleppo. Government troops and *Shabiha* militia responded in kind with aerial bombing, shelling, and indiscriminate killing. Atrocities were committed on all sides. The Syrian conflict became, and remains, a war of attrition.

While the UN Security Council grappled with its response to the conflict, it became clear that a crucial barrier to an R2P intervention was that the Syrian political opposition and rebel military movements were deeply divided. Any possibility of a Western or Arab incursion in favour of the rebels was set back by profound concern as to the composition and agendas of the many different military and militia factions of which the opposition was comprised. At the heart of that concern was the fundamentalist, Salafist character of Syrian and foreign rebel groups. Principal amongst the latter were Jabhat al-Nusra, a jihadist element closely connected to Al-Qaeda and, later, its competitor and successor ISIS. The problem for those advocating some form of humanitarian intervention, therefore, was that the armed opposition had become primarily jihadist in character. None of the countries that might have participated in a peacekeeping or coercive intervention, whether Western or Arabic, wished the outcome of a rebel victory to be hardline Islamist rule.

At the political level, the civilian Syrian National Coalition, formed in November 2012 as a notionally representative grouping of Syrian opposition actors, was moderate and received substantial political support from Western nations and the Arab League alike.[48] It made initial attempts to engage the Syrian government, minus President Al-Assad, in peace negotiations. However, it had next to no control of the military and militant groups doing the fighting on the ground. And its members too were often at odds. This was unhelpful to potential interveners and, in the end, it was always likely to be the people with guns, rather than the more distantly involved and largely symbolic political leadership, that would determine the final shape of the Syrian State when the fighting finally ended.[49] The Syrian National Coalition drifted steadily into irrelevancy.

Syria, unlike Libya, was intensely enmeshed in its region. Until, and for a long time after, the protests began, the Al-Assad government was perceived by its neighbours as a strong and stable country in the midst of a volatile region. Not all of its policies may have been endorsed but Middle Eastern governments regarded Syria as an important trading partner, an influential political force, and in many cases, an essential strategic ally. Syria's web of alliances in the Middle East served as a strong disincentive to Security Council condemnation and action.

Critically, military intervention, even if directed only at the protection of civilians, was likely to have severe adverse effects on the stability of the entire Middle East. That consequence arose principally from Syria's geographical position, bordering five other nations almost all of which were volatile. Western intervention would certainly incite Syria's ally Hezbollah in Lebanon, thousands of whose members had already crossed the border to fight. It would fan the flames of sectarianism in Lebanon, thereby risking the downfall of the fragile Lebanese government, and possibly prompting civil war there.[50] Syria's relations with Turkey had worsened as a result of huge cross-border refugee flows from Syria's North. Early in 2013, approximately 170,000 Syrians had fled to camps in Turkey. The Turkish Prime Minister, Mr Erdoğan, made it clear that Turkey would not make the

---

[48] Patrick Seale, 'Syria's New Opposition Coalition Still has its Old Problems', *The Guardian*, 14 November 2012.   [49] Ramzy Mardini, 'After Assad. Chaos?', *The Guardian*, 3 February 2013.
[50] Roula Khalaf, 'Lebanon's Complex Part in Syrian Conflict', *Financial Times*, 29 October 2011.

smallest concession in its oppositional stance on Syria. In Iraq, rebel victory might have emboldened the country's Sunni minority and exacerbated tensions with its Shia majority. There was not yet a civil war in Iraq but the signs of enduring sectarian conflict were increasing and persistent. Jordan was already home to more than a million Palestinian and Iraqi refugees and was stretched to the limit by the arrival of a further 300,000 Syrians. This had the potential to create significant political instability in Jordan, whose ruling royal family had become increasingly unpopular.[51]

If there were a Western-led military intervention, the probability that Iran might engage, whether indirectly through its Lebanese and Palestinian allies, or directly would be high. Iran had much at stake in Syria. Should the Assad regime fall, its likely replacement by a Sunni-led government would have meant that Syria could move closer to Tehran's adversaries in the Gulf. The Syrian conflict had metamorphosed into a highly dangerous proxy war between Iran and its principal regional antagonists, Saudi Arabia, Qatar, and Turkey.

Russia was the principal opponent of any direct international action against Syria.[52] It was not difficult to discern the country's significant political, economic, and strategic investment in Syria. Syria remained a major purchaser of exports of Russian arms and defence equipment. It hosted a strategically positioned Russian naval base at Tartus on the West coast, its only one outside the former Soviet Union. Russia's largest intelligence-gathering organization situated on foreign soil was located in Latakia also on Syria's west coast. The Russian government continued to send weapons to Syria throughout the period of the crisis. It was unsurprising given these important connections that the Russians did not wish to see them disturbed by the replacement of the Al-Assad regime. Its veto at the Security Council, exercised on eight occasions, provided it with political power it needed to forestall any such possibility.

Israel, meanwhile, had become extremely concerned about Syria's arsenal of chemical weapons, particularly since Al-Qaeda and other extremist militants had joined the war against President al-Assad. Both Israel and the United States drew a red line under the use of chemical weapons, threatening military intervention should such weapons be deployed.[53] In the event, however, no such intervention materialized as the Assad regime deployed sarin gas and barrel bombs.

The Security Council split (Dergham, 2016, ch 35.1). By 2017, first Russia and China and then Russia alone had vetoed eight draft resolutions proposed by France, Britain, and the United States.[54] No agreement could be reached even on the creation of humanitarian corridors to ferry life-saving supplies to a war-torn and impoverished civilian population. The reality was that Russia would veto any measures adverse to the Syrian government despite breath-taking levels of savagery, unrelenting aerial bombardment, the indiscriminate shelling of areas populated by civilians, and the use of chemical weapons. As of September 2017, approximately 500,000 people, the majority civilians, had been killed. About half of Syria's population had been displaced and more than five million of them had sought refuge abroad, initiating the refugee crisis that then broke out across Europe. A World Bank report issued in 2017 estimated the country's lost economic output during the first six years of the war at $US 226 billion.

[51] Nicholas Pelham, 'Jordan Starts to Shake', The New York Review of Books, 8 December 2011.
[52] David Herszenhorn and Nick Cumming-Bruce, 'Putin Defends Stand on Syria and Chastises U.S. on Libya Outcome', Financial Times, 20 December 2012.
[53] Carla Seaquist, 'Obama's Principled Red Line on Syria', Huffington Post, 21 September 2013.
[54] UN News Centre, 'Russia Blocks Security Council Action on Reported Use of Chemical Weapons in Syria's Khan Shaykhun', 12 April 2017.

The Council's paralysis had become complete. Then, in 2015, Russia unilaterally deployed its own military forces to fight on the side of the regime. It used the pretext that its military was there to combat ISIS. The reality appeared to be that Russian forces were attacking the opposition rebel groups that were fighting Syrian President Assad's armies.[55] The Russian intervention had made decisive humanitarian focused action by the Security Council next to impossible. It was ironic, then, that the external military intervention most likely to bring the Syrian conflict to an end was the one that had been undertaken by Russia, R2P's most strident opponent.

In an article published in May 2017, Charles Glass, perhaps the best journalist presently writing on Syria, concluded, in a manner fully consistent with the philosophy of R2P but presently, operationally unattainable, that:

> What matters is giving the Syrian people a viable future. No party to the conflict—not the United States, Saudi Arabia, Qatar, Turkey, Israel and hundreds of jihadist militias on one side, or Russia, Iran Hezbollah and the Syrian army on the other—cares how many Syrians die. While the conflict endures, all seek power at the expense of ordinary citizens. Militarists in the White House, Congress and the US media call for escalation against Assad and Vladimir Putin, but they might serve Syria's beleaguered population better by seeking an accord with the Russians and the Iranians. Until then, there will be more war crimes, and more war.[56]

C. CENTRAL AFRICA

In December 2013, violent internal conflicts broke out in two Central African countries: South Sudan and the Central African Republic (CAR). Within weeks it was clear that crimes against humanity and war crimes were being committed with impunity by all sides, in both places. Thousands were killed within a month. The significant majority of these were innocent civilians. The UN had peacekeeping and monitoring missions in South Sudan and CAR but neither had predicted an outbreak of violence and the commission of mass atrocities on the scale that occurred so precipitately. Both were completely overwhelmed, being reduced almost instantly to undertaking a residual, albeit critical role in protecting civilians by housing and shielding them in UN facilities. All the preconditions for the international community, through the Security Council, to take action to halt the violence in accordance with the responsibility to protect doctrine were present. And yet, 12 months later, fighting continued to spiral out of control and international crimes continued unabated (Zifcak, 2015).

In South Sudan, the war had been fought between two major parties, the Sudan People's Liberation Movement/Sudan People's Liberation Army (SPLM/A) in government, led by the President, Salva Kiir, and SPLM/A in opposition, led by Rick Machar.[57] Kiir is a Dinka man and Machar is a Nuer. The ferocious fighting between the two had been the principal threat to peace in the country.[58] The parties' arming of local communities on the basis of tribal affiliation had continued to fuel widespread violence. The tribal undercurrent of the conflict, the collapse of the economy, and the continuing importation of arms and related

[55] BBC, 'Russia Joins in War in Syria: Five Key Points', 1 October 2015,

[56] Charles Glass, 'In the Horrorscape of Aleppo', *New York Review of Books*, 25 May 2017.

[57] 'Two Elephants Trample the Grass', *The Economist*, 21 December 2013; 'The descent into civil war', *The Economist*, 27 December 2013; 'Two Tribes', *The Economist*, 24 January 2014.

[58] As to the background see Human Rights Watch, 'They Are Killing Us: Abuses Against Civilians in South Sudan's Pibor County' (Report, September 2013).

material by both sides magnified the threat. Several peace agreements had been reached. Every one of them had been broken, sometimes within days. Some 50,000 people had been killed in the four years since the conflict's commencement. Furthermore, threats against the UN and international humanitarian personnel increased in number and brutality. As at September 2016, 59 national and international aid workers had been killed.

More than 3.8m South Sudanese had been forced to escape their homes. This exodus included 1.97m people who had been internally displaced and more than 1.89m people who fled as refugees to neighbouring countries. 218,000 people had sought safety in seven UN protection of civilian sites. As at September 2017, 6m people, half the population, were severely food insecure.[59]

In early 2017, the death toll in CAR was more than 5,000 and rising. The security situation remained precarious. Heightened intercommunal tensions persisted and materialized in the form of continuous clashes between Seleka (Muslim) militias and anti-balaka (Christian) militias. Combat between armed groups across the country had been motivated by internal power struggles, attempts to gain territory, competition over natural resources, and inter-religious disputation. The presence of the UN mission, MINUSCA, had been unable to eliminate the threat of armed groups in huge swathes of the country. MINUSCA itself became the target of armed attack. Several peacekeepers were killed during 2016. An estimated 467,000 people, the majority of them Muslim, remained refugees in neighbouring countries and a further 384,3000 were internally displaced. Half of the estimated 4.6m citizens remained dependent on humanitarian assistance. Some two million people had become food insecure.[60]

So, as the civil war in Syria raged and Libya began to unravel, from December 2013 the ethnic and sectarian conflicts in South Sudan and CAR intensified dramatically and on a huge scale. At the same time, however, unlike the political and military complexities that beset the Libyan and Syrian conflicts, these two internecine civil wars appeared to be ideal candidates for the application of R2P.

There were three reasons for this. First, early in each conflict, it became clear that mass atrocities were occurring. Moreover, State authorities were manifestly failing to exercise their responsibility to protect their own citizens. Pursuant to the doctrine, therefore, the international community assumed a moral and political responsibility to take collective action to protect civilian populations from war crimes and crimes against humanity. Secondly, in contrast to Libya and Syria, neither in South Sudan nor CAR was a dangerous proxy war amongst regional rivals likely to develop. The two conflicts had been relatively self-contained. Further, unlike the Libyan and Syrian cases, none of the P-5 had a substantial strategic interest in the outcomes of these faraway African conflicts. So, it was far less likely a Security Council veto would be wielded. Thirdly, both countries were poor. They had neither the military nor civil institutions nor resources to resist any substantial, external, protective intervention, whether economic or military.

Nevertheless, even given these positive indicators, the international community, through the UN, had not managed to prevent a dramatic escalation in the commission of mass atrocity crimes in either country during the four years since the conflicts' commencement. Security Council action was too little and too late. The question is, why? Several obstacles may readily be identified.

[59] See generally, UN Doc S/2016/793, *Report of the Panel of Experts on South Sudan established pursuant to Security Council Resolution 2206 (2015)*, 19 September 2016.

[60] See generally, *Report of the Secretary-General on Central African Republic*, UN SCOR, UN Doc S/2013/677 (15 November 2013); *Statement of the Under-Secretary-General/Special Adviser on the Prevention of Genocide, Mr Adama Dieng on the Human Rights and Humanitarian Situation in the Central African Republic*, 1 November 2013; 'A Catastrophe in the Making?', *The Economist*, 23 November 2013.

The tyranny of distance played a significant part in the failure to attract international diplomatic and political attention to the unfolding crises in Central Africa. Even in the corridors of UN headquarters in New York, informed diplomats had paid very little attention to developments in CAR prior to 2014. This was not surprising. Many other hotspots in regions of significant strategic interest preoccupied them. Terrorism related events in Mali, the DRC, Kenya, and Nigeria ranked more highly. By comparison, CAR was low priority. What happened there was of little serious diplomatic concern:

> Almost no one could place CAR on a map. Who cared about the country? The general impression is that it is a hopeless kind of place. The Security Council's initial reaction to it was that it was a bit of mess, but not worth taking any significant action about. Slowly, however, it became more apparent that its civilian population might need international protection.[61]

The second retardant to decisive international action to stop mass atrocities in Central Africa was the difficulty involved in the effective deployment of peacekeeping contingents. To make a decision to deploy peacekeepers was one thing. The politics and logistics of doing so quickly and effectively were quite another (Holt and Berkman, 2006; Thakur, 2011, p 161). In the preceding decade, developed nations, with the notable exception of France, had largely deserted the peacekeeping arena. Rich countries had become averse to the loss of life in foreign military ventures. This aversion was magnified where countries to which peacekeepers were to be sent seemed of distant relevance to developed nations' domestic, political concerns. The large-scale military interventions in Afghanistan and Iraq had burnt the USA badly at home and abroad. European nations had demonstrated a distinct reluctance to fill the void that the withdrawal of American troops and resources had left. With the flight of rich nations from peacekeeping, the burden of assuming them fell on poorer nations. In South Sudan, for example, surge peacekeepers were recruited from Ethiopia, Ghana, Kenya, Rwanda, Tanzania, Pakistan, Bangladesh, Nigeria, and Nepal.

Western countries, with highly effective, well organized, well armed, well resourced, and battle-ready battalions, no longer provided them. It was developing countries, with modestly effective, minimally armed, moderately trained, relatively inexperienced, and substantially under-resourced battalions, that were now asked to meet the call for peacekeeping operations. One serious consequence of this contributory imbalance was that it took considerably longer to deploy troops for peacekeeping from developing nations than it had done from developed ones. The UN Security Council authorized the establishment of a peacekeeping force of 12,500 in South Sudan in May 2014. The full complement had not arrived more than 12 months later.

The third obstacle to early and effective intervention lay within the Security Council itself. The Security Council is responsible for authorizing peacekeeping operations (Berdal, 2008, ch 7). Yet there were divisions within it as to the rules of engagement that should be set down in the relevant mandates.[62] Western member States of the Security Council had become seriously concerned about the passivity of peacekeepers in the face of attacks on civilians. For this reason, Britain and France argued that peacekeeping mandates should be framed more assertively to authorize the use of force. And they should be more explicit as to the circumstances in which armed force could be used to repel the attackers. Other member States, in particular Russia and China, were more cautious about legitimizing the use of force by peacekeepers. They expressed a preference for prevention and robust

[61] Interview with European Ambassador to the United Nations (New York, May 2014).

[62] UN Office of Oversight Services, *Evaluation of the Implementation and Results of Protection of Civilians Mandates in United Nations Peacekeeping Operations*, UN Doc A/68/787 (7 March 2014).

political negotiation as the more desirable course. On this view, the use of force should be authorized solely for the protection of UN missions and to protect civilians shelter-ing within UN facilities. The weakness of this position was that it had led to situations in which peacekeepers stood by as civilians whom they were charged with protecting were killed, maimed, or violated by armed militias involved in the fighting.[63] This was a particu-lar problem in South Sudan. In July 2014, for example, more than 300 people were killed in several locations in Pibor County, while peacekeepers refrained from forcible interven-tion. Overall, peacekeeping forces in South Sudan took immediate action to protect civil-ians under attack in only 10 per cent of cases.[64]

An urgent question, therefore, remained. Should the UN, an organization founded for the fundamental purpose of promoting peace, protect civilians only by peaceful means or should UN peacekeepers be authorized as a last resort to use force against combatants in order to ensure that civilians were not heedlessly or needlessly killed or injured.

Partly in response to such passivity, in 2013 the Security Council framed a new, more assertive resolution for the Democratic Republic of the Congo specifically entitling peace-keepers there to use force to separate combatants and quell violence against innocent citi-zens.[65] In doing so, peacekeepers would take on the character of 'intervention brigades'. The Council authorised such 'brigades' to engage in targeted offensive operations against armed groups as one element of a comprehensive approach to addressing the root causes of the conflict. Russia and China, however, continued to express reservations about such an approach. Their firmly held view was that peacekeepers should focus on prevention and pre-emption rather than extending their remit to enforcement. As long as the Council remained divided on such questions, the negotiation of peacekeeping mandates was likely to be protracted. Because of that, as in South Sudan and CAR, many lives may be lost as deadly conflicts burn out of control pending the outcome of the Council's politically com-plex and contentious deliberations.[66]

Generally speaking, the member States of the Security Council converged as to their perspectives and actions with respect to the South Sudanese and CAR conflicts. Security Council resolutions were adopted without dissent and members across the board ex-pressed continuous frustration with the disingenuous and erratic behavior of the political leaderships. Nevertheless, obvious cleavages remained. As just noted, Security Council members had been divided about the appropriateness of the use of force by peacekeepers. Russia and China insisted that peacekeeping be conducted defensively. That is, peacekeep-ing contingents in both countries should be confined to the protection of civilians, to pro-viding corridors for the receipt and distribution of humanitarian aid, and to monitoring and reporting on human rights abuse.

A similar dividing line emerged as to what action, if any, should be taken against politi-cal and military leaders engaged in internationally criminal actions. Targeted sanctions against identified political and military leaders in South Sudan were discussed but not imposed because Russia and China signalled their opposition. Western nations were more inclined to support stronger action in this regard. So too were there suggestions that the leaders of South Sudan should be referred to the International Criminal Court to deter-mine whether a case existed for their prosecution for crimes against humanity. In South

---

[63] For an illuminating recent discussion of the dilemmas with the protection of civilians see Thakur, 2013.
[64] UN Office of Oversight Services, *Evaluation of the Implementation and Results of Protection of Civilians Mandates in United Nations Peacekeeping Operations*, UN Doc A/68/787 (7 March 2014), p 19.
[65] SC Res 2098 (2013), UN SCOR, 6943rd mtg, UN Doc S/RES/2098 (2013) (28 March 2013).
[66] See further *Report of the Secretary-General on Protection of Civilians in Armed Conflict*, UN SCOR, UN Doc S/2013/689 (22 November 2013); and UN SCOR, 7019th mtg, UN Doc S/PV.7019 (19 August 2013).

Sudan that would have sent a strong message to Mr Kiir and Mr Machar that a continuation of inter-communal violence was unacceptable and that they might be brought to judicial account for their actions. Again, Russia, China, and a handful of other Security Council members determined that they would not favour such a reference.

It was most unfortunate, finally, that the early deliberations in the Security Council as to what actions might constructively be taken to dampen down the civil wars in South Sudan and CAR had to take place beneath the shadow of the serious political and military upheavals in Ukraine. The conflict there hardened the contending positions of Russia and the US/European alliance in relation to a host of contentious global issues. That fallout was felt as far as Central Africa, where the means and methods of international intervention to halt mass atrocity crimes fell for discussion. As a result of Ukraine, Russia and China on the one hand, and the P-3 on the other, had become far less inclined to compromise on any issues that divided them. This significantly reduced the prospect of agreement on the measures that might constructively be taken by the international community to halt the commission of extensive and grave international crimes in both South Sudan and CAR. Four years on, the commission of crimes continued.

D. SUMMATION AND SYNTHESIS

On any interpretation, an R2P-based intervention to prevent mass atrocity crimes has not so far been successful in Libya and Syria or in South Sudan and CAR. Crimes against humanity and war crimes still take place in all four countries. Should one conclude, therefore, that the doctrine of the responsibility to protect has failed? After all, if it has not been applied effectively in poverty stricken, militarily weak, politically chaotic, and strategically inconsequential nations such as those in Central Africa, are there any conditions or locations in which its success might realistically be anticipated?

In my view, any such conclusion suggesting failure would be premature.[67] The lead-time for the effective implementation of such a transformative change to the conduct of international relations will inevitably be lengthy. And already much has been learnt. The progressive experience of R2P's execution across all three Pillars, and the learning derived from it through time, may still have the capacity to inform the conceptualization and practice of this ethical, political doctrine so that, eventually, R2P may move incrementally yet steadily from setback to success. So, in what follows, I provide a summation and interpretation of what appears to have been learnt in R2P's first decade:

- A necessary precondition for a humanitarian intervention is that early warning signs of impending mass atrocities are recognized by the international community, through the Security Council, and that the international community's sympathy for and attention to potential victims is engaged. States, similarly, should become more willing than at present to place country situations on the agendas of regional and international organisations before they reach crisis point. In this respect, recent work done by the UN Office on Genocide Prevention and the Responsibility to Protect may prove valuable. The Office has produced a detailed 'framework for the analysis for mass atrocity crime'. This identifies critical risk factors that might signal impending sectarian, ethnic, or inter-tribal violence. Armed with such systematic analysis, the Security Council and other relevant intergovernmental organisations may be placed in a better position to act early and decisively.

---

[67] For a contradictory perspective see Hehir, 2012, ch 9.

- When effectively implemented, strategies for capacity-building in nations under threat can play a very substantial part in averting the likelihood of mass atrocity crime. Capacity-building may be directed at the creation of effective, legitimate, and inclusive government. It may include the development of laws and social mores designed to protect the rights of ethnic, religious, cultural, and linguistic minorities. It should include mechanisms to ensure respect for and protection of fundamental human rights and freedoms. It should encourage the development of local forms and structures for mediation and conflict resolution and include the creation of an impartial and independent judiciary. Security sector reform aimed at the establishment of strong and effective law enforcement bodies to take the lead in the protection of vulnerable populations is crucial.

- Peacekeeping operations are unlikely to prevent the commission of mass atrocity crimes, unless they are undertaken early in a conflict and where the number of peacekeepers deployed is sufficient to the scale of the task and the resources to provide for them are adequate. It follows that international incursion is less likely to be successful where it is borne upon the shoulders of, and conducted by, the soldiers of nations whose military forces and police are themselves minimally trained and equipped. Further, international intervention when limited to the deployment of peacekeepers is unlikely to be successful unless rules of engagement are clear and agreed between troop-contributing nations, and where peacekeepers are authorized to use force to prevent or cease the indiscriminate killing and maiming of civilians.

- Prior to approving a coercive intervention, in the interests of underpinning national sovereignty and independence, the Security Council will need to be satisfied that every feasible diplomatic solution to a crisis has been exhausted. Furthermore, the Security Council will need to be satisfied, first, that the intervention is likely to achieve its protective objective within the country concerned; secondly, that an intervention is likely to result in the maintenance or creation of a stable and legitimate government; and, thirdly, that intervention is highly unlikely to result in wider regional destabilization. Within the Security Council, international intervention is more likely to be acceptable where it is limited to the protection of civilians and the provision of humanitarian assistance. It is highly unlikely that the Security Council will approve a coercive intervention if its explicit or implicit objective is regime change.

- A Security Council resolution mandating a coercive intervention is likely, in future, to require continuous monitoring of the intervention's implementation on the ground. If the mandate is no longer regarded as sufficient or if the Council determines that it has been exceeded, the conduct of the intervention will likely return to the Security Council for further discussion and review. Given that a Security Council mandate for a Pillar 3 intervention is likely to have as its principal objective the protection of civilians, it is probable that the Security Council will in future require that the position of an intervening force be one of strict neutrality as between the contending parties. A Pillar 3 intervention should, in all aspects, conform to the dictates of international law, and, in particular, international humanitarian law.

- Where a contemplated coercive intervention runs contrary to the core political or strategic interests of a member of the P-5, it is highly unlikely to proceed. Deeply regrettably, the scale of genocide, crimes against humanity, and war crimes being committed within a nation remains an insufficient condition or incentive for the international community, through the UN Security Council, to engage in collective, coercive action to stop the carnage. For this reason, the problem of the Security Council veto must be addressed. There is now a concerted movement, initiated by civil society organizations and adopted by a substantial and increasing number of members of the UN General Assembly, to implement a new Security Council code of practice. Pursuant to this, member States of the United Nations would agree, voluntarily, not to exercise the veto in situations where the commission of genocide, crimes against humanity, or war crimes is to be considered. Encouragingly, as at October 2017, 114 nations had signed on to the code.[68]

- The responsibility to protect will not be implemented successfully unless, after co-ercive action has been taken, the UN, rich nations, and foreign donors commit to long-term political and economic rebuilding in the nation that has been damaged.

- Beneath all of these factors there lies still the fundamental clash between the essential political and legal principle of State sovereignty—and the moral principle that un-derpins the international community's responsibility to prevent the commission of mass atrocity crimes. On the Security Council, this divides Britain, France, and the UK, from Russia and China and the significant and increasingly influential BRICS nations, from an array of other smaller ones—those in the S-5 for example.[69] In the present context this clash of principle is the source of deep division as to the extent and limits of the strategies to be employed in peacekeeping operations, and on the justification or otherwise of coercive forms of international intervention designed to diminish, if not eliminate, the actual or anticipated commission of crimes against humanity. Where the balance between intervention and sovereignty should properly lie remains R2P's most significant dilemma. The failure even to approach an answer remains a cause of untold suffering and the waste of innumerable innocent lives.

The ethical challenge facing the international community, which is to prevent the commis-sion of genocide, crimes against humanity, war crimes, and ethnic cleansing, is formida-ble. As will have become apparent, making a real difference in this work involves tackling immensely complex and variegated problems in highly divergent contexts. It is, of course, too much to expect that one overarching framework or mechanism, like R2P, could ever meet that challenge. That does not mean, however, that within that framework, incremen-tal, constructive, and influential advances in mass atrocity prevention are unachievable.

So, the more that is learnt about R2P's failures and successes; about its plans and their misconceptions; about implementation and its errors; about its politics and conflicting in-terests; about national, regional, political, economic, and cultural differences in its spheres of application, the better the chance will be that practical, innovative, astute, and diverse forms of humanitarian intervention to protect civilian lives will, over time, become ever more effective.[70]

VIII. THE RESPONSIBILITY TO PROTECT AS INTERNATIONAL LAW

Politically speaking, it is fair to say that until the point at which NATO forces intervened in the Libyan conflict there had been a progressive convergence of opinion amongst member States of the United Nations that they bore a responsibility individually and collectively to protect their peoples from the commission of mass atrocity crimes. That broad consensus,

---

[68] As to the use of the veto in cases of mass atrocity crime see Security Council Report (2015), Research Report, 'The Veto', October 2015.

[69] The S-5 consists of Jordan, Costa Rica, Singapore, Lichtenstein, and Switzerland.

[70] Two informed and fair assessments of R2P's present and future are Evans, 2016 and Welsh, 2016.

at least in relation to Pillar 3 intervention, was partially fractured by events in Libya and Syria. Despite this, whether R2P in whole or in part may be regarded as having attained the status of a norm of international law remains a matter of interest and contention in diplomatic and academic circles (Stahn, 2007). For the following reasons, the preferable conclusion is that it has not (see similarly Thakur, 2011c; Burke-White, 2012; Vashadmake, 2012).

The responsibility to protect is not embodied in any treaty.[71] Consequently, the most likely way that it could be considered as a norm of international law would be by way of its acceptance as part of customary international law. A doctrine or principle will form part of customary law if two broad conditions are met. First, it must be a matter of State practice and that practice must be recurrent and widely observed. Secondly, there must be a conviction among nations that the practice is sufficiently consistent and of sufficiently general application to be regarded as a compulsory rule.[72] In other words, it should come to be understood that the practice is dictated by international law (*opinio juris*).

A. STATE PRACTICE

Applying these conditions to R2P, it is evident immediately, first, that State practice in conformity with the doctrine is nascent and second, that following the Security Council disagreements concerning the Libyan and Syrian cases, such State practice as there is, is neither recurrent nor widely observed.

It could perhaps be argued that State practice in relation to prior humanitarian interventions should also be taken into account, thereby providing a stronger foundation for a claim for R2P's normative standing. Given, however, that the new doctrine's sponsors have been at great pains to distinguish it from humanitarian intervention, and that many in the General Assembly have repudiated the latter, the argument cannot be accorded much weight.[73]

Still, there is one current of thought that suggests that the existence of well-settled State practice may not be absolutely critical in the formation of customary rules. So for example, within the framework of international humanitarian law, an imperative of moral behaviour and the dangers attendant upon its abuse may be such as to make the observance of a particular rule of war absolutely necessary even prior to recurrent State practice having been established. In this case, 'the laws of humanity' and the 'dictates of public conscience' are put on the same footing as State practice in the formation of international law (Cassese, 2005, pp 160–1).

In that context it might reasonably be accepted that the principle that States have an individual and collective responsibility to protect their peoples from genocide, war crimes, crimes against humanity, and ethnic cleansing is a 'law of humanity' of a similar kind and standing (see Teitel, 2011). But that is still far from affirming that in its practical operation R2P will be accorded similar force and legal effect.

---

[71] The doctrine, however, is closely related to the objectives and provisions of existing international treaties including, for example, the International Convention on the Prevention and Punishment of the Crime of Genocide (1948), the Geneva Conventions (1949), and the Rome Statute of the International Criminal Court (2002).

[72] *North Sea Continental Shelf, Judgment, ICJ Reports 1969*, p 3, para 77.

[73] See Ban Ki-Moon, 'Responsible Sovereignty: International Co-operation for a Changed World', Speech delivered in Berlin, 15 July 2008; M Sahnoun, 'Africa: Uphold Continent's Contribution to Human Rights', *AllAfrica.com.* 21 July 2009; G Evans, Statement delivered to the UN General Assembly Interactive Thematic Dialogue on the Responsibility to Protect, 23 July 2009.

B. *OPINIO JURIS*

The second condition to be met is that there should be a mutual conviction among nations that the doctrine or principle in question should have the character of a binding rule of law. In the present case, the existence of this '*opinio juris*' is difficult to discern or to justify. Certainly, R2P has been the subject of consideration, elaboration, and recommendation by international commissions of stature. It has been embodied, though not without considerable prior political division, in the resolutions of the most important summit of world leaders held in the last dozen years. It has been referred to, and endorsed in general terms, on numerous occasions in subsequent Security Council resolutions. And at least in relation to its core components, it has generated a surprising measure of acceptance at all eight General Assembly dialogues on R2P.

Yet the idea that it might constitute a legal rule that binds nations to it by common consent is not a position that has yet been reached. This has been demonstrated clearly by the reservations expressed within the Security Council in the aftermath of the Libyan intervention and the Council's paralysis in relation to the adoption of any resolution at all with respect to Syria.

It is clear, further, that although the three-Pillar model for R2P's operation is now widely accepted, there remain significant areas of uncertainty as to their scope, meaning, and effect. Many conceptual as well as operational questions remain to be addressed and resolved in the light of practical experience. It is difficult to contend in such circumstances that some new, generally accepted legal norm governing the conduct of nations has come to fruition.

On this basis the best that can be said, in my view, is that R2P is a political doctrine that at most constitutes but a fledgling rule of international customary law. It has quite some considerable way to go before it can be regarded as having been adopted in practice and obtained the requisite international acceptance to be considered as fully formed. As Mindia Vashadmake (2012, pp 1222–3) concluded:

> (R2P) is a multifaceted concept that lacks the quality of a specific legal norm at this stage of its development. However, the concept may have identified certain areas of international law where there is some potential for normative change. Thus, the concept may not be a binding legal instrument *per se;* however, it has legal implications in international relations and may serve as a platform for a slow normative change in the long term.

It is also worth recalling in this regard that R2P sits closely alongside existing legal obligations to prevent mass atrocity crimes which may, in certain aspects and circumstances, provide it with legal heft. So, for example, all States have an extraterritorial obligation to take all reasonable measures to prevent genocide. States Parties to the Rome Statute of the International Criminal Court are legally obliged to assist the Court. This includes an obligation to detain and surrender individuals indicted by it. Common Article 1 of the 1949 Geneva Conventions sets out an obligation not just to abide by its terms but also to ensure respect for the Conventions in all relevant circumstances. Additional Protocol 1 (1977) to the Geneva Conventions establishes a duty for States to act, jointly or individually, in cooperation with the United Nations and in conformity with the UN Charter, in situations of serious violations of the Geneva Conventions and Protocol (Article 89).

C. SECURITY COUNCIL PRACTICE

One final legal matter should be considered. As explained at the commencement of this chapter, the UN Charter's provisions, and in particular the terms of Articles 2(4) and 2(7), have proven exceptionally difficult to reconcile with any doctrine of external intervention in a nation's domestic affairs. Article 2(7) relevantly provides however that this principle of non-interference is not to prejudice the application of enforcement measures under Chapter VII. Chapter VII enforcement measures may be pursued where the Security Council has determined the existence of any threat to the peace, breach of the peace, or act of aggression. It has generally been assumed that any such threat must be to international peace and security, as Chapter VII measures are authorized in accordance with Articles 41 and 42 only to restore international peace and security.

However, the sole arbiter of whether there exists a threat to international peace and security remains the Security Council itself. And in recent years it has become apparent that the Council is now more willing than it has been previously to determine the existence of such a threat even where conflict or strife is taking place entirely within the boundaries of one State.

Generally speaking, the Council has made such a determination only where, for example, the 'international dimension' is constituted by some cross-boundary ramification of the primary conflict such as massive consequential refugee flows. In the past two decades or so, however, it has seemed prepared to go one step further where a humanitarian disaster is in prospect and declare a threat even where cross-boundary consequences have not plainly been in evidence. The Council's resolutions in relation to Somalia, Rwanda, Bosnia-Herzegovina, and, more recently, Libya and Côte d'Ivoire provide relevant examples.[74] In the absence of a power of judicial review of Security Council decision-making, the Council will continue to have very considerable flexibility when determining whether threats to international peace and security are present. And, further, it does not need to give reasons for its decisions.

This broad exercise of Security Council discretion in humanitarian cases suggests, consequently, that there may be one further, legally recognized way in which the competing demands of sovereignty and the prevention of atrocity may eventually be capable of reconciliation within the framework of the UN Charter. On the basis of the emerging trend, it could over time become standard Security Council practice to interpret the threshold requirement of a threat to peace and security as existent in situations of humanitarian crisis, even where the crisis is contained entirely within a State. Were this practice to become recurrent and internationally recognized as necessary and appropriate, a new customary rule, as embodied in Council practice, may eventually crystallize as part of international law.[75] This rule would allow for an exception to Article 2(4) by sanctioning intervention by the international community to prevent a humanitarian catastrophe occurring entirely within the boundaries of one State pursuant, first, to a preliminary determination by the Security Council under Article 39 of a threat to international peace and security, followed, secondly, by authorized international intervention in accordance with Articles 41 and 42.

This is not to suggest that international law has arrived at such a normative recognition yet. Security Council practice in the relevant respect has neither solidified nor attained the requisite measure of consistency and international acceptance. And to achieve recognition as institutional custom, a large stretch in the interpretation of the language of the Charter would still be required. Nevertheless, it is not unreasonable to observe that in

---

[74] See SC Res 794 (3 December 1992) (Somalia); SC Res 770 (13 August 1992) (Bosnia-Herzegovina); SC Res 929 (22 June 1994) (Rwanda), SC Res 1973 (17 March 2011) (Libya), SC Res 1975 (30 March 2011) (Côte D'Ivoire); and Chesterman, 2001, pp 140–51.

[75] In an analogous case, the International Court of Justice determined in an Advisory Opinion that the United Nations had international legal personality partly based on the practice of the United Nations in concluding international conventions. See *Reparation for Injuries Suffered in the Service of the United Nations, Advisory Opinion, ICJ Reports 1949*, p 174.

an increasingly interconnected and interdependent world, few conflicts or catastrophes remain entirely local in their ramifications.

The promise of eventual legal recognition is there but, for the moment, that hope rests on fragile and uncertain foundations.

REFERENCES

ADAMS, S (2012), *Libya and the Responsibility to Protect* (New York: Global Centre for the Responsibility to Protect).

ALSTON, P and MACDONALD, E (2008), 'Sovereignty, Human Rights, Security: Armed Intervention and the Foundational Problems of International Law', in P Alston and E MacDonald (eds), *Human Rights, Intervention, and the Use of Force* (Oxford: Oxford University Press), p 1.

BELLAMY, A (2008), *The Responsibility to Protect* (Cambridge: Polity Press).

BELLAMY, A (2011), 'Libya and the Responsibility to Protect: The Exception and the Norm', 23 *Ethics and International Affairs* 263.

BELLAMY, A and WILLIAMS, P (2016), 'Libya', in S von Einseidel, D Malone, and B Stagno Ugarte, *The UN Security Council in the 21st Century* (London: Lynne Renner Publishers), ch 34.

BERDAL, M (2008), 'The Security Council and Peacekeeping', in V Lowe, A Roberts, J Welsh, and D Zaum (eds), *The United Nations Security Council and War* (Oxford: Oxford University Press), ch 7.

BURKE-WHITE, W (2012), 'Adoption of the Responsibility to Protect' in J Genser and I Kotler (eds), *The Responsibility to Protect: The Promise of Stopping Mass Atrocities in Our Time* (Oxford: Oxford University Press), ch 2.

CASSESE, A (1999), 'Follow Up: Forcible Humanitarian Countermeasures and opinio necessitas', 10 *EJIL* 791.

CASSESE, A (2005), *International Law* (Oxford, Oxford University Press).

CHESTERMAN, S (2001), *Just War or Just Peace: Humanitarian Intervention and International Law* (Oxford: Oxford University Press).

CHINKIN, C (2000), 'The Legality of NATO Action in the Former Republic of Yugoslavia (FRY) under International Law', 49 *ICLQ* 910.

CORTEN, O (2008), 'Human Rights and Collective Security: Is there an Emerging Right to Humanitarian Intervention?' in Alston and MacDonald, *Human Rights, Intervention, and the Use of Force*, p 87.

DERGHAM, R (2016), 'Commentary: The Council's Failure on Syria', in von Einseidel, Malone, and Stagno Ugarte, *The UN Security Council in the 21st Century*, ch 35.1.

EVANS, G (2006), 'From Humanitarian Intervention to the Responsibility to Protect', 24 *Wisconsin ILJ* 703.

EVANS, G (2008), The Responsibility to Protect: Ending Mass Atrocity Crimes Once and for All (Washington, DC: The Brookings Institution Press), ch 1.

EVANS, G. (2011), 'End of the Argument' (December 2011) *Foreign Policy*.

EVANS, G (2012), 'R2P and RWP after Libya and Syria', Keynote Address to Global Centre for the Responsibility to Protect and the Stanley Foundation, *The Responsibility While Protecting: What Next?* Rio De Janeiro, 23 August 2012.

EVANS, G (2016), 'R2P: The Next Ten Years' in A Bellamy and T Dunne, *The Oxford Handbook of the Responsibility to Protect* (Oxford: Oxford University Press).

FABRI, H (2008), 'Human Rights and State Sovereignty: Have the Boundaries been Significantly Redrawn?', in Alston and MacDonald, *Human Rights, Intervention, and the Use of Force*, p 33.

FOCARELLI, C (2008), 'The Responsibility to Protect and Humanitarian Intervention: Too many Ambiguities for a Working Doctrine', 13 *Journal of Conflict and Security Law* 191.

GAZZINI, T (2005), *The Changing Rules on the Use of Force in International Law* (Manchester: Manchester University Press).

GLASS, C (2017), 'In the Horrorscape of Aleppo', *New York Review of Books*, 25 May 2017.

GRAY, C (2018), *International Law and the Use of Force* (4th edn, Oxford: Oxford University Press).

HEHIR, A (2012), *The Responsibility to Protect: Rhetoric, Reality and the Future of Humanitarian Intervention* (Basingstoke: Palgrave Macmillan).

HOLT, V and BERKMAN, T (2006), *The Impossible Mandate: Military Preparedness, the Responsibility to Protect and Modern Peace Operations* (Stimson Centre).

HOLZGREFE, J (2003), 'The Humanitarian Intervention Debate', in J Holzgrefe and R Keohane (eds), *Humanitarian Intervention* (Cambridge: Cambridge University Press), p 53.

INDEPENDENT INTERNATIONAL COMMISSION ON KOSOVO (2000), *Kosovo Report, Conflict, International Response, Lessons Learned* (Oxford: Oxford University Press).

LUCK, E (2009), 'Sovereignty, Choice and the Responsibility to Protect', 1 *Global Responsibility to Protect* 1.

PETERS, A (2009), 'Humanity as the Alpha and Omega of Sovereignty', 20 *EJIL* 513.

SIMMA, B (1999), 'NATO, the UN and the Use of Force: Legal Aspects' (1999) 10 *EJIL* 1.

STAHN, C (2007), 'Responsibility to Protect: Political Rhetoric or Emerging Legal Norm?' 101 *American Journal of International Law* 99.

TEITEL, R (2011), *Humanity's Law* (Oxford: Oxford University Press).

THAKUR, R (2011), 'R2P and the protection of civilians in armed conflict', in R Thakur, *The Responsibility to Protect: Norms, Laws and the Use of Force in International Politics* (Abingdon: Routledge), ch 11.

THAKUR, R (2011a), 'Kosovo, Humanitarian Intervention and the Challenge of World Order', in Thakur, *The Responsibility to Protect,* ch 3.

THAKUR, R (2011b), 'R2P, Libya and International Politics as the Struggle for Competing Normative Architectures', in A Stark (ed), *The Responsibility to Protect: Challenges and Opportunities Following the Libyan Intervention,* e-International Relations, 13 (December 2011) *Foreign Policy,* http://www.e-ir.info/2011/11/21/the-responsibility-to-protect-challenges-opportunities-in-light-of-the-libyan-intervention/.

THAKUR, R (2011c), 'Normative Contestation, Incoherence and Inconsistency', in Thakur, *The Responsibility to Protect,* ch 12.

THAKUR, R (2013), 'Protection Gaps for Civilian Victims of Political Violence', 20(3) *South African Journal of International Affairs* 321.

VASHADMAKE, M (2012), 'The Responsibility to Protect', in B Simma, D Erasmus-Kahn, G Nolte, and A Paulus, *The Charter of the United Nations: A Commentary* (Oxford: Oxford University Press).

WEISS, T (2007), *Humanitarian Intervention* (Cambridge: Polity Press).

WELSH, J (2004), 'Conclusion: The Evolution of Humanitarian Intervention in International Society', in J Welsh (ed), *Humanitarian Intervention and International Relations* (Oxford: Oxford University Press), ch 10.

WELSH, J (2008), 'The Security Council and Humanitarian Intervention', in Lowe, Roberts, Welsh, and Zaum, *The United Nations Security Council and War,* ch 24.

WELSH, J (2016), 'R2P's Next Ten Years: Deepening and Extending the Consensus', in Bellamy and Dunne, *The Oxford Handbook of the Responsibility to Protect,* ch 53.

Wheeler, N (2004), 'The Humanitarian Responsibilities of Sovereignty: Explaining the Development of a New Norm of Military Intervention for Humanitarian Purposes in International Society', in Welsh, *Humanitarian Intervention and International Relations*, ch 3.

Zifcak, S (2009), *United Nations Reform: Heading North or South?* (London: Routledge).

Zifcak, S (2012), 'The Responsibility to Protect after Libya and Syria', 13 *Melbourne Journal of International Law* 59.

Zifcak, S (2015), 'What Happened to the International Community? R2P and the Conflicts in South Sudan and Central African Republic', 16 *Melbourne Journal of International Law* 52.

FURTHER READING

International Commission on Intervention and State Sovereignty (2001), *The Responsibility to Protect: Report of the International Commission on Intervention and State Sovereignty*, Ottawa, International Development Research Centre: the Canadian Commission Report in which the Responsibility to Protect was first conceptualized.

Report of the Secretary-General (2009), *Implementing the Responsibility to Protect*, UN Doc A/63/677: the UN Secretary-General's most comprehensive elaboration of the core elements of the Responsibility to Protect.

Alston, P and MacDonald, E (2008), (eds), *Human Rights, Intervention, and the Use of Force* (Oxford: Oxford University Press): a fine contemporary overview of the inter-relationship between sovereignty, armed intervention, and human rights under international law.

Bass, G (2008), *Freedom's Battle: The Origins of Humanitarian Intervention* (New York: Alfred A. Knopf): the best history of the concept.

Bellamy, A and Dunne, T (eds) (2016), *The Oxford Handbook of the Responsibility to Protect* (Oxford: Oxford University Press): an extensive new collection of articles on R2P.

Chesterman, S (2001), *Just War or Just Peace: Humanitarian Intervention and International Law* (Oxford: Oxford University Press): the most lucid overview of the law with respect to humanitarian intervention.

Evans, G (2008), *The Responsibility to Protect: Ending Mass Atrocity Crimes Once and for All* (Washington, DC: The Brookings Institution Press): a key text in the field written by the first of two principal authors of the ICISS report in which the Responsibility to Protect was first formulated.

PART VI

RESPONDING TO BREACHES OF INTERNATIONAL OBLIGATIONS

17

COUNTERMEASURES
AND SANCTIONS

Nigel D White and Ademola Abass

SUMMARY

The issue of enforcement by means of non-forcible measures is one of the least developed areas of international law. Two legal regimes are relatively clear—non-forcible countermeasures taken by States (countermeasures) and non-forcible measures taken by international organizations (sanctions). The development of a restricted doctrine of countermeasures as the modern accepted form of self-help is considered, along with the partial centralization of coercion in international organizations. The problems within each of these regimes are examined, along with the limitations that have been placed upon their application. The coexistence of countermeasures based on a traditional view of international relations, alongside the post-1945 development of centralized institutional responses, is explored. Moreover, the range of State and institutional practice that seems to lie somewhere between the basic right of a State to take countermeasures to remedy an internationally wrongful act, and the power of international organizations to impose sanctions in certain circumstances, is considered. The legality of the continued use by States of non-forcible reprisals, retorsion, and wider forms of economic coercion is explored, as is the issue of collective countermeasures imposed either multilaterally or institutionally.

I. INTRODUCTION: SELF-HELP IN INTERNATIONAL LAW

Traditionally, States coexist in a legal system that is essentially consensual. States, no matter their disparities in size or strength, are sovereign and equal. Obligations are accepted by States either in treaty or custom by consent; they are not imposed by any higher authority. In its purest form such a legal condition existed in the eighteenth and nineteenth centuries. This period was one of self-help, in that if a State breached one of its obligations, the victim State(s) of such a breach could take both non-forcible and forcible measures to remedy or to punish that breach. Forcible measures could range from measures short of war, such as armed reprisals,[1] or could take the form of war.

---

[1] *Naulilaa* case (1928) 2 *RIAA* 1052.

War itself could be a relatively minor exchange of fire, even mere confrontation without hostilities, or it could be a full-scale bloody conflict the causes of which could be relatively minor.

Before this period of absolute sovereignty and its accompanying self-help regime of enforcement, theories of natural law argued for a hierarchy of norms within the concept of an international society (Bull, 1992, pp 71–2). Moving forward to the advent of the League of Nations in 1919, created in the aftermath of the failure of the system of self-help, there emerged structures as well as norms that were again suggestive of a more hierarchical approach. The Covenant of the League of Nations purported to regulate, if not prohibit, war, and the organization it established potentially had weak authority over States. Brierly argued that the League was based on the principles of consensuality and voluntarism (Brierly, 1946, p 92), a view that would suggest that the organization did not upset the pre-existing order. McNair on the other hand thought that the League marked a move away from a system of purely private law between consenting States towards a system of public law (McNair, 1930, p 112) indicating a more hierarchical system of regulation.

The idea of an international organization, with some measure of authority over States, took an even firmer grip on the imagination of States during the Second World War. The UN was created in 1945, its Charter containing in Article 2(4) a basic rule prohibiting the threat or use of force in international relations, and creating machinery to promote and restore international peace and security. The prohibition of force, which itself formed a core norm in an emerging corpus of peremptory norms of international law (*jus cogens*) from which States could not derogate, immediately cut back on the type of measures a State could lawfully take in response to a breach of international law. Self-help was reduced to half its former size by the UN Charter. Although States were still permitted to take forcible action in self-defence in response to an armed attack against them, forcible measures beyond that were prohibited by the new legal regime initiated by the Charter. Although some States and writers have repeatedly tried to resurrect the concept of armed reprisals (Bowett, 1972a) there does not appear to be any general acceptance of an erosion of the statement of law made by member States of the UN in 1970—'States have a duty to refrain from acts of reprisal involving the use of armed force.'[2]

The prohibition in 1945 of forcible measures of self-help left the position of non-forcible measures untouched but at the same time unclear. Clarity was lacking because the doctrines that had emerged over the centuries were inevitably subject to many interpretations. In addition, the UN itself was given significant power to impose on member States obligations to impose non-forcible measures against miscreant member States by virtue of Article 41 of the Charter. The developing Inter-American system of collective security also provided for the application of such measures,[3] a trend that was to be followed by some other regional organizations. A self-help system of non-forcible measures deriving from an earlier period of international relations, had to coexist with a system of centralized 'sanctions' based on notions of hierarchy and governance. In addition to the uncertainty that existed between the institutional level and the customary level, there was also a lack of clarity in the relationship between the universal organization (the United Nations) and other organizations. Article 53(1)

---

[2] *Declaration on Principles of International Law concerning Friendly Relations and Co-operation among States in Accordance with the Charter of the United Nations*, UN Res 2625 (XXV) (24 October 1970).

[3] Articles 8, 17, and 20 Rio Treaty, 1947, 21 UNTS 77.

[4] *Air Services Agreement* case (1978) 54 ILR 303.

of the UN Charter seems to provide that any non-forcible measures taken by regional organizations that amounts to 'enforcement action' requires the authorization of the Security Council.

The concept of lawful non-forcible measures survived the new world order of the post-1945 period. Article 2(4) of the Charter prohibited the 'threat or use of force', and this was clearly construed as military force (but see Paust and Blaustein, 1974, p 417). State practice in the immediate post-1945 period provided evidence of the continuation of the concept of non-forcible measures. As Elagab states: '[r]egardless of whether the conditions of legality had been complied with in each case, the crucial feature was the very fact of such claims being staked at all. This provides a presumption of continuity of counter-measures as a viable mode of redress' (Elagab, 1988, p 38). In the first decade after the UN Charter the USA adopted, *inter alia*, measures freezing the assets of China, Bulgaria, Romania, and Hungary. The coinage of the term 'countermeasures' in the *Air Services Agreement* case of 1978[4] and the codification of countermeasures by the International Law Commission (ILC), culminating in Chapter III of the Articles on State Responsibility of 2001,[5] represent its consolidation in the structures of international law.

Despite the proliferation of international institutions since 1945, the ILC was confident in asserting in 2001 that countermeasures are inherent in a decentralized system where 'injured States may seek to vindicate their rights and to restore the legal relationship with the injured State which has been ruptured by' an unlawful act.[6] As noted by Alland, 'countermeasures are a mechanism of private justice', the result of which are 'contradictions inherent in a self-assessed (ie auto-interpreted or auto-appreciated) decentralized policing of an international *ordre public*' (Alland, 2002, pp 1223, 1235). Provost is even more explicit in depicting the weaknesses of such a system when he writes that 'the right of states unilaterally to assess a breach by another state and to validate what would otherwise be an illegal act has the potential of significantly destabilizing international relations' (Provost, 2002, p xv). A recent example of this involved Gulf States imposing an embargo in June 2017 against Qatar for allegedly supporting terrorism, including the demand that Qatar close the Al-Jazeera media network as well as desist in its support for Hamas, the Muslim Brotherhood, and Hezbollah, and cease its relations with Turkey and Iran. Although these are problematic as countermeasures in the narrow sense described later, they are nonetheless non-forcible measures of self-help taken by Saudi Arabia, the UAE, Bahrain, and Egypt, which demonstrate the weaknesses of self-declared victim States acting as judge, jury, and executioner.

While injured States remain entitled to take certain non-forcible actions within a bilateral context against States responsible for a breach of international law, sanctions imposed by the UN and other international organizations create a hierarchical relationship between the organization and the implementing States (Gowlland-Debbas, 2001, p 2). After 1945, and arguably in a weaker sense after 1919 (but see Brierly, 1932, p 68), there no longer exists a pure system of self-help, and this has affected practice, as will be seen. States wanting to take measures against a responsible State may go to international bodies for authority/ legitimacy; indeed it could be argued that they ought to do this when they are not the direct victims of the unlawful act.

---

[5] See Report of the International Law Commission on the work of its Fifty-third Session, UN Doc A/56/10, adopted 9 August 2001. The Articles and the Commentary are found in Crawford, 2002. The Articles will be referred to as ARSIWA (Articles on Responsibility of States for Internationally Wrongful Acts). The references to the Commentary are to Crawford's text.

[6] Crawford, 2002, p 281.

II. COUNTERMEASURES

A. DEFINITION OF COUNTERMEASURES

Since the first use of the term in 1978 by the arbitral tribunal in the *Air Services Agreement* case, the term 'countermeasures' has been used to indicate non-forcible measures. However, the following discussion will illustrate that this has not necessarily clarified the matter, for the related doctrines of retorsion, reprisals (in a non-forcible sense), economic coercion, and economic sanctions remain. In effect, after the ILC Articles of 2001 the concept of countermeasures is a fairly narrow one at one end of a spectrum of non-forcible measures that may be taken in international relations. At the other end of the spectrum are sanctions undertaken by international organizations. In between there is something of a grey area where regulation is rudimentary, indeed, arguably, non-existent. In this section, the focus is on countermeasures on the grounds that they have become perhaps the most clearly defined type of non-forcible measures, having been the subject of many years of study by the ILC. The ILC's concept of countermeasures is the one portrayed here, though it must be noted that it may well constitute an example of the ILC progressively developing international law. It should be noted that the ILC's Special Rapporteur on the matter, James Crawford, commented only a few years before the adoption of the Articles that 'at present there are few established legal constraints on non-forcible counter-measures' (Crawford, 1994, p 65). As Bederman suggests, 'the central conceptual mission' of the ILC's Articles on countermeasures is 'the search for a polite international society' (Bederman, 2002, p 819). Further he contends that the articles on countermeasures represent a 'profound impulse toward social engineering for international relations . . . imagining a time in international life when unilateral and horizontal means of enforcement through robust self-help will be a thing of the past' (Bederman, 2002, p 831). Nevertheless, while the ILC purports to define and constrain countermeasures, in so doing it leaves question marks hanging over the legality of a large segment of State practice on wider non-forcible measures.

Countermeasures 'are intrinsically unlawful, but are justified by the alleged failing to which they were a response' (Alland, 2002, p 1221). In its final Articles on State Responsibility of 2001, the ILC defined countermeasures as non-forcible measures taken by an injured State in response to a breach of international law in order to secure the end of the breach and, if necessary, reparation.[7] Non-forcible countermeasures may only be taken in response to an internationally wrongful act, and only against the State responsible for that act.[8] If such measures are taken without fulfilling these conditions, they themselves will constitute an internationally wrongful act, giving rise to State responsibility and possible countermeasures. According to the ILC, countermeasures are limited to the temporary non-performance of one or some of the international obligations of the injured State owed to the responsible State.[9] Cassese's summation is perhaps stronger than that of the ILC, but useful nonetheless. He states that 'in the event of a breach of international law, the injured State is legally entitled to disregard an international obligation owed to the delinquent State' (Cassese, 2005, p 302). In ILC terms, countermeasures are not intended to be punishment for illegal acts but as 'an instrument for achieving compliance with the obligations of the responsible State'. Countermeasures are taken 'as a form of inducement, not punishment'. The ILC's definition does not restrict States taking countermeasures to suspension of performance of the same or very similar obligation. However, countermeasures

---

[7] Ibid.
[8] Article 49(1) ARSIWA. See also *Gabčíkovo-Nagymaros Project (Hungary/Slovakia), Judgment, ICJ Reports 1997*, p 7, paras 83–5.　　　　　　　　　　　　　　　　　　　[9] Article 49(2)(3) ARSIWA.

are more likely to accord with the conditions of proportionality and necessity if they are so taken. Such measures, which correspond to the obligation breached by the responsible State, are sometimes called 'reciprocal countermeasures'.[10]

The suspension or temporary non-performance of a treaty obligation, quite often the suspension of a trade agreement, and the freezing of the assets of a State under international obligations are primary examples of countermeasures.[11] In ILC terms the paradigmatic case is the *US-French Air Services Arbitration* of 1978. This case concerned the application of a bilateral air services agreement that existed between the two countries. France had objected, as being incompatible with the treaty, to the so-called 'change of gauge' or change of type of aircraft by PanAm on its flight from the USA to Paris via London. The French authorities prevented PanAm passengers from disembarking in Paris. By the time of arbitration, the USA had initiated (but had not implemented) measures which would have prohibited certain French flights to the USA. The arbitral tribunal found that the change of gauge by PanAm was permitted under the treaty and that the US retaliatory measures were permissible countermeasures, which were not disproportionate to the violative actions taken by France. The arbitral tribunal stated: '[i]f a situation arises, which in one State's view, results in the violation of an international obligation by another State, the first State is entitled, within the limits set by general rules of international law, pertaining to the use of armed force, to affirm its rights through "countermeasures".[12] Of course, the case reveals the inherent problem with countermeasures, indeed with measures of self-help more generally, in that the crucial element, the determination of the initial wrongful act, is a subjective one. As Alland makes clear, it is this 'self-assessed' aspect of countermeasures which 'manifests the danger they represent in the international legal order: they open the possibility to all States to take prejudicial measures contrary to the obligations incumbent on them on the basis of subjective unilateral claims' (Alland, 2010, p 1129).

Countermeasures are distinct from suspension or termination of treaty obligations due to material breach of a treaty within the meaning of Article 60 of the 1969 Vienna Convention on the Law of Treaties (VCLT). Measures taken under Article 60 affect the substantive legal obligations of the State parties while countermeasures are concerned with the responsibility that has arisen as a result of the breach. The aim of countermeasures is to rectify the legal relationship and their application should always be temporary.[13] Article 60 of the VCLT deals with 'material breach' of a treaty, countermeasures may be taken in response to any breach, as long as they are proportionate. Article 60 specifies a procedure for suspension or termination of treaty obligations for material breach, which differs from the procedures required to take countermeasures. Action under Article 60 of the VCLT must be confined to the treaty being breached, while countermeasures are not so confined (Elagab, 1988, p 164). Article 60 of the VCLT provides for the possibility of termination of the treaty, or obligation, while, in principle, countermeasures are only temporary.

It is possible that a non-forcible measure taken by a State can be classified as both a response to a material breach and a countermeasure if it meets the different set of requirements for each. The International Court of Justice considered arguments concerning countermeasures and material breach in 2011 in a case involving a dispute between the Former Yugoslav Republic of Macedonia (FYR Macedonia) and Greece over violations of an Interim Accord agreed in 1995 by the two States in the context of the dissolution of Yugoslavia. The Court found that Greece had violated the Accord by objecting to FYR Macedonia's admission to NATO in 2008. Greece attempted to justify this action as

---

[10] Crawford, 2002, pp 282–6.   [11] Ibid, p 286.

[12] *Air Services Agreement* case (1978) 54 ILR 303, 337.   [13] Crawford, 2002, p 282.

a response to a material breach of the Interim Accord by FYR Macedonia and as a countermeasure to the same breach. The Court did find that FYR Macedonia had breached the
Accord by the use of a symbol (the 'Sun of Vergina'). The Court dismissed the argument
that Greece's actions could be justified as a response to a material breach under Article
60 of the Vienna Convention on the basis that it was not a serious enough breach, and
also because the violation by FYR Macedonia had ceased in 2004 so that Greece's action
in 2008 could not be seen as a response to that breach. Neither could Greece's actions be
justified as a countermeasure because such measures are taken for the purposes of achieving a cessation of a wrongful act, and Macedonia had ceased its wrongful act in 2004.[14]

B. COUNTERMEASURES AGAINST ORGANIZATIONS

Given the growth of international organizations possessing international legal personality,
with rights and duties under international law, there appears no reason why countermeasures cannot be taken by States or other organizations against international organizations
that have committed internationally wrongful acts, or by organizations that are the victims of internationally wrongful acts. In principle countermeasures should be available to
any entity possessing international legal personality, though in the current state of international legal development such actors are generally confined to States and a significant
number of intergovernmental organizations. The ILC's work on the responsibility of international organizations, started in 2002, made good progress until it came to the issue of
countermeasures in its 2008 report.[15] Although certain draft articles on countermeasures
were posited in the report,[16] there was clearly some disagreement among the members
of the ILC as to the value of including articles on countermeasures by and against international organizations.[17] Nonetheless, the final Articles, adopted in 2011 and taken note
of by the General Assembly, contain articles on countermeasures against and by international organizations,[18] most of which are similar in content to those governing State
responsibility. The final Articles of 2011 try to balance the logic of countermeasures being
available to counter unlawful acts committed by international organizations (as international legal persons) and the desire to prevent member States precipitously taking unilateral countermeasures against the organization for perceived internationally wrongful or
ultra vires acts. Given the problems the UN has been faced with in the past, with France
and the Soviet Union withholding their peacekeeping contributions on the basis of the
alleged *ultra vires* actions of the General Assembly in mandating peacekeeping forces in
the Middle East and the Congo in the late 1950s and early 1960s, and the US practice of
withholding financial contributions in the 1980s and 1990s, there is clearly a potential
problem in recognizing that member States can take countermeasures against organizations in response to perceived unlawful acts (but see Tzanakopoulos, 2011, pp 189–92).

Arguably, however, States that believe they are victims of unlawful actions by an organization (for example being subjected to economic sanctions) have very limited options to challenge the legality of such measures (with no access to the International Court
of Justice, for instance). Without giving member States means of holding organizations
to account, arguably they should have the right to take countermeasures against the

---

[14] *Application of the Interim Accords of 13 September 1995 (the Former Yugoslav Republic of Macedonia v
Greece), ICJ Reports 2011*, p 644, paras 162–4.   [15] ILC Report of Sixtieth Session (2008), A/63/10.
[16] Ibid, paras 141–4.   [17] Ibid, paras 148, 163.
[18] Articles on the Responsibility of International Organizations, Articles 51–7, UN Doc A/66/10 (2011);
taken note of in GA Res 66/100 (2011).

organization (O'Connell, 2008, pp 267, 271). Organizations, on the other hand, normally possess a number of means of controlling their members—expulsion, suspension, other non-forcible measures such as sanctions, and, as international legal persons, countermeasures (Dopagne, 2011, pp 178–91).

Ultimately, the 2011 Articles on the Responsibility of International Organizations came down on the side of the organization by providing a number of restrictions on when countermeasures can be taken against it. The Articles permit an injured State or organization to take countermeasures against an international organization for an internationally wrongful act, but contain a number of limitations in addition to the normal conditions attaching to countermeasures. A number of those additional limitations are aimed at reducing the over-use of countermeasures by disgruntled member States of the UN and other organizations. These limitations include a general one that provides that 'countermeasures shall, as far as possible, be taken in such a way as to limit their effects on the exercise by the responsible international organization of its functions'. Furthermore, countermeasures against a responsible organization: shall not be inconsistent with the rules of the organization; shall not be used where other appropriate means are available for inducing compliance; and, most significantly, shall not be taken by an injured State which is a 'member of a responsible international organization against that organization in response to a breach of an international obligation under the rules of the organization unless such countermeasures are provided for by those rules'.[19] The 'rules of the organization' are defined as 'the constituent instruments, decisions, resolutions and other acts of the international organization adopted in accordance with those instruments, and established practice of the Organization'.[20] These rules would clearly include the obligation to pay expenses under Article 17(2) of the Charter and equivalent provisions in the constituent treaties of the UN's specialized agencies. Certainly, the views of UNESCO on these restrictions suggest that UN organizations are not too concerned that the Articles will open them up to a rash of countermeasures by disgruntled member States: 'for international organizations of quasi-universal membership such as those of the United Nations system, the possibility for their respective Member States to take countermeasures against them would either be severely limited by the operation of the rules of those organizations, rendering it largely virtual, or would be subject to a *lex specialis*—thus outside the scope of the draft articles—to the extent that the rules of the organization concerned do not prevent the adoption of countermeasures by its Member States.'[21]

C. REPRISALS AND RETORSION

The ILC's definition of countermeasures has internal coherency. But its failure to address the related concepts of non-forcible reprisals and retorsion leaves the impression that other types of non-forcible action taken by States remain unregulated and, on one view of international law, therefore permitted.[22] This means that, in reality, while States can engage in countermeasures that are quite specific, they may also be able to engage in wider non-forcible measures. Such measures may punish the responsible State (reprisals) as opposed to inducing it into compliance (countermeasures). On the other hand, it could be argued that this approach, essentially permitting other non-forcible measures to be taken by States, makes something of a nonsense of the painstaking process of defining

---

[19] Articles on the Responsibility of International Organizations, 2011, Articles 51(1) 51(4), 52(1), 52(2).
[20] Ibid, Article 2(b).   [21] ILC Report of the Sixty-third Session, UN Doc 66/10 (2011), pp 151–2.
[22] See 'Lotus', Judgment No 9, 1927, PCIJ, Ser A, No 10, p 18.

countermeasures. Why spend so many years defining lawful countermeasures, unless it is based on a presumption that wider action by States is unlawful? There was certainly a move by the ILC away from conflating countermeasures and reprisals, and countermeasures and sanctions.[23] The separation of these concepts though is not, by itself, concrete evidence that unilateral non-forcible measures, not coming within the ILC's doctrine of countermeasures, are unlawful. This issue will be returned to in particular when looking at the wider concept of economic coercion.

Retorsion is conduct that does not involve the suspension of international obligations owed by the injured State to the responsible State, even though usually taken in response to unlawful acts on the part of the responsible State. 'Acts of retorsion may include the prohibition of or limitations upon normal diplomatic relations or other contacts, embargoes of various kinds or withdrawal of voluntary aid programs.'[24] Countermeasures could take the form of a suspension of a trade agreement, whereas acts of economic retorsion are based on a State's freedom to trade or not to trade (or deal more generally) with other States, although embargoes may well be both punitive and breach principles of international law, such as the principle of non-intervention. In general, an 'act of retorsion is an unfriendly but nevertheless lawful act by the aggrieved party against the wrongdoer. As such retorsion is not circumscribed by the international legal order' (Zoller, 1984, p 5). Some writers, however, see countermeasures as encompassing both non-forcible reprisals and retorsion (Abi-Saab, 2001, p 38, citing Schachter, Virally, and Leban in support). In general Abi-Saab sees them as 'reactions permitted in international law to illegality' (Abi-Saab, 2001, p 37). However, that view was not adopted by the ILC, which, at least in its final Articles, keeps the concepts distinct and only concerns itself with delimiting countermeasures, keeping them apart from retorsion. Furthermore, the ILC, together with the International Court of Justice, distinguish countermeasures from reprisals by saying that countermeasures are instrumental while reprisals are punitive.[25]

Thus, non-forcible measures taken by a State may constitute countermeasures if they arise as a result of the suspension of international obligations owed to the responsible State. If they are not the result of the non-fulfilment of an international obligation owed to the responsible State, then they may be acts of retorsion. Whether this means that victim States have freedom to impose sanctions against States that have violated international law will be considered later. At first sight it seems odd that acts of retorsion, which could be more damaging than countermeasures, may be acceptable but this seems to reflect the underdeveloped state of international law in this area. It is the case that acts of retorsion, while not governed by a specific bilateral legal relationship between the responsible State and the injured State, are still governed by the limitations of necessity and proportionality, and by general principles of international law, such as those prohibiting intervention or violation of basic human rights norms. Furthermore, if the ILC's doctrine of countermeasures is to make complete sense, retorsion arguably should be viewed as a residual remedy in the case of a State injured by a breach of international law where the injured State does not have any existing specific obligations to the responsible State that it is able to suspend. It may, in these circumstances, take limited proportionate non-forcible measures of retorsion that are an attempt to remedy that breach. Such a suggestion, however, is clearly *de lege ferenda*.

Cassese defines retorsion as 'any retaliatory act by which a State responds, by an unfriendly act not amounting to a violation of international law, to either (a) a breach of

---

[23] See the writings of earlier ILC Rapporteurs where these terms were used without real distinction: Arango-Ruiz, 1994, p 21; Ago, 1979, p 47.   [24] Crawford, 2002, p 281.
[25] *Gabčíkovo-Nagymaros Project (Hungary/Slovakia), Judgment, ICJ Reports 1997*, p 7, paras 83–5.

international law or (b) an unfriendly act, by another State'. He gives examples of the breaking off of diplomatic relations, discontinuance or reduction of trade/investment, withholding economic assistance, expulsion of nationals, heavy fiscal duties on goods from the offending State, or strict passport regulations (Cassese, 2005, p 310). As can be seen, these measures may be much more damaging than the fairly restrictive doctrine of countermeasures.

D. LIMITATIONS UPON COUNTERMEASURES AND OTHER NON-FORCIBLE MEASURES TAKEN BY STATES

The doctrine of countermeasures as defined by the ILC is specific. First of all the response to an unlawful act can only be the suspension of an international obligation owed to the responsible State. This distinguishes countermeasures from reprisals and retorsion. Further, there are numerous other limitations governing the form and extent of that suspension. Countermeasures must not be forcible. This clearly applies to other types of non-forcible measures.[26] Furthermore, 'anticipatory non-forcible counter-measures are unlawful; since by definition they precede actual occurrence of breach' (Elagab, 1988, p 63). The same principle must be applicable to all non-forcible measures taken by States, since they are based on the occurrence of unlawful or unfriendly acts. Countermeasures should be directed against the responsible State and not third party States.[27] This too seems applicable to other non-forcible measures.

Countermeasures are temporary and should, whenever possible, be reversible so the future legal relations between victim State and responsible State can be restored.[28] If the measures taken punish the responsible State by inflicting irreparable damage on it, then they are not countermeasures.[29] Such punitive measures would appear to be non-forcible reprisals, the legality of which is not discussed by the ILC, but that body's movement away from the notion of punishment as the rationale for countermeasures indicates uncertainty about the legality of reprisals. This is supported by the International Court's statement in the *Gabčíkovo* case that the purpose of countermeasures is to 'induce the wrong-doing State to comply with its obligations under international law, and that the measures must therefore be reversible'.[30] It is noticeable that James Crawford, then Rapporteur, stated that the 'international community has moved away from the classical terminology of reprisals and towards the notion of countermeasures as temporary, reversible steps' (Crawford, 2001, p 66). As with many changes in international law it is not possible to draw a clear line between the demise of one concept or principle and the emergence of another; the transition is gradual.

Countermeasures must be proportionate. According to the ILC, they 'must be commensurate with the injury suffered, taking account of the gravity of the internationally wrongful act and the rights in question'.[31] Disproportionate countermeasures give rise to the responsibility of the State taking them.[32] Taking a different approach, Franck asserts

---

[26] Article 50(1)(a) ARSIWA; Article 2(4) UN Charter; *Declaration on Principles of International Law Concerning Friendly Relations and Co-operation among States in Accordance with the Charter of the United Nations*, UN Res 2625 (XXV) (24 October 1970).

[27] Article 49(1)(2) ARSIWA.   [28] Articles 49(2)(3), 53 ARSIWA.   [29] Crawford, 2002, p 287.

[30] *Gabčíkovo-Nagymaros Project (Hungary/Slovakia), Judgment, ICJ Reports 1997*, p 7, paras 56–7.

[31] Article 51 ARSIWA.

[32] Crawford, 2002, p 294. See *Naulilaa* case (1928) 2 *RIAA* 1052 (disproportionate); *Gabčíkovo-Nagymaros Project (Hungary/Slovakia), Judgment, ICJ Reports 1997*, p 7, para 87 (disproportionate); *Air Services Agreement* case (1978) 54 ILR 303 (proportionate).

that the response must be proportionate to the initial unlawful act, equivalent to the biblical eye for an eye, tooth for a tooth approach (Franck, 2008, pp 715, 763). However, there appear to be difficulties in both the approaches of the ILC and Franck. The issue ought not to be one of proportionality to the unlawful act or the injury it causes, because this would suggest that countermeasures are taken to punish the responsible State, thus confusing countermeasures with reprisals. As Cassese states, 'in current international law the purpose of countermeasures must be seen . . . in impelling the offender to discontinue its wrongful conduct or to make reparation for it. If this is so, the proportionality must be appraised by establishing whether the countermeasure is such as to obtain this purpose.' This should mean that in certain cases a weak State may be subject to countermeasures that are quantitatively less than the injury suffered by a powerful State, if the measures are sufficient to bring an end to the illegal act (Cassese, 2005, p 306). The International Court has found that non-forcible countermeasures were disproportionate in the *Gabčíkovo-Nagymaros* case, though it provided little by way of explanation of why Czechoslovakia's assumption of control of part of the Danube in response to Hungary's violation of a treaty obliging it to undertake construction to aid shipping, energy development, and flood control on the section of the Danube shared by both countries was disproportionate.[33] This adds to the impression of indeterminacy in the principle of proportionality despite its possible elevation to a general principle of international law (Franck, 2008, p 716).

According to the ILC, countermeasures must not violate basic obligations under international law (namely those prohibiting the threat or use of force, protecting fundamental human rights,[34] or concerning obligations of a humanitarian character), and those arising under *jus cogens*. Countermeasures should not affect dispute-resolution procedures that are applicable. Countermeasures cannot be taken to impair consular or diplomatic inviolability.[35] Diplomatic law provides its own legal regime for dealing with illicit activities by members of diplomatic or consular missions.[36] 'If diplomatic or consular personnel could be targeted by way of countermeasures, they would in effect constitute resident hostages against perceived wrongs of the sending State, undermining the institution of diplomatic and consular relations.'[37] Countermeasures must follow an unsatisfied demand by the injured State that the responsible State comply with its international obligation(s). The injured State must also notify the responsible State that it intends to take countermeasures and offer to negotiate, except in the case of urgent countermeasures necessary to preserve the injured State's rights (eg temporary staying orders or the temporary freezing of assets).[38] Furthermore, they must be suspended if the wrongful act has ceased and the dispute has been submitted to a tribunal with binding authority.[39]

The limitations discussed in this section are arguably applicable to other more controversial claims to non-forcible measures, with the exception of the suspension of diplomatic relations that seems to be an accepted act of retorsion in international relations.

---

[33] *Gabčíkovo-Nagymaros Project (Hungary/Slovakia), Judgment, ICJ Reports 1997*, p 7, para 87. See also Scobbie, 2004, p 1129 for discussion as to whether Israel's construction of a security wall is better analysed as a purported non-forcible countermeasure rather than the purported exercise of the right of self-defence, dismissed by the International Court in *Legal Consequences of the Construction of a Wall in the Occupied Palestinian Territory, ICJ Reports 2004*, p 136, paras 139–40.

[34] Especially the non-derogable rights contained in the International Covenants—Crawford, 2002, p 289. See also CESCR General Comment No 8 (1997), UN Doc E/C.12/1997/8, 5 December 1997, paras 1 and 5.

[35] Article 50(1)(2) ARSIWA.

[36] *United States Diplomatic and Consular Staff in Tehran, Judgment, ICJ Reports 1980*, p 3, paras 84–6.

[37] Crawford, 2002, pp 292–3.   [38] Ibid, p 299.

[39] ARSIWA, Article 52. See also *Application of the Interim Accord of 13 September 1995 (the Former Yugoslavia Republic of Macedonia v Greece), ICJ Reports 2011*, p 644, para 164.

This seems to contradict the 'resident hostages' argument mentioned earlier. This is illustrative of the problem in defining countermeasures without addressing the issue of retorsion. In general, Elagab states that in the case of a 'self-contained regime', where such a regime 'possesses its own mechanism for redressing the wrongful conduct, countermeasures should not be imposed' (Elagab, 1988, p 218). He refers to diplomatic law, but the same can be said of the WTO's procedures for dispute settlement, followed, if necessary, by a form of institutionalized countermeasures. Although they look like countermeasures, they are not measures imposed by dint of custom but by reason of the GATT treaty regime. They are thus similar in appearance to countermeasures, but the source of the rights and duties is the special treaty regime, and the limitations may be different (but see Gazzini, 2006, pp 737–41).

Thus, countermeasures may be excluded by special rules (eg a treaty which states that its provisions cannot be suspended)[40] or by a regime that dictates the way in which measures are taken by victim States (the primary example is the WTO).[41] Countermeasures are thus said to be 'residual' remedies,[42] reflecting the fact that States may choose to move away from a decentralized system of self-help by developing treaty regimes with their own processes of enforcement.

E. COUNTERMEASURES AND THIRD STATES

We turn now to the question of whether countermeasures as defined by the ILC can be taken by States other than the State directly injured. According to the ILC, countermeasures are normally taken by a State injured by an internationally wrongful act of another State. However, responsibility may be invoked by States other than the injured State acting in the collective interest.[43] Responsibility is not invoked by these third States as a result of injury to themselves but as a result of breach of an obligation to a group of States of which it is a member—obligations *erga omnes partes* (eg regional environmental or human rights regimes), or to the international community as a whole—obligations *erga omnes* (eg laws prohibiting genocide, aggression, slavery, racial discrimination, and self-determination).[44]

However, the ILC is careful to distinguish third States invoking responsibility from them taking countermeasures. The latter issue is left much more open. Such third States can demand cessation and performance in the interests of the injured States or the beneficiaries of the obligation breached.[45] 'The question is to what extent these States may legitimately assert a right to react against unremedied breaches',[46] *viz* by taking countermeasures against the responsible State. One problem in taking collective countermeasures is that of proportionality, though it is difficult to prove a violation of this principle if the aim is to stop a breach of an obligation owed *erga omnes*. In the absence of institutional sanctions imposed, for example, by the UN Security Council under Chapter VII of the Charter,[47] the legality of such measures is in doubt, though there seems to be some State and institutional practice to support the proposition that such measures are allowed (Katselli Proukaki,

---

[40] EU treaties provide for their own system of enforcement—Crawford, 2002, p 291.

[41] The WTO system requires authorization from the Dispute Settlement Body before a member can take measures against another—Crawford, 2002, p 291.

[42] Crawford, 2002, p 283.   [43] Ibid, p 276.

[44] Article 48(1) ARSIWA. See *Barcelona Traction, Light and Power Company, Limited, Second Phase, Judgment, ICJ Reports 1970*, p 3, paras 33–4; *East Timor (Portugal v Australia), Judgment, ICJ Reports 1995*, p 90, para 29.

[45] Article 48(2) ARSIWA.   [46] Crawford, 2002, p 302.   [47] Ibid.

2010, pp 90–209). However, practice is inconsistent, making the drawing of any conclusions as to *opinio juris* extremely difficult, if not impossible.

Further, it is inaccurate to portray such 'collective' countermeasures as a replacement for centralized collective action through an international organization. The term 'collective countermeasures' gives the 'illusion of concerted action when in reality such collective countermeasures are individual initiatives—even though there is more than one such initiative at the same time' (Alland, 2002, p 1222). In addition, the subjective assessments of States as to whether to impose such countermeasures undermine the enforcement of these crucial norms (Alland, 2002, p 1237). However, it is true to say that to expect international institutions such as the UN Security Council to replace this subjective assessment with something more objective when considering whether to impose non-forcible measures under Chapter VII of the UN Charter would, in reality, 'be replacing one subjectivity (of states) by another (of the Security Council)' (Klein, 2002, p 1249). It is thus premature to argue that the UN Security Council's sanctioning machinery has, or indeed should, replace a system of collective countermeasures even though that system is very weak. In reality there currently exist two weak systems of non-forcible sanctions for the enforcement of community norms, one decentralized and one (partly) centralized.

Indeed, the practice coming from the decentralized system mentioned in the ILC's commentary leads it to conclude that 'the current state of international law on countermeasures taken in the general or collective interest is uncertain. State practice is sparse and involves a limited number of States. At present there appears to be no clearly recognized entitlement of [third] States . . . to take countermeasures in the collective interest'[48] (but see Sicilianos, 2010, p 1148). Hence Article 54 of the ILC Articles states that a third State's right to take 'lawful' measures is not prejudiced by any of its other provisions on countermeasures. What are lawful measures in this context is an issue that is, in effect, left open (Klein, 2002, pp 1253–5; but see Alland, 2002, p 1233). Bederman's summary of the ILC's position on collective countermeasures characterizes it as the 'only possible political solution', which was 'to defer debate to another day and to allow customary international lawmaking processes to elaborate any conditions on the use of collective countermeasures' (Bederman, 2002, p 828).

The ILC mentions the US prohibition in 1978 of export of goods and technology to Uganda and all imports from Uganda in response to alleged genocide by the government of Uganda.[49] This certainly appears to be a response to a breach of an obligation owed *erga omnes*, but it did not only concern the suspension of US treaty obligations, and therefore went beyond countermeasures as defined by the ILC. The US response appeared to be unilateral non-forcible measures, in effect sanctions, imposed to enforce community norms. The ILC also refers to measures taken by Western States against Poland and the Soviet Union in 1981 in response to internal repression by the Polish government. Measures included suspension of treaty landing rights for scheduled civilian aircraft. These actions seemed to take the form of countermeasures but were they a response to a breach of an obligation owed *erga omnes*? It is still difficult, though not impossible, to argue for a right to democracy in the twenty-first century, but in 1981 such an argument was mainly a political, not legal, one. The US countermeasures in the form of the suspension of treaty landing rights against South African airlines in 1986 seem to be a clearer example given the odium attached to the system of apartheid, and its categorization as a crime against humanity.

---

[48] Ibid, p 305.   [49] Ibid, pp 302–4.

The examples cited by the ILC of non-forcible measures imposed by regional organizations, mainly the EC, illustrate the even greater legal confusion when the analysis of such measures is elevated from the purely bilateral. In 1982 the EC, along with Australia, Canada, and New Zealand, adopted trade sanctions against Argentina in response to its invasion of the Falklands. Before the GATT, the EC justified these as measures taken by the 'Community and its Member States' on the basis of their 'inherent rights', meaning the right of self-defence (Zoller, 1984, p 105). In 1990 (before the UN Security Council imposed sanctions) the EC and USA imposed trade sanctions and froze Iraqi assets in response to Iraq's invasion of Kuwait. In both of these episodes the non-forcible measures were in response to a breach of an obligation owed *erga omnes* (not to commit aggression) but they seemed to extend beyond mere countermeasures to take the form of multilateral economic sanctions. In 1998, in response to the crimes against humanity being committed in Kosovo, the EC imposed a flight ban and froze Yugoslav assets in response to the humanitarian crisis in Kosovo. In some countries the flight ban was a product of the suspension of treaty rights. The suspension of treaty rights and the freezing of assets seemed to be clear examples of countermeasures undertaken in response to a breach of a fundamental norm. Nevertheless, the EC has not limited itself to clear countermeasures in other instances. In response to violence and human rights violations that marred the run-up to the Presidential elections in Zimbabwe in March 2002, the EU imposed a travel ban, a freeze on financial assets, and an arms embargo. The Commonwealth, on the other hand, simply suspended Zimbabwe from membership, a power that is purely institutional. Both institutional responses do show, however, that there is practice that suggests that denial of democracy/democratic rights could now be seen as a breach of an obligation owed *erga omnes*. However, it is too early to state that this has crystallized into a rule of customary law given the uncertainty about the legal status of third party countermeasures.

There is, however, growing practice that shows that States frequently resort to collective or third party non-forcible measures when there are clear breaches of community norms protected by obligations owed *erga omnes*, especially when the UN Security Council has been unable to act, for example Western States' measures against Russia in response to its military interventions in Ukraine starting in 2014, and EU, Arab League, and other third party non-forcible measures in response to the Syrian regimes crimes against humanity committed there since 2011 (Dawidowicz, 2017, pp 3–5).

What the examples we have described illustrate is that State and institutional practice is confused in a number of ways. First the wrongful acts involved are not always clearly breaches of obligations owed *erga omnes*. Secondly, non-forcible measures, especially trade sanctions, are not always a product of non-performance of existing obligations. Thirdly, some of the practice is institutional rather than by individual States, though the line between them is not clear. Zoller expresses doubts about the imposition of sanctions by regional organizations, in the sense of whether they are actually deploying sanctions as international legal persons, or whether, in reality 'the organization acts less as an organization than as a collectivity of the member States as a whole. When countermeasures are undertaken under these circumstances, it is legally hazardous to consider that they can genuinely be attributed to the organization as such' (Zoller, 1984, p 104). Zoller views the EC measures taken against Argentina in 1982 following its invasion of the Falklands, and against the Soviet Union in 1981 following the imposition of martial law in Poland, as a product of political cooperation by States, despite the fact that the measures against Argentina were imposed by a regulation adopted under Article 113 of the EEC Treaty (Zoller, 1984, pp 104–5). The line between countermeasures and sanctions can be unclear though the justification for the latter 'does not derive from general international law' (as with countermeasures), 'but from the constituent instrument of the organization' (Alland, 2010, p 1135).

Crawford casts doubts on the role in international law of obligations *erga omnes*. The ICJ inspired the concept in the *Barcelona Traction* case but in a dictum wholly inapplicable to the case. When the Court was faced in the *Second South West Africa*[50] and the *East Timor* cases with concrete arguments based on *erga omnes*, it shied away from the application of the concept (Crawford, 2001, p 64). This may indicate doubts about the legal basis of collective measures taken outside the UN, by other organizations or third States. In reality they are a modern form of non-forcible measure or sanction that are taken outside the narrowly defined countermeasures regime. They are, in essence, in the grey area between the doctrine of countermeasures as defined by the ILC, and the imposition of centralized sanctions. In that grey area the failure by the UN Security Council to impose sanctions when community norms against aggression and crimes against humanity are being breached is leading States and other organizations increasingly to take non-forcible measures against the responsible State.

Cassese suggests that in the case of countermeasures taken by third States in response to 'aggravated responsibility' (ie breach of fundamental rules), a precondition is that they have sought to bring the matter before an international organization. This can be the UN or a regional organization, with a view to settlement or the adoption of sanctions. This precondition is 'dictated by the inherent nature of this class of responsibility. This responsibility arises out of a gross attack on community or "public" values. The response to the wrongdoing must therefore be as much as possible public and collective.' However, 'if those bodies take no action, or their action has not brought about cessation of the wrong or adequate reparation . . . all States are empowered to take peaceful countermeasures on an individual basis' (Cassese, 2005, p 274). Although this seems to be a useful suggestion, it is more by way of *de lege ferenda*, given that States do not always report to IGOs first. It also shows that Cassese certainly does not think that regional or indeed individual countermeasures are subject to any need for prior UN *authorization*.

It certainly seems to be the case that regional organizations have in their practice taken non-forcible measures against member and non-member States without seeking authority from the Security Council. Practice by the OAS against Cuba and Venezuela in the early 1960s and against Haiti in the early 1990s, as well as the measures taken by the EC against Yugoslavia in the 1990s, all without UN authority or preceding UN measures, suggest that the requirement in Article 53 of the UN Charter that 'enforcement action' needs the authorization of the Security Council does not cover non-military, as opposed to military, coercive measures (see Charron and Portela, 2015, p 1369 (on the African Union)). Of course, if the Security Council goes on to take non-forcible measures under Article 41 of the UN Charter after determining that the situation is a threat to the peace, the Security Council 'takes over', and individual States may only take action to the extent allowed by the UN Charter (individual or collective self-defence), or recommended, authorized, or decided upon' by the Security Council (Cassese, 2005, p 275). This is achieved by dint of Article 25 of the Charter, which makes Security Council decisions binding on members of the UN. Article 103 gives obligations arising out of the UN Charter pre-eminence over obligations arising under any other international treaty, although it is not clear that this affects member States' customary duties (see Brzoska, 2015, p 1339).

---

[50] *South West Africa, Second Phase, Judgment, ICJ Reports 1966*, p 6.

III. ECONOMIC COERCION

While the ILC has defined lawful countermeasures with a high degree of abstraction and in quite a narrow way, thereby implicitly excluding reprisals, the reality of international relations seems to be very different. Powerful States do not always appear to be constrained by the niceties of the requirements of countermeasures, they do not simply suspend obligations, they do not simply seek to remedy the illegality; what they seek is coercion and punishment by the application of sanctions often of an economic nature. While preferring a collective umbrella for these actions if possible, the USA, for example, is prepared to go it alone if necessary. Its sanctions regimes against Iran first imposed in 1979 and those against the Soviet Union in 1980 are cases in point. Neither could be authorized by the Security Council, and so the USA imposed them unilaterally. This has led one leading US commentator to state that 'the suggestion that economic sanctions are unlawful unless approved by the Security Council (or by a regional organization such as the OAS) is obsolete'. Furthermore, he states that 'sanctions have become sufficiently common—and often better than the alternatives—to have become tolerated (not to say accepted) as a tool of foreign relations' (Lowenfeld, 2001, p 96). Furthermore, US practice includes the imposition of extraterritorial sanctions (Beaucillon, 2016, p 103).[51] Even when the Security Council does agree on sanctions, for instance against North Korea for WMD proliferation,[52] the USA's own non-forcible measures, though largely similar, make no reference to them.[53]

This reflects a view of international law that existed before 1945. Writing in 1933, Lauterpacht stated that 'in the absence of explicit conventional obligations, particularly those laid down in commercial treaties, a state is entitled to prevent altogether goods from a foreign state from coming into its territory'. The prevention of trade going the other way from the victim State to the responsible State seemed equally permissible in the pre-Charter period. Further, this is justified on the basis that 'in a community from which war in its technical sense has been eliminated and which has not reached the stage of moral perfection, pacific means of pressure are unavoidable. To prohibit them would mean to court the more radical remedy of war' (Lauterpacht, 1933, pp 130, 140). In a modern sense this still appears to be the case, subject to the requirements of the multilateral regime of the WTO. Non-forcible measures, ranging from countermeasures in the ILC sense to punitive economic sanctions, can be justified under the view that 'restrictions upon the independence of States cannot be presumed',[54] in other words on the basis of a State's freedom to trade. However, this basic tenet of sovereignty has to be balanced against another tenet—that of non-intervention. The sovereign freedom of a State must always be balanced against the infringement of the sovereignty of other States.

To take two obvious instances—the Arab oil embargo of 1973–4, and the US embargo against Cuba in place since 1962: these were much more coercive, hurtful, and intrusive than the regimes of countermeasures or acts of retorsion outlined by the ILC. Their motivations were political—to support the Palestinians and to undermine a communist regime respectively—they were not simply about the suspension of obligations in response to an illegal act in order to try and remedy that act.

---

[51] See, for example, US Helms-Burton Act 1996 and the D'Amato-Kennedy Act 1996 discussed in Cassese, 2005, p 305.

[52] See, for example, SC Res 1874 (12 June 2009) and, more recently, SC Res 2371 (5 August 2017).

[53] Executive Order 13466, promulgated by President Bush on 26 June 2008, renewed by President Obama on 24 June 2009.   [54] 'Lotus', Judgment No 9, 1927, PCIJ, Ser A, No 10, p 18.

Such embargoes appear to breach the law as stated in several General Assembly resolutions that prohibit coercive economic intervention that is intended to undermine the territorial integrity or political independence (and arguably other sovereign rights) of the target States.[55] It is interesting to note too that the General Assembly has regularly called for the ending of the US economic, commercial, and financial embargo against Cuba and, in doing so, it recalls the principle of non-intervention.[56] The problem is that State practice does not appear in conformity with this law (Bowett, 1972b, p 4). Lillich outlines a 'general principle that serious and sustained economic coercion should be accepted as a form of permissible self-help only when it is also compatible with the overall interests of the world community, as manifested in the principles of the UN Charter or in decisions taken or documents promulgated thereunder' (Lillich, 1975, p 366). However, this is suggested by way of *de lege ferenda*. Furthermore, the approach advocated by Lillich and Bowett is that non-forcible, principally economic activity and measures must be presumed to be lawful unless there is evidence of intent by the sanctioning State—'measures not illegal per se may become illegal only upon proof of an improper motive or purpose' (Bowett, 1972b, pp 3–7). Given the unclear state of international law, that presumption could equally be replaced by the opposite proposition that such measures that interfere with the sovereign rights of another State are unlawful—that is certainly the General Assembly's view.[57]

Elagab considers State practice and Assembly resolutions and concludes rather ambivalently (but perhaps accurately) that 'there are no rules of international law which categorically pronounce either on the prima-facie legality or prima-facie illegality of economic coercion'. However, he is of the opinion that this does not leave economic coercion unregulated by international law; rather that 'individual rules of international law may be applied to determine the legality of economic conduct on a given occasion'. He seems to suggest that while non-forcible measures may involve some element of coercion, their regulation is subject to a separate legal regime (Elagab, 1988, pp 212–13), though this regime is subject to limitations including principles of international law. Thus the sanctions against Cuba by the USA go far beyond countermeasures (and, indeed, reprisals and retorsion); they amount to coercion (White, 2015, pp 125–54). This is then subject to applicable rules of international law, such as *jus cogens* and fundamental human rights standards, and, it is argued here, to the principle of non-intervention, which (despite significant erosion over the years) has a core element, prohibiting coercion of political independence (Boisson de Chazournes, 2010, pp 1209–11).

If a State wishes to overcome the principle of non-intervention and subject another State to sanctions then it has to seek authority from an international organization, even in the case of breaches of obligations owed *erga omnes*, unless the State confines itself to countermeasures. The UN Security Council clearly has the competence to override the domestic jurisdiction limitation in Article 2(7) of the UN Charter when acting under Chapter VII. The extent of this competence and the issue of whether other international organizations also possess it will now be turned to.

---

[55] GA Res 2131 (21 December 1965: Non-intervention); GA Res 2625 (24 October 1970: Friendly Relations); GA Res 3171 (17 December 1973: Permanent Sovereignty over Natural Resources); GA Res 3281 (12 December 1974: Charter of Economic Rights and Duties of States).

[56] Starting with GA Res 47/19 (24 November 1992).

[57] See also GA Res 69/180 (18 December 2014, Human Rights and Unilateral Coercive Measures).

IV. SANCTIONS

A. DEFINITION OF SANCTIONS

Non-forcible countermeasures, reprisals, and acts of retorsion clearly continue to occur in international relations. Analysis so far has raised a presumption against the legality of non-forcible measures wider than countermeasures as defined by the *Air Services* case, unless they are imposed for breaches of community norms (*erga omnes*), normally through institutional mechanisms. Reprisals are therefore illegal if they are imposed with the purpose of punishment or coercion of the sovereign will of the target State, and by means that are designed to achieve these ends. Punitive measures and deeper coercion than necessary to force the responsible State to stop its illegal act are best seen as sanctions. Of course, in a general sense all measures designed to enforce the law can be seen as sanctions. Kelsen sees law as essentially a coercive order, an organization of force, a system of norms providing for sanctions (Kelsen, 1945). Brown-John argues that 'in a juristic sense a sanction is a hyphen between prescribed law and law enforcement, although certainly sanctions tend to be more closely related to enforcement than a prescribed law' (Brown-John, 1975, p 2). But despite the fact that sanctions exist under international law, their nature is less precise compared to sanctions under the domestic system, a disparity that has led to controversy about whether sanctions exist at all in international law.

Brierly notes that the 'real difference . . . between municipal and international law is not that one is sanctioned and the other is not, but that in the one the sanctions are organized in a systematic procedure and that in the other they are left indeterminate. The true problem for consideration is therefore not whether we should try to create sanctions for international law, but whether we should try to organize them in a system' (Brierly, 1932, p 68). Similarly Kunz observes that:

> the alleged absence of sanctions has been and is today the principal argument of those who deny that the rules of international law have the character of legal rules. But general international law *has* sanctions . . . This is not a unique feature of international law, but it is common to all primitive, highly decentralized legal orders, whether municipal or international. Such legal orders have no central organs either for the making or application of legal rule or for the determination of the delict or the execution of sanctions. All these functions must be left to the members of the legal community; in international law, to the sovereign states. There are no collective but only individual sanctions, carried out by way of self-help; there is no monopoly of force at the disposal of a central law-enforcing organ; there is no distinction between criminal and civil sanctions; the sanctions are based on collective, not individual responsibility. (Kunz, 1960, p 324)

While Kunz was writing at the height of the Cold War, with no real practice by the UN on sanctions, in the post-Cold War period it might be argued that there now exists a central sanctioning organ—the Security Council.

Schachter attributed the decentralized nature of sanctions under international law to an indifferent attitude in the international legal community to enforcement in general rather than to a formal system of structuring between law and politics. Accordingly,

> for a long time compliance and enforcement were on the margins of UN concern. Like somewhat backward members of a family, their place was vaguely recognized, but not much was expected from them. The busy world of UN law-making and law applying carried on pretty much without serious consideration of means of ensuring compliance. Some prominent international lawyers dismissively referred to enforcement as a political matter

outside the law. Within UN bodies comfort was taken in the pious hope that governments which acknowledged their legal obligations would carry them out, at least most of the time. It was far from evident that they generally did so in some areas, but measures such as compulsory jurisdiction, mandatory fact finding and coercive sanctions were not considered acceptable or feasible. (Schachter, 1994, pp 9–10)

Schachter, though, also points to the progress made on enforcement and compliance in the post-Cold War period.

Sanctions are different from countermeasures. Zoller is clear on this when she states that '[a]s opposed to countermeasures, sanctions are very specific measures. A countermeasure is a measure which has temporary effects and a coercive character, while a sanction has final effects and a punitive character. Moreover, sanctions have an exemplary character directed at other countries which countermeasures do not have' (Zoller, 1984, p 106). For instance, the Security Council, through Resolution 1343, imposed sanctions on Liberia in 2001 following its determination that its government was supporting the Revolutionary United Front (RUF) in Sierra Leone, in violation of SC Resolution 1132 which had imposed sanctions against the rebel group. This was the first time the Security Council had imposed sanctions against a country because of its refusal to comply with sanctions against another country (Cortright and Lopez, 2002, p 82). Zoller further argues that '. . . countermeasures should always be temporary measures, they draw a line between the consequences of unlawful conduct in international law; they underline the difference between them and those measures which impose a final harm on the defaulting party and which could properly be designated by the term "sanctions"'. For this reason, '[c]ountermeasures . . . have to be placed within reparation and outside punishment' (Zoller, 1984, p 75).

To be clearly lawful, sanctions have to be pursued by international organizations, representing the 'centralized mechanisms' hinted at by Brierly (Gowlland-Debbas, 2001, p 6). The issue is not simply how many States were involved in the decision to impose sanctions but rather whether the decision was taken by those States acting under the auspices of an organization competent to do so. The British Royal Institute of International Affairs recognized the element of collectivity when in 1938 it defined sanctions as 'action taken by members of the international community against an infringement, actual or threatened, of the law' (Brown-John, 1975, p 5), though it is uncertain whether 'international community', as used in this context, equates to international organizations for the purpose of establishing the legality of sanctions. Abi-Saab defines sanctions as 'coercive measures taken in execution of a decision of a competent social organ, ie an organ legally empowered to act in the name of the society or community that is governed by the legal system'. He distinguishes them sharply from 'coercive measures taken individually by States or group of States outside a determination and a decision by a legally competent social organ', including countermeasures. These 'are manifestations of "self-help" or "private justice", and their legality is confined to the very narrow limits within which "remnants" of "self-help" are still admitted in contemporary international law' (Abi-Saab, 2001, p 32).

Cassese notes that the trend in the 'international community is for international bodies, principally international organizations, to react to gross breaches of international law' by means of sanctions (Cassese, 2005, pp 310–11). This practice became more evident after the end of the Cold War. One common trait of this practice is the utilization of sanctions by international organizations to counter unconstitutional removals of governments among their membership. Sanctions were first used by the OAS against the military junta in Haiti in 1992, and there were similar scenarios with regard to ECOWAS in Liberia (1989–97) and Sierra Leone (1997–2001). This practice has been further entrenched by the use of sanctions by ECOWAS, for example, to reverse unconstitutional governmental take-overs in Togo in February 2005, and separately in Mali and Guinea-Bissau in 2012.

While countermeasures are taken by individual States, sanctions are imposed within a collective context, normally an international organization. This development corresponds to the growth in recognition of community interests, representing the 'creation of international institutional responses to violations of such core norms' (Gowlland-Debbas, 2001, p 7). However, the distinction between countermeasures and sanctions should not be read as suggesting that countermeasures can only be taken on an individual basis. Countermeasures, like sanctions, can also be taken collectively. Elagab recognizes this possibility with regard to countermeasures taken by international institutions although he doubted that there is a 'generalized theory of countermeasures taken by international institutions' (Elagab, 1988, p 1).

Sanctions imposed by the Security Council under Article 41 of the Charter can include full or partial trade, financial, commercial, and arms embargoes, and are therefore, generally, of an economic nature. Schachter states that 'sanctions under Article 41 have come to be seen as quintessential type of international enforcement. The language of Article 41 is broad enough to cover any type of punitive action not involving use of armed force' (Schachter, 1994, p 12). Gowlland-Debbas argues that although Chapter VII measures imposed by the Security Council were not intended to be restricted to cases of non-compliance with international law, the practice of the Council has moved considerably towards dealing with responsibility of States for breaches of international law (Gowlland-Debbas, 2001, p 9; cf Zoller, 1984, pp 106–7). The determination of Iraq's guilt for its invasion of Kuwait, and the requirement for it to pay compensation, is a case in point.[58] Before taking action under Chapter VII, the Council is required by Article 39 of the UN Charter to determine the existence of a 'threat to the peace', 'breach of the peace', or 'act of aggression'. The Council can thus deal with threats to or breaches of the peace that do not constitute internationally wrongful conduct. Aggression would appear to be more a determination of breach of international law, although the history of the definition of aggression shows that there is a reluctance to delimit the Security Council's competence in purely legal terms. Thus it is true to say that sanctions imposed by the UN serve much wider purposes than the concept of unilateral, or even collective, countermeasures as defined by the ILC.

It is relevant to ask whether economic measures taken by regional organizations are subject to the legal regime governing sanctions (as with the UN) or the legal regime governing countermeasures. Economic sanctions based on Chapter VII are to be distinguished from economic countermeasures in that the latter are bilateral, imposed in peacetime, and generally considered to be lawful unless prohibited by national law (Kondoch, 2001, p 269). Countermeasures are not punitive; they are taken to ensure that the responsible State ceases its violation, and, if applicable, provides reparation. They are instrumental—their aim is to achieve a restitution of a legal relationship (Crawford, 2001, p 61). Thus there is clear autonomy for regional organizations to authorize the imposition of countermeasures against a State for breach of either regional or international community norms. Action taken by the regional organization outside its membership must be justified as countermeasures for breach of an international community rule, not merely a regional one.

Given the requirements of Article 53 of the UN Charter, question marks may be raised against action beyond countermeasures, for example measures taken by regional

---

[58] SC Res 687 (3 April 1991).

organizations that are designed to be punitive or aimed at achieving a change in regime (Sossai, 2017, ch 17). Such actions beyond countermeasures blur the distinction between sanctions and countermeasures. The imposition of measures designed to achieve regime change in another country is an action beyond the doctrine of countermeasures since the original action by the target State may not necessarily constitute a breach of an obligation owed to any of the imposing States. In March 2005, ECOWAS imposed sanctions against Togo in order to reverse the unconstitutional take-over of government in that country. Clearly these were coercive measures designed to achieve regime change, albeit in response to an earlier unconstitutional regime change in that country. It could be argued, however, that the sanctions imposed by ECOWAS on Togo were not illegal under Article 53 of the Charter since Togo, as an ECOWAS member State, had agreed to an ECOWAS treaty that empowers ECOWAS to take such measures against any member State under specific circumstances (see Abass, 2004, p 163). This is different to a situation where a regional organization imposes sanctions on a non-member State. The imposition of sanctions by the EU, for example, on Zimbabwe in 2002 seems to breach Article 53 given that Zimbabwe is not an EU member State, although there may be arguments of violations of obligations owed *erga omnes* (Gestri, 2016, p 70). However, there is institutional practice by the EC and OAS, reviewed earlier in this section, on which it may be argued that Article 53 does not pose an absolute prohibition on unauthorized regional action of a non-forcible kind, subject to the caveat that the Security Council still has the power to condemn autonomous regional activity as a breach of the Charter.

B. LIMITATIONS UPON SANCTIONS

One effect of Article 103 of the UN Charter seems to be that mandatory sanctions adopted by the Security Council under Article 41 of the UN Charter can result in obligations for member States that prevail over obligations arising for them from other international treaties. The Security Council has adopted Article 41 sanctions in a number of instances (eg Southern Rhodesia, South Africa, Iraq, the Federal Republic of Yugoslavia, Libya, Somalia, Haiti, Sudan, UNITA areas of Angola, Liberia, Sierra Leone, Rwanda, Afghanistan, and more lately North Korea, Iran, and Syria) (White, 2017, pp 176–9). Sanctions regimes have proliferated since the end of the Cold War, with the comprehensive regime against Rhodesia (1966–79) and the arms embargo against South Africa (1977–94) being the only instances of *mandatory* sanctions imposed by the Security Council during the Cold War. It has also adopted measures directed at stopping assistance to terrorists in the wake of the attacks against the USA on 11 September 2001,[59] and has followed this up with general measures aimed at preventing the spread of weapons of mass destruction, especially to non-State actors.[60] These measures are binding on all States and are directed at *activities* (for example financing terrorists) rather than the past sanctions regimes that were binding on all States but were targeted at *certain States*, including those allegedly supporting terrorism (for example, Libya, Sudan, and Afghanistan). This apparent expansion in the legislative powers of the Security Council has caused considerable discussion (Happold, 2003; Talmon, 2005).

As a consequence of UN sanctions regimes, member States may be required to suspend some of their treaty relations with the target State—eg trade treaties or civil aviation treaties. Article 103 of the Charter provides a dispensation for implementing States from the performance of these treaty obligations (Gowlland-Debbas, 2001, p 18). The justification

---

[59] SC Res 1373 (28 September 2001).   [60] SC Res 1540 (28 April 2004).

for this must be that the UN was established, or has become recognized, as having the competence to uphold and protect community norms, and can therefore direct a collection of States to take measures which would otherwise be unlawful. This partial constitution-alization would also suggest that non-members should also comply with UN directives, certainly to the extent that the Council requires them to take action to combat breaches of fundamental rules. Requiring non-member States to take action beyond that is problem-atic, although Article 2(6) of the Charter suggests that non-member States should comply if this is deemed necessary to maintain international peace and security. It is questionable whether other organizations have this competence in theory, though they may take collec-tive countermeasures within their region on the basis of regional laws (*erga omnes partes*). In practice, regional organizations have taken wider non-forcible measures or sanctions to enforce obligations owed *erga omnes* as well as *erga omnes partes*, though this practice can be said to have only taken hold because the UN has ultimately not condemned it either specifically or in a general sense.

If the Security Council or the General Assembly only recommend sanctions, it is ques-tionable whether this entitles States (if they choose) to suspend treaty obligations. Since there are no legal obligations created by a recommendatory resolution (except perhaps a duty to consider), Articles 25 and 103 of the UN Charter do not come into play, although some commentators argue that the authority of the UN is sufficient to entitle member States to breach trade agreements (Lowenfeld, 2001, p 97). Even mandatory sanctions imposed by the Security Council do not *ensure* that all members comply. The sanctions committees established by the Council to oversee implementation try to ensure this but there has been little attempt to force non-complying States into action.

There is generally no real investigation into the effective execution of sanctions by those States purportedly complying with Council decisions though there are indications that more supervision is occurring. In 2001, Charles Taylor's government in Liberia reported that it was no longer supporting the RUF following the adoption of SC Resolution 1343. Liberia's claim was independently confirmed by an ECOWAS delegation which reported that Liberia 'seemed serious in meeting the demands of the Security Council' (Cortright and Lopez, 2002, p 84). Furthermore, with respect to the effect of the sanctions imposed by SC Resolutions 1127 and 1178 on Angola/UNITA, both the mission headed by the Canadian Representative to the UN, Robert Fowler, and the panel of experts reported on the effectiveness of the sanctions against UNITA (Cortright and Lopez, 2002, p 63). Additionally, in relation to the non-forcible measures directed against terrorism after 11 September 2001, the Counter Terrorism Committee established by the Security Council is actively supervising their implementation (Ward, 2003).

It is only with the adoption of comprehensive regimes, especially that imposed against Iraq in the period 1990–2003, that the focus has turned to the limitations upon sanctions in terms of their effects (White, 2017, 179–84). The Committee on Economic, Social and Cultural Rights' General Comment of 1997 made it clear that sanctions regimes should not violate basic economic, social, and cultural rights, on the basis that unlawfulness of one kind should not be met with unlawfulness of another.[61] In 2000, the Bossuyt Report, which emerged at the behest of the Sub Commission on the Promotion and Protection of Human Rights, proposed six tests for evaluating the effectiveness of sanctions.[62] Like a study com-missioned by the UN Department of Humanitarian Affairs in 1998,[63] the Bossuyt Report recommended that sanctions be based on a valid reason, specifically target the parties

[61] General Comment No 8, UN Doc E/C.12/1997/8, (1998) 5 *IHRR* 302.
[62] The Adverse Consequences of Economic Sanctions on the Enjoyment of Human Rights (The Bossuyt Report), E/CN4/Sub.2/2000/33, 21 June 2000. [63] Bruberlin, 1998; cited by Kondoch, 2001, p 273.

responsible for the threat or breach of peace, exclude the targeting of humanitarian goods, and be imposed for a limited time.

The UN may impose sanctions not on the basis of a breach of international law but with the aim of restoring peace and security. It must be the case that in these situations, *a fortiori*, it must protect the human rights of the target State's population. If the International Court actively reviews a sanctions regime in the future—a possibility raised by the *Lockerbie* cases, 'considerations of proportionality might be examined by the Court'. 'If a particular form of sanctions results in injury to innocent civilians or causes serious harm to the environment and has no discernible impact on the targeted delinquent regime, would it be improper for the Court to say that the measures taken are disproportionate to the goals to be achieved?' (Dugard, 2001, pp 88–9). In reality there are two limitations here, namely those of human rights norms as well as the general principle of proportionality, although the two are closely related. Sanctions regimes must not cause serious human rights violations, though causation is notoriously difficult to prove in these situations, especially when sanctions regimes always contain an exception for humanitarian supplies. In addition, they must be proportionate to the end being aimed at, either the restoration of peace and security by the withdrawal of an aggressor State,[64] or some specific acts that would lead to the termination of a threat to the peace. For example in the case of Libya, this amounted to the handing over of the two suspects and the renunciation of terrorism by Libya.[65] In the case of Rhodesia, the first attempt by the UN at a comprehensive sanctions regime,[66] the aim was to end white-minority rule in that country.

C. TARGETED OR SMART SANCTIONS

To adapt Zoller's words, it is true to say that '[i]n the field of countermeasures and law enforcement, the international legal order has not yet reached a very advanced stage. Most of the time, as the rain in the New Testament, [sanctions] draw no distinction between the just and the unjust; they affect both the state and its citizens, or more precisely the state through its citizens. This situation is a direct result of the primitive doctrine of collective responsibility' (Zoller, 1984, p 101). The Iraqi citizens suffered from the effects of sanctions in the period 1990–2003 because of the guilt of their government. The response has been to modify and target sanctions more accurately on those who are really responsible—the leaders of the regimes, or non-State actors responsible, for example, for acts of terrorism or for supporting terrorism (White, 2017, pp 184–8). While the Security Council has tempered its general sanctions regimes out of concern for the human rights of the general population, preferring instead targeted or smart sanctions against individuals, those more directed measures can also be seen as falling foul of human rights protections of the targeted individuals (Happold, 2016, pp 92–8).

Since 1999, starting with Resolution 1267, the Security Council has in place a scheme of targeted measures, under Chapter VII of the Charter,[67] whereby an individual whose name is placed on the Security Council's list of individual members, or supporters, of the Taliban or Al-Qaeda has his assets and funds frozen by member States, as

---

[64] SC Res 661 (6 August 1990) (Iraq).   [65] SC Res 748 (31 March 1992).

[66] SC Res 253 (29 May 1968).

[67] SC Res 1267 (15 October 1999, against the Taliban) and SC Res 1333 (19 December 2000, against Al-Qaeda). SC Res 1267 (15 October 1999) and 1989 (17 June 2011) established what is now the UN Security Council Al Qaeda Sanctions Committee to oversee an 'Al-Qaeda sanctions list', composed of individuals and entities which it considers pose threats to international peace and security due to their links with Al-Qaeda. SC Res 2170 (15 August 2014) extended this list to members of the so-called Islamic State.

well as being subject to a travel embargo. Although there is some debate as to whether these sanctions are 'administrative' rather than 'criminal', 'preventive' rather than 'punitive' (Bianchi, 2006, pp 905–7), thereby causing uncertainty as to the human rights of the individuals listed, there seems to be increasing judicial recognition that such measures, without any safeguards, violate the human rights of the individuals concerned (Keller and Fischer, 2009, p 257). In the *Kadi* judgment of 2008 the European Court of Justice found that the EU's incorporation of obligations under SC Resolution 1267 violated the European fundamental rights of Mr Kadi, who had been listed by the Council's 1267 Committee and therefore had his assets frozen without recourse to a remedy, but the Court gave the European bodies the chance to redraft the regulations in a way that was human rights-compliant.[68] The argument that Article 103 of the Charter means that the obligations created by Resolution 1267 prevailed over human rights treaty obligations did not succeed, at least in that case (Cardwell, French, and White, 2009, p 237; de Wet, 2013, p 787; Willems, 2014, p 39).

The development of 'smart sanctions' (Cortright and Lopez, 2000, pp 4–5), both against regime elites and non-State actors (White, 2016, p 127), is a recent one, and the question of whether they will be effective in achieving their aims by targeting the regimes and leaders of States as well as individuals such as terrorist suspects while alleviating the suffering of the civilian population remains to be seen. Indeed, in terms of success, sanctions in their raw form rarely achieve their primary purposes. Sometimes it is the combination of economic and military measures that produces the required change in the targeted State; for example Rhodesia in 1979 (guerrilla campaign); Haiti in 1994 (threat of force by the USA); Serbia in 1995 (use of force by NATO and Muslim/Croat army); and Iraq in 1991 (Coalition action). On other occasions it is the combination of sanctions plus diplomacy, as in the majority of other cases of sanctions mentioned in this section. Thus it appears that economic sanctions are not by themselves an alternative to military coercion (or indeed diplomacy), but must be used in combination with other foreign policy tools. Normally, they must be used in combination with diplomacy; only exceptionally should they be used in combination with military action when States are acting under the right of self-defence or under the authority of the UN. The UN Secretary-General recognized this when he observed that 'sanctions, as preventive or punitive measures, have the potential to encourage political dialogue, while the application of rigorous economic and political sanctions can diminish the capacity of the protagonists to sustain a prolonged fight' (Cortright and Lopez, 2000, p 2).

V. CONCLUSION

This chapter has demonstrated that there are two areas of legal clarity in the area of sanctions and countermeasures. First, countermeasures taken under the doctrine enunciated by the ILC and the *Air Services* case are lawful (subject to limitations concerning, *inter alia*, human rights and proportionality). Secondly, non-military sanctions imposed by the UN Security Council under Chapter VII are lawful (subject to the limitations of human

---

[68] See decision of the European Court of Justice in *Kadi and Al Barakaat International Foundation* v *Council*, Joined Cases 402/05 and 415/05, [2008] ECR I-6351. See also the decision of the UN Human Rights Committee in *Sayadi and Vinck* v *Belgium* (2009) 16 *IHRR* 16; the decision of the European Court of Human Rights in *Nada* v *Switzerland*, no 10593/08, Judgment of 12 September 2012; and the decision of the European Court of Human Rights in *Al-Dulimi and Montana Management Inc.* v *Switzerland*, [GC] no 5809/08, ECHR 2016.

rights and proportionality). This would suggest that the topic dealt with under the title of this chapter is straightforward—unfortunately it is not. The clashes between the continuance (at least in the non-forcible realm) of self-help with greater centralization in the post-Charter era, combined with the perennial clash between States' freedom of action and the principle of non-intervention, mean that much of the area in the middle between countermeasures and UN sanctions is unclear.

This chapter demonstrates that measures in that space are, on balance, illegal, with the probable exceptions of countermeasures imposed by third States for breaches of obligations owed *erga omnes* or *erga omnes partes*, and retorsion in a residual sense. Such measures can be taken through organizations other than the UN, as can more punitive or coercive economic sanctions, subject to censure by the Security Council or, arguably, the General Assembly. In convincing the world of the legality and therefore the legitimacy of non-forcible measures, States are best advised to stick to the doctrine of countermeasures. If they want to take deeper, more punitive or coercive measures, they should seek authority of a regional organization, and preferably, though not necessarily, the UN. The requirement of convincing an organization helps to ensure that such measures are taken for the purpose of protecting a community norm, and are not taken out of pure self-interest. Thus, although there may be remaining doubts about some of the legal conclusions drawn here, there is no doubt that the legitimacy of non-forcible measures in international relations is vastly increased if they are channelled through a competent international organization.

REFERENCES

ABASS, A (2004), *Regional Organisations and the Development of Collective Security. Beyond Chapter VIII of the UN Charter* (Oxford: Hart Publishing).

ABI-SAAB, G (2001), 'The Concept of Sanction in International Law', in Gowlland-Debbas, *United Nations Sanctions and International Law*, p 38.

AGO, R (1979), 'Eighth Report', *YBILC*, vol II, part one, 47.

ALLAND, D (2002), 'Countermeasures of General Interest', 13 *EJIL* 1221.

ALLAND, D (2010), 'The Definition of Countermeasures', in Crawford, Pellet, and Olleson, *The Law of International Responsibility*, p 1127.

ARANGIO-RUIZ, G (1994), 'Countermeasures and Dispute Settlement: The Current Debate within the ILC', 5 *EJIL* 20.

BEAUCILLON, C (2016), 'Practice Makes Perfect, Eventually? Unilateral State Sanctions and the Extraterritorial Effects

of National Legislation', in N Ronzitti (ed), *Coercive Diplomacy, Sanctions and International Law* (Leiden: Brill Nijhoff), p 103.

BEDERMAN, DJ (2002), 'Counterintuiting Countermeasures', 96 *AJIL* 817.

BIANCHI, A (2006), 'Assessing the Effectiveness of the UN Security Council's Anti-terrorism Measures: The Quest for Legitimacy and Cohesion', 17 *EJIL* 881.

BOISSON DE CHAZOURNES, L (2010), 'Other Non-derogable Rights', in Crawford, Pellet, and Olleson, *The Law of International Responsibility*, p 1205.

BOWETT, DW (1972a), 'Reprisals Involving Recourse to Armed Force', 66 *AJIL* 1.

BOWETT, DW (1972b), 'Economic Coercion and Reprisals by States', 13 *Virginia JIL* 1.

BRIERLY, JL (1932), 'Sanctions', 17 *Transactions of the Grotius Society* 68.

BRIERLY, JL (1946), 'The Covenant and the Charter', 23 *BYIL* 83.

BROWN-JOHN, LC (1975), *Multilateral Sanctions in International Law: A Comparative Analysis* (New York: Praeger).

BRUBERLIN, C (1998), 'Coping with the Humanitarian Impact of Sanctions', http://www.reliefweb.int/ocha_ol/pub/sanctions.html.

BRZOSKA, M (2015), 'International Sanctions Before and Beyond UN Sanctions', 91 *International Affairs* 1339.

BULL, H (1992), 'The Importance of Grotius in the Study of International Relations', in H Bull et al (eds), *Hugo Grotius and International Relations* (Oxford: Oxford University Press), p 65.

CARDWELL, PJ, FRENCH, D, and WHITE, ND (2009), 'Yassin Abdullah Kadi', 58 *ICLQ* 229.

CASSESE, A (2005), *International Law* (2nd edn, Oxford: Oxford University Press).

CHARRON, A, and PORTELA, C (2015), 'The UN, Regional Sanctions and Africa', 91 *International Affairs* 1369.

CORTRIGHT, D and LOPEZ, GA (2000), *The Sanctions Decade: Assessing UN Strategies in the 1990s* (Boulder, CO: Lynne Rienner).

CORTRIGHT, D and LOPEZ, GA (2002), *Sanctions and the Search for Security: Challenges to UN Action* (Boulder, CO: Lynne Rienner).

CRAWFORD, J (1994), 'Counter-Measures as Interim Measures', 5 *EJIL* 65.

CRAWFORD, J (2001), 'The Relationship between Sanctions and Countermeasures', in Gowlland-Debbas, *United Nations Sanctions and International Law*, p 57.

CRAWFORD, J (2002), *The International Law Commission's Articles on State Responsibility* (Cambridge: Cambridge University Press).

CRAWFORD, J, PELLET, A, and OLLESON, S (eds) (2010), *The Law of International Responsibility* (Oxford: Oxford University Press, 2010).

DAWIDOWICZ, M (2017), *Third Party Countermeasures in International Law* (Cambridge: Cambridge University Press).

DE WET, E (2013), 'From *Kadi* to *Nada*: Judicial Techniques Favouring Human Rights over United Nations Security Council Sanctions', 12 *Chinese JIL* 787.

DOPAGNE, F (2011), 'Sanctions and Countermeasures by International Organizations', in R Collins and ND White (eds), *International Organizations and the Idea of Autonomy: Institutional Independence in the International Legal Order* (Abingdon: Routledge), p 178.

DUGARD, J (2001), 'Judicial Review of Sanctions', in Gowlland-Debbas, *United Nations Sanctions and International Law*, p 8.

ELAGAB, OY (1988), *The Legality of Non-Forcible Counter-Measures in International Law* (Oxford: Clarendon Press).

FRANCK, TM (2008), 'On Proportionality of Countermeasures in International Law', 102 *AJIL* 715.

GAZZINI, T (2006), 'The Legal Nature of WTO Obligations and the Consequences of their Violation', 17 *EJIL* 723.

GESTRI, M (2016), 'Sanctions Imposed by the European Union: Legal and Institutional Aspects', in N Ronzitti (ed), *Coercive Diplomacy, Sanctions and International Law* (Leiden: Brill Nijhoff), p 70.

GOWLLAND-DEBBAS, V (ed) (2001), *United Nations Sanctions and International Law* (The Hague: Kluwer).

HAPPOLD, M (2003), 'Security Council Resolution 1373 and the Constitution of the United Nations', 16 *Leiden JIL* 593.

HAPPOLD, M (2016), 'Targeted Sanctions and Human Rights', in M Happold and P Eden, *Economic Sanctions in International Law* (Oxford: Hart).

KATSELLI PROUKAKI, E (2010), *The Problem of Enforcement in International Law: Countermeasures, the Non-Injured State and the Idea of International Community* (London: Routledge).

KELLER, H and FISCHER, A (2009), 'The UN Anti-terror Sanctions Regime under Pressure', 9 *Human Rights Law Review* 257.

KELSEN, H (1945), *General Theory of Law and State* (Cambridge, MA: Harvard University Press).

KLEIN, P (2002), 'Responsibility for Serious Breaches of Obligations Deriving From Peremptory Norms of International Law and United Nations Law', 13 *EJIL* 1241.

KONDOCH, B (2001), 'The Limits of Economic Sanctions under International Law: The Case of Iraq', 7 *International Peacekeeping* 267–94, also available at http://www.casi.org.uk\info\kondoch01.pdf.

KUNZ, LK, (1960), 'Sanctions in International Law', 54(2) *AJIL* 324.

LAUTERPACHT, H (1933), 'Boycott in International Relations', 14 *BYIL* 125.

LILLICH, RB (1975), 'Economic Coercion and the International Legal Order', 51 *International Affairs* 358.

LOWENFELD, AF (2001), 'Unilateral versus Collective Sanctions: An American Perception', in Gowlland-Debbas, *United Nations Sanctions and International Law*, p 95.

MCNAIR, AD (1930), 'The Functions and Different Legal Character of Treaties', 11 *BYIL* 100.

O'CONNELL, ME (2008), *The Power and Purpose of International Law* (Oxford: Oxford University Press).

PAUST, J and BLAUSTEIN, AP (1974), 'The Arab Oil Weapon—A Threat to International Peace', 68 *AJIL* 410.

PROVOST, R (2002), *State Responsibility in International Law* (Aldershot: Ashgate).

SCHACHTER, O (1994), 'United Nations Law' 88 *AJIL* 1.

SCOBBIE, I (2004), 'Smoke, Mirrors and Killer Whales: the International Court's Opinion on the Israeli Barrier Wall', 5 *German Law Journal* 1107.

SICILIANOS, L-A (2010), 'Countermeasures in Response to Grave Violations of Obligations Owed to the International Community', in Crawford, Pellet, and Olleson, *The Law of International Responsibility*, p 1137.

SOSSAI, M (2017), 'UN Sanctions and Regional Organizations: An Analytical Framework', in L van den Herik (ed), *Research Handbook on Sanctions and International Law* (Cheltenham: Elgar), ch 17.

TALMON, S (2005), 'The Security Council as World Legislature', 99 *AJIL* 175.

TZANAKOPOULOS, A (2011), *Disobeying the Security Council: Countermeasures against Wrongful Sanctions* (Oxford: Oxford University Press).

WARD, CA (2003), 'Building Capacity to Combat International Terrorism: The Role of the United Nations Security Council', 8 *Journal of Conflict and Security Law* 289.

WHITE, ND (2015), *The Cuban Embargo Under International Law: El Bloqueo* (London: Routledge).

WHITE, ND (2016), 'Sanctions Against Non-State Actors', in N Ronzitti (ed), *Coercive Diplomacy, Sanctions and International Law* (Leiden: Brill Nijhoff), p 127.

WHITE, ND (2017), *The Law of International Organisations* (Manchester: Manchester University Press).

WILLEMS, A (2014), 'The European Court of Human Rights on the Individual Counter-Terrorist Sanctions Regime: Safeguarding Convention Rights and Harmonising Conflicting Norms in *Nada v. Switzerland*', 83 *Nordic JIL* 39.

ZOLLER, E (1984), *Peacetime Unilateral Remedies: An Analysis of Countermeasures* (Dobbs Ferry, NY: Transnational).

FURTHER READING

CORTRIGHT, D and LOPEZ, GA (2000), *The Sanctions Decade: Assessing UN Strategies in the 1990s* (Boulder, CO: Lynne Rienner): a very good examination of the issues and problems of recent and current UN sanctions regimes.

CRAWFORD, J (2002), *The International Law Commission's Articles on State Responsibility: Introduction, Text and Commentaries* (Cambridge: Cambridge University Press): an essential collection of International Law Commission materials necessary for an understanding of the nature, role, and function of countermeasures.

DAWIDOWICZ, M (2017), *Third Party Countermeasures in International Law* (Cambridge: Cambridge University Press): an excellent recent analysis of practice.

ELAGAB, OY (1988), *The Legality of Non Forcible Counter-Measures in International Law* (Oxford: Clarendon Press): a very thorough exposition of the history and development of countermeasures.

FARRALL, JM (2007), *United Nations Sanctions and the Rule of Law* (Cambridge: Cambridge University Press): a thorough review of sanctions practice by the Security Council and an evaluation of its legal shortcomings.

GOWLLAND-DEBBAS, V (ed) (2001), *United Nations Sanctions and International Law* (The Hague: Kluwer): an excellent collection of essays, exploring, *inter alia*, the boundaries between countermeasures and sanctions.

O'CONNELL, ME (2008), *The Power and Purpose of International Law* (Oxford: Oxford University Press): a clear reconsideration of the theory and practice of the enforcement of norms of international law, by both forcible and non-forcible means.

RONZITTI, N (2016), *Coercive Diplomacy, Sanctions and International Law* (Leiden: Brill Nijhoff): an excellent contextual and conceptual reconsideration of the place and role of sanctions in international law.

SICILIANOS, L-A (1990), *Les Réactions Décentralisées à l'Illicite: Des Contre-Mesures à la Légitime Défense* (Paris: Librairie Générale de Droit et de Jurisprudence): leading non-English text on the subject matter of countermeasures.

ZOLLER, E (1984), *Peacetime Unilateral Remedies: An Analysis of Countermeasures* (Dobbs Ferry, NY: Transnational): a useful conceptual analysis of countermeasures.

18

THE MEANS OF DISPUTE SETTLEMENT

John Merrills

SUMMARY

The peaceful settlement of disputes occupies a central place in international law and international relations. A range of methods of handling international disputes has been developed and this chapter explains what the relevant techniques and institutions are, how they work, and when they are used. Because important distinctions are to be found between the various diplomatic means of settlement (negotiation, mediation, inquiry, and conciliation) and the legal means of arbitration and judicial settlement, the two categories are examined separately. Also considered is the role of the United Nations and regional organizations.

In the light of current international practice two main conclusions emerge: first that enormous progress has been made in refining and developing the means available for dealing with disputes; and secondly that while the various methods have distinctive features which determine how and when they are likely to be used, the key to resolving disputes often lies in their use in combination and interaction.

I. INTRODUCTION

The idea that international disputes should be settled by peaceful means rather than by the use of force has a long history. The attempt to construct institutions and develop techniques with this objective is a more recent phenomenon, however, much of what exists today having been created in the twentieth century and a significant proportion since 1945. This chapter is concerned with the result of that effort in the form of the means currently available for resolving international disputes peacefully. Initially, though, and to put the present arrangements in context, two questions need to be considered: what we mean by an 'international dispute', and what the law has to say about States' obligations.

A 'dispute' is a disagreement about something and an 'international dispute' is a disagreement, typically but not exclusively between States, with consequences on the international plane. However, a dispute is not just any disagreement, but a disagreement about something fairly specific. So the Arab–Israeli problem, for example, is not really a dispute, but because it is so complex is better described as a 'situation'. Of course, 'situations' generally contain specific disputes within them and the international community has to be concerned with both.[1] Nevertheless, this chapter is mainly concerned with methods for dealing with disputes, rather than situations, so the distinction is worth bearing in mind.

What sort of specific disagreements qualify as disputes? Or to put the question another way, what is the subject matter of disputes? This is easily answered. International disputes can be about almost anything. A dispute within the EU, for instance, about the need for closer political integration, would be a dispute about policy. In contrast, most disputes about boundaries or territorial issues involve a disagreement about legal rights. Disputes can also sometimes be about issues of fact. Where was State A's ship when it was intercepted by State B? What was it doing there? Did it have permission? And so on. Clearly these various sources of disagreement (fact, law, and policy) are not mutually exclusive and in many disputes are mixed up together. Separating the different elements, as we shall see, may be a key move in dealing with such disputes effectively.

What, then, are States' legal obligations in this field? A comprehensive statement can be found in an important resolution of the UN General Assembly, the 1982 Manila Declaration on the Peaceful Settlement of International Disputes,[2] which confirms and elaborates the relevant provisions of the UN Charter and the General Assembly's earlier Declaration on Principles of International Law concerning Friendly Relations and Co-operation among States of 1970.[3] Thus paragraph 2 of Section I of the Manila Declaration, like Article 2(3) of the Charter, requires every State to 'settle its international disputes exclusively by peaceful means in such a manner that international peace and security and justice, are not endangered'. And paragraph 5, echoing Article 33, lists the means available, calling for States to 'seek in good faith and in a spirit of co-operation an early and equitable settlement of their international disputes by any of the following means: negotiation, inquiry, mediation, conciliation, arbitration, judicial settlement, resort to regional agencies or arrangements or other peaceful means of their own choice including good offices'. Acknowledging the range of contingencies, the paragraph then concludes: 'In seeking such a settlement the parties shall agree on such peaceful means as may be appropriate to the circumstances and the nature of their dispute.'

It should also be noted that the Declaration says that in the event of the failure of the parties to reach an early solution 'they shall continue to seek a peaceful solution' and 'consult forthwith on mutually agreed means' (para 7), adding in the next paragraph that the parties to a dispute and other States 'shall refrain from any action whatsoever which may aggravate the situation so as to endanger the maintenance of international peace and security and make more difficult or impede the peaceful settlement of the dispute'. The obligation, then, is not just to give peaceful methods a try, but to persevere for as long as necessary, while at the same time avoiding action which could make things worse. In other words, if a dispute cannot be settled, States must at least manage it and keep things under control. What the various methods are and how they are used will therefore now be considered.

---

[1] On the significance of 'situations' with particular reference to the role of the UN, see Koufa, 1988.

[2] GA Res 37/10 (15 November 1982) 21 ILM 449.

[3] GA Res 2625 (XXV) (24 October 1970) 9 ILM 1292. See further Merrills, 1994.

II. DIPLOMATIC METHODS

A. NEGOTIATION

The methods of peaceful settlement listed in the Manila Declaration are not set out in order of priority, but the first mentioned, negotiation, is the most widely used way of dealing with international disputes.[4] In fact, negotiation is used more often in practice than all the other methods put together. Often, indeed, negotiation is the only means employed, not just because it is normally the first to be tried and is often successful, but also because its advantages may appear so great as to rule out other methods, even where the chances of a negotiated settlement are slight. When other methods are chosen, negotiation is not supplanted but used to resolve instrumental issues—the terms of reference for an inquiry commission, for instance, or the arrangements for implementing an arbitral award.

Since negotiation allows the parties to retain control of a dispute without involving third parties, it is not surprising that governments find it so attractive. However, the decision to negotiate can itself be controversial, acknowledging as it does both the other party's standing and the legitimacy of its interests. Consequently, on sensitive subjects such as sovereignty, if it is possible to negotiate at all, it may be necessary to restrict discussions to relatively uncontentious issues at least to start with, leaving the bigger problems until later. In 1973, for example, the UK succeeded in negotiating an Interim Agreement during its fishing dispute with Iceland,[5] and following the Falklands War of 1982 it was likewise able through diplomatic contact to establish a *modus vivendi* with Argentina (Evans, 1991; Churchill, 1997). It would therefore be a mistake to see negotiation as concerned only with settling international disputes. Its function in 'managing' disputes, ie containing them in order to preserve other aspects of the parties' relationship, may be equally significant.

Because negotiation is fundamental it should be thought of not so much as a first stage in the conduct of virtually all disputes, but rather as an option available to the parties at any time, for use either alongside, or as part of, other processes. Thus, as the International Court indicated in the *Aegean Sea Continental Shelf* case, the fact that negotiations are being pursued during litigation is no bar to the exercise of the Court's powers and vice versa.[6] As a result, it is not at all uncommon for cases to be resolved by negotiation in the course of litigation, as happened in 2013 in the *Ecuador-Colombia Aerial Herbicide Spraying* case.[7] Similarly, a State may decide to take a dispute to a political body like the Security Council or General Assembly but at the same time continue bilateral discussions. Such twin-track approaches, employing both public and private diplomacy, are perfectly permissible and show the adaptability of negotiation.

Important though negotiation is, it cannot guarantee that a dispute will be settled, or even managed, because it is limited in various ways. It may be impossible if the parties refuse to speak to each other and it will be ineffective if their positions are too far apart, although in both situations, as we shall see, mediation or good offices can help. If a procedure for dealing with the dispute, such as arbitration, has already been agreed, one party may see no point in further negotiation, especially if it is confident of its legal position. More generally, the objective of resolving disputes 'equitably' and in accordance with justice, as the Manila Declaration prescribes, sits uneasily with the prospect of having to negotiate in a situation of grossly unequal political power. Accordingly, though negotiation is often called for by the strong, the weak may be justified in declining the invitation.

---

[4] For more detailed discussion of negotiation see Merrills, 2017, ch 1.
[5] See *Fisheries Jurisdiction (United Kingdom v Iceland), Merits, Judgment, ICJ Reports 1974*, p 3, paras 37–9.
[6] See *Aegean Sea Continental Shelf, Judgment, ICJ Reports 1978*, p 3, para 29.
[7] *Aerial Herbicide Spraying (Ecuador v Colombia), Order of 13 September 2013, ICJ Reports 2013*, p 278.

Negotiation, however, is not always a matter of free choice. Quite apart from the force of circumstances which may mean that refusing to negotiate is not an available option, a State may bind itself to negotiate in a treaty, or find that an obligation to negotiate arises under the general law. In the *North Sea Continental Shelf* cases, for instance, the International Court decided that according to customary international law the delimitation of continental shelf boundaries between neighbouring States 'must be effected by agreement in accordance with equitable principles'.[8] Of course, an obligation to negotiate on this or any other subject is not the same as an obligation to agree, nor does it exclude recourse to other procedures. What the Court wished to emphasize was simply that as each party had rights in the disputed area, the boundaries in question were not subject to unilateral determination, and unless resolved by another procedure, had to be settled by negotiation.

The duty to negotiate sometimes laid down in treaties may be compared with related, but lesser, obligations which are an alternative. The 1994 World Trade Organization (WTO) Agreement requires its parties to 'enter into consultations' over trade issues when requested by another party,[9] which is an obligation to negotiate, whereas the 1982 Law of the Sea Convention calls only for the parties to a dispute to 'proceed expeditiously to an exchange of views' as to the means of settlement to be used.[10] It is, however, worth stressing that just as there is no general duty to consult before taking action which may affect others, so there is no general duty to seek negotiated settlements. The various methods of settlement available in international law are listed as alternatives. Negotiation is simply one possibility and in the absence of a specific duty to negotiate, such as in the WTO Agreement, States can use it or not as they see fit.

Despite this essential qualification, negotiation is an extremely important means of dealing with disputes and international relations would be unimaginably different without it. In almost all cases diplomatic exchanges will have to take place before a disagreement becomes specific enough to be described as a dispute—that is in order for the parties to establish what, if anything, they disagree about. And once it is clear a dispute exists, negotiation will often provide the best prospect of a solution, whether permanent or provisional, and for cases involving major differences as well as routine friction. It is evident, however, that although negotiation must be regarded as basic, it may not be sufficient, without more, either to resolve a dispute or even to supply a *modus vivendi*. The other methods mentioned in the Declaration must therefore now be considered.

B. MEDIATION

Mediation is essentially an adjunct of negotiation and involves a third party. If the latter does no more than encourage the protagonists to resume negotiations, or simply acts as a channel of communication, the role is described as one of 'good offices'. A mediator, on the other hand, is an active participant, authorized, and indeed expected, to advance fresh ideas and to interpret, as well as to transmit, each party's proposals to the other.[11] Mediation therefore has much in common with conciliation, although a mediator usually makes proposals informally and on the basis of information supplied by the parties, rather than through independent investigations which are a feature of conciliation. In practice,

---

[8] *North Sea Continental Shelf, Judgment, ICJ Reports 1969*, p 3, para 85.

[9] WTO Understanding on Rules and Procedures Governing the Settlement of Disputes (1994), Article 4(3). Text in (1994) 33 ILM 1226.

[10] United Nations Convention on the Law of the Sea (1982), Article 283(1). Text in (1982) 21 ILM 1245.

[11] For more detailed discussion of mediation see Bercovitch and Rubin, 1992; Greenberg, Barton, and McGuiness, 2000; Merrills, 2017, ch 2.

however, these distinctions tend to be blurred. In a given case it may therefore be difficult to draw the line between mediation and conciliation, or to say exactly when good offices ended and mediation began.

Mediation can only take place if the parties to a dispute consent and a mediator willing to act in that capacity is available. The UN and several regional organizations are charged with the resolution of disputes as an institutional objective and as a result the Secretary-General and his regional counterparts often find themselves providing good offices and mediation. Non-governmental organizations too, such as the International Committee of the Red Cross, can act as mediators. Since it offers an opportunity to become involved in a dispute and to influence its outcome, the role of mediator also has attractions for States, or individuals, with the necessary qualifications. Accordingly, it is not unusual for the course of intractable international disputes to be punctuated by offers of mediation from one or more outside sources.

Since mediation cannot be forced on the protagonists, unless they take the initiative and invite outside involvement, an unwillingness even to consider this form of assistance may frustrate the efforts of would-be mediators. If a party is unwilling to negotiate, or to contemplate any modification of its position, its acceptance of mediation (which would imply the opposite) is clearly very unlikely. On the other hand, States normally have an interest in resolving their disputes and while the terms of any settlement are plainly important, intransigence may be too expensive politically for a blank refusal of mediation to be feasible. In 1982, for example, Argentina and the UK were willing to accept good offices from the UN Secretary-General, and then mediation from the USA, because neither government could afford to alienate potential supporters.[12] It was clear at the time that something of a miracle would be needed to avoid further conflict, but for the sake of appearance, if for no other reason, they had to show willing.

Once mediation has been accepted, the task of the mediator is to devise or promote a solution which both sides can accept. Here much can be achieved by simply providing good offices and facilitating communication, especially if the parties are unable to deal with each other directly. This was the situation in both the Falklands crisis and the Diplomatic Hostages dispute of 1980, where Algeria acted as intermediary between Iran and the USA (Sick, 1985). As well as acting as a channel for information, a mediator can remind the parties of their real objectives, or encourage rethinking, and devise suitable compromises, as the Papal mediator in the Beagle Channel dispute eventually succeeded in doing (Laudy, 2000). A powerful mediator may also be able to influence the parties by offering inducements to agree in the form of rewards, or indicating that a failure to do so will be costly.

Normally, a mediator's main concern is only to find terms the parties can accept; in some types of mediation, however, any settlement must also meet certain external criteria. Thus, according to Article 38 of the European Convention on Human Rights, one of the functions of the European Court of Human Rights is to 'place itself at the disposal of the parties concerned with a view to securing a friendly settlement of the matter *on the basis of respect for human rights*' as defined in the Convention and its Protocols. In this provision, which has its counterpart in other human rights treaties, the Court is, in effect, required to act as mediator, while at the same time respecting the Convention's basic values. A significant number of individual claims have been resolved using the friendly settlement procedure,[13] demonstrating that mediation with a substantive requirement is both workable and appropriate in the human rights field.

As a means of dispute settlement mediation is clearly subject to important limitations. A mediator must be available, and the parties must be willing to accept mediation. When

---

[12] For an account of these initiatives and the subsequent efforts of the President of Peru, see Freedman and Gamba-Stonehouse, 1990, pp 150–323.

mediation has begun the prospects of success rest largely on the parties' readiness to com-promise, which means that timing is often crucial. In both the Diplomatic Hostages cri-sis and the Beagle Channel dispute mediation occurred at an opportune moment and a peaceful resolution of the situation was achieved. In the Falklands crisis, on the other hand, the aims of Britain and Argentina were diametrically opposed and as neither was willing to yield on the crucial issue of sovereignty, the matter was eventually decided by armed conflict.

Mediation, then, is as effective as the disputants allow it to be and their attitudes are likely to be governed by their immediate situation. This restricts the possibilities of me-diation, but does not destroy its value. A mediator does more than perfect an inchoate settlement. By facilitating the parties' dialogue, providing them with information and sug-gestions, identifying and exploring their aims, and canvassing possible solutions, interces-sion may be vital in moving them towards agreement. Success will often be incomplete and failure sometimes unavoidable. The mediator, however, must spare no effort and trust that the parties reciprocate.

C. INQUIRY

Inquiry in the context of dispute settlement is a term used in two distinct, but related senses. In the broader sense it refers to the process performed whenever a court or other body attempts to resolve a disputed issue of fact. Since most international disputes raise such issues, even if questions of law or policy are also present, it is clear that inquiry in this operational sense must play a large part in arbitration, conciliation, the work of interna-tional organizations, and other methods of peaceful settlement. Inquiry can, however, also be used in a narrower sense, not as a process of general relevance and application, but as a specific institutional arrangement which may be selected instead of arbitration or other techniques to establish the facts. In its institutional sense, then, inquiry refers to a particu-lar type of international tribunal, known as the commission of inquiry and introduced by the 1899 Hague Convention.[14]

The delegates to the first Hague Peace Conference were prompted to address the issue of fact-finding by an incident the year before in which the unexplained destruction of the US battleship *Maine* had precipitated a Spanish-American war. In an effort to minimize such problems in the future the Conference suggested the appointment of international commissions of inquiry for impartial fact-finding and arrangements to this effect were in-corporated in the 1899 Hague Convention. Soon afterwards in 1904 they were used for the first time in a curious episode known as the Dogger Bank incident when the Russian fleet, wrongly believing it was under attack, fired on and damaged a number of British trawlers. A commission of inquiry appointed by the two governments established that a mistake had been made and on payment of suitable compensation the incident was declared closed (Bar-Yaacov, 1974, pp 72–81).

The Dogger Bank episode was a striking example of the value of fact-finding in the set-tlement of international disputes. However, it also revealed certain weaknesses in the pro-visions of the Hague Convention which were conspicuously lacking in detail. Accordingly, the Hague Convention of 1907 expanded the earlier scheme with a series of Articles de-voted to organization and procedure. These arrangements were then used in a group of cases over the next two decades involving incidents at sea, where once again establishing

---

[13] For an account of practice under Article 38 (ex 28) of the European Convention, see Merrills and Robertson, 2001, pp 279–82, 318–19. See also Koopmans, 2008, pp 184–99.

[14] For more detailed discussion of inquiry see Bar-Yaacov, 1974; Merrills, 2017, ch 3.

the facts enabled the disputes to be disposed of.[15] This was also the outcome in the *Red Crusader* case[16] in 1962 in which the UK and Denmark set up an inquiry commission to deal with a dispute arising out of an attempt to arrest a British trawler.

Following the 1907 Hague Convention the USA concluded treaties with France and Great Britain, known as the Taft treaties, providing for commissions of inquiry with expanded powers and a further series, known as the Bryan treaties, featuring further variations. A number of other States concluded agreements along similar lines. All this treaty practice failed to produce a sequence of inquiries like those generated by the Hague Conventions, although in 1992 one of the Bryan treaties was used in the *Letelier and Moffitt* case[17] to resolve a dispute over compensation between the USA and Chile. But if in terms of case law the significance of these bilateral treaties was negligible, they were important more generally, because the idea of combining inquiry with the power to make recommendations produced the institutional arrangement known as conciliation described further in Section II D.

Inquiry is clearly a very flexible method, having been used both for 'pure' fact-finding, as in some of the early cases, and for situations where legal questions were prominent, as in *Letelier and Moffitt*. Why, then, is it so rarely used? One explanation is that today when an inquiry is needed it can sometimes be carried out through an international organization without using the Hague Conventions. The Security Council, for example, sets up fact-finding commissions from time to time, as do the Specialized Agencies, and in 1993 the World Bank introduced a unique Inspection Panel procedure[18] to investigate development projects. These institutional developments account, at least in part, for the relatively small number of cases using the Hague procedure. There is, however, a more fundamental explanation.

All forms of third party settlement have proved less popular than was once anticipated. The root of the problem is that States are often less interested in settling a dispute than in having their own views prevail. It is therefore only when certain special conditions are satisfied that there is usually scope for setting up an inquiry commission. These are that the disputed issue is largely one of fact, that no other procedure is being employed, and, most important of all, that the parties are willing to accept that their version of events may be shown to be wrong. Such a combination evidently does not occur very often. When it does, the highly satisfactory outcome of the *Red Crusader* episode shows that the international commission of inquiry can still produce useful results.

D. CONCILIATION

Conciliation has been defined as:

> A method for the settlement of international disputes of any nature according to which a Commission set up by the Parties, either on a permanent or an ad hoc basis to deal with a dispute proceeds to the impartial examination of the dispute and attempts to define the terms of a settlement susceptible of being accepted by them, or of affording the Parties with a view to its settlement, such aid as they may have requested.[19]

---

[15] For a summary of these cases see Bar-Yaacov, 1974, pp 141–79.

[16] The text of the Commission's Report can be found in 35 ILR 485. For discussion of the case see Bar-Yaacov, 1974, pp 179–96.

[17] *Letelier and Moffitt* case (Chile-USA), 88 ILR 727 and (1992) 31 ILM 1. For comment see Merrills, 2017, ch 3.

[18] See Gowlland Gualtieri, 2001; Koopmans, 2008, pp 212–17; and French and Kirkham, 2010, pp 68–72. The Inter-American Bank and the Asian Development Bank have established similar panels.

[19] The quotation is from Article 1 of the Regulations on the Procedure of International Conciliation, adopted by the Institute of International Law in 1961. For more detailed discussion of conciliation see Cot, 1972; Bar-Yaacov, 1974, pp 198–248; Merrills, 2017, ch 4; and Koopmans, 2008.

If mediation is essentially an extension of negotiation, conciliation puts third party intervention on a formal footing and institutionalizes it in a way comparable, but not identical, to inquiry or arbitration—for the fact-finding exercise that is the essence of inquiry may or may not be present in conciliation, while the search for terms 'susceptible of being accepted by the parties', but not binding on them, contrasts sharply with arbitration and forms a link between conciliation and mediation.

Like other institutional methods, conciliation is normally entrusted to commissions containing several members. However, it is also possible to refer a dispute to a single conciliator and this procedure was adopted in 1977 when Kenya, Uganda, and Tanzania asked the experienced Swiss diplomat, Dr Victor Umbricht, to make proposals for distributing the assets of the former East African Community (EAC). As the extent of the assets was unknown, the conciliator had to begin by conducting a wide-ranging inquiry, first to identify and then to value the assets, after which he could consider their distribution. Although in the final negotiated settlement the division of assets differed slightly from that proposed by Dr Umbricht, it is clear that his activities, which included mediation as well as conciliation and inquiry, and extended over seven years, made a vital contribution to the eventual settlement (Umbricht, 1984).

A more straightforward dispute which was resolved at about the same time involved a commission of the type familiar from previous conciliations. In 1980 Iceland and Norway set up a commission to make recommendations with regard to the dividing line for the area of continental shelf between Iceland and Jan Mayen Island. The Commission was instructed to take into account Iceland's 'strong economic interests' in the sea areas in question, along with various other factors. Following a detailed investigation of geological and other evidence, the Commission proposed both a boundary line and a joint development agreement for the area where oil deposits might exist (Richardson, 1988). This recommendation, typical of the kind of constructive compromise which conciliation can generate, was accepted by the parties and in 1981 was incorporated in a treaty which ended the dispute.

Bilateral agreements providing for the reference of future disputes to conciliation were quite common in the League of Nations era after the First World War, but are now quite rare. When States use conciliation in a bilateral treaty today it is therefore usually in order to deal with a specific dispute, as in the two cases just mentioned. Multilateral treaties, however, show a quite different pattern and in recent practice agreements providing for conciliation, often in conjunction with other procedures, have been concluded on a variety of topics. Among treaties demonstrating the relevance of conciliation to dispute settlement in different fields are the 1969 Vienna Convention on the Law of Treaties, the 1981 Treaty establishing the Organization of Eastern Caribbean States, the 1982 Convention on the Law of the Sea, and the 1992 Convention on Biological Diversity.[20]

The 1987 Montreal Protocol on Substances that Deplete the Ozone Layer is also worth mentioning here as it establishes a novel 'non-compliance procedure', constituting a special kind of conciliation. Under the procedure an Implementation Committee consisting of ten parties to the Protocol hears submissions relating to a party's non-compliance which may be put forward by the Secretariat or any other party. The Committee may then make recommendations 'with a view to securing an amicable solution of the matter on the basis of respect for the provisions of the Protocol'. Chinkin (1998, p 129) points out that a process such as this, dealing as it does with disputes both 'in-house' and informally,

---

[20] See also the 1997 UN Convention on the Law of the Non-Navigational Uses of International Watercourses, Article 33 of which provides for Commissions charged with inquiry and conciliation.

is particularly suitable for an evolving regulatory regime, as it can reflect the expectations and understandings of the parties, but at the same time avoid crystallizing the law in a fast changing area. Following the example of the Montreal Protocol, non-compliance procedures have been included in a number of other environmental treaties, including the 1997 Kyoto Protocol, the 1998 Aarhus Convention, and the 2000 Cartagena Protocol on Biosafety (Scott, 2010).

The Law of the Sea Convention, which includes conciliation as part of elaborate arrangements for the settlement of disputes, lays down the procedure to be followed in setting up commissions, together with details of their organization and jurisdiction.[21] Other multilateral treaties contain similar provisions, though with various differences of detail. For States wishing to establish an ad hoc commission the UN General Assembly has produced a set of model rules covering all aspects of conciliation which were approved in 1995. In the following year the Permanent Court of Arbitration produced its own optional rules for States wishing to use the Court and the UN Commission on International Trade Law (UNCITRAL) adopted rules in 1980 for conciliation in international commercial disputes.[22]

Although conciliation is now regularly included in provisions on dispute settlement, the number of cases in which it has actually been used remains very small. Moreover, since a commission's proposals are not binding, even when conciliation is attempted, there can be no guarantee it will be successful. Conciliation, nevertheless, has a value. Compulsory procedures of any kind, by their very existence, tend to discourage unreasonable claims, while conciliation in practice has proved particularly useful for disputes like the *Jan Mayen* case where the main issues are legal, but the parties are seeking an equitable compromise. Like inquiry, the process from which it developed, conciliation offers a procedure adaptable to a variety of needs and shows the advantage to be gained from a structured involvement of outsiders in the settlement of international disputes.

III. LEGAL METHODS

A. ARBITRATION

The oldest of the legal methods of dispute settlement is arbitration, the origins of which in current international practice can be traced back to the 1794 Jay Treaty between Great Britain and the USA. A distinctive feature of arbitration is that the parties themselves set up a tribunal to decide a dispute, or a series of disputes, usually on the basis of international law, and agree to treat its decisions as binding. Since form is subordinate to function in international relations, variations on the basic pattern are possible, but the standard form of arbitration is now well established and regularly used for many kinds of international disputes.[23]

Traditionally, arbitration has been used for disputes in which the issues are legal and the need to remove an obstacle to good relations makes the idea of a binding settlement attractive. Territorial and boundary disputes, for example, often fall into this category. Because the parties define the question to be answered and can specify the basis of the

---

[21] For analysis of these arrangements and their relation to the Convention's other provisions see Merrills, 2017, ch 8.

[22] See the Annex to GA Res 35/52 (4 December 1980) and Collier and Lowe, 1999, p 31.

[23] For useful surveys of the development and current role of arbitration see: Simpson and Fox, 1959; Gray and Kingsbury, 1992; Collier and Lowe, 1999, pp 189–279; Merrills, 2017, ch 5.

decision, they exercise a degree of control over the process, which is a further advantage. Moreover, the parties are entitled to choose the arbitrators. Although this, like other elements of an arbitration, requires agreement and so may cause delay, it means that the dispute will eventually be decided by a tribunal which the parties believe they can trust, a factor of fundamental importance in international litigation. Over the years the reference of disputes to arbitration has generated a significant and influential case law, prominent awards including those in the *Tinoco* case (1923),[24] the *Island of Palmas* case (1928),[25] and the *Trail Smelter* case (1938–41).[26] More recently, the value of arbitration has been further demonstrated in the *Abyei* case (2009),[27] where a land boundary was in issue, the *Guyana/Suriname* case (2007)[28] involving a maritime boundary, and the two-stage *Red Sea Islands* case (1998–9)[29] between Eritrea and Yemen, where territorial sovereignty and maritime delimitation were both in issue. Among notable arbitrations where boundary issues were not involved are the two arbitrations in the *Rainbow Warrior* case (1986 and 1990)[30] between France and New Zealand, the *OSPAR (Article 9)* case (2003)[31] between Ireland and the UK, and the *Indus Waters* case (2013) between Pakistan and India.[32]

Arbitration, like conciliation, is a method which can be employed ad hoc when a dispute arises, or provided for in advance by appropriate arrangements in a treaty. It is therefore to be found in the dispute settlement provisions of multilateral and bilateral conventions on a wide variety of subjects, as either an optional or a compulsory procedure, and often in combination with other methods. The 1982 Law of the Sea Convention, for example, gives a very prominent role to arbitration, as do the 1992 Stockholm Convention on Conciliation and Arbitration within the CSCE and a number of recent conventions concerned with the environment.[33] In the WTO's dispute settlement system, similarly, though the general emphasis is on panel proceedings (described in Section III C), arbitration is also an option and for certain disputes is even mandatory.

The use of arbitration to decide inter-State disputes must be distinguished from its use in a related context, to deal with disputes between a State on one side and an individual or corporation on the other. In cases of this type, known as mixed arbitrations,[34] the tribunal's jurisdiction may derive from a contract rather than a treaty, but in either event has international implications that are likely to be significant. The Iran-USA Claims Tribunal,[35] for example, was set up in 1981 to handle a large number of disputes arising from the Islamic revolution in Iran and has jurisdiction over both inter-State and private claims. Its decisions, which now run to more than 30 volumes, not only show the value of arbitration as a procedure for resolving serious and complex disputes of a commercial character, but, because the Tribunal has had to address issues such as expropriation and State responsibility, have also made a significant contribution to international law.

In the process known as 'investment arbitration', the home State of an investor and the host State (where the investment is located) are parties to an investment treaty containing a dispute settlement clause. Such a treaty may be a bilateral investment treaty (BIT), or a multilateral investment treaty (MIT), such as the North American Free Trade Agreement (NAFTA). In either case arbitration may be employed by the private investor without the

---

[24] 1 *RIAA* 369.   [25] 2 *RIAA* 829.   [26] 3 *RIAA* 1905.   [27] (2009) 48 ILM 1254.
[28] (2008) 47 ILM 164.   [29] (2001) 40 ILM 900 and 983.   [30] 74 ILR 241 and 82 ILR 499.
[31] (2003) 42 ILM 330.   [32] *In re Indus Waters Kishenganga Arbitration* (2014) 108 *AJIL* 308.
[33] See Merrills, 2017, chs 5 and 8.
[34] For a good account of mixed arbitration, including the work of the International Centre for the Settlement of Investment Disputes (ICSID), and the related topic of international commercial arbitration, see Collier and Lowe, 1999, pp 45–84.
[35] For a more detailed account of the Tribunal and its work see Brower, 1998.

involvement of the investor's home State. As this is plainly not inter-State litigation, it is not necessary to go into the complex topic of investment arbitration in detail (see Subedi, Ch 23 of this book). However, since this use of arbitration is increasingly important, it certainly deserves to be mentioned here.

Arbitration, then, is an important means of handling international disputes. It does, however, have significant limitations. As we shall see in Section III B, States are reluctant to make general commitments to judicial settlement and for much the same reasons often resist the idea of arbitration. When a specific dispute arises, however, negotiation or another diplomatic method may be preferred on the ground that it keeps the solution firmly in the hands of the parties. Another limitation concerns enforcement. Although arbitration produces a binding decision, it can be difficult to ensure that the losing party carries out the award. This does not mean that arbitral decisions are widely disregarded, but nonetheless is a real weakness. Ways of encouraging compliance are available and can be useful, but the answer really lies with the protagonists. Arbitration, like other means of settling disputes in a world of sovereign States, relies for its effectiveness on responsible behaviour from the parties.

B. THE INTERNATIONAL COURT OF JUSTICE

Judicial settlement involves the reference of disputes to permanent tribunals for a legally binding decision. It is listed in the Manila Declaration after arbitration, from which it developed historically, and is currently available through a number of courts with general or specialized jurisdiction. The only court of general jurisdiction is the International Court of Justice (ICJ) at The Hague (for a detailed consideration see Thirlway, Ch 19 of this book). Courts with specialized jurisdiction include human rights courts and various tribunals considered in Section III C, and the European Court of Justice (ECJ), a regional organ with extensive powers over the Member States of the European Community, Community organs, and natural or legal persons. It is interesting to note that the ECJ and the other specialized courts have all been created since 1945 and reflect the increasing complexity of international relations. Our review must begin, however, with the ICJ.[36]

The Court's authority to decide cases is conferred by its Statute and is based on the principle of consent. It is therefore open to States to agree to take future disputes, or any particular dispute, to the Court by concluding a treaty in appropriate terms, or to make a unilateral acceptance of jurisdiction in the form of a declaration under Article 36(2) of the Statute, known as the Optional Clause.[37] In the event of a disagreement as to whether jurisdiction has been accepted the matter is decided by the Court, whose decision, according to Article 36(6), is final. Only States may be parties in cases before the Court, although under Article 65 it may also give advisory opinions on legal questions for the benefit of international organizations.

The Court is composed of 15 judges who are elected for nine-year terms by the Security Council and General Assembly of the UN. The Statute requires the judges to be broadly representative of 'the main forms of civilization and of the principal legal systems of the world', but they sit as independent judges, not as representatives of their national States. However, if a party to a dispute does not currently have a judge of its nationality on the Bench, it is entitled to appoint an ad hoc judge who becomes a member of the Court for that case only.

---

[36] For more detailed treatment of the International Court and its work see Merrills, 2017, chs 6 and 7; Collier and Lowe, 1999, pp 124–89; Tams and Sloan, 2013; and Hernández, 2014.

[37] For discussion of the Optional Clause, with particular reference to recent State practice, see Merrills, 2009 and for an earlier survey, Merrills, 2002.

Cases are normally heard by the full Court, but if the parties wish, they can instead refer it to a smaller chamber (normally five judges). The composition of a chamber is in practice determined by the parties, making the process similar in this respect to arbitration.[38]

The Court's function is described in Article 38(1) of the Statute as 'to decide in accordance with international law such disputes as are submitted to it' and the list of materials which follows, beginning with 'international conventions' and ending with 'judicial decisions' and 'the teachings of publicists', has come to be seen as the core of modern international law. As well as interpreting and applying the law, the Court must, of course, also resolve any issues of fact that may be necessary and for this purpose receives and assesses documentary or other evidence brought forward by the parties, the quantity of which may sometimes be extremely large. This may include the evidence of witnesses or experts and the Court itself may decide to visit the scene, as happened in 1997 in the *Gabčíkovo-Nagymaros Project* case.[39]

Under Article 38(2) of the Statute the Court may at the request of the parties give a decision *ex aequo et bono* instead of on the basis of law. However, this provision, which blurs the distinction between adjudication and conciliation, has never been used. A less drastic alternative is to refer a case to the Court for a decision on an agreed basis. Like the chambers procedure, this again brings adjudication close to arbitration, although the Court's powers must always be exercised within the Statute. A further possibility is for the Court to extend its function on its own initiative by utilizing equitable considerations of various kinds. While this is not a licence for freewheeling judicial legislation, it introduces an element of flexibility into the Court's decisions which can sometimes be useful.

When the Court decides a case, its judgment is binding on the parties and is final and without appeal. Whether it actually resolves the dispute, however, depends partly on whether the parties accept it, that is are prepared to treat it as binding, and partly on the precise question referred. States may, for example, decide to use the Court only to obtain a ruling on applicable rules and principles,[40] or to determine whether a dispute is subject to compulsory arbitration,[41] and in cases such as these further steps may be needed to achieve a final settlement. As regards the acceptance of decisions, difficulties can sometimes arise, especially where the unsuccessful party has sought to challenge the Court's jurisdiction. On the other hand, disputes are often taken to the Court and resolved there without acrimony because the States concerned want a settlement. In such cases repudiation of the decision would merely return the dispute to the political arena and therefore be self-defeating.

C. OTHER COURTS AND TRIBUNALS

Among the various courts with specialized jurisdiction the most spectacular developments have unquestionably been those associated with human rights tribunals, notably the European Court of Human Rights at Strasbourg and the Inter-American Court in San José. Before 1970 the former was rarely employed, and the American Court was not inaugurated until 1979. Today, however, the European Court, which was reconstructed in 1998, has a flourishing jurisprudence[42] and although the American Court

---

[38] For discussion of this and other aspects of the chambers procedure see Ostrihansky, 1988.

[39] *Gabčíkovo-Nagymaros Project (Hungary/Slovakia), Order of 5 February 1997, Judgment, ICJ Reports 1997,* p 7. [40] As in the *North Sea Continental Shelf, Judgment, ICJ Reports 1969,* p 3.

[41] As in *Ambatielos, Merits, Judgment, ICJ Reports 1953,* p 10.

[42] For an account of the Court and its work, including the changes made in 1998, see Merrills and Robertson, 2001.

is not as busy, it has made its mark with both contentious cases and advisory opinions. The work of these courts stems mainly from cases brought by individuals, but both courts have jurisdiction over inter-State disputes and deal with such cases from time to time. More importantly, as human rights are now an international issue, procedures for adjudicating claims help to promote friendly relations whether or not they are brought by States. The activities of human rights courts thus certainly fall within the Manila Declaration.

Courts with specialized jurisdiction of a quite different type are to be found in the 1982 Law of the Sea Convention, for among several new institutions created by the Convention is a new court, the International Tribunal for the Law of the Sea (ITLOS), and a separate subsidiary organ, the Sea-Bed Disputes Chamber (SBDC).[43] ITLOS reflects the preference which many States had for a special tribunal to handle disputes arising out of the new law contained in the 1982 Convention, and the Court is developing its own distinctive jurisprudence. In the same way, the SBDC was set up because the complex arrangements in the Convention for exploiting the deep sea-bed were thought unsuitable for adjudication in the main Tribunal. In 2011 the SBDC decided its first case when it gave an Advisory Opinion at the request of the International Seabed Authority.[44]

The arrangements pertaining to the organization and jurisdiction of ITLOS and the SBDC and the choice of law to be applied are set out in great detail in the 1982 Convention and show the thinking behind their creation. Among points particularly worth noting are that the jurisdiction of ITLOS is based on the principle of free choice of means, since it depends upon States making a declaration nominating the Tribunal as their preferred option. The SBDC, on the other hand, has a jurisdiction which is automatically accepted by all the parties to the Convention. Both tribunals, unlike the International Court, are open not just to States, but also to other entities, including organizations, and each is permitted to split into smaller chambers, in order to provide the parties, if they wish, with some of the advantages of arbitration.

Functioning in a quite different sphere of operation is the dispute settlement system of the WTO, set up when the Organization was created in 1994. This complex system exists to deal with disputes concerned with trade agreements and utilizes consultations between the parties, mediation, conciliation, and arbitration in elaborate provisions, details of which must be sought elsewhere.[45] At the centre of the system is an arrangement for referring disputes to panels made up of independent experts whose role resembles that of arbitrators. Panel reports are then liable to review by the members of an organ called the Appellate Body, which further emphasizes the juridical nature of the process.

A feature of the WTO system is that the principle of free choice of means, normally so important in dispute settlement, is largely absent. While States are encouraged to settle disputes by agreement, if they fail to do so, the complaining party is entitled to request a panel. When the panel has reported, recourse to the Appellate Body is again a matter of right, and when the litigation stage is complete, a political organ, called the Dispute Settlement Body, takes over to ensure implementation. Notice also that by subscribing to the WTO Agreement States not only forgo the remedy of self-help, but also undertake to use its procedures exclusively. So, for example, if a dispute could be

---

[43] On the arrangements relating to ITLOS and its place in the dispute settlement arrangements of the Convention, see Klein, 2005, and Merrills, 2017, ch 8.

[44] *Responsibilities and Obligations of States Sponsoring Persons and Entities with Respect to Activities in the Area*, Advisory Opinion, ITLOS Reports 2011, nyr, (2011) 50 ILM 458.

[45] There is already a large literature on the WTO system, including Palmeter and Mavroidis, 2004 and a detailed treatment by Petersmann, 1997. For a more concise treatment see Merrills, 2017, ch 9.

dealt with either through the WTO or through a regional system, the former should be given priority.

Although the WTO system is relatively new, it is in constant use and regularly proves its worth. Trade disputes are complex, often involve shifts in economic and political forces, and are capable of arousing strong passions. If this makes peaceful methods for resolving such disputes essential, it also means that methods which encourage accommodation are no less important than those that seek to enforce rules. That is why the WTO system features diplomatic as well as legal processes. Moreover, in international trade law, as elsewhere, adjudication works best when rules are not just applied impartially, but also command general acceptance. As the fairness of trade rules depends on the policies of the major players in the WTO, their responsibility as legislators underpins its system for dealing with disputes.

D. THE PLACE OF LEGAL METHODS

To understand the significance of arbitration or other legal methods and how they are used in practice it is important to appreciate at the outset that courts and tribunals do not operate in isolation, but regularly interact with political institutions and processes. So, for example, the reference of a dispute to the ICJ may be prompted by the efforts of a regional organization, negotiations may be necessary to establish the question asked, and may well continue on substantive matters once litigation is in progress. At the post-adjudication stage, likewise, technical assistance from the UN, or further negotiations, perhaps assisted by a mediator, may be needed to deal with boundary demarcation, or similar issues concerning implementation.[46]

It is as well to recognize that courts and tribunals have no all-embracing ability to solve international problems, but occupy a specialized place among the instruments of dispute settlement. Not only are they limited to deciding disputes and so lack competence to deal with broader 'situations', but as their normal function is to decide cases by applying law, many problems are unsuited to adjudication because they do not raise legal issues. Thus the International Court has indicated that as a general rule it cannot deal with issues requiring, say, a political or economic assessment, rather than a legal decision, and by the same token it will decline to answer questions which are moot or only of historical interest.[47] What, then, is the value of legal methods? Because the decisions of courts and tribunals are binding, litigation is a good way of disposing of troublesome issues the resolution of which is considered to be more important than the actual result. Conversely, when the result is all-important adjudication is likely to be unattractive because it is simply too risky, a point which is reinforced by the fact that adjudication is not merely dispositive, but tends to produce a winner-takes-all type of solution. This explains why States are notoriously reluctant to make a general commitment to take their disputes to the International Court, but may be willing to do so in individual cases. It also explains the popularity of ITLOS and the WTO panels system, which are designed for a specific purpose, where the parties' commitments are defined and the judges have special expertise. It is worth bearing in mind, however, that when arrangements of this kind are set up they are not mutually exclusive. Consequently, an unavoidable effect is to

---

[46] For discussion of the issue of compliance and implementation generally see Paulson, 2004 and Schulte, 2004. For a wider perspective Shany, 2014. On the decision to employ litigation see Klein, 2014.

[47] See *Haya de Torre, Judgment, ICJ Reports 1951*, p 71; *Northern Cameroons, Preliminary Objections, Judgment, ICJ Reports 1963*, p 15; *Nuclear Tests (Australia v France), Judgment, ICJ Reports 1974*, p 253, and *Nuclear Tests (New Zealand v France), Judgment, ICJ Reports 1974*, p 457. See also Lowe, 2012.

create situations of overlapping competence, where several courts or tribunals may have jurisdiction over the same dispute, or different aspects of it. If, as may happen in such circumstances, the parties elect to refer a dispute to different legal bodies, difficult questions can arise as to which, if either, should have priority (Shany, 2003; Merrills, 2007; Crawford and Nevill, 2012).

Are international courts capable of deciding disputes with a strong political element? The answer is to be found in a firmly established principle which is really quite basic to international adjudication. It is that courts and tribunals are set up to resolve legal issues and so, provided a case presents a legal issue, they are not prevented from deciding it merely because it also has political elements.[48] It is easy to see that such an attitude is essential if adjudication is to function. All disputes between States have political elements because States are political bodies. Therefore to concede that a case could not be decided if it had political elements would be to enable any case to be blocked. Quite rightly, this absurd conclusion has been rejected.

Since international disputes often have both a legal and a political dimension, it is no surprise to find that on occasion disputes are referred to legal and political institutions simultaneously. The Tehran hostages dispute, for example, between the USA and Iran was considered by both the ICJ and the UN Security Council in 1980 and there have also been cases involving regional organizations. Such cases clearly raise the question of the relation between the legal and the political process, on which the Court's view, as might be expected, is that each has its own sphere and neither is entitled to priority as a matter of principle.[49] This is useful as far as it goes, but leaves open questions such as how far the legality of the Security Council's actions may be challenged before the Court, a problem to which as yet there is no clear answer.[50]

When the parties to a dispute decide to employ adjudication by, for example, concluding an arbitration agreement or jointly referring a case to the International Court they are, in effect, agreeing that the legal and political aspects of the dispute should be separated. When, on the other hand, a case is referred unilaterally, it may be because the parties view the dispute differently, the applicant seeing the legal aspect as paramount, but the respondent emphasizing its political aspects and so regarding it as unsuitable for adjudication. As already noted, a court can decide such a case, notwithstanding the conflict of characterization, but it does so by isolating the legal element, thereby effecting a 'depoliticization' which the parties were unable to achieve consensually.

The point just made is critical because it means that although courts and tribunals are competent to deal with disputes which present legal issues, however complex their political background, the party whose concerns are with the non-legal elements of the dispute may be unwilling to accept the decision. This limits the contribution which adjudication can make to the resolution of international disputes in practice. It is also why appreciating the interaction of legal and political processes is so vital and why, when describing the WTO system, we noticed the role of consultation and the need for trade rules which all States can regard as legitimate. It is not enough to have courts and tribunals capable of handing down legal decisions. Persuading States to use them, and making their decisions effective, are problems grounded in the political context.

---

[48] For discussion of the cases in which this point has been made, including the *Diplomatic Staff in Tehran* case and the *Nicaragua* case, see Merrills, 2017, ch 7.

[49] For discussion of the 1993 *Genocide* case and earlier cases in which this point has been made see Merrills, 2017, ch 10.

[50] For discussion of the *Lockerbie* cases which raised this point see Akande, 1997; White, 2002, pp 119–30; Merrills, 2017, ch 10.

IV. INTERNATIONAL ORGANIZATIONS AND DISPUTE SETTLEMENT

A. REGIONAL ORGANIZATIONS

The reference in the Manila Declaration to 'resort to regional agencies or arrangements' relates to bodies such as the Organization of American States (OAS); the African Union (AU), formerly the Organization of African Unity (OAU); NATO; and the EEC, which are recognized in Article 52(2) of the UN Charter as relevant to the settlement of local disputes.[51] There is no reference in the Declaration's list to the UN's own procedures, although these are covered in some detail in later provisions which, as well as mentioning the ICJ, deal also with the Security Council and the General Assembly. Thus the Declaration acknowledges the role of international political organizations in dispute settlement at both the regional and universal levels.

One of the main functions of regional organizations is to provide governments with opportunities for diplomatic contact in a structured setting. Although such contact serves many purposes, it is something which may be particularly useful when there are disputes between member States because it can provide them with an opportunity to discuss their differences when tension may have disrupted normal communication. Such contact, moreover, is by no means restricted to the speech-making and formal proceedings of the organization, but also includes behind the scenes activity where the real work is often done. Indeed, informal contact of this kind may well be more valuable for parties with a dispute since it enables other States to use their influence without having to take a public position.

Negotiations, whether formal or informal, are the basic method of dealing with disputes, but, as noted earlier, may benefit from the presence of an outsider to encourage the dialogue and keep it going, or to make an independent contribution. Regional organizations provide opportunities for both good offices and mediation, as may be seen, for example, in the OAU which frequently provided these services in disputes between African States (Maluwa, 1989) and the EU which attempted mediation during the break-up of Yugoslavia. Some of these efforts, including the last, were unsuccessful, but then mediation, it will be recalled, is about facilitating negotiations, not imposing solutions.

More formal than mediation are the other diplomatic methods—inquiry and conciliation—and these too can be used by regional organizations. Inquiry, as we have seen, is essentially a fact-finding exercise, whereas conciliation involves presenting the parties with specific recommendations. Both processes need an individual or a commission to do the necessary fact-finding or conciliation and the two can sometimes be combined. In 1929, for example, the Conference of American States established a body called the Chaco Commission to investigate a dispute between Bolivia and Paraguay and to make proposals for a settlement. This involved both inquiry and conciliation and the Commission produced recommendations which the parties accepted, so demonstrating the value of this type of initiative (Bar-Yaacov, 1974, pp 199–211). So far we have really been considering ways in which disputes can be handled *through* regional organizations, rather than ways in which they can be handled *by* them. Negotiation and the other diplomatic methods are all processes which States can, and often do, employ on their own initiative without involving a regional organization at all. This does not make such organizations irrelevant because they may provide the spur to make things happen. It does, however, prompt the question

---

[51] On the role of regional organizations in general see Fawcett and Hurrell, 1995 and in relation to disputes specifically Merrills, 2011, ch 11.

whether there is action in relation to disputes which only organizations can take. Is there, in other words, a contribution from regional organizations that is uniquely their own?

The answer is yes, as may be seen from the following examples. First, a collective declaration of policy, such as the OAU's 1964 Declaration on respecting African boundaries,[52] can both reduce the likelihood of disputes and provide a basis for dealing with them when they arise. Secondly, though the powers of regional organizations are subject to international law and not unlimited, in some circumstances they are entitled to impose sanctions on a recalcitrant member.[53] And thirdly, regional organizations can play a role in international peacekeeping,[54] or in support of action by the Security Council under Chapter VII of the Charter. Such measures show how collective action may be used to pursue goals not open to States acting separately and the variety of ways in which regional organizations may be involved in international dispute settlement.

B. THE UNITED NATIONS

Article 1 of the UN Charter sets out the purposes of the UN, which are: to maintain international peace and security; to develop friendly relations among nations; to achieve international cooperation in solving problems of an economic, social, cultural, or humanitarian character and in promoting human rights; and to be a centre for harmonizing the actions of States in attaining these ends. These are inter-related purposes, but the maintenance of international peace and security occupies a primary place, the UN having a responsibility to bring about cessation of conflict whenever it occurs and to assist the parties to international disputes to settle their disputes by peaceful means. Clearly, then, dealing with disputes is a central function of the Organization according to the Charter.[55]

How is this to be done? The Charter assigns a key role to the Security Council and gives it the relevant powers in Chapter VI, which is wholly concerned with the peaceful settlement of disputes. Although the Council may make recommendations with a view to the settlement of any dispute, if all the parties so request, and under Article 34 can investigate any dispute or threatening 'situation', its general competence is limited to disputes 'the continuation of which is likely to endanger the maintenance of international peace and security'. It is therefore clear that although Article 2(3) imposes a quite general obligation on member States to settle disputes by peaceful means, only the more serious disputes, or those which may become serious, are regarded as the Council's concern.

The particular role of the Security Council is further emphasized in Article 33(1) which provides that the parties to a dispute within its remit should 'first of all' seek a solution by negotiation or another peaceful means of their own choice, and Article 52(2), which provides that members of regional arrangements or agencies 'shall make every effort to achieve peaceful settlement of local disputes' through such arrangements or agencies before referring them to the Security Council. However, despite these priorities, the Council has the right under Article 36(1) to recommend appropriate procedures at any time. Moreover, its authority to consider these issues comes from the relevant provisions of

---

[52] See on the declaration Zartman, 1991. Another example is the adoption in 1991 of a common policy on recognition towards the States of Eastern Europe by the members of the EU, on which see Warbrick, 1992.

[53] For an example see Macdonald, 1963–4, pp 367–72.

[54] For a general survey see McCoubrey and Morris, 2000. An interesting illustration of such activity is provided by the operations carried out by the Commonwealth of Independent States (CIS) in several parts of the former Soviet Union, which are described by Webber, 1996.

[55] From the vast literature on the UN the following relate specifically to the issues discussed in the text: Peck, 1996; White, 1997; Merrills, 2017, ch 10.

the Charter. Thus, unlike a court of arbitration or conciliation commission, the Security Council does not require the consent of the States concerned in order to become involved.

A final point to make about Chapter VI is that the provisions in this part of the Charter, which are all concerned with encouraging States to use peaceful methods of settlement, need to be read alongside those of Chapter VII, which give the Security Council power to impose sanctions. The structure of the Charter can therefore be seen as designed first and foremost to help States with their problems, but in the last resort to back this up with coercive measures in disputes or situations which lead to a 'threat to the peace, breach of the peace or act of aggression'. How well this has worked in practice is another matter, but in theory at least the Charter equips the Security Council with enforcement powers to use when they are needed.

Because the Charter envisages the Security Council playing the main role in UN dispute management, there is nothing as elaborate as Chapter VI or Chapter VII conferring powers on the General Assembly or Secretary-General. However, these organs too are given a role. Thus the General Assembly has broad powers of discussion and recommendation under Articles 10 to 14. These are wide enough to cover, for example, the recommendation of 'measures for the peaceful adjustment of any situation, regardless of origin, which it deems likely to impair the general welfare or friendly relations among nations' (Article 14), although this provision, like others relating to the General Assembly, is subject to Article 12, which preserves the primacy of the Security Council.

The role of the Secretariat is set out in Articles 98 and 99 of the Charter, which, though brief, are very important. Article 98 speaks of the Secretary-General performing secretarial (ie administrative) functions for the General Assembly, the Security Council, and the other principal organs and performing 'such other functions as are entrusted to him by these organs'. Under this provision, then, tasks relating to disputes and other matters may be delegated to the Secretariat. Article 99, on the other hand, refers to the Secretary-General bringing 'to the attention of the Security Council any matter which in his opinion may threaten the maintenance of international peace and security'. Here, therefore, the Secretary-General is given a power of initiative which, as will be seen, has proved highly significant.

C. THE CHARTER SYSTEM IN PRACTICE

The UN is often criticized for failing to solve the world's problems and the validity of this criticism, at least in relation to disputes, is something we must consider. Before doing so, however, something should be said about what the UN has been able to achieve, beginning with the work of the political organs. As noted earlier, both the General Assembly and the Security Council are entitled to make recommendations and both organs have used this power extensively, to try to calm disputes, to urge the use of particular methods, or in some cases to recommend specific terms for a settlement. As these are merely recommendations, they can be, and often are, ignored. On the other hand, such UN involvement has the effect of bringing diplomatic pressure to bear and is sometimes helpful in providing States which may be locked on a collision course with a way out of their difficulty.

It was pointed out earlier that the existence of regional organizations stimulates negotiation by bringing States together in a setting where diplomatic contact is easy and can be encouraged by others. The UN functions in a similar way, with the advantage that at the UN diplomacy is possible not just among States which are neighbours, but on a worldwide scale. Providing a setting for diplomatic contacts is useful in itself, but it is often possible to go further and use the Organization's own machinery to facilitate negotiations. One rather formal method is to appoint a committee of selected member States to assist negotiations, as was done for discussions on Indonesia's independence in 1947. Another is to use individuals as mediators or conciliators, which has been one of the Secretariat's most significant activities.

The contribution which fact-finding can make to the resolution of certain types of disputes has also already been mentioned. This too is a matter on which the UN may be able to help and there are many examples of the Security Council or the General Assembly creating subsidiary organs for this purpose.[56] As we have seen, this is something which the States concerned could do for themselves utilizing the inquiry procedure of the Hague Conventions, but this requires the parties to agree and by the time a dispute reaches the UN it is usually plain they are not going to do so. The Organization's contribution is therefore to fill this gap by promoting the necessary investigation, in an attempt to bring the parties closer together.

If the political organs cannot help directly, or do not wish to do so, they can refer a dispute to another body—a regional organization, for example, or another UN organ. So long as it is not merely a way of evading responsibility (as it can sometimes be), passing a dispute on in this way may be a desirable step. A case in point is legal disputes, which Article 36(3) says should 'as a general rule' be referred to the International Court. The General Assembly and the Security Council may also ask the Court for advisory opinions and this power is potentially very important in disputes like that in the *Western Sahara* case[57] which involve decolonization or other UN policies. Accordingly, the Court responded positively to the requests from the General Assembly for advisory opinions on the effects of Kosovo's declaration of independence and on the legal consequences of Israel's construction of a security barrier in the occupied Palestinian territory.[58] It cannot be said, however, that the political organs use the Court as often as they might, with the result that opportunities to engage it in their work have been somewhat neglected.

The political organs, and the Security Council in particular, though active in the ways described, have frequently been slow to act; however, the same cannot be said for the Secretary-General, whose work under Articles 98 and 99 has often formed the main, or even the only, element in a UN response (Chesterman, 2007). As regards Article 98, one of the most important contributions has been to provide good offices and mediation when the authorizing organ perceives a need to help the parties with negotiations (Franck and Nolte, 1993; Skjelsbaek and Fermann, 1996). In such cases, introduction of the Secretary-General as a neutral third party, supported by the Security Council or the General Assembly, can be a constructive move. Among the many examples of such involvement are Secretary-General Waldheim's creation of a fact-finding and conciliation commission, together with the provision of good offices, in the Diplomatic Hostages crisis of 1979, and the good offices of Secretary-General Boutros-Ghali following the invasion of Kuwait in 1990.

The powers of initiative possessed by the Secretary-General under Article 99 have been interpreted broadly which has made this provision just as important in practice as Article 98. Consequently, a similar range of activities has been undertaken. It is important to

---

[56] For a review of early UN practice, see Plunkett, 1968–9. For recent practice see White and Saul, 2010 and Cogan, 2015.

[57] *Western Sahara, Advisory Opinion, ICJ Reports 1975*, p 12. See also the *Namibia* case, *Legal Consequences for States of the Continued Presence of South Africa in Namibia (South West Africa) notwithstanding Security Council Resolution 276 (270), Advisory Opinion, ICJ Reports 1971*, p 16.

[58] *Accordance with International Law of the Unilateral Declaration of Independence in Respect of Kosovo, Advisory Opinion, ICJ Reports 2010*, and *Legal Consequences of the Construction of a Wall in the Occupied Palestinian Territory, Advisory Opinion, ICJ Reports 2004*, p 136.

appreciate, however, that even when exercising initiative under Article 99, the Secretary-General has always been careful to coordinate his work with that of the political organs, especially the Security Council (Perez de Cuellar, 1993). This underlines the point that the primary responsibility for making the UN system work lies with the member States. If they fail to play their part it is pointless expecting the Secretary-General to fill the gap and blaming him when things go wrong. The Secretary-General has a key role, but cannot carry the whole burden of dispute management for the UN.

D. THE VALUE AND LIMITATIONS OF ORGANIZATIONS

Enough has been said to indicate that political organizations can make a useful contribution to the management and resolution of international disputes. However, various factors which can limit their activity must now be noted. To take regional organizations first, one very obvious limitation is that they are unlikely to be very effective in disputes which cross regional boundaries, ie in disputes between States from different regions. Another, no less significant, limitation is that regional organizations are often reluctant to become involved in disputes within States, for example, civil wars and other internal conflicts. A further limitation is that most regional organizations lack resources and so may simply be unable to undertake the more expensive kinds of institutional activities such as peacekeeping.

Turning to the UN, its involvement in disputes has tended to reflect the extent to which the major States have seen UN action as something which is in their interests. This means that in many disputes there has been little UN involvement, or its contribution has been only marginal. Where the UN has been involved, the record underlines the point made at the beginning about the need to manage international disputes when they cannot be settled. Not many disputes have been settled through the UN, compared with the large number which have been managed, in the sense of being dealt with in some way, through the Organization's processes. This is particularly clear in the case of peacekeeping operations, for example, which have almost always been concerned with stabilizing situations, so as to create conditions in which other processes can be used.

To see why all this is so is to begin to understand the nature and limitations of the UN system. The Organization is a reflection of the social and political relations of States. Although constructive steps have sometimes been taken, effective action is usually possible only insofar as States are prepared to relinquish claims to exclusive control and seek assistance. When things become sufficiently serious, a UN presence or other initiative may be acceptable, but unless what is wanted is simply a face-saving arrangement, settling the basic problem is likely to be much more difficult. As a consequence, in very many cases prophylactic measures may be all that is politically possible, yet the fact that a festering dispute remains unresolved will be accounted another failure of the Organization.

In *An Agenda for Peace*,[59] his 1992 report to the Security Council, Secretary-General Boutros-Ghali examined the potential of the UN in the fields of preventive diplomacy, peacekeeping, peacemaking, and post-conflict peacebuilding. The report described what the Secretary-General saw as the contribution which regional organizations could make to resolving disputes, emphasizing, as might be expected, that they must act in a manner consistent with the Charter and that the Security Council has primary responsibility for maintaining international peace and security. However, provided these constitutional limitations are respected, regional action could lighten the Security Council's burden and 'contribute to a deeper sense of participation, consensus and democratization in international affairs'.[60]

---

[59] SC Doc S/24111, 17 June 1992. Text in (1992) 31 ILM 953.   [60] Ibid, para 64.

As the Secretary-General indicated, cooperation between regional organizations and the UN is particularly useful in situations which call for peacekeeping forces or related action, and recent events have demonstrated how institutions can perform complementary functions when the political atmosphere is favourable. In the complex situation in Central America in the 1980s, for example, the main diplomatic work was carried out through the regional Contadora process, but when security arrangements were needed, a UN force (ONUCA) was established by the Security Council (White, 1993, pp 226–7). Similarly, in the Liberian crisis of 1990 peacekeeping forces were supplied by the local sub-regional organization (ECOWAS) and subsequently supported both politically and on the ground by the UN (White, 1996, pp 217–19). It is scarcely necessary to add that cooperation between organizations presents many difficulties and is not a panacea. But if there is still far to go before we can speak of a global-regional peacemaking system, what *An Agenda for Peace* calls 'this new era of opportunity'[61] makes it worth working for.

The Charter, as already noted, puts the Security Council at the centre of the collective security system. It was therefore fitting that following the controversial invasion of Iraq in 2003, which lacked explicit authorization from the Council, Secretary-General Kofi Annan established a High Level Panel to bring forward new ideas on collective security, including a re-evaluation of the role of the principal organs of the UN (Slaughter, 2005). The Panel's report,[62] which appeared in 2004, adopted a radical approach, proposing, among other steps, that the Security Council should employ five criteria to guide its decisions on the use of force. In response, the Secretary-General produced his own report, *In Larger Freedom: Towards Development, Security and Human Rights for All*,[63] in which he largely endorsed the Panel's conclusions. However, the UN World Summit in September 2005 did not support the five criteria, although another of the Panel's proposals, the concept of a 'responsibility to protect', was accepted (Gray, 2007). Collective security is, of course, only one aspect of dispute settlement. Likewise, the prominence of the Security Council in this field should not prevent the potential of other organs from being recognized. The report of the High Level Panel and the response of the Secretary-General are nonetheless important for both their content and as a reminder of how hard it can be to secure political support for institutional changes.

One final point. Institutions exist to help with disputes which States are incapable of dealing with themselves. It follows that these will tend to be the more difficult cases and it should be no surprise if even moderate success is often elusive. However, whether a dispute is referred to an organization or not, the primary responsibility remains with the governments concerned. Organizations are valuable and worth improving, but institution building is no more a substitute for responsible behaviour internationally than it is in domestic affairs.

V. CONCLUSION

International law requires States to resolve their disputes peacefully and the primary means available for them to do so remains negotiation, sometimes assisted by good offices and mediation from third parties, and including today new forms of diplomacy associated with the ever-expanding role of international organizations. With the introduction of inquiry and conciliation we find third party assistance formalized in processes which provide the benefit of independent findings or recommendations, but with no prior

[61] Ibid, para 63.   [62] *A More Secure World: Our Shared Responsibility*, UN Doc A/59/565.
[63] UN Doc A/59/2005.

commitment to accept the result. The non-binding character of these methods means they should be thought of more as ways of moving a dispute forward than of settling it, but their value and flexibility may be seen in international practice.

States which are prepared to relinquish control over their disputes can reap the additional advantages of judicial settlement or arbitration. Legal means, including the dispute settlement system of the WTO and an increasing number of specialized courts, provide a way of obtaining binding decisions for individual cases, or whole classes of disputes. Moreover, access to such procedures need not, as hitherto, be confined to States, but is now sometimes available to international organizations, companies, or individuals. Important as they are, however, courts and tribunals are not suitable for all disputes and even when available may not always be utilized, or be effective. Thus legal methods must be seen in their political context.

Organizations are also important. However, the UN is not a world government, but essentially a body through which pressure and influence can be exerted on States when their disputes come before the Organization. Of course, many disputes never reach the UN, while many of those that do remain unsettled. Regional organizations can sometimes help by providing a diplomatic forum, or involving regional neighbours in the capacity of mediators or conciliators. There is also now the possibility of combining regional action with action by the UN. In both fora though, institutional action will often be less important in practice than the parties' own initiatives. Organizations, then, bring new possibilities, but for much of the time are no more than a further arena in which the sovereign State can exercise its traditional power to settle, or not to settle, its international disputes.

No student of current affairs needs to be told that dispute settlement is a subject on which the gulf between rhetoric and reality is conspicuously wide. All too often governments express support for general propositions like those to be found in the UN Charter, the Declaration on Friendly Relations, and the Manila Declaration, only to follow quite different precepts in their international behaviour. But realism is not cynicism and any dispassionate observer must recognize that since the landmark 1899 Hague Convention enormous progress has been made in refining the methods available for resolving international disputes and in developing States' obligations. The challenge for the twenty-first century is to see that current arrangements, which unquestionably provide the means for dealing with disputes, continue to be used in international practice.

REFERENCES

AKANDE, D (1997), 'The International Court of Justice and the Security Council: Is there Room for Judicial Control of Decisions of the United Nations?', 46 *ICLQ* 309.

ANDO, N, McWHINNEY, E, and WOLFRUM, R (eds) (2002), *Liber Amicorum Judge Shigeru Oda* (The Hague: Kluwer).

BAR-YAACOV, N (1974), *The Handling of International Disputes by Means of Inquiry* (Oxford: Oxford University Press).

BERCOVITCH, J (ed) (1996), *Resolving International Conflicts: The Theory and Practice of Mediation* (London: Lynne Rienner).

BERCOVITCH, DJ and RUBIN, JZ (eds) (1992), *Mediation in International Relations* (London: St Martin's Press).

BROWER, CN (1998), *The Iran-United States Claims Tribunal* (The Hague: Kluwer).

CHESTERMAN, S (ed) (2007), *Secretary or General? The UN Secretary-General in World Politics* (Cambridge: Cambridge University Press).

CHINKIN, C (1998), 'Alternative Dispute Resolution under International Law', in Evans, *Remedies in International Law: The Institutional Dilemma*, p 123.

CHURCHILL, RR (1997), 'Falkland Islands: Maritime Jurisdiction and Co-operative Arrangements with Argentina', 46 *ICLQ* 463.

COGAN, JK (2015), 'Stabilization and the Expanding Scope of the Security Council's Work', 109 *AJIL* 324.

COLLIER, J and LOWE, AV (1999), *The Settlement of Disputes in International Law* (Oxford: Oxford University Press).

COT, J-P (1972), *International Conciliation* (London: Europa).

CRAWFORD, J and NEVILL, P (2012), 'Relations between International Courts and Tribunals The "Regime Problem"', in Young, *Regime Interaction in International Law*, p 260.

DENG, FM and ZARTMAN, IW (eds) (1991), *Conflict Resolution in Africa* (Washington, DC: The Brookings Institute).

EVANS, MD (1991), 'The Restoration of Diplomatic Relations between Argentina and the United Kingdom', 40 *ICLQ* 473.

EVANS, MD (ed) (1998), *Remedies in International Law: The Institutional Dilemma* (Oxford: Hart Publishing).

FAWCETT, L and HURRELL, A (eds) (1995), *Regionalism in World Politics* (Oxford: Oxford University Press).

FRANCK, TM and NOLTE, G (1993), 'The Good Offices Function of the Secretary-General', in Roberts and Kingsbury, *United Nations, Divided World. The UN's Roles in International Relations*, p 143.

FREEDMAN, L and GAMBA-STONEHOUSE, V (1990), *Signals of War: The Falklands Conflict of 1982* (London: Faber & Faber).

FRENCH, D and KIRKHAM, R (2010), 'Complaint and Grievance Mechanisms in International Dispute Settlement', in French, Saul, and White, *International Law and Dispute Settlement*, p 57.

FRENCH, D, SAUL, M, and WHITE, ND (eds) (2010), *International Law and Dispute Settlement* (Oxford: Hart Publishing).

GOWLLAND GUALTIERI, AN (2001), 'The Environmental Accountability of the World Bank to Non-State Actors: Insights from the Inspection Panel', 72 *BYIL*, 213.

GRAY, C (2007), 'A Crisis of Legitimacy for the UN Collective Security System?', 56 *ICLQ* 157.

GRAY, C and KINGSBURY, B (1992), 'Developments in Dispute Settlement: Inter-State Arbitration since 1945', 63 *BYIL* 97.

GREENBERG, MC, BARTON, JH, and McGUINESS, ME (eds) (2000), *Words over War. Mediation and Arbitration to Prevent Deadly Conflict* (Lanham, MD: Rowman and Littlefield).

HERNÁNDEZ, G I (2014), *The International Court of Justice and the Judicial Function* (Oxford: Oxford University Press).

KLEIN, N (2005), *Dispute Settlement in the UN Convention on the Law of the Sea* (Cambridge: Cambridge University Press).

KLEIN, N (2014), *Litigating International Disputes* (Cambridge: Cambridge University Press).

KOOPMANS, SMG (2008), *Diplomatic Dispute Settlement* (The Hague: TMC Asser Press).

KOUFA, KK (1988), 'International Conflictual Situations and their Peaceful Adjustment', 18 *Thesaurus Acroasium* 7.

LAUDY, M (2000), 'The Vatican Mediation of the Beagle Channel Dispute', in Greenberg, Barton, and McGuiness, *Words over War. Mediation and Arbitration to Prevent Deadly Conflict*, p 293.

LOWE, V (2012), 'The Function of Litigation in International Society', 61 *ICLQ* 209.

LOWE, V and WARBRICK, C (eds) (1994), *The United Nations and the Principles of International Law* (London: Routledge).

McCOUBREY, H and MORRIS, J (2000), *Regional Peace-keeping in the Post Cold War Era* (The Hague: Kluwer).

The history of the Permanent Court during the inter-war period was generally a sat-isfactory one; it gave a number of judgments and advisory opinions, some on matters of acute political or legal delicacy, and its operation inspired increasing confidence. The fact of its existence was also a force for peaceful settlement, since the possibility that a dispute might be brought before it, with the attendant publicity, was an inducement to reach a negotiated settlement. However, although it was not formally an organ of the League, its fortunes were bound up with those of the League; and the paralysis of the League caused by the outbreak of the Second World War had already impeded the Court's work even before the German invasion of the Netherlands, where the Court had its seat, brought it completely to a halt.

The Allies' plans for a new post-war international organization included provision for a judicial body; the possibility of keeping the Permanent Court in being was considered, but it was thought better to let it disappear with the League of Nations, and set up a new Court to continue its work. However, the new International Court of Justice was not only to take over the premises and archives of the pre-war Court, but also, so far as possible, to inherit its jurisdiction. Numerous treaties had been concluded providing for settlement of disputes by the Permanent Court; the Statute of the new Court provided that, as between parties to that Statute, such treaties should be read as referring to the new Court.[2]

III. STRUCTURE AND COMPOSITION

The Court consists of 15 judges, elected by the Security Council and the General Assembly (voting separately) for terms of nine years; the elections are staggered so that five judges complete their terms of office every three years. A judge may be re-elected (and this has frequently occurred), but the system thus ensures that a regular renewal of the Bench is possible, while at the same time preserving continuity. Judges are elected as individuals, not as representatives of their countries, and are required to make a solemn declaration in open court of impartiality in the exercise of their functions. Article 16 of the Statute requires that they do not engage in any other occupation 'of a professional nature' during their period of office.[3]

No two members of the Court may be of the same nationality.[4] The Statute (Article 9) directs that the election be such as to ensure the representation of 'the main forms of civilization and of the principal legal systems of the world'. There is no official allocation of seats on this (or any other) basis, but it is a long-standing convention that the candidate of each of the permanent members of the Security Council will always be elected, and the other seats are unofficially distributed between various regions of the world.

The salaries of the judges, and the other expenses of the Court, are borne by the UN, as part of the regular budget. The seat of the Court is at The Hague, in the Peace Palace,

---

[2] Similarly, pre-war 'optional clause' jurisdiction was preserved, so far as possible: see n 22 in this chapter. These provisions of the Statute did not specifically regulate the position of States parties to the Statute of the Permanent Court who did not become members of the UN, and thus parties to the Statute of the new Court, until many years after the Permanent Court had ceased to exist. For the handling of lacunas of this kind, see *Temple of Preah Vihear, Preliminary Objections, ICJ Reports 1961*, p 17; *Barcelona Traction, Light and Power Company, Preliminary Objections, ICJ Reports 1964*, p 6.

[3] During a period when the Court had few cases before it, it became accepted that a member of the Court could properly sit as an arbitrator, or member of an arbitral tribunal. Some concern may be felt that this practice has continued, notwithstanding the fact that the number and size of the cases being handled by the Court would suggest that the full participation of every member is now continuously required.

[4] But a judge ad hoc (see later) may have the same nationality as an elected member of the Court.

where the Court occupies premises under an agreement between the UN and the Carnegie Foundation, the owner of the building. The President of the Court (elected triennially by his or her colleagues) is to 'direct the work and supervise the administration of the Court' (Rules, Article 12). The day-to-day administration of the Court is the responsibility of the Registry, headed by a Registrar, elected by the Court for a seven-year term.

Cases are heard by the full Court unless the parties to a case agree that it shall be heard by a chamber of the Court (see later). A judge is not required to withdraw if a case is brought by the State of which he is a national; on the contrary, he is bound to sit in all cases before the full Court, unless there are special reasons, other than the mere fact of nationality, why it would be inappropriate for him to sit. (If, however, the President of the Court is a national of one of the parties to a case, he does not preside in the case, but hands over the presidency to the Vice-President or senior judge.) The disqualification or withdrawal of a judge from a case is dealt with by Articles 17 and 24 of the Statute: the commonest reason for exclusion is that the judge has, prior to his election, already been involved in the case, for example, as having advised one of the parties.

The possible presence on the Bench of a judge of the nationality of one of the parties was seen, when the Statute was drafted, as suggestive of inequality, despite the fact that members of the Court are required to act impartially. This view is defended on the ground that the presence of a 'national judge', even one bound to decide impartially, is still valuable for ensuring justice for the State of which he is a national, since he can ensure that the case presented by his country is fully understood. Rather than requiring withdrawal of the judge in such circumstances, the Statute ensures equality by enabling the other party to a case of this kind to nominate a person to sit as judge solely for that case, with the title of judge ad hoc.[5] The Statute also provides, consistently with the idea of the benefit of a 'national judge', that in a case where neither party has a judge of its nationality on the Bench, and thus there is no inequality between the parties, each party still has the right to choose a judge ad hoc. In such cases, the parties, however, quite often agree that neither of them will exercise this right.

Elected members of the Court not infrequently vote against the State of their nationality, but to date judges ad hoc have nearly always voted in favour of the State that appointed them; and it is often too much to expect that they should do otherwise.

In addition to certain standing chambers (in practice virtually never used),[6] a chamber may be formed by the Court to deal with a specific case, if the parties so request. The number of judges to constitute such a chamber is determined by the parties, but the individual judges to be members of it are elected by the Court, and the composition of the chamber is thus, theoretically, outside the control of the parties. In practice, however, it has become accepted that if the parties indicate that certain names would be acceptable, the Court is virtually certain to elect them, if only because the creation of a chamber composed otherwise than as desired by the parties would be likely to result in the case being withdrawn and referred to some other method of settlement.[7]

---

[5] There is, however, no requirement that the judge ad hoc be of the nationality of the party appointing him, and this is frequently not the case. For an analysis of the function of a judge ad hoc, see the Dissenting Opinion of Judge ad hoc Franck in the case of *Sovereignty over Pulau Ligitan and Pulau Sipadan, ICJ Reports 2002*, p 625, paras 9–12, quoting the Separate Opinion of Judge ad hoc Elihu Lauterpacht in the *Application of the Convention on the Prevention and Punishment of the Crime of Genocide, Provisional Measures, Order of 13 September, ICJ Reports 1993*, p 325, at pp 408–9, paras 4–6.

[6] The experience with special chambers suggests that the reason for the neglect of the standing chambers is probably that their composition is determined in advance by the Court, and the parties have no say in it.

[7] The first request for a special chamber, by the USA and Canada in the *Gulf of Maine* case, was made pursuant to a treaty which provided explicitly that the case would be transferred to arbitration if the Chamber was not formed as the parties wished. Subsequent approaches to the Court have been more tactful.

Reference of a case to a special chamber of the Court, a procedure long neglected, became more popular between 1984 and 2002, but may now be in decline.[8] To some extent the use of chambers makes for greater flexibility and thus tends toward speedier settlement of cases; but simultaneous operation of two chambers is only practicable for this purpose if no member of one chamber is also a member of the other. In tribunals where the chambers are established by the tribunal itself, as sub-units (eg the International Criminal Tribunal for the Former Yugoslavia and the International Criminal Court), this can be arranged; but where the membership of chambers is in effect left to the parties to determine, experience shows that overlapping membership is often inevitable. The use of chambers has thus not appreciably accelerated the procedure of the International Court.

IV. PROCEDURE

The procedure before the Court is regulated primarily by its Statute. Under Article 30 of the Statute the Court has power to make rules 'for carrying out its functions', including rules of procedure. The Rules of Court adopted in 1946 were modelled closely on those drawn up by the Permanent Court; they were revised in part in 1972, and more radically in 1978. Further revisions of detail have been effected in more recent years. The Court has recently found it useful to regulate detailed matters of procedure in a more informal way, by issuing 'Practice Directions' interpreting and implementing the Statute and Rules. The hierarchy of norms is of course that Practice Directions cannot be inconsistent with the Rules or the Statute, and the Rules cannot depart from the Statute.[9] Generally, the extent to which the broad lines of the procedure laid down in the Statute of the Permanent Court, and in the Rules adopted by that body, have been found satisfactory and thus maintained, is a tribute to the work of the jurists of the inter-war period. The official languages of the Court are French and English.

The proceedings in contentious cases are set in motion in one of two ways. If the parties have concluded an agreement (*compromis* or special agreement) to bring the dispute before the Court, the case begins with the notification of this to the Court. If not, one State may file an application instituting proceedings against another State, and the Registrar communicates this to that State. In either event, all other States entitled to appear before the Court are notified of the institution of proceedings. The procedure thereafter represents something of a blend of the continental system of extensive written pleadings, and the Anglo-American common law system in which the hearing, the 'day in court', is the essential element. In a first stage, the parties exchange written pleadings (Memorial by the applicant, Counter-Memorial by the respondent; in some cases followed by a Reply (applicant) and a Rejoinder (respondent), but these additional pleadings are now exceptional). There then follows a series of hearings, which in the past might have taken up several weeks, but are usually limited to a few days, at which the parties address their arguments to the Court in the same order: a presentation by the applicant, followed by a presentation by the respondent, and a much briefer 'second round' devoted to refutation of the opponent's

---

[8] The following cases have been decided by chambers: *Gulf of Maine* (1984); *Frontier Dispute (Burkina Faso/Mali)* (1986); *Elettronica Sicula* (1989); *Land, Island and Maritime Frontier Dispute* (1992); *Application for Revision of the Judgment of 11 September 1992 in the Land, Island and Maritime Frontier Dispute* (2003); *Frontier Dispute (Benin/Niger)* (2005).

[9] For an example of a challenge to a provision in the Rules on the ground that it was inconsistent with the Statute, see the Dissenting Opinion of Judge Shahabuddeen in the *Land, Island and Maritime Frontier Dispute, (El Salvador/Honduras), Application to Intervene, Order of 28 February 1990, ICJ Reports 1990*, p 3 at pp 18ff.

contentions. When the case is brought by special agreement, rather than by a unilateral application filed by one State against another, neither party is, strictly speaking, in the position of applicant or respondent; the order of speaking is determined by the Court, taking into account the views of the parties.[10] The hearing is open to the public, and is usually broadcast on the Court's website and the UN television channel; the Court has power to hold a closed hearing (Statute, Article 46), but has done so only on two occasions.[11] The written pleadings are normally made available to the public (in particular, on the Court's website) at the time of the opening of the oral proceedings (Rules, Article 53(2)), and transcripts (and a videocast) of the hearings are also available.

Evidence is normally submitted in the form of documents, though it may of course take other forms (eg photographs, physical objects); witnesses may give written evidence, or appear at the hearing to give their evidence orally, in which case they may be cross-examined by the other party. The procedure in this respect is modelled broadly on Anglo-American practice. Hearsay evidence does not carry weight;[12] and in the case of *Military and Paramilitary Activities in and against Nicaragua* the Court expressed some reservations as to the value of evidence of government ministers and other representatives of a State, who could be taken to have some personal interest in the success of their government's case.[13]

The burden of proof of fact, in accordance with general procedural principles, rests upon the party alleging the fact. In accordance with the principle *iura novit curia* (the law is known to the Court), the parties are not required to prove the existence of the rules of international law that they invoke; the Court is deemed to know such rules. An exception to this is where a party relies on a customary rule which is not one of general law (local or special custom): in this case, the party must 'prove that this custom is established in such a manner that it has been binding on the other Party'.[14] In practice, particularly where the existence of a particular rule of general law is controversial, States will devote much argument to demonstrating that it does, or does not, exist, citing the facts of State practice in support.

The sources of international law to be applied by the Court, enumerated in Article 38 of the Statute, have been discussed in Chapter 4 of this book: international treaties and conventions; international custom; general principles of law; and the subsidiary sources, ie decisions of tribunals[15] and opinions of jurists.

The decision of the Court is adopted by majority vote; a judge is not permitted to abstain. The President of the Court has a casting vote in the event of a tie. Every judge has the right to append to the decision an individual statement of his views, normally entitled 'separate opinion' if he agrees in the main with the decision, or 'dissenting opinion' if he does not (the term 'declaration' is also used). Until 1978, the way in which a judge had voted would not become public unless he chose to attach such an opinion; but the revised Rules of Court adopted in that year provided that in future the decision would indicate not only the numbers of the votes on each side, but also the names of the judges voting for and against.

---

[10] The order of speaking is different in proceedings on preliminary objections or requests for the indication of provisional measures; these proceedings are explained later.

[11] *South West Africa, Pleadings, Oral Arguments, Documents*, Vol VIII, p 4; *Legal Consequences for States of the Continued Presence of South Africa in Namibia (South West Africa) Notwithstanding Security Council Resolution 276 (1970) Pleadings, Oral Arguments, Documents*, Vol II, p 3. In the latter case, the verbatim record of the closed sitting was later made public (ibid).

[12] Cf *Corfu Channel, Merits, Judgment, ICJ Reports 1949*, p 4 at pp 16–17; *Military and Paramilitary Activities in and against Nicaragua (Nicaragua v USA), Merits, Judgment, ICJ Reports 1986*, p 42, para 68.

[13] Ibid, para 70.   [14] *Asylum, Judgment, ICJ Reports 1950*, p 266 at p 276.

[15] For the treatment by the Court of its own decisions, see Section VII of this chapter.

V. THE COURT'S JURISDICTION

Emphasis has already been laid on the fact that the jurisdiction of the Court, like that of any international judicial or arbitral body, is based upon the consent of States. The application of this principle is, however, complicated as a result of the fact that the Court is a permanent institution.

In the first place, the Court is a treaty-based institution, created and regulated by the UN Charter and the Statute of the Court (which is in fact an 'integral part' of the Charter: see Article 92); this means that the general scope of its jurisdiction, and the conditions of its exercise, are defined *ne varietur* by those instruments. Jurisdiction in this sense, relating to access to the Court, and to the general nature of the powers it possesses, is thus a function of the will of the body of States parties to the Charter and Statute, not of the will of the specific parties to a given dispute. The consent of the parties to the dispute cannot therefore abrogate or modify statutory provisions of this kind;[16] it is in fact those provisions that determine how, for example, the necessary consent may be given for the creation of jurisdiction in specific cases.

Secondly, the jurisdiction of the Court may be, and frequently is, asserted on the basis of treaty instruments of a general nature conferring future jurisdiction over a range or category of disputes. When the instrument was concluded, no such disputes may yet have been in existence, but the possibility that such might arise will have been foreseen, and consent given in advance to the binding determination of them by the Court. When a dispute is subsequently brought before the Court on the basis of a clause of this kind, that advance consent creative of jurisdiction is still operative (assuming that the treaty has not been denounced), but it may well not be accompanied, at the time that the matter is brought to the Court, by actual contemporary consent or willingness to have that particular dispute settled by decision of the Court. The respondent State may therefore seek to deny that the general consent given in the past applies to the specific dispute, because, for example, it does not really fall within the category of disputes contemplated, or because any conditions attached to it have not been met in the specific case. The Court, in order to be satisfied that consent to its dealing with the dispute has actually been given, will have to analyse, in sometimes painstaking detail, the provisions of the relevant instruments in order to trace a link between the consent given, often in wide general terms, by the respondent and the facts of the particular case. The principle remains simple: has the respondent State given consent to jurisdiction? Its application may, however, involve much subtle and complex argument.

A. JURISDICTION: STRUCTURAL LIMITATIONS

The most basic limitation on the Court's jurisdiction is that provided in Article 38 of the Statute: 'Only States may be parties to cases before the Court'. The reference is of course to sovereign States in the sense of the principal category of subjects of international law, and excludes the component States of federations, for example. A case could not be brought by or against a non-State entity, such as an individual, a non-governmental organization, or a multinational, even if the other party were a State and consented to

---

[16] Discussing Article 35, para 2, of the Statute, the Court has observed that 'it would have been inconsistent with the main thrust of the text to make it possible in the future for States to obtain access to the Court simply by the conclusion between themselves of a special treaty . . .': *Legality of the Use of Force (Serbia and Montenegro v Belgium), Judgment, ICJ Reports 2004*, p 319, para 102.

the case being brought.[17] Nor can an intergovernmental international organization (not even the UN itself) be a party, though the major ones are empowered to ask the Court for advisory opinions.

To be a party to a case, a State must also be one of those to which the Court is 'open', or having 'access' to the Court, under Article 35 of the Statute. The principal category of States with such access is that of parties to the Statute of the Court (Article 35(1)); this category automatically includes the members of the UN.[18] There is also provision, in Article 93(2) of the UN Charter, for a State to become a party to the Statute without joining the UN, but the quasi-universal membership of the UN has made this practically obsolete.[19] The application of these requirements is normally simple, inasmuch as it is generally evident at the outset of a case whether the parties are States, and whether they are States having access to the Court;[20] and if one of them is not, then the case cannot proceed, even with the consent of the other party. If, for example, an individual attempts to bring a case before the Court (as frequently happens), the Registrar draws his attention to the provisions of Article 38, and no further action is necessary.

A similar limitation is imposed by the provisions of the Statute concerning the nature of the Court's judgment, which is 'final and without appeal'. The Court cannot, even at the request of the parties, give a provisional or conditional judgment (though it can give a

[17] The position is apparently different in advisory proceedings, in which there are strictly speaking no 'parties': cf the participation by Palestine in the case concerning *Legal Consequences of the Construction of a Wall in the Occupied Palestinian Territory, ICJ Reports 2004*, p 136, para 4; Order of 17 October 2008 in the case of *Accordance with International Law of the Unilateral Declaration of Independence by the Provisional Institutions of Self-Government of Kosovo*. The Court has also indicated in Practice Direction XII that where an international non-governmental organization submits a statement in advisory proceedings, while 'it is not to be considered part of the case-file', the Court may refer to it as 'a publication readily available', and it may thus be referred to by, and before, the Court.

[18] UN Charter, Article 93, para 1. Paragraph 2 of Article 35 of the Statute contains an obscure reference to 'the special provisions contained in treaties in force'. At the provisional measures stage of the *Bosnia* v *Yugoslavia* case, the Court took the view that this might authorize proceedings against a State which was not a party to the Statute and had not complied with the conditions laid down by the Security Council: *Application of the Convention on the Prevention and Punishment of the Crime of Genocide, Provisional Measures, Order of 8 April 1993, ICJ Reports 1993*, p 3, paras 18–19. The Court, however, took the opposite view in the NATO cases: see for example *Legality of the Use of Force (Serbia and Montenegro* v *Belgium), Judgment, ICJ Reports 2004*, p 279, paras 113–14.

[19] Article 93(2) of the Charter provides that the conditions for this are to be laid down by the General Assembly, on the recommendation of the Security Council. Furthermore, under Article 35(2) of the Statute, the Security Council is empowered to lay down the conditions on which other States not parties to the Statute may have access to the Court. Security Council Resolution 9 (1946) implements this provision, and provides for the deposit with the Secretary-General of a declaration accepting the jurisdiction of the Court and undertaking to comply with its decisions.

[20] An exception is the case of the *Application of the Convention on the Prevention and Punishment of the Crime of Genocide*. Following the break-up of the former Socialist Federal Republic of Yugoslavia, for a time the new Republic of Yugoslavia (Serbia and Montenegro) was treated by the UN as the successor of the old Yugoslavia, and on that basis it was made respondent to the proceedings before the Court. On 1 November 2002, however, after the Court had indicated certain provisional measures in the case, and had given judgment dismissing certain preliminary objections, the new Yugoslavia was admitted to the UN as a new member. Yugoslavia filed an Application for Revision of the Court's judgment on the preliminary objections on the basis that this admission showed that it had not previously been a party to the Statute. The Court, however, dismissed the Application on the ground that this event was not a 'new fact' within the meaning of Article 61 of the Statute (see Section VI C of this chapter). The question then arose again in the cases brought by Yugoslavia against ten member States of NATO: at a late stage in the proceedings, Yugoslavia withdrew its claim to have been a party to the Statute (and to the Genocide Convention) and invited the Court 'to decide on its jurisdiction'. The Court ruled that Yugoslavia had not been a member of the UN when its Application was filed, and consequently declined jurisdiction: *Legality of the Use of Force*, eight judgments dated 15 December 2004.

declaratory judgment, confined, for example, to certain aspects of a dispute). For example, parties to a case before the Permanent Court of International Justice requested the Court to give an informal and non-binding indication of how it was minded to decide, so that they could negotiate a settlement on that basis; but the Court declined, on the basis that it had no power to give a ruling of this kind, which would be dependent for its implementation on the wishes of the parties.[21]

B. JURISDICTION IN PARTICULAR CASES

1. Special agreements and compromissory clauses

The simplest means of putting into effect the principle that jurisdiction is conferred on the Court by the consent of the parties is for two States that wish a dispute to be settled by the Court to enter into an agreement to that effect. This is the classic *compromis* or special agreement, used for many years prior to the establishment of the Court for the submission of a dispute to arbitration. Such an agreement will define the dispute and record the agreement of the parties to accept the Court's decision on it as binding—this last being theoretically unnecessary in view of the provisions of the Charter and Statute. It may also contain provisions as to the procedure to be followed (number and order of written pleadings, possibly waiver of the right to appoint judges ad hoc, etc). Normally no jurisdictional problems arise in a case brought before the Court by special agreement, since the consent of the parties is real and contemporaneous, rather than given in advance and in general terms.[22] When a special agreement has been concluded, the procedural step by which a case is brought before the Court—in technical language the 'seising' of the Court—is the notification of the agreement to the Court. Whether this is done by one party or by both parties jointly, the essence of a case of this kind is that it is a joint approach to the Court, not an action commenced by one party against the other.

Where jurisdiction is asserted on the basis of some instrument other than a special agreement, the Court is seised unilaterally, by an application, indicating the subject of the dispute and the parties. The applicant State claims that the other party to the dispute has in the past consented to settlement of disputes of a particular category being referred unilaterally to the Court for settlement, and that the current dispute falls into that category. In a case of this kind, the consent creative of jurisdiction will, according to the applicant, have been given in advance. It may take the form of a compromissory clause, that is to say a clause in a treaty providing that all disputes relating to the application or interpretation of the treaty may be brought by one or the other party before the Court by unilateral application. Alternatively, the treaty itself may have been concluded for the purpose of making advance provision for the settlement by the Court of all disputes (or certain categories of disputes) that may subsequently arise between the parties: a treaty of judicial settlement (often combined with a treaty of friendship or commercial relations).

If a case is brought before the Court by unilateral application, there is thus normally a pre-existing title of jurisdiction in the form of a treaty between the parties of this kind, or

---

[21] *Free Zones of Upper Savoy and the District of Gex, Order of 6 December 1930, PCIJ, Ser A, No 24*, p 14. In a more modern case, however, concerning a treaty contemplating a complex project, which had not been completed, each party asserting breach of the treaty by the other, the Court decided (*inter alia*) that the parties 'must negotiate in good faith in the light of the prevailing situation, and must take all necessary measures to ensure achievement of the objectives' of the treaty: *Gabčíkovo-Nagymaros Project (Hungary/Slovakia), Judgment, ICJ Reports 1997*, p 7, para 155(2)(c).

[22] There may, however, be limitations on the exercise of jurisdiction: see *Monetary Gold Removed from Rome in 1943, Judgment, ICJ Reports 1954*, p 19; Section VII of this chapter.

in the form of acceptances of jurisdiction under the 'optional clause', to be discussed later. This does not mean, however, that an application that fails to specify such a pre-existing title is invalid; the Statute of the Court (Article 40) only requires an application to specify 'the subject of the dispute and the parties', and the Rules of Court (Article 38(2)) only require that it indicate 'as far as possible' the basis of jurisdiction relied on. Consequently, an application may be made which in effect invites the State named as respondent to consent to jurisdiction simply for the purposes of that particular case, a process known as *forum prorogatum*. At one time this possibility was being abused for political ends, applications being made simply for publicity purposes against States whose known attitude to judicial settlement made it certain that no such consent would be forthcoming. As a result, a special provision (Article 38(5)) was included in the Rules of Court in 1978 whereby an application of this kind is treated for procedural purposes as ineffective until the consent of the named respondent is forthcoming—usually it is not, but in two recent cases, both brought against France, following applications on this basis, France later gave its consent to ad hoc jurisdiction.[23] *Forum prorogatum* can in theory also result from the simple participation in the proceedings of a respondent State which has not previously accepted jurisdiction, but only if such participation amounts to 'an unequivocal indication' of acceptance of jurisdiction in a 'voluntary and indisputable' manner.[24]

2. The 'optional clause' system

At the time of the drafting of the Statute of the Permanent Court in 1920, it was first envisaged that the new Court would have universal compulsory jurisdiction, in the sense that any State party to the Statute could bring before the Court, by unilateral application, any dispute whatever with another State party to the Statute. The necessary consent conferring jurisdiction would thus be given simply by accession to the Statute. However, as noted earlier, it was soon realized that the majority of States were not ready for so radical an innovation, and the optional clause system was devised as being the furthest that it was then possible to go in the direction of compulsory jurisdiction. This system was carried over, without change of substance, into the Statute of the post-war Court, and it is in that context that it will be examined here.[25]

Under Article 36(2) of the Statute, a State may deposit with the UN Secretary-General a declaration that it accepts the jurisdiction of the Court for disputes in respect of all or some of a number of matters enumerated in Article 36 (in effect, all international legal disputes), 'in relation to any other State accepting the same obligation'. The intended effect of this was that those States that were ready to accept compulsory jurisdiction could do so among themselves, while other States would have to rely on obtaining the consent ad hoc of any State with which they might have a dispute, if that dispute were to be brought before the Court. There would be two classes of 'clients' of the Court, those within the 'optional clause' system and those outside it. This simple vision became complicated,

---

[23] See *Certain Criminal Proceedings in France (Republic of the Congo v France)*, (2003), which was later withdrawn (see *Certain Criminal Proceedings in France (Republic of the Congo v France), Order of 16 November 2010, ICJ Reports 2010*, p 635) and *Certain Questions of Mutual Assistance in Criminal Matters (Djibouti v France), Judgment, ICJ Reports 2008*, p 177; see paras 39–43 and 63–95 for the complications involved in ascertaining the precise extent of such jurisdiction.

[24] *Armed Activities on the Territory of the Congo (New Application: 2002) (Democratic Republic of the Congo v Rwanda), Jurisdiction and Admissibility, Judgment, ICJ Reports 2006*, p 6, paras 19–22.

[25] Article 36(5) of the Statute of the post-war Court preserves, as between parties to that Statute, any declarations of acceptance of jurisdiction made under the PCIJ Statute: cf *Military and Paramilitary Activities in and against Nicaragua (Nicaragua v USA), Jurisdiction and Admissibility, Judgment, ICJ Reports 1984*, p 392, para 14. (See also n 2 in this chapter.)

however, as a result of the recognition by Article 36 of the possibility of making reservations to an optional clause declaration. Specifically, the reservations foreseen were 'a condition of reciprocity on the part of several or certain States' and acceptance 'for a certain time'. The simplicity of the system was already compromised by this facility; but the question soon arose whether any *other* reservations were effective (eg the exclusion of disputes of a specified type, or of disputes arising before or after a specified date). No reservation was challenged before the Permanent Court as being unauthorized by the Statute, and the inclusion of reservations became standard State practice. The prevailing view became that, since a State was free to decide to accept or not to accept the optional clause jurisdiction in its entirety, it was also free to accept it subject to whatever reservations it saw fit to make.[26]

Furthermore, Article 36(2) of the Statute employed the term 'reciprocity', and provided for acceptances of jurisdiction 'in relation to any other State accepting *the same obligation*'. If a State which had made a reservation to its acceptance brought proceedings against a State which had made none, was the jurisdiction of the Court affected by the reservation? The Permanent Court held that it was; that the respondent State could invoke the applicant State's reservation, or to put it another way, that the Court's jurisdiction was defined by the narrower of the two acceptances.[27] Some of the cases concern reservations that must necessarily operate bilaterally, for example the reservation limiting jurisdiction to disputes arising after a certain date: if a dispute arises after such date for one party to it, then it must equally do so for the other.[28] A more striking example of the application of this principle is afforded by the *Certain Norwegian Loans* case, in which the reservation made by France, the applicant, excluding disputes within the domestic jurisdiction of France could be turned against it by Norway, the respondent, so as to exclude a dispute on the ground that it was within the domestic jurisdiction of Norway.[29]

The consequence was that, instead of the simple system of universal compulsory jurisdiction within a limited group of States foreseen by the draftsmen of the Statute, the jurisdiction of the Court under Article 36(2) became a complex network of bilateral relationships. The fact that two States have each made a declaration of acceptance no longer signifies that any dispute between them can be brought by either of them unilaterally before the Court, unless both acceptances are entirely without reservations. If that is not so, it is necessary to find the lowest common denominator of the jurisdiction *not* excluded by reservations on each side, and consider whether the particular dispute falls within it.

---

[26] See the statement in the report of Subcommittee IV/1/D of the San Francisco Conference that drafted the Statute of the post-war Court: UNCIO, vol 13, pp 391, 559. The League Assembly had taken the view as early as 1928 that reservations were not limited to those specifically contemplated in the Statute: see the resolution of the Assembly quoted in *Aerial Incident of 10 August 1999 (Pakistan v India), Jurisdiction, ICJ Reports 2000*, p 12, para 37.

[27] *Electricity Company of Sofia and Bulgaria, Judgment, 1939, PCIJ, Ser A/B, No 77*, p 64 at p 81; see also *Certain Norwegian Loans, Judgment, ICJ Reports 1957*, p 9 at p 24. For a fuller examination of the problem, see Thirlway, 1984.

[28] See, eg, the Orders on provisional measures in the cases concerning the *Legality of Use of Force*, brought by Yugoslavia against the member States of NATO: eg *Yugoslavia v Belgium, Provisional Measures, Order of 2 June 1999, ICJ Reports 1999*, p 124, paras 22ff.

[29] *Certain Norwegian Loans, Judgment, ICJ Reports 1957*, p 9: the reservation was in fact of the 'Connally' type (see later). Cf also the *Aegean Sea Continental Shelf, Judgment, ICJ Reports 1978*, p 3, where a reservation made by Greece (applicant) excluding matters of the 'territorial integrity' of Greece applied to exclude a matter concerning the territorial integrity of Turkey (respondent), though this case related not to Article 36(2) of the Statute, but to the 1928 General Act for the Pacific Settlement of International Disputes.

Another disruptive development, though one that has now more or less passed out of use, was the invention of the 'self-judging' reservation, designed to retain control of the extent of the jurisdictional obligation in the hands of the State making the declaration. In the form pioneered by the USA, and known as the 'Connally reservation', this was a reservation excluding matters within the domestic jurisdiction of the reserving State *as determined by the reserving State*. This reservation apparently enabled the reserving State to declare, even after the Court had been seised of a dispute on the basis of the optional clause declaration, that the dispute was a matter of domestic jurisdiction, and that the Court had therefore no jurisdiction. It was generally felt that a reservation of this kind was objectionable as being incompatible with the system of Article 36, and in particular with the principle of the *compétence de la compétence* stated in Article 36(6) (see later), but the Court nevertheless gave effect to the reservation. It has been convincingly argued that to rule that the reservation was invalid would lead to the consequence that the whole declaration of acceptance was invalid, so that the reserving State would still be able to escape the jurisdiction of the Court.[30]

There is, however, nothing illicit about attaching even extensive reservations to an acceptance of jurisdiction. The Court has had occasion to emphasize the 'fundamental distinction between the acceptance by a State of the Court's jurisdiction and the compatibility of particular acts with international law'.[31] The fact that a reservation to an optional clause declaration excludes jurisdiction over acts of which the legality may be doubtful does not render the reservation invalid; the reservation may have been made specifically because there is doubt about the matter, and this does not mean that the reserving State is claiming a licence to commit wrongful acts with impunity. This is another application of the principle that, since a State is free not to accept the jurisdiction of the Court at all, it must also be free to decide for itself what limitations it will impose on such acceptance as it does consent to make.

C. JURISDICTION AND ITS EXERCISE

In principle, if the Court finds that it has jurisdiction to entertain a particular case, it is under a duty to exercise that jurisdiction, to the extent that it has been conferred and to the extent of the claims of the parties before it (the rule *ne ultra petita*). In a few cases, the Court has, however, found that, even before inquiring into the existence of jurisdiction, it sees reasons for not exercising it. One example of a category of cases of this kind is where to decide the case would involve deciding the legal situation of a State not a party to the case (the *Monetary Gold* principle, examined further in Section VII of this chapter). Another is where any judgment given would be ineffective, because the legal situation is such that the decision would have no 'forward reach',[32] or because the claims of the applicant have in effect been satisfied, so that the case has become 'without object' or 'moot'.[33]

---

[30] See *Certain Norwegian Loans, Judgment, ICJ Reports 1957*, p 9, Separate Opinion of Judge Lauterpacht, p 34 at pp 56ff. This was on the basis that it would not be proper to 'sever' the reservation from the acceptance, since to do so would be to impose on the State concerned an obligation that it had clearly not consented to accept. The European Court of Human Rights, on the basis of a virtually identical provision in its constituent instrument, has, however, taken a different view on this point: see *Belilos v Switzerland, Judgment of 29 April 1988, Ser A, no 132*; 10 EHRR 418, and *Loizidou v Turkey (Preliminary Objections), Judgment of 23 March 1995, Ser A, no 310*, 20 EHRR 99.

[31] *Fisheries Jurisdiction (Spain v Canada), Jurisdiction of the Court, Judgment, ICJ Reports 1998*, p 432, para 55.

[32] *Northern Cameroons, Judgment, ICJ Reports 1963*, p 15 at p 37.

[33] *Nuclear Tests (Australia v France), Judgment, ICJ Reports 1974*, p 253, paras 55ff.

Since a refusal to exercise jurisdiction would normally be a renunciation of the very function of the Court, these cases are, however, highly exceptional.[34]

D. VERIFICATION OF JURISDICTION AND ADMISSIBILITY: PRELIMINARY OBJECTIONS

A well-established principle of the law relating to international arbitral and judicial proceedings is that a tribunal (arbitral or judicial) has power to decide, with binding effect for the parties, any question as to the existence or scope of its jurisdiction.[35] This principle is known as that of the *compétence de la compétence*, the jurisdiction to decide jurisdiction. It is in fact inherent in the concept of consensual jurisdiction: if a party, having consented to dispute-settlement by a third party, were then to claim the right to determine for itself the extent of the third party's jurisdiction, it would be in effect withdrawing the consent given.

The principle is stated as applicable to the Court by Article 36(6) of the Statute: 'In the event of a dispute as to whether the Court has jurisdiction, the matter shall be settled by the decision of the Court.' The text makes it clear that if the two parties agree on the extent of jurisdiction, the Court can and must accept that agreement (provided the question is one of consensual jurisdiction—see earlier); and that the decision of the Court on a jurisdictional question is binding on the parties.[36] The matter is, however, not merely one of application of the Statute: the principle of the *compétence de la compétence* is a general one, which would operate even if Article 36(6) were not included in the Statute.[37]

The Court must exercise this power in any case in which the existence of its jurisdiction is disputed. It is not merely debarred from *deciding* a case in which the parties have not conferred jurisdiction upon it by consent: it may not even entertain it, that is to say begin to receive written or oral argument upon it. The existence of a special agreement will of course guarantee jurisdiction; in the case of an application, the ground of jurisdiction relied on will normally be indicated (and if it is conceded that there is no pre-existing jurisdiction, the case will not proceed, as explained earlier). Sometimes the attitude of the respondent State in disputing jurisdiction is fully justified: the applicant State may be trying to extend a limited acceptance of jurisdiction by its opponent to cover a dispute of a kind that was never contemplated in the instrument relied on. Sometimes, on the other hand, the respondent is trying to evade its obligation to accept settlement of the dispute by the Court because the ruling, or even any discussion of the matter before the Court, is likely to cause political embarrassment. The Court has also indicated that if the jurisdictional issue is one that cannot be waived by agreement of the parties (tacit or otherwise), then it is 'one which the Court is bound to raise and examine, if necessary, *ex officio*'.[38]

---

[34] When a point of this kind was raised in the cases concerning the *Aerial Incident at Lockerbie*, the Court declined to deal with it as a preliminary issue (and the cases were subsequently discontinued). See *Questions of Interpretation and Application of the 1971 Montreal Convention arising from the Aerial Incident at Lockerbie (Libyan Arab Jamahiriya v United Kingdom), Preliminary Objections, Judgment, ICJ Reports 1998*, p 9, paras 46–50.

[35] It even extends to ruling on a claim that the tribunal itself has no legal existence: see the decision of the Appeals Chamber of the ICTY in *Prosecutor v Dusko Tadić, Decision on the Defence Motion for Interlocutory Appeal on Jurisdiction (Interlocutory Appeal)*, Case No IT-94-1-AR72 (2 October 1995).

[36] Note that the matter is 'settled' by a 'decision', and under Article 59 of the Statute the decision has 'binding force' for the parties in respect of that particular case.

[37] Consequently it is equally applicable in advisory proceedings: cf the PCIJ Advisory Opinion on *Interpretation of the Greco-Turkish Agreement of December 1 1926, PCIJ Ser B, No 16*, p 20.

[38] *Application of the Convention on the Prevention and Punishment of the Crime of Genocide (Bosnia and Herzegovina v Serbia and Montenegro), Judgment, ICJ Reports 2007*, p 43, para 122. The Court had, however, in that case not in fact done so, or at least not explicitly. Cf Article 79, para 8, of the Rules of Court.

A State named as respondent that considers that the case has been brought without a jurisdictional title will normally raise this at an early stage, and the usual procedure is to file a 'preliminary objection', defined by the Rules of Court as 'Any objection by the respondent to the jurisdiction of the Court or to the admissibility of the application, or other objection the decision upon which is requested before any further proceedings on the merits . . .' (Article 79(1)).[39] Such an objection is usually presented in response to the Memorial filed by the applicant (though it may be filed earlier). Objections to jurisdiction are of course denials that the respondent State ever gave its consent to the particular dispute being brought before the Court, or denials that the particular dispute falls within a category of disputes for which it did accept jurisdiction. Objections to admissibility are less easy to define, except negatively, as contentions that are neither matters of jurisdiction nor questions of the merits. Examples are the contention that the applicant lacks *locus standi* (ie has no legally protected interest), that remedies available within the respondent State (local remedies) have not been exhausted; that the case is, or has become, 'without object' or moot; that the presence as a party of a third State is essential to the proceedings (see Section VII of this chapter), etc.

In accordance with the principle mentioned in this section, the effect of a preliminary objection is that the proceedings on the merits of the case (the actual dispute brought before the Court) are suspended (Rules, Article 79(3)), and will never be resumed if an objection to jurisdiction is upheld (some objections to admissibility may be 'curable' and make the continuation of the proceedings possible after certain steps have been taken). A separate phase of the proceedings is opened to deal with the objection: the applicant has the opportunity of responding in writing to the objection, in a pleading entitled 'Observations', and in the subsequent oral proceedings the respondent speaks first to present its objection, and the applicant replies. This is the application of a principle of procedural law, *in excipiendo reus fit actor* (by submitting an objection the defendant becomes the plaintiff). The Court may uphold an objection or reject it; but it may also 'declare that the objection does not possess, in the circumstances of the case, an exclusively preliminary character' (Article 79(7)). This possibility, introduced in the revision of the Rules of 1978, was at first somewhat obscure, but it is now clear that its effect is that the objection is not determined at the preliminary stage, but may be re-presented and re-argued along with the merits.[40]

VI. OTHER INCIDENTAL PROCEEDINGS

A. REQUESTS FOR THE INDICATION OF PROVISIONAL MEASURES

The power of a tribunal to determine its own jurisdiction is one that belongs to all national judicial bodies, and its attribution to international judicial and arbitral organs is not in doubt. More controversial is the question whether the power, also enjoyed by most, if not all, municipal courts, to issue binding interim injunctions, that is to say directives

---

[39] It was at one time unclear whether a State that failed to present a timely preliminary objection was to be taken to have renounced the objection; but in the *Avena* case the Court made it clear that 'a party failing to avail itself of the [preliminary objection] procedure may forfeit the right to bring about a suspension of the proceedings on the merits, but can still argue the objection along with the merits' (*Avena and other Mexican Nationals (Mexico v United States of America), ICJ Reports 2004*, p 12, para 24).

[40] See the Judgments on preliminary objections in the cases concerning *Questions of Interpretation and Application of the 1971 Montreal Convention arising from the Aerial Incident at Lockerbie (Libyan Arab Jamahiriya v United Kingdom) (Libyan Arab Jamahiriya v United States of America), ICJ Reports 1998*, pp 9, 115.

requiring or prohibiting certain action pending settlement of the case before the court, is also a necessary and essential part of the armoury of international courts and of the International Court of Justice in particular. The Statute (Article 41) does in fact include a power of the Court to 'indicate, if it considers that circumstances so require, any provisional measures which ought to be taken to preserve the respective rights of either party'; the debate is therefore in this instance not about the existence of *some* power of this kind, but whether the measures so indicated create an obligation to respect them, binding on the States addressed. The wording of the Statute is, to say the least, ambiguous, inasmuch as it uses such mild terms as 'indicate' and 'measures which ought to be taken' (rather than 'direct' or 'order', and 'measures which shall be taken'); and the trend of the *travaux préparatoires* of the drafting of the PCIJ Statute is rather such as to suggest that, like universal compulsory jurisdiction, a power of the new Court to indicate binding measures at a preliminary stage may have been regarded as more than States were ready to accept. Some scholars have been ready to appeal to the idea that a power to indicate binding measures is bound up with the power to settle disputes by binding final decisions, and thus belongs in principle to all international judicial bodies; from this they conclude that the power conferred by Article 41 must be interpreted in this sense.

The question long remained unsettled; but in the *LaGrand* case, the Court decided that provisional measures addressed to the USA, which had not been complied with, had created a legal obligation, the breach of which gave rise to a duty of reparation, independently of the rights and duties of the parties in respect of the original dispute.[41] It did not, however, base this conclusion on any general principle, analogous to that of the *compétence de la compétence*, but rather on an interpretation of Article 41 as having been intended to achieve that result.[42] The finding that an order indicating measures is binding has been welcomed in many quarters. However, it should not be overlooked that the fact that an order (or, indeed, a judgment) is binding on the parties does not ensure that it will in fact be complied with; and, as explained later in this chapter (Section VII), there is no procedure for enforcement of decisions of the Court.

There is no doubt that the Court has incidental jurisdiction under Article 41 to indicate measures; but a question that has given rise to some difficulty is the relationship between this incidental jurisdiction and the jurisdiction of the Court to hear and determine the merits of the case in which measures are requested. The problem only arises at the international level, because of the principle that international jurisdiction rests on consent, and consent has therefore to be proved in each case. If an indication of measures is requested in a case in which the respondent State has already made it clear that it denies the existence of jurisdiction over the merits, what is the relevance of this circumstance to the exercise of the power to indicate measures? At one extreme, it might be argued that if the Court has no jurisdiction to hear the case at all, then it has no power to indicate measures; at the other extreme, it might be said that, since Article 41 confers an independent power (and contains no reference to the question of merits jurisdiction), the Court could indicate measures, if it saw fit, in a case where it was very doubtful whether it had any jurisdiction over the merits, or even where it was almost certain that it had none.

The first view has the obvious defect that it tends to rob the provisional measures procedure of all meaning: if no measures can be indicated until the disputed question of merits jurisdiction has been thrashed out, then the measures cannot serve to meet the urgent

---

[41] *LaGrand (Germany v United States of America), Merits, Judgment, ICJ Reports 2001*, p 466, paras 98ff.

[42] In the light of the *travaux préparatoires* and of the general trend of interpretation of the text in practice, this view of Article 41 may be regarded as somewhat revolutionary: see Thirlway, 2001, pp 114ff.

needs that they were designed for.[43] The second view may, however, be seen as a threat to the principle of consensual jurisdiction, or even to the sovereign independence of States, if a State can be subjected to an order indicating measures that it is bound to comply with, in a case in which it asserts (justifiably, as it later turns out) that it has never consented to the Court having any jurisdiction at all.[44]

A middle solution has therefore become established in the jurisdiction of the Court: the possibility or probability of establishing jurisdiction over the merits is one of the factors to be weighed by the Court when considering whether to indicate measures. Several different formulae have been employed to express this relationship. It is, however, clear that, on the one hand, the Court is not debarred from indicating measures by the existence of an objection to jurisdiction, even one which seems prima facie likely to be upheld; and on the other, that it is open to the Court to decline to indicate measures because there is a 'manifest lack of jurisdiction', or even a serious doubt as to the existence of merits jurisdiction. In some of the cases brought by Yugoslavia against members of NATO, the Court found, when examining the request for provisional measures, that it 'manifestly lack[ed] jurisdiction' to entertain the application instituting proceedings; it not only rejected the request for measures, but decided to remove the case from the list at that stage.[45] If the Court's eventual finding on jurisdiction contradicts the expectations on which its decision on provisional measures was founded, this will not retrospectively invalidate that decision: thus if it considers it justified to indicate measures on the basis of a likelihood of jurisdiction over the merits, a subsequent finding against jurisdiction will simply cause the measures to lapse, but they will have been valid until then.[46] If the Court refuses measures because of doubts as to jurisdiction, a subsequent finding upholding jurisdiction might justify a renewed request for measures, but the original refusal would not be undermined.

The purpose of the indication of provisional measures is, as stated in Article 41, 'to preserve the respective rights of either party'; and this has been understood to mean the rights that are in issue in the proceedings, and no others. Thus in a case concerning the formal validity of an arbitral award defining a maritime boundary, the Court declined to indicate measures directed to the conduct of the parties in the maritime areas concerned, since the only question before the Court was the validity or otherwise of the award, not the legal correctness of the boundary indicated.[47] However, in cases where measures were requested in the context of a request for interpretation of an earlier decision (where it might be thought that the only relevant rights were limited to obtaining an interpretation) the Court has shown itself ready to adopt a wider interpretation of its powers, especially where hostilities or other threat to human life were concerned.[48]

---

[43] This view was nevertheless put forward by dissenting judges in the *Nuclear Tests* case in 1974, but has not been heard of since.

[44] The difficulty is exacerbated by the ruling in *LaGrand* that the measures indicated constitute an independent legal obligation, one which exists even in face of a later finding of lack of jurisdiction, at least up to the moment that that finding is made. Provisional measures lapse when judgment on the merits is given, the obligations of the judgment being substituted for those under the measures. In the *Avena (Interpretation)* case, provisional measures were indicated forbidding the execution of five named individuals, and in its judgment refusing the Request the Court unanimously found that the execution of one of them had been a breach of the obligations of the USA under the provisional measures Order (see Judgment of 19 January 2009, para 61(2)).

[45] See, eg, *Legality of Use of Force (Yugoslavia v United States of America), Provisional Measures, Order of 2 June 1999, ICJ Reports 1999*, p 916, para 29. Removal of a case from the list, without any decision even on jurisdiction, is an exceptional step, only taken in particular circumstances: see, eg, *Legality of the Use of Force (Serbia and Montenegro v Belgium), ICJ Reports 2004*, p 279, para 33.

[46] See the 2009 decision on the Request for Interpretation in the *Avena* case.

[47] *Arbitral Award of 31 July 1989, Provisional Measures, Order of 2 March 1990, ICJ Reports 1990*, p 64.

[48] See the Orders made in the *Avena (Interpretation)* and *Temple of Preah Vihear (Interpretation)* cases cited in n 61 in this chapter.

The indication of measures is an interlocutory measure justified by urgency: there must be a threat to the rights of a party that is immediate in the sense that the final decision in the case may come too late to preserve those rights. If therefore it is to be expected that the case will have been decided before irreparable injury is caused, no measures will be indicated.[49] The workload of the Court is currently such that this is a much less likely situation than in the past; and pending a decision the respondent may not better its legal position by making modifications to the status quo, of which the Court might thus, if it upheld the applicant's claim, order the reversal.

B. PARTIES: JOINDER OF CASES; INTERVENTION BY THIRD STATES

Contentious proceedings before the Court are normally brought either by two States jointly (by special agreement), or by one State against another (by application); in either case there are only two parties to the proceedings. It is, however, possible for two or more States to bring proceedings as joint applicants against another State. In practice, it has been more frequent for two States to bring independent proceedings against the same respondent; and the Court then has power, if it sees fit, to 'direct that the proceedings . . . be joined' (Rules, Article 47). The cases are then heard and determined together, by a single judgment; and the Court may 'direct that the written or oral proceedings . . . be in common'. A joinder of this kind was ordered in the two *South West Africa* cases (*Liberia* v *South Africa*; *Ethiopia* v *South Africa*), and in the two *North Sea Continental Shelf* cases (brought by two special agreements: *Denmark/Federal Republic of Germany*; *Netherlands/Federal Republic of Germany*). Joinder has, however, become less common: it was not ordered in the two *Fisheries Jurisdiction* cases (*UK* v *Iceland*; *FRG* v *Iceland*), the two *Nuclear Tests* cases (*Australia* v *France*; *New Zealand* v *France*), or in subsequent 'pairs' of cases.

Similarly, it is possible for a State to bring proceedings against two or more States as joint respondents, though this has never yet occurred. The legal claim of Nauru against Australia in the case of *Certain Phosphate Lands in Nauru* was in fact asserted also against New Zealand and the UK, who had constituted, jointly with Australia, the administering authority under a UN Trustee Agreement for Nauru; but Nauru did not choose to bring proceedings against all three States, probably because it was uncertain of being able to establish jurisdiction against the other two. The absence of the other two States was in fact raised by Australia as an objection to the admissibility of the claim, but the Court ruled it admissible.[50] In the two cases concerning the *Lockerbie* incident,[51] and the ten cases brought by Yugoslavia against the NATO States,[52] the contentions against each respondent in each set of cases were virtually identical, but the applicants nevertheless chose to bring parallel cases, and the Court did not see fit to join them.[53]

---

[49] When Finland complained that the construction by Denmark of a bridge over a particular seaway would block the passage of ships and thus prevent Finland from exercising its rights to pass through the seaway, the Court declined to indicate measures because the timetable for the bridge-works was such that there would be no interference with passage within the time likely to be required for the Court to decide the case: *Passage through the Great Belt, Provisional Measures, Order of 29 July 1991, ICJ Reports 1991*, p 12.

[50] *Certain Phosphate Lands in Nauru (Nauru v Australia), Preliminary Objections, Judgment, ICJ Reports 1992*, p 240, para 457.

[51] *Questions of Interpretation and Application of the 1971 Montreal Convention arising from the Aerial Incident at Lockerbie (Libya v UK, Libya v USA).*

[52] *Legality of Use of Force (Yugoslavia v Belgium, Yugoslavia v Canada, Yugoslavia v France, Yugoslavia v Germany, Yugoslavia v Italy, Yugoslavia v Netherlands, Yugoslavia v Portugal, Yugoslavia v Spain, Yugoslavia v UK, Yugoslavia v USA).*

[53] A controversial question is whether the existence of parallel cases which have not been joined affects the right to appoint a judge ad hoc: see the Joint Declaration of Judges Bedjaoui, Guillaume, and Ranjeva in the *Lockerbie* cases, *ICJ Reports 1998*, pp 32ff.

Where cases are brought in parallel in this way, but no formal joinder is effected, the Court does, for example, hold hearings in quick succession, deliberate on both cases, and issue several judgments on the same day; and the judgments are often identical in much of their reasoning and construction.

The choice of States to be parties is normally therefore in the hands of the State or States commencing proceedings; but it may happen that another State wishes to become involved in the case. The Statute provides two possibilities in this respect. Under Article 63, 'Whenever the construction [ie interpretation] of a convention to which States other than those concerned in the case are parties is in question' in a case, the other parties to the convention have to be notified, and may choose to intervene in the proceedings: however, it is provided that if they do so, the interpretation of the convention given by the Court will be binding upon them. Possibly as a result of this provision, the faculty of intervention under Article 63 has been very little used. In any event, the interpretation by the Court of a multilateral convention will enjoy authority beyond the parties to the case in which it is given.

Under Article 62, a State may request the Court to permit it to intervene in a pending case if it 'consider[s] that it has an interest of a legal nature which may be affected by the decision in the case'. One specific type of dispute has made intervention under this Article particularly attractive to third States. In a number of cases the Court was asked to rule on the delimitation of seabed areas in a dispute between two States, but in a geographical situation in which the possible rights or interests of other States might be infringed in some way—even if in strict law the decision of the Court would be *res inter alios acta* for those States. These cases showed that application of Article 62, which had long remained virtually unused, gives rise to a number of problems. First of all, what sort of interest is contemplated, and how may it be 'affected' by the decision, given that the judgment is only binding on the parties? Secondly, must the original parties agree to the intervention, and if not, does an objection on their part affect the matter? Thirdly, does the State permitted to intervene become a 'party' to the case, and as such bound by the judgment; or if it is not a party, may it still be bound by the decision? The most controversial question has, however, been that of the 'jurisdictional link'.

The problem was illustrated by the attempted intervention of Fiji in the *Nuclear Tests* cases. Australia and New Zealand had brought proceedings against France asserting the illegality of atmospheric nuclear tests in the Pacific, and had been able to cite as bases of jurisdiction the French acceptance under the 'optional clause', and a 1928 Treaty. Fiji sought to join in the proceedings, in effect as co-plaintiff, but could not point to any jurisdictional title available to it: it was not a party to the 1928 Treaty, and it could not rely on the optional clause declaration because it had not deposited one of its own. Accordingly, Fiji could not validly have brought a separate case against France; could it therefore be allowed to reach the same result by taking advantage of the fact that Australia and New Zealand had brought proceedings? The cases came to a premature end before the Court was called upon to decide the point, but some of the judges felt strongly enough to indicate their views upon it in separate or dissenting opinions.[54]

After some judicial hesitation, a chamber of the Court ruled, in the case of the *Land, Island and Maritime Boundary Dispute* between El Salvador and Honduras, that no jurisdictional link was required for an intervention which did not confer the status of party; and that the objection of the original parties was to be taken into account, but was not

---

[54] A further complication was introduced by the introduction into the new Rules of Court, adopted in 1978, of a text which was (apparently deliberately) ambiguous on the issue (Article 81(2)(c)).

decisive.[55] These findings were approved by the full Court in the subsequent cases of *Land and Maritime Boundary between Cameroon and Nigeria*[56] and *Sovereignty over Pulau Ligitan and Pulau Sipadan*.[57] It appears that intervention as a party is also possible, either with the consent of the original parties,[58] or if there exists a jurisdictional title such that the intending intervener could have brought independent proceedings against each of them.[59] If, however, the intervener is not a party, the chamber in the *El Salvador/Honduras* case held that it is not bound by the judgment, but similarly cannot invoke it against the original parties.[60] These decisions have also clarified the significance of the 'legal interest' and how it was to be 'affected'.

C. INTERPRETATION AND REVISION OF JUDGMENTS

Article 60 of the Court's Statute provides that '[t]he judgment is final and without appeal'. The text, however, continues: 'In the event of dispute as to the meaning or scope of the judgment, the Court shall construe it upon the request of any party'.[61]

Article 61 further qualifies the finality of a judgment, by providing that:

An application for revision of a judgment may be made only when it is based upon the discovery of some fact of such a nature as to be a decisive factor, which fact was, when the judgment was given, unknown to the Court and to the party claiming revision, always provided that such ignorance was not due to negligence.

The fact is then referred to in paragraph 2 as 'the new fact'; this expression has been a source of confusion, as the fact must be an old fact newly discovered. In the case between Bosnia and Yugoslavia, the Court distinguished between a fact of this kind and 'the legal consequences' as to a pre-existing state of affairs drawn from 'facts subsequent to the Judgment';[62] but the distinction is not entirely convincing.

---

[55] *Land, Island and Maritime Frontier Dispute (El Salvador/Honduras), Application to Intervene, Judgment, ICJ Reports 1990*, p 92.

[56] *Land and Maritime Boundary between Cameroon and Nigeria, Application to Intervene, Order of 21 October 1999, ICJ Reports 1999*, p 1029.

[57] *Sovereignty over Palau Ligitan and Pulau Sipidan (Indonesia/Malaysia), Application to Intervene, Judgment of 23 October 2001, ICJ Reports 2001*, p 575, paras 35–6.

[58] In *Land and Maritime Boundary between Cameroon and Nigeria (Cameroon v Nigeria: Equatorial Guinea Intervening), Judgment, ICJ Reports 2002*, p 303, para 12, the Court took note of the fact that the parties had no objection to the intervention of Equatorial Guinea, but that State was not seeking to intervene as a party.

[59] The only case to date in which intervention as a party has been specifically requested was the intervention applied for by Honduras in the *Territorial and Maritime Dispute (Nicaragua v Colombia), Application of Honduras to Intervene, Judgment of 4 May 2011, ICJ Reports 2011*.

[60] The intending intervener (Nicaragua) had in fact announced in advance that it would accept the Judgment as binding, but the chamber did not find this acceptance legally effective.

[61] *Request for Interpretation of the Judgment of 20 November 1950 in the Asylum case, Judgment, ICJ Reports 1950*, p 395; *Application for Revision and Interpretation of the Judgment of 24 February 1982 in the Case concerning the Continental Shelf (Tunisia/Libyan Arab Jamahiriya) (Tunisia v Libyan Arab Jamahiriya), Judgment, ICJ Reports 1985*, p 192; *Request for Interpretation of the Judgment of 11 June 1998 in the Case concerning the Land and Maritime Boundary between Cameroon and Nigeria (Cameroon v Nigeria), Preliminary Objections (Nigeria v Cameroon), Judgment, ICJ Reports 1999*, p 31; *Request for Interpretation of the Judgment of 31 March 2004 in the Case concerning Avena and Other Mexican Nationals (Mexico v United States of America), Judgment, ICJ Reports 2009*, p 3; *Request for Interpretation of the Judgment of 15 June 1962 in the case concerning the Temple of Preah Vihear (Cambodia v Thailand), Order of 18 July 2011*.

[62] *Application for Revision of the Judgment of 11 July 1996 in the Case concerning Application of the Genocide Convention (Bosnia and Herzegovina v Yugoslavia), Preliminary Objections (Yugoslavia v Bosnia and Herzegovina), ICJ Reports 2003*, p 7, para 69.

Requests for interpretation or for revision were formerly comparatively rare, but recent years have seen an increase in their frequency.[63] In particular, requests for interpretation have been employed to bring an issue before the Court which would not be covered by any existing title of jurisdiction, as no independent title is required for such a request, which is treated as ancillary to the original proceedings leading to the judgment to be interpreted. A remarkable example is the request made for interpretation of the Judgment in the case of the *Temple of Preah Vihear*, made nearly 50 years after the Judgment was given![64]

VII. EFFECT OF THE DECISIONS OF THE COURT

A judgment of the Court is binding upon the parties to the case in which it is given. As noted earlier, under Article 60 of the Statute, the judgment is 'final and without appeal', and Article 59 provides that '[t]he decision of the Court has no binding force except between the parties and in respect of that particular case', implying *a contrario* that, between the parties and in respect of the particular case, it is binding. Furthermore, under Article 94(1), of the Charter, '[e]ach Member of the United Nations undertakes to comply with the decision of the International Court of Justice in any case to which it is a party'.[65]

If, however, a judgment is not complied with, there is no possibility for the winning party to come back to the Court to compel the other party to comply. The only provision for what might be termed enforcement is Article 94(2) of the Charter:

> If any party to a case fails to perform the obligations on it under a judgment rendered by the Court, the other party may have recourse to the Security Council, which may, if it deems necessary, make recommendations or decide upon measures to be taken to give effect to the judgment.

Very little use has been made of this faculty, which does not confer any additional powers on the Security Council; the political implications of any attempt to enforce a judgment by this means need not be gone into here.

There is a clear obligation of treaty law to treat a judgment of the Court as binding and to comply with it. In legal theory, however, the judgments of the Court are in principle declaratory of the rights and obligations of the parties, not creative of new rights and obligations.[66] If therefore the Court decides, for example, that under a provision in a treaty, the

---

[63] *Application for Revision and Interpretation of the Judgment of 24 February 1982 in the Case concerning the Continental Shelf (Tunisia/Libyan Arab Jamahiriya) (Tunisia v Libyan Arab Jamahiriya), Judgment, ICJ Reports 1985*, p 192; *Application for Revision of the Judgment of 11 July 1996 in the Case concerning Application of the Genocide Convention (Bosnia and Herzegovina v Yugoslavia) (Yugoslavia v Bosnia and Herzegovina), Judgment, ICJ Reports 2003*, p 7; *Application for Revision of the Judgment of 11 September 1992 in the Case concerning the Land, Island and Maritime Frontier Dispute (El Salvador v Honduras: Nicaragua Intervening) (Honduras/El Salvador), Judgment, ICJ Reports 2003*, p 392.

[64] The unsuccessful party in the original proceedings, Thailand, had never accepted the Court's decision to allocate the Temple to Cambodia; and the situation had become acute as a result, ironically enough, of the proposal to adopt the Temple as a World Heritage Site! See the Court's Order of 18 July 2011 on the request of Cambodia for the indication of provisional measures.

[65] This commitment does not, as such, apply to parties to the Statute that are not UN members, or to States admitted to appear without being parties to the Statute. However, when the General Assembly admits a State, under Article 93 of the Charter, to become a party to the Statute, it always attaches as a condition '[a]cceptance of all the obligations of a Member of the United Nations under Article 94 of the Charter' (see GA Res 91 (I)), 11 December 1946 (Switzerland); 3 GA Res 63 (IV), 1 December 1949 (Liechtenstein); GA Res 806.

[66] With the possible exception of orders indicating provisional measures: see Section VI A of this chapter.

correct interpretation of which is disputed, one of the parties is under a particular obligation, that obligation results from the treaty (as authoritatively interpreted), but is backed
by the obligation to comply with the judgment. The only special status that the existence of
the judgment confers on the original obligation is confirmation that it exists, in the sense
that no alternative interpretation of the treaty provision is legally possible. The fact that
the judgment is binding on the parties does not mean that they may not, by agreement
between themselves, depart from it—unless of course the obligation found by the Court to
exist is one of *jus cogens*.[67] All it means is that neither party may unilaterally act as though
the legal situation were other than as declared by the Court.

Some of the relevant texts refer to the 'judgment' of the Court (Statute, Article 60;
Charter, Article 94(2)) and others to the 'decision' of the Court (Statute, Article 59;
Charter, Article 94(1)). The question has therefore sometimes been raised whether an
order of the Court is binding on the parties. Most orders are procedural, and any sanction
for compliance is also procedural: if a party fails to file a pleading within the time-limit
fixed by an order, it may lose the right to file that pleading. A special case is, however, that
of provisional measures, which are invariably indicated in the form of an order. Now that
the Court has decided (see Section VI A of this chapter) that the measures themselves
constitute a legal obligation, the formal question of the effect of the order as a 'decision' has
perhaps lost much of its pertinence.

Article 59 thus excludes any formal impact of the judgment on third parties; and on
this basis the Court has, for example, been willing to draw a boundary line between two
States in an area where a third State might have valid claims, reasoning that the decision of
the Court, like a delimitation agreement between the two States before the Court, would
be *res inter alios acta* for the third State, and could not therefore prejudice its position.[68]
Other cases, however, have given rise to a distinction: if the Court finds that the rights and
obligations of a third State would not merely be affected by the decision, but would form
the very subject matter of the decision, the Court takes the view that it should decline
to exercise its jurisdiction. The classic case on the point was that of the *Monetary Gold
Removed from Rome in 1943*.[69] The parties to the case were Italy as applicant, and the UK,
France, and the USA as respondents. The disputed gold had been removed from Rome by
the Germans during the Second World War, but was subsequently found by an arbitrator
to have belonged to Albania. Italy and the UK, however, each claimed that gold, on the
basis of legal claims by those two States against Albania. The Court found that in order
to determine the validity of Italy's claim, it would have to 'determine whether Albania has
committed any international wrong against Italy', and thus to 'decide a dispute between
Italy and Albania'. However, Albania was not before the Court as a party to the proceedings, and had not consented to the dispute being settled by the Court:

> To adjudicate upon the international responsibility of Albania without her consent would
> run counter to a well-established principle of international law embodied in the Court's
> Statute, namely that the Court can only exercise jurisdiction over a State with its consent.[70]

It was urged that, under Article 59 of the Statute, the decision would not be binding on
Albania; but the Court held that where 'the vital issue to be settled concerns the international responsibility of a third State, the Court cannot, without the consent of that third

---

[67] On the concept of *jus cogens*, see Roberts and Sivakumaran, Ch 4 of this book.

[68] *Frontier Dispute*, ICJ Reports 1986, p 554, paras 46ff. The position is apparently different in the case of
maritime delimitations: see, eg, *Land and Maritime Boundary between Cameroon and Nigeria (Cameroon v
Nigeria: Equatorial Guinea Intervening)* ICJ Reports 2002, p 424, para 245.

[69] *Monetary Gold Removed from Rome in 1943, Judgment*, ICJ Reports 1954, p 19.   [70] Ibid, p 32.

State, give a decision on that issue binding upon any State, either the third State, or any of the parties before it'.[71]

The possibility of intervention (see Section VI B of this chapter) has been raised in connection with the principle laid down in the *Monetary Gold* line of cases. If a State, not a party to a case, did not wish its rights and duties to be discussed before the Court in its absence, it was open to such a State, it was said, to intervene. The Court, however, drew a distinction: if the interests of the absent State would merely *be affected* by the decision, then if that State chose not to exercise its right to request intervention, the proceedings could continue to judgment; but if the legal interests of the absent State 'would form the very subject matter of the decision', then the Court could not exercise its jurisdiction in the absence of that State.[72]

VIII. ADVISORY PROCEEDINGS

In addition to its function of settling international disputes in accordance with international law, the Court is empowered by its Statute to give advisory opinions. The provision to that effect included in the Statute of the Permanent Court was something of an innovation: some, but by no means all, national supreme courts possessed a power of this kind; and on the international level, arbitration proceedings, from which the concept of an international tribunal sprang, were essentially means of reaching a binding settlement of a dispute. It was the organs of the League of Nations that were expected to feel a need for such an opinion, and from the beginning it was only such international organs, and not States, that were to be entitled to ask for advice in this form.

The essence of an advisory opinion is that it is advisory, not determinative: it expresses the view of the Court as to the relevant international legal principles and rules, but does not oblige any State, nor even the body that asked for the opinion, to take or refrain from any action. The distinction, clear in theory, is less so in practice: if the Court advises, for example, that a certain obligation exists, the State upon which it is said to rest has not bound itself to accept the Court's finding, but it will be in a weak position if it seeks to argue that the considered opinion of the Court does not represent a correct view of the law.

The essentially non-binding character of an advisory opinion has in the past given rise to some doubts as to the legal effect of a treaty commitment whereby an opinion of the Court is to be accepted, by the parties to the treaty, as binding. One field in which treaty provisions of this kind have proved useful is the relations between international organizations, particularly the UN itself, and States. Since an international organization cannot be a party to proceedings before the Court, a dispute between an organization and a State cannot be settled by contentious proceedings. A device that has been used to meet the difficulty is to provide in a convention (for example the 1946 Convention on the Privileges and Immunities of the UN) that, in the event of a dispute of this kind, the General Assembly (or other organ concerned) will ask the Court for an advisory opinion on the point at issue, and that it is agreed in advance that the Court's opinion will be accepted as 'decisive' by the State and the organization. It is established that since the essentially non-binding character of the opinion itself is not affected, there is no legal obstacle to the conclusion of an agreement of this kind.

Under the Charter, Article 96(1), the General Assembly and the Security Council are entitled to request the Court 'to give an advisory opinion on any legal question'. This is

---

[71] Ibid, p 33.   [72] Ibid, p 32.

purely a faculty: nowhere in the Charter is there any obligation to seek the advice of the Court, and the Court has no power to offer it unasked. A proposal during the drafting of the Charter to give the Court responsibility for authoritative interpretations of the Charter was not adopted.

Article 96(2) provides that '[o]ther organs of the United Nations and specialized agencies, which may at any time be so authorized by the General Assembly, may also request advisory opinions of the Court on legal questions arising within the scope of their activities'.[73] Such authorizations have in fact been given to the Economic and Social Council and to practically all the specialized agencies. The restriction as to the type of questions to be put was, however, held to debar the World Health Organization (WHO), which had received a general authorization from the General Assembly to request opinions, from asking for an opinion on the question whether the use of nuclear weapons by a State would be a breach of its obligations under international law 'including the WHO Constitution'. The Court held that under the 'principle of speciality' the WHO could not deal with matters beyond what was authorized by its Constitution; that the question of the legality of nuclear weapons was outside that Constitution; and accordingly that the question was not one 'arising within the scope' of the activities of the Organization.[74] In another case, the question was raised whether a subsidiary organ of the General Assembly, whose sole function was in fact to ask for advisory opinions (on the validity of judgments of the UN Administrative Tribunal), had any 'activities' of its own for the purposes of this text; the Court ruled in the affirmative.[75]

The provision in the Statute that corresponds to this Charter text is Article 65, which provides that '[t]he Court may give an advisory opinion on any legal question' at the request of any authorized body. The use of the word 'may' signifies, as the Court has repeatedly emphasized, that the Court is not bound to give an opinion, but may decline to do so if it considers that course appropriate. It has never in fact done so,[76] but has on a number of occasions considered the possibility of refusal. From the resulting jurisprudence it is clear that the reply of the Court, itself an organ of the UN, 'represents its participation in the activities of the Organization and, in principle, should not be refused'; and that only compelling reasons would justify a refusal.[77]

A special problem, however, arises if the question put to the Court is related to an inter-State dispute, and one of the States concerned in that dispute objects to the Court giving the opinion. The consent of the States parties to a dispute is the basis of the Court's jurisdiction in contentious cases; but since the Court's reply to a request for an advisory opinion has no binding force, 'it follows that no State . . . can prevent the giving of an Advisory Opinion which the United Nations considers to be desirable in order to obtain enlightenment as to the course of action it should undertake'.[78] The consent of any State party to a

---

[73] The wording of paras 1 and 2 of Article 96 suggests that a request from the Security Council or General Assembly can relate to a question not 'within the scope of their activities', but there are dicta of the Court suggesting that this approach may be too wide: see *Legal Consequences of the Construction of a Wall in the Occupied Palestinian Territory, Advisory Opinion, ICJ Reports 2004*, p 136, para 16, and references there cited.

[74] *Legality of the Use by a State of Nuclear Weapons in Armed Conflict, Advisory Opinion, ICJ Reports 1996*, p 66.

[75] *Application for Review of Judgment No 158 of the United Nations Administrative Tribunal, Advisory Opinion, ICJ Reports 1973*, p 166.

[76] The refusal, referred to in the preceding paragraph, of the opinion requested by WHO was not a matter of discretion but a matter of lack of jurisdiction following the lack of competence of WHO to ask for an opinion on the subject.

[77] See, eg, *Western Sahara, Advisory Opinion, ICJ Reports 1975*, p 12, para 23.

[78] *Interpretation of Peace Treaties with Bulgaria, Hungary and Romania, First Phase, Advisory Opinion, ICJ Reports 1950*, p 65 at p 71.

dispute underlying a request for advisory opinion is thus not necessary for the opinion to be given; but, as the Court declared in a later case, that concerning *Western Sahara*, 'lack of consent might constitute a ground for declining to give the opinion requested', in the exercise of the Court's discretion, 'if, in the circumstances of a given case, considerations of judicial propriety should oblige the Court to refuse an opinion'.[79] The Court offered as an instance of this (and probably the most compelling instance), 'when the circumstances disclose that to give a reply would have the effect of circumventing the principle that a State is not obliged to allow its disputes to be submitted to judicial settlement without its consent'.[80] This might be so if the object of the requesting organ (*in casu* the General Assembly) were 'to bring before the Court, by way of a request for advisory opinion, a dispute or legal controversy, in order that it may later, on the basis of the Court's opinion, exercise its power and functions for the peaceful settlement of that dispute or controversy'.[81] This criterion appears, however, to have been tacitly abandoned in the *Wall* case.[82] In no case up to the present has the Court declined to give an opinion on this ground, or any other discretionary ground. It did not even refuse in the case of a dispute between the General Assembly and a State, in which the Assembly, unable to obtain a binding advisory opinion under the provisions of the Convention on the Privileges and Immunities of the UN, because of a reservation to that Convention made by the State concerned, sought and obtained a non-binding opinion of the Court on the point in dispute.[83]

A further difficulty that has arisen in connection with requests for advisory opinions in cases involving, or related to, existing international disputes is the extent to which a party, or the parties, to such a dispute should be treated as though they were parties to a contentious case, and in particular should be able to appoint a judge ad hoc. Article 68 of the Statute provides that:

> In the exercise of its advisory functions the Court shall further be guided by the provisions of the present Statute which apply in contentious cases to the extent to which it recognizes them to be applicable.

The Permanent Court had recognized that in some cases States should be treated as 'parties' to the extent of appointing judges ad hoc. The Rules of Court make no direct provision for this, but Article 102(2) repeats the text of Article 68, and adds: 'For this purpose, it shall above all consider whether the request for the advisory opinion relates to a legal question actually pending between two or more States.'

Practice has shown that the implementation of these texts in specific cases in relation to the appointment of judges ad hoc is not always straightforward. In the *Namibia* case, South Africa, which had a very special interest in the proceedings, and could claim that there was a 'legal question actually pending' between itself and nearly every other State, was not permitted to appoint a judge ad hoc.[84] In the *Western Sahara* case, Morocco and Mauritania each claimed the existence of special legal ties with the territory, and contested the arguments of Spain, the former colonial power: Morocco was permitted to appoint a

[79] *Western Sahara, ICJ Reports 1975*, p 12, para 32.
[80] Ibid, para 33. This passage was later criticized, by Judge Kooijmans in the *Wall* case, as containing 'purely circular reasoning': *Legal Consequences of the Construction of a Wall in the Occupied Palestinian Territory, ICJ Reports 2004*, p 227, para 27.   [81] *Western Sahara, Advisory Opinion, ICJ Reports 1975*, p 12, para 29.
[82] See the Separate Opinion of Judge Higgins, *Legal Consequences of the Construction of a Wall in the Occupied Palestinian Territory, Advisory Opinion, ICJ Reports 2004*, p 136 at p 210, paras 12–13.
[83] *Applicability of Article VI, Section 22, of the Convention on the Privileges and Immunities of the United Nations, Advisory Opinion, ICJ Reports 1989*, p 177, para 38.
[84] *Legal Consequences for States of the Continued Presence of South Africa in Namibia (South West Africa) notwithstanding Security Council Resolution 276 (1970), Order of 29 January 1971, ICJ Reports 1971*, p 12, and Advisory Opinion, p 16, paras 35ff.

judge ad hoc, but Mauritania was not.[85] In the *Wall* case one of the parties to the dispute (Palestine) was not a State for the purposes of the Statute.[86]

IX. THE COURT PAST AND PRESENT: AN ASSESSMENT

For the first 20 years of its existence, the International Court of Justice seemed destined to play a part on the international scene similar to that played by its predecessor, the Permanent Court of International Justice. Cases were submitted to it in a small but regular flow, and a series of requests were made by the General Assembly for advisory opinions; the decisions and advisory opinions given were on the whole well received, and the Court's contribution to the development of law, though necessarily marginal, was significant. While the creators of the Permanent Court, and their successors at the San Francisco Conference in 1946, might have hoped for a more spectacular contribution to international dispute-settlement, the experiment begun in 1920 could be regarded as successful.

In the 1960s and 1970s, a marked change was observed. For reasons which need not be gone into here, but which must include the Court's 1966 decision in the *South West Africa* case (which had a devastating effect on the Court's reputation with the developing countries), doubts began to be expressed about the future of the Court, as fewer and fewer States seemed inclined to bring their disputes before it. For a brief period, the Court had no cases whatever on its list. Little by little, however, the situation improved, particularly as a result of the increasing need for impartial settlement of seabed delimitation disputes, where the Court had shown the way in the *North Sea Continental Shelf* case (1969). The formation of a special chamber according to the wishes of the parties in the *Gulf of Maine* case (1984) offered an attractive alternative to submission to the full Court, and it was striking that the next request for such a chamber came from two developing countries in sub-Saharan Africa (Burkina Faso and Mali in the *Frontier Dispute*, 1986).

Today, the Court is busier than it has ever been before. Disputes have been submitted to it not only by its more established 'clients', but by States of: Latin America;[87] Eastern Europe;[88] Asia;[89] and Africa.[90] On the other hand, China has so far remained aloof, and the USA now shows distinct coolness toward the Court, marked by the withdrawal of

---

[85] *Western Sahara, Order of 22 May 1975, ICJ Reports 1975*, p 6.

[86] See the Separate Opinion of Judge Owada, *Legal Consequences of the Construction of a Wall in the Occupied Palestinian Territory, Advisory Opinion, ICJ Reports 2004*, p 136 at p 267, para 19. The problem remained hypothetical, as Israel did not claim the right to appoint a judge ad hoc.

[87] *Military and Paramilitary Activities in and against Nicaragua (Nicaragua v USA), Border and Transborder Armed Actions (Nicaragua v Honduras, Nicaragua v Costa Rica), Land, Island and Maritime Frontier Dispute (Honduras/El Salvador, Nicaragua intervening), Territorial and Maritime Dispute (Nicaragua v Colombia); Maritime Delimitation between Nicaragua and Honduras in the Caribbean Sea; Avena and other Mexican Nationals (Mexico v USA); Territorial and Maritime Dispute (Nicaragua v Colombia)*.

[88] *Gabčíkovo-Nagymaros Project (Hungary/Slovakia), Application of the Convention on the Prevention and Punishment of the Crime of Genocide (Bosnia and Herzegovina v Serbia and Montenegro), Legality of Use of Force (Yugoslavia against 10 NATO countries); Application of the Convention on the Prevention and Punishment of the Crime of Genocide (Croatia v Serbia); Maritime Delimitation in the Black Sea (Romania v Ukraine)*.

[89] *Aerial Incident of 10 August 1999 (Pakistan v India); Sovereignty over Pulau Ligitan and Pulau Sipadan (Indonesia/Malaysia); Sovereignty over Pedra Blanca/Pulau Batu Pateh, Middle Rocks and South Ledge (Malaysia/Singapore)*.

[90] *Frontier Dispute (Benin/Niger); Ahmadou Sadio Diallo (Republic of Guinea v Democratic Republic of the Congo); Armed Activities on the territory of the Congo (Democratic Republic of the Congo v Rwanda); Arrest Warrant of 11 April 2000 (Democratic Republic of the Congo v Belgium); Armed Activities on the Territory of the Congo (Democratic Republic of the Congo v Burundi; v Rwanda; v Uganda); Certain Criminal Proceedings in France (Republic of the Congo v France)*.

various long-established bases of jurisdiction, avowedly in response to what it regards as unjustifiedly extensive interpretation by the Court of its jurisdiction over the USA.[91] There has, however, been increasing use of the possibility of requesting an advisory opinion, including the request by both WHO and the General Assembly for an opinion on the legality of nuclear weapons,[92] and by the General Assembly on an aspect of the Israel/Palestine problem.[93]

On the practical level, there are signs that the Court is becoming a victim of its own success. The principle that all cases are heard by the full Court unless the parties agree to a chamber means that there is a limit to the number of cases that can be heard and determined each year; and although the Registry has been enlarged and some of the Court's working methods improved, there are signs of an overload. Judicial settlement has never been a speedy means of resolving disputes, but it is to be feared that States considering bringing a case to the Court may be put off by the likely delay before a decision is given, due to the presence of so many other cases in the queue.

A consistently high standard has, however, been maintained in the quality of the Court's decisions, even though they have, as always, been exposed to healthy criticism. The bringing of more cases has meant more opportunities for contribution to the development of the law; on a number of occasions, for example, the Court has been able to supplement the work of the International Law Commission by settling authoritatively the customary-law status of a rule embodied in a treaty or other text emanating from the ILC.

Considerable use has been made of the possibility of requesting the indication of provisional measures, *inter alia* in situations of armed hostilities. It remains to be seen, however, whether the ruling in the *LaGrand* case, that provisional measures give rise to a binding obligation of compliance, may conceivably have a negative influence on advance acceptance of jurisdiction. The provisional measures procedure has always offered a temptation to States to commence proceedings on a shaky jurisdictional foundation in the hope of getting at least the short-term benefit of an order for provisional measures, and this is all the more attractive when the order is recognized to be immediately binding, even if unenforceable. The only defence against such tactics is to limit generalized acceptances of jurisdiction that may be misused; but there is no sign at present of any generalized flight from potential jurisdiction, in terms of withdrawal of acceptances or denunciation of settlement treaties.

Nevertheless, the prospects as regards acceptance of jurisdiction must otherwise be regarded as mixed: existing treaties for dispute settlement, compromissory clauses, and optional dispute-settlement protocols continue to provide a background of potential jurisdiction, but there seem to be few fresh treaties of this kind concluded, and such clauses seem to appear less frequently in new multilateral treaties.[94] Nor does the optional clause system seem to be thriving. The number of States having filed declarations of acceptance (currently 67 out of 193 UN members) is not increasing, and the declarations that have

---

[91] The cases of *Armed Activities in and against Nicaragua, Oil Platforms*, and *Avena and other Mexican Nationals* may be mentioned.

[92] Opinions differ, however, as to the wisdom of using the advisory opinion procedure in an area of this kind (see, eg, *Legality of the Threat or Use of Nuclear Weapons, Advisory Opinion, ICJ Reports 1996*, p 226, Dissenting Opinion of Judge Oda, p 330).

[93] *Legal Consequences of the Construction of a Wall in the Occupied Palestinian Territories, Advisory Opinion, ICJ Reports 2004*, p 136.

[94] According to the information on the Court's website, derived from registrations of treaties with the UN Secretariat, only three new bilateral treaties providing for ICJ jurisdiction have been concluded since 1991; and no multilateral treaties with such provisions have been registered since 2003.

been filed are much qualified by reservations. Some disquiet has also been caused by what is perceived as a trend whereby the Court, in order to comment on legal questions of substantial current importance, has been over-generous in its interpretation of texts conferring jurisdiction. The decision in the *Oil Platforms* case,[95] in particular, has been criticized on this ground.[96] The development of a coherent system of intervention has been valuable, since many modern international disputes are plurilateral rather than bilateral. The Court is clearly alive to the need to review its own procedures, as is shown by the recent revision of Articles 79 and 80 of the Rules, and the use of Practice Directions.

All in all, the prospects for the future role of the Court in the settlement of international disputes are encouraging. While it may not be such a World Court as idealists might like to envisage, in its present structure and operation it remains a real force for peaceful settlement of disputes, and the furthest extension of judicial power to the affairs of States that is likely to be acceptable to the members of the present-day international community.

CITATION OF ICJ CASES

Although cases brought before the Court are numbered consecutively on the Court's General List (Rules, Article 26(1)(b)), these numbers are not used for purposes of citation. The official title of each case is determined by the Court at the outset of the proceedings, on the basis of the document instituting proceedings; considerations of avoiding any appearance of pre-judgment lead to such titles often being somewhat unwieldy. The names of the parties are sometimes included in the official title, particularly when the same title is used for more than one case. Abbreviated titles are therefore often used by scholars in books and articles; unfortunately, there is no generally recognized system for these.

REFERENCES

SMALL, D (2004), 'The Oil Platforms Case: Jurisdiction through the—Closed—Eye of the Needle', 3 *Law and Practice of International Courts and Tribunals* 113.

THIRLWAY, H (1984), 'Reciprocity in the Jurisdiction of the International Court', 15 *NYBIL* 97.

THIRLWAY, H (2001), 'The Law and Procedure of the International Court of Justice 1960–1989, Part Twelve', 72 *BYIL* 37.

FURTHER READING

BOWETT, D et al (1997), *The International Court of Justice: Process, Practice and Procedure* (London: BIICL (British Institute of International and Comparative Law)): based on the work of a Study Group set up by the British Institute of International and Comparative Law, this study focuses on the practical aspects of the Court's work and procedures.

---

[95] *Oil Platforms (Islamic Republic of Iran v United States of America), Judgment, ICJ Reports 2003*, p 161.
[96] Cf the opinion of Judge Kooijmans in that case, ibid, p 257, para 35, and Small, 2004.

KOLB, R (2013), *The International Court of Justice* (Oxford: Hart Publishing): an up-to-date and encyclopedic survey of the Court and its work. Although probably too detailed for student use, it is valuable for the clarity with which it is written.

ROSENNE, S (1997), *The Law and Practice of the International Court, 1920–1996* (The Hague: Martinus Nijhoff): this is the most complete and authoritative survey of the Court.

THIRLWAY, H (2013), *The Law and Procedure of the International Court: Fifty Years of Jurisprudence* (Oxford: Oxford University Press): an assemblage of the articles contributed by this author to the *British Year Book of International Law*, 1989–2012.

THIRLWAY, H (2016), *The International Court of Justice* (Oxford: Oxford University Press): an extended exploration of the work and working of the Court.

A Commentary on the Statute of the International Court of Justice (April 2006): a joint publication of the Max-Planck-Institut, Heidelberg, the Institut für Völker- und Europarecht, Humboldt University, Berlin, and the Walter-Schücking-Institut, University of Kiel.

International Court of Justice: Yearbook: this annual publication contains a wealth of information on current cases and on points of practice and procedure; the current issue is No. 68 (2014–15).

The International Court of Justice Handbook: this useful handbook is published periodically by the Registry of the Court, and distributed jointly by the Court and the UN Department of Public Information. It was most recently updated in 2013.

The International Court of Justice: Questions and Answers about the Principal Judicial Organ of the United Nations (2000), UN Sales No E.99.I.25: this sets out basic facts concerning the Court.

WEBSITES

http://www.icj-cij.org

The Court's website contains the text in the two official languages (English and French) of the Statute, Rules of Court and Practice Directions, the other texts governing jurisdiction, and full texts of all recent decisions, press releases, and other materials. Once the Court has decided that the pleadings in a case are to be made public, these and the oral arguments will also be on the website, but only in the language in which they were presented. The translations of judges' separate and dissenting opinions may also not be available until some time after the decision itself is given.

20

THE USE OF FORCE AND THE INTERNATIONAL LEGAL ORDER

Christine Gray

SUMMARY

This is one of the most controversial areas of international law. States are divided as to the interpretation of the fundamental rules on the use of force in the UN Charter. The prohibition of the use of force in Article 2(4) is directed at inter-State conflicts; there is disagreement as to whether this allows the use of force for humanitarian intervention or 'responsibility to protect'. The application of Article 2(4) to intervention in civil wars is also problematic. The main exception to the prohibition on the use of force is the right to self-defence under Article 51. It is controversial whether this is a narrow right, available only in response to an armed attack, or whether it allows force in protection of nationals abroad or in response to terrorist attacks. The UN Charter also establishes a collective security system whereby the Security Council may respond to threats to the peace, breaches of the peace, and acts of aggression. This chapter examines the use of enforcement action and the institution of UN peacekeeping as well as the power of regional organizations to assist in peacekeeping and enforcement action.

I. INTRODUCTION

The law on the use of force is one of the most controversial areas of international law and one where the law may seem ineffective. The UN Charter prohibits the use of force by States in Article 2(4), but this has not prevented the occurrence of more than 100 major conflicts since 1945 and the deaths of more than 20 million people. Difficult questions arise as to how far international law in fact influences State behaviour. In practice States are clearly anxious to avoid condemnation for their use of force and they generally use the language of international law to explain and justify their behaviour—not as the sole justification but as one of a variety of arguments. Thus NATO based its use of force in 'humanitarian intervention' over Kosovo (1999) on a mixture of political, moral, and legal arguments. It is tempting to dismiss legal arguments in justification of the use of force by States, especially powerful States, as merely self-interested manipulation of the rules, but in the absence of clear empirical evidence about the nature of decision-making within States this remains an assumption. It may underestimate the genuine differences of viewpoint between opposing States and the commitment of the vast majority of States, especially small, weak States, to the prohibition on the use of force.

A. THE UN CHARTER SCHEME

The UN Charter is the starting point for any discussion of international law on the use of force (Simma, 2012). It was concluded after, and in response to, the experiences of the Second World War, in the same way as the League of Nations Covenant was a response to the First World War. There is disagreement as to whether the prohibition of the use of force in the UN Charter was a revolutionary new provision or whether customary law had already developed along the lines of Article 2(4) by the time of the creation of the UN (Brownlie, 1963, p 66). The Charter aims not only to prohibit the unilateral use of force by States by Article 2(4), but also to centralize control over the use of force in the Security Council, acting under Chapter VII.

The Preamble of the Charter begins: 'We the peoples of the United Nations determined to save succeeding generations from the scourge of war', and the first purpose of the UN set out in Article 1 is '[t]o maintain international peace and security, and to that end: to take effective collective measures for the prevention and removal of threats to the peace and for the suppression of acts of aggression or other breaches of the peace'. The original scheme was that the Security Council should respond to threats to the peace, breach of the peace, and acts of aggression, if necessary through its own standing UN army. However, this plan foundered during the Cold War because the veto possessed by the five permanent members of the Security Council—the USA, the USSR (now succeeded by Russia), China, France, and the UK—obstructed effective decision-making by the Security Council (Patil, 1992).

The original Charter scheme has not been implemented; the action taken by the Security Council under Chapter VII has been different from that originally planned. 'Coalitions of the willing' have replaced the plan for a standing UN army: member States have been authorized to use force in major enforcement operations which are perceived to be beyond the resources of the UN. Also the institution of peacekeeping which grew up as a partial substitute for Security Council enforcement action during the Cold War did so without express provision in the Charter.

There is broad agreement between States on the core of the law on the use of force, as set out in the UN Charter and also in regional and collective self-defence treaties. However, early divisions between developed and developing States emerged on the interpretation of the brief provisions of the Charter. The UN General Assembly adopted resolutions on the use of force to elaborate on the Charter, and where these were adopted by consensus they are generally regarded as statements of customary international law or as authoritative interpretations of the UN Charter. But often these resolutions were deliberately ambiguous. The consensus in favour of the *Definition of Aggression*,[1] the *Declaration on Friendly Relations*,[2] and the *Declaration on the Non-Use of Force*[3] masked the divisions between States on questions such as the scope of the right of self-defence. These divisions were

---

[1] *Definition of Aggression*, GA Res 3314 (XXIX) (14 December 1974).

[2] *Declaration on Principles of International Law concerning Friendly Relations and Co-operation among States in Accordance with the Charter of the United Nations*, GA Res 2625 (XXV) (24 October 1970).

[3] *Declaration on the Enhancement of the Effectiveness of the Principle of Refraining from the Threat or Use of Force in International Relations*, GA Res 44/22 (18 November 1987).

apparent in the debates leading up to the resolutions. The central concerns of developing States have been with disarmament, nuclear weapons, and economic coercion; in general they have favoured a stricter interpretation of the prohibition of the use of force than developed States.

Also important in the interpretation and application of the UN Charter rules on the use of force are the resolutions of the General Assembly and of the Security Council passed in reaction to specific instances of the use of force by States. Of course these are political bodies, but it is generally accepted that a condemnation of a use of force is strong evidence of its illegality. In contrast, a failure to condemn may not be conclusive evidence that the action in question was lawful, given the variety of motives influencing States. The International Court of Justice (ICJ) has also played a significant part in the identification and development of the rules on the use of force in the *Nicaragua* case,[4] the *Legality of the Threat or Use of Nuclear Weapons* Advisory Opinion,[5] the *Oil Platforms* case,[6] and the *Case Concerning Armed Activities on the Territory of the Congo (DRC v Uganda)*.[7]

II. THE PROHIBITION OF THE USE OF FORCE IN ARTICLE 2(4) UN CHARTER

Article 2(4) is the basic prohibition on the use of force by States. It provides that '[a]ll Members shall refrain in their international relations from the threat or use of force against the territorial integrity or political independence of any State, or in any other manner inconsistent with the Purposes of the United Nations'. Clearly this is directed at the inter-State use of force, although as it has turned out, civil conflicts have been more common than traditional inter-State conflicts since the Second World War. Under Article 2(6) there is a duty on the UN to ensure that even States which are not UN members act in accordance with these principles so far as may be necessary for the maintenance of international peace and security. This brief prohibition of the use of force in Article 2(4) is accepted as representing customary international law, as was acknowledged by the ICJ in the *Nicaragua* case.[8] But its interpretation has given rise to much debate. General Assembly resolutions give some limited guidance, but gloss over the more fundamental disagreements.

A. THE USE OF FORCE IN 'INTERNATIONAL RELATIONS'

Article 2(4) prohibits the use of force in 'international relations'; certain States have therefore tried to argue that they were justified in the use of force to recover what they claimed to be their own territory. Thus, Argentina invaded the Falkland Islands in 1982 in order to seize them back from the UK, whose title to the territory it rejected.[9] Iraq invaded Kuwait in 1990 on the basis that it had pre-colonial title and therefore was not violating Article 2(4) because the territory belonged to it.[10] These invasions were strongly condemned by

---

[4] *Military and Paramilitary Activities in and against Nicaragua (Nicaragua v United States of America), Merits, Judgment, ICJ Reports 1986*, p 14.

[5] *Legality of the Threat or Use of Nuclear Weapons, Advisory Opinion, ICJ Reports 1996*, p 226.

[6] *Oil Platforms (Islamic Republic of Iran v United States of America), ICJ Reports 2003*, p 161.

[7] *Armed Activities on the Territory of the Congo (Democratic Republic of the Congo v Uganda), Judgment, ICJ Reports 2005*, p 168.

[8] *Military and Paramilitary Activities in and against Nicaragua (Nicaragua v United States of America), Merits, Judgment, ICJ Reports 1986*, p 14, para 190.　　　　　　　　　　　　　　[9] 1982 *UNYB* 1320.

[10] 1991 *UNYB* 189.

the international community; the actions of Argentina and Iraq were inconsistent with the duty under Article 2(3) of the UN Charter to settle disputes, including territorial and boundary disputes, peacefully. This duty was further elaborated in the *Definition of Aggression* and the *Declaration on Friendly Relations*. Nevertheless, China does not exclude the right to use force to recover the island of Taiwan on the basis that it is part of China, while other States have called for a peaceful settlement of the controversy.

Another problem with the interpretation of 'international relations' has arisen over the categorization of conflicts: is the situation an inter-State conflict to which Article 2(4) applies or is it an internal conflict governed by different rules? This issue of categorization was crucial in the Vietnam and Korean Wars during the Cold War; Western States argued that these were inter-State wars initiated when an aggressor Communist State invaded its neighbour and that the international community was able to respond in collective self-defence or collective action under Chapter VII of the UN Charter. The Communist bloc position was that Vietnam and Korea were both unitary States engaged in struggles against colonial intervention. Disagreements as to whether the conflict was a civil war or an inter-State conflict also arose with regard to the break-up of the former Yugoslavia.[11]

B. THE MEANING OF 'THREAT OR USE OF FORCE'

Developed and developing States were divided on the meaning of 'force' during the Cold War: the former maintained that this meant only armed force, whereas developing States claimed that it covered also economic coercion. However, this division is today perhaps more of symbolic than of practical importance; economic coercion is now expressly prohibited in General Assembly resolutions, such as the *Declaration on Friendly Relations*. More recently, commentators have debated whether cyber-attacks can be classified as a use of force (Roscini, 2014).

The pronouncements of the ICJ in the *Nicaragua* case are of central importance with regard to the interpretation of 'force'. The ICJ was called on to categorize the various actions of the USA aimed at the overthrow of the government of Nicaragua. It held that not only the laying of mines in Nicaraguan waters and attacks on Nicaraguan ports and oil installations by US forces but also support for the opposition forces—the *contras*—engaged in forcible struggle against the government could constitute the 'use of force'. The arming and training of the *contras* involved the unlawful use of force against Nicaragua. The mere supply of funds did not in itself amount to a use of force, but could constitute unlawful intervention.[12] This categorization is clearly significant for the assessment of the legality of assistance to opposition forces in the civil war that started in 2012 in Syria. States including Saudi Arabia, Qatar, Turkey, and the USA have supplied money, arms, training, and intelligence support to a diverse range of groups.

The prohibition of the 'threat of force' has attracted less discussion than the actual 'use of force'. The ICJ in the *Nicaragua* case and in the Advisory Opinion on the *Legality of Nuclear Weapons* was faced with questions as to the meaning of 'threat of force' but offered little by way of guidance, limiting itself to the not very surprising conclusion that a threat of force is unlawful where the actual use of the force threatened would itself be unlawful;

---

[11] See Gray, 1996. See also ICTY, Appeals Chamber, *Prosecutor v Dusko Tadić, Decision on the Defence Motion for Interlocutory Appeal on Jurisdiction (Interlocutory Appeal)*, Case No IT-94–1-AR72 (2 October 1995).

[12] *Military and Paramilitary Activities in and against Nicaragua (Nicaragua v United States of America), Merits, Judgment, ICJ Reports 1986*, p 14, para 228.

the Court refused to find that the mere possession of nuclear weapons was an unlawful threat of force.

C. THE USE OF FORCE 'AGAINST THE TERRITORIAL INTEGRITY AND POLITICAL INDEPENDENCE OF ANY STATE, OR IN ANY OTHER MANNER INCONSISTENT WITH THE PURPOSES OF THE UNITED NATIONS'

The most fundamental debate on the interpretation of Article 2(4) is whether it is an absolute prohibition on the use of force or whether it should be interpreted to allow the use of force for aims which are consistent with the purposes of the UN. Can there be a use of force which does not harm the territorial integrity or political independence of a State? There have been debates as to whether the use of force to rescue nationals, to promote democracy, and to further self-determination could be compatible with Article 2(4). States were divided as to whether NATO's forcible humanitarian intervention in Kosovo in 1999 was prohibited by Article 2(4).

During the Cold War some, mostly US, writers argued that Article 2(4) represents only a limited prohibition; they maintained that it should be interpreted in the context of the whole Charter and thus that the prohibition of force depends on the functioning of the Charter scheme for collective security under Chapter VII. In the Cold War the Security Council could not use its powers effectively and therefore Article 2(4) should be interpreted to allow the use of force to further the principles and purposes of the UN. Others rejected this approach, arguing that Article 2(4) should be strictly construed; the non-functioning of the UN system made it all the more important that States should not use force except in self-defence. The debate as to whether Article 2(4) is a wide or a narrow prohibition on the use of force has outlasted the Cold War.

In practice few States openly relied on a narrow interpretation of Article 2(4) to justify their use of force during the Cold War. The apparent adoption of the restrictive argument on Article 2(4) by the UK in the *Corfu Channel* case was exceptional; the UK argued that its forcible intervention in Albanian territorial waters to recover evidence (as to which State was responsible for laying naval mines that had led to the destruction of two British warships) did not violate Article 2(4) because its action did not threaten the territorial integrity or political independence of Albania.[13] The Court rejected this claim, but there was some debate as to whether this was merely a limited rejection of the UK claim on the particular facts or a total rejection of the narrow interpretation of Article 2(4). The ICJ in the *Nicaragua* case seems to have taken the latter view of the ruling.[14] In later incidents the USA and Israel also expressly took a narrow view of Article 2(4) as not prohibiting the rescue of nationals. This was argued by Israel to justify its rescue of nationals on a hijacked plane from Entebbe in Uganda (1976) and by the USA in its more extensive operation in Grenada (1983), but this was not the sole justification for the use of force and was not taken up by other States. In these cases other justifications were also offered by the USA and Israel for their use of force; they did not rely solely on the controversial narrow interpretation of Article 2(4). So express reliance on the argument that Article 2(4) should be interpreted to allow the use of force if this was consistent with the aims of the UN remained exceptional.

[13] *Corfu Channel, Merits, Judgment, ICJ Reports 1949*, p 4 at p 34.
[14] *Military and Paramilitary Activities in and against Nicaragua (Nicaragua v United States of America), Merits, Judgment, ICJ Reports 1986*, p 14, para 202.

1. Force in pursuit of self-determination

During the era of decolonization States were divided as to whether force could be used by colonial peoples in pursuit of the right of self-determination (Wilson, 1988). Former colonies and developing States maintained that Article 2(4) did not prohibit such use of force; Western and former colonial powers did not accept this and voted against the General Assembly resolutions which expressly affirmed a right to use force. Those resolutions which were adopted by consensus, such as the *Definition of Aggression* and the *Friendly Relations Resolution*, were deliberately ambiguous. They spoke of the right of peoples with the right to self-determination to 'struggle' for that end; by this developing States understood armed struggle and the developed States peaceful struggle. There was agreement, however, that force should not be used against a people with the right of self-determination. Even though many groups continue to invoke self-determination and to turn to armed force in pursuit of independence, there is no support by States for any legal right to use force other than in pursuit of decolonization. The virtual end of decolonization therefore means that the legal debate does not have great practical significance today, except in the context of the struggle of the Palestinians for self-determination to end the illegal occupation by Israel of the West Bank and Gaza Strip. Even in this context there was little public debate of this legal issue with regard to the series of conflicts in Gaza.

2. Force in pursuit of democracy

The claim that pro-democratic force—the use of force to restore a democratic government—is not prohibited by Article 2(4) has been put forward by writers such as D'Amato (1990), but not by States. It is notable that when the USA invaded Panama in 1989 it specifically disavowed any legal doctrine of pro-democratic invasion, preferring to rely instead on self-defence. When the former President Noriega refused to stand down after defeat in the election the USA intervened, claiming that it was acting in self-defence of its nationals in Panama. It distinguished between its political interest in the protection of democracy and its legal justification for intervention.[15] Although the UN may have a power to authorize force to restore democratic government in exceptional cases, such as that of Haiti after its first democratically elected government was overthrown in a coup in 1991, it is not possible to extrapolate from this a right of unilateral intervention by States. It is significant that, even though the 2006 *US National Security Strategy* produced during the presidency of George W Bush devoted considerable attention to the promotion of democracy, it did not support the use of force for this end. Nor did Western States invoke any such doctrine in the context of the uprisings of the Arab Spring as a legal justification for their interventions against the governments of Libya and Syria.

D. HUMANITARIAN INTERVENTION AND RESPONSIBILITY TO PROTECT

The NATO action over Kosovo in 1999 led to prolonged debate as to whether Article 2(4) allowed the use of force for humanitarian intervention, and produced a fundamental split between NATO States on the one hand and China, Russia, and the Non-Aligned Movement on the other.[16] Acting in response to Yugoslavia's repression and displacement of ethnic Albanians in Kosovo, NATO conducted a 78-day air campaign starting in March 1999. Although NATO did not offer a fully elaborated legal argument for its air campaign, it seemed to put forward in justification a mixture of implied authorization by the Security

---

[15] 1989 *UNYB* 172.   [16] 1999 *UNYB* 332.

Council and humanitarian arguments. Member States set out their legal arguments in the Security Council debates and in their pleadings in the *Legality of Use of Force* case brought by Yugoslavia before the International Court of Justice against NATO States.[17]

The UK more than any other State has developed a doctrine of humanitarian intervention as an autonomous institution. It has argued that the interpretation of Article 2(4) has changed over time; that international law in this field has developed to meet new situations. This apparently new doctrine was first put forward with regard to US and UK action over Iraq. After Iraq invaded Kuwait in 1990 and was driven out by coalition forces in *Operation Desert Storm*, the UN Security Council established a binding cease-fire which was accepted by Iraq. However, the cease-fire regime in Resolution 687 failed to make provision for the protection of human rights in Iraq; Iraq turned on the Kurds of the north and the Shiites and Marsh Arabs of the south. In response the Security Council passed Resolution 688[18] asking Iraq to end its repression and to allow access to humanitarian agencies. This resolution was not a binding resolution passed under Chapter VII; it expressly refers to Article 2(7) UN Charter which provides that nothing in the Charter authorizes UN organs to intervene in matters which are essentially within the domestic jurisdiction of States; it did not authorize force. The USA, the UK, and, to a lesser extent, France nevertheless intervened in Iraq to protect the endangered civilians and subsequently proclaimed no-fly zones over north and south Iraq. The legal basis for this was not made clear at first, but the UK subsequently developed the doctrine of humanitarian intervention. To justify the use of force to protect the no-fly zones over north and south Iraq, the UK said: 'We believe that humanitarian intervention without the invitation of the country concerned can be justified in cases of extreme humanitarian need.' In contrast, the USA and France did not offer humanitarian intervention as the justification for their use of force in Iraq. States became polarized over the legality of the operations in the no-fly zones which continued for over ten years until *Operation Iraqi Freedom* (2003). France withdrew its initial support; China and Russia did not accept the legality of the no-fly zones (Gray, 2002).

Those who support a doctrine of humanitarian intervention often rely on earlier, pre-Iraq, practice; they invoke as precedents India's intervention to end repression and support self-determination in Bangladesh (1971), Tanzania's intervention which overthrew the regime of Idi Amin in Uganda (1979), and Vietnam's use of force which ended the murderous rule of Pol Pot in Cambodia (1978). But in these episodes the States using force did not actually invoke a doctrine of humanitarian intervention; they preferred to rely on the better-established right to self-defence. Several States said that violations of human rights could not justify the use of force. Some commentators attempt to re-write history in order to try to justify the action in Kosovo. This requires that we ignore what the States in question actually said, and therefore seems inconsistent with the approach of the ICJ in the *Nicaragua* case. The Court, in considering whether a new doctrine of forcible intervention to help opposition forces to overthrow the government had emerged through State practice, put great stress on the fact that neither the USA itself, nor other States, had actually claimed such a right.[19]

As regards Kosovo there was little express support from States for an autonomous doctrine of humanitarian intervention, other than from the UK. However, Belgium in

---

[17] *Legality of Use of Force (Yugoslavia v Belgium), Provisional Measures, Order of 2 June 1999, ICJ Reports 1999*, p 124.

[18] SC Res 688 (5 April 1991). This was adopted with ten votes in favour, three against, and with two abstentions.

[19] *Military and Paramilitary Activities in and against Nicaragua (Nicaragua v United States of America), Merits, Judgment, ICJ Reports 1986*, p 14, paras 206–9.

its arguments to the ICJ did resort to this doctrine on the interpretation of Article 2(4). It said that the NATO campaign was an action to rescue a population in danger and was not directed against the territorial integrity or political independence of Yugoslavia. Other States such as Germany and France stressed the unique nature of the NATO operation and made clear that they did not regard it as a precedent for future humanitarian intervention. Most States arguing in support of the NATO campaign in the Security Council and before the ICJ did not rely on humanitarian intervention alone as an autonomous justification for the use of force; they seemed to rely on a combination of humanitarian intervention and implied authorization by the Security Council.

Those against the NATO bombing argued that Article 2(4) should be construed strictly. It was an absolute prohibition of the use of force and it was for the Security Council under Chapter VII to authorize the use of force; unilateral action by NATO was illegal. Yugoslavia's pleadings argued that there was no right of humanitarian intervention in international law. The practice of States after the creation of the UN did not justify any argument that there had been a change in the meaning of Article 2(4). General Assembly resolutions such as the *Definition of Aggression* and the *Declaration on Friendly Relations* excluded intervention in absolute terms. However, the attempt to secure a Security Council resolution condemning the NATO action was rejected—an indication of considerable political sympathy for NATO, if not conclusive as to the legality of its action.

Therefore, even if a legal doctrine of humanitarian intervention could be said to have emerged from the NATO action in Kosovo, its scope was far from clear (Chesterman, 2001). Is humanitarian intervention an autonomous right or does it depend on a prior determination by the Security Council under Chapter VII? Must it always be collective action and, if so, how many States should be involved? Can a bombing campaign amount to humanitarian action? Yugoslavia argued that, even if there is a right of humanitarian intervention, the modalities chosen were inconsistent with humanitarian aims: a high-level bombing campaign and the wide range of targets chosen put the population of the whole of Yugoslavia at risk.

There have been attempts by the UK and by scholars to develop a detailed framework for humanitarian intervention.[20] Moreover, Article 4(h) of the African Union Constitutive Act (2000) includes provision for humanitarian intervention pursuant to a decision of the African Union (AU) Assembly. But there is still no significant support for a right of unilateral intervention. Many States in many different fora within and outside the UN after the NATO campaign have made a point of condemning the NATO action in Kosovo as illegal. The Non-Aligned Movement rejects humanitarian intervention as having no legal basis in the Charter. The doctrine therefore remains very controversial. It is noteworthy that it was not used to justify the use of force against Afghanistan in *Operation Enduring Freedom* or against Iraq in *Operation Iraqi Freedom*, despite the choice of names for these operations. During the Syrian conflict it was only the UK that expressly invoked this doctrine as a justification for intervention in response to the alleged use of chemical weapons by the Assad government.[21]

In recent years attention has shifted away from humanitarian intervention to the concept of the 'responsibility to protect' (Stahn, 2007 and see Zifcak, Ch 16 in this book). Provision for this was included in the 2005 UN World Summit Outcome Document which

---

[20] See, for example, (2000) 71 *BYIL* 644, and the *Report of the International Commission on Intervention and State Sovereignty, The Responsibility to Protect* (2001).

[21] See (2013) 84 *BYIL* 806, and Henderson, 2015. When President Trump ordered a missile attack on Syrian government targets in April 2017 in response to the use of chemical weapons, the USA did not offer a clear legal justification.

was adopted unanimously by States. This responsibility arises in cases of international crimes such as genocide and ethnic cleansing. When a State fails to act to protect its own citizens, the international community has a responsibility to act, by force if necessary. But the action should be taken through the UN Security Council. There was no agreement on a right of unilateral intervention. The 2011 military intervention in Libya was hailed by many as a successful implementation of the 'responsibility to protect', in that it led to the overthrow of Colonel Gaddafi and the end to his regime's violent actions against the opposition, but this operation was seen by others as discrediting the concept. The African Union opposed the military intervention. The Security Council Resolution authorizing the military intervention did refer to 'responsibility to protect', but only to that of Libya rather than that of the international community. The actual legal basis for the use of force was a Security Council authorization under Chapter VII. Many States, including Russia and China, regarded the invocation of 'responsibility to protect' with regard to Libya as a pretext for regime change; accordingly they refused to support forcible intervention under the doctrine of 'responsibility to protect' in the subsequent civil war in Syria.

III. INTERVENTION, CIVIL WARS, AND INVITATION

The prohibition of the use of force in the UN Charter is directed at inter-State conflict, but apart from the many minor border incidents since the Second World War the most common use of force has been civil war, sometimes purely internal and sometimes fuelled by outside involvement. The rules against forcible intervention in civil conflict have been developed by General Assembly resolutions which elaborate on the Charter provisions on the use of force and complement the prohibitions of intervention in the constitutions of regional organizations. Thus the *Friendly Relations Declaration* (1970) makes clear that every State has the duty to refrain from organizing, instigating, assisting, or participating in acts of civil strife in another State and the duty not to foment, incite, or tolerate subversive, terrorist, or armed activities directed towards the violent overthrow of the regime of another State. There is a general consensus between States as to the principles to be applied to forcible intervention in civil conflicts, but their application in particular conflicts has caused fundamental disagreement (Doswald Beck, 1985; Roth, 1999).

The *Nicaragua* case set out the general doctrine in this area.[22] Nicaragua brought this case against the USA not only for unlawful use of force but also for unlawful intervention against the government through its support for the military and paramilitary operations of the *contra* forces. The ICJ affirmed that the principle of non-intervention involves the right of every State to conduct its affairs and to choose its own form of government without outside interference; it acknowledged that breaches of this principle were common but nevertheless found that the principle was customary international law. It held that the USA through 'recruiting, training, arming, equipping, financing, supplying and otherwise encouraging, supporting, aiding and directing military and paramilitary actions in and against Nicaragua' had violated international law.

In this case the Court distinguished between assistance to the government of a State and assistance to an opposition forcibly to overthrow the government. The former is allowed, the latter is forbidden. If forcible assistance to the opposition were allowed, nothing would remain of the principle of non-intervention. The Court stressed that States in practice had not claimed such a right to help opposition forces against the government outside the

---

[22] *Military and Paramilitary Activities in and against Nicaragua (Nicaragua v United States of America)*, Merits, Judgment, ICJ Reports 1986, p 14, paras 202–9.

context of national liberation movements seeking the right of self-determination, and that in the *Nicaragua* case the USA itself had not invoked a right to intervene but had relied on collective self-defence to justify its use of force against Nicaragua. The ICJ reaffirmed this approach in 2005 in *Armed Activities in the Territory of the Congo*.[23]

During the Cold War States which assisted opposition forces generally did so covertly; they also tended to challenge the legitimacy of the governments they were trying to over-throw. Thus when the USA assisted the opposition forces in Angola, Cambodia, and Afghanistan its use of force was covert, and it challenged the legitimacy of the government in all these cases. No objective determination of the status of governments by the Security Council was possible in the Cold War. It is clear that States manipulated the rules in pur-suit of their own interests. Certain States attempted to justify their intervention by claim-ing that it was in response to a prior foreign intervention against the government. The USSR interventions in Czechoslovakia in 1968 and in Afghanistan in 1979 are examples of such claims. In both cases the claim that there had been an invitation was a fiction because the USSR had itself installed the government whose invitation it claimed to rely on, and in both the intervention was condemned by the General Assembly.

Since the end of the Cold War it is sometimes possible for the Security Council to de-termine which is the lawful government and to distinguish between it and the opposition, for example in the context of arms embargoes. In the case of the complex conflict which broke out in the Democratic Republic of Congo (DRC) in 1998 the Security Council dis-tinguished between those States lawfully in the DRC at the invitation of the government and those unlawfully assisting opposition forces. In Syria also it is possible to distinguish between assistance to the government and that to armed opposition forces. When the 2011 uprising against the Assad government turned into a sectarian civil war, many States in-tervened in the conflict. Saudi Arabia, Qatar, Turkey, the USA, and others provided assis-tance to armed opposition groups. In so doing they tried to distinguish between moderate opposition groups and Islamist terrorists as recipients of assistance, they provided covert aid through intermediaries, or they claimed that their aid was 'non-lethal'. However, these interventions in support of opposition forces are open to condemnation on the basis of the rules established in the *Nicaragua* case, and the intervening States did not expressly challenge these rules.

As for military intervention at the request of a government, the ICJ in *Nicaragua* said simply that this was allowed. The *Definition of Aggression* acknowledges that a State may invite a foreign army into its territory. The right to use force to keep a government in power or to maintain domestic order has been taken for granted if the level of unrest falls below the threshold of civil war. France repeatedly intervened in its former colonies in Africa, ostensibly to maintain order. Similarly the USA denied military intervention in the long-lasting civil war in Colombia, but maintained that it was merely assisting the govern-ment to fight the drugs trade and terrorism. In 2011 the government of Bahrain invited troops from Saudi Arabia to suppress domestic protests. This last example illustrates that, although forcible intervention to assist a government may not violate the law on the use of force, it may be open to challenge on other grounds. Similarly, the right of the Assad gov-ernment to invite direct military assistance from Russia and Iran in Syria was attacked on political rather than legal grounds by Western States, but such an invitation cannot justify violations of human rights or international humanitarian law. There was also controversy about the legality of the interventions by Russia in Crimea (2014) and Saudi Arabia in Yemen (2013), as both relied on invitations by presidents who had been overthrown.

---

[23] *Armed Activities on the Territory of the Congo (Democratic Republic of the Congo v Uganda), Judgment, ICJ Reports 2005*, p 168.

In some recent conflicts, intervening States have justified their actions as designed to assist the inviting government against terrorists, rather than to intervene in a civil war. Thus, France gave this explanation for its military intervention in support of the government of Mali (2013); Iraq invited help from a number of States to enable it to resist the dramatic seizure of territory by ISIS (2014); the USA continues its long-lasting counter-terrorism operations in Afghanistan on the basis of an agreement with the government. The legality of these operations has not been contested. More controversially, the USA has justified its drone strikes in Yemen and Somalia as part of the war on Al-Qaeda, and thus as military assistance to governments in their struggle with terrorists, rather than as intervention in a civil war.

IV. SELF-DEFENCE

The main exception to the prohibition on the use of force in Article 2(4) is the right of self-defence. There are deep divisions between States and between scholars as to whether this right of self-defence is a wide or a narrow right (Corten, 2010). The controversy as to the scope of the right has intensified following the terrorist attacks of 11 September 2001. The basic UN Charter provision on self-defence is Article 51, which provides:

> Nothing in the present Charter shall impair the inherent right of individual or collective self-defence if an armed attack occurs against a Member of the United Nations, until the Security Council has taken measures necessary to maintain international peace and security. Measures taken by Members in the exercise of this right of self-defence shall be immediately reported to the Security Council and shall not in any way affect the authority and responsibility of the Security Council under the present Charter to take at any time such action as it deems necessary in order to maintain or restore international peace and security.

As a matter of treaty interpretation, the debate centres on whether Article 51 is an exhaustive statement of the right to self-defence or whether there is a wider customary law right of self-defence going beyond the right to respond to an armed attack. Those supporting a wide right of self-defence argue, first, that the reference to 'inherent right' in Article 51 preserves a customary law right of self-defence and, second, that such a customary law right is wider than Article 51 and allows self-defence other than against an armed attack (Bowett, 1958; Arend and Beck, 1993). They argue for a right of anticipatory self-defence and of protection of nationals abroad. Those against a wide view of self-defence argue that this interpretation deprives Article 51 of any purpose; Article 51 imposes restrictions on the right of self-defence in response to armed attack, and so it would be strange at the same time to preserve a wider right of self-defence unlimited by these restrictions. Also, as the right of self-defence is an exception to the prohibition on the use of force, it should be narrowly construed (Brownlie, 1963, p 251). Those arguing for a narrow right of self-defence also deny that customary law in 1945 included a wide right of self-defence which was preserved by Article 51. Given this fundamental disagreement on the proper interpretation of the UN Charter, State practice since 1945 is crucial for an understanding of the scope of the right of self-defence.

A. THE SCOPE OF SELF-DEFENCE: NECESSITY AND PROPORTIONALITY

Despite the fundamental disagreement on the scope of the right of self-defence, all are agreed that self-defence must be necessary and proportionate. This requirement of necessity and proportionality is not explicit in the UN Charter but is part of customary international law. It is generally taken as limiting self-defence to action which is necessary to recover territory or repel an attack on a State's forces and which is proportionate to this end. These customary law requirements of necessity and proportionality have been reaffirmed in the *Nicaragua* case,[24] the *Nuclear Weapons* Advisory Opinion,[25] the *Oil Platforms* case,[26] and *Armed Activities on the Territory of the Congo*.[27] The agreement between States that all self-defence should be necessary and proportionate makes it possible for them to reject many claims to self-defence on this basis without going into the more controversial doctrinal debates such as the existence of a right to anticipatory self-defence or the right to protect nationals or self-defence against terrorism.

B. THE MEANING OF 'ARMED ATTACK'

Article 51 specifies that self-defence is permissible in response to an armed attack. The definition of armed attack is left to customary international law. The most straightforward type of armed attack is that by a regular army of one State against the territory or against the land, sea, or air forces of another. The meaning of armed attack at sea was considered in some detail in the recent *Oil Platforms* case; mine and missile attacks aimed at US-flagged military ships could constitute 'armed attacks', but attacks on US-owned ships did not amount to attacks on the State. Recently there have been extensive but inconclusive debates as to whether cyber-attacks can constitute armed attacks; commentators are divided as to whether physical harm to people or property is necessary. States have yet to agree on rules to govern this special area.

'Armed attack' extends beyond attacks by regular forces; it can also cover attacks by armed bands, irregulars, and mercenaries. In the *Nicaragua* case the ICJ used the *Definition of Aggression* paragraph 3(g) to help interpret the meaning of armed attack in customary international law. It held that an armed attack must be understood as including 'the sending by or on behalf of a State of armed bands, groups, irregulars or mercenaries, which carry out acts of armed force against another State of such gravity as to amount to an actual armed attack, or its substantial involvement therein'. But the ICJ did not consider that the concept of armed attack stretched as far as assistance to rebels in the form of the provision of weapons or logistical or other support.[28] The Court's conception of armed attack clearly requires a significant degree of government involvement.

However, it has been argued that the 9/11 terrorist attacks by Al-Qaeda on the World Trade Center and Pentagon in the USA have further expanded the notion of armed attack to cover the use of force by terrorist organizations, even in the absence of State involvement in the attack. The Security Council stopped short of an express pronouncement that the terrorist attack amounted to an 'armed attack', preferring to characterize it as a 'threat to the peace', but it did affirm the right of self-defence in the preambles to Resolutions 1368 and 1373 condemning the terrorist attacks;[29] this may amount to an implicit acceptance

---

[24] *Military and Paramilitary Activities in and against Nicaragua (Nicaragua v United States of America), Merits, Judgment, ICJ Reports 1986*, p 14, para 194.

[25] *Legality of the Threat or Use of Nuclear Weapons, Advisory Opinion, ICJ Reports 1996*, p 266, para 141.

[26] *Oil Platforms (Islamic Republic of Iran v United States of America), ICJ Reports 2003*, p 161.

[27] *Armed Activities on the Territory of the Congo (Democratic Republic of the Congo v Uganda), Judgment, ICJ Reports 2005*, p 168.

[28] *Military and Paramilitary Activities in and against Nicaragua (Nicaragua v United States of America), Merits, Judgment, ICJ Reports 1986*, p 14, para 195. These types of assistance could nevertheless constitute unlawful intervention.   [29] SC Res 1368 (12 September 2001); SC Res 1373 (28 September 2001).

that the terrorist attacks on the USA were armed attacks, but it leaves unclear the exact nature of Afghanistan's involvement in the actions of Al-Qaeda terrorists. Similar questions arose about Hezbollah's attacks on Israel from Lebanon, Hamas' rocket attacks on Israel from Gaza, and attacks by the PKK (Kurdish terrorists) on Turkey from Iraq: could these be classified as armed attacks giving a right to use force in response? What degree of State involvement is necessary to allow self-defence against Lebanon and Iraq? The law on this question remains controversial, and the ICJ deliberately avoided pronouncing on it in *Armed Activities on the Territory of the Congo*.[30]

C. THE USE OF FORCE IN PROTECTION OF NATIONALS

One controversy as to the scope of self-defence concerns the right of States to use force to protect their nationals abroad (Ronzitti, 1985). This right has been asserted by developed States such as the USA, the UK, and Israel under Article 51. It has been exercised in practice by the USA in the Dominican Republic (1965), Grenada (1983), and Panama (1989); by the UK in Suez (1956); and by Israel in Entebbe (1976). Most recently it has been invoked by Russia to justify its use of force against Georgia (2008). Developing States are more doubtful about the existence of this right. Where the host State consents or acquiesces or where there is no effective government, there is not usually a hostile response by other States if the forcible action is limited to the evacuation of nationals and not a pretext for more far-reaching intervention.

One of the most discussed and most controversial examples of the use of force to protect nationals abroad was by the USA in the small Caribbean island of Grenada.[31] The USA relied on a series of justifications for sending forces into Grenada in response to a coup which brought a socialist government to power. One of its arguments was that US nationals were under threat and that the operation was designed to rescue them. But there was considerable doubt as to the existence of the danger, and the use of force was condemned by the UN General Assembly. In the Security Council the USA vetoed the resolution condemning its intervention. One of the grounds for doubt about the legality of the US operation, insofar as it was based on protection of nationals, was that the use of force went beyond what was necessary and proportionate. All too often the protection of nationals is a mere pretext to mask the real intent of overthrowing the government; this was the case in all the episodes listed earlier, with the exception of the Entebbe intervention. Even here a majority of States did not accept the legality of the intervention, though there was sympathy for Israel's position.[32]

When Russia invoked the protection of nationals to justify its use of force against Georgia, Western States did not oppose this doctrine as a matter of principle. Instead they challenged Russia's motives and the proportionality of its action. In August 2008 Georgia mounted a military action to assert control over separatists in the region of South Ossetia.[33] Russia's response was to send troops into South Ossetia to protect its nationals; many ethnic Ossetians held Russian passports. The conflict spread to Abkhazia, another area of separatist conflict, and Russia went on to attack military bases and transport links throughout Georgia. Georgia was forced to withdraw its forces from South Ossetia and Abkhazia, which subsequently proclaimed their independence. Western States asserted that Russia's intervention was unlawful because it was not limited to the protection of its

---

[30] *Armed Activities on the Territory of the Congo (Democratic Republic of the Congo v Uganda), Judgment,* ICJ Reports 2005, p 168, para 147.   [31] 1983 *UNYB* 211.

[32] 1976 *UNYB* 315.

[33] 2009 Report by Independent International Fact-Finding Mission http://www.ceiig.ch/Report.html.

nationals, but was really designed to lead to the dismemberment of Georgia and the independence of South Ossetia and Abkhazia.

D. ANTICIPATORY OR PRE-EMPTIVE SELF-DEFENCE

Another major controversy over the scope of self-defence concerns the right of 'anticipatory' self-defence; that is, does the right of a State to self-defence arise only after an armed attack has started under Article 51 or is there a wider right to anticipate an *imminent* attack? Is there even a right of pre-emptive self-defence where there is no imminent attack? The controversy over the legality of anticipatory self-defence was so strong that no provision on self-defence could be included in the UN General Assembly resolutions such as the *Definition of Aggression* and the *Declaration on Friendly Relations*. States such as the USA, the UK, and Israel have claimed a wide right of self-defence, but the doctrine is so controversial that such claims have been rare in practice. Although the USA has sometimes adopted wide Rules of Engagement which allow its own forces to use force in response to demonstrations of 'hostile intent' by opposing forces rather than requiring them to wait for an actual armed attack, it has tended to play down any anticipatory element in operations such as those by its naval convoys in the Gulf during the 1980–88 Iran/Iraq War, and those by its aircraft over the no-fly zones proclaimed in Iraq to protect the civilian population after Iraq invaded Kuwait in 1990. Thus, in the case of the shooting down of the civilian Iran Airbus by the *USS Vincennes* in 1988, an incident which may be taken to show the hazards of anticipatory self-defence, the USA argued that it had acted in the context of an ongoing armed attack on its naval convoy in the Gulf to respond to what it (mistakenly) believed to be imminent attack by a hostile Iranian military aircraft. Iran took the case to the ICJ, but it was settled without the need for the Court to make any authoritative pronouncement on anticipatory self-defence. Similarly in the *Oil Platforms* case the USA preferred to rely on an extensive notion of armed attack rather than claim any right of anticipatory self-defence.

The express invocation of self-defence by Israel to justify its pre-emptive attack on an Iraqi nuclear reactor in 1981 was therefore unusual. Israel (itself a nuclear weapons State) argued that the Iraqi reactor under construction was designed to produce nuclear weapons for use against Israel and therefore that it was entitled to take pre-emptive action. This attack was condemned by both the Security Council and by the General Assembly, but the resolutions do not directly address the fundamental doctrinal issue; it is left open to question whether the condemnation should be taken as a total rejection of anticipatory self-defence (as many States had argued) or just a rejection on the particular facts (as was the position of the USA).[34]

Those in favour of a right to anticipatory self-defence against an imminent attack argue that it is not realistic to expect States to wait for an attack before responding; those against argue that anticipatory self-defence involves a risk of escalation in that the State may mistake the intentions of the other or react disproportionately. The ICJ in the *Nicaragua* case deliberately left the matter unresolved.[35] It did so again in *Armed Activities on the Territory of the Congo* (2005), a clear indication of the controversial nature of the doctrine.[36]

---

[34] 1981 *UNYB* 275.

[35] *Military and Paramilitary Activities in and against Nicaragua (Nicaragua v United States of America)*, Merits, Judgment, *ICJ Reports 1986*, p 14, para 194.

[36] *Armed Activities on the Territory of the Congo (Democratic Republic of the Congo v Uganda)*, Judgment, *ICJ Reports 2005*, p 168, para 143.

E. THE IMPACT OF THE TERRORIST ATTACKS OF 9/11 ON THE LAW OF SELF-DEFENCE

The attacks by Al-Qaeda on the World Trade Center and the Pentagon on 11 September 2001 brought a revolutionary challenge to the doctrine of self-defence.[37] Before 9/11 the use of force in response to terrorist attacks had been controversial; only Israel and the USA had expressly claimed such a right, and this was generally exercised in response to attacks on nationals abroad. There was no general support for such a right. In response to the 9/11 attacks on US territory, the USA began *Operation Enduring Freedom* with the aim of disrupting the use of Afghanistan as a terrorist base. It relied on self-defence as the basis for its use of force against Afghanistan; in its report to the Security Council under Article 51 the USA claimed to be acting in self-defence. This claim may seem controversial in the light of the previous doubts as to whether the right to self-defence could extend to action against past terrorist attacks, but *Operation Enduring Freedom* received massive support and the action was almost universally accepted as self-defence. NATO invoked Article 5 of the NATO Treaty for the first time; this provides that an attack on one member State is an attack on all. Other collective self-defence organizations, including the Organization of American States (OAS), also took the view that the attack was an armed attack for the purposes of collective self-defence. The EU, China, Russia, Japan, and Pakistan supported this view. Many States played a role in the military campaign. Only Iran and Iraq expressly challenged the legality of the operation. In the preambles of Resolution 1368 condemning the attacks and Resolution 1373 on measures against international terrorism the Security Council recognized the right of self-defence in general terms. This was the first time that the Security Council had implicitly recognized the right to use force in self-defence in the context of terrorist action, and several States regarded this Security Council backing as crucial to the US claim to self-defence.

This use of force against Afghanistan raised many questions about the traditional model of self-defence. First, did the response to 9/11 widen the concept of armed attack? The USA and the UK in their letters to the Security Council accused the government of Afghanistan of support for Al-Qaeda, but there was uncertainty about the degree of State complicity required to justify a military response to terrorist attacks. Second, did State practice following 9/11 support anticipatory or pre-emptive self-defence against future attacks? Both the USA and the UK in their letters to the Security Council said that their military action was in response to the attack on the World Trade Center and the Pentagon; for the USA the aim was to deter further attacks on the USA, for the UK 'to avert the continuing threat of attacks from the same source'. That is, although the initial attack had ended and thus it would be difficult to invoke self-defence against that attack, the USA and the UK clearly felt the need to avoid the appearance of punitive (and unlawful) reprisals. Third, questions arose as to necessity and proportionality. The USA at the start of *Operation Enduring Freedom* warned that the 'global war on terror' could take many years. In a campaign to prevent future terrorist attacks it is difficult to identify an appropriate end to the action, but the longer it continues and the more destruction it involves the more difficult it is to argue that it is proportionate. If the use of force proves ineffective in deterring terrorist attacks, it is also difficult to argue that it is necessary. *Operation Enduring Freedom* finally terminated at the end of 2014, but a substantial US counter-terrorism force remains in Afghanistan on the basis of a continuing right of self-defence against Al-Qaeda.

The drafters of Article 51 originally envisaged self-defence against an attack by a State, and those invoking the right generally took care to attribute responsibility to a State. After

---

[37] See account of the facts in (2002) 96 *AJIL* 237, and editorial comments in (2001) 95 *AJIL* 833.

9/11 some States argued that the words of Article 51 are wide enough to mean that a terrorist attack on a State's territory by a non-State actor may be an armed attack which justifies a response against the State which harboured those responsible. However, considerable uncertainty remained as to the degree of State involvement required, and as to whether force could be used in self-defence against terrorists in a State which was not complicit in the terrorist attack (Becker, 2006). The ICJ did not elaborate on the law in this controversial area in *Armed Activities on the Territory of the Congo* and the *Wall* Advisory Opinion, but some commentators took an extensive view of the legal significance of 9/11 and its aftermath (Tams, 2009).

Since 9/11 the USA has developed a wide doctrine of self-defence in counter-terrorism operations.[38] First, the drone warfare initiated by President Bush and expanded by President Obama involved the 'targeted killing' of members of Al-Qaeda and affiliated groups not only in Afghanistan, but also in States such as Pakistan, Somalia, and Yemen which were at that time (according to the USA) 'unwilling or unable' to act against the terrorists. The USA then applied this doctrine to justify its military intervention against ISIS in Syria. In 2014 it claimed that it was acting in collective self-defence of Iraq to protect it against attacks by ISIS from Syria; it also claimed individual self-defence to protect itself from 'imminent' terrorist attacks. Its legal argument was that self-defence was necessary because Syria was unwilling or unable to act against ISIS. Several other States participated in the military operations, but only Australia, Canada, and Turkey gave their express support to the 'unwilling or unable' doctrine. France, which joined in the military operations against ISIS after the November 2015 terrorist attacks on Paris, did not adopt this doctrine. It regarded this military operation as an exceptional case: it did not generally support the doctrine of self-defence against non-State actors (Alabrune, 2016). Other States that joined in the military action against ISIS in Syria attached critical importance to Security Council Resolution 2249 (2015) passed in response to the Paris attacks. Although this did not authorize force under Chapter VII of the UN Charter and did not mention self-defence, it identified ISIS as a global and unprecedented threat to international peace and security, and called on States to take all necessary measures, in compliance with international law, against ISIS.

The 'unwilling or unable' doctrine is problematic in its application to the Syrian conflict and in general. Syria asserts that it is not unwilling to act against ISIS. Nor does the inability of a State to act mean that it is no longer possible to seek its consent for military intervention against terrorists on its territory. This is clearly a subjective doctrine that does not impose effective constraints on a State's use of force, and one that is difficult to reconcile with the prohibition on the use of force in Article 2(4) and with the Charter principle of the equality of States. It effectively enables rather than limits the use of force.

The USA has also taken a very wide view of the meaning of 'imminence' in its targeted killing programme and in its wider counter-terrorism policy. The focus is no longer on imminence in time: several other factors are also to be taken into account, including the likely scale of the attack and of the injury likely to result and the likelihood that there will be other opportunities to undertake action in self-defence. The absence of specific evidence of where an attack will take place or of the precise nature of an attack does not preclude the conclusion that an armed attack is imminent. This interpretation of imminence clearly offers an extremely wide discretion to the State claiming the right to use force in self-defence.

---

[38] Legal and Policy Frameworks Guiding the US Use of Military Force and Related National Security Operations, 5 December 2016, https://obamawhitehouse.archives.gov/sites/whitehouse.gov/files/documents/Legal_Policy_Report.pdf.

It is unlikely that the US counter-terrorism doctrine of self-defence represents custom-ary international law. It does not have the widespread and uniform support necessary to limit the fundamental prohibition on the use of force in Article 2(4). It is true that few States are willing to speak out openly against the USA, but the Non-Aligned Movement (of 120 States) has since 9/11 consistently reaffirmed its view that Article 51 is restrictive and should not be rewritten or reinterpreted.[39]

F. A 'BUSH DOCTRINE' OF PRE-EMPTIVE SELF-DEFENCE AGAINST THE PROLIFERATION OF NUCLEAR WEAPONS?

After it had initiated *Operation Enduring Freedom* in Afghanistan, the USA shifted its focus in the 'global war on terror' to the threat posed by the 'Axis of Evil': Iran, Iraq, and North Korea. In the light of the alleged new dangers facing it after 9/11, the USA developed a new *National Security Strategy* (2002): the USA must be prepared to stop rogue States and global terrorists from threatening to use weapons of mass destruc-tion against it.[40] Accordingly it asserted that there was a need to re-examine the law of self-defence. The USA had always taken the wide view that anticipatory self-de-fence was lawful in the case of an imminent armed attack, but now it argued that the requirement of imminence should be reconsidered. However, it did not make clear what would trigger such pre-emptive (or preventive) action. The 2006 US *National Security Strategy* repeated the commitment to pre-emptive self-defence, but did not elaborate further.

There is little sign of support for a fundamental transformation of self-defence along the lines suggested in the US *National Security Strategy* under President Bush. The UN set up a High-level Panel of Experts to respond to the new challenges to the collective security system after 9/11; in its Report of December 2004 it accepted the controversial right of anticipatory self-defence, but firmly rejected the doctrine of pre-emptive self-defence.[41] It said that there is no right to self-defence if the threat of armed attack is not imminent. If there are good arguments for preventive military action, with good evi-dence to support them, they should be put to the Security Council which can authorize action if it chooses to. A unilateral right of pre-emptive self-defence would be danger-ously destabilizing. Similarly, the ICJ in *Armed Activities on the Territory of the Congo* (2005) said that Article 51 may justify a use of force in self-defence only within the strict confines there laid down. It does not allow the use of force by a State to protect perceived security interests beyond those parameters. Other means are available to a concerned State, including recourse to the Security Council.[42] Thus, the UK supports anticipatory self-defence but rejects a wider doctrine of pre-emptive self-defence. The USA has not ruled out the use of force against Iran or North Korea to prevent their development of nuclear weapons, but it has not attempted to provide any legal justification for such ac-tion. The destabilizing effects of this doctrine were apparent in the 2017 exchanges of threats between North Korea and the USA.

---

[39] UN Doc S/2014/573, para 299. It reaffirmed this position in 2016.   [40] (2002) 41 ILM 1478.

[41] Report of the Secretary-General's High-level Panel on Threats, Challenges and Change, UN Doc A/59/565. The UN Secretary-General in his response to the High-level Panel, 'In Larger Freedom' (March 2005), also accepted this previously controversial doctrine, although in more cautious terms, saying that 'imminent threats are fully covered by Article 51' (UN Doc A/59/2005). The Non-Aligned Movement reaffirmed its rejection of a wide doctrine of self-defence.

[42] *Armed Activities on the Territory of the Congo (Democratic Republic of the Congo v Uganda), Judgment, ICJ Reports 2005*, p 168.

G. COLLECTIVE SELF-DEFENCE

The express provision for collective self-defence in Article 51 of the UN Charter is generally seen as an innovation, included in response to the desire of Latin American States
to retain regional autonomy. The right of collective self-defence formed the basis for the
NATO Treaty and the Warsaw Pact and for many regional treaties after the Second World
War; these treaties provided that an attack on one was an attack on all and provided for a
collective response. As mentioned earlier, NATO invoked Article 5 for the first time with
regard to the 9/11 attacks. However, the USA chose not to act through NATO (or the UN).
It took the major role in *Operation Enduring Freedom* against Afghanistan, but it received
some assistance from other States acting in collective self-defence. Opinion is divided as
to whether collective self-defence is a valuable safeguard for small States or a dangerous
doctrine justifying intervention by distant and powerful States in remote conflicts. It was
not often invoked during the Cold War and the few instances where it was invoked—such
as the USA in the Vietnam War (1961–75) and in Nicaragua, and the USSR interventions
in Hungary (1956), Czechoslovakia (1968), and Afghanistan (1979)—were controversial.
In all these cases there was dispute as to whether there had been an armed attack or a
genuine request for help from the victim State.

The *Nicaragua* case played a crucial role in establishing the scope of the right of collective self-defence. The USA had attempted to justify its use of force against Nicaragua by
relying on collective self-defence, but the ICJ held that the use of force by the USA did not
satisfy any of the criteria for legitimate collective self-defence. There had been no armed
attack by Nicaragua on Costa Rica, El Salvador, or Honduras, no declaration by any of
these States that it was the victim of an armed attack, and no invitation by them to the
USA to come to their aid. Finally, the mining of harbours and bombing of ports by the
USA was not necessary to repel alleged attacks by Nicaragua on El Salvador, and was not
proportionate. The USA had not reported its actions to the Security Council under Article
51. The ICJ decision was controversial at the time, but accurately reflects State practice on
collective self-defence.

The protracted conflict in Syria demonstrated the complexities of collective self-defence. First, Iraq asked the USA and other States for military help against ISIS not only on
its own territory but also in Iraq. But some of the States coming to its aid also claimed to
be acting in individual self-defence. Second, France also invited assistance against ISIS in
Syria after the Paris terrorist attacks. Like the USA after 9/11, it chose not to act through
NATO, but instead turned to individual EU Member States for bilateral help. The States
taking part in the military operations in Syria did not always make clear the exact nature
of their involvement. The question whether their operations were in collective self-defence
of Iraq or of France, or individual self-defence to protect themselves against attacks from
ISIS, is important because it affects the type of action to be taken, and the question which
State can decide on the scope of military action and determine when there is no further
need for self-defence.

H. THE ROLE OF THE SECURITY COUNCIL

In theory the Security Council has a central role with regard to individual and collective
self-defence: under Article 51 States must report their use of force in self-defence to the
Security Council immediately and the right of the State to self-defence is temporary until
the Security Council takes the measures necessary to maintain international peace and
security. In practice the Security Council does not generally make pronouncements on
the legality of claims to self-defence. Thus in the case of inter-State conflict between Iran

and Iraq (1980–88) and Ethiopia and Eritrea (1998–2000) the Security Council did not initially attribute responsibility for the start of the conflict, and did not decide who had the right of self-defence. In contrast when Iraq invaded Kuwait in 1990 the Security Council did expressly uphold the right of Kuwait to self-defence.

States have taken care to report their self-defence to the Security Council, especially since the *Nicaragua* case where the Court held that the failure by the USA to report its use of force to the Security Council was an indication that the USA was not itself convinced that it was acting in self-defence. This approach was followed in *Armed Activities on the Territory of the Congo*[43] and by the Eritrea/Ethiopia Claims Commission.[44] In the past there has been some controversy as to whether the right to self-defence has been terminated because the Security Council has taken action and thus has taken 'measures necessary to maintain international peace and security'. It seems to be generally accepted that it is not enough for the Security Council simply to pass a resolution or even to impose economic measures if the aggressor is left in occupation of territory it has seized illegally. This was the argument of the UK with regard to the Falkland Islands (Islas Malvinas); it claimed the right to use force in self-defence when Argentina seized the Falklands despite the Security Council resolutions calling for a peaceful resolution. The UK argued that it retained its right to self-defence until Argentina was driven out.[45] Unless the Security Council has expressly passed a binding resolution declaring the right to be terminated, there will be room for doubt on this issue. If a State wishes to make the position clear, it should try to secure an express recognition of its right by the Security Council. Thus in the Iraq/Kuwait conflict, even when economic measures were taken by the Security Council, in the same resolution it affirmed the right of self-defence;[46] and in regard to the 9/11 attacks the Security Council expressly referred to the continuing right to self-defence.[47]

V. THE USE OF FORCE UNDER CHAPTER VII OF THE UN CHARTER

The original intent behind the UN Charter was that control over the use of force would lie with the Security Council which would have a standing army at its disposal to enable it to take enforcement action against aggression in order to restore international peace and security. This ambitious plan has not been realized and the original Charter scheme has been modified through practice. Under Article 24 of the UN Charter the Security Council has the primary responsibility for the maintenance of international peace and security, but during the Cold War the veto possessed by the five permanent members of the Security Council under Article 27 generally blocked effective action by the Security Council. Chapter VII sets out the framework for its enforcement powers; under Article 2(7) these powers are not limited by the normal duty on the UN not to intervene in matters essentially within the domestic jurisdiction of States. Thus Chapter VII gives very wide powers to the Security Council. For many years the Council typically did not make express reference to specific Articles within Chapter VII; it more commonly made a reference to Chapter VII in general terms (Sarooshi, 1999). However, since the use of force against Iraq in 2003, it has become more common for the Security Council to refer to Article 41; certain members of the Security Council have ensured that its resolutions on

---

[43] *Armed Activities on the Territory of the Congo (Democratic Republic of the Congo v Uganda), Judgment, ICJ Reports 2005*, p 168, para 145.   [44] See Ethiopia's *Ius ad Bellum* claims 1–8 (2006) 45 ILM 430.
[45] 1982 *UNYB* 1320.   [46] SC Res 661 (16 August 1990).
[47] SC Res 1368 (12 September 2001), 1373 (14 November 2001).

Iran and North Korea (concerning the proliferation of nuclear weapons) refer expressly to specific Charter Articles, in order to prevent any invocation of those resolutions to justify the use of force.

Under Article 39 the Security Council is 'to determine the existence of any threat to the peace, breach of the peace or act of aggression' and then to make recommendations or decide measures under Articles 41 and 42. The Council has been reluctant to find an act of aggression under Article 39; rare examples are resolutions condemning South Africa (under the apartheid regime) and Israel for attacks on neighbouring States. It has determined the existence of a breach of the peace only in cases of inter-State conflicts as in the 1980–88 Iran/Iraq conflict and in response to the 1990 Iraqi invasion of Kuwait.

The Security Council has consistently taken a wide view of 'threat to the peace' and has been prepared to identify such a threat as arising out of internal conflicts such as those in the DRC and Somalia, overthrow of democratic government as in Haiti, and refusal to act against terrorism in the cases of Libya, Sudan, and the Taliban regime in Afghanistan. It is not clear whether any other body such as the ICJ would have the power to challenge a finding under Article 39 by the Security Council. The Court has never made an authoritative ruling on the matter; it avoided the issue in the *Lockerbie*[48] and *Bosnia-Herzegovina Genocide* cases.[49]

Article 40 provides for provisional measures and the Security Council has invoked this as the basis for its call for cease-fires as, for example, in Resolution 598 (1987) with regard to the 1980–88 Iran/Iraq conflict.

A. MEASURES UNDER ARTICLE 41

Article 41 allows the Security Council to decide on measures not involving the use of armed force to give effect to its decisions; these include 'complete or partial interruption of economic relations and of rail, sea, air, postal, telegraphic, radio, and other means of communication, and the severance of diplomatic relations'. Article 41 was little used in the Cold War: only in the comprehensive trade embargo on the illegal white minority government in Rhodesia (now Zimbabwe) in a series of resolutions from 1965 and in the arms embargo on South Africa in 1977. But there has been a massive increase in the use of Article 41 since then (Gray, 2018, p 275). Since the comprehensive embargo on Iraq under Resolution 687 (1991) there has been increasing concern about the effects of trade embargoes on 'innocent' populations and the Security Council has attempted to develop 'smart' sanctions, targeted on those responsible for any non-compliance with its decisions. The official position is that Article 41 measures are not punishment, but should be designed to secure compliance with decisions of the Security Council. They have been imposed on States, and also on non-State actors that obstruct peace processes, and on individual members of terrorist groups such as Al-Qaeda and ISIS. Recently they were imposed on Iran and North Korea in an attempt to halt their development of nuclear weapons; these resolutions refer expressly to Article 41 in order to prevent any argument that they could be invoked to justify the use of force. In many civil wars the imposition of an arms embargo is the immediate response of the Security Council to calls for it to act; thus arms embargoes were imposed in response to civil war in Yugoslavia, Somalia and Rwanda, and Libya.

---

[48] *Questions of Interpretation and Application of the 1971 Montreal Convention arising from the Aerial Incident at Lockerbie (Libyan Arab Jamahirya v United States of America), Preliminary Objections, Judgment, ICJ Reports 1998*, p 115.

[49] *Application of the Convention on the Prevention and Punishment of the Crime of Genocide, Provisional Measures, Order of 8 April 1993, ICJ Reports 1993*, p 3, *Order of 13 September, ICJ Reports 1993*, p 325.

B. THE USE OF FORCE UNDER CHAPTER VII OF THE UN CHARTER

In cases where Article 41 measures would not be sufficient or had proved insufficient to maintain or restore international peace and security, the original Charter scheme under Articles 42–9 was that the UN would have its own standing army able to take measures involving armed force. Member States were to make agreements to put troops at the disposal of the Security Council which would 'take such action by air, sea or land forces as may be necessary to maintain or restore international peace and security' under Article 42. But in practice member States did not conclude agreements to put troops at the disposal of the UN under Article 43 and no standing army was created. Cold War divisions help to explain this failure to implement the Charter scheme, but even today States remain unwilling to hand over control of troops for enforcement action. Because of the failure of States to conclude agreements under Article 43 there was a doctrinal debate as to whether the whole Charter scheme was therefore frustrated and Article 42 was inoperative (Simma, 2012, p 1337).

However, the Security Council interpreted Chapter VII flexibly to authorize the establishment of a UN force in Korea in 1950. Although it did not make clear the exact constitutional basis for its actions, it referred to Chapter VII in general terms. When North Korea invaded South Korea in 1950 the Security Council intervened, although neither was a member State; it recommended member States to 'furnish such assistance to South Korea as may be necessary to repel the armed attack and to restore international peace and security in the area'. There was heated debate at the time as to the legal basis for this action, especially as the Security Council was able to act only because the USSR had stayed away from the relevant meeting in protest at the representation of China by the Taiwan government rather than the effective Communist government. Commentators disagreed as to whether this was collective security under Article 39, 42, or Chapter VII generally, or whether it was only an authorization of collective self-defence. The debate leading to the Security Council decision sheds no light on this dilemma and it appears to have little practical significance.

No further forcible action was authorized under Chapter VII until the end of the Cold War. When Iraq invaded Kuwait in 1990 the Security Council passed Resolution 678 (1990) authorizing member States to use 'all necessary means to secure the withdrawal of Iraqi troops and to restore international peace and security in the area'.[50] It is clear from the Security Council debates that the phrase 'all necessary means' was intended to cover the use of force. The action against Iraq in *Operation Desert Storm* was seen at the time as the beginning of a new era for the Security Council, the start of a New World Order. In contrast with Korea the force did not operate under the UN flag, but it did act under the authorization of the Security Council, even if the precise constitutional basis was again unclear.

This use of Chapter VII to authorize member States to use force has been repeated many times in many different situations. It has certainly become clear that Chapter VII action is not limited to collective self-defence. The Security Council has not again authorized force against an aggressor State, but it has authorized force in internal conflicts, for example in response to non-cooperation with UN-brokered cease-fires; to secure the delivery of humanitarian aid as in Somalia and in Yugoslavia; to protect safe havens and enforce no-fly zones in Bosnia-Herzegovina; to restore democracy in Haiti; to act against Somali pirates; to support the government of Mali in recovering control of its territory from terrorists and armed groups; as well as to secure the implementation of economic measures under Article 41. A controversial recent instance of the authorization of force by the Security Council was

---

[50] SC Res 678 (29 April 1990).

in Libya. In Resolution 1973 (2011) the Security Council authorized member States to use 'all necessary means' to protect civilians and civilian populated areas under threat of attack. There were deep divisions between States as to whether the ensuing military operations went beyond the scope of this authority (Ulfstein and Christiansen, 2013). The Security Council has also authorized substantial member State forces to maintain order and engage in peacebuilding after the end of conflicts in East Timor, Kosovo, Afghanistan, and Iraq.

The UN Secretary-General recognizes that the UN does not itself have the resources for enforcement action, and that it will have to continue to turn to 'coalitions of the willing' or to regional organizations, but he acknowledges that there is a danger that the UN may be sidelined. The Security Council has made greater attempts to keep some control of the member State forces since *Operation Desert Storm* when it set no time-limit for the operation against Iraq. The mandates authorizing member States to use force are now usually for a fixed period and they may stress the need for impartiality; States are required to report regularly to the Security Council.

C. IMPLIED OR REVIVED AUTHORIZATION OF FORCE?

More controversial than the express authorization of member States to use force under Chapter VII has been the issue of implied or revived authorization (Lobel and Ratner, 1999). States seeking legitimacy for their use of force but unable or unwilling to obtain a Chapter VII resolution have sought to rely on implied or revived authorization. NATO's legal justification for its 1999 air campaign against the government of Yugoslavia to end repression in Kosovo was brief, but there were indications that it claimed implied authorization under Security Council Resolutions 1160 (1998), 1199 (1998), and 1203 (1998). Those impatient with the difficulty of securing agreement from China and Russia to the use of force even after the end of the Cold War argued that there was no need for express authorization of the use of force. It was enough that the resolutions identified a threat to international peace and security under Chapter VII, made certain demands on Yugoslavia, and determined that it had violated international agreements. This interpretation of the relevant Security Council resolutions was strongly resisted by Russia and China as a distortion of the words of the resolutions, not justified in the light of the Security Council debates, and a dangerous threat to the authority of the Security Council.

1. Operation Iraqi Freedom (2003)

These arguments arose again over *Operation Iraqi Freedom* in March 2003. Deep divisions as to the legality of the use of force against Iraq existed not only between the USA and China and Russia, but also within NATO and Europe. The USA, the UK, and Australia (with the support of a 'coalition' of about 45 other States including Spain, Poland, and others from eastern Europe) undertook *Operation Iraqi Freedom* to secure the disarmament of Iraq of weapons of mass destruction. The legal justification they offered was that they were acting on the basis of Security Council authority under a combination of three resolutions (678, 687, and 1444) adopted under Chapter VII of the Charter.[51] They claimed that military operations were necessary because of the threat posed by Iraq's alleged development of weapons of mass destruction in violation of its disarmament obligations. Other States such as Russia, China, France, and Germany argued for the continuation of UN weapons inspections; military action was not necessary.

---

[51] For the UK case, see 52 *ICLQ* (2003) 811. The US position has been set out in Taft and Buchwald, 2003, p 553. For a description of the sequence of events, see Murphy, 2003, p 419.

Only the USA invoked (pre-emptive) self-defence as a possible basis for *Operation Iraqi Freedom* and it did not provide any detailed justification of this position; the UK and Australia did not rely on this doctrine. After *Operation Iraqi Freedom* drove Saddam Hussein from power in April 2003 it became apparent that Iraq did not possess weapons of mass destruction or the immediate capacity to produce them. Serious doubts emerged about the intelligence on the basis of which the use of force had been justified, and for many this provided a dramatic illustration of the dangers of pre-emptive action.

The argument as to the legality of *Operation Iraqi Freedom* turned on the interpretation of the three Security Council resolutions. Resolution 1441 was passed unanimously in November 2002 to give Iraq a 'final opportunity' to comply with its disarmament obligations imposed under the cease-fire regime.[52] The Security Council recalled its earlier resolutions and, acting under Chapter VII, decided that Iraq had been and remained in material breach of its obligations under Resolution 687 (1991), the cease-fire regime imposed by the Security Council requiring Iraq to disarm its weapons of mass destruction and to cooperate with UN weapons inspectors.[53] The UN weapons inspectors were to return to Iraq under an enhanced system of weapons inspection and Iraq was to provide a complete declaration of all aspects of its weapons programme; any omissions would constitute a further material breach by Iraq. In the event of reports of non-compliance the Security Council would reconvene to consider the situation. Resolution 1441 clearly did not expressly authorize force against Iraq; several permanent members of the Security Council were not willing to agree to such authorization.

Following this resolution Iraq produced a lengthy declaration on the state of its weapons programme and UN weapons inspectors returned to Iraq. The USA and the UK argued that Iraq was in material breach of its obligations, but there was no such formal determination by the Security Council itself. The USA and the UK tried to secure a second resolution expressly authorizing force against Iraq, but failed to convince other member States that military action was justified. They then proceeded to argue that no second resolution was necessary: Resolution 1441 had not expressly required a second resolution; its effect was to revive the authority to use force given in Resolution 678 (1991) in the event of material breach by Iraq of disarmament requirements under the cease-fire regime established by Resolution 687.

The main problems with this line of argument are, first, that it relies on the revival of Resolution 678, passed 12 years earlier in response to Iraq's invasion of Kuwait. Those supporting *Operation Iraqi Freedom* argued that the authorization to use force in Resolution 678 could be revived as it had been suspended but not terminated by the cease-fire in Resolution 687. Resolution 678 did not contain any time-limit and Iraq continued to pose a threat to international peace and security. Second, the 'coalition' case assumed that it was possible for them unilaterally to determine that there had been a material breach by Iraq and that the use of force was justified. States opposed to the use of force, such as Russia and China, argued that such decisions were exclusively for the Security Council; this was also the view of the UN Secretary-General.

VI. UN PEACEKEEPING

A. THE INCEPTION OF PEACEKEEPING

UN peacekeeping is not expressly provided for in the UN Charter; it developed through practice during the Cold War (Higgins, 1969–81). When the UN Security Council proved

---

[52] SC Res 1441 (8 November 2002).   [53] SC Res 687 (3 April 1991).

unable to take action in response to breaches of the peace, threats to the peace, and acts of aggression, because its decision-making was obstructed by the divisions between the Western and Eastern blocs, peacekeeping was developed as a partial substitute. The General Assembly initially took on a (controversial) role in this area under the *Uniting for Peace Resolution* (1950)[54] which allowed it to call emergency meetings and make recommendations to States on the use of force when the Security Council was prevented from acting by the lack of unanimity of the permanent members. The *Certain Expenses* Advisory Opinion[55] considered the constitutionality of a force set up by the General Assembly: could member States be required to pay the expenses of such operations? The ICJ held that, although the Security Council had primary responsibility for the maintenance of international peace and security under Article 24, this was primary and not exclusive; it was open to the General Assembly to recommend peacekeeping but not to decide on enforcement action which was the exclusive province of the Security Council.

In practice it has been the Security Council which has subsequently exercised the main responsibility for peacekeeping. The UN Charter does not make any express provision for peacekeeping and its precise constitutional basis remains unclear, but discussion now centres on the nature rather than on the legality of the institution. There was initially a clear distinction between peacekeeping and Chapter VII enforcement action, but the peacekeeping label has come to cover a wide range of operations and the distinctions between peacekeeping and enforcement action have blurred. From 1948 to 1988 15 peacekeeping forces were created (United Nations, 1996). The first major force was UNEF, established by the General Assembly in the Middle East from 1956 to 1967; the principles on which this operation was based provided guidelines for future operations. UNEF was established with the consent of the host State and was terminated when Egypt withdrew its consent; it was an impartial and neutral force and used force only in self-defence. Like UNEF, most Cold War peacekeeping operations functioned between States, and most were limited operations mandated only to monitor cease-fires or borders. The five permanent members of the Security Council generally did not take part in peacekeeping forces in order to insulate peacekeeping from Cold War divisions, and States with historic or geographical interests in the conflict were also excluded.

ONUC was the second major peacekeeping operation and it departed to some extent from the guidelines described earlier. It operated within the Congo which had descended into chaos on the withdrawal of the colonial power in 1960. The original mandate of ONUC was expanded to allow the use of force beyond self-defence; the Security Council used the language of Chapter VII in authorizing force to prevent the occurrence of civil war and the secession of the province of Katanga, but made no express reference to it.

Five of the first 15 peacekeeping forces are still in existence: three in the Middle East, one in Kashmir, and one in Cyprus; this reflects the danger that a peacekeeping force may simply freeze a situation.

B. PEACEKEEPING AFTER THE END OF THE COLD WAR

After the end of the Cold War the Security Council expanded its peacekeeping functions and there is now a continuing debate about the nature of peacekeeping. Over 50 new peacekeeping forces have been created, most within States. UN peacekeeping forces played a role in the settlement of Cold War conflicts in Namibia, Angola and Mozambique, Afghanistan, Cambodia, and Central America. These forces are sometimes called the

---

[54] GA Res 377 (V), (3 November 1950).
[55] *Certain Expenses of the United Nations, Advisory Opinion, ICJ Reports 1962*, p 151.

second generation of peacekeeping; they were generally ambitious operations going be-yond military and humanitarian operations to bringing about national reconciliation and re-establishing effective government. They met with mixed success and faced serious problems of non-cooperation in Angola and Cambodia.

New conflicts broke out after the Cold War in the former Yugoslavia, the former USSR, and Africa, and more peacekeeping forces were created. The Security Council took an innovative approach in many ways: the distinction between peacekeeping and enforce-ment action was blurred; peacekeeping forces were expected to carry out their functions at the same time as member State enforcement forces; UN peacekeeping was combined with regional peacekeeping. A third generation of peacekeeping was conceived in 1999 when UNMIK was established in Kosovo and UNTAET in East Timor. The UN Secretary-General said that these were qualitatively different from almost any other the UN had ever undertaken; in each place the UN formed the administration responsible for fulfilling all the functions of a State (Wilde, 2008). There are currently 15 peacekeeping operations (of which half are in Africa), ranging from traditional observer missions to large multidimen-sional forces.

C. CHALLENGES TO PEACEKEEPING: YUGOSLAVIA, SOMALIA, AND RWANDA 1991–5

The peacekeeping operations in Yugoslavia and Somalia posed a major challenge to the traditional principles governing peacekeeping—the principles that peacekeeping is dis-tinct from enforcement action under Chapter VII of the Charter, and that a peacekeeping force should be impartial, use force only in self-defence, and operate with the consent of the host State. In Yugoslavia UNPROFOR was created as a peacekeeping force, initially without reference to Chapter VII. However, there was no effective cease-fire and no real cooperation from the parties on the ground. UNPROFOR was given an ambitious and unrealistic mandate 'to create the conditions of peace and security required for the ne-gotiation of a settlement'. This mandate was incrementally expanded in a long series of resolutions, most of which were passed under Chapter VII. These gave UNPROFOR the power to use force to secure the delivery of humanitarian aid, to enforce no-fly zones and to protect safe havens declared to protect Bosnian Muslims in Bosnia-Herzegovina. This authority to use force brought UNPROFOR into conflict with the Bosnian Serbs. But member States were not willing to provide enough troops to enable UNPROFOR to carry out its wide mandate. Instead the UN turned to NATO air forces to take enforcement ac-tion under Chapter VII.

The UN had a similar experience in Somalia. The Security Council was slow to get involved in the civil war which broke out in 1991. It established a peacekeeping force, UNOSOM, to provide security for those delivering humanitarian aid. When this met non-cooperation on the ground it was supplemented by a US-led member State force. Both were later replaced by UNOSOM II, the first UN peacekeeping operation which was actually created under Chapter VII. But UNOSOM II was drawn into the conflict and proved unable to carry out its mandate. In both Yugoslavia and Somalia UN peacekeep-ing forces on the ground had to try to operate at the same time as member State forces authorized to use force under Chapter VII. This combination proved unworkable during these conflicts.

The peacekeeping forces subsequently created in Georgia, Liberia, and Tajikistan were not established under Chapter VII, and were not given powers under Chapter VII. This looked like a return to traditional peacekeeping in response to the experience of Yugoslavia and Somalia. However, events in Rwanda led to further reappraisal of peacekeeping.

The demands of the major operations in Yugoslavia and Somalia made developed States reluctant to intervene in Rwanda in 1994 when the Hutu government turned on the Tutsis and massacred over 500,000 people in three months. The relatively small UN peacekeeping force in Rwanda was not authorized or equipped to prevent the genocide. The UN was subjected to serious criticism for the failure, and there were calls for more robust peacekeeping in the protection of civilians.

E. PEACEKEEPING AFTER THE *BRAHIMI REPORT*

In response to the experiences in Yugoslavia, Somalia, and Rwanda, the UN set up a panel to carry out the first comprehensive review of peacekeeping since its inception. The panel presented the *Brahimi Report* at the 2000 UN Millennium Summit, making proposals for major reform.[56] The most important called for an increase in resources for the UN Department of Peacekeeping to enable it properly to manage complex and demanding peacekeeping operations. The Report also stressed the need for the Security Council to provide a clear and realistic mandate for peacekeeping forces, and suggested that no resolution creating a peacekeeping force be passed until the Security Council has commitments from member States for troops. It supported robust peacekeeping under Chapter VII where necessary, taking the view that action against 'spoilers' who were violating peace agreements did not undermine the impartiality of peacekeeping forces. The Report also called for better cooperation between the Security Council and troop-contributing countries; this raises issues about control of the force and the balance of power between the Security Council with its primary responsibility for the maintenance of international peace and security and those States contributing troops.

But the most serious problem facing UN peacekeeping remains one of resources. There was a major surge in peacekeeping in 2003. This reflects the success of peacekeeping as the 'flagship of the UN', but the increased demand created by the establishment of complex, multi-dimensional forces in difficult environments such as the DRC, Mali, and South Sudan has placed an enormous strain on UN resources and on the ability of member States to provide funds, troops, and equipment. The reforms which followed the *Brahimi Report* proved insufficient to cope with these increased demands, and a further reform programme is underway in accordance with a 2015 Report, *Uniting Our Strengths For Peace*.[57] This re-examined the traditional principles of peacekeeping in the light of the challenges facing peacekeeping operations, and of the novel mandates given to the peacekeeping forces in the DRC, Mali, and South Sudan. It took a cautious approach. Although the principles should not stand in the way of effective action, and should not be used as an excuse for failure to protect civilians, UN peacekeeping forces should in general not be mandated to undertake 'conflict management' in situations of violent conflict and in the absence of a viable peace process. Nor were they suited to take the lead in military counter-terrorism operations. In order to cope with the increasing demands the UN is turning increasingly to regional organizations as first responders.

VII. REGIONAL ACTION UNDER CHAPTER VIII OF THE UN CHARTER

The Charter provides for UN action to be supplemented by regional action under Chapter VIII: 'regional arrangements or agencies' are to deal with such matters relating to the

---

[56] (2000) 39 ILM 1432.   [57] UN Doc S/2015/446.

maintenance of international peace and security as are appropriate for regional action, provided that their actions are consistent with the purposes and principles of the UN (Article 52). Any enforcement action should be authorized by the Security Council; the Security Council may choose to utilize regional arrangements for enforcement action (Article 53). The Charter does not define 'regional arrangements or agencies', but the UN has accepted that the main regional organizations, the African Union (AU), the Organization of American States (OAS), and the Arab League come within this heading. Also certain sub-regional organizations not originally set up under Chapter VIII have taken on peace-keeping powers and have drawn up new constitutional instruments to regulate this. These include the Economic Community of West African States (ECOWAS), the Southern African Development Community (SADC), and the Intergovernmental Authority on Development (IGAD). In its resolutions the Security Council has taken a flexible, non-formalistic approach to the issue of which organizations come within Chapter VIII.

A. A GREATER ROLE FOR REGIONAL ORGANIZATIONS

Since the end of the Cold War regional organizations have become much more active, and there has been a significant increase in cooperation between regional organizations and the UN.[58] UN and regional or sub-regional forces have combined in Georgia, Tajikistan, Liberia, Sierra Leone, Côte d'Ivoire, the DRC, and Chad/Central African Republic and have undertaken complementary roles. Regional organizations may possess the advantages of proximity, an informed understanding of the causes of conflicts and of local norms; they may be able to deploy quickly when the UN Security Council is unable or unwilling to act.[59] The 2015 Report on *Uniting Our Strengths for Peace* recognized that regional organizations were essential as first responders in situations of ongoing conflict. Developed States have given significant financial assistance, logistical support, and military training to regional and sub-regional organizations in Africa. They have encouraged the AU in particular to take an increased role in peacekeeping. The AU has developed its own legal framework and institutions for this purpose. It has deployed peacekeeping forces in Burundi, Darfur (Sudan), Somalia, Mali, and the Central African Republic. The first hybrid AU-UN operation was established in Sudan in December 2007. But the AU still faces serious resource problems and depends on outside support for its peacekeeping operations. Its forces have struggled to cope with the extremely challenging conditions in Darfur and Somalia (Omorogbe, 2011), and more recently in Mali and the Central African Republic (2013), where regional forces were later replaced by UN peacekeeping operations.

Since the end of the Cold War regional organizations have been authorized to use enforcement action under Chapter VII; in Yugoslavia the Security Council authorized 'member States acting nationally or through regional agencies or arrangements' to use force to implement economic embargoes imposed under Article 41. A similar resolution was passed with regard to the enforcement of economic measures against Haiti after the 1991 anti-democratic coup. Although the Security Council did not expressly refer to Article 53, or specify exactly which regional organization was envisaged, it seems that these are the first instances of authorization in accordance with Article 53. The Security Council has since gone further: acting under Chapter VII it has authorized States acting through regional arrangements or agencies to use force to facilitate the delivery of humanitarian aid in Yugoslavia, to ensure compliance with the ban on flights over Bosnia-Herzegovina,

---

[58] UN Secretary-General's Reports on UN/regional relations, UN Doc S/2006/590, S/2008/186, S/2014/560, S/2015/229.   [59] UN SC Res 2167 (2014).

and to protect the safe havens; it has also authorized the member States of ECOWAS to use force in Côte d'Ivoire and Liberia. Since 2003 the EU has taken on an increasing role under its Common Defence and Security Policy; it has been authorized by the Security Council to conduct targeted operations in the DRC, Chad, and the Central African Republic. Under Security Council Resolution 2240 (2015) it was to carry out naval operations against the smuggling of migrants from Libya after the 2011 military intervention had left that State without an effective central government. The Security Council has also authorized the AU to establish AMISOM in Somalia and, in cooperation with ECOWAS, to send an African-led force to help the government of Mali to regain control of its territory. In 2013 it authorized the deployment of an AU force to the Central African Republic to restore order after a coup had reduced that State to anarchy.

B. CONTROVERSY AS TO THE INTERPRETATION OF CHAPTER VIII

During the Cold War and subsequently, the distinction between regional peacekeeping action with the consent of the host State, for which no Security Council authorization was necessary, and regional enforcement action which required such authorization in accordance with Article 53 has been problematic. When the OAS intervened against Cuba (1962) and the Dominican Republic (1965) there was controversy as to whether this was legal under the UN Charter (Akehurst, 1967). The Eastern and Western blocs were divided as to whether economic measures constituted enforcement action requiring authorization; more recently it seems to have been implicitly accepted that Security Council authorization is not needed for regional economic sanctions. The other main question which arose as to the legality of the OAS actions with regard to Cuba and to the Dominican Republic was whether acquiescence or failure to condemn by the Security Council amounted to authorization of enforcement action under Article 53. Such claims seem far-fetched where it is the veto or the threat of a veto by a permanent member which has led to the failure to condemn.

During the Cold War there was sometimes suspicion that major powers were manipulating regional organizations to further their own ends. For example, there was doubt as to whether the Syrian-dominated Arab League intervention in Lebanon (1976–83) was truly impartial peacekeeping in accordance with the purposes and principles of the UN. There were also concerns about the relation between the USA and the OAS and about the sub-regional Organization of East Caribbean States (OECS) intervention in Grenada in 1983. This provoked lengthy discussion in the Security Council as to whether the action was legitimate peacekeeping or whether it amounted to unlawful interference in the domestic affairs of a State in order to overthrow an unsympathetic government.[60] There was a coup in 1983 and a pro-Cuban government seized power. The USA, which was not itself a member of the OECS, led an OECS intervention and oversaw the installation of a new government. It offered a variety of legal justifications for its use of force, including an argument that the intervention was regional action under Chapter VIII at the request of the Governor-General of Grenada. Many States did not accept that the Governor-General had such power to represent the State of Grenada, but the main reason for their criticism of the invasion was that the action went beyond peacekeeping and constituted unlawful intervention. The UN General Assembly and the OAS condemned the intervention; in the Security Council the USA vetoed a resolution calling for the withdrawal of foreign troops from Grenada (Gilmore, 1984).

[60] 1983 *UNYB* 211.

C. REGIONAL PEACEKEEPING AFTER THE COLD WAR

Questions about the distinction between peacekeeping and enforcement action and concerns about the impartiality of regional action continue to arise after the Cold War, in particular with regard to the CIS operations in Georgia and Tajikistan in the former USSR and also with regard to ECOWAS operations in Liberia (1990–97) and Sierra Leone (1997–2000). ECOWAS, a sub-regional organization of 15 member States, established in 1975 and originally concerned with economic matters, took a major role in attempting to end civil wars in Sierra Leone and Liberia through its Economic Community of West African States Monitoring Group (ECOMOG) force. Commentators expressed doubts as to whether there were genuinely impartial peacekeeping forces or whether the major regional power, Nigeria, was pursuing its own agenda through ECOWAS. In both conflicts ECOMOG seemed to go beyond limited peacekeeping action, but ECOWAS did not openly claim wide powers or seek authorization in accordance with Article 53 by the Security Council. Its official position was that ECOMOG used force only in self-defence or to secure implementation of a UN economic embargo. The Security Council acquiesced in the ECOMOG action; it avoided discussion of legality under the UN Charter, leading some commentators to argue that these operations marked the inception of a new wide right of regional action to restore democracy or to undertake humanitarian intervention. However, the Security Council itself was cautious and did not expressly approve any use of force going beyond self-defence or in performance of the provisions of peace agreements. It is difficult to read approval for any radical change in the doctrine of regional peacekeeping into its resolutions. But some commentators have argued for a reinterpretation of the UN Charter in the light of these developments (Franck, 2002, 162). Subsequent regional operations do not support such claims: all enforcement action has been expressly authorized by the Security Council, and this authorization was expressly requested by the AU in Mali and the Central African Republic. States including China and Russia stress the need for regional action to be conducted strictly in accordance with the Charter framework.

VIII. CONCLUSION

The UN Charter provisions on the use of force by States, Article 2(4) on the prohibition of force and Article 51 on self-defence, have produced fundamental divisions between States. There is disagreement as to whether the prohibition on force should be interpreted strictly or whether it allows humanitarian intervention, as in Kosovo. There is also disagreement as to whether the right of self-defence is wide or narrow. The response to the 9/11 terrorist attacks has led to an unresolved disagreement about the law in this area. As regards collective security, the original scheme of the UN Charter for the Security Council to play a primary role in the maintenance of international peace and security through its own standing army has not been fully implemented. Instead the UN has turned to member States to use force under Security Council authority in 'coalitions of the willing'. It is extremely controversial in the light of *Operation Iraqi Freedom* whether member States may ever use force without express authority. Also, UN peacekeeping has developed through practice. UN peacekeeping forces deployed in ongoing conflicts face a tension between impartiality and effectiveness. The relationship between peacekeeping operations and Chapter VII has yet to be satisfactorily resolved.

REFERENCES

AKEHURST, M (1967), 'Enforcement Action by Regional Agencies, with Special Reference to the OAS', 41 *BYIL* 175.

ALABRUNE, F (2016), 'Fondements juridiques d'intervention militaire française contre Daech', 41 *RGDIP* 41.

AREND, A and BECK, R (1993), *International Law and the Use of Force* (London & New York: Routledge).

BECKER, T (2006), *Terrorism and the State* (Oxford: Hart Publishing).

BOWETT, D (1958), *Self-Defence in International Law* (Manchester: Manchester University Press).

BROWNLIE, I (1963), *International Law and the Use of Force by States* (Oxford: Oxford University Press).

CHESTERMAN, S (2001), *Just War or Just Peace? Humanitarian Intervention and International Law* (Oxford: Oxford University Press).

CORTEN, O (2010), *The Law against War* (Oxford: Hart Publishing).

D'AMATO, A (1990), 'The Invasion of Panama was a Lawful Response to Tyranny', 84 *AJIL* 516.

DOSWALD BECK, L (1985), 'The Legal Validity of Military Intervention by Invitation of the Government', 56 *BYIL* 189.

FRANCK, T (2002), *Recourse to Force* (Cambridge: Cambridge University Press).

GILMORE, W (1984), *The Grenada Intervention* (London: Mansell).

GRAY, C (2002), 'From Unity to Polarisation: International Law and the Use of Force against Iraq', 13 *EJIL* 1.

GRAY, C (2018), *International Law and the Use of Force* (4th edn, Oxford: Oxford University Press).

HENDERSON, C (2015), 'The UK Government's Legal Position on Forcible Measures in Response to the Use of Chemical Weapons by the Syrian Government', 64 *ICLQ* 179.

HIGGINS, R (1969–81), *United Nations Peacekeeping*, vols I–IV (Oxford: Oxford University Press).

LOBEL, J and RATNER, M (1999), 'Bypassing the Security Council: Ambiguous Authorizations to Use Force, Cease-fires and the Iraqi Inspection Regime', 93 *AJIL* 124.

MURPHY, SD (ed) (2003), 'Contemporary Practice of the United States relating to International Law', 97 *AJIL* 419.

OMOROGBE, E (2011), 'Can the African Union Deliver Peace and Security?', 16 *Journal of Conflict and Security Law* 35.

PATIL, A (1992), *The UN Veto in World Affairs 1946–1992* (London: Mansell).

RONZITTI, N (1985), *Rescuing Nationals Abroad* (Dordrecht: Martinus Nijhoff).

ROSCINI, M (2014), *Cyber Operations and the Use of Force in International Law* (Oxford: Oxford University Press).

ROTH, B (1999), *Governmental Illegitimacy in International Law* (Oxford: Oxford University Press).

SAROOSHI, D (1999), *The United Nations and the Development of Collective Security* (Oxford: Clarendon Press).

SIMMA, B et al (eds), (2012), *The Charter of the United Nations: A Commentary* (3rd edn, Oxford: Oxford University Press).

STAHN, C (2007), 'Responsibility to Protect', 101 *AJIL* 99.

TAFT, WH and BUCHWALD, TF (2003), 'Preemption, Iraq and International Law', 97 *AJIL* 553.

TAMS, C (2009), 'The Use of Force against Terrorists', 20 *EJIL* 359.

ULFSTEIN, G and CHRISTIANSEN, C (2013), 'The Legality of the NATO bombing in Libya', 62 *ICLQ* 159.

UNITED NATIONS (1996), *The Blue Helmets* (3rd edn, New York, NY: United Nations Dept of Public Information).

WILDE, R (2008), *International Territorial Administration* (Oxford: Oxford University Press).

WILSON, H (1988), *International Law and the Use of Force by National Liberation Movements* (Oxford: Oxford University Press).

FURTHER READING

General textbooks

BROWNLIE, I (1963), *International Law and the Use of Force by States* (Oxford: Oxford University Press).

CHINKIN, C and KALDOR, M (2017), *International Law and New Wars* (Cambridge: Cambridge University Press).

CORTEN, O (2010), *The Law against War* (Oxford: Hart Publishing).

FRANCK, T (2002), *Recourse to Force* (Cambridge: Cambridge University Press).

GRAY, C (2018), *International Law and the Use of Force* (4th edn, Oxford: Oxford University Press).

WELLER, M (ed) (2015), *Oxford Handbook of the Use of Force in International Law* (Oxford: Oxford University Press).

WHITE, N and HENDERSON C, (eds) (2013), *Research Handbook on International Conflict and Security Law* (Cheltenham: Edward Elgar Publishing).

The interpretation of article 2(4)

BANNELIER-CHRISTAKIS, K (2016), 'Military Interventions against ISIL in Iraq, Syria and Libya', 29 *Leiden JIL* 743.

CHESTERMAN, S (2000), *Just War or Just Peace? Humanitarian Intervention and International Law* (Oxford: Oxford University Press).

GRAY, C (2015), 'The Limits of Force', 376 *Hague Recueil des Cours* 101.

REISMAN, M (1984), 'Coercion and Self-determination: Construing Charter Article 2(4)' and the reply by O Schacter (1984), 'The Legality of Pro-democratic Invasion', 78 *AJIL* 642, 646.

STÜRCHLER, N (2007), *The Threat of Force in International Law* (Cambridge: Cambridge University Press).

Self-defence

BECKER, T (2006), *Terrorism and the State* (Oxford: Hart Publishing).

CORTEN, O (2016), 'The Unwilling or Unable Test: Has It Been or Could It Be Accepted?', 29 *Leiden JIL* 777.

LUBELL, N (2010), *Extraterritorial Use of Force against Non-state Actors* (Oxford: Oxford University Press).

NOLTE, G (2013), 'Multipurpose Self-defence: Proportionality Disoriented', 24 *EJIL* 75.

O'CONNELL, M-E (2007), 'The Ban on the Bomb—and Bombing', 78 *Syracuse Law Journal* 497.

RONZITTI, N (1985), *Rescuing Nationals Abroad* (Dordrecht: Martinus Nijhoff).

RUYS, T (2010), *Armed Attack and Article 51 of the UN Charter* (Cambridge: Cambridge University Press).

SCHACTER, O (1989), 'Self-defence and the Rule of Law', 83 *AJIL* 259.

UN enforcement and peacekeeping

BLOKKER, N and SCHRIJVER, N (2005), *The Security Council and the Use of Force* (Leiden/Boston: Martinus Nijhoff Publishers).

GRAY, C (2016), 'The 2015 Report on Uniting Our Strengths for Peace', 15 *Chinese JIL* 193.

GREENWOOD, C (1992), 'New World Order or Old? The Invasion of Kuwait and the Rule of Law', 55 *MLR* 153.

KONDOCH, B (ed) (2007), *International Peacekeeping* (Aldershot: Ashgate Publishing).

KOOPS, J et al (eds), (2015), *Oxford Handbook of UN Peacekeeping* (Oxford: Oxford University Press).

LOWE, AV, ROBERTS, A, WELSH, J, and ZAUM, D (eds) (2008), *The UN Security Council and War* (Oxford: Oxford University Press).

MATHESON, M (2006), *The Council Unbound* (Washington DC: US Institute of Peace Press).

ZACKLIN, R (2010), *The UN Secretariat and the Use of Force in a Unipolar World* (Cambridge: Cambridge University Press).

WEBSITES

http://www.un.org
The United Nations website

http://www.africa-union.org
The African Union website

http://www.ecowas.int
ECOWAS website

http://www.nato.int
NATO website

PART VII

THE APPLICATION OF INTERNATIONAL LAW

21

THE LAW OF THE SEA

Malcolm D Evans

SUMMARY

Historically, the principal division in the law of the sea has been between the territorial seas, which form a part of the territory of a State but within which other States enjoy a number of restricted rights, and the high seas, which are open to use by all. This has now changed, with the development and recognition of new zones of functional and resource-oriented jurisdiction, accompanied by complex realignments of jurisdictional competences which cut across—and, in the eyes of some, threaten to undermine—the traditional principles of governance at sea. This chapter traces these developments. It also provides an introduction to the principal zones of maritime jurisdiction, as well as looking at the rules concerning the construction of baselines—which is foundational to the entire subject—and to the problem of determining boundaries where entitlements to maritime zones overlap.

I. INTRODUCTION

The law of the sea is regulated in a complex yet subtle manner, providing an interesting contrast to the rather absolutist approach to questions concerning sovereignty and jurisdiction which still hold sway in other areas of international law. Sovereignty and jurisdiction are, of course, the basic building blocks of the law of the sea, providing the basis upon which all else is founded. Over time, however, they have been moulded and melded in an extremely sophisticated manner in order to better reflect the changing nature of the competing interests at stake in the utilization of the seas.

The earliest doctrinal debates concerned whether the seas could be made subject to the exclusive sovereignty of a single State. In the middle ages, before State-sponsored exploration of the oceans and the intensification of international trade by sea, this was, in truth, not really a question at all. It was in the fifteenth and sixteenth centuries that the question became significant, and the arguments advanced largely mirrored the prevailing interests of the sovereigns concerned. Those who argued that the seas should be 'closed' and subject to the jurisdiction of a single (usually the coastal) State did so either for reasons of security (to keep threatening forces at a distance) or for reasons of trade (to operate profitable customs regimes). Those that argued in favour of the seas being 'open' did so in order to foster and facilitate their developing long-distance overseas trading interests. The balance that finally emerged reflected both concerns: whereas States were to enjoy sovereignty over those waters proximate to their coasts, reflecting their interests in security and control, in the waters beyond, where trade and navigation issues assumed a greater significance, the principle of the freedom of the seas—famously argued for by Grotius in his work *Marem Liberum*—prevailed (Anand, 1983; O'Connell, 1982, pp 18–30).

This, then, established the basic division that has dominated the law of the sea for some 400 years; between the territorial sea, which was subject to the jurisdiction of the coastal State, and the high seas beyond, which were open to all. At the same time, this division also reflected a belief that the seas were to be used purposively, and thus the balance struck should reflect the needs of those seeking to do so. Inevitably, then, as strategic interests have changed and as economic and technological developments have increased the ability to access and harvest the resources of the sea and seabed, new accommodations between competing interests have had to be made (see Posner and Sykes, 2010). The challenges presented by these changes have been made more complex in recent years by the rapid expansion of the number of States, significant shifts in the balance of political power, the recognition of international community interests in the seas and the increasing awareness of the need to conserve and protect the resources of the seas and the marine environment.

In the early years of the twentieth century ambitious plans were made to 'codify' much of international law, including the law of the sea. Although the overall project made little headway, one positive outcome was the 1930 'Hague Codification Conference'. Whilst this did not produce any finished text on the law of the sea it did provide useful experience which was extensively drawn on when, after the Second World War, the International Law Commission (ILC) decided to examine the subject. In 1956 the ILC produced sets of draft Articles which were considered at the First UN Conference on the Law of the Sea (UNCLOS I) held in Geneva in 1958. This conference produced the four 'Geneva Conventions' on the Law of the Sea,[1] which in part reflected customary international law but which also contained much that was 'progressive development'.

Although impressive in their scope, the Geneva Conventions left some important issues open. The most significant of these concerned the vexed question of the breadth of the territorial sea. In 1960 a second UN Conference was convened in Geneva (UNCLOS II) to address this and other related questions but it ended without agreement. One reason for this failure was the mounting pressure for a more fundamental review of the law of the sea which would take account of the growing demands for access to resources and, in the process, erode the rigidity of the territorial sea/high seas dichotomy. Admittedly, the four 1958 Conventions themselves represented a limited break with the past. Two of those conventions reflected the traditional divisions, one dealing with the territorial sea (and contiguous zone) and another with the high seas. The other two 1958 Conventions reflected new concerns, these being the continental shelf and fisheries conservation and management. Although the fisheries convention did not gain much international support, and elements of the continental shelf convention have since been jettisoned, adopting 'general' conventions on these 'functional' issues indicated that the way forward did not lie only in fixing on new outer limits for the territorial sea and further refining the relationship between the territorial seas and high seas. Rather, it showed that the future lay in creating new zones and new forms of jurisdictional competence that would co-exist alongside them. UNCLOS II had attempted to go down this path by suggesting that, rather than extend the territorial sea to 12 nautical miles (n. miles), States be permitted to exercise exclusive jurisdiction over fishing in a 6 n. mile belt beyond a 6 n. mile territorial sea.

---

[1] These being the Convention on the Territorial Sea and Contiguous Zone (TSC); Convention on the High Seas (HSC); Convention on the Continental Shelf (CSC); and the Convention on Fisheries and Conservation of the Living Resources of the High Seas (CFC).

Moreover, this general approach was endorsed by the International Court of Justice (ICJ) in the *North Sea*[2] and *Fisheries Jurisdiction*[3] cases, where the emergence of the continental shelf and exclusive fisheries zones was acknowledged and accepted.

The basic idea underlying the distinction between the territorial seas and high seas was that it differentiated between those maritime spaces over which a single State exercised jurisdiction and control and those over which no single State exercised jurisdiction or control. As a result, therefore, the resources of the high seas were available for unilateral exploitation by anyone and everyone. As will be seen later, the extension of coastal State jurisdiction over resources located in the seabed and subsoil beyond the territorial sea was already having the effect of breaking down this clear distinction. In 1967, however, a fundamental challenge to this traditional approach was made when, at the prompting of Arvid Pardo, the Maltese ambassador to the UN, the UN General Assembly adopted the first of a series of resolutions[4] in which it recognized that the resources of the seabed in areas beyond national jurisdiction should be considered to be the 'Common Heritage of Mankind' and be exploited for the benefit of the international community as a whole (Schmidt, 1989, pp 18–30).

There was, then, a complex matrix of unresolved issues and emerging agendas which needed to be addressed and these were considered at the third UN Conference on the Law of the Sea (UNCLOS III), which met in the period 1974–82 and culminated in the adoption of the 1982 Convention on the Law of the Sea (LOSC).

Negotiations at UNCLOS III were tortuous and the 1982 Convention attempted to balance a myriad of competing interests in a 'package deal' that ultimately satisfied few. Although by the early 1990s the number of ratifications approached the 60 required by LOSC Article 308 for the Convention to enter into force there was relatively little support from developed States, whose acceptance was critical to its success. This focused the minds of all concerned and, assisted by changes in the world political order at that time following the collapse of communism in eastern Europe, a rather euphemistically entitled 'Implementation Agreement' was agreed in July 1994. This, in fact if not in name, amended Part XI of the Convention (the provisions concerning the 'Common Heritage' and seabed mining in the area beyond national jurisdiction) in order to make it acceptable to a broader range of States (Anderson, 1993; 1995; Harrison, 2011, pp 85–99). The LOSC entered into force on 16 November 1994 and at the time of writing there are 168 States parties (including the EU). The Implementation Agreement entered into force in July 1996 and currently has 150 States parties. However, Article 7 of the 1994 Agreement allowed for its provisional application pending its entry into force and so for those States party to both the 1982 Convention and the 1994 Agreement, the 'original' version of Part XI as set out in the 1982 Convention never became binding on them at all.

Much of the 1982 Convention now reflects customary law (Roach, 2014) and so is relevant to the increasingly small number of States which are not bound by it as a matter of treaty law.[5] As a result, it provides the starting point for any presentation of the contemporary law of the sea and is likely to do so for many years to come (Churchill, 2015, p 45). However, parts of the Convention are of a 'framework' nature and it has been

---

[2] *North Sea Continental Shelf, Judgment, ICJ Reports 1969*, p 3.

[3] *Fisheries Jurisdiction (United Kingdom v Iceland), Merits, Judgment, ICJ Reports 1974*, p 3.

[4] See UNGA Res 2340 (XII) (18 December 1967) which established an 'Ad Hoc Committee to Study the Peaceful Uses of the Sea-Bed and the Ocean Floor beyond the Limits of National Jurisdiction' and, in particular, the 'Declaration of Principles Governing the Sea-Bed and the Ocean Floor, and the Subsoil thereof, Beyond the Limits of National Jurisdiction', UNGA Res 2749 (XXV) (17 December 1970).

[5] Including, for example, the USA and Turkey, who are not States parties to the LOSC.

supplemented by a number of other major conventions addressing certain issues in greater detail. Developments in other areas of international law have also had an impact on the Convention framework and customary law continues to play an important role by further supplementing and amplifying its provisions (Boyle, 2005; Harrison, 2011). As a result, the 1982 Convention is very much a 'living treaty' and is not to be approached or understood in a 'static' fashion (see Barrett, 2016; Barnes, 2016).

Since a chapter of this length cannot be comprehensive, it aims to give a flavour of the Convention's approach and illustrate the manner in which competing interests are accommodated in some key areas.

II. CONSTRUCTING BASELINES

A. INTRODUCTION: THE NORMAL RULE

International law parcels the sea into various zones in which States enjoy a variety of juris-dictional competences. The general approaches is that coastal States exercise the greatest degree of jurisdictional competence over those zones that lie closest to them. Logically enough, a State exercises full powers of territorial sovereignty within areas of water which are 'internal'. This obviously includes lakes and rivers but also includes harbours and other areas of water which are landward of 'baselines' from which the various zones of seawards jurisdiction are generally[6] measured.

Determining baselines is, then, very important and a number of detailed rules were set out in the 1958 TSC and largely repeated in the 1982 LOSC. Most of these rules reflect customary law. Since the further seawards a coastal State is able to 'push' its baselines the further seawards its jurisdiction will extend, the practical application of these rules often gives rise to controversy. It should also be remembered that islands, defined in LOSC Article 121(1) as 'a naturally formed area of land, surrounded by water, which is above water at high tide', have baselines which generate maritime zones, no matter how small, miniscule even, they might be.

However, LOSC Article 121(3) provides the important exception that '[r]ocks which cannot sustain human habitation or economic life of their own shall have no exclusive eco-nomic zone or continental shelf'. In 2012 the ICJ finally concluded that 'the legal régime of islands set out in UNCLOS Article 121 forms an indivisible régime, all of which . . . has the status of customary international law',[7] thus finally ending doubts concerning the custom-ary law status of Article 121(3).

Nevertheless, the precise scope of this provision remains uncertain, as the terms 'rock' and the concepts of 'human habitation' and 'economic life' are not expressly de-fined (Charney, 2000; Lavalle, 2004; Prescott and Schofield, 2005, pp 61–89). In 2016, the Arbitral Tribunal in the *South China Seas Arbitration* explored the meaning of these terms at length. It confirmed that, under the 1982 Convention, all features above the water at high tide were entitled to maritime zones unless this was precluded by LOSC Article 121(3). Controversially, it took the view that 'human habitation' 'implies a non-transient presence of persons who have chosen to stay and reside on the feature in a settled man-ner'.[8] Equally controversially, it took the view that 'economic life of its own' referred to the

---

[6] The continental shelf is, in part, an exception to this. See later in this chapter.

[7] *Territorial and Maritime Dispute (Nicaragua v Colombia), Judgment of 19 November 2012*, para 139. But cf Tanaka, 2015, pp 68–9 who argues that there is insufficient consistent State practice to justify such a conclusion.

[8] *South China Seas Case (Philippines v China)*, Arbitral Tribunal constituted under annex VII of the UN Law of the Sea Convention, Award of 12 July 2016, PCA Case No 2013–19, para 489.

economic life and livelihoods of those living on the feature, and not based on the more general economic value of the surrounding waters or extractive activities on the feature itself.[9] This is a high threshold which might not even be met by some very small island States. It remains to be seen whether this highly restrictive interpretation wins widespread recognition.

Whether island or mainland territory, '... the normal baseline for measuring the breadth of the territorial sea is the low-water line along the coast as shown by the appropriate symbols on charts officially recognized by the coastal state' (LOSC Article 5). Although relatively easy to apply, this method can produce unwieldy results when a coastline is not comparatively straight and/or there are a considerable number of islands in the vicinity of a mainland coast. Therefore, a number of rules have been devised which address some exceptional situations. States do not have to adopt one method of drawing baselines but may use those methods most appropriate for each portion of their coast (LOSC Article 14).

B. STRAIGHT BASELINES

In the *Anglo-Norwegian Fisheries* case[10] the UK challenged the right of Norway to claim a territorial sea which was drawn not from the low-water line but from a series of artificial lines linking the outermost points of the 'skaergaard' (a fringe of rocks and islands) that lay off the Norwegian coast. The Court noted that it might be inconvenient to use the low-water mark as the baseline in such geographically complicated circumstances and accepted the legitimacy of drawing 'straight baselines' under certain circumstances. The judgment was reflected in TSC Article 4, the essence of which was repeated in LOSC Article 7 (Reisman and Westerman, 1992; Kopela, 2013, ch 2).

Straight baselines may only be drawn if a coastline is 'deeply indented and cut into' or 'if there is a fringe of islands along the coast in its immediate vicinity' (LOSC Article 7(1)). If these criteria are not met, the normal rule applies. Even if straight baselines *may* be drawn, there are limitations upon *how* they are to be drawn. These include restrictions on the use of Low Tide Elevations,[11] that straight baselines 'must not depart to any appreciable extent from the general direction of the coast', and that 'the sea areas lying within the lines must be sufficiently closely linked to the land domain to be subject to the regime of internal waters' (LOSC Article 7(4)). This latter, rather impressionistic, requirement is particularly important. Waters on the landward side of a straight baseline are by definition internal waters over which the coastal State enjoys full territorial jurisdiction and control (subject to an exception to be considered later) and straight baselines must not be used to bring into the territorial domain waters which lack an intrinsic nexus with the coast. That nexus might be established by non-geographic criteria: in keeping with the *Anglo-Norwegian Fisheries* case, LOSC Article 7(5) permits local and well-established economic interests to be taken into account when establishing particular baselines, but only in those situations where the geographical threshold criteria set out in Article 7(1) are met.

C. BAYS

A further exception to the 'normal' rule concerns bays and is addressed by LOSC Article 10, which is generally considered to reflect customary law (Westerman, 1987). The motivation for departing from the normal rule here is not so much based on convenience but

---

[9] Ibid, para 543.   [10] *Fisheries, Judgment, ICJ Reports 1951*, p 116.
[11] A 'Low Tide Elevation' is 'a naturally formed area of land which is surrounded by and above water at low tide but submerged at high tide' (LOSC Article 13).

to avoid situations in which the territorial sea—or even fingers of high seas—penetrate the mouths of bays and intrude into areas intrinsically connected with the land domain. The problem is greatest where entrances to bays are relatively narrow but open out into broader expanses of water. The aim is to differentiate areas of water which are essentially of an 'internal' nature from those which are not and this is achieved by drawing 'closing lines' across the mouth of bays and using that 'closing line' as the baseline from which the territorial sea and other zones of jurisdiction are measured.[12]

Once again, there are two stages to this process. First, the distance between the 'natural entrance points' of a bay is measured, and a semi-circle is drawn along a line of that length. The area of this semi-circle is then compared to the area of water on the landward side of the closing line. If the area of the semi-circle is less than that of the area of water, the indentation is, for the purposes of baseline construction, a bay; if the area of the semi-circle is greater than the area of the water on the landward side of the closing line, the indentation is not—for legal purposes—a bay. The second stage is to draw a closing line. If the distance between the natural entrance points used for the previous calculation is less than 24 n. miles, the closing line may be drawn between them. If that distance exceeds 24 n. miles, then a closing line of up to that length can be drawn 'within the bay in such a manner as to enclose the maximum area of water that is possible with a line of that length' (LOSC Article 10(6)). This seemingly simple provision is very complex to apply in practice, with the identification of the natural entry points being a particular problem,[13] and the bay being a 'well marked indentation' another.[14]

It may be the case that the coastline of a bay belongs to more than one State. This poses an additional difficulty since the exceptional rule in LOSC Article 10 only applies to those bays whose coasts belong to a single State. However, in the *Land, Island and Maritime Frontier Dispute* the ICJ identified a concept of a 'pluri-State' bay, where the coasts belong to a number of States yet a closing line might still be drawn.[15] The Tribunal in the *Slovenia/Croatia Arbitration* in 2017 adopted the same approach in relation to the Bay of Piran.[16] Both cases concerned situations where a juridical bay had been established prior to a territorial separation, at a time when the coastline of the bay had indeed belonged to a single State. Whilst this may be an appropriate response in such situations where there is a compelling historical justification, it is difficult to justify its more general use, if only because the waters behind the closing line would be 'internal' to all of the States concerned and this would simply generate a further need to differentiate between them. It seems to create more problems than it solves and is not reflective of general State practice.

In any case, LOSC Article 10(6) expressly renders the Convention regime inapplicable to 'historic bays', these being indentations claimed by the coastal State as a part of its internal waters on the basis of a long-standing claim, assertion of jurisdiction, and acquiescence by others (O'Connell, 1982, ch 11). This offers an alternative route for States wishing to make claims in respect of indentations which cannot fulfil the criteria set out in the

---

[12] It is important to remember that a bay closing line and a straight baseline are legally speaking two very different types of line, though both have the same general function.

[13] See, eg, *Post Office v Estuary Radio* [1968] 2 QB 740. See also Marston, 2002.

[14] See, eg, the US Supreme Court judgment in *United States v Alaska* 545 US 17 (2005), pp 17–20.

[15] *Land, Island and Maritime Frontier Dispute (El Salvador/Honduras: Nicaragua) Judgment of 11 September 1992, ICJ Reports 1992*, p 351, para 395. The entire concept was roundly criticized by Judge Oda in his Dissenting Opinion, p 732, paras 1–26.

[16] *Arbitration under the Arbitration Agreement between the Government of the Republic of Croatia and the Government of the Republic of Slovenia, signed on 4 November 2009 (Croatia/Slovenia)*, Award of 17 July 2017, PCA case no 2012–04, paras 881–3.

Convention. Whilst it is said that 'the concept of a historic bay is well understood in international law',[17] such claims are difficult to substantiate and will often meet with considerable protest, as was the case with the Libyan claim to the Gulf of Sirte, a 'bay' nearly 300 n. miles in extent (Ahnish, 1993, ch 7).

D. ARCHIPELAGOES

The 1951 *Anglo-Norwegian Fisheries* case also addresses what might be called 'coastal archipelagoes'. But what of States composed wholly or partly of groups of islands? Should the waters between them be enclosed and treated as internal? What of the navigational rights of third States? At UNCLOS III the interests of archipelagic States, such as Indonesia and the Philippines, and the concerns of adjacent maritime neighbours, such as Australia, combined to produce a particular regime, set out in Part IV of the Convention, applicable to 'archipelagic states' (see Davenport, 2015). Rather self-referentially, LOSC Article 46 defines an archipelagic State as a State 'constituted wholly by one or more archipelagoes' and other islands, where an 'archipelago' is itself further defined as a group of islands, or parts of islands, and their interconnecting waters which are so closely interconnected as to form, or be regarded as forming, an intrinsic entity, or which have been historically regarded as such. Therefore Indonesia, the Philippines, Fiji, Japan, and the UK are archipelagic States for Convention purposes and so are entitled to draw archipelagic baselines, whereas island groups such as the Azores (belonging to Spain) and the Galapagos (belonging to Ecuador) are not. Although it has been argued that non-coastal dependent archipelagos might be entitled to draw straight baselines in a manner akin to archipelagic baselines (Kopela, 2013), this suggestion was decisively rejected by the Arbitral Tribunal in the *South China Seas Arbitration*.[18] It remains to be seen whether its views gain general acceptance.

However, not all archipelagic States are able to construct archipelagic baselines since such baselines must conform to strict criteria, the principal elements of which are that they must link the main islands of the group; no baseline may be more than 100 n. miles long, except that 3 per cent of the total may be up to 125 n. miles in length; they must follow the general configuration of the island grouping; and, most importantly, they must fulfil the requirement that the ratio of water to land within the baselines must be not less than 1:1 and not more than 9:1 (LOSC Article 47). The result is both that those archipelagic States which primarily consist of a few large islands (such as Japan and the UK) and those which are composed of very small and widely spaced islands (such as Kiribati) are unable to draw archipelagic baselines even though they fall within the definition of an archipelagic State. It is the latter category of small and scattered island States which stood to gain most from the concept, but they were unable to influence the negotiations in their favour and the details of the regime found in the Convention favour the interests of the larger archipelagic States. It may be that, in time, State practice and customary law might develop in a fashion which is somewhat less rigid than the Convention regime.

The waters within archipelagic baselines are 'archipelagic waters' rather than internal waters and are subject to special rules concerning, *inter alia*, fishing and navigation which will be considered later (LOSC Articles 49–53). Once again, and whatever its shortcomings, the archipelagic regime offers another example of the manner in which the Convention sought to forge a new approach to the division of jurisdictional competences, and moved away from a strict approach based on the distinction between the territorial and high seas.

---

[17] *South China Seas Case (Philippines v China)*, Arbitral Tribunal constituted under annex VII of the UN Law of the Sea Convention, Award of 12 July 2016, PCA Case No 2013–19, para 205.

[18] Ibid, paras 575–6.

III. THE INTERNAL WATERS, TERRITORIAL SEA, AND CONTIGUOUS ZONE

A. INTRODUCTION

The idea that States are entitled to exercise authority over the waters beyond their land territory (and internal and archipelagic waters) is deeply entrenched in international legal thinking. Although it was once argued that the competences States enjoyed within waters off their coasts fell short of territorial sovereignty and had to be positively asserted,[19] it is now clear that this authority flows automatically from the sovereignty exercised over land territory and so all coastal States do in fact have a territorial sea.[20] Practically speaking, however, States need to make some form of pronouncement, if only to determine the extent of their jurisdiction.

The breadth of water over which a State might legitimately exercise sovereign jurisdiction has been the subject of lengthy debate down the ages, but at the dawn of the twentieth century the preponderance of known practice fixed that distance at 3 n. miles. The conflict between those who favoured broadening this zone, in order to enhance coastal State security or to increase control over navigation and resources, and those who opposed this in the name of freedom of navigation (and of fishing on the high seas) not only underpinned the development of the various functional maritime zones which will be considered shortly but was also responsible for the failure of UNCLOS I and II to settle the issue. By the time of UNCLOS III, however, it seemed clear that an expansion of territorial seas to 12 n. miles was inevitable and the only question was the price that its opponents could extract from its proponents. LOSC Article 3 now recognizes the right to establish a territorial sea of up to 12 n. miles, the overwhelming majority of States—some 140—have done so, and this is now the position under customary international law.[21] Although described as the territorial sea, the sovereignty of the State extends to the airspace above and the seabed and subsoil beneath (LOSC Article 2(2)).

It is important that States make their position clear since possession of a territorial sea not only entails rights but also duties: in his Separate Opinion in the *Fisheries Jurisdiction* case Judge Fitzmaurice pointed out that coastal States were obliged to maintain navigational aids within their territorial sea[22] and could be held responsible for damage flowing from the failure to do so. Clearly, the scope of this obligation depends on the extent of the territorial sea.

B. JURISDICTION OF THE COASTAL STATE

Although the coastal State exercises 'sovereignty' within its territorial sea, this sovereignty is circumscribed in a number of ways which will be considered in this section. It is also helpful to consider the jurisdiction enjoyed by a State within its territorial sea alongside that which it may exercise within its internal waters and in the contiguous zone that lies beyond, since these together represent a progression from the strongest to the weakest form of jurisdictional competences over maritime spaces which are grounded upon territorial sovereignty.

---

[19] This view found reflection—somewhat unexpectedly—in *R v Keyn* (1876) 2 Ex D 63, the substance of which was subsequently reversed by the 1878 Territorial Waters Jurisdiction Act.

[20] A view expressed by Judge McNair in his Dissenting Opinion in *Fisheries, Judgment, ICJ Reports 1951*, p 116 at p 160.

[21] See, eg, *Territorial and Maritime Dispute (Nicaragua v Colombia), Judgment of 19 November 2012*, para 177.

[22] *Fisheries Jurisdiction (United Kingdom v Iceland), Jurisdiction of the Court, Judgment, ICJ Reports 1973*, p 3 at p 27.

1. Internal waters

Predictably, a coastal State exercises sovereignty to its fullest extent within its internal waters. No State is obliged to allow foreign vessels into its internal waters, except in cases of distress, and, exceptionally, where drawing straight baselines has the result of enclosing as internal waters not previously considered as such, the right of innocent passage (described later) remains (LOSC Article 8(2)). Otherwise, coastal States are free to restrict or impose whatever conditions they wish upon entry into internal waters, including entry into their ports,[23] the waters of which form part of their 'internal waters'.

Once a foreign vessel has entered internal waters it is subject to the domestic legislation of that State which can, in principle, be enforced against it.[24] On entering a port, the port State (as the coastal State then becomes known) is particularly well-placed to take enforcement action against vessels, if only because it can prevent them from leaving (see generally Molenaar, 2015). The expansion of 'port State jurisdiction' over vessels is a feature of contemporary law, particularly as regards vessels which have breached health and safety regulations or have been causing pollution outside of the territorial sea of the State concerned (eg LOSC Articles 218–20, and see Özçayir, 2001; Marten, 2013). Indeed, there is an increasing trend to encourage the use of port State jurisdiction as a means of addressing the failures of flag States to exercise jurisdiction over vessels acting in breach of international standards (see Molenaar, 2006; 2015, pp 289–93) and as regards fishing, see also Section VII B 3 in this chapter). However, States generally exercise restraint in enforcing local law over incidents taking place on board foreign vessels in their ports, limiting this to matters such as the infringement of customs laws, or activities which threaten to disrupt the peace of the port. This may include offences such as murder,[25] which have an intrinsic gravity that on-board scuffles between crew members lack. Such restraint reflects the temporary nature of the vessel's presence in a port and the fact that the flag State of the vessel itself has the right to exercise jurisdiction and that it is often more appropriate for it do so. States will, however, generally exercise jurisdiction over incidents occurring whilst the vessel is in port and which also involve non-crew members, as these concern more than the 'internal economy' of the vessel, and also in situations where the captain requests intervention.

2. Territorial sea

The dominant view is that coastal State jurisdiction automatically extends to the territorial sea, with the logical corollary that the entire body of State law applies there. However, this does not mean that the coastal State has an unfettered discretion regarding the content of that legislation since international law imposes a number of important restrictions upon what activities the coastal State might render unlawful within the territorial sea, the most important of which concerns vessels exercising the right of innocent passage, considered later. Moreover, logic does not necessarily make for practicality and the full rigours of this approach (assuming it to be doctrinally correct) are mitigated by a more restrictive approach to the enforcement of domestic law within the territorial sea, irrespective of whether a vessel is engaged in innocent passage or not.

---

[23] Whether vessels have a right of access to a port of a third State is a matter of controversy. For a helpful summary see Klein, 2011, pp 65–7.

[24] No enforcement action may be taken against foreign warships, however, as they enjoy immunity from local jurisdiction. See LOSC Article 32 and 'ARA Libertad' (Argentina v Ghana), Provisional Measures, Order of 15 December 2012, ITLOS Reports 2012, para 95.

[25] Eg United States v Wildenhaus, 120 US 1 (1887), concerning the assertion of jurisdiction by the local courts over a murder on board a Belgian vessel in New York harbour.

It would be odd if States were to enforce their criminal law over vessels merely passing through their territorial seas in circumstances which would not have triggered enforcement within internal waters. Therefore, LOSC Article 27(1) exhorts States to refrain from investigating or arresting those suspected of offences committed on board a vessel in its territorial sea unless: the consequences extended to the coastal State; it was of a kind to disturb the peace of the country or the good order of the territorial sea; assistance was requested; or it was necessary for the suppression of illicit traffic in drugs (LOSC Article 27(1)(a)–(d)). If the vessel has just left the State's internal waters it need show no such restraint (LOSC Article 27(2)), but in all cases the coastal State is to have 'due regard to the interests of navigation' when deciding whether, or how, to carry out an arrest within the territorial sea. These provisions apply to the criminal jurisdiction of the State. There are further exhortations against the exercise of jurisdiction over vessels in respect of civil matters, the chief of which is that vessels should not be stopped in order to exercise civil jurisdiction over an individual or with regard to actions *in rem*, rather than in respect of the activities of the vessel itself (LOSC Article 28). Finally, and unsurprisingly, coastal States are not permitted to arrest a warship or other vessels being used for governmental purposes which belong to another State. Rather, such vessels may be 'required' to leave the territorial sea immediately (LOSC Article 30) and it is implicit in this that the requisite degree of force necessary to ensure compliance with such a request might be used.

3. Contiguous zone

Traditionally, where the territorial sea ended, the high seas began and the laws of the coastal State no longer applied. However, policing maritime zones is no easy matter and, unlike land boundaries, they are simple to cross. It is therefore easy for vessels to commit offences within the territorial sea but to evade arrest by moving just a little further seawards. The answer was to permit coastal States to arrest vessels outside their territorial seas in connection with offences that either had been committed or which it was suspected were going to be committed within their territorial sea. Under LOSC Article 33 (and following a compromise first agreed upon in the 1958 TSC Article 24), the coastal State is permitted to 'prevent' and 'punish' infringements of some, but not all, of its laws (those concerned being 'customs, fiscal, immigration or sanitary laws and regulations') in a zone which might be up to 24 n. miles from the baselines (thus permitting a State with a three mile territorial sea to have a contiguous zone of up to 21 n. miles). Not all States have declared a contiguous zone, but their usefulness is such that an increasing number do so.[26]

The ability to 'punish' means that vessels that have committed such offences within the territory of the State may be arrested even though they have left the territorial seas. The ability to 'prevent' suggests that a State might stop a vessel from entering its waters when it has reason to believe that such an offence would be committed should that vessel enter. This is clearly open to abuse. Indeed, the entire concept represents a not insignificant extension of coastal State authority and there is a tendency for States to assert jurisdiction for a more ambitious range of matters than those mentioned in the Convention text.

C. NAVIGATION IN THE TERRITORIAL SEA

The desire of coastal States to assert their jurisdiction in the waters off their coasts is matched by the needs of the international community to ensure that the seas remain open to navigation. Once again, there has been progressive development in both the range and

---

[26] Approaching 90 States currently claim contiguous zones for a variety of purposes (not all in compliance with the LOSC) and the overwhelming majority are of 24 n. miles.

the content of regimes applicable to navigation within waters over which coastal States exercise sovereignty. The principal regime concerns innocent passage through the territorial sea and the manner in which that regime has sought to balance the relevant competing interests has shifted over time. In addition, some entirely new regimes of passage have been developed that reflect other developments.

1. Innocent passage

Ships of all States enjoy a right of 'innocent passage' through the territorial seas of coastal States. For these purposes, 'passage' means that the vessel is in the process of travelling through the territorial sea and is doing so in a 'continuous and expeditious' fashion, though there are exceptions for stops which are 'incidental to ordinary navigation' or as a result of *force majeure* (LOSC Article 18). Thus a ship loitering within the territorial sea or traversing in a circuitous manner would not be engaged in 'passage' at all.

Not all passage is 'innocent'. According to the 1958 TSC Article 14(4), 'Passage is innocent so long as it is not prejudicial to the peace, good order or security of the coastal state.' It is, however, unclear who is to make that determination. In the *Corfu Channel* case[27] the ICJ adopted a fairly objective approach, suggesting that the innocent nature of passage was capable of objective assessment, that the opinion of the coastal State was not decisive, and that the mere fact that a violation of local law had occurred was not in itself sufficient to demonstrate prejudice to the interests of the coastal State. The difficulty that faced the Court was that it needed to allow coastal States sufficient scope to decide whether to take measures against vessels exercising the right of innocent passage but it also needed to guard against their acting in an arbitrary and capricious fashion. The approach adopted in the *Corfu Channel* case seemed to favour the interests of ships in passage over that of the coastal State. The balance struck by the 1958 TSC seemed to adopt a rather more subjective and coastal-State oriented approach. It also provided for two special cases in which the very manner of passage would be enough to result in the loss of innocence, irrespective of whether there was in fact any prejudice to the coastal State or not: these concerned infringements by foreign fishing vessels of local legislation concerning fishing in the territorial sea (TSC Article 14(5)) and the requirement that submarines were to 'navigate on the surface and show their flag' (TSC Article 14(6)). Such activities were deemed to be incompatible with 'innocent passage' altogether.

These provisions in the 1958 TSC were widely regarded as unsatisfactory, particularly given the trend towards establishing increasingly broad belts of territorial seas and they were revisited at UNCLOS III. Although LOSC Article 19(1) endorses the general principle established in TSC Article 14(1), it takes a more objective approach to the determination of innocence by setting out in Article 19(2) a considerably longer list of activities and circumstances in which innocence is deemed to be lost, irrespective of whether there is any actual prejudice or infringement of local law. Moreover, these heads are themselves rather open textured, particularly the final catch-all provision of 'any other activity not having a direct bearing on passage' (LOSC Article 19(2)(j)). At first sight this might suggest that the right of innocent passage has been limited even further by the LOSC. This has to be balanced against the argument that the list of exceptions is now exhaustive and closed, an argument forcefully put by the USA and former USSR in a joint statement in 1989. However, the wording of the Convention is ambiguous on this matter, to say the least. Churchill and Lowe also point out that Article 19(2) refers to 'activities' and so the mere 'presence' of a vessel may no longer be sufficient to deprive it of innocence (Churchill and Lowe, 1999, p 85). It is clear that there is still considerable controversy surrounding

---

[27] *Corfu Channel, Merits, Judgment, ICJ Reports 1949*, p 4 at pp 30–1.

this Article, but it would be consonant with the general thrust of the Convention if it were to be understood as representing a modest move towards enhanced, but objectively verifiable, coastal State control over passage through the territorial sea.[28]

Even this assessment must be balanced against developments concerning the other plank of the innocent passage regime. Being engaged in innocent passage does not exempt a vessel from the need to comply with coastal State legislation, but the coastal State may only legislate for the range of issues that are set out in LOSC Article 21. These concern the safety of navigation, cables, and pipelines; the conservation of living resources and prevention of infringements of fisheries laws; matters concerning the preservation of the environment and marine pollution; marine scientific research; and prevention of infringements of customs, fiscal, immigration, and sanitary laws. By way of checks and balances, however, the coastal State may not use these legislative competences in ways which hamper innocent passage by, for example, imposing onerous or discriminatory requirements (LOSC Article 24(1)). Moreover, such laws 'shall not apply to the design, construction, manning or equipment of foreign ships unless they are giving effect to generally accepted international rules or standards' (LOSC Article 21(2)), increasingly referred to as 'GAIRS', in this instance these being those agreed under the auspices of the International Maritime Organization (IMO). The coastal State does have the power to 'suspend temporarily' innocent passage in specified areas, but only if this is non-discriminatory, is 'essential for the protection of its security', and is duly publicized (LOSC Article 25(3)).[29]

Vessels violating such laws are liable to arrest in accordance with LOSC Article 27 even though they may be exercising the right of innocent passage through the territorial sea. It would, of course, be in breach of international law for a coastal State to enforce laws on matters other than these upon a vessel simply because it ceased to be engaged in innocent passage by reason of entering internal waters. The more exacting standards that can be applied to ships not engaged in innocent passage can only be enforced against those whose passage ceased to be innocent *whilst in the territorial sea* and in accordance with Article 27.

A final question concerns the range of vessels which are entitled to exercise innocent passage. The Convention texts refer to 'ships' and in the *Passage through the Great Belt* case[30] Denmark questioned whether the regime was applicable to structures such as oil rigs. The better view is that a broad, purposive approach should be taken in unusual cases such as this, but the most controversial issue is whether warships can exercise a right of innocent passage. No agreement could be reached on this issue at UNCLOS I or III, and the matter is not dealt with directly by the TSC or the LOSC. The major maritime powers favour warships enjoying the right of innocent passage, but this is opposed by many smaller States or those in strategically sensitive locations.

There are three schools of thought: that the passage of warships requires the prior authorization of the coastal State; that such passage must be notified to the coastal State, though no express authorization need be requested or given; or that such passage is possible provided that it conforms to the general rules on innocent passage as set out in the Convention. For some, this last approach is implausible since they consider the mere presence of a foreign warship within a territorial sea to be prejudicial to the coastal State's interests. However, the move towards focusing upon 'activities' rather than the presence of

[28] See further Rothwell and Stephens, 2016, p 232, where they also note, however, that 'there is little State practice to suggest that this provision has in fact been misused'.

[29] Notifications made to the UN Secretary-General are publicized on the UN website at http://www.un.org/depts/los.

[30] *Passage Through the Great Belt (Finland v Denmark), Provisional Measures, Order of 29 July 1991, ICJ Reports 1991*, p 12.

ships within the territorial sea in the LOSC makes this argument unpersuasive (see Klein, 2011, p 31). Moreover, the Convention texts provide some support for warships enjoying innocent passage: the general rules are set out in a section headed 'Rules Applicable to all Ships'; some of the activities listed in Article 19(2) as leading to the loss of innocence can only (or largely) be undertaken by warships; and submarines, most (but not all) of which are warships, can exercise that right if surfaced and showing their flag (Churchill and Lowe, 1999, p 89; Rothwell and Stevens, 2016, pp 237–88). None of these arguments is wholly convincing and State practice is as diverse as it is predictable, with major maritime powers such as the UK and the USA (joined by the USSR in their 1989 Joint Statement)[31] arguing in favour of warships enjoying the right of innocent passage and less powerful coastal States enacting legislation requiring authorization or notification (Tanaka, 2015, pp 89–93). Despite the growing trend towards increased coastal State dominance of off-shore areas, the imperatives of essential military interests would suggest that this is likely to remain a matter of controversy for some time to come, though on a day-to-day basis pragmatic approaches are usually found which respect the positions of all concerned.

2. Straits

The regime of innocent passage is a concession by coastal States to accommodate the interests of navigation but, as has been seen, the coastal State still enjoys a formidable array of jurisdictional competences. Whilst this might be acceptable where there is no real need, other than convenience or desire, to enter the territorial seas, different consider-ations apply to narrow straits wholly comprised of territorial seas but which are also used for international navigation, such as the straits of Dover, Gibraltar, and Hormuz. In such cases, international law shifts the balance somewhat in favour of the freedom of navigation (Rothwell, 2015, p 115 and see generally Nandan and Anderson, 1989; Jia, 1998; Caminos and Cogliati-Bantz, 2016).

In the *Corfu Channel* case the ICJ concluded that, irrespective of the position more gen-erally, warships were entitled to exercise a right of innocent passage through straits used for international navigation and that coastal States were not entitled to 'suspend' innocent passage within such straits for any form of ship.[32] This variant on innocent passage only applied in straits which linked one part of the high seas with another and which were ac-tually used as a route of international navigation. Importantly, the existence of a relatively convenient alternative (in this case, around the western side of the Island of Corfu) did not deprive it of this status. Arguably, this was an overly generous approach to the interests of the international community at the expense of the coastal State but it was nevertheless reflected in 1958 TSC Article 16(4), which further expanded the regime by applying it to straits linking the high seas with the territorial sea of a third State at the head of a Gulf (this being intended to facilitate access to the Israeli port of Eilat at the head of the Gulf of Aqaba). This latter gloss did not reflect customary law, and was rejected by Arab States, but it was retained in Article 45 of the LOSC which reflects the TSC approach, though now expanded to take account of the Exclusive Economic Zone (EEZ).

Under the LOSC, the *Corfu Channel* regime of 'non-suspendable innocent passage' has something of a residual flavour, now applying only to straits not covered by the new re-gime of transit passage, considered later. However, there is no doubting the customary law status of the *Corfu Channel* regime which provides an assured minimum guarantee of passage though international straits for all vessels, including warships.

---

[31] USA-USSR Uniform Interpretation of Norms of International Law Government Innocent Passage (1989), 14 *Law of the Sea Bulletin* 12. See Schachte, 1993, pp 182–3.

[32] *Corfu Channel, Merits, Judgment, ICJ Reports 1949*, p 4 at p 28.

3. Transit passage

A major problem facing UNCLOS III concerned the consequences of the breadth of the territorial sea increasing from 3 to 12 n. miles. This meant that many major strategic waterways which had previously been high seas, such as the Straits of Dover, could become entirely territorial seas and at best be subject to the regime of non-suspendable innocent passage. During the Cold War, when super-power security was thought to depend in part on relatively undetectable submarine-based nuclear missiles, the idea that submarines should surface and show their flags when prowling the oceans was an additional concern. The result was a compromise that sought to further reduce the ability of coastal States to restrict passage within their territorial seas.

The LOSC regime of transit passage applies to all straits connecting high seas or EEZs with other areas of high seas or EEZs and which are used for international navigation unless there is a corridor of high seas or EEZ running through it (LOSC Article 36) or the strait is formed by an island which belongs to the coastal State and seawards of which there is an alternative route (LOSC Article 38(1)). In cases covered by this latter rule, known as the 'Messina Strait' exception (after the Straits between Sicily and mainland Italy), the *Corfu Channel* regime of non-suspendable innocent passage continues to apply. Straits covered by particular treaty regimes, such as the Turkish Straits (the Dardanelles and the Bosphorus), are also expressly excluded from the scope of the provisions concerning transit passage (LOSC Article 35(c)).

Whereas innocent passage only applies to ships and submarines, transit passage also applies to aircraft which are accorded the right of overflight. Although not expressly stated, the regime applies to military ships and aircraft, and submarines may proceed submerged. Ships or aircraft must 'proceed without delay' and 'refrain from any threat or use of force' against the States bordering the strait (thus, for example, hurrying through the Straits of Gibraltar to conduct military activities in the eastern Mediterranean would be permissible). Although ships and aircraft must comply with generally accepted international regulations regarding safety matters (LOSC Article 39), coastal States may themselves only regulate a very circumscribed list of activities: maritime safety (including traffic separate schemes); internationally approved regulations concerning discharges of oil, oily waste, and noxious substances in the strait; with respect to fishing vessels, prevention of fishing, and the stowage of fishing gear; and loading and unloading in connection with customs, fiscal, immigration, or sanitary laws (LOSC Article 42(1)). The balance struck clearly favours the freedom of navigation. The customary law status of transit passage has long been challenged (de Yturriaga, 1991) and remains unclear, although State practice outside the Convention framework increasingly reflects these provisions.[33] Whilst the increasing numbers of States party to the LOSC has taken some of the heat out of this debate, it remains the case that maritime powers which are not party to the Convention, including the USA, may need to rely on the customary status of transit passage in order to be assured of passage for warships and overflight of aircraft through or over straits of key strategic significance.

4. Archipelagic sea lane passage

Drawing archipelagic baselines converts vast tracts of waters which were previously either high seas or territorial seas into 'archipelagic waters'. LOSC Article 52 provides that the right of innocent passage applies throughout such waters and, moreover, Article 53

---

[33] Cf Tanaka, 2016, p 109, who suggests that there is insufficient State practice to justify the conclusion that transit passage is a part of customary international law.

provides for a right of 'archipelagic sea lane passage' in 'corridors' to be designated by the archipelagic State. Archipelagic sea lane passage is similar to transit passage, meaning that the jurisdiction of archipelagic States over a wide range of matters in waters within their baselines is substantially reduced.[34] As a result, the demands of international navigation have been given precedence over local control.

IV. THE HIGH SEAS

A. THE FREEDOMS OF THE SEAS

The idea that beyond the territorial seas lie the high seas which are free for use by all lies at the heart of the law of the sea. Both the 1958 HSC and the LOSC proclaim the high seas to be free and open to vessels of all States and give non-exhaustive lists of freedoms. The HSC mentions navigation, fishing, overflight, and cable laying (HSC Article 2), and the LOSC adds the construction of artificial islands and marine scientific research. All are to be enjoyed with 'due regard' (in the HSC, 'reasonable regard') to the interests of others (LOSC Article 87).

It has already been seen how that space has been eroded by the expansion of the territorial seas, and some of the balances that have been struck as a consequence. Later sections will look at how the high seas have been further eroded by the creation of zones of functional jurisdiction. This section considers how freedom of navigation on the high seas has fared.

The key to regulating activities within the high seas is the concept of flag-State jurisdiction (see generally Barnes, 2015). All vessels must be registered according to the laws of a State and, in consequence, are subject to its legislative jurisdiction and, whilst on the high seas or within its own territorial sea or EEZ, to its enforcement jurisdiction. In principle, a flag State enjoys exclusive jurisdiction over its vessels, although there are exceptions. However, if a ship is stateless, or flies more than one flag so that its true State of registry is not clear, then any State can exercise jurisdiction over it.[35]

Although the content of domestic laws applicable to vessels will vary considerably, there are an increasingly large number of international conventions relating to matters such as pollution control, resource management, and health and safety at sea which seek to ensure as common an approach as possible. Beyond this lies the problem of enforcement. A State is obliged to 'effectively exercise its jurisdiction and control' over ships operating under its flag (LOSC Article 94(1)) but this is often easier said than done. Many States simply do not have the capacity to enforce their laws over vessels flying their flag (many of which may only rarely, if ever, put into port in their State of registry), whilst others simply lack the will to do so. Moreover, States are entitled to set their own conditions for registering ships, and although a 'genuine link' must exist between the vessel and State (LOSC Article 91),[36] attempts to lend greater precision to this requirement have not been successful. Indeed, in the 'Virginia G' case, the ITLOS itself adopted a most minimalist position, observing that '... once a ship is registered, the flag State is required, under article 94 of the Convention, to

---

[34] The first example of a designation was that of Indonesia. See Indonesian Government Reg No 37 on the Rights and Obligations of Foreign Ships and Aircraft Exercising the Right of Archipelagic Sea Lane Passage through Designated Archipelagic Sea Lanes, 28 June 2002 (2003) 52 *Law of the Sea Bulletin* 20.

[35] See, eg, *Molvan v Attorney General for Palestine* [1948] AC 351.

[36] But cf Tanaka, 2015, p 164 who wonders if it is really possible for a State to refuse to recognize the nationality on a vessel in the absence of a 'genuine link'.

exercise effective jurisdiction and control over that ship in order to ensure that it operates in accordance with generally accepted international regulations, procedures and practices. This is the meaning of "genuine link".[37] As a result, the problem of vessels being registered under 'flags of convenience', which exercise little effective control over their activities, remains (Guilfoyle, 2015, pp 215–16). It is against this background that the subtle but steady erosion of the exclusive jurisdictional competence of the flag State over its registered vessels must be assessed.

B. THE EXCEPTIONS TO FLAG-STATE JURISDICTION

1. Visit

It is axiomatic that the authorities of one State may not board a vessel flying the flag of another without the consent of the flag State. There is, however, an increasingly long and increasingly detailed list of exceptions to this general principle. These exceptions will be outlined later, but since it will not always be immediately apparent whether such action is permissible, international law recognizes an intermediary position in which the authorities of a non-flag State are entitled to board a vessel on the high seas in order to verify whether their suspicions are justified (see generally Guilfoyle, 2009; Papastavridis, 2013). These instances arise where there are reasonable grounds for suspecting that a ship is engaged in piracy, the slave trade, or unauthorized radio broadcasting (LOSC Article 110(1) (a)–(c)), the consequences of which are considered later. In addition, a ship might be visited to confirm that it is either stateless or, in cases of doubt, that it is in fact of the nationality of the visiting authorities, meaning that the visiting authority can assert its jurisdiction on the basis of the principles outlined in the previous section. In all of these cases a visit and any subsequent action may only be undertaken by a warship or other vessel or aircraft duly authorized and clearly marked (LOSC Articles 110(5) and 107), but the right of visit cannot be exercised in respect of a warship of another State or any other non-flag State vessel entitled to immunity.

2. Piracy

Under both customary international law and the 1958 and 1982 Conventions all States may take action on the high seas, or in any other place beyond the national jurisdiction of a State, against individuals or vessels involved in acts of piracy. Those committing acts of piracy are often said to have rendered themselves 'enemies of all mankind' and piracy is the oldest and most well-attested example of an act which attracts universal jurisdiction.[38] However, the LOSC definition of piracy is comparatively narrow, covering only 'illegal acts of violence or detention, or any act of depredation, committed for private ends by the crew or passengers of a private ship or private aircraft and directed (i) on the high seas, against another ship[39] or aircraft, or against persons or property on board such a ship or aircraft;

---

[37] M/V 'Virginia G' (Panama/Guinea-Bissau), Judgment, ITLOS Reports 2014, p 4, para 113.

[38] See, eg, Arrest Warrant of 11 April 2000 (Democratic Republic of Congo v Belgium), Preliminary Objections and Merits, Judgment, ICJ Reports 2002, p 3. Separate Opinion of Judges Higgins, Kooijmans, and Buergenthal, para 61; Separate Opinion of President Guillaume, para 5.

[39] The importance of the action being taken against another ship (or aircraft) was highlighted by the Arctic Sunrise Arbitration, which made it clear that action against a fixed platform could not be piracy as a fixed platform was not a 'ship'. See Arctic Sunrise Arbitration (Netherlands v Russia), Arbitral Tribunal constituted under annex VII of the UN Law of the Sea Convention, Award on the Merits, 14 August 2015, PCA Case No 2014–02, para 238.

(ii) against a ship, aircraft, persons or property in a place outside the jurisdiction of any State' (LOSC Article 101(a)).[40]

This definition conjures up a vision of pirates roaming the seas in their own private and unregistered vessels, beyond the reach of any flag State, and preying on other vessels whose own flag State may not be in a position to react or respond. Whilst this may seem something of a caricature, reflecting historical experience (and Hollywood stereotypes), it still resonates with the current reality in a number of regions and, in particular, where weak or failing States have produced the forms of legal vacuum in which piracy flourishes. The situation off the coast of Somalia has given rise to particular concern in recent times. In June 2008 the UN Security Council, with Somalia's consent and acting under Chapter VII of the UN Charter, adopted Resolution 1816 which called on States to cooperate in tackling piracy off the coast of Somalia and authorized them to enter Somalia's territorial seas in order to exercise enforcement jurisdiction over acts of piracy or armed robbery which had occurred either in international waters or in the territorial sea itself[41] (Guilfoyle, 2008). Later that year, in Resolution 1846, the Security Council went further and authorized States to take action against vessels reasonably suspected of involvement in piracy.[42] Shortly afterwards the Council went further again, calling on States to take all necessary measures within the territory of Somalia itself to suppress piracy and armed robbery at sea[43] (Guilfoyle, 2009, pp 61–78; Treves, 2013). In response to these calls, an unprecedentedly complex web of multilateral arrangements have been entered into in order to protect shipping from attack and to apprehend, try, and punish those suspected of piracy (see generally Giess and Petrig, 2011; Guilfoyle, 2013; Petrig, 2015). Importantly, the response was not limited to States, with the EU playing a major role through its Operation Atlanta (see Gosalbo-Bono and Boelaert, 2014). It seems likely, however, that this unusually innovative and expansive response to piracy off Somalia has been driven by the particular situation within that country and does not offer a more general model for tackling piracy.[44]

Previous responses to the shortcomings of the definition of piracy in LOSC 110 have also left an enduring legacy, even if they have fallen short of what was required to address the problems posed by piracy off the coasts of Somalia. The *Achille Lauro* incident in the mid-1980s concerned a situation in which a group of passengers turned hijacker and seized control of an Italian cruise liner, and subsequently killed one of the other passengers. Although those responsible were clearly susceptible to, *inter alia*, Italian jurisdiction, this incident prompted the adoption of the 1988 Rome Convention on the Suppression of Unlawful Acts Against the Safety of Maritime Navigation (known as the 1988 SUA Convention). Following the pattern of numerous other international conventions, it sets out an extensive range of offences which States parties must make criminal under their domestic law and obliges them either to extradite or to submit the cases of those suspected of committing such acts to their prosecuting authorities. Although the SUA Convention does not grant

---

[40] It also includes voluntarily participating in operating a ship or aircraft, in the knowledge that it is being used for the purposes of piracy and inciting or intentionally facilitating piracy (LOSC Article 101(b) and (c)). In US v Ali, the US Court of Appeals, District of Colombia (11 June 2013) decided that, whilst the definition embraces aiding and abetting piracy, it does not extend to conspiracy to commit acts of piracy, which, it believed, fell outside the scope of piracy as defined under international law. For an excellent appraisal of LOSC Article 101 see Churchill, 2014.

[41] SC Res 1816 (2 June 2008). This authorization was for a period of six months from the date of the resolution.

[42] SC Res 1846 (2 Dec 2008), extending the authorizations given in SC Res 1816 for a further 12 months. This has been extended for further 12-month periods annually, most recently by SC Res 2383 (7 November 2017).

[43] See SC Res 1851 (8 December 2008).

[44] It has, however, inspired similar responses in relation to migrant smuggling and people trafficking through Libya. See SC Res 2240 (9 October 2014), most recently renewed for one year by SC Res 2380 (5 October 2017).

States parties further jurisdictional competencies at sea, it does oblige them to extend and use their domestic law against those who imperil the freedom of navigation. Moreover, Article 17 of the SUA Convention sets out a highly developed framework for facilitating cooperation between contracting States, including procedures for flag States to authorize the boarding and searching of vessels suspected of prohibited activities by those requesting to do so. These provisions have been built upon in other contexts, as will be described later.

3. Hot pursuit

The problem of how to deal with vessels which commit offences within internal waters or the territorial sea but evade arrest by moving outside the zones of coastal State jurisdiction has already been mentioned and one response—that of the contiguous zone—has already been noted. The doctrine of 'hot pursuit' provides another means of addressing the same problem and forms another exception to the principle of exclusive flag-State jurisdiction. According to this doctrine, the rather complex details of which are set out at length in LOSC Article 111, warships or military aircraft of a coastal State which have commenced the pursuit of a vessel within their territorial sea (or within their the contiguous zone or EEZ, if the offence in question is one for which an arrest might have been made there) may continue that pursuit outside of it provided that the pursuit is continuous, although the actual ship or aircraft involved in the pursuit might change: indeed, practice suggests that ships or aircraft of several nationalities may cooperate in arresting a vessel in the exercise of a right of hot pursuit.[45]

A further variant on this is 'constructive presence'. Rather than commit an offence within the territorial sea, some vessels choose to remain just outside the territorial sea and dispatch smaller boats, for example, to take illegal goods ashore. A variant of this occurred in the *Arctic Sunrise* case,[46] which concerned the dispatch of environmental protestors in small boats to a Russian oil rig located in its EEZ. Under such circumstances, the 'mother' vessel might be chased and arrested even though it has never entered the territorial sea (or, in the case of the *Arctic Sunrise*, the 500-metre safety zone around the rig within which Russia was entitled to exercise jurisdiction) and the pursuit of the 'mother vessel' begins outside of it. The same is true should boats be sent out from the coastal State to meet the 'mother' vessel: in both cases there has been teamwork that implicates the vessel operating outside of the territorial seas with those committing offences within it.

How far can this approach be taken? In *R v Mills*, the *Poseidon*, a vessel registered in St Vincent, transferred a consignment of drugs on the high seas to a trawler sailing from Ireland to the UK. Following the arrest of the trawler in the UK, the *Poseidon* was also arrested, this being justified on the basis of 'constructive presence' (Gilmore, 1995). Taken to extremes, this suggests that any vessel which whilst at sea colludes with another vessel in the commission of an illegal act within the jurisdiction of a State is liable to arrest by that State anywhere on the high seas. Though not irreconcilable, this expansive approach sits rather uneasily with the caution expressed by the International Tribunal on the Law of the Sea (ITLOS) in *M/V Saiga (No 2)* which stressed the need for a strict approach to be taken to the application of LOSC Article 111.[47]

---

[45] In 2003 the *Viarsa 1* was arrested following a pursuit lasting some 21 days and extending over some 3,900 km, and which involved vessels from Australia, South Africa, and the UK. See Molenaar, 2004.

[46] *Arctic Sunrise Arbitration (Netherlands v Russia)*, Arbitral Tribunal constituted under annex VII of the UN Law of the Sea Convention, Award of 12 July 2015, Award on the Merits, 14 August 2015, PCA Case No 2014–02.

[47] *M/V Saiga No 2 (St Vincent and the Grenadines v Guinea)*, Case No 2, Judgment of 1 July 1999, paras 146–52. Cf also *M/V Louisa (St Vincent and the Grenadines v Spain), Case No 18, Judgment, 28 May 2013*, paras 86–7 for a further example of ITLOS taking a strict approach to a similar question.

4. Broadcasting

In the 1960s elements of the international community became agitated about the rise of commercial broadcasting into a country from foreign registered vessels on the high seas and over which they could not exercise any control (or extract revenues).[48] Regional State practice to address this problem in the North Sea through cooperative measures was subsequently built on, with the result that LOSC Article 109 permits the arrest and prosecution of any person engaged in 'unauthorized radio broadcasting' from ships or installations on the high seas by a range of States, including the State where the transmissions are received (Anderson, 2006, pp 340–1). A perhaps unexpected consequence of this arose in the early 1990s when a vessel called the *Goddess of Democracy* planned to broadcast messages of solidarity and support for those arrested in the pro-democracy demonstrations in Beijing. The Chinese authorities made it clear they would arrest the vessel if it did so, and the mission was aborted.

5. Slavery

The rather heavy-handed approach taken in respect of unauthorized broadcasting contrasts with the comparatively feeble manner in which other, more pressing, issues were tackled. The international prohibition of slavery is well established in international law yet the 1982 Convention does not permit the arrest of vessels engaged in slave trading by non-flag States; it merely provides that a State 'shall take effective measures to prevent and punish the transport of slaves in ships authorized to fly its flag' (LOSC Article 99). Admittedly, that Article also provides that any slave fortunate enough to escape and take refuge on a non-flag State vessel 'shall *ipso facto* be free' and since there is a right to visit vessels suspected of being involved in slave trading (LOSC Article 110(1)(b)) this should not be difficult to manufacture. Nevertheless, it remains difficult to see why those involved in the slave trade, and their vessels, should not be susceptible to arrest under such circumstances without the express authorization of the flag State. More attention has been paid to the related practice of smuggling migrants across borders and the 'Migrant Smuggling Protocol' to the UN Convention against Transnational Organized Crime adopted in 2000 follows the model of the 1988 Vienna Convention against Illicit Traffic in Narcotics (considered later) in constructing a regime to encourage and facilitate the acquisition of flag-State consent to board and undertake other 'appropriate measures' to 'prevent and suppress' migrant smuggling.[49] In addition, and as has already been noted, specific measures have also been authorized by the UN Security Council to address specific situations of migrant smuggling, such as that relating to Libya.

6. Drugs trafficking

As with slavery, the LOSC provisions concerning drugs trafficking have also been found wanting. Article 108 is an anodyne provision which merely provides that States 'shall co-operate' in the suppression of the drugs trade by vessels on the high seas and that a State which suspects a vessel flying its flag is involved in trafficking 'may request the co-operation of other states to suppress such traffic'. This states the obvious. The 1988 Vienna Convention Against Illicit Traffic in Narcotic Drugs and Psychotropic Substances takes the matter further, developing and institutionalizing a more detailed framework for

---

[48] See generally Guilfoyle, 2009, ch 7. The film *The Ship that Rocked* (2008) provides an entertaining account of the issues as seen at the time.

[49] The Protocol entered into force in 2004. See generally Guilfoyle, 2009, pp 184–226 for this and a consideration of related State practice.

cooperation, but boarding a vessel still requires flag-State authorization and there is no right of visit under LOSC Article 110. This was vividly illustrated in *R v Charrington* where irregularities in the manner in which the UK Customs and Excise obtained the consent of the Maltese authorities to board a vessel carrying £15m of cannabis resulted in the collapse of the domestic prosecution (Gilmore, 2000). State practice has gone further and, building on the model provided by the 1988 Convention, arrangements for mutual enforcement and assistance have been concluded in a number of spheres, particularly fishing. In addition, the UK has concluded bilateral arrangements permitting US authorities to board British vessels suspected of drugs offences on the high seas within the Caribbean region and has concluded a regional treaty to facilitate more widespread cooperation.[50]

Once again, it may be that long-standing dogmas have stood in the way of devising rather more effective means of tackling a matter of major international concern.

7. Terrorism and weapons of mass destruction

The 1988 SUA Convention was drafted in the wake of a terrorist outrage akin to piracy and so it was not surprising that the response was tailored to that form. As new concerns have emerged they too have been addressed within the model that the SUA provides; that is, through the identification and definition of additional forms of unlawful conduct and the utilization of cooperative arrangements to enable flag-State consent to be more readily obtained for boarding, search and, if necessary, arrest of vessels by non-flag States. In October 2005 the International Maritime Organization adopted a Protocol to the SUA which would make it an offence under the Convention to engage in an extremely broad range of activities at sea when the purpose of the activity, given its nature and context, is intended to 'intimidate a population, or to compel a government or an international organization to do or to abstain from any act', or to knowingly transport persons who have committed such unlawful acts.[51] Moreover, the Protocol permits participating States to notify the IMO Secretary-General in advance that permission for boarding and searching is to be presumed if no reply is given to a requesting State within four hours of a request being made. This goes a long way to creating a presumption in favour of boarding by those States with reasonable grounds for suspicion and a heavy onus on those flag States that might seek to deny such a request. Although the 2005 Protocol entered into force in 2010, it has not been widely ratified as yet.[52]

The 2005 Protocol had already been prefigured by the 'Proliferation Security Initiative' (PSI), instigated by the USA in 2003 and which provides an enhanced framework for cooperation between its now more than 100 participating States when seeking to undertake an interdiction at sea (see Byers, 2004; Guilfoyle, 2009, ch 9; Klein, 2011, pp 193–208; Papastavridis, 2013, ch 5). The USA has also entered into reciprocal bilateral treaties with a number of States which, like the 2005 Protocol, provide for a presumption that a request

[50] Agreement Concerning Co-operation in Suppressing Illicit Maritime and Air Trafficking in Narcotic Drugs and Psychotropic Substances in the Caribbean Area, 10 April 2003. See Gilmore, 2005. For a more general review of the topic see Guilfoyle, 2009, ch 5; Papastavridis, 2013, ch 7.

[51] These acts not only embrace the use or discharge of any explosive, radioactive material, or BCN (biological, chemical, nuclear) weapon in a manner that causes or is likely to cause death or serious injury or damage but also include the transportation of explosive or radioactive materials in the knowledge that they are intended to be so used, knowingly transporting a BCN weapon, and a further range of related activities including the transportation of any equipment, materials, or software or related technology that significantly contributes to the design, manufacture, or delivery of a BCN weapon with the intention that they will be used for such purposes. See 2005 Protocol, adding Article 3*bis* to the SUA. See generally Klein, 2011, pp 170–84.

[52] The Protocol has 41 States parties, compared to the 166 parties to the 1988 SUA, although those ratifying the Protocol account for 39 per cent of registered shipping.

for boarding has been granted if no response if given within a limited period of time.[53] Once again, these developments are consonant with the traditional principles of high seas and flag-State jurisdiction, but point to a reality very different from that which those principles suggest for those willing to accept them through participating in the SUA Protocol, PSI, or other bilateral arrangements. However, there is as yet no evidence to suggest that such broad-ranging rights and facilitative arrangements for boarding and search—even in this context—are reflective of customary international law.

C. CONCLUSION

The freedom of navigation has, then, been the subject of some whittling away, both by reason of the increasing breadth of the territorial sea, outlined in Section III, and by the erosion of exclusive flag-State jurisdiction outlined earlier. However, the modifications to the regime of innocent passage and the regime of transit passage, as well as the limited and piecemeal nature of the increased jurisdictional competence over non-flag-State vessels, all point in the direction of the continuing significance of the freedom of navigation, albeit that this is 'freedom under the law' (Anderson, 2006, p 345). This is further underscored by the remaining sections of this chapter, which chart the rise of functional zones of jurisdiction which, although representing a marked diminution in other freedoms of the high seas, have had a lesser impact on the freedom of navigation and ensured that the increase in the breadth of the territorial sea was kept within modest bands.

V. RESOURCE JURISDICTION

A. THE CONTINENTAL SHELF

During the opening decades of the twentieth century improvements in technology made the exploration and exploitation of seabed and subsoil resources beyond the territorial sea—particularly oil and then natural gas—both increasingly possible and economically viable. In theory, these deposits were available to all since legally speaking they were high seas resources. However, orderly and effective development required some degree of involvement by a proximate coastal State and in the Truman Proclamation (1945), the US President declared 'the natural resources of the subsoil and seabed of the continental shelf beneath the high seas but contiguous to the coasts of the US as appertaining to the US, subject to its jurisdiction and control'.[54] Following consideration by the ILC, the 1958 CSC provided that '[t]he coastal state exercises over the continental shelf sovereign rights for the purpose of exploring it and exploiting its natural resources' and did so independently of express acts or declarations (Articles 2(1) and 2(3)). In the *North Sea* cases the ICJ recognized this as a statement of customary law, stressing that these rights existed '*ipso facto and ab initio*'.[55] LOSC Article 77 reiterates this approach.

---

[53] The USA has so far concluded nine such bilateral agreements, with Antigua and Barbuda (2010), the Bahamas (2008), Belize (2005), Croatia (2005), Cyprus (2005), Liberia (2004), Malta (2007), Marshall Islands (2004), Mongolia (2007), Panama (2004), and St Vincent and the Grenadines (2010). See Klein, 2011, pp 184–90. These States account for much of the registered shipping in the world. The time period for notification before the presumption in its favour takes effect in these agreements is the even shorter period of two hours.

[54] 1 *New Directions in the Law of the Sea* 106.

[55] *North Sea Continental Shelf, Judgment, ICJ Reports 1969*, p 3, paras 19, 39, and 43.

Natural resources include both mineral and other non-living resources of the seabed and subsoil as well as 'sedentary species' (CSC Article 2(4); LOSC Article 77(4)). Thus pearling is clearly covered by this definition, whereas jurisdiction over wrecks is not. Whether crabs and lobsters are continental shelf resources is more controversial, although the EEZ now provides an alternative means of securing coastal State jurisdiction over such resources.

The most vexed question concerns the outer limit of continental shelf jurisdiction. The seabed off a coast may not be a 'continental shelf' in a geophysical sense at all: the coast may swiftly plunge to great depths, as it does off the western coasts of much of South America, or merely be shallow indentations into which water has flooded, as in the Gulf region of the Middle East. The continental shelf proper is merely a component of the 'continental margin' which comprises the gently sloping shelf, which gives way to a steep slope which then levels off into the continental rise that emerges from the ocean floor (sometimes rather prosaically described as the 'Abyssal Plain'). The 1958 CSC did not draw directly on any of these concepts and defined the continental shelf, for legal purposes, as comprising the seabed and subsoil adjacent to the coast but outside the territorial sea, extending to the point where the waters above were 200 metres deep, or as far seawards as it was possible to exploit (CSC Article 1). This was most unsatisfactory since it permitted States to claim ever more distant areas as technology rapidly developed. Moreover it ran into the claim advanced in the late 1960s that the deep seabed was the 'common heritage' of all mankind and not subject to single State jurisdiction. It was, then, necessary to place some limit on the seawards expansion of continental shelf jurisdiction.

In the *North Sea* cases the ICJ argued that the continental shelf represented the 'natural prolongation' of the landmass into and under the sea,[56] implying some limit to its seawards expansion. However, this still did not address the claims of States which had no 'natural prolongation' as such, but which nevertheless sought jurisdiction over offshore seabed and subsoil resources and therefore argued that the continental shelf should be a fixed distance, measured from the baselines, irrespective of the nature of the seabed. This approach was opposed by some of the so-called 'broad shelf' States which already exercised jurisdiction on the basis of 'natural prolongation' beyond the most likely fixed limit of 200 n. miles.

This conundrum was resolved by the complex compromise found in LOSC Article 76(1), according to which the continental shelf extends (a) to the outer edge of continental margin (this being seen as the natural prolongation), or (b) to a distance of 200 n. miles from the baselines from which its territorial sea is measured, whichever is the further. LOSC Article 76(2)–(7) then set out details of how the outer edge of the continental margin is to be calculated. This is to be done with reference to the 'foot' of the continental slope, this being the point where the continental slope gives way to the continental rise. From this point, a State might either exercise jurisdiction for a further 60 n. miles seawards, or as far as a point where the depth of the 'sedimentary rock' (loose, rather than bedrock) overlying the continental rise is more than 1 per cent of the distance of that point from the foot of the slope. These outer lines are then subject to one of two alternative limitations: they cannot be drawn more than 350 miles from the baselines of a State, or more than 100 miles from a point at which the depth of the water is 2,500 metres.

This complicated formula is difficult to apply and its customary law status unclear. In the *Territorial and Maritime Boundary Dispute (Nicaragua v Colombia)*, the ICJ confirmed that Article 76(1) was customary law, but reserved its position as regards the remainder of

---

[56] Ibid, para 18. For an extended discussion see Hutchinson, 1985.

that Article, noting that it was not necessary to decide on its customary law status for the purposes of the case.[57] This resonates with the view that the continental shelf is composed of two elements: an 'inner shelf' of 200 n. miles to which all coastal States are entitled, and an 'outer shelf', where its continental margin extends beyond that distance.[58] A controversial question which then arises is whether the 'inner' shelf provided for in Article 76(1) takes precedence over a claim to an 'outer' shelf made by another State, and this is currently being considered by the ICJ in a case concerning Nicaragua and Colombia.[59] Others, however, have taken the entirely different view that 'Article 76 of the Convention embodies the concept of a single continental shelf' and so the question does not arise.[60]

Irrespective of the views taken on this question, it is vital to determine the outer limit of each State's continental shelf since, if there is no overlap with another State, the seabed beyond the continental shelf forms part of the 'area', which is governed by its own legal regime (considered in Section V D in this chapter). LOSC Article 76(8) establishes the Commission on the Limits of the Continental Shelf, to which States parties must submit details of their claims to outer limits beyond 200 n. miles from their baselines. The role of the Commission is to examine these submissions and to make recommendations to States 'on the basis of which' the State establishes its final boundary (see generally Cook and Carlton, 2000). This is clearly opaque—for example, it is unclear what happens should the State reject the Commission's recommendations. The Commission issues recommendations, only summaries of which are made public, and which reveal the extremely complex nature of its task.[61] What is clear is that the entire regime reflects a careful balancing act between the interests of coastal States with varied geophysical relationships to the sea; to the economic interests of the international community as a whole; and to the interests of the freedom of navigation and of the high seas, which it leaves substantially untouched.

B. THE EXCLUSIVE FISHING ZONE

As States watched the international community recognize and legitimate coastal State jurisdiction over the resources of the seabed and subsoil, it was inevitable that the argument would be made that resources of the water column be treated likewise. This was always going to be controversial since the seabed was, by and large, chiefly of potential economic importance, whereas high seas fishing was already of very real economic importance and excluding foreign-flagged fishing vessels from waters beyond narrow belts of territorial seas would have serious consequences for many communities and economies. However,

---

[57] *Territorial and Maritime Dispute (Nicaragua v Colombia), Judgment of 19 November 2012*, para 118. Whilst both parties had accepted that Article 76(1) reflected customary international law, Colombia had contested Nicaragua's claim that Articles 76(2)–(7) were also rules of customary international law.

[58] For consideration of this see Colson, 2003; Nelson, 2009, Magnusson, 2015.

[59] See *Question of the Delimitation of the Continental Shelf between Nicaragua and Colombia beyond 200 Nautical Miles from the Nicaraguan Coast (Nicaragua v Colombia), Preliminary Objections, Judgment, ICJ Reports 2016*, p 100. For an early discussion of this problem see Evans, 1993.

[60] See *The Bay of Bengal Maritime Boundary Arbitration (Bangladesh v India)*, Arbitral Tribunal constituted under annex VII of the UN Law of the Sea Convention, Award of 7 July 2014, PCA Case No 2010–16, para 77, supporting the view of ITLOS in *Delimitation of the Maritime Boundary in the Bay of Bengal (Bangladesh/Myanmar), Judgment, ITLOS Reports 2012*, p 4 and supported by the subsequent decision of the Special Arbitral Tribunal in the *Delimitation of the Maritime Boundary in the Atlantic Ocean (Ghana/Côte d'Ivoire), Judgment, ITLOS Reports 2017, nyr*, para 490.

[61] This might account for why the Commission is only able to produce only some three or four Recommendations per year, meaning that at current rates there is a ten-year backlog of submissions. See Subedi, 2011. For an overview of the practice of the Commission see Rothwell and Stevens, 2016, pp 116–23; see also the essays in Vidas, 2010, Pt V; Parson, 2016.

the increased capacity of vessels to harvest fish was putting stocks at risk and so there was a tension between maximizing access to resources and promoting effective conservation. Viewed in this light, increased coastal State control appeared more beneficial than high seas freedoms and this was reflected in the developing law of fisheries. This will be considered further in Section VII but it is important to note here the emergence of the Exclusive Fishing Zone (EFZ) as an autonomous zone of resource jurisdiction.

Neither UNCLOS I nor II could agree upon the establishment of an EFZ but State practice moved steadily in the direction of recognizing the right of a coastal State to assert jurisdiction over fisheries within 12 n. miles of its baselines and in the 1974 *Fisheries Jurisdiction* case the ICJ recognized this as reflecting customary law.[62] By this time claims for zones of up to 200 n. miles were being advanced yet the Court was unwilling to go further and endorse Iceland's claim for an EFZ of up to 50 n. miles. It did, however, suggest that a State might exceptionally be entitled to preferential access to the high seas resources within such a distance under certain circumstances.[63] Such hesitations were subsequently swept away by the development of the EEZ and, although there is no mention of the EFZ as an autonomous regime within the LOSC, it is clear that customary law now recognizes EFZ claims of up to 200 n. miles.[64]

C. THE EXCLUSIVE ECONOMIC ZONE

The previous sections have already identified the reasons why during the 1960s and 1970s many coastal States wanted to have exclusive access to the resources of the seabed and the water column but were reluctant to extend the breadth of their territorial seas. In order to balance the competing interests, Latin and South American States advanced the claim that there should be a single zone of up to 200 n. miles in which the coastal State enjoyed sovereign rights over all natural living and non-living resources but within which the other freedoms of the seas, and in particular navigation, would be unaffected. Over time, this claim became refined into what is now known as the EEZ, which became recognized as reflecting customary international law during the UNCLOS III process[65] and, of course, is established as a matter of treaty law by the LOSC itself.[66]

Under the regime established by the Convention, States may claim an EEZ of up to 200 n. miles (LOSC Article 57) within which the range of matters reserved for the coastal State are so extensive that the Zone is composed of neither territorial seas nor high seas but is considered to be 'sui generis' and subject to a distinct jurisdictional framework (LOSC Article 55). First and foremost, coastal States exercise sovereign rights within the EEZ for the purposes of 'exploring and exploiting, conserving and managing' both living and non-living natural resources (LOSC Article 56(1)(a)). Although this may seem to be an amalgamation of the jurisdictional capacities which States already were able to enjoy on the basis of the continental shelf and the EFZ regimes, the EEZ does in fact embrace additional elements, including the harnessing of wind and wave power. The coastal State also has jurisdiction, subject to the other provisions of the Convention, over the establishment and use of artificial islands and installations, marine scientific research, and the preservation of the marine environment, as well as a range of other matters (LOSC Article 56(b) and (c)).

---

[62] *Fisheries Jurisdiction (United Kingdom v Iceland), Merits, Judgment, ICJ Reports 1974,* p 3, para 53.

[63] Ibid, paras 55–60.

[64] See *Maritime Delimitation in the Area between Greenland and Jan Mayen, Judgment, ICJ Reports 1993,* p 316, accepting uncritically the Norwegian claim to an EFZ of this distance.

[65] See *Continental Shelf (Libyan Arab Jamahiriya/Malta), Judgment, ICJ Reports 1985,* p 13.

[66] For general studies of the origins and background of the EEZ see Attard, 1986; Orrego-Vicuna, 1989.

Despite its *'sui generis'* nature, the EEZ is pulled in a number of different directions. As regards jurisdiction over the resources of the seabed and subsoil, it is closely aligned with the continental shelf (LOSC Article 56(3)). Article 58 provides that three of the freedoms of the seas expressly mentioned in the Convention—navigation, overflight, and laying cables and pipelines, and related activities—are to be exercised by all States within an EEZ in accordance with the general framework for the high seas, as provided for in Articles 87–116. Thus, of the six high seas freedoms identified in the Convention, three pass to the predominant control of the coastal State within its EEZ whilst three remain open to the international community at large. This list of freedoms is not exhaustive and in situations not specifically provided for the question of whether a matter falls within the jurisdiction of the coastal State 'should be resolved on the basis of equity and in the light of all the relevant circumstances, taking into account the respective importance of the interests involved to the parties as well as to the international community as a whole' (LOSC Article 59).

The heart of the EEZ concerns jurisdiction over fisheries and this is considered in Section VII in this chapter. However, it should be noted here that coastal States enjoy broad-ranging legislative jurisdiction (LOSC Article 63(4)) and may take measures including 'boarding, inspection, arrest and judicial proceedings' which are necessary to enforce laws and regulations concerning its sovereign right to 'explore, exploit, conserve and manage' living resources of the EEZ (LOSC Article 73). This is not without difficulties, and the *M/V Saiga (No 2)* illustrates the type of problem that might arise. Guinea arrested a vessel in its EEZ and argued, *inter alia*, that it was entitled to do so because the vessel had been 'bunkering' (transferring oil to) a fishing vessel and thereby avoiding customs duties. If the bunkering had occurred within the territorial sea, and the arrest taken place within internal waters, the territorial sea, or a contiguous zone, the legitimacy of the arrest would not have been in doubt. The ITLOS found it unnecessary to decide this point at the time,[67] but in a subsequent case, the *'Virginia G'*, it took the view that a State is entitled to regulate the bunkering of a fishing vessel within its EEZ since the coastal State exercises jurisdiction within the EEZ over fisheries.[68] This does not, however, extend to the bunkering of non-fishing vessels. Similar difficult questions have arisen in other cases.[69]

The Convention also balances the potentially intrusive power of the coastal State over vessels within its EEZ against the risk of abuse by requiring that vessels or crew arrested 'shall be promptly released upon the posting of reasonable bond or other securities' and by restricting the nature of the penalties to which they might be subject (LOSC Article 73). Moreover, the International Tribunal on the Law of the Sea enjoys an automatic jurisdiction over claims concerning the prompt release of vessels arrested for contravening coastal State law relating to the exploitation of living resources of the EEZ (LOSC Articles 292 and 73) and this has generated a considerable number of cases.

---

[67] *M/V Saiga No 2 (St Vincent and the Grenadines v Guinea), Case No 2, Judgment of 1 July 1999*, paras 56–9.

[68] *M/V 'Virginia G' (Panama/Guinea-Bissau), Judgment, ITLOS Reports 2014*, p 4, paras 222–3. In the 1986 *Franco-Canadian Fisheries Arbitration* ((1986) 90 *RGDIP* 713) it was thought that a vessel engaged in processing fish at sea fell outside the range of activities over which the coastal State was entitled to exercise and enforce jurisdiction. This has been subject to criticism (Churchill and Lowe, 1999, p 291) and in the light of the *'Virginia G'* decision might not be decided in the same way today.

[69] See *Arctic Sunrise Arbitration (Netherlands v Russia)*, Arbitral Tribunal constituted under annex VII of the UN Law of the Sea Convention, Award on the Merits, 14 August 2015, PCA Case No 2014–02 and also *'Enrica Lexie' Incident (Italy v India), Provisional Measures, Order of 24 July 2015, ITLOS Reports 2015*, p 176, both of which again illustrate the tension between the exercise of the freedom of navigation within the EEZ and the legislative and enforcement jurisdiction of the coastal State.

D. THE DEEP SEABED

The final zone of resource jurisdiction which has been carved out of the high seas is the most dramatic in both kind and extent. The claim that the seabed beyond the limits of national jurisdiction form the 'common heritage of mankind', fuelled initially by some near fantastical estimates of the potential mineral wealth at stake, has already been noted. The difficulty lay in translating that idea into a workable regime: the developed world favoured a loosely structured international agency to oversee and regulate activities of those wishing to conduct mining whereas the developing world generally favoured creating a strong international mechanism that would itself undertake mining activity and distribute the proceeds as appropriate, taking account of the needs of developing countries and developing land-based producers. Negotiations at UNCLOS III were tortuous and produced an outcome—Part XI of the LOSC—which satisfied few and was considered completely unacceptable by the developed world in general and the USA in particular (Schmidt, 1989).

Even at the time of its adoption, it was clear that the Convention text would need to be modified in some way in order to accommodate the interests of the major industrialized powers whose support would be necessary for the regime to become a practical reality. Some concessions were made in Resolutions I and II which were appended to the Final Act of the Conference. These granted certain privileges to 'pioneer investors', States and companies registered in States which had already made a significant investment in seabed mining. This, however, proved to be too little too late. The breakthrough came in the early 1990s when the likelihood of the Convention's entry into force, coupled with the demise of communism and changing economic and geo-political factors, produced a climate in which it was possible to revisit the Convention text, sweep away some of the more bureaucratic and arcane layers of regulation, and strike a new balance between the interests of those States and those companies which were already practically engaged in activities relating to mining the deep seabed and the more general interests of the international community as a whole. Far-reaching changes were made in the 1994 Implementation Agreement which paved the way for widespread ratification of the Convention (Section I of this chapter; Harrison, 2011, ch 5). Underlying this change of approach was the realization that the financial rewards were likely to be considerably less than originally thought.[70]

Under the current arrangements, resource exploration and exploitation of the seabed and subsoil beyond the limits of national jurisdiction, known as the 'Area', is administered by the International Seabed Authority (ISA) to which applicants must submit 'plans of work'. These must identify two areas of roughly equal mining potential, one of which is to be mined by the applicant whilst the other will be 'reserved' for exploitation by the international community. In the original Convention scheme, exploitation of the 'reserved' site would be undertaken by the 'Enterprise', an independent commercial mining arm of the ISA, but under the 1994 Agreement the 'Enterprise' was given a considerably reduced role and, at least initially, might only engage in joint ventures. If the Enterprise does not undertake the mining of a reserved site within 15 years, the original applicant may do so. Moreover, if it does seek to mine the site, the original applicant is to be offered the chance to participate in the joint venture. The reality is that the Enterprise does not yet exist as an entity, and the ISA is currently fulfilling its functions. In the meanwhile, the Authority

[70] Indeed, commercial interest was already switching away from polymetallic nodules, primarily located beyond national jurisdiction in the Area, and becoming more focused on polymetallic sulphides which are more usually found within areas of continental shelf and EEZ under national jurisdiction, further lessening the significance of the Deep Seabed regime.

has since 2001 entered into a number of 15-year contracts with a range of governments,[71] government entities, and commercial consortia, whose activities are largely focused on exploration and research at present, in the Clarion-Clipperton Zone in the Pacific Ocean and the Central Indian Ocean Basin.

The details of the regime, and the manner in which it balances the interests of various interest groups—including consumer States, investing States, producing States, developing States, landlocked States, and others—is such as to defy easy and succinct description and may be pursued elsewhere.[72] For current purposes what is significant is the manner in which the international community—after a number of false starts—was able to agree that the resource potential of the seabed and subsoil should no longer be considered as a part of the high seas regime and that yet another 'bespoke' regime of resource jurisdiction should be created, whilst preserving the integrity of the general jurisdictional framework applicable to the law of the sea.

An important problem has, however, emerged. The discovery of new forms of resource potential in hydrothermal vents, and the marine genetic resources associated with them, is posing new challenges to the division between the seabed/subsoil and water column beyond national jurisdiction, it being unclear whether such resources are best understood as a resource of the 'Area' or of the high seas (see generally Leary, 2006 and Vidas, 2010, Pt IV). Their interdependence is such that, in fact, they are a resource of both and in 2015 the UN General Assembly decided in GA Resolution 69/292 (19 June 2015) to commence the process of drafting a new 'international legally binding instrument under the United Nations Convention on the law of the sea on the conservation and sustainable use of marine biological diversity of areas beyond national jurisdiction' (see Freestone, 2016, pp 232–43). It remains to be seen quite what the scope of any new instrument adopted as a result of this process actually is, this being deliberately opaque in the work of the preparatory commission.[73]

VI. DELIMITATION OF MARITIME ZONES BETWEEN OPPOSITE OR ADJACENT STATES

It will often be impossible for States to extend their jurisdiction as far seawards as international law permits because of the claims of other States. The resulting problem of delimiting maritime zones between coastal States whose claims overlap is extremely difficult and has given rise to more cases before the ICJ than any other single subject, as well as having generated a considerable number of ad hoc arbitrations.[74]

A. EQUIDISTANCE OR EQUITABLE PRINCIPLES?

LOSC Article 15 provides that, in the absence of agreement to the contrary, States may not extend their territorial seas beyond the median, or equidistance line, unless there are historic or other 'special' circumstances that dictate otherwise. This 'equidistance/special

[71] States may also sponsor commercial applicants. See further *Responsibilities and Obligations of States Sponsoring Persons and Entities with Respect to Activities in the Area, Advisory Opinion, ITLOS Reports 2011*, p 10 and see Evans and Okowa, 2013, pp 127–36.

[72] For details see the information available on the International Sea Bed Authority website: http://www.isa.org.jm. For a helpful overview of its early work, see Nandan, 2006 and for an excellent summation of its work to date, see Lodge, 2015.

[73] For the latest Report of the Preparatory Commission see UN Doc A/AC.287/2017/PC4/2 (31 July 2017).

[74] For an overview of the major decisions see Fietta and Cleverly, 2016.

circumstances' rule has been accepted by the ICJ as customary international law[75] and it is clear that only in exceptional cases will the equidistance line not form the basis of the boundary between overlapping territorial seas, although there have been examples of such exceptions in recent practice.[76]

Article 6 of the 1958 CSC adopted the same approach to the delimitation of overlapping continental shelves but its application in this context has had a more chequered history (see generally Evans, 1989; Weil, 1989; Antunes, 2003; Tanaka, 2006; Cottier, 2015). In the *North Sea* cases Denmark and the Netherlands argued that Article 6 represented customary law and so bound Germany, a non-State party. Applying this rule mechanically to the concave German coastline sandwiched between Denmark and Norway restricted Germany to a modest triangle of continental shelf, to the substantial benefit of its neighbours. Rather than ameliorate this outcome by arguing that the concave nature of the coast was a 'special circumstance' justifying another line, the ICJ decided that Article 6 did not reflect customary law, and that customary law required continental shelf delimitation to be conducted on the basis of equitable principles and taking account of relevant circumstances.[77]

This ushered in a period in which supporters of the more formulaic 'equidistance/special circumstances' approach vied with supporters of the relatively more flexible 'equitable principles/relevant circumstances' approach—though it is doubtful whether there was ever much to choose between them.[78] At UNCLOS III groups of States championed the approach they considered best suited their interests and, as no consensus could be found, an anodyne formula, applicable to both continental shelf and EEZ delimitation, was adopted in the dying days of the conference. Thus LOSC Articles 74(1) and 83(1) both provide that such delimitations are to be 'effected by agreement on the basis of international law, as referred to in Article 38 of the Statute of the International Court of Justice, in order to achieve an equitable solution'. This avoids mentioning equidistance, equitable principles, special or relevant circumstances—and is virtually devoid of substantive content, other than to seek an agreed outcome.[79]

Around this time the ICJ delivered a trilogy of judgments, all of which emphasized the role of equity at the expense of equidistance, though in varying degrees.[80] Perhaps these

---

[75] *Maritime Delimitation and Territorial Questions Between Qatar and Bahrain (Qatar v Bahrain), Merits, Judgment, ICJ Reports 2001*, p 40, paras 175–6. Cf Separate Opinion of Judge Oda, paras 13–21, who challenged the Court's views of customary law. The Court reaffirmed its view in *Territorial and Maritime Dispute between Nicaragua and Honduras in the Caribbean Sea (Nicaragua v Honduras), Judgment, ICJ Report 2007*, p 659, paras 268 and 281.

[76] In the *Territorial and Maritime Dispute between Nicaragua and Honduras in the Caribbean Sea (Nicaragua v Honduras), Judgment, ICJ Reports 2007*, p 659, paras 268–81 the ICJ, whilst emphasizing that equidistance remained the general rule, took the view that both the configuration and unstable nature of the relevant coastal area made it impossible to identify basepoints and construct a provisional equidistance line at all. This amounted to a 'special circumstance' justifying the use of an alternative method, the use of a line which bisected two lines drawn along the coastal fronts of the two States. Also in that year the Annex VII Arbitration Award in the case concerning *Guyana/Suriname*, 17 September 2007, paras 323–5 concluded that historical and navigational issues amounted to special circumstances justifying a departure from the use of the equidistance line for the territorial sea.

[77] *North Sea Continental Shelf, Judgment, ICJ Reports 1969*, p 3, para 101(c)(1).

[78] Thus the 1977 *Anglo-French Arbitration*, Cmnd 7438, 18 ILM 397, generally considered to lean towards the equitable principles school of thought, proceeded on the basis that although CSC Article 6 and custom were different the practical result of their application would be the same.

[79] See the comments of the ICJ in the *Maritime Delimitation in the Indian Ocean (Somalia v Kenya), Preliminary Objection, ICJ Reports 2017*, nyr, paras 90 and 97, where it said that the article did not prescribe a method and merely called for settlement by negotiation.

[80] *Continental Shelf (Tunisia/Libyan Arab Jamahiriya), Judgment, ICJ Reports 1982*, p 18; *Delimitation of the Maritime Boundary in the Gulf of Maine Area, Judgment, ICJ Reports 1984*, p 246; *Continental Shelf (Libyan Arab Jamahiriya/Malta), Judgment, ICJ Reports 1985*, p 13.

cases were too close in time to UNCLOS III to shake off the ideological hostility to equidistance. By 1993, however, the Court was prepared to declare in the *Jan Mayen* case that, '[p]rima facie, a median line delimitation between opposite coasts results in general in an equitable solution'[81] (Evans, 1999) and in 2002 it confirmed, in the *Cameroon v Nigeria* case,[82] that equidistance would provide the starting point in cases in adjacency too. Thus after 35 years of hesitation, the ICJ finally accepted what it had rejected in the *North Sea* cases, that the equidistance/special circumstances approach reflected customary international law (Evans, 2006). It has subsequently confirmed this is the case for the delimitation of the territorial sea,[83] for the delimitation of the continental shelf, the EEZ, or when drawing a single delimitation line.[84]

The matter seemed to be settled beyond all doubt when in 2009 in the *Black Sea* case the ICJ Court set out a three-stage approach: (a) a provisional line will be drawn, which 'will be' an equidistance line, 'unless there are compelling reasons that make this unfeasible in the particular case';[85] (b) it will then 'consider whether there are factors calling for the adjustment or shifting of the provisional equidistance line in order to achieve an equitable result';[86] finally, (c) it will 'verify that the line (a provisional equidistance line which may or may not have been adjusted by taking into account the relevant circumstances) does not, as it stands, lead to an inequitable result by reason of any marked disproportion between the ratio of the respective coastal lengths and the ratio between the relevant maritime area of each State by reference to the delimitation line'.[87] This three-stage test was subsequently endorsed by the ITLOS in the *Myanmar/Bangladesh* case,[88] by the ICJ in the *Nicaragua v Colombia* case,[89] by the ICJ in the *Peru v Chile* case,[90] and by the Tribunal in the *Bangladesh v India* Arbitration.[91] Most recently, the Special Chamber of ITLOS in the *Maritime Boundary in the Atlantic Ocean* case said that 'in the absence of any compelling reasons that make it impossible or inappropriate to draw a provisional equidistance line, the equidistance/relevant circumstances method should be chosen for maritime delimitation'.[92] Despite this seemingly settled state of affairs, all these cases set out the three-stage test in rather different terms and offer differing views on when, or why, the method is to be applicable (see Evans, 2015 and 2016). Indeed, the Special Chamber itself went on to stress that 'the overarching objective of maritime delimitation is to achieve an equitable solution'.[93] To that extent, a degree of uncertainty concerning its applicability remains.

---

[81] *Maritime Delimitation in the Area between Greenland and Jan Mayen, Judgment, ICJ Reports 1993*, p 316, para 64, a position affirmed in the *Eritrea-Yemen Arbitration, Second Phase, Award of 17 December 1999*, para 131.

[82] *Land and Maritime Boundary between Cameroon and Nigeria (Cameroon v Nigeria: Equatorial Guinea Intervening), Merits, Judgment, ICJ Reports 2002*, p 303, para 288. See also *Barbados/Trinidad and Tobago*, Award of 11 April 2006, paras 242–4 and 306.

[83] *Territorial and Maritime Dispute between Nicaragua and Honduras in the Caribbean Sea (Nicaragua v Honduras), ICJ Reports 2007*, p 659, paras 262–98.

[84] *Guyana/Suriname*, Award of 17 September 2007, paras 376–92; *Maritime Delimitation in the Black Sea (Romania v Ukraine)*, Judgment of 2 February 2009, para 116.

[85] *Maritime Delimitation in the Black Sea (Romania v Ukraine)*, Judgment of 2 February 2009, para 116.

[86] *Ibid*, para 120.   [87] *Ibid*, para 122.

[88] *Delimitation of the Maritime Boundary in the Bay of Bengal (Bangladesh/Myanmar), Judgment, ITLOS Reports 2012*, p 4, para 240.

[89] *Territorial and Maritime Dispute (Nicaragua v Colombia), Judgment of 19 November 2012*, paras 190–4.

[90] *Maritime Dispute (Peru v Chile), Judgment, ICJ Reports*, p 3, para 180.

[91] *Bay of Bengal Maritime Boundary Arbitration (Bangladesh v India)*, Arbitral Tribunal constituted under annex VII of the UN Law of the Sea Convention, Award of 7 July 2014, PCA Case No 2010–16, para 348.

[92] *Delimitation of the Maritime Boundary in the Atlantic Ocean (Ghana/Côte d'Ivoire), Judgment, ITLOS Reports 2017*, nyr, para 289. See also para 310 where it is described as 'the internationally established approach'.

[93] *Ibid*, para 409.

Endorsement and applicability does not, however, imply application and some recent decisions have applied the three-stage approach in such a fashion as to cast very serious doubt upon the weight to be given to equidistance in practice; in the Bay of Bengal cases, both the ITLOS[94] and Arbitral Tribunal[95] also emphasized the importance of the equitable solution and ultimately set equidistance aside in favour of an angle-bisector methodology,[96] and the ICJ, whilst purporting to apply it,[97] has produced outcomes which bear so little relationship to the 'provisional' equidistance line with which it started as to cast doubt up on its real place within the delimitation process, other than being a point of departure. In short, it appears that 'equity' rather than 'equidistance' may be re-emerging, yet again, as the dominant approach.

B. FACTORS AFFECTING DELIMITATION

It has always been clear that even if equidistance provides the starting point, this does not mean it will be the finishing line. All formulations of the rule accept that it can be modified to take account of other factors. Although the categories of potentially relevant factors are never closed, the potential relevance of some factors—and the comparative irrelevance of others—is well attested (Crawford, 2012, pp 288–9; Tanaka, 2015, pp 209–24). The overriding focus is on the 'geographic configuration of the coasts',[98] with close attention usually paid to ensuring that areas appertaining to each State are not disproportionate to the ratio between the lengths of their 'relevant coasts' adjoining the area. Likewise, the presence of islands capable of generating claims to a continental shelf or EEZ is a complicating factor[99] and their impact upon an equidistance line can be reduced or discounted in numerous ways (Jayawardene, 1990). On the other hand, geological factors are not considered relevant where the distance between the coasts is less than 400 n. miles[100] and economic factors are generally considered irrelevant by courts and tribunals, although they probably play a significant role in negotiated boundary agreements (Cottier, 2015; Evans, 2018).

It is difficult to go beyond this with certainty, and it is certainly not possible to predict how the various factors will be taken into account. Courts and tribunals increasingly refrain from indicating how—or why—the factors considered relevant combine with the chosen methodology to produce the final line. Some earlier judgments seem to do little more than 'split the difference' between competing claims (Churchill and Lowe, 1999, p 191). However, in the *Cameroon* v *Nigeria* case the ICJ dismissed the relevance of all the various factors put forward by the parties and used an equidistance line in an unmodified

---

[94] *Delimitation of the Maritime Boundary in the Bay of Bengal (Bangladesh/Myanmar), Judgment, ITLOS Reports 2012*, p 4, para 235.

[95] *Bay of Bengal Maritime Boundary Arbitration (Bangladesh v India)*, Arbitral Tribunal constituted under annex VII of the UN Law of the Sea Convention, Award of 7 July 2014, PCA Case No 2010–16, para 339, see also para 397.

[96] *Delimitation of the Maritime Boundary in the Bay of Bengal (Bangladesh/Myanmar), Judgment, ITLOS Reports 2012*, p 4, para 334; *Bay of Bengal Maritime Boundary Arbitration (Bangladesh v India)*, Arbitral Tribunal constituted under annex VII of the UN Law of the Sea Convention, Award of 7 July 2014, PCA Case No 2010–16, para 478. See further Evans, 2016.

[97] *Territorial and Maritime Dispute (Nicaragua v Colombia), Judgment of 19 November 2012*, para 199; *Maritime Dispute (Peru v Chile), Judgment, ICJ Reports*, p 3, para 185.

[98] *Delimitation of the Maritime Boundary in the Atlantic Ocean (Ghana/Côte d'Ivoire), Judgment, ITLOS Reports 2017*, nyr, para 452.

[99] This posed particular problems in the 2012 *Nicaragua v Colombia* case, where it was the presence of Colombian islands proximate to the coast of Nicaragua which generated the overlap of maritime zones which the Court was called on to address.

[100] *Continental Shelf (Libyan Arab Jamahiriya/Malta), Judgment, ICJ Reports 1985*, p 13, para 39.

fashion, despite the presence of a number of factors that might have been thought to have some claim to consideration.[101] In the *Black Sea* case the ICJ also dismissed the relevance of all factors put forward by the parties,[102] as did the Special Chamber in the *Maritime Boundary in the Atlantic Ocean* case.[103] Predictably perhaps, in the light of their more equity-driven approaches, the judgments from ITLOS and the ICJ in the *Myanmar/Bangladesh* and *Nicaragua* v *Colombia* cases and of the Arbitral Tribunal in the *India* v *Bangladesh* case have all altered the provisional line to take account of relevant circumstances. What does seem clear is that there is need for caution and clear reasoning, particularly when presenting claims which call for a departure from the equidistance line on grounds other than factors flowing from coastal geography (see Tanaka, 2004; Evans, 2006).[104] Overall, it seems that despite the endorsement of the three-stage test, recent decisions have introduced a heightened degree of unpredictability into the delimitation process.

VII. FISHERIES

A. THE BASIC SCHEME OF REGULATION

Given its significance, it is perhaps surprising that the LOSC does not address fisheries as a discrete topic. However, the manner in which the seas are divided for jurisdictional purposes means that one has to look at how fisheries are regulated in each particular maritime zone. The basic scheme seems simple enough; the coastal State exercises sovereignty over the territorial seas and sovereign right to explore, exploit, conserve, and manage fishing in any EEZ or EFZ that it might claim. In the high seas the freedom of fishing remains and fish stocks are open to all, but the activities of fishing vessels are subject to the jurisdiction and control of their flag State. The problems are, however, enormous. Overfishing has endangered many fish stocks and there is a pressing need to agree upon and implement effective strategies for conservation and management in the increased threat from 'Illegal, Unreported and Unregulated' (IUU) fishing. At the same time, the economic and nutritional needs of communities must be borne in mind. The result is that the piecemeal approach to regulation is under increasing pressure and a more holistic approach, built around the idea of sustainable development, may be in the process of emerging (see Edeson, 1999; Orrego-Vicuna, 1999). However, any system that is ultimately dependent upon flag-State enforcement will be vulnerable to abuse.

One particularly noteworthy trend is the establishment of Regional Fisheries Bodies (RFBs) and Regional Fisheries Management Organizations (RFMOs) which provide means through which States may work together in the conservation, management, and development of fishing in particular areas or of particular stocks (see generally Rayfuse, 2016). Multilateral treaty practice is moving beyond merely encouraging States to participate in such regimes and is increasingly requiring them to do so in order to have access to such stocks (Serdy, 2011). However, such obligations only bind States which become a party to such agreements and many major fishing States simply choose not to do so and continue to claim the right to fish these stocks as an aspect of the freedom of the high seas. An alternative response is to extend coastal State jurisdiction still further seawards but this

[101] *Land and Maritime Boundary between Cameroon and Nigeria (Cameroon v Nigeria: Equatorial Guinea Intervening), Merits, Judgment, ICJ Reports 2002*, p 303, paras 293–306.

[102] *Maritime Delimitation in the Black Sea (Romania v Ukraine)*, Judgment of 2 February 2009, paras 185–218.

[103] *Delimitation of the Maritime Boundary in the Atlantic Ocean (Ghana/Côte d'Ivoire), Judgment, ITLOS Reports 2017*, nyr, para 480.

[104] See also *Barbados/Trinidad and Tobago*, Award of 11 April 2006, paras 233–40. But cf n 48 in this chapter.

also runs into fierce opposition. Some years ago Canada adopted a slightly different approach, by asserting its right to enforce conservation and management measures adopted by the relevant regional body (NAFO) over non-flag-State vessels fishing beyond its 200 n. mile EEZ. The subsequent arrest in 1995 of the Spanish registered *Estai* on the high seas prompted a serious incident between the EC and Canada[105] and illustrated the difficulty of pursuing the unilateral route. For the moment, then, we can merely chart the trends in this direction whilst outlining the major elements of the regimes applicable beyond the limits of the territorial seas.

B. MANAGING FISHERIES

1. EEZ

Some 80–90 per cent of all fishing takes place within EEZs. The coastal State does not enjoy a completely unfettered right to exploit the fisheries resources of the EEZ under the LOSC (though this may not be the position in customary law). LOSC Article 61(1) requires the coastal State to 'determine the allowable catch' (known as the TAC) of living resources. A number of factors feed into this determination, including the need to 'ensure through proper conservation and management measures that the maintenance of the living resources . . . is not endangered by over-exploitation' (Article 61(2)). At the same time, these measures must themselves be designed 'to maintain or restore populations of harvested species at levels which can produce the maximum sustainable yield' (Article 61(3)). This, then, looks to conserving stocks, but Article 62(1) switches to the obligation to 'promote the objective of optimum utilization of the living resources of the EEZ' by requiring the coastal State 'to determine its capacity to harvest' them. Where the harvestable capacity falls short of the TAC, the coastal State is to give other States access to that surplus (Article 62(2)), with particular regard being given to the requirements of developing States in the area (Article 62(3)), as well as the interests of landlocked and geographically disadvantaged States (Articles 69 and 70; Vasciannie, 1990) in determining to whom access will be offered.[106] Despite these provisions, since coastal States have their hands on both levers—determining both the TAC and the harvestable capacity—their control over EEZ fisheries is hardly troubled by these latter provisions, which have more symbolic than substantial significance. If it were otherwise, the attraction of declaring an EEZ rather than an EFZ (in which these provisions would not apply) would be significantly diminished.

The Convention also provides special rules for particular categories of species, including anadromous stocks, such as salmon, which spend most of their time at sea but spawn in freshwater rivers (LOSC Article 66); catadromous stocks, such as eels, which spawn at sea but spend most of their lives in fresh water (LOSC Article 67), which again reflect the theme of reconciling the interests of the State of origin with the established interests of others; and marine mammals (LOSC Article 65). The situation regarding 'straddling stocks' and 'highly migratory species' (LOSC Articles 63 and 64) will be considered later.

Although the coastal State in principle enjoys complete control over fishing within the EEZ, this has not prevented overfishing. Some States refuse to accept the need for

---

[105] See Davies, 1995. Spain subsequently brought a case against Canada before the ICJ which the Court was unable to consider because Canada had previously removed such disputes from the scope of its consent to the Court's jurisdiction. (See de LaFayette, 1999.)

[106] Such access can, of course, be subject to licensing and fees and is more generally regulated by LOSC Article 64. For a succinct statement of this as the position under the Convention see *South China Seas Case (Philippines v China)*, Arbitral Tribunal constituted under annex VII of the UN Law of the Sea Convention, Award of 12 July 2016, Case No 2013–19, paras 735–40.

conservation of fish stocks in the face of more pressing and immediate economic or political interests, whilst others are simply unable to control the fishing activities of foreign-flagged vessels within their EEZ, both licensed and illegal. Whilst the flag State has a responsibility of due diligence to ensure that those fishing under its flag within the EEZ of another State do so in accordance with local law, the International Tribunal of the Law of the Sea has taken the view that 'the flag State is not liable if it has taken all necessary and appropriate measures to meet its "due diligence" obligations to ensure that vessels flying its flag do not conduct IUU fishing activities in . . . exclusive economic zones'.[107] This failure to hold flag States themselves accountable may seem to exacerbate, rather than help address, the problem of illegal fishing within an EEZ. Much now turns on the extent of the obligation of due diligence. In the *South China Seas Arbitration* China was found to have been in breach of its due diligence obligation.[108] However, this was hardly controversial since Chinese government vessels had escorted its fishing vessels during—and may even have organized—their illegal fishing in the Philippines, EEZ. The Arbitral Tribunal noted that in many cases it would be 'far from obvious what the flag state could realistically have done' to prevent illegal fishing.[109] This casts the burden back on the coastal State, which may be ill-equipped to address it.

2. High seas

It is sometimes forgotten that the freedom of fishing upon the high seas is not unfettered. The 1958 Convention on Fishing and Conservation of the Living Resources of the High Seas (CFC) had recognized the 'special interest' of the coastal State in fishing activities in areas adjacent to its territorial waters and sought to reflect that through cooperative arrangements with States engaged in high seas fishing in the interests of conservation and management (CFC Article 6). LOSC Article 116(b) now expressly subjects that freedom to the interests that coastal States have in the particular classes of species identified in LOSC Articles 63–7 as well as the more general obligation to conserve the living resources of the high seas by setting total allowable catches, based on the maximum sustainable yield (LOSC Article 119). It has to be said that, to the extent that this implies unilateral determinations and self-imposed restrictions, this is little short of wishful thinking. How can the practice of a single State significantly affect the overall pattern when its self-restraint may simply make more space for others to over-exploit?

The key lies in coordinated and cooperative activities by all involved in fishing a given stock or region and LOSC Article 118 recognizes this by requiring that States 'whose nationals exploit identical living resources, or different living resources in the same area, shall enter into negotiations with a view to taking the measures necessary for the conservation of the living resources concerned. They shall, as appropriate, co-operate to establish sub-regional or regional fisheries organizations to this end.' This approach is not new, having echoes in the 1958 CFC, and, as mentioned earlier, a considerable number of RFBs and RFMOs have been established.[110] Some have been relatively successful, notably the Northwest Atlantic Fisheries Organization (NAFO) and the Commission for the Conservation of Antarctic Marine Resources (CCAMLR), though even these have

---

[107] *Request for Advisory Opinion submitted by the Sub-Regional Fisheries Commission, Advisory Opinion, 2 April 2015, ITLOS Reports 2015*, p 4, paras 147–8.

[108] *South China Seas Case (Philippines v China)*, Arbitral Tribunal constituted under annex VII of the UN Law of the Sea Convention, Award of 12 July 2016, Case No 2013–19, para 757.

[109] Ibid, para 754.

[110] The distinguishing feature of an RFMO is that, unlike a RFB, it is able to adopt measures which are binding on its members. For a helpful overview see Harrison, 2011, pp 227–33.

suffered from poor records of enforcement at times. Others have been less successful, such as the 1993 Commission for the Conservation of Southern Bluefin Tuna (CCSBT), where some years ago the failure of the three States parties (Japan, Australia, and New Zealand) to agree a TAC and the introduction of an 'experimental fishing programme' by Japan prompted a case under the LOSC dispute settlement provisions (Churchill, 2000; Boyle, 2001). This gives a flavour of the difficulties which need to be overcome.

It is difficult to resist the conclusion that the problems of over-utilization of the living resources of the high seas will remain until the right to exploit them is made conditional upon participation in a unified international regulatory framework. However, the experience of creating the International Seabed Authority suggests this might also be a route to paralysis and is bound to be fraught with difficulties. Unless there is a further expansion of coastal State jurisdiction—itself no panacea since some coastal States have themselves fished their own resources to near extinction—it is difficult to see what the international community can do except continue to press the case for cooperation and coordination. This it continues to do. For example, in November 2009 the FAO built on the trend of utilizing port State jurisdiction by adopting the Agreement on Port State Measures to Prevent, Deter and Eliminate Illegal, Unreported and Unregulated Fishing (Harrison, 2011, pp 221–4; Kopela, 2016) which entered into force in 2016.[111] It remains to be seen whether moving towards a more enforcement-oriented approach is more successful than reliance on restraint, cooperation, and self-regulation.

3. Straddling stocks and highly migratory species

Fish do not respect man-made boundaries and many stocks 'straddle' the limits of maritime zones. Where stocks straddle boundaries the LOSC provides that those States concerned in the fisheries should, either directly or through appropriate organizations if they exist, agree upon appropriate measures of conservation and development (LOSC Article 63). Other stocks, such as tuna, are highly mobile and travel great distances in the course of their regular life cycle, migrating through both EEZs and high seas making them particularly vulnerable to predatory exploitation as they pass. Once again, the Convention's response is to call for cooperation with respect to a list of species contained in Annex I to the Convention, with the objective of optimum utilization, and also calls for the establishment of appropriate regional organizations where none exist (LOSC Article 64).

These rather open-textured provisions have since been built upon by the 1995 UN Agreement on Straddling Stocks and Highly Migratory Species (SSC).[112] This, *inter alia*, obliges States parties fishing for such stocks either to become members of those fisheries management organizations that exist for the relevant region or stock, or to agree to apply the measures which such an organization establishes, and States parties to the Agreement which do not do so are debarred from having access to the stock (SSC Articles 8(3) and (4)). In other words, States parties to the Agreement may not fish for such stocks outside of the framework established by any such organization (SSC Article 17). Since most fishing undertaken on the high seas involves either straddling stocks or highly migratory species, this is an extremely significant self-denying ordinance. Moreover, where RFMOs exist, SSC Article 21 permits the authorized inspectors of any State party to board and inspect fishing vessels flying the flag of other States parties in order to ensure compliance with the conservation and management measure that the organization has established and, in cases where there are 'clear grounds' for suspecting that 'serious violations' have occurred, the

---

[111] Forty-nine States and the European Union are currently parties to the Agreement.
[112] See Davies and Redgwell, 1996; Orrego-Vicuna, 1999, chs 5–9; Stokke, 2001 and Harrison, 2011, pp 99–113.

vessel might be taken to the nearest appropriate port—though it should be noted that in both cases enforcement action against the vessel can only be taken by the flag State or with the flag State's consent.

Once again, it is possible to see in this how the international community is striving to address a complex problem by incremental diminutions in the freedom of the high seas in favour of communal responses, backed by equally incremental incursions into the principle of flag-State jurisdiction. However, this is entirely dependent upon States choosing to fetter themselves in this way and many remain reluctant to do so and remain free to take advantage of the self-restraint of others.[113] Whether the current process to conclude a treaty on marine bio-diversity, mentioned earlier, expands to embrace this issue remains to be seen.

VIII. CONCLUSION

There are a great many important topics that have not been touched upon in this chapter, including, *inter alia*, marine scientific research, pollution and the marine environment, military uses of the seas, and the dispute settlement provisions of the LOSC. Although a number of these topics are considered elsewhere in this volume, these omissions remain regrettable. However, by focusing in some detail on a number of foundational aspects of the division of ocean space and its principles of governance, this chapter introduces the complexities that must be grappled with and the manner in which this has been attempted. The underlying tension remains the same as ever: balancing the competing demands of access to ocean space whilst recognizing the need to preserve order and good governance. The law of the sea has undergone a remarkable transformation in the last 70 years, yet more still needs to be done if that balance is to be achieved. Perhaps at the end of the day the problem is the perception, uttered by the ICJ in the *North Sea* cases in the context of the delimitation of maritime boundaries, that 'the land dominates the sea'.[114] We are coming to realize that, in many ways, it is the sea that dominates the land and, as they are projected seawards, our concepts of sovereignty, rights, and jurisdiction, no matter how subtle or sophisticated their application, seem increasingly cumbersome instruments for addressing the resulting issues. But for the moment, they remain the best we have.

REFERENCES

AHNISH, FA (1993), *The International Law of Maritime Boundaries and the Practice of States in the Mediterranean Sea* (Oxford: Clarendon Press).

ANAND, RM (1983), *Origin and Development of the Law of the Sea* (The Hague: Martinus Nijhoff).

ANDERSON, DH (1993), 'Efforts to Ensure Universal Participation in the UN Convention on the Law of the Sea', 42 *ICLQ* 654.

ANDERSON, DH (1995), 'Legal Implication of the Entry into Force of the UN Convention on the Law of the Sea', 44 *ICLQ* 313.

---

[113] The SSC entered into force in December 2001. At the time of writing 87 States and other entities (including the European Community) have become a party to it.

[114] *North Sea Continental Shelf, Judgment, ICJ Reports 1969*, p 3, para 96.

ANDERSON, DH (2006), 'Freedoms of the High Seas in the Modern Law of the Sea', in Freestone, Barnes, and Ong (eds), *The Law of the Sea: Progress and Prospects*, p 327.

ANTUNES, NM (2003), *Towards the Conceptualisation of Maritime Delimitation* (The Hague: Martinus Nijhoff).

ATTARD, D (1986), *The Exclusive Economic Zone* (Oxford: Clarendon Press).

BARNES, R (2015), 'Flag States', in Rothwell et al (eds), *Oxford Handbook of the Law of the Sea*, ch 14.

BARNES, R (2016), 'The Continuing Vitality of UNCLOS', in Barrett and Barnes (eds), *Law of the Sea: UNCLOS as a Living Treaty*, ch 16.

BARRETT, J (2016), 'The United Nations Convention on the Law of the Sea: A "Living Treaty"?', in Barrett and Barnes, *Law of the Sea: UNCLOS as a Living Treaty*, ch 1.

BARRETT, J and BARNES, J (eds) (2016), *Law of the Sea: UNCLOS as a Living Treaty* (London: British Institute of International and Comparative Law).

BOYLE, A (2001), 'The Southern Bluefin Tuna Arbitration', 50 *ICLQ* 447.

BOYLE, A (2005), 'Further Development of the Law of the Sea Convention: Mechanisms for Change', 54 *ICLQ* 563.

BYERS, M (2004), 'Policing the High Seas: the Proliferation Security Initiative', 98 *AJIL* 526.

CAMINOS, H and COGLIATI-BANTZ, V (2014), *The Legal Regime of Straits: Contemporary Problems and Solutions* (Cambridge: Cambridge University Press).

CHARNEY, J (2000), 'Rocks that Cannot Sustain Human Habitation', 96 *AJIL* 863.

CHURCHILL, RR (2000), 'The Southern Bluefin Tuna Cases', 49 *ICLQ* 979.

CHURCHILL, RR (2014), 'The Piracy Provisions of the UN Convention on the Law of the Sea—Fit for Purpose?', in P Koutrakos and A Skordas (eds), *The Law and Practice of Piracy at Sea* (Oxford: Hart Publishing), ch 1.

CHURCHILL, RR (2015), 'The United Nations Convention on the Law of the Sea', in Rothwell et al, *Oxford Handbook of the Law of the Sea*, ch 2.

CHURCHILL, RR and LOWE, AV (1999), *The Law of the Sea* (3rd edn, Manchester: Manchester University Press).

COLSON, D (2003), 'The Delimitation of the Outer Continental Shelf between Neighbouring States', 97 *AJIL* 91.

COOK, PJ and CARLTON, C (2000), *Continental Shelf Limits* (Oxford: Oxford University Press).

COTTIER, T (2015), *Equitable Principles of Maritime Boundary Delimitation: The Quest for Distributive Justice in International Law* (Cambridge: Cambridge University Press).

CRAWFORD, J (2012), *Brownlie's Principles of Public International Law* (8th edn, Oxford: Oxford University Press).

DAVENPORT, T (2015), 'The United Nations Convention on the Law of the Sea', in Rothwell et al, *Oxford Handbook of the Law of the Sea*, ch 7.

DAVIES, PGG (1995), 'The EC/Canadian Fisheries Dispute in the Northwest Atlantic', 44 *ICLQ* 933.

DAVIES, PGG and REDGWELL, C (1996), 'The International Legal Regulation of Straddling Fish Stocks', 67 *BYIL* 199.

DE LAFAYETTE, L (1999), 'The Fisheries Jurisdiction Case (*Spain* v *Canada*)', 48 *ICLQ* 664.

DE YTURRIAGA, JA (1991), *Straights Used for International Navigation* (Dordrecht: Martinus Nijhoff).

EDESON, W (1999), 'Towards Long-term Sustainable Use: Some Recent Developments in the Legal Regime of Fisheries', in A Boyle and D Freestone (eds), *International Law and Sustainable Development* (Oxford: Oxford University Press), p 165.

EVANS, MD (1989), *Relevant Circumstances and Maritime Delimitation* (Oxford: Clarendon Press).

Evans, MD (1993), 'Delimitation and the Common Maritime Boundary', 64 *BYIL* 283.

Evans, MD (1999), 'Maritime Delimitation after *Denmark v Norway*. Back to the Future?', in GS Goodwin-Gill and S Talmon (eds), *The Reality of International Law* (Oxford: Clarendon Press), p 153.

Evans, MD (2006), 'Maritime Boundary Delimitation: Where Do We Go From Here?', in Freestone, Barnes, and Ong, *The Law of the Sea: Progress and Prospects*, p 137.

Evans, MD (2015), 'Maritime Boundary Delimitation', in Rothwell et al, *Oxford Handbook of the Law of the Sea*, ch 12.

Evans, MD (2016), 'Maritime Boundary Delimitation: Whatever Next?', in Barrett and Barnes, *Law of the Sea: UNCLOS as a Living Treaty*, ch 2.

Evans, MD (2018), 'Relevant Circumstances', in Oude Elferink, A, Henriksen, T and Busch, S (eds) *Maritime Boundary Delimitation: The Case Law* (Cambridge: Cambridge University Press), ch 9.

Evans, MD and Okowa, PN (2013), 'Approaches to Responsibility in International Courts', in M Evans and P Koutrakos (eds), *The International Responsibility of the European Union: European and International Perspectives* (Oxford: Hart Publishing), p 101.

Fietta, S and Cleverly, S (2016), *A Practitioner's Guide to Maritime Boundary Delimitation* (Oxford: Oxford University Press).

Freestone, D (2016), 'Governance of Areas Beyond National Jurisdiction: An Unfinished Agenda?', in Barrett and Barnes, *Law of the Sea: UNCLOS as a Living Treaty*, ch 9.

Geiss, R and Petrig, A (2011), *Piracy and Armed Robbery at Sea* (Oxford: Oxford University Press).

Gilmore, W (1995), 'Hot Pursuit: The Case of *R v Mills* and Others', 44 *ICLQ* 949.

Gilmore, W (2000), 'Drugs Trafficking at Sea: The Case of *R v Charrington* and Others', 49 *ICLQ* 477.

Gilmore, W (2005), *Agreement Concerning Co-Operation in Suppressing Illicit Maritime and Air Trafficking in Narcotic Drugs and Psychotropic Substances in the Caribbean Area, 2003* (London: TSO).

Gosalbo-Bono, R and Boelaert, S (2014), 'The European Union's Comprehensive Approach to Combatting Piracy at Sea: Legal Aspects', in Koutrakos and Skordas, *The Law and Practice of Piracy at Sea*, ch 5.

Guilfoyle, D (2008), 'Piracy off Somalia: UN Security Council Resolution 1816 and IMO Regional Counter-Piracy Efforts', 57 *ICLQ* 690.

Guilfoyle, D (2009), *Shipping Interdiction and the Law of the Sea* (Cambridge: Cambridge University Press).

Guilfoyle, D (ed) (2013), *Modern Piracy: Legal Challenges and Responses* (Cheltenham: Edward Elgar).

Guilfoyle, D (2015), 'The High Seas', in Rothwell et al, *Oxford Handbook of the Law of the Sea*, ch 10.

Harrison, J (2011), *Making the Law of the Sea* (Cambridge: Cambridge University Press).

Hutchinson, D (1985), 'The Seawards Limit to Continental Shelf Jurisdiction in Customary International Law', 56 *BYIL* 133.

Jayawardene, H (1990), *The Regime of Islands in International Law* (Dordrecht: Martinus Nijhoff).

Jia, BB (1998), *The Regime of Straits in International Law* (Oxford: Clarendon Press).

Klein, N (2011), *Maritime Security and the Law of the Sea* (Oxford: Oxford University Press).

Kopela, S (2013), *Dependent Archipelagos in International Law* (Leiden: Martinus Nijhoff Publishers).

Kopela, S (2016), 'Port State Jurisdiction, Extraterritoriality and the Protection of Global Commons', 47 *ODIL* 83.

Lavalle, R (2004), 'Not Quite a Sure Thing: The Maritime Areas of Rocks and Low Tide Elevations under the UN Convention on the Law of the Sea', 19 *IJMCL* 43.

Leary, D (2006), *International Law and the Genetic Resources of the Deep Sea* (Leiden: Martinus Nijhoff).

Lodge, M (2015), 'The Deep Seabed', in Rothwell et al, *Oxford Handbook of the Law of the Sea*, ch 11.

Magnusson, BM (2015), *The Continental Shelf Beyond 200 Nautical Miles: Delineation, Delimitation and Dispute Settlement* (Leiden: Brill Nijhoff).

Marston, G (2002), 'Redrawing the Territorial Sea Boundary in the Firth of Clyde', 51 *ICLQ* 279.

Marten, D (2013), *Port State Jurisdiction and the Regulation of International Merchant Shipping* (Heidelberg: Springer).

Molenaar, E (2015), 'Port and Coastal States', in Rothwell et al, *Oxford Handbook of the Law of the Sea*, ch 13.

Molenaar, EJ (2004), 'Multilateral Hot Pursuit and Illegal Fishing in the Southern Ocean: The Pursuits of the *Viarsa 1* and *South Tomi*', 19 *IJMCL* 19.

Molenaar, EJ (2006), 'Port State Jurisdiction: towards Mandatory and Comprehensive Use', in Freestone, Barnes, and Ong, *The Law of the Sea: Progress and Prospects*, p 137.

Nandan, SM (2006), 'Administering the Mineral Resources of the Deep Sea Bed', in Freestone, Barnes, and Ong, *The Law of the Sea: Progress and Prospects*, p 75.

Nandan, SM and Anderson, DH (1989), 'Straits Used for International Navigation', 90 *BYIL* 159.

Nelson, D (2009), 'The Settlement of Disputes Arising from Conflicting Outer Continental Shelf Claims', 24 *IJMCL* 409.

O'Connell, DP (1982), *The International Law of the Sea*, vol I (Oxford: Clarendon Press).

Orrego-Vicuna, F (1989), *The Exclusive Economic Zone* (Cambridge: Cambridge University Press).

Orrego-Vicuna, F (1999), *The Changing Law of High Seas Fisheries* (Cambridge: Cambridge University Press).

Özçayir, ZO (2001), *Port State Control* (London: LLP Professional Publishing).

Papastavridis, E (2013), *Interception of Vessels on the High Seas* (Oxford: Hart).

Parson, L (2016), 'Observations on the Article 76 Process: Coastal States' Submissions and he Work Outstanding for the Commission on the Limits of the Continental Shelf', in Barrett and Barnes, *Law of the Sea: UNCLOS as a Living Treaty*, ch 4.

Petrig, A (2015), 'Piracy', in Rothwell et al, *Oxford Handbook of the Law of the Sea*, ch 37.

Posner, E and Sykes, A (2010), 'The Economic Foundations of the Law of the Sea', 104 *AJIL* 569.

Prescott, V and Schofield, C (2005), *The Maritime Political Boundaries of the World* (2nd edn, Leiden: Martinus Nijhoff).

Reisman, WM and Westerman, GS (1992), *Straight Baselines in International Maritime Boundary Delimitation* (London: Macmillan).

Rayfuse, R (2015), 'Regional Fisheries Management Organisations', in Rothwell et al, *Oxford Handbook of the Law of the Sea*, ch 20.

Roach, A (2014), 'Today's Customary International Law of the Sea', 45 *ODIL* 239.

Rothwell, D (2015), 'International Straits', in Rothwell et al, *Oxford Handbook of the Law of the Sea*, ch 6.

Rothwell, D, Oude Elferink, A, Scott, K, and Stephens, T (eds) (2015), *Oxford Handbook of the Law of the Sea* (Oxford: Oxford University Press).

ROTHWELL, DR and STEVENS, T (2016), *The International Law of the Sea* (2nd edn, Oxford: Hart Publishing).

SCHACHTE, WL (1993), 'International Straits and Navigational Freedoms', 24 *ODIL* 179.

SCHMIDT, M (1989), *Common Heritage or Common Burden?* (Oxford: Clarendon Press).

SERDY, A (2011), 'Postmodern International Fisheries Law, or We Are All Coastal States Now', 60 *ICLQ* 387.

STOKKE, OV (ed) (2001), *Governing High Seas Fisheries* (Oxford: Oxford University Press).

SUBEDI, S (2011), 'Problems and Prospects of the CLCS in Dealing with Submissions by Coastal States in Relation to Ocean Territory beyond 200 N Miles', 26 *IJMCL* 413.

TANAKA, Y (2004), 'Reflections on the Maritime Delimitation in the Cameroon/Nigeria Case', 53 *ICLQ* 369.

TANAKA, Y (2006), *Predictability and Flexibility in the Law of Maritime Delimitation* (Oxford: Hart Publishing).

TANAKA, Y (2015), *The International Law of the Sea* (2nd edn, Cambridge: Cambridge University Press).

TREVES, T (2013), 'Piracy and the International Law of the Sea', in D Guilfoyle (ed), *Modern Piracy: Legal Challenges and Responses* (Cheltenham: Edward Elgar), p 117.

VASCIANNIE, SC (1990), *Land-Locked and Geographically Disadvantaged States in the Law of the Sea* (Oxford: Clarendon Press).

VIDAS, D (ed) (2010), *Law, Technology and Science for Oceans in Globalisation* (Leiden: Martinus Nijhoff).

WEIL, P (1989), *The Law of Maritime Delimitation—Reflections* (Cambridge: Grotius).

WESTERMAN, G (1987), *The Juridical Bay* (Oxford: Clarendon Press).

FURTHER READING

BARRETT, J and BARNES, J (eds) (2016), *Law of the Sea: UNCLOS as a Living Treaty* (London: British Institute of International and Comparative Law): an exploration of the manner in which the Law of the Sea Convention has adapted over time as is to be understood as a 'living treaty'.

CHARNEY, JI and ALEXANDER, LM (eds), *Maritime Boundary Agreements*, vol I (1993), vol II (1993), vol III (1998); Charney JJ and Smith RW (eds), vol IV (2002); Colson, D (ed), vol V (2005); Colson, D and Smith, RW (eds), vol VI (2011) (The Hague: Martinus Nijhoff): a compendium of State practice, with commentaries and an excellent series of essays relating to boundary delimitation.

CHURCHILL, RR and LOWE, AV (1999), *The Law of the Sea* (3rd edn, Manchester: Manchester University Press): this remains the essential *vade mecum* to the subject.

FIETTA, S and CLEVERLY, S (2016), *A Practitioner's Guide to Maritime Boundary Delimitation* (Oxford: Oxford University Press): a valuable digest and analysis of the leading cases on maritime delimitation.

HARRISON, J (2011), *Making the Law of the Sea* (Cambridge: Cambridge University Press): a very helpful survey of the development of the law of the sea, focusing on the period following the conclusion of the 1982 Law of the Sea Convention.

KLEIN, N (2011), *Maritime Security and the Law of the Sea* (Oxford: Oxford University Press): an important survey of the Law of the Sea considered from the perspective of maritime security.

NORDQUIST, MN ET AL, *United Nations Convention on the Law of the Sea 1982: A Commentary*, vol I (1985), vol II (1993), vol III (1995), vol IV (1990), vol V (1989), vol VI (2002), vol VII (2011) (The Hague: Martinus Nijhoff): this is an excellent source of reference, tracing and commenting upon the evolution of each Article of 1982 Law of the Sea Convention.

O'CONNELL, DP, *The International Law of the Sea*, vol I (1982), vol II (1984) (Oxford: Clarendon Press): although now considerably out of date, this remains a classic and magisterial point of reference.

PRESCOTT, V and SCHOFIELD, C (2005), *The Maritime Political Boundaries of the World* (2nd edn, Leiden: Martinus Nijhoff): an excellent overview of the construction of maritime boundaries.

ROTHWELL, D, OUDE ELFERINK, A, SCOTT, K, and STEPHENS, T (eds) (2015), *Oxford Handbook of the Law of the Sea* (Oxford: Oxford University Press): an invaluable collection by leading scholars on a broad range of key issues in the law of the sea today.

22

INTERNATIONAL ENVIRONMENTAL LAW

Catherine Redgwell

SUMMARY

The development of international environmental law is typically divided into three periods. The first demonstrates little genuine environmental awareness but rather views environmental benefits as incidental to largely economic concerns such as the exploitation of living natural resources. The second phase demonstrates a significant rise in the number of treaties directed to pollution abatement and to species and habitat conservation. Here an overt environmental focus is evident, yet the approach is still largely reactive and piecemeal. The final phase, which characterizes current international environmental law, demonstrates a precautionary approach to environmental problems of global magnitude such as biodiversity conservation and climate change. Concern transcends individual States, with certain global problems now considered the common concern of humankind. This chapter first defines international environmental law, its key sources and actors, and the difficulties of enforcement, before embarking on a sectoral examination of the extensive treaty law applicable in this field.

I. INTRODUCTION: WHAT IS INTERNATIONAL ENVIRONMENTAL LAW?

This chapter addresses one of the more recent areas of development in international law, international environmental law.[1] It is an area of public international law marked by the application of principles which have evolved in the environmental context, such as the precautionary and no harm principles, yet also forms part of, and draws from, the general corpus of public international law elaborated elsewhere in this text such as the sources of public international law, principles of the exercise of State jurisdiction, and State responsibility. This is well illustrated by cases involving environmental issues which also involve issues of general international law, such as the extensive discussion of the law of treaties,

---

[1] For discussion of *why* the environment is protected, see Gillespie, 1997.

State responsibility, and international watercourses in the first contentious case involving environmental matters before the ICJ, the *Gabčíkovo-Nagymaros* case.[2] International environmental law should thus be viewed as part and parcel of general public international law and not an entirely separate, self-contained discipline (Birnie, Boyle, and Redgwell, 2009; Crawford, 2012, p 353). In this sense it is analogous to, say, international human rights law, the law of the sea, or international economic law, all applications of international law addressed in this volume. Institutionally it is less well-developed than these fields: there is no 'global environmental organization' with competence over environmental matter analogous to, say, the World Trade Organization (WTO), or a dispute settlement body analogous to the WTO's Dispute Settlement Body or the Law of the Sea Convention's International Tribunal for the Law of the Sea.

There has been significant growth in the body of general and particularized rules governing State conduct in respect of the environment. A 'broad range of issues [are] now addressed by international environmental law, including conservation and sustainable use of natural resources and biodiversity; conservation of endangered and migratory species; prevention of deforestation and desertification; preservation of Antarctica and areas of outstanding natural heritage; protection of oceans, international watercourses, the atmosphere, climate and ozone layer from the effects of pollution; safeguarding human health and the quality of life' (Birnie, Boyle, and Redgwell, 2009). While it may be debated whether a general customary law obligation on States to protect and preserve the environment per se has emerged, this breadth and depth of coverage means that no State may ignore its responsibilities to protect and preserve (elements of) the environment. This is buttressed by a negative obligation found in customary international law—the no harm principle, or the obligation imposed on States not to allow their territory to be used in a such a manner so as to cause significant harm to the territory of other States, or to the global commons, which may be traced back to the seminal *Trail Smelter Arbitration*.[3] Positive obligations remain largely sectoral in focus, the most outstanding examples being the obligation in Article 192 of the 1982 Law of the Sea Convention to protect and preserve the marine environment[4] and the obligation in Article 2 of the 1991 Protocol on Environmental Protection to the 1959 Antarctic Treaty comprehensively to protect the Antarctic environment and dependent and related ecosystems. But as for a general obligation to protect and preserve the environment wherever situated, one looks in vain. This is partly explained by the piecemeal development of the subject, elaborated in the next section. Early international regulation of environmental activities dealt with conservation of common property resources subject to over-exploitation and customary international law first developed to restrain State actions causing transboundary harm—primarily economic harm—in the territory of another State. International environmental regulation of State behaviour penetrating *within* the State has been less rapid to develop, particularly since it encounters the twin yet related obstacles of State sovereignty and permanent sovereignty over natural resources. Nonetheless it is possible to detect the impact of international environmental law on the

---

[2] *Gabčíkovo-Nagymaros project (Hungary/Slovakia), Judgment, ICJ Reports 1997*, p 7. For discussion of its significance as a landmark case in public international law, see Boisson de Chazournes and Mbengue, 2017.

[3] (1939) 33 *AJIL* 182 and (1941) 35 *AJIL* 684; see also Principle 21 of the 1972 Declaration of the UN Conference on the Human Environment (Stockholm) and Principle 2 of the 1992 Declaration of the UN Conference on Environment and Development (Rio) reproduced in Birnie and Boyle, 1995, at pp 1 and 9 respectively.

[4] See also the *Chagos Marine Protected Area Arbitration (Mauritius v United Kingdom), Award of 18 March 2015, PCA Case No 2011-13* and the *South China Sea Arbitration (Philippines v China), Award of 12 July 2016, PCA Case No 2013-19*.

evolution of the principle of permanent sovereignty over natural resources, most notably in the concept of sustainable development, importing duties as well as rights in respect of natural resource management (Schrijver, 1997). Undoubtedly one of the challenges facing international environmental law in the twenty-first century is achieving a holistic and integrated approach to environmental regulation which applies within as well as between and beyond States. The 1992 UN Convention on Biological Diversity is one example of a treaty instrument moving in this direction.

What does 'the environment' mean for our purposes? It is an amorphous term that has thus far proved incapable of precise legal definition save in particular contexts. Even the Law of the Sea Convention, which comprehensively defines pollution of the marine environment, does not define the marine environment as such. A rare exception is Article 2(10) of the 1993 Council of Europe Convention on Civil Liability for Damage Resulting from Activities Dangerous for the Environment. It defines the environment to include 'natural resources both abiotic and biotic, such as the air, water, soil, fauna, and flora and the interaction between the same factors; property which forms part of the cultural heritage; and the characteristic aspects of the landscape'. This broad definition encompasses natural and cultural heritage protection (regulated by the 1972 UNESCO Convention for the Protection of the World Cultural and Natural Heritage, for example); species and habitat protection (see, for example, the 1992 UN Convention on Biological Diversity); and pollution prevention (regulated, *inter alia*, by the 1972 London (Dumping) Convention and the 1979 UN ECE Convention on Long-Range Transboundary Air Pollution (LRTAP)). As will be seen shortly, this in fact encapsulates the development of international law, especially treaty law, in the field of the environment: from sectoral pollution and conservation treaties to ecosystem and holistic environmental protection, with increasing attention to issues of liability, compensation, and compliance.

II. THE DEVELOPMENT OF INTERNATIONAL ENVIRONMENTAL LAW

Although the origins of international environmental regulation may be traced to the nineteenth century,[5] the modern development of the subject dates from the post-Second World War era. Indeed, the development of international environmental law shares much in common with the development of domestic environmental law which arose concomitantly with concerns about environmental degradation highlighted especially in the 1960s. A turning point was undoubtedly the UN-sponsored 1972 Stockholm Conference on the Human Environment which produced a non-binding Declaration of Principles and a Programme for Action. Subsequently not only did national departments of environmental protection proliferate, but the UN established a specialized subsidiary body of the UN General Assembly—the UN Environment Programme (UNEP), headquartered in Nairobi. Today UNEP remains the only international body exclusively concerned with environmental matters, although many other specialized bodies within the UN family concern themselves with environmental matters as part of their broader remit, such as the fisheries conservation efforts of the Food and Agriculture Organization (FAO) in Rome and the marine environmental protection activities of the International Maritime Organization (IMO) in London.

---

[5] See for example the *Behring Fur Seals Arbitration* (1898) 1 Moore's Int Arbitration Awards 755.

The UN General Assembly has also played a significant role in shaping international environmental law and policy, notwithstanding the absence of any mention of the environment in the UN Charter. Undoubtedly dynamic interpretation of the Charter—especially of Articles 1 and 55—and the implied powers approach adopted by the ICJ in the *Reparations* case[6] would support reading environmental matters into the competence of the UN. The establishment of UNEP following the Stockholm Conference in 1972, and of the UN Commission on Sustainable Development (1992–2012)[7] following the 1992 Rio Conference on Environment and Development, is ample testament to the suppleness of the Charter treaty text. Today a number of significant global treaties has resulted from UN auspices, including the 1992 Conventions on Climate Change and Biological Diversity and their subsequent protocols and agreements. The UN has also played a significant role in regional developments through, for example, the regional seas programme of UNEP and the UN's economic commissions. The UN Economic Commission for Europe (ECE) has been particularly active in the environmental field and is responsible for two significant procedural treaties addressing environmental impact assessment (the 1991 Espoo Convention on Environmental Assessment in a Transboundary Context) and access to environmental information, public participation, and access to justice (the 1998 Aarhus Convention on Access to Information, Public Participation in Environmental Decision-Making, and Access to Justice in Environmental Matters), as well as for sectoral pollution regulation (the 1979 Convention on Long-Range Transboundary Air Pollution and the 1992 Conventions on the Transboundary Effects of Industrial Accidents, and on the Protection and Use of Transboundary Watercourses and International Lakes).

It is common to divide the development of international environmental law into three (Francioni, 1994) or four (Sands and Peel, 2012; Fitzmaurice, 2001) stages. The first predates the 1972 Stockholm Conference and is characterized by piecemeal and reactive responses to particular problems of resource use and exploitation (eg the 1946 International Convention for the Regulation of Whaling), including shared resources (eg the 1909 Treaty Between the USA and Great Britain Respecting Boundary Waters Between the USA and Canada), and pollution (eg the 1954 International Convention for the Prevention of Pollution of the Sea by Oil). Some writers sub-divide this first stage into two, commencing the second stage with the creation of international institutions from 1945 and seeing its culmination in the 1972 Stockholm Conference on the Human Environment inaugurating on this analysis the third phase of development. It produced a Declaration[8] and an Action Programme, a template followed by the 1992 Rio Conference on Environment and Development 20 years later. In addition, the run-up to and conclusion of the Stockholm Conference stimulated a great deal of regional and global treaty-making activity, much of it directed towards protection of the marine environment. The 1972 London (Dumping) Convention dates from this period, as does the regional seas programme of UNEP which from 1976 onwards has led to the conclusion of a number of regional seas agreements including environmental protection provisions. The terrestrial environment was also the focus of attention, with the conclusion of major treaties regarding the natural and cultural heritage (the 1972 UNESCO Convention Concerning the Protection of the World Cultural and Natural Heritage), species and habitat protection (eg the 1971 Ramsar

---

[6] *Reparations for Injuries Suffered in the Service of the United Nations, Advisory Opinion, ICJ Reports 1949,* p 174.

[7] See UN GA Res 47/191 (1992) in Birnie and Boyle, 1995, p 658 and the Report of the UN Secretary-General, Lessons Learned from the Commission on Sustainable Development UN Doc A/67/757, 26 February 2013.

[8] For seminal analysis of the Stockholm Declaration on the Human Environment, see Sohn, 1973.

Convention on Wetlands of International Importance Especially as Waterfowl Habitat, the 1973 Convention on International Trade in Endangered Species, and, in direct response to a recommendation at Stockholm, the 1979 Bonn Convention on the Conservation of Migratory Species of Wild Animals). With one or two exceptions, such as the 1980 Convention on the Conservation of Antarctic Marine Living Resources with its novel ecosystem approach, this period of international legislative activity is characterized by a sectoral and fragmented approach to achieving environmental protection.

The third (or fourth) period witnesses instruments adopting a holistic approach to environmental protection and seeks to marry such protection with economic development, embraced in the concept of sustainable development. This was the theme of the 1992 Rio Conference on Environment and Development which, in addition to producing a Declaration of Principles[9] and a programme of action for the twenty-first century (Agenda 21) saw the conclusion of two major treaties under UN auspices—the 1992 Framework Convention on Climate Change and the 1992 Convention on the Conservation of Biological Diversity. It was hoped also to adopt binding texts relating to forests and to deserts, but in the event only a soft law text on forests was adopted (the 'Non-Binding Authoritative Statement of Principles for a Global Consensus on the Management, Conservation and Sustainable Development of all Types of Forest').[10] In 1994 the Convention to Combat Desertification was adopted, as was the International Tropical Timber Agreement (ITTA) (replacing a 1983 agreement and itself superseded by a new agreement in 2006). While paying greater attention to sustainable development than its predecessors, the 2006 ITTA is largely concerned with facilitating sustainable timber trade and not with forest biodiversity per se, which thus falls under the remit of the Biodiversity Convention. Both forests and deserts have proved resistant to international regulation largely owing to concerns about the infringement of State sovereignty. Nonetheless the general outcome of the Rio Conference, and the conclusion of the Biodiversity and Climate Change Conventions in particular, marked a new phase in international environmental regulation with the acknowledgement that the conservation of biological diversity and the prevention of further adverse changes in the earth's climate are the common concern of humankind. However, proposals further to develop the institutional framework of international environmental law to reflect these common and intergenerational concerns have not yet made any significant headway. Suggestions for revamping the UN Trusteeship Council to address global commons issues became linked with broader and more vexed questions of UN institutional reform. The ten-year follow-up to the Rio Conference, the 2002 Johannesburg World Summit on Sustainable Development, neither achieved environmental institutional reform nor resulted in significant multilateral law-making, though making a significant contribution, *inter alia*, to developments within the Southern African region.[11] The 2012 UN Conference on Sustainable Development, dubbed 'Rio+20', provided an opportunity to assess the limited progress towards achieving sustainable development since 1992, and produced a political outcome document entitled 'The Future We Want'.[12] Amongst other things, the Commission on Sustainable Development, viewed as largely ineffectual, was replaced in 2013 by a High-Level Political Forum (HLPF) on Sustainable Development, with a renewed emphasis on the science and policy interface. While major institutional reform as part of this process is highly unlikely, the first report of the HLPF calls for a 'UN

---

[9] For article-by-article commentary see Viñuales, 2015.   [10] See generally Eikermann, 2015.
[11] See the Johannesburg Declaration on Sustainable Development and Plan of Implementation, http://www.johannesburgsummit.org.
[12] 'The Future We Want', UN Doc A/RES/66/288 available at http://sustainabledevelopment.un.org/futurewewant.html.

institutional platform for sustainable development models and scenarios' as support for the production of the Global Sustainable Development Report called for in the Rio+20 outcome document.[13]

The past decades have witnessed an evolution in law-making focus from environmental regulation incidental to the primary focus, such as economic regulation of a resource, to an holistic approach to environmental protection within and beyond State borders. These stages are not necessarily sequential, however, with evidence in the present of international rules reflecting each of these stages of evolution. This is particularly evident in the tension between permanent sovereignty over natural resources and the common concern of humankind contained in the Biodiversity Convention, and in the continuing resistance to robust international regulation of forest and desertification issues because of the perceived threat to State sovereignty. Moreover, what is absent from the corpus of international rules thus developed is a comprehensive codification of the basic rules and principles applicable to international regulation of the environment analogous to the 1948 Universal Declaration of Human Rights or the 1982 Law of the Sea Convention.[14] The Stockholm and Rio Declarations were political attempts to articulate such principles, though some of the principles contained in them are of a sufficiently norm-creating character, and enjoy the widespread and consistent State practice and buttressing *opinio juris*, for recognition as customary international law. That said, given the wide range of environmental issues confronting humankind, many of which require a detailed, standard-setting regulatory response, it is not surprising that the vast bulk of international environmental regulation is found in tailor-made treaty arrangements. Nonetheless, as discussed in Section IV of this chapter, certain key customary law principles have also emerged. The parallels with human rights and law of the sea are again apparent.

III. KEY ENVIRONMENTAL ACTORS

While States remain the central actors in environmental law-making and enforcement activities, they are not the exclusive actors. Participation at the 1992 and 2012 Rio and 2002 Johannesburg summits is but one example of a further feature of international environmental law, which is the increased participation of non-State actors, in particular non-governmental organizations (NGOs). Witness the range of actors identified in Section 3 of the Earth's Action Plan (Agenda 21) agreed at Rio in 1992: women, youth, indigenous peoples, NGOs, local authorities, workers and trade unions, business and industry, the scientific and technological community, and farmers. Of course this is not a unique feature of the environmental field, though it is particularly marked within it (and in the human rights area, as Ch 26 of this book attests). The role of NGOs in particular has been significant both in shaping the treaty-negotiating process and also in stimulating subsequent developments within treaty regimes.[15] Perhaps the outstanding example is the influence of the International Council for Bird Preservation (ICBP) and the International Waterfowl and Wetlands Research Bureau (IWRB) in the conclusion and implementation of the 1971 Ramsar Convention, for which the International Union for the Conservation

---

[13] Ibid, para 85k. See the Global Sustainable Development Report—Executive Summary (New York: United Nations Department of Economic and Social Affairs, Division for Sustainable Development, 2014) available at http://sustainabledevelopment.un.org/globalsdreport.

[14] One such attempt is the *International Union for the Conservation of Nature's Draft International Covenant on Environment and Development* (5th edn, IUCN, 2015).   [15] See further Chinkin and Boyle, 2007.

of Nature (IUCN), a unique union of governmental and non-governmental actors, acts as the secretariat.

NGO influence is achieved primarily through the mechanism of participation, viz as observers in international organizations, at treaty negotiations, and within treaty institutions. This may be expressly provided for in the treaty text, or in the rules of procedure or through practice. For example, the meetings of the conference of the parties to the 1992 Climate Change Convention and its subsidiary bodies provide for the participation of NGO representatives to observe with limited scope for active participation (Yamin and Depledge, 2004). These reflect the diverse constituencies of the Convention including business and industry NGOs (principally the major natural resource companies), environmental and local government NGOs, and indigenous peoples' organizations. These developments may be viewed as a wider trend towards viewing international society in terms broader than a community of States alone and as a recognition of community interest.[16] This is recognized in recent environmental treaties such as the Climate Change and Biodiversity Conventions, where we have seen that the global climate and biological diversity respectively are expressly recognized as the common concern of humankind (Soltau, 2016; French, 2016). However, as yet there is limited participation of non-State actors as treaty parties. A notable exception is the European Union[17] which possesses international legal personality coupled with the requisite internal constitutional competence to participate in international treaties alongside the Member States. Thus, for example, the EU is a party to the 1992 Climate Change Convention, the 1997 Kyoto Protocol, and the 2015 Paris Agreement which expressly provide for the participation of regional economic integration organizations.[18] Yet it is not a party to the 1973 Convention on International Trade in Endangered Species, because the treaty text does not presently make provision for non-State participation. Thus only the Member States may become parties in their individual capacities. This has not prevented the EU from regulating trade in endangered species, but it does so in the exercise of internal legal competence over the matter and not in furtherance of an expressly undertaken international obligation.[19]

In addition to participation in international environmental law-making, non-State actors may play a significant role in enforcement, whether through transnational litigation before national courts, in treaty compliance procedures (where permitted, as under the Aarhus Convention procedure), or in the indirect enforcement of environmental norms through human rights litigation. Civil liability regimes are concerned with the liability of non-State actors—shipowners under oil pollution liability; nuclear operators under the nuclear liability regimes, for example. Increasing attention is also being paid to corporate environmental accountability; however, corporations are not directly bound by environmental treaties or customary international law, and national courts have not been highly receptive to international environmental law arguments, especially in horizontal litigation.[20] Corporations may nonetheless voluntarily adhere to environmental standards (eg ISO 14000 series environmental standards) as a form of corporate self-regulation;[21]

---

[16] See, eg, the Commission on Global Governance, 1995; Benvenisti and Nolte, 2018.

[17] Prior to the Treaty of Lisbon, which entered into force on 1 December 2009, it was the European Community which enjoyed international legal personality.

[18] The European Court of Justice has recognized that an environmental treaty to which the EU is a party may be directly effective in the Member States 'so that any interested party is entitled to rely on those provisions before national courts': see *Syndicat professionnel coordination des pêcheurs de l'étang de Berre and de la région* v *Électricité de France (EDF)*, Case C-213/03, [2004] ECR I-7357, para 47.

[19] See, eg, Council Regulation (EC) No 338/97 on the protection of species of wild fauna and flora by regulating trade therein.   [20] See Anderson and Galizzi, 2002.

[21] See Muchlinski, 2007.

corporate social responsibility discussions also evidence an environmental dimension, illustrated by three of the ten principles of the non-binding UN Global Compact[22] and Part VI of the OECD Guidelines for Multinational Enterprises.[23]

IV. SOURCES OF INTERNATIONAL ENVIRONMENTAL LAW

Since international environmental law is concerned with the application of general international law to environmental problems, it is not surprising that its sources include the traditional ones enumerated in Article 38 of the Statute of the International Court of Justice. However, four features should be highlighted in this context. The first is the relative importance of treaty regimes for the articulation of primary and secondary (subsidiary) norms of international environmental law.[24] The process of regime building is a dynamic one, with an ongoing succession of treaties, protocols, and related instruments on the same subject an increasingly common phenomenon. The adoption of consensus and 'package-deal' approaches to treaty negotiation have been particularly beneficial in the environmental context, permitting States to reach agreement on issues such as transboundary air pollution, climate change, and the conservation of biological diversity, even in the face of sharp differences of view about the very existence of the problems and about their solution.

The second feature is that this norm generation process is pluralized and decentralized (Gehring, 2007) with a particularly distinctive role for institutions and non-State actors. The third is the relative importance of informal normative sources—non-legally binding instruments or soft law—in the environmental context. Indeed, sometimes environmental treaties are preceded by a non-binding instrument—for example, the UNEP Guidelines which preceded the 1989 Basel Convention and the UNEP and FAO Guidelines and Code which preceded the 1998 Rotterdam Convention on the Prior Informed Consent Procedure for Certain Hazardous Chemicals and Pesticides in International Trade. Finally, international environmental law is a clear illustration of the permeability of categories of sources: treaties may codify or generate custom; general principles may be articulated in treaty texts, reflect custom, fit within the Article 38(1)(c) category of general principles, or be found in soft law (Redgwell, 2017a).

A. TRADITIONAL SOURCES OF INTERNATIONAL ENVIRONMENTAL LAW

The vast bulk of environmental law is contained in treaty texts which are given dynamic force in part because they usually provide an institutional mechanism for their implementation (Churchill and Ulfstein, 2000; Jacur, 2013). A common format is to provide for regular meetings of the Conference of the Parties (COP),[25] a number of subsidiary Committees reporting to the COP, most commonly comprising at least a Committee for Scientific and Technical Advice, and a Secretariat to provide support at and between

---

[22] Principles 7 (precautionary principle), 8 (environmental responsibility), and 9 (environmentally friendly technologies): see http://www.unglobalcompact.org.

[23] The fifth and more recent update, on 25 March 2011, is available at: http://www.oecd.org/daf/inv/mne/oecdguidelinesformultinationalenterprises.htm.

[24] On environmental treaty-making, see Redgwell, 2000, and generally, Boyle and Chinkin, 2007.

[25] For analysis of the role of the COP, including in compliance procedures, see Brunee, 2002 and Jacur, 2013.

meetings of these bodies. The dynamic force of many environmental treaties derives from the need to respond to changes in the physical environment regulated thereby and is most generally effected through the COP via a subsidiary scientific body. A significant number of environmental treaties adopt a framework approach to facilitate more rapid change than is generally the case through the normal (and time-consuming) process of treaty amendment. This approach enables the treaty to contain general principles and set forth the organizational structure of the treaty bodies (the framework), while further protocols and/or annexes embody specific standards and are generally subject to a more flexible amendment process.

An excellent example of a framework treaty is the regional 1979 ECE Convention on Long-Range Transboundary Air Pollution, now accompanied by eight protocols. More flexible amendment procedures were pioneered by the International Maritime Organization with the use of the 'tacit acceptance amendment procedure' with its 1973/78 Convention for the Prevention of Pollution from Ships (MARPOL), to which there are now six annexes. Changes to the annexes come into force for *all* contracting parties within a minimum of 16 months of adoption of the change unless objection is lodged within a certain time period (ten months) by one-third of the contracting parties or by the number of contracting parties whose combined merchant shipping fleets represent at least 50 per cent of world gross tonnage. A more recent and further example of this framework approach is the 1992 Convention for the Protection of the Environment of the North-East Atlantic (OSPAR), where the Convention is accompanied by five annexes and three appendices, with the latter embodying matters exclusively of a technical, scientific, or administrative nature. Both appendices and annexes are more readily amended and modified than the Convention text itself, thus permitting the Convention more readily to grow and adapt to changing scientific and other data.[26]

Further flexibility is found in recent treaty texts that allow for differentiation in the implementation obligations for States taking on treaty commitments (French, 2000; Cullet, 2003; Rajamani, 2006). For example, Article 3(1) of the 1992 Climate Change Convention recognizes the common but differentiated responsibilities and respective capabilities of States in implementing the obligation to protect and preserve the climate system for the benefit of present and future generations (Rajamani, 2000). Developed country parties 'should take the lead in combating climate change and the adverse effects thereof'; indeed, under the 1997 Kyoto Protocol it is only Annex I (developed country) parties which are subject to specific targets and timetables for greenhouse gas emission reductions. As the climate regime has evolved, however, there is a trend towards symmetry—obligations for 'all Parties' under the 2015 Paris Agreement—with a key issue for negotiation of the post-2020 legal framework having been the basis for, and extent of, differentiation in the application of the common but differentiated responsibilities principle first enshrined in the 1992 Convention (Rajamani, 2013; Bodansky et al, 2017). Other instruments adopt similar methods of differentiation based on the parties' capabilities. For example, a number of the substantive treaty obligations of States parties to the 1992 UN Convention on Biological Diversity are qualified by the words 'in accordance with [each contracting party's] particular conditions and capabilities'.

While the vast majority of the rights and obligations of States with respect to the environment derive from voluntarily assumed treaty obligations, it would be wrong to infer from this that no customary international law norms govern State conduct. State practice

---

[26] For further discussion of the legal implications of such flexible amendment procedures under OSPAR, see de la Fayette, 1999.

has given rise to a number of customary law principles, buttressed by the process of treaty and customary law interaction (see generally De Sadeleer, 2002; Roberts and Sivakumaran, Ch 4 of this book). Of these the most significant is the 'good neighbour' or so-called 'no harm' principle, pursuant to which States have a duty to prevent, reduce, and control pollution and significant transboundary environmental harm (Redgwell, 2015). It has been enunciated in judicial decisions as well as soft law declarations. Thus, for example, in the *Pulp Mills* case, which involved the siting of a pulp mill on a shared watercourse, the River Uruguay, the ICJ observed that '[a] State is thus obliged to use all the means at its disposal in order to avoid activities which take place in its territory, or in any area under its jurisdiction, causing significant damage to the environment of another State.'[27] Far from imposing an absolute prohibition on any transboundary harm, as the 'no harm' shorthand appears to suggest, the obligation to prevent significant transboundary harm is widely viewed as imposing an obligation of due diligence. The ILC Commentary to the Draft Articles on Prevention of Transboundary Harm for Hazardous Activities thus accurately reflects current international law in stating that 'the obligation of the State of origin to take preventive or minimization measures is one of due diligence.'[28]

State practice further supports the customary law obligation to consult and to notify of potential transboundary harm where there are shared resources or ultrahazardous activities being carried out, and the requirement to conduct a prior transboundary environmental impact assessment. In the *Pulp Mills* case, the ICJ found the requirement to conduct a transboundary environmental impact assessment (EIA) to be a distinct and freestanding obligation in international law where significant transboundary harm is threatened. Although the specific content of such an EIA is left to the State's discretion, international law requires that an EIA is conducted and that it bears a relation to the 'nature and magnitude of the proposed development and its likely adverse impact on the environment.'[29]

Other relevant principles of customary international law include the principle of preventive action and equitable utilization of shared resources. More controversial is the customary law status of the precautionary principle or approach (Birnie, Boyle, and Redgwell, 2009), the principle of sustainable development per se (Lowe, 1999) and of its buttressing principles (eg sustainable use; intergenerational equity; integration of the environment into economic and development projects; and common but differentiated responsibilities) (Paradell-Trius, 2000; French, 2005), and the polluter-pays principle (Birnie, Boyle, and Redgwell, 2009). Arguments range from lack of normative content to the absence of a uniform understanding of the meaning of the principles, and widely varying consequences of their application depending on the specific context. While such principles may lack legally binding force as customary international law, their impact may nonetheless be considerable when further concretized in a treaty text (eg the precautionary principle under the 1995 Straddling Fish Stocks Agreement) or used as a 'general guideline' or aid to judicial interpretation of treaty obligations between the parties (eg the concept of sustainable development and the bilateral agreement between Hungary and Slovakia in the

---

[27] *Pulp Mills on the River Uruguay (Argentina v Uruguay), Judgment, ICJ Reports 2010*, p 14, para 101. See also Article 2 of the ILC's 2001 Draft Articles on Prevention of Transboundary Harm from Hazardous Activities (ILC Yearbook 2001, Vol II Part 2, p 152).

[28] ILC Yearbook 2001, Vol II Part 2, 154, commentary to Article 3, para (7).

[29] *Pulp Mills on the River Uruguay (Argentina v Uruguay), Judgment, ICJ Reports 2010*, p 14, para 205. See also *Responsibilities and Obligations of States Sponsoring Persons and Entities with Respect to Activities in the Area, Advisory Opinion, ITLOS Reports 2011*, p 10, paras 145–8; *Indus Waters Kishenganga Arbitration (Partial Award)* (Pakistan v India), *Partial Award of 20 December 2013*, PCA Case No 2011–01, para 450; and *Certain Activities carried out by Nicaragua in the Border Area (Costa Rica v Nicaragua); Construction of a Road in Costa Rica along the San Juan River (Nicaragua v Costa Rica), ICJ Reports 2015*, p 665, paras 104 and 153.

Gabčíkovo-Nagymaros case). In a wide-ranging assessment of the environmental impact of deep seabed mining activities, the Seabed Disputes Chamber of the International Tribunal for the Law of the Sea in an Advisory Opinion affirmed the obligation of sponsoring States to apply a precautionary approach, relying *inter alia* on provisions of the Nodules and Sulphides Regulations.[30] It was prepared to go further, noting that 'the precautionary approach is also an integral part of the general obligation of due diligence of sponsoring States, which is applicable even outside the scope of the Regulations'.[31] Apart from this Advisory Opinion, instances of international judicial recognition of the principle are muted and few. For example, there was no mention of it by the ICJ in the *Gabčíkovo-Nagymaros* case, nor was it generally recognized as a principle of customary international law in the *Pulp Mills* case where the Court considered that 'a precautionary approach *may be relevant in the interpretation and application of the Statute*' between the parties.[32] This statement is correctly regarded as 'fall[ing] well short of any confirmation as to the requirement of precaution in customary law' (Sands and Peel, 2012). In the *Beef Hormones* case, the WTO Appellate Body found the legal status of the precautionary approach to be uncertain in general international law,[33] and eight years later in the *EC-Biotech* case, a WTO Panel still found its status 'unsettled'.[34]

General principles of law are also of significance in the environmental context, though a distinction needs to be made between the general principles of law referred to in Article 38(1)(c) of the ICJ Statute, and general principles such as those found in the Stockholm and Rio Declarations in international environmental law. To the extent that the former embraces general principles found in national law, these are of limited utility in the international environmental context (though relied on in the seminal *Trail Smelter Arbitration*). If Article 38(1)(c) includes general principles recognized at international law, then the scope is potentially significant. These operate to influence the interpretation of (but do not override) treaty provisions and the application of custom, and influence judicial decisions (Redgwell, 2017b). This is the 'architectural function' performed by principles in shaping 'a norm, a treaty (or an identifiable part of it), or a legally linked set of treaties' (Viñuales, 2016). The reference to 'the concept of sustainable development' by the ICJ in the *Gabčíkovo-Nagymaros* case[35] is a well-known example of the influence an internationally recognized principle of international environmental law may wield. There the Court observed that 'the Treaty is not static, and is open to adapt to emerging norms of international law',[36] with its approach grounded in the evolutionary language of the treaty text itself.[37]

In practice, environmental principles may be derived from general international law (eg the principle of good neighbourliness), from other specialized areas of international

---

[30] *Responsibilities and Obligations of States Sponsoring Persons and Entities with Respect to Activities in the Area, Advisory Opinion*, ITLOS Reports 2011, paras 121–2 and 125–7.   [31] Ibid, para 131.

[32] *Pulp Mills on the River Uruguay (Argentina v Uruguay), Judgment*, ICJ Reports 2010, (I) p 14, para 164 (emphasis added).

[33] *European Communities—Measures Concerning Meat and Meat Products* (1998), WTO Doc WT/DS26/AB/R; WT/DS48/AB/R (Appellate Body Report), paras 120–5.

[34] *European Communities—Measures Affecting the Approval and Marketing of Biotech Products* (2006), WTO Doc WT/DS291/R (Panel Report), para 7.89.

[35] *Gabčíkovo-Nagymaros Project (Hungary/Slovakia), Judgment*, ICJ Reports 1997, p 7, para 140.

[36] Ibid, para 112. See also *Iron Rhine Arbitration (Belgium/Netherlands) Award of 24 May 2005*, PCA Case No 2003-02, para 80; *Pulp Mills on the River Uruguay (Argentina v Uruguay), Judgment*, ICJ Reports 2010, (I) p 14, para 205.

[37] Ibid (1996) *ICJ Reports*, para 88; for recent, less ambiguous, invocation, see the *Indus Waters Kishenganga Arbitration (Partial Award), (Pakistan v India), Partial Award of 20 December 2013*, PCA Case No 2011-01, para 452.

law (eg human rights, especially participatory rights), and principles which are specific to international environmental law (eg the principle of common but differentiated responsibility; the precautionary principle) (Atapattu, 2015, p 75).

As noted earlier, general principles also have an influential role to play through their authoritative articulation in non-binding declarations, such as the 1992 Rio Declaration on Environment and Development. This has stimulated the development of new general principles of direct environmental relevance, particularly the precautionary principle, the polluter-pays principle, common but differentiated responsibilities, and sustainable development. While, as already stated, their customary law status may be doubtful or disputed, they have influence to varying degrees, particularly as modifiers of existing rules and treaties, and on treaty negotiations.

Although not a formal source of international law as such, judicial decisions provide important authoritative evidence of what the law is, with a growing number of judicial and arbitral awards of importance in the environmental field. These include judgments and advisory opinions of the ICJ[38] and ITLOS[39] and judgments of the PCA[40] and other arbitral awards[41] and the decisions of human rights courts.[42]

B. SOFT LAW

In addition to the traditional sources of international law identified earlier, a variety of non-binding instruments such as codes of conduct, guidelines, resolutions, and declarations of principles may be resorted to by States and non-State actors alike.[43] As discussed earlier (Boyle, 1999, ch 5), these are non-binding instruments, non-compliance with which does not entail international responsibility. Soft law may be employed because its origins are not law-creating either because the body promulgating the 'law' does not have law-making authority (eg an autonomous treaty supervisory body or an NGO) or because a law-making body chooses a non-binding instrument with which to embody a statement of particular principles (eg States at the 1992 Rio Conference on Environment and Development adopting the binding 1992 Climate Change Convention and the non-binding 1992 Rio Declaration of Principles on Environment and Sustainable Development). International environmental law is a particularly fertile area for soft law norms, since it allows agreement on collective but non-binding action where, for example, the scientific evidence is inconclusive or the economic costs uncertain. It may, and not infrequently does, lead to 'hard' law, such as the UNEP Guidelines mentioned earlier, although as the discussion of the climate change regime in Section VI of this chapter illustrates, this process is not necessarily a linear one. An example is the relationship between soft and hard

---

[38] See, eg, *Gabčíkovo-Nagymaros Project (Hungary/Slovakia), Judgment, ICJ Reports 1997*, p 7; *Legality of the Threat or Use of Nuclear Weapons, Advisory Opinion, ICJ Reports 1996*, p 226; *Pulp Mills on the River Uruguay (Argentina v Uruguay), Judgment, ICJ Reports 2010*, p 14.

[39] See, eg, *MOX Plant Case (Ireland v United Kingdom), Provisional Measures, Order of 3 December 2001, ITLOS Reports 2001*, p 95; *Responsibilities and Obligations of States Sponsoring Persons and Entities with Respect to Activities in the Area, Advisory Opinion, ITLOS Reports 2011*, nyr; (2011) 50 ILM 458.

[40] *MOX Plant Arbitration (Ireland v United Kingdom), Jurisdiction and Provisional Measures*, PCA, 16 June 2003; *Iron Rhine Arbitration (Belgium/Netherlands), Award of 24 May 2005*, PCA Case No 2003-02, para 58; *Chagos Marine Protected Area Arbitration (Mauritius v United Kingdom), Award of 18 March 2015*, PCA Case No 2011-13; *South China Sea Arbitration (Philippines v China), Award of 12 July 2016*, PCA Case No 2013-19.

[41] See, eg, *Trail Smelter Arbitration*, (1939) 33 *AJIL* 182; *Metalclad Corporation v United Mexican States* (ICSID Case No ARB(AF)/97/1), Award of 30 August 2000.

[42] See, eg, *Fadeyeva v Russia*, no 55723/00, ECHR 2005-IV and, generally, Boyle, 2012.

[43] See Chinkin and Boyle, 2007, and Shelton, 2000; on the interaction of treaty and soft law, see Boyle, 1999.

law in the climate regime, which has not been a simple linear trajectory but rather has meandered from hard to soft, and, with the adoption of the 2015 Paris Agreement, back to hard (French and Rajamani, 2013). Informal cooperation (eg in the conclusion of the Copenhagen Accord, and interaction in settings such as the Major Economies Forum) has played an important role in the climate regime 'as necessary alternatives, or complements, to the protracted and cumbersome negotiations in the multilateral UNFCCC context'. What is also striking is the 'incorporation' of informal agreements within the wider UNFCCC framework—the transition of the Copenhagen Accords from 'minilateralism' by five States to incorporation within the UNFCCC framework, albeit over the objections of one State[44]—and the apparent commitment (though to be sure, not necessarily exclusively) to multilateralism.

V. ENFORCEMENT OF INTERNATIONAL ENVIRONMENTAL LAW

A question of over-arching importance is what happens in the event of the breach of an environmental obligation?[45] Here the traditional rules regarding State responsibility (see Crawford and Olleson, Ch 14 of this book) would apply. Yet these rules are of only limited assistance in the environmental field for a number of reasons (Redgwell, 2013). One is that responsibility rules generally operate once damage has already occurred, rather than to prevent damage from occurring in the first place. A second difficulty, illustrated particularly well by the climate change example, is that harm may be incremental and difficult to link to the specific actions or omissions of another State.[46] Problems of causation and proof will loom large. The generally non-reciprocal character of international environmental obligations will also render it difficult to meet the requirement of breach of an obligation owed to another State. Both the *Trail Smelter Arbitration* between the USA and Canada[47] and the *Gabčíkovo-Nagymaros Dam* dispute between Hungary and Slovakia[48] saw the application of traditional rules on State responsibility because of the bilateral character of the dispute and of the obligations thereunder. Had it proceeded to the merits, the ICJ case brought in 1974 against France by Australia and New Zealand regarding French atmospheric nuclear testing in the South Pacific would have likewise largely fit within this bilateral model.[49] But what of the example of a breach by a State of its obligation to conserve biological diversity, expressly acknowledged as 'the common concern of humankind'? A complainant State is required to show that the obligation is owed to it and (usually) that injury has resulted to it in order for standing requirements to be satisfied; there is no such thing (yet) under international law as an *actio popularis* whereby a State may bring an action on behalf of

---

[44] Bolivia. Similarly, the Conference of the Parties serving as the meeting of the parties to the Protocol (COP/MOP) agreed a second commitment period under the Kyoto Protocol to 2020 (albeit with binding emission reductions for a small group of States) over objections from Russia. See Rajamani, 2014.

[45] See the contributions to the edited volume by Francioni and Scovazzi, 1991; Wetterstein, 1997; and Wolfrum, 1999.

[46] From a burgeoning literature see Verheyn, 2005; Fitzmaurice, 2010; Tomuschat, 2011; Lefebre, 2012.

[47] *Trail Smelter Arbitration* (1939) 33 AJIL 182 and (1941) 35 *AJIL* 684.

[48] *Gabčíkovo-Nagymaros Project (Hungary/Slovakia), Judgment, ICJ Reports 1997*, p 7.

[49] *Nuclear Tests (Australia v France), Interim Protection, Order of 22 June 1973, ICJ Reports 1973*, p 99; *Judgment, ICJ Report 1994*, p 253; *Nuclear Tests (New Zealand v France), Interim Protection, Order of 22 June 1973, ICJ Reports 1973*, p 135; *Judgment, ICJ Reports 1994*, p 457.

[50] *South West Africa, Second Phase, Judgment, ICJ Reports 1966*, p 6.

the international community.[50] There are glimmerings of such an approach in Articles 42 and 48 of the 2001 Articles on State Responsibility drafted by the International Law Commission, wherein the possibility exists for a State party to a multilateral treaty to complain of breach of a multilateral obligation by another State party.[51] While there has not yet been international judicial recognition of this possibility in the environmental context, in the 2012 *Obligation to Prosecute or Extradite* case (*Belgium v Senegal*), the ICJ explicitly recognized that the Convention against Torture imposed obligations *erga omnes partes* giving rise to a common interest in compliance and 'the entitlement of each State party to the Convention to make a claim concerning the cessation of an alleged breach by another State party'.[52]

There are several consequences of the inadequacies of traditional rules of State responsibility for the development of international environmental law. The first is the historic paucity of cases at the international level in which environmental matters have figured largely.[53] Recourse to the dispute settlement under international environmental treaties is rare, with few dispute settlement clauses in such treaties providing for compulsory third party settlement of inter-State claims (Brus, 1995). Sparse examples include the Ozone Layer Convention and the Montreal Protocol, and the Framework Convention on Climate Change (FCCC) and the Kyoto Protocol. A second consequence has been pressure further to develop the rules of State responsibility, including standing. Few environmental treaties address standing; rarer still is to provide for reciprocal standing for non-State actors.[54]

A third consequence is the development of alternatives to traditional dispute settlement techniques under specific treaty instruments directly to address the issue of non-compliance with treaty obligations from both a facilitative and a coercive point of view. The 1987 Montreal Protocol is pioneering in this regard, establishing the first non-compliance procedure in an environmental agreement. A handful of other treaty instruments have established implementation and compliance procedures, including the 1997 Kyoto Protocol to the 1992 Framework Convention on Climate Change, the 1989 Basel Convention on the Transboundary Movement of Hazardous Wastes and their Disposal, the 2000 Cartagena Protocol to the 1992 Convention on the Conservation of Biological Diversity, and the 1998 Aarhus Convention on Access to Information, Public Participation in Decision-Making, and Access to Justice in Environmental Matters. These generally exist alongside traditional dispute settlement clauses and are suspended in the event of the invocation of traditional dispute settlement procedures (Fitzmaurice and Redgwell, 2000). Finally, a further consequence of the inadequacies of State responsibility in the environmental field is the development of liability regimes which side-step the necessity to rely on the route of inter-State claims. As we will see, the development of specific liability instruments has been particularly marked in the field of activities with transboundary consequences (eg nuclear activities, vessel-source oil pollution, and hazardous waste movements) and in the protection of common spaces (eg liability arising from environmental emergencies in Antarctica under the 2005 Annex to the 1991 Environmental Protocol to the 1959 Antarctic Treaty, and the responsibility and liability of seabed contractors for environmental damage in the 2000 regulations on prospecting and exploring for polymetallic modules promulgated by the International Seabed Authority under the 1982 LOSC).

---

[51] 2001 Articles on State Responsibility, Article 48; for analysis see Peel, 2001.

[52] *Questions relating to the Obligation to Prosecute or Extradite (Belgium v Senegal), Judgment of 20 July 2012,* para 69.   [53] See the examples at n 42.

[54] A rare example is Article 3 of the 1974 Nordic Environmental Protection Convention.

VI. SUBSTANTIVE INTERNATIONAL ENVIRONMENTAL LAW

From the foregoing it will already be apparent that there exists a considerable body of international rules applicable to environmental protection. The breadth of regulatory activity is enormous, ranging from liability and compensation for oil pollution damage through to licensing regimes for the transboundary movement of hazardous waste and the listing of sites important for wild birds or for protection of the natural and cultural heritage. The purpose of this section is to provide a flavour of the breadth and depth of international law pertaining to the environment particularly as developed through multilateral standards-setting conventions.

A. PROTECTION OF THE MARINE ENVIRONMENT

The protection of the marine environment[55] was one of the key issues at the 1972 Stockholm Conference, and is clearly reflected in the flurry of law-making in this area which occurred in the early 1970s in particular. The negotiation of the 1982 LOSC, which commenced in 1973, likewise had an influence upon (and was influenced by) these developments. Thus Part XII of the resulting 1982 Convention—with its 46 Articles devoted to the marine environment—implicitly acknowledges existing marine environment treaties in the areas of dumping at sea[56] and vessel-source pollution in particular. Pollution of the oceans, and concerns about their limited absorption capacity, formed a key thrust of these 1970s law-making activities: both the global 1972 London (Dumping) Convention and the regional 1972 Oslo Dumping Convention date from this period, as does the 1973 Convention on the Prevention of Pollution from Ships (MARPOL 73/78). UNEP, established, it will be recalled, after the Stockholm Conference, undertook the establishment of regional seas programmes for which the 1976 Barcelona Convention for the Protection of the Mediterranean Sea Against Pollution, and subsequent protocols, formed the prototype for many other regional seas areas (only the Baltic, the North-east Atlantic/North Sea, Antarctic, and Arctic oceans are regulated by regional instruments outside UNEP's programme). The Protocols to the Barcelona Convention range in subject matter from pollution caused by dumping, land-based sources, and seabed activities, to cooperation in emergencies, specially protected areas and biodiversity, transboundary movement of hazardous waste, and integrated coastal zone management. Other regional seas agreements following the Barcelona Convention pattern are comprehensive in their inclusion of sources of marine pollution, but the extent to which further protocols have been adopted varies. The Convention was substantially revised in 1995[57] following the Rio Conference, the impact of which is observable in many other areas of regulatory activity where such 'second generation agreements' have been adopted. As the list of Protocols to the Barcelona Convention attests, regulation for marine environmental protection extends beyond pollution to include area-based management tools, such as the designation of marine protected areas (MPAs) and the integrated management of the marine environment.[58]

---

[55] For succinct treatment of the extensive law in this area, see Birnie, Boyle and Redgwell, 2009, ch 7; Tanaka, 2015, ch 8; Rothwell and Stephens, 2016, ch 15; and generally Harrison, 2017.

[56] For analysis of the relationship between the 1982 LOSC and both prior and subsequent treaties regulating ocean dumping, see Redgwell, 2006a and 2016a.

[57] 1995 Convention for the Protection of the Marine Environment and the Coastal Region of the Mediterranean.

[58] A number of regional agreements provide for the designation of MPAs, with the largest MPA to date declared in 2016 by CCAMLR for the Ross Sea in the Antarctic. MPAs have been established for high seas areas under both the OSPAR and the Barcelona Conventions.

Dumping is one area of regulatory activity where this progression is particularly marked. Initially, regional and global dumping conventions adopted the regulatory approach of listing prohibited, dangerous, and other substances, relying on nationally implemented licensing schemes for their enforcement. Coastal States exercised the jurisdiction afforded them under international law to do so: territoriality and nationality (of the vessel). There was no presumptive ban operating in respect of dumping at sea, with the regulatory approach essentially one of 'permitted unless prohibited'. Wastes were divided into three categories: Annex I, the 'black list', contained a list of substances prohibited from dumping; Annex II, the 'grey list', those substances the dumping of which required a prior special permit; for all other substances, Annex III (the 'white list') required a prior general permit. However, with the replacement of the 1972 Oslo Convention (and 1974 Paris Convention for the Prevention of Marine Pollution from Land-Based Sources) by the 1992 Convention on the Protection of the Marine Environment of the North-east Atlantic (OSPAR) and the negotiation of the 1996 Protocol to the 1972 London Convention, this philosophy has been replaced by a 'prohibited unless permitted' approach. Dumping is not permitted unless it falls within one of the permitted exceptions to a general ban on dumping. The list is quite restrictive, including bulky matter such as dredged material and sewage sludge and (at least for the moment) offshore installations. A precautionary approach is very much in evidence here, with a significant shift in the burden of proof to the polluter to demonstrate that dumping at sea will not have significant harmful consequences for the marine environment. There has also been a noticeable shift away from an approach based on pollution prevention and control, the focus of the 1982 LOSC, to a more integrated approach to marine protection under these instruments (Sands and Peel, 2012). The nimbleness of this regime is further evidenced by amendments addressing new technologies—carbon capture and storage and ocean iron fertilization (Redgwell and Rajamani, 2014).

Vessel-source pollution, though a relatively minor contributor to marine pollution, has nonetheless been subject to extensive international regulation following highly publicized oil spills such as the *Torrey Canyon* in 1967. MARPOL 73/78 adopts a framework approach in that six accompanying annexes embody the technical details of regulating oil discharges (Annex I), noxious liquids in bulk (Annex II), harmful packaged substances (Annex III), sewage (Annex IV), garbage (Annex V), and air pollution (Annex VI). Any State wishing to become a party to MARPOL 73/78 must also adopt Annexes I and II as a minimum. Annex I reflects a particular preoccupation with vessel-source oil pollution, focusing on limiting discharges of oil as part of routine tanker operations. It sets forth oil discharge and tanker design criteria[59] and requires coastal States to provide adequate reception facilities for oily residues. Some maritime areas have been designated as 'special areas' under MARPOL in which no discharge is permitted, including areas such as the North-west Atlantic Ocean, the Mediterranean Sea, and the Antarctic Southern Ocean. Indeed, there has been a marked increase in the designation of 'particularly sensitive sea areas'[60] where specific measures can be used to control the maritime activities in that area, such as routing measures; strict application of MARPOL 73/78 discharge and equipment requirements for ships, such as oil tankers; and installation of Vessel Traffic Services (VTS).[61]

[59] Thus constituting the 'generally accepted international rules or standards' which coastal States may apply to third party shipping traversing the territorial sea in accordance with LOSC Article 21(2). See, generally, Redgwell, 2016a.
[60] See IMO Res A.982(24) *Revised Guidelines for the Identification and Designation of Particularly Sensitive Sea Areas* (2005).   [61] Seventeen PSSAs have been designated to date: see http://pssa.imo.org/#/intro.

A key regulatory device under MARPOL is the use of standardized International Oil Pollution Prevention Certificates, the issuance of which is linked to regular surveying and inspection of vessels. This is supplemented by a requirement for tankers and other ships to carry an Oil Record Book itemizing all operations involving oil. In addition to the requirement that this record may be inspected by any other party to MARPOL, it is these documents which in certain circumstances coastal and port States are entitled to inspect under the 1982 LOSC, whether or not a party to MARPOL.[62] Coastal States' enforcement powers are also enhanced under the 1982 LOSC, including the power to investigate, inspect, and, in limited circumstances, to arrest vessels navigating in the Exclusive Economic Zone (EEZ) when a violation of applicable international rules and standards for the prevention, reduction, and control of pollution from vessels, eg MARPOL 73/78, has occurred which threatens or causes significant pollution of the marine environment.[63] Thus MARPOL 73/78, like the other marine pollution conventions, relies on general international law and the 1982 LOSC in particular for the exercise of legislative and enforcement jurisdiction. As Ch 21 of this book makes clear, the LOSC constitutes a significant innovation in the development of port State enforcement jurisdiction upon which the success of MARPOL 73/78 has largely rested. Improved exercise of flag State jurisdiction has likewise had beneficial impact on the number of pollution incidents at sea.

The oil tanker catastrophes of the 1960s and 1970s also led to the development of separate liability conventions, the 1969 Convention on Civil Liability for Oil Pollution Damage (CLC) and the 1971 Convention on the Establishment of an International Fund for Compensation for Oil Pollution Damage (Fund Convention). These follow a pattern also found in the nuclear civil liability conventions, which is to limit and channel liability. Risk is assumed by, and liability is channelled through, the shipowner, which is strictly liable for oil pollution damage as defined under the conventions. A monetary ceiling on liability is fixed, enabling the shipowner to obtain insurance cover in the market through P & I Clubs. If this ceiling is exceeded under the CLC, then the Fund Convention may provide a further source of compensation funds for claimants. The Fund is based on levies from oil-importing countries, thus spreading the risk between the shipowner and the risk-creating States. The advantage for claimants in States parties to the CLC/Fund regime is the ability to obtain compensation swiftly without recourse to the courts in their own or another State. Both conventions were updated by Protocols in 1992 with an increase in the compensation limits (further increased in 2000 and 2003), an extension of geographic coverage (to incidents in the EEZ), and the inclusion of pollution prevention costs in the recoverable heads of damage. In 2001, a further convention was concluded on pollution damage from bunker fuel from ships, the International Convention on Civil Liability for Bunker Oil Pollution Damage. Modelled on the CLC, it entered into force in 2008.

Further responses to catastrophic oil spills are reflected in the 1969 Convention Relating to Intervention on the High Seas in Cases of Oil Pollution Casualties—which permits the coastal State to intervene beyond its territorial sea—and the 1990 Oil Pollution Preparedness and Response Convention (OPRC) which requires, *inter alia*, the preparation of emergency response plans for oil spill incidents. These were international legislative responses to the 1967 *Torrey Canyon* and 1989 *Exxon Valdez* oil spill emergencies respectively. In recognition of the fact that the threat to the marine environment from vessel-source pollution extends beyond petroleum, in 1973 the Intervention Convention was extended to apply to hazardous substances other than oil and, in 2000, the OPRC was

---

[62] Article 218 LOSC.   [63] Article 220, especially paras (3), (5), and (6).

extended by Protocol to cover hazardous and noxious substances.[64] Emergency response is also the subject of the first binding instrument adopted by Arctic States under the auspices of the Arctic Council.[65]

Related to the pollution context, a further threat to the marine environment arises from the introduction of invasive alien species through ballast water (Rayfuse, 2007), which is now regulated under the 2004 International Convention for the Control and Management of Ships' Ballast Water and Sediments. It uses techniques familiar from the oil pollution context, including the requirement to implement a management plan, carry a 'Ballast Water Record Book', and for port State inspection.

Despite this extensive legislative activity, significant gaps remain in marine environmental protection. Since the 1990s, over-fishing (see Evans, Ch 21 of this book), loss of marine biological diversity, and degradation of marine ecosystems have all become more apparent, as has the impact of climate change and ocean acidification.[66] Two notable gaps in the current regulatory framework are robust global regulation of the largest source of marine pollution, land-based pollution, and international regulation of the marine environment in areas beyond national jurisdiction. The former is the subject of weak provision in the 1982 LOSC and addressed in protocols to four UNEP regional seas agreements, and in the 1992 Baltic Convention, but there is no present prospect of further global regulation, not least because regulating this source of marine pollution most heavily intrudes on a wide range of human activities under the sovereignty of States. In contrast, marine protection in areas beyond national jurisdiction was part of the remit of the Ad Hoc Open-ended Informal Working Group to study issues relating to the conservation and sustainable use of marine biological diversity beyond areas of national jurisdiction, established by UN General Assembly resolution in 2006. As discussed in Ch 21, this led to the establishment of a Preparatory Commission[67] which in 2017 made substantive recommendations to the UN General Assembly on the elements of an internationally legally binding instrument under the 1982 LOSC addressing the conservation and sustainable use of marine biological diversity of areas beyond national jurisdiction in order to fill this high seas 'marine biodiversity gap' (Oral, 2012).

B. PROTECTION OF THE ATMOSPHERE

There are three principal areas of international regulatory activity in respect of protection of the atmosphere—transboundary air pollution, ozone depletion, and climate change. All share a transboundary or global dimension, and in no case are the existing rules of customary law, including those on State responsibility, adequate to address the problem. In particular the persistence, scope, and intertemporal nature of environmental problems such as climate change necessitate global (preventative) action. A classic case for international regulation, it would seem. Yet in the case particularly of transboundary air pollution

---

[64] The 1996 International Convention on Liability and Compensation for Damage in Connection with Carriage of Hazardous and Noxious Substances by Sea (HNS), also modelled on the CLC, has not entered into force and in 2010 was amended by the HNS Protocol, which to date has attracted eight signatures and one ratification (Norway).

[65] The 2013 Agreement on Cooperation on Marine Oil Pollution Preparedness and Response in the Arctic. The IMO has also developed a 'Mandatory Code for Ships Operating in Polar Waters', ie for both Arctic and Antarctic waters, requiring amendments to SOLAS and to MARPOL 73/78, and which entered into force on 1 January 2017.

[66] UN, Report of the Secretary-General, *Oceans and the Law of the Sea*, GAOR/A/72/70 (2017).

[67] Established by UN General Assembly Res 69/292, it met in four sessions in 2016–17. The final report of PrepCom is available at http://www.un.org/depts/los/biodiversity/prepcom.htm#69/292.

and of climate change, there was some scepticism regarding the existence and scope of the problem. Moreover, unlike the marine context discussed in Section VI A, there is no single instrument where the general 'law of the atmosphere' is codified, nor is this picture likely to change. In 2013 the International Law Commission adopted the topic of 'Protection of the atmosphere' in its programme of work but with express caveats including that: (a) this work would not interfere with political negotiations, including on climate change, ozone depletion, and long-range transboundary air pollution; and (b) the outcome of the work will be draft guidelines which do not seek to impose on existing treaty regimes legal principles not already contained therein.[68]

1. Transboundary air pollution

The *Trail Smelter* Arbitration referred to in Section V of this chapter was an early instance of an inter-State claim arising in respect of the harmful transboundary effects of airborne pollutants.[69] Yet this case involved a single detectable source of air pollution (sulphur dioxide emissions from the smelter) causing quantified harm to health and property; today it would most likely be resolved through transnational litigation by access to national courts. What if the sources of air pollution are far more diffuse and its harmful effects upon the environment are widespread? These were the difficulties confronting States in negotiating the 1979 LRTAP Convention, added to which was the initial scepticism of some parties as to the very existence and nature of the problem. In fact it remains the only major regional agreement addressed to air pollution, a reflection both of the severity of the problem in Europe (though Canada and the USA are also parties[70]) and the difficulty in achieving international regulation of an activity impacting on sovereign energy and other choices.

The purpose of LRTAP is to prevent, reduce, and control transboundary air pollution from both new and existing sources. 'Air pollution' is defined in terms reminiscent of the marine pollution definition of the 1982 LOSC, and includes harm to living resources, ecosystems, and interference with amenities and legitimate uses of the environment. 'Long-range transboundary air pollution' is defined as adverse effects in the jurisdiction of one State resulting from emissions originating in the jurisdiction of another State yet the individual source of which cannot necessarily be distinguished. The framework character of LRTAP resulted in the absence of specific reduction targets in the treaty itself; rather, an environmental monitoring programme was first put in place pursuant to the first Protocol to LRTAP, in order to gather data to assess the extent of the problem, followed by the negotiation of further protocols to reduce emissions of specific air pollutants. In this respect the LRTAP Convention is a good example of the interaction of monitoring and reporting obligations on the one hand and flexible treaty structures, easily adapted to changes in scientific knowledge, on the other. The framework approach of the Convention has allowed a step-by-step approach by States allowing 'agreement' at the outset even where there is no consensus regarding the concrete steps to be taken to address a particular environmental problem. To date eight protocols on monitoring and on specific air pollutants with specific reduction targets and timetables[71] have been added to the initial framework convention, significantly expanding the scope of the parties' commitments. Although there are provisions on notification and consultation in cases of significant risk of transboundary pollution, LRTAP does not itself contain provisions on liability nor on compliance. But in 1994

---

[68] See http://legal.un.org/ilc/texts/8_8.htm.

[70] As noted in Section III of this chapter, LRTAP is one of five environmental treaties concluded under the auspices of the UN's Economic Commission for Europe, membership of which comprises 56 States within Europe (east and west), the CIS and North America: see http://www.unece.org.

[71] For texts see http://www.unece.org/env/lrtap.

a second sulphur protocol was adopted with a non-compliance procedure influenced by the experience of the 1987 Montreal Protocol to the Ozone Convention. In 1997, this procedure was subsumed within a broader Implementation Committee established, *inter alia*, to review compliance by parties with the reporting obligations of the Convention and any non-compliance with the Protocols.[72]

2. Ozone depletion

It was UNEP which in 1981 initiated negotiations for the conclusion of a treaty to protect the ozone layer,[73] culminating in the adoption of the 1985 Vienna Convention for the Protection of the Ozone Layer (Yoshida, 2001). Like LRTAP, the initial treaty contained little by way of substantive obligations, focusing rather on the need to assess the causes and effects of ozone depletion and cooperation in the exchange of relevant information and technology. This 'largely empty framework' treaty was a result of the divergent interests of States: the USA, having taken steps for domestic reduction, was concerned to ensure a level playing field in respect of ozone-depleting substances regulation; developing States were concerned to ensure that any restraints on the use of such substances did not adversely affect industrial development and that if imposed, appropriate access to alternative technology would be assured; while the EU, where many producers were located, was concerned regarding the potential cost of steps to be taken and unconvinced of the scientific case for the harmful effects of the substances (Birnie, Boyle, and Redgwell, 2009).

The 1987 Montreal Protocol—like the 1997 Kyoto Protocol to the Climate Change Convention—radically altered this picture in several respects. In addition to introducing specific targets for the reduction and eventual elimination of ozone-depleting substances, subsequent adjustments or amendments of the Protocol have introduced financial (the Multilateral Fund) and technical incentives to encourage developing country adherence to the Protocol. Implementation and compliance is further secured through the establishment of a non-compliance procedure, the first mechanism of its kind but which is now found in a number of other agreements (see Section V of this chapter). This is a form of 'soft enforcement' designed to address non-compliance by essentially self-implicating States through both facilitation (access to the Multilateral Fund, provision of technical assistance) and/or sanction (issuing of cautions and/or suspension of the Article 5 privilege of delay in implementation for which some 148 developing States are currently eligible[74]). In fact compliance by developed States has been high, and it has been largely former Soviet and East European States which have experienced difficulties with full compliance, largely owing to financial and technical constraints. Successive amendments to the Protocol have also set more stringent targets and timetables and added to the list of ozone-depleting substances such that recovery of the ozone layer, including the hole above Antarctica, is hoped for by the mid-twenty-first century. This projected recovery of the ozone layer, combined with wide participation in the Protocol, high compliance rates, and the dynamic and flexible operation of the treaty regime which has continued over time to strengthen controls over ozone-depleting substances, constitutes the Montreal Protocol as an all-too-rare success story in addressing environmental problems through international cooperation. Yet there may be factors impeding long-term success, including the emergence of new

---

[72] Decision 1997/2. The Implementation Committee's terms of reference were most recently updated in 2012 (Decision 2012/25). For the most recent available (nineteenth) report by the Implementation Committee, Body on non-compliance cases considered by the Implementation Committee, see ECE/EB.AIR/2016/7, 6 October 2016, available at http://www.unece.org/env/lrtap/ic/reports.html.

[69] See generally Okowa, 2000.

[74] For the complete list see http://ozone.unep.org/new_site/en/parties_under_article5_para1.php.

ozone-depleting substances not covered by the Protocol, and the fact that it encourages resort to substituting substances some of which (eg HFCs) are greenhouse gases covered by the Kyoto Protocol (Annex A) (Birnie, Boyle, and Redgwell, 2009). This led the contracting parties in 2016 to adopt an amendment to the Protocol requiring an 80 per cent reduction in HFC emissions over a 30-year period and their replacement by more 'planet friendly' substances.[75]

3. Climate change

It will be recalled that the 1992 UN Framework Convention on Climate Change[76] was one of two treaties adopted at the Rio Conference. Negotiations followed upon recognition by the General Assembly that the atmosphere is 'the common concern of mankind' and the work of the Intergovernmental Panel on Climate Change (IPCC) in providing the scientific guidance necessary to regulate the emission of greenhouse gases on the international level.[77] The principal objective of the Convention is 'stabilization of greenhouse gas concentrations in the atmosphere at a level that would prevent dangerous anthropogenic interference with the climate system'. Although framework in character, the Convention contains specific commitments in Article 4 addressed to all parties and, additionally, specifically to developed country parties. All 197 parties have the obligation to produce inventories of greenhouse gas sources and sinks, to formulate national and, where appropriate, regional programmes to reduce global warming, to cooperate in preparing for adaptation to the impacts of climate change, and to promote scientific research. Since these obligations are addressed to developing as well as developed country parties, the Convention qualifies these obligations by permitting parties to 'tak[e] into account their common but differentiated responsibilities and their specific national and regional development priorities'. No such qualification is made of the obligations for developed country parties and other parties (countries with economies in transition)—the 'Annex I' parties to the Convention. For these States, Article 4 sets forth the obligation to develop national policies and measures to mitigate the adverse effects of climate change indicating that developed country parties are to take the lead in modifying longer-term trends in anthropogenic emissions. Detailed reports on such policies are to be provided 'with the aim of returning individually or jointly to their 1990 levels ... of carbon dioxide and other greenhouse gases not controlled by the Montreal Protocol'. It is also the responsibility of developed country parties to provide new and additional financial resources to meet the agreed full costs incurred by developing country parties in complying with their Convention obligations. The financial mechanism under the Convention is the Global Environmental Facility (GEF), administered jointly by the World Bank (as trustee), UNEP, and the UN Development Programme. The GEF is also the financial mechanism under the Biodiversity Convention.

Notwithstanding the obligations contained in Article 4, it was not until the negotiation of the 1997 Kyoto Protocol that developed country parties committed themselves to explicit, unambiguous targets and timetables for the reduction of the chief greenhouse gases and to the development of international mechanisms for ensuring the fulfilment of

---

[75] The 2016 Kigali Amendment will enter into force on 1 January 2019.

[73] See, generally, Benedick, 1998; Yoshida, 2001; Anderson and Sarma, 2002, and http://www.ozone.unep.org.

[76] On the negotiation of the convention see Bodansky, 1993; on the protocol see Freestone and Streck, 2005, and on the climate regime see Depledge and Yamin, 2004. For recent comprehensive analysis of the climate regime to date, see Bodansky et al, 2017. For current status and text see http://www.unfccc.int.

[77] The Fifth Assessment Report (AR5) was released 2013–14, comprising four volumes (reports of the three working groups and a synthesis report) available at http://www.ipcc.ch.

these commitments. It marked a 'regulatory phase' in the evolution of the climate regime
marked by four features: a top-down regulatory approach, sharp differentiation between
developed and developing States, a legally binding instrument with a robust compliance
system,[78] and market mechanisms for cost-effective implementation (Bodansky et al,
2017). The core obligation of the Protocol is contained in Article 3(1), which states that
Annex I parties 'shall, individually or jointly, ensure that their aggregate anthropocentric
carbon dioxide equivalent emissions' of specific greenhouse gases 'do not exceed their assigned amounts' and that overall emissions of such parties are reduced 'by at least 5 per
cent below 1990 levels in the commitment period 2008–2012'. To ensure its effectiveness
the Protocol could only enter into force when adhered to by 55 States including Annex
I parties representing 55 per cent of that group's 1990 carbon dioxide emissions. Annex
I party participation was contingent on satisfactory elaboration of the three 'flexibility
mechanisms' in the Protocol for achieving these targets and timetables, namely, joint
implementation (projects between Annex I parties), the clean development mechanism
(between Annex I and non-Annex I parties), and emissions trading. At COP7 (2001) significant breakthrough had been achieved in realizing the details of implementation such
that both Canada and Russia announced at the Johannesburg summit in 2002 that they
would ratify the Protocol. The participation of both States was essential for the attainment
of the entry into force threshold of the Protocol given the USA's stated determination to
remain outside the Protocol. The Protocol duly entered into force on 16 February 2005,[79]
leaving less than eight years remaining for Annex I parties to achieve the reductions mandated for the first commitment period (2008–12).

In consequence of this time-limited commitment period, attention turned in 2005 to
the post-2012 legal framework. Negotiations continued along two tracks, one under the
Convention and the other under the Protocol. At COP13 in 2007 the parties agreed the
Bali Plan of Action with the aim of reaching agreement on a post-2012 governance framework by COP15/MOP5 that was to be held in Copenhagen at the end of 2009.[80] Two
ad hoc working groups—on long-term cooperation action under the Convention, and
on further commitments of the Annex I parties to the Protocol—prepared draft texts for
consideration at Copenhagen, which was the intended end point for these parallel negotiations. In the event a controversial non-binding 'Copenhagen Accord' was concluded
by representatives of major economics and regions, which was not based on the Working
Group drafts, and of which the COP decision to which it was attached as an unofficial
document 'took note'.[81] Unlike the Kyoto Protocol, the Accord did not contain binding
targets for emissions reduction but rather relied on a 'bottom-up' approach of pledged reductions. Nonetheless, over 141 States made pledges, representing 87.24 per cent of global
emissions.

The uncertain status of the Copenhagen Accord was addressed at COP16 in Cancun
(2010) where agreements were concluded on each of these tracks, and 'note taken' of the
mitigation targets agreed at Copenhagen. Important areas of disagreement remained,
however, including most notably over long-term global emissions targets and whether
to extend the Kyoto Protocol beyond 2012. At COP17 in Durban in 2011, agreement
was reached on a second commitment period, to 2020, but not on what legal form future

---

[78] The Protocol has a Compliance Committee, with both a facilitative branch and an enforcement branch,
to facilitate, promote, and enforce compliance with the Protocol. For discussion and comparison with the
Montreal Protocol compliance procedure, see Werksman, 1998; see also Fitzmaurice and Redgwell, 2000.

[79] It presently has 192 parties including the EU (but not the USA). Canada announced its withdrawal from
the Protocol in 2011, which pursuant to Article 27(1) of the Kyoto Protocol took effect from 15 December 2012.

[80] On the legal implications of the possible outcomes, see Rajamani, 2009.   [81] See Decision 2/CP.15.

commitments would take, with some States continuing to register opposition to the conclusion of a 'second Kyoto Protocol' (eg Japan, Russia, and Canada—in the latter case unsurprising given the announcement of its withdrawal from the Kyoto Protocol with effect from 15 December 2012).

The possibility of a legally binding outcome remained on the table owing to careful drafting of the Durban outcome, the 'Durban Platform for Enhanced Action', which launched 'a process to develop a protocol, another legal instrument or an agreed outcome with legal force under the Convention' by 2015.[82] This deadline was achieved with the adoption at COP21 of the legally binding Paris Agreement on 12 December 2015. It entered into force on 4 November 2016 and to date has 173 parties. Such rapid entry into force is the product of the momentum generated at Paris and a reflection of the framework character of the Agreement, with much of the legal framework it creates yet to be fleshed out. Central to the Agreement is its aim in Article 2 to limit temperature increases to below 2 degrees C and the ambition to pursue efforts to limit temperature increase even further to 1.5 degrees C. It continues the trajectory in climate negotiations away from the sharp differentiation of the Kyoto Protocol towards symmetry of obligations with, for example, reference in Article 3 to 'all parties' with respect to undertaking and communicating nationally determined contributions (NDCs) to the global response to climate change (Article 3). At the same time, there is recognition of the need to support developing country parties in both mitigation and adaptation measures and provision in the Agreement for providing financial resources and capacity building, and for loss and damage (a particular concern of small island ocean states). The Agreement reflects a hybrid architecture combining a bottom-up approach of nationally-determined contributions to mitigation (Article 4.2)[83] with international oversight to promote 'ambition and accountability'. Accountability is enhanced through requirements of transparency (Article 13) and a 'global stocktake' every five years (Article 14), in the light of NDCs, to form a collective assessment of whether national efforts 'add up' to what is necessary to limit temperature increases to below 2 degrees C. This 'progression over time' is a key feature of the Agreement, with much hard work remaining to be done to ensure effective national implementation with international oversight (Bodansky et al, 2017).

C. NUCLEAR RISKS

The nuclear sector has been the subject of considerable regulatory activity at the international level.[84] Given that nuclear energy activities are ultrahazardous in character with potentially devastating transboundary implications, this degree of international regulatory activity is unsurprising. The first international agreements, at both global and regional level, were concerned with regulating liability and compensation for nuclear damage largely with a view to rendering a fledgling energy industry commercially viable. They also reflected the generally unsatisfactory nature of the general customary international law principles in respect of State responsibility discussed earlier, as well as the magnitude of the potential harm to humans and the environment.

At the regional level, the 1960 Paris Convention on Third Party Liability in the Field of Nuclear Energy and the 1963 Brussels Supplementary Convention were adopted under

---

[82] Establishment of an Ad Hoc Working Group on a Durban Platform for Enhanced Action 2011, available at http://unfccc.int/2860.php. For analysis see Rajamani, 2012.

[83] 152 intended NDCs of 182 States had been submitted by 1 December 2015; to date, parties' NDCs cover 99 per cent of global emissions.

[84] For succinct overview, see Ghaleigh in Birnie, Boyle, and Redgwell, 2009, ch 6; Handl, 2015; and Redgwell, 2016b, section E.

the auspices of the Nuclear Energy Agency of the Organization for Economic Cooperation and Development (OECD). These are designed to elaborate and harmonize legislation relating to third party liability to ensure that compensation is paid for persons suffering nuclear damage, while at the same time ensuring that the development and use of nuclear energy remains commercially feasible. Channelling and limiting liability achieves both of these aims, with the nuclear operator initially liable, then the State of operation and, finally, all contracting parties. Financial limits for liability, which is strict, are set for each level. In 2004, amendments to the Paris/Brussels regime (not yet in force) were made which increase compensation levels, enhance operator liability, and enlarge their geographic scope. The definition of nuclear damage thereunder includes not only personal injury and damage to property, but also economic losses such as the cost of preventive measures and of measures to reinstate an impaired environment, which may constitute the major portion of the damage caused by a nuclear incident. However, there has not yet been a serious test of these provisions within Europe. The Chernobyl incident in 1986 did not fall under the Paris/Brussels regime since, as a non-OECD member, the Soviet Union was not a party to the Convention (nor is the Russian Federation now) and the convention does not apply to incidents outside convention States. In 1988 a Joint Protocol was concluded which links this regional system with the similar global regime, the 1963 Vienna Convention on Civil Liability for Nuclear Damage, with a further 1997 Supplemental Convention (in force 2003) increasing the amount of compensation available for nuclear damage.

These global instruments have been concluded under the auspices of the International Atomic Energy Agency (IAEA), a UN body which was established in 1957 to facilitate the peaceful development of nuclear energy and adherence to non-proliferation safeguards. Following the Chernobyl accident in 1986, the IAEA concluded two further international treaties addressed to early notification (1986 Convention on Early Notification of a Nuclear Accident or Radiological Emergency) and to assistance in the event of an international nuclear incident (1986 Convention on Assistance in the Case of a Nuclear Accident or Radiological Emergency). The former embraces in treaty form the customary law obligation to notify in the event of serious transboundary harm. In more preventive vein, a further IAEA convention, the 1994 Convention on Nuclear Safety, is designed to ensure the safe design, operation, and decommissioning of land-based nuclear power plants. The effectiveness of this instrument came under scrutiny following the Fukushima Daiichi nuclear plant incident in Japan in 2011 (Kus, 2011). An extraordinary meeting of the parties to the Convention was held in 2012 to consider the implications of the Fukushima incident for the Convention, which identified several key weaknesses including the non-binding peer review mechanism for national reports submitted under the Convention. Procedural changes have been instituted to strengthen peer review and transparency, which unlike treaty amendment may have immediate effect, with a working group established to consider further strengthening through amendment of the Convention.[85] In 2015, a Diplomatic Conference to consider a Swiss amendment to the Convention resulted in the (non-binding) Vienna Declaration on Nuclear Safety.[86]

Safety and security issues form an increasingly important area of the IAEA's activities with the object, *inter alia*, of protecting humans and the environment from harmful radiation exposure. In 1997 a further Joint Convention on the Safety of Spent Fuel and Radioactive Waste Management was concluded, modelled on the 1994 Convention, to ensure high safety standards and the prevention of accidents in the disposal of nuclear waste.

---

[85] For the outcome of the second extraordinary meeting of the parties to the Convention on Nuclear Safety, see http://www-ns.iaea.org/conventions/nuclear-safety.asp?s=6&l=41.

[86] Text available at https://www.iaea.org/sites/default/files/cns_viennadeclaration090215.pdf.

In many respects these recent developments of both the OECD and IAEA regimes demonstrate parallels with the regulation of oil pollution liability: preventive concern to ensure that the activity is carried out to minimize or avert pollution consequences; emergency response and notification systems; and a liability regime which increasingly acknowledges the environmental costs of prevention and of reinstatement.

Despite the extent of legislative activity at the global level and regional levels, a significant gap remains in the legal regime for disposal of radioactive waste. In addition to the recognition of the Antarctic continent as the first 'nuclear waste free zone' (Antarctic Treaty 1959 Article 5), it is widely recognized that the disposal of radioactive waste on or below the seabed is prohibited by international law. This flows either from specific treaty prohibition (ie London Convention Article IV(1)(a); London Protocol Article 4(1); OSPAR Article 3, Annex II), or from the more general treaty and customary international law duty to protect the marine environment (eg LOSC Article 192), with which such disposal is regarded as inconsistent. While this leaves States with the exclusive option of land-based disposal, international law continues to play a role in the regulation of safe disposal of nuclear material, largely through the work of the IAEA. However, it is unclear whether the existing nuclear liability regime would extend to geological or subsurface disposal of high-level waste and spent nuclear waste. This is because (strict) liability is channelled through the operator of a 'nuclear installation' upon proof of nuclear damage, but the definition of 'nuclear installation' under the 1963 Vienna Convention on Civil Liability for Nuclear Damage appears to include only a nuclear reactor, a nuclear factory, or 'any facility where nuclear material is stored' (Article I(j))—there is no explicit reference to disposal. While there is a clear technical distinction between storage, however long term, and permanent disposal,[87] the legal distinction between them is less clear: does 'storage' include 'disposal' for the purposes of the application of the liability regime? Legal certainty could be achieved, for example, were a determination made by the Steering Committee for Nuclear Energy of the OECD that a disposal facility with nuclear fuel or radioactive products or waste is an 'installation' for the purposes of the liability regime. Whether it should be so extended is another question, given that geological disposal of high-level nuclear waste and spent fuel raises issues different from even the long-term storage of nuclear waste, and may thus require a bespoke legal response (Redgwell and Rajamani, 2014).

D. OTHER HAZARDOUS SUBSTANCES AND ACTIVITIES

Apart from the nuclear sector there has also been considerable regulation of other hazardous activities and substances, focusing on environmentally sound management and regulation of the transboundary movement of such substances.[88] Four instruments are of particular importance in this area, three of which are of relatively recent origin. The 1989 Basel Convention on the Transboundary Movement of Hazardous Wastes and their Disposal[89] was the first to occupy the field and was the international response to 'toxic traders' seeking to avoid the increasingly high costs of hazardous waste disposal in developed countries through cheaper disposal in developing and East European countries. It has had an influence on the scope and application of two other instruments with which

---

[87] IAEA, *The Long Term Storage of Radioactive Waste: Safety and Sustainability, A Position Paper of International Experts* (2003) 3, stressing permanence with no intention to remove.

[88] See, generally, Pallemaerts, 2003; Wirth, 2007.

[89] Regional regulation is found in the 1991 Bamako Convention on the Import into Africa and the Control of Transboundary Movement and Management of Hazardous Wastes within Africa and in Protocols to the Regional Seas Agreements discussed in Section VII A of this chapter.

it is closely linked, namely, the 1998 Rotterdam Convention on Prior Informed Consent Procedure for Certain Hazardous Chemicals and Pesticides in International Trade and the 2001 Stockholm Convention on Persistent Organic Pollutants. Together these three instruments are intended to provide for the environmentally sound management of hazardous chemicals throughout their life-cycle, and reflect international consensus that the toxic or highly dangerous substances regulated by them may *a priori* be deemed significantly harmful. A fourth instrument, the 2000 Cartagena Protocol to the 1992 Biodiversity Convention, is addressed to the transboundary movement of living modified organisms, on the hazardous character of which there is as yet no international consensus. Further linkages between these instruments are provided by UNEP, which functions as the secretariat for each of the four instruments (jointly with the Food and Agriculture Organization (FAO) in the case of the Rotterdam Convention).[90] UNEP is also responsible for the most recent multilateral environmental agreement to be concluded on hazardous substances, the 2013 Minamata Convention on Mercury, which is brought within the Basel framework through, *inter alia,* the definition of mercury as 'waste' for the purposes of the latter.

1. 1989 Basel Convention on the Transboundary Movement of Hazardous Wastes and their Disposal

The Basel Convention[91] has achieved widespread adherence with 184 parties at present, including significant developing country participation which was facilitated by the early establishment of a Trust Fund and a Technical Cooperation Fund. It is concerned both with regulating the transboundary movement of hazardous waste and ensuring sound environmental management in respect of its disposal. This is reflected in the annexes to the Convention which address not only the categories of waste controlled (Annex I) or requiring special consideration (Annex II) but seek to standardize the definition of hazardous characteristics (Annex III), regulate disposal operations (Annex IV), and ensure adequate information is provided about hazardous characteristics, etc (Annex V). There is also provision for arbitration (Annex VI) and, concluded in 1999 but not yet in force, a Protocol on Liability and Compensation for Damage (including environmental damage). The Convention affirms the sovereign right of States to prohibit imports of hazardous waste and ensures the corresponding export prohibition will be respected by other States parties. Where transboundary movement does take place it must be grounded in the prior consent of the importing State (and any transit States), with both importing and exporting States obliged to ensure that waste is managed in an environmentally sound manner. Trade with non-parties is prohibited; moreover hazardous waste disposal from OECD to non-OECD countries is also now prohibited under the Convention. This move to prohibition is characteristic of other pollution treaties, most notably in the case of dumping at sea under both the global 1996 London Protocol and under the regional 1992 Convention for the Protection of the Marine Environment of the Northeast Atlantic. These treaties also share with the Basel Convention (and with the Stockholm and Minamata Conventions) an increasing focus on sound environmental management seeking to eliminate waste generation at source through best environmental practices and available techniques, signalling a shift in emphasis from remediation to prevention. The Basel Convention parties are also increasingly focused on the effective implementation and enforcement of the regulatory framework established over the decade of the 1990s. The Convention joins an increasing number of environmental treaties to address not only the liability of non-State actors and compensation for, *inter alia,* environmental damage (the 1999 Protocol), but also

90 See the joint portal for the conventions at http://www.brsmeas.org.
91 For a thorough analysis see Kummer, 2000.

compliance by States with their Convention obligations. In 2002 the Basel Convention established a compliance mechanism to facilitate early detection of implementation and compliance problems such as illegal trafficking or meeting reporting obligations, a move possible only through the establishment of concrete norms and standards against which to benchmark State compliance and the political will of the parties to achieve more effective implementation of its provisions.[92]

2. 1998 Rotterdam Convention on Prior Informed Consent and the 2001 Stockholm Convention on Persistent Organic Pollutants

Conclusion of the Rotterdam and Stockholm Conventions[93] was stimulated by Chapter 19 of Agenda 21 which highlighted the regulatory gap in respect of substances that are 'toxic, persistent and bio-accumulative and whose use cannot be controlled'. Like the Basel Convention, soft law guidance in the form of UNEP/FAO Guidelines preceded their negotiation, with both instruments fairly rapidly entering into force with relatively widespread adherence by States. The Rotterdam Convention (PIC) was applied provisionally from its conclusion in 1998 until its entry into force on 24 February 2004, and currently has 156 parties. It establishes a prior informed consent regime in respect of the importation of toxic substances, many of which are also subject to the Stockholm Convention. It does not ban outright the import/export of hazardous chemicals and pesticides but rather subjects them to a regime of the prior informed consent of the importing party before export of a banned or severely restricted chemical or severely hazardous pesticide to which the convention applies may take place between parties. These are listed in Annex III of the Convention, which provides a mechanism for amending the list of substances through the Conference of the Parties, on the recommendation of the Convention's Chemical Review Committee. Ultimately of course the Convention relies on exchange of information among parties about potentially hazardous chemicals that may be exported and imported and requires national decision-making processes to be established regarding import and compliance by exporters with these decisions. The 2001 Stockholm Convention entered into force on 17 May 2004 and presently has 181 parties. It initially addressed environmentally sound management of a so-called 'dirty dozen' toxic substances, to which a further nine chemicals were added at COP4 in 2009. Indeed, as under the Rotterdam Convention, there is regular review of POPs by the Convention's Persistent Organic Chemicals Review Committee, with has led to the inclusion of a further five chemicals at subsequent COPs. The fundamental objective is to protect human health and the environment from persistent organic pollutants (POPs), which remain intact in the environment for long periods, becoming widely distributed geographically, and accumulate in the fatty tissues of living organisms thus posing a toxic threat both to humans and to wildlife. The Stockholm Convention seeks to eliminate or reduce the release of POPs into the environment through controls over the production or use of intentionally produced POPs (ie industrial chemicals and pesticides), management and reduction of stockpiles, and minimization and elimination of unintentionally produced POPs (eg industrial by-products such as dioxins and furans). Unlike the PIC Convention, POPs explicitly relies on a precautionary approach (Article 1).

3. 2000 Cartagena Protocol on Living Modified Organisms

The Cartagena Protocol on Living Modified Organisms (LMOs)[94] to the 1992 Convention on Biological Diversity was concluded in 2000 and entered into force on 11 September

---

[92] For reports of the Compliance Committee to date, see http://www.basel.int/legalmatters/compcommitee.

[93] See further http://www.pic.int and http://chm.pops.int, respectively.

[94] See further Redgwell, 2006b; McKenzie et al, 2003; and http://www.cbd.int/biosafety.

2003. It presently has 171 parties. The focus of the Protocol is upon the transboundary movement of LMOs which may have adverse effects on biological diversity and human health. 'LMO' is defined as 'any living organism that possesses a novel combination of genetic material obtained through the use of modern biotechnology'. In fact the Protocol addresses two general categories of LMO: (i) those intended for release into the environment (eg seeds for cultivation or animal breeding stock); and (ii) those intended for use in food or feed, or for processing (eg corn, cotton, and soy). The latter were of particular concern to exporters of genetically modified crops (including the USA, though not a party to the Protocol) and are subject to a less onerous regime (Article 11) than that applicable to LMOs intended for direct release into the environment (Articles 7–10). The chief regulatory technique employed under the Protocol is the 'advanced informed agreement' (AIA) procedure, which is designed to ensure that contracting parties are provided with the information necessary to make informed decisions before agreeing to the import of LMOs into their territory. AIA marks the Protocol out from the 'prior informed consent' procedures of the 1989 Basel and 1998 Rotterdam Conventions, which are based on prior multilateral agreement on the hazardous substances to be regulated and which are set out in annexes. No such agreement exists regarding LMOs; in consequence, a marked feature of the Protocol is its overtly precautionary approach, with Article 1 making express reference to the precautionary approach contained in Principle 15 of the 1992 Rio Declaration. To facilitate information exchange and to assist with national implementation, a Biosafety Clearing-House has been established. Facilitative financing is also available through the Global Environmental Facility (the financial mechanism for the parent Convention on the Conservation of Biological Diversity (CBD) as well). A Compliance Committee, expressly contemplated under the Protocol to address problems of implementation and non-compliance, was established at the first meeting of the parties,[95] to consider specific instances of non-compliance and to review compliance in general terms based on national reports submitted by the parties. In common with many similar mechanisms in other environmental treaties, it is intended to be principally facilitative and non-adversarial in function,[96] with more coercive measures (eg the issuing of cautions and the publication of non-compliance details in the Biosafety Clearing-House) left to the decision of the Meeting of the Parties under the Protocol.

Article 27 of the Cartagena Protocol provided for the further elaboration of international rules and procedures in the field of liability and redress for damage resulting from transboundary movements of living modified organisms. In 2010, the Nagoya-Kuala Lumpur Supplementary Protocol on Liability and Redress to the Cartagena Protocol on Biosafety was adopted and entered into force on 5 March 2018 upon the deposit of the fortieth ratification. Damage is defined, *inter alia*, as an adverse effect on the conservation and sustainable use of biological diversity, taking into account risks to human health, and must be significant, a threshold also defined in the Convention (Article 2).

4. The 2013 Minamata Convention on Mercury

In 2009 the process of negotiating a new Convention[97] to address mercury pollution was initiated under UNEP's auspices, and in October 2013 the text was formally opened for signature in Minamata, Japan, the location of serious mercury poisoning and loss of life caused by consumption of fish and shellfish contaminated by industrial wastewater from

[95] For reports of the Compliance Committee to date, see https://bch.cbd.int/protocol/cpb_art34_info.shtml.
[96] The supportive role of the Committee has been particularly emphasized: see COP-MOP Decision BS-V/1.
[97] Final text of the Convention together with the Report of the fifth and final negotiation session is available at http://www.unep.org/hazardoussubstances/Mercury/Negotiations/INC5/INC5Report/tabid/3496/Default.aspx.

a chemical factory. It entered into force on 16 August 2017 and presently has 86 parties. The objective of the Convention 'is to protect human health and the environment from anthropogenic emissions and releases of mercury and mercury compounds' (Article 1). It addresses the reduction of mercury emissions to the air from power plants and other point sources (Articles 8 and 9), adopting a 'menu of options' approach to mercury emissions (Article 8(5)) and releases (Article 9(5)) in deference to varying national circumstances. Similarly, Article 8(5) uses mandatory language—'shall include' and 'shall implement'— but permits a choice of measures ('one or more of the following measures') with ample scope for national differentiation ('taking into account its national circumstances, and the economic and technical feasibility and affordability of the measures').

In addition to mercury emissions and releases, the Convention addresses the use of mercury in products and industrial processes (Articles 4 and 5), mercury supply and trade (Article 3), and the severe and growing problem of mercury use in artisanal gold mining (Article 7). Safe interim storage and sound management of mercury, and management of contaminated sites, is also emphasized. Indeed, in common with the instruments noted earlier, the Minamata Convention employs environmental tools such as best environmental practices and best available techniques (both defined in Article 2), and makes provision for capacity-building, technical assistance, and technology transfer (Article 14). From the outset, a financial mechanism is to be established to support effective implementation of the Convention, although notably resources may come from domestic funding as well as relying on the Global Environmental Facility Trust Fund (Article 13). Building on the experience of other instruments, the Minamata Convention provides for an Implementation and Compliance Committee, duly established at COP1 in 2017, and requires review of the effectiveness of the Convention no later than six years after its entry into force.

E. CONSERVATION OF NATURE

The evolution of treaties for the protection of species and habitat reflects in many respects the evolution of international environmental law itself. Some of the earliest treaties in the environmental field were concerned with the incidental regulation of wildlife, though their primary purpose was economic, eg the 1902 Paris Convention on the Protection of Birds Useful to Agriculture and the 1911 Treaty of Washington on the Protection of Fur Seals. One of the first cases to consider (and reject) the concept of coastal State stewardship over common property resources on the adjacent high seas likewise concerned fur seals, the 1898 *Bering Fur Seals Fisheries Arbitration*.[98] There are now dozens of bilateral, regional,[99] and multilateral treaties concerned with species and habitat protection, ranging from the protection of seals, bears, whales, and turtles, to holistic environmental regulation of the Antarctic environment.[100] For present purposes it is not intended exhaustively to scrutinize the detailed legal mosaic of species and habitat regulation at the bilateral and regional levels, but rather to focus upon the 'big five' of multilateral species and habitat treaties, namely, the 1971 Ramsar Convention on Wetlands of International Importance Especially As Waterfowl Habitat (Ramsar Convention); the 1972 UNESCO Convention Concerning the Protection of the World Cultural and Natural Heritage (WHC); the 1973 Convention

---

[98] *Bering Fur Seals Fisheries Arbitration (Great Britain v US)* (1893) *Moore's International Arbitrations* 755.

[99] In particular the 1968 African Convention on the Conservation of Nature and Natural Resources (revised 2003, not yet in force), the 1979 Council of Europe Convention on the Conservation of European Wildlife and Natural Habitats (Berne Convention).

[100] Eg the 1991 Environmental Protocol to the 1959 Antarctic Treaty on which see Redgwell, 1994; Rothwell, 1996, ch 9.

on International Trade in Endangered Species of Wild Fauna and Flora (CITES); the 1979 Bonn Convention on the Conservation of Migratory Species of Wild Animals (Bonn Convention); and the 1992 Convention on the Conservation of Biological Diversity (see Bowman, Davies, and Redgwell, 2010).

1. 1971 Convention on Wetlands of International Importance (Ramsar Convention)

The Ramsar Convention[101] is the only global environmental treaty addressed to a particular ecosystem, the conservation and wise use of wetlands primarily as habitat for wild birds. The mission of the Convention has broadened over time, so that today 'wise use' is interpreted to mean 'sustainable use' and the concept of wetlands now embraces fish as well as bird species and habitat. Integration of the conservation of wetland biodiversity with sustainable development, considered as synonymous with the Convention's concept of 'wise use', is at the heart of the current strategic plan for the Convention. There are currently 169 contracting parties to the Ramsar Convention, with 2,293 sites designated for the List of Wetlands of International Importance covering a total surface area of nearly 286 million hectares (larger than the combined surface area of France, Germany, and Switzerland).

Much has been accomplished under a convention of initially rather unpromising beginnings. It is still an extraordinarily brief instrument of only 13 articles, but these have been subject to extensive elaboration through the Guidelines issued by the Regular Meetings of the COP. The chief regulatory device of the Convention is the listing of sites for protection that is then afforded such sites under national laws. Each contracting party is required to designate 'suitable wetlands' within its territory for inclusion on the List of Wetlands of International Importance, the 'flagship' of the Convention. Indeed, a State is not considered a full party to the Convention unless and until a site has been designated (in contrast with the World Heritage Convention, for example). So long as the proposed site fulfils one of the Criteria for Identifying Wetlands of International Importance and has been designated by the appropriate national authority it will be added to the list. Contracting parties are required to submit triennial reports on the implementation of the treaty to the contracting parties, thus providing an opportunity for review of national implementation measures.

Once designated, Ramsar sites are to be protected under national law but also acquire recognition under international law as being significant for the international community as a whole. Failure to promote the conservation of wetlands on the list and their wise use may lead to listing on the 'Montreux Record of Ramsar sites requiring priority attention', established in 1990, and which highlights threats to designated sites. The ultimate sanction is de-listing because of the irremediable loss of the values which led to Ramsar listing in the first instance. This has never occurred; nor have any sites been deleted owing to 'urgent national interests' as provided for in the Convention.[102] The only instance of removal was of three sites designated before the development of the Criteria which they then failed to meet, and they were replaced with other designations.

Sites requiring priority attention may not formally be added to the Record without the consent of the State concerned. There are currently 49 sites which have been added to

---

[101] See http://www.ramsar.org; Ramsar Convention Secretariat, 2007, *Ramsar Handbooks for the Wise Use of Wetlands*, 3rd edn; Bowman, Davies, and Redgwell, 2010, ch 13.

[102] Article 2.5 provides that in the urgent national interest the boundaries of a site may be deleted or restricted. Parties have invoked the 'urgent national interest' clause to *restrict* the boundaries of a Ramsar site on three occasions only: Belgium in the 1980s, Australia in 1997 (though not ultimately implemented), and Germany in 2000. Further guidance on implementation of Article 2.5 is found in Resolution VIII.20 (2002).

the Montreux Record with such consent.[103] An additional and facilitative feature of the Ramsar Convention is the awareness that failure to conserve wetlands may result from lack of capacity. Thus, a Small Grants Fund for Wetland Conservation and Wise Use was also established in 1990 with the express purpose of facilitating compliance, along with other forms of technical assistance, and the Ramsar Advisory Mission was established as a technical assistance mechanism to provide further advice regarding the problems or threats which have caused Montreux listing to be contemplated. Site visits are an integral part of this mechanism and, as with the Montreux listing procedure itself, are conditional upon the agreement of the contracting party concerned. For sites covered by both Ramsar and the World Heritage Convention, such visits may be requested and carried out jointly. For example, Ichkeul National Park in Tunisia is on both the Ramsar Montreux Record and the WHC Heritage in Danger List owing to the impact of dam projects on the river flowing into Ichkeul.[104] Conservation efforts may be assisted by listing on the Montreux Record with consequent access to technical assistance and facilitative financing under the Convention and elsewhere: the listing of the Azraq Oasis in Jordan assisted in obtaining funding from the Global Environmental Facility and of the Austrian Donau-March-Thaya-Auen in obtaining European Commission funding.

2. The World Heritage Convention

The World Heritage Convention (WHC)[105] was adopted on 16 November 1972 under UNESCO auspices, mere months after the 1972 Stockholm Conference. There are presently 193 States parties to the Convention. Participation by developing States in particular is enhanced through the World Heritage Fund, a trust fund constituted by compulsory and voluntary contributions made by States parties to the Convention. The purpose of the WHC is the identification, protection, conservation, presentation, and transmission to future generations of cultural and natural heritage of outstanding universal value. The WHC is thus unusual in its express linkage of nature conservation and preservation of cultural properties, seeking to achieve a balance between the two. Protection of designated natural and cultural heritage is conferred by inscription on the World Heritage List of natural and cultural sites satisfying the inscription criteria under the Convention. At present there are 1,073 properties on the list: 832 cultural, 206 natural, and 35 mixed properties in 167 States parties. However, unlike under the Ramsar Convention, it is not necessary to have a site listed to become a full participating party to the WHC.[106] The effectiveness of the Convention is thus dependent upon States parties offering up sites for designation since UNESCO has no independent listing power. Independent evaluation of proposed sites is carried out by two advisory bodies, the International Council on Monuments and Sites (ICOMOS) in respect of cultural properties and the World Conservation Union (IUCN) in respect of natural properties. The criteria for inscription on the World Heritage List are set forth in *Operational Guidelines* which are revised regularly by one of the Convention bodies, the World Heritage Committee, in order to reflect changes in the concept of world heritage.[107]

Listing applications must include details of how the site is managed and protected under national legislation. Subsequent protection is thus a task for national law, subject to

[103] See http://www.ramsar.org; and Bowman, Davies, and Redgwell, 2010, ch 13.
[104] In fact, the Park is one of a few sites which are protected by listing under three agreements: Ramsar (1980), WHC (1979), and Biosphere Reserve (1977). Details of listings can be found on the Ramsar website: http://www.ramsar.org.   [105] For commentary on the Convention, see Francioni with Lenzerini, 2008.
[106] For a full list by country and property, see http://whc.unesco.org.
[107] Last updated in 2017: see http://whc.unesco.org/en/guidelines/.

the general treaty obligation already indicated to protect and preserve such heritage. The Convention makes clear that *international* protection of the world cultural and natural heritage is limited to 'the establishment of a system of international cooperation and assistance designed to support States parties to the convention in their efforts to conserve and identify that heritage'. The chief regulatory tools at the disposal of the Convention organs for the achievement of such international protection are monitoring entry to and departure from listed status of sites of world natural and/or cultural heritage based on the data supplied by States parties in their national inventory and implementation reports and providing international assistance, including access to the resources of the World Heritage Fund.

In addition to stipulating the criteria for listing, published in the *Operational Guidelines*, the World Heritage Committee is also responsible for establishing the 'List of World Heritage in Danger', the latter designation signalling that major operations are necessary to conserve the site, for which assistance has been requested under the Convention. The ultimate consequence of a State's failure to fulfil its obligations under the Convention is deletion from the World Heritage List. Unlike Ramsar, there have been two deletions from the World Heritage List: the Arabian Oryx Sanctuary in Oman (2007) and the Dresden Elbe Valley in Germany (2009). Danger listing may be perceived either as a form of 'name and shame' or as a means of highlighting for the international community difficulties in conserving heritage values and seeking assistance in addressing them. Whatever the perception, the clear expectation upon danger listing is that steps will be taken by the State party concerned to reduce and/or eliminate the danger posed to world cultural and natural heritage, often in consultation with the key stakeholders in the site and activities related thereto. At present there are 54 properties on the danger list.

3. 1973 Convention on International Trade in Endangered Species

Unlike the other treaties considered here, the direct purpose of the 1973 Convention on International Trade in Endangered Species (CITES)[108] is not the protection of animal and plant species or habitat per se. Rather, its objective is to control or prohibit trade in species or their products where those species are in danger of extinction. It addresses one of the reasons for species decline apart from loss of habitat, which is increased exploitation to which commercial trade is a contributory factor. Roughly 5,800 animal species 'from leeches to lions' and 30,000 plant species 'from pine trees to pitcher plants' are now covered in the 183 States presently parties to CITES.

The Convention controls the import and export of endangered species and products on a global scale through a permitting system operated by designated national authorities, a procedure familiar from the discussion of the dumping conventions in Section V A of this chapter. Three appendices are used. Appendix I forbids trade in the listed species which are in danger of extinction, subject to some exceptions which are controlled by export, re-export, and import permits as required. Appendix II permits trade subject to certain restrictions in the species listed therein which are not threatened with extinction but may become so if trade is not controlled and monitored. Here only export (or re-export) permits apply. Appendix III encompasses species covered by national regulation where a State seeks international cooperation in controlling (external) trade, in which case an export permit is required. As may be expected, much of the controversy surrounding CITES has focused on listing (and de-listing) in the Appendices, with the listing of the African elephant particularly contentious. The African elephant was moved to Appendix I in 1990,

---

[108] See http://www.cites.org; and Bowman, Davies, and Redgwell, 2010, ch 15.

but the adverse socio-economic consequences for Range States led to a partial relaxation in the ban in an attempt to seek a compromise between wildlife protection and human development. Populations in Botswana, Namibia, South Africa, and Zimbabwe were moved to Appendix II in 1990, with one-off sales of existing ivory stocks permitted in 1997 and 2007 (following the establishment of baseline data on poaching and wild populations[109]).

In common with the other treaties examined here, the effectiveness of CITES is dependent on national implementation. Each party is required to establish at least one Management Authority and Scientific Authority to implement the permitting scheme, while the CITES Secretariat is responsible for monitoring the overall operation of the Treaty and facilitating exchange of information obtained through performance of States' monitoring and (annual) reporting obligations. NGOs also play a significant role under CITES in monitoring trade, such as the Wildlife Trade Monitoring Unit and IUCN/WWF's TRAFFIC (Trade Records Analysis of Flora and Fauna in Commerce). CITES' compliance review process is based on infractions reports by the Secretariat to the COP with the effective sanction for non-compliance being suspension of trade in specimens of CITES-listed species with the non-complying party. Presently there are 29 States subject to a recommendation to suspend trade in certain species, which can include non-parties (eg Haiti). In practice this has been a potent tool for ensuring proper national implementation of CITES' obligations to enact legislation, develop work plans, control legal/illegal trade, and/or improve the basis for government decision-making (Yeater and Vasquez, 2001). It has also encouraged participation in CITES, with recent accession by three States subject to trade suspensions while non-parties (Bahrain, Iraq, and Tajikistan).

4. 1979 Convention on the Conservation of Migratory Species

The Convention on the Conservation of Migratory Species (Bonn Convention)[110] is not quite a pygmy amongst the giants of the other 'big five' species and habitat treaties, but it certainly has the lowest profile. This is in part due to its relatively slow start; however, today there are 126 parties, of whom about half are developing countries. Activity under the Convention was also hampered by the failure of many States parties to pay their contributions and expenses, which led to the Bonn Secretariat being chronically short-staffed and underfunded. Nonetheless the Bonn Convention has achieved some modest success in its primary objective, which is to conserve habitat and protect migratory species threatened with extinction. The need for such regulatory action was highlighted in the Stockholm Action Plan in 1972, offering an holistic approach to protection of both land-based and marine migratory species not readily afforded by other international instruments. The two techniques employed under the Convention are first to impose obligations on Range States to protect migratory species through restoration of habitat and removing obstacles to migration of species listed in Appendix I as endangered throughout all or a significant portion of their range. Taking of such species must be prohibited under domestic law. Secondly, the Convention provides for the conclusion of conservation 'AGREEMENTS' (including Memoranda of Understanding) between Range States for the conservation and management of migratory species listed in Appendix II as having 'unfavourable conservation status' requiring international agreement,[111] or at least which would benefit

---

[109] Pursuant to the establishment under CITES of ETIS (Elephant Trade Information System) and MIKE (Monitoring the Illegal Killing of Elephants).

[110] See, generally, http://www.cms.int and Bowman, Davies, and Redgwell, 2010, ch 16.

[111] For an example of such international cooperation see the 1991 Agreement on the Conservation of Small Cetaceans of the Baltic and North Seas (ASCOBANS). For a full list of the Agreements and Memoranda of Understanding concluded within the framework of the Bonn Agreement see http://www.cms.int.

significantly from international cooperation. The Bonn Convention thus has a framework character, encouraging Range States to conclude regional or global agreements in respect of Appendix II species. In practice it is possible for dual-listing of species under the Bonn Convention and for species also to be subject to protection under other existing international agreements (marine mammals in particular fall into this category). Thus, in concluding agreements, parties to the Bonn Convention are to ensure that rights and obligations under other treaties are not affected.

5. 1992 UN Convention on Biological Diversity

Notwithstanding the extent of international environmental regulation of species and habitat protection outlined earlier, a gap persisted:[112] no global instrument regulated the interaction of species and habitat, and of ecosystems, in a holistic rather than a piecemeal manner.[113] The closest perhaps is the regional Convention on the Regulation of Antarctic Marine Living Resources which expressly adopts an ecosystem approach, but this applies only to the Southern Ocean and, at the time of the adoption of the CBD in 1992, had yet successfully to operationalize its novel ecosystem approach. UNEP perceived this 'biodiversity gap' and initiated negotiations to conclude a Convention on Biological Diversity (CBD) in time for signature at Rio. This was duly accomplished, and the Convention entered swiftly into force a mere 18 months later. Today it has virtually universal support with 196 parties (including the EU and all of its Member States). This includes significant developing country participation, crucial to the effectiveness of the Convention given that the most biologically rich parts of the planet are located within developing equatorial States. Participation is facilitated through funding (the GEF is the funding mechanism for the CBD) and differentiation of implementation obligations through 'according to respective capabilities' language. The Convention also provides a framework for national regulation of access to biological resources ('bioprospecting') on mutually agreed terms and benefit-sharing where such resources are exploited for commercial benefit, further elaborated upon in the Nagoya Protocol. The role of indigenous peoples' knowledge and the application of traditional intellectual property rights principles remain areas of acute controversy under the Convention though without impairing developing country participation. Here it is developed States, in particular the USA, which expressed concerns regarding the intellectual property and technology transfer provisions of the Convention (Articles 15 and 16) and it has remained outside the Convention regime.

In its role as 'biodiversity gap-filler' the CBD defines biodiversity broadly to encompass the variability among living organisms from all sources, including, *inter alia*, terrestrial, marine, and other aquatic ecosystems and the ecological complexes of which they are part. The CBD's objectives are: the conservation of biological diversity; sustainable use of its components; and fair and equitable sharing of the benefits arising out of the utilization of genetic resources, including by appropriate access to genetic resources, transfer of relevant technologies, taking into account all rights over those resources, and funding. Each is addressed in further detail in the body of the CBD. Significant reliance is placed upon national measures for implementation, in accordance with each State's particular conditions and capabilities. It is thus up to individual contracting parties to determine the manner of implementation of their obligations, subject to scrutiny of national implementation by the

---

[112] See, generally, http://www.cbd.int; Bowman, Davies, and Redgwell, 2010, ch 17; Bowman et al, 2016; and the CBD Handbook, 3rd edn, available at http://www.cbd.int/handbook. For discussion of the 2000 Cartagena Protocol to the CBD, see Section VI D 3 of this chapter.

[113] For contributions placing the CBD in its broader context, see Bowman and Redgwell, 1996; Bowman et al, 2016.

COP through the reporting requirements of the Convention. National implementation is further guided by decisions of the COP such as the adoption of the Strategic Plan for Biodiversity 2011–20, including the Aichi Biodiversity Targets, implementation of which was the focus of the fifth round of national reports in 2014.[114] Nonetheless, concrete obligations are few and far between in the Convention, a reflection both of the resistance to binding targets, lists, and the identification of species and sites for protection (though some States such as France preferred to adopt the listing model of the WHC for the CBD) and of the realization that there already exist a number of conventions with concrete obligations in respect of species and habitat such as Ramsar and the WHC. Indeed, cooperation with other closely linked treaty regimes has been facilitated by the conclusion of memoranda of understanding between secretariats. In addition, the CBD COP and its subsidiary organs have continued to supplement the treaty text principally through seven thematic work programmes comprising: marine and coastal biodiversity; mountain biodiversity; agricultural biodiversity; forest biodiversity; inland waters biodiversity; dry and sub-humid lands biodiversity; and island biodiversity. These are buttressed by a number of cross-cutting issues such as access to genetic resources and benefit-sharing, alien species, biodiversity and tourism, and sustainable use of biodiversity. As discussed in Section VI D 3 of this chapter, the 2000 Cartagena Protocol addresses one of the issues outstanding from Rio, namely, the impact upon biological diversity of the transboundary movement of living modified organisms. A second Protocol to the Convention was added in 2010; the Nagoya Protocol on Access to Genetic Resources and the Fair and Equitable Sharing of the Benefit Arising from their Utilization was concluded, and entered into force on 12 October 2014, with 104 parties presently. It restates and elaborates upon the principles in Article 15 of the Convention, fleshing out access and benefit-sharing commitments including benefits arising from traditional knowledge (though only in accordance with domestic legislation). Monitoring of genetic resources accessed from other parties is also required in order, *inter alia*, to ensure compliance with the requirements for prior informed consent. It piggy-backs on the institutional and financial arrangements under the Convention, as does the Cartagena Protocol.

The CBD constitutes an important milestone in its preambular recognition of the intrinsic value of biodiversity and of the conservation of biodiversity as a 'common concern of humankind'. However, it should be observed that this falls far short of any internationalization of biological resources either in their ownership or in their control—common concern is thus not akin to the 'common heritage of mankind' concept applicable to the resources of the deep seabed. Indeed, there is an inherent tension in the CBD in that the Preamble also reaffirms States' permanent sovereignty over their natural resources. Linkage between these concepts is found in the responsibility of States for conserving their biological diversity and for using their biological resources in a sustainable manner (Glowka et al, 1994). Permanent sovereignty is thus responsible sovereignty under the CBD, a theme which pervades many of the instruments discussed earlier in this chapter.

F. CONSERVATION OF MARINE LIVING RESOURCES

Regulation of marine living resources was one of the first areas of international environmental regulatory activity, stimulated by the need to regulate common property resources of significant economic value such as seals, whales, and fish stocks. Of course in the nineteenth and early twentieth centuries, most coastal States claimed only a 3-mile

---

[114] Available at https://www.cbd.int/sp/.

territorial sea, with the seas beyond regarded as high seas open to exploitation of the resources therein. The *Bering Fur Sea Arbitration* established that adjacent coastal States had no legal interest in the protection of living resources beyond their initial belt of territorial sea. Today the picture is rather different, particularly with the development of the 200 mile Exclusive Economic Zone which accords coastal States exclusive rights over the living resources of this zone (see Evans, Ch 21, Section V C of this book). International regulation of marine living resources tends to focus on areas beyond national jurisdiction—high seas fisheries, for example—and/or fish stocks which are straddling or highly migratory, spending at least part of their life-cycle beyond coastal State zones. In 1995 the Straddling Stocks Agreement (SSA) was concluded to address this problem, supplementing not only the 1982 LOSC but also the myriad regional fisheries organizations (RFOs) regulating such stocks (see Ch 21, Section VII B 2–3 of this book). Of particular note in the latter context is the 1949 North Atlantic Fisheries Convention and the 1980 Convention on the Regulation of Antarctic Marine Living Resources (CCAMLR) with its ecosystem approach.

The approach of most fisheries treaties is to establish a fixed quota (a total allowable catch) for particular stocks, regulate fishing methods (eg stipulated mesh size, open and closed fishing seasons and/or areas, and the prohibition of certain methods such as drift or purse seine nets), and to require monitoring and reporting obligations to be observed. Some form of inspection system is also common, as is the establishment of a scientific body to assess catch data and generally to advise on sustainable levels of fishing activity. In the Antarctic context the determination of permissible fishing effort is related not only to an analysis of the individual stocks but also of the interaction between predator and prey, in order to set a level of catch consistent with maintenance of the marine ecosystem as a whole. Common to all these instruments, however, is the persistent problem of illegal fishing, usually by 'free riders' outside the relevant treaty and thus exercising the high seas freedom to fish. The 1995 SSA seeks to encourage participation in RFOs where established for the areas in question, though here again such provision depends on the free rider States being party to the SSA. The FAO has also had a role to play, first through the adoption of guidelines and then more recently with the entry into force on 5 June 2016 of the 2009 Agreement on Port State Measures (PSMA) to Prevent, Deter and Eliminate Illegal, Unreported and Unregulated (IUU) Fishing. There have also been unilateral attempts to address illegal fishing, whether by States parties to an RFO (eg Canada's arrest of the Spanish trawler the *Estai* outside its 200-mile EEZ for violation of NAFO measures)[115] or by coastal States exercising control over landing rights the exercise of which are crucial in ensuring transit of fresh fish to lucrative European and other markets.[116] Particular fish stocks, such as highly migratory tuna stocks,[117] are the subject of species specific regulation as are a wide range of marine mammals such as dolphins,[118] seals,[119] and whales (which are also protected under CITES).[120] Here we see a shift in regulatory focus, for whilst fisheries regulation continues to be primarily concerned with conserving the economic value of the resource through good fisheries management practices, there is no doubt the 1946 International Convention for the Regulation of Whaling has seen a shift in approach from regulation of the (over) exploitation of an economic resource to a

---

[115] For analysis see Davies, 1995; more generally on straddling stocks, Davies and Redgwell, 1996.

[116] See the Special Chamber of the ITLOS established on 20 December 2000 in the *Case Concerning the Conservation and Sustainable Exploitation of Swordfish Stocks in the South-Eastern Pacific Ocean (Chile/European Community)* (proceedings suspended by agreement).

[117] See the 1949 Convention for the Establishment of an Inter-American Tropical Tuna Commission.

[118] See, eg, the 1991 ASCOBANS, n 86.

[119] Such as the 1972 Convention on the Conservation of Antarctic Seals.

[120] See, generally, Jefferies, 2016.

moratorium on whaling based at least in part on the more diffuse anthropocentric concern to protect the species.[121]

VIII. CONCLUSION

The breadth and scope of international environmental law is of course much greater than that briefly introduced in this chapter. For example, regional regulation of the Antarctic has contributed much to international environmental protection of both marine living resources and the terrestrial Antarctic environment; the regulation of the non-navigable uses of international watercourses has been codified and rests alongside extensive regional and bilateral regulation of riparian uses, including those which may have significant environmental impact; and marine living resources, from fish to mammals, have been subject to a myriad of global, regional, and bilateral arrangements only touched on here. Fertile areas for further exploration are the intersection of international environmental law with other areas addressed in this volume, most notably human rights (including access to environmental justice and public participation in environmental decision-making) and trade, as well as the effect of armed conflict on the environment.

With its development over the last several decades, international environmental law has been transformed from mere incidental regulation of the environmental effects of human activities, to holistic regulation of global issues of common and intertemporal concern reaching both within and beyond the State. Its maturation is reflected in present concerns regarding State compliance with international obligations, reflected in the growing number of treaty-based compliance mechanisms, and in the crucial importance of effective national implementation and enforcement. Future developments will therefore see significant emphasis upon the effective enforcement of international environmental law at the global, regional, national, and local levels, with less emphasis on the generation of new rules.

REFERENCES

ANDERSON, M and GALIZZI, P (eds) (2002), *International Environmental Law in National Courts* (London: British Institute of International and Comparative Law), ch 1.

ANDERSON, S and SARMA, K (eds) (2002), *Protecting the Ozone Layer: The United Nations History* (London: Earthscan Publications Limited).

ATAPATTU, S (2015), 'The Significance of International Environmental Law Principles in Reinforcing or Dismantling the North–South Divide', in A Alam et al (eds) *International Environmental Law and the Global South* (Cambridge: Cambridge University Press).

BENEDICK, R (1998), *Ozone Diplomacy: New Directions in Safeguarding the Planet* (enlarged edn, Cambridge, MA: Harvard University Press).

BENVENISTI, E and NOLTE, G (2018), 'Community Interests Across International Law: Introduction', in E Benvenisti and G Nolte (eds) *Community Interests Across International Law* (Oxford: Oxford University Press, 2018).

---

[121] See Birnie, 1997; Bowman, Davies, and Redgwell, 2010, ch 6; *Whaling in the Antarctic (Australia v Japan: New Zealand Intervening), Judgment, ICJ Reports 2014*, p 226 and generally Fitzmaurice, 2015.

BIRNIE, P (1997), 'Are Twentieth Century Marine Conservation Conventions Adaptable to Twenty-First Century Goals and Principles?', 12 *IJMCL* 307 and 488.

BIRNIE, P and BOYLE, A (1995), *Basic Documents on International Law* (Oxford: Oxford University Press).

BIRNIE, P, BOYLE, A, and REDGWELL, C (2009), *International Law and the Environment* (3rd edn, Oxford: Oxford University Press).

BODANSKY, D (1993), 'UN Convention on Climate Change', 18 *Yale ILJ* 451.

BODANSKY, D, BRUNNÉE, J and RAJAMANI, L (2017), *International Climate Change Law* (Oxford: Oxford University Press).

BOISSONS DE CHAZOURNES, L and MBENGUE, M (2017), '*Gabčikovo-Nagymaros Project (Hungary/Slovakia)* (1997) in E Bjorge and C Miles (eds) *Landmark Cases in Public International Law* (Oxford: Hart Publishing).

BOWMAN, M and REDGWELL, C (eds) (1996), *International Law and the Conservation of Biological Diversity* (The Hague: Kluwer).

BOWMAN, M, DAVIES, P, and REDGWELL, C (2010), *Lyster's International Wildlife Law* (2nd edn, Cambridge: Cambridge University Press).

BOWMAN, M, DAVIES, P, and GOODWIN, E (eds) (2016), *Research Handbook on Biodiversity and Law* (Cheltenham: Edward Elgar Publishing).

BOYLE, A (1999), 'Some Reflections on the Relationship of Treaties and Soft Law', 48 *ICLQ* 901.

BOYLE, A and CHINKIN, C (2007), *The Making of International Law* (Oxford: Oxford University Press).

BOYLE, A (2012), 'Human Rights and the Environment: Where Next?', 23 *EJIL* 613.

BRUNNEE, J (2002), 'COPing with Consent: Law-Making under Multilateral Environmental Agreements', 15 *Leiden JIL* 1.

BRUS, M (1995), *Third Party Dispute Settlement in an Interdependent World* (The Hague: Martinus Nijhoff).

CHINKIN, C and BOYLE, A (2007), *The Making of International Law* (Oxford: Oxford University Press).

CHURCHILL, RR and ULFSTEIN, G (2000), 'Autonomous Institutional Arrangements in Multilateral Environmental Agreements: A Little-Noticed Phenomenon in International Law', 94 *AJIL* 623.

Commission on Global Governance (1995), *Our Global Neighbourhood* (Oxford: Oxford University Press).

CRAWFORD, J (2012), *Brownlie's Principles of Public International Law* (8th edn, Oxford: Oxford University Press).

CULLET, P (2003), *Differential Treatment in International Environmental Law* (Aldershot: Ashgate).

DAVIES, PGG (1995), 'The EC/Canadian Fisheries Dispute in the Northwest Atlantic', 44 *ICLQ* 933.

DAVIES, PGG and REDGWELL, C (1996), 'The International Legal Regulation of Straddling Fish Stocks', LXVII *BYIL* 199.

DE LA FAYETTE, L (1999), 'The OSPAR Convention Comes into Force: Continuity and Progress', 14 *IJMCL* 247.

DEPLEDGE, J and YAMIN, F (2004), *The International Climate Change Regime: A Guide to Rules, Institutions and Procedures* (Cambridge: Cambridge University Press).

DE SADELEER, N (2002), *Environmental Principles: From Political Slogans to Legal Rules* (Oxford: Oxford University Press).

EIKERMANN, A (2015), *Forests in International Law: Is There Really a Need for an International Forest Convention?* (Heidelberg: Springer International Publishing).

FITZMAURICE, M (2001), 'International Environmental Protection of the Environment', 293 *Recueil des Cours* 13.

FITZMAURICE, M (2010), 'Responsibility and Climate Change', 53 *German Yearbook of International Law* 89.

FITZMAURICE, M (2015), *Whaling and International Law* (Cambridge: Cambridge University Press).

FITZMAURICE, M and REDGWELL, C (2000), 'Environmental Non-Compliance Procedures and International Law', XXXI NYIL 35.

FRANCIONI, F (1994), 'Developments in Environmental Law from Sovereignty to Governance: The EC Environmental Policy', in B Markesinis (ed), *The Gradual Convergence: Foreign Ideas, Foreign Influences, and English Law on the Eve of the 21st Century* (Oxford: Clarendon Press), p 205.

FRANCIONI, F with LENZERINI, F (eds) (2008), *The 1972 World Heritage Convention: A Commentary* (Oxford: Oxford University Press).

FRANCIONI, F and SCOVAZZI, T (eds) (1991), *International Responsibility for Environmental Harm* (Dordrecht: Kluwer).

FREESTONE, D and STRECK, C (eds) (2005), *Legal Aspects of Implementing the Kyoto Protocol* (Oxford: Oxford University Press).

FRENCH, D (2000), 'Developing States and International Environmental Law: The Importance of Differentiated Responsibilities', 49 ICLQ 38.

FRENCH, D (2005), *International Law and Policy of Sustainable Development* (Manchester: Juris Publishing/Manchester University Press).

FRENCH, D (2016), 'Common Concern, Common Heritage and Other Global(-ising) Concepts: Rhetorical Devices, Legal Principles or a Fundamental Challenge?' in M Bowman, P Davies, and E Goodwin (eds) *Research Handbook on Biodiversity and Law* (Cheltenham: Edward Elgar Publishing).

FRENCH, D and RAJAMANI, L (2013), 'Climate Change and International Environmental Law: Musings on a Journey to Somewhere', 25 *Journal of Environmental Law* 4.

GEHRING, T (2007), 'Treaty-Making and Treaty Evolution', in D Bodansky, J Brunnee, and E Hey (eds) *The Oxford Handbook of International Environmental Law* (Oxford: Oxford University Press).

GILLESPIE, A (1997), *International Environmental Law, Policy and Ethics* (Oxford: Oxford University Press).

GLOWKA, L et al (1994), *A Guide to the Convention on Biological Diversity*, IUCN Environmental Policy and Law Paper No 30.

HANDL, G (2015), 'Transboundary Risks of Harm from Peaceful Nuclear Activities: The Evolving Legal Regime', in S Jayakumar, T Koh, R Beckman, and HD Phan (eds) *Transboundary Pollution: Evolving Issues of International Law and Policy* (Cheltenham: Edward Elgar Publishing).

HARRISON, J (2017), *Saving the Oceans Through Law: The International Legal Framework for the Protection of the Marine Environment* (Oxford: Oxford University Press).

IUCN (2000), *Draft International Covenant on Environment and Development* (2nd edn, IUCN).

JACUR, FR (2013), *The Dynamics of Multilateral Environmental Agreements: Institutional Architectures and Law-Making Processes* (Naples: Editoriale Scientifica).

JEFFERIES, CSG (2016), *Marine Mammal Conservation and the Law of the Sea* (Oxford: Oxford University Press).

KUMMER, K (2000), *International Management of Hazardous Wastes* (Oxford: Clarendon Press).

KUS, S (2011), 'International Nuclear Law in the 25 Years between Chernobyl and Fukushima and Beyond', 87 *Nuclear Law Bulletin* 7.

LEFEBRE, R (2012), 'Climate Change and State Responsibility', in R Rayfuse and SV Scott (eds) *International Law in the Era of Climate Change* (Cheltenham: Edward Elgar).

LOWE, AV (1999), 'Sustainable Development and Unsustainable Arguments', in AE Boyle and D Freestone (eds) *International Law and Sustainable Development: Past Achievements and Future Challenges* (Oxford: Oxford University Press).

McKenzie, R et al (2003), *An Explanatory Guide to the Cartagena Protocol on Biosafety* (Gland: IUCN Environmental Policy and Law Paper No 46).

Muchlinski, P (2007), *Multinational Enterprises and the Law* (2nd edn, Oxford: Oxford University Press).

Okowa, P (2000), *State Responsibility for Transboundary Air Pollution in International Law* (Oxford: Oxford University Press).

Oral, N (2012), '1982 UNCLOS+30: Confronting New Complexities in the Protection of Biodiversity and Marine Living Resources in the High Seas', in *Proceedings of the 106th Annual Meeting of the American Society of International Law* (Washington: ASIL), p 403.

Pallemaerts, M (2003), *Toxics and Transnational Law* (Oxford: Hart Publishing).

Paradell-Trius, L (2000), 'Principles of International Environmental Law: an Overview', 9:2 *RECIEL* 93.

Peel, J (2001), 'New State Responsibility Rules and Compliance with Multilateral Environmental Obligations—Some case studies of how the new rules might apply in the international environmental context', 10:1 *RECIEL* 82.

Rajamani, L (2000), 'The Principle of Common but Differentiated Responsibility and the Balance of Commitments under the Climate Regime', 9 *RECIEL* 120.

Rajamani, L (2006), *Differential Treatment in International Environmental Law* (Oxford: Oxford University Press).

Rajamani, L (2009), 'Addressing the "Post-Kyoto" Stress Disorder; Reflections on the Emerging Legal Architecture of the Climate Regime', 58 *ICLQ* 803.

Rajamani, L (2012), 'The Durban Platform for Enhanced Action and the Future of the Climate Regime', 61 *ICLQ* 501.

Rajamani, L (2013), 'Differentiation in the Emerging Climate Regime', 14:1 *Theoretical Inquiries in Law* 151.

Rajamani, L (2014), 'The Warsaw Climate Negotiations: Emerging Understandings and Battle Lines on the Road to the 2015 Agreement', 63 *ICLQ* 721.

Rayfuse, R (2007), 'Biological Resources', in D Bodansky, J Brunnee, and E Hey (eds) *The Oxford Handbook of International Environmental Law* (Oxford: Oxford University Press).

Redgwell, C (1994), 'Environmental Protection in Antarctica: the 1991 Protocol', 43 *ICLQ* 599.

Redgwell, C (2000), 'Multilateral Environmental Treaty-Making', in V Gowlland-Debbas (ed) *Multilateral Treaty-Making: The Current Status of Challenges to and Reforms Needed in the International Legislative Process* (The Hague: Martinus Nijhoff), p 89.

Redgwell, C (2006a), 'From Permission to Prohibition: the 1982 LOSC and Protection of the Marine Environment', in D Freestone, R Barnes, and D Ong (eds) *The Law of the Sea: Progress and Prospects* (Oxford: Oxford University Press), p 180.

Redgwell, C (2006b), 'Biotechnology, Biodiversity and International Law', in J Holder (ed), *Current Legal Problems* (Oxford: Oxford University Press), p 543.

Redgwell, C (2015), 'Transboundary Pollution: Principles, Policy and Practice', in S Jayakumar, T Koh, R Beckman, and HD Phan (eds) *Transboundary Pollution: Evolving Issues of International Law and Policy* (Cheltenham: Edward Elgar Publishing).

Redgwell, C (2016a), 'The Never Ending Story: The Role of GAIRS in UNCLOS Implementation in the Offshore Energy Sector', in J Barrett and R Barnes (eds) *Law of the Sea: UNCLOS as a Living Treaty* (London: The British Institute of International and Comparative Law).

Redgwell, C (2016b), 'International Regulation of Energy Activities', in MM Roggenkamp et al, *Energy Law in Europe* (3rd edn, Oxford: Oxford University Press).

REDGWELL, C (2017a), 'Sources of International Environmental Law: Formality and Informality in the Dynamic Evolution of International Environmental Norms', in S Besson and J d'Aspremont (eds) *The Oxford Handbook on the Sources of International Law* (Oxford: Oxford University Press).

REDGWELL, C (2017b), 'General Principles in International Law', in S Weatherill and S Vogenauer (eds) *General Principles in European and Comparative Law* (Oxford: Hart Publishing).

REDGWELL, C and RAJAMANI, L (2014), 'Energy Underground: What's International Law Got To Do With It?', in D Zillman et al (eds) *The Law of Energy Underground* (Oxford: Oxford University Press).

ROTHWELL, D (1996), *The Polar Regions and the Development of International Law* (Cambridge: Cambridge University Press).

ROTHWELL, D and STEPHENS, T (2016), *The International Law of the Sea* (2nd edn, London: Hart Publishing).

SANDS, P and PEEL, J (2012), *Principles of International Environmental Law* (3rd edn, Cambridge: Cambridge University Press).

SCHRIJVER, N (1997), *Sovereignty Over Natural Resources: Balancing Rights and Duties* (Cambridge: Cambridge University Press).

SHELTON, D (ed) (2000), *Commitment and Compliance: The Role of Non-Binding Norms in the International Legal System* (Oxford: Oxford University Press).

SOHN, L (1973), 'The Stockholm Declaration on the Human Environment', 14 *Harv ILJ* 423.

SOLTAU, F (2016), 'Common Concern of Humankind', in C Carlane, KR Gray, and RG Tarasofsky (eds) *The Oxford Handbook on International Climate Change Law* (Oxford: Oxford University Press).

TANAKA, Y (2015), *The International Law of the Sea* (2nd edn, Cambridge: Cambridge University Press).

TOMUSCHAT, C (2011), 'Global Warming and State Responsibility' in H Hestermeyer et al (eds) *Law of the Sea in Dialogue* (Berlin: Springer-Verlag).

VERHEYEN, R (2005), *Climate Change Damage and International Law: Prevention Duties and State Responsibility* (Netherlands: Brill Academic Publishers).

VIÑUALES, J (ed) (2015), *The Rio Declaration on Environment and Development: A Commentary* (Oxford: Oxford University Press).

WERKSMAN, J (1998), 'Compliance and the Kyoto Protocol: Building a Backbone into a "Flexible" Regime', 9 *YBIEL* 48.

WETTERSTEIN, P (ed) (1997), *Harm to the Environment: The Right to Compensation and the Assessment of Damages* (Oxford: Clarendon Press).

WIRTH, D (2007), 'Hazardous Substances and Activities', in D Bodansky, J Brunnee, and E Hey (eds) (2007), *The Oxford Handbook of International Environmental Law* (Oxford: Oxford University Press).

WOLFRUM, R (1999), 'Means of Ensuring Compliance with and Enforcement of International Environmental Law', 272 *Recueil des Cours* 9.

YAMIN, F and DEPLEDGE, J (2004), *The International Climate Change Regime: A Guide to Rules, Institutions and Procedures* (Cambridge: Cambridge University Press), ch 3.

YEATER, M and VASQUEZ, J (2001), 'Demystifying the Relationship between CITES and the WTO', 10:3 *RECIEL* 271.

YOSHIDA, O (2001), *The International Legal Regime for the Protection of the Stratospheric Ozone Layer* (The Hague: Kluwer).

FURTHER READING

BIRNIE, P, BOYLE, A, and REDGWELL, C (2009), *International Law and The Environment* (3rd edn, Oxford: Oxford University Press): of the general textbooks on international environmental law, this is one of the most thorough. A second edition is forthcoming in late 2018.

BODANSKY, D, BRUNNEE, J, and HEY, E (eds) (2007), *The Oxford Handbook of International Environmental Law* (Oxford: Oxford University Press): this edited volume follows the pattern of this work, with chapters submitted by the leading authorities in the international environmental field. An invaluable source to supplement the standard texts and specialized edited collections. A second, substantially revised, edition is under preparation by a new editorial team for publication in 2020.

BOWMAN, M, DAVIES P, and REDGWELL, C (2010), *Lyster's International Wildlife Law* (2nd edn, Cambridge: Cambridge University Press): the second edition of a highly readable account of the principal treaties concerned with wildlife protection.

BOYLE, A and ANDERSON, M (eds) (1996), *Human Rights Approaches to Environmental Protection* (Oxford: Clarendon Press): an excellent overview of the issues arising from the intersection of human rights and the environment.

BOYLE, A and FREESTONE, D (eds) (1999), *International Law and Sustainable Development: Past Achievements and Future Challenges* (Oxford: Oxford University Press): a valuable resource not only for discussion of sustainable development but for contextual analysis drawing on many topical international environmental issues.

FITZMAURICE, M (2001), 'International Protection of the Environment', 293 *Recueil des Cours* 13: these Hague Academy lectures on international environmental law provide a helpful overview of the subject with case studies of the ozone layer protection and international watercourses.

FRANCIONI, F (ed) (2001), *Environment, Human Rights and International Trade* (Oxford: Hart Publishing): this contains a number of stimulating contributions not only on the general issue but also examining the compatibility of specific environmental treaties, in particular the Cartagena Protocol, with the WTO agreements.

HURRELL, A and KINGSBURY, B (eds) (1992), *International Politics of the Environment* (Oxford: Clarendon Press): this places environmental issues in their international relations context.

SANDS, P and PEEL, J (2012), *Principles of International Environmental Law* (3rd edn, Cambridge: Cambridge University Press): another very useful textbook with detailed treatment of principles and of specific treaty regimes, with a 4th edition due in 2018.

The principal treaty texts are compiled with useful commentary and guidance for further reading in BIRNIE, P and BOYLE, A (1995), *Basic Documents on International Law and the Environment* (Oxford: Oxford University Press) and in Galizzi, P, and Sands, P (2004), *Documents in International Environmental Law* (Cambridge: Cambridge University Press).

WEBSITES

Those searching for access to the web pages of the key environmental treaties will find the UNEP (http://www.unep.org) and IMO (http://www.imo.org) sites useful gateways.

23

INTERNATIONAL INVESTMENT LAW

Surya P Subedi

SUMMARY

This chapter explores what international investment law is, how it has changed over time, and the state of the law today. In order to do so, it will present the evolution of the law of foreign investment, international efforts to regulate foreign investment, the main principles of the international law of foreign investment governing international economic relations among States, regulation under bilateral investment treaties, free trade agreements and regional trade and investment agreements, and the case law developed by various international courts and tribunals, including the International Court of Justice and the International Centre for the Settlement of Investment Disputes. The aim is to provide an understanding of current and evolving principles of the law of foreign investment, and the interplay between law and politics in regulating foreign investment.

I. INTRODUCTION: WHAT IS INTERNATIONAL INVESTMENT LAW?

International investment law governs relations between foreign investors, including private and State-owned companies, and investor-receiving States (known as host States), as well as between investor States and investment receiving States. The law of foreign investment is one of the oldest and most complex areas of international law. Attempts have been made in the past 70 or so years (both within and outside of the UN) to codify and develop rules of international law in a number of areas. Consequently, there is now a sizeable body of treaty law dealing with different areas of international activity. However, there is as yet no single comprehensive treaty on the law of foreign investment. While there is a comprehensive treaty, the 1982 Convention on the Law of the Sea, governing the activities of States in the seas and oceans of the world, there are a number of core international treaties in the fields of human rights and environmental protection that constitute the core body of law in the subjects concerned. However, this is not the case in international investment law. Most of the law of foreign investment is still based on customary international law, which has evolved out of diplomatic exchanges, the jurisprudence of international courts and tribunals, bilateral investment treaties, and a host of 'soft law' instruments adopted under the auspices of the UN and its specialized agencies (see generally Dolzer and Schreur, 2012; Subedi, 2016).

Attempts were made within the UN in the 1970s and 1980s to adopt a comprehensive code of conduct for transnational corporations. However, when in the early 1990s political and economic events overtook these efforts, the efforts were abandoned. The Organisation for Economic Cooperation and Development (OECD) tried in the late 1990s to conclude a multilateral agreement on investment (MAI), but it too resulted in failure. The World Trade Organization (WTO) then decided to include foreign investment in its agenda for the Development Round of trade negotiations through the Doha Declaration of November 2001. In July 2004 the WTO decided to set aside the project. It was too complex an area also for the WTO, since there existed among the WTO members an unwieldy number of differences of opinion as to the nature, scope, and desirability of the conclusion of an international treaty on such a matter under the auspices of the WTO.

However, the absence of a global comprehensive treaty on foreign investment does not mean that there is no identifiable or generally accepted body of law regulating foreign investment. To begin with, there is a set of generally accepted rules of international law providing protection to foreign investors. They are based, *inter alia*, on the rules of customary international law, various subject or sector-specific international treaties, several human rights treaties providing protection to right to property, and the doctrine of State responsibility. Next are thousands of bilateral investment treaties (BITs) or free trade agreements (FTAs) (which include substantial and substantive provisions dealing with investment) as well as regional trade and investment treaties that regulate foreign investment, provide protection for foreign investment, and include a dispute resolution mechanism. Finally, there is a burgeoning body of case law of international courts and tribunals that have fleshed out the provisions in both customary international law and treaty law.

II. EVOLUTION OF INTERNATIONAL INVESTMENT LAW

The law of foreign investment has developed over several centuries in response to changing political and economic events. It has evolved in response to the challenges brought about by the industrial revolution during which the people of the industrial world ventured out to new territories to invest in the acquisition of exotic products and raw material; the wave of independence of the Latin American colonial territories, seeking to assert economic sovereignty and to re-write the law of foreign investment following their political independence; the challenges brought by the Bolshevik revolution in Russia to foreign-owned property in that country; the attempts made by the Asian, African, and Latin American States in the immediate aftermath of the Second World War when these States were seeking to assert permanent sovereignty over their natural resources; the attempts made by the developing countries to bring about fundamental changes to the law on international economic relations under the notion of the New International Economic Order, and the subsequent wave of expropriations and nationalization in the 1960s and 1970s; the end of the Cold War, the collapse of the old political order, and the ideological triumph of the West; and the excesses of foreign investors undermining the very State authority that accorded them their protection in the first place.

Since time immemorial people have travelled abroad to invest and to engage in business. When European traders began to sail to Asia, Africa, and Latin America to trade with the people in local communities, it was held that the local law could not be applied to the traders since they were already subject to the law of their respective home countries.

This argument was based on the assumption that the businessmen carried the law of the country of their nationality with them wherever they went and were thus not subject to the local law. Foreigners coming from European countries sought special and superior treatment from the local population in much of Asia, Africa, and Latin America. The implication of this attitude was that their assets could not be expropriated or nationalized through legislation enacted by the local population. Since local law was 'inferior', it could not apply to the foreigners who were subject to the 'superior' body of law of their home countries.

Thus, in the early years of the development of the law of foreign investment it was understood that no State could expropriate or nationalize foreign assets. States could not invoke national laws as a reason for avoiding their international obligations arising from the notion of an international minimum standard. Only in the next phase of development when the number of independent States grew did it come to be accepted that States could expropriate the assets of foreigners under narrowly defined conditions and against the payment of compensation.

A. NATIONAL TREATMENT V THE INTERNATIONAL MINIMUM STANDARD

When colonial territories began to gain independence, they started to challenge the concept that foreigners residing and conducting business in those countries could not be governed by the local law. Relying on the doctrine of sovereignty and sovereign equality, they asserted that every sovereign State had the right to expropriate or nationalize foreign assets provided that the foreign investor was provided with compensation. The very notion of sovereignty meant that foreigners residing within the national borders of the country were subject to the law of the land. For instance, Article 9 of the Convention on the Rights and Duties of States (one of the first international instruments to support the idea of national treatment), signed at the Seventh Pan-American Conference, provided that:

> The jurisdiction of states within the limits of national territory applies to all the inhabitants. Nationals and foreigners are under the same protection of the law and the national authorities and the foreigners may not claim rights other or more extensive than those of the nationals.[1]

The Latin American countries were the first group of States to gain independence from their colonial rulers. After independence these States began to assert that foreign investors were not entitled to any greater protection than those accorded to the nationals of the country, under the law of the land. If the host States treated foreign investors on a par with the nationals of the country, the host States were acting within the norms of international law. Consequently, the right to expropriate the assets of foreign companies with compensation was accepted as an appropriate corollary to State sovereignty. However, it was submitted that if the local law were considered not well developed, or it failed to meet the standards of justice and equity, the international minimum standard rather than national law would apply to foreign investors. The assertion was that as international law provided for the international minimum standard, all States had to conform to the international minimum standard by bringing their national laws up to this standard. Consequently, the focus was on interpreting what constituted the international minimum standard (Oppenheim, 1992, pp 931–5).

---

[1] The Convention on the Rights and Duties of States (Montevideo Convention, 1933), 165 LNTS 19. For text see (1976) 70 *AJIL* 445.

One of the advocates of applying an international minimum standard to the question of the treatment of aliens (including foreign investors) was Elihu Root. He was a leading American international lawyer who in 1910 argued that there existed a standard of justice that formed a part of international law. Any national law dealing with the treatment of aliens had to conform to this general international standard:

> If any country's system of law does not conform to that standard, although the people of the country may be content or compelled to live under it, no other country can be compelled to accept it as furnishing a satisfactory measure of treatment to its citizens.[2]

A prominent British international lawyer, Schwarzenberger, added his voice in support of this argument:

> The national standard cannot be used as a means of evading international obligations under the minimum standard of international law. Even if the standard of national treatment is laid down in a treaty, the presumption is that it has been the intention of the parties to secure to their nationals in this manner additional advantages, but not to deprive them of such rights as, in any case, they would be entitled to enjoy under international customary law or the general principles of law recognised by civilised nations.[3]

Scholarly views such as these have been supported by the decisions of international courts and tribunals. For instance, in the *Barcelona Traction* case, the International Court of Justice (ICJ) stated that:

> When a state admits into its territory foreign investments of foreign nationals, whether natural or juristic persons, it is bound to extend to them the protection of the law and assumes obligations concerning the treatment to be afforded them.[4]

When it was submitted that the international minimum standard rather than national law was applicable to foreign investment, an attempt was made to define the international minimum standard in the light of the general principles of justice and equity, the practice of States on the treatment of foreign investment, and the existing rules of both conventional and customary international law of human rights. In other words, human rights principles, including the right to property, were also invoked to define what constituted the international minimum standard. Under the evolving principles of international human rights law, every individual, both physical and juridical and whether national or alien, residing within any country, was entitled to their basic human rights (including property rights) as protected by law. Consequently, when it came to defining what constituted the minimum international standard, not only the law of foreign investment, but also the law of human rights (including the property rights of the individuals, whether national or alien) had to be taken into account (Borchard, 1940, p 445).

B. THE CALVO DOCTRINE

Those who were opposed to accepting the law of the investor countries in the name of the international minimum standard were of the view that no State should be required to offer greater protection to foreign investors than that accorded to its own nationals. There had to be equality of treatment. If the State in question were not discriminating against foreign investors, it was not violating any rules of customary international law. The argument was

---

[2] Root, 1910, pp 521–2.   [3] Schwarzenberger, 1957, p 248.
[4] *Barcelona Traction, Light and Power Company, Limited, Second Phase, Judgment, ICJ Reports 1970*, p 3, para 33.

that to accord a higher standard of treatment to foreign investors would be difficult for some countries, such as those which are newly independent, have not attained the level of economic development required, or have not acquired a developed legal system.

At the forefront of the argument in favour of national treatment of foreign investors and the right of States to expropriate the assets of foreign companies was a leading nineteenth-century Latin American jurist, Carlos Calvo of Argentina, who articulated the position dependent on the doctrine of economic sovereignty of States in the following terms:

> It is certain that aliens who establish themselves in a country have the same right to protection as nationals, but they ought not to lay claim to a protection more extended. If they suffer any wrong, they ought to count on the government of the country prosecuting the delinquents, and not claim from the state to which the authors of the violence belong any pecuniary indemnity.
>
> The rule that in more than one case it has been attempted to impose on American states is that foreigners merit more regard and privileges more marked and extended than those accorded even to the nationals of the country where they reside. The principle is intrinsically contrary to the law of equality of nations.[5]

The central element of the Calvo doctrine was to require that aliens submit disputes arising in a country to that country's courts. As deduced by Verwey and Schrijver (1984, p 23), the Calvo doctrine basically stipulates that the principle of territorial sovereignty of the State entails the principle of absolute equality before the law between nationals and foreigners, the exclusive subjection of foreigners and their property to the laws and juridical regimes of the State in which they reside or invest, and strict abstention from interference by other governments, notably the governments of the States of which the foreigners are nationals, in disputes arising over the treatment of foreigners or their property (ie abstention from diplomatic protection). In simple terms, according to the Calvo doctrine land and other natural resources belong to the State by virtue of the doctrine of sovereignty and no foreign entity can permanently own land in the host States.[6]

C. THE HULL FORMULA

After the Communist Revolution in Russia in 1917 and the agrarian revolution in Mexico at around the same time, the governments of these countries proclaimed State ownership of land. The assets of foreign companies were expropriated and nationalized without proper compensation, through invoking the sovereignty of States. The actions of the Soviet and Mexican governments were opposed by the Western States, who held the view that although sovereign States had the right to expropriate the assets of foreign companies, they could do so only under certain narrowly defined conditions stipulated in international law and especially under prompt, adequate, and effective compensation.

After years of negotiations a bi-national claims commission was established in 1927 between the USA and Mexico to consider the claims of those US foreign investors whose assets (mainly land) had been expropriated by Mexico. However, since not a single claim had been adjusted or paid by 1938, the USA in that year intensified its diplomatic efforts. The US Secretary of State, Cordell Hull, began a series of diplomatic exchanges with the Mexican government; the content of these diplomatic exchanges, in which Hull articulated the US views on compensation, came to be known as the 'Hull formula' in the international law of foreign investment. Outlining the US position on the issue of expropriation

---

[5] Translated and quoted from Calvo's work which was written in Spanish by Shea, 1995, pp 17–19.
[6] See, generally, Lipstein, 1945; Freeman, 1946.

and the nature of compensation under international law, Secretary Cordell Hull stated that the taking of property without compensation was not expropriation: it was confiscation. He went on to state that:

> If it were permissible for a government to take the private property of the citizens of other countries and pay for it as and when, in the judgment of that government, its economic circumstances and local legislation may perhaps permit, the safeguards which the constitutions of most countries and established international law have sought to provide would be illusory. Governments would be free to take property far beyond their ability or willingness to pay, and the owners thereof would be without recourse. We cannot question the right of a foreign government to treat its own nationals in this fashion if it so desires. This is a matter of domestic concern. But we cannot admit that a foreign government may take the property of American nationals in disregard for the rule of compensation under international law. Nor can we admit that any government unilaterally and through its municipal legislation can, as in this instant case, nullify this universally-accepted principle of international law, based as it is on reason, equity and justice.

However, the Mexican Foreign Minister disagreed with Hull's views on international law applicable to the subject matter. He replied by stating that there was in international law:

> [N]o rule universally accepted in theory nor carried out in practice, which makes obligatory the payment of immediate compensation nor even of deferred compensation, for expropriations of a general and impersonal character like those which Mexico has carried out for the purpose of redistribution of the land.

Rejecting the arguments advanced by the Mexican Foreign Minister and his interpretation of the status of foreign investment in international law, Secretary Hull responded in the following terms:

> The Government of the United States merely adverts to a self-evident fact when it notes that the applicable precedents and recognised authorities on international law support its declaration that, under every rule of law and equity, no government is entitled to expropriate private property, for whatever purpose, without provision for prompt, adequate and effective payment thereof. In addition, clauses appearing in the constitutions of almost all nations today, and in particular in the constitutions of the American republics, embody the principle of just compensation. These, in themselves, are declaratory of the like principles in the law of nations.[7]

In his response the Mexican Foreign Minister rejected Secretary Hull's assertion and justified the Mexican expropriations as being a move designed to achieve social justice in the country. However, just before the Second World War spread to the Western hemisphere, Mexico and the USA reached an agreement to establish a commission to determine the compensation for the US nationals affected by the Mexican agrarian expropriations that took place after 30 August 1927. A deal designed to compensate the US investors was struck between the two countries.

III. THE EFFORTS TO REGULATE FOREIGN INVESTMENT BY THE UN

The attempt to regulate foreign investment immediately after the establishment of the UN was a fundamental struggle between the defenders of the old law and the proponents of the new. The area of conflict lay between the sanctity of the existing agreements and the

---

[7] See the correspondence between the US and Mexican Foreign Secretaries in (1938) 32 *AJIL* supp 181–207.

attempt to rewrite the law by introducing certain new principles, such as the permanent sovereignty of States over their natural resources. With the establishment of the UN, a new world order, both economic and political, was envisaged for the world. While the UN was seen primarily as a political body, the World Bank and the International Monetary Fund were established as financial and monetary institutions respectively. Part of this grand vision for a new world order was the establishment of an international organization dealing with international trade. Accordingly, a UN conference on Trade and Employment was held at Havana, Cuba, between 21 November 1947 and 24 March 1948.

The draft Havana Charter submitted to the Conference contained no provision on regulating foreign investment. One of the reasons for this deliberate omission seems to have been the fear on the part of the USA that investment provisions negotiated at a multilateral conference might express the lowest common denominator of protection to which any of the participants would be willing to agree. Nevertheless, when a chapter on economic development was added to the initial draft Charter proposed by the USA, a number of provisions making reference to foreign investment were included. In the end, the Charter itself never came into effect due, *inter alia*, to the US decision to abandon it in 1950. The States participating in the Havana Conference had decided, through Chapter VII of the Charter, to establish the International Trade Organization (ITO) whose functions could have included making recommendations for and promoting bilateral and multilateral agreements on measures designed 'to assure just and equitable treatment for the enterprise, skills, capital, arts and technology brought from one member country to another'.[8] However, the ITO itself never came into existence and the Charter remained merely a document of historical interest.

A. PERMANENT SOVEREIGNTY OF STATES OVER THEIR NATURAL RESOURCES

When the colonial territories of Asia, Africa, and other parts of the world gained political independence their priority was to assert economic independence. Many newly independent States had inherited a situation under which the natural resources of the country were controlled or being exploited by foreign companies under concessions or other agreements concluded by the previous colonial administration. The people of the newly independent States had their hopes of a better standard of living; the political leaders had to strive hard to realize these hopes. When looking around for means of economic development, one of the first actions these States could take was to devise a policy to utilize the natural resources of the country for the benefit of the people. However, the newly independent States relied on the doctrine of economic sovereignty to claim permanent sovereignty of States over their natural resources, since such natural resources were being exploited by foreign companies under the existing concessions and other agreements. The idea was that once the permanent sovereignty of States over their natural resources (PSNR) was acknowledged, sovereign States would be able to negotiate their way out of the old agreements and concessions.

While the well-established principle expressed in the maxim *pacta sunt servanda* (ie treaties must be respected in good faith) of the law of treaties required States to respect the sanctity of the existing agreements, an equally (if not more) powerful doctrine of international law had to be deployed to allow States to take back the control over their natural resources into their own hands. To this end, the doctrine of PSNR was claimed, relying on one of the most powerful doctrines of international law—the sovereignty of States.

---

[8] Havana Charter (1948), Article 11(2)(a).

It was an attempt not to rewrite the law completely, but to give a new direction to the law of foreign investment on the basis of certain rules of public international law, including economic sovereignty and the right to the self-determination of States. Indeed, without achieving economic sovereignty States would not be fully sovereign. Although these States could also invoke the right to expropriate the assets of foreign companies, this right is limited in scope, is technical in character, and comes with a number of conditions: it would not have allowed States to achieve full economic sovereignty vis-à-vis their natural resources. Rather, the idea was to strengthen and expand, *inter alia*, the right not only to expropriate the assets of foreign investment, but also other rights of States flowing from the doctrine of sovereignty through the principle of PSNR.

It was against this background that the General Assembly adopted Resolution 1803 (XVII), on 14 December 1962, on the Permanent Sovereignty of States over their Natural Resources. The Resolution provides, *inter alia*, that:

1. The right of peoples and nations to permanent sovereignty over their natural wealth and resources must be exercised in the interest of their national development and of the well-being of the people of the state concerned;

2. The exploration, development and disposition of such resources, as well as the import of the foreign capital required for these purposes, should be in conformity with the rules and conditions which the peoples and nations freely consider to be necessary or desirable with regard to the authorisation, restriction or prohibition of such activities;

3. In cases where authorisation is granted, the capital imported and the earnings on that capital shall be governed by the terms thereof, by the national legislation in force, and by international law. The profits derived must be shared in the proportions freely agreed upon, in each case, between the investors and the recipient state, due care being taken to ensure that there is no impairment, for any reason, of that state's sovereignty over its natural wealth and resources;

4. Nationalisation, expropriation or requisitioning shall be based on grounds or reasons of public utility, security, or the national interest which are recognised as overriding purely individual or private interests, both domestic and foreign. In such cases the owner shall be paid appropriate compensation, in accordance with the rules in force in the state taking such measures in the exercise of its sovereignty and in accordance with international law. In any case where the question of compensation gives rise to a controversy, the national jurisdiction of the state taking such measures shall be exhausted. However, upon agreement by sovereign states and other parties concerned, settlement of dispute should be made through arbitration or international adjudication.[9]

Thus, Resolution 1803 of the General Assembly sought to strike a balance between the interests of both the hosts' and the investors' home countries by incorporating into one single instrument the issues of vital concern for both of these groups of States. For instance, when outlining principles applicable to the nationalization or expropriation of foreign investment, the Resolution conforms neither to the Hull formula nor to the Calvo doctrine yet contains elements of both. While it seeks to limit the conditions under which nationalization or expropriation can take place, it lists enough conditions to enable a country to embark upon nationalization and expropriation when necessary. It speaks of appropriate compensation rather than of prompt, adequate, and effective compensation,

[9] GA Res 1803 (XVII) (14 December 1962). For the record of its adoption see UN Doc A/C.2/SR.835.

and of remaining in accordance with international law. Although the principle of PSNR represented an attempt to develop certain new rules in favour of the developing countries on the basis of the extant and evolving rules of international economic law, it was accepted by the international community with little opposition from any quarter. Indeed, the UN General Assembly Resolution to this effect has been regarded as a good compromise between the developed and developing countries, stating the law acceptable to both sides. This principle has in some decisions of international courts and tribunals been regarded as reflecting customary international law. Thus in the *Texaco* v *Libya* case, for example, the arbitrator held that Resolution 1803 reflected the state of customary international law existing in this field.[10]

B. THE CONCEPT OF A NEW INTERNATIONAL ECONOMIC ORDER

When the developing countries gained a numerical majority in the UN, they sought to use the UN system to introduce a much more fundamental reform of the law governing international economic relations among States. The developing countries introduced the agenda of a new international economic order (NIEO) within the UN as they were encouraged and influenced by the oil crisis of the early 1970s and disappointed at the lack of progress in addressing the issues of economic equality and prosperity for all. One of the items on the agenda was concerned with regulating foreign investment in a manner more favourable to developing countries (Hossain, 1980). Accordingly, the UN General Assembly adopted a Declaration on the Establishment of a New International Economic Order,[11] and a Programme of Action on the implementation of the Declaration.[12]

Article 4 of the Declaration listed the principles on which the NIEO had to be founded. One included in sub-Article (e) relates to the question of PSNR and the issue of expropriation and nationalization. It recognized the 'full permanent sovereignty of every State over its natural resources and all economic activities'. It went on to add that:

> In order to safeguard these resources, each state is entitled to exercise effective control over them and their exploitation with means suitable to its own situation, including the right to nationalisation or transfer of ownership to its nationals, this right being an expression of the full permanent sovereignty of the state. No state may be subjected to economic, political or any other type of coercion to prevent the free and full exercise of this inalienable right.

As part of the drive for an NIEO, and in order to restructure the legal order for the world economy, the General Assembly adopted the Charter of Economic Rights and Duties of States on 12 December 1974.[13] The Charter of Economic Rights and Duties of States is perhaps the most comprehensive international instrument outlining the economic rights and duties of States. However, it is not a 'hard law' instrument, since it was adopted by means of a General Assembly resolution and the powers of the General Assembly are limited by the UN Charter to the making of recommendations. Moreover, it was adopted by a vote of 120 in favour, with six against and ten abstentions (see Chatterjee, 1991). Thus, although it is an instrument of limited legal significance, it was seen as an instrument of far-reaching implications by a vast majority of States who voted in favour of the resolution of the General

---

[10] *Texaco Overseas Petroleum Co* v *Libyan Arab Republic*, Arbitral Award (1977), 53 ILR 389, para 87. For similar views see *Kuwait* v *American Independent Oil Co* ('*Aminoil*' case) (1982), 66 ILR 518; 21 ILM 976, paras 143, 144.   [11] GA Res 3201(S-VI) (1 May 1974).
[12] GA Res 3202 (S-VI) (1 May 1974).   [13] GA Res 3281 (XXIX) (12 December 1974).

Assembly; it has since its adoption had a measure of influence on the development of international legal order. For instance, in the *Texaco* v *Libya* case the arbitrator was not prepared to accept that this provision of CERD reflected customary international law.[14]

C. THE UN DRAFT CODE OF CONDUCT FOR TRANS-NATIONAL CORPORATIONS

The NIEO resolutions cited earlier in Section III B, on The Concept of a New International Economic Order had called for the adoption of two codes of conduct: one on the transfer of technology and another on the regulation of trans-national corporations (TNCs). One of the achievements of the NIEO bandwagon was the establishment in 1974 of the UN Commission on Trans-national Corporations (CTC) by the Economic and Social Council to consider proposals for the regulation of multinational enterprises.[15] The activities of the CTC were linked to the efforts to realize the ideals of the NIEO. Much of the debate throughout the 1970s and 1980s focused on the content of a code of conduct for TNCs and whether it should be a voluntary or a mandatory code of conduct (see Horn, 1980). When the CTC in 1988 finally formulated a draft code of conduct for TNCs it became clear that there remained so many areas of major disagreement among States that the CTC itself seemed resigned to the possibility of adopting an internationally agreed code. Consequently, through a letter of 31 May 1990 to the President of the ECOSOC,[16] the Chairman of the reconvened special session of the CTC forwarded the Draft Code of conduct.[17] In sum, nothing much came out of this endeavour as the world moved on in the aftermath of the events of 1989–90; then, the economic and political landscape of the world was transformed by the collapse of the Soviet Union, the demise of Communism in Europe, the fall of the Berlin Wall, and the consequent and subsequent disarray in Third World solidarity.

IV. THE INVOLVEMENT OF OTHER ACTORS

As seen in the preceding paragraphs, the failings of the UN to offer a final or definitive word on foreign investment law left the door open for other actors to enter the stage. Some of the international bodies that tried to become involved are the World Bank, the OECD, the WTO, and the Human Rights Council.

A. THE ROLE OF THE WORLD BANK

The World Bank has had a long-standing interest in promoting foreign investment for economic development and has associated itself with a number of initiatives in this area. Among the initiatives are: the Convention for the Settlement of Investment Disputes of 1965; the Convention Establishing the Multilateral Investment Guarantee Agency of 1985, and the 1992 Guidelines on the Treatment of Foreign Direct Investment (see Shihata, 1991).

1. The International Convention on the Settlement of Investment Disputes

Foreign investors wish to have legal certainty when making investment decisions. One of those certainties is to have a credible mechanism for the settlement of investment disputes.

---

[14] *Texaco Overseas Petroleum Co v Libyan Arab Republic*, Arbitral Award (1977), 53 ILR 389, para 88.
[15] ECOSOC Resolutions 1908 (LVII) (2 August 1974) and 1913 (LVII) (5 December 1974).
[16] UN Doc E/1990/94 (12 June 1990).   [17] UN Doc E/1988/39/Add.1.

The perceived wisdom is that if foreign private investors are assured that, in the event of a dispute between them and the State in question, the dispute can be referred to an independent international tribunal, they would be encouraged to invest in that State. Foreign investors would generally be unwilling to invest in countries where the judiciary is not fully independent and the political situation is unstable. However, such investors would be encouraged to invest in such States if the State in question has agreed through an international agreement to settle any investment dispute with potential foreign investors. Accordingly, the International Convention on the Settlement of Investment Disputes between States and nationals of other States (ICSID) was concluded in 1965 (see Schreuer, 2001). Its aim was of establishing an international centre for the settlement of investment disputes and encouraging States to refer investment disputes with foreign private investors to an international arbitration tribunal. Under this Convention, the Bank is the host of the International Centre for the Settlement of Investment Disputes, which is similar in many respects to other international arbitration centres in existence. Under Article 25(1) the jurisdiction of the Centre is as follows:

> The jurisdiction of the centre shall extend to any legal dispute arising directly out of an investment, between a contracting state (or any constituent subdivision or agency of a contracting state designated to the centre by that state) and a national of another contracting state, which the parties to the dispute consent in writing to submit to the centre. When the parties have given their consent, no party may withdraw its consent unilaterally.

The provision in Article 42(1) is perhaps one of the most important ones because it stipulates the law applicable to a dispute submitted to the arbitration tribunal of the ICSID Centre:

> The Tribunal shall decide a dispute in accordance with such rules of law as may be agreed by the parties. In the absence of such agreement, the Tribunal shall apply the law of the contracting state party to the dispute (including its rules on the conflict of laws) and such rules of international law as may be applicable.

The adoption of the ICSID signalled that other positive developments relating to the law of foreign investment could also take place outside of the UN framework and away from politics.

2. The Multilateral Investment Guarantee Agency

In addition to legal certainty, potential foreign investors need some sort of guaranteed protection of their investment when they invest in developing countries. Many individual developed countries have their own respective internal systems of investment guarantee for those investing in developing countries and investment risks could also be covered through private insurance, yet it was thought desirable to have an international system of investment guarantee against non-commercial risks, such as expropriation, nationalization, and other political risks.

This would be in order to promote foreign investment in general and private foreign investment in particular. Of course, protection was available to foreign investors under bilateral investment treaties, international law principles relating to the treatment of foreign investment, and diplomatic channels; however, it was considered desirable to have an additional mechanism designed to alleviate concerns related to non-commercial risks. This would promote the flow of foreign investment to developing countries. Therefore, as a measure complementary to already existing national and regional investment guarantee programmes and to private insurers of non-commercial risks, as well as supplementary to the activities of the World Bank Group, the Convention Establishing the Multilateral Investment Guarantee Agency (MIGA) was in 1985 adopted.

3. The 1992 Guidelines on the Treatment of Foreign Direct Investment

As stated earlier, the promotion of foreign investment has long been an area of interest for the World Bank. It was joined by the MIGA, whose constituent document states that it is supposed to carry out research, undertake activities to promote investment flows, and disseminate information on investment opportunities in developing member countries. Accordingly, the Development Committee, a joint committee of the World Bank and the International Monetary Fund (IMF) in 1991 requested the MIGA to prepare a 'legal framework' to promote foreign direct investment. In 1992, the Development Committee adopted a set of Guidelines on the Treatment of Foreign Direct Investment.[18] It should be noted here that neither the Bank nor the IMF nor the MIGA has the competence to adopt any legally binding instrument for the international community, nor to modify the existing rules of international law on the subject matter. Strictly speaking, these organizations lack the capacity even to adopt 'soft law' instruments for the international community. Nevertheless, the document adopted as a result of the work carried out under the auspices of these three important financial organizations does carry certain weight and thus merits examination.

B. THE OECD GUIDELINES AND THE MULTILATERAL AGREEMENT ON INVESTMENT

The 1976 Declaration of the OECD on International Investment and Multinational Enterprises includes Guidelines for Multilateral Enterprises. As a next step in consolidating the rules governing foreign investment protection, the OECD in 1998 sought once again to conclude a multilateral agreement on investment (MAI).[19] However, the OECD attempt was abandoned when the draft MAI came under criticism from some member States and civil society for not being a balanced document that would protect the interests of both foreign investors and investor-receiving countries. After failing in its attempt to adopt a legally binding MAI, the OECD in 2000 adopted a set of revised guidelines for multinational enterprises (MNEs).[20] The OECD issued new updated Guidelines in 2011. They provide non-binding principles and standards for responsible business conduct in a global context consistent with applicable laws and internationally recognized standards. The updated Guidelines and the related Decision were adopted by the 43 adhering governments on 25 May 2011 at the OECD's 50th Anniversary Ministerial Meeting. The updated Guidelines include:

- a new human rights chapter which is consistent with the Guiding Principles on Business and Human Rights: Implementing the United Nations 'Protect, Respect and Remedy' Framework;

- a new and comprehensive approach to due diligence and responsible supply chain management representing significant progress relative to earlier approaches;

- important changes in many specialised chapters, such as on Employment and Industrial Relations; Combating Bribery, Bribe Solicitation and Extortion, Environment, Consumer Interests, Disclosure and Taxation;

- clearer and reinforced procedural guidance to strengthen the role of the National Contact Points (NCPs) improve their performance and foster functional equivalence; and

---

[18] *Legal Framework for the Treatment of Foreign Investment, Volume II: Guidelines*, available at http://www-wds.worldbank.org/servlet/WDSContentServer/WDSP/IB/1999/11/10/000094946_99090805303082/Rendered/PDF/multi_page.pdf.   [19] OECD DAFEE/MAI (98)7/REV1 (22 April 1998, footnotes omitted).
[20] 40 ILM 237 (2000).

- a proactive implementation agenda to assist enterprises in meeting their responsibilities as new challenges arise.[21]

This was an attempt to reconcile investment protection with other competing principles of international law, including environmental protection. This was also one of the first major attempts to give some practical meaning to the UN 'Guiding Principles on Business and Human Rights: Implementing the UN "Protect, Respect and Remedy" Framework' developed by the UN Special Representative on business and human rights, Professor John Ruggie, to be discussed in Section III D.

C. THE WTO AND FOREIGN INVESTMENT

After the failures of the OECD and the CTC of the UN to formulate a balanced and comprehensive set of standards on foreign investment, efforts were made by the EU at the Doha Ministerial Conference. Although efforts had been made during various GATT Rounds of Trade Negotiations to include investment onto the international trade agenda and the WTO itself had since 1997 been engaged in analysis and debate about the relationship between international trade and investment, it was only at the Doha conference that the WTO committed itself to including investment as part of its main agenda.[22] However, when the State members of the WTO met in July 2004 to agree on the work programme for the Doha Development Round, they too decided to set aside the idea of negotiating an international agreement on foreign investment under the auspices of the WTO. A decision taken by the General Council of the WTO on 31 July 2004, known as the 'July Package', stated that a number of issues, including the relationship between trade and investment, would not form part of the Work Programme of the Doha Development Round.[23]

Thus, the idea of adopting an international treaty regulating foreign investment was, once again, effectively removed from the scope of action of an inter-governmental body for the time being. Having said this, the 1994 TRIMS Agreement of the WTO does deal with certain aspects of foreign investment. It prohibits governments from requiring foreign investors to purchase inputs locally or to sell their output domestically rather than exporting it.[24]

D. THE UN HUMAN RIGHTS COUNCIL

Although the UN itself is not at present actively engaged in efforts to regulate foreign investment as such, some of its agencies, such as the UN Human Rights Council, are looking at the interaction between business and human rights. The UN Special Representative on the Issues of Human Rights and Trans-national Corporations and Other Business Enterprises, appointed by the Secretary-General, submitted a series of reports on business and human rights. In March 2011, he submitted his final report to the UN Human Rights Council, appending a document entitled 'Guiding Principles on Business and Human Rights: Implementing the United Nations "Protect, Respect and Remedy" Framework'[25] containing a set of 31 standards to support the implementation of the UN 'Protect, Respect and Remedy' policy framework and in June 2011 the UN Human Rights Council unanimously endorsed the Guiding Principles.[26]

---

[21] *Guidelines for Multinational Enterprises, 2011 edn*, available at http://dx.doi.org/10.1787/9789264115415-en.
[22] WT/MIN(01)/DEC/W/1 (14 November 2001).   [23] WT/GC/W/535 (1) (31 July 2004).
[24] See World Trade Organization, 1999, pp 143–6 at p 146.   [25] UN Doc A/HRC/17/13 (21 March 2011).
[26] UN Doc A/HRC 17/14 (6 June 2011).

The UN Special Representative identified three core principles: 'the state duty to protect against human rights abuses by third parties, including business; the corporate responsibility to respect human rights; and the need for more effective access to remedies'. He argued that the State had a duty to protect because it lies at the very core of the international human rights regime and the corporate responsibility entailed respecting human rights by companies because it is the basic expectation society has of business. Although this UN document is not legally binding, its endorsement by the Human Rights Council has established the Guiding Principles as the authoritative global reference point for business and human rights. When it endorsed the Guiding Principles, the Human Rights Council also established a Working Group composed of five independent experts on business and human rights to promote the implementation of the Guiding Principles, as well as an annual forum on business and human rights under the guidance of the Working Group.

V. GENERAL PRINCIPLES OF THE INTERNATIONAL LAW OF FOREIGN INVESTMENT

A. CUSTOMARY INTERNATIONAL LAW

On the basis of the foregoing account of the evolution of international law, it can be submitted that certain aspects of the law on regulating foreign investment are settled in international law. In addition to the Calvo doctrine and the Hull formula governing expropriation, there are a number of other principles deeply rooted in international law and practice that govern the relations among nations concerning foreign investment. Accordingly, among the settled rules of customary international law on foreign investment, the following are the major principles:

1. Host States are entitled to expropriate or nationalize the assets of foreign companies, but expropriation or nationalization can take place only if the following four main conditions are met: (a) it must be for a public purpose; (b) it must be non-discriminatory; (c) it must be against fair and equitable compensation, and (d) it must be in accordance with the law.

2. The compensation must be equivalent to the fair market value of the investment expropriated, immediately before the expropriation or before the impending expropriation became public knowledge, whichever is the earlier, shall include interest at a commercially reasonable rate until the date of payment, shall be made without unreasonable delay, be effectively realizable, and be freely transferable.

3. The affected investor has the right, in conformity with the laws of the host State that makes the expropriation, to the prompt review, by a judicial or other independent authority of that State, of its case, in order to decide if the expropriation and assessment of its investment have been adopted pursuant to the principles of international law.

4. Foreign investors and their investment enjoy the protection of the principle of non-discrimination.

5. They should be accorded the most-favoured-nation treatment (MFN).

6. Once admitted into the country foreign investors are entitled to national treatment; and

7. Foreign investors enjoy the protection accorded under the principle of fair and equitable treatment.

8. Non-discriminatory regulatory measures by a host that are designed and applied to protect legitimate public welfare objectives including the protection of public health, safety, and environment do not constitute expropriation or nationalization, except in rare circumstances, where those measures are so severe that they cannot be reasonably viewed as having been adopted and applied in good faith for achieving their objectives.

9. Actions and awards by judicial bodies of a host State that are designed, applied, or issued in public interest including those designed to address public health, safety and environmental concerns, do not constitute expropriation or nationalization.

10. Multinational companies have a duty to respect human rights in the countries where they do their business.

Ensuring non-discrimination in the conduct of international business is the underlying idea behind these principles. They are employed in international practice to secure a certain level of treatment for foreign investment in host countries. The purpose of the MFN principle is to grant foreign investors treatment comparable to the foreign investors from third countries operating in the host country, but the object of the national treatment principle is to grant treatment comparable to domestic investors operating in the host country itself. The principle of fair and equitable treatment brings in the elements of fairness and equity drawn from international law, especially the principle of international minimum standard, and practice as well as municipal law principles in the overall treatment of foreign investment in a host country. The problem with this principle is that it is difficult to define in concrete terms and is open to different interpretations. The precise meaning of the phrase 'fair and equitable treatment' has been the subject of interest and often controversy both in literature and in the case law dealing with the treatment of foreign investment.

B. THE BILATERAL INVESTMENT TREATIES

States have traditionally welcomed foreign investment for a variety of reasons. Foreign investment has been regarded as an engine of economic growth; a source of foreign currency income; a stimulator of the local economy; and a source of foreign skills, information, and know-how, among other features. Foreign investment takes place in different forms, including, through committing capital resources abroad either directly or through portfolio investment, by licensing the use of technology, and through managerial know-how.

Because of the form such investment takes, it requires special protection under the law of the country concerned. This is because foreigners who purchase land and other immovable property or enter into joint ventures to create a new company cannot leave the host country as and when they want. Their commitment to the host country is long-term, hence the need for long-term protection under special laws. Traditionally, such protection has been sought under international law and lately under bilateral investment treaties (BITs).

1. The origins of bilateral investment treaties

Unlike local laws on foreign investment, which can also offer adequate protection and incentives to foreign investors but are liable to change with a change of government, no State can unilaterally change international law or the provisions of BITs. Such treaties are of long duration, usually ten years, with a provision for automatic renewal unless and until the contracting parties agree otherwise. The formal safeguards and guarantees that BITs provide on non-commercial risks have acted as an incentive to potential investors and as a useful reassurance to those with existing investments in the signatory States. Therefore, when it comes to promoting foreign investment, States have sought additional safeguards and guarantees under international law; BITs are designed to set standards of protection. Any protection provided for foreign investment is always under the law of the host country; however, this law has to conform to the commitments undertaken by the State concerned either under BITs, FTAs, or other principles of international law.

A bilateral investment treaty is a relatively recent phenomenon, a German development of the late 1950s perfected over the years by other leading capital exporting countries such as the USA and the UK. Initially, BITs were seen as a challenge to international efforts by developing countries in order for them to regulate foreign investment through an international instrument adopted under the auspices of the UN. The Federal Republic of Germany was the first country to conclude BITs with certain developing countries in order to protect German investment in these countries. Outlining the utility of a BIT, a Presidential communication to Congress stated the main US objectives in the conclusion this BIT in the following words:

> Investment of nationals and companies of one Party in the territory of the other Party (investments) receive the better of the treatment accorded to domestic investments in like circumstances (national treatment), or the treatment accorded to third country investments in like circumstances (most-favoured-nation (MFN) treatment), both on establishment and thereafter, subject to certain specified exceptions:
>
> — Investments are guaranteed freedom from performance requirements, such as obligations to use local products or export goods;
>
> — Companies which are investments may hire top managers of their choice, regardless of nationality;
>
> — Expropriation can occur only in accordance with international law standards: in a non-discriminatory manner; for a public purpose; and upon payment of prompt, adequate, and effective compensation;
>
> — Investment-related funds are guaranteed unrestricted transfer in a freely usable currency; and
>
> — Nationals and companies of either Party, and their investments, have access to binding international arbitration in investment disputes with the host government, without first resorting to domestic courts.[27]

These are the main reasons why States conclude BITs with other countries and especially those in which their nationals have made foreign direct investment or are likely to invest. The BITs offer an added layer of protection to the regime of protection already in existence by virtue of customary international law or other treaties existing between the countries concerned.

2. The content of bilateral investment treaties

Most BITs follow a standard format whereby they provide a definition of investment and investors; the standards of protection of investment, which include protection against expropriation (both direct and indirect expropriations) and nationalization; compensation in the event of expropriation; the principles of non-discrimination; most-favoured-nation treatment; national treatment; fair and equitable treatment, and an international dispute resolution mechanism. More recent BITs have also started to include provisions for regulatory expropriation primarily in favour of environmental protection.

---

[27] US Treaty Doc 103–2, Focus—32 of 48 Documents, 1991 UST LEXIS 176.

The host States have, by and large, accepted the Hull formula and agreed to the provisions favoured by the home or investor countries when it came to negotiating bilateral investment treaties, regardless of the negotiating position taken by various States on international platforms. While the debate was taking place within the UN about the codification and progressive development of the law of foreign investment, the business of regulating foreign investment through bilateral investment treaties gathered pace outside of the UN. Those developed countries who wanted to protect investment by their nationals in foreign countries also wanted to conclude BITs of *sui generis* or *lex specialis* character rather than wait for international legislation under the auspices of the UN. Most of these treaties incorporated provisions more akin to the traditional position taken by the developed countries such as the Hull formula. When new regional trading blocs such as NAFTA were created to promote the free flow of capital, goods, and services among the countries of the region they, too, followed the pattern of bilateral investment treaties.

The practice of conforming to the Hull formula and offering as many incentives as possible to foreign investors through a BIT was confined to the treaties concluded not only between one developed country and another, but also between the developed and developing countries. Therefore, the law on foreign investment has been understood in many quarters to be the law as incorporated in the modern bilateral and regional investment treaties. When the international efforts to conclude an internationally acceptable treaty or a mandatory code of conduct within the UN remained unsuccessful, increasing numbers of States (including those leading developing countries which had championed the international regulation of foreign investment) also started concluding bilateral investment treaties along the pattern favoured by the developed countries. This is one reason why greater weight has been accorded to the content of such treaties in determining what the law is on foreign investment.

When the developing countries themselves started competing with each other for foreign direct investment that was flowing from developed countries into developing countries, they were in competition to offer greater incentives to foreign investors. Thus, they agreed to provisions designed to strengthen the position of foreign investors. The term 'investment' itself was defined as broadly as possible so as to accord protection to all conceivable forms of investment under the treaties, including asset-based investments (eg portfolio investment). Of course, there are some BITs that exclude portfolio investment from the definition of the term 'investment', but the general trend seems to be to include it. For instance, a bilateral investment treaty concluded between Jordan and the USA in July 1997 defines the term 'investment' as comprehensively as possible in Article I (d) in the following terms:

> '[I]nvestment' of a national or company means every kind of investment owned or controlled directly or indirectly by that national or company, and includes investment consisting or taking the form of:
>
> (a) a company;
> (b) shares, stock, and other forms of equity participation, and bonds, debentures, and other forms of debt interests, in a company;
> (c) contractual rights, such as under turnkey, construction or management contracts, production of revenue-sharing contracts, concessions, or other similar contracts;
> (d) tangible property, including real property; and intangible property, including rights, such as leases, mortgages, liens, and pledges;
> (e) intellectual property rights, including copyrights and related rights, industrial property rights, patents, rights in plant varieties, utility models, industrial designs or models, rights in semiconductor layout design, indications of origin, trade

secrets, including know-how, confidential business information, trade and service marks, and trade names; and rights conferred pursuant to law, such as licenses and permits.

With regard to the treatment and protection of investment, the Jordan–USA treaty is illustrative of the practice of States. The provisions included in Article II of the treaty are typical of the trend of the 1990s:

Treatment and protection of investment
With respect to the establishment, acquisition, expansion, management, conduct, operation and sale or other disposition of covered investments, each contracting party shall accord treatment no less favourable than that it accords, in like situations, to investments in its territory of its own nationals or companies (hereinafter 'national treatment') or investments in its territory or nationals or companies of a third country (hereinafter 'most favoured nation treatment'), whichever is most favourable (hereinafter 'national and most favoured nation treatment'). Each contracting party shall ensure that its state enterprises, in the provision of their goods or services, accord national and most favoured nation treatment to covered investments. . .

The Jordan–USA BIT goes on to state that each contracting party 'shall at all times accord to covered investments fair and equitable treatment and full protection and security, and shall in no case accord treatment less favourable than that required by international law'. With regard to expropriation and nationalization the BIT provides the following protection:

1. Neither contracting party shall expropriate or nationalize a covered investment either directly or indirectly through measures tantamount to expropriation or nationalisation ('expropriation') except for a public purpose; in a non-discriminatory manner; upon payment of prompt, adequate and effective compensation; and in accordance with due process of law and the general principles of treatment provided for in Article II(3).
2. Compensation shall be paid without delay; be equivalent to the fair market value of the expropriated investment immediately before the expropriatory action was taken ('the date of expropriation'); and be fully realisable and freely transferable. The fair market value shall not reflect any change in value occurring because the expropriatory action had become known before the date of expropriation.[28]

However, a bilateral investment treaty concluded in 1994 between India and the UK varies slightly from other BITs. The Indo–UK Treaty does not fully subscribe to the Hull formula in respect of every type of expropriation or nationalization. Rather, it speaks of 'fair and equitable compensation' as opposed to 'prompt, adequate and effective' compensation with regard to most forms of foreign investment and 'prompt, adequate and effective' compensation only with regard to compensation for foreign shareholders in an expropriated company. The provision concerning the nationalization and expropriation of foreign investment admits the possibility of expropriation and nationalization not simply for 'a public purpose', but for 'a public purpose related to the internal requirements for regulating economic activity'.[29]

3. Dispute resolution

One of the main reasons why foreign investors wish to see the conclusion of a BIT is for a separate or distinct international dispute resolution mechanism for disputes arising out of

---

[28] 36 ILM 1498 (1997).   [29] 34 ILM 935 (1995).

the interpretation or application of the provisions of the treaty. A demand of this nature springs from a vote on the part of foreign investors of no confidence in the ability of the national judiciary to provide impartial, speedy, and effective justice in the event of a dispute between a host State and a foreign investor. Indeed, the judiciary in many developing countries, especially those not fully democratic or lacking a long tradition of democracy, is not always as independent as it should be, and may be full of political cronyism, corruption, and inefficiencies.

Foreign investors who invest in such countries with weaker reputations, especially those who make longer-term investments and commit sizeable capital to such countries, seek an assurance against political risks; one of the means of providing that assurance is through a promise to remove a dispute with the host government out of the jurisdiction of that country, thus to an international court or tribunal that is generally independent and impartial and can provide effective, speedy, and efficient justice. Against this background most BITs provide for an international dispute settlement mechanism. There are two kinds of disputes that can arise in relation to BITs: first, between a foreign investor and investor-receiving country also known as a host country and, second, between the contracting parties themselves. With regard to the former kinds of disputes most BITs include a provision for settlement of such disputes by international investment tribunals. For instance, one of the recent BITs concluded by India and Nepal in 2011 provides the following mechanism:

Article 9: Settlement of Disputes between an Investor and a Contracting Party

(1) Any dispute between an investor of one Contracting Party and the other Contracting Party in relation to an investment of the former under this Agreement shall, as far as possible, be settled amicably through negotiations between the parties to the dispute.

(2) Any such dispute which has not been amicably settled within a period of six months may, if both parties agree, be submitted:
  (i) for resolution, in accordance with the law of the Contracting Party which has admitted the investment to that Contracting Party's competent judicial, arbitral or administrative bodies; or
  (ii) to international conciliation under the Conciliation Rules of the United Nations Commission on International Trade Law.

(3) Should the parties fail to agree on a dispute settlement procedure provided under paragraph (2) of this Article or where a dispute is referred to conciliation but conciliation proceedings are terminated other than by signing of a settlement agreement, the dispute may be referred to Arbitration.[30]

This is an elaborate and flexible mechanism with a number of options for the settlement of disputes between, on the one hand, an Indian investor and the government of Nepal and, on the other, a Nepalese investor and the Indian government. The emphasis is very much on a negotiated settlement of disputes. Only when negotiations fail to produce a mutually satisfactory outcome will the other options, including referring the matter to an international arbitration, arise. Only when the options of negotiation and conciliation fail to produce a mutually satisfactory outcome and both of the disputing parties have failed to agree to refer the matter to national judicial, arbitral, or administrative bodies of either country can a dispute be referred to an international arbitration. Even then it is not mandatory to

---

[30] See in SP Subedi, India's New Bilateral Investment Promotion and Protection Treaty with Nepal: A New Trend in State Practice', 28(2) *ICSID Review: Foreign Investment Law Journal* (Oxford University Press, Fall, 2013), pp 384–404 at 397.

refer the matter to permanent arbitration mechanisms such as ICSID. The matter can be referred to any permanent or ad hoc arbitration operating under the rules of UNCITRAL.

4. Free trade agreements

The newest generation of trade and investment treaties concluded by the USA with other States are the so-called 'free trade agreements'. These are some of the most ambitious and comprehensive bilateral treaties ever concluded in the history of international economic relations. For instance, the massive 800-page treaty concluded with Chile in June 2003 and the even longer 1,400-page treaty with Singapore in May 2003 contain detailed provisions on foreign investment, spelling out many of the key terms and phrases whose definition has dogged the debate on the law of foreign investment for so long.[31]

5. The significance of bilateral investment treaties

In the view of many international tribunals and publicists, the law on foreign investment at this juncture seems to be the law supported, albeit not created, by the provisions of the BITs and regional treaties such as NAFTA. Indeed, although the individual BITs could be regarded as *lex specialis*, it is difficult to deny that the practice of States in concluding such treaties is capable of strengthening the rules of customary international law on the subject matter. These treaties have been regarded by international tribunals in various cases as a source of law.

The BITs concluded since the introduction of ICSID in the mid-1960s made investor-to-State dispute resolution possible for the first time. Under a typical BIT, an investor is entitled to take a host State to a binding, third party arbitration, typically under the rules of the ICSID, to settle any disputes involving the interpretation of the application of the BIT. Should the host State refuse to participate, the BIT made provision for an appointing authority to appoint arbitrators on behalf of the host State to enable the arbitration to proceed even without the cooperation of the host State. This constituted an innovation in the history of dispute settlement at the international level.

Thus, the BITs allow the home or investor countries to extricate themselves from involvement in private investment disputes without diminishing the effectiveness of the remedies available to investors. This is because prior to the BIT era, investors from a country had to look to the government of their own country for assistance when their investment was expropriated or unlawfully impaired by a foreign government. Diplomatic protection was the only avenue open to such investors since there were no binding, third party dispute settlement mechanisms available for foreign investors and host States could invoke sovereign immunity and the act of State doctrine before any municipal courts. The dispute acquires a political character when the State machinery decides to espouse a claim and pursue a remedy on behalf of its private investors through diplomatic channels or international arbitration or to impose economic sanctions on the alleged wrongdoer.

There is no need for government intervention and the politicization of investment disputes when an effective dispute settlement mechanism such as the ICSID is available to private foreign investors. Thus, one of the major positive contributions made by the BITs is the 'depoliticization' of investment disputes.

C. REGIONAL INVESTMENT TREATIES

In the absence of a global treaty on foreign investment, both BITs and regional treaties have sought to fill the vacuum and lead the way. This is especially the case with the North American Free Trade Agreement (NAFTA). At the time of its adoption, the provisions of

---

[31] For text see http://www.ustr.gov/new/fta/chile.htm.

this regional treaty provided far more protection to foreign investors than accorded hitherto in customary international law. The NAFTA set the trend for much greater protection
of foreign investment throughout the 1990s, whether it be through the BITs, the TRIMS
agreement of the WTO, or other regional treaties.

The Energy Charter Treaty of 1994 includes equally greater protection for foreign investment than that accorded under customary international law. In the absence of a global
treaty, bilateral investment treaties have been the main instruments regulating foreign investment. They have been used successfully by investor countries constantly to expand the
level of protection accorded to foreign investors by host States. There is some evidence to
suggest that BITs have increased foreign investment; they certainly have instilled a sense
of security in foreign investors. These treaties have provided the assurance to foreign
investors that should something go wrong within the host States due to governmental
interference then they have an international legal remedy. BITs have made a significant
contribution to the development of the international law of foreign investment.

D. THE CASE LAW ON THE TREATMENT
OF FOREIGN INVESTMENT

The jurisprudence developed by international courts and tribunals with regard to the standard of treatment of foreign investors, with particular focus on issues concerning expropriation in its various forms, have played a crucial role in the development of the law of
foreign investment. Some of the standard-setting decisions of the International Court of
Justice, the Iran–USA Claims Tribunals, and other ad hoc tribunals, such as those established under the ICSID, have had far-reaching implications for the development of international investment law. This is because, in the absence of a global comprehensive treaty
on the regulation of foreign investment, the decisions of international courts and tribunals
have 'fleshed out' the customary international law principles of the law of foreign investment on, *inter alia*, the definition of expropriation and nationalization, and the determination of the quantum of compensation. In doing so, they have extended the frontiers of the
law especially in relation to expropriation and compensation.

Where the main principles pertaining to the area are not fully settled and the State
practice and the efforts made within and outside of the UN point in conflicting directions,
the decisions of international courts and tribunals on these matters have been relied upon
to deduce the rules applicable not only to expropriation and compensation, but also to
the meaning of the terms 'fair and equitable treatment', the 'due process of law', and 'full
protection and security'.

Traditionally, international courts, claims commissions and tribunals have relied upon
the international law of State responsibility regarding the treatment of aliens to provide
legal remedy to foreign investors when their investments were expropriated or unlawfully impaired by a foreign government. For instance, supporting the idea behind diplomatic protection, the Permanent Court of International Justice held in the *Mavrommatis
Palestine Concessions case* that:

> It is an elementary principle of international law that a state is entitled to protect its sub-
> jects, when injured by acts contrary to international law committed by another state, from
> whom they have been unable to obtain satisfaction through the ordinary channels.[32]

Cases such as the *Neer* claim *(US v Mexico)* support the notion that international law required
States to treat aliens according to an international minimum standard. Indeed, the *Neer* claim

---

[32] *Mavrommatis Palestine Concessions, Judgment No 2, 1924, PCIJ, Ser A, No 2, p 12.*

decided by the Mexico–US General Claims Commission in 1926 has been relied upon to support the doctrine of an international minimum standard of treatment of foreign investors in international law.[33] The classic and often cited case pronouncing the standard of treatment to be accorded to foreign investors is the *Chorzów Factory* case, in which the Permanent Court of International Justice relied on the doctrine of State responsibility to provide legal remedy to Germany. After finding that Poland had violated the Geneva Convention of 1922 between Germany and Poland on Upper Silesia, the Court held that 'it is a principle of international law, and even a general conception of law, that any breach of an engagement involves an obligation to make reparation'. The Court held that:

> The essential principle contained in the actual notion of an illegal act—a principle which seems to be established by international practice and in particular by decisions of arbitral tribunals—is that reparation must, as far as possible, wipe out all the consequences of the illegal act and re-establish the situation which would, in all probability, have existed if that act had not been committed.[34]

The opinion of the court in this case has been relied upon heavily by international courts and tribunals established in later years, among which the Iran–USA Claims Tribunal is a prominent example. There is a great deal of literature on defining what constitutes a 'taking of property', commonly known as expropriation or nationalization. The meaning of these terms has also been the preoccupation of international courts and tribunals on a number of cases referred to them. Some of the more recent cases seek to cover not only direct, express or outright cases of the compulsory taking of foreign property, but also indirect 'constructive taking' or 'creeping expropriation' such as that considered by the ICJ in the *ELSI* case.[35]

Many of the decisions of international tribunals, especially those of the Iran–USA Claims Tribunal, have followed the definition of taking of property in various decisions of the PCIJ and the ICJ. For instance, in the *Starrett Housing Corporation* v *Iran (interlocutory order)* the Tribunal held that since the Starrett company, an American company, had been deprived of the effective use, control, and benefits of their property rights by the Government of Iran in the aftermath of the Islamic Revolution, this amounted to 'creeping' or 'constructive' expropriation:

> It is recognised in international law that measures taken by a state can interfere with property rights to such an extent that these rights are rendered so useless that they must be deemed to have been expropriated, even though the state does not purport to have expropriated them and the legal title to the property formally remains with the original owner.[36]

In the *Amoco International Finance Corporation* v *Iran* case, the issue involved was the nationalization of the Iranian oil industry under the Single Article Act in the aftermath of the Islamic Revolution during which *Khemco*, an Iranian company jointly owned and managed by Amoco, was also nationalized. In delivering its award the Tribunal held that:

> Expropriation, which can be defined as a compulsory transfer of property rights, may extend to any right which can be the object of a commercial transaction i.e. freely sold and bought, and thus has a monetary value. It is because Amoco's interests under the Khemco Agreement have such an economic value that the nullification of those interests by the Single Article Act can be considered as a nationalisation.[37]

---

[33] *Neer* claim (*US* v *Mexico*) (1926), 4 *RIAA* 60.
[34] *Factory at Chorzów, Merits, Judgment No 13, 1928, PCIJ, Ser A, No 17*, p 29.
[35] *Elettronica Sicula SpA (ELSI), Judgment, ICJ Reports 1989*, p 15, para 119.
[36] *Starrett Housing Corporation* v *Iran (Interlocutory Order)* 23 ILM 1090 (1984); 4 *Iran–US CTR* 122 (1983).
[37] *Amoco International Finance Corporation* v *Iran*, 15 *Iran–US CTR* 189 (1987).

Thus, the lawful taking of foreign property is expropriation which would attract compensation, but illegal expropriation or confiscation such as that which occurred in relation to *Chorzów Factory* would give rise to State responsibility and attract reparation or restitution.

The ICSID tribunals have in recent years made their own contribution to clarifying the standard of treatment and nature of compensation available to foreign investors. For instance, in the *SD Myers Inc.* v *Canada* case, an ICSID tribunal sitting under the NAFTA drew, citing the *Chorzów* pronouncements, a clear distinction between the standard of compensation for otherwise lawful expropriation, on the one hand, and on the other the measure of damages for unlawful expropriation resulting from discrimination or violation of treaty obligations.[38]

In the *Asian Agricultural Products Ltd* v *Republic of Sri Lanka* case an ICSID tribunal established Sri Lanka's State responsibility for failing to take the appropriate precautionary measures to protect the interests of Asian Agricultural Products, a British company having its business in an area where fighting was taking place between the government and rebel forces.[39]

VI. CONCLUSION

After witnessing steady growth in the law of foreign investment designed to protect the interests of foreign investors in the past 50 years or so, the law of foreign investment appears to be going through a particularly interesting phase in its development at this juncture and this phase is characterized by the tension between public and private interests in international investment arbitration and the perceived need to secure effective remedies for investment-related human rights violations (van Harten, 2007; Sornarajah, 2015a and b). The tension that has been witnessed in recent years between the law of foreign investment, which guarantees investors' protections and legitimate expectations, on one hand, and the need not to unduly restrict the right of host governments to implement their public policy, including the protection of the environment and human rights, and the promotion of social and economic justice within the host country, on the other, is the result of the growing concern about the trend in jurisprudence in this area of law, about the gradual dissatisfaction with the investor-State dispute settlement mechanism itself and the gradual rejection of the institution of bilateral investment agreements or international investment agreements.[40]

There seems to be a new trend in State practice which has been characterized by various scholars as the revival of the Calvo doctrine or the return of the New International Economic Order (NIEO), considered long dead by many. Whether the new trend is described as 'the end of history', the return to the Calvo doctrine, or the advent of 'neo-NIEO', the law of foreign investment is taking a new turn. After nearly 50–60 years of practice of concluding BITs or IIAS, there is a momentous change taking place within this body of law characterized by many States' gradual rejection of such treaties with an ISDS mechanism and withdrawal from ICSID itself by a number of States. The momentum against ISDS in its current form is gathering pace not only within the developing world but also in the developed world, especially in relation to the debate on the draft Transatlantic Trade and Investment Partnership (TTIP) agreement with an ISDS mechanism between the EU and

---

[38] https://www.italaw.com/cases/969; NAFTA Ch 11 Arbitration Tribunal, 2000–2002.

[39] *Asian Agricultural Products Ltd* v *Republic of Sri Lanka* (1991) 30 ILM 577.

[40] See for example UNCTAD, 'Reforming the International Investment Regime: An Action Menu' (June 2015); Waibel et al, 2010).

the US.[41] Whether it is in the context of TTIP or another IIA or BIT, the general public, academics, journalists, and civil society organizations too have all expressed their concern about including an ISDS mechanism in such treaties.

Various independent UN human rights experts too have intervened in the matter and presented their critical views of the ISDS mechanism. For instance, the UN independent expert on the promotion of a democratic and equitable international order, Alfred de Zayas, stated in his report submitted to the UN Human Rights Council in September 2015 that the ISDS mechanism 'has mutated into a privatized system of "justice" incompatible with Article 14(1) of the International Covenant on Civil and Political Rights, whereby three arbitrators are allowed to override national legislation and the judgments of the highest national tribunals, in secret and with no possibility to appeal. This constitutes a grave challenge to the very essence of the rule of law.'[42] These all are indications that the current state of affairs is not satisfactory or sustainable and new ways should be found to reconcile competing interests and principles within international investment law.

Over the centuries the law of foreign investment has evolved in response to both the economic and political realities of the world. The developing countries sought in the 1960s, 1970s, and 1980s to regulate foreign investment through an international instrument, rather than leaving the matter to international customary law. The idea was to impose certain conditions on foreign investors, including TNCs, requiring them, among other duties, to use local raw material, to employ local people, and to refrain from interfering in the internal affairs of the host States.

However, in the 1990s these very developing countries became reluctant to support the notion of the regulation of foreign investment under the auspices of the WTO. When the developing countries sought to regulate foreign investment under the auspices of the UN, many developed countries resisted the attempt, perhaps fearing that such an international instrument would be more in the interests of host States than of the home States. An attempt was made through the OECD to adopt an international agreement on foreign investment; the developing countries opposed it, fearing that the instrument would be in the greater interest of home States than of the host States. This is also the reason why many developing countries were opposed to the regulation of foreign investment under the auspices of the WTO.

Thanks to globalization neither the host nor home countries are able to regulate or control the activities of foreign investors in general or the multinational enterprises (MNEs) in particular. While the people in developing nations are concerned about violations of human rights and degradation of the environment by the MNEs, those in the developed countries are concerned that MNEs are relocating or outsourcing their business operations to developing countries in order to avoid tax, to escape from environmental compliance and other regulatory regimes, to exploit cheap labour, and to pursue profit at the expense of other responsibilities. The interests of both developed and developing countries seem to be converging gradually towards the adoption of an international agreement to regulate foreign investment.

---

[41] It was in July 2013 that the EU and the US launched negotiations for a Transatlantic Trade and Investment Partnership (TTIP) Agreement with a view to reaching a comprehensive economic agreement between two major trading partners in the world. Its proponents have argued that it offers great opportunities for liberalizing trade and investment and regulatory convergence. See Geiger, 2014.

[42] Report of the UN Independent Expert on the promotion of a democratic and equitable international order: UN Doc A/HRC/30/44 of 14 July 2015; News Release of the UN Office of the High Commissioner for Human Rights: 'UN Expert: UN Charter and Human Rights Treaties Prevail Over Free Trade and Investment Agreements', 17 September 2015.

What is required is to balance the interests of both host and home countries. There is a plausible case in favour of the conclusion of a comprehensive international treaty on foreign investment. Unless there is a chance perhaps within the WTO to revive the negotiations for a treaty on foreign investment, the matter should be referred back to the UN, after which either the ECOSOC or UNCTAD should be entrusted with the task of developing and negotiating such a treaty.

REFERENCES

BORCHARD, E (1940), 'The Minimum Standard of Treatment of Aliens', 38 *Mich LR* 445.

CHATTERJEE, SK (1991), 'The Charter of Economic Rights and Duties of States: An Evaluation after 15 Years', 40 *ICLQ* 669.

DOLZER, R and SCHREUR, C (2012), *Principles of International Investment Law* (Oxford: Oxford University Press).

FREEMAN, AV (1946), 'Recent Aspects of the Calvo Doctrine and the Challenge to International Law', 40 *AJIL* 131.

GEIGER, R (2014), 'The Transatlantic Trade and Investment Partnership: A Critical Perspective', in *Columbia FDI Perspectives* (Vale Columbia Centre on Sustainable International Investment), No 119.

HORN, N (ed) (1980), *Legal Problems of Codes of Conduct for Multinational Enterprises* (Deventer: Kluwer).

HOSSAIN, K (ed) (1980), *Legal Aspects of a New International Economic Order* (London: Frances Pinter).

LIPSTEIN, K (1945), 'The Place of the Calvo Clause in International Law', 24 *BYIL* 130.

OPPENHEIM, L, JENNINGS, SIR R, and WATTS, SIR A (1992) (eds), *Oppenheim's International Law* (9th edn, Harlow: Longmans).

ROOT, E (1910), 'The Basis of Protection to Citizens Residing Abroad', 4 *AJIL* 517.

SCHREUER, C (2001), *The ICSID Convention: A Commentary* (Cambridge: Cambridge University Press).

SCHWARZENBERGER, G (1957), *International Law as Applied by International Courts and Tribunals* (3rd edn, London: Stevens and Sons).

SHIHATA, IFI (1991), *The World Bank in a Changing World: Selected Essays* (Dordrecht: Martinus Nijhoff).

SORNARAJAH, M (2015a), *The International Law on Foreign Investment* (4th edn, Cambridge: Cambridge University Press).

SORNARAJAH, M (2015b), *Resistance and Change in the International Law of Foreign Investment* (Cambridge: Cambridge University Press).

SUBEDI, SP (2016), *International Investment Law: Reconciling Policy and Principle* (3rd edn, Oxford: Hart Publishing).

VERWEY, WD and SCHRIJVER, NJ (1984), 'The Taking of Foreign Property under International Law: A New Legal Perspective?', XV *Netherlands Yearbook of International Law* 3.

WAIBEL, M, KAUSHAL, A, CHUNG, K, and BALCHIN, C (eds) (2010), *The Backlash Against Investment Treaty Arbitration: Perceptions and Reality* (The Hague: Kluwer).

WORLD TRADE ORGANIZATION (1999), *The Legal Texts: The Results of the Uruguay Round of Multilateral Trade Negotiations* (Cambridge: Cambridge University Press).

FURTHER READING

Higgins, R (1982), 'The Taking of Property by the State' (1982-III) 176 *Recueil des Cours* 259.

McLachlan, C, Shore, L, and Weiniger, M (2007), *International Investment Arbitration: Substantive Principles* (Oxford: Oxford University Press, 2007).

Montt, S (2011), *State Liability in Investment Treaty Arbitration: Global Constitutional and Administrative Law in the BIT Generation* (Oxford: Hart Publishing).

Puvimanasinghe, SF (2007), *Foreign Investment, Human Rights and the Environment: A Perspective from South Asia on the Role of Public International Law* (The Hague: Martinus Nijhoff).

Salacuse, W (2010), *The Law of International Investment Treaties* (Oxford: Oxford University Press).

Shea, DR (1955), *The Calvo Clause: A Problem of Inter-American and International Law and Diplomacy* (Minneapolis: University of Minnesota Press).

Tudor, I (2008), *The Fair and Equitable Treatment Standard in International Foreign Investment Law* (Oxford: Oxford University Press).

UNCTAD (1999), *Most-Favoured-Nation Treatment* (UNCTAD series on issues in international investment agreements) (New York and Geneva: UN).

UNCTAD (1999), *Fair and Equitable Treatment* (UNCTAD series on issues in international investment agreements) (New York and Geneva: UN).

UNCTAD (1999), *National Treatment* (UNCTAD series on issues in international investment agreements) (New York and Geneva: UN).

Van Harten, G (2007), *Investment Treaty Arbitration and Public Law* (Oxford: Oxford University Press).

WEBSITES

UNCTAD BITs Online:

http://unctad.org/en/pages/DIAE/International%20Investment%20Agreements%20(IIA)/IIA-Tools.aspx
This website contains a search engine which enables one to find BITs and investment dispute-related cases online.

www.ita.law.uvic.ca
Provides access to all publicly available investment treaty awards and information and resources relating to investment treaties and investment treaty arbitration.

http://www.worldbank.org/icsid
This is the website of ICSID which was established under the Convention on the Settlement of Investment Disputes between States and Nationals of Other States. Most of the ICSID awards are available here.

24

INTERNATIONAL
CRIMINAL LAW

Robert Cryer

SUMMARY

This chapter deals with international crimes in the narrow sense. These are crimes which are directly criminalized by international law. It therefore discusses the material and mental aspects of the four crimes that qualify as such crimes: genocide, crimes against humanity, war crimes, and aggression. As international criminal law directly criminalizes those offences, this chapter also covers some of the general principles of liability and defences that are of particular relevance to international crimes. Therefore it explains and critiques joint criminal enterprise, co-perpetration, command responsibility, and the defence of obedience to superior orders. The chapter then looks at the international and, briefly, the national prosecution of international crimes. It covers, in particular, the Nuremberg and Tokyo Trials, the International Criminal Tribunals for former Yugoslavia and Rwanda, and the International Criminal Court. Reference is also made, *inter alia*, to the Special Court for Sierra Leone, the Special Tribunal for Lebanon, the Iraqi High Tribunal, and purely national prosecutions such as that of Adolf Eichmann in Israel. As prosecution is not the only, or predominant, response to international crimes, the chapter concludes with a discussion, and evaluation, of alternatives and complements to prosecution, such as amnesties and truth and reconciliation commissions.

I. INTRODUCTION

There are various different ways of defining international criminal law (Kreβ, 2015). These include those aspects of international law involving the allocation of jurisdiction, or international cooperation in criminal matters (Schwarzenberger, 1950). However, international criminal law, for the purposes of this chapter, is the branch of public international law that deals with the direct criminal responsibility of individuals. It can be summed up in the famous statement of the Nuremberg International Military Tribunal (IMT) that '[i]ndividuals have international duties which transcend the national obligations of obedience imposed by the individual State . . . crimes against international law are committed by men, not by abstract entities, and only by punishing individuals who commit such crimes can the provisions of international law be enforced'.[1] For international crimes, the locus of

---

[1] Nuremberg IMT, 'Judgment and Sentence' (1947) 41 *AJIL* 172, 221, 223.

the criminal prohibition is the international legal order (although such crimes may also be criminalized in domestic legal orders). There are only four clear examples of international crimes in this sense (often called the 'core' international crimes): genocide, crimes against humanity, war crimes, and aggression.

Some suggest that there are other core international crimes, most notably terrorism and individual acts of torture (Cassese et al, 2013, ch 8). Indeed, the Appeals Chamber of the Special Tribunal for Lebanon (over which Cassese presided) asserted in 2011 that international law had developed to the point that there was a customary international crime of terrorism.[2] The Special Tribunal's decision, however, is largely considered unpersuasive (Saul, 2011; *contra* Ventura, 2011). Terrorism or torture may fall under the definitions of other international crimes (in particular crimes against humanity or war crimes), and when they do so they may be prosecuted as those crimes. However, as it stands, there is insufficient acceptance by States of the idea that they exist as separate categories of customary international crimes (Simma and Paulus, 1999, p 313; Saul, 2006, ch 4).

In addition to their overlap with core crimes, terrorism and individual acts of torture are regulated by international law. There are numerous treaties covering aspects of terrorism,[3] and individual acts of torture are dealt with by the 1984 UN Convention Against Torture.[4] However, these are examples of what are known as 'transnational crime' conventions (Boister, 2003; 2012). These do not in themselves create direct liability international crimes, but require States to create domestic crimes.

It is sometimes thought that the question of whether torture is an international crime turns, at least in part, on whether the Torture Convention has achieved customary status (Cassese et al, 2013, p 132). However, since the Convention itself does not create a direct criminal prohibition, if the Torture Convention is customary, then all States are obliged to prohibit torture domestically, rather than accept that international law directly criminalizes torture.

Sometimes international crimes are referred to as '*jus cogens* crimes' (eg Sadat, 2007, p 231). Although there is considerable overlap between *jus cogens* norms and international crimes (genocide, for example, has been authoritatively determined to be 'assuredly' contrary to a *jus cogens* prohibition[5]), the term '*jus cogens* crime' can be apt to mislead. An international crime is created when international law directly criminalizes something. It is not required that the rule doing so has *jus cogens* status. Indeed, international crimes arose at the very latest in the Nuremburg and Tokyo IMTs, nearly 25 years before the concept of *jus cogens* was adopted in the Vienna Convention on the Law of Treaties.[6]

Similarly, that a prohibition has reached *jus cogens* status does not mean that it is automatically an international crime. Torture is contrary to a *jus cogens* norm;[7] however, that does not, in and of itself, mean that torture is an international crime. Still, the vast majority of international criminal law finds its basis in customary international law, and thus is applicable throughout the world. There are those that question the cultural sensitivity of this

---

[2] *Interlocutory Decision on the Applicable Law: Terrorism, Conspiracy, Homicide, Perpetration, Cumulative Charging, STL-11–01/I/AC/R176bis*, Appeals Chamber, 16 February 2011.

[3] Eg Convention for the Suppression of Unlawful Seizure of Aircraft, 860 UNTS 105; International Convention for the Suppression of the Financing of Terrorism, GA Res 54/109 (9 December 1999).

[4] 1465 UNTS 85.

[5] *Armed Activities on the Territory of the Congo (New Application: 2002) (Democratic Republic of the Congo v Rwanda), Jurisdiction and Admissibility, Judgment, ICJ Reports 2006*, p 6, para 64. This case was also the first time the ICJ had used the term *jus cogens*.   [6] 1155 UNTS 331, Article 53.

[7] *Questions relating to the Obligation to Prosecute or Extradite (Belgium v Senegal), Judgment of 20 July 2012*, para 99; ICTY, *Prosecutor v Furundzija*, Judgment, Case No IT–95–17/1–T, Trial Chamber II (10 December 1998), para 153.

(Clarke, 2009). However, there is very considerable agreement about the relevant norms,[8] even if the way in which they are implemented and enforced is sometimes the matter of more debate.

A. INTERNATIONAL AND CRIMINAL LAW

International criminal law is an amalgam of international and criminal law. As such its sources are those of international law, which has its own ways of thinking, and criminal law, which also has its own approach (see, eg, Robinson, 2008; Robinson, 2015). An appreciation of both is necessary for a full understanding of international criminal law. Sometimes, the dual nature of international criminal law has led to critique, particularly from those in civil law systems where the principle of non-retroactivity of criminal law prohibits reliance on unwritten law (*nullum crimen sine lege scripta*) (eg Djuro-Degan, 2005, p 67). However, the *nullum crimen sine lege* principle, at the international level, does not prohibit the use of custom (Gallant, 2008, p 354), and the International Criminal Tribunal for the former Yugoslavia (ICTY), in particular, has made considerable use of customary law.[9] Furthermore, Article 21(1)(b) of the Rome Statute of the ICC permits that Court, *inter alia*, to refer to 'the principles and rules of international law'.[10] There are also those that assert that treaties cannot suffice to provide for individual criminal liability (Mettraux, 2008, pp 7–9). This is, however, contradicted by nearly 80 years of practice, and the fundamental nature of the ICC Statute, which, after all, is a treaty. The relation between treaty and custom in international criminal law is not always simple, though, especially in relation to non-State parties to the Rome Statute (Milanovic, 2011, 2012).

II. THE CRIMES

As mentioned earlier, there are four undoubted international crimes: genocide, crimes against humanity, war crimes, and aggression.

A. GENOCIDE

Genocide, said by some to be the 'crime of crimes' (Schabas, 2009), is also possibly the youngest international crime. The term itself was coined by Raphaël Lemkin in 1944 to describe the Holocaust (Lemkin, 1944) by combining the Greek 'genos' (people, or race) and the Latin 'cide' (to kill). This provides an insight into the focus of the crime. It focuses on threats to the existence of groups. Although the term was referred to in the Nuremberg IMT indictment, the first time the term genocide was used as a term of art in positive international law was in General Assembly Resolution 96(I) (1946). The label of genocide is an exceptionally potent one. As such, debates over whether particular atrocities amount to genocide are often politically contentious (Luban, 2006–7; Akhavan, 2010; Scheffer, 2012, ch 2). It must be said that, for the most part, in spite of the controversy over the Darfur situation, genocide has not played a large role in the practice of the ICC to date. Whether this will change if the situation relating to Daesh/ISIS and its actions with respect to minorities

---

[8] But see Kelsall 2009, chs 3–5.

[9] See, in particular, ICTY Appeals Chamber, *Prosecutor v Tadić, Decision on the Defence Interlocutory Appeal on Jurisdiction*, Case no IT-94-1-AR72, 2 October 1995 (hereafter cited as '*Tadić* Appeal'). Some go as far as to say that its jurisdiction is limited to customary crimes (Shahabuddeen, 2012, pp 61–70).

[10] On which see Bitti, 2015.

is dependent on the political will to refer the matter to the ICC, and as such is speculative (Sadat, 2015).

The accepted definition of genocide as an international crime came about in the 1948 Genocide Convention. Three years later the ICJ, in the *Reservations* case, determined that 'the principles underlying the Convention are principles which are recognized by civilized nations as binding on States, even without any conventional obligation'.[11] As discussed in Section I of this chapter, the ICJ has also made clear that the prohibition has achieved *jus cogens* status.

Article II of the Genocide Convention (which is repeated essentially verbatim in the ICTY, International Criminal Tribunal for Rwanda (ICTR), and International Criminal Court (ICC) Statutes) defines genocide as:

> any of the following acts committed with intent to destroy, in whole or in part, a national, ethnical, racial or religious group, as such:
>
> (a) Killing members of the group;
> (b) Causing serious bodily or mental harm to members of the group;
> (c) Deliberately inflicting on the group conditions of life calculated to bring about its physical destruction in whole or in part;
> (d) Imposing measures intended to prevent births within the group;
> (e) Forcibly transferring children of the group to another group.

Genocide is characterized in particular by its mental element, but it is also worth looking at the controversies that have surrounded the conduct element.

1. Conduct element

The paradigmatic example of genocide's conduct element is killing. This has not caused too many difficulties in practice, and it is generally accepted that the killing has to be intentional. Genocide may also be committed in other ways, which are provided for in Article II. The second means of committing genocide is causing serious bodily or mental harm. The former was given a progressive (but entirely defensible) interpretation by the ICTR in the *Akayesu* case.[12] There the ICTR accepted that rape and other forms of sexual violence are covered by Article II. The ICC's Elements of Crimes (EoC) agree.[13] Deliberately inflicting conditions of life designed to destroy a group, like most of the acts of genocide, tracks Nazi policies. The EoC for the ICC provide that '[t]he term "conditions of life" may include, but is not necessarily restricted to, deliberate deprivation of resources indispensable for survival, such as food or medical services, or systematic expulsion from homes'.[14] It is not enough that these conditions are imposed, they must also be calculated to destroy the group, which is a mental element.

The inclusion of 'imposing measures intended to prevent births within the group' was also a response to Nazi policies. The EoC do not contain much elaboration of this crime; however, the ICTR has made clear that the measures may be physical or mental.[15] Finally, Article II also includes transferring children of a group to another group. For this purpose, children are those under 18 years old, and 'forcible' includes physical force and mental coercion, 'such as that caused by fear of violence, duress, detention, psychological oppression

---

[11] *Reservations to the Convention on the Prevention and Punishment of the Crime of Genocide, Advisory Opinion, ICJ Reports 1951*, p 15 at p 23.

[12] ICTR Trial Chamber I, *Prosecutor* v *Akayesu*, Judgment, Case No ICTR-95–4-T, 2 September 1998, para 731 (hereafter cited as '*Akayesu*').   [13] Elements of Crimes for Article 6(b), footnote 3.

[14] Elements of Crimes for Article 6(c), footnote 4.   [15] *Akayesu*, paras 507–8.

or abuse of power, against such person or persons or another person, or by taking advantage of a coercive environment'.[16] This last phrase is rather vague, and will need judicial interpretation, although to date, there have been no authoritative rulings on this point.

The final part of the external aspect of genocide is provided for in the EoC: this is that '[t]he conduct took place in the context of a manifest pattern of similar conduct directed against that group or was conduct that could itself effect such destruction'.[17] It is controversial whether this is something inherent in the concept of genocide, or a non-customary addition to the crime solely for the purposes of the ICC. The ICTY in the *Krstić* case took the view that the element was not customary.[18] However, a Pre-Trial Chamber in the ICC, while not determining the customary status of the element, has applied it as it was not in 'irreconcilable contradiction' with the ICC Statute.[19] What is notable, however, is that a 'manifest pattern of similar conduct' is not the same as a genocidal policy, as the term 'conduct' was chosen carefully to avoid that implication (Oosterveld, 2001, pp 47–8), and a single, large-scale act (for example the detonation of a weapon of mass destruction) can also fulfil the element.

2. Mental element

The factor that distinguishes genocide from 'mere' mass killing is the 'intent to destroy, in whole or in part, a national, ethnical, racial or religious group, as such'. This aspect of the definition is contested between those who would interpret the mental element broadly, to legally label more killings and the like as 'genocide' so it reflects the popular concept of genocide more closely, and those who take the view that it must be kept narrow, for fear of diluting the opprobrium that attaches to conduct legally classified as genocide (Schabas, 2009, pp 10–11).

The first question is whether 'intent' in the definition means motive, direct intention, or indirect intention.[20] The ICJ, ICTY, and ICC have taken the view that although proof of motive is not required, direct intention is necessary for genocide; indirect intent is insufficient.[21] In part as a result of this, proving genocidal intent is difficult, and the ICJ only found genocidal intent in former Yugoslavia in Srebreniča.[22] These difficulties have led the tribunals into controversial waters, as some have claimed that indirect intention should suffice, and the approach of the ad hoc tribunals in particular has often been to use modes of liability that require lower mental elements to circumvent the high thresholds they have otherwise set (Greenawalt, 1999). Either way, proof of intent often depends on circumstantial factors. The ICTR has identified, *inter alia*, the following as useful evidence:

> The overall context in which the crime occurred, the systematic targeting of the victims on account of their membership in a protected group, the fact that the perpetrator may have targeted the same group during the commission of other criminal acts, the scale and scope

---

[16] Elements of Crimes for Article 6(e), element 5 and footnote 5.

[17] Eg Elements of Crimes for Article 6(a), element 4.

[18] ICTY Appeals Chamber, *Prosecutor v Krstić, Judgment*, Case No IT-98–33-A, 19 April 2004, para 224 (hereafter cited as '*Krstić* Appeal').

[19] ICC Pre Trial Chamber 1, *Prosecutor v al-Bashir*, Case No 02/05–01/09, 4 March 2009, para 132 (hereafter '*al-Bashir*').

[20] Direct intention requires wanting something to occur; indirect intention is when a person, whilst not wanting something to occur, accepts it as a virtually certain consequence of their conduct.

[21] *Application of the Convention on the Prevention and Punishment of the Crime of Genocide (Bosnia and Hercegovina v Serbia and Montenegro), Merits Judgment, ICJ Reports 2007*, para 189 (hereafter cited as '*Bosnian Genocide*'); ICTY Appeals Chamber, *Prosecutor v Jelesić, Judgment*, Case No IT-95–10-A, 5 July 2001, para 49; *al Bashir*, para 114; ICTY Trial Chamber II, *Prosecutor v Kupreškić*, Judgment, Case No IT-95–16-T, 14 January 2000, para 636 (hereafter cited as '*Kupreškić*').   [22] *Bosnian Genocide*, paras 278–97.

of the atrocities committed, the frequency of destructive and discriminatory acts, whether the perpetrator acted on the basis of the victim's membership in a protected group and the perpetration of acts which violate the very foundation of the group or considered as such by their perpetrators.[23]

The second controversy is whether the intention to destroy the group refers to physical or cultural destruction. Some support the idea of 'cultural genocide',[24] but this has been rejected as a matter of law, probably most authoritatively by the ICJ in the *Bosnian Genocide* case.[25] Still, as it said in that case, adopting the ICTY's view, 'where there is physical or biological destruction there are often simultaneous attacks on the cultural and religious property and symbols of the targeted group as well, attacks which may legitimately be considered as evidence of an intent to physically destroy the group'.[26] Equally, the means of genocide of transfer of children to other groups has links to cultural destruction.

Some of the thorniest issues relating to genocide concern the definitions of the protected groups and what those groups should be (Nersessian, 2010). Although one Trial Chamber in the ICTR argued that the Convention protects all stable and permanent groups,[27] this remains a minority view. As the ICJ has said: 'the essence of the intent is to destroy the protected group, in whole or in part, as such. It is a group which must have particular positive characteristics—national, ethnical, racial or religious . . .'[28] On this basis the ICJ, more controversially, also rejected the idea that a group could be defined negatively, such as 'all non-Serbs'.[29]

The question of the existence of a group protected from genocide and its membership is also complex. In *Akayesu* the ICTR tried to define all four terms separately. This proved to be problematic, not least as on the definitions the Trial Chamber gave, there was no relevant distinction in the Rwandan context between Hutus and Tutsis. A more satisfactory approach was taken by the ICTY in the *Krstić* case, where the ICTY explained:

> The preparatory work of the convention shows that setting out such a list was designed more to describe a single phenomenon, roughly corresponding to what was recognized, before the second world war, as 'national minorities', rather than to refer to several distinct prototypes of human groups. To attempt to differentiate each of the named groups on the basis of scientifically objective criteria would thus be inconsistent with the object and purpose of the Convention.[30]

Part of the difficulty is that groups exist, at least partially, at the level of (often fostered) perception, rather than objective fact (Wilson, 2011, ch 7). In addition, even against this backdrop, group membership is complex, as some people may not consider themselves to belong to a group, but others may do so, and vice versa (Schabas, 2009, pp 124–9). Owing to this, the better view is that if such a group is considered to exist in the relevant cultural context, then the perception of the perpetrator that the victim is a member of that group suffices for them to be considered a member for the purposes of genocide.[31] The ICJ has noted this approach.[32]

Finally, as can be seen from the language of the Genocide Convention, it suffices if the perpetrator intended to destroy a part of the group. It therefore becomes very important to

---

[23] ICTR Trial Chamber III, *Prosecutor v Ncamihigo, Judgment*, Case No ICTR-01-63-T, 12 November 2008, para 331.   [24] See the discussion in Schabas, 2009, pp 207–21.

[25] *Bosnian Genocide*, para 344.   [26] Ibid.   [27] *Akayesu*, para 516.

[28] *Bosnian Genocide*, para 193.   [29] Ibid. See *contra* Shahabuddeen, 2012, pp 193–5.

[30] ICTY Trial Chamber I, *Prosecutor v Krstić, Judgment*, Case No IT-98-33-T, 2 August 2001, para 556.

[31] See, eg, ICTR Trial Chamber I, *Prosecutor v Semanza, Judgment*, Case No ICTR-97-20-T, 15 May 2003, para 317.   [32] *Bosnian Genocide*, para 191.

define what the group is and what size a part of the group has to be. The ICTY has tended to take the view that it is all members of the group in the country. So, for example, in the *Krstić* case, the prosecution argued that the relevant group was the Bosnian Muslims of the Srebreniča area. The ICTY disagreed, saying that the relevant group was the Bosnian Muslims, and the Bosnian Muslims of the Srebreniča area were a part of the group.[33] They also determined that the part of the group must be 'substantial',[34] something the ICJ has also accepted.[35]

B. CRIMES AGAINST HUMANITY

Crimes against humanity, although they arguably existed prior to 1945 and few would question their heinous nature (Bassiouni, 2011, chs 4–6), were first defined in Article 6(c) of the London Charter, which set up the Nuremberg Tribunal, as 'murder, extermination, enslavement, deportation, and other inhumane acts committed against any civilian population, before or during the war; or persecutions on political, racial or religious grounds in execution of or in connection with any crime within the jurisdiction of the Tribunal, whether or not in violation of the domestic law of the country where perpetrated'. Since then there have also been definitions in, *inter alia*, the Statutes of the Tokyo IMT (Article 5(c)), ICTY (Article 5), ICTR (Article 3), and SCSL (Article 2). Unfortunately none of them are identical. This has led to calls for a comprehensive convention on crimes against humanity (Bassiouni, 1994). There are current non-governmental drafts of such a treaty (Sadat, 2011). The International Law Commission is currently working on the possibility of such a convention,[36] but, to date, it is not clear that such efforts will come to fruition.[37] The most widely ratified treaty-based definition of crimes against humanity is contained in Article 7 of the ICC Statute. This reads:

1. For the purpose of this Statute, 'crime against humanity' means any of the following acts when committed as part of a widespread or systematic attack directed against any civilian population, with knowledge of the attack:

   (a) Murder;

   (b) Extermination;

   (c) Enslavement;

   (d) Deportation or forcible transfer of population;

   (e) Imprisonment or other severe deprivation of physical liberty in violation of fundamental rules of international law;

   (f) Torture;

   (g) Rape, sexual slavery, enforced prostitution, forced pregnancy, enforced sterilization, or any other form of sexual violence of comparable gravity;

   (h) Persecution against any identifiable group or collectivity on political, racial, national, ethnic, cultural, religious, gender . . . or other grounds that are universally recognized as impermissible under international law, in connection with any act referred to in this paragraph or any crime within the jurisdiction of the Court;

   (i) Enforced disappearance of persons;

---

[33] *Krstić* Appeal, para 12.   [34] Ibid.   [35] *Bosnian Genocide*, para 198.
[36] UN International Law Commission, 'Crimes Against Humanity', UN Doc A/Cn.4/L 892, 27 May 2017.
[37] Report of the International Law Commission, 69th Session, UN Doc A/72/10, Chapter IV.

(j) The crime of apartheid;

(k) Other inhumane acts of a similar character intentionally causing great suffering, or serious injury to body or to mental or physical health.[38]

Crimes against humanity is a complex crime, and there are many definitional controversies. The crime has conduct, contextual, and mental elements.[39] It is worth noting, though, that such crimes have formed the bulk of the early work of the ICC, which has engaged in significant judicial treatment of the nuances of the crime, although not all of its decisions have passed without critical comment (Sadat, 2013).

1. Conduct element

For reasons of space, it is not possible to deal with all of the conduct elements in great detail. Article 7(2) and the EoC provide further elaboration of the varied conduct amounting to crimes against humanity. For example, Article 7(2)(c) defines enslavement as 'the exercise of any or all of the powers attaching to the right of ownership over a person and includes the exercise of such power in the course of trafficking in persons, in particular women and children'. One of the more controversial definitions was that of enforced pregnancy. Article 7(2)(f) defines that crime as 'the unlawful confinement of a woman forcibly made pregnant, with the intent of affecting the ethnic composition of any population or carrying out other grave violations of international law. This definition shall not in any way be interpreted as affecting national laws relating to pregnancy'. The additional intent requirement, as well as the last sentence, were added at the insistence of some States, who thought that this crime could potentially be used to condemn domestic laws limiting or prohibiting abortion (von Hebel and Robinson, 1999, p 100). The additions render the crime narrower than customary law (Cryer, 2005, p 258).

Another controversial addition to the requirements set by customary law is the condition in Article 7(1)(h) that persecutive crimes against humanity can only be prosecuted if they occur 'in connection with any act referred to in this paragraph or any crime within the jurisdiction of the Court'. This was included on the basis that some States felt that some of their family laws could be interpreted as contrary to the prohibition of gender-based persecutions.[40] It remains the case, however, that this limitation also makes the Rome Statute's definition of crimes against humanity more restrictive than customary law.[41]

2. Contextual element

The core of crimes against humanity, the thing that renders conduct which generally amounts to a domestic crime (such as rape and murder) into an international crime, is the context in which it occurs. This context has been the subject of conflicting definitions. For example, in the Nuremberg and Tokyo IMT's definitions there was a requirement of the existence of an armed conflict.[42] This is no longer the case (if it ever was) in customary law,[43] and it does not appear in any later definitions other than that in the ICTY Statute. In that context, the limitation has been explained on the basis that the Security Council simply wished to grant the ICTY jurisdiction over a limited subset of crimes against humanity rather than make an assertion about customary law (Shahabuddeen, 2012, p 65).

---

[38] Although it must be noted that this definition is not necessarily entirely reflective of customary international law on the point: Cassese, 2013, pp 123–6.

[39] The question of whether or not genocide has a contextual element is controversial: see Section II B 2 of this chapter.

[40] The definition of gender was similarly controversial (von Hebel and Robinson, 1999, p 101).

[41] *Kupreškić*, para 580.   [42] London Charter, Article 6(c); Tokyo IMT Charter, Article 5(c).

[43] *Tadić* Appeal, para 141.

The core of the customary contextual element is that the conduct occurs in the context of a widespread or systematic attack on a civilian population. As the ICTY has said,
"'Widespread" refers to the large-scale nature of the attack and the number of victims,
while the phrase "systematic" refers to the organized nature of the acts of violence and the
improbability of their random occurrence.'[44] In Rome the question arose of whether the
terms 'widespread' and 'systematic' ought to be included in the alternative or cumulatively
(ie whether it was widespread and systematic or widespread or systematic). The latter was
chosen, however, as part of the compromise; Article 7(2) defines an attack on the civilian population as being 'a course of conduct involving the multiple commission of acts
referred to in paragraph 1 against any civilian population, pursuant to or in furtherance of
a State or organizational policy to commit such attack'.

This definition means that if the prosecution seeks to prove a crime against humanity
on the basis that it was widespread they will also have to prove a (perhaps) more limited
form of the systematic element (a 'policy') while if they seek to prove the crime against
humanity on the basis that the attack was systematic, they will have to prove a more limited version of the widespread requirement (Robinson, 1999, pp 450–1). The ICTY has
expressly rejected the customary basis of the policy requirement in the *Kunarac* case,[45]
although the rather conclusionary nature of the discussion in that case has been criticized
(Schabas, 2008, pp 958–69). There are considerable disagreements about whether there
ought to be such a requirement, and, if so, what level of organization an entity needs before it can be considered sufficiently organized to have such a policy (Kreβ, 2010; Halling,
2010; Schabas, 2010; Werle and Burghardt, 2012).

The question of what amounts to a civilian population, and who can be a victim of a
crime against humanity have also proved divisive. On the former point, the ICTY has
adopted the view that:

> the use of the word population does not mean that the entire population of the geographi-
> cal entity in which the attack is taking place must have been subjected to that attack. It is
> sufficient to show that enough individuals were targeted in the course of the attack, or that
> they were targeted in such a way to satisfy the Chamber that the attack was in fact directed
> against a civilian population, rather than against a limited and randomly selected number
> of individuals.[46]

Furthermore, the presence of some non-civilians in a population does not render that
population non-civilian so long as it is 'predominantly' so.[47] In wartime situations, who
is a civilian is to be interpreted in accordance with the relevant applicable humanitarian
law.[48] It was often thought that only civilians can be the victims of crimes against humanity. However, what is required is that the attack is against the civilian population, not that
all of the victims are civilians. As a result, the ICTY has held that those non-civilians who
are hors de combat (such as PoWs) may also be the victims of crimes against humanity
so long as the attack as a whole is directed at a civilian population.[49] Precisely how the
elements of an attack, and against whom it must be directed, may be proved is far from
uncontroversial.

---

[44] ICTY Appeals Chamber, *Prosecutor v Kunarac, Kovać and Vuković, Judgment*, Case No IT-96–23/1-A,
12 June 2002, para 94 (hereafter cited as '*Kunarac* Appeal'). The ICC has, so far, agreed: see *al-Bashir*, para 81.
[45] Ibid, para 98.   [46] *Kunarac* Appeal, para 90.
[47] ICTY Trial Chamber II, *Prosecutor v Tadić*, Opinion and Judgment, Case No IT-94–1-T, 7 May 1997,
para 638.
[48] ICTY Appeals Chamber, *Prosecutor v Blaškić*, Judgment, Case No IT-95–14-A, 29 July 2004, paras 113–15.
[49] ICTY Appeals Chamber, *Prosecutor v Martić* Judgment, Case No IT-95–11-A, 8 October 2008, para 313.

3. Mental element

The mental element applicable to crimes against humanity is, first, that the person had the mental element required for the underlying crime (murder, etc.). Second, they had knowledge of the broader context in which their crimes are committed, in other words, that they took place in the context of a widespread or systematic attack on the civilian population, or intended it to be. There is nothing which excludes a personal motive from co-existing with this knowledge, though.[50] For persecutive crimes against humanity there is an additional mental element that the perpetrator has to intend to discriminate against the victims.[51] The EoC require that the perpetrator 'targeted' the members of the relevant group, which implies the same.

C. WAR CRIMES

The law of war crimes is, in essence, the criminal phase of humanitarian law (Sivakumaran, 2012, pp 77–83). As such, war crimes are parasitic upon that law (for which see Turns, Ch 27 of this book). The relationship between them, however, is not simple or uncontested (Stahn, 2017), although it is tolerably clear that no war crime can exist in the absence of a violation of the law of armed conflict/humanitarian law.

As with humanitarian law more generally, the law of war crimes differs depending on whether the armed conflict is international or non-international. In international armed conflicts, there are treaty-based and customary norms that are relevant. Of the treaty-based norms, possibly the most important are grave breaches of the Geneva Conventions (see Symposium, 2009); these are explained in Article 8(2)(a) of the ICC Statute as being:

> any of the following acts against persons or property protected under the provisions of the relevant Geneva Convention [essentially the wounded, sick, shipwrecked, PoWs and interned civilians and civilians in occupied territory] . . .:

> (i)   Wilful killing;
> (ii)   Torture or inhuman treatment, including biological experiments;
> (iii)   Wilfully causing great suffering, or serious injury to body or health;
> (iv)   Extensive destruction and appropriation of property, not justified by military necessity and carried out unlawfully and wantonly;
> (v)   Compelling a prisoner of war or other protected person to serve in the forces of a hostile Power;
> (vi)   Wilfully depriving a prisoner of war or other protected person of the rights of fair and regular trial;
> (vii)   Unlawful deportation or transfer or unlawful confinement;
> (viii) Taking of hostages.

Outside the ICC, such acts are also subject to mandatory extradition or prosecution on the basis of universal jurisdiction (eg Geneva Convention I, Article 49). There are also grave breaches provisions in Additional Protocol I (Article 85, see Sandoz, Swiniarski, and Zimmerman, 1987, pp 899ff), although the extent to which universal jurisdiction inheres in those grave breaches depends on their customary status (which is likely, but not guaranteed: see Henckaerts and Doswald-Beck, 2005).

The Nuremberg (Article 6(b)) and Tokyo IMTs (Article 5(b)), as well as the ICTY (Article 3) were given jurisdiction over an open-ended list of war crimes, and were thus able to

---

[50] ICTY Appeals Chamber, *Prosecutor v Tadić*, Judgment, Case No IT-94–1-A, 15 July 1999, para 248.
[51] ICTY Trial Chamber II, *Prosecutor v Krnojelac*, Judgment, Case No IT-97–25-T, 13 March 2002, para 435.

prosecute any applicable customary war crime. The ICC, on the other hand, has only been granted jurisdiction over (in addition to grave breaches of the Geneva Conventions (Article 8(2)(a)) a closed list of 26 customary crimes, which include those relating to a limited number of weapons offences (eg Article 8(2)(b)(xviii) (employing chemical weapons contrary to the 1925 Geneva Gas Protocol)), declaring no quarter (Article 8(2)(b)(xii)), sexual offences (Article 8(2)(b)(xxii)), attacking civilians (Article 8(2)(b)(i)), using human shields (Article 8(2)(b)(xxiii)), and launching an attack which will cause disproportionate collateral damage (Article 8(2)(b)(iv)). The definitions in, and the inclusions and exclusions from, the list of crimes in the Rome Statute were extremely controversial (Cullen, 2011, p 148).

Turning to non-international armed conflict, the ICTR (Article 4), SCSL (Article 3), and ICC (Article 8(2)(c)) all have jurisdiction to prosecute violations of common Article 3 to the Geneva Conventions,[52] which reads (in relevant part):

[T]he following acts are and shall remain prohibited at any time and in any place whatsoever with respect to the above-mentioned persons [persons taking no active part in hostilities]:

(a) violence to life and person, in particular murder of all kinds, mutilation, cruel treatment and torture;

(b) taking of hostages;

(c) outrages upon personal dignity, in particular humiliating and degrading treatment;

(d) the passing of sentences and the carrying out of executions without previous judgment pronounced by a regularly constituted court, affording all the judicial guarantees which are recognized as indispensable by civilized peoples.

The ICTR (Article 5) and SCSL (Article 3) also have jurisdiction over violations of Additional Protocol II, as those States were parties to that treaty before the beginning of the respective Courts' jurisdictions. The Special Court for Sierra Leone had jurisdiction over three named offences that may be committed in non-international armed conflict (Article 4—attacking civilians, attacking peacekeepers entitled to protection as civilians, and conscripting, enlisting, or using child soldiers). The ICC has a closed list of 12 customary war crimes for non-international armed conflicts (Article 8(2)(e)). In addition to those included in the SCSL Statute, these include prohibitions on pillage (Article 8(2)(e) (v)), perfidy (Article 8(2)(e)(ix)), and sexual offences (Article 8(2)(e)(vi)). In 2010, the parties to the Rome Statute adopted an amendment to the Statute to harmonize its weapons prohibitions in international and non-international armed conflicts. The amendment came into force in September 2012, and currently has 16 parties.[53] As identified *inter alia* in the *Tadić* decision, there is a body of customary war crimes law, applicable to both types of conflicts, that goes beyond what has been included in the Rome Statute.

As with many of the activities that amount to crimes against humanity, many war crimes would also amount to domestic crimes, and domestic crimes also occur in times of armed conflict and occupation. As a result, for conduct to amount to a war crime, there has to be a 'nexus' to the armed conflict. The ICTY has explained the position as follows: 'what distinguishes a war crime from a purely domestic offence is that a war crime is shaped by and dependent upon the environment—the armed conflict—in which it was committed.'[54] This means that:

The armed conflict need not have been causal to the commission of the crime, but the existence of an armed conflict must, at a minimum, have played a substantial part in the perpetrator's ability to commit it, his decision to commit it, the manner in which it was committed or the purpose for which it was committed . . .[55]

---

[52] The ICTY also has jurisdiction over this, as it interpreted Article 3 of its Statute to cover all applicable humanitarian law in force during the Yugoslav wars of dissolution, *Tadić* Appeal, paras 86–93.

[53] RC/Res 5 (10 June 2010).   [54] *Kunarac* Appeal, para 58.   [55] Ibid, paras 58–9.

As such, conduct such as a brawl that occurs in an occupied territory is not a war crime simply because of the fact that it occurs in that situation.

D. AGGRESSION

Aggression was first prosecuted (as 'Crimes Against Peace') before the Nuremberg IMT. The prosecution proceeded on the basis of Article 6(a) of the Nuremberg IMT Charter, which criminalized 'planning, preparation, initiating or waging of a war of aggression, or a war in violation of international treaties, agreements or assurances, or participation in a common plan or conspiracy for any of the foregoing'. That Article (to which Article 5(a) of the Tokyo IMT's Statute essentially conforms) does not provide a definition of aggression. It is also highly doubtful that aggression was criminal prior to the war; although the Kellogg-Briand pact rendered recourse to non-defensive force unlawful, it did not contain any hint of criminal responsibility for its breach (Schwarzenberger, 1947, pp 346–8). That did not stop those tribunals (and other post-War courts) from convicting people of that offence.

Unfortunately neither the Nuremberg or Tokyo IMTs (nor the later Control Council Law 10 trials) provided a direct definition of aggression, although all made determinations of whether or not particular conflicts were aggressive or not, thus giving sufficient evidence from which to induct a customary definition.[56] However, the project for a permanent international criminal court stalled in the 1950s in part owing to disagreements about the definition of aggression. Even after the General Assembly created a definition of the concept (not necessarily the crime) of aggression in 1974 in Resolution 3314, this did not settle the question. None of the ICTY, ICTR, or SCSL were given jurisdiction over aggression. The matter was deeply controversial in the negotiations for the Rome Statute. As a result Article 5(1) of the Rome Statute included aggression as a crime in the jurisdiction of the ICC. But Article 5(2) declares that the ICC may not exercise jurisdiction over the crime of aggression unless and until a definition is included by an amendment to the Statute. In spite of the difficulties in finding agreement, the 2010 Kampala Review Conference of the Rome Statute adopted an amendment to the Statute containing a definition of aggression (Kreβ and Barriga, 2017).

The definition is 'the planning, preparation, initiation or execution, by a person in a position effectively to exercise control over or to direct the political or military action of a State, of an act of aggression which, by its character, gravity and scale, constitutes a manifest violation of the Charter of the United Nations'.[57] This is supplemented by a set of acts of aggression drawn from Resolution 3314.

Some of the aspects of this definition, such as that the perpetrator must be in a high leadership position, are relatively uncontroversial (although see Heller, 2007). However, others, such as what amounts to a 'manifest' violation of the UN Charter, or what 'gravity, character and scale' mean and how they interrelate, are the subject of controversy (Special Issue, 2012). Other issues relating to specific aspects of the definition remain deeply contested (Kreβ and Barriga, 2017).

In part, but not only because of this, the ICC, when it was created, was initially unable to exercise its statutory jurisdiction over aggression. The controversies in the area were deferred until the Assembly of States Party to the Rome Statute determined, pursuant to that Statute's Article 5(2), and its provisions relating to its revision (ie those in Article 121), that its jurisdiction over aggression was to be operationalized. These conditions were fulfilled in December 2017, when the Assembly activated the ICC's jurisdiction over aggression from July 2018. This

---

[56] *R v Jones et al* [2006] UKHL 16, para 19.   [57] RC/Res 6 (10 June 2010), (Article 8*bis*).

is, however, in a manner that differs from the other crimes over which the ICC has jurisdiction, absent a Security Council referral of the matter to the Court, only when both the alleged victim and aggressor States have ratified the Kampala amendments on aggression.[58]

III. PRINCIPLES OF LIABILITY AND DEFENCES

International law also provides for principles of liability and defences (see generally van Sliedregt, 2012). Many of them, such as aiding, abetting, duress, and self-defence, will be familiar to those who have a grounding in domestic criminal law.[59] However, international law does have a number of specialized forms of liability and defences that are worthy of note, although they have been criticized on the basis that they do not have strong doctrinal foundations (Fletcher, 2012). On the liability side, these are joint criminal enterprise, co-perpetration, and command responsibility. For defences, superior orders are controversial.

A. JOINT CRIMINAL ENTERPRISE

It is a characteristic of many (although not all) international crimes that they tend to be committed by groups of people, some of whom are remote from the actual scene of the commission of the actual crime. As a result, the ICTY has adopted a theory of liability, claimed to exist in customary law, of joint criminal enterprise. The *actus reus* is made up of three aspects, set out authoritatively in the *Tadić* case as being:

   i. A plurality of persons.
   ii. The existence of a common plan, design or purpose which amounts to or involves the commission of a crime provided for in the Statute.
   iii. Participation of the accused in the common design involving the perpetration of one of the crimes provided for in the Statute.[60]

The *mens rea* is an intention that the group commit the crime or, more controversially,

> the *intention* to participate in and further the criminal activity or the criminal purpose of a group and to contribute to the joint criminal enterprise or in any event to the commission of a crime by the group. In addition, responsibility for a crime other than the one agreed upon in the common plan arises only if, under the circumstances of the case, (i) it was *foreseeable* that such a crime might be perpetrated by one or other members of the group and (ii) the accused *willingly took that risk*.[61]

The last part, often known as 'type three' joint criminal enterprise, expands liability a long way, although it is noteworthy that it still requires a subjective mental element. This, alongside the fact that the direct perpetrators of the offences do not have to be a part of the joint criminal enterprise, ensures that the doctrine provides for liability of policy-makers, but also renders the doctrine, for some, to be excessively broad and vague.[62] Given the closure of the ad hoc tribunals, and the scepticism of the ICC towards using (at least directly) the outer ambits of such a form of liability, it is quite possible that the edges of this form of liability may evanesce.

---

[58] Draft Resolution on the Activation of the Jurisdiction of the International Criminal Court over the Crime of Aggression, ICC-ASP/16/L.10 14 December 2017. The Resolution was adopted by consensus on that date. There are, as of December 2017, 35 parties to the amendment. On jurisdiction see also Article 15*bis*,15*ter*.
[59] See ICC Statute, Articles 25 and 31.   [60] *Tadić* Appeal, para 227.   [61] Ibid, para 228.
[62] See, eg, Ohlin, 2007; Danner and Martinez, 2005; although for a contrary view see Cassese, 2007.

756 ROBERT CRYER

B. CO-PERPETRATION

It is notable that the ICC has not adopted joint criminal enterprise in the way the ICTY has. They have, instead, relied on 'co-perpetration', including 'indirect perpetration' (where the perpetration is done through other people). This form of liability, which is said to have its basis in Article 25(3)(a) rather than customary law,[63] has two objective aspects, and three subjective ones.

The objective aspects are the existence of an explicit or implicit agreement or common plan between the co-perpetrators and a coordinated essential contribution by the suspect for the commission of the objective elements of the crime.[64] This contribution can be made through control of a hierarchically structured organization in which interchangeable subordinates can be relied upon to carry out orders.[65]

In relation to *mens rea*, it is necessary that the defendant has the *mens rea* of the relevant offence, the co-perpetrators realize that the common plan will result in that crime,[66] and the defendant is aware of the circumstances that allow them to jointly control the crime.[67] This is similar to, but narrower than, joint criminal enterprise. The basis of liability that has been adopted for co-perpetration, joint control of the crime, has been the subject of considerable critique[68] (Ohlin, Sliedeght, and Wiegend, 2013; Jain, 2014), not least as a number of opinions of the ICC have relied specifically on doctrinal studies from one jurisdiction (Germany).

C. COMMAND/SUPERIOR RESPONSIBILITY

Command responsibility is the liability of those who have effective control over subordinates for offences committed by such persons, where they failed to prevent or punish them. It received its modern judicial confirmation in the *Yamashita* case in 1945.[69] The current treaty-based statement of this principle of liability comes in Article 28 of the Rome Statute, which does not entirely reflect custom. Article 28 reads:

(a) A military commander or person effectively acting as a military commander shall be criminally responsible for crimes within the jurisdiction of the Court committed by forces under his or her effective command and control, or effective authority and control as the case may be, as a result of his or her failure to exercise control properly over such forces, where:

(i) That military commander or person either knew or, owing to the circumstances at the time, should have known that the forces were committing or about to commit such crimes; and

(ii) That military commander or person failed to take all necessary and reasonable measures within his or her power to prevent or repress their commission or to submit the matter to the competent authorities for investigation and prosecution.

---

[63] ICTY Appeals Chamber, *Prosecutor v Stakić*, Judgment, Case No IT-97-24-A, 22 March 2006, para 62.

[64] ICC Pre-Trial Chamber I, *Prosecutor v Lubanga*, Decision on the Confirmation of Charges, Case No ICC-01/04–01/06, 29 January 2007, paras 343–8 (hereafter cited as '*Lubanga*, confirmation of charges').

[65] ICC Pre-Trial Chamber, *Prosecutor v Katanga and Ngudjolo*, Decision on the Confirmation of Charges, Case No ICC-01/04–01/07, 30 September 2008, paras 500–10.

[66] ICC Pre-Trial Chamber II, *Prosecutor v Bemba Gombo*, Decision on the Confirmation of Charges, Case No ICC-01/05–01/08, 15 June 2009, paras 352–69 (hereafter cited as '*Bemba Gombo*').

[67] *Lubanga*, confirmation of charges, paras 349–67.

[68] *Prosecutor v Lubanga*, Judgment Pursuant to Article 74 of the Statute, Case No ICC-01/04–01/06, 14 March 2012, Separate Opinion of Judge Fulford; *Prosecutor v Ngudjolo Chui*, Judgment Pursuant to Article 74 of the Statute, Case No ICC-01/04–02/12, 18 December 2012, Concurring Opinion of Judge van den Wyngaert. For support of this approach see Wirth, 2012.   [69] *US v Yamashita* 327 US 1 (1945).

(b) With respect to superior and subordinate relationships not described in paragraph (a), a superior shall be criminally responsible for crimes within the jurisdiction of the Court committed by subordinates under his or her effective authority and control, as a result of his or her failure to exercise control properly over such subordinates, where:

    (i) The superior either knew, or consciously disregarded information which clearly indicated, that the subordinates were committing or about to commit such crimes;

    (ii) The crimes concerned activities that were within the effective responsibility and control of the superior; and

    (iii) The superior failed to take all necessary and reasonable measures within his or her power to prevent or repress their commission or to submit the matter to the competent authorities for investigation and prosecution.

The ICTY has elaborated the requirements of command responsibility under customary law. These are a superior/subordinate relationship; the 'mental element'; and a failure to take reasonable measures to prevent or punish international crimes.[70] The Rome Statute also requires that a failure of the defendant's command had a causal relationship to the commission of the crimes.

The superior/subordinate relationship is characterized, for both military and civilian superiors, as being 'effective control', although it is accepted that the manner in which such control is exercised may differ between those superiors. Effective control means 'a material ability to prevent or punish criminal conduct', alongside a formal, or informal hierarchy.[71] A legal position is unnecessary, but may be useful evidence of effective control.[72]

The mental element of command responsibility is a matter of contention. Early cases, such as *Yamashita,* took the view that it was sufficient that the defendant 'knew, or should have known', of the offences. The ICTY, however, interpreted the standard in its Statute (Article 7(3)) that the defendant knew, or had reason to know, of the offences, as being:

> where: (1) he had actual knowledge, established through direct or circumstantial evidence, that his subordinates were committing or about to commit crimes . . . or (2) where he had in his possession information of a nature, which at the least, would put him on notice of the risk of such offences by indicating the need for additional investigation in order to ascertain whether such crimes were committed or were about to be committed by his subordinates.[73]

This standard is the one accepted by later cases both in the ICTY and ICTR;[74] it is somewhat narrower than the 'should have known' standard, and, in the view of many, customary law (eg Kolb, 2000, p 301). The ICC, with respect to military superiors, has taken the view that the 'should have known' standard in Article 28 of the Rome Statute is broader, including negligent failures to obtain information, something not covered by the ICTY's formula.[75] The Rome Statute does, for the first time, expressly distinguish military and civilian superiors. The *mens rea* for civilian superiors, that they 'knew, or consciously disregarded information that clearly indicated' that offences occurred, or were going to, is a novelty in international law, and not necessarily a welcome one.

---

[70] ICTY Trial Chamber II, *Prosecutor v Delalić, Mučić, Delić and Landžo,* Judgment, Case No IT-96–21-T, 16 November 1998, para 344 (known as, and hereafter cited as, '*Čelebići*').

[71] ICTY Appeals Chamber, *Prosecutor v Delalić, Mučić, Delić and Landžo* Judgment, Case No IT-96–23-A, 20 February 2001, para 256 (known as, and hereafter cited as, '*Čelebići* Appeal'). See generally Mettraux, 2009.

[72] *Čelebići* Appeal, para 197.   [73] Ibid, paras 223 and 241.   [74] *Blaškić* Appeal, paras 58–64.

[75] *Bemba Gombo,* paras 432–4.

What the precise measures that the superior has to take in relation to subordinates have been said by the ICTY to be those which:

> can be taken within the competence of a commander as evidenced by the degree of effective control he wielded over his subordinates . . . What constitutes such measures is not a matter of substantive law but of evidence.[76]

Relevant evidence on this point, according to the ICC, building upon ICTY jurisprudence, includes activities:

> (i) to ensure that superior's forces are adequately trained in international humanitarian law; (ii) to secure reports that military actions were carried out in accordance with international law; (iii) to issue orders aiming at bringing the relevant practices into accord with the rules of war; (iv) to take disciplinary measures to prevent the commission of atrocities by the troops under the Superior's command.[77]

When it comes to punishment, it is possible that the superior is unable to punish the person personally. Where this is the case it can be sufficient that the superior 'submit[s] the matter to the competent authorities for investigation and prosecution'.[78]

As mentioned earlier in this section, the ICC Statute adds a requirement that the offences occur as a result of the superior's failure to exercise control. This creates a difficult issue relating to causation (Robinson, 2012). The ICTY has consistently rejected such a requirement;[79] the Rome Statute, however, is clear on the point. The ICC, has, nonetheless, done its best to minimize this requirement, by saying that:

> There is no direct causal link that needs to be established between the superior's omission and the crime committed by his subordinates. Therefore, the Chamber considers that it is only necessary to prove that the commander's omission increased the risk of the commission of the crimes charged in order to hold him criminally responsible under Article 28(a) of the Statute.[80]

This requirement also relates to the nature of command responsibility. Early case law considered it a form of liability for the underlying crimes (Meloni, 2007, pp 621–3); however, amongst the judges in the ICTY, there is an increasing view that command responsibility is a *sui generis* form of liability, in that '[c]ommand responsibility imposes responsibility on a commander for failure to take corrective action in respect of a crime committed by another; it does not make the commander party to the crime committed by that other.'[81] This is deeply contested (Meloni, 2007; Shahabuddeen, 2012, pp 213–16; Robinson, 2012), but nonetheless has implications for the ambit of command responsibility, as the ICTY accepted, in particular in relation to the question of whether a commander could be responsible for failing to punish offences that occurred prior to the superior taking up post.

D. DEFENCES

Defences are sometimes a taboo amongst international criminal lawyers (Eser, 1996, p 251). However, the defences that are applicable to international crimes, such as self-defence, duress, necessity, insanity, and intoxication,[82] are similar to those in most

---

[76] *Blaškić* Appeal, para 72.   [77] *Bemba Gombo*, para 438.

[78] Rome Statute, Articles 28(a)(ii) and 28(b)(iii).

[79] ICTY Appeals Chamber, *Prosecutor v Hadžihasanović and Kubura*, Judgment, Case No IT-01-47-A, 22 April 2008, para 39 (hereafter cited as '*Hadžihasanović* Appeal').

[80] *Bemba Gombo*, paras 424–5.

[81] *Hadžihasanović* Appeal, Judge Shahabuddeen, para 33. See also ICTY Appeals Chamber, *Prosecutor v Orić*, Judgment, Case No IT-03-68-A, 3 July 2008.   [82] See ICC Statute, Article 31.

domestic systems.[83] The defence that has caused most comment in international criminal law is obedience to superior orders.[84] The first major international document dealing with superior orders was the Nuremberg IMT's Charter, Article 8 of which excluded reliance on the defence, a position that was questionably consonant with the pre-existing customary position. However, the defence was also excluded in the Tokyo IMT's Statute (Article 7). The ICTY (Article 7(4)), ICTR (Article 6(4)), and SCSL (Article 6(4)) Statutes also exclude the defence. The ICC Statute, on the other hand, permits the defence in narrow circumstances for war crimes (Article 33), as follows:

1. The fact that a crime within the jurisdiction of the Court has been committed by a person pursuant to an order of a Government or of a superior, whether military or civilian, shall not relieve that person of criminal responsibility unless:
   (a) The person was under a legal obligation to obey orders of the Government or the superior in question;
   (b) The person did not know that the order was unlawful; and
   (c) The order was not manifestly unlawful.

2. For the purposes of this article, orders to commit genocide or crimes against humanity are manifestly unlawful.

The provision is quite tightly drafted, and all three conditions (that the person was under a duty to obey orders, that they did not know it was unlawful, and that it was not manifestly unlawful) have to be fulfilled before the defence may be relied on. Not all issues are entirely clear; for example, like earlier formulations this provision does not clarify to whom the illegality must be manifest. The customary status of Article 33 is contested (Gaeta, 1999; Garraway, 1999).

IV. PROSECUTION OF INTERNATIONAL CRIMES

A. THE NUREMBERG AND TOKYO IMTS[85]

Prosecutorial responses to international crimes have occurred at both the national and international levels, with varying degrees of success. The first international tribunal was the Nuremberg IMT, which sat between 1945 and 1946 to prosecute high-ranking Nazis. It was set up by France, the UK, the USA, and the USSR. Pursuant to Article 6 of its Charter, the Tribunal had jurisdiction over crimes against peace (aggression), crimes against humanity, and war crimes. Articles 9 and 10 of the Charter also permitted it to make declarations of criminality against organizations, which would permit domestic prosecutions of their members for that membership. Six such organizations were prosecuted (the SS, SD, SA, High Command, Leadership Corps of the Nazi party, and the Gestapo) alongside 24 individuals. They were chosen for their representative nature of the Nazi party, the Army, the Navy, and civilian supporters of the regime. The most famous of the defendants was Hermann Göring.

Three of the indicted organizations were acquitted (the SA, High Command, and Leadership Corps). Three of the defendants (Hjalmar Schacht, Hans Fritzsche, and Franz von Papen) were also acquitted. All the other defendants were convicted, although not of all charges laid against them. The judgment is a seminal document in international

---

[83] One difference to UK law though is that duress is not a priori excluded for intentional killings (Article 31(d)), although the ICTY has, by a bare majority, taken a different view: ICTY Appeals Chamber, *Prosecutor v Erdemović*, Judgment, Case No IT-96-22-A, 7 October 1997.   [84] See, eg, Dinstein, 1965.

[85] See, eg, Taylor, 1993; Boister and Cryer, 2008.

criminal law, and, although not without its flaws, the trial process was basically fair. There were critiques of the Nuremberg Trial, many of which focus on the crimes against peace charge, which was novel in 1945 (Schwarzenberger, 1947, pp 346–8), and the fact that allegations of war crimes by Allied forces were not heard. This latter claim has some validity, but this is not generally thought to entirely undermine the legitimacy of the Nuremberg Trial.

There was a lesser-known counterpart to Nuremberg in Tokyo, designed to prosecute the leaders of martial Japan. It was set up by Australia, Canada, China, India, France, the Netherlands, New Zealand, the Philippines, the UK, the USA, and the USSR, all of whom appointed one judge. Article 5 of the Tokyo IMT's Charter gave the Tribunal jurisdiction over crimes against peace, crimes against humanity, and war crimes. The indictment charged 28 Japanese leaders, both military and civilian, with crimes against peace, war crimes, and murder. These last charges were based on the prosecution's theory that killings in aggressive wars were not covered by belligerent privilege, and were therefore, simply, murder. The Tribunal considered these charges as overlapping with the crimes against peace charges, so did not pronounce on their validity.[86]

The majority judgment, which was delivered in 1948, largely followed the Nuremberg judgment on issues of law such as the criminality of crimes against peace and the exclusion of superior orders,[87] but, also dealt with command responsibility, including of civilians.[88] It found a large-scale conspiracy on the part of the defendants (all of whom who lived through to the judgment were convicted, although not of all counts) to dominate Asia as far back as 1928, and various war crimes. The judgment was not unanimous, though, and there were various separate and dissenting opinions. One of the judges, Judge Bernard (France), thought that the proceedings were so flawed that he could not determine the charges against the defendants.[89] Judge Jaranilla, on the other hand, was of the view that the Tribunal had been too lenient both in terms of the charges that were not pronounced upon, and the sentences imposed.[90] Judge Webb, who presided over the trial, used his opinion to criticize the absence of the Emperor of Japan from the dock.[91]

Judge Röling doubted the existence of a crime against peace in international law at the time, but argued that those responsible for such offences could lawfully be interned in the interests of international security.[92] He also raised factual doubts about some of the convictions.[93] The largest, and most famous, dissent was that of the Indian justice, Judge Pal. Pal denied the existence of crimes against peace,[94] found that there was no conspiracy,[95] and found that none of the war crimes found were attributable to the defendants.[96] He would have acquitted them all, and accused the prosecuting States of hypocrisy owing to their colonialism and use of the atomic bomb.[97] The critiques of the Tokyo IMT are similar to those of the Nuremberg IMT, although there has also been significant, and not unjustifiable, criticism of the running of the trial.[98]

B. THE ICTY AND ICTR (1993–2017)[99]

There were no international proceedings after the Nuremberg and Tokyo IMTs until after the end of the Cold War. Then in 1993 the Security Council, responding to atrocities in the former Yugoslavia, created the ICTY under its powers under Chapter VII of the UN

---

[86] Tokyo IMT Judgment, p 48,449.   [87] Ibid, pp 48,437–48,439.   [88] Ibid, pp 48,443–48,447.
[89] Dissenting Opinion of the Member from France, pp 18–23.
[90] Concurring Opinion of the Member from the Philippines, pp 7–10, 32–5.
[91] Separate Opinion of the President, pp 18–20.
[92] Opinion of the Member for the Netherlands, pp 10–53.   [93] Ibid, pp 178–249.
[94] Dissenting Opinion of the Member for India, Parts 1 and 2.   [95] Ibid, Part 4.   [96] Ibid, Part 6.
[97] Ibid, Recommendation.   [98] On such critiques, see Boister and Cryer, 2008, ch 4.
[99] See generally Schabas, 2006.

Charter, in Resolution 827 (25 May 2003).[100] The Tribunal was granted jurisdiction over grave breaches of the Geneva Conventions (ICTY Statute, Article 2), other war crimes (Article 3), crimes against humanity (Article 4), and genocide (Article 5) committed in former Yugoslavia since 1 January 1991. The ICTY had primacy over national courts.[101] This means that the Tribunal may require States to defer any proceedings they were contemplating or undertaking to it.[102] The Chapter VII basis of the Tribunals meant that as a matter of law, the Tribunal may also order, as a matter of law, any UN member State to cooperate with the Tribunal.[103]

The early practice of the ICTY was hampered by the refusal to cooperate of a number of the ex-Yugoslav States. Of those States, only the central government in Bosnia was supportive of the ICTY. Owing to a general, although not universal, lack of cooperation, early cases at the court tended to be of low-ranking soldiers, which caused criticism (Verrijn Stuart and Simons, 2009, p 53). These early cases did, however, allow the ICTY to considerably develop their processes and also international law, in particular in the *Tadić* case.[104] By 2001, though, the political situation had altered such that significant (albeit not perfect) cooperation had been obtained from all parties.

One of the problems that occurred to the various stakeholders around this time was that it was realized that in the heady days of 1993, not all long-term impacts had been fully thought through, By the turn of the millennium, the judges realized that their work could take at least 15 more years. As a result they asked the Security Council to ensure a 'completion strategy' to speed up its processes (which may not have always been effective). The Tribunal issued its final Appeals Judgment in November 2017,[105] and formally closed its doors at the end of 2017. Now any further appeals (of which there are a small, but important,[106] number) will be dealt with by what is known as the residual mechanism (shared between the ICTY and ICTR), which is a skeletal version of the Tribunals it replaces and is also known by its acronym MICT (Symposium 2011), and which will also serve to supervise sentences, parole, and deal with any new facts that come to light and lead to appeals against conviction (see also Mulgrew, 2013). The ICTY itself has set out a number of its achievements.[107] These are, *inter alia,* that it has promoted accountability rather than impunity, including of leaders; established the facts of the crimes in former Yugoslavia; brought justice to victims and given them a voice; developed international law; and strengthened the rule of law. The Tribunal has, to some extent, fulfilled these goals, although critiques of the Tribunals suggest that they are neither quick nor cheap (Zacklin, 2004, pp 543–4). Shortly after the creation of the ICTY, the Security Council created the ICTR, to prosecute international crimes committed in Rwanda in 1994. Notably, Rwanda was at the time a non-permanent member of the Security Council. Although it was initially supportive of the creation of the ICTR, owing to the refusal of other members to include the death penalty in the sentencing regime of the Court, it voted against the Resolution that established the Court.[108] The ICTR has jurisdiction over genocide (ICTR

---

[100] The legality of this was doubted by some (Rubin, 1994) but confirmed by the ICTY in the *Tadić* Appeal.
[101] ICTY Statute, Article 9(1).
[102] Eg *In the Matter of a Proposal for a Formal Request for Deferral to the Competence of the Tribunal Addressed to the Republic of Bosnia and Herzegovina in Respect of Radovan Karadzic, Ratko Mladic and Mico Stanisic*, IT-95-5-D, Trial Chamber (16 May 1995).   [103] ICTY Statute, Article 28.
[104] *Tadić* Appeal.
[105] *Prosecutor* v *Prlić et al*, Judgment, IT-04-74,-A, (29 November 2017). As an aside, the judgment was somewhat overshadowed by the very public suicide of one of the defendants, Slobodan Praljak, just after his sentence was confirmed.   [106] The Appeals of Radovan Karadzić and Ratko Mladić remain to be determined.
[107] http://www.icty.org/sid/324.   [108] SC Res 955 (8 November 1994).

Statute, Article 2), crimes against humanity (Article 3), and some war crimes—violations of common Article 3 and Additional Protocol II (Article 4). It has the same powers in relation to primacy and cooperation as the ICTY. They also have a joint appeals chamber, to ensure consistency of their jurisprudence.[109]

Unlike the early practice of the ICTY, some African States were quick to cooperate with the ICTR, although Rwanda was not always amongst them. This was a problem, as most of the evidence and witnesses, and many of the suspects, were in Rwanda. The ICTR was, initially, slow to move, there were staffing problems, and a damning report on the management and administration of the ICTR in 1997 was highly damaging.

Things appeared to improve in 1998, when the ex-Prime Minister of Rwanda, Jean Kambanda, pleaded guilty to genocide, admitting that this had occurred in Rwanda. The first trial, of a Mayor, Jean-Paul Akayesu, proceeded to judgment in September 1998. 1999 proved more difficult. In protest at a decision of the Appeals Chamber in the *Barayagwiza* case to release a defendant whose human rights had been violated in pre-trial detention in Cameroon,[110] Rwanda refused to cooperate with the ICTR at all. This practically caused trials to stop. The Appeals Chamber revisited its decision in early 2000, and determined that Barayagwiza should remain in detention and be sent for trial.[111] Rwanda resumed cooperation as a result. Some have suggested that this showed the extent to which Rwanda was able to guide the practice of the Court (Schabas, 2000, p 565).

In 2003 the ICTR also was given a very similar completion strategy by the Security Council in the same Resolutions. The ICTR has now closed its doors, and the remaining cases and appeals are to be dealt with by the residual mechanism it shares with the ICTY or domestic courts. Unlike the ICTY, the ICTR has three high-ranking fugitives not yet in custody, which may render the role of the MICT highly important were they to be found. (The ICTY has no suspects that are at large.)

There have been criticisms of the ICTR for failing to prosecute possible offences committed by the Rwandan Patriotic Front (RPF), particularly in the aftermath of the genocide, and it has been suggested that this is because the RPF, having defeated the génocidaires in 1994, became the government of Rwanda, and controlled cooperation with the ICTR. The prosecutor argued, on the other hand, that the allegations are less serious than those against Hutu defendants and because of the completion strategy, there was no time to engage in prosecution of allegations against the RPF (Peskin, 2008, ch 8; Thalman, 2008, pp 1001–2). As such, some have questioned the impartiality of the ICTR (Peskin, 2008).

With both Tribunals now having now largely wound down, discussions have tended to turn to the legacy that they have left (Symposium, 2016). Whilst views may differ, and their output and practice may be the subject of both approbation and criticism, few could deny that they revived and reinvigorated international criminal law as a whole.

C. THE INTERNATIONAL CRIMINAL COURT (ICC)

Probably the most important development in international criminal law, at least since Nuremberg, was the creation of the ICC.[112] The ICC's Statute was finalized in 1998 in difficult negotiations in Rome. The ICC actually came into being in 2002, when the required 60 ratifications were obtained. There are currently 123 States parties to the ICC Statute.

---

[109] ICTR Statute, Article 12(2).

[110] ICTR Appeals Chamber, *Prosecutor* v *Barayagwiza*, Decision, ICTR-97–19-AR72, 19 November 1999.

[111] ICTR Appeals Chamber, *Prosecutor* v *Barayagwiza*, Decision (Prosecutor's Request for Review or Reconsideration) ICTR-97–19-AR72, 31 March 2000.

[112] See generally Triffterer and Ambos, 2016; Schabas, 2017.

The Court has jurisdiction over genocide, crimes against humanity, and a closed list of war crimes (ICC Statute, Articles 5–8).[113] The ICC also has jurisdiction over the crime of aggression. The Statute also contains a detailed treatment of the general principles of criminal law such as principles of liability and defences (Articles 25, 28, 30–3).

Other than for aggression (on which, see earlier) the jurisdiction of the Court is over crimes committed by nationals of States parties or on their territories (Article 12), or over any situation referred to it by the Security Council (Article 13(b)). The jurisdiction of the ICC is prospective; it began, for its States parties at that date, in 2002, when the Statute came into force (Article 11(1)). For States that were not parties then, unless they make a specific declaration that it may, the ICC can only exercise its jurisdiction in relation to the relevant offences committed after the entry into force of the Statute for them (Article 11(2)).

There are three ways for the prosecutor to initiate an investigation: the first is after the referral of the situation by a State party to the Rome Statute (Article 12(a)). Contrary to expectations, this provision has led to the practice of 'self referrals' where States refer the situations in their own territories to the ICC (Arsanjani and Reisman, 2005). This has happened, and there is nothing in law to prevent this, but there have been suggestions that in accepting such self-referrals, the ICC may become too close to governments who wish it to only prosecute crimes by rebels. The next method of the ICC beginning an investigation is that the prosecutor may, with the consent of a Pre-Trial Chamber, initiate an investigation on his own motion (Article 15). This was controversial at Rome, but has been invoked, *inter alia*, by the prosecutor in relation to post-election violence in Kenya, Georgia, and Afghanistan. All have proved controversial, but this does not necessarily render any decision on point unlawful, rather than, perhaps, impolitic. It ought to be remembered that the ICC, like all international criminal courts, operates at the cusp of international law and politics.

This is also shown by the fact that the Security Council also has the power to refer a situation anywhere in the world to the ICC (Article 13(b)). The Security Council has, contrary to expectation, done this twice: referring the situation in Darfur, Sudan, to the ICC in Resolution 1593 (31 March 2005) (see Cryer, 2006), and the Libyan situation in Resolution 1970 (26 February 2011). The Council has, however, been very wary of taking enforcement measures in support of the ICC and its orders. The Security Council has the power under Article 16 of the ICC Statute to require the prosecutor to defer investigation or prosecution for a one-year period that can be renewed indefinitely. Its practice under this Article, in Resolutions 1422 (12 July 2002) and 1487 (12 June 2003) were heavily criticized (Jain, 2005), although these Resolutions now seem to have been relegated to the annals of history, having not been renewed for some years now.

In contrast to the ICTY and ICTR, who enjoy primacy over national courts, the ICC's jurisdiction is said to be 'complementary' to domestic jurisdictions (Article 1).[114] This means that the ICC can only exercise jurisdiction where it determines that a competent national court is 'unwilling or unable genuinely' to prosecute a case itself (Article 17). Unwillingness is elaborated upon by Article 17(3):

(a) the proceedings were or are being undertaken or the national decision was made for the purpose of shielding the person concerned from criminal responsibility for crimes within the jurisdiction of the court referred to in Article 5;

---

[113] Owing to concerns about the possible limiting effect of the Statute's definitions on customary law, Article 10 of the Statute provides: '[n]othing in this Part shall be interpreted as limiting or prejudicing in any way existing or developing rules of international law for purposes other than this statute.'

[114] See generally Kleffner, 2008; Stahn and El-Zeidy, 2011.

    (b) there has been an unjustified delay in the proceedings which in the circumstances is inconsistent with an intent to bring the person concerned to justice;

    (c) the proceedings were not or are not being conducted independently or impartially, and they were or are being conducted in a manner which, in the circumstances, is inconsistent with an intent to bring the person concerned to justice.

Inability is the subject of Article 17(3), which reads: 'In order to determine inability in a particular case, the Court shall consider whether, due to a total or substantial collapse or unavailability of its national judicial system, the State is unable to obtain the accused or the necessary evidence and testimony or otherwise unable to carry out its proceedings.' The precise interpretation of these terms will be an important task for the Court. This is a process which is currently embryonic, although the Appeals Chamber has made clear that where there is inactivity by the relevant State, the case is admissible without the necessity of determining unwillingness or inability.[115] What has proved controversial is the definition of a 'case', or a 'situation' with respect to complementarity, and there have been suggestions that the ICC has not always been consistent in its interpretations of the, somewhat elastic, terms of Article 17 (Stahn and el-Zeidy, 2011).

D. REACTIONS TO THE CREATION AND PRACTICE OF THE ICC

Whilst the (probably vast) majority of commentators support the creation and existence of the ICC, there have been both legal and political critiques of the ICC. It is sometimes the case that the former reflect the latter. The main legal challenge, which was first raised by the US government, is the allegation that as the ICC can exercise its jurisdiction over nationals of non-State parties (where they commit international crimes on the territory of States parties), the Rome Statute violates international law (Scheffer, 1999, p 71; Newton, 2016; *contra*, Stahn, 2016; O'Keefe, 2016). The most sophisticated version of this critique does not deny that States can exercise their own territorial jurisdiction over non-nationals, but says they cannot delegate that power to an international organization (Morris, 2001, pp 26–52). However, there is no existing prohibition of this in international law (Akande, 2003, pp 625–34).

    Some of the early practice of the Court, in particular the fact that the situations before the ICC were initially all in Africa, has led to criticism from some quarters, alleging that the prosecutor is acting selectively by not confronting powerful (especially Western) countries (see generally Ambos, 2013). The Office of the Prosecutor has responded strongly, arguing that they are only applying the law, that the situations chosen are the most serious, and that the critique ignores African victims.[116] Whether the opening of investigations into situations outside Africa, such as into Georgia and Afghanistan (albeit not, as yet, leading to any indictments), will blunt such criticisms remains to be seen, but the African Union remains at best ambivalent to the Court.

---

[115] ICC Appeals Chamber, *Prosecutor v Katanga and Chui*, Judgment on the Appeal of Mr Germain Katanga against the Oral Decision of Trial Chamber II of 12 June 2009 on the Admissibility of the Case, Case No ICC-01/04–01/07, 25 September 2009, paras 1–2.

[116] Deputy Prosecutor's Remarks, 'Introduction to the Rome Statute Establishing the ICC and Africa's Involvement with the ICC', 14 April 2009.

E. 'INTERNATIONALIZED' AND NATIONAL COURTS

There are also a diverse group of courts which come under the heading of 'internationalized' courts.[117] Some, such as the SCSL and the Special Tribunal for Lebanon, are more akin to international courts than domestic courts, as their founding documents are treaties or Security Council resolutions rather than domestic legislation. Others, such as the Iraqi High Tribunal and the Extraordinary Chambers in the Courts of Cambodia, are far closer to ordinary domestic courts, as their jurisdiction was initially founded on domestic law; they simply have some form of international support, usually in the form of international staff. Each such court is rather different, both in the level of internationalization and jurisdiction. The SCSL, for example, was described by the Secretary-General as 'a treaty-based *sui generis* court of mixed jurisdiction and composition'.[118] It had jurisdiction over international crimes, such as crimes against humanity and some war crimes (SCSL Statute Articles 2–4) and domestic offences, such as arson (Article 5). The Special Tribunal for Lebanon, on the other hand, has jurisdiction over Lebanese domestic crimes only, although it uses international law principles of liability (STL Statute, Articles 2–3). The Iraqi High Tribunal and Extraordinary Chambers prosecute domestic crimes, but which are based on implementations of international criminal law. The diversity of these courts makes generalizations about them often unhelpful.

As the principle of complementarity attests to, the bulk of prosecutions of international crimes are intended to be in domestic courts. States are entitled to assert universal jurisdiction over genocide, crimes against humanity, and war crimes,[119] insofar as they are contrary to customary law (there may be some exceptions for parties to treaties that create war crimes that may not be customary, or where domestic definitions of the other crimes are broader than that which customary law accepts). However, in spite of a number of well-known trials, such as the *Eichmann* trial,[120] for the most part domestic courts have been slow to react to international crimes. Often political difficulties in the territorial or nationality jurisdiction impede prosecutions, and other States are unwilling to become involved, with the bulk of prosecutions being of Nazis, former Yugoslav, and Rwandan accused, where there is almost unanimous agreement on the need for prosecution (Langer, 2011). There are some signs that there is an increased willingness of domestic courts to prosecute international crimes. Part of the reason for this is a positive side-effect of the complementarity provisions of the ICC Statute, which create an incentive for domestic authorities to prosecute international crimes rather than see them prosecuted internationally. Nonetheless, the effect of the Rome Statute is still, it seems, to be taken by many State officials as a suggestion, rather than a requirement.

V. NON-PROSECUTORIAL RESPONSES TO INTERNATIONAL CRIMES

Although there is an increasing swing towards prosecution of international crimes, both historically and currently there are other methods of dealing with international crimes. The lawfulness of some of them are increasingly being contested, however; at least some of

---

[117] See generally, Cryer, Friman, Robinson, and Wilmshurst, 2014, ch 9. On their promise, see Dickinson, 2003. For a more sombre analysis, see McAuliffe, 2013. On the Special Court for Sierra Leone, see Jalloh, 2015.

[118] Report by the Secretary-General on the Establishment of a Special Court for Sierra Leone, UN Doc S/2000/915 (4 October 2000), para 9. [119] See Staker, Ch 10 of this book.

[120] *Attorney-General of the Government of Israel* v *Eichmann* (1961) 36 ILR 5.

them can be seen as complementary to prosecution, although others (such as amnesties) have to be seen as alternatives.

A. AMNESTIES

Amnesties are conferred by a law that blocks criminal action against people in the State in which it is passed. At the end of a conflict, the practice was frequently, at least until recently, to offer an amnesty to all of those who committed crimes. They were very controversial in the 1980s when various military regimes granted themselves amnesties, or required them as a condition for handing over power. The most well-known amnesty offered in the recent past was that in South Africa, following truth and reconciliation proceedings after the end of apartheid.

There are various types of amnesties,[121] which go from those granted by regimes to themselves to those which are voted upon by the population. Although the latter are usually thought more legitimate than the former, it must also be said that often there is little practical choice for the electorate.[122] A further distinction must be made between 'blanket' amnesties, which prevent legal proceedings against all persons without distinction, and those, such as the South African amnesty legislation, which required certain conduct (often full confession of crimes) and/or certain motivations for the crimes (usually political ones) before an amnesty was granted. The latter seem to obtain a greater level of support.

The legality of amnesties is hotly contested. There are those who argue that amnesties are inevitably unlawful (Orentlicher, 1991). These arguments tend to rely on either human rights concerns, or the assertion that there is an all-encompassing duty to prosecute international crimes. It is true that there are certain treaties that impose a duty to prosecute certain international crimes, such as the Geneva Conventions grave breaches regime (eg Geneva Convention 1, Article 49), the Genocide Convention (Articles IV, VI), and the Torture Convention (Article 5). However, these do not cover, for example, crimes against humanity or war crimes other than grave breaches. Therefore, authors supporting the existence of this duty tend to revert to customary law. However, there is not sufficient State practice yet to assert that customary law imposes a duty to prosecute all international crimes, and certainly not on the basis of universal jurisdiction.[123]

Looking to the human rights arguments, The Inter-American Court of Human Rights and Commission have been the most strident in declaring amnesties unlawful:

> [A]ll amnesty provisions, provisions on prescription and the establishment of measures designed to eliminate responsibility are inadmissible, because they are intended to prevent the investigation and punishment of those responsible for serious human rights violations such as torture, extrajudicial, summary or arbitrary execution and forced disappearance, all of them prohibited because they violate non-derogable rights recognized by international human rights law.[124]

However, it is by no means clear that this is reflective of a more general principle of human rights law, and probably has much to do with the particular context of Latin America

---

[121] For a detailed survey see Mallinder, 2008.   [122] Osiel, 1997, p 138.
[123] SCSL Appeals Chamber, *Prosecutor v Kallon and Kamara*, Decision on Challenge to Jurisdiction: Lomé Amnesty Accord, SCSL-2004–15-AR72(E) and SCSL-2004–16-AR72(E), 13 March 2004, para 82. But see Akhavan, 2010.
[124] Inter American Court of Human Rights, *Chumbipuma Aguirre* et al v *Peru (Barrios Altos Case)*, Judgment, 14 March 2001 Series C No 75, [2001] IACHR 5, para 41. See Binder, 2011.

and the fact that the Peruvian amnesty under discussion was granted by a regime to itself in a developed State.[125] The other regional human rights courts, and the Human Rights Committee have not gone so far as the inter-American Court, and so despite the fact that the scope for lawful amnesties appears to be narrowing, it has not been completely removed.[126] Where offences are subject to the jurisdiction of other States (on the basis of universal or more limited jurisdiction in international law, or before an international tribunal), any domestic law amnesty is simply inapplicable, as a matter of basic international law. As such, although it may be questioned whether amnesties are consistent with international law, they merely domestic acts, therefore do not bind other States who lawfully have jurisdiction over the conduct which has been immunized, and, owing to the fact that liability arises for such conduct under international law, it does not lie within the grant of any single State to exempt any person of such liability.

B. TRUTH AND RECONCILIATION COMMISSIONS

A frequently used response to international crimes is a truth and reconciliation commission (TRC). These have been defined as bodies that '(1) focus on the past, rather than ongoing, events; (2) investigate a pattern of events that took place over a period of time; (3) engage directly and broadly with the affected population, gathering information on their experiences; (4) are temporary bodies, with the aim of concluding with a final report; and (5) are officially authorized by the State under review' (Hayner, 2011, pp 11–12). One of the most famous of these was the South African TRC. However, there have also been TRCs in, for example, Guatemala, Liberia, and Sierra Leone. In the latter case, difficulties were encountered, as there were also proceedings ongoing before the SCSL, and the TRC wanted testimony from some of those indicted before the Tribunal. This led to tensions as the Special Court was unwilling to allow this on the terms the Commission wanted.[127]

The success or otherwise of TRCs depends on various factors, including the terms of reference that they have and the personal qualities of the commissioners. A great deal depends on the quality of the information that they can obtain. This can be difficult, as perpetrators are unlikely to be willing to fully confess their activities without some promise of amnesty or immunity, and victims may be unwilling to talk about sensitive matters. Although sometimes the hearings can be cathartic affairs, this is not always the case, and some victims are not satisfied with truth without more. It has also been questioned whether truth-telling does lead to reconciliation (Hayner, 2011, ch 13). Similarly, it has been doubted if truth and reconciliation are congruent goals. Most take the view that there is a relationship, albeit though, one which can be tense (2011, ch 13).

C. OTHER RESPONSES

One way in which some countries have dealt with large-scale criminality is by lustration, which is the compulsory removal of people from their jobs.[128] This is usually done on a mass, rather than individual, basis and as such has fallen from favour, as the innocent are punished alongside the guilty. There were elements of lustration involved in the de-Baathification of Iraq, which was, in itself, subject to criticism.

---

[125] Siebert-Fohr, 2009, p 109.
[126] SCSL Appeals Chamber, *Prosecutor v Kondewa*, Decision on Lack of Jurisdiction/Abuse of Process: Amnesty provided by the Lomé Accord, SCSL-2004-14-AR72(E) 25 May 2004, para 48: but see Bell, 2008, pp 240–1.   [127] *Report of the Truth and Reconciliation Commission for Sierra Leone*, vol 3b, ch 6.
[128] See generally Teitel, 2002, ch 5.

In some countries civil claims relating to international crimes are permitted. For example, there has been a series of civil suits in the USA against alleged human rights violators (including international criminals) under its Alien Tort Claims Act where their conduct occurred outside the USA. The first such case, *Filártiga* v *Peña-Irala*,[129] was considered groundbreaking in this regard, and has led to a large number of civil claims in US courts. However, more recent cases have put significant limitations on this line of authority,[130] in particular the extraterritorial applicability of the Act, which has been significantly curtailed.[131]

Whether these are sufficient is sometimes the subject of doubt, but in the absence of prosecutions such proceedings can find the facts and provide some measure of justice for victims, even if, where they occur outside the *locus delicti*, enforcing such awards can be very difficult. Immunities can also be a problem in third States where government behaviour is at issue. In many societies where there have been international crimes, there simply are insufficient resources to satisfy claims. In some societies, it is suggested that rather than prosecution, people ought to undergo culturally appropriate traditional justice mechanisms aimed at reconciliation rather than prosecution. Local justice mechanisms are supported by many, on the basis that they 'may have greater legitimacy and capacity than devastated formal systems, and they promise local ownership, access and efficiency' (Waldorf, 2006, p 4). However, critics of such a position have said that they can also be exclusionary and, in fact, authoritarian actors use such arguments, on a solely strategic basis (Drumbl, 2005, p 549). As is very often the case, a great deal depends on the particular process and its context, making sweeping acceptances or rejections of such measures ill-advised.

REFERENCES

AKANDE, D (2003), 'The Jurisdiction of the International Criminal Court Over Nationals of Non-Parties: Legal Basis and Limits', 1 *JICJ* 618.

AKHAVAN, P (2010), 'Whither National Courts? The Rome Statute's Missing Half: Towards an Express and Enforceable Obligation for the National Repression of International Crimes', 8 *JICJ* 1245.

AKHAVAN, P (2012), *Reducing Genocide to Law: Definition, Meaning and the Ultimate Crime* (Cambridge: Cambridge University Press).

AMBOS, K (2013), 'Expanding the Focus of the "African Criminal Court"', in WA Schabas, Y McDermott, and N Hayes (eds), *The Ashgate Research Companion to International Criminal Law: Critical Perspectives* (Farnham: Ashgate).

ARSANJANI, M and REISMAN, R, (2005), 'The Law-in-action of the International Criminal Court', 99 *AJIL* 385.

BASSIOUNI, MC (1994), 'Crimes Against Humanity: The Need for a Specialized Convention', 31 *Columbia Journal of Transnational Law* 457.

BASSIOUNI, MC (2011), *Crimes Against Humanity* (Cambridge: Cambridge University Press, 2011).

BELL, C (2008), *On the Law of Peace: Peace Agreements and the Lex Pacificatoria* (Oxford: Oxford University Press).

---

[129] *Filartiga* v *Peña-Irala*, 630 F2d 876 (2nd Cir 1980).
[130] Eg *Sosa* v *Alvarez-Machain* (2004) 542 US 692; although this may not have affected claims relating to allegations of international crimes.
[131] *Kiobel* v *Royal Dutch Petroleum Co*, 133 S Ct 1659 (2013). See 'Symposium' (2014).

BINDER, C (2011), 'The Prohibition of Amnesties by the Inter-American Court of Human Rights', 12 *German Law Journal* 1203.

BITTI, G (2015), 'Article 21 and the Hierarchy of Sources of Law Before the ICC' in C Stahn (ed), *The Law and Practice of the International Criminal Court* (Oxford: Oxford University Press).

BOISTER, N (2003), 'Transnational Criminal Law?', 14 *EJIL* 953.

BOISTER, N (2012), *An Introduction to Transnational Criminal Law* (Oxford: Oxford University Press).

BOISTER, N and CRYER, R (2008), *The Tokyo International Military Tribunal: A Reappraisal* (Oxford: Oxford University Press).

CASSESE, A (2007), 'The Proper Limits of Criminal Liability Under the Doctrine of Joint Criminal Enterprise', 5 *JICJ* 109.

CASSESE, A et al (2013), *Cassese's International Criminal Law* (Oxford: Oxford University Press).

CLARKE, KM (2009), *Fictions of Justice: The International Criminal Court and the Challenge of Legal Pluralism in Sub-Saharan Africa* (Cambridge: Cambridge University Press).

CRYER, R (2005), *Prosecuting International Crimes: Selectivity and the International Criminal Law Regime* (Cambridge: Cambridge University Press).

CRYER, R (2006), 'Sudan Resolution 1593 and International Criminal Justice', 19 *Leiden JIL* 195.

CRYER, R, FRIMAN, H, ROBINSON, D, and WILMSHURST, E (2014), *An Introduction to International Criminal Law and Procedure* (3rd edn, Cambridge: Cambridge University Press).

CULLEN, A (2011), 'War Crimes', in WA Schabas and N Bernaz (eds), *Routledge Handbook of International Criminal Law* (London: Routledge).

DANNER, AM and MARTINEZ, JS (2005), 'Guilty Associations: Joint Criminal Enterprise, Command Responsibility and the Development of International Criminal Law', 93 *California Law Review* 75.

DICKINSON, L (2003), 'The Promise of Hybrid Courts', 97 *AJIL* 295.

DINSTEIN, Y (1965), The Defence of 'Obedience to Superior Orders', in *International Criminal Law* (Leyden: A W Sijthoff).

DJURO-DEGAN, V (2005), 'On the Sources of International Criminal Law', 4 *Chinese JIL* 45.

DRUMBL, M (2005), 'Collective Violence and Individual Punishment: The Criminality of Mass Atrocity', 99 *Northwestern University Law Review* 539.

ESER, A (1996), 'Defences in War Crimes Trials' in Y Dinstein and M Tabory (eds), *War Crimes in International Law* (Dordrecht: Martinus Nijhoff), p 251.

FLETCHER, G (2012), 'The Theory of Criminal Liability and International Criminal Law', 10 *JICJ* 1029.

GAETA, P (1999), 'The Defence of Superior Orders: The Statute of the International Criminal Court Versus Customary International Law', 10 *EJIL* 172.

GALLANT, K (2008), *The Principle of Legality in International and Comparative Law* (Cambridge: Cambridge University Press).

GARRAWAY, C (1999), 'Superior Orders and the International Criminal Court: Justice Delivered or Justice Denied?', 836 *International Review of the Red Cross* 785.

GREENAWALT, AKA (1999), 'Rethinking Genocidal Intent: The Case for a Knowledge-Based Interpretation', 99 *Columbia Law Review* 2265.

HALLING, M (2010), 'Push The Envelope Watch It Bend: Removing the Policy Requirement and Extending Crimes Against Humanity', 23 *Leiden JIL* 829.

HAYNER, P (2011), *Unspeakable Truths: Confronting State Terror and Atrocity* (2nd edn, London: Routledge).

HELLER, KJ (2007), 'Retreat From Nuremberg: The Leadership Requirement in the Crime of Aggression', 18 *EJIL* 477.

Henckaerts, J-M, and Doswald-Beck, L (2005), *Customary International Humanitarian Law* (Cambridge: Cambridge University Press).

Jain, N (2005), 'A Separate Law for Peacekeepers; the Clash between the Security Council and the International Criminal Court', 16 *EJIL* 239.

Jain, N (2014), *Perpetrators and Accessories in International Criminal Law: Individual Modes of Liability for Collective Crimes* (Oxford: Hart Publishing).

Kelsall, T (2009), *Culture Under Cross-Examination: International Justice and the Special Court for Sierra Leone* (Cambridge: Cambridge University Press).

Kleffner, J (2008), *Complementarity in the Rome Statute and National Criminal Jurisdictions* (Oxford: Oxford University Press).

Kolb, R (2000), 'The Jurisprudence of the Yugoslav and Rwandan Criminal Tribunals on Their Jurisdiction and on International Crimes', 69 *BYIL* 259.

Kreβ, C (2010), 'On the Outer Limits of Crimes against Humanity: The Concept of Organization within the Policy Requirement: Some Reflections on the March 2010 ICC Kenya Decision', 23 *Leiden JIL* 855.

Kreβ, C (2015), 'International Criminal Law' in Wolfrum, R (ed). *Max Planck Encyclopaedia of Public International Law* (Oxford: Oxford University Press)

Kreβ, C and Barriga, S (2017), *The Crime of Aggression: A Commentary, Vols I-II,* (Cambridge: Cambridge University Press).

Langer, M (2011), 'The Diplomacy of Universal Jurisdiction: The Political Branches and the Transnational Prosecution of International Crimes', 105 *AJIL* 1.

Lemkin, R (1944), *Axis Rule in Occupied Europe* (New York: Carnegie Endowment for International Peace).

Luban, D (2006–7), 'Calling Genocide by Its Rightful Name: Lemkin's Word, Darfur, and the UN Report', 7 *Chicago JIL* 303.

Mallinder, L (2008), *Amnesty, Human Rights and Political Transitions: Bridging the Gap in International Law* (Oxford: Hart).

McAuliffe, P (2013), 'Hybrid Courts in Retrospect: Of Lost Legacies and Modest Futures', in Schabas, McDermott, and Hayes, *The Ashgate Research Companion to International Criminal Law.*

Meloni, C (2007), 'Command Responsibility: Mode of Liability for Subordinates or Separate Offence of the Superior?', 5 *JICJ* 619.

Mettraux, G (2008), *International Crimes and the* ad hoc *Tribunals* (Oxford: Oxford University Press).

Mettraux, G (2009), *The Law of Command Responsibility* (Oxford: Oxford University Press).

Milanovic, M (2011), 'Does the Rome Statute Bind Individuals? (And Why we Should Care)' 9 *JICJ* 25.

Milanovic, M (2012), 'Aggression and Legality', 10 *JICJ* 165.

Morris, M (2001), 'High Crimes and Misconceptions: The ICC and Non-Party States', 64 *Law and Contemporary Problems* 131.

Mulgrew, R (2013), *Towards the Development of the International Penal System* (Cambridge: Cambridge University Press).

Nersessian, DL (2010), *Genocide and Political Groups* (Oxford: Oxford University Press).

Newton, M (2016), 'How the International Criminal Court Threatens Treaty Norms', 49 *Vanderbilt Journal of Transnational Law* 371.

Ohlin, J (2007), 'Three Conceptual Problems with the Doctrine of Joint Criminal Enterprise', 5 *JICJ* 69.

O'Keefe, R. (2016), 'Quid, not Quantum: A Comment on "How the International Criminal Court Threatens Treaty Norms"', 49 *Vanderbilt Journal of Transnational Law* 433.

Ohlin, J, Van Sliedreght, E, and Weigend, T. (2013). 'Assessing the Control-Theory', 26 *Leiden JIL* 725.

OOSTERVELD, V (2001), 'Context of Genocide', in R Lee et al (eds), *The International Criminal Court: Elements of Crimes and Rules of Procedure and Evidence* (Ardsley: Transnational).

ORENTLICHER, D (1991), 'Settling Accounts: The Duty to Prosecute Violations of a Prior Regime', 100 *Yale Law Journal* 2537.

OSIEL, M (1997), *The International Criminal Court: Elements of Crimes and Rules of Procedure and Evidence* (Ardsley: Transnational).

PESKIN, V (2008), *International Justice in Rwanda and the Balkans: Virtual Trials and the Struggle for State Cooperation* (Cambridge: Cambridge University Press).

ROBINSON, D (2008), 'The Identity Crisis of International Criminal Law', 21 *Leiden JIL* 925.

ROBINSON, D (2012), 'How Command Responsibility Got So Complicated: A Culpability Contradiction, Its Obfuscation, and a Simple Solution', 12 *Melbourne JIL* 1.

ROBINSON, D (2015) 'Inescapable Dyads: Why the ICC Cannot Win', 28 *Leiden JIL* 323.

ROBINSON, G (1999), *Crimes Against Humanity: the Struggle for Global Justice* (London: Penguin).

RUBIN, A (1994), 'An International Criminal Tribunal for Former Yugoslavia', 6 *Pace International Law Review* 7.

SADAT, L (2007), 'The Effect of Amnesties Before Domestic and International Tribunals, Law, Morality, Politics', in E Hughes, W Schabas, and R Thakur (eds), *Atrocities and International Accountability: Beyond Transitional Justice* (Tokyo: UN University Press).

SADAT, L (ed) (2011), *Forging a Convention on Crimes Against Humanity* (Cambridge: Cambridge University Press).

SADAT, L (2013) 'Crimes Against Humanity in the Modern Era', 107 *AJIL* 334.

SADAT, L (2015) 'Genocide in Syria: International Legal Options, International Legal Limits, and the Serious Problem of Political Will', *Impunity Watch Law Journal* 1.

SANDOZ, Y, SWINIARSKI, C, and ZIMMERMANN, B (eds) (1987), *Commentary on the Additional Protocols of 8 June 1977* (Geneva: ICRC/Martinus Nijhoff).

SAUL, B (2006), *Defining Terrorism in International Law* (Oxford: Oxford University Press).

SAUL, B (2011), 'Legislating from a Radical Hague: The United Nations Special Tribunal for Lebanon Invents an International Crime of Transnational Terrorism', 24 *Leiden JIL* 677.

SCHABAS, W (2000), 'Prosecutor v. Barayagwiza', (2000) 94 *AJIL* 563.

SCHABAS, W (2006), *The UN International Criminal Tribunals: Yugoslavia, Rwanda, Sierra Leone* (Cambridge: Cambridge University Press).

SCHABAS, W (2008), 'The State Policy as an Element of International Crimes', 98 *Journal of Criminal Law and Criminology* 953.

SCHABAS, W (2009), *Genocide In International Law: The Crime of Crimes* (2nd edn, Cambridge: Cambridge University Press).

SCHABAS, W (2010), 'Prosecuting Dr Strangelove, Goldfinger and the Joker at the International Criminal Court: Closing the Loopholes', 23 *Leiden JIL* 850.

SCHABAS, W (2017), *An Introduction to the International Criminal Court*, 5th edn (Cambridge: Cambridge University Press).

SCHEFFER, D (1999), 'The International Criminal Court: The Challenge of Jurisdiction', 63 *ASIL Proceedings* 68.

SCHEFFER, D (2012), *All The Lost Souls: A Personal History of the War Crimes Tribunals* (Princeton: Princeton University Press).

SCHWARZENBERGER, G (1947), 'The Judgment of Nuremberg', 21 *Tulane Law Review* 329.

SCHWARZENBERGER, G (1950), 'The Problem of an International Criminal Law', 3 *Current Legal Problems* 263.

SHAHABUDDEEN, M (2012), *International Criminal Justice at the Yugoslav Tribunal: A Judge's Recollection* (Oxford: Oxford University Press).

SIEBERT-FOHR, A (2009), *Prosecuting Serious Human Rights Violations* (Oxford: Oxford University Press).

SIMMA, B and PAULUS, A (1999), 'The Responsibility of Individuals for Human Rights Violations in Internal Conflicts: A Positivist View', 93 *AJIL* 302.

SIVAKUMARAN, S (2012), *The Law of Non-International Armed Conflict* (Oxford: Oxford University Press).

SPECIAL ISSUE (2012), 'After Kampala, Aggression', 10 *JICJ* 1.

STAHN, C (2016), 'The ICC, Pre-Existing Treaty Regimes and the Limits of the Nemo Dat Quod non Habet Doctrine', 49 *Vanderbilt Journal of Transnational Law* 443.

STAHN, C (2017), 'Between "Constructive Engagement", "Collusion", and "Critical Distance": The International Committee of the Red Cross and the Development of International Criminal Law', in R Geiß, A Zimmermann, and S Haumner (eds), *Humanizing the Laws of War* (Cambridge: Cambridge University Press).

STAHN, C and EL-ZEIDY, M (eds) (2011), *The International Criminal Court and Complementarity* (Cambridge: Cambridge University Press).

SYMPOSIUM (2009), 7 *JICJ* 653.

SYMPOSIUM (2011), 9 *JICJ* 787.

SYMPOSIUM (2014), 12 *JICJ* 539.

SYMPOSIUM (2016), 110 *AJIL* 171.

TAYLOR, T (1993), *The Anatomy of the Nuremberg Trial* (London: Bloomsbury).

TEITEL, R (2002), *Transitional Justice* (New York: Oxford University Press).

THALMAN, V (2008), 'French Justice's Endeavours to Substitute for the ICTR', (2008) 6 *JICJ* 995.

TRIFFTERER, O, and AMBOS, K (eds) (2016), *Commentary on the Rome Statute of the International Criminal Court* (Oxford: Hart).

VAN SLIEDREGT, E (2012), *Individual Criminal Responsibility in International Law* (Oxford: Oxford University Press).

VENTURA, MJ (2011), 'Terrorism According to the STL's Interlocutory Decision on the Applicable Law: A Defining Moment or a Moment of Defining?', 9 *JICJ* 1021.

VERRIJN STUART, H and SIMONS, M (eds) (2009), *The Prosecutor and the Judge: Benjamin Ferencz and Antonio Cassese: Interviews and Writings* (Amsterdam: Amsterdam University Press).

VON HEBEL, H and ROBINSON, D (1999) 'Crimes Within the Jurisdiction of the Court', in R Lee (ed), *The International Criminal Court* (The Hague: Martinus Nijhoff).

WALDORF, L (2006), 'Mass Justice for Mass Atrocity: Rethinking Local Justice as Transitional Justice', 79 *Temple Law Review* 1.

WERLE, D and BURGHARDT, B (2012), 'Do Crimes Against Humanity Require the Participation of a State or 'State-Like' Organization?', 10 *JICJ* 1151.

WILSON, RA (2011), *Writing History in International Criminal Trials* (Cambridge: Cambridge University Press).

WIRTH, S (2012), 'Co-Perpetratorship in the *Lubanga* Trial Judgment', 10 *JICJ* 971.

ZACKLIN, R (2004), 'The Failings of ad hoc International Tribunals', 2 *JICJ* 541.

FURTHER READING

ALVAREZ, J (1999), 'Crimes of Hate/Crimes of State, Lessons from Rwanda', 24 *Yale JIL* 365: this is a lengthy, but sophisticated analysis of the law and politics of the creation and early practice of the ICTR,

and of international criminal justice more generally.

AMBOS, K (2013–16), *A Treatise on International Criminal Law Volumes I–III:* (Oxford: Oxford University Press): these volumes are a comprehensive treatment of international criminal law from a systematic perspective. It is a comprehensive work, steeped in German criminal law theory.

BASSIOUNI, MC (ed) (2008), *International Criminal Law Volumes I–III* (3rd edn: The Hague: Martinus Nijhoff): this collection is one of the foundational works in international criminal law, overseen by one of the leading lights of the discipline. It covers the entire area of both substantive law, including what would be called transnational crime, and procedure.

CASSESE, A, GAETA, P, and JONES, J (eds) (2002), *The Rome Statute: A Commentary* (Oxford: Oxford University Press): an early, very advanced set of essays on the Rome Statute of the ICC, which is amongst the standard reference works on point. Whilst, owing to the timing of its publication, it does not deal in detail with the practice of the ICC, it contains highly insightful analyses of the Statute.

CASSESE, A et al (eds) (2008), *The Oxford Companion to International Criminal Justice* (Oxford: Oxford University Press): the *Companion* is, in many ways an encyclopedia of international criminal law. It includes conceptual essays, and commentaries on cases, ideas, and people involved in the area.

GREENWOOD, C (1996), 'International Humanitarian Law and the Tadić Case', (1996) 7 *EJIL* 265. A very thoughtful evaluation of probably the classic case for which the ICTY will be remembered, which at the time the ICTY issued its views was deeply controversial.

GUILFOYLE, D (2016), *International Criminal Law* (Oxford: Oxford University Press): the book is a very readable, succinct, and thoughtful book on international criminal law. Its brevity belies its close, careful analysis of the subject. An ideal way into the subject.

MINOW, M (1998), *Between Vengeance and Forgiveness* (Boston: Beacon Press): this is an exceptionally thoughtful rumination on the question of what to do with respect to international crimes, written by a leading scholar. It is subtle and humane.

O'KEEFE, R (2015) *International Criminal Law* (Oxford: Oxford University Press): a very detailed, scholarly, work on the subject, that concentrates, in particular, on national approaches to the prosecution of international crimes, including jurisdiction and immunities.

SADAT, L (2002), *The International Criminal Court and the Transformation of International Law: Justice for a New Millennium* (Ardsley: Transnational Publishers): a thoughtful reflection on the relation between the Rome Statute and general international law. It is optimistic, and comprehensively referenced.

SCHABAS, W (2015), *The International Criminal Court: A Commentary on the Rome Statute* (2nd edn, Oxford: Oxford University Press): this is an extraordinary work, that discusses, Article by Article, the Rome Statute of the ICC, written by a leading scholar in the area. That one person could write such a work is breathtaking.

WERLE, G and JESSBERGER, F (2014), *Principles of International Criminal Law* (3rd edn, Oxford: Oxford University Press): an outstanding textbook on international criminal law, with an emphasis on the criminal law aspects. It is very well referenced, and is a fount of well-informed commentary.

ZAPPALÀ, S (2003), *Human Rights in International Criminal Proceedings* (Oxford: Oxford University Press): a very helpful work that applies international human rights law to the conduct of international criminal proceedings, an issue which is sometimes rather overlooked.

25

INTERNATIONAL HUMAN RIGHTS LAW

Sir Nigel Rodley

Sir Nigel Rodley had agreed to contribute to this volume before his untimely death in 2017. With the kind permission of Dr Rodley, his contribution to the previous edition has been reproduced as a tribute to him. Sir Nigel was a founder of the contemporary system of international human rights law, whose wisdom and guidance is greatly missed in a world which much needs it. The chapter has been lightly edited to reflect recent factual developments, but the ideas and views expressed remain his own.

SUMMARY

The human rights idea developed as a non-clerical counterweight to the increasing power of the emerging modern State, establishing limits to the imposition of State power over individuals. Despite nineteenth-century concern with slavery, especially the slave trade, human rights did not become a full-fledged issue of international concern until the advent of the UN Charter, which made the advancement of human rights a purpose of the UN. The Charter paved the way for the adoption of the International Bill of Human Rights which framed human rights as an issue of general international law, as well as giving treaty form to specific obligations and providing machinery for monitoring compliance with the treaties' provisions. The main categories of human rights—civil and political/economic and social— are addressed by international law. The former, classic, human rights are mainly about the freedom and autonomy of the individual within the larger society, whereas economic and social rights typically require State action to guarantee them. However, to an extent, civil and political rights require action by the State to protect people from the actions of others in society (including corporations). The bearers of human rights remain individuals and the duty to safeguard them remains with the State. Human rights are accepted, at least as a matter of law, to represent universal obligations; they are not the privilege of inhabitants of States with a 'Western' culture. Civil and political rights include both intellectual freedom (conscience, expression, association, assembly) and physical freedom (liberty and security of person, movement, prohibition of slavery). Human dignity, an underlying principle in the International Bill of Human Rights, is the main value protecting physical integrity and life. From the 1960s a substantial network of treaty-based and UN-Charter-based machinery developed to lend international protection for internationally recognized human rights.

I. INTRODUCTION[1]

The original notion of human rights referred to those rights that the individual might assert against the organized power of the State (Freeman, 2011, pp 15–36). It is a notion that grew in the West in the seventeenth and eighteenth centuries, at a time when feudalism was being replaced by mercantilism and religion had begun to lose its position as a counterweight to royal power that was giving way to the emergent, industrializing State. Indeed, it was the State that claimed a monopoly of the use of physical force with a view to protecting people from each other (Weber, 1919). It was the Leviathan that would tame the dangerous, predatory jungle.[2] But it too required taming and from Locke[3] to Rousseau[4] and Thomas Paine,[5] from Magna Carta and the English Bill of Rights to the Virginia Bill of Rights[6] and the *Déclaration des droits de l'homme et du citoyen*,[7] the idea of an individual human *domaine réservé* was born and consecrated.[8] The human gift of conscience was now not only of equal worth and respect as the duty to obey the sovereign,[9] but also, in some limited but basic respect, superior to that duty, whether the sovereign be hereditary or institutional/constitutional. The social contract, by which each individual ceded some of his or her naturally endowed autonomy to ensure the meeting of shared needs, did not require the total surrender of that autonomy. Human rights marked the boundary of the cession. The individual retained sovereignty too.

At this point we are dealing with a philosophical construct. For it to be materialized, it had to be translated into law and would sometimes assume constitutional form. It took time, but nowadays hardly a constitution exists that does not recognize human rights. The international human rights project was mainly a post-World War II development, but so was the coming into existence of a majority of the world's States (principally through the process of decolonization). As a result, many constitutional bills of rights owe much to the Universal Declaration of Human Rights, the International Covenant on Civil and Political Rights, and the European Convention on Human Rights (see the next section). It is the legal rather than the philosophical manifestation of human rights that is the focus of this chapter.

A brief section on the historical origins of international human rights law is followed by a discussion of the basis of obligation in the field. Then there is a consideration of various modes of human rights classification that have been put forward and in which 'core' economic and social rights are identified. A summary treatment of the almost outdated political discourse as to whether human rights are truly universal or culturally specific precedes a more extensive elaboration of the major substantive principles of civil and political rights and the values underlying them. The main universal machinery for monitoring or

---

[1] The text of this introduction is borrowed from Rodley, 2013, ch 29.

[2] The Leviathan was Hobbes' image for that 'man or assembly of men' to whom each vulnerable individual member of society would surrender 'all their power and strength' for 'our peace and defence'. See Hobbes, 1651, ch XVII. [3] Eg Locke, 1689.

[4] Rousseau, 1762, especially Book I, ch 4 on the limits of sovereign power (that democratically reflects the General Will).

[5] Paine, 1791. [6] (English) Bill of Rights (1689), Virginia Bill of Rights (1776).

[7] *Déclaration des droits de l'homme et du citoyen* (1789).

[8] See Henkin, 1978, pp 3–13. On the history of human rights generally, see Ishay, 2008, pp 63–116.

[9] The primacy of conscience is sometimes sourced to Antigone, who had to choose between obedience to her king and her obligation to bury her brother (Weston, 1989, p 13). In fact, even though she chose the latter, Sophocles at any rate does not seem to make clear that this was the morally superior stance: Sophocles, *Antigone* (442 bce, trans Jebb, RC, http://classics.mit.edu/Sophocles/antigone.html).

implementing human rights, both treaty-based and UN-Charter-based, as well as regional machinery, is then reviewed.

II. HISTORICAL ORIGINS OF INTERNATIONAL HUMAN RIGHTS LAW (IHRL)

It is not surprising that human rights entered the domain of international law only relatively late and slowly.

International law was and remains a system of law designed to make inter-State coexistence as smooth as possible: its function is to provide the norms and means to attenuate transnational friction. Like any legal system, its overall goal has been the avoidance and resolution of conflict, the pursuit of peace. During most of its life, international law was predicated on a notion of the sovereign independence of States that excluded any consideration of the 'internal affairs' of States, which were seen as matters of domestic jurisdiction. After all, international law was the normative expression of international relations, just as much as national law can be said to be the normative expression of any national political dispensation. According to perhaps the most influential school, international relations are about the pursuit of the national interest (the maximization of power) in economic, trade, territorial, political, military areas, with international law as a means of securing a non-violent balance of the aggregate of national interests.[10] Indeed, factoring human rights into the mix of material interests that are the traditional content of international relations would, it has been asserted, make matters of principle (human rights) merely another commodity to be traded in the market of national interests.[11]

Human rights are inherently intra-State matters and that means that in the international context they are capable of becoming additional sources of friction between States, rather than balm, thus multiplying the challenge to the international legal system. They seemed to be a cuckoo in the nest of the doves of peace, even if the hawks of war had little affinity for them either. To vary the metaphor, human rights may well have been felt by diplomats and international civil servants to be grit thrown into the oil designed to lubricate the cogs of the machinery of international discourse.

Nevertheless, as early as the nineteenth century, one human rights issue, slavery, entered the domain of international law. Starting with Britain in 1807, the major European slave-owning and slave-trading nations abandoned the practice and then worked to strangle other States' slave-trading practices.[12] By the time of the 1926 Slavery Convention, chattel slavery and its associated trade were largely historical relics,[13] but until the early twentieth century, action was focused more on the international trade in slaves than on the practice of slavery. Escaping slaves might find freedom in States that did not recognize or no longer recognized the status of slaves, but the slavery-free were not insisting that international law required that the status of slavery be abolished in those jurisdictions that retained it.

The advent of the League of Nations after the First World War brought further developments. Recognizing that the denial of national minority aspirations had been a factor

---

[10] The realist school (*Realpolitik*) whose most influential exponent was Hans Morgenthau. See Morgenthau, 1967, chs 1 and 6 and *passim*.

[11] See the observations of Ernst Haas concerning the (then) new Carter Administration's human-rights-focused foreign policy: 'The United States has embarked on the most naïve and moralistic campaign since Woodrow Wilson' (Haas, 1977, p 72).

[12] Abolition of the Slave Trade Act. In 1811, the trade was made a felony in the British Empire.

[13] It has managed to be abolished three times in Mauritania, in 1905, 1981, and 2007: see Corrigan, 2007.

leading to the war—the assassination by Serb nationalists of the Archduke Franz Ferdinand of Austria is generally considered the spark that set fire to the European tinder box—the League presided over the creation of a series of treaties concerned with minorities, aimed at avoiding a repetition of the problem. Of course, it was not all minorities that would be protected, only those in the Balkans and eastern Europe, so this was a limited human rights incursion into international law.[14]

Also limited was the inclusion of human rights clauses into the mandates given by the League to some colonial powers to administer the former colonies of the defeated powers, notably the Germans. This was no general project of incorporating human rights into the administration of colonies as a whole, still less one aimed at decolonization, but it must have been perceived as a signal that those subjected to colonialism deserved to have their human rights respected.[15]

The most significant post-World War I development in the field of human rights was the creation in 1919 of the International Labour Organization (ILO). Here was established an organization designed to promote and protect a certain category of rights—freedom of association—at least as regards the rights of trade unionists. This development too was a response to political events, notably the 1917 Russian Revolution, which led to the withdrawal of Russia from the global conflict of World War I. The ILO was effectively an enlightened response aimed at showing workers that their interests could be met by something less radical than communist revolution. With its imaginative tri-partite structure (States, trade union organizations, and employers' organizations) and its serious machinery for addressing allegations of violations of workers' unionists' rights, particularly the Committee on Freedom of Association, it was a real example of the possibility of the international protection of human rights (Swepston, 2013, ch 20).

A. CHARTER OF THE UN

The foundations of modern international human rights law are to be found in the Charter of the United Nations. One of the goals of the UN laid down in its Article 1 is the achievement of 'international cooperation in … promoting and encouraging respect for human rights and fundamental freedoms for all without distinction as to race, sex, language or religion'. It was far from inevitable that human rights would figure prominently, if at all, in what was to become the nearest thing to a world constitution. It took intense lobbying by what we now call civil society, especially American non-governmental organizations (NGOs). The argument that prevailed was that a paradigm-changing lesson had to be learned from the Second World War (Lauren, 2011, chs 5 and 6). Nazi Germany's genocide of Jews and Roma and other crimes against humanity, and its territorial aggressiveness, were seen as part of the same phenomenon. A ruthless, lawless regime that could commit carnage in parts of its own population and brutally repress any opposition to it was seen to be part and parcel of a project of violent deployment of force internationally. The frontier between the previous hermetically sealed realms of the inter-State and the intra-State was now seen to be porous. Once in the Charter, human rights had, in one leap, become a matter of international concern and, thus, of international legal relevance.

---

[14] See *Treatment of Polish Nationals and Other Persons of Polish Origin or Speech in the Danzig Territory, Advisory Opinion, 1932, PCIJ Series A/B, No 44*, p 4.

[15] Mandates were allocated pursuant to Article 22, League of Nations Covenant; see *South West Africa, Second Phase, Judgment, ICJ Reports 1966*, p 6; *Legal Consequences for States of the Continued Presence of South Africa in Namibia (South West Africa) notwithstanding Security Council Resolution 276 (1970), Advisory Opinion, ICJ Reports 1971*, p 16.

III. THE BASIS OF OBLIGATION IN INTERNATIONAL HUMAN RIGHTS LAW

The UN Charter language of 'cooperation' for 'promoting and encouraging respect' for human rights was not exactly a demand for the immediate *observance* of human rights. However, later provisions came closer to this. Thus, Article 55 of the Charter requires that, '[w]ith a view to the creation of conditions of stability and well-being which are necessary for peaceful and friendly relations among nations,'[16] the UN 'shall promote ... universal respect for and observance of, human rights for all without distinction as to race, sex, language or religion.' Here we at least had the goal of securing respect for, and observance of, human rights on a universal basis. This still fell short of imposing direct human rights obligations on States, but Article 56 did address this point: '[a]ll members pledge themselves to take joint and separate action in cooperation with the Organization for the achievement of the purposes set forth in Article 55.' So, States had to work not only jointly but each on their own to achieve promotion of respect for, and observance of, human rights.

In the early decades of the UN, there was disagreement as to whether this language should be read as an exhortation or a direct obligation (Schwelb, 1972). By 1971, the answer for the International Court of Justice (ICJ) was that the provisions involved a directly binding obligation and that South Africa had, by applying its apartheid system in South-West Africa under the mandate it was given by the League of Nations, violated these provisions.[17] It might still have been possible to interpret this decision as being restricted to the obligation to respect human rights 'without distinction as to race' and so on (Humphrey, 1979, p 36), but if so, the ICJ certainly put paid to that notion in the later *Teheran Hostages* case, where it affirmed:

> Wrongfully to deprive human beings of their freedom and to subject them to physical constraint in conditions of hardship is in itself manifestly incompatible with the principles of the Charter of the United Nations, as well as with the fundamental principles enunciated in the Universal Declaration of Human Rights.[18]

The reference to the Universal Declaration of Human Rights (UDHR) is important for two reasons: first, the UN Charter itself provided no elaboration of what was meant by the term 'human rights and fundamental freedoms'; second, the UDHR was, as will be seen, contained in a resolution of the General Assembly and so not per se binding.

A. THE INTERNATIONAL BILL OF HUMAN RIGHTS

The first task of the UN Commission on Human Rights, established pursuant to Article 68 of the Charter,[19] was the drafting of an International Bill of Human Rights that would consist, first, of a declaration of human rights principles (this would become the UDHR), followed by obligations consecrated in treaty form. The purpose of the treaties would be both to give clear legal force and more precision to the UDHR and to provide machinery for

---

[16] Thus echoing the lesson learned in Article 1.

[17] *South West Africa, Second Phase, Judgment, ICJ Reports 1966*, p 6, para 131: 'To establish instead, and to enforce, distinctions, exclusions, restrictions and limitations exclusively based on grounds of race, colour, descent or national or ethnic origin which constitute a denial of fundamental human rights is a flagrant violation of the purposes and principles of the Charter.'

[18] *United States Diplomatic and Consular Staff in Tehran, Judgment, ICJ Reports 1980*, p 3.

[19] The only 'Functional Commission' of ECOSOC that was specifically to be established under Article 68 was the one on human rights.

monitoring the implementation of the substantive provisions. The latter will be returned to in Section VII.

To the extent that the eventual treaties were perceived to be needed, not only for the creation of monitoring procedures but also for legal specificity, did that mean that the UDHR was devoid of force? The matter was controversial from the beginning. There were those who held that it had no legal force. Under Article 14 of the Charter, the General Assembly had only the power to make recommendations; it was not intended to be a world legislature. Moreover, by its very terms, the UDHR purported to be no more than a 'common standard of achievement for all peoples and all nations'.[20] On the other side, whatever the legal status of the UDHR as such, it contained the catalogue of human rights and fundamental freedoms that were referred to by UN Charter articles on human rights, especially Articles 1, 55, and 56. So, to the extent that these provisions contained binding obligations, it was to the UDHR that one would have to look to discover their content (de Schutter, 2012, p 39).

The arguments began to be finalized by the time of the 1968 UN International Conference on Human Rights which adopted the Proclamation of Teheran. According to paragraph 2 of that Proclamation, the UDHR 'states a common understanding of the peoples of the world concerning the inalienable and inviolable rights of members of the human family and constitutes an obligation for members of the international community'.[21] A quarter of a century later, a World Conference on Human Rights would declare: 'Human rights and fundamental freedoms are the birthright of all human beings; their protection and promotion is the first responsibility of governments'.[22] From that point on one rarely heard a challenge to the idea that States had human rights obligations other than by virtue of human rights treaties. By the time of the UN Millennium Declaration in 2000, the General Assembly was able to resolve to 'respect fully and uphold the Universal Declaration of Human Rights' and in 2005 the World Summit Conference could proclaim:

> We recommit ourselves to protect and promote human rights, the rule of law and democracy, and recognize that they are interlinked and mutually reinforcing and that they constitute together universal and indivisible core values and principles of the United Nations, and call upon all parts of the United Nations system to promote human rights and fundamental freedoms.[23]

B. GENERAL INTERNATIONAL LAW

Because of the quasi-constitutional nature of the UN Charter, it would be misleading to conceive of the human rights obligations it contains as merely themselves treaty obligations. The better approach is to understand them in the same way as the State obligations on the use of force, that is to say, as norms of general or universal international law (Charney, 1993). They are norms of customary international law, generally binding on all States and often rooted in all three major sources of international law, customary international law, treaty law, and general principles of law (see Roberts and Sivakumaran, Ch 4 of this book).

---

[20] GA Res 217A III (10 December 1948), proclamatory paragraph.

[21] Proclamation of Tehran, proclaimed by the International Conference on Human Rights at Tehran, 22 April–13 May 1968, UN Doc A/CONF.32/41, para 2.

[22] Vienna Declaration and Programme of Action, adopted by World Conference on Human Rights, Vienna, 14–25 June 1993, UN Doc A/CONF.157/23, para 1.

[23] UN Millennium Declaration, GA Res 55/2 (2000), para 25; World Summit Outcome Document, GA Res 60/1 (24 October 2005), para 98.

Some of the rules have firmly become rules of *jus cogens* (Bianchi, 2008). After the prohibition of genocide[24] the most evident would be the prohibition of torture that is non-derogable in universal and regional human rights treaties and has been recognized as a rule of *jus cogens* by the ICJ, a body generally cautious about attributing that status to specific rules of customary or general international law.[25] Logic would suggest that the Charter-based exclusion of (implicitly adverse) distinctions based on race, sex, language, or religion would enjoy *jus cogens* status. The prohibition of racial discrimination would certainly seem to fall into the category;[26] although there is less manifest authority for the proposition as regards discrimination on grounds of language or religion, if only because they have not received the same amount of attention. This cannot be said as regards discrimination on grounds of sex, which, like racial discrimination, has been addressed in widely ratified treaties. So far, the ICJ has not been called upon to express its view.

Not too much should be made of the distinction between a norm of general international law and one of *jus cogens*. The origins of the distinction lie in that between traditional customary international law and *jus cogens*. The point about ordinary rules of international law is that they may not be binding on 'persistent objectors', or may be departed from by means of regional custom, or by treaty. It is the latter dimension that *jus cogens* addresses directly: treaties may not depart from rules of *jus cogens*.[27] In reality, the possibilities of evading or modifying rules of customary international law discussed earlier arise out of the synallagmatic nature of most of the traditional customary international law rules.[28] International human rights law is by nature non-synallagmatic; its rules are, by definition, *erga omnes*.[29] It is instructive in this respect to note the great range of UN Human Rights Council 'special procedures' which have come to deal with most of the rights contained in the UDHR, in the expectation that all States are bound to respect them. In fact, as will appear later, the area of potential dispute nowadays lies not in whether States are bound to respect most if not all, of the rights contained in the UDHR, but in differences about the scope and nature of those rights. That is to say, there may be some room for interpretation of the obligation implied in the right in question.

C. TREATY LAW

The advantage of treaties as a source of international legal obligation over other sources is that there is generally no dispute as to the existence of a legal obligation. In principle, the only question to be answered is not whether there is a rule, but only whether the facts in question do or do not conform to the stated rule. After all, the State party to a treaty will be expected to have freely undertaken its obligations as a solemn act of sovereign power. And, as with other fields of international law, treaties in the field of human rights have been widely resorted to.

---

[24] See *Armed Activities on the Territory of the Congo (New Application: 2002) (Democratic Republic of the Congo v Rwanda), Jurisdiction and Admissibility, Judgment, ICJ Reports 2006*, p 6, para 64.

[25] *Questions relating to the Obligation to Prosecute or Extradite (Belgium v Senegal), Judgment of 20 July 2012*, para 99.

[26] Eg the Draft Articles on the Responsibility of States for Internationally Wrongful Acts, with Commentaries, Yearbook of the International Law Commission, 2001, Vol II, Part 2, Article 40, Commentary, para 4.

[27] Vienna Convention on the Law of Treaties (1969), Article 53.

[28] Ie a series of bilateral relationships.

[29] Ie opposable to the whole community of States or, in the case of treaties, States parties to the treaty. See Human Rights Committee, General Comment No 31, 'The Nature of the General Legal Obligation Imposed on States Parties to the [International] Covenant [on Civil and Political Rights]', UN Doc CCPR/C/21/Rev.1/Add.13 (2004), para 2.

The speedy adoption in 1948 of the Genocide Convention[30] was a necessary response to the holocaust of Jews and Roma. It took until 1966 for the International Bill of Human Rights to be completed, by adding to the UDHR (also 1948) the International Covenants on Economic, Social and Cultural Rights (ICESCR) and on Civil and Political Rights (ICCPR), together with the (first) Optional Protocol to the ICCPR. In fact, the process of adopting the Covenants was so protracted that a subject-specific treaty was adopted a year earlier, namely the 1965 International Convention on the Elimination of All Forms of Racial Discrimination (ICERD). Other subject-specific treaties followed and there are now nine 'core' UN human rights treaties.[31]

Meanwhile, regional treaties came into existence, sometimes preceding the UN treaties, sometimes following them. The most influential and long-standing general ones are the European and American Conventions on Human Rights and the African Charter on Human and Peoples' Rights. There are also regional subject-specific ones, such as the Inter-American Convention to Prevent and Punish Torture[32] and the African Charter on the Rights and Welfare of the Child.

IV. CATEGORIES OF RIGHTS

If the original notion of human rights connoted the limits of governmental power over the individual, and so concerned the rights of the individual against the State, there have been further claims to the title of human rights. A common set of categorizations of such claims, in addition to individual human rights as traditionally understood and commonly denominated civil and political rights (considered later in this chapter), is collective and group rights.[33]

Collective rights would be those that are needed by, or that pertain to, segments of the population, particularly the most vulnerable, and demand government action. The term 'economic and social rights' is typically used to encompass such rights, which consist essentially of expectation of the fulfilment of claims on governments (or society as a whole) to meet basic human needs, such as health, food, shelter, and education. What distinguishes them conceptually is that the centre of gravity of the idea of civil and political rights is individual freedom *from* government, while that of economic and social rights

---

[30] Convention on the Prevention and Punishment of the Crime of Genocide, GA Res 260A III (9 December 1948).

[31] The core treaties are: International Convention on the Elimination of all Forms of Racial Discrimination (ICERD), 66 UNTS 195 (21 December 1965); International Covenant on Economic, Social and Cultural Rights (ICESCR), GA Res 2200 A (XXI) (16 December 1966); International Convention on Civil and Political Rights (ICCPR), GA Res 2200 A (16 December 1966); Convention on the Elimination of All Forms of Discrimination against Women (CEDAW), GA Res 34/180 (18 December 1979); Convention against Torture and Other Cruel, Inhuman or Degrading Treatment or Punishment (UNCAT), GA Res 39/46 (10 December 1984); the Convention of the Rights of the Child (CRC), GA Res 44/25 (20 November 1989); International Convention on the Protection of All Migrant Workers and Members of Their Families (CMW), GA Res 45/158 (18 December 1990); the Convention on the Rights of Persons with Disabilities (CRPD), GA Res 61/106 (13 December 2006); and the International Convention for the Protection of All Persons from Enforced Disappearance (ICED), GA Res 61/177 (20 December 2006).

[32] There is also the 1987 European Convention for the Prevention of Torture and Inhuman or Degrading Treatment or Punishment (ECPT), (CETS No 126); it is non-normative, confining itself to establishing a Committee for the Prevention of Torture (CPT) which visits places of detention in States parties.

[33] The eminent commentator Karel Vasak once described these three categories as the 'three generations of human rights' (Vasak, 1977). This catchy term did little service to clarity of thought about human rights.

is the claim for action *by* governments. What they have in common is that those subject to governmental authority are the rights-bearers and governments are the duty-bearers.

'*Group rights*' are a wholly different species. They are said to inhere not in the individual but in populations. They seem to cover such issues as self-determination, development, a clean and healthy environment, and peace.[34] The asserted rights in question may not even be within the power of the State to respect. Rather, at least implicitly, their centre of gravity involves the claims by the State vis-à-vis the international community or even the rights of States against their own populations and the individual constituting the latter.[35] Space does not allow for an analysis of the legal existence or content of any of these asserted rights. It is evident that there is nothing in the structure of international law that would prevent such groups having rights, even if at present the amount of discussion and writing about them seems in inverse proportion to any agreed content. The point is that to call them 'human rights' is a misnomer that totally denatures a term that should be limited to denoting the rights of individual human beings in relation to the State.

However, one of them must be addressed, if only because of its juridical pedigree, before we move on, and that is the right of all peoples to self-determination—for is not the right specified as the first article of both the ICESCR and the ICCPR? At first sight that of itself would appear to lay to rest any objection to its existence as a human right. In fact, as is often the case, first sight is misleading, requiring a second look. It is evident from the structure and organization of the Covenants that the right to self-determination is apart from other rights. Each Covenant is divided into five parts. Part I has Article 1 on the right to self-determination standing alone. Part II provides general jurisdictional and obligational articles. Only Part III sets out specific human rights. Part IV deals with monitoring procedures and Part V has the Final Clauses. This structure, separating the right to self-determination from the rights-articulating part by a non-rights-articulating part, compels the conclusion that the right to self-determination is contextual to other rights rather than a self-standing Covenant-protected right.[36] It is neither a civil nor political, nor economic nor social human right.

Similarly, it cannot be ignored that States have adopted a Declaration on the Right to Development that specifically refers to its subject as 'an inalienable human right'.[37] The provisions of this instrument, most of which use the hortatory 'should', are so devoid of specificity or precision as to make their meaning, if any, elusive. The other asserted 'group rights' are even more vacuous, making them still more doubtful candidates for the title of 'rights', much less 'human rights'. What follows will therefore focus on civil and political rights, and on economic and social rights, more or less as reflected respectively in the ICCPR and the ICESCR.

[34] For self-determination and development, see next paragraph; for environment see, eg, African Charter on Human and Peoples' Rights, Article 23; for peace: Article 24 and Protocol of San Salvador to the American Convention on Human Rights, Article 11.

[35] Thus, Algeria invokes an asserted right to peace to justify avoidance of accountability and perpetuate impunity for its brutal repression in the 1990s of an Islamist revolt involving thousands of enforced disappearances. Eg Human Rights Committee, *Guezout et al v Algeria* (Communication No 1753/2008), UN Doc CCPR/C/105/D/1753/2008 (2012), para 4.6.

[36] Thus, the Human Rights Committee took account of the article in interpreting Article 25 (right to participate in government); in fact, it found that the exclusion of certain French and other foreign citizens (persons not resident for the previous ten years) from participating in a referendum on self-determination for New Caledonia did not violate Article 25 read together with Article 1: *Gillot et al v France* (Communication No 932/2000), UN Doc CCPR/C/75/D/932/2000 (2002), para 13.4. This was a case of external self-determination from colonial control, pursuant to the General Assembly Declaration on the Granting of Independence to Colonial Countries and People, GA Res 1514 (XV) (14 December 1960). It is unclear whether or how the right may apply in internal situations.   [37] GA Res 41/128 (4 December 1986), Article 1.

A. CIVIL AND POLITICAL/ECONOMIC AND SOCIAL

According to the 1993 Vienna Declaration and Programme of Action, all human rights are 'indivisible and independent and interrelated'. This does not mean that they are indistinguishable. Certainly, the (necessarily exaggerated) paradigm indicated earlier—that civil and political equals freedom from government action, while economic and social equals demand for such action—can be misleading. For example, the 'freedom from' idea is often thought of as requiring abstention or *negative* action, while the 'demand for' idea is seen as involving *positive* action. In reality, much in the civil and political rights domain also requires positive action, for example, a decent system of administration of justice, including a humane penitentiary system, or an effective, clean law enforcement apparatus. Similarly, access to economic and social goods can sometimes be facilitated by State *inaction*, for instance, by not standing in the way of humanitarian assistance.

However, the similarities should not mask the reality of dissimilarities. The financial cost of a system of decent government capable of respecting the rule of law is surely infrastructural to the whole rights project and so, arguably, *prior* to the costs of guaranteeing any particular right. Deduct these costs from the 'price' of ensuring civil and political rights and not so much remains. And much of what does remain is in the realm of the so-called horizontal obligations of States (considered in Section IV B), whereas the major costs of meeting people's needs are so central to the economic and social rights project that States have shied away from assuming the same type of legal obligation.

Thus, whereas Article 2 ICCPR pledges States 'to respect and to ensure' the rights recognized by the Covenant, the comparable Article 2 ICESCR requires them only 'to take steps, individually and through international assistance and cooperation … to the maximum of its available resources, with a view to achieving progressively the full realization of the rights recognized' by the Covenant. Even discounting the muddying of the nature of the duty-bearer (international cooperation is not within the gift of the State party in question), an obligation on a State to 'take steps', within 'available' resources to achieve rights 'progressively' cannot be equated with the peremptory notions of 'respect and ensure'.

The Committee on Economic, Social and Cultural Rights (see later) has noted that the obligation of non-discrimination is of immediate effect,[38] even though the same obligation would anyway apply to a State party to the ICCPR (Article 26). The same Committee has insisted that there is 'a minimum core obligation to ensure the satisfaction of, at the very least, minimum essential levels of each of the rights' of the Covenant.[39] So, where 'a significant number of individuals is deprived of essential foodstuffs, of essential primary health care, of basic shelter and housing, or of the most basic forms of education', the State in question 'is *prima facie* failing to discharge its obligations under the Covenant'.[40] This observation would have been more helpful to the individuals concerned had it not been accompanied by a further observation that acknowledges the legitimacy of the State's 'failure to meet at least its minimum care obligations' on the basis of a 'lack of available resources' provided that it has made every effort to satisfy the obligations.[41] Ten years later, the Committee, in a General Comment on the Right to Health, affirmed the following core obligations:

(a) To ensure the right of access to health facilities, goods and services on a non-discriminatory basis, especially for vulnerable or marginalized groups;

---

[38] General Comment No 3 (1990) (The nature of States parties' obligations (Article 2, para 1 of the Covenant)), Committee on Economic, Social and Cultural Rights, Fifth Session, Report (UN Doc ESCOR 1991, Supp 3), Annex III, para 1.   [39] Ibid, para 10; see generally, Chapman and Russell, 2002.
[40] General Comment No 3, ibid, para 10.   [41] Ibid, para 10.

(b) To ensure access to the minimum essential food which is nutritionally adequate and safe, to ensure freedom from hunger to everyone;

(c) To ensure access to basic shelter, housing and sanitation, and an adequate supply of safe and potable water;

(d) To provide essential drugs, as from time to time defined under the WHO Action Programme on Essential Drugs;

(e) To ensure equitable distribution of all health facilities, goods and services.[42]

It also required States to 'adopt and implement a national public health strategy and plan of action'.[43] This peremptory language tracks that of Article 4 of the ICCPR, which makes certain rights in that Covenant non-derogable. There is no comparable language in the ICESCR itself.

Much attention has been given to whether or not economic and social rights are justiciable, in the sense that they are the sorts of subject matter that are suitable for judicial rather than policy decision by legislatures and executives. There is a certain artificiality to the discussion insofar as any polity may grant any functions to its courts. Certainly, at the international level, it will be interesting to follow the work of the Committee on Economic, Social and Cultural Rights under the 2008 Optional Protocol that grants the right of individual petition to it for violations of obligations under the Covenant. The challenge for the Committee will be to identify specific violations on the basis of such unclear obligational requirements.

B. VERTICAL AND HORIZONTAL OBLIGATIONS

A sub-species of positive obligations is in the domain of 'horizontal' obligations of States. If the paradigmatic human rights construct envisages a vertical relationship—the State vis-à-vis the individuals subject to the States' jurisdiction—there is nevertheless a 'horizontal' dimension, in the sense that there is also an expectation that the State will protect individuals from other individuals (or groups or legal entities). This is not the same as saying that individuals can violate the human rights of other individuals. As the Human Rights Committee has affirmed, ICCPR obligations are binding on States and 'do not, as such, have *direct* horizontal effect as a matter of international law'.[44] But, the Committee goes on to state that:

> the positive obligations on States Parties to ensure Covenant rights will only be fully discharged if individuals are protected by the State, not just against violations of Covenant rights by its agents, but also against acts committed by private persons or entities that would impair the enjoyment of Covenant rights in so far as they are amenable to application by private persons or entities.[45]

First, this passage recognizes that, even in the area of civil and political rights, States have positive obligations of protection. This goes beyond the provision of a clean, rule-of-law-respecting system of governance (see earlier). Thus, for example, the right to life and the prohibition of torture require the State to investigate allegations of violations of those provisions and bring perpetrators to justice (especially State officials who have inflicted or acquiesced in the harm in question).[46] Similarly, States may be in violation of their

---

[42] General Comment No 14 (2000) (the right to the highest attainable standard of health (Article 12 of the ICESCR)), para 43(a)–(e).   [43] Ibid, para 43(f).

[44] Human Rights Committee, General Comment No 31 (n 29), para 8 (emphasis added).

[45] Ibid.   [46] Ibid, para 18.

obligations to ensure such rights as a result of 'permitting or failing to take appropriate measures or to exercise due diligence to prevent, punish, investigate or redress the harm caused by such acts by private persons or entities'.[47] The attraction of this approach is that it allows holding the State accountable when it seeks to use private persons or entities to inflict the harm (or to claim that private persons or entities are responsible for inflicting the harm); while it may not be possible to attribute direct responsibility to the State, it will remain possible to attribute indirect responsibility for failure to discharge its positive obligations.

The obligation to use 'due diligence' to protect against harms is not restricted to those areas where there may be conceded State responsibility (for acts that must otherwise have served governmental interests). The Human Rights Committee frequently reminds governments, for example, of their obligation to use due diligence to prevent domestic violence. Here the harm will rarely, if at all, have been inflicted in pursuit of a governmental interest, but that does not mean that there is no foundation of responsibility on any State to protect people from threats to life or limb at the hands of others.

Equally, these positive obligations are not open-ended to the point of losing the vertical paradigm dimension in favour of the horizontal dimension to prevent any harm inflicted by one person on another. This is what is meant by the phrase 'in so far as [the rights in question] are amenable to application by private persons or entities'. An evident example of a right that *is* so amenable is that offered by the Human Rights Committee itself: 'In fields affecting basic aspects of ordinary life, such as work or housing, individuals are to be protected from discrimination within the meaning of Article 26'.[48]

C. RIGHTS-HOLDERS AND DUTY-BEARERS

As has been seen, the only conceptually consistent and generally accepted rights-holders are individuals. States or comparable collectivities may have rights under international law, but not human rights. However, there is an extensive discourse, to the point of polemic, as to whether other entities may be human rights duty-bearers, that is, bound to respect human rights, failing which they would be considered human rights violators (Clapham, 2006; Rodley, 2013).

For instance, there is little resistance to the notion that intergovernmental organizations (IGOs) are capable of violating human rights. Conceptually, it should be self-evident that, if a State acting alone can commit a human rights violation, then a group of States pooling their powers and acting in the same way should be similarly capable of violating human rights. Indeed, the opposite would be subversive of the whole project: States would merely have to act collaboratively to relieve themselves of their human rights obligations. That IGOs were capable of having rights and obligations under international law has been acknowledged since the 1949 *Reparations Case*. Here the ICJ held that an IGO, the UN, must protect its own personnel and must accordingly have the power to bring a claim against States for harm done by them to such personnel.[49] As the UN has found itself increasingly involved not only in peacekeeping, but also in peace-enforcement and peacebuilding operations, the UN slowly came to accept that it

---

[47] Ibid, para 8.

[48] Ibid. Article 26 provides for equality under the law and non-discrimination 'on any ground such as race, colour, sex, language, religion, political or other opinion, national or social origin, property, birth or other status'.

[49] *Reparation for Injuries Suffered in the Service of the United Nations, Advisory Opinion, ICJ Reports 1949*, p 174 at p 183.

too would have obligations of a general international humanitarian law and general international human rights law nature.[50]

The precedent of the *inter*-State organization having duties and responsibilities hardly serves to justify the claim that (other) *non*-State actors (NSAs) can and do have human rights obligations. Yet claims are made in respect of various NSAs, including armed opposition groups, organized crime gangs, transnational business enterprises, and even individuals. One cannot look to human rights treaties to clarify the situation, since these only bind the States that become party to them. This drives us to look to customary or general international law for guidance. Here too we have a dearth of authority. It would be plausible to apply the criterion that human rights treaty bodies invoke to establish State responsibility: is the State in effective control?[51] *Pari passu*, we could ask the same question in respect of the other candidates for potential human rights violation status.

So, it would be consistent at least with the principles of international humanitarian law to consider armed opposition groups (typically called terrorists by the governments in question) as capable of having international human rights law obligations. If such a group has the attributes of a party to an armed conflict, which would normally involve, if not territorial control (as in international armed conflict),[52] at least similar exclusive de facto control of parts of a population, then it would not do violence to the international human rights law project to consider the group as being required also to respect at least those human rights for which that the level of control permits it to incur responsibility. In the absence of such status, then the acts of the group are no more than any government would consider them to be, namely, criminal acts, which the government would be expected to seek to repress. To dignify their perpetrators as anything more than criminal seems to serve no purpose. For international human rights law to pipe up 'me too' with the State in question will hardly serve to ameliorate the harms inflicted or offer any redress. Of course, this is without prejudice to the (limited) role of international criminal law as regards crimes against humanity. However, to the extent that the group whose members may have committed crimes against humanity fails to meet the criteria of a party to an armed conflict, it must still have sufficient organizational density and structure to be in a position to meet the threshold test for crimes against humanity, that is, that there be an attack against a civilian population, that the acts be committed on a widespread or systematic basis, and that they be committed pursuant to an organizational policy.[53] Close as this may come to

---

[50] See UN Secretary-General, Secretary-General's Bulletin: Observance by UN Forces of International Humanitarian Law, 6 August 1999, UN Doc ST/SGB/1999/13; Remarks of the UN Legal Counsel, Nicolas Michel, to the Security Council meeting on 'Strengthening International Law: Rule of Law and Maintenance of International Peace and Security', UN Doc S/PV.5474 (2006), pp 3–5; UN Secretariat, 'Human Rights Due Diligence Policy on UN Support to non-UN Security Forces' (HRDDP) (July 2012), which confirms 'the Organization's Purposes and Principles in the Charter and its *obligations under international law to respect*, promote and encourage respect for *international* humanitarian, *human rights* and refugee *law*' (emphasis added).

[51] See, eg, Human Rights Committee, General Comment No 31, 'The Nature of the General Legal Obligation Imposed on States Parties to the [International] Covenant [on Civil and Political Rights]', UN Doc CCPR/C/21/Rev.1/Add.13 (2004), para 10.

[52] Article 3 common to the four Geneva Conventions of 12 August 1949 does not specify the attributes of a non-State party to an armed conflict. Additional Protocol II to the Conventions, relating to the protection of victims of armed conflict refers to 'dissident armed forces or other organized armed groups which, under responsible command, exercise such control over a part of [a state's] territory as to enable them to carry out sustained and concerted military operations and to implement this Protocol', Article 2(1). Common Article 3 is not generally interpreted to require such a high threshold for an entity to be considered a party to a non-international armed conflict.

[53] See International Criminal Court, Elements of Crimes, UN Doc PCNICC/2000/1/Add.2 (2000), Article 7, Introduction.

being a party to an armed conflict within the meaning of international humanitarian law (IHL), it is not clear what the 'value added' would be of calling the groups human rights violators. Certainly, there is little legal authority for the proposition.[54]

All these arguments apply *a fortiori* as regards ordinary criminal gangs and yet more so for individuals. The most cited latter manifestation would be domestic violence. According to a feminist critique, the traditional human rights paradigm relates to the public sphere and is therefore male-oriented. Apparently this fails to take account of the reality of the millions of women round the world who are kept in the private sphere and out of the public sphere. It is hard to give credence to a critique that would appear to legitimate a situation that inherently violates the rights and power of women to act autonomously and in the public sphere, on terms of equality with men. To the extent that they are denied that right and the State has not exercised due diligence to address that deprivation, this is a matter of State responsibility (see earlier) and should, of course, be vigorously addressed as such.

As to the suggestion that business enterprises, transnational or otherwise, may be considered as bodies having direct human rights responsibilities under international law, it is certainly true that these are sometimes perceived as having more power than governments, at least insofar as the availability or otherwise of their investments and business activity can have major consequences for a State's economy. However, except perhaps in the area of personnel policy or security measures, their activities pose limited *direct* challenge to human rights. Rather it is the territorial State that is most likely to be the direct violator. Indeed, few States would deny that it is *their* responsibility to protect people from harms committed by business enterprises and thus should exercise the appropriate due diligence to that end. It is certainly the case that the international legal evidence is consistent with that approach.

Thus, in 2003 the UN Sub-Commission on the Promotion and Protection of Human Rights submitted to the Commission on Human Rights (see later) a draft text entitled 'Norms on the Responsibilities of Transnational Corporations and Other Business Enterprises with regard to Human Rights'.[55] The Norms purported to vest in the corporations and enterprises 'the obligation to promote, secure the fulfilment of, respect, ensure respect of and protect human rights recognized in international ... law'.[56] Even though the Norms acknowledged the 'primary responsibility' of States to ensure that the corporations and enterprises respect human rights,[57] the Norms' acceptance of the principle that international law would target such enterprises directly led to their being abandoned.

Eight years later, the UN Human Rights Council (successor to the Commission, see later) was able to adopt by consensus a new text of 'Guiding Principles on Business and Human Rights', drafted by Professor John Ruggie,[58] and the Council even established a Working Group to promote the Principles.[59] There is no mystery as to what led to the changed reception. The Ruggie Principles, as they are known, focus heavily on the responsibility of *States* to ensure that business enterprises respect human rights. To the

---

[54] However, Ben Emmerson QC, the UN Human Rights Council's Special Rapporteur on the promotion and protection of human rights while countering terrorism, has rejected this approach as 'legalistic' though he cites no primary sources to sustain the refutation: UN Doc A/HRC/20/14 (2012), para 13.

[55] UN Doc E/CN.4/Sub.2/2003/12/Rev.2 (13 August 2003).

[56] Ibid, para 1.   [57] Ibid.

[58] Human Rights Council Res 17/4 (16 June 2011), para 1; the Principles are contained in Professor Ruggie's final report: UN Doc A/HRC/17/31, Annex (25 May 2011); see Principles 11–24.

[59] Human Rights Council Res 17/4 (16 June 2011), para 6.

(important) extent that the Principles address businesses directly, it is mainly to encourage them to respect human rights by avoiding activities with potentially adverse human rights impacts.[60] The introductory commentary to the Principles expressly eschews their creating 'new international law obligations'. Hopefully, the Principles will be a catalyst to encourage further State activity to hold their corporations, whether acting domestically or abroad, to a human rights-respecting posture and to permit civil society and shareholders to put the political spotlight on non-rights-respecting enterprises.[61]

V. HUMAN RIGHTS: UNIVERSAL OR CULTURALLY SPECIFIC

For some decades a view was propounded that human rights was a Western notion that was being foisted on the rest of the world. For example, 'Asian values' would be invoked by some States of that region in opposition to the idea of a universal concept of human rights. While the problem still inspires academic discussion (Freeman, 2013), it has little of relevance to say from the perspective of international human rights law. As we have seen, human rights and fundamental freedoms are thoroughly grounded in the UN Charter and most States of all regions of the world have freely become parties to most of the core international human rights treaties (see earlier), including the ICCPR and the ICESCR. At some time or another, they will all vote for (or join a consensus on) resolutions taking up human rights issues in other countries.

In fact, as early as 1993, the Vienna Declaration and Program of Action was untypically direct on the issue, declaring in its first paragraph: 'The universal nature of these rights and freedoms is beyond question.'

The same document, while insisting on the duty of States to promote and protect human rights, did nevertheless signal delphically that 'the significance of national and regional particularities and various historical, cultural and religious backgrounds must be borne in mind' (para 5). This should not be seen as clawing back the general orientation of universality; rather it is indicating that, as with any international norms, the method of securing compliance with them is a matter for any State's internal legal system. It may also be a signal that there may be some limited margin for the interpretation of the content of rights (see later).

The relativist argument is also specious. It ignores the fact that one very Western construct, the modern State, is gratefully adopted by some non-Western societies, however alien to their indigenous cultures. Since respect for human rights has become a feature of the modern State—a means of limiting the overweening power of the State—it is not convincing to claim a right to exercise the powers of statehood without accepting the constraints needed to ensure that the State represents, rather than subjugates, those within its jurisdiction.

Meanwhile, a robust debunking of culturally relative approaches to human rights was given as early as 1978 by the late Senator José Diokno of the Philippines: speaking of a cultural justification for Asian authoritarianism, he pointed out that this meant that 'the Asian conception of freedom differs from that in the West; that, in short, Asians are not

---

[60] Principles 11–24.

[61] [Editor's Note: Human Rights Council Res 26/9 (26 June 2014) established an open-ended intergovernmental working group, mandated 'to elaborate an international legally binding instrument to regulate, in international human rights law, the activities of transnational corporations and other business enterprises with respect to human rights'. The 3rd Session of the Working Group took place in October 2017.]

fit for democracy'; this he dismissed as 'racist nonsense'.[62] Indeed, insofar as States are the effective power-holders responsible for human rights violations, it is axiomatic that it is only at the State level that human rights can be guaranteed.

What international law does not dictate is how this guarantee is to be achieved and, as with all international law rules, that is a matter for the State. For instance, in principle, monist States will permit international law obligations generally, or international human rights obligations in particular, to be directly justiciable in their courts, whereas in principle, dualist States will not allow their courts to adjudicate international law or IHRL issues, unless they have in some way, typically by legislative act, been incorporated into national law. For example, the courts of the (more or less) dualist UK could not directly apply the provisions of the European Convention of Human Rights until the Human Rights Act 1998 directly incorporated it into UK law.[63] By contrast, the courts of generally monist Netherlands had been doing just that (de Wet, 2008, ch 5).

In reality, the two paradigms tend to be caricatural. The courts of States considering themselves dualist may well be willing at least to seek to interpret national law in a manner consistent with international law.[64] Meanwhile, monist States are rarely totally monist: they may be restricted to adjudicating treaty law rather than customary international law or they may treat a treaty provision as ordinary legislation that can be varied by subsequent legislation.[65] The courts themselves may clip their own wings by adopting doctrines such as the non-self-executing treaty, by which they decide that the particular treaty or treaty obligation is not one that was intended to be justiciable without legislation.[66] In any event, lawyers and or judges may just be unfamiliar or uncomfortable with international (human rights) law and so avoid invoking or applying it. These are only some of the points on a continuum between the monist and dualist paradigms.

In practice, human rights treaty bodies will not typically expect the provisions of their treaties to be expressly incorporated into national law.[67] However, as the Human Rights Committee has put it, 'Covenant guarantees may receive enhanced protection in those States where the court is automatically or through specific incorporation part of the domestic legal order.'[68] Whatever the level of incorporation, the judiciary may, like the other branches of government, be capable of placing a State in violation of its international human rights law obligations.[69]

---

[62] Quoted in Shue, 1980, p 66.

[63] Even under the Act, the Courts cannot strike down legislation that they cannot reconcile with the ECHR; they may only issue a certificate of incompatibility that then would require the amending legislator to repair the incompatibility (s 4).

[64] An early UK (Scottish) example not involving human rights is *Mortensen v Peters* (1906) 14 *Scots Law Times* 227. It took until the 1990s before the Courts would feel comfortable with ECHR-based arguments for interpretive purposes: see Besson, 2008, p 48; the ICCPR is generally overlooked.

[65] This is US practice: *Whitney v Robertson* 124 US 190 (1888) (Supreme Court).

[66] See, eg, *Foster and Eelam v Neilson*, 2 Pet 253 (1829) (US Supreme Court); also the refusal of the courts of clearly monist Senegal to try exiled Chadian President Hissène Habré in the absence of legislation implementing the universal jurisdiction clauses of the UNCAT: *Questions relating to the Obligation to Prosecute or Extradite (Belgium v Senegal), Judgment of 20 July 2012*, para 18.

[67] See, eg, Human Rights Committee, General Comment No 31 (n 29), para 13. Note, however, the practice of the Committee against Torture under UNCAT, which maintains that States are obliged to incorporate into domestic law the crime of torture, containing the elements of torture as defined in UNCAT Article 1: see Committee against Torture General Comment No 2 (Implementation of Article 2 by States parties), UN Doc CAT/C/GC/2 (2008), para 8.

[68] General Comment No 31, para 13.   [69] See, eg, Rodley, 2008.

VI. PRINCIPLES OF INTERNATIONAL
HUMAN RIGHTS LAW

It is not in the nature of international law to articulate the conceptual premises on which its elements are based. This is also true of international human rights law, and whereas we can look to notions of national law and social contract theory for the origins of human rights thinking in the West, the international level offers no such explanatory sources. The one idea that recurs in the preambles of the UDHR and the two Covenants that constitute the International Bill of Human Rights is that of human dignity. Thus, the first preambular paragraphs of the UDHR and the Covenants, echoing similar language from the UN Charter,[70] announce that 'recognition of the inherent dignity and of the equal and inalienable rights of all members of the human family is the foundation of freedom, justice and peace in the world'. The Covenants then proclaim that 'these rights *derive* from the inherent dignity of the human person'.[71] In the UDHR, the first article continues the invocation: 'All human beings are born free and equal in dignity and rights. They are endowed with reason and conscience and should act towards one another in a spirit of brotherhood'. The notion of 'reason' perhaps resonates with that of reason that underlies natural law whether theist or non-theist in doctrine.[72] Clearly, in addition to human dignity, other deep principles are freedom, equality, justice, and brotherhood. Yet others are identifiable, although not spelled out, notably fairness and impartiality (of which equality is a dimension), participation, and accountability.[73] Between them they can be considered to embrace most, if not all, internationally recognized human rights. Some rights will be more associated with one principle than another. Evidently a key value underlying the core economic and social rights is that of brotherhood, but as will be seen to be the case with civil and political rights, most could fall within more than one of these deep values.

What follows in this section is limited to civil and political rights, as the key economic and social rights have already been identified. It is also the case that virtually all the jurisprudence at the universal level at this stage concerns civil and political rights. As noted, the work of the Committee on Economic, Social and Cultural Rights under its Optional Protocol could affect the picture.

A. FREEDOM

The notion of freedom has two broad connotations: *intellectual* freedom and *physical* freedom. Under the former fall most of the so-called fundamental freedoms that are the hallmark of a free civil society: freedom of opinion and expression; of thought, conscience, and religion; of association; and right of peaceful assembly. It is hard to imagine a society in which all these freedoms are broadly respected that could be characterized as repressive.

There may, of course, be some limitations on such freedoms, especially where the rights of the individual and those of the group are not clearly compatible: indeed, giving the lie to the communitarian taunt that these traditional liberal freedoms connote a privileging of the individual over the legitimate needs of a society are the so-called 'claw-back' clauses that permit restrictions necessary to preserve such group values as national security, public order, and the

---

[70] Preambular para 2.

[71] Common preambular para 2. For an examination of the notion, see Jeremy Waldron, 'Is Dignity the Foundation of Human Rights?' (3 January 2013); available at SSRN http://ssrn.com/abstract=2196074.

[72] See Friedman, 1960, pp 58–9 (on St Thomas Aquinas) and 64–5 (on Grotius).

[73] I have here borrowed from the taxonomy I have previously used in Rodley, 2012, p 106.

rights of others.[74] Of course, any such restrictions must be the minimum necessary to achieve the declared goal and must not be such as to render the rights nugatory. Expression invoking incitement to racial hatred may well require to be restricted,[75] but evidently there is no justification for restricting the distribution of copies of the UDHR on Human Rights Day![76]

It is also not uncommon to speak of 'balancing', in the sense of balancing the right of an individual with the group value[77] or balancing the apparent demands of one right with another.[78] This implies an element of subjectivity that would allow anyone to make what would effectively be a 'judgement call'. A better conception is that of identifying the correct *scope* of each right internally and vis-à-vis other rights. The notion is captured vividly by the famous aphorism: 'the right to swing my fist ends where the other man's nose begins'.[79] It is not always possible to highlight so clearly the frontier between the rights and other recognized (group) values or between the rights themselves, but tests of necessity and proportionality that are integrated to the analytical process are a guide to the delimitation of the proper scope of the particular right in the context of the particular facts.[80]

The primordial instance of a right engaging *physical* freedom is, axiomatically, the right to liberty and security of person and its obverse, the prohibition of arbitrary detention. While not raising the same kinds of conceptual issues as the intellectual fundamental freedoms, there are areas of potential uncertainty in the notion of what is arbitrary. That a detention be provided for by law is not sufficient to dispose of the matter. For the Human Rights Committee, 'arbitrariness' connotes 'elements of inappropriateness, injustice and lack of predictability'.[81] Issues also arise in relation to 'security of person' which, for the European Court of Human Rights, is inseparable from deprivation of liberty, whereas the Human Rights Committee considers it to cover threats, such as death threats. Such threats come close to engaging freedom of movement. This latter freedom is evidently another physical freedom right and one that raises especially difficult issues when it comes to the rights of aliens lawfully within a State's territory: it touches a raw nerve under a traditional principle under international law that permits States the sovereign right to determine which aliens may be within their territory.[82]

A final freedom right is found in the prohibition of slavery and while chattel slavery may thankfully be of merely historical interest, other 'contemporary forms of slavery' persist, such as that associated with human trafficking, and may require strenuous action by States to protect its victims.

---

[74] See ICCPR Article 19(3) (freedom of opinion and expression); Article 18(3) (freedom of thought, conscience and religion); Article 22(2) (freedom of association); and Article 21, second sentence (right of peaceful assembly).

[75] Human Rights Committee General Comment No 34 (Article 19: Freedoms of Opinion and Expression), UN Doc CCPR/C/GC/34 (2011), paras 50–2.

[76] *Velichkin* v *Belarus* (Communication No 1022/2001), UN Doc CCPR/C/85/D/1022/2001 (2005).

[77] Eg *Coleman* v *Australia* (Communication No 1157/2003), UN Doc CCPR/C/87/D/1157/2003 (2006), ICCPR Article 19 being violated by 'disproportionate' reaction (fine and imprisonment) to public speaking in a shopping mall without a permit: para 7.3. Note the joint concurring opinion of Committee Members Nisuke Ando, Michael O'Flaherty, and Walter Kälin to the permit system allowing the authorities to 'strike a balance' between freedom of expression and 'countervailing' interests: ibid, Appendix.

[78] *Ross* v *Canada* (Communication No 736/1997), UN Doc CCPR/C/70/D/736/1997 (2000), upholding restrictions placed on a teacher in a school district with Jewish children, who publicly expressed anti-Jewish sentiments.

[79] Commonly attributed to the great nineteenth-century American jurist and judge, Oliver Wendell Holmes Jr.

[80] See General Comment No 31 (n 29), paras 33–7.

[81] *Van Alphen* v *Netherlands* (Communication No 305/1988), UN Doc CCPR/C/39/D/305/1988 (1990), para 5.8.

[82] Thus, under ICCPR Article 13, such an alien is provided only with procedural, rather than normative, protections.

B. FAIRNESS AND IMPARTIALITY: EQUAL TREATMENT AND NON-DISCRIMINATION

It is hard to think of anything that so offends one's sense of justice than to be treated differently from others for reasons extraneous to the issue at stake and on the basis of attributes that are, or are felt to be, beyond choice. Hence, the UN Charter's constant mention of 'without distinction as to race, sex, language or religion'. The first three criteria are evidently beyond all choice while the same may not be true in quite the same way for religion, since freedom of religion involves a right to 'adopt' a religion, evidently implying choice. Nevertheless, the inclusion of religion here was inevitable in that it was the inseparable link between race and religion that was the basis for the Jewish holocaust perpetrated by Nazi Germany. This genocide, as we have seen, was pivotal to the inclusion of human rights in the UN Charter. A further factor must have been that it is in the nature of religion or similar profoundly held beliefs as to the nature and purpose of humanity that the holder feels him or herself to be impotent simply to abandon such beliefs.

By the time of the adoption of the UDHR, other prohibited criteria of discrimination were added: 'colour, as well as political or other opinion, national or social origin, property, birth or other status'.[83] Again, most of these attributes are not a matter of individual choice, just ones that the individual was simply 'landed with'. This is also the case for property at birth, but not necessarily in later life when the acquisition or loss of property may be very much a matter of choice. As to political or other opinion, there is more personal freedom of choice, at least in respect of the decision to *express* one's political or similar opinions. The point is captured in the very freedom itself: under Article 19 ICCPR, there is a right to hold opinions without interference; it is only the expression of them that may, as noted, be restricted on certain grounds. What then of the notion of 'other status'? Assuming the *ejusdem generis* rule applies,[84] the question arises as to what amounts to 'the same kind'. The underlying idea seems to be that of attributes that are biologically or psychologically beyond choice. Thus, sexual orientation has come to be recognized as falling within the prohibited categories of discrimination.[85] In one major respect, the ICCPR goes beyond the UN Charter and UDHR, in the sense that it has a free-standing non-discrimination article. The earlier texts required the rights protected to be enjoyed without discrimination,[86] but Article 26 of the ICCPR requires equality under the law generally and non-discrimination on the listed grounds in respect of *all* legal rights. The Human Rights Committee, as other treaty bodies, accepts that offensive discrimination may be indirect as well as direct, but that some distinctions may be made as long as they are reasonable and objective.[87]

The same principles of fairness, impartiality, and equality also underlie the protection of the rights of (members of) ethnic, linguistic, or religious minorities found in Article 27 ICCPR. It is not clear to what extent this provision goes beyond the provisions on non-discrimination, direct or indirect (Rodley, 1995).

---

[83] Article 2.

[84] That is, the rule of interpretation that open clauses after a list should be understood as limiting further examples to those 'of the same kind' as those specified in the list.

[85] Nowak correctly points out that a specific decision of the Committee involving the criminalization of homosexual behaviour was found to violate Article 17(1) (private life) together with Article 2(1) (on the basis of the word 'sex'). The Committee did not explain this deviation from the issue as it was litigated, namely, as an Article 26 issue in relating to 'other status'; Nowak, 2005, referring to *Toonen v Australia* (Communication No 488/1992), UN Doc CCPR/C/50/D/488/1992 (1994).   [86] And, indeed, ICCPR, Article 2(1).

[87] See General Comment 18 (1989) (Non-discrimination), paras 10 and 13 respectively.

C. HUMAN DIGNITY

While the human dignity value appears to underlie the whole corpus of international human rights law, some rights are especially associated directly with this value. Thus the UN Declarations against Torture and other Cruel, Inhuman or Degrading Treatment or Punishment, and against Enforced Disappearance both consider their subject matter to be 'an offence to human dignity'.[88] The only international treaty on the right to life, the Second Optional Protocol to the ICCPR, aiming at the abolition of the death penalty, affirms that abolition 'contributes to the enhancement of human dignity'.[89]

Indeed, few human rights issues have received as much attention as the prohibitions of torture and ill-treatment and of enforced disappearance, which are prohibited by every general human rights treaty.[90]

Enforced disappearance, while not specifically addressed in general human rights conventions, violates many of the rights contained in those conventions, most evidently the prohibition of arbitrary arrest and detention/right to liberty and security of person and the prohibition of torture and similar ill-treatment. To at least this extent, that links the latter right directly to the human dignity value, as well as the freedom value. In addition to the just-mentioned Declaration there are now a universal and a regional convention on this abhorrent violation.[91] Even though the UN Conventions define the notions of torture and enforced disappearance, there remain outstanding issues of scope, such as whether pain or suffering for 'torture' has to be more severe than for 'inhuman treatment' or whether enforced disappearance requires, beyond refusal to acknowledge the detention and/or the whereabouts of the person, an additional element involving placing the person outside the protection of law.[92]

The right to life, while non-derogable, is not absolute in the sense that not all deprivations of life will be considered arbitrary and thus violating the right. Accordingly, deployment of potentially lethal force in international armed conflict permissible under IHL would also be consistent with international human rights law. Similarly, law enforcement officials may use such force to protect life and limb if no other means are available. Once again, as with restrictions on fundamental freedoms, we see notions of necessity and proportionality at work. An especially difficult area is posed by the continuing existence of the death penalty in some national jurisdictions, despite the fact that there are one universal and three regional abolitionist protocols to treaties whose original texts expressly contemplate the death penalty as an exception to the right to life, albeit subject to certain important restrictions.[93] Meanwhile, with (so far) increasing majorities, the UN General Assembly has been urging States to adopt moratoria on the use of the death penalty.[94]

---

[88] GA Res 3452 (9 December 1975), Article 2 (torture); GA Res 47/133 (18 December 1992), Article 1 (enforced disappearance).

[89] GA Res 44/128 (15 December 1989), preambular para 1; see also African Charter on Human and Peoples' Rights, Article 5, and American Convention on Human Rights, Article 5.

[90] ICCPR, Article 7; ECHR, Article 3; ACHR, Article 5; ACHPR, Article 5; Arab CHR, Article 8; see generally Rodley and Pollard, 2009, ch 2.

[91] International Convention for the Protection of All Persons from Enforced Disappearance, GA Res 61/177 (20 December 2006) and Inter-American Convention on the Forced Disappearance of Persons, OAS General Assembly, Twenty-fourth Regular Session, 9 June 1994, OAS TS A-60.

[92] See Rodley and Pollard, 2009, pp 85–124 (torture) and 332–7 (enforced disappearance).

[93] Second Optional Protocol to the ICCPR, GA Res 44/128 (15 December 1989); Protocol No 6 (1982), CETS No 114 and 13 (2013), CETS No 187 to the European Convention on Human Rights, and Protocol to the American Convention on Human Rights to Abolish the Death Penalty (1990), OAS TS 73.

D. JUSTICE AND LEGALITY

In broad terms, the justice value connotes fairness and equality, as indicated earlier. It also has the specific connotation in the sense of administration of justice: the legal justice system. If that system acts arbitrarily or without integrity, there can be no secure legal rights. The right to a fair trial or hearing—due process of law—is thus infrastructural. The relevant article of the ICCPR is Article 14, and Human Rights Committee General Comment 32 deals with it at length. One noteworthy element is the increasing scepticism as to the ability of military or special courts to deliver justice either to those who are accused of crime or those who may be the victims of crimes committed by military or security personnel.[95] Unless one has the means of knowing the content of one's legal obligations and the consequence of non-compliance, any notion of legality—and so justice—is fatally undermined. The principle of non-retroactivity of crime and punishment (*nullum crimen, nulla poena sine lege*) is found in the non-derogable Article 15 ICCPR.

E. PARTICIPATION

Intellectual fundamental freedoms represent both a condition and a means of meaningful participation in society. The right to participate in the government of one's society is evidently a direct manifestation of this value (Article 25 ICCPR). It covers a range of issues, from equality of access to the civil service to the right to choose a State's political leaders or indeed to stand for election. To the extent that competitive democratic elections have become the system of choice since the end of the Cold War, the Human Rights Committee has felt able to find the requirement that candidates for political office should belong to parties or to specific parties to be an 'unreasonable restriction on the right to participate in public affairs'.[96] Like the European Court of Human Rights, it has also found a blanket prohibition on prisoners' voting to violate the right.[97]

F. ACCOUNTABILITY

Numerous rights that respond to other values also respond to the value of accountability. Obvious examples would be the right to freedom to receive and impart information (a dimension of freedom of opinion and expression) and hold elected representatives accountable by voting for others (see the preceding paragraph). Especially important are the provisions for remedies in case of violation of rights. While the right to compensation is the standard means, it can go much further to include an obligation on the State to investigate criminal violations of human rights and bring perpetrators to justice.[98]

---

[94] Most recently at the time of writing, GA Res 67/176 (20 December 2012): 111 for, 41 against, 34 abstaining (UN Doc A/67/PV.60, pp 16–17).

[95] See Human Rights Committee General Comment No 32 (2007) (Article 14: Right to equality before courts and tribunals and to a fair trial), UN Doc CCPR/C/GC/32, para 22 (civilians before military or special courts); *Kholodova v Russian Federation* (Communication No 1548/2007), UN Doc CCPR/C/106/D/1548/2007 (2012) (public officials acquitted by military tribunal for murder of a journalist).

[96] General Comment No 25 (1996), UN Doc CCPR/C/21/Rev.1/Add.7, para 17.

[97] *Yevdokimov and Rezanov v Russian Federation* (Communication No 1410/2005), UN Doc CCPR/C/101/D/1410/2005 (2011), following *Hirst v United Kingdom* (74025/01) ECHR 6 October 2005.

[98] Human Rights Committee, General Comment No 31 (n 29), paras 15 and 18.

G. THE PRIVATE SPHERE

The right to be left undisturbed in one's home and to a private life is not a typical mani-festation of the freedom value, but although precisely not in the public domain, it could be considered a form of freedom to be insulated from social intrusion.[99] It certainly con-nects up with freedom of expression, on the scope of which it represents a limitation. The protection of the family and childhood[100] are primary positive obligations on the State and are not easily assignable to one of the core values. They may be seen as preconditions to the full flourishing of the human personality, without which the other rights and the values on which they are based cannot be meaningfully enjoyed.

VII. INTERNATIONAL MACHINERY ON HUMAN RIGHTS

Anyone attending the principal UN political human rights organ, the Human Rights Council, would find it difficult to credit the difference between it and its predecessor, the Commission on Human Rights, in the latter's early years. Nowadays, States and NGOs routinely make oral interventions (under certain agenda items) on any human rights issue or any country. NGOs also routinely submit written information for circulation as UN documents on the same issues. It was only in the late 1970s and early 1980s that it came to be accepted that the previous pervasive silence on specific human rights cases and situ-ations in member States could be left behind. There is now a substantial network of what are usually called Charter-based human rights procedures.

A. UNIVERSAL CHARTER-BASED HUMAN RIGHTS PROCEDURES

1. UN Commission on Human Rights

The Commission established by the Economic and Social Council (ECOSOC) pursuant to Article 68 of the UN Charter understood its early role to be one of standard-setting. Very early in its existence, in 1947, it decided 'that it has no power to take any action in regard to any complaint concerning human rights', a stance confirmed by ECOSOC Resolution 75 V (1947). A confidential list of complaints, without details, was to be compiled by the UN Secretariat, with original texts of the complaints being made accessible to members. No public discussion of the complaints took place, nor, even in closed discussion, did members raise alleged human rights violations in other States.

a. Country-specific procedures

A breakthrough came two decades later in 1967, when the Commission and its Sub-Commission[101] were authorized by ECOSOC Resolution 1235 XLII to make 'a thorough study' of alleged consistent patterns of human rights violation and investigate gross human rights violations. Examples given were the human rights situation in southern Africa, that is, South Africa, Southwest Africa (now Namibia) and secessionist Southern Rhodesia.

---

[99] See ICCPR, Article 17.

[100] See ICCPR, Articles 23 and 24.

[101] A body of up to 26 individual experts, then known as the Sub-Commission on Prevention of Discrimination and Protection of Minorities, later re-named Sub-Commission on the Promotion and Protection of Human Rights, until it was dissolved at the same time as the parent inter-governmental Commission on Human Rights.

When in 1968 the Sub-Commission took this mandate seriously, forwarding material from NGOs not only on the southern African situation, but also on the independent sovereign States of Greece (after a 1967 military coup) and Haiti (languishing under the dictatorship of President-for-life Dr François (Papa Doc) Duvalier), the Commission, unwilling to let NGOs dictate its agenda, established a confidential complaints procedure reflected in ECOSOC Resolution 1503 XLVIII (27 May 1970) ('the 1503 procedure'). This was a confidential procedure, whereby the confidential list of communications[102] would be examined by a working group on communications of five members of the Sub-Commission ('working group on communications'). The working group could forward to the full Sub-Commission communications 'which appear to reveal a consistent pattern of gross and reliably attested violations of human rights'. The Sub-Commission could then send on any such situation to the Commission.

The Commission in turn established its own working group ('working group on situations'), composed of five of its members, to recommend to the Commission what action to take. Such activity occasionally involved a 'thorough study' carried out by a special rapporteur appointed by the Commission,[103] sometimes a request to the UN Secretary-General to report to the next annual session of the Commission. Usually, the Commission would merely decide to keep the situation 'under review' from year to year. On occasion it would simply decide to drop consideration of the situation, regardless of its seriousness. It never used its power under Resolution 1503 to establish an investigative committee.

However, the '1503 procedure' dictated how 'communications' from private sources, including NGOs, should be treated. It did not constrain individual members of the Commission, nor of the Sub-Commission. If they wanted to raise situations of their own motion, they could. Already a working group on southern Africa had been established in 1967. Its mandate was extended briefly to cover the territories occupied by Israel in the June 1967 war—until the General Assembly itself established a working group on that situation. Public consideration of human rights country problems at the UN only moved beyond southern Africa and the Israeli-occupied territories (IOT) in 1975 in response to international concern with a friendless military government in Chile that had brutally seized power in 1973 from a constitutionally elected government.

Slowly after this other countries were taken up in public session, with a special rapporteur[104] usually appointed to examine the situation, provided the State in question was not too influential. There are at the time of writing some 13 country mandates. Despite the appalling record of the military government of Argentina in the latter half of the 1990s, whose barbarities included thousands of enforced disappearances, there was insufficient political will to initiate a study of the situation in that country. This lamentable situation in fact led to a positive development. If the Commission could not examine the situation in Argentina, perhaps it could consider the phenomenon that most characterized that situation, that is, enforced disappearance (Kramer and Weissbrodt, 1981).

---

[102] By ECOSOC Res 728F (30 July 1959), the Secretariat had been authorized to prepare a confidential list of communications (complaints) alleging human rights violations in specific countries, the list being circulated to members of the Sub-Commission and the Commission. This list became the basis for the '1503 procedure'.

[103] The term 'special rapporteur' is a portmanteau term for individual experts charged with a specific function by a UN body and expected to report to the body. Here, we are talking about experts mandated to investigate or fact-find for the body appointing them.

[104] Sometimes the term 'special representative' (usually, then, to be appointed by the Secretary-General) or 'independent expert' would be used. The terminology was no guide to the function.

b. Thematic special procedures

The outcome was the establishment of the first of the thematic special procedures, the Working Group on Enforced or Involuntary Disappearances (1980). Its initial mandate was merely to study the phenomenon of enforced disappearances and it was created for a year. However, the Working Group's first report, in 1981, was something of an institutional earthquake. It provided a summary of all the cases it had received and transmitted to the governments impugned, as well as summaries of any replies from them. It also began the practice of making urgent appeals where people had been detained in circumstances indicating that they might be at risk of enforced disappearance. The Working Group did not draw any conclusions regarding State responsibility, considering its role to be humanitarian and non-judgmental, albeit there was nothing requiring such caution in the resolution setting it up. It also began undertaking country visits, the reports of which evidently struggled, none too successfully, to avoid judgment.

The next thematic mechanisms to be created were those of the Special Rapporteurs on extra-judicial, summary and arbitrary executions (1982) and on torture and ill-treatment (1985) (see Rodley, 1986). Their reports followed the style of those of the Working Group. There are now some 44 thematic mandates.[105] Some (mainly in the field of civil and political rights) are more action-oriented, based on individual case work; others (mainly in the field of economic and social rights) are more study-oriented. But there is no hard and fast dividing line, as evidenced by the joint work of a number of civil and political rights mandates with that on the right to health in respect of the situation in the US Naval Station at Guantánamo Bay, Cuba. Only one, the Working Group on Arbitrary Detention, is expressly mandated to make individual case-specific conclusions. However, the other original mandates have long since abandoned any pretence of not arriving at country-specific evaluations.

2. UN Human Rights Council

The 'double-standards' implied in the politically grounded selection of countries for public consideration by the Commission had been noted from the early days of focus on the IOT and southern Africa exclusively. The inability to address the situation in Argentina directly has already been noted. Another high-profile example was the impunity of Iraq under the bloody dictatorship of President Saddam Hussein. Even after the gas bombing of 5,000 of its own people in Halabja in 1988, it was not possible to get a majority to vote for public consideration. Indeed, Iraq even managed to get itself dropped from the confidential 1503 procedure. Two years later, after Iraq invaded Kuwait, the Commission could then appoint a special rapporteur on the human rights situation in Iraq.[106]

Yet it was not until 2004 that a High-Level Panel on Threats, Challenges and Change, established by Secretary-General Kofi Annan, found that the Commission had become discredited and should eventually be replaced by another body.[107] The political selectivity matter was the key issue. One reason for this, it was suggested, was that States with poor human rights records were more inclined to stand and work hard for election to this 53-member State body[108] so as to deflect possible attention from themselves.

---

[105] [Editor's Note: the number of thematic mandates in the text has been updated from the 36 at the time of the previous edition in 2014.]

[106] And another one on occupied Kuwait. See Commission on Human Rights Res 1991/74 (6 March 1991), para 5 (Iraq) and 1991/67 (6 March 1991), para 9 (occupied Kuwait).

[107] UN Doc A/59/565 (2004).   [108] Ibid, para 283.

The solution of the High-Level Panel was to have a body, either at Charter level or, at any rate, reporting to the General Assembly, that would be universal in membership. It would thus not be a distorted cross-section of the UN membership and it would have instantly enhanced status by reporting directly to the Assembly rather than to ECOSOC. The Secretary-General, with strong support from the USA, came out in favour of a smaller body elected by the General Assembly, with a two-thirds majority vote (implicitly guaranteeing that States with poor human rights records would not be elected).[109] After an extensive negotiation General Assembly Resolution 251/60 was adopted in 2006 and a 47-member Human Rights Council elected by a simple majority of the General Assembly was created; it would report direct to the Assembly, not to ECOSOC.

Even if there is no competition for regional slots, any candidate has to secure a majority of positive votes in the General Assembly rather than obtain the seat by acclamation. Moreover, no State may have more than two successive three-year terms. The Council is also required to institute a system of universal periodic review (UPR) of the human rights of all UN member States. It is easier to call special sessions to deal with urgent situations (one-third of Council members can request, not over a half as before) and, anyway, the Council meets much more frequently than the one annual six-week session of the Commission. Meanwhile, the Council inherits the system of special procedures and a 'complaints mechanism' modelled on the '1503 procedure'. Of particular significance, there is the UPR.

It is too early to attempt an authoritative evaluation; the Council is a work-in-progress. At first, it looked as though it would be retrogressive. The institution-building package that emerged after its first year was not encouraging.[110] While the use of country rapporteurs was continued, they were limited in practice to those that had already been taken up by the Commission; two, Belarus and Cuba, were even dropped as part of the political deal to get the package.[111] By 2011, a willingness to take up new situations emerged (Côte d'Ivoire, Syria), with others following (Eritrea, 2012; Mali, 2013). Others that had been dropped earlier reappeared (Iran, 2011; Belarus, 2012), one, Sudan, as early as 2009.[112]

The earliest special sessions were overwhelmingly focused on the IOT (and Israel's 2006 incursion into Lebanon). An apparent breakthrough on the situation in Sri Lanka proved illusory when the Council adopted an uncritical resolution proposed by Sri Lanka itself.[113] The Council retrieved itself by adopting resolutions in 2012 and 2013 expressing concern at various grave human rights violations,[114] a concern confirmed late in 2013 by the High Commissioner for Human Rights.[115] A convincing indication of real moving away from political selectivity or 'double-standards' would be if the Council were to appoint a special rapporteur on Sri Lanka's (at the time of writing) continuously deteriorating situation.[116] On the other hand, after the Sri Lanka setback, there were significant

---

[109] *In Larger Freedom: Towards Development, Security and Human Rights for All*, Report of the Secretary-General, UN Doc A/59/2005, para 183.   [110] Human Rights Council Res 5/1 (18 June 2007).

[111] Human Rights Council Dec 1/102 (30 June 2006); for the background, see Boyle, 2009, pp 28–44.

[112] [Editor's Note: Only one new country rapporteur has since been established, for the Central African Republic in 2013. There are currently 12 such mandates.]

[113] Human Rights Council Res S-11/1 (27 May 2009).

[114] Human Rights Council, Res 19/2 (22 March 2012) and 22/1 (21 March 2013).

[115] Opening remarks by UN High Commissioner for Human Rights at a press conference during her mission to Sri Lanka, Colombo, 31 August 2013: http://www.ohchr.org/EN/NewsEvents/Pages/DisplayNews.aspx?NewsID=13673&LangID=Es.

[116] Ibid. [Editor's Note: Such a mechanism has not been established.]

special sessions on Côte d'Ivoire (2010), Libya (2011), and Syria (three in 2011 and one in 2012).[117]

Meanwhile, although UPR does not lead to country-specific evaluations by the Council as such,[118] it is generally thought to be playing a role that encourages States to make pledges, such as to ratify unratified human rights treaties or to issue standing invitations to special procedures to visit the country in question. Also, the very process of having to face questions and recommendations, based on the report submitted by the country and reports prepared by the Office of the High Commissioner for Human Rights (OHCHR), on the concerns of special procedures and treaty bodies (see next section), and on those expressed by 'stakeholders' (national human rights institutions and NGOs), can be at least a means of nudging the State towards improving its performance to some extent.

B. UNIVERSAL TREATY BODIES

As already indicated, the presumption in the early days of the UN was that only by treaty adherence could States' human rights behaviour be submitted to international scrutiny. What follows is a consideration of the 'system' of the nine treaty bodies (Committees) established pursuant to the 'core' human rights treaties referred to earlier.[119] There are in fact ten treaty bodies, as a second one on torture was created by an Optional Protocol to UNCAT (OPCAT), that is, the Sub-Committee on Prevention of Torture (SPT). Its functions are innovative and will be briefly touched on at the end. The first one, the Committee against Torture (CAT) established under UNCAT, has more usual functions.

The treaty bodies are composed of between 10 and 25 members, with the mean being 18. The members are expected to be experts and are nominated by the States parties to the respective treaty to serve in their individual capacities. They are typically elected to four-year terms and may be re-elected without limit under some treaties, while two mandates are the maximum under other (more recent) ones. The expertise required is that of the subject matter, not necessarily law, although their job is to seek to interpret and apply a legal instrument that normally falls to be interpreted according to the law of treaties, a discipline likely to be more familiar to persons with legal training. In principle it may be easier for persons who are not government members to act in a genuinely individual capacity. Nevertheless, some treaty body members are government officials, often senior diplomats.[120] In practice, the discourse that takes place reflects far more that of individual expertise than intergovernmental negotiation.

---

[117] [Editor's note: subsequent Special Sessions have been held concerning: the Central African Republic (2014); IOT (2014); ISIS in Iraq and the Levant (2014); Boko Haram (2015); Syria (2016); South Sudan (2016); and the Rohingya in Rakhine State, Myanmar (2017).]

[118] The UPR process outcome consists of recommendations made by other States together with the response of the examined State to each recommendation; there is no corporate conclusion or recommendation made by the Council as a whole.

[119] Committee on the Elimination of Racial Discrimination (CERD), Committee on Economic, Social and Cultural Rights (CESCR) (uniquely, established by ECOSOC, the body originally provided for by ICESCR to perform the monitoring function), Human Rights Committee (HRC), Committee on the Elimination of Discrimination against Women (CEDAW Committee), the Committee against Torture (CAT), the Committee on the Rights of the Child (CRC Committee), the Committee on the Protection of All Migrant Workers and Members of Their Families (CMW Committee), the Committee on the Rights of Persons with Disabilities (CRPD Committee), and the Committee on Enforced Disappearances (CED).

[120] It is a long-standing practice of most committees, now enshrined in the 'Guidelines on the Independence and Impartiality of Members of Human Rights Treaty Bodies ("the Addis Ababa Guidelines")', adopted by the Twenty-fourth annual meeting of chairs of the treaty bodies (UN Doc A/67/222 (2012) Annex), for members to refrain from participating in work on their own countries.

1. Functions

a. State reports

In respect of all but the Committee on Enforced Disappearances (CED) and evidently the Subcommittee for the Prevention of Torture and Inhuman or Degrading Treatment or Punishment (SPT), the States parties to a treaty are required to submit periodic reports to the Committees and reviewing these State reports is the one common function across the nine core treaty bodies. The periodicity of reports, when specified, is between two and five years. For the Human Rights Committee, the treaty body of the ICCPR, it is when the Committee specifies, but in practice the Committee uses a range of three to six years depending on the seriousness of the situation. The outlier CED only receives as of right and automatically an initial report, after which it is up to the Committee to decide whether it wants further reports. This doubtless reflects the fact that most States parties will not engage in the practice of enforced disappearance and should not be required to report unnecessarily.

Several of the Committees put written questions before the hearing to the State, in the form of a 'list of issues' (LOI), requesting States to respond in writing, so that when the actual oral hearing takes place with a delegation from the State, the process of information clarification is already underway. Some have gone further and offered States wishing to ease what the latter call the 'reporting burden' the option of 'focused reporting', that is simply responding to a 'list of issues prior to reporting' (LOIPR) once the initial reports of the States has been examined.[121] After the written and oral exchange, the Committee will adopt 'concluding observations'; these are mainly a list of concerns about areas of possible non-compliance with treaty provisions and recommendations to address the concerns. Concluding observations began only in 1992.[122] Some Committees have also established a follow-up procedure consisting of a further round of exchanges, under the guidance of a special rapporteur, on a number of the recommendations. The Committees refer to the overall process as the 'constructive dialogue'.[123]

Many States become overdue in submitting their reports, some for up to two decades. This has led some Committees to institute a procedure of considering a situation in the absence of a report, applied to the most seriously overdue. Here usually the Committee will announce its intention to initiate the procedure. As is intended, this may often result in the State in question submitting a report. If it does not, the Committee may draft an LOI and, again, the State may respond. In the absence of a response then the hearing will go ahead, the State being invited to send a delegation, which the State may well do. The least satisfactory (and rarest) outcome will be an actual hearing in the absence of any written contribution from the State or any delegation. A constant problem for the Committees is that they generally have a backlog of reports submitted but yet to be considered, while also faced with overdue reports; if the latter were to be submitted, the backlog would be even greater.[124]

---

[121] See Rodley, 2013, pp 621, 627 (LOI) and 629–30 (LOIPR). [Editor's Note: Following the adoption by the General Assembly of Res 68/268 (9 April 2014) on 'Strengthening and enhancing the effective functioning of the Un human rights treaty body system' (paras 1 and 2), all treaty bodies are encouraged to offer States the possibility of using what is now called the 'Simplified Reporting Procedure'. This is increasingly being used.]

[122] Before that there was no agreement that the bodies could interpret their powers as including the issuance of country-specific evaluations: ibid, 628–9.

[123] See, eg, Report by Navanetham Pillay, *Strengthening the United Nations Human Rights Treaty Body System: A Report by the United Nations High Commissioner for Human Rights* (22 June 2012) section 3.1.1 (available at http://www.ohchr.org/EN/HRBodies/HRTD/Pages/TBStrengthening.aspx).

[124] [Editor's Note: in response to this problem UN GA Res 68/268 (9 April 2014) substantially increased the amount of meeting time available to treaty bodies to deal with the backlog of reports and, whilst not entirely eliminated, the problem of backlog for many Committees is now significantly reduced. The problem of late or non-reporting, however, remains.]

b. General comments

The Committees have developed a practice of issuing 'general comments', consisting of guidance to States on the Committees' understanding of what States' obligations under the respective treaty may be. These were developed by the Human Rights Committee in the early 1980s, during the Cold War, when there was no agreement to issue country-specific evaluation of the sort found in what are now called 'concluding observations'. These are seen as authoritative interpretations of the treaties, developed on the basis of extensive experience of reviewing periodic reports and of examining individual cases (see following section). General comments are now typically the result of protracted discussion over several sessions of the Committee in question. The practice of consulting civil society and governments during the process has also emerged over time.

c. Individual complaints

It was not by oversight that the only obligation States were willing to assume from the beginning was that of reviewing periodic reports submitted by governments. This process was in effect the lowest common denominator of what States were prepared to accept by way of international supervision of their compliance with their human rights obligations. Nevertheless, from the beginning the idea of a court that would hear individual complaints was advanced by some.[125] Yet outside the European and, later, Inter-American regions there was no political will for such a radical idea. What was, however, in the realm of the possible was an optional system of having individual complaints submitted to the Committees. This was first made available by States making declarations under Article 14 ICERD and Article 22 UNCAT or by their ratifying the (First) Optional Protocol to the ICCPR. Later other treaty bodies were given the same power to consider individual complaints, either by an optional declaration under a new treaty or by ratifying an optional protocol, usually adopted later. The Convention on the Elimination of All Forms of Discrimination Against Women (CEDAW) was the first of these with its Optional Protocol and now it is or will be possible for all treaty bodies to receive individual complaints. So far, it is the Human Rights Committee that has most practice on such complaints, followed by CAT and then the CEDAW Committee and CERD.

Although the 'views' that are the outcome of the Committees' deliberations on individual complaints are not per se legally binding on the States in question, the (written, confidential) process by which they are adopted is modelled on judicial practice. Both parties are given full opportunity to respond to each other's pleadings and the Committees' deliberations are indistinguishable from those of a court. The views are adopted 'in a judicial spirit'.[126] The 'jurisprudence' or 'case law' emanating from the cases is in the public domain and widely resorted to by international lawyers seeking authoritative interpretation of the treaties. Some Committees have also established a follow-up procedure, whereby the good offices of a special rapporteur are used to seek compliance with the adverse findings of the Committee.

The practice has emerged, similar to that of the ICJ and the European Court of Human Rights, of seeking interim measures to discourage action by the State party that would render the process nugatory. Thus, if 'irreparable harm' appears imminent, such as the application of the death penalty or the deportation of someone to a State where they face torture or other prohibited ill-treatment, the State will be requested to refrain from taking

---

[125] Eg Lauterpacht, 1950, ch 3, discussing the possibility of amending Article 34 of the Statute of the International Court of Justice to permit individuals, rather than just States, to seize the Court.

[126] The language of the Human Rights Committee: General Comment No 33 (2008) (The Obligations of States Parties under the Optional Protocol to the [ICCPR]) UN Doc CCPR/C/GC/33, para 11.

the action, pending consideration of the case. Non-compliance with the request will be considered a violation of the instrument providing for the right of individual petition.[127]

d. Inter-State complaints

A number of treaties provide for inter-State complaints, that is, on a reciprocal basis, the consideration of complaints by one State against another. Uniquely within the UN treaty bodies system, ICERD makes such complaints an automatic possibility (Article 12). The others, like that under Article 41 ICCPR are all optional on a reciprocal basis. The procedure has not once been used and so will not further detain us here.

e. Inquiries

The drafters of UNCAT introduced a novel function for a UN human rights instrument. Provision was made for undertaking inquiries into the alleged systematic practices of torture (Article 20). The innovation was sufficiently controversial that a special provision had to be made for States to be able to opt out of the procedure by means of a reservation at the time of ratification (Article 28). Even without availing themselves of the 'opt out', States could refuse to permit the treaty body to have access to their territories when undertaking an inquiry.[128] Subsequently, other instruments came to envisage a similar power, starting with the Optional Protocol to CEDAW. The principal practice to date is that by UNCAT, followed by CEDAW. The UNCAT practice has been more limited than was expected at the time of drafting, consisting of only eight published inquiry reports.[129]

f. Other functions

Committee on Enforced Disappearances

No doubt reflecting the especial gravity of the phenomenon of enforced disappearances, the CED is empowered to refer serious situations—apparent systematic or widespread practices of enforced disappearance—to the attention of the General Assembly (Article 34). It may also request urgent action (not just requests for interim measures) in respect of a feared enforced disappearance (Article 30).

Sub-Committee for the Prevention of Torture and Other Cruel, Inhuman or Degrading Treatment or Punishment (SPT)

As indicated earlier, OPCAT establishes a wholly novel body. It has no similarity with the other treaty bodies. Modelled broadly on the functions of the Committee for the Prevention of Torture and Inhuman or Degrading Treatment or Punishment (CPT) established under the 1987 European Convention of the same name, the SPT has the right without further permission to undertake periodic missions to States parties and visit places of detention. The idea is that institutions subject to visits will be deterred from engaging in the prohibited practices. Unlike the CPT, there is no express power for it to undertake ad hoc visits, though it may be that the dearth of available resources for frequent visits will be more of an obstacle to the achievement of this deterrent function.[130]

---

[127] Ibid, para 19, following *Piandiong et al v The Philippines* (Communication No 869/1999), UN Doc CCPR/C/70/D/869/1999 (2000), para 5.2.

[128] UN Doc A/51/44 (1996), paras 216–18 (refusal of Egypt—no other refusal of a CAT visit is known to have occurred).

[129] [Editor's Note: the number of Inquiry Reports published by the CAT has increased to ten, with Reports being published concerning Lebanon (2014) and Egypt (2017).]

[130] [Editor's Note: When this was written, the SPT had only been able to undertake an average of three or four visits per year. The SPT is now able to undertake approximately ten visits per year following increased resourcing in the wake of UN GA Res 68/268 (9 April 2014).]

However, the OPCAT also provides for States parties to establish their own national preventive mechanisms (NPM), whose function would be the same as the SPT or, for that matter, the CPT. This dimension may then suggest that the principal contribution of the SPT in practice will be in its ability to support and so enhance the effectiveness of the NPMs.

2. The legal nature of treaty body outputs

In some ways, the human rights treaty drafters sought to steer clear of endowing the treaty bodies with the same power to issue binding decisions or judgments as courts would have. Nevertheless, the output of a body provided for *within* a treaty and appointed by States parties to the treaties, operating in a judicial spirit, must have the sort of juridical authority that governments could not simply dismiss as merely recommendatory. The point could not have been stated more clearly, in respect of the Human Rights Committee, by the ICJ:

> Since it was created, the Human Rights Committee has built up a considerable body of interpretative case law, in particular through its findings in response to the individual communications which may be submitted to it in respect of States parties to the first Optional Protocol, and in the form of its 'General Comments'. Although the Court is in no way obliged, in the exercise of its judicial functions, to model its own interpretation of the Covenant on that of the Committee, it believes that it should ascribe great weight to the interpretation adopted by this independent body that was established specifically to supervise the application of that treaty. The point here is to achieve the necessary clarity and the essential consistency of international law, as well as legal security, to which both the individuals with guaranteed rights and the States obliged to comply with treaty obligations are entitled.[131]

3. Proposals for improvements to the system

The core treaty bodies are thought to represent a reporting burden on States, thus giving a reason for delays in reporting, and, as noted earlier, there are backlogs that would increase with removal of the delays in reporting. There are also elements of duplication across the treaty bodies: many of the subjects of the topic-specific treaties also fall within the scope of the general treaties (the Covenants). There are also possibilities in the latter areas for contradictions in the outputs of the treaty bodies.

Various proposals have been mooted to address these issues: a single, unified treaty body,[132] a consolidated report for submission to all the bodies,[133] and a comprehensive reporting calendar.[134] There is no space here to analyse why, so far, none of these solutions has been able to overcome assorted legal or political obstacles. It remains the case that most improvements are made by the treaty bodies themselves, sometimes individually and sometimes collectively.[135] Thus, the treaty bodies have developed the LOI and LOIPR, as well as the consideration of situations in the absence of a report. It is instructive that the latest proposal from the High Commissioner for Human Rights—the comprehensive

---

[131] *Ahmadou Sadio Diallo (Republic of Guinea v Democratic Republic of the Congo), Merits, Judgment, ICJ Reports 2012*, p 639, para 66.

[132] See Report of Philip Alston, *Effective Functioning of Bodies Established Pursuant to United Nations Human Rights Instruments: Final Report on Enhancing the Long-Term Effectiveness of the United Nations Human Rights Treaty System* (27 March 1997), UN Doc E/CN.4/1997/74.

[133] *Strengthening of the United Nations: An Agenda for Further Change: Report of the Secretary-General*, UN Doc A/57/387 (9 September 2002), para 54.

[134] *Strengthening the United Nations Human Rights Treaty Body System: A Report by the United Nations High Commissioner for Human Rights*, (22 June 2012), pp 37–46. [135] Ibid.

reporting calendar (or 'master calendar') is predicated on the now optional LOI and LOIPR procedures being made compulsory and operating together with the procedure of a review in the absence of a report.

At the time of writing, it seems that it will remain necessary for the treaty bodies to continue their own initiatives to increase the efficiency of their procedures. The main obstacle to their attempts in this direction is the constant limitation on their resources, aggravated by periodic financial crises.[136]

4. The special procedures and the treaty body system

The treaty bodies were created, it will be recalled, because in the early decades of the UN it was thought that international scrutiny of States' human rights performance could only be engaged in by means of freely accepted treaty obligations. The development of the special procedures of the Human Rights Council did not impede their development.

Under the circumstances, it is surprising that there is not more overlap and even competition between the two systems. So far, there is more complementarity than competition between them. The special procedures do not engage in reviews of State periodic reports. Even the advent of UPR that could have been at odds with that core function of the treaty bodies has not turned out that way, since UPR does not lead to corporate conclusions and recommendations like those of the treaty bodies. On the contrary, treaty body concluding observations have proved a fertile source of recommendations by Council members to States undergoing UPR (Rodley, 2012, pp 328–30).

Similarly, except for the Working Group on Arbitrary Detention, special procedures do not routinely come to conclusions about specific individual allegations of human rights violations. Apart from the CED, it is left to the special procedures to undertake urgent appeals. It will be interesting to see how the CED and Working Group on Enforced or Involuntary Disappearances deal with their overlapping powers to make such appeals.

One area of definite potential overlap is that of inquiries into systematic practices. However, while such inquiries, typically involving country visits, are routine for the special procedures, they have not yet attained the same standard practice for even those treaty bodies with the power to pursue such inquiries. In any event, as long as the inquiries do not take place at the same time, it is possible that they can still be complementary, with each inquiry able to build on the previous one (Rodley, 2012, p 339–40).

C. REGIONAL BODIES

If the universal system was slow to get off the ground, there was progress at the regional level, no doubt reflecting a sense of shared priorities and a preference to settle issues, as it were, *en famille*.

The first was the European Convention on Human Rights (ECHR). This is the only human rights instrument that establishes a court to which any individual can call to account the State exercising jurisdiction over him or her, and expect a legally binding decision on the case. This radical development emerged relatively recently. When the ECHR was adopted in 1950, there was not even an automatic right to individual petition: the Convention created a European Commission of Human Rights and a European Court of

[136] [Editor's Note: UN GA Res 68/268 (9 April 2014) brought about significant changes to the practical operation of the treaty bodies. Meeting time was substantially increased and as a result backlogs have declined. Streamlined and aligned procedures have been encouraged to improve efficiency and effectiveness. Nevertheless, the system is still affected by significant resource constraints and a further review of the system is due to occur in 2020.]

Human Rights. The Commission could consider inter-State complaints as of right. It could only deal with individual complaints in respect of States that chose to make the requisite declaration.[137] The Court's jurisdiction was also optional.

Moreover, even when States parties to the ECHR accepted the Court's jurisdiction, that did not entitle the individual directly to seize the court of a complaint. Any complaint was first considered by the Commission. Once the Commission had issued its report, it could itself refer the case to the Court if the State party concerned had accepted the court's jurisdiction.[138] Moreover, the State party concerned could also choose to refer the case to the Court,[139] in effect giving the defendant State a right of appeal not enjoyed by the individual applicant, albeit the State of nationality of the applicant, if the applicant were not a national of the accused State, could also refer the case of its national to the Court.

It was only in 1990 that Protocol 9 to the ECHR was adopted to permit individuals from States that chose to accept this Protocol to refer a case to the Court. It took Protocol 11 (1994) that had to be accepted by all States parties to the ECHR before the Commission was dissolved and all individuals from all States parties could apply directly to the Court for a remedy.[140] All members of the Council of Europe are parties to the Convention and adherence to it is now a condition of membership for new candidates to join the Council of Europe. This in turn means that 820 million citizens and others within the jurisdiction of the 47 States now have direct access to a human rights court outside their own countries' legal systems. This has resulted in the Court's having a major challenge in dealing with its docket.[141]

The Court, as mentioned, has jurisdiction to hear inter-State complaints in respect of any State party to the ECHR (Article 33). There have been only four of these.[142] It was vested with a new power pursuant to Protocol 11 (1994) by which it could issue advisory opinions at the request of the Committee of Ministers, the body representing all member States of the Council of Europe (Article 47). Neither of the two so far requested has concerned the interpretation of substantive Convention rights.

The next regional system to come into being was the inter-American one, first, directly under the Charter of the Organization of American States (OAS) and later by virtue of the American Convention on Human Rights (ACHR). The latter Convention incorporated the Inter-American Commission on Human Rights that had earlier been established by the political organs of the OAS, and examined cases in respect of alleged violations of the American Declaration on the Rights and Duties of Man. There is an automatic right of individual petition by anyone in the 35 member States of the OAS.[143] In respect of the 23 States parties to the ACHR, the Commission (now a treaty body) applies the provisions of the Convention. The Commission retains its original jurisdiction over the other 12 member States, applying the Declaration.

Unlike the European system where inter-State complaints were always possible in respect of all parties to the ECHR, inter-State complaints to the Inter-American Commission are optional requiring separate acceptance, by both the State against which the complaint is made

---

[137] Article 25.   [138] Article 48.

[139] Ibid; the State of the alleged victim's nationality could also refer the case to the Court.

[140] In force 1 November 1998.

[141] See Lord Woolf et al, Review of the Working Methods of the European Court of Human Rights, December 2005, 49.

[142] There were others dealt with by the European Commission, including the landmark *Greek Case* (1969) 12 *Yearbook of the European Commission of Human Rights* 468. [Editor's Note: The Court has now also determined on the merits a fifth inter-State complaint and three others are currently pending before the Court, marking a notable increase in the use of the inter-State procedure.]

[143] The population of the Americas is estimated at 953 million.

and the State making the complaint. Also, unlike in the European system, the Commission may also, *propio motu*, investigate *situations* of apparent violations of human rights.

Meanwhile, paralleling the earlier practice of the ECHR, the ACHR established an Inter-American Court of Human Rights. Its jurisdiction is optional and individuals from the 18 States that have accepted the jurisdiction of the Court do not have a right to refer their case directly to the Court. Rather, the Commission must first consider the case and only then may it be referred whether by the Commission itself or the State concerned, to the Court.

The Court may also issue advisory opinions, at the request of a number of entities established by the Charter of the OAS. Individual member States, regardless of whether they are parties to the ACHR, may also request advisory opinions (Article 64). This function was an original part of the Court's work and, unlike its later arrival under the ECHR, it has been used.

Following its European and inter-American predecessors (the ECHR and ACHR), the African Charter on Human and Peoples' Rights (ACHPR, 1981) creates an expert body, the African Commission on Human and Peoples' Rights (ACNHPR), composed of 11 African personalities of the highest reputation.[144] The Commission mainly deals with complaints both of individual and general practices of violations of human rights, on the basis of communications submitted by individuals and NGOs, and like its UN counterparts it reviews periodic reports.

By a 1998 Protocol, the OAU established an African Court of Human and Peoples' Rights of 11 judges.[145] Twenty-six of the States parties to the Charter have ratified the Protocol.[146] The Commission, the States parties concerned, and African IGOs may refer cases to the Court, after they have been considered by the Commission. A major step is the possibility of NGOs or individuals bringing cases directly to the Court, by-passing the Commission, if the State concerned has accepted its jurisdiction.[147]

To date, five States have accepted this jurisdiction.[148] The Court may also issue advisory opinions, at the request of OAU member States, the OAU or any of its organs, or 'any African organization recognized by the OAU' (Article 4). This element of the jurisdiction has not to date been used.[149]

Other regional systems have been created but have not so far sufficiently advanced to indicate the need for detailed consideration. Thus, the revised Arab Charter on Human Rights (2004), which entered into force in 2008 and established a seven-member Arab Human Rights Committee, only provides the Committee with a power to review State reports. This procedure has not to date yielded any public outcome (Rishmawi, 2013, pp 52–3).[150] Expectations are not high for the ASEAN Intergovernmental Commission on Human Rights, composed of State representatives. A recent authoritative review of the system described it as 'nascent rather than well-established' (Muntarbhorn, 2013).

---

[144] Article 31.

[145] Protocol to the African Charter on Human and Peoples' Rights on the Establishment of an African Court of Human Rights, Article 12 (in force 2004). The Court will merge with the proposed African Court of Justice after 15 African Union member States have ratified the 2008 Protocol on the Statute of the African Court of Justice and Human Rights; three had done so at the time of writing. [Editor's Note: the number of ratifications has now risen to six.]   [146] [Editor's Note: the number of ratifications has now risen to 30.]

[147] Protocol to the African Charter on Human and Peoples Rights on the Establishment of an African Court or Human Rights, Articles 5 and 34(6).

[148] [Editor's Note: the number accepting the jurisdiction of the Court has now risen to eight.]

[149] [Editor's Note: by the end of 2017 the Court had now issued six Advisory Opinions.]

[150] [Editor's Note: a number of Reports following the consideration of country situations are now available at http://blogs.lse.ac.uk/vaw/regional/arab-league/arab-human-rights-committee/.

VIII. CONCLUSION

Human rights really entered the corpus of international law only after their promotion became a purpose of the UN Charter. There had been forerunners: the abolition of slavery and, especially the slave trade, in the nineteenth century, and the protection of freedom of association for labour; the rights of minorities in the Balkans; and the rights of residents in League of Nations mandate territories after World War I.

The notion of human rights in the crucial, classical sense of being the limits of States' authority over those subject to their jurisdiction, was a product of the European Enlightenment. If the church had been a counterweight to the feudal State, human rights were the non-clerical counterweight to the emergent, industrializing modern Western State that spread all over the world with the end of the colonial period. It took the cataclysm of World War II, characterized by aggression externally and crimes against humanity (genocide, systematic and widespread gross violations of human rights) internally and externally, for the world to accept that human rights was not something that could be left in the *domaine réservé* of States.

After some early doubt about whether the UN Charter's human rights clauses were merely hortatory or peremptory, it gradually became accepted that the latter was true. The Universal Declaration of Human Rights may formally only have had the status of a resolution of the General Assembly, that is, a recommendation, but it came to be accepted as reflecting the actual content of human rights and fundamental freedoms of which the UN Charter spoke. It also took time for the Charter provisions to be accepted as containing obligations to comply with human rights. The early decades of the UN assumed that the UN could not address allegations of human rights violations other than by treaty obligation.

The UDHR from the beginning aimed to address, not only freedom from fear (human rights as traditionally understood), but also freedom from want (requiring State action to secure economic and social needs). So-called group rights (eg to self-determination, development, a healthy environment, and even peace), whatever their status may be under international law, cannot qualify as human rights, as the latter have to be seen to be the rights of the individual in relation to the State, unless the term is to be deprived of all content.

There have been hypocritical and self-serving attempts to separate the modern State from its obverse side—human rights—in the name of asserted local cultural traditions. While the idea may still be heard in political discourse, international human rights law has nailed the issue: human rights are universal.

The nature and content of economic and social rights has been somewhat elusive. Authoritative statements affirm that there are identifiable core obligations: ensuring the right of non-discriminatory access to health facilities, goods, and services; to minimum essential, nutritionally adequate food and freedom from hunger; to basic shelter, housing, and sanitation and potable water; to essential drugs; and to ensure equitable distribution of health facilities, goods, and services.

Even if, paradigmatically, economic and social rights imply (extensive) State action, while civil and political rights imply State abstention, both conceive of human rights such that the rights-holders are individuals and the duty-bearers are States (or States acting together in IGOs). The idea that corporations, bands of organized criminals, or politically motivated armed opposition groups may also be duty-bearers directly under international law (they remain subject to national law) is incompatible with the basic conception of human rights and unsupported by persuasive authority.

The standard civil and political rights reflect a number of basic values: intellectual freedom (conscience, expression, association, and assembly); physical freedom (liberty and security of person/prohibition of arbitrary arrest and detention; freedom of movement;

and prohibition of slavery); fairness (equal treatment, non-discrimination and protection of rights of minority members); human dignity (personal integrity, including prohibition of torture and ill-treatment, and right to life); justice and legality (due process, no retroactive crime or punishment); participation (especially in government); accountability (right to remedy); and the legitimacy of a non-public or private sphere (respect for home and private life).

Slowly a broad network of monitoring, supervisory, and complaints mechanisms developed. The first to be recognized, being juridically unchallengeable, were bodies established by treaty. Later, the main political organ of the UN dealing with human rights—formerly the Commission on Human Rights, later the Human Rights Council—created a web of country-specific and thematic 'special procedures'. Generally, their activities are complementary, with the main area of overlap between some treaty bodies and most special procedures being the power of country visits. The record of treaty bodies in this respect is too limited to suggest the existence of extensive duplication. The potential for overlap and even competition in the area of periodic review conducted by treaty bodies and the Human Rights Council has not, so far, materialized.

At the regional level, there has been more progress, both with regard to the power to examine individual complaints by expert treaty bodies and to have them adjudicated by human rights courts.

REFERENCES

BESSON, S (2008), 'The Reception Process in Ireland and the United Kingdom', in H Keller and A Stone Sweet (eds), *A Europe of Rights: The Impact of the ECHR on National Legal Systems* (Oxford: Oxford University Press).

BIANCHI, A (2008), 'Human Rights and the Magic of *Jus Cogens*', 19 *EJIL* 491.

BOYLE, K (2009), *New Institutions for Human Rights Protection* (Oxford: Oxford University Press).

CHAPMAN, A and RUSSELL S (eds) (2002), *Core Obligations: Building a Framework for Economic, Social and Cultural Rights* (Antwerp/Oxford: Intersentia).

CHARNEY, JI (1993), 'Universal International Law', 87 *AJIL* 529.

CLAPHAM, A (2006), *Human Rights Obligations of Non-State Actors* (Oxford: Oxford University Press).

CORRIGAN, T (2007), 'Mauritania Made Slavery Illegal Last Month', South African Institute of International Affairs website: http://www.saiia.org.za/opinion-analysis/mauritania-made-slavery-illegal-last-month.

DE SCHUTTER, O (2012), 'The Status of Human Rights in International Law', in C Krause and M Scheinin (eds), *International Protection of Human Rights. A Textbook* (2nd edn, Turku: Åbo Akademi University Institute of Human Rights).

DE WET, E (2008), 'The Reception Process in the Netherlands and Belgium', in Keller and Stone Sweet, *A Europe of Rights: The Impact of the ECHR on National Legal Systems*.

FREEMAN, M (2011), *Human Rights: An Interdisciplinary Approach* (2nd edn, Cambridge: Polity Press).

FREEMAN, M (2013), 'Universalism of Human Rights and Cultural Relativism', in S Sheeran and N Rodley (eds), *Routledge Handbook on International Human Rights Law* (London: Routledge).

FRIEDMAN, W (1960), *Legal Theory* (4th edn, London: Stevens and Sons).

HAAS, E (1977), 'Human Rights: A New Policy by a New Administration', in *Proceedings of the Annual Meeting of the American Society of International Law, 21–23 April 1977*, 71 *AJIL* 68.

HENKIN, L (1978), *The Rights of Man Today* (London: Stevens and Sons).

HOBBES, T (1651), *Leviathan* (M Oakeshott (ed) (1957)) (Oxford: Blackwell).

HUMPHREY, JP (1979), 'The Universal Declaration of Human Rights: Its History, Impact and Juridical Character', in BJ Ramcharan (ed), *Human Rights: Thirty Years after the Universal Declaration* (The Hague: Martinus Nijhoff).

ISHAY, M (2008), *The History of Human Rights: From Ancient Times to the Globalization Era* (Berkeley: University of California Press).

KRAMER, D and WEISSBRODT, D (1981), 'The 1980 UN Commission on Human Rights and the Disappeared', 3 *Human Rights Quarterly* 18.

KRAUSE, C and SCHEININ, M (eds) (2009), *International Protection of Human Rights. A Textbook* (2nd edn, Turku: Åbo Akademi University Institute of Human Rights).

LAUREN, PG (2011), *The Evolution of International Human Rights: Visions Seen* (3rd edn, Philadelphia: University of Pennsylvania Press).

LAUTERPACHT, H (1950), *International Law and Human Rights* (London: Stevens and Sons).

LOCKE, J (1689) *A Letter Concerning Toleration* (W Popple, (ed) (1983)) (Indianapolis: Hackett Publishing Corporation).

MORGENTHAU, HJ (1967), *Politics Among Nations: The Struggle for Power and Peace* (4th edn, New York: Alfred A Knopf).

MUNTARBHORN, V (2013), 'The South-East Asia System for Human Rights Protection', in Sheeran and Rodley, *Routledge Handbook on International Human Rights Law*.

OWEN, D and STRONG, TB (eds) (2004), *Max Weber, The Vocation Lectures: Science as a Vocation—Politics as a Vocation* (trans R Livingstone) (Indianapolis: Hackett Publishing Corporation).

PAINE, T (1791), *Rights of Man* (M Philp (ed) (2008)) (Oxford: Oxford University Press).

RAMCHARAN, BJ (ed) (1979), *Human Rights: Thirty Years after the Universal Declaration* (The Hague: Martinus Nijhoff).

RISHMAWI, M (2013), 'The League of Arab States in the Wake of the "Arab Spring"', *Cairo Institute of Human Rights, Annual Report 2013*, 52–3; available at http://www.cihrs.org.

RODLEY, NS (1986), 'U.N. Action Procedures against "Disappearances", Summary or Arbitrary Executions, and Torture', 8 *Human Rights Quarterly* 700.

RODLEY, NS (1995), 'Conceptual Problems Concerning Minorities—International Legal Developments', 17 *Human Rights Quarterly* 48.

RODLEY, NS (2008), 'The *Singarasa* Case: *Quis Custodiet* …? A Test for the Bangalore Principles of Judicial Conduct', 41 *Israel Law Review* 500.

RODLEY, NS (2012), 'UN Treaty Bodies and the Human Rights Council', in H Keller and G Ulfstein (eds), *UN Human Rights Treaty Bodies: Law and Legitimacy* (Cambridge: Cambridge University Press).

RODLEY, NS (2013), 'The Role and Impact of Treaty Bodies', in D Shelton (ed), *The Oxford Handbook of International Human Rights* (Oxford: Oxford University Press).

RODLEY, NS (2013), 'Non-State Actors and Human Rights', in Sheeran and Rodley, *Routledge Handbook on International Human Rights Law*.

RODLEY, NS and POLLARD, M (2009), *The Treatment of Prisoners under International Law* (3rd edn, Oxford: Oxford University Press).

ROUSSEAU, J-J (1762), *The Social Contract* (trans GDH Cole 1782) http://www.constitution.org/jjr/socon.htm.

SCHWELB, E (1972), 'The International Court of Justice and the Human Rights Clauses of the Charter', 66 *AJIL* 350–1.

SHEERAN, S and RODLEY, N (eds) (2013), *Routledge Handbook on International Human Rights Law* (London: Routledge).

SHUE, H (1980), *Basic Rights: Subsistence, Affluence and U.S. Foreign Policy* (2nd edn, Princeton NJ: University of Princeton Press).

SWEPSTON, L (2013), 'The International Labour Organization and the International Human Rights System', in Sheeran and Rodley, *Routledge Handbook on International Human Rights Law*.

VASAK, K (1977), 'Human Rights: A Thirty-Year Struggle', in *UNESCO Courier* 30:11 (Paris, UNESCO, November 1977).

WEBER, M (1919), *Politics as a Vocation*, reproduced in D Owen and TB Strong (eds) (2004), *Max Weber, The Vocation Lectures: Science as a Vocation—Politics as a Vocation* (trans R Livingstone) (Indianapolis: Hackett Publishing Corporation).

WESTON, B (1989), 'Human Rights', in RP Claude and B Weston (eds), *Human Rights in the World Community* (Philadelphia: University of Pennsylvania Press).

FURTHER READING

DE SCHUTTER, O (2010), *International Human Rights Law: Cases, Materials, Commentary* (Cambridge: Cambridge University Press).

DONNELLY, J (2012), *International Human Rights: Dilemmas in World Politics* (4th edn, Boulder, CO: Westview Press).

FREEMAN, M (2011), *Human Rights* (2nd edn, Cambridge: Polity Press).

ISHAY, M (2008), *The History of Human Rights: from Ancient Times to the Globalisation Era* (Berkeley: University of California Press).

KÄLIN, W and KÜNZLI, J (2009), *The Law of International Human Rights Protection* (New York: Oxford University Press).

KRAUSE, C and SCHEININ, M (2012), *International Protection of Human Rights: A Textbook* (2nd rev edn, Turku: Abo Akademi University Institute for Human Rights).

MARKS, S and CLAPHAM, A (2005), *International Human Rights Lexicon* (Oxford: Oxford University Press).

MOECKLI, D, SHAH, S, SIVAKUMARAN, S, and HARRIS, D (2013), *International Human Rights Law* (2nd edn, Oxford: Oxford University Press).

NIFOSI, I (2005), *The UN Special Procedures in the Field of Human Rights* (Antwerp/Oxford, Intersentia).

NOWAK, M (2005), *UN Covenant on Civil and Political Rights: CCPR Commentary* (2nd edn, Kehl am Rhein: Engel).

OBERLEITNER, G (2007), *Global Human Rights Institutions* (Cambridge: Polity Press).

RODLEY, NS and POLLARD, M (2009), *The Treatment of Prisoners under International Law* (3rd edn, Oxford: Oxford University Press).

SHEERAN, S and RODLEY, NS (2013), *The Routledge Handbook on International Human Rights Law* (London: Routledge).

SHELTON, D (2013), *The Oxford Handbook of International Human Rights Law* (Oxford: Oxford University Press).

SMITH, RKM (2011), *Textbook on International Human Rights* (5th edn, Oxford: Oxford University Press).

WEISSBRODT, D and DE LA VEGA, C (2007), *International Human Rights Law: An Introduction* (Philadelphia: University of Pennsylvania Press).

26

INTERNATIONAL REFUGEE AND MIGRATION LAW[1]

Geoff Gilbert and Anna Magdalena Rüsch

SUMMARY

Refugees are defined under international law as being outside their country of nationality owing to a well-founded fear of persecution for one of five grounds and unable or unwilling to avail themselves of its protection. This chapter explores that definition, its scope and limitations, and consequent protection gaps for those forcibly displaced, including internally displaced persons (IDPs), who have crossed no international border. There is, though, no equivalent definition for migrants, but like refugees, asylum-seekers, and IDPs, international human rights law provides a framework for their protection. The chapter explains the difference between refugee status and asylum, focusing on *non-refoulement* in international law. It discusses some of the rights that are guaranteed during displacement, particularly those pertaining to detention, along with assistance and humanitarian relief. Given that refugee status is intended to be temporary, the final section looks at cessation and durable solutions, either following voluntary return to the country of nationality, through local integration in the hosting State, or by resettlement in some third State.

I. INTRODUCTION

Fundamentally, public international law is the law regulating States, and if a person's flight results in movement across an international border, then the obligations of two States may be engaged—the State where their rights were violated so that they were forced to flee, and the State where they seek refuge. In addition, rights and obligations are also accorded to the refugees themselves, who are—as individuals—traditionally not subjects of international law. The protection of refugees in international law focuses on the State of refuge: what are its obligations under international and regional refugee instruments and human rights law?[2] That is not to say, however, that the source State is wholly irrelevant to dealing with the displacement, because one durable and sustainable solution is voluntary repatriation.

---

[1] The views expressed in this chapter are those of the authors and do not necessarily reflect those of any organization with which they are or have been associated.

[2] Article 2(1) International Covenant on Civil and Political Rights (ICCPR), UNGA Res 2200A (XXI), UN Doc A/6316 (1966), 999 UNTS 171.

This chapter will focus on the protection of refugees and asylum-seekers under international law, which requires that they have crossed an international border and are unwilling or unable to avail themselves of the protection of their country of nationality.[3] The chapter will address other individuals of concern to the United Nations High Commissioner for Refugees (UNHCR):[4] conflict-driven internally displaced persons (IDPs), and stateless persons, especially where statelessness is the consequence or cause of displacement, and migrants, too. However, given space constraints, the situation of migrants will concentrate on how displacement affects their rights.[5]

Applying for and even acquiring refugee status does not deny, surrender, or relinquish nationality, but one consequence is that UNHCR then has the unique mandate to provide international protection until a durable and sustainable solution can be achieved. By contrast, IDPs and stateless persons, both of whom are within UNHCR's mandate, may remain within the State of nationality or habitual residence, although both, in time, may become refugees after crossing an international border. The international law pertaining to displacement emphasizes the pervading Westphalian character of international law as it brings to the fore the obligations of at least two States and their interaction with international organizations.

Finally, it should be noted at the outset that there is no international refugee court akin to the Human Rights Committee's role as regards the International Covenant on Civil and Political Rights. This chapter cannot pretend to look at domestic law and procedure in every State carrying out refugee status determination. However, courts do draw on the interpretations from other jurisdictions[6] and UNHCR has a supervisory function[7] that allows it to provide guidelines on the meaning of the Convention. Thus, reflecting the way that the law has developed, the chapter refers to cases from around the world and to UNHCR guidelines.

II. LEGAL FRAMEWORKS FOR PROTECTION

The protection of refugees and asylum-seekers in international law draws not just on international refugee law, but on international human rights law, international criminal law, in part, the international law of armed conflict, and law of the sea, as well as various other sub-disciplines, along with regional systems, too. The interplay of these branches is complex[8] and it is not always the case that interpretations from one would be directly applicable in the field of refugee protection: the term 'persecution' in Article 1A.2 1951 Convention, for

---

[3] Convention relating to the Status of Refugees, 1951, 189 UNTS 137 (28 July 1951), Article 1A.2 (1951 Convention); and 1967 Protocol, 606 UNTS 267 (16 December 1966).

[4] See Statute of the Office of UNHCR, UNGA Res 428 (V) (14 December 1950) para 1, and http://www.refworld.org/idps.html. See also Türk and Eyster, 2010.

[5] The International Convention on the Protection of the Rights of All Migrant Workers and Members of Their Families (CMW), UNGA Res 45/158, Annex, UN Doc A/45/49 (1990), like the Convention on the Rights of the Child, UNGA Res 44/25, Annex, UN Doc A/44/49 (1989) or the International Convention on the Protection and Promotion of the Rights and Dignity of Persons with Disabilities, UNGA Res 61/106, Annex I, UN Doc A/61/49 (2006), is general international human rights law made specific to a particular group. See also reports of the Special Rapporteur on the Human Rights of Migrant. The concept of international protection in this area can be traced back to the Capitulations with the Ottoman Empire that started in the fifteenth century. See Gilbert, 1999 and Chetail, 2018.

[6] See, eg, *Al-Sirri and DD (Afghanistan)* v *Secretary of State for the Home Department* [2012] UKSC 54, citing Canadian and German case law.

[7] See para 8(a) of the Statute, and Article 35 1951 Convention. See also Kälin, 2003.

[8] 'Like a pair of water-skiers being towed separately but in parallel across a lake, the wake from one speedboat will affect the skier behind the other boat, but both continue on their chosen course.' See Gilbert and Rüsch, 2014, at fn 4.

example, cannot have the same meaning as that set out in Article 7(2)(g) of the 1998 Rome Statute of the International Criminal Court given the humanitarian character of the former treaty as opposed to the latter, which is drafted so as to impose individual responsibility for the most serious crimes. As with much of international refugee law, it must be given an autonomous meaning appropriate to an international humanitarian measure.[9]

A. THE RIGHT TO SEEK AND ENJOY ASYLUM

There is no right to asylum in international law. Asylum is in the gift of the State. While one speaks of asylum-seekers, they are more likely applying for refugee status and the State, if it were to offer protection, might subsequently under its domestic legislation grant asylum, which has a more permanent character—refugee status is, as will be seen, tempo- rary, it lasts for as long as protection is required. Article 14 of the Universal Declaration of Human Rights (UDHR) 1948, though, provides that everyone has the right to seek and enjoy asylum.[10] The standing of Article 14 in international law, however, is not absolutely clear-cut. The UDHR is a mere declaration of the General Assembly and is not, therefore, binding in and of itself. Equally, unlike many other provisions of the UDHR, Article 14 was not incorporated in either the International Covenant on Civil and Political Rights or the International Covenant on Economic, Social and Cultural Rights (ICESCR).[11] Nevertheless, Article 14 is recognized as reflecting customary international law and, as such, is binding on all States.[12]

Thus, international human rights law imposes an obligation on States to allow individu- als to seek protection from another State and there is a clear interplay with international refugee law in that the State where asylum is sought may have a duty to grant refugee status. Article 14 UDHR is a humanitarian exception to the general rule of international law that States can control their borders—they have to allow individuals to seek asylum from per- secution through proving they fall within the definition of a refugee in international law.[13]

B. INTERNATIONAL LAW AS IT RELATES TO DISPLACEMENT[14]

Refugee status as defined in the 1951 Convention provides that a refugee is a person with a well-founded fear of persecution based on one of five grounds—race, religion, nationality, membership of a particular social group, or political opinion—who is unable or unwilling

---

[9] See Lord Steyn in *R v Secretary of State for the Home Office, ex parte Adan and Aitseguer* [2001] 2 AC 477, at 517. In practice, it is left to national courts, faced with a material disagreement on an issue of interpretation, to resolve it. But in doing so it must search, untrammelled by notions of its national legal culture, for the true autonomous and international meaning of the treaty. *And there can only be one true meaning [of the Convention]* ... (emphasis added).   [10] UNGA Res 217A (III), UN Doc A/810, 71 (1948).

[11] UNGA Res 2200A (XXI), UN Doc A/6316 (1966), 993 UNTS 3.

[12] See, eg, UNSC Res 1624 (14 September 2005), Preamble para 7, adopted during the 2005 World Summit, most recently affirmed in UNSC Res 2368 (20 July 2017):

Recalling in addition the right to seek and enjoy asylum reflected in Article 14 of the Universal Declaration and the *non-refoulement* obligation of States under the Convention relating to the Status of Refugees adopted on 28 July 1951, together with its Protocol adopted on 31 January 1967 ...

[13] The extraterritorial application of Article 14 is less clear, so it may be legitimate for States to patrol close to the edge of territorial waters of another State so as to prevent persons reaching their own territory, but the obligation not to *refoule* in international refugee law requires States not to return anyone to the frontiers of a territory where their life or freedom would be threatened, and that applies even on the high seas. See *Hirsi Jamaa v Italy* [GC], no 27765/09, ECHR 2012.

[14] See Goodwin-Gill and McAdam, 2007 and Hathaway and Foster, 2014.

to avail themselves of the protection of their country of nationality or, if stateless, country of habitual residence—Article 1A.2.[15] They must also be outside their country of nationality or habitual residence. The Convention, therefore, imposes a series of interrelated hurdles for applicants to clear: they will be unwilling or unable to avail themselves of protection because the fear is well-founded; the five grounds indicate the persecutory nature of the treatment that gives rise to the fear.

Before looking at the detail of Article 1A.2, there is one further point to note. The Convention nowhere lays down the procedure that States should adopt when carrying out refugee status determination.[16] Nor is there any international refugee court to oversee State practice and procedure.[17] While the lack of any rules on procedure means one cannot be categorical, the position should be that both the applicant and the decision-maker share the burden of proof as to whether the criteria of Article 1A.2 are met: given the nature of a refugee status determination hearing, there will usually only be the personal evidence of the applicant and generic country of origin information on which to base the decision, so credibility is a huge factor (Noll, 2005).

1. Outside

A person cannot seek refugee status while in their country of nationality,[18] not even in an embassy of another country,[19] but the reason for being outside need not be the well-founded fear that prompts their desire not to return—refugees *sur place* are those who have left for a different reason, work or education for instance, and who cannot now return because of a well-founded fear. Stateless persons must be outside their country of habitual residence, but, having been wrongly deemed stateless, could be part of the evidence of

---

[15] In the original 1951 text of the Convention before the 1967 Protocol, there were two additional limitations. First, the fear had to arise as a result of 'events occurring before 1 January 1951'. While it was possible to read some events back to the persecution arising during the Second World War and to the creation of the Soviet Bloc in its aftermath, it became extremely tenuous when dealing with persons fleeing persecution outside Europe. That though, points to the second limitation in the original text: under Article 1B, a State could limit the definition to 'events occurring in Europe before 1 January 1951'. Over time, States dropped this limitation, but there was no uniform practice. In 1967, therefore, States promulgated the Protocol to the Convention, which removed the temporal limitation and only allowed States that had made the European declaration to maintain it—Article I.3. As of 4 August 2017, Congo, Madagascar, Monaco, and Turkey preserved the European limitation, although in the light of the Syrian conflict, Turkey agreed to admit Syrians fleeing the conflict. The 1967 Protocol is unusual in that it is open to signature by non-parties to the 1951 Convention, the obligations of which they thereby accept under Article I.1—the USA, for example, has only ratified the 1967 Protocol.

[16] Handbook and Guidelines on Procedures and Criteria for Determining Refugee Status under the 1951 Convention and the 1967 Protocol relating to the Status of Refugees, Reissued Geneva, December 2011, para 189 (hereafter 1979 Handbook).

[17] It is worth noting that the European Court of Human Rights has held that the fair trial obligations under the European Convention for the Protection of Human Rights and Fundamental Freedoms (1950), ETS 5 (hereafter ECHR) do not apply to deportation hearings and, thus, those related to refugee status determination. See *Maaouia v France* [GC], no 39652/98, ECHR 2000-X. The Human Rights Committee in General Comment 32, CCPR/C/GC/32, 23 August 2007, holds at para 17 that the guarantee of access to a fair and independent hearing in Art 14.1 ICCPR (n 2), does not extend to 'expulsion and deportation procedures' (see also *Zundel v Canada*, (Communication No 1341/2005), UN Doc CCPR/C/89/D/1341/2005 (2006), para 6.7, para 6.7), although Article 13 may apply if the alien is lawfully on the territory—General Comment 32, para 62.

[18] Where a person has more than one nationality, they must be outside all of them and have a well-founded fear of persecution in all of them if they want refugee status—a dual national fearing persecution in one country of nationality could just go to the other one.

[19] They are still physically in the territory of their own country, the embassy is just immune from the jurisdiction of that State. Cf *Asylum, Judgment, ICJ Reports 1950*, p 266.

persecution in what ought to be their country of nationality.[20] The hurdles are intricately interrelated.

2. Well-founded fear

As a standard of proof, a well-founded fear is unusual in law regardless of legal system. The traditional understanding is that it combines a subjective and an objective dimension: the applicant, by seeking refugee status, is prima facie indicating a fear, one that should be assessed in relation to that applicant, that is, a child refugee will have a different level for a rational fear than an adult, but the fear must still be 'well-founded', one that would be recognized as reasonable for such an applicant. It relates to what could happen if the applicant returns to their country of nationality, although previous experience will help validate the well-founded character of the fear.[21] There is an added complication to do with the language and structure of the 1951 Convention. Article 1A.2 sets out the criteria for refugee status, but at least on arrival in another State, the refugee most wants not to be returned to their country of nationality—*non-refoulement*. The guarantee of *non-refoulement*, discussed later, is set out in Article 33.1 and draws on refugee status under Article 1A.2, except that the standard of proof is different: it requires that the refugee's 'life or freedom *would be* threatened'. Courts in most countries fuse the tests so that someone recognized as a refugee owing to a well-founded fear of persecution would be able to show that their life or freedom would be threatened for the purposes of *non-refoulement*.[22]

3. Persecution

It is too simplistic to confine persecution to human rights violations. For sure, violations of human rights standards indicate persecution, but the term is broader and is not, therefore, confined to the activities of a State—refugee status depends on a well-founded fear of persecution where the asylum-seeker is unwilling or unable to avail themselves of the protection of the country of nationality, but the source of the persecution is not tied inextricably to the State:[23]

> The term 'persecution' cannot be seen in isolation from the increasingly sophisticated body of international law on human rights generally. In recognition of the adaptable nature of the refugee definition to meet the ever changing needs of protection UNHCR recognises an important link between persecution and the violation of fundamental human rights. In this context the focus of any enquiry is to establish whether there has been a failure of domestic protection and therefore a need for surrogate international protection.

To deem it otherwise is to confuse the persecution with the persecutor. That said, fear of torture, inhuman, or degrading treatment or punishment, threats to life, and fear of slavery or other non-derogable human rights standards will be recognized as persecution. The violation of other civil and political rights could constitute persecution if sufficiently

---

[20] See Convention relating to the Status of Stateless Persons (1954), 360 UNTS 117; Convention on the Reduction of Statelessness (1961), 989 UNTS 175.

[21] See *Canada (Attorney General)* v *Ward* [1993] 2 SCR 689; *HJ (Iran) and HT (Cameroon)* v *Secretary of State for the Home Office* [2010] UKSC 31, paras 17ff.

[22] See *R* v *Secretary of State for the Home Office, ex parte Sivakumaran and Conjoined Appeals (UNHCR Intervening)* [1988] AC 958, 993, where the then House of Lords referred to well-founded fear requiring a 'reasonable degree of likelihood', less than the balance of probabilities. The United States has adopted two different tests for Articles 1A.2 and 33.1—*INS* v *Cardoza-Fonseca* v *INS* 480 US 401 (1987); *INS* v *Stevic* 467 US 407 (1984).

[23] *Urim Gashi, Astrit Nikshiqi* v *Secretary of State for the Home Department*, HX-75677–95, HX/75478/95, 1996 UKIAT No 13695, 14.

severe. Picking up on language from the European Court of Human Rights,[24] if there were to be a 'flagrant denial' of freedom of religion, for example, that could constitute persecution.[25] As for economic, social, and cultural rights, again, a very high standard would be demanded, one approximating to torture, or inhuman or degrading treatment or punishment.[26] The most complicated element of persecution, however, is its overlap with discrimination. Discrimination in and of itself is not persecution—it may indicate that one of the five grounds for persecution under Article 1A.2 has been satisfied, or it may combine with another aspect of failed protection to constitute persecution.[27] On the other hand, cumulative discrimination may constitute persecution (Dowd, 2011). Cumulative discrimination could be as a result of several different forms of discriminatory treatment, none of which on their own would amount to persecution, or different discriminatory experiences based on one aspect of that person's identity.[28]

The final aspect of persecution to consider concerns who can persecute. Since States assume international human rights obligations, traditionally only States can violate them. However, the 1951 Convention speaks of persecution and separately of an inability or unwillingness to avail oneself of the protection of one's country of nationality or habitual residence. Thus, there is no need for persecution to emanate from State actors.[29] In passing, it is worth noting, though, the correlation with being unable or unwilling to avail oneself of the protection of one's country of nationality and the concept of the internal protection/flight alternative.

4. Five grounds

It is not enough to be outside one's country of nationality with a well-founded fear of persecution, it must be based on one of five grounds: race, religion, nationality, membership of a particular social group, or political opinion. That is why fleeing generalized violence has on occasions been deemed not to give rise to refugee status under the 1951 Convention.[30] There is clearly overlap between the grounds. 'Race' has to be understood in the light of the subsequent definition set out in Article 1 of International Convention on the Elimination of All Forms of Racial Discrimination 1965, which includes ethnic origin.[31] Race under CERD also includes national origin, which ties in with 'nationality'. It may seem odd that refugee status requires the applicant to be outside their country of nationality, yet persecution can be based on nationality, too. Nationality again includes ethnicity, but if a State were to be occupied and the invading forces then target the national population, that could trigger refugee status, while nationality must include 'lack of

---

[24] *Soering v United Kingdom, Judgment of 7 July 1989, Ser A, No 161*, para 113.

[25] *R (on the application of Ullah) v Special Adjudicator, Do v Secretary of State for the Home Department* [2004] UKHL 26.

[26] *Urim Gashi, Astrit Nikshiqi v Secretary of State for the Home Department*, HX-75677–95, HX/75478/95, 1996 UKIAT No 13695.

[27] *Urim Gashi, Astrit Nikshiqi v Secretary of State for the Home Department*, HX-75677–95, HX/75478/95, 1996 UKIAT No 13695. And see the 1979 Handbook, para 54.

[28] See 1979 Handbook, paras 53–5.

[29] See *Islam v Secretary of State for the Home Department, R v Immigration Appeal Tribunal and Another, ex parte Shah* [1999] 2 AC 629; *2 BvR 260/98* and *2 BvR 1353/98*, German Federal Constitutional Court, 10 August 2000—the authors are grateful to Anja Klug of UNHCR for her note on this decision.

[30] See later in this chapter on Special Cases on Armed Conflicts and the regional mechanisms' extended definitions, along with the 1979 Handbook, paras 164–6. See also UNHCR, *Guidelines on International Protection No 12: Claims for refugee status related to situations of armed conflict and violence under Article 1A.2 of the 1951 Convention and/or 1967 Protocol and the regional refugee definitions*, 2 December 2016, HCR/GIP/16/12.

[31] UNGA Res 2106 (XX), UN Doc A/6014 (1966), 660 UNTS 195 (CERD).

nationality,[32] especially where the stateless persons are being arbitrarily denied a nationality to which they are entitled. Persecution on grounds of 'religion', also, must be read as specific to the persecution, not as a general context: the persecution targets a faith group or atheists *qua* group or their manifestation of a faith/no-faith.[33] Just because the persecutors are motivated by their faith, if the applicant, too, is an adherent of that faith, it is less likely that persecution is on the ground of religion, rather it might be your membership of a less orthodox particular social group—divisions within a faith group add to the complexities of this ground. In those States where there is a close connection between the religious and governing authorities, the potential for persecution associated with religion is greater, but it could equally be that the persecution is based on membership of a particular social group. Political opinion is broader than simply supporting the policies of a particular political party or group. It includes perceived views that the applicant might hold regarding parties to an armed conflict[34] or, alternatively, what might be deemed central to upholding freedom of expression.[35] As will be seen, living a particular lifestyle can be seen as an expression of a political opinion.

The remaining ground, membership of a particular social group (MPSG), is possibly the most complex.[36] It is the one part of the refugee definition not found in the 1950 Statute.[37] There is not space here to go into it in detail, but note that it is the fourth of the five grounds, not the last, and there is no justification for treating it as a catch-all. MPSG has to be read in the light of the other grounds. As will be seen, parallel with the development of international human rights law standards, MPSG has been used to include groups not otherwise covered who suffer persecution. The most widely accepted understanding was provided by *AG Canada* v *Ward*:[38]

> The meaning assigned to 'particular social group' in the Act should take into account the general underlying themes of the defence of human rights and anti-discrimination that form the basis for the international refugee protection initiative . . .
>
> (1) groups defined by an innate or unchangeable characteristic;
> (2) groups whose members voluntarily associate for reasons so fundamental to their human dignity that they should not be forced to forsake the association; and
> (3) groups associated by a former voluntary status, unalterable due to its historical permanence.
>
> The first category would embrace individuals fearing persecution on such bases as gender, linguistic background and sexual orientation, while the second would encompass, for example, human rights activists. The third branch is included more because of historical intentions, although it is also relevant to the anti-discrimination influences, in that one's past is an immutable part of the person.

Ward makes clear that membership does not always require a voluntary association and that MPSG is to be interpreted in line with the other grounds for persecution, but it leaves open the possibility for further development to meet protection gaps in the 1951 Convention.

---

[32] *Sejdić and Finci* v *Bosnia and Herzegovina* [GC], nos 27996/06 and 34836/06, ECHR 2009.

[33] See UNHCR, *Guidelines on International Protection No. 6: Religion-Based Refugee Claims under Article 1A.2 of the 1951 Convention and/or the 1967 Protocol*, 28 April 2004, HCR/GIP/04/06. See also Musalo, 2004.

[34] *MZ (PSG—Informers—Political Opinion) Colombia* v *Secretary of State for the Home Department*, CG [2002] UKIAT 02465.

[35] *Klinko* v *Canada (Minister of Citizenship and Immigration)*, [2000] 3 FC 327.

[36] UNHCR, *Guidelines on International Protection No 2: 'Membership of a Particular Social Group' Within the Context of Article 1A.2 of the 1951 Convention and/or its 1967 Protocol*, 7 May 2002, HCR/GIP/02/02.

[37] Statute, para 6B.   [38] *Canada (Attorney General)* v *Ward* [1993] 2 SCR 689, 739.

Finally, persecution can relate to more than one ground. People may have a political opinion imputed to them because of their ethnicity or religion. That raises the concomitant issue of imputation—when deciding whether the persecution relates to one of the five grounds, the mindset of the persecutor is just as relevant to the determination.[39]

5. Unable or unwilling

This final element of the definition is tied closely to the well-foundedness of the fear and the context of the persecution. Where an authoritarian State is persecuting a section of its population, then refugee status will be easier to assert than if the fear relates to treatment by a rebel group not in full control of the territory of the State.[40] That said, persecution can emanate from non-State actors, but it may be that the asylum-seeker will fail because there is an internal flight or protection alternative (IFA/IPA) to a part of the State where the government is still in control and can offer protection. It is not part of the *travaux préparatoires* of the 1951 Convention, but courts in the global north have promulgated the IFA/IPA.[41] According to UNHCR, refugee status can only be denied because the applicant can be returned to another part of the country of nationality and obtain the protection of its government, where (i) the area of relocation is practically, safely, and legally accessible to the individual, (ii) the claimant would not be exposed to a risk of being persecuted or other serious harm upon relocation, and (iii) the claimant, in the context of the country concerned, can lead a relatively normal life without facing undue hardship.[42] Such requirements tell against returning anyone to a place where there is an ongoing armed conflict.

6. Summary

The 1951 Convention provides a complex definition of refugee status that has developed over the years through State practice, UNHCR guidance, and the decisions of the disparate courts in various countries—and, of course, there is no international refugee court to try and draw these threads together and provide a definitive interpretation. Under international law, not everyone who is forcibly displaced qualifies as a refugee: that does not mean that they receive no protection, just that the 1951 regime is but one, although a very large, part of the picture.

C. REGIONAL PROTECTION MECHANISMS

The 1951 definition arose out of the horrors of World War II and the expansion of the Soviet Bloc into central and eastern Europe. Subsequent events, such as decolonization,

---

[39] *Olimpia Lazo-Majano v INS*, 813 F.2d 1432 (9th Cir 1987).

[40] *MZ (PSG—Informers—Political Opinion) Colombia v Secretary of State for the Home Department*, CG [2002] UKIAT 02465.

[41] *Dyli v Secretary of State for the Home Department* [2000] UKIAT 00001. And see Directive 2011/95/EU of the European Parliament and of the Council of 13 December 2011 on Standards for the Qualification of Third-Country Nationals or Stateless Persons as Beneficiaries of International Protection, for a Uniform Status for Refugees or for Persons Eligible for Subsidiary Protection, and for the Content of the Protection Granted (Recast), OJ L 337/9, 20 December 2011 (EUQD), Articles 6 and 7.

[42] Taken from para 7, UNHCR, *Guidelines on International Protection No 4: 'Internal Flight or Relocation Alternative' Within the Context of Article 1A.2 of the 1951 Convention and/or 1967 Protocol*, 23 July 2003, HCR/GIP/03/04. Whether the persecution emanates from the State or a non-State actor is also relevant to the decision.

did not fit neatly within Article 1A.2. Regional refugee mechanisms have developed in Africa, the Americas, South-East Asia, and Europe. While all of them extend protection, it would be wrong to think of them as identical. Africa has the 1969 Convention Governing the Specific Aspects of Refugee Problems in Africa,[43] while the 1984 Cartagena Declaration[44] applies in Central and South America—it is not binding in and of itself, but has been incorporated into the domestic laws of 14 States in the region.[45] In South-East Asia, the Bangkok Principles of 2001 can be applied, although they describe themselves as declaratory and non-binding.[46] All of them uphold the 1951 Convention definition, but then provide an expanded definition that focuses on the cause of displacement rather than the grounds for fear: Article I.2 1969 Convention talks of refugees as those compelled to flee 'external aggression, occupation, foreign domination or events seriously disturbing public order';[47] the Cartagena Declaration includes 'persons who have fled their country because their lives, safety or freedom have been threatened by generalized violence, foreign aggression, internal conflicts, massive violation of human rights or other circumstances which have seriously disturbed public order'. The language is different and broader. Both stem from the massive displacements seen in each region.[48] Beyond not requiring a ground for persecution, how far they go beyond the 1951 Convention is not clear—there is nothing in that text that demands refugee status be based on individual determination, that is more the consequence of the judicialization of the process in the global north, an issue discussed later when considering those fleeing armed conflict.[49] The European Union Qualification Directive (Recast) is different. The refugee definition is not extended, indeed it is arguable that some of the glosses put on terms within Article 1A.2 narrow parts of it.[50] Nevertheless, the EUQD Recast establishes that 'subsidiary protection' will be available to those not qualifying as refugees, but who face a 'real risk of serious harm', which includes 'serious and individual threat to a civilian's life or person by reason of indiscriminate violence in situations of international or internal armed conflict'(paras 2f and 15c). The 2011 recast tries to harmonize the protection available to refugees and those receiving subsidiary protection, but categorizing them as non-refugees and including only third-country nationals challenges the living and dynamic character of the 1951 Convention.

---

[43] 1001 UNTS 45 (1969 Convention).

[44] 22 November 1984, Annual Report of the Inter-American Commission on Human Rights, OAS Doc OEA/Ser.L/V/II.66/doc 10, rev 1, 190–3 (1984–85).

[45] Expert roundtable: Interpretation of the extended refugee definition contained in the 1984 Cartagena Declaration on Refugees, held at Montevideo, Uruguay, 15 and 16 October 2013, 'Summary Conclusions on the interpretation of the extended refugee definition in the 1984 Cartagena Declaration', para 2.

[46] Asian-African Legal Consultative Organization (AALCO), Bangkok Principles on the Status and Treatment of Refugees (Bangkok Principles), 31 December 1966, as adopted on 24 June 2001 at the AALCO's 40th Session, New Delhi. See Notes, Comments and Reservations Made by the Member States of AALCO, Introductory Remarks, para 2.   [47] The Bangkok Principles mirror this language.

[48] See UNHCR, *Guidelines on International Protection No 11: Prima Facie Recognition of Refugee Status*, 24 June 2015, HCR/GIP/15/11, para 5.

[49] See Guideline No 12. Where UNHCR carries out refugee status determination for a State in these regions, it uses the broader definitions in line with the State's obligations.

[50] And that is without taking account of its application only to third-country nationals. See also Article 5.3 EUQD and UNHCR's recommendations during consultation on the Recast—UNHCR comments on the European Commission's proposal for a Directive of the European Parliament and of the Council on minimum standards for the qualification and status of third-country nationals or stateless persons as beneficiaries of international protection and the content of the protection granted (COM(2009)551, 21 October 2009), July 2010.

D. SPECIAL CASES

The 1951 Convention is a living and dynamic instrument.[51] As such, its interpretation has developed to include those needing protection who were not necessarily expressly envisaged as refugees in 1951 or where the Convention's language has had to be clarified in an inclusive fashion. Examples of this include the protection of women, those persecuted on grounds of their sexual orientation and/or gender identity (SOGI), and those fleeing armed conflict and generalized violence.

1. Women and girls

Despite referring to the UDHR in its Preamble, the five Convention grounds do not include gender. Persecution based on gender is not, therefore, an automatic gateway to status, at least as regards the Convention language. Moreover, while some States have laws that do discriminate against women,[52] a lot of the persecution is by private actors, often in the home, but where the authorities do not intervene. If women cannot obtain protection from domestic violence from their own government, then they may need to seek international protection through refugee status. The UK case of *Islam and Shah*[53] concerned two Pakistani women who feared being killed by their husbands' relatives after they had been accused of adultery. The House of Lords held they could not obtain effective protection in Pakistan and accorded them refugee status on the ground that their persecution was based on MPSG in line with *Ward*.[54] There is nothing exceptional in extending the Convention definition in that way, rather it is the fact that this would ever be thought to be a question.[55] Where States are unwilling or unable to provide protection to their nationals being persecuted because of their gender, then that is clearly in keeping with the object and purpose of the 1951 Convention.[56] It is also central to granting refugee status to victims of human trafficking.[57]

2. Sexual orientation and gender identity[58]

The LGBTIQ community suffer persecution and lack of protection in many countries across the world. They often suffer multiple discrimination from individuals and the State.[59] Again, in the light of the developments under international human rights law as regards sexual orientation and gender identity, it is not exceptional that refugee status should be available where persecution is on the basis of MPSG. What is worthy of note is how international refugee law now deals with discretion on the part of the victims of

---

[51] See *Sepet* and *Bulbil v Secretary of State for the Home Department* [2003] UKHL 15, para 6, per Lord Bingham. And see Foreword by UNHCR Assistant High Commissioner for Protection, Dr Volker Türk, to the 1979 Handbook.

[52] See the reservations to the Convention on the Elimination of All Forms of Discrimination Against Women, UNGA Res 34/180, UN Doc A/34/46.

[53] *Islam v Secretary of State for the Home Department, R v Immigration Appeal Tribunal and Another, ex parte Shah* [1999] 2 AC 629.   [54] *Canada (Attorney General) v Ward* [1993] 2 SCR 689.

[55] Cf *Sanchez-Trujillo et al v Immigration and Naturalization Service*, 801 F.2d 1571 (1986).

[56] See also *González et al. ('Cotton Field') v Mexico, Preliminary Objections, Merits, Reparations and Costs, Judgment of 16 November 2009*, Ser C, No 205.

[57] UNHCR, *Guidelines on International Protection No 7: The Application of Article 1A.2 of the 1951 Convention and/or 1967 Protocol to Victims of Trafficking and Persons at Risk of Being Trafficked*, 7 April 2006, HCR/GIP/06/07.

[58] UNHCR, *Guidelines on International Protection No 9: Claims to Refugee Status based on Sexual Orientation and/or Gender Identity within the context of Article 1A.2 of the 1951 Convention and/or its 1967 Protocol*, 23 October 2012, HCR/GIP/12/01.

[59] A trans woman may suffer discrimination because she is a woman, for her gender identification, and for her imputed or real sexual orientation.

persecution. It is not just SOGI; several of the grounds can be concealed so as to avoid persecution if returned to the country of nationality. However, something that is so fundamental to a person's identity[60] should never have to be hidden for fear of persecution, so in those cases refugee status should be accorded, a principle just as pertinent to religious profession or political opinion.[61]

3. Armed conflict and generalized violence

Most forcibly displaced persons are fleeing conflict or violence, yet the Handbook, first published in 1979, provided that '[p]ersons compelled to leave their country of origin as a result of international or national armed conflicts are not *normally* considered refugees under the 1951 Convention or 1967 Protocol' (paras 164–6, emphasis added). The reasoning was that they were not suffering persecution, they were just caught up in dangerous circumstances, and that was not enough for Article 1A.2. The consequence was confusion and obfuscation of responsibility. Of course, this analysis was far too simplistic and armed conflict and generalized violence could always create 1951 Convention refugees, although the regional instruments expanding the definition for Africa and the Americas indicate that the applicability of Article 1A.2 to armed conflicts was not without problem. The increasing number of non-international armed conflicts and the targeting of civilians as a means of warfare towards the end of the twentieth century made it easier to prove refugee status within the meaning of Article 1A.2 of the 1951 Convention.[62] While the 1979 Handbook has not been amended, UNHCR issued Guideline No 12 in December 2016 on claims for refugee status related to situations of armed conflict and violence, in part to clarify paragraph 164. When dealing with persons who fear return to a situation of armed conflict or generalized violence, Article 1A.2 can readily address protection needs. Events in such situations can easily amount to persecution within the meaning of the 1951 Convention, and, given their erratic nature and progression, it will be difficult to show there is an IFA/IPA;[63] given that the 1951 Convention seeks to proffer protection to those who are unable or unwilling to obtain it from their own government, the source of the persecution is irrelevant, whether it be the State or non-State actors.[64] The fact that the person seeking refugee status is but one of many in a group targeted for a Convention reason does not prevent Article 1A.2 from applying—there is no need to be singled out for special treatment.[65] Therefore, protection under Article 1A.2 of the 1951 Convention ought to be available to most persons fleeing armed conflict or generalized violence, such that in situations of mass influx, prima facie status should be the default rather than trying to rely on judicialized mechanisms that already often fail to cope with numbers arriving in peacetime.[66] Furthermore,

---

[60] See *Canada (Attorney General)* v *Ward* [1993] 2 SCR 689, 739.

[61] See *HJ (Iran) and HT (Cameroon)* v *Secretary of State for the Home Office* [2010] UKSC 31, para 110, and *RT (Zimbabwe) et al* v *Secretary of State for the Home Office* [2012] UKSC 38.

[62] Canadian Immigration and Refugee Board, *Chairperson Guideline 1: Civilian Non-Combatants Fearing Persecution in Civil War Situations*.

[63] *NB* The Article I.2 1969 Convention, reference to 'in either part or whole of the country of origin' suggests that IFA/IPA might be deemed irrelevant in Africa, but IFA/IPA goes to protection available, not the scope of the conflict. And the existence of an IDP camp should never indicate an IFA/IPA is available given their precarious nature in situations of armed conflict—cf *Januzi* v *Secretary of State for the Home Department* [2006] UKHL 5. See also Gilbert and Rüsch, *Creating Safe Zones*.

[64] On gang violence and refugee status, see UNHCR, *Guidance Note on Refugee Claims Relating to Victims of Organized Gangs*, 31 March 2010.

[65] See also *Case C-465/07, Elgafaji* v *Staatssecretaris van Justitie* (ECJ Grand Chamber), 17 February 2009, dealing with subsidiary protection.   [66] Guideline No 11.

over time, UNHCR's mandate has expanded under its Statute and through its good offices, alongside the regional mechanisms and the EUQD's subsidiary protection.[67]

E. EXCLUSION[68]

Exclusion is a huge topic that is deserving of its own section, and it provides a useful link with armed conflicts, with displacement, and with the next major section on
non-refoulement. The 1951 Convention holds that certain persons who would otherwise
meet the Article 1A.2 criteria, nevertheless are not deserving of refugee status. The focus
will be on Article 1F, although it is not the only article that regulates under which conditions the 1951 Convention should not be applied: under Article 1D the Convention shall
not apply to persons receiving 'protection or assistance' from other UN organs, which
today means Palestinians within the UN Relief and Works Agency (UNRWA) area,[69]
that is, Jordan, Lebanon, Syria, and the OPT (Gaza Strip and the West Bank, including East Jerusalem)—Palestinians outside that area do fall within the 1951 Convention.
Further, according to Article 1E, once a person has been recognized as having the rights
of a national in the State in which they now take residence, then the 1951 Convention
does not apply.

Article 1F provides as follows:

> The provisions of this Convention shall not apply to any person with respect to whom
> there are serious reasons for considering that
>
> (a) He has committed a crime against peace, a war crime, or a crime against humanity,
>   as defined in the international instruments drawn up to make provision in respect
>   of such crimes;
> (b) He has committed a serious non-political crime outside the country of refuge prior
>   to his admission to that country as a refugee;
> (c) He has been guilty of acts contrary to the purposes and principles of the United
>   Nations.[70]

The subsections overlap. According to the *travaux préparatoires*, two purposes were
sought to be achieved: serious transgressions prior to entry should disbar an applicant
from refugee status and no-one who had committed such crimes should escape prosecution through obtaining refugee status.[71] To international human rights law, where everyone receives protection, exclusion is an alien concept. Given that Article 1F is a limitation
on a humanitarian provision, it must be interpreted narrowly.[72] However, as will be seen,

---

[67] Statute, para 9, and UNGA Res 1167 (XII), 1957. On UNHCR's extended mandate, see Türk and Eyster,
2010, p 163. See also the 1969 Convention (n 43), the Cartagena Declaration (n 45), and the Bangkok Principles
(n 46), along with subsidiary protection under the EUQD, para 15c.

[68] See UNHCR, *Guidelines on International Protection No 5: Application of the Exclusion Clauses: Article 1F
of the 1951 Convention*, 4 September 2003, HCR/GIP/03/05. See also Geoff Gilbert, 2003; 2014a; 2014b and
Gilbert and Rüsch, 2014.

[69] See materials at https://www.unrwa.org.   [70] See also para 7d 1950 Statute.

[71] See Standing Committee of the Executive Committee of the High Commissioner's Programme, 'Note
on the Exclusion Clauses', 47th session, UN Doc EC/47/SC/CRP.29, 30 May 1997, para 3, and Conference of
Plenipotentiaries on the Status of Refugees and Stateless Persons, Summary Record of the 24th meeting, UN
Doc A/CONF.2/SR.24, 27 November 1951, statements of M. Herment, Belgium, and Mr Hoare, UK.

[72] 1979 Handbook, para 149. *Gurung v Secretary of State for the Home Department* [2002] UKIAT 04870,
para 151.1. *Gurung* was overruled in *JS (Sri Lanka) v Secretary of State for the Home Department* [2010] UKSC
15, but not on this point—para 2.

if it applies, courts have held that there is no scope for any balancing exercise vis-à-vis the potential consequences of a loss of protection.[73]

It is important to consider the specific crimes, the standard of proof, the required degree of participation, and the role of proportionality and expiation, as well as the relationship with Article 33.2 and regional variations. Sub-paragraph (a) refers to international instruments defining the crimes. At the time of drafting, the Nuremberg Charter was still operative and the Geneva Conventions of 1949 on the laws of armed conflict had just set out the grave breach provisions.[74] However, they are limited in that the London Charter was not universal, and the Geneva Conventions only covered grave breaches in time of armed conflict—and sub-paragraph (a) only applies where the crimes are defined in international instruments. There never has been a convention dealing with crimes against humanity[75] and war crimes are broader than just grave breaches.[76] The position is clearer after the Rome Statute and especially the Kampala amendments of 2010 defining the crime of aggression, but there are several unanswered questions surrounding the definitions and their applicability to non-parties to the Rome Statute, given that it does not always reflect customary international law. Sub-paragraph (b) speaks of serious non-political crimes—like a lot of the 1951 Convention, the concept is peculiar to that treaty. It draws on the concept of political crimes in extradition law, where a fugitive would not be extradited if their crime were of a political character (Gilbert, 2006, ch 5), so only if the crime is not political in character and is sufficiently serious should refugee status be denied. The political character ordinarily depends not so much on motive, but on whether the crime was part of and in furtherance of a political disturbance, not too remote from the ultimate goal of the organization to which the applicant belongs and proportionate.[77] The seriousness of the non-political crime is not specified in the Convention. Nevertheless, given that it is part of sub-paragraph (b) and comes between 'crimes against humanity, war crimes, crimes against peace' and 'acts contrary to the purposes and principles of the United Nations', the ordinary meaning in context should suggest crimes of a similar magnitude. As for sub-paragraph (c), exclusion follows on from there being serious reasons for considering that the applicant is guilty of acts contrary to the purposes and principles of the United Nations:[78] they are to be found in the Preamble and Articles 1 and 2 of the UN Charter, as expanded by the Security Council and General Assembly.[79] Not all the purposes and principles could render an individual 'guilty' and, having regard to paragraph 7d of the 1950 Statute, the

---

[73] Note that Article 33.2 1951 Convention, discussed later in the chapter, appears similar in effect, but it only withdraws the *non-refoulement* guarantee, it does not deprive the refugee of status and UNHCR can continue to offer protection.

[74] Agreement for the Prosecution and Punishment of the Major War Criminals of the European Axis, and Charter of the International Military Tribunal, London, 8 August 1945; see also the four Geneva Conventions, for the Amelioration of the Condition of the Sick, Wounded and Shipwrecked, the Treatment of Prisoners, and the Protection of Civilians, along with the two Additional Protocols for international and non-international armed conflicts of 1977 (AP1 and AP2).

[75] The ILC is currently undertaking work on crimes against humanity.

[76] See *Prosecutor v Tadić*, Decision on the Defence Motion for Interlocutory Appeal on Jurisdiction (Interlocutory Appeal), Case No IT–94–1–AR72 (2 October 1995).

[77] *T v Secretary of State for the Home Department* [1996] 2 All ER 865; *In re Nappi* (Swiss Fed Trib, 1952), 19 ILR 375; *Watin v Ministère Public Fédéral* (Swiss Fed Trib, 1964), 72 ILR 614; *In re Pavan* [1927–28] Ann Dig 347, 349.

[78] The 1969 Convention adds acts contrary to the purposes of what is now the African Union—Article I.5(c).

[79] Eg UNSC Res 1373 (28 September 2001) deeming international terrorism as a threat to international peace and security.

drafters probably considered that it reflected Article 14.2 UDHR, violations of inter-national human rights law not amounting to crimes against humanity. Nevertheless, it has been interpreted more broadly and applied more widely than to persons in senior government positions who might be recognized as having responsibilities vis-à-vis the Charter.[80]

The burden of proving that there are serious reasons for considering that an applicant is excluded lies on the State. 'Serious reasons for considering' does not come anywhere near proving guilt for a criminal trial, but it 'sets a standard above mere suspicion'.[81] There is clearly an expectation of individual involvement,[82] but indirect participation might suffice, either through aiding or abetting or, possibly, joint criminal enterprise.[83] Nevertheless, it should be noted that Article 1F does not expressly take into account that the applicant has already served a sentence for their prior crime—however, it is arguable in the light of developments in international human rights law that expiation should negate exclusion.[84]

The final element of exclusion to be dealt with under displacement concerns the tim-ing of the crime or act—should it be prior to entry as an applicant for refugee status or can it be retrospectively applied after according status under Article 1A.2?[85] The text of sub-paragraph (b) states that the serious non-political crime must be committed 'prior to . . . admission to that country as a refugee'. Therefore, the 1Fb crime must pre-date entry and application for status.[86] However, there is no similar text in Articles 1Fa or 1Fc. Thus, as the Exclusion Guidelines set forth, a refugee can be excluded under sub-paragraphs (a) and (c) after being granted Article 1A.2 status.[87] This overlaps with Article 33.2, consid-ered later in the context of *non-refoulement*, and will be returned to there. In that regard, since the EUQD also melds Article 1F with Article 33.2, its approach to exclusion is part of that analysis. Although Article 1F goes to status and Article 33.2 to protection against *refoulement*, given the fundamental centrality of *non-refoulement* to refugee status, and that exclusion cuts across both, several of these issues are revisited there where a full com-parison can be made.

---

[80] *Georg K* v *Ministry of the Interior*, Austrian Admin Court, 1969, 71 ILR 284; *Al-Sirri and DD (Afghanistan)* v *Secretary of State for the Home Department* [2012] UKSC 54.

[81] *Yasser Al-Sirri* v *Secretary of State for the Home Department* [2009] EWCA Civ 222, para 33; *Al-Sirri and DD (Afghanistan)* v *Secretary of State for the Home Department* [2012] UKSC 54, para 75, following UNHCR's guidance in the 2003 Guidelines.

[82] *JS (Sri Lanka)* v *Secretary of State for the Home Department* [2010] UKSC 15 overruling *Gurung* v *Secretary of State for the Home Department* [2002] UKIAT 04870 on this point; *Al-Sirri and DD (Afghanistan)* v *Secretary of State for the Home Department* [2012] UKSC 54; and *Bundesrepublik Deutschland* v *B* (C-57/09), *D* (C-101/09) [2010] ECR I-10979.

[83] Article 25(3) Rome Statute, and *Prosecutor* v *Mrkšić and Šljivančanin*, Judgment, Case IT-95–13/1A, Appeals Chamber (5 May 2009); *Prosecutor* v *Lukić and Lukić*, Judgment, Case IT-98–32/1-A, Appeals Chamber (4 December 2012); *Prosecutor* v *Perišić*, Judgment, Case IT-04–81-A, Appeals Chamber (28 February 2013), paras 37–40, 42, and 73; *Prosecutor* v *Šainović, Pavković, Lazarević and Lukić*, Judgment, Case IT-05–87A, Appeals Chamber (23 January 2014); *Prosecutor* v *Taylor*, Case No SCSL-03–01-A, Appeals Chamber, Judgment of 26 September 2013, paras 466ff.

[84] Cf *Febles* v *Canada (Citizenship and Immigration)* [2014] 3 SCR 431.

[85] This places the question as part of both according status and *non-refoulement*, so much so that some of these questions will be dealt with later in the chapter.

[86] Article 12.2b EUQD lays down that 'prior to admission as a refugee' means 'the time of issuing a residence permit based on the granting of refugee status'. This is clearly contrary to the text of the 1951 Convention and may place EU Member States in conflict with their international obligations—granting refugee status is declaratory, not constitutive, as noted, ironically, in EUQD Recast Preamble (21).

[87] Exclusion Guidelines, para 6. Of course, this is separate from occasions where the evidence of prior crimes only comes to light after status has been accorded.

F. INTERNALLY DISPLACED PERSONS[88]

Since Article 1A.2 1951 Convention requires that persons seeking refugee status be outside their country of nationality, IDPs require a different legal regime. Clearly, like everyone else in the territory and jurisdiction of the State, they enjoy the human rights obligations undertaken by that State, but in 1998 the Guiding Principles were launched.[89] The Guiding Principles are not binding in international law in and of themselves, but they assert that they reflect and are consistent with international human rights law and international humanitarian law.[90] Moreover, since 1998 it is arguable that at least in part they reflect customary international law, especially given the number of States where they have been incorporated into domestic law and their referencing by the Security Council and General Assembly.[91] They provide guidance to the Human Rights Council's Special Rapporteur on the human rights of internally displaced persons, States with IDPs, 'all other authorities, groups and persons in their relations with internally displaced persons and Intergovernmental and non-governmental organizations when addressing internal displacement'. To the extent that they now reflect customary international law, the question arises as to how far they bind non-State actors. Given that non-international armed conflicts are a primary cause of internal displacement, the relevance of the Guiding Principles for rebel groups is significant and overlaps with international humanitarian law applicable under Additional Protocol 2.

The Guiding Principles provide a description, rather than a definition,[92] of an IDP:

> For the purposes of these Principles, internally displaced persons are persons or groups of persons who have been forced or obliged to flee or to leave their homes or places of habitual residence, in particular as a result of or in order to avoid the effects of armed conflict, situations of generalized violence, violations of human rights or natural or human-made disasters, and who have not crossed an internationally recognized State border.

Clearly, there is no requirement to be outside, but there are also no grounds, no requirement of fear, and the conditions prompting flight, akin to the expanded regional refugee definitions, include, as well, natural, or human-made disasters. While an IDP could become a refugee if they subsequently cross an international border, it is possible that refugees and asylum-seekers can also fall within the Guiding Principles if they are subsequently internally displaced, for example by a natural disaster affecting the refugee camp.

The Guiding Principles set out a series of rights for IDPs dealing with protection from displacement; rights during displacement; principles relating to return, resettlement, and reintegration; and principles relating to humanitarian assistance. Some of these are similar to rights for refugees in the country of refuge, discussed later, but the Guiding Principles are broader and establish obligations, in line with paragraph 3 of the Introduction, to provide and permit humanitarian assistance. As such, the Guiding Principles go beyond what is provided for under the 1951 Convention. To that extent, this chapter's focus is on the

---

[88] See the Guiding Principles on Internal Displacement 1998 (Guiding Principles), and African Union Convention for the Protection and Assistance of Internally Displaced Persons in Africa (Kampala Convention), 22 October 2009. See also Kälin, 2000.

[89] There was no international conclave of States to adopt them and, at the outset, they were challenged by several States as lacking any authority. See Cohen, 2004, p 460.

[90] Guiding Principles, Introduction, para 3. Of course, the Kampala Convention, which mirrors a lot of the Guiding Principles, but with a very different structure, does establish binding international obligations.

[91] See http://www.refworld.org/idps.html.

[92] Kälin, 2000, pp 2–3. There is no equivalent of the exclusion clause in the Guiding Principles.

protection of refugees and other displaced persons in international law, rather than simply international refugee law, which covers only a part of how international law responds to displacement. Before moving on to this broader understanding of and approach to protection with respect to displacement, the primary 'right' of refugees, *non-refoulement*, needs to be addressed.

III. *NON-REFOULEMENT*

The primary concern of an asylum-seeker who has sought refuge outside their country of nationality is not to be returned to where they fear persecution, thus *non-refoulement* stands at the very heart of the 1951 Convention.

> Article 33—Prohibition of expulsion or return ('*refoulement*')
>
> 1. No Contracting State shall expel or return ('*refouler*') a refugee in any manner whatsoever to the frontiers of territories where his life or freedom would be threatened on account of his race, religion, nationality, membership of a particular social group or political opinion.

While it is written as an obligation of States, *non-refoulement* is a right of individuals. Since the promulgation of the 1951 Convention, it has developed into a customary international law right, which, in specific circumstances, may even qualify as a peremptory norm of international law.[93] Before considering that broader principle of *non-refoulement*, though, the Convention definition will be addressed.

Refugees, as defined in Article 1A.2, qualify for Article 33 *non-refoulement*. The five grounds are identical and although the reference is to 'life or freedom', that is interpreted synonymously with 'persecution'. The standard of proof, though, is different: 'would be threatened', not 'well-founded fear'. As was indicated earlier,[94] the standard of proof for *non-refoulement* is stricter than for refugee status, but courts pragmatically fuse the two questions given the centrality of Article 33.1 to asylum-seekers—the decision-maker is looking for a reasonable degree of likelihood that the persecution will occur if returned. One other substantial difference between Articles 1A.2 and 33 relates to scope of application. A person can only claim refugee status in the country of asylum.[95] However, Article 33.1, being drafted as an obligation on States parties, is not so limited: 'No Contracting State shall expel or return ("*refouler*") a refugee *in any manner whatsoever to the frontiers of territories* . . .' (emphasis added). As Blackmun J explained, dissenting in the United States Supreme Court:[96]

> Article 33.1 is clear not only in what it says, but also in what it does not say: It does not include any geographical limitation. It limits only where a refugee may be sent 'to,' not where he may be sent from. This is not surprising, given that the aim of the provision is to protect refugees against persecution.

---

[93] Lauterpacht and Bethlehem, 2003, para 216; Allain, 2002. We do not go that far because, while freedom from torture might be *jus cogens*, it is not necessarily the case that peripheral rights have the same status.

[94] Eg *R v Secretary of State for the Home Office, ex parte Sivakumaran and Conjoined Appeals (UNHCR Intervening)* [1988] AC 958.

[95] *R v Immigration Officer at Prague Airport and another, ex parte European Roma Rights Centre and others* [2004] UKHL 55.

[96] *Sale and ors v Haitian Centers Council, Incorporated and ors*, 509 US 155 (1993), Blackmun J, dissenting, 193. See also, Goodwin-Gill and McAdam, 2007, pp 244ff.

Since refugee status is declaratory, not constitutive, if State authorities have jurisdiction over an individual, whether within the territory or not,[97] then any asylum-seeker must be treated as a refugee and benefit from *non-refoulement*, even if found on the high seas.[98] States have control of their borders, but that is limited by other obligations undertaken or assumed under international law, such as the right to seek asylum under Article 14 UDHR and *non-refoulement*.[99] Moreover, although Article 33.1 refers to returning a refugee to the 'frontiers of a territory where his life or freedom would be threatened', it covers those cases where the refugee would not obtain protection from *refoulement* in a State to which they could be returned, so-called chain *refoulement*.[100]

On the other hand, *non-refoulement* is much broader than Article 33.1. As already stated, the principle is part of customary international law, binding on all States, not just parties to the 1951 Convention. In part, that reflects international human rights law obligations that have embraced *non-refoulement*, either explicitly or through extraterritorial application.[101] Article 3 of the 1984 United Nations Convention Against Torture provides as follows:[102]

> 1. No State Party shall expel, return ('*refouler*') or extradite a person to another State where there are substantial grounds for believing that he would be in danger of being subjected to torture.

Torture is defined in Article 1 in such a way that it requires 'such pain or suffering is inflicted by or at the instigation of or with the consent or acquiescence of a public official or other person acting in an official capacity', although the Committee Against Torture has interpreted it more broadly.[103] What is certain is that Article 3 does not extend to 'cruel,

---

[97] See Human Rights Committee General Comment No 31, Nature of the General Legal Obligation on States Parties to the Covenant, para 10, UN Doc CCPR/C/21/Rev.1/Add 13 (2004).

[98] See Bostock, 2002; Schloenhardt, 2002; Pallis, 2002; Willheim, 2003; Edwards, 2003; Magner, 2004; Goodwin-Gill and McAdam, 2007, pp 246–6 and 371–4; Higgins 2017. See also Committee Against Torture, *JHA v Spain,* No 323/2007, decision of 21 November 2008, CAT/C/41/D/323/2007., and Wouters and den Heijer, 2010. It is interesting that even the Australian government, when defending its turn-back policies by its navy, makes clear that none of the people found in the boats sought refugee status—see BBC News website, 'Chinese men sent home in Australia people-smuggling probe', http://www.bbc.co.uk/news/world-australia-41091403. UNHCR has regularly decried Australia's refugee policies.

[99] *Chahal* v *the United Kingdom*, 15 November 1996, *RJD* 1996-V, para 73. See also the decision of the Human Rights Committee in *Shirin Aumeeruddy-Cziffra and 19 other Mauritian women* v *Mauritius* (Communication No 35/1978), UN Doc CCPR/C/12/D/37/1978 (1981).9.2(b)2(ii)3 . . . Though it might be justified for Mauritius to restrict the access of aliens to their territory and to expel them therefrom for security reasons, the Committee is of the view that the legislation which only subjects foreign spouses of Mauritian women to those restrictions, but not foreign spouses of Mauritian men, is discriminatory with respect to Mauritian women and cannot be justified by security requirements.The Committee Against Torture has also acknowledged this point in *Agiza v Sweden*, Communication No 233/2003, decision of 20 May 2005, CAT/C/34/D/233/2003.13.1 . . . The Committee acknowledges that measures taken to fight terrorism, including denial of safe haven, deriving from binding Security Council Resolutions are both legitimate and important. Their execution, however, must be carried out with full respect to the applicable rules of international law, including the provisions of the Convention, as affirmed repeatedly by the Security Council (United Nations Security Council Res.1566 (2004), at preambular paragraphs 3 and 6, Res.1456 (2003) at paragraph 6, and Res.1373 (2001) at paragraph 3(f).

[100] *In Re Musisi, R* v *Secretary of State for the Home Office, ex parte Bugdaycay* [1987] AC 514, 532, per Lord Bridge.

[101] And international human rights law has influenced how one interprets 1951 Convention, Article 33.1.

[102] UNGA Res 39/46, UN Doc A/39/51 (1984). And see *Tahir Hussain Khan* v *Canada*, decision of 15 November 1994, A/50/44, p 46.

[103] *Elmi* v *Australia*, No 120/1998, decision of 14 May 1999, CAT/C/22/D/120/1998.

inhuman or degrading treatment or punishment', despite Article 16: the drafts of the Convention included these broader terms, but they were rejected before the final text was agreed, so it is not possible to reintroduce them through interpretation. Regional human rights bodies have no explicit guarantee against *refoulement*, but the treaty bodies have read their freedom from torture guarantees so as to prevent people's return to violative treatment. Building on its decision in *Soering*,[104] the European Court of Human Rights has held that no-one can be returned if there is a real risk that they would face torture, inhuman, or degrading treatment or punishment contrary to Article 3.[105] This has been used where refugee status might not be available because the applicant may fall within Article 1F,[106] would fall within Article 1B's geographic limitation,[107] may simply be fleeing generalized, non-directed violence,[108] or fail any of the other specific requirements of the 1951 Convention's definition of a refugee.[109] Jurisprudence of the Human Rights Committee and the Inter-American Court of Human Rights provides similarly.[110] Other human rights than freedom from torture, inhuman, or degrading treatment or punishment could also be the basis for *non-refoulement*, such as the right to life or freedom from slavery.[111]

While *non-refoulement* cannot technically apply to IDPs, the idea of no forcible return to their home, if that is unsafe, is part of the Guiding Principles:

Principle 15 Internally displaced persons have:

(a) The right to seek safety in another part of the country; . . .
(b) The right to be protected against forcible return to or resettlement in any place where their life, safety, liberty and/or health would be at risk.

Sub-paragraph (c) reaffirms the right to seek asylum in another country. Thus, the essence of 'seeking asylum' and '*non-refoulement*' are seen as central to protection for everyone who is displaced, whether across or within international borders.

Finally in this section, the concept of exclusion must be revisited. If Article 1F is applied, Article 33.1 is inapplicable as that person is no longer considered to be a refugee. On the other hand, someone falling within Article 33.2 remains a refugee and within the mandate of UNHCR: however, they can be returned to the frontiers of a territory where their life or freedom would be threatened. Article 33.1 thus needs to be read in the light of not just Article 1F, but also Articles 32 and 33.2.

Article 32 deals with expulsion of refugees lawfully in the territory, which is only permitted on the basis of 'national security or public order'. Despite the seriousness of national security and public order, the prohibition on *non-refoulement* must still be respected under Article 32, which further requires due process of law, and that the 'Contracting

---

[104] *Soering* v *United Kingdom, Judgment of 7 July 1989, Ser A, No 161*.
[105] *Chahal* v *the United Kingdom*, 15 November 1996, *RJD* 1996-V.
[106] Ibid. *Saadi* v *Italy* [GC], no 37201/06, ECHR 2008.
[107] *Jabari* v *Turkey*, no 40035/98, ECHR 2000-VIII.
[108] *NA* v *the United Kingdom*, no 25904/07, 17 July 2008.
[109] *D* v *the United Kingdom*, 2 May 1997, RJD 1997-III.
[110] Human Rights Committee, *Alzery* v *Sweden* (Communication no 1416/2005), UN Doc CCPR/C/88/D/1416/2005 (2006), paras 11.4, 11.5; Inter-American Court of Human Rights, *Pacheco Tineo Family* v *Plurinational State of Bolivia, Preliminary Objections, Merits, Reparations and Costs, Judgment of 25 November 2013, Ser C, No 272*.
[111] And other rights where the fear is that the denial in the country of nationality would be flagrant in character—*Soering* v *United Kingdom, Judgment of 7 July 1989, Ser A, No 161*. Note that human rights treaty bodies might, on occasion, reject deportation for reasons other than *non-refoulement*, such as preserving the right to family life.

States shall allow such a refugee a reasonable period within which to seek legal admission into another country'.[112]

Article 33.2 is as follows:

> The benefit of the present provision may not, however, be claimed by a refugee whom there are reasonable grounds for regarding as a danger to the security of the country in which he is, or who, having been convicted by a final judgment of a particularly serious crime, constitutes a danger to the community of that country.

The standard of proof is only 'reasonable grounds for regarding', not 'serious reasons for considering', so being in a position to *refoule* is, at first blush, easier under Article 33.2. On the other hand, the second limb of Article 33.2 requires conviction by a 'final judgment of a particularly serious crime' and, then, that they also constitute a danger to the community of the country of refuge. Additionally, while 'danger to the security' of the country of refuge is vaguer and is open to a broader interpretation, by way of analogy with Article 32, it ought to reflect a more serious threat than that posed by risks to national security, since they do not obviate the requirement of *non-refoulement*.

Two matters make Articles 1F and 33.2 more complicated to apply than should be the case. First, as discussed, the 2003 Exclusion Guidelines provide that sub-paragraphs (a) and (c) can be applied post-status. The EUQD (Recast) gloss on Article 1Fb aside, given the difference in language between sub-paragraph (b) and sub-paragraphs (a) and (c) permits the difference in interpretation set out in the Exclusion Guidelines at paragraph 6,[113] that still presents States with a choice as to how to proceed with someone who has refugee status, but where the country of refuge no longer wants to provide protection under the 1951 Convention.[114] Article 1F requires 'serious reasons', rather than the less demanding reasonable grounds, but the second limb of Article 33.2 requires the country of refuge to prosecute and convict the refugee, unless of course some third State has already done that—if a refugee were to leave the country of refuge, commit a 1Fa crime while overseas, and be convicted there, then the second limb of Article 33.2 would be satisfied, but only if that renders the refugee 'a danger to the community' of the country of refuge as well. Further, while commission of some Article 1Fa crimes might render the refugee 'a danger to the security of the country in which he is', it would have to be a very significant and substantial crime, not just a particularly serious one. Thus, denying a refugee the *non-refoulement* guarantee under either method is demanding, which is how it should be.

Secondly, greater cause for concern arises where Article 33.2 is applied at the time of the application for refugee status because Articles 1F and 33.2 are fused in domestic legislation or the process is expedited, as is the case under the EUQD (Recast). The text of the 1951 Convention presumes any pre-entry crime should be dealt with under Article 1F, which requires 'serious reasons'. Nevertheless, technically an asylum-seeker

---

[112] See also Article 13 ICCPR which provides that an alien lawfully in the territory may be expelled therefrom only in pursuance of a decision reached in accordance with law and shall, except where compelling reasons of national security otherwise require, be allowed to submit the reasons against his expulsion and to have his case reviewed by, and be represented for the purpose before, the competent authority or a person or persons especially designated by the competent authority. That has to be read, though, in the light of the General Comment 32 and the right to a fair trial.

[113] While the interpretation cannot be gainsaid, whether UNHCR, whose mandate is to provide international protection to refugees under paragraph 1 of the Statute (n 4), should have been the one to point out is questionable—the *travaux préparatoires* clearly saw Article 1F as applying as a whole to pre-entry crimes.

[114] Of course, it may be that even if *non-refoulement* protection is lost under the Convention, the person can still not be deported because of international human rights law obligations.

with a conviction for a particularly serious crime could be granted refugee status if Article 1F were not fulfilled, but then be immediately returned if the rest of Article 33.2 is satisfied simply because there are reasonable grounds for considering that person a 'danger to the community of that country'. The position is even worse in the EU because the process is fused under Articles 12 and 14. The traditional view is that ordinarily 'inclusion' should precede 'exclusion',[115] if only because that way the whole scenario is considered, and there would be no need to exclude someone who fails to satisfy Article 1A.2. Moreover, proportionality should be intrinsic to any application of Article 1F since it removes the humanitarian protections found in the Convention and to Article 33.2 given the customary character of *non-refoulement*. It can only be applied properly where the entire set of facts and circumstances are known to the decision maker that can only come to light during the process to determine whether the applicant qualifies under Article 1A.2.[116]

Article 14 EUQD (Recast) adds further problems (Peers, 2016, pp 270–3). First, sub-paragraph (4) provides that 'the status granted to a refugee' may be revoked, ended, or renewal refused where the two limbs of Article 33.2 of the Convention are met, whereas the Convention simply denies *non-refoulement* whilst leaving the person a refugee. On the other hand, sub-paragraph (6) provides that persons who fall within sub-paragraph (4) are still entitled to the rights set out in or similar to, *inter alia*, Article 33 of the Convention.[117] And there is greater concern where refugee status can be denied, not under Article 12 EUQD (Recast) because there are 'serious reasons for considering that' they have committed one of the crimes or are guilty of acts contrary to the purposes and principles of the UN, but simply because there are just 'reasonable grounds for regarding them as a danger to the security of the Member State in which they are present', a much vaguer, less precise, and less demanding ground to prove.

Finally in *non-refoulement*, as stated, exclusion plays no part with respect to complementary protection under international human rights law. However, once again the EUQD (Recast) muddies the waters. Subsidiary protection is a form of complementary protection to refugee status for displaced persons, but Article 17 allows for exclusion, and the grounds are wider.

> Article 17.1. A third-country national or a stateless person is excluded from being eligible for subsidiary protection where there are serious reasons for considering that:
>
> (a) he or she has committed a crime against peace, a war crime, or a crime against humanity, as defined in the international instruments drawn up to make provision in respect of such crimes;
>
> (b) he or she has committed a serious crime;
>
> (c) he or she has been guilty of acts contrary to the purposes and principles of the United Nations as set out in the Preamble and Articles 1 and 2 of the Charter of the United Nations;
>
> (d) he or she constitutes a danger to the community or to the security of the Member State in which he or she is present.

---

[115] See Exclusion Guidelines, para 31—cf Article 14(5) EUQD. The authors are grateful to Dr Sibylle Kapferer, Director of Protection and National Security Section, Division of International Protection, UNHCR, for discussions on this point. Needless to add, the views expressed and any errors are the authors' alone.

[116] Exclusion Guidelines, para 31, and Background Note, paras 76–8.

[117] One interpretation might be that Article 14 refers only to the loss of refugee status as regards the EUQD, but they remain refugees for the purposes of the 1951 Convention. The authors are grateful for their discussions with Professor Steve Peers on this matter. Needless to add, the views expressed and any errors are the authors' alone.

While sub-paragraphs (a) and (c) mirror Article 1F, (b) applies to any serious crime committed at any time, while (d) incorporates Article 33.2 in much broader fashion, in that there is no replication of the requirement that they have been convicted by a final judgment of a particularly serious crime akin to its second limb. Fortunately, all member States of the EU are bound by the ECHR, so persons falling within Articles 12, 14, or 17 would be protected thereby.[118]

Lastly, despite European Union law that provides for the return to the country where the person could have first sought refugee status in the EU, the so-called Dublin Regulation,[119] international law does not recognize a general obligation to receive non-citizens, even if they subsequently entered a third State via that State: the 'safe third country' concept for deporting someone who qualifies as a refugee but could have sought refugee status in another country through which they had previously passed is dependent on an agreement between the States in question.[120]

IV. RIGHTS DURING DISPLACEMENT

The modal average length of a displacement situation is just under 20 years.[121] At the outset, the most pressing issue might be *non-refoulement*, but that soon develops into needing to access education, health care, employment, housing, and other legal services. Most refugees do not live in camps, so to be able to operate within the State of refuge as fully as possible, initial documentation and registration are so important.[122] Clearly, IDPs should enjoy all the usual rights accorded in the State because they have not crossed an international border. Indeed, the Guiding Principles are designed to apply those rights more effectively in the context of internal displacement. Some rights might be constrained as a consequence of displacement, such as freedom of movement, but even here, Principle 12, for example, sets out that IDPs shall only be confined to a camp or interned in 'exceptional circumstances' where it is 'absolutely necessary' and 'it shall not last longer than required by the circumstances'. In addition, the Guiding Principles also make clear in Principles 5–9 that persons shall be protected from internal displacement, drawing on international human rights law and international humanitarian law.

The position is more complicated when dealing with refugees, despite the fact that like everyone else on the territory and within the jurisdiction of the State, they should enjoy the human rights obligations it has assumed. Additionally, the 1951 Convention sets out, in a manner that was ground-breaking at the time, a series of rights for refugees. Nevertheless, refugees are not nationals of the State in which they find themselves, they may have entered contrary to the State's immigration laws, and the 1951 Convention itself

---

[118] Preamble (15) is wrong to state that those allowed to stay who do not qualify for refugee status or subsidiary protection do so 'on a discretionary basis on compassionate or humanitarian grounds'—they do so because of a treaty obligation predating the creation of the EEC, let alone the EU.

[119] Regulation (EU) No 604/2013 of the European Parliament and of the Council of 26 June 2013 establishing the criteria and mechanisms for determining the Member State responsible for examining an application for international protection lodged in one of the Member States by a third-country national or a stateless person. See also Peers, 2016.   [120] See EU-Turkey Statement of 18 March 2016, EU press release 144/16.

[121] Some persons may spend that time displaced, but the fluidity of the situation and lack of detailed individual data makes it impossible to give accurate figures for the modal average time any person is displaced—see Xavier Devictor and Quy-Toan Do, 'How many years do refugees stay in exile?', World Bank, 15 September 2016 http://blogs.worldbank.org/dev4peace/how-many-years-do-refugees-stay-exile.

[122] On documentation and its relationship to employment, see the related situation under Article 35 and Part IV CMW (n 5).

differentiates between refugees at different stages of their recognition by the host State. To start with the last point, while the 1951 Convention imposes obligations on the host State regarding access to education, employment, housing, social security, and the courts, to name but a few, not every asylum-seeker qualifies. For instance, while *non-refoulement* and access to the courts are available to all refugees/asylum-seekers, Article 17 only accords to refugees 'lawfully staying in their territory the most favourable treatment accorded to nationals of a foreign country in the same circumstances . . . the right to engage in wage-earning employment'. Self-employment is open to refugees 'lawfully in the territory' (Article 18). While anyone seeking refugee status is, at one level, 'lawfully staying in the territory' during the determination process, clearly the 1951 Convention is differentiating between refugees in a more settled relationship with the host State. The Convention does not define these terms,[123] so States are open to limit access to employment and social security, but not in such a manner that the asylum-seeker is left destitute and unable to remain in the host State pending the determination process—constructive *refoulement*. In passing, the 1951 Convention does not accord a right to family reunification,[124] but it is to be found in some regional systems.[125]

Turning to international human rights law, while some rights are limited to citizens,[126] most are available to all individuals within the State's territory and subject to its jurisdiction. Articles 12 and 13 ICCPR have particular pertinence to refugees and asylum-seekers. Article 13 deals with the expulsion of an alien lawfully on the territory and was discussed with respect to *non-refoulement*.[127] Article 12 states that everyone lawfully in the territory shall have liberty of movement. While General Comment No 12 refers to refugees in relation to sub-paragraph (4) on the right to return, it makes no mention as regards sub-paragraph (1).[128] Thus, detention of asylum-seekers or restricting refugees to camps ought to be susceptible to the same criteria as would be used for a citizen of the State who is detained. Indeed, General Comment No 35 on Article 9 states that liberty of the person applies to everyone, including 'aliens, refugees and asylum seekers'.[129] The 1951 Convention also deals with detention, but is not limited to those lawfully in the territory.

Article 31—Refugees unlawfully in the country of refuge

1. The Contracting States shall not impose penalties, on account of their illegal entry or presence, on refugees who, coming directly from a territory where their life or freedom was threatened in the sense of article 1, enter or are present in their territory without authorization, provided they present themselves without delay to the authorities and show good cause for their illegal entry or presence.

2. The Contracting States shall not apply to the movements of such refugees' restrictions other than those which are necessary and such restrictions shall only be applied until their status in the country is regularized or they obtain admission into another country.

Article 31 speaks to the need for asylum-seekers to enter countries sometimes without following the proper immigration procedures, for example, because the persecution they feared meant they had to leave without warning. There is nothing expressly on detention,

---

[123] UNHCR has an internal document, 'Lawfully Staying—A Note on Interpretation', from 1988—in the possession of the authors.

[124] See Executive Committee (ExCom) of UNHCR, Family Reunification, Conclusion No 24 (XXXII), 21 October 1981; UNHCR *Guidelines on Determining the Best Interests of the Child*, May 2008.

[125] See EUQD, Article 23.   [126] Eg Article 25 ICCPR, on political participation.

[127] General Comment 32.   [128] CCPR/C/21/Rev.1/Add.9, 1 November 1999.

[129] CCPR/C/GC/35, para 3, 16 December 2014.

but it is implicit in the prohibition on penalties.[130] The requirement that they come 'directly from a territory where their life or freedom was threatened' does not mean that it only applies in the first country they reach outside the country of nationality if countries they passed through were unsafe. The requirement that they present themselves 'without delay' also needs to take account of the personal characteristics of the asylum-seeker. According to UNHCR's Guidelines, any detention must respect the right to seek asylum, it must be in accordance with and authorized by law, it must not be arbitrary and indefinite detention is arbitrary, it must not be discriminatory, there must be legally prescribed limits on detention, decisions to detain must be subject to procedural safeguards, the conditions must be humane and dignified,[131] and it should be independently monitored. Moreover, while the particular needs of certain asylum-seekers need to be especially taken into account, Guideline 4 provides in general that:

4.1 Detention is an exceptional measure and can only be justified for a legitimate purpose.[132]

4.2 Detention can only be resorted to when it is determined to be necessary, reasonable in all the circumstances and proportionate to a legitimate purpose.

4.3 Alternatives to detention need to be considered.

Detention of refugees is practised by most States and it is an area where the lack of a supranational treaty body to which individual complaints could be brought regarding State practice under the 1951 Convention is most keenly felt.

V. ASSISTANCE AND RELIEF

The popular perception of refugees is individuals in camps receiving relief and assistance from the international community, particularly UNHCR. At so many levels that image is inaccurate. To start, most displaced persons are not in camps, but live in urban settings, which are to be preferred, but where monitoring and protection are less straightforward. Moreover, apart from Articles 23 and 24 of the 1951 Convention dealing with public relief and social security for refugees lawfully staying in the contracting State, there is nothing on assistance for refugees. Moreover, UNHCR's mandate is to provide international protection, not relief and assistance.[133] Nevertheless, the interplay between assistance and protection (Morris, 1997), along with the UNHCR expansion of mandate during the past seven decades, means that there is law, policy, and practice pertaining to assistance and relief to refugees (Türk and Eyster, 2010).

At the most general level, Article 11 ICESCR provides a right to an adequate standard of living for everyone, including adequate food, clothing, and housing. While the ICESCR has no derogation clause, it is recognized that States might not be able instantly to provide the full realization of the right, particularly in the face of a massive cross-border influx.

Article 2.1 Each State Party to the present Covenant undertakes to take steps, individually and through international assistance and co-operation, especially economic and technical, to the maximum of its available resources, with a view to achieving progressively the

---

[130] UNHCR, *Guidelines on the Applicable Criteria and Standards relating to the Detention of Asylum-Seekers and Alternatives to Detention*, 2012. The Council of Europe is, at time of writing, drafting its own guidelines—see McGregor, 2017.   [131] See *MSS v Belgium and Greece* [GC], no 30696/09, ECHR 2011.

[132] Such as to protect public order, public health, or national security.

[133] See Statute, para 1. Cf UNRWA mandate.

full realization of the rights recognized in the present Covenant by all appropriate means, including particularly the adoption of legislative measures.

This raises questions on responsibility sharing, discussed later.

The existence of an ongoing conflict also makes the provision of relief and assistance more complicated, but it is a clear parallel obligation to international protection: they are inextricably intertwined. The international law of armed conflict places obligations on parties to the conflict in this scenario. AP1 on international armed conflicts and AP2 on non-international armed conflicts both make limited provision in relation to humanitarian assistance,[134] but neither establishes a right to access such supplies. Under AP1, relief actions are 'subject to the agreement of the Parties concerned'.[135] Under AP2, where a civilian population is suffering 'undue hardship', exclusively humanitarian and impartial relief actions should be undertaken 'subject to the consent of the High Contracting Party concerned'.[136] The ICRC asserts that customary international humanitarian law applicable in international and non-international armed conflicts reflects the same obligation, with the same limitation: 'The parties to the conflict must allow and facilitate rapid and unimpeded passage of humanitarian relief for civilians in need, which is impartial in character and conducted without any adverse distinction, *subject to their right of control*' (Henckaerts and Doswald-Beck, 2005, Vol I, Rule 55). In practice, of course, humanitarian organizations seeking to deliver humanitarian assistance in non-international armed conflicts will also need the consent of any non-State actors who are party to the conflict.[137] Thus, since the consent of parties to the conflict (whether international or non-international) is required and conditions can be imposed under both Additional Protocols, access could potentially be denied. Furthermore, to ensure that only humanitarian relief supplies were being transported along a safe corridor, a party to the conflict could legitimately dismantle a refrigerated lorry carrying medicines and foodstuffs, even if that meant that those supplies were damaged.[138] The Guiding Principles provide stronger guarantees for IDPs.

> Principle 25.3—All authorities concerned shall grant and facilitate the free passage of humanitarian assistance and grant persons engaged in the provision of such assistance rapid and unimpeded access to the internally displaced.

While paragraph 3 of the Introduction states that the Guiding Principles 'reflect and are consistent with international human rights law and international humanitarian law', this goes beyond what even the ICRC claims is customary international law.

Turning to UNHCR, its Statutory mandate is to provide international protection to refugees and assist governments by seeking permanent solutions for refugees. UNHCR does not have a mandate to provide relief and assistance. Indeed, paragraphs 8i and 10 make it clear that its role is to facilitate 'the co-ordination of the efforts of private organizations concerned with the welfare of refugees' and 'administer any funds, public or private, which he receives for assistance to refugees, and shall distribute them among the private and, as appropriate, public agencies which he deems best qualified to administer such assistance'. Of course, UNHCR operates camps for refugees, asylum-seekers, IDPs, and other individuals of concern to the High Commissioner around the world under its extended

---

[134] See AP1, Article 70 and AP2, Article 18.2, along with Article 23 Fourth Geneva Convention 1949 (n 74).
[135] AP1, Article 70.1.   [136] AP2, Article 18.2.
[137] See 'Syria conflict: Russia proposes safe corridors for Aleppo', *BBC News* (online), 1 December 2016, http://www.bbc.co.uk/news/world-middle-east-38172477.
[138] See generally, Henckaerts and Doswald-Beck, 2005, pp 193–200. The only case in which there might be an absolute obligation on parties to the conflict to provide humanitarian access would be if there were a siege and a civilian population were starving.

mandate (Türk and Eyster, 2010). Through the work of ExCom, which is comprised of States, UNHCR has developed policies and practice with respect to camps so as to ensure refugees' safety.[139] The starting point is ExCom Conclusion No 48 (XXXVIII) of 1987:

> *Predicating* this Conclusion on the assumption, *inter alia*, that refugee camps and settlements have an *exclusively civilian and humanitarian character* and on the principle that the grant of asylum or refuge is a peaceful and humanitarian act that is not to be regarded as unfriendly by another State; hoping to assist in guaranteeing the safety of refugees and asylum-seekers, as well as to reinforce their rights, obligations and responsibilities and those of States and international organizations pursuant to relevant rules and principles of international law; and underlining that the rights and responsibilities of States pursuant to the Charter of the United Nations and relevant rules and principles of international law, including international humanitarian law, remained unaltered.[140]

While the Conclusion assumes that refugee camps are located across a border and that the people in it are refugees, the same principles apply by analogy to camps within a State where an armed conflict is occurring. While it is certainly easier to maintain the non-political and neutral character of a camp when it is located beyond a conflict zone in another country, decades of experience with camps for IDPs suggest that the ideas are transposable.

ExCom Conclusion No 94 (LIII) of 2002 provides the greatest guidance on the nature of refugee camps. Promulgated after UNHCR's experience in the former Yugoslavia and in the Great Lakes Region of Africa, it provides 'that all actors, including refugees themselves, have the obligation to cooperate in ensuring the peaceful and humanitarian character of refugee camps and settlements'.[141] Furthermore, camps can best demonstrate their humanitarian, neutral, demilitarized, and civilian character if there are no armed elements in the camp, if no recruitment or training by any party to the conflict takes place, and if they are not mixed with populations of internees or prisoners of war. All this might seem obvious, but in an ongoing armed conflict, it may prove difficult to preserve these important preconditions.[142]

In 2016, States emphasized in the New York Declaration for Refugees and Migrants that:

> host States have the primary responsibility to ensure the civilian and humanitarian character of refugee camps and settlements. We will work to ensure that this character is not compromised by the presence or activities of armed elements and to ensure that camps are not used for purposes that are incompatible with their civilian character. We will work to strengthen security in refugee camps and surrounding local communities, at the request and with the consent of the host country.[143]

---

[139] ExCom currently consists of 101 States, not only parties to the 1951 Convention but also those most affected by refugee movements. Amongst other things, ExCom adopts by consensus Conclusions proposed by UNHCR on refugee protection, which means that the Conclusions carry a great deal of authority. UNHCR's 'entirely non-political [and] humanitarian' character (UNHCR Statute (n 4), para 2) is an asset that will support its credibility and legitimacy with the parties to the conflict.

[140] ExCom, 'Military or Armed Attacks on Refugee Camps and Settlements' No 48 (XXXVIII) (12 October 1987) (emphasis added). See also UNSC Res 1208 (19 November 1998), para 3.

[141] ExCom, 'Conclusion on the Civilian and Humanitarian Character of Asylum' No 94 (LIII) (8 October 2002), Preamble.

[142] See the need for the UN to establish in 1982 the UN Border Relief Organization on the Thai–Cambodian border because the camps there were being used by the Khmer Rouge to continue the armed conflict with the government in Phnom Penh. For UNBRO's principles, see Thai/Cambodia Border Refugee Camps 1975–99 Information and Documentation Website, UNBRO: The United National Border Relief Operation (2 August 1989).

[143] New York Declaration, UN Doc A/RES/71/1, para 73.

These ideas are complemented by the obligations of parties to the conflict in relation to neutralized zones, non-defended localities, and demilitarized zones.[144]

In sum, although the principal documents of international refugee law do not explicitly provide for assistance and relief, they are so bound up with protection in practice that, drawing on international human rights law and international humanitarian law, UNHCR has developed policies and best practice to ensure protection that provides appropriate assistance.

VI. CESSATION AND DURABLE SOLUTIONS

Refugee status is meant to be temporary, required only while refugees cannot rely on the protection of their country of nationality due to a well-founded fear of persecution. Under Article 1C, refugee status can come to an end. It deals with clear-cut cases where refugees have voluntarily re-established themselves in the country of nationality and re-availed themselves of its protection, or they have obtained another nationality and enjoy that State's protection. There are difficult cases where a refugee needs to obtain documents from his country of nationality or makes short trips back there, and in these cases refugee status should not necessarily be lost. The most difficult situation, and one where UNHCR's supervisory function has the largest role, relates to Article 1C.5.[145]

> This Convention shall cease to apply to any person falling under the terms of section A if:
>
> . . .
>
> (5) He can no longer, because the circumstances in connection with which he has been recognized as a refugee have ceased to exist, continue to refuse to avail himself of the protection of the country of his nationality;
>
> Provided that this paragraph shall not apply to a refugee falling under section A (I) of this article who is able to invoke compelling reasons arising out of previous persecution for refusing to avail himself of the protection of the country of nationality.

Determining that the circumstances have ceased to exist is not something that should be left to the countries most affected by the displacement. Equally, there will need to be a tripartite memorandum of understanding between the country of asylum and the country of nationality along with UNHCR that still has a protection mandate under its Statute towards these refugees until they have properly re-established themselves. Simply re-entering the country of nationality does not end refugee status. Such memoranda need to explicitly guarantee access by UNHCR to the refugees as they return and uphold their human rights.[146]

---

[144] See Geneva Convention relative to the Protection of Civilian Persons in Time of War (n 74), Article 15; AP1, Articles 59–60. See also Gilbert and Rüsch, *Creating Safe Zones*, pp 8–9, from which some of this text is taken.

[145] See UNHCR, *Guidelines on International Protection No 3: Cessation of Refugee Status under Article 1C(5) and (6) of the 1951 Convention relating to the Status of Refugees (the 'Ceased Circumstances' Clauses)*, 10 February 2003, HCR/GIP/03/03. See also Article I.4 of the 1969 Convention, which repeats this and adds two further cessation clauses: Article I.4(g) holds the 1969 Convention shall cease to apply to a refugee who 'has seriously infringed the purposes and objectives of this Convention'—given that Article III prohibits subversive activities against another AU member State, this has the potential to restrict legitimate political activities in the host State if interpreted too broadly. Even more disconcerting is Article I.4(f), which ends refugee status under the 1969 Convention if the refugee 'has committed a serious non-political crime outside the country of refuge *after* to his admission to that country as a refugee' (emphasis added)—this reverses the intention of Article 1Fb 1951 Convention.

[146] See Amnesty International, *RWANDA Human Rights Overlooked in Mass Repatriation*, esp. 17, AI Index AFR 47/02/97, 14 January 1997; and *GREAT LAKES REGION Still in Need of Protection: Repatriation, Refoulement and the Safety of Refugees and the Internally Displaced*, esp. 5, AI Index AFR 02/07/97, 24 January 1997. Cf Morris, 1997, pp 494–5.

Durable and sustainable solutions for refugees and other displaced persons require States to accept the responsibilities they assume under the 1951 Convention and customary international law, alongside the obligation to share the responsibility among the international community as a whole. It is worth noting that 84 per cent of all refugees live in developing countries, almost 30 per cent in the least developed.[147] The classic durable solutions are voluntary repatriation, local integration, and resettlement. As regards the last, resettlement in a third country is only for the most vulnerable refugees, especially given that for the 65.6 million persons of concern to UNHCR, there were only 189,300 resettlement places in 2016.[148] Local integration in the host State may happen by default in protracted situations of displacement. Given, though, that the vast majority of displaced persons are in developing countries, proper responsibility sharing as agreed to in the 2016 New York Declaration is essential; the poorest States on the planet who already house the refugee populations cannot be expected to be in a position to integrate thousands more people into their economies without massive investment in infrastructure and education programmes.[149] It is important that asylum-seekers and refugees are given access to education and employment during displacement if they are to be in a position to integrate if that is the preferred durable solution. Finally, voluntary repatriation, if possible, is usually seen as the preferred solution: displaced populations want to return home, host States want the protection responsibility to come to an end, and a voluntary return suggests the country of nationality has stabilized and is in transition.[150] The danger is that voluntary repatriation becomes more 'safe return' because the host State is not receiving sufficient support from the international community, the displaced persons cannot return home because their home has been destroyed or has been occupied by others in the intervening period, and for the grandchildren of the refugees born during displacement, this never was home. The international law pertaining to refugees and migration is replete with gaps in the protection structures and failure by States to meet the obligations they have assumed because of clashes between law, policy, and domestic politics.

VII. CONCLUSION

The protection of refugees and other displaced persons draws on specific treaties such as the 1951 Convention and its 1967 Protocol, but also international human rights law, the international law of armed conflict, international humanitarian law, and international criminal law. It depends on State cooperation and responsibility sharing: alongside that, the work of international organizations and other humanitarian actors facilitates that protection and the implementation of rights for displaced persons. It is simultaneously paradigmatic of the Westphalian approach to international law, yet in practice it cuts across international borders for the promotion and the protection of individuals and their rights.

---

[147] UNHCR, *Global Trends: Forced Displacement 2016*, 2.   [148] *Global Trends*, 3.

[149] New York Declaration. See 'Annex 1, Comprehensive refugee response framework: 1. The scale and nature of refugee displacement today requires us to act in a comprehensive and predictable manner in large-scale refugee movements. Through a comprehensive refugee response based on the principles of international cooperation and on burden- and responsibility-sharing, we are better able to protect and assist refugees and to support the host States and communities involved.' See also the 2015 Sustainable Development Goals, 'Transforming our world: the 2030 Agenda for Sustainable Development' GA Res 70/1 (25 September 2015), with its aim that no-one is left behind, which would include displaced persons. See also the decision of the CJEU on responsibility sharing within the EU in *Slovakia and Hungary v Council of the European Union* (Decision (EU) 2015/1601), Joined Cases C-643/15 and C-647/15, 6 September 2017.

[150] See UNHCR, *Framework for Durable Solutions for Refugees and Persons of Concern*, May 2003, available at http://www.refworld.org/docid/4124b6a04.html.

REFERENCES

ALLAIN, J (2002), 'The *Ius Cogens* Nature of Non-Refoulement', 13 *IJRL* 533.

BOSTOCK, C (2002), 'The International Legal Obligations Owed to the Asylum Seekers on the MV Tampa', 14 *IJRL* 279.

CANTOR D and DURIEUX, J-F (eds) (2014), *Refuge from Inhumanity: War Refugees and International Humanitarian Law* (The Hague: Martinus Nijhoff).

CHETAIL, V (2018), *International Migration Law* (Oxford: Oxford University Press).

COHEN, R (2004), 'The Guiding Principles on Internal Displacement: An Innovation in International Standard Setting', 10 *Global Governance* 459.

DOWD, R (2011), 'Dissecting Discrimination in Refugee Law: An Analysis of its Meaning and its Cumulative Effect', 23 *IJRL* 28.

EDWARDS, A (2003), 'Tampering with Refugee Protection: The Case of Australia', 15 *IJRL* 192.

FELLER, E, TÜRK, V, and NICHOLSON, F (2003), *Refugee Protection in International Law* (Cambridge: Cambridge University Press).

GILBERT, G (2003), 'Current Issues in the Application of the Exclusion Clauses', in E Feller, V Türk, and F Nicholson (eds), *Refugee Protection in International Law* (Cambridge: Cambridge University Press), p 425.

GILBERT, G (2006), *Responding to International Crime* (The Hague: Martinus Nijhoff).

GILBERT, G (2014a), 'Exclusion under Article 1F since 2001: Two Steps Backwards, One Step Forward', in V Chetail and C Bauloz (eds), *Research Handbook on International Law and Migration* (Cheltenham: Edward Elgar), p 519.

GILBERT, G (2014b), 'Exclusion is Not Just about Saying "No": Taking Exclusion Seriously in Complex Conflicts', in D

Cantor and J-F Durieux (eds), *Refuge from Inhumanity: War Refugees and International Humanitarian Law* (The Hague: Martinus Nijhoff), p 155.

GILBERT G and RÜSCH, AM (2014), 'Jurisdictional Competence through Protection: To What Extent Can States Prosecute the Prior Crimes of Those to Whom They Have Extended Refuge?', 12 *JICJ* 1093.

GOODWIN-GILL, G S and McADAM, J (2007), *The Refugee in International Law* (3rd edn, Oxford: Oxford University Press).

HATHAWAY, J and FOSTER, M (2014), *The Law of Refugee Status* (2nd edn, Cambridge: Cambridge University Press).

HENCKAERTS, J-M and DOSWALD-BECK, L (2005), *Customary International Humanitarian Law* (Cambridge: Cambridge University Press).

HIGGINS, C (2017), *Asylum by Boat: Origins of Australia's Refugee Policy* (Sydney: New South Wales University Press).

KÄLIN, W (2000), *Guiding Principles on Internal Displacement: Annotations*, ASIL Studies in Transnational Legal Policy No. 32.

KÄLIN, W (2003), 'Supervising the 1951 Convention relating to the Status of Refugees: Article 35 and Beyond', in Feller, Türk, and Nicholson, *Refugee Protection in International Law*, p 613.

LAUTERPACHT, SIR ELIHU and BETHLEHEM, D (2003), 'The Scope and Content of the Principle of Non-Refoulement: Opinion', in Feller, Türk, and Nicholson, *Refugee Protection in International Law*, p 87.

McGREGOR, L (2017), 'An Appraisal of the Council of Europe's Draft European Rules on the Conditions of Administrative Detention of Migrants', https://www.ejiltalk.org/an-appraisal-of-the-council-of-europes-draft-european-rules-on-the-conditions-of-administrative-detention-of-migrants/.

MAGNER, T (2004), 'A Less than "Pacific" Solution for Asylum Seekers in Australia', 16 *IJRL* 53.

MORRIS, N (1997), 'Protection Dilemmas and UNHCR's Response: A Personal View from within UNHCR', 9 *IJRL* 492.

MUSALO, K (2004), 'Claims for Protection Based on Religion or Belief', 16 *IJRL* 165.

NOLL, N (2005), *Proof, Evidentiary Assessment and Credibility in Asylum Procedures* (The Hague: Martinus Nijhoff).

PALLIS, M (2002), 'Obligations of States towards Asylum Seekers at Sea: Interactions and Conflicts Between Legal Regimes', 14 *IJRL* 329.

PEERS, S (2016), *EU Justice and Home Affairs Law* (4th edn, Oxford: Oxford University Press).

SCHLOENHARDT, A (2002), 'To Deter, Detain and Deny: Protection of Onshore Asylum Seekers in Australia', 14 *IJRL* 302.

TÜRK, V and EYSTER, E (2010), 'Strengthening Accountability in UNHCR', 22 *IJRL* 159.

WILLHEIM, E (2003), 'MV Tampa: The Australian Response', 15 *IJRL* 159.

WOUTERS, W and DEN HEIJER, M (2010), 'The *Marine I* Case: A Comment', 22 *IJRL* 1.

FURTHER READING

BURSON, B and CANTOR, D (2016), *Human Rights and the Refugee Definition* (The Hague: Martinus Nijhoff).

COSTELLO, C (2016), *The Human Rights of Migrants and Refugees in European Law* (Oxford: Oxford University Press).

GIBNEY, M (2010), *Global Refugee Crisis* (2nd edn, Santa Barbara: ABC-CLIO).

GILBERT, G and RÜSCH, AM, *Creating Safe Zones and Safe Corridors in Conflict Situations: Providing protection at home or preventing the search for asylum?*, available at http://www.kaldorcentre.unsw. edu.au/sites/default/files/Policy_brief_ Creating_safe_zones_and_safe_corridors.

pdf?mc_cid=6e9bb775e9&mc_eid=fb55c2 c7c4&cn=bWVudGlvbg%3D%3D.

HURWITZ, H (2009), *The Collective Responsibility of States to Protect Refugees* (Oxford: Oxford University Press).

MORENO-LAX, V and EFTHYMIOS PAPASTAVRIDIS, E (2016), *'Boat Refugees' and Migrants at Sea: A Comprehensive Approach* (The Hague: Martinus Nijhoff).

SLINGENBERG, L (2014), *The Reception of Asylum Seekers under International Law: Between Sovereignty and Equality* (Oxford: Hart Publishing).

WEBSITES

UNHCR's REFWORLD http://www.refworld.org

UNHCR http://www.unhcr.org

HUDOC https://hudoc.echr.coe.int/eng#%7B%22documentcollectionid2%22:%5B%22J UDGMENTS%22,%22DECISIONS%22,%22ADVISORYOPINIONS%22%5D%7D

27

THE LAW OF ARMED CONFLICT (INTERNATIONAL HUMANITARIAN LAW)

David Turns

SUMMARY

The international law of armed conflict (also known as international humanitarian law, also known as the law of war) regulates the conduct of hostilities—including the use of weaponry—and the protection of victims in situations of both international and non-international armed conflict. Rooted in customary law, often of very great antiquity, since the late nineteenth century it has become one of the most intensively codified areas of international law. The 1949 Geneva Conventions, which form the cornerstone of contemporary humanitarian law, have been ratified by every single State on the face of the planet; yet implementation and enforcement are, if anything, even more problematic in this than in other areas of public international law, which has led to a symbiotic link between international humanitarian and international criminal law. Indeed, it was the creation of international criminal tribunals to deal with the aftermath of appalling atrocities in the former Yugoslavia and Rwanda, in the early 1990s, which sparked a renewal of interest in substantive humanitarian law, leading to its reaffirmation and development. This chapter outlines the scope of application of the law, issues of personal status (combatants and civilians), the conduct of hostilities (methods and means of warfare, including choice of weapons and targeting operations), the protection of victims (sick, wounded, shipwrecked, prisoners of war, and civilians), and various ways of securing the law's implementation and enforcement.

I. INTRODUCTION

It is a fact of life that armed conflict—the resort to organized force between States or within States—is, and always has been, an integral part of the human condition. Disregarding such indicia as the duration or intensity of the fighting, the number of casualties incurred or whether hostilities are active or 'frozen', there are currently some 50 situations in the world where there is either an actual armed conflict or a degree of tension so heightened that there is a real risk of resort to force. Given this state of affairs, coupled with the increase in humanitarian activism, the so-called 'CNN effect' of constant televised reporting from conflict zones, and enhanced mechanisms for securing the international legal liability of both governments (under the doctrine of State responsibility) and individuals (under the doctrine of individual criminal responsibility), it is unsurprising that international humanitarian law (IHL) has re-emerged from the shadows of public international law during the last three decades. The well-known aphorism, 'If international law is in some ways at the vanishing point of law, the law of war is, perhaps even more conspicuously, at the vanishing point of international law' (Lauterpacht, 1952, p 382), may have been accurate enough 60 years ago, but it is certainly no longer so today. Although the First Gulf War (1991) was the first modern armed conflict of which it could be said that '[d]ecisions were impacted by legal considerations at every level, [the law] proved invaluable in the decision-making process',[1] the law of war—now more commonly referred to as IHL or, alternatively, the law of armed conflict (LOAC)[2]—is of very much greater antiquity (Green, 2008, pp 26–45).

For much of its existence, the primary purpose of the law of war was to regulate in a technical sense the conduct of hostilities between belligerents. During the Middle Ages in Europe, war was regarded as a kind of game played by princes, nobles, and knights on horseback; like any game, it had to have a set of rules. The Second Lateran Council's ban on crossbows in 1139, for instance, was formulated not by reason of the pain and suffering which the weapon might cause to anyone unfortunate enough to be struck by one of its bolts, but because, by enabling a man to strike from a distance without himself being struck, the crossbow was considered a disgraceful and ignoble weapon which violated the rules of chivalry (Draper, 1965, pp 18–19).

The 'rules of the game' that constituted the laws of war at this time, however, were of little relevance to the feudal peasants who constituted the foot soldiery of European armies, nor were they believed to be of any application to wars against 'uncivilized enemies'—infidels and 'primitive peoples'. By the time of the Peace of Westphalia (1648), war had become a more public activity, in which increasingly regularized, standing armies fought on behalf of their countries, rather than as a time-limited feudal service obligation to their overlords. This contributed during the eighteenth century to the growth of the concept of reciprocity: captured enemy soldiers, for example, should be well treated because there was a vested interest in having the adverse party accord the same treatment to one's own soldiers who were captured on the battlefield.

The law at this time was almost exclusively customary in nature, encompassing a wide variety of rules and practices that had been mutually observed by warring forces for many centuries. By the mid-nineteenth century and such conflicts as the Crimean (1853–5) and Franco-Austrian (1859) Wars, the exponential growth in human suffering, caused by a combination of developing military technology and inadequate provision for military medical facilities, together with increased reporting of the battlefield (the latter enhanced further by the expansion of war photography in the American Civil War, 1861–5), led to the rise of humanitarianism as a major concern in the regulation of conflicts. This desire to provide for the protection of victims of hostilities in turn encouraged the increasing use of multilateral treaties to codify the existing rules—and develop new ones.

Today IHL is very largely codified in a series of some 58 multilateral treaties. However, the customary laws of war continue to retain considerable significance, in part because of the recognition (as long ago as 1899)[3] that treaties could not cover every eventuality that might

---

[1] General Colin Powell, Chairman of the US Joint Chiefs of Staff, cited in US Department of Defense, *Final Report to Congress on the Conduct of the Persian Gulf War, Appendix O* (1992) 31 ILM 615.

[2] The terms 'IHL' and 'LOAC' are synonymous and are used interchangeably throughout this chapter. The term 'law of war', while still appropriate in an historical context, has been generally abandoned in the contemporary legal discourse.

[3] In the 'Martens Clause', Preamble to The Hague Convention II with Respect to the Laws and Customs of War on Land (1899).

arise in an armed conflict; the International Committee of the Red Cross (ICRC) reinforced this with the publication of a major piece of research identifying 161 'rules' of customary international humanitarian law and collating the evidence (examples of State practice and *opinio juris sive necessitatis*) on which they are based (Henckaerts and Doswald-Beck, 2005). Furthermore, the 1949 Geneva Conventions are now so widely accepted—they attained their 196th accession (by Palestine) in 2014[4]—that they are considered to have passed in their entirety into customary international law. This enabled them to be applied in arbitration proceedings between Ethiopia and Eritrea relating to their 1998–2000 conflict: Eritrea, having attained independence only five years before the commencement of hostilities, had not at the relevant time become a party to the Geneva Conventions. Nevertheless, it accepted their application *ex post facto* on the basis of their universal acceptance as customary law.[5]

For all their etymological similarity to each other, and notwithstanding the fact that the language of many provisions of humanitarian law relating especially to non-international armed conflicts is clearly influenced by the language of human rights,[6] it is important to emphasize that international humanitarian law and international human rights law are not the same thing at all. If humanitarian law has been characterized by the International Court of Justice (ICJ) as the *lex specialis* applicable in situations of armed conflict and mostly concerned with how belligerent States treat nationals of adverse and neutral parties, human rights law is better viewed as a *lex generalis* broadly applicable in all situations—both peace and war—and mostly concerned with how States treat their own nationals. In relation to situations of armed conflict, humanitarian law is almost invariably more detailed and comprehensive than the law of human rights.[7] That said, the application of these two bodies of law has become increasingly blurred, largely in consequence of a complaint brought to the European Court of Human Rights (ECtHR) in relation to the bombing of the Federal Republic of Yugoslavia (FRY) by air forces of the North Atlantic Treaty Organization (NATO) in 1999, and the *lex specialis* doctrine has not been accepted by all commentators (Milanovic, 2011).

The applicants in the *Banković* case sought to argue that the NATO States had violated the right to life of Serbs in the FRY in the conduct of their bombing campaign, specifically in relation to the destruction of the Serbian Radio and Television studios in Belgrade. In dismissing the application, the ECtHR found that FRY nationals were not 'within the jurisdiction' of the NATO States in the terms of Article 1 of the European Convention of Human Rights (ECHR) because, *inter alia*, bombing an area from 30,000 feet did not amount to having 'effective control' of that area for the purposes of applying human rights obligations.[8] An aerial bombing campaign, however, is distinguished for the purposes of ECHR application from a military occupation: thus, Turkey has been held responsible for the application of the ECHR in the 'Turkish Republic of Northern Cyprus' because it has 'effective control' over that territory.[9] A subsequent series of decided cases in the UK and

---

[4] The Conventions do not apparently apply to Hong Kong, since in 1997 the UK's ratification ceased to have effect for that territory upon its reversion to Chinese sovereignty. The Beijing government has not extended its ratification of the Conventions to Hong Kong, although it did so in respect of Macao (in 1999).

[5] Ethiopia-Eritrea Claims Commission, *Partial Awards on the Claims Relating to Prisoners of War* (2003) 42 ILM 1056 and 1083.

[6] This is especially the case in respect of Additional Protocol (AP) II (1977).

[7] *Legality of the Threat or Use of Nuclear Weapons, Advisory Opinion, ICJ Reports 1996*, p 226, paras 24–5.

[8] *Banković et al v Belgium et al* (Dec) [GC], no 52207/99, paras 67–81, ECHR 2001-XII; 123 ILR 94. For detailed discussion of this and other cases concerning extraterritorial jurisdiction under the ECHR, see Byron, 2007, pp 869–78.

[9] *Loizidou v Turkey (Preliminary Objections), Judgment of 23 March 1995, Ser A, No 310*, 20 EHRR 99, paras 56–64. On the applicability of human rights law in territory under belligerent occupation, see *Legal Consequences of the Construction of a Wall in the Occupied Palestinian Territory, Advisory Opinion, ICJ Reports 2004*, p 136, paras 105–13.

the European Court of Human Rights has indicated that human rights law *is* applicable in respect of certain situations that may arise during military operations overseas, most notably where forces are in occupation of territory or have physical custody of individuals (which the House of Lords in *Al-Skeini* likened to having extraterritorial 'effective control' of a prison).[10] All this is not to say, however, that human rights law regulates prima facie the conduct of soldiers during active hostilities on the battlefield; indeed, it would be entirely counterintuitive to reach that conclusion. One of the most basic human rights is the right to life; yet it is precisely this right that may, with certain limitations, lawfully and violently be taken away in armed conflicts. Humanitarian law has evolved highly detailed and technical provisions to govern soldiers' and civilians' conduct in such situations, and it continues to be the primary body of law applicable in all situations of armed conflict.

II. SCOPE OF APPLICATION OF HUMANITARIAN LAW

The international law of armed conflict applies in all armed conflicts, however they are characterized, and applies to all parties in a conflict, irrespective of the legality of the resort to force. There is no doctrinal relationship between *jus ad bellum* and *jus in bello*: the application of the latter in no way depends upon the former, and the legality of a conflict as such has no bearing whatsoever on the use of IHL, although justifications publicly offered by States for their military operations in recent years have increasingly tended to blur the boundaries between these two bodies of international law, especially in the tendency to base actions like drone strikes on the right of individual or collective self-defence under Article 51 of the United Nations Charter (or customary international law) (Turns, 2017). It would thus be quite incorrect to suggest that, for instance, every individual attack (such as an airstrike) undertaken as part of an operation illegal under the *jus ad bellum* is *ipso facto* also illegal under the *jus in bello*, or conversely, that the victim of an act of aggression has the right to attack the civilian population of the aggressor.[11] The question, however, of when and how humanitarian law applies ('scope of application') is not as straightforward as it might initially seem. This is partly because of some uncertainties surrounding the definition of armed conflict itself, and partly because of the different types of armed conflicts that are recognized in the contemporary law.

Traditionally, application of the law of war was triggered by a declaration of war, which had the legal effect of suspending most peacetime legal relations between belligerent States. Although a declaration of war did not invariably precede the actual start of hostilities,[12] it usually followed in due course once hostilities were under way; conversely, although there did not need to be active hostilities in progress at all times after a declaration of war had been issued, the existence of such a declaration was conclusive evidence as to the existence of a formal state of war. The state of war would normally be terminated only by a peace treaty, at which point the international law of peacetime relations would resume and the

---

[10] *Al-Skeini and others* v *United Kingdom* [2011] ECHR 1093; [2011] 53 EHRR 18; *Al-Jedda* v *United Kingdom* [2011] ECHR 1092; [2011] 53 EHRR 23; *Al-Saadoon and Mufdhi* v *United Kingdom* [2010] ECHR 285; [2010] 51 EHRR 9; see also *Secretary of State for Defence* v *R (Smith)* [2009] EWCA Civ 441; [2009] 3 WLR 1099; *Smith* v *Ministry of Defence* [2013] UKSC 41; *Hassan* v *United Kingdom* [GC], no 29750/09, ECHR 2014.

[11] Some advocates of the Palestinian cause aver that, because Israel is illegally occupying Palestinian land, it is legitimate to target Israeli civilians: see, eg, *The New York Times*, 5 May 2009.

[12] Eg the Japanese surprise attacks on the Imperial Russian Far East Squadron in Port Arthur (1904) and the US Pacific Fleet in Pearl Harbor (1941).

law of war would no longer be operative.[13] However, as has been suggested in recent years, with some understatement:

> Developments in international law since 1945, notably the United Nations (UN) Charter, including its prohibition on the threat or use of force in international relations, may well have made the declaration of war redundant as a formal international legal instrument.[14]

In point of fact, there have been no formal declarations of war since the Soviet declaration of war on Japan in August 1945; the association of such declarations with the appearance of an unlawful use of force under the Charter, or an act of aggression, has led to the procedure becoming defunct. The kind of confusion implicit in British Prime Minister Anthony Eden's statement in 1956, that the UK was not at war with Egypt during the Suez Crisis but merely in a state of armed conflict with that country,[15] is now a thing of the past in international law: the term 'armed conflict' is preferred to the term 'war',[16] as the former is a purely factual description of a situation, without connotations of right and wrong as regards the *jus ad bellum*. It is additionally often perceived to be in a State's interest to refrain from such an unequivocal declaration of hostile intent, as the *status mixtus*—simultaneously observing the law of war for some purposes and the law of peace for others—affords more room to manoeuvre, both diplomatically and politically. This may be the case especially in a 'low-intensity conflict', wherein neither side provokes the other into escalation, resulting in a conflict that is relatively limited and easily contained, from which belligerents may back away without necessarily appearing to have been defeated in a military sense (Green, 2008, pp 91–3). During Indonesia's policy of *Konfrontasi* ('Confrontation') with Malaysia from 1962 to 1966, British troops were actively engaged in armed hostilities against Indonesian forces in North Borneo, but diplomatic and commercial relations between the UK and Indonesia continued throughout the four years over which the Confrontation persisted.[17]

In any event the application of humanitarian law in no way affects the legal status of parties to a given conflict; it depends on neither the legality of the initial resort to force, nor the formal recognition of a state of war or armed conflict by the belligerents. The Geneva Conventions, for example, are expressly stated to apply to 'declared war or any other armed conflict'.[18] In 1982 during the Falklands War, the UK publicly denied that it was at war with Argentina, yet it applied the law of armed conflict in all its military operations.[19]

---

[13] The lack of peace treaties between Israel and its Arab neighbours (with the exception of Egypt and Jordan) could be said to imply that those countries remain in a state of war with each other, as the Armistice Agreements of 1949 did not terminate hostilities, but merely suspended them: Maoz, 2005, pp 36–44. A similar point may be made in relation to the situation between North and South Korea since the armistice agreement suspending hostilities in the Korean War in 1953.

[14] House of Lords Select Committee on the Constitution, Fifteenth Report of Session 2005–6, *Waging War: Parliament's Role and Responsibility, Volume I: Report* (HL Paper 236-I, 27 July 2006), para 10.

[15] See *Hansard, HC Debs*, 1 November 1956, vol 558, cols 1639–43. Regarding legal characterization of the Korean War, see Jessup, 1954.

[16] On the official characterization of hostilities between the UK and Iraq in 2003 as 'armed conflict' but not 'war', see *Amin v Brown* [2005] EWHC 1670 (Ch).

[17] See Hansard, HL Debs, 14 November 1963, vol 253, cols 153–5.

[18] Geneva Conventions (GC), Common Article 2 (1949).

[19] See, eg, Hansard, HC Debs, 26 April 1982, vol 22, col 616 (on the treatment of Argentine prisoners of war—the Prime Minister's statement that they were not prisoners of war because the UK was 'not at war' with Argentina was subsequently retracted, and all captured Argentine military personnel were treated in accordance with GCIII); ibid, 11 June 1982, vol 25, col 170W (on the treatment and repatriation of Lieutenant-Commander Alfredo Astiz of the Argentine Navy); ibid, 14 June 1982, col 611 (on the establishment by the ICRC of a neutralized zone in Port Stanley, in accordance with GCIV Article 15).

The difficulty lies in the fact that the law of armed conflict nowhere defines precisely what an 'armed conflict' is for the purposes of application of the law, despite the use of the phrase in the Geneva Conventions and other treaties that constitute this body of law. The ICRC indicated that '[a]ny difference arising between States and leading to the intervention of members of the armed forces is an [international] armed conflict' (Pictet, 1952, vol I, p 32), but this is problematic because it implies that even a very limited military operation of only a few hours' duration and not followed by any other hostilities would have to be considered an armed conflict, a position which is not supported by State practice. Although there are court decisions on point from various national jurisdictions (including the UK),[20] these invariably have been concerned with defining 'war' in municipal law for such purposes as interpreting liability exclusion clauses in insurance contracts, rather than having anything to do with IHL. In 1995 the International Criminal Tribunal for the Former Yugoslavia (ICTY) held that:

> an armed conflict exists whenever there is a resort to armed force between States or protracted armed violence between governmental authorities and organized armed groups or between such groups within a State. International humanitarian law applies from the initiation of such armed conflicts and extends beyond the cessation of hostilities until a general conclusion of peace is reached; or, in the case of internal conflicts, a peaceful settlement is achieved. Until that moment, international humanitarian law continues to apply in the whole territory of the warring States or, in the case of internal conflicts, the whole territory under the control of a party, whether or not actual combat takes place there.[21]

The statement in *Tadić* has since come to be widely accepted as a useful formulation of the concept of an armed conflict in customary international law. At least implicit in the formulation is the requirement that hostilities be 'substantial', 'protracted', and 'large-scale'.[22] Thus, it is doctrinally possible for a very brief or limited military operation to take place, yet for there to be no armed conflict between the States involved, as in the Entebbe Raid (1976), when Israel mounted a military operation to rescue hostages being detained by hijackers on Ugandan territory. Although Ugandan soldiers did resist the Israelis and there were some exchanges of fire between them, resulting in casualties on both sides and the destruction of several Ugandan Air Force fighters, it was never accepted that there was an armed conflict between Israel and Uganda.[23] Similarly, armed incidents across international borders in connection with the civil war in Syria, such as repeated exchanges of artillery fire between Turkish and Syrian government forces and the shooting down of a Turkish reconnaissance jet by Syrian anti-aircraft artillery in 2012, and the shooting down of a Russian attack aircraft by a Turkish fighter jet in 2015, have not been treated as constituting an armed conflict between those States. A maritime law enforcement operation involving the use of force might also not qualify as an armed conflict, even if it meets with armed resistance (ICRC, 2016, para 227). Nevertheless, it would surely be wrong to argue that States in such circumstances should actually be free to disregard substantive rules of IHL on the grounds that there is no formal situation of armed conflict; thus, in the last-named incident, the killing of one of the Russian pilots by ground fire attributed to the Free Syrian Army was a violation of customary IHL, at the very least (Henckaerts and

[20] Eg *Kawasaki Kisen Kabushiki Kaisha of Kobe* v *Bantham Steamship Co* [1939] KB 544.

[21] *Prosecutor* v *Duško Tadić*, Decision on the Defence Motion for Interlocutory Appeal on Jurisdiction (Interlocutory Appeal), Case No IT–94–1–AR72 (2 October 1995) 35 ILM 35, para 70.

[22] Ibid.

[23] Invocations of international law in the UN debates concerning the Israeli intervention at Entebbe were couched exclusively in terms of the *jus ad bellum*: see *Repertoire of the Practice of the Security Council* (1975–1980), pp 286–90.

Doswald-Beck, 2005, Rule 48). The ICRC continues to maintain its position with regard to unilateral uses of force and *de minimis* situations such as minor skirmishes (ICRC, 2016, paras 222–3 and 236–44).

Notwithstanding the possibility that military forces might be deployed on active operations absent a state of armed conflict, the military doctrine of many major military powers today requires that their armed forces comply with the spirit and principles of LOAC in all their operations, irrespective of whether they are formally considered to be in a state of armed conflict.[24] It is not necessary for there to be actual fighting at all times in an armed conflict for the law to be applicable. Some of the treaties that constitute LOAC also apply in situations where actual fighting may no longer be taking place: eg prisoners of war continue to benefit from protection under the law until their final release and repatriation,[25] while the law relevant to military occupation and protection of the civilian population continues to apply as long as an occupation subsists, even if other substantive military operations ceased at an earlier date.[26] The Geneva Conventions are silent as to the end of armed conflict, but Convention IV's mention (in Article 6) of 'the general close of military operations' has acquired great practical significance with the modern decline in the practice of concluding treaties of peace (ICRC, 2016, paras 274–84).

Until the mid-twentieth century, international law only recognized armed conflicts between States as being subject to its legal regulation. This was partly because of the dominant concept of State sovereignty over internal affairs and partly because of the then prevalent view that international law was concerned only with the regulation of international relations between States. Possibilities for extending the reach of international law to non-international conflicts were traditionally limited although some did exist, even before 1949 (Moir, 2002, pp 4–18). In that year, Common Article 3 of the Geneva Conventions extended certain basic humanitarian rules of protection to 'armed conflicts not of an international character'; these were supplemented in 1977 by Additional Protocol II. A trend has also emerged whereby certain rules are extended to all types of armed conflict, irrespective of their classification (Henckaerts and Doswald-Beck, 2005).[27] This trend is particularly apparent in, though not limited to, the treaties regulating weaponry (Turns, 2006).[28] While fulfilment of the trend would have the virtue of simplifying greatly the legal standards and their consistent application in all armed conflicts, however, the distinction between international and non-international conflicts retains its traditional importance in respect of several key legal provisions. 'Grave breaches' of the Geneva Conventions, for example, exist and may be punished exclusively in the context of international armed conflicts;[29] the qualifications of combatant and prisoner of war (POW) status do not exist in non-international armed conflicts.

Armed conflicts today, therefore, are normally classified into one of two types: international or non-international. The latter type may be further sub-classified into those conflicts that are internal to the territory of a State, and those that are not so confined but have cross-border, 'spillover' or 'transnational' effects (ICRC, 2016, paras 465–82). In addition, a non-international armed conflict may become 'internationalized' in certain circumstances

---

[24] Eg US Department of Defense, Directive 2311.01E, 9 May 2006, *DoD Law of War Program*, para 4.1.

[25] GCIII Article 5.

[26] GCIV Article 6.

[27] *Prosecutor* v *Duško Tadić*, Decision on the Defence Motion for Interlocutory Appeal on Jurisdiction (Interlocutory Appeal), Case No IT–94–1–AR72 (2 October 1995), paras 97–127; cf ibid, Separate Opinion of Judge Abi-Saab.

[28] Eg UN Convention on Conventional Weapons (1981), Amended Article 1 (2001).

[29] *Prosecutor* v *Duško Tadić*, Decision on the Defence Motion for Interlocutory Appeal on Jurisdiction (Interlocutory Appeal), Case No IT–94–1–AR72 (2 October 1995), paras 79–84.

by the participation of forces from another State (Byron, 2001) or by a change in the legal personality of one of the parties, eg if a secessionist insurgency becomes recognized as a new State. The *lex lata* essentially restricts the internationalizing effect of interventions to cases where the foreign State is intervening on the side of *insurgents* (or exercising effective control, according to the ICJ—or overall control, according to the ICTY—over them) in an internal conflict, because then the requirement of an international armed conflict, for two or more *States* to be in conflict with each other, is met. On the other hand, situations where a State intervenes in an internal conflict by providing assistance to *government* forces fighting against insurgents are said to remain non-international in nature, because the intervening State is not fighting against the host State, although this position is not unanimously accepted. Thus, the UK technically considered itself to be engaged in a non-international armed conflict in Afghanistan once the Taliban were displaced as the de facto government of that country in December 2001.[30] The international law basis for this somewhat counterintuitive position derives exclusively from the practice of the Coalition States operating in Afghanistan and admittedly is supported by a strict interpretation of the wording of Common Article 2 of the Geneva Conventions, but otherwise lacks any doctrinal support in decided case law and is not unproblematic, in that the 'inviting' government may actually lack the legitimacy genuinely to invite foreign forces onto the State's territory. It also takes no account of the UN Security Council's role in 'internationalizing' a previously internal situation. In some contemporary conflicts, a single State intervenes (as with France in Mali, 2012–14); in others, an international organization mandates the intervention (as with the African Union Mission in Somalia since 2009); in yet others, an ad hoc coalition of interested States collectively intervenes on one side or the other (as with the Saudi-led coalition in Yemen since 2015). The multifaceted complexity of such conflicts as the Syrian Civil War, with its proliferation of multilaterally engaged State and non-State parties, has led some commentators to adopt an approach focusing on the 'fragmentation' of the law, whereby international and non-international armed conflicts exist in parallel to each other in the same geographical and temporal space, but with different bodies of law applicable to different parties to the conflict (Ferraro, 2015; Lubell, 2017).

Under the Geneva Conventions an international armed conflict is defined as 'all cases of declared war or of any other armed conflict which may arise between two or more of the High Contracting Parties, even if the state of war is not recognized by one of them', and also as 'all cases of partial or total occupation of the territory of a High Contracting Party, even if the said occupation meets with no armed resistance';[31] thus, such long-running situations as the Israeli occupation of Palestinian Territories since 1967[32] and the Moroccan occupation of Western Sahara since 1975[33] are correctly considered to be international armed conflicts, as is the unopposed Russian occupation of the Crimea since 2014.[34] An armed conflict 'not of an international character' simply has to occur 'in the territory of one of the High Contracting Parties'.[35] The rather formalistic requirement that the conflict be between two or more 'High Contracting Parties' was a direct descendant of the stipulation, in the 1899 and 1907 Hague Conventions, that their provisions applied only 'between contracting Powers, and then only if all the belligerents are parties to the Convention'.[36]

---

[30] *GS v Secretary of State for the Home Department* [2009] UKAIT 00010.

[31] Common Article 2.

[32] Although Israel disputes the formal applicability *de jure* of GCIV to the occupation of the West Bank, it applies the Convention's humanitarian provisions on a *de facto* basis (Shamgar, 1971, pp 262–6).

[33] See UN Doc A/RES/34/37, 21 November 1979, para 5.

[34] See UN Doc A/68/PV.80, 27 March 2014, 1 and 8.   [35] Common Article 3.

[36] The Hague Convention (HC) IV, Article 2 (1907).

These *si omnes* or 'all-participation' clauses had to some extent already been discredited by notable abuse by Germany and Japan during World War II, when the Germans refused to apply the 1929 Geneva Convention on the Treatment of Prisoners of War vis-à-vis the Soviet Union, ostensibly on the grounds that the latter was not a party to that instrument.[37] Japan, also not a party to the Geneva Convention, punctiliously sent diplomatic notifications to the governments responsible for Allied forces in the Far East, stating that it would nevertheless apply the terms of that Convention, *mutatis mutandis*—and then went on to treat captured Allied nationals with casually systematic cruelty.[38] With both the Geneva Conventions and The Hague Regulations considered as customary international law, however, the 'all-participation clauses' are considered redundant today: IHL is truly universal in its application once there is a factual situation of armed conflict.

The scope of application provisions of the two 1977 Additional Protocols, which added to the definitions of armed conflicts, have been a major reason for some States' unwillingness to sign or ratify those instruments. Article 1(4) of Protocol I extends the Protocol's scope of application to include:

> armed conflicts in which peoples are fighting against colonial domination and alien occupation and against racist regimes in the exercise of their right to self-determination, as enshrined in the Charter of the United Nations and the Declaration on Principles of International Law concerning Friendly Relations and Co-operation among States in accordance with the Charter of the United Nations.

Article 96(3) of the Protocol further provides that an 'authority' representing a people engaged in such an armed conflict may unilaterally undertake to apply the Geneva Conventions and the Protocol by means of a declaration to that effect.

With the stroke of a pen, the Protocol thus made armed struggles that had previously been seen as internal to individual States, matters for international regulation. After 1977, acts of violence committed by non-State actors could be viewed as legitimate acts of war if the persons committing them claimed to be acting in the name of national liberation or self-determination. Naturally enough, those States that are engaged in armed struggles against such groups have opposed the imposition of international regulation for their conflicts against what they often style mere 'criminals' or 'terrorists'. In many cases this has resulted in important military powers either not becoming parties to the Protocol at all,[39] or becoming parties, but with substantial reservations that have the specific effect of negating the expanded scope of application. The Irish Republican Army (IRA), in its long armed struggle against the UK security forces in Northern Ireland during 'the Troubles', sought to claim that it was acting in pursuit of Irish self-determination, to 'liberate' Northern Ireland from 'illegal British occupation', and was thus engaged in an international armed conflict against the UK. This led the IRA to demand prisoner of war (POW) status for its captured operatives. The UK, for its part, consistently denied that there was an armed conflict of any kind in Northern Ireland[40]—and specifically denied the entitlement of captured IRA members to POW status, preferring to regulate their activity under national law and to regard them as nothing more than common criminals (Walker, 1984). Concern about

---

[37] *The Trial of German Major War Criminals*, 1946, Judgment, pp 46–8. A 1941 Soviet offer to apply the Geneva Convention *mutatis mutandis* was left unanswered by Germany.

[38] *International Military Tribunal for the Far East*, 1948, Judgment, pp 1096–106.

[39] Eg the USA, Turkey, Israel, India, Pakistan, and Indonesia. On the official US attitude to the Protocol, see President Ronald Reagan, *Message to the Senate Transmitting a Protocol to the 1949 Geneva Conventions* (1987) 26 ILM 561.

[40] See, eg, Hansard, HC Debs, 14 December 1977, vol 941, col 237W.

attempts to apply the Protocol to Northern Ireland contributed to the UK's decision to delay ratification of the Protocol: although it signed the instrument in 1977, the UK did not ratify it until 1998. Moreover, upon ratification, the UK was careful to enter the following 'statement of understanding' in respect of Articles 1(4) and 96(3):

> It is the understanding of the UK that the term 'armed conflict' of itself and in its context denotes a situation of a kind which is not constituted by the commission of ordinary crimes including acts of terrorism whether concerted or in isolation.
>
> The UK will not, in relation to any situation in which it is itself involved, consider itself bound in consequence of any declaration purporting to be made under [Article 96(3)] unless the UK shall have expressly recognised that it has been made by a body which is genuinely an authority representing a people engaged in an armed conflict of the type to which [Article 1(4)] applies.[41]

There has to date been no successful attempt to invoke Article 1(4) as the basis for applying the law of international armed conflict to any situation, although in 1989 the Palestine Liberation Organization (PLO) notified the Swiss government (as the depositary of the Geneva Conventions and the Additional Protocols) of its decision to adhere to those instruments. The Swiss government declined to confirm that the PLO's decision was a valid accession to the instruments, '[d]ue to the uncertainty within the international community as to the existence or the non-existence of a State of Palestine'.[42]

If the expanded definition of international armed conflicts has proved controversial, that of non-international conflicts has been all but unworkable. The *Tadić* case and subsequent decisions from the ICTY and other international criminal courts and tribunals had established the customary law requirement that in order for a situation to be characterized as a non-international armed conflict, the fighting must have a certain level of intensity and the parties to the conflict must have a sufficient degree of organization.[43] Article 1 of Protocol II defines non-international armed conflicts to which it applies as:

> all armed conflicts which are not covered by Article 1 of Protocol I and which take place in the territory of a High Contracting Party between its armed forces and dissident armed forces or other organised armed groups which, under responsible command, exercise such control over a part of [the State's] territory as to enable them to carry out sustained and concerted military operations and to implement this Protocol.
>
> This Protocol shall not apply to situations of internal disturbances and tensions, such as riots, isolated and sporadic acts of violence and other acts of a similar nature, as not being armed conflicts.

Quite apart from the fact that States with internal conflicts on their territories have been unsurprisingly reluctant to submit to international legal regulation of their violent struggles against 'bandits' or 'terrorists', the main problem with the definition of non-international conflicts, which has largely sabotaged attempts to apply the Protocol in practice, is the requirement for the dissident party to be in control of territory. Illogically enough, this requirement is placed at a higher threshold than is required for national liberation movements in Additional Protocol I, which do not have to control any territory in order to have their struggle legally classified as an *international* armed conflict. The requirement that dissident movements be able to carry out 'sustained and concerted military operations' and to implement the Protocol has been a gift to States seeking to deny the Protocol's

[41] Roberts and Guelff, 2000, p 510.

[42] Ibid, p 362. The State of Palestine, as proclaimed by the PLO in 1988 and granted 'non-member observer State' status at the UN in 2012, acceded to the Geneva Conventions and API in 2014.

[43] *Prosecutor* v *Duško Tadić*, Opinion and Judgment, Case No IT–94–1–T (7 May 1997), para 562.

applicability to their own internal conflicts, as rebel movements are rarely in such a strong position and rarely have any incentive to apply international humanitarian law in their operations.[44] In effect, the definition of a non-international armed conflict under Protocol II has a threshold so high as to preclude the vast majority of armed rebellions from being subject to its regulation. To date fewer than half a dozen States, and even fewer insurgent movements, have indicated any willingness to be bound by the Protocol in the conduct of their respective internal conflicts (Moir, 2002, pp 119–32). During the Sri Lankan Civil War (1983–2009), the Liberation Tigers of Tamil Eelam (LTTE) undeniably controlled substantial parts of the north-east of the country and mounted 'sustained and concerted' military operations against government forces; yet Sri Lanka is not a party to Protocol II and neither the government nor the LTTE showed any effective application of IHL.[45]

The technicalities of the definitions of international and non-international armed conflicts make it difficult for military personnel to know when to treat irregular opponents as legitimate combatants, civilians directly participating in hostilities, 'dissident armed forces' under Protocol II, a national liberation movement under Protocol I, or common criminals engaged in violence and entitled to no specific protections under IHL. This has led to an increase in the importance of governmental determinations as to the classification of armed conflicts in which regular forces are engaged and as to the applicable scope of application of IHL. Unfortunately, as the official US reaction to the events of 11 September 2001 in terms of the treatment of detainees captured in the course of the new 'Global War on Terror' showed, such determinations may do more harm than good. The US Administration of George W Bush persisted in viewing the 'War on Terror' as an international armed conflict within the LOAC paradigm, albeit one in which captured enemy combatants could be detained until the end of 'active hostilities'[46] but were not entitled to be treated as POWs under Geneva Convention III.[47] The US Supreme Court, however, took a radically different view in one of its more celebrated decisions regarding the status and treatment of detainees captured by US forces and held in Guantánamo Bay, Cuba. The plurality of the court held, obiter, that because the conflict between the USA and Al-Qaeda terrorists was neither against a High Contracting Party to the Geneva Conventions, nor in the territory of one such party, it was by default an 'armed conflict not of an international character' in the terms of Common Article 3.[48]

It is worth noting that virtually no other State agreed with the US legal approach to this situation and, indeed, the Administration of Barack Obama abandoned such contortions of logic from its first days in office in January 2009. In Israel it has been suggested that such conflicts are better viewed as being in the nature of international armed conflicts, to which the fullest possible extent of IHL should be applied, by reason of the transnational nature of such conflicts—ie the fact that they cross international borders—and the military capabilities of modern terrorist organizations.[49] In the UK, determinations about the existence

[44] Cf Sivakumaran, 2006.

[45] See UN, *Report of the Secretary-General's Panel of Experts on Accountability in Sri Lanka* (31 March 2011), http://www.un.org/News/dh/infocus/Sri_Lanka/POE_Report_Full.pdf.

[46] GCIII Article 118.

[47] GCIII Article 5 requires that if there is any doubt as to a detainee's status under LOAC, s/he shall be treated as a POW until their status is determined by a competent tribunal. Cf President Bush, *Military Order: Detention, Treatment and Trial of Certain Non-Citizens in the War Against Terrorism* (2001) 41 ILM 252; Attorney-General Alberto Gonzales, *Memorandum to the President re Application of the Geneva Convention on Prisoners of War to the Conflict with Al Qaeda and the Taliban* (2002) (reproduced in Greenberg and Datrel, 2005, p 118).

[48] *Hamdan v Rumsfeld* 548 US 557 (2006).

[49] *Public Committee against Torture in Israel* v *Government of Israel (targeted killings)* HCJ 769/02; (2006) 46 ILM 375.

and characterization of an armed conflict are made as a matter of policy, depending on the facts on the ground and the status of the parties to the conflict.[50] It follows that the UK does not accept that there is a single armed conflict between itself and Al-Qaeda; rather, there were discrete conflicts in theatres such as Iraq (until the withdrawal of British forces in 2009) and Afghanistan (until the termination of British combat operations in 2014). Current operations against the so-called 'Islamic State' in Iraq and Syria since 2014 are treated as discrete conflicts. IHL was and is applied by British forces in all such military operations.

The spectrum of conflict is well illustrated by the case of Iraq since 2003: after an initial phase of international armed conflict (March–April 2003) to which the fullest extent of LOAC applied, there followed a period of belligerent occupation (April 2003–June 2004) during which certain parts of IHL (notably Geneva Convention IV) continued to be applicable. After the formal end of occupation, however, the legal position became substantially less clear in that Coalition forces were operating extraterritorially against non-State actors; this resulted in the haphazard application of an ad hoc hodgepodge of rules cobbled together from the laws relating to both international and non-international armed conflicts, supplemented by a dose of human rights law and overshadowed by the significance of UN Security Council resolutions regarding the rights of foreign forces in Iraq.

Finally, it is worth noting that broadly the same rules apply in all domains of conflict: land, sea, air, outer space, and cyberspace. Although the bulk of the law was formulated with land warfare in mind, the centuries-old customary law of maritime warfare continues to be applicable: it was largely codified in 1907[51] and in the 1930s,[52] and has since been comprehensively restated in the International Institute of Humanitarian Law's *San Remo Manual on International Law Applicable to Armed Conflicts at Sea* (1994). Aerial warfare has been a feature of armed conflicts since 1911, but has to date not been the subject of a specific adopted treaty; although the rules on targeting in API clearly apply to air warfare, it was only in 2009 that the *Manual on International Law Applicable to Air and Missile Warfare* was produced by the Harvard Program on Humanitarian Policy and Conflict Research, containing a comprehensive restatement of the law in such operations.[53] Considerable attention has been devoted to cyber warfare recently, following the cyber operations (attributed to Russia) which were targeted at Estonia in 2007 and Georgia in 2008; this has culminated in another manual produced by an international group of experts under NATO auspices, the *Tallinn Manual on the International Law Applicable to Cyber Warfare*. It should be noted that all these manuals are the work of academic specialists and legal practitioners working in a personal capacity; this did not matter so much in the cases of the *San Remo* and *Harvard Manuals*, but the extent to which the *Tallinn Manual* in particular will be generally accepted by a convincing number of States as *lex lata* remains very uncertain. In 2017 a UN Group of Governmental Experts (GGE) on Developments in the Field of Information and Telecommunications in the Context of International Security, which had been meeting since 2004, collapsed without adopting a final report because certain States (most notably China, Cuba, and Russia) rejected the proposed application of some of the most fundamental norms of international law to cyberspace, including even any express mention of IHL (Schmitt and Vihul, 2017).

---

[50] UK Ministry of Defence, 2004, paras 3.1–13.   [51] The Hague Conventions VI–XI and XIII.
[52] The London Procès-verbal on Submarine Warfare (1936); the Nyon Agreement (1938).
[53] See https://www.researchgate.net/profile/Claude_Bruderlein/publication/264036862_Manual_on_
International_Law_Applicable_to_Air_and_Missile_Warfare/links/59a911d50f7e9b27900e2f0e/Manual-on-
International-Law-Applicable-to-Air-and-Missile-Warfare.pdf.

III. THE ACTORS IN HUMANITARIAN LAW

Once the scope of application of IHL has been determined, the crucial feature of the modern law in international armed conflicts is the distinction between combatants and civilians. The former may legitimately participate and be targeted in military operations, while the latter—subject to certain exceptions[54]—may not. Conversely, and as a direct consequence of their status, the former are entitled to certain rights and privileges upon capture, while the latter are not. Therefore, in the planning and execution of military operations, a distinction must always be made between combatants on the one hand, and civilians on the other. This was an easy enough task when battles were fought by organized armies on discrete (mostly rural) battlefields largely denuded of their civilian inhabitants; however, the proliferation of irregular forces in modern warfare, which also is frequently conducted in an urban environment where the civilian population remains present, has made distinction exceedingly difficult in practice.

Historically, the laws of war did not provide a definition of the concept of a 'combatant'. Warfare was carried on by soldiers, who generally were easily distinguishable from the civilian population. This was so even before the issue of standardized uniforms to European armies began to become common practice in the late seventeenth century. Although a concept of lawful combatancy was present in the literature by the late eighteenth century (Green, 2008, pp 125–8), and the need to regulate unconventional warfare made an early appearance in Section IV of the *Lieber Code* (1863), there was little controversy in practice before the Franco-Prussian War (1870–71). In that conflict, the swift advance of Prussian forces into French territory led to the definition of two new categories of persons whose proper combatant status was initially a matter of some legal uncertainty: *francs-tireurs* and the *levée en masse*. The latter category ('mass levy') had been recognized since its use by the French Republic in 1793[55] and referred to the spontaneous requisitioning of the civilian population of an invaded—but unoccupied—territory, without time for military organization; its members are regarded as combatants, provided they 'carry arms openly and . . . respect the laws and customs of war'.[56] They are entitled to POW status upon capture.[57]

The former category ('free-shooters'), on the other hand, referred to civilians who—whether in occupied territory or not—take up arms on their own initiative to fight, independently of any governmental or military control, against an invading army. In 1870, members of rifle clubs or unofficial paramilitary shooting societies in eastern France formed irregular bands that carried out ambushes and attacks on Prussian lines of communication, isolated military posts and reconnaissance patrols; nominally under the control of the French Ministry of War, they were in fact entirely outside any military discipline, wearing no uniforms and electing their own officers. Prussian practice was to treat captured *francs-tireurs* as non-combatants found illegally participating in hostilities, and to execute them as such. Their activities also often led to reprisal actions being conducted against nearby French villages. This pattern of conduct, which was repeated in Belgium and France in World War I, occasioned real legal controversy when, in World War II, the Germans treated members of Resistance movements in occupied territory as *francs-tireurs* not entitled to any protection under the laws of war, while the Allies insisted that their

[54] Principally, if civilians directly participate in hostilities, they lose their protected status and may legitimately be targeted 'for such time' as they do so: see ICRC, *Interpretive Guidance on the Notion of Direct Participation in Hostilities under International Humanitarian Law* (2008) 90 IRRC 991.
[55] French National Convention, Decree of 23 August 1793.
[56] The Hague Regulations (HR), Article 2 (1907).
[57] GCIII Article 4(A)(6).

degree of organization and allegiance to their respective Governments-in-Exile entitled them to POW status upon capture. Although one subsequent war crimes trial of German generals found that captured partisans in the Balkans had been correctly subjected to the death penalty as *francs-tireurs*,[58] treaty law since has endorsed the contrary position.

As it was generally understood at the turn of the twentieth century that members of regular armies were combatants who were subject to the rights and duties of the laws of war, the main legal issue became how to define others who might be so entitled. Article 1 of the 1907 Hague Regulations accordingly provides that:

> The laws, rights, and duties of war apply not only to armies, but also to militia and volunteer corps fulfilling the following conditions:
>
> 1. To be commanded by a person responsible for his subordinates;
> 2. To have a fixed distinctive emblem recognizable at a distance;
> 3. To carry arms openly; and
> 4. To conduct their operations in accordance with the laws and customs of war.

Apart from designating those persons who can lawfully use force (and themselves be attacked) in wartime, the other principal significance of the concept of lawful combatancy is that it entitles a person, on capture, to the benefit of treatment as a POW. In 1949, Article 4 of Geneva Convention III expanded entitlement to POW status to the following principal groups:

1. members of the regular armed forces,[59] and of militias or volunteer corps forming part of the armed forces, of a party to the conflict;[60]

2. members of other militias or volunteer corps of a party to the conflict, including organized resistance movements, provided that they satisfy the requirements for lawful combatancy listed in Article 1 of The Hague Regulations;

3. authorized persons who accompany the armed forces without actually being members thereof, eg war correspondents,[61] supply contractors, members of military labour units, etc; and

4. participants in a *levée en masse*.

Military medical and religious personnel, on the other hand, are non-combatant members of the armed forces. They may if captured be retained by the Detaining Power in order to assist POWs, and benefit from the protections of the Convention, but are not formally considered POWs.[62]

This comparatively simple regime was supplemented in 1977 by the controversial provisions of Additional Protocol I, which set up a new regime with regard to lawful combatant and POW status; this inevitably is distinctly favourable to the national liberation movements whose conflicts were recognized by the Protocol as being international in nature. Article 43 of the Protocol defines the armed forces, and accordingly lawful combatants, as, 'all organized armed forces, groups and units which are under a command responsible

---

[58] *The Hostages Trial (United States of America v Wilhelm List and Others)* [1949] VIII Law Reports of Trials of War Criminals 38.

[59] Including paratroopers, marine commandos, or other special forces, as long as they fight in their correct uniform and with the appropriate unit badges: see Parks, 2003.

[60] The criterion of belonging to a State has been used to deny POW status to captured guerrillas: *Prosecutor v Kassem* (1969) 42 ILR 470.

[61] Journalists not formally accredited as war correspondents are treated as civilians: API Article 79 (1977).

[62] GCIII Article 33.

to [a Party to the conflict] for the conduct of its subordinates, even if that Party is represented by a government or an authority not recognized by an adverse Party'. This shifts the
irrelevance of recognition from the existence of a state of armed conflict, as stipulated in
Common Article 2 of the 1949 Conventions, to the representation of a party to the conflict: a change very much to the benefit of non-State actors, who are seldom if ever legally
recognized by the States against which they are fighting. It is not hard to see why certain
States continue to object to this formulation.

Lawful combatants, as defined in Article 43, are entitled on capture to POW status,[63]
subject to the following:

> In order to promote the protection of the civilian population from the effects of hostilities,
> combatants are obliged to distinguish themselves from the civilian population while they
> are engaged in an attack or in a military operation preparatory to an attack. Recognizing,
> however, that there are situations in armed conflicts where, owing to the nature of the
> hostilities an armed combatant cannot so distinguish himself, he shall retain his status as a
> combatant, provided that, in such situations, he carries his arms openly:
>
> (a) during each military engagement; and
> (b) during such time as he is visible to the adversary while he is engaged in a military
>   deployment preceding the launching of an attack in which he is to participate.[64]

The first sentence relaxes the pre-existing standard in that it does not specify the way in
which combatants must distinguish themselves from civilians (as opposed to The Hague
Regulations' requirement of a 'fixed, distinctive sign'); it also requires such distinction
to have effect only during 'an attack or . . . a military operation preparatory to an attack'
(whereas the Regulations contain no temporal element as regards lawful combatancy).
The second sentence, however, goes even further towards accommodating guerrillas, and
remains deeply controversial for several States. Its assumption that there are situations in
which a combatant cannot distinguish himself from the civilian population is of limited
application,[65] and the interpretation that arms need only be carried openly immediately
before opening fire (as opposed to continually while visible to the enemy and moving into
an attack position) has received little support in the literature or State practice.[66] States not
party to the Protocol continue to be bound only by the stricter standards from The Hague
Regulations and Geneva Convention III.

Thus, there are effectively two different legal standards for the determination of lawful
combatancy; the undesirability of this situation was plainly demonstrated by the conflict
in Afghanistan after 2001. US President Bush's determination that Al-Qaeda and Taliban
fighters captured by US forces were 'unlawful combatants' who were not entitled to POW
status and could be detained indefinitely without charge and (eventually) prosecuted for
war crimes generated enormous controversy in theory and proved unworkable in practice.[67]

---

[63] API Article 44(1).   [64] Ibid, Article 44(3).
[65] The UK considers that such situations can only arise in occupied territory or in respect of national
liberation movements: see Roberts and Guelff, 2000, p 510.
[66] For the UK position on this point, see ibid.
[67] *Military Order*. In *Rasul v Bush* (2004) 542 US 466 the US Supreme Court held that detainees were
entitled to challenge in the US courts the legality of their detention by US forces. In *Hamdan v Rumsfeld* 548
US 557 (2006) the Court held that the Military Commissions established by the Bush Administration for the
trial of 'unlawful combatants' did not meet the requirements of the Geneva Conventions. On 4 June 2007 the
original charges in the first two substantive cases to be tried by Military Commissions, *United States v Hamdan*
and *United States v Khadr*, were both dismissed for lack of jurisdiction on the grounds that the defendants'
status under LOAC had not been properly determined: 1 MC 6 & 152.

The detention facility at Guantánamo Bay, Cuba, continues to operate, although the eventual fate of its remaining inmates has still not been determined.

Any 'person who takes part in hostilities' without being a combatant under the terms of the Protocol shall upon capture be presumed to be a POW and therefore entitled to protection under IHL, unless and until a competent tribunal decides otherwise.[68] This provision is in essence the same as that in Article 5 of Geneva Convention III, but its scope of application is more controversial. It applies a presumption of actual POW status (as opposed to Article 5's assertion that a captive of doubtful legal status will be treated as if he were a POW until a competent tribunal determines his actual status) to all persons participating in hostilities in armed conflicts covered by the Protocol. The overall effect of Articles 43–5 is to shift the balance of presumptions and entitlements very much in favour of a captive who, prior to the Protocol, would not have had such benefits under traditional LOAC but would have been automatically subject to trial merely for illegally participating in hostilities. Now the Protocol necessitates charges of specific criminal conduct, as opposed to mere participation in hostilities, if any trial is to take place.

Although in mediaeval Europe and until the advent of mass-recruited citizen-armies in the eighteenth century the use of mercenaries was lawful and indeed widespread,[69] the post-1945 decolonization period saw large numbers of demobilized professional soldiers from Western nations enrolling for financial gain in the armies of colonial powers in Africa who were fighting against NLMs claiming self-determination (or, as in the Congo and Nigeria, for secessionist rebellions). Condemnation of mercenarism consequently became widespread and it is not surprising that special provision for it was eventually made in Additional Protocol I, Article 47 of which removes any possibility of mercenaries being regarded as lawful combatants entitled to POW status if captured. The salient features of the definition of a mercenary are that his motivation is the desire for private gain, and that he is neither a national nor a resident of a party to an armed conflict, nor a member of the armed forces thereof. This was subsequently added to by the UN General Assembly's International Convention against the Recruitment, Use, Financing and Training of Mercenaries, which extended the Protocol's definition of a mercenary to include the purpose of 'participating in a concerted act of violence aimed at overthrowing a government or otherwise undermining the constitutional order . . . or . . . the territorial integrity of a State'.[70] The Convention offence is committed even if a person recruited as a mercenary does not actually take part in a conflict—a departure from Article 47's requirement that he take a direct part in hostilities.

These provisions have not managed to prevent or deter the repeated use of mercenaries since the early 1990s in conflicts such as those in the former Yugoslavia and Sierra Leone.[71] The issue continues to be pertinent in light of the 'privatization of war' in the first decade of the twenty-first century: since the occupation of Iraq in 2003–04, several States have increasingly outsourced many military services and types of expertise to a growing array of private contractors or 'private military security companies' (PMSCs). These are generally composed of former military personnel who undertake a range of duties from

---

[68] API Article 45(1).

[69] A unique survivor of this tradition is the Pontifical Swiss Guard, since 1506 the *de facto* military force of the Vatican, which recruits exclusively Catholic Swiss citizens. Mercenaries are not to be confused with the foreign professional soldiers traditionally used in certain armies, eg the British Army's Brigade of Gurkhas and the French Foreign Legion. These units are regularly constituted and subject to the discipline of the armies in which they serve and are lawful combatants.

[70] GA Res 44/34 (1989), Article 1(2)(a).

[71] The UN Convention on Mercenaries entered into force in 2001 but still has only 33 States parties.

serving as bodyguards for political leaders and diplomats, through the provision of training and advice in the reorganization of State military capabilities in countries from Nigeria
to Bulgaria, to actual military missions in countries such as Colombia (where they have
piloted aircraft and helicopter gunships engaged in the destruction of coca crops). Their
tendency, exhibited in Iraq, to be somewhat 'trigger-happy' has attracted considerable no-
toriety.[72] US and British PMSCs operate under national regulation[73] but their legal position under LOAC is uncertain. The UN General Assembly has condemned them as one of
'the new modalities of mercenarism',[74] but they could also arguably be assimilated in certain circumstances to 'supply contractors' who benefit from POW status,[75] and their right
to use force in self-defence is lawfully mandated under their contracts of employment.
Ultimately, their status under LOAC is most likely to be that of civilians, since they are not
part of the armed forces and cannot be regarded as militia; the legal issue is then whether
or not their precise function in a given situation involves direct participation in hostilities.

It is a tragic reality of modern warfare, particularly in certain parts of Africa, that child
soldiers form a significant part of the combatant forces. This has been notably evident
in such cases as the Lord's Resistance Army in Uganda and the Revolutionary United
Front in Sierra Leone; in the latter country especially, many of the worst atrocities in the
conflict were committed by children (Happold, 2005).[76] Article 77 of Protocol I requires
States to 'take all feasible measures in order that children who have not attained the age
of fifteen years do not take a direct part in hostilities and, in particular, [to] refrain from
recruiting them . . .'. Measures for the protection of children in armed conflicts are repeatedly called for by the UN Security Council[77] and provided for in legal terms also by
the 1989 UN Convention on the Rights of the Child and its 2000 Optional Protocol on
the Involvement of Children in Armed Conflict, although these instruments use a higher
cut-off age of 18 years.

IV. CONDUCT OF HOSTILITIES

The 1907 Hague Regulations, together with certain provisions of 1977 Additional Protocol
I, are the modern sources of the law on the conduct of hostilities—a topic often referred
to as 'methods and means of warfare'—but their much older genesis lies in the interaction
of the customary principles of humanity, chivalry, and military necessity. Nowhere is this
truer than in the context of the law of targeting, which is dominated by what the ICJ has
termed the two 'cardinal' principles of IHL: the rule of distinction, and the prohibition of
the use of weapons causing unnecessary suffering or superfluous injury.[78] The law on the
conduct of hostilities also determines the difference between battlefield practices that are
forbidden, and those that are permitted, although it should be noted that even if a given

[72] In *United States* v *Slough et al*, three former employees of the PMSC Blackwater Worldwide were
convicted of manslaughter, and one of murder, in connection with the killing of 14 unarmed Iraqi civilians in
Baghdad, and sentenced to 30 years and life imprisonment, respectively: *The Washington Post*, 13 April 2015.
[73] In the USA, PMSCs are now subject to the Uniform Code of Military Justice: HR 5122, John Warner
National Defense Authorization Act for Fiscal Year 2007, Section 552. In the UK, s 370 and Sch 15 to the
Armed Forces Act 2006 make civilians accompanying the armed forces in certain circumstances subject to
military law.
[74] GA Res 62/145 (4 March 2008).   [75] GCIII Article 4(A)(4).
[76] *Prosecutor* v *Sesay, Kallon & Gbao*, Trial Chamber Special Court for Sierra Leone, Judgment of 25
February 2009, pp 482–519.
[77] Eg SC Res 1882 (4 August 2009).
[78] *Legality of the Threat or Use of Nuclear Weapons, Advisory Opinion, ICJ Reports 1996*, p 226, para 78.

practice is allowed under international LOAC, it may well be prohibited under the national law of the belligerents. Thus, while The Hague Regulations do not forbid such classic wartime activities as espionage or sabotage, a spy or saboteur who is captured out of uniform will be tried as such and, under the national laws of many States, may be sentenced to death.[79] Other practices, such as perfidy—'[a]cts inviting the confidence of an adversary to lead him to believe that he is entitled to, or is obliged to accord, protection under the rules of [LOAC], with intent to betray that confidence'[80]—and denial of quarter,[81] are clearly forbidden under LOAC.

A. DISTINCTION AND PROPORTIONALITY

Given the importance which attaches to personal status in international armed conflicts, it is logical that the principle of distinction should lie at the heart of the modern LOAC, notably in relation to targeting operations; as such it forms part of customary international law, although it is codified in Article 48 of Additional Protocol I. It requires belligerents at all times to distinguish between combatants and military objectives on the one hand, and civilians and civilian objects on the other, and to attack the former only (subject to certain exceptions which will be detailed later in this section). Basically, anyone who is not a combatant is a civilian, but because in contemporary warfare the two categories are not always clearly distinguishable from each other, the principle of distinction is moderated by a proportionality test. The law recognizes the permissibility of civilian casualties or damage to civilian objects, during an otherwise lawful attack on a military target, by the grim but functional doctrine of 'collateral damage': such casualties or damage is proportionate if it is not clearly excessive in relation to the concrete and direct military advantage anticipated from the attack.[82] In effect, the law accepts that at least *some* civilian casualties and/or *some* damage to civilian objects will be inevitable in most military operations, however carefully conducted.

In both World Wars it was considered acceptable to attack the enemy civilian population's morale as such, but such practices would be clearly illegal today: Article 51(2) of Protocol I prohibits direct (deliberate) attacks on the civilian population and those which are designed primarily to spread terror among the civilian population. In light of these prohibitions and Article 48's requirement that military operations be directed 'only against military objectives', the key question is: what constitutes a military objective? Article 52(2) of the Protocol defines military objectives as 'those objects which by their nature, location, purpose or use make an effective contribution to military action and whose total or partial destruction, capture or neutralization, in the circumstances ruling at the time, offers a definite military advantage'. Thus, while certain objects—such as an air force base—are intrinsically military in nature, others—an apartment block, for example—may be located, or used by the enemy, in such a way that they make an effective contribution to military action. On the other hand, blanket determinations of military significance for objects which are not intrinsically military but clearly have some military uses in wartime, such as roads, railways, or bridges, are not allowed. The Protocol requires a presumption, in case of doubt as to whether a civilian object is actually being used to make an effective contribution to military action, that it is not in fact being so used;[83] it

---

[79] Eg *Ali* v *Public Prosecutor* [1969] 1 AC 430.

[80] API Article 37(1). Examples of perfidious conduct include feigning intent to surrender, incapacitation by wounds or sickness, or non-combatant status.

[81] HR Article 23(d).   [82] API Article 57(2).

[83] Certain objects may never be attacked (unless they are being abused by the enemy): eg medical facilities, personnel and transport, and cultural property.

also requires the commander to take all feasible precautions in planning and launching an attack, to warn the civilian population of an impending attack and to cancel or suspend an attack if it becomes apparent that the object is not a military objective or that the attack cannot be executed without disproportionate civilian casualties or damage to civilian objects.[84] A particularly important aspect of these provisions is the heavy burden they place on the attacking commander: the law to some extent expects him to place the safety of the civilian population ahead of that of his own troops or his legitimate military objectives: despite widespread condemnation of Israeli operations in the Gaza Strip since 2000, on a number of occasions Israeli military commanders have cancelled planned airstrikes that would have eliminated senior Palestinian militant leaders, when it became apparent that Palestinian civilians were flocking to the area in question in an attempt to shield the target.[85] The obligations of the defending commander to take precautions to protect the civilian population under his control against the effect of attacks, on the other hand, rarely attracts comparable attention.

With so-called 'dual-use objects', a case-by-case determination must be made as to whether a definite military advantage would be obtained by attacking that object, not tomorrow or the day after, but today. It would also be reasonable, however, to take into account longer-term military advantages and effects on the civilian population, such as the eventual strategic consequences of an attack, or impairment of the civilian population's means of survival.[86] The Protocol unhelpfully does not mention dual-use objects as such, but the principles for determining the legality of an attack on such targets are the same as those of general application. The critical issue will generally be whether the anticipated collateral damage (if any) would be proportionate to the military advantage expected. In 1999 NATO treated the Serbian Radio and Television building in Belgrade as a military target, because in addition to its normal function of providing entertainment and information to the civilian population, it also in wartime served as a back-up communications network for the Serbian armed forces. As it was located in the middle of Belgrade, the required assessment of collateral damage had to estimate how many civilians were likely to become casualties in the attack, and whether such casualties would be proportionate to the military advantage which would be gained by knocking out a back-up military communications network. In the event, NATO proceeded with the attack in the middle of the night, when the smallest possible number of civilian employees was likely to be present in the building: in the event, 16 civilians died and broadcasting resumed from a back-up transmitter in a secret location within 24 hours. Although it was unfortunate that 16 civilians died, NATO took the required precautions in attack and made a proper assessment of likely collateral damage and proportionality. The circumstances disclosed no prima facie violation of LOAC on NATO's part.[87]

It is important to emphasize that there is no mathematical formula for deciding what would, or would not, be a proportionate level of collateral damage in any given case. Everything depends on the circumstances ruling at the time and the operational context; the decision whether or not to attack a given target is that of the commander, who must

[84] API Article 57.　　[85] *The Jerusalem Post*, 19 November 2006.

[86] API Article 56 prohibits attacks on dams, dykes, and nuclear electrical generating stations if such attack is likely to release dangerous forces which would cause severe losses to the civilian population. These sorts of considerations are likely to assume enhanced importance in situations of cyber conflict, where the interconnected nature of many networks and the likelihood of unforeseen consequences of a computer network attack could have dire effects on the civilian population.

[87] See ICTY, *Final Report to the Prosecutor by the Committee Established to Review the NATO Bombing Campaign Against the Federal Republic of Yugoslavia* (2000) 39 ILM 1257, paras 71–9.

base his assessment on the intelligence that is reasonably available to him, in the light of recommendations by his military legal adviser. It is wrong, therefore, to assume that any case of civilians being killed in a military operation ipso facto constitutes a war crime: as long as the target was a military objective or a dual-use object and the attacking force undertook the required precautions in attack to the best of their ability in the circumstances ruling at the time, the relevant rules of IHL have been complied with. By the same token, cases of civilian casualties caused by honest mistakes, such as attacks on the wrong target due to faulty intelligence or misunderstood battle instructions, are not violations of IHL: thus, Colonel Georg Klein of the *Bundeswehr* was cleared by German prosecutors of criminal responsibility for the deaths of 60–180 Afghans in an airstrike that he ordered on two fuel tankers at Kunduz that had been captured by Taliban fighters, because he had feared that they would be used to attack a German camp nearby and it was found that he could not have known, on the basis of the intelligence available to him, that civilians were in the vicinity of the target.[88] Civilian deaths or damage to civilian objects in armed conflicts is always a tragedy; but it is one that the law factors into its strictures.

B. WEAPONS

Article 22 of The Hague Regulations lays down a general principle that [t]he right of belligerents to adopt means of injuring the enemy is not unlimited'. From this, and from the principle of distinction, flow two specific customary rules affecting the choice of weaponry in armed conflicts:

1. it is forbidden to employ methods or means of warfare that may be expected to cause superfluous injury or unnecessary suffering;[89] and

2. it is forbidden to employ methods or means of warfare that are indiscriminate, ie cannot be directed against a specific military objective.[90]

In addition, there are specific treaty obligations not to use methods and means of warfare that are intended or may be expected to have negative effects on the environment.[91]

The first rule, in particular, has prompted many treaties banning specific weapons. The Hague formula prohibits weapons 'calculated to cause' unnecessary suffering, while its more modern counterpart in Protocol I uses the phrase 'of a nature to cause' such injury or suffering. The latter is the better formulation in practice, as it relies less on the intention with which a weapon is used—any weapon can be used in such a way as to cause unnecessary suffering—and more on its intrinsic nature. This is the case with white phosphorus, which is not currently prohibited by LOAC but can certainly have very deleterious burning or asphyxiating effects if used directly against human beings; nevertheless, it is in the armoury of many States, including Russia, Israel, the USA, and the UK, for use against military objectives because of its obscurant or illuminating effect. Its use as an anti-personnel weapon, to flush out Iraqi insurgents in Fallujah in 2004, was therefore probably a violation of the rule.[92] It is important, however, to remember that suffering is an integral part of war, and therefore the concept of *unnecessary* suffering is inevitably both subjective and relative. The difficulties have been well expressed in the following terms:

---

[88] *Deutsche Welle*, 19 April 2010.   [89] HR Article 23(e), API Article 35(2).
[90] API Article 51(4).   [91] Ibid. Article 55.
[92] See *US Defends Use of White Phosphorus Munitions in Iraq* (2006) 100 *AJIL* 487; cf Israeli Ministry of Foreign Affairs, *The Operation in Gaza: Factual and Legal Aspects*, July 2009, paras 406–30.

The law does not specify the permissible level of disablement. In contemporary military operations, while the killing of enemy combatants is still contemplated, so is wounding them to put them out of action. This may cause them permanent injury. In either case suffering is implicit. But the law does not define unnecessary suffering, and views can differ markedly. Some are horrified by the prospect of blindness, others by the blast injuries caused by mines, and many regard burn injuries as particularly serious, but it is difficult to compare one type of injury with another and say that it necessarily signifies unnecessary suffering . . . [T]herefore, all that can be done, in very general terms, is to try and balance the military utility of weapons with the wounding and incidental effects that they have.[93]

The ban on indiscriminate weapons is a corollary of the rules on protection of civilians, discussed earlier in this section. It serves to prohibit such practices as area bombardment—treating an entire area as a military target, as was done by the German deployment of V1 and V2 rockets against southern England in World War II, and Iraq's use of Scud missiles against large areas of the desert in Saudi Arabia and heavily populated Israel in 1991.

In addition to these general principles, treaty provisions exist to ban or restrict the use of the following specified weapons, *inter alia*:

1. explosive bullets or projectiles under 400 grammes weight;

2. dum-dum bullets;

3. poison and poisoned weapons;

4. asphyxiating and poison gases, along with bacteriological and chemical weapons;

5. weapons causing injury by fragments in the human body undetectable by X-ray;

6. anti-personnel landmines and booby-traps;

7. incendiary weapons;

8. blinding laser weapons; and

9. cluster munitions.

The 1977 Environmental Modification Treaty also prohibits the deliberate manipulation of the environment as a method of warfare. Although the deliberate use of weapons that are specifically and unequivocally banned is comparatively rare in contemporary warfare, the Syrian Civil War has seen multiple uses of several chemical weapons (eg nerve agent sarin, chlorine gas, and sulfur mustard) since 2013 by various parties to the conflict;[94] in 2017, a particularly deadly nerve gas attack at Khan Shaykhun prompted the US to launch missile strikes against the Syrian Air Force base at Shayrat, in an action implied to be a belligerent reprisal,[95] although it is doubtful that the US was party to an international armed conflict with Syria at the relevant time.

The one type of weapon that is conspicuous by its absence from explicit regulation in LOAC is nuclear weapons, the use of which is not forbidden by any treaty. Whether

---

[93] UK Ministry of Defence, 2004, para 6.1.2.

[94] See, eg, *Report of the United Nations Mission to Investigate Allegations of the Use of Chemical Weapons in the Syrian Arab Republic on the alleged use of chemical weapons in the Ghouta area of Damascus on 21 August 2013*, UN Doc A/67997-S/2013/553, 16 September 2013; UN Human Rights Council, *Report of the Independent International Commission of Inquiry on the Syrian Arab Republic*, A/HRC/27/60, 13 August 2014, paras 115–18; Organization for the Prohibition of Chemical Weapons, *Third Report of the OPCW Fact-Finding Mission in Syria*, S/1230/2014, 18 December 2014.

[95] US Central Command, *Statement from Pentagon Spokesman Capt. Jeff Davis on US Strike in Syria*, Release No 17–135, 7 April 2017.

customary law prohibits the use of nuclear weapons is less obvious: their use has been condemned on many occasions by the UN General Assembly, which in 1994 requested an Advisory Opinion from the ICJ on the subject. The resulting Opinion,[96] which saw the Court split down the middle with seven votes in favour and seven against (one chair on the Court being vacant at the time the Opinion was rendered, due to the death of the previous incumbent), was widely derided as an exercise in evasiveness. The ICJ found that, while there was no specific prohibition or permissive rule in international law regarding the use of nuclear weapons, their use nevertheless would have to comply with 'the principles and rules' of IHL—in particular the rules relating to unnecessary suffering, in light of the injuries caused by radiation. In that context, the Court found that it would 'generally be contrary' to IHL to use nuclear weapons,[97] an opaque conclusion that has drawn considerable criticism. In fairness to the ICJ, it should be mentioned that its credibility would have suffered irreparable damage had it ruled conclusively either for or against legality: in the former case, non-nuclear States, which constitute a large majority in the world, would have condemned it as out of step with world opinion. But in the latter case, the nuclear weapons States would surely have simply ignored the Advisory Opinion. The UK's position, for instance, is that none of the rules of Additional Protocol I have any effect on, regulate, or prohibit, the use of nuclear weapons.[98] The ICRC, in its *Customary Law Study*, declined to express any position on the matter, ostensibly because it was *sub judice* the ICJ at the time of research for the Study (Henckaerts and Doswald-Beck, 2005, p 255). The most recent efforts to regulate nuclear weapons have centred on arms control: although an attempt by the Marshall Islands at litigation against nuclear weapons States in the ICJ failed on procedural grounds,[99] the UN General Assembly subsequently adopted by 122 votes a Treaty on the Prohibition of Nuclear Weapons.[100] While the Treaty is certain to achieve the 50 ratifications required for it to enter into force, it seems unlikely that it will ever achieve much more than a moral effect, given that nearly one third of UN member States (including all the nuclear weapons States) refused even to participate in the vote.

In fact, it is difficult to see how the use of such tremendously destructive weapons could ever be IHL-compliant, given also the inestimable military advantage that their use would create for the party using them. The two sides of the equation would therefore seem to cancel each other out. However, it is conceivable that a tactical nuclear weapon, deployed for instance by a submarine against an enemy surface fleet on the high seas, could be targeted against a purely military objective and be both necessary and proportionate in terms of IHL. Conversely, the use of a nuclear weapon against a civilian population would clearly be unlawful, not because of the nature of the weapon, but because of its deliberate use against civilians. The use of such weapons in a setting where their effects would be indiscriminate—for example, against military installations located near civilian population centres—would violate the ban on indiscriminate weapons generally, rather than any specific rule on nuclear weapons.

The first decade of the twenty-first century saw the rise to prominence of unmanned aerial vehicles (UAVs, or 'drones') as a 'weapon of choice' for technologically advanced

---

[96] *Legality of the Threat or Use of Nuclear Weapons, Advisory Opinion, ICJ Reports 1996*, p 226.

[97] Ibid, para 105(2)(E).

[98] Roberts and Guelff, 2000, p 510.

[99] *Obligations Concerning Negotiations Relating to Cessation of the Nuclear Arms Race and to Nuclear Disarmament (Marshall Islands v United Kingdom), Preliminary Objections, ICJ Reports 2016*, nyr. Identical cases brought by the Marshall Islands in the ICJ against India and Pakistan were dismissed for essentially the same reasons on the same date, and a further case in the US domestic courts was thrown out as non-justiciable: *Republic of the Marshall Islands v United States of America et al*, USCA 9th Circuit, 31 July 2017.

[100] UN Doc A/CONF.229/2017/8, 7 July 2017.

States in asymmetric conflicts; the US, in particular, uses them to carry out 'targeted killings' of 'terrorists' in such lawless territories as Yemen, Syria, Afghanistan, and the Tribal
Areas of Pakistan. While only a dozen countries are known to have used drones, some 20
more have them in service and around 50 more around the world are believed to possess
drone technology; their use has widely been condemned as unlawful, usually because of
the civilian casualties that they often cause and the perception that their use against named
individuals amounts to 'extrajudicial execution' or prohibited assassination.[101] The UK justifies its drone strikes principally by reference to the right of self-defence.[102] However, criticisms and responses alike tend to conflate paradigms of *jus ad bellum*, human rights, and
humanitarian law. It should be noted that UAVs are not inherently illegal under LOAC;
indeed, they are not really even a weapon as such, merely a platform for the delivery of a
weapon (ie a missile). They are attractive to commanders as they permit several important
military functions (principally intelligence-gathering and the application of lethal force)
to be executed with no risk to their own troops, since the UAVs are remotely piloted.
However, the real issues in terms of their compliance with LOAC are: (1) whether the
persons targeted are in fact combatants; and (2) whether any resulting collateral damage is
actually excessive in relation to the corresponding military advantage. In the background
lurks the admittedly sinister question of whether fully autonomous battlefield systems will
be introduced—killing machines without humans 'in the loop' or 'on the loop' to apply
IHL when they authorize the application of deadly force. No such systems are currently
known to exist for use in combat operations, and expert technical opinion is divided as
to how far off they are, but unless a pre-emptive ban can be achieved their introduction
seems to be only a matter of time.[103] Nevertheless, if and when they are introduced, the
legal questions surrounding their compliance with IHL will remain identical; the moral
and ethical questions will be much harder to resolve.

V. PROTECTION OF VICTIMS

For the purposes of legal protection, IHL defines three categories of person as 'victims'
of armed conflicts, in the sense that they have specific rights as a consequence of their
status. These categories are: the wounded and sick (including persons shipwrecked at sea),
prisoners of war, and civilians. Each is subject to a detailed separate regime of legal protection; in the case of the wounded and sick on land, the treaty in question is the oldest in the
canon of contemporary humanitarian law.

A. THE WOUNDED AND SICK

The Geneva Convention for the Amelioration of the Condition of the Wounded in Armies
in the Field (1864), which famously resulted from Henri Dunant's experiences at the Battle
of Solferino (1859) and the subsequent foundation of the ICRC (1863), was the first treaty
to make specific provision for the protection of soldiers who had become *hors de combat*

---

[101] Eg UN Human Rights Council, *Report of the Special Rapporteur on Extrajudicial, Summary or Arbitrary
Executions, Philip Alston—Addendum: Study on Targeted Killings*, UN Doc A/HRC/14/24/Add.6, 28 May 2010.

[102] Eg UN Doc S/2015/688, 7 September 2015.

[103] A prominent forum for discussion of issues relating to lethal autonomous weapons is the Review
Conference of High Contracting Parties to the 1980 UN Convention on Certain Conventional Weapons:
see Fifth Review Conference, *Report of the 2016 Informal Meeting of Experts on Lethal Autonomous Weapons
Systems (LAWS)*, UN Doc CCW/CONF.V/2, 10 June 2016.

by virtue of wounds or sickness. The foundation principles of this area of the law, as laid down in the 1864 Convention and expanded in subsequent Geneva Conventions,[104] are:

1. relief must be provided for the wounded and sick without distinction as to status, allegiance or nationality;

2. the inviolability of medical personnel, establishments and units must be respected; and

3. the distinctive protective signs must be recognized and respected.

Enemy wounded may not be attacked,[105] but must be collected and cared for, with the same access to medical treatment as the State's own wounded.[106] The same protection from attack extends to enemy medical transports, units, and hospitals, provided they do not forfeit this protection by being used to commit hostile acts; even then, they may be attacked only after due warning.[107] Although attacks on medical units and installations have been a feature of armed conflicts since the advent of air power in the second decade of the twentieth century, when the Ottoman Red Crescent Society complained that their field hospitals in Libya had been bombed by Italian aircraft during the Italo-Turkish War (1911–12), the 'fog of war' often makes it difficult to determine the exact circumstances of such attacks: when a US airstrike in Afghanistan hit a Trauma Centre operated by *Médecins Sans Frontières* (MSF) at Kunduz in 2015, resulting in more than 250 casualties, the personnel involved apparently thought they were attacking a Taliban-held compound nearby since the hospital was on a No Strike List, while the Afghan National Forces who called in the airstrike claimed that Taliban fighters were present in the hospital, a claim which was hotly denied by MSF. The subsequent investigation concluded that, 'this tragic incident was caused by a combination of human errors, compounded by process and equipment failures', and despite referring to failures to comply with the Rules of Engagement and LOAC, declined to find that any war crime had been committed.[108] Medical personnel may carry weapons for their own defence and that of the wounded and sick in their care; neither they nor those in their care may be the object of reprisals. The Red Cross and its associated protective signs[109] may be used only for marking the personnel, transports, and establishments of the ICRC, military medical services, and other medical bodies (eg national Red Cross societies) specifically authorized to use the emblems. Misuse of any of the emblems will normally constitute a criminal offence under national law, and may additionally amount to the war crime of perfidy.

---

[104] GCI (1929); GCI (1949) (wounded and sick on land); GCII (1949) (wounded, sick, and shipwrecked at sea).

[105] In 2013 a British marine, Sergeant Alexander Blackman, was convicted by court-martial of the murder of a wounded Taliban fighter in Afghanistan: *BBC News*, 8 November 2013.

[106] Suggestions that wounded Taliban fighters captured in Afghanistan should not be treated in the same field hospitals as wounded British soldiers would, if implemented, have amounted to a violation of GCI Article 12 or Common Article 3: *The Guardian*, 23 January 2009.

[107] GCI Article 21. The same is true in respect of individual medical personnel.

[108] US Central Command, *Summary of the Airstrike on the MSF Trauma Center in Kunduz, Afghanistan on October 3, 2015; Investigation and Follow-on Actions* (28 April 2016).

[109] Since 1929 many (though not all) Islamic States have used the Red Crescent as a recognized alternative to the Red Cross—its use originated in the Russo-Turkish War (1877–8), when Ottoman medical units adopted it for protection. Persia used its own (equally recognized) traditional emblem of the Red Lion and Sun from 1922, and reserves the right to use it still, although its use was discontinued after the 1979 Islamic Revolution because of its association with the former Shah's regime. Israel's unrecognized use of the Red Shield of David eventually contributed to the adoption of Additional Protocol III (2005), which provides for a third, universal protective emblem devoid of potential religious or national symbolism: the Red Crystal.

B. PRISONERS OF WAR

Since the advent of the nation-State and regularly conscripted citizen-armies in the late seventeenth century, it has been accepted that soldiers who surrender to the enemy are under the protection of the enemy State and not at the mercy of the individual enemy commander. The sole reason for detaining them was that they should not be able to re-join the enemy's forces and thereby negate the military advantage accrued by their removal from the field, although it was common for prisoners to be 'paroled', whereby they were released on a promise not to re-enlist and resume fighting. The notion of reciprocity as a principle underpinning the law of war also provided an incentive for States to ensure that enemy soldiers taken prisoner should be well treated. Geneva Conventions II (1929) and III (1949) have since ensured that this aspect of IHL is particularly highly regulated, with many technical provisions deriving from the grant of POW status.

An essential aspect of the protection of POWs is that the State which has captured them (the Detaining Power) is responsible in international law for their good treatment.[110] A POW is neither a criminal (although he may be prosecuted for crimes committed before capture)[111] nor a hostage. The Detaining State is under an absolute duty to ensure that POWs are not murdered, tortured, ill-treated,[112] or otherwise abused (eg by exposure to insults and public curiosity).[113] POWs cannot be the object of reprisals and no considerations of military necessity can justify their ill-treatment; thus, it would be unlawful to use them as human shields, 'to render certain points or areas immune from military operations'.[114] Equally, although the Detaining Power has a legitimate interest in questioning POWs in order to obtain intelligence, they are obliged to provide only their name, rank, date of birth, and military number, and it is illegal to coerce them to provide any other information.[115] They must be held in special camps located away from the combat zones; although the Detaining Power may transfer them to the custody of another State party to the Convention,[116] the State that originally captured them may remain responsible for their good treatment. POWs must be released and repatriated after the cessation of active hostilities,[117] although this requirement is not interpreted as authorizing forcible repatriation of POWs who do not wish to be repatriated: after the 1991 Gulf War many Iraqi POWs chose to remain in Saudi Arabia rather than return to Iraq.

---

[110] GCIII Articles 12–13.

[111] Usually, though not invariably, for violations of IHL committed during the conflict in which he was captured. Cf the American trial of General Manuel Noriega for drug trafficking prior to the 1989 US invasion of Panama, *United States* v *Noriega* (1992) 808 F.Supp 791 (SD Fla), and the British refusal to prosecute Astiz, captured on South Georgia during the Falklands War, for crimes committed during the 'Dirty War' in Argentina in the late 1970s: see Meyer, 1983.

[112] During the 2003 Gulf War there were instances of Iraqi POWs being beaten by American soldiers: *The Guardian*, 6 January 2004.

[113] In the 2003 Gulf War some Coalition POWs were shown being questioned on Iraqi television, while Western networks also carried footage of blindfolded Iraqi POWs: *The Christian Science Monitor*, 26 March 2003. See also Rogers, 2004, pp 52–3. British practice is not to broadcast such images if they enable any POW to be individually recognized. Broadcasting pictures of the captured Saddam Hussein undergoing medical and dental examination, however, were arguably justified as a factual demonstration of his capture.

[114] GCIII Article 23. Iraq clearly violated this provision in its treatment of Coalition POWs during the 1991 Gulf War: Rowe, 1993, pp 196–7.

[115] GCIII Article 17.

[116] See, eg, arrangements for transfer of British-captured POWs in the 1991 Gulf War to US custody, reprinted in Rowe, 1993, pp 348–9.

[117] GCIII Article 118.

C. CIVILIANS

The definition of civilians in IHL is a negative one: a civilian is anyone who is not a combatant as defined by Geneva Convention III and, for those States that are party to it, Additional Protocol I. Much of the emphasis of contemporary IHL is on the protection of the civilian population and individual civilians: this is achieved both by safeguarding them in most circumstances from the direct effect of hostilities (as discussed earlier) and by providing for the specific protection of civilians who are in the power of a State of which they are not nationals. Unlike the sick and wounded or POWs, civilians were not previously covered by LOAC; while this was mainly because the nature of warfare prior to the early twentieth century was such that civilians were rarely subjected to direct attack and specific measures of protection were thus not thought necessary, the experience of 'total war' in the various conflicts of the 1930s and 1940s made it clear that development of the law in this direction was urgently required. The result was the entirely innovative Geneva Convention IV (1949).

The Convention protects nationals of one belligerent who find themselves in the power of another belligerent, either through being in the territory of an enemy State or in territory under belligerent occupation. It does not protect nationals of neutral States caught up in a conflict,[118] unless they are in occupied territory, in which case they benefit from the general protections accorded to all civilians in such territory. Thus, British citizens in Kuwait at the time of the Iraqi invasion in 1990 were covered by the Convention but those in Iraq itself were not, since the UK at that time was not a party to any conflict with Iraq and the UK still had diplomatic relations with that State. Only when Coalition military action started in 1991 did British citizens in Iraq come under the protection of the Convention. Civilians in the territory of an enemy State should normally be allowed to leave the State at any time during the conflict, although permission to leave may be refused if their departure would be contrary to the national interests of the State;[119] they may even be interned if absolutely necessary for security reasons,[120] although this would not authorize the mass internment of members of specific ethnic groups. If internment does occur, civilians are entitled to a standard of treatment effectively analogous to that accorded POWs. Civilians must not be subjected to reprisals or collective punishments,[121] held hostage,[122] or otherwise ill-treated.

D. BELLIGERENT OCCUPATION

Similar legal standards govern the treatment of civilians in occupied territory, who additionally must not be deported to any other State (including the Occupying Power).[123] The Occupying Power also has various detailed obligations concerning maintenance of the physical welfare of the civilian population, respect for private property, and the administration of law and order (Benvenisti, 1993).[124] While these provisions of the Convention were adopted as a reaction to the systematic abuse of occupied territories by the Axis Powers in World War II, they built upon legal foundations already instituted by The Hague Regulations (1907). The greatest contemporary controversies surrounding their implementation have been in relation to the Israeli occupation of the Palestinian Territories (OPT) since 1967, and the Coalition occupation of Iraq (2003–04).

Although Israel denies the formal applicability of Convention IV to the West Bank on the grounds that it was not legally recognized as 'the territory of a High Contracting Party' (ie

---

[118] GCIV Article 4(2).   [119] Ibid, Article 35.   [120] Ibid, Article 42.
[121] Ibid, Article 33.   [122] Ibid, Article 34.   [123] Ibid, Article 49.   [124] Ibid, Articles 50–78.

Jordan) prior to 1967, as required by Article 2 of the Convention, this argument has never been accepted by the international community; in any event, Israel claims to apply the provisions of the Convention on a de facto basis.[125] The principal criterion for the applicability of the law of belligerent occupation, as stated in Article 42 of The Hague Regulations, which as customary law is binding on Israel, is that territory be 'actually placed under the authority of the hostile army . . . where such authority has been established and can be exercised'. The legal status of the territory prior to occupation is therefore irrelevant: the test for determining the existence of an occupation is the factual one of effective control.[126] By the same token, de facto annexation or other changes to the legal status of the occupied territory—as were effected by Israel in East Jerusalem and parts of the Golan Heights in 1967, by Argentina in the Falkland Islands in 1982 and by Iraq in Kuwait in 1990—cannot affect the *de jure* application of the law of belligerent occupation.[127] Those parts of the West Bank that are under the jurisdiction of the Palestinian Authority since the implementation of the Oslo Accords in 1993 are technically no longer under belligerent occupation; neither, since Israel's withdrawal in 2005, is the Gaza Strip, although uncertainty persists in relation to the latter, in light of Israel's continuing control over its borders, coast, and airspace (Shany, 2006). Further controversy was caused by the naval blockade which Israel imposed on Gaza in 2009 to prevent weapons from being landed in the territory, where they might be used by Hamas to attack targets in Israel. Although Israel was harshly criticized for its violent enforcement of the blockade on the high seas against a Turkish and international aid flotilla bound for the Gaza coast in 2010, a subsequent UN inquiry found that in the *sui generis* continuing state of de facto international armed conflict between Israel and Gaza, the former was entitled under international law to institute the blockade and to enforce it, albeit not in an unreasonable and excessive manner.[128]

The comparatively brief occupation of Iraq gave rise to a different set of concerns under IHL. Although the USA and the UK, as the leading members of the Coalition Provisional Authority (CPA), formally accepted that they were *de jure* Occupying Powers within the meaning of Geneva Convention IV, the situation in Iraq from April 2003 was one of debellatio—the total defeat and extinction of authority in the occupied territory, a situation that had not occurred since the unconditional surrender of Germany in 1945. Occupying Powers are under an obligation to respect, 'unless absolutely prevented', the laws previously in force in the occupied territory,[129] because belligerent occupation in no way grants legal title to the Occupying Power and cannot affect the legal status of the territory under general international law: thus, Iraq continued to be a sovereign State in international law, although its powers of government were temporarily exercised by the CPA. The latter, however, substantively changed Iraqi law on a number of matters, most notably by the wholesale privatization of Iraq's previous centrally planned economy and opening it up to foreign investment, providing tax incentives for foreign corporations wishing to do business in the country and suspending all trade tariffs. The CPA also amended Iraqi criminal law by providing for the immunity of foreign contractors in Iraqi courts. The CPA's delegation to the Iraqi Governing Council of the power to create a special civilian court for the trial of officials of Saddam Hussein's regime was also problematic, as the Occupying

---

[125] *Legal Consequences of the Construction of a Wall in the Occupied Palestine Territory, Advisory Opinion, ICJ Reports 2004*, p 136, paras 90–101.

[126] Cf *Armed Activities on the Territory of the Congo (Democratic Republic of the Congo v Uganda), ICJ Reports 2005*, p 168, paras 172–8.

[127] See, on Israel, SC Res 681 (20 December 1990); on Iraq, SC Res 670 (25 September 1990).

[128] See UN, *Report of the Secretary-General's Panel of Inquiry on the 31 May 2010 Flotilla Incident*, September 2011, http://www.un.org/News/dh/infocus/middle_east/Gaza_Flotilla_Panel_Report.pdf.

[129] HR Article 43.

Power may only create 'non-political military courts' for offences committed against the Occupying Power,[130] or for breaches of the laws and customs of war.[131]

The experience of occupation in Iraq also demonstrated the significance of involvement by the UN Security Council in mandating the occupation regime. The Council gave an *ex post facto* mandate to the CPA[132] which in some respects, as noted in the preceding paragraphs, went further than the traditional law of belligerent occupation would permit (Scheffer, 2003; Kaikobad, 2005; Roberts, 2006).

VI. THE LAW IN NON-INTERNATIONAL ARMED CONFLICTS

A substantial majority of the armed conflicts that have taken place since 1945 have been non-international in nature, yet none of the substantive LOAC applied to such conflicts before the adoption of Common Article 3 of the Geneva Conventions in 1949 and the concept of liability for war crimes committed in such conflicts was not enunciated until the ICTY's 1995 decision in *Tadić*. In that case, the Appeals Chamber opined that '[w]hat is inhumane, and consequently proscribed, in international wars, cannot but be inhumane and inadmissible in civil strife'.[133] Neither Common Article 3 nor the 1977 Additional Protocol II included any provision for individual criminal responsibility; nor did they purport to regulate methods and means of warfare, but focused exclusively on the protection of victims.

Common Article 3 has been described as 'a Convention in miniature' (Pictet, 1952, p 48) and 'a minimum yardstick' of humanitarian protection in all armed conflicts, whatever their characterization.[134] It requires that persons taking no part in hostilities, including those who have surrendered or are *hors de combat*, be treated humanely and without adverse discrimination; to that end, it prohibits 'violence to life and person', hostage-taking, humiliating and degrading treatment, and 'the passing of sentences and the carrying out of executions without previous judgment pronounced by a regularly constituted court . . .'. Within three decades recognition of the generality and vagueness of these provisions resulted in more detailed provision for fundamental guarantees, treatment of the wounded and sick, and protection of the civilian population in Additional Protocol II.

However, with a mere 15 substantive articles (compared to 84 in Protocol I), and no concept of grave breaches or compulsory enforcement, Protocol II is widely viewed as lacking teeth. It took a horrified Security Council's response to the Rwandan genocide to secure the Protocol's enforcement by criminal prosecutions, and even that was on a strictly ad hoc basis.[135] The *Tadić* decision played a seminal role in expanding, and providing some detail on, the rules of customary IHL applicable in non-international armed conflicts; a charge to which the ICRC returned with its 2005 *Study on Customary International Humanitarian Law*. Although these creative approaches have not been uncontroversial, largely due to methodological concerns in the deduction of customary norms of international law (Wilmshurst and Breau, 2007), and the fact that certain States not party to the Protocols have seen the Study in particular as an attempt to import various rules contained

---

[130] GCIV Article 66.   [131] Ibid, Article 70.

[132] SC Res 1483 (22 May 2003), 1511 (16 October 2003), and 1546 (8 June 2004).

[133] *Prosecutor v Duško Tadić*, Decision on the Defence Motion for Interlocutory Appeal on Jurisdiction (Interlocutory Appeal), Case No IT–94–1–AR72 (2 October 1995), para 516.

[134] *Military and Paramilitary Activities In and Against Nicaragua (Nicaragua v United States of America)*, ICJ *Reports 1986*, p 14, para 218.

[135] SC Res 955 (8 November 1994).

in those instruments into customary law 'by the back door',[136] they have served the valuable function of ensuring that the question of detailed legal regulation of conduct in non-international armed conflicts does not become a dead letter. Much recent attention has focused on the legal power to detain individuals captured by States in non-international armed conflicts, which is not mentioned in Protocol II despite wording which assumes the fact of detention taking place in such conflicts by providing for humane treatment of detainees. In *Serdar Mohammed v Secretary of State for Defence*,[137] the UK Supreme Court held that there is no legal authority to detain under either treaty or customary law in IHL during non-international armed conflicts, although such authority may be inferred from UN Security Council resolutions mandating military operations in situations like Afghanistan (2001–15), as long detention is required for imperative reasons of security.

As noted in relation to the scope of application of IHL, there is a spectrum of conflict: apart from internal disturbances and tensions—including, in the British interpretation, acts of terrorism—which are not subject to LOAC at all, the lowest level is conflict 'not of an international character', which is governed by Common Article 3. If non-State forces have sufficient control of territory to satisfy the requirements of Protocol II, non-international conflicts are governed by the Protocol in addition to Common Article 3; finally, if other States intervene on the side of insurgents against the State party, the conflict may become 'internationalized', leading to the application of the Geneva Conventions in full, plus Protocol I if the States concerned are parties thereto.

VII. IMPLEMENTATION AND ENFORCEMENT

Notwithstanding chronic weaknesses in the enforcement of international law generally, there are several methods by which compliance with IHL may be secured. In roughly ascending order of impact and effectiveness, these are:

1. recourse to belligerent reprisals;
2. States' responsibility for violations committed by their armed forces;
3. States' duty to disseminate IHL and provide for its instruction to their armed forces;
4. commanders' duty to supervise conduct and repress violations;
5. States' duty to implement IHL and provide criminal sanctions for its violation in their national legal systems;
6. criminal investigation and, where appropriate, prosecution of individuals accused of violations; and
7. external scrutiny and pressure by third parties.

A. REPRISALS

Belligerent reprisals—not to be confused with armed reprisals under the *jus ad bellum*—are violations of LOAC which may be permitted in response to prior violations by the enemy, as long as they are proportionate to those prior violations and have no other object than securing the cessation of illegal activity by the adverse party (Kalshoven, 1971). Historically they were seen as a not only legitimate, but often quite effective, method of forcing an

---

[136] See US Departments of State and Defense, *Letter to International Committee of the Red Cross Regarding Customary International Law Study* (2006) 46 ILM 514; also Parks, 2005.

[137] *Serdar Mohammed v Secretary of State for Defence* [2017] UKSC 2.

enemy to comply with the law; however, the extent to which they have survived modern trends in both warfare and law since 1949 is doubtful. The Geneva Conventions prohibit reprisals against any persons protected by those instruments[138] and Protocol I additionally prohibits them against the civilian population and civilian objects generally.[139] Although these treaty provisions are clear, the extent to which reprisals are prohibited in customary law remains uncertain. Their last documented substantial use in an international armed conflict was during the Iran-Iraq War (1980–88), when each belligerent attacked the other's cities and claimed that they were engaged in limited reprisals to stop similar attacks by the enemy (Henckaerts and Doswald-Beck, 2005, vol I, pp 521–2). The ICRC's *Study on Customary International Humanitarian Law* asserted that reprisals are also prohibited in non-international armed conflicts, a position which is arguably difficult to maintain in the light of State practice and *opinio juris* (Wilmshurst and Breau, 2007, pp 370–2).

The essential problem with reprisals is the risk that, 'far from enforcing the law, [they] can produce an escalating spiral of atrocities completely undermining respect for the law' (Greenwood, 1989, p 36), thereby achieving precisely the opposite effect to what was intended. The British use of poison gas on the Western Front in 1915, for instance, although intended as retaliation for the German use of the weapon in the Second Battle of Ypres, simply resulted in its adoption on all fronts and by all belligerents for the duration of World War I.

Today, while many States expressly reserve the right to take belligerent reprisals, they generally do so with stringent conditions attached and subject to political approval at the highest level.[140]

B. STATE RESPONSIBILITY

As a general rule of public international law, States are legally responsible, and liable to pay compensation, for violations of LOAC committed by their armed forces. The rule is enunciated with reference to international armed conflicts in Article 3 of The Hague Convention IV (1907), and reparations have been required from defeated enemies in respect of their troops' depredations: for example, Part VIII of the Treaty of Versailles (1919), requiring Germany to pay compensation to the Allied Powers, was based upon the notion of German responsibility for the tremendous damage inflicted on Allied lives and property during World War I. In 1991, the Security Council confirmed Iraq's legal responsibility for depredations of its troops during the occupation of Kuwait and established a UN Compensation Commission to process claims and allocate compensation for losses resulting therefrom.[141] Following the conclusion of their 1998–2000 conflict in the Horn of Africa, Ethiopia and Eritrea agreed the establishment of a joint Claims Commission to arbitrate all claims for loss or damage, including violations of IHL, which had occurred in the conflict.[142] States have been much more reluctant, however, to accept legal responsibility for the actions of their forces when deployed abroad in multinational peacekeeping, peace support, or enforcement operations under UN mandate. Years of litigation were necessary before the Dutch courts would accept partial State responsibility of the Netherlands for the massacre of some 8,000 Bosnian Muslims by Bosnian Serb troops in the UN 'safe haven' of Srebrenica in 1995[143] (after Bosnian Muslim claimants lost a separate case aimed at finding that the UN bore legal responsibility for their relatives'

---

[138] GCI Article 46, GCII Article 47, GCIII Article 13 and GCIV Article 33.

[139] API Articles 51(6), 52(1), 53(c), 54(4), 55(2), and 56(4).

[140] UK Ministry of Defence, 2004, paras 16.16–19.   [141] SC Res 687 (3 April 1991).

[142] See, eg, *Partial Awards on Prisoners of War (Ethiopia's Claim 4)* (2003) 42 ILM 1056; *Eritrea's Claim 17*, ibid, 1083.

[143] *The New York Times*, 27 June 2017.

deaths[144] and the 'Dutchbat' soldiers were equally found not to be individually criminally responsible for the atrocity);[145] the German courts have refused to find Germany liable at all for the 2009 Kunduz airstrike in Afghanistan (the airstrike was executed by US aircraft on the orders of a German Colonel).[146]

The doctrinal weakness of the State responsibility doctrine in the armed conflict context is that it does not cover responsibility for violations committed by non-State actors: it is easy to hold States to account for their armed forces' actions in asymmetric conflicts, but their irregular opponents fall outside the framework of State responsibility (unless they win the war and the new government subsequently adopts legal responsibility for their actions, as was done by the State of Israel in respect of the assassination of Count Folke Bernadotte by members of the Stern Gang in 1948).

C. DISSEMINATION AND SUPERVISION

In order to ensure that soldiers are aware of their rights and duties under international law, the Geneva Conventions and Protocol I impose obligations upon States parties to disseminate their provisions to their armed forces, and as widely as possible among the civilian population at large.[147] Most armed forces, therefore, have training programmes which include instruction in LOAC, both internally and by way of attendance at external (often academic) courses. Dissemination is usually undertaken by the military legal advisory services of the armed forces themselves,[148] but in the case of States that lack the relevant in-house military legal expertise, the ICRC plays a crucial and extensive role by providing seminars, training materials, consultancy, and other assistance.

Arguably the most crucial aspect of ensuring compliance in the armed forces is military discipline and the role of the commander in the supervision of conduct and repression of violations. Article 43(1) of Protocol I requires that armed forces 'shall be subject to an internal disciplinary system which, *inter alia,* shall enforce compliance with the rules of international law applicable in armed conflict'. The key component in this system is the commander, who must ensure that the troops under his command comply with LOAC, and must therefore himself be familiar with his rights and responsibilities. The contemporary law of command responsibility, which in modern terms is based on Article 86(2) of Protocol I, holds the commander liable in a variety of ways, if he:

1. personally sees or hears of illegal acts being committed;

2. receives reports of the illegal conduct of his troops through his subordinates, staff, or chain of command, yet fails to act to put a stop to their violations; or

3. is so negligent or reckless in the discharge of his command as to amount to a dereliction of duty in that he unaware of the conduct of his troops.[149]

Article 87 requires commanders to prevent and suppress violations of the law and report them to the appropriate authorities; it requires, however, that commanders be 'aware' of violations.[150]

---

[144] *Association of Citizens 'Mothers of Srebrenica' et al v State of the Netherlands and the United Nations,* Supreme Court of the Netherlands, Case no 10/04437, 13 April 2012.

[145] *Mustafić-Mujić and Others v The Netherlands (Dec),* no 49037/15, 30 August 2016

[146] *Deutsche Welle,* 6 October 2016.

[147] GCI Article 47, GCII Article 48, GCIII Article 127, GCIV Article 144, and API Article 83.

[148] The requirement to have such military legal advisory services is itself an obligation of API Article 82.

[149] See *The High Command Trial* [1949] XII Law Reports of Trials of War Criminals 1, 76.

[150] A commander who gives an illegal order or himself commits a criminal act is of course equally liable, but not under the doctrine of command responsibility, which is concerned only with acts of omission.

In a famous precedent in 1946, the former Commander-in-Chief of Japanese forces in the Philippines was executed as a war criminal despite his lack of knowledge, due to a breakdown in communications and the chain of command, of atrocities committed by troops under his overall command in Manila;[151] the modern doctrine, however, requires that a commander have actual effective control—not merely nominal or titular authority—over troops and actual knowledge of, or information concerning, crimes being committed,[152] a position which arguably gives rise to a concept of the 'reasonable commander'. Thus the standard of knowledge has shifted from a 'should have known' to a 'knew or had reason to know' test, a position which is undoubtedly fairer to the individual commander. In addition, the modern doctrine of command responsibility requires the existence of a superior-subordinate relationship and effective control of the commander over his subordinates.[153]

D. IMPLEMENTATION AND PROSECUTION

The most dramatic, although not the most effective, way of securing compliance with LOAC is to investigate and punish violations after they have occurred, through either international or national criminal courts. Acceptance of individual criminal responsibility for such crimes has been uncontroversial since the Nuremberg and Tokyo Trials after World War II. On the international level, the creation of the ICTY (1993) and International Criminal Tribunal for Rwanda (1994), followed by the establishment of other specialized criminal tribunals to deal with atrocities in Sierra Leone and Cambodia, among others, heralded a new age of activism in this respect. The first decade of the twenty-first century saw the establishment of the world's first permanent International Criminal Court.

For centuries States have asserted the right to prosecute both captured enemy nationals for violations of the laws and customs of war and their own soldiers for similar offences charged under national military or criminal law. Violations of the laws and customs of war, generically described as war crimes, are subject to universal criminal jurisdiction in customary international law; other types of offences specifically relevant, though not limited, to armed conflicts are crimes against humanity and genocide. States will usually have recourse to international war crimes law only when prosecuting foreign nationals; violations committed by their own troops will normally be treated as offences under the ordinary national criminal or military law. Thus, Lieutenant William Calley was charged with four counts of premeditated murder in violation of Article 118 of the US Uniform Code of Military Justice for his role in the massacre of Vietnamese civilians at My Lai in 1968. In respect of war crimes, the Geneva Conventions and Protocol I place all States parties under a duty to investigate and prosecute grave breaches of those instruments, or extradite suspects to another State; they must also enact legislation implementing these offences in their national criminal law.[154] In the UK, as in many other countries, there is special legislation in force to give effect to these obligations.[155] The degree of scrupulousness with which States investigate and prosecute violations committed by their own armed

---

[151] *Application of Yamashita* (1946) 327 US 1.

[152] *Prosecutor* v *Hadžihasanović & Kubura*, Judgment, Case No IT-01-47-T, Trial Chamber II, (15 March 2006).

[153] See *Prosecutor* v *Delalić, Mučić, Delić and Landžo*, Judgment, Case No IT-96-21-T, Trial Chamber II (16 November 1998), [1999] 38 ILM 57.

[154] GCI Article 49, GCII Article 50, GCIII Article 129, GCIV Article 146, API Articles 85, 86(1), 88, and 89.

[155] Geneva Conventions Act 1957, Geneva Conventions (Amendment) Act 1995, International Criminal Court Act 2001, Geneva Conventions and United Nations Personnel (Protocols) Act 2009.

forces varies considerably, but it has certainly been a significant aspect of the response to violations committed by British forces in Iraq in 2003–04.[156]

Liability for war crimes applies throughout the military hierarchy. As discussed in Section VII C, commanders are responsible for the acts of their subordinates; conversely a soldier cannot plead, in defence to a war crimes charge, that he was following superior orders—in the UK as in many other States, soldiers are clearly forbidden to obey illegal orders. This represents a shift from the widely held pre-1944 position that superior orders were an absolute defence to a war crimes charge and a soldier would be liable to court-martial if he refused to obey an order,[157] and is clearly preferable in that otherwise, the vast majority of perpetrators would invariably be able to escape liability for their acts. It is equally no defence to claim that a war crime was committed for reasons of military necessity: allowance for the exigencies of military necessity is already made in many LOAC treaties, so that conduct that would otherwise constitute a violation may be permitted in certain circumstances. But if the rule is an absolute one, such as the prohibition of the wilful killing of protected persons, a plea of military necessity would be rejected.[158]

Prosecutions are an imperfect tool for enforcing LOAC: the difficulties of securing reliable evidence in respect of incidents occurring in combat conditions—leading many cases to be abandoned or dismissed—cannot be underestimated. It is also true that war crimes trials are often derided as 'victor's justice', in the sense that the defeated party does not have a chance to hold its enemies to account for ill-conduct, although this is a much less valid criticism in relation to standing courts established by the international community acting as a whole. Nevertheless, they are often the prism through which consciousness of IHL is embedded in the general public.

E. EXTERNAL SCRUTINY

The proliferation of media reporting of abuses in armed conflicts since the early 1990s has had the effect of greatly increasing the importance of external scrutiny of States' forces' conduct and pressure for investigations. Sometimes this comes from public opinion, but more frequently it is prompted by reports from non-governmental organizations like Human Rights Watch or international organizations like the UN and its specialized agencies.[159] This sort of external pressure is not mandated by the law, but it can help to generate an independent process of internal scrutiny, which in turn can contribute to increased respect for the law. The Geneva Conventions and Protocol I, however, in any event make provision for monitoring compliance with IHL by the mechanisms of the Protecting Power system and the International Humanitarian Fact-Finding Commission.

The Protecting Power system pre-dates World War II and in its current form is contained in all four 1949 Conventions.[160] It was instituted to enable a belligerent in an international armed conflict to designate another State, the Protecting Power, to represent its interests and those of its nationals vis-à-vis enemy belligerents in matters relating to the conflict. The Protecting Power has rights of access to POW and detention camps, may

[156] See UK Ministry of Defence, *The Aitken Report—An Investigation into Cases of Deliberate Abuse and Unlawful Killing in Iraq in 2003 and 2004*, 25 January 2008.
[157] Although this would not be the case if the order was manifestly illegal: see *The Llandovery Castle* (1921) 16 *AJIL* 708.
[158] *The Peleus Trial* [1945] I Law Reports of Trials of War Criminals 1.
[159] Eg UN Human Rights Council, *Report of the United Nations Fact-Finding Mission on the Gaza Conflict*, UN Doc A/HRC/12/48, 25 September 2009; Res A/HRC/RES/S-12/1.B, 16 October 2009.
[160] GCI, GCII, GCIII Article 10; GCIV Article 11.

attend trials of POWs and civilians held by the enemy belligerent, and may make representations to the enemy belligerent concerning compliance with LOAC generally. In the Falklands War the UK designated Switzerland, and Argentina designated Brazil, to act as their respective Protecting Powers; but on the whole the system has been underused in contemporary conflicts, usually because one side is reluctant to agree to the other side's nominee. Neither the Iran-Iraq War nor the Second Gulf War saw the appointment of any Protecting Powers. Indeed, since 1949, only four international armed conflicts have seen Protecting Powers designated by both parties (Wylie, 2006, p 13).[161]

The International Humanitarian Fact-Finding Commission (IHFFC), which became operational in 1991, is mandated by Article 90 of Protocol I to investigate allegations of violations of the Protocol and the Conventions, but it may only act at the invitation of a State that has recognized its competence and only against a State that has indicated the same acceptance (to date 76 of the States parties to the Protocol have done so). Its reports are confidential to the parties concerned and it has no power of enforcement. In 2017 the IHFFC was invited to conduct its first investigation since its establishment in 1991.

Finally, it is pertinent to mention the invaluable role of the ICRC, which not only seeks to provide humanitarian assistance to the victims of armed conflicts, but also is an indefatigable advocate of IHL and, in particular, of the Geneva Conventions and their Additional Protocols. The ICRC operates under very strict limitations as to publicity—its reports on unrestricted inspection visits to POW and detention camps are confidential, although one on ill-treatment of Iraqi detainees held by the Coalition in 2004 was famously leaked to the public—and also depends on the consent of the parties to the conflict for their voluntary cooperation, although the latter must accept any offer by the ICRC to fulfil the humanitarian functions of a Protecting Power where none is appointed. It usually restricts itself to making confidential representations to the parties concerned, to urge them to comply with their obligations under IHL. Nevertheless, it does sometimes issue public reminders to all parties in a conflict to respect IHL, and generally commands unrivalled respect and efficacy in improving compliance with the law in armed conflicts.

REFERENCES

BENVENISTI, E (1993), *The International Law of Occupation* (Princeton: Princeton University Press).

BYRON, C (2001), 'Armed Conflicts: International or Non-International?', 6 *JCSL* 63.

BYRON, C (2007), 'A Blurring of the Boundaries: The Application of International Humanitarian Law by Human Rights Bodies', 47 *Virginia JIL* 839.

DRAPER, GIAD (1965), 'The Interaction of Christianity and Chivalry in the Historical Development of the Law of War', 46 *Int Rev Red Cross* 3.

FERRARO, T (2015), 'The ICRC's Legal Position on the Notion of Armed Conflict Involving Foreign Intervention and on Determining the IHL Applicable to this Type of Conflict', 97 (900) *Int Rev Red Cross* 1227.

GREEN, LC (2008), *The Contemporary Law of Armed Conflict* (3rd edn, Manchester: Manchester University Press).

GREENBERG, KJ and DATREL, JL (2005), *The Torture Papers* (Cambridge: Cambridge University Press).

GREENWOOD, C (1989), 'The Twilight of the Law of Belligerent Reprisals', 20 *Neth YBIL* 35.

---

[161] Since the 2008 conflict between Russia and Georgia, Switzerland has acted as Protecting Power for both States.

HAPPOLD, M (2005), *Child Soldiers in International Law* (Manchester: Manchester University Press).

HENCKAERTS, J-M and DOSWALD-BECK, L (eds) (2005), *Customary International Humanitarian Law* (Cambridge: Cambridge University Press).

ICRC (2016), *Commentary on the First Geneva Convention: Convention (I) for the Amelioration of the Condition of the Wounded and Sick in Armed Forces in the Field* (2nd edn, Cambridge: Cambridge University Press).

JESSUP, PC (1954), 'Should International Law Recognize an Intermediate Status between Peace and War?', 48 *AJIL* 98.

KAIKOBAD, KH (2005), 'Problems of Belligerent Occupation', 43 *ICLQ* 253.

KALSHOVEN, F (1971), *Belligerent Reprisals* (Leiden: Nijhoff).

LAUTERPACHT, H (1952), 'The Problem of Revision of the Law of War', 29 *BYIL* 382.

LUBELL, N (2017), 'Fragmented Wars: Multi-Territorial Military Operations against Armed Groups', 93 *Int Law Studies* 215.

MAOZ, A (2005), 'War and Peace—an Israeli Perspective', 24 *Constitutional Forum* 35.

MEYER, MA (1983), 'Liability of Prisoners of War for Offences Committed Prior to Capture: The Astiz Affair', 32 *ICLQ* 948.

MILANOVIC, M (2011), *Extraterritorial Application of Human Rights Treaties: Law, Principles, and Policy* (Oxford: Oxford University Press).

MOIR, L (2002), *The Law of Internal Armed Conflict* (Cambridge: Cambridge University Press).

PARKS, WH (2003), 'Special Forces' Wear of Non-Standard Uniforms', 4 *Chicago JIL* 493.

PARKS, WH (2005), 'The ICRC Customary Law Study: a Preliminary Assessment', 99 *ASIL Proceedings* 208.

PICTET, J (ed) (1952), *Commentary on the Geneva Convention (I) for the Amelioration of the Condition of the Wounded and Sick in Armed Forces in the Field* (Geneva: ICRC).

ROBERTS, A (2006), 'Transformative Military Occupation: Applying the Laws of War and Human Rights', 100 *AJIL* 580.

ROBERTS, A and GUELFF, R (2000), *Documents on the Laws of War* (3rd edn, Oxford: Oxford University Press).

ROGERS, APV (2004), *Law on the Battlefield* (2nd edn, Manchester: Manchester University Press).

ROWE, PJ (ed) (1993), *The Gulf War 1990–91 in International and English Law* (London: Routledge).

SCHEFFER, DJ (2003), 'Beyond Occupation Law', 97 *AJIL* 842.

SCHMITT, MN (2013), *Tallinn Manual on the International Law Applicable to Cyber Warfare* (Cambridge: Cambridge University Press).

SHAMGAR, M (1971), 'The Observance of International Law in the Administered Territories', 1 *Israel YBHR* 262.

SHANY, Y (2006), 'Faraway, So Close: The Legal Status of Gaza After Israel's Disengagement', 8 *YBIHL* 369.

SIVAKUMARAN, S (2006), 'Binding Armed Opposition Groups', 55 *ICLQ* 369.

TURNS, D (2006), 'Weapons in the ICRC Study on Customary International Humanitarian Law', 11 *JCSL* 201.

TURNS, D (2017), 'The United Kingdom, Unmanned Aerial Vehicles, and Targeted Killing', 21(3) *ASIL Insights*.

UNITED KINGDOM MINISTRY OF DEFENCE (2004), *The Manual of the Law of Armed Conflict* (Oxford: Oxford University Press).

WALKER, CP (1984), 'Irish Republican Prisoners—Political Detainees, Prisoners of War or Common Criminals?', XIX *The Irish Jurist* 89.

WILMSHURST, E and BREAU, S (eds) (2007), *Perspectives on the ICRC Study on Customary International Humanitarian Law* (Cambridge: Cambridge University Press).

WYLIE, N (2006), 'Protecting Powers in a Changing World', 40 *Politorbis* 6.

FURTHER READING

The literature on this area of law has grown exponentially in the past 15 years. What follows is a necessarily selective list of suggestions for further reading in the area; all the works cited either provide insightful general commentary on international humanitarian law, or focus detailed analysis on specific topics within the area.

General

FLECK, D (ed) (2008), *The Handbook of International Humanitarian Law* (Oxford: Oxford University Press).

GREENWOOD, C (1987), 'The Concept of War in Modern International Law', 36 *ICLQ* 283.

GREENWOOD, C (1996), 'International Humanitarian Law and the *Tadić Case*', 7 *EJIL* 265.

NEFF, S (2005), *War and the Law of Nations: A General History* (Cambridge: Cambridge University Press).

SCHMITT, MN (2007), '21st Century Conflict: Can the Law Survive?', 8 *Melb JIL* 443.

Scope of application

GREEN, LC (1951), 'The Nature of the 'War' in Korea', 4 *ILQ* 462.

GREENWOOD, C (2003), 'War, Terrorism and International Law', 56 *Current Legal Problems* 505.

ROBERTS, A (2005), 'Counter-terrorism, Armed Force and the Laws of War', 44 *Survival* 7.

STEWART, JG (2003), 'Towards a Single Definition of Armed Conflict in International Humanitarian Law: A Critique of Internationalized Armed Conflict', 850 *Int Rev Red Cross* 313.

TURNS, D (2007), 'The "War on Terror" Through British and International Humanitarian Law Eyes: Comparative Perspectives on Selected Legal Issues', 10 *NY City LR* 435.

Conduct of hostilities

BOOTHBY, WH (2009), *Weapons and the Law of Armed Conflict* (Oxford: Oxford University Press).

CORN, GS (2005), '"Snipers in the Minaret—What is the Rule?" The Law of War and the Protection of Cultural Property: A Complex Equation', July, *The Army Lawyer* 28.

CRYER, R (2002), 'The Fine Art of Friendship: *Jus in Bello* in Afghanistan', 7 *JCSL* 37.

DINSTEIN, Y (2004), *The Conduct of Hostilities under the Law of International Armed Conflict* (Cambridge: Cambridge University Press).

GREENWOOD, C (1988), 'Belligerent Reprisals and the 1977 Protocols to the Geneva Conventions of 1949', 37 *ICLQ* 818.

SCHMITT, MN (2005), 'Precision Attack and International Humanitarian Law', 859 *Int Rev Red Cross* 445.

SCHMITT, MN (2010), 'Military Necessity and Humanity in International Humanitarian Law: Preserving the Delicate Balance', 50 *Virginia JIL* 795.

SCHMITT, MN (2010), 'Deconstructing Direct Participation in Hostilities: The Constitutive Elements', 42 *NYU J Int'l Law & Politics* 697.

SCHMITT, MN and VIHUL, L (2017), 'International Cyber Law Politicized: The UN GGE's Failure to Advance Cyber Norms', https://www.justsecurity.org/42768/international-cyber-law-politicized-gges-failure-advance-cyber-norms/.

Protection of victims

DÖRMANN, K (2003), 'The Legal Situation of "Unlawful/Unprivileged Combatants"', 850 *Int Rev Red Cross* 45.

HAMPSON, FJ (1991), 'The Geneva Conventions and the Detention of Civilians and Alleged Prisoners of War', 4 *Public Law* 507.

ROBERTS, A (2005), 'The End of Occupation: Iraq 2004', 54 *ICLQ* 27.

Implementation and enforcement

BANTEKAS, I (1999), 'The Contemporary Law of Superior Responsibility', 93 *AJIL* 573.

GARRAWAY, C (1999), 'Superior Orders and the International Criminal Court: Justice Delivered or Justice Denied?', 836 *Int Rev Red Cross* 785.

ROGERS, APV (1990), 'War Crimes Trials under the Royal Warrant: British Practice 1945–1949', 39 *ICLQ* 780.

INDEX

Contents

Photo Taken By: Nina Rizzo

From Kathleen's Perspective...

This book was born not long after my first textbook for Prentice Hall/Pearson entitled *Fashion Design on Computers*. I approached the idea of rendering fashion on computers as concept-specific versus software-specific. The idea was to learn the basics and then apply that knowledge to any given software.

It seemed obvious to me that anyone using either vector or raster software would clearly be able to recognize the major commonalities between brands of software. Much like car companies, both off-the-shelf and proprietary software companies developed products that would each accomplish similar tasks and use similar tools.

At the time of that book, both the industry and educational communities as a whole had not yet settled on a definitive software solution.

In addition, in the not so distant past, most fashion done digitally was initially done by a graphic artist who had the necessary computer skills, while the educational community on a whole was slow to garner these needed skills in order to better prepare the next generation of designers. Since digitally rendering textiles both in the classroom and within the industry is still in its infancy, we soon found out that the lines were blurred between graphic and fashion when it comes to executing ideas digitally.

The idea was to teach the educational community to think outside the box and consider learning to be concept-specific instead of software-specific. The goal was to prepare the designer to make the quantum leap from any vector and raster off-the-shelf software to proprietary used within the industry and then apply that macro-level knowledge to any type, brand, or version of design software with only a limited learning curve. Since the inception of my first text, both the industry and educational community seem to agree that one company and one software program was clearly emerging as a favorite—Adobe. So, it was only a natural for me to follow-up my first book with a micro-examination of the leading design software—Adobe® Photoshop®!

For the fashion designer, knowledge of the basic tools and techniques of Adobe® Photoshop® is a must. You will soon discover you will be using 20% of the tools 80% of the time. For that reason, it is hard to say that this is a version-specific book. The truth is most of the exercises in this text can be accomplished easily both in older and later versions of Photoshop. With very few exceptions the exercises apply to all versions of Photoshop except for a few exercises limited to version 7 and beyond.

The challenge was to prepare a text that covered all facets of digitally rendering fabric and prints. To date, this issue had only been addressed in a very limited and generic way. There was no one book for digital printing know-how nor was there one Adobe® Photoshop® how-to book that recognized and catered to the fashion and textile design industry.

To do the subject matter justice, it didn't take long to realize that it needed another set of eyes, ears, and expertise to do the job right!

As in most industries, the circle of movers and shakers is surprisingly small. There will be names you will hear over and over again when you begin to do your research. While working on my first book, I met one such individual—Steve Greenberg.

Steven brought industry insight and sensibilities to my first book, so it was a given he would be just the person to collaborate with on this book.

Deciding what should be included in the book was difficult. I wanted to create a straightforward, user-friendly book that would touch on all the important concepts a digital designer would need to know. My desire was for both the newbie digital designer as well as the experienced graphic designer to benefit from the insights we have included in the text.

At the same time, both Steve and I heard people say to us over and over again that in order to correctly render fabric and prints, designers need to have a working knowledge of textiles, graphic design, and technology. Students in particular need a good working knowledge of fabric and textiles before rendering them digitally.

So it was only natural for us to include a short refresher on the foundations for textiles, design basics, and Photoshop. We then placed a concerted effort into the tricks and techniques that would be useful for rendering fashion, fabric, and prints in the remaining chapters.

We make no promises other than that we have done the best we could do to make this book realistic and down-to-earth with practical applications.

My heart as an educator shows in the plethora of literal goodies that have been prepared in the accompanying CDs. Believe me when I tell you that it is filled with just about everything you will need to get started including trial software from Adobe.

What you do with this information is up to you. We invite you to read the book in its entirety in order to have a better understanding of the design process. We value your feedback, so don't forget to contact us at our Website: www.ComputersandFashion.com to tell us what you think. Thank you for choosing our text and we trust it will be a practical asset to you in your journey of digitally rendering fashion, fabric, and prints!

Enjoy!

From Steve's Perspective…

This is no ordinary instruction book. It has been derived from the dedication and talents that only come with many years of experience. Not just my own, but the vast knowledge of many of the amazing people I have had the pleasure of working with over time.

For the last 13 years I have spent my days helping apparel and textile designers wade through the enlightening but sometimes confusing world of digital design—first as a designer, then as a trainer, now as a director at a textile software company. At times when I was designing, I spent much of my time showing others how to create digitally what they had done traditionally, saving them time, money, and frustration.

"You should write a book" was a phrase constantly thrown at me. I ignored it, not believing that there could not be a resource out there already. I was wrong. After collaborating with Kathy on Chapter 13 of her first book, I began to realize that no such resource existed or one that was written in easy terms anyone could follow. After much research, (a deep thank-you to the World Wide Web) approaching Kathy about the idea was an easy choice because she had already been very successful at testing the waters, as well as easy to work with.

She had already been developing a similar idea for Prentice Hall when we both agreed that this type of book was a missing link. Something was needed to help the designer of today get started as well as help others along and beyond what they thought would be possible with digital design. As the need for graphic and creative designers grows, many students and designers alike have jumped into the fashion industry. This was a place where a graphic artist could adapt their well-defined computer skills and enjoy their job. The drawback was that many do not possess the textile or apparel knowledge that a graduate of a fashion design school would have.

I wanted to write a book that appealed to every level of designer. It had become very clear that Adobe® Photoshop® was a link between designers throughout the industry, as well as an easy place for someone to start before graduating to a proprietary software like Pointcarré. We hope this book will help guide anyone with an interest in designing digitally and rendering textiles and prints—from the current student to the seasoned designer, no matter their level of design or knowledge of the industry. This book and its CDs should start them on their way or direct them to the next step.

Important Announcement and Disclaimer…

When developing the main exercise chapters for this text, every care has been given to write the steps in a clear and understandable fashion for our reader. Although this book covers concepts that range from elementary to advanced, it is assumed that you already have a working knowledge of Adobe® Photoshop® *and* of textiles. Therefore, we strongly urge you to read the early chapters and then work through the early chapter exercises and develop a comfortable working knowledge of all the material covered in Chapters 1 through 6 before tackling the advanced rendering exercises in the later chapters.

You will find that the later chapter exercises are based on having a working knowledge of these elementary techniques. To write the exercises in any other manner would have belabored the information and increased the number of written steps to the point of actually causing unnecessary confusion to the reader. All of these exercises have been written to give you ample opportunity to experience the wide range of techniques that can be used.

The purpose of the exercises is to reinforce the basic skills of Adobe® Photoshop® as would be applied by a fashion, textile, or interior designer. If you come to this book having learned the tools of Adobe® Photoshop® in a different context, you may need to put aside what you already think you know about how something should be done and be willing to learn another way to accomplish a task. We heartily encourage you to make notes in the book as you complete each exercise and note what works best for you. Frequently, you will discover that there is not necessarily a right or wrong way to do something, but more of a good, better, best scenario. For example, in Chapter 8 on rendering plaids, there are several ways that are short and sweet but others involve steps that appear to be a bit more tedious. In reality, sometimes taking the longer route affords you more control over the design process. Should the shortcuts work for you, terrific! Use them; by all means apply them to your work!

When a technique or method is preferred over another, we will give notice to that. Therefore, the use of the designer's critical thinking skills to modify the exercises to suit a given project is to be expected. If you find that you are experiencing extreme difficulty following along in any exercises, we suggest that you go back and review the basic tools and techniques covered in the earlier chapters and then attempt the practical application exercise. Frequently, a student or designer may attempt to rush the design process without adequately knowing the software, and the results can be a disappointment or an unnecessary time of frustration.

The last thing you need to do is to become frustrated. Try getting up from the computer for a small break, or perhaps go on to another exercise and come back to the one that is challenging. If you have the luxury of discussing the outcome objectives with someone who has successfully mastered the assignment, this can help considerably. Trying to go on to more difficult exercises before you are ready is like trying to build upper floors without successfully completing the structural foundation first.

Although these exercises have been classroom tested, we welcome your feedback via e-mail found at our Website www.ComputersandFashion.com.

It is impossible to write a book of this scope without the assistance of some amazing people.

This book took months to research and without the kind support of information, interviews, and even sample products we could never have completed such a daunting task. We can't even begin to thank everyone for all your help. In our humble attempt to give everyone equal acknowledgment, we have listed in alphabetical order the names of the people and companies that caught our vision for this book!

We would like to offer a special thanks to our reviewers for all of your valuable input into this project. We appreciate all comments and suggestions. We have done our best to reflect them in the text.

Thank you!

Adobe—how do you begin to say thank you to everyone who supported and believed in this project? We are indebted to the BETA Team management, the legal department, and so many more folks we have pitched to along the way, especially….

Anjali Ariathurai	Kakul Srivastava
Heather Forte	Gwyn Weisberg
Tasha Mulvihill	

AGE Technology—Alain Bélair

AlienSkin/Xeneoflex Software—Amedeo Rosa

Apple Computer Corp.

Artsville Images—Jane Nelson

Art Institute—Kathy's bosses, Bob—thanks for cooperation with my schedule and the toll writing a book takes on a full-time teacher <*sigh*>, also to *Jesus*— hard to believe it has been 20+ years—your kindness, support, and friendship mean more than everything! I appreciate you!

Art Institute Students—who participated, named or anonymous who have helped or inspired exercises:

Katherine Bárcenas	Andrea Knaub
Yvette Basetti	Heather Dalzell-Kolsky
Brittany O'Conner	Shawntelle Kulmann
Megan Cedro	Judith Kruger
Natalie Chachin	Lori Lagasse
Nandi Chin	Denis Lates
Nathalie Duberanet	Jerry Martinez
Emily Fiorella	Jessica Medina
Farah Ishmael	Lisa Valle
Maayan Keren	Efi Viradaki
Yvonne Kinnie	

Bond's—Thanks for believing in me and all the long-distance calls to prove it!— love, K.

ColorSpan—**MacDermid**—Dinah Weigle

Craig Crawford—of Liz Claiborne….thanks!

Dani Locastro— *Design Works.* (You are a special blessing!)

DuPont—John Kane and Adrian F. Newell (John, you're the best!)

Emily Bush—Carlisle Publishers Services—You are in the will! Thank you for everything including making this process as painless as possible.

FabriCAD—Alison Hardy

First 2 Print and **Design Works**—management and staff!

Graph to Graphics—Ivette Principe (Maria and Peter)

Greenberg Family—again Randi—thanks for "sharing Steve" all these many months, and to Jake and Ben, you have a great legacy—your dad is the best!

Hewlett Packard—Shivan Kortanta

Human Software USA. Co Inc

Imagine That!

Jean Parsons, PhD.—Iowa State University

Joanne O'Reilly—textile artist extraordinaire!

J. R. Campbell—& students at Iowa State University

Liza Niles—artisan-educator

Lyson—Simon Guest and Alison Starkweather

Mimaki—Conrad R Simoneau, Sy Simoneau, Fran Gardino, Mark Trimble

Pantone

Paul Kane—you are such a mench! Thanks for the great cover!

Peter—you can have the dining room table back, at least until the next book. I will not be using it as my flat file for awhile!—thanks for the tea, the chocolate, and the love, K.

Pointcarré—you guys are the best!

Punto Software—*including Karen Stevens, great artwork!*

Richard Lerner

Robert Manning

SaraLee Corp—Tibby Marton

Schacht Spindle Co., Inc.

Snap Fashun—Wendy Bendoni, Bill Glazer

SoftTeam USA, George Brecht

Spinwave Software—Dawn Ginn

Stoll—USA and Germany Regine Schlagowski and Stefan Schaed—you both are awesome! We deeply appreciate all your help!

SuperSample—thanks David, Robert, and everyone for your insight and time!

TechExchange—Tc2

Teri Ross

Thorsten Lemke—Lemke Software

UMAX

Wacom—Will Reeb

Wasatch—Jay Griffin (and Alison Hyman for getting everything ok'd—thanks)

Xaos Tools— Andrew Hathaway & Brian Jones

1 The Fundamentals

Part One—Fiber Fundamentals

Terms to look for:

Absorbency	Elastic	Pilling
Affinity to Dyes	Fabric	Protein
Balling	Face	Resiliency
Bias	Findings	Selvage
Cellulose	Greige Goods	Static
Converter	Hand	Synthetic
Crimp	Jobber	Textile
Crinkle	Luster	Texture
Crocking	Mill	Thread
Density	Mineral	Yarn
Dull	Muslin	

You might be wondering why a book on using Adobe Photoshop has its first two chapters exclusively about textiles? In our years of teaching, doing workshops, and writing on the subject of fashion design and Adobe Photoshop, we often found more than half of our clients and students struggling to understand how to translate the information they learned in a basic textiles class into practical rendering of fibers, yarns, and fabrics on the computer.

In addition, numerous graphic designers have been or will be employed within the fashion industry simply because they have stronger computer skills. However, graphic designers usually have limited working knowledge about fabrics. Therefore, when they are called upon to render a twill fabric, for example, they have nowhere to turn for insight. Soon it became apparent that we had to include this information early in the text in order to facilitate the learning process and increase the learning curve for digitally rendering fabric.

Thus, the primary function of the next two chapters is to be a textile primer for the graphic artist and a refresher course for the fashion designer. Digital designers must have a comfortable working knowledge of fibers and fabrics. Therefore, a complete overview of the study of textiles is provided in *everyday* language. Every new segment that pertains to fabric will address the topic with a simple overview, followed by a practical application in Adobe Photoshop and a glossary. So let's begin!

Textiles—Five Basic Units of Study

According to the ATMI (American Textile Marketing Industry), "if the annual U.S. textile mills were made into strips of cloth one yard wide, that strip would be enough to circle the earth at the equator approximately 500 times or make 26 round trips to the moon." In fact, one in four jobs today in the United States are related to the textile and apparel industry! So how can a computer graphic designer begin to grasp the implications of converting fabric images digitally? We begin our overview of textiles by breaking down our topic into five units of study. The five basic units to categorize the study of textiles are:

1. Fibers
2. Yarns
3. Fabric Structure
4. Finishes
5. Color

Beginning with the production process for most of today's textiles, Figure 1–1 shows the common sequence from start to finish.

Before you ever begin to render a fabric, it is essential that you understand the distinguishing characteristics that identify a given fiber or fabric. Simply stated, fibers are the building blocks that fabric is made from.

Let's begin by taking a closer look at how fibers are further divided and categorized. (See Figure 1–2.)

Unit #1: Fibers

Fibers are the basic building blocks for making yarn and fabrics. A fiber is a hairlike substance that is either natural or chemically engineered. Natural fibers are classified as being either vegetable (cellulosic), mineral, or protein (animal or insect). The four major natural fibers are *cotton, linen, wool,* and *silk.* Synthetic fibers are classified into two groups that are derived or adapted from cellulose (vegetable) or from noncellulosic fibers, commonly referred to as man-made fiber or synthetics. The most common synthetic fibers are *acrylic, acetate, modacrylic, nylon, polyester, rayon, spandex,* and *triacetate.* According to the Federal Trade Commission, fibers are assigned generic names and are classified by their organic composition. In addition to generic names, hundreds of trade names or trademarks are granted to indicate a distinctive fiber producer or product. The subject of fiber is covered later in this chapter.

Unit #2: Yarns

Terms to look for:

Blends	Multifilament	Spun
Monofilament	Novelty	Stretch

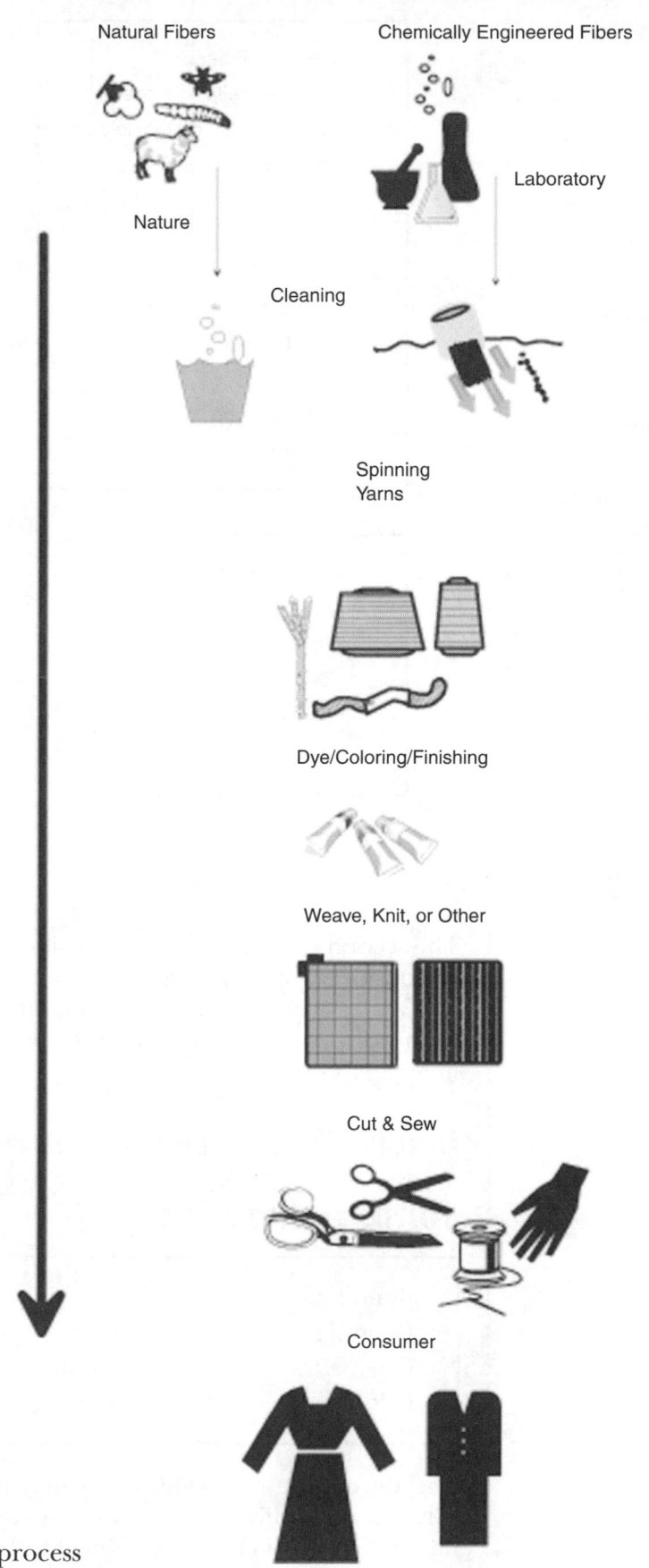

Natural Fibers

Chemically Engineered Fibers

Laboratory

Nature

Cleaning

Spinning
Yarns

Dye/Coloring/Finishing

Weave, Knit, or Other

Cut & Sew

Consumer

FIGURE 1–1
Production process

Natural Plant Fibers
    Cotton—cellulosic-seed
    Linen/Ramie–cellulosic-bast
    Minor Vegetable Fibers:
        Coir
        Jute
        Raffia
        Sisal
        Rubber
        Grass
        Bamboo
        Abaca

Natural Animal Fibers
    Wool
    Silk
    Leather
    Skins
    Feather/Down
    Furs
    Other:
        Angora
        Alpaca
        Cashmere
        Camel
        Llama
        Mohair
        Rabbit
        Vicuna

Natural Mineral Fibers
    Asbestos
    Gold/Silver
    Aluminum
Synthetic Mineral Fibers
    Aramid

Petroleum Plastic Fibers/Synthetic
    Acrylic
    Nylon
    Modacrylic
    Olefin
    Polyester
    Spandex
    Vinyl

Synthetic Cellulosic Fibers
    Acetate
    Rayon
    Tencel
    Triacetate
    Viscose

FIGURE 1–2
Types of fibers

Notes . . .

The second stage of textile production is yarn. Yarn is made from fibers that can be considered short (*staple* or *tow*) or by using long fibers, which are known as *filaments*. These fibers or filaments are laid together in varying amounts of twist to form yarns. Later in this chapter we will cover the subject of yarns and finishing in greater detail.

Unit #3: Fabric Construction Methods

Terms to look for:

Bonding	Film	Netting
Braiding	Foam	Tufting
Crocheting	Knitting	Weaving
Felting	Knotting	

The third stage of textile production is making cloth, or fabric construction. There are basically three ways to construct cloth: *knit, weave,* or *other.* The method known as other includes a gambit of techniques such as bonding, laminating, felting, and other nonwoven techniques. Listed below is a quick reference chart for categorizing fabrics. Fabric construction methods will be discussed in more detail in Chapter 2.

Unit #4: Methods of Finishing Fabrics

Terms to look for:

Anti: Bacteria, Static, Shrink, and Moth/Insect	Couching	Napping
Appliqué	Embroidery	Plissé
Beading	Flame Resist,	Quilting
Bleaching	flameproof	Scotch Guard
Calendaring	Flocking	Shearing
Cire	Glazing	Teflon
	Moiré	Water Resist, waterproof

The term *finish* refers to anything that will alter the hand, appearance, or performance of a fabric. This means that, like color, a finish can be added at *any* time in the production process. The subject of finishing is covered extensively in Chapter 2.

Unit #5: Methods of Adding Color

Terms to look for:

Batik	Hand Painting	Tie Dye
Dye Sublimation	Roller Printing	Transfer Printing
Dying	Screen Printing	

Color refers to the application, retention, or removal of color to a fiber, yarn, fabric, or garment. This topic is so significant to the graphic and fashion designer that it will require a complete chapter in order to adequately cover the subject matter.

Now that we have introduced the fundamentals, this chapter will deal with the discussion of the first two categories of textile studies: fiber and yarns. Chapter 2 will deal with construction methods and finishing. Chapter 3 introduces using Adobe Photoshop and Chapter 4 begins our transition into the graphic section of our text as we take a closer look at color and print concepts.

The Fiber Story: Unit #1

All of today's fibers used in textile production have their roots in the four most common and popular natural fibers—cotton, linen, wool, and silk. For thousands of years clothing was made from these four fibers, historically on a weaving loom.

However, most of today's generation cannot recall a time without the use of man-made or synthetic fibers. It is important to remember that many of the synthetic fibers were originally designed less than 100 years ago, and most in the last 50 years, to be a reflection of the natural fiber they were designed to replace or mirror. The goal was to minimize cost and care for the consumer without sacrificing quality or appearance. To that extent they have served us well. We begin by making a simple distinction between the types of synthetic fibers available. Basically there are two groups of fibers—those with cellulose base ingredients and those with noncellulose base ingredients. Cellulose refers to things derived from vegetable or plant matter. In the case of synthetics, the primary ingredient is wood pulp from trees. Many synthetic fibers are considered to be a (long) filament fiber that can be "cut" or blended with natural fibers to ensure the best characteristics of both fibers to be found in yarns or fabrics.

Why not test your knowledge by having another look at Figure 1–2. How many fibers could you immediately recognize? Looking ahead, Figure 1–10 on page 13 expands on Figure 1–2 by labeling the fiber name, what the fiber is most commonly known for with the consumer, and which fibers are used in substitution.

Physical Properties of Fibers

All fibers possess intrinsic qualities that will determine their overall appeal and performance with the consumer. Whether or not the consumer makes a conscious decision when purchasing a garment, the following qualities are part of the mix. Everyone likes the hand of natural fibers such as cotton, but we also want the easy care that we find if the garment has a blend of polyester. The following categories of qualities describe a given fiber performance and hand. You will discover that fibers behave much like human hair. There are certain inherent qualities that can be enhanced or altered but also have specific limitations. Several ways that fibers are quantified are by the following qualities:

Microscopic—longitude and cross-sectional shapes

Thermal Qualities—measured responses to heat

Chemical—measured responses to alkalis, acids, and solvents

Biological—insect, microorganism's susceptibility

Tactile Qualities—the actual surface texture and hand, including the longitude and cross-sectional shapes

Optical Qualities—refers to the color or luster of a fiber

Understanding Fiber Characteristics for Digital Rendering

Textile fibers are very much like human hair. Each of the fibers used in the construction of fabrics has a distinctive appearance that is evident when viewing a cross section of the individual fiber. The shape of the fiber helps to determine and distinguish the physical properties. (See Figure 1–3.) These characteristics will determine the amount of luster a fiber has, as well as how resilient the fiber will be. There are many types of cross sections of fibers including: trilobal, t-Y, multilobal, cruciform, KX, pentalobal, star, i-beam, ribbon, square, triangular, elliptical, and hollow.

Notes...

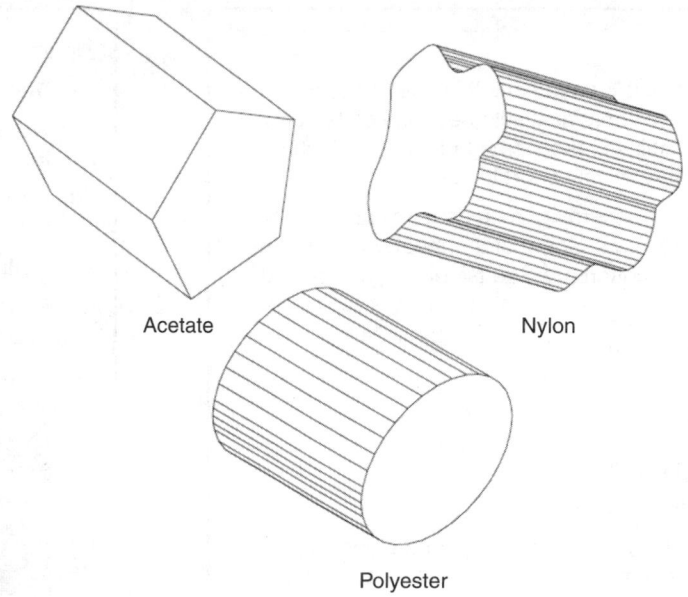

Acetate

Nylon

Polyester

FIGURE 1–3
Fiber cross sections

Understanding the Natural Fiber Production Process

Natural fibers constitute any fiber derived from nature with textile utility. The production processes vary depending on the fiber selected. We have put together brief snapshots of each of the four major natural fibers and how they get from their natural origins to the consumer in the form of textile products. Each of the natural fibers has a unique production story, which we have encapsulated for you in the production charts, relevant terms, and accompanying photos, starting with cotton in Figure 1–4 and ending with wool in Figure 1–7.

Understanding the Synthetic Fiber Production Process

Synthetic fibers can best be understood by how the synthetic fibers are chemically engineered in the laboratory. There are basically five steps in the production of most manufactured synthetic fibers:

1. A chemical process of combining components

2. Optional adding of color to fiber

3. The spinning process to produce the fiber

4. Twisting the cut fibers and/or filaments into yarns

5. Weaving, knitting, or other processes to produce the fabric

The initial process of taking a syrupy, chemically engineered substance and solidifying it into a fiber is done by spinning. A *spinneret* is a showerhead-like devise with hundreds of holes through which the solvent is forced. (See Figure 1–8.)

The distinctive size and shape of the holes as well as the chemical ingredients used in the process will determine the final fiber produced. The term *denier* is often

Cotton

Cotton is a cellulosic seed fiber. It is one of the most desirable natural fibers available because of its soft hand and versatility. Cotton is a staple fiber, which means it has a relatively short length.

Cotton is graded according to its genetics or heredity, its spinnability factors. Some of the most common better grades of cotton are Sea Island, Egyptian, and Pima cottons.

The basic production process for cotton:

- Plant
- Harvest
- Cleaning process
- Combing or detangling
- Bleaching, dyeing, finishing (these steps can also be done at different intervals other than at this stage)
- Blending and/or spinning
- Weaving, knitting, or other
- Cutting, sewing
- Shipped and marketed
- Sold to consumer

Important terms associated with production of cotton:

1. **Staple** = short fiber
2. **Wicking** = natural ability to draw moisture away from the body
3. **Carding/combing** = detangling and smoothing the fiber
4. **Cellulose** = vegetable fiber (seed)
5. **Pima, Sea Island, Egyptian** = better grade of cotton fiber

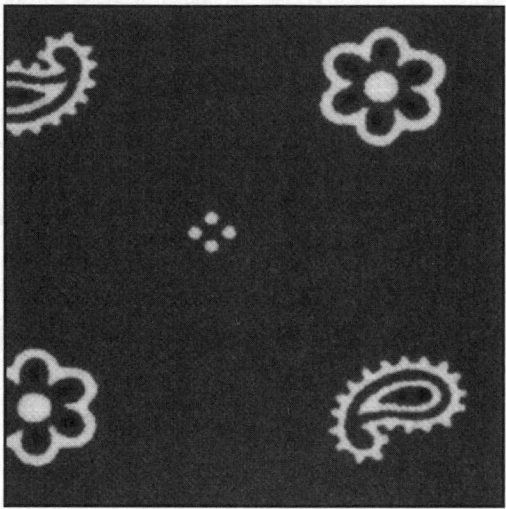

FIGURE 1–4

Cotton—the undisputed king of fibers and a real consumer favorite for comfort and quality!

Notes...

used in conjunction with the manufacturing of synthetic fibers. Denier refers to the fineness or thickness of the monofilament of the fiber produced. For example, 12-denier refers to the thickness used for pantyhose.

Denier is based on:

- Luster
- Hand
- Performance
- Ingredients used to produce fibers
- Size of holes in the spinneret
- Shape of hole on the spinneret
- Method of spinning and/or hardening of fiber
- End use: for example, nylon for tires or pantyhose

Linen and Ramie

Linen and ramie are bast (cellulose) fibers that have a history of being woven into cloth for thousands of years. The Egyptian civilization raised the weaving of linen muslin to an art of the sheerest and finest quality of fabrics. Linen has a distinctively soft, crisp hand and slubbed appearance in the yarns.

Linen also is known for easily wrinkling. Because of this factor, anyone in the know considers linen a prestige fiber that can be referred to as "rich wrinkles." This is a case where the consumer does not mind the wrinkling because it has become synonymous with linen.

One of the best attributes of linen is its ability to repel dirt and soil as well as actually improving with laundering. It should be noted that linen is very slow drying and is easily subject to mildew and insect damage.

Unfortunately linen has a long, costly production process that inhibits its availability and price. Ramie, on the other hand, is a less expensive substitute with a coarser hand and appearance.

The production process for linen:

- Plant
- Harvest
- Very time-consuming cleaning process—a series of soaking and drying to separate the stalk from the fiber
- Combing or repeated detangling
- Hammering to soften plant
- Bleaching, dyeing, finishing (these steps can also be done at different intervals other than at this stage)
- Blending and/or spinning
- Weaving, knitting, or other
- Cutting, sewing
- Shipped and marketed
- Sold to consumer

Important terms associated with linen:

1. **Beetle** = a form of hammering to soften linen
2. **Hackle** = detangling the linen fibers from one another
3. **Cambric** = fine quality of linen used for fine apparel
4. **Cellulose/bast** = a stalklike plant with textile utility
5. **Line** = longer lengths of linen fibers. Linen is still considered to be a staple or short fiber but does come in longer lengths based on heredity of the plants.
6. **Linen** = a commonly misunderstood or misused term for flax
7. **Flax** = processed into tow or short fibers as well as line, which are longer, more uniform and finer yarns

FIGURE 1–5

Linen—the wrinkles the fashion industry loves!

Notes . . .

Silk

Silk has a long history of being a premier prestige fiber. Silk is also the only natural filament (long) fiber. Silk comes from silkworms. The industry originated in China, and silk production was swathed in mystery for thousands of years. Silk is a protein fiber that comes from the cocoon of the silkworm.

Silkworms have a relatively short life span and go through a series of stages beginning with the larva, worm, cocoon, and finally the moth life cycle.

Each individual cocoon can vary in diameter (approx. 1.5 inches) and vary in thickness (about the diameter of human hair). It is not uncommon for an unbroken cocoon to produce a single strand of fiber that can be typically from 1,500 yards to up to 1 mile in length!

Broken cocoons where the silkworm is permitted to break through and live produce a series of short fibers that obviously will vary in lengths and must be spun into yarns that will produce a characteristically textured hand and surface appearance.

The production process for silk:

- Cocoon
- The cocoon is dropped into solution to protect the silk from the worm being permitted to live and break open the cocoon. Cocoons that are broken have a much more tedious process of recovering the split ends of fibers.
- An additional cleaning process removes the sticky, gumlike sericin from the fiber.
- Detangling the fiber into one long continuous filament
- Cleaning and drying the fiber
- Combing and/or repeated detangling
- Spinning into yarn
- Weaving, knitting, or other
- Cutting, sewing
- Shipped and marketed
- Sold to consumer

Important terms associated with silk:

1. **Cultivated silk** = worms feed exclusively on mulberry leaves
2. Silkworms that dine in the wild on scrub oak produce a **wild** or **Tussah** silk
3. **Douppioni** (Italian for double) = silk where two moths produce one cocoon, resulting in an unusual silk that is considered more costly because it is irregular in appearance but still possesses the distinctive silk sheen
4. **Weighted silk** = silk that has been degummed and has been weighted artificially with metal salts that form a permanent bond to the silk protein molecule
5. **Raw silk** = silk that has been unscoured and contains **sericin,** which is the gumlike protein substance that naturally coats silk
6. **Silk noil** = the short fiber that comes from a broken or damaged cocoon and results in a slubbed appearance to the fabric surface
7. **Thrown** = silk from a broken cocoon

FIGURE 1–6

Silk—the fashion secret kept for thousands of years!

Notes . . .

Wool

Wool is a protein (hair) fiber. One of the biggest misconceptions about wool is that it comes from just sheep. This is absolutely incorrect; wool encompasses a variety of hair or protein fibers used in the production of textiles.

Another misconception is that wool is heavy and scratchy. In fact, for thousands of years wool has been one of the most versatile fibers available. Gabardine or Hebrew cloth was the fabric that Moses supposedly wore in the desert. What better fiber to literally go from day (heat) to night (cold)! Wool also is extremely versatile in the thickness in which the yarn can be spun; wool can be spun as fine as Voile or as thick as a Melton coat.

Because wool is typically derived from the hair of an animal, wool is frequently graded and sorted according to its quality and end use. Wool fibers are generally spun into either woolen fiber yarns or into worsted fiber yarns.

Wool possesses a variety of excellent characteristics preferred by consumers, including its ability to hold moisture without feeling wet, as well as its resiliency and its ability to breathe.

The production process for wool:

- Shear or collect from animal
- Sort and grade
- Scour and remove by-products such as lanolin
- Combing or repeated detangling
- Bleaching, dyeing, finishing (these steps can also be done at different intervals other than at this stage)
- Blending and/or spinning
- Weaving, knitting, or other
- Cutting, sewing
- Shipped and marketed
- Sold to consumer

Important terms associated with wool:

1. **New** or **virgin wool** = the first shearing of wool, which is considerably softer
2. **Recycled wool** = reclaimed wool
3. **Garneting** = reclaiming wool
4. **Shetland** = higher grade of wool
5. **Merino** = higher grade of wool
6. **Felting** = nonwoven method of making cloth using heat, adhesion, and pressure
7. **Woolen** = shorter, less uniform wool fibers used in making sweaters
8. **Worsted** = longer, more uniform fibers used in the making of wool suits

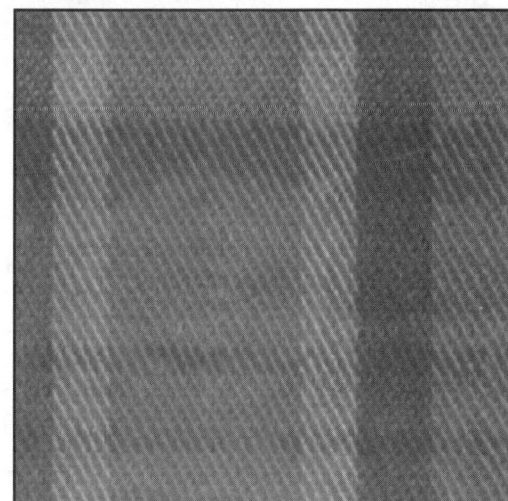

FIGURE 1–7
Wool—it's not just about sheep!

Notes . . .

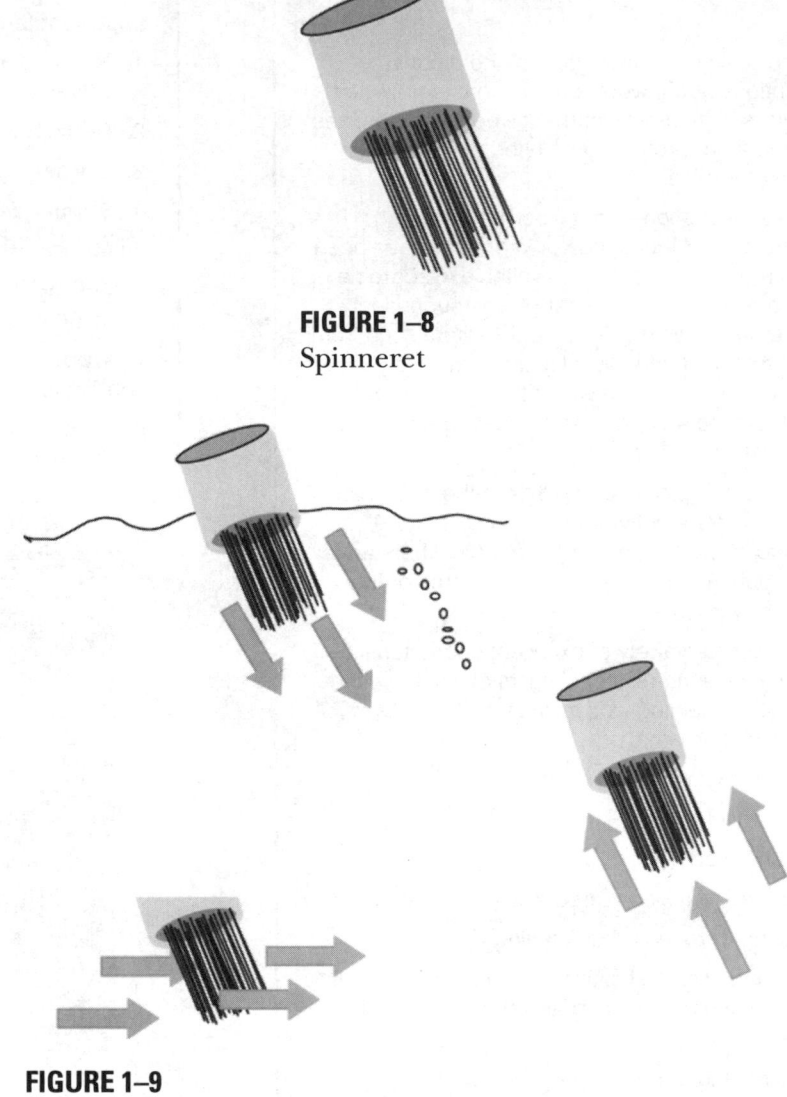

FIGURE 1–8
Spinneret

FIGURE 1–9
Synthetic hardening processes

Unlike natural fibers, chemically engineered fibers are long continuous filaments that must be solidified into a fiber. This process of hardening the liquid is known as spinning. There are several variations of hardening the fiber depending on the actual fiber to be manufactured. (See Figure 1–9 for examples of several hardening processes.)

Synthetic fibers are by nature a filament fiber; however, there are times when the filament fibers are collected and cut and bundled into shorter fibers, known as tow. These bundles can be crimped or have other finishing techniques applied in order for the fiber to more closely imitate its natural fiber counterpart. This technique is also useful when blending combinations of synthetic and natural fibers. This results in counterbalancing characteristics of each fiber used in the yarn, which consumers come to appreciate. An example is a combination of the softness found in cotton and the easy care found

Natural Fiber Name	Known For	Most Common Substitute
Cotton	Comfort, wicking	Polyester
Linen	"Rich" wrinkles	Polyester or rayon
Ramie	China grass	Linen
Silk	Luxurious hand	Polyester, acetate, rayon, nylon
Wool	Protein/hair	Acrylic, polyester

- These natural fibers can be categorized as being either a cellulose or protein fiber.
- With the exception of silk (which is a filament), all the natural fibers are considered short or staple.
- There are also a variety of other minor vegetable fibers such as sisal, hemp, and piña, just to name a few.

FIGURE 1–10
Review of natural fibers

Synthetic Fiber Name	Known For	Most Common Substitute
Acetate	After-five /cellulose	Silk
Acrylic	Faux wool	Wool
Metallic	Lamé, glitter	Gold and silver
Modacrylic	Faux fur	Fur
Nylon	Strongest synthetic fiber	Silk
Olefin	Wicking	Cotton
Polyester	Industry workhorse	EVERYTHING
Rayon	1st m/m fiber	Silk, linen
Spandex	Stretch	Rubber
Tencel	Newest synthetic fiber	Cotton
Triacetate	Holding pleats/ cellulose	Silk

FIGURE 1–11
Review of synthetic fibers

in polyester. The percentage of the blends will depend on the specific qualities the designer is attempting to achieve as well as the final price of the garment or fabric.

To summarize, natural fibers are fibers found in nature with textile utility, and synthetic fibers are chemically engineered to reflect the natural fibers while offsetting any undesirable quality at an affordable cost to the consumer. (See Figure 1–10 for a short review of natural fibers and Figure 1–11 for a review of synthetic fibers.)

Fiber-Related Terms

Abrasion: Refers to a fabric's ability to resist or withstand everyday normal rubbing, friction, or abrasion.

Absorbency: A fiber or fabric's ability to retain moisture; also referred to as moisture regain or the percentage of moisture on a dry fiber from the air under normal or standard conditions of moisture and temperature.

Affinity to Dyes: A fiber or fabric's ability to attract color; does not imply colorfastness.

Balling: Also known as Pilling; small split ends of the yarn fibers break off and form small balls on the surface of the fabric.

Bias: Diagonal stretch or give on a piece of fabric.

Blend: (1) The combination of two or more fiber contents in a yarn. (2) The combination of two or more fiber contents in yarns used in woven or knitted fabrics. For example, in woven fabric the warp is made from fiber a, while the weft yarn is from fiber b.

Cellulose: From plant or vegetable; found in fibers or filaments with textile utility.

Colorfast: A fiber or fabric's ability to retain color.

Converter: An individual or organization that sells and finishes, dyes, prints, or performs other textile processes to produce greige goods, including yarns.

Crimp: The waviness either occurring naturally or artificially to produce fibers or yarns.

Crinkle: Wrinkling or puckering of fabric done by heat, chemicals, or mechanical means.

Crocking: Color cracking and peeling from the surface of a fabric when exposed to heat, chemicals, or abrasion.

Denier: The fiber or yarn size as defined in a weight of grams.

Density: Weight or quantity by volume of an area of fibers or yarns.

Dimensional Restorability: Ability of a fiber to return to its original shape after laundering.

Dimensional Stability: Ability of a fiber, yarn, or garment to maintain its shape through normal wear and tear, including laundering; typically a finish added to a fabric or garment to prevent either shrinkage or growth in normal use or care.

Dull: A fiber exhibiting low luster or limited degree of shine.

Dye: Uniformly adding color to a fiber or fabric using synthetic or natural coloring.

Elastic: One-way stretch and recovery of a fiber, yarn, or fabric.

Fabric: Same as cloth, material, textile, greige goods, good, or stuff.

Face: The surface or front of the fabric.

Findings: Also known as Notions, including buttons, zippers, thread, etc.

Finish: Anything that alters the hand, appearance, or performance of a fiber, yarn, or fabric when subjected to everyday wear; may be added at any stage of the textile production process and in no way implies that it is applied at the end of the process, although in some cases it can be the final step.

Generic: No name or trademark for a fiber; for example, the name polyester is the generic name but the name Dacron® polyester indicates ownership or trademark.

Greige Good: Unfinished cloth. (Pronounced *gray* good.)

Hand: Description for the tactile characteristics of a fiber, yarn, or fabric.

Hydrophilic: The measured rate at which a fiber is able to draw liquid or moisture.

Hydrophobic: Fiber that repels moisture or liquid.

Jobber: An individual or organization that represents fibers, yarns, or yard good overruns to resell in smaller quantities to companies who cannot meet traditionally large minimum-quantity orders.

Luster: The degree of shine a fiber or yarn exhibits naturally or after value-added finishing.

Microfibers: Sometimes referred to as second-generation synthetic fibers with the hand, appearance, or performance of the natural fiber they were intended to simulate.

Mill: Building or business in which fabrics are manufactured.

Mineral: Fibers that come from minerals may have special textile applications, for example, asbestos, glass, or metals.

Muslin: Represents a varied degree of quality and weights of greige good or plain woven fabrics sold for a variety of apparel and nonapparel applications.

Notions: Includes buttons, zippers, thread, etc. (See Findings.)

Pilling: (See Balling.)

Protein: Fibers or filaments that are derived from hair or insects for textile application purposes.

Resiliency: A fiber or yarn's ability to recover to its original shape after being stretched, twisted, or crushed.

Selvage: The tightly woven fabric edging that runs parallel to the warp.

Static: The degree of electrical charge that a fiber, yarn, or fabric exhibits or conducts.

Synthetic: Chemically engineered fibers; previously referred to as man-made fibers.

Textile: Latin term for to weave.

Texture: The surface characteristics or qualities assigned to describe the surface hand of a fiber, yarn, or fabric.

Thread: A general term that frequently refers to tightly twisted, thin, continuous fibers or filaments that are made into a corded yarn.

Trade: Common name for anyone working in the apparel industry.

Wicking: A unique moisture-absorbent feature of cotton, where the fiber actually draws moisture away from the body.

Yarn: The second stage of textile production involving the combination of fibers or filaments laid together in varying amounts of twist.

In this section we address the importance of understanding how yarns are made and how it will have an impact on their final appearance and performance in fabric. In rendering fabric it is critical to capture the essence of the surface appearance as well as the tactile qualities of a given yarn.

The Second Stage of Textile Production: Unit #2: Yarns

Terms to look for:

Bobbin	Hackle	Skein
Bouclé	Knit de Knit	Slub
Bulk	Loop	Spindle
Card	Measurement	Spinning
Chenille	Metallic	Spinning Wheel
Comb	Mule	Spool
Cone	Noil	Spot
Cord	Nub	Spun
Corkscrew	Ply	Staple
Crepe	Reeled	Woolen
Curl	Ring	Worsted
Denier	"S" twist	"Z" twist
Filament		

Yarn is the second stage of textile production. The twisting or combining of natural fibers (spun) and (synthetic) filaments to form yarns is one way in which blends combine the best properties of natural fibers and synthetic fibers for aesthetics, performance, and hand. The best method of yarn production is based on the fiber used.

The process of *twisting* or *drawing out* the fibers or filaments together is called *spinning*. The original implements used for centuries to produce yarn were the distaff and the spindle (Figure 1–12). The *spindle*, which is held at opposite ends from the distaff, is a long, smooth wooden stick approximately 9 to 15 inches in length; the spindle has a notch on it where the fiber is attached. The spinner whirls or rolls the weighted spindle. Another stick called the *distaff* holds the newly twisted yarn.

In ancient times, a stone or clay bowl known as a *whorl* was also used to help make the spindle spin like a top. During the Middle Ages, the spinning process became mechanized by the invention of a spinning wheel (Figure 1–12).

By the late 1700s, additional spinning inventions such as the *spinning jenny* by Sir James Hargreaves[1] and the *mule* by Samuel Compton[2] significantly in-

---

[1] Spinning Jenny /Hargreaves *Encyclopaedia Britannica*. Encyclopaedia Britannica Premium Service, 22 Sep, 2003 http://www.britannica.com/eb/article?eu=115279(22 September 2003).
[2] "Textile," *Encyclopaedia Britannica*. Encyclopaedia Britannica Premium Service (22 September 2003).

FIGURE 1–12
A spindle and a spinning jenny
(Photo courtesy of Schacht Spindle Co., Inc.)

creased the capabilities of the spinning process. Both methods increased production because they could spin more than one yarn at a time. By the beginning of the twentieth century, the Industrial Revolution saw the advent of power looms that quickly and economically produced fabric and yarn in much larger quantities.

Modern Spinning Methods

The basis of all yarns is the fiber or filaments selected. In the case of natural fibers the process of aligning and drawing the fibers out into yarns depends on the actual natural fiber selected. For example, in cotton spinning the short or staple cotton fibers go through a process of being carded on huge roller teeth to detangle the fibers. Then the cotton fibers are re-rolled on top of each other to form slivers. *Slivers* make the cotton take on the appearance of large ropes ready to be spun into yarns. In today's process of spinning fibers or filaments these slivers or rovings are fed into machines with rollers that do the drawing and twisting.

You may recall that in the linen process converting and cleaning linen fiber is known as *hackling*, which is the same as the combing used for cotton fibers. (Refer back to Figure 1–5.)

Making silk yarns begins with the unwinding of raw silk filaments that come directly from the cocoon. Fibers that come from a broken cocoon are referred to as *thrown*. (Refer back to Figure 1–6.)

Other natural fibers such as wool yarns are spun based on the final end product. Wool has two main systems—the woolen and the worsted. The *woolen system* is used for high bulk, less tightly twisted fibers, which are used most often for sweaters. *Worsted* yarns that have been more finely as well as tightly twisted are used in suiting materials. (Refer back to Figure 1–7.)

The spinning method of synthetic fibers such as polyester or rayon depends on the final end use of the yarn. Polyester that used to imitate cotton must be chopped or "cut" first in order to begin to take on the actual appearance of cotton. The process of causing the loose fibers to lay parallel and form a condensed uniform thickness is referred to as *carding*. This untwisted strand is called a sliver. Loose, twisted slivers form rovings. This roving process is also used for blended combinations of cotton and polyesters.

Basic Yarn Spinning Directions

Before describing the most common spinning techniques, it should be noted that all methods of spinning yarns could first be categorized by the direction the fibers are twisted.

There are two main directions of twisting yarn. Yarn twisted to the left is known as an "S" twist. Twisting to the right is known as a "Z" twist. (See Figures 1–13 and 1–14.)

The tightness of the twist will determine the strength and appearance of the yarn. Combinations of these two types of twisting are the cable, which is an "SZS," and "ZSZ," or the Hawser, which produces a firm twisted yarn "SSZ" or "ZZS" combination.

Yarn is determined to be balanced if it has no kinks in it and forms a "U" when untwisted. Unbalanced yarn forms a "figure 8" when untwisted. (See Figure 1–15.)

Common Spinning Techniques

Common spinning techniques are:

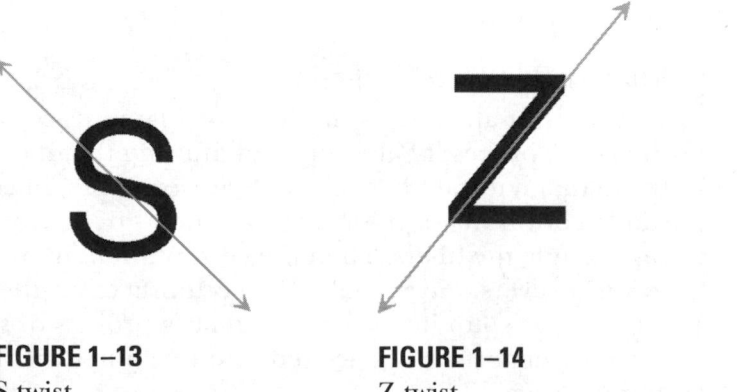

FIGURE 1–13
S twist

FIGURE 1–14
Z twist

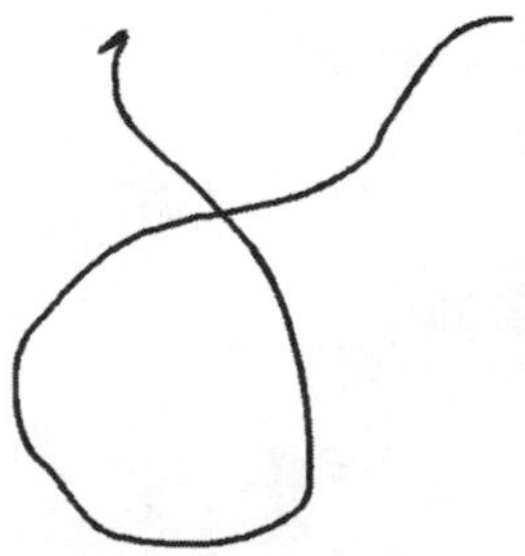

FIGURE 1–15
Figure 8 twist

- Warp spinning
- Ring spinning
- Rotor spinning (Open-End)
- Air-jet spinning

In *warp spinning*, the bundles of a large number of individual fibers are laid parallel, and then wrapped tightly in a spiral fashion. Yarns spun with this technique are considered to be dense and strong. In *ring spinning*, fibers are tightly twisted alone without the use of a wrapper or binder yarn. In *open-end spinning*, the individual fibers are irregular and not necessarily laid in a parallel fashion, but instead are bound by some irregular fiber wraps to secure the main bundle. *Air-jet spinning* uses compressed air to wrap fiber around a core fiber to form yarn.

Types of Yarns

Most yarns fall into four basic categories regardless of fiber content.

- Single
- Ply (folded)
- Cord (including cable and hawser)
- Novelty

A *single yarn* is comprised of fibers that are spun or twisted into a single strand of yarn (Figure 1–16).

Ply yarns are combinations of two or more single yarns, which are further twisted together. For example, if a yarn is labeled as a 3-ply yarn, it will be a combination of three separate yarns twisted together to form one yarn (Figure 1–17).

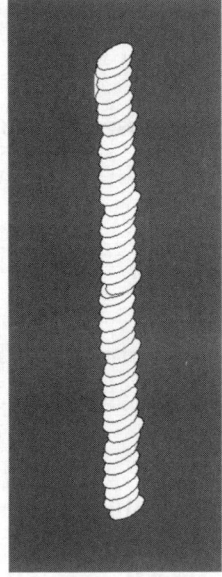

FIGURE 1–16
Single strand of yarn

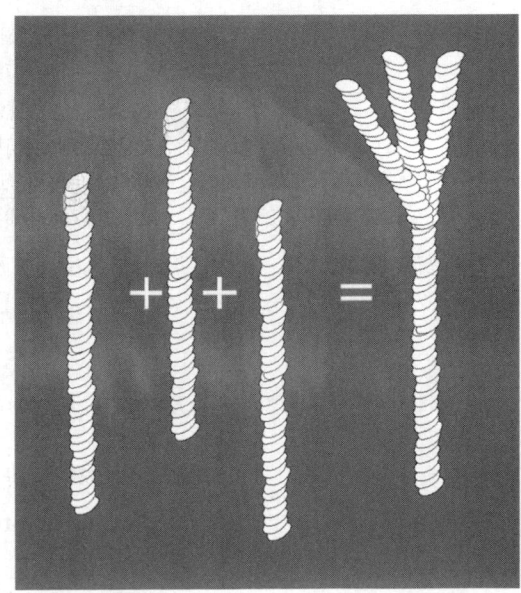

FIGURE 1–17
Ply yarn

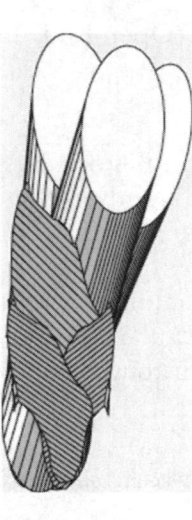 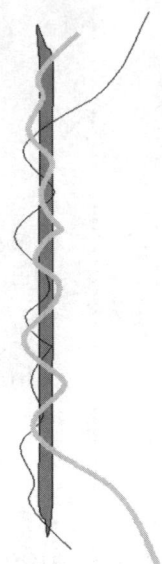

FIGURE 1–18
Cord yarn

FIGURE 1–19
Yarn parts

Cord yarns are strands of yarn that have been twisted in a braidlike manner to make yarn (Figure 1–18).

Novelty yarns are made to showcase an unusual effect, texture, or appearance. There are scores of possibilities as well as dozens of reasons why this is done. Some of the more traditional reasons are aesthetics, performance, prestige, and cost. Typically novelty yarns are comprised of three parts—the *core,* the *effect,* and the *binder.* This is easy to understand by looking at Figure 1–19.

Yarns can be described as being comprised of short or long fibers. By nature, yarns can be a single filament or continuous monofilament comprised of more than two. Yarn can consist of the following:

Staple (short or cut yarn)

Cut-Staple = short, fuzzy, natural fibers of discontinuous (cut) filament fibers

Staple Yarn = aligned, combined, and twisted together to form a single yarn

Conventional Filament

Monofilament = single filament

Continuous Monofilament = continuous smooth strands of two or more monofilaments twisted together

Texturized Filament

Low-twist nonparallel fibers arranged for bulk and surface interest

Adding Texture, Stretch, and Special Effects to Yarns and Yarn Blending

There are several variations on mixing yarns, as well as a wide variety of finishing techniques that are applied to yarns. All of these are based on the final end use of the yarn. Yarns are used for a wide variety of different reasons. The most common end uses for yarns are:

- Threads
- Yarn for weaving and knitting in production of cloth
- Hand knitting and crafts
- Cordage

Adding Texture to Yarns

Texture is added when a yarn has been modified so that both its physical and surface properties have been altered. Not unlike the way we can add texture to human hair, fibers and yarns are given added texture to the hand. This is accomplished by several different methods, including using *mechanical means, chemicals, and/or heat.* Variations of the degree of twist to the fiber or yarns can also cause the yarn to kink or crimp, which will produce different variations of light reflected on the finished fabric hinting at degrees of coloration, shading, and luster.

Adding Finishes

The basis for adding finishing is also determined by end usage of the yarn. Yarn finishes are applied for aesthetic purposes, as well as functional finishes. These changes in the final appearance of the yarn can be done through a variety of different methods including mechanical, heat, or use of chemicals, as well as by fiber blending. Each of these methods will ultimately affect the hand, appearance, and performance of the yarn.

Adding Bulk

One of the most basic goals of adding texture to a yarn is to increase insulation, volume, and loft. Bulk creates air spaces. Bulk occurs naturally in wool. Bulk improves ventilation, giving the garment the ability to breathe, as well as absorbency and other thermal qualities. Bulk can be accomplished by adding crimps, curls, coils, and loops mechanically by twisting or false twisting (such as *knit de knit,* using heat to unravel knitted cloth, which then packages as yarn). Bulk can also be added by applying chemicals, steam, or high-pressured jets of air to the yarn.

Adding Stretch

Similar to bulking methods, yarns can be given a boost in elasticity by several techniques—starting with blending, tightly twisted heat-set yarns that have been untwisted, or by adding a chemical process that will cause the yarns to crimp or pucker.

Blended Yarn Combinations

Yarn blending is also done to modify the physical appearance and/or performance of a yarn. Some of the most common blending, finishing, and texturing methods are to add bulk (coverage), stretch (*movement*), or surface interest *(aesthetic hand)*. Blends are also used to reduce cost (i.e., *poly-cotton blends*), laminated (or covered yarn to improve hand), and to simplify care (*performance such as reduce shrinkage*).

FIGURE 1–20
Examples of novelty, textured, and complex yarns

Adding Special Effects

Special effects are applied to yarns to add surface interest as well as to improve performance. For example, a *metallic* yarn can be flat or round with an outer shell with a novelty core that has been coated with film, lacquer, or laminate. In the case of the metallic yarn, a special coating of the yarns is done to offset the scratchy hand often associated with metallics.

Now, let's take a closer look at several of the more common types of novelty and textured yarns available today. Figures 1–20 and 1–21 provide a visual representation of the most popular yarns used in apparel production.

There are many types of novelty, textured, and complex yarns, such as crepe, bouclé, chenille, corkscrew, loop-curl, spiral, noil, nub, slub, spot and/or knot, seed, thick-thin, metallic, space-dyed, and fasciated yarns. Figure 1–21 illustrates some examples of these yarns.

Measurement Systems for Yarns

Yarn is bought and sold by the pound. The numbering system is based on the unit length and weight. There are two systems—direct and indirect.

Direct Systems

- The Denier System is a direct system that uses metrics to define weight in grams and meters of filament yarn or fiber. The weight per unit measures

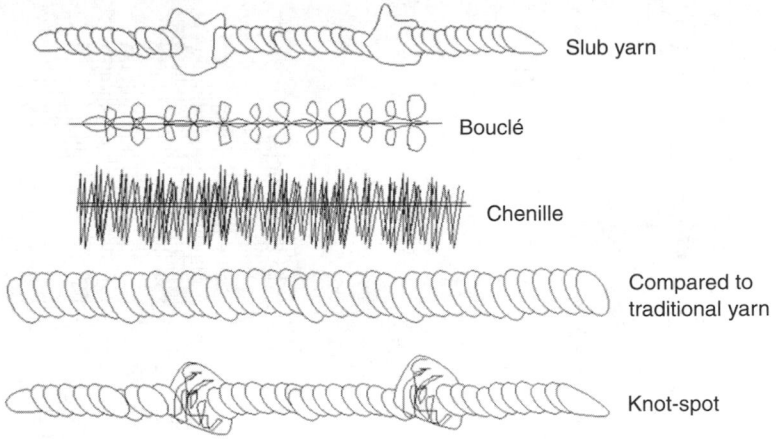

Slub yarn

Bouclé

Chenille

Compared to traditional yarn

Knot-spot

FIGURE 1–21
Novelty yarns

any linear material. For example, in the case of filament, the lower the number, the finer the yarn. This direct numbering system is employed mostly within the United States.

- The Tex System is another direct system that is used primarily outside the United States.

Indirect System

This method of measuring yarn is based on traditional English-American weights and measurements such as feet, pounds, ounces, etc. All indirect systems are based on the number of yards in a pound. In the case of weight, the packaging as well as the fiber content come into consideration. For example, the cotton-sizing system of yarns is called the "yarn count" or the "cotton count." Most spun yarns are considered to be in the cotton system. Using the indirect system, the higher the number, the finer the yarn.

Yarn Packaging

Traditionally yarns are sold in one of the following types of yarn packages (Figure 1–22):

- Spools
- Cones
- Bobbins
- Hanks (skeins)
- Prims

Notes...

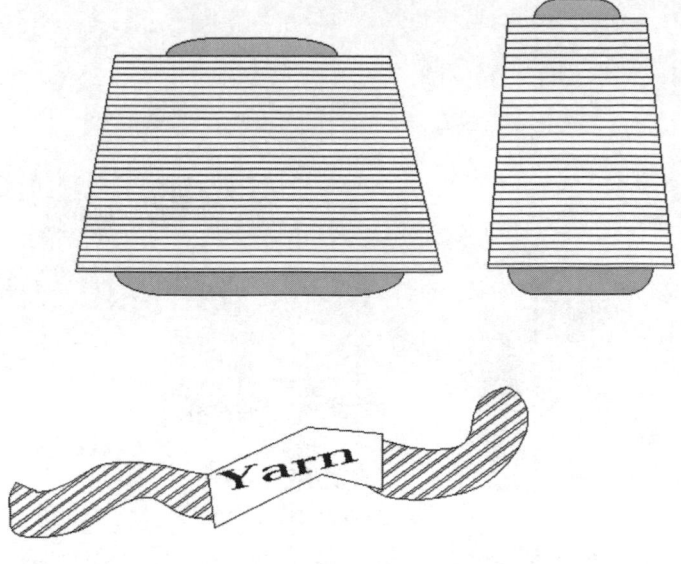

FIGURE 1–22
Packages of yarn

Relevant Yarn Terms

Bobbin: Hollow spool that holds thread or yarn.

Bouclé: Nubby, looped yarn used for woven or knitted fabric.

Bulky Yarn: Yarn that has been given an added texture to increase bulk or fullness without adding additional weight.

Carding: The separating or cleaning process for converting cotton, wool, and some silk and synthetic fibers.

Chenille: The French word for caterpillar used to describe a pile yarn.

Combing: The first step in refining and detangling cotton and synthetic fibers; fibers are combed to lay parallel and the shorter fibers are removed while the longer, smoother fibers are later twisted into yarns.

Cord: A heavy strand of tightly twisted or braided thread or yarn.

Corkscrew: Yarn that has been twisted into forming the shape of a corkscrew and used as a novelty or textured yarn for sweaters or suits.

Crepe: An uneven surface of yarn or fabric that has been produced by heat, chemical, or mechanical means.

Curl: Texturing by a heated blade to add curl to a fiber or filament.

Denier: (1) Unit of measurement of yarn; the lower the number, the finer the fiber or yarn. (2) Indicates the thickness of a synthetic fiber.

Filament: Extremely long continuous silk or synthetic fibers.

Hackle: Similar to the carding process, used to prepare the longer flax fibers for combing.

Knit de knit: Yarn that has been knitted to add crimp, then the knit is unraveled, and the crimped yarn is repackaged.

Metallic: Typically these are yarns made from plastic-coated foil that has been cut into strips to be used as yarns for weaving, knitting, or other purposes.

Mule: Spinning frame invented by Samuel Compton in 1782.

Noil: Knots on the surface of yarn created by the broken cocoon used in the making of silk yarns.

Nub: An irregularity in yarns that produces texture or buildup of fibers on the surface of a yarn.

Ply: Combinations of two or more single yarns that are further twisted together to make a stronger yarn.

Ring: This occurs when fibers are tightly twisted alone without the use of a wrapper or binder yarn.

"S": The direction that yarn is twisted to the left, known as an "S" twist.

Skein: Type of bundling or packaging of yarn used for resale.

Slub: Yarn with a thick-thin appearance produced by tight and then loose twisting of the fibers randomly on the surface of the yarn.

Spindle: An ancient device that is held upright as a slender rotating rod used to spin fibers into yarns.

Spinning Wheel: A wooden device used for centuries to twist fibers together in the preparation of making yarns.

Spool: Usually a symmetrical or conical shaped cardboard, metal, or wood device used to hold yarns or threads.

Spot: Yarn that has been created by accentuating a given area with additional twists of fibers or contrasting colored yarn to call attention to an area of surface interest in a yarn.

Spun: Refers to the twisting fibers or filaments to make yarns.

Staple: Short fibers used in the production of making yarns.

Woolen: Short wool fibers spun into yarns used for sweaters.

Worsted: Longer wool fibers spun and tightly twisted in yarns used typically for wool suiting materials.

"Z": The direction that yarn is twisted to the right, known as a "Z" twist.

Fabric Structure— Understanding How Fabric Is Made

Part One—Woven

Terms to look for:

Balance of Cloth	Herringbone	Satin
Count	Jacquard	Shuttle
Dobby	Leno	Twill
Ends	Loom	Warp
Filling	Picks	Weft
Floats	Pile	

Now that an overview of fibers and yarns has been provided, we turn our attention to Unit #3 on fabric structure. This chapter covers the fundamentals of how most fabric is constructed. This chapter provides insight for the designer to increase comprehension of construction methods in order to more accurately render fabric digitally. It is important to understand and know the subtle nuances between woven or knitted patterns as well as how skillfully rendered woven count and knitted gauge will further the final application of your work. It will change your work from ordinary to extraordinary because of your expertise in this arena. Understanding how a fabric is made is every bit as important as knowing what a fabric is made from. The construction of cloth will determine how a fabric is used and how it should be cared for, and most importantly what tools you will need to accurately render it by using Adobe Photoshop.

Fabric structure is most commonly divided into three categories—*woven, knits,* or *other.* The majority of cloth being made today is woven cloth.

Woven Cloth

The most widely used method of making fabric has always been weaving. Regardless of culture, woven fabric has been the foundation of making cloth for thousands of years. The Latin word *textile* simply means to weave. The most widely accepted definition for *weaving* is fabric that is formed by two yarns that *interlace* at right angles.

Many ancient writings include a significant amount of references to weaving and the making of cloth. For example, in the Middle Eastern writings[1] of Solomon, a

---

[1] Prov. 31: 10–31 NKJ

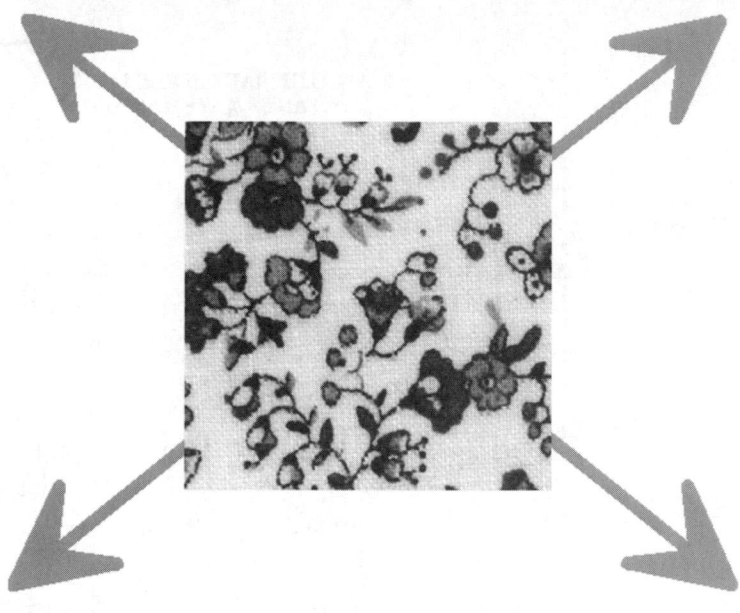

FIGURE 2–1
Bias

woman who could spin, weave, and dye her own fabric was considered to be an ideal wife.

In some Latin American cultures one female deity was a weaver. Weavers were so highly regarded that weaving instruments were given to females at birth and then buried with the woman upon her death![2]

It is fairly easy to recognize a piece of woven fabric; typically a woven fabric only "stretches" on the *bias*. This means that the fabric will have its "give" on the diagonal, the movement is felt when pulling from corner to corner (Figure 2–1).

Traditionally, all weaving is done on a device called a *loom*. Almost every culture has its own version of a loom. Most looms began as simple portable frames; for example, in the culture of South America they used a harness-like devise known as a backstrap loom (Figure 2–2). Their European or North American counterpart used a conventional or traditional 4-harness, freestanding (floor) version of a loom (Figures 2–3 and 2–4). Even traditional basket weaving uses the same type of construction.

Fabric is comprised of a series of vertical yarns and *interlaced horizontal yarns.* Yarns placed on the loom in a vertical fashion are called the *warp* or *end yarns* (Figure 2–5). Think of it this way, the term *warp* ends in the letter "**p**," so just remember that the warp are the up and down yarns!

The rows of weft yarns are transported or "*laced*" across the warp yarns horizontally by using a device called a *shuttle* (Figure 2–6). These series of horizontal yarns are referred to as the *filling, picks,* or *weft yarns.* These are also very easy to remember because they fill in and are transported from w**eft** to w**ight**!!!! Sorry for the bad joke but it *will* really help you remember the difference! (See Figure 2–7.)

---

[2] Dr. Patricia Anawart.

**THE BACKSTRAP LOOM:
PARTS & TOOLS USED:**

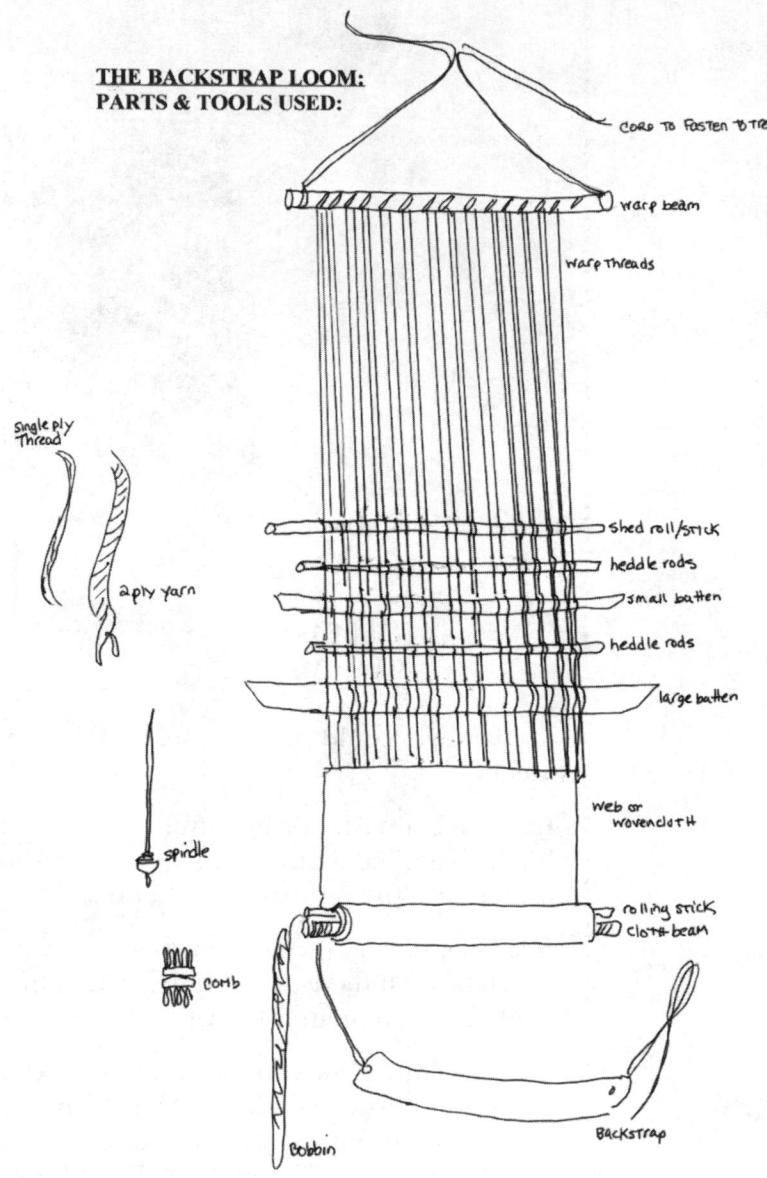

cord to fasten to tree

warp beam

warp threads

single ply thread

2 ply yarn

shed roll/stick

heddle rods

small batten

heddle rods

large batten

web or woven cloth

spindle

rolling stick
cloth beam

comb

Bobbin

Backstrap

FIGURE 2–2
Backstrap loom

FIGURE 2–3
Example of floor loom
(Photo courtesy of Schacht Spindle Co., Inc.)

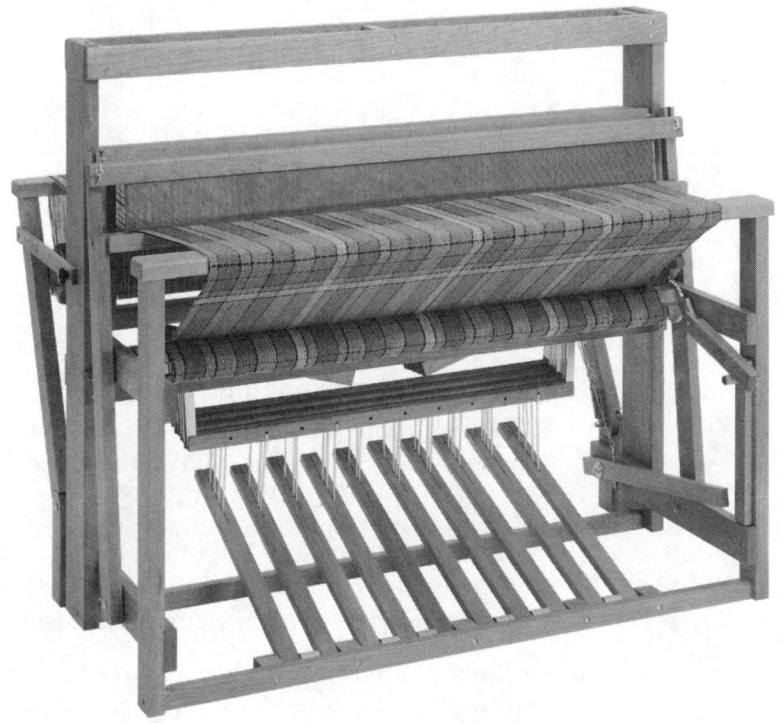

FIGURE 2–4
Example of standard loom
(Photo courtesy of Schacht Spindle Co., Inc.)

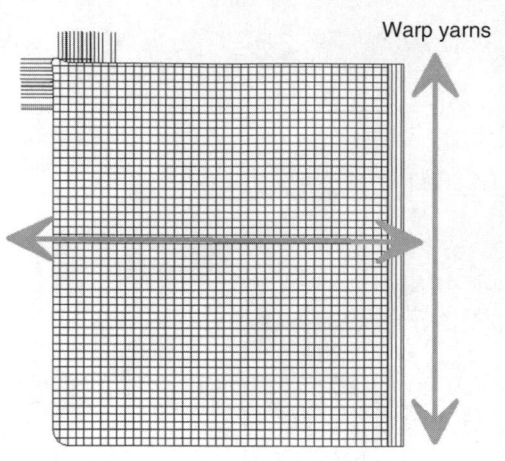

FIGURE 2–5
Warp yarns

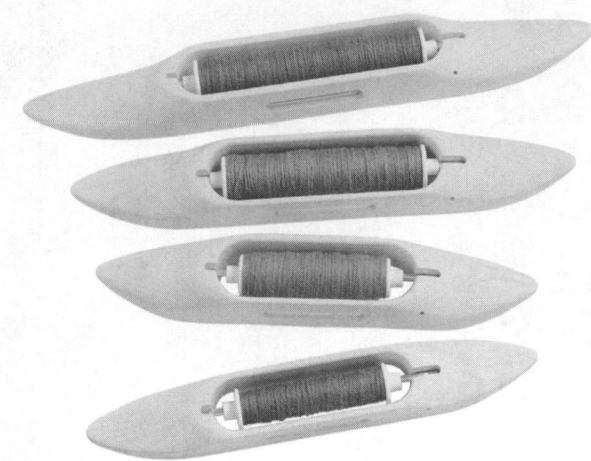

FIGURE 2–6
Shuttles
(Photo courtesy of Schacht Spindle Co., Inc.)

Notes...

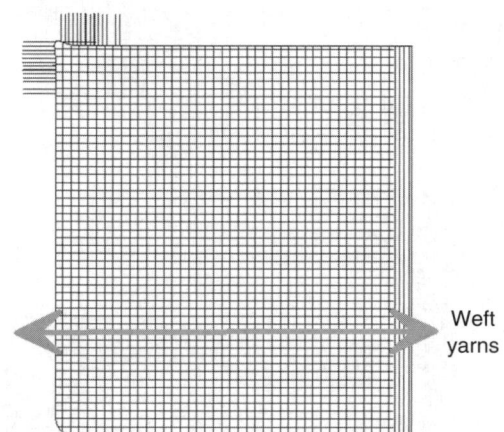

FIGURE 2–7
Weft yarns

Basic Steps in Weaving

Even with today's industrial looms nothing has changed from the foundation of warp and weft yarns. We still use the same four basic steps in weaving—shedding, pickings, beating, and takeoff.

Woven cloth is constructed on a loom. It uses a series of yarns that first are placed vertically on the loom (warp) (Figure 2–8) and then horizontal yarns (weft or filling) are inserted in a back and forth fashion.

In the making of woven fabric, a device known as a *reed*, which is a comb-like bar with metal prongs or dents, is used to properly align the yarns—a process known as *beating* or *battening*.

Today most 2- or 4-harness handlooms still require the use of a shuttle. These handlooms are considered to be *nonautomatic* or *hand-replenished*. On the other hand, today's industrial looms are considered to be *replenished*.

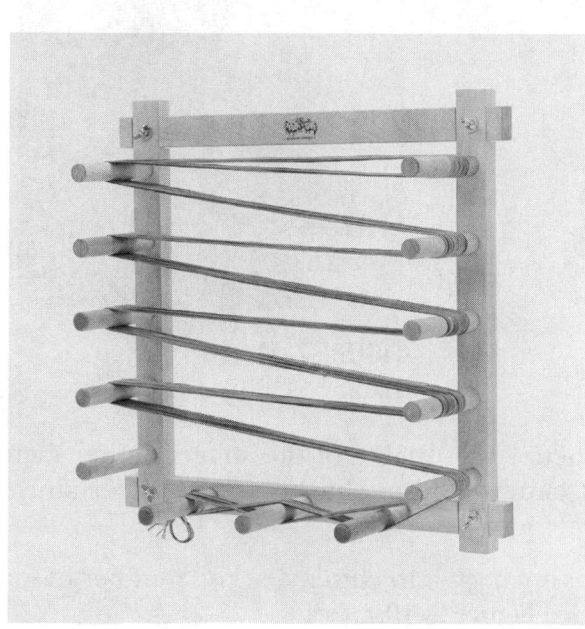

FIGURE 2–8
Preparing the yarn for the warp

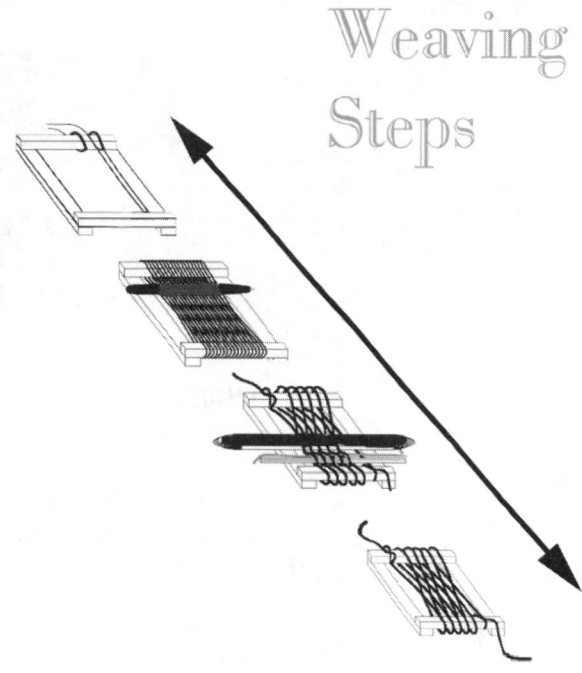

FIGURE 2–9
Weaving steps

Notes...

There are three types of shuttleless replenishment methods: *rapier* (rigid rods or flexible steel tapes that transport yarn), *dummy* (a projectile that contains no weft yarn but passes through and leaves a trail of weft yarn behind it), and the *air-* or *water-jet* (propels the weft yarn through the shed).

The next step in the weaving process is the movement of the heddles. *Heddles* are long needle-like metal rods that are attached to the top and bottom of the harness. A hole known as an eye is in the middle of each heddle and is used to secure the yarn to the loom. When the harness is raised, the warp yarns are strung. These heddles are raised up and down to facilitate a given pattern to be created by the shuttle carrying the weft yarns. Most industrial looms can be considered to be *shuttleless,* because the weft yarns are frequently transported crosswise by jets of air or water. The raising and lowering is called *shedding.*

The final step in the weaving process is the letting off of the ends from the beam in the back of the loom by taking up the finished fabric on the roller from the front of the loom. (See Figure 2–9.)

Woven cloth is described by weight in ounces, by thread count, by tactile surface quality, and by end use. The surface quality is frequently a direct result of the yarns that are used or the pattern of the weave. *Count* refers to the exact number of weft and warp yarns in an inch of cloth. Frequently the term count is used in sheeting or domestic fabrics. Sheets are often sold and marketed as being either 180, 200, or 250 count. Obviously, the higher the number, the

FIGURE 2–10
Pick glass

FIGURE 2–11
Balanced cloth

tighter the weave, and the better the quality of the sheets. Other factors are considered in the quality of better bedding, but the count is certainly one of the most important.

Designers use a tool known as a *pick glass* to better view the number of warp and weft threads that intersect. (See Figure 2–10.)

Cloth with a similar *count* or number of warp threads and weft threads intersecting one another within 10 is said to be a *balanced cloth*. An example of a piece of balanced cloth is gingham. (See Figure 2–11.)

Woven Patterns

Woven patterns fall into two main categories—a *basic weave* or a *complex or fancy weave*. The basic woven patterns are:

1. Plain (Tabby)
   a. Basket
   b. Rib

2. Twill
   a. Right
   b. Left
   c. Herringbone

3. Satin

Plain Weaves

The most basic pattern is a *plain* (*tabby*) weave. The yarns used to form this simple pattern are typically considered to be a *1 + 1*, or the weft yarn transverses the loom in a horizontal interlacing of *(1) yarn over, (1) yarn under* to form its design pattern. (See Figure 2–12.) This cloth is most widely used for adding prints due to its stability and limited distortion of the final print.

There are several variations of the plain weave. The first is known as a *basket weave*. Basket weaves are formed by a *2 + 2* pattern of weft yarns that interlace *(2) over and (2) under*. There are several other variations including *1 + 2, 2 + 2,* or *4 + 4* combinations. This pattern is a flat design, which is considered to be

FIGURE 2–12
Plain weave

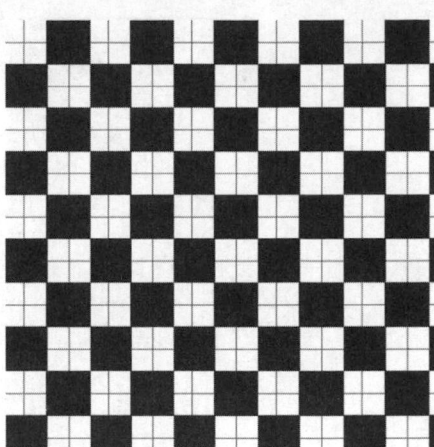

FIGURE 2–13
Basket weave

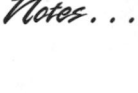 *Notes...*

FIGURE 2–14
Rib weave

porous in nature, and it can cause the fabric in some cases to easily snag, to lose its shape, to wrinkle, or to even cause the fabric to shrink. (See Figure 2–13.)

The next variation is the *rib* weave. (See Figure 2–14.) A rib weave is easily recognizable by both eye and touch. The rib weave has a thicker or novelty filling yarn than the weft yarn. This causes the filling yarn to have a slightly raised appearance and hand even though the construction is still a basic *1 + 1 pattern*. Several examples of rib weaves with a distinctive crosswise rib that is discerned by the touch are most taffetas, grosgrain, poplins, ottoman silks, and faille fabrics. Vertical ribs can be found in most seersucker fabrics.

Twill Weaves

The next basic weave is a *twill* weave. A twill weave consists of yarns that form a distinctive "right" or "left" pattern design. A common variation of a twill weave is a *herringbone,* known for a combination of "right *and* left" patterns. (See Figure 2–15.)

Twill weaves are also described by the *degree* or *steep of the angle* in which the pattern takes shape. (See Figure 2–16.) Several examples of twill weave fabrics are denim, gabardine, and houndstooth (Figure 2–17).

Satin Weave

The last basic weave is a *satin* weave. Satin weaves are formed when the "weft" yarns *float* across the face of the fabric in intervals. These floats create a "*satiny*" appearance on the surface of the fabric. Satin weaving is used to enhance the natural reflection or shine of the filament yarn used to make the satin fabric. (See Figure 2–18.) Satin weaves have several variations, which include filling-faced, warp-faced, and crepe-backed. Although the fabric's primary distinction is the shiny surface created by floats left on the surface, the actual weave or pattern can still be constructed using either a plain or twill pattern. Although the face of the fabric will display a distinctive satin, the reverse will reveal the pattern combination with which the cloth was woven.

Other Woven Variations

There are several other variations of woven cloth. For example, *double cloth* is produced by two sets of filling yarns that are binding. This fabric is often used for in-

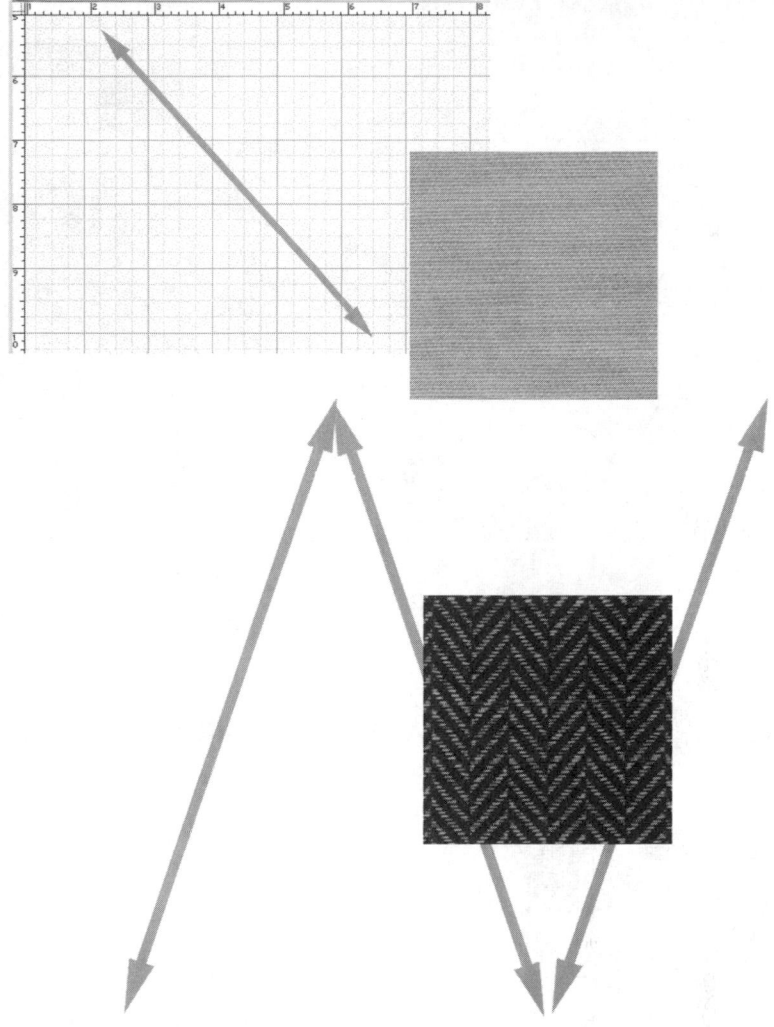

FIGURE 2–15
Twill and herringbone

creased insulation and warmth. The main quality of this fabric is that it cannot be separated into two distinct pieces of cloth. *Double-faced cloth* also uses additional yarns for its construction; however, unlike double cloth, double-faced cloth can be separated into two distinct fabrics.

Fancy Woven Patterns

The categories of fancy woven patterns include:

1. Pile

2. Dobby

3. Jacquard

4. Leno

5. Swivel

6. Lappet

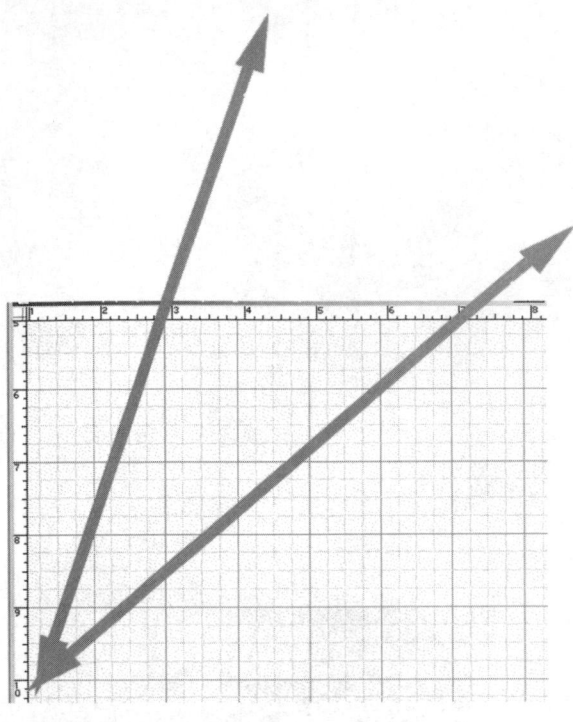

FIGURE 2–16
Degree

FIGURE 2–17
Examples of twill

FIGURE 2–18
Satin

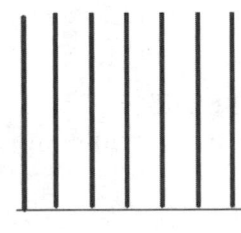 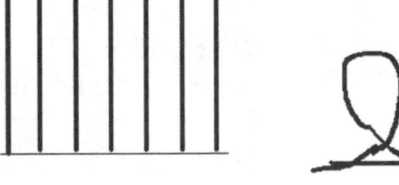

FIGURE 2–19
Cut and uncut loops

 *Notes...*

Pile weaves are formed by leaving "loops" of yarn or thread on the surface or face of the fabric. The loops or floats can be "cut" as in a velvet or left "uncut" as in a terry cloth. (See Figure 2–19.)

A *dobby* weave is frequently described as a small geometric repeat pattern, such as a "diamond-like design," formed by yarns on the surface of the fabric. Examples of a dobby weave are bird's-eye and piqué. (See Figure 2–20.)

It is important to point out that knitted fabric has its own version of *piqué*. Don't confuse a piqué knit with a woven piqué. These fabrics are made from two very different methods of construction. (See Figure 2–21.) Remember a woven piqué will only stretch on the bias. What these fabrics may share in

FIGURE 2–20
Dobby weave

FIGURE 2–21
Woven piqué and piqué knit

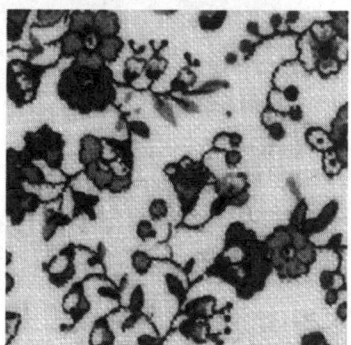

FIGURE 2–22
Floral jacquard vs. floral print

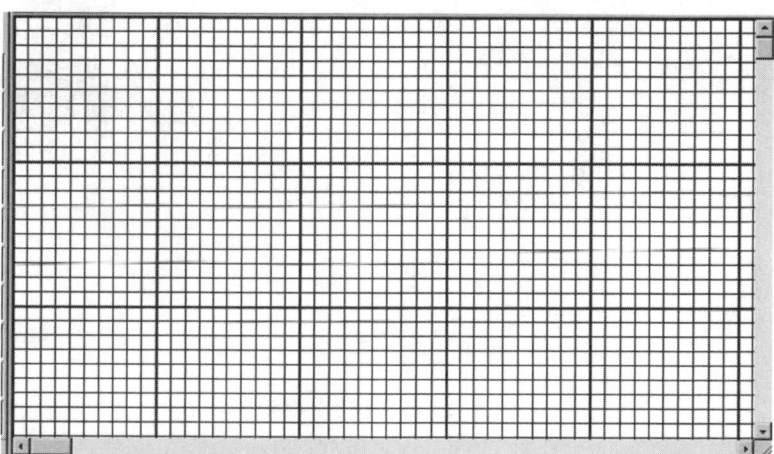

FIGURE 2–23
Digital graph
(Courtesy of Pointcarré)

Notes...

common is a geometric (often a diamond-like texture) pattern formed on the surface of the cloth.

A woven *jacquard* is a complex pattern that is formed during the weaving process and requires a special type of loom (Figure 2–22). In the early nineteenth century, Joseph Marie Jacquard developed a programmable punch-card system of "zeros and ones" in the pattern making for the woven fabric for which his name has been associated. Jacquard was a forerunner in the development and understanding of the fundamental principles (0–1) used in computers.

The jacquard looms were originally adapted as a primary form of computer input. Therefore, this system is widely recognized today by the computer world. Originally most woven patterns were designed on graph or point papers. Today the designs are created digitally on a simulated graph. (See Figure 2–23.)

For example, if the cloth has a floral pattern, it is frequently a design printed on a plain weave fabric. However, in a woven jacquard, the floral pattern is woven *into* the cloth. The result is that anyone who handles a woven jacquard fabric should be able to *feel* as well as see the texture of the design on the surface of the fabric.

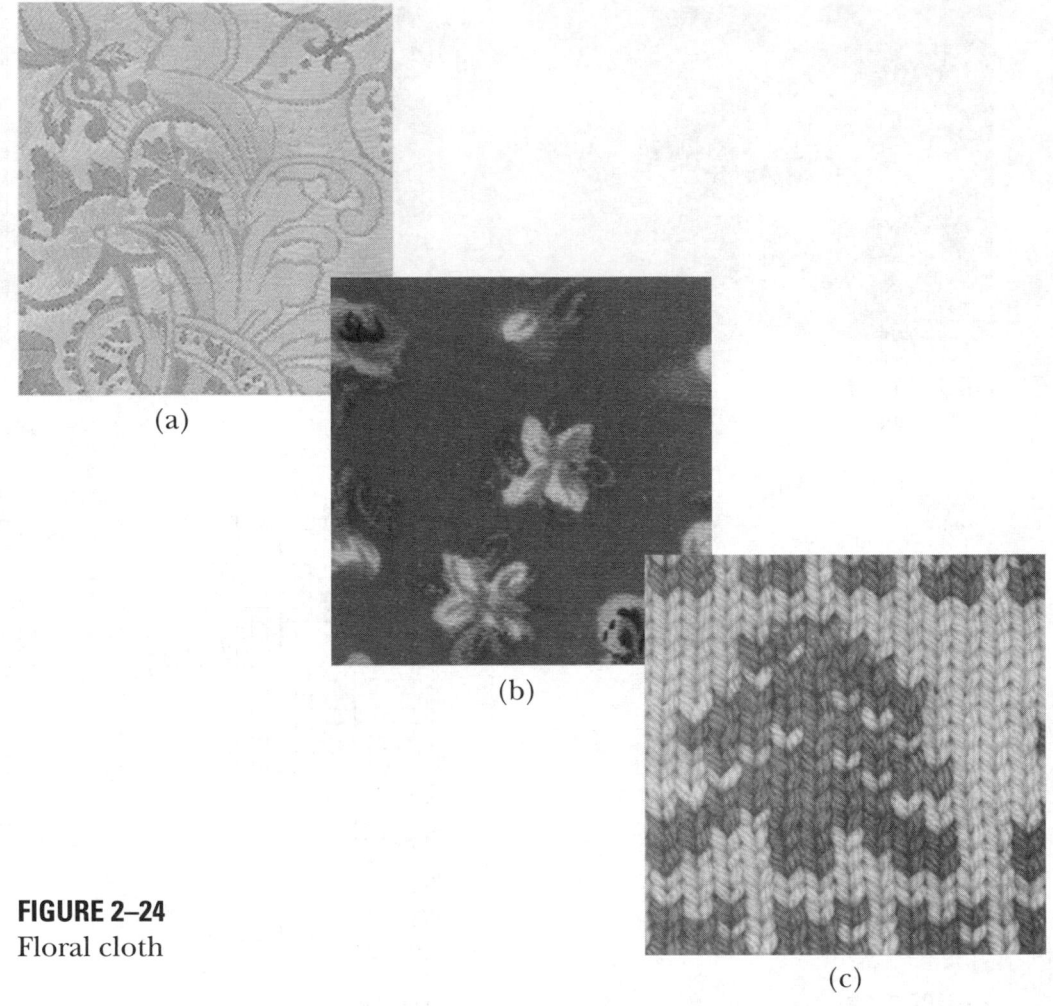

FIGURE 2–24
Floral cloth

(a)

(b)

(c)

(See Figure 2–24, which shows the differences between (a) a print, (b) a knit jacquard, and (c) a woven jacquard.)

Jacquard weaves have several variations:

- *Brocade* is made of contrasting colors in the background with no visible floats.

- *Tapestry* is comprised of multiple colors of yarns that intersect to form scenes portraying figures, flora, and/or fauna.

- *Damask* is a reversible jacquard, comprised of contrasting colors and threads with matt and glossy appearance.

- *Matelassé* has a distinctive puckered, blistered, or quilted surface design.

- A tone-on-tone lightweight *jacquard* is frequently found in women's blouses or in sleepwear and lingerie.

Later in this chapter, you will encounter the term jacquard again in the creation of knitted fabrics. The difference between the two fabrics is the construction method. However, both woven and knitted jacquards are typically considered to be complex patterns.

A *leno* weave is characterized by the appearance of a figure 8 in the pattern. This pattern is also called a *doup* weave because it requires the use of a *doup attachment* to form the pattern in the fabric. The warp yarns are used to form crosswise pairs. These pairs are then held together to avoid a slipping of the pattern. This fabric will result in a light, airy appearance.

The *swivel* weave uses extra weft yarns, which are carried across the loom to form "groups" of warp yarns that are later clipped. Swivel weave forms spots on the surface of the fabric.

In the *lappet* pattern, which is not a very common pattern, you will find the extra yarns used in a warp direction. The yarns are fastened or knotted to the base fabric and then cut to form the appearance of an eyelash effect.

Several additional variations include a *spot* or *clipped* weave, which is comprised of a clipped decorative pattern done in intervals across the entire width and length of the fabric. *Uncut floats* between the patterns, which are not cut, form the *spot*, creating weaves or uncut dot weaves. (See Figure 2–25.)

After studying the most common types of woven patterns, you should now understand that there is more significance to a piece of cloth than just the pattern that was implemented. The selection of the fibers *and* the yarns are as critical as the selection of the woven pattern.

Let's closely examine an example of a simple plain weave fabric—lamé. In Figure 2–26, you can clearly see that lamé requires the use of more warp yarns. Typically the warp yarns selected are a nylon filament, which is used to add stability to the fabric. This will prevent slippage of the slippery weft metallic (lamé) filling yarns

FIGURE 2–25
Spot or clipped weave

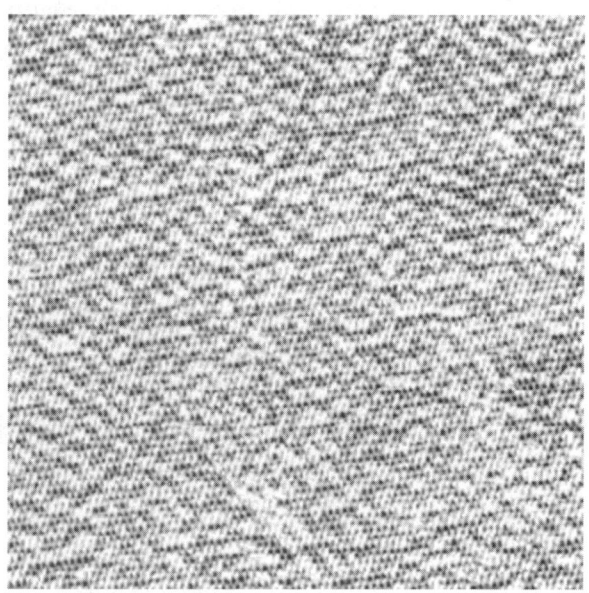

FIGURE 2–26
Lamé

that are used. This is one of many examples of blending and problem solving that is done by a designer. As a designer you will be responsible for making the garment not only appealing but serviceable as well.

Perhaps you are beginning to notice that while studying the textile section of this book you are learning to train your eye. Being able to recognize and make distinctions between the available fibers and fabrics is an immeasurable portion of a fashion designer's responsibility.

Although we live in a time with an overwhelming number of choices, knowing the basics is really the key to good design. A solid textile foundation will be useful when you are ready to work on computer-aided designing. Taking the time to study and handle fabrics, as well as learning to discern the subtle differences and similarities between fabrics will be very useful when you are ready to render them digitally.

The most common pattern in woven cloth is a plain weave. Surprisingly, even if you can design almost anything you want, notice that it is the basics that are used over and over. Aren't you glad you don't have to overdesign or reinvent the wheel even when it comes to creating woven patterns? Designers not only create, they problem solve—so a good foundation of textiles will help you go a long way!

You will soon discover that creating any woven fabric on the computer utilizes the same design concepts and drawing tools used in most vector-or raster-based programs. Industrial-based software/systems have integrated additional tools and options to enhance a woven design so that the design is *translatable* for transmuting the computer-generated pattern to the loom used in the actual production of cloth.

As you continue to study fabrics more closely, you may notice that sometimes the best-kept secret is simplicity, such as subtle selection of fibers, yarn weight, textures, or colors. Another way we blend fibers is through weaving creatively and choosing unusual blends of fibers for the warp and weft yarns.

One of the fastest ways to differentiate cloth construction is through comparing and contrasting. In the Fabric Glossary Section of your CD, you will find a fabric worksheet designed to help you discern and comprehend the different types of weaves.

Go to CD> Goodie Folder> Chapter 2> Woven worksheet

Relevant Weaving Terms

Balance of Cloth: A woven fabric in which the number of warp and weft threads that intersect within a given area is equal within 10.

Bias: The diagonal stretch or give on a piece of woven fabric.

Chevron: A twill weave pattern with a "zigzag" appearance similar to a herringbone pattern.

Chino: A firmly woven fabric, typically trousers, made from cotton.

Chintz: A semigloss fabric.

Corduroy: A soft, raised lengthwise pile rib woven fabric.

Count: The number of warp and weft threads that intersect within a given area (usually one inch). For example, sheets may be sold according to count such as 180, 200, or 250. Therefore, the higher number is usually given to indicate a higher quality of the weave.

Denim: A popular, durable twill weave fabric; often synonymous with jeans.

Dobby: A woven pattern with the appearance of a small geometric repeat pattern.

Ends: Another name for the warp yarns.

Ethnic: Also folk; a type of design or inspiration from a traditional national or regional costume.

Fabrication: How a design is made (knit, woven, other) and whether a design is made from natural or synthetic fibers.

Filling: Another name for the weft yarns.

Flannel: This fabric was originally made from wool and has come to be known as a brushed fabric, which can also be made from cotton or synthetic fibers. The term flannelette was given to a flannel-look fabric made from cotton.

Float: These are the weft yarns intentionally left on the surface face of a piece of woven cloth.

Floral: A repeat pattern of flora and fauna. Floral patterns may also be woven into a jacquard fabric.

Greige Goods: Unbleached or unfinished fabric without a finishing treatment. An example is muslin.

Herringbone: A twill weave pattern with a distinctive right and left pattern.

Jacquard: A complex weave that is created on a loom of the same name. This weave has the pattern constructed into the fabric. The design is a texture that can be seen as well as "felt."

Lappet: This fancy weave is constructed of warp yarns that form an "eyelash effect" on the surface of the fabric.

Leno: This fancy weave has the appearance of a figure 8 within the pattern.

Loom: A device used in the making of woven cloth.

Loop: Also known as a "pick glass," or a magnifier used in the inspection of a piece of woven cloth.

Muslin: A fabric that is generally a plain weave. This fabric is typically considered a greige good made from cotton.

Picks: This term is another name for the filling or weft yarns used in the construction of woven fabric.

Pile: This woven pattern is made from "loops" on the surface of the weave that are intentionally left *cut or uncut*.

Plaid: A checked pattern that is formed by the colored warp and weft yarns in a weave that can be either a plain or twill weave.

Plain: The most basic woven pattern that is formed by a 1 + 1 or 2 + 2 pattern of warp and weft yarns.

Point Paper: Typically a graph paper used in the plotting of a woven pattern. The size of the paper in terms of the number of blocks or series of grids to the inch may vary.

Satin: A basic weave formed by floats that are left in intervals on the face surface of a fabric.

Selvage: The right edge of the fabric made from warp-wise finished edges or "self-edges."

Shuttle: This device moves the warp yarns across the weft yarns in the making of woven fabric. The standard, historical type of wooden shuttle as well as more traditional "shuttleless" versions, such as "air-jet" and "water-jet," "propel" the threads.

Suiting: Fabrics associated with the construction of suits for men and women. They can be categorized as a bottom or tropical weight fabric typically of worsted wool.

Swivel: This fancy weave is made from "groups" of warp yarns that are later clipped in woven cloth.

Tabby: Another name for a plain weave.

Textile: Fabric, cloth, goods, and/or stuff; but not findings. This term is Latin for "to weave."

Thread Count: (See Count)

Twill: A basic weave with a distinctive right-or left-angled pattern.

Warp: The vertical yarns placed on the loom in woven fabrics.

Weaving: The interlacing of two yarns at right angles to make fabric.

Weft: The filling or horizontal yarns used in the making of woven fabric.

Part Two—Knits

Terms to look for:

Cable	Float	Jacquard
Circular	Full Fashioned	Jersey
Courses	Gauge	Knitting
Cut	Grin Thru	Pointelle
Double Knit	Intarsia	Purl

Racking akacible	Tuck	Weft Knit
Single	Wales	
Tricot (French to Knit)	Warp Knit	

Knits are more popular today than ever before. Knits have become synonymous with comfort and stretch. Unfortunately, until recently very few young people actually knew how to knit. This however is beginning to change. In a recent article from the Associated Press,[3] columnist Miranda Leitsinger comments that celebrities such as Julia Roberts and Daryl Hannah have been spotted knitting on the set, which has "sparked a resurgence of interest in the craft." The same article noted stats from the Craft and Yarn Council of America stating that "knitters and crocheters under age 35 have soared from 3 percent nationwide in 1998 to 15 percent in 2000." Young people today are rediscovering the joys as well as the therapeutic qualities of knitting. In fact hand knitting is enjoying a 400 percent increase! Regardless whether you knit or don't knit, it is essential that you possess a basic understanding of how knits are made or how a knit differs from a woven. Distinguishing a knit from a woven and the different patterns used in knits will be very helpful when you are asked to create these designs digitally on the computer.

Let's begin with the basics of how you can recognize and distinguish a knit from a woven. It is very simple to determine—"Where is the stretch?" Typically, woven fabrics only stretch on the bias, but knits usually stretch in a third direction—either side-to-side or top-to-bottom. (See Figure 2–27.)

Another way to distinguish between knits and woven cloth—"Knits run. Wovens fray." (See figure 2–28.) Now anyone who is wondering about all the different exceptions to such a broad statement, *relax*! This is merely presented as a *general statement* of how these two methods of fabric construction *usually* differ.

Officially, knitting is defined as the "*interloping*" of yarns at right angles. Weaving is referred to as the "*interlacing*" of yarns.

According to most encyclopedias,[4] knitting was originally done by hand knitters who used a pair or a series of needles and yarn, probably beginning with nomads in the Arabian Desert around 100 B.C. (See Figure 2–29.)

Then during the Middle Ages knitting spread throughout the Middle East and Egypt through Europe where it became a thriving trade of knitting guilds, especially in Italy and France. The first attempt to mechanize the knitting method of making cloth was the invention of the frame-knitting machine[5] in 1589.

---

[3] Miranda Leitsinger, Associated Press, "Knitting soothes young nerves," *Sun Sentinel*, April 2, 2001.

[4] "Textile," *Encyclopaedia Britannica* 2003. Encyclopaedia Britannica Premium Service, 22 Sep, 2003 http://www.britannica.com/eb/article?eu=115281[rtgt] (22 September 2003).

[5] Ibid.

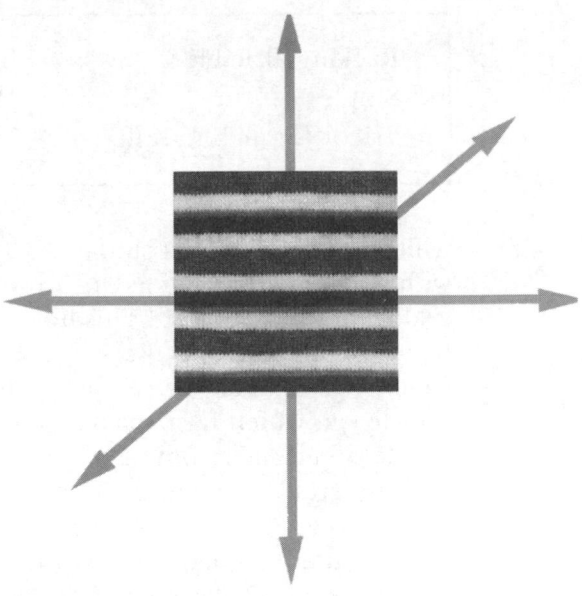

FIGURE 2–27
Stretch in knits

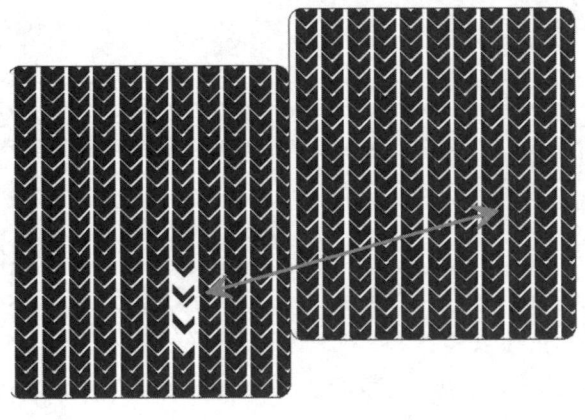

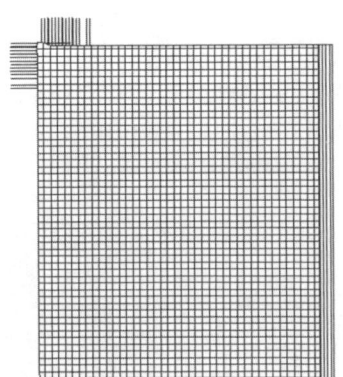

FIGURE 2–28
Knits run. Wovens fray.

FIGURE 2–29
Hand knitting

Some of the names for the machines that are used for creating knitted fabric are *frame, flat bed,* and *circular machines.* (See Figure 2–30.)

Most knitting machines consist of the *bed,* the *needles,* the *sinker post,* and the *threader.*

Today there are two basic machines that make knitted fabric—the *weft* knitting machine and the *warp* knitting machine. *Weft knits* are constructed of loops or stitches and rows that are made *sequentially. Warp knits* are constructed of several yarns that loop in a simultaneous fashion. The weft knit will appear to be vertical rows of "v's" while most warp knits will appear to be horizontal rows of "v's." (See Figure 2–31.)

Let's take a closer look at each type of knit, starting with the most common—weft knits.

FIGURE 2–30
Frame-Knitting Machines
(Courtesy of Stoll Knitting Machines)

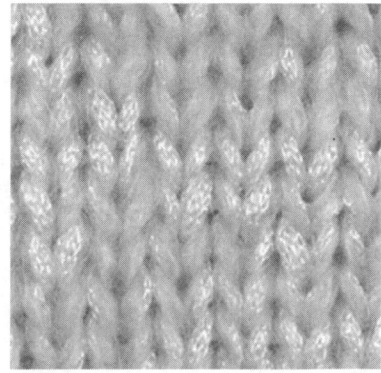

FIGURE 2–31
Weft knit

Weft Knitting

Originally knitting was done by hand and knitted fabric was made by two or more needles looping yarn to form *stitches*. Stitches are the building blocks of all knitted fabric. Knits are formed stitch by stitch and row upon row. Machine-made stitches are created on a bed of needles, each knitting independently from one another, but the fabric is still built row by row.

The two basic types of stitches for weft knits are either a *knit* (Figure 2–32) or a *purl* (Figure 2–33). When these stitches are knitted sequentially, the *horizontal rows*

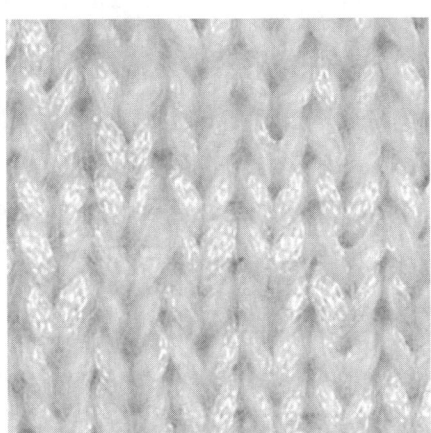

FIGURE 2–32
Knit

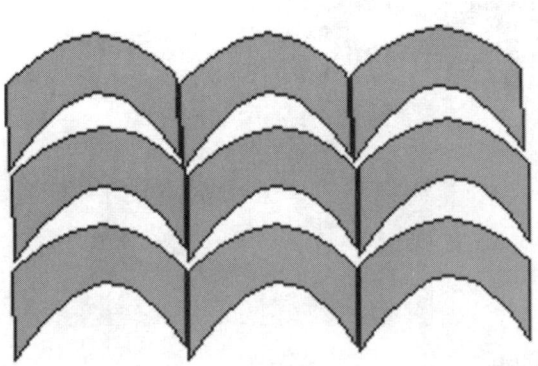

FIGURE 2–33
Purl

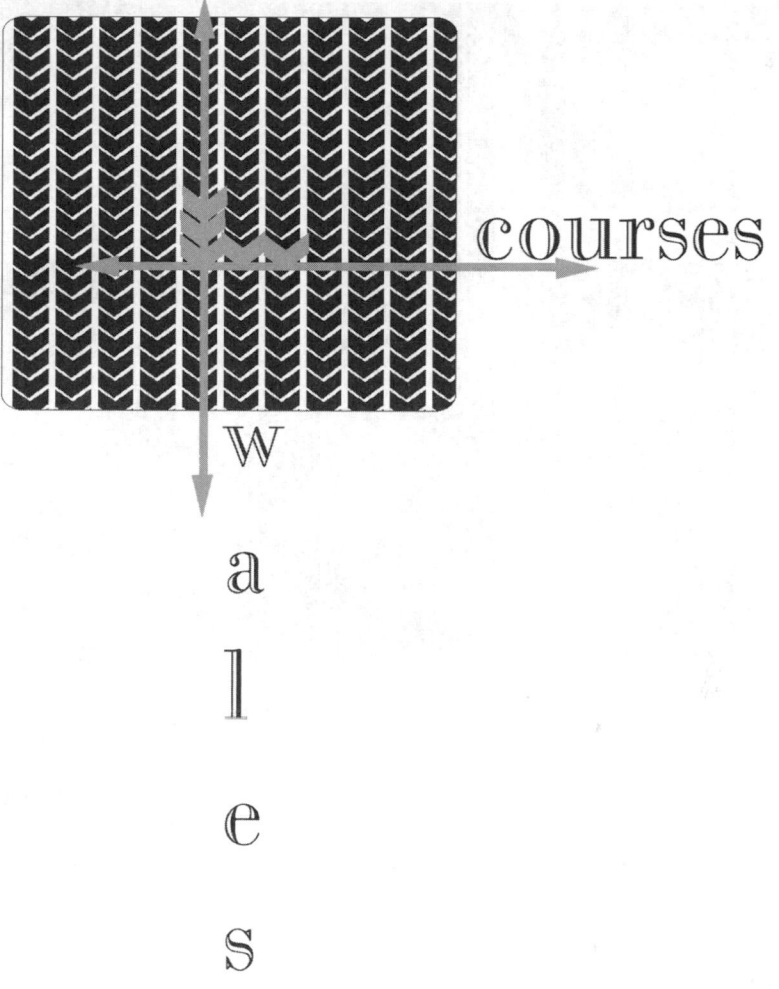

courses

wales

FIGURE 2–34
Courses and wales

will look like rows of the letter "v." These horizontal rows are known as *courses* and the *vertical columns* of rows that look like ladders of the letter "v" are known as *wales* (Figure 2–34.)

A distinguishing characteristic of weft knits is that they easily "run" or unravel when the fabric is cut or snagged. Although they offer plenty of movement and flexibility, weft knits can have limited hanger appeal and tend to sag unless they are properly laundered or stored.

Hand knits are usually made with two needles to form flat panels or pieces of cloth. If tubular knits are needed, sewing the seams together joins the fabric. In order to knit circular fabric without seams, more than two needles are required. Machines now can make circular fabric by using the double-facing beds on a circular knitting machine. The obvious advantages of the machine are speed, quality, and fabric weight. Machine knits can be made in a much finer and tighter weight than a hand knit.

The weight or tightness of the knitted stitches to one another is measured. This measurement of the horizontal and vertical rows of stitches in relationship to one

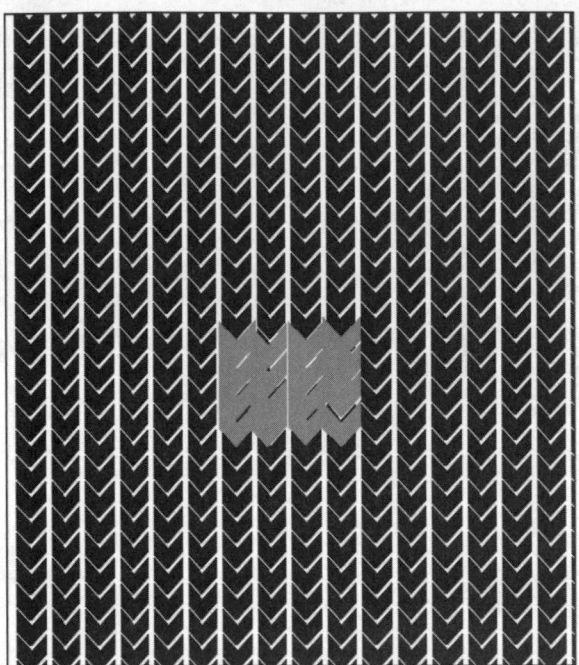

FIGURE 2–35
Cut

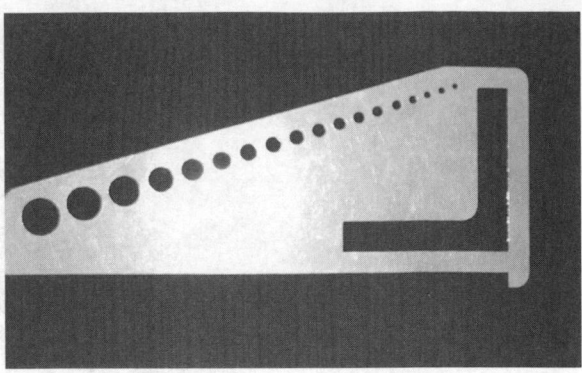

FIGURE 2–36
Gauge

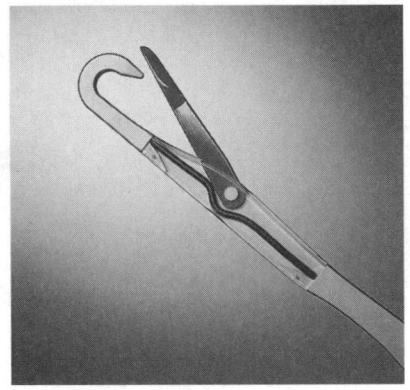

FIGURE 2–37
Latch needle

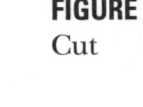

Notes . . .

another is known as the *gauge* of the knits. The tightness of the knit quality, the amount of elasticity in the fibers used, and the stitch pattern selected are also measured in *count* or *gauge*. For example, a hand-knit sweater may be said to be 5 gauge (indicates the number of stitches within a set area) in contrast to a higher number such as an 80 gauge (the gauge used in the making of hosiery).

The term *cut* refers to the number of actual needles per inch used in the construction of the knit. Both cut and gauge will determine the appearance and performance of the knit including the amount of give or resiliency. (See Figures 2–35 and 2–36.) For example, you can have a cut of five stitches horizontally and seven rows vertically.

Even though woven fabric only stretches on the bias, weft knits will stretch on the bias *and* from side to side as well as top to bottom. Hand knits must be bound off or they can easily unravel, while woven fabric will fray on the ends instead. Hand knits are less stable than woven fabric. This means that knits can sag, bag, and snag more readily than woven fabric. In addition, most knits require more care in handling and storage and often have far less hanger appeal than woven goods.

The processes of making a hand knit and a machine weft knit are very similar. In the production of machine-made knit two types of needles are used—the *bearded spring needle* or the *latch needle*. (Figure 2–37.) The common *latch or self-acting needle* can knit a variety of weights used in weft knits.

Types of Weft Knit Manufacturers

Weft knits are generally made by two types of knitwear manufacturers. The first type of knitwear manufacturer is known as a *direct knitter*. Direct knit manufacturers make the fabric *and* sell the finished knitted product.

The second type of knitwear manufacturer, called a *contract knitter,* specializes in making a particular type of knit product on behalf of another company. Contract knitters make the cloth and/or garment as a second party who specializes in volume. The contract knitter will then resell the final product back to the company whose name will ultimately appear on the label. One of the best examples of contract knitting is T-shirt underwear fabric. It is not uncommon for a T-shirt to be made by a contract knitter to be packaged, sold, and distributed by two independent T-shirt labels. Contract knitters can make knits cost-effective to produce and sell.

Both contract and direct knitters can make and sell knitted fabric in the form of yard goods (knitted panels) or fully or partially formed garments. (See Figure 2–38.) Garments constructed directly on a knitting machine are easily recognizable from yard goods that have been cut and sewn into knitted garments. (See Figure 2–39.)

Garments that have been shaped on the machine and assembled either by hand or on a device known as a looping machine are said to be *fully fashioned.* (See Figure 2–40.) Full-fashioned knits are readily identifiable by the fashion marks (Figure 2–41), which are formed during construction of the knitted garments. Fashion marks are created during the increasing or decreasing that gives the garment shape directly on the machine. Such marks are an indication of a quality knitted garment.

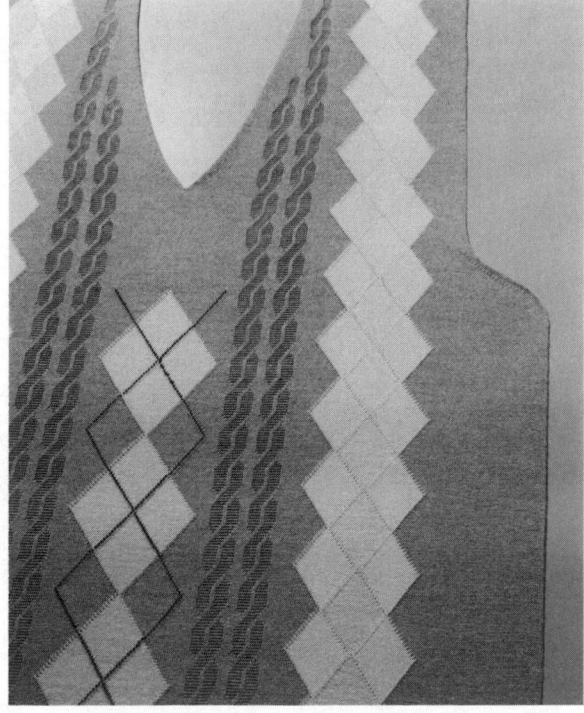

FIGURE 2–38
Full fashion marks on partially formed garment front
(Courtesy of Stoll Knitting Machines)

FIGURE 2–39
Various knitting machines
(Courtesy of Stoll Knitting Machines)

FIGURE 2–39
Continued
(Courtesy of Stoll Knitting Machines)

FIGURE 2–40
Looping machine
(Courtesy of Stoll Knitting Machines)

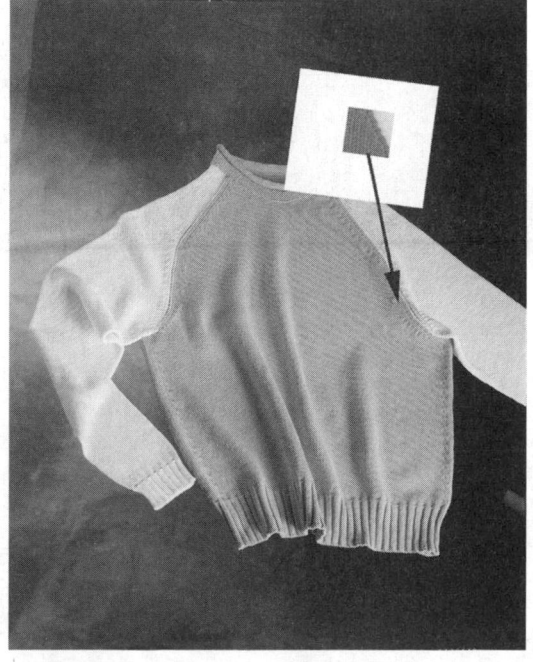

FIGURE 2–41
Fashion marks
(Courtesy of Stoll Knitting Machines)

FIGURE 2–42
Circular machine
(Courtesy of Stoll Knitting Machines)

FIGURE 2–43
Weft-knitted pattern

Classifying Weft Knits

Weft knitting machines may further be classified as flat bed (also known as flat plate), as a double bed, or as a circular machine (Figure 2–42).

Naturally there are different uses for each of these machines. Most tubular knitted goods such as hosiery or underwear are made on a circular machine, but interlock or double knits are generally made on a double-bed mechanism.

Common Weft Patterns and Stitches

Weft-knitted patterns can be constructed either by using combinations of stitch variations or by adding color to convey a design. (See Figure 2–43.)

The basic weft patterns used today are single knits, double knits, and interlock knits.

A *single knit* is the most common knit. Single-knit fabric is comprised of rows of knitted stitches on the face of the fabric. The reverse of this fabric is comprised of all purl stitches. This fabric is known by several other names such as *jersey, sweater knit, weft knit, plain knit,* or *stockinet.* (See Figure 2–44.)

A *double knit* is a way of knitting fabric so that both sides of the fabric are the right side of the piece, and when color is used to form the pattern, the images are the reverse of each other. Double knitting is really a way of working both sides in one row. For each grid in a stitch graph there is a knit stitch for the side facing you of the color shown and a purl stitch for the other side of the color not shown. It is really like knitting two fabrics at once, back-to-back, on the same needle at the same time.

Interlock is a stable compound fabric and is limited to having only crosswise stretch. Interlock weft-faced is produced by two sets of needles on a double bed or on a circular knitting machine.

Variations of a Single Knit

One of the most common variations of a single knit is to add color. The stitch combination of face knit and reverse purl is maintained while a pattern is formed

Notes. . .

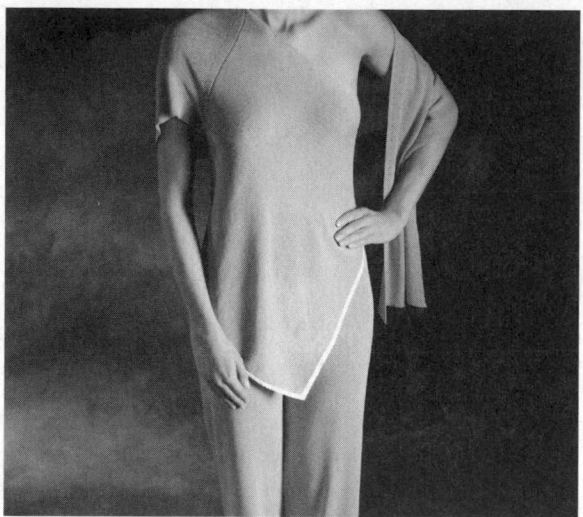

FIGURE 2–44
Single knit
(Courtesy of Stoll Knitting Machines)

FIGURE 2–45
Jacquard front

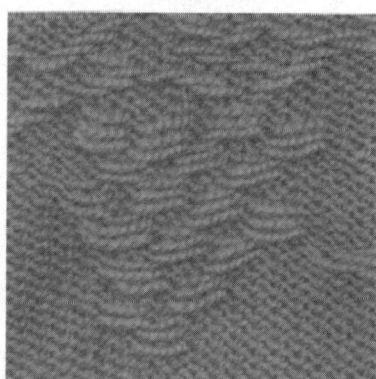

FIGURE 2–46
Jacquard back

by a change in the color of the yarn. Notice that each fabric listed below has its own identity or stitch name, yet the pattern base is clearly a single-knit jersey.

- Color changes in jacquard fabric are made by an attachment with the same name added to the machine. This method is sometimes known as knit-in. On the reverse side of the yard good or garment there will be a series of floats, which represent the different colors of yarn that are used to construct the pattern. (See Figures 2–45 and 2–46.) There are several variations of knitted jacquards, which depend on the type of knitting machine used. Some jacquards are made with the floats secured by an addition of a chain stitch on the reverse of the fabric. This is known as a ladder-back jacquard.

- When additional colors used to knit the pattern are clearly visible on the face of the fabric, this is known as grin thru.

- The distinguishing feature of *intarsia* is on the reverse side of the cloth, which does not have floats or yarns that are carried across the back of the cloth. (See Figure 2–47.)

- *Stripe* (See Figure 2–48.)

- *Argyle* (See Figure 2–49.) Both an argyle and a houndstooth can be a variation of an intarsia or a jacquard.

- *Houndstooth* (See Figure 2–50.)

- *Plaiting* uses two different yarns simultaneously. One yarn appears only on the face while the other appears on the reverse.

- *Purl knit* (also known as a reverse jersey) can be made in two ways. (1) Knitting rows of only knit stitches will make a double-faced purl fabric. (2) The other option is to use the reverse side of a weft knit as the face side. (See Figure 2–51.)

- The *rib stitch* is a combination of vertical rows of alternating knit and purl stitches. (See Figure 2–52.) This stitch pattern is most often used as a trim on sweaters in the form of a waistband or as cuffs.
  1×1 (Sometimes this fabric is known as double-faced or interlock when it is made as compound fabric.)
  2×2
  2×1
  3×2
  5×1

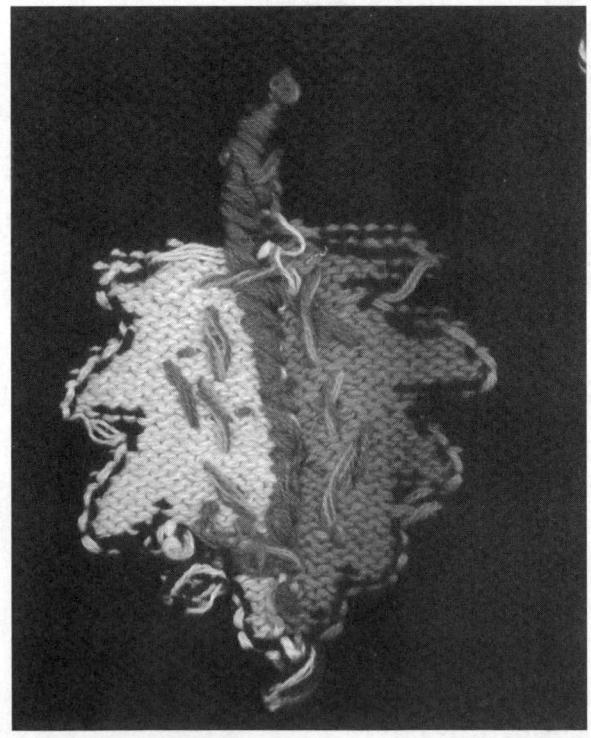

FIGURE 2–47
Reverse of intarsia

FIGURE 2–48
Stripe

FIGURE 2–49
Argyle
(Courtesy of Stoll Knitting Machines)

FIGURE 2–50
Houndstooth

FIGURE 2–51
Purl knit

FIGURE 2–52
Rib stitch

- Shaker sweaters are made of only a rib pattern and usually in a loose gauge.

- Another combination of knit and purl stitches is known as a seed stitch. In a seed stitch, knits and purls are alternated not only in knit and purl rows but also in the knit and purl column.

Other types of weft-knitted patterns involve the use of textures and spacing.

- *Racking* is a popular stitch that can look like a herringbone pattern on the face of knitted fabric. To get this effect, the stitches are mounted on the needle bed as if to knit, then the *stitches* are transferred. A common variation of this technique is also known as cables. (See Figure 2–53.) *Cables* are formed by moving and transforming the stitches from one location to another on the needle bed. It should be noted that the stitches are transferred literally by crossing over one another. On the other hand, the racking technique will move the stitch from side to side to form a zigzag pattern.

- *Tuck* stitches are made by loops that are accumulated on the needles of the machine and then secured to form a textured surface. This technique

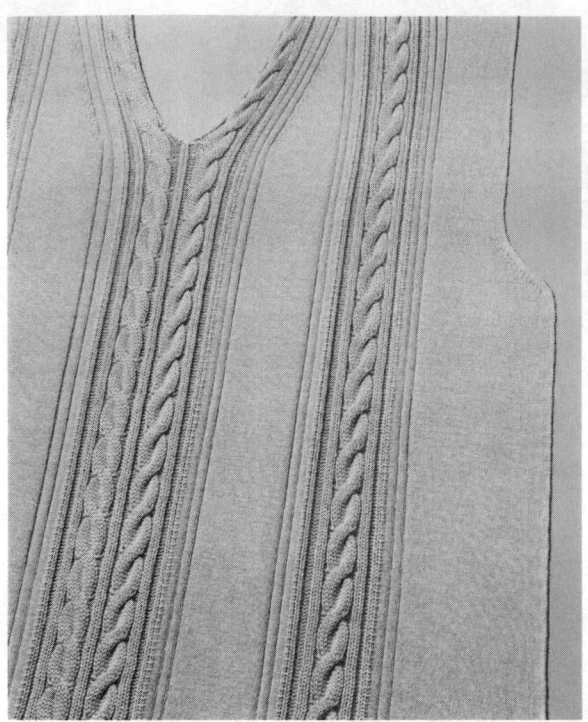

FIGURE 2–53
Cables
(Courtesy of Stoll Knitting Machines)

FIGURE 2–54
Tuck stitches
(Courtesy of Stoll Knitting Machines)

Notes . . .

creates texture on the fabric in the form of blisters, puckers, bobbles, and welts that appear on the surface face of the knit. (See Figure 2–54.)

- *Lace* is another type of weft knit jersey. This type of knit merely gives the impression of lace but is not considered true lace. (See Figure 2–55.)

  As you can see, this knit has a similar appearance that closely simulates eyelets or holes. Relocating stitches onto its adjacent neighbor creates these holes; this process forms a miss stitch or a hole. This combination of making holes is known as *miss stitch, eyelet,* or *pointelle.* (See Figure 2–56.)

- *Pile knit* is made of loops of yarn that are accumulated on the surface of the knit.

This is by no means an exhaustive look at weft-knitted patterns but it is a great starting point for the new designer to begin. Most knitted patterns take their inspiration from woven fabric. In fact, a great majority of the patterns are originally generated on graph paper first, just like the point paper used in woven patterns. (See Figure 2–57.)

Most of today's digitally created knits begin on a screen version of graph or point paper. In a later chapter you will be shown how to actually design these knitted patterns.

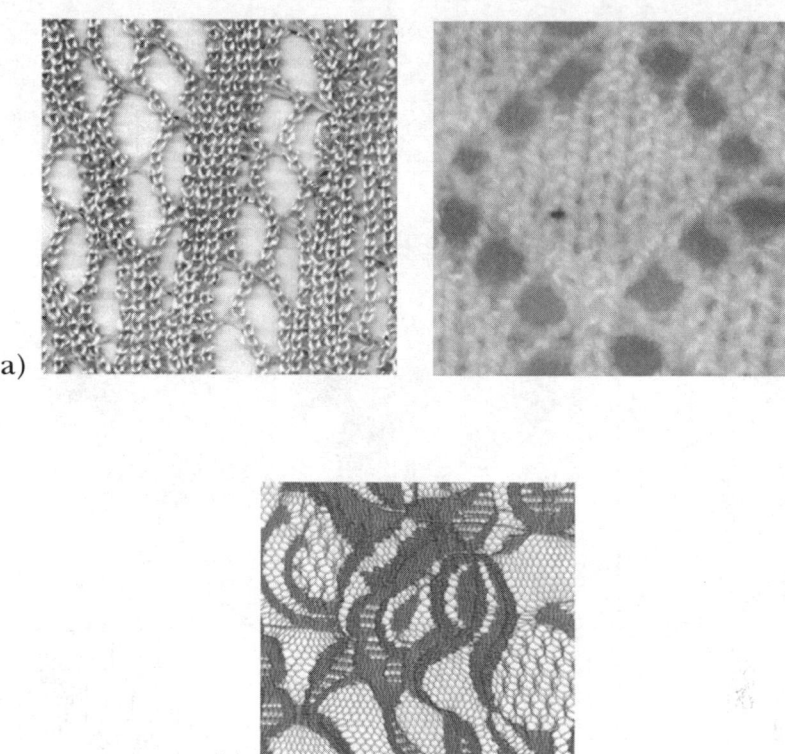

(a)

(b)

FIGURE 2–55
(a) Weft knit lace vs. (b) warp knit lace

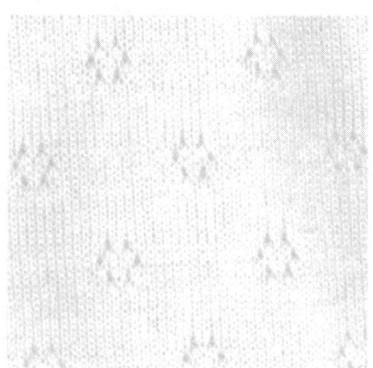

FIGURE 2–56
Eyelet woven vs. eyelet knit

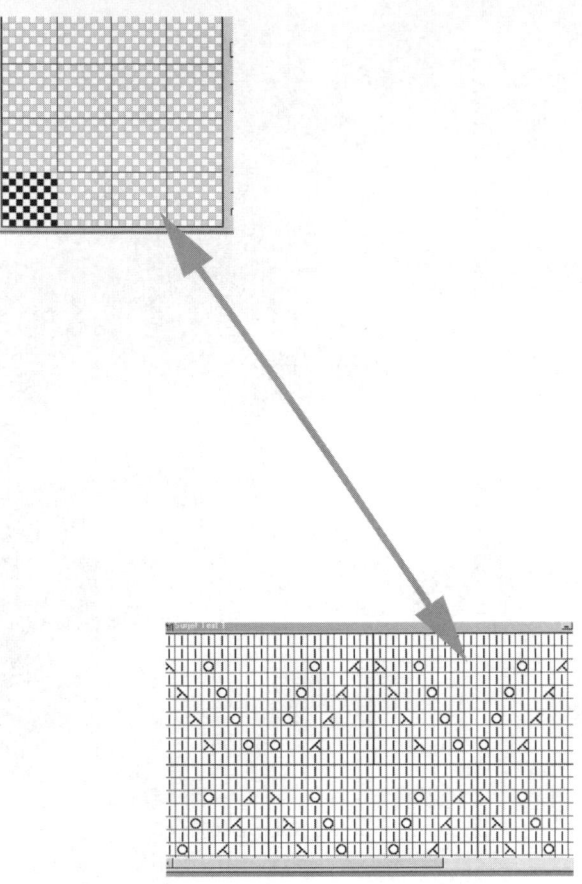

FIGURE 2–57
Pattern on graph paper

Knitted Trivia

Notice in Figure 2–58 that the circles are not true circles. The close-up of the graph clearly shows the illusion of a rounded corner.

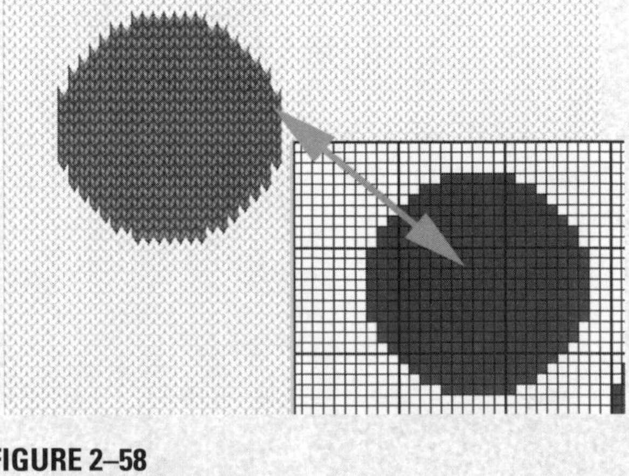

FIGURE 2–58
Rounded edges

Review of Weft Knits

- Knitting machines are known as looms, frames, or beds.

- The two basic stitches or loop formations used in weft knitting are knit and purl.

- Horizontal rows of knitted stitches are called courses.

- Vertical rows of knitted stitches are called wales.

- Gauge refers to the numbers of stitches that intersect in rows of stitches in a given measurement.

- Cut refers to the number of needles per inch used on the loom and gauge is referred to as the number of stitches horizontally and the number of rows vertically to an inch.

- Knits can be classified (and made on machines of the same name) as either a warp knit (simultaneously formed loops) or a weft knit (sequentially formed loops).

- Knits can be made and sold as yard goods or complete garments.

- Knits can also be either flat or circular.

- Knits can be manufactured by direct (from the manufacturers) or by contract knitters (knitters for hire).

Determining Quality of a Weft Knit

Several factors are involved in determining the quality of a knitted fabric, including:

- The type of machine used

- The number and type of needles used

- The fiber content and/or blend of the yarns

- The type, size, or denier of the yarn

- The stitch pattern selected

- What kinds of knitting attachments were employed (for example, jacquard)

- The numbers of colors involved to form a pattern or design

- Finishing process applied to the knit (for example, napping)

Warp Knits

Another category of knitted fabric used today is known as warp knits. Warp knits are complex knits that cannot be duplicated by hand. Typically warp knits have great dimensional stability. Their appearance has smooth flat edges that do not run or unravel when snagged or cut. Warp knitting machines date back to the late 1700s. Warp knitting machine needles move side to side and front to back in a simultaneous, interlocking zigzag pattern. Warp knits typically have a characteristic appearance of rows of the letter "v" on its side. (See Figure 2–59.)

FIGURE 2–59
Warp knit

FIGURE 2–60
Tricot

Warp knits differ greatly in appearance from the more traditional weft knits and can vary in appearance from lace to power stretch knits and even carpeting. Warp knits can take on the appearance of crocheting, netting, dramatic surface inlays, or even woven fabric.

There are (four) types of warp knitting machines:

Tricot (French for knit) Tricot is made on a springboard needle with one needle bar and from one to three guide bars. The face of tricot has the appearance of a traditional jersey knitted fabric, but the reverse will display the characteristic sideways "v" associated with warp knits. (See Figure 2–60.) This fabric has little or no stretch horizontally, which gives the fabric great dimensional stability. Tricot fabric is most often made from fine filament yarns, which results in a finer weight fabric.

Raschel In this version of warp knitting, the needles move the ground bar. The loops are prevented from moving up and down in a simultaneous coordinating series of actions. A typical raschel knit has a more coarse texture than other warp knits. (See Figure 2–61.) Raschel knits are also known as open-structured knits.

Simplex Simplex warp knits are similar in appearance to a tricot knit and they are used in the manufacturing of gloves and handbags.

Milanese Milanese warp knits are less popular and are generally replaced with tricot knits.

Common Warp Knit Patterns are listed below

- Sliver knit
- Single machine
- Pile/plush
- Interlock
- Milanese

Notes...

FIGURE 2–61
Warp lace and tulle

- Raschel
  Lace
  Tulle
  Netting

- Kettenraschel

- Tricot

- Weft insertion warp

To aid you in better comprehending the differences between knitted and woven fabric, we have included a quick cross-reference (Table 2–1) on what makes them different from one another.

TABLE 2–1   Knit vs. Woven Fabric

Quality	Weft Knit	Warp Knit	Wovens
Cost to Produce	(−)	(−)	(+)
Stretch	(+)	(+)	(−)
Movement	(+)	−/+	−/+
EZ Care	(+)	(+)	−/+
Stability	−/+	(+)	(+)
Hanger Appeal	(−)	(−)	(+)
Snag	(−)	(+)	(+)
Bag	(−)	(−/+)	(+)
Resist: Shrink	(−/+)	(+)	(−/+)
Resist: Static	(+)	(+)	(−/+)
Wrinkle	(+)	(+)	(−)
Pilling	(−/+)	(−/+)	(−/+)
Insulation	(+)	(+)	(−/+)
Fray	(−)	(−)	(+)
Run-Snag	(+)	(+)	(−)

Relevant Knitting Terms

Argyle: A knitted pattern that generally is comprised by a diamond repeat intersected by narrow stripes.

Cable: A weft-knitted pattern of stitches that form a "crisscross" or twisted cable appearance on the surface of the fabric.

Chevron: A repeat "v" design used on prints or in knitted patterns.

Circular: A term used to describe fabric or garments that are knitted in "the round" or in an unbroken circular or tubular fashion.

Course: Horizontal rows of knitted stitches.

Cut: (See Gauge.)

Cut and Sew: Refers to a yard good made from jersey that is "cut and sewn" to make a finished garment.

Double Knit: A reversible knitted fabric that was constructed on a weft-knitting machine.

Ends: Warp yarns. These are the vertical yarns on a piece of woven cloth.

Fair Isle: A knitted pattern that can consist of two or more colors to create a repeat pattern.

Float: When using two or more colors of yarn in a weft knit, the colored threads are carried across the reverse of the fabric in intervals of color, forming a float made by the yarn not currently being knitted.

Full Fashioned: In hand or machine knitting, portions of the garment are actually shaped or fashioned to fit against another garment piece, which has also been shaped or fashioned to fit. For example, a raglan sleeve has been fashioned to fit against the raglan shaping of the body of the sweater. The pieces are joined by means of sewing. Knitted garments that are not full fashion are said to be "cut and sewn."

Garter Stitch: A reversible weft-knitted stitch consisting of alternating rows of knit and purl.

Gauge: A knitting term indicating the number of stitches and/or rows to an inch. The gauge of a swatch or a garment is measured by the size or closeness of the stitches or needles. For example, seven stitches to an inch generally indicates the appearance of a hand-knit sweater and fifteen implies a finer machine gauge (cut) knit.

Grin Thru: In a double-knit fabric with a colored pattern, grin thru is the amount of color that is visible on the reverse side of the fabric.

Hand Loom: A loom used in making a hand-woven fabric. This is not a knitting loom used for making knitted yard goods or completed garments.

Intarsia: A weft-knitted design made of two or more colors. Unlike a jacquard that "floats" the color across the row on the reverse side of the fabric, in an intarsia these yarns are broken and knotted on the reverse side of the fabric, eliminating floats and bulk.

Jacquard: A complex weaving loom created in 1805 by Joseph Jacquard, which used a punch-card system.
  - Woven: Originally, this was a complex design of texture, surface interest, and color woven into fabric.
  - Knitted: In knitting this is a pattern of two or more colors that are carried across in floats on the reverse of the fabric.

Jersey Knit: Single, stockinet, or weft knit. The face of the cloth is constructed of all knit stitches and the reverse is constructed of all purl.

Knitting: The interlooping of yarn to form fabric.

Motif: A single or repeat pattern or design that can be "knitted" into a knitted fabric. A motif can also be added as a direct print.

Pile Knit: Taking its cue from weaving, this is a knitted pattern of loops left on the surface of the fabric, which are cut or left uncut.

Pin-Tuck: Horizontal rows of tubular relief on the surface of the knitted fabric.

Piqué: A term we often associate with woven fabric. A piqué knit is constructed by a "tuck-like" stitch, which gives a puckered appearance on the surface of the fabric. This stitch is very common in men's golf shirts.

Plating: Using two yarns simultaneously in knitting, one yarn will appear on the surface and the other yarn will only appear on the reverse side of the cloth.

Pointelle: A mesh or open work constructed of "missed" weft stitches; sometimes called lace.

Popcorn: Bobble or bubble stitch. This stitch is made by isolating groups of stitches that will form a popcorn-like appearance on the surface of the fabric.

Purl: One of the two basic stitches in weft knitting; has the appearance of a horizontal ridge loop formed across the surface of the fabric.

Rib: Alternating rows of knit and purl form vertical ridges that provide additional surface interest as well as stretch. This stitch pattern is primarily used for cuffs and waistbands. This stitch is also called a shaker knit when the entire body of the sweater is made of alternating rows of knit and purl.

Single: (See Jersey).

Tuck: This stitch is made by a series of "incomplete stitches" formed on the surface of the fabric, causing a pucker-like textured appearance in the knit.

Wales: Vertical rows of knitted stitches.

Warp: A specific type of knitting loom and/or knitting machine used in the construction of knitted fabric. Typically, warp knits are considered run-resistant when snagged.

Weft: One of the most common types of knit available. It is constructed from a combination of two basic stitches—knit and purl. Generally, weft knits can easily snag or run.

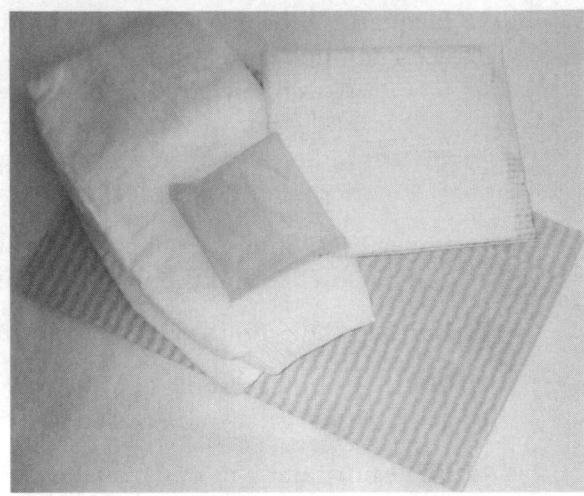

FIGURE 2–62
Examples of Other Fabrics
(Courtesy of Stoll Knitting Machines)

In the following chapters, you will be digitally rendering both woven and knit patterns in a variety of different ways. To begin with, most patterns for knits are created on graph paper similar to woven fabric. The design is then knitted into the fabric being made and is signified by a change in color. However, knits can also have a design printed or applied directly to the yarn prior to knitting. Prints can be applied to the finished knitted fabric as well as to the finished knitted garment.

Other Methods of Making Cloth

Obviously there are other types of fabric that have not been constructed by either weaving or knitting. In fact, any fabric *not* categorized as either a knit or a woven is placed into a group referred to as *other*. Although this can be somewhat confusing, these are fabrics that we come in contact with every day. (See Figure 2–62.)

Other is a name that may seem nondescript, yet it encompasses several versions as well as many diverse methods of fabric construction. The following is a list of many of the "other" fabrics we use or encounter every day:

Felts:—crafts, apparel, pool tables

Disposables:—wipe cloths, personal care, airline, and hospital

Nondisposable:—facings, inner-linings, industrial sheeting (roads)

Laminates:—include several types of wipe-off tablecloths or placemats

Tufting:—some types of carpets

Bonding:—items that have been fused together to form cloth

Each of these techniques forms cloth using very different construction methods. Many of these fabric groups (with the exception of tufting and crochet) share several common characteristics:

- They are made directly from nonaligned fibers or filaments.
- They have no grain.

- They do not unravel, run, or fray.

- They are secured by combinations of heat, chemicals, adhesions, or other ingredients such as foams, films, or laminates, with any combination of entanglement and/or pressure or other mechanical processes.

- They are less costly to produce than traditional fabrics.

- They can be categorized as being either durable (everything from interfacing to carpet backs) or disposable (everything from diapers to coffee filters) depending on the fibers used and the end use of the cloth.

A partial listing of uses for these fabrics:

Advertising	Health Care
Agricultural	Home Furnishing
Airline	Household
Apparel	Hygiene (Personal Care)
Automotive (Figure 2-63)	Industrial
Cleaning	Leisure
Construction	Medical
Cosmetics	Military
Crafts	Millinery
Culinary	Office Supplies
Engineering	Outer Space
Games	

FIGURE 2–63
Automotive use of fabric

FIGURE 2–64
Crochet

The other category of making fabric must also include the more traditional handcrafted categories:

Bobbin Lace

Braiding

Crewel

Crochet (See Figure 2–64.)

Embroidery

Macrame

Needlepoint

Quilting

Tatting

Examples of popular types of lace are:

Alencon	Battenberg
Allover	Beading
Antique	Belgian
Argentan	Binche

Bobbin

Brussels

Chantilly

Cluny

Crochet-Fillet Lace

Hairpin

Irish

Nottingham

Pointelle

Renaissance

Tatting

Valenciennes

Venetian

Unit #4 Enhancing Fabric Through Finishes

A widely accepted definition of *finish* is anything that alters the hand appearance or performance of a fiber, yarn, or fabric. Interestingly enough a finish is not done at the end or in the final stage of textile production, although it can be. Frequently it is a preparatory process that is done at the fiber stage of the textile production process.

Another name for finishing is *converting*. Generally speaking, an unfinished piece of cloth is referred to as a greige good. An example of a well-known greige in the fashion design world is muslin.

Finishing Categories

It can be said that all finishes are either *visible* or *invisible*. Finishes can also be categorized by *when* the finishes are added, *why* they are added, and *how* they are added. Most finishes can be categorized as:

- General, preparatory
- Functional or performance measured
- Aesthetic

All finishes are added to fibers or fabrics by either *mechanical* or *chemical* (including *wet, dry,* or *heat*) processes.

All finishes are measured by their degree of permanence:

- Permanent (no change in fiber or fabric life span)
- Durable
- Temporary (diminish quickly and uncertain)
- Renewable

Greige Good Conversions

1. Boil off
2. Dying (done at several intervals to remove moisture by use of centrifuges, vacuums, and dryers, carefully controlling heat and/or temperatures)
3. Moisture
4. Roller print

5. Application of special finishes

6. Drying

7. Tenter (process that stretches the fabric on a frame and passes through a heated chamber to the fabric's final dimensions)

8. Perching (inspection of newly made garments)

9. Color removal of inherent colors/bleach

10. Add inherent shine/optical brightness/apparent whiteness

11. Flatten—Calendar

12. Add strength and shine

    Mercerize (added to cotton)

    Beetle (hammering to soften linen)

Preparatory Finishes

Preparatory finishes are finishes that are added at the beginning of the textile production process. Below is a list of several common finishes, which are added at the fiber or fabric stage, along with their definitions:

- *Beetle* (hammer to soften linen)

- *Bleach* (strips color)

- *Burling* (applied to wools, rayons, and cotton fibers to remove remaining foreign matter)

- *Decating* (heat-or steam-set process applied to wool, some synthetics and blends, and double knits, which adds a crisp lustrous hand to the fabric)

- *Degum* (removal of sticky sericin from the silk filament fiber)

- *Deluster* (process done to synthetics such as polyester to remove excess shine)

- *Drying* (method of using a fiber-forming solution that is hardened (or dried) in a heating chamber)

- *Felting* (adding heat, pressure, and/or adhesions to make cloth)

- *Fulling* (adding heat and pressure to mat and shrink fibers while maintaining fullness to a fabric)

- *Mercerizing* (adding strength and shine to cotton with sodium hydroxide)

Functional Finishes

Many times functional finishes may or may not be able to be easily seen by looking at the fabric. However, they serve a significant purpose in the overall performance or function of the fiber, yarn, or fabric.

Stabilizing finishes can be done either pre-or post-textile production. Stabilizing finishes ensure the overall performance stability of the final textile product. Here is a brief list of the most common stabilizing finishes that consumers may take for granted, but are very glad they are there!

- Heat set
- Preshrink
- Shrinkage control
- Durable press
- Wash-and-wear, chemically treated fabrics
- Relaxation
- Texture retention
- Sizing
- Soil release or stain release
- Antistatic

Functional finishes *also* include finishes that are added to offset the negative inherent qualities of some fibers:

- Reduce microbial action/antibacterial/antifungal or moths or other insects (such as silverfish)
- Perspiration resistant
- Wrinkle resistant
- Crease resistant
- Resistant to pilling
- Resist fading
- Resist crushing

Legislation of Finishes

Since 1972 the United States has had legislation in place to produce fiber, fabrics, and clothing that do not burn easily. This is especially important for infant clothing.

HINT: *Go to GOODIES FOLDER> CHAPTER EXERCISES> Chapter 2 laundry chart*

Functional Safety Finishes

- Reduces flammability
  Fire resistant
  Flame repellant

- Increasing or decreasing moisture absorption
  Water resistant
  Water repellant

The last group of functional finishes has a good deal of overlap with aesthetic finishes. You may notice that in the list of functional finishes many times a fiber's overall performance value may be linked to its hand or appearance (aesthetic qualities).

Pile Orientation Finishes

- Beetle (Done to cottons or linens by pounding or hammering the fabric to add surface shine and softness)

- Brushing

- Burn out

- Calendar (A process of adding heat and pressure to fabrics to impart a glossy smooth surface to fabric)

- Crushed

- Direction (The lay or sweep and height, as well as hand and appearance)

- Felting

- Flatten/luster

- Fulling

- Glaze

- Heat set

- Mercerize

- Napping (A process to raise a velvety soft surface to wools, cottons, spun silks, and rayon knitted or woven cloth)

- Optical brighteners

- Parchmentize (A permanent stiffener added to ultrasheer fabric such as organdy)

- Polish

- Singeing (A process that passes yarns and yard goods over a gas flame or heated copper plates to remove fuzz. This process is sometimes referred to as gassing)

Aesthetic Finishes

Aesthetic finishes are finishes that may or may not have s specific performance or added value function to the consumer.

However, most fabric choices that consumers make outside of care are most frequently associated with touch or the hand and the overall appearance of the fabric or garment. Listed below are some of the most common aesthetic finishes. Notice how many have a combination of function and preparatory as well as aesthetic purposes.

- *Crabbing*

- *Creping* (a variety of processes that cause a blister or puckered effect to the surface of the cloth either by adding steam hot rollers or using caustic soda to pucker a given area of the cloth)

- *Embellishing* (most done to finished fabric by hand or by machine)

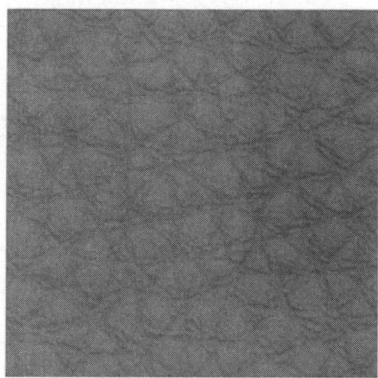

FIGURE 2–65
Emboss

- *Emboss* (See Figure 2–65.)

- *Flocking*

- *Moiré* (See Figure 2–66.)

- *Plissé or Creping* (See Creping)

- *Softening*

- *Tenter*

One of the most interesting finishes is the application of an embellishment to a fabric or garment. The following is a brief list of embellishments you may be called upon to digitally render. (See Figure 2–67.)

- *Beading*

- *Embroidery*

- *Quilting*

- *Smocking*

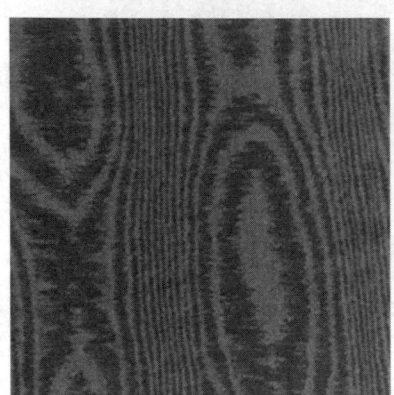

FIGURE 2–66
Moiré

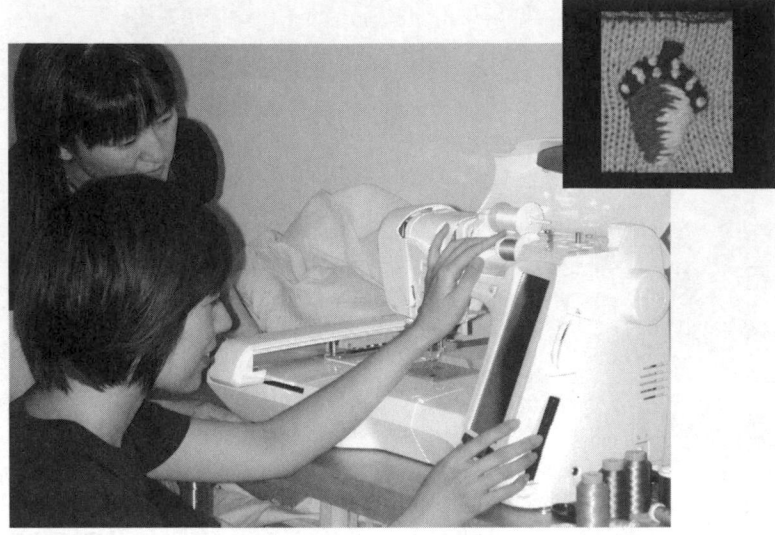

FIGURE 2–67
Examples of embroidery
(Courtesy of First 2 Print/Neil Breslali)

Some Final Thoughts on Finishing

When it comes to using digitally printed fabric, adding a finishing takes on new meaning. Frequently when using this new media, the design has a myriad of alternatives to consider. Several of these choices involve the ability to add laminates that can withstand ultraviolet light and even most weather conditions.

The most important factor to consider is the handling of the finished cloth in postprinting. Fabric that has been printed through digital methods will often require additional finishing methods such as steaming to fix or adhere the ink/dyes to the fabric.

Please refer to this section on fabric basics as you encounter these issues. Now more than ever you can see how a firm foundation of understanding fabric properties and behaviors can come in handy when designing!

Practical Knowledge Application for Digitally Rendering Fabric

Meet several designers using technology today to render fabric and prints.

The following is a story of a young lady who graduated with an associate's degree in Fashion Design, and was able to make a successful transition from traditional fashion designer into a digital textile designer.

Combining State of the Art Digital Design and State of the Art Finishing Techniques
Meet Ivette Principe: Owner of Graph to Graphics Inc.

Located in Ft. Lauderdale, Florida

Ivette (see Figure 2–68) began her business in the late 1990s armed with degrees in business, fashion, and chemistry. Ivette saw the potential for an emerging market in digital textiles.

Ivette began her small business in the graphic design and sign and banner industry. She even recruited several of her peers from college to become part of this new venture of digitally printing felt for gaming tables. According to Ivette, financial backing was not as difficult as overcoming some challenges that Graph to Graphics experienced in color management and in finishing.

We will go into more detail about the issues of color and color management for digital textiles in Chapters 5, 6, and 12. However, with regards to finishing, Ivette was able to set her company apart from the other printers in the gaming industry by securing several patents for her fabric finishes. Ivette's patented finishing incorporates aluminum backing to the felt along with other surface-applied finishes, which results in a gaming felt that is far superior to any of her competitors' (see Figure 2–69). In addition, the patented finish maintains the aesthetic integrity of the cloth by resisting damage by liquid (such as alcohol) as well as damage by fire (accidental cigarette burns).

FIGURE 2–68
Ivette Principe and her work
(Courtesy of Ivette Principe)

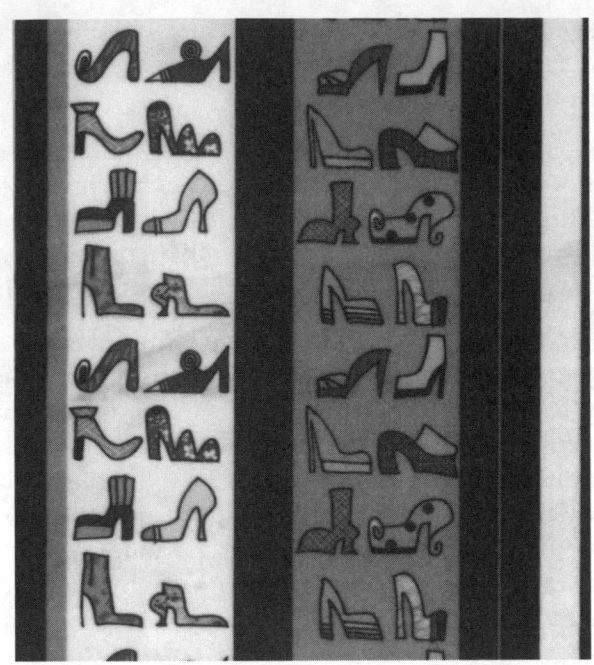

FIGURE 2–69
Sample of Ivette's work on felt
(Courtesy of Ivette Principe)

Ivette's customers include many of the major gaming industry giants such as Trump Casino, Caesar's Palace, and Carnival Cruise Line, just to name a few!

Committed to Excellence in Education and Design
Meet Designer Liza Niles

Liza Niles (see Figure 2–70) is a textile designer and consultant. She received a BFA in textiles with a concentration in screen printing and traditional surface design techniques. For the last 10 years Liza has been living in New York and has been working in the commercial industry, teaching and pursuing international research. She develops original prints for various apparel companies as well as expedites designs from concept to mill production.

Most of her apparel work has been developed in CAD and she is now a consultant for the software company, Pointcarré. In the home furnishing industry, Liza develops original collections for bedding and bath (see Figures 2–71 and 2–72) and frequently oversees the printing production. As an adjunct professor at Parsons School of Design in both the Textile and Digital Design Departments, Liza has been a visiting faculty member and has received grant support to travel in Asia, South America, and the Caribbean. While traveling, she became aware of the challenges and needs of grassroots textile organizations in developing countries.

Consequently, she has devoted part of her time as a representative for Aid to Artisans, an NGO that supports craft throughout the world. As a consultant, Liza is invited to the host country and works with the artisans to improve their working conditions and to revise their product development for the U.S. market.

FIGURE 2–70
Liza Niles
(Courtesy of Liza Niles)

FIGURE 2–71
Example of Liza's bedding collections
(Courtesy of Liza Niles)

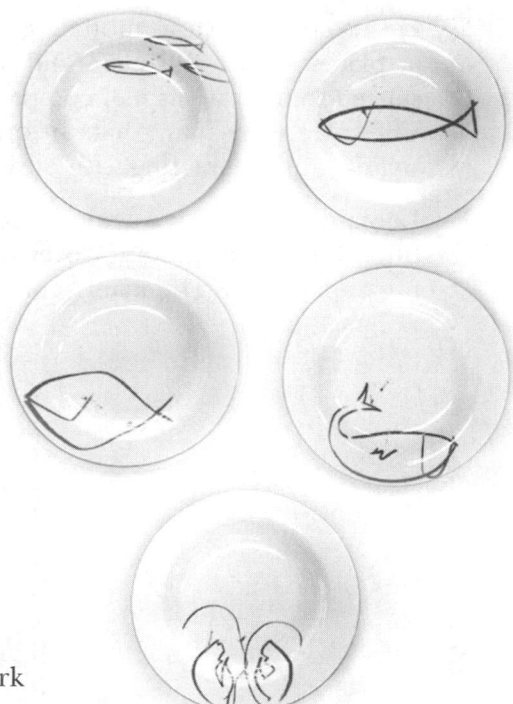

FIGURE 2–72
Sample of Liza's work
(Courtesy of Liza Niles)

For the future, Liza is concentrating on designing more products by combining traditional textile techniques and digital technology. She hopes to continue in international development work, whether it is as a consultant to the handicraft industry, as a supervisor in textile printing production, or promoting all of the above in education.

PO Box 1795 New York City 10013 212.431.6567 tel.fax nilesl@newschool.edu

Craig Crawford, Director of Design Technologies at Liz Claiborne, Inc.

It is amazing how many people in the fashion and apparel industry did not start their careers there. Always having a goal in mind is necessary, but adapting yourself and your goals to the changing world around you is an awesome feat that not everyone can follow. Craig is one of the people who can (see Figure 2–73).

Craig and his team are responsible for the research, development, and implementation of technology in the areas of color, textile, and apparel (specifications technologies) as they are used to design products at Liz Claiborne.

A long list of products at Liz Claiborne include, among many others, DKNY Jeans, DKNY City, Laundry by Shelli Segal, Sigrid Olsen, Lucky Brand Jeans, Kenneth Cole, and Liz Claiborne brands.

The road to Liz Claiborne was a long one for Craig, with over a 10-year history in the Design Technologies field. Craig graduated from the University of Virginia with a BA in Rhetoric & Communication Studies and a BA in English Literature. Upon graduation he looked forward to being a writer or reporter. That's when his direction changed. Computers were not as common then as they are today. As a writer for a newspaper, Craig became involved in a new industry—desktop publishing. Craig was not only writing but became involved in the archiving, typesetting, and backing up of data at a newspaper.

He also began a short modeling career, as well as working in a retail environment at places such as Barney's and Macy's. Continuing on the fashion track, Craig started to work at a small company that designed a bridge line of women's wear. There he wore many hats in quality control, merchandising, public relations, styling, and interacting with buyers.

Looking for a change again, Craig landed a job at the American Institute of Certified Public Accountants, overseeing data management, data entry, and a training department. The management experience he acquired there would take him

FIGURE 2–73
Craig Crawford
(Courtesy of Craig Crawford)

onto his next endeavor—The GAP. This is where all his past experiences started to add up. The GAP was looking for someone who could work and manage a computer design system as well as have the retail, design, and styling background to understand what the market needed.

Craig was a perfect fit and The GAP took a chance on him. Soon Craig was designing for boys' wear, men's active wear, women's wear, and Baby GAP, among others. Two and a half years later he moved to GAP Warehouse, which became Old Navy. At Old Navy he was in charge of building an entire computer-aided design (CAD) department, directing all technology and workflow.

In his spare time, Craig had taken a job as a CAD training instructor at Parsons School of Design in New York City, which is where he met Kathryn Shipman, who was starting a new job at Liz Claiborne, Inc. She was so enticed by Craig's knowledge of CAD systems that she immediately tried to hire him at Liz. Soon enough Craig left the GAP for Liz Claiborne and became their CAD administrator and started his climb to the position of director of design technologies. The challenge of the job has kept him there ever since.

When asked about the industry today, Craig says that he is seeing more and more interns and new hires who already possess the computer design skills he had to develop on his own over the years. It is easy to see why there is a strong interest from schools to teach the skills a designer will need in the industry today and that schools are serious about computer-aided design along with the apparel and textile design skills. Craig stated, "It is easy enough on the job to teach someone to use a computer, but you cannot teach them aesthetics."

As chairman of the Computer Integrated Textile Design Association (CITDA), Craig feels that designers and studios today need to design more with the product in mind. It is easy enough with the advancement of computer design software to develop a pattern or print in repeat, in the proper colors as well as that design's end use. He also feels that many companies underrate their CAD designers as computer operators.

At Liz Claiborne, Craig also manages a digital fabric printing area. It is going along well, but there are still some issues to be addressed. Correct color is one of the biggest issues that needs attention. "You still cannot go from a Scan to Monitor to Paper to Fabric to Web and have continuous color." It may be close but it can still be a guessing game. Considering the Web, communicating files through available bandwidth is another issue that needs help. Web catalogs and consumer kiosks are being created, but it will be so much better if these issues are correctly addressed.

To anyone starting in this industry, Craig advises spending the time to acquire the right skills for the job. If you want to be a fashion designer, you need to have the artistic skill but also know how to work in a team, deal with stressful situations, and remember that it is design by committee. Something may start as your idea, but then many will have their hands in it to get the product to market.

Craig also serves on the board of the University of Wisconsin at Madison, the Fashion Institute of Technology faculty advisory committee, lectures at Savannah College of Arts and Design, Philadelphia University, and is a member of Fashion Group International.

Notes . . .

So Where's Unit 5? Discovering How to Color and Print Fabric. . . .

Chapters 1–2 have covered the first four units introduced in Chapter 1. Because so much has changed in the method of coloring and printing fabric in the last 5–7 years, the issue of color and prints warrants its own chapter. Chapter 5 will cover the coloring and printing of fabric in detail.

Before discussing coloring and printing further, Chapter 3 will provide you with an introduction to recent developments in Adobe Photoshop for the fashion professional. Following this introduction, you will be able to apply your knowledge of Adobe Photoshop and the basics of what makes a good design with exercises using Adobe Photoshop. Chapter 5 will then discuss in more detail the new innovations in the textile world for rendering prints and patterns.

You will begin to see the quiet revolution of converting prints traditionally to digitally and everything in between! So let's get ready and head to the computer for your review of Adobe Photoshop.

3 "Photoshop Basics"

Anti-aliased	"Hidden" Tools	Reverse Jersey
Bitmapped	Indexed	RGB
Cable	Jersey	Rib
CMYK	Menu Items	Satin
Color Palettes	Mode	Stitches
Colorways	Motif	Structures
Contiguous	Opacity	Toolbox
Effects	Pattern	Tool Short Cut
Engineered	Plain	Twill
Filter	Printed	Use All Layers
Flow	Repeat	Woven

Chapter 3 makes extensive use of the CD that accompanies this book. Step-by-step directions can be followed, using the files on the CD. Each lesson on the CD is followed by the final version of the steps to use.

Computers have forever changed the way designers do things. From sketches to line sheets, from concepts to final design, we have the ability to edit designs, save color palettes, archive design elements, and shorten turnaround time—no more markers going dry, no more tracing paper or making multiple copies of a single sketch at different percentages on the copy machine or colors shifting around from it.

One of the most outstanding programs a designer will use is Adobe Photoshop. This software has long been considered the industry standard. Chapter 4 looks at many of the tools and features specifically available through the use of Photoshop. Adobe Photoshop consists of numerous tools and menu items, so it can have a steep learning curve to master. Our approach to Photoshop focuses on showing you how these tools and menu items are best viewed for use in textile design. Therefore, we will not be going through every tool or feature here. That would take another whole book. This book will concentrate only on those with specific textile and fabric design functions. In addition, we will introduce you to several available plug-ins that will enhance Photoshop's abilities.

Although Photoshop is ever evolving and is primarily marketed for the photo retouching and graphic design industries, it will never truly address the full needs of the textile market. However, it is a great stepping-stone for designers to begin their journey into computer-aided design.

Welcome to Adobe® Photoshop®

Overall Product Highlights*

- File Browser for previewing and managing images

- Healing Brush effortlessly removes artifacts such as dust, scratches, blemishes, and wrinkles while preserving shading, lighting, and texture

- New Auto Color Command for reliable color correction

- New Painting Engine to simulate traditional painting techniques

- Pattern Maker-Generator plug-in to create realistic or abstract patterns simply by selecting a section of an image

- Built-in spell checker for search-and-replace operations in multiple languages within the same file

- Enhanced Picture Package to allow you to print multiple images on one page, choose different page sizes, and add custom labels, such as copyright notices or captions

- Tool with customizable workspace presets to allow you to personalize your settings and work more efficiently

First, every tool in Photoshop has a name and a shortcut. Names and shortcuts can be viewed by touching the pointer to any tool. After a 2-second delay, the name and shortcut will appear on the screen. Second, any tool with a page turn in the bottom right corner notifies the designer that there are "hidden" tools that can be selected by a click of the mouse on the tool.

On the following pages are the tools and menu items chosen for discussion. A brief description of their "textile or apparel" use is also provided.

The most important issue to consider when using any of these tools or menu options is. How will you utilize these tools most successfully as a textile designer? Therefore, even though there will be several options that can accomplish a given task, why not determine the best choice to serve your needs and your time. Annotate these choices as good, better, and best. Often the ranking of these choices will be determined by the final objective of the project. Let's look at Photoshop's toolbox (Figure 3–1) and the menu items you will be accessing.

Tools for Textiles

Selection of Tools

Figure 3–2 (M) Marquee: Rectangular/Round/Single Row/Column should be used to select any area of the design. Once selected, that area is the only "active" area in the design. It can then be manipulated in any way and leave the unselected area unchanged. The rectangular and round selections allow a large area to be active. By holding the shift key, continuous areas can be selected and joined by overlaps. The option key subtracts the selected area. Whether selecting a stripe or a

---

*Information gleaned from the Adobe.com/products/new features website.

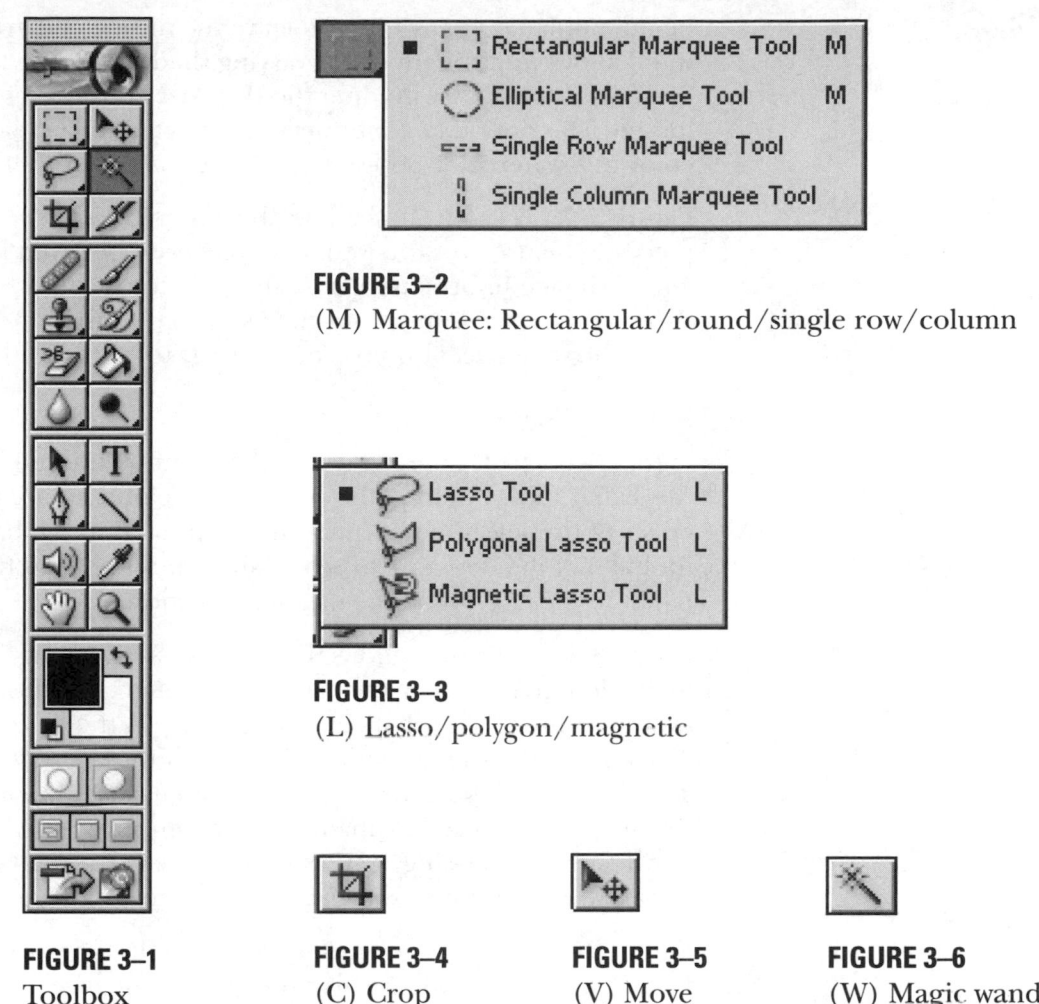

FIGURE 3–2
(M) Marquee: Rectangular/round/single row/column

FIGURE 3–3
(L) Lasso/polygon/magnetic

FIGURE 3–1
Toolbox

FIGURE 3–4
(C) Crop

FIGURE 3–5
(V) Move

FIGURE 3–6
(W) Magic wand

repeat of a design, these selection tools are some of the most used tools in the software.

Figure 3–3 (L) Lasso/Polygon/Magnetic should be used to select any area of the design. Once selected, that area is the only "active" area in the design. It can then be manipulated in any way and leave the unselected area unchanged. The free-hand lasso allows a large area to be active, using the polygon or magnetic lasso, specific areas can be selected very quickly. By holding the shift key, continuous areas can be selected and joined by overlaps. The option key subtracts the selected area.

Figure 3–4 (C) Crop allows an adjustable marquee to be used to cut out an area of a design. If designing a large area, this tool allows easy clipping of the needed area from the design and discards the rest of the page.

Figure 3–5 (V) Move allows the user to easily move a layer or selected area in the design or onto another window. This is especially necessary when building storyboards and moving flats around in their positions, from within the same page or from page to page.

Figure 3–6 (W) Magic Wand should be used to select any area of the design. Once selected, that area is the only "active" area in the design. The area can then be manipulated in any way and leave the unselected area unchanged. The magic wand allows adjustment of the varying shades of a hue to be easily selected in one or multiple clicks. By holding the shift key, continuous areas can be selected and joined. The option key subtracts the selected area. Selecting large tonal areas of color in a watercolor design is made easy with this tool.

Figure 3–7 (K) Slice Tool allows the designer to divide a large image into smaller pieces to be used on the web. Each slice can be given its own url, rollover effect, and alt image information. The slice select tool allows the designer to select any slice in the image. This allows the user to enter the information for the url and alt text. The slice select Toolbar has settings to control how the slices appear.

Painting Tools

Figure 3–8 (J) Healing Brush is like a combination of the Clone stamp tool and the Patch tool. It allows the designer to clone an area to another but then the edges of the selection are smoothly blended into the background. The (J)Patch tool allows the designer to select an area to be "patched" and then to drag the patch to the "fill" to fix the original selection.

Figure 3–9 (B) Brush allows the designer a wide range of methods to apply color to the design. It is one of the many pressure-sensitive tools. The edges are smoothed by anti-aliasing so it will create extra colors in the design that may not be wanted. Flats can be drawn freehand and look as if they were drawn by true brush strokes. The (B) Pencil tool allows the designer a wide range of methods to apply color to the design. It is one of the many pressure-sensitive tools. The edges are hard and not affected by anti-aliasing, so it will not create extra colors in the design. It is a great choice when painting a specific color and shades or edge smoothing is not needed.

Figure 3–10 (S) Clone Stamp allows the designer to select and reproduce one part of a design or texture, like the ground, in another area of the design with no seams showing. The trick is to use the option key with the stamp to select the area to be defined in the toolbar and then release the option key and use the stamp like a brush. The (S) Pattern Stamp allows the designer to select and reproduce one part of a design or texture, which has been predefined as a pattern, in another area of the design with no seams showing. Select the pattern to be defined in the toolbar at the top of the screen and then use the stamp like a brush.

Figure 3–11 (Y) History Brush is an ingenious tool that allows the designer to "erase history." It is used to remove part of the edits to a design by defining the time they were added. Used in conjunction with the History Window, the time in the past may be selected on the left and then the tool can be used to erase back to that stage in the design only where needed. It is like having an "unlimited undo." The (Y) Art History Brush acts like the History Brush but it replaces the original area with a "painter's effect" that is preselected in the menu bar.

FIGURE 3–7
(K)Slice

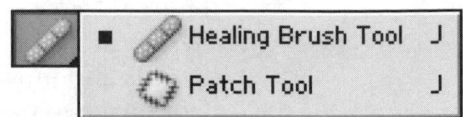

FIGURE 3–8
(J)Healing brush and patch

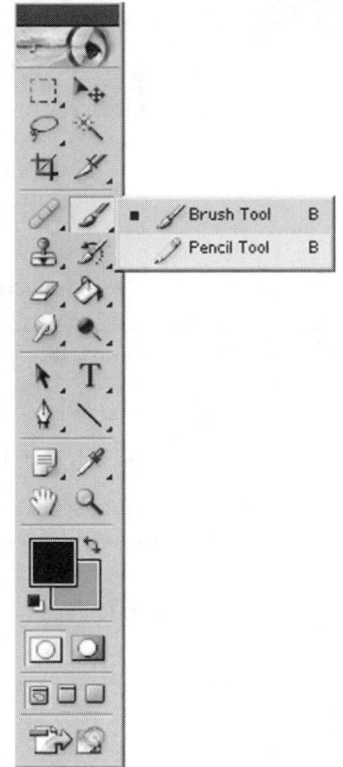

FIGURE 3–9
(B) Brush and pencil

FIGURE 3–10
(S) Clone stamp and pattern stamp

FIGURE 3–11
(Y) History brush and art history brush

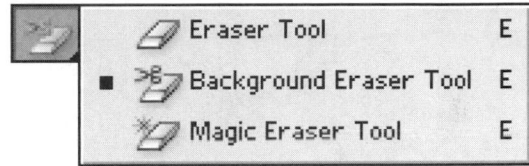

FIGURE 3–12
(E) Eraser, background eraser, and magic eraser

FIGURE 3–13
(G) Paint bucket/gradient bucket

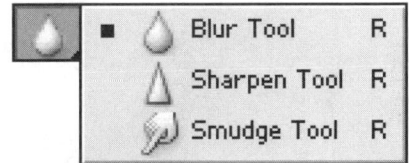

FIGURE 3–14
(R) Blur/sharpen/smudge

Figure 3–12 (E) Eraser will remove any area and replace it with the background color. Background Eraser will erase to transparency. Magic Eraser allows the designer to erase as if using a magic wand to select a hue range to be removed or erased.

Figure 3–13 (G) Paint Bucket/Gradient Bucket allows the use of pouring a color, pattern, or gradient into a specific area. Opacity, tolerance, and other top bar features can be used to modify the results. It is a favorite tool to fill in patterns or solids into flats and sketches.

Figure 3–14 (R) Blur/Sharpen/Smudge allows the special effects of these tools to be used almost anywhere. They create extra colors because they are anti-aliasing tools. Making a fabric appear fuzzy or brushed can be accomplished with them.

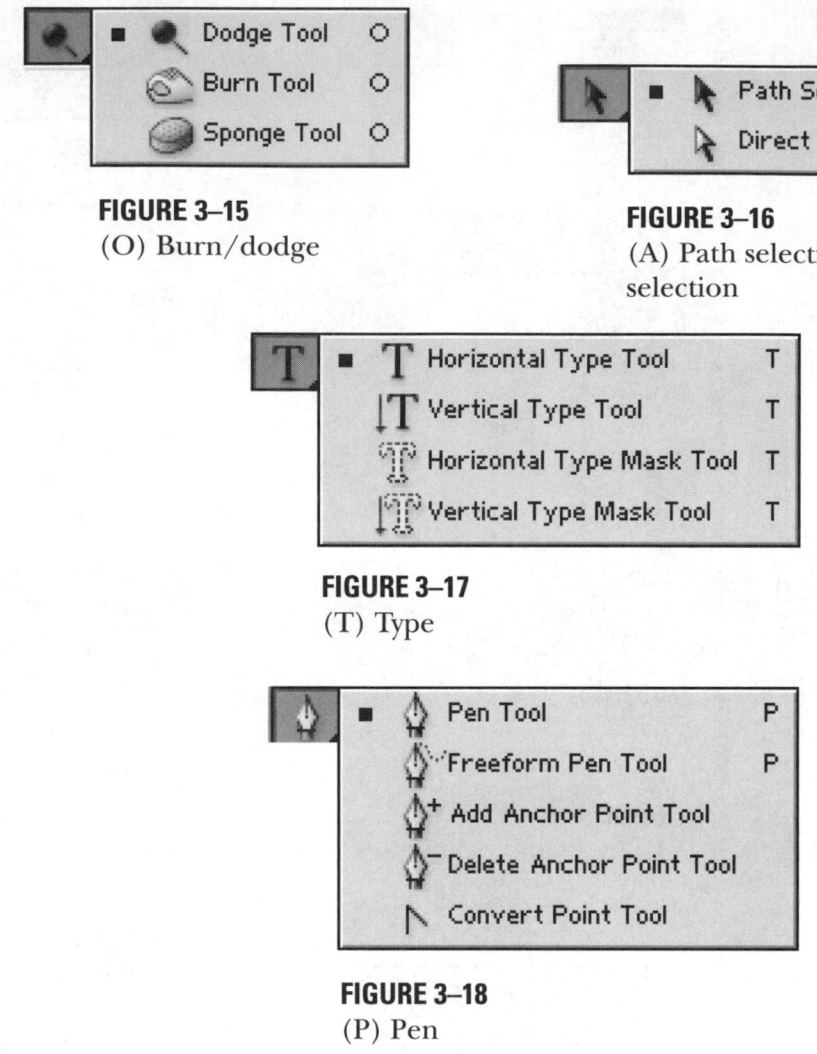

FIGURE 3–15
(O) Burn/dodge

FIGURE 3–16
(A) Path selection/direct
selection

FIGURE 3–17
(T) Type

FIGURE 3–18
(P) Pen

Figure 3–15 (O) Burn/Dodge is a nice tool for touching up a photo for draping. Its ability lies in adjusting a photo that is either over- or underexposed.

Path Tools

Figure 3–16 (A) Path Selection/Direct Selection is the tool used to select or manipulate a path previously drawn with the Pen tool. This is done by editing any drawn croquis or flats as well as objects that were drawn with the Pen. The Path Selection tool will activate the entire drawn line while the Direct Selection tool only activates and moves single anchor points.

Figure 3–17 (T) Type sets, manipulates, and edits any text. Storyboard titles and other type are easily typed and edited on a separate layer. The layer can then be flattened to the background when done.

Figure 3–18 (P) Pen is the ideal tool for drawing and editing "vector" line art. It is similar to the Pen tool in Illustrator and is used in the same way. Freeform/Add/Delete/Convert tools allow the user to continuously edit and update the drawn line.

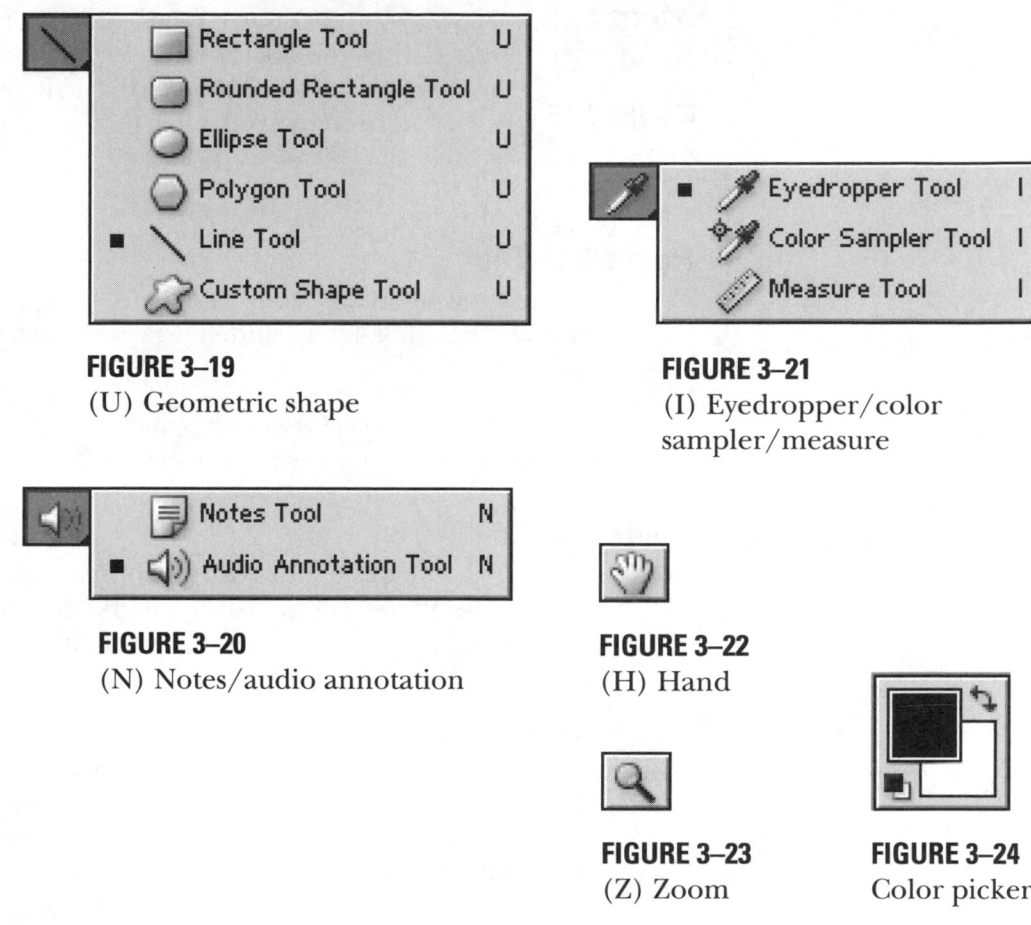

FIGURE 3–19
(U) Geometric shape

FIGURE 3–21
(I) Eyedropper/color
sampler/measure

FIGURE 3–20
(N) Notes/audio annotation

FIGURE 3–22
(H) Hand

FIGURE 3–23
(Z) Zoom

FIGURE 3–24
Color picker

Figure 3–19 (U) Geometric Shape helps you to draw out any basic or custom shape from the geometric menu.

Figure 3–20 (N) Notes/Audio Annotation is an amazing yet simple feature of applying notes to any design or image. It is used frequently to pass a design around the office for feedback and comments. The Audio Annotation tool allows the designer to record into a microphone any comments to be heard.

Figure 3–21 (I) Eyedropper/Color Sampler/Measure makes it easy to find and select a specific color pixel in a design. Its sampler feature measures and displays the color values of the selected pixel.

Figure 3–22 (H) Hand allows the quick and simple use of scrolling around a large design or texture without much trouble, even on a small monitor. When using any other tool, holding the space bar is a shortcut to access the hand to quickly move an image and then releasing the space bar returns the designer back to the previous tool.

Figure 3–23 (Z) Zoom allows the quick and simple ease of magnifying or enlarging an area in the design for editing and viewing purposes.

Figure 3–24 Color Picker allows the designer to quickly use two colors at once, for example, the foreground color and the background color. A number of tools allow the designer to switch between these colors for easy editing.

Notes . . .

FIGURE 3–25
Mask

Figure 3–25 Mask tool is used to fill in or paint over an area to be protected when the right part is selected. Once ready, the left tool is chosen and creates a selection of the active area, which is the reverse of what had been masked. Only this active area can now be edited.

Menu Items for Textiles

Figure 3–26 File

- New is used to create a new canvas. A design of any size and resolution can be created. They've added a Preset Sizes pop-up menu to the New dialog box.

- Import is used to access scanning plug-ins. Most scanners have a Photoshop plug-in that allows a designer to scan directly into Photoshop for easy editing.

Figure 3–27 Edit

- Paste allows the designer to drop a copied selection into the center of the design. This pasted file is floating on its own layer and can now be edited separately. This can be applied when creating a design with multiple files or images.

- Paste Into allows the designer to drop a copied selection into the center of a selected area of the design. This pasted file is floating on its own layer and can now be edited separately. Boundaries are defined by the original selection. This feature is priceless when pasting a design into a croquis for positioning and designing.

FIGURE 3–26
File

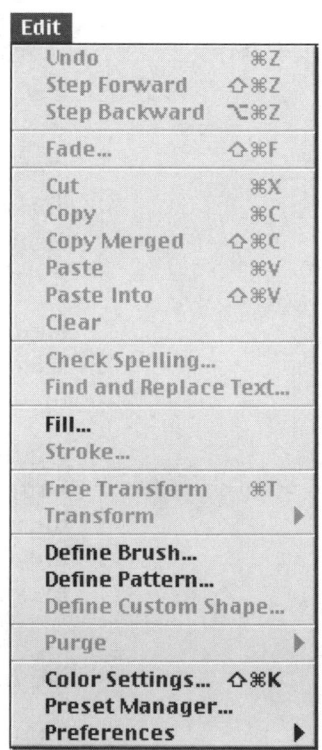

FIGURE 3–27
Edit

- Fill is used to place a foreground color, background color, or pattern into a specific area or selected color. This makes color blocking of a design or flat easy to do. Be sure anti-aliasing is turned off or extra colors will be created.

- Define Brush allows the designer to create a custom brush from any selected area of a design. The area is first selected and then Define Brush is chosen and named. This is a great tool for developing a seamless ground in a design when combined with the Rubber Stamp tool.

- Define Pattern allows the designer to create a custom pattern from any Marquee selected area of a design. The area is first selected and then Define Pattern is chosen and named. Although only a square or rectangular shape can be defined as a pattern, this feature helps to create great repeats and designs.

Figure 3–28 Image

- Mode is used to switch the design between Indexed, RGB, and CMYK color modes.

- Adjustments can be used to edit a photograph or repair poor scan quality. These features are used in techniques later in the book.

- Image Size is an important tool for editing the size and resolution of a design.

- Canvas Size allows the designer to adjust the canvas area. It will become an invaluable tool for editing the repeat edges of a design or image.

Figure 3–29 Layer

The designer can create layers in a file so parts of a design do not interfere with each other. This is a priceless feature for the creation and edits of storyboards.

FIGURE 3–28
Image

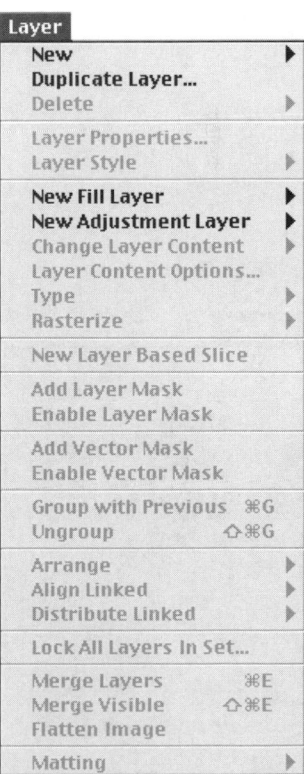

FIGURE 3–29
Layer

Figure 3–30 Select

Color Range allows a designer to specifically select and edit a single color or a range of hues in a design. This is especially valuable in the color reduction process or editing of a watercolor design.

Figure 3–31 Filter

- Blur is used to create a brushed or felted effect in a design.

- Noise creates a cotton or wool texture.

- Texture allows the designer to add a finish texture, like a seersucker, to a design.

- Other hides the limited but useful offset functions in Photoshop. These functions allow a designer to create a custom repeat of a design.

Figure 3–32 View

Print Size shows the design on the monitor in the exact size it will output to a printer. This is a useful tool for previewing a design's width and height before sending it to a printer, especially if outputting to fabric or other expensive substrates.

Figure 3–33 Window

This menu allows the designer to view feature windows from brushes to layers all at one time. These windows can be hidden and recalled to view at any time. Quick access is the key in Adobe Photoshop. Some of the important main windows are listed and described below.

- Color allows the designer fast access to custom color chip swatches.

- Swatches allows the designer to store an unlimited number of frequently used chips.

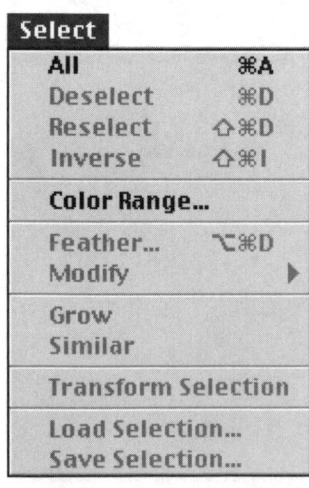

FIGURE 3–30
Select

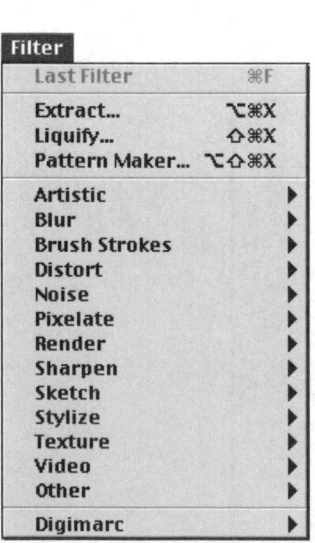

FIGURE 3–31
Filter

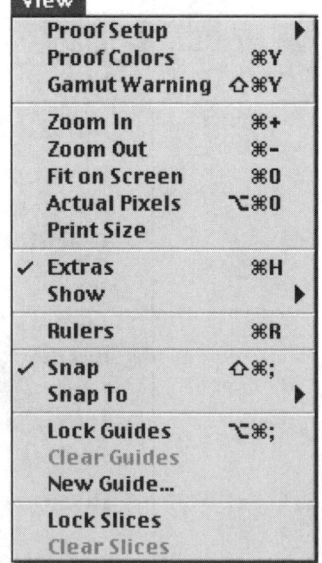

FIGURE 3–32
View

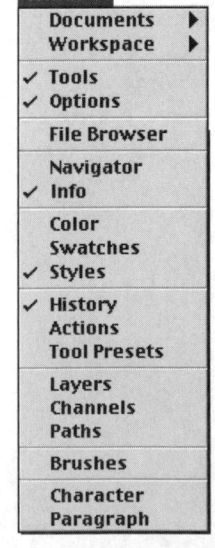

FIGURE 3–33
Window

- History accesses a limited number of past actions and allows the editing of them.

- Layers allows a designer the ability to work on separate areas of the design without affecting others. Overlapping designs and applying filters separately are strong areas when this feature is used.

- Brushes accesses all the custom brushes available in Photoshop. Brushes can be easily created in one design and then used on another.

Naming, Saving, and Exporting Files

The excitement of creating a design can be ruined by closing the design software, only to realize that the design, edits, or changes made were not saved. The most important rule of designing on a computer is *save, Save, Save*. Once a file or canvas is created, it is important to get into the habit of saving the design at every important addition or edit to the design. To accomplish this easy task, a design can be saved over the original by using the **File > Save** option or renamed as a new file by selecting **File > Save As. . . .**

When saving any file it is also important to name the file in a logical way. After awhile you could easily end up with 12 files named "Untitled 1," "Untitled 2," etc. Telling them apart from a small thumbnail is often difficult. Opening them all up again is time wasted. So naming files in a descriptive way will save a designer much trouble in the future.

Another way to save a file is to "Export" it. This feature is accessed through **File > Export** and is used primarily for bringing a Photoshop file into Illustrator for continued editing in Postscript. But, both Save and Save As are the best options to use.

Exercise: Saving over the Original File

Step 1. Go to the **File** menu and select **File > New** (Figure 3–34).

Step 2. Name the image "New Design 1." Select the file size to be 5 inches in the Width field and 5 inches in the Height field.

Step 3. Draw into the new canvas with a simple brush design.

Step 4. Choose **File > Save**. Select the destination to be the Desktop. The canvas has now been saved to the Desktop folder (Figure 3–35).

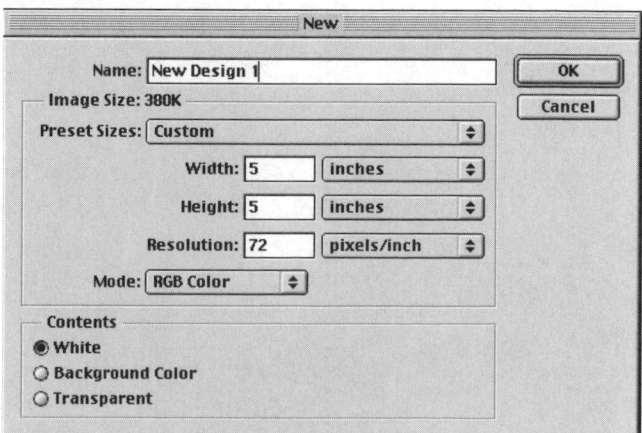

FIGURE 3–34
New dialogue window

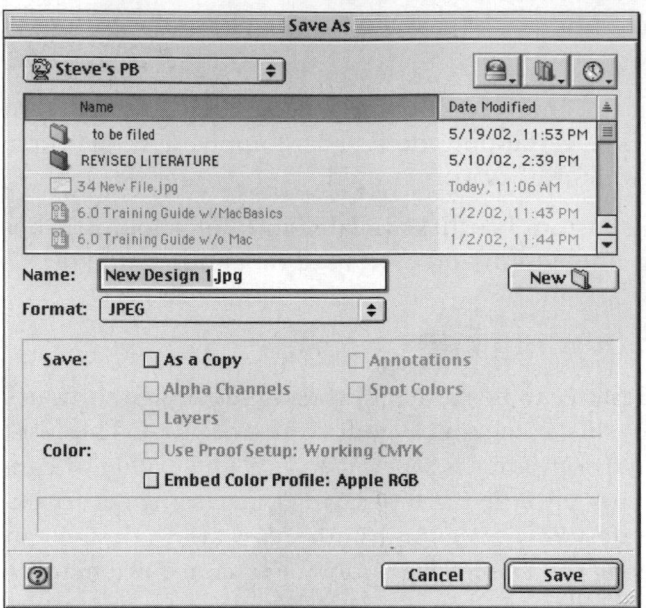

FIGURE 3–35
Save as

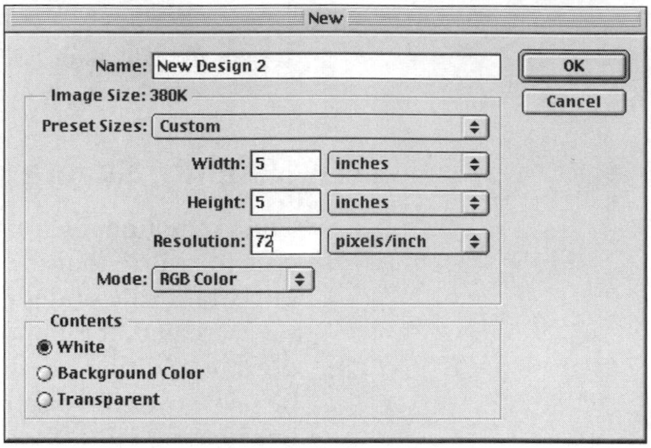

FIGURE 3–36
Saving a new file

Exercise: Saving a New File

Step 1. Go to the **File** menu and select **File > New.**

Step 2. Name the image "New Design 2." Select the file size to be 5 inches in the Width field and 5 inches in the Height field (Figure 3–36).

Step 3. Draw into the new canvas with a simple brush design.

Step 4. Choose **File > Save As. . . .** Select the destination to be the Desktop. Rename the file "New Design 3." The canvas has now been saved to the Desktop folder under an entirely new name (Figure 3–37).

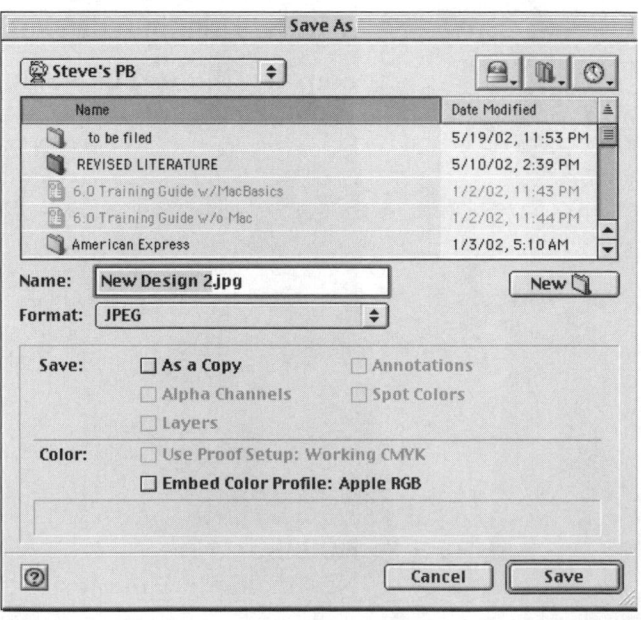

FIGURE 3–37
Save as

Color, Color Everywhere

The following exercises walk a designer through setting up a color palette—a basic beginning of design.

How to Select Colors

When designing for any reason, the first step in the process is to build a palette of seasonal colors. How a designer arrives at their choice of colors depends on many variables. Trends, shopping the market in the United States and abroad, as well as previous years' "hot" colors, all make an impression on what is going to happen in color for the next season. Once colors are determined, a designer gathers all of their fabrics, prints, swatches, and such that represent the color stories to be forecast. These colors need to be interpreted into the computer to be used for design generation. For ease of use, the colors are compiled into a custom color palette, which can then be shared with anyone involved in the design process.

Trial-and-Error Color Selection

The "poor man's" way is trial and error. Mix a color and print it out; if it is not correct, try again. This can take a designer five or more tries before getting the color right. Once a designer has a color they like, the designer needs to save the color in a palette for safekeeping and later use. The basics of creating a custom palette are described below.

Building Color Palettes

Color palettes in Photoshop are very user-friendly. Adding color and deleting or naming chips are a few of the options. Custom palettes can be saved and opened whenever needed as well as appended to each other to create larger palettes of color.

Palette View Options

Palettes can be viewed as small thumbnails (Figure 3–38) or small lists of colors (Figure 3–39). The advantages of each are up to the designer. Thumbnails allow the user to easily see many colors at once while the designer is adding, deleting, and selecting the chips. The list view allows the user to see the name of the color swatch next to the chips while the user scrolls down through a list.

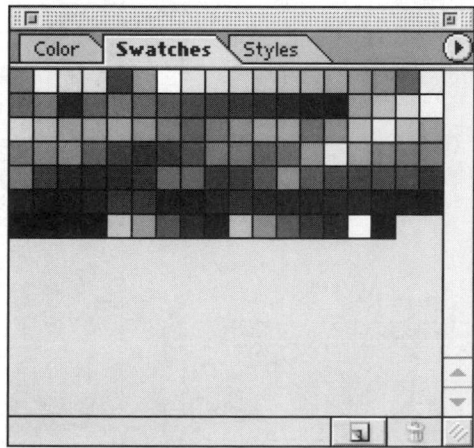

FIGURE 3–38
Thumbnails

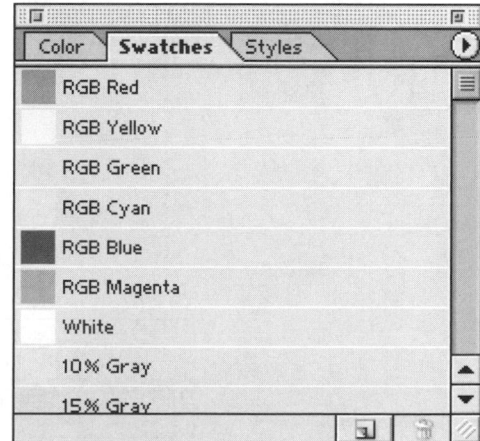

FIGURE 3–39
List

Creating a New Palette and Naming the Chips

Begin creating a new palette.

Step 1. Go to the **Window** menu and select **Swatches.**

A default palette shows up (Figure 3–40).

Step 2. Colors can be added here by simply having the chosen color as the foreground color, then dragging the mouse over a white area of the custom palette.

Step 3. A bucket will appear. Clicking the mouse will show a window to name the color chip (Figure 3–41).

Step 4. Enter a name and choose **OK.** The color is added to the palette (Figure 3–42).

Removing a Color from the Palette

Step 1. To remove a color from the palette, hold down the Apple key on a Mac mouse or the Control key on a PC mouse to see a scissors tool (Figure 3–43).

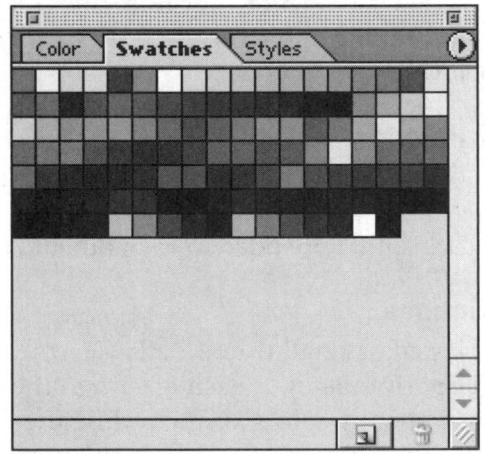

FIGURE 3–40
Default color palette

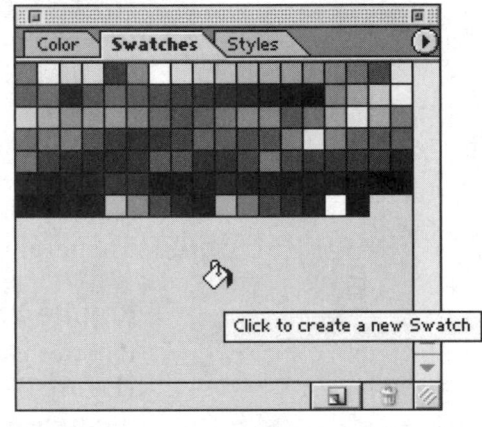

FIGURE 3–41
Fill color chip

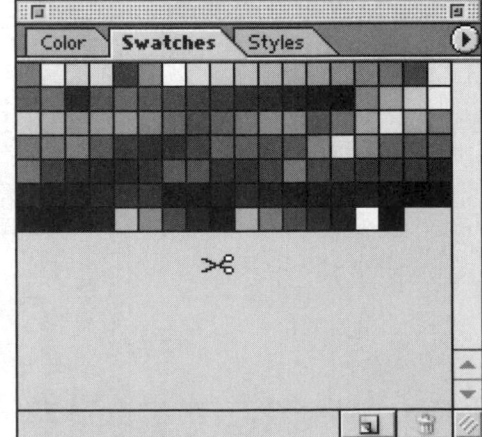

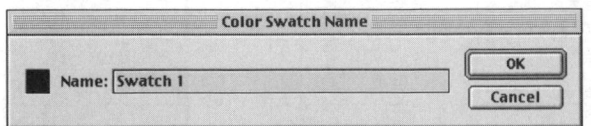

FIGURE 3–42
Name chip

FIGURE 3–43
Remove chip

Step 2. Click on the color to be removed and it is cut out.

Selecting a Color from a Swatches Palette

Step 1. To select a color from the palette, just drag the mouse over the chip to be selected. An eyedropper appears (Figure 3–44).

Step 2. Click the mouse on the chip and the color is now the new foreground color.

Loading Palettes and Swatches

Step 1. To load a new palette, select in the **Palette** window by using the right-hand options arrow (Figure 3–45).

Step 2. If no swatch palettes are available in the selector, select **Load Swatches.**

Step 3. In the **Load** window, find and open the Adobe Photoshop folder (Figure 3–46).

Step 4. In this folder, find the **Presets** folder (Figure 3–47).

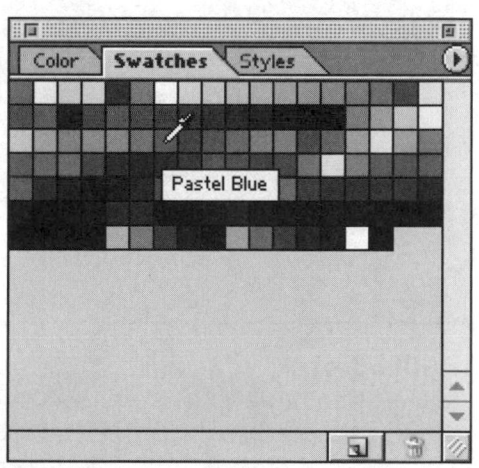

FIGURE 3–44
Select color chip

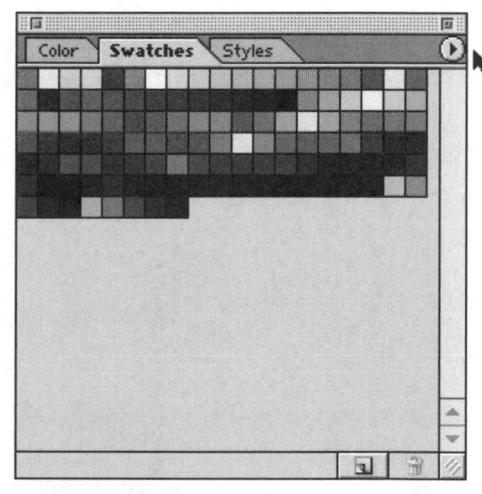

FIGURE 3–45
Palette option

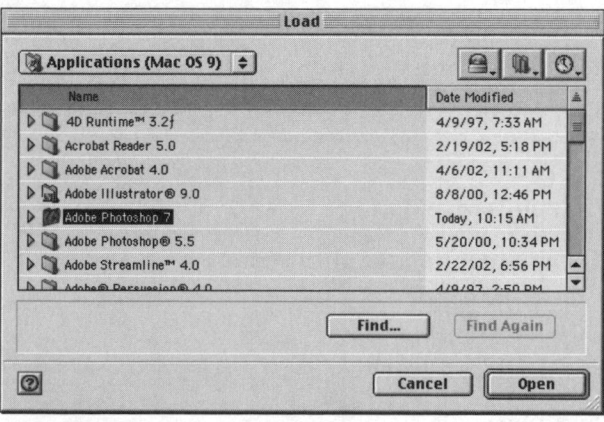

FIGURE 3–46
Palette selection

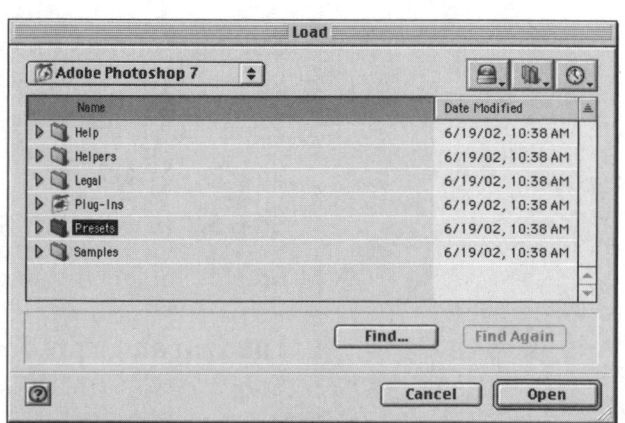

FIGURE 3–47
Presets

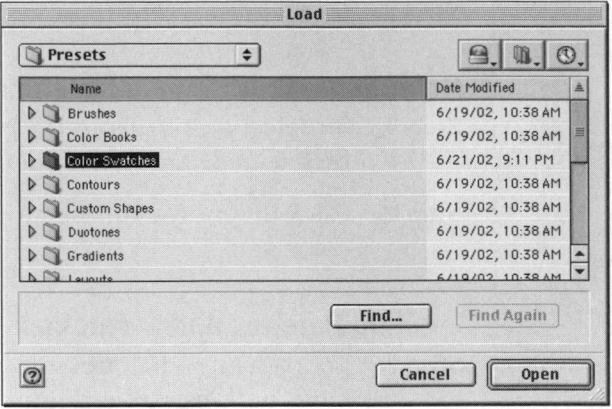

FIGURE 3–48
Color swatches

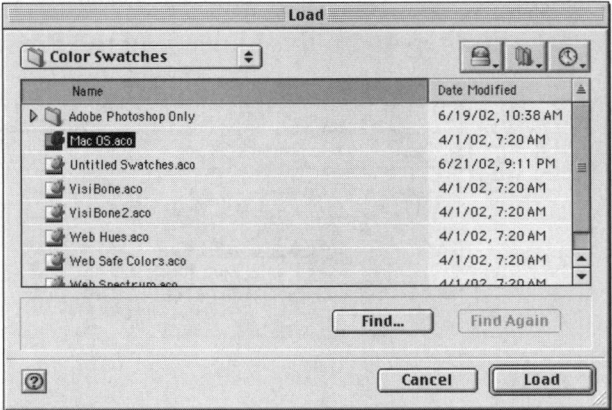

FIGURE 3–49
Select swatches

Step 5. In this folder, find the **Color Swatches** folder (Figure 3–48).

Step 6. Double-click on the palette to open (Figure 3–49).

Saving Palettes and Swatches

Step 1. To save a new palette, select the right-hand options arrow in the **Palette** window.

Step 2. Select **"Save" Swatches** option.

Step 3. In the **File > Save** window, name the palette (Figure 3–50).

Step 4. Select the swatch folder for the palette and choose **Save.**

Loading an Empty Swatch Palette

Step 1. Go to the **Window** menu and select **Swatches.**

Step 2. This will open a default Swatches palette.

Step 3. In the swatch options on the top right, choose **Replace Swatches.**

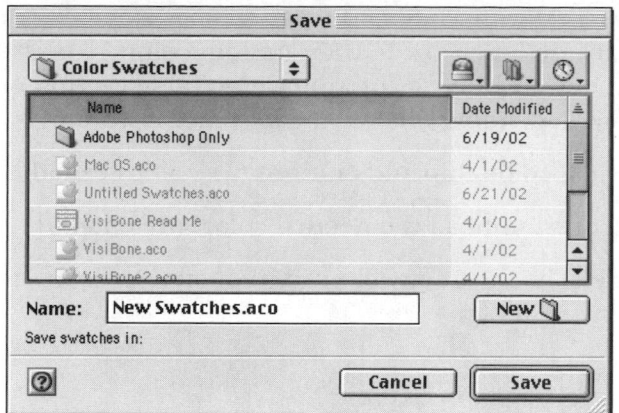

FIGURE 3–50
Save swatches

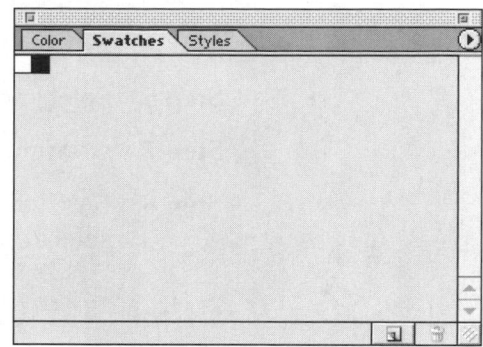

FIGURE 3–51
New swatches

Notes . . .

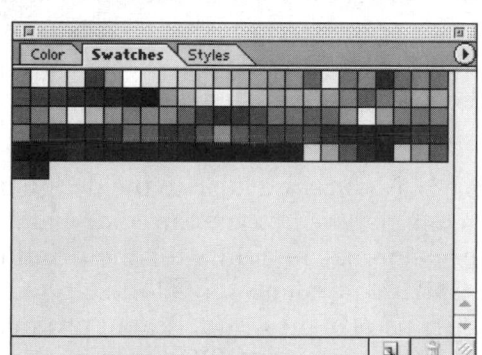

FIGURE 3–52
Default palette

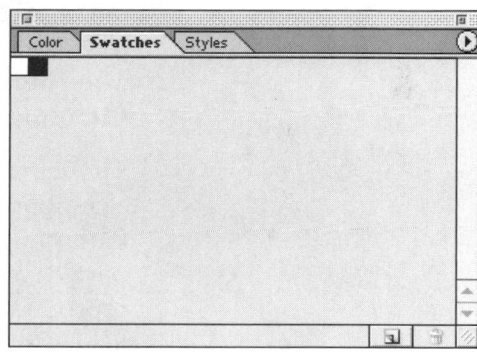

FIGURE 3–53
New swatches

Step 4. Select the **New Swatches** file on the CD that came with this book (Figure 3–51).

Step 5. This **New Swatches** window is now ready for new colors.

Let's Try It!

Building a Seasonal Palette from Scratch

Many designers prefer to set up a color palette from the beginning of the season and then continue to use and edit this palette as the season progresses. To create a palette, follow these steps:

Step 1. Go to the **Window** menu and select **Show Swatches.**

Step 2. This will open a default Swatches palette (Figure 3–52).

Step 3. In the swatch options on the top right, choose **Replace Swatches.**

Step 4. Select the **New Swatches** file on the CD that came with this book (Figure 3–53).

Step 5. This window starts off with white and black. The Swatches window is now empty for any designer to add their custom colors to be saved. This palette can now be opened into the Color Table window or the Swatches window, depending on how the designer is working.

Step 6. Select an individual color chip and enter in the color needed.

Step 7. Continue this process until all the needed colors are entered.

Step 8. SAVE this palette! The designer will need to open the file in order to select these colors to design.

Other Methods of Color Selection

Matching Color for Design and Printout

Matching color and matching color from monitor to printout are two different avenues. Most designers seem content to be "in the ballpark" when viewing color on the screen and then seeing the result at output. Those designers I have worked with in the textile industry seem to realize that the final output is what people are going to see, so they keep a palette of colors and how the colors print for easy reference when building the next season's palette. How they get these colors is another story. Choosing colors in any program can be intense. There are many ways to do this.

There are also many products available to the designer to select color. Pantone® is a company that seems to have become the color-matching standard in the industry. Pantone develops color-matching inks for the printing and textile industry. They have developed CMYK equivalents for colors selected so those colors can be easily reproduced in other parts of the world. Recent products from Pantone allow you to load a Textile Color Picker onto your PC or Macintosh and access their color-matching libraries (Figure 3–54). This electronic format of color is accessible through the Adobe Photoshop Color Picker. Pantone color values and names export to other applications when moving an image around from application to application.

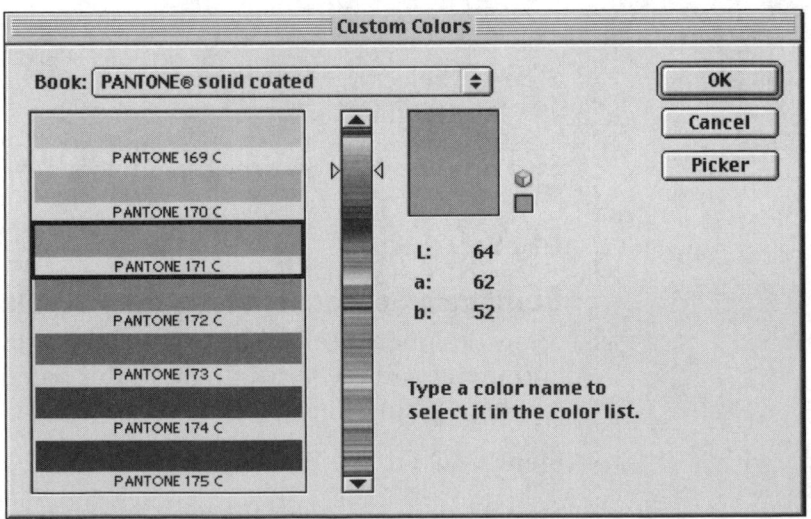

FIGURE 3–54
Pantone picker
(Pantone® and other Pantone, Inc. trademarks are the registered property of Pantone, Inc. PANTONE trademarks and copyrights used with permission of Pantone, Inc.)

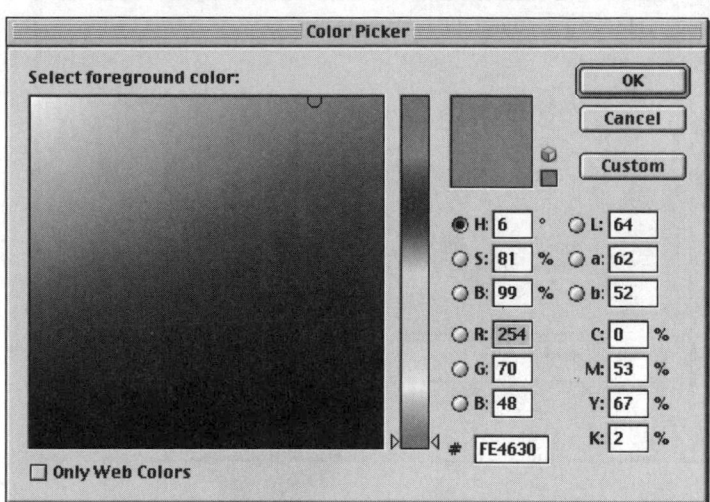

FIGURE 3–55
Adobe color picker

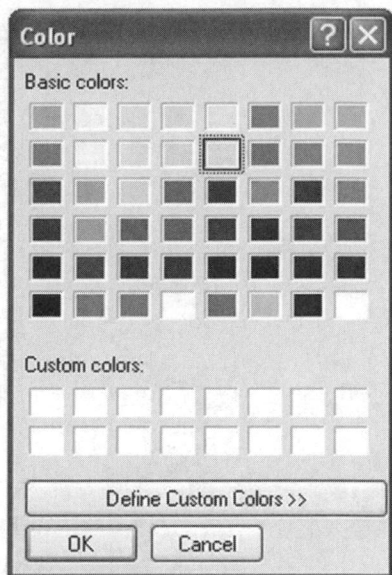

FIGURE 3–56
PC color picker

Selecting Pantone Libraries

- To see the Pantone selection window for selecting colors, in Photoshop 5.5 and earlier, go to the **File** menu and select **Preferences, General** or in Photoshop 6.0 and later, go to the **Edit** menu and select **Preferences, General.**

- In the window, select the option for Color Picker.

Here are the choices:

1. To access the **Adobe Color Picker,** the window in Figure 3–55 will show when a color is to be selected. The Adobe Color Picker will allow the entering of CMYK values, RGB values, Lab values, HSB values, and Pantone® ink selections by clicking on the **Custom** button in the right-hand corner.

2. On the **PC** the color picker in Figure 3–56 is first available when selecting the picker in the **Preferences** window.

3. The **Apple Color Picker** can be accessed by selecting the picker in the **Preferences** window. When chosen, the window in Figure 3–57 will show when a color is to be selected.

4. **Pantone** libraries can be accessed by selecting the **Custom** button on the right-hand side of the Adobe Color Picker. In this window, a designer can enter a color by using any Pantone Paper numbers (Figure 3–58) or Pantone Textile colors (Figure 3–59).

A Back-to-Front Color System

Another choice is doing a back-to-front system in which a set of palettes is created on the system to be used. These colors are then output to the same printer on which

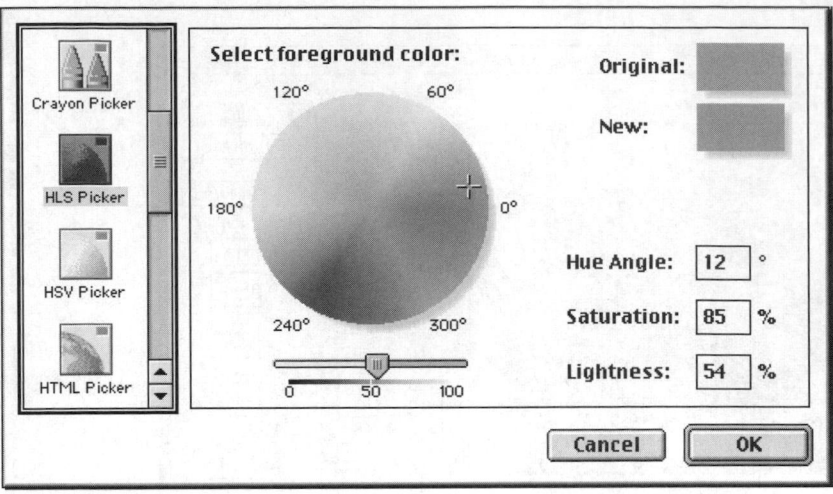

FIGURE 3–57

Apple color picker

(Courtesy of Apple Computer, Inc.)

FIGURE 3–58

Pantone paper

(Pantone® and other Pantone, Inc. trademarks are the registered property of Pantone, Inc. PANTONE trademarks and copyrights used with permission of Pantone, Inc.)

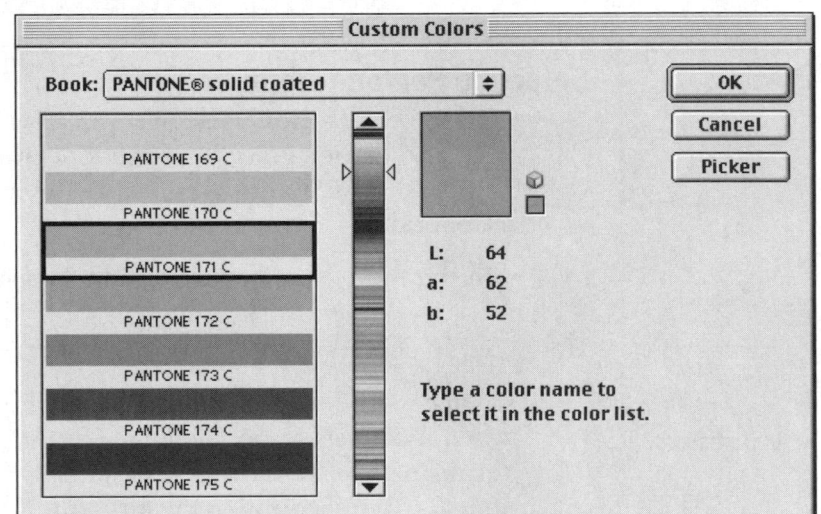

FIGURE 3–59

Pantone textile

(Pantone® and other Pantone, Inc. trademarks are the registered property of Pantone, Inc. PANTONE trademarks and copyrights used with permission of Pantone, Inc.)

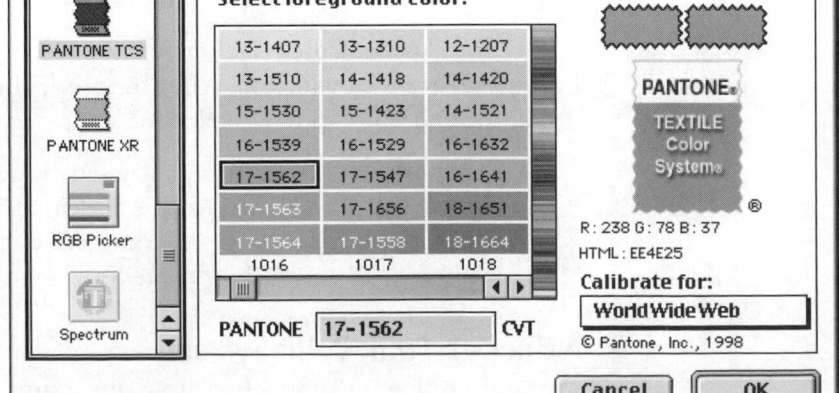

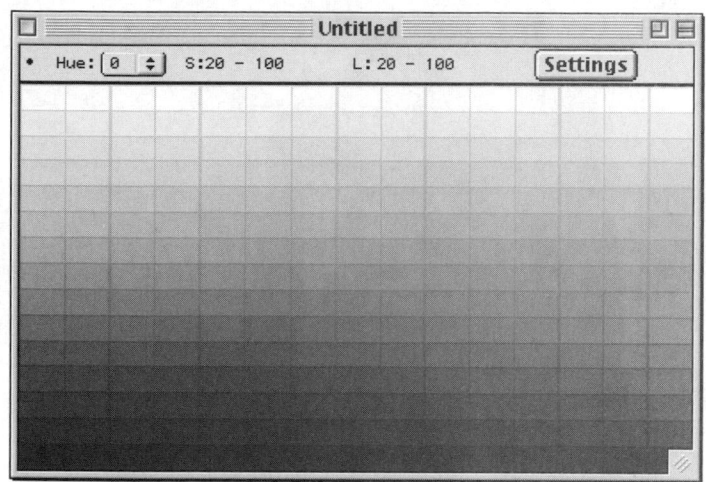

FIGURE 3–60
Screen shot of color charter

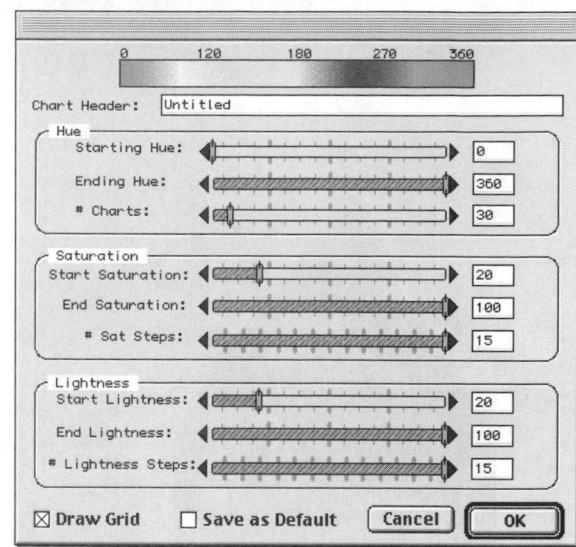

FIGURE 3–61
Color charter setup

all other artwork will be printed. This creates a predictable set of colors that can be re-entered into the palette of any artwork so that predictable color will be achieved.

If the software cannot easily develop and print out palettes of color, then a third-party software like **Color Charter** can be used. (See Figure 3–60.) Color Charter is one of many products that allows a designer to develop the charts of any color values needed and to print the color values out with the hue, saturation, and lightness values of every chip. Then the designer will have a true printout of what colors their desktop printer can manage as well as the color values to enter back in to get a reproducible color. The one drawback here is that the monitor may not be a perfect match. Matching the monitor is done by using a monitor calibrator to build a profile. This calibrator attaches directly to the screen and measures the light waves (gamma) received off the screen.

To use Color Charter, follow these steps:

Step 1. Open Color Charter software and select the **Settings** button on the top right.

Step 2. Set the settings to the desired range of hues. Also select the correct range of lightness and saturation. (See Figure 3–61.) Hue charts that are in between can be generated later as well.

Step 3. Choose **OK** and **Save As . . .** (Figure 3–62).

- Name the folder of charts.
- Choose the **Format** as "Separate Picts."
- Select the **Resolution** to be 72 DPI.
- Select the **Page** size of 8.5″ × 11″ or 11″ × 17″.
- Choose **Save.**

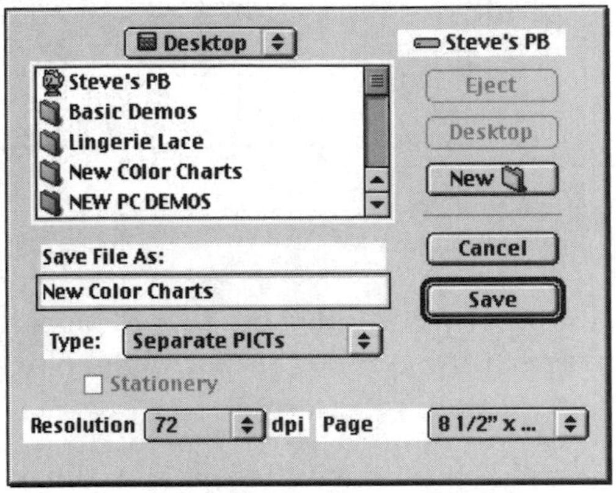

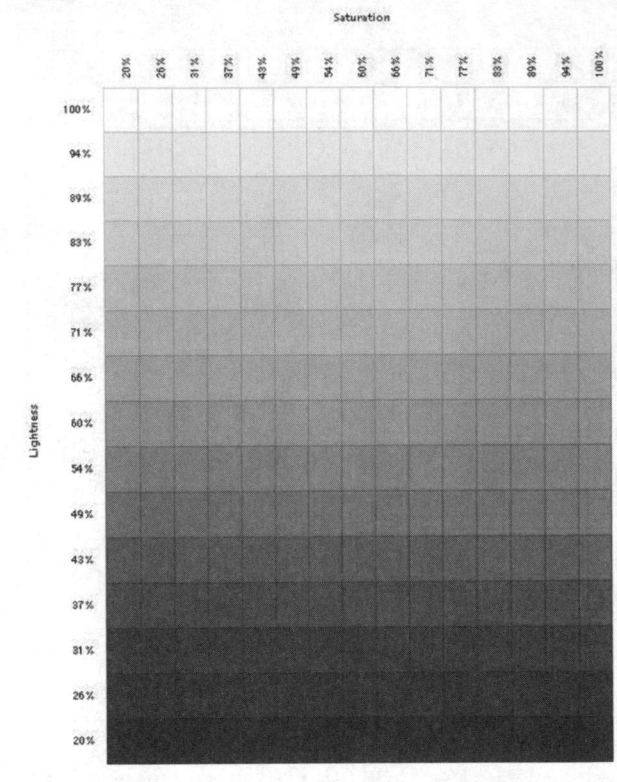

FIGURE 3–63
Sample color chart from color charter software

FIGURE 3–62
Save charts

Notes...

The hue charts can now be opened into any software that accepts Pict files. They can be printed from any design software and used as predictable color charts (Figure 3–63).

Profiling and Color Calibration

A third way to match color is to use a spectrophotometer like X-Rite's Digital Swatchbook. This device allows a designer to "zap" or sample a color on a chip, fabric swatch, or any object. It then averages the color it sees and creates a very close representation of it on the screen. These color chips can now be used in any program that works with the X-Rite palettes. For simple, functional color measurements the Digital Swatchbook is accurate, and can be utilized with Macintosh or Windows computers to utilize measured spectrophotometer readings with color software called ColorShop. The ColorShop Palette window is shown in Figure 3–64.

The Monitor Optimizer is X-Rite's monitor calibration instrument that assures on-screen color accuracy. It is used to calibrate the white-point and gamma of your display, or to create custom monitor profiles. The slight drawback to this system is the setup. There is always a need to have the same printer, monitor, and paper stock for this to work well, as any change in the process can throw off the color match. It is also recommended to do the calibration at least once a week. The basic spectrophotometer is used in the following way:

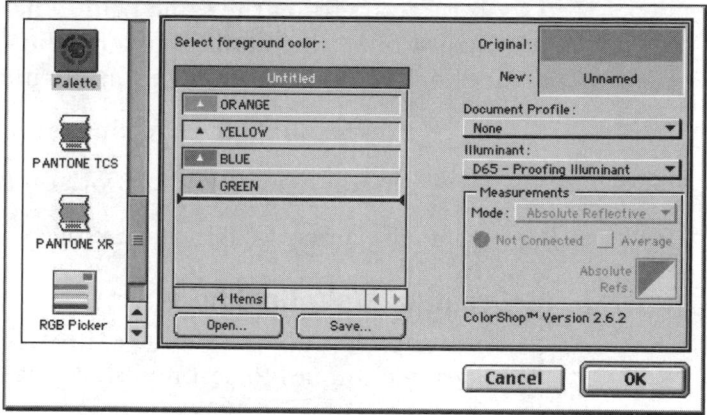

FIGURE 3–64
Screen shot of palette window in digital swatchbook
(Courtesy of X-Rite)

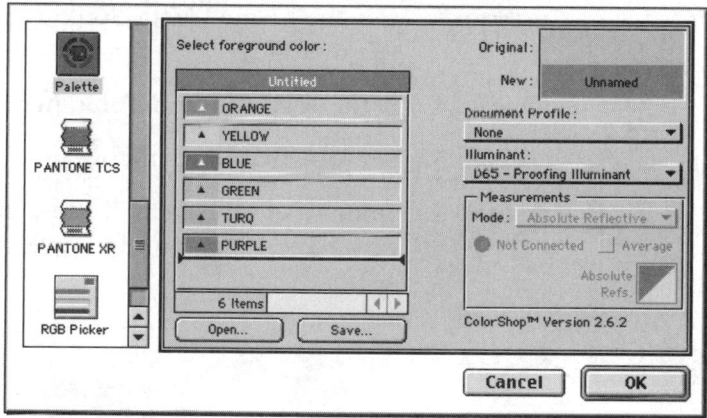

FIGURE 3–65
Screen shot of color chips in swatchbook (this screen shot
is to show chips that are "zapped in" after the calibration)
(Courtesy of X-Rite)

Step 1. Following the X-Rite Monitor Optimizer instructions, calibrate the monitor.

Step 2. Select the proper printer profile from the library of profiles that comes with the software.

Step 3. Using the Digital Swatchbook handheld device, select color chips that are to be matched and individually "zap" them to load each one into the custom color palette, adding the chips, like the one shown in Figure 3–65. The palette can then be saved.

These colors can now be used in any designs and accessed through the Photoshop color picker.

This sounds easy, but the real catch is setting up the spectrophotometer with the monitor and printer profiles correctly set. If any changes in the process occur, all color matching is thrown off, so it is important to keep the settings the

Notes...

same, always using the same printer and the same paper stock. Other variables in color matching actually involve the designer's working space. Keeping these in check will ensure your red in the morning is the same red in the afternoon:

- Prevent sunlight reflecting off the monitor or changing light.
- Do not hang bright artwork on the walls near the monitor.
- Use a neutral gray for the desktop instead of a wild desktop design.

Creating Multiple Colorways

Photoshop has no tool for the express development of colorways. The fastest and easiest techniques to accomplish this task are as follows:

Technique #1

Step 1. Open the file **"Textile Print 1"** on the enclosed CD (Figure 3–66).

Step 2. Use the **Bucket** and brushes to edit individual colors.

Step 3. Use the **Magic Wand,** double-click on the tool to see the options (Figure 3–67).

Step 4. Set the **Magic Wand Tolerance** to "0."

Step 5. Set **Anti-aliased** to unchecked.

Step 6. Select **Use All Layers,** if there are layers in the image and the color to be selected is on another layer.

FIGURE 3–66
"Textile print 1"

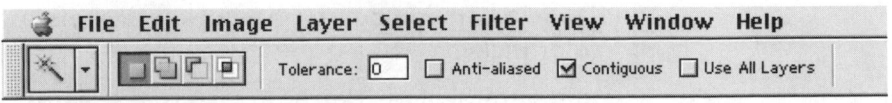

FIGURE 3–67
Magic wand options

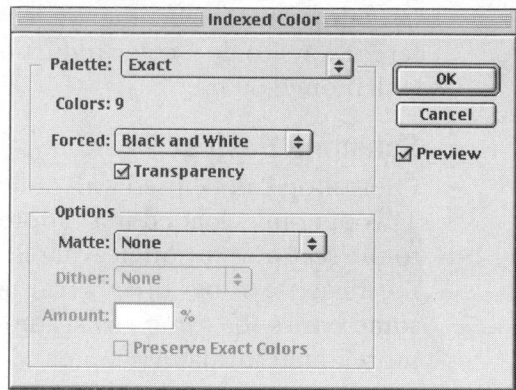

FIGURE 3–68
Indexed color

Step 7. Select **Contiguous,** if the area of color to be selected is a single shape of color. If the color to be selected is in many separate areas of the design, deselect **Contiguous.**

Step 8. Use the **Magic Wand** to select the area of color to be edited. For instance, select the RED hue. Once selected, the area can be filled with the **Fill** command or **Bucket** tool, painted in with brushes, drawn in, or otherwise edited.

Step 9. Continue **Select/Edit** until all color edits are done.

Technique #2

A second technique to edit a color of a file is done "globally," using **Indexed** mode and the **Color Table.**

Step 1. Open the file **"Textile Print 2"** on the enclosed CD.

Step 2. The image is in **RGB** mode, so change it to **Indexed** mode. To do this, go to the **Image** menu, select **Mode,** and then **Indexed** mode. Choose **OK.** (See Figure 3–68.)

Step 3. Going back to the **Image** menu, select **Mode** and go to **"Color Table."**

Step 4. In the open Color Table, select the color to be edited by clicking on it with the mouse.

Step 5. The active color picker will show. Enter the needed color.

HINT: If the color can be targeted in the **Color Table,** click on it in the image using the eyedropper from the **Color Table.** The selected color will be changed to a transparent color to "show" that it can now be edited freely.

Scanning a Fabric for Color Reduction

When scanning in a fabric for color reduction, you must take into consideration the technique used to scan the fabric. A 32-bit scan is going to give you more pixel information than an 8-bit scan. Also, remember that scans of a fabric tend to be tougher to clean up than a scan of flat art. The more color information and detail in the original image, the longer the cleanup process will be. There are a few different ways to do a color reduction in Photoshop and the image itself will dictate which one you use.

Scanning Basics

Photoshop can be used with almost any scanner that has its own plug-in software. This plug-in is loaded into Photoshop's Import/Export folder and allows access to the scanner without leaving Photoshop. Saving time is a great benefit, because the image can be directly scanned into Photoshop this way. The following are some basics for using any scanning software. Advanced scanning is discussed in more detail in a later chapter.

Step 1. Place the image to be scanned on the scanner bed.
- Be sure that the image is as flat as possible. If it is wrinkled fabric, iron it.
- Be sure the image is as straight as possible on the scanner bed. It is much easier to straighten it before scanning than figuring out in Photoshop the exact degree to rotate the image back to being straight.

Step 2. In Photoshop, go to **File > Import** and select the plug-in software for the scanner.

Step 3. Always select **Preview** first. Preview in any scanner software gives the designer the opportunity to see if the image is scanning well and is positioned right.

Step 4. After **Preview** is done, set the correct modes as needed:
- Select **Color** (32 bit) or **Black & White** (1 bit).
- Select the **Resolution** (usually a minimum of 150 DPI).
- Select any **Filters** for removing moiré effects.
- Set **Scale** to 100%.

Step 5. Choose **Scan.** When finished, the scanned images will appear as a new window in Photoshop. Every scanner is a little different, but they all have the same basic features. Be sure to read the manual that is included with your scanner. A little time invested now in becoming familiar with your scanner's features will save you much time later.

Preparing Fabric Scans for Color Reduction

Fabric scans can be a bit tricky because the scanner can pick up much of the texture of the weave or knit. Before reducing color in the fabric you should try a few filters to remove this texture.

Step 1. Open the file **"Textile Print 3"** on the enclosed CD.

Step 2. Go to the **Filter** menu and select **Blur > Gaussian Blur** (Figures 3–69 and 3–70).

Step 3. Set the **Radius** to 0.3 pixels; this will remove much of the texture without clouding detail in the image. Using the **Preview** button, the designer can see if the effect is what they want. If 0.3 is not high enough to remove the texture, use a higher number. Be careful not to go too high and blur out any detail that is to be kept.

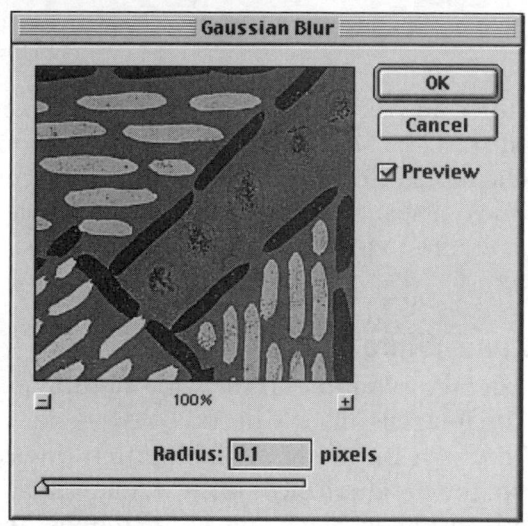

FIGURE 3–69
Before blur

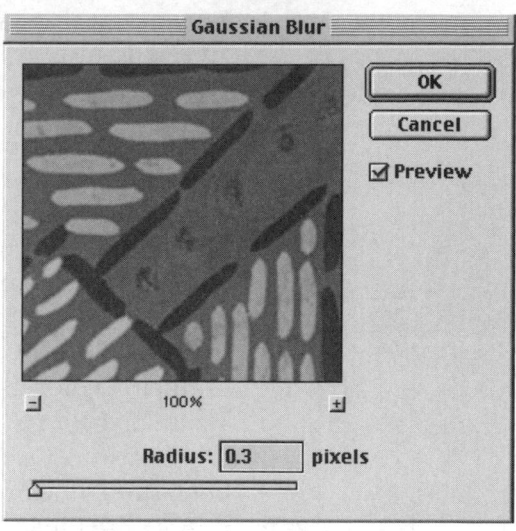

FIGURE 3–70
After blur

Notes . . .

Step 4. Choose **OK.** With the texture removed, one of the options listed in the next section for scanned artwork and photographs can be utilized to have a color-reduced image.

Color Reduction of a Scanned Image

Color reduction is an interesting process. Many designers ask why there is a need to reduce the colors when the original is an 8-or-12 color design. Scanning an image into the computer is the real issue. When an image is scanned into the computer, the scanner sees more color than is there. It sees the overlap of printed colors, where colors mix, shadows of colors from fabric texture, and if on fabric, even how the colors are reflected from the fabric they are printed on. That 8-or-12 color print is now almost 200 colors in the scan. Try to do a colorway on a 200-color design! So color reducing is necessary to color or design using scanned images. Just for a preview of how we will proceed, look at the images in Figure 3–71 and 3–72. Figure 3–71 is the original scan,

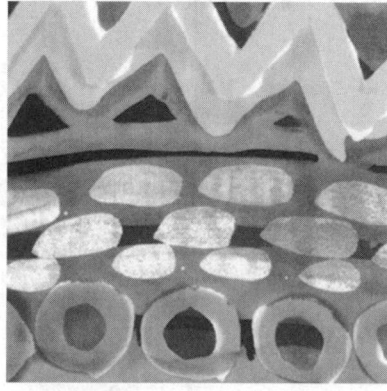

FIGURE 3–71
256-Color original

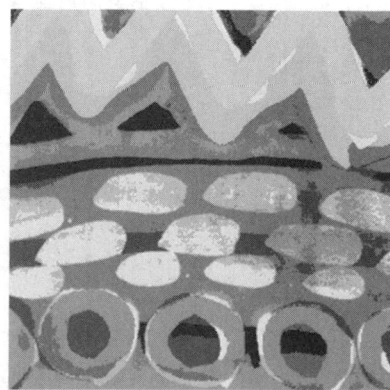

FIGURE 3–72
Reduced to 12 colors

containing 256 colors. Figure 3–72 is the new color-reduced version, with only 12 colors in it.

When scanning in a fabric for color reduction, you must also consider the technique used to scan the fabric. A 32-bit scan is going to give you more pixel information than an 8-bit scan. The more info you have, the harder the color reduction will be. Look for a feature on your scan software called "scan as art." This feature may remove much of the pixel info that is unnecessary for your use. Let's look at ways to reduce color.

Color Reducing to Black-and-White Line Art

Reducing color in line art can be very simple. If the scan was done in a Black and White or 1-Bit mode, then the image is already in two colors—black and white. If there was no Black and White or 1-Bit mode available, then the scan may have been done in Grayscale. If so, the design is most likely in many shades of gray. To reduce the file to two colors, most likely black and white, follow these steps. (See Figures 3–73 and 3–74.)

Step 1.   Select in the **Image** menu, **Mode,** and then select **Grayscale.** Choose **OK** when asked to "Discard Color Information." (See Figure 3–75.)

Step 2.   Choose **Mode > Bitmap.** Select the **Output** to 150 pixels per inch. (See Figure 3–76.)

Step 3.   Select for **Method** and use **50% Threshold.** This will allow only black and white to be used. On a scale of contrast from 1 to 100, any gray value from 1 to 50 will become white, and any gray value from 51 to 100 will become black.

Step 4.   Choose **OK.** The image should now be all black-and-white line art.

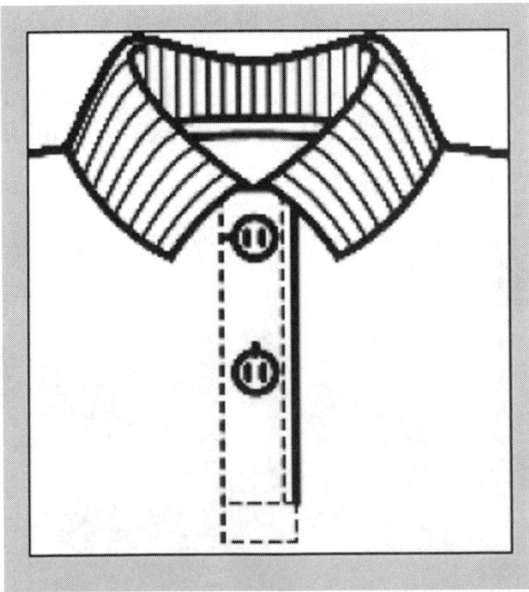

FIGURE 3–73
Original flat line art
(Courtesy of Teri Ross, Imagine That! Consulting Group, Inc.)

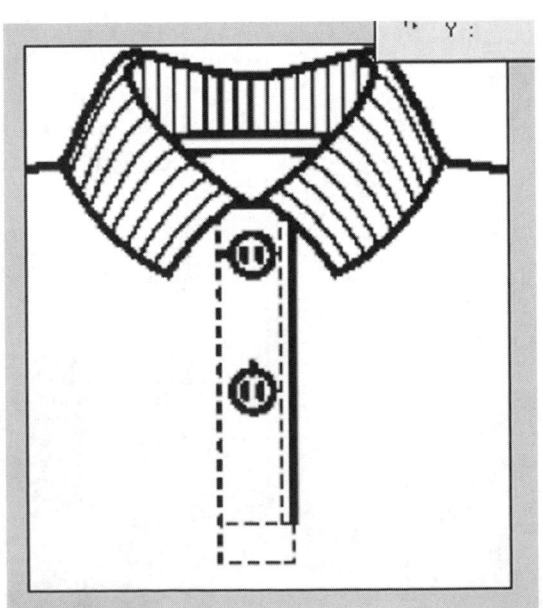

FIGURE 3–74
Two-color art
(Courtesy of Teri Ross, Imagine That! Consulting Group, Inc.)

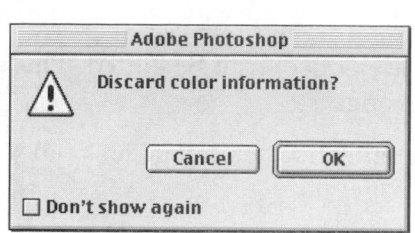

FIGURE 3–75
Discard color information

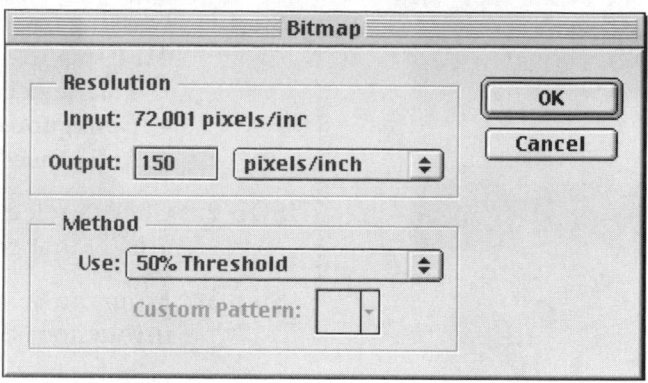

FIGURE 3–76
Bitmap dialog

Color-Reducing Scanned Color Artwork and Photographs

There are a few techniques for color-reducing a scanned color image or artwork. Every scanned or painted image is different. Once an image is opened, the technique to be used will need to be determined. Only practice and patience will allow the designer to determine the outcome. Remember how the design looked a few minutes ago in Figures 3–71 and 3–72? This scanned design is a real example of what the final design can look like before and then after color reduction.

Techniques for Using Adobe® Photoshop® for Color Reduction

Technique #1—Selection Tools

This first technique is used when there are areas of color that can easily be selected with the Magic Wand tool. Double-click on the Magic Wand tool (Figure 3–77). Setting the options of this tool can adjust it to select "like" hues of the color to be selected. The Tolerance and Contiguous options will allow the selection to grow and select a large range of the same hue. These options are defined as follows:

- **Tolerance**—This option, as it is increased, will select more and more color "like" the original selected area.

- **Contiguous**—This option, when selected, will select only the continuous area of "like" color. So if the need is to select the same color in the overall design, then this option should NOT be selected.

- **Anti-Aliased**—As usual, this option is NOT to be selected, because it will create halos of color when the selections and editing are done.

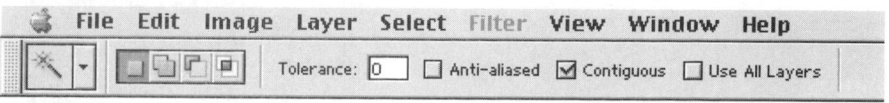

FIGURE 3–77
Magic wand prefs

Step 1. Looking on the CD, open the image named **Color Reduction Exercise #1.** Using the **Magic Wand** tool, set the options as below.
- **Tolerance:** 25
- **Contiguous:** Checked
- **Anti-aliased:** Checked

Step 2. Click to select an area of color to be edited. This will be the **"sample"** area of that color range.

Step 3. From the **Select** menu choose **Similar.** This will select that color range throughout the image.

Step 4. Choose a color to replace this area as the foreground color and select **Edit > Fill.**

Step 5. All selected areas will be replaced with a solid fill of the chosen color.

Technique #2—Edit by Mode

Step 1. Looking on the CD, open the image named **Color Reduction Exercise #2.**

Step 2. Select the **Image** menu and choose **Mode.** Select **Indexed** mode. Figure 3–78 will appear.

Step 3. Choose **Palette: Adaptive (Local).**

Step 4. Select for **Color** and enter the number of colors needed, 9. Here is an important step. Check the **Preview** box to the far right. When a specific number of colors are entered in the color box, the image will update instantly. The designer then is seeing exactly what the image will look like with that exact number of colors. Play with different color numbers and see the difference in the detail and clarity of the image.

Step 5. Select for **Forced: None.**

Step 6. Select for **Options.** Choose **"None"** for **Dither.**

Step 7. Choose **OK.**

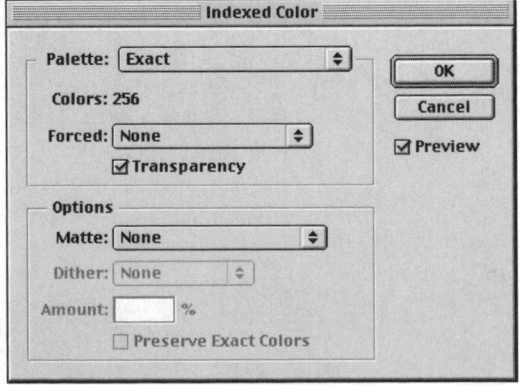

FIGURE 3–78
Indexed color window

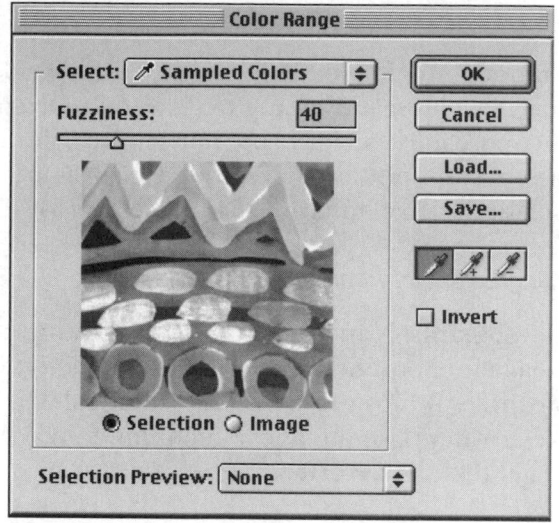

FIGURE 3–79
Color range

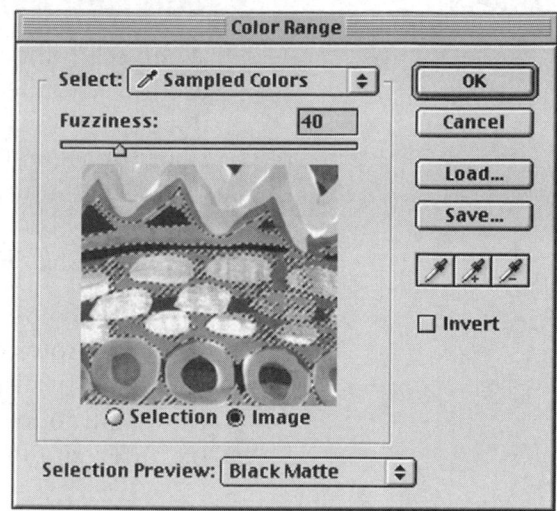

FIGURE 3–80
Color range

Notes...

HINT: Now the design can be edited further using Technique #1.

Technique #3—Color Range

Step 1. Looking on the CD, open the image named **Color Reduction Exercise #3.**

Step 2. From the **Select** menu, choose **Color Range**. (See Figure 3–79.)

Step 3. Select **Image** at the bottom of the window to preview the image to be worked on.

Step 4. Select the **Preview** as Black Matte. This will black out any area NOT selected so the designer can view exactly what color range is being edited.

Step 5. Using the eyedropper tool on the right, the designer can create the selection by clicking on the colors in the image window or directly on the image file. (See Figure 3–80.) The plus eyedropper will add colors to the selection; the minus eyedropper will subtract hues from the selection.

Step 6. The **Fuzziness** option controls the growing of the hue color selection. Start on 0 and drag it higher to see the difference. (See Figure 3–81.)

Step 7. With the tools, select all the colors in the range. Select **OK.** The area color range needed is now specifically selected and can be filled or edited.

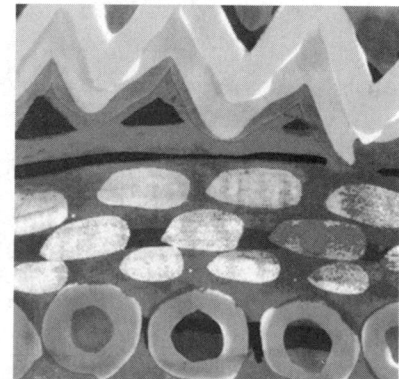

FIGURE 3–81
Color range results

Color Reduction of a Fabric

When scanning in a fabric for color reduction, you must consider the technique used to scan the fabric. A 32-bit scan is going to give you more pixel information than an 8-bit scan. The more info you have, the harder the color reduction will be. Look for a feature on your scan software that is called "scan as art" or 8-bit. This feature may remove much of the pixel info that is unnecessary for the designer's use.

A Note on Color Reducing/Editing of Photographs

Reducing colors in photographs is an interesting idea. Editing and manipulating color in photos can make them useful for storyboards. A designer needs to think ahead about just how these photos will be used. When color is reduced, photos can begin to look like artwork. Use the above techniques to edit the photos and try different filters to get the desired effect.

Design Tips for Using Color

1. Don't overdesign; keep your files clean and simple. (KISS—Keep it sweet and simple!)

2. For processing time and disk space, keep files as small as possible.

3. Be sure you save "versions" of your files.

4. Make a backup of whatever you give to someone else!

5. Don't cover mistakes or changes with white boxes. Delete the items you don't want instead!

6. Pay attention to the file format, so others can reopen the file easily. In fact, ask the person who will be printing the file what file format and version they want.

7. Don't forget, vector images can be scaled easier than raster or bitmap.

8. Check the page layout, color mode, and font selection; include a note with the file listing these specifications to avoid any unnecessary surprises.

9. Always supply a service bureau with a "rough" printout or hard copy of the design.

10. EPS file font should be converted to outlines, so there is no need to supply the font files.

11. Check, double-check, and check again that you have done all of the above!!!

Creating Repeats

Working with a Repeat of a Pattern

Definitions
- **Motif:** The most basic element from which a pattern can be created.
- **Repeat:** One design motif of a pattern.
- **Pattern:** A tiling of a repeat.

A pattern for almost any surface design will need to be "in repeat." This means that the elements of the original area repeat across in a specific motion, to fill out the area to be tiled. From apparel to home furnishings, every design needs to repeat throughout the area of the garment, bed linen, tablecloth, etc.

The following exercises will illustrate how this is easily accomplished.

Technique #1—"Straight" Repeat

Straight repeat takes a single design or motif and tiles it out, side to side and top to bottom.

Step 1. Open the **Repeat Exercise #1** file on the CD that was enclosed with this book (Figure 3–82).

Step 2. Using the square **Crop** tool, select one of the icons. When selecting the area, keep in mind that the final repeat will go from edge to edge on the selection, so only select what is to be seen in the final repeat (Figure 3–83).

Step 3. Choose **Select > All.**

Step 4. Choose **Edit > Define Pattern.** You have now designated the selected motif as a fill pattern. Any fill pattern defined this way is automatically set in a straight repeat. Multiple patterns can be created and saved, ready for use. Each pattern is added to the Pattern Picker in the Toolbar (Figure 3–84).

Step 5. Name the pattern (Figure 3–85).

FIGURE 3–82
Crop pattern repeat

FIGURE 3–83
Pattern repeat

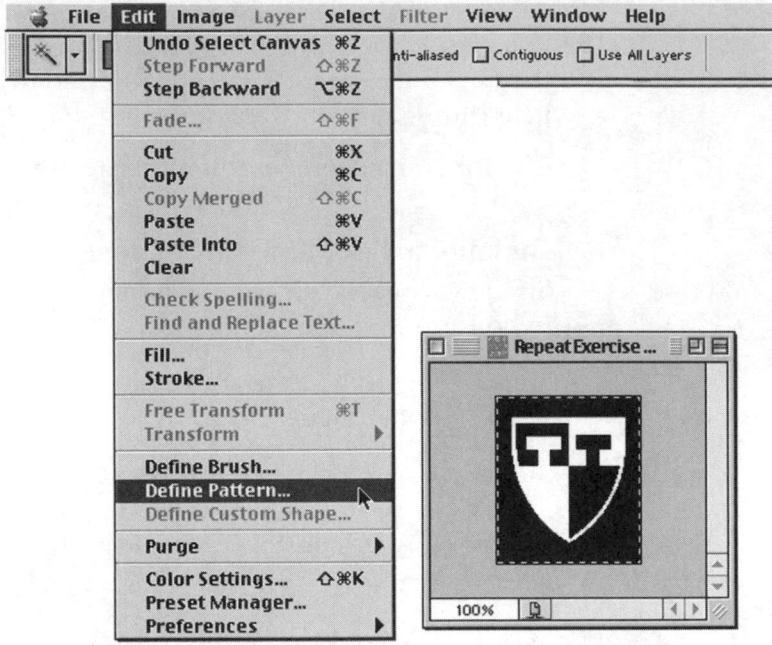

FIGURE 3–84
Edit > define pattern

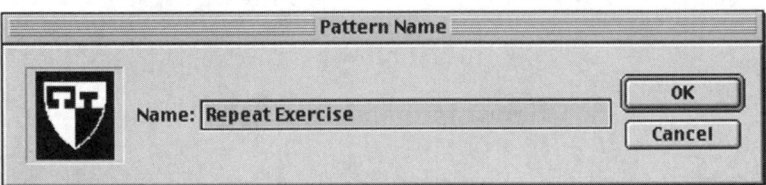

FIGURE 3–85
Name pattern

Now let's view what this repeat looks like:

Step 1. Create a **New File,** 5″ × 5″ at **72** DPI and select a **White** ground.

Step 2. Select the **Edit > Fill** command.

Step 3. In the dialog set:
- **Contents to Use:** Pattern
- **Mode:** Normal
- **Opacity:** 100%

The design that was designated as the repeat will tile side by side filling out the open canvas.

Technique #2—Toss Repeat

Step 1. Open the **Repeat Exercise #2** file on the CD that was enclosed with this book.

Step 2. Select the **Crop** tool, then select and double-click on one of the images in the file (Figure 3–86).

FIGURE 3–86
Crop pattern

FIGURE 3–87
Magic wand pattern

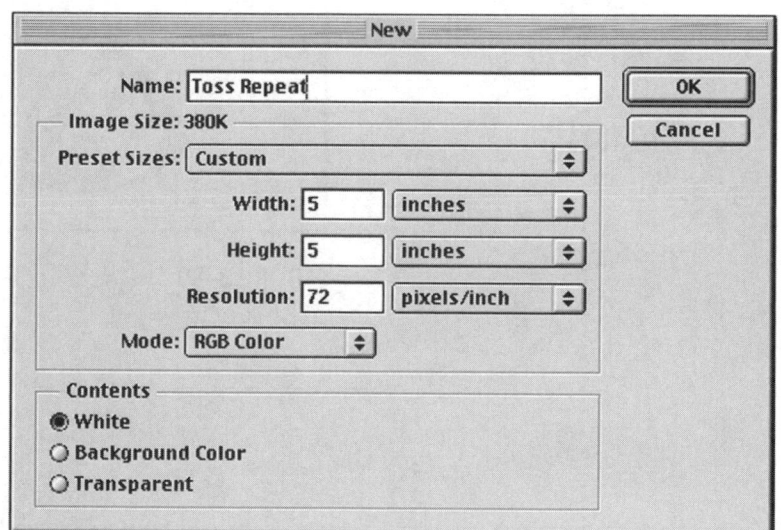

FIGURE 3–88
New file

Step 3.   With the **Magic Wand** tool select only the black area of the image (Figure 3–87).

Step 4.   Create a **New File,** 5″ × 5″ at **72** DPI and select a **White** ground (Figure 3–88).

Step 5.   With both windows open, side by side, use the **Move** tool to drag the "image" onto the new page.

Step 6. Use the **Option** key to **copy and drag** the shield to a new position. This copy can now be rotated to a new position or edited in many ways. Continue this process until you have filled all 5″ of the space. The total area of 5″ × 5″ is your tossed repeat (Figure 3–89). Do not drag the icon off the edge of this repeat area yet, or it will get cut off.

Step 7. The design will continue the "toss" across the repeat edges by using the **Offset Filter** to shift the edges from the outside to the middle (Figure 3–90).

Step 8. Go to the **Filter** menu and select **Other > Offset.** The **Offset Filter** window will show.

FIGURE 3–89
Toss repeat

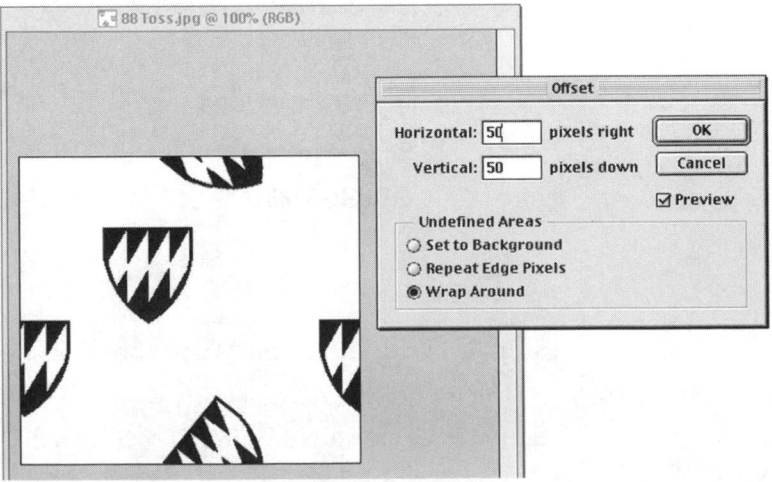

FIGURE 3–90
Offset filter window

Step 9. Make the selections:
- Horizontal: **180 pixels right**
- Vertical: **180 pixels down**
- Check the **Preview** option
- Undefined Areas: Select **Wrap Around**
- Select **OK**

This will give the design a perfect swap of the top and bottom areas. For this design 180 pixels were chosen, because that was the exact number in half of the design. (See Figures 3–91 and 3–92.)

Any part of the design that was in the original area is now repeating over the edges of the 5″ × 5″ canvas. Any part of the design that was on the edges (the empty canvas area) is now in the center. This empty area can now be edited and filled in as the original area was with more icons of the design.

Step 10. Select another image area with the **Magic Wand** and continue to **Option > Copy > Drag** the image to fill out the remaining empty spaces (Figure 3–93).

Technique #3—Offset (1/2 Drop) Repeat

Step 1. Open the **Repeat Exercise #3** file on the CD that was enclosed with this book.

Step 2. Using the square **Marquee** tool, select one of the icons. When selecting the area, keep in mind that the final repeat will go from edge to edge on the selection, so only select what is to be seen in the final repeat. Choose **Crop** (Figure 3–94).

Step 3. Go to **Select > All**.

Step 4. Choose **Edit > Copy**.

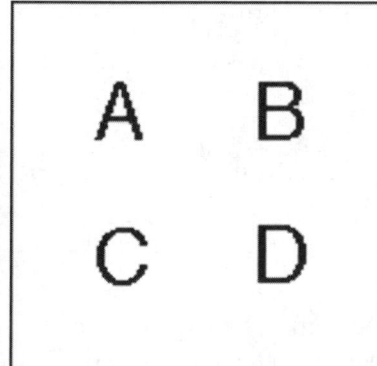

FIGURE 3–91
Diagram of design before top and bottom swap

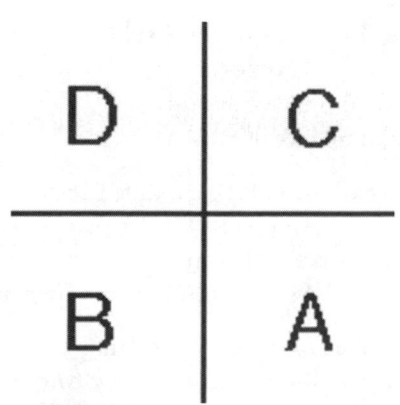

FIGURE 3–92
Diagram of design after top and bottom swap

FIGURE 3–93
Final toss repeat

FIGURE 3-94
Crop selected area

Notes . . .

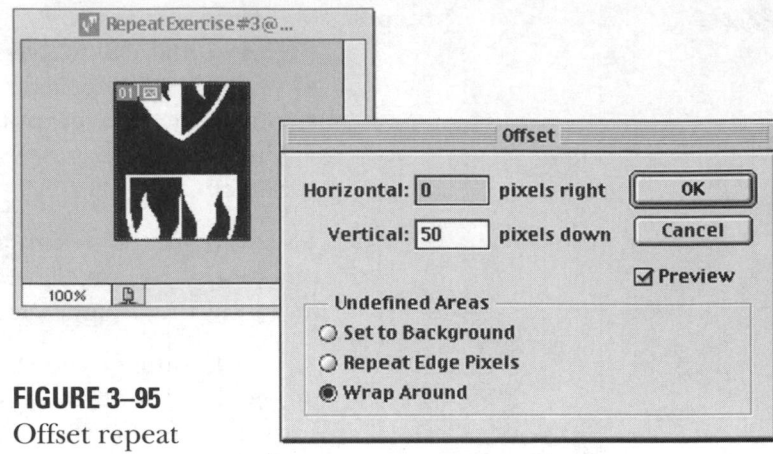

FIGURE 3-95
Offset repeat

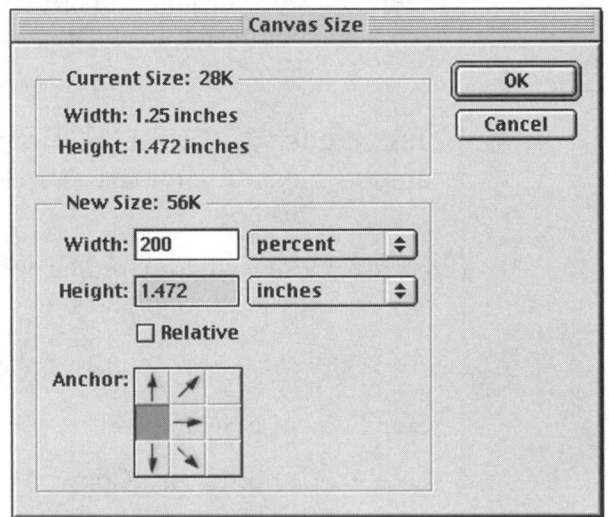

FIGURE 3-96
Canvas size

Step 5. Go to the **Filter** menu and select **Other > Offset** (Figure 3–95). Make the selections as below:
  • Horizontal: **0** pixels right
  • Vertical: **50** pixels down

  HINT: If you check the exact file width in pixels, you can enter in the numbers for a perfect 1/2 drop.
  • Check **Preview** option
  • Undefined Areas: Select **Wrap Around**

Step 6. Select **Canvas Size** from the **Image** menu and make the canvas twice as wide (Figure 3–96). An easy way to do this without calculating (we all know as designers we hate to do any math) is to select percentages on the right of the Width and enter 200%.
  • Choose the far left as an **Anchor** point.
  • Select **OK.**

FIGURE 3–97
Added canvas

FIGURE 3–98
Selected canvas

Notes...

FIGURE 3–99
Final offset repeat

Step 7. Use the **Magic Wand** to select the **added** canvas area (Figure 3–97) and choose **Edit > Paste Into** to place the copy in the center of the selected area. It will be placed into the center of the area. Because the original design has already been shifted down, the added copy creates the 1/2 drop repeat (Figure 3–98). To see the full repeat tiled out follow these easy steps.

To Tile the Repeat Out:

Step 1. **Select > All** on the new design repeat.

Step 2. Choose **Edit > Define Pattern.**

Step 3. Create a **New File,** 5″× 5″ at **72** DPI and select a **White** ground.

Step 4. Select the **Edit > Fill** Command and choose "fill with **pattern**" into the canvas. Be sure the new pattern is showing in the Toolbar. The design that was designated as the repeat will tile side by side filling out the canvas in the 1/2 drop (Figure 3–99).

Defining a Custom Brush

Defining a custom brush can be very useful in textile and apparel design. Designers have always cut or changed the physical appearance of a paintbrush to create a different technique or texture. Here it can be done digitally and easily, as long as a few steps are followed.

First, a Few Rules

- Custom brushes can be defined with any selection tool.

- A brush can be created using color, but when used the brush will translate those colors into gray tones of the color being painted.

Exercise to Define a Custom Brush

Step 1. Open the image or design from which the brush will be created. If there is no image readily available, draw out a custom "brush shape" using black on a white ground.

Step 2. Use a selection tool to select an area to be defined as a brush.

Step 3. Go to **Edit > Define Brush**.

Step 4. **Name** the brush. The brush can now be accessed through the **Brush** window. A tool that uses brushes must be selected or the **Brush** window will be grayed out. **Advanced Brush Attributes** can be applied to any defined brush. **Distorted Shape, Scattering,** or **Texture** from a defined pattern can be used.

Defining a Custom Pattern

Defining a custom pattern in Photoshop can be an extremely useful feature. Any part of an image when selected with the **Marquee** can be easily saved as a pattern for later use in the current image or a different image. Only the **Marquee** tool can be used to select a pattern. Any of the other selection tools, like **Lasso** or **Magic Wand,** will not activate the **Pattern** menu choice. Also, when selecting the area, keep in mind that the final pattern will go from edge to edge on the selection, so only select what is to be seen in the final pattern fill.

Exercise to Define a Custom Pattern

Step 1. Open the file named **Custom Pattern.**

Step 2. Use the square **Marquee** tool to select any part of a design.

Step 3. Choose **Select > All.**

Step 4. Choose **Edit > Define Pattern.**

Step 5. **Name** the pattern.

You have now designated that motif as a fill pattern. Any fill pattern defined this way is readily accessed through the pattern palette in the toolbox at the top of the **Design** window. Be sure that **Pattern** is chosen as the fill to view the pattern choices.

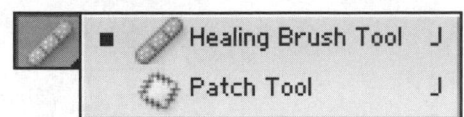

FIGURE 3–100
Healing brush

The Healing Brush

As with the **Stamp** tool, the **Healing Brush** allows an area to be corrected with a sample from another place in a design (Figure 3–100). The big difference is that the **Healing Brush** also matches the texture, lighting, and shading of the area being repaired. Follow these easy steps to use the **Healing Brush.**

Step 1. Select the **Healing Brush** tool.

Step 2. Set the **Brush** options for **Diameter, Hardness,** and **Spacing.**

Step 3. Choose **Replace** as the **Blend** mode from the options bar. This will help match the qualities of the blend from the sampled pixels to the source pixels.

Step 4. Choose the sample area to be used. Select **"Alt + Mouse Click"** on Windows or **"Option + Mouse Click"** on Mac.

Step 5. Use the brush on the destination area. Each release of the mouse will show the progress.

Layers: Their Use and Function in Design

Layers add to any design program the ability to work in a single design, but have images on separate "pages" or "layers." Layers add the ability to overlap images, and move them from place to place as well as above and below each other. The most widely used function of layers is for the creation of storyboards. The following will briefly describe layers and their use, but will go into more detail in Chapter 11.

No More Cutting and Pasting! Using Layers in Photoshop

The most important function of layers is to lay out or present multiple images on a board or page and have the ability to continually edit and update those images. Using layers does this well and also allows the user to output the board on a single printout for presentation.

Exercise for Layers

Step 1. From the enclosed CD, open the folder named **Flats, Flat #1** and **Flat #2.** These will both open as individual windows. They have been pre-filled with a solid color for this specific exercise in **Layers.**

Step 2. Open a **New File** and create a page the size of your final output. This can be 8.5″ × 11″ or 11″ × 17 ″, whatever the final size needs to be (Figure 3–101).

Step 3. Using the **Move** tool, select each image and drag or move it from the original window to the new page window. Dragging between windows makes this process very quick and easy.

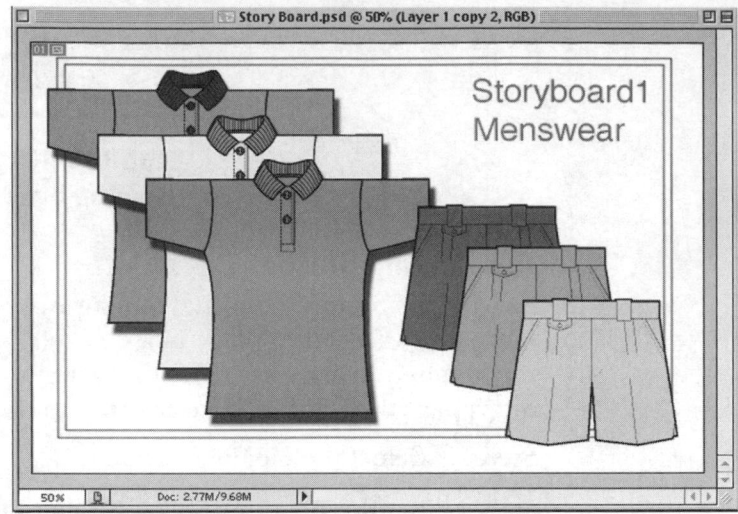

FIGURE 3–101
Preview of 8.5″ × 11″ final presentation board with shadows

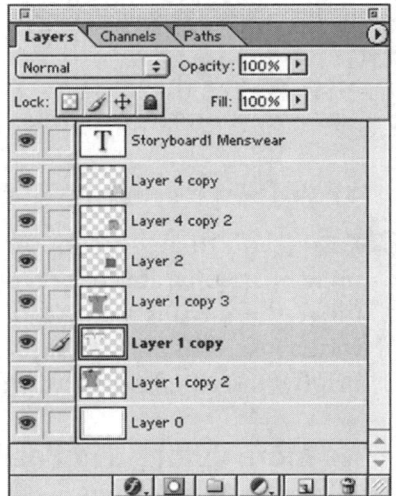

FIGURE 3–102
Layers palette

Step 4. Each time an image is dragged from window to window, a new layer is formed. This makes it easy to access each flat or design for continuous editing and moving.

Step 5. Once all the images are dragged, choose to save the file.

Step 6. Once a **layer** is active in the **Layers Palette** (Figure 3–102), that image can be edited or moved wherever the designer sees fit. Layers can also be dragged above and below each other.

Step 7. Using the **Move** tool, click on a layer and move that flat to a different spot on the page. To see which layer is active, look at the thumbnails in the **Layers Palette.**

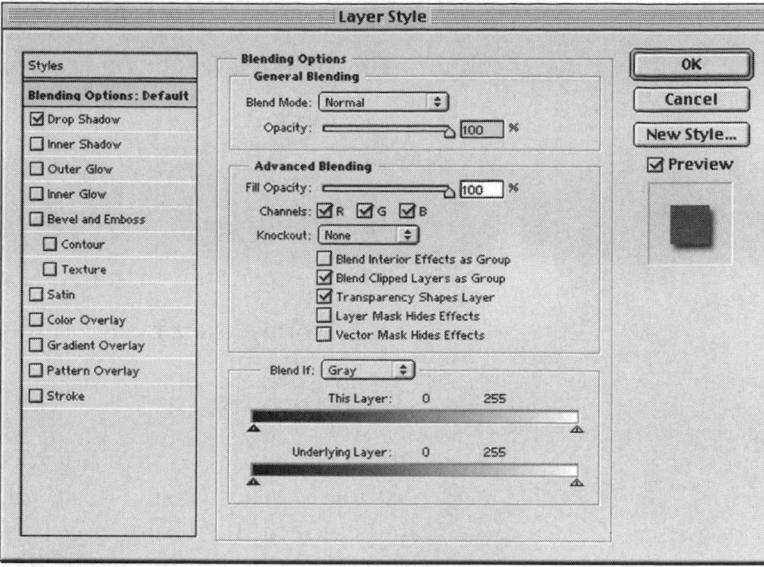

FIGURE 3–103
Layer style options

Step 8. Any text can be added on its own layer as well. Creating titles and labels for the boards becomes an easy task.
- Select the **Text** tool.
- Begin typing on the canvas. A new layer is automatically added.
- Text can be moved and edited just like any other image.
- The color of the text is determined by the foreground color.

Step 9. Other attributes of **Layers** can be edited by a double-click on the layer in the **Layers Palette** (Figure 3–103).

Step 10. SAVE the file.

Step 11. To print this page, choose **Layers > Flatten Layers.** Printing a page with so many layers and such a large size may slow down printing. Now that the file has been saved with **Layers,** the designer can always return to the original for any editing.

Here is a brief review of the use of layers. Layers can be used to:

1. Create additional layers

2. Perform basic editing functions to modify layers

3. Isolate one layer or one object on a layer at a time or *all* at the same time

4. Change the order of layers

5. Change the order of objects on a layer

6. Delete layers or objects from layers

7. Use as multiple viewing option of layers such as show, hide, and view multiple layers

8. Lock or protect layers

9. Group as well as link

10. Delete layers or objects from layers

11. Organize layers

12. Name and save individual layers

13. Print specific layers

14. Merge down, flatten, and other consolidation options

15. Modify layers by use of modes, masks, and opacity

Blending Modes

Blending modes control how pixels are affected by the tools that are used when editing or painting in a design. Each mode involves a *base color*, which is the original color in the design, a *blend color*, which is the applied color, and a *result color*, which is the color in the end. The following is a brief description of these effects. For more details, look in the Photoshop manual under "blending modes."

- **Normal**—Paints each pixel to the resulting color.

- **Dissolve**—The resulting color is a random color based on the opacity chosen at that time.

- **Behind**—Edits only on the transparent layer in a design.

- **Clear**—Edits the pixels to transparency.

- **Darken**—Makes the base color darker for each pixel.

- **Multiply**—Multiplies the base color by the blend color. The result is always a darker color.

- **Color Burn**—Darkens the base color to reflect the blend color.

- **Linear Burn**—Darkens the base color to reflect the blend color by decreasing brightness.

- **Lighten**—Selects the lightest color of the base or blend. Pixels darker than the chosen color are replaced and anything lighter stays the same.

- **Screen**—Multiplies the inverse of the blend and base colors. The result is always a lighter color.

- **Color Dodge**— Brightens the base color to reflect the blend color by decreasing the contrast.

- **Linear Dodge**—Brightens the base color to reflect the blend color by increasing the brightness.

- **Overlay**—Pattern or color overlays the existing color but preserves its highlights and shadows.

- **Soft Light**— Darkens or lightens the color. Similar to using the Dodge and Burn tool.

- **Hard Light**— Multiplies or screens the colors. Useful for shadow effects.

- **Vivid Light**— Burn or Dodge colors by increasing or decreasing the contrast of the blend color.

- **Linear Light**— Decreases or increases the brightness of the blend color.

- **Pin Light**— Replaces the color depending on the blend color.

- **Difference**— Subtracts the blend color from the base or the base from the blend, depending on the one with the greater Brightness value.

- **Exclusion**—Similiar results as the "Difference Mode" with a lesser effect.

- **Hue**—Resulting color has the luminance and saturation of the base color with the hue of the blend color.

- **Saturation**—Resulting color has the luminance and hue of the base color with the saturation of the blend color.

- **Color** —Resulting color has the luminance of the base color with the hue and saturation of the blend color.

- **Luminosity**—Resulting color has the hue and saturation of the base color with the luminance of the blend color.

Color Modes

- **Bitmap**— Uses black or white to represent pixels in an image.

- **Grayscale**—Uses up to 256 shades of gray to represent pixels in an image

- **Duotone**—Creates a duotone (two colors), tritone (three colors), or quadtone (four colors) grayscale image using two to four custom inks.

- **Indexed**—Uses 256 colors at the most, when designing an image.

- **RGB**—Uses three colors or channels—red, green, and blue—to produce images with up to 16.7 million colors on screen.

- **CMYK**—Color usage based on light-absorbing inks. Known as four-color process; cyan, magenta, yellow, and black are combined to reproduce colors.

- **Lab Color**—An intermediate color model used by Photoshop when switching between other modes. Also used to edit the luminance and color values independently.

- **Multichannel**—Uses 256 levels of gray in each channel for specialized printing.

- **Bit Depth** or **Color Depth**—Defines how much color information is available for a pixel to print or display. The greater the bit depth, the more colors are available to describe a pixel to the printer or screen. The higher the bit depth is set, the finer the color distinction, but also the larger the file size.

- **8-Bits**—Most widely used bit depth in designing many images.

- **16-Bits**—Has finer color detail but is a file twice the size of 8-bit.

FIGURE 3–104
Opacity

Notes . . .

Opacity

Opacity is the maximum amount of paint coverage applied by a tool. A number of tools in Photoshop use this feature (Figure 3–104). The brush, bucket, and stamp tool are a few examples. Opacity can be very useful in designing textures and fabrics. Overlaying colors and effects can be a useful way to create some really lifelike designs.

Opacity Exercise

Step 1. Open the **Opacity Exercise** file on the enclosed CD.

Step 2. Choose a brush and brush size.

Step 3. Select a color to paint with.

Step 4. With the **Opacity** setting at 100%, paint across the design.

Step 5. Now change the **Opacity** to 50%, paint again.

Try choosing multiple colors to see the results.

What Is a Filter?

A filter is an option in a design program that allows the user to easily create a special effect or illusion out of the design. A variety of filters are available in Photoshop for just this purpose. To create the effect a designer is looking for, filters can be applied multiple times to the same image as well as the use of additional filters on the same design. Many versions of design software have different sets of filters. The best way to know how they will react is to really play with each one to see the effect. Filters will affect the entire image or only the selected area.

Photoshop is probably one of the most well-known off-the-shelf design programs. It is widely used for the Filter menu and the variety of effects. Trial and error is one of the best ways to get to know what each filter is capable of as well as the faults. Just going into the Filter menu shows the variety of effects that can be achieved through Photoshop. Keep in mind that filters can always be applied again and again as well as multiple filters being used together.

In most software, a brief description of each filter installed is available by choosing About plug-in the Apple menu (Macintosh) or the Help menu (Windows), then selecting the plug-in from the submenu. To use a filter is as easy as selecting it in the Filter submenu. If there are options to adjust the filter, adjust it to the desired settings. Many filters also have a Preview option. When this option is selected, the filter's adjustments are updated instantly in the image or selected area. In some software, filters will not work in some modes For example in Photoshop, they will not be available in Indexed or Bitmap modes. Modes allow a designer to work on different image types.

Just a reminder:

- **Bitmapped** mode is black and white.

- **Indexed** mode is a maximum of 256 colors in a palette.

- **RGB** mode is millions of colors in an image using **R**ed, **G**reen, and **B**lue light.

- **CMYK** mode for printing and separations uses **C**yan, **M**agenta, **Y**ellow, and **B**lack.

Applying the Filter Effects

Now that we have an idea of how filters can help achieve realistic results, let's look closer at them. Filters and effects can be used individually or together to achieve the desired results. The following list briefly describes what filter or effect to use to get a particular effect. Any of these filters can be added to create a realistic texture. The settings in any particular filter or effect can also be adjusted to get just the look needed. Try using some different ones together.

Color Ideas

HINT: Options for Hue, Color, or Luminosity generally work well. The choice depends on the colors used as well as the effect you want to get. Also, the filter allows the user to create real textural effects. Remember, for a brushed effect, try the Blur Filter combined with the Wind Filter. For a wool effect, try the Noise Filter combined with the Blur Filter.

Applying a Filter

Filters are easily applied to an entire image or layer, even just a specific selected area.

Step 1. Select the area to be affected. Again, if there is no selection, then the entire image will be edited.

Step 2. Go to the **Filter** menu and select the desired effect.

Step 3. If a dialog box appears, choose the option(s) desired.

Step 4. Select **Preview**, if available in the **Filter** options. This allows the designer to see the effect instantly before selecting OK.

Step 5. Choose **OK**.

> **NOTE:** If a designer wants to see a specific area of the design in the options dialog, the image in the dialog preview can be clicked on and dragged around to the correct area. Some filters also have Zoom options as well.

Filters simulate a variety of surface interests that can be applied to a digital image or to a vector rendering. These filters represent a wide range of texture types and styles, which include some of the following:

- Embossed surface

- Fabric-related surface textures—knits, brushed, puckered, etc.

- Tiled effects including Mosaic and Pixelated

- Motion/Directional effects, including "Wind-swept"

- Distortion and stylized effects

- Perspective effects

- Lighting effects

- Degree of intensity

- Shine—Finishes from glossy to matte

- Grain effects

- Glass effects, including Opaque and Stained Glass

- Artistic effects to make your work resemble different artistic styles or movements such as van Gogh, Impressionist, or Fresco

- Ink Pen and Outlined effects

Suggested Filter and Effects in Photoshop

The following are some chosen filters and a few popular textile/print applications each can serve. There are many filters and more are added with every release. The best way to know each effect is to try it. You can add your own remarks for future reference.

Name of Filter:	Textile/Print Effect	Your Comments Here:
Artistic	Watercolor	
Blur	Gaussian Blur: Polar Fleece	
Brush Strokes	Sprayed Strokes: Ikat	
Distort		
Noise	Add Noise: Cotton	
Pixelate	Pointillize: Terry	
Render		
Sharpen		
Sketch		
Stylize	Wind: Woven Effect	
Texture	Texturizer: Any Scanned Texture	
Other	Offset: Drop Repeats	

Next, we have provided some filter effects and their use for textile design. Try each exercise to get a feeling for each individual effect. Then try combining them to see how they react together.

Figure 3–105 is the Original design provided on the CD enclosed with the book. It is named "Original for Filters." Open it and try each of the following effects.

Artistic Cutout

1. Open the "Original for Filters" design.

2. Go to **Filter > Artistic > Cutout** (Figure 3–106).

FIGURE 3–105
Original

FIGURE 3–106
Artistic > cutout

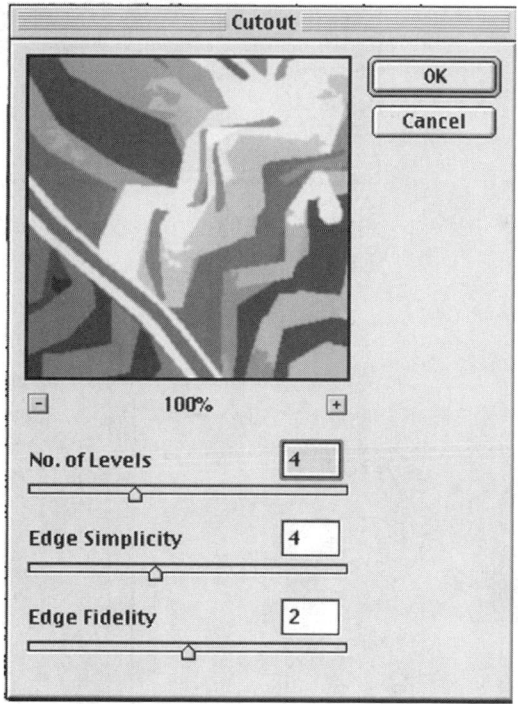

FIGURE 3–107
Dialogue

FIGURE 3–108
Artistic > film grain

3. Enter the variables as shown in Figure 3–107.

4. Choose **OK.**

Artistic Film

1. Open the "Original for Filters" design.

2. Go to **Filter > Artistic > Film Grain** (Figure 3–108).

3. Enter the variables as shown in Figure 3–109.

4. Choose **OK.**

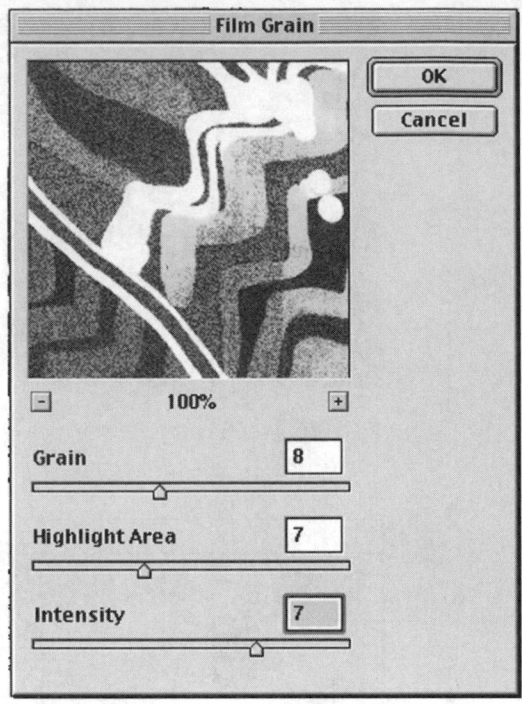

FIGURE 3–109
Enter variables

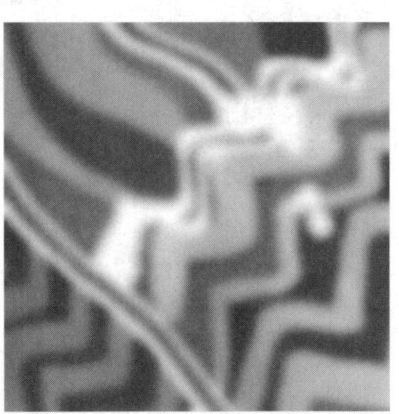

FIGURE 3–110
Blur > gaussian blur

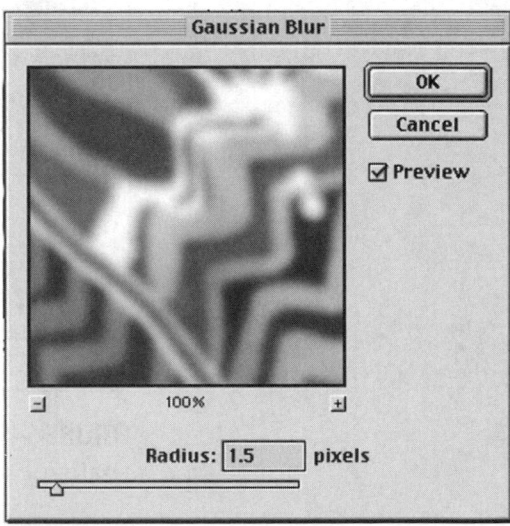

FIGURE 3–111
Blur > gaussian blur dialogue

Gaussain Blur

1. Open the "Original for Filters" design.

2. Go to **Filter > Blur > Gaussian Blur** (Figure 3–110).

3. Enter the variables as shown in Figure 3–111.

4. Choose **OK.**

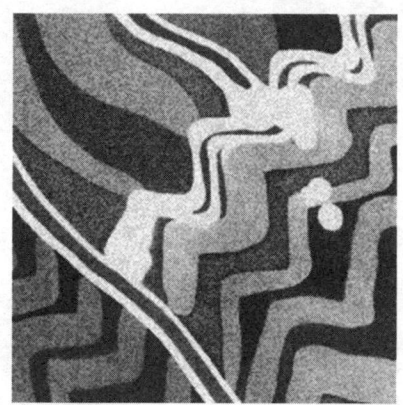

FIGURE 3–112
Add noise

FIGURE 3–113
Add noise dialogue

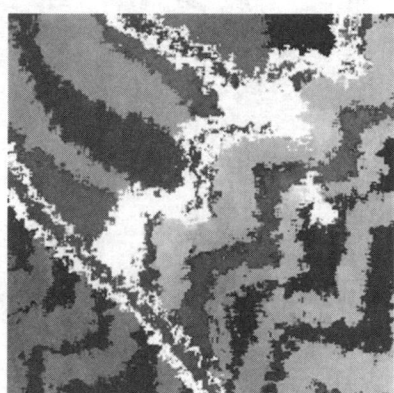

FIGURE 3–114
Brush strokes > spatter

Notes . . .

Add Noise

1. Open the "Original for Filters" design.
2. Go to **Filter > Noise > Add Noise** (Figure 3–112).
3. Enter the variables as shown in Figure 3–113.
4. Choose **OK.**

Brush Strokes > Spatter

1. Open the "Original for Filters" design.
2. Go to **Filter > Brush Strokes > Spatter** (Figure 3–114).
3. Enter the variables as shown in Figure 3–115.
4. Choose **OK.**

Brush Strokes > Sprayed Strokes

1. Open the "Original for Filters" design.
2. Go to **Filter > Brush Strokes > Sprayed** (Figure 3–116).
3. Enter the variables as shown in Figure 3–117.
4. Choose **OK.**

Distort > Diffuse Glow

1. Open the "Original for Filters" design.
2. Go to **Filter > Distort > Diffuse Glow** (Figure 3–118).

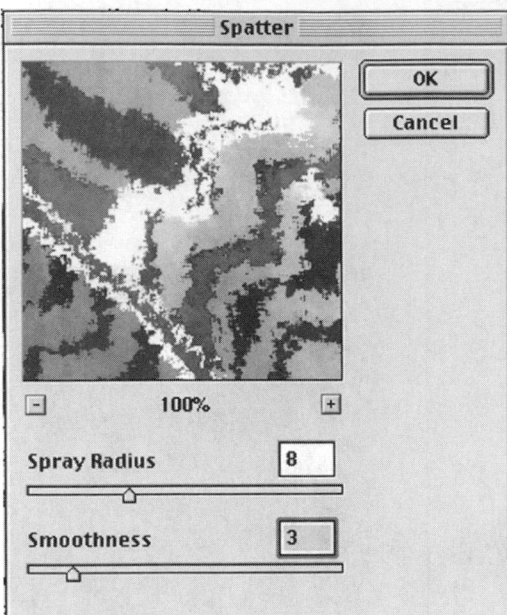

FIGURE 3–115
Spatter dialogue

FIGURE 3–116
Brush strokes > sprayed

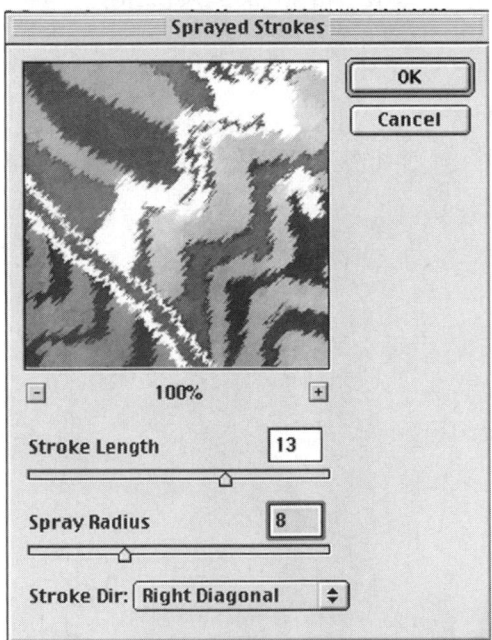

FIGURE 3–117
Sprayed dialogue

FIGURE 3–118
Distort > diffuse glow

3. Enter the variables as shown in Figure 3–119.

4. Choose **OK.**

Stylize > Trace Contour

1. Open the "Original for Filters" design.

2. Go to **Filter > Stylize > Trace Contour** (Figure 3–120).

3. Enter the variables as shown in Figure 3–121.

4. Choose **OK.**

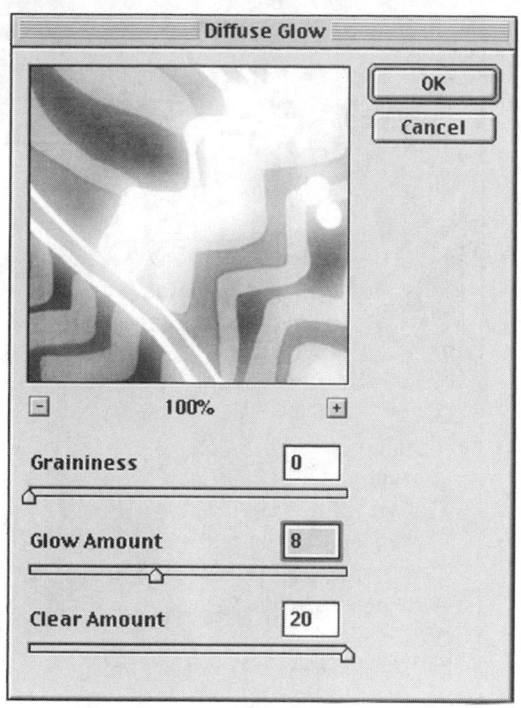

FIGURE 3–119
Distort > diffuse glow dialogue

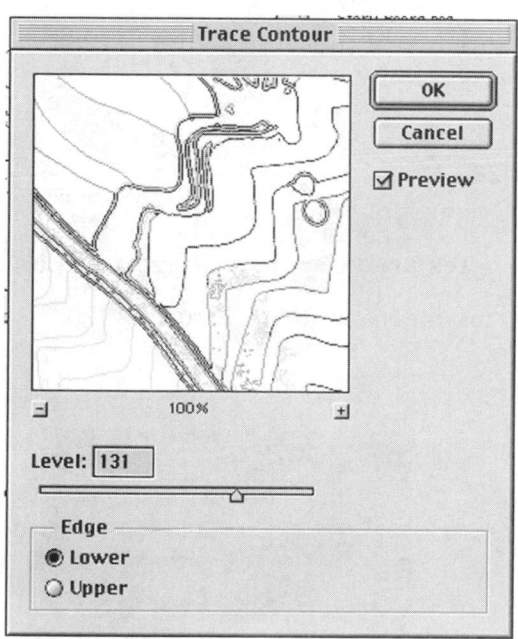

FIGURE 3–121
Trace contour dialogue

FIGURE 3–120
Stylize > trace contour

FIGURE 3–122
Stylize > wind

Stylize > Wind

1. Open the "Original for Filters" design.

2. Select **Filter > Stylize > Wind** (Figure 3–122).

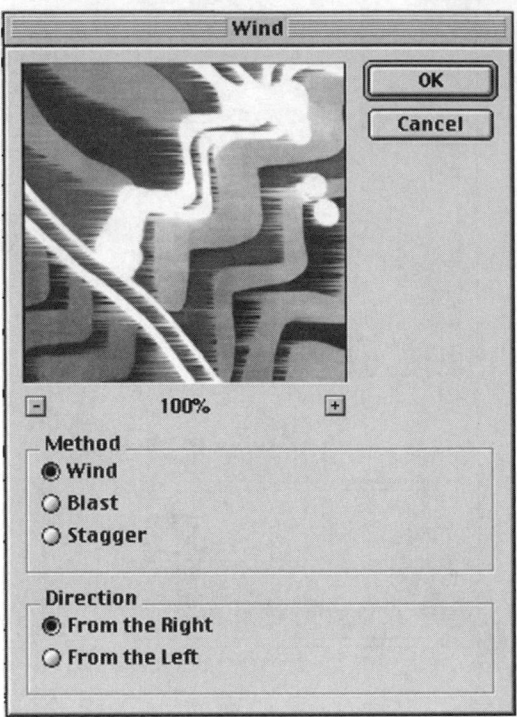

FIGURE 3–123
Stylize > wind dialogue

3. Choose the variables as shown in Figure 3–123.

4. Choose **OK.**

Texture > Texturizer

1. Open the "Original for Filters" design.

2. Select **Filter > Texture > Texturizer** (Figure 3–124).

3. Choose the variables as shown in Figure 3–125.

4. Choose **OK.**

FIGURE 3–124
Texture > Texturizer

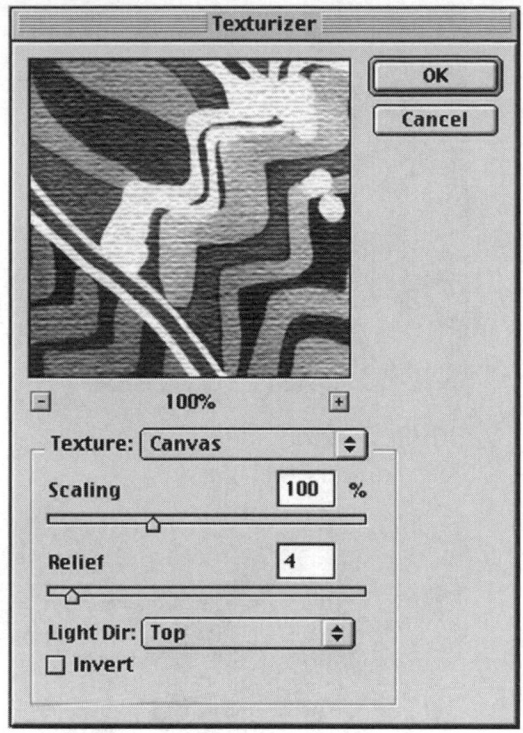

FIGURE 3–125
Texturizer dialogue

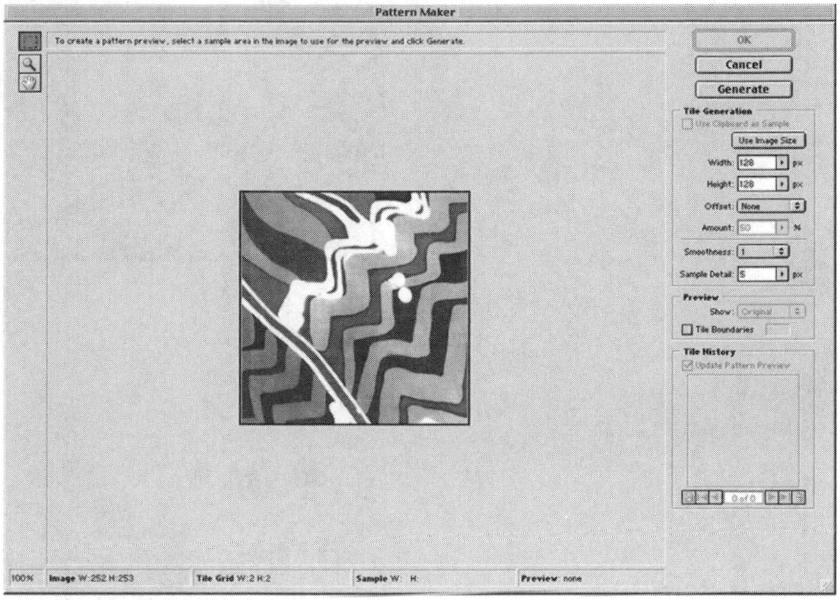

FIGURE 3–126
Pattern maker window

Notes...

The Pattern Generator

The Pattern Maker works by creating a tile out of a designated pattern from the clipboard (Figure 3–126). The pixels of the selected area are rearranged to create a randomly tiled pattern. This pattern can be regenerated (Generate Again) over and over to get a different tile effect each time.

1. Open the design that has the pattern in it.
2. Go to **Filter > Pattern Maker**.
3. Use the mouse to **Marquee** a section of the design to select the pattern tile. This filter only works with a square or rectangular selection.
4. Set the final tile size and any offset, if needed.
5. Choose **Generate.**
6. Choose **OK.**

Here are some examples of different settings with the same image. After practicing with these settings, use the Original Design or any of the other Textile Prints on the CD to be creative and try your own effects (Figure 3–127).

Pattern Maker #1/Figure 3–128
Settings:
    Image Size: 350 × 350
    Offset: None
    Sample Detail: 3

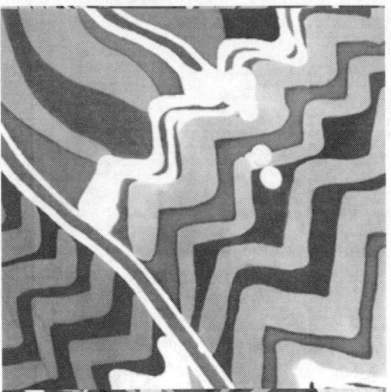

FIGURE 3–127
Pattern maker original

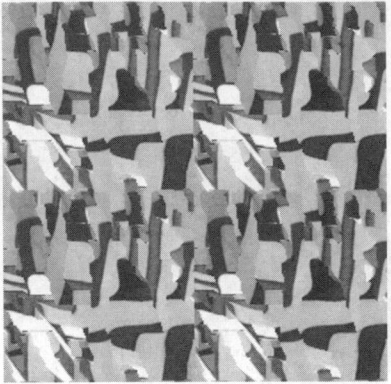

FIGURE 3–128
Pattern maker #1

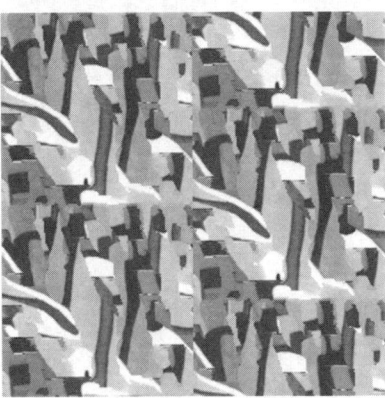

FIGURE 3–129
Pattern maker #2

FIGURE 3–130
Pattern maker #3

Pattern Maker #2/Figure 3–129

Settings:
    Image Size: 350×150
    Offset: Vertical
    Sample Detail: 10

Pattern Maker #3/Figure 3–130

Settings:
    Image Size: 748×760
    Offset: Horizontal
    Sample Detail: 21

A Brief How-to on Using Masks in Adobe® Photoshop®

In its most basic form, *Masking* allows a designer to isolate parts of a design so they are protected when using many of the editing tools. By selecting a part of an image, the part that is selected is "masked" and cannot be edited. To create a "Quick Mask" do the following.

FIGURE 3–131
Mask tool

1. Open the **"Quick Mask Exercise"** file on the enclosed CD.

2. Select in the toolbox on the right half of the **Quick Mask** tool (Figure 3–131). This will activate the tool.

3. Using any drawing tool, create a "mask" on the area to be protected or not edited. The tool will paint in a 50% tone of red.

4. When finished, select the left half of the **Quick Mask** tool and the painted area has become selected.

5. Edit the design. The masked area is now uneditable. The masked area can be updated and added to by going back into "quick mask" mode at any time. When all editing is done, choose deselect.

Archiving Swatches and Images

Adobe Photoshop now contains a File Browser. Archiving files and folders can be easily managed and constantly edited through this browser. Files can be named, renamed, sorted, deleted, moved, copied, and just about any other type of file management. The following are some of the most used features of the browser (Figure 3–132). For more details, see the Photoshop 7 manual.

1. File information

2. File browser palette menu

3. File information pop-up menu

4. Sort by pop-up menu

5. View by pop-up menu

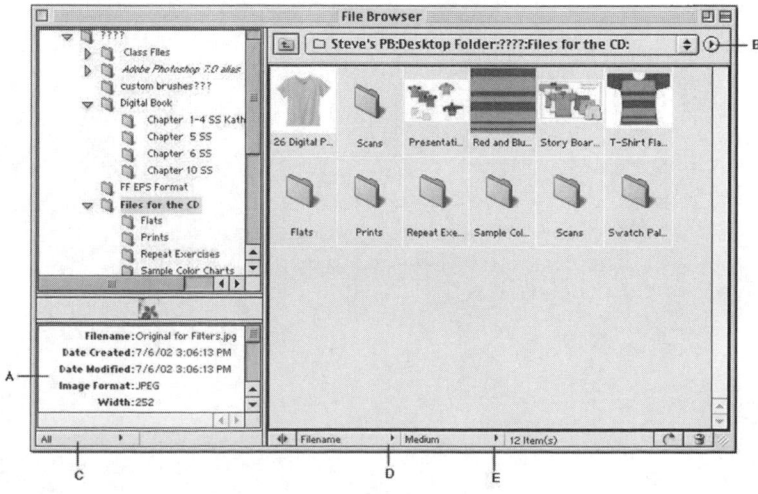

FIGURE 3–132
File browser dialogue

To Display the File Browser

Choose **File > Browse** or **Window > File Browser**. The browser can now be clicked and dragged out, if it is docked in the menu bar.

- A folder can be double-clicked to view its contents.

- The View By pop-up menu can sort the files by any of the following:
  - Small, Medium, Large
  - Large with Rank, Details

- The Sort By pop-up menu can be selected by:
  - File Name, Rank
  - Width, Height
  - File Size, Resolution, File Type
  - Color Profile, Date Created, Date Modified
  - Copyright

- Rank allows the designer to manually control the sorting of files.
  - To specify Rank choose the Large Thumbnail with Rank display.
  - Click in the Rank field and enter in a letter.
  - Choose **Enter** (Windows) or **Return** (Mac).
  - Select **Sort By Rank.**

What Next?

Next we will discuss the importance of having a good working knowledge of design basics. Having the knowledge of Adobe Photoshop tools coupled with a great sense of design basics will go a long way in helping you to succeed as a designer.

4 Design Basics and Workflow Strategies with Adobe® Photoshop®

Terms to look for:

Asymmetrical	Eye flow	Rectilinear
Axis	Field	Repetition
Background	Focal point	Rhythm
Balance	Foreground	Scale
Collage	Harmony	Shape
Composition	Juxtaposition	Space
Contrast	Line	Symmetrical
Depth	Mass	Theme
Design basics	Motion	Unity
Elements	Perspective	Value
Emphasis	Plane	Volume

The most important aspect of designing digitally is using the basic principles of design used in conjunction with good planning.

Overdesigning is one of the biggest mistakes that designers can make. Overdesigning (o-d) occurs when a designer is new or first starting to convert from hand rendering to digital designing, and the new designer succumbs to using too many features of the software instead of good planning and good designing. We have all seen examples of a design that is so overwhelming with effects that the original intent is lost.

Our goal in Chapter 4 is to help you review and apply design basics to your digital creations. We will share with you the simple secrets of planning as well as other workflow strategies you will want to incorporate for creating successful designs digitally. You can work smarter instead of harder, rendering designs with minimum effort, angst, and time! It all starts with a little savvy know-how!

So What Is Design Basics?

Design basics can be defined as creative planning and problem solving. Creativity is problem solving in a practical *and* in an aesthetic manner that is clearly understood by your intended viewer. A great design is accomplished by using the basic principles of good design.

Why Study and Review Design Basics?

We all know that today's consumer can be *very* fickle, *but* they also can be *very* loyal. Therefore, your job as a designer is to stay tuned into both the demographics *and* the psychographics of your primary and secondary target markets. Your designing is about giving the consumer reasons to buy and *continue buying from you!*

Every successful design uses the principles of design basics. The truth is unless you are the one controlling the shots within the design process, chances are good that you *must* answer to *someone* or *many someones.* Your ultimate consumer is the most important *someone* or individual to consider in the design process. Everything starts with knowing your customer, everything!

The Principles of Design Basics

Let's begin by looking at the basic principles and elements used in design, starting with design principles. The basic principles of design are:

1. Proportion
2. Balance
3. Emphasis
4. Rhythm
5. Harmony and Unity

These principles are presented in both text and visual format for you to review. When you look at these principles, ask yourself how you have addressed each of these in your current work. Never underestimate the significant impact each of these principles will have in the success or failure of rendering your ideas.

In addition, we have provided an area in which you can jot down any insights you may have as you review these principles.

Principles of Design

Proportion

- Pertains to scale, size, and ratios (Figure 4–1)
- Repetitive—pyramid, step, or zigzag

Personal Insight:

_____

_____

_____

_____

Balance (Equilibrium)

- Formal
- Informal

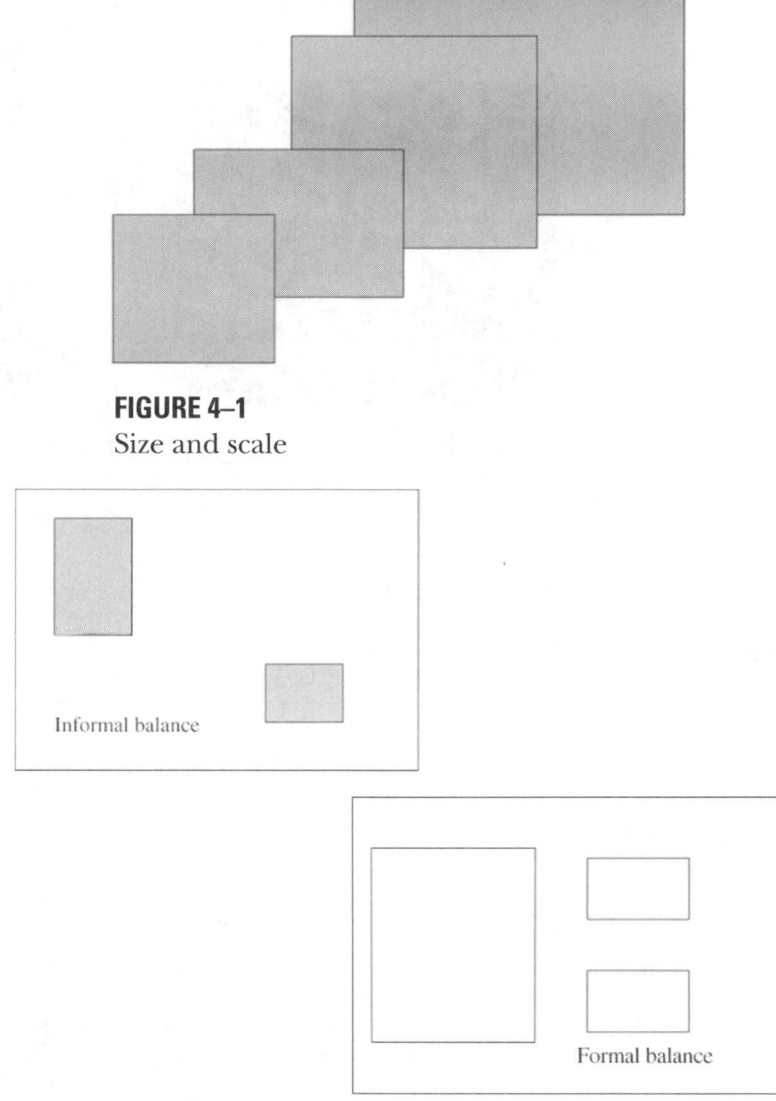

FIGURE 4–1
Size and scale

Informal balance

Formal balance

FIGURE 4–2
Informal balance vs. formal balance

- Symmetry

- Can indicate weight, quantity, force, or tension

Balance typically pertains to the distribution of weight. In every design the eye looks for the axis of the overall composition. The eye will immediately notice anything out of balance. (See Figure 4–2.)

Mastering this concept is vitally important to every designer, especially the textile designer. One of the more common patterns used in rendering prints is known as crystallographic, also known as an allover or toss pattern. (See Figure 4–3.) Here, the best use of equilibrium is an essential mainstay in textile designing.

FIGURE 4–3
Toss pattern

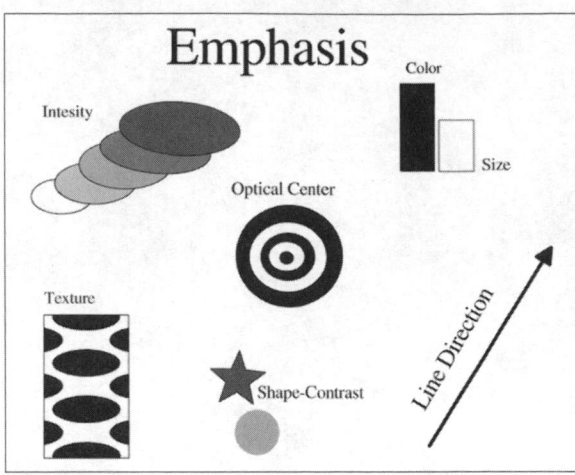

FIGURE 4–4
Emphasis

Personal Insight:

_____

_____

_____

_____

Emphasis

- Focal point can be achieved by use or manipulation of color, line, shape, contrast, texture, and movement, including intensity, optical center, and/or object placement or detail. (See Figure 4–4.)

- Focal point can be achieved by one focal point, no specific focal point, or all elements of equal emphasis.

Personal Insight:

_____

_____

_____

_____

Rhythm

- Rhythm can convey a feeling or emotion as well as a sense of sound or sense—achieved through line, color, and movement.

- Repetition or altering of lines, colors, or trims indicates contour, gesture, and quality. (See Figure 4–5.)

FIGURE 4–5
Rhythm

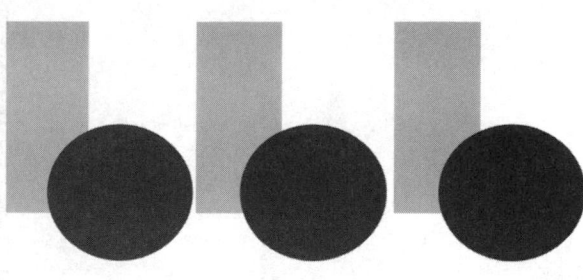

FIGURE 4–6
Harmony

Personal Insight:

_____

_____

_____

_____

Harmony

- Harmony is the *unity* of all the elements to convey a message.

- The whole dominates the parts in implying agreement visually or conceptually.

- Such elements refer to lines, shapes, size, color, texture, ideas, or themes.

- Harmony is achieved through proximity, isolation, or variation of the elements.(See Figure 4–6.)

Personal Insight:

_____

_____

_____

_____

Notes...

Understanding these basic principles of design is at the heart of *any* good design including rendering fabric and textile prints.

Design Elements

Every design contains several ingredients; these ingredients are collectively known as elements. *Elements* can include parts of a design or a combination of several elements

FIGURE 4–7
Design elements

that make the sum total of a design. Elements convey concepts and ideas—visually. How you use these elements *within* the principles of design will determine how successful your design will be. (See Figure 4–7.) The division of space and boundaries includes: *background, foreground,* and the following list of specific elements:

1. *Lines* (geometric or organic)

2. *Shapes* (objects, images, symbols)

3. *Texture* (indicating tactile or visual qualities—such as rough or smooth—collage, patterns, or trompe l'oeil)

4. *Color* (pertaining to emotion, mood, space, balance, perspective, contrast, temperature, or other use of symbolism)

5. *Type* (classic or contemporary used as text, objects, or symbols)

Visual Communication

All rendering takes place on a desktop; that desk can be a traditional surface or a virtual surface. (See Figure 4–8.) On the computer, as with designing on traditional surface, the paper space is known as the *field* and its *boundaries*. (See Figures 4–9 and 4–10.) Incorporating the basic principles and elements of design is known as *visual communication*.

As the designer begins to introduce new elements to the field, these elements are referred to as *events*. The area between events is known as *space*, while the surrounding area is considered to be "inside or outside" of the event. The relationship of additional elements is the *intersection*. (See Figure 4–11.)

The Importance of Line

Two of the most important elements found in every design—good *or* bad—are line and color. The significance of the correct use of lines cannot be underestimated. The following list elaborates on the definition of lines by use as well as the function of line in good design. Lines include thickness, movement, and direction, including eye flow. (See Figure 4–12.)

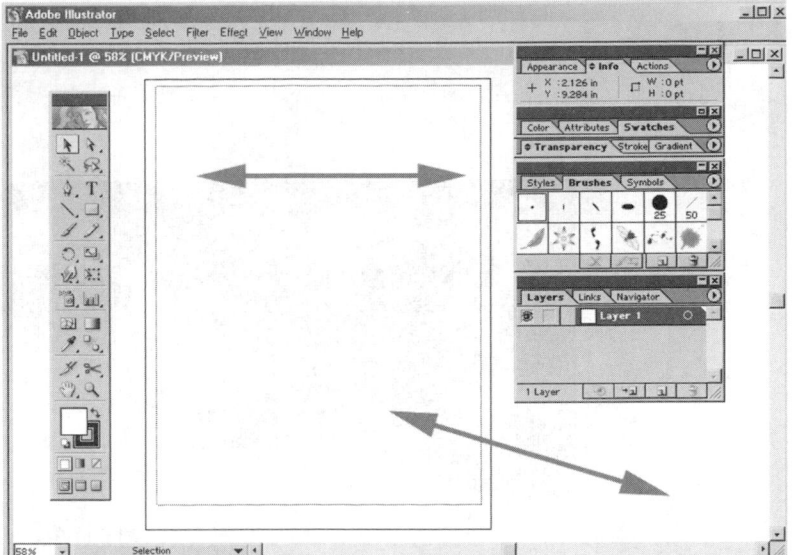

FIGURE 4–8
Virtual surface

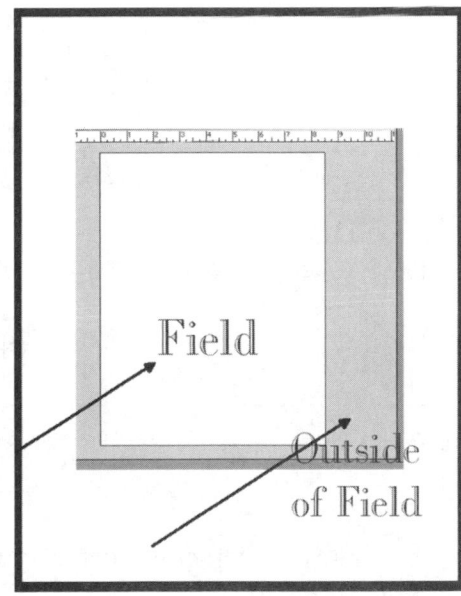

FIGURE 4–9
Field

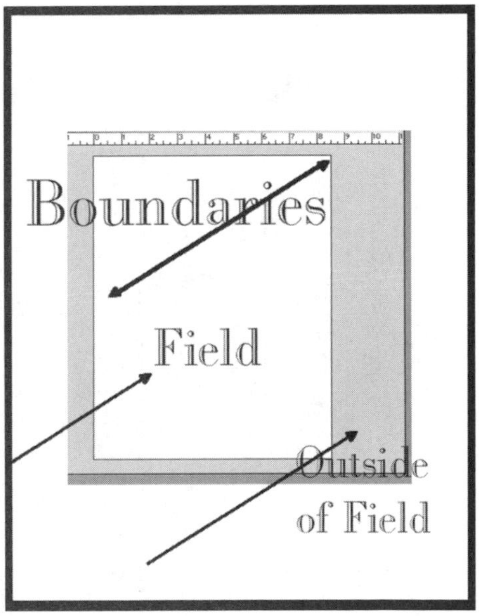

FIGURE 4–10
Boundaries

1. Lines can be thick, thin, or anywhere in between.

2. Lines can be straight, curved, broken, or bent.

3. Lines can be vertical, horizontal, diagonal, zigzag, or ogee (S), as well as being equal, continuous, graduated, or progressive.

4. Lines can be linear and/or radial.

5. Lines convey mood, convey gesture or movement, add or subtract weight, as well as form silhouettes.

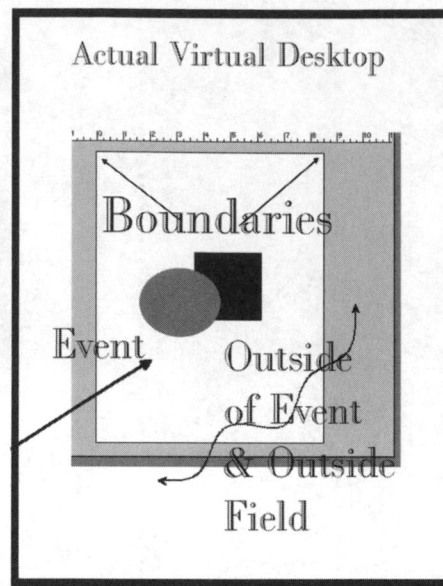

FIGURE 4–11
Intersection

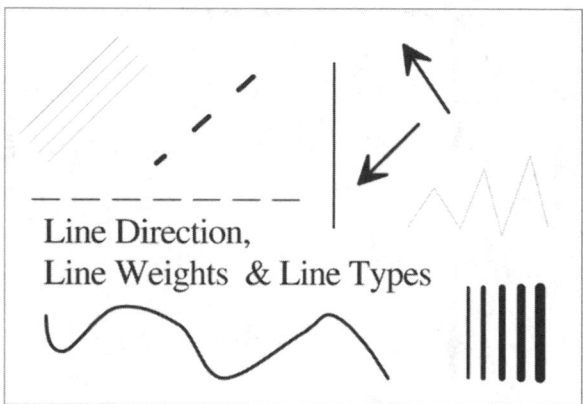

FIGURE 4–12
Line

6. Lines also convey texture by depicting surface interest and surface qualities that imply types of fabrications.

7. Lines comprise and showcase details or specific areas of interest and emphasis.

8. Lines guide the eye and can also create optical illusions.

Decisions, Decisions, Decisions

Your selection of how and where you create lines can have a negative or a positive impact on your message. Regardless, if you are consciously aware of making these design decisions, the choices you make or fail to make will greatly impact your design. In Figure 4–13, you can see the result of eliminating the lines when rendering denim. Denim just isn't denim without the diagonal twill lines within the construction of the cloth. To visually ignore these will result in sending a confusing or mixed message to your reader.

FIGURE 4–13
Denim with and without lines

FIGURE 4–14
Top ten strategies for designers

Now that you have reviewed the principles and elements of design you are ready for some secret strategies to apply these concepts.

Best-Kept Secrets of Design

As we promised earlier, everything starts with a little know-how. We are sharing with you our "top ten commandments" for good design. Consider it our version of divine designing inspiration for keeping your life simple and successful!

Top Ten Commandments (Strategies) for Designers!

In this section we will look at the practical as well as the human side of strategies to successful design (Figure 4–14).

Strategy #1: Know Thy Customer—Know Thy Company

It should be a given that you know the styles and rules of the business for which you are working. So, if you are a freelance designer and must design for many different

Notes...

clients, be sure you are designing in context for the company, as well as for their consumers. We cannot say it often enough, if you do not know who your ultimate consumers are, you will *not* be a successful designer. Your job title should really say "problem solver."

It does not matter if you are giving the fashion-forward contemporary shopper a design reflecting the latest trend or if you are designing a print that will visually shave off ten years *or* ten pounds for the baby boomer missy market—your job is to know thy customer and what makes them tick—or better yet, what makes them buy, and then give it to them in your designs!

You cannot afford to be wrong, not when someone is going to manufacture a thousand dozen of your creations. What if they do not sell? Can you afford to be wrong?

The solution is to immerse yourself in your customer, learn everything you can about them, go to the stores *where* they shop, watch *what* they buy, *how much* they buy, as well as ask yourself *why* they are making this purchase.

Review your notes from your college marketing class. Go on-line and surf the Internet for facts and trends. Learn to listen with your eyes as well as with your ears!

Next, take the information you have gleaned from your research and begin to apply it to your next design. It always comes down to giving the customer what they want, and *then* they will give you what you want!

You *must* know your customer. Period! No if's, and's, or but's. A great design geared to the wrong customer is *not* a great design.

Strategy #2: Know Thyself!

Have you ever stopped to consider that stubbornness and persistence *do not* mean the same thing. Stubbornness is trying to do things *your* way and making little or no progress on a project. On the other hand, persistence is being productive and making progress, both in time and with approval rate. (See Figure 4–15.)

When it comes to designing, you must begin by being honest and knowing who you are. Challenges you encounter as a designer are not really design-related issues at all. Often the challenges you face may be personality issues we sometimes wish we could ignore. Take the following test and answer the questions with honesty and candor.

1. What are your time management skills really like?

2. How would you rate your work ethic?

3. What is your designing style? Do you sit down to plan first and then design or do you sit down and just begin designing?

4. How are your communication skills? How well do you listen? *Really listen?*

5. Do you work smarter instead of harder? How much planning really goes into your designing?

Ouch! Perhaps we are treading on sacred ground here, but when you include these issues in the designing process, you will be amazed how simple your job will become, and how few changes you will have to make in the finished design.

FIGURE 4–15
Persistence

The Role of Listening in Good Designing

Listening is essential to good designing. Part of the secret to knowing yourself is to determine your listening skill quotient. How well do you listen and take suggestions? Soliciting, listening, and integrating the information you gleaned will almost always result exponentially in the success of any design. By asking *very* specific questions of those other individuals who are also involved in the design process and then incorporating the input of others into your designs, you can actually save yourself grief, and improve your reputation within the company!

So, if a project is taking far too long or if you are struggling to complete the task, it could just be a red flag to you that perhaps you are being stubborn in some area. So be flexible and really get to know thyself a little better.

Input from other design team members can improve the entire outcome of the project—a satisfied customer!

Soon you will begin to enjoy a sense of accomplishment that comes from just a little humble planning and a lot of active listening on your part. This leads us to our next strategy—knowing who your friends are.

Strategy #3: Know Thy Friends

No, we are not talking about who you spend your free time with. The kind of friend we are talking about is someone who is close enough to you to give you honest feedback. This can be a personal friend but often is a trusted peer at work. This friend cares enough about you to tell you *the truth.*

Let's face it, most designers struggle with being able to emotionally divorce themselves from their creations. When someone critiques his or her design, the criticism frequently gets lost in the translation. It is unfortunate that some designers take the criticism personally, as a personal attack, when this is not the case at all.

So know who your *real* friends are; they will tell you the truth if you are confusing stubbornness with persistence. If they say you do sometimes get the two confused, you are not alone—trust us, even the most successful designers have had to learn this lesson!

An ancient proverb states "wounds from a friend are better than kisses from an enemy." Anyone who takes the time to attempt to constructively improve your work is your real friend, even if it's the boss!

Strategy #4: The Advantages of Planning and Making Thumbnails

Everyone knows that time *is* money, right? But are you making the best use of your time?

Perhaps in your world the word *plan* is just a four-letter word in your vocabulary! However, ask any successful designer and they will tell you that when it comes to designing, one of the best-kept secrets *is* planning.

Without good planning, the top way to waste time is to "o-d" or "over-design." Let's face it, we have all given in to over-designing at one time or another in an attempt to impress a boss or client with our computer savvy. We succumb to the trap of attempting to incorporate too many design features of the software into our design. Remember, sometimes more is just more!

Often this goes hand-in-hand with another time-wasting trap that many designers fall into, that is, "designing as you go," instead of adequately preparing and planning first, and *then* designing.

No matter how long you have been a designer or how creative a designer you are, *everyone* can benefit from a little planning. Why not consider doing a rough sketch or *thumbnail* of your proposal to show your supervisor, *before* you begin designing (Figure 4–16)? It is not a sign of weakness on your part to include your supervisor, other decision-makers, or other staff members in the design process. Doing things this way can be not only a time saver, but a temper saver as well.

Planning Means Making Templates

One smart technique for planning involves the use of templates. Templates can be an extension of making a thumbnail. Templates may involve taking your time to mock up a page layout using only grids, guides, rulers, and geometric shapes in order to plan out your message before you begin to add the actual elements of your design. (See Figure 4–17.)

Consider it to be good planning when you use a template. We have observed that many designers as well as students are easily distracted in the design process and frequently struggle from overuse of the tools, especially when digitally rendering. Over-designing can spoil and distract. Unfortunately, it is usually symptomatic of poor planning. That is why at the end of this chapter we have included a set of exercises for you to practice, which include planning, making templates, and using the basic principles of design.

Strategy #5: Know Thy Resources

Do your homework first! Many companies are known for having a *signature look* or style they wish to convey to the consumer (see Figure 4–18). This signature look is used to distinguish their product from other products on the market by offering a consistent type of design that is easily recognizable to the consumer as being exclusively *their product or style*. They specialize in color, fabric, or designing key items that are updated every design season.

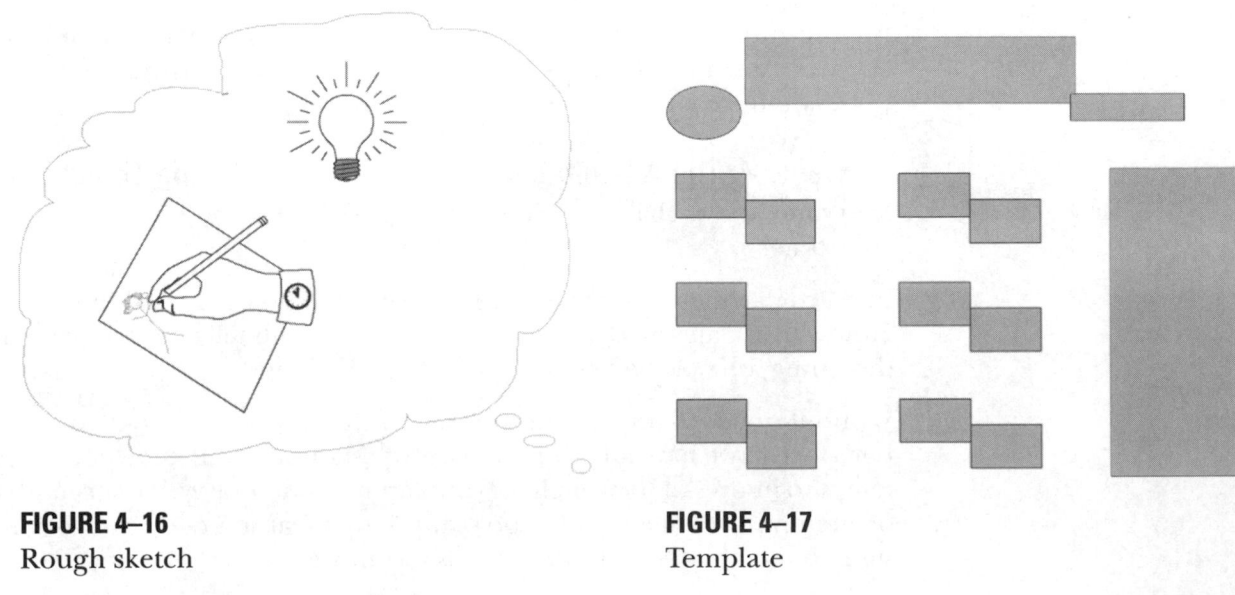

FIGURE 4–16
Rough sketch

FIGURE 4–17
Template

FIGURE 4–18
Know thy resources

FIGURE 4–19
Designing is not divining

Therefore, most designers begin by looking at previous sales within the company while synthesizing simultaneously the latest industry and consumer trends. Your resources can be as varied and creative as you are. Several of the most obvious places to begin your research are:

1. Key staff in-house

2. Trade publications

3. Trade shows

4. Industry peers or mentors

5. The library

6. The company's Intranet

7. The Internet

Thanks to Intranets and the Internet, many designers can accomplish multiple tasks via their keyboard in minutes. This means you can log on and do *informational* as well as *inspirational research* for your next proposal.

Designing Is not Divining

Who would you trust? When it comes to designing, management may not understand or trust the feelings or hunches you have. Even if you are very perceptive when it comes to trends or concepts, we suggest that it's better to back up those hunches with some cold hard facts (see Figure 4–19).

Today, you can find everything you need—from quotes to stats—easily and quickly on-line.

When relaying your ideas to others, convey your ideas visually. Make your proposal using the right text and the right images. Not quantifying your ideas by stats and images leaves too much to chance or confusion.

Be sure to include creditable facts or stats to back up your perceptions. A little extra resourcing on your part will pay off in getting the response you want for your ideas.

Strategy #6: Know Thy Message

It may seem that this book is starting to sound like a book about marketing or advertising, but the truth is "knowing what you are saying, saying what you mean, and meaning what you say" is everything in a good design. That's the problem-solving part—taking an old idea and updating it, in a new and creative way. Thousands of years ago King Solomon may have said, "there is nothing new under the sun," but let's face it, a good designer can make it look like there is!! Here's what we mean:

1. *Creatively* state your message.

2. Be sure you are stating your message *clearly*. Use words, images, color, and layout geared to your intended customer. Your message should be one they will understand *and* relate to. Avoid sending mixed messages with your design.

3. Is your message *complete*? Did you include everything? Does it anticipate problems or questions *and* solve them?

4. Is your message *consistent* with your company profile, your customer profile, and your intended message?

5. Are you saying your message *confidently*? Don't be shy about using strong images, colors, and text to convey your message where appropriate.

Design basics is every bit as much about being creative as it is about making sure your visual message is complete, consistent, and clear. Being confident about your product (design) and satisfying your client is the purpose of a good design!

This book is about helping you technically render your designs, maintaining good design and good product knowledge, and staying focused on satisfying your consumer. Oh yes, trust us—you will keep the boss happy too in the process!

Strategy #7: Know Thy File Management and File Formats—Practical Workflow Strategies

Everyone wants to work smarter instead of harder. One of the best-kept secrets is having good practical workflow strategies (see Figure 4–20). This always includes good file management.

FIGURE 4–20
Practical workflow strategies

File Management

Everyone at one time or another has misplaced their keys or their wallet. Perhaps we were tired or distracted when we put these objects down. Happily these items always seem to turn up. But what happens if what you misplaced is a file? Now what??? Ugh! How much time do you spend looking for improperly managed data?

Answering a few simple questions up front can make the difference between success and frustration.

Important Questions to Ask Before You Begin

(HINT: You may wish to make copies of this page and use it for each project.)

1. Who will be sharing these files?

2. On what platform will they be viewing the files?

3. What software do they have available and what version are they using?

4. What color mode will you be working in? (RGB, CMYK, Index, etc.)

5. What will be the final output of the design? (print, fabric, Web, etc.)

6. How will you be sharing the files? (CD, Internet, hard copy)

7. Where will you be storing or archiving the data?

8. How will you be storing and archiving the data? Do you have a system of managing files that *everyone* agrees on and will be using?

9. How much space has been allotted to archiving the data?

_____

_____

10. Who else will be responsible for editing your work?

_____

_____

11. How important will naming the file be? Is there a system for naming files that is agreed upon by everyone in the design process? It is critical that the file can quickly and easily be located, especially when it comes to locating files months after production.

_____

_____

12. What will be the size of the page? Are you working in pixels or inches?

_____

_____

13. What resolution will you need? What is the intended output of the file?

_____

_____

14. What will be the orientation of the final printable page layout?

_____

_____

15. How important is file size to the project? What should the file size be?

_____

_____

16. What deadlines are you working on? How flexible are they?

_____

_____

17. Will there be any other time or budget constraints you need to consider with this project?

_____

_____

18. Ask your supervisor what additional questions (not listed here) would be relevant within your company and jot them down in the space provided.

_____

_____

19. Each project and company is unique. What other considerations must you have? Feel free to jot them down here.

_____

_____

Knowing the answers to these questions will go a long way in saving you and your company time, money, and angst.

Strategy #8: Know Thy Software

Do you know the differences between vector- and raster-based software? Knowing which type of software to use and when is every bit as important as knowing which software type to choose.

We have included a copy of an article written by author Kathleen Colussy for TechExchange.com. The article is a compilation of information gleaned from her first book: *Fashion Design On Computers* © 2001 also for Prentice Hall.

The Software Fundamentals of Fashion Design

Getting It Right the First Time!

M. Kathleen Colussy

As both an educator and industry professional, I cannot tell you how many times I have observed designers starting out in either graphic or fashion design who fail to lay a proper foundation. This foundation requires a solid understanding of the basic software programs used by the industry. The key to successful results lies in differentiating between vector and raster based software—two unique software formats, each of which provides for unique advantages and disadvantages.

When it comes to software for the fashion industry there are several choices in off-the-shelf software, or software that is readily available to anyone, such as Adobe Photoshop®, Adobe Illustrator® or CorelDraw®. Proprietary software, software that is specifically designed for use within a given industry, is often a hybrid which allows the user to use a traditional off-the-shelf software in conjunction with an industry software frequently sold as a "plug-in." This kind of software has been adapted to work with the off-the-shelf software and includes features useful to the industry.

Regardless of which software application is used to develop apparel and textile designs, there still remains the most fundamental choice of will you be using a vector-based program or a raster-based program to accomplish the task? These two types of drawing formats are the crux of most design operations and are the foundations I was referring to earlier.

Vector Image Drawing Programs

Features of Vector Image Drawing /Illustration (Graphic) Programs

What is a vector-drawing program?	Drawing or Illustration Programs
What does a vector-drawing program do?	Creates vector images based on mathematically defined curves and lines.
Disadvantages?	Not well suited for editing or creating realistic images.
Advantages?	No "Jaggies" or stair-step appearance, just smooth looking graphics
	Fonts are better recognized
	Can be saved as a bitmap file format
	Higher quality output
	Can manipulate objects freely and still access them individually.
Usage parameters:	Flat renderings of garments, some motifs or logos
Vendors:	Corel Corp. (CorelDraw and Designer), Adobe Corp. (Illustrator), and Macromedia (Freehand)
How to save a vector-drawing program:	Native Formats such as .ai for Adobe Illustrator or .cdr in CorelDraw, or universal file formats such as EPS, PICT, and WMF

Vector drawings, also known as "object-oriented" drawings, are images defined by curves and lines or mathematical formulas. Basically, this means a vector program stores each image as a series of instructions on just how to draw the image. These graphical representations of objects usually consist of line drawings or other primitives such as lines, rectangles, ellipses, arc, spline, and curves. In many cases type set is generally simpler and can be highly compressed (made smaller).

The most important feature of vector-based images is the resolution or clarity of the drawing. Vector images are resolution independent and always render at the highest resolution an output device can produce. That means the higher the resolution of the monitor or printer the sharper the object-oriented image will appear.

What this means to the fashion designer is that these drawings are easy to select, color, move, re-size (without degradation of image), re-order, overlap with other images, access individual objects, and re-format (i.e., change color or fill).

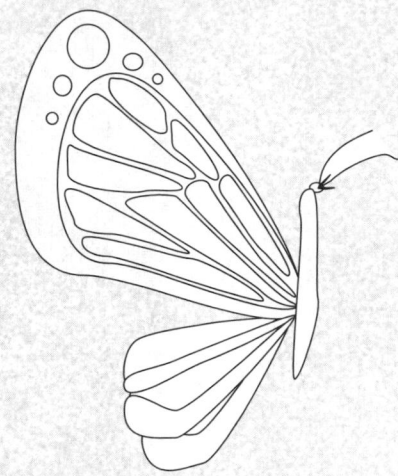

FIGURE 4–21
Vector graphic

Vector graphics are also much smaller files than raster/bitmap files (Figure 4–21). Vector files can be re-sized without degrading the file in any way. This is not true of raster images.*

Vector images are best used when working with small type and bold, smooth, crisp graphics requiring curves and lines. They are considered the most flexible and use relatively little memory for storage. The downside is that vector-based images are not as realistic as raster-based images, which can hold a lot more data. Furthermore, they are known for having a flat versus dimensional appearance when compared to a raster-based image.

Raster-Based Programs

Features of Raster-Based Software Application Programs

What is a raster-based program?	Image Editing Program (Also known as paint programs)
What does a raster-based program do?	Raster or Bit Map or REALISTIC Images based on pixels.
Disadvantages:	Can't create crisp, bold, smooth graphics
Usage parameters:	Primarily used working with photographs and other realistic images, i.e., clip art.
Vendors:	Examples: Corel Corp. (CorelPHOTO PAINT and Painter), Adobe Corp. (Photoshop)
How to save a raster-based program:	Native Formats such as .psd for Adobe Photoshop, or universal formats such as TIFF, BMP, PCX, BMP, JPEG, and GIF

*Notice the image can be sized up or down without losing quality. Design done in Adobe Illustrator.

FIGURE 4-22
Raster baby

Raster images create realistic or *real-world* images. (See Figure 4–22.) These types of drawing programs allow the designer to refine details, make dramatic changes with special effects options, and are noted for providing a greater degree of subtlety than vector-based graphics.

Raster/bitmap: or realistic images such as photographs can be transformed by using image editing filters to create a wide range of special effects and natural looks. These programs work with pixels or bitmapped images that can be enhanced with vector-style painting options.

Let's take a moment and give you an overview of what a bitmap is and what it does. Bitmap is a collection of picture elements or dots, also known as pixels. Bitmapped images are resolution-dependent. Basically this means you *must* specify a resolution. If you create the image and then change the resolution, you "de-grade" the image. Scaling up can be a real disaster; scaling the image smaller sometimes yields better results. In fact, the raster image is referred to as a bitmap image because it contains information that is directly mapped to the display grid of x (horizontal) and y (vertical) coordinates.

In scanned images the computer views as 1 and 0. These bitmap squares can be independently accessed but are difficult to edit. They can be toggled on and off. The 1 represents "on" and the 0 represent "off."

Figure 4–23 shows the same original vector image (Figure 4–21) in a raster-based program. Notice the "pixelation" of the image.

Bitmapped images are resolution dependent; that is, the best images to use are with continuous tone images like photographs that can be modified with great detail because you can manipulate each pixel. If you are scanning a hand-drawn image that you plan to modify, you will want to save it as a raster image. Bitmapped images are difficult to modify and to re-size as well as difficult to freely access objects individually.

Advantages and disadvantages of raster images include:

- Enlarging—Suffers from "aliasing" or blurred appearance when enlarged.

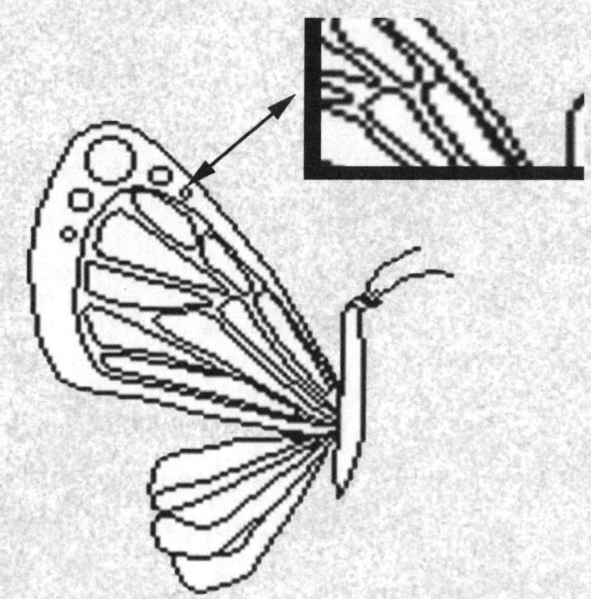

FIGURE 4–23
"Pixelation" of image

- Pixels or squares make a "jaggie" stair-step appearance.

- Reduction of image can result in interpolation or indiscriminate discarding of pixels.

- Can modify individual pixels or large groups of pixels.

- Requires huge amounts of memory. Usually larger than a vector file, which means they should be compressed to store.

- Data compression can shrink the size of the pixel data.

- Slows down the reading, rendering, and printing.

Adobe Photoshop is one of the most widely used image-editing programs. Another leading painting program you can use to edit and enhance photos is Corel Painter. Fashion designers love Painter because it simulates natural mediums such as charcoals, chalks, oils, and acrylics to enhance their photographic images.

Now that you have a better understanding of what each of these programs are and what they do, the next step is to have a better understanding of how you should share and save your files.

Common File Formats

Each image created will need to be saved in a specific file format that is native to the application. Naming and saving an image along with the file format extension will make it easy for other users of the images to identify the type of drawing it is and what applications may be used to open it.

Typically this extension is added to a file automatically in its own default known as a native format. As in the case of using Adobe Illustrator, the file will be saved automatically with an ".ai" extension unless you assign the file another extension.

The challenge arises when the native file is not always readable in another application. This means after you name a file, you have to give the file a special identifying code after its name that will enable you to open the file, no matter what program or platform you use.

Below is a list of common universal file formats used in saving vector- and raster-based images, most of which are inter-application and cross-platform compatible. This is by no means an inclusive list, but merely a description of some of the most common formats used by most fashion designers.

TIFF: Tagged Image Format

Characteristics include:

- Versatile
- Reliable
- Suppose bitmap including full-color
- Can contain multiple images
- Great for scanners, frame grabbers, and paint/image-editing programs
- Transfer cross-platform

PICT: This picture format is native to a Mac.

Characteristics include:

- This format is used with bitmap.
- Object-oriented drawings
- Great for raster printers

EPS: Encapsulated PostScript

Characteristics include:

- Cross-platform: Mac and PC
- Great for high resolution PostScript illustrations/vector images
- Files can be imported into other documents.
- Can be scaled and cropped
- May not be editable beyond scale and crop
- Requires a PostScript printer for output
- Bitmap images may require tracing to convert images.
- Vector images compress well in this format.

BMP: A file format for bitmapped images

Characteristics include:

- Stored in Windows as grid of dots or pixels

- Important for color information/color coded as 1, 4, 8, 16, 24 bits, which means a 24-bit image can contain more than 16 million different colors!

JPEG: Joint Photographic Experts Group

Characteristics include:

- Interchangeable format is great for photos working with layers.

- Each layer is independent of the others, which means each layer can be edited. Individual layers can be preserved for additional editing.

- Designed for compressing up to 1/20th of file's original size

- Designed to be used for full-color, grayscale, and real-world images

- Great for sending in e-mail attachments because you can control the file size and therefore the download time.

As you can see there really is a difference when choosing which type of designing software will best suit your designing needs. You will probably want to refer back to this section as you begin to design.

Notes . . .

Strategy #9: Know Thy Color Wheel
The Role of Color in Good Designing

Many times designing is color driven. Translation—while the designing of a print may involve specific shapes and motifs, typically what is noticed most and most often noticed first *is* color. Volumes have been written on the psychological impact of color and its effect on everything from stimulating moods to stimulating consumer purchasing!

Color is typically defined as the presence or absence of light as it is reflected from a surface or not reflected. Color is basically wavelengths of light. When we describe color, we refer to a color by its *hue*, which is merely another name for color. Color is also described by *chroma* or *intensity*, which signifies the degree of *saturation*. The term *value* is the "range of grays from white to black." Those closest to white are called *tints* and those closest to black are called *shades*.

We are all familiar with the basic color wheel as seen in Figure 4–24. (See also a color version of this figure in the color insert.) Colors are divided by the primary colors (chromatic colors)—the red, blue, and yellow from which all colors come.

Achromatic hues are the essence of neutrals such as black, white, and gray. We further break hues into *secondary colors, monochromatic, analogous, triadic,* and so on. Figure 4–25 shows complementary colors (a), triadic (b), monochromatic (c), and split (d).

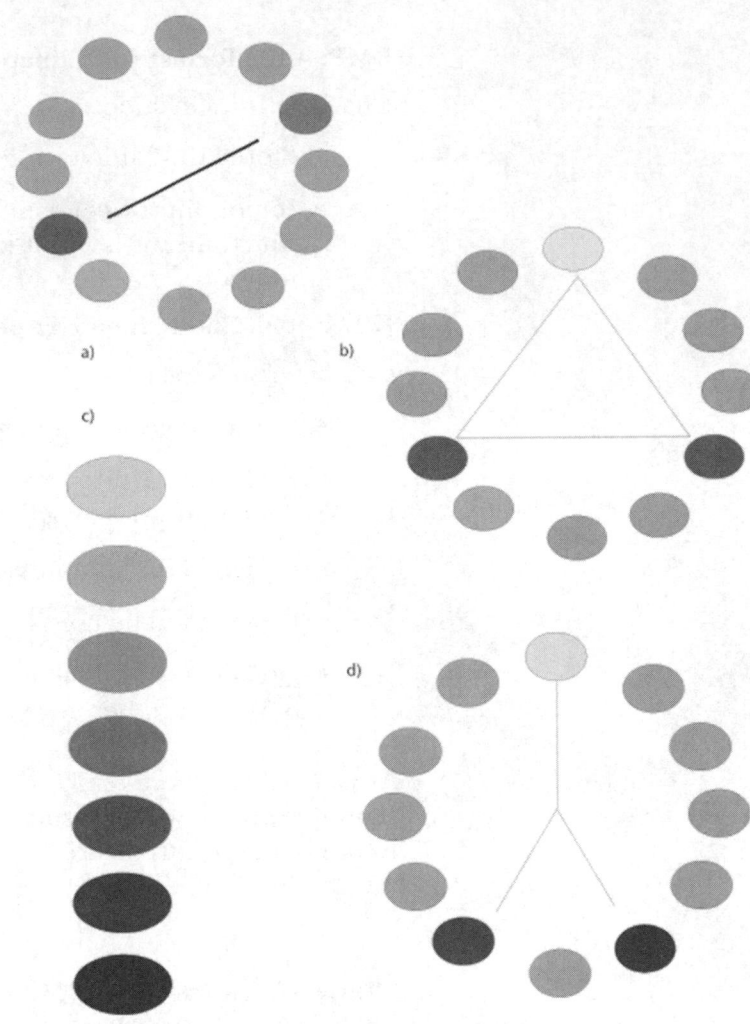

FIGURE 4–24
Color wheel

FIGURE 4–25
Complementary colors

Notes...

The ability to select colors as well as choose color combinations is an integral part of a designer's job. We cannot underestimate a designer's knowledge of which colors work best together and why. So why not take a few moments to reacquaint yourself with the color wheel before we put you to the test with a mini-quiz on color.

Putting Color to the Test

Now it's time for a pop quiz. Test your color savvy by answering the following color questions. You don't need paper or pencil, just a quick trip to your local shopping mall.

Are you ready? Well, here goes—

1. Start by examining several visual (window) displays. Can you discern the color scheme they are presenting?

2. Continue by visiting several of the major department stores and begin to evaluate several of the top designers within the store. Can you clearly de-

termine the theme of the line that is currently presented? Next, is it discernible if the designer has a signature color story presented this season? If so, what is the color story and how does it coincide with the theme?

3. As you discover the dominating season color palette, begin to compare and contrast how this palette is translated between different market segments and price points. Do different market segments mute or intensify the colors?

4. Next, as you continue to walk through the mall, begin to discern which visual displays grab your attention and why.

5. How many of these displays are driven by color?

6. Think about the last two years. What color combinations have you seen that dominate the market segment that your purchases represent?

7. What were the major color schemes you noticed while doing this test?

8. Do you think these colors will carry into the next season? If so, how?

9. Now, think about *your* last five purchases. How many were motivated by color?

10. Finally, do you have a signature color range you gravitate to? If so, what is it based on?

11. Begin to select three color schemes for the upcoming season and jot them down in the space provided.

Personal Notes:

_____

_____

_____

_____

Well, how did you do? Did the answers come naturally? Do you find you instinctively make these kinds of observations on color, prints, or fabrications? If so, consider yourself a good candidate for designing textiles.

Notes . . .

What's in a Name?

Now that you have selected several colors that appeal to you, our next step is to choose a name for these colors. Color naming is important to color selection (Figure 4–26). Nowhere is the naming of colors more evident than when you purchase everything from makeup, including lipstick and nail polish, to paint for the walls of your home.

Designers *love* to give attitude to names of colors—for example, it's not red, it's barn red; it's not black, it's noir; it's not gray; it's dove gray; it's not blue, it's Wedgwood—you get the idea!

Take some time to make a handy reference list of color names in the spaces we have provided on the following pages.

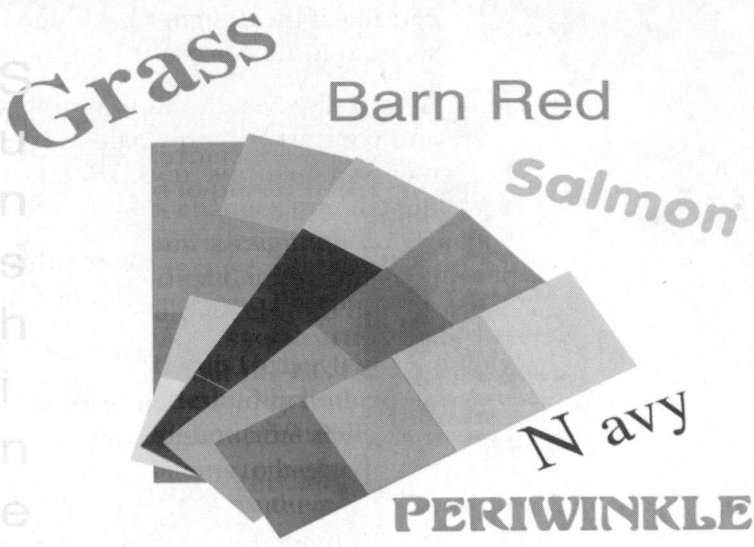

FIGURE 4–26
Color naming

Finally, we have also provided a quick reference to color trends to which you can continue to add your favorites!

Most Frequently Used Color Names Reference Chart

White	Ivory	Gray	Brown	Black
Winter	Beige	Dove	Cocoa	Noir
Pale	Pebble	Pearl	Chocolate	Midnight
Snow	Sahara	Slate	Coffee	Ink
Blanco	Sand	Frost	Chinchilla	Boot Black
Opalescence	Eggshell	Taupe	Mahogany	Granite
Mist	Buff	Putty	Cognac	Gun Metal
Milk	Mushroom	Stone	Cordovan	Saddle
White Opal	Honey	Pacific Fog	Carmel	Night Sky
Linen	Cream	Smoke	Nutmeg	Raven

Warm Color Names

Red	Orange	Yellow
Ruby	Pumpkin	Sunflower
Barn	Spice	Daisy
Apple	Mango	Lemon

Geranium	Cantaloupe	Marigold
Brick	Peach	Maize
Cherry	Salmon	Buttercup
Cardinal	Sonoran Desert	Dandelion
Cabernet	Poppy	Prairie

Cool Color Names

Blue	**Green**	**Purple**	**Pink**
Wedgwood	Grass	Periwinkle	Powder
Military/Navy	Parrot	Grape	Shocking
Iroquois	Forrest	Berry	Pale
Robin's Egg	Emerald	Amethyst	Cranberry
Azure	Mint	Lilac	Taffy
Turquoise	Sage	Plum	Peppermint
Powder Blue	Hunter	Mauve	Tulip
French Blue	Loden	Lavender	Hot
Cadet	Kelly	Wisteria	Lullaby

Notice how a color name can convey a geographical location or an emotion, age, or gender. Frequently, color names take their cue from nature.

Everybody gets into the act of color naming. Even an episode on the NBC TV sitcom *Frasier* depicts the two brothers, Frasier and Niles (TV's version of reputed fashion experts) in a repartee about the subtle nuances of color names for off-white carpeting! So continue to add to the list. You will be amazed at how frequently you will refer back to it in the future as a reference source.

Color Research Resources

URL	Company Name	Comment
www.Pantone.com	Pantone	
www.ColorMatters.com	Color Matters	
www.Dupont.com	Dupont (also check other fiber companies for similar services)	
www.Tobe.com	Tobe-Forecasting Services	
www.WGSN-EDU.com	Worth Global Style Network—forecasting	
www.Promostyle.com	Promostyle forecasting services	
www.BillGlazer.com	Bill Glazer and Associates—multiservice forecasting	

www.HuePoint.com   Hue Point

www.Kodak.com   Kodak

Personal Notes:

_____

_____

_____

_____

Notes...

Strategy #10: Know Thy Terminology

The defining moment in being included in any group is when you find yourself using their language. So, if nothing else, by now we should have realized the advantages of knowing your terminology!

As always, we have included a list of working terms frequently associated with design basics for you to review.

Design Basics Terminology

Asymmetrical: Having no balance or symmetry.

Axis: Point of balance the eye gravitates to.

Background: The ground *behind* a design. Sometimes referred to as the *blotch*.

Balance: Identical weight throughout a design.

Collage: Any grouping of related materials (such as newspaper, magazine tear sheets, fabric, wallpaper) fixed on a surface or board that conveys a message or theme.

Composition: To arrange or organize a series of design or art elements in a given body or work.

Contrast: Emphasis on a difference in color.

Depth: A measure of distance in a design based on an observation point.

Design Basics: Defined as *creative planning* and *problem solving*.

Elements: Include parts of a design or a combination of several elements that make up the sum total of a design.

Emphasis: Forcefulness of expression that gives importance to an element singled out.

Eye Flow: Direction the eye moves within a design, typically from left to right or top to bottom.

Field: The area of page defined by its boundaries.

Focal Point: A highly visible area in a presentation, where the eye flow will begin to be directed.

Foreground: Part of a design that is nearest the viewer.

Harmony: The unity of all the elements to convey a message.

Juxtaposition: To be placed side by side in near proximity.

Line: In design, an imaginary position of reference.

Mass: A group of elements that create a design.

Motion: In design, a flow of the elements in a design.

Perspective—Aerial, linear, vertical, multiple: The relationship of elements in a design.

Plane: Continuous 2D surface with only one direction.

Rectilinear: Moving in, consisting of, bounded by, or characterized by a straight line (wallpaper patterns).

Repetition: The repeating of elements in a design.

Rhythm: Movement characterized by the regular recurrence or alternation of elements.

Scale: The proportion used in determining the dimensions of a design.

Shape: The outline or contour of a design.

Space—Positive, Negative: A defined area of a design; can be of the elements (positive) or the background (negative).

Symmetrical: A design having proportion or equal weight in all its parts.

Theme: Development and application of a sustained series of related concepts or topics.

Unity: In design, a feeling of singleness of all the elements.

Value: Graduation of tone from light to dark (from white to gray to black).

Volume: The amount of space of a design and its elements.

Sample Exercises for Templates and Design Basics
Practical Application of Design Basics Principles
How to use design basics in Adobe Photoshop:

Step 1. Open up the files labeled **Design Basics** (Figure 4–27).

Step 2. Next open a **New File**, 11 × 8.5, **Landscape**, 72 dpi, **RGB**, White background.

Step 3. Review the images on the second layer of the file, entitled Figure 4–27. Drag this new layer onto your new file.

Step 4. Make several copies of this object or layer.

Step 5. Using the **Edit> Free** transform to scale, as well as using the **Move** tool, begin to select the layer objects.

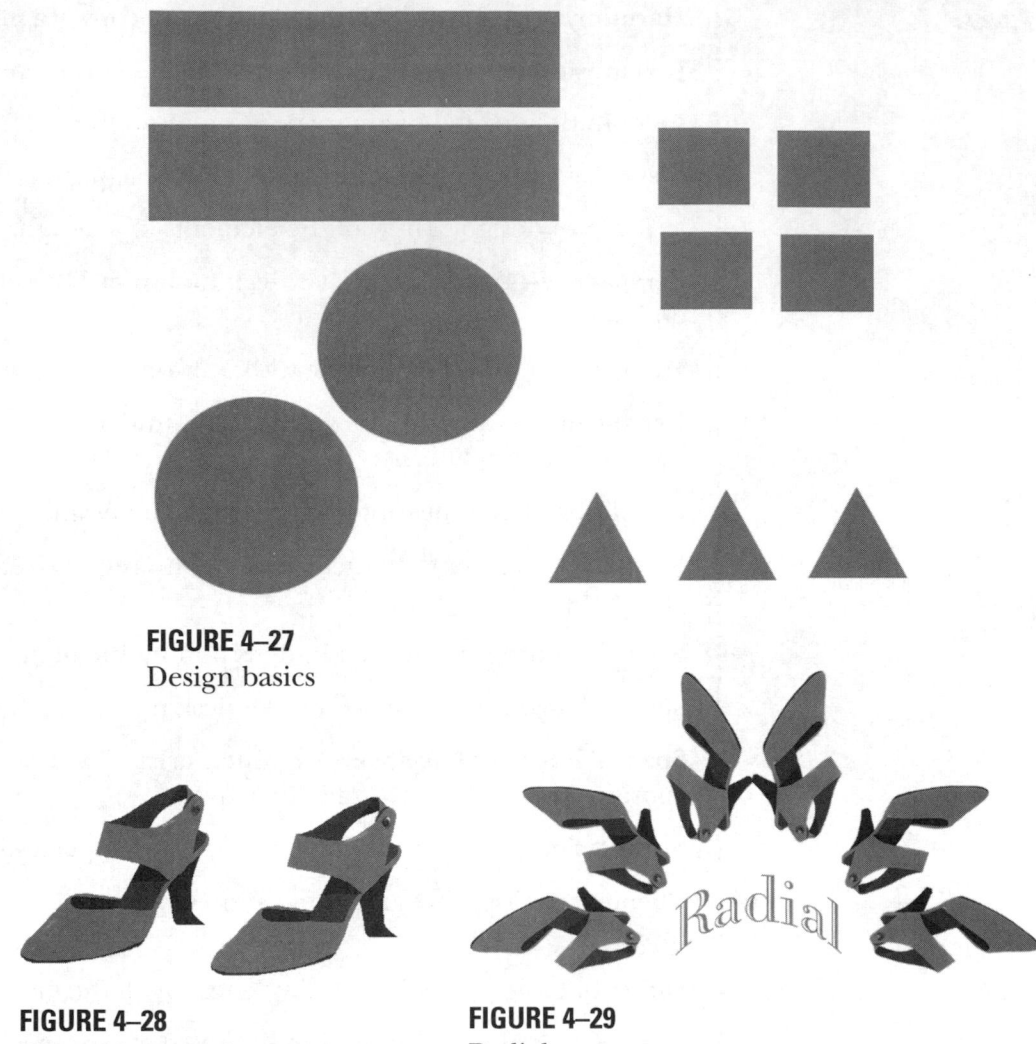

FIGURE 4–27
Design basics

FIGURE 4–28
Formal balance image

FIGURE 4–29
Radial repeat

Step 6. Proceed to experiment with the following design basics to make the following:

    a. Formal Balance Image—Your work might look something like Figure 4–28.

    b. Informal Balance

    c. Radial Repeat—See Figure 4–29.

    d. Continue to experiment, only this time change the colors of the object to see what impact color will have on the overall design.

As you can see, practicing with nondescript objects really helps divorce your thinking from over-designing to focusing on the basics of design and page layout.

Personal Notes:

_____

_____

_____

_____

Design Template for Laying out a Technical Drawing Board:

Step 1. Open **Adobe Photoshop>** Open the **Goodies CD>** Open **Template Folder>** Open file entitled>**Technical Drawing Sample Template**.

Step 2. Notice that the file is in layers. You may opt to drag and drop these layers on to a new file *or*

Step 3. Opt to place your front and back technical sketches on top of the templates.

Step 4. Continue to add the text, which also includes your title, season, *company logo*, and your name.

Step 5. Turn off the template layers on the red boxes or discard them completely.

Step 6. Assign the file a new name and save.

Step 7. See Figure 4–30.

Personal Notes:

_____

_____

_____

_____

Implementing these principles and elements of design basics is the creative challenge that designers thrive on. A simple review of each of these principles can often eliminate disappointment or disaster.

We included a simple visual review of concepts relevant to the basic principles and elements of design you will want to consider the next time you sit down to design.

In addition, we have included a practical checklist of questions you want to be sure that your design will answer affirmatively.

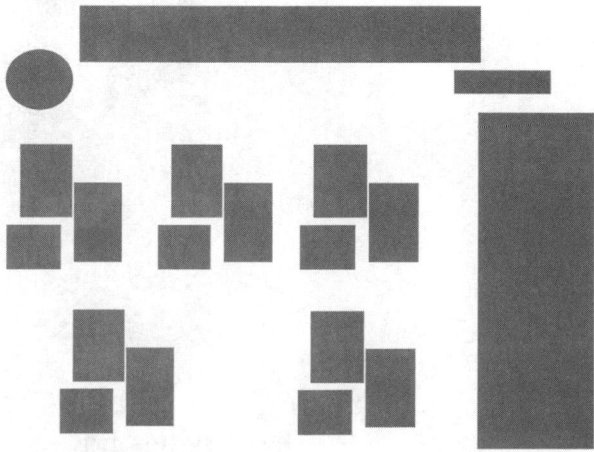

FIGURE 4–30
Design template

1. What mood am I trying to convey in my selection of colorways?

2. Is the background dominating the foreground?

3. Have I used the principles of design to control the reader's eye flow?

4. Is my design complete?

5. Am I inferring any mixed messages in my design?

Personal Notes:

_____

_____

_____

_____

Notes . . .

Advantages of Making a Template in Designing

Finally, we recommend that *before* you begin designing start by making two separate files in Adobe Photoshop for the purpose of making a practice template.

We have included a sample of both a 14″ × 11″ *landscape* file and a 11″ × 14″ file on the CD. (See Figure 4–31.)

HINT: *Each of these files comes with a series of layers that have solid fill objects for you to experiment with and practice moving and resizing. If you are not comfortable using Adobe Photoshop 7, we suggest you jump ahead to Chapter 5, the Adobe Photoshop Primer, and become better acquainted with the program before tackling the next set of exercises.*

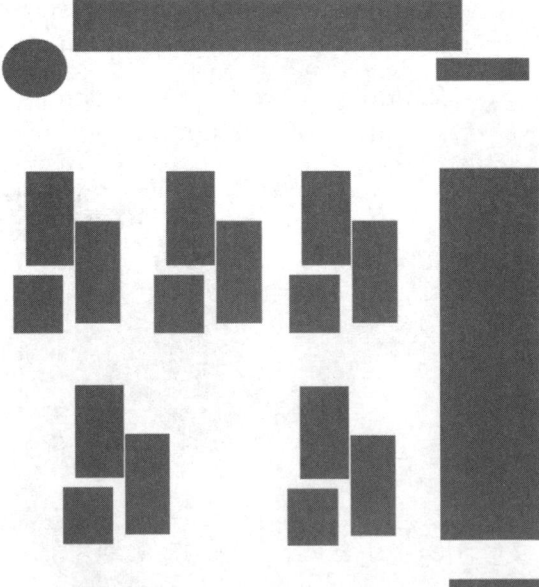

FIGURE 4–31
Portrait template

Unit #5: Color— Understanding Common Color Methods

Part One—Understanding How to Add Color to Cloth—Traditional and Digital Dyeing Methods

Terms to look for:

Affinity to dyes	Dyes	Short-run production
Color	Garment dyed	Solution dyed
Colorfast	Mass dyed	Space dyed
Converter	Ombré	Union dyed
Cross-dyed	Pigment	Vat dyed
Doped dyed	Screen print	Yarn dyed

This chapter is pivotal in transferring from traditional fabric dyeing and printing methods to digital. As a digital textile designer you will need to have complete working knowledge of how fabric is dyed and printed. In today's ever-changing economy of doing business, you may encounter one or all of the following scenarios.

Digital Printing Fabric Scenarios

1. Sample fabric designed and printed in-house digitally, but artwork files prepared for roller, screen, or other traditional industrial printing methods

2. Sample fabric designed and printed digitally in-house and artwork files are prepared for short-run off-site (up to 1,000 yds) printed digitally

3. Sample fabric designed and printed digitally in-house and artwork files prepared for digital printing larger runs at digital printing mill or bureau

4. Designed in-house artwork and printed in sample or short-run quantities by service bureau
   a. All of the above can be any combination of hand to digital conversion of artwork
   b. Including hand rendering, digitally inputted and colored

To help you better comprehend the methods of adding color to fabric, we need to get real for just a moment. Let's consider a simple analogy that will help you better visualize this next step in the textile production process.

Be honest, have you ever colored your hair for *any* reason? If you are a fashion designer, don't lie; many of you would have to answer yes! Perhaps it was youthful rebellion or you are a hard-core fashion nut which made you go to hair color extremes. Either way, you should be acquainted with various products on the market to accomplish the task.

Let's pose a hypothetical question—let's say you were born with dark black hair, but you have decided to become a blond. How easy would that be to achieve? For anyone familiar with the process, obviously you would have to first *remove* the original color, before you could *add* the new color. This would be followed by some maintenance on your part to retain the color. *Why?* Before you begin, there are several things to think about. For example, how well will your specific type of hair accept the color as well as how long can you expect it to be able to hold or maintain the color?

In addition, pretreatment and finishing would be done to improve the hand, appearance, and performance of the hair quality *before*, *during*, and *after* the coloring process!

In textile production, we can add color at any stage of the textile production cycle, including the fiber or filament stage, the yarn or fabric stage, or even to complete garments. If you recall from Chapter 1, we officially described *color* as the *removal, application, and/or the retention of color to a fiber, yarn, fabric, or garment.*

When adding color to textiles, we have several considerations:

- When is the best time to add color?

- What is the best method of color?

Therefore, the type of fiber used will determine its affinity to dyes as well as the colorfastness of the color that is applied. *Affinity to dyes* along with *dye penetration* implies a fiber's ability to completely absorb color. *Colorfastness* refers to the fiber's ability to keep its color when subjected to laundering, heat, chemicals, ultraviolet light, and abrasion. As a consumer, your biggest concern is the *degree of reliability* or *permanence* that a fiber or fabric has. I am sure everyone remembers laundering something red by accident with a load of whites! Ah, the horror and shock of discovering a washer now filled with "pinks"!

Typically greige goods are fibers or fabrics before coloring is added. The collective process of adding color as well as the person responsible for adding color is known as a converter. A *converter* is a highly trained and skilled individual who is responsible for monitoring the color process and assuring quality and standards dictated by federal standards. Converting can be an in-house process or it can be *subcontracted* out to a specialist who matches the right method of adding color to the right fiber.

Figure 5–1 lists the process of color converting.

Adding color to a fiber or fabric can be accomplished in several ways, including:

1. Pigments (which are not water soluble)

2. Prints (which is color added to the surface of the cloth)

- Preparation—scouring and cleaning
- Bleaching and stripping unwanted color
- Adding of optical bleaches and brighteners such as fluorescent dyes
- Drying and/or singeing and burning off unwanted fuzz
- Pretreating fabric
- Dye and/or print fabric

FIGURE 5–1
Greige good process of color converting

3. Dyes that can be either *natural* or *synthetic*—typically, color producing compounds are *not* water soluble
   a. *Disperse*
   b. *Reactive*

Pigments are finely ground color substances that are either natural or synthetic. Typically, pigments are added at the solution stage of synthetic fibers, which makes them extremely colorfast. Dyes used for prints often include chemical adhesions to fasten the color. Pigment dyes are *not* water soluble.

According to the *Hoest Dictionary*, pigments can be used in place of dyes for prints. Resins are used to cure the print after the application of color to the fabric to make the colors brighter.

Typically, *dyes* refer to adding a solid color to a fiber, yarn, fabric, or garment. Dyes originally came from natural sources such as plants (i.e., colors like saffron) or animals, shellfish, and mollusks (colors like purple) or rocks and minerals (reds). Today's dyes are chemically engineered in the laboratory.

Common Methods of Adding Color to Textiles

Solution dyed is adding color to synthetic fibers at the liquid or spinneret stage. Color added at this time is considered to be extremely colorfast.

Vat dyed is generally used for cellulose fibers.

Stock dyed is adding color at the fiber stage to a natural fiber. This is also frequently referred to as *fiber dyed, packaged dyed, dyed in the wool,* or *skin dyed.* A good example of a fiber-dyed fabric would be leather.

Yarn dyed is adding color at the yarn stage of the textile process. Yarn-dyed fabrics are easily recognizable because they involve fabrics with two or more colors such as most stripes, checks, plaids, and jacquards. Fabrics would also include most solid-color silks and wools.

Piece or *garment dyed* is the result of consumer demand for the latest colors. Color is added at the fabric stage or as late as the garment stage. This method of adding color has proven to be cost-effective for both the producer and the consumer. A good example of garment-dyed goods would be T-shirts, some sweaters, socks, and hosiery.

Cross-dyeing is adding one color to two or more fibers. The fibers may have different dye absorption and affinity, so the effect might be the appearance of different shades of color within the same fabric. Two fibers that may be combined and have different affinities to dyes might be cotton and nylon blends.

Union dyed is using two different fibers to make a solid-colored cloth. The color will be uniform in appearance.

Color or *mass dyed* is adding color to synthetic tow fibers or yarns. Adding pigments into the polymer is sometimes referred to as *dope dyed*.

Spaced dyed is adding several colors in irregular intervals to yarns or fabrics in the knit de knit or warp printing process. Yarns that utilize this method are sometimes called ombré yarns.

Thermal fixation is adding or infusing color to polyester by means of adding dry heat to the fabric.

Figures 5–2 through 5–4 are examples of fabric that are yarn dyed, piece dyed, and solution dyed.

The next method of adding color to a fabric is known as printing. Most printing involves adding color to the surface of the cloth.

FIGURE 5–2
Yarn dyed

FIGURE 5–3
Piece dyed

FIGURE 5–4
Solution dyed

Part Two—Understanding Print Making Methods (Including Intro into Digital Printing Methods)

Terms to look for:

1-Way	Half-drop	Repeat
2-Way	Hand printing	Roller printing
4-Way	Jet printing	Screen printing
Blotch	Mirror	Strike-off
Continuous	Motif	Sublimation
Converter	Print	Tossed
Emphasis	Print house	Transfer printing
Engineered	Print mill	Warp printing
Flop-over		

In the previous section of this chapter the focus was on color and color application. We looked at *when, why,* and *how* color was added to a fiber, yarn, fabric, or garment. Now we will focus on the design aspect of using color to render prints or patterns.

Most of today's fabric incorporates the use of applying surface prints directly to the fabric. Prints can draw inspiration from a variety of different designs, patterns, or motifs. Single and repeat prints are used in all facets of design— not just for apparel. Figure 5–5 shows other markets involved in the design and use of prints—all of which can be rendered on the computer. The market is wide open for digital textile and print designers to make their mark in this industry.

Interior Design Markets
- Home/domestics
- Bath
- Bedding/domestics
- Wall coverings
- Flooring
- Window treatment
- Dinnerware
- Stem or glassware

Apparel Design
- All types of apparel including: men's, women's, and children's.
- In addition we can include: accessories, purses, and shoes.

Other Textile Design and Print Design Uses
- Luggage
- Office furniture
- Auto industry
- Industrial prints for disposable consumables such as diapers, and other paper products

FIGURE 5–5
Other markets involved in the design and use of prints

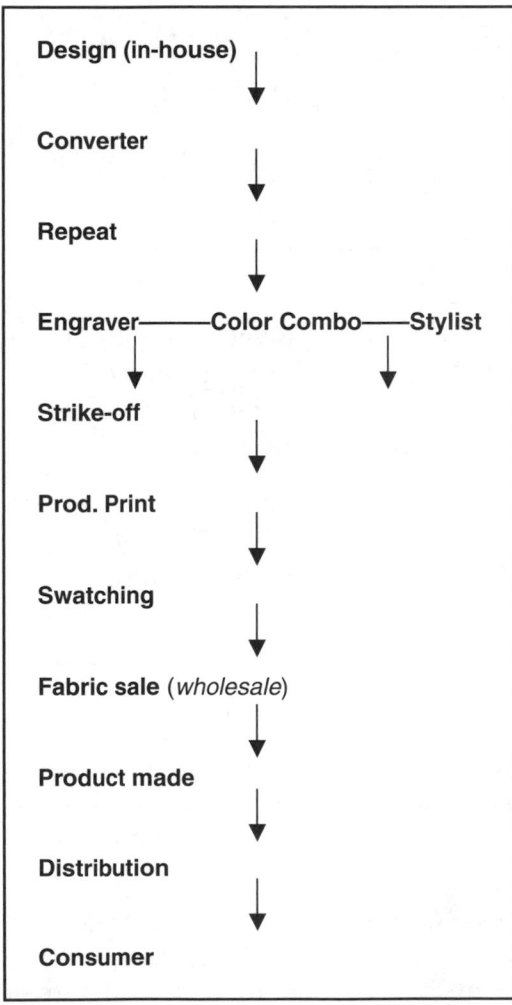

FIGURE 5–6
Traditional print production process

Originally, the term *print* implied a design or pattern applied to the surface of the fabric. However, for our purposes, the term *print* refers to the process of creating or adapting artwork either by hand or digitally for the purpose of printing on fabric.

Prints are comprised of several elements as they pertain to the background and foreground of the design. Typically, a print can consist of a single design or *motif*. These motifs are then used in a variety of combinations that form a *repeat* of a pattern. These designs are not limited exclusively to prints. Design motifs or patterns can be adapted for use in woven or knitted fabrics, or for surface embellishment such as embroidery or flocking.

The process of taking an original design from concept to consumer begins with the designer and then moves on to an individual known as a converter. The converter is a person who "converts" the greige goods into finished cloth by adding the color and/or print to the fabric. A print house or printing mill does the process of applying a printed design to the fabric.

Although the print house has been the traditional location of adding prints, with the advent of digital printing all this is changing. Figure 5–6 shows the typical steps in the design process of creating traditional prints. Figure 5–7 shows typical steps in the digital process of creating prints.

Compare and contrast the two methods.

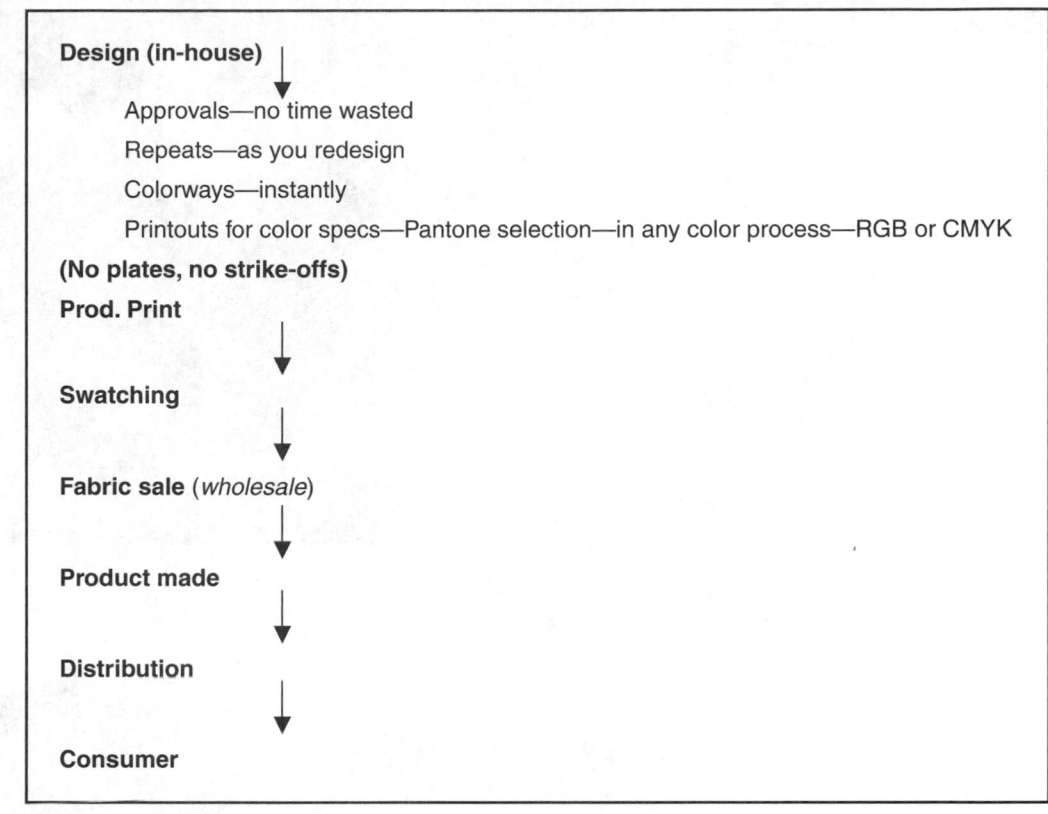

FIGURE 5–7
Digital print production process

1. Relief including rubber stamp and woodblock
2. Resist printing
3. Roller printing
4. Warp printing
5. Screen printing/stencil
6. Heat transfer printing
7. Jet/ink jet/sublimation
8. Discharge printing
9. Burnt-out
10. Photographic
11. Hand
12. Combination

FIGURE 5–8
Types of printing methods

Types of Print Processes

Several methods of printing processes are used today.

Prints have been used in fabrics for thousands of years and were handcrafted. As the industry evolved and technology improved, so did the printing methods.

The digital designer should be acquainted with the printing methods that are in use today. Figure 5–8 shows the most common printing methods.

Figures 5–9 through 5–11 show several fabric examples of the most popular methods used.

Notes...

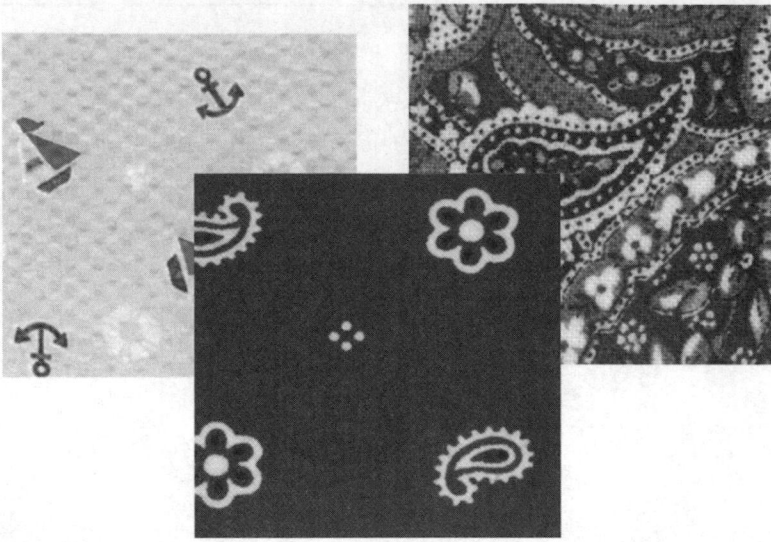

FIGURE 5–9
Direct print

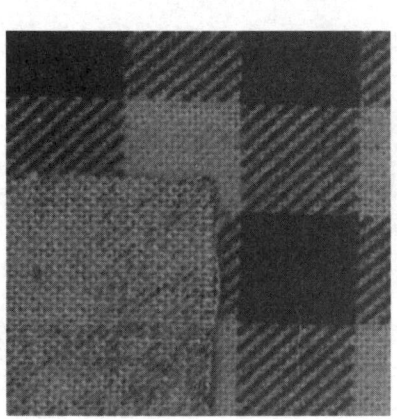

FIGURE 5–10
Direct print to simulate yarn dyed

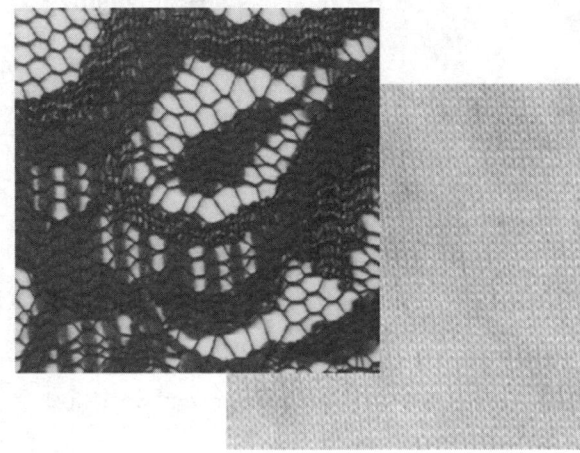

FIGURE 5–11
Examples of piece-dyed garments

Common Printing Categories

To better comprehend printing, we have simplified the various methods into five basic categories:

1. Direct

2. Discharge

3. Resist

4. Other Methods

5. Digital

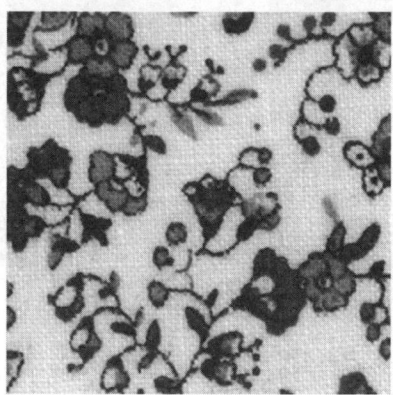

FIGURE 5–12
Direct print

Direct Prints

One of the most popular methods of printing used today is direct printing. Most *direct printing* involves applying color to a white or solid ground fabric. Most direct prints are applied to the surface of the fabric. They are generally fine line designs created by either *roller* or *screen* techniques. (See Figure 5–12.)

There are several variations for creating direct prints; the first is known as overprinting. What distinguishes *overprinting* is that a new foreground color is applied to the previously predyed ground color with the end result having tonal shaded qualities. This method is also referred to as *top printing*.

Another type of direct print is *print on print*, which applies additional colors and/or patterns on a preprinted fabric. This overlapping print on print is used most often for large, colorful, floral or allover designs.

The *blotch printing* method begins with a dyed ground color and then applies either a block, screen, or roller printing technique to overprint the foreground design.

An interesting variation of a direct print is photo printing. Also known as *photographic printing, photo printing* is done by coating the fabric first with light-sensitive chemicals. Next, a photo engraving technique is used to transfer the design or print to the fabric. This technique is considered an exception and is usually listed under category 4 of *other* methods because it is *not* accomplished by either a screen or roller. Typically it is transferred directly onto the screen used in silk screening. This method is considered costly and is often used in the high-end interior design market for wallpaper prints.

Discharge Printing

Our next official category is discharge printing. *Discharge prints* use chemicals to destroy or bleach color from predyed fabric. This extracting method can be done either by roller or screen printing methods. The most common variations of this method are *white discharge*, sometimes known as *extract printing*, and *color discharge printing*.

White discharge prints are easily recognizable; typically they are white dots (bleached) on a solid-color ground. Color discharge printing is like white discharge with a twist. Color discharge prints begin with a solid-color fabric and then

FIGURE 5–13
Color discharge printing

use bleaching agents to remove selected amounts of color to form a print. Typically this might be a lighter shade background and a solid-color series of dots in the foreground. (See Figure 5–13.)

Let's focus on several specific types of discharge printing, beginning with roller printing. *Roller* (also known as *calendar* or *cylinder*) *printing* is used mostly for prints that will be large or have long runs as well as for high quality. Roller prints begin with each individual color or parts of the design being created by a series of engraved rollers, which will represent a corresponding pattern and/or color. Roller-printed fabric can have a large number of colors within the design. Each roller has its own dye-dispensing unit along with a blade that is used to remove any excess dye from the surface of the cloth.

Screen printing has several variations; the most common method can be done either manually or mechanically. The screen printing process involves a series of separate frames or screens created for only one color and one portion of the design or repeat. Then, color is added sequentially over the cloth to create the print. Screen printing can also be accomplished by *flat bed screen* or *rotary screen* methods. Handcrafted screen prints and manually *stenciled prints* also fall under this category.

Several variations of screen printing, which are becoming very popular today, are burnt-out printing and flock printing. It should be noted that some people tend to categorize each of these methods of printing as finishing techniques rather than as a printing technique. However, each of these special effects is created through printing methods. *Burnt-out prints* utilize chemicals to dissolve the fiber or color application. *Flock printing* uses adhesives or an electrostatic charger to apply short fiber to produce a raised surface design.

Duplex or *register printing* passes fabric through roller printing machines so that fabric is printed on both sides of the cloth, often to simulate a complex woven pattern.

Resist Printing

Our next category of printing methods is resist prints. A *resist print* is created using an engraved roller and a resist paste. The fabric is then placed in a dye bath

Notes . . .

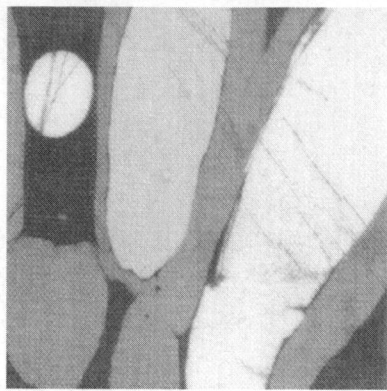

FIGURE 5–14
Batik

and the areas covered with the resist paste reject the color. Although this sounds more like a dyeing method of adding color to the fabric because the first stage uses roller printing, it is categorized as a resist print.

One of the better-known methods of resist printing is batik. *Batik* is one of the most labor-intensive printing methods. It involves the use of dyes, resins, or wax. This is a multistep process of adding wax, dyeing, and then removing the wax to create a print. (See Figure 5–14.)

Other Traditional Printing Methods

Although the next few methods seem to defy a category heading, they clearly can be considered prints. *Warp printing* is accomplished by adding color to only warp yarns that will later be woven with solid-colored filling yarns to create a unique and distinctive effect.

Another subheading of the direct print category is transfer printing. *Transfer* or *heat transfer printing* is the application of a design to fabric using a paper substrate that has been preprinted with a design. The pattern is then transferred to the fabric using dry heat or other press-on methods to affix the design to the fabric. Another common variation of this method is *iron-on* or *press-on* prints used in applying isolated patterns or emblems to fabric or a garment.

Combinations are also used in printing, including rotary screen prints. *Rotary screen printing* is a combination of roller and screen that forces color from the interior through a perforated cylindrical screen onto the cloth.

Our last technique pays homage to the artisan who designs and creates a *hand-painted print* design or employs other time-honored handcrafted methods known as *relief prints*. Unlike hand painting, which is a free-flowing design, a relief print results from a pattern etched into a woodblock or a rubber stamp that creates relief prints. Dye is applied to the image and the block is pressed against the surface of the fabric.

Today's Designers—Merge the Traditional with the Digital

Making the transition from hand to digital designing is a process. We have included a student success story so you can see the benefits of understanding both

FIGURE 5–15
Joanne O'Reilly—textile artist
(Courtesy of Joanne O'Reilly)

traditional and digital techniques and then make the transition from hand to computer. Meet freelance textile designer Joanne O'Reilly. (See Figures 5–15 through 5–19 for samples of her work.)

Our final technique *gauffage* also falls into the *other* category. Gauffage is a technique that is considered to be both a printing technique and a finishing process. This ancient technique has been updated by master textile designer Sabina Braxton. Sabina is considered to be one of today's leading fabric designers within both the couture fashion and the haute couture interior design communities. Her textile work has been used by several leading designers including Bill Blass and the house of Dior. Her gauffage fabrics were also used in the popular Harry Potter movies. Figure 5–20 shows a sample of gauffage.

FIGURE 5–16
Sample of textile designer business card
(Courtesy of Joanne O'Reilly)

FIGURE 5–17
Storyboard of technical drawings of purses
(Courtesy of Joanne O'Reilly)

FIGURE 5–18
Sample of 1940s retro-look prints done on cotton fabrics
(Courtesy of Joanne O'Reilly)

FIGURE 5–19
Storyboard showing fabric and colorways for purses
(Courtesy of Joanne O'Reilly)

Notes . . .

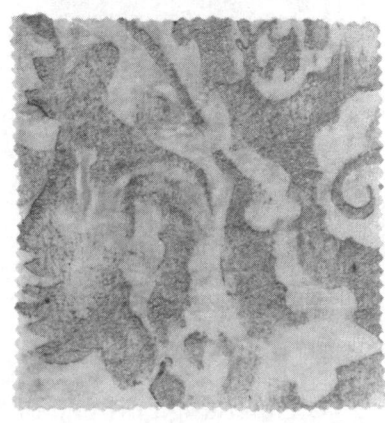

FIGURE 5–20
Gauffage

Digital Printing

So what is digital printing anyway? According to the experts from the Digital Printing and Imaging Association, "Digital imaging is a means to an end . . . a process rather than a product . . . a creative and cost-effective approach to managing data . . . including graphics using the computer and electronic technologies."

Let's now apply that definition to digital textile printing—the process begins when a designer creates or converts an image digitally to be adopted for use in a printed product. For our purposes, this end product typically will be an apparel- or interior-related textile.

Therefore, *digital printing* is the actual process of transforming a digital design to fabric and is accomplished when microsized droplets of dye are placed on the desired substrate through an ink-jet print head. The print system utilizes software that interprets and manages the data or file supplied by the designer. The printer software will then control the droplet output so that image quality and color control will be exactly as the designer intended.

The original image can be rendered by hand or digitally created from scratch. This process does not replace the designer's pens, watercolors, or markers. Instead designers are using today's software. The designer has the freedom to choose which method or which combination of traditional and digital methods will work best for their client's timeline and budget. (See Figures 5–21 and 5–22.)

FIGURE 5–21
Digital design printed on felt

FIGURE 5–22
Digital design printed on jersey

According to Teri Ross, president of Imagine That!, "The undisputed king of commercial applications is Adobe Photoshop. Even with several production shortcomings, savvy designers are making recommendations to management for purchasing a new breed of proprietary software plug-ins that offset any textile design-related limitations Adobe Photoshop may have."

Efforts from such organizations as CITDA (Computer Integrated Textile Design Association) are eliminating other barriers to entry by establishing industry file format standards. With 88 percent of the commercial graphic market using Adobe Photoshop, the natural "save as options" adopted is TIFF 6.0.

Digital Printing: Convergence of Craft, Production, and Technology

Digital textile printing is converting the traditional textile and apparel design industry. A growing number of designers, visionaries, and entrepreneurs are driving the momentum. Propelling this movement is the trend to mass customization. *Mass customization* is the ability to design and render small or large quantities of fabric or garments that have been individually customized. This process of digital rendering on fabric has revolutionized how companies develop products responding to consumer preferences. This ability to act in a timely fashion is also known as *immediate response*, and in today's fast-paced and fickle consumer market this allows for short-run production while still providing uniqueness of design.

As we stated earlier, prints evolved from several variations of handcrafted methods. There is another evolution occurring within the industry and that is the conversion to digital production for prints. As with any new technology the trend has experienced several barriers. Such barriers can be emotional as well as rational. The perceived fear is often based on a lack of experience and/or training to use this new technology. Other very real factors to consider include color matching and reproductive issues. All of these can be difficult challenges and therefore we will cover them in greater detail in Chapter 6.

However, another significant factor is helping to fuel enthusiasm for this emerging industry—the artisans themselves. Both the graphic artist and the fine artist see the creative potential, not to mention the timesaving potential. The industry is making strides to adopt or at least adapt—thanks to investors, entrepreneurs, and retailers in the apparel supply chain who can't help but smell profit and see dollar signs!

Industry Winners

The real winner in this emerging industry is the consumer. Emerging technologies such as 3D body scanning and other related new technologies, and the uniqueness or "customized" design that digital prints provide all converge to satisfy the customer who has an appetite for form, fit, function, and uniqueness!

No longer is the manufacturer or the designer limited by the inherent nature of the screen printing process. It is now possible to engineer a print design according to the actual shape of the garment and include other customized design elements. Now, a consumer can opt to become part of the design process by selecting his or her own personal print preferences as well as selecting personal unique colorway interpretations!

Finally, this new technology is expanding the job market beyond traditional apparel or the sign and banner (flag) business. Now "digitally trained" textile designers are needed for the field of entertainment—costumes, backdrops, sporting apparel—and the interior design world of fabrics and wall, floor, and window coverings.

Relevant Digital Printing Terminology

Digital images are produced on a wide range of output devices. We will have a closer look at who is producing and distributing these output devices in Chapter 12. Suffice it to say that the technology these printers utilize can range from modest priced off-the-shelf software and hardware that utilizes available industry plug-ins to more costly proprietary software and hardware considerations. Every output device and related software have important features and associated jargon. The most widely used technologies today are liquid ink-jet, electrostatic, solid ink-jet, and photographic.

In order to better comprehend the technique as well as the technology, we have provided you with a glossary of relevant terminology on digital printing. In the course of our research we discovered an easy way to understand the terms posted on the website of the Digital Printing and Imaging Association. This organization provides a complete list and a detailed explanation of the related terms frequently associated with digital printing. For further information, please refer to www.DPI.org.

Acid dyes: Commercial dyes that are typically used for adding color to fabric in organic or inorganic acid dye solutions. Most commonly used on the natural fibers of wool and silk, as well as for synthetic fibers such as acrylic, nylon, and polypropylene and blended combinations.

Blotch printing: In this method of printing, the ground color is printed rather than dyed. This fabric is easily distinguishable because the reverse of the fabric will be white.

Colorfastness: Will always refer to the degree of permanence and performance of a dye or ink after repeated exposure to ultraviolet light and repeated laundering.

Digital printing: A form of printing where microsized droplets of dye are placed onto a given substrate through an ink-jet print head. This is accomplished when the print software interprets the data supplied by a digital image file. The software controls the droplet output and determines the final image color and quality.

Disperse dyes: These are synthetic and nearly water-insoluble dyes used for dyeing synthetic fibers such as acetate, nylon, and polyesters.

Dye sublimation: Similar to thermal transfer, sublimation dyes are transferred from a carrier roll and applied through the use of heat. When a controlled amount of heat is applied, the dye is vaporized and then transferred to the medium or fabric. This term also refers to the amount of dye loss due to evaporation of the solid without formation of a liquid phase.

Electrostatic: Special media are imaged with an electronic charge that attracts toner particles. Typically electrostatic printers image each color individually.

Fixing, Fixation, or Finishing: All three terms are relevant when discussing the method of setting the dye to the fabric. This postprinting process is usually accomplished through several methods including steaming, hot wash, or chemicals.

Heat transfer printing: Uses heat and pressure to fixate an image to a fabric or garment.

Ink-jet: There are several alternatives:

- **Continuous**—The ink is applied continuously under pressure from a stream of droplets. The droplets required to form the image are channeled to the media, while the unused droplets are recycled.
- **Drop on demand**—The ink is released by applying pressure to force a drop of ink onto the media as needed to create the image.
- **Thermal**—Here a gas bubble is created in the nozzle that creates pressure to force a droplet of ink onto the media.
- **Solid**—The ink is stored in a solid format, and then is melted as needed and applied to the media using methods similar to liquid ink-jet (wax ink).

Spray jet: Individual ink colors are applied directly to the media through a spray nozzle.

Thermal wax or **resin transfer:** Wax or resin is applied to a film carrier, which is usually in a roll format. The wax or resin is then transferred to the media using heat. However, each color must be transferred individually.

Now you should have a better working knowledge of the different types of printing. Let's identify the individuals who are the driving force behind this exciting new industry.

In the world of digital textiles two major forces propelling this emerging technology are the fine artists and the fashion industry insiders. Both types of individuals are always searching for new forms and mediums of expression. Even though their underlying motivations to produce may be very different, the results of their work often provide the catalyst for change within the way of doing business or the usual way of producing art.

In the last section of this chapter we are going to showcase profiles of two individuals who, in their own right, are leading this revolution.

We would like you to meet Teri Ross, of Imagine That! and Techexchange, whose global insights have had a profound impact on the digital textile and designing community (see Figure 5–23).

Teri Ross is a writer, speaker, and consultant focusing on CAD/CAM technology and process improvement strategies for the sewn products industry. She is owner and president of Imagine That! Consulting Group, previous owner of the award-winning techexchange.com. (Kindly note at the time of printing, the Techexchange website had been purchased by TC2.)

It shouldn't take long for anyone interested in the business of digital textiles and production to come across the name Teri Ross. Teri's impact is felt in every corner

FIGURE 5–23
Teri Ross
(Courtesy of Teri Ross)

of the fashion community. In the world of fashion, many people may fancy themselves as industry "mavens," but Teri Ross truly is the definitive maven in this cutting-edge industry.

Teri has graciously consented to grant us permission to include one of her more prophetic explanations on digital textile production. The following article succinctly explains this emerging industry's impact on today's fashion.

A Primer in Digital Textile Printing

by Teri Ross, May 2001

The rapidly evolving world of digitally printed textiles is a reflection of several unique and contrasting business models that create challenges, threats, and opportunities to the future of the textile printing market.

The traditional textile industry looks at it from their traditional mass production business models and complains it is too slow and too expensive relative to the conventional screen printing technologies most commonly used in the market today. For these companies, digital textile printing has proven to be a tremendous cost savings in sampling only, while moving to conventional methods for their mass production needs.

With textile seminars and exhibits being presented on in increasingly frequent basis at wide format printing and graphics trade shows, it is apparent that other industries are looking at this technology with an eye towards what it can do, as opposed to what it can't do. Since these industries already support short-run and customization business models as a reflection of their technology driven businesses, textiles simply represent a new market to which they can sell their excellent command of printing technology as well as their ability to produce short-run production with quick turn-around—a business practice that is foreign to the conventional printing industry as a result of the analog technology on which it is founded.

So, is the wide-format printing industry a threat to the conventional textile printing industry? Yes and no. If the textile industry waits for the technology to evolve in order to adopt it as a production tool, then yes, they will have lost many opportunities to new players. If, on the other hand, they can re-engineer their businesses to support the growing consumer demand for customized product, then they can lessen the probability of market erosion.

The wide-format printers are not without their challenges to the new market opportunities. While most have mastered the basics of printing on paper, vinyl and even plastics, printing on textiles that vary in fiber content, weight, thickness, ink absorbency, and yarn size, that must be washable, light fast, crock resistant, and wearable and require multiple ink sets can present a whole new set of challenges, if not at least a learning curve. Satisfying a textile industry that is accustomed to the color accuracy that spot color offers is yet another challenge.

With an eye towards the growing number of wide-format printers, graphic artists, and entrepreneurs who see the market opportunities, we offer a primer in digital textile printing.

The Textile Printing Market, Textile Types and Suppliers

According to research offered by Dupont, cotton is the most commonly printed substrate (48% of printing production), followed by cotton/polyester blends (19%), polyester (15%), and viscose (13%). From a worldwide perspective, other substrates (e.g., polyamide, polyacrylic, wool, and silk) play just a minor role.

Printing of woven substrates is the most important activity worldwide. The knits and nonwovens are quickly advancing, although at the expense of wovens. Nonwovens show great progress. Their share is now almost 8 times the original value. Of the 26 billion linear meters printed annually, the majority are 60″ wide and printed using six to eight spot colors.

Printed textiles offer some unique variables not found in the paper world, including:

1. More than a half dozen common types of synthetic and natural fibers, each with its own ink compatibility characteristics

2. Dealing with a stretchable, flexible, often highly porous and textured surface

3. Extreme use requirements including light, waterfastness (sweat, too) through finishing operations and often outdoor use, heavy wear, abrasion, and cleaning

4. For some apparel applications, challenging registration requirements since separate pieces need to be assembled

5. Not just sight, but also touch requirements

6. Much greater absorbency, requiring many times the ink volume compared with printing on papers

While most equipment manufacturers will boast the ability to print in all fabrics, with the exception of those with high naps or piles that leave lint in the ink heads, direct ink-jet printing to fabric (as distinguished from heat transfer printing) requires that the fabric be pre-treated in order to achieve the highest quality of ink absorbency and color vibrancy. There are a growing number of vendors offering a broad range of both stock fabrics as well as custom coating services. For a list of vendors, search the techexchange.com database under "Manufacturing—Textile Fabrics and Supplies (digital)."

Ink Types and Applications

Fabric, unlike paper, is a three-dimensional structure and the ink and colorant requirements vary over a large range. Practical limitations exist on the range of fabrics and colors that can be produced with a single ink set. On some fibers that are absorbent, like wool and cotton, the ink is absorbed quickly and easily, so bleeding of the water-like ink-jet ink is minimized even without a pretreatment. Unlike the thick, paste-like ink used in conventional screen-printing, these water-like inks will bleed badly on nonporous fibers like polyester and nylon. A mechanism to control bleeding must be incorporated to avoid the ink wicking along the nonporous fibers of the textile. This also is important in applications that require print-through on the design to give nearly equal color on both sides of the fabric. In traditional printing this is controlled by the high viscosity of the inks used. With ink-jet printing, preheating the textile or addition of a fabric pretreatment may help control these effects. The binding mechanism of the pigment to the textile and the reaction of the dyes with the fibers usually require a complimentary pretreatment chemistry and/or post-treatment to achieve the optimum result. The bottom line is that the ink, textile, and the printing system must be designed to control bleeding while achieving the hand and correct colorfastness required by the intended application.

The operative here is "intended application." Printed textiles are sold to many different market segments for a variety of end uses, including fashion textiles, home textiles, and soft signage (flag and banner). The target market and end use will ultimately determine the fabric, ink, and post processing requirements.

- Solvent-based inks
- Ink chemistry fibers post-processing markets supported
- Dye polyester (not often used in ink-jet printers—only currently used in the Gretag Carolina printer) none soft signage
- Pigment vinyl, polyester, nylon none outdoor signage
- Water-based inks
- Ink chemistry fibers post-processing markets supported
- Acid dyes silk, nylon, wool steam/wash, can be dry-cleaned fashion textiles, indoor soft signage (not flame retardant)
- Disperse dyes (sublimation) polyester (flame retardant or nonflame retardant) Heat fixation fashion textile, indoor & outdoor soft signage, home textile (wash fast and durable, not very UV resistant)
- Reactive dyes natural fibers: Cotton, silk, rayon, wool steam/wash, can be dry-cleaned fashion textiles, indoor soft signage (not flame retardant)
- Direct dyes all fibers steam/wash, can be dry-cleaned fashion textiles
- Cotton, polyester none flame retardant soft signage

- Cotton, polyester, nylon, rayon, silk none not flame retardant soft signage

- Pigments without binder, all fibers dry heat indoor and outdoor soft signage, home textile

- Pigments with binder cotton and possibly polyester dry heat indoor and outoor soft signage, home textile

Source: 3P Ink-Jet Textiles

As printing technology advances, progress must and will be supported by ink chemistry improvements. The important trend to follow is the development of pigment systems or alternative chemistry for textiles. Pigment systems have not been easily adapted for the textile ink-jet environment and early introductions have been criticized for color brilliance and fastness. For the sewn products industry, the pigment trend is significant for a couple of reasons. In contrast to dye-based systems in which dye class must be matched with fiber type, pigments are substrate independent.

They can be used for printing a wide range of fibers and fabrics including blends. This will have a great deal of interest for producers of home furnishings, bed linens, and certain apparel products. In addition, pigments and alternative chemistry that do not require steam fixation will simplify the path between printing and cutting. A dry fixation unit could potentially be mounted between a printer and single-ply cutting unit. In contrast, the steaming process required by dye-based systems presents a barrier to integration. Steaming requires a separate process and may cause changes in dimension and shape that make part recognition more difficult during the cutting procedure.

Spot vs. Process Color

There is not an issue more widely contested in the emerging digital textile printing market than the issue of spot versus process colors. Each has its advantages and disadvantages, as outlined below. Some experts argue that the best solution will be one that supports the ability to print both spot and process colors, which will support no color gamut problems, perfect color matching, color gradation similar to screen printing, for spot tones and color gradation better than screen printing for halftones.

- Ink-jet process colors screen printed spot colors (analog printing)

- Advantages—Theoretically four basic colors, actual use of seven to twelve colors depending on print head

- Higher productivity due to bigger drops

- A color change on the fabric does not require a physical color change on the machine.

- Better coverage due to bigger drops

- Theoretically an unlimited number and range of colors for printing available

- Easy setting of desired color tones

- Less chemical/dyestuff usage

- Normal work processes can be kept.

- Environmentally friendlier

- Exact color reproduction

- Wider tolerance permitted for fabric structure as well as for mechanical engineering

- Disadvantages—Difficult color adjustment on "flat" colors

- Colors must be premixed (color kitchen).

- Strong dependence on dyestuffs and fabric structure

- Color change requires washing and changing of colors (environmental issue plus 40% ink waste in the wash).

- As the single color drops, it must be placed on the fabric at exact spots. Maximum preciseness is required for the printing machine manufacturer.

- High resolution (up to 760 dpi) is required to avoid color areas from appearing granular and pixel-like. The resolution value however does not represent the delicateness actually achieved on the fabric, as several colors drop together to form "super pixels."

- Higher resolution leads to lower output speed.

- Penetration varies depending on how many process colors are used.

The Advantages of Digital Textile Printing

To date, the key drivers in adopting digital textile printing technology for traditional textile printers has been the reduction of sampling costs and time to market. In conventional textile screen printing, the development cost for strike-offs and samples are $4,000 to $8,000 (USD) per design, with the cost fluctuating based upon the number of spot colors used in a design. The development of these screens and strike-offs takes from two to five weeks. With digital textile printing there are no screen costs, and a sample can be printed upon demand.

However, with the textile industry using this technology only for strike-offs, while moving to conventional screen printing for their production needs, it is failing to incorporate many of the key benefits and design opportunities that the new technology provides. These benefits include the ability to use an unlimited number of colors, excellent reproduction of continuous tone images, unlimited repeat sizes and the ability to print engineered designs across multiple seam lines.

What Will Drive the Market?

By eliminating wet post processing, ink-jet pigment printing has the potential to make "agile manufacturing" much more attractive. "Agile manufacturing" refers to an integrated, on-demand order and fulfillment process that includes the textile printing and product fabrication manufacturing processes. To implement "agile manufacturing" one must have the ability to print, cut, sew, and ship immediately on demand. This capability can dramatically change the way sewn product and other printed textiles are produced.

Freedom from the requirement of using wet chemicals along with "agile manufacturing" will facilitate "distributed printing." "Distributed printing" refers to a small textile fabrication facility that receives the design and product information electronically, then produces product at or near the retail outlet. With these capabilities, along with the digital design, the potential cost savings in the supply chain and the reduction in inventory and design risk, the availability of digital ink-jet pigment printing should drive conversion of some parts of the textile printing industry away from conventional screen printing.

Another key driver is printing speed. While all printers available on the market to date have been too slow to support mass production speed requirements, two recent product launches from BMT Technologies (dye sublimation/heat transfer printing) and Dupont boast digital textile printing speeds that can match the speeds of conventional rotary screen printing. While increasing speeds will certainly increase the likelihood of adaptation by the conventional printing industry, this solution merely supports the application of technology to existing business models, and provides no incentive to develop the mass customization business opportunities that the technology will support.

The greatest challenge to digital textile printing adaptation is the conventional textile printing industry itself, which continues to place analog restrictions on digital printing. They are looking at this new technology through the existing workflow and output of a 30-year-old printing technology and trying to replace these analog processes and products with the digital ones. The result is a mind-set that is focused more on what the digital technology can't do than what it can do.

Implementing digital printing effectively means rethinking the overall system. It means designing different types of products that leverage the advantages of digital printing. It means sales and marketing strategies that leverage short-run production. It means thinking about your business from the perspective of mass customization as opposed to mass production.

The single most costly element in today's soft goods business is the holding of product and parts in anticipation of a sale. This process supports the maxim that the best way to create profit is to mass-produce and discount the surplus. To make this gamble work, the apparel delivery system has developed a cumbersome structure designed to stockpile the inventory in staged production surpluses, then to sell finished product in tiered discount and therefore reduce the risk for each participant.

While this process has in fact lowered cost, it has also lowered profit and customer choice. In many ways this solution has made a badly weakened segment of the U.S. economy even weaker. The solutions to profit erosion and lack of consumer choice are the same—individualized mass production and delivery. Digital textile printing offers the technology to deliver mass customized product.

And therein lies the heart of the problem—as well as the opportunity. Screen printing was developed in the industrial age when the economies of scale demanded a mass production business model. The technology itself, with the tremendous time and cost of screen development, has demanded large production runs. The economic models of the conventional printing industry are based upon the volume of yardage that can be printed each year. Digital printing, in its current state of development, does not support this business model.

However, when looked at from the perspective of the wide-format printing industry, an industry that is based on short-run customized production, textiles represent nothing more than a new media and a new market. This industry doesn't look at digital textile printing from the perspective of what it can't do, but rather all of the new markets it will allow them to enter. The challenge to these people is in learning the textile industry, whereas the challenge to the textile industry is in learning both the digital printing technology as well as a new business model under which to sell their products.

Bottom line, digital printing for short-run production requires thinking outside the box. It requires an entirely new approach with new products and new marketing strategies that leverage not just printing technology, but CAD systems, cutting systems, information systems, and even the Internet. Since the traditional industry has repeatedly demonstrated its lack of desire to change its ways and its fear of new technology, digital textile printing applications are as likely to come from outside the industry as they are from the inside.

You will learn more about the industry in the final chapter of this text. For now this is a great primer for you to better understand what is involved and why color and managing color is so critical to our industry.

Our last interview on color is from one of the leading industry experts on dealing with color management from traditional textile coloring methods to digital content with color.

Meet Richard Lerner of RSL Digital Consultants

Offices in New York City and Connecticut, Working Worldwide

Richard is a very well-known and respected consultant in digital imaging and color-managed workflows. Richard is also an accomplished internationally published professional photographer. His roots stretch back through manufacturing, textile dyeing, screen printing, and color matching. He is a charter member of CITDA's Color Committee, attempting to quantify, codify, and set standards for the textile and apparel companies in cooperation with CAD vendors.

Richard has an eclectic combination of talents and skills. We have included in our interview of Richard a sampling of his interesting projects and clients from over the last 15 years.

FIGURE 5–24
Richard Lerner
(Courtesy of Richard Lerner)

Richard's sensibilities and well-developed empathy for others can be traced back to his years when he attended Clark University studying psychology. Richard put his communication and people-skills to good use when he started his working life in a family business owned by his uncles—*Liberty Die and Button Mold Company*.

Richard never could have known that his brief contact with the apparel industry in the form of buttons would start him on the path to becoming a well-known digital color consultant in the textile and home furnishings industries and beyond into publishing including on the Web. After two and a half years of the button business, Richard left to pursue a stint as a photography assistant. This led to joining up with a longtime photographer friend, Brian Haviland. They opened Haviland/Lerner, a professional photography studio, which they successfully operated for 10 plus years. Following this association Richard had his own shot at several national advertising and billboard campaigns for such notable clients as *Onkyo Stereo, DiMario Guitars*, and *ABC News*, just to name a few.

Then approximately 13 years ago, Richard began doing pioneer work in CAD when he partnered with Joni Johns, Gene Mignola, and C. L. Hundley to form another new company entitled, *Fabric Effects, Inc.*, in 1990. This company was groundbreaking in small production and design development. Their studio combined fabric dyeing, hand-painted fabric, silk screening, and computer-aided designing. At this point Richard decided that he needed to step into digital design with both feet. Thankfully, he had purchased a Macintosh. Why do we say thankfully? At the time when Richard opened his studio, his other choice in a graphics desktop computer was the Commodore and, as history has shown us, for most of the graphic design industry, Mac, Adobe Photoshop, and Adobe Illustrator have become the industry standards! These were his first steps in developing a process for computer to screen artwork for many of the top fashion design houses in the country.

With the help of Joni, who is an accomplished textile and costume hand-painter, along with Gene Mignola, a successful screen printer and fabric dyer, Richard quickly absorbed the textile and color knowledge that he now applies to his business today.

This combined talent of dyeing, silk screening, hand-painting, and CAD has led to creating digital techniques for quick development, including sample and small production runs of fabric that are needed for the textile, apparel, theater, and motion picture industries.

Typically, a fabric would have a dyed ground for the major sections of the motifs to be silk-screened and the smaller detail hand-painted onto fabric for design development, sample yardage, and small production runs. This led to faster production of designs, and the output from computer files produced the film positives, which were then used to burn the screens for screen prints.

Fabric Effects next started to experiment with proprietary textile software. Then they teamed up with *Monarch Design Systems*, where Richard helped to develop software specifically for the textile, apparel, and home furnishings industries. This was done to overcome some of the challenges Richard encountered in his design experience. Today, Monarch's design software has grown into *Pointcarre, USA*.

Naturally for Fabric Effects, direct digital printing to fabrics would be just on the horizon. Fabric Effects' growing textile and apparel clientele along with Richard's industry contacts throughout the technology marketplace positioned him for a prime opportunity to acquire a textile printer (an Iris's 4700 HS), which helped to launch Fabric Effects into custom coating fabrics. Throughout the early to mid-1990s Fabric Effects also experimented with film, dot angles, and other technical issues. Sadly, however, in 1995 one partner, C. L. Hundley, passed away, which caused the remaining partners to reevaluate their work goals. At that time many of the principals decided to pursue individual interests.

Richard parlayed his new design knowledge and practical experience with computer-aided design, digital imaging, and color management and formed *RSL Digital Consultants.*

As a result, many of Richard's earlier textile and apparel clients immediately began to call to inquire if he could help them improve their digital image workflow and control colors throughout the design process. Richard continued working with Monarch Design Systems to begin development of a process for predictable color management from computer monitor to where it really counted—at the printer. Simultaneously, Richard continued to work closely with end users and technology developers as well as consult with *E-Color*, based in San Francisco. E-Color has its own unique technology that allows them to control color on the Web and deliver accurate color to individual desktops.

One opportunity led to another as a result of this association, including working on projects for Bloomingdales and L'Oreal in New York and Paris.

Richard never left his roots and also continued to work closely with the Apple corporation. Through this affiliation, Richard attended numerous meetings that Apple held with customers on color management and color technology.

From one such meeting with Apple, Richard was introduced to *Nourison Rugs*, the largest manufacturer of handmade rugs in the world, hiring him to build a digital photography studio for them as part of their largest showroom. This was followed by the training of staff and instituting of color-managed workflows for both their catalogs and their website. Ever the problem solver, Richard's input enabled Nourison to have vastly greater control of their process and saved large amounts of money while improving the quality of their output.

When we inquired about several of the other aspects of his work, Richard said that he "enjoys tremendously working with artists of many varied disciplines. One such artist is the painter Christopher Wool. Much of Christopher's art is hand silk-screened." For Christopher, much of his design "pre-Richard" involved a lot of hand work in the preparation stages and in multiple stats and collaging.

Much of the work had to be sent out to be photographed to create film to go to the next stage, which was creating screens. This process has now been brought into submission with the aid of the computer. Now all this work is done with greater control and a superior ability to experiment. The end result is a file from which film is directly produced and then screens are burned.

When asked about his biggest challenge through the years, Richard replied, "attempting to explain color management and often correcting the misperception held by many people from designers right through to production people. Many designers are looking for a push button solution that will produce *dead on color.*

Not only is color highly subjective, changing even as an individual gets tired, but getting the correct color input from a yarn or color swatch into the computer can be a tremendous hurdle. The spectrophotometer reading on a yarn that is twisted will be different on a yarn of the same color that is not twisted.

There will always be a large color appearance difference between two garments woven or knit from the same yarn based on a difference in construction. Also a swatch of fabric will often appear to be different shades when viewed under different light sources. There are many variables that designers should not need to think about when they think of color management.

When color management is properly implemented, it should be virtually transparent to the user, neither limiting nor changing their color choices. It is difficult to compare the old methods of trial-and-error color matching to a well-managed color workflow. In the past, you had to keep changing your file to get a good printout of your printer and who knows what that is doing to the file when you need to present it elsewhere and except for sophisticated software doing color swapping, forget about your computer display and your print matching.

Now you can use a spectrophotometer to capture, zap in, your color from a color chip or whatever into the computer, use this color value in your design and get a good representation out of your printer. It can become a new, more accurate, efficient and fun process."

There are, of course, challenges inherent in digital fabric printing at the design level. There is the danger of producing in design and sampling fabrics not easily reproducible at the mill level. This necessitates the continued effort on the CAD artist's side, where a design needs to be scanned, color reduced, and then edited before any color matching can be added, to get an in-house proof.

According to Richard,

> the color process begins long before any designs are created. It is always a real pleasure to see a company truly grasp potential of the technology available to them. Running a pilot program as a proof of concept can lead to true and company-wide utilization of these new techniques. The fruits of this labor can be realized, by producing mill-ready colors in the design process and accurately sampling them before cutting any screens or moving further towards production until feedback is received!

It seems that one of Richard's greatest assets is his ability to problem solve. Gliding back and forth through numerous related industries, Richard seems to have no problem absorbing the knowledge and learning and creating the techniques needed to help others to succeed and therefore succeeding himself.

When asked about someone starting out in this industry his response was this, "Learn as much as possible about traditional design techniques, as that will give you the best possible base for working with today's technology. Many students come into the industry with the CAD abilities, but without the basics of how design and color development evolved. Knowledge of textile history and development as well as traditional design and production methods allow people not only to design intuitively in CAD but to make the most of these modern tools. Create a situation where unique designs come out of modern tools and merge smoothly with the ability to produce them. Some of my most valuable lessons in photography were learned in the numerous hours spent in a darkroom trying to get just the right color and effect in my photographs. The pre-visualization of the images then allows for the move into actually shooting them. The time spent in the darkroom finishes bringing them to life. It is that experience in traditional methods that has helped me to maximize and see unusual uses of such modern tools as digital cameras and Photoshop."

When asked about the industry today, Richard replied, "Companies need to take advantage of technology to sharpen their competitive design and production edge. I feel that companies must embrace digital printing and color management to increase accuracy, allow for more experimentation in design and lower costs. This increased efficiency will help in coping with the communication delays inherent in the increasing amount of offshore manufacturing. Additionally, we all must deal with the pressure created by the increased rate that product needs to get to market, i.e., shorter runs, more new styles or seasons, more often."

As you can clearly see from Richard's interview it was only appropriate that we devote a complete chapter to contend with the color issues as they pertain to computer-aided designing.

In Chapter 6, we will walk you through several important areas that Richard touched on in his interview, along with several other topics you are likely to encounter in your journey through designing digitally with color.

Contending with Computer Color Issues

Terms to look for:

Anti-aliasing	Indexed	ppi
BMP	Jaggies	PSD
CMYK	JPEG	Resampling
Color gamut	Lossy	Resolution
Color mapping	Palettes	RGB
Color reduction	Pantone®	Scanning
Colorways	PICT	TGA
dpi	Pixelization	TIFF
Export		

Let's Continue with Color

In our last chapter we defined *color* as the presence or absence of light as it is reflected from a surface or not reflected. Color is basically wavelengths of light. When we describe color, we refer to its *hue*, which is merely another name for color. Color is also described by *chroma* or *intensity*, which signifies the degree of *saturation*. The question is how does this information apply to computers?

Designers use a variety of imaging devices to accomplish this, such as scanners, displays, and printers that use a subset of all visible colors. The color subset that a device is capable of handling is called its *color gamut*.

You will find that the colors you typically view on your *output profile*, which means a monitor or printed hard copy, when compared to your original or s*ource profile* do not always match. Here is where you might encounter the terms color gamut and color mapping; color gamut refers to image devices such as scanners, monitors, and printers that can only display a *subset* of all visible colors. On the other hand, *color mapping* is the technology that permits the "best match" in appearance to the "source image."

Therefore, the challenge is converting color from a source device to a destination device with as little loss of color as possible.

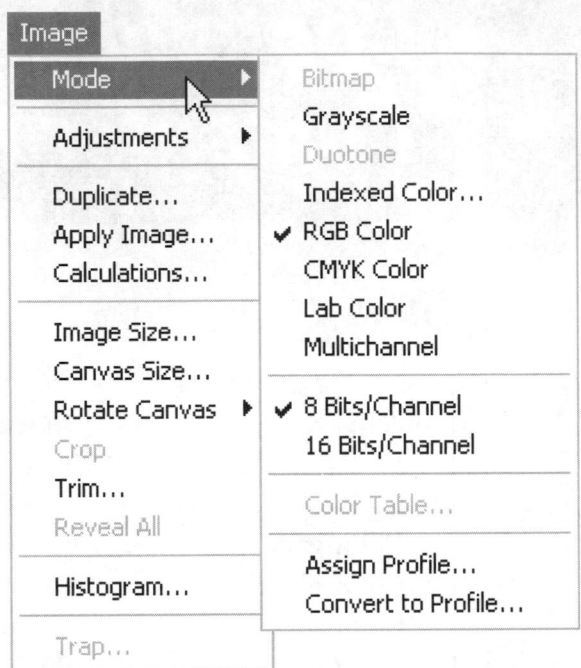

FIGURE 6–1
List of modes

WYSIWYG??? Is What You See What You'll Get?

Further frustration arises for designers who are "driven by color" in trying to match the colors they see. The fact is that the human eye can detect a wider color gamut, than the computer; so no wonder some designers go prematurely gray in the attempt!

Information about software solutions for these challenges is included later in this book.

You may need to select your colors based on a matching system such as Pantone or Trumatch for process printing. Trumatch involves matching color by using a numbering system and not trusting your eye to what you see on the screen.

As a designer you can choose from a *premixed swatch* on the computer, or you can mix "your own percentage of gray," or mix *process color*, using *CMYK*—cyan, magenta, yellow, black—or using *RGB*—red, green, blue.

The following is a list of several choices of color palettes available for depicting color on the computer along with a brief explanation of each. These color choices are frequently referred to as *color modes* or *models*. (See Figure 6–1.)

Color Modes Found in Adobe Photoshop®

Bitmap Mode: Uses one of two color values such as black and white to represent the pixels in an image. Images in bitmapped mode have a bit depth of 1. Pixels are 100% black or white.

Grayscale: Uses up to 256 shades of gray. Each pixel of a grayscale image has a brightness value range from (0), which is black, to (255), which is white. Grayscale can also be measured in percentages. Pixels are black, white, or up to 255 shades of gray.

Duotone: Printing method using two or more plates to add depth to grayscale.

Indexed Color: Uses the most color (256). For example, Adobe Photoshop builds a color lookup table that stores and indexes color in an image. If the original color does not appear in the table, the program will automatically choose the closest color or simulate it from the colors that are available. One channel and a color table up to 256 colors.

RGB: Numeric values are represented for the primary colors—**R**ed, **G**reen, and **B**lue. When all three colors are combined at maximum value, the result is white. When none of the colors are present or have a zero value for each, the result is black. Most widely used.

CMYK: **C**yan = light blue, **M**agenta, and **Y**ellow. While RGB is additive, CMYK is known as subtractive. This model is also elected and controlled numerically. In CMYK, each color has a numeric value assigned. Theoretically, when all three (CMY) are combined at 100%, the result should be black. However, on screen it may appear as a dreadful looking muddy brown. In addition, when 0% of each (CMY) is eliminated, the result is white. Oh yes, where's the "K"? The **K** value or true black is added to compensate for ink impurities in color printing. Used for PostScript level printers, professional quality in-house printing.

Lab Color: Three channel mode, which can be known for WYSIWYG.

Multichannel: The 256 multiple level grayscale channels.

HLS: **H**ue, **L**ight, **S**aturation color model. If you start with black, you can choose grayscale by leaving the saturation at zero and changing the degree of lightness. The hue value for the primary colors are:
- Red = (0)
- Yellow = (60)
- Green = (120)
- Cyan = (180)
- Blue = (240)
- Magenta = (300)

The standard setting for a hue is 50% lightness and 100% saturation.

Additional Digital Color Terms

As a designer there are other terms with which you should be familiar when working digitally with color. The above default color modes in Photoshop tend to allow the designer some advantage to selecting or entering the correct color. When working with color in the traditional sense, we are all used to comparing lab dips or matching our swatches to Pantone and Scotdik colors. Digital color allows the designer to take more control and go that one step further—to get the color they want. Halftone, gamut, opacity, and saturation are just a few of the ways that color can be digitally edited or "tweaked."

Brightness: The relative lightness or darkness of the color. It is measured in percentages of black as 0% and white as 100%.

Channel: Image components that contain the pixel information for any given color. Grayscale = 1; RGB = 3; and CMYK = 4.

Color Mapping: The technology that permits the "best match" in appearance to the "source image."

Gamut: Refers to image devices such as scanners, monitors, and printers that can only display a "subset" of all visible colors. Colors that you see on the monitor can be closely matched to the colors that will be printed out if the devices can "see" the same gamut.

Gradient: Color in shades from one starting point to another and gradually blending in between.

Halftone: Lightness of a color independent of its hue and saturation.

Hue: Color reflected from or transmitted through an object. It is a measured location on a standard color wheel and it is expressed in degrees of 0 to 360.

Intensity: Degree of color saturation.

Opacity: The density of a color or shade. Ranging from transparent to opaque.

Resolution: The measurement of the fineness of detail. The higher the resolution, the finer the detail.

Saturation: Another name is chroma, which is strength or purity of a color. Saturation represents the amount of gray in proportion to a hue. It is measured in percentages of 0% gray to 100% (fully saturated).

A list of color-related terminology is provided to better prepare you to use and discuss color in an intelligent way for digital design. You may be familiar with some terms because they are frequently mentioned whenever a designer is developing an image on a computer.

Color-Related Terminology

Achromatic: A design without color or hue. Therefore, it is in neutral grays, white, or black.

Analogous: Similar or alike in elements or design.

B/W: Black and white.

Brightness: The dimension of a color that represents its similarity to one of a series of achromatic colors.

Channel: A frequency or band that represents color value, such as CMYK or RGB.

Chroma: The aspect of color in the Munsell color system by which a sample appears to differ from a gray of the same brightness or lightness that corresponds to saturation of the perceived color.

Color Balance: A state of equilibrium between colors in a design.

Color Book: A hard copy of your colors calibrated for your printer and useful in color matching.

Color Characteristics: Features of defining a specific hue.

Color Emphasis: Singling out a specific hue or range of hues.

Color Mapping: To depict specific colors based on their characteristics.

Color Modes: An arrangement or order of colors, such as CMYK, RGB, or Lab.

Color Properties: Characteristic attributes possessed by individual hues.

Color Scheme: A specific outline of color in a design.

Color Space: The gamut or range of colors that can be seen in the chosen color picker.

Color Wheel: The color picker that is used on the Macintosh to display the entire range of color space available.

Colorway: A series of color choices made by the designer to indicate the "season's" color selection for the line.

Complementary: A color directly opposite another on the color wheel and providing the greatest chromatic contrast to it.

Cool Colors: Greens, blues, and violet.

Duotone: Any design or print created by using two shades of the same hue.

Earth Tones: Hues that are representative of earthy colors, such as browns and reds.

Gamut: The range of hues that a device can output.

Gradient: A graded change in a hue.

Halftone: A design created by the gradations of the same hue.

Hue: A particular gradation of a color; a shade or tint.

Intensity: The strength of a color.

Jewel Tones: Hues that are representative of bright jewel colors, such as golds and blues.

Monochromatic: A design appearing to have only one color and gradations of that color.

Monotone: Having a single color.

Neutral: A color that lacks hue.

Ombré: The blending and gradation of multiple colors to create a continuous blend of the differing hues.

Opacity: The reduction of light through a color.

Pastels: Soft, delicate hues.

Primary Colors: RGB. The true colors developed from a solar beam that can be mixed in many percentages to get secondary and tertiary colors.

Notes...

Resolution: The dpi or dots per inch of a design. Measured by how many dots or pixels are in one inch of a design.

Saturation: Vividness of a hue.

Shade: The degree a color is mixed with black.

Spectrum: A range of values of hues in a set.

Tint: A shade or gradation of a color.

Value: The relative darkness or lightness of a color.

Warm Colors: Reds, yellow, orange.

Inputting Color: Option # 1 Scanning

Scanning: What Is It and How Do We Do It?

To begin to design in any software, an idea is needed first. Whether that idea is referenced from something seen or thought of is up to the designer. Most ideas are generated through the research of market trends and forecasts. Once inspirational images or designs are found, they need to be digitized or entered into the software. The best way to do this is by scanning.

Scanning is the process of taking an image—paper, photo, fabric, or other dimensional object—and reading it into the computer for further editing and manipulation of the design and color.

Almost any scanner with a plug-in product can work with Photoshop. The software is loaded into the Plug-ins folder and placed in the Import/Export folder. The scanning software can now be accessed through the File > Import menu selection (Figure 6–2).

If there is not a plug-in available to work with Photoshop, the scan can be made with the software that was supplied with the scanner and then the file can be opened later in Photoshop to be edited.

Scanning is an easy way to avoid drawing images into the computer. First, let's look at the terms used in the scanning process. Most scanning software will need some or all of these settings adjusted before the image can be scanned. Knowing what they mean will help you understand the results of the scan.

FIGURE 6–2
File import
(Courtesy of UMAX Data Systems: Used with permission)

Scanning Terms

B/W: Black-and-white image or drawing.

Brightness: Setting the overall "whiteness" of an image.

Contrast: The comparing of light and dark on an image, such as low = gray (light).

Dithering: Creating dots to "fool the eye" into seeing shades of gray.

DPI: The measurement of an image resolution in dots per inch, such as 300 dpi or 150 dpi.

Grayscale: The range of grays from white to black.

Halftone: Used in the making of black-and-white images to appear to have shades of gray.

Image: Usually a photograph that is "translated into a bitmapped" image by scanning.

Image Type: This could refer to the options of B/W, gray, or color.

Original: Art, photograph, transparency, or other item to be scanned.

Pixel: A single dot on a monitor or on a digital image.

Previous Size: Used to control the size of an image to reduce size and/or scanning time.

Resolution: Measuring the fineness or detail of an image. The higher the resolution, the finer the detail.

Scanning Basics: From Black and White to Full Color

Before scanning, a few questions need to be answered. Make notes below while going through these questions.

1. Is the scan going to be color or black and white?

2. If color, is it 8 bit (indexed) or 32 bit (fill color)?

3. What will the dpi be?

4. What format does it need to be saved in?

5. Where will the file be saved?

Once these questions are answered, the rest is easy. By following a few basic guidelines, the process of scanning will become as natural as drawing with a pencil. To begin the process, we have provided a design to scan (Figure 6–3). Simple in design, with a crisp line art, this image can be used to practice scanning.

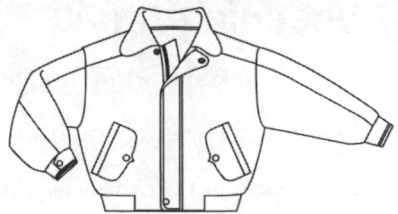

FIGURE 6–3
Black-and-white line art

As a Reminder, When Scanning Black-and-White Line Art:

- Keep original hand drawings crisp and clean or use a fine felt-tip pen.

- Scan in B & W drawing mode and use at least 150 to 300 dpi.

- Unless drawings are for catalog use, they may require additional considerations such as converting the file from grayscale to RGB; file format, size, storage, and hardware requirements; platforms to be used; file transfer considerations; or any other miscellaneous editing needs.

Scanning Basics—Let's Scan

Step 1. Place the image on the scanner bed, making sure it is as flat as possible. If the image or paper is "see-through," place a black cardboard behind it so the scanner light does not pass through. This would otherwise cause the scan to be too light and detail would be lost.

Step 2. Open up **Photoshop** by double-clicking on the icon.

Step 3. Go to the **File** menu and go to **Import** to select the scanning plug-in on your computer.

Step 4. Once open, select **Preview**. Preview is an important step. Some scans may take a few minutes due to their size and resolution choices. A preview is a low-res "quick scan" done solely for placement and to be sure the image is straight (Figure 6–4).

Step 5. Once the **Preview** is OK, enter the other variables (Figure 6–5).
- **Mode**—Black & White
- **Resolution**—Generally start with 150 dpi and see if it provides enough detail and clarity.

Step 6. Then increase it to 200 or 300 dpi to see what is really needed. Remember, the lower the resolution, the smaller the file size. Very large files will be slow to edit on *any* computer.

Step 7. Choose **Scan**.

Once the image is scanned, **Save** it.

Scanning in a color image is similar to black and white, with a few additional thoughts to the process.

Notes . . .

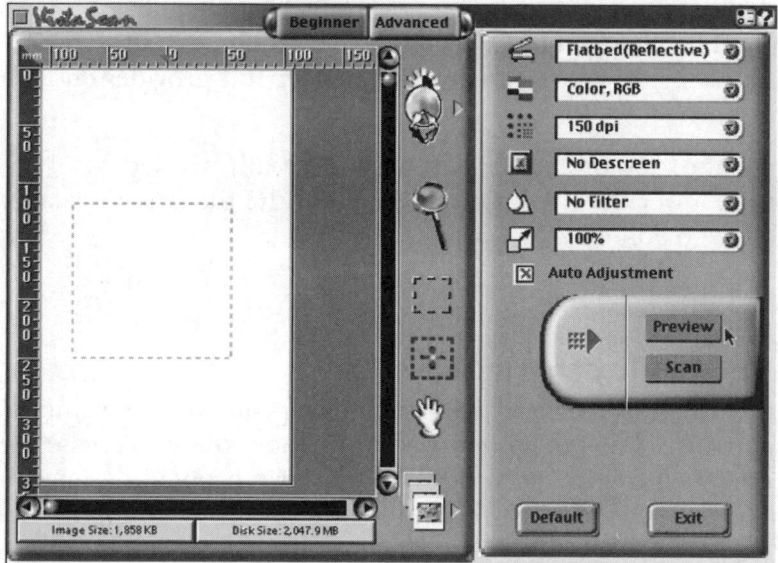

FIGURE 6–4
Preview scan
(Courtesy of UMAX Data Systems: Used with permission)

FIGURE 6–5
Color modes
(Courtesy of UMAX Data Systems: Used with permission)

Notes . . .

Color Photographs or Slides

- Pay attention to Color Settings that describe the type of photograph to be scanned.

- Typically, for color photographs, you will use sharp millions of color.

- Typically, 300 dpi will suffice. Remember, the better the resolution, the larger the file size, and the bigger the storage capacity needs to be!

- Typically, you will always save your file as a TIFF.

To scan in a color design, proceed as follows:

Color Rendering

Step 1. Place the image on the scanner bed, making sure it is as flat as possible. If the image or paper is "see-through," place a black cardboard behind it so the scanner light does not pass through. This would otherwise cause the scan to be too light and detail would be lost.

Step 2. Open up **Photoshop** by double-clicking on the icon.

Step 3. Go to the **File** menu and go to **Import** to select the scanning plug-in on your computer.

Step 4. Once open, select **Preview**. Preview is an important step. Some scans may take a few minutes due to their size and resolution choices. A preview is a low-res "quick scan" done solely for placement and to be sure the image is straight.

Step 5. Once the **Preview** is OK, enter the other variables as needed.
- **Mode** should be changed to Color (Indexed—8 bit or RGB—32 bit).
- **Resolution.** Generally start with 150 dpi and see if it provides enough detail and clarity.

Step 6. Then increase it to 200 or 300 dpi to see what is really needed. Remember, the lower the resolution, the smaller the file size. Very large files will be slow to edit on *any* computer..

Step 7. Choose **Scan.** Once the image is scanned, **Save** it.

Scanning Fabric and Other Textured Images

Scanning fabrics or other textured images poses their own problems for scanning. Once scanned, these textures need to be removed or further edited to create the designs that are needed. Textures in a scan can add their own problems even with simple editing of color. Use the following basic guidelines when scanning fabrics and textured images. (See Figure 6–6.)

Scanning Fabric Guidelines

- Be sure to determine the appropriate color setting.

- Be prepared, because some files may require you to limit the number of colors to be used. This is one area you may encounter and may want to seek out good advice as well as experiment with and/or practice.

- Typically, 150 dpi is sufficient. Don't forget that the larger the dpi, the larger the file size.

- Save fabric scan files as a TIFF.

- Take the time to learn to use *all* the tools in Adobe Photoshop to manipulate color. Be sure you are not afraid to experiment and practice. There are, however, other great shortcuts.

- Don't be afraid to use the **Filters** menu in Adobe Photoshop to clean up your fabric. Surprisingly, these filters such as **Blur** or **Noise** can actually help you work smarter.

FIGURE 6–6
Textured image

• Don't trust your memory—make notes! Make any additional notes *every* time you learn something new about scanning.

When scanning any image with a texture, follow the same principles already discussed and add the additional following steps to the final scan. Once mastered, these techniques will help you in a variety of design ideas. When scanning in a fabric for color reduction, you must consider the technique used to scan the fabric. A 32-bit scan is going to give you more pixel information than an 8-bit scan. Also, scans of a fabric tend to be tougher to clean up than a scan of flat art. The more color information and detail in the original image, the longer the cleanup process will be. There are a few different ways to do a color reduction in Photoshop and the image itself will dictate which one you use.

Scanning Fabrics with Textures

Step 1. Place the image on the scanner bed, making sure it is as flat as possible. If the image or paper is "see-through," place a black cardboard behind it so the scanner light does not pass through. This would otherwise cause the scan to be too light and detail would be lost.

Step 2. Open up **Photoshop** by double-clicking on the icon.

Step 3. Go to the **File** menu and go to **Import** to select the scanning plug-in on your computer.

Step 4. Once open, select **Preview**. Preview is an important step. Some scans may take a few minutes due to their size and resolution choices. A preview is a low-res "quick scan" done solely for placement and to be sure the image is straight.

Step 5. Once the **Preview** is OK, enter the other variables.
  • **Mode**—Black & White
  • **Resolution**—Generally start with 150 dpi and see if it provides enough detail and clarity. Then increase it to 200 or 300 dpi to see what is really needed. Remember, the lower the resolution, the smaller the file size. Very large files will be slow to edit on *any* computer.

Step 6. Once scanned in, view the file in **Photoshop**.

Step 7. If the Fabric has a lot of **texture** to it, such as a knit or heavy weave, then now is the time to use the **Blur** filter to hide this texture. The **Gaussian Blur** works best for this.

Step 8. To access the **Gaussian Blur** filter—go to the **Filter** menu and select **Blur**.

Step 9. In the **Blur** submenu, select **Gaussian Blur**. (See Figure 6–7.)

Step 10. Choose the settings for **Gaussian Blur** by sliding the **Radius** button to the right.

Step 11. The farther right it slides, the more blur is created. Be sure not to slide it too high or detail in the design will be lost.

Step 12. Always select **Preview** so the update of the design can be immediately seen.

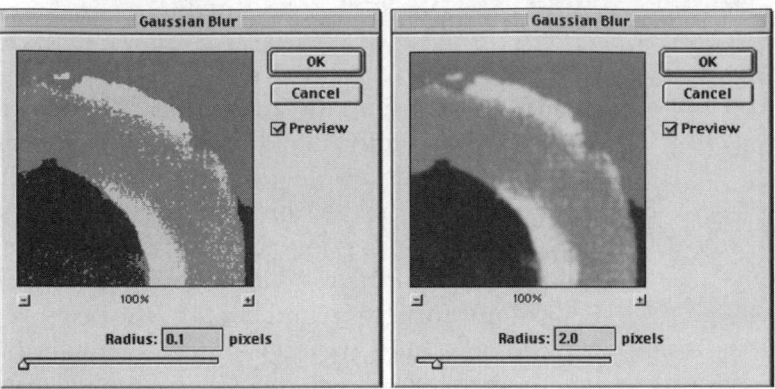

FIGURE 6–7
Gaussian blur

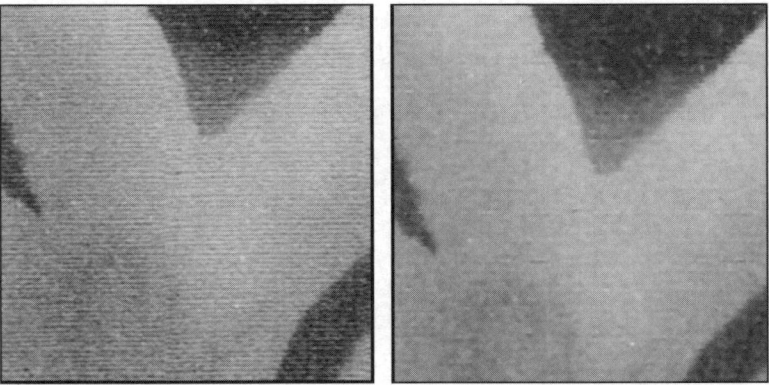

FIGURE 6–8
Despeckle filter

HINT: The **Despeckle** filter helps as well. (See Figure 6–8.)

1. Go to the **Filter** menu and select **Despeckle**.

2. Small specks will be gradually eliminated if the filter is chosen consecutively.

Scanning an image into the computer has many advantages to traditional design. Along with these advantages come details that must be addressed in order to get as good a quality image as possible from the computer. Color output or reproduction is the next topic. We will discuss several of the solutions including correcting dpi, file size, and format, among others.

From the view of a designer, computers have forever changed the way we do things. From sketches to line sheets, from concepts to final design, we have the ability to edit designs, save color palettes, archive design elements, and shorten turnaround time. No more markers going dry, no more tracing paper, or making multiple copies of a single sketch at different scales on the copier. No need for spray mount or rubber cement, because an entire storyboard can be created on-screen, edited, and updated until the very last minute. Best of all, you can visualize your ideas and concepts without ever sending a design out to be painted in six colorways and getting back only three that you like. In later chapters we will take you through these concepts, so by the end you will feel confident to boot up that computer and be more creative than you ever have, because there is always **Undo**.

Now that you know how to scan an image, details and explanations are needed of what choices were discussed and made to create a scan. The next section describes in detail the reasons for such choices. Following these details will make you a scanning pro in no time at all.

Color Output

Resolution and DPI (Dots per Inch)

Before beginning to scan an image, we need to define a few terms so you can understand the process. There are a few different types of *resolution* when working with digitized images. *Bit resolution* is a definition of how many "bits of data" are storing the color information of the image. The higher the bit "depth," the more color details in the image. For example, a 1-bit image is only black and white, and a 32-bit image is a full-color photograph. *Device resolution* is the number of pixels defining the image as it is viewed on the monitor. Most monitors used for design are 72 *pixels per inch (ppi)* or *dots per inch (dpi)*. *Image resolution* is defined as the specific number of pixels per inch in the image. The more pixels per inch in an image, the larger the file size. *Output resolution* is defined as the dpi or number of dots per inch that the printer outputs when printing the image.

We begin our discussion with the bit resolution. This *dpi* or *dots per inch* is the unit of measurement for defining detail when scanning an image into the computer. It represents the density of information in the file. It is shown in either *pixels per inch* (*ppi*) or dots per inch (dpi).

All scanners ask you to choose a dpi or resolution for your scan. Many times designers select either the default resolution of 72 dpi or the highest resolution the scanner will apply, which may be 600 dpi or higher. Both choices are wrong. At this point designers need to make an intelligent choice of what resolution to scan at. Once scanned, an image can be edited to some extent, but there are some rules to follow in digital textile design.

First, determine what is the best resolution to scan at. If scanning at a resolution that is low, pixelization of the image will occur and the image will appear to have "**jaggy**" edges, like in Figure 6–9, as opposed to clear edges, like in Figure 6–10. Scanning at a higher resolution than needed will create an overly large file size. A large file size can cause print problems and use hard drive space as well as increase the need for more RAM, thus slowing down the program. When in doubt, always **scan** at a higher resolution than you think you may need, just not too high. Some scanners actually have dpi choices that are higher than the scanner itself can use. In these instances, the scanner is actually making up the pixel information.

Second, it is important to realize that editing the resolution, after the scanning, has implications as well. Lowering the resolution will remove information (detail) from the design, adding to the "jagginess" of the image. Increasing the resolution does not necessarily add detail, but allows the software to add the detail on its

FIGURE 6–9
Low resolution

FIGURE 6–10
High resolution

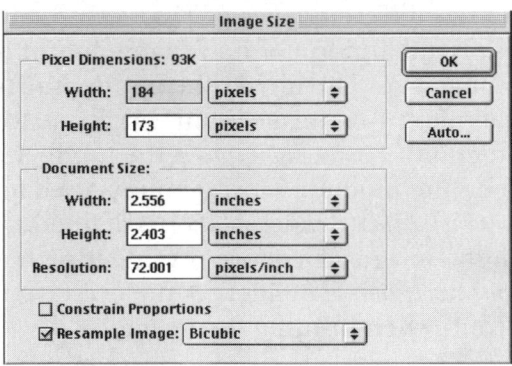

FIGURE 6–11
Image size

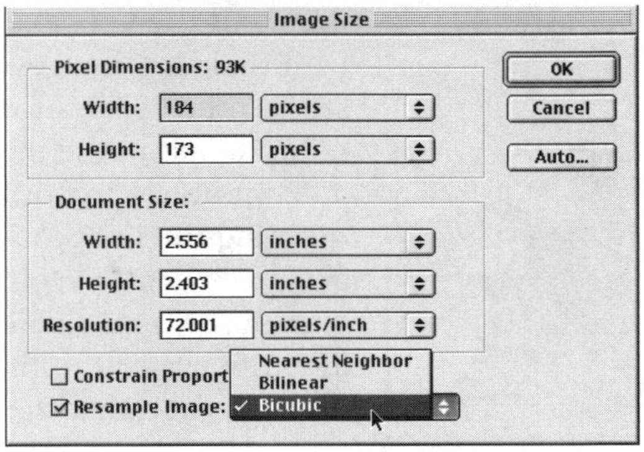

FIGURE 6–12
Options

Notes . . .

own. This can cause the image to become blurry because it is adding pixels to the design where it chooses. Either way, this process is called resampling and is an option at the bottom left of the **Image Size** window (Figure 6–11).

The Importance of Resampling

Resampling means allowing the software to decide which pixels of color to remove or which to add. In Adobe Photoshop this can be controlled to a degree. In the preferences, under the **File** menu, you can select your method of *interpolation*, the process Photoshop uses to add or delete pixels. The choices for interpolation are **Bicubic**, **Nearest Neighbor**, and **Bilinear**. Bicubic is the best choice. Through a series of calculations, Photoshop adds or removes the best choice pixels. This is also the slowest option, but well worth it. Nearest Neighbor is fast but least precise in adjusting pixels, and Bilinear is of average quality. So, all said, it is suggested to set the preference to Bicubic and leave it there. (See Figure 6–12 for the above choices.)

Most important of all is that the quality of the original document, whether a photo, fabric, or artwork, determines the quality of a scan. Starting with an original painting that is of poor quality will only be emphasized in the scan. The better the original, the better the scan.

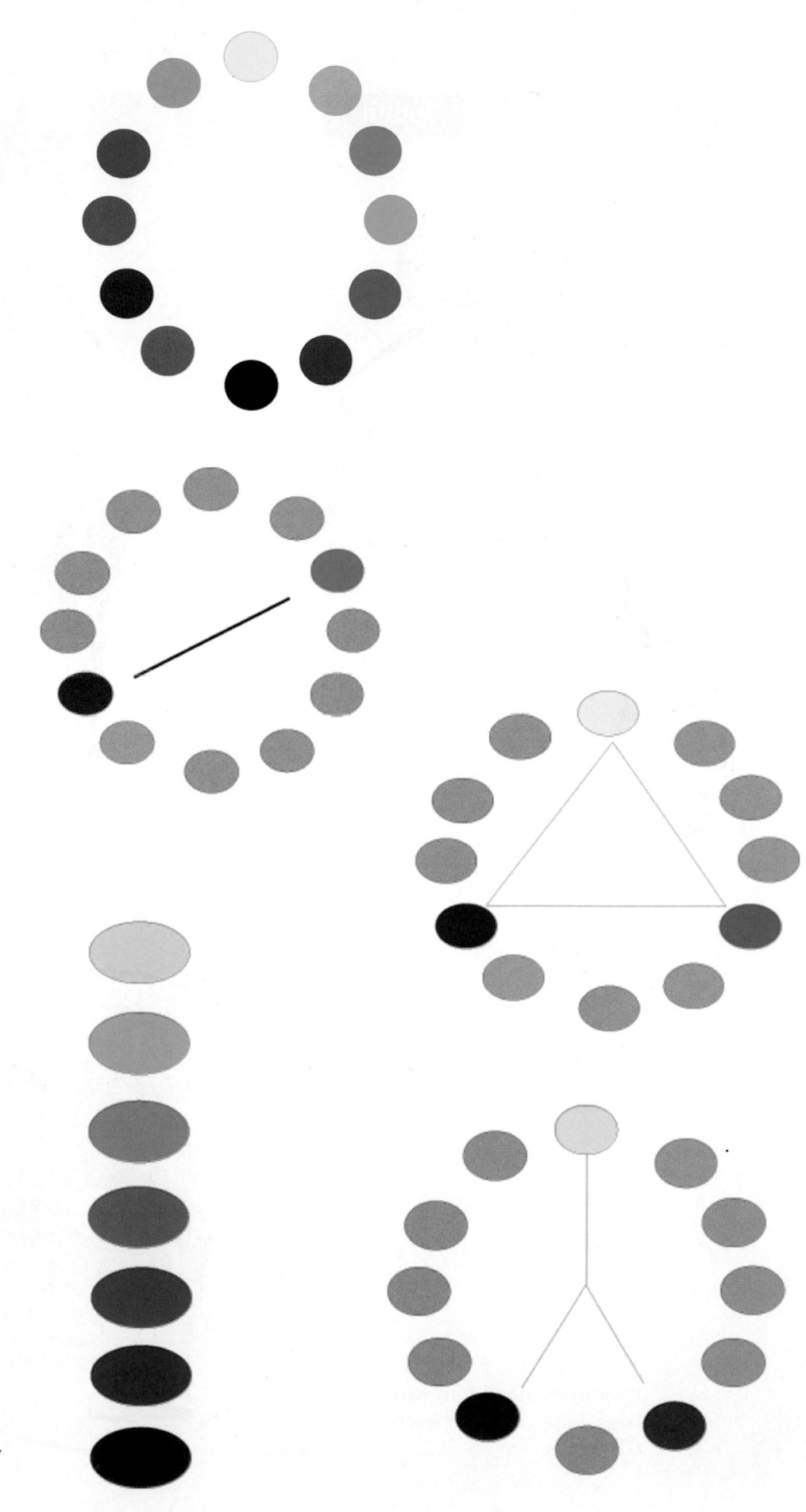

Color wheel, complementary
color harmonies

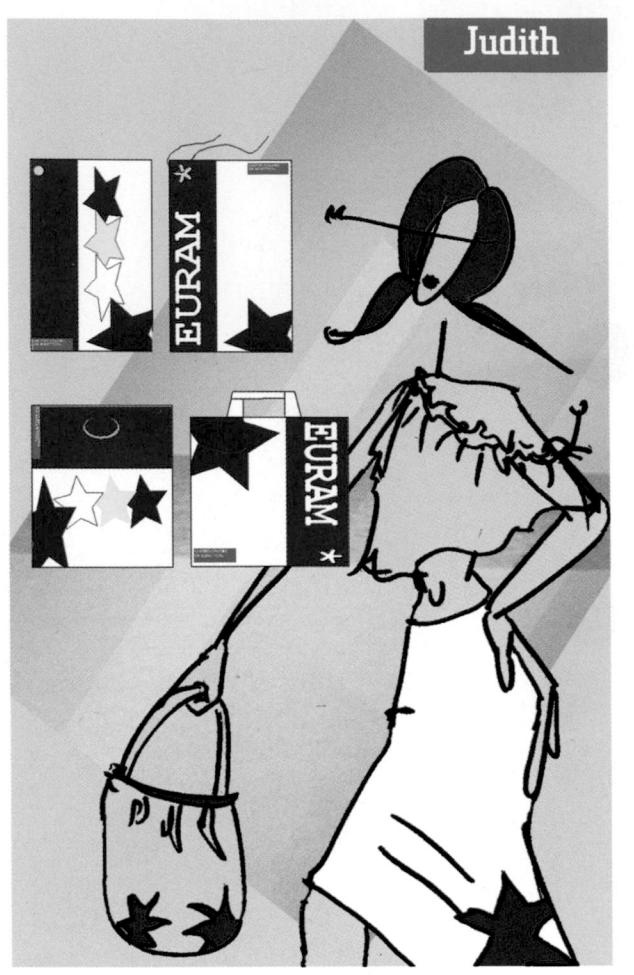

Examples of student work,
bags, tags, booklet covers, and
CD labels

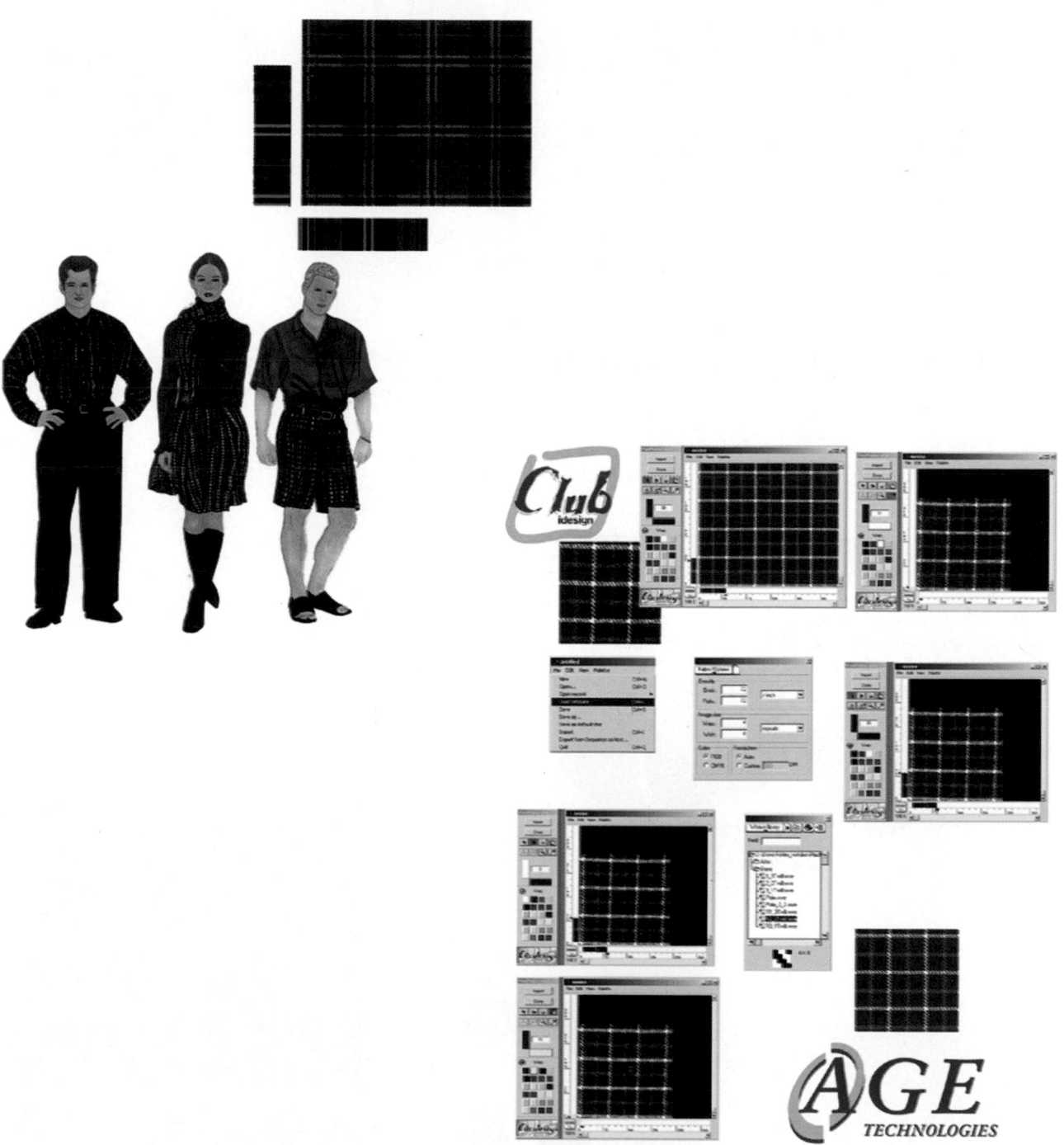

Plaid plug-in by AGE Technologies
(Courtesy of AGE Technologies)

Single and repeat motif variations

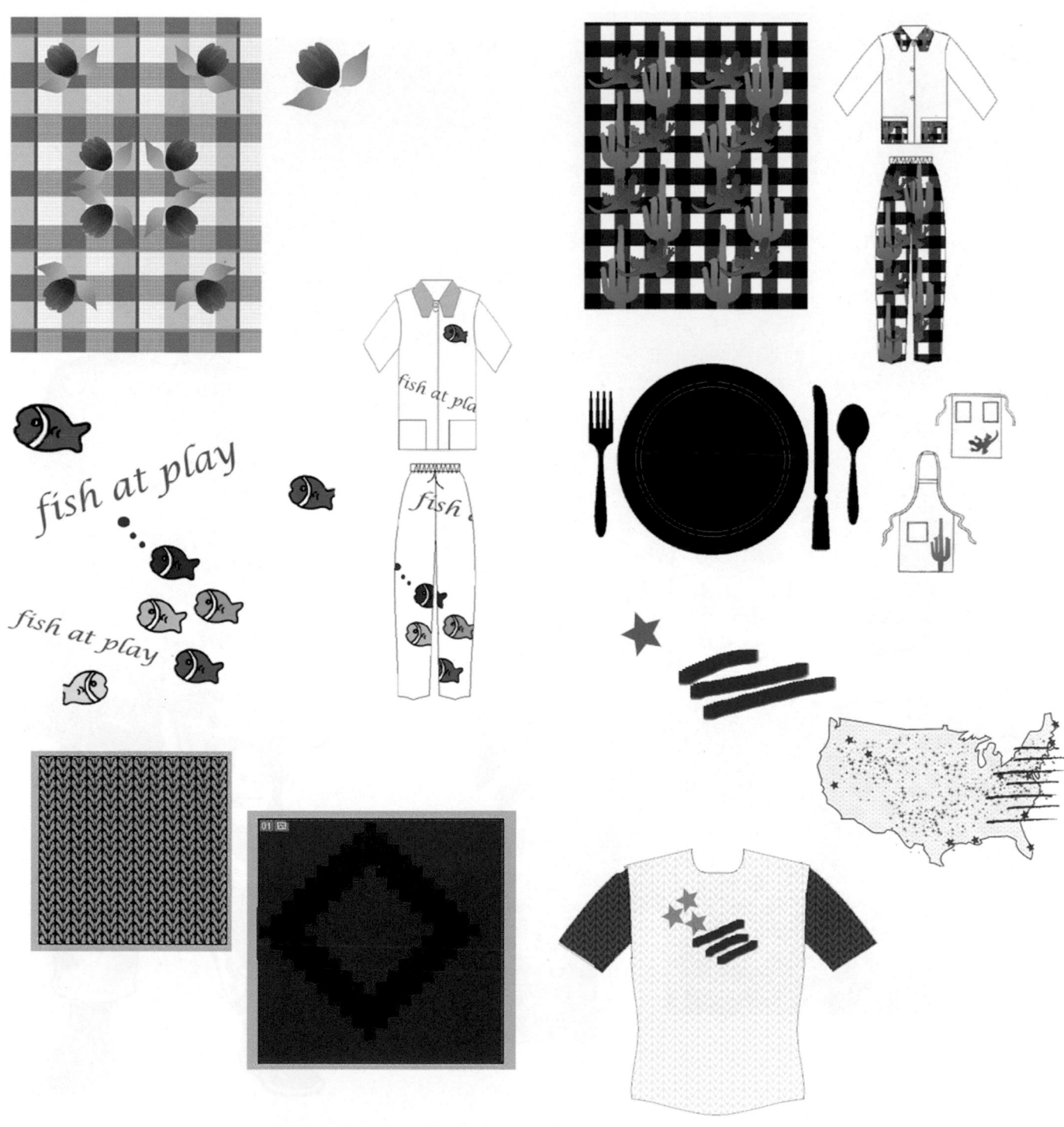

Samples of various design applications
(Courtesy of Pointcarré)

Animal print variations

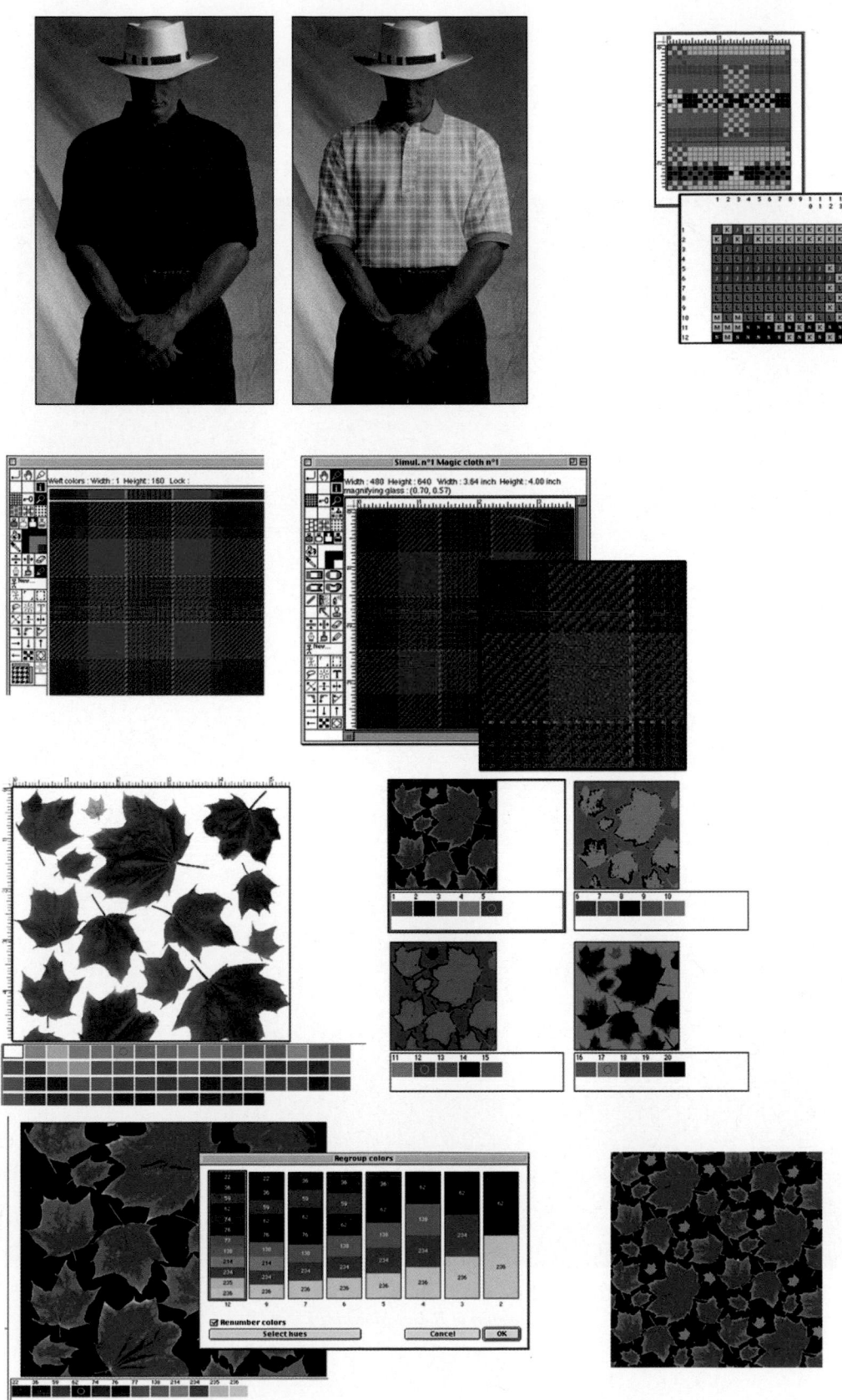

Pointcarré software textile design applications
(Courtesy of Pointcarré)

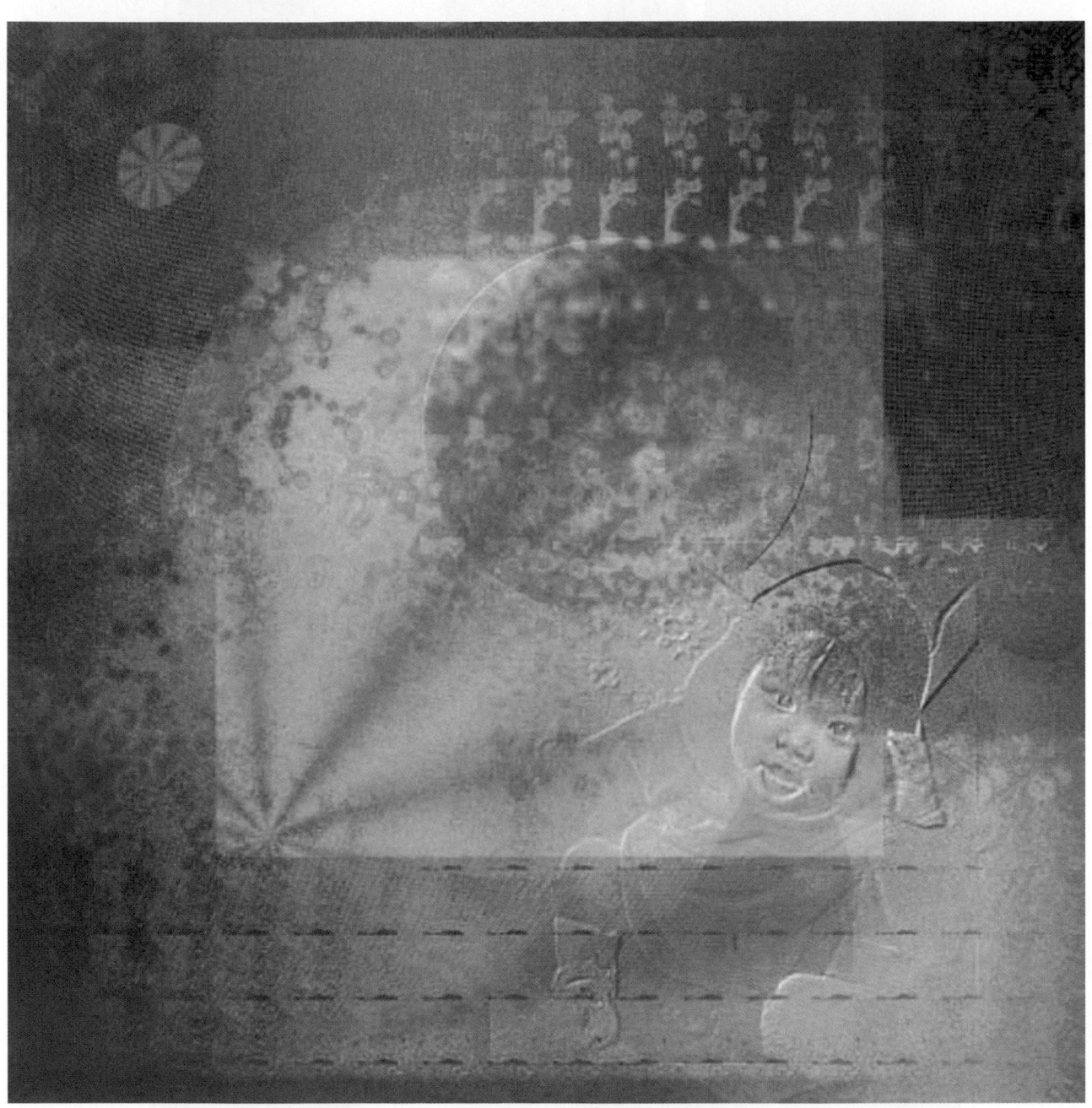

Textiles as fine art, Lili by Robert Manning
(Courtesy of Robert Manning)

Summer—front and back
(Courtesy of J. R. Campbell)

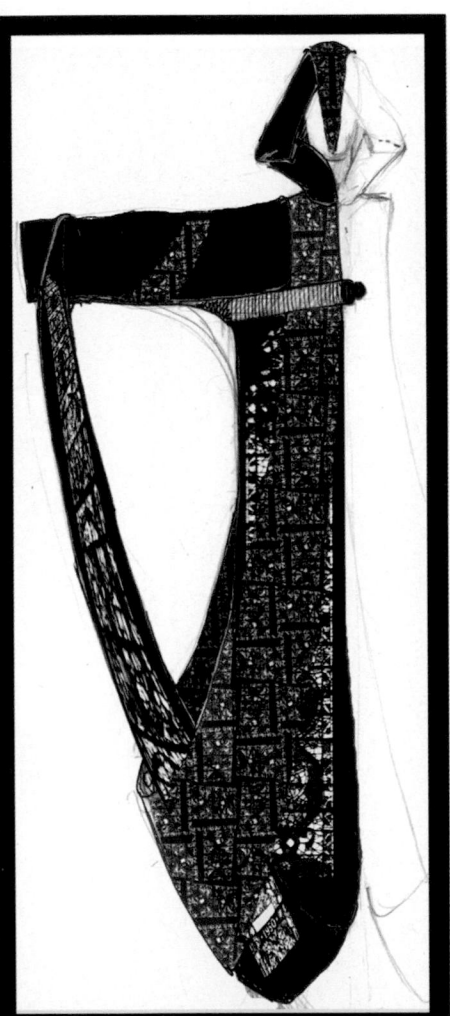
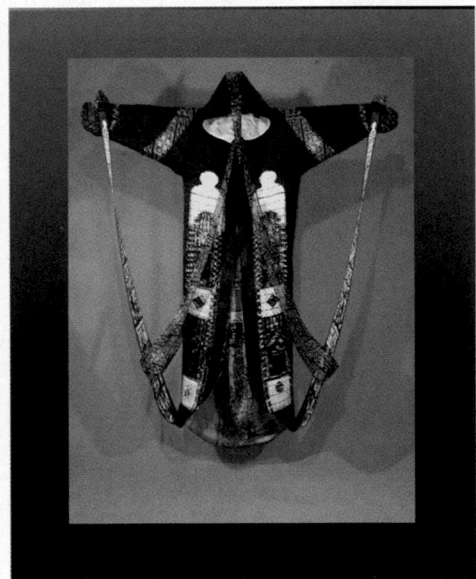

Digital Textiles: From inspiration to digital fine art application
(Courtesy of Dr. Jean Parsons)

Student samples of presentation boards and "raster" baby
(Top image courtesy of Nandi Chin)

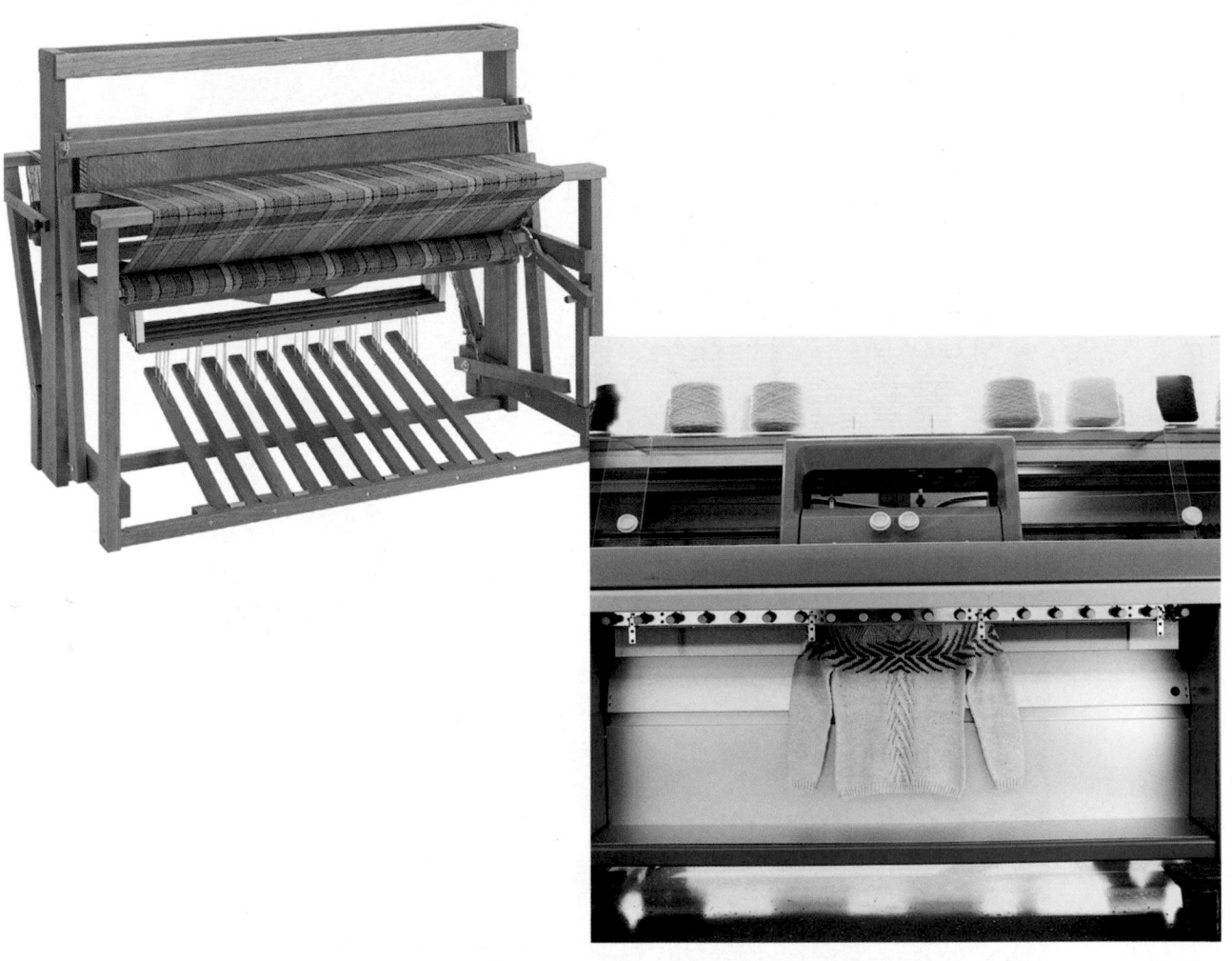

Weaving and knitting loom
(Top image Courtesy of Schacht Spindle Co., Inc.; Bottom image Courtesy of Stoll Knitting Machines)

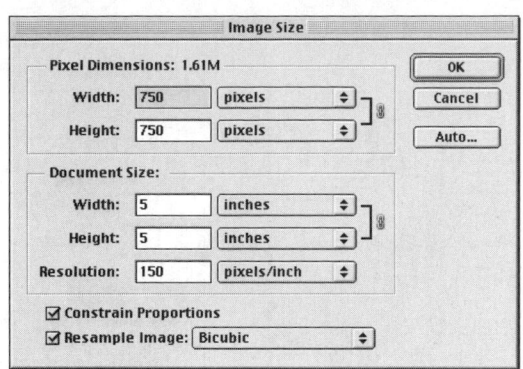

FIGURE 6–13
Image size

FIGURE 6–14
5″ × 5″ textile design

The next lesson to be learned is about file size. A number of factors determine the true file size of any design. A "get info" will not always provide the true file size due to compression when images are saved in different formats.

Facts about File Size—Changes via Resizing

It is important to remember that when you change the resolution of an image, in effect, the file size is changed as well. Increasing or decreasing the size of an image can increase or decrease the resolution of the file. Not being aware of this can have a detrimental effect on the printed image. The changes will not be noticed on the monitor, but will be noticed when the image is finally printed. Important to remember as well is to save a file over its original so there is no way to go back so easily. Doing a "**Save As**" and renaming the design will always be the best bet. In the end, delete any unwanted versions of the design. File size can be adjusted by using the **Image Size** option. Photoshop allows easy control of this feature. In the screen shot in Figure 6–13 there is an image that is a 5″ × 5″ square at 150 dpi and 1.61M (megabytes).

Step 1. On the CD enclosed with this book, open the file named "**5 × 5 Textile Design**" (Figure 6–14).

Step 2. Go to the **Image** menu and select **Image Size** (Figure 6–15).

Step 3. Make a note of the **Pixel Dimensions** and the **Document Size** (Figure 6–16).

Step 4. Be sure that **Constrain Proportions** and **Resample Image** are checked (Figure 6–17).

Step 5. Change the **Resolution** from 72 to 36 (Figure 6–18).

Step 6. Now compare the **Pixel Dimensions** and the **Document Size** with that in Figure 6–16. (See Figure 6–19.)

Notice how the file size stayed at 5″ × 5″ but the image size decreased from 1.61M to 380K. By lowering the resolution we are increasing the document size. By constraining the image size, we are keeping the file at 5″ × 5″. By resampling the file, we are allowing Photoshop to determine what color pixels to remove or add to keep the clarity of the design. Notice the options of Bicubic, Nearest Neighbor,

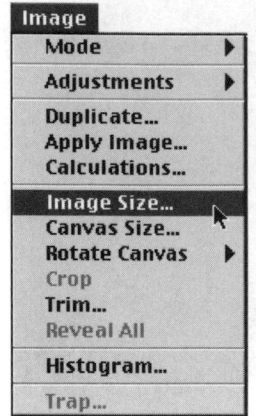

FIGURE 6–15
Image menu

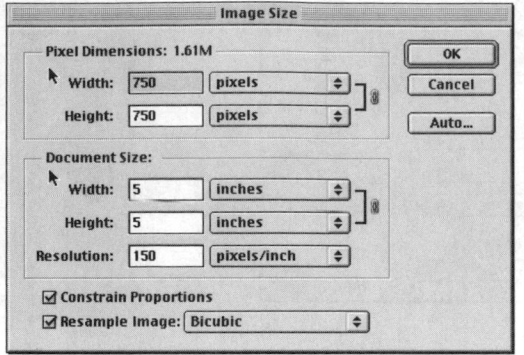

FIGURE 6–16
Pixel dimensions and document size

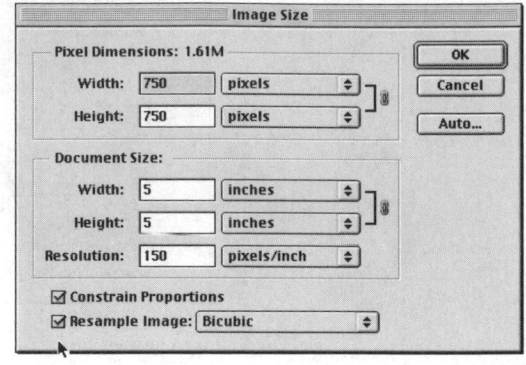

FIGURE 6–17
Constrain proportions and resample image

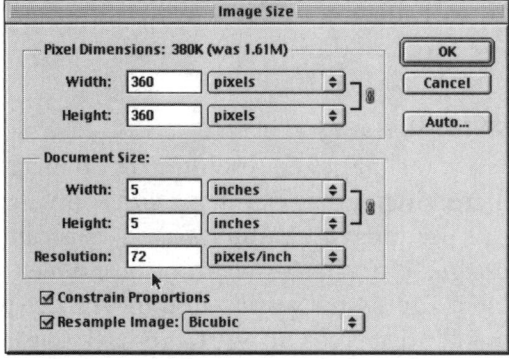

FIGURE 6–18
Resolution

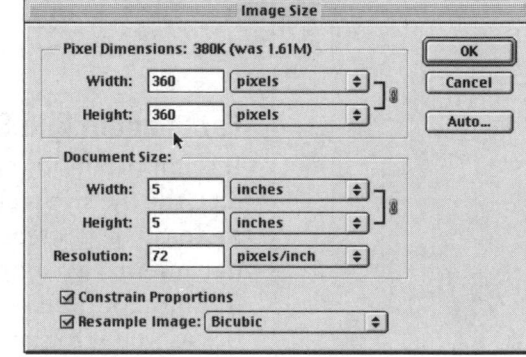

FIGURE 6–19
Pixel dimensions and document size

Notes . . .

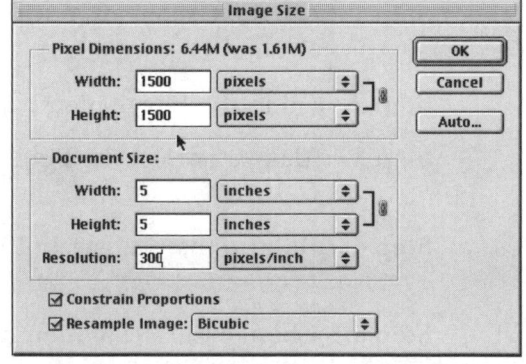

FIGURE 6–20
Increase resolution

and Bilinear. Again, keep Bicubic because that will generate the best-quality image possible. Another option available is Constrain Proportions. If the image resolution is increased, the file size would increase (Figure 6–20). Compare the images resulting from these changes.

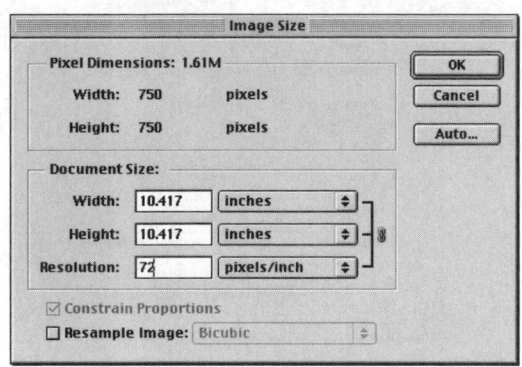

FIGURE 6–21
Deselect constrain

FIGURE 6–22
5″ × 5″ textile design

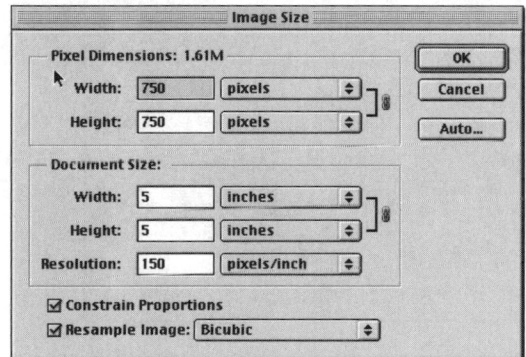

FIGURE 6–23
Image size

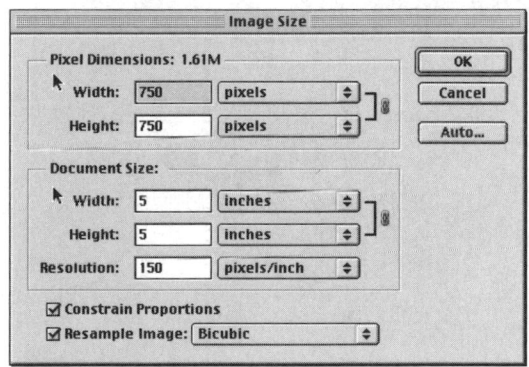

FIGURE 6–24
Pixel dimensions and document size

Notes . . .

What would happen if Constrain Proportions and Resample image were not selected? Notice in Figure 6–21 that the width and height have doubled. This happens when decreasing the resolution of the image by half. Notice that the image still has the same number of pixels describing the detail, but it now has less of those pixels per inch to display it. So, in effect it scales up the image because it has not been constrained in size.

Step 1. On the CD enclosed with this book, open again the file named "**5 × 5 Textile Design**" (Figure 6–22).

Step 2. Go to the **Image** menu and select **Image Size** (Figure 6–23).

Step 3. Make a note of the **Pixel Dimensions** and the **Document Size** (Figure 6–24).

Step 4. Be sure the **Constrain Proportions** and **Resample Image** are NOT checked (Figure 6–25).

Step 5. Change the **Resolution** from 72 to 36 (Figure 6–26).

Step 6. Now compare the **Pixel Dimensions** and the **Document Size** with that in Figure 6–24. (See Figure 6–27.)

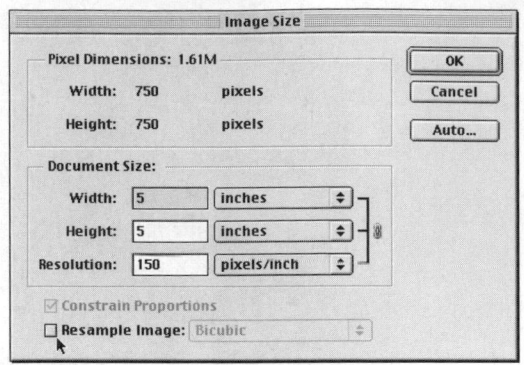

FIGURE 6–25
Check constrain proportions and
resample image

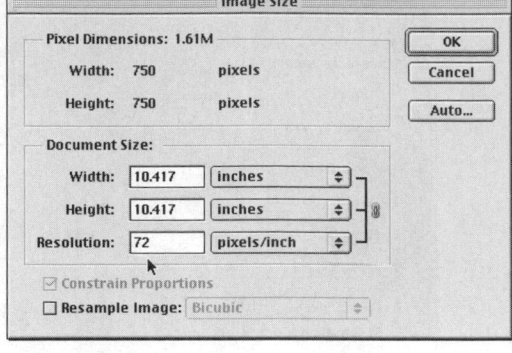

FIGURE 6–26
Change resolution

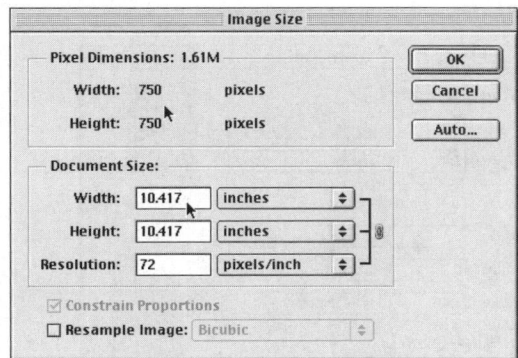

FIGURE 6–27
Compare pixel dimensions and document size

By selecting or deselecting these options, notice the visual feedback from Photoshop, where it has drawn a "link" between the width and height and the resolution. Again, this works with increasing the resolution as well. If an image needs to be the same size, but the dpi increased, Photoshop can handle it by selecting Constrain Proportions and Resample Image. Also, if the image size needs to be increased and the resolution is to remain the same, then this can be easily accomplished as well.

Decide on the resolution best suited to each image's needs and stick with it. Determining just what that resolution is has been a quest for many designers. Experience has shown that for most scans 150 dpi is perfect. It scans enough detail so the image is clean and crisp and it does not take up too much file space.

An important note to make is that it is always better to start with a high-resolution image and go lower. Taking a low-resolution image and increasing the dpi generally does not work as well with Photoshop making the choices of which pixels to edit. So again, try to work with 150 dpi and see how it goes.

Scanning versus Printer DPI
Why Scan at 150 dpi but the Printer Outputs at 300 dpi?

If a designer is scanning at 150 dpi, why are the scans printing at 300 dpi? Is there a difference between the image dpi and printing dpi? The answer to this is yes.

FIGURE 6–28
Screen shot of 150 dpi

FIGURE 6–29
Screen shot of 300 dpi

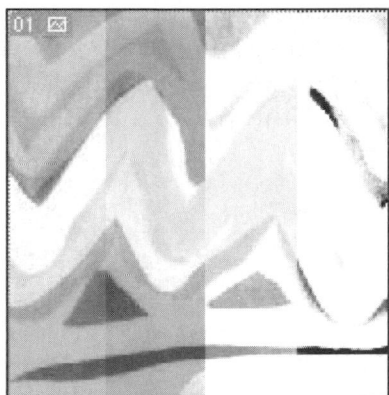

FIGURE 6–30
Screen shot of scanned "Printed" area showing CMYK dots of different sizes

Scanning an image at 150 dpi means that for every inch of the scan there are 150 pixels to describe the detail of the image. Now, most desktop printers print at 300 dpi or more. One recent, popular printer—the Epson—can print up to 1440 dpi and an Iris prints at 300 dpi. When that image is sent to the printer, the printer driver "emulates" the 150 dpi, while putting down 300 dots or whatever the resolution of that printer may be. *Emulating* is the ability of the printer to create the printed image using more dots than in the original file information. It does this by using dots of different sizes to create the detail.

On the screen, the image is 150 dpi and the dots are all the exact same size, the size of a pixel. When the image is printed, these pixels are broken down into different sizes to create the detail in the image, so there are really more than 150 per inch—300 to be exact or the resolution that a particular printer prints in the printed image. (See Figures 6–28 through 6–30.)

Scanning the image at the proper resolution or dpi is crucial in getting out a design with the detail and clarity as close to the original as possible. With a little trial and error, any designer can master the art of scanning. Try the following exercise, so the difference in resolution will become clear.

Comparing and Contrasting dpi
Let's Go Through This Visually, So We Can See the Results

Step 1. Select an image that needs to be scanned and place it on the scanner bed.

Step 2. Set the scanner for 72 dpi in **Color** mode.

Step 3. Scan the image and save it to the desktop.

Step 4. Now scan the same file at 150 dpi and save this to the desktop.

Step 5. Scan it a third time, but at 300 dpi and save.

Step 6. Open all three files and print them.

HINT: Can you tell the difference between the different resolutions. The file that was scanned at 72 dpi will most likely have more "jaggies" than the others. This is generally the lowest resolution you need. The files scanned at 150 and 300 dpi will probably look very similar in detail. This also is the point in time when we need to think about file size, because the 300 dpi file is much larger than the 150 dpi file. (See Figures 6–31 and 6–32.)

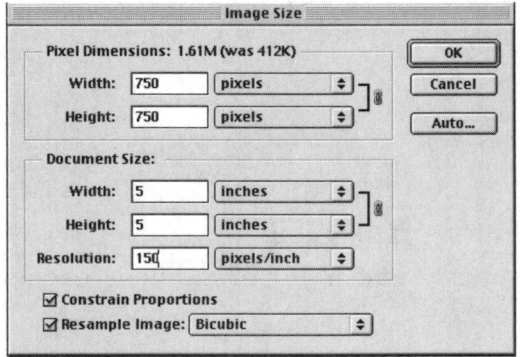

FIGURE 6–31
150 dpi

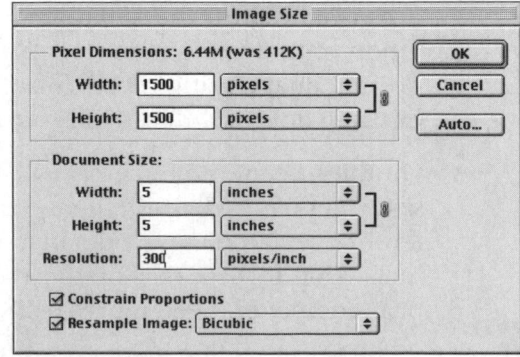

FIGURE 6–32
300 dpi

If the 150 dpi image is nice, then there is no reason for scanning at 300 dpi and loading up the hard drive with information, which may even slow down the computer. On the following pages we will discuss these differences as well as other details to be aware of when scanning in any art or fabric.

Bit Depth and Scanning
Scanning in a Design or Flat Art

There are many ways to utilize a scanner with the computer. Scanning an image directly into the computer is a fast way to start designing. Once the image is in the computer, manipulating it and editing it can take a designer in unlimited directions. One single scan of an image can easily bring forth a dozen new designs. Multiple images when combined practically leave the designer with an unlimited amount of designs that can be created, from companion prints to new designs.

Many designers when starting out in doing digital designs do not realize some important decisions they need to make when scanning. Once these parameters are figured out, there is no longer any worry if scanning is being done right. The following are some principles of scanning using basic scanning software from *UMAX* called *MagicScan.*

How to Scan Correctly

Step 1.   Place the image to be scanned on the scanner bed.

Step 2.   Open **Adobe Photoshop** and go to the **File** menu > **Import** (Figure 6–33).

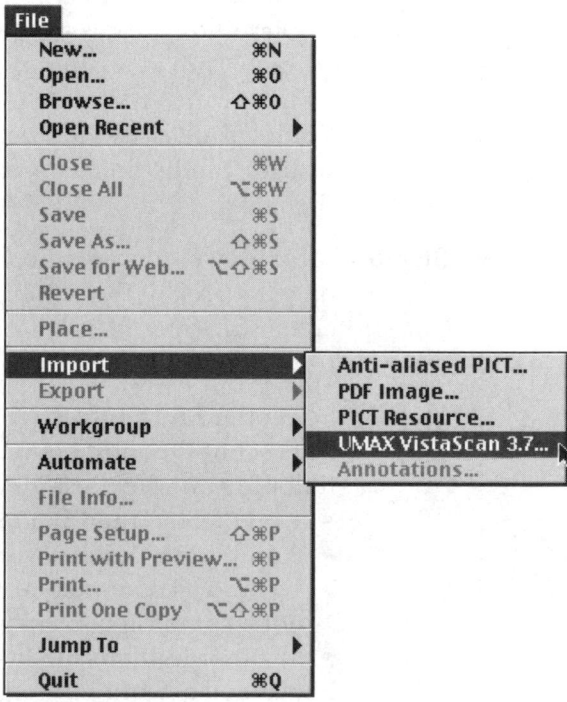

FIGURE 6–33
Import menu
(Courtesy of UMAX Data Systems: Used with permission)

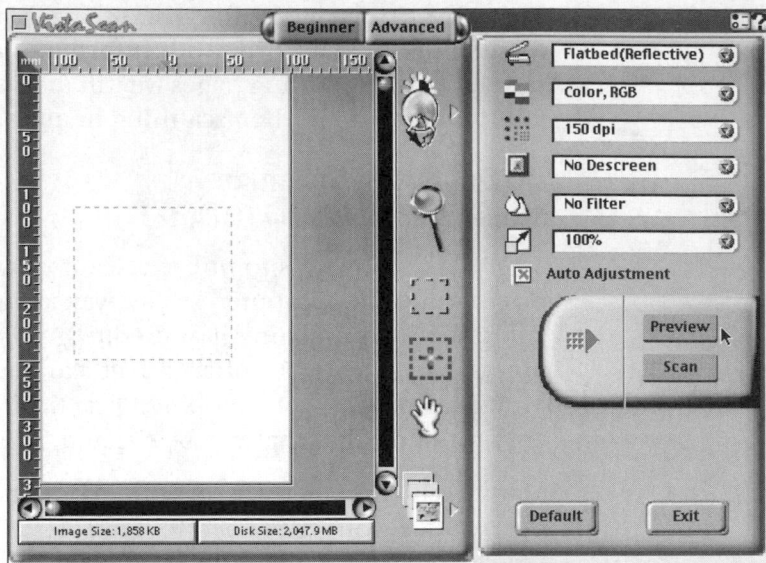

FIGURE 6–34
MagicScan window
(Courtesy of UMAX Data Systems: Used with permission)

Step 3. Select **MagicScan** for the submenu (Figure 6–34).

Step 4. Select a **Preview** of the scan, always.

Step 5. In this screen the **Preview** button is in the lower left corner. Preview is a quick and easy way to see if the image is placed on the scanner correctly, not at an angle. This gives you the opportunity to crop and scan only the area you need. Again, it is another way to save file space. Editing time is also reduced, because rotating an image to be perfectly straight can be time-consuming as well as disrupting to the pixels in the image.

Step 6. After previewing, use the **Crop** or **Marquee** tool (Figure 6–35) to select only the area of the scan that is needed. Selecting more than needed creates a bigger file size, which will take up more hard drive space on the computer.

Step 7. Select the **Bit Depth** or type of scan. Many scanners call this many things, but the most common terms are Scan Type or Bit Depth. The following are the most common choices (Figure 6–36).
- 1 Bit or **Black and White** is used primarily for line art.
- 8 Bit or **256 Colors** is used for artwork and paintings.
- 16 Bit or **Thousands of Colors** is used for artwork and paintings, but not a common choice on most scanners.
- 32 Bit or **Millions of Colors** is used to scan almost anything, especially detailed art and photographs, the most common choice.
- Grayscale is also an option on many scanners. This can also be used for scanning in sketches when there is no choice for black-and-white scans.

Step 8. Select the dpi or path. The dpi or path of a scan is the resolution it will scan at. Knowing to set the resolution of the scanner to 150 dpi is key.

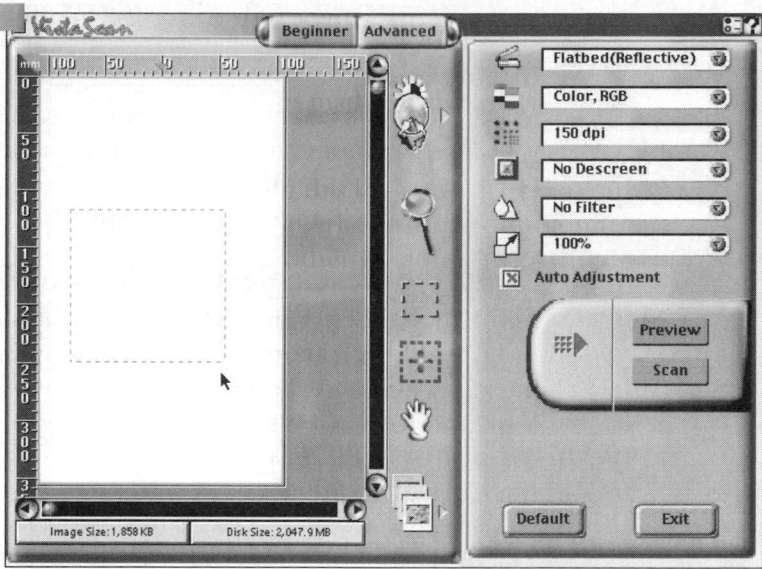

FIGURE 6–35
MagicScan crop tool
(Courtesy of UMAX Data Systems: Used with permission)

FIGURE 6–36
Color modes
(Courtesy of UMAX Data Systems: Used with permission)

Anything lower will create a low-resolution file; anything higher will create a large file size that is unnecessary. Designers want to scan the detail as needed, without adding to file space on the computer.

Step 9. Don't spend a lot of time adjusting the contrast and brightness of the image. As in Figure 6–35 the **Contrast** and **Brightness** are located in the center. Any scanned image most likely will be used as a reference or updated to be the designer's own.

Step 10. Scaling should generally be at 100%. The image size will remain the same as the original.

Inputting Color: Option # 1 Tablet Rendering

Sketch It in!

Many times the image needed is not available for scanning or does not exist. In this case the designer needs to draw or sketch directly into the design software. Once done a few times this becomes very easy for the designer to do. Additions like a Wacom® Tablet make drawing into any software easy.

Sketching into the Computer Instead of Scanning

Some digital designers prefer to draw directly into the computer, using a mouse or stylus like a Wacom Tablet. Designers can sketch right into the many software packages available. Drawing by hand gives a designer the ability to keep that fresh look and feel, as well as quickly getting their ideas into the software. Some programs like Photoshop are also pressure sensitive. Once the artwork is in digital form, then editing is an easy next step.

Wacom Tablet Rendering—*Tracing and Rendering Made Easy*

Today's designers no longer consider this to be a luxury option—every computer station where textile designing occurs must include a tool like a Wacom Pen and Tablet. Designers have a wide variety of products from which to select. Each product is based on the particular needs of the designer. Conveniently located on the Wacom website (www.wacom.com) is a specific questionnaire, which was designed to eliminate confusion over which tablet is best for them personally and why. (See Figure 6–37.)

For our exercises we have chosen to include the use of the Wacom 12″ × 18″ tablet. This product comes complete with all the necessary installation software, drawing tablet, a pen that includes an eraser, and a 4-button puck. (See Figure 6–38.) The software is very user-friendly and will guide the user though the installation process. The software is compatible with most vector and raster design programs for Mac or PC, including Adobe Photoshop 7.

Once installed, the software is activated by attaching the tablet through an open USB port on your computer. In order to activate the Wacom pen, you will need to turn over to disable your existing resident mouse. The Wacom Tablet has numerous features that will enhance the design process and overall experience for the designer.

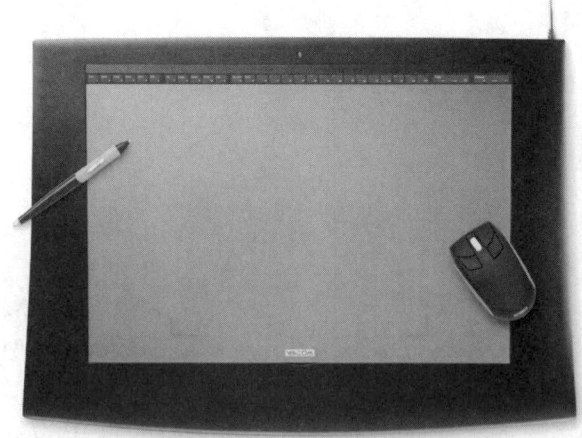

FIGURE 6–37
Wacom logo
(Wacom Technology Corp. Used with permission)

FIGURE 6–38
Wacom 12″ × 18″ tablet
(Wacom Technology Corp. Used with permission)

Features that are easily accessed directly on the tablet include:

- Ability to also modify the speed
- Modify the pressure sensitivity of the pen and eraser
- Change and set preferences
- Access productivity tools and more (See Figure 6–39.)

For our exercises on tracing we suggest that you have access to a digital drawing tablet. Many of the steps or features may be similar, so feel free to follow along in this next exercise. If you do not have access to a drawing tablet, you may want to try the same exercise by using the Paintbrush tool and mouse.

Tracing Functions

There are several function features of the pen and puck with which you will want to familiarize yourself before you begin.

The *4-button puck* (or optical mouse) is both cordless and batteryless, which allows for effortless movement and flexibility. Each button can be programmed for specific functions. Using the pen successfully means becoming familiar with the positions and pointers with the specific software program you are operating. For example, the angle as well as the type of movements used will vary from program to program. It is recommended that you do the following:

Step 1. Always use a Wacom pen with a Wacom tablet—do not substitute pens.

Step 2. Point with the mouse when you first access the on-screen cursor.

Step 3. Next, employ the *pick-up and roll* action when changing locations of cursor.

Step 4. *Clicking* means tapping the pen on the tablet.

Step 5. *Dragging* means pressing and rolling the pen.

Step 6. Accessing and pressing the side switch on the pen can be programmed for a variety of other functions as determined by the designer.

Step 7. Experiment with *tilt sensitivity* with the *gripper*. (See Figure 6–40.)

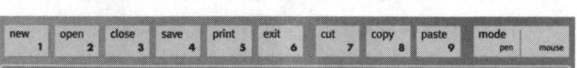

FIGURE 6–39
Access productivity tools
(Wacom Technology Corp. Used with permission)

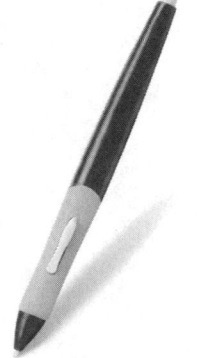

FIGURE 6–40
Wacom pen
(Wacom Technology Corp. Used with permission)

_____

_____

_____

Another use of the tablet is for tracing artwork that has already been drawn by hand. A designer can place the artwork or sketch on the tablet surface. Some tablets have a clear overlay attached to them for the artwork to slide under. The design, artwork, or sketch can then be used as a template and drawn directly into Photoshop.

Now that the image has been properly scanned or sketched and is ready to be edited, it needs to be saved. Just how to do that is determined by where it is going to go when it is finished. Is the image going to be printed in-house or at a service bureau? Will it be e-mailed or sent on a CD to another computer? Determining the correct file format in which to save the image is a critical point in the design process. It can be a disaster if the design that was sent out on a deadline to be printed out or viewed on another computer would not even open up for anyone to see.

Managing Color and File Type— Saving the File in the Correct Format

Choosing the file format for the image to be saved is an important issue. *File format* refers to the type of file the chosen design programs can read. There are many different formats out there. Be sure to know what formats your application will open, so there will be no problems later. Some common formats are PICT, TIFF, TGA, BMP, PSD, and JPEG. These are defined as follows.

Review of File Formats

- PICT—Picture File: This file is read as only RGB and is a compressed format used on the Macintosh to save space.

- TIFF—Tagged Image File Format: This format is similar to PICT but saves as a larger file size. It can be an RGB or CMYK file and can only be compressed if the program you are working in subscribes to Adobe's LZW Compression.

- BMP—Bitmap: Primarily a PC format for saving low-resolution images.

- TGA—Targa: This format is only PC and is used for large color images.

- PSD: This is Photoshop proprietary format. When saved in this format, only Photoshop can open these files.

- JPEG: A popular Web format that saves images in a compressed format by discarding file information that is not needed to view the image. Due to the small size, this format has become popular primarily for images to be viewed on web pages.

CITDA (Computer Integrated Textile Design Association) has designated TIFF as the standard format for all design applications. In effect this makes sure, no matter what software a designer is utilizing, that the image files can also be used in other software, even proprietary or off-the-shelf. www.citda.org

File Compression

A note on compressed file formats: When a saving format compresses an image, the decompressed file is referred to as a *lossy* file. This means that it has lost some detail from the original in order to create the smaller file size, but the human eye very rarely sees the loss in detail. Also most compressed formats automatically decompress when opened. No special tools or software are needed as long as the software can read that compressed file format.

At times a file that has been saved as one format needs to be in a different format. Transferring a file from one format to another is an easy task with Photoshop. Especially today, a file can go between Macs and PCs very easily and even on the same network.

File Transfers—Saving an Image in a Specific Format from Another

There will be times when a designer needs to transfer or export a file to other applications. For example, placing an image in Adobe Illustrator can be useful for masking the design into a flat or sketch. For this use, the image can be a PICT, TIFF, or EPS. This is just one example of when a different file format is needed. The designer needs to know which format is necessary for the image to be opened into another application. Always ask the other computer users if the file format is not known. A transfer of files between programs is made easy with Photoshop. Photoshop can save a file in the most widely used formats. To save images into another format, do the following:

Transferring File Formats

Step 1. With the file open in **Photoshop**, go to **Save As** or **Save for Web** in the **File** menu. There will be a list of the many different formats to select for the Mac or PC. (See Figure 6–41.)

Step 2. Select the format needed.

Step 3. Enter a file name.

Step 4. Select a destination for the image.

Step 5. Choose **Save**.

Exporting a File

Another way to select other formats is in the File menu, using **Export**. Exporting a file is another way of saving a file but with advanced options. (See Figure 6–42.) Here, a designer can export a Photoshop Pen tool path as an Adobe Illustrator Path so it may be opened directly into Illustrator. Exporting a file as an EPS file with JPEG compression to save on space can be accomplished as well. More options are given for image quality and image size than a basic save as an EPS file.

There is other software on the market that do only file conversions and offer a multitude of formats from which to choose. Graphic Converter®, from Lemke Software, is another program that is used in this fashion (Figure 6–43). It is amazing for "batch" converting files all at one time, as well as its impressive list of 57 formats, and counting, for converting these images. It is a piece of shareware that is well worth the low cost to have on hand.

FIGURE 6–41
File formats

FIGURE 6–42
Export

FIGURE 6–43
Graphic converter
(Courtesy of Thorsten Lemke, Lemke Software)

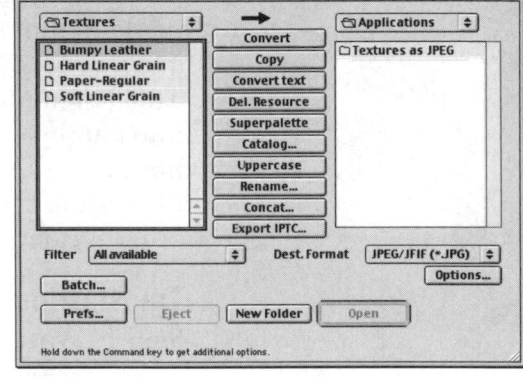

FIGURE 6–44
Convert
(Courtesy of Thorsten Lemke, Lemke Software)

Using Graphic Converter

Step 1. Open **Graphic Converter** (Figure 6–43).

Step 2. Go to the **File** menu and select **Convert** (Figure 6–44).

Step 3. On the left side column of the window, highlight the file to be converted.

Step 4. On the right side column of the window, open the destination folder for the image in the new format.

Step 5. Choose the top button **Convert**. The files have now been saved in the new format and have been directed to the chosen folder as well. (See Figure 6–45.)

Color is possibly one of the most important factors in designing, if not the most important. Photoshop allows any designer to work and design in a variety of color "modes." These modes allow the designer to access different features of the software or to avoid using some features if chosen. For instance, CMYK and RGB modes allow all the features of Photoshop to be accessed, whereas Indexed mode limits the designer by locking out anti-aliasing features that will add unnecessary color to the design.

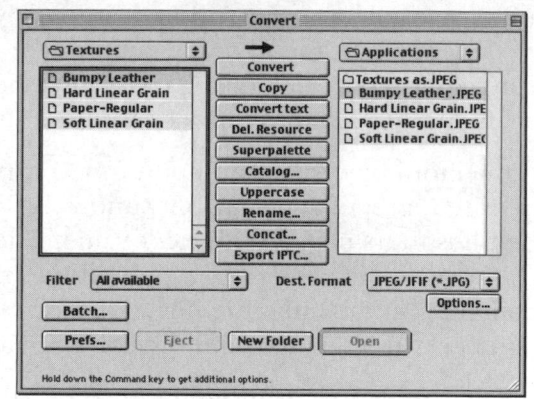

FIGURE 6–45
Converted
(Courtesy of Thorsten Lemke, Lemke Software)

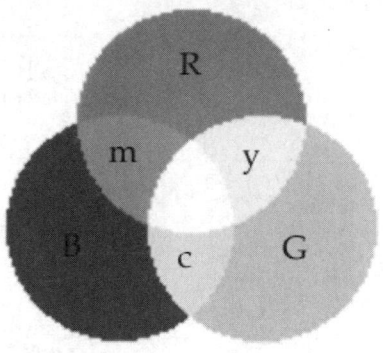

RGB/CMY Mix

FIGURE 6–46
Screen shot of RGB/CMY mix

Understanding Color Mode Selection

RGB or CMYK?

As designers we understand color theory—that the primary colors are additive and are red, green, and blue. Secondary colors are subtractive and made from an equal mix of primary colors. For example, a green image is reflecting green light and absorbing red and blue light. Other colors are a combination of the percentages of RGB color the object reflects. White is reflecting equal amounts of RGB; an object that is black reflects no color. Secondary colors are cyan, magenta, and yellow, which are the opposites of the primary colors and are made up of equal amounts of the primary colors that they are between. By combining the three primary colors (red, green, and blue) in different percentages, a designer can mix a wide range of colors (Figure 6–46).

Did you ever wonder why we design on a computer in RGB but we print designs in CMYK (cyan, magenta, yellow, and black)? This brings up the issue of monitor and printer color.

Monitors display color with RGB light; there's no way around that. Printers use CMYK inks; can't change that either. So, in order to design around this color issue, most programs convert any output into CMYK colors when it sends the file to the printer. This is usually the job of the printer driver. The driver takes the colors it is given and converts or "rips" them into CMYK values. This is why what you see is not necessarily what you get.

Printer Color vs. Monitor Color— Is What You See, What You'll Get???

The human eye breaks down light into red, green, and blue data. A computer monitor successfully imitates and reproduces the color data the same way we perceive color. Through additive color a monitor can accomplish showing us what we would perceive with our eyes. However, printers cannot create the color spectrum from just printing red, blue, and green, so a system of using subtractive colors— CMYK or cyan, magenta, yellow, and black—has been devised.

When two subtractive colors are overprinted, an additive color is created. So, by using CMYK a designer can theoretically reproduce millions of colors on their printer. In true color practice just mixing CMY would be enough to create the color, but in reality black is needed to create a crisper and sharper color.

Let's look at the monitor first. All computer monitors project light. These lights are made up of red, green, and blue phosphors. A differing electrical charge to each of these phosphors changes its color value. These RGB colors, as they are known, can be used to mix a seemingly unlimited range of colors. When designing on the computer and editing the hue, lightness, saturation, and other values of RGB, a designer can ultimately find the color needed.

Now, let's look at the printer. Getting these colors to match the CMYK printout can be a challenge. All desktop printers use cyan, magenta, yellow, and black (CMYK). Some newer printers are called 6-color printers. They use CMYK plus a light cyan and a light magenta, creating the ability to get even more depth out of your colors. So, as can be seen, there is a missing link between the RGB of the screen and the CMYK of the printer. Most printers do a good job of printing colors. They all have ways to get close color by simulating the RGB on the screen by mixing percentages of CMYK (Figures 6–47 through 6–53).

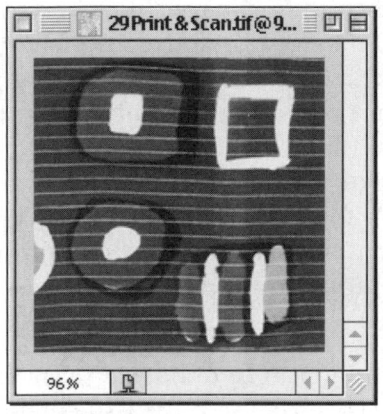

FIGURE 6–47
Design with RED channel

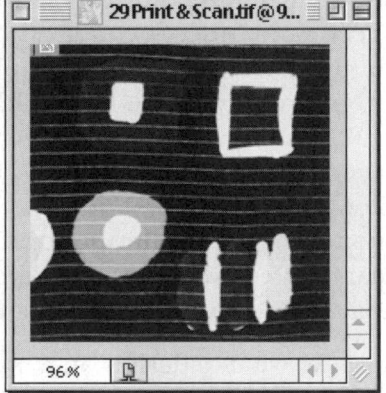

FIGURE 6–48
Design with GREEN channel

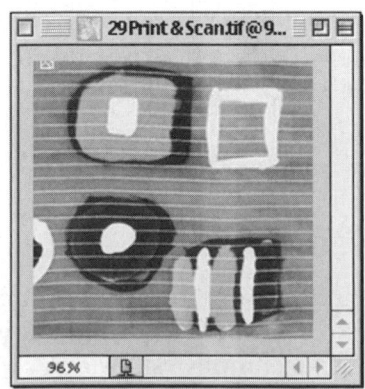

FIGURE 6–49
Design with BLUE channel

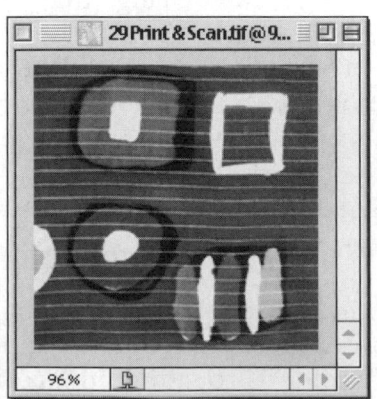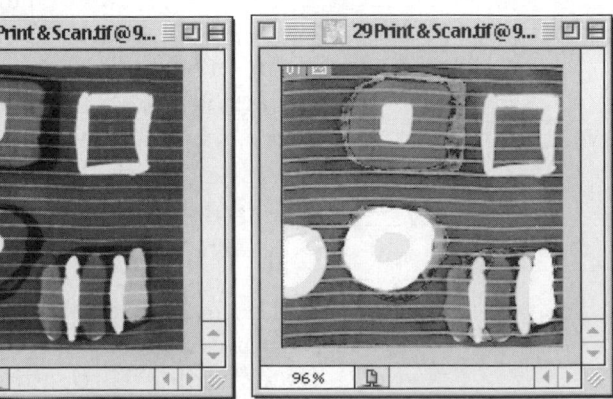

FIGURE 6–50
Design with CYAN channel

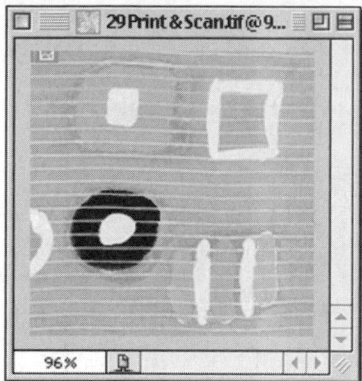

FIGURE 6–51
Design with MAGENTA channel

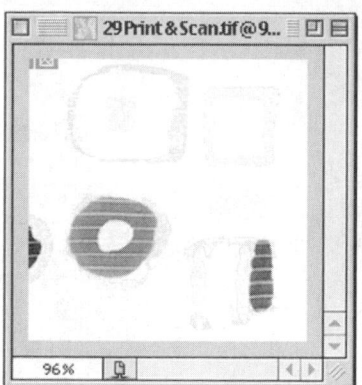

FIGURE 6–52
Design with YELLOW channel

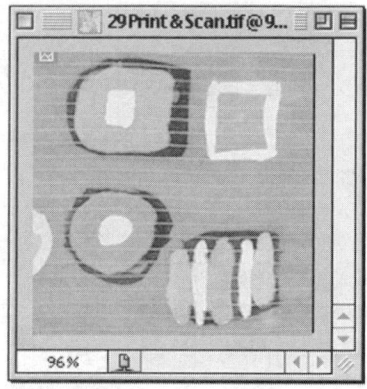

FIGURE 6–53
Design with BLACK channel

Notes . . .

So how do we get the color we see on the monitor to be on the printout? Calibrating monitors to printers has long been the Holy Grail of the designer. There are many ideas that may get "in the ball park" color, but the ones that get it closer will cost more.

Methods for Color Matching for Design or Printout

Matching color and matching color from monitor to printout are two different avenues. Most designers seem content to be "in the ball park" when seeing color on the screen and then the result at output. Those I have worked with in the textile industry seem to realize that the final output is what people are going to see, so they keep a palette of colors and how they print so they have an easy reference when building the next season's palette. How they get these colors is another story. Choosing colors in any program can be intense. There are many ways to do this.

Accessing Color Libraries in Adobe Photoshop— Including Pantone Digital Color Libraries

There are also many products available to the designer to select color. Pantone, Inc. is a company that seems to have become the color-matching standard in the industry. Pantone, Inc. develops color-matching standards for the printing and textile industry. They develop CMYK equivalents for print colors to be selected, so those colors can be easily reproduced when printed in other parts of the world. Recent products from Pantone, Inc. allow a designer to load a Pantone Textile Color Picker onto the PC or Macintosh and access their color-matching libraries for textiles. This electronic format of color is accessible through the Adobe Photoshop Color Picker when installed on the Macintosh or through separately accessed software that can be installed on any PC. So how are these Pantone colors accessed or selected? Adobe Photoshop has a Pantone Digital Color Library inherent in the program. It is easily accessed through the Color Picker on a Mac or PC. (See Figures 6–54 and 6–55.)

Selecting Pantone Digital Color Libraries

Step 1. See the selection windows in Figures 6–56 through 6–59 to allow access to select PANTONE Colors.

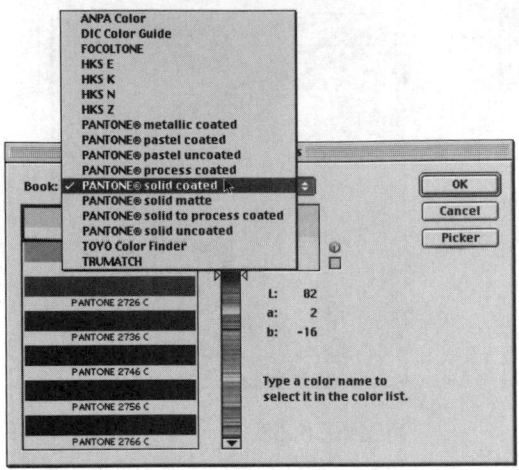

FIGURE 6–54
PANTONE on Apple Macintosh
(Pantone® and other Pantone, Inc. trademarks are the registered property of Pantone, Inc. PANTONE trademarks and copyrights used with permission of Pantone, Inc.)

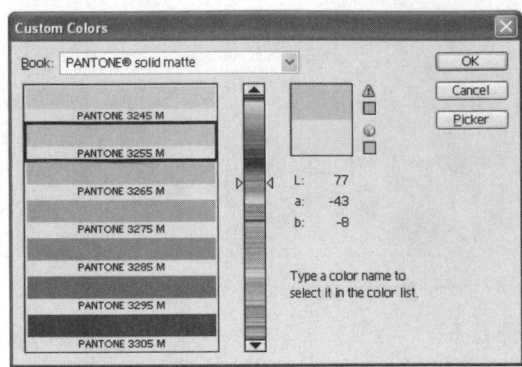

FIGURE 6–55
PANTONE on a PC
(Pantone® and other Pantone, Inc. trademarks are the registered property of Pantone, Inc. PANTONE trademarks and copyrights used with permission of Pantone, Inc.)

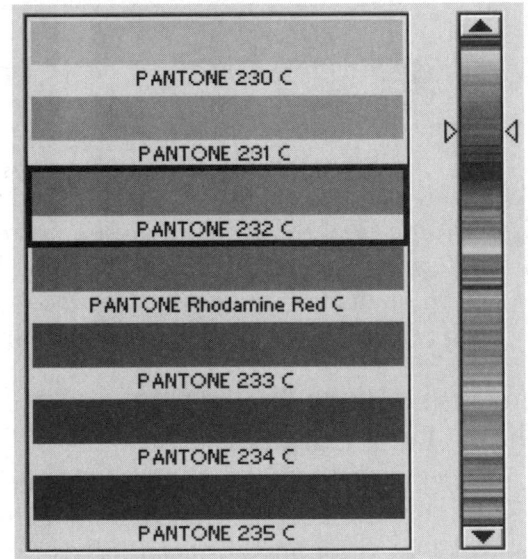

FIGURE 6–56
Color picker
(Pantone® and other Pantone, Inc. trademarks are the registered property of Pantone, Inc. PANTONE trademarks and copyrights used with permission of Pantone, Inc.)

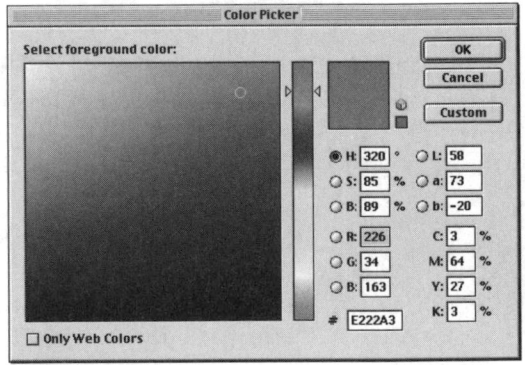

FIGURE 6–57
Custom

Notes...

Step 2. In Adobe Photoshop 5.5 and earlier, go to the **File** menu and select **Preferences, General**. In Adobe Photoshop 6.0 and later, go to the **Edit** menu and select **Preferences, General**.

For Access on a PC:

Step 3. In the **Preferences** window, set the **Color Picker** option for **Adobe**.

Step 4. Now, when the Color Picker is clicked on, the Color window in Figure 6–60 will show.

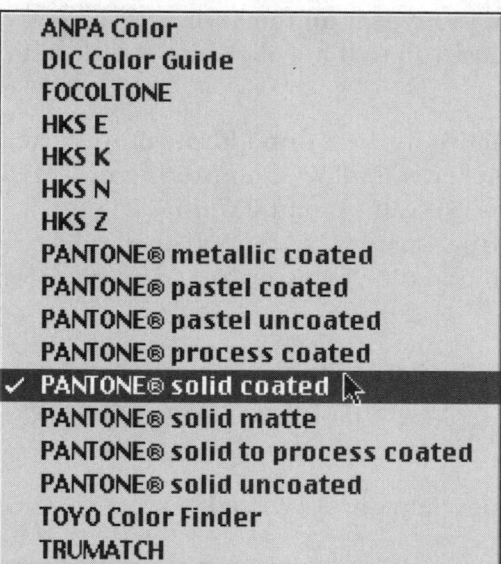

FIGURE 6–58
PANTONE digital color library selection
(Pantone® and other Pantone, Inc. trademarks are the registered property of Pantone, Inc. PANTONE trademarks and copyrights used with permission of Pantone, Inc.)

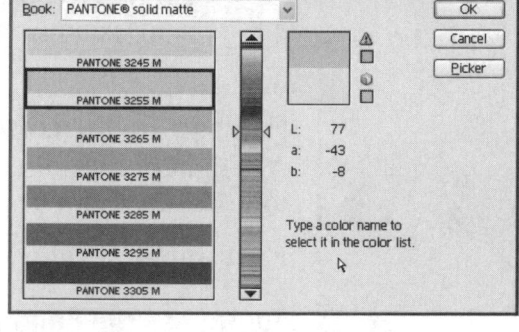

FIGURE 6–59
PANTONE digital color library selection by number
(Pantone® and other Pantone, Inc. trademarks are the registered property of Pantone, Inc. PANTONE trademarks and copyrights used with permission of Pantone, Inc.)

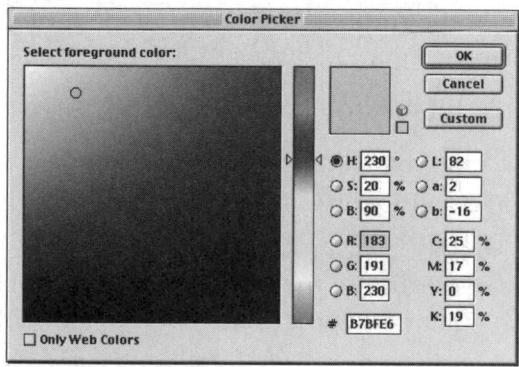

FIGURE 6–60
Adobe color picker

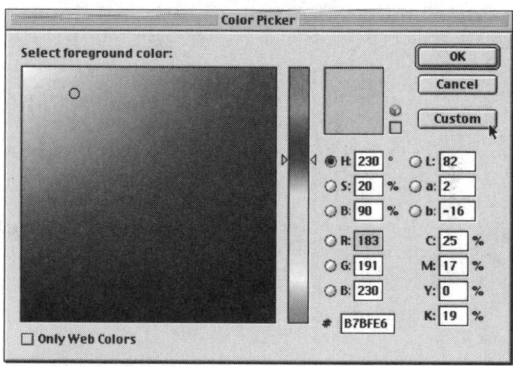

FIGURE 6–61
Custom button selection

Notes...

For Access on a Mac:

Step 1. In the **Preferences** window, set the **Color Picker** option for **Adobe**.

Step 2. Now, when the Color Picker is clicked on the color, the Adobe Color Picker will show.

To Access the Pantone Digital Color Libraries:

Step 1. Select the **Custom** button on the right side of the Adobe Photoshop Picker (Figure 6–61).

Step 2. All the Adobe Photoshop and Pantone Digital Color Libraries will be seen in the top list. Select the book to be used.

Step 3. If the Pantone number is known, just type it on the keyboard. The Pantone Digital Color Library will scroll to that color or to the closest numerical match.

Step 4. Choose **OK**. The color is now active in the Adobe Photoshop Picker. The Adobe Photoshop Color Picker will allow the entering of CMYK values, RGB values, Lab values, HSB values, and Pantone Digital Color selections by clicking on the **Custom** button in this window. In this window, a designer can enter a color by using any of these color values.

Pantone Textile Library—Pantone Textile Color Chooser

A designer can enter any Pantone Textile Colors, if they have purchased the Pantone Textile Color Chooser, as follows.

For Pantone Textile selection, the dialogues below are accessed.

To Access the Pantone Textile Library

On a Mac:

Step 1. In Adobe Photoshop, be sure to set the Preferences for the Color Picker to Apple Picker.

Step 2. Scroll down on the left side of the Apple Picker, until the Pantone Textile Color Chooser is visible (Figure 6–62).

Step 3. Select it. The Pantone Textile Library will be shown.

Step 4. If the Pantone Textile color number is known, just type it on the keyboard. The Pantone Textile Library will scroll to that color or to the closest numerical match.

Step 5. Choose **OK** and the color is now active in the Adobe Photoshop Picker. Choose **OK** and the color will be in the foreground color of the toolbox.

On a PC:

Step 1. In Adobe Photoshop, the Color Picker Preferences can be Adobe or Windows. Access to enter an RGB value is all that is needed.

Step 2. On the desktop, open the Pantone Textile Color Chooser (Figure 6–63).

FIGURE 6–62

Pantone textile color chooser on a Mac

(Pantone® and other Pantone, Inc. trademarks are the registered property of Pantone, Inc. PANTONE trademarks and copyrights used with permission of Pantone, Inc.)

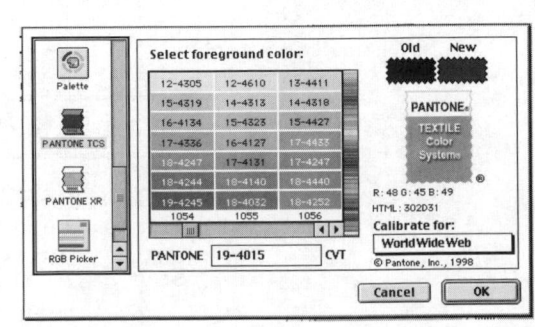

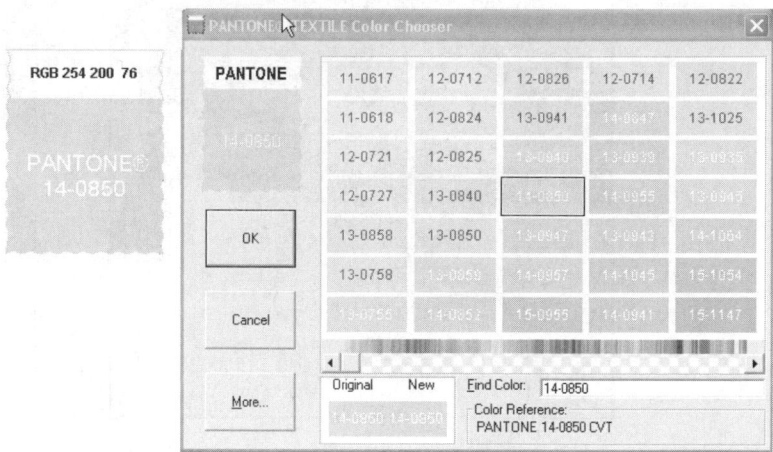

Notes...

FIGURE 6–63
Pantone textile color chooser on a PC
(Pantone® and other Pantone, Inc. trademarks are the registered property of Pantone, Inc. PANTONE trademarks and copyrights used with permission of Pantone, Inc.)

Step 3. Select the color needed.

Step 4. If the Pantone Textile color number is known, just type it on the keyboard. The Pantone Textile Library will scroll to that color or to the closest numerical match. A swatch of the selected color will show on the desktop.

Step 5. Enter the given RGB values into the Adobe Photoshop Picker and choose **OK.** The color should now be in the foreground color of the toolbox.

Trial-and-Error Color Selection

The "poor man's" way to select color is trial and error. Mix a color and print it out; if it is not correct, try again. This can take a designer five or more times before getting it right. Once a designer has a color that they like, they would need to save it into a palette for safekeeping and later use.

Creating Custom Colors—
Including Several How-to Examples

Creating a Custom Color Palette

Step 1. Go to the **Window** menu and select **Show Swatches.** A default palette will open (Figure 6–64).

Step 2. Colors can be removed from this default palette by selecting the Alt key on the PC or the Option key on the Mac.

Step 3. Colors are added simply by having the needed color selected as the foreground color, and by dragging the mouse over the blank area of the palette. A bucket will appear (Figure 6–65). Clicking the mouse will show a window on which to name the color chip (Figure 6–66).

Step 4. Enter a name and choose **OK.** The color is added to the palette (Figure 6–67).

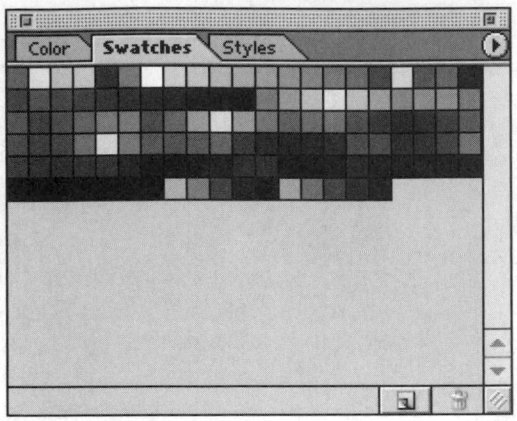

FIGURE 6–64
Default palette

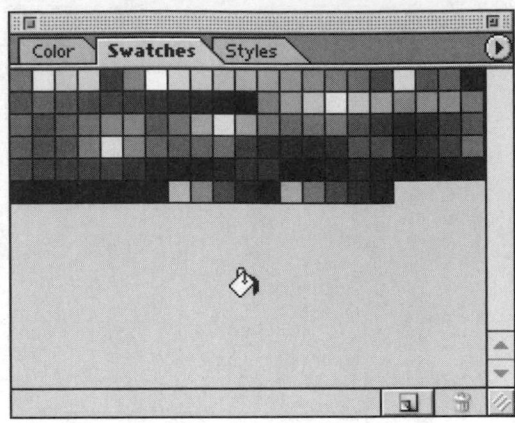

FIGURE 6–65
Bucket on palette

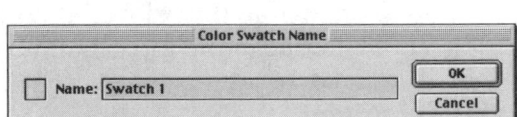

FIGURE 6–66
Name chip

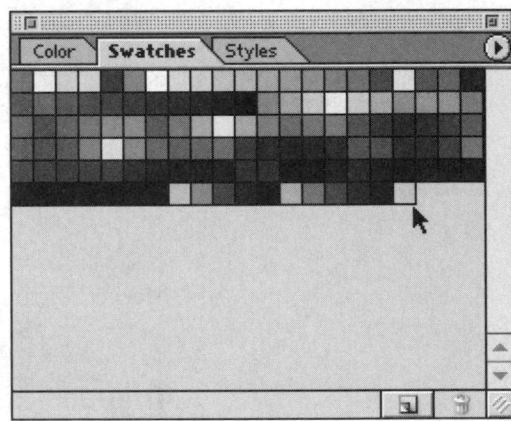

FIGURE 6–67
Palette with new chip

Notes...

Back-to-Front Method

A second way to create custom colors is doing a back-to-front system, in which a set of palettes is created in the program to be used. These colors are then output to the same printer on which all other artwork will be printed. This creates a predictable set of colors that can be reentered into the palette of any artwork and predictable color will be achieved.

Step 1. Create or set up the color charts.

Step 2. Print out each chart with all color values.

Step 3. Using the printouts, colors can be selected and reentered into the swatch palette.

Step 4. Colors selected on the printouts will always match the output.

If the software cannot easily develop and print out palettes of color, then a third-party software like Color Charter (Macintosh only) can be used (Figure 6–68). This is one of many products that allow a designer to develop the charts of any

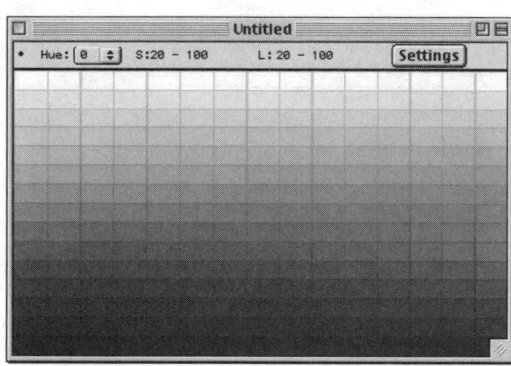

FIGURE 6–68
Color charter

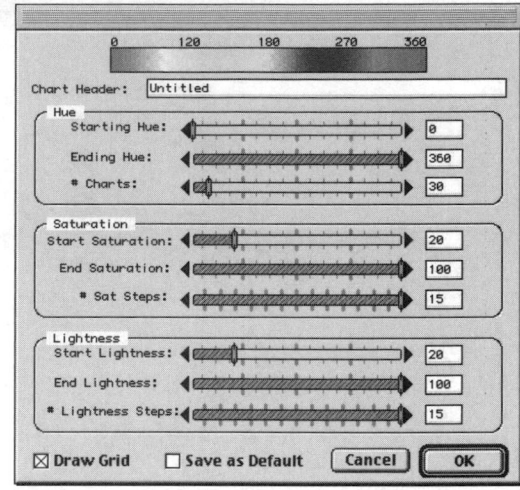

FIGURE 6–69
Settings

Notes...

color values needed and print them out with the hue, saturation, and lightness values of every chip.

Step 1. Open **Color Charter** to create or set up the color charts, a red chart will appear.

Step 2. Choose the **Settings** button in the top right of the window (Figure 6–69).

Step 3. Select the starting hue number from 0–360.

Step 4. Select the ending hue number from 0–360.

Step 5. Select the number of charts from 0–360.

Step 6. Choose **File > Save As...** and in that window name the folder in which the charts are to be saved. Also, be sure to choose the desktop for the destination of the folder.

Step 7. Make the **Format > Separate Picts**.

Step 8. Make the **Resolution** 72 dpi.

Step 9. Choose **Save.**

HINT: Once the folder of charts has been saved, these charts can be individually opened into any design software that accepts PICT files. They can then be printed out from that software and used to enter color values that will print the same way.

How to Print a Color Chart for Color Matching

Step 1. Open the first chart in the design software, by using **File > Open.**

Step 2. Open and print out each chart (Figure 6–70).

Step 3. Using the printouts, colors can be selected and reentered into the swatch palette using their HSL values.

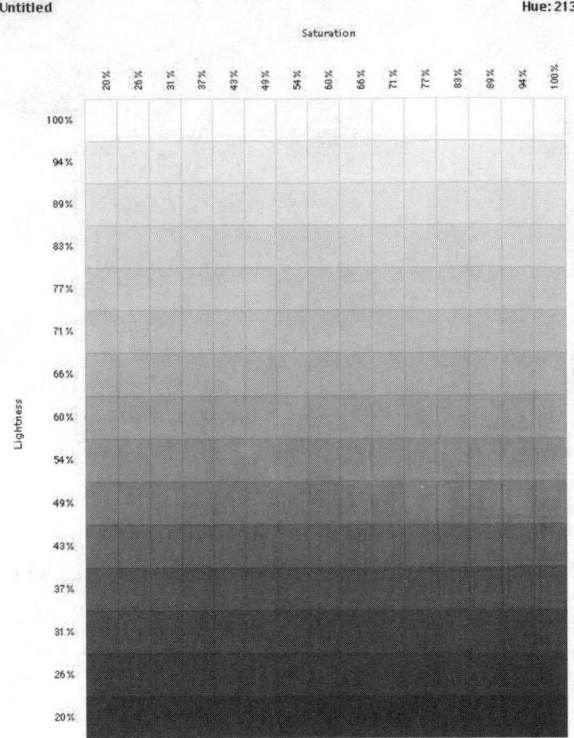

FIGURE 6–70
Sample of printed page from color charter

Step 4. Colors selected from the printouts will always match the output because they were printed out of the same design software.

The designer then has a true printout of what colors their desktop printer can manage, as well as the color values to enter back in to get a reproducible color. The one drawback here is that the monitor may not be a perfect match.

Matching the monitor can be done by creating a monitor profile, using a monitor calibrator. This is a device that attaches directly to the screen and measures the light waves (gamma) received off the screen.

Digital Swatchbook Method

The third way to create custom colors is to use a spectrophotometer, like X-Rite's Digital Swatchbook. This device and its software allow a designer to "zap" or sample a color on a chip, fabric swatch, or any object. It then averages the color it sees and creates a very close representation of the color on the screen. This color chip can now be used in any program that works with the X-Rite palettes. The only drawback to this system is the setup. There is always a need to have the same printer, monitor, and paper stock for this to work well, because any change in the process can throw off the color match. The spectrophotometer is used the following way:

Notes . . .

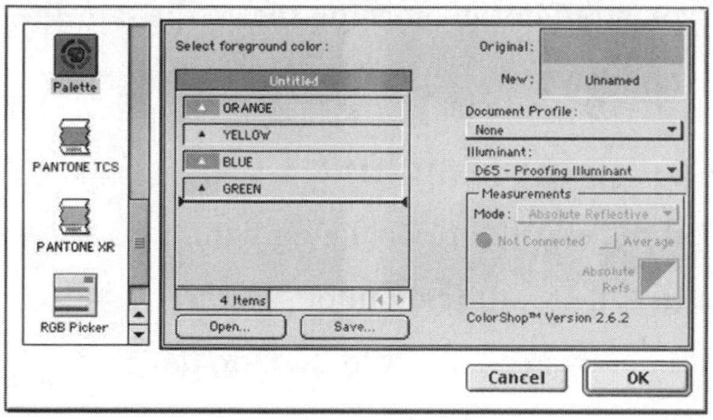

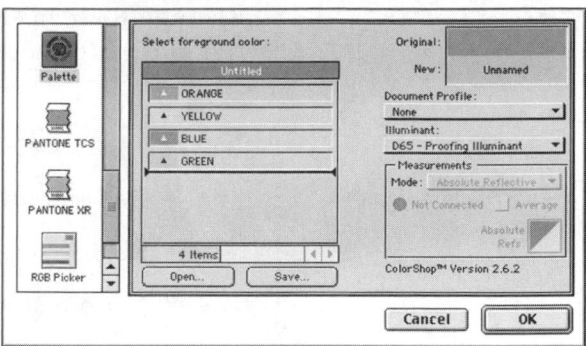

FIGURE 6–71
Palette window for X-Rite® Colorshop
(Courtesy of X-Rite)

FIGURE 6–72
Color palette with added colors
(Courtesy of X-Rite)

Notes . . .

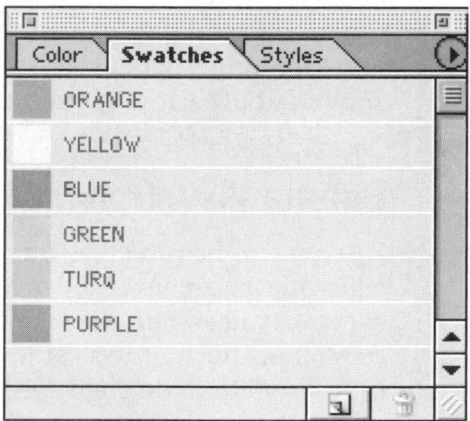

FIGURE 6–73
Color palette with colors in Photoshop picker
(Courtesy of X-Rite)

Step 1. Following the device's instructions, calibrate the monitor to the printer that is using the X-Rite software. This creates a monitor profile (Figure 6–71).

Step 2. Select the proper printer profile from the library of profiles that comes with the software. If one does not exist for the printer being used, then you will need to create one, again using the X-Rite software.

Step 3. Any color chips that are to be matched are individually "zapped" and read into a custom color palette, which is then saved (Figure 6–72).

Step 4. These colors can now be used in any design and accessed through the Photoshop Color Picker (Figure 6–73).

HINT: This sounds easy, but the real catch is setting up the spectrophotometer and having the monitor and printer profiles set right. If any changes in the process occur, all color matching is thrown off, so it is important to keep the settings the same, always using the same printer and the same paper stock. Other variables in color matching actually involve the designer's working space.

Keeping these in check will ensure you a red in the morning that is the same red in the afternoon.

Successful Timesaving Secrets for Matching Color

- Reduce sunlight reflecting off the monitor or changing light.

- Remove bright artwork on the walls near the monitor.

- Use a neutral gray for the desktop instead of a wild desktop design.

Building Color Palettes

If you recall earlier in Chapter 3, we walked you through the process of building a generic color palette using Adobe Photoshop. In this section, we will apply this information further for the textile designer's use. Color palettes in Photoshop are very user-friendly. Adding, deleting, and naming color chips are a few of the options. Custom palettes can be saved and opened when they are needed, as well as appended to each other to create larger palettes of color.

Palette View Options

Palettes can be viewed as small chip thumbnails or as lists of colors. The advantages of each are up to the designer. Thumbnails allow the user to easily see many colors at once when they are adding, deleting, and selecting the chips. The list view allows the user to see the name of the color swatch right next to the chips as they scroll down through a list.

To View the Palette Options:

Step 1. Go to the **Window** menu and select **Swatches.**

Step 2. In the **Swatch** window, select the arrow in the top right-hand corner.

Step 3. Select the viewing preference of **Small Thumbnail** or **Small List** (Figure 6–74).

To Create Names for the Chips:

Step 1. To view the swatch window for editing, go to the **Window** menu and select **Swatches.** A default palette will open.

Step 2. Double-clicking on a color chip will allow the designer to name the chip (Figure 6–75).

Step 3. Choose **OK** and the name is listed.

To Create a Custom Color Palette:

Step 1. Go to the **Window** menu and select **Swatches.** A default palette will open (Figure 6–76).

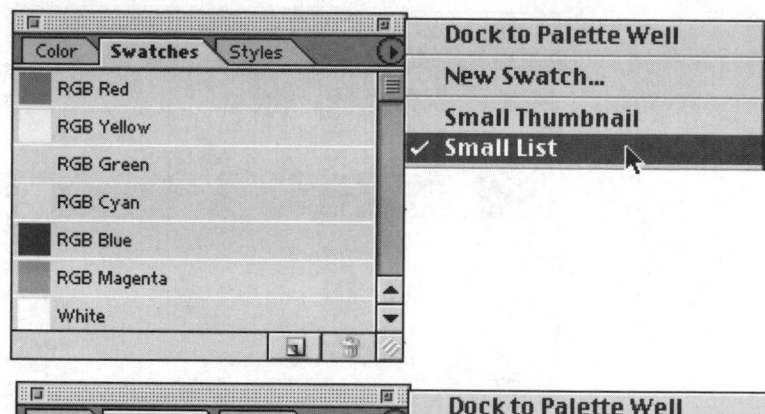

FIGURE 6–74
Show swatch window

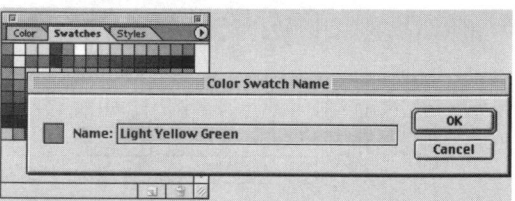

FIGURE 6–75
Show swatch window

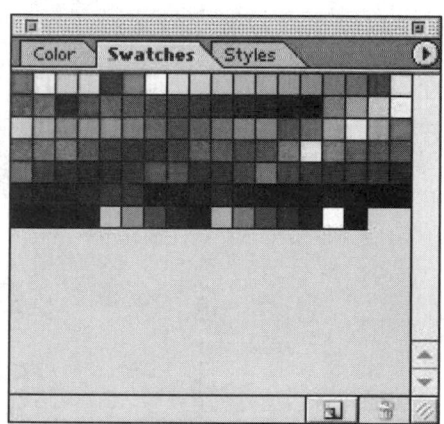

FIGURE 6–76
Default palette

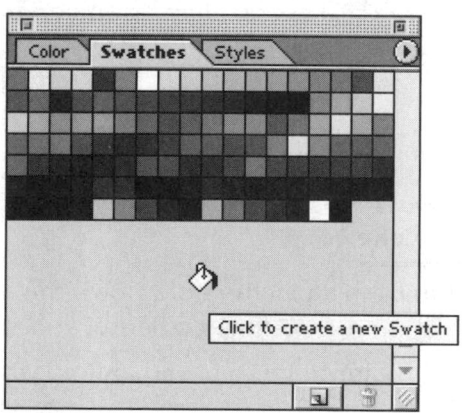

FIGURE 6–77
Bucket on palette

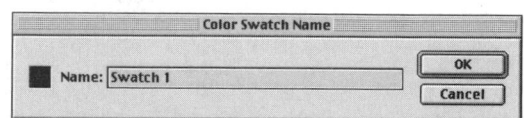

FIGURE 6–78
Name chip

Notes . . .

Step 2. Colors can be removed from this default palette by selecting the Alt key on the PC or the Option key on the Mac.

Step 3. Colors are added simply by having the needed color selected as the foreground color and by dragging the mouse over the blank area of the palette. A bucket will appear (Figure 6–77). Clicking the mouse will show a window to name the color chip.

Step 4. Enter a name and choose **OK.** The color is added to the palette (Figure 6–78).

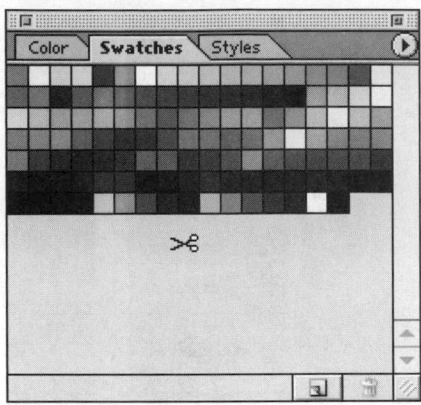

FIGURE 6–79
Scissor tool

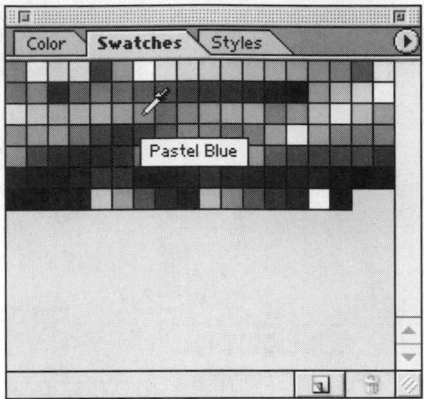

FIGURE 6–80
Eyedropper

Notes...

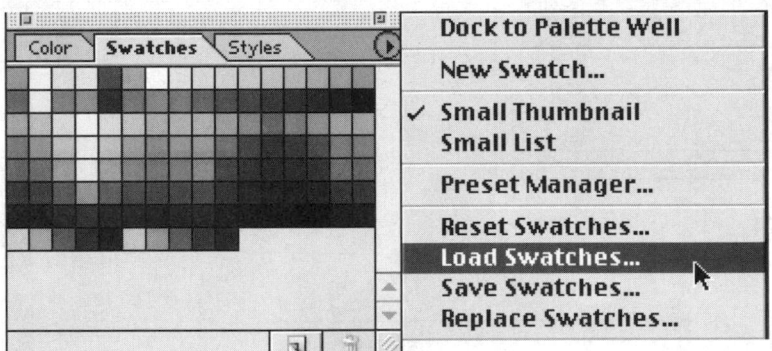

FIGURE 6–81
Load swatches

To Remove a Color from the Palette:

Step 1. To remove a color chip from a palette, hold down the Apple key on a Mac or the Control key on the PC to get a Scissor tool (Figure 6–79).

Step 2. Click the Scissor on the color to be removed and it is cut out.

To Select a Color out of a Swatch Palette:

Step 1. To select a color chip from the palette, just drag the mouse over the chip to be selected. An Eyedropper will appear (Figure 6–80).

Step 2. Click on the mouse and the color is now the new foreground color.

To Load Palettes and Swatches:

Step 1. To load a new palette, select **Load** in the palette window by using the right-hand options arrow.

Step 2. If no swatch palettes are available in the selector, select **Load Swatches** (Figure 6–81).

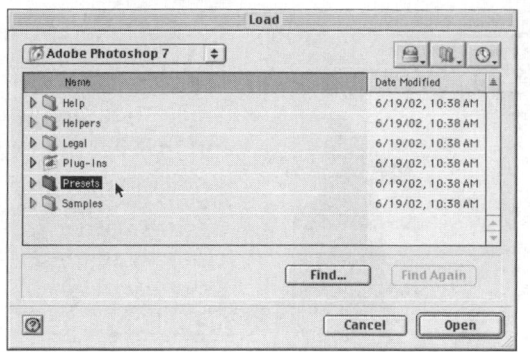

FIGURE 6–82
Presets folder

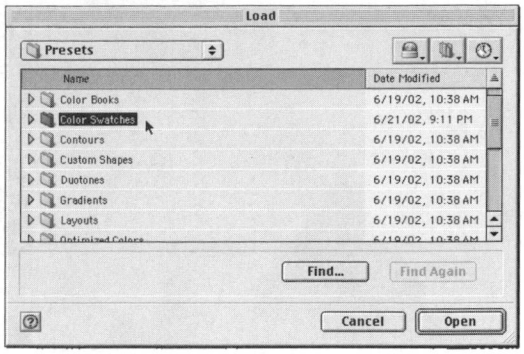

FIGURE 6–83
Color swatches folder

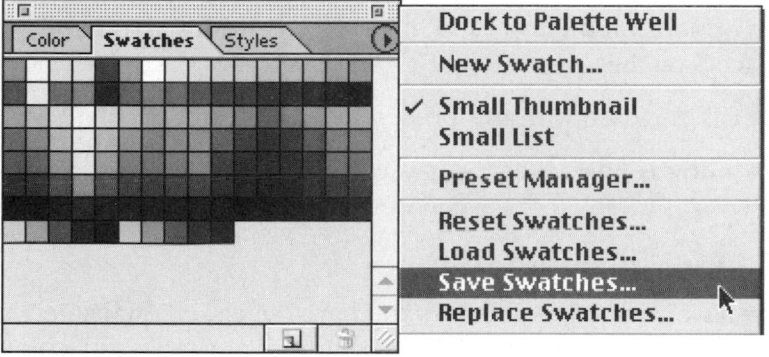

FIGURE 6–84
Save swatches

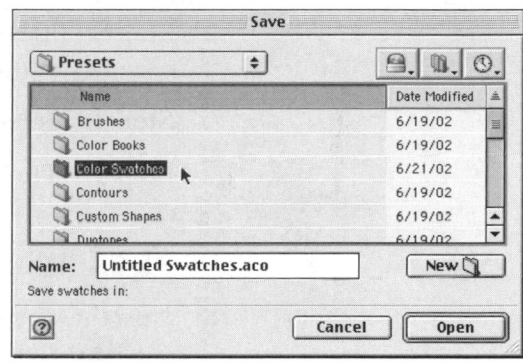

FIGURE 6–85
Save

Notes . . .

Step 3. In the **Open** window, find and open the Adobe Photoshop folder.

Step 4. In this folder, find the **Presets** folder (Figure 6–82).

Step 5. In this folder, find the **Color Swatches** folder (Figure 6–83).

Step 6. Double-click on the palette to open.

To Save Palettes and Swatches:

Step 1. To save a new palette, select **Save** in the **Palette** window by using the right-hand options arrow.

Step 2. Select the **Save Swatches** option (Figure 6–84).

Step 3. In the **Save** window, name the palette (Figure 6–85).

Step 4. Select the swatch folder for the palette and choose **Save.**

To Load an Empty Swatch Palette:

Step 1. Go to the **Window** menu and select **Show Swatches**. This will open a default swatch palette.

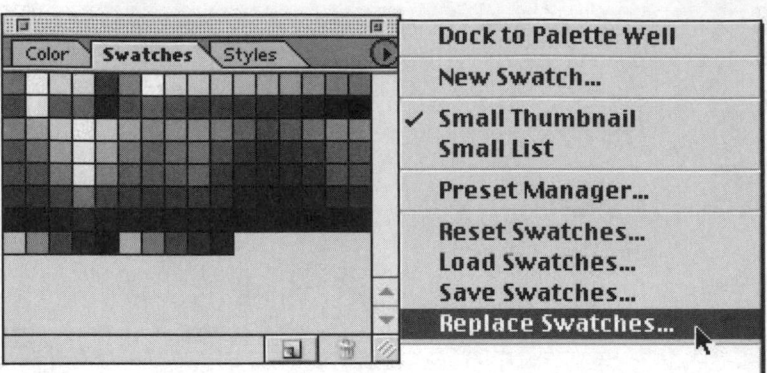

FIGURE 6–86
Replace swatches

Step 2. In the swatch options on the top right, choose the options arrow and choose **Replace Swatches** (Figure 6–86).

Step 3. Select on the CD enclosed with this book the "**New Swatches**" file.

Step 4. The **Swatch** window is now ready for new colors.

The Importance of Color Reduction

Now that the designers have selected their colors and have built a seasonal palette, the next step to develop any image further is to contend with any necessary color reduction. When the original source of the design was scanned earlier, it had many colors in it. In fact, it has even more colors than the original design was created with. Color reduction is a process to remove these added colors.

Color Reduction Issues for Scanned Images

Color reduction is an interesting process. Many designers ask why is there a need to reduce the colors anyway when the original is an 8- or 12-color design. Scanning an image into the computer is the real issue. When an image is scanned into the computer, the scanner sees more color than is there. It sees the overlap of printed colors, where colors mix, shadows of colors from fabric texture, and, if on fabric, even how the colors are reflected from the fabric they are printed on. That 8- or 12-color print is now almost 200 colors in the scan!

Try to do a colorway on a 200-color design! So color reducing is necessary to color or design using scanned images.

For a preview of how we will proceed, refer to the images in Figures 6–87 and 6–88. Figure 6–87 is the original scan, containing 70 colors. Figure 6–88 is the new color-reduced version, with only 12 colors in it.

Let's continue and see how this reduction was accomplished.

Color Reducing B/W Line Art and Sketches

Reducing color in line art can be very simple. If the scan was done in a black-and-white or 1-bit mode, then the image is already in two colors — black and white. If

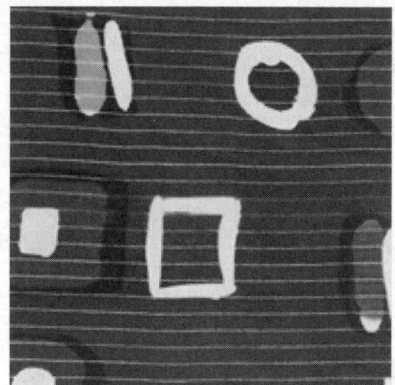

FIGURE 6–87
Original scan with 70 colors

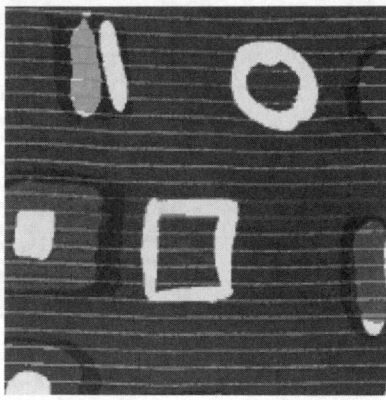

FIGURE 6–88
After reduction with 12 colors

FIGURE 6–89
B/W sketch

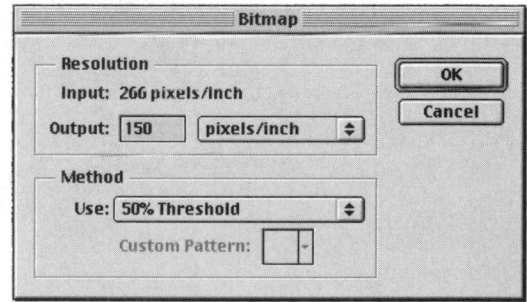

FIGURE 6–90
Bitmap mode

there was no black-and-white or 1-bit mode available, then the scan may have been done in grayscale. If so, the design is most likely in many shades of gray. To reduce the file to two colors, most likely black and white, follow these steps:

Step 1. Open the file on the CD named "**B/W sketch.**" (See Figure 6–89.)

Step 2. Select in the **Image** menu > **Mode Grayscale.**

Step 3. Select in the **Image** menu > **Mode Bitmap.** (See Figure 6–90.)

Step 4. Select the **Output** to 150 pixels per inch.

Step 5. Select for **Method: Use: 50% Threshold.** This will allow only black and white to be used. On a scale of contrast of 1–100, any gray value from 1–50 will become white, and gray value for 51–100 will become black (Figure 6–91).

Step 6. Choose **OK.** The image will now be all black-and-white line art.

Preparing Fabric Scans for Color Reduction

(In order to follow along you will need to open the scanned fabric from the Goodies CD, Chapter Exercise Folder.)

FIGURE 6–91
50% threshold

FIGURE 6–92
Before

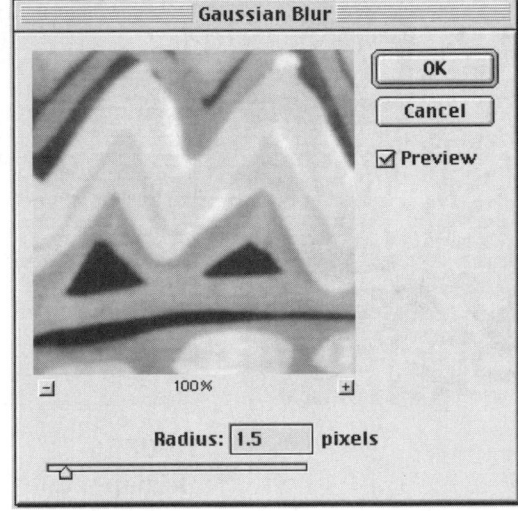

FIGURE 6–93
Gaussian blur settings

FIGURE 6–94
After

Fabric scans can be a bit tricky because the scanner can pick up much of the texture of the weave or knit. Before reducing color in the fabric, it is recommended to try a few filters to remove this texture.

Step 1.   Open the scanned fabric. (See Figure 6–92.)

Step 2.   Go to the **Filter** menu and select **Blur > Gaussian Blur** (Figure 6–93).

Step 3.   Set the **Radius** to 0.3 pixels; this will remove much of the texture without clouding detail in the image. Using the **Preview** button, the designer can see if the effect is what they want. If 0.3 is not high enough to remove the texture, try a higher number. Be careful not to go too high and blur out any detail you need to keep.

Step 4.   Choose **OK**. (See Figure 6–94.)

HINT: With the texture removed, one of the options listed in the section for scanned artwork and photographs can be utilized to have a color-reduced image.

FIGURE 6–95
Magic wand tool

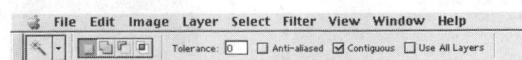

FIGURE 6–96
Setting the options

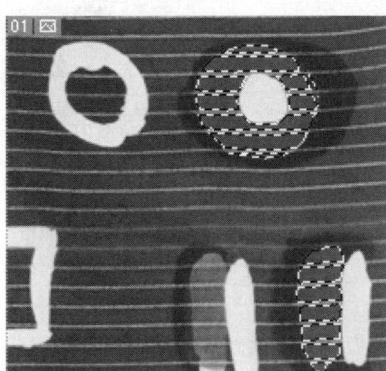

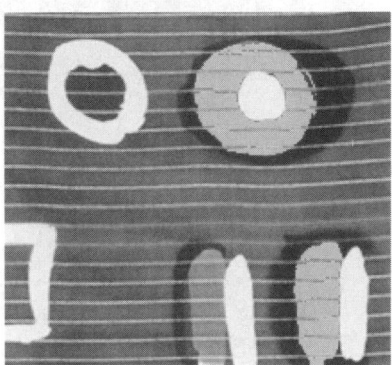

FIGURE 6–97
Select similar

FIGURE 6–98
New color added

Color Reducing Scanned Color Artwork and Photographs

There are a few techniques for color reducing a scanned color image or artwork using Adobe Photoshop. Each technique has its own merits and after awhile the designer will know which one works best for different designs and scans.

Technique #1 — Selection Tools

This first technique is used when there are areas of color that can easily be selected with the Magic Wand tool.

Step 1. Double-click on the **Magic Wand** tool (Figure 6–95).

Setting the options of the tool can adjust it to select "like" hues of the color to be selected. The Tolerance and Contiguous options will allow the selection to grow and select a large range of the same hue (Figure 6–96). These are defined as follows:
- **Tolerance**—This option as it is increased will select more and more color "like" the original selected area.
- **Contiguous**—This option when selected will select only the continuous area of "like" color. So, if the need is to select the same color in the overall design, then this option should NOT be selected.
- **Anti-Aliased**—As usual, this option is NOT to be selected, because it will create halos of color when we do the selections and editing.

Step 2. With the Magic Wand tool, select the options needed as listed above. Click to select the area of color to be edited. This will be the "sample" area of that color range.

Step 3. From the **Select** menu, choose **Select Similar**. This will select that color range throughout the image (Figure 6–97).

Step 4. Choose the color to replace this area as the foreground color and select **Fill** from the **Edit** menu (Figure 6–98).

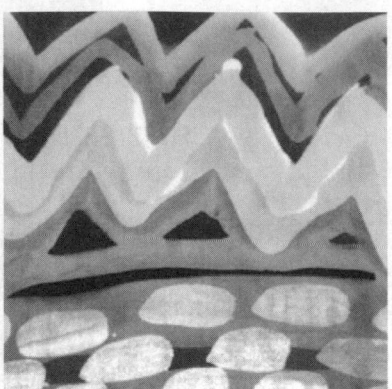

FIGURE 6–99
Original

FIGURE 6–100
Reduced 12 colors

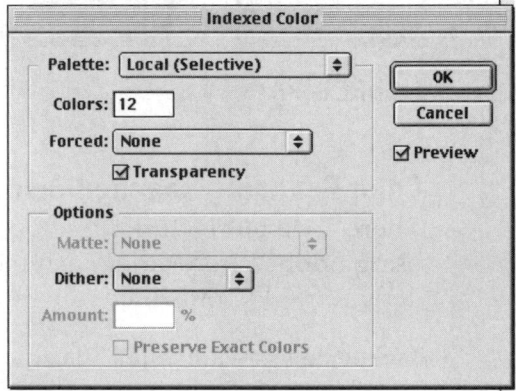

FIGURE 6–101
Adaptive selection window

Step 5. All selected areas will be replaced with a solid fill of the chosen color.

Technique #2—Edit by Mode

Step 1. Open the scanned image.

Step 2. Select the **Image** menu and choose **Mode.**
- If the Mode is already RGB, select **Indexed Mode** (Figure 6–99).
- If the Mode is Indexed Mode, select **RGB Mode**, and then reselect **Indexed Mode** (Figure 6–100).

Step 3. Make the following choices in the **Mode** window:
- Choose **Palette: Adaptive.** (See Figure 6–101.)
- **Colors:** Enter the desired final number of colors. Check the Preview box to the far right. When a specific number of colors is entered in the Colors box, the image will update instantly. The designer then is seeing exactly what the image will look like with that exact number of colors. Play with different color numbers and see the difference in the detail and clarity of the image.
- **Forced:** None.
- **Dithering:** None.

Notes . . .

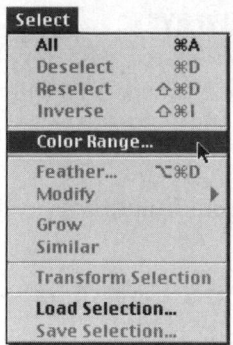
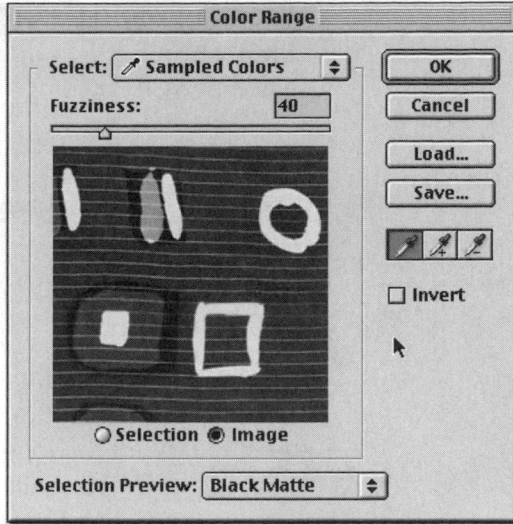

FIGURE 6–102
Color range

Step 4. Choose **OK.**

Technique #3—Color Range

Step 1. Open the scanned image.

Step 2. From the **Select** menu, choose **Color Range** (Figure 6–102).

Step 3. Make the following selections:
- **Image** is selected at the bottom of the window to see the image to be worked on.
- **Preview** is selected as **Black Matte.** This will black out any area NOT selected so the designer can view exactly what color range is being edited.

Step 4. Using the eyedropper tool on the right, the designer can create the selection by clicking on the colors in the image window or directly on the image file. The plus eyedropper will add colors to the selection; the minus eyedropper will subtract hues form the selection.

Step 5. The **Fuzziness** option controls the growing of the hue color selection. Start on 0 and drag it higher to see the difference.

Step 6. Select all the colors in the range necessary and choose **OK.** The area color range needed is now specifically selected and can be filled or edited.

A Note on Color Reducing/Editing of Photographs

Reducing colors in photographs is an interesting idea. Editing and manipulating color in photographs can make them useful for storyboards. A designer needs to think ahead about just how these photos will be used. When color reduced they can begin to look like artwork. Use the above techniques to edit the photos and try different filters to get the desired effect intended.

Creating Multiple Colorways

Photoshop has no tool for the express development of colorways. The fastest and easiest way to accomplish this task is as follows:

Technique #1

Step 1. Go to the **Image** menu and choose **Duplicate** to create a copy of the image.

Step 2. Using the Bucket, Brushes, and Selection tools edit individual areas of colors.

Step 3. Using the Magic Wand tool (Figure 6–103), double-click on the tool to see the options:
- Set the Magic Wand **Tolerance** to "0."
- Set **Anti-aliased** to unchecked.
- Select **Use All Layers,** if there are layers in the image and the color to be selected is on all layers.
- Select **Contiguous** if the area of color to be selected is a single shape of color. If the color to be selected is in many separate areas of the design, deselect contiguous.

Step 4. Using the wand, select the area of color to be edited

Step 5. Once selected, the area can be filled with the Fill command or Bucket tool, painted in with brushes, drawn in, or otherwise edited.

Technique #2

A second way to edit a color in a file is "globally," using Indexed Mode and the Color Table.

Step 1. Have the image to be edited open.

Step 2. If the image is in RGB Mode, change it to Indexed Mode. To do this, go to the Image menu, select **Mode** and select **Indexed Mode.**

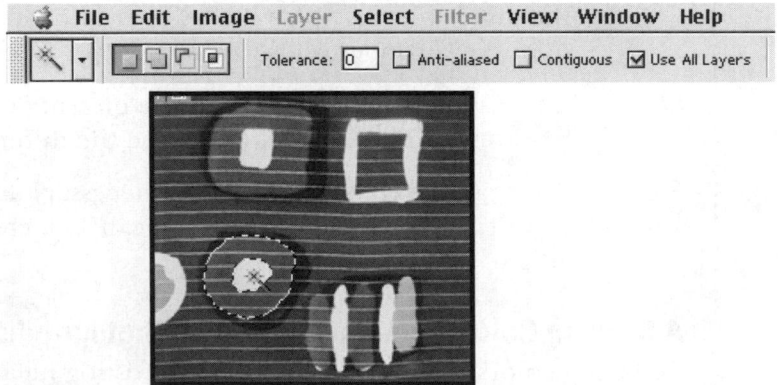

FIGURE 6–103
Magic wand selection

Notes...

Step 3. Going back to the **Image** menu, select **Mode** and go to **Color Table** (Figure 6–104).

Step 4. In the open **Color Table**, select the color to be edited by clicking on it with the mouse (Figure 6–105).

Step 5. The active Color Picker will show. Select the needed color.

HINT: If the color can be targeted in the Color Table, click on it in the image using the Eyedropper from the Color Table. The selected color will be highlighted.

Building a Seasonal Palette from Scratch

Many designers prefer to set up a color palette in the beginning of the season and then continue to use and edit this palette as the season progresses. To create a palette, follow these steps:

Step 1. Go to the **Window** menu and select **Show Swatches**.

Step 2. This will open a default swatch palette (Figure 6–106).

Step 3. In the swatch options on the top right choose **Replace Swatches**.

Step 4. Select on the CD enclosed with this book the **New Swatches** file (Figure 6–107).

Step 5. This window starts off with white and black (Figure 6–108). The Swatch window is now empty so the designer can add any custom colors to be saved. This palette can now be opened into the Color Table window or the Swatch window, depending on how the designer is working.

Step 6. Select an individual color chip and enter in the color needed.

Step 7. Continue this process until all the needed colors are entered.

Step 8. Save this palette. The designer will need to open it to select the colors with which to design.

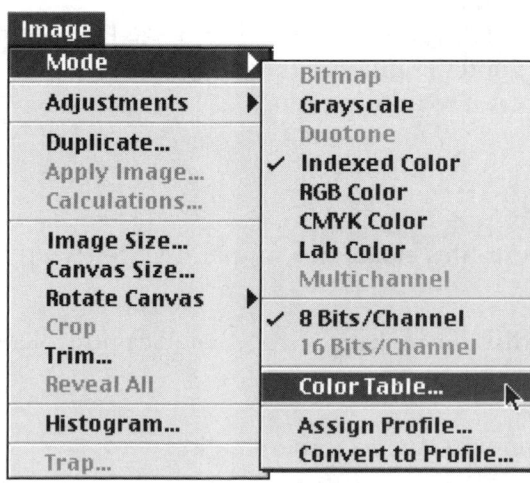

FIGURE 6–104
Color table mode

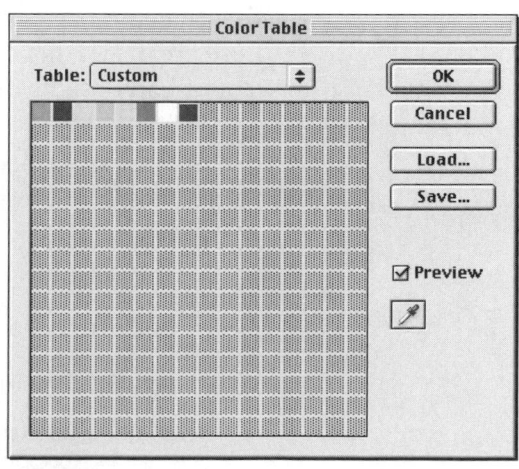

FIGURE 6–105
Color table

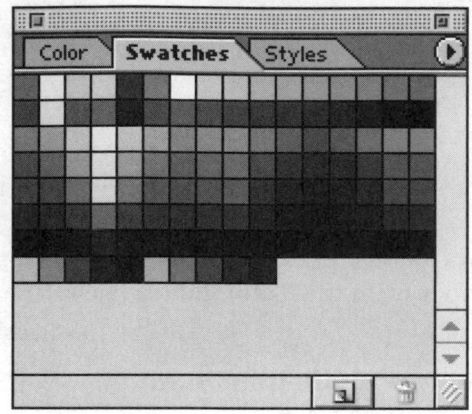

FIGURE 6–106
Default swatch palette

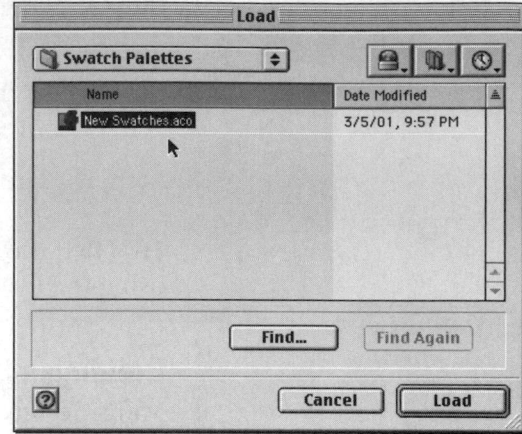

FIGURE 6–107
Select new swatches file

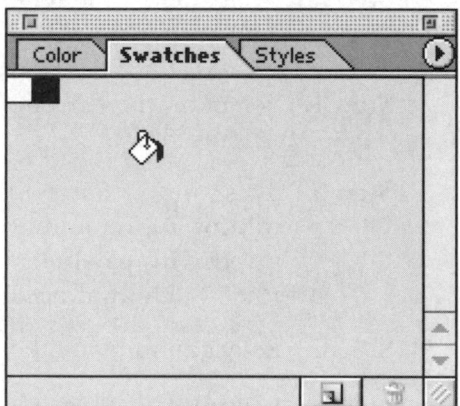

FIGURE 6–108
Empty swatch window

Now that the basics of designing with color in Photoshop have been discussed, there are a few rules to follow for good design that need to be reviewed. There are a lot of bad designs out there. Try not to add to them.

Design Tips for Using Color

- Don't overdesign, keep your files clean and simple. (KISS—Keep it sweet and simple!)

- For processing time and disk space, keep files as small as possible.

- Be sure you save "versions" of your files.

- Make a backup of whatever you give to someone else!

- Don't cover mistakes or changes with white boxes or otherwise. Delete the items you don't want instead!

- Pay attention to the file format, so others can reopen the file easily.

- In fact, ask the person printing what file format and version they want you to save in.

- Don't forget that vector images can be scaled easily, while raster or bitmap cannot.

- Check the page layout, color mode, and font selection. Include a note with the file with these specifications to avoid any unnecessary surprises.

- EPS file font should be converted to outlines.

- Send a preliminary hard copy with the file.

- Check, double-check, and check again that you have done all of the above!!!

Now a few tips on file size, compression, and conversion. Photoshop can be a great design tool, but it can be frustrating to the designer when they run into a file size issue or even a format issue. Remember these points, and time as well as aggravation will be saved.

File Size, Compression, and Conversion

- Remember only Adobe Photoshop native file format will allow you to save a file with all the layers open.

- EPS is a file format that is useful for sharing files between Photoshop, Illustrator, PageMaker, and QuarkXPress. This file can also be used to save a clipping path in Adobe Photoshop.

- When you convert a .psd or the Photoshop native file format to another file format, you will have to flatten the layers. Translation: You can no longer work on those layers. It is always good to make a backup of the .psd file in order to have editing access to the design if you need to!

- The most common file format is TIFF. TIFF is great for RGB and CMYK and is supported by both the Mac and PC. One additional thought: if you save your file as a TIFF and the file has layers, don't forget in earlier versions of Adobe Photoshop, TIFF will flatten all the layers. In version 7, be sure you check to include the layers in your file.

We thought it may be helpful at this time to provide you with a quick reference glossary of the relevant terminology associated with digital designing.

Computer Graphics Terminology

Aliasing: Also known as "jagged edges." The appearance of a "stair-step" or "jagged edges" on a bitmap image or text. In a drawing program, try drawing a diagonal line in a fairly wide pen point and you will notice the jagged stair-steps. (See also Bitmap and Dithering.)

Anchor Point: Also known as end points. This point can represent the beginning or end of a line segment. These can appear hollow when not selected or shaded when activated.

Application: A set of programs used to accomplish a specific task.

Bezier: This can refer to a pen/tool or a curved line. This tool option is found in most drawing programs. It permits the designer to create a line segment that when activated, can convert into a "curved line."

Bit: Basic unit of measurement.

Bitmap: A pixel-by-pixcl image created in a raster-based program. This can also be associated with file extension used for bitmap images such as TIFF, PICT, GIF, and some EPS files. The bitmap images often have gritty, grainy, or jagged outlines, because these images are created on a "fine grid system." A fine grid system is necessary to depict the image and all aspects of the image, including hue, color (RGB, CMYK), intensity, and saturation. Fonts may also be "bitmap." When the font is enlarged, you can clearly see the "stair-step jagged edges" on the lettering. (See also Aliasing.)

Blend: The progression of shapes, objects, or colors often associated with terms like gradient or fountain fills.

Cache: (Pronounced cash) This feature is the amount of fast memory that stores information that is frequently used, which translates into faster processing speeds.

CAD/CAM: Computer-aided designing, computer-aided manufacturing. Sometimes the terms are interchangeable. For example, in fashion designing, you can use the computer to both aid in the design of a garment or a line and set up detailed instructions for the computer to aid in the manufacturing of the garment or line.

Case Sensitive: Some programs are *very* sensitive to the way commands are typed. For example, the word "PASSWORD" and the word "password" are very different to a case-sensitive program. If you are working with a case-sensitive program and you do not enter data exactly, this may account for some frustration you may be experiencing in entering a program or in executing a command.

CD: A circular disk that stores programs and data.

CD-ROM: Compact disk, read-only memory. This is usually a drive on your computer and frequently is labeled the "M" drive.

Click: The action of depressing the mouse to activate or issue a command. This refers to accessing the right, left, and center buttons on the mouse including single- and double-click actions.

Clip Art: Figures that are available—included or sold separately and often stored on a CD or disk. Clip art can often be modified in a variety of ways to enhance a document or graph. Clip art can also be created by the designer and stored.

Clipboard: This is an area of storage used by the computer when using such commands as cut, copy, and paste.

Closed Path: Also known as shape.

CMYK: Cyan, magenta, yellow, and black.

Color Book: A hard copy of your colors calibrated for your printer and useful in color matching.

Colorway: A series of color choices made by the designer to indicate the "season's" color selection for the line.

Control Key: The abbreviation on this key is "Ctrl." There are usually two Control keys on the computer keyboard and they can be found on the right and left of the keyboard. This key is used with other keys to issue commands to the computer software programs.

Copy: This is a frequently used command in computers. The command will copy what you direct it to copy. For example, if you use a phrase over and over, rather than type the phrase each time you use it, you can drag the mouse over the phrase, command the computer to "copy" the phrase, and then you can "paste" the phrase where you want in the document.

Crosshair: X-like symbol used when cursor changes on the screen when drawing objects. (See also Cursor.)

Cursor: This is a symbol on the monitor that indicates where the user must begin or where the work stopped. The cursor can take the icon format of an "I" beam, an "arrow," a "pointer," a "hand," an "hourglass," a "question mark," or a "blinking underscore or I beam."

Cut: A process that cuts out text/data. If the user doesn't want to eliminate the section of text but simply wants to move it, the function is often combined with the paste function. This means that the user may cut out a section of text and then paste that text to another area in the document. This is a great time-saver and saves the user from retyping data.

Default: Actions or assumptions the computer will automatically make for you, unless you issue other instructions. For example, the default for most workspace is "portrait" or $8.5'' \times 11''$. There is also the ability to alter your Preferences and desktop tools. We suggest you refer to the Help menu or your software owner's manual to edit these options.

Default Drive: Sometimes this is known as the area of the computer automatically assigned for storage. Typically, it is an area, such as a hard drive or designated disk drive, that has been designated by the user for data storage.

Desktop: This can be a blank screen, background, or actual work space. It should be noted that when you open a new file in most graphic programs, the actual "blank page" and not the "gray area" will be what is saved to a disk or printed on a hard copy. The gray area outside the page is great for "practicing" and then moving that work onto the actual page to be saved or printed.

Dialog Box: See Menu.

Digitizer: A graphic input tool that converts an image into digital information for the computer to utilize.

Direction Handles: Used to reshape curves or curved points. Clicking the mouse on the object/line you wish to rotate its position can activate its handles.

Direction Points: Indicating the end on direction handles when reshaping curve segments.

Dithering: Smoothing the pixels (dots) of a black-and-white image to smooth out the "jagged edges." (See also Aliasing and Bitmap.)

Double-click: Firmly and rapidly depressing the mouse button twice. Used for activating a program icon or any other command that may require a yes or enter response.

Download: Transferal of information from one computer to another.

dpi: Dots per inch. This term is synonymous with scanners and printers. The higher the number, the clearer the resolution—for example, 300 dpi, 600 dpi.

Drag: Mouse motion of depressing the left or right buttons located on the mouse while simultaneously moving the mouse from one location to another.

Drag and Drop: A click and continuous depression of the mouse on an item, icon, or image will enable you to "drag" that selection and "drop" the selection to another location by releasing the mouse.

End Points: See Anchor Point.

Exit: To quit or shut down a program.

Export: Sending a file from one program, system, and/or computer to another.

File Extension: This refers to the three characters following the name of a file. This identifies what kind of file and the type of program used to generate the file.

File Format: This indicates how a file has been set up for retrieval, exporting, or printing. For example, if you are working in Adobe Photoshop, this program uses a "native" extension code of .psd.

Fill: Associated with an open or closed path (shape) frequently used to indicate "filling" with paint, color, or pattern.

Filter: A term associated with Adobe products that are special effects; these can be text or graphics used to overlap objects.

Fly-Out Menu: See Menu.

Font: Text character generated on the computer that can be categorized by (1) typeface or name, such as Ariel or Signature, (2) style, such as **BOLD,** or *italic*, and (3) weight and point size, such as 8, 14, 24.

Foreground: In the case of multitasking or multiple windows open, this indicates the window that is "activated." In a graphic program it can indicate an image, object, text, or fill.

Function Key: These keys, which are located on the top of your keyboard, are also called "hot keys." These are "shortcut" keys that issue commands such as "select-all" by merely touching just that one key. Check your computer and/or program for what each key represents.

Gouache: A heavy, strong opaque watercolor or other style paint.

Gradient: A type of fill of two or more colors, which can be graduated linearly or radially.

Graphics: Pictures or charts.

Greeking: Filling an area with text that is for the purpose of "showing text" not showing text for its content.

Grid: Useful option that is a series of dots that enable the designer to align or measure objects, images, or text. This option may be toggled on or off to lay out a design.

Group: Two or more objects that can be combined to form one object or one "idea."

Guide: This useful feature can be lines or rulers, which can be toggled on and off to view on the screen. It will assist the designer to align, position, or even measure distance between objects. They are "invisible" on hard copy.

Halftone: Usually this term is associated with a black-and-white image.

Handles: The selection icon is represented by "small black-filled boxes" outlining an image, object, or text. It can be activated for editing purposes.

Hierarchical Menu: These menus are sequential, which means you make one selection and then another selection (menu) appears. For example, in the case of "Save As," your next choice is where to save.

Hue: The name of a color such as red, blue, or green.

I-Beam: See Cursor.

Icon: A small picture or symbol on the screen representing a task or function.

Import: Bring data from one program into another.

Ink-jet Printer: A printer that uses a nozzle device to spray the ink onto the paper.

Input Devices: A device for inputting data into the computer. For example, keyboard, light pen, mouse, digitizer, or scanner, just to name a few.

Insertion Point: See Cursor.

Join: The process of connecting end points in lines within an object.

Kerning: Adding or deleting space between text characters.

Landscape: The orientation (direction) of a document or image. This is a horizontal document typically 11″ × 8.5″.

Laser Printer: A printer utilizing a beam of light to transfer information and images from the computer onto paper.

Layer: Computer concept that is comparable to a designer using acetate sheets to distinguish "layers" of a design that has been created in a series of steps. This feature can be edited, removed, or printed.

Light Pen: A graphic device that permits the designer/user to interface directly with the computer.

Line: An open path between two end points.

Line Art: Drawings that are created without halftones for the purpose of printing on low-resolution printers.

Marquee: This option, also known as a bounding box, is typically found by using the mouse to activate the "selection tool or pointer" and then dragging the cursor over and around the area, object, image, or text you want to isolate for editing purposes.

Mask: To cover or drape an object or character with an overlapping pattern.

Maximize: This option permits you to "enlarge a screen and/or window" to full size for viewing and editing purposes. It is typically indicated as a "clear block icon" on the top right of your screen and/or document. Clicking the mouse inside the "clear block icon" activates this option.

Menu: List of choices or options. There are several versions as well as a variety of different names associated with the term menu. Examples include:
- Pull-down
- Pop-up
- Fly-out
- Icon
- ? (Help) F4
- Item
- Bar
- Submenu
- List Box
- Message Box
- Dialog Box

Menu Bar: On-screen (visible) text or graphic list of options.

Message Box: This is a list of choices similar to a list box or dialog box.

Minimize: This option permits you to "shrink the size of a screen and/or window." This is generally an icon made to look like an "underscore or underline," located in the top portion of your screen and/or document.

Mouse: A handheld input device that rolls across a flat surface and is activated by a series of moves—drag and clicking operations to input and manipulate data, which correspond to the data viewed simultaneously upon the screen. Other terms associated with mouse are Mouse Button, Mouse Pad, and Mouse Action.

Object: A shape or line that can be manipulated and/or isolated to manipulate independently within the design.

Object-Oriented Drawing: The creation of a digital image that is mathematically represented as lines or shapes on a 2- or 3-dimensional space.

Open Path: A line or path with two end points.

Orientation: Used to indicate the direction of the work space/page layout. Landscape orientation means that the page is a horizontal layout; portrait orientation means that the page is used vertically.

Output Device: Equipment such as printers and plotters used to produce a tangible representation of work generated on the computer.

Path: A single line segment or a series of segments.

Pattern: A repeat design that can also be used for filling an object. Can be manually generated or an existing piece of clip art. This can also be converted for use as Pattern Tile.

Peripheral Equipment: External hardware attached to the computer.

Pixel: Smallest portion of the image—similar to a dot or point of light.

PMS: Pantone Matching System. This is an industry standard system for defining and matching color.

Pointer: See Cursor. This tool can be used to activate an area and is often referred to as the Selection Tool.

Portrait: The orientation (direction) of a document or image, using a vertical page layout or work space, typically 8.5″ × 11″.

Printers: Hardware used in "printing" a hard copy of what was viewed on the screen or saved on the computer. Types of printers include dot matrix, bubble jet, ink-jet, laser, or drum.

Pull-down Menu: Similar to a window shade, this menu when "pulled-down" offers a variety of functions or other options for the user to perform. In many graphics programs this menu can be left open on the screen. In addition, it often offers additional "fly-out" menus offering additional selections.

RAM: Random access memory. The computer's primary "working" memory. This information is stored and accessible but is lost when the computer is shut off. This is similar to our short-term memory.

Raster: Type of computer image. (See also Bitmap.)

Resolution: The clarity and quality of the viewing monitor, actual screen image display, or printer output. The range could be categorized as high or low.

RGB: The primary colors red, blue, and green.

ROM: Read-only memory. Unlike RAM (random access memory), ROM represents information that is permanently written on a computer chip and it will always remember the commands or functions it needs to perform.

Rotate: The ability to select an object or line to a specified number of degrees either by inputting a number such as 45 degrees or by manually "eyeballing" the amount of "tilt."

Ruler: These guides are located at the top and/or sides of the screen. They enable the designer to render an image that is perfectly aligned and scaled. These guides can be activated by a simple toggle on and off command and then accessed or "grabbed" to a specific on-screen location.

Scale: The ability to resize the object, line, or group of objects.

Scanner: Equipment that reads text, photos, or other images directly into the computer to be enhanced, manipulated, or modified by the designer/user. Files can be opened in a word processing program, graphics program, loaded on the Web, or sent electronically via e-mail or Fax.

Scroll: This action or option permits the designer to move through the screen, text, image, graphic, document, or page layout by using the cursor or keypad. Other terms or icons associated with the term scroll are:
- Page Up
- Page Down
- Home
- End
- The directional "Arrow keys"
- "Arrows"
- Icon
- Scroll Bar
- Scroll Box
- Select Browse Object
- Next Page

Selection Tool: This tool is often in the form of an "arrow" or "pointer" that activates an area by highlighting, which can be seen in the form of "shading, dotted outline, or a motion or flickering outline." Typically, the mouse is used to activate this tool. Keystrokes can also be used but they are considered cumbersome.

Service Bureau: Commercial printing service used to print a variety of files, but typically known for doing camera-ready work.

Shear: The skewing of an object. These handles permit you to slant the object a variety of different directions.

Skew: Alter the appearance of an image in diagonal or horizontal directions.

Software Programs: Application or instructions that tell the computer what to do.
- Shareware
- Public Domain
- Plug-In
- Freeware
- Proprietary
- Copyrighted
- Pirated
- Specific purpose software
- Integrated software

Status Bar: This can often be located on the top portion of your screen and can indicate everything from the font style selected to the drawing tool used.

Status Line: Generally located on the bottom of your screen, it indicates everything from the location of your mouse, last typed line/character of text, or even the tool you are currently using.

Storage: This indicates areas or devices that are designated for retaining information. They can be temporary or permanent. Examples include:

- Hard drive
- Floppy disk
- Zip disk
- Magnetic tape
- CD
- Servers

Style: A typeface alternative such as **bold,** underline/underscore, or *italic* that is used to enhance a font. (See also Font.)

Submenu: Additional options available that relate or are relevant to the previous menu.

Title Bar: The name of the program and file at the top of the screen.

Toolbar: In most programs this is where the "tools" used by the designer are located.

Tutorial: A sample of "how" the program works. This is usually a mini-exercise, using step-by-step instructions that walk you through the operation of a program. Like the Help menu, this feature comes with the program, but often is not installed because of the amount of space required on the hard drive to run such an application.

Tweak: To clean up, edit, modify, and cajole settings, images, and files.

Undo: This function can be your best friend, and it is done in most programs by selecting the Undo command to undo your last step, command, or function. Several graphic programs permit you to "go back" several functions.

Ungroup: To break apart an image or collection of objects in order to work with them individually.

Vector Images: These are object-oriented images that are either basic geometric shapes or objects created with a Bezier tool/curve. The result is objects or images that are clear regardless if resizing or other editing functions are performed on them. (Note: Typically, we contrast bitmapped images to vector. Each has a different function and purpose. Often we attempt to make them do something they are not designed to do or are not best suited for.)

White Space: The area of the document left blank to enhance the image by adding focal emphasis.

WYSIWYG: "What you see is what you get." What is on the screen/monitor is what will print.

X Axis: Object width.

Y Axis: Object height.

Zoom: The ability to view the artwork created "up close" to clean up details. This tool appears as an icon that resembles a magnifying glass because that is what it does—"magnifies the work."

You are now ready to tackle the actual rendering of fabric in our next chapter!

7 Rendering the Basics

Over the next four chapters we will take you on a journey of rendering fabrics, prints, and finishes using Adobe Photoshop 7. Each chapter is designed to build upon the skills and techniques you learned in the preceding chapters. In Chapter 7 you will learn how to render the basic fabrics including:

- Solid fabrics including knits, wovens, and other nonwovens
- Specific plains, twill, satins, and wovens
- Foundational knit patterns such as jersey, purl, rib, and cable knits
- Rendering novelty yarns

In Chapter 8 you will learn about rendering other common fabrics:

- Stripes
- Checks
- Plaids
- Advanced woven patterns and common fabric finishes

In Chapter 9 you will review the secrets of researching and rendering single motifs and repeat patterns for prints.

In Chapter 10 you will learn about more advanced techniques and prints such as:

- Furs
- Leathers
- Skins
- Other animal prints
- Camouflage

- Jacquards
- Simple motifs
- Florals
- Toiles
- Tessellation or geometric repeats

Important Announcement and Disclaimer

When developing these next few chapters and the accompanying series of practical exercises, every care has been given to write the procedures in a clear and understandable fashion. It is assumed that you already have worked through the early exercises in Chapter 4 and have a comfortable working knowledge of all the material covered in Chapters 3, 4, and 5.

To write the procedures in any other manner would have belabored the information and increased the number of written steps to the point of actually causing unnecessary confusion to the reader. All of these exercises have been written to give you ample opportunity to experience the wide range of techniques that can be used.

The purpose of the exercises is to reinforce the basic skills of Adobe Photoshop as applied by a fashion, textile, or interior designer. If you come to this book having learned Adobe Photoshop's tools in a different context, you may need to put aside what you already think you know—how something should be done—and be willing to learn another way to accomplish a task. We heartily encourage you to make notes in the book as you complete each exercise. Note what works best for you. Frequently, you will discover this is not necessarily the right or wrong way to do something, but rather a good, better, best scenario. For example, when you get to Chapter 8 on rendering plaids, there are several procedures that are short and sweet but others may involve steps that appear to be a bit more tedious. In reality, sometimes taking the longer route affords you more control over the design process. If the shortcuts work for you, by all means apply them to your work!

We will give notice about when a technique or method is preferred over another. Therefore, the use of the designer's critical thinking skills to modify the exercises to suit a given project is to be expected. If you find that you are experiencing extreme difficulty following along in any exercises, we suggest that you go back and review the basic tools and techniques covered in the earlier chapters and then attempt the practical application exercise. Frequently, a student or designer may attempt to rush the design process without adequately knowing the software, and the results can be a disappointment or an unnecessary time of frustration.

The last thing you need to do is to become frustrated. Try getting up from the computer for a small break, or perhaps go on to another exercise and come back later to the one that is challenging you. If you have the luxury of discussing the outcome objectives with someone who has successfully mastered the assignment, this to can help considerably. Trying to go on to more difficult exercises before you are ready is like trying to build upper floors without successfully completing the structural foundation first.

Although these exercises have been classroom tested, we welcome your feedback via e-mail at our website—www.ComputersandFashion.com.

Instead of the usual list of relevant terms to look for, we begin to learn actual digital application in Adobe Photoshop and include a specific list of fabrics you will be learning to render.

- Common Fabrics (cottons, linens, wools, and silks)

- Specific Methods of Construction (including rendering wovens and knits)

  - Plain weave
  - Rib weaves
  - Basket weaves
  - Twill
  - Herringbone
  - Dobby

  - Pile
  - Satin
  - Jacquards
  - Jersey
  - Ribs
  - Cables

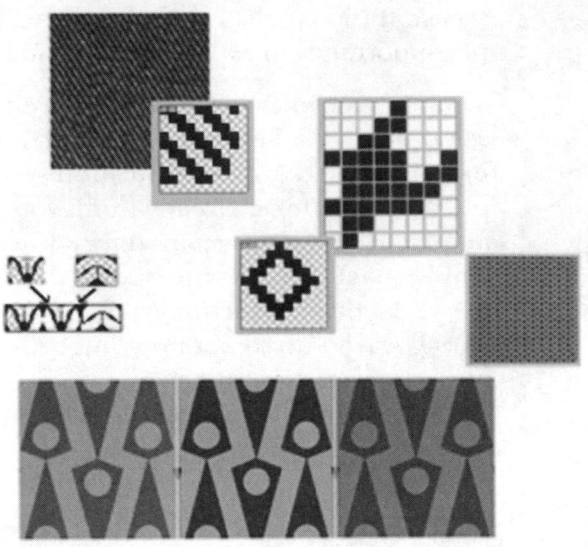

FIGURE 7–1
Examples of surface textures for fabric using Adobe Photoshop

- Surface Finishes and Yarns
  - Napped
  - Moiré
  - Embossed
  - Plissé

We have included a complete list of fabrics you will be rendering in the following three chapters. They are listed alphabetically and not necessarily according to fabric structure. (See Figure 7–1 for samples of what you will be learning in this chapter.)

Fabrics Included in this Section

- Batiste
- Brocade/damask-jacquard
- Burlap
- Camouflage
- Canvas
- Corduroy
- Cotton
- Crepe de chine
- Denim
- Dotted swiss
- Ethnic prints
- Faille
- Felts
- Flannels
- Furs
- Gabardine
- Gingham
- Herringbone
- Houndstooth
- Ikat
- Jersey
- Leathers
- Linen
- Madras
- Mock Croc
- Moiré

- Muslin
- Naugahyde
- Novelty prints
- Period prints
- Plissé
- Piqué
- Rib knit

- Satin
- Snakeskin
- Taffeta
- Tartan plaid
- Terry cloth
- Toile de Jouy
- Wool suiting

Beginning with the Basics—Rendering Solid-Colored Fabrics

Now the excitement begins. In this chapter you finally put to practice all that you have been learning these last few chapters. All of your textile savvy and Photoshop skills will be put to the test as you begin to render and create fabric digitally.

As you have discovered, many times fabrics used for prints are made from very specific types of yarns in addition to specific methods of fabric construction, such as a knit or woven. Therefore, careful attention to the subtle nuances is essential in re-creating each fabric's distinctive details.

In earlier chapters you learned that both fiber as well as yarns could be smooth, textured, or hairy. You further discovered that the type of weaves used in making cloth have very distinctive appearances that will have a direct outcome on the fabric's appearance, performance, and hand. This means you will need to capture the essence of these fabrics accurately in order to fool the viewer into "feeling" the cloth with their eyes. Therefore, as we begin this section, we have included several of the most common fabrics you may be called upon to render.

The fabrics we have selected to include are several of the more widely used fabrics for the apparel, accessories, footwear, domestics, and interior design industries.

Rendering fabrics has a variety of applications for the graphic artist, fashion designer, animator, or Webmaster. The fact is that fabric or textural elements *are* found today in ads, on greeting cards, shopping bags, in accurately rendering clothing for animation, and, of course, as backgrounds on web pages! Every designer is called upon at some point to render elements of the textural qualities found in fabric, and this text will be your reference guide in that process.

As you work through each of the exercises, we suggest that you jot down (in the note space provided) any other new ideas or applications of where or how you might apply these techniques. Don't forget to contact us at our website—tell us how you have been applying this information and share with us and our readers any new ideas you may have gleaned in your digital design journey (Figure 7–2).

www.ComputersandFashion.com

FIGURE 7–2
Website

Let's Start at the Beginning

A significant portion of fabric used in apparel applications is woven. In many cases, these fabrics are woven as a plain weave. This solid weave can then also serve as the ground for fabrics that will have a direct print applied to them later in the production process.

The most common choices for fabric constructions are plain and twill weaves, which enhance the realistic quality of your image. It is essential that your viewer understands the specific weave or yarn you are trying to convey. Simply filling a rendering with a solid blue color will certainly not convey the look or the feel of denim.

In the upcoming exercises, we will be guiding you through digitally rendering the tactile association of a fabric.

Rendering Woven Backgrounds for Fabric

The following set of instructions has been designed to aid you in the fabric construction method, such as in producing a knit or a woven fabric.

We have included a variety of exercises to help you apply your Photoshop knowledge with the textile information you learned in Chapters 1 through 4, to create realistic images that should impress even the most savvy of clients!

Rendering the Basic Woven Patterns

You may recall from Chapter 2 that a woven fabric is constructed of vertical (warp) yarns and horizontal (weft) yarns. These yarns are interconnected in a variety of different patterns on a loom to create the woven fabric. The most common woven patterns you will be called upon to render digitally are:

1. Plain weave, including basket and rib weaves
2. Twill weave, including a right twill, left twill, and herringbone
3. Satin
4. Pile
5. Dobby
6. Jacquard

Creating and Rendering Plain Weave Fabrics

The most common foundational pattern is a plain weave. Regardless of the woven pattern chosen, every substrate has its own distinctive hand and appearance. For example, plain weave cottons typically have a soft hand and smooth surface, whereas linens appear to have a slubbed or nubby textural quality to their appearance. Wools made in a plain weave generally have a napped or hairlike appearance. Capturing these qualities will be the focus of the next few exercises.

When you begin the exercises in Photoshop, don't forget to jot down any comments or insights you may glean in the space provided in the margin. You may want to save the file you are making into two separate file formats—the first as a native file format (.psd) with all the layers, and the second file as a JPEG file that you can use later for adding a digitally created surface print.

Each of the following exercises is designed to explore the capabilities of Adobe Photoshop and help you in digitally rendering the basic woven patterns. The techniques used in the exercises are a compilation of techniques you learned in Chapter 6—Photoshop Basics. The following exercises also employ the strategies of Chapter 4. Therefore, you must have a firm foundation of this knowledge in order to successfully go beyond replicating our examples. We trust that the combination of textile know-how and Photoshop skills will propel you in your progress to digitally render fabric and prints.

Adding Woven Structures

In the upcoming series of exercises you will discover how easy it is to add an already rendered fabric structure to your work. In several exercises you will be instructed to open the **Goodies Folder** on your CD and go to the **Sub Folder > Entitled > Fabric Structures**. There you will find several great examples of the basic woven and knitted structures you will be using on a regular basis when rendering fabric. The ability to transform a simple design into a specific fabric has been streamlined for you! You will also notice that in many of the exercises there are several alternative solutions for rendering a given fabric. Just as you may opt to use alternative roads to reach your destination, so too, when rendering fabric, you must decide what look you are going after and how much time is really necessary to render that feel or look.

One of the most unique features of this section on how to render fabrics and prints will be the way you will come to look at the software. You will soon discover that you will be rendering designs perhaps a little differently than a traditional graphic artist would. By applying the tools and techniques from Chapter 3 on the basics of Adobe Photoshop, however, we will be utilizing the tools and workflow strategies that best service a fashion or textile designer.

CD—Drag and Drop Fabric Structures

Another common way we will be adding texture to our images will require you to open the **CD> Goodies Folder> Fabric Structures Sub Folder>** and open a given fabric ground (Figure 7–3).

Often these files will be saved in a .psd or native Photoshop file format. These files will typically have two layers. The bottom ground layer will be in white and the second layer will be the actual fabric structure. These individual layers can be turned on or off so that you will be able to see the actual fabric structure in more detail.

You will then be instructed to drag and drop a copy of that fabric structure onto your actual follow-along project.

Other Applications and Insights:

_____

_____

_____

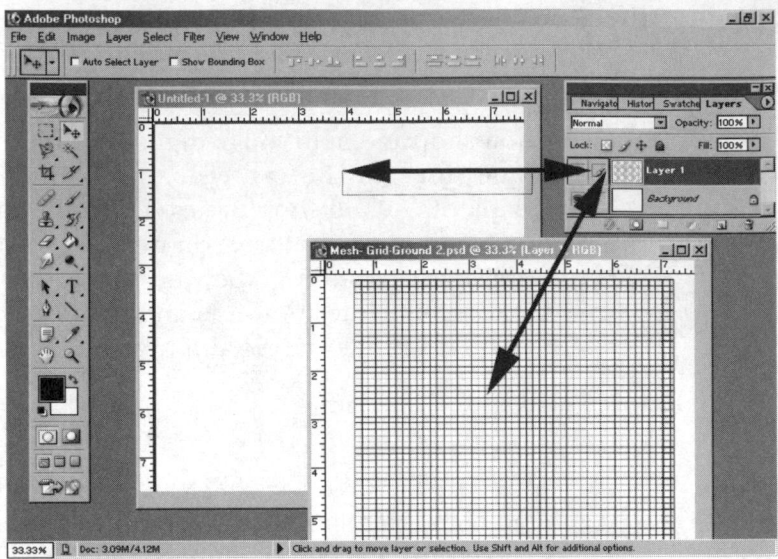

FIGURE 7–3
Fabric ground

Using Photoshop to Create Solids: A Review and Overview

Before we begin the exercises, we have included a brief review of how to begin to render solid-colored fabrics in Photoshop. Creating solid grounds is very fast and simple to do. We recommend that you keep in mind a few basics before you begin.

When it comes to filling your screen, be sure to always remember to buy yourself options for use later in the design process, such as the rules in Chapter 4 on workflow strategies. Always start new concepts on its own layer, save in layers that are labeled or annotated, save your files in versions, save often, and save in universal file formats.

When it comes to filling, the best tool to use is the Paint Bucket tool.

Beyond Making a Solid Color Fill:

Step 1. Start with a **New File** in the desired size in inches or pixels, 72–150 dpi, desired color mode—such as RGB, and start with a white background.

Step 2. Make a **New Layer** and name it **Ground**.

Step 3. Select the **Paint Bucket** tool. (See Figure 7–4.)

Step 4. Please note, if you are filling an object such as Flats, be sure to select each color to be used as Flats are being filled. The settings for the Paint Bucket tool need to be as follows: In 6.0 and later versions, the Attributes palette shows at the top of the window. In 5.5 and earlier versions, double-click on the Paint Bucket tool (Mac) or right-click on the tool (PC).
   a. **Fill**: Photoshop default will always fill with the foreground color, unless otherwise selected.
   b. **Mode: Normal**—Solid fill.
   c. **Opacity: 100%**—No transparency.

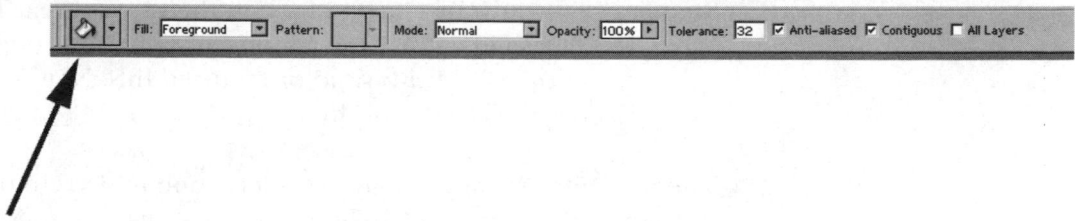

FIGURE 7–4
Paint bucket tool

FIGURE 7–5
Fill color

d. **Tolerance**: **0**—Fills only the color clicked on.

e. **Anti-aliased**: **OFF**—Will not anti-alias the edges of color (no blurs or blending where colors meet).

f. **Contiguous**: *Checked*—Will fill the color only into the specific area clicked on.

 Unchecked—Will fill the color in ALL the areas of the same color clicked on.

g. **Layers**: *Checked*—Will fill the color only on the active layer into the color clicked on.

h. *Unchecked*—Will fill the color on ALL the layers into the color clicked on. (See Figure 7–5.)

Step 5.   Click the **Paint Bucket** tool on the canvas area. The window will fill with a flat, solid color. This simple exercise shows how easy it can be to create multiple flats with solid or textured fills. Now, imagine building a whole presentation out of them.

The next alternative you may be called upon to do is to use the "Define Pattern," also covered in detail in Chapter 6. We have listed a quick review below:

Adding the Weave Structure or "Effect":

Step 1.   Open on the CD, the **Plain Weave** file in the **Structure** folder.

Step 2.   Choose **Select > All**.

Step 3.   Choose **Edit > Define Pattern**.

Step 4.   Add a new layer in between the two stripe layers.

Step 5.   Choose **Edit > Fill with Pattern**.

HINT: Try editing the weave with the options for Hue, Color, or Luminosity. The choice depends on the colors used, as well as the effect you want to get. The filter also allows the user to create real textural effects. For a brushed effect, try the Blur Filter combined with the Wind Filter. For a Wool effect, try the Noise Filter combined with the Blur Filter.

Other Applications and Insights:

_____

_____

_____

Freebies

The third method you may be using requires a series of very specific steps that require the incorporation of the Filter Menu alternatives, including using several of the leading off-the-shelf software plug-ins. Many of the most common plug-ins will be reviewed in more detail in Chapter 12.

However, because we recognize that many of you are already familiar with many of these companies, we determined that it was only logical to cite several examples of how these additional filters can enhance the Photoshop experience. There will be only minimal examples of this type of exercise, in order to better familiarize you with the other alternatives you have at your disposal as a designer.

Don't worry if you do not have the software on hand; many of the companies make the software at affordable prices. If you are currently a full-time student and can provide proof of attendance, you are eligible to purchase much of the software at considerably discounted prices at a company known as JourneyEd. Log on to www.JourneyEd.com and have a look! Or you can visit our website at www.ComputersandFashion.com. Sample trial versions of software are also located on the CD that comes with this text.

How to Render a Plain Weave 1
Rendering a solid-colored plain weave ground:
Plain Weaves

Begin by creating a simple horizontal stripe and a simple vertical stripe. These are the warp and weft of the plaid. The two files should be equal in size or divisible into each other. This will be so you end up with a complete repeat.

Step 1. Open a **New File** that is 5″ × 5″ or whatever the final repeat size of the stripe is needed. Select the bottom right corner of the window and drag to open the window so there is extra space around the paper area (Figure 7–6).

Step 2. Using the **Marquee** tool and starting from outside the canvas area, create a vertical selection across the space. To do this, start the click and drag from outside the paper area. This technique ensures selecting the area from the very top edge pixel to the very bottom edge (Figure 7–7).

Step 3. Fill the selection with a solid color using the Paint Bucket tool. Continue across the canvas to select narrow vertical stripes and to fill each with a color. The rulers can be used as a guide for the width of each stripe. This is the vertical column of the weave.

Step 4. Repeat Steps 1, 2, and 3 to create a horizontal stripe. It is done in the same way, but the Marquee stripes are selected horizontally. This will be the horizontal row of the weave (Figure 7–8).

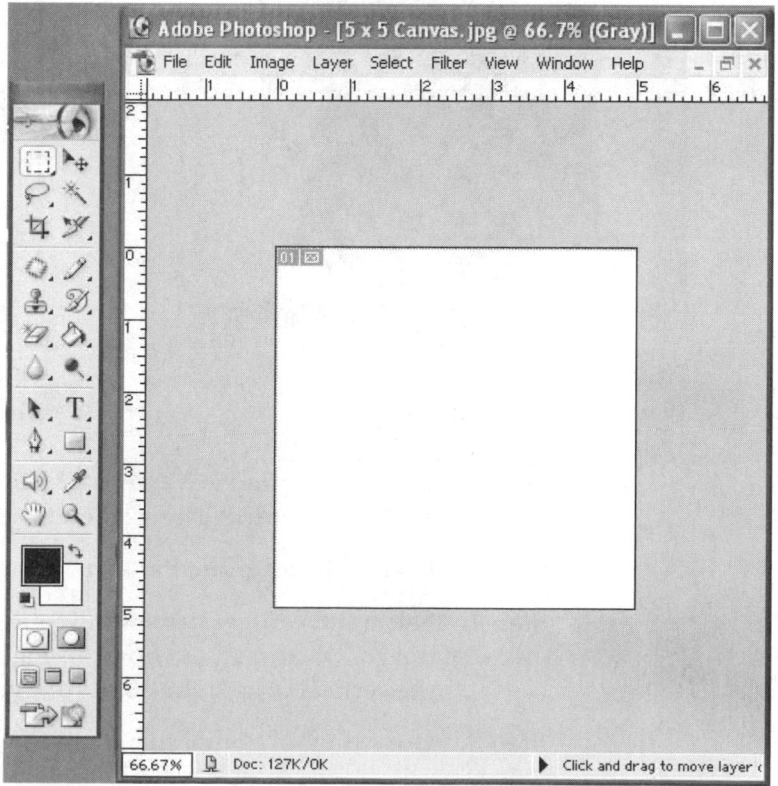

FIGURE 7–6
Open canvas

FIGURE 7–7
Drag of vertical marquee

FIGURE 7–8
Horizontal row of weave

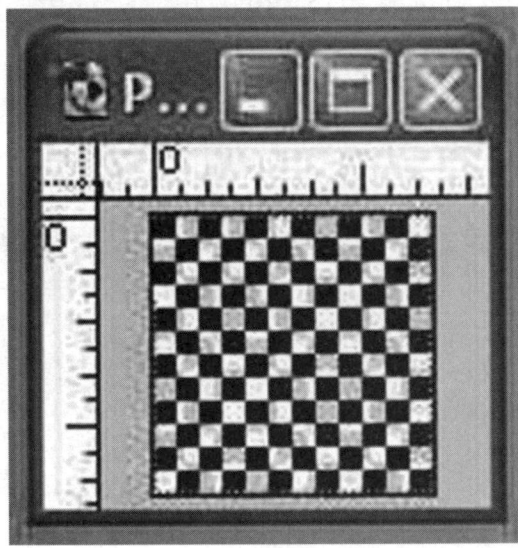

FIGURE 7–9
Plain weave structure

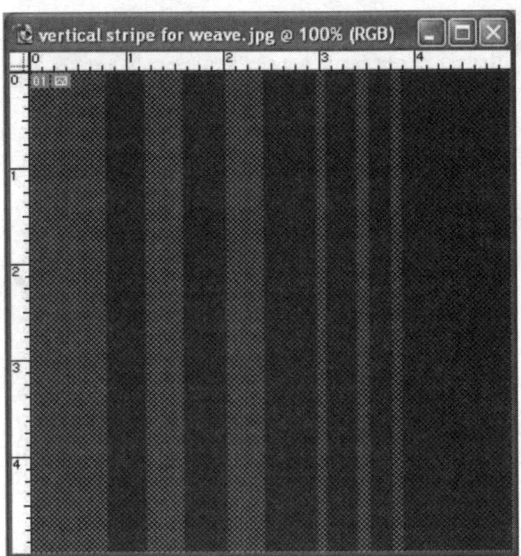

FIGURE 7–10
Vertical stripe

Step 5. Open the **Plain Weave** file in the **Structure** folder on the CD. In the open structure window, choose **Select>All** (Figure 7–9).

Step 6. Go to **Edit > Define Pattern**.

Step 7. Select the vertical stripe window and choose **Edit > Fill with Pattern**. The image will appear as shown in Figure 7–10 with the weave filling in over the vertical stripe. The colors of the stripe are showing through the weave.

Step 8. Go to the horizontal stripe window, choose **Select > All**, then **Edit > Copy**.

Step 9. Going back to the vertical stripe window, select the **Magic Wand** settings to uncheck **Contiguous** and **Anti-aliased**. Select "one area" of the black plain weave structure. All of the black "structure" should now be selected.

Step 10. Choose **Edit > Paste Into**. The weave is now complete.

HINT: Try editing the weave with the options for Hue, Color, or Luminosity. The choice depends on the colors used, as well as the effect you want to get. The filter also allows the user to create real textural effects. For a brushed effect, try the Blur Filter combined with the Wind Filter. For a Wool effect, try the Noise Filter combined with the Blur Filter.

Be sure to choose **Layers > Flatten** before adding any other filter effect on top of this layer or the whole weave will not be affected by them. You can opt to save the file as a JPEG and reopen the JPEG copy and begin to experiment with filter selections to add additional finishes or effects later, after you have completed the advanced instructions in the next two chapters.

How to Render a Plain Weave 2
Adding the Weave Structure or "Effect":

Step 1. Open the **Plain Weave** file in the **Structure** folder on the CD.

Step 2. Choose **Select > All**.

Step 3. Choose **Edit > Define Pattern**.

Step 4. Add a new layer in between the two stripe layers.

Step 5. Choose **Edit > Fill with Pattern**.

Step 6. Be sure to choose **Layers > Flatten** before adding any other filter effect on top of this layer if the filter will affect the entire design. Select a Filter to add a finish effect.

HINT: Options for Hue, Color, or Luminosity generally work well. The choice depends on the colors used, as well as the effect you want to get. Also the filter allows the user to create real textural effects. Remember, for a brushed effect, try the Blur Filter combined with the Wind Filter. For a Wool effect, try the Noise Filter combined with the Blur Filter.

Open Goodies CD > Fabric Structures > Plain Weave

Other Applications and Insights:

_____

_____

_____

How to Render a Plain Weave 3

Step 1. Open a **New File: 8.5 × 11 inches, RGB, 72–150 dpi, White Background**.

Step 2. Add a **New Layer** and fill with desired color. As you can see in Figure 7–11, we made a gradient of blue and white to add light and shadows to our fill.

Step 3. Go to **Filter > Texture > Texturizer** and select the following options: **Burlap > Scaling, 75 > Relief, 4 > Light Direction > Top**. Click **OK**. (See Figure 7–12.)

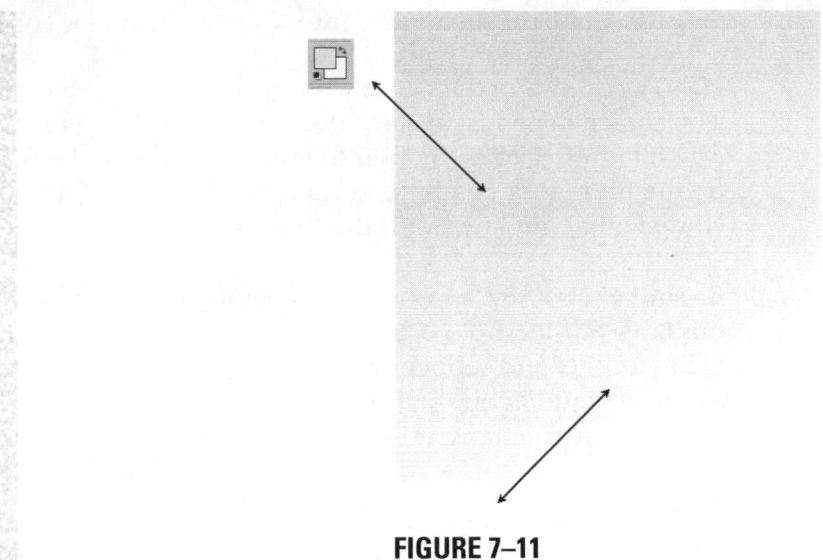

FIGURE 7–11
Gradient

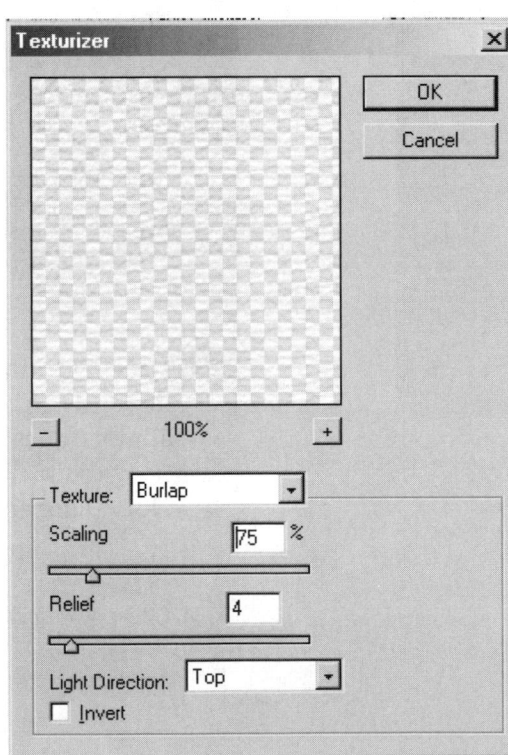

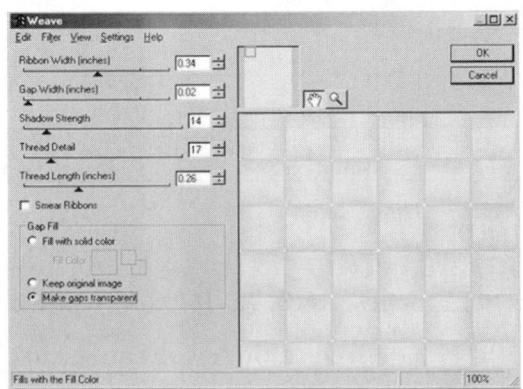

FIGURE 7–12
Plain weave 3

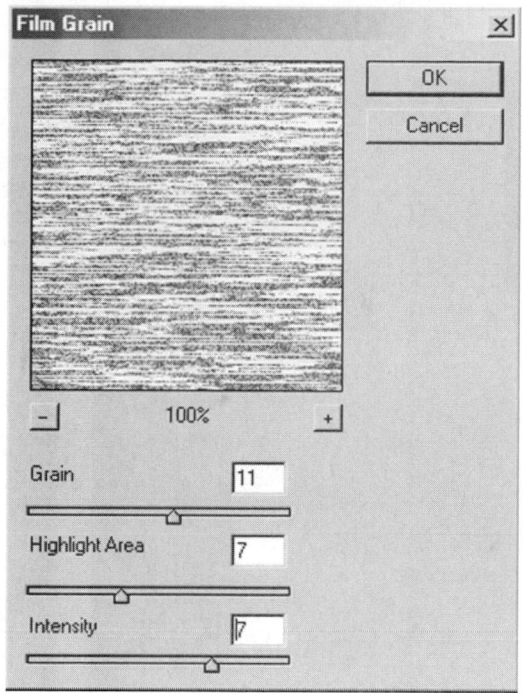

FIGURE 7–13
Film grain

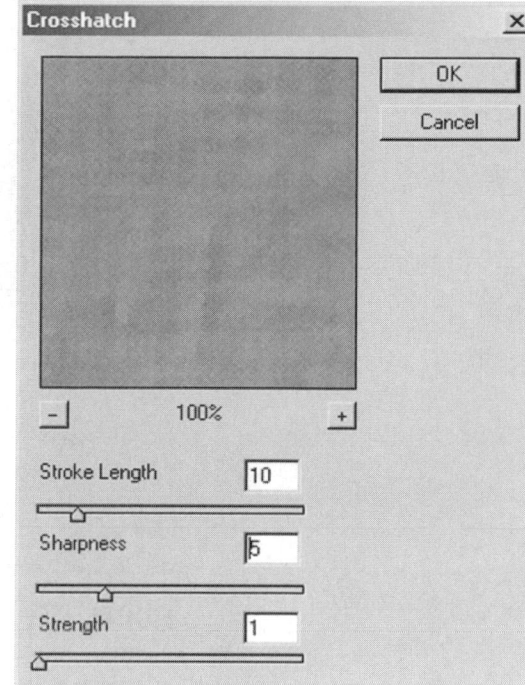

FIGURE 7–14
Crosshatch

Step 4. Name and save.

Other Applications and Insights:

_____

_____

_____

How to Render Cotton Batiste

Step 1. Open a **New File: 8.5 × 11 inches, RGB, 72–150 dpi, White Background.**

Step 2. Add a **New Layer** and fill with desired color.

Step 3. Duplicate Layer 2 and name **Plain Weave** in the **Layer Property** window.

Step 4. Go to **Filter** select **Artistic > Film Grain > Grain = 11, Highlighted Area = 7,** and **Intensity = 7.** Click **OK.** (See Figure 7–13.)

Step 5. From the **Filter** menu, select **Brush Strokes > Crosshatch > Stroke Length = 10, Sharpness = 5,** and **Strength = 1.** Click **OK.** (See Figure 7–14.)

Step 6. Name and save. (See Figure 7–15.)

Other Applications and Insights:

_____

_____

_____

FIGURE 7–15
Cotton batiste

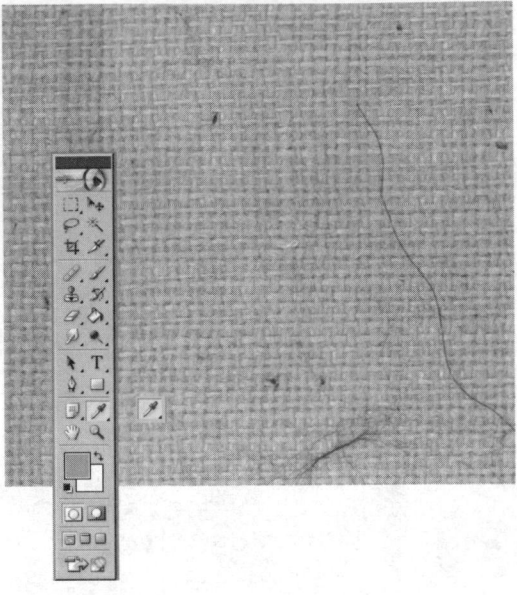

FIGURE 7–16
Eyedropper

How to Render Burlap

Step 1. Open a **New File** in the size needed for more than a repeat of the texture.

Step 2. Open the **Burlap Swatch** from the **Textile Swatch** CD and use the **Eyedropper** to pick up a similar color shade for your digital swatch. (See Figure 7–16.)

Step 3. Use the **Bucket Tool** to fill the window with the desired color.

Step 4. Go to **Filter > Texture** and select **Texturizer**.

Step 5. Select the settings to your preference. When selecting from the **Texture** options, select **Burlap**.

Step 6. Set **Scaling** to the size that the canvas texture will appear. The **Preview** window is a great guide for this. The higher the setting, the larger the texture.

Step 7. Select the desired **Relief** setting for the depth of the canvas texture. The higher the setting, the deeper the texture.

Step 8. Choose the **Light Direction**. Selecting from the left, right, top, or bottom will create a lined effect, where lighting from a corner, the bottom left for example, will have a crosshatch effect.

Step 9. The **Invert** option reverses the effect. Choose **OK**. (See Figure 7–17.)

Step 10. Name and save.

Other Applications and Insights:

_____

_____

_____

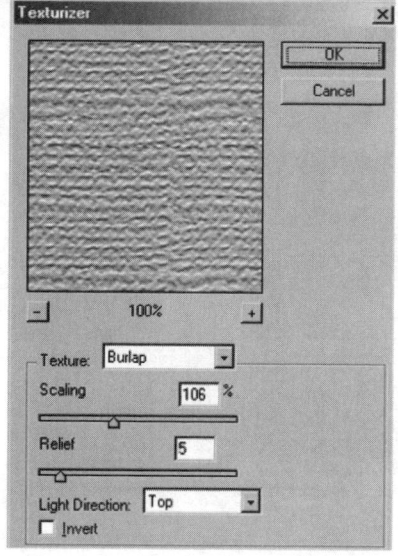

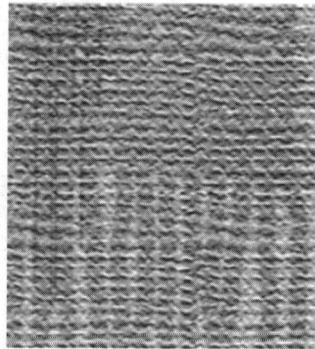

FIGURE 7–17
Invert

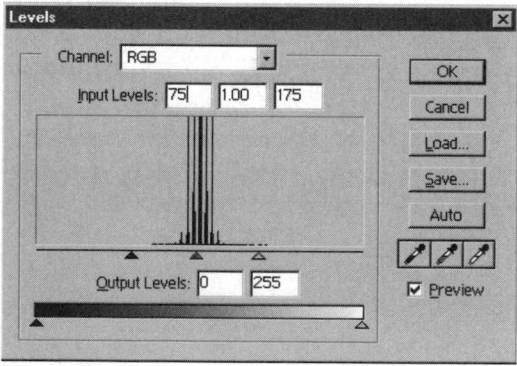

FIGURE 7–18
Adjust levels

How to Render Linen 1

Step 1. Open a **New File: 8.5 × 11 inches, RGB, 72–150 dpi, White Background**.

Step 2. Add a **New Layer** and fill with Black.

Step 3. Go to **Filter Noise > Monochromatic > Gaussian Blur 90 degrees**.

Step 4. From **Filter** select **Blur > Motion Blur > 90 degrees** and **50**.

Step 5. From **Filter** select **Blur > Motion Blur > 0 degree** and **50**.

Step 6. From **Filter** select **Stylize > Emboss > 133, 5, 170** and click **OK**.

Step 7. From **Image** select **Adjust Levels > 75, 1.00, 175**. Click **OK**. (See Figure 7–18.)

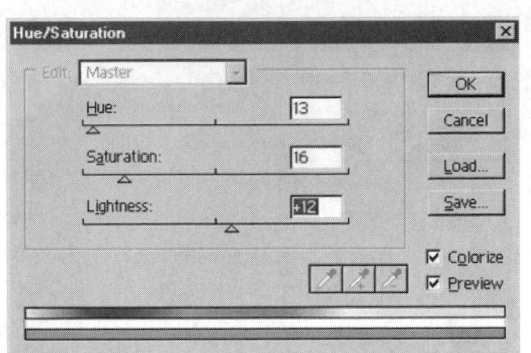

FIGURE 7–19
Hue/saturation

FIGURE 7–20
Dropping opacity

Step 8. From **Image** select **Adjust > Hue Saturation > Hue 13 > Saturation > 16 > Lightness > +12   35 > 3**. (See Figure 7–19.) Or adjust **Hue and Saturation** to suit.

Step 9. Experiment with dropping the opacity of the layer. (See Figure 7–20.)

Step 10. Name and save. (Do not flatten your file; instead, you may opt to save a JPEG copy for future use as ground fabric when rendering prints.)

Other Applications and Insights:

_____

_____

_____

How to Render Linen 2

Step 1. Open a **New File: 8.5 × 11 inches, RGB, 72–150 dpi, White Background.**

Step 2. Add a **New Layer** and fill with desired color.

Step 3. Make a **New Layer** and in the **Layer Property** menu, name the layer **Hatch Lines**.

Step 4. Use the **Color Picker** to select one shade darker than your original color from Layer 1.

Step 5. You can experiment with adding Marquee rectangles and fill with a deeper shade of your original color. Repeat this variation across the fabric—alternating vertical and horizontal boxes.

Step 6. Using the **Marquee** tool again, select the new group of hatch lines.

Step 7. Select **Edit** and **Define Pattern** and name the pattern **Linen Hatch Lines**.

Step 8. Make a **New Layer**, and select **Edit Fill** with the Hatch Lines pattern.

FIGURE 7–21
Rectangle
marquee tool

Step 9. You can opt to experiment with adding such Filters as **Noise > Add, Noise > Gaussian** and **Monochromatic**.

Step 10. Next, you may opt to experiment with **Opacity** on this new layer as well.

Step 11. Go to **Filter** and select **Blur > Motion Blur > Angle 0 > Distance 49** pixels.

Step 12. In Figure 7–21, you can see the results of choosing **Filter Menu > Texturizer > Burlap > Scaling 104 > Relief > 5, Light Direction > Top**.

Step 13. Name and save. (Do not flatten your file; instead, you may opt to save a JPEG copy for future use as ground fabric when rendering prints.)

Other Applications and Insights:

_____

_____

_____

How to Render Muslin

Step 1. Open a **New File: 8.5 × 11 inches, RGB, 72–150 dpi, White Background**.

Step 2. Add a **New Layer** and fill with desired natural eggshell color.

Step 3. Duplicate Layer 2 and name **Plain Weave** in the **Layer Property** window.

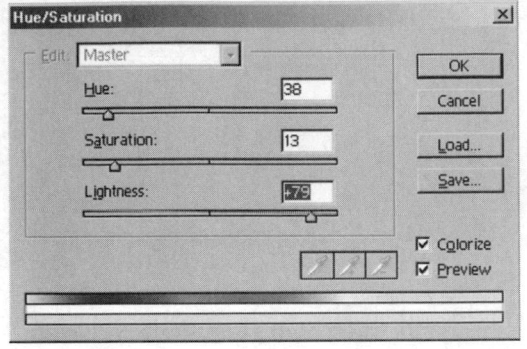

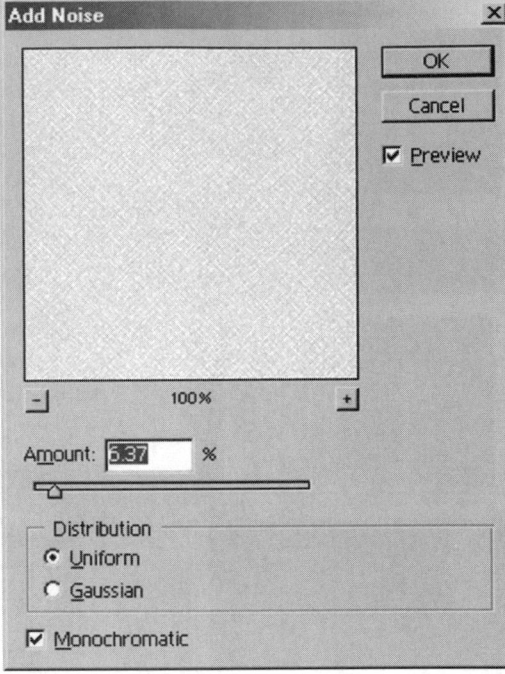

FIGURE 7–22
Adjust color

Step 4. Go to **Filter** and select **Artistic > Film Grain > Grain = 11, Highlighted Area = 7,** and **Intensity = 7.** Click **OK.**

Step 5. Select **Filter** and **Brush Strokes > Crosshatch > Stroke Length = 10, Sharpness = 5,** and **Strength = 1.** Click **OK.**

Step 6. We suggest that you adjust the color before attempting any other selections. Go to **Edit > Adjust > Hue & Saturation.** Click on the **Preview** button. Based on the shade of ivory we had originally, our choices were as follows: **Hue, 38 > Saturation, 13 > Lightness + 79.**

Step 7. Go to **Filter** and select **Noise > Add Noise.** Select **Experiment** with **Monochromatic** and **Gaussian** combinations. (See Figure 7–22.) Figure 7–22 shows what the fabric will look like after you adjust the color and add texture and noise.

Step 8. Name and save. You may again opt to make both a Native File format file and a JPEG copy to continue to experiment with additional filters and opacity options for later use.

Other Applications and Insights:

_____

_____

_____

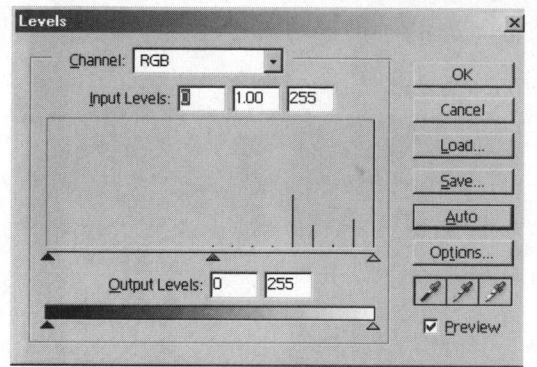

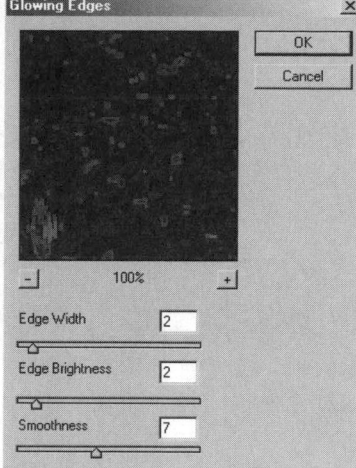

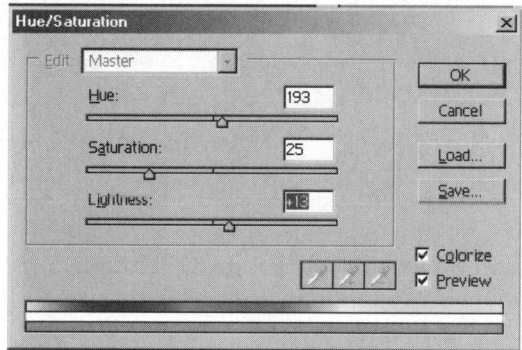

FIGURE 7–23
Filter

How to Render Worsted Wool Suiting 1
Rendering Traditional Gray Flannel Men's Suiting:

Step 1. Open a **New File: 8.5 × 11 inches, RGB, 150 dpi, White Background.** Name the file **Gray Flannel.**

Step 2. Add a **New Layer** and fill with White.

Step 3. Using the **Default Colors,** go to **Filter** and **Fill Render – Difference.** Select **Clouds** and **OK.**

Step 4. Go to **Filter** and select **Stylize > Find Edges.**

Step 5. From **Layers** select **Adjust Level,** hit the **Auto Button** and select **OK.**

Step 6. Duplicate Layer 2. (This will include all the steps completed from Steps 3 through 6.) (See Figure 7–23.)

Step 7. Go to **Filter** and select **Sharpen > Unsharpen Mask.** Choose **200%, Radius 1, Threshold to 0.**

Step 8. From **Filter** select **Stylize > Glowing Edges.** Choose **Edge Width > 2, Edge Brightness > 2,** and **Smoothness > 7.** (See Figure 7–23.)

Step 9. From **Filter** select **Blur > Motion Blur.** Choose **Angle 5,** and **Distance 4.** Click **OK.** (See Figure 7–24.)

FIGURE 7–24
Motion blur

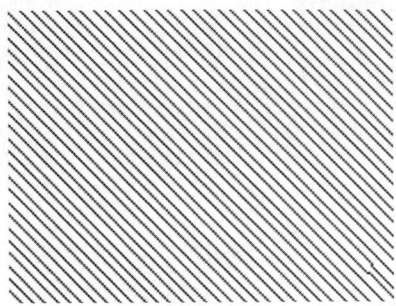

FIGURE 7–25
Drag and drop plain weave structure

Step 10. Open **Plain Structure** from the CD. Drag a copy to the top layer of your new file. Drop the Opacity. (See Figure 7–25.)

Step 11. Name and save.

Other Applications and Insights:

_____

_____

_____

_____

How to Create and Render a Basket Weave Ground

Step 1. Open the **Basket Weave** file from the **Structure** folder on the CD.

Step 2. In this **Structure** window, choose **Select>All**. Go to **Edit > Define Pattern**.

Step 3. Create a new window **5 × 5 inches** and using the **Paint Bucket** fill the window with a solid color.

Step 4. Select **Edit > Fill** with **Use: Pattern**. (See Figure 7–26.) Be sure the fill selected in custom pattern is the basket weave structure.

Step 5. To edit the "black" weave to another color, use the **Magic Wand** to select the black basket weave structure. Be sure to have **Contiguous** deselected so all of the structure is activated.

Step 6. Select the **Foreground** color to be used and choose **Edit > Fill Use: Foreground Color.** (See Figure 7–27.)

Step 7. Select a Filter to add a finish effect.

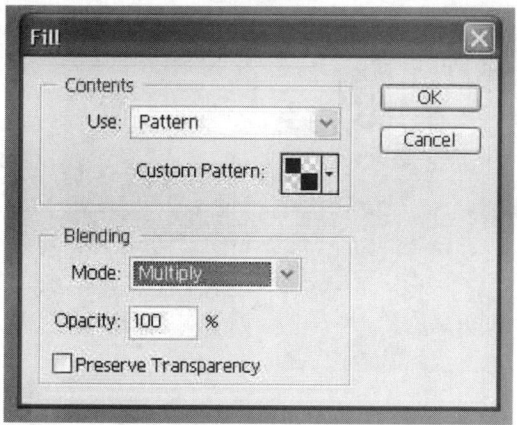

FIGURE 7–26
Fill dialogue window with pattern selection

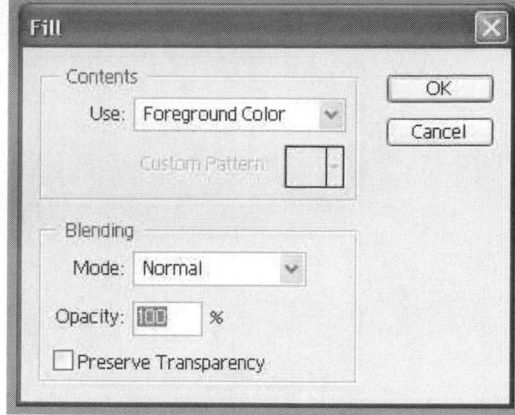

FIGURE 7–27
Fill dialogue window with foreground color selection

Other Applications and Insights:

_____

_____

_____

How to Render Canvas 1

Step 1. Open a **New File** in the size needed for more than a repeat of the texture. We suggest: 8″ × 8″, 150 dpi, RGB, white background.

Step 2. Once created, the edges of the texture will not match, so a larger area should be created.

Step 3. Open the **Swatch** folder and select the actual Canvas fabric swatch. Use the **Eyedropper** to select the nearest color.

Step 4. Using the **Paint Bucket**, fill the window with the desired color.

Step 5. Go to **Filter > Texture > Texturizer**. (See Figure 7–28.)

Step 6. Select the settings as follows: **Scaling 100%, Relief,** and **Light Direction Top**, check invert box.

Step 7. Select **Texture** and **Canvas**.

Step 8. Set **Scaling** to the size of the Canvas texture dialogue box. The **Preview** window is a great guide for this.

Step 9. The higher the setting, the larger the texture. Select the desired **Relief** setting for the depth of the canvas texture. Hint: The higher the setting, the deeper the texture.

Step 10. Choose the **Light Direction**. Selecting from the left, right, top, or bottom will create a lined effect; lighting from a corner, the bottom left, for example, will have a crosshatch effect.

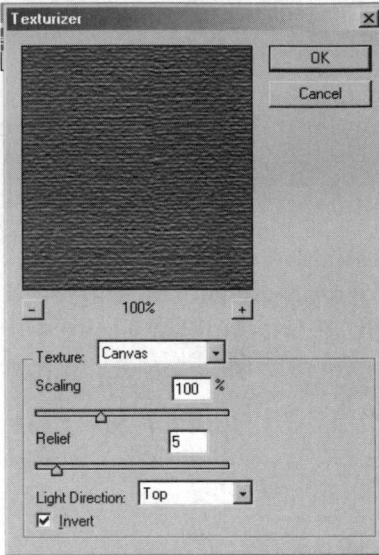

FIGURE 7–28
Texturizer dialogue window

Step 11. The **Invert** option reverses the effect.

Step 12. Choose **OK**, and save your file.

Other Applications and Insights:

_____

_____

_____

How to Render Canvas 2

Step 1. Open a **New File** in the size needed for more than a repeat of the texture.

Step 2. Once created, the edges of the texture will not match, so a larger area should be created.

Step 3. Open the **Swatch** folder and select the actual Canvas fabric swatch. Use the **Eyedropper** to select the nearest color.

Step 4. Using the **Paint Bucket**, fill the window with the desired color.

Step 5. Open the **Basic Rib Grid Sample** from the CD.

Step 6. Select with **Marquee** tool the one white square directly above the dark square and include the dark square in your selection.

Step 7. Go to **Edit > Define Pattern**. Name the pattern **Canvas**. (See Figure 7–29.)

Step 8. Above your solid color fill layer, make a **New Layer**.

Step 9. Go to **Edit > Fill > Pattern** and select **Canvas Fill**.

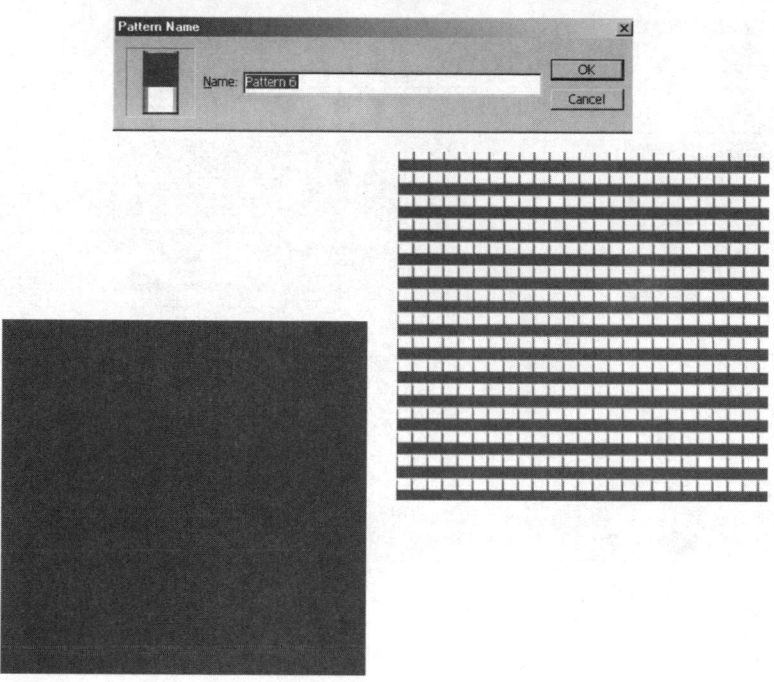

FIGURE 7–29
Zoom in

Step 10. Zoom in with **Magnifying Glass**. Select a small area of white. Go to **Select > Similar > Delete**.

Step 11. Drop the Opacity to approximately 50% and experiment with adding Filters.

Step 12. We suggest **Filter > Blur** and small amounts of **Motion Blur**.

Step 13. Name and save your work.

Rib Weaves:
How to Render Faille and Taffeta
Rendering Fine Rib Fabric:

Step 1. You will need to initially make two separate files:
File 1 will be **20 Pixels × 20 Pixels, 72 dpi, RGB, White Background**.
File 2 will be **8.5 × 11, RGB, 72–150 dpi, White Background**.

Step 2. On File 1, use the **Square Marquee** tool to select approximately half of the page horizontally in the form of a stripe.

Step 3. Fill with the color black. (See Figure 7–30.)

Step 4. Select **Edit > Define Pattern** and name the pattern **Faille**.

Step 5. Close File 1. (You can opt to name and save but this is already saved in the **Define Pattern** for future use.)

Step 6. Go to File 2 and make a **New Layer**.

Step 7. Fill with desired color and name this layer **Ground** under the **Layer Property** menu.

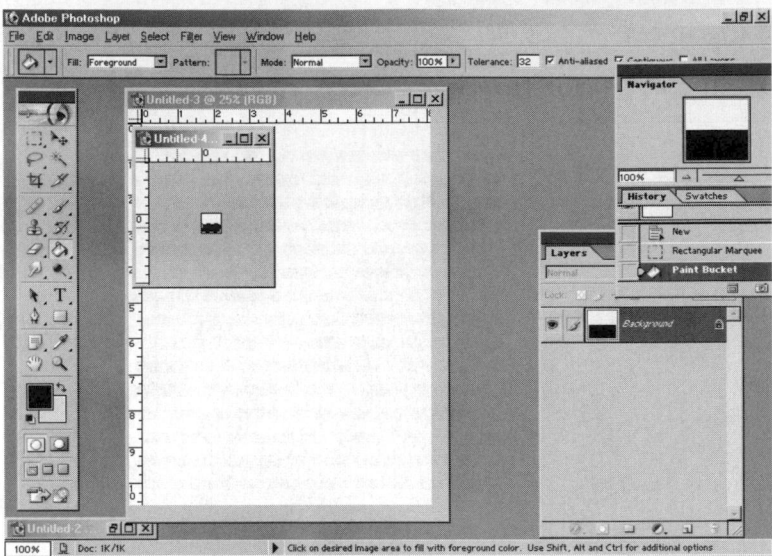

FIGURE 7–30
Fill with black

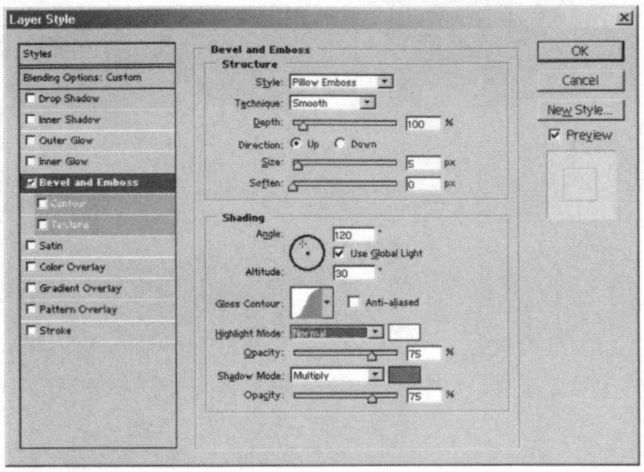

FIGURE 7–31
Embossing options

Step 8. Make a **New Layer** and fill with the **Pattern Fill** named **Faille**.

Step 9. Using the **Magic Wand**, select an area of white. Go to and select **Similar > Delete**.

Step 10. Name this new layer **Pattern Fill** in the **Layer Property** menu.

Step 11. On the **Layer Property** menu, select **Soft Light Mode**. Make **Opacity 94%**.

Step 12. You can now opt to add any type of additional texture to the Ground Layer of this file to simulate other fine vertical rib-textured fabric.

Step 13. For example, you may want to consider playing with the **Embossing Options** located under the **Layer Style** menu. (See Figure 7–31.)

Step 14. Then try **Filter > Blur > Motion Blur > Angle 32 > Distance 45**. Click **OK**. (See Figure 7–32.)

HINT: Be sure to switch the Mode to Normal and leave Opacity at approximately 50%.

Other Applications and Insights:

_____

_____

_____

Twill Weaves
Building a Twill Woven Structure

Earlier in this chapter, you learned how to make a simple plain weave structure. In this section we will walk you through several exercises designed to help you capture the distinctive diagonal appearance found in twill weaves. (See Figure 7–33.)

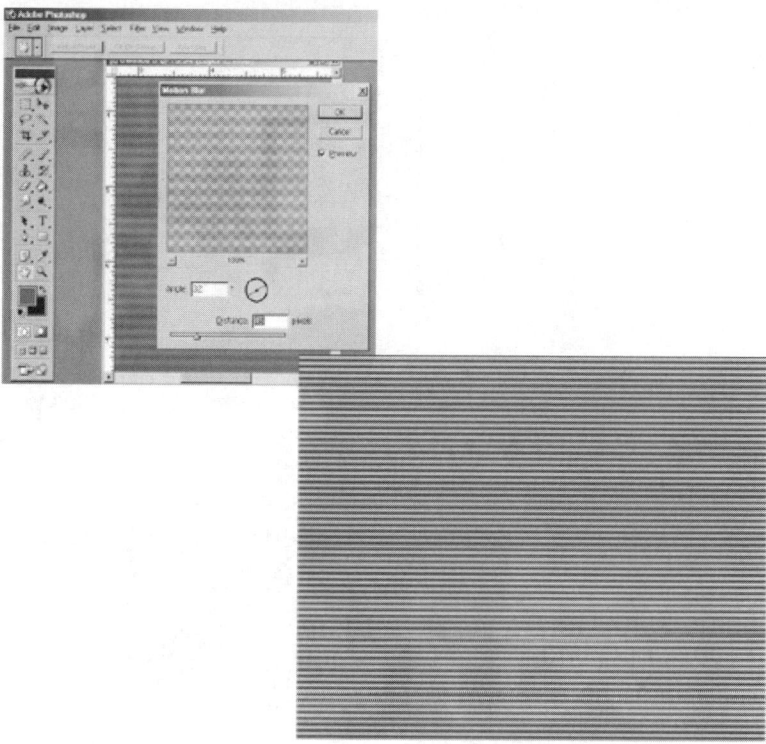

FIGURE 7–32
Motion blur

FIGURE 7–33
Twill weave

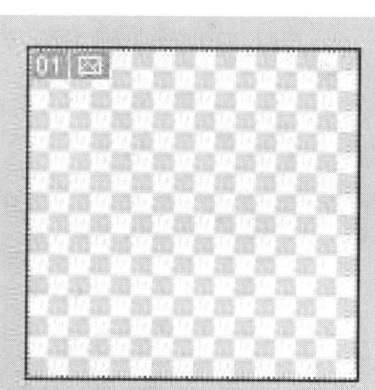

FIGURE 7–34
Zoom in

You will go through the steps of how to create the pattern using Adobe Photoshop and *then* you will learn how to apply these to a specific cloth later in this chapter.

Making a 2×2 Twill Structure

Step 1. Open a **New File: 8 pixels × 8 pixels, 72 dpi, RGB, Transparent Background.** The window created is very small; you will need to use the **Magnifying Glass** and zoom in, a lot. (See Figure 7–34.)

Step 2. Using a 1-pixel pencil and black as the color, begin to draw in a Twill Structure, pixel by pixel. (See Figure 7–35.)

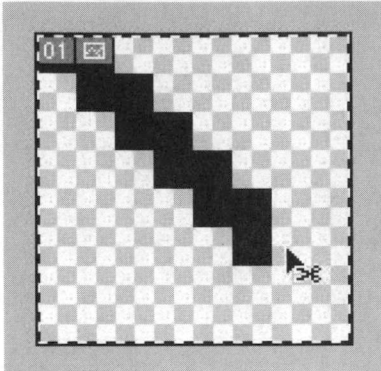

FIGURE 7–35
Twill structure

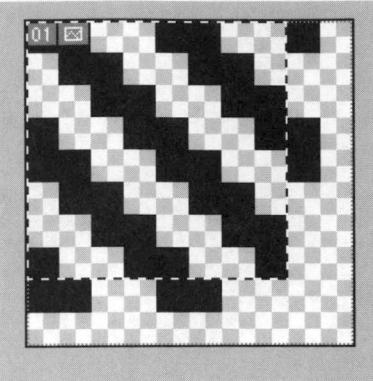

FIGURE 7–36
Weave structure

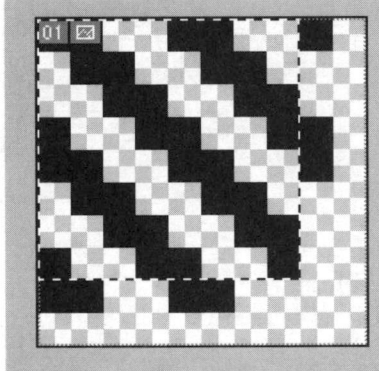

FIGURE 7–37
Final twill graph

FIGURE 7–38
Twill pattern

Step 3. Continue to draw in the Weave Structure as shown here. (See Figure 7–36.)

Step 4. The final graph of the Twill should appear as shown in Figure 7–37.

Step 5. As the designer, you have the control not only to design the step of the twill, but also to determine the direction, such as right or left.

Now you are ready to test to see if your design will properly repeat.

Making a Twill Ground Repeat Pattern Fill

Step 1. Select **All** in your new **Twill**.

Step 2. Then go to **Edit > Define Pattern**. In the title field name the pattern **Twill** and click **OK**.

Step 3. Create a **New File** twice as large: **16 × 16 pixels, 72 dpi, RGB, Transparent Background**.

Step 4. Select **Edit > Fill > Fill with Pattern**.

Step 5. Choose **Twill Pattern** to fill and click **OK**. (See Figure 7–38.)

HINT: If the repeat is incorrect, it will show up here in the pattern fill. It may be necessary to go back and correct the original pattern selected and retest again.

Other Applications and Insights:

_____

_____

_____

How to Render Chino
Or any 45-Degree Twill Stripe:

Step 1.   Open the file labeled **45-degree Twill** on the CD.

Step 2.   Open a **New File: 8.5 × 11 inches, 72–150 dpi, RGB, White Background.**

Step 3.   Make a **New Layer.**

Step 4.   With a **Paint Bucket,** fill with desired shade of khaki.

Step 5.   Drag the file from Step 1, entitled **45-degree Twill** onto a new layer in File 2. (See Figure 7–39.)

Step 6.   Go to **Filter** and adjust the Opacity controls to bring out the khaki.

Step 7.   Select **Blur > Gaussian Blur** to smooth the pattern.

Step 8.   Name and save.

Other Applications and Insights:

_____

_____

_____

How to Render Denim

Step 1.   Open a **New File: 8.5 × 11, RGB, 72–150 dpi, White Background.** Call the file **Digital Denim**.

Step 2.   Open the **Swatch** folder and open the file labeled **Denim** from the **Swatch Sample** folder on the CD. (See Figure 7–40.)

Step 3.   On your new **Digital Denim** file, start by adding a new layer using the **New Layer** icon and name it **Denim Blue.**

Step 4.   Go back to the **Digital Denim** file and use the **Color Picker** to match the color blue. Switching back to your image, use the **Paint Bucket** and fill the page with blue.

Step 5.   (Optional) Duplicate Layer 2 and name it **Texture.**

Step 6.   Go to **Filter** menu and **Noise > Add Noise** and make the amount approximately 7%. Check the boxes for **Gaussian** and **Monochromatic** and then click **OK.**

FIGURE 7–39
45-Degree twill

FIGURE 7–40
Denim

Step 7. Open the **Goodies Folder** from the CD and select **Right-Handed Twill** file.

Step 8. Drag this layer over to your **Digital Denim** file.

Step 9. Title this new layer as **Right-Handed Twill.**

Step 10. Zoom in on the new layer and using the **Magic Wand**, select one section of white, and then go to the **Select** menu and select **Similar.**

Step 11. Hit the Delete key to remove the white background.

Step 12. Go to the **Select** menu and select **Inverse.** Next, experiment with one of the following: a lighter shade of blue, a darker shade of blue, or white for the twill fill color.

Step 13. Next, hit the **Edit** menu, fill with **Foreground** or the shortcuts key to fill the twill with color.

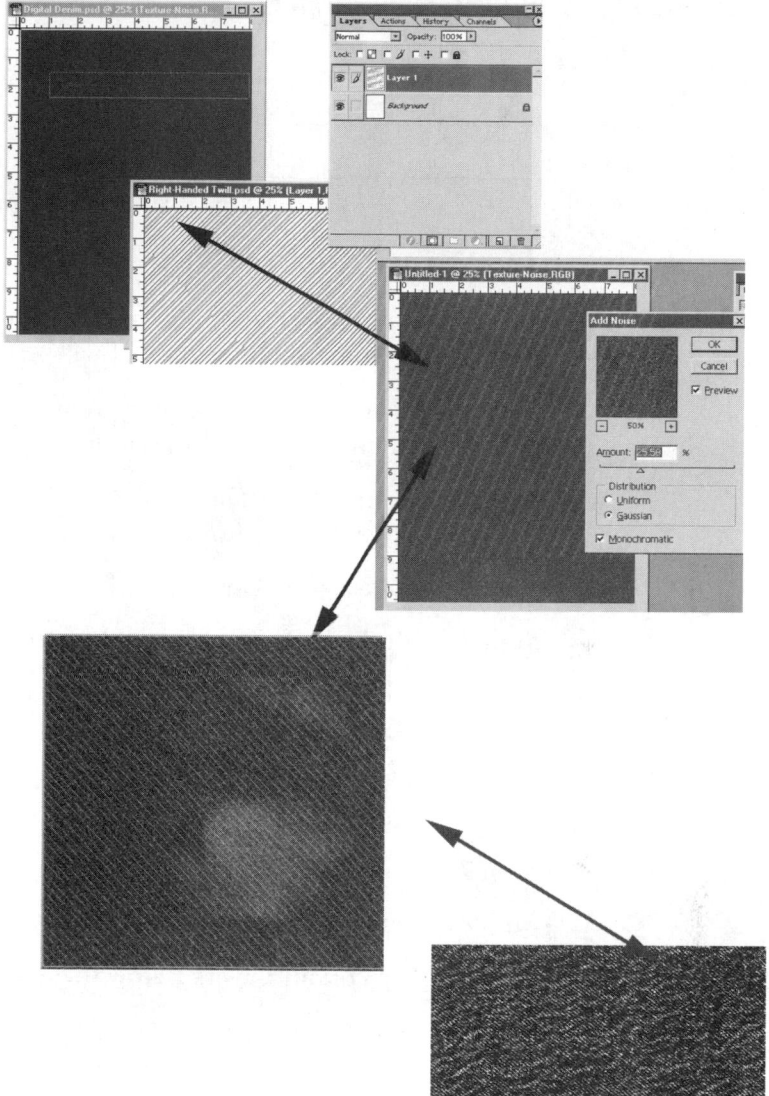

FIGURE 7–41
Duplicate layer

Step 14. Play with the Opacity slider to cause the twill to appear to be part of the fabric construction.

Step 15. On your duplicate layer of the Solid Blue Fill, try experimenting with adding texture. Go to the **Filter** menu, **Texturizer**, and from the drop-down menu, select **Canvas**, **Scaling 100%**, **Relief—4**, and **Light Direction—Top**. Then click **OK**.

Step 16. Name and save your work as a .psd.

HINT: You can also experiment with adding blotches of white on a fresh layer—try hitting **Motion Blur** and lowering the Opacity on that layer to give your denim a distressed look! (See Figure 7–41.) Figure 7–41 shows the steps from taking a solid fill to dragging and dropping a twill weave as well as motion blur to your fabric.

_____

_____

_____

How to Render Gabardine

The following steps are similar to creating worsted wool with the addition of the top layer of your twill pattern.

Step 1. Open actual **Gabardine Swatch** from the CD. Use the **Eyedropper** to match the color. (See Figure 7–42.)

Step 2. Open a **New File: 8.5 × 11 inches, RGB, 72–150 dpi, Blue** to match swatch background. Name the file **Blue Flannel.**

Step 3. Make a **New Layer.**

Step 4. Fill the new layer with **Blue** to match.

Step 5. Using the **Default Colors** go to **Filter, Fill Render – Difference > Clouds > OK.**

Step 6. Select **Image > Adjust > Hue & Saturation**. Turn on the **Preview** box and adjust the slider bar to the closet color selection to original swatch. Select **OK.**

Step 7. Open the file entitled **Twill** from your CD.

Step 8. Drag this file over to a **New Layer** in your **Gabardine** file.

Step 9. Turn off all **Layers Below** the Twill Pattern.

Step 10. Select **Edit > All.**

Step 11. Using the **Eyedropper**, select a color slightly darker than your gabardine fabric.

Step 12. Select **Edit > Fill > Foreground Color.**

FIGURE 7–42
Gabardine swatch

FIGURE 7–43
Opacity slider

FIGURE 7–44
Pattern fill

Step 13. Go to **Filter > Noise > Add Noise**. Click on the **Preview** button. Select **Uniform approx 17**. Click on **Monochromatic**.

Step 14. Turn on the **Layers Below**.

Step 15. Begin to experiment with the Opacity slider to cause your Twill Pattern to recede back into your digitally rendered Gabardine. (See Figure 7–43.)

Other Applications and Insights:

_____

_____

_____

How to Render a Herringbone Pattern Using Filters

Step 1. Open a **New File**: **8.5 × 11 inches, RGB, 72–150 dpi, White Background**.

Step 2. Make a **New Layer**.

Step 3. Using the **Square Marquee** tool, make two separate horizontal boxes and fill with desired color.

Step 4. **Marquee** these linear boxes and go to **Edit > Define Pattern**.

Step 5. Label the new pattern **Herringbone Fill**.

Step 6. Make a **New Layer** and label **Pattern Fill**. (See Figure 7–44.)

Step 7. Select **Edit > Fill > Herringbone** from the **Pattern Fill** options and fill the new layer. At this time, you may opt to duplicate this layer as many times as you would like in order to experiment with the Filters.

Step 8. First, select **Filter > Distort > Wave > Sine** for smooth. Second, select **Triangle** for a more defined herringbone pattern.

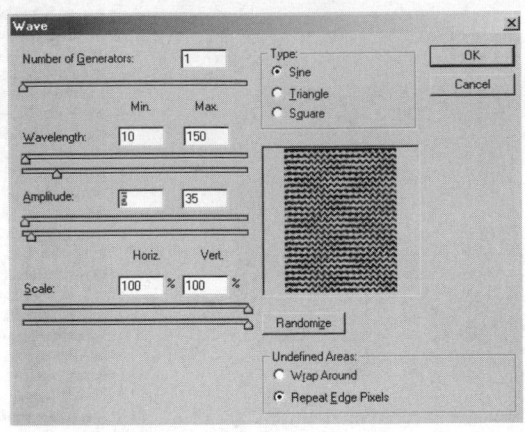

FIGURE 7–45
Wave dialogue window

FIGURE 7–46
Herringbone pattern

Settings should be **1 + Number of Generators; Wavelength** of **10 Mini-mum to 150 Maximum; Amplitude > 2, 35**; and **Scaling** at **100%.** Select **Repeat Pixels.** (See Figure 7–45.) Experiment with these settings in the **Preview** and adjust to suit.)

Step 9. Continue on one of the additional duplicate layers from Step 7. Experiment with other variations by using the Filter parameters from Step 8.

Step 10. Remember to record your findings so that you may duplicate this again in the future! (See Figure 7–46.)

Other Applications and Insights:

_____

_____

_____

How to Render a Herringbone Pattern Using Postscript

Step 1. This will require making two files.

Step 2. For File 1: Go to **File: Open> C Drive: > Program Files > Adobe > Adobe Photoshop > Preset > Patterns > Herringbone 1.** (See Figure 7–47.)

Step 3. Select **Image Size: 1 × 1 inch, RGB, 72–150 dpi,** check **Anti-Aliasing,** check **Constrain Proportions.** Click **OK.**

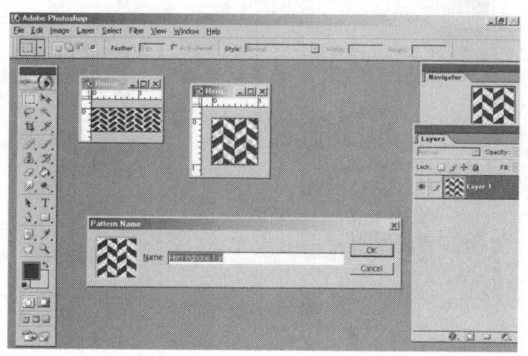

FIGURE 7–47
File #1

FIGURE 7–48
File #2

Step 4. Make a **Marquee** around the image. Choose **Edit > Define Pattern > Name Herringbone**. Click **OK**.

Step 5. Close the **PostScript Herringbone File 1**.

Step 6. For File 2: Open a **New File: 8.5 × 11, RGB, 72–150 dpi, White Background**. Go to **Edit > Fill**. Select **Pattern Fill**. Select **Herringbone Pattern 1** and click **OK**. (See Figure 7–48.)

Step 7. Make a **New Layer**. Fill with desired color.

Step 8. Go to **Layer** menu and select **Modes > Multiple**.

Step 9. Name and save your file.

OPTIONAL: You may wish to experiment with filters for adding texture or depth to your image.

Other Applications and Insights:

_____

_____

_____

How to Render a Houndstooth Pattern

Step 1. Open a **New File: 72–150 dpi, 8 pixels × 9 pixels**.

Step 2. Set up the pencil tool, so that it is 1 pixel in size.

Step 3. Draw in the houndstooth as shown in Figure 7–49.

Step 4. Once drawn, the single houndstooth can be selected and used as a custom stamp or brush to create the interlocking pattern as shown in Figure 7–50.

FIGURE 7–49
Single houndstooth motif

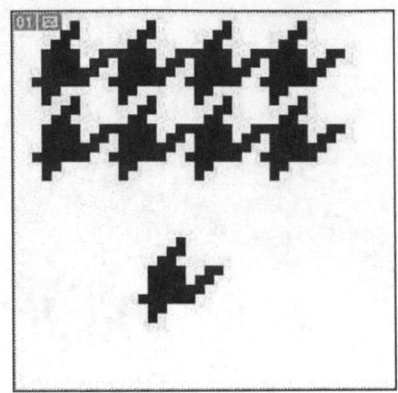

FIGURE 7–50
Houndstooth repeat motif

Step 5. Use caution to be sure that the white space is identical to the black space. If a houndstooth was created in a second color, it would be able to interlock right into the white space. (See Figures 7–49 and 7–50.)

Other Applications and Insights:

_____

_____

_____

Congratulations, you are doing great! By now you should be feeling fairly confident of how to render many of the basic fabrics. From here, the instructions will include additional woven backgrounds and fabrics that you will want to use in rendering fashion, or other projects.

How to Render a Satin Weave 1

Step 1. Open a **New File**: 8.5 × 11 inches, 72–150 dpi, RGB, White Background.

Step 2. Make a **New Layer** and fill with light color.

Step 3. Using the **Eyedropper** select a darker shade of the same color from Step 2.

Step 4. Select **Radial Gradient** of the two monochromatic shades from Steps 2 and 3.

Step 5. Go to the **Filter** menu and select **Blur > Motion Blur** at a right angle.

Step 6. Repeat as necessary Step 5.

Step 7. Another alternative is that you can opt to do the following: Go to the **Filter** menu and select **Liquify Menu,** and using the **Stir** option begin to fashion streaks on the diagonal.

FIGURE 7–51
Wind

Step 8. Next go to the **Filter** menu and select **Stylize Menu > Wind** and then select **Method > Wind > Direction > Right** to match Figure 7–51.

Step 9. Experiment with duplicating Layer 2 and adding **Noise, Monochromatic,**
and **Gaussian** in small amounts.

Step 10. Drop the Opacity of the duplicate layer.

Step 11. Name and save.

Other Applications and Insights:

How to Render a Satin Weave 2

In this variation, we have included the alternative method of using plug-in software
that works with Adobe Photoshop. This software is an additional purchase plug-in
that, when installed, will be available under the Filter menu of Photoshop. Although we recognize that not everyone has this software, we felt it was important
that we address the use of such software here in the step-by-step section of our text.
We will introduce you to several companies who provide such software in Chapter
12. It should be noted that trial versions of several of these plug-ins are included
on your CD or they can be obtained by logging on to the Alien Skin website and

selecting download—trial copy. (FYI: These download programs are limited in use and are typically for a preset determined period of time.)

Step 1. Open a **New File: 8.5 × 11 inches, 72–150 dpi, RGB, White Background**.

Step 2. Make a **New Layer** and fill with light color.

Step 3. Using the **Eyedropper**, select a darker shade of the same color from Step 2.

Step 4. Select **Radial Gradient** of the two monochromatic shades from Steps 2 and 3.

Step 5. Go to **Filter** menu and select **Eye Candy > Fire > Basic Tab > Column Length Inches > 7.62, Flame Width > 0.14, Side Taper > .30,** and **Movement > 54.** Check **Denser Flame** box and start from **Side Box, Random Seed 567.** (See Figure 7–52.)

Step 6. Under the Color Tab, leave **Natural Spectrum** unchecked, and select colors to match your gradient. (See Figure 7–53.) Then set **Opacity 80%** and click **OK.**

Other Applications and Insights:

_____

_____

_____

Rendering a Dobby Weave Effect

Step 1. Open a **New File** in Adobe Photoshop: **10 pixels × 10 pixels, 150 dpi, RGB, Transparent Background.**

Step 2. Using the **Pencil** tool on the smaller file, begin to render a dobby diamond or other pattern, as seen in Figure 7–54.

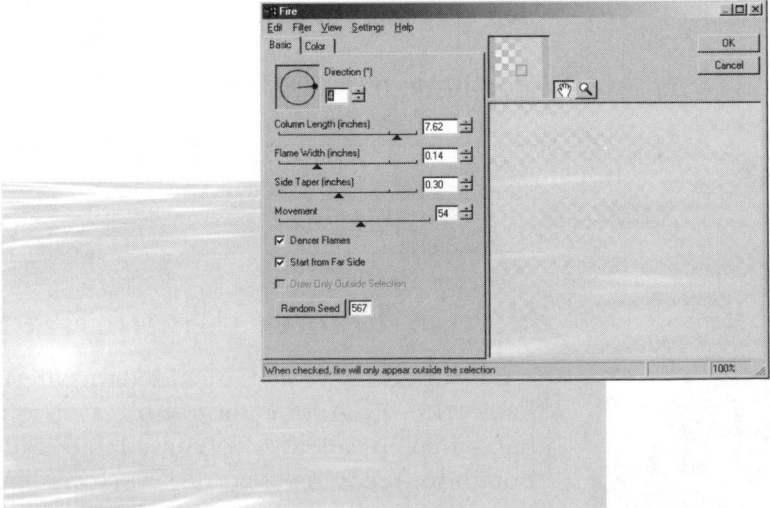

FIGURE 7–52
Fire dialogue window

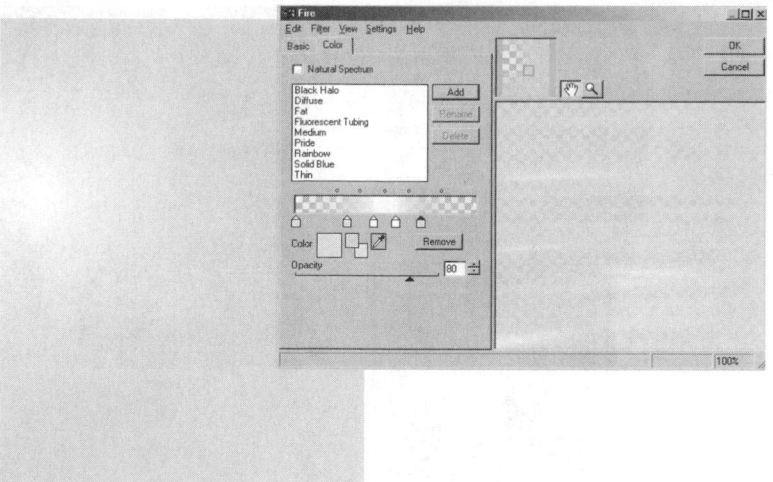

FIGURE 7–53
Color tab

FIGURE 7–54
Dobby diamond

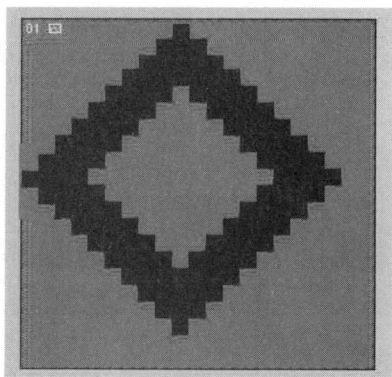

FIGURE 7–55
Edit image colors

Step 3. Place a **Marquee** around the image and go to **Edit > Define Pattern** and name the pattern **Dobby Weave.**

Step 4. Open a second file: **5 × 5, 150 dpi, RGB, White Background**. Add a **New Layer.**

Step 5. Go to **Edit > Fill > Pattern**. Select the **Dobby Weave.**

Step 6. At this point you can opt to edit the colors of the image from black and white to suit your needs. (See Figure 7–55.)

Step 7. Note: Also be sure that the two layers are kept separate and the top layer with the dobby has the transparent ground.

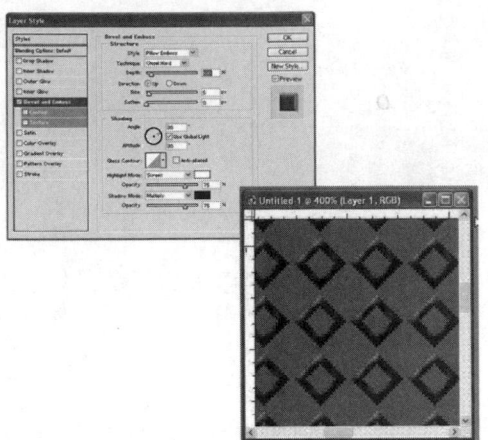

FIGURE 7–56
Layer property menu

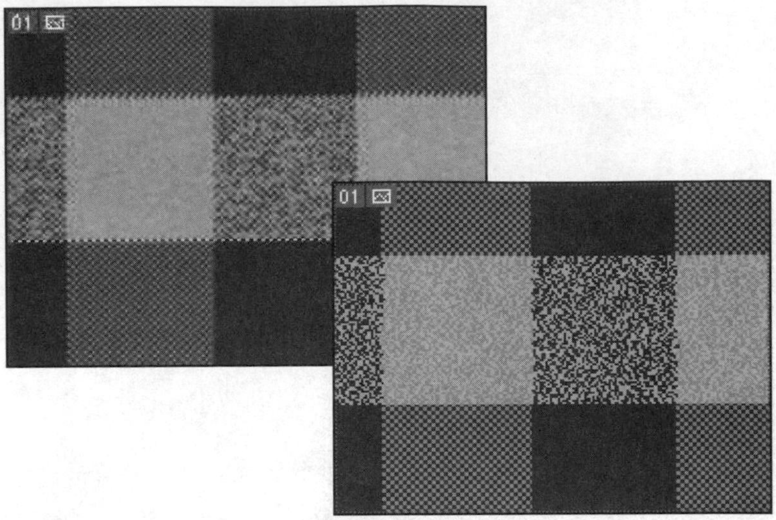

FIGURE 7–57
Ikat effect in a weave

Step 8. In the Layers palette, activate the **Dobby Layer**.

Step 9. Go to **Layer > Layer Style > Emboss** and experiment with the **Bevel Emboss** and the **Pillow Emboss** options. Experiment with the Layer Property Menu as seen in Figure 7–56 to suit your needs.

Step 10. Duplicate this layer and continue to experiment with adding **Noise** or **Motion Blur** Filters to create distinctive fabrics.

Other Applications and Insights:

_____

_____

_____

How to Render an Ikat Effect in a Weave 1

Step 1. Open the file **Ikat Weave Exercise** on the CD. This is the weave to start with.

Step 2. Use the **Marquee** tool to select the area of the weave to have an Ikat effect.

Step 3. Go to **Filter > Stylize >Wind > Stagger from Right.**

Step 4. Duplicate this weave as many times as you would like in order to experiment with the Filter. (See Figure 7–57.)

Other Applications and Insights:

_____

_____

_____

How to Render an Ikat Effect in a Weave 2

Step 1. Open the file **Ikat Weave Exercise** on the CD. This is the weave to start with.

Step 2. Use the **Marquee** tool to select the area of the weave to have an Ikat effect.

Step 3. Go to **Filter > Brush Strokes > Sprayed Strokes**.

Step 4. Duplicate this weave as many times as you would like in order to experiment with the Filter. (See Figure 7–57.)

Step 5. Choose the appropriate settings for **Stroke Length, Spray Radius**, and **Stroke Direction** (horizontal or vertical for an Ikat). The **Preview** is excellent for seeing what will occur.

Step 6. Select **OK.** To soften the effect, use the **Filter > Blur > Motion Blur.** Just keep the Angle set at 0 degrees.

Other Applications and Insights:

How to Render a Pile Weave/Terry Cloth

Step 1. Make a new window and fill it with the pattern or color of the final design.

Step 2. Open the file **Terry Cloth** from the enclosed CD. This file is a grayscale scan of actual terry cloth fabric. Any grayscale scan of a texture can be used in this technique. (See Figure 7–58.)

Step 3. Select **All** in the **Terry** and choose **Edit > Define Pattern**.

Step 4. In the design window, add a new layer and then double-click on the **Background Layer** to change the name to **Layer 0.**

Step 5. Activate the new layer and fill it with the pattern of the **Terry.**

Step 6. Drag the terry layer under the design layer.

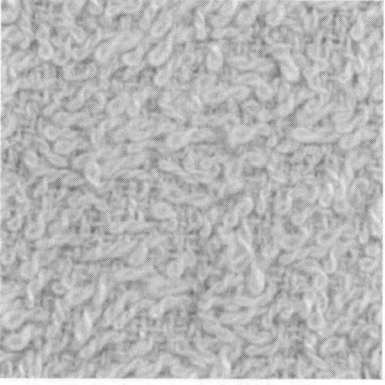

FIGURE 7–58
Terry cloth

Step 7. Set the design layer to **Overlay**.

Other Applications and Insights:

_____

_____

_____

How to Render a Corduroy Stripe

Step 1. You will need to initially make two separate files:
File 1 will be **20 pixels × 20 pixels, 72 dpi, RGB, White Background.**
File 2 will be **8.5 × 11, RGB, 72–150 dpi, White Background.**

Step 2. On File 1, using the **Square Marquee** tool, select approximately half of the page vertically in the form of a stripe.

Step 3. Fill with the color black. (See Figure 7–59.)

Step 4. Select **Edit > Define Pattern** and name the pattern **Corduroy**.

Step 5. Close **File 1**. (You can opt to name and save but this is already saved in the **Define Pattern** for future use.)

Step 6. Go to File 2 and make a **New Layer**. Fill with desired color and name this layer **Ground** under the **Layer Property** menu.

Step 7. Make a **New Layer** and fill with the **Pattern Fill** named **Corduroy**. (See Figure 7–60.)

Step 8. Name this new layer **Pattern Fill** in the **Layer Property** menu.

Step 9. On the **Layer Property** menu, select **Soft Light Mode**. Make **Opacity 94%**.

Step 10. (Optional) At this point you can now add any type of additional texture to the Ground Layer of this file to simulate corduroy or other fine vertical rib-textured fabric.

FIGURE 7–59
Fill color

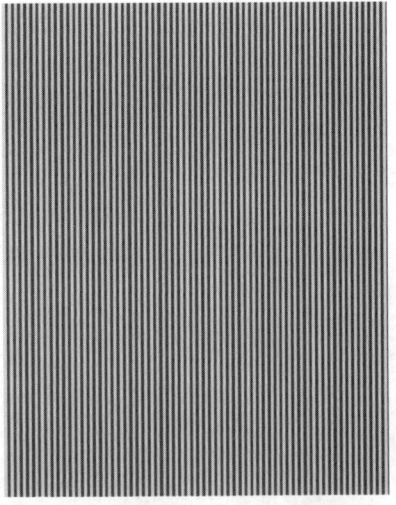

FIGURE 7–60
Corduroy

FIGURE 7–61
Jacquard woven

Other Applications and Insights:

_____

_____

_____

How to Render a Jacquard Woven—
Brocade or Damask

Step 1. Open or create a color-blocked version of the design to simulate as a Jacquard.

Step 2. Using the **Structures** on the enclosed CD, open each and define as a pattern. (See Figure 7–61.)

Step 3. Use the **Paint Bucket** to fill the first pattern into the necessary color-blocked area(s).

Step 4. Fill the black structure with a darker shade of the color-blocked area. This simulates the shadow of the yarn.

Step 5. Continue this process until the color areas are all filled with a structure and each structure is filled in a correct shadow color.

Step 6. Apply any finish effects with the Filters.

Other Applications and Insights:

_____

_____

_____

How to Render Knitted Fabric and Novelty Yarns

Jersey	Ombré Yarns
Rib	Marl Yarn
Purl or Reversible Jersey	Crepe and Bouclé Yarns
Cables	

Creating Knit Structures

A knit fabric is constructed of a series of stitches that loop together to form the fabric. There are some knit structures on the enclosed CD-ROM. To build a new or custom-knit structure, follow these steps. A designer can easily see how any design can be applied to this technique.

How to Render a Knitted Structure

Jersey Version #1:

Step 1. Open the scan of the **Jersey Knit Fabric** on the enclosed CD. (See Figure 7–62.)

Step 2. In the **Layer** menu, choose **New Layer.**

Step 3. Build the stitch with the **Pencil** tool, using dark and light grays for shadows, by drawing on top of the scan to trace the new stitch. The trick here is to draw in the shadows of the stitch, leaving the actual yarn area transparent where the image will appear, when the stitch is filled over a design.

Step 4. Delete the **Background Layer** to transparent.

Step 5. Crop out a single stitch. (See Figure 7–63.)

Step 6. Define the selection as a pattern. Go to **Edit > Define Pattern.** Use this pattern to fill over a design that needs to look like a knit.

Step 7. Name and save your file. In the next chapter you will learn to adapt additional finishes to your design.

HINT: Varying the stitch size is like changing the gauge of the stitch. Located on the CD are jersey, reverse jersey, and some other structures that have been created for your use. A designer can go as far as filling an empty window with the stitch and then filling in individual stitches to create the design.

Recreating a knit texture of a fabric can be a challenge. The combination of defining the knit as a pattern and then applying a filter to it can work well. Using Fil-

FIGURE 7–62
Jersey knit fabric

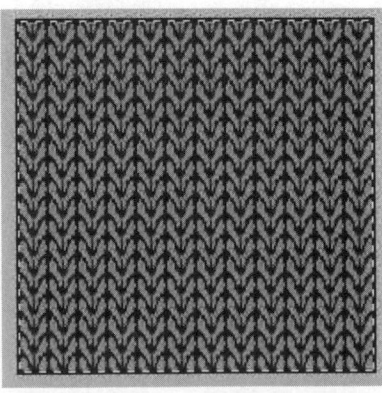

FIGURE 7–63
Crop out single stitch

ter options, brushed fabrics, hairy yarns, and fleece effects can all be created. We will be demonstrating how you do this in Chapter 8 on advanced woven patterns and finishes.

Other Applications and Insights:

_____

_____

_____

Jersey Version #2:

Step 1. Open a **New File** in Photoshop: **8.5 × 11, RGB, 150 dpi, White Background.** Name the file **Digital Jersey.**

Step 2. Make a **New Layer**. In the **Layer Property** menu, call this layer **Solid Color.**

Step 3. Open the **Swatch** folder and open **Jersey Scan** on the CD.

Step 4. Using the **Color Picker,** match the color used in your swatch.

Step 5. On your file on Layer 2, go to **Edit > Fill Menu** and select **Foreground Color > Dissolve, 25% Opacity.**

Step 6. Under the **Filter** menu, select **Blur > Motion Blur, 0 Angle, Distance 33**. Click **OK.**

Step 7. Open the CD and select **Jersey Pattern.**

Step 8. Drag a copy of the **Jersey Pattern** to your file and name the new layer, under the **Layer Property** menu: **Jersey Pattern.**

Step 9. Zoom in, using the **Magic Wand**. Select the Black outline. Go to the **Select** menu and select **Similar.**

Step 10. From the **Foreground Color** menu, select a slightly deeper shade of blue. (See Figure 7–64.)

Step 11. Now from the **Edit** menu, fill with **Foreground Color.**

Step 12. Experiment with dropping the Opacity levels.

Step 13. You may also wish to experiment with the **Motion Blur Filter** *or* the **Layer Style Emboss** options for your knit.

Step 14. Name and save your image. Do not flatten; instead make a JPEG copy for later use.

Other Applications and Insights:

_____

_____

_____

FIGURE 7–64
Foreground color menu

Jersey Version #3:

Step 1. Open a **New File** in Photoshop: **8.5 × 11, RGB, 150 dpi, White Background**. Name the file **Digital Jersey**.

Step 2. Make a **New Layer**. In the **Layer Property** menu, call this layer **Solid Color**.

Step 3. Open the **Swatch** folder and open **Jersey Scan** on the CD.

Step 4. Using the **Color Picker**, match the color used in your swatch.

Step 5. On your file on Layer 2, go to the **Edit > Fill Menu** and select **Foreground Color > Dissolve, 25% Opacity**.

Step 6. Under the **Filter** menu, select **Blur > Motion Blur, 0 Angle, Distance 33**. Click **OK**.

Step 7. Open the CD and select **Jersey Pattern**.

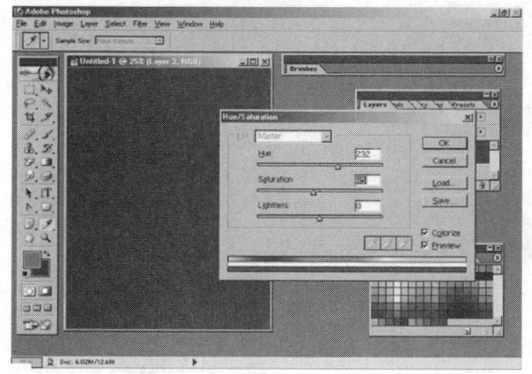

FIGURE 7–65
Foreground color menu

Step 8. Drag a copy of the **Jersey Pattern** to your file and name the new layer, under the **Layer Property** menu: **Jersey Pattern.**

Step 9. Zoom in, using the **Magic Wand.** Select the Black outline. Go to the **Select** menu and select **Similar**.

Step 10. From the **Foreground Color** menu, select a slightly deeper shade of blue. (See Figure 7–65.)

Step 11. Now from the **Edit** menu, fill with **Foreground Color**.

Step 12. Experiment with dropping the Opacity levels.

Step 13. You may also wish to experiment with the **Motion Blur Filter** *or* the **Layer Style Emboss** options for your knit.

Step 14. Name and save your image. Do not flatten; instead make a JPEG copy for later use.

Other Applications and Insights:

_____

_____

_____

How to Render Reverse Jersey

Step 1. Open the file of the **Reverse Jersey** on the enclosed CD. This file is already a cropped out repeat. (See Figure 7–66.)

Step 2. Define the selection as a pattern. Go to **Edit > Define Pattern.** Use this pattern to fill over a design that needs to look like a knit.

If a different type of stitch is needed, scan in a sample stitch from the actual fabric and follow the guidelines below to create the pattern file.

Step 1. Open the scan of the **Knit Fabric**.

Step 2. In the **Layer** menu, choose **New Layer**.

FIGURE 7–66
Reverse jersey

Step 3. Build the stitch with the **Pencil** tool, using dark and light grays for shadows, by drawing on top of the scan to trace the new stitch. The trick here is to draw in the shadows of the stitch, leaving the actual yarn area transparent where the image will appear, when the stitch is filled over a design.

Step 4. Delete the **Background Layer** to transparent.

Step 5. Crop out a single stitch.

Step 6. Define the selection as a pattern. Go to **Edit > Define Pattern**.

Use this pattern to fill over a design that needs to look like a knit.

Other Applications and Insights:

_____

_____

_____

How to Render a Cable Knit

Rendering a complex knit structure, such as a cable or a rib, can be complex and time-consuming. These simple steps will help to create the "effect" or "look" of the structure so that the design can be quickly visualized.

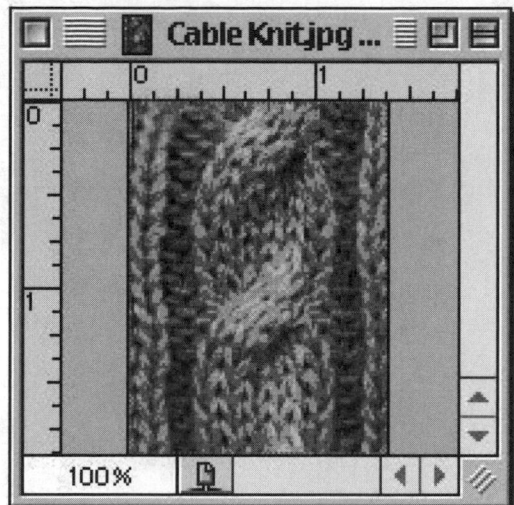

FIGURE 7–67
Cable scan file

Step 1. Open the **Cable Scan** file on the enclosed CD. (See Figure 7–67.) This file is a repeat of a grayscale scan of actual fabric. (FYI: Any grayscale scan of a texture can be used in this technique.)

Step 2. Choose **Edit > Define Pattern**.

Step 3. Open a **New File** in the size needed. In the design window, double-click on the **Background Layer** and change the name to **Layer 0**.

Step 4. Add a new layer and fill it with the pattern of the cable.

Step 5. Drag the cable layer under the design layer.

Step 6. Set the design layer to **Overlay.** Drawing in the design layer will now allow the cable to be seen as the stitch.

Other Applications and Insights:

_____

_____

_____

How to Render a Rib Knit

A rib is a combination of a jersey and a reverse jersey stitch. In the following steps, they will be combined to create the structure.

Step 1. Open the **Jersey Stitch** on the enclosed CD and define it as a pattern.

Open the **Reverse Jersey Stitch** on the enclosed CD and define it as a pattern.

Step 2. Open a **New File** that is 48 pixels wide by 16 pixels high. This is going to show two columns of jersey. (See Figure 7–68.)

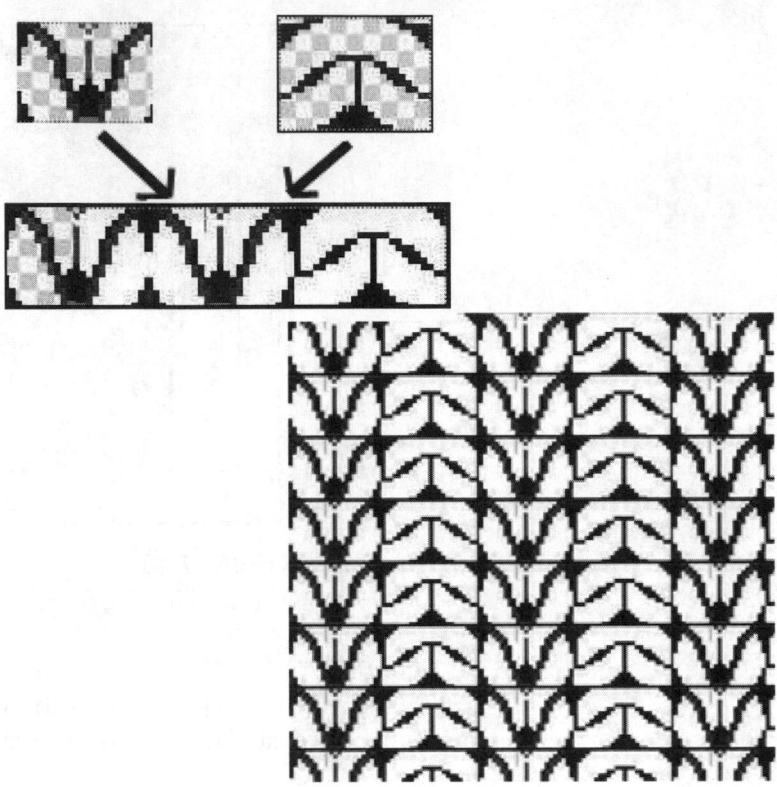

FIGURE 7–68
Rib knit

Step 3. Fill the new window with the previously defined Jersey Stitch.

Step 4. Go to **Image > Canvas Size** and edit the width in pixels to be 72 and anchor the design to the far left. Choose **OK.**

Step 5. In the space created, fill in the Reverse Jersey.

Step 6. Define the combined rib structure as a pattern.

Step 7. Open a design to overlay the new structure.

Step 8. In the design window, double-click on the **Background Layer** and change the name to **Layer 0**.

Step 9. Add a new layer and fill it with the pattern of the rib.

Step 10. Drag the rib layer under the design layer.

Step 11. Set the design layer to **Overlay.** Drawing in the design layer will now allow the rib to be seen as the stitch.

Other Applications and Insights:

_____

_____

_____

Creating a Space-Dyed Yarn, Marled, Ombré, Crepe, or Other Textured Yarns

Marled yarn generally consists of two to three colors of yarn twisted together. This can be simulated by following these steps.

Space-Dyed Yarns

Creating a yarn of similar hues:

Step 1. Create a **New File: 20 pixels × 20 pixels, 72–150 dpi, RGB, White Background**.

Step 2. Using the **Paint Bucket**, fill the window with a single main hue needed for the twist.

Step 3. Go to **Filter > Noise > Add Noise**. (See Figure 7–69.)

Step 4. Practicing with the percentage of Noise and the Distribution will create varying effects of the marl.

Step 5. Go to **Edit > Define Pattern**. This can now be filled into any of the knit stitches developed in the past exercises.

Step 6. Individual stitches can be filled by selecting the **Contiguous** option.

Step 7. Deselecting **Contiguous** will fill the marl into all areas of the selected color.

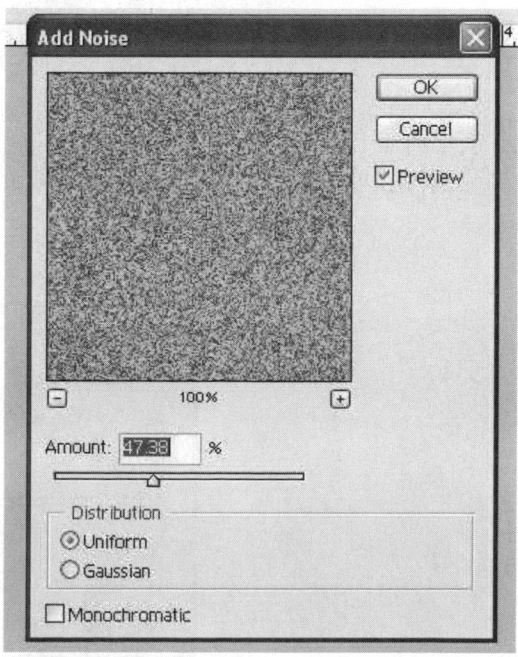

FIGURE 7–69
Adding noise

Creating a yarn of multiple hues:

Step 1. Create a **New File: 20 pixels × 20 pixels, 72–150 dpi, RGB, White Background**.

Step 2. Using the **Paint Bucket**, fill the window with a single main hue needed for the twist.

Step 3. Zoom in very close and draw in a mix of the colors needed for the twist.

Step 4. Go to **Filter > Texture > Grain.**

Step 5. Set the **Intensity**; the scale runs from 0 to 100 percent. For example, if using two colors in the yarn, 50 would be a perfect 50/50 mix of the colors. Experiment with the degree of Intensity to get varying degrees of a mix.

Step 6. Set the **Contrast** to **82**.

Step 7. Set **Grain Type** to **Stippled.** Choose **OK.** (See Figure 7–70.)

Step 8. Name and save your file.

HINT: Using the **Blur** tool is a great way to add a "brushing" effect to the knit, once the design is finished.

Other Applications and Insights:

_____

_____

_____

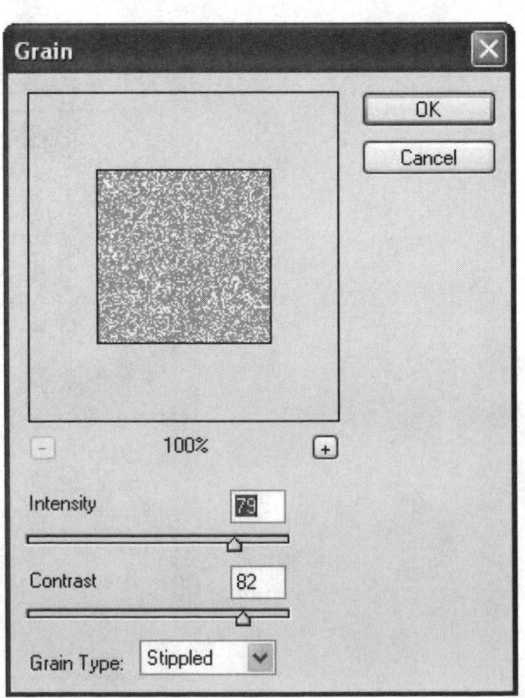

FIGURE 7–70
Stippled grain type

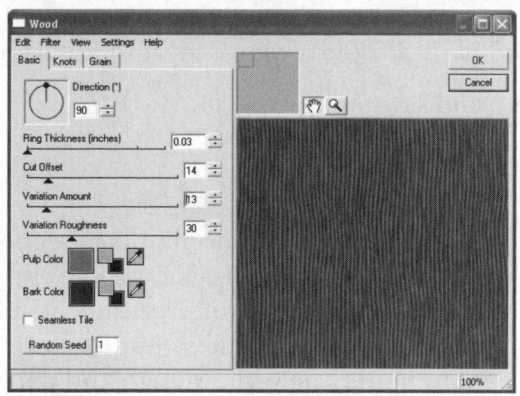

FIGURE 7–71
Make new layer

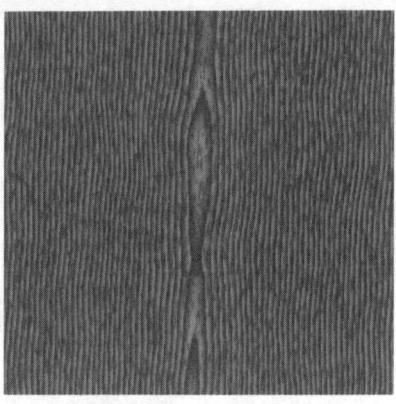

FIGURE 7–72
Crepe yarns

How to Render Crepe Yarns

Step 1. Open a **New File: 8.5 × 11 inches, 72–150 dpi, RGB, White Background.**

Step 2. Make a **New Layer** and fill with desired color.

Step 3. Go to **Filter > Eye Candy.** Select **Wood.**

Step 4. Select **Basic Tab > Ring Thickness > 0.07, Cut Offset > 14, Variation Amount > 13, Roughness > 30, Pulp Color.** Select a deeper shade of original color **Grain Color > Black, Bark Color > Deeper** shade of original color.

Step 5. Select **Knot Tab > Number of Knots > 0, Size > .14.**

Step 6. Select **Grain Tab > Grain Length > .19, Grain Width > .02, Grain Density 50%,** and **Grain Opacity 30%.** (See Figure 7–71.)

Step 7. Name and save your file. (See Figure 7–72.)

Other Applications and Insights:

_____

_____

Challenge—

How to render bouclé

Step 1. This is your first challenging exercise. We have provided you with a sample of bouclé yarn on your CD found in the Goodies Folder, Fabric Structures, Sub Folder and then listed as Yarns.

Step 2. Your assignment is to open a **New File** in Photoshop: **8 × 8, 72–150 dpi, RGB, White Background.**

Step 3. Using the techniques you have garnered in this chapter as well as using the drag and drop to obtain the yarn sample, begin to render this assignment. Be sure you annotate what you have done either on the file in the Layer Property menu or in the space provided on the next page!

Step 4. Name and save your work.

It's Your Turn

Now that we have completed the preliminary section on rendering the fabric ground, you should be more comfortable with several of the alternatives you have seen used. The idea was to practice different alternatives—some simple, some not so easy—and then take the techniques you first learned in Chapter 6 and apply them here. Combining this new knowledge and experience provides you with a real arsenal of techniques that work best for you. (See Figure 7–73 which depicts a collage of ideas you might want to try.)

We have provided you with ample room to jot down any last-minute thoughts or ideas. We have even included several questions to get you thinking about what worked and what did not. Typically, when it comes to rendering, the options really fall into a good, better, or best scenario. The purpose of the exercises was to experiment with as many different variations and then begin to determine your own signature style for rendering fabrics.

After you have pondered what you have learned, we would like to suggest that before you go on to the next chapter, why not take a minute and send us an e-mail to tell us what you think, and what you discovered. Log on to: www.Computers-andFashion.com. We will be happy to showcase your ideas on our site as well as acknowledge you as the designer!

FIGURE 7–73
Other examples of novelty and textured yarns

Let's Review

What works best for you?
   Drag and drop
   Filters
   Defining a pattern
   Defining a brush
   Menu alternative
   Layer property modes
   Layer style options
   Other

Where did the filters work best?
   On top of individual layers
   On top of a JPEG copy (or flatten file)
   Sandwiched in between layers and using the Multiple mode
   Other

Did you remember to use the annotation techniques and workflow strategies you learned in Chapter 4? If not, go back and take a quick review now!

Other observations and lessons learned:

Other Applications and Insights:

_____

_____

_____

Great job! Wasn't that easy? In Chapter 8, we will walk you through rendering most of the major pattern stripes and checks used in designing.

Advanced Rendering Fabric—Stripes, Checks, Plaids, and Advanced Fabric Finishes

In this chapter you will learn to create and render most of today's fabrics that are combinations of stripes and checks. We will also give careful attention to rendering several of the most important visually recognizable fabric finishes. (See Figure 8–1.)

Here is a list of what you will be learning to render:

Stripes:

Plain Woven/Vertical Tickings

Twill Weave Ticking

Seersucker

Rugby Stripes—Knitted Jersey Stripes

Chalk Pin Stripes—Worsted Wool Suiting

Checks:

Balanced Checks

Gingham

Argyle/or Diapered Fabric (See Chapter 10 for advanced rendering techniques)

Plaids:

Madras	Tartan (Advanced Plug-ins)
Tartan (Plain Weave)	Glen Plaid
Tartan (Twill Weave)	Windowpane Plaid

Advanced Finishes:

Napped—Corduroy	Moiré
Napped—Flannel	Embossed
Flocked—Dotted Swiss	Embroidered or Cross-Stitch

Important Announcement and Disclaimer

When developing these next few chapters and the accompanying series of practical exercises, every care has been given to write the steps in a clear and understandable fashion. It is assumed that you already have worked through the exercises in Chapter 4 and have a comfortable working knowledge of all the material covered in Chapters 3, 4, and 5.

FIGURE 8–1
Rendering recognizable fabric finishes

To write the steps in any other manner would have belabored the information and increased the number of written steps to the point of actually causing unnecessary confusion to the reader. All of these exercises have been written to give you ample opportunity to experience the wide range of techniques that can be used.

The purpose of the exercises is to reinforce the basic skills of Adobe Photoshop as applied by a fashion, textile, or interior designer. If you come to this book having learned Adobe Photoshop's tools in a different context, you may need to put aside what you already think you know—how something should be done—and be willing to learn another way to accomplish a task. We heartily encourage you to make notes in the book as you complete each exercise. Note what works best for you. Frequently, you will discover this is not necessarily the right or wrong way to do something, but rather a good, better, best scenario. For example, in this chapter on rendering plaids, there are several ways that are short and sweet but others may involve steps that appear to be a bit more tedious. In reality, sometimes taking the longer route affords you more control over the design process. If the shortcuts work for you, terrific! Use them; by all means apply them to your work!

When a technique or method is preferred over another, we will give notice to that. Therefore, expect to use critical thinking skills to modify the exercises to suit a given project. If you find that you are experiencing extreme difficulty following along in any exercises, we suggest that you go back and review the basic tools and techniques covered in the earlier chapters and then attempt the practical application exercise. Frequently, a student or designer may attempt to rush the design process without adequately knowing the software. The results can be a disappointment or an unnecessary time of frustration.

The last thing you need to do is to become frustrated. Try getting up from the computer for a small break, or perhaps go on to another exercise and come back later to the one that is challenging you. Discussing the outcome objectives with someone who has successfully mastered the assignment can help considerably. Trying the more difficult exercises before you are ready is like trying to build upper floors without successfully completing the structural foundation first.

Although these exercises have been classroom tested, we welcome your feedback via e-mail at our website—www.ComputersandFashion.com.

Insights Before You Begin

As we begin this chapter on using Adobe Photoshop to render stripes, checks, and plaids, you will find it necessary to draw upon the experiences you had in the previous chapter on building fabric structures as well as incorporating the basic tools and techniques of Photoshop covered in Chapter 3.

Each of the exercises has been designed to show you alternative ways to achieve the same goal. Be prepared to follow along and make plenty of notes of which techniques you found to be the most useful for your purposes. However, before we begin, we would like to introduce you to one designer who actually makes her living in sunny South Florida, designing and rendering stripes, checks, and plaids!

The "Sweet Smell of Success"

Meet: Tiborina K. Marton (see Figure 8–2)

Top Textile Designer for Sara Lee Corp. Located in Weston, Florida
Ok, so you are probably wondering what does a company that makes and sells pastries and dessert have a thing to do with rendering stripes, checks, and plaids?

One thing that never ceases to astound most people unfamiliar with fashion, is who owns what companies. The dessert and pastry giant of Sara Lee actually owns several major companies that design and manufacture a variety of clothing for some of the best-known brands in the industry.

FIGURE 8–2
Tiborina K. Marton
(Courtesy of Tiborina Marton)

Tibby studied fashion design in the 1990s at the Art Institute of Ft. Lauderdale where she got her first job designing at Sara Lee. Tibby got her big break when the company's design, advertising, and marketing divisions started to use computer-aided designing. For years the designers at Sara Lee had utilized the state-of-the-art proprietary software for marker making, pattern making, and grading. However, it wasn't long before textile rendering and designing proprietary software found its way into this environment, and Tibby was at the forefront!

Tibby came from the generation of fashion design students who had only limited exposure to computer-aided design. While she was in college, she was traditionally trained to illustrate and she experienced limited exposure to the graphic end of digitally rendering fashion. So as a result, Tibby was thrust like many "old-time" designers into the fray of having to learn, and to learn fast! There was no easy transition from hand to digital while at the same time keeping up with deadlines and productivity on the job. Thankfully, Tibby rose to the occasion and now her department boasts a respectable size staff of digitally trained designers! Therefore, it was only natural for Tibby to go back to her alma mater and hire students who received this new cutting-edge training, which has become available in recent years.

Tibby is one example of someone who used her talents, while continuing to stay current! In no time, her skills in design and communication opened the door for her to quickly move up the ranks.

Today, Tibby continues to enjoy her success as a designer and industry leader who is willing to give back to other fresh new talent, who also are willing to learn and grow with the times. So we suppose that you could say at Sara Lee, Tibby did find a "sweet" form of designing success. In our upcoming exercises, she has graciously provided us with inspiration samples for you to try!

Typically, at Sara Lee they use Adobe Photoshop for marketing boards as well as other forms of promotional materials. Although many of Tibby's textile designs have been generated in proprietary software, you will see how we have easily replicated them into exercises for you in Adobe Photoshop!

Rendering Stripes—Ticking (Ivory and White)

Part 1

Step 1. This project will require you to make two files. File 1: Begin by opening a **New File: 150 pixels × 150 pixels**, **72 dpi**, **RGB**, **White Background**. Do NOT name this file. This will be your pattern template.

Step 2. Open another **New File: 8.5 × 11 inches**, **72–150 dpi**, **RGB**, **White Background**. Name the file **Stripe**.

Step 3. Open the **CD**. Select the **Scan Swatch** folder and open the file entitled **Ticking**.

Step 4. Match the color from the Ticking swatch, using the Eyedropper tool. (See Figure 8–3.)

Step 5. Close the Ticking scanned original.

Part 2

Step 1. Go back to the first file, created from Step 1.

Step 2. Make a **Marquee** from outside the page, aproximately .5 inches wide and 1 inch high and fill with the color red you selected in Step 3. Don't forget when using the Marquee tool to open your window so that you may be able to select all of the area outside the printable page. This will ensure that an accurate selection of the area has been made into a Pattern Fill.

Step 3. Make a **Marquee** just to the right of the red stripe, the same size, and fill this area with white.

Step 4. Make a **Marquee** outside the image completely around both stripes.

Step 5. Go to the **Edit** menu. Select **Define Pattern** and name the pattern **Stripe #1**. Click **OK**. (See Figure 8–4.)

Step 6. Name this layer **Vertical Stripe** in the Layer Property box.

Step 7. Hint: On a PC, right-click on the layer. On a Mac, go to **Layer** menu, Layer Property flyout.)

Step 8. Drop the Opacity level to approximately 50%.

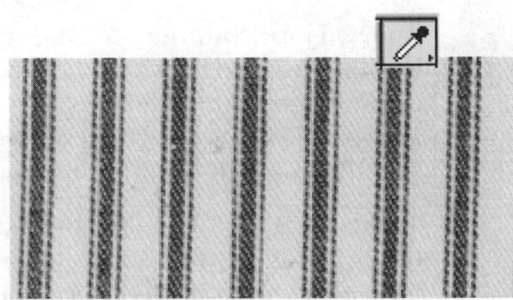

FIGURE 8–3
Rendering stripes

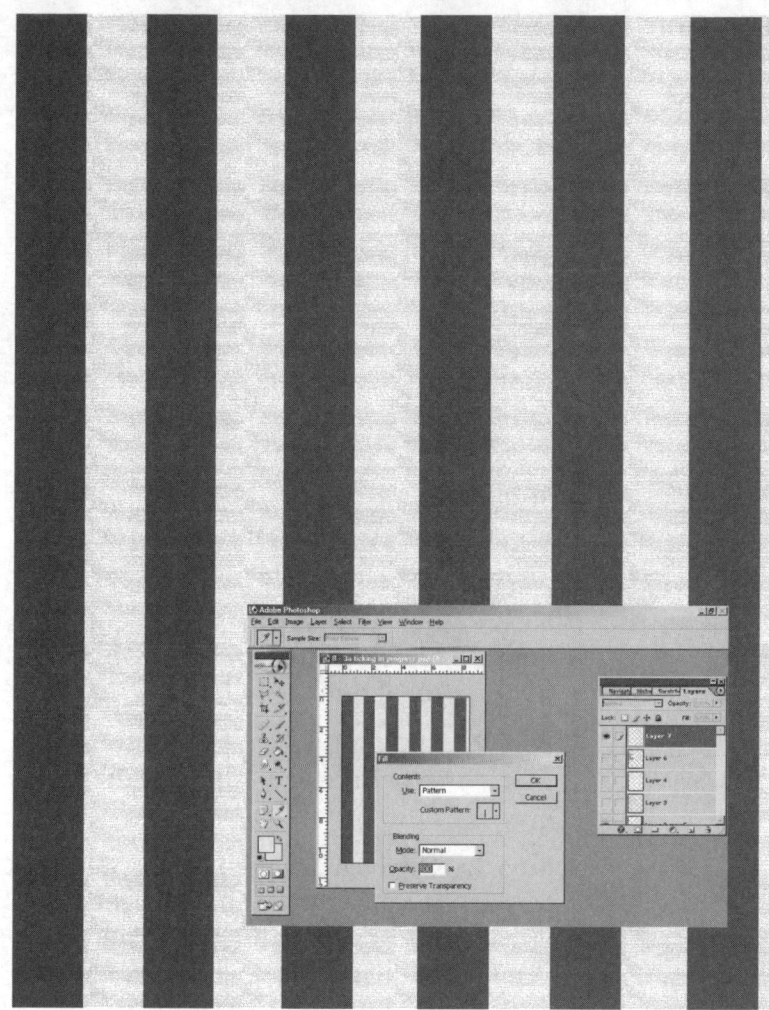

FIGURE 8–4
Define stripe pattern

Part 3

Step 1. Open the file entitled **Twill** on the enclosed CD.

Step 2. Drag a copy of the file entitled **Twill** onto your file entitled **Ticking**.

Step 3. You may need to move this layer to the top in case you dropped it out of order on the Layer Palette window.

Step 4. If the color of the Twill layer is not consistent, you may wish to zoom in with a **Magnifying Glass.** Using the **Magic Wand,** carefully select a section of the twill pattern. (See Figure 8–5.)

Step 5. Go to **Select > Select Similar** to select the complete twill pattern.

Step 6. Go to **Edit > Fill > Foreground Color** or a color of your choice to match.

We recommend that you experiment with different colors of the twill pattern, such as blue or eggshell, to see the different variations the simulated yarns can make. (See Figure 8–6.) Don't forget we have a sample of actual ticking fabric on the Goodies CD under **> Fabric Samples > Ticking.** This should make it easy for you to match the traditional blue and eggshell colors associated with ticking fabric.

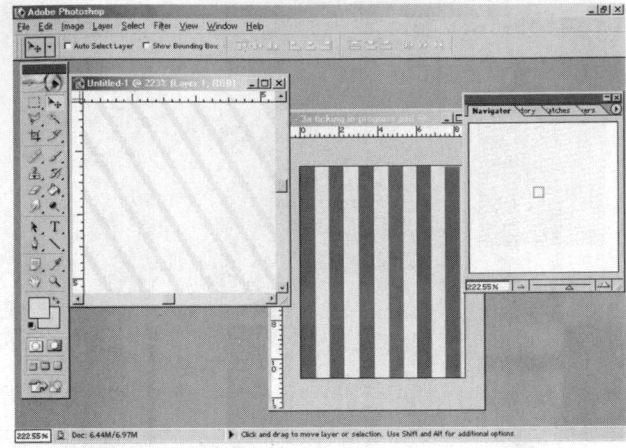

FIGURE 8–5
Select section of twill pattern

FIGURE 8–6
Experiment with color

Part 4
Next we suggest that you experiment with the following choices:

Step 1. Slide the Opacity Layer on the Twill Layer to make the twill recede into the fabric.

Step 2. Make a JPEG version of your file, and then reopen your JPEG copy and experiment by adding **Filter > Noise > Gaussian > Monochromatic** options to add textural effects.

Step 3. Or you may opt to make a duplicate layer of Stripe Layer #1 using the Duplicate Layer icon. Experiment with Filters to add texture and surface interest to only the background color. This can be accomplished by either adding **Filter > Noise > Gaussian > Monochromatic** or adding **Filter > Texturizer > Canvas** or **Burlap**. (See Figures 8–7 and 8–8.)

Step 4. A final example shows the steps and variations. (See Figure 8–9.)

Other Applications and Insights:

_____

_____

_____

_____

Rendering Seersucker

Step 1. This project will require you to make two files. File 1: Begin by opening a **New File: 150 pixels × 150 pixels, 72 dpi, RGB, White Background**. Do NOT name this file. This will be your pattern template.

Step 2. Open another **New File: 8.5 × 11 inches, 72–150 dpi, RGB, White Background**. Name the file **Seersucker**.

Step 3. Open the **CD.** Select the **Scan Swatch** folder and open the file entitled **Seersucker**.

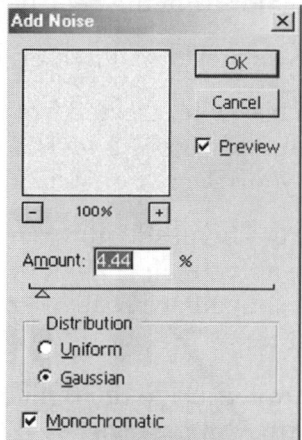

FIGURE 8–7
Filter > Noise > Gaussian

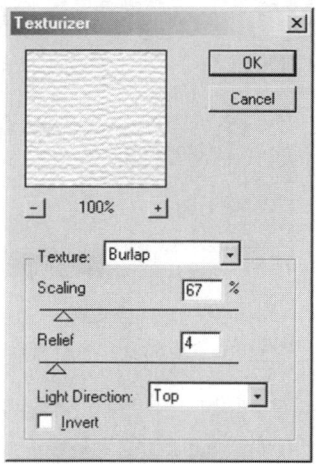

FIGURE 8–8
Filter > Texturizer > Burlap

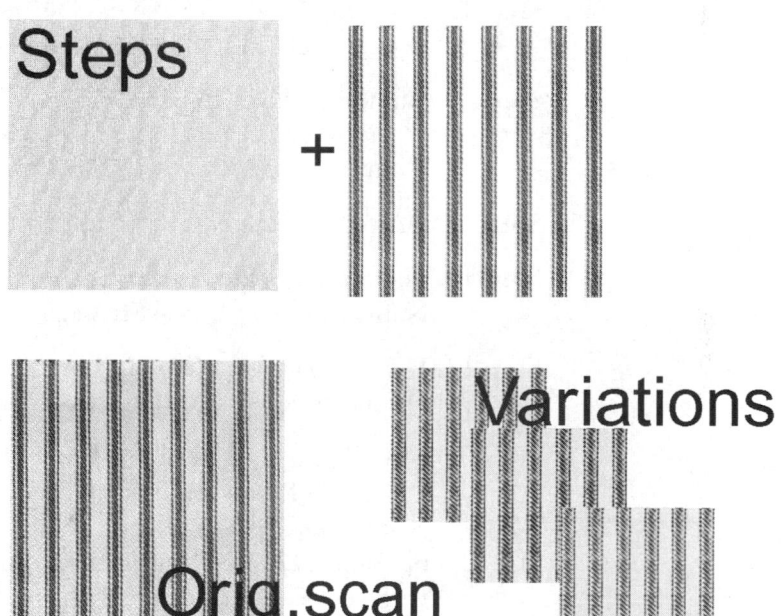

Steps

\+

Variations

Orig.scan

Practical
Application-
Storyboard

FIGURE 8–9
Steps and variations

Step 4. Match the color from the Seersucker swatch, using the Eyedropper tool.

Step 5. Close the Seersucker scanned original.

Step 6. Go back to **New File,** created from Step 1. Make a **Marquee** from outside the page, aproximately .5 inches wide and 1 inch high and fill with the color blue you selected in Step 3.

*Don't forget when using the Marquee tool to open your window so that you may be able to select all of the area outside the printable page. This will ensure that an accurate selection of the area has been made into a Pattern Fill.

Step 7. Make a **Marquee** just to the right of the blue stripe, the same size, and fill this area with white.

Step 8. Make a **Marquee** outside the image completely around both stripes and go to the **Edit** menu.

Step 9. From the **Edit** menu, select **Define Pattern** and name the pattern **Seersucker.** Click **OK.** (See Figure 8–10.)

Step 10. Name this layer **Vertical Stripe** in the Layer Property box. (Hint: On a PC, right-click on the layer. On a Mac, go to **Layer** menu, Layer Property flyout.)

Step 11. Drop the Opacity level to approximately 50%.

Step 12. Make a duplicate layer of **Stripe Layer #1,** using the Duplicate Layer icon. Name this layer **Plissé Stripe.**

Step 13. Using the **Magic Wand** and the Shift key, select **All** the blue stripes on the Duplicate Layer entitled **Plissé Stripe.**

Step 14. Select **Layer > Layer Style > Emboss.** (See Figure 8–11.) Check on as follows:
  a. **Style > Pillow Emboss > Technique > Hard Chisel > Depth 231 > Direction, Up > Size, 2.**
  b. **Angle, 120** and check on **Global Light > Altitude 30.**
  c. Select **Gloss Contour Box** and check off **Aliasing.**
  d. Select **Highlight mode, Normal > Opacity 75%.**
  e. Select **Shadow mode, Multiple > Color > slightly deeper blue than original stripe > Opacity, 75%.**
  f. Click **OK.**

Step 15. Make a **New Layer** directly above the newly embossed stripes. Fill with off-white.

Step 16. Go to **Filter > Noise > Select > Gaussian > Monochromatic** and select the range to suit your taste.
  a. Go to **Filter > Blur > Motion Blur > 4 degrees.** Move the slider bar to 150 pixels.
  b. **Filter > Texturizer > Burlap > Scaling 64 > Relief 4 > Light Direction > Top.** Click **OK.** Drop the Opacity level to 41% to clearly view the stripes.

Step 17. Name and save. (See Figure 8–12.)

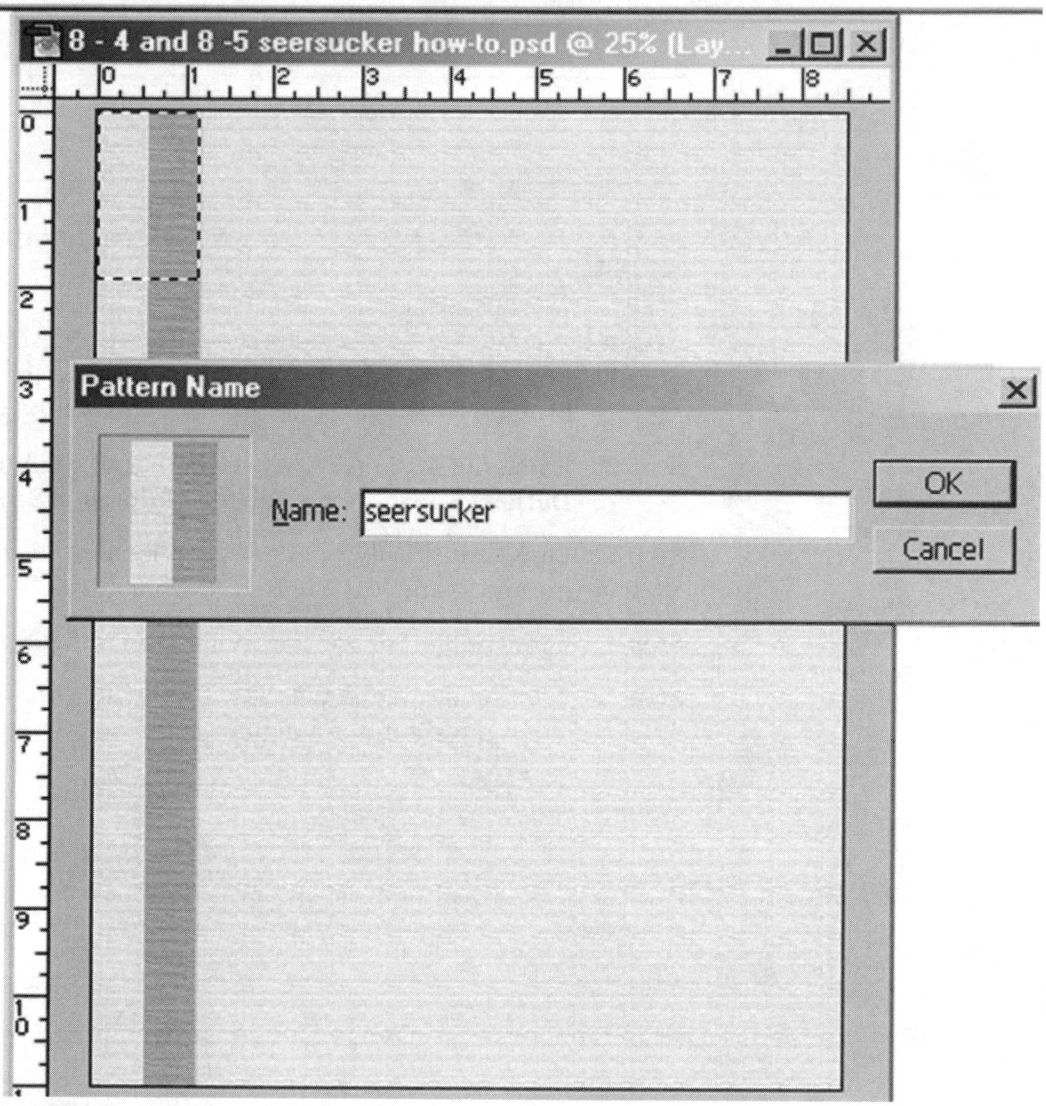

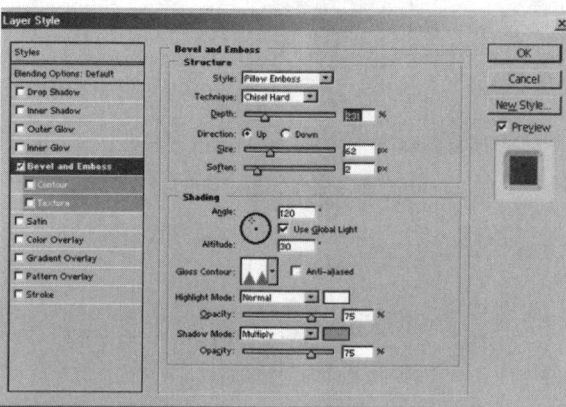

FIGURE 8–10
Layer style: emboss

FIGURE 8–11
Pillow emboss

FIGURE 8–12
Seersucker

Other Applications and Insights:

_____

_____

_____

_____

Rendering a Horizontal Stripe—Candy Stripe

Step 1. Open a **New File: 150 pixels × 150 pixels, 72 dpi, RGB, White Background.** Do NOT name this file. This will be your pattern template.

Step 2. Using the **Marquee** tool, select half of the horizontal area. Go to **Edit > Define Pattern**. Name the file **Horizontal Stripe**.

Step 3. Open another **New File: 8 × 8 inches, 72–150 dpi, RGB, White Background.** Name the file **Red & White Stripe**.

Step 4. Go to **Edit > Fill > w/Pattern > Horizontal Stripe**. (See Figure 8–13.)

Step 5. Name and save the file as **Candy Stripe.** You will need this file again when we begin to render a digital gingham.

Other Applications and Insights:

_____

_____

_____

_____

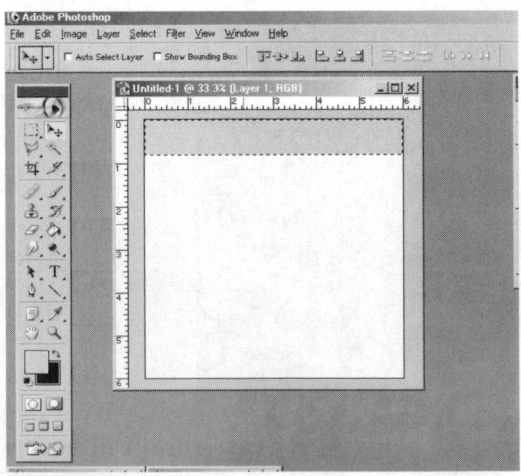

FIGURE 8–13
Edit > Fill > w/Pattern > Horizontal Stripe

Rendering a Rugby Stripe

Step 1. Open a **New File: 8.5 × 11 inches, 72–150 dpi, RGB, White Background.**

Step 2. Start a **New Layer** and label the file **Stripe #1.**

Step 3. Using the **Rectangle Marquee** tool, make a 2-inch wide horizontal stripe and fill with desired color.

Step 4. Make a copy of Layer #2 and fill the stripe with new color.

Step 5. Position the stripe directly below the existing stripe.

Step 6. Continue to either make copies of existing Stripe #1 or make additional layers with stripes in varying widths and color combinations. (See Figure 8–14.)

Step 7. Between the original background layer and the layers with the stripes, you can sandwich any of the previous textures created, such as a jersey knit or a plain weave.

Step 8. You may also opt to experiment with adding filters for additional textural surface interest. (See Figure 8–15.)

Other Applications and Insights:

_____

_____

_____

_____

FIGURE 8–14
Make copies of existing stripe

FIGURE 8–15
Rugby stripe

Creating Chalk Pin Stripes

Step 1. Open a **New File** in Adobe Photoshop: **8 × 8 inches, 72–150 dpi, RGB, White Background.**

Step 2. Make a **New Layer** and fill with gradient of two shades of dark navy color.

Step 3. Name the layer in the **Layer Property** menu, **Navy Ground.** Make a **New Layer** of two narrow vertical stripes using a **Marquee** tool.

Step 4. Fill the Box with off-white.

Step 5. Place a **Marquee** around both of the off-white stripes.

Step 6. Make a **New Layer.**

Step 7. Go to **Edit > Define Pattern.** Name the pattern **Chalk Stripes.**

Step 8. Make a **New Layer** and go to **Edit > Fill > Pattern** and fill with Chalk Stripe pattern.

Step 9. At this point, you can opt to make a copy of the newly filled stripe pattern because you will be experimenting with making the stripe to begin looking more like a chalk line than a solid stripe. (See Figure 8–16.)

Step 10. If you opt to make multiple copies, be sure to turn off the unselected copies by switching off the "Eye" On-Off button on the Layers palette. (See Figure 8–17.)

Step 11. Go to **Filter** menu, **Noise > Add Noise.** We suggest that you use a small amount of **Monochromatic > Gaussian** to give a simulated textural depth to the stripe. (See Figure 8–18.)

Step 12. Go to **Filter** menu, **Blur > Motion Blur** and experiment with adding slight motion to the stripe.

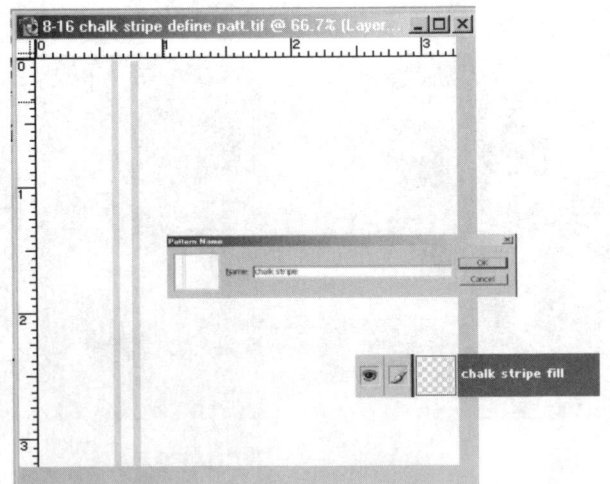

FIGURE 8–16
Chalk stripe pattern

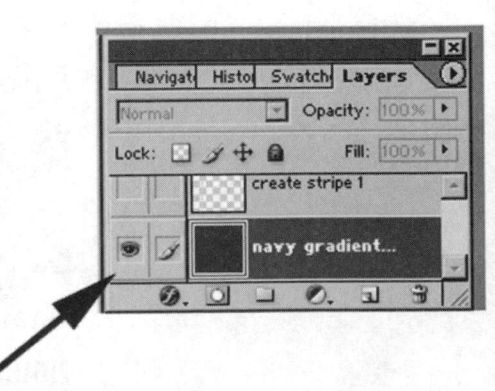

FIGURE 8–17
Eye button

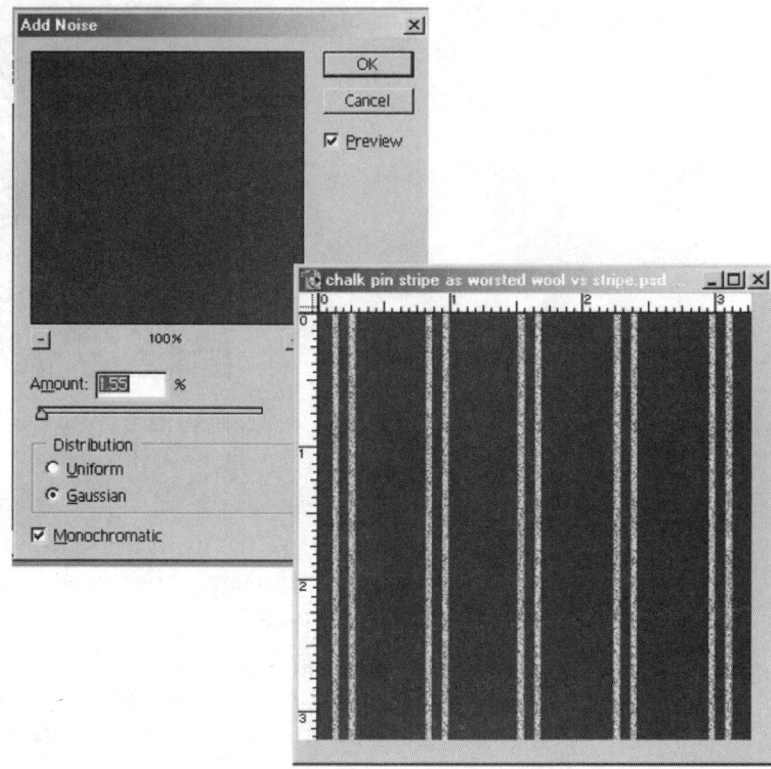

FIGURE 8–18
Add noise dialogue window

Step 13. Another alternative is to go to **Filter** menu, **Artistic > Plaster.**

Step 14. At this point, once you are satisfied with the stripe, we suggest that you turn off the stripe layer and move now to the gradient layer and begin to add texture and depth as follows:

Step 15. Begin by going to the **Filter** menu, **Noise > Add Noise** and again add only minimal amounts of **Monochromatic > Gaussian Noise.**

Step 16. Next, determine if you want the image to be a plain weave worsted wool suiting or a twill weave gabardine wool. If you wish to make the image a plain weave, follow Step 18. If you wish to make it a twill weave, go on to Step 19.

Step 17. Go to **Filter > Brush Strokes > Hatch Lines**. Next, go on to Step 22.

Step 18. Open the **Goodies Folder** in the CD and the file **Fabric Structures > Twill Weave**.

Step 19. Drag a copy of the twill pattern and place it between the solid navy gradient ground and the chalk stripe.

Step 20. You may need to change the color in the stripe to match your fabric. If this is the case, use the **Navigator** tool to zoom in and then take the **Magic Wand** to select a portion of the twill structure. Select **Similar;** then go to **Edit > Fill,** and choose a foreground color that will enhance the

FIGURE 8–19
Chalk pin stripes

twill pattern. Try using a lighter navy than the gradient ground color. Adjust the Opacity slider bar on the Layers palette to drop the ground into the image.

Step 21. Finally, you are ready to go back to the stripe layer and play with the Opacity slider to make the stripes appear to be more a part of the gradient gray ground.

Step 22. After you feel the image is complete, name and save the file. (See Figure 8–19.)

Step 23. Make a JPEG copy to open later when we choose to make this fabric appear to have more of a napped finish. We will reopen the JPEG in the finishing section later in this chapter.

Other Applications and Insights:

_____

_____

_____

_____

Notes...

Creating a Check Pattern

A check as a design is traditionally made up of only two color geometric squares that repeat in a pattern across the surface of the fabric. Checks come in several variations.

Plaid can be defined as a combination of lines and/or checks of more than two colors. Plaids can also be specific woven patterns or merely surface prints that are representative of a plaid.

Now we are ready to begin our section of checks and plaids, the subtle nuances of creating checks and plaids to fool the eye beginning with an excellent explanation of the connection between layers and opacity in Adobe Photoshop.

How to Render a Check

Step 1. Open your file entitled **Horizontal Candy Stripe.**

Step 2. Open a **New File: 8 × 8 inches, 72–150 dpi, RGB, White Background.**

Step 3. Drag the Horizontal Candy Stripe pattern to your new file.

Step 4. Place your **Magic Wand** on one of the white stripes and go to **Edit > Select > Similar** and hit **Delete.**

Step 5. Make a duplicate copy of the stripe.

Step 6. Repeat Step 4.

Step 7. Go to **Edit > Transform > Flip 90 degrees clockwise.**

Step 8. Open the **Fabric Swatch** folder on the CD and open the file **Gingham.** You will use this to help you more closely mimic the way gingham looks. (See Figure 8–20.)

Step 9. Begin to adjust the Opacity slider on Layers 2 and 3 to make your image appear to more closely resemble the actual gingham swatch of fabric. (See Figure 8–21.)

Step 10. You may opt to open the **Goodies Folder** on the CD and open **Fabric Structures > Plain Weave** to enhance your image even more. (See Figure 8–22.)

Step 11. Name and save your file **Gingham.**

Other Applications and Insights:

_____

_____

_____

_____

FIGURE 8–20
Gingham

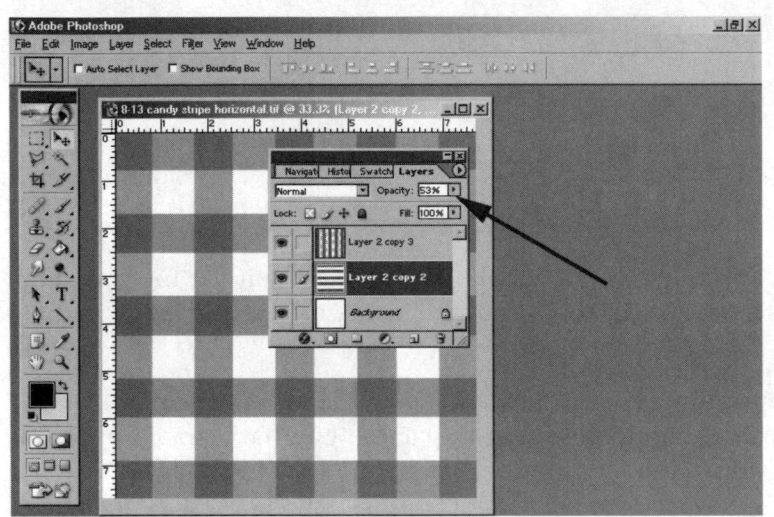

FIGURE 8–21
Adjust opacity slider

FIGURE 8–22
Adding a ground plain weave

FIGURE 8–23
Variations of gingham checks

Variations on Checks

In the last exercise we built on an existing file you had made in a previous exercise; however, you may also opt to make a gingham by making small pattern fill boxes consisting of horizontal and vertical stripes (Figure 8–23).

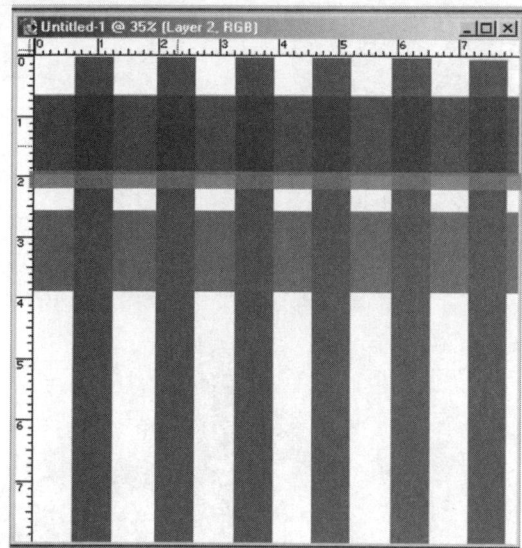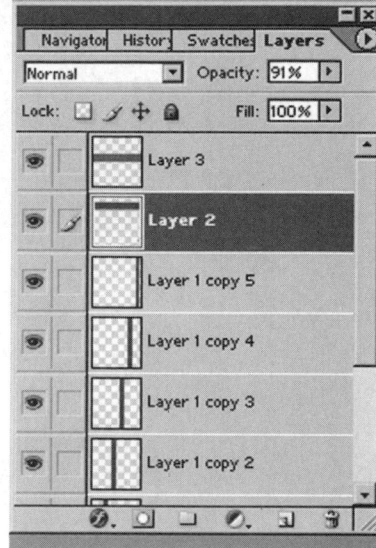

FIGURE 8-24
Creating stripes layer by layer

Another terrific way to create a check is a bit more time-consuming, but it will give the most options for you in the future. That method is creating the horizontal and vertical stripes layer by layer, making individual stripes each on their own layer. The advantage is that later you can opt to change the color as well as select a specific stripe to make wider or narrower for use in a plaid fabric. (See Figure 8-24.)

Rendering Plaids

Historically, we associate plaids with the Scottish Isles, noting that specific colors and pattern color combinations are representative of specific families and specific regions. In fact, in Figure 8-25 you can see an example provided of an actual Scottish family tartan (Dalziel) from one of Kathleen's former students, Heather Dalziel-Kolsky.

As you can see in Figure 8-25, one of the images was the actual scanned fabric. The second image is digitally rendered. Can you tell which one is which?

Secrets of Not "Going Mad" over Plaids!

Perhaps one of the easiest ways to re-create a plaid is to begin by trying to emulate a plaid in the exact same stripe order and color.

For example, we suggest that you open up the **Goodies Folder** on the CD and open the file **Swatches.** Choose **Tartan Plaid-Plain Weave** and then open **Tartan Plaid-Twill Weave.** Although both of these plaids have common colors, the fabric construction ground is very different. (See Figure 8-26.)

We suggest, as you walk through the following exercises, you follow this simple technique for simulating a plaid.

FIGURE 8–25
Scottish family tartan: can you tell the scanned original from the digitally created one?

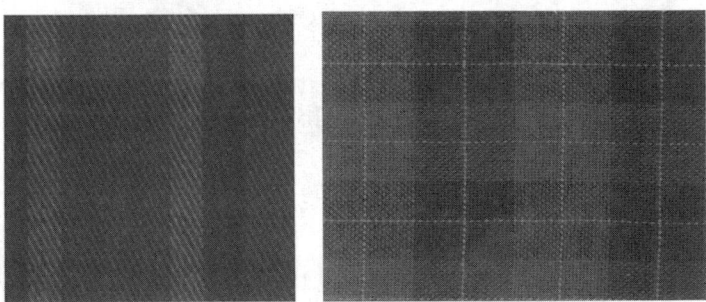

FIGURE 8–26
Tartan weaves

Overview—How to Render a Basic Plaid

Step 1. Open your original scanned swatch.

Step 2. Open a **New File** in Adobe Photoshop: **8 × 8 inches, 72–150 dpi, RGB, White Background**. Be sure to go to **View > Show Rulers.** This will be very helpful later when attempting to align the stripes both vertically and horizontally.

Step 3. Drag a copy of the scanned fabric into your new file, and close the original swatch. This will ALWAYS be the top copy of your layers. Therefore, every time you begin a New Layer, do it below the swatch.

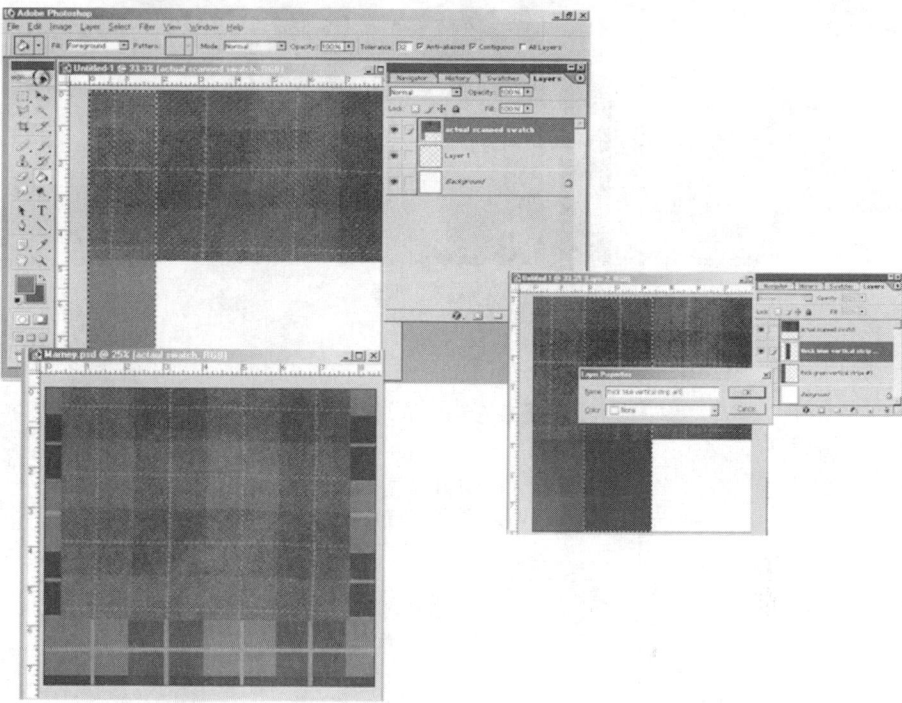

FIGURE 8–27
Aligning stripes

Step 4. Examine the pattern repeat. On a New Layer BELOW your swatch, use the **Marquee** tool to draw the first vertical stripe.

Step 5. Using the **Eyedropper,** match the color to the original swatch and fill the new stripe to match original.

Step 6. If this stripe repeats several times across the face of the pattern, continue to drag this layer to the **Layer > Copy** icon on the bottom of the Layers palette menu.

Step 7. Use the **Move** tool to align these stripes directly over the original.

Step 8. Continue in this manner for all the vertical and horizontal stripes until they are complete. (We suggest that you name each layer by the stripe's designated location. For example, Thick Vertical Blue Stripe number one, or Thin Green Horizontal Stripe number 2, and so on. This will make it easier to reorder the layers later.) (See Figure 8–27.)

Step 9. At this point you will need to access the layer order for the stripes. This will mean changing layer order to simulate the "over-under" motion of a real woven pattern. It will also mean that you will need to slide the Opacity slider bar on the Layer Property menu to enhance the appearance to be more like that of a traditional woven fabric.

Step 10. Finally, you will need to access the best way to add the actual fabric texture such as plain or twill weave. Because every plaid is different, you will need to apply critical thinking skills to determine the most effective method of doing this successfully.

FIGURE 8–28
Several variations of digitally
rendered plaids
(Courtesy of AGE Technologies)

FIGURE 8–29
Sample storyboard application
(Courtesy of Judith Kruger)

Adding texture and fabric structure to a plaid:

- For twill weaves, place the twill on the top layer and drop the Opacity.

- For plain weaves, sandwich the twill below the ground and all of the stripes layers. You can opt to open a fabric structure from the CD.

- Another way for plain weaves, make a JPEG copy before any texture has been added. Experiment with dragging and dropping an existing fabric structure from your Goodies Folder on the CD or play with the Filter menus.

In Figure 8–28 you can see several variations of plaids that were digitally rendered. In this section we will share with you the secrets of easily rendering plaids with Adobe Photoshop. In Figure 8–29 you can see a sample storyboard application.

FIGURE 8–30
Tartan plaid

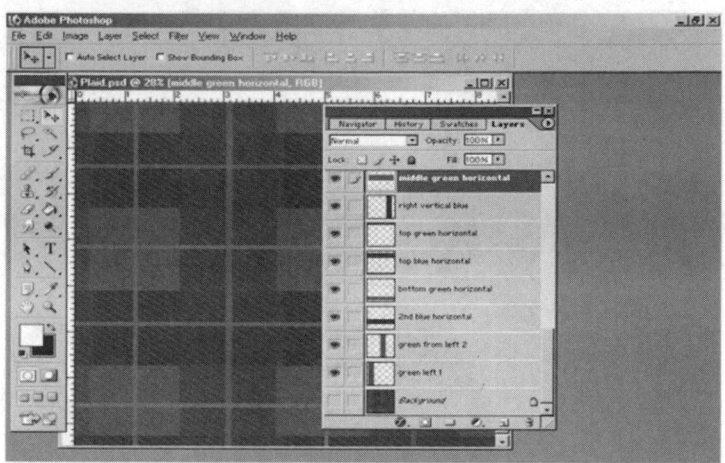

FIGURE 8–31
Layer property menu

How to Render a Tartan Plaid—Step-by-Step

Step 1. Open a **New File: 8.5 × 11 inches, RGB, 72–150 dpi, White Background.**

Step 2. Make a **New Layer.**

Step 3. Open from the CD in the Goodies Folder **Sample Exercise Folder > Tartan Plaid**. (See Figure 8–30.)

Step 4. Using the **Eyedropper,** begin to match the color of the widest stripe.

Step 5. Make a rectangle **Marquee** to match the width of the original scan and fill by using a **Paint Bucket** tool.

Step 6. Copy and paste additional rows of the stripe across the layer to match the original scan.

Step 7. Make a **New Layer** and begin to follow the thinner lines of the stripe found in the original fabric. Using the **Eyedropper** tool, match the colors and repeat Steps 5 and 6 for each segment of colors and lines of the original plaid.

Step 8. We recommend as you begin to build your layers that you name the stripes according to their position. This is done by right-clicking on the **Layer Property** menu. Then type the name of the layer in the Layer Property box and click **OK**. (See Figure 8–31.)

Step 9. Experiment with the layer position and the Opacity levels to resemble the original scan.

Step 10. Opt to open the weave patterns that you made earlier or access the examples from the CD to give the effect of a plain or twill weave fabric construction to your plaid.

Step 11. After you have filled in all of the stripes both horizontally and vertically, begin to shift the layers so that you can clearly see the stripes as they might appear in an actual woven fabric. This may also involve adjusting the Opacity slider on the layers so that you can view the layers from below.

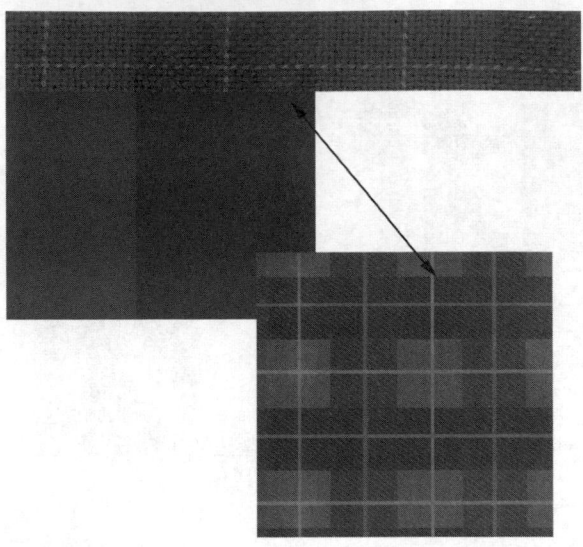

FIGURE 8–32
Variations

FIGURE 8–33
Added twill ground

Step 12. Finally, you can make a JPEG copy of your work to experiment with adding Filters and other options to enhance your design. We have included several variations created only with Photoshop for you to examine. (See Figure 8–32.) See also Figure 8–33 where we added a twill ground and **Filter > Noise** and **Motion Blur** to simulate a flannel tartan plaid.

Notes...

HINT: There are a variety of ways to overcome any special challenges found in complex pattern combinations, as you have just seen using the layer order. However, sometimes additional solutions need to be considered. Such was in the case of Heather's plaid, seen in Figure 8–33. She used the Define Brush to make a small stamp-style brush of the twill pattern to place over the top of areas where the twill appears in different colors from other segments of the design.

Adding Advanced Ground Techniques

In Chapter 7 you discovered the secrets to adding woven and knitted fabric structures to your rendering. However, there are times when you must enhance the image to really showcase the effects of two colors of yarns crossing over each other on the surface of a fabric. For times like these, it may be advantageous for you to make the size of the fabric structure the exact same size as the area you need to color. This is accomplished by creating a new brush.

How to Define a Brush for Texture
Although Adobe Photoshop7 does include this kind of brush, there are advantages to making a new brush to fit the exact proportions of a given twill. In this exercise, you will adapt a twill from the Goodies Folder in the CD to create and use to enhance your images.

Step 1. Open one of the fabric structure textures from your CD.

Step 2. For example, open in the Goodies Folder **Fabric Structures > Right-Handed Twill**.

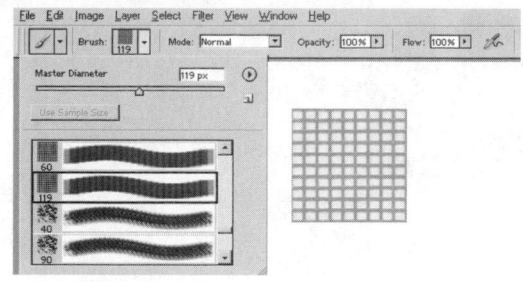

FIGURE 8–34
Select brush

Step 3. Place a square **Marquee** of the approximate size of the fabric brush size you will need. This may take you several tries to get it exact.

Step 4. Go to **Edit > Define Brush**.

Step 5. Go to the **Tool Box > Select the Brush** from the flyout menu.

Step 6. Go to the list of brushes on the **Brush** menu. Select your fabric brush.

Step 7. Select the desired color and begin to paint the extra texture to your image as needed.

Step 8. In Figure 8–34 you can see our example contrasted to the brush that is included in Adobe Photoshop7. You will also see an example of how you can easily change colors of your twill brush to enhance your designs.

Other Applications and Insights:

_____

_____

_____

_____

How to Render Madras

Step 1. Open the madras swatch from your CD.

Step 2. Make a **New File: 8.5 × 11 inches, 72–150 dpi, RGB, White Background.**

Step 3. Make a **New Layer** and name this layer > **Ground** in the Layer Property menu.

Step 4. Using the **Eyedropper,** select the yellow ground color.

Step 5. Using the **Paint Bucket,** fill the New Layer with the gold color.

Step 6. Starting a New Layer for each stripe in the plaid, use the **Eyedropper** to match the color of the stripes.

FIGURE 8–35
Adding puckered appearance to plaid

Step 7. Use the **Marquee** tool to make each stripe one at a time.

Step 8. After making each stripe and filling with corresponding color, go to **Filter > Distort > Wave** and experiment as shown in Figure 8–35 to give the puckered appearance to the plaid. This image also shows you a close-up of each of the steps you will be taking to render the madras, beginning with the actual inspiration swatch to the stripe-by-stripe fills, all the way until the Filters are added.

Step 9. When all the layers have been complete, you may need to reorder the layers to simulate the weave. Adjust each individual layer's Opacity slider bar to match original swatch for depth.

Step 10. Experiment by making a JPEG copy of this file.

Step 11. Reopen your JPEG copy and drag this copy to your actual step-by-step rendering.

Step 12. You may opt to make multiple copies of the JPEG to experiment with applying texture or surface interest to your file.

Step 13. You can opt to add a **Filter > Crosshatch** to the final file.

Step 14. Name and save your file.

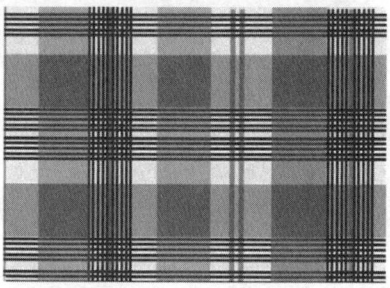

FIGURE 8–36
Glen plaid

Other Applications and Insights:

_____

_____

_____

_____

Making a Glen Plaid

Step 1. Open a **New File: 8.5 × 11 inches, RGB, 72–150 dpi, White Background.**

Step 2. Make a **New Layer.**

Step 3. Open from the CD in the Goodies Folder **Sample Exercise Folder > Glen Plaid.** (See Figure 8–36.)

Step 4. Using the concept of matching and layering stripes that we used in the tartan plaid exercise, use the **Eyedropper** to match colors and begin to make the vertical stripes. Be sure to give each stripe its own layer.

Step 5. Continue to use this process for the horizontal stripes, building row-by-row.

Step 6. Reorganize the rows and adjust individual layer Opacity levels to make your file align with your layer order similar to that in the tartan plaid exercise.

Step 7. Open the file **Fabric Structures** in the Goodies Folder and select the warp and weft files.

Step 8. Turn off Layer #3 and place a **Marquee** around the image and select **Edit > Define Pattern > Name the Pattern > Weft Lines.**

Step 9. Now, turn off Layer #2 and turn on Layer #3. Make a **Marquee** around the image. Go to **Edit > Define Pattern > Name the Pattern > Warp Lines.**

Step 10. Close the weft and warp fabric structure files and make a New Layer on top of your Glen Plaid file. Go to **Edit > Fill > Pattern > Weft Lines** and adjust the Opacity slider bar on the Layer Property menu to make your new lines fade into the fabric.

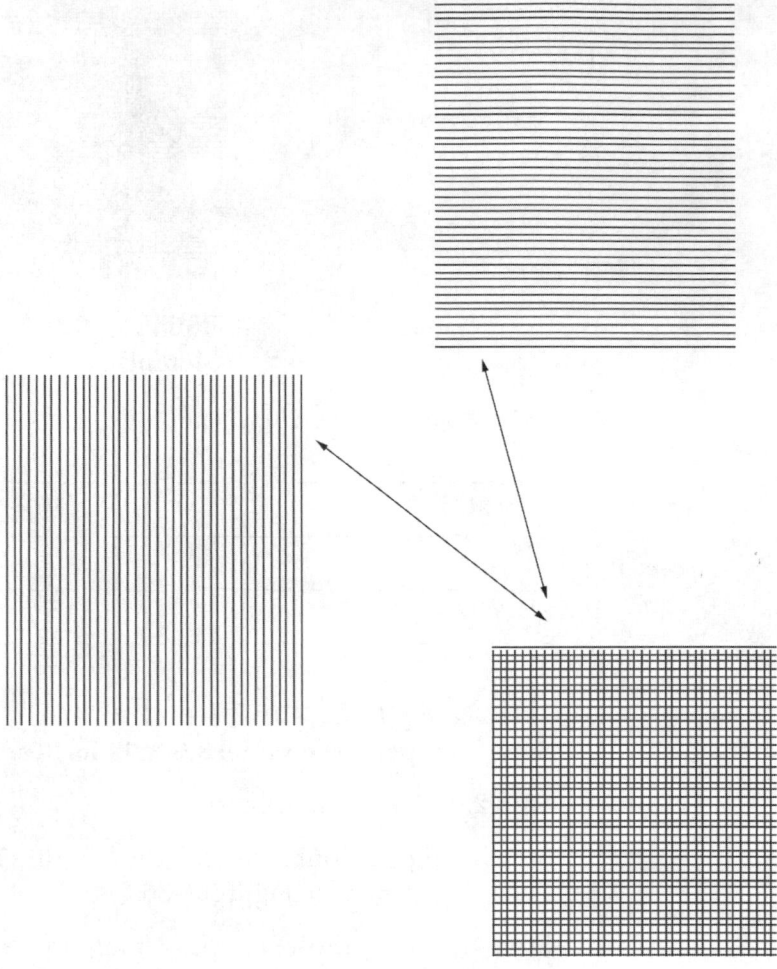

FIGURE 8–37
Adjust lines

Step 11. Make a **New Layer.** Go to **Edit > Fill > Pattern > Warp Lines** and adjust the Opacity slider bar on the Layer Property menu to make your new lines fade into the fabric. (See Figure 8–37.)

Step 12. Finally go to the **Filter** menu and select **Brush Strokes > Accent Edges > Width > 2 > Brightness > 35 > Smoothness > 2** and select **OK**. (See Figure 8–38.)

Step 13. At this point you may opt to flatten your image or save a JPEG copy. We will reopen this file later in this chapter when we are doing fabric finishing, and again in Chapter 10, when we will enhance the fabric further with feathers.

Notes . . .

Other Advanced Alternatives

A Quick Look into Plug-ins

In addition to teaching you the traditional methods for rendering plaids, we felt it appropriate to introduce you briefly to the advantages of working with plug-in software that can speed up the process of plaid rendering. If you recall from Chapter 7, we added exercises for using Alien Skin Eye Candy to our satin fabric. The software

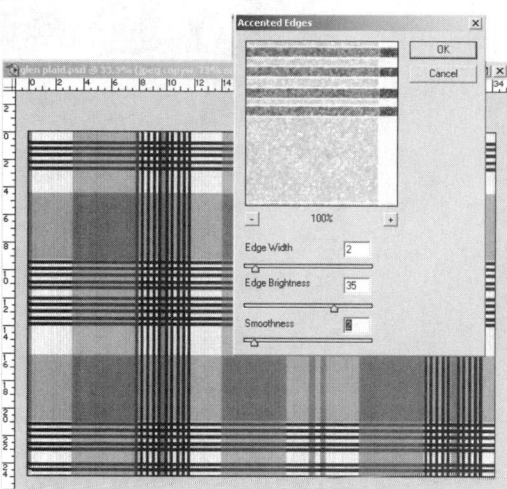

FIGURE 8–38
Accent edges

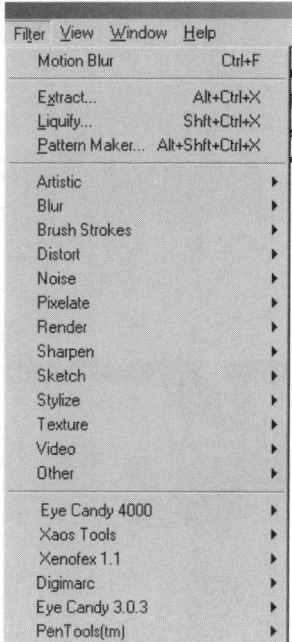

FIGURE 8–39
Flyout menu

typically is accessed through the Filter menu or as an Import flyout menu found on the File menu in Adobe Photoshop. (See Figure 8–39.) We will review and discuss in greater detail additional choices you have as a designer rendering fabric and prints.

How to Render a Tartan Plaid:

Using ClicDesign PlaidMaker Plus with Adobe Photoshop:
As you can clearly see, there are distinctive advantages for using additional plug-in programs with Adobe Photoshop. In this exercise for making plaids, you will have the opportunity to use the free-trial version of software that comes from AGE Technologies. Begin by installing the free-trial software from the Goodies Folder and select **Trial Software > Age Technology > Plaid.** (See Figure 8–40.) This exercise comes courtesy of AGE Technologies Tips and Tricks on the members segment of their website in June 2002. See Figure 8–41 for a visual sequence of steps using ClicDesign by AGE Technologies.

Creating your plaid or weaving fabric:
From PlaidMaker Plus, simply create your woven fabric and import into Photoshop.

Using the Noise filter:
From the Photoshop Filter menu, choose **Noise (>) Add Noise**. From the Option menu, choose **Gaussian Distribution** and **Monochromatic**. It is generally better to set up a small amount of Noise and redo the Noise to obtain the desired effect. Here's how: Set up the Noise amount to around 2% with the proper option mentioned above. Apply it to your plaid.

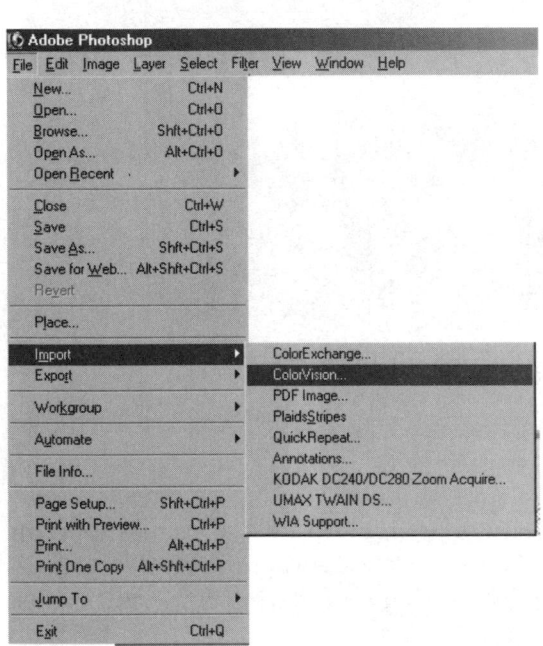

FIGURE 8–40
Installing software

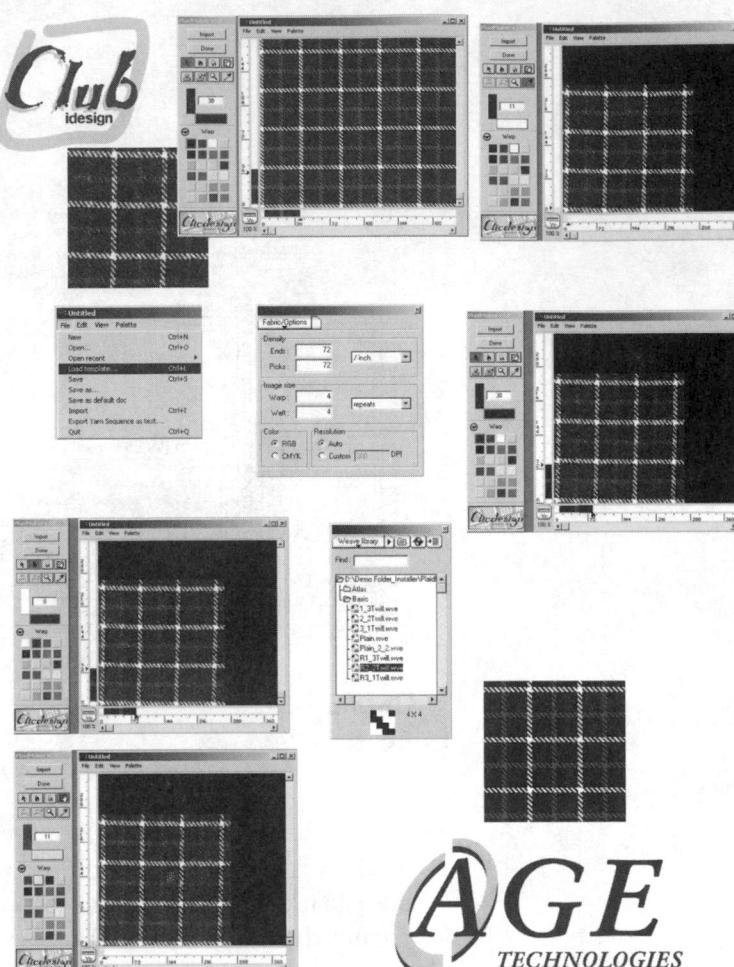

FIGURE 8–41
Tartan plaid steps using AGE Technologies's ClicDesigns
(Courtesy of AGE Technologies)

Using the last filter command from the Filter menu (Ctrl + F for Windows and Cmd + F for Mac OS) will reapply the Noise effect. You can then reapply the Noise until you have the desired effect.

Our suggestion to enhance your plaid is to add the Noise Filter several times to achieve the desired look of flannel. You can also opt to experiment using the Motion Blur filter.

Create your weave from a scanned file:

Step 1. Using PlaidMaker Pro, the newest addition to the ClicDesign modules family, you can use a scanned file of a woven fabric and use it as a guide. Furthermore, you can use your scanned file to set up your yarn colors. So, if you have a piece of fabric that you need to re-create digitally, Plaid-Maker Pro is the easiest way to do it.

Scan your fabric:

Step 2. Using Photoshop or a scanner software, scan your fabric the way you would normally scan it. Resolution is not a factor when working with

PlaidMaker Pro, so a low resolution of 72 dpi will do the trick. However, you can set up a higher resolution if needed.

Step 3. You then need to save your file as a Clicdesign or BMP file. Using Plaid-Maker Pro, you can load on those two types of files and use it as a template.

Load template:

Step 4. Once in PlaidMaker Pro, choose **Load Template** from the File menu and open your newly scanned file of your fabric. You can use the Move template tools to place your scanned file exactly where you want it inside the PlaidMaker window. You will then be able to start designing your yarn where you want it to start.

Fabric/Options palette:

Step 5. Using the Fabric/Options palette, you should set the Ends and Picks per inch according to the scanned fabric. This will ensure that the yarn sequence you draw matches the number of yarns in your fabric.

Eyedropper tool:

Step 6. Using the Eyedropper tool, you can set up the yarn color according to your scanned fabric.

Step 7. Click on the appropriate yarn position in the Yarn Color Selector and using the Eyedropper tool, click on the desired color located on your scanned fabric. You will see the yarn color in the Yarn Color Selector change according to the fabric color you have chosen.

Step 8. Choose the yarn colors from the scanned fabric using the Eyedropper tool.

Weave construction:

Step 9. Using the Weave library palette, choose the right weave construction file and double-click on it to use it for your fabric. If the construction file does not exist, you can simply create it using the Weave editor palette.

Step 10. Choose the fabric construction from the Weave library palette.

Draw your yarn sequence:

Step 11. Finally, all you need to do is to draw your yarn sequence using the New Yarn tools. Pick up the right color from the Yarn Color Selector and click and drag the New Yarn tool until the yarn sequence is equivalent to the number of yarns in your scanned fabric.

Step 12. Repeat the same process until all your yarns are drawn. In only a few minutes, we were able to re-create a piece of fabric, using the New Yarn tool and the scanned file as a guide. You can then apply all the color changes you want using the Yarn Control palette and then have a peek at what your fabric would look like in different colorways, or simply import it to Photoshop for use on a storyboard.

Adding Enhancement to Your Plaid Using Adobe Photoshop Filters

Noise definition

One easy way to give a more realistic look to your woven fabric created with Plaid-Maker Plus is by using a very simple filter plug-in available in Photoshop—the Noise filter. Using the Noise filter will give your fabric a more natural fiber look. The idea is to give the pixel creating your woven fabric the look of a real fiber yarn.

Step 1. Applying random pixels to an image will simulate the effect of shooting pictures on high-speed film. The Add Noise filter can also be used to reduce banding in feathered selections or graduated fills, or to give a more realistic look to heavily retouched areas.

Step 2. Options included with the Noise distribution are—Uniform, which distributes color values of Noise using random numbers between 0 and plus or minus the specified value for a subtle effect; and Gaussian, which distributes color values of Noise along a bell-shaped curve for a speckled effect. The Monochromatic option applies the filter to only the tonal elements in the image without changing the colors.

Other Applications and Insights:

_____

_____

_____

_____

Notes...

Rendering Fabric Finishes

In this section we examine multiple ways to realistically simulate several common fabric finishes using Photoshop. Many of these finishes can be added to most of the designs you have digitally created thus far.

Before we begin the actual step-by-step specifics, let's review for a moment. Where is the most logical place to add a finish to your designs in Adobe Photoshop? Perhaps you are already thinking that this is an easy question. The answer is under the Filter menu. Obviously that is correct! In Chapter 6, we spent time having you experiment with the Filter menu and we asked you to make your notes in the comment margin as you examined the outcome of applying the filters to a rendered image as well as to photographs.

As you proceed through this section, you may want to go back to those original notes and review the insights you may have gleaned. Perhaps you discovered a new technique that may work easier or more efficiently, and you may choose to apply it the next time you sit down to create.

Obviously, in Photoshop the ways to accomplish any task are almost infinite. The trick is finding one that saves the most time and energy without compromising the aesthetic outcome! We have listed several quick picks at the end of this section for you to continue your progress on rendering unusual fabrics and finishes.

Simulating Beaded Fabric

Step 1. Open a **New File** in Photoshop: **8.5 × 11 inches, 72–150 dpi, RGB, White Background.**

Step 2. Make a **New Layer** and fill with the color of your choice. In the Property menu, name this layer **Ground.**

Step 3. Make a **New Layer** and fill with white and in the Property menu name this layer **Beads.**

Step 4. On the new layer entitled **Beads,** select **Filter > Xenoflex > Eye Candy 4.0 > Constellation.**

Step 5. Next select **Star Size > 15, Sharpness > 43, Overdrive > 48, Random Seed > 68** and click **OK.** (See Figure 8–42.)

Step 6. Name and save.

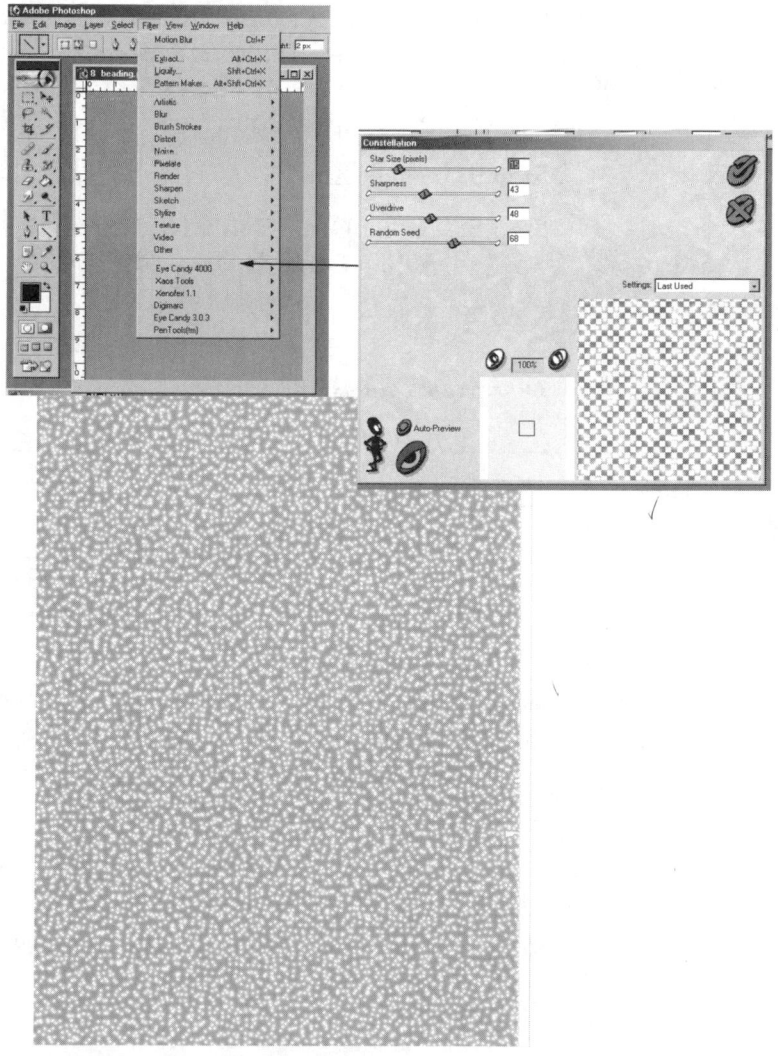

FIGURE 8–42

Select star size

(Courtesy of Alien Skin/Eye Candy)

Other Applications and Insights:

_____

_____

_____

_____

How to Render Crepe de Chine

Step 1. Open a **New File** in Photoshop: **8.5 × 11 inches, 72–150 dpi, RGB, White Background.**

Step 2. Make a **New Layer** and fill with the color of your choice.

Step 3. Select **Filter > Eye Candy 4.0 > Wood**.

Step 4. Then select **Basic Tab > Ring Thickness > 0.03, Cut Offset > 14, Variation Amount > 13, Roughness > 30, Pulp Color** and select a deeper shade of original color. Then select black for Grain color and a deeper shade of the original color for Bark color.

Step 5. Select **Knot Tab > Number of Knots > 0, Size > .07.**

Step 6. Select **Grain Tab > Grain Length .19 > Grain Width .04 > Grain Density 50% > Grain Opacity 30%**. (See Figure 8–43.)

Step 7. Name and save your file.

Other Applications and Insights:

_____

_____

_____

_____

How to Render Flocked Fabric—Dotted Swiss

Step 1. Open a **New File** in Photoshop: **8.5 × 11 inches, 72–150 dpi, RGB, White Background.**

Step 2. Add a **New Layer** using the New Layer icon on the Layers palette. Right-click on the New Layer and type the name **Dots** in the Layer Property dialogue box and click **OK.**

Step 3. Fill the layer with a solid color of your choice. (We selected pink.)

Step 4. Go to the **Filter** menu and select **Sketch > Halftone Pattern > Size 10 > Contrast 5 > Pattern > Dots** and click **OK.**

Step 5. Using the **Zoom** tool, zoom in and select only one dot in the contrast color. Select **Similar** and click the Delete key to remove the background.

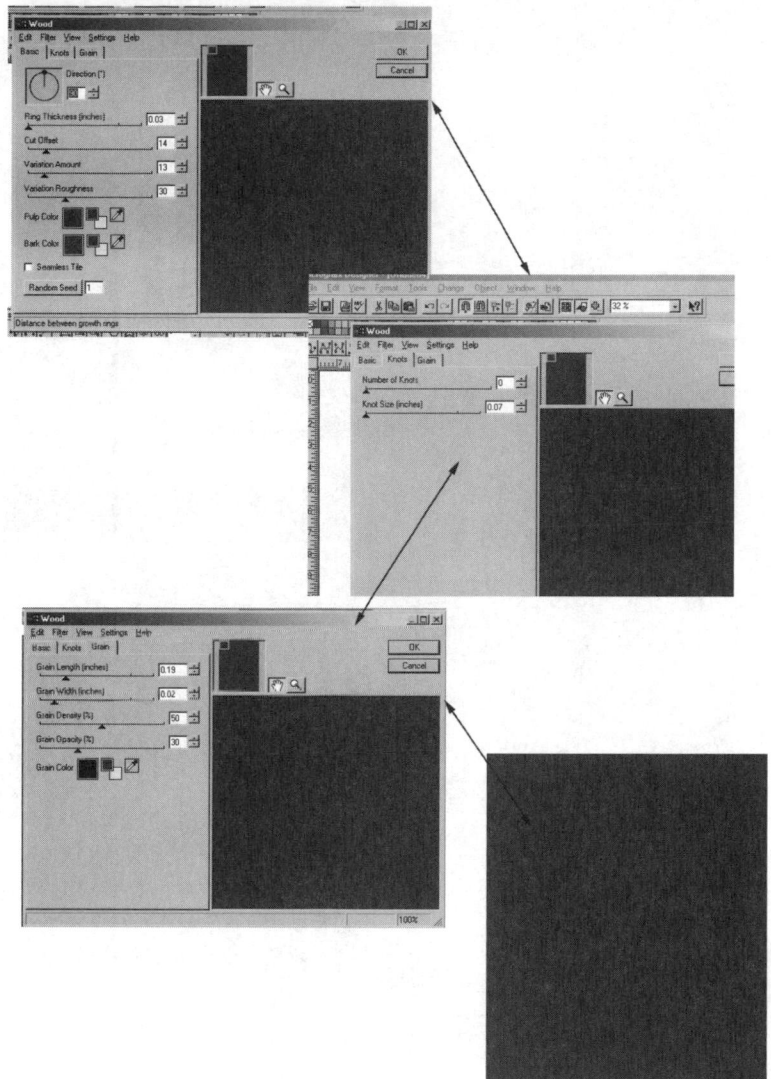

FIGURE 8–43
Grain options
(Courtesy of Alien Skin/Eye Candy)

Step 6. Add a **New Layer** below your layer entitled Dots and double-click on the New Layer. In the Layer Property box, type **Background** and click **OK.**

Step 7. (Optional) You may opt to add a textured weave ground to your fabric. We suggested that you open an earlier rendered fabric, such as Batiste or Linen. Drag a copy of this onto the Dotted Swiss File and adjust the Hue and Saturation accordingly.

Step 8. To add the flocked finish, on your layer entitled **Dots,** go to **Filter > Blur > Motion Blur > Angle 31 degrees > Pixels 20,** and click **OK.** (See Figure 8–44.)

Step 9. Name and save your work.

FIGURE 8–44
Dots

Other Applications and Insights:

_____

_____

_____

_____

How to Render Moiré Using Define Brush Filters

Step 1. Open the **Moiré Brush** from the CD.

Step 2. Open a **New File: 8.5 × 11 inches, 72–150 dpi, RGB, White Background.**

Step 3. Go to the **Brush** file and place a rectangle **Marquee** around the pattern.

Step 4. Select **Edit > Define Brush.**

Step 5. Open an existing file such as a JPEG—Plaid. (See Figure 8–45.)

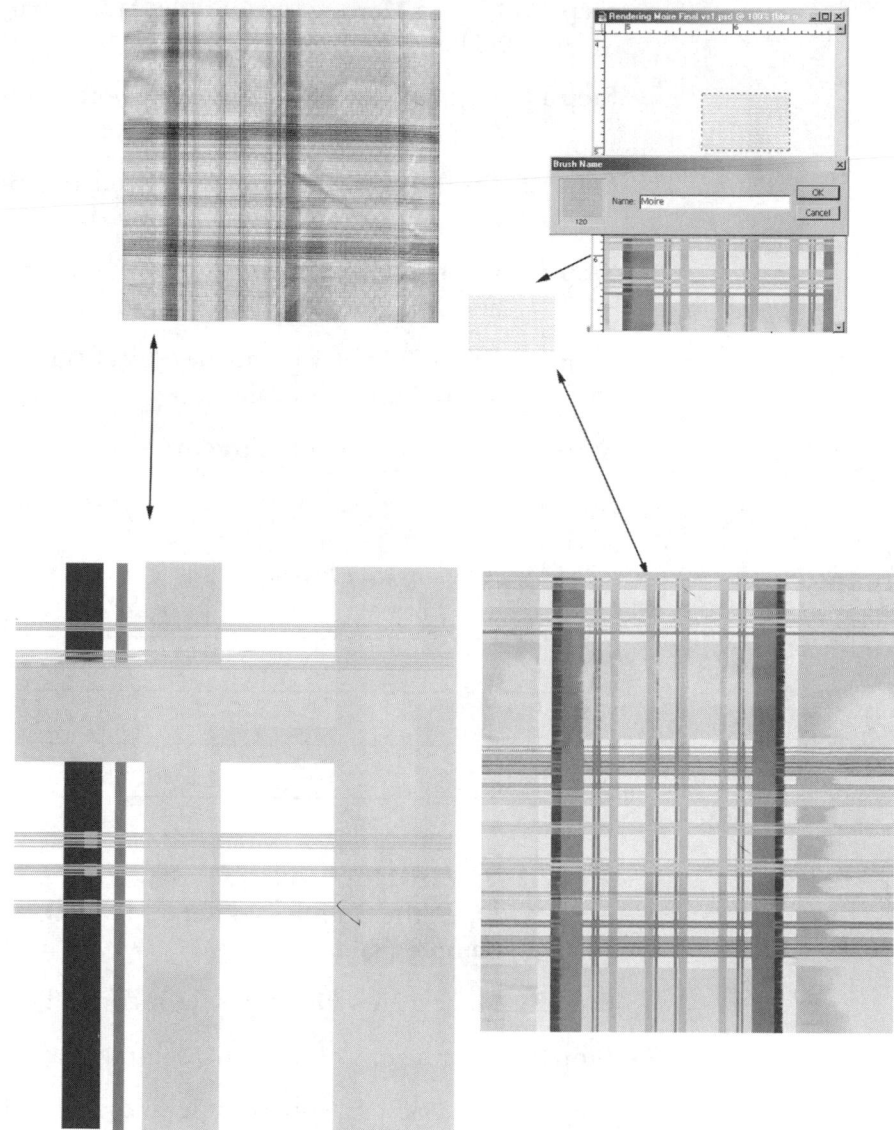

FIGURE 8–45
JPEG—plaid

Step 6. Drag a copy of the JPEG—Plaid to your New File.

Step 7. Using the layer-by-layer method along with the Eyedropper to match color, begin to build the plaid row-by-row and layer-by-layer as done in the tartan plaid exercise.

Step 8. Once you are finished, you can opt to add a plain weave, as well as flatten your finished file. We suggest to keep the original layers and make a JPEG copy.

Step 9. Now you are ready to make the Moiré finish brush. Go to the Goodies Folder on the CD and open **Fabric Structures**. Select **Moiré Brush > Next.**

Step 10. Make a **Marquee** around the Moiré Brush and go to **Edit > Define Brush > Name the Brush > Moiré**.

Step 11. Make a **New Layer** on top of your flattened JPEG—Plaid. Use the Eyedropper to select a soft color for the Moiré Pattern.

Step 12. Go to the **Brush** tool and from the Brushes palette, select the Moiré Brush. Make several strokes on the new layer.

Step 13. You may experiment with both adjusting the Opacity slider and/or you may opt to make additional improvements with Select.

Step 14. Go to the **Filter** menu and select **Blur > Motion Blur** to begin to add the Moiré Pattern to your design.

Step 15. You may also opt to use the **Smudge** tool to enhance the design.

Step 16. Name and save your work when satisfied.

Other Applications and Insights:

_____

_____

_____

_____

How to Render Moiré Pattern to an Image

Step 1. Open the **Goodies Folder** on the **CD** and select **Sample Exercises > JPEG Sample Plaid**.

Step 2. Make a **New File: 8.5 × 11 inches, 72–150 dpi, RGB, White Background.**

Step 3. Drag a copy of the JPEG sample plaid to your new file.

Step 4. Make several copies (at least 3) of this layer to experiment with.

Step 5. You may also opt to add a fabric structure to your image before adding the Moiré finish.

Step 6. Next, using the **Poly Lasso,** begin to isolate several areas of the plaid and copy them. (Note that Figure 8–46 is not the complete pattern.)

Step 7. Select **Filter > Twirl > Angle – 47.**

Step 8. Next move the Opacity slider to preview the effect of adding the simulated Moiré movement against the original plaid pattern.

Other Applications and Insights:

_____

_____

_____

_____

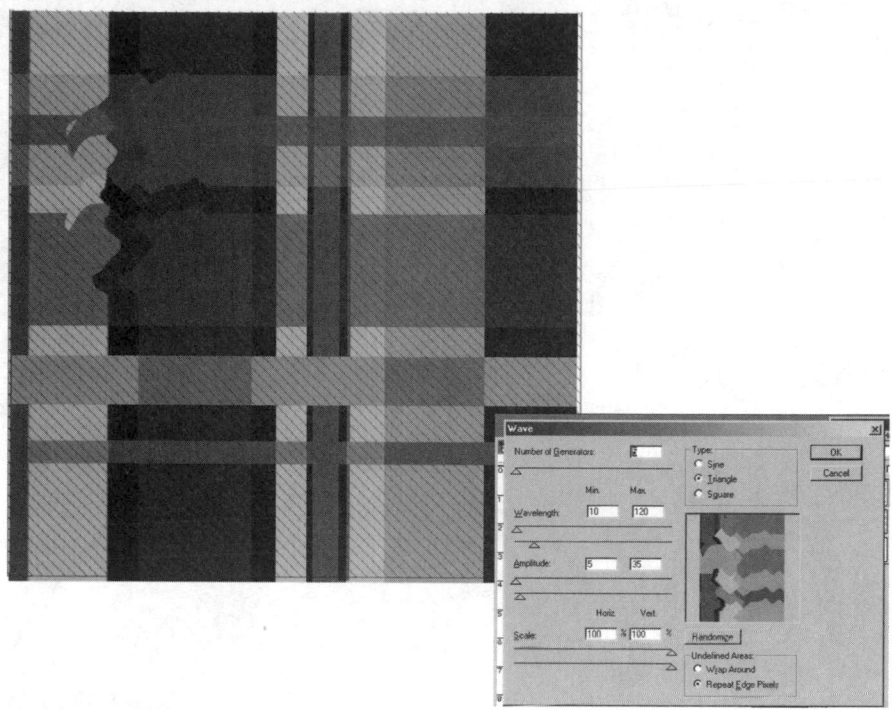

FIGURE 8–46
Moiré fabric variations

How to Render Moiré Pattern to an Image Using Eye Candy 1

Step 1. Open a **New File** in Photoshop: **8.5 × 11 inches, 72–150 dpi, RGB, White Background.**

Step 2. Open the **Goodies Folder** and select **SAMPLE > OPEN Plaid#2.**

Step 3. Drag a copy of the JPEG—Plaid onto your new file.

Step 4. Select **Filter > Eye Candy 4.0 > Marble.** Select **Vein Size > 3.29, Vein Coverage > 80%, Vein Thickness > 17, Vein Roughness > 92, Bedrock Color > White, Vein Color (we used gold), Seamless Tile, unchecked** and **Random Seed > 1,** Click **OK.** (See Figure 8–47.)

Step 5. Taking the **Magic Wand,** place on all the "white" sections of the Marble Layers and hit **Delete.** All that will remain is your "veins."

Step 6. Go to **Filter > Blur > Motion Blur** and make the following selections: **Blur 28 degree > 129.** Click **OK.** (See Figure 8–48.)

Step 7. Slide Opacity bar on Layer Property box to 50%.

Step 8. (Option) Go to **Filter > Noise > Add Noise > 10% Gaussian > Monochromatic** to add more surface interest.

Step 9. Name and save your work.

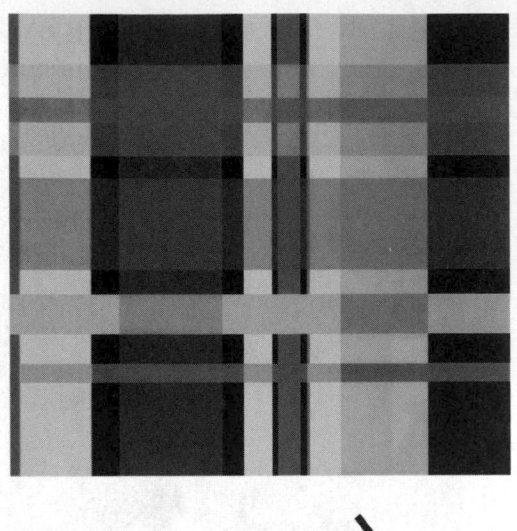

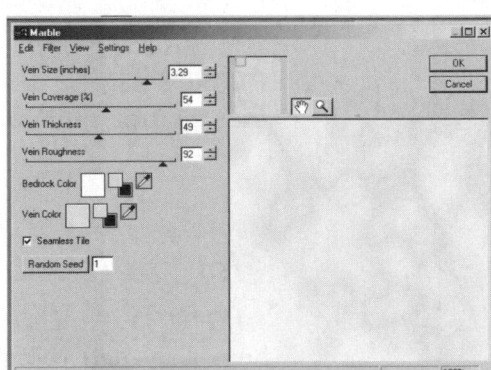

FIGURE 8–47
Moiré pattern using Eye Candy
(Courtesy of Alien Skin/Eye Candy)

Other Applications and Insights:

_____

_____

_____

_____

How to Render Moiré Using Eye Candy 2

Step 1.   Open a **New File** in Photoshop: **8.5 × 11 inches, 72–150 dpi, RGB, White Background.** Note that this image will be cropped later, so make the file about 50% larger than you will need.

Step 2.   Make a **New Layer** and fill with the color of your choice.

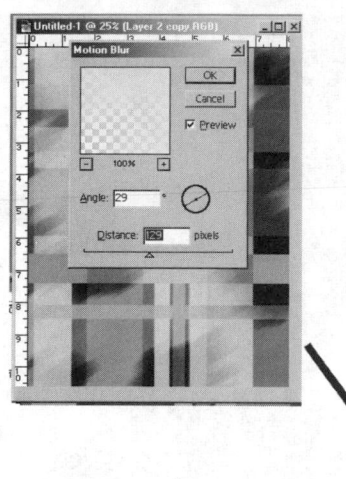

FIGURE 8–48

Using Adobe Photoshop Filter > Blur > Motion Blur
(Courtesy of Alien Skin/Eye Candy)

Step 3. Go to **Filter > Eye Candy 4.0 > Wood > Ring Thickness .03 > Cut Offset 14 > Variation Amount 13 > Variation Roughness 30.** (See Figure 8–49.)

Step 4. Go to **Knots 0 > Knot Size .07.**

Step 5. Then go to **Grain > Grain Length .19 > Grain Width .04 > Grain Density 47% > Grain Opacity 30%.** (Note that the color should be slightly deeper than the original color.)

Step 6. Crop the file to eliminate any unnecessary knottiness from this image.

Step 7. You can opt to add horizontal hatch lines. Go to **Layer > Bevel/Emboss** and select **Pillow Emboss** to make it a Moiré-Taffeta fabric.

Step 8. Name and save your work.

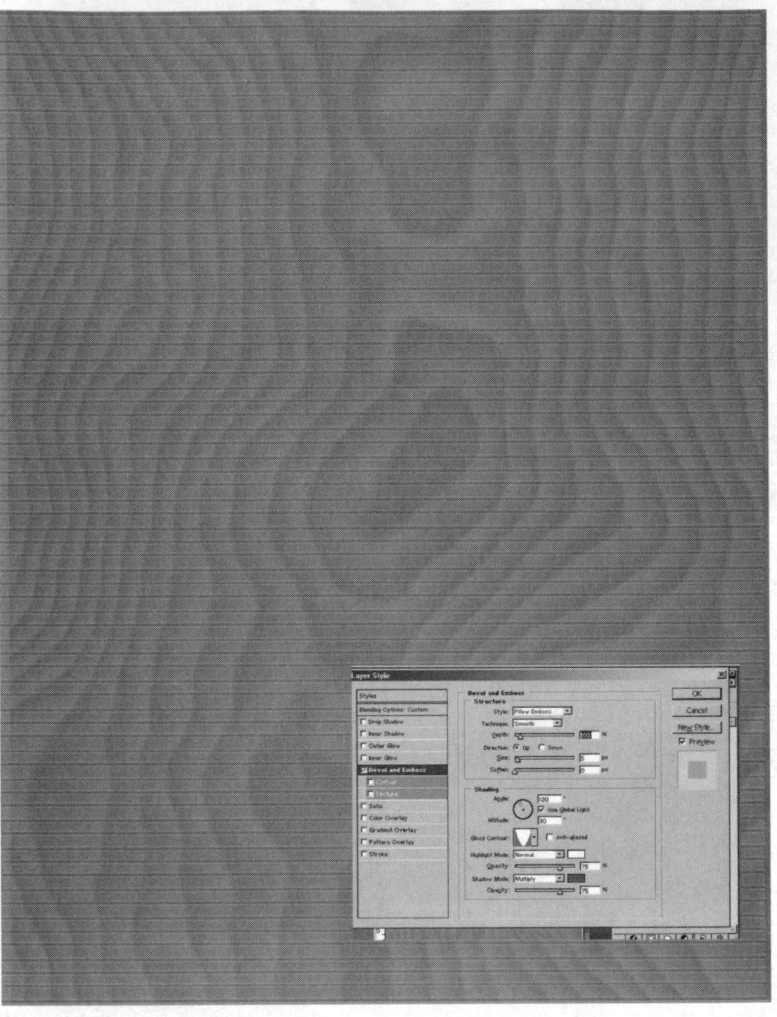

FIGURE 8–49
Moiré pattern using Eye Candy 2
(Courtesy of Alien Skin/Eye Candy)

Other Applications and Insights:

_____

_____

_____

_____

How to Render Napped Fabric—Flannel and Fleece

Step 1. Reopen the **JPEG Plaid File #1 or #2** from the Goodies Folder on the CD in the Samples file.

Step 2. Open a **New File: 8.5 × 11 inches, RGB, 150 dpi, White Background.** Name the file **Flannelette.**

Step 3. Drag a copy of the JPEG Flannel to your new file.

FIGURE 8–50
Flannel

Step 4. Open the file from your **Goodies Folder** on the **CD** and select **Fabric Structures** and **Twill > Next.**

Step 5. Make a **Marquee** around the Twill fabric structure and go to **Edit > Define Pattern > Name pattern > Twill.**

Step 6. Go to **Edit > Fill > Pattern > Twill** to make the twill lines match. You may need to zoom in on the lines and place the **Magic Wand** on the Twill Pattern. Go to **Select > Select Similar.**

Step 7. Use the Eyedropper to select a deeper shade of the plaid and then go to **Edit > Fill > Foreground color**. Opt to adjust the Opacity slider bar on the Layer menu to make the twill ground blend into the plaid to look more natural. (See Figure 8–50.)

Step 8. You can opt to make a JPEG copy of this new file.

Step 9. You can also go to **Image > Merge Down** to move the Twill layer to the Flannel layer.

Adding the finishing napped effect:

Step 10. Go to **Filter** and select **Blur > Gaussian Blur.** A low number will give a light brushed effect and a high number will look like polar fleece.

Step 11. Go to **Filter** and select **Noise > Add Noise.** Experiment with **Monochromatic** and **Gaussian** to achieve the desired effect.

Step 12. Name and save your work.

HINT: You can add this finished texture to provide a realistic look to any other digitally rendered woven or knit fabric.

Other Applications and Insights:

_____

_____

_____

_____

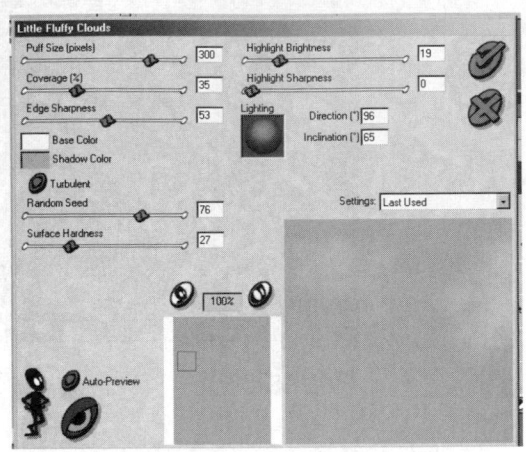

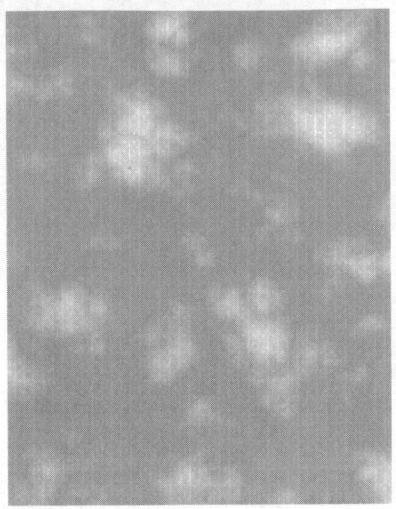

FIGURE 8–51
Select puff size
(Courtesy of Alien Skin/Eye Candy)

FIGURE 8–52
Adding knitted ground

How to Render Tie-Dye

Step 1. Open a **New File** in Photoshop: **8.5 × 11 inches, 72–150 dpi, RGB, White Background.**

Step 2. Make a **New Layer** and fill with the color of your choice.

Step 3. Select **Filter > Eye Candy 4.0 > Little Fluffy Clouds.**

Step 4. Select **Puff Size > 300, Coverage > 35%, Sharpness > 53, Base Color > White, Random Seed Amount > 76, Surface Hardness > 27, Highlight Brightness > 19, Highlight Sharpness > 0, Lighting Direction > 65, Lighting Inclination > 65.** Click **OK.** (See Figure 8–51.)

Step 5. In Figure 8–52, we opted to add knitted ground to our file.

Step 6. Name and save your work.

Other Applications and Insights:

_____

_____

_____

_____

How to Render Embossed Fabric—Vinyl

Step 1. Open a **New File** in Photoshop: **8 × 8 inches, 72–150 dpi, RGB, White Background.**

Step 2. Make a **New Layer** and fill with light blue or a desired color.

Step 3. Go to the **Filter** menu and select **Noise > Add Noise.** Input a small percentage of **Monochromatic** and **Gaussian Noise.** Select **OK.** (The

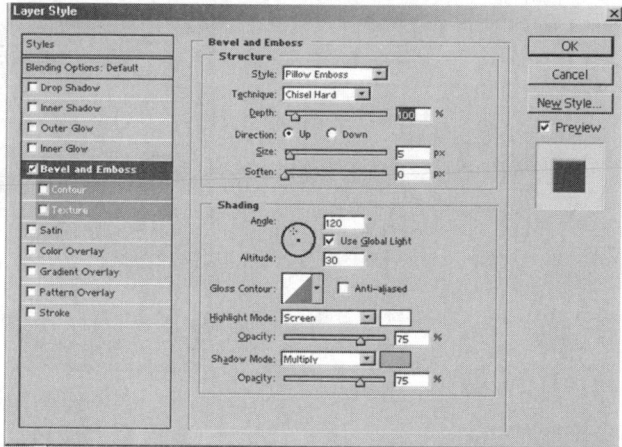

FIGURE 8–53
Layer style menu selections

amount is unimportant as long as you place a small percentage of Monochromatic and Gaussian.)

Step 4. Go to the **Filter** menu and select **Brush Strokes > Crosshatch.** Select **OK.**

Step 5. Go to the **Goodies Folder** in the **Fabric Structures** file. Select **Emboss Sample**.

Step 6. Drag a copy of this file onto your new file and adjust the Opacity slider bar on the Layers palette menu to 80%.

Step 7. Merge the Emboss layer with Fill layer.

Step 8. Go to the **Layer** menu and select **Layer Style > Bevel and Emboss.**

Step 9. See Figure 8–53 and follow the selections.

Step 10. Name and save your file. (See Figure 8–54.)

Other Applications and Insights:

_____

_____

_____

_____

Enhancing Your Jacquard

This is an opportunity for you to enhance the finish of the jacquard that you made in Chapter 7.

Step 1. Reopen your file from Chapter 7 entitled **Jacquard.** Or go to the **Goodies Folder** and select **Fabric Structures > Jacquard.**

Step 2. Using the **Magic Wand** tool or the **Poly Lasso** tool. Select the darker colored shaped outline.

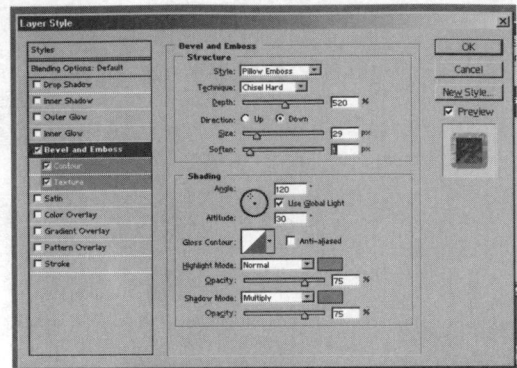

FIGURE 8–54
Vinyl

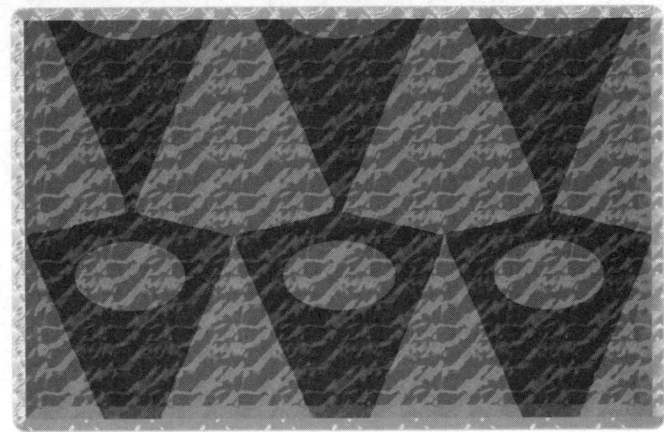

FIGURE 8–55
Select pillow emboss

Step 3. Go to **Layer** menu and select **Layer Style > Emboss**.

Step 4. Select **Pillow Emboss** as shown in Figure 8–55.

Step 5. Continue to make additional selections in the Emboss Dialogue box to simulate the existing design to have more of a textural surface interest quality.

Step 6. Record any changes you made or discovered in the space below.

Step 7. Name and save your work.

Other Applications and Insights:

_____

_____

_____

_____

How to Render Needlepoint Finishes

Step 1. This exercise utilizes several fun techniques that are easy to use. Begin by opening the **Goodies Folder** on the **CD** and select **Royalty Free Images.** Select the **City Café Image**.

FIGURE 8–56
City café image

FIGURE 8–57
Artistic > cutout

FIGURE 8–58
Texture > patchwork

Step 2. Place a **Marquee** around the bottom portion of the image to match Figure 8–56. Make a copy of this portion of the foliage.

Step 3. Open a **New File: 6 × 6 inches, 72–150 dpi, RGB, White Background.** Go to **Edit** and hit **Paste.** (See Figure 8–56.)

Step 4. Go to **Edit > Free Transform > Scale** to make the image fill the page.

Step 5. Go to the **Filter** menu and select **Artistic > Cutout.** This will make your image appear to look more like a drawing than a photo. (See Figure 8–57.)

Step 6. Go to the **Filter** menu and select **Texture > Patchwork.** (See Figure 8–58.)

Step 7. Voila! Now your work looks like a tapestry or needlepoint. You can apply this concept to almost any kind of photo or rendering.

Step 8. Name and save your work.

Other Applications and Insights:

_____

_____

_____

_____

Notes . . .

So far you accomplished a lot! You have applied the basics of fibers and fabric structures to your rendering. In Chapter 9, we will reflect on the advanced concepts of rendering single motifs and repeat motifs.

Be sure you are comfortable with all of the information up to this point before going forward. If you find you are struggling in any area, take the time to go back to Chapter 3 and review the basics. Often, when designers struggle they are rushing the exercises or even overlooking the importance of grasping the basic concepts thoroughly.

Therefore, take time to stop and reflect. Review is well worth the investment of your time!

Insights and Inspiration into Creating Repeats Using Adobe® Photoshop®

Sourcing Inspiration for Prints

So, where do designers begin when creating a motif or print for fabric? Obviously, the design process will begin by reflecting the company the designer is working for, the end use of the product, the season in which the print will be used, and the intended retail client who will purchase the product.

In the previous chapters we studied rendering simple fabric repetitions of woven patterns and knitted stitches, culminating in rendering the repeats of stripes, checks, and plaids. In this chapter we will focus on rendering a different kind of repetition—single motifs and variations on repeating or enhancing the original motif or design. Therefore, a print repeat is defined as a continuous patterning of a motif as it flows into itself.

There are other kinds of repeats, known as tessellations. Tessellations are repeating tiles of geometric shapes including fractals, geometrics, iterated sequences, and pattern definitions.

We closely examine the kinds of print repeats you may be called upon to execute, as well as how to accomplish this in Adobe Photoshop 7.

Inspiration for Prints

So, where do the ideas for prints come from? For centuries designers have been products of their own environment as well as of the times in which they live and work. Naturally, the designs created will be a reflection of these influences along with many other unseen stimuli.

Frequently, a design inspiration starts with the designer's own lifestyle. People and places become the motivator or the catalyst for the creative process to begin.

As you take a look at the following list, stop and think about how many times you have been moved or inspired by what you have seen or experienced.

Print Inspiration

- Nature
- Art—Museums and galleries
- Travel
- Folk or ethnic cultures
- Costume
- Media—including TV, music, print
- Books, magazines, greeting cards, posters, advertising

FIGURE 9–1
Styles and travel inspiration images

- People—Gender
- Lifestyles—Hobbies and sports
- Theatre—Dance
- Graffiti
- The past
- Arbiters of style
- Styles and types of art—Impressionist, animation, etc. (Figure 9–1)

All of these sources and many more create a rich tapestry of inspiration for the textile designer.

The reality is that most times you as the designer may not have the luxury of freely creating a design based on your own ideas or ideals. Instead, you may be called upon to research a specific theme, and then render a print that will reflect the market segmentation of the company you are designing for. This means that as a designer you must be familiar with the current trends in patterns, colors, and textures in order to reflect them in an aesthetic manner relevant to your company's ultimate consumer.

The choices of where you begin your research are sometimes not as obvious as you would imagine. Start by asking if your company has a textile library. Frequently, the company archives successful prints they have used in the past. If this is not being done, you may need to head to your local library or bookstore for ideas.

Another great alternative available to college and university students today is WGSN-EDU. This is an on-line forecasting and reporting service available in a fee-based format to the industry or as a limited but free time-delayed membership for students. This website has excellent up-to-the-minute reporting on all the latest trends in the apparel, accessory, and interior design industry, especially for reporting and forecasting trends in prints.

There are numerous other forecasting services that also provide this information to the trade; however, because this is a free service, we felt that it should be given special mention. Another forecasting service includes Bill Glazer Inc. Many of you may be familiar with Bill Glazer's textbook for Prentice Hall, entitled SnapFashun. Bill's company is located in California and it offers a wide array of services for the designer from up-to-the-minute forecasting, to e-zine, to trend and image books, to CDs, and beyond. All of these great companies can be found at your fingertips on-line!

You may recall from Chapter 4 that research is an integral part of what you will be doing as a designer. Much of this research happens today on-line. Both WGSN-edu.com and SnapFashun.com are great places to start!

As a designer you will need to source for information *and* inspiration. You must have a working knowledge of how prints are categorized and how to successfully render them in Photoshop, not to mention how to adapt them to other products or market segments.

In our next section, we walk you through the basics of understanding and categorizing prints, as well as how to lay them out for rendering in Adobe Photoshop.

Categorizing Prints

Prints are categorized by trend influences. Prints frequently are comprised of a simple or single motif that is repeated on the face of the fabric. Therefore, it is the subject matter or theme of the motif where you must begin your sourcing and thumbnails.

There are several common categories prints fall into. Look at Figure 9–2 to see how many you can recognize.

- **Nature: Floral and fauna—Botanicals** including *landscapes, scenic,* or *tropical,* depending on the subject matter.
- **Animals** and **insects**
- **Geometric** shapes and objects—*Foulards, paisleys, patchwork,* and *bandanas.*
- **Abstract**—Some geometric patterns.
- Geographical influences, including regional designs and symbols known as **ethnic,** sometimes referred to as *folk* and/or *cultural representation* (i.e., Asian, African, Mayan)
- **Historical** representations:
  (a) **Styles** or periods of time—*these often coincide with Art Movements,* i.e., *Art Nouveau, Deco,* or *Jacobean.* Furthermore, a print can represent a geographic location and/or company where a design originated, such as a *calico, country French, Provence, toile de Jouy,* or *liberty print.*
  (b) **Documentary** prints are also considered historical and are often associated with images from the Middle East or the Orient and depicting specific moments in time or a specific historical event.
- **Conversational**—the print tells a distinctive story. Sometimes called **novelty.**
  (a) *Specific themes,* i.e., romantic, holiday, or sports.
  (b) *Market segmentation,* i.e., children's, men's, etc.

FIGURE 9–2
Common print categories

Print Layout and Design Basics

It is as important for the designer to become familiar with the categories of prints as it is for the designer to recognize and utilize the most frequently used pattern layout. (See Figures 9–2 and 9–3.)

It can be said that print layout is generally arranged in an invisible grid that can be interlocked into geometric shapes. (See Figure 9–4.)

Prints are further classified by:

- **Style,** i.e., folkloric, botanical, historical, artistic movement, etc.
- **Interpretation:** Uniqueness, realistic, or stylized
- Degree of **complexity**
- **Artistic medium** *implies* watercolor, gouache, stipple, photocopy, batik, embroidery, tapestry, warp print, as well as graffiti!
- Available **technology** to render and/or produce the print
- **Scale** of the print (small to large) and size ratios
- **Foreground to background relationship**
- **Color scheme** (including all colors used in the print itself)
- Alternative **colorways** in which the print will be available
- **Motif direction**
- **Repeat ratios**
- *Number of elements* and *number of repeats* to be used as well as in what combinations including the use of borders

---

FIGURE 9–3
Subcategories of prints

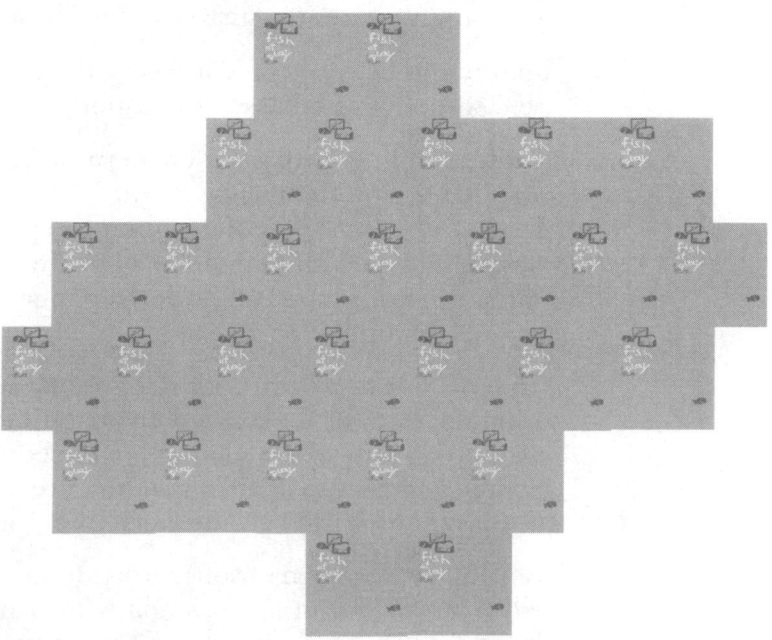

FIGURE 9–4
Print layout

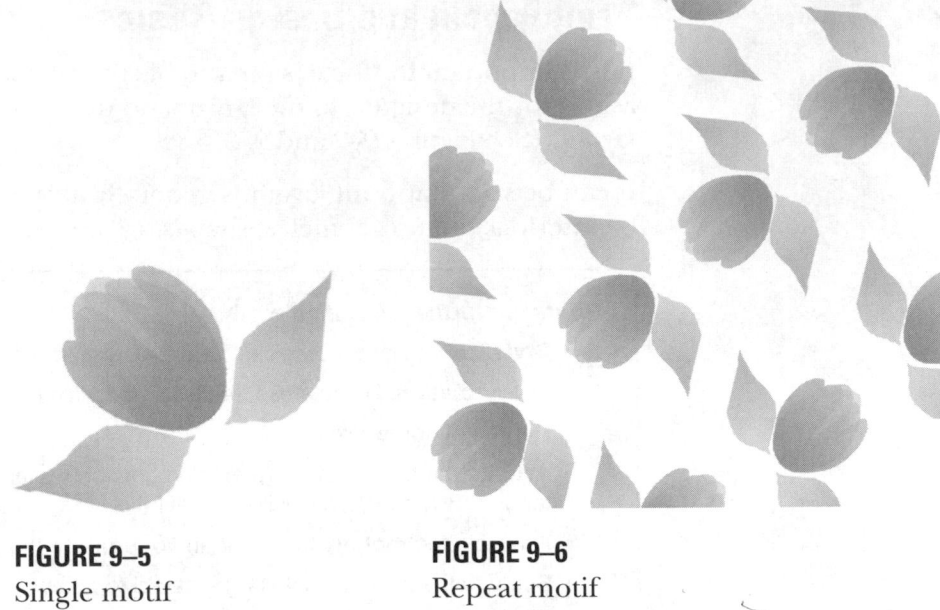

FIGURE 9–5
Single motif

FIGURE 9–6
Repeat motif

Applying the Elements of Design Basics to Prints

As we mentioned earlier in Chapter 4, the major elements involved in textile design can be broken down into the background, foreground, and unifying elements, in this case a single or repeat motif.

The term *repeat* implies a design that is repeated within a print for use on the fabric. The basis of a *repeat pattern* is a pattern comprised of a design or *motif* that "repeats itself" across the surface of the fabric. (See Figure 9–5.)

In order to be considered a repeat, the design must repeat and flow or "follow itself" without any breaks in the pattern.

Understanding the basics of pattern repeats is critical. The motif, pattern, or design has a continuous flow of the elements with no breaks in the design. The most important aspect of designing a repeat is to be sure that any element of the design that goes off to one side of the line of vision will come back on the opposite side. (See Figure 9–6.) The challenge is working over these *join lines*, without a visual disruption of the pattern.

To have *seamless* repeats, the designer either needs to work an image as a repeat from the start, or use many of the painting features and tools available in design software to hide or blend in where the edges of the repeats meet. Clone, Rubber Stamp, and Blur tools all help in this area. As a designer becomes more fluent in any program, it will become easier and faster to edit these join lines.

Repeats can come in various forms. Some repeats are random and others are *direction specific*. For instance, a home furnishing pattern may need to be used horizontally only. Still other designs need to be *nondirectional*, reading up or down. Next we will have a look at several other variations of the most commonly used repeats.

Common Print Variations

1. **1-Way motif**—one or more motifs that are right-side up and generally going in one direction. (See Figure 9–7.)

2. **2-Way motif**—one or more motifs used in two different directions, for example, up and down. (See Figure 9–8.)

3. **Mirror**—this is a simple variation of a 2-way motif. The design takes the original pattern and flips the pattern to be an exact reflection or mirror image of the original. Another variation is known as a " 1/2 swivel mirror." (See Figure 9–9.)

4. **Straight Repeat**—another common version of a pattern that is a continuous repeat of the motif. (See Figure 9–10.)

5. **Random or toss**—can be described as a random or irregular arrangement, including having no specific direction.

6. **Half-drop**—depicts the amount of drop in the pattern that follows the original. (See Figure 9–11.)

7. **5-Star layout**—most often characterized by its characteristic 5 pattern repeat.

FIGURE 9–7
1-way motif

FIGURE 9–8
2-way motif

FIGURE 9–9
1/2 swivel mirror

FIGURE 9–10
Straight column repeat

FIGURE 9–11
Half-drop repeat

Notes . . .

FIGURE 9–12
4-way motif

FIGURE 9–13
Stripe motif

8. **Continuous**—every object that optically goes off the top and the right must continue onto the left and the bottom. The pattern can also be described in the amount of drop in the repeat of the pattern as noted in the next category.

9. **4-Way motif**—literally goes in four different directions—north, south, east, west—and has several variations, including on the bias. Even within this style of print there are several variations such as a "4-way flopover" or "1/4 turning." (See Figure 9–12.)

10. **Stripe**—a band of solid color or a motif in rows. These rows can be vertical, horizontal, perpendicular, diagonal, or drop diagonal. (See Figure 9–13.)

FIGURE 9–14
Check repeat

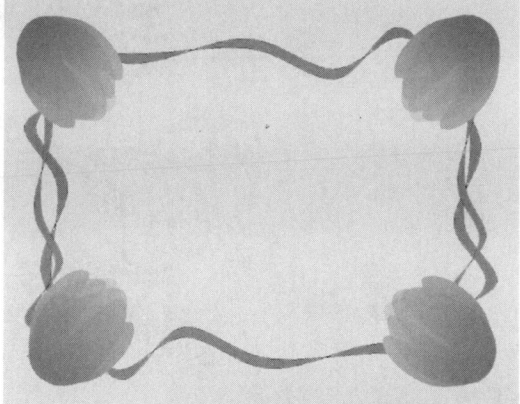

FIGURE 9–15
Plaid repeat

FIGURE 9–16
Border repeat

Notes . . .

11. **Checks**—another variation that is comprised of intersecting bands of color and/or lines, typically in two color combinations. (See Figure 9–14.)

12. **Plaids**—comprised of lines and square or rectangular shapes arranged in combinations of two or more color combinations. (See Figure 9–15.)

13. **Border**—print that is typically located on the selvage or around the edge of a fabric. (See Figure 9–16.)

14. **Engineered**—prints that are a set size or pattern for specific yardage used on a specific placement of a piece of fabric, or on a scarf or garment. (See Figure 9–17.)

15. **Chevron**—a mirror used more specifically in a knit. The mirror occurs, but the center pixel or stitch is not duplicated (as for an argyle pattern). It is almost like it mirrors on a half stitch or pixel. (See Figure 9–18.)

16. **Photo-Realistic**—uses photo images as a print. (See Figure 9–19.)

FIGURE 9–17
Engineered repeat

FIGURE 9–18
Chevron repeat

FIGURE 9–19
Photo-realistic repeat

All of these designs, once originally done by hand, can be accomplished using the computer.

Some Practical Design Considerations before You Begin!

Although you may be eager to start rendering a repeat print, there are other practical considerations that must be addressed. The choices you make can have far-reaching consequences if they are overlooked.

Textile Considerations

Beyond the design basics, today's fashion designer has to learn to think globally as well as sequentially. You are probably wondering just what does that mean?

Remember, everything is driven by the end product use by the consumer and production costs.

As you should now clearly see, the information covered in earlier chapters has some very real practical application in the decision-making process of designing prints.

Several critical determining factors such as what fabric will the print be printed on, which types of dyes will be utilized, and how the print will ultimately be used and cared for by the consumer are behind most of today's textile designing.

Your success as a designer often hinges on having a better understanding of textiles and fiber properties as well as the technical savvy to depict a given design. Understanding print design and textiles will obviously prepare you to become a better designer, regardless of your application of these prints.

The use of repeats and prints is found not only in the obvious areas such as interior design or apparel-related design industry, but also in commercial graphic design and web page backgrounds. (See Figures 9–20 and 9–21.)

As a digital textile or print designer there are several design considerations you should keep in mind as you begin the digital design process.

Ask the questions in Figure 9–22 and determine the significance of each answer before you begin to design.

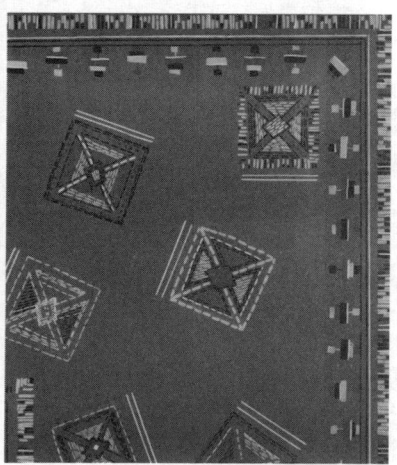

FIGURE 9–20
Commercial graphic design
(Courtesy of Artsville)

FIGURE 9–21
Web page background

1. What kind of *fiber* will the design ultimately be printed on?
   - Natural
   - Synthetic
   - Blend
2. What is the actual *fabric* the print will be viewed on?
3. Which specific *method of construction* will be used in the construction of the fabric? A plain weave? Twill weave? The fabric used will greatly determine the quality of the print.
4. Which *printing method* will be used?
5. What is the *intended end use* of the fabric? Apparel? Interior? The Web? Or other commercial graphic design applications?
6. What *type of dyes* will be used?
7. What *types of finishes* will be added to the fiber or fabric?
8. What *laundry considerations* will the consumer need to know for preserving the quality of the print?
9. The price point of the product will help determine some of the above criteria.

FIGURE 9–22
Design considerations

Design Basics Considerations:

Don't forget the basics of good designing. A print can be a simple two-color choice such as black and white or a print can explode with color. A designer must consider the basic unifying factors of the design. In order to better prepare the next generation of designers, we have dedicated Chapter 10 to making sure you can apply design basics to your digital designing.

Aesthetic	Color scheme
	Line (i.e., eye flow)
	Balance (i.e., use of negative space)
	Harmony (i.e., layout)

Finally, you must keep on a marketing hat along with your designer hat when creating prints. The consumer is the final critic of your success or failure. Did it sell? Figure 9–23 lists outcome objectives you will want to keep in mind as you begin digitally designing.

Ethical Considerations

When you begin to design a very specific pattern such as a floral, you will often be confronted with a very real practical consideration— "How do you accurately interpret a design without plagiarizing the design?" A brief discussion about plagiarism is very relevant to the topic of print design today. With the advent of digital designing, we can quickly transfer a design digitally and design is more than merely manipulating the shape and color of a design.

According to Elaine Polvinen in her paper entitled "The Ethics of Scanned Imagery for Textile Design," "The introduction of new technology to textile design has opened Pandora's box of questions regarding the ethics and originality of scanned

- Category/consumer/market segment
- Production cost
- Number of colors and how they will work to enhance the design, including background to foreground color interactions
- Number of elements to be used
- Number of repeats
- Distance in the repeat (size ratios) that vertical and horizontal is based on
- What is the fabric width?
- How much excess should be allotted for the design?
- Number or scale of the motif
- Number of available colorways
- Which color mode will your completed work be viewed in? For example, will it be viewed in RGB on the Web or will it be printed in CMYK for marketing purposes?
- What is the best way to begin the design? Render by hand or digital?
- Vector or Raster?

FIGURE 9–23
Other factors to consider

designs. . . . The primary function of the scanner is simply to transfer data for one form to another for further image manipulation. . . . Educators have a basic responsibility to make students aware of the extent and proper use of sources of inspiration." Professor Polvinen goes on to say that "true creativity lies not in hundreds of resources or techniques for subject matter. The true test of creativity lies in the challenge of creating design after design without the restrictive confines of the reality-based business world where you are limited to style, material, color, and time."

Therefore, Professor Polvinen concludes that "Students should be acquainted with the existence of copyright law, as well as be trained to follow ethical standards." We chose to address this topic because in most instances we learn to replicate before we create.

In fact, we typically have our students begin to design by first accurately replicating a pattern before they begin to convert the design into their own interpretation of the print selected.

Software Considerations

In Chapter 12 we will discuss in greater detail the alternatives available to the designer and the design firm who want to go beyond Photoshop. For now we need to merely address several of the very specific practical considerations a designer will need to address when working exclusively with Photoshop. We have listed these challenges in a topical format and will offer practice solutions within the individual exercises you will be completing.

- Creating seamless repeats
- Color reduction
- Color matching

- Color modes
- Scaling motifs
- Which type of program to render in—Vector or Raster

Practical Applications

We conclude this chapter with an example of a floral repeat. The print was taken from fabric purchased at a local retail fabric store by fashion design student Yvonne Kinne.

Within the context of the classroom environment, students were requested to digitally re-create the design on the computer by hand without the use of a scanner. The next task assigned to the students was to isolate the motif. From this point students were required to provide several variations of the motif to reflect their comprehension of the types of motif layout learned in class.

Finally, the students were required to generate their own digital interpretation based on original fabric and adapt it to a specific market segment. (See Figure 9–24.)

Grasping the Fundamentals

How to Digitally Generate the Basic Repeats in Photoshop

You are now ready to try your hand at rendering several of the most common repeat patterns using Adobe Photoshop 7. First, you will begin by practicing the general concepts with simple shapes. Next, you will perform the specific how-to steps to replicate advanced fabrications and prints. Finally, by the conclusion of this chapter you will be able to apply your newly acquired knowledge and experience to digitally create your own textile applications!

If you recall in Chapter 3, there was a discussion and exercises for advanced repeat development in Adobe Photoshop. The exercises in this chapter will review a few of the previous techniques on a simpler level. As your proficiency with Adobe Photoshop increases, you can refer back to Chapter 3 to fine-tune your ability.

It is vital that you are confident with the general concepts of prints and repeats before you move on to solving specific design applications using Adobe Photoshop. (See Figure 9–25.)

- Single floral motif
- Multifloral with foliage
- Floral with geometric
- Patchwork element using a floral motif
- Floral motif using a stripe and/or border
- Floral motif with a textured background

FIGURE 9–24
Floral variations

FIGURE 9–25
Examples of the alternatives you have for making a repeat

E-Z Ways to Render in Adobe Photoshop

- Straight Repeat

- Offset Repeat (1/2 drop)

- Tossed Repeat

- Single Motif

Creating Repeats in Photoshop Using the Basic Tools

You must have competent working knowledge of all of the menus and tools we explored in Chapter 6 on Photoshop basics, including:

- General concept rendering tools in Adobe Photoshop

- Fills

- Define pattern

- Define brush

- Using filters

- Layer manipulation

- Loading textures

- Selection and editing tools

- Modes and layer styles

Rendering Logos for a Repeat

We hope that your review was helpful and that you know how to accomplish these simple basics in Adobe Photoshop. We have designed a series of exercises for you to put these concepts into practice.

Traditionally, many of the most successful designers and design firms are instantly recognizable from their initials used as a logo—for example, Fendi, Chanel, and Bill Blass, just to name a few. An easy way to grasp the concept of rendering repeats is to keep it simple. We suggest that you type your initials as if they were to be used for a logo. The first exercise will show you how to design and use your logo using Adobe Photoshop. Think of the plethora of applications for these images—on hangtags, on tissue paper and shopping bags, on linings for jackets, on ties, or on purses—the list is endless. So let's begin.

Main Version

Step 1. Open a **New File: 5 × 5 inches**, **72–150 dpi**, **RGB**, **White Background**.

Step 2. Type any letter or character. (See Figure 9–26.)

Step 3. Place a Marquee around the letter, leaving some white space.

Continue following directions for the variations:

Version #1

Steps 1–3. Same as in Main Version.

Step 4. Select **All > Edit Copy > Edit Paste > Flip Horizontal**.

Step 5. You may need to pick up and move the letter to form a logo. Next make a Marquee around both characters, leaving some white space. (See Figure 9–27.)

Step 6. Select **Edit > Define Pattern**.

Step 7. Make a **New Layer** and name it **Logo Repeat** in the Layer Property menu.

Step 8. Go to **Edit > Fill** and select the logo pattern and click **OK** to fill.

Step 9. Name and save as **logo** and click **OK.**

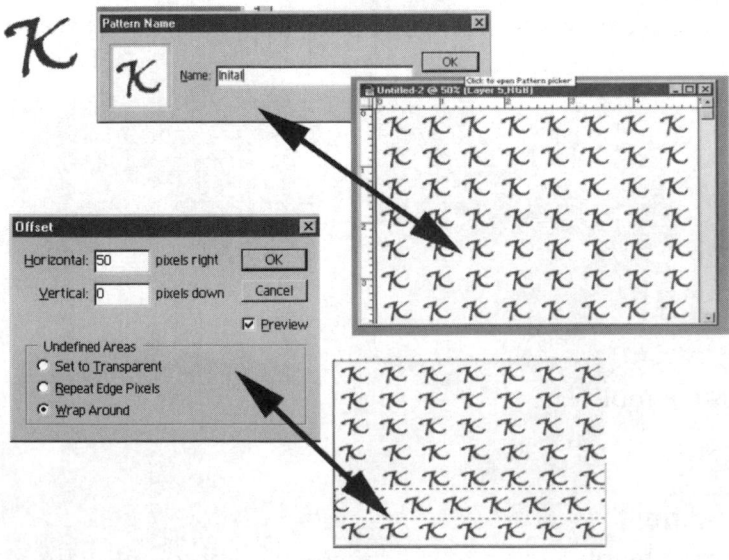

FIGURE 9–26
Type any letter or character

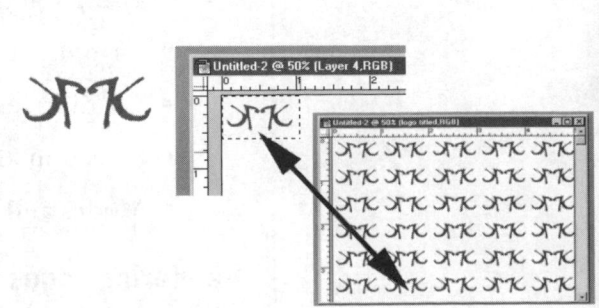

FIGURE 9–27
Make marquee

Version #2

Steps 1–4.   Same as in Version #1.

Step 5.   Make a Marquee around the single initial letter.

Step 6.   Select **Edit > Define Pattern** and name the pattern **Initial**.

Step 7.   Select **Edit > Fill > Pattern** and select your Initial pattern.

Version #3

Steps 1–4.   Same as in Version # 1.

Step 5. On the second row from the bottom, form a Marquee around the complete row from outside the page.

Step 6. Go to **Filter > Other > Offset** and select **Horizontal Offset > 50 pixels > Vertical > 0,** and click on **Wrap Around** and click **OK**.

Step 7. Make a Marquee around the bottom line, also outside on the gray, and choose **Filter > Other > Offset > Horizontal to 100 pixels > Vertical to 0** and click **OK**.

Step 8. Make a Marquee around the last three rows that you just adjusted. Choose **Edit > Define Pattern** and label **Offset Initials**.

Step 9. Add a **New Layer** and choose **Edit > Fill > Pattern > Offset Initials**.

Step 10. Name and save files. (See Figure 9–28.)

Other Applications and Insights:

_____

_____

_____

_____

Notes . . .

Rendering Prints in Photoshop Using Advanced Techniques
What Other Options Do You Have?

So far you have tackled rendering using several tools available in Photoshop. As we move to our advanced exercises, we want to reflect on several other options that are available to help you digitally render fabric.

In Chapter 4 and again in the first section of this chapter, you read that everything begins with inspiration and research. In the next several exercises, we will walk you through this process in a practical hands-on approach.

What You Need Before You Begin This Next Section

For this next section, you will need Internet access along with Adobe Photoshop in order to replicate the design process being demonstrated. You will also need either a "swipe" of an image or inspiration you may want to use for a motif or repeat.

You have been given a sample to follow along with in the Goodies Folder on the CD in the file **Inspiration-Chpt 9.**

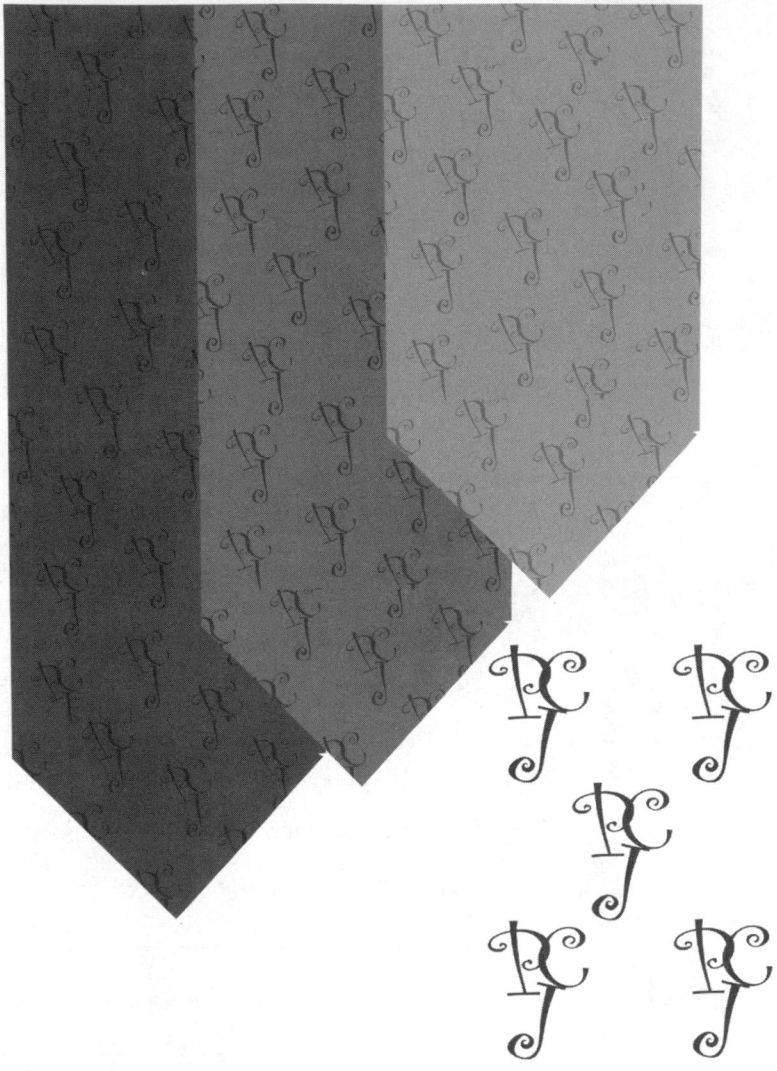

FIGURE 9–28
Logo repeats used for ties

Sourcing for Print Inspiration
Where Do You Source the Net for Ideas?

Earlier in this chapter you discovered that designers glean information and inspiration from everywhere their busy lives take them. Well, what do you do if you are working without any idea? Where do you turn? One place most designers turn to is the Internet. In this segment we will show you how to glean ideas from the Net for your next project!

The purpose of this segment is to demonstrate how a designer can source for inspiration on the fly using the Internet as a tool for locating a *swipe* for inspiration for rendering a single motif or repeat motif using Adobe Photoshop. A swipe can be defined as an object or image acquired by the designer for use in designing or for use on a storyboard.

Swipes can also be a photo of a sunset taken on your last vacation, or a button, a zipper, a swatch of fabric, a piece of yarn, a fall leaf collected from your yard, an oddly shaped seashell, or a clipping from a magazine. Swipes can be almost anything—whatever will motivate, captivate, or inspire you as the designer.

However, what happens if you do not have access to objects and you need an idea now? Where do you turn? Thank heaven for the Internet! In this next exercise we will walk you through obtaining ideas from the Internet for a floral print design.

Part 1—Internet Inspiration Swipes

Step 1. Open the Internet and go to your favorite search engine.

Step 2. We have several search engines that you may find easy to use:
   a. www.ASK.com
   b. www.Google.com
   c. www.AltaVista.com

Step 3. You may opt to go to several image bank sites:
   a. www.Ditto.com
   b. www.Corbis.com
   c. www.Comstock.com
   d. www.Artsville.com

Step 4. Once you arrive at the website, type in your request for an image: flowers.

Step 5. You may opt to narrow your search by asking for a specific flower such as a "rose" or a "daisy."

Step 6. Locate the image you want to use as your inspiration. You may accomplish this by paying the download image fee, if you are using an image bank such as Comstock, Eyewire, or similar image bank firm.

Step 7. After you have secured the image legally, you now have the option to utilize this image in your inspiration, mood, or storyboards. In addition, you can use the image for other marketing-related purposes. Read the licensing agreement from each firm, because the usage may vary from company to company or image to image.

Step 8. Did your notice use the phrase *legally obtained*? Obviously, you can sometimes obtain an image by snagging a quick copy, and it is clear to see why the term *swipe* is used in the design world. However, you do want to be in compliance with copyright laws—*don't you*?

So, for our purposes we will be using images that have been collected ethically for you from the folder on your CD entitled: Inspiration. Besides, did you know the images you "swipe" from the Web are extremely small—only several inches at best and are always of a poor pixel quality? This means for those of you considering "swiping" an image, it would not work anyway. FYI, most Web images are *only* 72 dpi—this is done in order to hasten the load time on the Web and will have a terrible print quality to it. So we sincerely appeal to your conscience *and* your logic— do not for any reason "swipe" the image. It will not work anyway!!!

Step 9. Open the Folder entitled **Inspiration.** Browse through and select an image to use and hit **Open.**

Part 2—Rendering Your Version of the Swipe

Here is where all the information on how to use Adobe Photoshop tools from Chapter 6 will really come in handy. Now you need to determine what is the best possible way to isolate the image you are looking for to use as inspiration in your print. We have listed below most of the major tools you will have to choose from. However, there is not a right or wrong answer of which tool to use. The solutions are more likely to come in the form of good, better, and best. Frequently, you will discover that as you become more experienced through practice with each of the tools, it will not be long before you will find which ones you are the most comfortable using for which job.

Sometimes the solution is obvious. For example, if there is sufficient contrast between an image and the background, often choosing to use the Magic Wand is the answer. Other times you will need to zoom in tight to the image and use the Magnetic Lasso. However, most of the time a combination of tools and patience should be used to extract or isolate the image you desire.

Isolating a motif on an illustration to be used as a repeat:

Step 1. Open the scanned image in Adobe Photoshop. Crop the portion of the illustration you want to isolate. (See Figure 9–29.)

Step 2. Open a **New File** in Photoshop to accommodate the anticipated final image size: **RGB, 150 dpi, White Background.**

Step 3. Paste the new cropped image for use on your new file.

Step 4. Duplicate the image to preserve the original.

Step 5. Next select **Filter > Noise > Median** and make the radius 3 or 4 pixels. This will begin to help you reduce the number of colors in the image.

Step 6. Next select **Image > Mode > Indexed Color.**

FIGURE 9–29
Crop step #1 by using the magic wand to delete the white background

Step 7. In the Index Color Dialogue box, choose the number of colors you wish to reduce to. For our example, we selected 8 as the number of colors and then **Matte & Dither > None.**

Step 8. At this point, if you have incorrectly anticipated the final canvas size for your design, you can opt to select **Image > Canvas Size** and adjust to desired size.

Step 9. Be sure you have your Rulers option turned on under **View > Rulers.**

Step 10. Make copies of the image and begin to lay out the copies of the motif as per figure.

Step 11. Next you will need to crop the additional portions of the image before you define a pattern, taking extra care to be sure you have isolated the repeat perfectly to avoid glitches in the joined seams.

Step 12. Use your Marquee tool to isolate your repeat and select **Edit > Define Pattern.**

Step 13. Name your pattern in the Dialogue box and select **OK.**

Step 14. Make a **New Layer** and select **Edit > Fill > with Pattern** and select your new pattern and click **OK.**

Step 15. It is important to keep in mind that some images will require additional manipulation to ensure a seamless pattern. There are several methods for accomplishing this, including copy and paste of missing print areas or using the Pattern Stamp option to eliminate disjointed seams.

Step 16. Finally, after you have concluded your print, you may continue to experiment with alternative colorways by choosing **Hue** and **Saturation** or **Image Adjust.**

Step 17. Don't forget, you can opt to isolate only one of the colors on your image by using the Magic Wand to exchange one color for another under Hue and Saturation. Just be sure that you have the Contiguous option turned off.

Other Applications and Insights:

_____

_____

_____

_____

Notes . . .

Now that you have accomplished obtaining an image for your motif, you need to consider what Photoshop options you should repeat.

In this next section, we have labeled most of the major tools and menu options you would be using for this task and have provided ample space to evaluate the pros and cons of each option. You will need to determine which tool and technique to use, when it is best suited, and what limitations you will encounter.

The Most Used Tools and Techniques for Prints in Adobe® Photoshop®

Figures 9–30 through 9–32 show some of the challenges, palettes, tools, and techniques you will be using in Adobe Photoshop. Why not open one of the images from the Goodies Folder on the CD and begin to use each of the tools and techniques listed. Make yourself some notes on which tools you prefer to use on which type of job.

Marquee

Isolate

Lasso

Wand-tolerance

Magnetic

Crop

Cut/copy/paste

Scan and then

Freehand trace

Vector trace

Wacom tablet trace

FIGURE 9–30

The most used techniques for rendering fashion, fabric, and prints in Photoshop

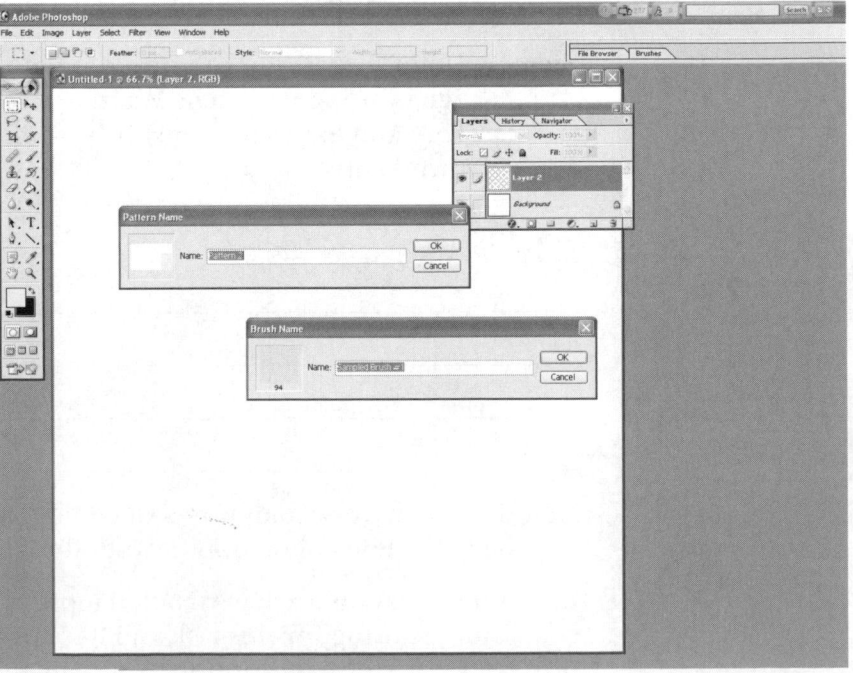

FIGURE 9–31

Most common palettes used in Photoshop

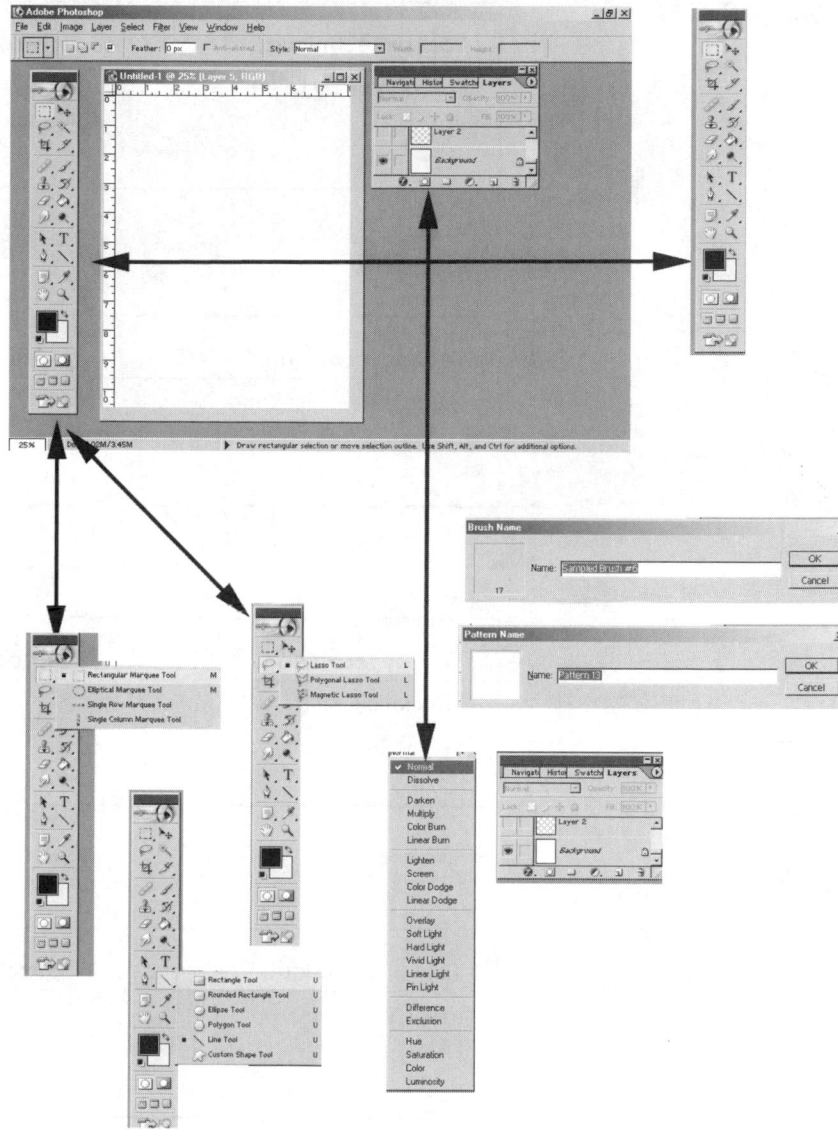

FIGURE 9–32

The most used palettes, tool bars, and menus in Photoshop

Student Tools and Techniques Work Reference Chart

Tool or Technique	Pros and Cons	Comments or Insights
Define Pattern		

Tool or Technique	Pros and Cons	Comments or Insights
Define Brush		

Notes...

Tool or Technique	Pros and Cons	Comments or Insights
Using the Poly Lasso		

Tool or Technique	Pros and Cons	Comments or Insights
Using the Magic Wand		

Tool or Technique	Pros and Cons	Comments or Insights
Magnetic Lasso		

Tool or Technique	Pros and Cons	Comments or Insights
Irregular Lasso		

Tool or Technique	Pros and Cons	Comments or Insights
Using the Paintbrush		

Tool or Technique	Pros and Cons	Comments or Insights
Using the Pencil		

Tool or Technique	Pros and Cons	Comments or Insights
Using the Vector drawing pen		

Tool or Technique	Pros and Cons	Comments or Insights
Using the Pattern Stamp		

Tool or Technique	Pros and Cons	Comments or Insights
Freehand—scan-trace		

Tool or Technique	Pros and Cons	Comments or Insights
Freehand—scan-trace		

Tool or Technique	Pros and Cons	Comments or Insights
Image—scan-trace		

Tool or Technique	Pros and Cons	Comments or Insights
Trace with Tablet		

Rediscovering the Magic of Filters

The Filter menu is possibly one of the most valuable menus for the textile designer. Although we covered the significance of this menu in Chapter 3, and you experienced the practical applications in Chapters 7 and 8, we have determined that this would be a perfect time for you to reflect on the menu's additional applications for your designs.

We have provided you with a close-up screenshot of each of the menu flyouts in Figure 9–33 and Figure 9–34 so you can make additional personal annotations on what you have learned so far!

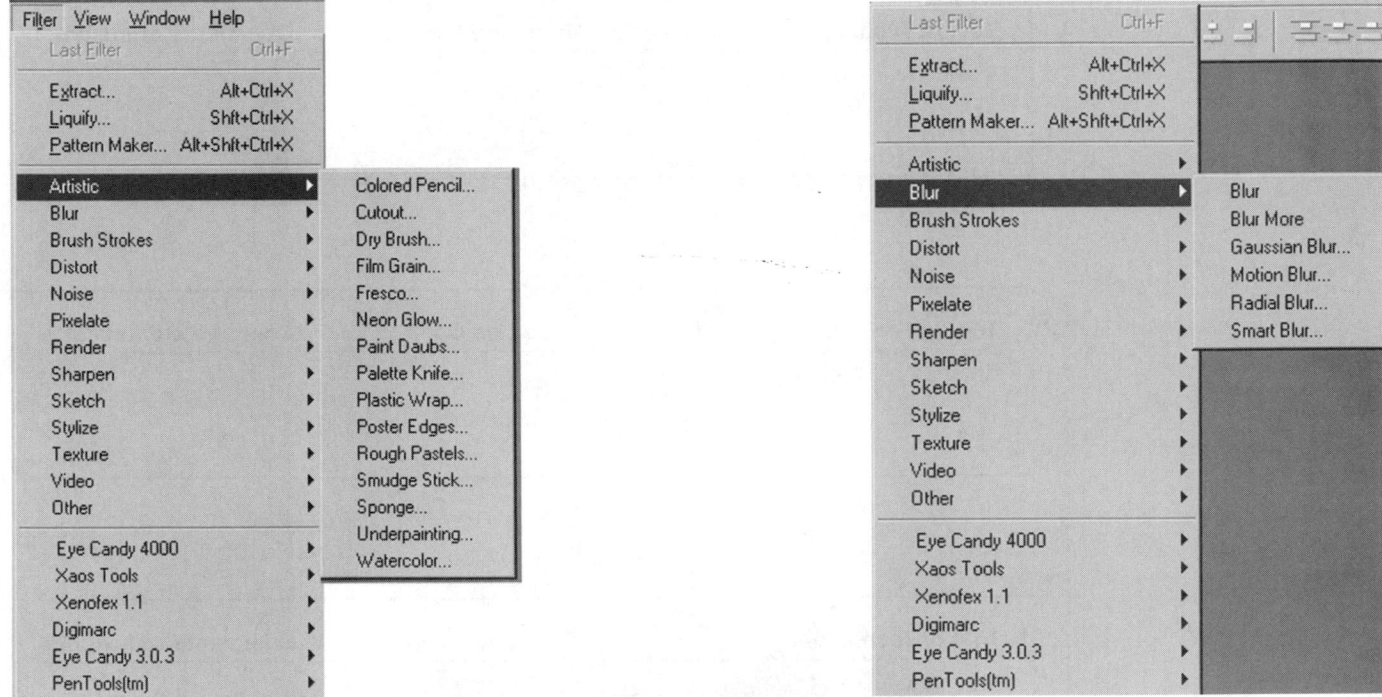

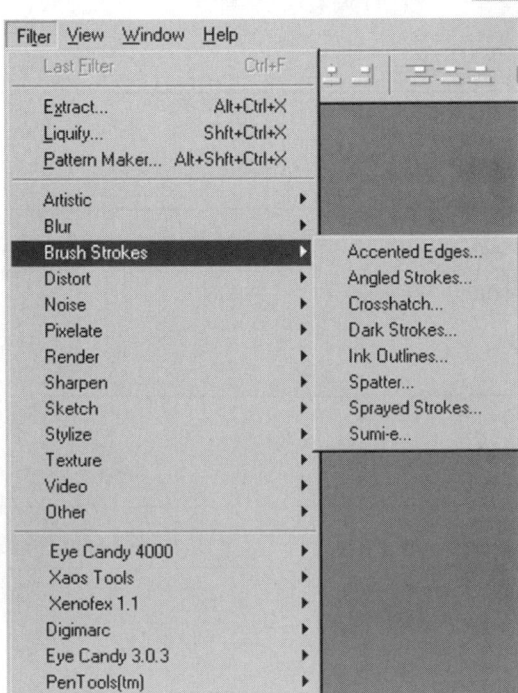

FIGURE 9–33
Menu flyouts

Notes . . .

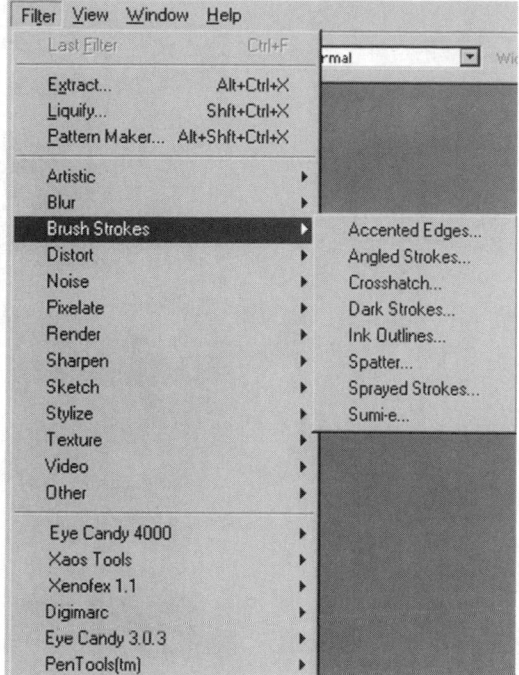

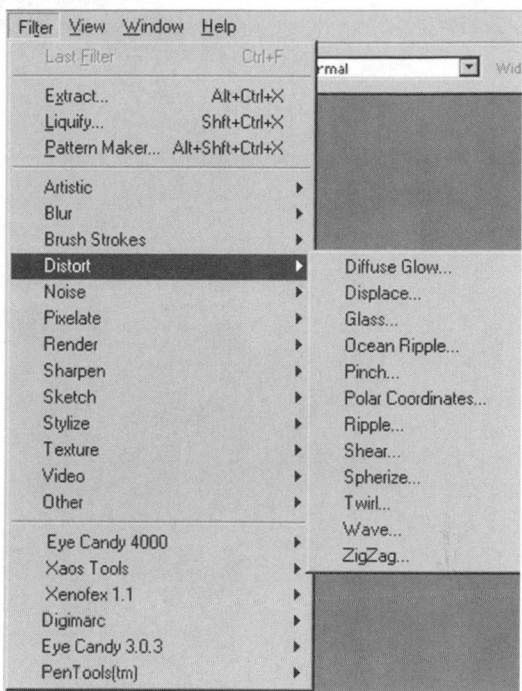

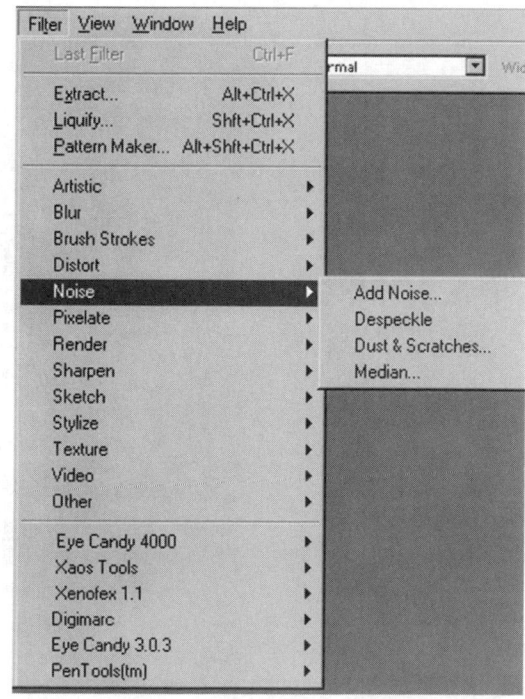

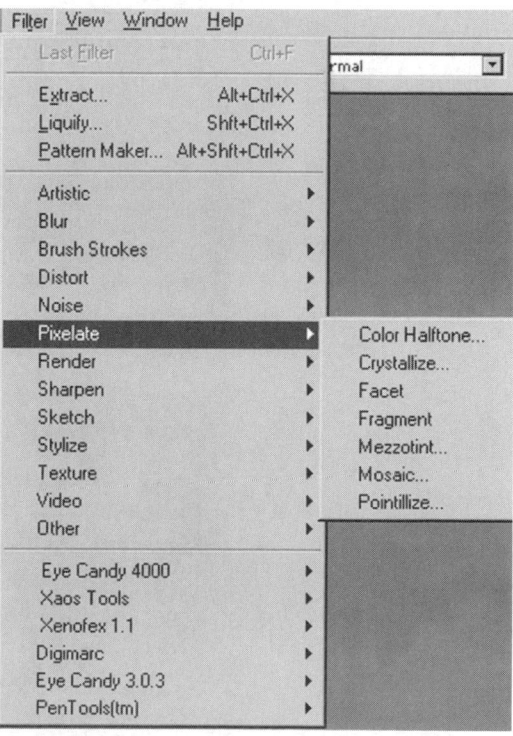

FIGURE 9–33

Menu flyouts *(continued)*

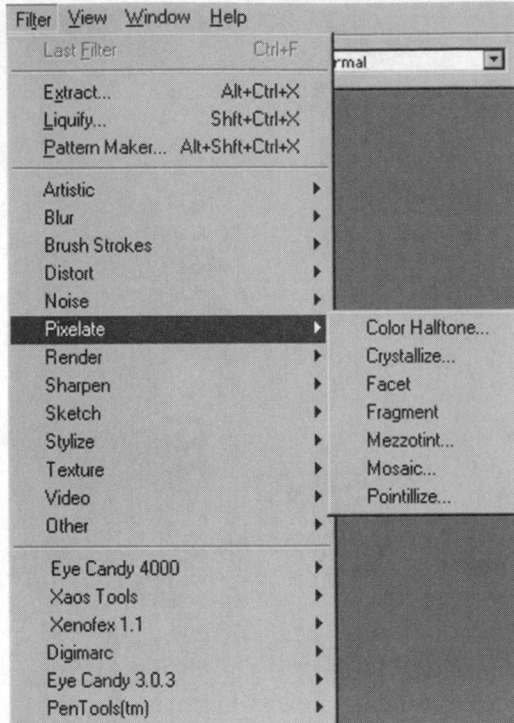

FIGURE 9–33
Menu flyouts *(continued)*

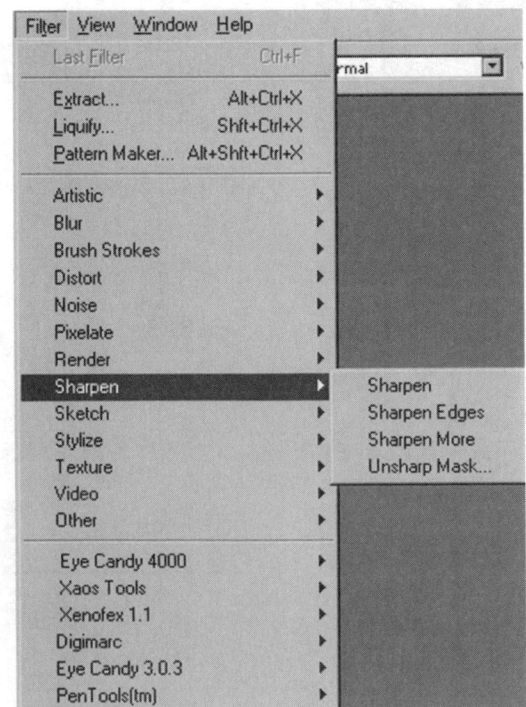

FIGURE 9–34
Menu flyouts

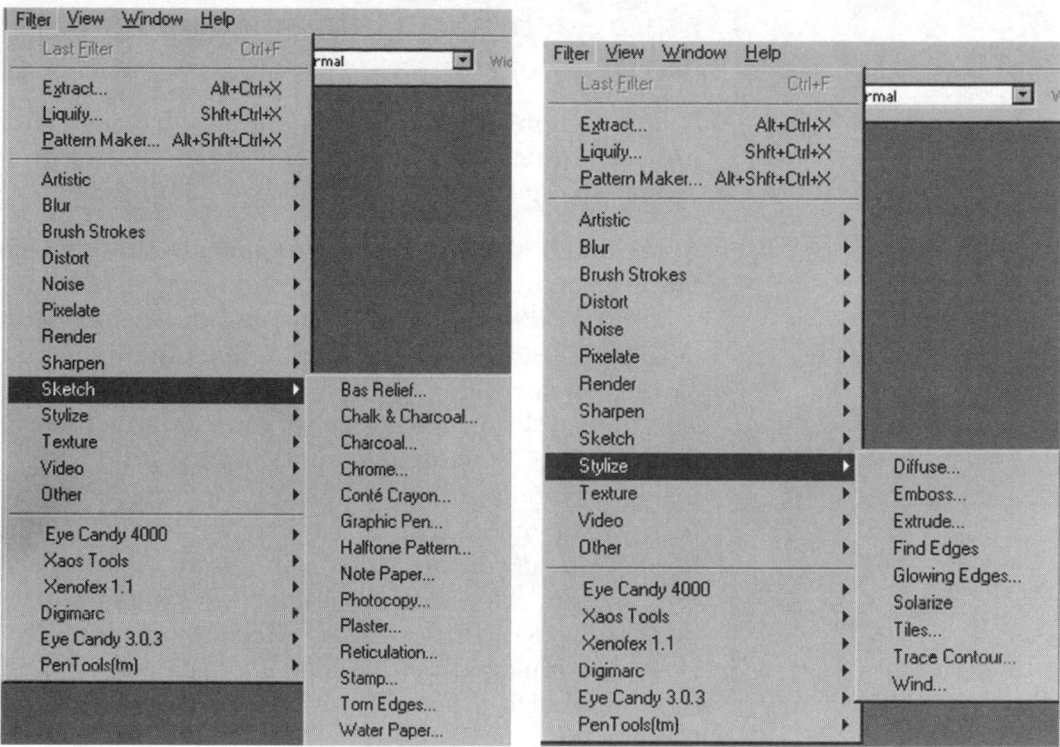

Notes...

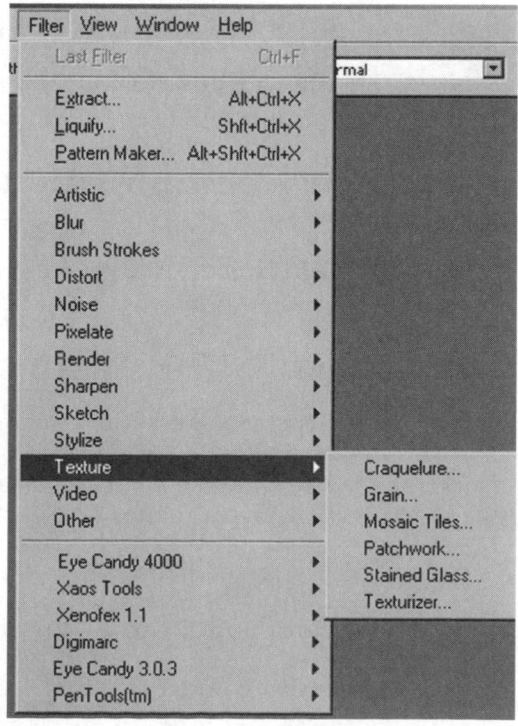

FIGURE 9–34
Menu flyouts *(continued)*

More Secrets and Strategies on Making the Most of Photoshop

In this section are several techniques we have not included as "specific" how-to projects. Instead we suggest that you test yourself to see how far you have progressed in digitally rendering fabrics and finishes!

At the end of this chapter we have included another Filter Review Comment section for you to jot down your latest discoveries. This is the perfect time to review what the Filters can do and how you can best utilize them to enhance your renderings. We strongly suggest that you continue to make notes in your text as you make new discoveries of the tools and menus. For example, as you spend time with the new Pattern Maker Filter you will soon discover all of its wonderful adaptations. However, perhaps you may notice as a textile designer that it has several major limitations. It will not take your existing image and maintain its original integrity to be repeated as the earlier tulip repeats we rendered manually in Adobe Photoshop. If you are looking for software to speed up and streamline this process, you will want to consider the plug-in software that accompanies this book, provided courtesy of Age Technology. Just like other plug-in software, it works in conjunction with Adobe Photoshop and not in place of Photoshop to assist your design process. We will cover this type of software in greater detail in Chapter 12.

Strategy #1—Making the Most of Filters

- **Artistic > Cut Out**—Looks like block printing

- **Artistic > Film Grain**—Creates a cotton texture

- **Blur > Gaussian Blur**—A low number will give a light brushing; a high number will look like polar fleece.

- **Blur > Motion Blur**—On plaids renders a flannel or napped surface effect.

- **Add Noise**—Adds a simulated surface texture. **Gaussian-Monochromatic** is a best bet!

- **Brush Strokes > Spatter**—Prints a terry effect.

- **Brush Strokes > Sprayed Strokes**—Produces an Ikat effect.

- **Brush Stroke > Crosshatch**, combined with **Monochromatic-Gaussian Noise**—Simulates linen and a plain weave effect.

- **Distort > Diffuse Glow**—Creates a cotton/wool effect.

- **Noise > Add Noise**—Produces a marled/multicolor yarn effect.

- **Stylize > Trace Contour**—Creates line art out of any design.

- **Stylize > Wind**—Produces a highly editable Ikat-like effect.

We have covered many more in the course of our exercises and we know you also have discovered many other wonderful applications. So be sure to jot them down here, so you don't forget what you have learned along the way!

Other Applications and Insights:

_____

_____

_____

_____

Other Applications for Your Ideas

If you are attempting to render fabric on the fly and do not have time to simulate the fabric structure, don't forget that you always have the option of opening one of our fabric scans from the Goodies Folder!

Simulating Prints and Repeats to an Existing Fabric:

Step 1. Open a **New File** in Adobe Photoshop: **6 × 6 inches**, **72–150 dpi**, **RGB**, **Transparent Background**.

Step 2. Go to the Goodies Folder and select the **Fabric Scan** folder and open **Denim**.

Step 3. Go to the Goodies Folder and select the **Exercise** folder and open **Chapter 9 > Tulips**.

Step 4. Drag a copy of the Denim fabric onto your New File. (This image will be on Layer #2.)

Step 5. Drag a copy of the Tulips onto your New File. (This image will be on Layer #3.)

Step 6. Voilà! Now you can preview what your print will look like on any fabric ground.

Step 7. You can opt to switch Layers 2 and 3 and experiment with the Multiple Mode by going to the Layer Property palette menu and selecting the Multiple Mode.

Step 8. Name and save your work. (See Figure 9–35.)

Other Applications and Insights:

_____

_____

_____

_____

FIGURE 9–35
Simulating prints and reprints
(Courtesy of Artsville)

Final Thoughts and Solutions

There are a variety of ways for adapting your artwork for other apparel and fashion applications, including converting your designs into jacquard woven, jacquard knit, or intarsia knitted patterns, as well as adapting the images for embroidery applications.

Here are several images from proprietary software applications that will assist you in creating or adapting your designs for other applications. (See Figures 9–36 and 9–37.) We will discuss these companies and their products in greater detail in Chapter 12. However, it is important that you recognize at this stage of designing that your creations have far greater applications than you can even begin to imagine!

FIGURE 9–36
Cat
(Courtesy of Punto)

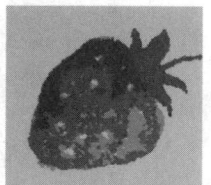

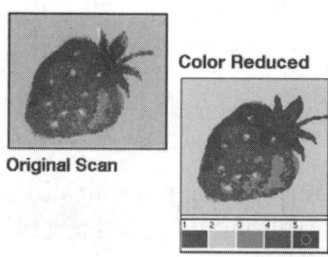

Original Scan   Color Reduced

FIGURE 9–37
Strawberries
(Courtesy of Punto)

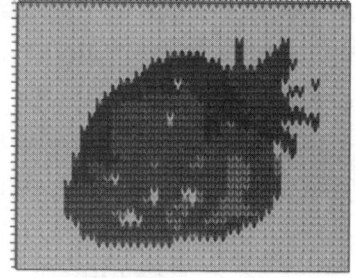

Notes . . .

FIGURE 9–38
From Artsville
(Courtesy of Artsville)

This is just the tip of the iceberg on how far your rendering can be applied. Think of the possibilities:

Interior design applications
    Wallpaper
    Borders
    Companion fabrics

Domestics
    Bedding
    Bath

Greeting cards

Wrapping paper and more!

It is exciting to think about how far your imagination and talents can take you. Before we begin our next chapter, we want to introduce you to another great product line that actually showcases the talents of a textile designer.

Regarding these other applications, we want to introduce you to a wonderful collection from Artsville, by the designer Jane Nelson. (See Figure 9–38.)

Stock Image Application Showcase

Artsville and Jane Nelson

Jane Nelson is a New York City artist, who finds inspirations for work while traveling to distant lands. Her original hand-painted backdrops have appeared in numerous high-profile magazines and television commercials. She is a member of the United Scenic Artists' Union. Nelson's career has also included extensive work in fashion and textile design. She has experimented with many processes, including batik techniques on silk, hand-painting fabrics, papermaking, silk screening, and photography, and as you will soon discover, the wonderful application of adapting these designs for digital applications.

You should be very excited by now about the future of digital design and should be more than up for the challenge of the final series of exercises. In our next chapter we include ideas from Jane Nelson for the Artsville collection of stock images entitled: Color Rhythms.

10 Advanced Fabric and Print Rendering

Terms to look for:

Abstract
Argyle
Art Deco-inspired print
Damask
Diapered
Ethnic
  African
  Oriental character
Fleur-de-lis
Flora and fauna
  Roses
  Leaves—tropical
  Historical variation—toile de Jouy
Geometric
  Mosaic
Novelty
  Venetian mask
  Holiday (Valentine)
  Women's shoes
  Found objects
Paisley
Patriotic
Photo-Realism
Stencil
Uniform—culinary and medical (pediatric—children)
Furs-Feathers-Skins and Leathers
  Astrakhan and fur
  Feathers
  Leather
    Cat-Tiger-Leopards
    Crock
    Snake
    Pony (Cow)(Dalmation)
    Giraffe
    Zebra
    Military—camouflage
  Tulle—lace

FIGURE 10–1
Typical geometric prints

Advanced Rendering of Prints

In this chapter on how to render fabric and prints you will further apply your Adobe Photoshop savvy to rendering some of the most common prints found in fashion and interior today. (See Figure 10–1.)

Each of these ideas can be adapted to almost any medium or application. The steps are written so you can follow along. Then these exercises can easily be adapted and modified for a variety of other design applications.

Be sure you annotate any additional filter or tool modifications you apply to these designs.

Important Announcement and Disclaimer

When developing these next few chapters and the accompanying series of practical exercises, every care has been given to write the steps in a clear and understandable fashion. It is assumed that you already have worked through the early exercises in Chapter 4 and have a comfortable working knowledge of all the material covered in Chapters 3, 4, and 5.

To write the steps in any other manner would have belabored the information and increased the number of written steps to the point of actually causing unnecessary confusion to the reader. All of these exercises have been written to give you ample opportunity to experience the wide range of techniques that can be used.

The purpose of the exercises is to reinforce the basic skills of Adobe Photoshop as would be applied by a fashion, textile, or interior designer. If you come to this book having learned Adobe Photoshop's tools in a different context, you may need to put aside what you already think you know about how something should be done and be willing to learn another way to accomplish a task. We heartily encourage you to make notes in the chapter as you complete each exercise and record what works best for you. Frequently, you will discover that there is not necessarily a right or wrong way to do something, but more of a good, better, best scenario. For example, in Chapter 8 on rendering plaids, there were several ways that were short and sweet but others involved steps that appeared to be a bit more tedious. In reality, sometimes taking the longer route affords you more control over the design process. Should the shortcuts work for you, terrific! Use them; by all means apply them to your work!

When a technique or method is preferred over another, we will give notice to that effect. Therefore, the use of the designer's critical thinking skills to modify the exercises to suit a given project is to be expected. If you find that you are experiencing extreme difficulty following along in any exercises, we suggest that you go back and review the basic tools and techniques covered in the earlier chapters and then attempt the practical application exercise. Frequently, a student or designer may attempt to rush the design process without adequately knowing the software and the results can be a disappointment or an unnecessary time of frustration.

The last thing you need to do is to become frustrated. Try getting up from the computer for a small break, or perhaps go on to another exercise and come back later to the one that is challenging you. If you have the luxury of discussing the outcome objectives with someone who has successfully mastered the assignment, this too can help considerably. Trying to go on to more difficult exercises before you are ready is like trying to build upper floors without successfully completing the structural foundation first.

Although these exercises have been classroom tested, we welcome your feedback via e-mail at our website www.ComputersandFashion.com.

How to Render a Geometric Abstract
Going in circles!

Step 1. Open a **New File: 8.5 × 11 inches, RGB, 72–150 dpi, White Background**.

Step 2. Figure 10–2 shows a series of circles each on their own layer.

Step 3. The circles have been formed by using the circle Marquee and then by filling the selection with color.

Step 4. The circles with the hollow centers are made by making a new "smaller" circle selection directly on top of a given circle and then hitting the Delete key.

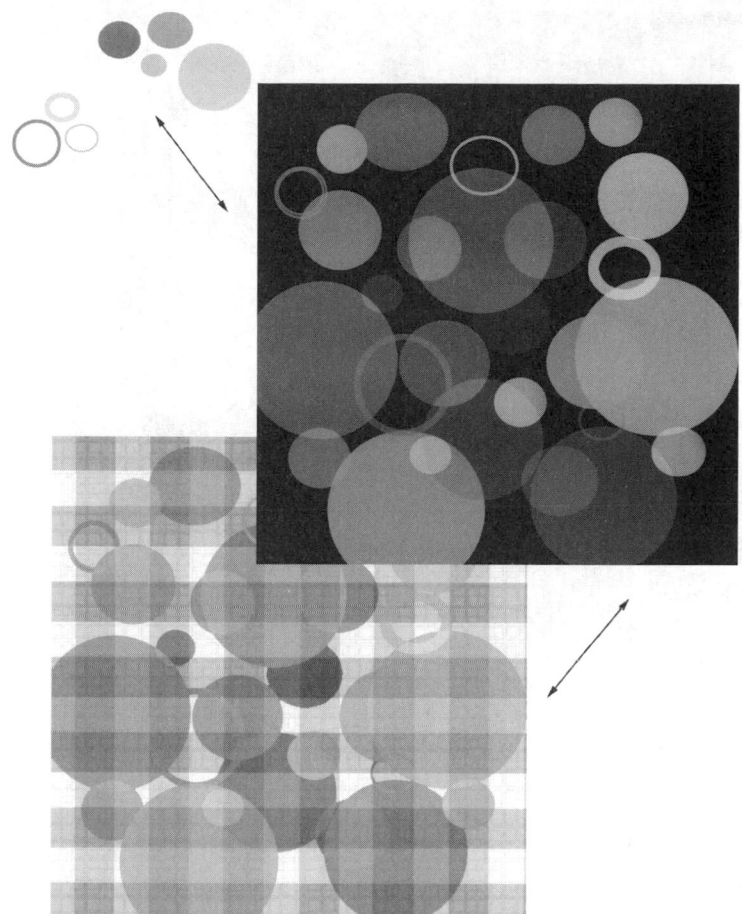

FIGURE 10–2
Circles in layers

Step 5. After you have completed your circles, you can opt to **Define a Pattern** and **Fill a New layer** or you may continue to make individual circles one at a time. The reason the circles are each on their own layer is to give you the option of resizing and relocating the circles to create your own variation pattern.

Step 6. When you are satisfied with your rendering, you can opt to flatten the layers or make a JPEG copy.

Step 7. If you make a JPEG copy, you can now reopen the JPEG copy and begin to experiment with colors and textures.

Step 8. In Figure 10–2 we have reopened our plaid fabric and placed this file copy below our circles to enhance the design in a mix-and-match fashion.

Other Applications and Insights:

_____

_____

_____

_____

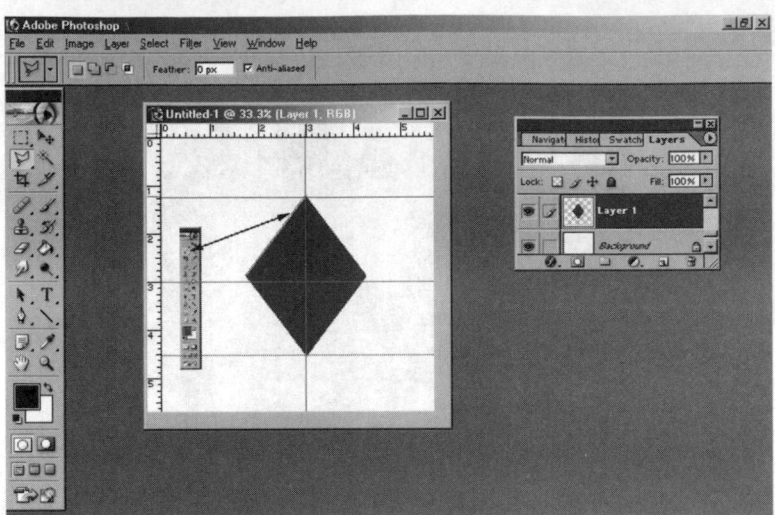

FIGURE 10–3
Use poly lasso tool

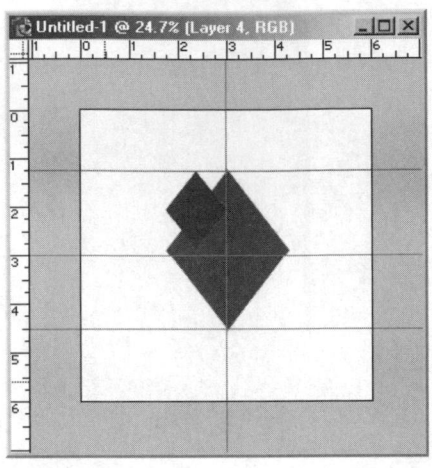

FIGURE 10–4
Copy of diamond motif

How to Render Argyle

Step 1. Open a **New File** in Adobe Photoshop: **8 × 8 inches**, **72–150 dpi**, **RGB**, **White Background.**

Step 2. Using the Vertical Rulers, place rulers approximately at 2, 3, and 4 inches.

Step 3. Then place Horizontal Rulers approximately at 1 1/2 inches and at 3 inches.

Step 4. Using the Poly Lasso tool, begin to shape a diamond. (See Figure 10–3.)

Step 5. Fill this new shape with desired color.

Step 6. Copy the diamond layer one more time and move the shapes as in Figure 10–4.

Step 7. You can now merge these layers and **Define** a pattern or continue to copy the layers and color each diamond independently as shown in Figure 10–5.

Step 8. Drag the burgundy-colored diamond and copy to New Layer.

Step 9. Using the Magic Wand tool, select the diamond and fill with a royal blue color.

Step 10. Go to **Edit > Free Transform** to match the shape in Figure 10–6.

Step 11. Make three copies of this new diamond shape and using the Move tool begin to place the diamond shapes in all four corners of the larger original diamond.

Step 12. Next using the Line tool from the Toolbox flyout menu, separate four diagonal lines in black to outline the main diamond pattern. Make the lines approximately 10 pixels wide.

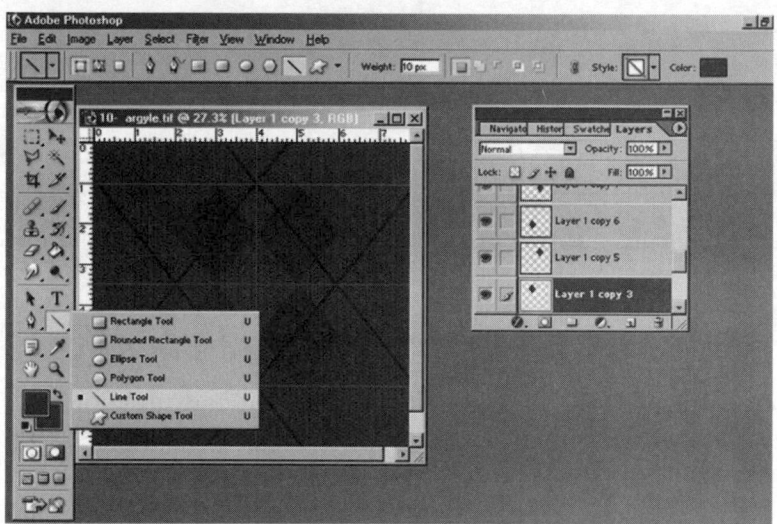

FIGURE 10–5
Merge layers

FIGURE 10–6
Match shape

FIGURE 10–7
Make a new layer

Step 13. Place your cursor on the bottom layer and go to **Layer > Make New Layer > Fill** and fill this new layer with forest green color.

Step 14. Open the Goodies Folder in the CD and select **Fabric Structures > Jersey Knit.**

Step 15. Marquee around the jersey shape and go to **Edit > Define Pattern.**

Step 16. Make a New Layer and go to **Edit > Fill > Pattern > Jersey**, and click **OK.** (See Figure 10–7.)

Step 17. You can now opt to flatten your image. We suggest that you make a JPEG copy and then add texture or filters to your image.

How to Render a Diapered Fabric Repeat

During the Gothic period, there was a favored repeat pattern known as a diapered fabric. This pattern typically was a single motif that was repeated to form a diamond pattern that would continue across the face of the fabric.

Step 1. Open a **New File** in Adobe Photoshop: **8 × 8 inches**, **72–150 dpi**, **RGB**, **White Background**.

Step 2. Follow Steps 1–3 in the argyle exercise to make your first diamond.

Step 3. Place a Marquee around the new diamond shape.

Step 4. Go to **Edit > Define Pattern** and name the pattern **Harlequin** and click **OK.**

Step 5. Make a New Layer and go to **Edit > Fill > Pattern**. Select **Harlequin** pattern and click **OK.**

Step 6. Using the Magic Wand, begin to select every other diamond and fill with new color.

Step 7. You may opt to add a textured ground such as a knit or woven pattern similar to the one in the argyle exercise. (See Figure 10–8.)

Step 8. Name and save your work.

FIGURE 10–8
Add textured ground

_____

_____

_____

_____

Rendering Mirrored Damask Pattern

Step 1. Open a **New File** in Adobe Photoshop: **8 × 8 inches, 72–150 dpi, RGB, White Background.**

Step 2. Open the Goodies Folder and select **Exercise Folder > Wheat-leaf sample.**

Step 3. Drag a copy of this file onto your New File.

Step 4. Make another copy of this image and go to **Edit > Transform > Flip Horizontally.**

Step 5. Go to **Layer > Merge Down** to make the wheat on one layer directly above the background layer.

Step 6. Make a Marquee around the two sheaves of wheat and go to **Edit > Define Pattern** and name the pattern **wheat.**

Step 7. Go to the Layer Property menu and select the New Layer icon.

Step 8. Go to **Edit > Fill > Pattern > Wheat** and click **OK.**

Step 9. Go to the Main menu and select a new color of your choice for the background.

Step 10. Place the Magic Wand on the background behind the wheat repeat. Hit the **Solid Color Fill** bucket.

Step 11. You may also opt to enhance or recolor the wheat sheaves.

Step 12. Do not add any texture or filters to your image at this time.

Step 13. Placing the Magic Wand again on the background color behind the wheat, select **Inverse** to capture all the wheat.

Step 14. Go to **Layer > Layer Style > Bevel and Emboss.**

Step 15. From the Bevel and Emboss Layer palette menu, you can begin to experiment with the degree of embossing you want to add to the wheat so that it begins to appear as if it is woven into the background. We suggest that you try the combination in Step 16.

Step 16. You may now reselect the solid-colored ground of the image and go to **Filter > Noise > Add Noise** to add a small amount of **Gaussian > Monochromatic** to your images.

Step 17. Then go to **Filter > Brush Strokes > Crosshatch.** (See Figure 10–9.)

Step 18. Name and save your work.

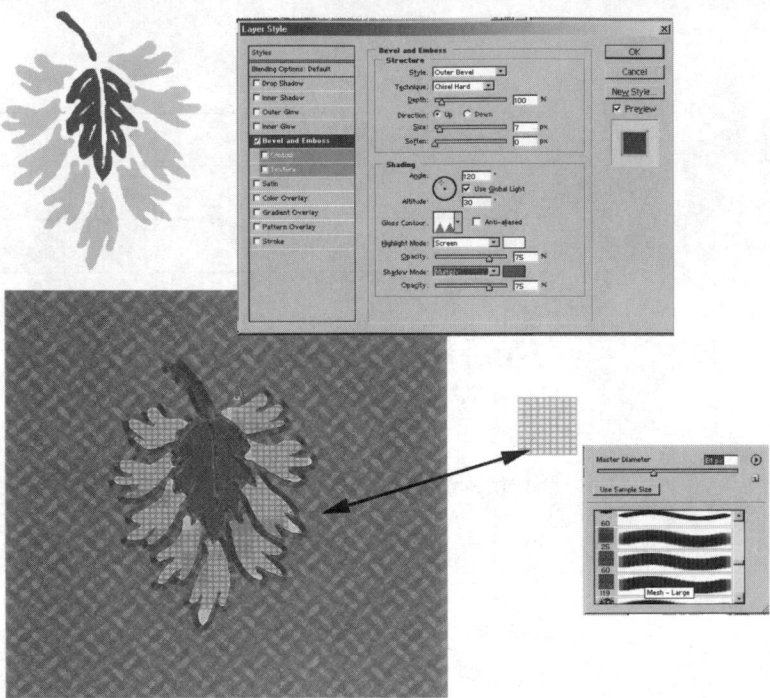

FIGURE 10–9
Mirrored damask pattern

Other Applications and Insights:

_____

_____

_____

_____

How to Render an Art Deco-Inspired Print

We have selected an Art Deco-inspired print as our example of a historical print that was motivated by architecture in New York City, including the quintessential symbols of America's tribute to the Art Deco movement—the Chrysler Building and the elements of the interior found in the Waldorf Hotel on Park Avenue.

The designs from the 1920s and 1930s are an eclectic mix of the Jazz Age and Ballet Russe fantasy, and include simple geometric elegance and polished streamline elements inspired by emerging technology reflected in everything considered new or modern. This style includes popular modes of transportation— in the "bullet-style" trains and luxury ocean passenger liners—and was reflected in South Beach Deco-inspired hotels as well as Egyptian motifs inspired by the discovery of King Tut's tomb, and, of course, the lovely movie sound sets of the 1930s musicals with Fred Astaire, Ginger Rogers, and Busby Berkeley's extravaganzas!

Step 1. Open a **New File: 8.5 × 11 inches, RGB, 72–150 dpi, White Background.**

Step 2. Using the Lasso tool to make straight lines, begin to make lines to match Figure 10–10 to form several crisp line silhouettes.

FIGURE 10–10
Use lasso tool to create lines

Step 3. The succeeding white lines were made individually by using the Rectangle Marquee and then filling the shapes with the color white. We suggest that you use your rulers to align the shapes, as well as consider making them on individual layers, in case you need to nudge them in any direction.

Step 4. Using the Magic Wand, select the shapes one at a time. Begin to fill with desired colors. We made our image in black and white and gray.

Step 5. Open the Goodies Folder and select **Sample Exercises > Antelope silhouette.**

Step 6. Drag a copy of the antelope onto your new file and make another copy of the same shape.

Step 7. Using the Move tool, place the shapes near the building, one on the right and one on the left. You will need to go to **Edit > Flip Horizontally** on one of the shapes so that they will be facing one another.

Step 8. Open the Goodies Folder and select **Fabric Structures.** Add a simple twill weave pattern as explained in the exercises in Chapter 7.

Step 9. Name and save your file. (See Figure 10–11 for another variation of this technique. We also included an example of a filter applied to this concept.)

Other Applications and Insights:

_____

_____

_____

_____

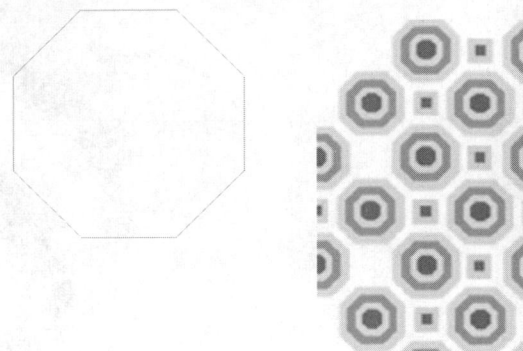

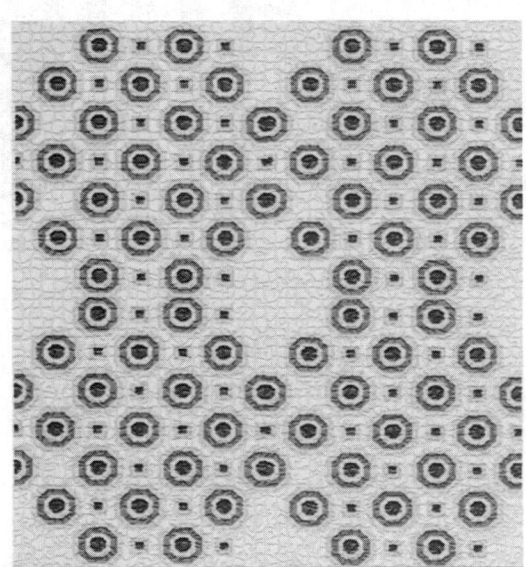
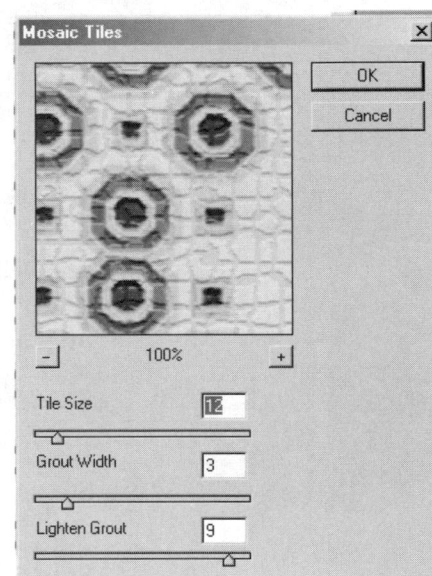

FIGURE 10–11
Variation of art deco-inspired print
(Artwork by F. Ishmael)

Ethnic-Inspired Prints
African Ethnic—by F. Ishmael

In this exercise you can opt to do several coloring methods:

(a) Use a Wacom tablet and hand paint.

(b) Select **Toolbox > Paintbrush > Hand Paint** with the mouse.

(c) Select **Tools > Paint Bucket > Gradient Fills.**

Step 1. Open a **New File: 8.5 × 11 inches, RGB, 72–150 dpi, White Background.**

Step 2. Go to the Goodies Folder on the CD and select **Exercise Images > Ethnic Color-up.** (See Figure 10–12.)

Step 3. Drag a copy of this image onto your New File and to Layer #2.

FIGURE 10–12
Ethnic color-up
(Courtesy of F. Ishmael)

FIGURE 10–13
Add texture
(Courtesy of F. Ishmael)

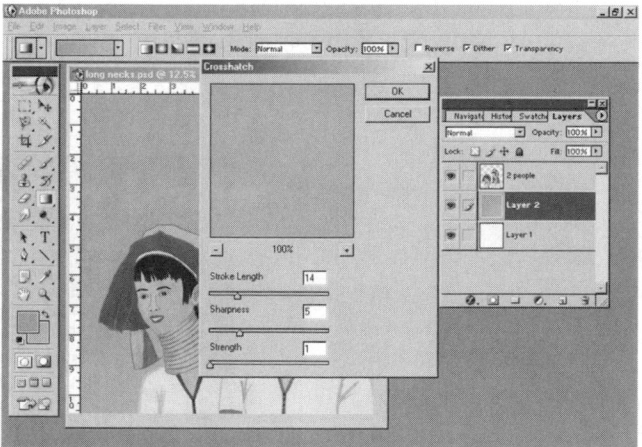

FIGURE 10–14
Adding texture to the merged down layer
(Courtesy of F. Ishmael)

Step 4. Begin to color the images using options listed above, including (a), (b), or (c).

Step 5. Make a New Layer below the drawing. Using the Eyedropper, select two different shades of the primary color used in the image.

Step 6. Fill this New Layer with a gradient of the two monochromatic shades.

Step 7. Go to **Filter > Brush Strokes > Crosshatch** and add texture to this image. (See Figure 10–13.)

Step 8. Next go to the layer with your colored rendering and repeat Step 7.

Step 9. Merge down your layers and name and save. (See Figure 10–14.)

Other Applications and Insights:

_____

_____

_____

_____

Adding an Oriental Character to a Print

Step 1. Open a **New File: 8.5 × 11 inches**, **RGB**, **72–150 dpi**, **White Background.**

Step 2. Using the Paint Bucket, fill the background with the color gray.

Step 3. Go to the Goodies Folder on the CD and select **Exercise Images > Brilliant Symbol.**

Step 4. Drag the copy of the symbol to your new file. Following the example shown in Figure 10–15, continue to drag additional copies to your image.

Step 5. Opt to make a complex pattern repeat. Also add fabric structure or filters to enhance your image.

Step 6. Name and save your file.

FIGURE 10–15
Drag copy of the symbol

FIGURE 10–16
Fleur-de-lis motif

FIGURE 10–17
Final pattern

How to Render a Fleur-de-lis

Step 1.   Open a **New File: 8.5 × 11 inches**, **RGB**, **72–150 dpi**, **White Background.**

Step 2.   Using the Paint Bucket, fill the background with the color gray.

Step 3.   Go to the Goodies Folder on the CD and select **Exercise Images > Fleur-de-lis shape.** (See Figure 10–16.)

Step 4.   Drag the copy of the fleur-de-lis to your image and make at least two copies and place the images suitable for defining a pattern. You may also opt to manually make additional copies of this shape and using the rulers and guides to lay out the pattern of your choosing.

Step 5.   If you do opt to define a pattern, place a Marquee around your image. Go to **Edit > Define Pattern** and name the pattern **Fleur-de-lis.**

Step 6.   Make a New Layer by using the New Layer icon from the Layer palette menu.

Step 7.   Go to **Edit > Fill > Pattern > Fleur-de-lis.**

Step 8.   As you can see from Figure 10–17, we have made the image so that it can be used for a variety of different applications, including scarves and ties.

Step 9.   You may opt to go to the Goodies Folder and add a fabric structure to your image.

Step 10. Name and save your work.

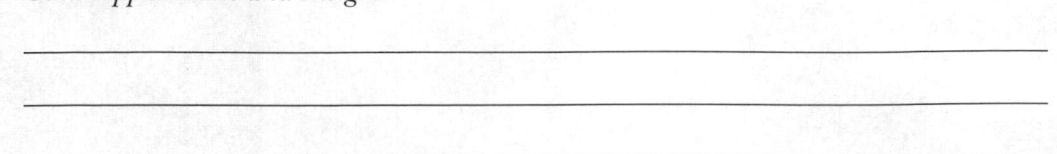

Other Applications and Insights:

_____

_____

_____

_____

Floral and Fauna

Version #1 — Everything is coming up roses — by Nandi Chin AIFL student

This exercise uses the flower on your CD for you to pen and color. However, if you are comfortable with your rendering skills, try using a Wacom tablet and stylist pen and attempt your own creation. Just be sure you close all the gaps in your image for adding color fills later!

Step 1. Open a **New File: 8.5 × 11 inches, RGB, 72–150 dpi, White Background.**

Step 2. Using the Paint Bucket, fill the background color with a light blue.

Step 3. Go to the Goodies Folder on the CD and select **Exercise Images > Nandi's Rose.** (See Figure 10–18.)

Step 4. Drag a copy of the rose to your file or opt to use an actual photo of a flower and trace the shape with a Wacom tablet.

Step 5. We suggest that you make an additional copy of your rose and turn off the layer. Name this layer **Floral Backup** on the Layer Property menu. This will be useful if you opt to make other variations later. It will save you a step later when reopening the image.

Step 6. Using the Magic Wand, begin to isolate individual sections of the flower for coloring. We suggest that you begin to fill the areas directly above the original selection. This will enable you to adjust the shading and

FIGURE 10–18
Nandi's rose
(Artwork by Nandi Chin)

FIGURE 10–19
Textured background

FIGURE 10–20
Striped background

opacity or even experiment with different style brushes when adding color to your flower.

Step 7. Once your rose is complete, we suggest that you consider adding different backgrounds and textures to your image. Have a look at Figures 10–19 and 10–20 for the actual process as well as your alternatives for adding other fabric combinations!

Step 8. Name and save your file.

Other Applications and Insights:

_____

_____

_____

_____

Floral and Fauna

Version 2—Tropical-leaves application

Step 1. Open a **New File** in Adobe Photoshop: **8 × 8 inches, 72–150 dpi, RGB, White Background.**

Step 2. Make a New Layer and fill the layer with a gradient color range found in your leaf—for example, a dark green to the deep burgundy found in the stem. The other alternative is to select two shades of deep ocean blue for a gradient. Fill the new layer with color and hit **Next.**

Step 3. Go to the Goodies Folder and select the following files: **Chapter Exercises > Chapter 10 > Scanned Leaf** and **Bamboo Image.** (See Figures 10–21 and 10–22.)

FIGURE 10–21
Bamboo image

FIGURE 10–22
Scanned leaf

Step 4. We took the bamboo shape and dragged several copies to our file and proceeded to alternately flip them vertically and horizontally. We did the same steps with the sea grape leaf.

Step 5. Go to the Filter menu and select **Artistic > Dry Brush** to enhance the image. Hint: Experiment with the Filter menu to Posterize or add other types of filters to cause your image to have very different feelings. You should experiment with these filters before you proceed.

Step 6. Add from the Filter menu and select **Noise > Add Noise** and small amounts of **Monochromatic > Gaussian Noise** to your image. (See Figure 10–23.)

Step 7. Finally you can add your desired choice of ground texture to your image. (See Figure 10–24.)

Step 8. Name and save your file.

Other Applications and Insights:

_____

_____

_____

_____

FIGURE 10–23
Noise

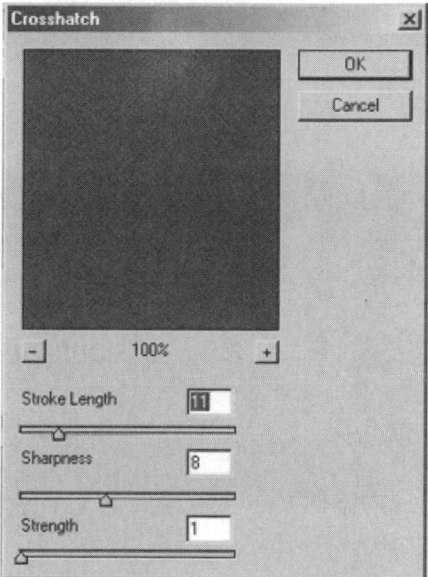

FIGURE 10–24
Add texture

Flora and Fauna—Toile de Jouy Historical Print

Version #1 Advanced for those with a Wacom Drawing tablet

Step 1. Open a **New File** in Adobe Photoshop: **8 × 8 inches**, **72–150 dpi**, **RGB**, **White Background.**

Step 2. Open the Goodies Folder and select **Chapter Exercises > Chapter 10** and open the following files: **Nandi's Rose, Leaves Background, Castle, Shields, Elizabeth.**

Step 3. First drag a copy of the background leaves to your new file. Depending on the size of your file, you may need to edit and Free transform your leaves to fit the background. Next, adjust the Opacity slider bar on the Layer Palette to approximately 50%.

Step 4. Drag a copy of the castle and Elizabeth onto your New File. Edit and free transform them to size.

Step 5. Next, go to the shield file and place a Marquee around the first shield and then go to **Edit > Define Brush** and name the brush **Shield #1**.

Step 6. Repeat Step 5 for the second shield.

Step 7. Using the newly created shield brush, make at least one shield on each of your files. (See Figure 10–25.)

FIGURE 10–25
Examples

Step 8. Drag a copy of the castle onto your New File and resize as needed.

Step 9. Drag a copy of Nandi's Rose to your New File. Resize and then select **Edit > Rotate**. Resize multiple copies of your rose for placement near the castle and near Elizabeth.

Step 10. Experiment with other variations. You may also opt to add texture to the background layer.

Step 11. Name and save your work.

We have given you two examples of our toile de Jouy in Figure 10–25 to use as an inspiration. Feel free to make your own combinations of images. For example, you can opt to open the fleur-de-lis pattern and use that as your background. Whatever choices you make, be sure to annotate your steps.

Other Applications and Insights:

_____

_____

_____

_____

Flora and Fauna—Toile de Jouy Historical Print
Version #2 Advanced for those with a Wacom Drawing tablet

Step 1. Open a **New File** in Adobe Photoshop: **8.5 × 11 inches, 72–150 dpi, RGB, White Background**.

Step 2. Using your Wacom Drawing tablet, begin to draw trees and leaves in various corners of your page. We suggest that you make a New Layer for each series of flora and fauna in case you opt to resize or enhance these images later.

Step 3. Next, render a simple female silhouette outline and fill with a solid color. Make two copies. Hint: Toile prints typically are rendered on a white background and each of the images are typically in black, red, or blue outlines. They are made to look like they have been etched or inked. So be sure you limit your colors and also which brush styles you select. (See Figure 10–25.)

Step 4. Next, go to the Goodies Folder and select **Exercise Images > Chapter 10** and select the **Oriental Character/Symbol**. Place a Square Marquee around the image.

Step 5. Go to **Edit > Define Brush** and name the brush **Oriental Symbol**. Click **OK**.

Step 6. Using the Ruler Guides to mark out the placement for your symbols, drag the guides to the desired location on your image.

Step 7. Next, go to the Brush flyout menu from the Main Toolbox menu and select the **Oriental Symbol** brush. Using the slider bar, size the brush to the scale you feel will best suit your rendering.

Step 8. Place several symbols throughout your image.

Other Applications and Insights:

_____

_____

_____

_____

Geometric

How to render a mosaic tile print

Step 1. Open a **New File: 8.5 × 11 inches**, **RGB**, **72–150 dpi**, **White Background**.

Step 2. Using the Straight-Line Lasso tool, begin to make several shapes as shown in Figure 10–26 to look like mosaic tile.

Step 3. After you have prepared your selection to match, place a Marquee around the desired tiles shapes and go to **Edit > Define Pattern** and name the pattern **Mosaic Tiles**.

Step 4. Make a New Layer and go to **Edit > Fill > Pattern > Mosaic Tiles** and click **OK**. (See Figure 10–27.)

Step 5. Using the Poly Lasso tool, begin to make an "S" silhouette to match Figure 10–28. Then make additional copies of the "serpentine shape" and go to **Edit > Transform > Rotate** and adjust the images to match Figure 10–29.

Step 6. Also shown in Figures 10–28 and 10–29 is an additional element of a star. This shape can be added by using the Straight-Line Lasso tool and filling the star shape with a golden hue.

FIGURE 10–26
Isolate the repeat with
straight-line lasso tool

FIGURE 10–27
New layer with fill repeat

FIGURE 10–28
Additional element

FIGURE 10–29
Adding surface texture

Step 7. Add texture by including fabric structures or filters to suit your taste. (See Figure 10–29.)

Step 8. Name and save your file.

Other Applications and Insights:

_____

_____

_____

_____

Bold Mix and Match of Patterns 101
Practical application of designing

You can clearly see how easy it is to render the most popular fabric and prints in Adobe Photoshop. In our next section we will explore the concepts of creating and rendering novelty prints as well as animal prints and more.

We believed it would be helpful at this time to remind you of the many different mix-and-match combinations you can create with your final designs.

In the next few exercises you can see just how simple it is to use color to mix and match and combine fabrics in many unique as well as traditional ways! (See Figures 10–30, 10–31, and Figure 10–32.)

FIGURE 10–30
Examples of companion fabrics

FIGURE 10–31
Technical drawings

FIGURE 10–32
Various digital fabric applications

Take a moment to reflect on all you have learned so far. Think of how you can take your designs to the next level by mixing and matching fabric patterns and prints. Jot down any thoughts you may have here.

_____

_____

_____

_____

Notes . . .

Novelty Prints

One of the most enjoyable prints to make is the novelty print. Here you can take your imagination and let it run free.

We underestimate just how often we see these prints in our everyday life. These colorful expressions of wit and whimsy brighten our day or color our world.

Here are just a few of the applications:

- Children's wear
- Lingerie
- Scarves
- Purses and bags
- Swimwear
- Wallpaper

- Holiday items
- Bedding and domestics
- Men's ties
- Shoes and socks
- Uniforms

We know you will enjoy thinking about the many different applications for your images too.

Rendering a Novelty Print—
Mardi Gras Mask–Updated

Version # 1 Meet: Farah Ismael

This talented young designer has a degree in Graphic Design and is currently pursuing an additional degree in Fashion Design.

Step 1. Open a **New File: 8.5 × 11 inches**, **RGB**, **72–150 dpi**, **White Background**.

Step 2. Open the Goodies Folder on the CD and select **Copyright-royalty free images > Smiling Face**. (See Figure 10–33.)

Step 3. Make a copy of the image and drag to your New File.

Step 4. Go to the Filter menu and select **Dry Brush** or **Cut Out** menu. Click **OK**.

Step 5. Using a Wacom tablet or a mouse, begin to manually redraw the image with color.

Step 6. Add additional elements to enhance the image.

Step 7. As you can see, the artist added each element on its own layer and then she experimented with Filters and Opacity to enhance the image.

Step 8. Name and save your work.

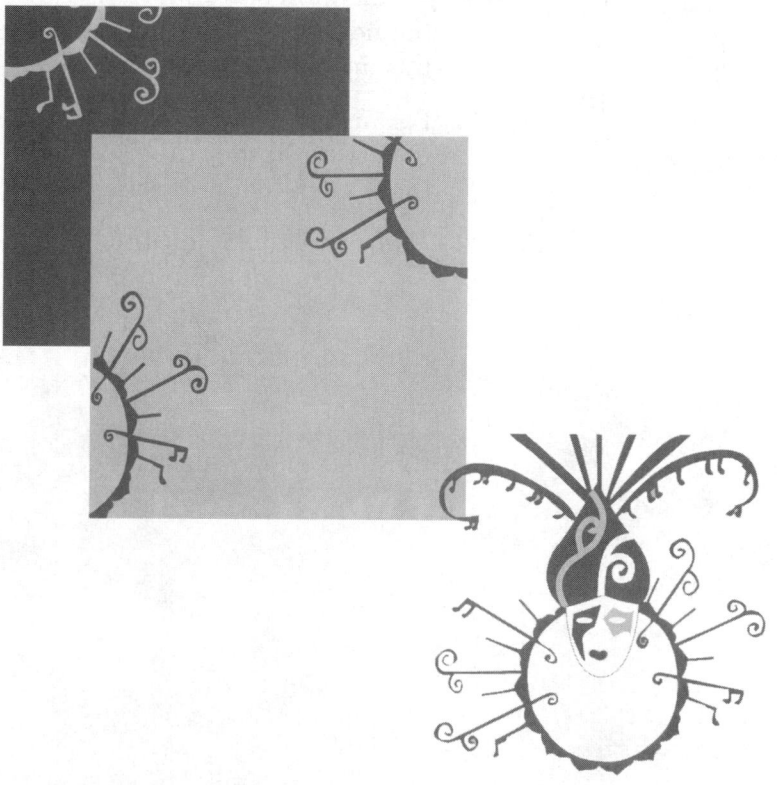

FIGURE 10–33
Smiling face
(Courtesy of F. Ishmael)

Other Applications and Insights:

_____

_____

_____

_____

Rendering a Holiday Novelty Print
Version #2 Hugs and kisses—valentine

Step 1. Open a **New File: 8 × 8 inches**, **RGB**, **72–150 dpi**, **White Background**.

Step 2. Go to the Goodies Folder on the CD and select **Chapter Exercise Images > Chapter 10**. Then select the **Lipstick** and **Kisses** templates.

Step 3. Drag a copy of each image on to your New File. Notice the images are each on their own layer for ease in copying.

Step 4. Experiment with making additional copies in various sizes or colors and repeat across the face of the page.

Step 5. Experiment with adding texture to the image. Use methods that are similar to those in Chapter 7.

Step 6. Add a border to your design by placing a Marquee box just inside the boundaries of the complete image. Hit **Select > Inverse > Fill** with contrasting color. (See Figure 10–34.)

Step 7. For fun, try experimenting with an airbrush from the Brush menu and make your lipstick tube appear as if it has just written a message, such as the X's & O's in our example.

Step 8. Name and save your file.

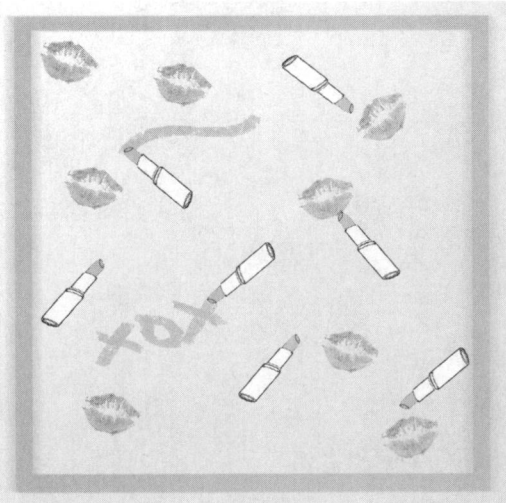

FIGURE 10–34
Fill with contrasting color

Other Applications and Insights:

_____

_____

_____

_____

_____

Rendering a Novelty Print
Version #3 Shoes, shoes, shoes

Step 1. Open a **New File: 8.5 × 11 inches**, **RGB**, **72–150 dpi**, **White Background**.

Step 2. If you recall from Chapter 4, we provided you with a sample shoe found in your Goodies Folder. Select **Sample Exercises > Shoe Master**. At this time you can open that shoe and begin to make a repeat pattern *or* you can do what we did in Figure 10–35. We used our Wacom tablet and instead opted to free-hand several different styles of shoes for use on our scarf. You can also free-hand your own shoe silhouettes using a drawing tablet, or by rendering the shoes by hand, or by scanning them into the computer per instructions in Chapter 5.

Step 3. We suggest that you make each shoe on its own layer so you can decide on placement and then flatten the image when you are satisfied or even

FIGURE 10–35
Shoe master

define a pattern if you choose to create a simple repeat. Take a moment to apply the techniques of pattern placement covered in Chapter 9 in order to determine the repeat pattern you like best.

Other Applications and Insights:

_____

_____

_____

_____

Rendering a Novelty Print
Version #4 Scanning found objects

This exercise is very easy and fun to do. Earlier we provided you with a copy of a Sea Grape Leaf for you to use in rendering a print. Now we are asking you to use your imagination and locate several everyday objects to use in a print. We opted to scan several strands of beads and pearls; you can use whatever you have available.

Step 1. Open a **New File** in Adobe Photoshop: **8 × 8 inches**, **72–150 dpi**, **RGB**, **White Background**.

Step 2. Next, we opted to scan several strands of costume jewelry beads we had and then dragged a copy of our scanned pearls and beads onto our New File.

Step 3. Next, we went to the Filter menu and selected **Artist > Poster Edges.** (See Figure 10–36.)

Step 4. Consider adding **Filter > Noise** or **Filter > Brush Strokes** or perhaps a fabric structure to your print to enhance the look. The important thing is to have fun; use your imagination and see where it takes you! (See Figure 10–37.)

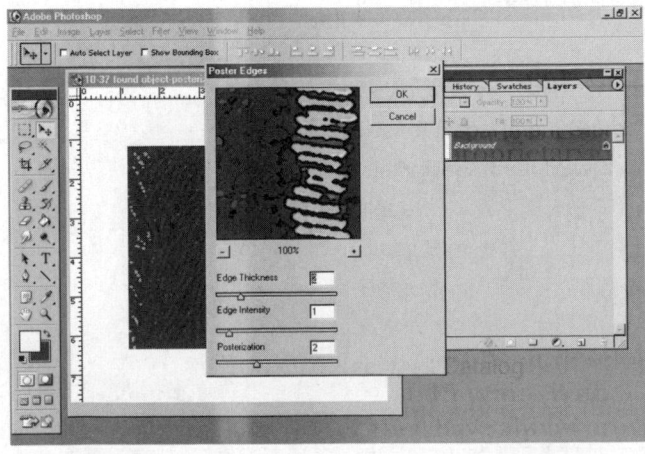

FIGURE 10–36
Poster edges

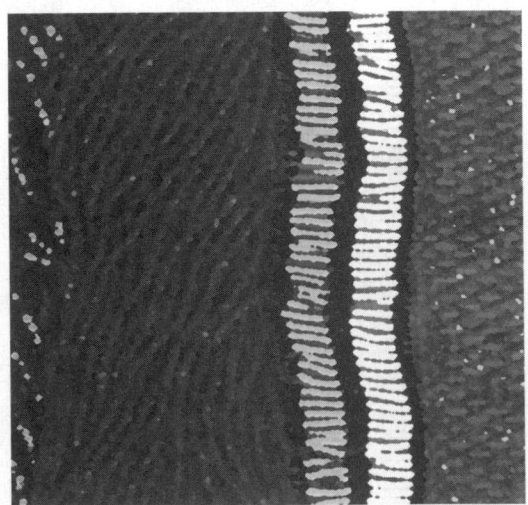

FIGURE 10–37
Add noise or brush strokes

Step 5. Be sure to make notes and annotate your findings.

Step 6. Name and save your work.

As you can see from our last exercise, rendering repeat motifs has endless possibilities.

Other Applications and Insights:

_____

_____

_____

_____

Rendering a Paisley Print

Version #1 Mosaic tile variation of paisley mosaic—from Farah Ismael

Step 1. Open a **New File: 8 x 8 inches**, **RGB**, **72–150 dpi**, **White Background**.

Step 2. Open the Goodies Folder on the CD and select **Paisley**. (See Figure 10–38.)

Step 3. Using this image as an example, drag a copy of the Paisley over to your New File.

Step 4. Make a New Layer for each series of strokes. Using a smooth-edged Paintbrush from the Toolbox flyout menu, begin to trace the Paisley.

FIGURE 10–38
Paisley
(Courtesy of F. Ishmael)

FIGURE 10–39
Use square marquee tool
(Courtesy of F. Ishmael)

FIGURE 10–40
Flatten image
(Courtesy of F. Ishmael)

Step 5. Open New Layers to indicate different brush types used or different thicknesses of brush strokes.

Step 6. When you are satisfied, make a JPEG copy of the file and name it **Paisley Version #1.**

Step 7. Open a **New File: 12 × 12 inches, 72–150 dpi, White Background.**

Step 8. Drag over a copy of the JPEG Paisley, and begin to make multiple copies. Experiment with the tiles going in different directions.

Step 9. Then, using the Square Marquee tool, begin to make vertical width boxes to indicate the "grout of the tile." Fill this area with the darkest shade of your tile. Make both horizontal and vertical stripes. (See Figure 10–39.)

Step 10. Flatten your image. Name and save your file as **Paisley Tiles.** (See Figure 10–40.)

Other Applications and Insights:

_____

_____

_____

_____

Paisley Variations

In Figure 10–41 you can see that we made a scan of an actual fabric, using the reduce color technique you learned in Chapter 5. We reduce the color and isolate

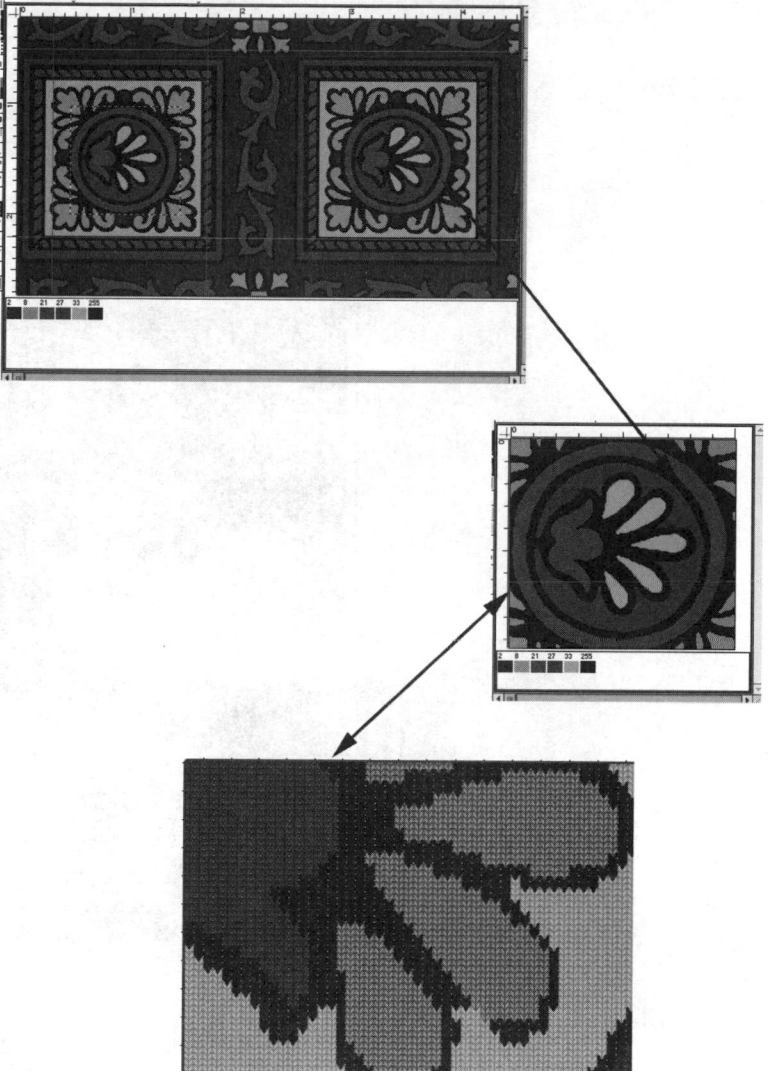

FIGURE 10–41
Scan of actual fabric

the image for Figure 10–42. The image for Figure 10–41 depicts isolating the motif, then converting it to a knit. In Figure 10–42 you can see where we made another variation on our paisley by changing the method of repeat from toss to column, as well as adding additional elements and converting the texture ground of several variations of repeat.

Other Applications and Insights:

_____

_____

_____

_____

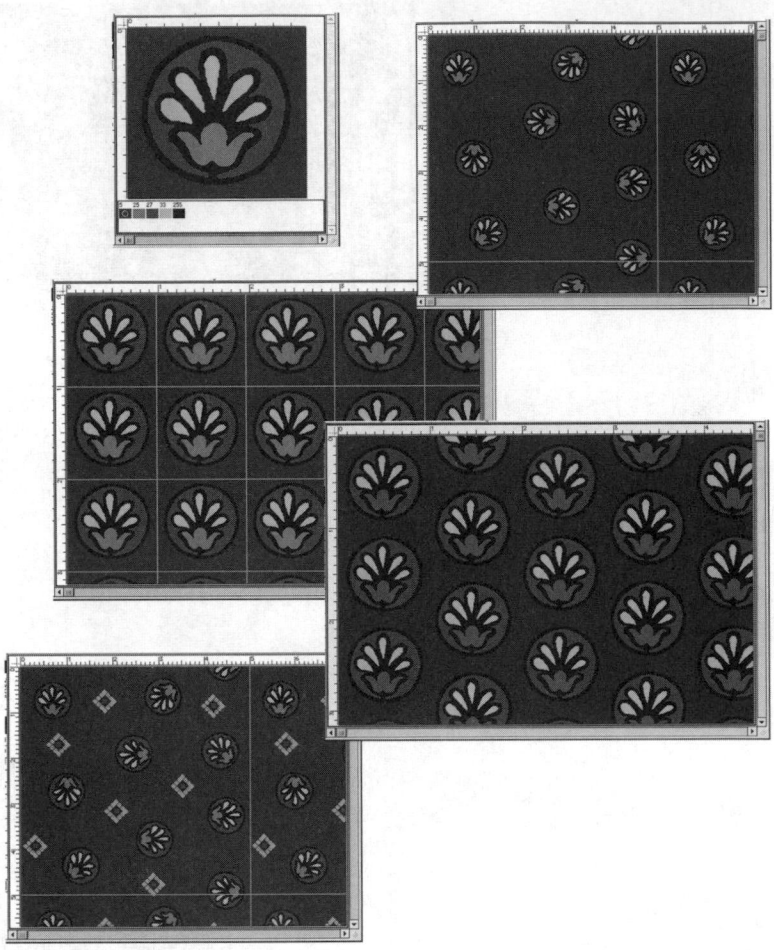

FIGURE 10–42
Changing method of repeat

How to Render a Patriotic Print

The inspiration for this exercise was first rendered by a former AIFL student Kelly Schiovo for a class assignment. It was then modified to suit the purpose of this exercise.

Background

During the aftermath of 9/11 in the United States, there has been a renewed sense of patriotism, and the result has been a resurgence of the familiar stars and stripes. This one was a takeoff of several ideas including one designed by fashion design student Kelly Schiovo.

Step 1.   Open a **New File: 8.5 × 11 inches, RGB, 72–150 dpi, White Background**.

Step 2.   Open the Goodies Folder and select **Images > Map**.

Step 3.   Drag a copy of the map onto your new file.

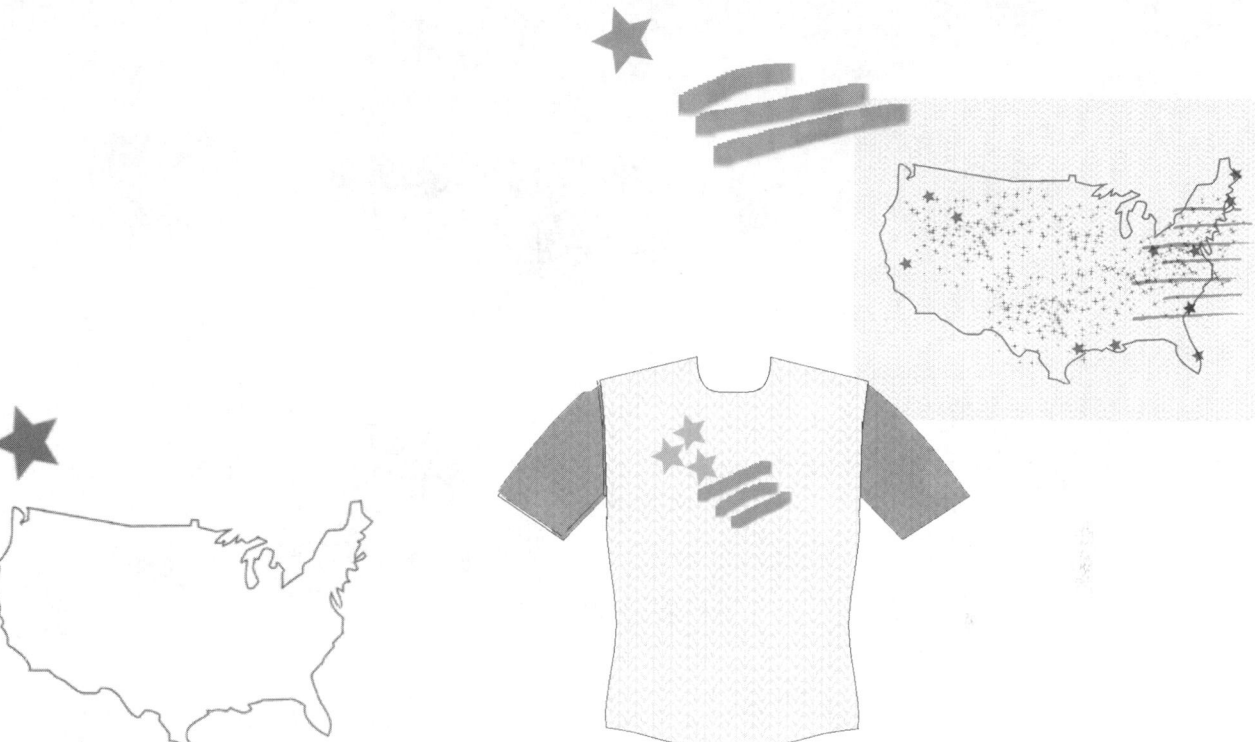

FIGURE 10–43
Star

FIGURE 10–44
Make series of smaller stars

Step 4. Open the Goodies Folder and select **Images > Star**. (See Figure 10–43.)

Step 5. Place a Marquee around the Star and go to **Edit > Define Brush** and name the brush **Star**.

Step 6. Make a New Layer and select the Brush tool from the Toolbox. Select the new Star Brush from the Brushes palette and begin to make a series of smaller stars across the face of the map. (See Figure 10–44.)

Step 7. Make another New Layer and then go back to the Brushes palette and select Brush #6, which makes a small cross-like star. Begin to add additional smaller stars across the face of the map.

Step 8. Make another New Layer and go back to the Brush Palette and select Brush # 63 and begin to make long, flowing horizontal stripes.

Step 9. The logic behind the individual layers was to give you the option to easily edit the image without sacrificing the integrity of the map.

Step 10. Add texture if desired. As you can see in Figure 10–45, we did other variations of this design and then added the pattern in a T-shirt clip art technical.

Step 11. You may opt to flatten your image. Name and save your work.

FIGURE 10–45
Add pattern

Other Applications and Insights:

_____

_____

_____

_____

_____

Adapting Photos as Fabric Print

What could be more exciting than incorporating photography and digital printed textiles? This new genre of designing is one of the hottest trends in fabric today. The junior and contemporary markets appear to have insatiable hunger for these unusual designs.

In the following exercises we will walk you through utilizing a photograph for an engineered design that can all be accomplished in Adobe Photoshop!

How to Adapt a Photo as Fabric Print
Travel postcard

Step 1. Go to the Goodies Folder on the CD and select **Royalty Free Images** and the image entitled **Monaco.**

Step 2. Go to **Select > All**.

Step 3. Go to **Edit > Copy**.

Step 4. Open a **New File: 8 × 8 inches, 72–150, dpi, RGB, White Background**.

Step 5. Open the Goodies Folder and select the Clip Art folder and the T-shirt example.

Step 6. Drag a copy of the T-shirt to your New File.

Step 7. Using the Magic Wand, isolate the body portion of the T-shirt.

Step 8. Go to **Edit > Paste Into** and go to **Edit > Transform** and scale the image to fit into the shirt.

Step 9. Using the Magic Wand, select one sleeve at a time. Using the Eyedropper, select a color from the photo. Using the Paint Bucket, fill the sleeves with a solid matching or contrasting color from the image. Add a knit ground, if desired. (See Figure 10–46.)

Step 10. Name and save your work.

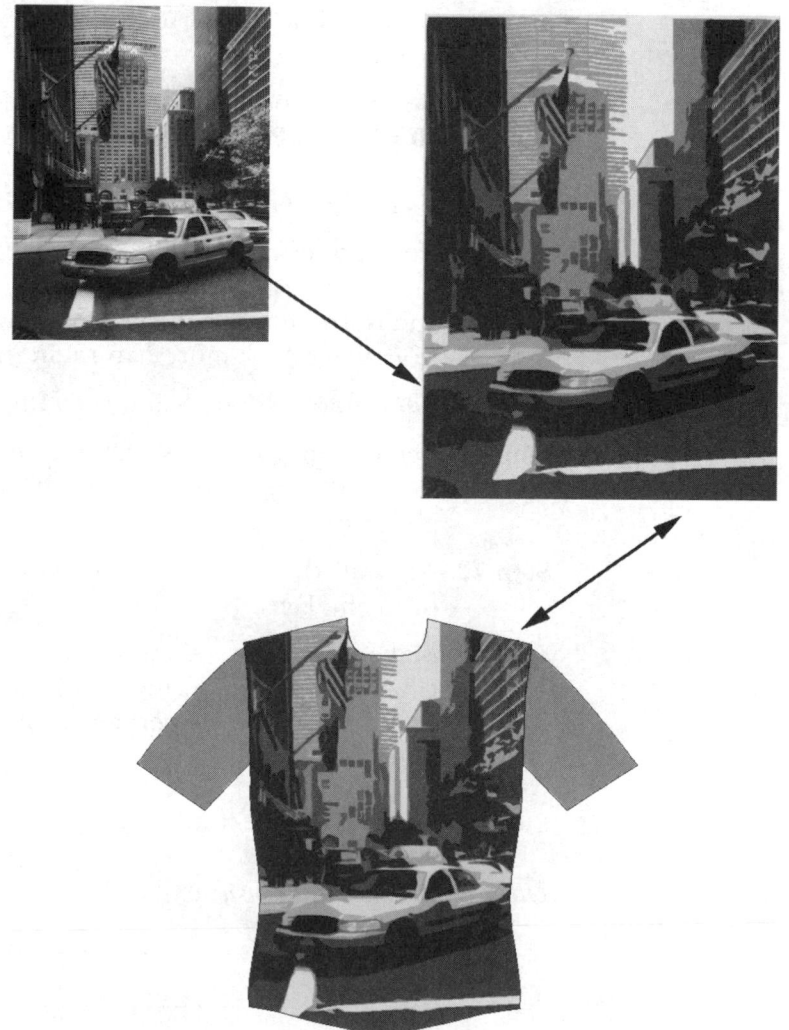

FIGURE 10–46

From a realistic to a stylized photo used for a photo-realistic pattern-filled t-shirt

Although this is an oversimplified explanation of how to adapt a photo for use in a garment for print, you will find a complete set of instructions on how to use Adobe Illustrator, Adobe Photoshop, and even proprietary pattern software to actually lay out and plot all the pattern pieces. You will then see how you can adapt and modify a photo to be "engineered" to fit into the individual pattern pieces, using Adobe Photoshop. This complete set of basic instructions will be covered in more detail in Chapter 12.

Other Applications and Insights:

_____

_____

_____

_____

How to Render a Stencil-Look Print

Step 1. Open a **New File** in Adobe Photoshop: **8 × 8 inches**, **72–150, dpi**, **RGB**, **White Background.**

Step 2. Go to the Goodies Folder and select **Sample Exercise Folder > Chapter 10 > Stencil Parts** (cherry and basket template). (See Figure 10–47.)

Step 3. Using the Magic Wand, select the cherry and go to **Edit > Copy**.

Step 4. Next, go to the New File and select **Edit > Paste.** Make several copies of the cherry. Also consider going to **Edit > Transform > Free Transform** and resize several cherries. You may also want to flip several cherries horizontally to look more natural in the bowl (See Figure 10–48.)

Step 5. Repeat Steps 2 and 3 and copy the basket to your new file.

Step 6. Begin to individually select the cherries, stems, and the basket and color to suit. We opted to make the cherries a solid color and the basket a simple gradient.

Step 7. After all the images have been colored, merge the bowl and cherries onto one layer.

Step 8. Make a new layer *below* the cherries and bowl. Using what you learned in Chapter 7 on rendering a twill weave—denim—fill the new layer to resemble a denim or perhaps a plain weave chambray fabric, similar to Figure 10–48.

Step 9. Name and save your work.

Other Applications and Insights:

_____

_____

_____

_____

FIGURE 10–47
Stencil parts

FIGURE 10–48
Add cherries

How to Render a Print for a Uniform
Focus: Culinary

We have decided to "spice" up a traditional gingham check used in most culinary uniforms with a little Tex-Mex flavor. We have given you a few ideas on ways to add interest to the everyday uniform worn by most cooks. You can follow along or even make your own version. Maybe you can do a pasta combo or perhaps even a break or treat confection! Either way, it will not be the same old uniform idea anymore!

FIGURE 10–49
Tex-mex sample

Step 1.	Open a **New File** in Adobe Photoshop: **8 × 8 inches, 72–150 dpi, RGB, White Background**.
Step 2.	Similar to the method of rendering gingham in Chapter 7, begin to render a black-and-white check gingham fabric background. We suggest that you do not make your gingham too large, but rather a smaller check similar to the popular style used for most culinary gingham trousers.
Step 3.	Go to the Goodies Folder and select **Sample Exercise > Chapter 10** and open the Tex-Mex sample files. (See Figure 10–49.)
Step 4.	Drag copies of the cactus and lizard to your new file.
Step 5.	Look at Figure 10–50 to get some inspiration about different variations you can have in your print. As you can see, the possibilities are endless!
Step 6.	As always we recommend that you annotate what you do so that you will later be able to replicate your "recipe" for success!

FIGURE 10–50
Variations of print

Other Applications and Insights:

_____

_____

_____

_____

How to Render a Print for a Uniform
Focus: Medical—Pediatrics print—Fish at Play
(fish inspired by student Judith Kreuger)
This is an example of an engineered print that can be used alone or in combination with other traditional uniform prints such as gingham.

Step 1. Open a **New File: 8.5 × 11 inches, RGB, 72–150 dpi, White Background**.

Step 2. Go to the Goodies Folder and open **Chapter Exercises > Chapter 10 > Fish at Play**.

Step 3. Following the sample in Figure10–51 begin to make several copies of the little fish in contrasting "crayon colors."

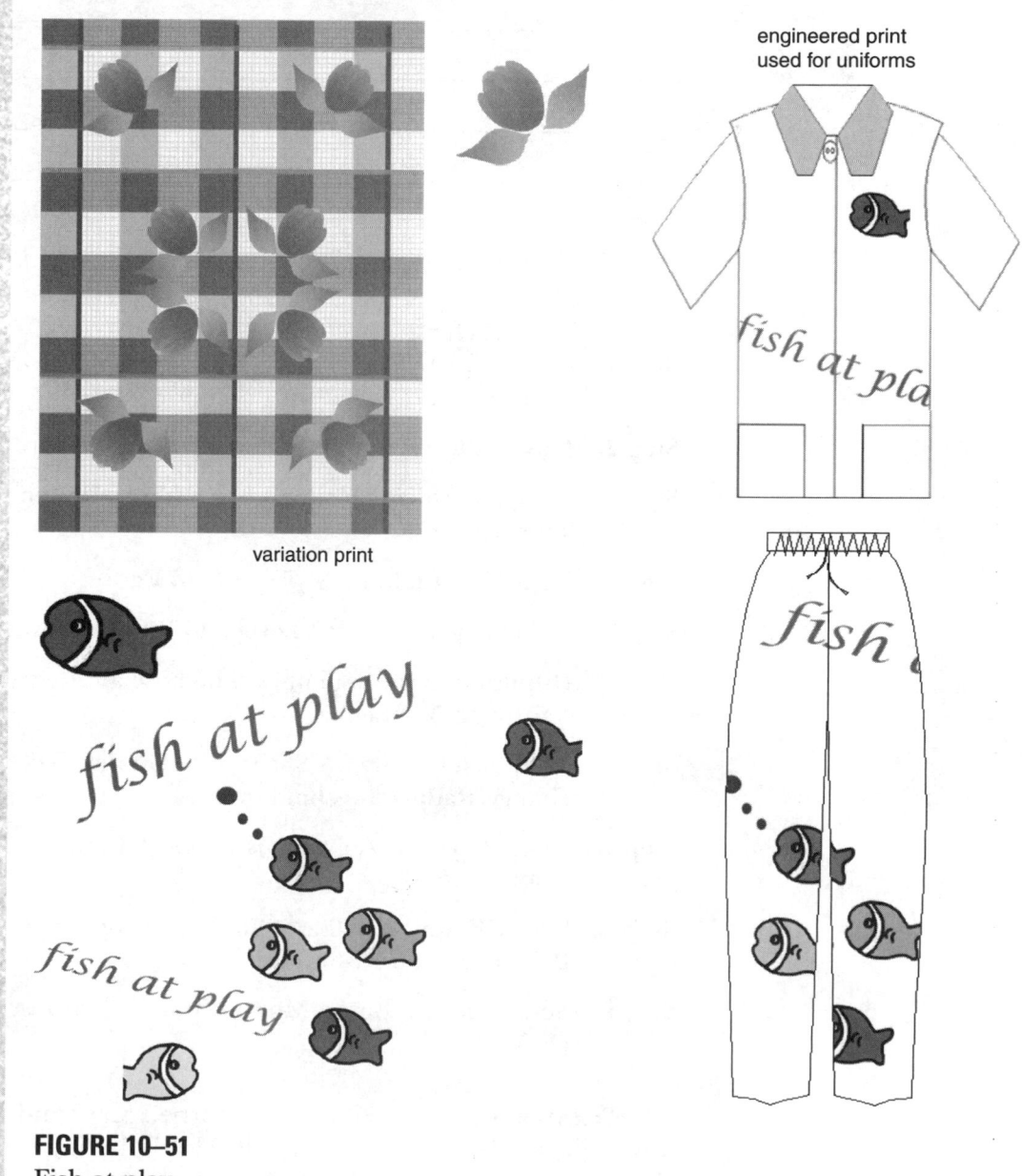

variation print

engineered print
used for uniforms

fish at play

FIGURE 10–51
Fish at play

Step 4. Flatten your work and opt to add a fabric texture, such as a plain or twill weave to enhance your image. For example, in the upper left-hand corner of Figure 10–51, we have used our gingham fabric you made earlier in Chapter 8 along with adding our tulip motif from Chapter 9 as a variation on the classic uniform design.

Step 5. Name and save your work.

Step 6. You can also opt to use traditional gingham prints with tulips or other images in place of the fish seen in Figure 10–51. The gingham plaid instructions were found in Chapter 8, while the tulip was found in Chapter 9.

Other Applications and Insights:

_____

_____

_____

_____

Rendering Leathers, Furs, and Skins

How to Render Fur (Astrakhan)

Step 1. Open a **New File: 8.5 × 11 inches**, **RGB**, **150 dpi**, **White Background.** Name the file **Astrakhan**.

Step 2. Make a New Layer and fill with White Background.

Step 3. Using the Default Colors, go to **Filter** > **Fill Render** > **Difference** > **Clouds**. Then click **OK**.

Step 4. Next, select **Filter > Stylize > Find Edges**.

Step 5. Select **Layers > Adjust Level** and hit **Auto Button** and select **OK**.

Duplicate Layer 2. (This will include all the steps completed from Steps 3 through 5.) (See Figure 10–52.)

Step 6. Then select **Filter > Sharpen > UnSharpen Mask**. Choose **200%** and change **Radius threshold to 0.**

Step 7. Go to **Layers > Adjust > Hue** and **Saturation** and experiment with the color to suit.

Step 8. Select **Filter > Stylize > Find Glowing Edges** and choose **2-Width, 2-Brightness,** and **7-Smooth.**

Step 9. Select Filter > Blur > Motion Blur and choose **5-Angle, Distance-4,** and click **OK**.

HINT: Experiment with Filter > UnSharpen Mask and gradient. Experiment with adjusting Hue and Saturation BEFORE finding the Glowing Edges—it changes the color of the glowing edges.

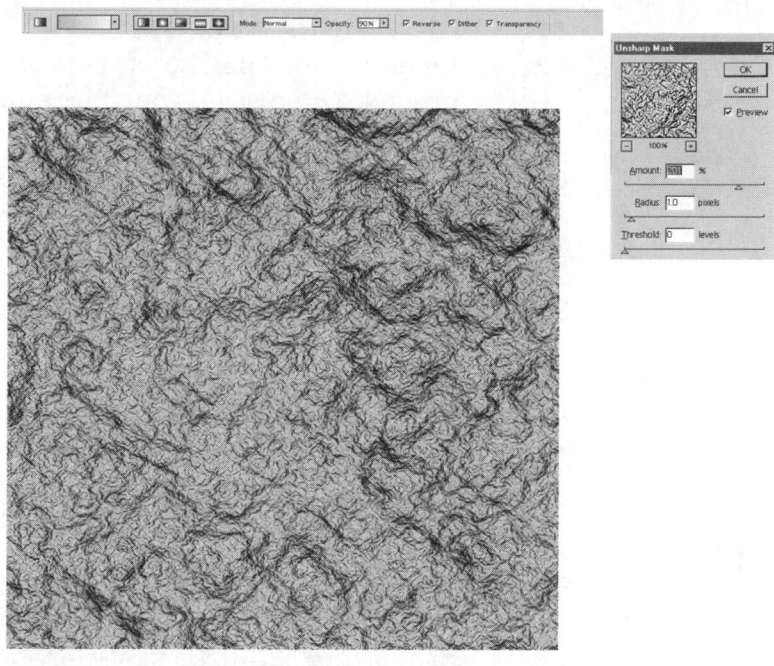

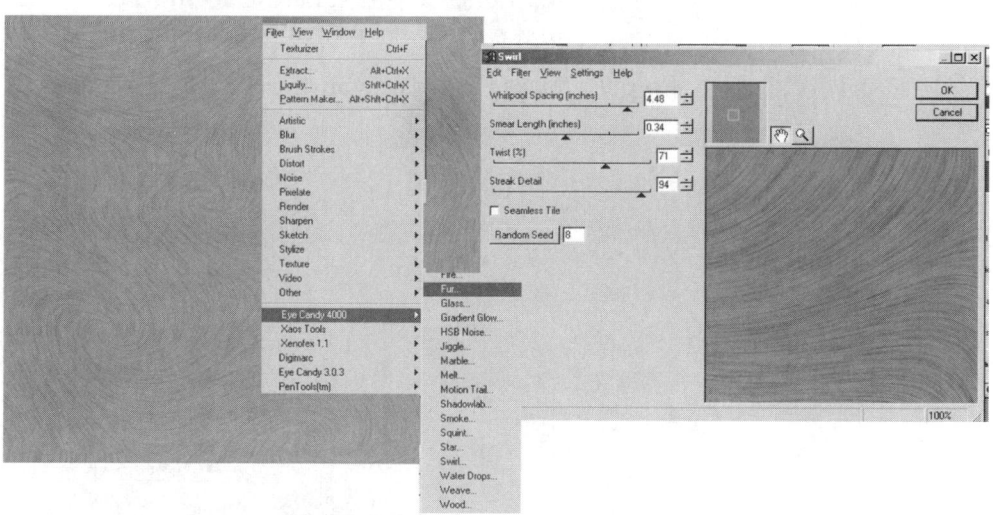

FIGURE 10–52
Adjusting levels and filters to render Astrakhan fur

Other Applications and Insights:

_____

_____

_____

_____

How to Render Feathers

Step 1. Open a **New File: 8.5 × 11 inches**, **RGB**, **72–150 dpi**, **White Background**. *Or* open up your file, entitled **Glen Plaid**, that you made in Chapter 7.

Step 2. If you notice on the Toolbox Brushes menu, there is a sample of several small feather-like brushes available. We have also included a feather template for you in the Goodies Folder of your CD.

Step 3. Go to the Goodies Folder and select **Chapter Exercises > Chapter 10 > Feathers**.

Step 4. Place a Square Marquee around the "feather" and go to **Edit > Define Brush** and name the brush **Feather 2**.

Step 5. Using the Eyedropper, select a lighter shade of the burgundy stripe of your Glen Plaid and begin to add feathers to your image.

Step 6. In Figure 10–53, one of Kathleen's students (Natalie Dubernet) opted to place her Glen Plaid into a handbag that was embellished with pink feathers. Very urban chic! You can opt to enhance anything with the feathers, or you can rescale the Feather 2 brush to a larger scale and make a feather repeat pattern fabric print.

Step 7. Name and save your work.

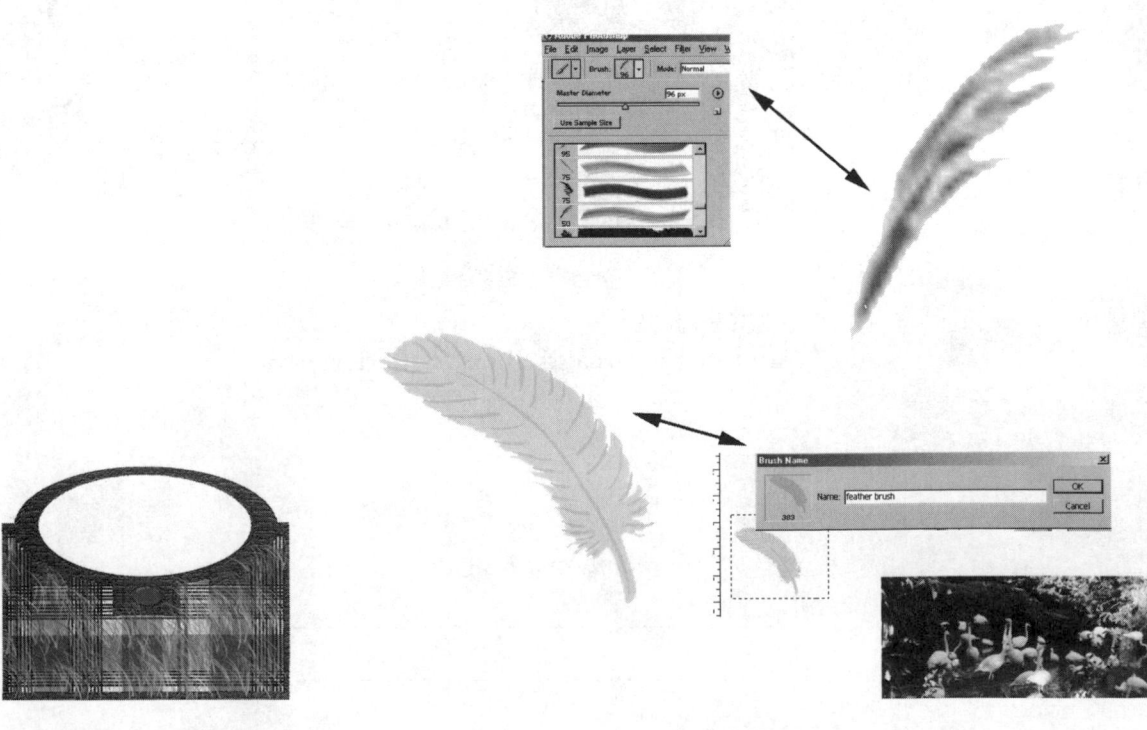

FIGURE 10–53
Glen plaid with feathers

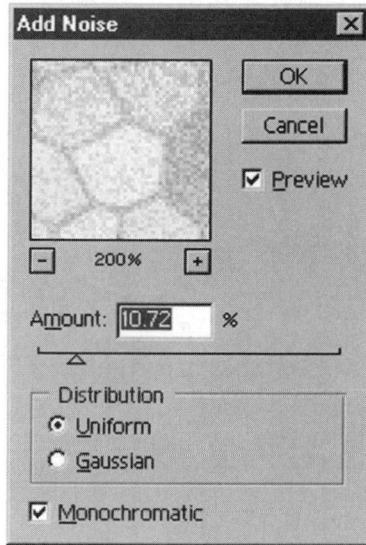

FIGURE 10–54
Drag copy of layer #1

Other Applications and Insights:

_____

_____

_____

_____

How to Render Snakeskin

Step 1. Open a **New File: 8.5 × 11 inches**, **RGB**, **72–150 dpi**, **White Background**.

Step 2. Then open the file entitled **Batiste**.

Step 3. From this file, drag a copy of Layer # 1 onto your New File. (See Figure 10–54.)

Step 4. Go to **Filter > Texture > Texturizer** and select **Canvas**. Then select **Scaling 100%, Relief-4** and **Direction from Top**. Choose **OK.**

Step 5. Go to **Filter > Texture > Texturizer** and choose **Stain Glass**. Select **Cell Size 10 > Border-3 > Light-3** and click **OK.**

Step 6. Select **Filter > Noise** and choose **Amount 10.75 > Uniform > Monochromatic**, and click **OK.**

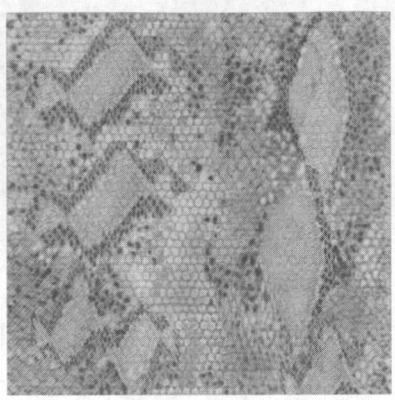

FIGURE 10–55
Snakeskin

Figure 10–55 is a much more complex version of snakeskin, using several techniques, including brush strokes and filter combinations.

Other Applications and Insights:

_____

_____

_____

_____

How to Render a Mock Crock

Step 1. Open a **New File: 8.5 × 11 inches**, **RGB**, **72–150 dpi**, **White Background**.

Step 2. We began by rendering a solid-colored background and then applied small amounts of **Filter > Noise > Add Noise > Gaussian > Monochromatic**. Click **OK**.

Step 3. Using a fine-tip brush and a Wacom tablet, free-hand draw several odd-shaped ovals and select **Define a Pattern** with our new shape. However, you can continue to free-hand draw the shapes to fill the page as well. When finished, your work will look something like Figure 10–56.

Step 4. Finally, you can experiment with the **Layer Style** menu and the **Bevel and Emboss** option if you want to further enhance the character of your mock crock.

Step 5. Name and save your work.

Other Applications and Insights:

_____

_____

_____

_____

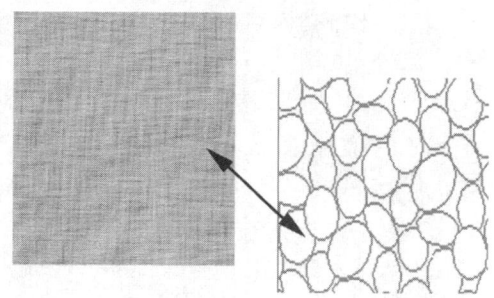

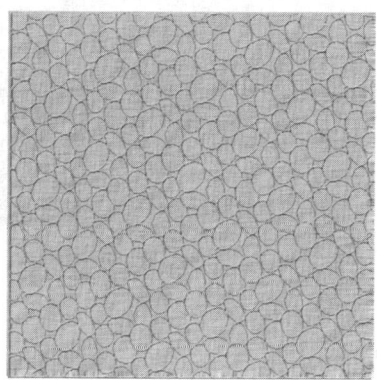

FIGURE 10–56
Mock crock

Leather

How to Render Leather
Version #1 (for handbags or shoes)

Step 1. Open a **New File: 8.5 × 11 inches, RGB, 72–150 dpi, White Background**.

Step 2. Make a New Layer and fill with solid light to medium blue color.

Step 3. Copy Layer #2 and select **Filter > Noise > Grain 5.46 Sprinkle**.

Step 4. Select **Filter > Texture > Sandstone 4** from top.

Step 5. You may want to experiment with **Filter > Blur > Motion Blur** and use a small percentage to enhance the texture. (See Figure 10–57.)

Step 6. Then go to **Filter > Add Noise > Noise > Uniform > 11% > Monochromatic**. Select **Texturizer > 100%** and **Sandstone > Relief Amount 4 thru 12 > Direction** from top.

Step 7. Name and save your work.

Other Applications and Insights:

_____

_____

_____

_____

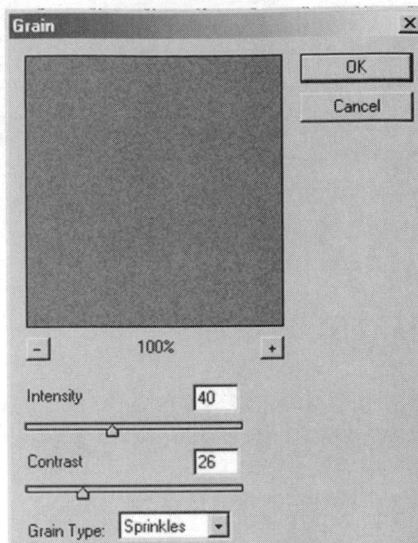
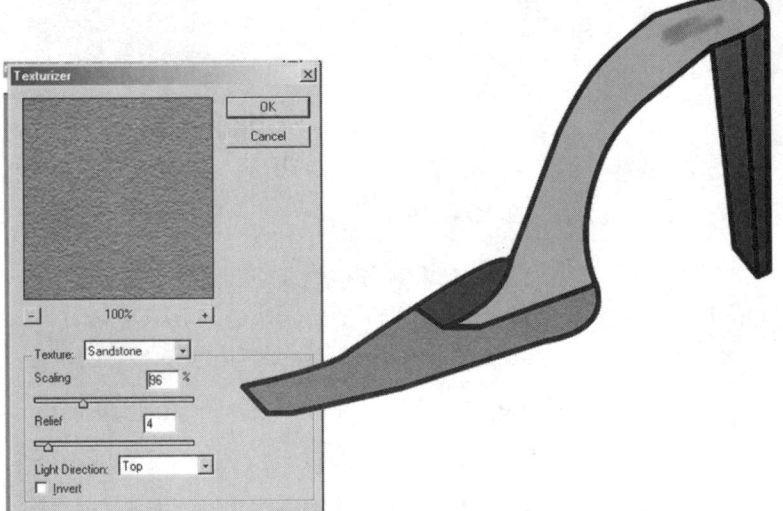

FIGURE 10–57
Render leather

How to Render Leather (Traditional Brown)
Version #2 (also used for Naugahyde and Vinyl)

Step 1. Open a **New File: 8.5 ×11 inches**, **RGB**, **72–150 dpi**, **White Background** and name the file **Leather**.

Step 2. Make a New Layer and fill with white.

Step 3. Using the Default Colors, go to **Filter > Fill Render > Difference Clouds**.

Step 4. Select **Filter > Stylize > Find Edges**.

Step 5. Select **Layers > Adjust Level** and hit **Auto Button**. Click **OK**.

Step 6. Duplicate Layer 2.

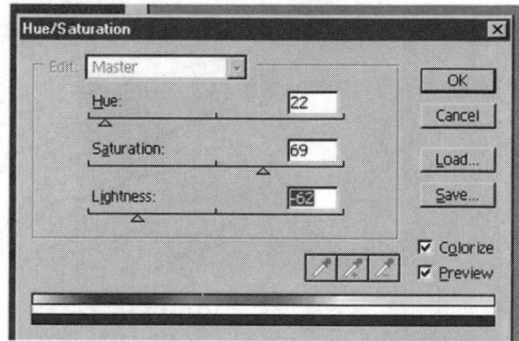

FIGURE 10-58

Render leather (traditional brown)

Step 7. Then go to **Filter > Noise > Gaussian > Monochromatic > 105%** and click **OK**.

Step 8. Select **Image > Adjust > Hue/Saturation** and check **Colorize** and select **22, 69,** and **−62**. Click **OK**. (See Figure 10–58.)

Step 9. Name and save your work.

Other Applications and Insights:

_____

_____

_____

_____

Animal Prints

These prints are all variations on a theme in nature and in how the prints are constructed. So begin with the cat print and then move on to one of the other prints.

How to Render Leopard (Cat-Animal Print)

Step 1. Open a **New File: 8 × 8 inches**, **RGB**, **72–150 dpi**, **White Background**.

Step 2. Go to the Goodies Folder and select **Chapter Exercises > Chapter 10 > Cat Outlines**. (See Figure 10–59.)

Step 3. Drag a copy of this file onto your New File.

Step 4. Using the Magic Wand, begin to isolate sections of the image and fill with color. (See Figure 10–60.) We used a combination of solid colors and gradients to simulate the naturally occurring color variations.

Step 5. When you are finished coloring in your image, merge all the layers to Layer #2. Make a duplicate copy of your merged cat print. Turn this layer off and save it to compare with later.

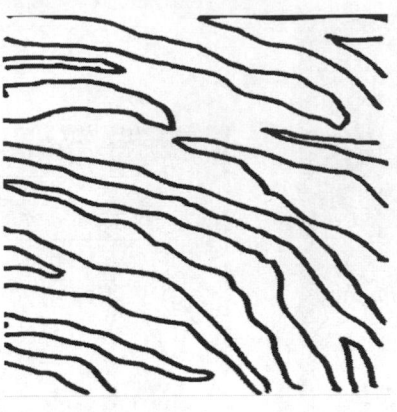

FIGURE 10–59
Cat outlines

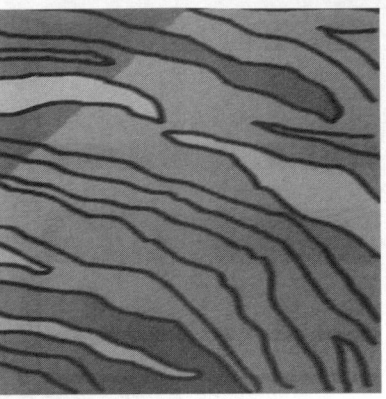

FIGURE 10–60
Isolate sections

FIGURE 10–61
Leopard print

Step 6. Going now to the Filter menu, begin to add **Noise > Gaussian > Monochromatic** in small amounts.

Step 7. Next go to **Filter > Blur > Motion Blur** to simulate the look of fur. Now, compare this to the original without filters. If you want you can continue to use the image without filters and experiment with other types of textures. When you are satisfied with your results, be sure to annotate your choices.

Step 8. Name and save your work. (See Figure 10–61.)

Step 9. Notice other examples of cat variations in Figure 10–62.

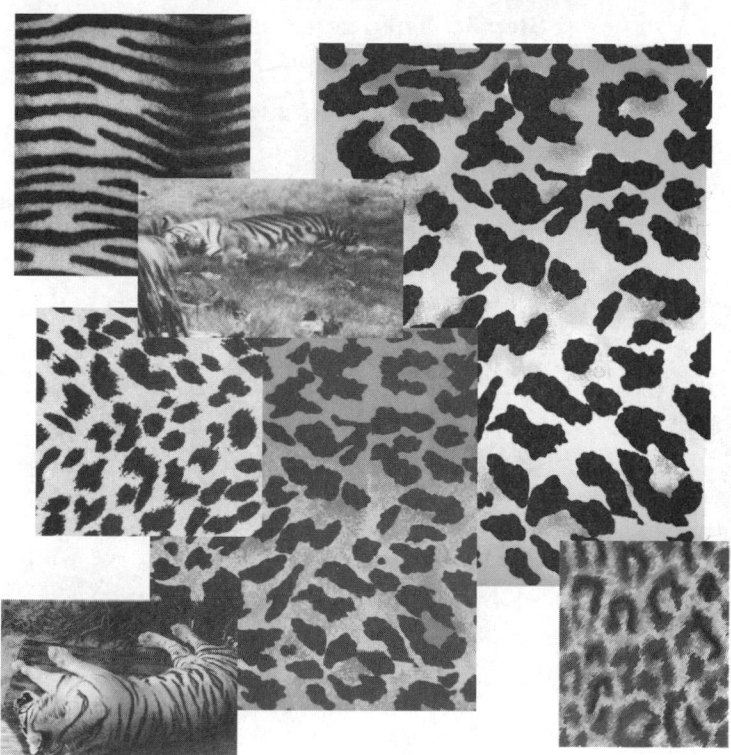

FIGURE 10–62
Cat variations

Other Applications and Insights:

_____

_____

_____

_____

How to Render a Pony Print

Step 1. Open a **New File: 8 x 8 inches**, **RGB**, **72–150 dpi**, **White Background**.

Step 2. Using the Lasso tool, begin to make irregular shapes similar to those "spots" found on horses.

Step 3. Fill the shapes with desired color. We filled our shapes in a chocolate brown.

Step 4. Then go to **Edit > Stroke** and outline in a deeper brown color, approximately 3 pixels.

Step 5. Next, when all the shapes are complete, merge all the shapes onto one layer.

Step 6. Add a slightly lighter shade of tan to the base or background color.

Step 7. Merge the "spots" onto the solid background.

Step 8. Go to the Filter menu and add **Noise > Gaussian > Monochromatic** in small quantities.

Step 9. Then go to the Filter menu and select **Blur > Motion Blur > 10 degree** about 18 pixels or less.

Step 10. Name and save your work.

Step 11. Your work should look something like Figure 10–63. When the color is adjusted, these instructions can also work for rendering a cow print or even a Dalmatian print.

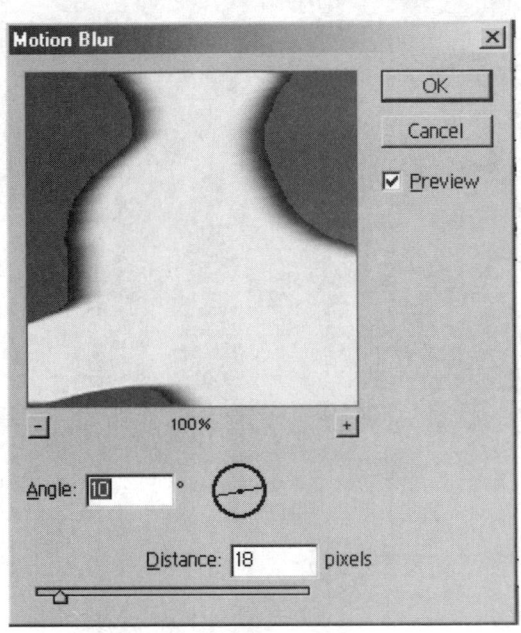

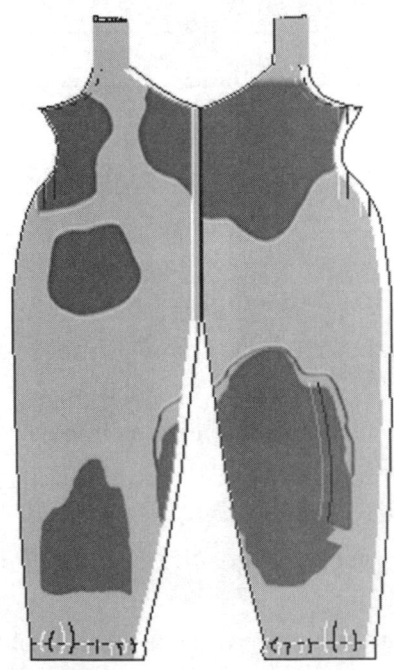

FIGURE 10–63
Pony print

Other Applications and Insights:

_____

_____

_____

_____

How to Render a Giraffe

Step 1. Open a **New File: 8 × 8 inches**, **RGB**, **72–150 dpi**, **White Background**.

Step 2. Fill the background with a slight hint of beige.

Step 3. Make a New Layer. Using the Lasso tool, similar to how you rendered your pony print, begin to make several irregular rectangle shapes and fill each with a solid color.

Step 4. Make a duplicate layer of the irregular rectangle shapes. Using the Magic Wand, select the shapes and begin to fill with a deeper gradient set of colors from those used in the solid fill.

Step 5. Experiment with the Opacity slider bar on the Layers palette.

Step 6. Once you have the shapes and colors you are satisfied with, you can flatten the file and begin to add **Filters > Noise > Motion Blur** similar to the steps used in the pony print. (See Figure 10–64.)

Other Applications and Insights:

_____

_____

_____

_____

How to Render a Zebra Print

Step 1. Open a **New File: 8 × 8 inches, RGB, 72–150 dpi, White Background.**

Step 2. Go to the Toolbox Brush menu and select the long thin brush similar to the one seen in Figure 10–65.

Step 3. Using the color black, begin to make several long close strokes to simulate the look of a zebra pattern.

Step 4. Continue to render the print on one layer to match Figure 10–65.

Step 5. Then go to the Filter menu and add small amounts of **Noise** and **Motion Blur** as you did in your pony print and giraffe print.

Step 6. Name and save your work.

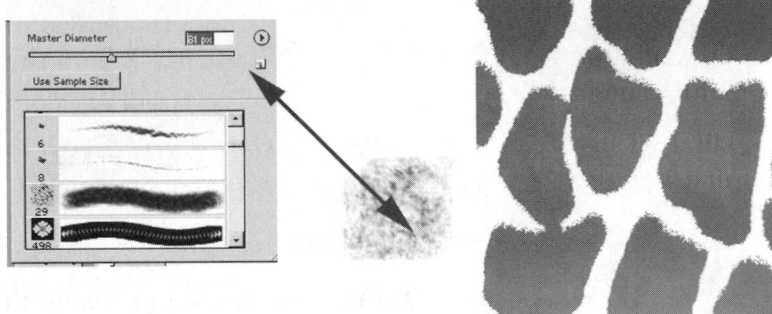

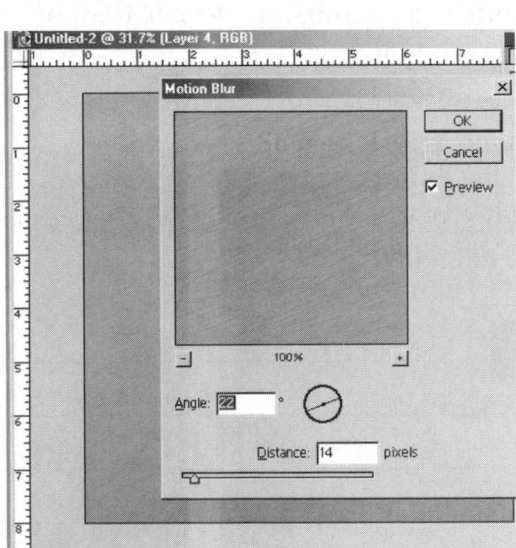

FIGURE 10–64
Giraffe print

Other Applications and Insights:

_____

_____

_____

_____

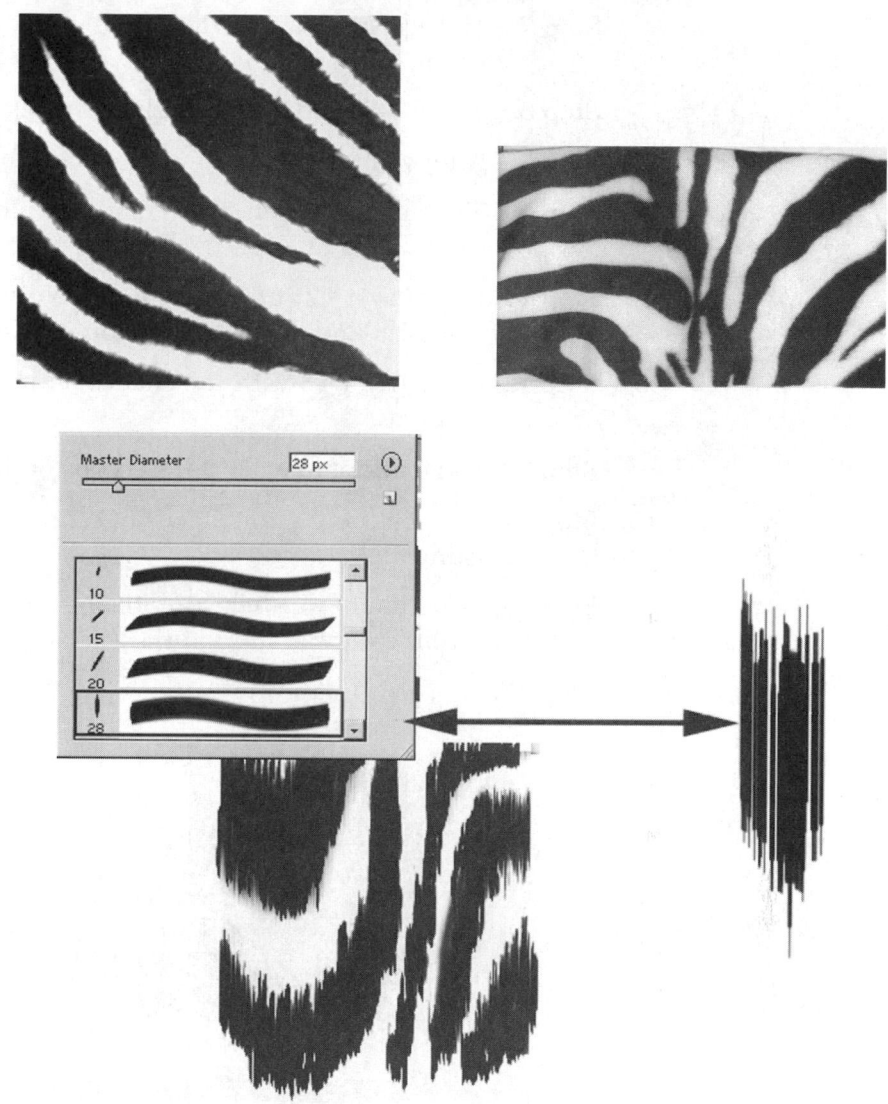

FIGURE 10–65
Zebra print

How to Render Camouflage

Step 1. Open a **New File: 8.5 × 11 inches, RGB, 72–150 dpi, White Background**.

Step 2. Make a New layer and fill with khaki color.

Step 3. Make a New Layer and name the layer **Large Shapes**.

Step 4. Using the same technique as for the previous leopard exercise, begin to make large shapes with the Poly Lasso tool and fill with colors.

Step 5. Make a New Layer and name the layer **Medium size**. Begin to make medium size shapes.

Step 6. Repeat Step 4 and fill with other color variations.

Step 7. Make a New Layer and, using the Poly Lasso tool, begin to make smaller irregular shapes.

Step 8. Select **Edit** and fill with lighter shades to match Figure 10–66.

Step 9. After you have made all the needed shapes, select **Layer**.

Step 10. Then merge Layers #3, #4, and #5 onto one layer. Be sure not to include the solid color Layer #2.

Step 11. Copy Layer #2 and select **Filter > Noise > Add Noise > Monochromatic > Gaussian** and select small amounts of each to suit.

Step 12. Copy Layer #3 with the shapes and select **Blur > Motion Blur** in small amounts.

Step 13. You may opt to make a JPEG copy of the file. Name the file **Camouflage**.

Step 14. Reopen the Camouflage JPEG copy and drag a copy to the original existing file.

Step 15. Experiment with selecting **Image > Adjust > Hue** and **Saturation** for different colorway alternatives. (See Figure 10–66.)

Step 16. Name and save your work.

FIGURE 10–66
Camouflage print

FIGURE 10–67
Actual lace fabric

Other Applications and Insights:

_____

_____

_____

_____

How to Render Lace or Tulle Netting

In our last exercise we will walk you through simulating the appearance of lace, tulle, or nylon netting. (See Figure 10–67 for an example of actual lace fabric.)

How to Render Tulle (Lace)

Step 1.   Open a **New File: 8.5 × 11 inches**, **RGB**, **72–150 dpi**, **White Background**.

Step 2.   On New Layer #2, fill with desired color and make a New Layer.

Step 3.   On New Layer #3, fill the ground with a right-handed twill weave.

Step 4.   Duplicate Layer #3. Go to **Edit >Transform > Flip Horizontal**.

Step 5.   Make a New Layer. Using a mouse or Wacom pen, go to **Toolbox > Pen**. Select a fine-point brush and using the Zoom tool, zoom in and draw a simple hexagon shape.

Step 6.   Place a Rectangle Marquee close to the shape and go to **Edit > Define Pattern** and name the new pattern **Tulle**. (See Figure 10–67.)

Step 7.   Make a New Layer and go to **Edit > Fill > Tulle Pattern**.

Step 8.   Make a New Layer.

Step 9.   Using a Mouse or Wacom pen, begin to free-hand draw a floral similar to the one in Figure 10–68. Continue rendering additional sections of the flower and leaves.

Step 10.   When you are satisfied, name and save your work.

FIGURE 10–68
Draw floral to simulate digitally rendered lace

Other Applications and Insights:

_____

_____

_____

_____

Fantastic job! You are really beginning to master the secrets of using Adobe Photoshop for rendering fashion, fabrics, and prints. In our last two chapters we will continue to share the industry insider secrets you will need to get your prints from computer to consumer.

11

Presentation Boards: Raster or Vector

Terms to look for:

Adobe Illustrator	Flats	Raster
Adobe Photoshop	Flatten	Sourcing
Adobe Streamline	Layers	Style Sheet
Color Stories	Object based	Template
Compound Path	Paste into	Texture Mapping
Croquis	Pitching Color	"Think in the right direction"
Drawing Tablet	Pixels	Trend Board
Engineered	Planagrams	Vector
Fabric Board	Presentation Boards	

Presentation Boards and More

Designers can be called upon to render everything from technical flats to full-blown marketing literature such as hangtags, logos, and catalogs. When it comes to making presentations, there is no better tool for the designer than Adobe Photoshop! Now that you have mastered the tools and techniques in Adobe Photoshop to render fabrics, we are ready to complete your repertoire of digital designing in Adobe Photoshop with how to create presentation boards.

So What Are Presentation Boards, Anyway?

In the world of graphic-speak, there are a variety of names used for all of the design and support material you will be creating in Adobe Photoshop. (See Figure 11–1.) The term *presentation board* is a fairly broad term that includes a wide range of elements:

- Mood Boards
- Story Boards
- Trend Boards
- Merchandise Boards
- Style Sheets
- Planagrams
- Color and Fabric Cards
- Swatches and Colorways

- Swipes
- Details, Embellishments, and Trims
- Technical Sketches or Flats
- Silhouettes
- Croquis or Minibodies
- Photos
- Hangtags, Logos, etc.
- Text

FIGURE 11–1
Presentation boards

Concept to Consumer—Understanding What the Presentation Boards Represent

Each of the design elements listed on page 447 is done at different intervals within the design process from concept to consumer. By the time all the presentation boards are complete, most of the design decisions including edits have been finalized. All that awaits is to present the end version of all your work for the buyer's approval, which hopefully will result in sales.

These boards need to instantly communicate to the buyers with visual images of the collection. Buyers need to be able to quickly understand the fabric and color choices of each style presented.

Presentation boards need to show the product, as it will be sold. They need to show colorways and text describing seasons and styles as well as any other important information. Some boards may contain texture-mapped photos of the garments and fabric and real-size printouts of the design being shown.

Therefore, we will spend a few moments reacquainting you with some of the most popular presentation materials you will probably be required to make. Let's begin a quick overview of the language used within the fashion industry, as well as the terms assigned to the graphical representation of the most widely used design support materials.

Fashion-Speak

Presentation boards are the final step in showing the line of designs to a buyer. Every presentation board will have its own version of fashion-speak. *Fashion-speak* is a collection of specific fashion-related terms used within the industry.

We have included in this next section a listing and brief explanation of many terms and phrases you are sure to encounter. Understanding and properly applying these terms will be useful as you begin to graphically render each of these items or elements in a later section of this chapter.

Collection or Line?

In today's American fashion scene, the term *line* is considered a collection of styles (garments, accessories, or shoes) by trims or detail. Some American designers will refer to their line as a collection; however, generally the term *collection* is associated with high-end European fashion.

In most cases the term *line* is widely accepted as a seasonal representation of garment groupings (*also known as styles*) presented by a designer or manufacturer. Hot-selling items that are updated each season are known as *key items*.

Another term used to describe a line that specializes in one or more specific items is referred to as an *item line*, whereas a line grouped around fabric, styles, or silhouettes is known as a "group line."

When a line is divided by six to eight garment groupings, each group is referred to as a *division*. In the U.S. design market, most companies or designers will produce up to four or five lines per year. The name of the line will often coincide with the *season* in which it is sold—for example, Spring, Summer, Transitional, Fall, Winter, Holiday, and Resort.

Lines are frequently subcategorized by classification. A *classification* is a grouping of items that are similar in nature or in use—for example, sweaters, pants, and coats each represent a classification. Within the retail world these items can also be called an *assortment* or *category* of items. These classifications are broken down further to include variations of the design or styles within the category. An example of the classification, pants, might include such styles as capri, bell-bottoms, cuffed, and so on.

Style—Style—Style

Hopefully, many of these terms are becoming more familiar to you. Depending on who you talk to or the context of the topic, the term *style* has the widest range of meanings and uses.

- Referring to a specific historic period of time

- Distinguishing features of a design or presentation

- Suggesting a category or mode of clothing, such as:
  - Classic
  - Sporty
  - Retro
  - Ethnic
  - Career
  - Bridal
  - Activewear
  - After-Five—Formal
  - Club wear
  - Couture
  - Contemporary
  - Trendy

By now you should be beginning to connect the dots between the type of merchandise that is created and the way the line will be depicted on presentation boards. This will have everything to do with the company's design philosophy and their ultimate target customer.

Your presentation boards will have to reflect the consumer's taste level. The consumer's taste level will reflect the consumer's preferences on how they choose to be perceived by others because they have chosen to purchase a given product. The image they may want to convey can be:

- Conservative and classic

- Updated and current

- Fashion forward—cutting edge and ahead of the crowd in recognizing the next fashion wave

The style in which you create your presentation boards should also denote the style of the company's signature look and the customer they cater to:

- High-end or designer

- Better or bridge

- A specific adaptation such as Missy or Petite

- Contemporary

- Junior trendy chic

Naturally, each of these considerations will be a sign of the type of store in which the design will be carried and the price point at which it will be sold. (See Figures 11–2 and 11–3.)

One of the greatest challenges a designer will have is to reflect and translate into the design the times and seasons in which they live. This naturally includes interpreting and reflecting effectively the image of the company for which they are designing. The ability to step outside of your own personal notions of style and understanding the needs and tastes of others can be a challenge.

Traditional Department Store
Specialty Department Store
Boutique
Specialty Stores
Off-Price
Outlet
Direct Mail/Catalog
On-line

FIGURE 11–2
Retail sources

Popular $
Moderate $$
Better $$$
Designer $$$$
Couture $$$$$+

FIGURE 11–3
Price point

This is especially true when you are 25-year-old contemporary who is attempting to design for a 40-something missy. The designer who masters this will always have an easier go of things, than the designer who confuses their opinions and taste with that of the company and misses the mark.

Your presentation boards will need to incorporate more than factual and creative information and designs. The elements on your boards will be a reflection of the tone and mood for your company and your client.

Elements of Presentation Boards

Assimilating all the information that we just covered and transmuting it into presentation boards that accurately reflect their company and client is the goal. Can you imagine trying to sell a series of visually stimulating high-tech and trendy presentation boards to a traditionally staunch conservative menswear company? Probably not!

As we begin to examine the elements you will be generating for your presentation boards, you will need to analyze how each element will clearly represent the company it will be symbolizing.

Key Elements of Presentation Boards

Presentation boards is an inclusive term for boards that convey everything from the mood or theme or the line to the specifics of colors and fabrics. Consisting mostly of flats, silhouettes, croquis, or minibodies (Figure 11–4), these boards are true representations of the seasonal lines being produced. Another name for flats is technical drawings. The term *croquis* can also be considered a flat; however, it can also refer to a rendering of a male or female form. (See Figure 11–5.)

Just as clothing is divided into market segmentation in order to better represent the market's taste level and lifestyle needs, it should be noted that one of the most

FIGURE 11–4
Jacket flat

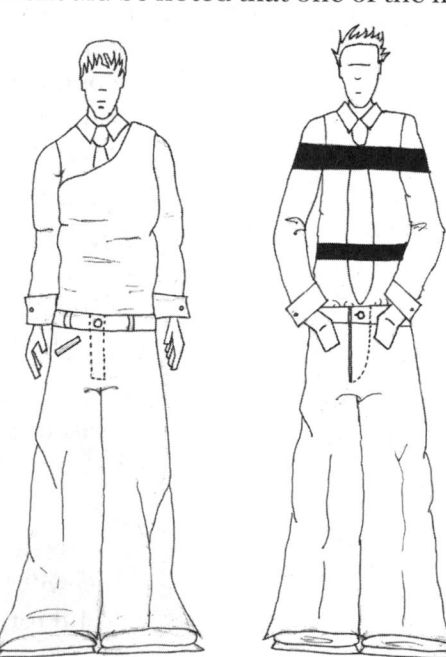

FIGURE 11–5
Rendering of male croquis

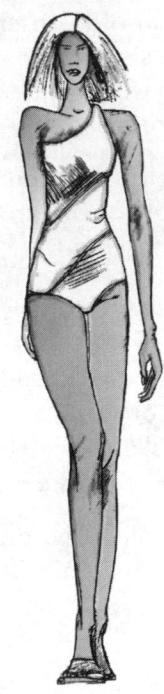

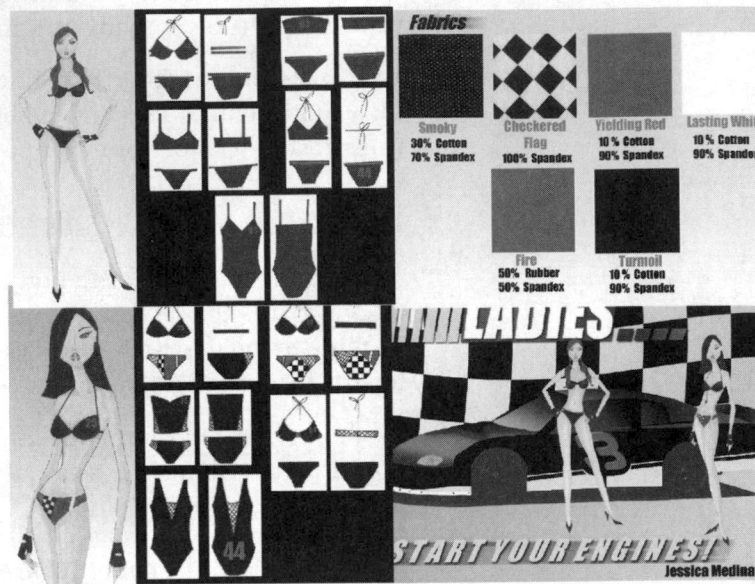

FIGURE 11–6

An example of a female croquis

FIGURE 11–7

Other examples of a female croquis used in presentation boards

unusual trends in illustration today is also beginning to reflect the market segmentations. In our classroom and training sessions, styles of rendering also reflect geographical and regional preferences. The style of rendering croquis has become indigenous to cities, age groups, and countries as evidenced in our collection of croquis created by students who were trained or reared in diverse geographical locations. We have captured the essence of this in an illustration done by a student as seen in Figure 11–6. Several other examples are included in the Goodies Folder on the CD in the file **Croquis Student samples.**

Just as there is a difference in illustration or rendering styles, there is also some difference in the terms associated with the renderings. Therefore, you may want to be sure you are using the agreed-upon term when discussing these items with other individuals in the design process to avoid any possible confusion. For our purposes, we will refer to the hand-drawn or computer-generated sketches of the garments as *flats*.

Once these images have been rendered, buyers will take these images and use them to sell product. Colors must be correct as well as assortments presented. Flats may be stylized to show them off.

Logos and graphics are also placed on the flats in appropriate positions and colors. Coordinates and groups are shown working together to show the buyer how they will look in the stores. Figure 11–7 shows several variations of logo layouts useful for hangtags.

The sequence of when these boards are done will be determined by your company and by you, the designer. The first place most designers begin is with inspiration for the new season.

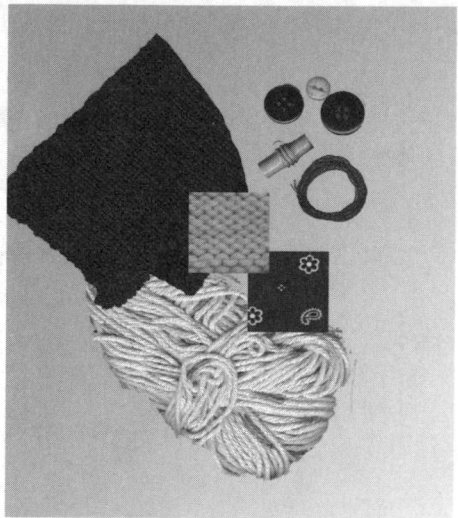

FIGURE 11–8
Swipes

FIGURE 11–9
Mood board
(Courtesy of Stoll Knitting Machines)

If you are like most designers, you are constantly accumulating objects and images for inspiration to be included on your presentation boards. *Swipes* refer collectively to items or objects that have been "swiped" for inspiration, evaluation, and observation. Swipes can be buttons, or other notions, yarn or fabric swatches, magazine images, photographs, and other found three-dimensional objects. (See Figure 11–8.)

Each of these items may find its way onto any combination of presentation boards that are usually titled according to their purpose. For example, a *mood board* often is an in-house board that conveys the general "overall" mood or theme for the upcoming collection. (See Figure 11–9.) *Theme boards* or mood boards reflect the tone of the collection conveyed with images and text.

FIGURE 11–10
Theme board

Next stop is the *trend board* that shows the newly developed styles and colors that are being predicted as the next best-sellers. Images and color discovered in the sourcing process, as well as any ideas from forecasting services are shown. Trend boards include a variety of images, including fabrics to be used directly in the design to be manufactured or simply for use as textural reference or inspiration. (See Figure 11–10.)

Sourcing is the term used when looking for the next season's colors or trends. Colors which will be later matched digitally are initially selected from artwork, paint chips, yarns, or nature, such as leaves, in fact from almost any source of inspiration. (See Figure 11–11.)

Throughout the design process, there are many steps that are taken to fine-tune the line and prepare it for production and for marketing. Boards of all types are produced. *Color stories* are first created from resources that the designers use to pitch colors. *Pitching colors* relates to the developing of color palettes for a line being designed. From apparel to home furnishings, deciding what colors to use is the first decision to be made.

The end result will be a series of *color cards* and *fabric cards* that can also be included on the presentation boards or as stand-alone storyboards, depending on the company. Some companies prefer to make their own boards or charts to convey this information, which will be shared later with buyers. (See Figures 11–12 and 11–13.) Fabric cards will often be a combination of digitally rendered prints and patterns in various colorways. Many times a designer will include the actual fabric swatches mounted directly on the board to add the tactile experience associated with fabric.

In later chapter exercises you will also be digitally rendering prints and patterns that can be printed directly onto the fabric! The use of computers to digitally render fabric prints and patterns has resulted in the flourishing mass-customization market.

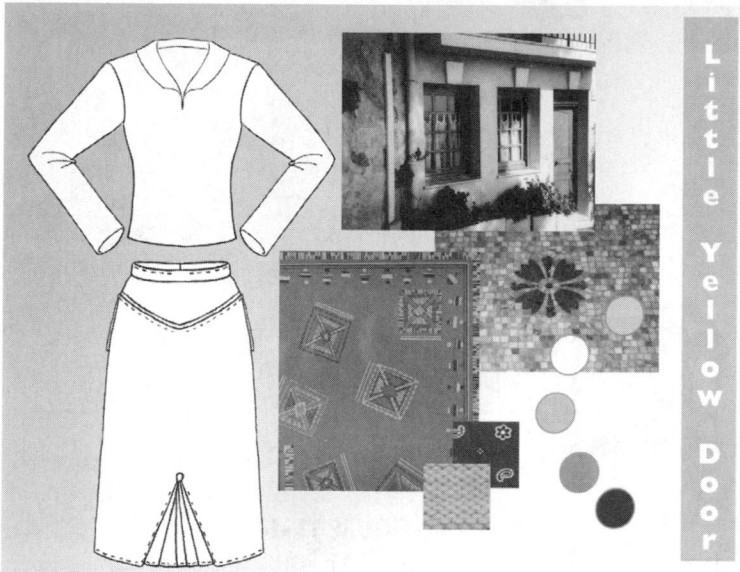

FIGURE 11–11
Sourcing

FIGURE 11–12
Fabric card

FIGURE 11–13
Fabric colorways

Style Sheets

Flat sketches of every garment are drawn by hand and then scanned into the software or digitally rendered so that the designers and buyers can easily build and view the style sheet. A style sheet is a black-and-white sketch of every style that is being approved for development of the line. It shows all the garments in a particular line being developed, including choices on fabric, color, and coordinating items. Style numbers, delivery dates, and other details are included.

Style sheets could include a list of details for each garment sketch and some include a simple rendition of the appropriate prints and embroideries, as well as mentioning the colorways of each item. Using this, the buyers, merchandisers, and designers can look at the line together and make changes and recommendations as well as decide on assortments and purchases.

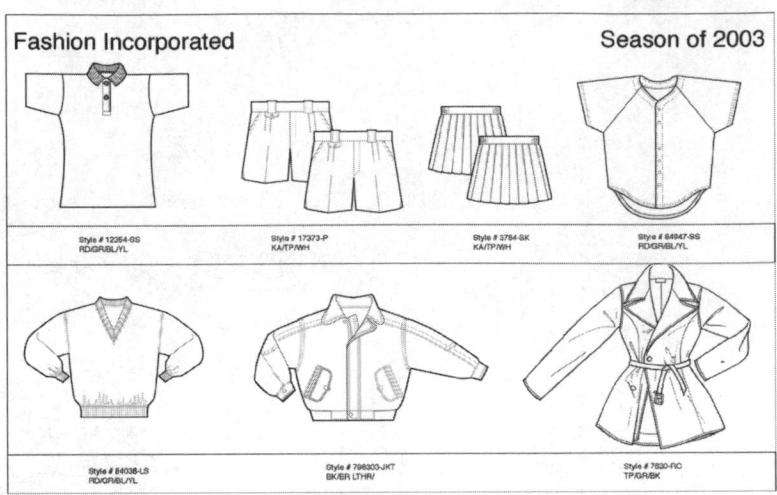

FIGURE 11–14
Style sheet

FIGURE 11–15
Merchandising boards

All other information is integrated at this point to give all involved a clear understanding of the direction of the line. (See Figure 11–14.) It is not uncommon for style sheets to be created in black and white; the reason is so that any new specific change in detail or silhouette will be easily discernable by the buyer. Colored style sheets can often mask the changes, drawing the eye to the color instead of the silhouette. Style sheets that do include color are primarily done by companies that are color-driven and they want to showcase the color variety within the line.

Another important series of boards are the *merchandising boards,* which depict a "final" combination of all of the above. Again, depending on the design firm these boards may also be referred to as storyboards. (See Figure 11–15.) These boards give the complete story or direction for chosen colors, styles, and fabrics that are going to be used in the line. These boards give the designer direction as well as give the buyer a real understanding of what they will be selling.

Planagrams

Taking the presentation idea a step further, designers can use these images for store planning or layout. (See Figure 11–16.)

Planagrams show preplanning of assortments or groups prepared to show recommendations for display of groups and assortments. Differences in the boards can show how a group will hang together or even how coordinates will look dressed together.

Sometimes color tells the story, and it is easy for the designers to direct how the assortments may need to be displayed. Planagrams are also helpful for store managers to get instant ideas on how to merchandise their deliveries and increase sales.

Texture Mapping

Our final trend in presentation boards is the use of texture mapping. *Texture mapping* is a fairly new digital technique of "draping" real or digitally rendered fabric onto a flat or photo. It is the latest and most cost-effective way of presenting. Texture mapping can be easily simulated in Adobe Photoshop or it can be accomplished with additional software—either plug-in or proprietary. The

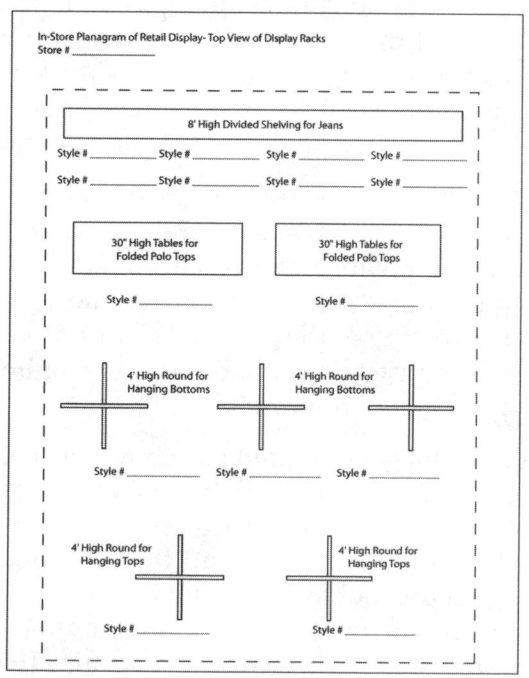
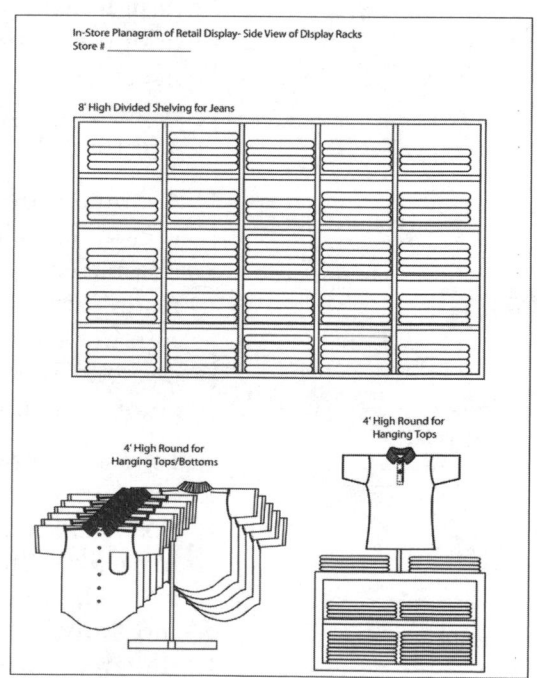

FIGURE 11–16
Store planning or layout

benefit is that designs can be realistically rendered for presentation as samples for buyers without the need to have samples made. Buyers can visualize different colors and details as they would appear on a finished garment. For small businesses this technique can be a real money saver.

In this chapter we will walk you through a variety of exercises designed to help you digitally generate each of these items!

In the end, the secret to designing these boards is planning and organization. Everything should be well-organized, concise, and clearly labeled and done in draftsman-like quality. The text, lettering, or fonts should reinforce the concepts as well as the company's image.

Therefore, the goal of each of these boards is to visually convey your collection with accuracy, interest, and simplicity!

In our next segment we will discuss where and how you begin to make these presentation boards in Adobe Photoshop.

Presentation Boards—Raster or Vector?

So, where do you begin? Although there are numerous types of design software out there, for the most part there are two main choices—raster- or vector-based software.

Some types of software do combine both. It is surprising how many designers who are starting to use CAD do not know why they are using a particular software. They are mostly using what they were "recommended" to use, when a different product would actually suit their needs better. The recommendation of a design product is truly in good faith. Sometimes though, we need to analyze the design situation and find the products best suited for that purpose. There will never be one software package that does it all or works for all other designers. A designer needs to know what they want to accomplish with design software and then decide how they can use it to get the final result they are looking for.

As you discovered in Chapter 5, most software can be defined as either raster or vector. *Raster* images are defined as images or designs of closely spaced dots or pixels on a computer monitor. One of the best examples of design software that uses raster images is Photoshop. When a designer is drawing, painting, or filling a design in this software, they are putting dots of color onto the screen to create the design. The dots of color are really squares on the monitor because the pixels of color on a monitor are square not round.

In raster software, the images designed are being created by the position of the pixels on the screen, blending and mixing. Pixel is short for picture element. Pixels are being colored and created with every stroke of the brush or tool being used. Effects can easily be created and the edge quality can be soft as well as hard, depending on the tool used. Digital images, scans, and other files of almost any format can be opened and fully edited in this type of software. Simply dragging brushes and colors can create amazing effects and designs. (See Figure 11–17.)

Vector can be defined as a design or image drawn by placing points on a screen or monitor and the connecting of those points creates a line segment. The computer

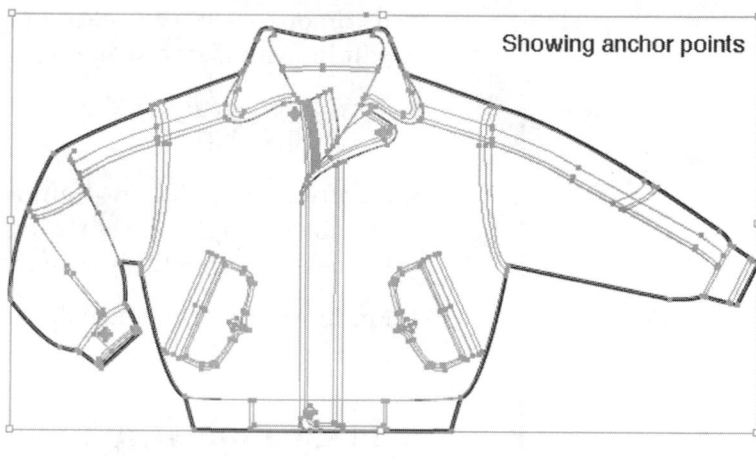

Showing anchor points

Hiding anchor points

FIGURE 11–17
Raster sketch

FIGURE 11–18
Vector sketch

Notes...

draws the line in pixels on the monitor by plotting the points of the line and mathematically redrawing them to the printer when they are sent for output. An example of vector software is Adobe Illustrator, but Photoshop also has a Pen tool that utilizes vector abilities. (See Figure 11–18.)

In vector-based software, images are drawn and created using precise line segments and filled or stroked to add detail. Another term for this type design is "object based." Object based means that any drawn shape is its own object or "piece" of the art. Here, any object can be continually moved and edited independent of the entire design. A crisp edge on the artwork is a given as well as precision shape and stroke. Resolution-independent images that can be easily scaled and edited are a plus with this type of drawing software. No loss of detail or quality is expected. Blends of colors can be created within objects as well as other effects. The hard-edged boundaries of the objects can be a drawback when a soft edge is desired. Software of this type is perfect for technical drawings of flats and croquis. Afterwards, these images can easily be opened into Photoshop for editing.

Cross-Software Compatibility Issues

When opening an image into different software from what it was created in, remember that features of the original software may not be supported by the opening software.

- If you open a vector image in a raster program, you will lose the ability to edit individual line segments.

- A raster image opened into a vector program cannot be edited for color or detail.

- A software that does not support layers will remove the layers and flatten an image to open it. Flattening an image creates a single editable drawing layer—no more multiple layers.

- Masking features are usually only supported in the software they were created in.

Think in the Right Direction

There are other specific features of software that can be worked around as long as the designer can "think in the right direction." This means knowing what software to use in each step and having the knowledge of what features or details in the design will become uneditable as a design passes through multiple software. A safe way to begin this process is for the designer to save all possible versions of a design as the work progresses, so if there is the need to go back a few steps or more, the design has been saved in various stages and software.

The advantage of learning how to work this way allows the designer to use tools or effects that do not exist in one software, but may be applied in another.

The Use and Development of Flats

In the apparel and fashion industry, flats or croquis of garments are widely used in the development and design of any line of clothing.

Clip Art Solutions

Throughout your journey as a designer you will be called upon to render your fabric and place a scaled-down version of the fabric either into a croquis or a technical drawing (flat), or simulate the image via a texture mapping process or program into a photo.

One of the most widely used methods is placing your print into a flat-technical drawing. There are several companies that provide such drawings in the form of editable clip art.

There are numerous companies who sell and supply vector-based work sketches or flats for industry use. Because these drawings are vector based, they are completely editable in such programs as Adobe Illustrator. Two great examples of clip art that you should know about come from (1) Bill Glazer, entitled Snap Fashun, and (2) Library Clip Art Fashion Findings by Imagine That! Productions. Both of these companies have graciously provided samples for you to review located on the Goodies Folder on the CD in the file **Entitled > Clip Art.**

Figure 11–19 shows you the start to finish process of using Bill Glazer's Snap Fashun clip art. Snap Fushun, has a wide assortment of clip art available that can be used by the designer to render fashion images. Included is a seasonal sampling of the latest trends along with historical examples from the past. All of these im-

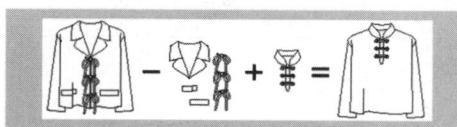

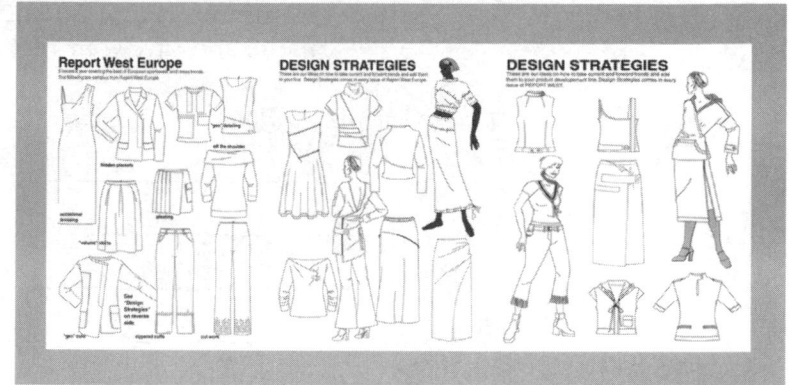

FIGURE 11–19
Bill Glazer's SnapFashun clip art
(Courtesy of Bill Glazer, SnapFashun)

Notes . . .

ages have been rendered in Adobe Illustrator with the ability to export the files in other file formats for use in other types of programs.

Sometimes the most stressful portion of a presentation is rendering the flats. Having them available in a vector-editable format relieves the pressure of time constraints often facing the designer. Furthermore, having the ability to return to the next season and make minor modifications really makes things a "snap" for the designer. Even designers who are accomplished at manual technical drawing prefer this alternative to sketching and scanning because of the time savings when the drawing requires only minor modifications.

Here is how the clip art is edited in Adobe Illustrator, and you can follow along with the steps as seen in Figure 11–19.

Snap Fashun Clip Art for Use in Adobe Illustrator and Adobe Photoshop:

Step 1. Open Adobe Illustrator and begin a **New File: 8.5 × 11 inches, RGB**.

Step 2. Name the file **Samples**.

Step 3. Next, open the CD that came with the book and go to the Goodies Folder and then go to the Snap Fashun subfolder. Open the file entitled **Womens**.

Step 4. Go to **Select All** and make a copy of the image and paste onto the new file.

Step 5. Go to **Edit > Direct Select Tool** to select one of the elements of the garment you want to modify.

Step 6. Your alternatives to modify include deleting and replacing the area with a new alternative. For example, in the case of a blouse you may want to replace the existing sleeves with a different sleeve type. You may also opt to isolate a segment of the garment to add additional points or nodes to reshape the garment, including adding length to a sleeve or hemline.

Step 7. There are endless possibilities of adapting the clip art to suit your needs—with the biggest plus being accuracy and time savings!

Step 8. Continue to experiment with clip art and master the alternatives, then name and save your file.

Other Applications and Insights:

_____

_____

_____

_____

Notes . . .

Similar to SnapFashun, the clip art from Imagine That! can also be carefully edited in Adobe Illustrator and the sections can be combined, edited, and re-edited over and over again. (See Figure 11–20.) The contents of the library include various kinds of cuffs, collars, buttons, snaps, zippers, pulls, and much more!

Scanning vs. Drawing in Flats

Getting the flats into the computer is the beginning. Hand-drawn sketches have been used for line sheets in the past, because this has been what the designers and buyers are used to seeing. Today, designers can have hand-drawn sketches scanned right into the computer, using the scanning methods for black-and-white scanning, as discussed in Chapter 5.

Hand-draw any sketches and then scan them in as black-and-white line art. These images can be placed into the line sheet template like the one in Figure 11–21. Images can be added and deleted as needed as the line is developed. For a more formal and editable line sheet, layers can be used in Photoshop. To speed up the process for each season, a designer can set up a template for each specific season or client, including logos and style names, and keep using it over and over.

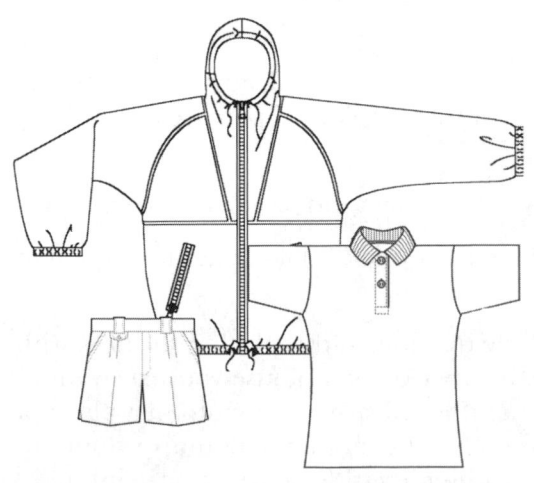

FIGURE 11–20
Imagine That! clip art
(Courtesy of Teri Ross, Imagine That! Consulting Group, Inc.)

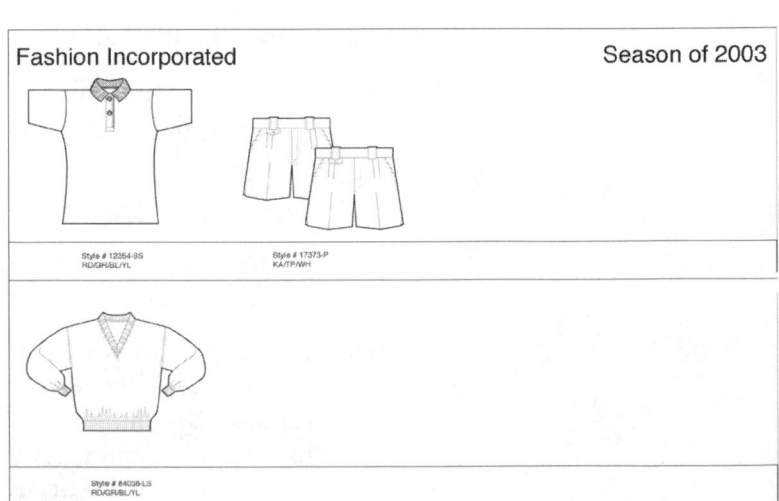

FIGURE 11–21
Line sheet template

Drawing Flats Directly into the Computer

If drawing the flats and croquis directly into the computer is necessary, then a designer can easily use many programs to accomplish the task. These sketches can be done in a few different ways.

Drawing in Illustrator

Adobe Illustrator has long been considered the norm for drawing technically correct and detailed flats. However, some industry individuals comment that the computer-generated flats have a sense of looking "too perfect." Regardless of your preference, if there is a hand-drawn flat that needs to be copied to look very technically correct, this flat can be used as a template in Illustrator and traced over for a great final result.

In the next section we include a brief set of follow-along instructions for those who have access to Adobe Illustrator. It is not important which version of the software you are working on, as long as you have access to utilizing a scanner in conjunction with the software. It also should be noted that if you only have access to another vector-based program such as CorelDraw or others, the steps in this exercise will remain consistent.

Let's Try It! Using Adobe Illustrator:

Step 1. Place the hand sketch on the scanner. (Any freehand drawing will do if the lines are clean and the ink is black. Be sure all of your lines are closed.)

Step 2. Scan in the sketch. This will be very similar to using the scanner exercises in Chapter 5.

Step 3. In Adobe Illustrator or other comparable vector-based software, go to **File > Open,** and select the sketch. (See Figure 11–22.)

Step 4. A selected sketch will open as a template. A template is an open file that cannot be edited for color or detail in any way, except for scaling or similar distortions. It is mainly used for tracing over the design or sketch.

Step 5. Select the flat and choose **Lock** in the object menu. The file cannot move now while it is being traced.

FIGURE 11–22
Select sketch

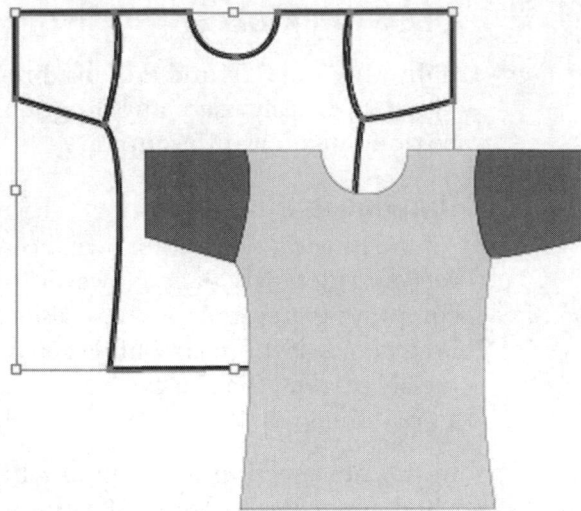

FIGURE 11–23
Flat and sketch

Step 6. Using the pen drawing tools, trace over the details of the entire flat.

Step 7. After tracing, select **Unlock All** in the object menu.

Step 8. Select and choose delete to remove the original scan. The traced drawing is left. (See Figure 11–23.)

Step 9. Save the sketch. This is now a vector drawing.

Other Applications and Insights:

_____

_____

_____

_____

Using Adobe Streamline to Generate a Sketch

Adobe Streamline is popular software for automatic tracing of a scanned or raster image. It easily converts the image into a vector graphic. The drawback is that it can create more lines or points than are needed, so some editing will still need to be done. There is also a looser feel to the drawing, so editing may be needed to tighten it up. We include the steps of how this is accomplished if you currently own a copy of Adobe Streamline.

Step 1. Open Streamline.

Step 2. Select **Options > Color/B&W Setup.** (See Figure 11–24).
   • Posterization should be set to **Black & White Only**.
   • Threshold should be **50%**.

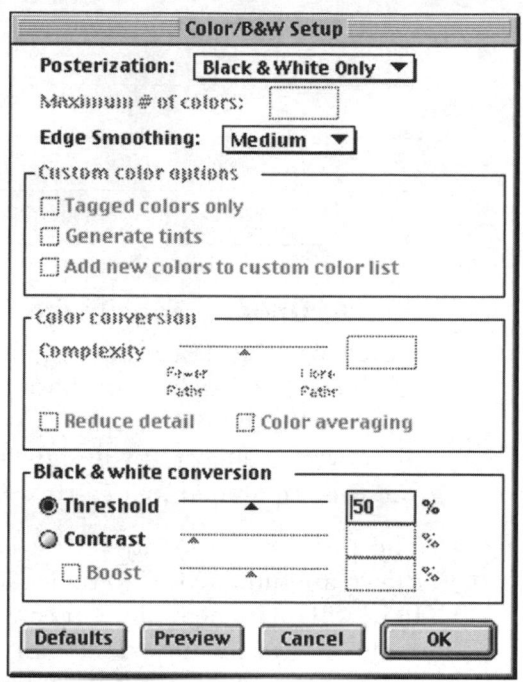

FIGURE 11–24
Color/B & W setup

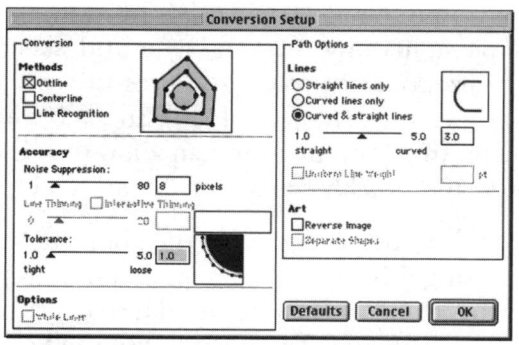

FIGURE 11–25
Conversion options
(Courtesy of Streamline)

FIGURE 11–26
Final image "vectorized"
(Courtesy of Streamline)

Step 3. Select **Options > Conversion Setup**. (See Figure 11–25.)
- For Conversion Method, **Outline** needs to be selected.
- For Accuracy, **Noise Suppression** should be set to **8.** If set too low, it will pick up every speck or pixel on the scan.
- Tolerance should be **1.0 (tight).**
- Path Options should be set to **Curved & straight lines**.

Step 4. Select **File > Convert**. The scanned file will now be redrawn as a vector image. (See Figure 11–26.) It can now be used and edited in Illustrator and for later use in Photoshop.

_____

_____

_____

_____

Notes . . .

Using a Drawing Tablet with Photoshop

A drawing tablet is an amazing tool for drawing directly into any computer. These products, like Wacom, are known as Intelligent Drawing Tablets. Whether on a Mac or a PC computer, these devices allow any designer to draw with a special pen directly into almost any design software. The pen attributes can be customized and even upgraded to an airbrush tool.

The pressure sensitivity of the Pen tool allows designers to have a truly hand-drawn and unique feel to their sketches. Pressing softly gives a light line; pressing hard will give a heavy line. It can even splatter the "ink." Selecting from the wide range of brushes and effects can keep a designer busy for hours. Photoshop goes to great lengths in using the pressure sensitivity settings of the tablet.

Simply picking up the pen and sketching is one way to begin using the tablet. The sketch in Figure 11–27 was quickly sketched in Photoshop using only a tablet and pen.

Drawing with Adobe Photoshop

Photoshop has always been widely used for drawing flats. Using the wide variety of tools complements any drawing style and sketches can be quickly accomplished. Stylus size, opacity, color, and pressure can all be easily varied as the designer sketches. Almost every tool in Photoshop allows these attributes to be edited on the fly. In addition, layers can allow the ability to easily open a photo or scanned sketch and quickly trace over the original for the final art.

The Pen tool in Photoshop increases the ability to sketch on a layer as if in a vector program. Using this tool, the designer can draw vector lines and move points until the sketch is done, and then flatten it to be used as a raster file. To draw flats directly into Photoshop you will need to use the Pen tool.

Using the Bezier Drawing Pen in Adobe Photoshop
Let's Continue and Draw a Flat Directly into Photoshop

The Pen tool is a Bezier drawing pen tool. To begin drawing, select the tool and click down a single point on the paper, release the mouse and move to where the second point will be, and click again. If you click and release the mouse, a straight line will have been drawn. If you click and drag the second point, a curved line will form. As you drag the mouse farther away, the curve will become deeper. This is how to control the curve. For what it is worth, this will take practice—so have patience and invest the time in mastering this tool! After releasing the mouse on a curved line, there are "anchor points" or "handles." The points can be clicked on and dragged to continually edit the curved line. (See Figures 11–28 and 11–29.)

In Figure 11–28 the Path tool is used to move anchor points and handles. It is accessed by selecting the Apple key on the Mac or Control key on the PC.

FIGURE 11–27
Raster sketch
(Wacom Technology Corp. Used with permission)

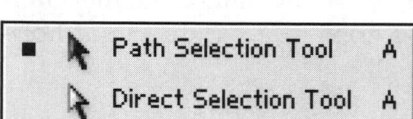

FIGURE 11–28
Path tool

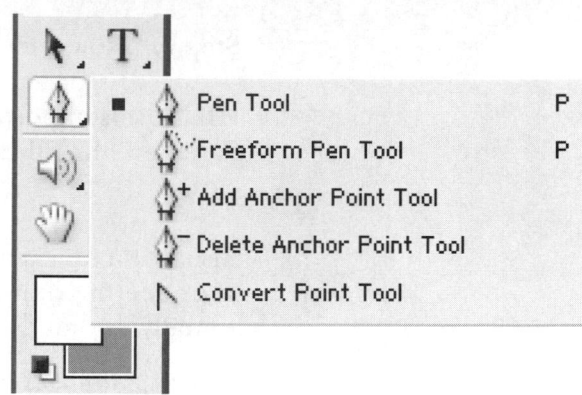

FIGURE 11–29
Tool icons

Notes...

Figure 11–29 shows the following tool icons:

- Pen Tool—Draws anchor points
- Freeform Pen Tool— Allows the designer to drag and sketch a line
- Add Anchor Tool—Adds anchor points
- Delete Anchor Tool—Deletes anchor points
- Convert Point Tool—Reverses between a curved anchor point and a corner anchor point

Using the Pen Tool to Draw a Flat:

Step 1. Using the Pen tool, start to sketch the shorts.

Step 2. Draw one "part" at a time and finish off the shape so it is a "closed" shape.

Step 3. For example, draw a pair of short pants. Create the drawing of the short body, legs, and waist. Add the details such as pockets and cuffs. Remember, to get a curved line, click and drag the tool.

Step 4. When finished, select all the parts.

Step 5. Choose from the Path Submenu **Make Selection.**

Step 6. Choose from the Edit menu **Stroke** and make a 2-pixel stroke on the "center" of the line. (See 11–30.)

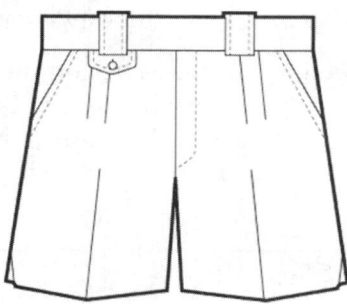

FIGURE 11–30
Sketched walking short

Step 7. Now select and delete the "paths."

HINT: It is important to draw a "closed path" every time. When the sketch is flattened, the fill can "leak" out if the line art of each object or shape is not closed.

Also, for a quicker and more symmetrical sketch, draw one-half of the flat, then Marquee the drawn half of the sketch and drag a copy to the right, flip it horizontally, and drag it back to match the opposite half.

Other Applications and Insights:

_____

_____

_____

_____

Notes . . .

Filling Designs into Flats

Now that the garments and croquis are designed, they need to be filled. Whether it is a solid-color blocking or a fancy print or weave, the flats need to be filled. One of the flashiest ways to present a design or line sheet is to drop the real designs into the flat of the garment on which it will be produced. Visualizing these flats helps a designer put together a line of apparel, wall coverings, and home furnishings. Buyers can also see the assortments and know how the designs will merchandise together, right from the beginning.

Let's Do It! Fill a Pattern into a Flat:

Step 1. Open the flat to be filled into Photoshop.

Step 2. Also open the design to be placed.

Step 3. In the design window, go to **Select > All**.

Step 4. Go to **Edit > Define Pattern**. Once defined as a pattern, any design will automatically fill as a straight repeat. If the design was developed as a half drop, this can be done as long as there is one full repeat to be selected.

Step 5. Select the window with the flat.

Step 6. Double-click on the Bucket tool to see its attributes. Select the settings as shown in Figure 11–31. The most important option is **Fill: Pattern**. Then select the pattern to be used from the Pattern menu.

FIGURE 11–31
Bucket options

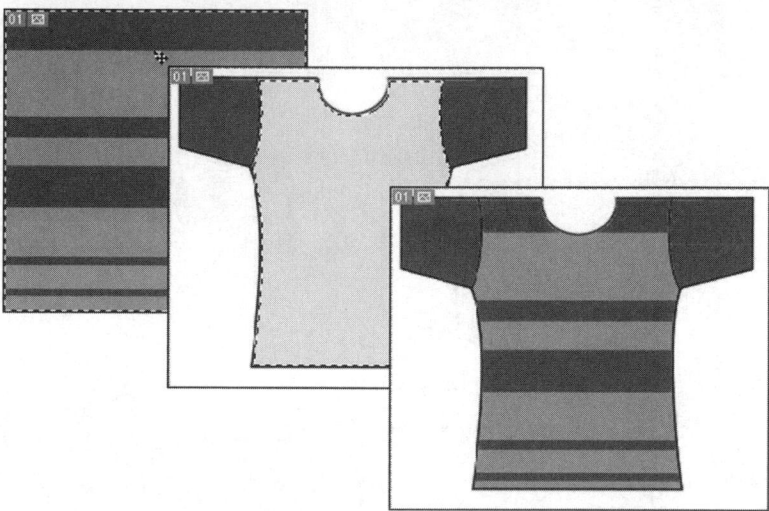

FIGURE 11–32
Caption

Step 7. Click the Bucket tool into the area the repeat needs to go. The design will fill into the area clicked on, flowing in repeat until hitting the edge of another color.

Step 8. Continue the Bucket fill until all areas are filled.

Other Applications and Insights:

_____

_____

_____

_____

Notes...

Placement of Engineered Designs

Designs can also be easily "engineered" into a flat. Engineering a design is the placement of a design into a garment when it is critical, such as in positioning the design in the exact place it will be sewn. Placing the design into the sleeves at just the right angle can be done as well. One of the best features of Photoshop, when filling flats, is the **Paste Into** function. A final flat with an engineered stripe may look like that shown in Figure 11–32.

Engineering a design into a flat can easily be done using Adobe Photoshop.

Let's Try It! Placing a Design into a Flat:

Step 1. Open the flat to be filled into the design program. On the CD open the file **Flat 1.** (See Figure 11–33.)

Step 2. Open the design to be used as the fill. On the CD open the file **Stripe for Fill.** (See Figure 11–34.)

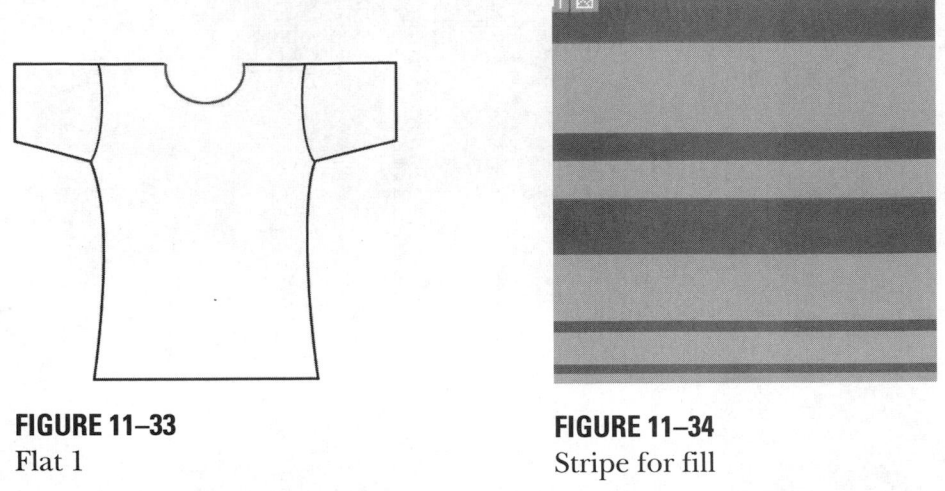

FIGURE 11–33
Flat 1

FIGURE 11–34
Stripe for fill

FIGURE 11–35
Magic wand selection

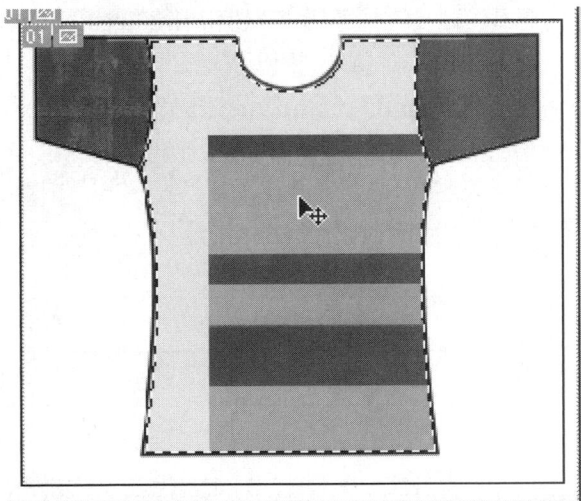

FIGURE 11–36
Move tool

Step 3. Scale the design to be in correct proportion to the flat.

Step 4. In the design window go to **Select** and choose **Select All.**

Step 5. In the Edit menu choose **Copy.**

Step 6. Go to the flat window and using the Magic Wand selection tool, set the defaults as shown and select the area to be filled. (See Figure 11–35.)

Step 7. Go to Edit and select **Paste Into.** Do not select **Paste,** because this will only paste the design on top of the whole window. **Paste Into** will paste the design *inside* the selected area. The key here is that the design is still active. A simple click on the design using the Move tool (Figure 11–36)

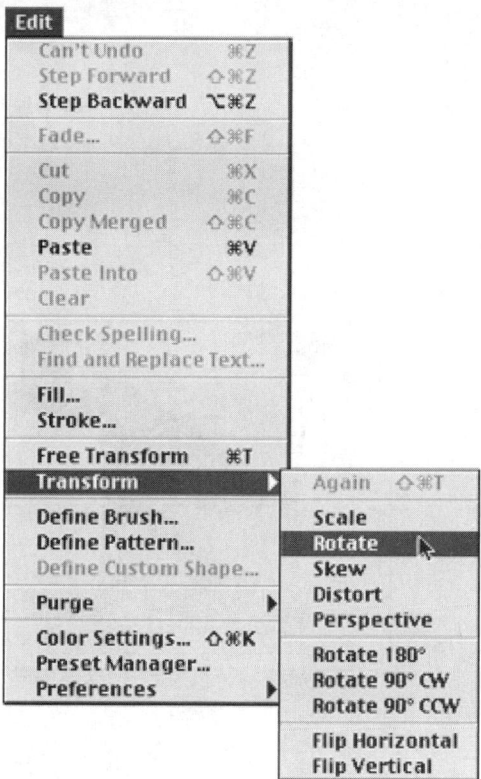

FIGURE 11–37
Rotate options

allows the designer to edit, move, and rotate the design until the position is perfect. This is engineering the design.

Other Applications and Insights:

_____

_____

_____

_____

Rotating a Design Inside a Flat:

Selecting **Edit > Free Transform** allows almost unlimited editing. Rotating and stretching the design can easily be done. (See Figure 11–37.)

Step 1. Select **Edit** and copy the design to be used.

Step 2. Using the Magic Wand, select the area to be filled with the design.

Step 3. Choose **Edit > Paste Into** to have the design placed into the area.

Step 4. Select **Edit > Free Transform.** Anchor points all around the area will become active.

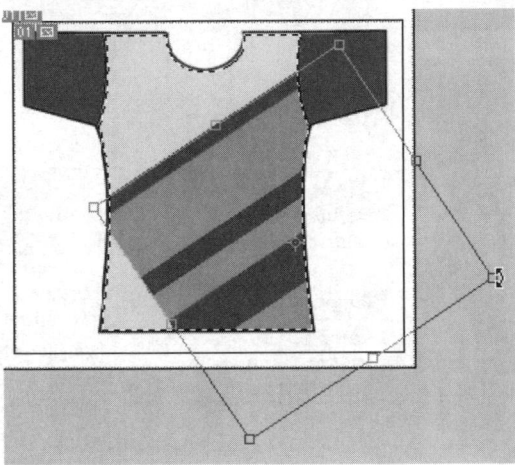

FIGURE 11–38
Rotate stripe

FIGURE 11–39
Flatten layers option

Step 5. Rotate the design by selecting just outside a corner point and dragging in a circular direction around the selected area. (The center of this area is the center of rotation.) (See Figure 11–38.)

Step 6. Select and drag the anchor points that show when **Free Transform** was chosen.

Other Applications and Insights:

_____

_____

_____

Notes...

It is important to understand that **Paste Into** also places the design in a mask on a separate layer. Layers are useful in keeping parts of a design separate so they can be continuously edited without affecting other parts of the image. If layers are not needed or it is easier to work without layers, choose to **Layer > Flatten** the image after each area is edited. **Flatten,** under the Layer menu, has the function to remove any layers or masks created when an image is edited. (See Figure 11–39.)

When the Repeat Is too Small for the Flat:

Be sure there is enough of the design to fill the flat and that it is in repeat. If not, edit the design so there is enough to repeat across the flat. See the previous chapters on creating a tiled repeat.

If the design is a single repeat and needs to be a larger repeat to go across the flat, open a new window in the software.

Step 1. Create a new window that is larger than the repeat size needed. (See Figure 11–40.)

Step 2. Define the design to be used as a pattern, by choosing **Select All > Edit >Define Pattern**. (See Figure 11–41.)

Step 3. Using the Bucket tool, fill the empty window. (See Figure 11–42.)

Other Applications and Insights:

_____

_____

_____

_____

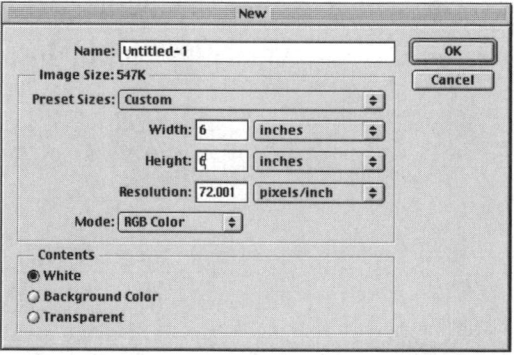

FIGURE 11–40
New window

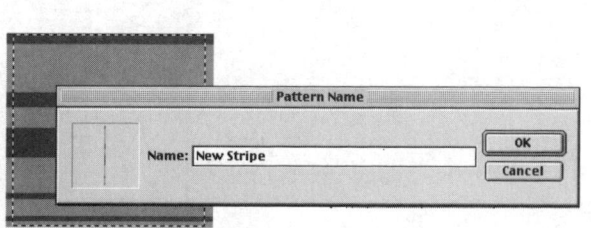

FIGURE 11–41
Edit define pattern

FIGURE 11–42
Filled flat

Creating a Texture-Mapped Version of the Fabric

For many years designers relied on paintings of a design, in multiple colorways, for selecting the final choices for the line. Waiting for artwork to be done at a service bureau or even longer for a sample to be printed is lost time. Texture mapping is a fantastic way to visualize a design in the final stage. It adds that extra punch of reality for a design to be displayed on a product in a photograph. Whether on a garment or a couch or even a wall, the ability to take a digital design the distance and place it in its final environment is an extremely useful sales and marketing tool.

Showing other designers or buyers what the design will actually look like on the product is a tremendous jump forward from seeing a flat printout or paintings of the designs. Adobe Photoshop can be used for texture mapping a photograph with almost any design.

Simulated Sample Making with Texture Mapping
Let's try it! Preparing the photo:

Step 1. Scan in the photograph to be used.

Step 2. If using a digital camera, download the photo to the computer.

Step 3. Open the photograph needed for texture mapping in Photoshop. (See Figure 11–43.)

Step 4. Using photo-retouching tools in Photoshop, edit the design for color and detail if needed. The Rubber Stamp tool is great for removing any text or details that were in the original photograph. (See Figure 11–44.)

When filled, it will tile automatically into the photograph.

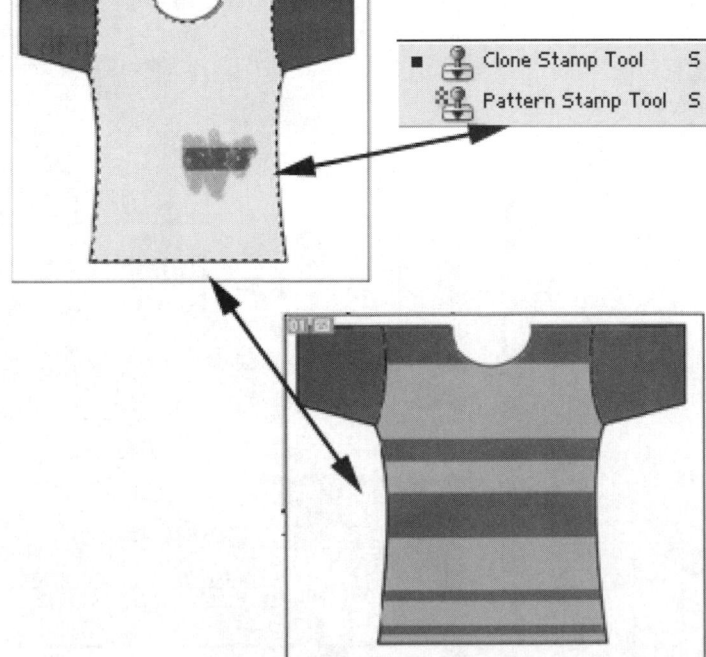

FIGURE 11–43
Digital photograph of garment

FIGURE 11–44
Rubber stamp tool

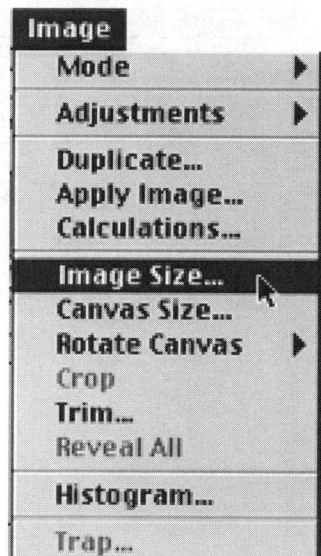

FIGURE 11–45
Image size

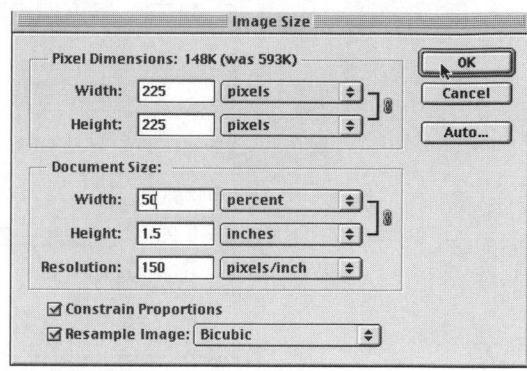

FIGURE 11–46
Constrain proportions and resample

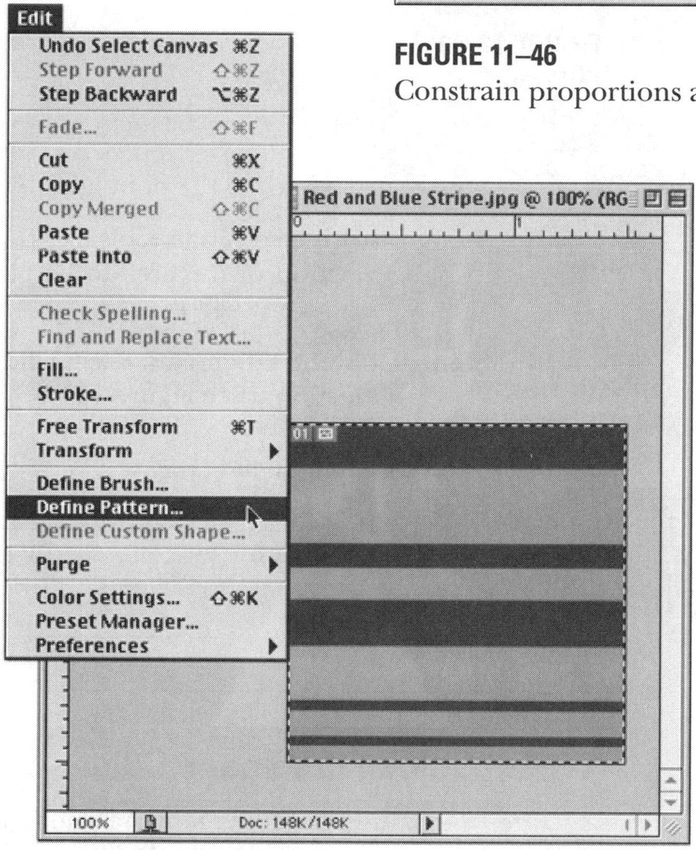

FIGURE 11–47
Define pattern

Adding the Design:

Step 5. Open and scale the design to the proportions of the photograph. Using the Image menu, select **Image Size.** (See Figure 11–45.)

Step 6. Be sure to Constrain Proportions and select the **Resample** option. (See Figure 11–46.)

Step 7. Once the scale is correct, go to **Select All** in the design window.

Select **Define Pattern** from the Edit menu. This creates a pattern in memory that will automatically be in a straight repeat when filled into the photograph. (See Figure 11–47.)

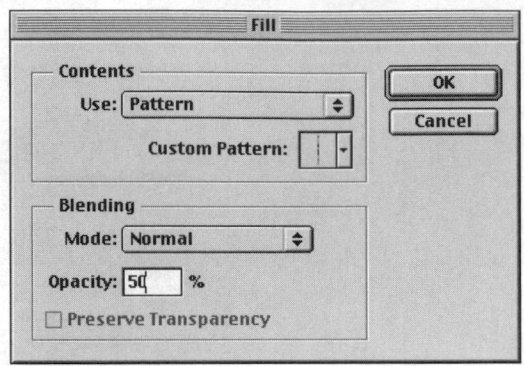
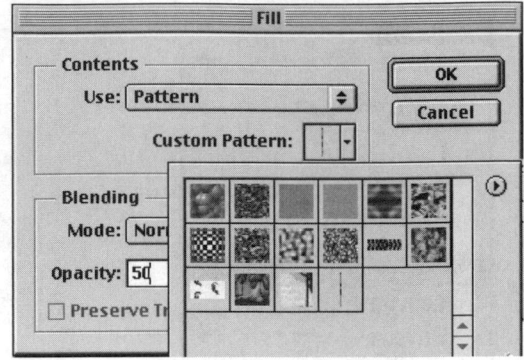

FIGURE 11-49
Fill options

FIGURE 11-48
Create a section to be filled

Step 8. Go back to the photograph window.

Step 9. Using selection tools like the Magic Wand and Lasso, create a selection of the area to be pattern filled in the photograph. (See Figure 11–48.)

Step 10. In the Edit menu, select **Fill.** Use the settings shown for the best selection. (See Figure 11–49.)

Other Applications and Insights:

_____

_____

_____

_____

Notes...

Retouching the Image Color

After the pattern has filled into the photograph, the user can edit the depth and detail of color by going to the Image menu and selecting **Adjustments.** The few options shown below are usually the best options.

- Select **Levels** and set the choices as shown in Figure 11–50. Choose **OK.**

- Select **Hue/Saturation** and set the choices as shown in Figure 11–51. Choose **OK.**

- Select **Brightness/Contrast** and set the choices as shown in Figure 11–52. Choose **OK.**

NOTE: For a little more of a fabric texture to the design set the Mode to **Multiply** when filling the selected area. Edit the settings as shown in Figure 11–53.

These settings can be adjusted and edited until the design and photo contrast are "alike." It is important to adjust the design that is added to the photograph so it blends into the image. If there is too much contrast, it will look too "cartoony." If

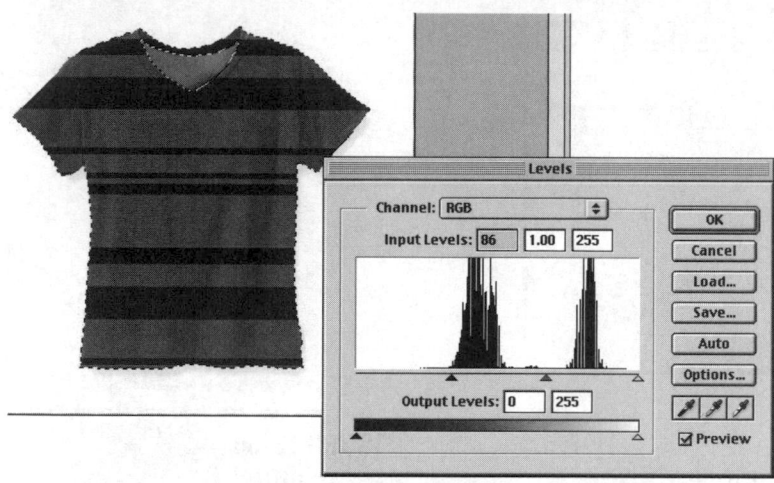

FIGURE 11–50
Levels

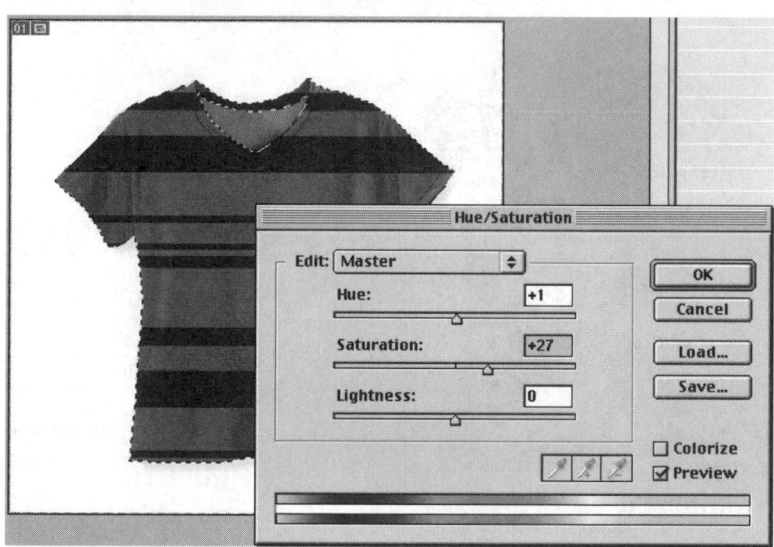

FIGURE 11–51
Hue/saturation

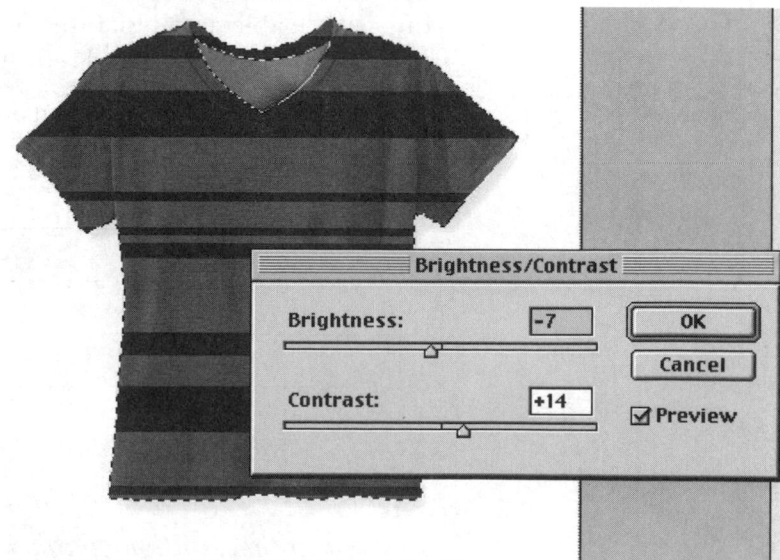

FIGURE 11–52
Brightness/contrast

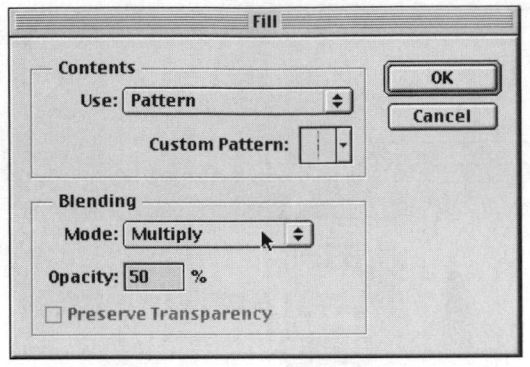

FIGURE 11–53
Mode window for multiply

FIGURE 11–54
Normal fill

FIGURE 11–55
Multiply fill

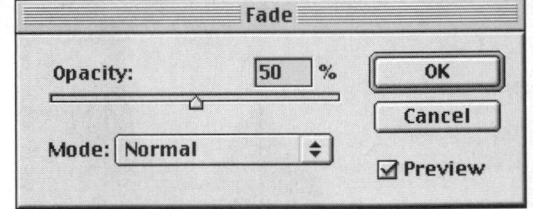

FIGURE 11–56
Fade fill

there is not enough contrast, it will be washed out. A little practice at this and no one will be able to tell that the design in the photograph is not a real garment or product, yet. (See Figures 11–54 and 11–55.)

- Select **Opacity Levels** and other choices as shown in Figure 11–56. Choose **OK.**

Other Applications and Insights:

_____

_____

_____

_____

Before We Begin . . . Presentation Boards— the Secret Is in the Layers

Designing presentation boards in Photoshop

Step 1. Create a new page in the final size of the board. This can be 8.5 × 11 to 11 × 17 for sell sheets printed on a desktop printer, or 20 × 30 for full-

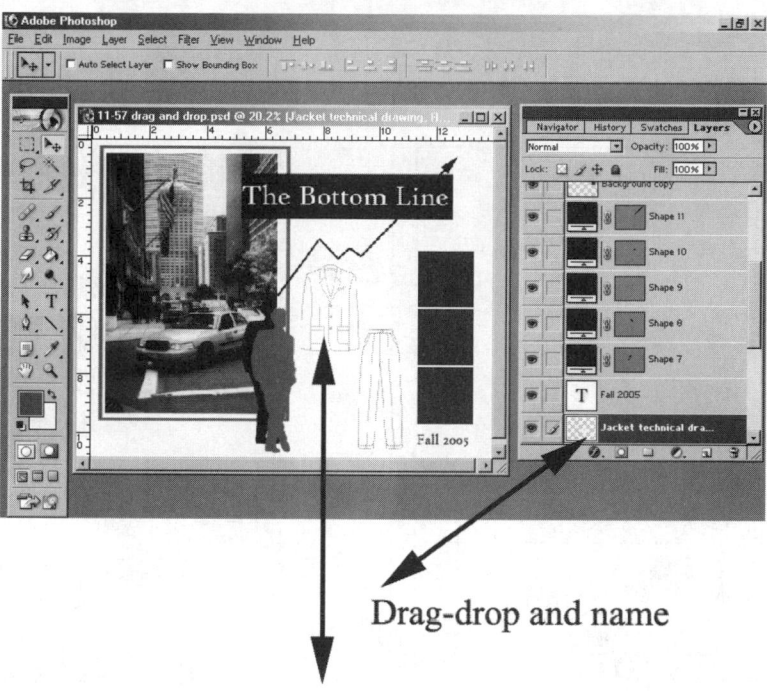

Drag-drop and name

FIGURE 11–57
Beginning of board

size presentation boards. If these are going to be printed on a plotter, 20 × 30 is a great size to present—no cutting and pasting your flats.

Step 2. Open every image, flat, or design to be used on this particular board.

Step 3. Select the Move tool and use it to drag each individual flat or design, one at a time, and drop each design into a position on the page layout. (See Figure 11–57.)

Step 4. Each drag and drop of a design will create a new layer that can be individually edited. Note: When you are making a storyboard that may include an illustration, you may opt instead to use a silhouette image in place of a rendering so that all the emphasis is shifted to the other portions of the board and not focused on the drawing. This is especially helpful if rendering figures is not a personal design strength.

Using Layers: Putting It All Together

Layers is one of Adobe Photoshop's strongest features. It allows a designer to continually edit images without affecting the underlying design. Here Layers is used to keep flats separate until ready to print. This allows the constant editing and moving that is normally done to create a presentation board. It almost simulates moving around cutout prints of each file as they are moved around on a piece of "foamboard."

Step 1. Now that all the needed images are placed on the page, the designer can move and reposition each one individually. The way to activate a certain flat or design is by using the Layers palette. (See Figure 11–58.)

Step 2. In the Layers palette, look for the thumbnail of the design to be moved.

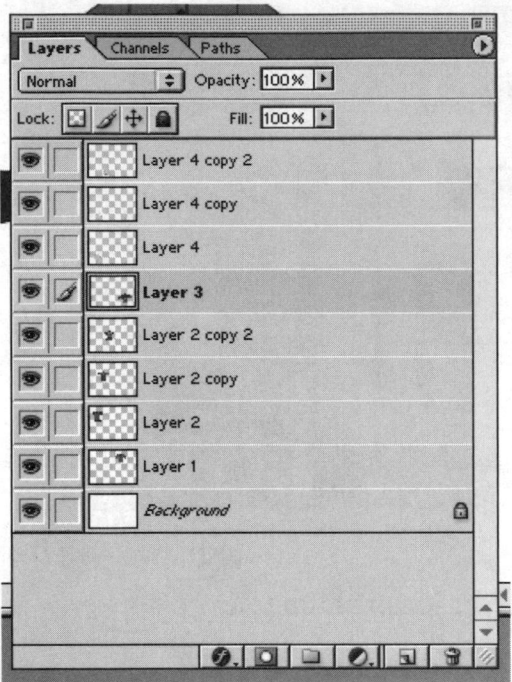

FIGURE 11–58
Layers detail palette

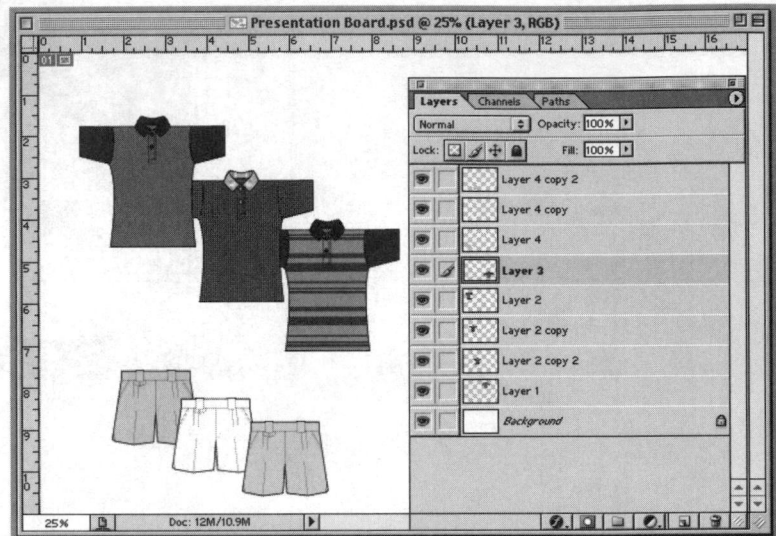

FIGURE 11–59
Layers palette with layers moved around

Step 3. Activate that Layer by selecting it with the mouse.

Step 4. Now go back to the presentation board and with the Move tool change the position of the design or flat.

Step 5. If the design or flat needs to be moved forward or backward on the board, use the Layers palette to do this as well. The Layers palette is set up with the topmost layer at the top of the palette. (See Figure 11–59.)

Step 6. Using the mouse, select the layer to move and drag it up the list to bring it forward on the page. Drag down the list to send an image to the back of the page.

Step 7. Text can be added using the Text tool. Text that was manipulated in other programs like Adobe Illustrator or Typestyler®can be imported as a graphic and used here as well.

Step 8. Save the file. (See Figure 11–60.)

Other Applications and Insights:

_____

_____

_____

_____

NOTE: *When sending a large presentation board to print, save the layered file, and then select* **Layers > Flatten.** *This option will decrease the file size and increase the print speed. The file can be saved as layers, but when printing layers there can be a tremendous amount of information sent to the printer. Flattening the file compresses this data.*

FIGURE 11–60
Final presentation board with text

Cross Section of Overlapping Layers File

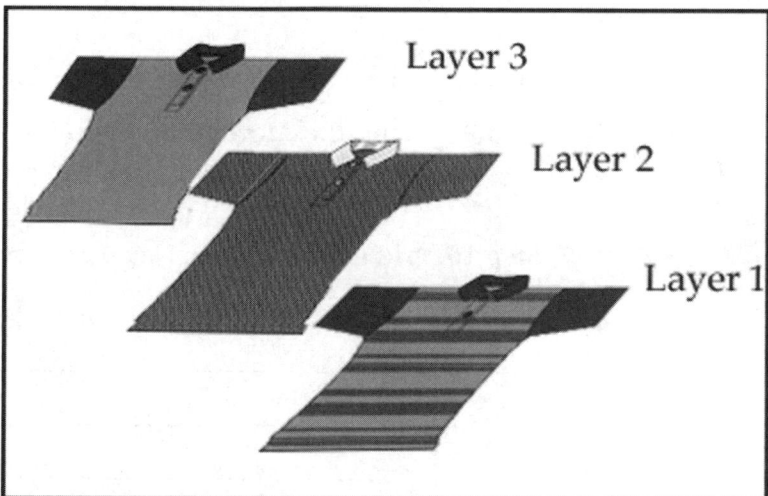

FIGURE 11–61
Cross section and close-up of labeled layers palette

Working with Layer Secrets (See Figure 11–61.)

- Layers in Photoshop can be hidden.
- Layers can be moved.
- Layer Modes can be applied.
- Layer Masks can be applied.
- Opacity can be altered.
- Layers can be annotated.

- Layers can be turned on or off.

- Layers can be color coded.

- Layers can be linked or merged.

Making a Color Board

Step 1. Open a **New File** in Adobe Photoshop: **14 × 11 inches, 150 dpi, RGB, White Background.**

Step 2. Open from the Goodies Folder in the Image subfolder the photo entitled **Pinking Shears.** (See Figure 11–62.)

Step 3. Drag and drop this photo to the New File and name the layer **Background.**

Step 4. Place a Magic Wand on Pinking Shears to resize to suit image and select **Edit > Free Transform.**

Step 5. Start a New Layer and begin to fill with color to match the storyline.

Step 6. Using the Eyedropper, select a defining color from the background photo. Begin to fill this new layer with that color.

Step 7. Make another new layer and continue to select a second color similar to Step 5.

Step 8. Repeat Steps 4–6 for a total of five colors.

Step 9. Using the Move tool, reposition each of the new color chips layer by layer. Notice also in this image you can use similar techniques to achieve a fabric board too! (See Figure 11–63)

Step 10. Add text to the file. Name and save this file.

Other Applications and Insights:

_____

_____

_____

_____

FIGURE 11–62
Pinking shears

Fabric Card 05

FIGURE 11–63
Fabric board

Making a Presentation Board

The goal of this board is to convey a complete story. (See Figures 11–64 and 11–65.) Presentation boards might include the following:

- Inspiration and theme
- The name of line and season
- The designer company name and/or logo
- Garment fronts and backs
- Fabric swatches
- Colorways or color story
- Patterns, prints, or motifs used
- Styles
- Silhouettes
- Details, including trims, embellishments, and findings

FIGURE 11–64
Presentation boards by Nandi Chin

FIGURE 11–65
Presentation board

Other Applications and Insights:

_____

_____

_____

_____

A Word about Words

What really makes a presentation have that extra kick to it? Is it the images that are chosen? Is it the magic of color? Or maybe, just maybe, it is the subtle inclusion of text and fonts infused into the presentation to give the added allure of the story being told.

Importance of Buzz Words

In our last exercise we had you add text phrases to enhance your images. We want to stop briefly to discuss the underlying importance of text, copy, and font selection.

Today's designers are without excuse for using the right font to punch up their presentation. If you have not taken a good class on managing text, you owe it to yourself and your boss to acquire this information.

Designers are skilled in the art of fashion and graphics, but incorporating words to accompany their images can sometimes be a real stretch to the new designer. Make good use of that sketch pad you always carry with you and jot down terms and phrases—the buzz words—on the day you encounter them.

We have noticed that in many of the popular magazines and catalogs you will find just the right phrase or description that captures the essence of what you want to convey visually with your graphics or your designs.

Just like you did in Chapter 4 with color names, jotting down popular phrases, a line from a song, or a quote from a movie or arbiter can go a long way in making your presentation boards have the distinction you desire to stand out from the crowd. Our next exercise will give you a head start on this.

Buzz Word Exercise

Step 1. Locate a website that specializes in movie clichés.

Step 2. Locate a website that specializes in quotes from famous people or authors.

Step 3. Jot down five quotes or phrases that accurately depict the following themes:
  a. Romance
  b. Patriotism
  c. Sophistication
  d. Business
  e. Leisure
  f. Geographical location

Step 4. Type in your answers for a–f in Adobe Photoshop or Adobe Illustrator.

Step 5. Annotate in the Layer Property menu the name of the font family you used.

Step 6. Make five copies of any one of the answers from Step 4 and begin to experiment with the effect that color changes will have on the word. Compare and contrast how color works in conjunction with the font family selection to enhance the message.

Wedding Bells

Western-Ho

Hot Tropical Nights

New York

JUNIOR PROM

Holiday Magic

Cyber-generation

LET'S DANCE

FIGURE 11–66
Font families

Step 7. Now go back to each reply for Step 3 and find a font family that captures your response by visually reenforcing your answer. (See Figure 11–66.)

Other Applications and Insights:

_____

_____

_____

_____

HINT: Here we have listed a few websites to give you a jump start on finding great phrases, clichés, and the like to enhance your mood boards.

Notes...

Suggested URLs for Quotes and Clichés:

www.quoteland.com   www.quotations.co.uk
www.quotations.about.com/cs/cliches/   http://www.cj5c.com
www.moviecliches.com   http://www.bartleby.com/99
www.sportscliches.com

Keeping a Journal

Most fashion designers will readily admit that they always carry a sketchbook-style journal with them at all times. Keeping a journal with names for colors as well as ideas for buzz words that can be used in making storyboards is always a plus. These words and phrases can be adapted for use in a variety of fashion presentation boards. These words are used to convey emotions, attitude, and inspiration for a collection.

Listed below are just a few examples of words and phrases that should give you some insight into exactly what we mean:

Textured accents	Modern classic
Sophisticated	Uptown-downtown
Graphic proportion	Casual comfort
Curvy charisma	Balanced perspective
Refined beauty	Old-world opulence
Lush beauty	Engaging infusion
Cosmopolitan flair	Subtle solutions
Glamour carefully orchestrated	Synergy
Minimalist appeal	Functional flair
Understated elegance	Sensible chic
Urban utopia	La dolce vita
Stylish solutions	Architectural influence
Strong silhouettes	Undiscovered style
Legacy	Generous proportions
Uncomplicated	Tranquility
Serenity	

Now it's your turn. Jot down several ideas here:

_____

_____

_____

_____

_____

_____

_____

_____

_____

_____

More Tricks of the Trade—
Special Workflow Strategies for Photoshop

As you will see, the system and/or software a designer uses can support a variety of time-constraining tasks including color reduction, color separations, creation of multiple colorways, rendering pattern motifs into repeats, or editing and adding additional elements to a design. However, although it is imperative that you can manage tools and techniques within a given software, there are several more tricks you will want to consider to empower yourself in your digital design journey.

In the last section of this chapter we will review the secrets to managing your presentations in Adobe Photoshop, including several special tricks of the trade for annotating your layers and files with valuable information you will need for future presentations!

If you have the space to archive your work, Adobe Photoshop has several excellent options you will surely want to consider when you begin your design.

#1 Always make a thumbnail and have it approved before you begin your design.

#2 Consider making a template for the elements you want to use in your design. Then place the elements where the geometric shapes were used as a placeholder. This will really be a time-saver and will enable you to divorce yourself from overdesigning and stay focused to the task at hand. (See Figure 11–67.)

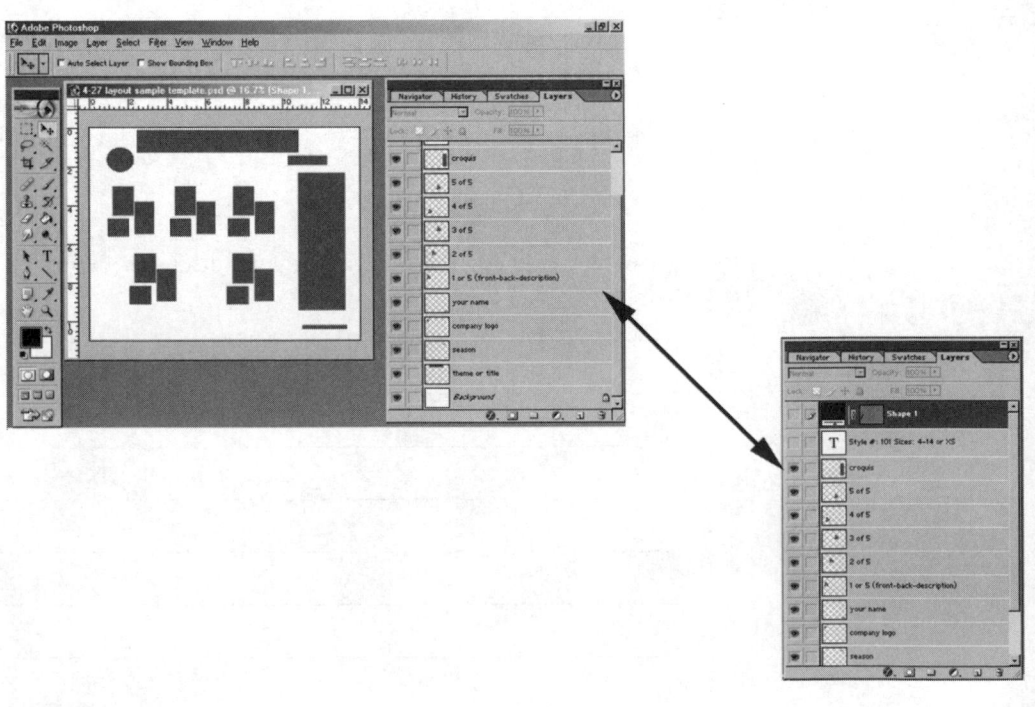

FIGURE 11–67
Making a template

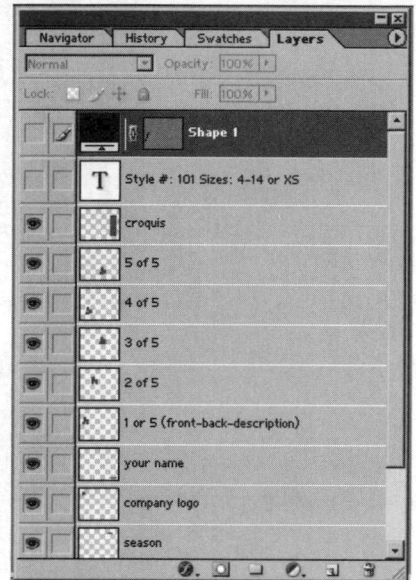

FIGURE 11–68
Save working versions

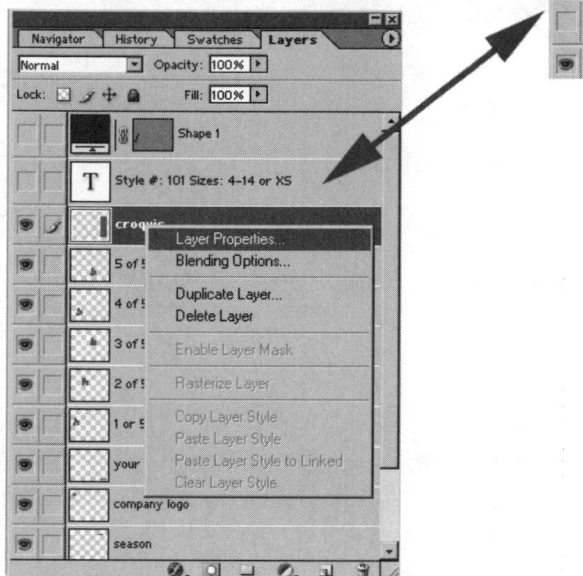

FIGURE 11–69
Layer properties

#3 Always save your work in versions. When you are designing, it may prove to a real time-saver if you name and save your work in versions. (See Figure 11–68.)

#4 It is also advisable to always save your work in layers. When you are designing, saving several ideas on different layers is a great way to go back and compare and contrast the different concepts you are working on. In addition, it is really a time-saver when showing your boss your ideas to have several layers of ideas turned off. (See Figure 11–69.) Your layers can be quickly turned on again for the boss to review the changes or suggestions you are sharing.

1. Make duplicate layers before any major editing or merging as a backup.
2. Always name your layers.
3. Always annotate your work and record the techniques you used. For example, you can opt to annotate your work in several ways:
   a. You can write your notes in the Layer Properties box. (See Figure 11–70.)
   b. You can type a layer of specific steps and then turn the layer off. (See Figure 11–71.)
   c. You can make a screen capture of your steps to make a visual record of pivotal techniques that are too time-consuming to write out. (See Figure 11–72.)

#5 Always archive the files in several formats for different uses. For example:

1. Saving files as a .psd will enable you to store ALL the layers for further use and editing.

Notes . . .

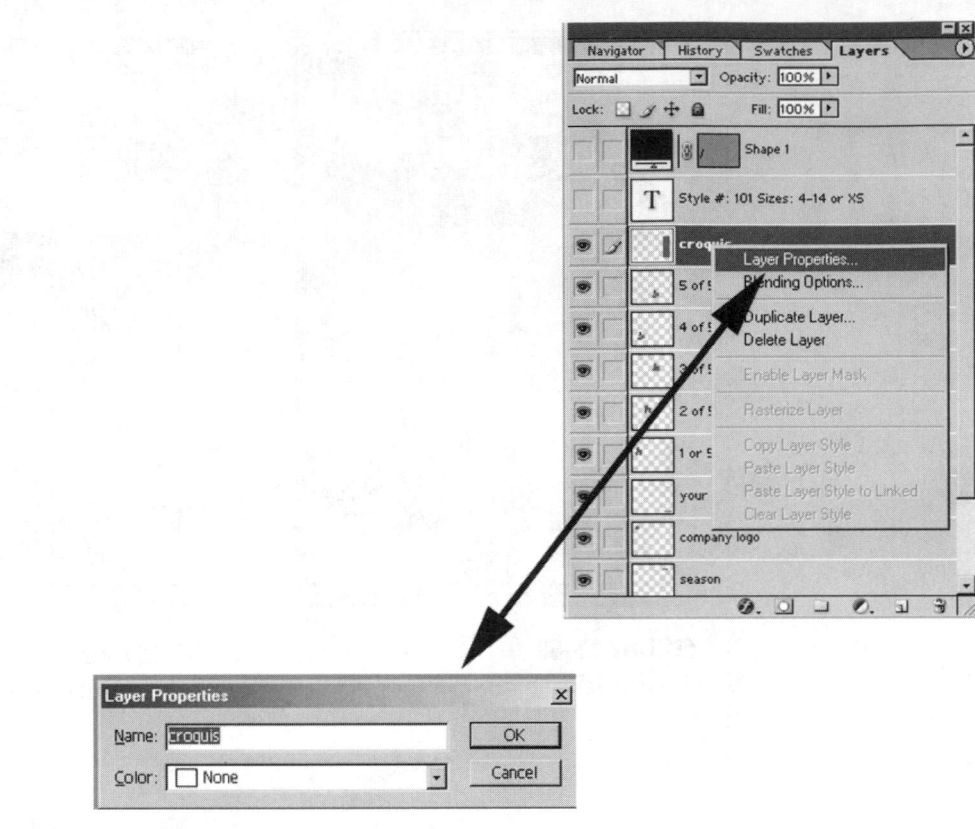

FIGURE 11–70
Layer properties box

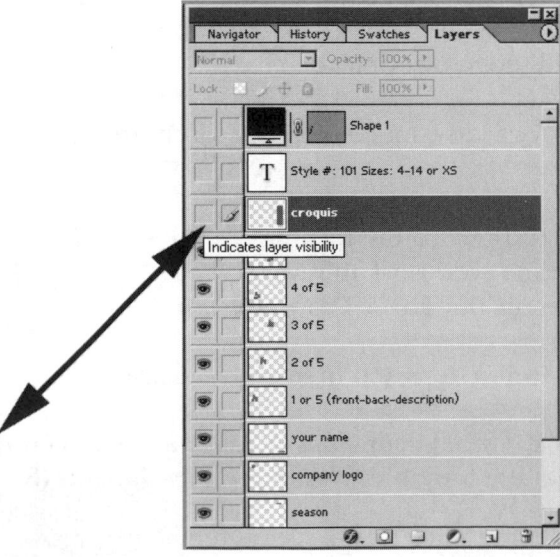

FIGURE 11–71
Turn layer off

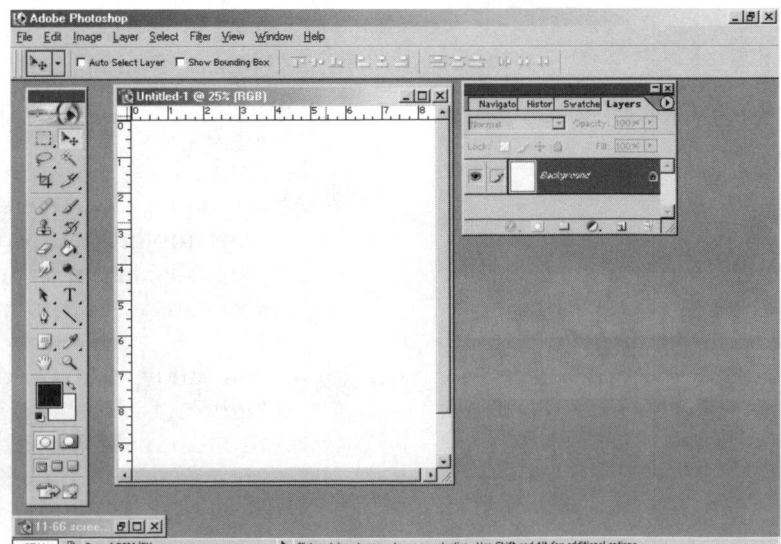

FIGURE 11–72
Make screen capture

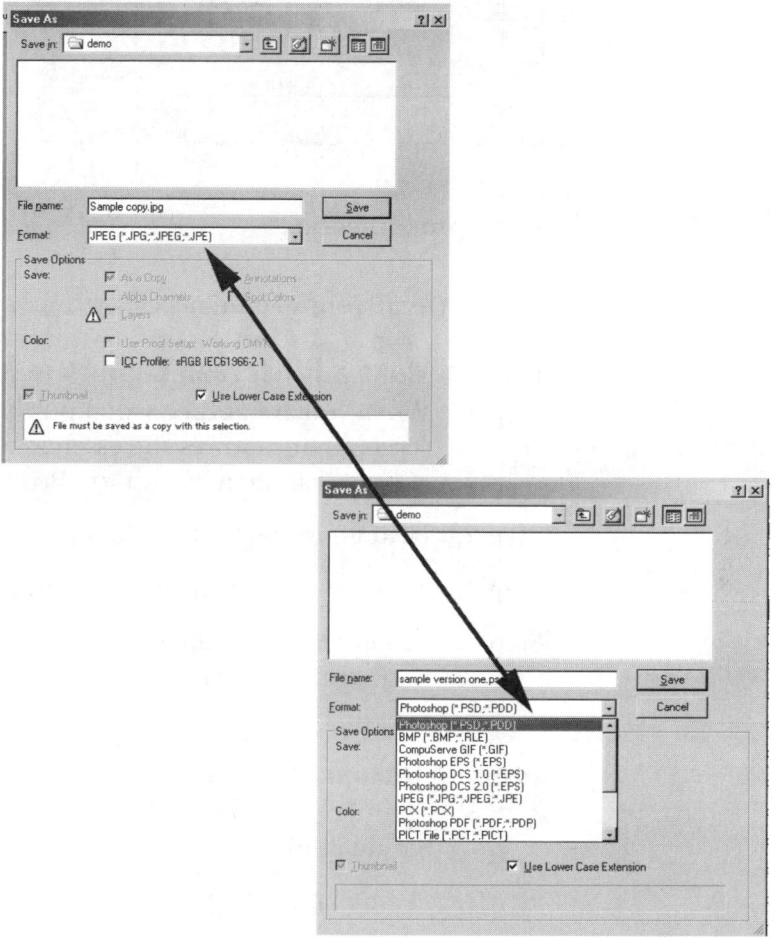

FIGURE 11–73
Save as JPEG

2. Saving the original as a .psd, then renaming as final version, and saving it as a TIFF creates the highest quality file for printing.
3. Save the file as a JPEG—highest quality. (See Figure 11–73.) You can then reopen this file, drag the JPEG copy to a new layer on the original file, and see what the filters will look like on a flattened copy of your work. This is an excellent way to test filters and other techniques without sacrificing flattening the original work.

Layer Naming and Annotation Methods

We recommend that you save your work in layers, name your layers, and annotate what techniques or changes you made. Therefore, we thought it would be beneficial at this time to show you how to annotate the Layer Property menu as well as how to make a screen capture in Adobe Photoshop.

How to Annotate Your Work in the Layer Property Box:

Step 1. Double-click on the layer you want to annotate. This will pop-up a new dialog box in which you type comments. (See Figure 11–74.)

Notes...

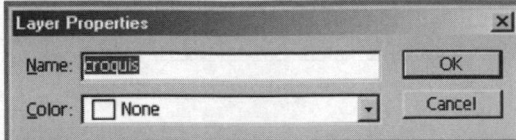

FIGURE 11–74
Layer properties box

Step 2. Type your comments clearly and specifically.

How to Make a PC Screen Capture in Adobe Photoshop:

Step 1. When you are at the pivotal point of your designing and have the screen that captures the essence of what you are attempting to accomplish, on a PC, hit the Print Screen key.

Step 2. Next go to the Edit menu and select **Paste.** (See Figure 11–75.)

Step 3. This will paste your screenshot on a new layer.

Step 4. You may want to name this layer in the Layer Property box *or* you may want to crop the image using one of the Selection tools or the Crop tool to capture only the screen you are interested in keeping. (See Figure 11–76.)

Graphic Design Insights

- Best rule of thumb—KISS—Keep it sweet and simple. Don't overdesign. (Sound familiar?)

- All emphasis is NO emphasis! Avoid clutter.

- Don't send mixed messages—be consistent.

- A great graphic design or marketing package has one goal—to convey a specific message and provoke a specific response!

- Headlines are for impact. Keep them short and concise and position at the head of the page and leave plenty of white space around the headline.

- Strive for contrast.

- Avoid negative white space.

- Don't mix too many font types.

- Strive for three dimensions—experiment with foreground, middle, and background.

- Consider the artful arrangement of all graphic elements, including text. Remember proportion, balance, and harmony.

- Keep subheadings short and in a similar font to the main headline. Also try bold or italic for emphasis.

- Keep captions less than three lines.

- Try to avoid widows and orphans in text.

- Experiment with frames around captions.

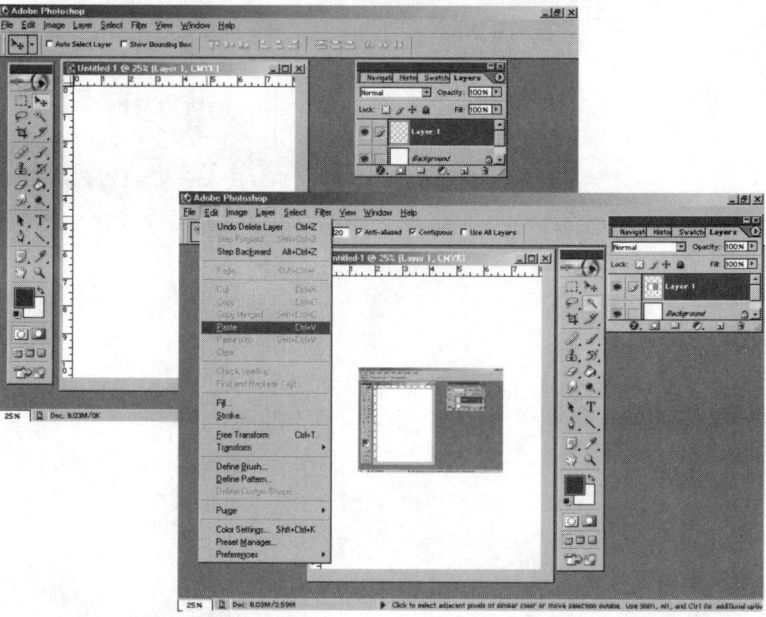

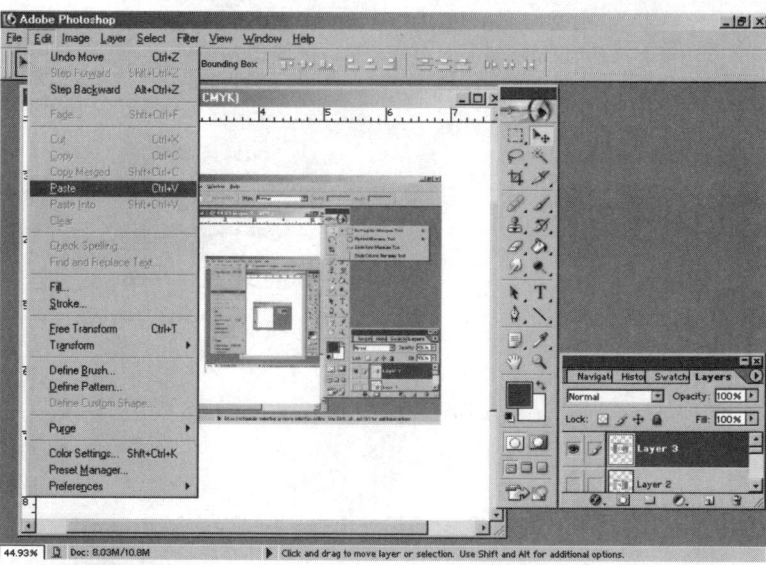

FIGURE 11–75
Select paste

- Use drop caps or initial caps for emphasis.

- Avoid hyphenations.

- Be sure your work is complete.

- Ask for input—have someone else evaluate it.

- Accept constructive "advice" from others.

Don't forget to set your work aside for a few days (if your deadline permits) and then come back to it. The perspective will do you *and* your work a world

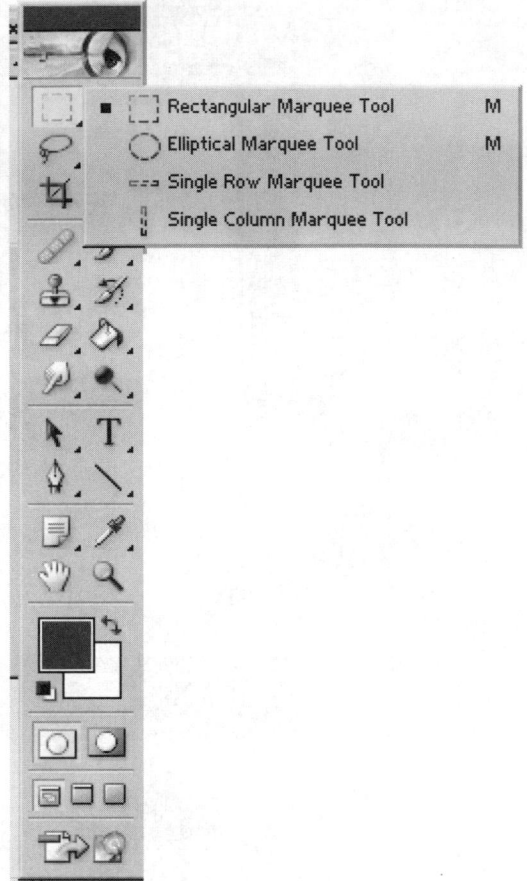

FIGURE 11–76
Cropping tools

of good. Then, when you pick it up again, see if your work answers the following questions.

Top Ten Questions to Ask Yourself:

1. What other factors must I consider?

2. Are there any budget restrictions I need to be aware of?

3. How accurate or flexible are the deadlines?

4. Who else is participating on this project? Does copywriting, printing, or distribution determine the final outcome of the design? This includes other individuals who will have their hands or their say on the final product (in-house, sales reps, buyers—consumers). Who do I really need to make "happy"?

5. Is there anyone I can go to for help or advice on the design to ensure its quality and accuracy?

6. Will the "reader" get the message right the first time? Will this piece grab their attention and keep it?

Notes . . .

7. In describing the features, did I stress the benefits of those features? Remember a feature describes the materials used in construction of a product. For example, cotton fiber content is a feature, so stress the "benefit" of wearing cotton—**Comfort!**

8. How will the reader best use this information?

9. Will the reader see what I want them to see?

10. Will the reader respond the way I want them to respond?

How and Where Do I Begin My Career in Design

In our final section we will help you put everything together to start your career in digitally rendering fabric and prints.

Putting It All Together:
Finding Jobs in This Field
Hottest Portfolio Presentation Trends

We will walk you through several great strategies to navigate today's digital design job market.

1. The current list of job titles

2. The skills necessary

3. The kinds of tasks that would be expected

4. Where to begin your job search—including on-line

5. Searching strategies and portfolio strategies

6. Student samples

Also included is a section on preparing digital CD presentations and insight into beginning to make the transition from the traditional to the digital portfolio. There are several great samples located on your Goodies CD.

Jobs in Design

Perhaps you are reading this book and wondering what to do with all of this new training you have just garnered.

The next direction you will want to take in becoming a designer is to begin to determine:

1. What are the possible job titles for this type of work?

2. Where do I begin my search for job leads?

We trust that what we have included in this section will help you to be on your way to a successful career in designing or rendering fabric and prints.

Here is an introduction to several possible job titles we have come across that are widely used by the industry.

List of Jobs:

Artist

Assistant Print Designer

CAD Artist

CAD Designer/Engineer/Operator

CAD/CAM Designer

Colorist

Converter

Decorative Artist or Designer

Design Assistant

Design Director

Design Editor

Designer

Design Technician

Fabric Development Specialist

Fashion Designer

Freelance Artist

Graphic Artist/Designer

Jacquard Designer (Knit or Woven)

Knitwear Designer

Lace Designer

Print Artist/Designer

Product Development Designer/Specialist

Repeat Artist

Sketcher

Stylist

Sweater Designer

Technical Artist/Designer/Assistant

Textile/Designer/Artist/Trainee

Textile Stylist

Textile Technologist

Tie or Print Designer

Wallpaper Designer

Woven Designer

Here is a list of what graphic/fashion designers may be expected to have knowledge of how to create:

- All other marketing aids
- Brochures
- Catalogs
- Direct mail pieces
- Fabric or wallpaper prints
- Garment flats
- Hangtags
- Labels
- Logos
- Mood or theme boards
- Patterns for knitting or weaving
- Personal promotion sheets
- Planagrams
- Spec sheets
- Storyboards
- Style sheets
- Web pages
- Worksheets

Textile Designer Qualifications

The duties of a textile designer can vary from company to company. It is widely accepted that the most important responsibility of a textile designer is problem solving. The textile designer should have excellent research skills and a thorough grasp of textiles, fibers, and fabric. The textile designer should possess a keenly developed sense of trend intuition and imagination, not to mention being an accomplished designer who knows computer-aided designing and rendering!

You may be called upon to render fabric both digitally and manually. This includes knowing how to adapt your designs for productions other than print—specifically, dobby loom, jacquard loom, jacquard knits, and beyond.

Often companies will prefer that the designer has had graduate-level courses on any or all of these subject areas. However, the good news is that a designer who is armed with a competent knowledge of CAD software can frequently bypass many of the requirement barriers to entry for this type of job.

As you have seen from the list of duties, which often require producing graphs and marketing support materials, the designer who has mastered Adobe Illustrator and Photoshop can go a long way in establishing a satisfying career.

Where Do I Begin My Job Search?

Naturally, the question you may be asking yourself is where do I begin to look for this type of opportunity?

Looking for the right job, in the right location, and at the right salary may seem a lot like mining for gold. You may start to wonder if you are ever going to find anything! However, a little persistence and patience really pays off when you begin to look in the right location!

So, where do you begin your search for the right job? Perhaps the most obvious place to begin to find the "perfect job" may be found in the more traditional locations. We have included a brief list of ideas of where you may want to search or mine for that job.

1. Determine if your college has an employment assistance department and then become their best friend! Visit them or that job posting bulletin board often!

2. Check out your local newspapers. Most larger cities have on-line versions of the want ads job list. Many will even have on-line career advice links. For example, in the greater metropolitan South Florida area, one terrific site includes a section entitled Career-Builder.com

3. Go to the local or college libraries and check out the trade publication want ads. For example, anyone searching in New York should go to the website WWD.

4. Become a member of related trade organizations. Frequently, a benefit is their membership roster of who's who names and addresses. For example, there are often recruitment services available through trade membership affiliations. We suggest you check out www.texi.org as well as the Register of Apparel and Textile Designers for great leads. (Be advised that many times membership or other fees may apply.)

5. Visit the corporate websites of the major companies to determine if they have employment links or insight for employment opportunities—for example, visit Wal-Mart or perhaps a visit to a designer, brand, or other manufacturing firm's website.

6. Lastly, there are a several great websites that cater specifically to a given design trade. We have included several that we recommend for graphic design and fashion-related sites.
   a. www.Jobsinfashion.com
   b. www.Fashionjobs.com
   c. www.TotalNY.com
   d. www.Careersinfashion.com
   e. www.WGSN-edu.com (gated site and requires membership)
   f. www.Adobe.com
   g. www.MacWorld.com
   h. www.TechExchange.com
   i. www.Citda.org (gated site and requires membership)
   j. www.Portfolio.com
   k. www.ApparelSearch.com
   l. www.WWD.com
   m. www.Fashion-career.com
   n. www.Careerbuilder.com
   o. www.careermosaic.com
   p. www.careerpath.com
   q. www.latpro.com (Hispanic Professional site—English-Spanish-Portuguese)
   r. www.Fashionpersonnel.com (UK)
   s. www.e-fashionsource.com
   t. www.careerthreads.com

It should go without saying that you begin by defining and refining your specific talents to match the job titles and descriptions you find within the want ads in your geographical location of choice. It is most important to keep a realistic expectation of your talents, the job pool, and the salary range for the job.

One final comment on finding the "ideal job"—there isn't a perfect job out there. There are ideal matches with talent and need. However, what it takes to succeed is a healthy, realistic attitude and work ethic that comes from within you. You can make the job fit perfectly when you choose to control these factors and let go of the ones you can't.

Finding a job, career, or destiny is a journey, not a destination. So relax, even a wrong choice can result in gleaning new insight that can be applied at your next job! Often you will discover that it is your second, third, or even fourth job that will be the one suited to who you are and to your designing style.

Don't forget to investigate the cost of living comparison if you plan on relocating to another city. Often the pay may seem too good to be true. Ask someone who wants to "live" and "work" in New York City; what may be a fantastic pay level for one city may be less than adequate in another. So when you surf online for the job, we suggest that you also research exactly what it will cost you to relocate!

The Interview and Beyond

What's next? Obviously it is deciding what should go into your portfolio and determining what information should be on your resume.

Many colleges offer classes in portfolio presentation for fashion designers that can help in the process of assembling and presenting your work. If your college does not, we recommend that you go on-line and garner some information about what others include in their portfolios. Ideally, it helps to keep in mind the following:

Before deciding which pieces to include and which ones to leave out, ask yourself a few questions:

1. What do I think this company would like?

2. Do I demonstrate that I understand their target market's needs? As well as the company signature look?

3. How do I feel about my portfolio in its present state?

4. Does it show variety and emphasize my strengths?

5. Can I speak confidently about what I've chosen to include as well as answer any questions or concerns that may be addressed within the interview?

6. Have I used discretion about content that may be considered objectionable or offensive to anyone?

Once you've decided what work needs to be done, get your portfolio ready for an interview. You will need to start taking out pieces and organizing the remainder in a way that displays your strengths. Don't worry about perfection—go for excellence. You shouldn't include every piece you have ever made—sometimes, more is just more. So look for strong themed pieces that showcase your strengths.

Most professional interviewers look at portfolios all the time and can determine the quality of your work from a few pieces. Try to start off with your strongest piece and develop an order based on a theme.

Interview Preparation

Part 1: Before the Interview

1. Research the company.

2. Do your homework. Know where the product is sold, what it looks like, what the advertising looks like, who the competition is. Find one thing you want to know about them. Ask the question at the interview. Be interested.

3. Don't interview at companies you aren't interested in. They will know.

4. Know why you want the job.

5. Know why you could make a difference and be prepared to explain. You'll be asked.

6. Be yourself! Let your personality come through.

The Basics

Companies will expect you to know something about them before you arrive. Taking time to research the company's website or reading a few current articles on them shows you're genuinely interested. Gaining some background information on the company will also help you decide if the company is right for you.

1. Always—always be on time! Interviewers hate nothing more than when an applicant is late and they have a full schedule of applicants to come. Leave early for the interview and check the location and best route beforehand.

2. This may seem obvious, but avoid chewing gum, eating, or smoking during the interview!

3. Dress accordingly. Look professional—take yourself seriously, so that your interviewer will too!

4. Be courteous to everyone you meet, including the receptionist and other applicants. You never know who might be asked what their first impression of you was and whether they think you would be right for the company. Receptionists and administrative assistants are gatekeepers, and often the boss will trust their instincts, so be sure you make a lasting impression on them for the good!

5. Take notice of your surroundings to get a feel for the place. Is it someplace you will want to invest your time? Remember, we often spend more hours on the job than with loved ones!

6. If the opportunity arises, always ask questions at the end of the interview. This is a simple means of confirming your enthusiasm and desire to work for the company. Plan which questions you would like to ask in advance. Even practice the interview "before" your interview—attempt to anticipate any questions they may ask you.

   In addition, be familiar with the kinds of work the company does and, if possible, attempt to discover which kinds of computers and software you will be working on. Once you pass the initial interview, you will be expected to sit down at the computer and "make something" in order to show your reaction to pressure as well as your time management and workflow strategies. (Yes, better go back and review Chapter 4 again!)

Part 2: After the Interview

Possibly the easiest thing you should consider doing after the interview is always, always follow up with the person or the company after the interview. One simple way to do that is the common courtesy of sending a thank-you note. Trust us when we tell you that this can go a long way in distinguishing you from the next applicant!

Finally, write down the interview questions where you did not perform well, and try to answer them again in case you do not get the job. You will not want to make the same mistake on the next interview. The more you can practice and refine your answers, the stronger your performance will be in future interviews.

Learn from Mistakes

Don't be shy; grasp every opportunity to improve your overall offering to potential employers. If you feel that an interview has gone badly because of your portfolio, ask the interviewer how they feel you could improve it. Many times the interviewers will be sympathetic and will be very willing to offer you advice. Don't be upset if it comes in the form of constructive criticism. There is an ancient proverb that states, "Wounds from a friend are better than kisses from an enemy!" So if they help you to do better the next time around, they have truly proved to be your friend! And who knows, your openness and obvious eagerness to learn from a bad situation may make them look at you in a new light as being humble and teachable.

Both of us will agree regardless if it is in a classroom or in an interviewing situation, we would grade higher or hire the person who is dependable and teachable over those with talent and arrogance of equal stature!

There are several secrets to helping stack the deck in your favor when it comes to putting together a good portfolio. We have gathered a few insights from several industry experts on what they are looking for both in the portfolio and in an applicant.

Portfolio Secrets and Contents

Most people looking at your portfolio will want to know your expertise in each of these areas:

- Concepts
- Merchandising
- Illustration—sketching digitally and by hand
- Research
- Use of colors/colorways
- Product development
- Construction of original fashion items
- Understanding of current fashion trends
- Styling and presentation—showcasing graphic design skills

Always attempt to put together a brief presentation specifically geared to the company you are interviewing with.

Top Ten Employers' Needs

1. Communication skills
2. Time management—dependability!
3. Interpersonal skills
4. Initiative
5. Self-starter
6. Problem-solving abilities
7. Good work ethic—honesty and integrity
8. Flexibility
9. Leadership skills
10. Technical skills

Have you noticed that YOU can have a lot of control over what goes into your portfolio? You can really flex your control in the personal attributes you will need to possess and exhibit in order to succeed.

The Hottest Trend in Presentations—Digital Portfolios!

The following information comes from an article written by the author, Kathleen Colussy, for WGSN-EDU (Worth Global Style Network—London).

Offering your portfolio in a digital format can score you vital points in the global hunt for your first job, and needn't take as much tech-savvy as you might think.

Not too long ago the traditional designer's portfolio was comprised of a series of carefully selected examples of storyboards, work sketches, and the like. It showcased a student's artistic talents—skills and inspiration carefully mounted and neatly bound in a briefcase or portfolio case.

But just how does one begin to transform a traditional portfolio into a digital one? Let me begin by explaining why you should consider making your portfolio digital. I have found you cannot assume that where a student studies fashion is necessarily the city where they get hired to create fashion. My students come from over 63 countries around the world. Naturally this led me to explore other options for preparing portfolio presentations that would transcend the traditional geographical challenges associated with my students' job searches.

It soon became obvious to me that anyone could easily convert a traditional portfolio into a digital portfolio.

All it took to start was a little computer savvy, the use of a scanner, and a variety of off-the-shelf software from such companies as Adobe or Corel and a student could be up and running in no time.

My advice to anyone who wants to convert their traditional portfolio into a digital one is to begin by starting at their computer comfort or skill level. Do not attempt to jump into a full-scale multimedia presentation when all you know how to do is type on a word processor!

Begin as you would any portfolio—start by assembling the pieces you want to include. Select pieces that will showcase your skills and your strengths, and always gear the presentation to the company you want to work for.

This means going to the library or getting on-line. Do your homework—research the company, know their product line, know their consumer. How can you say you want to work for someone you know nothing about? Besides, all the razzle-dazzle of a digital portfolio will not substitute having strong design skills and common-sense consumer marketing know-how. Remember if the designs you create do not sell, nobody wins.

Next, several other considerations for your digital portfolio include who will be ultimately viewing the portfolio and how they will be viewing it. Begin to ask some simple questions, such as who will see my digital portfolio—the marketing department, the design department, or management?

Next, find out what is the best way for them to open your files. Believe it or not, sometimes different departments use different computer platforms and programs within the same company. It is not uncommon for the business side of a company to work on a PC or Windows environment, while the graphic side of a company may be using a Mac.

Translation: What this means to you is that you will need to create and save your files in universal file formats so they can easily be opened and read on any computer platform and program by any department.

The best way to prepare and save your work digitally is to begin by saving digitally created drawings (also known as vector artwork) in an .EPS file format. Then save any painting or image editing (also known as raster) as a JPEG or as a TIFF file.

When it comes to packaging and presentation formats, students have several from which to choose. Some of the more popular software used today may include multimedia capabilities, such as Microsoft PowerPoint and Macromedia's Flash as well as Director. Even Adobe Photoshop 7 has several presentation capabilities that can be utilized to create a digital portfolio. The goal, however, is to make a portfolio that is compatible for most companies' computers. The Human Resource department in the company you are applying to are the primary "gatekeepers." It is vital that they can open your disk and view your work without a lot of problems or glitches. CDs that you generate should be self-running or have accompanying instructions that are simple to follow in order to open and view your work. Otherwise, all of your efforts to look techno-savvy have been in vain.

You should select the software program you are most comfortable using. You do not always have to use the most complex software to accomplish the task. For example, Microsoft PowerPoint has numerous multimedia capabilities—all in template format, which will more than suffice.

Remember to always include in your portfolio examples of scanned original artwork, original artwork that has been digitally enhanced, and examples of digitally created artwork.

Next, you must decide on presentation or what will be the best layout style for your work. Do you want it to look like a traditional portfolio, like a catalog, or like a website simulation? From there you should consider having the files burned onto a CD for distribution or to be sent out for mailing.

Although digital portfolios may never take the place of the traditional portfolio, this format really gives students a competitive edge in the marketplace.

Figure 11–77 showcases the diversity of student design inspiration and interpretation.

Visual Instructions for CD Booklet Layout

As you can see in Figure 11–78, we have shown you several methods to create a CD booklet layout in either Adobe Illustrator or in Adobe Photoshop. Once you have laid out the perfect scenario for your images, you can then place your images directly into the template and voilà!—you have a booklet for your CD!

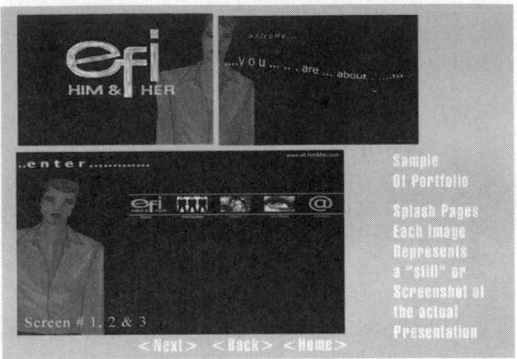

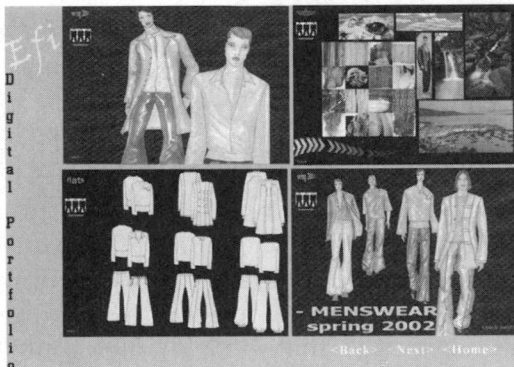

FIGURE 11–77
Diversity of student design information

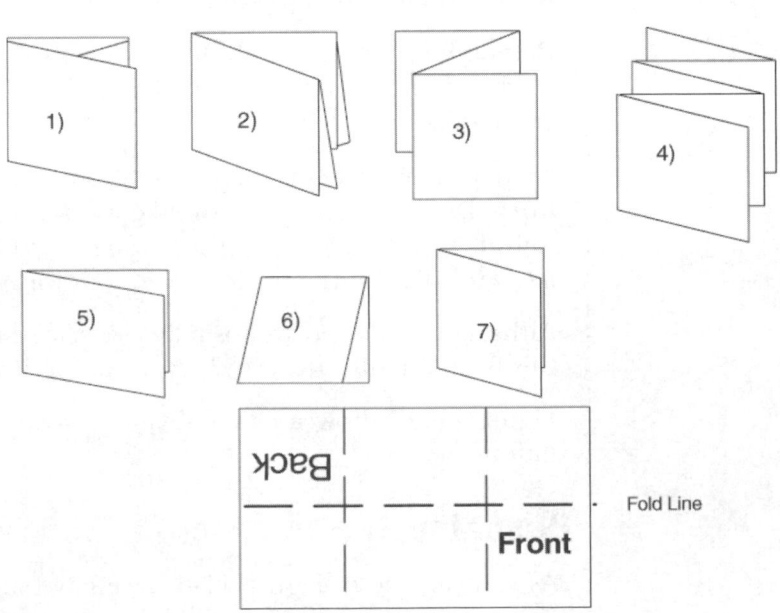

FIGURE 11–78
How to lay out booklet

Meet Fashion Design Student: Judith Kruger

In Figures 11–79 to 11–83, you can see the progression of how your booklet might look. These are examples from a young German fashion design student named Judith Kruger. Judith came to Ft. Lauderdale in the summer of 2002 as an exchange student from Trier, Germany, University of Applied Sciences. She came to study the secrets of digitally rendering fabric and prints in author Kathleen Colussy's classes at the Art Institute of Ft. Lauderdale. Kathleen was so impressed with Judith's work that she sent Judith on a Fall internship to work with co-author Steve Greenberg at the Pointcarré USA headquarters in New York City.

Currently, Judith is now back in Germany completing her degree in fashion design. We know she is one talented newcomer you will want to watch for!

Stock Images

Background Ideas Worth Looking Into

You may have noticed that behind the scenes in most of the examples of mood boards and storyboards is a subtle but effective tool that will truly enhance your presentations—actual photographic images.

These images can be obtained from a variety of sources, including leading stock image supply companies. Just type in the query for "stock images" in any search

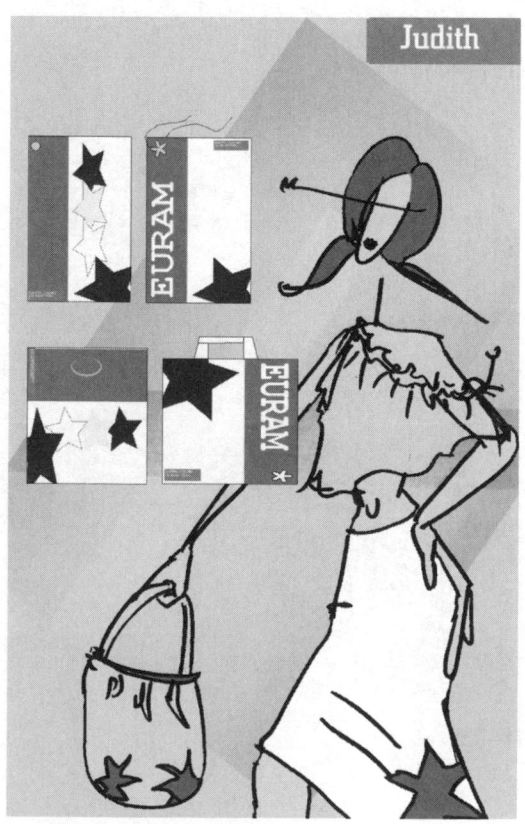

FIGURE 11–79
Samples of bags and tags

FIGURE 11–80
Example of tri-fold book layout

FIGURE 11–81
Examples of fabric booklet layouts

FIGURE 11–82
CD cover

Notes...

FIGURE 11–83
Actual CD

FIGURE 11–84
Stock images

engine—the list can be staggering. There are several that we have found to be of benefit to designers, which we would like to mention: www.Comstock.com and www.Eyewire.com. Both of these companies offer the kinds of images that are either sold individually or bundled in packages for you to use in your presentations. These images and the rights to use them in your presentation legally can enhance your presentations.

Free

If you are a student working on a limited budget, you may opt for a more cost-effective way to use professional images for backgrounds in your work. We truly understand how limited a student's budget can be so we have included several images that are copyright-AND royalty-free on the CD that accompanies this text. Simply go to the folder on the CD entitled **Goodies > IMAGES** and take the images for use on your boards. (See Figure 11–84.)

Great Image Types

As a designer it will be helpful to have several of the following images to use for backgrounds:

Water, ocean

City scenes

Country vistas, including seasonal images

Travel, landmarks

Flora and fauna

Animals and insects

Business-related objects or environments

Technology-related graphics

Dining—food, wine, markets

Nondescript backgrounds

Texture

People—various ages, gender, and ethnicity

You may also want to consider taking your own photos to use. As individuals who find themselves on the road for a considerable amount of time, we find it is helpful to always have a camera with us, loaded and ready to shoot!

Heart and "Stoll" Inspirations for Promoting Fashion

Our final example of mood boards, storyboards, and marketing boards comes courtesy of H. Stoll. If you recall, you were introduced to this terrific company in Chapter 2. There you learned about the concept of differentiating knits for rendering. These are actual photos used in Stoll's successful marketing campaigns. The company has graciously agreed to let us share them with you. In each of the photos you can clearly see how the images from nature inspired the knitted patterns used in the garments that were created. (See Figure 11–85.)

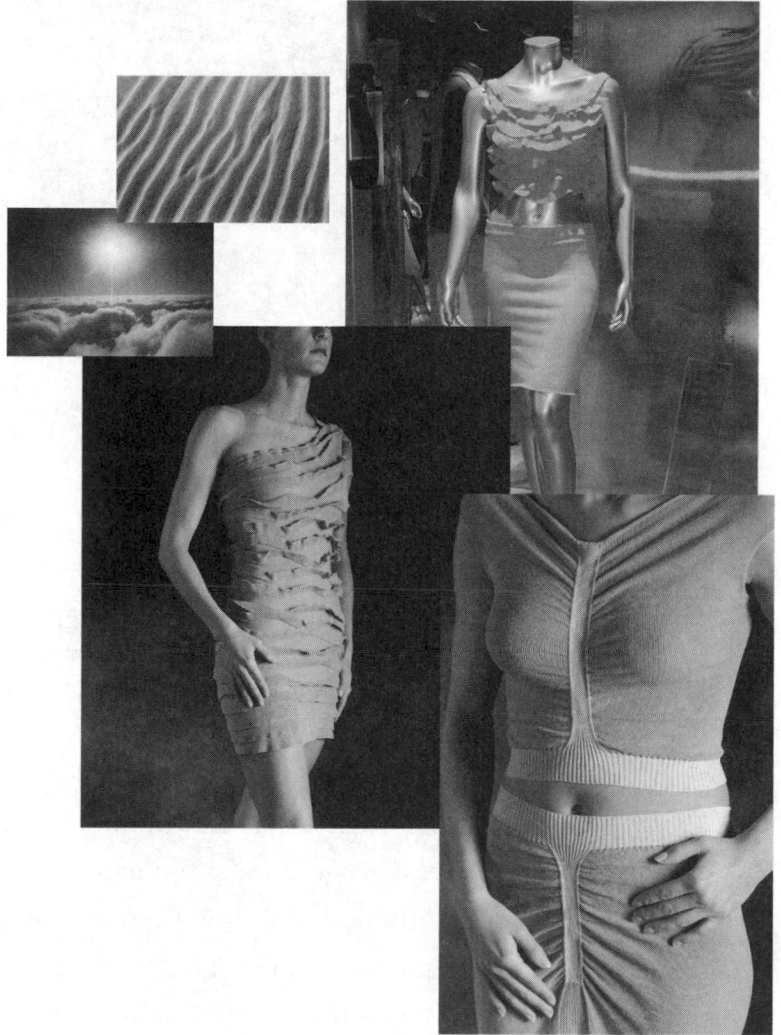

FIGURE 11–85
H. Stoll board
(Courtesy of Stoll Knitting Machines)

12 Taking It to the Next Level: Photoshop and Beyond

Terms to look for:

80/20 Rule	Demonstration	Plug-ins	Sourcing
CAD Designer	Design Process	Point Person	Techexchange.com
CAD Operator	Fabricad.com	Proprietary	Training
CAD Services	Off-the-Shelf	Ramp-Up Time	

Well by now, it seems that everyone agrees that Adobe Photoshop is the panacea for almost every challenge the digital designer faces today, but is there life beyond Photoshop? And if so, what do I need to know to get there? This and other topics such as:

- Evaluating Advanced Textile Design Software
- Sourcing Savvy—Trade Shows and Suppliers
- Design and Printer Testimonials
- Software and Printer Comparison Charts
- Traditional and Digital Printing Methods Reference Chart
- Service Bureau Alternatives
- What's Next?

will be addressed in this chapter.

The Great Divide—Photoshop—Plug-ins or Proprietary?

Plug-ins—What are They?

Plug-ins are software additions that are accessed in conjunction with another piece of hardware, such as a scanner or printer, or work with other software such as Adobe Photoshop. They are typically reasonably priced, but can only do a certain part of the design process. They can at times be an easy and affordable solution to create a special effect or detail for a design.

Once the plug-in software is loaded onto the computer, it is generally accessed through the **File > Import** menu of a software. However, in some cases, it may be accessed through the Filter menu in Adobe Photoshop. (See Figures 12–1 and 12–2.)

- Plug-ins generally work on the whole image.
- Plug-ins add specific features not in the original program.
- Plug-ins are industry specific.

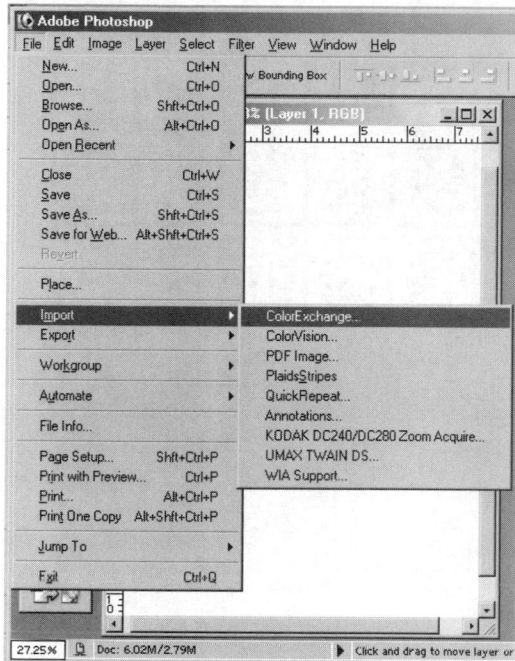

FIGURE 12–1

File > Import > Select plug-in such as Color Exchange

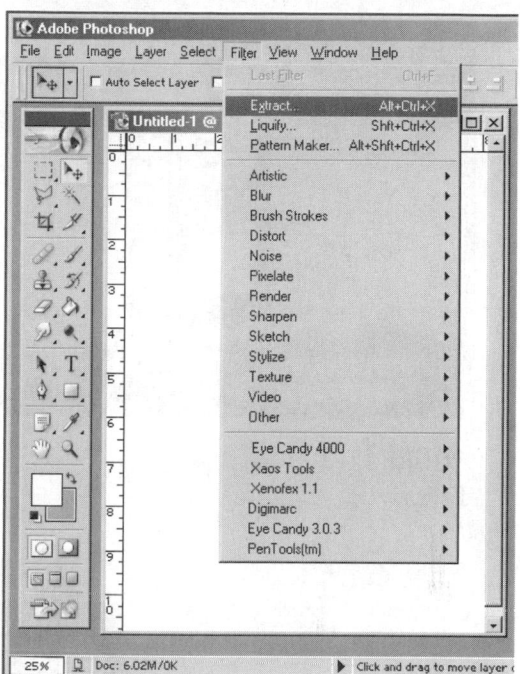

FIGURE 12–2

Using the Filter menu to access other Filter plug-ins > such as Eye Candy or Xaos tools

Notes . . .

Here is a short list of some plug-ins found to be useful for digital textiles and designing:

- AGE Technologies
  - **Plaid Maker**—Allows the user to develop basic plaids and stripes within Photoshop
  - **Repeat Maker**—Allows the user to design basic repeats within Photoshop
  - **Colorway Maker**—Allows the user to design basic colorways after reducing colors within Photoshop

- **Aridi's**   This is a popular collection of historically influenced decorative elements that have been hand-drawn in Celtic, Arabesque, Victorian, and Art Nouveau styles. The 18-volume library comes on a dual format CD-ROM. Mac images are available as EPS, Freehand, or 72 dpi PICT files; PC images are in .EPS, .BMP, and other popular formats. Most images are available in full-process color and black and white.

- **Eye Candy**   This is a set of 20 timesaving special effects that will enhance any film, video, animation, or multimedia project for Adobe Photoshop. Sophisticated texture, production, and distortion effects have never been easier—you'll be creating dazzling organic effects in a fraction of the time it used to require. Eye Candy automatically adapts to irregular floating objects, modifies layer opacity information, and allows users to draw outside layer boundaries without precomposing. Users can also apply effects based on transparency information from other layers. (See Figures 12–3 and 12–4.)

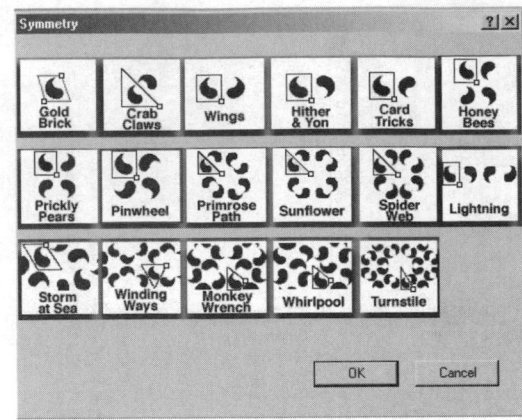

FIGURE 12–3
Terrazzo

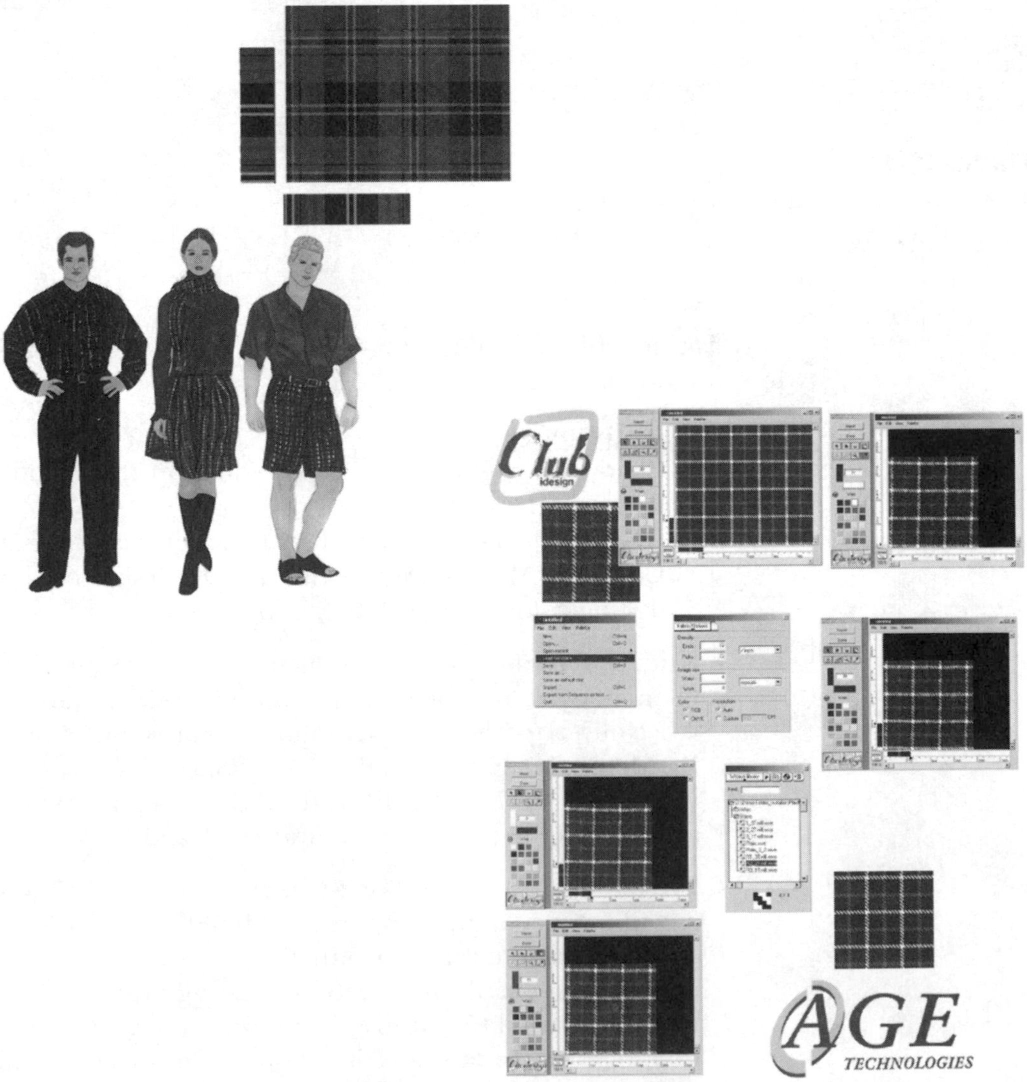

FIGURE 12–4
Using plug-ins by AGE Technologies including rendering plaids
(Courtesy of AGE Technologies)

Human Software Company—The Design Collection

The Design Collection contains:

- Textissimo v3—with more than 750 superb effects

- Squizz v3—professional distortion tools

- Ottopaths v1—warp and flow text in Photoshop

Very easy to use, more powerful than ever, Textissimo 3.0 filter plug-in for Adobe Photoshop/Corel PhotoPaint brings into your toolbox more than 700 prebuilt beautiful special effects! Distressed, fire, ice, smoke, shadows, chrome, lava—name one, you have it; just tap into the Library.

Squizz! filter plug-in for Adobe Photoshop/Corel PhotoPaint is the second generation of Human Software professional distortion tools within Photoshop and has more controls than ever. On top of the famous Squizz! distortion brush with jitter/pinch brush, displacement maps create any kind of geometrical meshes and warp your images!

Don't leave Photoshop to create text and objects, flow text along a curve, put a photo inside a rectangle, add a border or import, and manipulate artwork without leaving Photoshop. Ottopaths brings all the vector tools you need to quickly build gorgeous designs, blending artwork and images right inside Photoshop.

Warped headlines are now just one click away! Ottopaths is a selection plug-in available within Photoshop v4.0 or more.

- **KnockOut 2**   This product is owned by the Corel Corp. and lets you preserve fine image details that were once impossible to mask precisely. It's an ideal plug-in for Adobe Photoshop, speeding up the design process and helping you capture complex imagery such as hair, smoke, shadows, glass, liquid, and ice.

- **Digital Frontiers**   This product offers groundbreaking technology that reduces 24-bit images to 8 bits or less with no loss in quality.

- **JPEG Cruncher**   Take your enormous JPEG files and make them ready for the Web with 256 colors or less. Reach the perfect balance of size and quality using immediate reduction previews.

- **TypeStyler** is a powerhouse of spectacular special effects, yet it retains the friendly ease of use that made the original TypeStyler so popular. TypeStyler is the graphic designer's backroom secret weapon. Create dazzling Web graphics, headlines, ads, signs, posters, videos, titles, and more in minutes, instead of hours! TypeStyler is a complete stand-alone design, layout, and effects program, yet it also works seamlessly with Photoshop.

- **Deep Paint**   This product from Right Hemisphere brings rich artistic paint tools to Adobe Photoshop users. As a plug-in, Deep Paint maintains complete interface compatibility with Photoshop so that it is easy to master. Converting photos to almost any artistic style—from pastel sketches to realistic oil renditions—is practically effortless with a comprehensive set of tools such as wood, leather, stone, marbles, and more. Just plug them in and paint.

- A two-dimensional paint system offers dynamic three-dimensional lighting and texture control
- Convert photos and illustrations to any medium; thickly textured oils, bold acrylics, delicate watercolors, pearlescent pastels, and more
- Mix paint to any consistency
- Use an almost infinite variety of brush and paint combinations and presets, including a stunningly realistic airbrush tool
- Also functions as a stand-alone application
- Import detailed three-dimensional models, move them into any position, create lighting effects, control your camera view, and choose from a number of rendering effects–without leaving Adobe Photoshop or Adobe Illustrator.

- **XAOS Tools**   This product creates dazzling painterly effects, including Cubist, Oil Canvas, and custom styles, with a fast, flexible, and powerful special effects engine.

- **Kais Power Tools**   Another wonderful plug-in that offers interesting and unusual alternatives for the designer.

Stage 1: Converting to Digital Designing and Going beyond Photoshop with Proprietary Software

You Know You Need It

Design, recolor, edit, edit again. These are the repetitive processes that design software allows us to accomplish quickly and easily. Increased demand for CAD art as well as the need for quick turnaround in art and sampling has created a new area of design, the *CAD operator* or *CAD designer*. Today, these designers are armed with fantastic software tools that allow them to meet all these demands with smaller staff and hopefully less overtime. Finding the right tools for all their needs is the key.

When looking at the market, from off-the-shelf to proprietary, there are many software packages that allow a designer to do these tasks; however, there needs to be a focus on exactly what the design software will be used for. Off-the-shelf refers to design software like Adobe Photoshop or Illustrator. Proprietary refers to design software designed for a specific industry, like Pointcarré, Ned-Artworks, or U4ia. These proprietary design programs are written for the development of textile and apparel design. There will be a cost factor as well. Off-the-shelf is lower in initial cost than proprietary, but a designer may spend more time using off-the-shelf in the design stage than with proprietary. (See Figure 12–5.)

Spotlight—Pointcarré

Pointcarré has been developing proprietary apparel and textile design software for almost 15 years. With a diverse product line that is both Macintosh and PC based, they have always provided their clients with excellent service, training, and software support. Their New York office, Pointcarré USA, supports diverse clients such as Nautica, Tommy Hilfiger, Polo Ralph Lauren, Eddie Bauer, The Metropolitan Museum of Art, Town & Country Living, and Kmart.

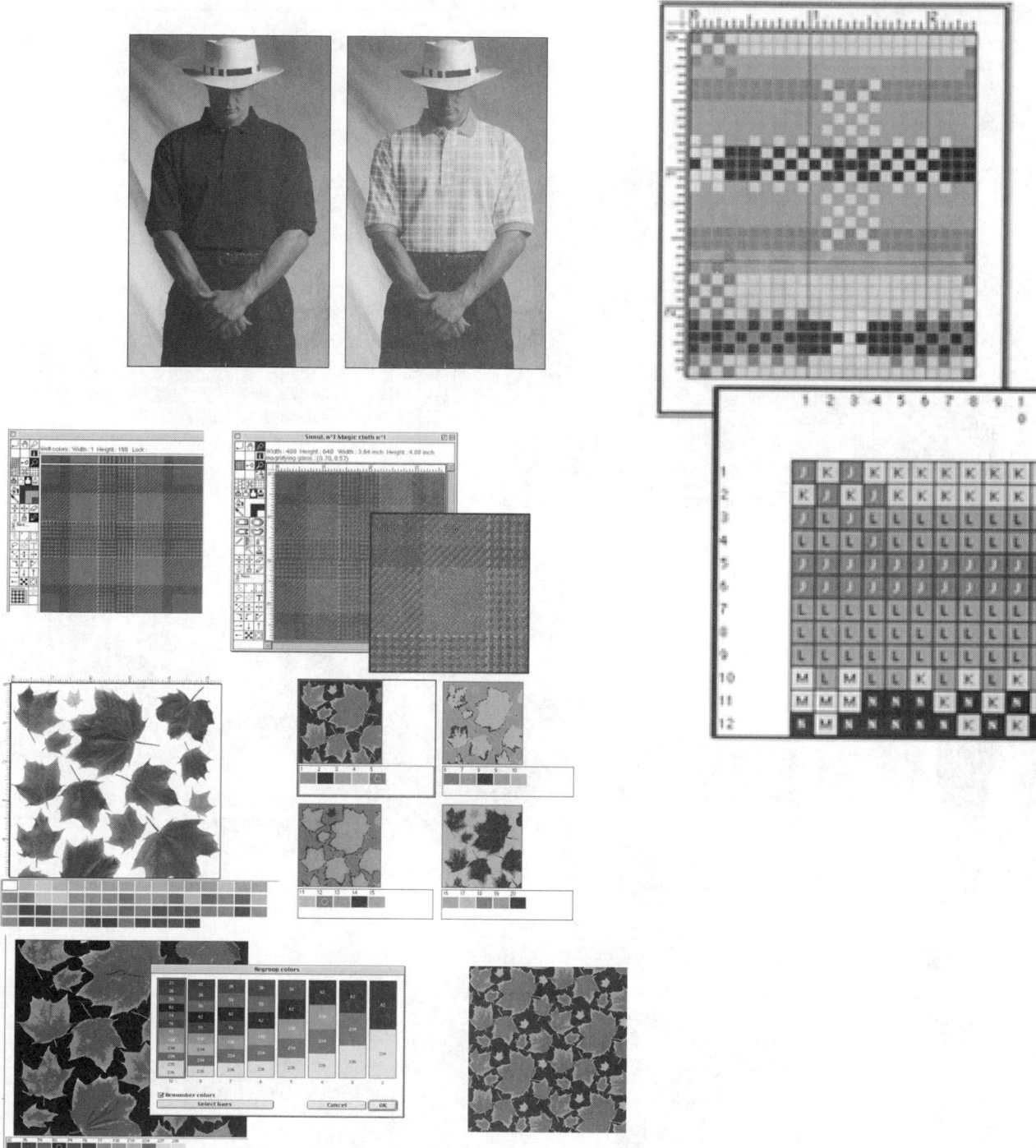

FIGURE 12–5
Collage Pointcarré
(Courtesy of Pointcarré)

Notes...

Pointcarré provides powerful, customizable, and user-friendly technology that designers find easy to use. That is what their solutions are about. Pointcarré USA provides CAD solutions at all levels for surface design. From woven and knits to textile prints, photo-realistic texture mapping and embroidery, they are well known for the amazing quality of the fabric simulations produced by their software.

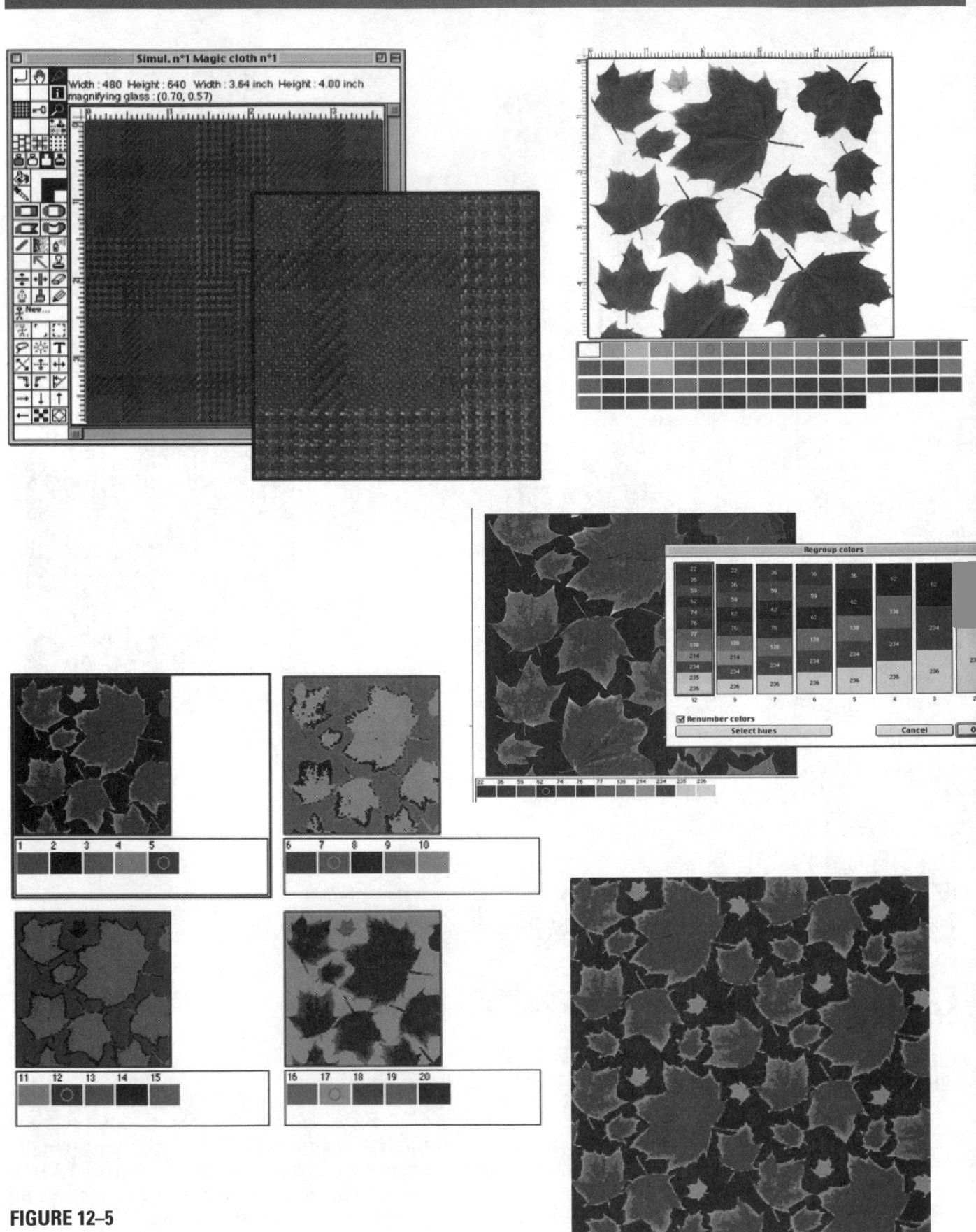

FIGURE 12–5

Continued

Fabric or surface design, merchandising, storyboards, and texture mapping are all different abilities and outcomes of any design project. Cost savings and turnaround time are also important to the company. The designer who will be using the software must evaluate the tasks they will be using the software for and then research all possible program options, to be sure it will fit their needs. Many designers will also find that there may not only be one software program that "does it all." They most likely will need to use a variety of two or three software packages to accomplish all their design needs. In this chapter we hope to give designers an easy-to-follow guide in the right direction, to find the design software best suited for their needs.

Pointcarré USA is also always committed to educating the fashion and textile designers of today and tomorrow. Colleges that use their software include North Carolina State University, Fashion Institute of Technology, Parsons School of Design, Philadelphia University, and Rhode Island School of Design.

There are other industry alternatives for rendering motifs and images beyond knits and wovens and prints.

Spotlight: SofTeam U.S.A. Punto Embroidery

SofTeam U.S.A. is a Baltimore-based company devoted to providing the best embroidery, sign-making, and engraving software available for the Macintosh and Windows platforms. One of their best products is Punto Designer for Macintosh and Windows. If you recall, you were briefly introduced to this product in Chapter 9 for other applications of single and repeat motifs.

Punto makes it easy to create wonderful embroideries directly on your computer. With powerful graphics tools you can follow your idea from the sketch to the finished design, all on your personal computer. Punto's capabilities include lifelike three-dimensional renderings and a catalogue feature. Punto allows you to prepare a database of your embroideries and to create lifelike images with fabric background that can be printed on any color printer. It also allows you to create lifelike images of embroidery designs with appliqué.

With Punto you can import a template with a scanner or any embroidery file format. You can also import paper-tape format embroidery design information with a paper-tape reader connected to the computer. Once you have produced your embroidery design, you can export it in an embroidery machine format, you can load it directly to the embroidery machine, or you can write it to a paper tape. (See Figure 12–6.)

Important Factors to Consider When It Is Time to Go beyond Photoshop

Let's face it, it seems unlikely you will ever NOT need Adobe Photoshop. However, in the world of design, production, and manufacturing, there are logical next steps you will need to know about as well as how to determine when it is time to make the transition. In the following section we have briefly included the answers to many of the questions and challenges you may be faced with.

Design Time

The typical design process is well known. Designers and merchandisers shop the market for trends and color. Seasonal palette and fabric development follow, with style development in close pursuit. Once lines are together, it continues with approvals, edits, more approvals, merchandising boards, samples, then strike-offs,

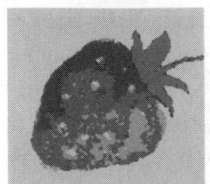

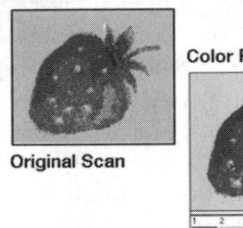

Original Scan

Color Reduced

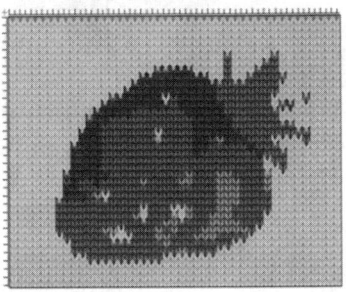

FIGURE 12–6
Punto

and final presentation. Throughout this development time, the design team is fully involved.

Now let's look closer to see where design software can help the designer accomplish these tasks so that designing, coloring, and styling times can be easily reduced. Creating and editing art on the computer easily saves time and money. When art is traditionally sent out to be developed or hand-painted, there are not only costs involved but there also needs to be time to get the art returned, and hopefully approved, without it needing to be edited again.

It is the same for sampling. When a design can be rendered or texture mapped as real fabric on a real photograph, the need for sampling decreases. Buyers and merchandisers have become more accepting, even demanding, of approvals on CADs. They know that colors and styles can be quickly edited or adapted to what they would like produced, and that the realistic value of a CAD can closely match the final product.

Cost Analysis

Design time is hard to define in terms of dollars, but a good cost-benefit analysis can help convince management of the need for design software. Expenses for outside painting and repeats are easy to track. Sending out for color copies, presentation board materials, and other expenses all add up. There will always be the expense of the designers, but the design expenses of the artwork and time can be controlled with the right software decision.

Know What Talents Are Needed

Buying software can be like hiring a new designer. Look at the product and check its qualifications. Can it do color editing easily? How about repeats? If so, how quickly or easily? If time and costs are factors, then a designer can focus on these attributes of software. If there is a need for simulation of fabrics, then this is the focus. Many times CAD is simply used as a means of quickly visualizing colorways and designs. The original art is then sent to the mills with directions on color and placement. Also there is the industrial software that allows a designer to not only create the basic image but to develop the information for mills to run separations on prints and to run looms for weaving and machinery for knitting. The important thing to keep in mind is that once a designer starts using software to develop, their creativity and abilities will increase due to the ease in which they can now visualize anything they need.

Involve the Designers

It amazes me how many times the MIS Director and the CFO decide what software the design team needs. Thousands of dollars become wasted on software. Then there is a team of designers being given software that may or may not meet their needs. "But it networks well with the rest of the company," they are told. This is a disaster in the making.

The importance of today's design team is very underestimated in many companies. In the past many designers were in the back room and were told what they needed to sketch by merchandisers and buyers. Today's designers are much more educated and knowledgeable about the design process. They are very involved in this process and are the ones to consult when decisions need to be made about what should be used to design.

Designate a Point Person

The best possible solution would be to pick a staff designer and ask that individual to be the point person on this endeavor. This point person for the project can go out and retrieve all the information necessary to make a proper decision. This will ensure accurate information as well as the integration of true design process knowledge. The point person should also know the company executive who will make the final decision, so any pertinent information can be passed to this person in a timely manner. Budget concerns should also be made known.

A follow-up process should be determined, as well as a time line by which the system needs to be purchased. This allows the point person adequate time to access all the resources and meet with the other designers to decide which software they will recommend to the decision maker. This will result in the best use of everyone's time as well as ensure that the software purchased truly meets the designers' and company's needs.

Where to Start

The best place to start looking for software information is on the Web. The Web has definitely become the best way of searching out any information. Websites, such as http://www.techexchange.com and http://www.fabricad.com, are excellent sites dedicated to textile CAD. Trade shows are next—from MacWorld or PC Expo to trade-specific shows like the CAD Expo or the IFFE(International Fabric Fashion Expo) show. These are all excellent routes to finding the software that fits the designers' needs. Publications like Bobbin Magazine, Apparel Industry Magazine, WWD, or DNR all run CAD sections a few times a year. These are great research tools.

Friends, family, and other designers are the next-best resource. If they have used a software, they are more inclined to give you a real working experience of a software and its abilities. Also, they may have only used a particular part of a software, so take all facts into consideration. There is an *80/20 rule* of software—80 percent of designers only use about 20 percent of any particular software. Even after years of using software, designers are sometimes using just enough of a particular software to do their job, but they never explore deeper into the software to see what else it can do.

Getting a "Real-World" Demonstration

One of the most important aspects of choosing a design software is seeing it in action, which would be a demonstration of the software. After narrowing down to a few selections, call each CAD company and set up a demo, either at their office or at your office. A software company should be accommodating to you, especially if everyone cannot be out of the office for a few hours. Have them come to you. This is a chance for everyone to see the software and ask questions they may have regarding how it will affect their design department, as well as higher managers to see what they will be getting for their money. A plus side is if the managers see the designers getting excited about how much the software will help them, then the managers will be more eager to purchase the software.

If there is no in-person demo available, then ask to be sent a demo CD. This demo CD can be a variety of things. Some are a quick-time movie of the product in action or a limited-use version of the software. It may even be a full working version of the program that has disabled the "Save" option or a "timed-out" version. Whichever it is, look it over and see if it will meet the design needs of the team.

One of the best ways to determine a software's ability is to use your own product as a "test." Bring your art and sketches to the demo. This way you can witness the process that you will need to go through, if you have that program. Watch for the complexity of the software, the number of steps it takes to do a task, and even the time involved. For the best knowledge gained, do not bring the toughest project you can think of, but bring something that is truly representative of the work you do every day, such as creating repeats, creating a weave or knit, or placing designs into minibodies. Have the person doing the demo of the software scan in your art and work with it. Have a firm goal in mind and make it known, so the demo person can achieve the results you want.

Have the demo person get you printouts at the end of the project so you can use these to compare not only printer output but, more importantly, software results. Printer quality is dependent on the printer, not the software, so be sure you are not misguided by that. Any software should be able to print well to any printer.

Training Time

Training time is an important consideration as well (Figure 12–7). How easy is the software to use? If training is needed, what is the general *ramp-up time* to be proficient enough to get the job done? Is advanced training available, when needed?

0

FIGURE 12–7
Time

What are the costs of training and are the trainers experts in their field? If the trainers are not knowledgeable with the design or apparel terms you are using, how are they going to help you in the future?

Also keep in mind that it takes about a week, after continuous usage, to be comfortable on any design software and up to 3 months to become truly proficient and realize an increase in personal productivity. This will be possible only if the designer is using the software. Whether off-the-shelf or proprietary, continuous use is the key.

To avoid distraction, the best possible training sessions are conducted out of the office—at a vendor site or a series of classes at a local college or training center. In-office sessions are often interrupted by phone calls, meetings the designers "need" to be in, etc. All detract from the learning process. A plus of any off-site session is that each designer can be on a separate computer. When going to these training sessions, always bring along real art that would be used in a day-to-day work session such as color palettes, fabric swatches, and photographs or flats if needed. This way the training can go through the entire design process from start to finish.

Do Not Be Foolish about Training or Support

Don't forget to budget for training when buying software. Whether you are buying off-the-shelf or proprietary software, designers need to know the basics and more if they are going to make the design and cost savings realistic. Many times I have seen or heard of designers who felt they could learn it "on their own," but those who are dedicated and knowledgeable enough to do that are few. If a company is willing to spend the money on software, correct training is the best way to ensure that the investment to cut costs and design time will continue as smoothly and quickly as possible.

Also keep those support numbers handy. When starting to use any new design software, there will be questions—about loading software or color palettes to scanning and drawing into the software. These topics all come up quickly in the beginning and those still unfamiliar with the process will need some hand-holding. Reference manuals and other software documentation only go so far.

Macintosh or PC?

At some point the decision will need to be made about what platform to use (Figure 12–8). There are software packages that run on Mac, some on PC, and a few that run on both. Deciding on the platform may take a meeting with the

FIGURE 12–8
Mac or PC?

designers as well as the MIS Director in the company to decide which is best. Some questions to be answered are:

- Will the design workstations be on the network?
- Will they be stand-alone?
- Do the designers prefer Mac or PC?
- Can the software run on both?
- Which employee will be doing the hardware support?
- Does the design software company offer software support?

Who's Who

Special Section on CAD Software and Printer Sourcing

It is always great to have the insider secrets to an endeavor, and shopping for software is no different. Sourcing of any kind is an integral part of the designer's job. *Sourcing* is a combination of research for the best suppliers and for the materials or resources needed. To help with the task we have put together a brief list of preliminary questions you will need to ask yourself before you begin your search.

Profile the specific leading companies who make and distribute printers, software, and other components of this digital printing revolution.

Questions to Ask/Discuss When Shopping for a CAD System

One of the first places you begin your search is by asking the right questions about your company's needs and budgetary requirements or restraints.

- What is your budget?

- What is your timeframe or goal to have the system installed and running? A system cannot be bought a week before a season begins. There is ramp-up time to consider.

- Which platform is the software for (Mac, PC, UNIX)?

- Who are the end users? We suggest that you involve them in the decision-making process to avoid any cognitive dissonance as well as passive resistance.

- What file format does the software save in? This will be important not just from an archiving standpoint, but from an accessing standpoint between departments. For example, the design department may prefer using Mac, while the marketing department uses PCs. If you are planning on sharing and transporting data between different software programs using different platforms in different physical locations, this information must be part of the consideration. Don't assume—research and ask.

- Are there many windows to go through? How do they facilitate ease of use?

- How long is the ramp-up time? This refers not only to the learning curve to learn new software, but to continue to maintain productivity on current projects while making the transition.

- Will there be training available? What are the options? What is the typical learning curve? Can you focus on complete training and is there custom training available?

- Where is the training held? Are there additional travel expenses that will need to be budgeted? How many people can be trained as part of the training package? Avoid training one person only, if they leave before you implement—you just paid for nothing! Also be sure you are sending "the right people" for the training. What is their computer learning curve track record? Will they be able to perform *and* also to train others in-house later when the company experiences growth as a result of upgrading its system?

- What are the hours of support? Consider time zone differences too!

- Do they have user group meetings? If so, how often?

- Is there a company website? Can it be used for support?

- Can you see a demo of the software using your own image?

- Always get references, and check them! This is an important investment—do your homework. Begin by soliciting insight and ideas from industry peers, go on-line, attend trade shows, and read trade publications. Don't forget the local educational community; how is the next generation of designers being trained? Interns or employees can be a valuable part of the resource pool for additional information.

Figure 12–9 provides a sample sourcing chart questionnaire and Figure 12–10 provides a software comparison chart to assist you in discovering what is the correct solution for you, your company, or your college.

Question:	Company Interviewed:	Contact Person:	Comments:

1. Costs involved
2. Platforms—PC/Mac/both
3. Training costs and availability
4. Support costs
5. Demo and trial versions
6. Specific needs addressed
7. List of satisfied clients:

1. Costs involved
2. Platforms—PC/Mac/both
3. Printers, RIP software, or other expenses
4. Training costs and availability
5. Support costs
6. Demo and trial versions
7. Specific needs addressed
8. List of satisfied clients:
9. Other insights gleaned:

1. Costs involved
2. Platforms—PC/Mac/both
3. Printers, RIP software, or other expenses
4. Training costs and availability
5. Support costs
6. Demo and trial versions
7. Specific needs addressed
8. List of satisfied clients:
9. Other insights gleaned:

1. Costs involved
2. Platforms—PC/Mac/both
3. Printers, RIP software, or other expenses
4. Training costs and availability
5. Support costs
6. Demo and trial versions
7. Specific needs addressed
8. List of satisfied clients:
9. Other insights gleaned:

1. Costs involved
2. Platforms—PC/Mac/both
3. Printers, RIP software, or other expenses
4. Training costs and availability
5. Support costs
6. Demo and trial versions
7. Specific needs addressed
8. List of satisfied clients:
9. Other insights gleaned:

FIGURE 12–9
Personal software resourcing information chart

Software Company	Corporate Owner/Parent	CAD Specialties	Platforms	Phone Number
AGE Technologies/Clic	AGE Technologies–Canada	Plug-ins for Adobe Photoshop w/Textile-Apparel Applications	Mac/Pc	1-888-862-1333
APSO USA		Design	PC	404-261-8113
AVA		Design/Weave	Mac	800-883-4555
Color Matters	Privately held Company		PC	212-695-0541
EAT, Inc.	EAT Germany	Weave	PC	704-329-0766
Gerber	Gerber Technologies	Pattern	PC	
Imagine That!	Teri Ross	CAD Consulting		
Infomax Corp.	Privately held Company	Mac/PC Hardware	Mac/PC	212-730-7930
Improved Technologies	Past IRIS Employees	Fabric Printers	Mac/PC	
JacqCAD Master	Privately held Company	Weave	Mac	603-878-4749
Kopperman	Privately held Company	Design	PC	310-229-5937
Lectra	Lectra Systems	Pattern/Design	PC	770-422-8050
Ned Graphics	Bought by Blue Fox NE	Design/Weave	PC	212-921-2727
Pointcarré USA	Pointcarré FR	Design/Weave/Knit/Embroidery	Mac/PC	212-627-2394
SofTeam USA	SofTeam Italy	Industrial Embroidery	Mac/PC	
SnapFashun, Inc.	Privately held Company	Garment Library	Mac/PC	
Sophis	Sophis FR	Design/Weave/Knit	PC	704-357-3580
Stork	Stork	Fabric Printers	PC	704-598-7171
Wasatch Computer Technology	Wasatch Computer Technology	RIP Software & Textile Repeat Software/Print Manangement	PC	800-894-1544

FIGURE 12–10
Who's who? Software comparison chart

Figure 12–10 is a highly simplified table that offers a brief description of the most well-known CAD vendors. We have intentionally not biased the chart with personal commentary on the company or the products. We instead recommend that you use this as a place to get started in the right direction. Every company or design firm is unique; therefore, as you begin to do your research and find answers to the questions we suggested that you ask, you will soon discover which companies, products, and prices will suit your needs.

Notes...

Stage 2: Going from Digital Design to Print

Other Significant Considerations for Converting to Digital Designing and Printing
Digital Printers, Papers, Fabrics, Inks and Dyes

Although selection of design software is one of the most important considerations you will make, deciding how to get your designs from your computer to the finished cloth also takes some major research and resourcing insights to determine where you should begin.

In this section we will attempt to remove much of the confusion and hopefully dispel any fears or concerns facing the designer, university, or company in reviewing the choices in converting to digitally rendering and printing textiles today.

Many of the leaders of this new movement in designing come from a variety of vantage points—designers, artists, manufacturers, and producers.

Digital Printing Industry

A Historical Overview: A Look Back, in Order to Better Define the Future

Even though this may seem like an unlikely place to discuss the history of digital printing, it will in fact serve as the backdrop to inform and educate you about the challenges and amazing opportunities that await you. In this section we will answer the following questions about digital textiles and designing.

- Who is involved?

- What is involved?

- What are the challenges or barriers to entry?

- What is at risk?

- What is at stake?

- Where do we go from here?

- Where do I begin?

Even though we have spent the greater portion of this text helping you acquire the knowledge and skills of digitally rendering fabric and prints, the question that now remains is what do I do with these designs? How do I get them from my computer onto the fabric? In this final section we will attempt to answer several questions often associated with digitally printing on fabric.

Sign and Banner Heritage

Let's take a quick look at the roots of digital textile printing. For years the graphic design world has had a significantly strong branch known as the sign and banner industry. In this industry there exists a series of service bureaus and production facilities that can create and print larger format signs and banners. Many of the signs and banners produced are designed to meet the specific needs of outdoor-style advertising. Obviously the mediums used vary from woods, metals, and paper to everything in between.

These highly skilled and creative men and women have approached their design work as a craft as well as an industry. They have been called upon as problem solvers for large-scale projects that can include billboards, bus panels, and trade show banners. Thanks to the sign and banner industry and the world of digital graphic designing, it is easy to see where much of digital textile printing owes its very existence.

For years this industry has been furthering the development of inks and substrates and finishes that withstand the elements and time. According to Teri Ross of

Imagine That!, the sign and banner industry has been "deploying this relatively new technology for years."

However, that does not negate the real barriers to entry facing the fashion and interior design textile industry or their justifiable concerns. In an on-line article from the TechExchange website, Teri Ross concludes, "There are two primary methods used for stabilizing and feeding fabric through an ink-jet printer, one is a paper backing and the other is a feed and take-up system. While many of the OEMs have developed feed and take-up systems that eliminate the need for backing on rolled goods, experts advise users to work closely with their equipment supplier and to test all fabrics to be used for either sampling or production.

Most fabrics used in ink-jet printing will require a pre-treated coating in order to prevent the ink colors from bleeding on the fabric. While some natural fiber fabrics do not require pre-treating, the colors produced on non-treated fabrics will end up very faded. The only way to obtain vibrant colors is by pre-coating the fabric; and for many applications it will also require a post-process step of steaming and washing of the fabric after printing."

Other Initial Roadblocks

So from the sign and banner industry to the fine artist, the digital textile industry has been more of a movement than anything else. However, there have been several barriers to entry. It is unfortunate that the conventional textile industry has resisted looking at digital printing for production, because most production business models can't support the slower speeds and higher costs of digital printing. The postprocessing requirements for steaming and washing of digital fabrics have also created barriers to entry.

Yet, there is a plus-side—a grassroots-level movement has been occurring, formed by a series of visionary pioneers including fine artists and the hand textile artisans who are always searching for new modes and mediums and enlarging the boundaries and scope of design.

Simultaneously, and thankfully, manufacturers of printers and inks caught the wind of change that represented a potentially profitable market expansion, which could include the fashion and interior textile industries. These companies began developing creative solutions to minimize or eliminate the challenges of taking this new field from concept to consumer.

The greatest challenges have been:

- Romantic, emotional attachments to the past way of doing business
- Fear of the unknown—resistance to change
- Initial steep learning curve for the new technology
- Color matching and a gamut of solutions
- Color converting issues and ink chemistry issues specifically contending with pigment process color used on paper to conventional spot color for fabrics
- Colorfastness and color penetration
- Need for industry to establish testing standards for the emerging ink-jet market

- Fabric stabilizing

- Cost-effective finishing—pre- and posttreatments

- Printer speed

- Capital investment and related production costs

Needless to say, these are all legitimate concerns that are slowly being addressed. Again, as cited by industry guru Teri Ross, "The conventional textile industry has slowly been reaping the rewards of digital printing for both sampling and presentation, where there is both a tremendous cost savings and reduction in time to market."

As we noted above, one of the greatest challenges for this new market has been that of ink chemistry. The wide format ink-jet printing vendors have been using pigmented process color inks for output to paper, but the textile market wants to use its conventional spot color inks, including reactive, acid, and dispersed dyes.

Printer vendors as well as several ink companies are developing and delivering inks and other solutions for the textile market. However, Ross goes on to say in her commentary that "the chemistry requires the finished fabric printed with reactive, acid and dispersed dyes to be steamed and washed if it is to be applied to an end use other than presentation, sampling or signage. Steaming will fix and enhance the color and the post-washing will get rid of excess ink that can adversely affect the finished hand. DuPont claims that their pigmented inks only require heat setting for production use on textiles."

Therefore, a deeper understanding of the textile fiber characteristics, when combined with the ink chemistry issue, is magnified when combined with the various chemical compositions of the different fabric coatings from the growing number of ink-jet fabric vendors.

The interesting thing we uncovered in our interviews and research is that individual vendors of printers and end users have each developed their own unique formula for finishing and printed textiles for commercial use. Several individuals have concentrated on color matching issues and developed their own RIP software, and one highly creative individual developed and patented her own brand of fabric finishing methods. The good news is that all of these individuals and companies are creating solutions that result in new products and new markets being made available at a record rate, taking the integration of digital textile printing and the apparel supply chain to new frontiers of providing an almost endless possibility of providing mass-customized printed products.

Because of the inherent nature of digital printing offering increased efficiency and flexibility, garments and products can be customized by size and colorways versions, and engineered prints can be quickly suited to meet the individual consumer's preferences and demands.

According to research conducted by Tony Hines of Management Research Group at LCF in an interview in the summer of 2002 for WGSN-EDU (Worth Global Style Network—global forecasting website>Future Fashion Link), "Projections on the viability of how much fabric will be digitally printed range between 12–15% and

50% in 10 years. It is estimated that the market will shift from 50 major textile printers to 500 smaller ones, many offering short-run customized solutions to satisfy more sophisticated customer demands." That is good news to the world of fashion and interior as well as to the economy and the consumer!

Perhaps it would be appropriate to introduce you to several of these individuals who are propelling this new textile movement further into the new millennium.

Before we begin with the showcase of experts, we felt that you would appreciate hearing information and testimonials from those companies and individuals who have crystallized the alternatives you have before you. Although our first few chapters were designed to give you a working knowledge of textiles, it is imperative that you really are comfortable not only with textile terminology but with the "tech-know" terms that are involved as well.

In this section, before you actually begin your research, we felt it would be helpful for you to be sure you are comfortable hearing and using the relevant terminology that accompanies this new medium.

Speaking the Lingo

It almost sounds humorous when you first notice that the acronym for color conversion software is referred to as RIP software (Figure 12–11). We are probably showing our age, but the term *RIP* at one time meant rest in peace. However, when it comes to color converting, the challenges and solutions do not conjure up restful or peaceful emotions!

Therefore, it would be of great comfort to you later in your research if you take the time to acquaint yourself with the relevant digital textile terminology that you will most likely encounter.

In order to streamline how this language is used in context, we have provided a digital printing chart in Figure 12–12 that we trust will clarify the terms and the technology for you.

FIGURE 12–11
RIP software

Method of Color	Explanation/Definition	Substrate Applied to: (Refers to the textile fiber, yarn, or fabric)	Method of Fixation: (Refers to method of setting the dye, typically involving heat via steam, hot wash, or chemicals)	Comments:
1. Acid Dyes	Commercially applied to fabric in organic or inorganic acid dye solutions.	Natural protein fibers: silk and wool. Synthetic fibers such as acrylic, nylon, and polypropylene blends.	Steam/wash	
2. Dispersed Dyes	Water-insoluble dyes. Sometimes referred to as sublimation, which refers to the loss of dye that occurs during evaporation, and is without formation of a liquid phase.	Acetates, nylons, and polyesters.	Hi-temp heat steam/wash	
3. Pigment Dyes	Combination of resin binders and insoluble dyes that are printed on the fabric.	All fibers or directly to fabric.	The adhesion properties of the resin in conjunction with the pigments are fixated through the application of dry heat.	
4. Reactive Dyes	Just like the name implies, this class of dyes react to chemically bond the color to the substrate they are applied to.	Primarily cottons and poly-cotton blends.	Steam/wash	

FIGURE 12–12
Traditional and digital textile terminology

Traditional and Digital Printing Methods

1. **Blotch Printing**—Printing instead of dyeing the ground color of a fabric. The result is that the reverse side of the fabric typically is white.

2. **Digital Printing**—Although this is a broad title, it typically refers to micro-sized droplets of inks or dyes that are placed directly onto the surface of the substrate via an ink-jet printhead. The substrate used and the amount of the droplets applied are directly determined by the data contained in the original image file and therefore translates into color quality of the print.

3. **Discharge Printing**—Using chlorine or other chemicals to remove areas of previously applied color on a fabric and replace with areas of white patterns on a colored ground.

4. **Dye Sublimation**—Printing that occurs when a sublimation of dyes are transferred from a carrier roll and applied to the fabric/substrate through the application of heat.

5. **Electrostatic**—Typically each color is printed individually via an electronic charge that actually attracts the toner (ink) particles.

6. **Heat Transfer Printing**—This method involves transferring patterns or prints that were previously preprinted on rolls of paper and applying the prints via relatively high-heat transfer printing machines directly to the surface of the fabric.

7. **Ink Jet**—Detailed explanation of digital printing involves the following:
   a. **Continuous** refers to ink that is continuously applied by channels of pressure forming steam droplets.
   b. **Drop-on-Demand** refers to images formed by ink droplets applied by pressure and released onto the substrate.
   c. **Thermal pressure** is created by a gas bubble within the nozzle that forces droplets of ink onto the substrate.
   d. **Solid inks** are stored and melted and applied as needed to the substrate.

8. **Rotary Screen Printing**—Hollow, perforated nickel screen cylinders are prepared for each individual pattern color involved in a design. Color is then forced through the metal rollers sequentially and directly to the surface of the fabric.

9. **Screen Printing**—Method of adding color to fabric, one color on one screen done one at a time.

10. **Spray Jet**—A spray nozzle individually applies color directly to the substrate.

11. **Thermal Wax**—Sometimes referred to as Resin Transfer wax or resin. Individual colors are then applied directly to the substrate via a roll format film carrier.

RIP—Wasatch

In Chapter 5 you were introduced to how important color management and RIP software is to textile designing. Therefore, we have included some visual information for you to review from one of the leading RIP software companies, Wasatch. You will also read articles by the Wasatch company Vice President who works closely with the industry in information and solutions to managing color. Wasatch provides several examples of textile printing solutions and support. The information you hear from our experts in this chapter will confirm the importance of doing it right the first time!

One such example of doing it right is with Wasatch SoftRIP™ for textile printing. This product allows the designer to manage a color database and swatchbook as well as customize print repeats for printing including engraving data support! (See Figures 12–13, 12–14, and 12–15.)

Digital Textiles—Roots in the Fine Art Community

The sign and banner industry was not the only one to catch the vision and potential of this new technology as a new medium of expression. Most of us own several versions of digital art expressed in the walking advertisement of an iron-on T-shirt. There is another expression of digital art that has existed for years—many fine artists have been experimenting on personal computers in simple resident

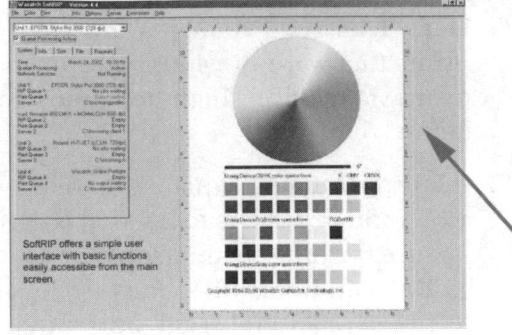

**RIP
Software**

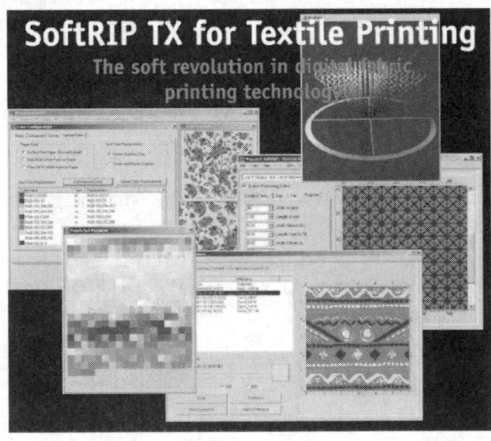

**Repeat
Software**

FIGURE 12–13
Wasatch RIP and Repeat software
(Courtesy of Wasatch Computer Technology)

paint programs to push the boundaries of hand and machine into defining a new medium of fine art.

Although many individuals lay claim to this natural, organic phenomenon, we are not laying that particular crown at anyone's feet, but rather to the collective fine artist, including the textile artist, who has early on braved this new world.

Notes . . .

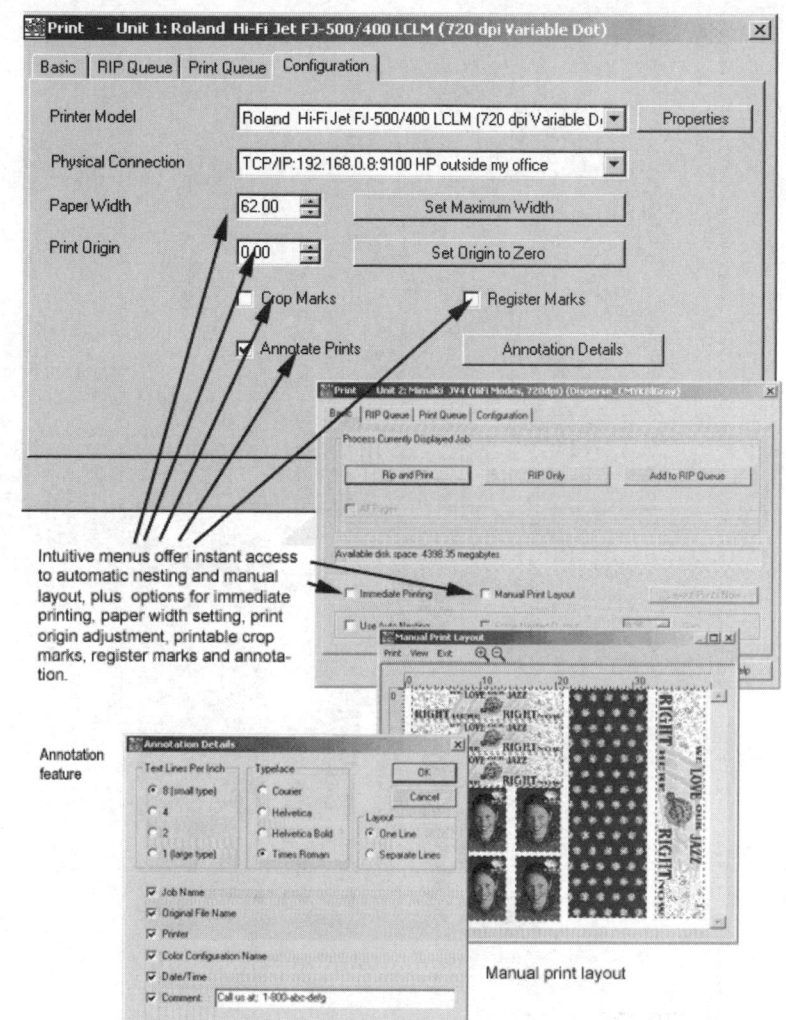

Intuitive menus offer instant access to automatic nesting and manual layout, plus options for immediate printing, paper width setting, print origin adjustment, printable crop marks, register marks and annotation.

Annotation feature

Manual print layout

FIGURE 12–14
Wasatch interactive menu
(Courtesy of Wasatch Computer Technology)

Many individuals venturing into this relatively new arena have experienced the brunt of the initial snobbery that came from many unsuspecting sources, including the educational and fine art community. Numerous times we have heard our peers who share our passion for digital designing lament about those in academia whose initial response was one of balking at computer imaging art as nothing more than "mindless computer manipulation." Opinions of how fine or far the chasm is between graphic design and fine art that is done on the computer certainly do stretch the gambit, yet no one can deny that the computer is as much a tool as a paintbrush in the hands of a skilled artist.

Thankfully, today many of us have been vindicated for our work using computer imaging as art, including photo-realistic textile design and art to wear. Many serious scholarly periodicals and societies are recognizing the impact of this new technology. Even at the time of writing this text, we received no less than two solicitations per week beckoning us to seminars conducted by serious surface design groups around the globe.

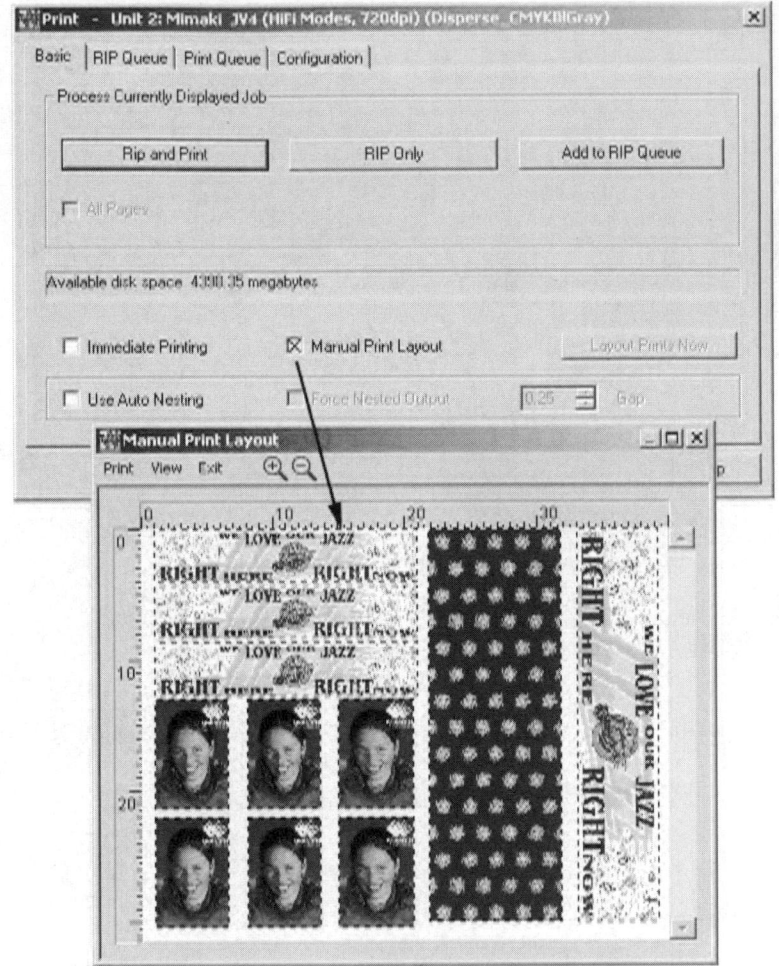

FIGURE 12–15
Wasatch print layout
(Courtesy of Wasatch Computer Technology)

Luckily for the textile and surface design community the initial opinions of disdain and skepticism many artists like myself have encountered have all but disappeared.

From Digital Imaging to Fine Art to Reproduction—Challenges

Figure 12–16 shows examples of photo-realism printed digitally in full-scale "life-size" on cotton canvas. This particular example comes from a series of digitally rendered gallery pieces, collectively entitled Lazarus by author Kathleen Colussy. The second image was also reproduced several additional times on a lightweight sheer chiffon to reproduce the gauze-like halo effect of discarded grave cloths.

The Process

Anyone will tell you that the process of making art is an integral part of the story. The original images for Lazarus were a series of digitally enhanced photographs that were initially conceived and manipulated on a computer using Adobe Photoshop and then printed electronically onto photo paper to be mounted and hung

FIGURE 12–16
Examples of digital surrealism

for a traditional gallery setting art show. However, the initial print appeared too flat, necessitating the need to explore other means of conveying the message in more dramatic and realistic fashion.

It was a challenge to discover alternative solutions to capture the essence of the original intent of the artist. The goal of the art was to represent the resurrection from the past into the present by a signal encounter in one moment in time. The challenge was to depict this transformation of the removal of the linen grave cloths that bound the subject matter. It soon became apparent that the work had to be printed in a larger scale or life-size format in order to capture the reality of this subject and the intensity and drama of the moment of enlightenment. The image was then reprinted on traditional "art canvas" fabric using a digital textile printer.

This meant locating and contacting nontraditional sources for reproducing the work. In order to show the transformation from death to life, the image had to be reprinted several times on a series of separate translucent or sheer fabrics. The main piece was printed life-size (6 feet by 3.5 feet) on cotton canvas, and the succeeding chiffon images were also the same size, but shredded and placed beneath the canvas original.

The image, on succeeding layers of sheer gauze, was strewn in a discarded fashion around the life-size canvas image, signaling the emerging transformation from death to life. (See Figure 12–16, Lazarus Come Forth.)

Other Examples from the Fine Art Community

Before looking at the practical side of digital printing from an industry standpoint, in this next section we will visit some very special artisans and educators who have elevated digital textile designing to new heights, while contributing to this relatively young medium. Like our authors, these artists have also overcome the challenges often accompanying digital designing.

FIGURE 12–17
Computer-aided design

FIGURE 12–18
Robert Manning's Silk Scarf with Feathers
(Courtesy of R. Manning/rob@supersample.com)

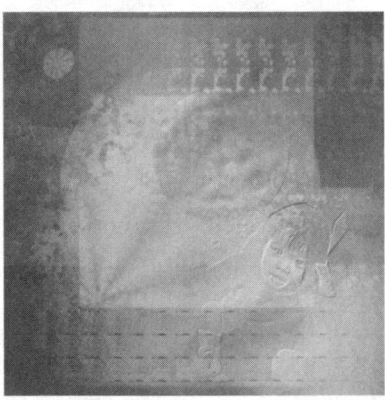

FIGURE 12–19
Robert Manning's Lili
(Courtesy of R. Manning/
rob@supersample.com)

FIGURE 12–20
Robert Manning's Flowers on
Gauze
(Courtesy of R. Manning/
rob@superSample.com)

Pushing the Envelope of Digital Designing
Meet Fine Artist: Robert Manning

Our first introduction is Robert Manning, who is a fine artist who works in New York. In the past Robert has used various mediums, from pen and ink to watercolors and oil paints. However, in the past couple of years, he has been exploring the exploding world of computer-aided design, particularly using Adobe Photoshop and printing directly onto fabric. (See Figure 12–17.)

Robert has successfully merged the fields of fine art and production to create unique and unusual prints. By using electronic imaging and digital rendering done with Adobe Illustrator and Adobe Photoshop, Robert can print his multicolor, complex patterns and designs on a wide variety of substrates, including papers and fabrics.

As an artisan, Robert has interacted with the SuperSample Corporation to create one of a kind prints. His designs are suitable for display or conversion for apparel and accessory application. However, his primary joy as a fine artist is in pushing the traditional boundaries from painting to pixels to produce unique artwork that is showcased in fine art gallery environments.

His inspiration comes from the little girl he is raising, who was adopted from China. (See Figures 12–18, 12–19, and 12–20.)

917–523–3976 meglartin@aol.com   rob@supersample.com

Next Up—Educational Digital Visionaries and Revolutionaries: J. R. Campbell and Jean Parsons

Although it may seem that New York or perhaps London or other cosmopolitan fashion giants are leading the charge in digital designing, there is a quiet revolution of art and design taking place in the Midwest. Located at the Iowa State University is the classroom of J. R. Campbell and Jean Parsons.

Meet: J. R. Campbell

J. R. holds a Bachelor of Science in Environmental Design and a Master of Fine Arts in Textile and Costume Design from the University of California at Davis. He is currently developing research/creative activity in digital capture, development, and surface application to textile art and design as an assistant professor in Textiles and Clothing at Iowa State University.

He explores the visual, cultural, and technological aspects of digital textile printing as he creates connections between two-dimensional print design and three-dimensional garment forms. He regularly shows artwork in national and international juried exhibitions.

J. R. is also conducting evaluation-based research on the colorfastness of a variety of digitally printed fabrics when tested for wash-fastness and light-fastness.

Meet: Jean L. Parsons

Jean holds a Ph.D. in Costume History from University of Maryland and is currently an assistant professor at Iowa State University. She has worked as both a fashion designer and costume designer, and currently teaches apparel design and illustration.

In her own design work, she explores draping techniques for manipulating fabric to produce apparel that does not follow traditional seam placement, and is currently investigating the integration of three-dimensional apparel design with digital textile technology for art-to-wear.

In their classroom, students are creating garments and digital textile prints unsurpassed anywhere we have discovered in our research.

Many of us in the industry have known J. R. from his writings and lectures on the subject of digital designing. J. R. has graciously agreed to work with us on this project by providing us with several insights into how he empowers his students to discover the world of digital textile designing.

J. R. has also graciously provided us with not only inspiration but also information on how to achieve similar results in your studio or classroom. He has provided the necessary step-by-step explanation of how this groundbreaking designing is accomplished in his classroom.

We felt it would be appropriate to hear from an educator's vantage point on how they view the impact of technology on textile designing. Therefore, the following information is from a compilation of interviews, workshops, and writings done by J. R. Campbell for a variety of educational and trade seminars and publications.

Excerpts from a paper by J. R. Campbell © 6/11/2001

Overview of Digital Textile Printing and How It Affects the Approach to Textile Design

Digital color printing technology is sparking a fundamental change in the textile and apparel industry. Traditionally, to create printable designs for fabric, color separations and screens or rollers had to be used for the transfer of designs to fabric.

This revolution in digital image processing has necessitated new ways of thinking about textile design and production.

A large percentage of the research involving the digital printing of textiles has focused on how the technology will affect marketing and merchandising strategies in the textile and apparel industry. However, we have found little research on the design capabilities of digital textile printing.

The purpose of this study was to examine the impact that digital color printing has had on textile design. The objectives were to assess the current state of digital textile printing technology, investigate how the technology is actually used in the industry, and address the new design issues related to the potentials and limitations of digital textile printing.

The following issues were evaluated according to how they affect design approach: (1) printing on fabrics of similar structure, but differing fiber content, (2) printing on textiles of various texture and structure, (3) repeat design versus non-repeating image creation, (4) photo-realistic imagery, (5) variations in size/scale, (6) changes in visual perception of motifs and imagery due to change of scale and repeat, (7) garment style and repeat print design integration, (8) limits of file size/transportability with contemporary software and hardware, (9) color matching and processing, (10) allowance for design correction and modification at any time without significant schedule delays or cost increases.

Digital textile printing affects the apparel industry by: (a) reducing the time-cycle for product development, (b) reducing the time required to produce to order, and (c) changing textile design techniques and capabilities. Industry experts predict that the textile and apparel industry will adopt digital textile printing when the systems can meet economic and performance standards that will allow firms to meet their customers' needs and produce profit (IT Strategies Inc., 97).

The design factors of digital textile printing ultimately affect the economic and performance standards of these printers by providing new opportunities for niche market products that include image enhancements not previously possible in traditional textile printing. The biggest plus of digital printing of fabric—especially for small textile companies—is that they can get a strike-off done at a very reasonable cost. If they were to do it the traditional way with offset printing, they would spend anywhere from $200 to $1,000 on film separations before they even print it . . . , they might only pay $200 to $1,000 for the final product with digital printing methods (Getting a Grip on Digital Printing, IT Strategies). Future research will include evaluation of these issues and of design approaches that companies in the industry have adopted for the use of digital textile printing technology.

Physical, chemical, and economic limitations are challenging those who are developing direct digital printing technology for textile applications. Some involve refinements to current technologies, while others involve the development of new digital printing methods. Strategies involve not only changes to the printing mechanism, but also to the substrate, inks, software, printing environment, material handling, and curing equipment. Both chemical and physical processes are used in different digital printing technologies that have never been designed with textile printing in mind. Issues that are inherent to ink jet printing include:

1. Color calibration and management

2. Production rates

3. Print quality

4. Chemistry

5. Materials handling

6. Environmental controls

7. Reliability

8. Consistent color supply

9. System integration

Change of Design Effect by Printing Fabrics of Similar Structure, But Different Fiber Content

The complexity of textile printing, with its variety of fiber contents, textures, finishes and inks, requires special technology depending on the application (Teri Ross 1997). Issues of colorfastness related to crocking (the rubbing off of color), wash-fastness (color transfer or loss in water), fading (due to sunlight or ultra-violet light) are very important factors when attempting to print on fabrics of varying fiber content. Metamerism (the color defect in which printed or dyed surfaces appear to change colors under different lighting situations) may also cause problems. Encad's digital textile printing system produces industry-standard performance in wet- and dry-crocking values on light, medium, and dark shades. The results are extremely good on cellulose, polyester, silk, and wool, and the process is water resistent and can be presented as a proposed product applicable to many textile design communities worldwide (Encad 1998, Encad: Digital Textile Printing System).

Change of Design Effect by Printing on Textiles of Different Structure and Texture

Other key factors may rely more on how well the fabric feeds through the printer without losing stability, stretching or distorting the design, or drastically impeding the transfer of color to the cloth. Questions such as, "Can pile fabrics like velvet and velveteen be printed digitally?" are common and the responses are mixed. Head height might be an issue on pile fabrics or highly textured surfaces, so it must be possible for the user to easily adjust the head height. For example, the ENCAD 1500TX wide-format ink jet printer can be adjusted, but only by a small variance, so very heavy weight fabrics are not likely to be able to pass through the printer.

What happens to designs visually as they are printed on fabrics that have a rough textural surface?" Do the ink-jet scatter patterns of dye or in dispersal work to aid in the quality of printed textured fabrics, or would another dispersal pattern be more appropriate? The answers to these questions are yet to be determined. Seiren, a textile printing company from Japan, has developed a digital printing system that can be used with any type of fabric—both synthetics and naturals—including sheers, lace, textures, knits and pile fabrics such as velvets and velours. Their digital textile printing system, called Viscotec, does incredibly sharp printing on velour, and in Japan, digitally printed velour wall hangings, some with photographic images, are popular (Raye Rudie 1998 Seiren's New Take on Digital Printing).

Use of Repeat Designs Versus Non-Repeating Image Creation

Decorative fabrics, which tend to be used in greater lengths, will be better able to take advantage immediately of digital printing's freedom from repeats. Currently, the size of a design is limited to the size of the screen on the rotary printer. After the drum has made one revolution, the pattern is repeated. Because digital printing has no screens, a sheet, bedspread, carpet, or window treatment can be printed in which the elements of the design are never repeated. For example, instead of the current offspring of Disney movie characters repeated every 18 inches, a sheet or bedspread could be created from an actual scene in the movie. In fact, Disney Studios may already be on to this idea. Home furnishings experts who saw Disney's Toy Story, the first movie to be completely computer generated, may have noted that the visual "Buzz Lightyear" bedspread created for the boy's room was a single design that filled the entire bedspread. In today's reality of rotary printing, that bedspread could not have been commercially mass-produced (IT Strategies: The Future for Digital Textile Printing). In Seiren's factory in Japan, there is a textile wall hanging containing an image captured during one of the Apollo missions, an 18-foot-long continuous view of the world (Raye Rudie 1998 Seiren's New Take on Digital Printing).

The Use of Photo-Realistic Imagery

Photo-realism opens the possibility for layered imagery, ghosting effects, an extended color gamut, and a number of possibilities that would not have been cost effective or even possible to produce through traditional printing methods. In creating digitally printable imagery for textiles, the designer can incorporate the use of high-resolution images to push the limits of photo-realistic printing. The use of high-resolution images is a technically limited issue that relates to the ease of use with currently available hardware and software and the current (and yet constantly changing) storage and transport media for dealing with large file sizes. ENCAD guarantees that their printer can be used with "today's most popular Mac and PC software." This has yet to be fully tested and verified, simply due to the relative infancy of the technology as is it being used for textile printing.

Variations in Size/Scale That Are Possible with Digital Printing

There is a generally accepted range of motif sizes that are currently compatible for use in apparel and are traditionally understood to relate to the size of the human form. How will the perceptions change with the use of a technology that can essentially ignore those limits and produce yardage of fabric where the printed design need never repeat? Entire garments, sofas, curtains, bedspreads, etc., could be printed with one single large-scale motif as the design effect. Perhaps a designed product could have only a portion of a motif, where the intention is to view that product with others as a means for recognizing the overall motif.

Garment Style Pattern and Repeat Print Design Integration

Through the integrated use of textile and apparel design software, printable designs can be tailored directly to pattern pieces for a garment. By registering the textile print designs to each pattern shape and graded size for a garment, fabric designs can become more personalized and body specific. [TC]^2 has already begun research in this realm in their effort to integrate body scanning technology, digital textile printing and computer-aided design into the apparel manufacturing industry. By registering perfectly the textile print designs to each pattern shape and graded size for a garment, fabric designs can become more personalized and body specific. The printed fabric yardage would appear as though it has finished garment parts, colored and sized to fit, that can simply be cut out and sewn together to create a finished garment.

Limits of File Size with Contemporary Software and Hardware and Transportability of Files to the Digital Printer

Usability of the software and hardware involved in digital textile printing is determined by how well the systems can handle the large computer files that are needed to be able to print large images. Many of the rasterization and spooling software packages that have been developed are specific to an operating platform, so files must be converted and saved in formats that are acceptable across platforms (Mac, Windows, UNIX, etc.). This may ultimately affect the design capabilities of digital printing for textiles as it relates to the file formats that are specific to the more industry specific textile design software packages.

Changes in Color Processing Resulting from a Non-Separation Process of Printing

From the design standpoint, digital printing presents none of the color limitations of traditional printing. Seiren's Viscotec system offers a pallet of 16.7 million colors. An infinite amount of colors can be added to a print without added expense—with almost photographic quality on certain fabrics (Raye Rudie 1998 Seiren's New Take on Digital Printing). Color is also an issue from the standpoint of both color control and color models. CAD users already have learned the inherent problem of color discrepancies between the computer monitor and proofs printed on paper. Printing on textiles adds even more variables, as colors can shift with both the type of ink used as well as the fiber content and structure of the fabric (Teri Ross 1997).

It is important to remember, though, that process color printing has a smaller color gamut that produces less accurate color matches than spot or flat color printing (Teri Ross 1997). Recently, ColorSpan has released their wide format printer for textiles, dubbed the FabriJet. This 12 color printer addresses the need for a wider color gamut by allowing the user to either add extended colors for process printing, such as orange, blue or green; or the extra color cartridges (beyond the regular CMYK) can be used to print a simulated spot color (printing only that color on a given area). ColorSpan has been partnering with Rupert, Gibbon and Spider, creators of Jacquard® products, to develop both acid and reactive dye-based inks for the printer.

Allowance for Design Correction and Modification at Any Time without Significant Schedule Delays or Cost Increases

The transformation of digital design ideas into production items will allow wider access for those who wish to experiment with the design process, in education and the design industry (CAD Infinitum). A design idea can be drastically changed almost instantly, and then simply removed with an "undo" command, allowing for less emotional stress in the changing of and experimenting with the design. This potential for creative design exploration is inherently available with digital printing technology for textiles. A designer can test their design variation immediately by sending their digital file to printing machinery and witnessing the unveiling of their design on fabric. If the design is not a success, the print job can be halted, and a new variation created. This is an incredible difference from previous methods of proofing designs on fabric, because there is no need for the production or changing of patterned screen or rollers (Printing Prospects for the Textile Industry).

J. R.'s work represents collaborative efforts within the educational community (his peers), his students, and the industry.

Intersecting Two Design Problems to Create Multiple Points of Exploration

Both artists approached the project with specific goals related to their own discipline. These goals were:

1. To create a short jacket style through manipulation of geometric fabric shapes on a dress form. The goal was to create a semi-fitted jacket with intersecting angles and minimal use of darts. Garment sizing and shape would allow it to be worn by a variety of size and body types. The primary design concept was to develop structural seams with a strong emphasis on diagonal line.

2. To use digital printing technology to manipulate the printed design by changing/distorting the scale of the imagery to match the directional lines on the garment pieces.

According to J. R., " historically, printed fabrics for apparel have primarily been developed with repeating designs that are of a repeat-unit size less than sixteen inches long. Only decorative fabrics, which tend to be used in greater lengths, were more likely to have large repeat sizes or singular image prints. The decorative fabrics industry is now able to take advantage of digital printing's freedom from repeats without causing exorbitant price increases in the production of the printed imagery. The goal of the investigators for this project was to apply the potential for non-repeating imagery to a garment, not just as a singular print on the front or back of a garment, but as continuous imagery that continues across the seams."

The use of photo-realistic imagery opens the possibility for layered imagery, ghosting effects, an extended color gamut, and a number of possibilities that would not have been cost-effective or even possible to produce through traditional printing methods. In creating digitally printable imagery for textiles, the designer can incorporate the use of high-resolution images to push the limits of photo-realistic printing. The use of high-resolution images is a technically limited issue that relates to the ease of use with currently available hardware and software and the current (and yet constantly changing) storage and transport media for dealing with large file sizes.

Through the integrated use of textile and apparel design software, printable designs can be tailored directly to pattern pieces for a garment. By registering the textile print designs to each pattern shape and graded size for a garment, fabric designs can become more personalized and body specific. [TC]2 has already begun research in this realm in their effort to integrate body scanning technology, digital textile printing and computer-aided design into the apparel manufacturing industry. By registering perfectly the textile print designs to each pattern shape and graded size for a garment, fabric designs can become more personalized and body specific. The printed fabric yardage would appear as though it has finished garment parts, colored and sized to fit, that can simply be cut out and sewn together to create a finished garment.

There were several significant design considerations, including that it was decided that for this initial collaboration we would allow the three-dimensional design to control the two-dimensional printed imagery. Thus the printed design was created after the garment pattern was developed. Issues that were considered in the creation of the three-dimensional form were as follows: its potential relationship to surface design, the type of fitting and shaping lines desired, and the actual fit of the garment.

Throughout the design development phase, the initial garment design evolved through an experimental draping process, rather than through the use of sketching. Because the goal was development of shapes that did not necessarily correspond to traditional seam placement, it was decided that this was the best technique.

The chosen print designs were inspired by the construction lines used in the garment. They were directly manipulated on the computer from digital images of photographs taken in the early 1900s. The strong visual lines integrated well with the radiating arrangement of garment pieces. In an effort to abstract the imagery from direct photographic representation, several of the images were layered and blended together. The color was then adjusted so that the resulting composition retained normal sky colors but all other hues were modified. The pattern pieces with imagery attached were then printed directly to a lightweight quality wool fabric.

Once the garment design was completed, the final pattern was digitized into the computer using PAD pattern-making software. The final patterns were then exported from PAD in an Adobe Illustrator format, then opened in Illustrator and copied and pasted into an Adobe Photoshop file, where the surface design could be applied to the garment pieces.

Technical Issues

1. **Fabric sourcing:** None of the vendors who offer fabrics pre-treated for digital printing carried a lightweight wool. We sourced an acceptable wool tricotine from Gstreet Fabrics on-line and decided to purchase it with the intention of pre-treating ourselves. Our pre-treatment process consisted of warm water wash cycle with the application of a surfactant. We chose not to apply any further preparatory chemicals. In order to stabilize the fabric

for feeding through the printer the tricotine was spray mounted to 60" wide paper.

2. **Technical considerations** that arose from this use of this fabric included potential skew problems in mounting it to paper, possible printing defects from loose fibers clogging print heads, shrinkage problems during steam-setting, and the retention of satisfactory color saturation.

3. **Pattern considerations:** We had to modify and shorten some of the pattern pieces because of perceived file size and capacity problems. Second, the process for digitizing the patterns for ultimate importation into Adobe Photoshop had to be developed.

4. **Garment Assembly:** The primary issue was matching the imagery at the seams due to some skew and stretching of the fabric.

5. **Summary** The execution of this project showed that one constraint to the process of integrating engineered surface design imagery to match garment pieces occur in the problems with file sizes on the computer, causing temporary halts to the design process. The solution of changing the scale of the garment downward for working with the imagery and then re-sizing back to original size proved to be an effective one, because the RIP software did very well in re-sampling the digital information to print out the imagery at a larger scale.

Figures 12–21 through 12–27 show the steps from completed garment to the rendering process, first in industrial software and then exported into Adobe Illustrator to Adobe Photoshop. You will also see the variations on this technique.

FIGURE 12–21
ChangeofAtmosphere

FIGURE 12–22
Close-up of man's shirt
ChangeofAtmosphere
(Courtesy of J. R. Campbell)

FIGURE 12–23
Example of a garment marker plotted out in Adobe Illustrator
(Courtesy of J. R. Campbell)

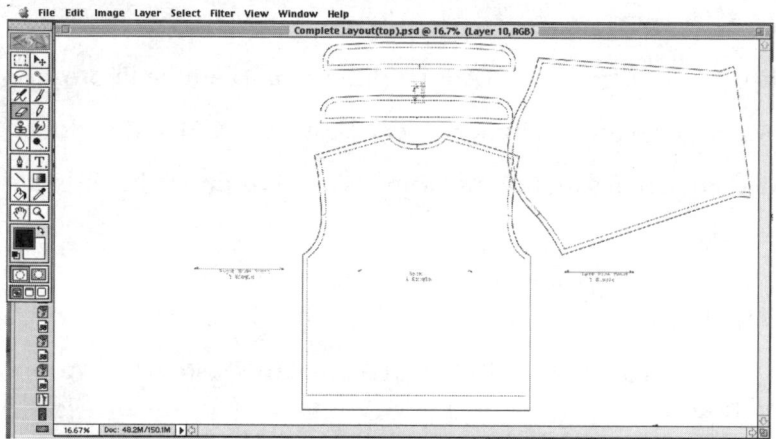

FIGURE 12–24

All garment pieces laid out in Adobe Illustrator
(Courtesy of J. R. Campbell)

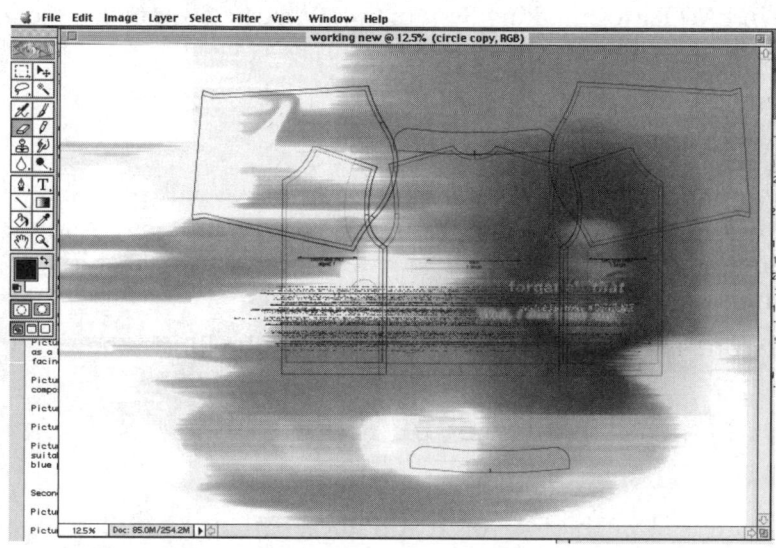

FIGURE 12–25

Preliminary artwork set onto garment maker
(Courtesy of J. R. Campbell)

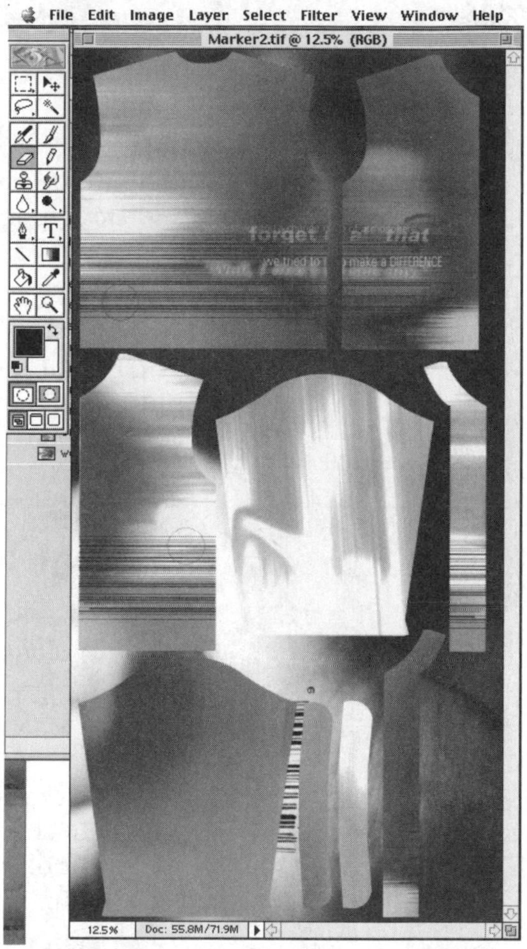

FIGURE 12–26

Final artwork laid out in Adobe Illustrator
(Courtesy of J. R. Campbell)

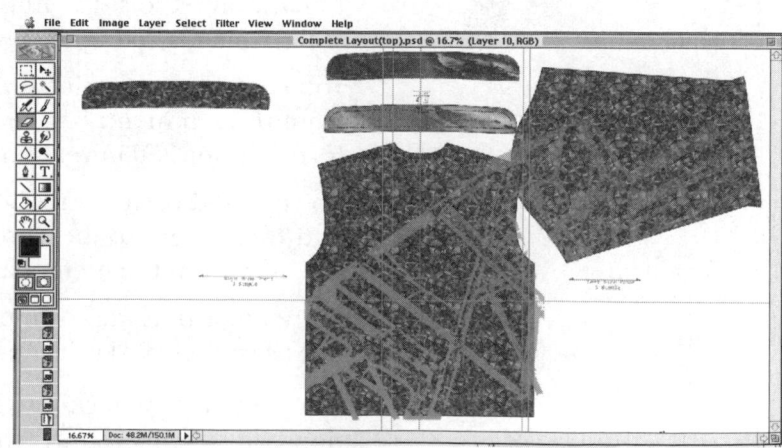

FIGURE 12–27

Pattern variation can also be viewed and
simulated in Adobe Illustrator
(Courtesy of J. R. Campbell)

Notes...

From Industry to Illustrator to Photoshop

Transition from industry pattern grading to Adobe Illustrator to Adobe Photoshop

This next exercise can be re-created in almost every classroom across the globe!

Here we have included an actual assignment from J. R.'s class on Digital Textiles and Designing:

How-To Instructions

The Digital Apparel Design Process from PAD Patternmaking System®, to Adobe Illustrator, to Adobe Photoshop
by J. R. Campbell, Iowa State University. All reproductive rights reserved. © 2001.

Exporting from PAD Patternmaking System® to Adobe Illustrator:

1. Save the work in PAD Patternmaking System® first, maybe even make a second copy for backup.

2. Go to File menu, go to Export.

3. Export as an Adobe Illustrator file 88 option.

4. Click the option button. It will ask for "plan" or "pieces," pick pieces, and check the boxes for all three sub-options: Piece, Grain, and Sewing lines. Hit okay. It will ask for a file name, choose one and give it an .ai suffix, to help in later transfers.

5. Quit PAD Patternmaking System®, and then open Adobe Illustrator.

Exporting Pattern Pieces from Adobe Illustrator to Adobe Photoshop:

1. Do a file open, and select the file you just named. (filename.ai, the icon should have an 88 on it.)

2. If your pieces are all in one file, you might want to create new files for each piece. You will need to increase the size of the pieces from 10% (PAD® automatically exports the Illustrator 88® files to 10% of actual size) to quarter scale, which is 250%.

3. You can do this by selecting the object, choosing Object, Transform, Scale from the top menu bar. In the Scale dialog box choose/checkmark "Uniform." Enter 250 in that box, and hit okay.

4. To copy and paste to Adobe Photoshop, select the piece, do an Edit, Copy, and then open Adobe Photoshop. When Adobe Photoshop opens, select file, new from the menu bar to make a new document.

5. Remember that Photoshop will automatically make the new file the same size as your copied selection from Illustrator.

6. Name the new file, choose RGB mode instead of CMYK, make sure resolution is at 300 pixels/inch (or whatever your desired print resolution will ul-

timately be). You can set the background color to transparent, white or black, whichever is your preference, and then hit okay.

7. Do a File, Paste, and it will ask you if you want to paste as pixels, or paths. Chose pixels, and turn anti-alias on. If the file is too big to open, try it with the anti-alias off. Don't worry about fonts.

8. One of the problems that might occur, some of the lines closest to the edges might have a tendency to get chopped off in the transfer process (the copy and paste function is not absolutely perfect at the very edges from vector to raster files), so zoom in and check them all. If you have some lines that are chopped, you will need to use the line tool to re-draw them.

9. Choose the grain line and type and do a copy, cut, and paste to move it to another layer.

10. When you are happy with the file in Adobe® Photoshop®, go back to Adobe® Illustrator®, and you may wish to quit and not save the enlargements you made of the pieces. This will save them in their original imported form, which will take less memory.

Applying Imagery to Pattern Pieces in Adobe® Photoshop®:

1. Back in Adobe® Photoshop® if you have a pattern selected, you can fill the inside of the entire pattern, by choosing the layer with the pattern piece in it, and use the magic wand tool to choose the negative space around the outside of the pattern.

2. Then invert the selection with Select, Inverse from the menu bar.

3. Create a new layer; the active selection will then transfer to the new layer. You can then choose to fill that space with the pattern. You may need to adjust the scale of the pattern fill if it is too large or small; you can do so by going back to the original repeat, and changing its image size. (Make sure you constrain proportions.)

4. You then need to Define the Pattern again. Return to the file with the garment shape/outline, delete the old pattern fill, and put the new fill in.

5. For placing a single image into the garment segment, do an Edit, Copy of the original, and then go to the Garment Document, and do an Edit, Paste. This will create a new layer, and will place the image at its original size in the pattern.

6. You can then enlarge or decrease the image with the transform tool. When you are done tweaking it, hit enter or double click. Don't worry about getting some stuff outside the garment edges, it can be trimmed off later.

7. One of the ways you can extend the image is with the rubber stamp tool. There are other ways to do this. Experiment with the different ways, and choose which is best for you.

8. To trim, hide the image layer, by clicking its eye icon in the layers toolbox.

9. Go to the layer with the pattern outline in it and use the magic wand to select negative space around the outside of the garment pattern.

10. Go back to the layer with your image in it, and hit the Delete key, which will cut everything within the selected area.

11. If you want to match image edges on different pattern pieces, increase the canvas size, then rotate the piece to the best angle to line up with another pattern piece.

12. Overlap the two adjoining garment parts so that the stitch lines are superimposed directly on top of each other (remember the images must match up along the stitch line, not the edge of the seam allowance).

13. Then fill the two pattern pieces with the imagery while the pattern pieces are overlapping. Finally, move the patterns back into an orientation so that they are back in alignment with their grainline.

14. Save the file.

In Figures 12–28 to 12–30 you can see the concept from draping, drafting, and sewing up a muslin, next how the images will be placed into a marker, and finally how the completed garment will look.

FIGURE 12–28
Actual photo of bridge used for inspiration
(Courtesy of J. R. Campbell)

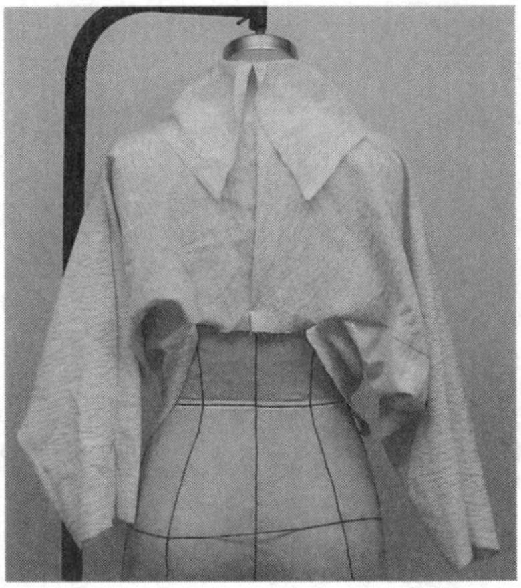

FIGURE 12–29
Muslin sample of garment made first to verify fit
(Courtesy of J. R. Campbell)

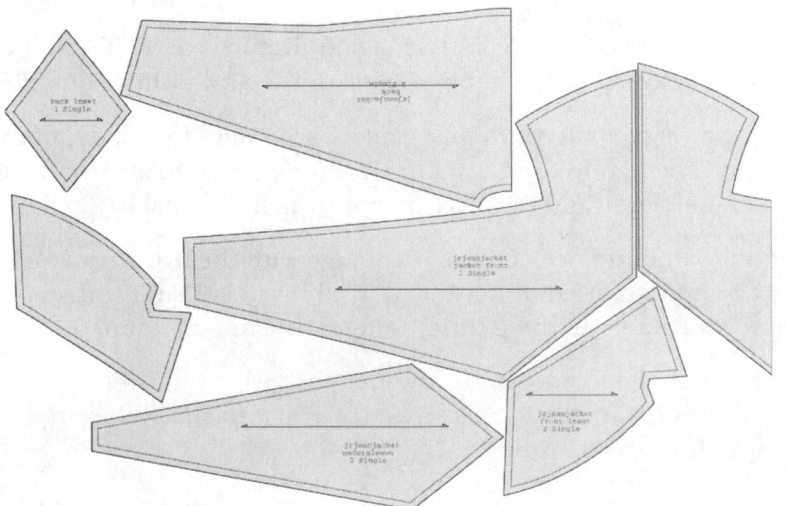

FIGURE 12–30
Digital garment pieces to be used for adding the finished digital design

Wasn't that an exciting exercise? Doesn't it give you the inspiration to want to run to your nearest computer and start designing? We have included three final photo samples from the Iowa State University collaboration that will simply overwhelm you by their sheer beauty and artistry.

Several of the images you are about to see are a compilation of several collaborative projects between several artists, educators, and students reprinted by permission from J. R. Campbell.

The works showcase the combined design talents of technical design, draping, CAD, costume history, and beyond!

In Figures 12–31 to 12–36, you can see how the seasons of spring and then summer have influenced the artisans. The images show details of the garments—both front and back as well as detailed steps of rendering and placing the images into a marker in Adobe Photoshop.

In Figures 12–37 and 12–38 you can see how a stained glass window starts the design process—first in the illustration, then into markers, and finally into a gallery-quality piece. These creations were from a collaborative project at Iowa State University, under Dr. Jean Parsons. (See Figure 12–39.)

In our final image (Figure 12–40) you can clearly see the progression from inspiration to marker and to final garment.

FIGURE 12–31
Spring front
(Courtesy of J. R. Campbell)

FIGURE 12–32
Spring back
(Courtesy of J. R. Campbell)

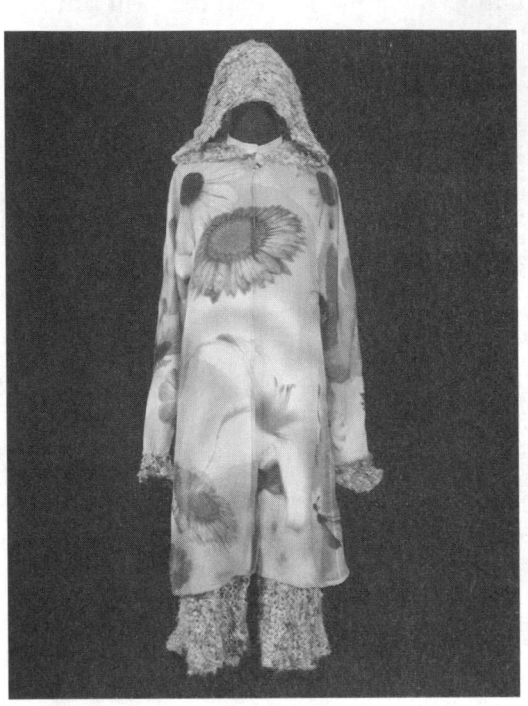

FIGURE 12–33
Summer front
(Courtesy of J. R. Campbell)

FIGURE 12–34
Summer back
(Courtesy of J. R. Campbell)

FIGURE 12–35
Close-up of digital flower detail
(Courtesy of J. R. Campbell)

FIGURE 12–36
Marker layout for placement of digitally enhanced floral print
(Courtesy of J. R. Campbell)

FIGURE 12–37
Illustration of actual stained
glass window used for
inspiration

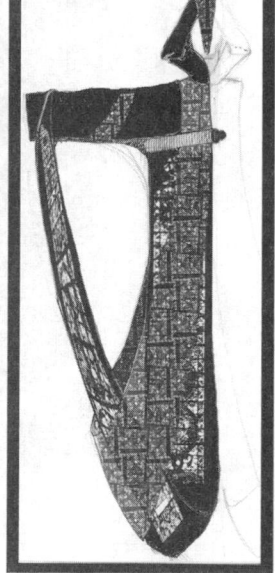
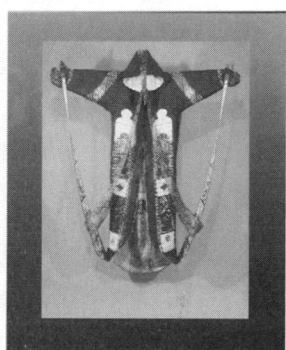

FIGURE 12–38
The process of inspiration to illustration to actual garment
completion
(Courtesy of Dr. Jean Parsons)

FIGURE 12–39
Accomplished artist and professor Dr. Jean
Parson's draping of a muslin on a dress form
(Courtesy of Dr. Jean Parsons)

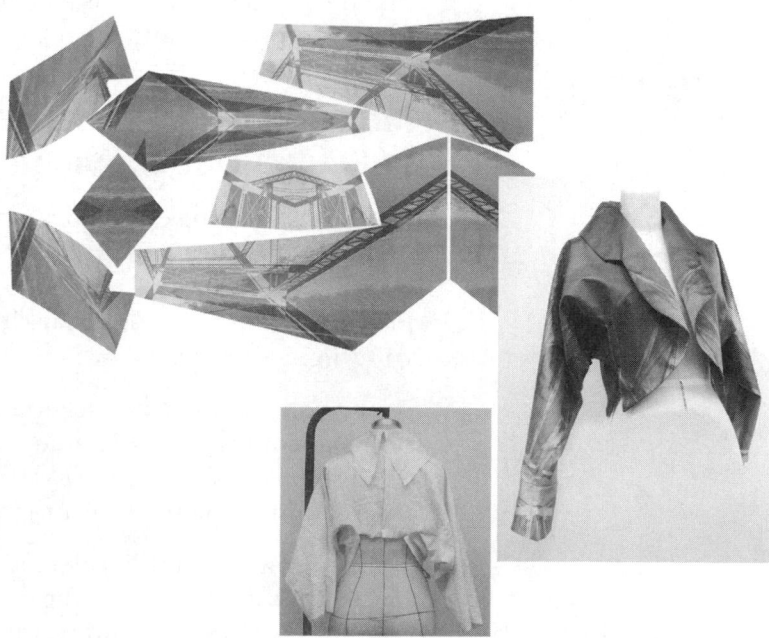

FIGURE 12–40
Photo image of the bridge placed in marker for the muslin
jacket sample and the final jacket with digital image
(Courtesy of J. R. Campbell)

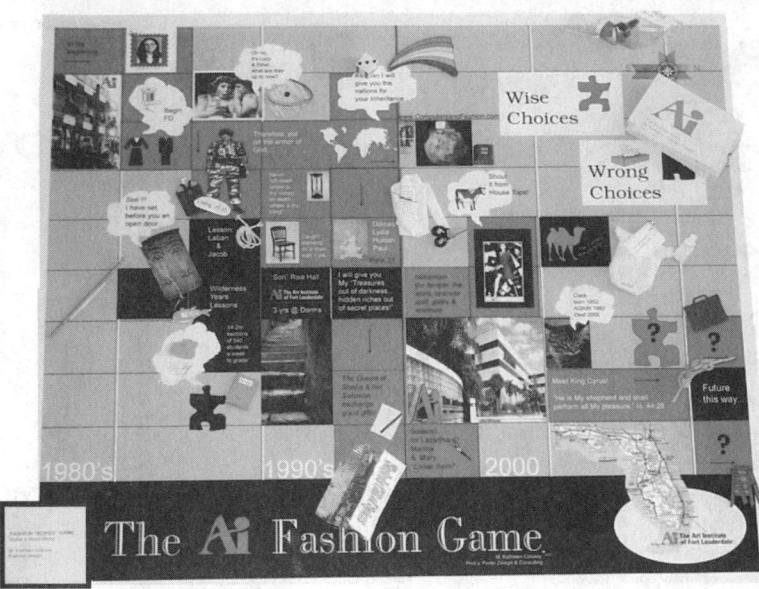

FIGURE 12–41
Fashion bored game

Before hearing from the industry experts, we have included one last image from education, showing that fashion can be fun. In Figure 12–41 (entitled Fashion Bored Game) author Kathleen Colussy showcases her sense of humor in an original graphical piece that displays how you can bridge the gap into the fine art realm (originally shown as a faculty art show piece to reflect her 20-year teaching career and then adapted back for textile application as a scarf).

Industry Digital Visionaries: Companies, Corporations, and Individuals Changing the Way We Look at Digital Design

Now you should be even more familiar with the digital textile heritage and the relevant terminology and language that is associated with the printing. In this section we would like to introduce you to several leading digital experts. They will provide you with the necessary information and insight you might need to begin your digital journey.

At the conclusion of this section we have also provided you with a chart of several of the major printer companies in existence today. In our testimonial of expert advice we have opted to showcase three of these companies as a cross-sectional representation of the major printer companies currently on the market.

The criteria we used to select a printer were based on profiling companies that have application for small businesses, on large corporations, and the educational community as well. As always, when a company is not included, it should in no way be assumed that noninclusion is an indictment or indication of their insignificance in market stature or contributions.

We have also taken into consideration what software applications might be paired with the printers involved. The choices enable you, the reader, to consider your own individual abilities and budgetary limitations when you begin to make your purchasing selections.

- Industry testimonial from one company that uses Adobe Photoshop in conjunction with MacDermid's ColorSpan digital textile printer—meet the team of SuperSamples Corp.

- Representing the industry large-run production solutions is DuPont's 3020 known for its speed and large production capabilities. (Represents large-run production for industry)

- Mimaki known for its short production speed with proprietary software, and Pointcarré (representing freelance designer and service bureaus). Included in this section is information from IT (Improved Technologies) and FabriCAD's Alison Hardy for one-stop shopping solutions.

- Hewlett-Packard, bridging between sign and banner industry and textiles for apparel
- Other printing alternatives—service bureau solutions

MacDermid's ColorSpan Digital FabricJet Printer

Our first textile printer profile comes via a successful company from Manhattan—SuperSamples. These gentlemen have built a tremendously successful operation using MacDermid's ColorSpan digital textile printer with Adobe Photoshop. (See Figures 12–42 to 12–45.

Of all our interviews, the following interview with the gentlemen of SuperSamples proved to be the most inspirational as well as the most informational, not to mention thoroughly enjoyable and memorable.

FIGURE 12–42
MacDermid's trade show booth
(Courtesy of MacDermid ColorSpan, Inc.)

FIGURE 12–43
ColorSpan display fabric jet printer
(Courtesy of MacDermid ColorSpan, Inc.)

FIGURE 12–44
Printer roller bars
(Courtesy of MacDermid ColorSpan, Inc.)

Notes . . .

FIGURE 12–45
ColorSpan provides inks and software
(Courtesy of MacDermid ColorSpan, Inc.)

Meet the Team of SuperSample, Inc.

David Kushner is the founder of SuperSample. He truly is a pioneer in the development and application of digital ink-jet textile printing, as a technology *and* as a business. Nine years ago, already an experienced textile printing professional, he became one of the very first to recognize the potential of digital ink-jet in textile printing. In 1993 he performed initial experiments in digital ink-jet textile printing using a simple "home" deskjet printer.

The success of these early efforts led to the establishment of SuperSample Corporation. Through his vast experience in traditional textile printing, he understood that one practical and profitable application of the new technology was the production of the sample prints that would be necessary in the successful sale of patterns and goods. In consideration of this potential market, he named his new company SuperSample Corporation.

According to David, "The dominant technology in commercial textile printing is the process known as *rotary screen*, a method designed for high-volume production." Rotary screen is a large-scale industrial technology in which pre-production expenses often comprise a considerable percentage of the total cost of an order.

The high expense, in money and time, is a persistent economic problem associated with the preproduction process of rotary screen. Costly volume minimums required for sample making resulted in Mr. Kushner's realization that digital ink-jet was the ideal solution for the small-run textile sample market, being particularly effective in relatively low volumes—fully capable of printing a superb facsimile of a textile printed by rotary screen, and in a far shorter time, and a proportionately far lower cost.

Through progressive experimentation, it was discovered that the key to superior quality in digital ink-jet textile printing was control of the colors themselves. Previously, digital ink-jet color sets were limited to the pallets of ink offered by the manufacturers and suppliers. SuperSample has successfully adapted existing technology, making possible the creation of customized inksets, with colors especially mixed for particular designs.

SuperSample has also become a pioneer in the application of "steaming and washing" techniques to digital ink-jet. Steaming is a postprinting process that significantly enhances such coloristic qualities as depth and brilliance. Through the additional process of washing, printed textiles are made colorfast, and can be actually washed in water without running and fading.

Colorfastness made digital ink-jet suitable for various additional applications and markets, including printing done especially for fashion product prototypes, and for the manufacture of limited high-fashion lines.

In 1994, from its first shop location in Great Neck, New York, SuperSample established itself as a provider of advantageous sample printing services for renowned clients such as Victoria's Secret, Old Navy, Gap, Fisher-Price, Clinique, Oshkosh, and Disney.

While David was expounding on the company's initial success story, he acknowledged that unforeseen challenging times affect every business at one time or another.

On the brink of expansion of their production of a line of original design, one-of-a-kind, high-fashion scarves, the young company suffered a serious setback in the form of a fire in its Great Neck shop. As a result, during its process of rebuilding and relocating, SuperSample became associated with a digital textile print design service bureau, and subsequently developed a specialty in printing samples and prototypes of products such as sheets, bedding, quilts, and tablecloths for the home furnishing industry, doing so successfully despite seriously limited facilities.

Without a water supply, the wet-processing techniques previously used to enhance vividness became impossible. SuperSample solved this problem by enhancing the vividness of printed textiles to an equivalent degree through a technique of printing on a specially treated fabric.

An additional technical achievement was the production of digital ink-jet textile prints that meet commercial standards of quality, using only those manufactured inks available for the CMYK process. Among its clients during this period were Crown Crafts Home Furnishings, Croscill (Royal Home Fashions), I Appel, Artex (tablecloth), and F. Schumacher & Co.

As in any company expansion, there was a critical need for additional talents to complement those of the company founder. In 1998, SuperSample relocated into a new facility with a water supply where wet-processing was again possible. During this time, fine artist Rob Manning came on board as a partner. Mr. Manning is a digital and video artist and entrepreneur who has worked closely with David Kushner in the establishment of SuperSample's full-featured wet-printing operation, and the eventual development of Multichrome and Popcolor. Rounding out the SuperSample team are digital graphics programming and systems expert Bob Hoffman, print production manager Brian Douglas, and master color chemist Rajenda Joshi.

The core of SuperSample digital technology comes in the form of primary digital designing being accomplished in Adobe Photoshop, RIP software being developed in-house, and all printing accomplished with MacDermid's Fabric Jet-Textile Ink Printer. (See Figures 12–46 through 12–50.)

As you can see, this company's growth potential was met with the right partners and staff, provided at the right time, with the technical skill and knowledge base to provide the right solutions for their clients' needs!

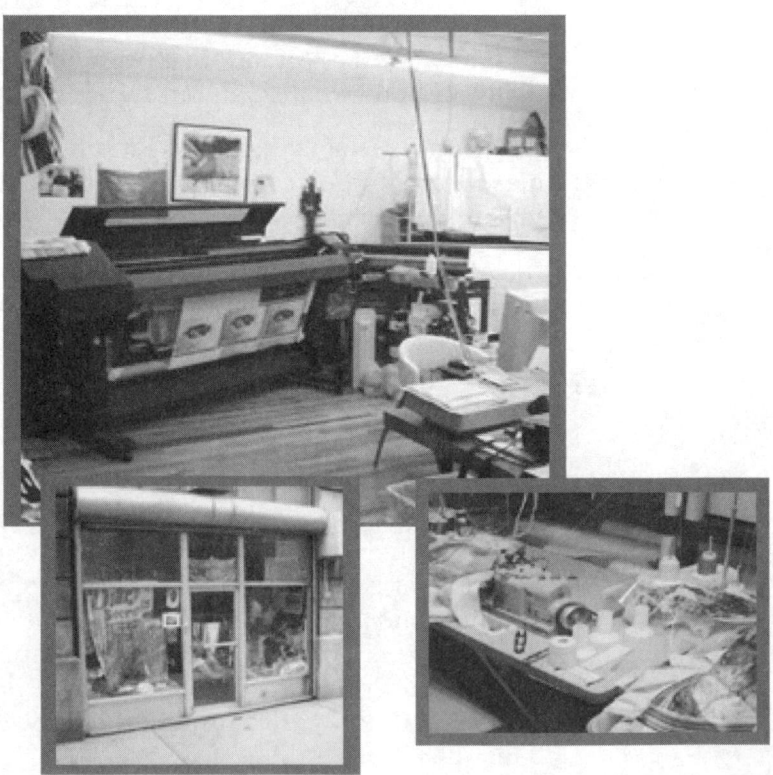

FIGURE 12–46
SuperSample offices in New York City
(Courtesy of SuperSample, Inc.)

FIGURE 12–47
Samples of whole clients by SuperSamples
(Courtesy of SuperSample, Inc.)

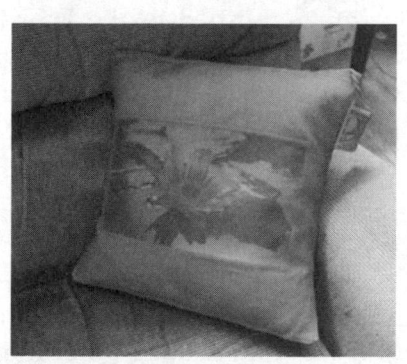

FIGURE 12–48
Fine art reproduction and interior design
client made up by Supersample
(Courtesy of SuperSample, Inc.)

FIGURE 12–49
Apparel and retail clients of
SuperSample
(Courtesy of SuperSample, Inc.)

SuperSample

 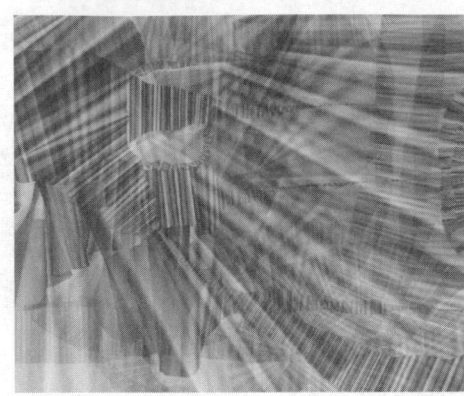 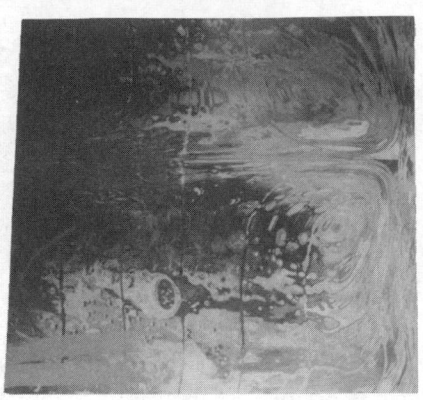

FIGURE 12–50
Three examples of digitally created fine art printed for clients by SuperSample
(Courtesy of Robert Manning)

Notes...

Meet Several Leading Printing Experts

Mimaki Printers

Our next printer showcase is Mimaki. In our effort to put faces to companies, one familiar face came to mind: Alison Hardy. Alison is a freelance consultant as well as a representative for Improved Technologies of New Hampshire (www.itnh.com).

Meet Alison Gruider Hardy, President of FabriCAD

Many of us within the industry or educational community recognize Alison for her groundbreaking research on salary satisfaction published in the FabriCad trade publication article. (See Figure 12–51.) This article is still available from her website at: www.FabriCAD.com. Alison also coordinated the first ever research findings seminar on digital color matching sponsored by the CADEXPO/Yarn Fair Trade Event held in the summer of 2001 in New York City.

At FabriCAD.com a designer can post job openings, equipment for sale, and freelance needs or services for free. A calendar of events and tradeshows as well as a consulting service to provide accurate, up-to-date information when researching for a CAD system is available. This allows a designer to spend less time gathering critical background information and more time making other important decisions.

FabriCAD is in the marketplace every day researching new products and their uses. Their staff combines the best of a fashion background with a business education. They are active members of the Computer Integrated Textile Design

FIGURE 12–51
FabriCAD
(Courtesy of Alison Gruider Hardy/FabriCAD)

Association (CITDA) and frequent speakers on the subject of CAD. In addition, FabriCAD Consulting has written numerous articles for leading industry publications.

Improved Technologies

Today Alison also works for Improved Technologies. They are one of several distributors for the Mimaki printer. IT is a technology, materials, and support company for digital printing. At IT they combine cutting-edge technology with proven consumables, and the result is an uncompromised digital printing solution. From wide-format digital imaging, consumables, and service and support, IT provides it all.

IT sells and supports IRIS and CreoScitex digital imaging equipment, as well as equipment from Mutoh, Mimaki, Roland, Polaroid, Epson, Gretag, X-rite, and others. Software systems are available from ColorBurst, ColorByte, CreoScitex, and Monaco. IT can provide the right integrated system for a start-up operation or a master printmaker.

All these printers are compatible with the many design programs available, like Pointcarré Design software, which can be used to develop designs in repeat and multiple colorways, then send them to the RIP software on the print server.

The Mimaki JV-4 printer, seen in Figure 12–52, is a Piezo drop-on-demand ink-jet that prints on paper-backed fabric. Using dye, pigment, or disperse dye–sub inks, this high-speed printer can print 290 sq ft/hr at 360 dpi and high-quality printing speeds up to 240 sq ft/hr at 540 × 360 dpi. Its two sets of print heads, when loaded with different ink sets, allow this printer to be two printers in one. The difference with the JV-4 over other printers is that it uses the Epson 10000 heads (for quality). When both ink sets are loaded with the same type of ink, it is faster than any printer out there, thus, combining print speed with higher quality. (See Figures 12–53 and 12–54.)

The Mimaki TX2, also Piezo drop-on-demand ink-jet, prints on almost any nonpaper-backed fabric. They can both use acid, reactive, or dispersed dyes. The TX2 can print at speeds up to 308.7 sq ft/hour and at resolutions up to 720 dpi for high-quality prints.

The latest Mimaki printers also have the ability to adjust and eliminate "banding," which tends to be a problem on many ink-jet printers.

Hewlett-Packard—Bridging the Gap between the Sign and Banner Industry and Fashion!

Providing speedy turnaround with uncompromising image quality is vital for print service providers (PSPs), GIS professionals, and those in the graphics industry.

Today, the newly introduced HP Designjet 5500 (see Figure 12–55) has a new large-format printer combining high productivity, image quality, and simplified operation for streamlined workflows and unattended printer operation, which is also getting the attention of colleges and universities around the globe for use in textile sample making.

The HP Designjet 5500, a follow-up to the popular HP Designjet 5000, is the first large-format device to offer direct file submission via the Web. Using HP Designjet

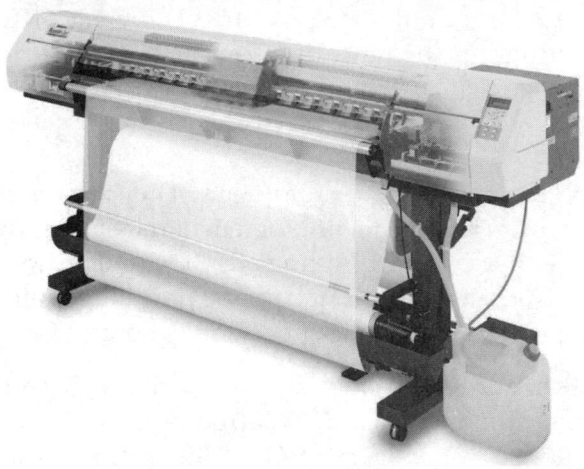

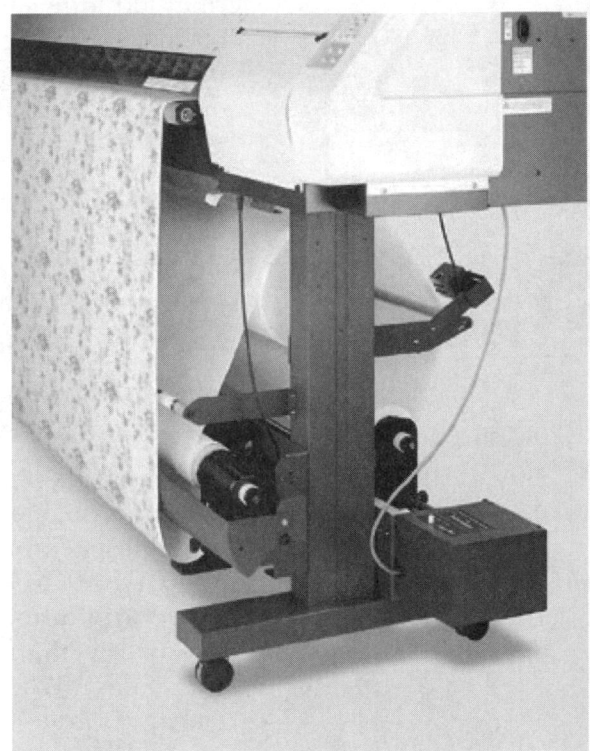

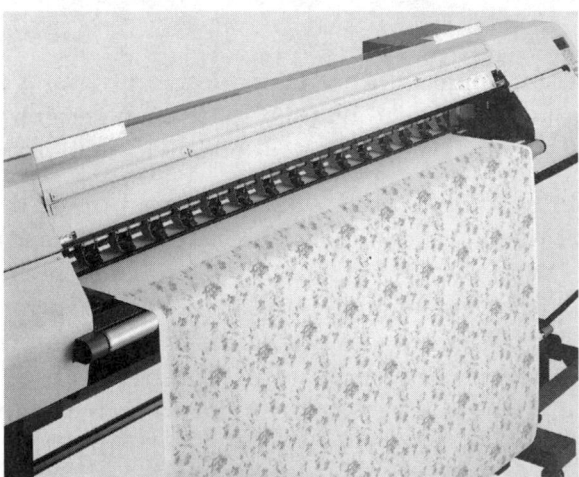

FIGURE 12–52
Example of textile printer front and side roller bars
(Courtesy of Mimaki)

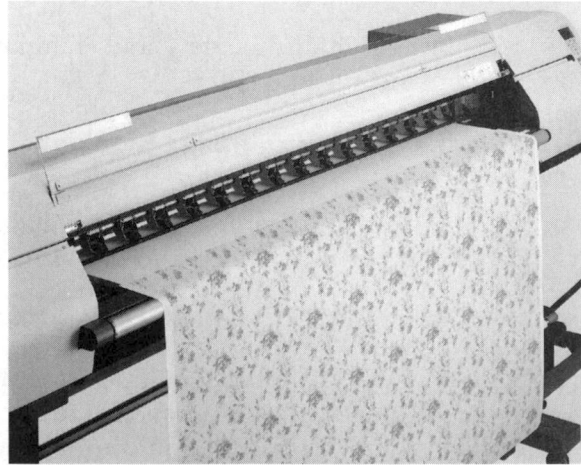

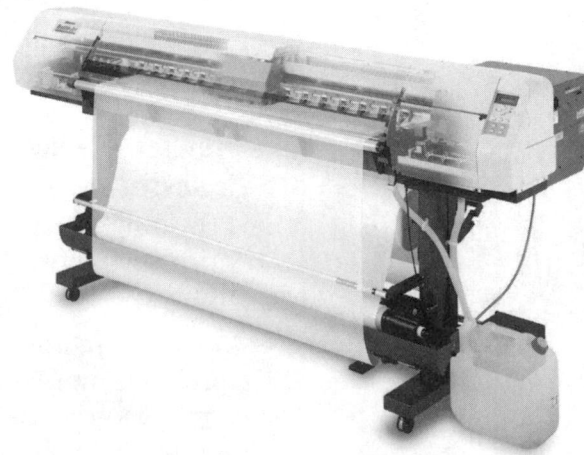

FIGURE 12–53
Close-up of textile printer head in motion
(Courtesy of Mimaki)

FIGURE 12–54
Mimaki JV-4 Printer
(Courtesy of Mimaki)

FIGURE 12–55
Photo realistic images on fabric
(Courtesy of Hewlett Packard)

Web access, users can submit up to seven file formats, including Adobe® PDF, TIFF, and JPEG, without the need for a driver or the application. It also offers a new 40 Gb hard disk drive so that files can be permanently stored and maintained in the printer.

"The printer's performance is outstanding from all points of view," says Maria Pla, head of automatic cartography at the Insitut Cartografic de Catalunya, the official mapping agency of the government of Catalonia in Spain. "The image quality is exceptional and turnaround is incredibly fast. Plus, the printer is easy to integrate into our work environment."

To enhance productivity, the Designjet 5500 printer offers new production print modes for high-speed, professional, ready-to-sell, or distributed images. Arnau Sallent, general manager of Propaganda, a print service provider in the food sector, is particularly impressed. "The new printer's performance is outstanding. Powerful processing power and extremely fast print speeds using the new production print mode meets our requirement for high volume printing of large-format point-of-purchase materials."

An innovative heater, coupled with the production print modes, provides maximum performance without sacrificing image quality. Remote printer management is also made fast and easy from any standard Web browser through HP Designjet WebAccess. WebAccess gives users the ability to conveniently manage and configure alerts for printer status or ink and media usage information.

The HP Designjet 5500 series supports a wide range of printing material, too—from CAD media to the new Instant Dry Glossy and 225-foot heavyweight coated productivity printing material. Dye-based inks and pigment-based UV inks are also available and interchangeable in the HP Designjet 5500 printer's six-color modular ink system. Fabrics can also be adapted for use in the apparel industry for sample making.

"This new series is ideally suited for today's high-pressure design and printing environments," says Manel Martinez, large-format marketing operations manager, Inkjet Commercial Division. "The large-format Designjet 5500 printer provides stunning output at high speeds to meet the needs of a wide variety of businesses who want to maintain their competitive edge."

Key enhancements for the HP Designjet 5500 include:

Increased productivity

- Production print modes provide ready-to-sell, high-quality output at 100 sq ft/hr on glossy media and 189 sq ft/hr on coated printing material

- Fast data transmission speeds through HP Jetdirect 615n print server (up to 4.5 megabytes per second)

- New productivity category media support

- Up to two times the performance in total print time versus the Epson Stylus Pro 10000 at maximum image quality

- Up to two times the performance of the predecessor HP Designjet 5000 printer in day-to-day production image quality modes

- Direct driverless printing path

Ink and media flexibility for CAD and graphics applications

- Support for CAD media, including Bright White, coated paper for line drawings, clear film, and vellum

- Smaller margin requirements (5 mm) to support CAD applications

Additional features include:

- Choice of RIP-ready or embedded Adobe PostScript RIP models

- Top speed at 569 sq ft/hr

- Six-ink, CMYK color

- HP Color Layering Technology creates continuous tones and smooth color transitions

- Automatic closed-loop color calibration ensures consistency, print after print

- Brilliant output at 1200×600 dpi

- Offset emulations for EuroScale, SWOP, DIC, TOYO, and JMPA and ICC profiles for Microsoft®, Windows®, and Mac

- Up to 256 Mb RAM memory

- Modular ink delivery system supports both dye-based and pigment-based UV inks

- 42-inch and 60-inch printing

DuPont

Meet DuPont's John Kane

We soon discovered that John Kane is one of the best-known movers and shakers in the world of digital textiles. Like the name Teri Ross, it seemed John's name coupled with DuPont's was popping up literally everywhere we did our research.

From the moment we contacted John for information, he immediately jumped into action to provide us with information above and beyond the call of duty. As our interviews progressed, we discovered that John had extensive knowledge and vision about the direction in which the digital textile industry was moving.

John Kane is currently new business development manager for DuPont Ink Jet, where he is responsible for sales and marketing activities in the Americas Region for Textile Printing. Prior to this role, he was the product manager for the integrated digital textile printing systems developed by DuPont.

Kane started with DuPont in 1992 as a process engineer in the company's Automotive Finishes business. He later joined the R&D organization of the printing and publishing business, and also worked in the company's nylon fibers unit.

Kane earned a B.S. in chemical engineering from Villanova University in 1992 and an MBA from Wilmington College in 1999. He is a senior member of the AATCC, and is a frequent speaker at conferences around the world on the subject of digital textile printing. John resides in Newark, Delaware, with his wife and three children.

At the time of publication of this text, John was in the middle of preparation for a major digital textile trade event that DuPont was co-sponsoring in Turkey. According to John, DuPont has a long history in textiles and has been working behind the scenes to shape the future of fashion. DuPont has a 200-plus-year history of transforming the fashion industry. Defining moments that have touched our lives are such milestones as the introduction of nylon hosiery at the New York World's Fair in 1939 to the revolutionary discovery of Lycra® brand stretch fiber. DuPont has modeled a commitment to technological innovation, scientific discovery, and strong customer focus. DuPont continues to deliver innovative products that will satisfy the needs of their customers and help differentiate themselves in an increasingly competitive environment.

One natural evolution is DuPont's venture in Textile Printing Systems. The printers and printing systems deliver several innovative components, including the fastest state-of-the-art printers, as well as inks and color control systems. (See Figures 12–56 through 12–60.)

FIGURE 12–56
DuPont 3030 printer
(Courtesy of DuPont)

FIGURE 12–57
DuPont textile printing system includes
software and hardware
(Courtesy of DuPont)

FIGURE 12–58
DuPont specializes in inks/dyes
which are specifically designed
for fabric printing solutions
(Courtesy of DuPont)

FIGURE 12–59
DuPont fabric printer at
showroom headquarters
(Courtesy of DuPont)

FIGURE 12–60
DuPont printing solution for drying and
finishing fabric
(Courtesy of DuPont)

For example, DuPont's 2020 Ink Jet Printer model is capable of a typical speed of 35 square meters per hour and prints at speeds exceeding 60 square meters an hour. The printer can handle fabric up to 2.0 meters in width. It can also handle most fabric types including knits, nonwovens, and stretch material. It also has the latest industrial-designed 16-head printheads on two adjustable height carriages. The easy-to-replace ink delivery system has minimal parts and comes with a single ink channel for every color. Translation: the user can allow for mixed ink chemistries.

The 2020 also comes with an integrated fabric dryer! The color management software enables the user to predict and match what traditional screen printers can achieve within the mill's unique color gamut. Therefore, it provides unparalleled color matching capabilities, but also repeatability and consistency from run to run.

We asked John to summarize what benefits a consumer could expect from DuPont's digital textile printing technology. His response is listed below:

Digital Textile Printing Customer Benefits

- Lower production and manpower costs vs. other digital solutions
- Provide numerous samples with little advanced planning
- Change designs and colors "on the fly" to meet customer demands
- Get samples to customers before the competition
- Improve inventory turns
- Eliminate closeouts due to changing market trends
- Shorten order-to-delivery cycles
- Meet last-minute deadlines
- Print one-of-a-kind, limited-edition products
- Open up new product and market opportunities

Figure 12–61 provides a few interesting stats on digital printing.

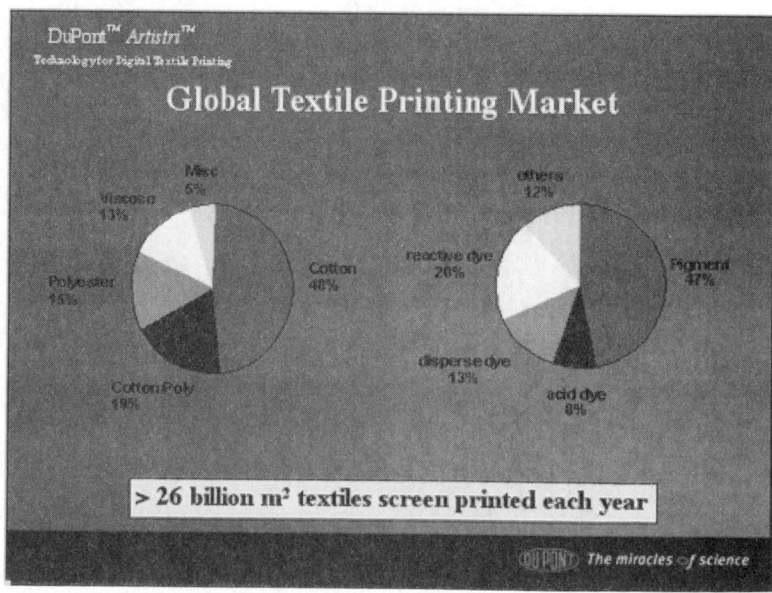

FIGURE 12–61
Stats on digital printing
(Courtesy of DuPont)

Service Bureaus and Other Printing Alternatives

Where to Turn for Help When You Can't Afford a Printer Just Yet
Your Next-Best Friend Could Just be Your Local Service Bureau

Naturally, when we began our section on digital printing alternatives, it soon became apparent we had to include interviews from the folks at First to Print and Design Works of New York City.

These two companies, under one umbrella of ownership, provide a unique blend of creative design and technical skill that makes them leading resources for textile design today. (See Figure 12–62.)

We caught up with one of the principals of Design Works, owner and president, Neil Breslau, for his insights into "closing the loop on digital textile design challenges."

Since 1989, Design Works International has been providing design services to customers, producing anything from home furnishings to apparel. Design Works provides a wide array of services through the product development process and closing the loop on the production cycle. According to Neil Breslau, "we currently deal with over 225 customers' designers. Each one is different, so it is important we have a feel for the way they think and the way they work. We create the art to fit the product. Supplying the resources, whether computerized or hand painting techniques to give them solutions they are looking for. Our aim is to create something that shows the ultimate customer what he's going to get from the finished article. Using digital technology and a variety of off-the-shelf and proprietary software, the design team create and render designs in series of colorways and samples matched to fit their client's needs.

FIGURE 12–62
Design Works
(Courtesy of Danielle Locastro, Design Works)

The speed of getting to market is particularly important for customers in the fashion business. Traditionally it takes from eight to ten weeks, however now with the design team approach we can save them something like four to six weeks! There is tremendous saving from cutting screens and printing minimum lengths of textiles. The bottom line—we save our customers valuable time and money!"

We found that at Design Works there is a unique blend of creativity, artistry, and professionalism making extensive use of the most modern digital electronic systems and devices to take any company from concept to consumer with quality assurance.

Forging New Frontiers for Many Clients

Meet: Danielle Locastro of First to Print

It doesn't take long to discover that the highly successful company of Design Works–First to Print employs another secret weapon besides the latest technology. This secret weapon we are referring to comes in the form of a petite powerhouse by the name of Danielle (Dani) Locastro.

While my co-author Steve has known Dani professionally for years, I personally first met Dani when she was a scheduled speaker for a CADEXPO conference in New York City. Perhaps the most accurate description of Dani's speech was that she spoke with the vision of a prophet and the zeal of an evangelist, but with the humility of an educator. It was clear to all that Dani's passion was to inform, to educate, *and* to serve anyone wanting to know more about digital designing!

Systematically, Dani walked the audience through the nuances of how to navigate the new frontier of digital printing and reproduction issues. At the same time she offered simple and profound solutions to what she refers to as "streamlining the process" and "closing the loop in the production process." (See Figures 12–63, 12–64, and 12–65.)

The Design World according to Dani!

Here is an encapsulated summary, "digital gospel" according to Dani. "Seeking a service bureau is not about contracted production; it is about on-going mutually benefiting relationships."

According to Dani, "it is all about trust *and* good communication—asking question, lots of questions—by both parties as well as listening will result in sensibly and creatively responding to project as well as challenges!"

Dani concedes, you have to begin with questions, in order to determine end results. It is important to be sure you and the client are both speaking the same language. Textile needs vary greatly from graphic needs. Dani provided us with a list of several types of client needs such as:

1. Sampling and design proof

2. Pre-line or sales samples

3. Showroom and marketing samples

4. One-of-a-kind products

FIGURE 12–63
Example of a typical Design
Works bureau office
(Courtesy of Danielle Locastro, Design Works)

FIGURE 12–64
The design team at Design Works
(Courtesy of Danielle Locastro, Design Works)

FIGURE 12–65
Dani giving a trade show presentation for the industry
(Courtesy of Danielle Locastro, Design Works)

5. Costumes

6. Photo shoot materials

7. Outdoor sign and banners—soft signage

8. Backdrops

9. Trade show signage and products

10. Short-run apparel

11. Interior design applications

12. Replacing "strike-offs"

Dani's list of the numerous other variables you will need to consider when seeking a service bureau should be familiar. It is similar to our earlier list of challenges that face this new industry as a whole. It includes very specific issues that need to be addressed on a more personal basis between a service bureau and a client. (See Figure 12–66.)

1. Substrate-related issues

2. Pretreatment

3. Dyes vs. inks vs. medium used

4. Color issues—color gamut and color matching

5. Color saturation

6. Color fixation—reducing bleeding

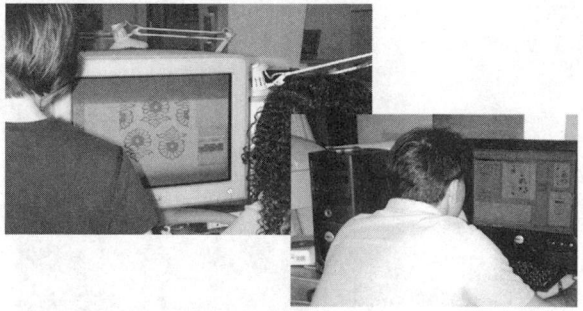

FIGURE 12–66
At Design Works, typical digital print goes from hand rendered images to digital images on screen and then finally to fabric
(Courtesy of Danielle Locastro, Design Works)

7. Including postprinting finishing aesthetic and performance issues

8. Quantities

9. Quality

10. Size

11. Budget

12. Timeline—speed

So now that you have heard from one of the best in the industry today, you may be beginning to wonder if there is a "service bureau life outside of New York City." Of course, there is. With a little bit of research you should be able to locate companies that have similar services in your area.

Take the time to research and determine if the companies you have located can service *your* specific needs. As always, in this section, we have taken the liberty of providing you with a specific criteria sheet to help you conduct your own informed interviews with companies who specialize in digital textile printing in your area.

FIGURE 12–67

At Design Works, quality control staff measure and compare color outputs both by machine and ultimately by the human hand and eye.

(Courtesy of Danielle Locastro, Design Works)

FYI

It should be noted that the companies you begin to interview may not in fact be listed in your local business phone directory as "fabric-related." Instead, you may need to refer back to the roots of textile printing and seek out the experts in your local sign and banner or graphic design service bureaus.

Where Do You Begin

Everything starts with the software you or someone else will be using to create the artwork. Therefore, it is very helpful when you know who will be working on your files. Are you speaking the same language in file formats? This information, as you will recall, has been explained to you in great detail in the earlier chapters of this text. Making sure that the software and platforms are compatible can mean success or failure in your printed results.

Here is a list of what you should expect from the companies you are interviewing:

Interviewing a Potential Service Bureau Checklist

- Don't be shy, ask for references—and then check on them!

- Ask to see samples of the work they have done.

- Be sure to discuss the hardware/cross-platform issues.

- Don't forget software compatibility challenges.

- Ask about color matching, file conversion, and file size.

- Especially, ask about fonts, if text is involved. Don't assume they have what you selected—ASK!

- Solicit their advice on cost-effective ways to handle your design needs.

- Shop around for quality, quality, quality—then price. Remember it's your name and career on the line.

These people should be your best friend. They can make you look really good or really bad!

Don't walk, run, if they don't want to give you the customer service you need. One more thing—there is no such thing as a dumb question. They're the experts, and you will be paying for their work as well as their advice, so don't be afraid to ask questions!

Beyond the boundaries of digital printing, points you *must* remember:

- The computer cannot solve design problems. Only you can. "Garbage in = garbage out!"

- The computer has not replaced the pencil or human brain, so use both, nor will the computer replace the traditional methods of fabric printing. There is enough business out there for everyone.

- Be calm, have a plan, know the limitations of the computer—know that the power and creativity are in you, not the technology or the equipment.

- Go to every seminar you can. Join relevant professional organizations or network for more insights.

- Go on-line. Surf the Net. It is a storehouse of useful ideas!

- Spend your spare time at the computer, and don't be afraid to experiment.

- When it comes to designing digitally, RAM is EVERYTHING! You can never have enough— so don't skimp on RAM!

- Color matching, colorfastness, and hand and fiber performance issues can make or break you—don't be afraid to deal with them head-on.

- Time is money—regardless if it is your investment into purchasing proprietary software or if you share the profits with a quality service bureau who will print your work. In the long run, it will be worth making purchases that streamline your design time.

- Great software and printers can easily pay for themselves in no time. They can be the best "staff" you ever hire—they can do the work of several employees!

Now that you know your choices for additional software and hardware, you can make informed decisions that will best reflect you or your company and your clients' needs.

At this time we are including several potential resource alternatives for you to further conduct your search.

Digital Printer Directory

Okay, you have met the experts and know the lingo. Now, where do you begin your quest for a digital textile printer? Fortunately we have included another of our handy reference charts (Figure 12–68)—this time focusing on the leading textile printers sold at the time of publication.

Digital Support Suppliers: Inks and Fabric Suppliers

As you can see, providing you with insight into software, as well as printer and printing service bureau solutions, is only part of the textile printing mix. By now, it should have become apparent to you that there is a variety of support materials you will need to know about. Fortunately, there is a plethora of other supplies and suppliers around the globe to meet the needs and challenges you may be facing.

Some of the most obvious and critical questions concern the leading suppliers who make and/or provide different kinds of inks and dyes, paper backing, and substrates to complete the digital production loop. (See Figure 12–69.)

We have also included one final chart for you to cross-reference, which is the most important chart on software suppliers. These include the majority of the top proprietary software on the market today. (See Figure 12–70.)

Manufacturer	Model	Media Width	Print Method	Paper-Backed Fabric/ NonPaper-Backed Fabric	Type of Inks	Inks	Resolution	Print Speed	Price	Website
Mimaki	JV4/TX2	52″/62″/73″	Water-based Piezo Ink Jet	Paper-Backed Fabric/ NonPaper-Backed Fabric	Acid/Reactive/ Disperse Dyes	6 and 8 color	1440×1440	10–20 YPH	$25–30,000	www.mimaki.com
Mutoh	Falcon 4300/6300	42.9″/63″	Water-based Piezo Ink Jet	Paper-Backed Fabric	Acid/Reactive/ Disperse Dyes	6 color	1440×1440	2.5 YPH	$9–14,000	www.mutoh.com
Encad	Novajt	60″	Water-based Thermal	Paper-Backed Fabric	Acid/Reactive/ Pigment Dyes	4 and 8 color	600×600	2.5–5 YPH	$15–25,000	www.encad.com
Hewlett-Packard	Design Jet 2000 Series	36″	Water-based Thermal	Paper-Backed Fabric	Pigment Dyes	4 color	600×600		Ask Distributor	www.hp.com
Epson	7000, 9000, 10000	44″	Water-based Piezo Ink Jet	Paper-Backed Fabric	Acid/Reactive/ Disperse Dyes	6 color	1440×720		Ask Distributor	www.epson.com
Roland	Hi-Fi Jet	53″/63″	Water-based Piezo Ink Jet	Paper-Backed Fabric	Acid/Reactive/ Disperse Dyes	7 color variable dot	1440×1440	2.5 YPH	$18–25,000	www.rolanddga.com
Dupont	Artistri 3012	3.2 meters	Water-based Textile Pigment*	NonPaper-Backed Fabric	Pigment	8 color	720×720	30 YPH	Available Fall 2002	www.dupont.com
Raster Graphics	Carolina Textile Press	52″	Solvent-based Pigment	Outdoor Fabric Banners	Disperse Dyes	6 color	720×720	15 YPH	$60,000+	www.rgi.com

Note: Most new printers seem to have the ability of using Pigment or Acid Dyes in their system.
The Mimaki allows the designer to load both ink sets in different heads, so switching between sets is quick and easy.
* Water-based Textile Pigment is nonpermanent at this time.

4-Color printers use cyan, magenta, yellow, and black.
6-Color printers use cyan, magenta, yellow, black, light cyan, and light magenta
8-Color printers use cyan, magenta, yellow, black, light cyan, light magenta, orange, and green.

Cyan, magenta, yellow, and black are the four colors used by all printers. Adding light magenta and light cyan improves gradations between colors.
Adding orange and green widens the color gamut of the printer.

This chart was compiled with the help of Digital Fabric Solutions, Inc.

FIGURE 12–68
Digital printer directory

Fabric and Ink Suppliers	Location	Contact	Fabrics	Digital Printers	Website/Email	Telephone
Digital Fabric Solutions	GA	Mark Trimble	Large Selection of Natural and Synthetics	Mimaki, Mutoh	trimsilk@bellsouth.net	404-408-3268
DigiFab	NY/LA	Call for Service	Large Selection of Natural and Synthetics	Mimaki, Mutoh	www.digifab.com	877-DIGIFAB
Encad	CA	Call for Service	Synthetic	Encad	www.encad.com	800-45ENCAD
Jacquard	CA	Neal Stone	Silk and Cotton	NA	neal@jacquardproducts.com	800-444-0455
TestFabrics, Inc.	PA	Call for Service	Large Selection of Natural and Synthetics	NA	www.testfabrics.com	570-603-0432

Although this is not a complete list of suppliers, we have listed those suppliers we have had success in dealing with on a professional basis. They are excellent contacts for someone just starting to get involved with digital printing.

FIGURE 12–69
Fabrc and ink suppliers

Software Company	Corporate Owner/Parent	CAD Specialty	Platforms	Phone Number
APSO USA		Design	PC	404-261-8113
AVA	Privately held company	Design/Weave	Mac	800-883-4555
Color Matters	Privately held company	Design/Weave/Knit	PC	212-695-0541
EAT, Inc.	EAT Germany	Weave	PC	704-329-0766
Gerber	Gerber Technologies	Pattern	PC	800-826-3243
Imagine That!	Teri Ross	CAD Consulting		952-544-3046
Infomax Corp.	Privately held company	Mac/PC Hardware	Mac/PC	212-730-7930
Improved Technologies	Past IRIS Employees	Digital Fabric Printers	Mac/PC	781-826-0200
JacqCAD Master	Privately held company	Weave	Mac	603-878-4749
Kopperman	Privately held company	Design	PC	310-229-5937
Lectra	Lectra Systems	Pattern/Design	PC	770-422-8050
Ned Graphics	Bought by Blue Fox NE	Design/Weave	PC	212-921-2727
Pointcarré USA	Pointcarré FR	Design/Weave/Knit/Embroidery	Mac/PC	212-627-2394
SofTeam USA	SofTeam Italy	Industrial Embroidery	Mac/PC	800-305-8326
SnapFashun, Inc.	Privately held company	Garment Library	Mac/PC	323-882-6620
Sophis	Sophis FR	Design/Weave/Knit	PC	704-357-3580
Stork	Stork	Digital Fabric Printers	PC	704-598-7171
Digital Fabric Solutions	Mark Trimble	Digital Fabric Printers		404-408-3268

FIGURE 12–70
Software suppliers

Notes...

Spotlight Lyson

One such supplier is Lyson (Figure 12–71). Formed in 1988, Lyson Specialist Fluids is a leading manufacturer of Ink-Jet inks and solutions in the world market. A privately owned enterprise, Lyson employs over 100 people globally. The company operates two manufacturing facilities in Stockport, United Kingdom, and Chicago, in addition to a sales and marketing company servicing mainland Europe, located near Dusseldorf, Germany.

Lyson maintains a particularly diverse customer base ranging from industrial manufacturers to graphics printers, sign makers, textile designers, ink-jet cartridge recyclers, and photographic and fine art professionals. A network of national and local distributors in over 30 countries provides additional sales and support assistance. (See Figures 12–72 and 12–73.)

Lyson Textile Inks

There are three ranges of Lyson Textile Ink. These inks work with numerous printers, including Mimaki, Encad, Epson, and many others.

1. Lyson Reactive
2. Lyson Subliming
3. Lyson Super Subliming

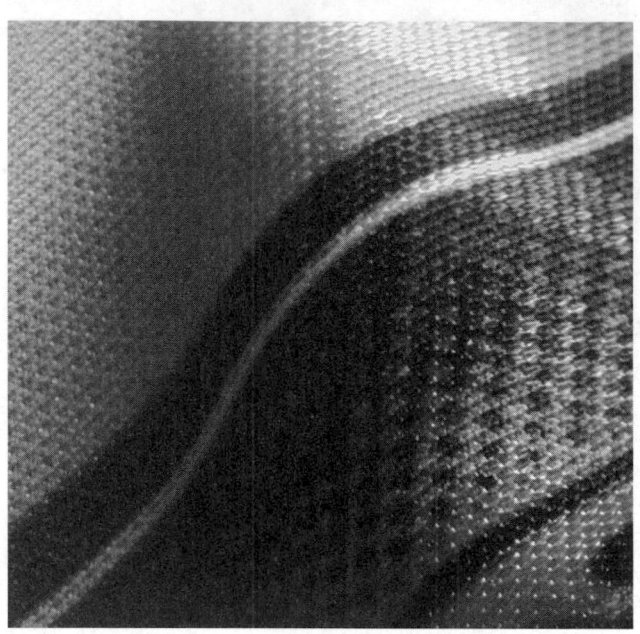

FIGURE 12–72
Lyson ink cartridges
(Courtesy of Lyson Ltd.)

FIGURE 12–71
Sample fabric using Lyson ink
(Courtesy of Lyson Ltd.)

FIGURE 12–73
Lyson reactive ink cartridges
(Courtesy of Lyson Ltd.)

Notes. . .

In addition to inks, Lyson also carries Presstex Heat Transfer Paper for subliming ink.

Lyson Presstex Heat Transfer Paper is the perfect complementary item for the Lyson Subliming and Super Subliming products. Designed for the Epson, Mutoh, Roland, or Mimaki printer, Lyson Presstex Heat Transfer Paper is a high-quality digital transfer paper designed for exceptionally demanding applications. It offers unsurpassed transfer yield, excellent contour, and fine detail printing. (See Figures 12–74 and 12–75. See also Figures 12–76, 12–77, and 12–78 for great samples of completed images.)

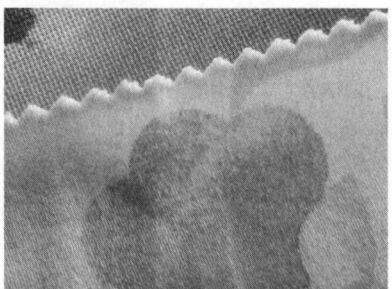

FIGURE 12–74
Lyson has great dye penetration for textile printing
(Courtesy of Lyson Ltd.)

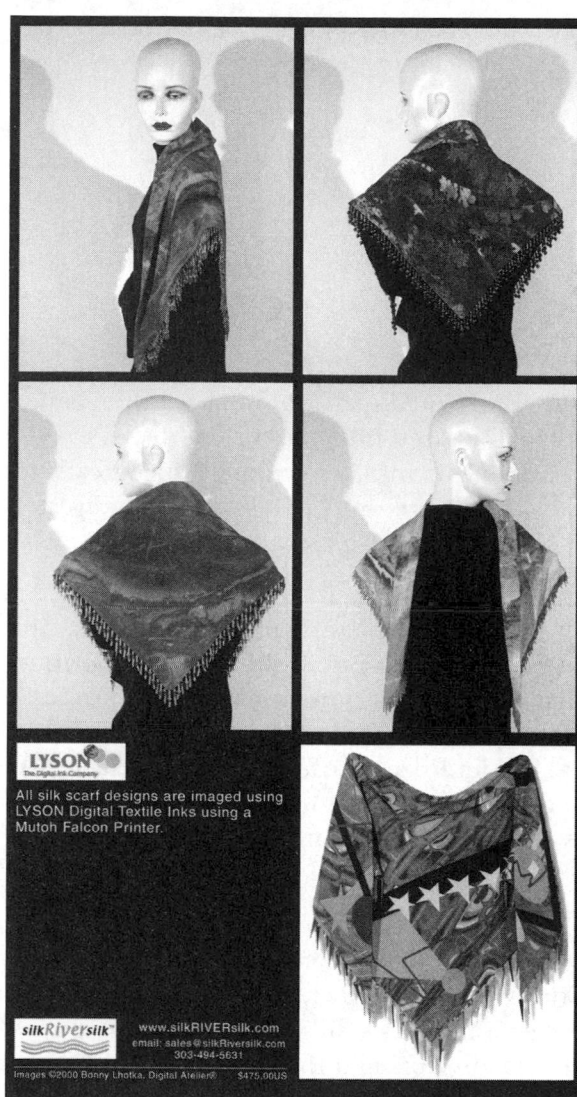

All silk scarf designs are imaged using LYSON Digital Textile Inks using a Mutoh Falcon Printer.

www.silkRIVERsilk.com
email: sales@silkRiversilk.com
303-494-5631
Images ©2000 Bonny Lhotka, Digital Atelier® $475.00US

FIGURE 12–75
Sample of designs by Bonnie Lhotka for SilkRiverSilk.com using Lyson inks
(Courtesy of Lyson Ltd.)

Notes . . .

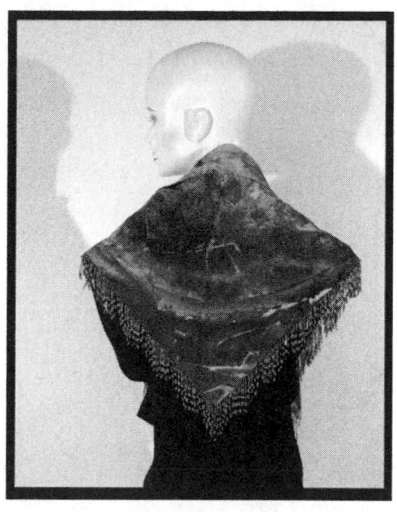

FIGURE 12–76
Close-up detail of the front of Bonnie's silk scarves printed with Lyson inks
(Courtesy of Lyson Ltd.)

FIGURE 12–77
Close-up detail of the side view of Bonnie's silk scarves printed with Lyson inks
(Courtesy of Lyson Ltd.)

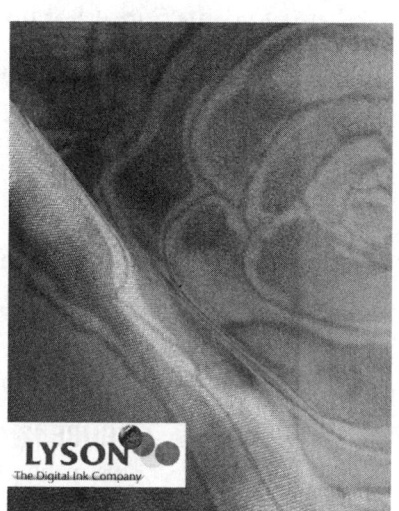

FIGURE 12–78
Lyson inks logo on polyester fabric
(Courtesy of Lyson Ltd.)

Notes...

Lyson Presstex Heat Transfer Paper is available in 42 cm, 91.4 cm, and 160 cm widths.

- Superior transfer yield
- Vibrant color
- Excellent detail
- Consistent printing
- Lightweight and durable

According to Simon Guest at Presstex, a high-quality digital heat transfer paper was developed for ink-jet printing with water-based inks containing disperse sublimation dyestuffs. Lyson's own Super Subliming inks are designed specifically to print onto Presstex before transferring the image onto polyester and polyester blend textiles. Transfer to other media, such as metal, glass, and ceramics, may be achieved if a polyester coating is applied first.

In the digital sublimation transfer process, an image is ink-jet printed onto Presstex and, using heat and pressure from a heat press, the image is bonded onto the substrate at the molecular level. Sublimation transfer with Presstex on polyester fabrics promises performance that far exceeds conventional cold or hot peel transfer where traditional ink-jet inks are used in conjunction with a transfer paper that has been coated simply with a polymer layer. This layer, along with the image, is transferred to the substrate and, even though it provides adhesion and a degree of protection, stability and color vibrancy are relatively poor.

Presstex Heat Transfer Paper offers significant advantages in comparison with regular matte ink-jet paper, which is designed to simply receive and bind inks to the paper after printing. Presstex also accommodates inks at printing, but it goes one step further by releasing those inks cleanly during transfer onto the substrate. After heat pressing, the paper is left carrying barely a shadow of the original print, and an overall reduction in ink consumption is achieved. It can therefore produce vibrant, deep shades successfully and economically on the textile. Transfer yield is influenced by both transfer time and temperature. When using Presstex and Lyson's Super Subliming inks and transferring onto textiles, a temperature of 21°C and a time of 30 seconds is recommended.

Presstex Heat Transfer Paper is suitable for all Piezo ink-jet printing techniques and has been tested extensively on most brands of printers used in digital sublimation transfer. With Super Subliming inks, it is ideal for short or long fabric runs, product sampling procedures, and a host of other decorative options.

Presstex, is lightweight and durable and ensures superior transfer yield, vibrant colors, sharp detail, and consistent printing—all benefits that put standard ink-jet papers in the shade.

Simon Guest went on to note that to really discover and appreciate the beauty of the Lyson product line, take a look at the outcome of items designed and executed using the Lyson inks and papers.

Notes . . .

Full details on Lyson—Presstex Heat Transfer Paper and Super Subliming ink-jet inks— are available from Lyson Ltd., 7 Barton Road, Heaton Mersey Industrial Estate, Stockport SK4 3EG. Tel: O161 442 2111. Fax: O161 442 2611. E-mail: simong@lyson.com. *Website:* www.lyson.com *or contact: Alison Starkweather at Lyson Limited, tel: 44 161 442 2111, or by e-mail at Alison @Lyson .com.*

We follow this section with some practical information organizations to help you secure the information you will need to begin textile designing from your business or college.

Additional Resourcing Solutions and Trade Shows

CAD Trade Shows

Your next stop for gathering information is through utilizing the valuable resources of related trade sources. Below we have listed several good places to begin this search.

Show Name and Information:	Date of Show

International Fabric Fashion Expo. This show has a special section just for CAD vendors to show their software. www.fabricshow.com

New York City, Jacob J. Javits Center . . . . March

New York City, Jacob J. Javits Center . . . . October

The Bobbin Show. This show is dedicated to the knit and sew industry. CAD vendors are found spaced throughout the show floor. www.bobbin.com

Georgia World Congress Center, Atlanta, GA . . . . September

Material World. This show is dedicated to the textile industry. CAD vendors are found spaced throughout the show floor. www.materialworld.com

Miami, FL . . . . September or October

LA International Textile Show. This is show of trimmings, fabrics, and accessories for textile design. They have a CAD aisle with all the major vendors that serve the Los Angeles area.

The California Mart, Los Angeles . . . . May

The California Mart, Los Angeles . . . . October

CAD Expo. This is a show within the Yarn Fair, dedicated to textile CAD software companies.

New York, New York *(Location Varies)* . . . . July or August

CITDA— Computer Integrated Textile Design Association. Association, seminars, and show for designers, product managers, and textile specialists. www.citda.org

Charlotte, North Carolina . . . . Spring

Notes...

CAD Services—Surfing the Net for Information

CAD software information can be found all over the Internet. Going to any search engine and typing in "CAD" or "Textile" or "Apparel" can achieve mind-boggling results. Going through all of these sites is impossible. As a part of helping your search, we are including several insider secrets on where to start. The sites we have included have a great reputation for staying current with technology as well as being on top of other relevant industry news. Staying current is everything in fashion. In fact, the only constant in the design industry is that it is *always* changing. There is an endless stream of mergers and acquisitions—today's designers need to stay informed and current about what is happening on the front line. The sites listed below are the best places to begin.

Technical Research Websites

TechExchange.com is originally published by Imagine That! Consulting Group, Inc.
2229 Sherwood Court, Minnetonka, MN 55305 USA
952/593–0776 Direct Phone
612/677–3671 Fax
612/384–7206 Cell

FYI: At the time of this book's printing, the company has been bought by TC2 (in the fall of 2002).

www.techexchange.com/

Computer Integrated Textile Design Association
An association dedicated to CAD/CAM technology and research
PO Box 849
Burlington, NC 27217
(910) 226–1852
www.citda.com

Other Important Resources:

American Association of Textile Chemist and Colorist
www.AATCC.com

American Fiber Manufacturers Association, Inc. (AFMA)
AFMA offices are located at
1150 17th Street, N.W.
Suite 310
Washington, D.C. 20036
phone: 202–296–6508
FAX: 202–296–3052
www.fibersource.com/afma/afma.htm

American Printed Fabric Council, Inc.
1440 Broadway
NYC, NY 10018

American Society for Testing and Materials
www.ASTM.org

American Textile Partnership
http://apc.pnl.gov:2080/AMTEXWWW/Amtex.html

American Yarn Spinners Association
http://aysa.org

Apparel and Textile Network
www.at-net.com

Apparel Exchange
www.apparelex.com

Apparel Mart
www.apparelmart.com

Apparel Mfg. Sourcing Web
www.Halper.com/sourcingweb/
sweb.html

Apparel Net
www.apparel.net

**Association of Non-Woven
Fabrics Industry**
Bobbin
www.Bobbin.com

Cashmere Market
Computer Integrated Textile
Design Association
www.CITDA.org

Cotton Inc. Corp.
www.cottoncorp.com
www.cottoninc.com

DPI
www.dpia.org

Fabric Link
www.fabriclink.com

Fashion
www.Fashionat.com

Fashion Group International
www.fgi.org

Fashion Net
www.fashion.net

Fed Trade Commission
www.ftc.gov

International Cotton
www.icac.org

International Fabric Care Council
www.ifi.org

**International Fashion Fabrics
Exhibition /IFFE**
www.fabricshow.com

International Linen Promotion
www.mastersoflinen.com

International Wool Secretariat
www.woolmark.com

**Intimate Apparel Salon INTIMA
America Group—NYC**
www.intimateapparelsalon.com

Knitted Textile Association
www.kta-usa.org

Mohair Council of America
www.mohairusa.com

National Cotton Council
www.cotton.org

National Needlework Association
www.tnna.org

National Textile Center
www.ntcresearch.org

Non-Woven Association
Phone (919)233–1210
Fax (919)233–1282
PO Box 1288
Cary, NC 27512–1288
www.Inda.org

Office of Textile and Apparel
otexa.ita.doc.gov

Planet Photoshop
www.PlanetPhotoshop.com

Screenprinters Association
www.Screenprinters.net

Sign and Banner Industry
www.SignIndustry.com

Surface Design Association
www.surfacedesign.org

**Tc2/Textile Clothing
Technology Corporation**
www.Tc2.com

Textile Color Card Association
200 Madison Ave.
NYC, NY 10020

Textile Designer's Guild
30 East 20th Street
NYC, NY 10003

Tech Exchange
www.Techexchange.com

Textile Information
www.texinfo.com

Textile Institute (also know as
the **Textile Organization**)
www.texi.org

Textile Scholars
http://Isu.edu/itaahom.html

Texture Yarn Association
www.tyaa.org

Wool Bureau
www.wool.com

WoolMark
www.woolmark.com

Concluding Thoughts

The fashion and textile design industry is organic and ever-changing. There is always new opportunities and challenges on the horizon and we trust that we have helped to better prepare you for what the future holds. We have taken you from concept to consumer and everywhere in between in our journey to rendering fabric and prints.

So, for now, our final words of advice—relax and enjoy the journey. Remember to keep a journal, take advantage of mentors and informational interviews, and definitely keep networking. Before long you will be well on your way to discovering a place for you and your special talents! Don't ever forget the ancient proverb that states, "A man's gifts (talents) will make room for him." Concentrate on refining your talents and it won't be long before your talents and gifts are opening doors for you!

All the best,

Kathleen and Steven!

Important References and Resources for Digitally Rendering Fabrics

*The information in this section is from Kathleen Colussy's workshops and seminars on digital textile designing.

Suggested Fabric List

Antique Taffeta	Felt	Paisley
Bandana	Flannel	Percale
Batik	Flannelette	Peau de Soie
Batiste	Fleece	Piqué
Bouclé	Foulard	Plissé
Broadcloth	Gabardine	Poplin
Brocade	Gauze	Quilted Fabric
Buckram	Georgette	Raw Silk
Burlap	Gingham	Sailcloth
Burned-Out Fabric	Glen Plaid	Sateen
Calico	Grosgrain	Satin
Cavalry Twill	Herringbone	Seersucker
Challis	Hopsack	Shantung
Chambray	Houndstooth	Taffeta
Charmeuse	Ikat	Tapestry
Chiffon	Interlock	Tartan Plaid
Chino	Jacquard	Terry Cloth
Chintz	Jersey	Ticking
Corduroy	Lace	Tie Dye
Crepe	Lamé	Tricot
Crepe-Backed Satin	Leno	Tropical Weight Wool
Crepe de Chine	Linen-Look	Tulle
Damask	Lining Fabric	Tweed
Denim	Madras	Twill
Dotted Swiss	Melton	Ultrasuede
Double Knit	Moiré	Velour
Drill	Muslin	Velvet
Duck	Naugahyde	Velveteen
Eyelet	Organdy/Organza	Voile
Faille	Ottoman	Vinyl
Faux Fur	Oxford Cloth	Windowpane Plaid

Notes...

Natural:	Synthetic/Man-Made:	
Cotton	Acetate	Polyester
Jute	Acrylic	Rayon
Linen	Metallic	Spandex
Ramie	Modacrylic	Tencel
Silk	Nylon	Triacetate
Wool	Olefin	

Sample Swatch Card

The information has been provided in this next section from support materials created by Kathleen Colussy for use in her consulting workshop on Digital Textile and Designing.

Below is the master page for your fabric swatch journal:

Photo:

Name of Fabric: _____

Description of Fabric: _____

Probable Fiber Content: _____

Method of Fabric Construction: _____

Method of Color: _____

Finishes: _____

Misc: _____

_____

_____

Actual Swatch   **Digital Swatch**

Digital Swatch Notes: _____

Software Used: _____

Techniques Used: _____

Misc. _____

Fabric Construction Methods Referenced and Detailed

Common Plain Weave

Bandana	Crepe	Muslin
Batiste	Dotted Swiss	Ottoman
Bouclé	Douppioni	Percale
Buckram	Duck	Plaid
Burlap	Eyelet	Plissé
Calico	Faille	Sailcloth
Canvas	Flannel	Seersucker
Chambray	Flannelette	Shantung
Chiffon	Gingham	Taffeta
China Silk	Madras	Tissue Silk
Chintz	Moiré	Voile

Common Twill Weaves

Broadcloth	Flannel	Houndstooth Plaid
Chevron	Gabardine	Sharkskin
Denim	Glen Plaid	Tartan Plaid
Drill	Herringbone	Ticking

Common Satin Weaves

Antique Satin	Satin
Charmeuse	Warp Sateen

Common Jacquard Weave

Bird's-eye	Damask	Matelassé
Brocade	Jacquard	Tapestry

Common Pile Weaves

Chenille	Plush Velvet	Velvet
Corduroy	Terry Cloth	Velveteen
Frieze	Velour	

Common Dobby Weaves

Piqué

Fibers at a glance:

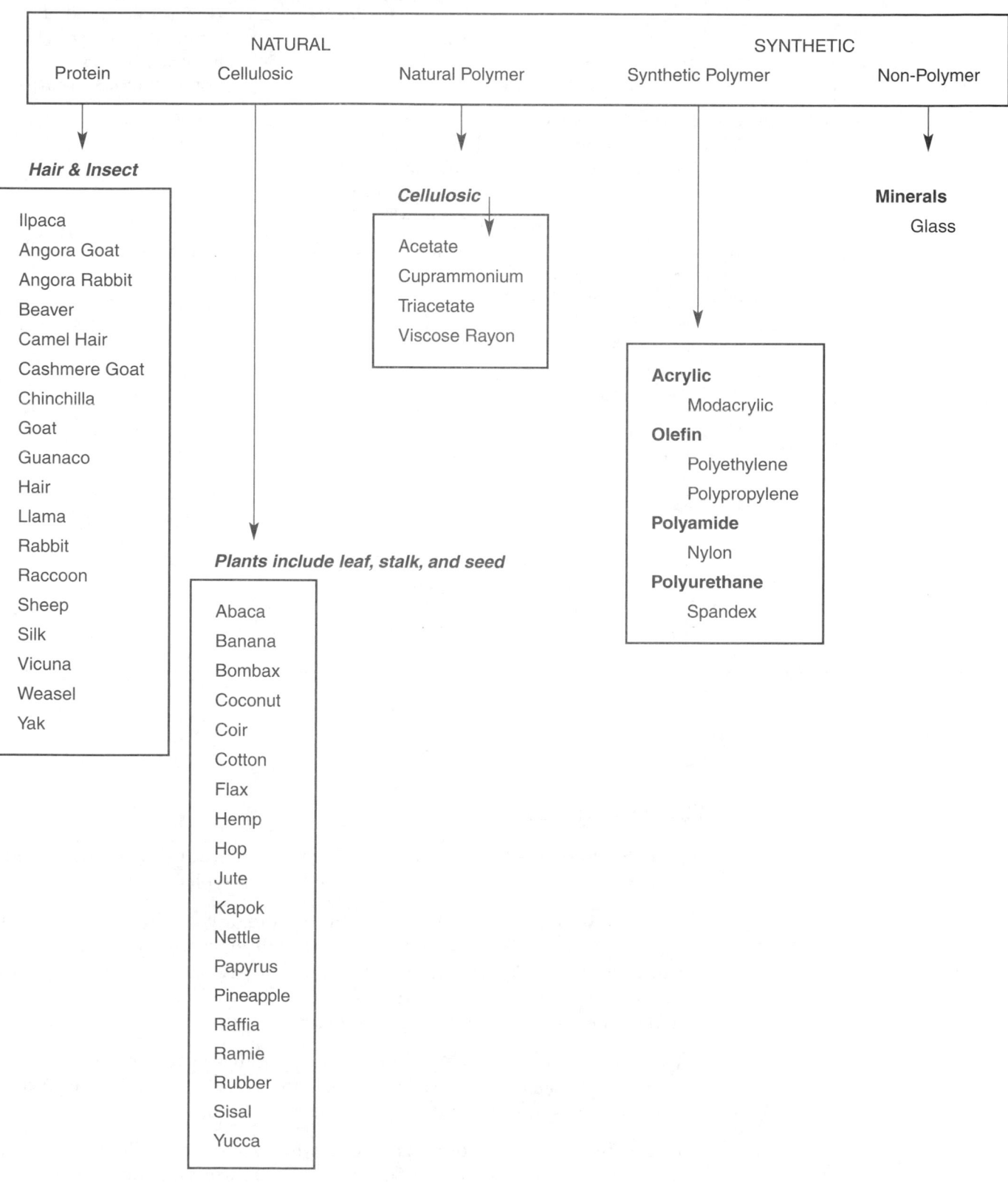

NATURAL			SYNTHETIC	
Protein	Cellulosic	Natural Polymer	Synthetic Polymer	Non-Polymer

Hair & Insect

Ilpaca
Angora Goat
Angora Rabbit
Beaver
Camel Hair
Cashmere Goat
Chinchilla
Goat
Guanaco
Hair
Llama
Rabbit
Raccoon
Sheep
Silk
Vicuna
Weasel
Yak

Cellulosic

Acetate
Cuprammonium
Triacetate
Viscose Rayon

Plants include leaf, stalk, and seed

Abaca
Banana
Bombax
Coconut
Coir
Cotton
Flax
Hemp
Hop
Jute
Kapok
Nettle
Papyrus
Pineapple
Raffia
Ramie
Rubber
Sisal
Yucca

Acrylic
   Modacrylic
Olefin
   Polyethylene
   Polypropylene
Polyamide
   Nylon
Polyurethane
   Spandex

Minerals
Glass

Method of Color	Explanation /Definition	Substrate Applied to: (Refers to the textile fiber, yarn, or fabric)	Method of Fixation: (Refers to method of setting the dye typically involving heat via steam, hot wash or chemicals)
1. Acid Dyes	Commercially applied to fabric in organic or inorganic acid dye solutions.	Natural protein fibers: silk and wool. Synthetic fibers such as acrylic, nylon, and polypropylene blends.	Steam/Wash
2. Disperse Dyes	Water-insoluble dyes. Sometimes referred to as sublimation, which refers to the loss of dye that occurs during evaporation, and is without formation of a liquid phase.	Acetate, nylons, and polyesters	Hi-temp heat steam/Wash
3. Pigment Dyes	Combination of resin binders and insoluble dyes that are printed on the fabric.	All fibers or directly to fabric.	The adhesion properties of the resin in conjunction with the pigments are fixated through the application of dry heat.
4. Reactive Dyes	Just like the name implies, this class of dyes reacts to chemically bond the color to the substrate it is applied to.	Primarily cottons and poly-cotton blends.	Steam/Wash

Notes...

Review of Printing Methods:

Traditional and Digital

1. **Blotch Printing**—Printing instead of dying the ground color of a fabric. The result is that the reverse side of the fabric is typically white.

2. **Digital Printing**—Although this is a broad title, it typically refers to micro-sized droplets of inks or dyes that are placed directly onto the surface of the substrate via an ink-jet printhead. The substrate used and the amount of the droplets applied are directly determined by the data contained in the original image file and therefore translate into color quality of the print.

3. **Discharge Printing**—Using chlorine or other chemical to remove areas of previously applied color on a fabric and replace with areas of white patterns on a colored ground.

4. **Dye Sublimation**—Printing that occurs when a sublimation of dyes is transferred from a carrier roll and applied to the fabric/substrate through the application of heat.

5. **Electrostatic**—Typically each color is printed individually via an electronic charge that actually attracts the toner (ink) particles.

6. **Heat Transfer Printing**—This method involves transferring patterns or prints that were previously preprinted on rolls of paper and applying the prints via relatively high-heat transfer printing machines directly to the surface of the fabric.

7. **Ink Jet**—Detailed explanation of digital printing involves the following:
   a. *Continuous* refers to ink that is continuously applied by channels of pressure forming steam droplets.
   b. *Drop-on-demand* refers to images formed by ink droplets applied by pressure and released onto the substrate.
   c. *Thermal pressure* is created by a gas bubble within the nozzle that forces droplets of ink onto the substrate.
   d. *Solid inks* are stored and melted and applied as needed to the substrate.

8. **Rotary Screen Printing**—Hollow, perforated nickel screen cylinders are prepared for each individual pattern color involved in a design. Color is then forced sequentially through the metal rollers directly to the surface of the fabric.

9. **Screen Printing**—Method of adding a print via one color per screen, one at a time

10. **Spray Jet**—A spray nozzle individually applies color directly to the substrate.

11. **Thermal Wax**—Sometimes referred to as Resin Transfer, it is wax or resin. Individual colors are then applied directly to the substrate via a roll format film carrier.

Burn Chart

Burn Test for Fiber/Fabric Identification

Fiber	Flame	Odor	Residue	Comment:
Cotton	Holds flame, and will ember when extinguished.	Wood or paper	Edges will be soft with soft gray ashes.	
Flax (Linen)/Ramie	Similar to cotton.	Paper or wood	Edges are soft with soft gray ashes.	
Pure Silk	Self-extinguishing, difficult to burn.	Human hair or feathers	Small brittle bead forms from surface area, turns to powder when pressed.	
Weighted Silk	Difficult to burn and the cloth or strand turns to carbon.	Faint smell of human hair.	Residue is black carbon.	
Wool	Self-extinguishing, difficult to burn.	Hair or feathers. Very sour smell like vinegar.	Brittle beaded edge that turns to grit between your fingers when pressed.	*(Continued)*

Fiber	Flame	Odor	Residue	Comment:
Acetate	Sparks when it burns.	Sour	Hard beaded edge.	
Acrylic	Easily burns and melts.		Hard beaded edge.	
Modacrylic	Self-extinguishing, will not support flame. Gray smoke.	Sour	Hard bead.	
Nylon	Melts quickly and may carry flame.	Cooked celery	Hard, dark gray bead.	
Polyester	Melts rapidly with black smoke.	Can smell sweet or like a chemical.	Hard black bead.	
Spandex				
Triacetate	Sparks and melts.	Sour	Hard curled edge.	

Notes...

Descriptive Fabric List

Antique Taffeta: Primarily a crisp, slubbed-yarn, heavy ribbed weave fabric used for after-five apparel.

Astrakhan: High-quality Persian wool often called Karakul. Lustrous, tight, curly appearance similar in weight to Melton and used in heavy winter coats.

Bandana: Originally a Hindi cloth tied or knotted, bleached, and dyed. Now available in an irregular pattern with dots and paisley combinations and used in handkerchiefs or scarves.

Batik: A muslin cloth printed with a series of applications and removal of wax or other resins and dyes in strategic areas to add color and patterns with a distinctive crackled appearance.

Batiste: Originally, a French fabric of finely mercerized combed cotton that is used for blouses or foundations.

Billiard Cloth: Fine knit Merion wool used for billiard or gaming tables, known for its distinctive green appearance.

Blanket Cloth: Usually made from wool and derived from the French word *blankete*. This is undyed wool used in the making of a wool blanket with a densely napped surface.

Blazer Cloth: This wool fabric is often made in a solid color or striped satin weave fabric used in the making of men's wool blazers with crested signature appliqués.

Bouclé: Tightly looped and curled yarn that is used in the making of suits or sweaters.

Broadcloth: A heavy ribbed fabric used in skirts and dresses, also known as poplin.

Brocade: A nonreversible fabric, typically richly figured jacquard woven cloth with sateen, plain, or twill background.

Notes...

Buckram: Cotton or linen plain weave fabric stiffened with resin or flour paste to add stiffness or shape to garments. Similar to a nonwoven inner facing.

Burlap: Made from a minor cellulosic fiber named jute. This coarse plain weave fiber is used for crafts and for carpet backings.

Burned-Out Fabric: This method of printing fabric is frequently associated with velvet fabrics that have a raised pattern contrasted to a sheer ground fabric that has been created by a chemical to remove the pile or nap of fabric to reveal or create the pattern.

Calico: A plain weave lightweight muslin fabric printed with a solid-color ground and small floral repeat foreground.

Cavalry Twill: A 63-degree steep wool twill fabric made from tightly twisted wool fibers, originally used in the making of cavalry officers' uniforms.

Cambric: A close, lightweight, opaque plain weave fabric that is known for its slight luster in appearance and soft hand. It was originally made from linen or cotton and is used in blouses or dresses.

Cashmere: Synonymous with luxury hand and appearance, this wool from goats is used in making prestigious sweaters and jackets.

Challis: Soft napped fabric originally made of wool or silks into a fluid and drapeable fabric used in skirts or dresses.

Chenille: From the French word for *caterpillar,* this soft pile yarn is used in plain weave and plain knit fabrics.

Chambray: A lightweight to medium-weight plain weave fabric, made from tightly twisted combed weft yarns to add a firm hand. Most often made with contrasting pale blue weft and white warp yarns, which are found in men's shirts or denim style garments. Minus the twill weave and rigid hand.

Charmeuse: Fine, fluid satin weave surface with a dull appearance on the reverse side. Typically used in lingerie or blouses.

Chevron: A herringbone or zigzag pattern fabric. The pattern may be woven or knitted into the cloth, or the pattern is printed on the surface of the fabric.

Chiffon: A fluid and sheer, lightweight plain weave fabric known for its drape.

Chino: A rugged twill weave summer-weight fabric used most often in men's casual trousers, often mistakenly called khaki, because of the colors used in dyeing the cloth.

Chintz: A plain weave fabric with a glazed or waxed surface finish, frequently printed with patterns that consist of birds and/or flowers, used on dresses or toss pillows.

Corduroy: Vertical weft float pile or twill weave combinations of cottons or polyblends for pants or jumpers.

Crepe: Any fabric that has a crinkled, puckered, or pebbly or grainy surface. This texture can be created by heat, chemical, or mechanical means. Originally crepe was made from wool and crepe de chine was made from silk.

Crepe-Backed Satin: The distinguishing characteristic of this fabric is that it is a reversible satin weave fabric made from crepe twist yarns woven in a satin float pattern.

Crepe de Chine: Plain weave fabric with a shiny surface appearance made with crepe warp and/or weft yarns.

Damask: A reversible jacquard weave fabric.

Denim: Bottom-weight twill weave fabric made with a white and blue set of warp and weft cotton yarns.

Dotted Swiss: A soft surface polka dot repeat found on lightweight muslin, lawn, or voile fabrics. Originally made with a swivel lappet loom; now a more cost-effective version is available by applying the dots with a flocked finish to the surface of the fabric.

Double Knit: Version 1 can be a jacquard in which the fabric is double-faced and the floats are hidden during the construction on a double-bed knitting machine. Version 2 frequently is a reversible knitted fabric that was constructed on a weft-knitting machine.

Douppioni: From the Italian word for *double,* this fabric is formed from the silk of two silkworms that come from the family of wild or tussah silk.

Drill: A 3 to 1 twill weave made from hard-twist greige good cotton yarns, similar in hand and weight to denim. Sometimes called dungaree or sailcloth.

Duck: A heavyweight basket (plain) weave fabric made from cotton, and like drill typically sold as a greige good. When color is added to this fabric, it is most often referred to as canvas. This is the fabric that is used in the making of Ked's®-styled tennis shoes.

Duchesse Satin: A warped-faced satin fabric.

Eyelet: This is typically an embroidered woven fabric that will have cutouts and holes to form the pattern. The eyelet also refers to an open-hole pattern used in knitted fabric. However, this fabric is more accurately referred to as pointelle.

Faille: A lightweight ribbed weave fabric.

Faux Fur: Made for synthetic fibers such as acrylic or modacrylic, these pile-friendly fibers are used in making knits or woven pile fabrics for coats and for children's stuffed toys.

Felt: A nonwoven napped fabric used in the making of hats or sold for crafts.

Flannel: Originally from the country of Wales, it is available today and is often associated with plaid shirts that are made from such fibers as wool, polyester, and trans-seasonal cotton fiber blends.

Flannelette: A plain or twill weave or knitted fabric made from cotton for use in shirts and children's sleepwear. Sold as a replacement for wool flannel, the *ette* suffix was added at the end to indicate the cotton fiber content.

Fleece: This fabric originally represented the first complete crop or clip of lamb's wool. Today, fleece fabrics are usually knitted fabrics referred to as sweatshirt fabric.

Foulard: 2 × 2 twill weave fabric often used in scarves and ties.

Gabardine: This uniform, tightly woven diagonal twill fabric was originally named Hebrew cloth. Today, this smooth hand fabric is most often used in men's trousers or suits.

Gauze: Shear but stable plain weave fabric that originated from Gaza-Palestine. When the fabric is less stable in hand and appearance and bleached white, it is known as cheesecloth.

Georgette: A crepe effect hard-twisted yarn woven into a a plain weave fabric.

Gingham: Originating in India and made from silk or cotton, this two-colored check cloth is known as a balanced cloth, because the warp and weft cloth are the same in number or count within 10 picks.

Glen Plaid: A fabric that is comprised of a two-colored series of checks and plaids, originally from the highlands of Scotland. It is used as men's wool suiting material.

Grosgrain: A large grain rib weave fabric used for ribbon.

Herringbone: One of the common variations of a twill weave is a "herringbone," known for a combination of "right *and* left" twill patterns.

Home Spun: Traditionally this handwoven cloth was considered a common rough and coarse fabric for everyday use in apparel.

Hopsack: A course basket weave that can have apparel applications such as in men's slacks.

Houndstooth: Sometimes called Dog's tooth or Shepherd's check, this two-colored 2 up 2 down or 4 + 4 twill is most often used as suiting material.

Interlock: Is a stable compound fabric and is limited to only having crosswise stretch. Interlock weft-faced is produced by two sets of needles on a double-bed or on a circular knitting machine.

Jacquard : There are several versions of a jacquard fabric. The first is a knit that refers to the color changes made by an attachment of the same name added to the machine. This method is sometimes known as Knit-In. One characteristic of this type of knitted fabric is the reverse side of the yard good or garment will have a series of floats, which represent the different colors of yarn that are used to construct the pattern. There are several variations of knitted jacquards depending on the type of knitting machine used. Some jacquards are made with the floats secured by the addition of a chain stitch on the reverse of the fabric. This is known as a ladder-back jacquard. The second version of a Jacquard is a woven. This is a complex weaving loom created in 1805 by Joseph Jacquard. This loom used a punch card system. Originally, woven Jacquards were complex designs of texture, surface interest, and color woven into fabric.

Jersey: Originally from the Channel Islands between Britain and France, this fisherman's wool knit pattern has a distinctive knitted face and purl stitch reverse pattern.

Khaki: Through the years the term khaki has evolved from the color of dye used in the making of military fatigues or in safari-styled clothing. Today, most chino fabric when it is found in a khaki color assumes the name khakis; however, originally khaki was merely a color not a fabric!

Lace: The first laces were traditionally made by hand on a series of bobbins. However, over time the cost became prohibitive and an alternative was sought in the form of a second category of lace known as weft knit jersey, which is sometimes known as lace. This type of knit merely gives the impression of lace but is not considered true lace. This knit has a similar appearance that closely simulates eyelets or holes. Relocating stitches onto its adjacent neighbor creates these holes; this process forms a miss stitch or a hole. This combination of making holes is known as Miss stitch, Eyelet, or Pointelle. Today's laces are made as warp knits. In this version of warp knitting, the needles move the ground bar. The loops are prevented from moving up and down in a simultaneous coordinating series of actions. The appearance of a typical raschel knit has a coarser texture than most other warp knits. Raschel knits are also known as open-structured knits.

Lamé: This is a fabric made from strips of plastic-coated aluminum foil that can be woven or knitted. Typically, when woven, it is blended by using a nylon warp yarn and a lamé weft yarn to give the fabric stability.

Lawn: Finer and crisper than voile, this sheer lightweight plain weave fabric is similar in appearance and hand to organdy.

Leno: A leno weave is formed by the appearance of a "figure eight" in the pattern. This pattern is also called a doup weave because it requires the use of a doup attachment to form the pattern in the fabric.

Linen: Typically a plain woven fabric used in blouses and suits. Known for easily wrinkling and its slubbed-yarn appearance.

Linen-Look: Made from polyester to resemble the appearance of linen but without the wrinkles.

Lining Fabric: This lightweight plain weave fabric is usually made from acetate.

Madras: This lightweight plain weave check or plaid fabric came from India. The distinguishing characteristic was the vegetable dyes originally used to add color to the yarns that would easily bleed or run when hot water was applied in laundering. Today, madras is found most often in men's summer shirts, children's or junior apparel, and thankfully the yarns used are now colorfast!

Melton: One of the most extremely dense woven pile fabrics used for coats and suits.

Merino: A better grade of wool that is most often used in fine sweaters.

Mohair: Wool yarn from angora goats used in sweaters, suits, coats, and rugs. It has an ultrasoft napped hand and fine lustrous appearance.

Moiré: A fine rib cord to heavier weight rib weave fabric.

Muslin: Unbleached cotton available in light- to medium-weight plain weave fabric, also known as toile.

Naugahyde: This synthetic fabric often has an embossed surface that resembles leather.

Organdy/Organza: Spelled organdy or organdie, this shear yet firm tightly twisted light weave yarn is woven into a plain weave fabric. Originally organdie was made from cotton, and organza was made from silk. Today most commercially sold organdie or organza is made from polyester.

Ottoman: Firm, lustrous plain weave corded-effect fabric.

Oxford Cloth: Taken from the name of the famous university, this fine warp yarn plain weave-soft hand fabric is found in men's dress shirts. Like chambray, when the fabric is sold in colors, the warp and weft yarns will be contrasting colors—one set of yarns will have the color and the other set of yarns will be white.

Paisley: This fabric originated in shawls dating from the early 1800s. The distinctive woven or printed pattern shawls were originally made from Kashmir wool.

Panne Velvet: Shaggy, long pile velvet fabric.

Percale: This fine and tightly twisted yarn is woven into a plain weave fabric and sold as sheeting material. The density of the warp and weft threads that intersect is referred to as the count. Therefore, sheets that are sold with a higher count such as 250, 300, or higher indicates a better-quality product that is less likely to pill over time.

Peau de Soie: Most often used in wedding gowns, this is a smooth, heavyweight reversible satin with a dull sheen appearance.

Pinstripe: A narrow vertical-striped fabric frequently made of wool or other suiting materials. The most common is found on a solid black, gray, or navy ground with a white or thin chalk vertical stripe.

Piqué: This honeycomb or waffle-like dobby-weave pattern found on the surface of the fabric is most often sold in the color white. Originally used for men's waistcoats, today it is sold as cool summer apparel items in a variety of colors as well as white.

Plaid: The generic term *plaid* typically represents fabric that consists of a multi-colored horizontal and vertical stripe combination.

Plissé: A crinkle crepe plain weave fabric that has permanent puckers across the surface of the cloth, which were made by heat set, caustic soda, or other chemicals.

Plush: Representing dense or high-pile fabrics of wool, acrylic, or modacrylic fibers and used today to make pile coats, pile fabrics, or stuffed toys.

Pongee: Irregular course silk-slubbed yarn fabric. Typically the warp yarn is finer than the weft.

Poplin: (See Broadcloth) When this fabric is woven into a lighter weight weave it is most often sold as English poplin and is used for men's dress shirts.

Quilted Fabric: Three layers of fabric that are held together by a running stitch. The first layer generally is a cotton or poly-cotton blend lightweight plain weave; the second is a fiber fill, feathers, or other batting materials; the third layer can be a warp knit mesh or another layer of a plain weave.

Raw Silk: This is a natural silk that has not been degumed of a sticky substance, known as sericin.

Sailcloth: This is often a medium-weight basket or plain weave cotton canvas cloth similar to duck.

Sateen: This 5×8 float satin weave fabric is made from cotton, giving it a soft hand and moderately dull pile appearance.

Satin: Shiny, dense warp float threads comprised of a satin weave fabric from which the fabric gets its name.

Seersucker: Implying the phrase "milk and sugar," this lightweight crinkled striped fabric is sold for summer-weight garments for children and used in the traditional pale blue-and-white-striped men's summer sports coat.

Serge: Originally made from silk, this strong $2 + 2$ twill fabric has a lightweight hand and a smooth face.

Shantung: Wild silk fibers with a rough uneven texture make a fabric that is thicker than a pongee silk.

Sharkskin: A small-step fine twill fabric with a shiny appearance that is used most often for suiting fabrics.

Shetland: The finest quality wool from the northern tip of Scotland, which varies from coarse to fine hand and is typically used for sweaters.

Surah: Close, heavy twill weave that is lustrous on both sides of the fabric, originally made from silk.

Taffeta: Stiff, crisp ribbed weave fabric.

Tapestry: Made from heavy spun yarns in a ribbed or jacquard scene or design. It is used for upholstery, wall hangings, luggage, or handbags.

Tartan Plaid: Typically this is a twill weave fabric but also made in plain weave. It is available in color combinations that signify the distinctive Highland family clans or Scottish regiments. Some of the most well known are Anderson, Armstrong, Barclay, Cunningham, Douglas, Elliot, Gordon, Graham, Keith, Kennedy, Logan, MacAlister, MacArthur, MacDonnell, MacFarlane, Mackintosh, MacHaughton, Morrison, Nicholson, Ogilvie, Ross, Scott, Stewart, and Wallace to the lesser recognized Dalziel, seen in Chapter 7.

Tattersall: This fabric is also known as windowpane plaid for its distinctive large, bold check design.

Terry Cloth: Also known as towel, this primarily cotton fabric can be woven in a rough uncut pile face or with a cut-pile surface.

Ticking: Traditionally a 2×2 twill stripe color that is water repellant and used to cover bedding such as mattresses or pillows.

Tie Dye: Plain weave or jersey knit cotton fabric that has been twisted, tied, or folded and the bound fabric was dyed and dried to make a distinctive hallo-like series of patterns on the fabric.

Tricot: Vertical wale crosswise rib knit with a purl reverse fabric.

Tropical Weight Wool: Finely twisted lightweight wool used for suits.

Tulle: Hexagon mesh knit often called nylon net.

Tussah: Wild silk with a course or stiff hand generally available in ecru, yellow, or other natural greige good colors.

Tweed: Sometimes referred to as Harris Tweed, this medium weight 2 + 2 twill can be made into solids, stripes, or plaids.

Twill: A diagonal woven pattern that repeats from left to lower right.

Ultra Suede: This is synthetic suede made into a nonwoven polyester napped cloth.

Velour: Pile-knitted velvet fabric, used in place of traditional velvet when stretch is needed.

Velvet: A pile weave cut warp fabric with a dense thick tuft fabric.

Velveteen: A pile weave napped cotton fabric used in after-five apparel. Like the term *flannelette,* velveteen indicates to the buyer that the fiber content should be cotton.

Vicuna: This yarn from the llama or alpaca is a prestige fiber generally spun in its natural color or earth tones and used in suits and sweaters.

Vinyl: A thick vinyl or vinyon-based fabric that has been coated.

Viyella: A blend of wool and cotton woven cloth used in the making of shirts ands sleep shirts.

Voile: A sheer, lightweight plain weave fabric originally made from wool or cotton.

Windowpane Plaid: (See Tattersall).

Software Company	Corporate Owner/Parent	CAD Specialty	Platforms	Phone Number
APSO USA		Design	PC	404-261-8113
AVA		Design/Weave	Mac	800-883-4555
Color Matters	Privately held company	Design/Weave/Knit	PC	212-695-0541
EAT, Inc.	EAT Germany	Weave	PC	704-329-0766
Gerber	Gerber Technologies	Pattern	PC	800-826-3243
Imagine That!	Teri Ross	CAD Consulting		952-544-3046
Infomax Corp.	Privately held company	Mac/PC Hardware	Mac/PC	212-730-7930
Improved Technologies	Past IRIS Employees	Digital Fabric Printers	Mac/PC	781-826-0200
JacqCAD Master	Privately held company	Weave	Mac	603-878-4749
Kopperman	Privately held company	Design	PC	310-229-5937
Lectra	Lectra Systems	Pattern/Design	PC	770-422-8050
Ned Graphics	Bought by Blue Fox NE	Design/Weave	PC	212-921-2727
Pointcarré USA	Pointcarré FR	Design/Weave/Knit/Embroidery	Mac/PC	212-627-2394
SofTeam USA	SofTeam Italy	Industrial Embroidery	Mac/PC	800-305-8326
SnapFashun, Inc.	Privately held company	Garment Library	Mac/PC	323-882-6620
Sophis	Sophis FR	Design/Weave/Knit	PC	704-357-3580
Stork	Stork	Digital Fabric Printers	PC	704-598-7171
Digital Fabric Solutions	Mark Trimble	Digital Fabric Printers		404-408-3268

Manufacturer	Model	Media Width	Print Method	Paper Backed Fabric/ Non-Paper Backed Fabric	Type of Inks	Inks	Resolution	Print Speed	Price	Website
Mimaki	JV4/TX2	52"/62"/73"	Waterbased Piezo Ink Jet	Paper Backed Fabric/ Non-Paper Backed Fabric	Acid/Reactive/ Disperse Dyes	6 and 8 color	1440×1440	10–20 YPH	$25–30,000	www.mimaki.com
Mutoh	Falcon 4300/6300	42.9"/63"	Waterbased Piezo Ink Jet	Paper Backed Fabric	Acid/Reactive/ Disperse Dyes	6 color	1440×1440	2.5 YPH	$9–14,000	www.mutoh.com
Encad	Novajt	60"	Waterbased Thermal	Paper Backed Fabric	Acid/Reactive/ Pigment Dyes	4 and 8 color	600×600	2.5–5 YPH	$15–25,000	www.encad.com
Hewlett Packard	Design Jet 2000 Series	36"	Waterbased Thermal	Paper Backed Fabric	Pigment Dyes	4 color	600×600		Ask Distributor	www.hp.com
Epson	7000, 9000, 10000	44"	Waterbased Piezo Ink Jet	Paper Backed Fabric	Acid/Reactive/ Disperse Dyes	6 color	1440×720		Ask Distributor	www.epson.com
Roland	Hi-Fi Jet	53"/63"	Waterbased Piezo Ink Jet	Paper Backed Fabric	Acid/Reactive/ Disperse Dyes	7 color variable dot	1440×1440	2.5 YPH	$18–25,000	www.rolandga.com
Dupont	Artistri 3012	3.2 meters	Waterbased Textile Pigment*	Non-Paper Backed Fabric	Pigment	8 color	720×720	30 YPH	Available Fall 2002	www.dupont.com
Raster Graphics	Carolina Textile Press	52"	Solvent based Pigment	Outdoor Fabric Banners	Disperse Dyes	6 color	720×720	15 YPH	$60,000+	www.rgi.com

Note: Most new printers seem top have the anility of using Pigment or Acid Dyes in their system.

The Mimaki allows the designer to load both ink sets in different heads so switching between sets is quick and easy.

* Water based Textile Pigment is non-permanent at this time.

4 Color printers use cyan, magenta, yellow, and black.

6 Color printers use cyan, magenta, yellow, black, light cyan and light magenta

8 Color printers use cyan, magenta, yellow, black, light cyan, light magenta, orange and green.

Cyan, magenta, yellow, and black are the four colors used by all printers. Adding light magenta and light cyan improves gradations between colors. Adding Orange and Green widens the color gamut of the printer.

This chart was compiled with the help of Digital Fabric Solutions, Inc.

Fabric and Ink Suppliers	Location	Contact	Fabrics	Digital Printers	Website/Email	Telephone
Digital Fabric Solutions	GA	Mark Trimble	Large Selection of Natural and Synthetics	Mimaki; Mutoh	trimsilk@bellsouth.net	404-408-3268
DigiFab	NY/LA	Call for Service	Large Selection of Natural and Synthetics	Mimaki; Mutoh	www.digifab.com	877-DIGIFAB
Encad	CA	Call for Service	Synthetic	Encad	www.encad.com	800-45ENCAD
Jacquard	CA	Neal Stone	Silk and Cotton	n/a	neal@jacquardproducts.com	800-444-0455
TestFabrics, Inc.	PA	Call for Service	Large Selection of Natural and Synthetics	n/a	www.testfabrics.com	570-603-0432

Although this is not a complete list of suppliers, we have listed those suppliers we have had success in dealing with on a professional basis. They are excellent contacts for someone just starting to get involved with digital printing.